O'CONNOR'S TEXAS PROPERTY CODE PLUS

AUTHORS

ROSEMARY B. JACKSON

STEVEN E. KENNEDY

RICK MCELVANEY

JEFFREY J. TOMPKINS

O'CONNOR'S

HOUSTON, TEXAS

O'CONNOR'S ANNOTATED CODES SERIES

Suggested cite form: ***O'Connor's Texas Property Code Plus*** (2017-18)

Product List

O'CONNOR'S®

Mailing address:
P.O. Box 3348
Houston, TX 77253-3348

Shipping address:
9364 Wallisville Rd., Ste. 150
Houston, TX 77013

Phone: (713) 335-8200
(800) OCONNOR (626-6667)
Fax: (713) 335-8201

www.oconnors.com

Print date: July 21, 2017
Printed in the United States of America

ISBN 978-1-59839-276-0

This book is intended to provide attorneys with current information about selected Texas cases, rules, and statutes. The information in this book, however, may not be sufficient in dealing with a client's particular legal problem, and O'Connor's, Michol O'Connor, Rosemary Jackson, Steven Kennedy, Rick McElvaney, and Jeffrey Tompkins do not warrant or represent its suitability for this purpose. Attorneys using this book do so with the understanding that the information published in it should not be relied on as a substitute for independent research using original sources of authority.

Subscription Notice: By ordering this book, you are enrolled in our subscription program, which entitles you to a lower annual price. Before we send you an updated book, we send you a letter and reply card confirming that you want the new edition. You have the option at that time to change or cancel your order. If you do not change or cancel your order, the book will be shipped to you. If you decide to return the book, the return postage is your responsibility. You can change your subscription status at any time in writing. If you want to order a product but do not wish to enroll in the subscription program, please call 1-800-OCONNOR for pricing details.

ABOUT THIS BOOK

O'Connor's Texas Property Code Plus contains a comprehensive, up-to-date collection of statutes and case annotations on real-estate and property law. It includes the entire Property Code as well as statutes covering annexation, land use, takings, property taxes, judgment interest, water rights, hazardous conditions, antiquities, and secured transactions. Also included are the Texas Title Examination Standards; charts listing attorney-fee provisions, statutes of limitations, and injunction provisions; timetables for eviction and condemnation suits; derivation and disposition tables for the Property Code; and the Federal Fair Housing Act. We are confident that you will find ***O'Connor's Texas Property Code Plus*** to be the most useful—and most used—property-law book in your library.

TRCP AMENDMENTS

TRCP 502.3. TRCP 502.3 was amended to require a party making a claim of inability to afford court costs in justice court to file a Statement of Inability to Afford Payment of Court Costs. If the Statement is accompanied by the certificate of a legal-aid provider meeting certain requirements, the Statement cannot be contested. These changes took effect September 1, 2016. Tex.Sup.Ct. Order, Misc. Docket No. 16-9122 (eff. Sept. 1, 2016).

TRCP 501.2, 502.4, 502.6, 504.1, 506.1, 506.4, 510.7 & 510.9. TRCP 501.2, 502.4, 502.6, 504.1, 506.1, 506.4, 510.7, and 510.9 were amended to make reference to the newly created Statement of Inability to Afford Payment of Court Costs. These changes took effect September 1, 2016. Tex.Sup.Ct. Order, Misc. Docket No. 16-9122 (eff. Sept.1, 2016).

CURRENCY

The statutes in this book are current through the 85th Legislature, Regular Session (2017). The case law is current through April 2017.

At the time of printing, the 85th Legislature had convened a special session to address certain sunset provisions and potentially 19 other items identified by the governor. If any Property Code sections are affected by laws passed during this session, you can receive an update to the code if you register to be notified at www.oconnors.com. Customers who subscribe to O'Connor's Online will be able to access the revised code sections before they take effect at www.oconnors.com/online.

CONVENTIONS & LEGISLATIVE CONFLICTS

In this book, 2017 legislative changes are marked with Ⓐ or Ⓔ, depending on whether the section was amended or enacted. Statutory language added by the Legislature is <u>underlined</u>, and language removed by the Legislature is shown in ~~strikethrough~~ text. Italicized editor's notes explain the effect of legislative changes (e.g., effective dates, savings clauses). 2016 rule changes are marked with ⑯.

Occasionally, the Legislature enacts multiple code sections with the same number. The identically numbered sections are marked with ☠ and accompanied by an editor's note describing the duplicate numbering. Each section is also labeled with a bracketed letter (e.g., [A*]) to help distinguish it. Likewise, when the Legislature passes a bill that amends a section or subsection without reference to another bill's conflicting amendment to the same section or subsection, both versions of the section or subsection are presented. Each version is marked with ☠ and accompanied by an editor's note describing the conflict.

When multiple amendments to the same section or subsection are enacted during the same legislative session, the amendments should be harmonized unless they are irreconcilable. Tex. Gov't Code §311.025(b); ***Burke v. Union Pac. Res.***, 138 S.W.3d 46, 75 (Tex.App.—Texarkana 2004, pet. denied). Conflicting amendments are irreconcilable only if both provisions cannot be complied with at the same time. ***State v. Jackson***, 370 S.W.2d 797, 800 (Tex. App.—Houston [1st Dist.] 1963), *aff'd*, 376 S.W.2d 341 (Tex.1964). In that circumstance, the amendment enacted last will prevail. Tex. Gov't Code §311.025(b). For this reason, the editor's note accompanying each conflict includes the date each bill was enacted, which in most cases is the date of the last vote on the bill (not the bill's effective date). *See* Tex. Gov't Code §311.025(d), (e).

To determine whether conflicting statutory provisions can be harmonized, you should review the text carefully and consult the Code Construction Act (Government Code ch. 311), the canons of statutory construction, and the legislative history for those provisions. Legislative history for recent bills can be found on the Texas Legislature Online (TLO) website at www.capitol.state.tx.us. To find a bill analysis on TLO, select the correct legislative session in the drop-down box under "Search Legislation," enter the bill number (e.g., HB 387) in the box below that, select "Go," click on the "Text" tab, and then select the latest document under the "Bill Analysis" column. Other legislative history, such as passed and rejected amendments, floor journals, fiscal notes, and audio or video recordings of hearings, can also be found on the TLO website.

Because some conflicting versions of sections and subsections persist beyond the following legislative session, editor's notes may contain references to session laws (e.g., Acts 2003, 78th Leg., ch. 213 …) rather than bill numbers. To find a bill number from past session laws, use the "Bill-chapter cross reference" function on the Legislative Reference Library website at www.lrl.state.tx.us.

ABOUT THE AUTHORS

Rosemary B. Jackson has practiced real estate law with distinction statewide since 1982. She is board-certified in Residential Real Estate Law by the Texas Board of Legal Specialization and a member of the Texas College of Real Estate Attorneys. She is the managing shareholder of Rosemary B. Jackson, P.C., which focuses on community associations, real property development, and real estate litigation, and has served as general counsel to over 400 condominium and property owners' associations. Her firm is designated AV Preeminent by Martindale-Hubbell Peer Review.

Ms. Jackson is a frequent presenter for the State Bar of Texas Advanced Real Estate Law and Drafting Courses, webcasts, and other professional development programs. Her more recent publications include: Governing Documents for POAs: Distinguishing Roles for Declaration, Rules, and Bylaws: Advanced Real Estate Law Course, 2016; Fair Housing Issues: Advanced Real Estate Law Course, 2015; Architectural Guidelines for Property Owners Associations: Advanced Real Estate Drafting Course, 2015; Drafting Covenants, Conditions and Restrictions Under the New Laws for Property Owners' Associations: Advanced Real Estate Drafting Course, 2013; Property Owners' Association Foreclosures and The New Expedited Foreclosure Process (with Marc Markel): State Bar of Texas Webcast, October 25, 2012; Expedited Foreclosure for Property Owners' Associations (with Marc Markel): State Bar of Texas Webcast, January 19, 2012; Established Subdivisions Without Mandatory HOAs – Adding HOAs "After the Fact": Advanced Real Estate Law Course, 2011; and Property Owners' Association "Reform Laws" – An Overview of the 2011 Texas Legislative Session: Houston Bar Association, 2011.

She received her Juris Doctor from St. Mary's University School of Law in San Antonio, Texas, and Bachelor of Arts, *magna cum laude*, from The Ohio State University in Columbus, Ohio.

Steven E. Kennedy received his law degree from Southern Methodist University in 1987. Mr. Kennedy holds a Bachelor of Architecture degree from the University of Arkansas. He is a shareholder and director of the firm of McGuire, Craddock & Strother, P.C., where his practice is concentrated in the area of construction law, contract disputes, and commercial litigation. Mr. Kennedy is a frequent speaker on the subject of construction law and related issues to both industry and professional groups. He is a member of the State Bar of Texas Construction Law Section and has served on the Governing Counsel of the section. He is also a member of the Dallas Bar Association Construction Law Section, immediate past Chair for the section, the American Bar Association, the Construction Law Forum, and the College of the State Bar of Texas. Mr. Kennedy is Board Certified in Construction Law by the Texas Board of Legal Specialization.

Rick McElvaney, Clinical Associate Professor, is the Director of the Consumer Law Clinic and the Texas Consumer Complaint Center at the University of Houston Law Center, where he also teaches consumer dispute resolution, landlord and tenant law, law practice strategies, poverty law practice, Texas consumer law and Texas procedure. He received a B.S. in Economics from The Pennsylvania State University in 1982 and a J.D. from the University of Houston Law Center in 1986, where he was an Associate Editor of the Houston Journal of International Law.

Professor McElvaney practiced as a legal aid attorney for 20 years in the areas of housing, consumer, and bankruptcy law at Gulf Coast Legal Foundation and Lone Star Legal Aid. He is licensed to practice law by the Supreme Court of Texas, the U.S. District Court for the Southern District of Texas, the U.S. Fifth Circuit Court of Appeals, and the U.S. Supreme Court, and is board-certified in consumer and commercial law by the Texas Board of Legal Specialization.

Professor McElvaney is a past Chair of the State Bar of Texas – Consumer & Commercial Law Section, a board member of the Tenants' Council of Houston, and a frequent lecturer at legal seminars and community service events on housing, consumer, and bankruptcy law. In 2004, he received the Phi Alpha Delta Legal Fraternity – Hickman Chapter Outstanding Alumnus Award and was named Professor of the Year at the University of Houston Law Center by the Order of the Barons in 2009.

He has worked in the Consumer Protection Division and State and County Affairs Division of the Texas Attorney General's Office, as a mediator for the Neighborhood Justice Center (now Dispute Resolution Center), and is a veteran of the United States Navy.

Jeffrey J. Tompkins began practicing law in December 1972 as an associate with Fulbright & Jaworski. He later practiced with the law firm of Roy H. Bray & Associates, where he was involved in all types of real estate law issues, including reviewing and examining title files, preparing loan and other closing documents, curing title defects, conducting nonjudicial foreclosures, and overseeing business entity formations. In 1977, he and his two law partners formed the law firm of Walsh, Squires & Tompkins, P.C., which engaged in all phases of sophisticated residential and commercial real estate transactional work on behalf of developers, builders, banks, and savings and loans. Mr. Tompkins is presently a sole practitioner with his practice primarily in the areas of general business, business entities, real estate, real estate finance, and business litigation. In the past he has taught land development law and real estate finance law at South Texas College of Law as an adjunct professor of law. He has also been active in the formation of homeowners' and condominium owners' associations and the creation of their respective declarations, bylaws, and rules and regulations. Mr. Tompkins has also been involved in the interpretation and enforcement of restrictive covenants by conducting litigation on behalf of homeowners and associations.

Mr. Tompkins received a B.A. in Business Education from the University of Northern Iowa in 1970, and a J.D. from the University of Houston, Bates College of Law, in 1972. He was an Associate Editor of the law school newspaper, the Advance Sheet; member of the Phi Alpha Delta legal fraternity; co-author of *Bordersville: In Our Opinion*, December 1971 (unpublished real estate work in Bates College of Law Library); and researcher on the law school's Legal Research Service staff. He is a member of the Texas Association of Bank Counsel and the Houston Bar Association. He is licensed to practice in Texas and before the U.S. District Court for the Southern District of Texas, the U.S. Fifth Circuit Court of Appeals, and the U.S. Supreme Court.

ACKNOWLEDGMENT

We would like to thank the National Conference of Commissioners on Uniform State Laws for use of the official comments to uniform acts adopted by the Texas Legislature.

YOUR SUGGESTIONS

We welcome your comments. If you think we should have included (or excluded) something, or if you see anything that needs to be corrected, please let us know. Send your comments to the mailing address or fax number shown on the copyright page, or by e-mail to Jessica Field, Managing Legal Editor, at jfield@oconnors.com.

CAVEAT

This book provides citations to important opinions that interpret the Texas Property Code, as well as timetables that outline the order and deadlines for various procedures and charts summarizing various topics. Because you may disagree with the choice of cases for the various codes and rules in this book or with the information presented in the timetables and charts, you should use this book only as a research guide. Read the codes, rules, and cases in full and make your own evaluation of them.

EDITORIAL & PRODUCTION STAFF

As always, the staff of O'Connor's worked hard to prepare this publication, both in its substance and in its layout. The people who worked on this edition of ***O'Connor's Texas Property Code Plus*** are listed below.

MANAGING LEGAL EDITOR
Jessica Younger Field, J.D.

CONTENT EDITOR
Douglas Rosenzweig, J.D.

LEGAL EDITORS
Blake Freeny, J.D.
Rachel L. Grier, J.D.
Jessica Ryan Luna, J.D.
Jamie Milne, J.D.
Courtney Drake Shaarawi, J.D.

LEGAL EDITORIAL ASSISTANTS
Eunjeong Jen Choi
Fabio Dworschak, J.D.
Leah Rush Easterby, J.D.
Erin Gage, J.D.
Victoria R. Guzman, J.D.
Erwin K. Kristel, J.D.
Brittany Lok
Patrick M. Miller, J.D.
Colin K. Morrison, J.D.
Alejandro Mota, J.D.
Amanda D. Pesonen, J.D.
Christian Eric Engelbrecht Ryholt

PRODUCTION MANAGER
Clare Jensen

PRODUCTION EDITOR
Emily J. Viehman

PRODUCTION STAFF
Sara Rhodes Bean
Evan Gabriel Bernard
Nicole E. Hammond
Rachel L. Jobe
Sara C. Rolater
Sarah M. Rutledge
Daniel Spence
Donna E. Vass
Annabelle M. Wilde

PROOFREADERS
Sara Rhodes Bean
Evan Gabriel Bernard
Clare Jensen
Rachel L. Jobe
Kathryn A. Ritcheske, J.D.
Sarah M. Rutledge
Emily J. Viehman
Annabelle M. Wilde

O'CONNOR'S
Houston, Texas

Master Table of Contents

PROPERTY CODE SECTIONS AFFECTED BY LEGISLATION

Abandoned personal property – designation of representative. Property Code §§72.1021 and 73.103 were enacted and §§74.101, 74.1011, and 74.103 were amended to allow owners of mutual funds and safe-deposit boxes to designate a representative for escheatment purposes in cases of abandoned personal property.

Commercial tenancies – termination of tenant's right of possession. Property Code §93.013 was enacted to provide a method for property owners to evict businesses that are engaging in human trafficking or prostitution.

Conveyances – equitable-interest disclosure. Property Code §5.086 was enacted to require a person selling an option or assigning an interest in real property to disclose that the person does not have legal title to the property.

Conveyances – seller's disclosure. Property Code §5.008(b) was amended to require a seller to provide information to the public and to purchasers of real property about the impact of the property's proximity to a military installation.

Eviction – access to residence. Property Code ch. 24A was amended to allow a court to issue a temporary ex parte writ authorizing entry and property retrieval to a residence if the current occupant poses a clear and present danger of family violence to an applicant or the applicant's dependent. Personal property that may be retrieved under a writ authorizing entry and retrieval was also expanded to include copies of electronic records containing legal or financial documents.

Eviction – nonlawyer representation. Property Code §24.011 was amended to authorize a nonlawyer to represent an owner in an appeal of an eviction suit for nonpayment of rent in a county or district court.

Liens – agricultural. Property Code ch. 70, subch. E, was amended to specify that an agricultural lien is a lien against the applicable crop and to change the value of the crop from the reasonable value to the market value on the date of transfer or delivery. The amendments also establish that an agricultural producer who delivers or transfers a crop has a lien against the crop for the market value of the crop on the date of delivery or transfer or, if there is a series of deliveries, on the date of the first delivery.

Liens – disposal of motor vehicle. Property Code §54.901 was enacted to allow a person authorized to dispose of property subject to a landlord's lien to dispose of motor vehicles in certain situations covered by the statute.

Liens – public sale. Property Code §51.002 was amended to move the statutorily required date for a public sale of real property to the first Wednesday of the month if the first Tuesday falls on January 1 or July 4.

Lis pendens – motion to expunge. Property Code §12.0071 was amended to clarify that the effect of a notice of lis pendens and any information derived from it also includes information that could have been derived from the notice. The amendment also states that an interest in the real property is authorized to be transferred or encumbered free of all matters asserted or disclosed in the notice.

Partition – Uniform Partition of Heirs' Property Act. Property Code ch. 23A was enacted to require a court, in an action to partition real property, to determine whether the property is the heirs' property and, if it is, to require partition of the property as provided for in the Act unless the cotenants otherwise agree.

Property management – investment funds. Property Code §142.004 was amended to allow a next friend or guardian ad litem to deposit the proceedings of a lawsuit in an Achieving a Better Life Experience account for the benefit of the minor or incapacitated person.

Public records – personal information. Property Code §11.008 was amended to allow a county clerk to omit or redact a judge's personal information from a deed or deed of trust on receipt of a written request from the judge.

Residential tenancies – emergency assistance. Property Code §92.015 was amended to expand the protection of a tenant's rights from being based on summoning police or emergency assistance for family violence to being based on the tenant's belief that an individual needs intervention or emergency assistance.

Self-service storage-facility liens – public sale. Property Code §§59.044 and 59.045 were amended to authorize the public sale of property seized from a self-service storage facility to be conducted through a publicly accessible website.

Trusts – appointment of agents. Property Code §113.018 was amended to allow a trustee to grant an agent powers over the property of the trust. The statute lists the duties and powers that a trustee may delegate to an agent.

Trusts – class gifts. Property Code §112.011 was enacted to clarify the time period for determining the persons who are class members for class gifts.

Trusts – definitions. Property Code §112.071 was amended to clarify the definitions of "full discretion," "limited discretion," and "presumptive remainder beneficiary."

Trusts – digital assets. Property Code §113.031 was enacted to allow trustees to access digital assets.

Trusts – exception to power of distribution. Property Code §112.085 was amended to allow an authorized trustee to exercise a power to distribute principal of the trust even if it materially impairs the right of a beneficiary.

Trusts – forfeiture clause. Property Code §112.038 was amended to establish that statutory provisions relating to forfeiture clauses in a trust are not intended to and do not repeal any law.

Trusts – notice. Property Code §112.074 was amended to establish that a trustee exercising a power of distribution need not give notice to the attorney general or certain beneficiaries if that requirement has been waived.

Trusts – reformation. Property Code §112.054 was amended to authorize a court to order that the terms of a trust be reformed on the petition of a trustee or beneficiary if reformation is necessary or appropriate under certain circumstances listed in the statute.

Unclaimed restitution payments – process. Property Code ch. 77 was enacted to establish a process for handling unclaimed restitution payments that are presumed abandoned. The chapter sets out provisions relating to the form, filing, and required contents of the property report as well as the claims process for unclaimed restitution payments.

Uniform Disclaimer of Property Interests Act – notice. Property Code §240.0081 was amended to establish that a trustee disclaiming an interest in property need not give notice to the attorney general or certain beneficiaries if that requirement has been waived.

SUMMARY OF LEGISLATION

PROPERTY CODE SECTIONS AFFECTED BY LEGISLATION

Legend: (A) Amended (E) Enacted

CODE SECTIONS AFFECTED BY 2015 LEGISLATION EFFECTIVE 2017

§	HEADING	ACTION
	Abandonment of Personal Property	
72.1021	Shares of mutual fund; designation of representative for notice	E
73.103	Designation of representative for notice	E
74.101	Property report	A
74.1011	Notice by property holder required	A
74.103	Retention of records	A

CODE SECTIONS AFFECTED BY 2017 LEGISLATION

§	HEADING	ACTION
	Conveyances	
5.008	Seller's disclosure of property condition	A
5.086	Equitable interest disclosure	E
5.202	Certain private transfer fee obligations void	A
	Public Records	
11.008	Personal information in real property records	A
12.0011	Instruments concerning property: original signature required for certain instruments	A
12.0071	Motion to expunge lis pendens	A
	UPHPA	
23A.001	Short title	E
23A.002	Definitions	E
23A.003	Applicability; relation to other law	E
23A.004	Service; notice by posting	E
23A.005	Commissioners	E
23A.006	Determination of value	E
23A.007	Cotenant buyout	E
23A.008	Partition alternatives	E
23A.009	Considerations for partition in kind	E

CODE SECTIONS AFFECTED BY 2017 LEGISLATION

§	HEADING	ACTION
	UPHPA (continued)	
23A.010	Open-market sale, sealed bids, or auction	E
23A.011	Report of open-market sale	E
23A.012	Uniformity of application & construction	E
23A.013	Relation to Electronic Signatures in Global & National Commerce Act	E
	Forcible Entry & Detainer	
24.011	Nonlawyer representation	A
	Access to Residence to Retrieve Personal Property	
24A.001	Definitions	A
24A.002	Writ authorizing entry & property retrieval; peace officer to accompany	A
24A.0021	Temporary ex parte writ authorizing entry & property retrieval	E
24A.003	Authorized entry procedures; duties of peace officer	A
24A.004	Immunity from liability	A
24A.005	Offense	A
24A.006	Hearing; review	A
	Use of Deceased Individual's Information	
26.005	Ownership after death of individual	A
	Provisions Applicable to Liens	
51.002	Sale of real property under contract lien	A
	Disposal of Motor Vehicles Subject to Lien	
54.901	Disposal of certain motor vehicles subject to lien	E
	Enforcement of Self-Service Storage Facility Liens	
59.044	Notice of sale	A
59.0445	Notice to owner & lienholders	A
59.045	Conduct of sale	A

PROPERTY CODE SECTIONS AFFECTED BY LEGISLATION

CODE SECTIONS AFFECTED BY 2017 LEGISLATION		
§	**HEADING**	**ACTION**
Manufactured Home Lien		
63.005	Conversion of lien from a personal property lien to a real property lien for the debt for the new improvements thereon	A
Possessory & Agricultural Liens		
70.006	Sale or disposal of motor vehicle, motorboat, vessel, or outboard motor	A
70.401	Definitions	A
70.402	Lien created	A
70.403	When lien attaches	A
70.404	Applicability of other law; effect on other law	A
70.4045	Perfection & priority of agricultural lien on crops	A
70.406	Effect of lien; recovery	A
70.407	Discharge of lien	A
70.410	Waiver of certain rights prohibited	A
Abandonment of Personal Property		
72.1021	Shares of mutual fund; designation of representative for notice	A
Abandoned Property Claims Process		
74.501	Claim filed with comptroller	A
Process for Unclaimed Restitution Payments		
77.001	Applicability	E
77.051	Property report	E
77.052	Notice by holder required	E
77.053	Signed statement	E
77.054	Confidentiality of property report	E
77.055	Exception to liability	E
77.101	Notice	E
77.102	Publication	E
77.151	Delivery of property to comptroller	E
77.152	Responsibility after delivery	E

CODE SECTIONS AFFECTED BY 2017 LEGISLATION		
§	**HEADING**	**ACTION**
Process for Unclaimed Restitution Payments (continued)		
77.201	Claim filed with comptroller	E
77.202	Claims not assignable	E
77.203	Claim filed with holder	E
77.204	Appeal	E
77.205	Limitation of liability	E
77.206	Fee for recovery	E
77.251	Unclaimed restitution payments	E
77.252	Use of money	E
77.253	Excess claims	E
77.301	Rules	E
77.302	Examination of records	E
77.303	Authority to take testimony & issue administrative subpoenas	E
77.304	Enforcement of subpoenas	E
77.305	Venue for pre-compliance review	E
77.306	Assistance in enforcement	E
77.307	Penalty	E
77.308	Waiver or abatement of penalty	E
Residential Tenancies		
92.015	Tenant's right to summon police or emergency assistance	A
92.025	Liability for leasing to person with criminal record	A
Commercial Tenancies		
93.013	Certain unlawful uses of premises; termination of tenant's right of possession	E
Texas Trust Code		
111.0035	Default & mandatory rules; conflict between terms & statute	A
112.011	Posthumous class gifts membership	E
112.035	Spendthrift trusts	A

PROPERTY CODE SECTIONS AFFECTED BY LEGISLATION

§	HEADING	ACTION
	Texas Trust Code (continued)	
112.038	Forfeiture clause	A
112.054	Judicial modification, reformation, or termination of trusts	A
112.058	Conversion of community trust to nonprofit corporation	A
112.071	Definitions	A
112.072	Distribution to second trust: trustee with full discretion	A
112.074	Notice required	A
112.078	Court-ordered distribution	A
112.085	Exceptions to power of distribution	A
113.018	Employment & appointment of agents	A
113.031	Digital assets	E
115.001	Jurisdiction	A
115.002	Venue	A

§	HEADING	ACTION
	Attorney General Participation & Charitable Trusts	
123.003	Notice	A
123.005	Breach of fiduciary duty: venue; jurisdiction	A
	Management of Property Recovered in Suit	
142.004	Investment of funds	A
	Institutional Funds	
163.011	Applicability of other parts of code	A
	Residential Property Owners Protection Act	
209.00592	Voting; quorum	A
	UDPIA	
240.002	Definitions	A
240.0081	Notice required by trustee disclaiming certain interests in property; effect of notice	A

PROPERTY CODE

TABLE OF CONTENTS

PROPERTY CODE

TABLE OF CONTENTS

TABLE OF CONTENTS

PROPERTY CODE

TABLE OF CONTENTS

TABLE OF CONTENTS

PROPERTY CODE

TABLE OF CONTENTS

TABLE OF CONTENTS

PROPERTY CODE

TABLE OF CONTENTS

TABLE OF CONTENTS

PROPERTY CODE

TABLE OF CONTENTS

TABLE OF CONTENTS

PROPERTY CODE

TABLE OF CONTENTS

TABLE OF CONTENTS

PROPERTY CODE

TABLE OF CONTENTS

TITLE 9. TRUSTS

Subtitle A. Provisions Generally Applicable to Trusts

Chapter 101. Provisions Generally Applicable to Trusts

Subtitle B. Texas Trust Code: Creation, Operation, & Termination of Trusts

Chapter 111. General Provisions

Chapter 112. Creation, Validity, Modification, & Termination of Trusts

Subchapter A. Creation

Subchapter B. Validity

Subchapter C. Revocation, Modification, & Termination of Trusts

Subchapter D. Distribution of Trust Principal in Further Trust

Chapter 113. Administration

Subchapter A. Powers of Trustee

TABLE OF CONTENTS

PROPERTY CODE

TABLE OF CONTENTS

TABLE OF CONTENTS

PROPERTY CODE

TABLE OF CONTENTS

TABLE OF CONTENTS

PROPERTY CODE

TABLE OF CONTENTS

TABLE OF CONTENTS

TITLE 1. GENERAL PROVISIONS

CHAPTER 1. GENERAL PROVISIONS

PROP §1.001. PURPOSE OF CODE

(a) This code is enacted as a part of the state's continuing statutory revision program begun by the Texas Legislative Council in 1963 as directed by the legislature in Chapter 448, Acts of the 58th Legislature, Regular Session, 1963 (Article 5429b-1, Vernon's Texas Civil Statutes). The program contemplates a topic-by-topic revision of the state's general and permanent statute law without substantive change.

(b) Consistent with the objectives of the statutory revision program, the purpose of this code is to make the law encompassed by this code more accessible and understandable by:

(1) rearranging the statutes into a more logical order;

(2) employing a format and numbering system designed to facilitate citation of the law and to accommodate future expansion of the law;

(3) eliminating repealed, duplicative, unconstitutional, expired, executed, and other ineffective provisions; and

(4) restating the law in modern American English to the greatest extent possible.

History of Prop. Code §1.001: Acts 1983, 68th Leg., ch. 576, §1, eff. Jan. 1, 1984.

PROP §1.002. CONSTRUCTION OF CODE

The Code Construction Act (Chapter 311, Government Code) applies to the construction of each provision in this code, except as otherwise expressly provided by this code.

History of Prop. Code §1.002: Acts 1983, 68th Leg., ch. 576, §1, eff. Jan. 1, 1984. Amended by Acts 1985, 69th Leg., ch. 479, §70, eff. Sept. 1, 1985.

PROP §1.003. INTERNAL REFERENCES

In this code:

(1) a reference to a title, chapter, or section without further identification is a reference to a title, chapter, or section of this code; and

(2) a reference to a subtitle, subchapter, subsection, subdivision, paragraph, or other numbered or lettered unit without further identification is a reference to a unit of the next larger unit of this code in which the reference appears.

History of Prop. Code §1.003: Acts 1983, 68th Leg., ch. 576, §1, eff. Jan. 1, 1984.

CHAPTER 2. NATURE OF PROPERTY

PROP §2.001. MANUFACTURED HOUSING

(a) Except as provided by Subsection (b), a manufactured home is personal property.

(b) A manufactured home is real property if:

(1) the statement of ownership and location for the home issued under Section 1201.207, Occupations Code, reflects that the owner has elected to treat the home as real property; and

(2) a certified copy of the statement of ownership and location has been filed in the real property records in the county in which the home is located.

(c) In this section, "consumer," "document of title," "first retail sale," "manufactured home," and "mobile home" have the meanings assigned by Chapter 1201, Occupations Code.

(d) to (h) Repealed by Acts 2003, 78th Leg., ch. 338, §52(2), eff. June 1, 2003.

(i) This section does not require a retailer or retailer's agent to obtain a license under Chapter 1101, Occupations Code.

History of Prop. Code §2.001: Acts 1995, 74th Leg., ch. 978, §15, eff. Sept. 1, 1995. Amended by Acts 2001, 77th Leg., ch. 899, §5 (eff. Sept. 1, 2001), ch. 1055, §5 (eff. Jan. 1, 2002); Acts 2003, 78th Leg., ch. 338, §§41-43, 52(2) (eff. June 1, 2003), ch. 1276, §14A.802 (eff. Sept. 1, 2003).

See also Occ. Code §1201.207.

ANNOTATIONS

W.H.V., Inc. v. Associates Hous. Fin., LLC, 43 S.W.3d 83, 93-94 (Tex.App.—Dallas 2001, pet. denied). "By its express provisions, [Prop. Code] §2.001 establishes the character of manufactured housing in this state; it does not purport to change, much less address, how liens against manufactured homes are perfected. [¶] We hold that a lienholder must comply with the Texas Manufactured Housing Standards Act [Occ. Code ch. 1201] to perfect a lien against a mobile home."

PROP §2.002. DRY FIRE HYDRANTS: AGREEMENT IS PERSONAL

(a) An agreement between an owner, lessee, or occupant of real property and a fire-fighting agency relat-

ing to the connection of a dry fire hydrant to a source of water on the property or the installation of a dry fire hydrant on the property may not bind a subsequent owner, lessee, or occupant of the real property.

(b) In this section:

(1) "Dry fire hydrant" means a fire hydrant that is connected to a stock tank, pond, or other similar source of water from which water is pumped in case of fire.

(2) "Fire-fighting agency" means any entity that provides fire-fighting services, including:

(A) a volunteer fire department; and

(B) a political subdivision of this state authorized to provide fire-fighting services.

History of Prop. Code §2.002: Acts 1997, 75th Leg., ch. 437, §2, eff. Sept. 1, 1997.

Chapters 3 & 4 reserved for expansion

TITLE 2. CONVEYANCES

CHAPTER 5. CONVEYANCES

SUBCHAPTER A. GENERAL PROVISIONS

PROP §5.001. FEE SIMPLE

(a) An estate in land that is conveyed or devised is a fee simple unless the estate is limited by express words or unless a lesser estate is conveyed or devised by construction or operation of law. Words previously necessary at common law to transfer a fee simple estate are not necessary.

(b) This section applies only to a conveyance occurring on or after February 5, 1840.

History of Prop. Code §5.001: Acts 1983, 68th Leg., ch. 576, §1, eff. Jan. 1, 1984. Source: TRCS art. 1291.

See also ***Real Estate Forms***, FORM 1:12.

ANNOTATIONS

Jackson v. Wildflower Prod. Co., 505 S.W.3d 80, 88 (Tex.App.—Amarillo 2016, pet. denied). "An absolute or 'fee simple' estate is one entitling the owner to the benefits of that estate during his life and descending to his heirs, devisees, and legal representatives on his death. One can own a fee simple estate in both legal and equitable property interests."

Union Pac. R.R. v. Ameriton Props. Inc., 448 S.W.3d 671, 684-85 (Tex.App.—Houston [1st Dist.] 2014, pet. denied). Grantor "reserved to herself timber rights in the land conveyed. If [grantee] obtained a mere easement, it would have had no right to do anything to the timber on the land, except as reasonably necessary for the full enjoyment of the easement, unless such rights were expressly granted in the deed. The deed's reservation of timber rights was thus unnecessary if the deed conveyed only an easement or right of way. We must assume the parties did not intend any provision of the deed to be meaningless. The reservation of timber rights implies that the deed conveyed an estate that would, but for the reservation, have included those rights. That is, the reservation implies that the deed conveyed a fee estate."

In re Estate of Friesenhahn, 185 S.W.3d 16, 20 (Tex.App.—San Antonio 2005, pet. denied). "[C]ourts have generally found contractual wills where the gift to the surviving spouse is limited to a life estate. [Decedent's] will uses the words, 'shall pass to and vest in my wife' and, 'hereby devise said real property to her' without any restrictions. … Based on the express language of the will, and the law's presumption that an estate in fee simple is devised unless expressly limited, we hold that [decedent's] will conveys the [real] property to [surviving spouse] as an absolute and unconditional gift in fee simple."

Deviney v. Nationsbank, 993 S.W.2d 443, 448 (Tex.App.—Waco 1999, pet. denied). "Estates may be limited by conditions precedent or subsequent. '[I]f a condition precedes or is incorporated into the [devise], [the vesting of the estate is contingent upon] a condition precedent; but if the condition is added after a vested gift is made, the [estate] is vested subject to divestment.' Texas law favors a construction allowing vesting at the earliest possible time. We will not construe an interest as contingent when it reasonably can be construed as vested." *See also* ***Russell v. City of Bryan***, 919 S.W.2d 698, 705-06 (Tex.App.—Houston [14th Dist.] 1996, writ denied); ***Smith v. Bynum***, 558 S.W.2d 99, 101 (Tex.App.—Tyler 1977, writ ref'd n.r.e.).

Zint v. Crofton, 563 S.W.2d 287, 290 (Tex.App.—Amarillo 1977, writ ref'd n.r.e.). The language—bequeath and devise all of the residue of my property and estate to my beloved son with personal instructions to him for my four grandchildren—"indicates a clear intent by [testator] to devise all of the residue property in fee simple absolute to her son … if he survives her. *At 291:* Had she intended to limit the estate to her son to less than a fee simple estate by creating an express trust, or even by attempting to express an oral trust outside the will, it would have been a very simple matter to so state explicitly. Instead, the language of the will specifically disavows an intent to create a trust." *Compare* ***Disabled Am. Veterans v. Mullin***, 773 S.W.2d 408, 409-11 (Tex.App.—San Antonio 1989, no writ) ("with full power to sell or dispose of same as to her may seem best" intends outright bequest of home in fee simple), *with* ***Taliaferro v. Mayer***, 681 S.W.2d 882, 884-85 (Tex.App.—Fort Worth 1984, no writ) ("shall have complete charge" of home and its contents construed as conveying life estate).

PROP §5.002. FAILING AS A CONVEYANCE

An instrument intended as a conveyance of real property or an interest in real property that, because of this chapter, fails as a conveyance in whole or in part is enforceable to the extent permitted by law as a contract to convey the property or interest.

History of Prop. Code §5.002: Acts 1983, 68th Leg., ch. 576, §1, eff. Jan. 1, 1984. Source: TRCS art. 1301.

ANNOTATIONS

Magee v. Young, 198 S.W.2d 883, 885 (Tex.1946). "[C]ourts, under proper facts, will treat an instrument in writing, having the form of a deed but which cannot be given effect as such, as if it were a contract to convey. This principle has become [§5.002]."

Smith v. Davis, No. 12-12-00169-CV (Tex.App.—Tyler 2013, no pet.) (memo op.; 6-5-13). "A purchaser takes title to real property solely through a deed. An instrument that does not operate as a present conveyance of title to real property is a contract to convey rather than a deed. A contract to convey real property contemplates further acts leading up to the actual conveyance of title in the deed. Before a deed is presented to convey title, it is the purchaser's obligation and responsibility to point out any defects in title, so that the seller may cure them. A purchaser cannot complain of defects in the title if those defects could and would have been cured at closing by the seller."

PROP §5.003. PARTIAL CONVEYANCE

(a) An alienation of real property that purports to transfer a greater right or estate in the property than the person making the alienation may lawfully transfer alienates only the right or estate that the person may convey.

(b) Neither the alienation by deed or will of an estate on which a remainder depends nor the union of the estate with an inheritance by purchase or descent affects the remainder.

History of Prop. Code §5.003: Acts 1983, 68th Leg., ch. 576, §1, eff. Jan. 1, 1984. Source: TRCS art. 1290.

See also ***Real Estate Forms***, FORM 1:12.

ANNOTATIONS

Easements

McKenna v. Caldwell, 387 S.W.3d 830, 834 (Tex. App.—Eastland 2012, no pet.). "An easement is a nonpossessory interest in land that authorizes its holder to use the property for a particular purpose. The holder or dominant estate may only make such use of the easement as is 'reasonably necessary[ ] to fairly enjoy the rights expressly granted,' lest the easement effectively become a possessory land interest. *At 836:* '[A]s a general rule, the questions of whether the use of an easement by the dominant estate is reasonably necessary and convenient and of whether the use is as little burdensome as possible on the servient estate are questions of fact for the trial court or jury.'" *See also* ***Greenwood v. Lee***, 420 S.W.3d 106, 111-12 (Tex.App.—Amarillo 2012, pet. denied).

Gleason v. Taub, 180 S.W.3d 711, 713-14 (Tex. App.—Fort Worth 2005, pet. denied). "When an easement is dedicated to the public, possession and control of the surface are surrendered to the public, but ownership is not surrendered. [¶] The land on which the trespass allegedly occurred is entirely within a public floodway, drainage, and utility easement. [D] contends that because a public easement is superior to the right of the individual who owns the fee, only the public ... can bring a suit for trespass on the public easement. *At 715:* [D] entered [Ps'] property and removed dirt, allegedly damaging their property. [Ps] have standing to sue because they own the property and their property rights have been aggrieved by the alleged wrong."

McWhorter v. City of Jacksonville, 694 S.W.2d 182, 184 (Tex.App.—Tyler 1985, no writ). "An easement appurtenant attaches to the land or dominant estate and passes with it. Therefore, an easement appurtenant would pass to a subsequent grantee with the passage of title of the dominant estate. Accordingly, [subsequent grantee] did not need to secure an additional deed to acquire the easement. However, since [subsequent grantee] had already conveyed Tract B to [another party], his attempt to convey the easement to the church would fail since he could not grant an easement over land which he no longer owned. Generally, where property has been conveyed by the owner, a subsequent conveyance transfers no title."

Quitclaim Deeds

Jackson v. Wildflower Prod. Co., 505 S.W.3d 80, 88-89 (Tex.App.—Amarillo 2016, pet. denied). "Both deeds and quitclaim deeds convey the grantor's interest in the property described to the grantee. What typically distinguishes a deed from a quitclaim deed is that the granting clause in a deed purports to grant and convey the described property, whereas the granting clause in a quitclaim deed only purports to grant and convey whatever 'right, title, and interest' the grantor has in that property at the time the instrument is executed and delivered. [¶] Effectively, a quitclaim deed is only a release and assignment of the grantor's claims to the property because it contains no covenant of seisen or representation of title in the grantor. By itself, a quit-

claim deed does not establish any title in the grantee but instead merely passes the interest of the grantor in the property described. [F]or a quitclaim deed to serve as a conveyance of title, the grantor must hold title to the property itself. [¶] Typically, a quitclaim deed is used when the interest of the grantor is unknown or uncertain and the grantor wants to limit or extinguish potential liability arising from any claim the grantee might assert against the grantor pertaining to the grantor's ownership interest." *See also* ***Enerlex, Inc. v. Amerada Hess, Inc.***, 302 S.W.3d 351, 354 (Tex.App.—Eastland 2009, no pet.).

Abraham v. Crow, 382 S.W.2d 756, 758 (Tex. App.—Amarillo 1964, no writ). "Where property has been conveyed by the owner, his subsequent conveyance conveys no title. *At 759:* [T]he deed from [grantor] to [D] clearly shows that [grantor] only attempted to transfer whatever interest he had in the property and that said deed was a quitclaim. When [grantor] transferred the property to [D], he had no title as he had transferred whatever title he had to [previous grantee] and could transfer no better title than he had."

PROP §5.004. CONVEYANCE BY AUTHORIZED OFFICER

(a) A conveyance of real property by an officer legally authorized to sell the property under a judgment of a court within the state passes absolute title to the property to the purchaser.

(b) This section does not affect the rights of a person who is not or who does not claim under a party to the conveyance or judgment.

History of Prop. Code §5.004: Acts 1983, 68th Leg., ch. 576, §1, eff. Jan. 1, 1984. Source: TRCS art. 1295.

ANNOTATIONS

Mosby v. Post Oak Bank, 401 S.W.3d 183, 185 (Tex.App.—Houston [14th Dist.] 2011, pet. denied). "An execution-sale purchaser asserted a trespass-to-try-title action, claiming that she held title to the property. A bank purchased the property at a subsequent foreclosure sale on the bank's deed-of-trust lien in the property. The bank disputed the purchaser's assertion of title and sought to remove what it asserts was a cloud on its title caused by the execution deed. Both parties filed motions for summary judgment. The trial court rendered judgment in favor of the bank and denied all relief sought by the execution-sale purchaser. *At 187:* [T]he Bank is asserting its rights as purchaser at the Foreclosure. The Bank is not a party to any conveyance in the Execution Deed, nor does the Bank claim under a party to any such conveyance. Likewise, the Bank is not a party to the [previous judgment], nor does the Bank claim under a party to this judgment. Therefore, we conclude that, under §5.004(b), §5.004(a) does not affect the Bank's rights. Accordingly, §5.004(a) does not give [execution-sale purchaser] title to the Property."

Williams v. National Credit Corp., 405 S.W.2d 858, 859 (Tex.App.—Fort Worth 1966, writ dism'd). "The 1959 judgment of foreclosure was one to which [P] was a party. It directed the divestiture of her title and a sheriff's sale. There was such a sale and it was under and by reason thereof that [D's] predecessor acquired title. However, there was no attempt to acquire possession until after the expiration of five years. When [there was, P] filed suit in the form of trespass to try title and plead the five year statute of limitation premised upon instruments in the chain of title up to the time of the prior foreclosure suit. Pursuant to [D's] motion therefor, summary judgment was rendered. The only question before this court is whether [P's] plea in reliance on the five year statute of limitation inhibited entry of the decree. In accord with the holding of the trial court we likewise hold that [P] may not rely thereon. Summary judgment was properly rendered."

PROP §5.005. ALIENS

An alien has the same real and personal property rights as a United States citizen.

History of Prop. Code §5.005: Acts 1983, 68th Leg., ch. 576, §1, eff. Jan. 1, 1984. Source: TRCS art. 166a.

ANNOTATIONS

HL Farm Corp. v. Self, 877 S.W.2d 288, 292 (Tex. 1994). "The classification created in [Tax Code] §23.56(3) is based upon ownership by a corporation that is required by federal law or rule to register its ownership or acquisition of land and whose majority interest is owned by a nonresident alien and/or a foreign government. *At 313:* A 'foreign corporation' owned by a nonresident alien may contribute to the preservation of open-space land as well as any Texas individual or legal entity. However, under §23.56(3), if [Virginia corporation owned by a nonresident alien] sold its property in Kaufman County to another Virginia corporation which was not owned by a nonresident alien, the new owner would qualify for the open-space land designation while [seller] would not. In fact, under §23.56(3), if the majority interest of a Texas corporation was owned by a

nonresident alien, it would not qualify for an open-space land designation. No rational basis exists for denying an open-space land designation to [seller], a 'foreign corporation' owned by a nonresident alien. We conclude that the classification drawn by §23.56(3) is not rationally related to the promotion and preservation of open-space land. Consequently, we hold that §23.56(3) … violates [Tex. Const. art. 1, §3]." *See also* ***Henderson Cty. Appr. Dist. v. HL Farm Corp.***, 956 S.W.2d 672, 675-76 (Tex.App.—Eastland 1997, no pet.) (follows rule in ***Self***).

PROP §5.006. ATTORNEY'S FEES IN BREACH OF RESTRICTIVE COVENANT ACTION

(a) In an action based on breach of a restrictive covenant pertaining to real property, the court shall allow to a prevailing party who asserted the action reasonable attorney's fees in addition to the party's costs and claim.

(b) To determine reasonable attorney's fees, the court shall consider:

(1) the time and labor required;

(2) the novelty and difficulty of the questions;

(3) the expertise, reputation, and ability of the attorney; and

(4) any other factor.

History of Prop. Code §5.006: Acts 1983, 68th Leg., ch. 576, §1, eff. Jan. 1, 1984. Source: TRCS art. 1293b.

See also Prop. Code chs. 201-211.

ANNOTATIONS

Anticipatory Breach

Davis v. Canyon Creek Estates Homeowners Ass'n, 350 S.W.3d 301, 311 (Tex.App.—San Antonio 2011, pet. denied). "[D] sought attorney's fees under §5.006 … contending [P] had engaged in anticipatory breach of the restrictive covenants, thereby entitling [D] to attorney's fees. *At 313:* A restrictive covenant is a contract subject to the same rules of construction and interpretation as any other contract. With regard to anticipatory breaches of a contract, it has long been the law in Texas that before there can be an anticipatory breach, there must be an unconditional declaration of an intention not to perform the contract. The repudiation must be a distinct, positive, unequivocal, and absolute refusal to perform the contract in the future. The party who is alleged to have committed an anticipatory breach must show a fixed intention to abandon, renounce, and refuse to perform the contract."

"Based On"

Radney v. Clear Lake Forest Cmty. Ass'n, 681 S.W.2d 191, 199 (Tex.App.—Houston [14th Dist.] 1984, writ ref'd n.r.e.). "The statute allows the recovery of attorney's fees in an action *based on* a restrictive covenant. We believe that the fraudulent conveyance action was in part based on and related to the breach of the restrictive covenant. … The fraudulent conveyance action would not have been necessary if [Ds] had not conveyed the property in order to avoid the suit to enforce the restriction. In this situation, the entire suit was based on the breach of the restriction."

Notice

Tees v. East Lake Woods Homeowners Ass'n, No. 12-04-00020-CV (Tex.App.—Tyler 2006, no pet.) (memo op.; 1-18-06). "[T]he Association did provide notice in a letter…. The letter was sent to [owners] by the Association's legal counsel. It informed [owners] that if they did not commence construction on a residence or commence demolition of the existing structure within 30 days of the date of the letter, the Association would commence litigation. It also stated that, if successful, the Association would be entitled to recover its attorney's fees and court costs. … Therefore, the trial court did not err in awarding attorney's fees to the Association."

Prevailing Party

Zuehl Land Dev., LLC v. Zuehl Airport Flying Cmty. Owners Ass'n, 510 S.W.3d 41, 48 (Tex.App.—Houston [1st Dist.] 2015, no pet.). The Texas Supreme Court has "held that a party prevails if the court awards it monetary or equitable relief—in other words, 'something that materially alters the parties' legal relationship.' *At 49:* This case presents the unusual circumstance of an order that purports to deny all causes of action and requests for injunctive relief but, at the same time and as a result of a settlement agreement between the parties, prohibits the very conduct alleged to constitute a breach…. [¶] Thus, the parties resolved by settlement what the landowners were seeking to achieve through trial. That the case resolved favorably for [the landowners] through a settlement and consent decree instead of a jury trial and a finding of breach does not prevent the landowners from having prevailed. *At 50:* Based on the agreed order, it cannot be said that the landowners 'received nothing of value of any kind' or 'left the courthouse empty-handed.' The agreed order 'materially alter[ed] the legal relationship between

the parties' by prohibiting the association from placing another fence in the objected-to area."

Norton v. Deer Creek Prop. Owners Ass'n, No. 03-09-00422-CV (Tex.App.—Austin 2010, no pet.) (memo op.; 7-22-10). "[U]nder federal law, a plaintiff 'prevails' when actual relief on the merits of his claim materially alters the legal relationship between the parties by modifying the defendant's behavior in a way that directly benefits the plaintiff. Based on this federal test, the [Texas Supreme Court] held that [P] could not be considered a 'prevailing party' because it recovered no damages, secured no declaratory or injunction relief, obtained no settlement in its favor, and received none of the relief sought in its petition. [Here, P] did not leave the courthouse empty-handed. Rather, [P] obtained the injunctive relief that it sought, materially altering the legal relationship between the parties. In ordering [D] not to return the gazebo to her back deck and to comply with all [Covenants, Conditions, and Restrictions] in the future, the court ordered [D] to modify her behavior in a way that directly benefited [P]. As a result, [P] qualifies as a 'prevailing party' under §5.006." (Internal quotes omitted.)

Anderson v. New Prop. Owners' Ass'n, 122 S.W.3d 378, 390 (Tex.App.—Texarkana 2003, pet. denied). "Only a party who successfully prosecutes a claim alleging breach of a restrictive covenant is entitled to recover attorney's fees." *See also* ***Pebble Beach Prop. Owners' Ass'n v. Sherer***, 2 S.W.3d 283, 291-92 (Tex. App.—San Antonio 1999, pet. denied); ***City of Houston v. Muse***, 788 S.W.2d 419, 424 (Tex.App.—Houston [1st Dist.] 1990, no writ).

Musgrave v. Brookhaven Lake Prop. Owners Ass'n, 990 S.W.2d 386, 403 (Tex.App.—Texarkana 1999, pet. denied). "The failure of the trial court to condition the award of fees on the success of the prevailing party does not require a reversal of the judgment, but requires a reformation of the judgment to reflect that appellate fees are only awarded in the event that the prevailing party at trial also prevails on appeal."

Briargrove Park Prop. Owners, Inc. v. Riner, 867 S.W.2d 58, 61 (Tex.App.—Texarkana 1993, writ denied). "Even if it can be said that by recovering a judgment *in rem* rather than a personal judgment, [petitioner] did not prevail on all phases of its claim, it did prevail on the essential claim that the restrictive covenants had been breached by nonpayment of the assessments. That is sufficient to make it a prevailing party within [§5.006]." *See also* ***Inwood N. Homeowners' Ass'n v. Meier***, 625 S.W.2d 742, 744 (Tex. App.—Houston [1st Dist.] 1981, no writ) (Legislature intended attorney fees to prevailing party to be mandatory).

Reasonableness

Gorman v. Countrywood Prop. Owners Ass'n, 1 S.W.3d 915, 918 (Tex.App.—Beaumont 1999, pet. denied). "Although the decision to award [properly pleaded and proved] attorney's fees to the prevailing party under §5.006 is not discretionary, the amount to be awarded must nonetheless be reasonable." *See also* ***Sloan v. Owners Ass'n of Westfield, Inc.***, 167 S.W.3d 401, 405 (Tex.App.—San Antonio 2005, no pet.) (fact that fees were based on contingent-fee agreement does not in itself make fees requested or awarded unreasonable); ***Mitchell v. Laflamme***, 60 S.W.3d 123, 130 (Tex. App.—Houston [14th Dist.] 2000, no pet.) (pleading incorrect or inapplicable theory or statute does not preclude award); ***Musgrave v. Brookhaven Lake Prop. Owners Ass'n***, 990 S.W.2d 386, 401 (Tex.App.—Texarkana 1999, pet. denied) (no requirement for expert testimony on reasonableness of attorney fees).

Beere v. Duren, 985 S.W.2d 243, 249 (Tex.App.—Beaumont 1999, pet. denied). "[T]he determination of the amount to be awarded as a reasonable attorney's fee is a question of fact to be determined by the trier of fact and the award, if any, must be supported by competent evidence. However, whether attorneys fees are authorized in a particular case is a question of law to be determined by the court." *See also* ***Fonmeadow Prop. Owners' Ass'n v. Franklin***, 817 S.W.2d 104, 105 (Tex. App.—Houston [1st Dist.] 1991, no writ) (trial-court determination reviewed under abuse-of-discretion standard); ***Knopf v. Standard Fixtures Co.***, 581 S.W.2d 504, 507 (Tex.App.—Dallas 1979, no writ) (factors considered in determining the reasonableness of attorney fees).

PROP §5.007. VENDOR & PURCHASER RISK ACT

(a) Any contract made in this state for the purchase and sale of real property shall be interpreted as including an agreement that the parties have the rights and duties prescribed by this section, unless the contract expressly provides otherwise.

(b) If, when neither the legal title nor the possession of the subject matter of the contract has been transferred, all or a material part of the property is de-

stroyed without fault of the purchaser or is taken by eminent domain, the vendor may not enforce the contract, and the purchaser is entitled to recover any portion of the contract price paid.

(c) If, when either the legal title or the possession of the subject matter of the contract has been transferred, all or any part of the property is destroyed without fault of the vendor or is taken by eminent domain, the purchaser is not relieved from the duty to pay the contract price, nor is the purchaser entitled to recover any portion of the price already paid.

(d) This section shall be interpreted and construed to accomplish its general purpose to make uniform the law of those states that enact the Uniform Vendor and Purchaser Risk Act.

(e) This section may be cited as the Uniform Vendor and Purchaser Risk Act.

History of Prop. Code §5.007: Acts 1989, 71st Leg., ch. 1002, §1, eff. Sept. 1, 1989.

See also *Real Estate Forms*, FORMS 1:2, 1:3, 1:5.

A PROP §5.008. SELLER'S DISCLOSURE OF PROPERTY CONDITION

The amended text in §5.008 is effective for transfers of property that occur on or after Sept. 1, 2017. Transfers in which the contract binding the purchaser to purchase the property is executed before Sept. 1, 2017, are governed by the former law in effect at that time.

(a) A seller of residential real property comprising not more than one dwelling unit located in this state shall give to the purchaser of the property a written notice as prescribed by this section or a written notice substantially similar to the notice prescribed by this section which contains, at a minimum, all of the items in the notice prescribed by this section.

(b) The notice must be executed and must, at a minimum, read substantially similar to the following:

SELLER'S DISCLOSURE NOTICE

CONCERNING THE PROPERTY AT

____

(Street Address and City)

THIS NOTICE IS A DISCLOSURE OF SELLER'S KNOWLEDGE OF THE CONDITION OF THE PROPERTY AS OF THE DATE SIGNED BY SELLER AND IS NOT A SUBSTITUTE FOR ANY INSPECTIONS OR WARRANTIES THE PURCHASER MAY WISH TO OBTAIN. IT IS NOT A WARRANTY OF ANY KIND BY SELLER OR SELLER'S AGENTS.

Seller ___ is ___ is not occupying the Property.

If unoccupied, how long since Seller has occupied the Property? __________

1. The Property has the items checked below:

Write Yes (Y), No (N), or Unknown (U).

___	Range	___	Oven	___	Microwave
___	Dishwasher	___	Trash Compactor	___	Disposal
___	Washer/Dryer Hookups	___	Window Screens	___	Rain Gutters
___	Security System	___	Fire Detection Equipment	___	Intercom System
		___	Smoke Detector		
		___	Smoke Detector – Hearing Impaired		
		___	Carbon Monoxide Alarm		
		___	Emergency Escape Ladder(s)		
___	TV Antenna	___	Cable TV Wiring	___	Satellite Dish
___	Ceiling Fan(s)	___	Attic Fan(s)	___	Exhaust Fan(s)
___	Central A/C	___	Central Heating	___	Wall/Window Air Conditioning
___	Plumbing System	___	Septic System	___	Public Sewer System
___	Patio/Decking	___	Outdoor Grill	___	Fences
___	Pool	___	Sauna	___	Spa
				___	Hot Tub
___	Pool Equipment	___	Pool Heater	___	Automatic Lawn Sprinkler System
___	Fireplace(s) & Chimney (Woodburning)			___	Fireplace(s) & Chimney (Mock)
___	Natural Gas Lines			___	Gas Fixtures

___ Liquid Propane Gas: ___ LP Community (Captive) ___ LP on Property

Garage: ___ Attached ___ Not Attached ___ Carport

Garage Door Opener(s): ___ Electronic ___ Control(s)

Water Heater: ___ Gas ___ Electric

Water Supply: ___ City ___ Well ___ MUD ___ Co-op

Roof Type: ____________ Age: ___ (approx)

Are you (Seller) aware of any of the above items that are not in working condition, that have known defects, or that are in need of repair?

_____ Yes _____ No _____ Unknown.

If yes, then describe. (Attach additional sheets if necessary):______________________

____

____

2. Does the property have working smoke detectors installed in accordance with the smoke detector requirements of Chapter 766, Health and Safety Code?*

_____ Yes _____ No _____ Unknown.

If the answer to the question above is no or unknown, explain. (Attach additional sheets if necessary): ______________________

____

____

* Chapter 766 of the Health and Safety Code requires one-family or two-family dwellings to have working smoke detectors installed in accordance with the requirements of the building code in effect in the area in which the dwelling is located, including performance, location, and power source requirements. If you do not know the building code requirements in effect in your area, you may check unknown above or contact your local building official for more information. A buyer may require a seller to install smoke detectors for the hearing impaired if: (1) the buyer or a member of the buyer's family who will reside in the dwelling is hearing impaired; (2) the buyer gives the seller written evidence of the hearing impairment from a licensed physician; and (3) within 10 days after the effective date, the buyer makes a written request for the seller to install smoke detectors for the hearing impaired and specifies the locations for installation. The parties may agree who will bear the cost of installing the smoke detectors and which brand of smoke detectors to install.

3. Are you (Seller) aware of any known defects/malfunctions in any of the following?

Write Yes (Y) if you are aware, write No (N) if you are not aware.

___ Interior Walls ___ Ceilings ___ Floors

___ Exterior Walls ___ Doors ___ Windows

___ Roof ___ Foundation/ Slab(s) ___ Basement

___ Walls/ Fences ___ Driveways ___ Sidewalks

___ Plumbing/ Sewers/ Septics ___ Electrical Systems ___ Lighting Fixtures

Other Structural Components (Describe): ______

____

____

If the answer to any of the above is yes, explain. (Attach additional sheets if necessary): __________

____

____

4. Are you (Seller) aware of any of the following conditions?

Write Yes (Y) if you are aware, write No (N) if you are not aware.

___ Active Termites (includes wood-destroying insects) ___ Previous Structural or Roof Repair

___ Termite or Wood Rot Damage Needing Repair ___ Hazardous or Toxic Waste

___ Previous Termite Damage ___ Asbestos Components

___ Previous Termite Treatment ___ Urea Formaldehyde Insulation

___ Previous Flooding ___ Radon Gas

___ Improper Drainage ___ Lead Based Paint

___ Water Penetration ___ Aluminum Wiring

___ Located in 100-Year Floodplain ___ Previous Fires

___ Present Flood Insurance Coverage ___ Unplatted Easements

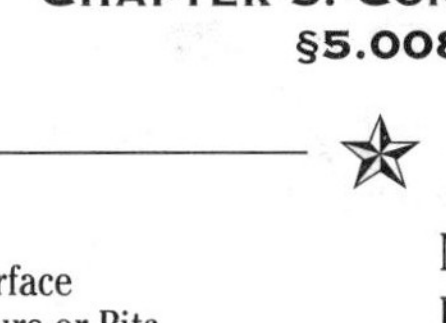

___ Landfill, Settling, Soil Movement, Fault Lines

___ Subsurface Structure or Pits

___ Single Blockable Main Drain in Pool/Hot Tub/Spa*

___ Previous Use of Premises for Manufacture of Methamphetamine

If the answer to any of the above is yes, explain. (Attach additional sheets if necessary): ______________

____

____

* A single blockable main drain may cause a suction entrapment hazard for an individual.

5. Are you (Seller) aware of any item, equipment, or system in or on the property that is in need of repair? ___ Yes (if you are aware) ___ No (if you are not aware). If yes, explain (attach additional sheets as necessary). ______________________________

6. Are you (Seller) aware of any of the following? Write Yes (Y) if you are aware, write No (N) if you are not aware.

___ Room additions, structural modifications, or other alterations or repairs made without necessary permits or not in compliance with building codes in effect at that time.

___ Homeowners' Association or maintenance fees or assessments.

___ Any "common area" (facilities such as pools, tennis courts, walkways, or other areas) co-owned in undivided interest with others.

___ Any notices of violations of deed restrictions or governmental ordinances affecting the condition or use of the Property.

___ Any lawsuits directly or indirectly affecting the Property.

___ Any condition on the Property which materially affects the physical health or safety of an individual.

___ Any rainwater harvesting system located on the property that is larger than 500 gallons and that uses a public water supply as an auxiliary water source.

___ Any portion of the property that is located in a groundwater conservation district or a subsidence district.

If the answer to any of the above is yes, explain. (Attach additional sheets if necessary): ______________

____

____

7. If the property is located in a coastal area that is seaward of the Gulf Intracoastal Waterway or within 1,000 feet of the mean high tide bordering the Gulf of Mexico, the property may be subject to the Open Beaches Act or the Dune Protection Act (Chapter 61 or 63, Natural Resources Code, respectively) and a beachfront construction certificate or dune protection permit may be required for repairs or improvements. Contact the local government with ordinance authority over construction adjacent to public beaches for more information.

8. This property may be located near a military installation and may be affected by high noise or air installation compatible use zones or other operations. Information relating to high noise and compatible use zones is available in the most recent Air Installation Compatible Use Zone Study or Joint Land Use Study prepared for a military installation and may be accessed on the Internet website of the military installation and of the county and any municipality in which the military installation is located.

__________ ______________________

Date Signature of Seller

The undersigned purchaser hereby acknowledges receipt of the foregoing notice.

__________ ______________________

Date Signature of Purchaser

(c) A seller or seller's agent shall have no duty to make a disclosure or release information related to whether a death by natural causes, suicide, or accident unrelated to the condition of the property occurred on the property or whether a previous occupant had, may have had, has, or may have AIDS, HIV related illnesses, or HIV infection.

(d) The notice shall be completed to the best of seller's belief and knowledge as of the date the notice is completed and signed by the seller. If the information required by the notice is unknown to the seller, the seller shall indicate that fact on the notice, and by that act is in compliance with this section.

(e) This section does not apply to a transfer:

(1) pursuant to a court order or foreclosure sale;

(2) by a trustee in bankruptcy;

(3) to a mortgagee by a mortgagor or successor in interest, or to a beneficiary of a deed of trust by a trustor or successor in interest;

(4) by a mortgagee or a beneficiary under a deed of trust who has acquired the real property at a sale conducted pursuant to a power of sale under a deed of trust or a sale pursuant to a court ordered foreclosure or has acquired the real property by a deed in lieu of foreclosure;

(5) by a fiduciary in the course of the administration of a decedent's estate, guardianship, conservatorship, or trust;

(6) from one co-owner to one or more other co-owners;

(7) made to a spouse or to a person or persons in the lineal line of consanguinity of one or more of the transferors;

(8) between spouses resulting from a decree of dissolution of marriage or a decree of legal separation or from a property settlement agreement incidental to such a decree;

(9) to or from any governmental entity;

(10) of a new residence of not more than one dwelling unit which has not previously been occupied for residential purposes; or

(11) of real property where the value of any dwelling does not exceed five percent of the value of the property.

(f) The notice shall be delivered by the seller to the purchaser on or before the effective date of an executory contract binding the purchaser to purchase the property. If a contract is entered without the seller providing the notice required by this section, the purchaser may terminate the contract for any reason within seven days after receiving the notice.

(g) In this section:

(1) "Blockable main drain" means a main drain of any size and shape that a human body can sufficiently block to create a suction entrapment hazard.

(2) "Main drain" means a submerged suction outlet typically located at the bottom of a swimming pool or spa to conduct water to a recirculating pump.

History of Prop. Code §5.008: Acts 1993, 73rd Leg., ch. 356, §1, eff. Jan. 1, 1994. Amended by Acts 2005, 79th Leg., ch. 728, §17.001, eff. Sept. 1, 2005; Acts 2007, 80th Leg., ch. 448, §1 (eff. Jan. 1, 2008), ch. 1051, §11 (eff. Sept. 1, 2007), ch. 1256, §22 (eff. Sept. 1, 2007); Acts 2009, 81st Leg., ch. 87, §20.001 (eff. Sept. 1, 2009), ch. 1178, §1 (eff. Jan. 1, 2010); Acts 2011, 82nd Leg., ch. 578, §1 (eff. Sept. 1, 2011), ch. 621, §1 (eff. Sept. 1, 2011), ch. 1131, §5 (eff. Sept. 1, 2011); Acts 2013, 83rd Leg., ch. 695, §6, eff. Sept. 1, 2013; Acts 2015, 84th Leg., ch. 524, §1, eff. Jan. 1, 2016; H.B. 890, §2, 85th Leg., eff. Sept. 1, 2017.

See also B&CC §27.01; Occ. Code §1101.155; ***Real Estate Forms***, FORM 1:5.

ANNOTATIONS

Generally

Myre v. Meletio, 307 S.W.3d 839, 843-44 (Tex. App.—Dallas 2010, pet. denied). "In the context of a real estate transaction, a seller is under a duty to disclose material facts that would not be discoverable by the exercise of ordinary care and diligence by the purchaser, or that a reasonable investigation and inquiry would not uncover. But a seller has no duty to disclose facts he does not know. Similarly, a seller is not liable for failing to disclose what he only should have known." *See also* ***Sherman v. Elkowitz***, 130 S.W.3d 316, 321 (Tex.App.—Houston [14th Dist.] 2004, no pet.) (broker has duty to come forward only when disclosures are believed false or inaccurate; broker liable only if statement in notice is shown untrue).

Bynum v. Prudential Residential Servs., 129 S.W.3d 781, 795 (Tex.App.—Houston [1st Dist.] 2004, pet. denied). "[B]ecause §5.008 requires only that the form be completed to the best of the seller's belief at the time the notice is completed and signed, [P's] argument that [D] had an obligation under §5.008 to provide continuing updates as to matters within the form is without merit."

"As Is" Contract

Prudential Ins. v. Jefferson Assocs., 896 S.W.2d 156, 161-62 (Tex.1995). An "as is" agreement will not bind a buyer who is induced to enter the agreement because of a fraudulent representation. *See also* ***Ritchey v. Pinnell***, 357 S.W.3d 410, 412-13 (Tex.App.—Texarkana 2012, no pet.) (buyer was clearly and explicitly relying on seller's disclosure notice, while buyer in ***Prudential*** acknowledged purchasing property while relying only on its examination of property).

Williams v. Dardenne, 345 S.W.3d 118, 124 (Tex. App.—Houston [1st Dist.] 2011, pet. denied). "An 'as is' clause that is induced by specific misrepresentations about the condition of property will not shield the seller from liability. *At 125-26:* The elements of fraud are that a material representation was made, the representation was false, the speaker knew the statement was false when made, the statement was made to induce reliance, it did induce reliance, the reliance was justifiable, and the relying party suffered injury as a result. [¶] Although the courts of appeals have articulated different tests for when a buyer's independent inspection will defeat causation and reliance as a matter

of law, the courts have consistently applied these tests such that a buyer's independent inspection precludes a showing of causation and reliance if it reveals to the buyer the same information that the seller allegedly failed to disclose. This is consistent with the principle that a party who has actual knowledge of specific facts cannot have relied on a misrepresentation of the same facts. [¶] The issue, then, is whether [Ps] presented any evidence of reliance to support their claim for fraudulent inducement. In the context of fraudulent inducement, this requires evidence that the claimant would not have entered into the contract but for the alleged misrepresentation or fraudulent non-disclosure."

Larsen v. Carlene Langford & Assocs., 41 S.W.3d 245, 251 (Tex.App.—Waco 2001, pet. denied). "The parties used a standard form earnest money contract for the transaction. The form was prepared by the Texas Real Estate Commission (TREC). The parties used TREC form no. 20-2. It was completed by [Ps]. In the earnest money contract, [Ps] contractually bound themselves to accept the house 'in its present condition.' [Buyer placed an 'X' by] the following section: ... '(1) Buyer accepts the Property in its present condition. Buyer shall pay for any repairs designated by a lender.' [¶] We have previously held this to be an agreement to purchase the property 'as is.'" *See also* ***McFarland v. Associated Brokers***, 977 S.W.2d 427, 431 (Tex.App.—Corpus Christi 1998, pet. granted, judgm't vacated w.r.m.) (P never expressly agreed to rely on inspection through "as is" clause, so inspector's failure to discover extent of defect did not preclude D's liability).

Structural Repair

Robertson v. Odom, 296 S.W.3d 151, 156 (Tex. App.—Houston [14th Dist.] 2009, no pet.). "The disputed portion of the Seller's Disclosure Notice derives from ... §5.008(b), which requires a seller to disclose 'Previous Structural or Roof Repair' of which he is aware. *At 157:* [W]e ... interpret the term 'structural repair,' as used in §5.008(b), as referring to repairs performed on the load-bearing portions of a residence."

PROP §5.009. DUTIES OF LIFE TENANT

(a) Subject to Subsection (b), if the life tenant of a legal life estate is given the power to sell and reinvest any life tenancy property, the life tenant is subject, with respect to the sale and investment of the property, to all of the fiduciary duties of a trustee imposed by the Texas Trust Code (Subtitle B, Title 9, Property Code) or the common law of this state.

(b) A life tenant may retain, as life tenancy property, any real property originally conveyed to the life tenant without being subject to the fiduciary duties of a trustee; however, the life tenant is subject to the common law duties of a life tenant.

History of Prop. Code §5.009: Acts 1993, 73rd Leg., ch. 846, §34, eff. Sept. 1, 1993. Renumbered from §5.008 by Acts 1995, 74th Leg., ch. 76, §17.01(42), eff. Sept. 1, 1995.

See also CPRC §§16.004, 37.005; Est. Code §401.004(e).

ANNOTATIONS

Montgomery v. Browder, 930 S.W.2d 772, 778 (Tex.App.—Amarillo 1996, writ denied). "A life tenant cannot alienate any greater interest in property than an interest that ceases with her life, even if the tenant expressly seeks to do so."

PROP §5.010. NOTICE OF ADDITIONAL TAX LIABILITY

(a) A person who is the owner of an interest in vacant land and who contracts for the transfer of that interest shall include in the contract the following boldfaced notice:

NOTICE REGARDING POSSIBLE LIABILITY FOR ADDITIONAL TAXES

If for the current ad valorem tax year the taxable value of the land that is the subject of this contract is determined by a special appraisal method that allows for appraisal of the land at less than its market value, the person to whom the land is transferred may not be allowed to qualify the land for that special appraisal in a subsequent tax year and the land may then be appraised at its full market value. In addition, the transfer of the land or a subsequent change in the use of the land may result in the imposition of an additional tax plus interest as a penalty for the transfer or the change in the use of the land. The taxable value of the land and the applicable method of appraisal for the current tax year is public information and may be obtained from the tax appraisal district established for the county in which the land is located.

(b) This section does not apply to a contract for a transfer:

(1) under a court order or foreclosure sale;

(2) by a trustee in bankruptcy;

(3) to a mortgagee by a mortgagor or successor in interest or to a beneficiary of a deed of trust by a trustor or successor in interest;

(4) by a mortgagee or a beneficiary under a deed of trust who has acquired the land at a sale conducted under a power of sale under a deed of trust or a sale under a court-ordered foreclosure or has acquired the land by a deed in lieu of foreclosure;

(5) by a fiduciary in the course of the administration of a decedent's estate, guardianship, conservatorship, or trust;

(6) of only a mineral interest, leasehold interest, or security interest; or

(7) to or from a governmental entity.

(c) The notice described by Subsection (a) is not required to be included in a contract for transfer of an interest in land if every transferee under the contract is:

(1) a person who is a co-owner with an owner described by Subsection (a) of an undivided interest in the land; or

(2) a spouse or a person in the lineal line of consanguinity of an owner described by Subsection (a).

(d) The notice described by Subsection (a) is not required to be given if in a separate paragraph of the contract the contract expressly provides for the payment of any additional ad valorem taxes and interest that become due as a penalty because of:

(1) the transfer of the land; or

(2) a subsequent change in the use of the land.

(e) If the owner fails to include in the contract the notice described by Subsection (a), the person to whom the land is transferred is entitled to recover from that owner an amount equal to the amount of any additional taxes and interest that the person is required to pay as a penalty because of:

(1) the transfer of the land; or

(2) a subsequent change in the use of the land that occurs before the fifth anniversary of the date of the transfer.

History of Prop. Code §5.010: Acts 1997, 75th Leg., ch. 174, §1, eff. Jan. 1, 1998.

See also *Real Estate Forms*, FORMS 1:2, 1:3, 1:5.

PROP §5.011. SELLER'S DISCLOSURE REGARDING POTENTIAL ANNEXATION

(a) A person who sells an interest in real property in this state shall give to the purchaser of the property a written notice that reads substantially similar to the following:

NOTICE REGARDING POSSIBLE ANNEXATION

If the property that is the subject of this contract is located outside the limits of a municipality, the property may now or later be included in the extraterritorial jurisdiction of a municipality and may now or later be subject to annexation by the municipality. Each municipality maintains a map that depicts its boundaries and extraterritorial jurisdiction. To determine if the property is located within a municipality's extraterritorial jurisdiction or is likely to be located within a municipality's extraterritorial jurisdiction, contact all municipalities located in the general proximity of the property for further information.

(b) The seller shall deliver the notice to the purchaser before the date the executory contract binds the purchaser to purchase the property. The notice may be given separately, as part of the contract during negotiations, or as part of any other notice the seller delivers to the purchaser.

(c) This section does not apply to a transfer:

(1) under a court order or foreclosure sale;

(2) by a trustee in bankruptcy;

(3) to a mortgagee by a mortgagor or successor in interest or to a beneficiary of a deed of trust by a trustor or successor in interest;

(4) by a mortgagee or a beneficiary under a deed of trust who has acquired the land at a sale conducted under a power of sale under a deed of trust or a sale under a court-ordered foreclosure or has acquired the land by a deed in lieu of foreclosure;

(5) by a fiduciary in the course of the administration of a decedent's estate, guardianship, conservatorship, or trust;

(6) from one co-owner to another co-owner of an undivided interest in the real property;

(7) to a spouse or a person in the lineal line of consanguinity of the seller;

(8) to or from a governmental entity;

(9) of only a mineral interest, leasehold interest, or security interest; or

(10) of real property that is located wholly within a municipality's corporate boundaries.

(d) If the notice is delivered as provided by this section, the seller has no duty to provide additional information regarding the possible annexation of the property by a municipality.

(e) If an executory contract is entered into without the seller providing the notice required by this section, the purchaser may terminate the contract for any reason within the earlier of:

(1) seven days after the date the purchaser receives the notice; or

(2) the date the transfer occurs.

History of Prop. Code §5.011: Acts 1999, 76th Leg., ch. 529, §1, eff. Jan. 1, 2000.

See also *Real Estate Forms*, FORMS 1:2, 1:3, 1:5, 10:8.

PROP §5.012. NOTICE OF OBLIGATIONS RELATED TO MEMBERSHIP IN PROPERTY OWNERS' ASSOCIATION

(a) A seller of residential real property that is subject to membership in a property owners' association and that comprises not more than one dwelling unit located in this state shall give to the purchaser of the property a written notice that reads substantially similar to the following:

NOTICE OF MEMBERSHIP IN PROPERTY OWNERS' ASSOCIATION CONCERNING THE PROPERTY AT (street address) (name of residential community)

As a purchaser of property in the residential community in which this property is located, you are obligated to be a member of a property owners' association. Restrictive covenants governing the use and occupancy of the property and all dedicatory instruments governing the establishment, maintenance, or operation of this residential community have been or will be recorded in the Real Property Records of the county in which the property is located. Copies of the restrictive covenants and dedicatory instruments may be obtained from the county clerk.

You are obligated to pay assessments to the property owners' association. The amount of the assessments is subject to change. Your failure to pay the assessments could result in enforcement of the association's lien on and the foreclosure of your property.

Section 207.003, Property Code, entitles an owner to receive copies of any document that governs the establishment, maintenance, or operation of a subdivision, including, but not limited to, restrictions, bylaws, rules and regulations, and a resale certificate from a property owners' association. A resale certificate contains information including, but not limited to, statements specifying the amount and frequency of regular assessments and the style and cause number of lawsuits to which the property owners' association is a party, other than lawsuits relating to unpaid ad valorem taxes of an individual member of the association. These documents must be made available to you by the property owners' association or the association's agent on your request.

Date: ________ ________________

Signature of Purchaser

(a-1) The second paragraph of the notice prescribed by Subsection (a) must be in bold print and underlined.

(b) The seller shall deliver the notice to the purchaser before the date the executory contract binds the purchaser to purchase the property. The notice may be given separately, as part of the contract during negotiations, or as part of any other notice the seller delivers to the purchaser. If the notice is included as part of the executory contract or another notice, the title of the notice prescribed by this section, the references to the street address and date in the notice, and the purchaser's signature on the notice may be omitted.

(c) This section does not apply to a transfer:

(1) under a court order or foreclosure sale;

(2) by a trustee in bankruptcy;

(3) to a mortgagee by a mortgagor or successor in interest or to a beneficiary of a deed of trust by a trustor or successor in interest;

(4) by a mortgagee or a beneficiary under a deed of trust who has acquired the land at a sale conducted under a power of sale under a deed of trust or a sale under a court-ordered foreclosure or has acquired the land by a deed in lieu of foreclosure;

(5) by a fiduciary in the course of the administration of a decedent's estate, guardianship, conservatorship, or trust;

(6) from one co-owner to another co-owner of an undivided interest in the real property;

(7) to a spouse or a person in the lineal line of consanguinity of the seller;

(8) to or from a governmental entity;

(9) of only a mineral interest, leasehold interest, or security interest; or

(10) of a real property interest in a condominium.

(d) If an executory contract is entered into without the seller providing the notice required by this section, the purchaser may terminate the contract for any reason within the earlier of:

(1) seven days after the date the purchaser receives the notice; or

(2) the date the transfer occurs as provided by the executory contract.

(e) The purchaser's right to terminate the executory contract under Subsection (d) is the purchaser's exclusive remedy for the seller's failure to provide the notice required by this section.

(f) On the purchaser's request for a resale certificate from the property owners' association or the association's agent, the association or its agent shall promptly deliver a copy of the most recent resale certificate issued for the property under Chapter 207 so long as the resale certificate was prepared not earlier than the 60th day before the date the resale certificate is delivered to the purchaser and reflects any special assessments approved before and due after the resale certificate is delivered. If a resale certificate that meets the requirements of this subsection has not been issued for the property, the seller shall request the association or its agent to issue a resale certificate under Chapter 207, and the association or its agent shall promptly prepare and deliver a copy of the resale certificate to the purchaser.

(g) The purchaser shall pay the fee to the property owners' association or its agent for issuing the resale certificate unless otherwise agreed by the purchaser and seller of the property. The property owners' association may require payment before beginning the process of providing a resale certificate requested under Chapter 207 but may not process a payment for a resale certificate until the certificate is available for delivery. The association may not charge a fee if the certificate is not provided in the time prescribed by Section 207.003(a).

History of Prop. Code §5.012: Acts 1999, 76th Leg., ch. 1420, §1, eff. Jan. 1, 2000. Amended by Acts 2011, 82nd Leg., ch. 1142, §1, eff. Jan. 1, 2012.

See also Prop. Code ch. 207; *Real Estate Forms*, FORMS 1:5, 6:16-6:18.

PROP §5.013. SELLER'S DISCLOSURE OF LOCATION OF CONDITIONS UNDER SURFACE OF UNIMPROVED REAL PROPERTY

(a) A seller of unimproved real property to be used for residential purposes shall provide to the purchaser of the property a written notice disclosing the location of a transportation pipeline, including a pipeline for the transportation of natural gas, natural gas liquids, synthetic gas, liquefied petroleum gas, petroleum or a petroleum product, or a hazardous substance.

(b) The notice must state the information to the best of the seller's belief and knowledge as of the date the notice is completed and signed by the seller. If the information required to be disclosed is not known to the seller, the seller shall indicate that fact in the notice.

(c) The notice must be delivered by the seller on or before the effective date of an executory contract binding the purchaser to purchase the property. If a contract is entered without the seller providing the notice as required by this section, the purchaser may terminate the contract for any reason not later than the seventh day after the effective date of the contract.

(d) This section applies to any seller of unimproved real property, including a seller who is the developer of the property and who sells the property to others for resale.

(e) In this section, "hazardous substance" and "hazardous waste" have the meanings assigned by Section 361.003, Health and Safety Code.

(f) A seller is not required to give the notice if:

(1) the seller is obligated under an earnest money contract to furnish a title insurance commitment to the buyer prior to closing; and

(2) the buyer is entitled to terminate the contract if the buyer's objections to title as permitted by the contract are not cured by the seller prior to closing.

History of Prop. Code §5.013: Acts 1997, 75th Leg., ch. 1239, §1, eff. Sept. 1, 1997. Renumbered from §5.010 by Acts 2001, 77th Leg., ch. 1420, §21.001(95), eff. Sept. 1, 2001.

See also *Real Estate Forms*, FORMS 1:3, 1:5, 10:11.

PROP §5.014. NOTICE OF OBLIGATIONS RELATED TO PUBLIC IMPROVEMENT DISTRICT

(a) A seller of residential real property that is located in a public improvement district established under Subchapter A, Chapter 372, Local Government Code, or Chapter 382, Local Government Code, and that consists of not more than one dwelling unit located in this state shall give to the purchaser of the property a written notice that reads substantially similar to the following:

NOTICE OF OBLIGATION TO PAY PUBLIC IMPROVEMENT DISTRICT ASSESSMENT TO (municipality or county levying assessment) CONCERNING THE PROPERTY AT (street address)

As a purchaser of this parcel of real property you are obligated to pay an assessment to a municipality or

county for an improvement project undertaken by a public improvement district under Subchapter A, Chapter 372, Local Government Code, or Chapter 382, Local Government Code. The assessment may be due annually or in periodic installments. More information concerning the amount of the assessment and the due dates of that assessment may be obtained from the municipality or county levying the assessment.

The amount of the assessments is subject to change. Your failure to pay the assessments could result in a lien on and the foreclosure of your property.

Date: ________ ____________________
Signature of Purchaser

(b) The seller shall deliver the notice required under Subsection (a) to the purchaser before the effective date of an executory contract binding the purchaser to purchase the property. The notice may be given separately, as part of the contract during negotiations, or as part of any other notice the seller delivers to the purchaser. If the notice is included as part of the executory contract or another notice, the title of the notice prescribed by this section, the references to the street address and date in the notice, and the purchaser's signature on the notice may be omitted.

(c) This section does not apply to a transfer:

(1) under a court order or foreclosure sale;

(2) by a trustee in bankruptcy;

(3) to a mortgagee by a mortgagor or successor in interest or to a beneficiary of a deed of trust by a trustor or successor in interest;

(4) by a mortgagee or a beneficiary under a deed of trust who has acquired the land at a sale conducted under a power of sale under a deed of trust or a sale under a court-ordered foreclosure or has acquired the land by a deed in lieu of foreclosure;

(5) by a fiduciary in the course of the administration of a decedent's estate, guardianship, conservatorship, or trust;

(6) from one co-owner to another co-owner of an undivided interest in the real property;

(7) to a spouse or a person in the lineal line of consanguinity of the seller;

(8) to or from a governmental entity;

(9) of only a mineral interest, leasehold interest, or security interest; or

(10) of a real property interest in a condominium.

(d) If an executory contract is entered into without the seller providing the notice required by this section, the purchaser may terminate the contract for any reason not later than the earlier of:

(1) the seventh day after the date the purchaser receives the notice; or

(2) the date the transfer occurs as provided by the executory contract.

(e) The purchaser's right to terminate the executory contract under Subsection (d) is the purchaser's exclusive remedy for the seller's failure to provide the notice required by this section.

History of Prop. Code §5.014: Acts 2005, 79th Leg., ch. 1085, §1, eff. Jan. 1, 2006. Amended by Acts 2009, 81st Leg., ch. 87, §20.002, eff. Sept. 1, 2009.

See also Loc. Gov't Code chs. 372, 382; ***Real Estate Forms***, FORM 1:5.

PROP §5.015. PROHIBITED FEES

A person who has a right of first refusal in real property that is a condominium subject to Chapter 81 or Chapter 82 may not charge a fee for declining to exercise that right, such as a fee for providing written evidence of the declination.

History of Prop. Code §5.015: Acts 2005, 79th Leg., ch. 825, §14, eff. Sept. 1, 2005. Renumbered from §5.014 by Acts 2007, 80th Leg., ch. 921, §17.001(63), eff. Sept. 1, 2007.

See also ***Real Estate Forms***, FORM 1:5.

PROP §5.016. CONVEYANCE OF RESIDENTIAL PROPERTY ENCUMBERED BY LIEN

(a) A person may not convey an interest in or enter into a contract to convey an interest in residential real property that will be encumbered by a recorded lien at the time the interest is conveyed unless, on or before the seventh day before the earlier of the effective date of the conveyance or the execution of an executory contract binding the purchaser to purchase the property, an option contract, or other contract, the person provides the purchaser and each lienholder a separate written disclosure statement in at least 12-point type that:

(1) identifies the property and includes the name, address, and phone number of each lienholder;

(2) states the amount of the debt that is secured by each lien;

(3) specifies the terms of any contract or law under which the debt that is secured by the lien was incurred, including, as applicable:

(A) the rate of interest;

(B) the periodic installments required to be paid; and

(C) the account number;

(4) indicates whether the lienholder has consented to the transfer of the property to the purchaser;

(5) specifies the details of any insurance policy relating to the property, including:

(A) the name of the insurer and insured;

(B) the amount for which the property is insured; and

(C) the property that is insured;

(6) states the amount of any property taxes that are due on the property; and

(7) includes a statement at the top of the disclosure in a form substantially similar to the following:

WARNING: ONE OR MORE RECORDED LIENS HAVE BEEN FILED THAT MAKE A CLAIM AGAINST THIS PROPERTY AS LISTED BELOW. IF A LIEN IS NOT RELEASED AND THE PROPERTY IS CONVEYED WITHOUT THE CONSENT OF THE LIENHOLDER, IT IS POSSIBLE THE LIENHOLDER COULD DEMAND FULL PAYMENT OF THE OUTSTANDING BALANCE OF THE LIEN IMMEDIATELY. YOU MAY WISH TO CONTACT EACH LIENHOLDER FOR FURTHER INFORMATION AND DISCUSS THIS MATTER WITH AN ATTORNEY.

(b) A violation of this section does not invalidate a conveyance. Except as provided by Subsections (c) and (d), if a contract is entered into without the seller providing the notice required by this section, the purchaser may terminate the contract for any reason on or before the seventh day after the date the purchaser receives the notice in addition to other remedies provided by this section or other law.

(c) This section does not apply to a transfer:

(1) under a court order or foreclosure sale;

(2) by a trustee in bankruptcy;

(3) to a mortgagee by a mortgagor or successor in interest or to a beneficiary of a deed of trust by a trustor or successor in interest;

(4) by a mortgagee or a beneficiary under a deed of trust who has acquired the real property at a sale conducted under a power of sale under a deed of trust or a sale under a court-ordered foreclosure or has acquired the real property by a deed in lieu of foreclosure;

(5) by a fiduciary in the course of the administration of a decedent's estate, guardianship, conservatorship, or trust;

(6) from one co-owner to one or more other co-owners;

(7) to a spouse or to a person or persons in the lineal line of consanguinity of one or more of the transferors;

(8) between spouses resulting from a decree of dissolution of marriage or a decree of legal separation or from a property settlement agreement incidental to one of those decrees;

(9) to or from a governmental entity;

(10) where the purchaser obtains a title insurance policy insuring the transfer of title to the real property; or

(11) to a person who has purchased, conveyed, or entered into contracts to purchase or convey an interest in real property four or more times in the preceding 12 months.

(d) A violation of this section is not actionable if the person required to give notice reasonably believes and takes any necessary action to ensure that each lien for which notice was not provided will be released on or before the 30th day after the date on which title to the property is transferred.

History of Prop. Code §5.016: Acts 2007, 80th Leg., ch. 1056, §1, eff. Jan. 1, 2008.

See also *Real Estate Forms*, FORM 1:10.

PROP §5.017. REPEALED

Repealed by Acts 2011, 82nd Leg., ch. 211, §2, eff. June 17, 2011.

PROP §5.018. DISCLOSURE OF ABSENCE OF CERTAIN WARRANTIES

(a) A seller of residential real property that is exempt from Title 16[1] under Section 401.005[1] shall give to the purchaser of the property a written notice that reads substantially similar to the following:

NOTICE OF NONAPPLICABILITY OF CERTAIN WARRANTIES AND BUILDING AND PERFORMANCE STANDARDS

The property that is subject to this contract is exempt from Title 16, Property Code,[1] including the provisions of that title that provide statutory warranties and building and performance standards.

(b) A notice required by this section shall be delivered by the seller to the purchaser on or before the effective date of an executory contract binding the purchaser to purchase the property. If a contract is entered into without the seller providing the notice, the purchaser may terminate the contract for any reason on or before the seventh day after the date the purchaser receives the notice.

(c) This section does not apply to a transfer:

(1) under a court order or foreclosure sale;

(2) by a trustee in bankruptcy;

(3) to a mortgagee by a mortgagor or successor in interest or to a beneficiary of a deed of trust by a trustor or successor in interest;

(4) by a mortgagee or a beneficiary under a deed of trust who has acquired the land at a sale conducted under a power of sale under a deed of trust or a sale under a court-ordered foreclosure or has acquired the land by a deed in lieu of foreclosure;

(5) by a fiduciary in the course of the administration of a decedent's estate, guardianship, conservatorship, or trust;

(6) from one co-owner to another co-owner of an undivided interest in the real property;

(7) to a spouse or a person in the lineal line of consanguinity of the seller;

(8) to or from a governmental entity; or

(9) of only a mineral interest, leasehold interest, or security interest.

1. **Editor's note:** Expired. See "Editor's note," p. 732.

History of Prop. Code §5.018: Acts 2007, 80th Leg., ch. 843, §1, eff. Sept. 1, 2007. Renumbered from §5.016 by Acts 2009, 81st Leg., ch. 87, §27.001(76), eff. Sept. 1, 2009.

See also *Real Estate Forms*, FORMS 1:3, 1:5.

PROP §5.019. NOTICE OF WATER LEVEL FLUCTUATIONS

(a) This section applies only to the sale of residential or commercial real property adjoining an impoundment of water, including a reservoir or lake, constructed and maintained under Chapter 11, Water Code, that has a storage capacity of at least 5,000 acre-feet at the impoundment's normal operating level.

(b) A seller of real property shall give to the purchaser of the property a written notice in substantially the following form:

NOTICE OF WATER LEVEL FLUCTUATIONS

The water level of the impoundment of water adjoining the property at ______________ (street address and city) or described as ______________ (legal description) fluctuates for various reasons, including as a result of:

(1) an entity lawfully exercising its right to use the water stored in the impoundment; or

(2) drought or flood conditions.

(c) The notice described by Subsection (b) shall be delivered by the seller to the purchaser on or before the effective date of an executory contract binding the purchaser to purchase the property.

(d) If a contract is entered into without the seller providing the notice within the period required by Subsection (c), the purchaser may terminate the contract for any reason within seven days after the date the purchaser receives:

(1) the notice described by Subsection (b) from the seller; or

(2) information described by the notice under Subsection (b) from any other person.

(e) After the date of the conveyance, the purchaser may bring an action for misrepresentation against the seller if the seller:

(1) failed to provide the notice before the date of the conveyance; and

(2) had actual knowledge that the water level described by Subsection (b) fluctuates for various reasons, including the reasons stated in Subsection (b).

History of Prop. Code §5.019: Acts 2015, 84th Leg., ch. 926, §1, eff. Sept. 1, 2015.

Section 5.020 reserved for expansion

SUBCHAPTER B. FORM & CONSTRUCTION OF INSTRUMENTS

PROP §5.021. INSTRUMENT OF CONVEYANCE

A conveyance of an estate of inheritance, a freehold, or an estate for more than one year, in land and tenements, must be in writing and must be subscribed and delivered by the conveyor or by the conveyor's agent authorized in writing.

History of Prop. Code §5.021: Acts 1983, 68th Leg., ch. 576, §1, eff. Jan. 1, 1984. Source: TRCS art. 1288.

See also B&CC §26.01; *Real Estate Forms*, FORMS 1:8-1:13, 1:16, 2:1, 2:15, 11:1, 11:2.

ANNOTATIONS

Generally

Wilson v. Fisher, 188 S.W.2d 150, 152 (Tex.1945). "In the absence of equities removing the case from the operation of the statute of frauds, ... it is well settled that before a court will decree the specific performance of a contract for the sale of land, or entertain a suit for damages for the breach thereof, the written agreement or memorandum required by the statute must contain the essential terms of a contract, expressed with such certainty and clarity that it may be understood without recourse to parol evidence to show the intention of the

parties; and no part of the instrument is more essential than that which identifies the subject matter of the agreement." *See also* ***Reiland v. Patrick Thomas Props., Inc.***, 213 S.W.3d 431, 436-37 (Tex.App.—Houston [1st Dist.] 2006, pet. denied).

Gordon v. West Houston Trees, Ltd., 352 S.W.3d 32, 43 (Tex.App.—Houston [1st Dist.] 2011, no pet.). "In essence, the instrument conveying the land must contain the essential characteristics of a deed. There is, however, no longer a requirement that a deed or instrument to effect the conveyance of real property must have all the formal parts of a deed recognized at common law or technical language. Rather, if (1) from the instrument as a whole a grantor and grantee can be ascertained and (2) there are operative words or words of grant showing an intention by the grantor to convey to the grantee title to a real property interest, (3) which is sufficiently described, and (4) the instrument is signed and acknowledged by the grantor, then the instrument of conveyance is a deed that accomplishes a legally effective conveyance." *See also* ***St. Paul Fire & Mar. Ins. v. Petroplex Energy, Inc.***, 474 S.W.3d 454, 460 (Tex.App.—Eastland 2015, pet. dism'd); ***Green v. Canon***, 33 S.W.3d 855, 858 (Tex.App.—Houston [14th Dist.] 2000, pet. denied).

Dedication of Road for Public Use

Shelton v. Kalbow, 489 S.W.3d 32, 44 (Tex.App.—Houston [14th Dist.] 2016, pet. denied). "Dedication is the act of appropriating private land to the public for any general or public use. 'Once dedicated, the owner of the land reserves no rights that are incompatible with the full enjoyment of the public.' 'There are two types of dedications, express and implied.' There are four elements to establish dedication, whether express or implied: (1) the person making the dedication must have the ability to do so—he must have fee simple title before he can dedicate his property; (2) there must be a public purpose served by the dedication; (3) the person must make either an express or implied offer; and (4) there must be an acceptance of that offer. Generally, an express dedication is accomplished by deed or other written document. *At 46:* [Ds] take issue with the fact that the … deed did not state the tract was to be used for a county road. The … deed substantively tracked the statutory form to convey a fee simple estate in real property. [Ds] did not provide, and we have not located, any authority requiring that a public dedication particularly describe or otherwise limit the public use. Indeed, where property is so generally dedicated, 'the public has a free hand in applying the property to such uses as it may desire,' such as a roadway." *See also* ***Baywood Estates Prop. Owners Ass'n v. Caolo***, 392 S.W.3d 776, 781 (Tex.App.—Tyler 2012, no pet.); ***McCulloch v. Brewster Cty.***, 391 S.W.3d 612, 616 (Tex.App.—El Paso 2012, no pet.).

Betts v. Reed, 165 S.W.3d 862, 868-69 (Tex.App.—Texarkana 2005, no pet.). "'In order to constitute dedication by estoppel or implication there must exist a clear and unequivocal intention on the part of the landowner to dedicate the same to public use and an acceptance thereby by the public.' There must be some evidence in addition to the owner's acquiescence that implies a donative intent. The additional evidence may include, but is not limited to: (1) permitting public authorities to grade, repair, or otherwise improve the roadway; (2) selling parcels of land from a plat or plan showing the roadway as a means of access to the parcels; (3) construction of facilities for general public use; (4) an express representation by the owner of a road to a land purchaser that the way is reserved for public use; (5) fencing off the roadway from the remainder of the land; or (6) obtaining a reduction in the purchase price commensurate with the area of the roadway. Direct evidence of a landowner's intent is not required. [¶] The long and continuous use of the road by the public raises a presumption of donative intent. When the origin of the road cannot be determined, evidence of long and continued use by the public raises a presumption that the landowner intended to dedicate the road. For this presumption to apply, the ownership of the land when the road originated must be 'shrouded in obscurity' so that no evidence of the intent of the owner is available. *At 870:* A landowner cannot revoke the dedication or use the property contrary to the original purpose of the dedication once a dedication is accepted. 'Once a road is dedicated to public use, that road remains subject to that use unless it is abandoned.'" *See also* ***Buffington v. DeLeon***, 177 S.W.3d 205, 210 (Tex.App.—Houston [1st Dist.] 2005, no pet.).

Delivery of Deed

Chambers v. Equity Bank, 319 S.W.3d 892, 900 (Tex.App.—Texarkana 2010, no pet.). "Conveyance by deed requires delivery of the deed. Delivery of a deed has two elements: (1) the grantor must place the deed within the control of the grantee (2) with the intention that the instrument become[s] operative as a convey-

ance. The question of delivery of the deed is controlled by the intent of the grantor, and it is determined by examining all the facts and circumstances preceding, attending, and following the execution of the instrument." *See also* ***Noell v. Crow-Billingsley Air Park L.P.***, 233 S.W.3d 408, 415 (Tex.App.—Dallas 2007, pet. denied).

Burgess v. Easley, 893 S.W.2d 87, 90-91 (Tex. App.—Dallas 1994, no writ). "What constitutes delivery of a deed is a question of law. Whether there has been a delivery is a question of fact. [¶] A trial court determines the question of delivery from all the facts and circumstances of the case. ... Although the trial court may presume delivery occurs on the date a grantor signs and acknowledges a deed, [grantee] could overcome this presumption by showing the grantor did not intend to deliver the deed on that date."

Description in Deed

AIC Mgmt. v. Crews, 246 S.W.3d 640, 645 (Tex. 2008). "To be valid, a conveyance of real property must contain a sufficient description of the property to be conveyed. A property description is sufficient if the writing furnishes within itself, or by reference to some other existing writing, the means or data by which the particular land to be conveyed may be identified with reasonable certainty. Like any other conveyance of property, a judgment for foreclosure of a tax lien upon real estate which fails to describe a definite tract of land is void. A tax judgment's property description must be sufficiently particular to allow a party to locate the specific land being identified." *See also* ***Hahn v. Love***, 394 S.W.3d 14, 25 (Tex.App.—Houston [1st Dist.] 2012, pet. denied).

Maupin v. Chaney, 163 S.W.2d 380, 383 (Tex. 1942). "The sole purpose of the description of property, as contained in a deed of conveyance, is to identify the subject matter of the grant. And in construing the deed the court endeavors to carry into effect the intention of the parties as expressed therein. [W]here the description specifies a property intended to be conveyed, and the instrument furnishes other sufficient means of determining the particular property covered ..., the description is legally sufficient." *See also* ***Wilson v. Fisher***, 188 S.W.2d 150, 152 (Tex.1945) (writing must furnish within itself or refer to another writing that identifies land with reasonable certainty); ***Apex Fin. Corp. v. Garza***, 155 S.W.3d 230, 237 (Tex.App.—Dallas 2004, pet. denied) (street address or commonly known name for property may be sufficient description if it is not confusing).

Reeder v. Curry, 426 S.W.3d 352, 359 (Tex.App.—Dallas 2014, no pet.). "A conveyance of property which fails to describe a definite tract of land is void. The writing does not have to list metes and bounds to be enforceable, but it must provide the necessary information to identify the property with reasonable certainty. An unidentifiable portion of a larger, identifiable tract is not sufficient to satisfy the statute of frauds. The legal description in the conveyance must not only furnish enough information to locate the general area as in identifying it by tract survey and county, it need contain information regarding the size, shape, and boundaries. Even when the record leaves little doubt that the parties knew and understood what property was intended to be conveyed, the knowledge and intent of the parties will not give validity to the contract and neither will a plat made from extrinsic evidence." (Internal quotes omitted.)

Easements

McKenna v. Caldwell, 387 S.W.3d 830, 834 (Tex. App.—Eastland 2012, no pet.). "When considering an express easement, we look to the language reserving it to determine the scope of the easement. Applying basic principles of contract construction and interpretation, we give the terms of the easement their plain and ordinary meaning when they are not expressly defined. We read the terms of an easement as a whole to determine the parties' intentions and to carry out the purpose behind the easement's creation." *See also* ***Vinson v. Brown***, 80 S.W.3d 221, 226-27 (Tex.App.—Austin 2002, no pet.).

Seber v. Union Pac. R.R., 350 S.W.3d 640, 647 (Tex.App.—Houston [14th Dist.] 2011, no pet.). "An implied easement is an exception to the rule that easements appurtenant must be created or transferred in writing. *At 648:* There are two forms of implied easement in Texas. The first is an easement by necessity, commonly called a 'way of necessity.' An easement by necessity is implied when the conveyed or retained parcel cannot be accessed except by traveling over the remaining tract of land. An easement by necessity has three requirements: (1) unity of ownership of both parcels prior to separation; (2) access must be a necessity and not a mere convenience; and (3) the necessity must exist at the time of severance. [¶] A second type of implied easement is based on prior use of the land

and is called an easement implied from a 'quasi-easement.' ... A party claiming an easement by prior use must prove that at the time of the severance: (1) both parcels were under unified ownership; (2) the use was apparent; (3) the use was continuous; and (4) the use was necessary to the use of the dominant estate. [¶] Texas courts routinely refer to implied easements based on prior use characteristics simply as 'implied easements.' The general term 'implied easement' is potentially confusing because, by definition, both an easement by necessity and an easement by prior use are implied." *See also* ***Harrington v. Dawson-Conway Ranch, Ltd.***, 372 S.W.3d 711, 722-23 (Tex.App.—Eastland 2012, pet. denied).

Martin v. Cockrell, 335 S.W.3d 229, 237 (Tex. App.—Amarillo 2010, no pet.). "[E]stoppel *in pais* holds that the owner of a servient estate may be estopped to deny the existence of an easement by making representations that have been acted upon by the owner of the dominant estate to his detriment ... and 'is grounded on the condition that justice forbids one to gainsay his own acts or assertions.' Each case in which equitable estoppel is sought to be applied must rest upon its own facts. [¶] Three elements are necessary to create an easement by estoppel: (1) a representation of the easement communicated, either by words or action, to the promisee; (2) the communication was believed; and (3) the promisee detrimentally relied on the communication. *At 237 n.11:* These elements apply at the time the communication creating the alleged easement is made. *At 237-38:* Further, once created, an easement by estoppel is binding on the successors in title to the servient estate if reliance upon the existing easement continues." *See also* ***McClung v. Ayers***, 352 S.W.3d 723, 729-30 (Tex.App.—Texarkana 2011, no pet.).

Equitable Interests

Rankin v. Naftalis, 557 S.W.2d 940, 944 (Tex. 1977). "A constructive trust escapes the unquestioned general rule that land titles must not rest in parol, but to do so, there must be strict proof of a prior confidential relationship and unfair conduct or unjust enrichment on the part of the wrongdoer. 'It must be used with caution, especially where as here proof of the wrongful act rests in parol, in order that it may not defeat the purposes of the statute of wills, the statute of descent and distribution, or the statute of frauds.' Subjective trust, cordiality and the trust which prevails between businessmen which is the foundation of ordinary contract law, affords no basis for the imposition of an oral trust that thwarts the Statute of Frauds." *See also* ***Troxel v. Bishop***, 201 S.W.3d 290, 297-98 (Tex. App.—Dallas 2006, no pet.).

Jewell v. Jewell, 602 S.W.2d 315, 317 (Tex.App.—Texarkana 1980, no writ). "One may ... acquire an equitable interest in real estate without formal conveyance, which interest can be enforced by a court of equity as circumstances may justify. If real property is purchased or paid for by partnership funds but record title is in one of the partners only, a court of equity may, in a proper case, impress it with a constructive or resulting trust in favor of the partnership, under the doctrine of equitable conversion. Too, if one partner's individual funds or those of the partnership are used to improve the other partner's real estate, the court may compensate the wronged partner accordingly, but that is to be done in the adjustment of equities in the partnership accounting or winding up, and not by a transfer of title to an interest in the land."

Leases

White v. Harrison, 390 S.W.3d 666, 672 (Tex. App.—Dallas 2012, no pet.). "The elements of ratification are: (1) approval by act, word, or conduct; (2) with full knowledge of the facts of the earlier act; and (3) with the intention of giving validity to the earlier act. A party ratifies an agreement when—after learning all of the material facts—he confirms or adopts an earlier act that did not then legally bind him and that he could have repudiated."

2616 S. Loop L.L.C. v. Health Source Home Care, Inc., 201 S.W.3d 349, 355-56 (Tex.App.—Houston [14th Dist.] 2006, no pet.). "A lessor may validly lease property to another, despite the fact that the title to the property is in a third person, if the lessor lawfully possesses the property. In such a case, the lessee may enforce the lease against the lessor. But, this does not necessarily mean that the lessee can enforce the lease against the property owner. Although the lessee 'may have had a subjective, good faith belief' that the lessor was the owner or an agent of the owner, this is not enough to create an agency relationship between the lessor and the property owner that binds the owner to the lessor's agreement. In the absence of the owner's ratification of the lease or the lessor's actual or appar-

ent authority to act on the owner's behalf, there is no basis on which to enforce the lease against the property owner."

Kerrville HRH, Inc. v. City of Kerrville, 803 S.W.2d 377, 388-89 (Tex.App.—San Antonio 1990, writ denied). "A lease of real estate for a term of more than one year must be in writing and must be signed by the person to be charged. Generally, a modification of a lease required to be in writing must also be in writing. There are, however, exceptions to the general rule. If the oral modification is not *material*, that is, if the character or value of the underlying agreement is unaltered, the modification is enforceable. [Here,] the agreement ... was silent regarding the obligation to repair the irrigation system. The parties worked out a mutually satisfactory agreement that [lessee] would do the repair work and [lessor] would pay the costs of parts and materials. [Lessee's] possession was not disturbed and it continued to pay rent and conduct its business as best it could, given the condition of the irrigation system. Further, the modification was executed by [lessee]. It made the repairs in accordance with the agreement, remained on the leasehold and paid its rent. It cannot now raise the Statute of Frauds as a defense." *See also* ***McDonald v. Roemer***, 505 S.W.2d 698, 699 (Tex. App.—San Antonio 1974, no writ) (lease for one year not within statute).

Reservation of Mineral Interest

Philipello v. Nelson Family Farming Trust, 349 S.W.3d 692, 694 (Tex.App.—Houston [14th Dist.] 2011, pet. denied). "[T]he sole issue on appeal is the construction of the reservation in the Deed. *At 695:* We conclude that it is reasonable to construe the oil, gas, and other minerals as referring to the oil, gas, and other minerals in and under the Property. Shortly before the reservation paragraph, the Deed contains a paragraph with a detailed description of the Property. But, the Deed does not contain a statement or description of the fractional mineral interest that the [grantor] is conveying to the [grantees]. In this context, we conclude that it is not reasonable to construe the oil, gas, and other minerals as referring to the oil, gas, and other minerals in and under the undivided, fractional mineral interest conveyed by the [grantor] in the Deed. Therefore, under the Deed's unambiguous language, the [grantor] reserved for itself, for a period of ten years, one-eighth of the royalty in oil, gas, or other minerals in and under the Property."

PROP §5.022. FORM

(a) The following form or a form that is the same in substance conveys a fee simple estate in real property with a covenant of general warranty:

"The State of Texas,

"County of ____________.

"Know all men by these presents, That I, ____________, of the ____________ (give name of city, town, or county), in the state aforesaid, for and in consideration of ________________ dollars, to me in hand paid by ____________, have granted, sold, and conveyed, and by these presents do grant, sell, and convey unto the said ____________, of the ____________ (give name of city, town, or county), in the state of ________, all that certain ____________ (describe the premises). To have and to hold the above described premises, together with all and singular the rights and appurtenances thereto in any wise belonging, unto the said ____________, his heirs or assigns forever. And I do hereby bind myself, my heirs, executors, and administrators to warrant and forever defend all and singular the said premises unto the said ________, his heirs, and assigns, against every person whomsoever, lawfully claiming or to claim the same, or any part thereof.

"Witness my hand, this __________ day of __________, A.D. 19____.

"Signed and delivered in the presence of ________."

(b) A covenant of warranty is not required in a conveyance.

(c) The parties to a conveyance may insert any clause or use any form not in contravention of law.

History of Prop. Code §5.022: Acts 1983, 68th Leg., ch. 576, §1, eff. Jan. 1, 1984. Source: TRCS arts. 1292, 1293.

See also Prop. Code §5.001; ***Real Estate Forms***, FORM 1:8.

ANNOTATIONS

Shelton v. Kalbow, 489 S.W.3d 32, 44 (Tex.App.—Houston [14th Dist.] 2016, pet. denied). See annotation under Property Code §5.021, *Dedication of Road for Public Use*, p. 40.

PROP §5.023. IMPLIED COVENANTS

(a) Unless the conveyance expressly provides otherwise, the use of "grant" or "convey" in a conveyance of an estate of inheritance or fee simple implies only that the grantor and the grantor's heirs covenant to the grantee and the grantee's heirs or assigns:

(1) that prior to the execution of the conveyance the grantor has not conveyed the estate or any interest in the estate to a person other than the grantee; and

(2) that at the time of the execution of the conveyance the estate is free from encumbrances.

(b) An implied covenant under this section may be the basis for a lawsuit as if it had been expressed in the conveyance.

History of Prop. Code §5.023: Acts 1983, 68th Leg., ch. 576, §1, eff. Jan. 1, 1984. Source: TRCS art. 1297.

See also *Real Estate Forms*, FORMS 1:2, 1:3, 1:5, 1:8-1:13, 6:4.

ANNOTATIONS

Humber v. Morton, 426 S.W.2d 554, 556 (Tex. 1968). TRCS art. 1297, now Prop. Code §5.023, "relates to covenants of title which arise out of conveyances and not to collateral covenants such as the suitability of a house for human habitation. The presence of a collateral covenant of this type in a deed would be strange indeed. 'It is not the office of a deed to express the terms of the contract of sale, but to pass the title pursuant to the contract.' The article simply prescribes what covenants may be implied by the use of two designated words, 'grant' or 'convey.' The implied warranty of fitness arises from the sale and does not spring from the conveyance."

Orca Assets, G.P., L.L.C. v. JPMorgan Chase Bank, No. 05-13-01700-CV (Tex.App.—Dallas 2015, pet. argued 11-7-17) (memo op.; 8-11-15). Grantee "argues that even if any express warranty of title has been disclaimed, there was no disclaimer of the statutory implied covenant against prior conveyances [contained in §5.023(a)(1)]. [¶] [Grantee] contends the statutory covenant is 'separate and distinct from the warranty of title[.]' [Grantee] argues that the leases disclaim only 'warranties of any kind, either express or implied,' and ... the statutory 'covenant' is not the same thing as a 'warranty.' [¶] '[T]he very purpose of the warranty covenant is for the indemnity of the purchaser against a loss or injury he may sustain by a defect in the vendor's title. The warranty clause does not convey title nor does it determine the character of the title conveyed.' [¶] But the implied covenant on which [grantee] relies is a promise that the grantor has not conveyed the property interest to anyone else. [T]his covenant is included in the 'covenant of general warranty' and is the essence of the special warranty, both of which were emphatically excluded from this lease. ... While the [disclaimer] did not directly and specifically reference the possibility of a prior lease ..., its far-reaching breadth to any warranty of any kind is sufficient. [R]egardless of [grantee's] arguments that the covenant regarding prior conveyances is different from 'warranty of title' or implied by statute, [grantee's] disclaimer encompassed its claim and foreclosed it."

Natland Corp. v. Baker's Port, Inc., 865 S.W.2d 52, 60-61 (Tex.App.—Corpus Christi 1993, writ denied). "The statutory covenant against encumbrances, as provided by [§5.023] is implied from the use of the words 'grant' or 'convey' in a transfer of a fee simple estate, unless the express terms of the conveyance negate that implication. The covenant against encumbrances is distinct from a warranty of title and protects the grantee against interests in third persons which, though consistent with the fee being in the grantor, will diminish the value of the estate conveyed. Such a covenant is breached, if at all, upon the execution and delivery of the deed." *See also* ***McNary v. Reeves***, 461 S.W.2d 127, 130 (Tex.App.—Texarkana 1970, writ ref'd n.r.e.); ***Fannin Inv. & Dev. Co. v. Neuhaus***, 427 S.W.2d 82, 88 (Tex.App.—Houston [14th Dist.] 1968, no writ).

PROP §5.024. ENCUMBRANCES

"Encumbrance" includes a tax, an assessment, and a lien on real property.

History of Prop. Code §5.024: Acts 1983, 68th Leg., ch. 576, §1, eff. Jan. 1, 1984. Source: TRCS art. 1298.

PROP §5.025. WOOD SHINGLE ROOF

To the extent that a deed restriction applicable to a structure on residential property requires the use of a wood shingle roof, the restriction is void.

History of Prop. Code §5.025: Acts 1983, 68th Leg., ch. 576, §1, eff. Jan. 1, 1984. Source: TRCS art. 1293c.

ANNOTATIONS

Hoye v. Shepherds Glen Land Co., 753 S.W.2d 226, 228 (Tex.App.—Dallas 1988, writ denied). "'The practical disadvantages of other alternatives to wood shingles for a structure of a particular design do not establish that the restriction in question is void.' The fact that 51 of the 55 houses in the subdivision have wood shingle roofs is not proof as a matter of law that the practical effect of enforcing the covenant is to force homebuilders to use wood shingle roofs. Even if this Court were to strike out the portion of the covenant dealing with wood shingles, [homebuilders] can still use 'slate or other permanent type' of materials."

PROP §5.026. DISCRIMINATORY PROVISIONS

(a) If a restriction that affects real property, or a provision in a deed that conveys real property or an interest in real property, whether express or incorporated by reference, prohibits the use by or the sale, lease, or transfer to a person because of race, color, religion, or national origin, the provision or restriction is void.

(b) A court shall dismiss a suit or part of a suit to enforce a provision that is void under this section.

History of Prop. Code §5.026: Acts 1983, 68th Leg., ch. 576, §1, eff. Jan. 1, 1984. Source: TRCS art. 1293a.

See also Fin. Code §341.401.

PROP §5.027. CORRECTION INSTRUMENTS: GENERALLY

(a) A correction instrument that complies with Section 5.028 or 5.029 may correct an ambiguity or error in a recorded original instrument of conveyance to transfer real property or an interest in real property, including an ambiguity or error that relates to the description of or extent of the interest conveyed.

(b) A correction instrument may not correct an ambiguity or error in a recorded original instrument of conveyance to transfer real property or an interest in real property not originally conveyed in the instrument of conveyance for purposes of a sale of real property under a power of sale under Chapter 51 unless the conveyance otherwise complies with all requirements of Chapter 51.

(c) A correction instrument is subject to Section 13.001.

History of Prop. Code §5.027: Acts 2011, 82nd Leg., ch. 194, §1, eff. Sept. 1, 2011.

PROP §5.028. CORRECTION INSTRUMENTS: NONMATERIAL CORRECTIONS

(a) A person who has personal knowledge of facts relevant to the correction of a recorded original instrument of conveyance may prepare or execute a correction instrument to make a nonmaterial change that results from a clerical error, including:

(1) a correction of an inaccurate or incorrect element in a legal description, such as a distance, angle, direction, bearing or chord, a reference to a plat or other plat information, a lot or block number, a unit, building designation, or section number, an appurtenant easement, a township name or number, a municipality, county, or state name, a range number or meridian, a certified survey map number, or a subdivision or condominium name; or

(2) an addition, correction, or clarification of:

(A) a party's name, including the spelling of a name, a first or middle name or initial, a suffix, an alternate name by which a party is known, or a description of an entity as a corporation, company, or other type of organization;

(B) a party's marital status;

(C) the date on which the conveyance was executed;

(D) the recording data for an instrument referenced in the correction instrument; or

(E) a fact relating to the acknowledgment or authentication.

(a-1) A person who has personal knowledge of facts relevant to the correction of a recorded original instrument of conveyance may prepare or execute a correction instrument to make a nonmaterial change that results from an inadvertent error, including the addition, correction, or clarification of:

(1) a legal description prepared in connection with the preparation of the original instrument but inadvertently omitted from the original instrument; or

(2) an omitted call in a metes and bounds legal description in the original instrument that completes the description of the property.

(b) A person who executes a correction instrument under this section may execute a correction instrument that provides an acknowledgment or authentication that is required and was not included in the recorded original instrument of conveyance.

(c) A person who executes a correction instrument under this section shall disclose in the instrument the basis for the person's personal knowledge of the facts relevant to the correction of the recorded original instrument of conveyance.

(d) A person who executes a correction instrument under this section shall:

(1) record the instrument and evidence of notice as provided by Subdivision (2), if applicable, in each county in which the original instrument of conveyance being corrected is recorded; and

(2) if the correction instrument is not signed by each party to the recorded original instrument, send a copy of the correction instrument and notice by first class mail, e-mail, or other reasonable means to each party to the original instrument of conveyance and, if applicable, a party's heirs, successors, or assigns.

History of Prop. Code §5.028: Acts 2011, 82nd Leg., ch. 194, §1, eff. Sept. 1, 2011. Amended by Acts 2013, 83rd Leg., ch. 158, §1, eff. Sept. 1, 2013.

ANNOTATIONS

Tanya L. McCabe Trust v. Ranger Energy LLC, 508 S.W.3d 828, 841 (Tex.App.—Houston [1st Dist.] 2016, pet. denied). See annotation under Property Code §5.029, this page.

PROP §5.029. CORRECTION INSTRUMENTS: MATERIAL CORRECTIONS

(a) In addition to nonmaterial corrections, including the corrections described by Section 5.028, the parties to the original transaction or the parties' heirs, successors, or assigns, as applicable may execute a correction instrument to make a material correction to the recorded original instrument of conveyance, including a correction to:

(1) add:

(A) a buyer's disclaimer of an interest in the real property that is the subject of the original instrument of conveyance;

(B) a mortgagee's consent or subordination to a recorded document executed by the mortgagee or an heir, successor, or assign of the mortgagee; or

(C) land to a conveyance that correctly conveys other land;

(2) remove land from a conveyance that correctly conveys other land; or

(3) accurately identify a lot or unit number or letter of property owned by the grantor that was inaccurately identified as another lot or unit number or letter of property owned by the grantor in the recorded original instrument of conveyance.

(b) A correction instrument under this section must be:

(1) executed by each party to the recorded original instrument of conveyance the correction instrument is executed to correct or, if applicable, a party's heirs, successors, or assigns; and

(2) recorded in each county in which the original instrument of conveyance that is being corrected is recorded.

History of Prop. Code §5.029: Acts 2011, 82nd Leg., ch. 194, §1, eff. Sept. 1, 2011.

ANNOTATIONS

Tanya L. McCabe Trust v. Ranger Energy LLC, 508 S.W.3d 828, 841 (Tex.App.—Houston [1st Dist.] 2016, pet. denied). "[Ds] contend that the revised mortgage documentation contained material corrections that did not comply with [Prop. Code] §5.029 because it was not executed by the proper parties. [P's] response has been that the revised documents were nonmaterial corrections of the legal description. [¶] To determine whether this case involves material or nonmaterial corrections, we compare the changes made by the … revised mortgage and deed of trust to [Prop. Code] §§5.028 and 5.029. Both the … revised mortgage and deed of trust had the primary effect of adding [two] leases to the exhibits that listed the properties as security for the loan or as subject to the deed of trust. [¶] The addition of land to a conveyance that correctly conveys other land is a material change. *At 842:* Further, a comparison of §5.028 to the changes made in the … revised documentation shows that none of the corrections are of the types identified as nonmaterial. For example, the correction instruments at issue did not change any of the identifying information or descriptions that were in the original documents … nor did they add, correct, or clarify a party's name or marital status, the date of execution of the conveyance, recording data for an instrument referenced in the correction instrument, or a fact relating to acknowledgment or authentication. Thus, the correction instruments at issue are not consistent with a nonmaterial correction pursuant to §5.028(a)."

PROP §5.030. CORRECTION INSTRUMENT: EFFECT

(a) A correction instrument that complies with Section 5.028 or 5.029 is:

(1) effective as of the effective date of the recorded original instrument of conveyance;

(2) prima facie evidence of the facts stated in the correction instrument;

(3) presumed to be true;

(4) subject to rebuttal; and

(5) notice to a subsequent buyer of the facts stated in the correction instrument.

(b) A correction instrument replaces and is a substitute for the original instrument. Except as provided by Subsection (c), a bona fide purchaser of property that is subject to a correction instrument may rely on the instrument against any person making an adverse or inconsistent claim.

(c) A correction instrument is subject to the property interest of a creditor or a subsequent purchaser for

valuable consideration without notice acquired on or after the date the original instrument was acknowledged, sworn to, or proved and filed for record as required by law and before the correction instrument has been acknowledged, sworn to, or proved and filed for record as required by law.

History of Prop. Code §5.030: Acts 2011, 82nd Leg., ch. 194, §1, eff. Sept. 1, 2011. Amended by Acts 2013, 83rd Leg., ch. 158, §2, eff. Sept. 1, 2013.

PROP §5.031. CORRECTION INSTRUMENTS RECORDED BEFORE SEPTEMBER 1, 2011

A correction instrument recorded before September 1, 2011, that substantially complies with Section 5.028 or 5.029 and that purports to correct a recorded original instrument of conveyance is effective to the same extent as provided by Section 5.030 unless a court of competent jurisdiction renders a final judgment determining that the correction instrument does not substantially comply with Section 5.028 or 5.029.

History of Prop. Code §5.031: Acts 2011, 82nd Leg., ch. 194, §1, eff. Sept. 1, 2011.

Sections 5.032-5.040 reserved for expansion

SUBCHAPTER C. FUTURE ESTATES

PROP §5.041. FUTURE ESTATES

A person may make an inter vivos conveyance of an estate of freehold or inheritance that commences in the future, in the same manner as by a will.

History of Prop. Code §5.041: Acts 1983, 68th Leg., ch. 576, §1, eff. Jan. 1, 1984. Source: TRCS art. 1296.

See also CPRC §64.092; Est. Code ch. 123, §§251.002, 255.001-255.003; Prop. Code §§5.003, 5.043, 23.003, 112.036, 181.082, ch. 240.

ANNOTATIONS

Cavazos v. Cavazos, 246 S.W.3d 175, 180 (Tex. App.—San Antonio 2007, pet. denied). The "instrument must clearly manifest the intention of the prospective heir to sell, assign or convey his expectancy or future interest."

Troxel v. Bishop, 201 S.W.3d 290, 296-97 (Tex. App.—Dallas 2006, no pet.). "The three elements constituting a gift are: (1) donative intent, (2) delivery of the property, and (3) acceptance of the property. All dominion and control over the property must be released by the owner. The one claiming the gift has the burden of establishing these elements. A gift of realty can be made in two ways: either by deed or by parol gift. [¶] Title to transferred property will vest upon execution and delivery of a deed. The question of delivery of the deed, being controlled by the intent of the grantor, is determined by examining all the facts and circumstances preceding, attending, and following the execution of the instrument. However, proof that a deed was filed of record establishes a prima facie case of delivery and the accompanying presumption that the grantor intended to convey the land according to the terms of the deed. On the other hand, this latter presumption—that a deed was intended to be operative as a conveyance according to its terms-may overcome by evidence that: (1) the deed was delivered or recorded for a different purpose, (2) fraud, accident, or mistake accompanied the delivery or recording, or (3) the grantor had no intention of divesting himself of title. [¶] There are three requisites to uphold a parol gift of realty in equity: (1) a gift in praesenti, (2) possession under the gift by the donee with the donor's consent, and (3) permanent and valuable improvements made on the property by the donee with the donor's knowledge or consent or, without improvements, the existence of such facts as would make it a fraud upon the donee not to enforce the gift. 'In praesenti' means at the present time; it is used in opposition to 'in futuro.' Thus, to be a gift in praesenti, the donor must, at the time he makes it, intend an immediate divestiture of the rights of ownership out of himself and a consequent immediate vesting of such rights in the donee. The donee's possession must be in the nature of an owner's right to control. An effective parol gift of real property is not in violation of the statutes of fraud."

PROP §5.042. ABOLITION OF COMMON-LAW RULES

(a) The common-law rules known as the rule in Shelley's case, the rule forbidding a remainder to the grantor's heirs, the doctrine of worthier title, and the doctrine or rule prohibiting an existing lien upon part of a homestead from extending to another part of the homestead not charged with the debts secured by the existing lien upon part of the homestead do not apply in this state.

(b) A deed, will, or other conveyance of property in this state that limits an interest in the property to a particular person or to a class such as the heirs, heirs of the body, issue, or next of kin of the conveyor or of a person to whom a particular interest in the same property is limited is effective according to the intent of the conveyor.

(c) Status as an heir or next of kin of a conveyor or the failure of a conveyor to describe a person in a con-

veyance other than as a member of a class does not affect a person's right to take or share in an interest as a conveyee.

(d) Subject to the intention of a conveyor, which controls unless limited by law, the membership of a class described in this section and the participation of a member in a property interest conveyed to the class are determined under this state's laws of descent and distribution.

(e) This section does not apply to a conveyance taking effect before January 1, 1964.

History of Prop. Code §5.042: Acts 1983, 68th Leg., ch. 576, §1, eff. Jan. 1, 1984. Amended by Acts 1999, 76th Leg., ch. 1510, §5, eff. Sept. 1, 1999. Source: TRCS art. 1291a.

ANNOTATIONS

Meduna v. Holder, No. 03-02-00781-CV (Tex. App.—Austin 2003, no pet.) (memo op.; 12-18-03). "We interpret §5.042(c) as allowing a conveyance to an unknown member of a class, *within the limits of the rule against perpetuities*."

PROP §5.043. REFORMATION OF INTERESTS VIOLATING RULE AGAINST PERPETUITIES

(a) Within the limits of the rule against perpetuities, a court shall reform or construe an interest in real or personal property that violates the rule to effect the ascertainable general intent of the creator of the interest. A court shall liberally construe and apply this provision to validate an interest to the fullest extent consistent with the creator's intent.

(b) The court may reform or construe an interest under Subsection (a) of this section according to the doctrine of cy pres by giving effect to the general intent and specific directives of the creator within the limits of the rule against perpetuities.

(c) If an instrument that violates the rule against perpetuities may be reformed or construed under this section, a court shall enforce the provisions of the instrument that do not violate the rule and shall reform or construe under this section a provision that violates or might violate the rule.

(d) This section applies to legal and equitable interests, including noncharitable gifts and trusts, conveyed by an inter vivos instrument or a will that takes effect on or after September 1, 1969, and this section applies to an appointment made on or after that date regardless of when the power was created.

History of Prop. Code §5.043: Acts 1983, 68th Leg., ch. 576, §1, eff. Jan. 1, 1984. Amended by Acts 1991, 72nd Leg., ch. 895, §16, eff. Sept. 1, 1991. Source: TRCS art. 1291b.

See also Prop. Code §§5.041, 112.036.

ANNOTATIONS

Meduna v. Holder, No. 03-02-00781-CV (Tex. App.—Austin 2003, no pet.) (memo op.; 12-18-03). "The rule against perpetuities is a rule of property and not one of construction. The interpretation of a written instrument or instruments, however, is ordinarily required for application of the rule. Texas law favors a construction allowing vesting at the earliest possible time. Furthermore, courts will not construe an interest as contingent when it reasonably can be construed as vested. If the instrument of conveyance is capable of two constructions, one of which will give effect to the whole of the instrument, while the other would defeat it in whole or in part, courts favor the construction that saves the validity of the instrument rather than one that renders it void. Courts may refer to the intention of the grantor, and if a doubt exists as to that intention, the interest or estate will be held to be vested if reasonably within the language of the instrument."

Maupin v. Dunn, 678 S.W.2d 180, 183 (Tex.App.—Waco 1984, no writ). "The rule against perpetuities provides that no interest is good unless it must vest, if at all, not later than 21 years after some life in being at the creation of the interest plus gestation period if gestation exists. For purposes of the rule, the word 'vest' means to give an immediate, fixed right of present for future enjoyment and may be described as an interest clothed with a present, existing, and legal right of alienation. [¶] [T]he law will presume the parties intended that it be exercised within a reasonable time. What that reasonable time would be depends upon the facts and circumstances."

Sections 5.044-5.060 reserved for expansion

SUBCHAPTER D. EXECUTORY CONTRACT FOR CONVEYANCE

PROP §5.061. DEFINITION

In this subchapter, "default" means the failure to:

(1) make a timely payment; or

(2) comply with a term of an executory contract.

History of Prop. Code §5.061: Acts 1995, 74th Leg., ch. 994, §2, eff. Sept. 1, 1995. Renumbered from §5.065 and amended by Acts 2001, 77th Leg., ch. 693, §1, Sept. 1, 2001. Source: TRCS art. 1301b, §1.

See also *Real Estate Forms*, FORM 1:21.

PROP §5.062. APPLICABILITY

(a) This subchapter applies only to a transaction involving an executory contract for conveyance of real property used or to be used as the purchaser's residence or as the residence of a person related to the purchaser within the second degree by consanguinity or affinity, as determined under Chapter 573, Government Code. For purposes of this subchapter, and only for the purposes of this subchapter:

(1) a lot measuring one acre or less is presumed to be residential property; and

(2) an option to purchase real property that includes or is combined or executed concurrently with a residential lease agreement, together with the lease, is considered an executory contract for conveyance of real property.

(b) This subchapter does not apply to the following transactions under an executory contract:

(1) the sale of state land; or

(2) a sale of land by:

(A) the Veterans' Land Board;

(B) this state or a political subdivision of this state; or

(C) an instrumentality, public corporation, or other entity created to act on behalf of this state or a political subdivision of this state, including an entity created under Chapter 303, 392, or 394, Local Government Code.

(c) This subchapter does not apply to an executory contract that provides for the delivery of a deed from the seller to the purchaser within 180 days of the date of the final execution of the executory contract.

(d) Section 5.066 and Sections 5.068-5.080 do not apply to a transaction involving an executory contract for conveyance if the purchaser of the property:

(1) is related to the seller of the property within the second degree by consanguinity or affinity, as determined under Chapter 573, Government Code; and

(2) has waived the applicability of those sections in a written agreement.

(e) Sections 5.066, 5.067, 5.071, 5.075, 5.079, 5.081, and 5.082 do not apply to an executory contract described by Subsection (a)(2).

(f) Notwithstanding any other provision of this subchapter, only the following sections apply to an executory contract described by Subsection (a)(2) if the term of the contract is three years or less and the purchaser and seller, or the purchaser's or seller's assignee, agent, or affiliate, have not been parties to an executory contract to purchase the property covered by the executory contract for longer than three years:

(1) Sections 5.063-5.065;

(2) Section 5.073, except for Section 5.073(a)(2); and

(3) Sections 5.083 and 5.085.

(g) Except as provided by Subsection (b), if Subsection (f) conflicts with another provision of this subchapter, Subsection (f) prevails.

History of Prop. Code §5.062: Acts 1995, 74th Leg., ch. 994, §3, eff. Sept. 1, 1995. Renumbered from §5.091 and amended by Acts 2001, 77th Leg., ch. 693, §1, eff. Sept. 1, 2001. Amended by Acts 2005, 79th Leg., ch. 978, §2, eff. Jan. 1, 2006; Acts 2015, 84th Leg., ch. 996, §1, eff. Sept. 1, 2015. Source: TRCS art. 1301b, §1.

See also *Real Estate Forms*, FORM 1:21.

ANNOTATIONS

Bryant v. Cady, 445 S.W.3d 815, 822-23 (Tex. App.—Texarkana 2014, no pet.). "In a typical real estate contract, the seller and purchaser mutually agree to complete payment and title transfer on a date certain, the closing date, at which time the purchaser generally obtains both title and possession. By contrast, in an executory contract, the purchaser is usually given immediate possession, but is required to satisfy numerous obligations over an extended period of time before the seller has an obligation to transfer actual title. [¶] Under an executory contract, the buyer has the right, but no obligation, to complete the purchase.... But, in a typical real estate contract, the buyer must complete the purchase."

Lugo v. Ross, 378 S.W.3d 620, 624 (Tex.App.—Dallas 2012, no pet.). "[Ds] argue that because they exercised the option to purchase the property, there is no longer a landlord-tenant relationship between the parties to support a forcible entry and detainer action. But under the express terms of [Prop. Code] §5.062(f), [Prop. Code] §5.0621(b) is not applicable. In addition, [Prop. Code] §5.081 entitled 'Right to Convert Contract,' does not apply. Section 5.081 permits a purchaser 'at any time' to 'convert the purchaser's interest in property under an executory contract into recorded, legal title in accordance with this section.' Thus, even under Subch. D, the purchaser does not obtain title until the purchaser tenders or delivers a promissory note for the balance of the purchase price due under the executory contract. We conclude that even if Subch. D applies to the parties' 'Lease to Purchase Option Agree-

ment,' there is no title dispute to be resolved and the justice court had jurisdiction to enter a judgment in [Ps'] forcible entry and detainer suit."

Marker v. Garcia, 185 S.W.3d 21, 25-26 (Tex. App.—San Antonio 2005, no pet.). "The statutory phrase 'used or to be used' is broad language. 'By its express terms, the [language] encompasses real property which is presently being used as the purchaser's residence as well as real property which will be so used in the future.' Thus, the language 'clearly encompasses executory contracts [for the] sale of real property which the purchaser may use as a residence in the future.'"

Dickey v. McComb Dev. Co., 115 S.W.3d 42, 45 (Tex.App.—San Antonio 2003, no pet.). "The term 'residence' has been construed as the place where one actually lives or has his home. 'Residence' connotes a home and a fixed place of habitation to which one returns when away. An individual does not, however, have to be physically present within the home in order to claim it as his residence. He may live temporarily in one place while maintaining his residence in another. In addition, the fact that an individual leases the abode while physically absent from it does not mean, by itself, that the abode is no longer his residence."

PROP §5.0621. CONSTRUCTION WITH OTHER LAW

(a) Except as provided by Subsection (b), the provisions of this subchapter and Chapter 92 apply to the portion of an executory contract described by Section 5.062(a)(2) that is a residential lease agreement.

(b) After a tenant exercises an option to purchase leased property under a residential lease described by Subsection (a), Chapter 92 no longer applies to the lease.

History of Prop. Code §5.0621: Acts 2005, 79th Leg., ch. 978, §3, eff. Jan. 1, 2006.

See also *Real Estate Forms*, FORM 1:21.

PROP §5.063. NOTICE

(a) Notice under Section 5.064 must be in writing and must be delivered by registered or certified mail, return receipt requested. The notice must be conspicuous and printed in 14-point boldface type or 14-point uppercase typewritten letters, and must include on a separate page the statement:

NOTICE

YOU ARE NOT COMPLYING WITH THE TERMS OF THE CONTRACT TO BUY YOUR PROPERTY. UNLESS YOU TAKE THE ACTION SPECIFIED IN THIS NOTICE BY (date) THE SELLER HAS THE RIGHT TO TAKE POSSESSION OF YOUR PROPERTY.

(b) The notice must also:

(1) identify and explain the remedy the seller intends to enforce;

(2) if the purchaser has failed to make a timely payment, specify:

(A) the delinquent amount, itemized into principal and interest;

(B) any additional charges claimed, such as late charges or attorney's fees; and

(C) the period to which the delinquency and additional charges relate; and

(3) if the purchaser has failed to comply with a term of the contract, identify the term violated and the action required to cure the violation.

(c) Notice by mail is given when it is mailed to the purchaser's residence or place of business. The affidavit of a person knowledgeable of the facts to the effect that notice was given is prima facie evidence of notice in an action involving a subsequent bona fide purchaser for value if the purchaser is not in possession of the real property and if the stated time to avoid the forfeiture has expired. A bona fide subsequent purchaser for value who relies upon the affidavit under this subsection shall take title free and clear of the contract.

History of Prop. Code §5.063: Acts 1983, 68th Leg., ch. 576, §1, eff. Jan. 1, 1984. Amended by Acts 1993, 73rd Leg., ch. 444, §1, eff. Sept. 1, 1993; Acts 1995, 74th Leg., ch. 994, §2, eff. Sept. 1, 1995. Renumbered from §5.062 and amended by Acts 2001, 77th Leg., ch. 693, §1, eff. Sept. 1, 2001.

See also *Real Estate Forms*, FORM 1:21.

ANNOTATIONS

Hall v. Parks, No. 07-08-0321-CV (Tex.App.—Amarillo 2009, no pet.) (memo op.; 5-19-09). "[D] asserts that his notice of default and foreclosure on the executory contract mailed to [assignor] was sufficient to give him good title to the property by virtue of his Trustee's Deed. Section 5.063 … requires that a notice of default 'be delivered by registered or certified mail, return receipt requested' to the purchaser's residence [or business]. Similarly, written notice of a foreclosure sale must be served on each debtor 'by certified mail.' In order for a trustee to lawfully undertake a foreclosure on real property, he or she is required to comply with the notice requirements set forth in the deed of trust and as prescribed by law."

Harbert v. Owen, 791 S.W.2d 627, 628 (Tex.App.—Beaumont 1990, no writ). "We hold that the contractual agreement to pay reasonable attorneys fees incurred by

reason of the purchaser's default is not rendered unenforceable by §5.063. The contract specifically provided for forfeiture in the event of failure to make any of the payments or to perform any of the covenants. It stated [sellers] could charge [purchaser] with their attorneys fees if she went into default. [Purchaser] was behind in her monthly payments when the attorney initiated collection efforts. She was informed of the existence and amount of attorneys fees before she paid the past due installments. Thus, [purchaser] failed to cure her default within the statutory period and [sellers] were entitled to declare the contract forfeited. Thus, [sellers] were entitled to judgment for possession of the property and recovery of their attorneys fees."

PROP §5.064. SELLER'S REMEDIES ON DEFAULT

A seller may enforce the remedy of rescission or of forfeiture and acceleration against a purchaser in default under an executory contract for conveyance of real property only if:

(1) the seller notifies the purchaser of:

(A) the seller's intent to enforce a remedy under this section; and

(B) the purchaser's right to cure the default within the 30-day period described by Section 5.065;

(2) the purchaser fails to cure the default within the 30-day period described by Section 5.065;

(3) Section 5.066 does not apply; and

(4) the contract has not been recorded in the county in which the property is located.

History of Prop. Code §5.064: Acts 1983, 68th Leg., ch. 576, §1, eff. Jan. 1, 1984. Amended by Acts 1995, 74th Leg., ch. 994, §2, eff. Sept. 1, 1995. Renumbered from §5.061 and amended by Acts 2001, 77th Leg., ch. 693, §1, eff. Sept. 1, 2001. Amended by Acts 2003, 78th Leg., ch. 959, §1, eff. Sept. 1, 2003; Acts 2015, 84th Leg., ch. 996, §2, eff. Sept. 1, 2015. Source: TRCS art. 1301b, §2.

See also ***Real Estate Forms***, FORM 1:21.

ANNOTATIONS

Reeder v. Curry, 294 S.W.3d 851, 856 (Tex.App.—Dallas 2009, pet. denied). "In an executory contract for the sale of land, such as the contract for deed in this case, the superior title remains with the seller until the purchaser fulfills its part of the contract. If the purchaser defaults under the contract, the seller is entitled to possession of the property. However, the rescission of a contract for deed with the forfeiture of the purchaser's payments and interest in the property is a harsh remedy not favored by the courts. Therefore, the seller's right to retake possession of the property under the contract's forfeiture provision may be defeated by the purchaser 'pleading and proving such facts as would make it inequitable to enforce it.'"

PROP §5.065. RIGHT TO CURE DEFAULT

Notwithstanding an agreement to the contrary, a purchaser in default under an executory contract for the conveyance of real property may avoid the enforcement of a remedy described by Section 5.064 by complying with the terms of the contract on or before the 30th day after the date notice is given under that section.

History of Prop. Code §5.065: Acts 1983, 68th Leg., ch. 576, §1, eff. Jan. 1, 1984. Amended by Acts 1995, 74th Leg., ch. 994, §2, eff. Sept. 1, 1995. Renumbered from §5.063 and amended by Acts 2001, 77th Leg., ch. 693, §1, eff. Sept. 1, 2001. Amended by Acts 2003, 78th Leg., ch. 959, §2, eff. Sept. 1, 2003.

See also ***Real Estate Forms***, FORM 1:21.

ANNOTATIONS

Harbert v. Owen, 791 S.W.2d 627, 628 (Tex.App.—Beaumont 1990, no writ). See annotation under Property Code §5.063, p. 50.

PROP §5.066. EQUITY PROTECTION; SALE OF PROPERTY

(a) If a purchaser defaults after the purchaser has paid 40 percent or more of the amount due or the equivalent of 48 monthly payments under the executory contract or, regardless of the amount the purchaser has paid, the executory contract has been recorded, the seller is granted the power to sell, through a trustee designated by the seller, the purchaser's interest in the property as provided by this section. The seller may not enforce the remedy of rescission or of forfeiture and acceleration after the contract has been recorded.

(b) The seller shall notify a purchaser of a default under the contract and allow the purchaser at least 60 days after the date notice is given to cure the default. The notice must be provided as prescribed by Section 5.063 except that the notice must substitute the following statement:

NOTICE

YOU ARE NOT COMPLYING WITH THE TERMS OF THE CONTRACT TO BUY YOUR PROPERTY. UNLESS YOU TAKE THE ACTION SPECIFIED IN THIS NOTICE BY (date) A TRUSTEE DESIGNATED BY THE SELLER HAS THE RIGHT TO SELL YOUR PROPERTY AT A PUBLIC AUCTION.

(c) The trustee or a substitute trustee designated by the seller must post, file, and serve a notice of sale and the county clerk shall record and maintain the no-

tice of sale as prescribed by Section 51.002. A notice of sale is not valid unless it is given after the period to cure has expired.

(d) The trustee or a substitute trustee designated by the seller must conduct the sale as prescribed by Section 51.002. The seller must:

(1) convey to a purchaser at a sale conducted under this section fee simple title to the real property; and

(2) warrant that the property is free from any encumbrance.

(e) The remaining balance of the amount due under the executory contract is the debt for purposes of a sale under this section. If the proceeds of the sale exceed the debt amount, the seller shall disburse the excess funds to the purchaser under the executory contract. If the proceeds of the sale are insufficient to extinguish the debt amount, the seller's right to recover the resulting deficiency is subject to Sections 51.003, 51.004, and 51.005 unless a provision of the executory contract releases the purchaser under the contract from liability.

(f) The affidavit of a person knowledgeable of the facts that states that the notice was given and the sale was conducted as provided by this section is prima facie evidence of those facts. A purchaser for value who relies on an affidavit under this subsection acquires title to the property free and clear of the executory contract.

(g) If a purchaser defaults before the purchaser has paid 40 percent of the amount due or the equivalent of 48 monthly payments under the executory contract, the seller may enforce the remedy of rescission or of forfeiture and acceleration of the indebtedness if the seller complies with the notice requirements of Sections 5.063 and 5.064.

History of Prop. Code §5.066: Acts 1995, 74th Leg., ch. 994, §3, eff. Sept. 1, 1995. Renumbered from §5.101 and amended by Acts 2001, 77th Leg., ch. 693, §1, eff. Sept. 1, 2001. Amended by Acts 2015, 84th Leg., ch. 996, §3, eff. Sept. 1, 2015.

See also Prop. Code §§5.063, 5.064, 51.002-51.005; ***Real Estate Forms***, FORM 1:21.

PROP §5.067. PLACEMENT OF LIEN FOR UTILITY SERVICE

Notwithstanding any terms of a contract to the contrary, the placement of a lien for the reasonable value of improvements to residential real estate for purposes of providing utility service to the property shall not constitute a default under the terms of an executory contract for the purchase of the real property.

History of Prop. Code §5.067: Acts 1991, 72nd Leg., ch. 743, §1, eff. Sept. 1, 1991. Amended by Acts 1995, 74th Leg., ch. 994, §2, eff. Sept. 1, 1995. Renumbered from §5.064 and amended by Acts 2001, 77th Leg., ch. 693, §1, eff. Sept. 1, 2001.

See also ***Real Estate Forms***, FORM 1:21.

PROP §5.068. FOREIGN LANGUAGE REQUIREMENT

If the negotiations that precede the execution of an executory contract are conducted primarily in a language other than English, the seller shall provide a copy in that language of all written documents relating to the transaction, including the contract, disclosure notices, annual accounting statements, and a notice of default required by this subchapter.

History of Prop. Code §5.068: Acts 1995, 74th Leg., ch. 994, §3, eff. Sept. 1, 1995. Renumbered from §5.093 and amended by Acts 2001, 77th Leg., ch. 693, §1, eff. Sept. 1, 2001.

See also ***Real Estate Forms***, FORM 1:21.

PROP §5.069. SELLER'S DISCLOSURE OF PROPERTY CONDITION

(a) Before an executory contract is signed by the purchaser, the seller shall provide the purchaser with:

(1) a survey, which was completed within the past year, or plat of a current survey of the real property;

(2) a legible copy of any document that describes an encumbrance or other claim, including a restrictive covenant or easement, that affects title to the real property; and

(3) a written notice, which must be attached to the contract, informing the purchaser of the condition of the property that must, at a minimum, be executed by the seller and purchaser and read substantially similar to the following:

WARNING

IF ANY OF THE ITEMS BELOW HAVE NOT BEEN CHECKED, YOU MAY NOT BE ABLE TO LIVE ON THE PROPERTY.

SELLER'S DISCLOSURE NOTICE

CONCERNING THE PROPERTY AT (street address or legal description and city)

THIS DOCUMENT STATES CERTAIN APPLICABLE FACTS ABOUT THE PROPERTY YOU ARE CONSIDERING PURCHASING.

CHECK ALL THE ITEMS THAT ARE APPLICABLE OR TRUE:

____ The property is in a recorded subdivision.

____ The property has water service that provides potable water.

____ The property has sewer service.

____ The property has been approved by the appropriate municipal, county, or state agency for installation of a septic system.

____ The property has electric service.

____ The property is not in a floodplain.

____ The roads to the boundaries of the property are paved and maintained by:

____ the seller;

____ the owner of the property on which the road exists;

____ the municipality;

____ the county; or

____ the state.

____ No individual or entity other than the seller:

(1) owns the property;

(2) has a claim of ownership to the property; or

(3) has an interest in the property.

____ No individual or entity has a lien filed against the property.

____ There are no restrictive covenants, easements, or other title exceptions or encumbrances that prohibit construction of a house on the property.

NOTICE: SELLER ADVISES PURCHASER TO:

(1) OBTAIN A TITLE ABSTRACT OR TITLE COMMITMENT COVERING THE PROPERTY AND HAVE THE ABSTRACT OR COMMITMENT REVIEWED BY AN ATTORNEY BEFORE SIGNING A CONTRACT OF THIS TYPE; AND

(2) PURCHASE AN OWNER'S POLICY OF TITLE INSURANCE COVERING THE PROPERTY.

__________ __________________

(Date) (Signature of Seller)

__________ __________________

(Date) (Signature of Purchaser)

(b) If the property is not located in a recorded subdivision, the seller shall provide the purchaser with a separate disclosure form stating that utilities may not be available to the property until the subdivision is recorded as required by law.

(c) If the seller advertises property for sale under an executory contract, the advertisement must disclose information regarding the availability of water, sewer, and electric service.

(d) The seller's failure to provide information required by this section:

(1) is a false, misleading, or deceptive act or practice within the meaning of Section 17.46, Business & Commerce Code, and is actionable in a public or private suit brought under Subchapter E, Chapter 17, Business & Commerce Code; and

(2) entitles the purchaser to cancel and rescind the executory contract and receive a full refund of all payments made to the seller.

(e) Subsection (d) does not limit the purchaser's remedy against the seller for other false, misleading, or deceptive acts or practices actionable in a suit brought under Subchapter E, Chapter 17, Business & Commerce Code.

History of Prop. Code §5.069: Acts 1995, 74th Leg., ch. 994, §3, eff. Sept. 1, 1995. Renumbered from §5.094 and amended by Acts 2001, 77th Leg., ch. 693, §1, eff. Sept. 1, 2001.

See also B&CC §§17.46, 17.50(h); ***O'Connor's Texas COA***, "DTPA Tie-In Statutes," chart 8-2, p. 224; ***Real Estate Forms***, FORM 1:21.

ANNOTATIONS

Morton v. Nguyen, 412 S.W.3d 506, 508 (Tex.2013). "The primary issue … is whether a buyer who exercised the statutory right to cancel and rescind a contract for deed must restore to the seller all benefits the buyer received under the contract. … Subchapter D's cancellation-and-rescission remedy contemplates mutual restitution of benefits among the parties. [T]he buyers here must restore to the seller supplemental enrichment in the form of rent for the buyers' interim occupation of the property upon cancellation and rescission of the contract for deed. *At 512:* While the buyer remains entitled to 'a full refund of all payments made to the seller,' cancellation and *rescission* of a contract also requires that the buyer restore to the seller the value of the buyer's occupation of the property."

PROP §5.070. SELLER'S DISCLOSURE OF TAX PAYMENTS & INSURANCE COVERAGE

(a) Before an executory contract is signed by the purchaser, the seller shall provide the purchaser with:

(1) a tax certificate from the collector for each taxing unit that collects taxes due on the property as provided by Section 31.08, Tax Code; and

(2) a legible copy of any insurance policy, binder, or other evidence relating to the property that indicates:

(A) the name of the insurer and the insured;

(B) a description of the property insured; and

(C) the amount for which the property is insured.

(b) The seller's failure to provide information required by this section:

(1) is a false, misleading, or deceptive act or practice within the meaning of Section 17.46, Business & Commerce Code, and is actionable in a public or private suit brought under Subchapter E, Chapter 17, Business & Commerce Code; and

(2) entitles the purchaser to cancel and rescind the executory contract and receive a full refund of all payments made to the seller.

(c) Subsection (b) does not limit the purchaser's remedy against the seller for other false, misleading, or deceptive acts or practices actionable in a suit brought under Subchapter E, Chapter 17, Business & Commerce Code.

(d) If the executory contract is recorded, the seller is not required to continue insuring the property.

History of Prop. Code §5.070: Acts 2001, 77th Leg., ch. 693, §1, eff. Sept. 1, 2001. Amended by Acts 2015, 84th Leg., ch. 996, §4, eff. Sept. 1, 2015.

See also B&CC §§17.46, 17.50(h); Tax Code §31.08; ***O'Connor's Texas COA***, "DTPA Tie-In Statutes," chart 8-2, p. 224; ***Real Estate Forms***, FORM 1:21.

ANNOTATIONS

Morton v. Nguyen, 412 S.W.3d 506, 511 (Tex.2013). "Allowing a buyer to recover all benefits bestowed upon the seller upon rescission without also requiring the buyer to surrender the benefits that he received under the contract would result in a windfall inconsistent with the general nature of Subch. D's cancellation-and-rescission remedy. '[R]escission is not a one-way street.' Rather, … '[rescission] requires a mutual restoration and accounting, in which each party restores property received from the other.' A seller's wrongdoing does not excuse the buyers from counter-restitution under the circumstances of this case. But here, … we similarly hold that notice and restitution or a tender of restitution are not prerequisites to the cancellation-and-rescission remedy under Subch. D, as long as the affirmative relief to the buyer can be reduced by (or made subject to) the buyer's reciprocal obligation of restitution."

City of Clarksville v. Drilltech, Inc., 353 S.W.3d 183, 187 (Tex.App.—Texarkana 2011, no pet.). "Both parties argue about [Tax Code §31.08's] meaning of the phrase 'indicat[ing] that no delinquent taxes, penalties, or interest are due.' On the certificates, the property was described by location, description, and situs address and contained a space for valuation for improvements. Because the improvement valuation was listed as '0,' [landowner] argued that the tax certificates showed no taxes owing. The Taxing Units argue that the tax certificate itself must contain a statement that no delinquent taxes, penalties, or interest are due. *At 188:* The tax certificates specifically certified and guaranteed that only the amounts listed were due 'for the above described property' and 'on the described property.' No indication of delinquent taxes owing for any improvements were shown. Therefore, the certificates 'erroneously indicate[d] that no delinquent taxes, penalties, or interest [were] due' with respect to any improvements. Therefore, we find [landowner] proved its entitlement to summary judgment as a matter of law."

PROP §5.071. SELLER'S DISCLOSURE OF FINANCING TERMS

Before an executory contract is signed by the purchaser, the seller shall provide to the purchaser a written statement that specifies:

(1) the purchase price of the property;

(2) the interest rate charged under the contract;

(3) the dollar amount, or an estimate of the dollar amount if the interest rate is variable, of the interest charged for the term of the contract;

(4) the total amount of principal and interest to be paid under the contract;

(5) the late charge, if any, that may be assessed under the contract; and

(6) the fact that the seller may not charge a prepayment penalty or any similar fee if the purchaser elects to pay the entire amount due under the contract before the scheduled payment date under the contract.

History of Prop. Code §5.071: Acts 1995, 74th Leg., ch. 994, §3, eff. Sept. 1, 1995. Renumbered from §5.095 and amended by Acts 2001, 77th Leg., ch. 693, §1, eff. Sept. 1, 2001.

See also ***Real Estate Forms***, FORM 1:21.

PROP §5.072. ORAL AGREEMENTS PROHIBITED

(a) An executory contract is not enforceable unless the contract is in writing and signed by the party to be bound or by that party's authorized representative.

(b) The rights and obligations of the parties to a contract are determined solely from the written contract, and any prior oral agreements between the parties are superseded by and merged into the contract.

(c) An executory contract may not be varied by any oral agreements or discussions that occur before or contemporaneously with the execution of the contract.

(d) The seller shall include in a separate document or in a provision of the contract a statement printed in 14-point boldfaced type or 14-point uppercase typewritten letters that reads substantially similar to the following:

__________	____________________
(Date)	(Signature of Seller)
__________	____________________
(Date)	(Signature of Purchaser)

THIS EXECUTORY CONTRACT REPRESENTS THE FINAL AGREEMENT BETWEEN THE SELLER AND PURCHASER AND MAY NOT BE CONTRADICTED BY EVIDENCE OF PRIOR, CONTEMPORANEOUS, OR SUBSEQUENT ORAL AGREEMENTS OF THE PARTIES. THERE ARE NO UNWRITTEN ORAL AGREEMENTS BETWEEN THE PARTIES.

(e) The seller's failure to provide the notice required by this section:

(1) is a false, misleading, or deceptive act or practice within the meaning of Section 17.46, Business & Commerce Code, and is actionable in a public or private suit brought under Subchapter E, Chapter 17, Business & Commerce Code; and

(2) entitles the purchaser to cancel and rescind the executory contract and receive a full refund of all payments made to the seller.

(f) Subsection (e) does not limit the purchaser's remedy against the seller for other false, misleading, or deceptive acts or practices actionable in a suit brought under Subchapter E, Chapter 17, Business & Commerce Code.

History of Prop. Code §5.072: Acts 2001, 77th Leg., ch. 693, §1, eff. Sept. 1, 2001.

See also B&CC §§17.46, 17.50(h); *O'Connor's Texas COA*, "DTPA Tie-In Statutes," chart 8-2, p. 224; *Real Estate Forms*, FORM 1:21.

ANNOTATIONS

Morton v. Nguyen, 412 S.W.3d 506, 511 (Tex.2013). See annotation under Property Code §5.070, p. 54.

PROP §5.073. CONTRACT TERMS, CERTAIN WAIVERS PROHIBITED

(a) A seller may not include as a term of the executory contract a provision that:

(1) imposes an additional late-payment fee that exceeds the lesser of:

(A) eight percent of the monthly payment under the contract; or

(B) the actual administrative cost of processing the late payment;

(2) prohibits the purchaser from pledging the purchaser's interest in the property as security to obtain a loan to place improvements, including utility improvements or fire protection improvements, on the property;

(3) imposes a prepayment penalty or any similar fee if the purchaser elects to pay the entire amount due under the contract before the scheduled payment date under the contract;

(4) forfeits an option fee or other option payment paid under the contract for a late payment; or

(5) increases the purchase price, imposes a fee or charge of any type, or otherwise penalizes a purchaser leasing property with an option to buy the property for requesting repairs or exercising any other right under Chapter 92.

(b) A provision of the executory contract that purports to waive a right or exempt a party from a liability or duty under this subchapter is void.

History of Prop. Code §5.073: Acts 1995, 74th Leg., ch. 994, §3, eff. Sept. 1, 1995. Renumbered from §5.096 and amended by Acts 2001, 77th Leg., ch. 693, §1, eff. Sept. 1, 2001. Amended by Acts 2005, 79th Leg., ch. 978, §4, eff. Sept. 1, 2005.

See also *Real Estate Forms*, FORM 1:21.

PROP §5.074. PURCHASER'S RIGHT TO CANCEL CONTRACT WITHOUT CAUSE

(a) In addition to other rights or remedies provided by law, the purchaser may cancel and rescind an executory contract for any reason by sending by telegram or certified or registered mail, return receipt requested, or by delivering in person a signed, written notice of cancellation to the seller not later than the 14th day after the date of the contract.

(b) If the purchaser cancels the contract as provided by Subsection (a), the seller shall, not later than the 10th day after the date the seller receives the purchaser's notice of cancellation:

(1) return to the purchaser the executed contract and any property exchanged or payments made by the purchaser under the contract; and

(2) cancel any security interest arising out of the contract.

(c) The seller shall include in immediate proximity to the space reserved in the executory contract for the

purchaser's signature a statement printed in 14-point boldface type or 14-point uppercase typewritten letters that reads substantially similar to the following:

YOU, THE PURCHASER, MAY CANCEL THIS CONTRACT AT ANY TIME DURING THE NEXT TWO WEEKS. THE DEADLINE FOR CANCELING THE CONTRACT IS (date). THE ATTACHED NOTICE OF CANCELLATION EXPLAINS THIS RIGHT.

(d) The seller shall provide a notice of cancellation form to the purchaser at the time the purchaser signs the executory contract that is printed in 14-point boldface type or 14-point uppercase typewritten letters and that reads substantially similar to the following:

(date of contract)

NOTICE OF CANCELLATION

YOU MAY CANCEL THE EXECUTORY CONTRACT FOR ANY REASON WITHOUT ANY PENALTY OR OBLIGATION BY (date).

(1) YOU MUST SEND BY TELEGRAM OR CERTIFIED OR REGISTERED MAIL, RETURN RECEIPT REQUESTED, OR DELIVER IN PERSON A SIGNED AND DATED COPY OF THIS CANCELLATION NOTICE OR ANY OTHER WRITTEN NOTICE TO (Name of Seller) AT (Seller's Address) BY (date).

(2) THE SELLER SHALL, NOT LATER THAN THE 10TH DAY AFTER THE DATE THE SELLER RECEIVES YOUR CANCELLATION NOTICE:

(A) RETURN THE EXECUTED CONTRACT AND ANY PROPERTY EXCHANGED OR PAYMENTS MADE BY YOU UNDER THE CONTRACT; AND

(B) CANCEL ANY SECURITY INTEREST ARISING OUT OF THE CONTRACT.

I ACKNOWLEDGE RECEIPT OF THIS NOTICE OF CANCELLATION FORM.

__________ ____________________
(Date) (Purchaser's Signature)

I HEREBY CANCEL THIS CONTRACT.

__________ ____________________
(Date) (Purchaser's Signature)

(e) The seller may not request the purchaser to sign a waiver of receipt of the notice of cancellation form required by this section.

History of Prop. Code §5.074: Acts 1995, 74th Leg., ch. 994, §3, eff. Sept. 1, 1995. Renumbered from §5.097 and amended by Acts 2001, 77th Leg., ch. 693, §1, eff. Sept. 1, 2001.

See also *Real Estate Forms*, FORM 1:21.

PROP §5.075. PURCHASER'S RIGHT TO PLEDGE INTEREST IN PROPERTY ON CONTRACTS ENTERED INTO BEFORE SEPTEMBER 1, 2001

(a) On an executory contract entered into before September 1, 2001, a purchaser may pledge the interest in the property, which accrues pursuant to Section 5.066, only to obtain a loan for improving the safety of the property or any improvements on the property.

(b) Loans that improve the safety of the property and improvements on the property include loans for:

(1) improving or connecting a residence to water service;

(2) improving or connecting a residence to a wastewater system;

(3) building or improving a septic system;

(4) structural improvements in the residence; and

(5) improved fire protection.

History of Prop. Code §5.075: Acts 1995, 74th Leg., ch. 994, §3, eff. Sept. 1, 1995. Renumbered from §5.098 and amended by Acts 2001, 77th Leg., ch. 693, §1, eff. Sept. 1, 2001.

See also *Real Estate Forms*, FORM 1:21.

PROP §5.076. RECORDING REQUIREMENTS

(a) Except as provided by Subsection (b), the seller shall record the executory contract, including the attached disclosure statement required by Section 5.069, as prescribed by Title 3 on or before the 30th day after the date the contract is executed.

(b) Section 12.002(c) does not apply to an executory contract filed for record under this section.

(c) If the executory contract is terminated for any reason, the seller shall record the instrument that terminates the contract.

(d) The county clerk shall collect the filing fee prescribed by Section 118.011, Local Government Code.

(e) A seller who violates this section is liable to the purchaser in the same manner and for the same amount as a seller who violates Section 5.079 is liable to a purchaser, except the damages may not exceed $500 for each calendar year of noncompliance. This subsection does not limit or affect any other rights or remedies a purchaser has under other law.

History of Prop. Code §5.076: Acts 1995, 74th Leg., ch. 994, §3, eff. Sept. 1, 1995. Renumbered from §5.099 and amended by Acts 2001, 77th Leg., ch. 693, §1, eff. Sept. 1, 2001. Amended by Acts 2015, 84th Leg., ch. 996, §5, eff. Sept. 1, 2015.

See also Loc. Gov't Code §§118.011, 118.013; Prop. Code §§5.069, 12.002; *Real Estate Forms*, FORM 1:21.

PROP §5.077. ANNUAL ACCOUNTING STATEMENT

(a) The seller shall provide the purchaser with an annual statement in January of each year for the term of the executory contract. If the seller mails the statement to the purchaser, the statement must be postmarked not later than January 31.

(b) The statement must include the following information:

(1) the amount paid under the contract;

(2) the remaining amount owed under the contract;

(3) the number of payments remaining under the contract;

(4) the amounts paid to taxing authorities on the purchaser's behalf if collected by the seller;

(5) the amounts paid to insure the property on the purchaser's behalf if collected by the seller;

(6) if the property has been damaged and the seller has received insurance proceeds, an accounting of the proceeds applied to the property; and

(7) if the seller has changed insurance coverage, a legible copy of the current policy, binder, or other evidence that satisfies the requirements of Section 5.070(a)(2).

(c) A seller who conducts less than two transactions in a 12-month period under this section who fails to comply with Subsection (a) is liable to the purchaser for:

(1) liquidated damages in the amount of $100 for each annual statement the seller fails to provide to the purchaser within the time required by Subsection (a); and

(2) reasonable attorney's fees.

(d) A seller who conducts two or more transactions in a 12-month period under this section who fails to comply with Subsection (a) is liable to the purchaser for:

(1) liquidated damages in the amount of $250 a day for each day after January 31 that the seller fails to provide the purchaser with the statement, but not to exceed the fair market value of the property; and

(2) reasonable attorney's fees.

(e) The requirements of this section continue to apply after a purchaser obtains title to the property by conversion or any other process.

History of Prop. Code §5.077: Acts 1995, 74th Leg., ch. 994, §3, eff. Sept. 1, 1995. Renumbered from §5.100 and amended by Acts 2001, 77th Leg., ch. 693, §1, eff. Sept. 1, 2001. Amended by Acts 2005, 79th Leg., ch. 978, §5, eff. Sept. 1, 2005; Acts 2015, 84th Leg., ch. 996, §6, eff. Sept. 1, 2015.

See also *Real Estate Forms*, FORM 1:21.

ANNOTATIONS

Flores v. Millennium Interests, Ltd., 185 S.W.3d 427, 434 (Tex.2005). "[W]e conclude that an annual statement that omits some of the information required by §5.077(b) does not invoke 'liquidated damages' under §5.077(c) unless the statement is so deficient as to be something other than a good faith attempt by the seller to inform the purchaser of the current status of their contractual relationship. We further conclude that these statutory damages are penal in nature and do not require actual harm as a predicate to recovery." *See also* ***Morton v. Nguyen***, 369 S.W.3d 659, 668-69 (Tex. App.—Houston [14th Dist.] 2012), *rev'd in part on other grounds*, 412 S.W.3d 506 (Tex.2013).

Burrus v. Reyes, 516 S.W.3d 170, 196-97 (Tex. App.—El Paso 2017, pet. filed 6-20-17). "The Property Code specifically states only that daily liquidated damages may be awarded when the seller has 'conducted two or more transactions under this section,' and it does not state what it intended by those terms. Obviously from the context, the 'transactions' in question must involve situations in which a seller sells the properties utilizing a contract for deed.... What is less clear is whether the Legislature intended that a purchaser would be required to prove that the executory contract for deed was enforceable in order to recover the daily liquidated damages. [¶] As part of its efforts to regulate this area of the law, the Legislature[, in adopting §5.077,] required sellers utilizing contracts for deed in [economically distressed] areas to provide an annual accounting statement to the purchaser in January of each year. Although the Legislature subsequently made changes to the penalties that apply when a seller fails to provide an annual accounting, the intent remains the same—to protect unsophisticated buyers in economically distressed areas from overreaching sellers. ... As such, we conclude that the Legislature intended to include voidable contracts for deed ... when it enacted the liquidated damages provision in [§5.077]."

Smith v. Davis, 462 S.W.3d 604, 612 (Tex.App.—Tyler 2015, pet. denied). "[Ds] argue that [CPRC] Ch. 41 applies to [Ps'] claim under [Prop. Code] §5.077, and that [Ps] failed to prove by clear and convincing evidence that they suffered actual damages.

[¶] [T]he Texas Supreme Court [has] expressly declined to decide whether §5.077's 'liquidated damages' are also 'exemplary damages' within the meaning of Ch. 41. *At 613:* Under Ch. 41, 'exemplary damages' means 'any damages awarded as a penalty or by way of punishment but not for compensatory purposes.' And the Texas Supreme Court has concluded that damages awarded under §5.077 are penal in nature. [¶] Chapter 41 requires proof of actual damages as a predicate to exemplary damages. Section 5.077 does not require proof of actual damages as a predicate to a recovery of liquidated damages. ... The legislature expressed its intent that Ch. 41 controls here, and we are not free to disregard the clear and unambiguous language expressed in the statute. [¶] We hold that §5.077 is subject to Ch. 41, and that a claimant must prove more than nominal damages as a predicate to recovery of liquidated damages under §5.077." *See also* ***Henderson v. Love***, 181 S.W.3d 810, 812 (Tex.App.—Texarkana 2005, no pet.).

PROP §5.078. DISPOSITION OF INSURANCE PROCEEDS

(a) The named insured under an insurance policy, binder, or other coverage relating to property subject to an executory contract for the conveyance of real property shall inform the insurer, not later than the 10th day after the date the coverage is obtained or the contract executed, whichever is later, of:

(1) the executory contract for conveyance and the term of the contract; and

(2) the name and address of the other party to the contract.

(b) An insurer who disburses proceeds under an insurance policy, binder, or other coverage relating to property that has been damaged shall issue the proceeds jointly to the purchaser and the seller designated in the contract.

(c) If proceeds under an insurance policy, binder, or other coverage are disbursed, the purchaser and seller shall ensure that the proceeds are used to repair, remedy, or improve the condition on the property.

(d) The failure of a seller or purchaser to comply with Subsection (c) is a false, misleading, or deceptive act or practice within the meaning of Section 17.46, Business & Commerce Code, and is actionable in a public or private suit brought under Subchapter E, Chapter 17, Business & Commerce Code.

(e) Subsection (d) does not limit either party's remedy for other false, misleading, or deceptive acts or practices actionable in a suit brought under Subchapter E, Chapter 17, Business & Commerce Code.

History of Prop. Code §5.078: Acts 2001, 77th Leg., ch. 693, §1, eff. Sept. 1, 2001.

See also B&CC §§17.46, 17.50(h); ***O'Connor's Texas COA***, "DTPA Tie-In Statutes," chart 8-2, p. 224; ***Real Estate Forms***, FORM 1:21.

PROP §5.079. TITLE TRANSFER

(a) A recorded executory contract shall be the same as a deed with a vendor's lien. The vendor's lien is for the amount of the unpaid contract price, less any lawful deductions, and may be enforced by foreclosure sale under Section 5.066 or by judicial foreclosure. A general warranty is implied unless otherwise limited by the recorded executory contract. If an executory contract has not been recorded or converted under Section 5.081, the seller shall transfer recorded, legal title of the property covered by the executory contract to the purchaser not later than the 30th day after the date the seller receives the purchaser's final payment due under the contract.

(b) A seller who violates Subsection (a) is liable to the purchaser for:

(1) liquidated damages in the amount of:

(A) $250 a day for each day the seller fails to transfer the title to the purchaser during the period that begins the 31st day and ends the 90th day after the date the seller receives the purchaser's final payment due under the contract; and

(B) $500 a day for each day the seller fails to transfer title to the purchaser after the 90th day after the date the seller receives the purchaser's final payment due under the contract; and

(2) reasonable attorney's fees.

(c) If a person to whom a seller's property interest passes by will or intestate succession is required to obtain a court order to clarify the person's status as an heir or to clarify the status of the seller or the property before the person may convey good and indefeasible title to the property, the court in which the action is pending may waive payment of the liquidated damages and attorney's fees under Subsection (b) if the court finds that the person is pursuing the action to establish good and indefeasible title with reasonable diligence.

(d) In this section, "seller" includes a successor, assignee, personal representative, executor, or administrator of the seller.

History of Prop. Code §5.079: Acts 1995, 74th Leg., ch. 994, §3, eff. Sept. 1, 1995. Renumbered from §5.102 and amended by Acts 2001, 77th Leg., ch. 693, §1, eff. Sept. 1, 2001. Amended by Acts 2015, 84th Leg., ch. 996, §7, eff. Sept. 1, 2015.

See also *Real Estate Forms*, FORM 1:21.

ANNOTATIONS

Shook v. Walden, 368 S.W.3d 604, 624 (Tex.App.—Austin 2012, pet. denied). "The pivotal question governing [Ps'] entitlement to relief ... is whether the Land Contract was an 'executory contract' within the meaning of ... §5.079. [¶] The linchpin of [Ps'] position is that 'executory contract' under subch. D must be given its ordinary, general meaning, denoting a contract 'that remains wholly unperformed or for which there remains something still to be done on both sides.' They insist that the Land Contract was 'executory' in this sense at all times before closing because both parties, by definition, had remaining obligations to perform. [¶] In [Ps'] view, their chief hurdle to recovery under §5.079 is subch. D's exclusion of an 'executory contract that provides for the delivery of a deed from the seller to the purchaser within 180 days of the date of the final execution of the executory contract.' [¶] Considering the context in which the Legislature used the term, 'executory contract,' in [D's] view, was intended to have a technical meaning basically synonymous with a contract for deed. *At 627:* While acknowledging that a contract for deed is one kind of 'executory contract' under subch. D, [Ps] insist that it is not the only kind. [N]o court to date has interpreted or applied 'executory contract' under subch. D as broadly as [Ps] urge here. Instead, the decisions are consistent with a recognition of what is apparent in the structure and wording of subch. D—that the 'executory contract' contemplated by the Legislature, whether or not extending beyond contracts for deed, contemplates that a purchaser satisfy a series of obligations over an extended period of time before the seller has an obligation to transfer title. The Land Contract, even considering the asserted modification on which [Ps] rely, is not this sort of contract. The district court did not err in concluding that §5.079 did not apply."

Zuniga v. Velasquez, 274 S.W.3d 770, 773 (Tex. App.—San Antonio 2008, no pet.). "In order to recover damages under §5.079 ..., [Ps] were required to prove they fulfilled the terms of the contract for deed, and [D] failed to convey title within 30 days after receiving the final payment. *At 774:* [Ps] maintain they overpaid [D] $200.00 [in late fees], which should offset any amount [D] claims was not paid under the contract for deed. ... The right of offset is an affirmative defense which must be pleaded and proved by the party asserting it. *At 775:* Section 5.079 imposes a harsh penalty on a noncomplying seller, and therefore [Ps] were required to demonstrate that they made all payments as called for under the contract for deed. [Ps] failed to meet this exacting burden of proof." *See also* ***Flores v. Millennium Interests, Ltd.***, 185 S.W.3d 427, 433 (Tex.2005) (noting that if statute is penal in nature, it would have to be strictly construed).

PROP §5.080. LIABILITY FOR DISCLOSURES

For purposes of this subchapter, a disclosure required by this subchapter that is made by a seller's agent is a disclosure made by the seller.

History of Prop. Code §5.080: Acts 1995, 74th Leg., ch. 994, §3, eff. Sept. 1, 1995. Renumbered from §5.103 and amended by Acts 2001, 77th Leg., ch. 693, §1, eff. Sept. 1, 2001.

See also *Real Estate Forms*, FORM 1:21.

PROP §5.081. RIGHT TO CONVERT CONTRACT

(a) A purchaser, at any time and without paying penalties or charges of any kind, is entitled to convert the purchaser's interest in property under an executory contract into recorded, legal title in accordance with this section, regardless of whether the seller has recorded the executory contract.

(b) If the purchaser tenders to the seller an amount of money equal to the balance of the total amount owed by the purchaser to the seller under the executory contract, the seller shall transfer to the purchaser recorded, legal title of the property covered by the contract.

(c) Subject to Subsection (d), if the purchaser delivers to the seller of property covered by an executory contract a promissory note that is equal in amount to the balance of the total amount owed by the purchaser to the seller under the contract and that contains the same interest rate, due dates, and late fees as the contract:

(1) the seller shall execute a deed containing any warranties required by the contract and conveying to the purchaser recorded, legal title of the property; and

(2) the purchaser shall simultaneously execute a deed of trust that:

(A) contains the same terms as the contract regarding the purchaser's and seller's duties concerning the property;

(B) secures the purchaser's payment and performance under the promissory note and deed of trust; and

(C) conveys the property to the trustee, in trust, and confers on the trustee the power to sell the property if the purchaser defaults on the promissory note or the terms of the deed of trust.

(d) On or before the 10th day after the date the seller receives a promissory note under Subsection (c) that substantially complies with that subsection, the seller shall:

(1) deliver to the purchaser a written explanation that legally justifies why the seller refuses to convert the purchaser's interest into recorded, legal title under Subsection (c); or

(2) communicate with the purchaser to schedule a mutually agreeable day and time to execute the deed and deed of trust under Subsection (c).

(e) A seller who violates this section is liable to the purchaser in the same manner and amount as a seller who violates Section 5.079 is liable to a purchaser. This subsection does not limit or affect any other rights or remedies a purchaser has under other law.

(f) On the last date that all of the conveyances described by Subsections (b) and (c) are executed, the executory contract:

(1) is considered completed; and

(2) has no further effect.

(g) The appropriate use of forms published by the Texas Real Estate Commission for transactions described by this section constitutes compliance with this section.

(h) This section may not be construed to limit the purchaser's interest in the property established by other law, if any, or any other rights of the purchaser under this subchapter.

History of Prop. Code §5.081: Acts 2005, 79th Leg., ch. 978, §6, eff. Sept. 1, 2005. Amended by Acts 2015, 84th Leg., ch. 996, §8, eff. Sept. 1, 2015.

See also *Real Estate Forms*, FORMS 1:21, 3:2.

ANNOTATIONS

Norton v. Norton, No. 07-08-0469-CV (Tex.App.—Amarillo 2010, no pet.) (memo op.; 7-19-10). "[P] argues that the Contract for Deed entered into for the purchase of the marital residence is an instrument for security for debts on real property akin to a lien. ... We agree with [P]. [¶] A contract for deed is an agreement by a seller to deliver a deed to property once certain conditions have been met. The seller is not obliged to deliver legal title to the property until the purchaser pays the purchase price in full. The legal effect of the contract is the same as that of a deed with a retained vendor's lien. Paramount title is in the purchaser and the seller retains a vendor's lien. [¶] [T]he record in the underlying case establishes that the seller ... retained a vendor's lien in the marital property as a matter of law. Therefore, the trial court abused its discretion in finding that the debt described in the contract for deed executed in connection with the purchase of the property ... was an unsecured debt to which the economic contribution statute did not apply."

PROP §5.082. REQUEST FOR BALANCE & TRUSTEE

(a) A purchaser under an executory contract, on written request, is entitled to receive the following information from the seller:

(1) as of the date of the request or another date specified by the purchaser, the amount owed by the purchaser under the contract; and

(2) if applicable, the name and address of the seller's desired trustee for a deed of trust to be executed under Section 5.081.

(b) On or before the 10th day after the date the seller receives from the purchaser a written request for information described by Subsection (a), the seller shall provide to the purchaser a written statement of the requested information.

(c) If the seller does not timely respond to a request made under this section, the purchaser may:

(1) determine or pay the amount owed under the contract, including determining the amount necessary for a promissory note under Section 5.081; and

(2) if applicable, select a trustee for a deed of trust under Section 5.081.

(d) For purposes of Subsection (c)(2), a purchaser must select a trustee that lives or has a place of business in the same county where the property covered by the executory contract is located.

(e) Not later than the 20th day after the date a seller receives notice of an amount determined by a purchaser under Subsection (c)(1), the seller may contest that amount by sending a written objection to the purchaser. An objection under this subsection must:

(1) be sent to the purchaser by regular and certified mail;

(2) include the amount the seller claims is the amount owed under the contract; and

(3) be based on written records kept by the seller or the seller's agent that were maintained and regularly updated for the entire term of the executory contract.

History of Prop. Code §5.082: Acts 2005, 79th Leg., ch. 978, §6, eff. Sept. 1, 2005.

PROP §5.083. RIGHT TO CANCEL CONTRACT FOR IMPROPER PLATTING

(a) Except as provided by Subsection (c), in addition to other rights or remedies provided by law, the purchaser may cancel and rescind an executory contract at any time if the purchaser learns that the seller has not properly subdivided or platted the property that is covered by the contract in accordance with state and local law. A purchaser canceling and rescinding a contract under this subsection must:

(1) deliver a signed, written notice of the cancellation and rescission to the seller in person; or

(2) send a signed, written notice of the cancellation and rescission to the seller by telegram or certified or registered mail, return receipt requested.

(b) If the purchaser cancels the contract as provided under Subsection (a), the seller, not later than the 10th day after the date the seller receives the notice of cancellation and rescission, shall:

(1) deliver in person or send by telegram or certified or registered mail, return receipt requested, to the purchaser a signed, written notice that the seller intends to subdivide or plat the property properly; or

(2) return to the purchaser all payments of any kind made to the seller under the contract and reimburse the purchaser for:

(A) any payments the purchaser made to a taxing authority for the property; and

(B) the value of any improvements made to the property by the purchaser.

(c) A purchaser may not exercise the purchaser's right to cancel and rescind an executory contract under this section if, on or before the 90th day after the date the purchaser receives the seller's notice under Subsection (b)(1), the seller:

(1) properly subdivides or plats the property; and

(2) delivers in person or sends by telegram or certified or registered mail, return receipt requested, to the purchaser a signed, written notice evidencing that the property has been subdivided or platted in accordance with state and local law.

(d) The seller may not terminate the purchaser's possession of the property covered by the contract being canceled and rescinded before the seller pays the purchaser any money to which the purchaser is entitled under Subsection (b).

History of Prop. Code §5.083: Acts 2005, 79th Leg., ch. 978, §6, eff. Sept. 1, 2005.

PROP §5.084. RIGHT TO DEDUCT

If a seller is liable to a purchaser under this subchapter, the purchaser, without taking judicial action, may deduct the amount owed to the purchaser by the seller from any amounts owed to the seller by the purchaser under the terms of an executory contract.

History of Prop. Code §5.084: Acts 2005, 79th Leg., ch. 978, §6, eff. Sept. 1, 2005.

PROP §5.085. FEE SIMPLE TITLE REQUIRED; MAINTENANCE OF FEE SIMPLE TITLE

(a) A potential seller may not execute an executory contract with a potential purchaser if the seller does not own the property in fee simple free from any liens or other encumbrances.

(b) Except as provided by this subsection, a seller, or the seller's heirs or assigns, must maintain fee simple title free from any liens or other encumbrances to property covered by an executory contract for the entire duration of the contract. This subsection does not apply to a lien or encumbrance placed on the property that is:

(1) placed on the property because of the conduct of the purchaser;

(2) agreed to by the purchaser as a condition of a loan obtained to place improvements on the property, including utility or fire protection improvements; or

(3) placed on the property by the seller prior to the execution of the contract in exchange for a loan used only to purchase the property if:

(A) the seller, not later than the third day before the date the contract is executed, notifies the purchaser in a separate written disclosure:

(i) of the name, address, and phone number of the lienholder or, if applicable, servicer of the loan;

(ii) of the loan number and outstanding balance of the loan;

(iii) of the monthly payments due on the loan and the due date of those payments; and

(iv) in 14-point type that, if the seller fails to make timely payments to the lienholder, the lienholder may

attempt to collect the debt by foreclosing on the lien and selling the property at a foreclosure sale;

(B) the lien:

(i) is attached only to the property sold to the purchaser under the contract; and

(ii) secures indebtedness that, at no time, is or will be greater in amount than the amount of the total outstanding balance owed by the purchaser under the executory contract;

(C) the lienholder:

(i) does not prohibit the property from being encumbered by an executory contract; and

(ii) consents to verify the status of the loan on request of the purchaser and to accept payments directly from the purchaser if the seller defaults on the loan; and

(D) the following covenants are placed in the executory contract:

(i) a covenant that obligates the seller to make timely payments on the loan and to give monthly statements to the purchaser reflecting the amount paid to the lienholder, the date the lienholder receives the payment, and the information described by Paragraph (A);

(ii) a covenant that obligates the seller, not later than the third day the seller receives or has actual knowledge of a document or an event described by this subparagraph, to notify the purchaser in writing in 14-point type that the seller has been sent a notice of default, notice of acceleration, or notice of foreclosure or has been sued in connection with a lien on the property and to attach a copy of all related documents received to the written notice; and

(iii) a covenant that warrants that if the seller does not make timely payments on the loan or any other indebtedness secured by the property, the purchaser may, without notice, cure any deficiency with a lienholder directly and deduct from the total outstanding balance owed by the purchaser under the executory contract, without the necessity of judicial action, 150 percent of any amount paid to the lienholder.

(c) A violation of this section:

(1) is a false, misleading, or deceptive act or practice within the meaning of Section 17.46, Business & Commerce Code, and is actionable in a public or private suit brought under Subchapter E, Chapter 17, Business & Commerce Code; and

(2) in addition to other rights or remedies provided by law, entitles the purchaser to cancel and rescind the executory contract and receive from the seller:

(A) the return of all payments of any kind made to the seller under the contract; and

(B) reimbursement for:

(i) any payments the purchaser made to a taxing authority for the property; and

(ii) the value of any improvements made to the property by the purchaser.

(d) A seller is not liable under this section if:

(1) a lien is placed on the property by a person other than the seller; and

(2) not later than the 30th day after the date the seller receives notice of the lien, the seller takes all steps necessary to remove the lien and has the lien removed from the property.

History of Prop. Code §5.085: Acts 2005, 79th Leg., ch. 978, §6, eff. Sept. 1, 2005.

See also B&CC §§17.46, 17.50(h); Prop. Code §5.001.

ANNOTATIONS

Morton v. Nguyen, 369 S.W.3d 659, 674 (Tex. App.—Houston [14th Dist.] 2012), *rev'd in part on other grounds*, 412 S.W.3d 506 (Tex.2013). "By its plain language, the purchaser's right to receive the 'value of improvements' under §5.085 is designed to compensate the purchaser for value that is added by the purchaser to the property, regardless of the reason, and that is retained by the seller after the purchaser properly cancels and rescinds the contract for deed. Unlike circumstances in which a claimant must exercise reasonableness when making necessary repairs to wrongfully damaged property for which reimbursement will be sought against another party, the circumstances contemplated by §5.085 involve a purchaser who spent his or her own money to improve property the purchaser contracted to own. As the statute measures the amount of recovery by the 'value' rather than the 'cost' of such improvements, we see no reason why [Ds] should be required to present evidence of reasonable costs."

E PROP §5.086. EQUITABLE INTEREST DISCLOSURE

Before entering into a contract, a person selling an option or assigning an interest in a contract to purchase real property must disclose to any potential buyer that the person is selling only an option or assigning an interest in a contract and that the person does not have legal title to the real property.

History of Prop. Code §5.086: Enacted by S.B. 2212, §4, 85th Leg., eff. Sept. 1, 2017.

Sections 5.087-5.090 blank

PROP §5.091. RENUMBERED

Renumbered as §5.062 by Acts 2001, 77th Leg., ch. 693, §1, eff. Sept. 1, 2001.

PROP §5.092. REPEALED

Repealed by Acts 2001, 77th Leg., ch. 693, §2, eff. Sept. 1, 2001.

PROP §§5.093, 5.094. RENUMBERED

Renumbered as §§5.068, 5.069 by Acts 2001, 77th Leg., ch. 693, §1, eff. Sept. 1, 2001.

PROP §5.095. RENUMBERED

Renumbered as §5.071 by Acts 2001, 77th Leg., ch. 693, §1, eff. Sept. 1, 2001.

PROP §§5.096 TO 5.100. RENUMBERED

Renumbered as §§5.073-5.077 by Acts 2001, 77th Leg., ch. 693, §1, eff. Sept. 1, 2001.

PROP §5.101. RENUMBERED

Renumbered as §5.066 by Acts 2001, 77th Leg., ch. 693, §1, eff. Sept. 1, 2001.

PROP §§5.102, 5.103. RENUMBERED

Renumbered as §§5.079, 5.080 by Acts 2001, 77th Leg., ch. 693, §1, eff. Sept. 1, 2001.

Sections 5.104-5.150 blank

SUBCHAPTER F. REQUIREMENTS FOR CONVEYANCES OF MINERAL OR ROYALTY INTERESTS

PROP §5.151. DISCLOSURE IN OFFER TO PURCHASE MINERAL INTEREST

(a) A person who mails to the owner of a mineral or royalty interest an offer to purchase only the mineral or royalty interest, it being understood that for the purpose of this section the taking of an oil, gas, or mineral lease shall not be deemed a purchase of a mineral or royalty interest, and encloses an instrument of conveyance of only the mineral or royalty interest and a draft or other instrument, as defined in Section 3.104, Business & Commerce Code, providing for payment for that interest shall include in the offer a conspicuous statement printed in a type style that is approximately the same size as 14-point type style or larger and is in substantially the following form:

BY EXECUTING AND DELIVERING THIS INSTRUMENT YOU ARE SELLING ALL OR A PORTION OF YOUR MINERAL OR ROYALTY INTEREST IN (DESCRIPTION OF PROPERTY BEING CONVEYED).

(b) A person who conveys a mineral or royalty interest as provided by Subsection (a) may bring suit against the purchaser of the interest if:

(1) the purchaser did not give the notice required by Subsection (a); and

(2) the person has given 30 days' written notice to the purchaser that a suit will be filed unless the matter is otherwise resolved.

(c) A plaintiff who prevails in a suit under Subsection (b) may recover from the initial purchaser of the mineral or royalty interest the greater of:

(1) $100; or

(2) an amount up to the difference between the amount paid by the purchaser for the mineral or royalty interest and the fair market value of the mineral or royalty interest at the time of the sale.

(d) The prevailing party in a suit under Subsection (b) may recover:

(1) court costs; and

(2) reasonable attorney's fees.

(e) A person must bring a suit under Subsection (b) not later than the second anniversary of the date the person executed the conveyance.

(f) The remedy provided under this section shall be in addition to any other remedies existing under law, excluding rescission or other remedies that would make the conveyance of the mineral or royalty interest void or of no force and effect.

History of Prop. Code §5.151: Acts 1999, 76th Leg., ch. 1200, §1, eff. Sept. 1, 1999.

Sections 5.152-5.200 blank

SUBCHAPTER G. CERTAIN PRIVATE TRANSFER FEES PROHIBITED; PRESERVATION OF PRIVATE REAL PROPERTY RIGHTS

PROP §5.201. DEFINITIONS

In this subchapter:

(1) "Encumbered property" means all property, including the property of a subsequent purchaser, subject to the same private transfer fee obligation.

(2) "Lender" means a lending institution, including a bank, trust company, banking association, savings and loan association, mortgage company, investment bank, credit union, life insurance company, and governmental agency, that customarily provides financing or an affiliate of a lending institution.

(3) "Payee" means a person who claims the right to receive or collect a private transfer fee payable under a private transfer fee obligation and who may or may not have a pecuniary interest in the obligation.

(4) "Private transfer fee" means an amount of money, regardless of the method of determining the amount, that is payable on the transfer of an interest in real property or payable for a right to make or accept a transfer.

(5) "Private transfer fee obligation" means an obligation to pay a private transfer fee created under:

(A) a declaration or other covenant recorded in the real property records in the county in which the property subject to the private transfer fee obligation is located;

(B) a contractual agreement or promise; or

(C) an unrecorded contractual agreement or promise.

(6) "Subsequent owner" means a person who acquires real property by transfer from a person other than the person who is the seller of the property on the date the private transfer fee obligation is created.

(7) "Subsequent purchaser" means a person who purchases real property from a person other than the person who is the seller on the date the private transfer fee obligation is created. The term includes a lender who provides a mortgage loan to a subsequent purchaser to purchase the property.

(8) "Transfer" means the sale, gift, conveyance, assignment, inheritance, or other transfer of an ownership interest in real property.

History of Prop. Code §5.201: Acts 2011, 82nd Leg., ch. 211, §1, eff. June 17, 2011.

A PROP §5.202. CERTAIN PRIVATE TRANSFER FEE OBLIGATIONS VOID

(a) Except as provided by this subchapter, a private transfer fee obligation created on or after the effective date of this subchapter is not binding or enforceable against a subsequent owner or subsequent purchaser of an interest in real property and is void.

(b) For purposes of this subchapter, the following payments are not considered private transfer fee obligations:

(1) consideration paid by a purchaser to a seller for an interest in real property transferred, including, as applicable, a mineral interest transferred, including additional consideration paid to a seller for the property's appreciation, development, or sale after the interest in the property has been transferred to the purchaser, if the additional consideration is paid only once and that payment does not bind successors in interest to the property to any private transfer fee obligation;

(2) a commission paid to a licensed real estate broker under a written agreement between a seller or purchaser and the broker, including an additional commission for the property's appreciation, development, or sale after the interest in property is transferred to the purchaser;

(3) interest, a fee, a charge, or another type of payment to a lender under a loan secured by a mortgage on the property, including:

(A) a fee payable for the lender's consent to an assumption of the loan or transfer of the property subject to the mortgage;

(B) a fee or charge payable for an estoppel letter or certificate;

(C) a shared appreciation interest or profit participation; or

(D) other consideration payable in connection with the loan;

(4) rent, reimbursement, a fee, a charge, or another type of payment to a lessor under a lease, including a fee for consent to an assignment, sublease, encumbrance, or transfer of a lease;

(5) consideration paid to the holder of an option to purchase an interest in property, or to the holder of a right of first refusal or first offer to purchase an interest in property, for waiving, releasing, or not exercising the option or right when the property is transferred to another person;

(6) a fee payable to or imposed by a governmental entity in connection with recording the transfer of the property;

(7) dues, a fee, a charge, an assessment, a fine, a contribution, or another type of payment under a declaration or other covenant or under law, including a fee or charge payable for a change of ownership entered in the records of an association to which this subdivision applies or an estoppel letter or resale certificate issued under Section 207.003 by an association to which this subdivision applies or the person identified under Section 209.004(a)(6), provided that no portion of the fee or charge is required to be passed through to a third party designated or identifiable in the declaration or other covenant or law or in a document referenced in the declaration or other covenant or law, unless paid to:

(A) an association as defined by Section 82.003 or 221.002 or the person or entity managing the association as provided by Section 82.116(a)(5) or 221.032(b)(11), as applicable;

(B) a property owners' association as defined by Section 202.001 or 209.002 or the person or entity described by Section 209.004(a)(6); or

(C) a property owners' association as defined by Section 202.001 that does not require an owner of property governed by the association to be a member of the association or the person or entity described by Section 209.004(a)(6);

(8) dues, a fee, a charge, an assessment, a fine, a contribution, or another type of payment for the transfer of a club membership related to the property;

(9) dues, a fee, a charge, an assessment, a fine, a contribution, or another type of payment paid to an organization exempt from federal taxation under Section 501(c)(3) or 501(c)(4), Internal Revenue Code of 1986, only if the organization uses the payments to directly benefit the encumbered property by:

(A) supporting or maintaining only the encumbered property;

(B) constructing or repairing improvements only to the encumbered property; or

(C) providing activities or infrastructure to support quality of life, including cultural, educational, charitable, recreational, environmental, and conservation activities and infrastructure, that directly benefit the encumbered property; or

(10) a fee payable to or imposed by the Veterans' Land Board for consent to an assumption or transfer of a contract of sale and purchase.

(c) The benefit described by Subsection (b)(9)(C) may collaterally benefit:

(1) a community composed of:

(A) [~~(1)~~] property that is adjacent to the encumbered property; or

(B) [~~(2)~~] property a boundary of which is not more than 1,000 yards from a boundary of the encumbered property; or

(2) with respect to a payment to a school for educational activities, property not described by Subdivision (1) if the encumbered property is located within:

(A) the school's assigned attendance zone; and

(B) a county with a population of more than 650,000 that is adjacent to two counties, each of which has a population of more than 1.8 million.

(d) Notwithstanding Subsection (c), an organization may provide a direct benefit under Subsection (b)(9) if:

(1) the organization provides to the general public activities or infrastructure described by Subsection (b)(9)(C);

(2) the provision of activities or infrastructure substantially benefits the encumbered property; and

(3) the governing body of the organization:

(A) is controlled by owners of the encumbered property; and

(B) approves payments for activities or infrastructure at least annually.

(e) An organization may provide activities and infrastructure described by Subsection (b)(9)(C) to another organization exempt from federal taxation under Section 501(c)(3) or 501(c)(4), Internal Revenue Code of 1986, at no charge for de minimis usage without violating the requirements of this section.

History of Prop. Code §5.202: Acts 2011, 82nd Leg., ch. 211, §1, eff. June 17, 2011. Amended by H.B. 755, §1, 85th Leg., eff. Sept. 1, 2017.

PROP §5.203. NOTICE REQUIREMENTS FOR CONTINUATION OF EXISTING PRIVATE TRANSFER FEE OBLIGATIONS

(a) A person who receives a private transfer fee under a private transfer fee obligation created before the effective date of this subchapter must, on or before January 31, 2012, file for record a "Notice of Private Transfer Fee Obligation" as provided by this section in the real property records of each county in which the property is located.

(b) Multiple payees of a single private transfer fee under a private transfer fee obligation must designate one payee as the payee of record for the fee.

(c) A notice under Subsection (a) must:

(1) be printed in at least 14-point boldface type;

(2) state the amount of the private transfer fee and the method of determination, if applicable;

(3) state the date or any circumstance under which the private transfer fee obligation expires, if any;

(4) state the purpose for which the money from the private transfer fee obligation will be used;

(5) notwithstanding Subsection (b), state the name of each payee and each payee's contact information;

(6) state the name and address of the payee of record to whom the payment of the fee must be sent;

(7) include the acknowledged signature of each payee or authorized representative of each payee; and

(8) state the legal description of the property subject to the private transfer fee obligation.

(d) A person required to file a notice under this section shall:

(1) refile the notice described by this section not earlier than the 30th day before the third anniversary of the original filing date described by Subsection (a) and within a similar 30-day period every third year thereafter; and

(2) amend the notice to reflect any change in the name or address of any payee included in the notice not later than the 30th day after the date the change occurs.

(e) A person who amends a notice under Subsection (d)(2) must include:

(1) the recording information of the original notice filed as required by this section; and

(2) the legal description of the property subject to the private transfer fee obligation.

(f) If a person required to file a notice under this section fails to comply with this section:

(1) payment of the private transfer fee may not be a requirement for the conveyance of an interest in the property to a purchaser;

(2) the property is not subject to further obligation under the private transfer fee obligation; and

(3) the private transfer fee obligation is void.

History of Prop. Code §5.203: Acts 2011, 82nd Leg., ch. 211, §1, eff. June 17, 2011.

PROP §5.204. ADDITIONAL COMPLIANCE REQUIREMENT: TIMELY ACCEPTANCE OF FEES PAID UNDER EXISTING PRIVATE TRANSFER FEE OBLIGATIONS

(a) The payee of record on the date a private transfer fee is paid under a private transfer fee obligation subject to Section 5.203 must accept the payment on or before the 30th day after the date the payment is tendered to the payee.

(b) If the payee of record fails to comply with Subsection (a):

(1) the payment must be returned to the remitter;

(2) payment of the private transfer fee may not be a requirement for the conveyance of an interest in the property to a purchaser; and

(3) the property is not subject to further obligation under the private transfer fee obligation.

History of Prop. Code §5.204: Acts 2011, 82nd Leg., ch. 211, §1, eff. June 17, 2011.

PROP §5.205. DISCLOSURE OF EXISTING TRANSFER FEE OBLIGATION REQUIRED IN CONTRACT FOR SALE

A seller of real property that may be subject to a private transfer fee obligation shall provide written notice to a potential purchaser stating that the obligation may be governed by this subchapter.

History of Prop. Code §5.205: Acts 2011, 82nd Leg., ch. 211, §1, eff. June 17, 2011.

PROP §5.206. WAIVER VOID

A provision that purports to waive a purchaser's rights under this subchapter is void.

History of Prop. Code §5.206: Acts 2011, 82nd Leg., ch. 211, §1, eff. June 17, 2011.

PROP §5.207. INJUNCTIVE OR DECLARATORY RELIEF; PROVIDING PENALTIES

(a) The attorney general may institute an action for injunctive or declaratory relief to restrain a violation of this subchapter.

(b) In addition to instituting an action for injunctive or declaratory relief under Subsection (a), the attorney general may institute an action for civil penalties against a payee for a violation of this chapter. Except as provided by Subsection (c), a civil penalty assessed under this section may not exceed an amount equal to two times the amount of the private transfer fee charged or collected by the payee in violation of this subchapter.

(c) If the court in which an action under Subsection (b) is pending finds that a payee violated this subchapter with a frequency that constitutes a pattern or practice, the court may assess a civil penalty not to exceed $250,000.

(d) The comptroller shall deposit to the credit of the general revenue fund all money collected under this section.

History of Prop. Code §5.207: Acts 2011, 82nd Leg., ch. 211, §1, eff. June 17, 2011.

Chapters 6-10 reserved for expansion

TITLE 3. PUBLIC RECORDS

CHAPTER 11. PROVISIONS GENERALLY APPLICABLE TO PUBLIC RECORDS

PROP §11.001. PLACE OF RECORDING

(a) To be effectively recorded, an instrument relating to real property must be eligible for recording and must be recorded in the county in which a part of the property is located. However, if such an instrument grants a security interest by a utility as defined in Section 261.001, Business & Commerce Code, the instrument may be recorded as required by Sections 261.004 and 261.006 of that code, and if such instrument is so recorded, the lien and the secured interest created by such instrument shall be deemed perfected for all purposes.

(b) If an instrument has been recorded in a proper county, the subsequent creation of a new county containing property conveyed or encumbered by the instrument does not affect the recording's validity or effect as notice. The county court of the new county shall at its own expense:

(1) obtain a certified transcript of the record of all instruments conveying or encumbering property in the new county;

(2) deposit the transcript for public inspection in the recorder's office of the new county; and

(3) make an index of the transcript.

History of Prop. Code §11.001: Acts 1983, 68th Leg., ch. 576, §1, eff. Jan. 1, 1984. Amended by Acts 1989, 71st Leg., ch. 999, §1, eff. Aug. 28, 1989; Acts 2007, 80th Leg., ch. 885, §2.32, eff. Apr. 1, 2009. Source: TRCS arts. 6630, 6661.

See also *Real Estate Forms*, FORMS 1:8-1:13.

ANNOTATIONS

Aston Meadows, Ltd. v. Devon Energy Prod. Co., 359 S.W.3d 856, 862 (Tex.App.—Fort Worth 2012, pet. denied). "We conclude and hold that the correct statutory construction of §11.001(a) is that when an instrument relates to a contiguous tract of land located in more than one county, the recording of that instrument in only one of the counties is sufficient to comply with the requirements of §11.001(a)."

Sanchez v. Telles, 960 S.W.2d 762, 767 (Tex. App.—El Paso 1997, pet. denied). "The recording laws in Texas were meant to protect innocent purchasers and creditors without notice of the prior transfer from being injured or prejudiced by their lack of knowledge of the competing claim."

PROP §11.002. ENGLISH LANGUAGE

(a) An instrument relating to real or personal property may not be recorded unless it is in English or complies with this section.

(b) An authenticated instrument not in English that was executed before August 22, 1897, may be recorded and operate as constructive notice from the date of filing if:

(1) a correct English translation is recorded with the original instrument; and

(2) the accuracy of the translation is sworn to before an officer authorized to administer oaths.

(c) An instrument acknowledged outside the United States or its territories in accordance with Section 121.001(c)(3), Civil Practice and Remedies Code, that contains a certificate, stamp, or seal of a notary public or other official before whom the acknowledgment was taken or an apostille relating to the acknowledgment, any portion of which is not in English, may be recorded and operate as constructive notice from the date of filing if:

(1) a correct English translation of any non-English portion of the certificate, stamp, seal, or apostille is recorded with the original instrument;

(2) the accuracy of the translation is sworn to before an officer authorized to administer oaths; and

(3) any apostille relating to the acknowledgment complies with the Hague Convention dated October 5, 1961, titled Convention Abolishing the Requirement of Legalisation for Foreign Public Documents.

History of Prop. Code §11.002: Acts 1983, 68th Leg., ch. 576, §1, eff. Jan. 1, 1984. Amended by Acts 1987, 70th Leg., ch. 891, §2, eff. Sept. 1, 1987. Source: TRCS art. 6629.

See also *Real Estate Forms*, FORMS 1:8-1:13, 11:1, 11:2.

PROP §11.003. GRANTEE'S ADDRESS

(a) An instrument executed after December 31, 1981, conveying an interest in real property may not be recorded unless:

(1) a mailing address of each grantee appears in the instrument or in a separate writing signed by the grantor or grantee and attached to the instrument; or

(2) a penalty filing fee equal to the greater of $25 or twice the statutory recording fee for the instrument is paid.

(b) The validity of a conveyance as between the parties is not affected by a failure to include an address of each grantee in the instrument or an attached writing.

(c) Payment of a filing fee and acceptance of the instrument by the county clerk for recording creates a conclusive presumption that the requirements of this section have been met.

History of Prop. Code §11.003: Acts 1983, 68th Leg., ch. 576, §1, eff. Jan. 1, 1984. Source: TRCS art. 6626(b).

See also *Real Estate Forms*, FORMS 1:8-1:13.

PROP §11.004. DUTY OF RECORDER

(a) A county clerk shall:

(1) correctly record, as required by law, within a reasonable time after delivery, any instrument authorized or required to be recorded in that clerk's office that is proved, acknowledged, or sworn to according to law;

(2) give a receipt, as required by law, for an instrument delivered for recording;

(3) record instruments relating to the same property in the order the instruments are filed; and

(4) provide and keep in the clerk's office the indexes required by law.

(b) A county clerk who violates a provision of this section and the sureties on the clerk's bond are liable for damages and, on motion in district court and after three days' notice to the clerk, for a civil penalty of not more than $500, half of which is payable to the county and half to the person who files the motion.

History of Prop. Code §11.004: Acts 1983, 68th Leg., ch. 576, §1, eff. Jan. 1, 1984. Amended by Acts 1989, 71st Leg., ch. 162, §1, eff. Sept. 1, 1989. Source: TRCS arts. 6633, 6652.

See also *Real Estate Forms*, FORMS 11:1, 11:2.

ANNOTATIONS

Tex. Atty. Gen. Op. No. JM-904 (1988). "If the requirements for recording have been satisfied, the county clerk is not liable for any substantive errors in the instrument."

PROP §11.0041. REVIEW OF CERTAIN INSTRUMENTS IN CERTAIN COUNTIES

(a) This section applies only to the county clerk of a county:

(1) that:

(A) is located on the international border; and

(B) has a population of less than 15,000;

(2) in which a colonia self-help center established under Section 2306.582, Government Code, is located; or

(3) that is served by a colonia self-help center described by Subdivision (2) in another county.

(b) Before accepting an instrument conveying real property for filing, the county clerk may send the instrument to the county attorney for review under this section. Not later than five business days after the date the county attorney receives an instrument under this subsection, the county attorney shall:

(1) review the instrument to determine whether the platting requirements prescribed by Sections 232.023, 232.025, and 232.031, Local Government Code, have been satisfied; and

(2) return the instrument to the county clerk with a statement of the county attorney's determination under Subdivision (1).

(c) Notwithstanding Section 11.004(a), the county clerk shall immediately notify the party that presented the instrument for recording that:

(1) the clerk is referring the instrument to the county attorney for review;

(2) the instrument will not be immediately recorded; and

(3) the clerk is not required to file an instrument the county attorney determines the clerk is not required to file.

History of Prop. Code §11.0041: Acts 2009, 81st Leg., ch. 1176, §1, eff. Sept. 1, 2009.

PROP §11.005. JUDGMENT PROVING AN INSTRUMENT OR CORRECTING A CERTIFICATE

(a) A person interested under an instrument that may be proved for record may bring an action in district court for a judgment proving the instrument.

(b) A person interested under a defectively certified instrument for which acknowledgement or proof of execution has been properly made may bring an action in district court for a judgment correcting the certificate.

(c) If a certified copy of a judgment in a suit under this section that shows proof of an instrument is attached to the instrument, the instrument may be recorded with the same effect as if it were acknowledged.

History of Prop. Code §11.005: Acts 1983, 68th Leg., ch. 576, §1, eff. Jan. 1, 1984. Source: TRCS arts. 6655-6657.

PROP §11.006. INSTRUMENT AFFECTING TITLE TO LAND IN ARCHER COUNTY

An instrument that in any manner affects title to land in Archer County, Texas, but was recorded in Jack

County on or after August 10, 1866, but no later than August 10, 1870, and was made under the hand and seal of the county clerk of Shackelford County, is admissible in evidence in any suit in which secondary evidence is admissible.

History of Prop. Code §11.006: Acts 1983, 68th Leg., ch. 576, §1, eff. Jan. 1, 1984. Source: TRCS art. 6658.

PROP §11.007. EFFECT OF CITATION TO REAL PROPERTY RECORDS

A reference in an instrument to the volume and page number, film code number, or county clerk file number of the "real property records" (or other words of similar import) for a particular county is equivalent to a reference to the deed records, deed of trust records, or other specific records, for the purpose of providing effective notice to all persons of the existence of the referenced instrument.

History of Prop. Code §11.007: Acts 1989, 71st Leg., ch. 161, §1, eff. May 25, 1989. Amended by Acts 1991, 72nd Leg., ch. 205, §1, eff. Aug. 26, 1991.

A PROP §11.008. PERSONAL INFORMATION IN REAL PROPERTY RECORDS

(a) In this section, "instrument" means a deed or deed of trust.

(b) An instrument submitted for recording is not required to contain an individual's social security number, and the social security number of an individual is not obtained or maintained by the clerk under this section. The preparer of a document may not include an individual's social security number in a document that is presented for recording in the office of the county clerk.

(c) Notwithstanding Section 191.007(c), Local Government Code, an instrument transferring an interest in real property to or from an individual must include a notice that appears on the top of the first page of the instrument in 12-point boldfaced type or 12-point uppercase letters and reads substantially as follows:

NOTICE OF CONFIDENTIALITY RIGHTS: IF YOU ARE A NATURAL PERSON, YOU MAY REMOVE OR STRIKE ANY OR ALL OF THE FOLLOWING INFORMATION FROM ANY INSTRUMENT THAT TRANSFERS AN INTEREST IN REAL PROPERTY BEFORE IT IS FILED FOR RECORD IN THE PUBLIC RECORDS: YOUR SOCIAL SECURITY NUMBER OR YOUR DRIVER'S LICENSE NUMBER.

(d) The validity of an instrument as between the parties to the instrument and the notice provided by the instrument are not affected by a party's failure to include the notice required under Subsection (c).

(e) The county clerk may not under any circumstance reject an instrument presented for recording solely because the instrument fails to comply with this section. Other than the duty to redact an individual's social security number as required by Section 552.147, Government Code, the county clerk has no duty to ensure that an instrument presented for recording does not contain an individual's social security number.

(f) The county clerk shall post a notice in the county clerk's office stating that instruments recorded in the real property or official public records or the equivalent of the real property or official public records of the county:

(1) are not required to contain a social security number or driver's license number; and

(2) are public records available for review by the public.

(g) All instruments described by this section are subject to inspection by the public. The county clerk is not criminally or civilly liable for disclosing an instrument or information in an instrument in compliance with the public information law (Chapter 552, Government Code) or another law.

(h) Unless this section is cited in a law enacted after September 1, 2003, this section is the exclusive law governing the confidentiality of personal information contained in the real property or official public records or the equivalent of the real property or official public records of a county.

(i) To the extent that federal law conflicts with this section, an instrument must contain the information required by and must be filed in a manner that complies with federal law.

(j) On receipt of a written request from a federal judge, state judge as defined by Section 572.002, Government Code, or spouse of a federal or state judge, the county clerk shall omit or redact from an instrument described by this section that is available in an online database made public by the county clerk, or by a provider with which the county commissioners court contracts to provide the online database, the social security number, driver's license number, and residence address of the federal judge, state judge, or spouse of the federal or state judge.

History of Prop. Code §11.008: Acts 2003, 78th Leg., ch. 715, §1 (eff. Sept. 1, 2003), ch. 960, §1 (eff. Sept. 1, 2003). Amended by Acts 2005, 79th Leg., ch. 45, §1, eff. May 13, 2005; Acts 2007, 80th Leg., ch. 3, §2, eff. Mar. 28, 2007; S.B. 42, §25, 85th Leg., eff. Sept. 1, 2017.

See also Loc. Gov't Code §191.007(c); ***Real Estate Forms***, FORMS 1:8-1:13.

Chapter 12. Recording of Instruments

Prop §12.001. Instruments Concerning Property

(a) An instrument concerning real or personal property may be recorded if it has been acknowledged, sworn to with a proper jurat, or proved according to law.

(b) An instrument conveying real property may not be recorded unless it is signed and acknowledged or sworn to by the grantor in the presence of two or more credible subscribing witnesses or acknowledged or sworn to before and certified by an officer authorized to take acknowledgements or oaths, as applicable.

(c) This section does not require the acknowledgement or swearing or prohibit the recording of a financing statement, a security agreement filed as a financing statement, or a continuation statement filed for record under the Business & Commerce Code.

(d) The failure of a notary public to attach an official seal to an acknowledgment, a jurat, or other proof taken outside this state but inside the United States or its territories renders the acknowledgment, jurat, or other proof invalid only if the jurisdiction in which the acknowledgment, jurat, or other proof is taken requires the notary public to attach the seal.

History of Prop. Code §12.001: Acts 1983, 68th Leg., ch. 576, §1, eff. Jan. 1, 1984. Amended by Acts 1989, 71st Leg., ch. 162, §2, eff. Sept. 1, 1989; Acts 1995, 74th Leg., ch. 603, §2, eff. June 14, 1995. Source: TRCS arts. 1294, 6626(a).

See also *Real Estate Forms*, FORMS 1:8-1:13, 11:1, 11:2.

Annotations

Haile v. Holtzclaw, 414 S.W.2d 916, 928 (Tex. 1967). "[A]s between a grantor and a grantee deeds are valid even without a valid acknowledgement." *See also* ***Apex Fin. Corp. v. Garza***, 155 S.W.3d 230, 237 (Tex. App.—Dallas 2004, pet. denied).

Thornton v. Rains, 299 S.W.2d 287, 288 (Tex. 1957). "[R]ecording of a deed is not essential to the conveyance of title, but without delivery title will not pass."

Adams v. First Nat'l Bank, 154 S.W.3d 859, 871 (Tex.App.—Dallas 2005, no pet.). "A correction deed is filed for the sole purpose of correcting some facial imperfection in the title. A correction deed has a definite legal effect. Proof of the fact that a correction deed was filed and recorded raises a prima facie presumption of the facts recited. Ordinarily, a correction deed relates back to the date of the document that it purports to express more accurately." *But see* ***Centerpoint Energy Houston Elec., L.L.P. v. Old TJC Co.***, 177 S.W.3d 425, 434 (Tex.App.—Houston [1st Dist.] 2005, pet. denied) (correction deed can do more than simply correct scrivener's error in description of property).

Author's comment: Attorneys drafting correction deeds should take extra care to avoid circumstances like those in ***Centerpoint Energy***.

Sanchez v. Telles, 960 S.W.2d 762, 767 (Tex. App.—El Paso 1997, pet. denied). "The general purpose of an acknowledgment is to authenticate an instrument as being the act of the person executing the instrument. In order to be recorded in the real property records, an acknowledgment is necessary. A contract for the sale and purchase of real estate which is not acknowledged by the grantor is not notice to subsequent purchasers, though it be acknowledged by the purchaser and recorded." *See also* ***Onwuteaka v. Cohen***, 846 S.W.2d 889, 895 (Tex.App.—Houston [1st Dist.] 1993, writ denied) (no requirement that appointment of trustee be acknowledged by notary public before it is effective); ***Martin v. Skelton***, 567 S.W.2d 585, 586-87 (Tex.App.—Fort Worth 1978, writ ref'd n.r.e.) (acknowledgment only makes an instrument recordable; it does not indicate when instrument was signed).

Pearson v. Wicker, 746 S.W.2d 322, 322 (Tex. App.—Austin 1988, no writ). Held: Purchaser's deed was void because joint agreement of owners was ac-

knowledged, giving purchaser constructive notice that neither venturer could sell the property without the other's consent. *See also* ***Turrentine v. Lasane***, 389 S.W.2d 336, 337 (Tex.App.—Waco 1965, no writ) (predecessor of §12.001(a) construed to authorize recordation of affidavits of heirship in light of policy that public records disclose all matters affecting land titles).

A PROP §12.0011. INSTRUMENTS CONCERNING PROPERTY: ORIGINAL SIGNATURE REQUIRED FOR CERTAIN INSTRUMENTS

(a) For the purposes of this section, "paper document" means a document received by a county clerk in a form that is not electronic.

(b) A paper document concerning real or personal property may not be recorded or serve as notice of the paper document unless:

(1) the paper document contains an original signature or signatures that are acknowledged, sworn to with a proper jurat, or proved according to law; or

(2) the paper document is attached as an exhibit to a paper affidavit or other document that has an original signature or signatures that are acknowledged, sworn to with a proper jurat, or proved according to law.

(c) An original signature may not be required for an electronic instrument or other document that complies with the requirements of Chapter 15 of this code, Chapter 195, Local Government Code, Chapter 322, Business & Commerce Code, or other applicable law.

(d) This section does not apply to a child support lien notice issued by the Title IV-D agency under Chapter 157, Family Code. For purposes of this subsection, "Title IV-D agency" has the meaning assigned by Section 101.033, Family Code.

(e) This section does not apply to a notice of sale under Section 51.065, Natural Resources Code, or a land award under Section 51.066, Natural Resources Code.

History of Prop. Code §12.0011: Acts 2007, 80th Leg., ch. 213, §1, eff. Sept. 1, 2007. Amended by Acts 2009, 81st Leg., ch. 87, §20.003 (eff. Sept. 1, 2009), ch. 767, §33 (eff. June 19, 2009); H.B. 3423, §4, 85th Leg., eff. Sept. 1, 2017.

See also ***Real Estate Forms***, FORMS 1:8-1:13, 11:1, 11:2.

PROP §12.0012. INSTRUMENTS CONCERNING REAL PROPERTY SUBJECT TO A FORECLOSURE SALE

(a) Notwithstanding Section 12.0011(b), the following documents received by the county clerk in the manner provided by Subsection (b) shall be recorded by the clerk and serve as notice of the matter document:

(1) an instrument appointing or authorizing a trustee or substitute trustee to exercise the power of sale in a security instrument;

(2) a notice of sale pursuant to which the sale under a power of sale occurred;

(3) a notice of default on which the sale evidenced by a deed conveying title from a trustee or substitute trustee to a purchaser occurred;

(4) documentation from the United States Department of Defense indicating that a debtor was not on active duty military service on the date of a foreclosure sale;

(5) a statement of facts regarding a foreclosure sale prepared by an attorney representing the trustee, substitute trustee, or mortgage servicer; or

(6) proof of service of the mailing of any notice related to a foreclosure sale.

(b) A document described by Subsection (a) shall be accepted for recording pursuant to Subsection (a) if it is attached as an exhibit to:

(1) a deed that conveys title from a trustee or substitute trustee to a purchaser at a foreclosure sale and that meets the requirements for recording under Section 12.0011(b); or

(2) an affidavit of a trustee or substitute trustee that meets the requirements for recording under Section 12.0011(b) and relates to a foreclosure sale.

(c) This section does not prevent the recording of documents in any other manner allowed by law.

History of Prop. Code §12.0012: Acts 2015, 84th Leg., ch. 653, §1, eff. Sept. 1, 2015.

PROP §12.002. SUBDIVISION PLAT; PENALTY

(a) The county clerk or a deputy of the clerk with whom a plat or replat of a subdivision of real property is filed for recording shall determine whether the plat or replat is required by law to be approved by a county or municipal authority or both. The clerk or deputy may not record a plat or replat unless it is approved as provided by law by the appropriate authority and unless the plat or replat has attached to it the documents required by Subsection (e) or by Section 212.0105 or 232.023, Local Government Code, if applicable. If a plat or replat does not indicate whether land covered by the plat or replat is in the extraterritorial jurisdiction of the municipality, the county clerk may require the person filing the plat or replat for recording to file with the clerk an affidavit stating that information.

(b) A person may not file for record or have recorded in the county clerk's office a plat or replat of a subdivision of real property unless it is approved as provided by law by the appropriate authority and unless the plat or replat has attached to it the documents required by Section 212.0105 or 232.023, Local Government Code, if applicable.

(c) Except as provided by Subsection (d), a person who subdivides real property may not use the subdivision's description in a deed of conveyance, a contract for a deed, or a contract of sale or other executory contract to convey that is delivered to a purchaser unless the plat or replat of the subdivision is approved and is filed for record with the county clerk of the county in which the property is located and unless the plat or replat has attached to it the documents required by Subsection (e) or by Section 212.0105 or 232.023, Local Government Code, if applicable.

(d) Except in the case of a subdivision located in a county to which Subchapter B, Chapter 232, Local Government Code, applies, Subsection (c) does not apply to using a subdivision's description in a contract to convey real property before the plat or replat of the subdivision is approved and is filed for record with the county clerk if:

(1) the conveyance is expressly contingent on approval and recording of the final plat; and

(2) the purchaser is not given use or occupancy of the real property conveyed before the recording of the final plat.

(e) A person may not file for record or have recorded in the county clerk's office a plat, replat, or amended plat or replat of a subdivision of real property unless the plat, replat, or amended plat or replat has attached to it an original tax certificate from each taxing unit with jurisdiction of the real property indicating that no delinquent ad valorem taxes are owed on the real property. If the plat, replat, or amended plat or replat is filed after September 1 of a year, the plat, replat, or amended plat or replat must also have attached to it a tax receipt issued by the collector for each taxing unit with jurisdiction of the property indicating that the taxes imposed by the taxing unit for the current year have been paid or, if the taxes for the current year have not been calculated, a statement from the collector for the taxing unit indicating that the taxes to be imposed by that taxing unit for the current year have not been calculated. If the tax certificate for a taxing unit does not cover the preceding year, the plat, replat, or amended plat or replat must also have attached to it a tax receipt issued by the collector for the taxing unit indicating that the taxes imposed by the taxing unit for the preceding year have been paid. This subsection does not apply if:

(1) more than one person acquired the real property from a decedent under a will or by inheritance and those persons owning an undivided interest in the property obtained approval to subdivide the property to provide each person with a divided interest and a separate title to the property; or

(2) a taxing unit acquired the real property for public use through eminent domain proceedings or voluntary sale.

(f) A person commits an offense if the person violates Subsection (b), (c), or (e). An offense under this subsection is a misdemeanor punishable by a fine of not less than $10 or more than $1,000, by confinement in the county jail for a term not to exceed 90 days, or by both the fine and confinement. Each violation constitutes a separate offense and also constitutes prima facie evidence of an attempt to defraud.

(g) This section does not apply to a partition by a court.

History of Prop. Code §12.002: Acts 1983, 68th Leg., ch. 576, §1, eff. Jan. 1, 1984. Amended by Acts 1987, 70th Leg., ch. 149, §22, eff. Sept. 1, 1987; Acts 1989, 71st Leg., ch. 624, §3.09, eff. Sept. 1, 1989; Acts 1991, 72nd Leg., ch. 570, §1, eff. June 15, 1991; Acts 1997, 75th Leg., ch. 583, §1, eff. Sept. 1, 1997; Acts 1999, 76th Leg., ch. 404, §27 (eff. Sept. 1, 1999), ch. 812, §1 (eff. Sept. 1, 1999), ch. 1382, §8 (eff. June 19, 1999); Acts 2005, 79th Leg., ch. 1126, §26 (eff. Sept. 1, 2005), ch. 1154, §1 (eff. Sept. 1, 2005); Acts 2007, 80th Leg., ch. 289, §1, eff. Sept. 1, 2007. Source: TRCS art. 6626(a).

See also Loc. Gov't Code §§192.0015, 212.004, 212.0105, 232.023, 232.072; *Real Estate Forms*, FORM 10:17.

ANNOTATIONS

State v. Walker, 195 S.W.3d 293, 300 (Tex.App.—Tyler 2006, no pet.). "Because the majority of the factors weigh in favor of requiring a culpable mental state and the punishment includes 90 days of confinement, we cannot say that [§12.002(b)] manifests an intent to dispense with a culpable mental state sufficient to overcome the presumption that one was required. Thus, we must conclude that a culpable mental state was required in the indictment."

PROP §12.003. INSTRUMENT IN GENERAL LAND OFFICE OR ARCHIVES

(a) If written evidence of title to land has been filed according to law in the General Land Office or is in the public archives, a copy of the written evidence may be recorded if:

(1) the original was properly executed under the law in effect at the time of execution; and

(2) the copy is certified by the officer having custody of the original and attested with the seal of the General Land Office.

(b) A court may not admit a title to land that was filed in the General Land Office as evidence of superior title against a location or survey of the same land that was made under a valid land warrant or certificate prior to the filing of the title in the General Land Office unless prior to the location or survey:

(1) the older title had been recorded with the county clerk of the county in which the land is located; or

(2) the person who had the location or survey made had actual notice of the older title.

History of Prop. Code §12.003: Acts 1983, 68th Leg., ch. 576, §1, eff. Jan. 1, 1984. Source: TRCS arts. 6625, 6628, 6634.

PROP §12.004. FOREIGN DEED

If written evidence of title to land has been filed outside the county in which the land is located or outside the state, a copy of the written evidence may be recorded in the county in which the land is located if:

(1) the original was properly executed and recorded under the law governing the recording; and

(2) the copy is certified by the officer having legal custody of the original.

History of Prop. Code §12.004: Acts 1983, 68th Leg., ch. 576, §1, eff. Jan. 1, 1984. Source: TRCS art. 6625a.

ANNOTATIONS

Jones v. P.A.W.N. Enters., 988 S.W.2d 812, 822 (Tex.App.—Amarillo 1999, pet. denied). TRCS art. 5330A, §5 "provided that '[a]ll deeds, mortgages, conveyances and all other instruments which would be valid under the laws of the State of Oklahoma[ ] shall be valid in Texas[ ]' and that such deeds 'shall be given the same force and effect in the State of Texas as [they] would have been given in the State of Oklahoma.' The statute also authorized the recording of those instruments in the Texas county in which the land was located. [Property Code] §12.004 … authorizes the recording of copies of deeds affecting title in Texas even if the original was filed in another state. [¶] [T]he only way a mineral interest owner could make their deeds effective, and fulfill the clear purpose of [TRCS art. 5330A], was to follow the procedure set out therein and record the deeds in the proper Texas county."

PROP §12.005. PARTITION

(a) A court order partitioning or allowing recovery of title to land must be recorded with the county clerk of the county in which the land is located in order to be admitted as evidence to support a right claimed under the order.

(b) A record of an order is sufficient under this section if it consists of a brief statement by the clerk of the court that made the order, signed and sealed by the clerk, that includes:

(1) the identity of the case in which the partition or judgment was made;

(2) the date of the case;

(3) the names of the parties to the case;

(4) a description of the land involved that is located in the county of the recording; and

(5) the name of the party to whom the land is decreed.

History of Prop. Code §12.005: Acts 1983, 68th Leg., ch. 576, §1, eff. Jan. 1, 1984. Source: TRCS arts. 6638, 6639.

PROP §12.006. GRANT FROM GOVERNMENT

A grant from this state or the United States that is executed and authenticated under the law in effect at the time the grant is made may be recorded without further acknowledgement or proof.

History of Prop. Code §12.006: Acts 1983, 68th Leg., ch. 576, §1, eff. Jan. 1, 1984. Source: TRCS art. 6624.

PROP §12.007. LIS PENDENS

(a) After the plaintiff's statement in an eminent domain proceeding is filed or during the pendency of an action involving title to real property, the establishment of an interest in real property, or the enforcement of an encumbrance against real property, a party to the action who is seeking affirmative relief may file for record with the county clerk of each county where a part of the property is located a notice that the action is pending.

(b) The party filing a lis pendens or the party's agent or attorney shall sign the lis pendens, which must state:

(1) the style and number, if any, of the proceeding;

(2) the court in which the proceeding is pending;

(3) the names of the parties;

(4) the kind of proceeding; and

(5) a description of the property affected.

(c) The county clerk shall record the notice in a lis pendens record. The clerk shall index the record in a direct and reverse index under the name of each party to the proceeding.

(d) Not later than the third day after the date a person files a notice for record under this section, the person must serve a copy of the notice on each party to the action who has an interest in the real property affected by the notice.

History of Prop. Code §12.007: Acts 1983, 68th Leg., ch. 576, §1, eff. Jan. 1, 1984. Amended by Acts 2009, 81st Leg., ch. 297, §1, eff. Sept. 1, 2009. Source: TRCS arts. 6640, 6641.

See also CPRC §125.002(g); Prop. Code §§12.008, 13.004; ***O'Connor's Texas Rules***, "Lis pendens notice," ch. 2-A, §4.4, p. 116; ***Real Estate Forms***, FORMS 10:19, 10:20.

ANNOTATIONS

Flores v. Haberman, 915 S.W.2d 477, 478 (Tex. 1995). Held: When only collateral issues may ultimately affect the parties' interest in the property, lis pendens is not appropriate. *See also* ***In re Wolf***, 65 S.W.3d 804, 805 (Tex.App.—Beaumont 2002, orig. proceeding); ***Garza v. Pope***, 949 S.W.2d 7, 8 (Tex.App.—San Antonio 1997, orig. proceeding).

City Nat'l Bank v. Craig, 257 S.W. 210, 211 (Tex. 1923). "The foundation of the rule of *lis pendens* … was the public policy to put an end to litigation by making it impossible to defeat adjudications by alienations pending suit."

Rosborough v. Cook, 194 S.W. 131, 132 (Tex.1917). "[A] *lis pendens* operates only during the pendency of the suit, and only as to those matters that are involved in the suit. It terminates with the judgment, in the absence of an appeal." *See also* ***R.I.O. Sys. v. Union Carbide Corp.***, 780 S.W.2d 489, 493 (Tex.App.—Corpus Christi 1989, writ denied) (final judgment renders lis pendens unnecessary).

In re Miller, 433 S.W.3d 82, 84 (Tex.App.—Houston [1st Dist.] 2014, orig. proceeding). "Generally speaking, the purpose of lis pendens notice is two-fold: (1) to protect the filing party's alleged rights to the property that is in dispute in the lawsuit and (2) to put those interested in the property on notice of the lawsuit. *At 85:* A lis pendens is not an independent claim; it has no existence separate from the litigation of which it notifies. A properly filed lis pendens is not itself a lien; rather it operates as constructive notice to the world of its contents. Although it does not prevent conveyance, it places a prospective purchaser on notice about the suit and the disputed title to the land." (Internal quotes omitted.) *See also* ***Werneke v. Seabury***, 720 S.W.2d 886, 887-88 (Tex.App.—Fort Worth 1986, no writ).

David Powers Homes, Inc. v. M.L. Rendleman Co., 355 S.W.3d 327, 339 (Tex.App.—Houston [1st Dist.] 2011, no pet.). Judgment debtor "does not dispute that the Affidavits contain all of the information required in [Prop.] Code §12.007(b) to constitute a notice of lis pendens. Instead, [judgment debtor] contends that the Affidavits contain too much information, namely, that a transfer of the real property described in the affidavit may be avoided by the court in the pending lawsuit pursuant to [Texas Uniform Fraudulent Transfers Act]. [Judgment debtor] intimates that this additional information transforms the Affidavits from a notice of lis pendens into a coercive threat levied for the purpose of harming [judgment debtor] economically. *At 340-41:* We conclude that because the Affidavits contain all of the information statutorily required to constitute a notice of lis pendens, the Affidavits filed by [judgment creditor] are instruments 'provided for by the … laws of this state' and are therefore presumed not to be fraudulent under [Gov't Code] §51.901(c)(2)(A). We hold that the trial court did not err in finding that the Affidavits are specifically provided for by specific state or federal statutes or constitutional provisions, and as a result, are not 'fraudulent' as defined in … §51.901."

In re Collins, 172 S.W.3d 287, 294-95 (Tex.App.—Fort Worth 2005, orig. proceeding). "[W]e hold that when the motion challenges the pleadings supporting the lis pendens, the trial court should examine the pleadings to determine whether the pleader has alleged facts that affirmatively demonstrate that the lis pendens is proper. *At 295 n.28:* If the pleadings affirmatively negate the existence of facts supporting the lis pendens, then the motion to remove the lis pendens may be granted without allowing the plaintiffs an opportunity to amend. *At 295:* If, however, a motion seeking the removal of a lis pendens challenges the existence of facts supporting the pleader's alleged interest in the property, the trial court should consider evidence relevant to the question of whether the alleged property interest is direct or collateral. In so doing, the trial court must not decide the merits of the parties' claims, but must confine itself to the evidence relevant to the issue of whether the alleged property interest is direct or collateral. [¶] If the evidence raises an issue of fact regarding whether the alleged

property interest is a direct interest, the motion should be denied and the issue must be resolved by the fact finder. If, however, the relevant evidence is undisputed, or fails to raise a fact question concerning the true nature of the alleged property interest, the trial court should rule on the validity of the lis pendens as a matter of law." *See also* ***In re Wolf***, 65 S.W.3d 804, 805-06 (Tex.App.—Beaumont 2002, orig. proceeding) (rejecting P's argument that requesting and praying for interest in real property is sufficient to support lis pendens). *But see* ***In re Jamail***, 156 S.W.3d 104, 107 (Tex.App.—Austin 2004, orig. proceeding) (purchaser's attempt to void obligation to buy three of 18 lots was not action involving establishment of interest in real property); ***First Nat'l Pet. Corp. v. Lloyd***, 908 S.W.2d 23, 25 (Tex.App.—Houston [1st Dist.] 1995, orig. proceeding) (P's petition requesting title and constructive trust on property was a direct interest and valid notice of lis pendens).

Abraham Inv. v. Payne Ranch, Inc., 968 S.W.2d 518, 527-28 (Tex.App.—Amarillo 1998, pet. denied). "[I]t is well established that any party who takes an interest in real property, when the title to the property is being litigated, and subsequent to the filing of a *lis pendens* notice, takes that interest subject to any judgment rendered in the pending cause." *See also* ***Hartel v. Dishman***, 145 S.W.2d 865, 868 (Tex.1940).

Cherokee Water Co. v. Advance Oil & Gas Co., 843 S.W.2d 132, 135 (Tex.App.—Texarkana 1992, writ denied). "The doctrine of *lis pendens* is based on the public policy that there should be an end to litigation. It accomplishes that policy by preventing alienations that would defeat the litigation and that would deprive the plaintiff of his relief by putting the property beyond the reach of the present action. The doctrine does not void a conveyance during the pendency of the suit. The interest of the grantor merely passes subject to the determination of the cause. If the grantor recovers the interest, the grantee succeeds to it; if not, the grantee acquires nothing. … The rule effectively prevents a grantee from being an innocent purchaser. It does not suspend or toll the statute of limitations on causes of action a property owner may have for trespasses, conversions, or other wrongful acts of which he has notice." *See also* ***Collins v. Tex Mall, L.P.***, 297 S.W.3d 409, 418 (Tex.App.—Fort Worth 2009, no pet.); ***Gene Hill Equip. Co. v. Merryman***, 771 S.W.2d 207, 209 (Tex. App.—Austin 1989, no writ).

Kropp v. Prather, 526 S.W.2d 283, 286 (Tex.App.—Tyler 1975, writ ref'd n.r.e.). "[Ps] contend that the recordation of a lis pendens notice is privileged and that therefore no cause of action for [slander] of title is stated. [T]he question presented is whether a notice of lis pendens recorded as authorized by [TRCS art. 6640, now Prop. Code §12.007,] is a publication in the course of a judicial proceeding. *At 287:* Because the recording of a lis pendens is specifically authorized by statute and has no existence separate and apart from the litigation of which it gives notice, we hold that the filing of a notice of lis pendens in this action is a part of the 'judicial proceeding.'" *See also* ***Chale Garza Invs. v. Madaria***, 931 S.W.2d 597, 600-01 (Tex.App.—San Antonio 1996, writ denied) (lis pendens privileged in tortious-interference-with-contract action); ***Prappas v. Meyerland Cmty. Imprv. Ass'n***, 795 S.W.2d 794, 797-98 (Tex. App.—Houston [14th Dist.] 1990, writ denied) (lis pendens privileged in slander-of-title action). *But see* ***International Shortstop, Inc. v. Rally's, Inc.***, 939 F.2d 1257, 1269 n.12 (5th Cir.1991) (court was not persuaded lis pendens is absolutely privileged).

Ⓐ PROP §12.0071. MOTION TO EXPUNGE LIS PENDENS

The amended text in §12.0071 is effective for certified copies of an order expunging a notice of lis pendens recorded on or after Sept. 1, 2017. Certified copies recorded before Sept. 1, 2017, are governed by the former law in effect at that time.

(a) A party to an action in connection with which a notice of lis pendens has been filed may:

(1) apply to the court to expunge the notice; and

(2) file evidence, including declarations, with the motion to expunge the notice.

(b) The court may:

(1) permit evidence on the motion to be received in the form of oral testimony; and

(2) make any orders the court considers just to provide for discovery by a party affected by the motion.

(c) The court shall order the notice of lis pendens expunged if the court determines that:

(1) the pleading on which the notice is based does not contain a real property claim;

(2) the claimant fails to establish by a preponderance of the evidence the probable validity of the real property claim; or

(3) the person who filed the notice for record did not serve a copy of the notice on each party entitled to a copy under Section 12.007(d).

(d) Notice of a motion to expunge under Subsection (a) must be served on each affected party on or before the 20th day before the date of the hearing on the motion.

(e) The court shall rule on the motion for expunction based on the affidavits and counteraffidavits on file and on any other proof the court allows.

(f) After a certified copy of an order expunging a notice of lis pendens has been recorded:

(1) [~~,~~] the notice of lis pendens and any information derived or that could be derived from the notice:

(A) [~~(1)~~] does not:

(i) [~~(A)~~] constitute constructive or actual notice of any matter contained in the notice or of any matter relating to the action in connection with which the notice was filed [~~proceeding~~];

(ii) [~~(B)~~] create any duty of inquiry in a person with respect to the property described in the notice; or

(iii) [~~(C)~~] affect the validity of a conveyance to a purchaser for value or of a mortgage to a lender for value; and

(B) [~~(2)~~] is not enforceable against a purchaser or lender described by Paragraph (A)(iii) [~~Subdivision (1)(C)~~], regardless of whether the purchaser or lender knew of the lis pendens action; and

(2) an interest in the real property may be transferred or encumbered free of all matters asserted or disclosed in the notice and all claims or other matters asserted or disclosed in the action in connection with which the notice was filed.

(g) The court in its discretion may require that the party prevailing in the expunction hearing submit an undertaking to the court in an amount determined by the court.

History of Prop. Code §12.0071: Acts 2009, 81st Leg., ch. 297, §2, eff. Sept. 1, 2009. Amended by S.B. 1955, §1, 85th Leg., eff. Sept. 1, 2017.

See also *Real Estate Forms*, FORMS 10:21-23.

ANNOTATIONS

County Inv. v. Royal West Inv., 513 S.W.3d 575, 581 (Tex.App.—Houston [14th Dist.] 2016, pet. denied). "[S]tatutory methods for nullifying a lis pendens are not exclusive—particularly considering that [Prop. Code] §12.0071 is available only to a 'party to an action in connection with which a notice of lis pendens has been filed,' whereas [Prop. Code] §12.008 is more broadly available to 'a party or other person interested in the result of or in property affected by a proceeding in which a lis pendens has been [recorded],' and even the latter is not exclusive."

In re Moreno, No. 14-14-00929-CV (Tex.App.—Houston [14th Dist.] 2015, orig. proceeding) (memo op.; 1-15-15). "Although §12.0071 was enacted only in 2009, subsection (c)(1) reflects the practice that existed prior to the enactment of that provision whereby a party could obtain cancellation of a lis pendens when the pleadings in the lawsuit to which the lis pendens relates did not contain an assertion of an interest in real property that fell within the categories for which the statute provides that a lis pendens may be filed. Therefore, cases dating from before the enactment of subsection (c)(1) remain instructive in applying this provision."

PROP §12.008. CANCELLATION OF LIS PENDENS

(a) On the motion of a party or other person interested in the result of or in property affected by a proceeding in which a lis pendens has been recorded and after notice to each affected party, the court hearing the action may cancel the lis pendens at any time during the proceeding, whether in term time or vacation, if the court determines that the party seeking affirmative relief can be adequately protected by the deposit of money into court or by the giving of an undertaking.

(b) If the cancellation of a lis pendens is conditioned on the payment of money, the court may order the cancellation when the party seeking the cancellation pays into the court an amount equal to the total of:

(1) the judgment sought;

(2) the interest the court considers likely to accrue during the proceeding; and

(3) costs.

(c) If the cancellation of a lis pendens is conditioned on the giving of an undertaking, the court may order the cancellation when the party seeking the cancellation gives a guarantee of payment of a judgment, plus interest and costs, in favor of the party who recorded the lis pendens. The guarantee must equal twice the amount of the judgment sought and have two sufficient sureties approved by the court. Not less than two

days before the day the guarantee is submitted to the court for approval, the party seeking the cancellation shall serve the attorney for the party who recorded the lis pendens a copy of the guarantee and notice of its submission to the court.

History of Prop. Code §12.008: Acts 1983, 68th Leg., ch. 576, §1, eff. Jan. 1, 1984. Source: TRCS art. 6643a.

See also Prop. Code §12.007; *O'Connor's Texas COA*, "Action to cancel lis pendens," ch. 18-C, §7.1, p. 571; ***Real Estate Forms***, FORMS 10:24-26.

ANNOTATIONS

County Inv. v. Royal West Inv., 515 S.W.3d 575, 581 (Tex.App.—Houston [14th Dist.] 2016, pet. denied). See annotation under Property Code §12.0071, p. 76.

PROP §12.009. MORTGAGE OR DEED OF TRUST MASTER FORM

(a) A master form of a mortgage or deed of trust may be recorded in any county without acknowledgement or proof. The master form must contain on its face the designation: "Master form recorded by (name of person causing the recording)."

(b) The county clerk shall index a master form under the name of the person causing the recording and indicate in the index and records that the document is a master mortgage.

(c) The parties to an instrument may incorporate by reference a provision of a recorded master form with the same effect as if the provision were set out in full in the instrument. The reference must state:

(1) that the master form is recorded in the county in which the instrument is offered for record;

(2) the numbers of the book or volume and first page of the records in which the master form is recorded; and

(3) a definite identification of each provision being incorporated.

(d) If a mortgage or deed of trust incorporates by reference a provision of a master form, the mortgagee shall give the mortgagor a copy of the master form at the time the instrument is executed. A statement in the mortgage or deed of trust or in a separate instrument signed by the mortgagor that the mortgagor received a copy of the master form is conclusive evidence of its receipt. On written request the mortgagee shall give a copy of the master form without charge to the mortgagor, the mortgagor's successors in interest, or the mortgagor's or a successor's agent.

(e) The provisions of the Uniform Commercial Code prevail over this section.

History of Prop. Code §12.009: Acts 1983, 68th Leg., ch. 576, §1, eff. Jan. 1, 1984. Source: TRCS art. 6626b.

See also ***Real Estate Forms***, FORM 3:2.

PROP §12.010. REPEALED

Repealed by Acts 1989, 71st Leg., ch. 945, §2(1), eff. Sept. 1, 1989.

PROP §12.011. CERTIFICATE OF REDEMPTION

An instrument issued by the United States that redeems or evidences redemption of real property from a judicial sale or from a nonjudicial sale under foreclosure of a lien, mortgage, or deed of trust may be recorded in records of conveyances in each county in which the property is located if the instrument has been issued according to the laws of the United States.

History of Prop. Code §12.011: Acts 1983, 68th Leg., ch. 576, §1, eff. Jan. 1, 1984. Source: TRCS art. 6644a.

PROP §12.012. ATTACHMENT

(a) If an officer files a writ of attachment on real property with a county clerk, the clerk shall record the name of each plaintiff and defendant in attachment, the amount of the debt, and the officer's return in full.

(b) A county clerk who receives a certified copy of an order quashing or vacating a writ of attachment shall record the order and the name of each plaintiff and defendant.

History of Prop. Code §12.012: Acts 1983, 68th Leg., ch. 576, §1, eff. Jan. 1, 1984. Source: TRCS art. 6662 (part).

PROP §12.013. JUDGMENT

A judgment of a court may be recorded if:

(1) the judgment is of a court:

(A) expressly created or established under the constitution or laws of this state or of the United States;

(B) that is a court of a foreign country and that is recognized by an Act of congress or a treaty or other international convention to which the United States is a party; or

(C) of any other jurisdiction, territory, or protectorate entitled to full faith and credit in this state under the Constitution of the United States; and

(2) the judgment is attested under the signature and seal of the clerk of the court that rendered the judgment.

History of Prop. Code §12.013: Acts 1983, 68th Leg., ch. 576, §1, eff. Jan. 1, 1984. Amended by Acts 1997, 75th Leg., ch. 189, §15, eff. May 21, 1997; Acts 2001, 77th Leg., ch. 668, §1, eff. Sept. 1, 2001. Source: TRCS art. 6635.

PROP §12.014. TRANSFER OF JUDGMENT OR CAUSE OF ACTION

(a) A judgment or part of a judgment of a court of record or an interest in a cause of action on which suit has been filed may be sold, regardless of whether the judgment or cause of action is assignable in law or equity, if the transfer is in writing.

(b) A transfer under this section may be filed with the papers of the suit if the transfer is acknowledged or sworn to in the form and manner required by law for acknowledgement or swearing of deeds.

(c) If a transfer of a judgment is filed, the clerk shall record the transfer appropriately. If a transfer of a cause of action in which a judgment has not been rendered is filed, the clerk shall note and briefly state the substance of the transfer on the court docket at the place where the suit is entered.

(d) A transfer filed under this section is notice to and is binding on a person subsequently dealing with the judgment or cause of action.

History of Prop. Code §12.014: Acts 1983, 68th Leg., ch. 576, §1, eff. Jan. 1, 1984. Amended by Acts 1989, 71st Leg., ch. 162, §3, eff. Sept. 1, 1989; Acts 2007, 80th Leg., ch. 628, §4, eff. Sept. 1, 2007. Source: TRCS art. 6636.

See also ***Real Estate Forms***, FORMS 11:1, 11:2.

ANNOTATIONS

Southwestern Bell Tel. Co. v. Marketing on Hold, Inc., 170 S.W.3d 814, 824 (Tex.App.—Corpus Christi 2005), *rev'd on other grounds*, 308 S.W.3d 909 (Tex.2010). "[D] contends that [§12.014] is an express effort by the legislature to limit assignability of causes of action to only after a suit is filed. [¶] We do not find that [§12.014] was a direct effort by the legislature to limit assignability of causes of action to only those situations where suit has already been filed, but, rather, that its purpose was to require adequate notice of any such assignment[.] *At 825:* We conclude that nothing in [§12.014] precludes or invalidates the assignments at issue in this matter simply because they were made prior to the filing of suit." *See also* ***Magill v. Watson***, 409 S.W.3d 673, 678 (Tex.App.—Houston [1st Dist.] 2013, no pet.); ***HSBC Bank USA v. Watson***, 377 S.W.3d 766, 776 (Tex.App.—Dallas 2012, pet. dism'd).

Vinson & Elkins v. Moran, 946 S.W.2d 381, 390 (Tex.App.—Houston [14th Dist.] 1997, pet. dism'd). "The general rule in Texas has been that causes of action are assignable absent a statutory bar. [However,] based upon public policy considerations, some causes of action are not subject to assignment. *At 391:* The Texas Supreme Court held other assignments invalid despite the language of §12.014. The court based holdings in these case[s] on public policy considerations. The policy reasons behind the rejection of certain assignments persist despite the existence of §12.014. That the supreme court did not specifically address §12.014 in these cases is unpersuasive." *See also* ***Wright v. Sydow***, 173 S.W.3d 534, 551 (Tex.App.—Houston [14th Dist.] 2004, pet. denied) (legal-malpractice claim not assignable); ***Tate v. Goins, Underkofler, Crawford & Langdon***, 24 S.W.3d 627, 633-34 (Tex.App.—Dallas 2000, pet. denied) (same); ***Baker v. Mallios***, 971 S.W.2d 581, 587 (Tex.App.—Dallas 1998) (public-policy concerns do not prohibit P from assigning a portion of proceeds recovered from his own legal-malpractice claim to a third party), *aff'd*, 11 S.W.3d 157 (Tex.2000).

River Consulting, Inc. v. Sullivan, 848 S.W.2d 165, 169 (Tex.App.—Houston [1st Dist.] 1992, writ denied), *disapproved on other grounds*, ***Formosa Plastics Corp. v. Presidio Eng'rs & Contractors, Inc.***, 960 S.W.2d 41 (Tex.1998). "A cause of action, assigned after the filing of suit, no longer belongs to the assignor, and neither the assignor, his debtor, nor the defendant, can dispose of the cause of action or pay money due thereon to a third person, depriving the assignee of the right thereto. An assignee may maintain in its own name any action that the assignor may have brought, and unless the assignor has retained some right or interest therein, the assignor is precluded from bringing suit."

PROP §12.015. JUDGMENT IN JUSTICE COURT

(a) On the application of a party interested in land that has been sold under an execution issued by a justice court, the justice of the peace having custody of the execution and the judgment under which it was issued shall make a certified transcript of the judgment, the execution, and the levy and return of the executing officer.

(b) A certified transcript under this section may be recorded in the same manner as a deed.

History of Prop. Code §12.015: Acts 1983, 68th Leg., ch. 576, §1, eff. Jan. 1, 1984. Source: TRCS art. 6637.

PROP §12.016. POWER OF ATTORNEY

A power of attorney may be recorded.

History of Prop. Code §12.016: Acts 1983, 68th Leg., ch. 576, §1, eff. Jan. 1, 1984. Source: TRCS art. 6633.

PROP §12.017. TITLE INSURANCE COMPANY AFFIDAVIT AS RELEASE OF LIEN; CIVIL PENALTY

(a) In this section:

(1) "Mortgage" means a deed of trust or other contract lien on an interest in real property.

(2) "Mortgagee" means:

(A) the grantee of a mortgage;

(B) if a mortgage has been assigned of record, the last person to whom the mortgage has been assigned of record; or

(C) if a mortgage is serviced by a mortgage servicer, the mortgage servicer.

(3) "Mortgage servicer" means the last person to whom a mortgagor has been instructed by a mortgagee to send payments for the loan secured by a mortgage. A person transmitting a payoff statement is considered the mortgage servicer for the mortgage described in the payoff statement.

(4) "Mortgagor" means the grantor of a mortgage.

(5) "Payoff statement" means a statement of the amount of:

(A) the unpaid balance of a loan secured by a mortgage, including principal, interest, and other charges properly assessed under the loan documentation of the mortgage; and

(B) interest on a per diem basis for the unpaid balance.

(6) "Title insurance company" means a corporation or other business entity authorized to engage in the business of insuring titles to interests in real property in this state.

(7) "Authorized title insurance agent," with respect to an Affidavit as Release of Lien under this section, means a person licensed as a title insurance agent under Chapter 2651, Insurance Code, and authorized in writing by a title insurance company by instrument recorded in the real property records in the county in which the property to which the affidavit relates is located to execute one or more Affidavits as Release of Lien in compliance with this section, subject to any terms, limitations, and conditions that are set forth in the instrument executed by the title insurance company.

(b) This section applies only to a mortgage on:

(1) property consisting exclusively of a one-to-four-family residence, including a residential unit in a condominium regime; or

(2) property other than property described by Subdivision (1), if the original face amount of the indebtedness secured by the mortgage on the property is less than $1.5 million.

(c) An authorized officer of a title insurance company or an authorized title insurance agent may, on behalf of the mortgagor or a transferee of the mortgagor who acquired title to the property described in the mortgage, execute an affidavit that complies with the requirements of this section and record the affidavit in the real property records of each county in which the mortgage was recorded.

(d) An affidavit executed under Subsection (c) must be in substantially the following form:

AFFIDAVIT AS RELEASE OF LIEN

Before me, the undersigned authority, on this day personally appeared (insert name of affiant) ("Affiant") who, being first duly sworn, upon his/her oath states:

1. My name is (insert name of Affiant), and I am an authorized officer of (insert name of title insurance company or authorized title insurance agent) ("Title Company").

2. This affidavit is made on behalf of the mortgagor or a transferee of the mortgagor who acquired title to the property described in the following mortgage:
(describe mortgage, the name of the mortgagor, and the property described in the mortgage)

3. (Insert name of Mortgagee) ("Mortgagee") provided a payoff statement with respect to the loan secured by the mortgage.

4. Affiant has ascertained that Title Company delivered to Mortgagee payment of the loan secured by the mortgage in the amount and time and to the location required by the payoff statement.

5. The mortgage relates to:

(A) property consisting exclusively of a one-to-four-family residence, which may include a residential unit in a condominium regime; or

(B) property, other than property described by Paragraph (A) above, for which the original face amount of the indebtedness secured by the mortgage on the property is less than $1.5 million.

6. Pursuant to Section 12.017, Texas Property Code, this affidavit constitutes a full and final release of the mortgage from the property.

Signed this ____ day of ________, ____.

____
(signature of affiant)

State of ________

County of ________

Sworn to and subscribed to before me on ________ (date) by ________ (insert name of affiant).

____
(signature of notarial officer)

(Seal, if any, of notary) ________

____
(printed name)

My commission expires:

____

(e) An affidavit filed under Subsection (c) or (f) must include the names of the mortgagor and the mortgagee, the date of the mortgage, and the volume and page or clerk's file number of the real property records where the mortgage is recorded, together with similar information for a recorded assignment of the mortgage.

(f) On or after the date of the payment to which the affidavit relates, the title insurance company or authorized title insurance agent must notify the mortgagee at the location to which the payment is sent that the title insurance company or authorized title insurance agent may file for record at any time the affidavit as a release of lien. If notice required by this section is not provided to the mortgagee, the title insurance company or authorized title insurance agent may not file for record the affidavit as a release of lien. The mortgagee may file a separate affidavit describing the mortgage and property and controverting the affidavit by the title insurance company or authorized title insurance agent as a release of lien on or before the 45th day after the date the mortgagee receives the notice if the mortgagee mails a copy of the mortgagee's affidavit to the title insurance company or authorized title insurance agent within that 45-day period.

(g) An affidavit under Subsection (c) operates as a release of the mortgage described in the affidavit if the affidavit, as provided by this section:

(1) is executed;

(2) is recorded; and

(3) is not controverted by a separate affidavit by the mortgagee in accordance with the requirements of Subsection (f).

(h) The county clerk shall index an affidavit filed under this section in the names of the original mortgagee and the last assignee of the mortgage appearing of record as the grantors and in the name of the mortgagor as grantee.

(i) A person who knowingly causes an affidavit with false information to be executed and recorded under this section is liable for the penalties for filing a false affidavit, including the penalties for commission of offenses under Section 37.02 of the Penal Code. The attorney general may sue to collect the penalty. A person who negligently causes an affidavit with false information to be executed and recorded under this section is liable to a party injured by the affidavit for actual damages. If the attorney general or an injured party bringing suit substantially prevails in an action under this subsection, the court may award reasonable attorney's fees and court costs to the prevailing party.

(j) A title insurance company or authorized title insurance agent that, at any time after payment of the mortgage, files for record an affidavit executed under Subsection (c) may use any recording fee collected for the recording of a release of the mortgage for the purpose of filing the affidavit.

(k) This section does not affect any agreement or obligation of a mortgagee to execute and deliver a release of mortgage.

History of Prop. Code §12.017: Acts 1993, 73rd Leg., ch. 1003, §1, eff. Aug. 30, 1993. Amended by Acts 2009, 81st Leg., ch. 997, §§1, 2, eff. Sept. 1, 2009.

See also *Real Estate Forms*, FORM 3:18.

PROP §12.018. TRANSFER BY RECEIVER OR CONSERVATOR OF FAILED DEPOSITORY INSTITUTION

If a bank, savings and loan association, savings bank, or other depository institution is placed in receivership or conservatorship by a state or federal agency, instrumentality, or institution, including the Banking Department of Texas, Department of Savings and Mortgage Lending of Texas, Office of the Comptroller of the Currency, Resolution Trust Corporation, Federal Deposit Insurance Corporation, Federal Savings and Loan Insurance Corporation, or their successors, a person at any time may record an affidavit or memorandum of a sale, transfer, purchase, or acquisition agreement between the receiver or conservator of the failed depository institution and another depository institution. If the sale, transfer, purchase, or acquisition agreement transfers or sells an interest in land or in a mortgage or other lien vested according to the real property records

in the failed depository institution, a recorded affidavit or memorandum under this section is constructive notice of the transfer or sale. The failure of the affidavit or memorandum to be executed by the record owner or of the affidavit, memorandum, or agreement to contain language of conveyance does not create a defect in title to the land or the lien.

History of Prop. Code §12.018: Acts 1993, 73rd Leg., ch. 1004, §1, eff. Aug. 30, 1993. Renumbered from §12.017 by Acts 1995, 74th Leg., ch. 76, §17.01(43), eff. Sept. 1, 1995. Amended by Acts 2007, 80th Leg., ch. 921, §6.064, eff. Sept. 1, 2007.

CHAPTER 13. EFFECTS OF RECORDING

PROP §13.001. VALIDITY OF UNRECORDED INSTRUMENT

(a) A conveyance of real property or an interest in real property or a mortgage or deed of trust is void as to a creditor or to a subsequent purchaser for a valuable consideration without notice unless the instrument has been acknowledged, sworn to, or proved and filed for record as required by law.

(b) The unrecorded instrument is binding on a party to the instrument, on the party's heirs, and on a subsequent purchaser who does not pay a valuable consideration or who has notice of the instrument.

(c) This section does not apply to a financing statement, a security agreement filed as a financing statement, or a continuation statement filed for record under the Business & Commerce Code.

History of Prop. Code §13.001: Acts 1983, 68th Leg., ch. 576, §1, eff. Jan. 1, 1984. Amended by Acts 1989, 71st Leg., ch. 162, §4, eff. Sept. 1, 1989. Source: TRCS arts. 1289, 6627.

See also ***Real Estate Forms***, FORMS 11:1, 11:2.

ANNOTATIONS

Generally

Haile v. Holtzclaw, 414 S.W.2d 916, 928 (Tex. 1967). "[A]s between a grantor and a grantee deeds are valid even without a valid acknowledgement." *See also* ***Apex Fin. Corp. v. Garza***, 155 S.W.3d 230, 237 (Tex. App.—Dallas 2004, pet. denied).

Thornton v. Rains, 299 S.W.2d 287, 288 (Tex. 1957). "[R]ecording of a deed is not essential to the conveyance of title, but without delivery title will not pass." *See also* ***Hooks v. Vanderburg***, 328 S.W.2d 467, 469 (Tex.App.—Fort Worth 1959, no writ) (title to real estate is conveyed by execution and delivery of deed).

Simonds v. Stanolind Oil & Gas Co., 114 S.W.2d 226, 235 (Tex.1938). "Delay in recording a deed or failure to assert ownership promptly will not divest one of title. The statutes of registration and limitation are intended to give protection against such negligence or indifference on the part of the land owner. … 'Silence or failure to assert title to land, while it is being adversely claimed, conveyed, or occupied, is not of itself sufficient to create an estoppel.'" *See also* ***Burris v. McDougald***, 832 S.W.2d 707, 709 (Tex.App.—Corpus Christi 1992, no writ).

Smith v. Sumeer Homes, Inc., No. 05-11-01632-CV (Tex.App.—Dallas 2013, pet. denied) (memo op.; 6-6-13). "Section 13.001(a), commonly referred to as the recording statute, states that a conveyance of real property is 'void as to a creditor or to a subsequent purchaser' without notice of the conveyance. But equitable title acquired independent of legal title is not subject to or governed by the recording statute. That is because equitable title arises by operation of law and exists independent of the execution of a deed; the recording of the deed is not essential to an effective conveyance of title. The 'superiority of such a title may be asserted against a judgment lien creditor even though he had no notice of the equitable title at the time of fixing his lien.' This rule makes sense because a judgment creditor … is not injured by the equitable interest held by another. If her lien fails to attach, she 'loses nothing.' She still retains her judgment in its full amount and a lien on any real property owned by [a judgment debtor]."

Sauceda v. Kerlin, 164 S.W.3d 892, 915 (Tex. App.—Corpus Christi 2005), *rev'd on other grounds*, 263 S.W.3d 920 (Tex.2008). "Estoppel by deed stands for the general proposition that 'all parties to a deed are bound by the recitals therein, which operate as an estoppel, working on the interest in the land if it be a deed of conveyance, and binding both parties and privies; privies in blood, privies in estate, and privies in law.' Estoppel by deed or contract precludes parties to a valid instrument from denying its force and effect. To determine whether the doctrine of estoppel by deed should apply to a deed and the recitals therein, we look to the intention of the parties to the instrument, to be determined from the writing itself by the consideration whether the recital was designed to furnish a basis of

action by the parties. In other words, whether the parties intended to bind themselves, to contract, as set forth in the instrument. [¶] Although estoppel by deed most commonly operates upon a grantor in favor of a grantee, the doctrine may be applied against a grantee in favor of a grantor through covenants of the grantee that run with the land purportedly conveyed. The general rule is 'that the grantee in a deed accepted by him is a party to the deed … and that he is concluded by recitals in the deed and by reservations contained therein in favor of the grantor.'" *See also* ***XTO Energy Inc. v. Nikolai***, 357 S.W.3d 47, 55-56 (Tex.App.—Fort Worth 2011, pet. denied).

Cadle Co. v. Butler, 951 S.W.2d 901, 913 (Tex. App.—Corpus Christi 1997, no writ). "Although an oral contract can be executed by performance, a parol agreement is logically incapable of being filed or recorded; there must be an instrument of some sort." *See also* ***Gaona v. Gonzales***, 997 S.W.2d 784, 786 (Tex.App.—Austin 1999, no pet.) (oral agreement to pay purchase price of land was for future performance; §13.001 has no effect on agreement).

Waggoner v. Morrow, 932 S.W.2d 627, 632 (Tex. App.—Houston [14th Dist.] 1996, no writ). "It is well settled that a purchaser is bound by every recital, reference, and reservation contained in or fairly disclosed by an instrument which forms an essential link in the chain of title under which he claims. The rationale of this rule is that any description, recital of fact, or reference to other documents in an instrument puts the purchaser upon inquiry, and he is bound to follow up this inquiry, step by step, from one discovery to another and from one instrument to another, until the whole series of title deeds is exhausted and a complete knowledge of all the matters referred to and affecting the estate is obtained."

Medley v. Medley, 683 S.W.2d 877, 879 (Tex. App.—Corpus Christi 1984, no writ). "A mere want of consideration is not ground for the avoidance of an executed deed. Consideration is only required for the junior deed. [¶] [I]n 1840, the legislature gave the benefit of the recording statute only to junior holders for consideration who were without notice. [¶] Because of this historical placement of the burden of proof, we will treat the invoking of [TRCS art. 6627, now Prop. Code §13.001,] as an affirmative defense." *See also* ***Dawson v. Bluhm***, 252 S.W.2d 515, 517 (Tex.App.—Beaumont 1952, no writ) (junior holder did not meet burden).

Bona Fide Purchaser

Madison v. Gordon, 39 S.W.3d 604, 606 (Tex.2001). "Status as a bona fide purchaser is an affirmative defense to a title dispute. A bona fide purchaser is not subject to certain claims or defenses. To receive this special protection, one must acquire property in good faith, for value, and without notice of any third-party claim or interest. … Actual notice rests on personal information or knowledge. Constructive notice is notice the law imputes to a person not having personal information or knowledge. [¶] One purchasing land may be charged with constructive notice of an occupant's claims. This implied-notice doctrine applies if a court determines that the purchaser has a duty to ascertain the rights of a third-party possessor. When this duty arises, the purchaser is charged with notice of all the occupant's claims the purchaser might have reasonably discovered on proper inquiry. The duty arises, however, only if the possession is visible, open, exclusive, and unequivocal." *See also* ***Jones v. Smith***, 291 S.W.3d 549, 554-55 (Tex.App.—Houston [14th Dist.] 2009, no pet.) (grantee not innocent purchaser even though she acquired title before obtaining notice of conflicting claim because she gave no consideration before obtaining notice); ***Fletcher v. Minton***, 217 S.W.3d 755, 760-61 (Tex.App.—Dallas 2007, no pet.) (grantee not innocent purchaser because agent had constructive notice of conflicting claim to property); ***Smith v. Morris & Co.***, 694 S.W.2d 37, 39 (Tex.App.—Corpus Christi 1985, writ ref'd n.r.e.) (grantee in quitclaim deed not innocent purchaser without notice but takes notice of all defects in grantor's title).

Hill v. Foster, 186 S.W.2d 343, 347 (Tex.1945). "The purchaser of land acquires no title as against a grantee of a deed previously executed and recorded to which is attached a defective certificate of acknowledgment, where such purchaser knew that the grantor had previously executed a deed in good faith to the same land, and also knew that the grantor did not claim any interest in such land. This rule rests on the ground that the purchaser who obtained a deed to such land with notice of the facts of the prior conveyance is not a bona fide purchaser for value, and acquired no interest in such land as against those claiming under the deed with the defective acknowledgment attached thereto. This rule also applies to those who purchased for an inadequate consideration."

Noble Mortg. & Invs. v. D&M Vision Invs., 340 S.W.3d 65, 77-78 (Tex.App.—Houston [1st Dist.] 2011, no pet.). "Whether [lender] is a bona fide mortgagee or purchaser turns largely on the issue of whether recording of a sale on an execution docket in compliance with [TRCP] 656 ... is a 'recording' for the purpose of putting subsequent creditors and purchasers on constructive notice under [Prop. Code] §§13.001 and 13.002.... [T]his presents an issue of first impression in Texas. *At 81:* Given that a civil County Court of Law execution docket is not a repository for chain-of-title documents, and given the 'well-established rule that a deed or instrument lying outside of his chain of title imports no notice,' ... we hold that recording on the execution docket of the county civil court of law is not a recording for purposes of importing constructive notice to subsequent creditors and purchasers."

City of Edinburg v. A.P.I. Pipe & Sup., 328 S.W.3d 82, 91 (Tex.App.—Corpus Christi 2010), *rev'd on other grounds sub nom.* ***Texas DOT v. A.P.I. Pipe & Sup.***, 397 S.W.3d 162. "[T]he 'good faith purchaser for value' doctrine is not merely an equitable doctrine—it is statutorily mandated, and no exception is made in the statute for governmental entities. In fact, other courts have applied the good faith purchaser for value doctrine as against a governmental entity. Thus, we reject the [Ds'] argument that they cannot be made subject to [P's] property interest as good faith purchasers for value because governmental entities are subject to the statutorily-imposed good faith purchaser for value doctrine."

McRae Expl. & Prod. v. Reserve Pet. Co., 962 S.W.2d 676, 682-83 (Tex.App.—Waco 1998, pet. denied). "Under the recording statutes, a bona fide purchaser must give value to be protected from prior unrecorded conveyances. [¶] Valuable consideration consists of some right, interest, profit or benefit accruing to one party, or some forbearance, loss, or responsibility given, suffered or undertaken by the other. [S]everal [cases] discuss the concept of issuing corporate stock as valuable consideration in exchange for other types of interests. In determining the value of corporate stock, however, book value is entitled to little, if any, weight, and many other factors must be taken into consideration to determine the value."

Boswell v. Farm & Home Sav. Ass'n, 894 S.W.2d 761, 766 (Tex.App.—Fort Worth 1994, writ denied). "[T]he determination that a grantee is a bona fide purchaser is a legal conclusion. [A] bona fide purchaser ... will prevail over the holder of a prior equitable title."

Unrecorded Instrument

Thornton v. Rains, 299 S.W.2d 287, 288 (Tex. 1957). See annotation under *Generally*, p. 81.

Apex Fin. Corp. v. Garza, 155 S.W.3d 230, 234 (Tex.App.—Dallas 2004, pet. denied). "A creditor's lien takes priority over an unrecorded deed, unless the creditor has notice of the deed at or before the time the lien attaches to the property. Such notice may be actual or constructive." *See also* ***Omohundro v. Jackson***, 36 S.W.3d 677, 682 (Tex.App.—El Paso 2001, no pet.) (immaterial that creditor may never have examined debtor's record); ***Gibraltar Sav. Ass'n v. Martin***, 784 S.W.2d 555, 558 (Tex.App.—Amarillo 1990, writ denied) (creditor has no duty to examine debtor's record).

Chicago Title Ins. v. Alford, 3 S.W.3d 164, 169 (Tex.App.—Eastland 1999, pet. denied). Section 13.001 has "provided that unrecorded instruments are void as to 'all creditors.' ... Texas courts have held 'all creditors' to mean: [A]ll creditors who have acquired liens without notice of the deed.... It is equally well settled, however, that an open, exclusive, and visible possession, maintained by the holder of the unrecorded deed when the right of the creditor attaches, is notice of the right under which it is held. [Owners'] possession of their home gave constructive notice to the judgment creditors ... even though their deed was unrecorded."

PROP §13.002. EFFECT OF RECORDED INSTRUMENT

An instrument that is properly recorded in the proper county is:

(1) notice to all persons of the existence of the instrument; and

(2) subject to inspection by the public.

History of Prop. Code §13.002: Acts 1983, 68th Leg., ch. 576, §1, eff. Jan. 1, 1984. Amended by Acts 2003, 78th Leg., ch. 715, §2 (eff. Sept. 1, 2003), ch. 960, §2 (eff. Sept. 1, 2003). Source: TRCS art. 6646.

See also ***Real Estate Forms***, FORMS 1:8-1:13.

ANNOTATIONS

Cosgrove v. Cade, 468 S.W.3d 32, 34 (Tex.2015). "[D]isputed in this case is whether ... §13.002 ... provides all persons, including the grantor, with notice of the deed's contents.... *At 38:* [Ps'] assertion that §13.002 only provides them with notice of the deed's existence and not the deed's contents defies common sense and clashes with our precedent that mineral interest owners bear a high duty of due diligence to protect their mineral interests. ... Reasonable diligence requires mineral interest owners to read and inspect

their deeds to ensure their mineral interests are properly reserved. [Ps'] ability to monitor information contained in public records to discover their injury prevents that information from being deemed undiscoverable. … When it comes to obvious deed omissions, the accrual of a deed-reformation claim is not delayed. Section 13.002 establishes a lack of diligence in the discovery of a mistaken omission in an unambiguous deed as a matter of law."

Ojeda de Toca v. Wise, 748 S.W.2d 449, 451 (Tex. 1988). In spite of Prop. Code §13.002, "Texas courts have never held that a purchaser's failure to search the deed records would bar his fraud action against the seller. [C]onstructive notice by itself will [not] bar a consumer's action for DTPA damages or for statutory fraud. Title to [owner's] house is not in issue, and we perceive no valid reason to allow [sellers] to escape damages liability arising out of fraud or conduct proscribed by DTPA §17.46(b)(23). There are defenses to a deceptive trade practices action …, but imputed notice under real property recording statutes is not one of them." *See also* ***Lewis v. Nolan***, 105 S.W.3d 185, 189 (Tex.App.—Houston [14th Dist.] 2003, pet. denied) (mere recording of abstracts of judgment is insufficient to establish as a matter of law that P discovered facts establishing DTPA claim); ***Johnson v. Prudential Relocation Mgmt.***, 918 S.W.2d 68, 70 (Tex.App.—Eastland 1996, writ denied) (mere recording of easements is insufficient to establish constructive notice of facts establishing DTPA claim).

Sun Expl. & Prod. v. Benton, 728 S.W.2d 35, 37 (Tex.1987). "The court of appeals held that the condition precedent, if any, was waived by [D's] acceptance and recordation of the lease. … A condition precedent may be waived, and the waiver of a condition precedent may be inferred from a party's conduct. We hold, however, that the mere acceptance and recordation of an oil, gas and mineral lease does not constitute such conduct inconsistent with claiming the right to approve title to the interest conveyed. The effect of recording an instrument is to give 'notice to all persons of the existence of the instrument.' Moreover, as between the parties to the instrument, recordation cannot alter the rights and obligations of the parties. Thus, recordation did not waive any right of [D] to check title in accordance with the language in the draft."

American Homeowner Pres. Fund, LP v. Pirkle, 475 S.W.3d 507, 519 (Tex.App.—Fort Worth 2015, pet. denied). "The expectation that parties exercise diligence and vigilance in their own affairs is a deeply rooted principle of equity. This fundamental notion of equity would be violated by permitting a subsequent purchaser to ignore the deed records that would put him on notice of the purported extinguishment of the property rights he seeks to acquire and then to collaterally attack the very deed that would have provided notice in advance of the acquisition. Instead, it would reward indolence and neglect."

Noble Mortg. & Invs. v. D&M Vision Invs., 340 S.W.3d 65, 76 (Tex.App.—Houston [1st Dist.] 2011, no pet.). "Recorded instruments in a grantee's chain of title generally establish an irrebuttable presumption of notice. [¶] 'Although a deed outside the chain of title does not impute constructive knowledge, a person may be charged with the duty to make a reasonable diligent inquiry using the facts at hand in the recorded deed.' 'Thus, every purchaser of land is charged with knowledge of all facts appearing in the chain of title through which he claims that would place a reasonably prudent person on inquiry as to the rights of other parties in the property conveyed.'" *See also* ***2327 Manana LLC v. Summit Elec. Sup.***, 316 S.W.3d 241, 244 (Tex.App.—Dallas 2010, pet. denied).

TMS Mortg., Inc. v. Golias, 102 S.W.3d 768, 771 (Tex.App.—Beaumont 2003, no pet.). "[N]othing in §13.002 creates an additional duty of disclosure or requires the holder of a superior lien to contact junior lienholders before conducting a trustee's sale."

PROP §13.003. INSTRUMENTS PREVIOUSLY RECORDED IN OTHER COUNTIES

The original or a certified copy of a conveyance, covenant, agreement, deed of trust, or mortgage, relating to land, that has been recorded in a county of this state other than the county where the land to which the instrument relates is located, is valid as to a creditor or a subsequent purchaser who has paid a valuable consideration and who does not have notice of the instrument only after it is recorded in the county in which the land is located. Recording a previously recorded instrument in the proper county does not validate an invalid instrument.

History of Prop. Code §13.003: Acts 1983, 68th Leg., ch. 576, §1, eff. Jan. 1, 1984. Source: TRCS art. 6631.

PROP §13.004. EFFECT OF RECORDING LIS PENDENS

(a) A recorded lis pendens is notice to the world of its contents. The notice is effective from the time it is

filed for record and indexed as provided by Section 12.007(c), regardless of whether service has been made on the parties to the proceeding.

(b) A transfer or encumbrance of real property involved in a proceeding by a party to the proceeding to a third party who has paid a valuable consideration and who does not have actual or constructive notice of the proceeding is effective, even though the judgment is against the party transferring or encumbering the property, unless a notice of the pendency of the proceeding has been recorded and indexed under that party's name as provided by Section 12.007(c) in each county in which the property is located.

History of Prop. Code §13.004: Acts 1983, 68th Leg., ch. 576, §1, eff. Jan. 1, 1984. Amended by Acts 2011, 82nd Leg., ch. 437, §1, eff. Sept. 1, 2011. Source: TRCS arts. 6642, 6643.

See also Prop. Code §§12.007, 12.008; *O'Connor's Texas Rules*, "Lis pendens notice," ch. 2-A, §4.4, p. 116.

ANNOTATIONS

B&T Distribs. v. White, 325 S.W.3d 786, 788-89 (Tex.App.—El Paso 2010, no pet.). Claimant "contends that the trial court erred in finding that the *lis pendens* barred [claimant] from levying a writ of execution on the property. [¶] '[Claimant's] claim would be as to the interest which [husband] had, if any, to the real property at the conclusion of [divorce] lawsuit. [Wife] filed her lis pendens [in] 2007. [Wife's] lis pendens was filed prior to [claimant] attempting, in any manner, to enforce its foreign judgment against [husband] in the State of Texas.' [¶] [Claimant] argues that a *lis pendens* does not create a lien, but is simply a warning to potential purchasers. *At 790:* [W]e conclude that [claimant's] interest in the [real] property was subordinate to the outcome of [the divorce] litigation because [wife's] *lis pendens* was filed before [claimant] took any action to enforce its judgment."

PROP §13.005. EFFECT OF RECORDING JUDGMENT OF JUSTICE COURT

A certified transcript of a justice court judgment recorded under Section 12.015 of this code has the same effect as a recorded deed. A court shall admit as evidence the transcript or a copy of the transcript, if the copy is certified with the signature and seal of the clerk of the county in which the transcript is recorded, in the same manner and with the same effect as the original judgment and execution.

History of Prop. Code §13.005: Acts 1983, 68th Leg., ch. 576, §1, eff. Jan. 1, 1984. Source: TRCS art. 6637.

See also Prop. Code §12.015; TRCP 505.1, 505.2.

CHAPTER 14. UNIFORM FEDERAL LIEN REGISTRATION ACT

NCCUSL Prefatory Comment*

This Act is a successor to the Revised Federal Tax Lien Registration Act as revised by the Conference in 1966 and does not make any drafting changes to the previous Act except as required to prescribe the method of perfecting the employer liability lien, provided by the Pension Reform Act, and any other similar liens.

Since most of the policy decisions made in drafting this Act were derived from the Revised Uniform Federal Tax Lien Registration Act as it was revised in 1966, it would appear helpful to include here the Prefatory Note which was included with the earlier Act in 1966.

"Section 6323 of the United States Internal Revenue Code of 1954, as amended by P.L. 89-719, Federal Tax Lien Act of 1966 provides that liens for an unpaid federal tax shall not be valid as against mortgagees, pledges, judgment creditors, purchasers and holders of other security interest until notice of the tax lien has been filed in an office designated by the law of the state in which the property subject to the lien is situated, or, in the absence of a valid state designation, in the federal district court for the place where the property is situated. Under federal law, personal property is deemed situated at the residence of the taxpayer regardless of its physical location.

"Thus the new federal act would invalidate any provision of a state law which required filing of liens for property other than real estate at more than one office or at any state office other than that associated with the residence of the taxpayer. State law requiring filing at the physical location of personal property or at both physical location and residence of the taxpayer is not permissible and if a state law includes such a provision the Internal Revenue Service would, for that state, file liens in the federal district court rather than in a state office.

"The new federal legislation provides for filing of certain types of certificates and notices affecting previously filed liens which some of the existing state legislation does not provide for. The effectiveness of these additional notices as a communication to interested persons depends on their being filed in the same office where the notice of lien is filed. It is necessary, therefore, that state law be broadened to permit filing and indexing of these additional notices.

"In addition to the above reasons for new state legislation, there is another reason for revising existing state laws concerned with federal tax liens. Many of the existing laws are no longer appropriate in the states (all but three in December 1966) which have enacted the Uniform Commercial Code. It is highly desirable that the place for filing and searching for federal tax liens be the same place as that designated by the state law under the Uniform Commercial Code for filing and searching for a security interest in the same property. Unfortunately, complete coordination of federal tax lien filing with the rules for filing under the Uniform Commercial Code cannot be fully achieved by state legislation. The United States Supreme Court has held that the Congressional permission to a state to designate the office for filing of federal tax liens cannot be taken advantage of by the states in such a way as to require the federal tax collector to specify the particular property to which the lien applies. *United States v. Union Central Life Insurance Company*, 363 U.S. 291 (1961). The Internal Revenue Service has interpreted this decision to preclude a state requirement for filing federal tax liens in conformity with the Uniform Commercial Code because of the Code's differing requirements for various types of property

* **Editor's note:**

The NCCUSL comments have been edited to reflect the Texas Legislature's omission of sections and changing of section numbers from the original uniform act. The Texas Legislature did not adopt the NCCUSL comments when it adopted the Uniform Federal Lien Registration Act. The full uniform act and comments can be found at www.uniformlaws.org.

and its requirement for filing in two offices in some cases. Rev. Rul. 64-170, 1964-1 Cum. Bull. 499. P.L. 89-719 continues this interpretation.

"Nevertheless, it is possible to go a long way toward bringing federal tax lien filing into conformity with the Uniform Commercial Code and it is highly desirable to do so in order to accommodate to commercial convenience so far as possible within the limitations of federal law. States which departed from the uniformity of the Commercial Code by amendment as to the place of filing may now wish to conform their Commercial Code to the original uniform version at the same time they change the federal tax lien requirements. The Act presented here calls for filing on taxpayers who are corporations or partnerships in the office of the Secretary of State and in all other cases in an office in the place where the taxpayer resides. No provision is possible calling for filing of the tax lien at the place where particular kinds of property are physically located. Any attempt to deviate from the proposed place of filing in this Code risks non-compliance with Federal Law. The federal act does permit filing of notices as to real property in an office at the place where the real property is situated. It has no such permission for other kinds of property. Section 14.001 of the Act contained herein complies with the federal requirement.

"The present Act was prepared in light of Public Law 89-719 of 1966 amending Section 6323 of the Internal Revenue Code of 1954. The Internal Revenue Service has reviewed the Act and believes it meets the requirement of federal law. The Conference recommends that it be adopted and that existing legislation concerning federal tax liens be repealed."

PROP §14.001. SCOPE

This chapter applies only to federal tax liens and to other federal liens notices of which under any Act of Congress or any regulation adopted pursuant thereto are required or permitted to be filed in the same manner as notices of federal tax liens.

History of Prop. Code §14.001: Acts 1989, 71st Leg., ch. 945, §1, eff. Sept. 1, 1989.

NCCUSL Comment*

This Act is a successor to the Revised Federal Tax Lien Registration Act as revised by the Conference in 1966. The changes made in the previous Act are brought about by the provisions of the Pension Reform Act which prescribes the method of perfecting the employer liability lien to be the same as for federal tax liens.

Therefore, the Act has been changed and now applies to the employer liability lien established by Section 4068(a) of the Pension Reform Act as well as a federal tax lien. Other similar liens that may be perfected like a federal tax lien, such as the provisions for collection of federal fines contained in proposed revisions to the federal criminal laws, are within the scope of this Act.

PROP §14.002. PLACE OF FILING

(a) Notices of liens, certificates, and other notices affecting federal tax liens or other federal liens must be filed in accordance with this chapter.

(b) Notices of liens upon real property for obligations payable to the United States and certificates and notices affecting the liens shall be filed in the office of the county clerk in the county in which the real property subject to the liens is situated.

(c) Notices of federal liens upon personal property, whether tangible or intangible, for obligations payable to the United States and certificates and notices affecting the liens shall be filed as follows:

(1) if the person against whose interest the lien applies is a corporation or a partnership whose principal executive office is in this state, as these entities are defined in the internal revenue laws of the United States, in the office of the secretary of state;

(2) in all other cases, in the office of the county clerk in the county where the person against whose interest the lien applies resides at the time of filing of the notice of lien.

History of Prop. Code §14.002: Acts 1989, 71st Leg., ch. 945, §1, eff. Sept. 1, 1989.

NCCUSL Comment*

1. In order to accommodate to commercial convenience so far as possible within the limitations of Section 6323 of the Internal Revenue Code, filing with the Secretary of State is provided for the lien on tangible and intangible personal property of partnerships and corporations (as those terms are defined in Section 7701 of the Internal Revenue Code of 1954 and the implementing regulations) thus including within "partnerships" such entities as joint ventures and within "corporations" such entities as joint stock corporations and business trusts.

Because most purchases and secured transactions involving personal property of natural persons relate to consumer goods or farm personal property, searches for liens against those persons are more likely to be made at the local level. Thus, with few exceptions a search for corporation federal tax liens with the Secretary of State and for natural persons with an officer in the county of residence will normally be in the same office as searches for security interests under the Uniform Commercial Code.

Section 6323 of the Internal Revenue Code "locates" all tangible and intangible personal property at the residence of the taxpayer even though it is physically located elsewhere in the same or in another state. State law cannot vary this requirement. State law does affect the result, however, in that state law determines the "residence" of a taxpayer. See IRC §6323(f)(2). Filing at the physical location of personal property of a taxpayer who is not a resident of the state of location of the property cannot be required.

2. The coverage of this Act now extends beyond federal tax liens as described in the Comment to Section 14.001.

3. In some jurisdictions, a question may be raised concerning the propriety of incorporating federal law by reference. In others, the place of filing described in this Act may not correspond to the place of filing under the Uniform Commercial Code. Alteration of this Act in these respects may create the peril that the notices will be filed in the federal district court, thus eliminating the benefits of this Act.

PROP §14.003. EXECUTION OF NOTICES & CERTIFICATES

Certification of notices of liens, certificates, or other notices affecting federal liens by the secretary of the treasury of the United States or his delegate, or by any official or entity of the United States responsible for filing or certifying of notice of any other lien, entitles them to be filed and no other attestation, certification, or acknowledgment is necessary.

History of Prop. Code §14.003: Acts 1989, 71st Leg., ch. 945, §1, eff. Sept. 1, 1989.

NCCUSL Comment*

This section addresses only the validity of the filing and not the validity of the lien.

PROP §14.004. DUTIES OF FILING OFFICER

(a) If a notice of federal lien, a refiling of a notice of federal lien, or a notice of revocation of any certificate described in Subsection (b) is presented to a filing officer who is:

* See footnote on p. 85.

(1) the secretary of state, he shall cause the notice to be marked, held or placed on microtext, and indexed in accordance with the provisions of Section 9.519, Business & Commerce Code, as if the notice were a financing statement within the meaning of that code; or

(2) any other officer described in Section 14.002, he shall endorse thereon his identification and the date and time of receipt and forthwith file it alphabetically in the real property records and if requested by the party submitting the document, in the personal property files or enter it in an alphabetical index for real or personal property, as appropriate, showing the name and address of the person named in the notice, the date and time of receipt, the title and address of the official or entity certifying the lien, and the total amount appearing on the notice of lien.

(b) If a certificate of release, nonattachment, discharge, or subordination of any lien is presented to the secretary of state for filing he shall:

(1) cause a certificate of release or nonattachment to be marked, held, and indexed as if the certificate were a termination statement within the meaning of the Uniform Commercial Code, but the notice of lien to which the certificate relates may not be removed from the files; and

(2) cause a certificate of discharge or subordination to be marked, held, and indexed as if the certificate were a release of collateral within the meaning of the Uniform Commercial Code.

(c) If a refiled notice of federal lien referred to in Subsection (a) or any of the certificates or notices referred to in Subsection (b) is presented for filing to any other filing officer specified in Section 14.002, he shall permanently attach the refiled notice or the certificate to the original notice of lien unless the document is on microtext and therefore not in the files of the filing officer and enter the refiled notice or the certificate with the date of filing in any alphabetical lien index on the line where the original notice of lien is entered.

(d) Upon request of any person, the filing officer shall issue his certificate showing whether there is on file, on a date and time specified by the filing office, but not a date earlier than three business days before the date the filing office receives the request, any notice of lien or certificate or notice affecting any lien filed under this chapter or filed under the Uniform Federal Tax Lien Registration Act (Subchapter C, Chapter 113, Tax Code) on or after January 1, 1972, naming a particular person, and if a notice or certificate is on file, giving the date and hour of filing of each notice or certificate. The amount of the fee for a certificate is the same as the amount of the fee provided by Section 9.525(d), Business & Commerce Code. Upon request, the filing officer shall furnish a copy of any notice of federal lien. The fee for a copy furnished under this section is in the amount provided by Section 405.031, Government Code.

(e) Section 9.523, Business & Commerce Code, applies to a federal lien filed under this chapter.

History of Prop. Code §14.004: Acts 1989, 71st Leg., ch. 945, §1, eff. Sept. 1, 1989. Amended by Acts 1999, 76th Leg., ch. 414, §2.34, eff. July 1, 2001; Acts 2009, 81st Leg., ch. 547, §10, eff. Sept. 1, 2009.

See also B&CC §9.519.

NCCUSL Comment*

1. It is the practice of the Internal Revenue Service to regard a "certificate of discharge" as primarily referable to specific pieces of property, so a certificate of discharge corresponds to a release under Section 9-406 of the Uniform Commercial Code. A "certificate of release" in tax practice is equivalent to a "termination statement" in Section 9-404 of the Uniform Commercial Code in the sense that it is a general statement applicable to all property or types of property referred to in the termination statement.

2. It is expected that the Pension Benefit Guaranty Corporation will adopt the same practices as the Internal Revenue Service or other practices as the circumstances may require.

PROP §14.005. FEE

The fee for filing and indexing each notice of lien or certificate or notice affecting the lien is $10. The filing of the same notice of lien or certificate or notice affecting a lien in both real property records and personal property files is two filings.

History of Prop. Code §14.005: Acts 1989, 71st Leg., ch. 945, §1, eff. Sept. 1, 1989.

NCCUSL Comment*

1. It is understood that the Treasury accepts the obligation to pay non-discriminatory filing fees for filing notice of tax liens but desires those payments to be on a monthly billing basis. For notice of tax lien on real property, the filing fee for a real estate mortgage may serve as a standard; for a filing fee on notice of tax lien on personal property the filing fee for filing a financing statement may serve as a standard. There is now no established practice concerning fees for other notices. The certificate of discharge is comparable to a satisfaction of a real estate mortgage and to release of collateral under Section 9-406 of the Uniform Commercial Code. Those instruments are usually filed by persons other than the Treasury, and a filing fee for filing them should be prescribed.

A different problem is presented by certificates of release or nonattachment. Sometimes those certificates serve the purpose of permitting the public filing official to clear his records, and for that purpose the filing fee perhaps should be low in order to induce filing. Sometimes those notices are filed for purposes of the taxpayer. Given the volume of notices of tax liens which are filed daily in large filing offices, it may serve the public interest to have filed certificates of release. From the standpoint of the Treasury, those certificates serve no important purpose, and the Treasury may not file them if the fee is large. In adoption of this Act, consideration should be given by the states to providing a substantially smaller fee for filing a certificate of release, so that when a tax case is closed the Treasury will file those releases in a routine manner in order to reduce the storage and administrative problem of the local and state filing officers.

2. It is understood that the Pension Benefit Guaranty Corporation will accept the same obligations as those imposed on the Treasury for federal tax liens.

---

* See footnote on p. 85.

PROP §14.006. UNIFORMITY OF APPLICATION & CONSTRUCTION

This chapter shall be applied and construed to effectuate its general purpose to make uniform the law with respect to the subject of this chapter among states enacting it.

History of Prop. Code §14.006: Acts 1989, 71st Leg., ch. 945, §1, eff. Sept. 1, 1989.

PROP §14.007. SHORT TITLE

This chapter may be cited as the Uniform Federal Lien Registration Act.

History of Prop. Code §14.007: Acts 1989, 71st Leg., ch. 945, §1, eff. Sept. 1, 1989.

CHAPTER 15. UNIFORM REAL PROPERTY ELECTRONIC RECORDING ACT

NCCUSL Prefatory Comment*

The status of electronic information technology has progressed rapidly in recent years. Innovations in software, hardware, communications technology and security protocols have made it technically feasible to create, sign and transmit real estate transactions electronically.

However, approaching the end of the 20th Century, various state and federal laws limited the enforceability of electronic documents. In response, the Uniform Electronic Transactions Act (UETA) was approved by the National Conference of Commissioners on Uniform State Laws (NCCUSL) in 1999. As of October 1, 2004, UETA had been adopted in 46 states, the District of Columbia, and the U.S. Virgin Islands. The federal Electronic Signatures in Global and National Commerce Act (E-Sign) was also adopted in 2000. The two acts give legal effect to real estate transactions that are executed electronically and allow them to be enforced between the parties to the transaction.

Even though documents resulting from electronic transactions are valid and enforceable between the parties, there is uncertainty and confusion about whether those electronic documents may be recorded in the various local land records offices in the several states. Legacy laws and regulations in many states purport to limit recordable documents to ones that are in writing or on paper or require that they be originals. Other laws and regulations require signatures to be in writing and acknowledgements to be signed. Being electronic and not written on paper, being an electronic version of an original paper document, or having an electronic signature and acknowledgement instead of handwritten ones, an electronic document might not be recordable under the laws of these states. The continuing application of these legacy laws and regulations remain uncertain (see Op. Cal. Atty. Gen. No. 02-112 (Sept. 4, 2002)).

* **Editor's note:**

The NCCUSL comments have been edited to reflect the Texas Legislature's omission of sections and changing of section numbers from the original uniform act. The Texas Legislature did not adopt the NCCUSL comments when it adopted the Uniform Real Property Electronic Recording Act. The full uniform act and comments can be found at www.uniformlaws.org.

Despite these uncertainties, recorders in approximately 40 counties in several states began recording electronic documents. These efforts depend, however, on the initiatives of individual recorders and the opportunities available under the laws of those states. They are piecemeal and offer only limited interoperability among the recording venues and across state lines. They do not provide a uniform legal structure for the acceptance and processing of electronic documents.

In response, a few states have convened study committees or task forces to consider the question of recording electronic documents (see Report of Iowa State Bar Ass'n, Real Estate Modernization Comm., draft of Ch. 558B—Iowa Electronic Recording Act (2001); Conn. Law Revision Comm., An Act Establishing the Connecticut Real Property Electronic Recording System (Conn. Gen Assembly, Judiciary Comm., Raised Bill No. 5664, 2004)). In 2002, a drafting committee was established by the NCCUSL Executive Committee to draft a Uniform Real Property Electronic Recording Act. The Committee's decision followed a recommendation of the NCCUSL Committee on Scope and Program. Their actions were in recognition of a strong recommendation from the Joint Editorial Board on Uniform Real Property Acts that a uniform act be drafted.

The Uniform Real Property Electronic Recording Act was drafted to remove any doubt about the authority of the recorder to receive and record documents and information in electronic form. Its fundamental principle is that any requirements of state law describing or requiring that a document be an original, on paper, or in writing are satisfied by a document in electronic form. Furthermore, any requirement that the document contain a signature or acknowledgment is satisfied by an electronic signature or acknowledgement. The act specifically authorizes a recorder, at the recorder's option, to accept electronic documents for recording and to index and store those documents.

If the recorder elects to accept electronic documents, the recorder must also comply with certain other requirements set forth in the act. In addition, the act charges an Electronic Recording Commission or an existing state agency with the responsibility of implementing the act and adopting standards regarding the receipt, recording, and retrieval of electronic documents. The Commission or agency is directed to adopt those standards with a vision toward fostering intra- and interstate harmony and uniformity in electronic recording processes.

This act does not state the means of funding the establishment or operation of an electronic recording system in the various recording venues. No single approach is inherently the best for funding electronic recording systems. This is especially true because of the range of taxation systems and cultures existing in the various states and recording venues and the diversity of the various states and recording venues in terms of population and resources. In fact, the best system for any state or recording venue might involve a combination of approaches.

The establishment, and perhaps the operation, of an electronic recording system might be funded from the general taxes and revenues of the state or county. Because of the relatively large "front end" expenses needed to set up an electronic recording system, this approach might be very appropriate for that purpose. Whether the funding is to be by the county or the state is an issue that should be resolved prior to the passage of this act. A related question is whether the funding should cover the entire cost of setting up the system or only part of it with the remaining costs to be paid by recording and searching fees dedicated to the establishment of the electronic recording system.

PROP §15.001. SHORT TITLE

This chapter may be cited as the Uniform Real Property Electronic Recording Act.

History of Prop. Code §15.001: Acts 2005, 79th Leg., ch. 699, §1, eff. Sept. 1, 2005.

See also *Real Estate Forms*, FORMS 1:8-1:13.

NCCUSL Comment*

This act applies to the recording of documents in the land records office maintained by a recorder. It applies both to the filing of, and the searching for, documents in the recorder's office by whatever term or terms those functions and offices are known locally.

PROP §15.002. DEFINITIONS

In this chapter:

(1) "Document" means information that is:

(A) inscribed on a tangible medium or that is stored in an electronic or other medium and is retrievable in perceivable form; and

(B) eligible to be recorded in the real property records maintained by a county clerk.

(2) "Electronic" means relating to technology having electrical, digital, magnetic, wireless, optical, electromagnetic, or similar capabilities.

(3) "Electronic document" means a document that is received by a county clerk in an electronic form.

(4) "Electronic signature" means an electronic sound, symbol, or process attached to or logically associated with a document and executed or adopted by a person with the intent to sign the document.

(5) "Paper document" means a document that is received by a county clerk in a form that is not electronic.

History of Prop. Code §15.002: Acts 2005, 79th Leg., ch. 699, §1, eff. Sept. 1, 2005.

See also ***Real Estate Forms***, FORMS 1:8-1:13.

NCCUSL Comment*

(1) "Document." A document consists of information stored on a medium, whether the medium be tangible or electronic, provided that the information is retrievable in a perceivable form. The traditional tangible medium has been paper on which information is inscribed by writing, typing, printing or similar means. It is perceivable by reading it directly from the paper on which it is inscribed. An electronic medium may be one on which information is stored magnetically and from which it may be retrieved and read indirectly on a computer monitor or a paper printout.

While a document recorded in a land records office will usually contain information affecting real property, it need not necessarily be so limited. It applies to any document that is recorded in the land records office maintained by the recorder. Deeds, grants of easements, and mortgages are documents subject to this act. Similarly, certificates and affidavits not directly affecting real property may be documents under this act if state law provides these documents are to be recorded in the land records office.

The definition of a document in this act is derived from the definition of the term "record" as contained in the Uniform Electronic Transactions Act (UETA) §2(13). In the terms of that act, a document is a record that is eligible to be recorded in the land records maintained by the recorder. In selecting the defined term "document" for use throughout this act, an explicit decision was made not to use "record" as a defined term. The term "record" has a different meaning in real estate recording law and practice than it has in UETA. If the term "record" were used generally in this act, it might lead to confusion and misinterpretation.

In UETA, the term "record" refers to information on a tangible or electronic medium as does the term "document" in this act. In this act, however, depending on syntax, the term "record" and its variations can have several meanings, all of which deal with document storage and not the information itself. For example, this act deals with the recording process through which a person can record a document. The government officer who oversees the land records office is the recorder. These terms are so ingrained in the lexicon of real estate recording law and practice that it would not be productive to attempt to change them by this act.

(2) "Electronic." The term "electronic" refers to the use of electrical, digital, magnetic, wireless, optical, electromagnetic and similar technologies. It is a descriptive term meant to include all technologies involving electronic processes. The listing of specific technologies is not intended to be a limiting one. For example, biometric identification technologies would be included if they affect communication and storage of information by electronic means. As electronic technologies expand and include other competencies, those competencies should also be included under this definition.

The definition of the term "electronic" in this act has the same meaning as it has in UETA §2(5).

(3) "Electronic document." An "electronic document" is a "document" that is in an "electronic" form. Both of these terms are previously defined. However, this definition adds an additional requirement not specifically stated in the individual definitions. In order to be an "electronic document" the document must be received by the county clerk in an "electronic" form. The character of a document as "electronic" or "paper" will be determined at the moment it is received by the county clerk.

Even though a document may have an existence in an "electronic" form prior or subsequent to being received by the county clerk it might not be an "electronic document" under this act. For example, the document may have been created by an electronic process or have existed in an electronic form before being converted to, and received by the county clerk in, a paper form. Thus, a document prepared on a computer by means of a word processing program may have been created electronically and may still exist electronically. If, however, the document is printed and submitted to the county clerk on paper, the submitted document is not an electronic document. Similarly, after arriving in the county clerk's office in a paper form, the document may be converted to an electronic form prior to, or as part of, the recording process. The paper document does not become an electronic document because of the post-receipt conversion. (For a definition of the term "paper document," see below.)

By comparison, a document received by the county clerk in an electronic form, but subsequently converted to a paper form, will be considered to be an electronic document. For example, if a document is received electronically and then printed in a paper form in the county clerk's office prior to storage, it is, nonetheless, an electronic document. Thus, a document received by the process commonly known as a facsimile or a FAX, is an electronic document. Issues common to electronic documents, such as security and integrity, also relate to a facsimile or FAX document.

In many cases a document may have originally been executed in a paper form with "wet signatures" and subsequently imaged and converted into an electronic format. This act provides that, if such a converted document is received by the county clerk in an electronic format, it will be considered to be an electronic document and may be recorded. (See Section 15.004(a).)

This act does not state or limit the type of electronic documents that may be accepted by the county clerk. Nor does it state the type of electronic signatures that are permissible. Those matters are subject to the standards adopted by the Texas State Library and Archives Commission pursuant to Section 15.006.

This act applies only to documents that are received by the county clerk in an electronic form and enables those documents to be recorded. The recordability of documents not received by the county clerk in an electronic form continues to depend on other state law.

(4) "Electronic signature." The term "electronic signature" is based on the definition of that term in UETA §2(8). However, this definition uses the word "document" instead of "record" to identify the instrument being signed. (See generally paragraph 1, above, for a discussion of the reasons).

(5) A "paper document" is one that is received by the county clerk in a form that is not "electronic." Despite the use of the word "paper," this document form is not limited to documents on a paper medium; the use of the word "paper" is merely a convenience. It applies to any non-electronic document that the county clerk is authorized to accept.

Just as with the definition of an "electronic document" of this act, the moment at which the character of the document will be determined is the moment it is received by the county clerk. If a document is received by the county clerk in a non-electronic form, it is a "paper" document regardless of whether it has a prior or subsequent existence as an electronic document.

* See footnote on p. 88.

PROP §15.003. UNIFORMITY OF APPLICATION & CONSTRUCTION

In applying and construing this chapter, consideration must be given to the need to promote uniformity of the law with respect to the subject matter of this chapter among states that enact a law substantially similar to this chapter.

History of Prop. Code §15.003: Acts 2005, 79th Leg., ch. 699, §1, eff. Sept. 1, 2005.

See also *Real Estate Forms*, FORMS 1:8-1:13.

NCCUSL Comment*

This section recites the importance of uniformity among the adopting states when applying and construing the act. It is more general than the uniformity stated in Section 15.006 for the Texas State Library and Archives Commission when implementing or adopting standards. This section seeks uniformity in all situations when the application or interpretation of the chapter itself is considered or under review.

PROP §15.004. VALIDITY OF ELECTRONIC DOCUMENTS

(a) If a law requires, as a condition for recording, that a document be an original, be on paper or another tangible medium, or be in writing, the requirement is satisfied by an electronic document that complies with the requirements of this chapter.

(b) If a law requires, as a condition for recording, that a document be signed, the requirement is satisfied by an electronic signature.

(c) A requirement that a document or a signature associated with a document be notarized, acknowledged, verified, witnessed, or made under oath is satisfied if the electronic signature of the person authorized to perform that act, and all other information required to be included, is attached to or logically associated with the document or signature. A physical or electronic image of a stamp, impression, or seal need not accompany an electronic signature.

History of Prop. Code §15.004: Acts 2005, 79th Leg., ch. 699, §1, eff. Sept. 1, 2005.

See also *Real Estate Forms*, FORMS 1:8-1:13, 11:1, 11:2.

NCCUSL Comment*

(a) Subsection (a) states the basic principle of this act—if a document would be recordable in a paper format, an electronic document with the same content and meeting the requirements of this act is also recordable. Any reference in a statute, regulation, or standard to a document as being on paper or a similar tangible medium in order to be recorded is superseded by this act. Similarly any statute, regulation, or standard that specifies that a document must be in writing in order to be recorded is also overruled by this act. Furthermore, since any paper-specific requirement such as the size of the paper or the color of the ink used for the document is inapplicable to an electronic document, those requirements do not prohibit or limit the recording of electronic documents.

This subsection also provides that any stipulation of state law requiring that a document be an original document is satisfied by an electronic document meeting the requirements of this act. For example, this section acknowledges that one form of electronic document is created by making an electronic duplicate of an original paper document. The duplicate is an electronic "picture" of the original document with all of its signatures and verifications. Under some existing state laws, the electronic duplicate may be considered to be a copy of the original paper document and not the original itself. The laws of the state may also provide that a copy of a document may not be recorded. This act corrects that circumstance and allows the electronic document containing the "picture" of the original document to be recorded. Of course, in order to be valid, the original paper document must be executed in accordance with law, including a signature and verification.

(b) Subsection (b) provides that any statute, regulation, or standard requiring that a document be signed in order to be recorded is satisfied by an electronic signature attached to an electronic document. The provisions of UETA and the federal Electronic Signatures in Global and National Commerce Act (E-Sign) provide that an electronic signature is not an impediment to the enforceability of an electronic document between the parties to the transaction. Similarly, this section provides that an electronic signature is not an impediment to the recording of the document.

(c) This section provides that any statute, regulation, or standard requiring that a notarization, acknowledgement, verification, witnessing, or taking of an oath be done on paper or similar tangible medium, that it be done in writing, or that it be signed, is satisfied by an electronic signature that is attached to, or logically associated with, the electronic document. It permits a notary public or other authorized person to act electronically without the need to do so on paper.

It also provides that any statute, regulation, or standard that requires a personal or corporate stamp, impression, or seal is satisfied by an electronic signature. These physical indicia are inapplicable to a fully electronic document. Thus, the notarial stamp or impression that is required under the laws of some states is not required for an electronic notarization under this act. Nor is there a need for a corporate stamp or impression as would otherwise be required under the laws of some states to verify the action of a corporate officer. Nevertheless, this act requires that the information that would otherwise be contained in the stamp, impression, or seal must be attached to, or logically associated with, the document or signature in an electronic fashion.

PROP §15.005. RECORDING OF DOCUMENTS

(a) A county clerk who implements any of the functions described by this section shall act in compliance with rules adopted by the Texas State Library and Archives Commission under Chapter 195, Local Government Code, and standards established by the Texas State Library and Archives Commission under Section 15.006.

(b) A county clerk may:

(1) receive, index, store, archive, and transmit electronic documents;

(2) provide for access to, and for search and retrieval of, documents and information by electronic means;

(3) convert paper documents accepted for recording into electronic form;

(4) convert into electronic form information recorded before the county clerk began to record electronic documents;

(5) accept electronically any fee or tax that the county clerk is authorized to collect; and

(6) agree with other officials of a state, a political subdivision of a state, or the United States on proce-

* See footnote on p. 88.

dures or processes to facilitate the electronic satisfaction of prior approvals and conditions precedent to recording and the electronic payment of fees and taxes.

(c) A county clerk who accepts electronic documents for recording shall:

(1) continue to accept paper documents; and

(2) place entries for paper documents and electronic documents in the same index.

History of Prop. Code §15.005: Acts 2005, 79th Leg., ch. 699, §1, eff. Sept. 1, 2005.

See also 13 T.A.C. §§7.71-7.79, 7.141-7.145; *Real Estate Forms*, FORMS 1:8-1:13.

NCCUSL Comment*

(a) Section 15.005 sets forth specific required or elective functions that apply to the recording of documents.

Implementation of any functions described in subsection (b) is optional and a decision to implement one or more of them is to be made by the county clerk. The act does not require that a county clerk implement any or all of those functions. It merely allows each county clerk to implement them when and if the county clerk decides to proceed with electronic recording.

However, under paragraph (a) if a county clerk does elect to implement any of the functions described in this section, the county clerk must do so in accordance with the standards established by the Texas State Library and Archives Commission. All aspects of the functions described in this subsection are subject to the standards of the commission.

(b)(1) Subsection (b)(1) provides that the county clerk may choose to implement electronic recording functions. Recording functions are varied and deal with obtaining and storing of documents in a recording system. Under this paragraph, the county clerk may elect to receive electronic documents. The county clerk may store those electronic documents, or the information contained in them, and create an index of the documents or information. The county clerk may also transmit electronic documents and communications to the recording party or to other parties. Finally, the county clerk may archive the electronic documents or the information in them as well as the index in order to preserve and protect them. This is an election to be made by the county clerk that is separate from the decision to provide electronic searching, as described in subsection (b)(2).

Since this act also applies to "Torrens" title registration systems, a county clerk who operates a title registration system may choose to implement the functions of receiving, indexing, storing, archiving, and transmitting electronic documents for the title registration system.

(2) Subsection (b)(2) provides that the county clerk may choose to implement electronic search and retrieval functions. Searching and retrieval functions include any process by which a title searcher obtains information from the land records system. The paragraph allows a county clerk to authorize persons to access documents or their information, including index information, electronically. In so doing, the county clerk may allow the accessing party to search the index and the stored documents or information electronically and to retrieve them in an electronic format. This is an election to be made by the county clerk that is separate from the decision to record electronic documents, as described in subsection (b)(1). A county clerk who operates a "Torrens" title registration system also may choose to implement the functions of accessing, searching, and retrieving documents or information in the title registration system.

(3) Subsections (b)(3) and (b)(4) relate to the conversion and storage of the text or information contained in paper documents in an electronic form. It does not concern the index information that is derived from those paper documents. The treatment of index information is described in the subsection (c).

Subsection (b)(3) relates to the conversion of "new" paper documents received by the county clerk after the implementation of an electronic recording system. It does not require that such newly-received paper documents be converted and stored in an electronic form. It does, however, permit the county clerk to make a conversion of those paper documents into an electronic form and store them with electronic documents received by the county clerk. If the paper documents are not converted into an electronic form, the county clerk must continue to store them and, as public documents, the county clerk must continue to provide a process for accessing them.

If the county clerk does not convert "new" paper documents into an electronic form, the usefulness and efficiency of the electronic recording system may be limited. A title examiner will have to obtain physical access to the paper document information in traditional ways. Since electronic documents are stored electronically, the examiner will have to access two different storage systems – one for paper documents and one for electronic documents.

(4) Subsection (b)(4) relates to the conversion of information from "old" paper documents recorded prior to the implementation of an electronic recording system. As with newly-received paper documents, the act does not require the county clerk to convert previously-recorded information into an electronic form. Such a conversion is, however, permitted under the act.

Dealing with "old" document information is more challenging than dealing with "new" documents simply because of the potentially large expenditure of time and money needed to convert a significant volume of paper information extending over many past years into an electronic form. The time period over which a fully-effective conversion would extend probably spans a period of forty to sixty or more years, depending on the customary period of search in the jurisdiction. Without the conversion, the usefulness and efficiency of the electronic recording system is limited, at least until the passage of a period after the adoption of the act that is equal to the customary period of search.

(5) Subsection (b)(5) provides that any fee or tax that is collected by the county clerk may be collected through an electronic payment system. Without a means of paying the applicable fees and taxes electronically, the achievement of a speedy and efficient electronic recording system would not be possible. Although the document could be submitted electronically, the fee would have to be paid by traditional means. The effective completion of the recording would be delayed until that payment is received by the county clerk.

The nature and operation of the electronic payment system is not specified. The selection is subject to standards set by the Texas State Library and Archives Commission and the choice of the county clerk. Among others, the alternatives might include a subscription service with a regular billing system, a prepayment system with recording and access charges applied against a deposited amount, or a payment per individual service system.

(6) Commonly, before a county clerk may accept a document for recording it must be approved by one or more other offices in order to assure compliance with the other office's requirements. The person submitting the document may also be required to pay fees or taxes to the other office or offices. If the prior approval and the fee or tax paying processes are not conjoined with the electronic recording process, it will not be possible to effectuate the speedy electronic recording envisioned by this act.

For example, a document may first need to be submitted to the county assessor or treasurer to determine whether prior real estate taxes have been paid or whether current ones are due. Under current practice that submission and approval might have to be accomplished in a physical process independent of the electronic recording process. If a tax or fee is due, that sum might also have to be paid by check or other non-electronic process to the treasurer. Procedures such as these will delay the electronic recording process and will limit the achievement of a speedy, efficient electronic recording system.

Subsection (b)(6) permits and encourages the county clerk to enter into agreements with other county and state offices for the purpose of implementing processes that will allow the simultaneous satisfaction of all conditions precedent to recording and the payment of all fees and taxes in a single transaction. Any fees and taxes paid by the recording party will be allocated among the county clerk and the other offices in accordance with their agreements.

(c) This act does not require that persons engaging in real estate transactions use electronic documents in order to have their documents recorded. It merely permits the county clerk to accept electronic documents if they are presented electronically. Economics, availability of technology, and human nature suggest that not everyone will begin to use electronic real estate documents immediately. It will likely be some time before the use of electronic documents becomes dominant and perhaps well beyond that before paper documents disappear altogether from the conveyancing process. In recognition of that fact, subsection (c) requires the county clerk to continue to accept paper documents even after establishing an electronic recording system. This is a mandatory and not an elective provision.

* See footnote on p. 88.

This paragraph also provides that the county clerk must index the paper documents together with electronic documents as part of a single indexing system. This will enable a title examiner to make a single search of one index for the purpose of ascertaining all relevant instruments that were recorded after the initiation of electronic recording. It avoids the inefficient and costly process of maintaining and searching two separate indexing systems—one for electronic documents and one for paper documents.

Efficiency also suggests that the unified index would be an electronic one. It would be more efficient to store the index information from paper documents in an electronic index than to convert and store the index information from electronic documents in a paper index system. Electronic index information can be sorted and managed more easily and efficiently than paper index information. In addition, an electronic index can be searched more quickly and without the searcher's physical presence in the county clerk's office. However, the act does not require the index chosen by the county clerk to be an electronic one.

PROP §15.006. UNIFORM STANDARDS

(a) The Texas State Library and Archives Commission by rule shall adopt standards to implement this chapter.

(b) To keep the standards and practices of county clerks in this state in harmony with the standards and practices of recording offices in other jurisdictions that enact a law that is substantially similar to this chapter and to keep the technology used by county clerks in this state compatible with technology used by recording offices in other jurisdictions that enact a law that is substantially similar to this chapter, the Texas State Library and Archives Commission, so far as is consistent with the purposes, policies, and provisions of this chapter, in adopting, amending, and repealing standards shall consider:

(1) standards and practices of other jurisdictions;

(2) the most recent standards promulgated by national standard-setting bodies, such as the Property Records Industry Association;

(3) the views of interested persons and governmental officials and entities; and

(4) the needs of counties of varying size, population, and resources.

History of Prop. Code §15.006: Acts 2005, 79th Leg., ch. 699, §1, eff. Sept. 1, 2005.

See also 13 T.A.C. §§7.71-7.79, 7.141-7.145; ***Real Estate Forms***, FORMS 1:8-1:13.

NCCUSL Comment*

(a) Subsection (a) delegates the duty to adopt standards to implement this act to an existing state agency. In some states this oversight of the recording process, and in some cases the electronic recording process, has already been delegated to an existing state agency. In like fashion, some state legislatures may wish to delegate these duties to an existing state agency instead of creating a new commission as is directed in Alternative A.

If the state agency has oversight of many diverse functions, it might prove useful for the agency to establish a subdivision to implement and adopt standards for this act. The agency or subdivision might also wish to establish a regular process to obtain advice from persons with expertise in the area of recordings, particularly in electronic recordings.

(b) The Texas State Library and Archives Commission is directed to adopt standards to implement the provisions of this chapter. As provided in Section 15.005, county clerks implementing any of the functions of this chapter must comply with those standards.

One of the objectives of this act is to facilitate the efficient use of electronic recording within the state and among the various adopting states. This subsection directs the Texas State Library and Archives Commission to seek to keep the standards and practices of the recording offices in states using electronic recording in harmony and uniformity with each other. Ease of user access and interoperability and the promotion of interstate commerce depend highly on a similarity of standards and operating processes among the various recording offices. However, differences in operating processes and their governing standards may be justified based on legitimate differences that exist from venue to venue. The commission is not required to adopt the same standards and practices that exist in other states, but must give them serious consideration.

When adopting, amending or repealing standards the commission or agency must consider the following factors:

(1) the standards and practices of other states adopting this uniform act or a substantially similar one. In many situations, Electronic Recording Commissions or state agencies of other states may have already considered the same issue. Their research and subsequent experiences may prove very helpful to the Texas State Library and Archives Commission in making its decision.

(2) the most recent standards promulgated by national standard-setting bodies, such as the Property Records Industry Association (PRIA). National standard-setting organizations such as PRIA will likely have considered the issue that is now before the commission or agency and have developed a protocol or standard to deal with it. Furthermore, since these bodies are national in scope, they will likely already have considered the needs of recording districts of varying size, population and resources when promulgating their standards.

(3) the views of interested parties. Among others, these persons should include county clerks and potential users of the electronic recording system such as real estate attorneys, mortgage lenders, representatives from the title and escrow industries, real estate brokers, and notaries public. It must also consider the views of governmental offices that may interact with the recording offices, such as clerks of court, taxing authorities, and the office of the Secretary of State. Also included might be potential suppliers of hardware, software and services for electronic recording systems.

(4) the needs of counties of varying size, population and resources. Because most states are quite diverse in the size, population and resources of their recording venues, it is important that the Texas State Library and Archives Commission consider all of their needs. Standards that are designed only for large, populous and well-funded recording districts may not promote the development of electronic recording in smaller, less-populous and not-as-well funded recording districts. This subsection recognizes that the standards should promote the overall good of the entire state and not just the good of certain types of recording venues. Thus, the commission is advised to consider the needs of the entire spectrum of recording districts.

PROP §15.007. RELATION TO ELECTRONIC SIGNATURES IN GLOBAL & NATIONAL COMMERCE ACT

This chapter modifies, limits, and supersedes the federal Electronic Signatures in Global and National Commerce Act (15 U.S.C. Section 7001 et seq.) but does not modify, limit, or supersede Section 101(c) of that Act (15 U.S.C. Section 7001(c)) or authorize electronic delivery of any of the notices described in Section 103(b) of that Act (15 U.S.C. Section 7003(b)).

History of Prop. Code §15.007: Acts 2005, 79th Leg., ch. 699, §1, eff. Sept. 1, 2005.

See also ***Real Estate Forms***, FORMS 1:8-1:13.

* See footnote on p. 88.

NCCUSL Comment*

This section responds to the specific language of the Electronic Signatures in Global and National Commerce Act and is designed to avoid preemption of state law under that federal legislation.

PROP §15.008. CONSTRUCTION WITH OTHER LAW

Except as otherwise provided by this chapter, Chapter 195, Local Government Code, and the rules adopted by the Texas State Library and Archives Commission under that chapter apply to electronic documents filed in accordance with this chapter.

History of Prop. Code §15.008: Acts 2005, 79th Leg., ch. 699, §1, eff. Sept. 1, 2005.

Chapters 16-20 reserved for expansion

TITLE 4. ACTIONS & REMEDIES

CHAPTER 21. EMINENT DOMAIN

* See footnote on p. 88.

SUBCHAPTER A. JURISDICTION

PROP §21.001. CONCURRENT JURISDICTION

District courts and county courts at law have concurrent jurisdiction in eminent domain cases. A county court has no jurisdiction in eminent domain cases.

History of Prop. Code §21.001: Acts 1983, 68th Leg., ch. 576, §1, eff. Jan. 1, 1984. Source: TRCS art. 3266, §1.

ANNOTATIONS

Concurrent Jurisdiction

State v. Gracia, 56 S.W.3d 196, 202 (Tex.App.—Fort Worth 2001, no pet.). The court of appeals declined "to adopt an interpretation of [Prop. Code] §21.013(b) placing exclusive jurisdiction in the county courts at law.... We conclude that the district court had concurrent jurisdiction with the [c]ounty courts at law over the State's condemnation suit, regardless of whether venue was proper in the district court or a county court at law. We further conclude that the filing of a condemnation petition in district court rather than a county court at law is a procedural issue, not jurisdictional."

Author's comment: Concurrent jurisdiction is a separate issue from venue, which may still be in the county courts at law. *See* Prop. Code §21.013.

Prerequisites to Jurisdiction

State v. Jackson, 388 S.W.2d 924, 925 (Tex.1965). "The jurisdiction of the County Court at Law was properly invoked by the State when it timely excepted to the

award of the Special Commissioners. By accepting the award of the Special Commissioners [owner] is precluded from contesting the State's right to take the property. ... After an award has been made, and the money deposited in the registry of the Court and the landowner has withdrawn the same, he cannot thereafter contend that the taking was unlawful. In legal contemplation, he has consented to such taking and will not be permitted to retain his compensation and at the same time assert that the condemning authority had no right to take his property under the eminent domain power."

Gulf Energy Pipeline Co. v. Garcia, 884 S.W.2d 821, 822-23 (Tex.App.—San Antonio 1994, orig. proceeding). See annotation under Property Code §21.003, p. 95.

Scope of Jurisdiction

Board of Regents of the Univ. of Houston Sys. v. FKM Prtshp., 178 S.W.3d 1, 6 (Tex.App.—Houston [14th Dist.] 2005), *aff'd*, 255 S.W.3d 619 (Tex.2008). "Because [condemnor's] amended petition sought to condemn only a smaller portion of the land originally described, and not add new or different land, the county court's jurisdiction remained intact. As to the smaller portion of land [condemnor] sought to condemn, the court should have continued to exercise its jurisdiction. *At 7:* [T]he fact that the commissioners evaluated only the larger tract of land in making their award does not strip the county court of jurisdiction to adjudicate the smaller tract of land."

In re Burlington N. & Santa Fe Ry., 12 S.W.3d 891, 898 (Tex.App.—Houston [14th Dist.] 2000, orig. proceeding). "[W]hen a county court already has jurisdiction over a controversy, either by the subject matter or amount in controversy, it has exclusive power to dispose of the controversy; this power includes the issuance of injunctions that are related to the controversy."

City of Garland v. Mayhew, 528 S.W.2d 305, 307 (Tex.App.—Tyler 1975, writ ref'd n.r.e.). "The county court at law is a court of general jurisdiction in eminent domain matters, and this jurisdiction by necessary implication includes the right to try and decide all questions which may arise in such controversies, including the right to determine whether the existing facts authorize the exercise of the power thus conferred. The county court's jurisdiction in a condemnation suit attaches immediately upon the filing of a petition containing the statutory allegations requisite to condemn property, ... and once that jurisdiction attaches, the county court is the only tribunal with the authority to determine in the first instance any objections raised in connection with the condemnation proceedings."

PROP §21.002. TRANSFER OF CASES

If an eminent domain case is pending in a county court at law and the court determines that the case involves an issue of title or any other matter that cannot be fully adjudicated in that court, the judge shall transfer the case to a district court.

History of Prop. Code §21.002: Acts 1983, 68th Leg., ch. 576, §1, eff. Jan. 1, 1984. Source: TRCS art. 3266a, §4.

ANNOTATIONS

AIC Mgmt. v. Crews, 246 S.W.3d 640, 643 (Tex. 2008). "Under [special statute's] plain language, the county civil courts at law in Harris County have exclusive jurisdiction over eminent-domain proceedings and may decide issues of title to real property."

City of Houston v. West, 520 S.W.2d 752, 754 (Tex. 1975). Section 21.002 "requires the transfer to the District Court of any eminent domain case involving an issue of title or any other matter which cannot be fully adjudicated in the County Court at Law. The right of access to the Airport runways is a property right which, if held by [owners] in present ownership, would constitute an interest in real estate. The adjudication of the nature of such rights, together with the resulting effect on the value of the property interest taken from [owners] by the City, are matters which may be fully adjudicated only in the District Court." *See also* ***In re Riley***, 339 S.W.3d 216, 219-20 (Tex.App.—Waco 2011, orig. proceeding).

PROP §21.003. DISTRICT COURT AUTHORITY

A district court may determine all issues, including the authority to condemn property and the assessment of damages, in any suit:

(1) in which this state, a political subdivision of this state, a person, an association of persons, or a corporation is a party; and

(2) that involves a claim for property or for damages to property occupied by the party under the party's eminent domain authority or for an injunction to prevent the party from entering or using the property under the party's eminent domain authority.

History of Prop. Code §21.003: Acts 1983, 68th Leg., ch. 576, §1, eff. Jan. 1, 1984. Source: TRCS art. 3269.

See also Gov't Code §25.1032(c).

ANNOTATIONS

State v. Giles, 368 S.W.2d 943, 947 (Tex.1963). "The district court has no jurisdiction to interfere with the progress of a condemnation proceeding before the Commissioners of condemnation because of the disqualification of one of the Commissioners."

Taub v. Aquila Sw. Pipeline Corp., 93 S.W.3d 451, 457 (Tex.App.—Houston [14th Dist.] 2002, no pet.). "The general grant of concurrent jurisdiction in [Prop.] Code §21.001 and the general grant of ancillary jurisdiction in [Prop. Code] §21.003 must yield to the specific grant of 'exclusive jurisdiction' over 'eminent domain proceedings, both statutory and inverse,' found in [Gov't] Code §25.1032(c)."

Gulf Energy Pipeline Co. v. Garcia, 884 S.W.2d 821, 822-23 (Tex.App.—San Antonio 1994, orig. proceeding). "An eminent domain proceeding is not within the general jurisdiction of the [district] court; any power to act is special and depends upon the eminent domain statute. The statute expressly gives the court administrative jurisdiction to appoint the commissioners, receive their opinion as to value, and render judgment based upon the commissioners' award. The parties may invoke the trial court's jurisdiction by timely objecting to the commissioners' findings. The proceeding then becomes a civil case, and the district court has jurisdiction to determine all issues in the suit. Without a timely filed objection, however, an eminent domain proceeding never becomes a civil case."

Coastal Indus. Water Auth. v. Houston Lighting & Power Co., 564 S.W.2d 389, 391 (Tex.App.—Houston [14th Dist.] 1978, no writ). "[A] district court lacks jurisdiction to enjoin condemnation proceedings instituted in a county court at law, even though the proceedings were begun after the filing of a suit for declaratory relief in the district court."

Sections 21.004-21.010 reserved for expansion

SUBCHAPTER B. PROCEDURE

PROP §21.011. STANDARD PROCEDURE

Exercise of the eminent domain authority in all cases is governed by Sections 21.012 through 21.016 of this code.

History of Prop. Code §21.011: Acts 1983, 68th Leg., ch. 576, §1, eff. Jan. 1, 1984. Source: TRCS art. 3264.

ANNOTATIONS

City of Austin v. Whittington, 384 S.W.3d 766, 777-78 (Tex.2012). "[T]he question of what is a public use is a question for the determination of the courts; however, where the legislature has declared a certain thing to be for a public use, such declaration of the legislature must be given weight by the courts. [W]here the Legislature declares a particular use to be public use the presumption is in favor of this declaration, and will be binding upon the courts unless such use is clearly and palpably of a private character. [¶] But the presumption favoring the legislative declarations that the property is being taken for public use and is necessary for that use does not abrogate judicial review. [T]he law is well established in this state that where the power of eminent domain is granted, a determination by the condemnor of the necessity for acquiring certain property is conclusive in the absence of fraud. [W]e have clarified that judicial review may nullify a taking where the condemnor's decision was fraudulent, in bad faith, or arbitrary and capricious. [¶] As the parties concede, this inquiry is an affirmative defense and the landowner bears the burden of proving his allegations as to this defense. ... The trial court should only submit the issue to a jury if the underlying facts are in dispute. If the court (or the jury when the underlying facts are in dispute) finds that the condemnor's determinations of public use or necessity were fraudulent, in bad faith, or arbitrary and capricious, the taking is invalid." (Internal quotes omitted.)

Amason v. Natural Gas Pipeline Co., 682 S.W.2d 240, 241-42 (Tex.1984). "When a party desires to condemn land for public use but cannot agree on settlement terms with the landowner, that party must file a statement seeking condemnation in the proper court, either district court or county court at law, of the county in which the land is located. Upon the filing of this statement, the trial court judge is to appoint three Special Commissioners who assess the damages and then file an award which, in their opinion, reflects the value of the sought-after land. The Special Commissioners' power, however, is limited to filing in the proper court an award of fair compensation for the condemnation. ... From the time the condemnor files the original statement seeking condemnation up to the time of the Special Commissioners' award, these initial proceedings are administrative in nature. [¶] Once the Special Commissioners file their award, the condemnor, if sat-

isfied with the award, must either pay the amount of the award to the condemnee or deposit that amount in the court's registry. If the condemnee is [dissatisfied] with the Special [Commissioners'] award, he must timely file his objections in the appropriate court. Upon the filing of objections, the Special Commissioners' award is vacated and the administrative proceeding converts into a normal pending cause in the court with the condemnor as plaintiff and the condemnee as defendant. While the condemnor becomes the plaintiff for the purpose of proving his right to condemn, the condemnee still must secure the service of citation on the condemnor. If the condemnee fails to secure the service of citation on the condemnor within a reasonable period of time, the trial court should dismiss the objections for want of prosecution and should also reinstate the Special Commissioners' award as the proper compensation for the condemnation of the condemnee's land. Once the service of citation on the condemnor is accomplished, however, the Special Commissioners' award cannot be reinstated." *See also* ***State v. Ellison***, 788 S.W.2d 868, 871-72 (Tex.App.—Houston [1st Dist.] 1990, writ denied).

Circle X Land & Cattle Co. v. Mumford ISD, 325 S.W.3d 859, 864-65 (Tex.App.—Houston [14th Dist.] 2010, pet. denied). "[T]he existence of another feasible plan not requiring condemnation is no evidence of an abuse of discretion. [I]t is not arbitrary or capricious to base a condemnation on a reasoned prediction of future need or demand. A condemnor also does not abuse its authority if it later changes its plans for the use of the land, and sells or devotes the excess to private use. [N]othing in the condemnation statute prohibits the condemnor from altering its specific plan for the property after the commissioners' hearing even if the new plan allegedly prejudices the landowner."

City of McKinney v. Eldorado Park, Ltd., 206 S.W.3d 185, 191 (Tex.App.—Eastland 2006, pet. denied). "[T]he party attempting to establish its right to condemn must show strict compliance with the law authorizing private property to be taken for public use. ... In condemnation proceedings, the property owner is given a single opportunity to recover damages for the taking of his property for public use. Therefore, the protections of the statutory condemnation procedures must be liberally construed for the benefit of the landowner." *See also* ***Brown v. State***, 984 S.W.2d 348, 349 (Tex.App.—Fort Worth 1999, pet. denied).

PROP §21.0111. DISCLOSURE OF CERTAIN INFORMATION REQUIRED; INITIAL OFFER

(a) An entity with eminent domain authority that wants to acquire real property for a public use shall, by certified mail, return receipt requested, disclose to the property owner at the time an offer to purchase or lease the property is made any and all appraisal reports produced or acquired by the entity relating specifically to the owner's property and prepared in the 10 years preceding the date of the offer.

(b) A property owner shall disclose to the entity seeking to acquire the property any and all current and existing appraisal reports produced or acquired by the property owner relating specifically to the owner's property and used in determining the owner's opinion of value. Such disclosure shall take place not later than the earlier of:

(1) the 10th day after the date of receipt of an appraisal report; or

(2) the third business day before the date of a special commissioner's hearing if an appraisal report is to be used at the hearing.

(c) An entity seeking to acquire property that the entity is authorized to obtain through the use of eminent domain may not include a confidentiality provision in an offer or agreement to acquire the property. The entity shall inform the owner of the property that the owner has the right to:

(1) discuss any offer or agreement regarding the entity's acquisition of the property with others; or

(2) keep the offer or agreement confidential, unless the offer or agreement is subject to Chapter 552, Government Code.

(d) A subsequent bona fide purchaser for value from the acquiring entity may conclusively presume that the requirement of this section has been met. This section does not apply to acquisitions of real property for which an entity does not have eminent domain authority.

History of Prop. Code §21.0111: Acts 1995, 74th Leg., ch. 566, §1, eff. Aug. 28, 1995. Amended by Acts 2011, 82nd Leg., ch. 81, §7, eff. Sept. 1, 2011.

CHARTS

See timetable, "Condemnation Procedure," p. 1536.

ANNOTATIONS

Pitts v. Sabine River Auth., 107 S.W.3d 811, 818 (Tex.App.—Texarkana 2003, pet. denied). "A market

study is different from an appraisal. ... Because §21.0111 only requires the disclosure of ***appraisals relating specifically to the owner's property*** before the beginning of a condemnation hearing, [owners] have failed to show that [condemnor] was in violation of this statutory requirement, and [owners'] point of error is overruled."

Tex. Atty. Gen. Op. No. OR-06675 (2006). Section 21.0111(a) "expressly requires a governmental body with eminent domain authority, at the time it makes an offer to purchase property, to furnish 'any and all ... *appraisal reports*' to the property owner. [W]hen a property owner requests an appraisal report under these circumstances, the requirements of §21.0111 prevail over the more general provisions of the [Public Information] Act."

Author's comment: "Any and all appraisal reports" may be limited to those "used in determining the ... offer."

PROP §21.0112. PROVISION OF LANDOWNER'S BILL OF RIGHTS STATEMENT REQUIRED

(a) Not later than the seventh day before the date a governmental or private entity with eminent domain authority makes a final offer to a property owner to acquire real property, the entity must send by first-class mail or otherwise provide a landowner's bill of rights statement provided by Section 402.031, Government Code, to the last known address of the person in whose name the property is listed on the most recent tax roll of any appropriate taxing unit authorized by law to levy property taxes against the property. In addition to the other requirements of this subsection, an entity with eminent domain authority shall provide a copy of the landowner's bill of rights statement to a landowner before or at the same time as the entity first represents in any manner to the landowner that the entity possesses eminent domain authority.

(b) The statement must be:

(1) printed in an easily readable font and type size; and

(2) if the entity is a governmental entity, made available on the Internet website of the entity if technologically feasible.

History of Prop. Code §21.0112: Acts 2007, 80th Leg., ch. 1201, §3, eff. Feb. 1, 2008. Amended by Acts 2009, 81st Leg., ch. 1145, §1, eff. Jan. 15, 2010.

PROP §21.0113. BONA FIDE OFFER REQUIRED

(a) An entity with eminent domain authority that wants to acquire real property for a public use must make a bona fide offer to acquire the property from the property owner voluntarily.

(b) An entity with eminent domain authority has made a bona fide offer if:

(1) an initial offer is made in writing to a property owner;

(2) a final offer is made in writing to the property owner;

(3) the final offer is made on or after the 30th day after the date on which the entity makes a written initial offer to the property owner;

(4) before making a final offer, the entity obtains a written appraisal from a certified appraiser of the value of the property being acquired and the damages, if any, to any of the property owner's remaining property;

(5) the final offer is equal to or greater than the amount of the written appraisal obtained by the entity;

(6) the following items are included with the final offer or have been previously provided to the owner by the entity:

(A) a copy of the written appraisal;

(B) a copy of the deed, easement, or other instrument conveying the property sought to be acquired; and

(C) the landowner's bill of rights statement prescribed by Section 21.0112; and

(7) the entity provides the property owner with at least 14 days to respond to the final offer and the property owner does not agree to the terms of the final offer within that period.

History of Prop. Code §21.0113: Acts 2011, 82nd Leg., ch. 81, §8, eff. Sept. 1, 2011.

See also Prop. Code §21.047(d).

ANNOTATIONS

City of Carrollton v. Singer, 232 S.W.3d 790, 800 (Tex.App.—Fort Worth 2007, pet. denied). "[T]he City could not *create* immunity from suit for [Ps'] claim for adequate compensation [for the City's acquisition of Ps' property] by contracting to purchase their property at an agreed upon valuation in fulfillment of the condition precedent to filing an eminent domain proceeding in court as set forth in [Prop. Code §21.012]." *But see* ***City of Midlothian v. ECOM Real Estate Mgmt.***, No. 10-09-00039-CV (Tex.App.—Waco 2010, pet. granted, judgm't vacated w.r.m.) (memo op.; 1-27-10) (agreeing with dissent in ***Singer*** that purchasing and taking property are two distinct rights, and agreement without a condemnation suit does not waive immunity).

PROP §21.012. CONDEMNATION PETITION

(a) If an entity with eminent domain authority wants to acquire real property for public use but is unable to agree with the owner of the property on the amount of damages, the entity may begin a condemnation proceeding by filing a petition in the proper court.

(b) The petition must:

(1) describe the property to be condemned;

(2) state with specificity the public use for which the entity intends to acquire the property;

(3) state the name of the owner of the property if the owner is known;

(4) state that the entity and the property owner are unable to agree on the damages;

(5) if applicable, state that the entity provided the property owner with the landowner's bill of rights statement in accordance with Section 21.0112; and

(6) state that the entity made a bona fide offer to acquire the property from the property owner voluntarily as provided by Section 21.0113.

(c) An entity that files a petition under this section must provide a copy of the petition to the property owner by certified mail, return receipt requested.

History of Prop. Code §21.012: Acts 1983, 68th Leg., ch. 576, §1, eff. Jan. 1, 1984. Amended by Acts 2007, 80th Leg., ch. 1201, §4, eff. Feb. 1, 2008; Acts 2011, 82nd Leg., ch. 81, §9, eff. Sept. 1, 2011. Source: TRCS art. 3264.

CHARTS

See timetable, "Condemnation Procedure," p. 1536.

ANNOTATIONS

Generally

State v. Brownlow, 319 S.W.3d 649, 655 (Tex. 2010). In the taking of an easement for a mitigation pond, "the State had the right to excavate the dirt from its easement ... in order to open and construct the mitigation pond.... [I]t could use the excavated dirt to maintain the pond. But the easement did not give the State the right to use the dirt for any other purposes...."

Harris Cty. Hosp. Dist. v. Textac Partners I, 257 S.W.3d 303, 316 (Tex.App.—Houston [14th Dist.] 2008, no pet.). "The term 'fraud' as applied to a condemnor's decision to institute condemnation proceedings means 'any act, omission or concealment, which involved a breach of legal duty, trust or confidence, justly reposed and ... injurious to another, or by which an undue and unconscientious advantage is taken of another.' The term 'arbitrary and capricious' as applied to the condemnor's action means 'willful and unreasoning action, action without consideration and in disregard of the facts and circumstances [that] existed at the time condemnation was decided upon, or within the foreseeable future.' If the purpose for which condemnation was sought could in reasonable minds in good faith be deemed to be a public one, then the condemnation proceedings are justifiable and lawfully authorized."

Dillard v. Austin ISD, 806 S.W.2d 589, 599 (Tex. App.—Austin 1991, writ denied). "We do not read §21.012 to create a cause of action for failure to negotiate in good faith, nor is there a general common-law duty of good faith."

Bona Fide Offer

City of Rosenberg v. State, 477 S.W.3d 878, 879 (Tex.App.—Houston [14th Dist.] 2015, pet. denied). "In [***Hubenak v. San Jacinto Gas Transmission Co.***, 141 S.W.3d 172 (Tex.2004)], the Supreme Court of Texas concluded that [Prop. Code] §21.012's requirements are not jurisdictional. *At 880:* [S]ince ***Hubenak*** was decided, the Legislature [added both Prop. Code §§21.012(b)(6) and] 21.0113, which require[] an entity with eminent-domain authority that desires to acquire real property for a public use to make a bona fide offer to the property owner [and state in its petition that it has done so]. The City argues that because §21.0113 makes a bona fide offer a 'requirement,' the condemnor's failure to make a bona fide offer deprives the trial court of subject-matter jurisdiction. [¶] [T]his issue appears to be an issue of first impression in Texas jurisprudence. Nonetheless, the ... amendments do not appear to have undermined the ***Hubenak*** analysis, which we conclude should be extended to the bona-fide-offer requirement."

Property Description

Hubenak v. San Jacinto Gas Transmission Co., 141 S.W.3d 172, 189 (Tex.2004). "It is the law in this state that the offer must be for the same tract of land described in the condemnation petition. *At 191:* Generally, it is sufficient that the parties negotiated for the same physical property and same general use that became the subject of the later eminent domain proceeding, even if the more intangible rights sought in the purchase negotiations did not exactly mirror those sought or obtainable by condemnation." *See also* **City**

of Dallas v. Pacifico Partners, 289 S.W.3d 371, 381 (Tex.App.—Dallas 2009, no pet.).

State v. Nelson, 334 S.W.2d 788, 792 (Tex.1960). "If the matter goes to judgment without amendment, the court should condemn only the property described in the statement. But when it develops during the trial on appeal that there are discrepancies in the description, the trial court has power to and should permit an amendment eliminating the same provided this can be done without material prejudice to the landowner. This assumes, of course, that the description as amended does not inject entirely new subject matter into the proceedings."

Purpose of Property

Circle X Land & Cattle Co. v. Mumford ISD, 325 S.W.3d 859, 865 (Tex.App.—Houston [14th Dist.] 2010, pet. denied). "[N]othing in the condemnation statute prohibits the condemnor from altering its specific plan for the property after the commissioners' hearing even if the new plan allegedly prejudices the landowner."

Lin v. Houston Cmty. Coll. Sys., 948 S.W.2d 328, 334 (Tex.App.—Amarillo 1997, writ denied). "[A] purpose statement that the condemnor wished to acquire a water line easement 'for the transportation of water and other facilities and uses incidental thereto' was adequate. If the purpose statement of a water authority [was sufficient] that it intended to condemn an easement for 'the transportation of water,' it would be sufficient for a college system to allege its intent to use property for 'school purposes.'" *See also* ***Coastal Indus. Water Auth. v. Celanese Corp.***, 592 S.W.2d 597, 600 (Tex.1979); ***Pizzitola v. Houston ISD***, No. 13-05-249-CV (Tex.App.—Corpus Christi 2006, no pet.) (memo op.; 5-18-06).

PROP §21.0121. CONDEMNATION TO ACQUIRE WATER RIGHTS

(a) In addition to the contents prescribed by Section 21.012(b), a condemnation petition filed by a political subdivision of this state for the purpose of acquiring rights to groundwater or surface water must state that the facts to be proven are that the political subdivision has:

(1) prepared a drought contingency plan;

(2) developed and implemented a water conservation plan that will result in the highest practicable levels of water conservation and efficiency achievable in the political subdivision's jurisdiction;

(3) made a bona fide good faith effort to obtain practicable alternative water supplies to the water rights the political subdivision proposes to condemn;

(4) made a bona fide good faith effort to acquire the rights to the water the political subdivision proposes to condemn by voluntary purchase or lease; and

(5) made a showing that the political subdivision needs the water rights to provide for the domestic needs of the political subdivision within the next 10-year period.

(b) A court shall deny the right to condemn unless the political subdivision proves to the court that the political subdivision has met the requirements of Subsection (a).

History of Prop. Code §21.0121: Acts 2003, 78th Leg., ch. 1032, §1, eff. Sept. 1, 2003.

See also Loc. Gov't Code §263.201; Prop. Code §21.012; Water Code §49.222.

PROP §21.013. VENUE; FEES & PROCESSING FOR SUIT FILED IN DISTRICT COURT

(a) The venue of a condemnation proceeding is the county in which the owner of the property being condemned resides if the owner resides in a county in which part of the property is located. Otherwise, the venue of a condemnation proceeding is any county in which at least part of the property is located.

(b) Except where otherwise provided by law, a party initiating a condemnation proceeding in a county in which there is one or more county courts at law with jurisdiction shall file the petition with any clerk authorized to handle such filings for that court or courts.

(c) A party initiating a condemnation proceeding in a county in which there is not a county court at law must file the condemnation petition with the district clerk. The filing fee shall be due at the time of filing in accordance with Section 51.317, Government Code.

(d) District and county clerks shall assign an equal number of eminent domain cases in rotation to each court with jurisdiction that the clerk serves.

History of Prop. Code §21.013: Acts 1983, 68th Leg., ch. 576, §1, eff. Jan. 1, 1984. Amended by Acts 1993, 73rd Leg., ch. 760, §1, eff. Sept. 1, 1993; Acts 1999, 76th Leg., ch. 756, §1, eff. June 18, 1999. Source: TRCS arts. 3264, 3266a, §§2, 3, 5.

CHARTS

See timetable, "Condemnation Procedure," p. 1536.

ANNOTATIONS

In re Transcontinental Rlty. Investors, Inc., 271 S.W.3d 270, 272 (Tex.2008). "[W]hen the Legislature

amended the permissive-venue statute to distinguish between a natural person's 'residence' and a business's 'principal office,' we do not think it intended to eliminate corporations and other legal entities from all statutes that refer to a place where one 'resides.' Undoubtedly, the Legislature could exclude corporations from §21.013. But until it does so, we hold that landowners who are businesses—just like landowners who are individuals—can insist on venue where they reside if the condemned property is partly located there."

Pinnacle Gas Treating, Inc. v. Read, 160 S.W.3d 564, 565 (Tex.2005). "This case presents the question whether a district judge had jurisdiction to sign orders in a condemnation case pending in another district court in the same county. The court of appeals held that the district judge did not have jurisdiction because there had been no exchange of benches. We hold there was jurisdiction.... *At 566-67:* [Property Code §21.013] does not purport to confer exclusive jurisdiction upon the court to which a case is assigned, and explicitly recognizes that jurisdiction can lie with multiple courts. ... The court of appeals noted that specific statutes control general ones, and concluded that [Prop. Code] §21.014 definitively established that only [the judge first assigned the case] could appoint the commissioners. However, §21.014 contains no language suggesting that it confers exclusive jurisdiction to appoint commissioners to the judge to which an eminent domain case is assigned, and might well conflict with district judges' constitutional right to exchange benches if it did."

State v. Gracia, 56 S.W.3d 196, 198 (Tex.App.—Fort Worth 2001, no pet.). Condemnor "filed a motion for nonsuit and verified plea to the jurisdiction seeking dismissal of the [condemnation] proceeding on the basis that the ... District Court lacked subject matter jurisdiction over the matter. Specifically, [condemnor] contended §21.013(b) ... places jurisdiction over eminent domain proceedings exclusively in the county courts at law in counties that have one or more county courts at law.... *At 202:* We decline to adopt [this] interpretation of §21.013(b).... We conclude that the district court had concurrent jurisdiction with the Tarrant County courts at law over State's condemnation suit, regardless of whether venue was proper in the district court or a county court at law. We further conclude that the filing of a condemnation petition in district court rather than a county court at law is a procedural issue, not jurisdictional."

PROP §21.014. SPECIAL COMMISSIONERS

(a) The judge of a court in which a condemnation petition is filed or to which an eminent domain case is assigned shall appoint three disinterested real property owners who reside in the county as special commissioners to assess the damages of the owner of the property being condemned. The judge appointing the special commissioners shall give preference to persons agreed on by the parties. The judge shall provide each party a reasonable period to strike one of the three commissioners appointed by the judge. If a person fails to serve as a commissioner or is struck by a party to the suit, the judge shall appoint a replacement.

(b) The special commissioners shall swear to assess damages fairly, impartially, and according to the law.

(c) Special commissioners may compel the attendance of witnesses and the production of testimony, administer oaths, and punish for contempt in the same manner as a county judge.

History of Prop. Code §21.014: Acts 1983, 68th Leg., ch. 576, §1, eff. Jan. 1, 1984. Amended by Acts 2011, 82nd Leg., ch. 81, §10, eff. Sept. 1, 2011. Source: TRCS arts. 3264, 3266, subdiv. 2.

CHARTS

See timetable, "Condemnation Procedure," p. 1536.

ANNOTATIONS

In re Lazy W Dist., 493 S.W.3d 538, 543 (Tex.2016). Condemnor "points to §21.014, requiring that when a condemnation case is filed, the court 'shall' appoint commissioners. [Condemnor] argues that this provision limits a court's jurisdiction from the time a condemnation case is filed until the commissioners' award issues to one thing: appointing commissioners. We disagree. [¶] Section 21.014 is certainly mandatory, but it is not restrictive. It requires the court to appoint commissioners, but it does not forbid any other action. *At 544:* We have never held that a trial court in a condemnation case is powerless to determine its own subject matter jurisdiction before appointing commissioners. The Property Code does not limit the trial court's power or responsibility to determine its jurisdiction, nor do we think it could. For the Legislature to attempt to authorize a court to act without subject matter jurisdiction would violate the constitutional separation of powers."

Amason v. Natural Gas Pipeline Co., 682 S.W.2d 240, 242 (Tex.1984). "The Special Commissioners' power ... is limited to filing in the proper court an award of fair compensation for the condemnation. For example, the Special Commissioners are powerless to decide whether the condemnor possesses the right to condemn the property in the first place."

PGP Gas Prods. v. Fariss, 620 S.W.2d 559, 561 (Tex.1981). Landowners "argue the procedures in [TCRS art. 3264, now Prop. Code §21.014,] are jurisdictional and cannot be waived. We disagree. Procedural irregularities in proceedings before the special commissioners can only be challenged on direct appeal ... and are waived if not properly preserved for appellate review."

City of Bryan v. Moehlman, 282 S.W.2d 687, 690 (Tex.1955). "[A] board of equalization is a quasi judicial body. The members of the board, although appointed, must act independently in the performance of their duties and are not subject to control or supervision by the city authorities. We believe, therefore, that they are not disqualified as a matter of law [to serve as special commissioners]."

In re Energy Transfer Fuel, LP, 250 S.W.3d 178, 181 (Tex.App.—Tyler 2008, orig. proceeding). "[W]here a trial court fails to enter a judgment conforming to the commissioners' award in a condemnation proceeding, that judgment is void."

In re State, 65 S.W.3d 383, 386 (Tex.App.—Tyler 2002, orig. proceeding). "Due to the absence of statutory authority for judicial oversight, a trial court may not become involved in the administrative phase of the proceeding. Rather, the special commissioners themselves may compel the attendance of witnesses and the production of testimony, administer oaths, and punish for contempt in the same manner as a county judge. The administrative phase of a condemnation proceeding implements a legislative policy to quickly award just damages to the landowner without the delays that occur in court proceedings. To allow the court to oversee the administrative phase would circumvent this policy."

Pape v. Guadalupe-Blanco River Auth., 48 S.W.3d 908, 911 (Tex.App.—Austin 2001, pet. denied). "[A]lthough [Prop. Code] §21.014 requires the trial judge to appoint special commissioners who 'shall swear to assess damages fairly, impartially, and according to the law,' and [Prop. Code] §21.015 requires the commissioners to set a hearing at the earliest practical time, ch. 21 does not state that the commissioners must take their oaths of office *before* setting the hearing. *At 912:* Setting a hearing date is not necessarily a judicial or quasi-judicial act; it is simply an act of scheduling and does not require a reminder to the special commissioners that they must assess damages fairly and in accordance with the law. Before conducting the hearing and receiving evidence, these special commissioners properly swore to assess damages fairly and impartially as required by law. Further, penalizing the condemning authority for actions taken by the commissioners would seem to imply that the authority had some control over the special commissioners, thus making them less than disinterested. Absent any statutory prohibition to the contrary, we hold that, once appointed, the special commissioners' mere housekeeping act of choosing the hearing date did not violate ch. 21."

PROP §21.015. HEARING

(a) The special commissioners in an eminent domain proceeding shall promptly schedule a hearing for the parties at the earliest practical time but may not schedule a hearing to assess damages before the 20th day after the date the special commissioners were appointed. The special commissioners shall schedule a hearing for the parties at a place that is as near as practical to the property being condemned or at the county seat of the county in which the proceeding is being held.

(b) After notice of the hearing has been served, the special commissioners shall hear the parties at the scheduled time and place or at any other time or place to which they may adjourn the hearing.

History of Prop. Code §21.015: Acts 1983, 68th Leg., ch. 576, §1, eff. Jan. 1, 1984. Amended by Acts 2011, 82nd Leg., ch. 81, §11, eff. Sept. 1, 2011. Source: TRCS art. 3264.

CHARTS

See timetable, "Condemnation Procedure," p. 1536.

ANNOTATIONS

Pape v. Guadalupe-Blanco River Auth., 48 S.W.3d 908, 911 (Tex.App.—Austin 2001, pet. denied). See annotation under Property Code §21.014, this page.

PROP §21.016. NOTICE

(a) Each party in an eminent domain proceeding is entitled to written notice issued by the special commissioners informing the party of the time and place of the hearing.

(b) Notice of the hearing must be served on a party not later than the 20th day before the day set for the hearing. A person competent to testify may serve the notice.

(c) A person who serves a notice shall return the original notice to the special commissioners on or before the day set for hearing. The person shall write a return of service on the notice that states how and when it was served.

(d) Notice may be served:

(1) by delivering a copy of the notice to the party or to the party's agent or attorney;

(2) if the property being condemned belongs to a deceased's estate or to a minor or other legally disabled person and the person or estate has a legal representative, by delivering a copy of the notice to the legal representative; or

(3) if the property being condemned belongs to a nonresident of this state and there has been no personal service on the owner, if the identity or the residence of the property owner is unknown, or if the property owner avoids service of notice by hiding, by publication in the same manner as service of citation by publication in other civil cases in the district courts or county courts at law.

History of Prop. Code §21.016: Acts 1983, 68th Leg., ch. 576, §1, eff. Jan. 1, 1984. Amended by Acts 2011, 82nd Leg., ch. 81, §12, eff. Sept. 1, 2011. Source: TRCS art. 3264.

CHARTS

See timetable, "Condemnation Procedure," p. 1536.

ANNOTATIONS

State v. Bristol Hotel Asset Co., 65 S.W.3d 638, 641 (Tex.2001). "All parties to the proceeding are entitled to notice of the time and place of the hearing, which must be served not later than 11 days [now 20 days] before the hearing date. Anyone competent to testify may serve notice, and must return the original notice plus a return of service to the commissioners on or before the hearing date. Unless notice has been properly served in accordance with [§21.016], the commissioners have no jurisdiction to assess damages or do anything that would declare a condemnation of the property. *At 642:* We therefore hold that a return of service of notice of a commissioners hearing that strictly complies with §21.016 … is prima facie evidence that the condemnee has been served with the notice in compliance with the statute. When the State introduces such a return, the condemnee must offer evidence that it was not served to raise a fact issue."

City of Houston v. Kunze, 262 S.W.2d 947, 951 (Tex.1953). TRCS art. 3264, §§5-10, now Prop. Code §21.016, "provides for the service of notice and the manner in which notice should be served. Notice to the owner of land sought to be condemned cannot be presumed from declarations or conclusions stated in any of the proceedings, but must be proved. [¶] The mere filing of the statement in condemnation does not determine jurisdiction. Notice to the landowner is necessary. [Landowner] has a right to appear before the Commissioners and until notice has been duly and properly served in accordance with the statute, the court is without jurisdiction, and the Special Commissioners have no authority to assess damages or perform any act which would declare a condemnation of his property."

Metropolitan Transit Auth. v. Graham, 105 S.W.3d 754, 759 (Tex.App.—Houston [14th Dist.] 2003, pet. denied). Condemnor "need not have served all owners in one proceeding, and that going forward without service on the Unserved Owners did not invalidate jurisdiction over the owners and their property interests who had been served. [¶] Nothing in the statutory scheme for condemnation actions prohibited [condemnor] from electing to proceed against only the Adjudicated Owners at the hearing, thereby impliedly abandoning its claims at that point against the Unserved Owners."

PROP §21.017. ALTERNATIVE PLEADINGS

(a) This state, a political subdivision of this state, a person, an association of persons, or a corporation that is a party to a suit covered by Section 21.003 of this code by petition, cross-bill, or plea of intervention may assert a claim to the property or, alternatively, seek to condemn the property.

(b) A plea under this section is not an admission of an adverse party's title to the property in controversy.

History of Prop. Code §21.017: Acts 1983, 68th Leg., ch. 576, §1, eff. Jan. 1, 1984. Source: TRCS art. 3269.

ANNOTATIONS

State v. Montgomery Cty., 338 S.W.3d 49, 56 (Tex. App.—Beaumont 2011, pet. denied). "[Ds] argue that the controversy presented here is not ripe because [P] 'did not first dismiss its fee simple title position and then assert an easement claim[.]' [P] has the right to urge a remedy that is inconsistent with the exercise of

eminent domain authority. In this case, the County Commissioners have determined the public necessity for the ... road-widening project through the subject property. Thus, the dispute concerning the statutory easement does not depend upon contingent or hypothetical events that have not yet come to pass; rather, the suit determines the parties['] existing rights."

PROP §21.018. APPEAL FROM COMMISSIONERS' FINDINGS

(a) A party to a condemnation proceeding may object to the findings of the special commissioners by filing a written statement of the objections and their grounds with the court that has jurisdiction of the proceeding. The statement must be filed on or before the first Monday following the 20th day after the day the commissioners file their findings with the court.

(b) If a party files an objection to the findings of the special commissioners, the court shall cite the adverse party and try the case in the same manner as other civil causes.

History of Prop. Code §21.018: Acts 1983, 68th Leg., ch. 576, §1, eff. Jan. 1, 1984. Source: TRCS arts. 3266, subdiv. 6, 3266a, §§2, 3, 5.

CHARTS

See timetable, "Condemnation Procedure," p. 1536.

ANNOTATIONS

Burden to Move Forward

Denton Cty. v. Brammer, 361 S.W.2d 198, 200-01 (Tex.1962). "Although the condemnee ... became [D], we construe [TRCS art. 3266, now Prop. Code §21.018,] to mean that the condemnee ... had the burden of causing the issuance of citation and the obtaining of service of such citation upon the condemnor.... While the condemnor ... as [P] had the burden of proving all the essentials necessary to show a right to condemnation ... and had the burden of going forward to trial, it was under no legal obligation to do so unless and until it had been served with citation. ... In the absence of citation, [condemnor's] suit could not have been dismissed for want of prosecution, and [condemnor] was under no obligation to voluntarily answer without the service of citation." *See also* ***James B. Bonham Corp. v. City of Corsicana***, ___ S.W.3d ___ (Tex.App.—Texarkana 2016, no pet.) (No. 06-16-00026-CV; 11-29-16).

Judgment in Absence of Objections

Pearson v. State, 315 S.W.2d 935, 939 (Tex.1958). "We hold ... when no timely objections to the award are filed, there is no right of appeal from the judgment subsequently entered in the proceedings even though the same does not conform to the award."

Need for & Effect of Citation

Amason v. Natural Gas Pipeline Co., 682 S.W.2d 240, 242 (Tex.1984). "If the condemnee is [dissatisfied] with the Special [Commissioners'] award, he must timely file his objections in the appropriate court. Upon the filing of objections, the Special Commissioners' award is vacated and the administrative proceeding converts into a normal pending cause in the court with the condemnor as plaintiff and the condemnee as defendant. While the condemnor becomes the plaintiff for the purpose of proving his right to condemn, the condemnee still must secure the service of citation on the condemnor. If the condemnee fails to secure the service of citation on the condemnor within a reasonable period of time, the trial court should dismiss the objections for want of prosecution and should also reinstate the Special Commissioners' award as the proper compensation for the condemnation of the condemnee's land. Once the service of citation on the condemnor is accomplished, however, the Special Commissioners' award cannot be reinstated." *See also* ***City of Tyler v. Beck***, 196 S.W.3d 784, 786 (Tex.2006); ***Musquiz v. Harris Cty. Flood Control Dist.***, 31 S.W.3d 664, 666-67 (Tex. App.—Houston [1st Dist.] 2000, no pet.).

Timing of Objections

John v. State, 826 S.W.2d 138, 141 (Tex.1992). Held: The time for making objections to the special commissioners' award is tolled if the parties are not given proper notice of the special commissioners' award.

State v. Titan Land Dev., Inc., 468 S.W.3d 705, 709 (Tex.App.—Houston [1st Dist.] 2015, pet. denied). "[T]he plain language of the statutory provisions reveals that only one provision governs when objections to the commissioners' award must be filed. That provision is [Prop. Code] §21.018(a). [¶] [Property Code] §21.048's language ... indirectly affects when a party's objections will be due. However, neither §21.018 nor §21.048 addresses the remedy, or any penalty, for the untimely filing of the commissioners' award, whether the untimely filing is made by the commissioners or by a party on the commissioners' behalf. [S]ection 21.018 serves to ameliorate the effect of an untimely filing by directly linking the period during which a party must object to the date the award is filed. [T]he party desiring to object has the full time period in which to object

even when the award is filed late. [¶] If it had intended either (1) to make the starting point for the objection period the same date that the award was required to be filed under §21.048 or (2) to restrict a party's ability to benefit from §21.018's objection period when that party played a role in causing the award to be filed late, the Legislature could have enacted such provisions. *At 710:* We are mindful that §§21.018 and 21.048 speak to the special commissioners filing the award in the trial court, rather than the State filing the award. However, … courts must enforce §21.018 as it is written, giving either party until the first Monday following the expiration of 20 days after the commissioners' award is filed to object."

Groves v. Wind Energy Transmission Tex., LLC, No. 11-12-00107-CV (Tex.App.—Eastland 2012, no pet.) (memo op.; 8-16-12). "The special commissioners held a hearing on October 25, 2011. They determined the amount of the condemnation award and filed the award with the trial court clerk on the same day…. However, the clerk did not send notice of the award until November 1, 2011. The Supreme Court of Texas has held that the time to file objections to a condemnation award is tolled until the clerk sends notice of the award. [¶] The statute does not require the party to be served with notice; it only requires that the clerk send the notice. [¶] The Supreme Court found that the clerk's duty to send notice was mandatory and, thus, tolled the time to file objections until the clerk fulfilled that duty. The Supreme Court did not hold that the clerk was required to serve the landowner with notice. Therefore, [condemnee] was not required to be served with notice of the award."

Waiver of Citation

Seals v. Upper Trinity Reg'l Water Dist., 145 S.W.3d 291, 295 (Tex.App.—Fort Worth 2004, pet. dism'd). Condemnee claimed condemnor's appearance to obtain a court order to allow preacquisition surveying removed the need to serve later-filed objections. The court disagreed and held: "We do not believe that [TRCP] 120's intent is to force condemnors to choose between the right to be informed when the condemnee challenges the special commissioners' award and the right to obtain access to the land subject to condemnation."

State v. Ellison, 788 S.W.2d 868, 873 (Tex.App.—Houston [1st Dist.] 1990, writ denied). "[T]he objecting party in an eminent domain case can be deemed to have abandoned the objections, properly resulting in a dismissal for want of prosecution, when the objecting party has failed to serve the other party with citation within a reasonable period of time."

Waiver of Error; Grounds for Objections; Jurisdiction

PR Invs. & Specialty Retailers, Inc. v. State, 251 S.W.3d 472, 478 (Tex.2008). "Petitioners argue that if [condemnor] is allowed to change the highway's lane design after the commissioners have ruled, this would render the legislatively mandated administrative proceeding before the special commissioners a meaningless step. [¶] It is true that [condemnor] itself changed the facts by changing its roadway plans for the condemned property, but condemning authorities are allowed to do so. *At 479:* Such a change of plans does not divest the trial court of jurisdiction to proceed after the special commissioners have ruled and to 'try the case in the same manner as other civil causes.' In these circumstances the statutory scheme does not require [condemnor] to start over with a new petition, a new hearing before the special commissioners, and payment to Petitioners of all the fees and expenses they incurred in the first administrative proceeding."

State v. Jackson, 388 S.W.2d 924, 925 (Tex.1965). "The jurisdiction of the County Court at Law was properly invoked by the State when it timely excepted to the award of the Special Commissioners. By accepting the award of the Special Commissioners[, condemnee] is precluded from contesting the State's right to take the property." *See also* ***Tigner v. City of Angleton***, 949 S.W.2d 887, 890 (Tex.App.—Houston [14th Dist.] 1997, no writ).

In re State, 85 S.W.3d 871, 876-77 (Tex.App.—Tyler 2002, orig. proceeding). "In the judicial phase, the trial court's actions relating to the administrative phase, as a general rule, become moot. Moreover, any error occurring during the administrative phase that affects the judicial phase typically can be reviewed in the trial de novo. Thus, Texas courts have routinely held that the right to appeal by trial de novo affords a party an adequate remedy for any error occurring in the administrative phase of the proceeding. Typically, mandamus is appropriate only when errors or irregularities before the special commissioners render the proceeding void. [¶] The administrative phase of the proceeding provides a means to quickly award just damages to the landowner without the delays that occur in court proceedings. Therefore, the right to an expedited hearing

during the administrative phase is a substantial right. The judicial phase is invoked and a trial de novo is conducted when a party files objections to the special commissioners' award. The objections 'wip[e] out entirely the award of the commissioners and preven[t] any judgment from being entered, based upon such award.' As a result, damages are determined in the trial de novo after any necessary review of errors occurring in the administrative phase. The right to an expedited hearing before the special commissioners and the right to a trial de novo for the determination of damages are equally essential to a prompt, fair award in a condemnation proceeding. Therefore, we conclude that the right to a trial de novo is also a substantial right in a condemnation proceeding."

Brown v. State, 984 S.W.2d 348, 350 (Tex.App.—Fort Worth 1999, pet. denied). "The trial court's appellate jurisdiction is limited to the parties and issues involved in the administrative proceeding before the special commission, as set out in the condemning authority's petition which is the only pleading required at that time. Although it is true that a condemning authority has a right to amend its petition to correct errors or to take *less* property, it can do so only as long as the exercise of the right *does not prejudice the landowner*. Allowing free amendment of pleadings to enlarge a taking after the special commissioners have assessed the damages to the property owner would allow a condemning authority to disregard the statutory requirements that a hearing be held before a special commission on the pleadings of the petition for condemnation. If the condemning authority amends its petition of condemnation to take more land or reduce the rights of the condemned property owner after the action is appealed to the trial court, then that court lacks jurisdiction to hear the case because the amendment enlarged the taking from the proposed taking that the special commissioners considered."

PROP §21.019. DISMISSAL OF CONDEMNATION PROCEEDINGS

(a) A party that files a condemnation petition may move to dismiss the proceedings, and the court shall conduct a hearing on the motion. However, after the special commissioners have made an award, in an effort to obtain a lower award a condemnor may not dismiss the condemnation proceedings merely to institute new proceedings that involve substantially the same condemnation against the same property owner.

(b) A court that hears and grants a motion to dismiss a condemnation proceeding made by a condemnor under Subsection (a) shall make an allowance to the property owner for reasonable and necessary fees for attorneys, appraisers, and photographers and for the other expenses incurred by the property owner to the date of the hearing.

(c) A court that hears and grants a motion to dismiss a condemnation proceeding made by a property owner seeking a judicial denial of the right to condemn or that otherwise renders a judgment denying the right to condemn may make an allowance to the property owner for reasonable and necessary fees for attorneys, appraisers, and photographers and for the other expenses incurred by the property owner to the date of the hearing or judgment.

History of Prop. Code §21.019: Acts 1983, 68th Leg., ch. 576, §1, eff. Jan. 1, 1984. Amended by Acts 1987, 70th Leg., ch. 483, §1, eff. Aug. 31, 1987. Source: TRCS art. 3265, subdiv. 6.

CHARTS

See timetable, "Condemnation Procedure," p. 1536.

ANNOTATIONS

Generally

Thompson v. Janes, 251 S.W.2d 953, 954-55 (Tex. 1952). "There is no doubt that a condemnor who has not taken possession of the land sought to be condemned has the right to dismiss the suit if the project is to be abandoned or the location changed, for an agency clothed with the power of eminent domain may not be forced to take land against its will. Likewise, the condemning agency is accorded the right to dismiss as to a portion of the land when it decides that its purpose may be accomplished with less land than was initially sought."

City of Wharton v. Stavena, 771 S.W.2d 594, 595-96 (Tex.App.—Corpus Christi 1989, writ denied). "The purpose of §21.019(b) is two-fold: (1) to compensate the landowner for expenses incurred during an abandoned condemnation proceeding ...; and (2) *to discourage the commencement and subsequent abandonment of condemnation proceedings*. Thus, when a condemnor initiates and then voluntarily dismisses a condemnation suit, §21.019(b) imposes a penalty or duty on the condemning authority to pay reasonable and necessary fees charged by the property owner's appraisers and attorneys for services rendered in preparation for the proceedings. The recovery of these fees

should *not* depend on the vagaries of any particular attorney-client agreement since such recovery is statutorily mandated."

Fees upon Dismissal

Brazos Elec. Power Coop. v. Weber, 238 S.W.3d 582, 583 (Tex.App.—Dallas 2007, no pet.). "[A]s to the attorney's fees portion of the award, the only criteria to be considered by the trial court is whether the fees are reasonable and necessary. Our review of the trial court's award, in turn, asks whether there was sufficient evidence that the fees awarded were in fact reasonable and necessary. *At 585-86:* The supreme court has directed us to evaluate the sufficiency of the evidence supporting an attorney's fees award by looking to the factors set forth in [Tex. Disciplinary Rules Prof'l Conduct R. 1.04]: '(1) the time and labor required, the novelty and difficulty of the questions involved, and the skill required to perform the legal service properly; (2) the likelihood ... that the acceptance of the particular employment will preclude other employment by the lawyer; (3) the fee customarily charged in the locality for similar legal services; (4) the amount involved and the results obtained; (5) the time limitations imposed by the client or by the circumstances; (6) the nature and length of the professional relationship with the client; (7) the experience, reputation, and ability of the lawyer or lawyers performing the services; and (8) whether the fee is fixed or contingent on results obtained or uncertainty of collection before the legal services have been rendered.' It is not mandatory that the record include evidence on each of these factors."

Taub v. Aquila Sw. Pipeline Corp., 93 S.W.3d 451, 459-60 (Tex.App.—Houston [14th Dist.] 2002, no pet.). "'We have held that the parties in a dismissed condemnation action brought in a county court at law should not be deprived of the opportunity to have a jury hear the evidence on the disputed fact issue of reasonable attorney fees and expenses. In our opinion, a party would be entitled to have a jury as fact finder on this issue *if the case were brought in district court in a county where the district court and the county court at law share concurrent jurisdiction over condemnation actions*. We do not think the legislature intended to deprive a party of that right by limiting condemnation actions to the exclusive jurisdiction of county courts at law in certain counties.'"

Urban Wilderness, S.A. v. City of San Antonio, 924 S.W.2d 410, 412 (Tex.App.—San Antonio 1996, writ denied). "It is apparent that the legislature intended to differentiate between voluntary dismissals and involuntary dismissals with regard to the condemning authority's responsibility to compensate the property owner for its fees and expenses. [¶] The legislature in this instance clearly intended to require a condemning authority in a voluntary dismissal to reimburse a property owner for fees and expenses incurred *to the date of the dismissal hearing*. The language of the statute is clear. We must presume that the legislature omitted the phrase 'or judgment' from §21.019(b) for a purpose, just as we must presume that the phrase was included in §21.019(c) for a purpose."

Loss of Right to Dismiss

Hooks v. Fourth Ct. of Appeals, 808 S.W.2d 56, 60 (Tex.1991). "A condemnor is entitled to dismiss a condemnation proceeding prior to taking possession of the property. ... In such circumstances, the condemnor's right of dismissal is fettered only by its obligation to reimburse the property owner for any 'reasonable and necessary fees for attorneys, appraisers, and photographers and for the other expenses incurred by the property owner' before dismissal. After a condemnor takes possession of the property it may dismiss the condemnation proceeding only if the landowner is not prejudiced or harmed as a result. *At 61:* Consistent with these principles, we conclude that a condemnor's right to dismiss a condemnation proceeding can be limited even if there was only a constructive taking of the property. It is possible that a landowner could be injured by a condemnor's right to possess the property, even if that right were never actually exercised. If the landowner cannot be restored to the position he enjoyed before the condemnation proceedings began, as for example by monetary compensation for his injury, the condemnor may be precluded from dismissing the action."

Murray v. Devco, Ltd., 731 S.W.2d 555, 557-58 (Tex.1987). A condemnor "may lose the right to dismiss 'by taking possession of the property.' A 'taking' is an actual physical invasion or an appropriation of the property. A taking is complete when the owner is prejudiced and the status quo cannot be restored. A landowner is prejudiced where the land is physically possessed and used by the condemnor. [¶] A condition precedent to the condemnor's right to dismissal is to re-

store the status quo by surrendering possession of the land to the condemnee. However, a condemnor is not required to take more land than it needs nor secure unnecessary easement rights in the absence of showing prejudice to the landowner."

Brazos River Conserv. & Reclamation Dist. v. Allen, 171 S.W.2d 842, 844-45 (Tex.1943). Condemnor "proceeded so far with the first condemnation suit that it would manifestly be unjust and would certainly be prejudicial to [condemnee] to permit [condemnor], against their consent, to dismiss or abandon the suit [and to allow a second condemnation suit on the same property]."

Riley v. City of Abilene, 834 S.W.2d 577, 578-79 (Tex.App.—Eastland 1992, writ dism'd). Condemnor "argues that, because ... §21.019 does not state a time frame for dismissing a case, a condemnor may dismiss at any time prior to the issuance of mandate by the appellate court. We disagree. [¶] [Condemnor] has cited no Texas authority to support its position that a condemnor can dismiss a condemnation suit after judgment has been entered and has been affirmed by the Court of Appeals and after application for writ of error has been denied by the Texas Supreme Court. We hold that [condemnor] can not, at this time, move to dismiss the underlying suit pursuant to §21.019."

Partial Dismissal

FKM Prtshp. v. Board of Regents of the Univ. of Houston Sys., 255 S.W.3d 619, 636 (Tex.2008). "We hold that an amended condemnation petition dismisses the proceedings within the meaning of §21.019(b) even if the condemnor does not completely dismiss or abandon the proceedings, but continues them in such manner that the amendment functionally abandons the original condemnation claim and asserts a different claim. *At 637:* There is no bright line that can be drawn here, and we add that §21.019(b) does not waive a condemning authority's immunity from liability for fees and expenses when just any downward adjustment in the size of the condemned property occurs. Other factors, such as whether the planned use of the smaller tract sought by amendment differs significantly from the tract originally sought and whether the potential future uses of the different tracts are similar, may be probative on the issue, in addition to the size of the reduced claim." *See also* ***Manning v. Enbridge Pipelines (E. Tex.) L.P.***, 345 S.W.3d 718, 726 (Tex.App.—Beaumont 2011, pet. denied); ***State v. Montgomery Cty.***, 338 S.W.3d 49, 58 (Tex.App.—Beaumont 2011, pet. denied).

State v. Tamminga, 928 S.W.2d 737, 740 (Tex. App.—Waco 1996, no writ). "While it is true that §21.019, literally read, requires that a motion to dismiss be filed before the trial court may order compensation for the landowner, we hold that the State's exclusion of [partitioned land] from its second amended petition effectively constituted a motion to dismiss within the meaning of §21.019. This amendment was not designed to reduce the amount of land to be taken at a single location or to clarify the interest to be taken. It had the effect of abandoning the State's right to condemn a tract of land separate and apart from the remaining property subject to condemnation—a tract originally the subject of an entirely separate proceeding."

PROP §21.0195. DISMISSAL OF CERTAIN CONDEMNATION PROCEEDINGS; TEXAS DEPARTMENT OF TRANSPORTATION

(a) This section applies only to the dismissal of a condemnation proceeding that involves the Texas Department of Transportation.

(b) The department may move to dismiss a proceeding it files, and the court shall conduct a hearing on the motion. The court may grant the motion only if the court determines that the property owner's interest will not be materially affected by the dismissal. The department may not dismiss the condemnation proceedings merely to institute new proceedings that involve substantially the same condemnation against the same property owner solely to obtain a lower condemnation award.

(c) If a court dismisses a condemnation proceeding on the motion of the department or as a result of the failure of the department to bring the proceeding properly, the court shall make an allowance to the property owner for the value of the department's use of the property while in possession of the property, any damage that the condemnation has caused to the property owner, and any expenses the property owner has incurred in connection with the condemnation, including reasonable and necessary fees for attorneys.

History of Prop. Code §21.0195: Acts 1997, 75th Leg., ch. 1171, §1.46(a), eff. Sept. 1, 1997.

CHARTS

See timetable, "Condemnation Procedure," p. 1536.

ANNOTATIONS

State v. Brown, 262 S.W.3d 365, 370 (Tex.2008). "Legislative intent is clear from the context of the caption of [Prop. Code §21.0195], the language of §21.0195(a) and the first phrase of §21.0195(c): fees, expenses and damages can be awarded under §21.0195(c) only if the condemnation proceeding is dismissed. In this case, the proceeding was not dismissed. [¶] [Condemnor] amended its pleadings to seek the same land it sought to condemn in its presentation to the special commissioners, albeit with a different configuration. The amended pleadings did not effect either an actual dismissal of its condemnation proceedings or the functional equivalent of a dismissal. Because the plain language of [Prop. Code] §21.019 requires a condemnation proceeding to be dismissed before fees and expenses may be recovered from the condemning authority, [property owner] is not entitled to recover fees and expenses." *See also* ***FKM Prtshp. v. Board of Regents of the Univ. of Houston Sys.***, 255 S.W.3d 619, 636-37 (Tex.2008) (no fees unless overwhelming change in compensation facts that functional dismissal of original condemnation suit had occurred).

PR Invs. & Specialty Retailers, Inc. v. State, 251 S.W.3d 472, 479 (Tex.2008). "Petitioners argue that the trial court had discretion to dismiss the case and award fees and expenses under [Prop. Code] §21.0195(c) ..., applicable to [condemnor]-related condemnation proceedings, because of [condemnor's] failure 'to bring the proceeding properly.' [Condemnor] did not fail to bring the proceeding properly. [Condemnor] may have failed to timely amend its discovery responses and/or may have failed to comply with the trial court's docket control orders, ... but such routine failures in the course of trial court proceedings are subject to the remedies available under the [TRCPs] automatically applicable to condemnation proceedings, which the court tries 'in the same manner as other civil causes' under [Prop. Code] §21.018(b). These lapses do not constitute a failure 'to bring the proceeding properly' in the first instance under §21.0195(c). [Condemnor] brought the condemnation suit properly by complying with all jurisdictional and procedural requirements for bringing the suit."

Eller Media Co. v. State, 51 S.W.3d 783, 786 (Tex. App.—Fort Worth 2001, no pet.). "Because ... the district court possessed subject matter jurisdiction over [condemnor's] condemnation suit, the court was required to follow the provisions governing the suit's dismissal in §21.0195(c). [¶] The language of §21.0195(c) is mandatory. The district court, therefore, had no discretion to refuse to award [property owner] its reasonable and necessary attorney's fees, if properly requested and proven."

PROP §21.020. REINSTATEMENT OF CONDEMNATION PROCEEDINGS

If a condemnor moves to dismiss a condemnation proceeding and subsequently files a petition to condemn substantially the same property interest from the same property owner, the court may not appoint new special commissioners but shall enter the award of the special commissioners in the first proceeding as the award in the second. The court shall award the property owner triple the amount of the expenses that were allowed the property owner prior to the dismissal of the first proceeding.

History of Prop. Code §21.020: Acts 1983, 68th Leg., ch. 576, §1, eff. Jan. 1, 1984. Source: TRCS art. 3265, subdiv. 6.

CHARTS

See timetable, "Condemnation Procedure," p. 1536.

ANNOTATIONS

Murray v. Devco, Ltd., 731 S.W.2d 555, 558 (Tex. 1987). Where the first condemnation "proceedings do not involve substantially the same property as the [later-filed] proceedings within the meaning of the Property Code[,] the penalty provision does not apply."

PROP §21.021. POSSESSION PENDING LITIGATION

(a) After the special commissioners have made an award in a condemnation proceeding, except as provided by Subsection (c) of this section, the condemnor may take possession of the condemned property pending the results of further litigation if the condemnor:

(1) pays to the property owner the amount of damages and costs awarded by the special commissioners or deposits that amount of money with the court subject to the order of the property owner;

(2) deposits with the court either the amount of money awarded by the special commissioners as damages or a surety bond in the same amount issued by a surety company qualified to do business in this state, conditioned to secure the payment of an award of damages by the court in excess of the award of the special commissioners; and

(3) executes a bond that has two or more good and solvent sureties approved by the judge of the court in which the proceeding is pending and conditioned to secure the payment of additional costs that may be awarded to the property owner by the trial court or on appeal.

(b) A court shall hold money or a bond deposited under Subdivision (1) or (2) of Subsection (a) to secure the payment of the damages that have been or that may be awarded against the condemnor.

(c) This state, a county, or a municipal corporation or an irrigation, water improvement, or water power control district created under legal authority is not required to deposit a bond or the amount equal to the award of damages under Subdivisions (2) and (3) of Subsection (a).

(d) If a condemnor deposits money with a court under Subdivision (2) of Subsection (a), the condemnor may instruct the court to deposit or invest the money in any account with or certificate or security issued by a state or national bank in this state. The court shall pay the interest that accrues from the deposit or investment to the condemnor.

History of Prop. Code §21.021: Acts 1983, 68th Leg., ch. 576, §1, eff. Jan. 1, 1984. Amended by Acts 1984, 68th Leg., 2nd C.S., ch. 18, §1(b), eff. Oct. 2, 1984. Source: TRCS art. 3268.

CHARTS

See timetable, "Condemnation Procedure," p. 1536.

ANNOTATIONS

Fort Worth Concrete Co. v. State, 400 S.W.2d 314, 317 (Tex.1966). "The fact that any or all of the parties to the condemnation are dissatisfied with the award at the time of the nonsuit or dismissal does not alone determine the prejudicial nature of such action. To deprive a condemnee of his right to possession without guaranteeing payment for the value of that right is prejudicial in itself. That guarantee is provided by compliance with [TRCS art. 3268, now Prop. Code §21.021], requiring the condemnor if it should desire to enter upon and take possession of the property, to pay the condemnee the amount of the damages awarded by the commissioners or to deposit an equal amount in the registry of the Court. Once an award is made and the amount thereof is placed in the registry of the court *to the order of the condemnees*, and the land is occupied by the condemning authority, the interest of each condemnee is established in and attaches to that fund as security for any possible damage suffered by reason of his dispossession. [T]he protection and guarantee for the condemnee is statutory, and those statutes are to be strictly complied with where prejudice might otherwise result."

City of Houston v. Culmore, 278 S.W.2d 825, 826 (Tex.1955). "By paying the amount of the award into the registry of the court[, condemnor] was authorized to take possession of the condemned right of way."

Whittington v. City of Austin, 456 S.W.3d 692, 700 (Tex.App.—Austin 2015, pet. denied). Condemnor "contends that if a condemning entity seeks to gain possession by paying the required deposit, trial courts are obligated under the [Property] Code to 'pay the interest that accrues from the deposit or investment to the condemnor.' [¶] [Condemnor's] reliance on this provision [in §21.021(d)] is misplaced. The provision instructing courts to award interest to a condemnor specifies that the instruction is limited to deposits made [under §21.021(a)(2)]. [¶] By only imposing this requirement on deposits made under §21.021(a)(2), the legislature has seemingly determined that the accrued interest on deposits required under §21.021(a)(1) does not belong to the condemnor. *At 701:* The limitation on interest accrued on [deposits made under §21.021(a)(2)] makes sense given that the deposit is designed to ensure that property owners will be able to recover any amount of the final judgment that exceeds the award made by the special commissioners. In other words, if the amount of the final judgment does not exceed the award of the special commissioners, no portion of the [§21.021(a)(2)] deposit is needed to fully compensate the property owner, and therefore, the property owner should not recover the accrued interest on the deposit. If the judgment amount does exceed the amount of the award, the limitation still makes sense because ... the property owner is entitled to recover prejudgment interest on the amount that exceeds the special commissioners' award in order to fully compensate the owner for the taking of his property. Accordingly, the property owner is made whole without needing to award him the interest accrued on the deposit."

City of Houston v. Texan Land & Cattle Co., 138 S.W.3d 382, 390 (Tex.App.—Houston [14th Dist.] 2004, no pet.). "Within the context of a condemnation case, prejudgment interest does not begin to accrue until the condemnor takes possession of the property. The condemnor has an election to make; he can either make

the requisite deposit and take immediate possession of the property, or he may await the jury's decision and leave the condemnee with possession during the pendency of suit. Additionally, any prejudgment interest that would accrue as a result of the condemnor's possession is tolled by the payment of the deposit. The rationale is that the condemnee may withdraw the deposit and use the money pending the court's determination of damages. *At 391:* Because there must be some independent basis for an award, [condemnee] is not entitled to prejudgment interest on the condemnation award merely because [condemnor] filed a condemnation counterclaim." *See also* ***Whittington v. City of Austin***, 174 S.W.3d 889, 907 (Tex.App.—Austin 2005, pet. denied) (accrual of prejudgment interest awards is not governed by common law).

Houston Lighting & Power Co. v. Klein ISD, 739 S.W.2d 508, 519 (Tex.App.—Houston [14th Dist.] 1987, writ denied). "The fact that [condemnor] entered upon the land knowing that the suit was pending is irrelevant. Section 21.021 covers such a situation with the language 'pending the results of further litigation.' As [condemnor] is not a trespasser that can be held liable for tort damages, punitive damages cannot be assessed."

City of Houston v. Wolfe, 712 S.W.2d 228, 230 (Tex.App.—Houston [14th Dist.] 1986, writ ref'd). Condemnor "argues that because it had placed into the registry of the court an amount equal to its estimation of the amount of the judgment award, the trial court erred by ordering [condemnor] to pay the judgment award directly to [property owner] and by awarding post-judgment interest on that award. [Condemnor] argues it is authorized to pay judgments into the registry of the court by ... §21.021.... We disagree. Section 21.021 merely allows a condemnor to pay into the registry of the court an amount equal to the Special Commissioners' Award so that the condemnor may take possession of the condemned property 'pending the results of further litigation.' This section does not purport to pertain to the payment of a *judgment*, the result of such further litigation. Therefore, the Clerk of the Court was unauthorized to accept [condemnor's] deposit."

PROP §21.0211. PAYMENT OF AD VALOREM TAXES

(a) A court may not authorize withdrawal of any money deposited under Section 21.021 unless the petitioner for the money files with the court:

(1) a tax certificate issued under Section 31.08, Tax Code, by the tax collector for each taxing unit that imposes ad valorem taxes on the condemned property showing that there are no delinquent taxes, penalties, interest, or costs owing on the condemned property or on any larger tract of which the condemned property forms a part; and

(2) in the case of a whole taking that occurs after the date the ad valorem tax bill for taxes imposed by a taxing unit on the property is sent, a tax receipt issued under Section 31.075, Tax Code, by the tax collector of the taxing unit that imposes ad valorem taxes showing that the taxes on the condemned property for the current tax year, prorated under Section 26.11, Tax Code, have been paid.

(b) For purposes of Subsection (a)(2), a "case of a whole taking" means a case in which the location, size, and boundaries of the property assessed for ad valorem taxes are identical to that of the condemned property.

History of Prop. Code §21.0211: Acts 2005, 79th Leg., ch. 1126, §27, eff. Sept. 1, 2005.

PROP §21.022. AUTHORITY OF COURTS

Laws that formerly governed the performance of functions by county clerks and judges in eminent domain proceedings are applicable to the clerks and judges of district courts and county courts at law.

History of Prop. Code §21.022: Acts 1983, 68th Leg., ch. 576, §1, eff. Jan. 1, 1984. Source: TRCS art. 3266, subdiv. 8.

PROP §21.023. DISCLOSURE OF INFORMATION REQUIRED AT TIME OF ACQUISITION

An entity with eminent domain authority shall disclose in writing to the property owner, at the time of acquisition of the property through eminent domain, that:

(1) the owner or the owner's heirs, successors, or assigns may be entitled to:

(A) repurchase the property under Subchapter E; or

(B) request from the entity certain information relating to the use of the property and any actual progress made toward that use; and

(2) the repurchase price is the price paid to the owner by the entity at the time the entity acquired the property through eminent domain.

History of Prop. Code §21.023: Acts 2003, 78th Leg., ch. 1307, §1, eff. Jan. 1, 2004. Amended by Acts 2011, 82nd Leg., ch. 81, §13, eff. Sept. 1, 2011.

CHARTS

See timetable, "Condemnation Procedure," p. 1536.

PROP §21.024. REPEALED

Repealed by Acts 2011, 82nd Leg., ch. 81, §23(b), eff. Sept. 1, 2011.

PROP §21.025. PRODUCTION OF INFORMATION BY CERTAIN ENTITIES

(a) Notwithstanding any other law, an entity that is not subject to Chapter 552, Government Code, and is authorized by law to acquire private property through the use of eminent domain is required to produce information as provided by this section if the information is:

(1) requested by a person who owns property that is the subject of a proposed or existing eminent domain proceeding; and

(2) related to the taking of the person's private property by the entity through the use of eminent domain.

(b) An entity described by Subsection (a) is required under this section only to produce information relating to the condemnation of the specific property owned by the requestor as described in the request. A request under this section must contain sufficient details to allow the entity to identify the specific tract of land in relation to which the information is sought.

(c) The entity shall respond to a request in accordance with the Texas Rules of Civil Procedure as if the request was made in a matter pending before a state district court.

(d) Exceptions to disclosure provided by this chapter and the Texas Rules of Civil Procedure apply to the disclosure of information under this section.

(e) Jurisdiction to enforce the provisions of this section resides in:

(1) the court in which the condemnation was initiated; or

(2) if the condemnation proceeding has not been initiated:

(A) a court that would have jurisdiction over a proceeding to condemn the requestor's property; or

(B) a court with eminent domain jurisdiction in the county in which the entity has its principal place of business.

(f) If the entity refuses to produce information requested in accordance with this section and the court determines that the refusal violates this section, the court may award the requestor's reasonable attorney's fees incurred to compel the production of the information.

History of Prop. Code §21.025: Acts 2011, 82nd Leg., ch. 81, §14, eff. Sept. 1, 2011.

Sections 21.026-21.040 reserved for expansion

SUBCHAPTER C. DAMAGES & COSTS

PROP §21.041. EVIDENCE

As the basis for assessing actual damages to a property owner from a condemnation, the special commissioners shall admit evidence on:

(1) the value of the property being condemned;

(2) the injury to the property owner;

(3) the benefit to the property owner's remaining property; and

(4) the use of the property for the purpose of the condemnation.

History of Prop. Code §21.041: Acts 1983, 68th Leg., ch. 576, §1, eff. Jan. 1, 1984. Source: TRCS art. 3265, subdiv. 1.

CHARTS

See timetable, "Condemnation Procedure," p. 1536.

ANNOTATIONS

Natural Gas Pipeline Co. v. Justiss, 397 S.W.3d 150, 159 (Tex.2012). "Because property owner testimony is the functional equivalent of expert testimony, it must be judged by the same standards. Thus, as with expert testimony, property valuations may not be based solely on a property owner's *ipse dixit*. An owner may not simply echo the phrase 'market value' and state a number to substantiate his diminished value claim; he must provide the factual basis on which his opinion rests. [T]he valuation must be substantiated; a naked assertion of 'market value' is not enough."

Reid Rd. MUD v. Speedy Stop Food Stores, 337 S.W.3d 846, 852-53 (Tex.2011). "[A] property owner is qualified to testify to the value of her property even if she is not an expert and would not be qualified to testify to the value of other property. [¶] Through their employees, entities are as capable of knowing the market value of their property as are individuals. ... Thus, we see no good reason to conclude that business organizations are any less familiar with the value of their property than are individual property owners, or to preclude them from coming within the Property Owner Rule and its presumption that a property owner is familiar with its property and the property's value. *At 854-55:* A reasonable balance as to who may testify under the Property Owner Rule on behalf of an entity is struck by allowing such testimony only from an officer in a management position with duties that at least in some part relate to the property at issue, or an employee of the en-

tity in a substantially equivalent position." *See also* ***Dallas Cty. v. Crestview Corners Car Wash (a Tex. Jt.V.)***, 370 S.W.3d 25, 41 (Tex.App.—Dallas 2012, pet. denied).

City of Pearland v. Alexander, 483 S.W.2d 244, 247 (Tex.1972). "[E]verything which affects the market value of the land itself, having due regard for past and probable future injuries, may be accurately reflected by ascertaining the difference in value, when all the legitimate testimony is properly submitted to the jury for consideration; and it is proper to admit evidence upon all matters which tend to increase or diminish the present market value. The landowner may recover damages which are reasonably foreseeable, and he may show the reasonably probable uses of the tract taken that are calculated to depress the value of the remainder tract and thus enhance the recovery of damages."

State v. Walker, 441 S.W.2d 168, 173 (Tex.1969). "Damages in condemnation proceedings are limited to damages to property. Property must be either taken or damaged. In considering whether or not tendered testimony is admissible it should be remembered that the purpose of the courts is to arrive ultimately at a measure of damages that will 'set up a yardstick for value that is broad enough and ultimate enough to include all elements of damages and all elements of values, to the end that just compensation for the land taken or damaged can first be paid to the landowner.'"

Sample v. Tennessee Gas Transmission Co., 251 S.W.2d 221, 223-24 (Tex.1952). "'The two most common species of proof in condemnation proceedings are—1st, the element of value; and 2d, the elements of damages. Under the first head is admitted everything which has a bearing on the value of the property; under the second, everything which enters into and makes part of the damage inflicted. These elements of damage and value are not the measure of damages. They go to the jury to throw light on the general question of depreciation.' [¶] The private preferences of a witness relative to the purchase of a tract of land cannot be used as proof of market value and depreciation in market value."

State v. Gaylor Inv. Trust Prtshp., 322 S.W.3d 814, 819 (Tex.App.—Houston [14th Dist.] 2010, no pet.). Held: Trial court has discretion to limit each side to one expert appraisal witness.

State v. Enterprise Co., 728 S.W.2d 812, 812 (Tex. App.—Houston [14th Dist.] 1986, writ ref'd n.r.e.). "[T]he Texas Constitution requires compensation for the full market value of the land taken. The value of any benefits to the condemnee's remaining land may not offset the amount paid for the part taken."

PROP §21.042. ASSESSMENT OF DAMAGES

(a) The special commissioners shall assess damages in a condemnation proceeding according to the evidence presented at the hearing.

(b) If an entire tract or parcel of real property is condemned, the damage to the property owner is the local market value of the property at the time of the special commissioners' hearing.

(c) If a portion of a tract or parcel of real property is condemned, the special commissioners shall determine the damage to the property owner after estimating the extent of the injury and benefit to the property owner, including the effect of the condemnation on the value of the property owner's remaining property.

(d) In estimating injury or benefit under Subsection (c), the special commissioners shall consider an injury or benefit that is peculiar to the property owner and that relates to the property owner's ownership, use, or enjoyment of the particular parcel of real property, including a material impairment of direct access on or off the remaining property that affects the market value of the remaining property, but they may not consider an injury or benefit that the property owner experiences in common with the general community, including circuity of travel and diversion of traffic. In this subsection, "direct access" means ingress and egress on or off a public road, street, or highway at a location where the remaining property adjoins that road, street, or highway.

(e) If a portion of a tract or parcel of real property is condemned for the use, construction, operation, or maintenance of the state highway system or of a county toll project described by Chapter 284, Transportation Code, that is eligible for designation as part of the state highway system, or for the use, construction, development, operation, or maintenance of an improvement or project by a metropolitan rapid transit authority created before January 1, 1980, with a principal municipality having a population of less than 1.9 million and established under Chapter 451, Transportation Code, the special commissioners shall determine the damage to the property owner regardless of whether the property owner makes a claim for damages to the remaining property. In awarding compensation or assessing the

damages, the special commissioners shall consider any special and direct benefits that arise from the highway improvement or the transit authority improvement or project that are peculiar to the property owner and that relate to the property owner's ownership, use, or enjoyment of the particular parcel of remaining real property.

(f) In awarding compensation or assessing damages for a condemnation by an institution of higher education, as defined by Section 61.003, Education Code, the special commissioners may not include in the compensation or damages any amount that compensates for, or is based on the present value of, an exemption from ad valorem taxation applicable to the property before its condemnation.

(g) Notwithstanding Subsection (d), if a portion of a tract or parcel of real property that, for the then current tax year was appraised for ad valorem tax purposes under a law enacted under Section 1-d or 1-d-1, Article VIII, Texas Constitution, and is outside the municipal limits or the extraterritorial jurisdiction of a municipality with a population of 5,000 or more is condemned for state highway purposes, the special commissioners shall consider the loss of reasonable access to or from the remaining property in determining the damage to the property owner.

History of Prop. Code §21.042: Acts 1983, 68th Leg., ch. 576, §1, eff. Jan. 1, 1984. Amended by Acts 1984, 68th Leg., 2nd C.S., ch. 29, §1, eff. Oct. 2, 1984; Acts 1989, 71st Leg., ch. 734, §5, eff. June 15, 1989; Acts 1997, 75th Leg., ch. 165, §30.244, eff. Sept. 1, 1997; Acts 2001, 77th Leg., ch. 669, §117, eff. Sept. 1, 2001; Acts 2003, 78th Leg., ch. 1266, §1.15, eff. June 21, 2003; Acts 2005, 79th Leg., ch. 281, §2.94, eff. June 14, 2005; Acts 2011, 82nd Leg., ch. 81, §15, eff. Sept. 1, 2011. Source: TRCS art. 3265, subdivs. 1-4.

Author's comment: The most substantive change to this section, made as part of Acts 2011, 82nd Leg., ch. 81, §10, concerns when access damages are compensable under subsection (d) and were intended to overturn case law on this issue, including at least part of the holdings in ***State v. Bristol Hotel Asset Co.***, 293 S.W.3d 170 (Tex.2009), ***State v. Dawmar Partners***, 267 S.W.3d 875 (Tex.2008), ***State v. Heal***, 917 S.W.2d 6 (Tex.1996), ***County of Bexar v. Santikos***, 144 S.W.3d 455 (Tex.2004), among other cases that had limited such recovery. The following is the legislative history for this statutory standard:

"REMARKS ORDERED PRINTED

...

Senator Hegar: Can you explain the effect of the new standard for recovery of access damages found in Property Code 21.042(d)...?

Senator Estes: In certain circumstances, we would want more landowners who are currently not recovering for loss of access under the 'material and substantial' test as that test is currently interpreted by the courts to recover for loss of access. We are acting here to change the current state of the law on that issue. We want the words in 21.042(d) to be interpreted such that if a property owner suffers a loss of access that is material – not trivial, nominal, imaginary, or speculative – and that loss affects the market value of the property, then the court must allow the factfinder to consider evidence on that loss when the factfinder determines what damages are due to the landowner. It's a lower standard than 'material and substantial' and a higher standard than 'any diminished access' proposed in the filed version of this bill."

S.J. of Tex., 82nd Leg., 12th Day R.S. 302 (2-9-11). There was a nearly identical exchange on the floor of the House of Representatives. H.J. of Tex., 82nd Leg., 55th Day R.S. 1731 (4-13-11) (also including: "[I]s 'material impairment of access,' as that term is used in the bill, a fact or a determination to be made by the special commissioners or, if their decision is appealed, by the jury?" Answer: "That's correct....").

See also Tex. Const. art. 1, §17.

CHARTS

See timetable, "Condemnation Procedure," p. 1536.

ANNOTATIONS

Generally

State v. Bristol Hotel Asset Co., 293 S.W.3d 170, 175 (Tex.2009). "In condemnation cases, the trial court must first determine if claimed damages are compensable, and admit evidence accordingly. If the damage award 'is based on evidence of both compensable and noncompensable injuries, the harmed party is entitled to a new trial.'" *See also* ***Interstate Northborough Prtshp. v. State***, 66 S.W.3d 213, 220 (Tex.2001). *But see* Author's comment, this page.

Elliott v. Joseph, 351 S.W.2d 879, 884 (Tex.1961). TRCS art. 3265, §3, now Prop. Code §21.042, "provides that where only a portion of the real estate is condemned the commissioners shall estimate the injuries sustained and the benefits received by the owner. The term 'owner' in this sense includes a lessee for years as well as any other person who has an interest in the property. The amount of rent is a factor in determining the damages suffered by the lessee in the taking of a portion of his lease, but it is not the only element."

City of Blue Mound v. Southwest Water Co., 449 S.W.3d 678, 684 (Tex.App.—Fort Worth 2014, no pet.). "[T]he general rule is that the taking by the government of a fee simple in real property does not entitle a property owner to compensation for loss of the value of his business as a going concern. [¶] [However,] utility systems are an exception to the ... general rule. [W]hen a governmental entity condemns an entire utility system for the purpose of taking it over and continuing its operation by the governmental entity, then the utility owner is entitled to be compensated for loss of the going-concern value of the utility system. *At 689:* [However,] if what is taken is not compensable under Texas's general condemnation statutes, then some specific statute or mechanism must exist authorizing compensation for that taking. *At 690:* Looking to the plain language of [the statutes in this case,] none of them grant eminent domain authority to the City to condemn the entire [property] as a going concern. *At 692:* We hold ... that the trial court properly granted summary judgment for [property owners] on the ground that as a

matter of law Texas's general condemnation statutes do not authorize the City's condemnation [of the property] as a going concern…."

State v. Momin Props., Inc., 409 S.W.3d 1, 10 (Tex.App.—Houston [1st Dist.] 2013, pet. denied). "Nothing in §21.042(d) addresses or alters the rule that a determination of whether a taking has occurred in an inverse condemnation case is resolved by courts as a matter of law."

Dallas Cty. v. Crestview Corners Car Wash (a Tex. Jt.V.), 370 S.W.3d 25, 39-40 (Tex.App.—Dallas 2012, pet. denied). "In condemnation cases, adequate compensation does not include profits generated by a business located on condemned land. However, income from a business located on the property may be considered in two situations: (1) where the taking, damaging, or destruction of property causes a material and substantial interference with access; and (2) where only a part of the land is taken and lost profits demonstrate the effect on the market value of the remaining land and improvements. [¶] [Expert] did not testify to lost profits as a separate element of damages. He presented evidence that the loss of inspection and detailing functions of the property will reduce what it would sell for in the market. Because [expert] did not use lost profits as an independent element of damages, his opinion of the market value of the remainder was relevant."

§21.042(b)—Market Value

Enbridge Pipelines (E. Tex.) L.P. v. Avinger Timber, LLC, 386 S.W.3d 256, 263 (Tex.2012). Condemnee "was entitled to have its land valued using its highest and best use. It is presumed that the land's highest and best use is that of its existing use, which in this case was the site of a gas processing facility. Indeed, it appears that the land was uniquely situated to be the site of a gas processing facility. The land had a 31 year history as a gas processing site with all the required permits, had over 15 separate natural gas pipelines running underneath it, each with its own easement, was connected to a high-voltage electricity line, and was located in one of Texas's most productive counties. The value of the land as a gas processing site is not exclusive to [condemnor]. Although [condemnee] was entitled to compensation for the distinct suitability of its land for a gas processing site, it was not entitled to be compensated for the land's unique value to [condemnor] as a result of the lease's terms. *At 264:* [T]he trial court … did abuse its discretion by admitting the portion of [landowner appraiser's] testimony premised on [condemnor's] obligation to remove the plant under the lease agreement, which violated the value-to-the-taker rule by impermissibly valuing the costs [condemnor] saved by condemning the land and avoiding the removal obligation of the lease." *See also* ***Hanford-Southport, LLC v. City of San Antonio***, 387 S.W.3d 849, 853-54 (Tex.App.—San Antonio 2012, pet. denied).

State v. Central Expressway Sign Assocs., 302 S.W.3d 866, 871 (Tex.2009). "Texas law allows income from a business operated on the property to be considered in a condemnation proceeding in two situations: (1) when the taking, damaging, or destruction of property causes a material and substantial interference with access to one's property …; and (2) when only a part of the land has been taken, so that lost profits may demonstrate the effect on the market value of the remaining land and improvements…. Absent one of these two situations, income from a business operated on the property is not recoverable and should not be included in a condemnation award. Courts have applied this rule for two reasons: first, because profits from a business are speculative and often depend more upon the capital invested, general market conditions, and the business skill of the person conducting it than it does on the business's location; and second, because only the real estate and not the business has been taken and the owner can presumably continue to operate the business at another location. [¶] Texas courts have refused to consider business income in making condemnation awards even when there is evidence that the business's location is crucial to its success. *At 873:* We are not inclined to create an exception for land on which a billboard is placed." *See also* ***State v. Clear Channel Outdoor, Inc.***, 463 S.W.3d 488, 497 (Tex.2015) (valuing billboards separately from land does not affect compensation due).

City of Harlingen v. Estate of Sharboneau, 48 S.W.3d 177, 182 (Tex.2001). "Market value is 'the price the property will bring when offered for sale by one who desires to sell, but is not obliged to sell, and is bought by one who desires to buy, but is under no necessity of buying.' The three traditional approaches to determining market value are the comparable sales method, the cost method, and the income method. [¶] Under a comparable sales analysis, the appraiser finds data for sales of similar property, then makes upward or downward adjustments to these sales prices based on differ-

ences in the subject property. [¶] Comparable sales must be voluntary, and should take place near in time to the condemnation, occur in the vicinity of the condemned property, and involve land with similar characteristics. Comparable sales need not be in the immediate vicinity of the subject land, so long as they meet the test of similarity." *See also* ***In re State***, 355 S.W.3d 611, 616 (Tex.2011) (discussing ***Sharboneau***'s analysis of "subdivision development method," a fourth valuation method); ***Religious of the Sacred Heart of Tex. v. City of Houston***, 836 S.W.2d 606, 615-17 & n.14 (Tex. 1992) (discussing three traditional approaches to determining market value); ***Williams v. State***, 406 S.W.3d 273, 284 (Tex.App.—San Antonio 2013, pet. denied) (same).

Callejo v. Brazos Elec. Power Coop., 755 S.W.2d 73, 76 (Tex.1988). "The measure of damages in a condemnation proceeding is the difference in market value of the land immediately before and immediately after the taking. Future condemnation cases should be submitted broadly in terms of the difference in value, rather than asking separate questions on pre-and post-taking values."

City of Fort Worth v. Corbin, 504 S.W.2d 828, 830 (Tex.1974). "The compensation for land taken by eminent domain is measured by the market value of the land at the time of the taking. This is the date upon which the condemnor lawfully takes actual possession or … takes constructively by a deposit of the special commissioners' award. [T]he landowners' compensation should under some circumstances or at some time cease to include enhancement due to the project which is itself the purpose of condemnation. *At 831:* The date upon which the market no longer allows project enhancement is delineated by variant tests. [U]nder Texas law: enhancement is allowed up to the time that the condemnor manifests a definite purpose to take the particular land. [¶] The determination of the cutoff date for project enhancement must be made by the court and not by the jury. That ruling must often precede the determination of comparability of sales as well as the admissibility of other evidence, which are matters for the judge to decide." *But see* ***Fuller v. State***, 461 S.W.2d 595, 598-99 (Tex.1970) (discussing exceptions to project-enhancement rule).

Hanford-Southport, LLC v. City of San Antonio, 387 S.W.3d 849, 858 (Tex.App.—San Antonio 2012, pet. denied). Condemnee "was not entitled to value the trees and other flora separately from the land. Rather, precedent states that although trees and other improvements on the land can be considered as possible enhancements to the value of the land (if they actually enhance the value), they cannot be valued separately, and the market value of the land as land is the proper method by which a condemnation award is determined."

Dallas Cty. v. Crestview Corners Car Wash (a Tex. Jt.V.), 370 S.W.3d 25, 37 (Tex.App.—Dallas 2012, pet. denied). "An expert's 'bald assurance' that he used a widely accepted appraisal method is not sufficient to demonstrate that his opinion is reliable. We must look beyond an expert's assertion that the data underlying his or her opinion are the type of data on which experts reasonably rely. Instead, the underlying data must be independently evaluated in determining if the opinion itself is reliable. [¶] We cannot find where [expert] applied the accepted appraisal methods to arrive at the fair market value of the remainder after the taking. Instead, [expert] simply took the market value of the whole before the taking and assumed—without any basis—that a willing buyer and willing seller would agree to reduce the market value by one-fifth for the loss of the perimeter lane. Thus, [expert] reached an unsupported conclusion on the damages to the remainder first, then applied that unsupported conclusion to the accepted appraisal methods he had done on the property as a whole."

Motiva Enters. v. McCrabb, 248 S.W.3d 211, 214 (Tex.App.—Houston [1st Dist.] 2007, pet. denied). Lessee "argues that, based on its reservation of the right to recover its 'special damages,' it is entitled to 'recover its damages for its lost leasehold….' [¶] A lessee is entitled, as a matter of law, to share in a condemnation award when part of its leasehold interest is lost by condemnation. Unless a lease provides that it terminates upon condemnation, the tenant will recover compensation for the unexpired term. But, if a lease provides that it terminates upon condemnation, the lessee has no interest in the condemnation award."

§21.042(c)—Portion of a Tract

In re State, 355 S.W.3d 611, 617 (Tex.2011). Condemnor "believes that the ideal economic unit is the entire condemned tract, the highest and best use of which is to hold as investment for future development. [Condemnor] is permitted under [***State v. Windham***, 837 S.W.2d 73 (Tex.1992),] to offer this testimony.

[Property owners here] believe that the condemned tract is an inferior economic unit. Where [property owner in ***Windham***] thought the proper unit was larger than the condemned tract, however, [property owners here] believe that the tract to be condemned contains several self-sufficient economic units. If they have non-speculative evidence to support this contention, they should be permitted to offer it at trial. Though [condemnor] has a right to define the property being taken, it does not have the power to constrain the owners' evidence of competing conceptions of the best economic unit by which the taken property should be valued."

County of Bexar v. Santikos, 144 S.W.3d 455, 462-63 (Tex.2004). "Damages to remainder property are recoverable only to the extent they arise from public use of the condemned land, not from public use of land the public already owns. [Condemnee] points out that the land taken here will be used to help raise the frontage road, while that taken in [***State v. Schmidt***, 867 S.W.2d 769 (Tex.1993),] was used not in elevating the main roadway but in widening a road below. The embankment here will be on the condemned property, but the elevated frontage road will not. The remainder property would be just as much 'in a hole' and no easier to access if the frontage road were supported by a wall or columns rather than a sloping shoulder." *But see* Author's comment, this page.

Exxon Pipeline Co. v. Zwahr, 88 S.W.3d 623, 628 (Tex.2002). "Texas law permits landowners to introduce testimony that the condemned land is a self-sufficient separate economic unit, independent from the remainder of the parent tract with a different highest and best use and different value from the remaining land. In this situation, the market value of the severed land can be determined without reference to the remaining land. But when the portion of the land taken by eminent domain cannot be considered as a separate economic unit, the before-and-after method requires determining market value by evaluating the taken land as a proportionate part of the remaining land." *See also* ***State v. Windham***, 837 S.W.2d 73, 76 (Tex.1992).

Author's comment: Note that the taken land should not be valued as a proportionate part of the larger tract if its value differs from the rest of the property. *See* ***DeWitt & Rearick, Inc. v. State***, 531 S.W.2d 862, 865 (Tex.App.—El Paso 1975, no writ); ***State v. Cherry***, 517 S.W.2d 337, 339 (Tex.App.—Dallas 1975, writ ref'd n.r.e.).

Interstate Northborough Prtshp. v. State, 66 S.W.3d 213, 218 (Tex.2001). "We calculate condemnation damages to remainder property when only part was taken for public use by ascertaining the difference between the market value of the remainder property immediately before the condemnation and the market value of the remainder property immediately after the condemnation, taking into consideration the nature of any improvements and the use of the land taken." *See also* ***State v. Meyer***, 403 S.W.2d 366, 371 (Tex.1966); ***City of Austin v. Cannizzo***, 267 S.W.2d 808, 812 (Tex. 1954); ***Coble v. City of Mansfield***, 134 S.W.3d 449, 455 (Tex.App.—Fort Worth 2004, no pet.).

State v. Schmidt, 867 S.W.2d 769, 778 (Tex.1993). The ***Campbell*** rule "'supported by better reason and the weight of authority is that the just compensation assured by the Fifth Amendment to an owner, a part of whose land is taken for public use, does not include the diminution in value of the remainder caused by the acquisition and use of adjoining lands of others for the same undertaking.' [¶] The Ninth Circuit has held that the ***Campbell*** rule should be applied unless: (1) the land taken from the condemnee landowner was indispensable to the ... project; (2) the land taken constituted a substantial (not inconsequential) part of the tract devoted to the project; and (3) the damages resulting to the land not taken from the use of the land taken were inseparable from those to the same land flowing from the condemnor government's use of its adjoining land in the ... project. This exception is based upon the analysis in ***Campbell*** and employed to allow landowners to recover in the circumstances described by the exception. We agree that this exception is a necessary qualification to the ***Campbell*** rule." *See also* ***Campbell v. U.S.***, 266 U.S. 368, 372 (1924); ***State v. Colonia Tepeyac, Ltd.***, 391 S.W.3d 563, 568 (Tex.App.—Dallas 2012, no pet.); ***City of San Antonio v. Kopplow Dev., Inc.***, 335 S.W.3d 288, 293-94 (Tex.App.—San Antonio 2010), *rev'd on other grounds*, 399 S.W.3d 532 (Tex.2013).

Cameron Cty. Drainage Dist. No. 5 v. Gonzales, 69 S.W.3d 820, 824 (Tex.App.—Corpus Christi 2002, no pet.). "When the tract taken is of an irregular shape, ... the preferable formula for calculating the damages is (1) the market value of the part taken, considered as severed land; (2) the market value of the entire tract before the taking; and (3) the market value of the remainder after the taking, giving consideration to the uses to which the condemned part is to be subjected. 'Under this approach, the total measure of damages is usually the difference between questions 2 and 3; how-

ever, if this difference is less than the answer to question 1 (indicating that the condemnation increased the value of the remainder), the landowner is entitled to the market value of the part taken.'"

§21.042(d)—Community Damages

Interstate Northborough Prtshp. v. State, 66 S.W.3d 213, 222 (Tex.2001). "[A] landowner's injury is not community simply because several landowners suffer similar injuries due to the condemnation. Rather, the nature of the injury and whether it affects the remainder in some special, unique way determines whether damages are community or special. *At 223:* [T]he difference in injury to [condemnee's] property is not one of degree, it is one of kind. [Condemnee] demonstrated that the building's [proximity to the new highway right-of-way] made its increased-proximity injury peculiar to its property and thus the increased-proximity damages are special not community."

Felts v. Harris Cty., 915 S.W.2d 482, 485 (Tex. 1996). "[I]njuries to property received or sustained in common with the community in which the property is situated, and resulting from the operation of a public work, are community in nature. Community damages are not connected with the landowner's use and enjoyment of property and give rise to no compensation. [¶] The only settled issue regarding noise and other annoyances attributable to highways is the non-recoverability of damages from noise, dust, increased traffic, and other inconveniences incident to the building of a highway. These temporary inconveniences are 'incident to city life and must be endured.' [¶] The fact that some damages may be greater if the property is in closer proximity to the roadway does not suffice to render such damages constitutionally compensable under [Tex. Const. art.] 1, §17."

State v. Schmidt, 867 S.W.2d 769, 781 (Tex.1993). "[T]he analysis of whether an injury or benefit was common to the community involved consideration of the location of the landowner's property, the condemnor's project, and the effects of the latter. However, the concept of community injury and benefit is not primarily geographical. It is always true that the injury or benefit from a public project increases with proximity. While injury to several landowners on the same street is not community injury simply because they all suffer alike, it is also not special injury simply because others farther away do not suffer at all. Whether an injury is community cannot be decided simply by setting the size of the relevant area. 'Community' in this context means not only where, but, more importantly, what kind. It is the nature of the injury rather than its location that is critical in determining whether it is community." *See also* ***Oddo v. State***, 912 S.W.2d 831, 833-34 (Tex. App.—Dallas 1995, writ denied).

Harris Cty. Flood Control Dist. v. Glenbrook Patiohome Owners Ass'n, 933 S.W.2d 570, 578 (Tex. App.—Houston [1st Dist.] 1996, writ denied). "When the government takes a servient estate that is burdened by an intangible property interest appurtenant to an adjacent dominant estate, the dominant estate owner's property interest in the servient estate is extinguished. Although the value of the property interest can only be determined by examining the effect of its absence on the dominant estate, we conclude this does not render the nature of the injury as community rather than special. Further, the injury is not rendered community merely because it is sustained by several individuals."

§21.042(e)—Highway Condemnation

City of LaGrange v. Pieratt, 175 S.W.2d 243, 246 (Tex.1943). "In a proceeding for the condemnation of a part of a tract of land for street or road purposes, it is presumed that the amount of damages allowed covers all lawful elements of damages, whether direct or consequential, that could reasonably have been foreseen and determined at the time of condemnation; and where a part of a tract of land is condemned for street or road purposes, the owner cannot recover in a subsequent proceeding for consequential damages to the remainder of the land which he ought reasonably have foreseen and presented in the condemnation proceeding."

State v. Enterprise Co., 728 S.W.2d 812, 812-13 (Tex.App.—Houston [14th Dist.] 1986, writ ref'd n.r.e.). "The language and the legislative history of [§21.042(e)] suggests that the Legislature might have intended to change the method for determining adequate compensation for land condemned for highway purposes. However, the Texas Supreme Court has held that 'adequate compensation' means the market price of the land actually taken without any reduction for estimated benefits to the condemnee's remaining land. If this principle is to be changed, it must be done directly and not merely by suggestive language. The Texas Constitution has been clearly interpreted as disallowing such a deduction."

PROP §21.0421. ASSESSMENT OF DAMAGES: GROUNDWATER RIGHTS

(a) In a condemnation proceeding initiated by a political subdivision under this chapter, the special commissioners or court shall admit evidence relating to the market value of groundwater rights as property apart from the land in addition to the local market value of the real property if:

(1) the political subdivision proposes to condemn the fee title of real property; and

(2) the special commissioners or court finds, based on evidence submitted at the hearing, that the real property may be used by the political subdivision to develop or use the rights to groundwater for a public purpose.

(b) The evidence submitted under Subsection (a) on the market value of the groundwater rights as property apart from the land shall be based on generally accepted appraisal methods and techniques, including the methods of appraisal under Subchapter A, Chapter 23, Tax Code.

(c) If the special commissioners or court finds that the real property may be used by the political subdivision to develop or use the rights to groundwater for a public purpose, the special commissioners or court may assess damages to the property owner based on:

(1) the local market value of the real property, excluding the value of the groundwater in place, at the time of the hearing; and

(2) the market value of the groundwater rights as property apart from the land at the time of the hearing.

(d) In assessing damages based on the market value of groundwater rights under Subsection (c)(2), the special commissioners or court shall consider:

(1) the amount of groundwater the political subdivision can reasonably be expected to produce from the property on an annual basis;

(2) the number of years the political subdivision can reasonably be expected to produce groundwater from the property;

(3) the quality of the groundwater;

(4) the location of the real property in relation to the political subdivision for conveyance purposes;

(5) any potential environmental impact of producing groundwater from the real property;

(6) whether or not the real property is located within the boundaries of a political subdivision that can regulate the production of groundwater from the real property;

(7) the cost of alternative water supplies to the political subdivision; and

(8) any other reasonable factor that affects the market value of a groundwater right.

(e) This section does not:

(1) authorize groundwater rights appraised separately from the real property under this section to be appraised separately from real property for property tax appraisal purposes; or

(2) subject real property condemned for the purpose described by Subsection (a) to an additional tax as provided by Section 23.46 or 23.55, Tax Code.

History of Prop. Code §21.0421: Acts 2003, 78th Leg., ch. 1032, §2, eff. Sept. 1, 2003.

ANNOTATIONS

Edwards Aquifer Auth. v. Bragg, 421 S.W.3d 118, 147 (Tex.App.—San Antonio 2013, pet. denied). "[T]akings claims fall into two distinct categories and occur at different times depending on whether the taking arises in the context of a statutory condemnation context or arises in an inverse condemnation context. In a statutory condemnation proceeding under [Prop. Code] §21.042, generally, the government compensates the owner before appropriating property, either by paying a mutually agreed price or by paying the value as determined at the statutory proceeding. … The assessment of damages when a portion of or an entire tract or parcel of real property is condemned is made 'according to evidence presented at the [condemnation] hearing.' These assessments are made at the time of trial because that is the time at which the government's authority to condemn is determined. *At 148:* On the other hand, if the government appropriates property without paying adequate compensation, the owner may recover the resulting damages in an 'inverse condemnation' suit. 'An inverse condemnation may occur when the government physically appropriates or invades the property, or when it unreasonably interferes with the landowner's right to use and enjoy the property, such as by restricting access or denying a permit for development.' Chapter 21 does not govern inverse condemnation claims brought by landowners. The assessment of damages in an inverse condemnation case that arises

from a regulatory taking is made, depending on the circumstances, either when the regulation is enacted or, as here, when the regulation was implemented or applied."

PROP §21.043. DISPLACEMENT FROM DWELLING OR PLACE OF BUSINESS

(a) A property owner who is permanently physically displaced from the property owner's dwelling or place of business and who is not entitled to reimbursement for moving expenses under another law may recover, in addition to the property owner's other damages, the reasonable expenses of moving the property owner's personal property from the dwelling or place of business.

(b) A recovery under this section may not exceed the market value of the property being moved. The maximum distance of movement to be considered is 50 miles.

History of Prop. Code §21.043: Acts 1983, 68th Leg., ch. 576, §1, eff. Jan. 1, 1984. Source: TRCS art. 3265, subdiv. 7.

ANNOTATIONS

G.P. Show Prods. v. Arlington Sports Facilities Dev. Auth., 873 S.W.2d 120, 123 (Tex.App.—Fort Worth 1994, no writ). "[A] 'property owner' is entitled to both a condemnation award and moving expenses. Further, in construing a statute, it is presumed that several provisions relating to the same subject were intended to be consistent and to operate in harmony. Therefore, considering our decision above, that 'property owner' as used in [Prop. Code] §21.042 includes a lessee for years, presuming the legislature used the term 'property owner' consistently, and concluding the term 'property owner' rather than 'owner' was used to symbolize the transfer of the provisions from the civil statutes to the Property Code, we hold 'property owner,' as used in [Prop. Code] §21.043, includes lessees for years."

PROP §21.044. DAMAGES FROM TEMPORARY POSSESSION

(a) If a court finally determines that a condemnor who has taken possession of property pending litigation did not have the right to condemn the property, the court may award to the property owner the damages that resulted from the temporary possession.

(b) The court may order the payment of damages awarded under this section from the award or other money deposited with the court. However, if the award paid to or appropriated by the property owner exceeds the court's final determination of the value of the property, the court shall order the property owner to return the excess to the condemnor.

History of Prop. Code §21.044: Acts 1983, 68th Leg., ch. 576, §1, eff. Jan. 1, 1984. Source: TRCS art. 3268.

CHARTS

See timetable, "Condemnation Procedure," p. 1536.

ANNOTATIONS

State v. First Interstate Bank, 880 S.W.2d 427, 430 (Tex.App.—Austin 1994, writ denied). "With regard to [Prop. Code] §21.044(b) ..., we find no similar justification for departing from the presumption that the term 'property owner,' as used therein, excludes mortgagees. Section 21.044(b) operates in conjunction with [Prop. Code] §21.021, the latter being a provision that allows a condemnor to acquire possession of the property pending further litigation after the commissioners' award. *At 431:* Given that a mortgagee ordinarily has no right of possession and, that the deposit is for the benefit of the condemnor who has sufficient means of protecting himself against any loss, we see no justifying rationale for our construing §21.044(b) contrary to its presumed meaning, which excludes mortgagees from its scope."

Eppoleto v. Bournias, 764 S.W.2d 284, 286 (Tex. App.—Waco 1988, orig. proceeding). "Plainly, a determination of the amounts that relators are entitled to recover as reasonable and necessary fees and expenses and damages to land presents questions of fact. We hold that relators are entitled to a jury on the trial of these issues."

Houston Lighting & Power Co. v. Klein ISD, 739 S.W.2d 508, 518 (Tex.App.—Houston [14th Dist.] 1987, writ denied). Section 21.044(a) "provides that if a court determines that a condemnor who has taken possession of property pending litigation did not have the right to condemn the property, the court may award the property owner the damages that resulted from the temporary possession. Texas courts have construed this language as limiting condemnation damages to the market value of the property itself." *See also* ***Southwestern Bell Tel. Co. v. Gordon***, 705 S.W.2d 767, 769 (Tex.App.—Houston [14th Dist.] 1986, writ ref'd n.r.e.) (§21.044 makes no provision for attorney fees and costs).

PROP §21.045. TITLE ACQUIRED

Except where otherwise expressly provided by law, the interest acquired by a condemnor under this chapter does not include the fee simple title to real property,

either public or private. An interest acquired by a condemnor is not lost by the forfeiture or expiration of the condemnor's charter and is subject to an extension of the charter or the grant of a new charter without a new condemnation.

History of Prop. Code §21.045: Acts 1983, 68th Leg., ch. 576, §1, eff. Jan. 1, 1984. Source: TRCS art. 3270.

ANNOTATIONS

Brunson v. State, 418 S.W.2d 504, 506 (Tex.1967). Condemnor "elected to condemn a lesser estate in the nature of a right-of-way easement over [condemnee's] land. The easement thus acquired carried with it the right of the State to remove any improvements on the land which would interfere with the full and beneficial use of the easement rights but did not take away the subsisting ownership of the landowner in the improvements and his right to remove them. [¶] 'Where the fee simple absolute title to land has been acquired the condemnor acquires all appurtenances thereto, buildings thereon, minerals lying beneath the surface, waters thereon.... Where only an easement is acquired the owner retains title to the land and all that is ordinarily considered part of the land.'"

Muhle v. New York, Tex. & Mexican Ry., 25 S.W. 607, 608 (Tex.1894). "[U]pon a permanent abandonment of the use for which the condemnation had been had, the land is 'relieved of the burden cast upon it, and the owner of the fee is restored to his complete dominion over it.' *At 609:* [P], as the owner of the fee, had the right to the dominion and control of the property, subject only to the use for which it had been condemned. So long as it was not appropriated to that use, [P] was entitled to its possession or enjoyment. It was not necessary for her to show a fee simple title in order to recover possession."

PROP §21.046. RELOCATION ASSISTANCE PROGRAM

(a) A department, agency, instrumentality, or political subdivision of this state shall provide a relocation advisory service for an individual, a family, a business concern, a farming or ranching operation, or a nonprofit organization that is compatible with the Federal Uniform Relocation Assistance and Real Property Acquisition Policies Act of 1970, 42 U.S.C.A. 4601, et seq.

(b) This state or a political subdivision of this state shall, as a cost of acquiring real property, pay moving expenses and rental supplements, make relocation payments, provide financial assistance to acquire replacement housing, and compensate for expenses incidental to the transfer of the property if an individual, a family, the personal property of a business, a farming or ranching operation, or a nonprofit organization is displaced in connection with the acquisition.

(c) A department, agency, instrumentality, or political subdivision of this state that initiates a program under Subsection (b) shall adopt rules relating to the administration of the program.

(d) Neither this state nor a political subdivision of this state may authorize expenditures under Subsection (b) that exceed payments authorized under the Federal Uniform Relocation Assistance and Real Property Acquisition Policies Act of 1970, 42 U.S.C.A. 4601, et seq.

(e) If a person moves or discontinues the person's business, moves personal property, or moves from the person's dwelling as a direct result of code enforcement, rehabilitation, or a demolition program, the person is considered to be displaced because of the acquisition of real property.

History of Prop. Code §21.046: Acts 1983, 68th Leg., ch. 576, §1, eff. Jan. 1, 1984. Amended by Acts 2011, 82nd Leg., ch. 81, §16, eff. Sept. 1, 2011. Source: TRCS art. 3266, §§1, 1A, 2.

ANNOTATIONS

Southwestern Bell Tel., L.P. v. Harris Cty. Toll Rd. Auth., 282 S.W.3d 59, 63-64 (Tex.2009). A telephone company that was forced to relocate its facilities due to road construction demanded reimbursement from the county and its toll-road authority. Held: Because telephone company was a licensee through Util. Code §181.082 and held no vested property interest, such as easement, the county was not required to pay for relocation of the telephone company's facilities.

PROP §21.047. ASSESSMENT OF COSTS & FEES

(a) Special commissioners may adjudge the costs of an eminent domain proceeding against any party. If the commissioners award greater damages than the condemnor offered to pay before the proceedings began or if the decision of the commissioners is appealed and a court awards greater damages than the commissioners awarded, the condemnor shall pay all costs. If the commissioners' award or the court's determination of the damages is less than or equal to the amount the condemnor offered before proceedings began, the property owner shall pay the costs.

(b) A condemnor shall pay the initial cost of serving a property owner with notice of a condemnation

proceeding. If the property owner is ordered to pay the costs of the proceeding, the condemnor may recover the expense of notice from the property owner as part of the costs.

(c) A court that has jurisdiction of an eminent domain proceeding may tax $10 or more as a reasonable fee for each special commissioner as part of the court costs of the proceeding.

(d) If a court hearing a suit under this chapter determines that a condemnor did not make a bona fide offer to acquire the property from the property owner voluntarily as required by Section 21.0113, the court shall abate the suit, order the condemnor to make a bona fide offer, and order the condemnor to pay:

(1) all costs as provided by Subsection (a); and

(2) any reasonable attorney's fees and other professional fees incurred by the property owner that are directly related to the violation.

History of Prop. Code §21.047: Acts 1983, 68th Leg., ch. 576, §1, eff. Jan. 1, 1984. Amended by Acts 2011, 82nd Leg., ch. 81, §§17, 18, eff. Sept. 1, 2011. Source: TRCS arts. 3266, subdivs. 3-5, 3267.

CHARTS

See timetable, "Condemnation Procedure," p. 1536.

ANNOTATIONS

In re Electric Transmission Tex., LLC, No. 13-15-00423-CV (Tex.App.—Corpus Christi 2015, orig. proceeding) (memo op.; 11-2-15). "[D] contends that ... §21.047(d) provides the trial court with jurisdiction and discretion to order a continuance of the condemnation proceeding. [D] argues that §21.047 was amended in 2011 to include subsection (d), and previous case law does not consider this section. [¶] In terms of the 2011 amendments adding section (d), we presume lawmakers enact statutes with complete knowledge of existing law. [¶] Nothing in the legislative text suggests that §21.047(d) contemplates judicial intervention before the appointment of the special commissioners. [¶] Further, nothing in the structure of the eminent domain statute as a whole suggests that §21.047(d) allows judicial intervention before the appointment of the special commissioners. The eminent domain statute is divided into three subchapters on jurisdiction, procedure, and damages and costs. Section 21.047 ... is not located in the subsections that pertain to jurisdiction and procedure. [¶] [W]e conclude that §21.047(d) does not vest the trial court with jurisdiction to [order a continuance of the condemnation proceeding]."

In re State, 85 S.W.3d 871, 875 (Tex.App.—Tyler 2002, orig. proceeding). "After reviewing the applicable law, we find no statute authorizing a trial court to award expenses to special commissioners during the administrative phase of a condemnation proceeding. Therefore, we hold that the order granting the Commissioners' recovery of their expenses from the State was an abuse of discretion because the trial court lacked jurisdiction to enter the order."

State v. Schmidt, 894 S.W.2d 543, 545 (Tex.App.—Austin 1995, no writ), *overruled in part on other grounds*, ***Hubenak v. San Jacinto Gas Transmission Co.***, 141 S.W.3d 172 (Tex.2004). "The obvious purpose of provisions such as §21.047(a) is to encourage the condemnor to offer the true value of the land and to discourage the property owner from making extravagant demands in their attempt to agree through negotiations *preceding* the filing of the statutory proceedings. [¶] The text of §21.047(a) fits the common pattern: the amount *finally* recovered by the property owner, as damages, determines the issue of adjudging costs. If the property owner finally recovers more than the condemnor's offer, whether by the administrative award of the special commissioner's or the judgment of the trial court, then 'the condemnor shall pay all costs'; but if the award of the commissioners or the trial court, whichever is final, is equal to or less than the amount of the condemnor's offer, 'the property owner shall pay the costs.' We see nothing ambiguous in the statutory text *when construed in light of the statutory purpose indicated*. The words 'all costs' reject the implication [condemnor] imputes to the text in order to argue for a division of costs in some manner, an implication that in our view contradicts both the statutory purpose and language."

PROP §21.048. STATEMENT OF DAMAGES & COSTS

After the special commissioners in an eminent domain proceeding have assessed the damages, they shall:

(1) make a written statement of their decision stating the damages, date it, sign it, and file it and all other papers connected with the proceeding with the court on the day the decision is made or on the next working day after the day the decision is made; and

(2) make and sign a written statement of the accrued costs of the proceeding, naming the party

against whom the costs are adjudged, and file the statement with the court.

History of Prop. Code §21.048: Acts 1983, 68th Leg., ch. 576, §1, eff. Jan. 1, 1984. Amended by Acts 1984, 68th Leg., 2nd C.S., ch. 18, §1(c), eff. Oct. 2, 1984. Source: TRCS arts. 3265, subdiv. 5, 3266, subdiv. 5.

CHARTS

See timetable, "Condemnation Procedure," p. 1536.

ANNOTATIONS

State v. Titan Land Dev., Inc., 468 S.W.3d 705, 709 (Tex.App.—Houston [1st Dist.] 2015, pet. denied). See annotation under Property Code §21.018, *Timing of Objections*, p. 103.

State v. Garland, 963 S.W.2d 95, 100 (Tex.App.—Austin 1998, pet. denied). "The trial court is specifically authorized to receive and file the commissioners' award and, upon the timely filing of a party's objections, to cite the adverse party and 'try the case in the same manner as other civil causes.' If the trial court is to carry out its statutory duty, and if an appeal to the trial court is to be an adequate remedy for errors committed during the proceedings before the commissioners, the court must, without interfering in those areas specifically delegated to the commissioners, be able to ensure that the appeal process is not thwarted by a failure to file the decision in court. [¶] [A] trial court has the power to order that the obligation to file the commissioners' decision in court be met. To allow a court to take such actions as are necessary to ensure the filing of the decision does not contravene any statutory language, does not interfere with those parts of the process specifically left to the commissioners' discretion, and furthers the purposes of protecting the landowner while simultaneously promoting condemnation proceedings as a swift alternative to the ordinary judicial processes available to the condemnor."

PROP §21.049. NOTICE OF DECISION OF SPECIAL COMMISSIONERS

The judge of a court hearing a proceeding under this chapter shall inform the clerk of the court as to a decision by the special commissioners on the day the decision is filed or on the next working day after the day the decision is filed. Not later than the next working day after the day the decision is filed, the clerk shall send notice of the decision by certified or registered United States mail, return receipt requested, to the parties in the proceeding, or to their attorneys of record, at their addresses of record.

History of Prop. Code §21.049: Acts 1984, 68th Leg., 2nd C.S., ch. 18, §1(d), eff. Oct. 2, 1984. Source: TRCS arts. 3265, subdiv. 5.

CHARTS

See timetable, "Condemnation Procedure," p. 1536.

ANNOTATIONS

John v. State, 826 S.W.2d 138, 140 (Tex.1992). Section 21.049 "must be construed as mandatory because it is part of the statutory scheme authorizing eminent domain actions and it is designed to protect the landowner. Moreover, since the language of the statute is clear and unambiguous, it should be enforced as written, giving its terms their usual and ordinary meaning, and without resorting to the rules of construction. Therefore, in condemnation cases, the clerk must comply with the notice provisions. *At 141:* [N]otice of the condemnation hearing is not sufficient notice that the landowners' time to object to the condemnation award has begun to run. In the case at bar, the clerk failed to notify [condemnee] that the special commissioners' award had been filed with the court until after the deadline to object had passed. As a result, [condemnee's] time to object to the special commissioners' award is tolled until the clerk sends the required notice pursuant to §21.049…." *See also* ***Oncor Elec. Delivery Co. v. Schunke***, No. 04-13-00067-CV (Tex.App.—San Antonio 2013, pet. dism'd) (memo op.; 12-18-13).

State v. Garland, 963 S.W.2d 95, 100-01 (Tex. App.—Austin 1998, pet. denied). "Because the commissioners' decision is to be filed within one working day of its issuance, and the court clerk is to send notice within one working day of filing, all parties should receive notice of filing from the court clerk within a few days after the commissioners issue their decision. If any party does not receive such notice within a short period, he is alerted to check on the filing of the decision and, if necessary, ask the trial court to use its powers—be they termed 'judicial' or 'administrative'—to compel the filing of the decision."

Sections 21.050-21.060 reserved for expansion

SUBCHAPTER D. JUDGMENT

PROP §21.061. JUDGMENT ON COMMISSIONERS' FINDINGS

If no party in a condemnation proceeding files timely objections to the findings of the special commissioners, the judge of the court that has jurisdiction of the proceeding shall adopt the commissioners' findings

as the judgment of the court, record the judgment in the minutes of the court, and issue the process necessary to enforce the judgment.

History of Prop. Code §21.061: Acts 1983, 68th Leg., ch. 576, §1, eff. Jan. 1, 1984. Source: TRCS art. 3266, §7.

CHARTS

See timetable, "Condemnation Procedure," p. 1536.

ANNOTATIONS

Pearson v. State, 315 S.W.2d 935, 938 (Tex.1958). TRCS art. 3266, §7, now Prop. Code §21.061, "requires the county judge, if no objections are filed within ten days, to cause the award to be recorded in the minutes and make the same the judgment of the court. No jurisdiction is conferred upon the court to do anything more than accept and adopt the award as its judgment, and this follows by operation of law and the ministerial act of the county judge. There is nothing which the court, as distinguished from the county judge in his administrative capacity, can hear and determine by the exercise of its judicial powers. It seems clear to us, therefore, that an order directing that the award be recorded and making the same the judgment of the court does not constitute a judgment in a civil case, and that there is no right of appeal therefrom."

PROP §21.062. WRIT OF POSSESSION

If a condemnor in a condemnation proceeding has taken possession of property pending litigation and the court finally decides that the condemnor does not have the right to condemn the property, the court shall order the condemnor to surrender possession of the property and issue a writ of possession to the property owner.

History of Prop. Code §21.062: Acts 1983, 68th Leg., ch. 576, §1, eff. Jan. 1, 1984. Source: TRCS art. 3268.

CHARTS

See timetable, "Condemnation Procedure," p. 1536.

PROP §21.063. APPEAL

(a) The appeal of a judgment in a condemnation proceeding is as in other civil cases.

(b) A court hearing an appeal from the decision of a trial court in a condemnation proceeding may not suspend the judgment of the trial court pending the appeal.

History of Prop. Code §21.063: Acts 1983, 68th Leg., ch. 576, §1, eff. Jan. 1, 1984. Source: TRCS art. 3268.

ANNOTATIONS

Town of Flower Mound v. Mockingbird Pipeline, L.P., 353 S.W.3d 230, 237-38 (Tex.App.—Fort Worth 2011, pet. granted, judgm't vacated w.r.m.). "Although [condemnee] argues that an interlocutory appeal is permissible here because [Prop.] [C]ode §21.063(a) states that '[t]he appeal of a judgment in a condemnation proceeding is as in other civil cases,' not all civil cases qualify for an interlocutory appeal—only those that meet the requirements set out in [CPRC] §51.014 or other statutory provisions permitting interlocutory appeals. And again, while the probate court may have been functioning with the same authority as a county or district court in this matter, we have found no authority to allow us to write 'probate court' into §51.014(a) to allow an interlocutory appeal from the probate court's decision to deny [condemnee's] plea to the jurisdiction. *At 241:* [B]ased on the plain language of §51.014(a), the 2005 amendments, and the new 2011 amendments, the legislature has clearly demonstrated that it knows how to modify the language of this particular statute when it so desires. This statutory background, combined with the legislature's history of expanding and then contracting the jurisdiction of the statutory probate court in Denton County, supports dismissing the appeal for want of jurisdiction."

State v. Blackstock, 879 S.W.2d 125, 129-30 (Tex. App.—Houston [14th Dist.] 1994, writ denied). Held: If objections to the award are struck, the trial court may return to its administrative capacity, having lost its judicial capacity, and may enter judgment on the award as if objections had not been filed.

PROP §21.064. INJUNCTIVE RELIEF

(a) A court hearing a suit covered by Section 21.003 of this code may grant injunctive relief under the rules of equity.

(b) Instead of granting an injunction under this section, a court may require a condemnor to provide security adequate to compensate the property owner for damages that might result from the condemnation.

History of Prop. Code §21.064: Acts 1983, 68th Leg., ch. 576, §1, eff. Jan. 1, 1984. Source: TRCS art. 3269.

ANNOTATIONS

Harris Cty. v. Gordon, 616 S.W.2d 167, 169 (Tex.1981). "The Court of Civil Appeals wrote that the [condemnor] did not have the authority to condemn for a fee simple, and on this basis granted the tempo-

rary injunction. However, this action ignores the landowner's remedy [that] provides for damages to the landowner for the use of the land when the condemnor does not have the right to condemn. The only limit on this award is the value of the property. [Landowners] have an adequate remedy at law if it is later determined that [condemnor] did not have authority to condemn for a fee simple. Therefore, the Court of Civil Appeals erred in granting the injunction on the grounds stated."

Tonahill v. Gulf States Utils. Co., 446 S.W.2d 301, 302-03 (Tex.1969). "The right of appeal affords petitioner an adequate remedy for anything that may occur in the condemnation proceedings up to and including the award of the special commissioners. There was no occasion then for the district court to enjoin the proceedings, and the temporary injunction was properly dissolved by the Court of Civil Appeals."

PROP §21.065. VESTED INTEREST

A judgment of a court under this chapter vests a right granted to a condemnor.

History of Prop. Code §21.065: Acts 1983, 68th Leg., ch. 576, §1, eff. Jan. 1, 1984. Source: TRCS art. 3271.

CHARTS

See timetable, "Condemnation Procedure," p. 1536.

Sections 21.066-21.100 blank

SUBCHAPTER E. REPURCHASE OF REAL PROPERTY FROM CONDEMNING ENTITY

PROP §21.101. RIGHT OF REPURCHASE

(a) A person from whom a real property interest is acquired by an entity through eminent domain for a public use, or that person's heirs, successors, or assigns, is entitled to repurchase the property as provided by this subchapter if:

(1) the public use for which the property was acquired through eminent domain is canceled before the property is used for that public use;

(2) no actual progress is made toward the public use for which the property was acquired between the date of acquisition and the 10th anniversary of that date; or

(3) the property becomes unnecessary for the public use for which the property was acquired, or a substantially similar public use, before the 10th anniversary of the date of acquisition.

(b) In this section, "actual progress" means the completion of two or more of the following actions:

(1) the performance of a significant amount of labor to develop the property or other property acquired for the same public use project for which the property owner's property was acquired;

(2) the provision of a significant amount of materials to develop the property or other property acquired for the same public use project for which the property owner's property was acquired;

(3) the hiring of and performance of a significant amount of work by an architect, engineer, or surveyor to prepare a plan or plat that includes the property or other property acquired for the same public use project for which the property owner's property was acquired;

(4) application for state or federal funds to develop the property or other property acquired for the same public use project for which the property owner's property was acquired;

(5) application for a state or federal permit to develop the property or other property acquired for the same public use project for which the property owner's property was acquired;

(6) the acquisition of a tract or parcel of real property adjacent to the property for the same public use project for which the owner's property was acquired; or

(7) for a governmental entity, the adoption by a majority of the entity's governing body at a public hearing of a development plan for a public use project that indicates that the entity will not complete more than one action described by Subdivisions (1)-(6) before the 10th anniversary of the date of acquisition of the property.

(c) A district court may determine all issues in any suit regarding the repurchase of a real property interest acquired through eminent domain by the former property owner or the owner's heirs, successors, or assigns.

History of Prop. Code §21.101: Acts 2003, 78th Leg., ch. 1307, §2, eff. Jan. 1, 2004. Amended by Acts 2011, 82nd Leg., ch. 81, §19, eff. Sept. 1, 2011.

PROP §21.102. NOTICE TO PREVIOUS PROPERTY OWNER REQUIRED

Not later than the 180th day after the date an entity that acquired a real property interest through eminent domain determines that the former property owner is entitled to repurchase the property under Section 21.101, the entity shall send by certified mail, return receipt requested, to the property owner or the owner's heirs, successors, or assigns a notice containing:

(1) an identification, which is not required to be a legal description, of the property that was acquired;

(2) an identification of the public use for which the property had been acquired and a statement that:

(A) the public use was canceled before the property was used for the public use;

(B) no actual progress was made toward the public use; or

(C) the property became unnecessary for the public use, or a substantially similar public use, before the 10th anniversary of the date of acquisition; and

(3) a description of the person's right under this subchapter to repurchase the property.

History of Prop. Code §21.102: Acts 2003, 78th Leg., ch. 1307, §2, eff. Jan. 1, 2004. Amended by Acts 2011, 82nd Leg., ch. 81, §19, eff. Sept. 1, 2011.

CHARTS

See timetable, "Condemnation Procedure," p. 1536.

PROP §21.1021. REQUESTS FOR INFORMATION REGARDING CONDEMNED PROPERTY

(a) On or after the 10th anniversary of the date on which real property was acquired by an entity through eminent domain, a property owner or the owner's heirs, successors, or assigns may request that the condemning entity make a determination and provide a statement and other relevant information regarding:

(1) whether the public use for which the property was acquired was canceled before the property was used for the public use;

(2) whether any actual progress was made toward the public use between the date of acquisition and the 10th anniversary of that date, including an itemized description of the progress made, if applicable; and

(3) whether the property became unnecessary for the public use, or a substantially similar public use, before the 10th anniversary of the date of acquisition.

(b) A request under this section must contain sufficient detail to allow the entity to identify the specific tract of land in relation to which the information is sought.

(c) Not later than the 90th day following the date of receipt of the request for information, the entity shall send a written response by certified mail, return receipt requested, to the requestor.

History of Prop. Code §21.1021: Acts 2011, 82nd Leg., ch. 81, §19, eff. Sept. 1, 2011.

PROP §21.1022. LIMITATIONS PERIOD FOR REPURCHASE RIGHT

Notwithstanding Section 21.103, the right to repurchase provided by this subchapter is extinguished on the first anniversary of the expiration of the period for an entity to provide notice under Section 21.102 if the entity:

(1) is required to provide notice under Section 21.102;

(2) makes a good faith effort to locate and provide notice to each person entitled to notice before the expiration of the deadline for providing notice under that section; and

(3) does not receive a response to any notice provided under that section in the period for response prescribed by Section 21.103.

History of Prop. Code §21.1022: Acts 2011, 82nd Leg., ch. 81, §19, eff. Sept. 1, 2011.

PROP §21.103. RESALE OF PROPERTY; PRICE

(a) Not later than the 180th day after the date of the postmark on a notice sent under Section 21.102 or a response to a request made under Section 21.1021 that indicates that the property owner, or the owner's heirs, successors, or assigns, is entitled to repurchase the property interest in accordance with Section 21.101, the property owner or the owner's heirs, successors, or assigns must notify the entity of the person's intent to repurchase the property interest under this subchapter.

(b) As soon as practicable after receipt of a notice of intent to repurchase under Subsection (a), the entity shall offer to sell the property interest to the person for the price paid to the owner by the entity at the time the entity acquired the property through eminent domain. The person's right to repurchase the property expires on the 90th day after the date on which the entity makes the offer.

History of Prop. Code §21.103: Acts 2003, 78th Leg., ch. 1307, §2, eff. Jan. 1, 2004. Amended by Acts 2011, 82nd Leg., ch. 81, §19, eff. Sept. 1, 2011.

CHARTS

See timetable, "Condemnation Procedure," p. 1536.

CHAPTER 22. TRESPASS TO TRY TITLE

Subchapter A. General Provisions

SUBCHAPTER A. GENERAL PROVISIONS

PROP §22.001. TRESPASS TO TRY TITLE

(a) A trespass to try title action is the method of determining title to lands, tenements, or other real property.

(b) The action of ejectment is not available in this state.

History of Prop. Code §22.001: Acts 1983, 68th Leg., ch. 576, §1, eff. Jan. 1, 1984. Source: TRCS art. 7364.

See also CPRC §§15.011, 16.024-16.034, 17.002, 37.004; Prop. Code ch. 24; TRCP 783-809.

ANNOTATIONS

Generally

Rogers v. Ricane Enters., 884 S.W.2d 763, 768 (Tex.1994). "A trespass to try title action is a procedure by which claims to title or the right of possession may be adjudicated. To recover in a trespass to try title action, the plaintiff must recover upon the strength of his own title. The plaintiff may recover (1) by proving a regular chain of conveyances from the sovereign, (2) by proving a superior title out of a common source, (3) by proving title by limitations, or (4) by proving prior possession, and that the possession has not been abandoned." *See also* ***Kennedy Con., Inc. v. Forman***, 316 S.W.3d 129, 135 (Tex.App.—Houston [14th Dist.] 2010, no pet.) (Ps must prevail based on strength of own title, not on weakness of D's title); ***Cullins v. Foster***, 171 S.W.3d 521, 532 (Tex.App.—Houston [14th Dist.] 2005, pet. denied) (P in trespass-to-try-title suit may rely on title acquired after institution of suit, if she asserts such title by amended pleading).

Dougherty v. Humphrey, 424 S.W.2d 617, 621 (Tex. 1968). "[I]f a person sues in trespass to try title and seeks to obtain relief which is unavailable to him in trespass to try title, he is not barred by that judgment from thereafter seeking proper relief." *See also* ***Ramirez v. Wood***, 577 S.W.2d 278, 286 (Tex.App.—Corpus Christi 1978, no writ) (judgment that attempts to adjudicate title would not be binding on any person who was not a party to suit).

I-10 Colony, Inc. v. Lee, 393 S.W.3d 467, 475 (Tex. App.—Houston [14th Dist.] 2012, pet. denied). "[W]hether or not title is awarded in a particular case, courts ... appear to agree that if resolution of a dispute does not require a determination of which party owned title at a particular time, the dispute could properly be raised in a declaratory judgment action; in other words, if the determination only *prospectively* implicates title, then the dispute does not have to be brought as a trespass-to-try-title action."

Teon Mgmt. v. Turquoise Bay Corp., 357 S.W.3d 719, 723 (Tex.App.—Eastland 2011, pet. denied). "[D] argues first that, because [P's] suit was primarily one to determine title to land, it was required to file a trespass to try title action rather than a suit for declaratory judgment. *At 724:* When the trial court found that [P's] leases were valid, the court was not resolving a question about the validity of those leases at the time of their execution or whether they were otherwise proper and enforceable. ... When the trial court found that [P] was the proper operator, it was because [P] had timely commenced reworking operations.... When it found that [P] and not [D] was entitled to the suspended runs, this was because [P's] leases were still in existence. Each of these decisions is a title determination. *At 727:* The dispositive question is: What is the nature of the dispute? [T]his case involved rival claims to the mineral estate, and every substantive issue was resolved when the trial court determined who owned the mineral estate. It was, therefore, a title determination, and [P] should have proceeded with a trespass to try title suit."

Aspenwood Apt. Corp. v. Coinmach, Inc., 349 S.W.3d 621, 636 (Tex.App.—Houston [1st Dist.] 2011), *rev'd in part on other grounds*, 417 S.W.3d 909 (Tex.2013). "[D]etermination of a right of possession is not a determination of title and, where the resolution of a title dispute is intertwined with the issue of possession, possession may not be adjudicated without first determining title. *At 637:* [D's] right of possession, if any such right existed, arose solely from the existence of some kind of leasehold. Thus, determination of [D's] right of possession necessarily required the resolution of the title questions surrounding the validity of the lease. [¶] The justice of the peace did not

have jurisdiction to determine [D's] ultimate right of possession under the lease. Thus, the proceedings in the justice court and the county court at law that allowed [D] to remain in possession of the [property] were not a determination of [D's] ultimate rights, if any, under the lease—they merely addressed the issue of immediate possession while [P] sought resolution of the issues surrounding the status of the original lease [in the instant trespass-to-try title suit]."

State v. BP Am. Prod., 290 S.W.3d 345, 352 (Tex. App.—Austin 2009, pet. denied). P's ouster "claim implicates sovereign immunity, [Ds] argue, because it seeks to adjudicate the validity of the State's claim to the disputed property and obtain a judgment that [P] owns the disputed property and is entitled to possession. In support of these contentions, [Ds] rely principally on ***State v. Lain***, … 349 S.W.2d 579 (Tex.1961). *At 357-58:* Under ***Lain***, a suit for land against a state official in his official capacity is not barred by sovereign immunity unless and until it is shown that the State actually has a superior right of possession in the property. [¶] The central holding of ***Lain*** … is that sovereign immunity does not bar a plaintiff from suing a state official in possession of property the plaintiff claims to determine, as between those parties, which party has the superior title or right of possession, and to recover possession of the property from the official if the plaintiff prevails. [T]he ***Lain*** court squarely rejected the notion that the mere fact the State *claimed* a right to possession controlled whether sovereign immunity applied. Instead, the trial court, according to ***Lain***, has not only subject-matter jurisdiction but the 'duty … to hear evidence on the issue of title and right of possession and to delay action on the plea until the evidence is in.'" *See also* ***Parker v. Hunegnaw***, 364 S.W.3d 398, 403 (Tex.App.—Houston [14th Dist.] 2012, no pet.); ***City of Dallas v. CKS Asset Mgmt.***, 345 S.W.3d 199, 203-04 (Tex.App.—Dallas 2011, pet. denied).

Florey v. Estate of McConnell, 212 S.W.3d 439, 449 (Tex.App.—Austin 2006, pet. denied). "A trespass-to-try title suit seeks title and possession of real property, and imposes unique and somewhat burdensome procedural requirements. [P's] suit, by contrast, seeks adjudication of the validity of [lien claimant's] deed of trust as it impacts his entitlement to proceeds from the sale of the … property. Although a declaration regarding the validity of the deed of trust could ultimately have impacted title and possessory rights to the property, we doubt that the legislature intended for the trespass-to-try title statute to displace or subsume every statutory or common law claim (*e.g.*, suits to rescind deeds) having such an impact."

Walston v. Lockhart, 62 S.W.3d 257, 262 (Tex. App.—Waco 2002, pet. denied). "If it is not proven that the defendant is a mere trespasser, the plaintiff must establish not only title to an undivided interest in the property but also that the defendant has no title to any interest in the property." *See also* ***Reed v. Turner***, 489 S.W.2d 373, 381 (Tex.App.—Tyler 1972, writ ref'd n.r.e.) (P should not include any land or interest in land except that which is in dispute at the time).

American S&L Ass'n v. Musick, 517 S.W.2d 627, 630 (Tex.App.—Houston [14th Dist.] 1974), *rev'd on other grounds*, 531 S.W.2d 581 (Tex.1975). "[W]hen a plaintiff in trespass to try title claims under a deed from the defendant, the defendant serves as the common grantor. The plaintiff does not have to prove title in the defendant at the time of the deed, and the defendant is estopped to deny it."

Adverse Possession

Natural Gas Pipeline Co. v. Pool, 124 S.W.3d 188, 192-93 (Tex.2003). "A mineral estate, even when severed from the surface estate, may be adversely possessed under the various statutes of limitations. Once severance occurs, possession of the surface alone will not constitute adverse possession of minerals. Generally, courts across the country including Texas courts have said that in order to mature title by limitations to a mineral estate, actual possession of the minerals must occur. In the case of oil and gas, that means drilling and production of oil or gas."

Rhodes v. Cahill, 802 S.W.2d 643, 645 (Tex.1990). "'[W]here a party relies upon naked possession alone as the foundation for his adverse claim, it must be such an actual occupancy as the law recognizes as sufficient, if persisted in for a long enough period of time, to cut off the true owner's right of recovery. [¶] [S]uch possession must not only be actual, but also visible, continuous, notorious, distinct, hostile (i.e., adverse), and of such a character as to indicate unmistakably an assertion of a claim of exclusive ownership in the occupant.' [¶] One seeking to establish title to land by virtue of the statute of limitations has the burden of proving every fact essential to that claim by a preponderance of the evidence. [¶] '[T]he possession must be of such character as to indicate *unmistakably* an as-

sertion of a claim of *exclusive* ownership in the occupant.' *At 646:* '[T]he question of adverse possession normally is a question of fact, so only in rare instances is a court justified in holding that adverse possession has been established as a matter of law.'" *See also* ***Tran v. Macha***, 213 S.W.3d 913, 914-15 (Tex.2006) ("hostile" use requires adverse possession, not just adverse beliefs; there must be intent to claim property as one's own to the exclusion of all others).

Rife v. Kerr, 513 S.W.3d 601, 616-17 (Tex. App.—San Antonio 2016, pet. denied). "'The adverse possession standard that courts apply to cotenants differs from the standard that courts impose between strangers.' 'Cotenants must surmount a more stringent requirement because acts of ownership which, if done by a stranger, would per se be a disseizin, are not necessarily such when co-tenants share an undivided interest.' In an adverse possession claim between cotenants, the proponent must prove ouster—unequivocal, unmistakable, and hostile acts the possessor took to disseize other cotenants. A cotenant's possession of property is not adverse until the tenancy has been repudiated, and 'notice of such repudiation has been brought home to the titleholder.'"

Conley v. Comstock Oil & Gas, LP, 356 S.W.3d 755, 765 (Tex.App.—Beaumont 2011, no pet.). "[P] argues that the doctrine of presumed lost deed is not a proper vehicle for asserting an adverse claim under a different chain of title. [P] distinguishes the doctrine of presumed lost deed from the adverse possession statutes. The doctrine of presumed lost deed or grant, which is also referred to as title by circumstantial evidence, has been described as a common law form of adverse possession. Its purpose is 'to settle titles where the land was understood to belong to one who does not have a complete record title, but has claimed a long time.' 'The rule is essential to the ascertainment of the very truth of ancient transactions. Without it, numberless valid land titles could not be upheld.' The doctrine has been applied to establish title in a party who failed to prove title under the adverse possession statutes. *At 766:* The long period of time in which the [original] grantees were claiming the neighboring land supports a conclusion that they acquiesced in the claims of the persons who claimed title under the 15 ancient surveys at issue in this case. Acquiescence is generally a fact issue but where 'the deeds are so ancient and the evidence is undisputed' it may be established as a matter of law."

Bernal v. Chavez, 198 S.W.3d 15, 19-20 (Tex. App.—El Paso 2006, no pet.). "[U]se of another individual's land with the acquiescence of the landowner does not ripen into adverse possession unless the evidence shows that the landowner was given notice of the adverse possession claim. [¶] Possession of a donee under a parol gift of land is generally regarded as hostile from its inception and indicates an intent to take as owner. Possession under such a gift is adverse and not permissive because it is unenforceable due to its violation of the statute of frauds." Held: Testimony that land had been a parol gift to claimant and the denial of permissive use of the property support trial court's award of title to claimant.

Cherokee Water Co. v. Freeman, 145 S.W.3d 809, 816 (Tex.App.—Texarkana 2004, pet. denied). "Real estate is considered to be unique. The fact that a party makes a claim of adverse possession to one lot does not require the party to assert an adverse possession claim to the adjoining lot or be forever barred. Essentially, [P] is arguing that, even though the previous suit sought to establish its ownership of [all land conveyed pursuant to that general warranty deed], [D] was required to pursue his adverse possession claim concerning [adjacent property], a separate lot. We disagree. [¶] We find that [adjacent property] is a separate and distinct parcel of real estate from [all land conveyed pursuant to that general warranty deed] and as such it does not involve the same subject matter as the previous litigation. Therefore, res judicata does not preclude [D] from asserting his adverse possession claim to [adjacent property]."

Harlow v. Giles, 132 S.W.3d 641, 646-47 (Tex. App.—Eastland 2004, pet. denied). "A party seeking to establish title to land by virtue of the statute of limitations has the burden of proving every fact essential to that claim by a preponderance of the evidence. The party claiming adverse possession must prove an actual and visible appropriation of the land for 10 or more consecutive years under the 10-year statute and for 25 or more consecutive years under the 25-year statute. The use of the land 'must constitute an actual and visible appropriation of the land such that the true owner is given notice of a hostile claim.' The possession must be 'actual, visible, continuous, notorious, distinct, hostile, and of such character as to indicate unmistakably an assertion of a claim of exclusive ownership in the occupant.' Sporadic, irregular, and occasional use of land

does not satisfy the adverse possession statutes. Exclusive possession of the land is required to support an adverse possession claim; the adverse possession claimant must wholly exclude the owner from the property. The question of adverse possession normally is a question of fact, so only in rare instances is a court justified in holding that adverse possession has been established as a matter of law." *See also* ***Tran v. Macha***, 213 S.W.3d 913, 914 (Tex.2006) (possession must indicate unmistakably an assertion of a claim of exclusive ownership in occupant).

Boundary Dispute

Texas Parks & Wildlife Dept. v. Sawyer Trust, 354 S.W.3d 384, 389-90 (Tex.2011). "[P] argues that the claims in this case constitute a boundary dispute and that '[CPRC] §37.004(c) can easily and logically be construed as a legislative waiver of any sovereign immunity that has ever in the past impeded private titleholders' efforts to litigate their boundary disputes against the State.' We disagree that the claims here constitute a boundary dispute. [¶] We need not decide whether §37.004(c) effects a waiver of the State's immunity from suit for boundary disputes because this controversy is not over the boundary between State-owned land and [P]-owned land; rather it is over whether the State owns any land at all. The case involves rival claims to ownership of the entire streambed. Consequently, [P's] suit in substance is one to determine title to land. Such a suit against the State is barred by sovereign immunity absent legislative consent. "

Plumb v. Stuessy, 617 S.W.2d 667, 669 (Tex.1981). "It is established that boundary disputes may be tried by a statutory action of trespass to try title. [¶] The proper test for determining if the case is one of boundary is as follows: If there would have been no case but for the question of boundary, then the case is necessarily a boundary case even though it might involve questions of title. [¶] Since this is a boundary dispute, it was not necessary for [P] to establish his superior title to the property in question in the manner required by a formal trespass to try title action to avoid losing title to his property." *See also* ***Plata v. Guzman***, 571 S.W.2d 408, 412 (Tex.App.—Corpus Christi 1978, writ ref'd n.r.e.) (P has burden to show by preponderance the location of boundary line on ground).

Howland v. Hough, 570 S.W.2d 876, 882 (Tex. 1978). "It is an established rule that the footsteps of the surveyor shall, if possible, be followed, and natural or artificial monuments are to be accepted as controlling over calls for course and distance. It is also permissible to run the calls in reverse order to ascertain the true lines and form a closure, since no greater dignity is accorded to the first call than the last." *See also* ***Zimmerman v. Hall***, 213 S.W.2d 89, 91 (Tex.App.—Eastland 1948, writ ref'd n.r.e.) (second surveyor not required to follow in footsteps of initial surveyor because no record made of boundary).

Great Plains Oil & Gas Co. v. Foundation Oil Co., 153 S.W.2d 452, 458-59 (Tex.1941). "[A]cquiescence in a line other than the true line will not support a finding of an agreement establishing the line as the boundary when there is no other evidence of agreement than acquiescence and when it is affirmatively shown that the use of the line resulted not from agreement but from a mistaken belief of the parties that it was the true line. Similarly, when the true location of the line is conclusively proven, mere acquiescence in another line in the mistaken belief that it is the true line will not support a finding that such other line is the true line." *See also* ***Kirby Lumber Corp. v. Lindsey***, 455 S.W.2d 733, 738-39 (Tex.1970); ***RDG Prtshp. v. Long***, 350 S.W.3d 262, 269 (Tex.App.—San Antonio 2011, no pet.).

Gulf Oil Corp. v. Marathon Oil Co., 152 S.W.2d 711, 714 (Tex.1941). "When there is uncertainty, doubt or dispute as to where the true division line between the lands of the parties may be, they may fix it by parol agreement, which will be mutually binding upon them, even though they were mistaken as to the true location of the line. This is true whether the mistake be of a matter of fact or of law. The existence of uncertainty, doubt or dispute is essential to the validity of such agreement. Actual dispute, however, between the parties is not necessary. It is enough that the location of the line had not been definitely established and is doubtful or uncertain." *See also* ***Higginbotham v. Bagley***, 346 S.W.2d 142, 144 (Tex.App.—Beaumont 1961, writ dism'd).

Stover v. Gilbert, 247 S.W. 841, 843 (Tex.1923). "[M]eander lines of surveys of land adjacent to or bounding upon a stream are not to be considered as boundaries, but they are to follow the general course of the stream, which in itself constitutes the real boundary."

Nabours v. Whiteley, 466 S.W.2d 62, 64 (Tex. App.—Austin 1971, writ ref'd n.r.e.). "[I]f … there is insufficient evidence to establish the line followed by the original surveyor, then ancient boundaries may be proved by evidence of common reputation."

State v. Horton, 454 S.W.2d 847, 853 (Tex.App.—Beaumont 1970, writ ref'd n.r.e.). "'The petition in a boundary suit should describe the land by metes and bounds, and this should be done by each party, *describing the lines by objects, if any, to be found on the ground*. Where the description in the field notes is doubtful, and the objects called for cannot be found on the ground, the pleadings should accurately describe the land as the lines actually exist, and allege that such description is correct.'"

Chain from Sovereign

Davidson v. Gelling, 263 S.W.2d 940, 942 (Tex. 1954). "The fact that [Ps] gratuitously assumed the burden of going back to the sovereignty and may have failed to carry it is no good reason to deprive them of the benefits of the common source rule." *See also* ***Spinks v. Estes***, 546 S.W.2d 390, 392 (Tex.App.—Tyler 1977, writ ref'd n.r.e.) (offer of proof from sovereign does not defeat claim of prior possession).

Coker v. Geisendorff, 370 S.W.3d 8, 13 (Tex. App.—Texarkana 2012, no pet.). "[Ps] argue that they conclusively proved that they had full title to the entirety of the property, showing a regular chain of title from the sovereignty of the soil into themselves. [Ps] provided evidence of transfers through an abstract. [¶] This Court has waded through the chain of title provided through the documentation as presented by [Ps]. Based on this review, we find that the abstract does indeed show a regular and uninterrupted chain of title from the sovereign to [Ps] as to the 131-acre tract. [D] argues that one of the deeds in the early part of the chain of title contains an error in the legal description that spoils the continuity of the chain of title upon which [Ps] rely. However, it is quite apparent that the flaw lies solely within an erroneous distance call…. [¶] Other than this flaw in a distance call in one deed, [D] does not maintain that [Ps'] chain of title is not complete or broken. We note (taking into account that the burden of proof did not rest with him) that in contrast with [Ps'] chain of title, [D's] chain of title has multiple gaps. Thus, we conclude that the trial court was correct in granting a [JNOV] on that jury question, because [Ps] conclusively proved title from the sovereign."

Common Source

Davidson v. Gelling, 263 S.W.2d 940, 942 (Tex. 1954). "Abstracts may … establish a case of common source." *See also* ***Moran Corp. v. Brashear***, 339 S.W.2d 557, 558 (Tex.App.—San Antonio 1960, writ ref'd).

Simmons Hardware Co. v. Davis, 27 S.W. 62, 63 (Tex.1894). "The theory of the doctrine of the common source is that proof of a claim of title by one under another is prima facie evidence, as against the claimant, that the title was at one time in that other; so that when the plaintiff shows that he has a valid chain of title from a certain grantor, and that the defendant claims under the same grantor, without proving what the defendant's title is, he shows prima facie that he is owner of the land, and it then devolves upon the defendant to show the authority of his own title." *See also* ***United Sav. Ass'n v. Villanueva***, 878 S.W.2d 619, 622 (Tex.App.—Corpus Christi 1994, no writ) (older title emanating from common source is generally superior); ***State v. Noser***, 422 S.W.2d 594, 600 (Tex.App.—Corpus Christi 1967, writ ref'd n.r.e.) (party not required to introduce all links set forth in pleadings if better title than adversary's can be shown); ***Abram v. Southeastern Fund***, 404 S.W.2d 673, 676 (Tex.App.—Tyler 1966, writ ref'd n.r.e.) (if D's title appears superior after P's evidence, P must continue and prove D's title is not superior).

Walters v. Pete, 546 S.W.2d 871, 875 (Tex.App.—Texarkana 1977, writ ref'd n.r.e.). "[P] relies on superiority of title out of a common source, but admits that her deed as written does not accurately describe the tract. Reformation, then, was a condition precedent to [P's] right of recovery. It is, however, within the power of the court to reform an instrument relied upon in trespass to try title when the deed contains a mutual mistake of fact, … provided the parties are before the court and limitation has not barred the action."

Gillum v. Temple, 546 S.W.2d 361, 364 (Tex.App.—Corpus Christi 1976, writ ref'd n.r.e.). "A common source may be established by pleadings, by agreement between the parties, or by proof at the trial." *See also* ***Jones v. Mid-State Homes, Inc.***, 356 S.W.2d 923, 924 (Tex.1962) (when parties stipulate, burden is on P to connect each party and to establish superior title). *Compare* ***Roberts v. Fraser***, 399 S.W.2d 211, 211-12 (Tex. App.—Beaumont 1966, writ dism'd) (P did not prove common source at trial), *with* ***Moran Corp. v. Brashear***, 339 S.W.2d 557, 558 (Tex.App.—San Antonio 1960, writ ref'd) (P proved common source at trial).

Best Inv. v. Hernandez, 479 S.W.2d 759, 762 (Tex. App.—Dallas 1972, writ ref'd n.r.e.). "In order for a plaintiff in a trespass to try title action to prove title from a common source it must (1) connect its title with a common source by a complete chain of title, (2) connect defendant's title to the same source, and (3) prove the superiority of its claim to that of the defendant."

Easements

City of Mission v. Popplewell, 294 S.W.2d 712, 714 (Tex.1956). "The plaintiff in a trespass to try title action must allege and prove the right to present possession of the land. The owner of an ordinary easement does not have such a possessory right and the remedy is not available to him. Injunction is a proper remedy."

Harrington v. Dawson-Conway Ranch, Ltd., 372 S.W.3d 711, 716-17 (Tex.App.—Eastland 2012, pet. denied). "A prescriptive easement is not well-regarded in the law. To obtain a prescriptive easement, one must use someone else's land in a manner that is open, notorious, continuous, exclusive, and adverse for a period of ten years or more. Exclusivity is not met when landowner and claimant both use the road. When a landowner and a claimant of an easement both use the same road, use by the claimant is not exclusive to the landowner's use and is not adverse. ... Joint use of a road, no matter for how long, cannot ripen into an easement by prescription. [¶] [D] contends that [P's] use of the road has been with his permission and that mere joint use, without more, will not establish a prescriptive easement. [P] concurs that this is a correct assertion of the law where there is joint use. *At 718:* Courts have analyzed the acquisition of an easement by prescription as being analogous to the acquisition of title by adverse possession. Therefore, a claim of prescription must be supported by proof of all of the elements that are involved in the statute of limitations for adverse possession. The hostile and adverse character of the use necessary to establish an easement by prescription is the same as that which is necessary to establish title by adverse possession. [¶] The party claiming an easement by prescription must give notice that its use of property is under a claim of right. Otherwise, the use (especially if joint) is presumed to be permissive, and a permissive use can never ripen into an easement by prescription. There must be an independent act of hostility to transform permissive use of an easement into an adverse use so as to begin the prescriptive period."

Roberson v. City of Austin, 157 S.W.3d 130, 135 (Tex.App.—Austin 2005, pet. denied). "Texas courts have often applied the [Uniform Declaratory Judgment Act (UDJA)] in construing the existence and scope of easements. [¶] Texas courts have also allowed parties to use trespass to try title actions to determine issues involving easements. [¶] In other cases, however, Texas courts have held that trespass to try title is not available where the property interest at issue is an easement or other nonpossessory interest. *At 136:* Although ***Martin*** [***v. Amerman***, 133 S.W.3d 262 (Tex.2004),] made explicit that boundary dispute claims are in fact trespass to try title claims and not UDJA claims, it made no mention of whether the existence and validity of easements may be determined by a declaration under the UDJA. What remains unclear is whether, under the ***Martin*** court's rationale, easement claims would be considered 'title' claims only. [W]e hold that they are not. *At 137:* For these reasons, we hold that [P] could properly bring his claims regarding the easement under the UDJA. *At 137 n.5:* ***Martin*** does not foreclose the resolution of easement disputes by means of a declaratory judgment under the UDJA."

Equitable Title

Binford v. Snyder, 189 S.W.2d 471, 474 (Tex.1945). "[W]e hold that [P] can recover an equitable title under the ordinary formal averments contained in a statutory action of trespass to try title without the necessity of specially pleading her equitable title." *See also* ***Tompkins v. Holman***, 537 S.W.2d 98, 99 (Tex.App.—Austin 1976, writ ref'd n.r.e.) (equitable right must be brought in separate suit, and once successful, party may proceed to recover title by trespass to try title).

Longoria v. Lasater, 292 S.W.3d 156, 165 (Tex. App.—San Antonio 2009, pet. denied). "An owner of a superior equitable title may recover in a trespass to try title action if the record shows the equitable title is superior to the defendant's bare legal title." *See also* ***Bagwell v. Lotspeich***, 561 S.W.2d 920, 924 (Tex.App.—Tyler 1978, no writ).

Cullins v. Foster, 171 S.W.3d 521, 533 (Tex.App.—Houston [14th Dist.] 2005, pet. denied). "'Equitable title may be shown when the plaintiff proves that he has paid the purchase price and fully performed the obligations under the contract. Upon such performance, he becomes vested with an equitable title to the property which is sufficient to allow him to maintain his action in trespass to try title.'" *See also* ***North East ISD v.***

Aldridge, 528 S.W.2d 341, 343 (Tex.App.—Amarillo 1975, writ ref'd n.r.e.) (equitable title distinguished from equitable right where P must set aside or reform deed not void to show title).

"Not Guilty" Plea

Brohlin v. McMinn, 341 S.W.2d 420, 422 (Tex. 1960). "In an action in trespass to try title, the answer of the defendant to the merits of the case by a plea of not guilty relieves the plaintiffs of the necessity of proving a trespass, since the plea constitutes an admission by the defendant for the purpose of the action that he was in possession of or claimed title to the premises sued for by the plaintiffs."

Gillum v. Temple, 546 S.W.2d 361, 363-64 (Tex. App.—Corpus Christi 1976, writ ref'd n.r.e.). "The burden of proof is ... on the plaintiff to establish a superior title in himself by an affirmative showing. ... Until the plaintiff presents such prima facie proof of title, the defendant is not required to offer evidence of title and the plaintiff may not rely on his failure to do so. Accordingly, defendant's possession entitles him to judgment against the plaintiff unless plaintiff shows a prima facie title. Under such circumstances, there is no necessity of determining the question of whether or not the defendant has title to the property." *See also* ***McShan v. Pitts***, 554 S.W.2d 759, 762 (Tex.App.—San Antonio 1977, no writ) (proof of legal title outstanding in third person constitutes defense to P's suit, even though D cannot connect with outstanding legal title).

Doria v. Suchowolski, 531 S.W.2d 360, 362 (Tex. App.—San Antonio 1975, writ ref'd n.r.e.). "Plaintiff, under a general allegation of ownership, may generally show whatever title he has to the property without special pleadings, except title by limitation, which must be specially pleaded. A plea of not guilty by the defendants is a denial of plaintiff's allegations and puts plaintiff on proof of all of the elements necessary to the maintenance of the suit and of his right to recover. The plaintiff is thereby put on proof of his title and right of possession. A plea of not guilty is a plea in bar against which plaintiff must show title and establish his right to possession of the property." *See also* ***McShan v. Pitts***, 554 S.W.2d 759, 763 (Tex.App.—San Antonio 1977, no writ) (no waiver of "not guilty" by specifically pleading limitations).

Prior Possession

Reiter v. Coastal States Gas Prod'g Co., 382 S.W.2d 243, 250 (Tex.1964). "Assuming that the plaintiff is relying upon prior possession, proof of title in the defendant unquestionably operates to rebut the inference of ownership arising from plaintiff's possession. On the other hand, proof that a grant has issued from the sovereign coupled with a showing that some third person holds the record title under such grant is insufficient to rebut the inference. [A] break in plaintiff's paper chain of title leaving an apparent outstanding title in a third person does not destroy plaintiff's case under the doctrine of prior possession. *At 251:* The doctrine of 'prior possession' ... proceeds upon the theory that one in possession should not be disturbed unless it be by one having a better title. ... '[T]he presumption of title arises from the possession, and, unless the defendant prove a better title, he must himself be ousted. Although he proves that some third person, with whom he in no manner connects himself, has title, this does him no good, because the prior possession of the plaintiff was sufficient to authorize him to maintain it as against a trespasser, and the defendant, being himself without title, and not connecting himself with any title, cannot justify an ouster of the plaintiff.'" *See also* ***House v. Reavis***, 35 S.W. 1063, 1065 (Tex.1896); ***Phillips v. Wertz***, 546 S.W.2d 902, 906 (Tex.App.—Dallas 1977, writ ref'd n.r.e.).

Land v. Turner, 377 S.W.2d 181, 186 (Tex.1964). "[T]o establish 'prior possession,' there must be an actual possession of the property which is exclusive, and peaceable. *At 187-88:* Once an actual possession of the land has been established, it must be continuous. But it may be continued by actual or constructive possession if there has been no abandonment of possession. [¶] [I]f the plaintiff does not have actual possession when ousted, but claims constructive possession, he must show the facts amounting to a constructive possession. If the land was apparently vacant when defendant entered, the plaintiff 'must go further and show that his actual possession was not abandoned; otherwise he cannot be said to have had even a constructive possession.'" *See also* ***Howland v. Hough***, 553 S.W.2d 162, 165 (Tex.App.—Eastland 1977), *rev'd on other grounds*, 570 S.W.2d 876 (Tex.1978).

Royalty Interest

Glover v. Union Pac. R.R., 187 S.W.3d 201, 211 (Tex.App.—Texarkana 2006, pet. denied). "A royalty interest is a nonpossessory interest. [Ps] are seeking damages for failure to account rather than attempting to gain possession of [property]. Because this dispute

does not concern possession of real property, [Ps] were not required to bring the action in trespass to try title."

Suit to Quiet Title

Ford v. Exxon Mobil Chem. Co., 235 S.W.3d 615, 618-19 (Tex.2007). "[A]n action to quiet title is never time-barred. [¶] Deeds obtained by fraud are voidable rather than void, and remain effective until set aside. Texas law is well settled that once limitations has expired for setting aside a deed for fraud, that bar cannot be evaded by simply asserting the claim in equity. If the rule were otherwise, limitations would rarely apply in real estate cases, as virtually every case could be recast as an action to remove cloud on title. Because [P's] legal claim for fraud was untimely, he cannot challenge [D's] facially valid deed by simply pleading it in equity."

Haskins v. Wallet, 63 Tex. 213, 218 (Tex.1885). "[O]ur courts have never regarded the legal remedy of ... trespass to try title[] as being the same in substance and effect as the equitable proceeding to cancel an opposing claim, or remove a cloud from the plaintiff's title. They originated in different ages of the history of the law; they were enforced in different tribunals, and proceeded on widely different principles. The one was a legal remedy which the plaintiff might demand as a matter of right in a court of law. The other was a prayer for relief by the plaintiff, in a court of equity, and in such cases the plaintiff must make his application within a reasonable time."

Montenegro v. Ocwen Loan Servicing, LLC, 419 S.W.3d 561, 567 (Tex.App.—Amarillo 2013, pet. denied). "In a suit to quiet title, the plaintiff must allege right, title, or ownership of the property with sufficient certainty to warrant judicial interference. A plaintiff has standing if he is 'the holder of the feeblest equity' and may use a quiet title action to 'remove from his way to legal title any unlawful [hindrance] having the appearance of better right.'"

Hahn v. Love, 321 S.W.3d 517, 531 (Tex.App.—Houston [1st Dist.] 2009, pet. denied). "'Any deed, contract, judgment or other instrument not void on its face that purports to convey an interest in or make any charge upon the land of a true owner, the invalidity of which would require proof, is a cloud upon the legal title of the owner.' [¶] The principal issue in a suit to remove a cloud from a title, or a suit to quiet title, is the existence of a cloud that equity will remove. An action to remove a cloud from title exists 'to enable the holder of the feeblest equity to remove from his way to legal title any unlawful hindrance having the appearance of better right.' In a suit to remove a cloud from his title, the plaintiff ... must prove, as a matter of law, right, title, or ownership in himself with sufficient certainty to enable the court to see that he has a right of ownership and that the alleged adverse claim is a cloud on the title that equity will remove. *At 532:* '[A] purchaser is bound by every recital, reference and reservation contained in or fairly disclosed by any instrument which forms an essential link in the chain of title under which he claims.'"

Sani v. Powell, 153 S.W.3d 736, 745 (Tex.App.—Dallas 2005, pet. denied). "Attorney's fees are not available in a suit to quiet title or to remove cloud on title."

Fricks v. Hancock, 45 S.W.3d 322, 327 (Tex.App.—Corpus Christi 2001, no pet.). "A suit to quiet title is an equitable action. A plaintiff in a suit to quiet title must prove and recover on the strength of his own title, not the weakness of his adversary's title." *See also* ***Wright v. Matthews***, 26 S.W.3d 575, 578 (Tex.App.—Beaumont 2000, pet. denied) (principal issue in suit to quiet title: if there is cloud, equity will remove); ***Bell v. Ott***, 606 S.W.2d 942, 952 (Tex.App.—Waco 1980, writ ref'd n.r.e.) (suit to quiet title allows holder of feeblest equity to remove unlawful hindrance appearing to have superior right).

PROP §22.002. TITLE SUFFICIENT TO MAINTAIN ACTION

A headright certificate, land scrip, bounty warrant, or other evidence of legal right to located and surveyed land is sufficient title to maintain a trespass to try title action.

History of Prop. Code §22.002: Acts 1983, 68th Leg., ch. 576, §1, eff. Jan. 1, 1984. Source: TRCS art. 7375.

See also TRCP 791-794.

ANNOTATIONS

Zobel v. Slim, 576 S.W.2d 362, 369 (Tex.1978). "In a trespass to try title suit, the general test for determining the sufficiency of a description of land is whether the tract can be identified with reasonable certainty."

City of Mission v. Popplewell, 294 S.W.2d 712, 717 (Tex.1956). "Parol evidence in the form of opinions and conclusions without documentary basis is inadmissible to establish [title to real property], and even if admitted without objection is of no probative force."

Ramsey v. Jones Enters., 810 S.W.2d 902, 904 (Tex.App.—Beaumont 1991, writ denied). "The trial court, over the objections of [Ds] allowed the testimony

of [the] title examiner, as to the sufficiency of [P's] title to the land in question. [¶] We hold that the trial court erred in allowing [P] to prove up title, in a trespass to try title action, by nothing more than the oral expert testimony of an attorney. *At 905:* To recover in trespass to try title, plaintiff must recover on the strength of his own title and not on the weakness of defendant's title, and may recover by proving: a regular chain of conveyances from the sovereign; superior title out of common source; title by limitation; or prior possession that has not been abandoned. [¶] [P] has failed in that burden in that [P] has come forward with no evidence that title resided in [P]. We cannot and do not consider the hearsay oral testimony of [P's] expert as any evidence whatsoever regarding the issue of title."

Jeffus v. Coon, 484 S.W.2d 949, 953 (Tex.App.—Tyler 1972, no writ). "In a trespass to try title action, where there is a missing link in the chain of title many years prior to time such issue is raised, there is a presumption [l]iberally indulged that a deed did exist covering the period. [¶] It is the established law in this State that title may be proved by other competent evidence, including circumstances."

W.T. Carter & Bro. v. Collins, 192 S.W. 316, 321 (Tex.App.—Beaumont 1916, writ ref'd). "It is the law of this state that where natural objects, as called for in the field notes, can be actually found and identified on the ground as showing the footsteps of the surveyor, both course and distance, when inconsistent therewith, must give way and be disregarded. The courts of this state have undertaken to grant the dignity of calls in field notes, and to attach to them different degrees of importance. The first in importance are natural objects, such as streams, hills, mounds, nature of soil, etc. Next in importance are artificial objects, such as stakes, mounds, marked trees, etc., and the least of all, course and distance. This classification and grade of calls, however, is only a rule of evidence. The primary purpose in all cases of the kind is to locate the survey as it was intended to be located on the ground by the original surveyor, and if this can be accomplished with more certainty under the circumstances of the case by the calls for course and distance, they will control. It has been determined, however, that only when the natural or artificial objects called for in the field notes can be found and identified on the ground with reasonable certainty will they control calls for course and distance." *See also* ***Coker v. Geisendorff***, 370 S.W.3d 8, 13 (Tex.App.—Texarkana 2012, no pet.).

PROP §22.003. FINAL JUDGMENT CONCLUSIVE

A final judgment that establishes title or right to possession in an action to recover real property is conclusive against the party from whom the property is recovered and against a person claiming the property through that party by a title that arises after the action is initiated.

History of Prop. Code §22.003: Acts 1983, 68th Leg., ch. 576, §1, eff. Jan. 1, 1984. Source: TRCS art. 7391.

See also TRCP 799, 800, 804, 807.

ANNOTATIONS

Dougherty v. Humphrey, 424 S.W.2d 617, 621 (Tex. 1968). "[I]f a person sues in trespass to try title and seeks to obtain relief which is unavailable to him in trespass to try title, he is not barred by that judgment from thereafter seeking proper relief. [Ps] had no rights under the 1939 will which they could assert against their father in trespass to try title. The only judgment that the trial court could have rendered in that suit was a take nothing judgment. The holdings in ***Permian Oil*** [***Co. v. Smith***, 73 S.W.2d 490 (Tex.1934),] ... have no application here because the parties in those cases asserted rights in trespass to try title which could be adjudicated. Consequently, adverse rulings in prior suits served as res judicata to prevent later suits over the issues which had already been decided. Whereas, in the case before us, the trespass to try title action in 1956 did not and could not adjudicate the rights of petitioners to the property under the 1939 will."

Permian Oil Co. v. Smith, 73 S.W.2d 490, 496 (Tex. 1934). Held: If P under the circumstances fails to establish her title, the effect of a take-nothing judgment against her is to vest title in D. *See also* ***Poth v. Roosth***, 202 S.W.2d 442, 444-45 (Tex.1947) (courts deciding effect of take-nothing judgment should construe judgment in light of pleadings); ***City of Houston v. Miller***, 436 S.W.2d 368, 372 (Tex.App.—Houston [14th Dist.] 1968, writ ref'd n.r.e.) (same).

Wolfe v. Devon Energy Prod. Co., 382 S.W.3d 434, 443 (Tex.App.—Waco 2012, pet. denied). "[A] plaintiff who has no interest at all in the land lacks standing to assert a trespass-to-try-title action. *At 453:* A plaintiff in a trespass-to-try-title suit may rely on a title acquired after the institution of suit if he asserts

such title by an amended pleading. Here, as admitted in his reply brief, [intervenor] did not amend his pleadings to assert his after-acquired title. Instead, [intervenor] raised the issue of after-acquired title for the first time when he filed his cross-motion for summary judgment on his trespass-to-try-title claim and again in his response to [Ds'] motions for summary judgment. When [intervenor] asserted his after-acquired title for the first time in his cross-motion for summary judgment and in his summary judgment response, [Ds] had two choices: they could object that his after-acquired title had not been pleaded, or they could respond on the merits and try the issue by consent. By choosing the latter course, the issue of [intervenor's] after-acquired title was placed squarely before the trial court. Therefore, [intervenor] has raised a fact issue as to his interest in the property and, thus, has standing."

Glenn v. Lucas, 376 S.W.3d 268, 274 (Tex.App.—Texarkana 2012, no pet.). "Upon the failure of a plaintiff to establish superior title in a trespass to try title suit, the proper course of action is for the trial court to enter a 'take-nothing' judgment. A take nothing judgment in a trespass to try title suit operates to divest the plaintiff of all its title to its interest in the lands in controversy and to vest the same in the defendant."

Houchins v. Scheltz, 590 S.W.2d 745, 749 (Tex. App.—Houston [14th Dist.] 1979, no writ), *disapproved on other grounds*, ***Roark v. Stallworth Oil & Gas, Inc.***, 813 S.W.2d 492 (Tex.1991). "A party [losing] under a valid judgment in a trespass to try title case is precluded thereby from asserting interest in the land in controversy through any fact which existed at the time the judgment was rendered." *See also* ***Browning v. West***, 557 S.W.2d 848, 851 (Tex.App.—Tyler 1977, writ ref'd n.r.e.) (earlier action had no effect on parties because none were parties to earlier action).

Bingham v. Boles, 458 S.W.2d 99, 100 (Tex. App.—El Paso 1970, writ ref'd n.r.e.). "[T]his is a trespass to try title suit, by [Ps] pleading for title and possession, and by the court's award of title to the land in controversy to [Ds]. In such a case the property must be described by the judgment with reasonable care and certainty. A judgment using a description that is uncertain in its terms and that cannot be made certain by reference to the pleadings in the case or to other extrinsic evidence is fatally defective."

Trigg v. Whittenburg, 129 S.W.2d 472, 474 (Tex. App.—Amarillo 1939, writ ref'd). TRCS art. 7391, now Prop. Code §22.003, "merely enacts into law the equitable rule that there should be an end to all litigation. ... No new and independent rights having accrued to him after such judgment he is not permitted to maintain another suit seeking to recover the same property upon some theory not advanced in the former action. To permit such a practice would be tantamount to the abolition of final judgments." *See also* ***State v. Sunray DX Oil Co.***, 503 S.W.2d 822, 828 (Tex.App.—Corpus Christi 1973, writ ref'd n.r.e.).

Houston Chronicle Publ'g v. Bergman, 128 S.W.2d 114, 116 (Tex.App.—Galveston 1939, writ dism'd). "[I]t is manifest that only one final judgment should be allowed in [a trespass-to-try-title] action, such judgment to be effective against whom it was rendered, and against all persons claiming to have acquired title through him, pendente lite. In the very nature of things the principle of lis pendens is essential to the effectiveness or finality of judgments. [I]t is universally held that for purposes of lis pendens, or its notice, an action does not begin until service of process, the Legislature must be taken to have intended, by the language it used, to adopt the common law rule as to lis pendens, in providing for finality of judgments in actions in trespass to try title."

PROP §22.004. EFFECT OF FORMER LAW

This chapter does not affect rights that existed before the introduction of the common law in this state. Those rights are defined by the principles of the law in effect at the time the rights accrued.

History of Prop. Code §22.004: Acts 1983, 68th Leg., ch. 576, §1, eff. Jan. 1, 1984. Source: TRCS art. 7392.

See also TRCP 808, 809.

Sections 22.005-22.020 reserved for expansion

SUBCHAPTER B. JUDGMENT & DAMAGES

PROP §22.021. CLAIM FOR IMPROVEMENTS

(a) A defendant in a trespass to try title action who is not the rightful owner of the property, but who has possessed the property in good faith and made permanent and valuable improvements to it, is either:

(1) entitled to recover the amount by which the estimated value of the defendant's improvements exceeds the estimated value of the defendant's use and occupation of and waste or other injury to the property; or

(2) liable for the amount by which the value of the use and occupation of and waste and other injury to the property exceeds the value of the improvements and for costs.

(b) In estimating values of improvements or of use and occupation:

(1) improvements are valued at the time of trial, but only to the extent that the improvements increased the value of the property; and

(2) use and occupation is valued for the time before the date the action was filed that the defendant was in possession of the property, but excluding the value resulting from the improvements made by the defendant or those under whom the defendant claims.

(c) The defendant who makes a claim for improvements must plead:

(1) that the defendant and those under whom the defendant claims have had good faith adverse possession of the property in controversy for at least one year before the date the action began;

(2) that they or the defendant made permanent and valuable improvements to the property while in possession;

(3) the grounds for the claim;

(4) the identity of the improvements; and

(5) the value of each improvement.

(d) The defendant is not liable for damages under this section for injuries or for the value of the use and occupation more than two years before the date the action was filed, and the defendant is not liable for damages or for the value of the use and occupation in excess of the value of the improvements.

History of Prop. Code §22.021: Acts 1983, 68th Leg., ch. 576, §1, eff. Jan. 1, 1984. Source: TRCS arts. 7389, 7393-7396.

See also TRCP 806, 807.

ANNOTATIONS

Cage Bros. v. Whiteman, 163 S.W.2d 638, 642 (Tex. 1942). When the trespass is done in bad faith, the measure of damages is "the value of the things mined at the time of severance without making deduction for the cost of labor and other expenses incurred in committing the wrongful act ... or for any value he may have added to the mineral by his labor.'"

Blanar v. Blanar, 598 S.W.2d 381, 382-83 (Tex. App.—Houston [14th Dist.] 1980, writ ref'd n.r.e.). "[Ps] assert that the trial court erred in awarding [Ds] compensation for the improvements because as a matter of law [Ds] were not good faith improvers. The defendant in a trespass to try title action may make a claim for improvements if he possessed the land in good faith. This is authorized under the statute and also under equitable principles. However, for one to qualify as a good faith improver under the equitable rule of betterments he must show not only that he believed that he was the true owner of the land but also that he had reasonable grounds for that belief.... [T]he improver must have examined the records to be in good faith." (Internal quotes omitted.) *See also* ***Miller v. Gasaway***, 514 S.W.2d 90, 93 (Tex.App.—Texarkana 1974, no writ).

Deal v. Carlton, 237 S.W.2d 1000, 1002 (Tex. App.—Galveston 1951, no writ). "[I]t is manifest that a defendant in a trespass to try title action has been provided with an adequate remedy at law by which he can assert, as against the claim of the plaintiff for damages, his equities to recover for improvements made in good faith. And so, if the party who asserts an equity for improvements made in good faith, deliberately suffers a judgment to be rendered against him, for damages in a trespass to try title action, he is not entitled to have the court, in a subsequent independent suit brought by him, enjoin the execution of the judgment pending the trial and determination of his independent suit for the value of improvements made in good faith."

Nilsen v. Bonugli, 220 S.W.2d 178, 180 (Tex. App.—San Antonio 1949, no writ). "[S]trict compliance with the statute is not necessary to obtain relief when the improvements are made with the full knowledge, acquiescence and consent of the owner of the land."

Humble Oil & Ref. Co. v. State, 162 S.W.2d 119, 136 (Tex.App.—Austin 1942, writ ref'd). "The particular wording employed in [TRCS arts. 7389 and 7395, now Prop. Code §22.021,] does not, we think, militate against the conclusion that the limitation of recovery for use and damages to the two-year period before suit is filed is a limitation and not a substantive right provision. Nor do we think that the fact that the two-year period is not required to be specially pleaded is important. The provisions only apply to trespass to try title actions. ... That this is the proper construction of these provisions was clearly recognized in [***Gulf, C. & S.F. Ry. v. Poindexter***, 7 S.W. 316 (Tex.1888)]: 'It may be necessary to state that, in suits of trespass to try title, the general law of limitation as to injury to the estate of an-

other does not apply. When the suit is strictly for damages to an estate or to land, the general law of limitation is applicable, but when the suit is in trespass to try title, the statute regulating such suits governs.'"

Bemrod v. Wright, 273 S.W. 938, 940 (Tex.App.—Amarillo 1925, no writ). "The measure of recovery for improvements by the defendant is the enhancement of the value of the land by reason of the improvements, and not the cost thereof, since it must be a benefit to the owner in enhanced value to estop him from denying the right of defendant to compensation for improvements."

PROP §22.022. WRIT OF POSSESSION

If in a trespass to try title action the plaintiff obtains a judgment for the contested property, but the defendant obtains a judgment for the value of the defendant's improvements in excess of the defendant's liability for use, occupation, and damages, the court may not issue a writ of possession until the first anniversary of the judgment unless the plaintiff pays to the clerk of the court for the benefit of the defendant the amount of the judgment in favor of the defendant plus interest.

History of Prop. Code §22.022: Acts 1983, 68th Leg., ch. 576, §1, eff. Jan. 1, 1984. Source: TRCS art. 7397.

See also TRCP 805, 807.

ANNOTATIONS

Zobel v. Slim, 576 S.W.2d 362, 369 (Tex.1978). "In a trespass to try title suit, the general test for determining the sufficiency of a description of land is whether the tract can be identified with reasonable certainty. More specifically, the judgment in a trespass to try title case must so identify the land that an officer charged with the duty of executing a writ of possession can locate the property without exercising judicial functions." *See also* ***Brown v. Eubank***, 378 S.W.2d 707, 714 (Tex.App.—Tyler 1964, writ ref'd n.r.e.).

PROP §22.023. FAILURE TO PAY

(a) If after a trespass to try title action a plaintiff does not pay a judgment awarded to a defendant, plus accrued interest, before the first anniversary of the judgment and if the defendant, before the sixth month after the first anniversary of the judgment, pays the value of the property, less the value of the defendant's improvements, to the clerk of the court for the benefit of the plaintiff, the plaintiff may not obtain a writ of possession or maintain any proceeding against the defendant or the defendant's heirs or assigns for the property awarded to the plaintiff in the trespass to try title action.

(b) If an eligible defendant does not exercise the option under this section, a plaintiff may apply for a writ of possession as in other cases.

History of Prop. Code §22.023: Acts 1983, 68th Leg., ch. 576, §1, eff. Jan. 1, 1984. Source: TRCS arts. 7398, 7399.

See also TRCP 804, 807.

PROP §22.024. PAYMENTS INTO COURT

If a party in a trespass to try title action makes a payment to the clerk of a court under this subchapter, the clerk shall enter a dated memorandum of the payment on the page of the record on which the judgment was entered. The clerk shall pay the money on demand to the person entitled to the payment, who shall indicate receipt of the payment by dating and signing the record on the same page on which the judgment was entered.

History of Prop. Code §22.024: Acts 1983, 68th Leg., ch. 576, §1, eff. Jan. 1, 1984. Source: TRCS art. 7401.

See also TRCP 804, 807.

Sections 22.025-22.040 reserved for expansion

SUBCHAPTER C. REMOVAL OF IMPROVEMENTS

PROP §22.041. PLEA FOR REMOVAL OF IMPROVEMENTS

(a) A defendant in a trespass to try title action who is not the rightful owner of the property in controversy may remove improvements made to the property if:

(1) the defendant, and those under whom the defendant claims, possessed the property, and made permanent and valuable improvements to it, without intent to defraud; and

(2) the improvements can be removed without substantial and permanent damage to the property.

(b) The pleadings of a defendant who seeks to remove improvements must contain:

(1) a statement that the defendant, and those under whom the defendant claims, adversely possessed the property, and made permanent and valuable improvements to it, without intent to defraud;

(2) a statement identifying the improvements; and

(3) an offer to provide a surety bond in an amount and conditioned as required by this section.

(c) Before removing the improvements, the defendant must post a surety bond in an amount determined by the court, conditioned on the removal of the im-

provements in a manner that substantially restores the property to the condition it was in before the improvements were made.

History of Prop. Code §22.041: Acts 1983, 68th Leg., ch. 576, §1, eff. Jan. 1, 1984. Source: TRCS art. 7401A, §§1-3.

ANNOTATIONS

Kennedy Con., Inc. v. Forman, 502 S.W.3d 486, 499 (Tex.App.—Houston [14th Dist.] 2016, pet. denied). "[D] challenges the trial court's denial of its request that the trial court delete from the judgment language giving [P] title to the improvements on the subject property, even though the judgment allows [D] to remove the improvements, as provided in … §22.041. [P] also asserts that [D] may disobey the trial court's judgment by refusing to remove the improvements, and therefore, [P] needs to own the improvements so that [P] will have a right to remove the improvements. But, the judgment gives [P] the right to have the improvements removed, and [P] has recourse to remedies available to enforce the judgment should [D] refuse to comply with the judgment. We conclude that the trial court erred by granting relief under … §22.041 while at the same time awarding [P] title to the improvements…. [¶] [D] also challenges the trial court's denial of its request [that] the trial court delete from the judgment language requiring [D] to remove the improvements from the subject property 'in a manner which allows [P] to fully utilize and access his Property….' [D] argues that this language is ambiguous and goes beyond the requirements of §22.041 … that [D] restore the subject property to its condition before the improvements were made. We agree that this language goes beyond the statute and might put [P] in a better position than he was before the events giving rise to this lawsuit. Therefore, we modify the judgment to delete this language."

PROP §22.042. REFEREE

A court that authorizes a defendant in a trespass to try title action to remove improvements shall appoint a referee to supervise the removal. The court may require the referee to make reports to the court concerning the removal.

History of Prop. Code §22.042: Acts 1983, 68th Leg., ch. 576, §1, eff. Jan. 1, 1984. Source: TRCS art. 7401A, §3.

PROP §22.043. RETAINED JURISDICTION

A court that authorizes a defendant in a trespass to try title action to remove improvements retains jurisdiction of the action until the court makes a final disposition of the case and a final determination of the rights, duties, and liabilities of the parties and sureties.

History of Prop. Code §22.043: Acts 1983, 68th Leg., ch. 576, §1, eff. Jan. 1, 1984. Source: TRCS art. 7401A, §3.

PROP §22.044. CONDITION FOR REMOVAL

Before a court in a trespass to try title action authorizes a defendant to remove improvements, the court may require the defendant to satisfy a money judgment in favor of the plaintiff that arises out of a claim of the plaintiff in the action.

History of Prop. Code §22.044: Acts 1983, 68th Leg., ch. 576, §1, eff. Jan. 1, 1984. Source: TRCS art. 7401A, §4.

PROP §22.045. CUMULATIVE REMEDIES

The remedy of removing improvements may be pleaded as an alternative to all other remedies at law or in equity.

History of Prop. Code §22.045: Acts 1983, 68th Leg., ch. 576, §1, eff. Jan. 1, 1984. Source: TRCS art. 7401A, §5.

CHAPTER 23. PARTITION

PROP §23.001. PARTITION

A joint owner or claimant of real property or an interest in real property or a joint owner of personal property may compel a partition of the interest or the property among the joint owners or claimants under this chapter and the Texas Rules of Civil Procedure.

History of Prop. Code §23.001: Acts 1983, 68th Leg., ch. 576, §1, eff. Jan. 1, 1984. Source: TRCS arts. 6082, 6101.

See also Fam. Code §9.201(a); TRCP 756-778.

ANNOTATIONS

Generally

Harrell v. Harrell, 692 S.W.2d 876, 876 (Tex.1985). "It has long been the rule in Texas that community property not partitioned or divided upon divorce is held by the former spouses as tenants in common or joint owners. It has likewise been the rule in Texas that a suit for partition of such former community property is a proper means of dividing said property between the tenants in common." *See also* ***Bass v. Bass***, 106 S.W.3d 311, 316 (Tex.App.—Houston [1st Dist.] 2003, no pet.);

Bishop v. Bishop, 74 S.W.3d 877, 879 (Tex.App.—San Antonio 2002, no pet.).

Phillips v. Phillips, 951 S.W.2d 955, 957 (Tex. App.—Waco 1997, no pet.). "Even if [Fam. Code §3.90, now §9.202,] applied to bar an enforcement action under the Family Code, that section would not operate to bar an otherwise valid partition under the Property Code. The *right to partition is absolute*."

First Nat'l Bank v. Texas Fed. S&L Ass'n, 628 S.W.2d 497, 498 (Tex.App.—Texarkana 1982, writ ref'd n.r.e.). "Three prerequisites are necessary to force a partition. First, the partitioners must be joint owners; second, they must be joint owners of the land to be partitioned or some interest therein; and third, the party seeking the partition must have an equal right to possess the land with the other joint owners." *See also* ***Texas Oil & Gas Corp. v. Ostrom***, 638 S.W.2d 231, 233 (Tex.App.—Tyler 1982, writ ref'd n.r.e.) (all owners of property must be joined).

Ferguson v. Ferguson, 189 S.W.2d 880, 881 (Tex. App.—Austin 1945, writ ref'd w.o.m.). "Obviously a partition suit is not in the nature of a suit in trespass to try title, nor to remove cloud from title. … 'Partition does not confer title; it effects the localization of undivided interests.' The trial court in such partition suit could, and did, determine the ownership as between the parties to the partition suit, a contested issue there. It was clearly not [trial court's] proper duty nor authority to determine merchantability of title as against anyone not a party to the partition suit, nor … to pass upon, nor correct, if such were necessary, outstanding claims, if any, against the property held by others not parties to that suit."

Agreement to Partition

Dimock v. Kadane, 100 S.W.3d 622, 625 (Tex. App.—Eastland 2003, pet. denied). "[J]oint owners may expressly or impliedly agree not to partition. [¶] In order to determine whether the parties impliedly agreed not to partition, the courts 'examine the particular contract involved and from the provisions thereof determine whether or not the parties impliedly contracted against partition.'" *See also* ***MCEN 1996 Prtshp. v. Glassell***, 42 S.W.3d 262, 263-64 (Tex.App.—Corpus Christi 2001, pet. denied) (express agreements not to partition will be honored); ***Dierschke v. Central Nat'l Branch of First Nat'l Bank***, 876 S.W.2d 377, 380 (Tex.App.—Austin 1994, no writ) (cotenants may voluntarily partition land by written agreement; all cotenants must participate in partition).

Spires v. Hoover, 466 S.W.2d 344, 346 (Tex. App.—El Paso 1971, writ ref'd n.r.e.). Under TRCS art. 6082, now Prop. Code §23.001, "the right to partition between joint owners is absolute. But this right can be waived or contracted away." *See also* ***Thomas v. McNair***, 882 S.W.2d 870, 878 (Tex.App.—Corpus Christi 1994, no writ).

Division

Sayers v. Pyland, 161 S.W.2d 769, 772 (Tex.1942). "[I]n partition proceedings the court may, if necessary, divide the property into shares of unequal value, and fix a lien on the larger share in favor of the party receiving the smaller share, for the difference. This difference is usually referred to as owelty. In such cases the owelty so assessed in adjusting the equities is recognized as being in the nature of purchase money secured by a vendor's lien on the larger tract. [¶] [O]ne of the inherent rights appertaining to the relation of cotenancy is that if the common property is such that it cannot be divided into equal shares without materially injuring the value thereof, it may be divided into unequal shares and a lien fixed for the difference against the larger share in favor of the recipient of the smaller share. This is a valuable right which each cotenant has, for otherwise the property might have to be sacrificed on an unfavorable market." *See also* ***Laster v. First Huntsville Props. Co.***, 826 S.W.2d 125, 131 n.3 (Tex.1991).

Barham v. McGraw, 342 S.W.3d 716, 719 (Tex. App.—Amarillo 2011, pet. denied). "The document at issue cannot be construed as a partition. The latter serves to divide property owned by co-tenants and concerns possession, not title. The record is clear that neither [D] nor [P] had a right to possession of any realty held in the trust. Right to possession resided in their mother, the trustee. … Consequently, the document [P] drafted and tendered to his remaining family members was not a partition irrespective of his unilateral belief."

Grant v. Clouser, 287 S.W.3d 914, 920 (Tex.App.—Houston [14th Dist.] 2009, no pet.). "Homestead rights can attach to property interests held by tenancy in common; however, such homestead rights may not prejudice the rights of a cotenant. The general rule is that homestead rights attaching to property interests held by a cotenant are subordinate to another cotenant's right to partition. *At 921:* The question arises whether the gen-

eral rule is applicable here in light of [heir's] argument that [Tex. Const.] art. 16, §50 … precludes a partition by sale because [P] acquired his cotenant interest in the property as [decedent's husband's] judgment creditor." Held: Yes.

Cecola v. Ruley, 12 S.W.3d 848, 855 (Tex.App.—Texarkana 2000, no pet.). "If the property can be divided in kind without materially impairing its value, a sale will not be ordered, but when dividing the land into parcels causes its value to be substantially less than its value when whole, the rights of the owners are substantially prejudiced. Substantial economic loss is one of the significant factors that would warrant a sale in lieu of a partition in kind. [B]ut even if the two parts are divided into equal value, if the value as a part of the larger tract has been greatly diminished, this also should be considered in determining whether or not a division in kind would be fair and equitable." *See also* ***Champion v. Robinson***, 392 S.W.3d 118, 123 (Tex.App.—Texarkana 2012, pet. denied); ***Humble Oil & Ref. Co. v. Lasseter***, 95 S.W.2d 730, 731 (Tex.App.—Texarkana 1936, writ dism'd).

Yturria v. Kimbro, 921 S.W.2d 338, 344 (Tex.App.—Corpus Christi 1996, no writ). "[W]e conclude that claims involving improvements to the property or other allegations that may favor awarding a particular tract to a particular party are equitable matters for the trial court and factfinder to determine before sending the matter to the commissioners with appropriate instructions thereon. However, whether to split each of several tracts equally among the parties or to divide the whole property to be partitioned by giving one whole tract to each party, or some combination of these methods, is a matter of property valuation and division which falls within the province of the commissioners and not the factfinder at trial." *See also* ***Rittgers v. Rittgers***, 802 S.W.2d 109, 113-14 (Tex.App.—Corpus Christi 1990, writ denied).

Limitations

Hipp v. Fall, 213 S.W.2d 732, 737 (Tex.App.—Galveston 1948, writ ref'd n.r.e.). "This is a suit for partition.... 'To such a claim, when thus asserted, the statute of limitations has … no application, because it is an incident to partition, and to an action for partition the statute does not apply.'" *See also* ***Carter v. Charles***, 853 S.W.2d 667, 671 (Tex.App.—Houston [14th Dist.] 1993, no writ) (fact that partition is barred two years from repudiation under Family Code does not bar partition under Property Code); ***Horrocks v. Horrocks***, 608 S.W.2d 733, 736 (Tex.App.—Dallas 1980, no writ) (limitations when cotenant on notice of adverse possession).

Parties & Standing

Laster v. First Huntsville Props. Co., 826 S.W.2d 125, 128-29 (Tex.1991). "The term 'joint owner' is utilized in the statute which authorizes partition of jointly held property. This term, however, is imprecise because its use does not signify any one type of ownership. The term has, in the past, been used to refer both to property held in joint tenancy, and property held in cotenancy. [¶] A cotenancy is formed when two or more persons share the unity of exclusive use and possession in property held in common. The present right to possession of the property is essential because one who is never entitled to possession of property held in common is not a cotenant. Therefore, [divorced spouses] did not hold the residence as tenants in common because the divorce decree gave [wife] the right to the use and possession of the residence to the exclusion of [husband]."

Manchaca v. Martinez, 148 S.W.2d 391, 391 (Tex.1941). "[A] party, in order to be entitled to compel partition, must not only own an interest in the land, but he must be entitled to possession of a portion thereof." *See also* ***Irons v. Fort Worth Sand & Gravel Co.***, 284 S.W.2d 215, 219 (Tex.App.—Fort Worth 1955, writ ref'd n.r.e.).

Simpson-Fell Oil Co. v. Stanolind Oil & Gas Co., 125 S.W.2d 263, 267 (Tex.1939). "[W]hen conveyance of a specific part of common property has been made by one tenant in common, the grantee has a right to have the whole property, and all interested parties, brought into a partition proceeding in order to determine whether or not in an adjustment of the equities of all parties he shall be entitled to receive from his grantor's interest the specific portion conveyed to him."

PROP §23.002. VENUE & JURISDICTION

(a) A joint owner or a claimant of real property or an interest in real property may bring an action to partition the property or interest in a district court of a county in which any part of the property is located.

(b) A joint owner of personal property must bring an action to partition the property in a court that has jurisdiction over the value of the property.

History of Prop. Code §23.002: Acts 1983, 68th Leg., ch. 576, §1, eff. Jan. 1, 1984. Source: TRCS arts. 6083, 6102.

See also CPRC §15.011.

ANNOTATIONS

Eris v. Giannakopoulos, 369 S.W.3d 618, 620-21 (Tex.App.—Houston [1st Dist.] 2012, pet. dism'd). "The language of §23.002 does not indicate a legislative intent that district courts have exclusive jurisdiction over partition actions; rather, the use of the word 'may' demonstrates a permissive, rather than mandatory, procedure. A statute merely providing that an action 'may' be brought in district court 'does not express an intention to grant *exclusive* jurisdiction to district courts,' but rather, 'to the extent that statutory courts share *concurrent* jurisdiction with district courts, nothing in [such a] statute limits or excludes that concurrent jurisdiction.' [¶] Harris County courts at law have jurisdiction concurrent with district courts, within a specified amount-in-controversy range. Thus, because §23.002 … grants district courts jurisdiction over partition actions, Harris County courts at law also have jurisdiction over partition actions, so long as the amount in controversy falls within the specified range." *See also* ***Schuld v. Dembrinski***, 12 S.W.3d 485, 489 (Tex.App.—Dallas 2000, no pet.).

PROP §23.003. EFFECT ON FUTURE INTERESTS

A partition of real property involving an owner of a life estate or an estate for years and other owners of equal or greater estate does not prejudice the rights of an owner of a reversion or remainder interest.

History of Prop. Code §23.003: Acts 1983, 68th Leg., ch. 576, §1, eff. Jan. 1, 1984. Source: TRCS art. 6098.

PROP §23.004. EFFECT OF PARTITION

(a) A person allotted a share of or an interest in real property in a partition action holds the property or interest in severalty under the conditions and covenants that applied to the property prior to the partition.

(b) A court decree confirming a report of commissioners in partition of real property gives a recipient of an interest in the property a title equivalent to a conveyance of the interest by a warranty deed from the other parties in the action.

(c) Except as provided by this chapter, a partition of real property does not affect a right in the property.

History of Prop. Code §23.004: Acts 1983, 68th Leg., ch. 576, §1, eff. Jan. 1, 1984. Source: TRCS arts. 6099, 6100.

See also TRCP 768.

PROP §23.005. FEES

The judge of a court that hears an action to partition real property shall examine the report of the commissioners appointed to partition the property and shall determine from the report and from evidence submitted by the parties the complexity and difficulty of making the partition. The court shall then award the commissioners, and any surveyor appointed by the court or retained by the commissioners, a reasonable fee for the services rendered. The fees awarded shall be taxed and collected as costs of court in the same manner as the other costs in the action.

History of Prop. Code §23.005: Acts 1983, 68th Leg., ch. 576, §1, eff. Jan. 1, 1984. Amended by Acts 1991, 72nd Leg., ch. 443, §1, eff. Sept. 1, 1991. Source: TRCS art. 6108.

See also TRCP 769, 778.

PROP §23.006. ACCESS EASEMENT FOR PARTITIONED PROPERTY

(a) Unless waived by the parties in an action to partition property under this chapter, the commissioners appointed to partition property shall grant a nonexclusive access easement on a tract of partitioned property for the purpose of providing reasonable ingress to and egress from an adjoining partitioned tract that does not have a means of access through a public road or an existing easement appurtenant to the tract. The order granting the access easement shall contain a legal description of the easement.

(b) Unless waived by the parties in writing in a private partition agreement, the property owner of a partitioned tract that has a means of access through a public road or an existing easement appurtenant to the tract shall grant in the private partition agreement a nonexclusive access easement on the owner's partitioned tract for the purpose of providing reasonable ingress to and egress from an adjoining partitioned tract that does not have a means of access through a public road or an existing easement appurtenant to the tract.

(c) The access easement may not be a width greater than a width prescribed by a municipality or county for a right-of-way on a street or road. The access easement route must be the shortest route to the adjoining tract that:

(1) causes the least amount of damage to the tract subject to the easement; and

(2) is located the greatest reasonable distance from the primary residence and related improvements located on the tract subject to the easement.

(d) The adjoining tract owner who is granted an access easement under this section shall maintain the easement and keep the easement open for public use.

History of Prop. Code §23.006: Acts 2001, 77th Leg., ch. 647, §1, eff. Sept. 1, 2001.

See also *Real Estate Forms*, FORM 9:1.

E CHAPTER 23A. UNIFORM PARTITION OF HEIRS' PROPERTY ACT

NCCUSL Prefatory Note*

Introduction and Summary

The Uniform Partition of Heirs Property Act is an act of limited scope which addresses a widespread, well-documented problem faced by many low to middle-income families across the country who have been dispossessed of their real property and much of their real property-related wealth over the past several decades as a result of court-ordered partition sales of tenancy-in-common properties. The highly unstable ownership these families experience stands in sharp contrast to the secure property rights wealthier families typically enjoy. Further, the loss of real property-related wealth these low to middle-income families have experienced has been particularly devastating to these families given the fact that real property constitutes by far the single greatest asset that these property owners typically own, unlike the much more diversified asset portfolios that wealthier families normally possess. In addition, the Act may be very helpful to a surprising number of wealthier families who own tenancy-in-common property under the default rules and who also experience great problems with this ownership form.

The law has made the tenancy in common, a common ownership structure under which two or more cotenants own undivided interests in particular property, the default ownership structure for two or more family members who inherit real property. In addition, the law presumes that two or more people who acquire undivided interests in real property by conveyance or devise take ownership to the property as tenants in common and not as joint tenants unless the intention to create a joint tenancy is very clear. But certain key features of tenancy-in-common ownership under the default rules create serious problems for those who seek to maintain ownership of their property for themselves and their relatives, or at least the wealth represented by such real estate holdings.

- Any tenant in common may sell his or her interest or convey it by gift during his or her lifetime without the consent of his or her fellow cotenants, making it easy for non-family members—including real estate speculators in a number of instances—to acquire interests in family real property. At a tenant in common's death, his or her interest in the tenancy in common property may be transferred under a will, or if the will is not probated in time or if there is no will, under the laws of intestacy.
- A significant feature of tenancy-in-common ownership—a feature that this Act does not disturb—is the universal right of any cotenant to file a lawsuit petitioning a court to partition the property, even if that cotenant only recently acquired its interest in property that the other cotenants had owned within their family for a long time and even if that interest is very small (e.g., a five percent or even smaller interest).
- In resolving a partition action, the two principal remedies that a court may order are partition in kind of the property into separate subparcels, with each subparcel proportionate in value to each cotenant's fractional interest or partition by sale, in which case the property is forcibly sold in its entirety with the proceeds of the sale distributed among the cotenants, again in proportion to their relative interests in the property. In the overwhelming majority of states, statutes governing partition mandate that partition in kind is the much preferred remedy because a forced sale of a person's property has always been viewed as an extraordinary remedy which undermines fundamental property rights.
- Despite the overwhelming statutory preference for partition in kind, courts in a large number of states typically resolve partition actions by ordering partition by sale which usually results in forcing property owners off their land without their consent. This occurs even in cases in which the property could easily have been divided in kind or an overwhelming majority of the cotenants had opposed partition by sale or even in some cases when the only remedy any cotenant petitioned the court to order was partition in kind and not partition by sale.
- A de facto preference for a partition by sale in many states has arisen in part because courts often only consider the theoretical beneficial economic effect of ordering a partition by sale as opposed to a partition in kind. The many courts that utilize this approach do not place much value on upholding basic property rights and do not take account of the noneconomic value which many owners place upon their property. These noneconomic values can be substantial as families often value their family real property for its ancestral and even historical significance or its capacity to provide shelter that in some cases may prevent homelessness.
- Further, courts typically order the property sold at an auction utilizing forced sale procedures that are notorious for yielding sales prices well below market value. A sale under these forced sale conditions normally harms the tenants in common economically by depriving them of the market value of their property but gives the buyer an unjustified windfall because the buyer acquires the property at a significant discount from its market value and often for fire sale prices. The forced sale conditions under which partition sales occur virtually guarantee that wealth will not be maximized for the tenants in common even though judges frequently order partition sales because they claim that a partition sale will be wealth maximizing for the cotenants.
- To make matters worse, in many states cotenants who unsuccessfully resist a request for a court-ordered partition by sale are then required to pay a portion of the attorney's fees and costs incurred by the cotenant who petitioned the court for a partition by sale, forcing them in effect to pay for the deprivation of their property rights and their resulting loss of wealth. These fees and costs are in addition to the attorney's fees they must pay the attorney they hired in their unsuccessful effort to resist the sale and maintain ownership of their property.
- Given these rules and practices which many courts utilize in partition actions, it is often the case that an unscrupulous real estate speculator purchases a very small interest in family-owned tenancy-in-common property with the sole purpose of seeking a court-ordered partition by sale. Often such a speculator submits the winning bid in the subsequent auction sale of the property even though the winning bid represents just a fraction of the property's market value.

For these reasons, estate planners and real estate lawyers believe that tenancy-in-common ownership under the default rules represents one of the most unstable forms of real property ownership. To address the dangers of this form of ownership, these professionals routinely advise their wealthy and legally savvy clients to enter into privately negotiated tenancy-in-common agreements with their fellow cotenants or work with their other cotenants to reorganize their ownership under a different ownership structure altogether such as a limited liability company. However, a substantial percentage of tenancy-in-common property owners are not able to afford the services of these professionals

---

The NCCUSL comments have been edited to reflect the Texas Legislature's omission of sections and changing of section numbers from the original uniform act. The Texas Legislature did not adopt the NCCUSL comments when it adopted the Uniform Disclaimer of Property Interests Act. The full uniform act and comments can be found at www.uniformlaws.org.

or are not aware of the legal benefits of hiring such professionals because they do not understand the inherent risks of owning property under the default rules of the tenancy in common.

Accordingly, this Act seeks to remedy the serious problems many of those who own family real property have faced in keeping their property and their wealth as a result of the application of the default rules governing tenancy-in-common property by providing a further set of coherent, default rules reforming the worst substantive and procedural abuses that have arisen in connection with the partition of tenancy-in-common property. Specifically, this Act imports certain core property preservation and wealth protection mechanisms already commonly used by wealthy and legally sophisticated family real property owners as well as protections legislatures and courts in other countries now afford co-tenants in partition actions as a result of modern reforms, and establishes those mechanisms as the default rules for the partition of real property owned by families under a tenancy in common. On the other hand, this Act does not seek to make wholesale changes to the law of partition. For example, this Act does not apply to any real property which is the subject of a written tenancy-in-common agreement which contains a provision governing the partition of the property (all such agreements typically contain such a provision) or which is owned under any other form of ownership (e.g., a joint tenancy, a limited liability company, a partnership, a limited partnership, a trust or a corporation) other than the tenancy in common.

Tenancy-In-Common Property Owners of Modest Means Are Particularly At Risk

There is a subset of tenancy-in-common property owners who are particularly vulnerable to losing their property and significant wealth as a result of court-ordered partition sales. Scholars and practitioners who have worked with poor and minority property owners have observed that a particularly high percentage of these owners tend to own their real property under the default rules governing tenancy-in-common ownership and not under a private agreement among the cotenants governing the ownership of the property. This phenomenon is explained in large part by the fact that many low to middle-income property owners transfer their real property by intestate succession instead of by will, which is consistent with studies that have documented low will-making rates among Americans of more modest economic means.

The more that property is transferred from one generation to the next by intestate succession, the more likely it is for an increasingly large number of people to acquire an interest in the property, resulting in increasingly unstable ownership given that each cotenant possesses an unfettered right to request a partition by sale of the entire property irrespective of the wishes of the other co-tenants. Given the prevalence of this pattern of property transfer, real property transferred from one generation to the next and held in a tenancy in common is referred to colloquially in many communities from those in the Southeast to those in Appalachia to those in Indian Country as "heirs property" or "heirs' property." Families who own tenancy-in-common property within these communities refer to their family real property holdings as heirs property whether some or all of the members of these families acquired their interests by intestate succession, by will, or by gift. Consistent with the widespread usage of the term within these communities, this Act utilizes the term "heirs property" and defines it under Section 2 consistent with how many communities throughout the country understand the term; therefore, the definition of heirs property is not limited to property in which one or more cotenants acquire their interests by intestacy as usage of the term "heirs" may suggest in some technical sense.

Many if not most of these heirs property owners have little or no understanding of the legal rules governing partition of tenancy-in-common property as studies have revealed, due to the fact that many of the rules are counterintuitive. For example, many of these owners believe that their property ownership is secure because they pay property taxes, they live on the land, and they make productive use of the land. They also believe that their property may only be sold against their will if a majority or more of their cotenants agree, which gives some of these families with a large number of members with an interest in the property false confidence that their ownership is extremely secure.

These families think it is inconceivable that one cotenant with a very small ownership interest can force a sale against the wishes of all other cotenants. Unfortunately, the first time that many of these owners are informed about the actual legal rules governing partition is after a partition action has been filed, and often after critical, early court rulings have been made against them. In contrast, there have been many well-documented cases in which an outside speculator who acquired a very small interest in a parcel of heirs property that had been owned by a family for decades has been able to convince a court soon after the speculator acquired its interest to order a partition by sale of the property despite the fact that the family opposed the request for a partition by sale and despite the family's longstanding ownership. In short, the law of partition often functions to give those cotenants who petition a court to force a sale upon their fellow cotenants an eminent domain-like power of condemnation. Unlike eminent domain, however, under a partition by sale, those who end up losing ownership of their property at the conclusion of the forced sale are not entitled to be paid fair market value compensation or any minimum level of compensation for that matter for having their property rights extinguished.

Partition Sales and Other Heirs Property Problems in Certain Select Communities

African-Americans have experienced tremendous land loss over the course of the past century. For example, although African-Americans acquired between sixteen and nineteen million acres of agricultural land between the end of the Civil War and 1920, African-Americans retain ownership of approximately just seven million acres of agricultural land today. Scholars and advocates who have analyzed patterns of landownership within the African-American community agree that partition sales of heirs property have been one of the leading causes of involuntary land loss within the African-American community. A considerable body of legal scholarship has highlighted the fact that partition sales have been a leading cause of African-American land loss. Many newspapers have published articles documenting the manner in which particular African-American families have lost land that had been in their families for generations after an outsider acquired a small interest from a family member and then in short order was able to convince a court to order the property sold at a partition sale. The Associated Press's 2001 award-winning series on African-American land loss, Torn from the Land, brought national attention to the manner in which partition sales have stripped African-American families of large amounts of land and wealth.

As a result of this legal scholarship and media attention, several years ago the American Bar Association's Section on Real Property, Trust and Estate Law established its Property Preservation Task Force. Along with the public interest and civil rights law firms and the community development and community-based organizations that have been working on heirs property issues for decades, the A.B.A.'s task force has been working to decrease the incidence of forced sales of heirs property that has so negatively impacted African-American and other poor and minority property owners. Nevertheless, the organizations that have been working tirelessly with families who wish to maintain their heirs property holdings or at least the wealth associated with such real estate holdings will continue to face nearly insurmountable obstacles in providing meaningful assistance to significant numbers of those with heirs property problems until the default rules governing the partition of tenancy-in-common ownership are reformed to make the law of partition more just and more sensible.

Although the issue of the substantial loss of African-American land due to partition sales has received more national attention than the land loss in other communities resulting from partition sales, it is important to recognize that forced partition sales have negatively impacted other communities as well, especially other low-income and low-wealth communities. For example, Mexican-Americans lost hundreds of thousands of acres of land in New Mexico and other states after a significant amount of their community-owned property was improperly classified as tenancy-in-common property and was then ordered sold under partition sales in the aftermath of the Mexican-American War. In most instances, the land was sold for a price that was far below the market value of the land. This occurred in part because, like heirs property owners today, the members of the community who had rights to the land prior to the partition sales were not able to bid effectively at the partition sale auctions because they were land rich but cash poor.

Property owners in other communities have been negatively impacted as well. For example, in parts of Appalachia, heirs property has been hypothesized to be correlated with, and a cause of, the persistence of poverty. Case studies suggest that heirs property owners in Appalachia are often concerned that one of their fellow cotenants might sell his or her interest to a wealthy buyer who will request a court to order the property partitioned by sale and then will purchase the property at the auction. Some American Indians also have had their family property sold against their will at partition sales.

Heirs property ownership has presented vexing problems to property owners in cities such as New Orleans. In New Orleans, many poor property owners were not able to draw upon governmental programs such as the "Road Home" program administered by the Department of Housing and Urban Development

which were established in the wake of Hurricane Katrina to provide financial assistance to property owners who had been harmed. A significant percentage of these poor property owners owned heirs property, which created merchantable title problems which needed to be resolved before the property owners could qualify for the governmental programs. These problems typically could not be resolved without hiring attorneys whom most of these property owners could not afford in contrast to the surprisingly large number of wealthy heirs property owners who were brought to light in the aftermath of Katrina who were able to hire attorneys to resolve their title problems. As in rural areas, partition sales have also resulted in the deprivation of property rights and the loss of wealth in urban areas undergoing gentrification.

As the post-Katrina New Orleans experience demonstrates, a surprising number of property owners who are not poor or minority also experience significant problems with heirs property ownership. In Maine, for example, heirs property is commonly referred to as "heirlocked property." Those who own such property in Maine experience many of the same problems that those who own heirs property elsewhere experience, including problems with unstable ownership. This has occurred in part because many properties that were not considered economically valuable in Maine fifty or sixty years ago increasingly lie in the path of development and because the ownership of many of these properties has become more fragmented with the passage of time as many interests in such property have been transferred by intestacy. Those who own heirs property in Maine also are often unable to manage their property in a rational way because some passive or uncooperative cotenants either do not contribute their share of the expenses needed to maintain ownership of the property or refuse to give their needed consent to plans that their more active fellow cotenants formulate to improve the management, stability, and utilization of the property. As is the case all across the country, many of those who own heirs property in Maine who are committed to maintaining ownership of the property within their families find themselves locked into a dysfunctional common ownership arrangement because there are no legal mechanisms to consolidate title to such property among family members who have been active and responsible owners.

Tenants in Common Often Lose Significant Wealth as a Result of Partition Sales

Those who own tenancy-in-common property under the default rules are not only at risk of losing their real property at a forced partition sale, but also are in danger of losing a significant portion of their wealth. In many states, a court will order a partition by sale under an "economics-only" test in which the court considers the hypothetical fair market value of the property in its entirety as compared to the fair market value of the subparcels that would result from a partition in kind. If the court finds that the fair market value of the property as a whole is greater than the aggregated fair market value of the subparcels, the court will order a partition by sale. Under this approach, the tenants in common theoretically should receive an economic benefit from the partition by sale.

In fact, most tenants in common are economically harmed when a court orders a partition by sale. First, the courts usually order the property sold at auctions in which the property is sold utilizing the procedures used for forced sales such as a sale under execution. These forced sales are notorious for selling property well below its fair market value which is ironic because judges often order the partition sale in the first instance because they claim that the cotenants will receive an economic benefit based upon an assumption that the sale will yield a fair market value price. When auction sales are challenged for yielding low sales prices, courts rarely overturn such sales as most courts utilize a "shock the conscience" standard to evaluate the sale. Under this standard, sales have been confirmed even though the property sold for twenty percent or less of its market value even though the court ordered a partition sale in the first instance because it indicated that a partition sale would likely provide the cotenants with an economic benefit.

Next, a number of fees and costs must first be paid to others before the remaining proceeds of a sale are distributed to the tenants in common. These fees often include costs incurred in selling the property including the fees of court-appointed commissioners or referees (often five percent or more of the sales price), surveyor fees, and attorney's fees which usually constitute ten percent of the sales price in the many states that permit such an attorney's fee award in a partition action. At the time a court orders a partition by sale under an economics-only test, these fees and costs are not taken into account although they can in fact be quite substantial and undermine any hypothetical economic benefit a cotenant would receive from a partition sale.

Poorer families who own heirs property are particularly at risk of having their property sold for a low sales price at partition sales. This phenomenon can be explained by the fact that these heirs property owners are not able to bid competitively at the partition sale auction because they are unable to secure any financing to make an effective bid and because they are cash poor. Banks and other lending institutions will not accept a partial interest in tenancy-in-common property as collateral to secure a loan and most of these heirs property owners cannot otherwise obtain financing because they often have few other assets to offer as collateral to secure a loan. Given that partition sales in general often attract few bidders, an auction of heirs property in which family members of limited economic means are unable to make any competitive bids is likely to yield a particularly low sales price as the winning bidder often needs only to submit a lowball bid in order to acquire the property as few if any other competitive bids are typically made in such cases.

Partition sales that result in an involuntary loss of property rights and in the loss of wealth may be very harmful, and even devastating to one or more of the cotenants and their relatives, depending on the facts of the particular case. The purpose of this Act is to ameliorate, to the extent feasible, the adverse consequences of a partition action when there are some cotenants who wish, for various reasons, to retain possession of some or all of the land, and other cotenants who would like the property to be sold. At the same time, the Act recognizes the legitimate rights of each cotenant to secure his, her, or its relative share of the current market value of the property and to seek to consolidate ownership of the property. Overall, the Act seeks to improve the law of partition with respect to cases involving family-owned tenancy-in-common property by ensuring that each cotenant in a partition action is treated in a fair and equitable manner.

PROP §23A.001. SHORT TITLE

This chapter may be cited as the Uniform Partition of Heirs' Property Act.

History of Prop. Code §23A.001: Enacted by S.B. 499, §1, 85th Leg., eff. Sept. 1, 2017.

PROP §23A.002. DEFINITIONS

In this chapter:

(1) "Ascendant" means an individual who precedes another individual in lineage, in the direct line of ascent from the other individual.

(2) "Collateral" means an individual who is related to another individual under the law of intestate succession of this state but who is not the other individual's ascendant or descendant.

(3) "Descendant" means an individual who follows another individual in lineage, in the direct line of descent from the other individual.

(4) "Determination of value" means a court order determining the fair market value of heirs' property under Section 23A.006 or 23A.010 or adopting the valuation of the property agreed to by all cotenants.

(5) "Heirs' property" means real property held in tenancy in common that satisfies all of the following requirements as of the filing of a partition action:

(A) there is no agreement in a record binding all the cotenants that governs the partition of the property;

(B) one or more of the cotenants acquired title from a relative, whether living or deceased; and

(C) any of the following applies:

(i) 20 percent or more of the interests are held by cotenants who are relatives;

(ii) 20 percent or more of the interests are held by an individual who acquired title from a relative, whether living or deceased; or

(iii) 20 percent or more of the cotenants are relatives.

(6) "Partition by sale" means a court-ordered sale of the entire heirs' property, whether by open-market sale, sealed bids, or auction conducted under Section 23A.010.

(7) "Partition in kind" means the division of heirs' property into physically distinct and separately titled parcels.

(8) "Record" means information that is inscribed on a tangible medium or that is stored in an electronic or other medium and is retrievable in perceivable form.

(9) "Relative" means an ascendant, descendant, or collateral or an individual otherwise related to another individual by blood, marriage, adoption, or law of this state other than this chapter.

History of Prop. Code §23A.002: Enacted by S.B. 499, §1, 85th Leg., eff. Sept. 1, 2017.

NCCUSL Comment*

1. Section 23A.002(1): In common usage, an ancestor is defined as "one from whom a person lineally descended." Wills v. Le Munyon, 107 A. 159, 161 (N.J. Ch. 1919). However, statutes of descent often narrow the term to "any one from whom an estate is inherited." *Id.* Thus, use of the term ancestor could be interpreted to exclude property acquired from a living person. In contrast, ascendant encompasses anyone who precedes an individual in lineage such as an individual's parents or grandparents, whether living or deceased. The term ascendant is used in a number of statutes encompassing many different subject matter areas. *See, e.g.*, ARK. CODE ANN. §28-9-202 (2009); CONN. GEN. STAT. §45a-755 (2010); IOWA CODE §428A.2 (2010); FLA. STAT. §732.403 (2009); LA. CIV. CODE ANN. art. 1301 (2009); MISS. CODE ANN. §93-13-253; P.R. LAWS ANN. TIT. 31 §2413 (209); TEX. ESTATES CODE ANN. §676 (Vernon 2009).

2. Sections 23A.002(1)-(3): The specific classes of people who may be considered ascendants, descendants, or collaterals shall be defined under state law.

3. Section 23A.002(5): Heirs property is defined in this Act to include only a subset of tenancy-in-common property. At minimum, for tenancy-in-common property to be considered heirs property, title must be acquired by at least one of the cotenants in an intergenerational transfer from a relative of that cotenant who was either that cotenant's ascendant, descendant, or collateral at the time title was transferred. Further, the Act does not apply to tenancy-in-common property in which all of the cotenants are subject to a binding agreement that governs the partition of the property, including binding agreements that run to successors and assigns. Tenancy-in-common property that is acquired by investors in part to qualify for federal like-kind exchange treatment under §1031 of the Internal Revenue Code and that is subject to an agreement governing the partition of the property is excluded from this Act. Furthermore the Act does not apply to "first generation" tenancy-in-common property established under the default rules and still owned exclusively by the original cotenants even if there is no agreement in a record among the cotenants governing the partition of the property. "First generation" tenancy-in-common property, however, may be converted into heirs property if a cotenant with an interest in such "first generation" tenancy-in-common property transfers all or a part of his or her interest to a relative provided that the other criteria for classifying property as heirs property are satisfied.

Joint tenancy property is not covered by this Act. In order for any real property that was initially owned by two or more individuals as joint tenancy property to be covered by this Act, one or more of the joint tenants must sever the joint tenancy in accordance with the requirements of state law. Once a joint tenancy is severed, this Act may apply if the property is determined to be heirs property at the time of the filing of a partition action even if two or more individuals who had formerly been joint tenants prior to severance of the joint tenancy remain joint tenants with each other after severance with respect to a particular interest in the tenancy in common. See 7-51 RICHARD R. POWELL, POWELL ON REAL PROPERTY §51.04(1)(a) (Michael Allen Wolf ed., 2009). See also Carmack v. Place, 535 P.2d 197 (Co. 1975).

4. Section 23A.002(5)(A): If tenants in common acquire their interests through a deed or a will that does not govern the manner in which the tenancy-in-common property may be partitioned, the deed or will alone shall not be construed to be an agreement in a record among all the tenants in common which governs the partition of the property within the meaning of §23A.002(5)(A).

5. Section 23A.002(8): Information that constitutes a "record" under this Act need not be recorded.

6. Section 23A.002(9): A relative as that term is defined under this Act does not include a person who is related to another person only by affinity. The definition of relative does encompass individuals who are determined to be relatives under state law even if, for example, it has not been established that these individuals are genetically related. For example, under the Uniform Parentage Act, a man may be determined to be the father of a child even if paternity has not been established by genetic testing.

7. Section 23A.002(9): In a partition action, a state court may apply the state's choice of law rules to determine whether two or more cotenants may be determined to be relatives. Under its choice of law analysis, the court could determine that two or more cotenants are relatives based upon application of the substantive law of another state because the law that applies under a state's choice of law rules would constitute "other law of this state" under §23A.002(9).

PROP §23A.003. APPLICABILITY; RELATION TO OTHER LAW

(a) In an action to partition real property under Chapter 23, the court shall determine whether the property is heirs' property. If the court determines that the property is heirs' property, the property must be partitioned under this chapter unless all of the cotenants otherwise agree in a record.

(b) This chapter supplements Chapter 23 and the Texas Rules of Civil Procedure governing partition of real property. If an action is governed by this chapter, this chapter supersedes provisions of Chapter 23 and the Texas Rules of Civil Procedure governing partition of real property that are inconsistent with this chapter.

History of Prop. Code §23A.003: Enacted by S.B. 499, §1, 85th Leg., eff. Sept. 1, 2017.

NCCUSL Comment*

1. Section 23A.003(a): A final order of a court in a partition action filed on or after the date this Act becomes effective is subject to challenge if the court failed to determine whether the real property in question is heirs property as that term is defined under this Act.

2. Section 23A.003(a): In a partition action, after a court has determined that the property in question is heirs property, all of the cotenants may agree to partition the property utilizing an agreed upon method or procedure that is different from the procedures required by this Act provided that the agreement is contained in a record.

* See footnote on p. 142.

PROP §23A.004. SERVICE; NOTICE BY POSTING

(a) This chapter does not limit or affect the method by which service of a petition in a partition action may be made.

(b) If the plaintiff in a partition action seeks citation by publication and the court determines that the property may be heirs' property, the plaintiff, not later than the 10th day after the date the determination is made, shall post, and maintain while the action is pending, a conspicuous sign on the property that is the subject of the action. The sign must state that the action has commenced and identify the name and address of the court and the common designation by which the property is known. The court may require the plaintiff to publish on the sign the name of the plaintiff and the known defendants.

History of Prop. Code §23A.004: Enacted by S.B. 499, §1, 85th Leg., eff. Sept. 1, 2017.

NCCUSL Comment*

1. Section 23A.004(b): In some instances, some states require by statute that a sign or notice be posted in a conspicuous place on real property that may be subject to a forced sale. *See, e.g.*, ARIZ. REV. STAT. ANN. §42-18266 (2010) (in connection with property that is subject to foreclosure for delinquent taxes, requiring in certain circumstances the placing of a sign in a conspicuous place on the property describing the property, indicating that the property is subject to foreclosure, and giving notice about the manner in which the owner may redeem the tax lien); CAL. CIV. CODE §2924f (West 2010) (in most nonjudicial foreclosures by power of sale, requiring that a copy of the notice of sale be posted in a conspicuous place on the real property in question and that the notice of sale contain relevant information about the power of sale foreclosure action).

PROP §23A.005. COMMISSIONERS

If the court appoints commissioners under Rule 761, Texas Rules of Civil Procedure, each commissioner, in addition to the requirements and disqualifications applicable to commissioners under that rule, must be impartial and may not be a party to or a participant in the action.

History of Prop. Code §23A.005: Enacted by S.B. 499, §1, 85th Leg., eff. Sept. 1, 2017.

PROP §23A.006. DETERMINATION OF VALUE

(a) Except as provided by Subsection (b) or (c), if the court determines that the property that is the subject of a partition action is heirs' property, the court shall determine the fair market value of the property by ordering an appraisal under Subsection (d).

(b) If all cotenants have agreed to the value of the property or to another method of valuation, the court shall adopt that value or the value produced by the agreed method of valuation.

(c) If the court determines that the evidentiary value of an appraisal is outweighed by the cost of the appraisal, the court, after an evidentiary hearing, shall determine the fair market value of the property and send notice to the parties of the value.

(d) If the court orders an appraisal, the court shall appoint a disinterested real estate appraiser to determine the fair market value of the property assuming sole ownership of the fee simple estate. On completion of the appraisal, the appraiser shall file a sworn or verified appraisal with the court.

(e) If an appraisal is conducted under Subsection (d), not later than the 10th day after the date the appraisal is filed, the court shall send notice to each party with a known address, stating:

(1) the appraised fair market value of the property;

(2) that the appraisal is available at the clerk's office; and

(3) that a party may file with the court an objection to the appraisal not later than the 30th day after the date notice is sent, stating the grounds for the objection.

(f) If an appraisal is filed with the court under Subsection (d), the court shall conduct a hearing to determine the fair market value of the property not earlier than the 30th day after the date a copy of the notice of the appraisal is sent to each party under Subsection (e), whether or not an objection to the appraisal is filed under Subsection (e)(3). In addition to the court-ordered appraisal, the court may consider any other evidence of value offered by a party.

(g) After a hearing under Subsection (f), but before considering the merits of the partition action, the court shall determine the fair market value of the property and send notice to the parties of the value.

History of Prop. Code §23A.006: Enacted by S.B. 499, §1, 85th Leg., eff. Sept. 1, 2017.

NCCUSL Comment*

1. Section 23A.006(a): Some states require that any property that may be subject to partition by sale shall first be appraised before a court decides whether to order partition in kind or partition by sale. *See, e.g.*, N.M. STAT. §42-5-7 (2009). Other states require that nearly all real property that is to be sold under an order or a judgment of a court must be appraised before the property is sold. *See, e.g.*, KY. REV. STAT. ANN. §426.520 (West 2010).

2. Section 23A.006(b): The court may not adopt a monetary value for the property that only some of the cotenants but not others have agreed upon or a valuation derived from an alternative method of valuation that only some of the cotenants have agreed upon even if the only cotenants that have not agreed to the value of the property or to another method of valuation are cotenants that are unknown, unlocatable, or otherwise remain unascertained.

* See footnote on p. 142.

3. Section 23A.006(b): The cotenants may agree that the property should be valued utilizing a less expensive method of valuation than an appraisal in situations, for example, in which the cotenants lack the expertise to value the property themselves. For example, the cotenants may agree to authorize two real estate brokers each to submit a broker's opinion of value and further may agree that the two valuation opinions should be averaged to determine the value of the property.

4. Section 23A.006(d): Under certain circumstances, some states require that property that is to be sold by partition by sale be appraised by one or more disinterested persons. *See, e.g.*, MINN. STAT. §558.17 (2009) (providing that property subject to partition by sale shall be appraised by two or more disinterested persons before the property is sold if the court orders the property sold at a private sale instead of at a public auction). In some instances, states require that certain court-appointed real estate appraisers must be state-certified and in good standing with the state appraisal authorities. *See, e.g.*, OKLA. STAT. tit. 52, §318.5 (2009).

5. Section 23A.006(d): State statutes and case law typically refer to one person's exclusive ownership of property as "sole ownership." *See, e.g.*, CAL. CIV. CODE §681 (2010) (designating the ownership of property by a single person as a sole or several ownership); FLA. STAT. §711.502 (2009) ("Only individuals whose registration of a security shows sole ownership by one individual ... may obtain registration in beneficiary form"); MONT. CODE ANN. 70-1-305 (2009); S.D. CODIFIED LAWS §43-2-10 (2009) ("The ownership of property by a single person is designated as a sole or several ownership."). *See also In re Robertson*, 203 F.3d 855, 860 (5th Cir. 2000) ("[T]he assets of which each former spouse acquires sole ownership is reclassified by law as the separate, exclusive property of that former spouse.").

PROP §23A.007. COTENANT BUYOUT

(a) If any cotenant requested partition by sale, after the determination of value under Section 23A.006, the court shall send notice to the parties that any cotenant except a cotenant that requested partition by sale may buy all the interests of the cotenants that requested partition by sale.

(b) Not later than the 45th day after the date notice is sent under Subsection (a), any cotenant except a cotenant that requested partition by sale may give notice to the court that the cotenant elects to buy all the interests of the cotenants that requested partition by sale.

(c) The purchase price for each of the interests of a cotenant that requested partition by sale is the value of the entire parcel determined under Section 23A.006 multiplied by the cotenant's fractional ownership of the entire parcel.

(d) After the period provided by Subsection (b) expires:

(1) if only one cotenant elects to buy all the interests of the cotenants that requested partition by sale, the court shall notify all the parties of that fact;

(2) if more than one cotenant elects to buy all the interests of the cotenants that requested partition by sale, the court shall:

(A) allocate the right to buy those interests among the electing cotenants based on each electing cotenant's existing fractional ownership of the entire parcel divided by the total existing fractional ownership of all cotenants electing to buy; and

(B) send notice to all the parties of that fact and of the price to be paid by each electing cotenant; or

(3) if no cotenant elects to buy all the interests of the cotenants that requested partition by sale, the court shall:

(A) send notice to all the parties of that fact; and

(B) resolve the partition action under Section 23A.008(a) or (b).

(e) If the court sends notice to the parties under Subsection (d)(1) or (2), the court shall set a date, not earlier than the 60th day after the date notice was sent, by which an electing cotenant must pay the cotenant's apportioned price into the court. After that date:

(1) if all electing cotenants timely pay their apportioned price into court, the court shall:

(A) issue an order reallocating all the interests of the cotenants; and

(B) disburse the amounts held by the court to the persons entitled to them;

(2) if no electing cotenant timely pays its apportioned price, the court shall resolve the partition action under Section 23A.008(a) or (b) as if the interests of the cotenants that requested partition by sale were not purchased; or

(3) if one or more but not all of the electing cotenants fail to pay their apportioned price on time, the court shall give notice to the electing cotenants that paid their apportioned price of the interest remaining and the price for all that interest.

(f) Not later than the 20th day after the date the court gives notice under Subsection (e)(3), any cotenant that paid may elect to purchase all of the remaining interest by paying the entire price into the court. After that period expires:

(1) if only one cotenant pays the entire price for the remaining interest, the court shall:

(A) issue an order reallocating the remaining interest to that cotenant;

(B) promptly issue an order reallocating the interests of all of the cotenants; and

(C) disburse the amounts held by the court to the persons entitled to the amounts;

(2) if no cotenant pays the entire price for the remaining interest, the court shall resolve the partition action under Section 23A.008(a) or (b) as if the inter-

ests of the cotenants that requested partition by sale were not purchased; or

(3) if more than one cotenant pays the entire price for the remaining interest, the court shall:

(A) reapportion the remaining interest among those paying cotenants, based on each paying cotenant's original fractional ownership of the entire parcel divided by the total original fractional ownership of all cotenants that paid the entire price for the remaining interest;

(B) promptly issue an order reallocating all of the cotenants' interests;

(C) disburse the amounts held by the court to the persons entitled to the amounts; and

(D) promptly refund any excess payment held by the court.

(g) Not later than the 45th day after the date the court sends notice to the parties under Subsection (a), any cotenant entitled to buy an interest under this section may request the court to authorize the sale as part of the pending action of the interests of cotenants named as defendants and served with the complaint but that did not appear in the action.

(h) If the court receives a timely request under Subsection (g), the court, after hearing, may deny the request or authorize the requested additional sale on such terms as the court determines are fair and reasonable, subject to the following limitations:

(1) a sale authorized under this subsection may occur only after the purchase prices for all interests subject to sale under Subsections (a) through (f) have been paid into court and those interests have been reallocated among the cotenants as provided in those subsections; and

(2) the purchase price for the interest of a nonappearing cotenant is based on the court's determination of value under Section 23A.006.

History of Prop. Code §23A.007: Enacted by S.B. 499, §1, 85th Leg., eff. Sept. 1, 2017.

NCCUSL Comment*

1. This Act includes a mechanism for the buyout of interests as the first preferred alternative to partition by sale to promote judicial economy, to encourage consolidation of ownership, and to accomplish the larger goal of establishing a default, statutory approach to partition of inherited property which mirrors the best practices used for family property owned by those who are wealthy and legally savvy. Private tenancy-in-common agreements, whether for family property or commercial property, virtually always provide that a cotenant that wishes to exit ownership must first offer his or her interest for sale to other cotenants.

Conducting the interest buyout process first may achieve sufficient consolidation of interests or alignment of interests among remaining cotenants that buyout eliminates the need for either partition in kind or partition by sale, and the relatively greater associated time, costs and complexities of the two latter remedies.

2. Although this section is one of the longer sections of the Act, it is streamlined compared to most, if not all, buyout provisions in written private agreements such as limited liability company operating agreements and tenancy-in-common agreements, and compared to buyout statutes in those states which have them. This streamlined buyout mechanism is consistent with the default rule nature of the overall Act.

Most of the detail of the section arises from the need to describe the procedural steps and mathematical proportions applicable at various stages in the buyout process, and to guide courts, that may not be familiar with buyout contracts or their corporate cousins, subscription agreements, including the possible outcomes of each step in a buyout and the next judicial action to assure an orderly process completed efficiently. Again, implementation of a buyout procedure in a given case is likely to be by far the fastest and simplest remedy to implement, both in comparison with partition in kind and partition by sale. Even allowing for motion practice, the expectation is that the mandatory buyout provisions of this Act could be and typically should be completed within a maximum of four to six months after the court establishes the value of the underlying real property (which must be done in any case under the Act).

3. Only those cotenants that seek partition by sale are mandatorily subject to the buyout. A cotenant who seeks partition by sale has already determined that he or she is willing to be divested of any interest in the real property owned in common in exchange for being paid money for any such divested interest. This is not necessarily true of cotenants that seek partition in kind or cotenants that are respondents in the partition proceeding. A principal historical justification for the remedy of a forced sale in many contexts has been to allow owners no longer desiring to participate in ownership to exit. A buyout mechanism such as the one in this section accomplishes this purpose without divesting owners who affirmatively indicate their preference for continuing ownership.

4. The buyout section gives a court, upon prompt motion, the discretion to conduct or not to conduct a second buyout process for the interests of cotenants who are respondents (a.k.a. defendants) in the action but do not file an appearance. In any case the first, mandatory buyout process for cotenants seeking partition by sale must be completed (and must result in a buyout) before the second, discretionary buyout process can begin. This ensures the best chance to consolidate interests in those cotenants who wish to continue to own a parcel of property together, by limiting the amount of money the purchasing cotenants need (just enough to purchase the interests of those who wish to partition the property by sale). Because banks and other institutional lenders virtually never lend on cotenancy interests, purchasers will need to use personal savings or other family capital to fund a buyout. In many cases, however, the interests (and value of interests) of those seeking partition by sale is relatively small and, if shared among several purchasing cotenants, will be within the means of many low to middle-income cotenants.

The section allows, in subsections (g) and (h), for the potential, discretionary buyout of cotenants who fail to appear in the action. This provision is intended to foster consolidation of interests among active cotenants (which makes any division in kind that may ultimately be needed easier for a court to accomplish), and to provide a fund of money based on a court-approved appraisal of land value, rather than a divided portion of land of potentially less certain value, for the benefit of those cotenants who cannot be located or who fail to appear and participate in the action. Courts should consider, however, that many small interest holders sometimes do not believe the court really has the power to take away their interests or sell property and that others believe that resisting any request for a partition by sale is futile notwithstanding the merits of any particular case. Other cotenants do not appear because they do not have the money to hire counsel or the persistence or capacity to read and respond to pleadings. Therefore, a court should exercise discretion in deciding when to treat nonappearance in an action as an indication of a cotenant's limited resources, true indifference, or free riding on other cotenants. Nonetheless, in the relatively common event where there are dozens or even scores of inactive or unlocatable cotenants, the discretionary buyout may be a valuable tool to consolidate ownership among active, engaged cotenants while still preserving property value for other cotenants.

Although it is always true that cotenants could buy and sell interests outside of a court proceeding, the statutory buyout provision has the benefit of (a) using an appraised, court-set valuation, and (b) outlining a clear process

* See footnote on p. 142.

with short timeframes. It thus eliminates two discussion points on which negotiations among cotenants often founder. The framework of the statutory buyout provision also creates a model which cotenants can use (and to which courts can direct the attention of litigants) to structure their own, private deals to value and sell interests in land among themselves without court involvement or as a supplement to judicial process.

5. The buyout section in the Act contemplates that the price for interests available for purchase (mandatorily or with leave of court) will be the simple result of multiplying the court-determined value of the entire real property (usually appraised value, but sometimes a value agreed on by all parties) by the partial interest available for purchase (whether expressed as a fraction or as a percentage).

So, for example, if John Smith owns a 10% cotenant interest in Greenacre, which is heirs property, he brings an action for partition by sale, and the appraised value of Greenacre accepted by the court is $100,000, then John Smith's cotenancy interest will be priced at $10,000 for statutory buyout purposes, and each of the other cotenants will have the right to purchase a pro rata share of John Smith's cotenancy interest for a pro rata share of the $10,000 price.

It is important to note that this likely overvalues John Smith's interest under classic concepts of valuation (because the $10,000 price disregards the discount for Smith owning only a 10%, minority interest, and disregards the further discount typically applied by valuators to interests in tenancy in common property due to its inherently unstable characteristics). The drafters concluded, however, that the simplicity of the math and the quid pro quo of somewhat enhanced value compensated for making Smith's interest mandatorily subject to the buyout by statute once he sought partition by sale.

6. In overview, the buyout section of this Act contemplates that the court will:

- establish the value of the entire real property;
- allow cotenants other than the petitioner for sale 45 days to express interest in purchasing the interests available for purchase (so the court can then determine pro rata shares and prices for each purchaser, using a simple mathematical ratio);
- give the purchasers who timely expressed interest in buying an additional, brief period to be determined by the court (at least 60 days, but preferably not much longer, due to the fact that property values are a function of market conditions over time) in which to pay the purchase price into court;
- if there is a failure of some purchasers to pay their apportioned price on time, the court will conduct a quick, 20-day, "savings" round in which any purchaser who timely paid can buy the entire remaining interest for which purchase money was not timely paid (and if more than one purchaser "saves" the buyout by paying such entire amount, then the cost and interest in question is split pro rata among those purchasers who act to save the buyout); and
- close the buyout, by paying the purchase price to the former cotenant who has been bought out, and issuing an order stating the new cotenancy interests among the remaining cotenants.

If the buyout fails for any reason or if there is any cotenant remaining at the conclusion of the buyout that has requested partition in kind, the Act contemplates that the court will then proceed to a partition in kind or a partition by sale (with a clear preference for a partition in kind).

7. The pro rata share any given cotenant may purchase is equal to his original share in the tenancy-in-common property divided by the total share of all those cotenants that elected to buy. In addition, the price to be paid by any given purchaser is that same fraction or percentage multiplied by the total value of the interest to be purchased.

So, continuing with the example begun in paragraph 5, above, we have John Smith, a 10% cotenant of Greenacre, who has filed a petition for partition by sale. John Smith's cotenancy interest is mandatorily subject to buyout by the cotenants who did not request partition by sale. The court determines the value of Greenacre pursuant to the Act and notifies the parties that John Smith's 10% interest is available to be bought out by his cotenants (the example assumes no other cotenant has sought partition by sale).

Next, assume Betty Smith Jones who owned 25% of Greenacre, George Smith who owned 20% of Greenacre, and Harriet Long who owned 15% of Greenacre, were the only cotenants of John Smith who timely notify the court of their election to purchase John Smith's 10% interest in Greenacre. The total percentage interest in Greenacre of all potential purchasers who timely gave notice of desire to buy is thus 60%. The owners of the other 30% cotenancy interests in Greenacre either did not wish to purchase or did not timely respond to the buyout notice and so become ineligible to participate in the buyout of John Smith's 10% interest.

In this example, Betty has a right to purchase 25/60ths of John Smith's interest, George has the right to purchase 20/60ths of John Smith's interest, and Harriet has the right to purchase 15/60ths of John Smith's interest. The court would determine these percentages and notify Betty, George, and Harriet of the interests they could purchase, and the related purchase price each of them would have to pay. Since John Smith's 10% interest in Greenacre was statutorily valued at $10,000 in the example in paragraph 5, the price to Betty is $10,000 x (25/60), or $4,166.67. The price to George is $10,000 x (20/60), or $3,333.33. The price to Harriet is $10,000 x (15/60), or $2,500. Obviously minor amounts of rounding will be required in some cases, as above with George and Betty.

Now further assume that the court orders that all purchasers pay their respective purchase price into court within 90 days after the court's determination of purchasers' interests and purchase prices is docketed, and that Betty and George timely pay their respective $4,166.67 and $3,333.33 into court, but that Harriet fails to do so. Under the buyout section of the Act, the court will then notify Betty and George that 15/60ths (i.e., one-quarter) of John Smith's 10% interest is still available for purchase and that either Betty or George may purchase the entire such interest for $2,500 by paying that further sum into court within 20 days (absent which the buyout will fail and the court will proceed to determine whether partition in kind is possible or whether only partition by sale is appropriate).

Assume that Betty and George each timely post another $2,500 with the court in the "savings" round (i.e., a further total of $5,000, in addition to the aggregate $7,500 already posted by Betty and George in the initial round). Under these circumstances, the court will allow Betty and George each to purchase a further pro rata share (meaning pro rata as between them) of Harriet's 15/60ths portion of John Smith's 10% interest. In the case of Betty she may purchase a 25/45ths share of the portion Harriet failed timely to buy (the numerator in the fraction is Betty's original percentage interest in Greenacre and the denominator in the fraction is the total original percentage interests of the two cotenants who timely posted money in both the first buyout round and the "savings" round, Betty's original interest of 25% plus George's original 20% interest). George, similarly, may purchase a further 20/45ths share. In this case, where Betty and George each posted the entire $2,500 needed to "save" the buyout, Betty will ultimately pay $1,388.89 and George will ultimately pay $1,111.11; the remaining amounts posted by each of them in the savings round will be returned to them ($1,111.11 will be returned to Betty and $1,388.89 will be returned to George).

The court then issues an order in which it reallocates John Smith's original 10% interest in Greenacre as follows: 5.556% to Betty (25/60ths plus [25/45ths x 15/60ths]) and 4.444% to George (20/60ths plus [20/45ths x 15/60ths]), pays to John Smith the $10,000 the court received for his bought-out interest from Betty and George, and leaves the percentage interests of Harriet (who attempted to participate in the buyout but did not come up with the cash) and the other cotenants who did not participate in the buyout unchanged. To complete the example, as a result of the order the interests of the remaining cotenants (who are satisfied to remain cotenants) are: 30% various cotenants who did not participate in the buyout and whose interests are unchanged by the buyout, 15% Harriet who attempted to participate in the buyout but could not come up with the necessary money, and whose interest therefore remains unchanged by the buyout, 30.556% Betty (her original 25% plus 5.556% formerly owned by John Smith) and 24.444% George (20% plus 4.444%).

PROP §23A.008. PARTITION ALTERNATIVES

(a) If all the interests of all cotenants that requested partition by sale are not purchased by other cotenants under Section 23A.007, or if after conclusion of the buyout under Section 23A.007 a cotenant remains that has requested partition in kind, the court shall order partition in kind unless the court, after consideration of the factors listed in Section 23A.009, finds that partition in kind will result in substantial prejudice to the cotenants as a group. In considering whether to order partition in kind, the court shall approve a request

by two or more parties to have the requesting parties' individual interests aggregated.

(b) If the court does not order partition in kind under Subsection (a), the court shall order partition by sale under Section 23A.010 or, if no cotenant requested partition by sale, the court shall dismiss the action.

(c) If the court orders partition in kind under Subsection (a), the court may require that one or more cotenants pay one or more other cotenants amounts so that the payments, taken together with the value of the in-kind distributions to the cotenants, will make the partition in kind just and proportionate in value to the fractional interests held.

(d) If the court orders partition in kind, the court shall allocate to the cotenants that are unknown, unlocatable, or the subject of a default judgment, if those cotenants' interests were not bought out under Section 23A.007, a part of the property representing the combined interests of those cotenants as determined by the court, and that part of the property shall remain undivided.

History of Prop. Code §23A.008: Enacted by S.B. 499, §1, 85th Leg., eff. Sept. 1, 2017.

NCCUSL Comment*

1. In many states, a court may order a partition in kind of part of the property and a partition by sale of the remainder. *See, e.g.*, CAL. CIV. PROC. CODE §872.830 (West 2010); NEB. REV. STAT. §25-21,103 (2009). However, in a limited number of other states a court may only order either a partition in kind or a partition by sale of the whole property. *See, e.g.*, *Fernandes v. Rodriguez*, 761 A.2d 1283, 1289 (Conn. 2000). This Act neither prescribes nor prohibits a partition in kind of part of the heirs property and partition by sale of the remainder. For example, there may be circumstances in which cotenants receiving part of the property in kind would receive substantially less than their pro rata share of the economic value of the whole property without a cash payment from the sale of the part of the property to be sold and might wish the court to retain jurisdiction for purposes of completing the partition by sale of the remaining portion of the property (rather than employing "owelty," discussed in the next comment). It is in circumstances such as the last-mentioned case that the court should consider exercising its equitable discretion to implement a mixed remedy and to fashion such appropriate procedures as justice may require. These procedures should draw upon the procedures and the property and wealth preservation principles of this Act, including the hierarchy of sales procedures that apply to the manner in which a partition by sale should be conducted under this Act. If a court decides to order such a mixed remedy, the court may consider whether, in such a process, there should or should not be a further right to buy out interests before ordering a partition by sale of part of the property.

2. Section 23A.008(c): This subsection provides for the remedy of "owelty" which is an equitable remedy. *See, e.g.*, CODE OF ALA. §35-6-24 (2010); CAL. CIV. PROC. CODE §873.250 (West 2009). Courts have the equitable power to order owelty payments when it is impractical to divide an estate in a just manner but monetary payments can be ordered to adjust for any variance in the value of the parcels from the interests in the property held by the respective cotenants. *Dewrell v. Lawrence*, 58 P.3d 223, 227 (Okla. Civ. App. 2002). In recent decades, courts have tended to underutilize the remedy of owelty which has resulted in more courts ordering partition by sale in instances in which partition in kind could have been ordered with an appropriate accompanying owelty order. *See, e.g.*, Faith Rivers, *Inequity in Equity: The Tragedy of Tenancy in Common for Heirs' Property Owners Facing Partition in Equity*, 17 TEMP. POL. & CIV. RTS. L. REV. 1, 76 (2007) (noting that heirs property owners could obtain fair and equitable divisions of property if courts stopped taking the easy option by ordering partition sales and utilized tools such as owelty payments). *See also* John G. Casagrande Jr., Note, *Acquiring Property Through Partitioning Sales: Abuses and Remedies*, 27 B.C. L. REV. 755, 778 (1986). A court in a partition action involving heirs property that may be practicably divided among the cotenants in a manner that preserves the fair value of each cotenant's ownership interest may not order owelty merely because a cotenant is willing to pay for a parcel that is more valuable than the fair economic value of that cotenant's ownership interest.

3. Section 23A.008(d): Several states have statutory provisions which permit a court to order a partition in kind and to designate a part of the property for cotenants who remain unknown or unlocatable at the conclusion of the action. *See, e.g.*, ALASKA STAT. §09.45.290 (2010); ARK. CODE ANN. §18-60-414 (2010); CAL. CIV. PROC. CODE §873.270 (West 2010); HAW. REV. STAT. §668-9 (2010); MICH. COMP. LAWS §3.402 (2010); N.D. CENT. CODE §32-16-12 (2010); OR. REV. STAT. §105.245 (2010); S.D. CODIFIED LAWS §21-45-15 (2010); UTAH CODE ANN. §78B- 6-1212 (2010); WASH. REV. CODE §7.52.080 (2010).

PROP §23A.009. CONSIDERATIONS FOR PARTITION IN KIND

(a) In determining under Section 23A.008(a) whether partition in kind would result in substantial prejudice to the cotenants as a group, the court shall consider the following:

(1) whether the heirs' property practicably can be divided among the cotenants;

(2) whether partition in kind would apportion the property in such a way that the aggregate fair market value of the parcels resulting from the division would be materially less than the value of the property if the property were sold as a whole, taking into account the condition under which a court-ordered sale likely would occur;

(3) evidence of the collective duration of ownership or possession of the property by a cotenant and one or more predecessors in title or predecessors in possession to the cotenant who are or were relatives of the cotenant or each other;

(4) a cotenant's sentimental attachment to the property, including any attachment arising because the property has ancestral or other unique or special value to the cotenant;

(5) the lawful use being made of the property by a cotenant and the degree to which the cotenant would be harmed if the cotenant could not continue the same use of the property;

(6) the degree to which the cotenants have contributed the cotenants' pro rata share of the property taxes, insurance, and other expenses associated with maintaining ownership of the property or have contributed to the physical improvement, maintenance, or upkeep of the property; and

* See footnote on p. 142.

(7) any other relevant factor.

(b) The court may not consider any one factor under Subsection (a) to be dispositive without weighing the totality of all relevant factors and circumstances.

History of Prop. Code §23A.009: Enacted by S.B. 499, §1, 85th Leg., eff. Sept. 1, 2017.

NCCUSL Comment*

1. Under this section, a court in a partition action must consider the totality of the circumstances, including a number of economic and noneconomic factors, in deciding whether to order partition in kind or partition by sale. In partition cases, a number of courts have utilized such a totality of the circumstances approach in deciding whether to order partition in kind or partition by sale. *See, e.g.*, *Delfino v. Vealencis*, 436 A.2d 27, 33 (Conn. 1980) ("It is the interests of all of the tenants in common that the court must consider; and not merely the economic gain of one tenant, or a group of tenants."); *Schnell v. Schnell*, 346 N.W.2d 713, 716 (N.D. 1984) (holding that economic and noneconomic factors, including sentimental value, should be weighed by a court in a partition action); *Eli v. Eli*, 557 N.W.2d 405, 409-411 (S.D. 1997) (citations omitted) (in adopting a totality of the circumstances test, the Supreme Court of South Dakota stated that "[o]ne's land possesses more than mere economic utility; it 'means the full range of the benefit the parties may be expected to derive from their ownership of their respective shares.' Such value must be weighed for its effect upon all parties involved, not just those advocating a sale."); *Ark Land Co. v. Harper*, 599 S.E.2d. 754, 761 (W. Va. 2004) ("[I]n a partition proceeding in which a party opposes the sale of property, the economic value of the property is not the exclusive test for deciding whether to partition in kind or by sale. Evidence of longstanding ownership, coupled with sentimental or emotional interests in the property, may also be considered in deciding whether the interests of the party opposing the sale will be prejudiced by the property's sale.").

2. Section 23A.009(a)(2): Under this subparagraph, among other possible considerations of the condition under which the property may be sold, the court must assess whether the cotenants would receive a greater economic benefit from a sale of the whole property due to possible economies of scale that would result from selling the whole property which could not be captured from partition in kind of the property. In conducting this assessment, a court must take into consideration the type of sales condition under which any court-ordered sale would occur as property that is sold at a forced sale – such as a sale upon execution or a foreclosure sale – typically results in property being sold at prices that are substantially below the fair market value of the property. Such a resulting discount from the fair market value of the property due to the forced sale conditions may render partition in kind to be as, or more, economically beneficial to the cotenants than partition by sale of the whole property even in instances in which economies of scale could be realized if the whole property were to be sold under fair market value conditions. *See generally*, Thomas W. Mitchell, Stephen Malpezzi, & Richard K. Green, *Forced Sale Risk: Class, Race, and The "Double Discount,"* 37 FLA. ST. U. L. REV. 589 (2010).

3. Section 23A.009(a)(3): Under this subparagraph, the court shall consider, among other considerations, longstanding possession of the property by any cotenant or certain predecessors in possession to that cotenant. Adverse possession, for example, raises this issue. Adverse possession statutes require possession over the course of a number of years before a person may actually take title to the property. *See, e.g.*, 735 ILL. COMP. STAT. 5/13-101 (2009) (requiring twenty years of adverse possession); WIS. STAT. §§893.25, 893.26 (2008) (requiring twenty years or ten years if color of title). Thus, because many states allow tacking of possession, it is possible that a cotenant may have acquired possession of the property from a relative who had been in possession of the property for many years despite the fact that the statute of limitations for adverse possession had not run, thereby preventing the relative in prior possession from obtaining valid title to the property.

4. Section 23A.009(a)(4): For many families or communities, real property ownership has important ancestral or historical meaning. *See, e.g.*, *Chuck v. Gomes*, 532 P.2d 657, 662 (Haw. 1975) (Richardson, C.J., dissenting): "[T]here are interests other than financial expediency which I recognize as essential to our Hawaiian way of life. Foremost is the individual's right to retain ancestral land in order to perpetuate the concept of the family homestead. Such right is derived from our proud cultural heritage.... [W]e must not lose sight of the cultural traditions which attach fundamental importance to keeping ancestral land in a particular family line." *See also* Phyliss Craig-Taylor, *Through a Colored Looking Glass: A View of Judicial Partition, Family Land Loss, and Rule Setting*, 78 WASH U. L.Q. 737, 766-68, 772-74 (2000); Thomas W. Mitchell, *From Reconstruction to Deconstruction: Undermining Black Landownership, Political Independence, and Community Through Partition Sales of Tenancies in Common*, 95 NW. U. L. REV. 505, 523-26 (2001).

5. Section 23A.009(a)(5): If a single cotenant is using the property in an unlawful way, for example by engaging in conduct that amounts to an ouster of one or more other cotenants, the court shall not recognize such unlawful use as a factor weighing in favor of the court's granting a request made by the cotenant in possession for a partition in kind of the property.

6. After considering the factors in this section, a court that decides to order a partition in kind may not divide the heirs property in a manner that modifies the pre-partition, fair economic value of any cotenant's ownership interest in the property unless the court issues an appropriate owelty order pursuant to §23A.008(c). This proscription is consistent with the approach that courts utilize in ordering partition in kind under general partition statutes.

PROP §23A.010. OPEN-MARKET SALE, SEALED BIDS, OR AUCTION

(a) If the court orders a sale of heirs' property, the sale must be an open-market sale unless the court finds that a sale by sealed bids or at an auction would be more economically advantageous and in the best interest of the cotenants as a group.

(b) If the court orders an open-market sale and the parties, not later than the 10th day after the date the order is entered, agree on a real estate broker to offer the property for sale, the court shall appoint the broker and establish a reasonable commission. If the parties do not agree on a broker, the court shall appoint a disinterested real estate broker to offer the property for sale and shall establish a reasonable commission. The broker shall offer the property for sale in a commercially reasonable manner at a price no lower than the determination of value and on the terms and conditions established by the court.

(c) If the broker appointed under Subsection (b) obtains within a reasonable time an offer to purchase the property for at least the determination of value:

(1) the broker shall comply with the reporting requirements of Section 23A.011; and

(2) the sale may be completed in accordance with state law other than this chapter.

(d) If the broker appointed under Subsection (b) does not obtain within a reasonable time an offer to purchase the property for at least the determination of value, the court, after hearing, may:

(1) approve the highest outstanding offer, if any;

(2) redetermine the value of the property and order that the property continue to be offered for an additional time; or

* See footnote on p. 142.

(3) order that the property be sold by sealed bids or at an auction.

(e) If the court orders a sale by sealed bids or at an auction, the court shall set terms and conditions of the sale. If the court orders an auction, the auction must be conducted in the manner provided by law for a sale made under execution.

(f) If a purchaser is entitled to a share of the proceeds of the sale, the purchaser is entitled to a credit against the price in an amount equal to the purchaser's share of the proceeds.

History of Prop. Code §23A.010: Enacted by S.B. 499, §1, 85th Leg., eff. Sept. 1, 2017.

PROP §23A.011. REPORT OF OPEN-MARKET SALE

(a) Unless required to do so earlier by other law governing the partition of real property, a broker appointed under Section 23A.010(b) to offer heirs' property for open-market sale shall file a report with the court not later than the seventh day after the date an offer is received to purchase the property for at least the value determined under Section 23A.006 or 23A.010.

(b) The report required by Subsection (a) must contain the following information:

(1) a description of the property to be sold to each buyer;

(2) the name of each buyer;

(3) the proposed purchase price;

(4) the terms and conditions of the proposed sale, including the terms of any owner financing;

(5) the amounts to be paid to lienholders;

(6) a statement of contractual or other arrangements or conditions of the broker's commission; and

(7) other material facts relevant to the sale.

History of Prop. Code §23A.011: Enacted by S.B. 499, §1, 85th Leg., eff. Sept. 1, 2017.

PROP §23A.012. UNIFORMITY OF APPLICATION & CONSTRUCTION

In applying and construing this chapter, consideration must be given to the need to promote uniformity of the law with respect to the subject matter of this chapter among states that enact a law based on the uniform act on which this chapter is based.

History of Prop. Code §23A.012: Enacted by S.B. 499, §1, 85th Leg., eff. Sept. 1, 2017.

PROP §23A.013. RELATION TO ELECTRONIC SIGNATURES IN GLOBAL & NATIONAL COMMERCE ACT

This chapter modifies, limits, and supersedes the Electronic Signatures in Global and National Commerce Act (15 U.S.C. Section 7001 et seq.) but does not modify, limit, or supersede Section 101(c) of that act (15 U.S.C. Section 7001(c)) or authorize electronic delivery of any of the notices described in Section 103(b) of that act (15 U.S.C. Section 7003(b)).

History of Prop. Code §23A.013: Enacted by S.B. 499, §1, 85th Leg., eff. Sept. 1, 2017.

CHAPTER 24. FORCIBLE ENTRY & DETAINER

+ See §91.001 Notice to terminate certain Tenancies

PROP §24.001. FORCIBLE ENTRY & DETAINER

(a) A person commits a forcible entry and detainer if the person enters the real property of another without legal authority or by force and refuses to surrender possession on demand.

(b) For the purposes of this chapter, a forcible entry is:

(1) an entry without the consent of the person in actual possession of the property;

(2) an entry without the consent of a tenant at will or by sufferance; or

(3) an entry without the consent of a person who acquired possession by forcible entry.

History of Prop. Code §24.001: Acts 1983, 68th Leg., ch. 576, §1, eff. Jan. 1, 1984. Amended by Acts 1989, 71st Leg., ch. 688, §1, eff. Sept. 1, 1989. Source: TRCS arts. 3973, 3974.

See also CPRC §§15.084, 16.003; TRCP 510; *O'Connor's Texas COA*, "Forcible Detainer—Eviction," ch. 16-B, p. 424.

CHARTS

See timetable, "Eviction," p. 1541.

ANNOTATIONS

Home Sav. Ass'n v. Ramirez, 600 S.W.2d 911, 913-14 (Tex.App.—Corpus Christi 1980, writ ref'd n.r.e.). The justice court "cannot adjudicate title to the land. The court merely resolves who is entitled to immediate possession. [¶] The forcible entry and detainer action provides a party with an immediate legal remedy to obtain possession. But, this cause of action does not prohibit the filing of related suits to determine the validity of the trustee's deed itself. The action is cumulative of other remedies, not exclusive. The party who is removed from the property may challenge the trustee's deed in a suit in the district court. [¶] If other legal remedies exist, then a party may not seek equitable relief through an injunction. The district court has no authority to issue an injunction restraining the enforcement of a judgment of the justice court (or county court as here) if that judgment solely resolves who is entitled to immediate possession. Additionally, applications for injunction seeking equitable relief are subject to strict construction due to the cumulative nature of this action. [¶] It is clear from an examination of the Legislature's intent in creating the action of forcible entry and detainer and case-law interpretation of the statute that the district court in the case before us abused its discretion. [T]he last actual, peaceable noncontested possession of the house was that adjudicated by the county court in favor of [P]. By issuing the injunction prohibiting the execution of the writ of restitution, the trial court abused its discretion by changing the status quo." *See also* ***Ward v. Malone***, 115 S.W.3d 267, 270-71 (Tex.App.—Corpus Christi 2003, pet. denied); ***Ogden v. Coleman***, 660 S.W.2d 578, 582-83 (Tex.App.—Corpus Christi 1983, no writ).

PROP §24.002. FORCIBLE DETAINER

(a) A person who refuses to surrender possession of real property on demand commits a forcible detainer if the person:

(1) is a tenant or a subtenant wilfully and without force holding over after the termination of the tenant's right of possession;

(2) is a tenant at will or by sufferance, including an occupant at the time of foreclosure of a lien superior to the tenant's lease; or

(3) is a tenant of a person who acquired possession by forcible entry.

(b) The demand for possession must be made in writing by a person entitled to possession of the property and must comply with the requirements for notice to vacate under Section 24.005.

History of Prop. Code §24.002: Acts 1983, 68th Leg., ch. 576, §1, eff. Jan. 1, 1984. Amended by Acts 1985, 69th Leg., ch. 200, §1, eff. Aug. 26, 1985; Acts 1989, 71st Leg., ch. 688, §2, eff. Sept. 1, 1989. Source: TRCS arts. 3973, 3975.

See also CPRC §16.003; TRCP 510; *O'Connor's Texas COA*, "Forcible Detainer—Eviction," ch. 16-B, p. 424.

CHARTS

See timetable, "Eviction," p. 1541.

ANNOTATIONS

Shields L.P. v. Bradberry, ___ S.W.3d ___ (Tex. 2017) (No. 15-0803; 5-12-17). "To establish a superior right to immediate possession, [landlord] had the burden to prove (1) [landlord] owns the property, (2) [tenant] is either a tenant at will, tenant at sufferance, or a tenant or subtenant willfully holding over after the termination of the tenant's right of possession, (3) [landlord] gave proper notice to [tenant] to vacate the premises, and (4) [tenant] refused to vacate the premises. … The only dispute is whether the record conclusively establishes that [tenant's] right of possession terminated. [¶] Disposition of that matter ultimately turns on the force and effect of the parties' nonwaiver agreement, which unequivocally precludes a defense of waiver premised on the landlord's acceptance of late

rental payments. [¶] [Landlord] contends [tenant] became a month-to-month holdover tenant [when tenant did not exercise the sublease's five-year option period because he was in default on his rent when the base lease expired], meaning [landlord] was entitled to terminate the tenancy at any time with proper notice. [¶] We agree with [landlord]. [¶] [Tenant] has not identified any conduct constituting waiver other than [landlord's] acceptance of late installments of rent without protest. Nor do we find in the record any other conduct 'unequivocally inconsistent' with [landlord] claiming its rights under the nonwaiver provision. Because the lease explicitly precludes acceptance of rental payments as constituting waiver of [landlord's] enforcement rights, [landlord] conclusively established all the elements of a forcible-detainer claim."

Coinmach Corp. v. Aspenwood Apt. Corp., 417 S.W.3d 909, 920 (Tex.2013). "We hold that [Prop. Code] ch. 24's procedural protections do not grant to tenants at sufferance any legal interests in or possessory rights to the property at issue; rather, the statute provides procedural protections that apply once the tenant has lost, or allegedly lost, all legal interests and possessory rights. Although the landlord must comply with the statute's procedural requirements to evict the tenant at sufferance, eviction is allowed only if the tenant has no remaining legal or possessory interest, which makes the tenant a tenant at sufferance. The [forcible-entry-and-detainer (FED)] action and judgment do not bar a separate action for trespass or for wrongful eviction, and if it is determined in that action that the tenant lacked any legal interest or right of possession, the tenant at sufferance is a trespasser. Nothing in the statute indicates that the procedural protections grant legal or possessory rights to a tenant at sufferance. To the contrary, the statute states that the 'person entitled to possession of the property' is not the tenant but the person seeking the eviction, that is, the one who 'must comply with the [procedural] requirements.' And, even more directly, the statute expressly provides that a suit for eviction under the FED statute 'does not bar a suit for trespass.' Thus, despite the so-called 'grace periods' and ch. 24's other procedural protections, the tenant at sufferance remains a trespasser on the property."

Federal Home Loan Mortg. Corp. v. Pham, 449 S.W.3d 230, 234 (Tex.App.—Houston [14th Dist.] 2014, no pet.). "[D] asserts that [the] third forcible detainer action is barred by res judicata. [¶] [P] argues that every time a notice to vacate and demand for possession is sent, and the occupant of the property fails to vacate, a new and independent cause of action for forcible detainer accrues. *At 235-36:* [C]onsidering the limited nature of a forcible detainer action and the statutory language of the Property Code, we conclude that a new and independent cause of action for forcible detainer arises each time a person refuses to surrender possession of real property after a person entitled to possession of the property delivers a proper written notice to vacate. Accordingly, res judicata would not bar a second suit based on the commission of a subsequent forcible detainer."

Clarkson v. Deutsche Bank Nat'l Trust Co., 331 S.W.3d 837, 839-40 (Tex.App.—Amarillo 2011, no pet.). "By attacking the notice to vacate and proof of the *prima facie* case to support the forcible detainer action, [tenants'] issues are actually attacking the underlying foreclosure procedure. A forcible detainer action is not the proper avenue to attempt such an action; rather, [tenants] should pursue those defects, if any, in a wrongful foreclosure action or suit to set aside the substitute trustee's deed. Here, [landowner] proved up its right of possession by presenting evidence of the foreclosure, substitute trustee's deed, and notice to vacate the premises. Accordingly, the trial court did not err in overruling [tenants'] objections based upon the alleged non-compliance with [Prop. Code §§24.002 and 24.005]." *See also* ***Shutter v. Wells Fargo Bank***, 318 S.W.3d 467, 471 (Tex.App.—Dallas 2010, pet. dism'd).

Yarto v. Gilliland, 287 S.W.3d 83, 87 (Tex.App.—Corpus Christi 2009, no pet.). "The fact that the Legislature found it necessary to reference both types of suits is an indication that the term 'forcible entry and detainer' does not subsume forcible detainer suits."

Salaymeh v. Plaza Centro, LLC, 264 S.W.3d 431, 435-36 (Tex.App.—Houston [14th Dist.] 2008, no pet.). "It has been long settled in Texas jurisprudence that a forcible detainer action is not exclusive. Forcible detainer actions are cumulative of any other remedy that a party may have in the courts of this state. The displaced party is entitled to bring a separate suit in the district court to determine questions of title. Forcible detainer suits in justice court may run concurrently with an action in another court—even if the other action involves adjudication of matters that could result

in a different determination of possession from the decision rendered in the forcible detainer suit." *See also* ***Aspenwood Apt. Corp. v. Coinmach, Inc.***, 349 S.W.3d 621, 635 (Tex.App.—Houston [1st Dist.] 2011), *rev'd in part on other grounds*, 417 S.W.3d 909 (Tex.2013); ***Harrell v. Citizens Bank & Trust Co.***, 296 S.W.3d 321, 325-26 (Tex.App.—Texarkana 2009, pet. dism'd); ***Ward v. Malone***, 115 S.W.3d 267, 270 (Tex.App.—Corpus Christi 2003, pet. denied).

Geldard v. Watson, 214 S.W.3d 202, 206 (Tex. App.—Texarkana 2007, no pet.). "[D]oes a homestead interest go to 'the merits of title' so as to defeat jurisdiction over the forcible detainer cause of action in the justice court ...? *At 208-09:* We find that a nonjoining spouse exercising the homestead right to his spouse's conveyance of a separate property homestead exerts a right to possession under the granting spouse's title. [¶] [T]he justice court adjudicated the merits of title in determining [P's] right to possession in her forcible detainer action. The justice court's judgment [is] void."

Murphy v. Countrywide Home Loans, Inc., 199 S.W.3d 441, 445 (Tex.App.—Houston [1st Dist.] 2006, pet. denied). "Generally, an occupant of the property holding over after execution of a deed is considered a permissive tenant whose right to possession is inferior to that of the party holding title."

Fandey v. Lee, 880 S.W.2d 164, 169 (Tex.App.—El Paso 1994, writ denied). "A tenant at will is one who holds possession of premises by permission of an owner, but without a fixed term. [¶] In the absence of a legally enforceable agreement, such as a lease or rental agreement or a contract to sell, an occupier of premises is at best a tenant at sufferance and at worst a trespasser. Under such circumstances, the record title owner of the premises would be entitled to possession, after notice and demand, by merely showing 'sufficient evidence of ownership to demonstrate a superior right to immediate possession.'"

Academy Corp. v. Sunwest N.O.P., Inc., 853 S.W.2d 833, 833-34 (Tex.App.—Houston [14th Dist.] 1993, writ denied). "We agree with [D] that [P] had the burden to prove that a landlord-tenant relationship existed between the parties. However, we do not agree with their contention that this proof is jurisdictional, and therefore reviewable by this court. This relationship is just one of the elements required by [Prop. Code] §24.002 to support a forcible detainer action. The proof of a landlord-tenant relationship is required to show who has the greater right of possession, and the question of possession is exactly what [Prop. Code] §24.007 says is not reviewable."

Caro v. Housing Auth. of Austin, 794 S.W.2d 901, 904 n.1 (Tex.App.—Austin 1990, writ denied). See annotation under Property Code §24.005, p. 158.

Johnson v. Fellowship Baptist Ch., 627 S.W.2d 203, 205 (Tex.App.—Corpus Christi 1981, no writ). "When a tenant defaults on rent payments, the landlord may bring an action of forcible detainer. Such an action requires a showing of the landlord-tenant relationship. [I]t was [D's] duty to present evidence that she was not the tenant of [P] because [P] lacked title. She did not claim ownership of the property and failed to properly show who did have title apart from [P]. ... The record does contain evidence of the existence of the landlord-tenant relationship in the form of a contract between [P] and [D] containing a promise by [D] to pay past due rent to [P]. Thus, the trial court was entitled to find that [P] was [D's] landlord and that the lower courts had jurisdiction."

Byrd v. Feilding, 238 S.W.2d 614, 616 (Tex.App.—Amarillo 1951, no writ). "The courts have held that the question of whether a person hiring rooms is a lodger or is a tenant depends upon the intention of the parties as evidenced by the contract of hiring. If the hirer is to have the exclusive possession of the premises as against the owner, an estate in the land is transferred and he is a tenant. An examination of authorities sets forth the following rules: Proof that the owner cares for the rooms, retains a key to the rooms, or resides on the premises in the course of a business of hiring out rooms, indicates a lodging contract; whereas, a showing that the hirer exercises complete control over the rooms indicates a lease."

PROP §24.003. SUBSTITUTION OF PARTIES

If a tenancy for a term expires while the tenant's suit for forcible entry is pending, the landlord may prosecute the suit in the tenant's name for the landlord's benefit and at the landlord's expense. It is immaterial whether the tenant received possession from the landlord or became a tenant after obtaining possession of the property.

History of Prop. Code §24.003: Acts 1983, 68th Leg., ch. 576, §1, eff. Jan. 1, 1984. Amended by Acts 1985, 69th Leg., ch. 891, §1, eff. Aug. 26, 1985. Source: TRCS art. 3975.

PROP §24.004. JURISDICTION; DISMISSAL

(a) Except as provided by Subsection (b), a justice court in the precinct in which the real property is located has jurisdiction in eviction suits. Eviction suits include forcible entry and detainer and forcible detainer suits. A justice court has jurisdiction to issue a writ of possession under Sections 24.0054(a), (a-2), and (a-3).

(b) A justice court does not have jurisdiction in a forcible entry and detainer or forcible detainer suit and shall dismiss the suit if the defendant files a sworn statement alleging the suit is based on a deed executed in violation of Chapter 21A, Business & Commerce Code.

History of Prop. Code §24.004: Acts 1983, 68th Leg., ch. 576, §1, eff. Jan. 1, 1984. Amended by Acts 1985, 69th Leg., ch. 891, §1, eff. Aug. 26, 1985; Acts 1997, 75th Leg., ch. 1205, §1, eff. Sept. 1, 1997; Acts 2011, 82nd Leg., ch. 958, §1 (eff. Jan. 1, 2012), ch. 1242, §3 (eff. Sept. 1, 2011); Acts 2013, 83rd Leg., ch. 161, §22.002(28), eff. Sept. 1, 2013. Source: TRCS art. 3973.

See also CPRC §15.084; Gov't Code §27.031; TRCP 500.3(d), 502.4(e), 510; ***O'Connor's Texas COA***, "Forcible Detainer—Eviction," ch. 16-B, p. 424; ***O'Connor's Texas Rules***, "Types of cases," ch. 2-F, §5.2, p. 172.

CHARTS

See timetable, "Eviction," p. 1541.

ANNOTATIONS

McGlothlin v. Kliebert, 672 S.W.2d 231, 233 (Tex. 1984). "The forcible entry and detainer action is not exclusive, but cumulative, of any other remedy that a party may have in the courts of this state. If all matters between the parties cannot be adjudicated in the justice court in which the forcible entry and detainer proceedings are pending due to the justice court's limited subject matter jurisdiction, then either party may maintain an action in a court of competent jurisdiction for proper relief." *See also* ***Aguilar v. Weber***, 72 S.W.3d 729, 732 (Tex.App.—Waco 2002, no pet.); ***Dormady v. Dinero Land & Cattle Co., L.C.***, 61 S.W.3d 555, 558 (Tex.App.—San Antonio 2001, pet. dism'd).

Guillen v. U.S. Bank, 494 S.W.3d 861, 865 (Tex. App.—Houston [14th Dist.] 2016, no pet.). "[P] argues that, because the title suit was removed to federal district court and decided in its favor, and [D's] appeal rests on the proposition that the title suit must be decided as a prerequisite to eviction, the appeal before us is moot. We reject this argument. First, the judgment of the federal court is not part of our appellate record. Second, the resolution of a title suit, even in the state courts, does not automatically eliminate the need for immediate possession to be adjudicated. On the contrary, the resolution of a title dispute may empower the justice court to assume jurisdiction over the forcible entry and detainer where it was previously unable to due to the pendency of the title suit."

Gonzalez v. Wells Fargo Bank, 441 S.W.3d 709, 713 (Tex.App.—El Paso 2014, no pet.). "[Ds] maintain that because they raised the issue of proper title in a collateral district court action, the justice court was precluded from acting on the forcible detainer suit until that title suit was resolved. However, merely raising the issue of title is not enough to defeat the justice court's original jurisdiction. The Property Code provides for parallel, separate title and possession suits in the justice courts and the county courts at law unless resolution of possession '*necessarily requires the resolution of a title dispute*.' Where property is sold at a nonjudicial foreclosure sale pursuant to a deed of trust, and where the deed of trust itself establishes a landlord and tenant-at-sufferance relationship between the purchaser and the former homeowners, we may uphold a writ of possession without ever reaching the issue of title on the independent basis of the landlord-tenant relationship established in the deed of trust."

Williams v. Bayview-Realty Assocs., 420 S.W.3d 358, 361-62 (Tex.App.—Houston [14th Dist.] 2014, no pet.). "Jurisdiction to hear a forcible-detainer action is expressly given to justice courts and, on appeal, to county courts for trial de novo. But, a justice court is expressly deprived of jurisdiction to determine or adjudicate title to land. The appellate jurisdiction of the county court is confined to the jurisdictional limits of the justice court. Accordingly, a county court at law has no jurisdiction to adjudicate title to real property in a de novo trial on appeal of a forcible-detainer action from a justice court. The only issue in a forcible-detainer action is the right to actual and immediate possession of the premises. To prevail in a forcible-detainer action, a plaintiff is not required to prove title, but is only required to show sufficient evidence of ownership to demonstrate a superior right to immediate possession. A justice court is deprived of jurisdiction only if resolution of a title dispute is a prerequisite to determination of the right to immediate possession of the premises. In a forcible-detainer action, if there is a landlord-tenant relationship between the plaintiff and the defendant, the justice court and county court at law have ju-

risdiction and may determine the right to actual possession of the premises, without determining who holds title to the premises." *See also* ***Goodman-Delaney v. Grantham***, 484 S.W.3d 171, 175 (Tex. App.—Houston [14th Dist.] 2015, no pet.) (no jurisdiction because justice court had to determine title to property before determining who had superior right to possession).

PROP §24.005. NOTICE TO VACATE PRIOR TO FILING EVICTION SUIT

(a) If the occupant is a tenant under a written lease or oral rental agreement, the landlord must give a tenant who defaults or holds over beyond the end of the rental term or renewal period at least three days' written notice to vacate the premises before the landlord files a forcible detainer suit, unless the parties have contracted for a shorter or longer notice period in a written lease or agreement. A landlord who files a forcible detainer suit on grounds that the tenant is holding over beyond the end of the rental term or renewal period must also comply with the tenancy termination requirements of Section 91.001.

(b) If the occupant is a tenant at will or by sufferance, the landlord must give the tenant at least three days' written notice to vacate before the landlord files a forcible detainer suit unless the parties have contracted for a shorter or longer notice period in a written lease or agreement. If a building is purchased at a tax foreclosure sale or a trustee's foreclosure sale under a lien superior to the tenant's lease and the tenant timely pays rent and is not otherwise in default under the tenant's lease after foreclosure, the purchaser must give a residential tenant of the building at least 30 days' written notice to vacate if the purchaser chooses not to continue the lease. The tenant is considered to timely pay the rent under this subsection if, during the month of the foreclosure sale, the tenant pays the rent for that month to the landlord before receiving any notice that a foreclosure sale is scheduled during the month or pays the rent for that month to the foreclosing lienholder or the purchaser at foreclosure not later than the fifth day after the date of receipt of a written notice of the name and address of the purchaser that requests payment. Before a foreclosure sale, a foreclosing lienholder may give written notice to a tenant stating that a foreclosure notice has been given to the landlord or owner of the property and specifying the date of the foreclosure.

(c) If the occupant is a tenant of a person who acquired possession by forcible entry, the landlord must give the person at least three days' written notice to vacate before the landlord files a forcible detainer suit.

(d) In all situations in which the entry by the occupant was a forcible entry under Section 24.001, the person entitled to possession must give the occupant oral or written notice to vacate before the landlord files a forcible entry and detainer suit. The notice to vacate under this subsection may be to vacate immediately or by a specified deadline.

(e) If the lease or applicable law requires the landlord to give a tenant an opportunity to respond to a notice of proposed eviction, a notice to vacate may not be given until the period provided for the tenant to respond to the eviction notice has expired.

(f) Except as provided by Subsection (f-1), the notice to vacate shall be given in person or by mail at the premises in question. Notice in person may be by personal delivery to the tenant or any person residing at the premises who is 16 years of age or older or personal delivery to the premises and affixing the notice to the inside of the main entry door. Notice by mail may be by regular mail, by registered mail, or by certified mail, return receipt requested, to the premises in question.

(f-1) As an alternative to the procedures of Subsection (f), a landlord may deliver the notice to vacate by securely affixing to the outside of the main entry door a sealed envelope that contains the notice and on which is written the tenant's name, address, and in all capital letters, the words "IMPORTANT DOCUMENT" or substantially similar language and, not later than 5 p.m. of the same day, depositing in the mail in the same county in which the premises in question is located a copy of the notice to the tenant if:

(1) the premises has no mailbox and has a keyless bolting device, alarm system, or dangerous animal that prevents the landlord from entering the premises to affix the notice to vacate to the inside of the main entry door; or

(2) the landlord reasonably believes that harm to any person would result from personal delivery to the tenant or a person residing at the premises or from personal delivery to the premises by affixing the notice to the inside of the main entry door.

(f-2) Notice to vacate under Subsection (f-1) is considered delivered on the date the envelope is affixed

to the outside of the door and is deposited in the mail, regardless of the date the notice is received.

(g) The notice period is calculated from the day on which the notice is delivered.

(h) A notice to vacate shall be considered a demand for possession for purposes of Subsection (b) of Section 24.002.

(i) If before the notice to vacate is given as required by this section the landlord has given a written notice or reminder to the tenant that rent is due and unpaid, the landlord may include in the notice to vacate required by this section a demand that the tenant pay the delinquent rent or vacate the premises by the date and time stated in the notice.

History of Prop. Code §24.005: Acts 1983, 68th Leg., ch. 576, §1, eff. Jan. 1, 1984. Amended by Acts 1985, 69th Leg., ch. 891, §1, eff. Sept. 1, 1985; Acts 1989, 71st Leg., ch. 688, §3, eff. Sept. 1, 1989; Acts 1997, 75th Leg., ch. 1205, §2, eff. Sept. 1, 1997; Acts 2015, 84th Leg., ch. 1198, §1, eff. Jan. 1, 2016. Source: TRCS art. 3975a.

See also TRCP 510; *O'Connor's Texas COA*, "Forcible Detainer—Eviction," ch. 16-B, p. 424.

CHARTS

See timetable, "Eviction," p. 1541.

ANNOTATIONS

Trimble v. Federal Nat'l Mortg. Ass'n, 516 S.W.3d 24, 31 (Tex.App.—Houston [1st Dist.] 2016, pet. filed 5-23-17). "Section 24.005 requires that, when notice to vacate is given by mail, notice be given 'to the premises in question.' It does not require receipt by any particular person. ... For this reason, we have rejected an argument that notice was improper because it was mailed to 'all occupants' and did not specifically identify a tenant's spouse. Addressing the notice to 'all occupants' and mailing it is sufficient to raise the presumption that the notice was delivered to the property." *See also* ***U.S. Bank v. Khan***, No. 05-14-00903-CV (Tex.App.—Dallas 2015, no pet.) (memo op.; 8-11-15).

Effel v. Rosberg, 360 S.W.3d 626, 631 (Tex.App.—Dallas 2012, no pet.). Tenant "argues that the ... notice was defective because it contained two allegedly false statements: that she had violated the lease agreement by building a fence and that she did not have a right to cure this purported act of default. [Tenant's] argument fails for two reasons. First, even assuming the statements are false, nothing in §24.005 requires the landlord to give in the notice to vacate either a reason for the eviction or an explanation of any right to cure. Second, because [tenant's] tenancy was at will, [landlord] could terminate the tenancy at any time regardless of whether [tenant] had defaulted under the terms of the lease. Accordingly, the claimed false statements were irrelevant to the sufficiency of the notice. The trial court correctly concluded that [landlord's] notice letter complied with the requirements of §24.005." *See also* ***AMC Mortg. Servs. v. Shields***, No. 05-06-01194-CV (Tex.App.—Dallas 2007, no pet.) (memo op.; 5-9-07).

Clarkson v. Deutsche Bank Nat'l Trust Co., 331 S.W.3d 837, 839-40 (Tex.App.—Amarillo 2011, no pet.). See annotation under Property Code §24.002, p. 154.

Russell v. American Real Estate Corp., 89 S.W.3d 204, 208 (Tex.App.—Corpus Christi 2002, no pet.). "When an owner acquires residential property by foreclosure, the Property Code requires that the new owner may not begin eviction proceedings—much less gain possession—before giving the tenant at sufferance 30 days' notice to vacate. Even after notice has been given, a tenant at sufferance continues to remain in possession until the remainder of the eviction process has been completed."

Caro v. Housing Auth. of Austin, 794 S.W.2d 901, 904 n.1 (Tex.App.—Austin 1990, writ denied). "The statutory cause of action for forcible detainer has never required a 'demand' for performance of the rent covenant as a prerequisite for termination of a leasehold. This is consistent, of course, with the theory that the statute is designed only as a summary remedy for one whose legal right to possession exists outside the statutory provisions. This kind of 'demand'—a demand for performance of the rent covenant—should not be confused with what the forcible-detainer statute *does* require—a demand for *possession*, which was an explicit element of the statutory cause of action between 1886 and May 6, 1957. It has since been superseded by the requirement of a 'written notice to vacate.'"

Santos v. City of Eagle Pass, 727 S.W.2d 126, 129 (Tex.App.—San Antonio 1987, no writ). "The language of [Prop. Code] §24.005(b) [now §24.005(e)], requires the landlord to delay sending a notice to vacate if the lease or applicable law requires him to give the tenant the opportunity to respond to a notice of proposed eviction. This language indicates that the length of the delay is determined by 'the period provided for the tenant to respond to the eviction notice.' We are not aware of any provision in the common law that sets forth a period for response by the tenant." *See also* ***Kennedy v. Andover Place Apts.***, 203 S.W.3d 495, 498 (Tex.App.—Houston [14th Dist.] 2006, no pet.).

PROP §24.0051. PROCEDURES APPLICABLE IN SUIT TO EVICT & RECOVER UNPAID RENT

(a) In a suit filed in justice court in which the landlord files a sworn statement seeking judgment against a tenant for possession of the premises and unpaid rent, personal service on the tenant or service on the tenant under Rule 742a, Texas Rules of Civil Procedure, is procedurally sufficient to support a default judgment for possession of the premises and unpaid rent.

(b) A landlord may recover unpaid rent under this section regardless of whether the tenant vacated the premises after the date the landlord filed the sworn statement and before the date the court renders judgment.

(c) In a suit to recover possession of the premises, whether or not unpaid rent is claimed, the citation required by Rule 739, Texas Rules of Civil Procedure, must include the following notice to the defendant:

FAILURE TO APPEAR FOR TRIAL MAY RESULT IN A DEFAULT JUDGMENT BEING ENTERED AGAINST YOU.

(d) In a suit described by Subsection (c), the citation required by Rule 739, Texas Rules of Civil Procedure, must include the following notice to the defendant on the first page of the citation in English and Spanish and in conspicuous bold print:

SUIT TO EVICT

THIS SUIT TO EVICT INVOLVES IMMEDIATE DEADLINES. A TENANT WHO IS SERVING ON ACTIVE MILITARY DUTY MAY HAVE SPECIAL RIGHTS OR RELIEF RELATED TO THIS SUIT UNDER FEDERAL LAW, INCLUDING THE SERVICEMEMBERS CIVIL RELIEF ACT (50 U.S.C. APP. SECTION 501 ET SEQ.), OR STATE LAW, INCLUDING SECTION 92.017, TEXAS PROPERTY CODE. CALL THE STATE BAR OF TEXAS TOLL-FREE AT 1-877-9TEXBAR IF YOU NEED HELP LOCATING AN ATTORNEY. IF YOU CANNOT AFFORD TO HIRE AN ATTORNEY, YOU MAY BE ELIGIBLE FOR FREE OR LOW-COST LEGAL ASSISTANCE.

History of Prop. Code §24.0051: Acts 1999, 76th Leg., ch. 1464, §1, eff. Sept. 1, 1999. Amended by Acts 2005, 79th Leg., ch. 712, §1, eff. Sept. 1, 2005; Acts 2007, 80th Leg., ch. 812, §1, eff. Sept. 1, 2007; Acts 2011, 82nd Leg., ch. 252, §1, eff. Jan. 1, 2012.

See also TRCP 510; *O'Connor's Texas COA*, "Forcible Detainer—Eviction," ch. 16-B, p. 424.

ANNOTATIONS

American Spiritualist Ass'n v. Ravkind, 313 S.W.2d 121, 124 (Tex.App.—Dallas 1958, writ ref'd n.r.e.). "In our opinion the Justice Court judgment was fatally defective because of a lack of proper service of citation. The original citation handed to the constable was accompanied by only one copy. The constable, endeavoring to comply with [TRCP] 742, left the one copy of the citation with a person over 16 years of age who was on the premises [in question]—he could leave only the one copy. But there were two [Ds] named in the citation, ... a corporation and [an individual]. It was necessary to serve a copy of the citation on each [D]."

PROP §24.00511. APPEAL BOND FOR CERTAIN EVICTION SUITS

(a) In a residential eviction suit for nonpayment of rent, the justice court shall state in the court's judgment the amount of the appeal bond, taking into consideration the money required to be paid into the court registry under Section 24.0053.

(b) In addition to meeting all other requirements of law, the bond must require the surety to provide the surety's contact information, including an address, phone number, and e-mail address, if any. If any of the contact information changes, the surety shall inform the court of the surety's new contact information.

History of Prop. Code §24.00511: Acts 2015, 84th Leg., ch. 1027, §1, eff. Jan. 1, 2016.

PROP §24.00512. CONTEST OF CERTAIN APPEAL BONDS

(a) This section does not apply to an appeal bond issued by a corporate surety authorized by the Texas Department of Insurance to engage in business in this state.

(b) If a party appeals the judgment of a justice court in a residential eviction suit for nonpayment of rent by filing an appeal bond, the opposing party may contest the bond amount, form of the bond, or financial ability of a surety to pay the bond by filing a written notice with the justice court contesting the appeal bond on or before the fifth day after the date the appeal bond is filed and serving a copy on the other party. After the notice is filed, the justice court shall notify the other party and the surety of the contest.

(c) Not later than the fifth day after the date the contest is filed, the justice court shall hold a hearing to hear evidence to determine whether to approve or disapprove the amount or form of the bond or the surety.

(d) If a party contests the amount or form of the bond, the contesting party has the burden to prove, by a preponderance of the evidence, that the amount or

form of the bond, as applicable, is insufficient. If a party contests the financial ability of a surety to pay the bond, the party filing the bond must prove, by a preponderance of the evidence, that the surety has sufficient nonexempt assets to pay the appeal bond. If the justice court determines that the amount or form of the bond is insufficient or the surety does not have sufficient nonexempt assets to pay the appeal bond, the justice court must disapprove the bond. If the surety fails to appear at the contest hearing, the failure to appear is prima facie evidence that the bond should be disapproved.

(e) Not later than the fifth day after the date the justice court disapproves an appeal bond, the party appealing may make a cash deposit, file a sworn statement of inability to pay with the justice court, or appeal the decision disapproving the appeal bond to the county court. If the party appealing fails to make a cash deposit, file a sworn statement of inability to pay, or appeal the decision disapproving the appeal bond, the judgment of the justice court becomes final and a writ of possession and other processes to enforce the judgment must be issued on the payment of the required fee.

(f) If an appeal is filed, the justice court shall transmit to the county court the contest to the appeal bond and all relevant documents. The county court shall docket the appeal, schedule a hearing to be held not later than the fifth day after the date the appeal is docketed, notify the parties and the surety of the hearing time and date, and hear the contest de novo. The failure of the county court to hold a timely hearing is not grounds for approval or denial of the appeal. A writ of possession may not be issued before the county court issues a final decision on the appeal bond.

(g) After the contest is heard by the county court, the county clerk shall transmit the transcript and records of the case to the justice court. If the county court disapproves the appeal bond, the party may, not later than the fifth day after the date the court disapproves the appeal bond, perfect the appeal of the judgment on the eviction suit by making a cash deposit in the justice court in an amount determined by the county court or by filing a sworn statement of inability to pay with the justice court pursuant to the Texas Rules of Civil Procedure. If the tenant is the appealing party and a cash deposit in the required amount is not timely made or a sworn statement of inability to pay is not timely filed, the judgment of the justice court becomes final and a writ of possession and other processes to enforce the judgment must be issued on the payment of the required fee. If the landlord is the appealing party and a cash deposit is not timely made or a sworn statement of inability to pay is not timely filed, the judgment of the justice court becomes final. If the appeal bond is approved by the county court, the court shall transmit the transcript and other records of the case to the justice court, and the justice court shall proceed as if the appeal bond was originally approved.

History of Prop. Code §24.00512: Acts 2015, 84th Leg., ch. 1027, §1, eff. Jan. 1, 2016.

PROP §24.0052. TENANT APPEAL ON PAUPER'S AFFIDAVIT[1]

(a) If a tenant in a residential eviction suit is unable to pay the costs of appeal or file an appeal bond as required by the Texas Rules of Civil Procedure, the tenant may appeal the judgment of the justice court by filing with the justice court, not later than the fifth day after the date the judgment is signed, a pauper's affidavit sworn before the clerk of the justice court or a notary public that states that the tenant is unable to pay the costs of appeal or file an appeal bond. The affidavit must contain the following information:

(1) the tenant's identity;

(2) the nature and amount of the tenant's employment income;

(3) the income of the tenant's spouse, if applicable and available to the tenant;

(4) the nature and amount of any governmental entitlement income of the tenant;

(5) all other income of the tenant;

(6) the amount of available cash and funds available in savings or checking accounts of the tenant;

(7) real and personal property owned by the tenant, other than household furnishings, clothes, tools of a trade, or personal effects;

(8) the tenant's debts and monthly expenses; and

(9) the number and age of the tenant's dependents and where those dependents reside.

(b) The justice court shall make available an affidavit form that a person may use to comply with the requirements of Subsection (a).

(c) The justice court shall promptly notify the landlord if a pauper's affidavit is filed by the tenant.

(d) A landlord may contest a pauper's affidavit on or before the fifth day after the date the affidavit is filed. If the landlord contests the affidavit, the justice

court shall notify the parties and hold a hearing to determine whether the tenant is unable to pay the costs of appeal or file an appeal bond. The hearing shall be held not later than the fifth day after the date the landlord notifies the court clerk of the landlord's contest. At the hearing, the tenant has the burden to prove by competent evidence, including documents or credible testimony of the tenant or others, that the tenant is unable to pay the costs of appeal or file an appeal bond.

(e) If the justice court approves the pauper's affidavit of a tenant, the tenant is not required to pay the county court filing fee or file an additional affidavit in the county court under Subsection (a).

1. **Editor's note:** This section refers to the filing of a pauper's affidavit and lists the required contents of the affidavit. In 2016, however, TRCP 502.3 and TRCP 510.9 were amended, in conjunction with TRCP 145, to require a plaintiff who is unable to afford court costs to file a Statement of Inability to Afford Payment of Court Costs. *See* Tex.Sup.Ct. Order, Misc. Docket No. 16-9122 (eff. Sept. 1, 2016). Instead of a sworn statement of inability to pay costs or an affidavit of indigence, a plaintiff must now use a form Statement approved by the Supreme Court or file a statement that includes the information required by the Court-approved form. *See* TRCP 502.3(b). The information specified in Property Code §24.0052(a) is now included in the Court-approved Statement. An electronic version of the Court-approved Statement can be found on the Texas Office of Court Administration website, www.txcourts.gov/rules-forms/forms.

History of Prop. Code §24.0052: Acts 2005, 79th Leg., ch. 1185, §1, eff. Sept. 1, 2005.

See also Prop. Code §24.007; TRCP 510.9(c)(1)-(4).

CHARTS

See timetable, "Eviction Appeal by Statement of Inability to Pay," p. 1545.

PROP §24.00521. CONTEST OF CERTAIN APPEAL BONDS IN COUNTY COURT

A contest under Section 24.00512 does not preclude a party from contesting the appeal bond in the county court after the county court has jurisdiction over the eviction suit. After the county court has jurisdiction over the eviction suit, the county court may modify the amount or form of the bond and determine the sufficiency of the surety.

History of Prop. Code §24.00521: Acts 2015, 84th Leg., ch. 1027, §2, eff. Jan. 1, 2016.

PROP §24.0053. PAYMENT OF RENT DURING APPEAL OF EVICTION

(a) If the justice court enters judgment for the landlord in a residential eviction case based on nonpayment of rent, the court shall determine the amount of rent to be paid each rental pay period during the pendency of any appeal and shall note that amount in the judgment. If a portion of the rent is payable by a government agency, the court shall determine and note in the judgment the portion of the rent to be paid by the government agency and the portion to be paid by the tenant. The court's determination shall be in accordance with the terms of the rental agreement and applicable laws and regulations. This subsection does not require or prohibit payment of rent into the court registry or directly to the landlord during the pendency of an appeal of an eviction case based on grounds other than nonpayment of rent.

(a-1) In an eviction suit for nonpayment of rent, if a tenant files a pauper's affidavit in the period prescribed by Section 24.0052 or an appeal bond pursuant to the Texas Rules of Civil Procedure, the justice court shall provide to the tenant a written notice at the time the pauper's affidavit or appeal bond is filed that contains the following information in bold or conspicuous type:

(1) the amount of the initial deposit of rent stated in the judgment that the tenant must pay into the justice court registry;

(2) whether the initial deposit must be paid in cash, cashier's check, or money order, and to whom the cashier's check or money order, if applicable, must be made payable;

(3) the calendar date by which the initial deposit must be paid into the justice court registry;

(4) for a court that closes before 5 p.m. on the date specified by Subdivision (3), the time the court closes; and

(5) a statement that failure to pay the required amount into the justice court registry by the date prescribed by Subdivision (3) may result in the court issuing a writ of possession without a hearing.

(a-2) The date by which an initial deposit must be paid into the justice court registry under Subsection (a-1)(3) must be within five days of the date the tenant files the pauper's affidavit as required by the Texas Rules of Civil Procedure.

(a-3) If a tenant files an appeal bond to appeal an eviction for nonpayment of rent, the tenant must, not later than the fifth day after the date the tenant filed the appeal bond, pay into the justice court registry the amount of rent to be paid in one rental pay period as determined by the court under Subsection (a). If the tenant fails to timely pay that amount into the justice court registry and the transcript has not yet been transmitted to the county court, the plaintiff may request a writ of

possession. On request and payment of the applicable fee, the justice court shall issue the writ of possession immediately and without a hearing. Regardless of whether a writ of possession is issued, the justice court shall transmit the transcript and appeal documents to the county court for trial de novo on issues relating to possession, rent, or attorney's fees.

(a-4) On sworn motion and hearing, the plaintiff in the eviction suit may withdraw money deposited in the court registry before the final determination in the case, dismissal of the appeal, or order of the court after final hearing. The county court shall give precedence to a hearing or motion under this subsection.

(b) If an eviction case is based on nonpayment of rent and the tenant appeals by filing a pauper's affidavit, the tenant shall pay the rent, as it becomes due, into the justice court or the county court registry, as applicable, during the pendency of the appeal, in accordance with the Texas Rules of Civil Procedure and Subsection (a). If a government agency is responsible for all or a portion of the rent under an agreement with the landlord, the tenant shall pay only that portion of the rent determined by the justice court under Subsection (a) to be paid by the tenant during appeal, subject to either party's right to contest that determination under Subsection (c).

(c) If an eviction case is based on nonpayment of rent and the tenant's rent during the rental agreement term has been paid wholly or partly by a government agency, either party may contest the portion of the rent that the justice court determines must be paid into the county court registry by the tenant under this section. The contest must be filed on or before the fifth day after the date the justice signs the judgment. If a contest is filed, not later than the fifth day after the date the contest is filed the justice court shall notify the parties and hold a hearing to determine the amount owed by the tenant in accordance with the terms of the rental agreement and applicable laws and regulations. After hearing the evidence, the justice court shall determine the portion of the rent that must be paid by the tenant under this section.

(d) If the tenant objects to the justice court's ruling under Subsection (c) on the portion of the rent to be paid by the tenant during appeal, the tenant shall be required to pay only the portion claimed by the tenant to be owed by the tenant until the issue is tried de novo along with the case on the merits in county court. During the pendency of the appeal, either party may file a motion with the county court to reconsider the amount of the rent that must be paid by the tenant into the registry of the court.

(e) If either party files a contest under Subsection (c) and the tenant files a pauper's affidavit that is contested by the landlord under Section 24.0052(d), the justice court shall hold the hearing on both contests at the same time.

History of Prop. Code §24.0053: Acts 2005, 79th Leg., ch. 1185, §1, eff. Sept. 1, 2005. Amended by Acts 2011, 82nd Leg., ch. 958, §2, eff. Jan. 1, 2012; Acts 2015, 84th Leg., ch. 1027, §3, eff. Jan. 1, 2016.

See also TRCP 510.9(c)(5).

CHARTS

See timetables, "Eviction Appeal," p. 1543; "Eviction Appeal by Statement of Inability to Pay," p. 1545.

ANNOTATIONS

Stevenson v. Housing Auth. of Austin, 385 S.W.3d 684, 686-87 (Tex.App.—El Paso 2012, no pet.). Tenant "argues that because he tendered the rent in an amount he calculated under §24.0053(d) …, he holds and asserts a meritorious claim to current, actual possession of the apartment. However, [tenant's] reliance on §24.0053(d) is misplaced because nothing in the record indicates that his rent has been wholly or partly paid by a government agency or that he even filed a motion to reconsider the amount of rent required to be paid into the court registry. The record contains no evidence affirming [tenant's] allegations that he continued to pay rent or tendered payment to [public-housing landlord]. [Tenant's] appellate brief fails to present any other basis for claiming a right to current, actual possession of the apartment. [¶] The record establishes that [tenant's] lease expired in October 2008. [Tenant] has not resided in the apartment since his eviction in May 2009, and [public-housing landlord] has leased the apartment at issue to another tenant. Because [tenant's] lease expired and because he presents no basis for claiming a current, actual right to possession of the premises, the issue of possession is moot."

PROP §24.0054. TENANT'S FAILURE TO PAY RENT DURING APPEAL

(a) During an appeal of an eviction case for nonpayment of rent, the justice court on request shall immediately issue a writ of possession, without hearing, if:

(1) a tenant fails to pay the initial rent deposit into the justice court registry within five days of the date the

tenant filed a pauper's affidavit as required by Rule 749b(1), Texas Rules of Civil Procedure, and Section 24.0053;

(2) the justice court has provided the written notice required by Section 24.0053(a-1); and

(3) the justice court has not yet forwarded the transcript and original papers to the county court as provided by Subsection (a-2).

(a-1) The sheriff or constable shall execute a writ of possession under Subsection (a) in accordance with Sections 24.0061(d) through (h). The landlord shall bear the costs of issuing and executing the writ of possession.

(a-2) The justice court shall forward the transcript and original papers in an appeal of an eviction case to the county court but may not forward the transcript and original papers before the sixth day after the date the tenant files a pauper's affidavit, except that, if the court confirms that the tenant has timely paid the initial deposit of rent into the justice court registry in accordance with Section 24.0053, the court may forward the transcript and original papers immediately. If the tenant has not timely paid the initial deposit into the justice court registry, the justice court on request shall issue a writ of possession notwithstanding the fact that the tenant has perfected an appeal by filing a pauper's affidavit that has been approved by the court. The justice court shall forward the transcript and original papers in the case to the county court for trial de novo, notwithstanding the fact that a writ of possession under this section has already been issued.

(a-3) Notwithstanding Subsections (a) and (a-2), the justice court may not issue a writ of possession if the tenant has timely deposited the tenant's portion of the rent claimed by the tenant under Section 24.0053(d).

(a-4) During an appeal of an eviction case for nonpayment of rent, if a tenant fails to pay rent into the justice court or county court registry as the rent becomes due under the rental agreement in accordance with the Texas Rules of Civil Procedure and Section 24.0053, the landlord may file with the county court a sworn motion that the tenant failed to pay rent as required. The landlord shall notify the tenant of the motion and the hearing date.

(b) If the county court finds that the tenant has not complied with the payment requirements of the Texas Rules of Civil Procedure and Section 24.0053, the county court shall immediately issue a writ of possession unless on or before the day of the hearing the tenant pays into the court registry:

(1) all rent not paid in accordance with the Texas Rules of Civil Procedure and Section 24.0053; and

(2) the landlord's reasonable attorney's fees, if any, in filing the motion.

(c) If the court finds that a tenant has failed to timely pay the rent into the court registry on more than one occasion:

(1) the tenant is not entitled to stay the issuance of the writ by paying the rent and the landlord's reasonable attorney's fees, if any; and

(2) the county court shall immediately issue a writ of possession.

(d) A writ of possession issued under Subsection (c) may not be executed before the sixth day after the date the writ is issued.

(e) In a motion or hearing under Subsection (a-4), or in a motion to dismiss an appeal of an eviction case in county court, the parties may represent themselves or be represented by their authorized agents, who need not be attorneys.

(f) During the appeal of an eviction case, if a government agency is responsible for payment of a portion of the rent and does not pay that portion to the landlord or into the justice court or county court registry, the landlord may file a motion with the county court requesting that the tenant be required to pay into the county court registry, as a condition of remaining in possession, the full amount of each rental period's rent, as it becomes due under the rental agreement. After notice and hearing, the court shall grant the motion if the landlord proves by credible evidence that:

(1) a portion of the rent is owed by a government agency;

(2) the portion of the rent owed by the government agency is unpaid;

(3) the landlord did not cause wholly or partly the agency to cease making the payments;

(4) the landlord did not cause wholly or partly the agency to pay the wrong amount; and

(5) the landlord is not able to take reasonable action that will cause the agency to resume making the payments of its portion of the total rent due under the rental agreement.

History of Prop. Code §24.0054: Acts 2005, 79th Leg., ch. 1185, §1, eff. Sept. 1, 2005. Amended by Acts 2011, 82nd Leg., ch. 958, §3, eff. Jan. 1, 2012.

See also TRCP 510.9(c)(5).

CHARTS

See timetables, "Eviction Appeal by Statement of Inability to Pay," p. 1545; "Writ of Possession & Warehouseman's Lien," p. 1547.

PROP §24.006. ATTORNEY'S FEES & COSTS OF SUIT

(a) Except as provided by Subsection (b), to be eligible to recover attorney's fees in an eviction suit, a landlord must give a tenant who is unlawfully retaining possession of the landlord's premises a written demand to vacate the premises. The demand must state that if the tenant does not vacate the premises before the 11th day after the date of receipt of the notice and if the landlord files suit, the landlord may recover attorney's fees. The demand must be sent by registered mail or by certified mail, return receipt requested, at least 10 days before the date the suit is filed.

(b) If the landlord provides the tenant notice under Subsection (a) or if a written lease entitles the landlord to recover attorney's fees, a prevailing landlord is entitled to recover reasonable attorney's fees from the tenant.

(c) If the landlord provides the tenant notice under Subsection (a) or if a written lease entitles the landlord or the tenant to recover attorney's fees, the prevailing tenant is entitled to recover reasonable attorney's fees from the landlord. A prevailing tenant is not required to give notice in order to recover attorney's fees under this subsection.

(d) The prevailing party is entitled to recover all costs of court.

History of Prop. Code §24.006: Acts 1983, 68th Leg., ch. 576, §1, eff. Jan. 1, 1984. Amended by Acts 1985, 69th Leg., ch. 891, §1, eff. Sept. 1, 1985; Acts 1989, 71st Leg., ch. 688, §4, eff. Sept. 1, 1989; Acts 1997, 75th Leg., ch. 1205, §3, eff. Sept. 1, 1997. Source: TRCS art. 3975b.

See also CPRC §38.001(8); TRCP 510; *O'Connor's Texas COA*, "Forcible Detainer—Eviction," ch. 16-B, p. 424; "Attorney Fees," ch. 45, p. 1399.

CHARTS

See timetable, "Eviction," p. 1541.

ANNOTATIONS

Stroman v. Tautenhahn, 465 S.W.3d 715, 718 (Tex.App.—Houston [14th Dist.] 2015, pet. dism'd). "[D] argues that recovery of fees [under §24.006] is automatic because subsection (c) states that a prevailing tenant is not required to give notice to recover attorney's fees under the subsection. ... Under this provision, the tenant has no corresponding obligation to notify the landlord that the tenant may be entitled to attorney's fees if the tenant prevails. [¶] We reject this contention because subsection (c) does not negate the tenant's obligation to request attorney's fees from the trial court. Having grounds to seek attorney's fees is not the same as requesting attorney's fees. Likewise, being entitled to attorney's fees is not the same as seeking to recover them. A request for affirmative relief requires positive action—an 'ask.'"

Washington v. Related Arbor Ct., LLC, 357 S.W.3d 676, 682 (Tex.App.—Houston [14th Dist.] 2011, no pet.). Landlord "delivered two notices to [tenant]—the first a notice of lease termination delivered on January 14, 2010, that required her to vacate her apartment by January 24, 2010, and the second a notice to vacate delivered on January 26, 2010, that required her to vacate within three days. [¶] Neither notice satisfies the requirements imposed by §24.006.... [Landlord] argues the January 14 lease-termination notice satisfies §24.006 because it urges [tenant] to 'avoid the expense and aggravation which litigation entails,' which [landlord] contends necessarily encompasses attorney's fees. We disagree. ... Accordingly, the January 14 notice failed to advise [tenant] she may be liable for attorney's fees if she failed to vacate by the termination date. [¶] The January 26 notice, on the other hand, specifically refers to attorney's fees, but its demand that [tenant] vacate in three days falls well short of the notice requirement imposed by §24.006...."

Hong Kong Dev., Inc. v. Nguyen, 229 S.W.3d 415, 454-55 (Tex.App.—Houston [1st Dist.] 2007, no pet.). "[P] prevailed in the forcible-detainer matter by having been awarded possession, entitling her to attorney's fees for counsel's work relating to the forcible-detainer allegations. But [P] also asserted [tort] claims ... and sought punitive damages and indemnity. [¶] Parties seeking to recover attorney's fees are required to segregate fees between claims for which [fees] are recoverable and claims for which they are not. [¶] A recognized exception to this duty to segregate arises when the attorney's fees rendered are in connection with claims arising out of the same transaction and are so interrelated that their prosecution or defense entails proof or denial of essentially the same facts. [¶] *Intertwined facts* do not make tort [attorney's] fees recoverable; it is only when *discrete legal services* advance both

a recoverable and unrecoverable claim that they are so intertwined that they need not be segregated." (Internal quotes omitted.)

PROP §24.0061. WRIT OF POSSESSION

(a) A landlord who prevails in an eviction suit is entitled to a judgment for possession of the premises and a writ of possession. In this chapter, "premises" means the unit that is occupied or rented and any outside area or facility that the tenant is entitled to use under a written lease or oral rental agreement, or that is held out for the use of tenants generally.

(b) A writ of possession may not be issued before the sixth day after the date on which the judgment for possession is rendered unless a possession bond has been filed and approved under the Texas Rules of Civil Procedure and judgment for possession is thereafter granted by default.

(c) The court shall notify a tenant in writing of a default judgment for possession by sending a copy of the judgment to the premises by first class mail not later than 48 hours after the entry of the judgment.

(d) The writ of possession shall order the officer executing the writ to:

(1) post a written warning of at least 8-½ by 11 inches on the exterior of the front door of the rental unit notifying the tenant that the writ has been issued and that the writ will be executed on or after a specific date and time stated in the warning not sooner than 24 hours after the warning is posted; and

(2) when the writ is executed:

(A) deliver possession of the premises to the landlord;

(B) instruct the tenant and all persons claiming under the tenant to leave the premises immediately, and, if the persons fail to comply, physically remove them;

(C) instruct the tenant to remove or to allow the landlord, the landlord's representatives, or other persons acting under the officer's supervision to remove all personal property from the rental unit other than personal property claimed to be owned by the landlord; and

(D) place, or have an authorized person place, the removed personal property outside the rental unit at a nearby location, but not blocking a public sidewalk, passageway, or street and not while it is raining, sleeting, or snowing, except as provided by Subsection (d-1).

(d-1) A municipality may provide, without charge to the landlord or to the owner of personal property removed from a rental unit under Subsection (d), a portable, closed container into which the removed personal property shall be placed by the officer executing the writ or by the authorized person. The municipality may remove the container from the location near the rental unit and dispose of the contents by any lawful means if the owner of the removed personal property does not recover the property from the container within a reasonable time after the time the property is placed in the container.

(e) The writ of possession shall authorize the officer, at the officer's discretion, to engage the services of a bonded or insured warehouseman to remove and store, subject to applicable law, part or all of the property at no cost to the landlord or the officer executing the writ.

(f) The officer may not require the landlord to store the property.

(g) The writ of possession shall contain notice to the officer that under Section 7.003, Civil Practice and Remedies Code, the officer is not liable for damages resulting from the execution of the writ if the officer executes the writ in good faith and with reasonable diligence.

(h) A sheriff or constable may use reasonable force in executing a writ under this section.

History of Prop. Code §24.0061: Acts 1985, 69th Leg., ch. 319, §1, eff. Sept. 1, 1985. Amended by Acts 1987, 70th Leg., ch. 314, §1 (eff. Sept. 1, 1987), ch. 745, §6 (eff. June 20, 1987), ch. 1089, §1 (eff. Aug. 31, 1987); Acts 1989, 71st Leg., ch. 2, §13.01 (eff. Aug. 28, 1989), ch. 688, §5 (eff. Sept. 1, 1989); Acts 1997, 75th Leg., ch. 1205, §4, eff. Sept. 1, 1997; Acts 2015, 84th Leg., ch. 355, §1, eff. Sept. 1, 2015.

See also CPRC §7.003; TRCP 510.13; ***O'Connor's Texas Appeals***, "Writ of possession," ch. 4-B, §2.1.2(2)(b), p. 175; "Writ of possession," ch. 4-B, §6.6.5, p. 187; ***O'Connor's Texas COA***, "Writ of possession," ch. 16-B, §3.1, p. 429.

CHARTS

See timetable, "Writ of Possession & Warehouseman's Lien," p. 1547.

ANNOTATIONS

Campos v. Investment Mgmt. Props., 917 S.W.2d 351, 355 (Tex.App.—San Antonio 1996, writ denied). Section 24.0061 "says that the property may not be *removed* while it is raining. The statute does not impose a duty on the landlord or its agent to stand guard over the property until it is retrieved by the owner. Likewise, we reject [tenant's] arguments that the 'spirit' of the

statute required [landlord] to protect the property after proper execution of a writ in compliance with §24.0061."

Kennedy v. Highland Hills Apts., 905 S.W.2d 325, 326 (Tex.App.—Dallas 1995, no writ). "If the justice court finds in favor of the landlord, the landlord is entitled to a judgment for possession and a *writ of possession. At 327:* Either party may appeal the justice court's judgment to the county court by filing an appeal bond or a pauper's affidavit. In a nonpayment of rent forcible detainer case, a tenant who has appealed by filing a pauper's affidavit pursuant to [TRCP] 749a is entitled to remain in possession of the premises *during the pendency of the appeal* to the county court if the tenant follows the procedures set out in [TRCP] 749b. First, the tenant must pay into the justice court registry one rental period's rent within five days of filing the pauper's affidavit. Second, during the appeal process, as the rent becomes due under the rental agreement, the tenant must pay the rent into the county court registry within five days of the date rent is due under the terms of the rental agreement. If the tenant fails to timely pay the rent into the county court registry, the landlord may file a notice of default in the county court. If the landlord shows the tenant defaulted under the rule, the court shall issue a *writ of restitution*."

PROP §24.0062. WAREHOUSEMAN'S LIEN

(a) If personal property is removed from a tenant's premises as the result of an action brought under this chapter and stored in a bonded or insured public warehouse, the warehouseman has a lien on the property to the extent of any reasonable storage and moving charges incurred by the warehouseman. The lien does not attach to any property until the property has been stored by the warehouseman.

(b) If property is to be removed and stored in a public warehouse under a writ of possession, the officer executing the writ shall, at the time of execution, deliver in person to the tenant, or by first class mail to the tenant's last known address not later than 72 hours after execution of the writ if the tenant is not present, a written notice stating the complete address and telephone number of the location at which the property may be redeemed and stating that:

(1) the tenant's property is to be removed and stored by a public warehouseman under Section 24.0062 of the Property Code;

(2) the tenant may redeem any of the property, without payment of moving or storage charges, on demand during the time the warehouseman is removing the property from the tenant's premises and before the warehouseman permanently leaves the tenant's premises;

(3) within 30 days from the date of storage, the tenant may redeem any of the property described by Section 24.0062(e), Property Code, on demand by the tenant and on payment of the moving and storage charges reasonably attributable to the items being redeemed;

(4) after the 30-day period and before sale, the tenant may redeem the property on demand by the tenant and on payment of all moving and storage charges; and

(5) subject to the previously stated conditions, the warehouseman has a lien on the property to secure payment of moving and storage charges and may sell all the property to satisfy reasonable moving and storage charges after 30 days, subject to the requirements of Section 24.0062(j) of the Property Code.

(c) The statement required by Subsection (b)(2) must be underlined or in boldfaced print.

(d) On demand by the tenant during the time the warehouseman is removing the property from the tenant's premises and before the warehouseman permanently leaves the tenant's premises, the warehouseman shall return to the tenant all property requested by the tenant, without charge.

(e) On demand by the tenant within 30 days after the date the property is stored by the warehouseman and on payment by the tenant of the moving and storage charges reasonably attributable to the items being redeemed, the warehouseman shall return to the tenant at the warehouse the following property:

(1) wearing apparel;

(2) tools, apparatus, and books of a trade or profession;

(3) school books;

(4) a family library;

(5) family portraits and pictures;

(6) one couch, two living room chairs, and a dining table and chairs;

(7) beds and bedding;

(8) kitchen furniture and utensils;

(9) food and foodstuffs;

(10) medicine and medical supplies;

(11) one automobile and one truck;

(12) agricultural implements;

(13) children's toys not commonly used by adults;

(14) goods that the warehouseman or the warehouseman's agent knows are owned by a person other than the tenant or an occupant of the residence;

(15) goods that the warehouseman or the warehouseman's agent knows are subject to a recorded chattel mortgage or financing agreement; and

(16) cash.

(f) During the first 30 days after the date of storage, the warehouseman may not require payment of removal or storage charges for other items as a condition for redeeming the items described by Subsection (e).

(g) On demand by the tenant to the warehouseman after the 30-day period and before sale and on payment by the tenant of all unpaid moving and storage charges on all the property, the warehouseman shall return all the previously unredeemed property to the tenant at the warehouse.

(h) A warehouseman may not recover any moving or storage charges if the court determines under Subsection (i) that the warehouseman's moving or storage charges are not reasonable.

(i) Before the sale of the property by the warehouseman, the tenant may file suit in the justice court in which the eviction judgment was rendered, or in another court of competent jurisdiction in the county in which the rental premises are located, to recover the property described by Subsection (e) on the ground that the landlord failed to return the property after timely demand and payment by the tenant, as provided by this section. Before sale, the tenant may also file suit to recover all property moved or stored by the warehouseman on the ground that the amount of the warehouseman's moving or storage charges is not reasonable. All proceedings under this subsection have precedence over other matters on the court's docket. The justice court that issued the writ of possession has jurisdiction under this section regardless of the amount in controversy.

(j) Any sale of property that is subject to a lien under this section shall be conducted in accordance with Section 7.210 and Subchapters D and F, Chapter 9, Business & Commerce Code.

(k) In a proceeding under this section, the prevailing party is entitled to recover actual damages, reasonable attorney's fees, court costs, and, if appropriate, any property withheld in violation of this section or the value of that property if it has been sold.

History of Prop. Code §24.0062: Acts 1985, 69th Leg., ch. 747, §1, eff. Sept. 1, 1985. Renumbered from §24.009 and amended by Acts 1987, 70th Leg., ch. 314, §2, eff. Sept. 1, 1987. Amended by Acts 1987, 70th Leg., ch. 745, §7, eff. June 20, 1987; Acts 1993, 73rd Leg., ch. 48, §1, eff. Sept. 1, 1993; Acts 1999, 76th Leg., ch. 414, §2.35, eff. July 1, 2001.

CHARTS

See timetable, "Writ of Possession & Warehouseman's Lien," p. 1547.

PROP §24.007. APPEAL

A final judgment of a county court in an eviction suit may not be appealed on the issue of possession unless the premises in question are being used for residential purposes only. A judgment of a county court may not under any circumstances be stayed pending appeal unless, within 10 days of the signing of the judgment, the appellant files a supersedeas bond in an amount set by the county court. In setting the supersedeas bond the county court shall provide protection for the appellee to the same extent as in any other appeal, taking into consideration the value of rents likely to accrue during appeal, damages which may occur as a result of the stay during appeal, and other damages or amounts as the court may deem appropriate.

History of Prop. Code §24.007: Acts 1983, 68th Leg., ch. 576, §1, eff. Jan. 1, 1984. Amended by Acts 1985, 69th Leg., ch. 891, §1, eff. Sept. 1, 1985; Acts 1997, 75th Leg., ch. 1205, §5, eff. Sept. 1, 1997; Acts 2011, 82nd Leg., 1st C.S., ch. 3, §2.02, eff. Jan. 1, 2012; Acts 2015, 84th Leg., ch. 1113, §1, eff. Jan. 1, 2016. Source: TRCS art. 3992.

See also TRAP 24.2(a)(2)(A); TRCP 510.13; *O'Connor's Texas Appeals*, "Writ of possession," ch. 4-B, §2.1.2(2)(b), p. 175; "Writ of possession," ch. 4-B, §6.6.5, p. 187.

ANNOTATIONS

Marshall v. Housing Auth., 198 S.W.3d 782, 786-87 (Tex.2006). Section 24.007 "provides that judgment in a forcible detainer action may not be stayed pending appeal unless the appellant timely files a supersedeas bond in the amount set by the trial court. Thus, if a proper supersedeas bond is not filed, the judgment may be enforced, including issuance of a writ of possession evicting the tenant from the premises. However, there is no language in the statute which purports to either impair the appellate rights of a tenant or require a bond be posted to perfect an appeal. [Tenant's] failure to supersede the judgment did not divest her of her right to appeal." *See also* ***Briones v. Brazos Bend Villa Apts.***, 438 S.W.3d 808, 812 (Tex.App.—Houston [14th Dist.] 2014, no pet.).

Olley v. HVM, L.L.C., 449 S.W.3d 572, 575 (Tex. App.—Houston [14th Dist.] 2014, pet. denied). "An appeal in a forcible detainer action becomes moot when the appellant ceases to have actual possession of the property, unless the appellant has a potentially meritorious claim of right to current, actual possession."

Whitmire v. Greenridge Place Apts., 333 S.W.3d 255, 260-61 (Tex.App.—Houston [1st Dist.] 2010, pet. dism'd). "The Rules of Appellate Procedure and the … Property Code both provide that, in setting the amount of the supersedeas bond requirement when the judgment involves a real property interest, the trial court must consider the value of rent or revenue likely to accrue during the pendency of an appeal. The sureties on the bond are subject to liability for all damages and costs that may be awarded against the judgment debtor, up to the amount of the bond, if the debtor does not pay the value of the property's rent or revenue during the pendency of the appeal. [¶] Generally, after the term in which we render a judgment expires, we lack plenary power to correct or alter that judgment, except for ministerial acts consistent with the judgment. … When we affirm the judgment of the trial court, we must also render judgment against the sureties on the supersedeas bond for the performance of the judgment and any costs taxed against the appellant. This is a mandatory duty, and our failure to do so in our initial judgment does not deprive us of the power to, at any time, even after our plenary power has expired, amend our judgment to reflect the sureties' liability. Rendering judgment against the sureties after we affirm a judgment is a ministerial act involving no judicial discretion, and thus we may amend our judgment, after the expiration of our plenary power, to operate against the sureties on the supersedeas bond."

Volume Millwork, Inc. v. West Houston Airport Corp., 218 S.W.3d 722, 729 (Tex.App.—Houston [1st Dist.] 2006, pet. denied). "Because [TRCP] 752 imposes no limits beyond those stated in the rule, a judgment may, therefore, exceed the jurisdictional-amount limitation that otherwise controls county-court adjudications on appeals by trial de novo from justice court.… We therefore agree that 'nothing in the rules limits the damage claims joined in the county court to the jurisdictional limits of the justice court.' [¶] Having sued for possession and prevailed in justice court, landlord properly relied on [TRCP] 752 to pursue its additional damages, reasonable attorney's fees, and costs, as authorized by that rule and [Prop. Code] §24.007 …, without regard to the amount-in-controversy limitation of justice court." *See also* ***Carlson's Hill Country Bev., L.C. v. Westinghouse Rd. Jt.V.***, 957 S.W.2d 951, 952-53 & n.6 (Tex.App.—Austin 1997, no writ) (finding §24.007 precluded review of issue of possession but allowed review of challenges to amount of damages and attorneys fees because award did not depend on issue of possession); ***A.V.A. Servs. v. Parts Indus.***, 949 S.W.2d 852, 853 (Tex.App.—Beaumont 1997, no writ) (finding no jurisdiction over points relating to judgment awarding possession, but reviewing monetary judgment).

Gibson v. Dynegy Midstream Servs., 138 S.W.3d 518, 521 (Tex.App.—Fort Worth 2004, no pet.). Section 24.007 "is not intended to preclude appellate review of all issues arising from an eviction proceeding involving commercial property, but only to limit review over appeals raising the issue of possession." *See also* ***Hong Kong Dev., Inc. v. Nguyen***, 229 S.W.3d 415, 431-32 (Tex.App.—Houston [1st Dist.] 2007, no pet.).

Rice v. Pinney, 51 S.W.3d 705, 708 (Tex.App.—Dallas 2001, no pet.). "Section 24.007 does not preclude appellate review of a county court at law's subject matter jurisdiction."

Fandey v. Lee, 880 S.W.2d 164, 167 (Tex.App.—El Paso 1994, writ denied). "It is [D's] contention that §24.007 … means what it says, that a judgment of a county court in a forcible detainer suit on the issue of possession is final and unappealable unless the property in question is being used strictly for residential purposes and nothing else. [¶] Taking the wording 'used for residential purposes only' at face value would mean that neither the landlord nor the tenant in a situation where the tenant used any part of the premises for commercial or business purposes, be it for occasional telephone calls to or from patients, clients or customers, piano lessons, tax services or whatever, would be able to appeal from an adverse judgment in the county court on the issue of possession. While we find it somewhat difficult to believe that the Texas Legislature intended to restrict the right to appeal so severely, we conclude that a literal reading of 'used for residential purposes only' cannot be interpreted any other way. If the legislature had intended otherwise, it would have been a simple matter to have restricted the right to appeal on the issue of possession to cases where the premises were used 'primarily' (or some other appropriate word) for residential purposes."

Academy Corp. v. Sunwest N.O.P., Inc., 853 S.W.2d 833, 833-34 (Tex.App.—Houston [14th Dist.] 1993, writ denied). See annotation under Property Code §24.002, p. 155.

Hughes v. Habitat Apts., 828 S.W.2d 794, 795 (Tex. App.—Dallas 1992), *rev'd on other grounds*, 860 S.W.2d 872 (Tex.1993). "[B]ecause an award of appellate attorney's fees is only a conditional award until the conclusion of the appeal, we hold that [tenant] cannot be compelled to post a supersedeas bond that includes the amount of that award while the appeal remains pending."

Mullins v. Coussons, 745 S.W.2d 50, 51 (Tex. App.—Houston [14th Dist.] 1987, no writ). Section 24.007 "prohibits appeal from final judgments of county courts in forcible entry and detainer suits or forcible detainer suits on the issue of possession unless the premises in question are being used for residential purposes only. A party to a forcible detainer suit in a county court cannot use a writ of mandamus to accomplish an appeal prohibited by this statute. To allow the use of a writ of mandamus to control the county court's non-appealable exercise of discretion would permit the very appeal … §24.007 was enacted to prohibit."

PROP §24.008. EFFECT ON OTHER ACTIONS

An eviction suit does not bar a suit for trespass, damages, waste, rent, or mesne profits.

History of Prop. Code §24.008: Acts 1983, 68th Leg., ch. 576, §1, eff. Jan. 1, 1984. Amended by Acts 1985, 69th Leg., ch. 891, §1, eff. Aug. 26, 1985; Acts 1997, 75th Leg., ch. 1205, §6, eff. Sept. 1, 1997. Source: TRCS art. 3994.

See also ***O'Connor's Texas COA***, "Related Causes of Action," ch. 16-B, §7, p. 440.

ANNOTATIONS

Coinmach Corp. v. Aspenwood Apt. Corp., 417 S.W.3d 909, 919 (Tex.2013). "[U]nder the common law a tenant at sufferance has no legal title or right to possession, and is thus a 'trespasser' who possesses the property 'wrongfully.' The question that [D] raises is whether the Legislature has altered the common law through the statute governing [forcible-entry-and-detainer (FED)] actions. The Legislature has itself answered that question, expressly providing in §24.008 that a suit for eviction under the FED statute 'does not bar a suit for trespass, damages, waste, rent, or mesne profits.' We held long ago that the remedies against a holdover tenant include a forcible detainer action for possession and an action for recovery of damages, including trespass damages. In §24.008, the Legislature made it clear that an FED action does not bar a suit to obtain these remedies."

Green v. Canon, 33 S.W.3d 855, 859 (Tex.App.—Houston [14th Dist.] 2000, pet. denied). "A litigant may pursue a forcible entry and detainer action in the justice court while simultaneously pursuing her other remedies in another court. … Courts have interpreted [§24.008] to mean that an action for eviction is not exclusive, but cumulative of any other remedy a party may have in other state courts."

Magcobar N. Am. v. Grasso Oilfield Servs., 736 S.W.2d 787, 797 (Tex.App.—Corpus Christi 1987), *writ dism'd*, 754 S.W.2d 646 (Tex.1988). "[S]uccessful prosecution of a forcible entry and detainer suit does not bar a later action for wrongful eviction. We hold that [D] may be held liable to [P] for lost profits proved with reasonable certainty, under [P's] cause of action for wrongful eviction."

Standard Container Corp. v. Dragon Rlty., 683 S.W.2d 45, 48 (Tex.App.—Dallas 1984, writ ref'd n.r.e.). Since tenant "had already recovered possession at the time suit was filed in the court below, the remedy it sought was recovery of damages for the wrongful holdover. In an action for damages for a tenant's wrongful holdover of a lease the landlord's proper measure of damages is the reasonable market value of the use of the land for the time the tenant held over."

Johnson v. Highland Hills Drive Apts., 552 S.W.2d 493, 494 (Tex.App.—Dallas 1977), *writ ref'd n.r.e.*, 568 S.W.2d 661 (Tex.1978). "[T]he legislative intent is clear that an action for damages is not barred by a judgment of possession in a forcible detainer action. … We conclude [that Prop. Code §24.008's language] with respect to 'damages' would be meaningless if we were to hold that an action for damages is barred. Accordingly, we hold that [TRCS art. 3994, now Prop. Code §24.008,] prevents a judgment of possession in a forcible entry and detainer action from barring a subsequent action for damages for wrongful eviction."

PROP §24.009. RENUMBERED

Renumbered as §24.0062 by Acts 1987, 70th Leg., ch. 314, §2 (eff. Sept. 1, 1987), ch. 745, §7 (eff. Sept. 1, 1987). Renumbered as §24.011 by Acts 1987, 70th Leg., ch. 167, §5.01(a)(49), eff. Sept. 1, 1987.

Section 24.010 blank

PROP §24.011. NONLAWYER REPRESENTATION

(a) In eviction suits in justice court for nonpayment of rent or holding over beyond a rental term, the parties may represent themselves or be represented by their authorized agents, who need not be attorneys. In any eviction suit in justice court, an authorized agent requesting or obtaining a default judgment need not be an attorney.

(b) In an appeal of an eviction suit for nonpayment of rent in a county or district court, an owner of a multifamily residential property may be represented by the owner's authorized agent, who need not be an attorney, or, if the owner is a corporation or other entity, by an employee, owner, officer, or partner of the entity, who need not be an attorney.

History of Prop. Code §24.011: Acts 1985, 69th Leg., ch. 891, §1, eff. Aug. 26, 1985. Renumbered from §24.009 by Acts 1987, 70th Leg., ch. 167, §5.01(a)(49), eff. Sept. 1, 1987. Amended by Acts 1997, 75th Leg., ch. 1205, §7, eff. Sept. 1, 1997; H.B. 3879, §1, 85th Leg., eff. Sept. 1, 2017.

See also TRCP 500.4; ***O'Connor's Texas COA***, "Filing & Responding to Suit," ch. 16-B, §5, p. 432.

CHAPTER 24A. ACCESS TO RESIDENCE OR FORMER RESIDENCE TO RETRIEVE PERSONAL PROPERTY

PROP §24A.001. DEFINITIONS [~~DEFINITION~~]

The amended text in §24A.001 is effective for applications filed on or after Sept. 1, 2017. Applications filed before Sept. 1, 2017, are governed by the former law in effect at that time.

In this chapter:

(1) "Electronic record" means a record created, generated, sent, communicated, received, or stored by electronic means.

(2) "Family violence" has the meaning assigned by Section 71.004, Family Code.

(3) "Peace[~~, "peace~~] officer" means a person listed under Article 2.12(1) or (2), Code of Criminal Procedure.

History of Prop. Code §24A.001: Acts 2015, 84th Leg., ch. 1076, §1, eff. Sept. 1, 2015. Amended by S.B. 920, §1, 85th Leg., eff. Sept. 1, 2017.

PROP §24A.002. WRIT [~~ORDER~~] AUTHORIZING ENTRY & PROPERTY RETRIEVAL; PEACE OFFICER TO ACCOMPANY

The amended text in §24A.002 is effective for applications filed on or after Sept. 1, 2017. Applications filed before Sept. 1, 2017, are governed by the former law in effect at that time.

(a) If a person is unable to enter the person's residence or former residence to retrieve personal property belonging to the person or the person's dependent because the current occupant is denying the person entry, the person may apply to the justice court for a writ [~~an order~~] authorizing the person to enter the residence accompanied by a peace officer to retrieve specific items of personal property.

(b) An application under Subsection (a) must:

(1) certify that the applicant is unable to enter the residence because the current occupant of the residence:

(A) has denied the applicant access to the residence; or

(B) poses a clear and present danger of family violence to the applicant or the applicant's dependent;

(2) certify that, to the best of the applicant's knowledge, the applicant is not:

(A) the subject of an active protective order under Title 4, Family Code, a magistrate's order for emergency protection under Article 17.292, Code of Criminal Procedure, or another court order prohibiting entry to the residence; or

(B) otherwise prohibited by law from entering the residence;

(3) allege that the applicant or the applicant's [~~minor~~] dependent requires personal items located in the residence that are only of the following types:

(A) medical records;

(B) medicine and medical supplies;

(C) clothing;

(D) child-care items;

(E) legal or financial documents;

(F) checks or bank or credit cards in the name of the applicant;

(G) employment records; [~~or~~]

(H) personal identification documents; or

(I) copies of electronic records containing legal or financial documents;

(4) describe with specificity the items that the applicant intends to retrieve;

(5) allege that the applicant or the applicant's dependent will suffer personal harm if the items listed in the application are not retrieved promptly; and

(6) include a lease or other documentary evidence that shows the applicant is currently or was formerly authorized to occupy the residence.

(c) Before the justice of the peace may issue a writ [an order] under this section, the applicant must execute a bond that:

(1) has two or more good and sufficient non-corporate sureties or one corporate surety authorized to issue bonds in this state;

(2) is payable to the occupant of the residence;

(3) is in an amount required by the justice; and

(4) is conditioned on the applicant paying all damages and costs adjudged against the applicant for wrongful property retrieval.

(d) The applicant shall deliver the bond to the justice of the peace issuing the writ [order] for the justice's approval. The bond shall be filed with the justice court.

(e) On sufficient evidence of urgency and potential harm to the health and safety of any person and after sufficient notice to the current occupant and an opportunity to be heard, the justice of the peace may grant the application under this section and issue a writ [an order] authorizing the applicant to enter the residence accompanied by a peace officer and retrieve the property listed in the application if the justice of the peace finds that:

(1) the applicant is unable to enter the residence because the current occupant of the residence has denied the applicant access to the residence to retrieve the applicant's personal property or the personal property of the applicant's dependent;

(2) the applicant is not:

(A) the subject of an active protective order under Title 4, Family Code, a magistrate's order for emergency protection under Article 17.292, Code of Criminal Procedure, or another court order prohibiting entry to the residence; or

(B) otherwise prohibited by law from entering the residence;

(3) there is a risk of personal harm to the applicant or the applicant's dependent if the items listed in the application are not retrieved promptly;

(4) the applicant is currently or was formerly authorized to occupy the residence according to a lease or other documentary evidence; and

(5) the current occupant received notice of the application and was provided an opportunity to appear before the court to contest the application.

History of Prop. Code §24A.002: Acts 2015, 84th Leg., ch. 1076, §1, eff. Sept. 1, 2015. Amended by S.B. 920, §1, 85th Leg., eff. Sept. 1, 2017.

See also *O'Connor's Family Forms*, FORMS 4B:27-29.

E PROP §24A.0021. TEMPORARY EX PARTE WRIT AUTHORIZING ENTRY & PROPERTY RETRIEVAL

(a) A justice of the peace may issue a writ under Section 24A.002 without providing notice and hearing under Section 24A.002(e)(5) if the justice finds at a hearing on the application that:

(1) the conditions of Sections 24A.002(e)(1)-(4) are established;

(2) the current occupant poses a clear and present danger of family violence to the applicant or the applicant's dependent; and

(3) the personal harm to be suffered by the applicant or the applicant's dependent will be immediate and irreparable if the application is not granted.

(b) A justice of the peace issuing a writ under this section may waive the bond requirements under Sections 24A.002(c) and (d).

(c) The justice of the peace may recess a hearing under Subsection (a) to notify the current occupant by telephone that the current occupant may attend the hearing or bring to the court the personal property listed in the application. The justice of the peace shall reconvene the hearing before 5 p.m. that day regardless of whether the current occupant attends the hearing or brings the personal property to the court.

(d) A temporary ex parte writ issued under Subsection (a) must state the period, not to exceed five days, during which the writ is valid.

History of Prop. Code §24A.0021: Enacted by S.B. 920, §1, 85th Leg., eff. Sept. 1, 2017.

PROP §24A.003. AUTHORIZED ENTRY PROCEDURES; DUTIES OF PEACE OFFICER

The amended text in §24A.003 is effective for applications filed on or after Sept. 1, 2017. Applications filed before Sept. 1, 2017, are governed by the former law in effect at that time.

(a) If the justice of the peace grants an application under Section 24A.002 or Section 24A.0021, a peace officer shall accompany and assist the applicant in making the authorized entry and retrieving the items of personal property listed in the application.

(b) If the current occupant of the residence is present at the time of the entry, the peace officer shall provide the occupant with a copy of the writ [~~court order~~] authorizing the entry and property retrieval.

(c) Before removing the property listed in the application from the residence, the applicant must submit all property retrieved to the peace officer assisting the applicant under this section to be inventoried. The peace officer shall create an inventory listing the items taken from the residence, provide a copy of the inventory to the applicant, provide a copy of the inventory to the current occupant or, if the current occupant is not present, leave the copy in a conspicuous place in the residence, and return the property to be removed from the residence to the applicant. The officer shall file the original inventory with the court that issued the writ [~~order~~] authorizing the entry and property retrieval.

(d) A peace officer may use reasonable force in providing assistance under this section.

(e) A peace officer who provides assistance under this section in good faith and with reasonable diligence is not:

(1) civilly liable for an act or omission of the officer that arises in connection with providing the assistance; or

(2) civilly or criminally liable for the wrongful appropriation of any personal property by the person the officer is assisting.

History of Prop. Code §24A.003: Acts 2015, 84th Leg., ch. 1076, §1, eff. Sept. 1, 2015. Amended by S.B. 920, §2, 85th Leg., eff. Sept. 1, 2017.

PROP §24A.004. IMMUNITY FROM LIABILITY

The amended text in §24A.004 is effective for applications filed on or after Sept. 1, 2017. Applications filed before Sept. 1, 2017, are governed by the former law in effect at that time.

A landlord or a landlord's agent who permits or facilitates entry into a residence in accordance with a writ [~~court order~~] issued under this chapter is not civilly or criminally liable for an act or omission that arises in connection with permitting or facilitating the entry.

History of Prop. Code §24A.004: Acts 2015, 84th Leg., ch. 1076, §1, eff. Sept. 1, 2015. Amended by S.B. 920, §3, 85th Leg., eff. Sept. 1, 2017.

PROP §24A.005. OFFENSE

The amended text in §24A.005 is effective for applications filed on or after Sept. 1, 2017. Applications filed before Sept. 1, 2017, are governed by the former law in effect at that time.

(a) A person commits an offense if the person interferes with a person or peace officer entering a residence and retrieving personal property under the authority of a writ [~~court order~~] issued under Section 24A.002 or 24A.0021.

(b) An offense under this section is a Class B misdemeanor.

(c) It is a defense to prosecution under this section that the actor did not receive a copy of the writ [~~court order~~] or other notice that the entry or property retrieval was authorized.

History of Prop. Code §24A.005: Acts 2015, 84th Leg., ch. 1076, §1, eff. Sept. 1, 2015. Amended by S.B. 920, §4, 85th Leg., eff. Sept. 1, 2017.

PROP §24A.006. HEARING; REVIEW

The amended text in §24A.006 is effective for applications filed on or after Sept. 1, 2017. Applications filed before Sept. 1, 2017, are governed by the former law in effect at that time.

(a) The occupant of a residence that is the subject of a writ [~~court order~~] issued under Section 24A.002 or 24A.0021, not later than the 10th day after the date of the authorized entry, may file a complaint in the court that issued the writ [~~order~~] alleging that the applicant has appropriated property belonging to the occupant or the occupant's dependent.

(b) The court shall promptly hold a hearing on a complaint submitted under this section and rule on the disposition of the disputed property.

(c) This section does not limit the occupant's remedies under any other law for recovery of the property of the occupant or the occupant's dependent.

History of Prop. Code §24A.006: Acts 2015, 84th Leg., ch. 1076, §1, eff. Sept. 1, 2015. Amended by S.B. 920, §5, 85th Leg., eff. Sept. 1, 2017.

CHAPTER 25. TRIAL OF RIGHT OF PROPERTY

PROP §25.001. JURISDICTION

A trial of the right of property is an action that applies only to personal property. A trial of the right of property must be tried in a court with jurisdiction of the amount in controversy.

History of Prop. Code §25.001: Acts 1983, 68th Leg., ch. 576, §1, eff. Jan. 1, 1984. Source: TRCS art. 7409.

See also TRCP 717-734.

ANNOTATIONS

Grocers Sup. Co. v. Powell, 775 S.W.2d 76, 77 (Tex.App.—Houston [14th Dist.] 1989, orig. proceeding). "A trial of the right of property must be tried in a court with jurisdiction of the amount in controversy. ... In a trial of the right of property, the value of the property is the amount in controversy."

PROP §25.002. DAMAGES

If a claimant in a trial of the right of property does not establish a right to the property, the court shall adjudge damages against the obligors in the claimant's bond equal to 10 percent of the lesser of:

(1) the property's value; or

(2) the amount claimed under the writ levied against the property.

History of Prop. Code §25.002: Acts 1983, 68th Leg., ch. 576, §1, eff. Jan. 1, 1984. Source: TRCS arts. 7417, 7418.

See also TRCP 717-734.

CHAPTER 26. USE OF A DECEASED INDIVIDUAL'S NAME, VOICE, SIGNATURE, PHOTOGRAPH, OR LIKENESS

PROP §26.001. DEFINITIONS

In this chapter:

(1) "Photograph" means a photograph or photographic reproduction, still or moving, videotape, or live television transmission of an individual in a manner that allows a person viewing the photograph with the naked eye to reasonably determine the identity of the individual.

(2) "Property right" means the property right created by this chapter.

(3) "Name" means the actual or assumed name used by an individual which, when used in conjunction with other information, is intended to identify a particular person.

(4) "Media enterprise" means a newspaper, magazine, radio station or network, television station or network, or cable television system.

History of Prop. Code §26.001: Acts 1987, 70th Leg., ch. 152, §1, eff. Sept. 1, 1987.

PROP §26.002. PROPERTY RIGHT ESTABLISHED

An individual has a property right in the use of the individual's name, voice, signature, photograph, or likeness after the death of the individual.

History of Prop. Code §26.002: Acts 1987, 70th Leg., ch. 152, §1, eff. Sept. 1, 1987.

PROP §26.003. APPLICABILITY

This chapter applies to an individual:

(1) alive on or after September 1, 1987, or who died before September 1, 1987, but on or after January 1, 1937; and

(2) whose name, voice, signature, photograph, or likeness has commercial value at the time of his or her death or comes to have commercial value after that time.

History of Prop. Code §26.003: Acts 1987, 70th Leg., ch. 152, §1, eff. Sept. 1, 1987.

PROP §26.004. TRANSFERABILITY

(a) The property right is freely transferable, in whole or in part, by contract or by means of trust or testamentary documents.

(b) The property right may be transferred before or after the death of the individual.

History of Prop. Code §26.004: Acts 1987, 70th Leg., ch. 152, §1, eff. Sept. 1, 1987.

PROP §26.005. OWNERSHIP AFTER DEATH OF INDIVIDUAL

(a) If the ownership of the property right of an individual has not been transferred at or before the death of the individual, the property right vests as follows:

(1) if there is a surviving spouse but there are no surviving children or grandchildren, the entire interest vests in the surviving spouse;

(2) if there is a surviving spouse and surviving children or grandchildren, one-half the interest vests in the surviving spouse and one-half the interest vests in the surviving children or grandchildren;

(3) if there is no surviving spouse, the entire interest vests in the surviving children of the deceased individual and the surviving children of any deceased children of the deceased individual; or

(4) if there is no surviving spouse, children, or grandchildren, the entire interest vests in the surviving parents of the deceased individual.

(b) The interests of the deceased individual's children and grandchildren are divided among them and exercisable on a per stirpes basis in the manner provided by Section 201.101, Estates ~~[43, Texas Probate]~~ Code, according to the number of the deceased individual's children represented. If there is more than one child of a deceased child of the deceased individual, the share of a child of a deceased child may only be exercised by a majority of the children of the deceased child.

(c) If the property right is split among more than one person, those persons who own more than a one-half interest in the aggregate may exercise the right on behalf of all persons who own the right.

History of Prop. Code §26.005: Acts 1987, 70th Leg., ch. 152, §1, eff. Sept. 1, 1987. Amended by S.B. 1488, §22.058, 85th Leg., eff. Sept. 1, 2017.

PROP §26.006. REGISTRATION OF CLAIM

(a) A person who claims to own a property right may register that claim with the secretary of state.

(b) The secretary of state shall provide a form for registration of a claim under this section. The form must be verified and must include:

(1) the name and date of death of the deceased individual;

(2) the name and address of the claimant;

(3) a statement of the basis of the claim; and

(4) a statement of the right claimed.

(c) The secretary of state may microfilm or reproduce by another technique a document filed under this section and destroy the original document.

(d) A document or a reproduction of a document filed under this section is admissible in evidence.

(e) The secretary of state may destroy all documents filed under this section after the 50th anniversary of the date of death of the individual whose property right they concern.

(f) The fee for filing a claim is $25.

(g) A document filed under this section is a public record.

History of Prop. Code §26.006: Acts 1987, 70th Leg., ch. 152, §1, eff. Sept. 1, 1987.

PROP §26.007. EFFECT OF REGISTRATION

(a) Registration of a claim is prima facie evidence of a valid claim to a property right.

(b) A registered claim is superior to a conflicting, unregistered claim unless a court invalidates the registered claim.

History of Prop. Code §26.007: Acts 1987, 70th Leg., ch. 152, §1, eff. Sept. 1, 1987.

PROP §26.008. EXERCISE OF OWNERSHIP FOR FIRST YEAR FOLLOWING DEATH OF INDIVIDUAL

(a) Except as provided by Subsection (b), for the first year following the death of the individual a property right may be exercised, if authorized by law or an appointing court, by the following persons who may be appointed by a court for the benefit of the estate of the deceased individual:

(1) an independent executor;

(2) an executor;

(3) an independent administrator;

(4) a temporary or permanent administrator; or

(5) a temporary or permanent guardian.

(b) For the first year following the death of the individual, an owner of a property right may exercise that right only if the owner registers a valid claim as provided by Section 26.006.

History of Prop. Code §26.008: Acts 1987, 70th Leg., ch. 152, §1, eff. Sept. 1, 1987.

PROP §26.009. EXERCISE OF OWNERSHIP AFTER FIRST YEAR FOLLOWING DEATH OF INDIVIDUAL

After the first year following the death of the individual, an owner of a property right may exercise that right whether or not the owner has registered a claim as provided by Section 26.006.

History of Prop. Code §26.009: Acts 1987, 70th Leg., ch. 152, §1, eff. Sept. 1, 1987.

PROP §26.010. TERMINATION

A property right expires on the first anniversary of the date of death of the individual if:

(1) the individual has not transferred the right; and

(2) a surviving person under Section 26.005 does not exist.

History of Prop. Code §26.010: Acts 1987, 70th Leg., ch. 152, §1, eff. Sept. 1, 1987.

PROP §26.011. UNAUTHORIZED USES

Except as provided by Section 26.012, a person may not use, without the written consent of a person who may exercise the property right, a deceased individual's name, voice, signature, photograph, or likeness in any manner, including:

(1) in connection with products, merchandise, or goods; or

(2) for the purpose of advertising, selling, or soliciting the purchase of products, merchandise, goods, or services.

History of Prop. Code §26.011: Acts 1987, 70th Leg., ch. 152, §1, eff. Sept. 1, 1987.

PROP §26.012. PERMITTED USES

(a) A person may use a deceased individual's name, voice, signature, photograph, or likeness in:

(1) a play, book, film, radio program, or television program;

(2) a magazine or newspaper article;

(3) material that is primarily of political or newsworthy value;

(4) single and original works of fine art; or

(5) an advertisement or commercial announcement concerning a use under this subsection.

(b) A media enterprise may use a deceased individual's name, voice, signature, photograph, or likeness in connection with the coverage of news, public affairs, a sporting event, or a political campaign without consent. Any use other than the above by a media enterprise of a deceased individual's name, voice, signature, photograph, or likeness shall require consent if the material constituting the use is integrally and directly connected with commercial sponsorship or paid advertising. No consent shall be required for the use of the deceased individual's name, voice, signature, photograph, or likeness by a media enterprise if the broadcast or article is not commercially sponsored or does not contain paid advertising.

(c) A person who is an owner or employee of a media enterprise, including a newspaper, magazine, radio station or network, television station or network, cable television system, billboard, or transit ad, that is used for advertising a deceased individual's name, voice, signature, photograph, or likeness in a manner not authorized by this section is not liable for damages as provided by this section unless the person:

(1) knew that the use was not authorized by this section; or

(2) used the deceased individual's name, voice, signature, photograph, or likeness in a manner primarily intended to advertise or promote the media enterprise itself.

(d) A person may use a deceased individual's name, voice, signature, photograph, or likeness in any manner after the 50th anniversary of the date of the individual's death.

History of Prop. Code §26.012: Acts 1987, 70th Leg., ch. 152, §1, eff. Sept. 1, 1987.

PROP §26.013. LIABILITY FOR UNAUTHORIZED USE

(a) A person who uses a deceased individual's name, voice, signature, photograph, or likeness in a manner not authorized by this chapter is liable to the person who owns the property right for:

(1) the amount of any damages sustained, as a result of the unauthorized use, by the person who owns the property right or $2,500, whichever is greater;

(2) the amount of any profits from the unauthorized use that are attributable to that use;

(3) the amount of any exemplary damages that may be awarded; and

(4) reasonable attorney's fees and expenses and court costs incurred in recovering the damages and profits established by this section.

(b) The amount of profits under Subsection (a)(2) may be established by a showing of the gross revenue attributable to the unauthorized use minus any ex-

penses that the person who committed the unauthorized use may prove.

History of Prop. Code §26.013: Acts 1987, 70th Leg., ch. 152, §1, eff. Sept. 1, 1987.

PROP §26.014. OTHER RIGHTS NOT AFFECTED

This chapter does not affect a right an individual may have in the use of the individual's name, voice, signature, photograph, or likeness before the death of the individual.

History of Prop. Code §26.014: Acts 1987, 70th Leg., ch. 152, §1, eff. Sept. 1, 1987.

PROP §26.015. DEFENSES TO LIABILITY

A person shall not be liable for damages under this chapter if he has acted in reliance on the results of a probate proceeding governing the estate of the deceased personality in question.

History of Prop. Code §26.015: Acts 1987, 70th Leg., ch. 152, §1, eff. Sept. 1, 1987.

CHAPTER 27. RESIDENTIAL CONSTRUCTION LIABILITY

PROP §27.001. DEFINITIONS

In this chapter:

(1) "Action" means a court or judicial proceeding or an arbitration.

(2) "Appurtenance" means any structure or recreational facility that is appurtenant to a residence but is not a part of the dwelling unit.

(3) "Commission" means the Texas Residential Construction Commission.

(4) "Construction defect" has the meaning assigned by Section 401.004[1] for an action to which Subtitle D, Title 16,[1] applies and for any other action means a matter concerning the design, construction, or repair of a new residence, of an alteration of or repair or addition to an existing residence, or of an appurtenance to a residence, on which a person has a complaint against a contractor. The term may include any physical damage to the residence, any appurtenance, or the real property on which the residence and appurtenance are affixed proximately caused by a construction defect.

(5) "Contractor":

(A) means:

(i) a builder, as defined by Section 401.003,[1] contracting with an owner for the construction or repair of a new residence, for the repair or alteration of or an addition to an existing residence, or for the construction, sale, alteration, addition, or repair of an appurtenance to a new or existing residence;

(ii) any person contracting with a purchaser for the sale of a new residence constructed by or on behalf of that person; or

(iii) a person contracting with an owner or the developer of a condominium for the construction of a new residence, for an alteration of or an addition to an existing residence, for repair of a new or existing residence, or for the construction, sale, alteration, addition, or repair of an appurtenance to a new or existing residence; and

(B) includes:

(i) an owner, officer, director, shareholder, partner, or employee of the contractor; and

(ii) a risk retention group registered under Article 21.54, Insurance Code,[2] that insures all or any part of a contractor's liability for the cost to repair a residential construction defect.

(6) "Economic damages" means compensatory damages for pecuniary loss proximately caused by a construction defect. The term does not include exemplary damages or damages for physical pain and mental anguish, loss of consortium, disfigurement, physical impairment, or loss of companionship and society.

(7) "Residence" means the real property and improvements for a single-family house, duplex, triplex, or quadruplex or a unit and the common elements in a multiunit residential structure in which title to the individual units is transferred to the owners under a condominium or cooperative system.

(8) "Structural failure" has the meaning assigned by Section 401.002[1] for an action to which Subtitle D, Title 16, applies and for any other action means actual physical damage to the load-bearing portion of a residence caused by a failure of the load-bearing portion.

(9) "Third-party inspector" has the meaning assigned by Section 401.002.[1]

(10) "Developer of a condominium" means a declarant, as defined by Section 82.003, of a condominium consisting of one or more residences.

1. **Editor's note:** Expired. See "Editor's note," p. 732.

2. **Editor's note:** Now Insurance Code ch. 2201.

History of Prop. Code §27.001: Acts 1989, 71st Leg., ch. 1072, §1, eff. Sept. 1, 1989. Amended by Acts 1993, 73rd Leg., ch. 797, §§1, 2, eff. Aug. 30, 1993; Acts 1999, 76th Leg., ch. 189, §1, eff. Sept. 1, 1999; Acts 2003, 78th Leg., ch. 458, §2.01, eff. Sept. 1, 2003; Acts 2007, 80th Leg., ch. 750, §1, eff. Sept. 1, 2007.

See also *O'Connor's Texas COA*, "Residential Construction Liability Act (RCLA)," ch. 32-I, §6, p. 1134.

ANNOTATIONS

In re Wells, 252 S.W.3d 439, 445-46 (Tex.App.—Houston [14th Dist.] 2008, orig. proceeding). "Because the applicable definition of 'contractor' in RCLA §27.001 incorporates the definition of 'builder' in [former Prop. Code] §401.003, which excludes an entity that replaces or repairs the roof of an existing home, [respondent] concludes [relator] is not a 'contractor' under the RCLA. [Relator] thus is not entitled, according to [respondent], to the benefits and protections of the RCLA notice and dismissal provisions contained in [Prop. Code] §27.004. We disagree. [¶] [Relator] is, indisputably, a person contracting with an owner, [respondent], for the construction of an alteration to an existing residence or for repair of an existing residence. So, while [relator] may not be a 'builder,' it is, as a matter of law, a 'contractor.'"

O'Donnell v. Roger Bullivant, Inc., 940 S.W.2d 411, 417 (Tex.App.—Fort Worth 1997, writ denied), *overruled on other grounds, **Perry Homes v. Alwattari***, 33 S.W.3d 376 (Tex.App.—Fort Worth 2000, pet. denied). "'Alteration' is defined as a 'change or modification made on a building that does not increase its exterior dimensions.' [¶] [F]or RCLA to apply … the design and construction of … foundation repair with concrete pilings would have to be an alteration or an addition to the … existing foundation. [¶] [T]he … pilings were alterations because they modified the design and function of the … foundation without increasing the house's exterior dimensions. The pilings were also additions because they were physically attached to the foundation and became a part of it."

PROP §27.002. APPLICATION OF CHAPTER

(a) This chapter applies to:

(1) any action to recover damages or other relief arising from a construction defect, except a claim for personal injury, survival, or wrongful death or for damage to goods; and

(2) any subsequent purchaser of a residence who files a claim against a contractor.

(b) Except as provided by this subsection, to the extent of conflict between this chapter and any other law, including the Deceptive Trade Practices-Consumer Protection Act (Subchapter E, Chapter 17, Business & Commerce Code) or a common law cause of action, this chapter prevails. To the extent of conflict between this chapter and Title 16, Title 16 prevails.

(c) In this section:

(1) "Goods" does not include a residence.

(2) "Personal injury" does not include mental anguish.

(d) This chapter does not apply to an action to recover damages that arise from:

(1) a violation of Section 27.01, Business & Commerce Code;

(2) a contractor's wrongful abandonment of an improvement project before completion; or

(3) a violation of Chapter 162.

History of Prop. Code §27.002: Acts 1989, 71st Leg., ch. 1072, §1, eff. Sept. 1, 1989. Amended by Acts 1993, 73rd Leg., ch. 797, §3, eff. Aug. 30, 1993; Acts 1999, 76th Leg., ch. 189, §2, eff. Sept. 1, 1999; Acts 2003, 78th Leg., ch. 458, §2.02, eff. Sept. 1, 2003; Acts 2007, 80th Leg., ch. 843, §2, eff. Sept. 1, 2007.

See also *O'Connor's Texas COA*, "Application of RCLA," ch. 32-I, §6.1, p. 1134.

ANNOTATIONS

Sanders v. Construction Equity, Inc., 45 S.W.3d 802, 804 (Tex.App.—Beaumont 2001, pet. denied). "We believe that a fraud claim does conflict with RCLA to some extent, and is governed by RCLA **to that extent**—for example, with respect to the type and amount of actual damages recoverable. However, we find no indication in RCLA that the Legislature intended to immunize residential construction contractors from the punitive consequences of fraud, if fraud exists. To read such a limitation into the statute would be to supply language that the Legislature did not provide and, further, would do so in a way that would seem contrary to the public policy of this State—which we believe is to discourage fraud by imposing punitive damages where fraud occurs."

Perry Homes v. Alwattari, 33 S.W.3d 376, 382 (Tex.App.—Fort Worth 2000, pet. denied). "In enacting the RCLA, the legislature specifically provided that the RCLA would prevail '[t]o the extent of conflict between this chapter and any other law, *including the Deceptive Trade Practices-Consumer Protection Act*.' [A] claim

that exists solely by virtue of alleged construction defects falls exclusively within the RCLA. A homeowner, however, may bring other claims that do not conflict with the remedial purpose of the RCLA." *See also* ***In re Anderson Constr. Co.***, 338 S.W.3d 190, 195 (Tex. App.—Beaumont 2011, orig. proceeding) (RCLA prevails to the extent it conflicts with any other law).

Bruce v. Jim Walters Homes, Inc., 943 S.W.2d 121, 123 (Tex.App.—San Antonio 1997, writ denied). "Section 27.002(a) provides that the RCLA prevails only *to the extent of conflict* between it and any other law. A common law cause of action for fraud does not conflict with the RCLA. [¶] The RCLA was enacted to promote settlement between homeowners and contractors and to afford contractors the opportunity to repair their work in the face of dissatisfaction. This purpose contemplates actual defects in construction, not willful misrepresentation regarding the construction, which can certainly exist independent of a construction defect. It is unreasonable to conclude that the legislature would deny a homeowner the opportunity to seek damages for fraud simply because he is also entitled to recover actual damages for construction defects pursuant to a statute. [¶] Moreover, the remedies available under an action for fraud and an action under the RCLA are separate and distinct. The RCLA limits the recovery of damages to those '*proximately caused by a construction defect*.' The damages available in an action for fraud are not premised on the construction defect, but on the act of misrepresentation."

PROP §27.003. LIABILITY

(a) In an action to recover damages or other relief arising from a construction defect:

(1) a contractor is not liable for any percentage of damages caused by:

(A) negligence of a person other than the contractor or an agent, employee, or subcontractor of the contractor;

(B) failure of a person other than the contractor or an agent, employee, or subcontractor of the contractor to:

(i) take reasonable action to mitigate the damages; or

(ii) take reasonable action to maintain the residence;

(C) normal wear, tear, or deterioration;

(D) normal shrinkage due to drying or settlement of construction components within the tolerance of building standards; or

(E) the contractor's reliance on written information relating to the residence, appurtenance, or real property on which the residence and appurtenance are affixed that was obtained from official government records, if the written information was false or inaccurate and the contractor did not know and could not reasonably have known of the falsity or inaccuracy of the information; and

(2) if an assignee of the claimant or a person subrogated to the rights of a claimant fails to provide the contractor with the written notice and opportunity to inspect and offer to repair required by Section 27.004 or fails to request state-sponsored inspection and dispute resolution under Chapter 428, if applicable, before performing repairs, the contractor is not liable for the cost of any repairs or any percentage of damages caused by repairs made to a construction defect at the request of an assignee of the claimant or a person subrogated to the rights of a claimant by a person other than the contractor or an agent, employee, or subcontractor of the contractor.

(b) Except as provided by this chapter, this chapter does not limit or bar any other defense or defensive matter or other defensive cause of action applicable to an action to recover damages or other relief arising from a construction defect.

History of Prop. Code §27.003: Acts 1989, 71st Leg., ch. 1072, §1, eff. Sept. 1, 1989. Amended by Acts 1993, 73rd Leg., ch. 797, §4, eff. Aug. 30, 1993; Acts 1999, 76th Leg., ch. 189, §3, eff. Sept. 1, 1999; Acts 2003, 78th Leg., ch. 458, §2.03, eff. Sept. 1, 2003.

See also *O'Connor's Texas COA*, "Not construction defect," ch. 32-I, §6.1.3(2), p. 1135.

PROP §27.0031. FRIVOLOUS SUIT; HARASSMENT

A party who files a suit under this chapter that is groundless and brought in bad faith or for purposes of harassment is liable to the defendant for reasonable and necessary attorney's fees and court costs.

History of Prop. Code §27.0031: Acts 1999, 76th Leg., ch. 189, §4, eff. Sept. 1, 1999.

PROP §27.004. NOTICE & OFFER OF SETTLEMENT

(a) In a claim not subject to Subtitle D, Title 16, before the 60th day preceding the date a claimant seeking from a contractor damages or other relief arising from a construction defect initiates an action, the claimant shall give written notice by certified mail, return receipt

requested, to the contractor, at the contractor's last known address, specifying in reasonable detail the construction defects that are the subject of the complaint. On the request of the contractor, the claimant shall provide to the contractor any evidence that depicts the nature and cause of the defect and the nature and extent of repairs necessary to remedy the defect, including expert reports, photographs, and videotapes, if that evidence would be discoverable under Rule 192, Texas Rules of Civil Procedure. During the 35-day period after the date the contractor receives the notice, and on the contractor's written request, the contractor shall be given a reasonable opportunity to inspect and have inspected the property that is the subject of the complaint to determine the nature and cause of the defect and the nature and extent of repairs necessary to remedy the defect. The contractor may take reasonable steps to document the defect. In a claim subject to Subtitle D, Title 16, a contractor is entitled to make an offer of repair in accordance with Subsection (b). A claimant is not required to give written notice to a contractor under this subsection in a claim subject to Subtitle D, Title 16.

(b) Not later than the 15th day after the date of a final, unappealable determination of a dispute under Subtitle D, Title 16, if applicable, or not later than the 45th day after the date the contractor receives the notice under this section, if Subtitle D, Title 16, does not apply, the contractor may make a written offer of settlement to the claimant. The offer must be sent to the claimant at the claimant's last known address or to the claimant's attorney by certified mail, return receipt requested. The offer may include either an agreement by the contractor to repair or to have repaired by an independent contractor partially or totally at the contractor's expense or at a reduced rate to the claimant any construction defect described in the notice and shall describe in reasonable detail the kind of repairs which will be made. The repairs shall be made not later than the 45th day after the date the contractor receives written notice of acceptance of the settlement offer, unless completion is delayed by the claimant or by other events beyond the control of the contractor. If a contractor makes a written offer of settlement that the claimant considers to be unreasonable:

(1) on or before the 25th day after the date the claimant receives the offer, the claimant shall advise the contractor in writing and in reasonable detail of the reasons why the claimant considers the offer unreasonable; and

(2) not later than the 10th day after the date the contractor receives notice under Subdivision (1), the contractor may make a supplemental written offer of settlement to the claimant by sending the offer to the claimant or the claimant's attorney.

(c) If compliance with Subtitle D, Title 16, or the giving of the notice under Subsections (a) and (b) within the period prescribed by those subsections is impracticable because of the necessity of initiating an action at an earlier date to prevent expiration of the statute of limitations or if the complaint is asserted as a counterclaim, compliance with Subtitle D, Title 16, or the notice is not required. However, the action or counterclaim shall specify in reasonable detail each construction defect that is the subject of the complaint. If Subtitle D, Title 16, applies to the complaint, simultaneously with the filing of an action by a claimant, the claimant must submit a request under Section 428.001. If Subtitle D, Title 16, does not apply, the inspection provided for by Subsection (a) may be made not later than the 75th day after the date of service of the suit, request for arbitration, or counterclaim on the contractor, and the offer provided for by Subsection (b) may be made not later than the 15th day after the date the state-sponsored inspection and dispute resolution process is completed, if Subtitle D, Title 16, applies, or not later than the 60th day after the date of service, if Subtitle D, Title 16, does not apply. If, while an action subject to this chapter is pending, the statute of limitations for the cause of action would have expired and it is determined that the provisions of Subsection (a) were not properly followed, the action shall be abated to allow compliance with Subsections (a) and (b).

(d) The court or arbitration tribunal shall abate an action governed by this chapter if Subsection (c) does not apply and the court or tribunal, after a hearing, finds that the contractor is entitled to abatement because the claimant failed to comply with the requirements of Subtitle D, Title 16, if applicable, failed to provide the notice or failed to give the contractor a reasonable opportunity to inspect the property as required by Subsection (a), or failed to follow the procedures specified by Subsection (b). An action is automatically abated without the order of the court or tribunal beginning on the 11th day after the date a motion to abate is filed if the motion:

(1) is verified and alleges that the person against whom the action is pending did not receive the written

notice required by Subsection (a), the person against whom the action is pending was not given a reasonable opportunity to inspect the property as required by Subsection (a), or the claimant failed to follow the procedures specified by Subsection (b) or Subtitle D, Title 16; and

(2) is not controverted by an affidavit filed by the claimant before the 11th day after the date on which the motion to abate is filed.

(e) If a claimant rejects a reasonable offer made under Subsection (b) or does not permit the contractor or independent contractor a reasonable opportunity to inspect or repair the defect pursuant to an accepted offer of settlement, the claimant:

(1) may not recover an amount in excess of:

(A) the fair market value of the contractor's last offer of settlement under Subsection (b); or

(B) the amount of a reasonable monetary settlement or purchase offer made under Subsection (n); and

(2) may recover only the amount of reasonable and necessary costs and attorney's fees as prescribed by Rule 1.04, Texas Disciplinary Rules of Professional Conduct, incurred before the offer was rejected or considered rejected.

(f) If a contractor fails to make a reasonable offer under Subsection (b), the limitations on damages provided for in Subsection (e) shall not apply.

(g) Except as provided by Subsection (e), in an action subject to this chapter the claimant may recover only the following economic damages proximately caused by a construction defect:

(1) the reasonable cost of repairs necessary to cure any construction defect;

(2) the reasonable and necessary cost for the replacement or repair of any damaged goods in the residence;

(3) reasonable and necessary engineering and consulting fees;

(4) the reasonable expenses of temporary housing reasonably necessary during the repair period;

(5) the reduction in current market value, if any, after the construction defect is repaired if the construction defect is a structural failure; and

(6) reasonable and necessary attorney's fees.

(h) A homeowner and a contractor may agree in writing to extend any time period described in this chapter.

(i) An offer of settlement made under this section that is not accepted before the 25th day after the date the offer is received by the claimant is considered rejected.

(j) An affidavit certifying rejection of a settlement offer under this section may be filed with the court or arbitration tribunal. The trier of fact shall determine the reasonableness of a final offer of settlement made under this section.

(k) A contractor who makes or provides for repairs under this section is entitled to take reasonable steps to document the repair and to have it inspected.

(*l*) If Subtitle D, Title 16, applies to the claim and the contractor's offer of repair is accepted by the claimant, the contractor, on completion of the repairs and at the contractor's expense, shall engage the third-party inspector who provided the recommendation regarding the construction defect involved in the claim to inspect the repairs and determine whether the residence, as repaired, complies with the applicable limited statutory warranty and building and performance standards adopted by the commission. The contractor is entitled to a reasonable period not to exceed 15 days to address minor cosmetic items that are necessary to fully complete the repairs. The determination of the third-party inspector of whether the repairs comply with the applicable limited statutory warranty and building and performance standards adopted by the commission establishes a rebuttable presumption on that issue. A party seeking to dispute, vacate, or overcome that presumption must establish by clear and convincing evidence that the determination is inconsistent with the applicable limited statutory warranty and building and performance standards.

(m) Notwithstanding Subsections (a), (b), and (c), a contractor who receives written notice of a construction defect resulting from work performed by the contractor or an agent, employee, or subcontractor of the contractor and creating an imminent threat to the health or safety of the inhabitants of the residence shall take reasonable steps to cure the defect as soon as practicable. If the contractor fails to cure the defect in a reasonable time, the owner of the residence may have the defect cured and may recover from the contractor the reasonable cost of the repairs plus attorney's fees and costs in addition to any other damages recoverable under any law not inconsistent with the provisions of this chapter.

(n) This section does not preclude a contractor from making a monetary settlement offer or an offer to purchase the residence.

(o) A notice and response letter prescribed by this chapter must be sent by certified mail, return receipt requested, to the last known address of the recipient. If previously disclosed in writing that the recipient of a notice or response letter is represented by an attorney, the letter shall be sent to the recipient's attorney in accordance with Rule 21a, Texas Rules of Civil Procedure.

(p) If the contractor provides written notice of a claim for damages arising from a construction defect to a subcontractor, the contractor retains all rights of contribution from the subcontractor if the contractor settles the claim with the claimant.

(q) If a contractor refuses to initiate repairs under an accepted offer made under this section, the limitations on damages provided for in this section shall not apply.

History of Prop. Code §27.004: Acts 1989, 71st Leg., ch. 1072, §1, eff. Sept. 1, 1989. Amended by Acts 1993, 73rd Leg., ch. 797, §5, eff. Aug. 30, 1993; Acts 1995, 74th Leg., ch. 414, §10, eff. Sept. 1, 1995; Acts 1999, 76th Leg., ch. 189, §5, eff. Sept. 1, 1999; Acts 2003, 78th Leg., ch. 458, §2.04, eff. Sept. 1, 2003; Acts 2007, 80th Leg., ch. 843, §3, eff. Sept. 1, 2007.

See also *O'Connor's Texas COA*, "RCLA damages," ch. 32-I, §3.3, p. 1133; "Requirements of RCLA," ch. 32-I, §6.2, p. 1136; "RCLA damages," ch. 32-J, §3.3, p. 1139.

ANNOTATIONS

Design Tech Homes, Ltd. v. Maywald, No. 09-11-00589-CV (Tex.App.—Beaumont 2013, pet. denied) (memo op.; 6-13-13). "[D] maintains that §27.004(g) provides the exclusive list of recoverable damages in a construction defect case. [Ps] are seeking to recover damages arising from a construction defect. [¶] Additional damages for 'knowing' violations under the DTPA are considered punitive in nature. Section 27.004(g) restricts economic damages, not punitive damages. RCLA does not bar additional damages under the DTPA for knowing violations."

In re Anderson Constr. Co., 338 S.W.3d 190, 196 (Tex.App.—Beaumont 2011, orig. proceeding). "Because [Prop. Code §27.004] is silent with respect to the amendment of pleadings to add new claims, there is no conflict between §27.004 and [TRCP 64, which] permits parties to amend their allegations after suit commences. [¶] In our opinion, abatement will allow the [Ps] to accomplish [§27.004's] procedures by giving them the ability to provide the required statutory notice of the newly added defects, while also giving [D] the opportunity to inspect the property within the statutorily prescribed period. *At 197:* If a settlement offer with respect to the additional defects is made, [Ps] will also be required to advise the contractor in writing and in reasonable detail why they consider that settlement offer to be unreasonable." *See also* ***F&S Constr. v. Saidi***, 131 S.W.3d 94, 99 (Tex.App.—San Antonio 2003, pet. denied) (RCLA timeline not followed, court allowed recovery because statutory procedures were implemented).

In re Kimball Hill Homes Tex., 969 S.W.2d 522, 525 (Tex.App.—Houston [14th Dist.] 1998, orig. proceeding). "The purpose of the notice requirement is to encourage pre-suit negotiations to avoid the expense of litigation. Forcing [relator] to trial without reviewing the propriety of an abatement under the RCLA will deprive [relator] of the opportunity to inspect the homes, make a reasonable settlement offer and present a defense to damages based on such an offer. [¶] A claimant seeking damages arising from a construction defect must give the contractor written notice of the defect 60 days before filing suit. If the claimant fails to give the required notice, the trial court, after a hearing, must abate the suit. The suit is automatically abated without court order on the 11th day after the date a verified plea in abatement is filed, if the claimant does not file a controverting affidavit before the 11th day."

Trimble v. Itz, 898 S.W.2d 370, 374 (Tex.App.—San Antonio 1995), *writ denied*, 906 S.W.2d 481 (Tex.1995). "[W]e conclude that failure to provide notice pursuant to [Prop. Code] §27.004(a) requires abating the action for 60 days in order to give the claimant time to comply with the statute and does not provide a basis for dismissing the claim or imposing [TRCP] 13 sanctions."

PROP §27.0041. MEDIATION

(a) If a claimant files suit seeking from a contractor damages arising from a construction defect in an amount greater than $7,500, the claimant or contractor may file a motion to compel mediation of the dispute. The motion must be filed not later than the 90th day after the date the suit is filed.

(b) Not later than the 30th day after the date a motion is filed under Subsection (a), the court shall order the parties to mediate the dispute. If the parties cannot agree on the appointment of a mediator, the court shall appoint the mediator.

(c) The court shall order the parties to begin mediation of the dispute not later than the 30th day after the date the court enters its order under Subsection (b)

unless the parties agree otherwise or the court determines additional time is required. If the court determines that additional time is required, the court may order the parties to begin mediation of the dispute not later than the 60th day after the date the court enters its order under Subsection (b).

(d) Unless each party who has appeared in a suit filed under this chapter agrees otherwise, each party shall participate in the mediation and contribute equally to the cost of the mediation.

(e) Section 154.023, Civil Practice and Remedies Code, and Subchapters C and D, Chapter 154, Civil Practice and Remedies Code, apply to a mediation under this section to the extent those laws do not conflict with this section.

History of Prop. Code §27.0041: Acts 1999, 76th Leg., ch. 189, §6, eff. Sept. 1, 1999.

See also CPRC §§154.023, 154.051-154.055, 154.071-154.073.

PROP §27.0042. CONDITIONAL SALE TO BUILDER

(a) A written agreement between a contractor and a homeowner may provide that, except as provided by Subsection (b), if the reasonable cost of repairs necessary to repair a construction defect that is the responsibility of the contractor exceeds an agreed percentage of the current fair market value of the residence, as determined without reference to the construction defects, then, in an action subject to this chapter, the contractor may elect as an alternative to the damages specified in Section 27.004(g) that the contractor who sold the residence to the homeowner purchase it.

(b) A contractor may not elect to purchase the residence under Subsection (a) if:

(1) the residence is more than five years old at the time an action is initiated; or

(2) the contractor makes such an election later than the 15th day after the date of a final, unappealable determination of a dispute under Subtitle D, Title 16, if applicable.

(c) If a contractor elects to purchase the residence under Subsection (a):

(1) the contractor shall pay the original purchase price of the residence and closing costs incurred by the homeowner and the cost of transferring title to the contractor under the election;

(2) the homeowner may recover:

(A) reasonable and necessary attorney's and expert fees as identified in Section 27.004(g);

(B) reimbursement for permanent improvements the owner made to the residence after the date the owner purchased the residence from the builder; and

(C) reasonable costs to move from the residence; and

(3) conditioned on the payment of the purchase price, the homeowner shall tender a special warranty deed to the contractor, free of all liens and claims to liens as of the date the title is transferred to the contractor, and without damage caused by the homeowner.

(d) An offer to purchase a claimant's home that complies with this section is considered reasonable absent clear and convincing evidence to the contrary.

History of Prop. Code §27.0042: Acts 2003, 78th Leg., ch. 458, §2.05, eff. Sept. 1, 2003.

PROP §27.005. LIMITATIONS ON EFFECT OF CHAPTER

This chapter does not create a cause of action or derivative liability or extend a limitations period.

History of Prop. Code §27.005: Acts 1989, 71st Leg., ch. 1072, §1, eff. Sept. 1, 1989. Amended by Acts 1999, 76th Leg., ch. 189, §7, eff. Sept. 1, 1999.

ANNOTATIONS

Sanders v. Construction Equity, 42 S.W.3d 364, 370 (Tex.App.—Beaumont 2001, pet. denied). "RCLA was amended in 1999 and now expressly provides that RCLA does not create a cause of action. Although no prior version of the statute contained that provision, we believe the prior law, like the current statute, did not create a cause of action. [¶] Chapter 27 modifies causes of action for damages resulting from construction defects in residences; but it does not provide the basis for a liability determination. The statute does not create a cause of action, but instead simply limits and controls causes of action that otherwise exist." *See also* ***Markel Am. Ins. v. Lennar Corp.***, 342 S.W.3d 704, 713 (Tex.App.—Houston [14th Dist.] 2011), *rev'd on other grounds*, 413 S.W.3d 750 (Tex.2013); ***Gentry v. Squires Constr., Inc.***, 188 S.W.3d 396, 404-05 (Tex.App.—Dallas 2006, no pet.).

PROP §27.006. CAUSATION

In an action to recover damages resulting from a construction defect, the claimant must prove that the damages were proximately caused by the construction defect.

History of Prop. Code §27.006: Acts 1993, 73rd Leg., ch. 797, §6, eff. Aug. 30, 1993.

See also *O'Connor's Texas COA*, "Plaintiff sought damages or other relief," ch. 32-I, §6.1.4, p. 1135.

PROP §27.007. DISCLOSURE STATEMENT REQUIRED

(a) A written contract subject to this chapter, other than a contract between a developer of a condominium and a contractor for the construction or repair of a residence or appurtenance to a residence in a condominium, must contain in the contract a notice printed or typed in 10-point boldface type or the computer equivalent that reads substantially similar to the following:

"This contract is subject to Chapter 27 of the Texas Property Code. The provisions of that chapter may affect your right to recover damages arising from a construction defect. If you have a complaint concerning a construction defect and that defect has not been corrected as may be required by law or by contract, you must provide the notice required by Chapter 27 of the Texas Property Code to the contractor by certified mail, return receipt requested, not later than the 60th day before the date you file suit to recover damages in a court of law or initiate arbitration. The notice must refer to Chapter 27 of the Texas Property Code and must describe the construction defect. If requested by the contractor, you must provide the contractor an opportunity to inspect and cure the defect as provided by Section 27.004 of the Texas Property Code."

(b) If a contract does not contain the notice required by this section, the claimant may recover from the contractor a civil penalty of $500 in addition to any other remedy provided by this chapter.

(c) This section does not apply to a contract relating to a home required to be registered under Section 426.003.

History of Prop. Code §27.007: Acts 1999, 76th Leg., ch. 189, §8, eff. Sept. 1, 2000. Amended by Acts 2003, 78th Leg., ch. 458, §2.06, eff. Sept. 1, 2003; Acts 2007, 80th Leg., ch. 750, §2 (eff. Sept. 1, 2007), ch. 843, §4 (eff. Sept. 1, 2007).

CHAPTER 28. PROMPT PAYMENT TO CONTRACTORS & SUBCONTRACTORS

PROP §28.001. DEFINITIONS

In this chapter:

(1) "Contractor" means a person who contracts with an owner to improve real property or perform construction services for an owner.

(2) "Improve" means to:

(A) build, construct, effect, erect, alter, repair, or demolish any improvement on, connected with, or beneath the surface of real property;

(B) excavate, clear, grade, fill, or landscape real property;

(C) construct a driveway or roadway;

(D) furnish any material, including trees or shrubbery, for the purpose of taking any action described by Paragraphs (A)-(C) of this subdivision; or

(E) perform any labor on or in connection with an improvement.

(3) "Improvement" includes all or any part of:

(A) a building, structure, erection, alteration, demolition, or excavation on, connected with, or beneath the surface of real property; and

(B) the act of clearing, grading, filling, or landscaping real property, including constructing a driveway or roadway or furnishing trees or shrubbery.

(4) "Owner" means a person or entity, other than a governmental entity, with an interest in real property that is improved, for whom an improvement is made, and who ordered the improvement to be made.

(5) "Real property" includes lands, leaseholds, tenements, hereditaments, and improvements placed on the real property.

(6) "Subcontractor" means a person who contracts to furnish labor or material to, or has performed labor or supplied materials for, a contractor or another subcontractor in connection with a contract to improve real property.

History of Prop. Code §28.001: Acts 1993, 73rd Leg., ch. 479, §1, eff. Sept. 1, 1993.

PROP §28.002. PROMPT PAY REQUIRED

(a) If an owner or a person authorized to act on behalf of the owner receives a written payment request from a contractor for an amount that is allowed to the contractor under the contract for properly performed

work or suitably stored or specially fabricated materials, the owner shall pay the amount to the contractor, less any amount withheld as authorized by statute, not later than the 35th day after the date the owner receives the request.

(b) A contractor who receives a payment under Subsection (a) or otherwise from an owner in connection with a contract to improve real property shall pay each of its subcontractors the portion of the owner's payment, including interest, if any, that is attributable to work properly performed or materials suitably stored or specially fabricated as provided under the contract by that subcontractor, to the extent of that subcontractor's interest in the owner's payment. The payment required by this subsection must be made not later than the seventh day after the date the contractor receives the owner's payment.

(c) A subcontractor who receives a payment under Subsection (b) or otherwise from a contractor in connection with a contract to improve real property shall pay each of its subcontractors the portion of the payment, including interest, if any, that is attributable to work properly performed or materials suitably stored or specially fabricated as provided under the contract by that subcontractor, to the extent of that subcontractor's interest in the payment. The payment required by this subsection must be made not later than the seventh day after the date the subcontractor receives the contractor's payment.

History of Prop. Code §28.002: Acts 1993, 73rd Leg., ch. 479, §1, eff. Sept. 1, 1993. Amended by Acts 1999, 76th Leg., ch. 805, §1, eff. Sept. 1, 1999.

ANNOTATIONS

St. Paul Mercury Ins. v. Stewart Builders, Ltd., No. 01-09-00276-CV (Tex.App.—Houston [1st Dist.] 2011, no pet.) (memo op.; 3-17-11). "Under [Prop. Code §28.002], a contractor must promptly pay a subcontractor after receiving payment from the owner. [¶] [Property Code §28.001] does not include an officer of a contractor. [Contractor], not [CEO of contractor], contracted with [owner] to perform construction on [owner's] property, and [contractor], not [CEO of contractor], contracted with [subcontractor]. Because [CEO of contractor] was not the contractor, ... the trial court erred by rendering judgment that [CEO of contractor], individually, was liable for ... interest under the Property Code."

PROP §28.003. EXCEPTION FOR GOOD FAITH DISPUTE; WITHHOLDING

(a) If a good faith dispute exists concerning the amount owed for a payment requested or required by this chapter under a contract for construction of or improvements to a detached single-family residence, duplex, triplex, or quadruplex, the owner, contractor, or subcontractor that is disputing its obligation to pay or the amount of payment may withhold from the payment owed not more than 110 percent of the difference between the amount the obligee claims is due and the amount the obligor claims is due. A good faith dispute includes a dispute regarding whether the work was performed in a proper manner.

(b) If a good faith dispute exists concerning the amount owed for a payment requested or required by this chapter under a contract for construction of or improvements to real property, excluding a detached single-family residence, duplex, triplex, or quadruplex, the owner, contractor, or subcontractor that is disputing its obligation to pay or the amount of payment may withhold from the payment owed not more than 100 percent of the difference between the amount the obligee claims is due and the amount the obligor claims is due. A good faith dispute includes a dispute regarding whether the work was performed in a proper manner.

History of Prop. Code §28.003: Acts 1993, 73rd Leg., ch. 479, §1, eff. Sept. 1, 1993. Amended by Acts 1999, 76th Leg., ch. 805, §2, eff. Sept. 1, 1999.

PROP §28.004. INTEREST ON OVERDUE PAYMENT

(a) An unpaid amount required under this chapter begins to accrue interest on the day after the date on which the payment becomes due.

(b) An unpaid amount bears interest at the rate of 1-½ percent each month.

(c) Interest on an unpaid amount stops accruing under this section on the earlier of:

(1) the date of delivery;

(2) the date of mailing, if payment is mailed and delivery occurs within three days; or

(3) the date a judgment is entered in an action brought under this chapter.

History of Prop. Code §28.004: Acts 1993, 73rd Leg., ch. 479, §1, eff. Sept. 1, 1993.

ANNOTATIONS

Gordon v. Leasman, 365 S.W.3d 109, 119 (Tex. App.—Houston [1st Dist.] 2011, no pet.). Workman "contends that his claim for payment against [homeowners] falls within the provisions of [Prop. Code] §28.002(a). [Homeowners] failed to pay him for carpentry work he performed as authorized on their real property even after he sent them two written invoices for payment. In his fourth amended petition, [workman] asked for prejudgment interest as provided by [Prop. Code] §28.004. Because his claim is for an overdue payment that a real property owner owed him for contracting work, it falls within the provisions of §28.002(a), the trial court should have awarded prejudgment interest at one and one-half percent per month as provided in §28.004(b)." *See also* ***Talley Constr. Co. v. Rodriguez***, No. 01-03-01147-CV (Tex. App.—Houston [1st Dist.] 2006, no pet.) (memo op.; 4-6-06).

AMX Enters. v. Master Rlty. Corp., 283 S.W.3d 506, 513-14 (Tex.App.—Fort Worth 2009, no pet.). "The fact that prejudgment interest under the [Prompt Payment to Contractors] Act is more than double the applicable rate of prejudgment interest gives contract debtors an additional incentive to pay promptly that would not exist but for the Act. ... Thus, allowing a contractor like [P] to recover 18% prejudgment interest under the Act but not common law prejudgment interest compensates the contractor for the loss of use of the unpaid money and provides an added incentive for prompt payment that would not exist but for the Act. On the other hand, to allow a contractor to collect both interest under the Act and common law prejudgment interest would allow a double recovery of two kinds of interest designed to promote the same two goals, namely, compensation for loss of use and the prompt payment of debts. [¶] [W]e hold that a contractor who is entitled to collect 18% interest under the Act is not also entitled to common law prejudgment interest...." *See also* ***RAJ Partners v. Darco Constr. Corp.***, 217 S.W.3d 638, 646-47 (Tex.App.—Amarillo 2006, no pet.); ***All Seasons Window & Door Mfg. v. Red Dot Corp.***, 181 S.W.3d 490, 497-99 (Tex.App.—Texarkana 2005, no pet.).

National Envtl. Serv. v. Homeplace Homes, Inc., 961 S.W.2d 632, 636 (Tex.App.—San Antonio 1998, no pet.). "Although §28.004 does not state who is entitled to receive interest on an unpaid amount, ... it is limited to contractors. Chapter 28 expressly requires an owner to pay a contractor. In turn, the contractor is required to pay the subcontractor the appropriate portion of the owner's payment 'including interest, if any.' Read as a whole, ch. 28 does not require an owner to pay a subcontractor the [principal] sum or any interest."

PROP §28.005. ACTION TO ENFORCE PAYMENT

(a) A person may bring an action to enforce the person's rights under this chapter.

(b) In an action brought under this chapter, the court may award costs and reasonable attorney's fees as the court determines equitable and just.

History of Prop. Code §28.005: Acts 1993, 73rd Leg., ch. 479, §1, eff. Sept. 1, 1993.

PROP §28.006. NO WAIVER

(a) Except as provided by Subsection (b), an attempted waiver of a provision of this chapter is void.

(b) A written contract between an owner and a contractor for improvements to or construction of a single-family residence may provide that the payment required under Section 28.002(a) be made not later than a date that occurs before the 61st day after the date the owner receives the payment request. Notwithstanding Section 28.004(b), an unpaid amount under contract subject to this subsection that allows payment later than the date otherwise required under Section 28.002(a) bears interest at the rate of 1-½ percent each month.

History of Prop. Code §28.006: Acts 1993, 73rd Leg., ch. 479, §1, eff. Sept. 1, 1993.

PROP §28.007. LEGAL CONSTRUCTION

(a) This chapter may not be interpreted to void a contractor's or subcontractor's entitlement to payment for properly performed work or suitably stored materials.

(b) Nothing in this statute shall be interpreted to change the rights and obligations set forth in Chapter 53, Property Code.

History of Prop. Code §28.007: Acts 1993, 73rd Leg., ch. 479, §1, eff. Sept. 1, 1993.

PROP §28.008. EXCEPTION FOR FAILURE OF LENDER TO DISBURSE FUNDS

The date of payment required of the owner pursuant to Section 28.002(a) shall change from the 35th day after the date the owner receives the payment request to the fifth day after the date the owner receives loan proceeds, in the event that:

(1) the owner has obtained a loan intended to pay for all or part of a contract to improve real property;

(2) the owner has timely and properly requested disbursement of proceeds from that loan; and

(3) the lender is legally obligated to disburse such proceeds to the owner, but has failed to do so within 35 days after the date the owner received the contractor's payment request.

History of Prop. Code §28.008: Acts 1993, 73rd Leg., ch. 479, §1, eff. Sept. 1, 1993. Amended by Acts 1999, 76th Leg., ch. 805, §3, eff. Sept. 1, 1999.

PROP §28.009. RIGHT TO SUSPEND WORK

(a) If an owner fails to pay the contractor the undisputed amount within the time limits provided by this chapter, the contractor or any subcontractor may suspend contractually required performance the 10th day after the date the contractor or subcontractor gives the owner and the owner's lender written notice:

(1) informing the owner and lender that payment has not been received; and

(2) stating the intent of the contractor or subcontractor to suspend performance for nonpayment.

(b) For purposes of Subsection (a), the contractor or subcontractor must give the owner's lender the written notice only if:

(1) the owner has obtained a loan intended to pay for all or part of the construction project;

(2) the lender has remitted funds, including acquisition funds, for construction purposes;

(3) the loan obtained:

(A) is evidenced by a promissory note secured by a deed of trust recorded in the real property records of the county in which the real property that is the subject of the contract is located; and

(B) is not only for the acquisition of personal property or secured only by a security instrument;

(4) the owner or lender, at the lender's option:

(A) securely posts not later than the 10th day after the date construction commences a sign on the project site in a prominent place accessible to each contractor, subcontractor, and supplier that states the lender's name, address, and the person to whom any notice should be sent; and

(B) maintains the sign during the pendency of the construction project;

(5) not later than the 10th day after the date construction commences, the owner or lender, at the lender's option, provides a written copy of the notice prescribed by Subdivision (4) to the contractor and any subcontractor or supplier identified by the contractor by depositing the notice properly addressed in the United States mail, first class, postage paid; and

(6) not later than the 10th day after the date a subcontractor or supplier performs labor or furnishes materials or equipment for the construction project, the owner, contractor, or subcontractor provides a written copy of the notice prescribed by Subdivision (4) to the subcontractor or supplier.

(c) A contractor or subcontractor who suspends performance as provided by this section is not:

(1) required to supply further labor, services, or materials until the person is paid the amount provided by this chapter, plus costs for demobilization and remobilization; or

(2) responsible for damages resulting from suspending work if the contractor or subcontractor has not been notified in writing before suspending performance that payment has been made or that a good faith dispute for payment exists.

(d) A notification that a good faith dispute for payment exists provided under Subsection (c) must include a list of specific reasons for nonpayment. If a reason specified includes labor, services, or materials provided by a subcontractor that are not provided in compliance with the contract, the subcontractor is entitled to a reasonable opportunity to:

(1) cure the listed items; or

(2) offer a reasonable amount to compensate for listed items that cannot be promptly cured.

(e) This section does not apply to:

(1) a contract for the construction of or improvements to a detached single-family residence, duplex, triplex, or quadruplex; or

(2) a contract to improve real property for a governmental entity.

(f) The rights and remedies provided by this section are in addition to rights and remedies provided by this chapter or other law.

History of Prop. Code §28.009: Acts 1999, 76th Leg., ch. 805, §4, eff. Sept. 1, 1999.

PROP §28.010. EXEMPTION FOR MINERAL DEVELOPMENT & OILFIELD SERVICES

(a) This chapter does not apply to any agreement:

(1) to explore, produce, or develop oil, natural gas, natural gas liquids, synthetic gas, sulphur, ore, or other

mineral substances, including any lease or royalty agreement, joint interest agreement, production or production-related agreement, operating agreement, farmout agreement, area of mutual interest agreement, or other related agreement;

(2) for any well or mine services; or

(3) to purchase, sell, gather, store, or transport oil, natural gas, natural gas liquids, synthetic gas, or other hydrocarbon substances by pipeline or by a fixed, associated facility.

(b) In this section:

(1) "Agreement" includes a written or oral agreement or understanding:

(A) to provide work or services, including any construction, operating, repair, or maintenance services; or

(B) to perform a part of the services covered by Paragraph (A) or an act collateral to those services, including furnishing or renting equipment, incidental transportation, or other goods and services furnished in connection with those services.

(2) "Well or mine services" includes:

(A) drilling, deepening, reworking, repairing, improving, testing, treating, perforating, acidizing, logging, conditioning, purchasing, gathering, storing, or transporting oil or natural gas, brine water, fresh water, produced water, condensate, petroleum products, or other liquid commodities, or otherwise rendering services in connection with a well drilled to produce or dispose of oil, gas, or other minerals or water; and

(B) designing, excavating, constructing, improving, or otherwise rendering services in connection with an oil, gas, or other mineral production platform or facility, mine shaft, drift, or other structure intended directly for use in exploring for or producing a mineral.

History of Prop. Code §28.010: Acts 1999, 76th Leg., ch. 805, §4, eff. Sept. 1, 1999.

CHAPTER 29. FORCED SALE OF OWNER'S INTEREST IN CERTAIN REAL PROPERTY AS REIMBURSEMENT FOR PROPERTY TAXES PAID BY CO-OWNER ON OWNER'S BEHALF

PROP §29.001. APPLICATION OF CHAPTER

This chapter applies only to real property that is not exempt from forced sale under the constitution or laws of this state and is:

(1) received by a person as a result of the death of another person:

(A) by inheritance;

(B) under a will;

(C) by a joint tenancy with a right of survivorship; or

(D) by any other survivorship agreement in which the interest of the decedent passes to a surviving beneficiary other than an agreement between spouses for community property with a right of survivorship; or

(2) owned in part by a nonprofit organization that is exempt from federal income tax under Section 501(a), Internal Revenue Code of 1986, and its subsequent amendments, by being listed as an exempt organization under Section 501(c)(3), Internal Revenue Code of 1986, and its subsequent amendments, that:

(A) has been incorporated in this state for at least one year;

(B) has a corporate purpose to develop affordable housing that is stated in the articles of incorporation or charter;

(C) has at least one-fourth of its board of directors residing in the county in which the property is located; and

(D) engages primarily in the building, repair, rental, or sale of housing for low-income individuals or families.

History of Prop. Code §29.001: Acts 1995, 74th Leg., ch. 981, §1, eff. Aug. 28, 1995. Amended by Acts 2001, 77th Leg., ch. 891, §1, eff. Sept. 1, 2001.

PROP §29.002. PETITION FOR FORCED SALE

(a) A person, including a nonprofit organization, that owns an undivided interest in real property to which this chapter applies may file in the district court in a county in which the property is located a petition for a court order to require another owner of an undivided interest in that property to sell the other owner's interest in the property to the person if:

(1) the person has paid the other owner's share of ad valorem taxes imposed on the property for any three years in a five-year period or, in the case of a nonprofit organization, has paid the other owner's share of ad valorem taxes imposed on the property for any two years in a three-year period; and

(2) the other owner has not reimbursed the person for more than half of the total amount paid by the person for the taxes on the owner's behalf.

(b) The petition must contain:

(1) a description of the property;

(2) the name of each known owner of the property;

(3) the interest held by each known owner of the property;

(4) the total amount paid by the petitioner for the defendant's share of ad valorem taxes imposed on the property; and

(5) if applicable, the amount paid by the defendant to the petitioner to reimburse the petitioner for paying the defendant's share of ad valorem taxes imposed on the property.

History of Prop. Code §29.002: Acts 1995, 74th Leg., ch. 981, §1, eff. Aug. 28, 1995. Amended by Acts 2001, 77th Leg., ch. 891, §1, eff. Sept. 1, 2001.

ANNOTATIONS

Ramos v. Unknown Heirs of Tomasa Gonzalez, No. 04-14-00667-CV (Tex.App.—San Antonio 2016, no pet.) (memo op.; 4-27-16). Property Code ch. 29 "does not expressly provide that the statutory scheme for seeking reimbursement for property taxes paid by a co-owner is exclusive; therefore, if the statute is meant to be exclusive, it would be by implication only. ... We do not believe that the legislature expressly declared or necessarily implied an intention to abrogate the common law remedy of reimbursement from a co-tenant. We conclude that the statutory action for reimbursement by means of forced sale of a co-tenant's interest in the property under Ch. 29 did not repeal the common law action, but instead provided a choice of remedies for a co-tenant who has incurred expenses in preserving a common property. [¶] Not only does the statutory scheme not trump common law recovery, but the statute speaks only to reimbursement for payment of ad valorem property taxes. The statute does not address monies expended for maintenance of and improvement to the common property."

PROP §29.003. HEARING ON PETITION FOR FORCED SALE

At a hearing on a petition filed under Section 29.002, the petitioner must prove by clear and convincing evidence that:

(1) the petitioner has paid the defendant's share of ad valorem taxes imposed on the property that is the subject of the petition for any three years in a five-year period or, in the case of a nonprofit organization, the petitioner has paid the defendant's share of ad valorem taxes imposed on the property that is the subject of the petition for any two years in a three-year period;

(2) before the date on which the petition was filed the petitioner made a demand that the defendant reimburse the petitioner for the amount of the defendant's share of ad valorem taxes imposed on the property paid by the petitioner; and

(3) the defendant has not reimbursed the petitioner more than half of the amount of money the petitioner paid on the defendant's behalf for the defendant's share of ad valorem taxes imposed on the property.

History of Prop. Code §29.003: Acts 1995, 74th Leg., ch. 981, §1, eff. Aug. 28, 1995. Amended by Acts 2001, 77th Leg., ch. 891, §1, eff. Sept. 1, 2001.

ANNOTATIONS

Ramos v. Unknown Heirs of Tomasa Gonzalez, No. 04-14-00667-CV (Tex.App.—San Antonio 2016, no pet.) (memo op.; 4-27-16). See annotation under Property Code §29.002, this page.

Gardner v. Estate of Trader, 333 S.W.3d 331, 336 (Tex.App.—El Paso 2010, no pet.). Petitioners "assert that §29.003(3) only requires a showing that the defendant did not reimburse the petitioner before suit was filed, and the defendant cannot avoid a forced sale of property by reimbursing the petitioner after the suit is filed. Section 29.003(2) includes the language 'before the date on which the petition was filed,' but §29.003(3) does not. [W]e construe §29.003(3) as requiring the petitioner to prove by clear and convincing evidence that the defendant had not reimbursed the petitioner more than half of the ad valorem taxes paid by the petitioner at any point before the hearing on the petition. *At 337:* [A] payment into the registry of the court under a reservation of rights or a conditional tender does not constitute 'payment.' It follows that an unconditional tender of payment into the court's registry can constitute payment of an obligation. [Ds'] tender of money into the court's registry was unconditional and made to satisfy the amount owed to [petitioners]. As such, it constituted payment of the reimbursement amount owed by them to [petitioners]."

PROP §29.0035. DEMAND TO UNKNOWN DEFENDANT

If the address or identity of the defendant is unknown, the demand of the petitioner for reimbursement from the defendant required by Section 29.003(2)

may be met by publication in a newspaper in the county in which the property is located once each week for four consecutive weeks, with the final publication occurring not later than the 30th day before the date on which the petition is filed. The publication must contain the demand for reimbursement and:

(1) a general description of the property involved;

(2) the legal description of the property according to the survey of the property, including the number of the lot and block or any other plat description that may be of record if the property is located in a municipality;

(3) the county in which the property is located;

(4) the interest of the defendant; and

(5) the name and address of the petitioner.

History of Prop. Code §29.0035: Acts 2001, 77th Leg., ch. 891, §2, eff. Sept. 1, 2001.

PROP §29.004. COURT-ORDERED SALE

On completion of the hearing on a petition filed under Section 29.002, if the court is satisfied that the petitioner has made the requisite proof under Section 29.003, the court shall enter an order that divests the defendant's interest in the real property that is the subject of the petition and that orders the petitioner to pay to the defendant an amount computed by subtracting the outstanding amount of money the defendant owes to the petitioner for payment of the defendant's share of ad valorem taxes imposed on the property from the fair market value of the defendant's interest in the property as determined by an independent appraiser appointed by the court. The court's order may also direct the defendant to execute and deliver to the petitioner a deed that conveys to the petitioner the defendant's interest in the property.

History of Prop. Code §29.004: Acts 1995, 74th Leg., ch. 981, §1, eff. Aug. 28, 1995.

CHAPTER 30. WRIT OF ASSISTANCE FOR REPOSSESSION OF AIRCRAFT

PROP §30.01. DEFINITIONS

In this chapter:

(1) "Aircraft" means a self-propelled motor vehicle that can be used to transport a person by flight in the air.

(2) "Repossession" means the recovery of an aircraft that has been sold under a security agreement containing a repossession clause authorizing the lender to recover the aircraft if the borrower defaults under the agreement.

(3) "Repossession agent" means an individual who is authorized to engage in a repossession for a lender.

History of Prop. Code §30.01: Acts 2015, 84th Leg., ch. 1125, §1, eff. Sept. 1, 2015.

PROP §30.02. WRIT OF ASSISTANCE FOR REPOSSESSION OF AIRCRAFT

(a) A writ of assistance for the repossession of an aircraft authorizes a peace officer to assist and protect a repossession agent in gaining possession of the aircraft while the agent:

(1) secures the aircraft on site; or

(2) prepares the aircraft, which may include a mechanical inspection, for removal from the site by flight or otherwise to another location.

(b) A writ of assistance for the repossession of an aircraft is valid for 30 days.

(c) A justice court may grant unlimited extensions of a writ of assistance issued under this chapter.

History of Prop. Code §30.02: Acts 2015, 84th Leg., ch. 1125, §1, eff. Sept. 1, 2015.

PROP §30.03. PETITION FOR WRIT OF ASSISTANCE

(a) A repossession agent may file a petition in a justice court for a writ of assistance for the repossession of an aircraft.

(b) The repossession agent is entitled to the writ if the repossession agent establishes that:

(1) the aircraft is subject to the proposed repossession; and

(2) the repossession agent is authorized to engage in the repossession.

(c) The petition for the writ must include a copy of:

(1) the security agreement relating to the aircraft;

(2) the notice of default under the security agreement sent by the lender to the borrower;

(3) the instrument in which a power of attorney for the repossession is granted to the repossession agent by the lender; and

(4) the results of a title search of the Federal Aviation Administration's records for the aircraft.

History of Prop. Code §30.03: Acts 2015, 84th Leg., ch. 1125, §1, eff. Sept. 1, 2015.

Chapters 31-40 reserved for expansion

Title 5. Exempt Property & Liens

Subtitle A. Property Exempt from Creditors' Claims

Chapter 41. Interests in Land

Subchapter A. Exemptions in Land Defined

Prop §41.001. Interests in Land Exempt from Seizure

(a) A homestead and one or more lots used for a place of burial of the dead are exempt from seizure for the claims of creditors except for encumbrances properly fixed on homestead property.

(b) Encumbrances may be properly fixed on homestead property for:

(1) purchase money;

(2) taxes on the property;

(3) work and material used in constructing improvements on the property if contracted for in writing as provided by Sections 53.254(a), (b), and (c);

(4) an owelty of partition imposed against the entirety of the property by a court order or by a written agreement of the parties to the partition, including a debt of one spouse in favor of the other spouse resulting from a division or an award of a family homestead in a divorce proceeding;

(5) the refinance of a lien against a homestead, including a federal tax lien resulting from the tax debt of both spouses, if the homestead is a family homestead, or from the tax debt of the owner;

(6) an extension of credit that meets the requirements of Section 50(a)(6), Article XVI, Texas Constitution; or

(7) a reverse mortgage that meets the requirements of Sections 50(k)-(p), Article XVI, Texas Constitution.

(c) The homestead claimant's proceeds of a sale of a homestead are not subject to seizure for a creditor's claim for six months after the date of sale.

History of Prop. Code §41.001: Acts 1983, 68th Leg., ch. 576, §1, eff. Jan. 1, 1984. Amended by Acts 1984, 68th Leg., 2nd C.S., ch. 18, §2(b), eff. Oct. 2, 1984; Acts 1985, 69th Leg., ch. 840, §1, eff. June 15, 1985; Acts 1993, 73rd Leg., ch. 48, §2, eff. Sept. 1, 1993; Acts 1995, 74th Leg., ch. 121, §§1.01, 2.01, eff. May 17, 1995; Acts 1997, 75th Leg., ch. 526, §1, eff. Sept. 1, 1997; Acts 2001, 77th Leg., ch. 516, §1, eff. Sept. 1, 2001. Source: TRCS arts. 3834, 3835, 3839.

See also Tex. Const. art. 16, §50; Prop. Code §§53.160, 53.254, 63.005; Tax Code §§11.13, 11.26, 11.431, 32.01, 32.05; ***O'Connor's Fam. Law Handbook***, "Protection from forced sale for payment of debt," ch. 2-E, §3.2, p. 185.

Annotations

Generally

Inwood N. Homeowners' Ass'n v. Harris, 736 S.W.2d 632, 635 (Tex.1987). "[W]hen the property has not become a homestead at the execution of the mortgage, deed of trust or other lien, the homestead protections have no application even if the property later becomes a homestead."

Fairfield Fin. Grp. v. Synnott, 300 S.W.3d 316, 320 (Tex.App.—Austin 2009, no pet.). "We [hold] that, other than the types [of encumbrances] listed in §41.001(b), judgment liens that have been properly abstracted nevertheless cannot attach to a homestead while that property remains a homestead. Under this rule, a judgment debtor may sell property claimed as homestead and pass title free of any judgment lien, and the purchaser may assert that title against the judgment creditor. A judgment lien may attach to the judgment debtor's interest, however, if he abandons the property as his homestead while he owns it and while there is a properly abstracted judgment lien against him." *See also* ***Cadle Co. v. Harvey***, 46 S.W.3d 282, 285 (Tex.App.—Fort Worth 2001, pet. denied).

Lot 39, Section C, N. Hills Subdiv. v. State, 85 S.W.3d 429, 432 (Tex.App.—Eastland 2002, pet. denied). "The forfeiture of real property based upon the owner's use of that property to conduct criminal activity ... is not a forfeiture for the payment of the owner's debts or the claims of creditors." Held: Homestead exemption does not protect a homestead from seizure or forfeiture under CCP ch. 59.

Sanchez v. Telles, 960 S.W.2d 762, 770 (Tex. App.—El Paso 1997, pet. denied). "A subsequent purchaser of homestead property, may assert the prior persons homestead protection against a prior lienholder so

long as there is no gap between the time of homestead alienation and recordation of his title. No estoppel can arise in favor of a lender or encumbrancer who has attempted to secure a lien on homestead property that is in actual use and possession of the homestead claimant, based solely upon declarations, whether written or oral, which state to the contrary. Moreover, when a homestead claimant is in actual occupancy of his homestead, it will be deemed that a lender or encumbrancer acted with knowledge of the occupant's right to invoke the rule of homestead." *See also* ***Dominguez v. Castaneda***, 163 S.W.3d 318, 330-31 (Tex.App.—El Paso 2005, pet. denied).

Patterson v. First Nat'l Bank, 921 S.W.2d 240, 245 (Tex.App.—Houston [14th Dist.] 1996, no writ). "A mortgage or lien is void if it is illegally levied against homestead property, and can never have any effect, even after the property is no longer impressed with the homestead character."

Tarrant Bank v. Miller, 833 S.W.2d 666, 667-68 (Tex.App.—Eastland 1992, writ denied). "Because the [judgment] lien is unenforceable as to the homestead does not mean that the lien does not cast a cloud on the title. To so hold would mean that only enforceable claims could create a cloud."

Painewebber, Inc. v. Murray, 260 B.R. 815, 822 (Bankr.E.D.Tex.2001). "When interpreting [homestead-exemption] provisions, a court must liberally construe them to protect the homestead. Indeed, a court must uphold and enforce the Texas homestead laws even though in so doing the court might unwittingly assist a dishonest debtor in wrongfully defeating his creditor." (Internal quotes omitted.)

Attorney Fees

In re Marriage of Banks, 887 S.W.2d 160, 164 (Tex.App.—Texarkana 1994, no writ). "Where a homestead cannot be partitioned, it is subject to sale and distribution of the proceeds to the parties; however, the trial court may not order that the proceeds from the sale of the parties' homestead be used to extinguish the liabilities due unsecured creditors. The attorney's fees are liabilities owed to general creditors. [¶] To order payment of the attorney's fees from the proceeds of the agreed sale ... circumvents the constitutional and statutory provisions protecting the homestead and proceeds from its sale from the reach of general creditors." *See also* ***Delaney v. Delaney***, 562 S.W.2d 494, 495-96 (Tex.App.—Houston [14th Dist.] 1978, writ dism'd).

Lien on Work & Materials

Jordan v. Hagler, 179 S.W.3d 217, 220 (Tex.App.—Fort Worth 2005, no pet.). "[T]he parties agreed to an order removing the liens and prohibiting [claimant] from filing further liens or affidavits claiming liens. Alternatively, the order gave [claimant] the option of staying removal of the liens by filing a $10,000 bond, which he did not do. [A] constructive trust is an equitable remedy created to prevent unjust enrichment that cannot be remedied by other legal theories; it is not a lien. [Claimant's] attempt to impose a constructive trust on materials affixed to the ... homestead property runs contrary to the plain language of [Prop. Code] §53.254, which details the method by which an encumbrance, a lien, may be fixed on a homestead. The constructive trust is thus outside the parameters of [Prop. Code] §§41.001 and 53.254...."

Purchase-Money Liens

McGoodwin v. McGoodwin, 671 S.W.2d 880, 881 (Tex.1984). "Does a divorce decree that approves a property settlement agreement by which the husband agrees to pay a sum of money as consideration for the wife's interest in a particular piece of real estate imply a vendor's lien in favor of the wife? The significance of this issue is clear. A vendor's lien is a lien for purchase money. If [wife] holds such a lien, she is entitled to enforce it through foreclosure notwithstanding [husband's] homestead claim. *At 882:* [W]hen no express lien is reserved in a deed and the purchase money is not paid, a lien nevertheless arises by implication in favor of the vendor to secure payment of the purchase money. That vendor's lien may be enforced in a suit brought for that purpose. [¶] During her marriage to [husband], [wife] owned an undivided one-half interest in the 22 acre tract of land. In the property settlement agreement, [wife] contracted to sell her interest to [husband] in exchange for [money]. That agreement was incorporated into the property division order of the final divorce decree. Because the purchase money was not paid at the time of the divorce decree, a vendor's lien arose in [wife's] favor against the undivided one-half interest she had sold. This purchase money lien is superior to [husband's] claim of homestead."

Gregory v. Sunbelt Sav., F.S.B., 835 S.W.2d 155, 160 (Tex.App.—Dallas 1992, writ denied). "Purchase-money liens on homestead property are not protected from forced sale under the Texas Constitution. Borrow-

ers often incur debt secured by a homestead and use only a portion of the proceeds to purchase or improve the homestead property. In such cases, a valid and enforceable lien may be created to the extent of the original purchase-money debt due upon the homestead. If the debt is later extended by giving new notes, the old lien may be perpetuated without losing its validity. Foreclosure under the valid portion of a deed is proper."

Fuller v. Preston State Bank, 667 S.W.2d 214, 219 (Tex.App.—Dallas 1983, writ ref'd n.r.e.). "[W]hen the parties to a simulated sale attempt to fix a lien on a homestead, the lien is invalid if the lender either (1) fails to pay additional consideration or (2) has knowledge or notice that the transaction is simulated. The homestead claimant need not establish both to avoid the lien."

Six-Month Grace Period After Sale

Hodes v. Diagnostic Experts, No. 03-09-00185-CV (Tex.App.—Austin 2010, no pet.) (memo op.; 7-23-10). "[D] contends that because the tract of land was part of her homestead, the proceeds obtained from the sale of the property are exempt from seizure by a creditor. [I]f the proceeds are not applied to the purchase of a new homestead within the six-month period, the exemption is lost. [D] appears to allege that the six-month deadline was tolled when the proceeds were placed in the trust and insists that she has not abandoned any right to those proceeds. [¶] Even assuming that the statutory period may be tolled, the few federal cases addressing this subject have explained that tolling is only permissible if a party specifically requests the court to toll the six-month statutory period before the expiration of the deadline." *See also* ***Taylor v. Mosty Bros. Nursery, Inc.***, 777 S.W.2d 568, 570 (Tex.App.—San Antonio 1989, no writ).

Tax Liens

U.S. v. Rodgers, 461 U.S. 677, 701 (1983). The appellate court "concluded that, if the homestead estate *both* was claimed by a nondelinquent spouse and constituted a property right under state law, then it *would* bar the Federal Government from pursuing a forced sale of the entire property. [¶] We disagree. If [the federal administrative levy for personal income taxes] is intended, as we believe it is, to reach the entire property in which a delinquent taxpayer has or had any 'right, title, or interest,' then state-created exemptions against forced sale should be no more effective with regard to the entire property than with regard to the 'right, title, or interest' itself."

Cornerstone Bank v. Randle, 869 S.W.2d 580, 587 (Tex.App.—Dallas 1993, no writ). "[W]e hold that state inheritance taxes … are not taxes on property for the purpose of [Tex. Const.] art. 16, §50…. Accordingly, as a matter of law, [assignee of State] is not entitled to foreclose upon [surviving spouse's] possessory homestead interest and force the sale of the property in question."

PROP §41.002. DEFINITION OF HOMESTEAD

(a) If used for the purposes of an urban home or as both an urban home and a place to exercise a calling or business, the homestead of a family or a single, adult person, not otherwise entitled to a homestead, shall consist of not more than 10 acres of land which may be in one or more contiguous lots, together with any improvements thereon.

(b) If used for the purposes of a rural home, the homestead shall consist of:

(1) for a family, not more than 200 acres, which may be in one or more parcels, with the improvements thereon; or

(2) for a single, adult person, not otherwise entitled to a homestead, not more than 100 acres, which may be in one or more parcels, with the improvements thereon.

(c) A homestead is considered to be urban if, at the time the designation is made, the property is:

(1) located within the limits of a municipality or its extraterritorial jurisdiction or a platted subdivision; and

(2) served by police protection, paid or volunteer fire protection, and at least three of the following services provided by a municipality or under contract to a municipality:

(A) electric;

(B) natural gas;

(C) sewer;

(D) storm sewer; and

(E) water.

(d) The definition of a homestead as provided in this section applies to all homesteads in this state whenever created.

History of Prop. Code §41.002: Acts 1983, 68th Leg., ch. 576, §1, eff. Jan. 1, 1984. Amended by Acts 1985, 69th Leg., ch. 840, §1, eff. June 15, 1985; Acts 1989, 71st Leg., ch. 391, §2, eff. Aug. 28, 1989; Acts 1999, 76th Leg., ch. 1510, §1 (eff. Jan. 1, 2000), ch. 1510, §2 (eff. Sept. 1, 1999). Source: TRCS art. 3833.

See also Tex. Const. art. 16, §51; *O'Connor's Fam. Law Handbook*, "Homestead Defined," ch. 2-E, §2, p. 183; "Claimant is single adult or head of family," ch. 2-E, §4.1.2, p. 191; "Overt acts of homestead usage," ch. 2-E, §4.3, p. 194.

ANNOTATIONS

Establishment

Norris v. Thomas, 215 S.W.3d 851, 857 (Tex.2007). "Movable chattels do not possess the characteristics of a fixture attached to real property and do not acquire the character of realty. '[I]t is their attachment to realty which gives them homestead character.' We hold that [D's] boat remains a movable chattel; it does not rest 'thereon' or 'on the land' as Texas homestead law clearly requires; it has not become a permanent part of the real estate; and it has not sufficiently attached to real property to merit homestead protection."

Wilcox v. Marriott, 103 S.W.3d 469, 472 (Tex. App.—San Antonio 2003, pet. denied). "The '[p]ossession and use of land by one who owns it and who resides upon it makes it homestead in law and in fact.' A party claiming homestead protection has the burden to establish that the property is homestead. To establish homestead rights, a party must show 'overt acts of homestead usage, and intention on the part of the owner to claim the property as homestead.' Once property has been dedicated as homestead, it can only lose such designation by abandonment, alienation, or death. After the party has established the homestead character of the property, the burden shifts to the creditor ... to disprove the continued existence of the homestead. In other words, a homestead is presumed to exist 'until its termination is proved.'" *See also* Tex. Const. art. 16, §50; ***First Interstate Bank v. Bland***, 810 S.W.2d 277, 283-84 (Tex.App.—Fort Worth 1991, no writ); ***Lifemark Corp. v. Merritt***, 655 S.W.2d 310, 314 (Tex.App.—Houston [14th Dist.] 1983, writ ref'd n.r.e.); ***Painewebber, Inc. v. Murray***, 260 B.R. 815, 822 (Bankr.E.D.Tex.2001).

Sanchez v. Telles, 960 S.W.2d 762, 770 (Tex. App.—El Paso 1997, pet. denied). "It must always be remembered that mere ownership alone is insufficient to constitute premises of a homestead[;] that merely residing in a house over a length of time alone does not convert it into a homestead[;] that occupancy of property does not ipso facto make the property a homestead[;] and that the word 'home' is not necessarily synonymous with 'homestead.'" *See also* **In re Mitchell**, 132 B.R. 553, 558 (Bankr.W.D.Tex.1991).

Farrington v. First Nat'l Bank, 753 S.W.2d 248, 250-51 (Tex.App.—Houston [1st Dist.] 1988, writ denied). "[A] homestead exemption may be established upon unoccupied land if the owner presently intends to occupy and use the premises in a reasonable and definite time in the future, and has made such preparations toward actual occupancy and use that 'are of such character and have proceeded to such an extent as to manifest beyond doubt the intention to complete the improvements and reside upon the place as a home.' A homestead claimant cannot claim both an urban and rural homestead. [¶] Good faith intention to occupy is the prime factor in securing the benefits of the homestead exemption, and preparatory acts collaborate this intention." *But see* ***Caulley v. Caulley***, 806 S.W.2d 795, 797 (Tex.1991) (while occupying property as homestead, one cannot establish a homestead right in another place by "attempting to live there in the future").

Fajkus v. First Nat'l Bank, 735 S.W.2d 882, 885 (Tex.App.—Austin 1987, writ denied). "[W]hether property claimed as homestead is in a rural or urban area is a question of fact. There is authority, however, indicating one must only prove the character of the property when that matter is subject to dispute. But, only slight evidence is necessary to raise the issue."

Johnson v. First S. Props., Inc., 687 S.W.2d 399, 401 (Tex.App.—Houston [14th Dist.] 1985, writ ref'd n.r.e.). "It is firmly established in Texas law that to create a homestead the person claiming the homestead must prove concurrent usage and intent to claim the property as homestead. This determination becomes somewhat complicated when the 'usage' follows the intent. During this interim period when the intention has not ripened into actual occupancy, the owner can, in effect, waive his homestead claim by making representations relinquishing that claim. Such representations can defeat a homestead without further reference to the homestead exemptions. *At 402:* The deed and the deed of trust represented that [homeowner] took the apartment *subject to* the declaration, which declaration designated that the homeowner's council had an assessment lien. This, of course, amounted to a prior relinquishment of [homeowner's] homestead claim. We therefore hold that the assessment lien constituted a valid pre-existing debt which would overcome the homestead claim."

Texas Commerce Bank v. McCreary, 677 S.W.2d 643, 646 (Tex.App.—Dallas 1984, no writ). "We hold

that permission by the corporation to use one of its buildings for living quarters does not establish an independent right to use the premises as a residence and does not divest the corporation of its exclusive right to possession under the lease. There is no evidence that the property was ever divided into income-producing and residential property. Thus, its uninterrupted use as rental property, regardless of [resident's] occupancy of a building, precludes its qualification for a homestead exemption."

Homestead Claimant

Brown v. Bank of Galveston, 963 S.W.2d 511, 515 (Tex.1998). "[P] asserts that the mechanic's lien is invalid because it was a lien against his wife's homestead that she did not sign.... [¶] [P's] statement that he was 'a single man' on at least three of the documents ... is enough to raise a fact question concerning [wife's] homestead rights. [P] did not conclusively establish [wife's] homestead rights, and he cannot rely upon them on appeal." *See also* ***Cadle Co. v. Ortiz***, 227 S.W.3d 831, 835-36 (Tex.App.—Corpus Christi 2007, pet. denied) (***Brown*** does not imply person is required to list spouse on real-property documents for homestead status to attach).

Laster v. First Huntsville Props. Co., 826 S.W.2d 125, 130 (Tex.1991). "[O]ne who holds only a future interest in property with no present right to possession is not entitled to homestead protection in that property. [¶] [I]n accordance with the general rule that one's homestead rights will not protect property in which no possessory interest is held, a non-possessory, future interest in property is not protected by the homestead right of the person with the present right to occupy the property."

Duran v. Henderson, 71 S.W.3d 833, 841 (Tex. App.—Texarkana 2002, pet. denied). "For over a century, within the context of homestead law, Texas courts have [followed the test in ***Roco v. Green***, 50 Tex. 483 (1878), which] held that the family relation is one of status; that the head of the family must be legally or morally obligated to support at least one other family member; and additionally there must be a corresponding dependence on the other member for this support. A family may include a parent and his or her adult child, provided that the parent is under an obligation to support the adult child and the child is dependent on the parent for support." *See also* ***Painewebber, Inc. v. Murray***, 260 B.R. 815, 827 (Bankr.E.D.Tex.2001) (test for dependency is whether dependent's position would be altered "but for" the support).

Rooms With a View, Inc. v. Private Nat'l Mortg. Ass'n, 7 S.W.3d 840, 849 (Tex.App.—Austin 1999, pet. denied). "Each spouse in a marriage has a separate and undivided possessory interest in their homestead property. Homestead rights vest in both spouses regardless of whether the property is owned by both spouses, by one spouse separately, or even by a third party." *See also* ***Renaldo v. Bank of San Antonio***, 630 S.W.2d 638, 639-40 (Tex.1982) (divorcing spouses may claim separate homesteads even if one spouse will not have full custody of children); ***Lindsley v. Lindsley***, 163 S.W.2d 633, 636 (Tex.1942) (surviving spouse has homestead rights in separate property of deceased spouse); ***Grissom v. Anderson***, 79 S.W.2d 619, 621 (Tex.1935) (if no joinder of both spouses, conveyance of homestead inoperative until abandonment or ratification); ***Painewebber, Inc. v. Murray***, 260 B.R. 815, 825 (Bankr.E.D. Tex.2001) (spouses cannot claim separate homesteads).

NCNB Texas Nat'l Bank v. Carpenter, 849 S.W.2d 875, 879-80 (Tex.App.—Fort Worth 1993, no writ). "The requirement of family is met whenever there is a group of people ... living together subject to one domestic government. *There must be a legal or moral responsibility on the head of the family for the rest of the members of the family, and a corresponding dependence of the others upon the head of the family.* A moral obligation for support and care exists where there is a necessity for such care and support, although that necessity need not be absolute. [¶] In addition to the situation involving a husband, wife, and minor children, Texas courts have found that a family exists for homestead exemption purposes in the following circumstances: (1) a divorcee and her mother constitute a family if the divorcee has a moral obligation to support and care for her mother, (2) brother and sister constitute a family when the brother has a moral obligation to support and care for his sister, (3) a father and minor son constitute a family—whether or not the father has custody of the child—because the father has a legal and moral obligation to support the child. In each of these instances, the court allowed the head of the family to claim a homestead exemption under [Tex. Const.] art. 16, §50...." *But see* ***L.E. Whitham & Co. v. Briggs' Estate***, 58 S.W.2d 49, 50 (Tex.Comm'n App.1933) (holding approved) (mother and adult son do not constitute a family).

In re Finkel, 151 B.R. 779, 785 (Bankr.W.D.Tex. 1993). "[T]he definition of 'family' ... has three requirements: (1) the family relation is one of status, (2) the head of the family must be legally or morally obligated to support at least one other family member, and (3) there must be a corresponding dependence on the supporting member. *At 786:* In ***Woods v. Alvarado***, [19 S.W.2d 35 (Tex.1929),] the Texas Supreme Court established the general rule that, where the head of a family is entitled to a homestead exemption, and thereafter, either by death or dispersion of its members, he ceases to have a family, the homestead will remain exempt as long as the surviving constituents of the family continue to use and occupy the property as homestead."

Loss of Homestead

Hruska v. First State Bank, 747 S.W.2d 783, 785 (Tex.1988). "A lien cannot be 'estopped' into existence. It is true that we have held that, in certain circumstances, a homestead claimant may be estopped to deny the validity of an *existing* lien. However, ***Lincoln*** [***v. Bennett***, 156 S.W.2d 504 (Tex.1941),] is not authority for the proposition that a lien may be created by oral representation.... The function of waiver or estoppel is to preserve rights, not to create independent causes of action. Waiver and estoppel are defensive in nature and operate to prevent the loss of existing rights. They do not operate to create liability where it does not otherwise exist."

Williams v. Williams, 569 S.W.2d 867, 868 (Tex. 1978). "The question presented by this cause is whether a premarital agreement to waive the constitutional and statutory rights of a surviving spouse to a homestead and other exempt property is valid." Held: Yes.

Estate of Montague v. Nat'l Loan Investors, L.P., 70 S.W.3d 242, 247 (Tex.App.—San Antonio 2001, pet. denied). "Whether a homestead claimant can be estopped to claim a homestead exemption based on a disclaimer depends on the circumstances. [¶] If the claimant owns only one piece of property which the claimant occupies and uses as his home, the claimant is not estopped to set up the homestead exemption notwithstanding declarations, whether written or oral, which state to the contrary. The refusal to estop the claimant is based on the theory that the fact of actual possession and use of the property as a home is so obvious at the time of the mortgage that the lender is charged with notice of the fact of the homestead. [¶] If a claimant owns two pieces of property, but only one piece of property could have been the homestead at the time of the mortgage, the lender again cannot shut his eyes to the fact that the mortgaged premises, which was being occupied at the time the deed of trust was executed, was the only property suitable for homestead purposes. If the court can determine as a matter of law that only one of the pieces of property was suitable for homestead purposes given the facts and circumstances surrounding the use of the properties, such as suitability for occupancy, the homestead claimant is not estopped from claiming the exemption despite declarations to the contrary. [¶] The ripest ground for the application of estoppel principles is where a claimant owns two or more pieces of property, each of which could constitute the claimant's homestead at the time the claimant mortgages one of the parcels for some reason other than for purchase money or improvements thereon. A claimant may be estopped under those circumstances from claiming the homestead exemption 'where physical facts open to observation lead to a conclusion that the property in question is not the homestead, the use of the property is not inconsistent with the claimant's representations that the property is disclaimed as the homestead, and the representations were intended to be and were actually relied upon by the lender.' Under these circumstances, 'ambiguous possession' is said to exist, which may enable a lender to successfully assert estoppel." *See also* ***Lincoln v. Bennett***, 156 S.W.2d 504, 506-07 (Tex.1941); ***Rutland Sav. Bank v. Isbell***, 154 S.W.2d 442, 445 (Tex.1941).

McFarland v. Rousseau, 667 S.W.2d 929, 931 (Tex. App.—Corpus Christi 1984, no writ). "The right to a homestead in a particular tract of land, having once vested by ownership and use, is presumed to continue until there is affirmative proof of abandonment. Abandonment is an affirmative defense. The person relying upon the affirmative defense of abandonment has the burden of establishing it. The party relying on abandonment of a homestead has the burden of showing that the homestead claimant moved from the homestead property with the intention of not returning to the property. The evidence relied on establishing abandonment of a homestead must make it 'undeniably clear' that there has been 'a total abandonment with an intention not to return and claim the exemption' before a homestead, once occupied as such, can be subjected to a forced sale. Neither temporary absence from a homestead nor even temporarily removing to another State

alone constitutes abandonment." *See also* ***Spiegel v. KLRU Endowment Fund***, 228 S.W.3d 237, 243-44 (Tex. App.—Austin 2007, pet. denied); ***Taylor v. Mosty Bros. Nursery, Inc.***, 777 S.W.2d 568, 569 (Tex. App.—San Antonio 1989, no writ).

In re Perry, 345 F.3d 303, 310 n.8 (5th Cir.2003). "Homestead status may be lost through alienation when the title to the property is transferred or conveyed to another, regardless of whether the grantor retains possession of the property." *See also* ***Resolution Trust Corp. v. Olivarez***, 29 F.3d 201, 207 (5th Cir.1994) (alienation may result in termination of homestead, even if abandonment by discontinuation of use is not shown).

In re Cole, 205 B.R. 382, 385 (Bankr.E.D.Tex.1997). "[T]here can be no more convincing proof that abandonment occurred than the sale of a homestead. Furthermore, when transfer of title occurs abandonment occurs even when the transferring party continues to occupy that property." *But see* ***Sullivan v. Barnett***, 471 S.W.2d 39, 43 (Tex.1971) (no abandonment because of intent to retain possession and use until sale was final).

In re Finkel, 151 B.R. 779, 783 (Bankr.W.D.Tex. 1993). "[T]he rules for abandonment of a business homestead and a residential homestead are precisely the same, i.e., the challenging creditor has the burden of proving an actual intent to abandon. The factual inquiry is different, however. With residential homesteads, we look for a voluntary intention to no longer reside on the property, and usually require as one of the subsidiary facts found that another property have been acquired as a new or substitute homestead. With business homesteads, we look for facts showing a voluntary discontinuance of the business, i.e., facts which demonstrate a cessation of any further intent to continue the business. The same fact might have no probative force were we speaking of abandonment of a residential homestead, but be of significant probative force in the case of business homesteads. For example, a financial inability to acquire another residence would not necessarily establish a lack of intent to claim a residential homestead, but a financial inability to engage in a business would tend to show a lack of intent to again engage in the business."

Rural Homestead

Youngblood v. Youngblood, 76 S.W.2d 759, 760 (Tex.1934). "[C]ontiguity of lots or parcels of land presents a 'situation … decidedly favorable for extending to the outside boundaries the homestead limits,' and, while the Constitution authorizes lots or parcels of land not contiguous to be united in one homestead, 'it would naturally require more distinct evidences of such destination in proportion to the inconvenience of using as parts of the same home lots remote from each other.'" *See also* ***Painewebber, Inc. v. Murray***, this page.

Riley v. Riley, 972 S.W.2d 149, 154 (Tex.App.—Texarkana 1998, no pet.). "If used for the purposes of a rural home, the homestead *may be in one or more parcels*. To establish a homestead claim in rural property, the claimant must reside on part of the property and use the property for purposes of a home, although the claimant need not reside on all the parcels so long as the other tracts are used for the support of the family. [¶] A homestead claimant *may* exclude part of a tract actually occupied to obtain more acreage in another tract. However, such claimant must show that the second tract satisfies the requirement that the land is used for support of the family."

In re Perry, 345 F.3d 303, 318 (5th Cir.2003). "Neither the Texas Property Code, nor the Texas Constitution, bar a rural resident from operating a business, per se, on the property on which he resides. Because the 'business' or 'calling' of rural residents has traditionally been agricultural, the Texas Supreme Court has not yet been presented with the opportunity to pass upon a case that involves (a) a rural resident, who claims (b) rural property, that is (c) on the same tract as his residence and (d) is used for non-agricultural business purposes, as part of his homestead. In the absence of a clear statement expressly limiting the scope of the rural homestead to property used for home or agricultural purposes, we cannot agree that the operation of a business, without more, necessarily forfeits a rural homestead interest."

Painewebber, Inc. v. Murray, 260 B.R. 815, 830 (Bankr.E.D.Tex.2001). "[I]n cases where the rural homestead consists of separate tracts of land, the mere establishment of a home on one tract may be insufficient to impress homestead character on the detached properties. For years, courts have drawn a distinction between those tracts that are contiguous and noncontiguous with the tract occupied by a residence. With a contiguous tract, one can logically extend the establishment of a home and the activities pertaining to the home to the outer boundaries of that tract. Only an imaginary line separates the residence tract from the

contiguous property. Hence, there is a presumption that such a tract is used for the purposes of a home. With a noncontiguous tract, more than an artificial boundary separates it from the home. Unless the noncontiguous tract somehow supports the home, it has no nexus with the residence tract and is nothing more than another piece of property. Thus, a claimant must demonstrate distinct evidence that the noncontiguous, piece of property is associated with the residence tract and that it is more than a separate plot of land. [¶] Most cases refer to the need to show that the separate tracts support the family without adequately addressing the kind of evidence that indicates support. While many of them presume that activities like cultivating crops, pasturing cows, or chopping wood constitute evidence of support, a few others suggest that acts on a detached property that contribute to the comfort, enjoyment, or convenience of the residence or the family may also represent distinct enough evidence of a rural purpose. Under this latter, more liberal view, comforting or convenient acts like taking a walk on the detached property or enjoying the property's aesthetic qualities could possibly impress a homestead. The two cases espousing this broader interpretation, however, concerned a separate tract that was utilized for sharecropping. Those separate tracts provided a form of support beyond mere aesthetic comfort or convenience. Accordingly, the notion that mere comforting or convenient acts may dedicate a homestead on a detached piece of property resonates less powerfully than one might originally believe." *See also* ***Youngblood v. Youngblood***, p. 196.

Urban Homestead

Ford v. Aetna Ins., 424 S.W.2d 612, 616 (Tex.1968). The business-homestead exemption "may extend to two non-contiguous lots when such lots are used as a place for the operation of the business of the head of a family, and both are essential to and necessary for such business, not merely being used in aid of the business."

Majeski v. Estate of Majeski, 163 S.W.3d 102, 109 (Tex.App.—Austin 2005, no pet.). "A business occupies a property owner's time, attention, or labor for purposes of profit or improvement. Renting or leasing property has generally not been considered a business or calling, even if rental income is an individual's sole source of income. Courts have instead viewed rental property as an investment that does not take up a large portion of the property owner's time, labor, or attention. Temporarily renting homestead property to another, however, does not change the property's homestead character. *At 110:* The evidence shows that some portion, indeed a substantial portion, of the land behind the fence is either not in use at all or is used by [claimant] for storage of his personal items and for his own use. The evidence is unclear about exactly what percentage of the property behind the fence is actually rented. [Claimant] acknowledged renting four housing units, but stated that several of the other houses or mobile homes are not rented and in fact are uninhabitable. [¶] Under the trial court's determination, the fence that [claimant] and his wife erected between [their business and home] and the remainder of the lot is the dividing line between what is homestead and what is not. This designation is arbitrary and begs the question of whether the line would shift if, on a whim, the 'temporary' fence had been placed ten feet in either direction or had been torn down altogether. [T]he uncontradicted evidence does not establish as a matter of law that [claimant's] homestead interest in all of the land behind the fence should be forfeited. Instead, there is a question of fact as to what portion of the tract, some of which is used by [claimant] for storage or is vacant, is deserving of homestead protection."

McKee v. Smith, 965 S.W.2d 52, 53 (Tex.App.—Fort Worth 1998, pet. denied). "The business homestead exemption was designed to protect property titled to a family member at which family 'members may pursue such business or avocation as may be necessary for the support and comfort of the family.' ... Consequently ... the business homestead exemption applies to real property titled to a family member but leased to a corporation wholly owned by a family member."

C.D. Shamburger Lumber Co. v. Delavan, 106 S.W.2d 351, 355-56 (Tex.App.—Amarillo 1937, writ ref'd). "The words 'calling' and 'business' are evidently used in the constitution in a very broad sense when taken together, but the signification of each one is uncertain; yet we are to infer that they were not used to designate the same thing. [¶] Taken together, they certainly embrace every legitimate avocation in life by which an honest support for a family may be obtained. [¶] The former was probably used in the sense of 'profession' or 'trade,' which would embrace all such employments as by course of study or apprenticeship in any of the learned professions, liberal arts, or mechanical occupations, a person has acquired skill or ability to

follow, and which has become practically a matter of personal skill, in its nature not temporary in existence. [¶] The latter word was probably used in contradistinction to the other, to denote ... that which occupies the time, attention and labor of men for the purpose of profit or improvement, and this may be temporary. [¶] The calling may exist as a fact, whether it be practiced or not; with the other, the actual employment in the given occupation furnishes the only means to determine whether the business exists or not. [¶] The law has never undertaken to restrict or define the kind or character of business in which the head of a family should engage, being satisfied to limit it only to legitimate business. The head of the family has the right to select any kind of business in which he chooses to embark, and, whatever may be the kind or character of business chosen by him, he is entitled to the same exemptions under the law as the man who is engaged in any other line of business." (Internal quotes omitted.)

Painewebber, Inc. v. Murray, 260 B.R. 815, 822 (Bankr.E.D.Tex.2001). "The Fifth Circuit ... has interpreted [§41.002(c)] as clarifying the test to determine homestead status rather than as a definitive measure of whether some property is rural or urban. Accordingly, §41.002(c) is but one of many factors that a court may consider to determine whether a homestead is rural or urban. Other factors include: '(1) the location of the land with respect to the limits of the municipality; (2) the situs of the lot in question; (3) the existence of municipal utilities and services; (4) the use of the lot and adjacent property; and (5) the presence of platted streets, blocks, and the like.'" *See also* **Smith v. Hennington**, 249 S.W.3d 600, 603 (Tex.App.—Eastland 2008, pet. denied).

In re Finkel, 151 B.R. 779, 781 (Bankr.W.D.Tex. 1993). "[T]o claim a business homestead exemption under [§41.002], two conditions must be met. First, the head of the family must have a calling or business to which the property is reasonably adapted and reasonably necessary. Second, the property must be used as a place to exercise the calling or business of the head of the family. *At 782:* In order for there to be a business homestead, there must be a calling or business being exercised on the property. In ***Waggener v. Haskell***, [35 S.W. 1 (Tex.1896),] the court defined 'calling' as 'the usual occupation, profession, or employment; [sic] vocation' of a party. The term 'business' is 'that which busies or occupies one's time, attention, and labor as his chief concern; that which one does for livelihood; occupation; employment.' The terms have been held to embrace every 'legitimate avocation by which honest support of a family may be obtained.' [¶] By the same token, not every activity that generates income constitutes a calling or business. For example, Texas courts have long held that the mere renting of property does not constitute a calling or business sufficient to provide a business homestead exemption. Such activity is classified as investment activity rather than a business or calling, because it requires little time and attention and does not comport with the general accepted notions of business."

PROP §41.0021. HOMESTEAD IN QUALIFYING TRUST

(a) In this section, "qualifying trust" means an express trust:

(1) in which the instrument or court order creating the express trust provides that a settlor or beneficiary of the trust has the right to:

(A) revoke the trust without the consent of another person;

(B) exercise an inter vivos general power of appointment over the property that qualifies for the homestead exemption; or

(C) use and occupy the residential property as the settlor's or beneficiary's principal residence at no cost to the settlor or beneficiary, other than payment of taxes and other costs and expenses specified in the instrument or court order:

(i) for the life of the settlor or beneficiary;

(ii) for the shorter of the life of the settlor or beneficiary or a term of years specified in the instrument or court order; or

(iii) until the date the trust is revoked or terminated by an instrument or court order recorded in the real property records of the county in which the property is located and that describes the property with sufficient certainty to identify the property; and

(2) the trustee of which acquires the property in an instrument of title or under a court order that:

(A) describes the property with sufficient certainty to identify the property and the interest acquired; and

(B) is recorded in the real property records of the county in which the property is located.

(b) Property that a settlor or beneficiary occupies and uses in a manner described by this subchapter and

in which the settlor or beneficiary owns a beneficial interest through a qualifying trust is considered the homestead of the settlor or beneficiary under Section 50, Article XVI, Texas Constitution, and Section 41.001.

(c) A married person who transfers property to the trustee of a qualifying trust must comply with the requirements relating to the joinder of the person's spouse as provided by Chapter 5, Family Code.

(d) A trustee may sell, convey, or encumber property transferred as described by Subsection (c) without the joinder of either spouse unless expressly prohibited by the instrument or court order creating the trust.

(e) This section does not affect the rights of a surviving spouse or surviving children under Section 52, Article XVI, Texas Constitution, or Part 3, Chapter VIII, Texas Probate Code.[1]

1. **Editor's note:** Now Estates Code chs. 102, 353.

History of Prop. Code §41.0021: Acts 2009, 81st Leg., ch. 984, §1, eff. Sept. 1, 2009.

See also *O'Connor's Fam. Law Handbook*, "When protected," ch. 2-E, §3.1.1, p. 184.

PROP §41.003. TEMPORARY RENTING OF A HOMESTEAD

Temporary renting of a homestead does not change its homestead character if the homestead claimant has not acquired another homestead.

History of Prop. Code §41.003: Acts 1983, 68th Leg., ch. 576, §1, eff. Jan. 1, 1984. Amended by Acts 1985, 69th Leg., ch. 840, §1, eff. June 15, 1985. Source: TRCS art. 3833.

See also Tex. Const. art. 16, §51.

ANNOTATIONS

In re Perry, 345 F.3d 303, 319 (5th Cir.2003). "Whether [debtor] temporarily rented portions of his homestead property or did so permanently in such a manner that he abandoned the property as his homestead is a question of fact."

PROP §41.004. ABANDONMENT OF A HOMESTEAD

If a homestead claimant is married, a homestead cannot be abandoned without the consent of the claimant's spouse.

History of Prop. Code §41.004: Acts 1985, 69th Leg., ch. 840, §1, eff. June 15, 1985.

See also Tex. Const. art. 16, §50; *O'Connor's Fam. Law Handbook*, "Abandonment," ch. 2-E, §6.1, p. 199.

PROP §41.005. VOLUNTARY DESIGNATION OF HOMESTEAD

(a) If a rural homestead of a family is part of one or more parcels containing a total of more than 200 acres, the head of the family and, if married, that person's spouse may voluntarily designate not more than 200 acres of the property as the homestead. If a rural homestead of a single adult person, not otherwise entitled to a homestead, is part of one or more parcels containing a total of more than 100 acres, the person may voluntarily designate not more than 100 acres of the property as the homestead.

(b) If an urban homestead of a family, or an urban homestead of a single adult person not otherwise entitled to a homestead, is part of one or more contiguous lots containing a total of more than 10 acres, the head of the family and, if married, that person's spouse or the single adult person, as applicable, may voluntarily designate not more than 10 acres of the property as the homestead.

(c) Except as provided by Subsection (e) or Subchapter B, to designate property as a homestead, a person or persons, as applicable, must make the designation in an instrument that is signed and acknowledged or proved in the manner required for the recording of other instruments. The person or persons must file the designation with the county clerk of the county in which all or part of the property is located. The clerk shall record the designation in the county deed records. The designation must contain:

(1) a description sufficient to identify the property designated;

(2) a statement by the person or persons who executed the instrument that the property is designated as the homestead of the person's family or as the homestead of a single adult person not otherwise entitled to a homestead;

(3) the name of the current record title holder of the property; and

(4) for a rural homestead, the number of acres designated and, if there is more than one survey, the number of acres in each.

(d) A person or persons, as applicable, may change the boundaries of a homestead designated under Subsection (c) by executing and recording an instrument in the manner required for a voluntary designation under that subsection. A change under this subsection does not impair rights acquired by a party before the change.

(e) Except as otherwise provided by this subsection, property on which a person receives an exemption from taxation under Section 11.43, Tax Code, is considered to have been designated as the person's home-

stead for purposes of this subchapter if the property is listed as the person's residence homestead on the most recent appraisal roll for the appraisal district established for the county in which the property is located. If a person designates property as a homestead under Subsection (c) or Subchapter B and a different property is considered to have been designated as the person's homestead under this subsection, the designation under Subsection (c) or Subchapter B, as applicable, prevails for purposes of this chapter.

(f) If a person or persons, as applicable, have not made a voluntary designation of a homestead under this section as of the time a writ of execution is issued against the person, any designation of the person's or persons' homestead must be made in accordance with Subchapter B.

(g) An instrument that made a voluntary designation of a homestead in accordance with prior law and that is on file with the county clerk on September 1, 1987, is considered a voluntary designation of a homestead under this section.

History of Prop. Code §41.005: Acts 1987, 70th Leg., ch. 727, §1, eff. Aug. 31, 1987. Amended by Acts 1993, 73rd Leg., ch. 48, §3 (eff. Sept. 1, 1993), ch. 297, §1 (eff. Aug. 1, 1993); Acts 1997, 75th Leg., ch. 846, §1, eff. Sept. 1, 1997; Acts 1999, 76th Leg., ch. 1510, §3, eff. Jan. 1, 2000. Source: TRCS arts. 3843, 3857.

See also Tex. Const. art. 16, §§50, 51; Tax Code §11.43; ***O'Connor's Fam. Law Handbook***, "Homestead designation," ch. 2-E, §4.4.2, p. 196; "Voluntary designation," ch. 2-E, §5.1, p. 197; ***Real Estate Forms***, FORMS 10:9, 10:10, 11:1, 11:2.

ANNOTATIONS

Lares v. Garza, No. 04-03-00546-CV (Tex. App.—San Antonio 2004, no pet.) (memo op.; 3-24-04). "The mere filing of a homestead designation is insufficient by itself to establish a homestead as a matter of law."

PROP §41.0051. DISCLAIMER & DISCLOSURE REQUIRED

(a) A person may not deliver a written advertisement offering, for a fee, to designate property as a homestead as provided by Section 41.005 unless there is a disclaimer on the advertisement that is conspicuous and printed in 14-point boldface type or 14-point uppercase typewritten letters that makes the following statement or a substantially similar statement:

THIS DOCUMENT IS AN ADVERTISEMENT OF SERVICES. IT IS NOT AN OFFICIAL DOCUMENT OF THE STATE OF TEXAS.

(b) A person who solicits solely by mail or by telephone a homeowner to pay a fee for the service of applying for a property tax refund from a tax appraisal district or other governmental body on behalf of the homeowner shall, before accepting money from the homeowner or signing a contract with the homeowner for the person's services, disclose to the homeowner the name of the tax appraisal district or other governmental body that owes the homeowner a refund.

(c) A person's failure to provide a disclaimer on an advertisement as required by Subsection (a) or to provide the disclosure required by Subsection (b) is considered a false, misleading, or deceptive act or practice for purposes of Section 17.46(a), Business & Commerce Code, and is subject to action by the consumer protection division of the attorney general's office as provided by Section 17.46(a), Business & Commerce Code.

History of Prop. Code §41.0051: Acts 2001, 77th Leg., ch. 341, §1, eff. Sept. 1, 2001. Amended by Acts 2003, 78th Leg., ch. 1191, §§1, 2, eff. Sept. 1, 2003.

See also B&CC §§17.46(a), 17.50(h); ***O'Connor's Texas Bus. & Com. Code***, "DTPA Tie-In Statutes Chart," chart 3, p. 998.

PROP §41.006. CERTAIN SALES OF HOMESTEAD

(a) Except as provided by Subsection (c), any sale or purported sale in whole or in part of a homestead at a fixed purchase price that is less than the appraised fair market value of the property at the time of the sale or purported sale, and in connection with which the buyer of the property executes a lease of the property to the seller at lease payments that exceed the fair rental value of the property, is considered to be a loan with all payments made from the seller to the buyer in excess of the sales price considered to be interest subject to Title 4, Finance Code.

(b) The taking of any deed in connection with a transaction described by this section is a deceptive trade practice under Subchapter E, Chapter 17, Business & Commerce Code, and the deed is void and no lien attaches to the homestead property as a result of the purported sale.

(c) This section does not apply to the sale of a family homestead to a parent, stepparent, grandparent, child, stepchild, brother, half brother, sister, half sister, or grandchild of an adult member of the family.

History of Prop. Code §41.006: Acts 1987, 70th Leg., ch. 1130, §1, eff. Sept. 1, 1987. Amended by Acts 1999, 76th Leg., ch. 62, §7.84, eff. Sept. 1, 1999.

See also Tex. Const. art. 16, §50; B&CC §§17.46, 17.50(h); ***O'Connor's Texas COA***, "DTPA Tie-In Statutes," chart 8-2, p. 224.

PROP §41.007. HOME IMPROVEMENT CONTRACT

(a) A contract for improvements to an existing residence described by Section 41.001(b)(3) must contain:

(1) the contractor's certificate of registration number from the Texas Residential Construction Commission if the contractor is required to register as a builder with the commission;

(2) the address and telephone number at which the owner may file a complaint with the Texas Residential Construction Commission about the conduct of the contractor if the contractor is required to register as a builder with the commission; and

(3) the following warning conspicuously printed, stamped, or typed in a size equal to at least 10-point bold type or computer equivalent:

"IMPORTANT NOTICE: You and your contractor are responsible for meeting the terms and conditions of this contract. If you sign this contract and you fail to meet the terms and conditions of this contract, you may lose your legal ownership rights in your home. KNOW YOUR RIGHTS AND DUTIES UNDER THE LAW."

(b) A violation of Subsection (a) of this section is a false, misleading, or deceptive act or practice within the meaning of Section 17.46, Business & Commerce Code, and is actionable in a public or private suit brought under the provisions of the Deceptive Trade Practices-Consumer Protection Act (Subchapter E, Chapter 17, Business & Commerce Code).

(c) A provision of a contract for improvements to an existing residence described by Section 41.001(b)(3) that requires the parties to submit a dispute arising under the contract to binding arbitration must be conspicuously printed or typed in a size equal to at least 10-point bold type or the computer equivalent.

(d) A provision described by Subsection (c) is not enforceable against the owner unless the requirements of Subsection (c) are met.

History of Prop. Code §41.007: Acts 1987, 70th Leg., ch. 116, §1, eff. Sept. 1, 1987. Renumbered from §41.005 by Acts 1989, 71st Leg., ch. 2, §16.01(30), eff. Aug. 28, 1989. Amended by Acts 1993, 73rd Leg., ch. 48, §4, eff. Sept. 1, 1993; Acts 2007, 80th Leg., ch. 843, §5, eff. Sept. 1, 2007.

See also Tex. Const. art. 16, §50; B&CC §§17.46; 17.50(h); Prop. Code §162.006; ***O'Connor's Texas COA***, "DTPA Tie-In Statutes," chart 8-2, p. 224.

ANNOTATIONS

Chubb Lloyds Ins. v. Andrew's Restoration, Inc., 323 S.W.3d 564, 577-78 (Tex.App.—Dallas 2010), *rev'd in part on other grounds sub nom.* ***Cruz v. Andrews Restoration, Inc.***, 364 S.W.3d 817 (Tex.2012). "[S]ection 41.007 ... does not provide that omission of the required warning makes a contract invalid or void. [S]ection 41.007 provides its own penalty for noncompliance: a failure to include the required warning in the contract is an actionable practice under the DTPA. [W]e conclude that the statutory consequence for noncompliance [with §41.007] is 'apparently ample' to insure observance. [Thus,] the agreement's noncompliance with §41.007(a) did not make the agreement void or unenforceable."

PROP §41.008. CONFLICT WITH FEDERAL LAW

To the extent of any conflict between this subchapter and any federal law that imposes an upper limit on the amount, including the monetary amount or acreage amount, of homestead property a person may exempt from seizure, this subchapter prevails to the extent allowed under federal law.

History of Prop. Code §41.008: Acts 1999, 76th Leg., ch. 1510, §4, eff. Sept. 1, 1999.

See also Tex. Const. art. 16, §51.

Sections 41.009-41.020 reserved for expansion

SUBCHAPTER B. DESIGNATION OF A HOMESTEAD IN AID OF ENFORCEMENT OF A JUDGMENT DEBT

PROP §41.021. NOTICE TO DESIGNATE

If an execution is issued against a holder of an interest in land of which a homestead may be a part and the judgment debtor has not made a voluntary designation of a homestead under Section 41.005, the judgment creditor may give the judgment debtor notice to designate the homestead as defined in Section 41.002. The notice shall state that if the judgment debtor fails to designate the homestead within the time allowed by Section 41.022, the court will appoint a commissioner to make the designation at the expense of the judgment debtor.

History of Prop. Code §41.021: Acts 1983, 68th Leg., ch. 576, §31, eff. Jan. 1, 1984. Amended by Acts 1985, 69th Leg., ch. 840, §1, eff. June 15, 1985; Acts 1987, 70th Leg., ch. 727, §2, eff. Aug. 31, 1987. Source: TRCS arts. 3845, 3846.

See also Tex. Const. art. 16, §50; ***O'Connor's Fam. Law Handbook***, "Involuntary designation," ch. 2-E, §5.2, p. 198.

PROP §41.022. DESIGNATION BY HOMESTEAD CLAIMANT

At any time before 10 a.m. on the Monday next after the expiration of 20 days after the date of service of the notice to designate, the judgment debtor may designate

the homestead as defined in Section 41.002 by filing a written designation, signed by the judgment debtor, with the justice or clerk of the court from which the writ of execution was issued, together with a plat of the area designated.

History of Prop. Code §41.022: Acts 1983, 68th Leg., ch. 576, §31, eff. Jan. 1, 1984. Amended by Acts 1985, 69th Leg., ch. 840, §1, eff. June 15, 1985. Source: TRCS arts. 3847, 3848.

See also Tex. Const. art. 16, §50; ***O'Connor's Fam. Law Handbook***, "Designation by debtor," ch. 2-E, §5.2.1(2), p. 198; ***Real Estate Forms***, FORMS 10:9, 10:10.

PROP §41.023. DESIGNATION BY COMMISSIONER

(a) If a judgment debtor who has not made a voluntary designation of a homestead under Section 41.005 does not designate a homestead as provided in Section 41.022, on motion of the judgment creditor, filed within 90 days after the issuance of the writ of execution, the court from which the writ of execution issued shall appoint a commissioner to designate the judgment debtor's homestead. The court may appoint a surveyor and others as may be necessary to assist the commissioner. The commissioner shall file his designation of the judgment debtor's homestead in a written report, together with a plat of the area designated, with the justice or clerk of the court not more than 60 days after the order of appointment is signed or within such time as the court may allow.

(b) Within 10 days after the commissioner's report is filed, the judgment debtor or the judgment creditor may request a hearing on the issue of whether the report should be confirmed, rejected, or modified as may be deemed appropriate in the particular circumstances of the case. The commissioner's report may be contradicted by evidence from either party, when exceptions to it or any item thereof have been filed before the hearing, but not otherwise. After the hearing, or if there is no hearing requested, the court shall designate the homestead as deemed appropriate and order sale of the excess.

(c) The commissioner, a surveyor, and others appointed to assist the commissioner are entitled to such fees and expenses as are deemed reasonable by the court. The court shall tax these fees and expenses against the judgment debtor as part of the costs of execution.

History of Prop. Code §41.023: Acts 1983, 68th Leg., ch. 576, §1, eff. Jan. 1, 1984. Amended by Acts 1985, 69th Leg., ch. 840, §1, eff. June 15, 1985; Acts 1987, 70th Leg., ch. 727, §3, eff. Aug. 31, 1987. Source: TRCS arts. 3850-3853, 3855.

See also Tex. Const. art. 16, §50; ***O'Connor's Fam. Law Handbook***, "Motion to appoint commissioner," ch. 2-E, §5.2.2, p. 198; ***Real Estate Forms***, FORMS 10:9, 10:10.

PROP §41.024. SALE OF EXCESS

An officer holding an execution sale of property of a judgment debtor whose homestead has been designated under this chapter may sell the excess of the judgment debtor's interest in land not included in the homestead.

History of Prop. Code §41.024: Amended by Acts 1985, 69th Leg., ch. 840, §1, eff. June 15, 1985; Acts 1987, 70th Leg., ch. 727, §4, eff. Aug. 31, 1987. Source: TRCS art. 3856.

See also Tex. Const. art. 16, §50.

CHAPTER 42. PERSONAL PROPERTY

PROP §42.001. PERSONAL PROPERTY EXEMPTION

(a) Personal property, as described in Section 42.002, is exempt from garnishment, attachment, execution, or other seizure if:

(1) the property is provided for a family and has an aggregate fair market value of not more than $100,000, exclusive of the amount of any liens, security interests, or other charges encumbering the property; or

(2) the property is owned by a single adult, who is not a member of a family, and has an aggregate fair market value of not more than $50,000, exclusive of the amount of any liens, security interests, or other charges encumbering the property.

(b) The following personal property is exempt from seizure and is not included in the aggregate limitations prescribed by Subsection (a):

(1) current wages for personal services, except for the enforcement of court-ordered child support payments;

(2) professionally prescribed health aids of a debtor or a dependent of a debtor;

(3) alimony, support, or separate maintenance received or to be received by the debtor for the support of the debtor or a dependent of the debtor; and

(4) a religious bible or other book containing sacred writings of a religion that is seized by a creditor

other than a lessor of real property who is exercising the lessor's contractual or statutory right to seize personal property after a tenant breaches a lease agreement for or abandons the real property.

(c) Except as provided by Subsection (b)(4), this section does not prevent seizure by a secured creditor with a contractual landlord's lien or other security in the property to be seized.

(d) Unpaid commissions for personal services not to exceed 25 percent of the aggregate limitations prescribed by Subsection (a) are exempt from seizure and are included in the aggregate.

(e) A religious bible or other book described by Subsection (b)(4) that is seized by a lessor of real property in the exercise of the lessor's contractual or statutory right to seize personal property after a tenant breaches a lease agreement for the real property or abandons the real property may not be included in the aggregate limitations prescribed by Subsection (a).

History of Prop. Code §42.001: Acts 1983, 68th Leg., ch. 576, §1, eff. Jan. 1, 1984. Amended by Acts 1991, 72nd Leg., ch. 175, §1, eff. May 24, 1991; Acts 1997, 75th Leg., ch. 1046, §1, eff. Sept. 1, 1997; Acts 2007, 80th Leg., ch. 444, §1, eff. Sept. 1, 2007; Acts 2015, 84th Leg., ch. 793, §1, eff. Sept. 1, 2015.

See also CPRC §31.002(f).

ANNOTATIONS

Stanley v. Reef Secs., Inc., 314 S.W.3d 659, 668 (Tex.App.—Dallas 2010, no pet.). "The general rule [under BOC §152.203(c)] is that, absent an agreement, a partner is not entitled to compensation for services rendered to the partnership no matter how valuable the services may be. Under appropriate circumstances, however, an agreement for compensation, express or implied, will be enforced. [¶] [The] partnership agreement does not contain any provision for compensating [debtor], previous years' tax returns indicate that [debtor] was never treated as an employee before or paid compensation, and there is no evidence that [debtor] has devoted any more time or attention to the business than was anticipated at its formation. Because the undisputed evidence shows that [debtor] is not [partnership's] employee, we conclude that the trial court did not abuse its discretion by concluding that the payments [debtor] receives and will receive from [partnership] are distributions of the partnership and not exempt wages." *See also* ***Schultz v. Cadle Co.***, 825 S.W.2d 151, 153 (Tex. App.—Dallas 1992), *writ denied*, 852 S.W.2d 499 (Tex.1993).

General Elec. Capital Corp. v. ICO, Inc., 230 S.W.3d 702, 706-07 (Tex.App.—Houston [14th Dist.] 2007, pet. denied). "When no contradictory contract language exists, we hold that a severance payment should be liberally construed as a bonus for satisfactory service, since such payments might be considered additional compensation for services previously rendered. [¶] [B]ecause of the general rule that we apply the exemption laws liberally, and because this contract does not clearly state that the severance payment was for something other than personal services, and because courts have found severance agreements to qualify as current wages for personal service, the trial court acted within its discretion when it found that the severance payment was in the nature of current wages for personal service."

Brink v. Ayre, 855 S.W.2d 44, 45 (Tex.App.—Houston [14th Dist.] 1993, no writ). "The general rule is that current wages for personal service are exempt from attachment, execution and seizure for the satisfaction of debts. Once wages are received by the debtor, they cease to be current wages and are not exempt from attachment, execution or seizure for the satisfaction of liabilities. However, the rule is different with regard to attorney's fees. The term 'current wages' implies a master and servant relationship. We have previously held that an attorney engaged in private practice is an independent contractor and does not receive current wages. Thus, attorney's fees are not current wages for purposes of the Turnover statute."

PROP §42.002. PERSONAL PROPERTY

(a) The following personal property is exempt under Section 42.001(a):

(1) home furnishings, including family heirlooms;

(2) provisions for consumption;

(3) farming or ranching vehicles and implements;

(4) tools, equipment, books, and apparatus, including boats and motor vehicles used in a trade or profession;

(5) wearing apparel;

(6) jewelry not to exceed 25 percent of the aggregate limitations prescribed by Section 42.001(a);

(7) two firearms;

(8) athletic and sporting equipment, including bicycles;

(9) a two-wheeled, three-wheeled, or four-wheeled motor vehicle for each member of a family or single

adult who holds a driver's license or who does not hold a driver's license but who relies on another person to operate the vehicle for the benefit of the nonlicensed person;

(10) the following animals and forage on hand for their consumption:

(A) two horses, mules, or donkeys and a saddle, blanket, and bridle for each;

(B) 12 head of cattle;

(C) 60 head of other types of livestock; and

(D) 120 fowl; and

(11) household pets.

(b) Personal property, unless precluded from being encumbered by other law, may be encumbered by a security interest under Subchapter B, Chapter 9, Business & Commerce Code, or Subchapter F, Chapter 501, Transportation Code, or by a lien fixed by other law, and the security interest or lien may not be avoided on the ground that the property is exempt under this chapter.

History of Prop. Code §42.002: Acts 1983, 68th Leg., ch. 576, §1, eff. Jan. 1, 1984. Amended by Acts 1991, 72nd Leg., ch. 175, §1, eff. May 24, 1991; Acts 1993, 73rd Leg., ch. 216, §1, eff. May 17, 1993; Acts 1997, 75th Leg., ch. 165, §30.245, eff. Sept. 1, 1997; Acts 1999, 76th Leg., ch. 414, §2.36 (eff. July 1, 2001), ch. 846, §1 (eff. Aug. 30, 1999).

See also B&CC §§9.201-9.210; Transp. Code §§501.111-501.117.

ANNOTATIONS

Mata v. Ellis, No. 11-14-00207-CV (Tex.App.—Eastland 2016, no pet.) (memo op.; 8-11-16). "When we determine whether property is exempt [under §42.002(a)(4)], we utilize a 'use' test. First, we determine whether the property is necessary to the debtor's trade, and then we consider whether such property is used with sufficient regularity for such purpose to indicate actual use by the debtor. [¶] In … portions of [debtor's] deposition, he admitted that he had not used the property in the construction business for some time and that he would only take another construction job if it were not too hard. [Debtor] has not met his burden to show that the property … was exempt under §42.002(a)(4)."

Leibman v. Grand, 981 S.W.2d 426, 435 (Tex. App.—El Paso 1998, no pet.). The Legislature added CPRC §31.002(f) "to the turnover statute in response to a line of cases that allowed the turnover of property that had lost its exempt status because a debtor had received it, such as paychecks, retirement checks, and other similar types of assets. Stripping the assets of their exempt status because the judgment debtor had received them was viewed as thwarting the purpose of the exemption. [¶] [A]n entirely different situation is presented where a judgment debtor … voluntarily liquidates exempt personal property, such as an automobile, and holds the funds for several months before investing them in an exempt annuity. A finding that the funds realized from the sale of the vehicle are not exempt, particularly where the judgment debtor has purchased a replacement vehicle, does not defeat the purpose of the exemption provided by [Prop. Code] §42.002(9). To hold otherwise would permit [debtor] to claim an exemption not only for his two automobiles but also for the funds realized from the sale of a third vehicle."

Segraves v. Weitzel, 734 S.W.2d 773, 775 (Tex. App.—Fort Worth 1987, writ ref'd n.r.e.). Texas case law interpreting §42.002 establishes conflicting liberal and restrictive views. The liberal view holds "that office furniture used by a professional person should be exempt. *At 776:* [The restrictive view holds that the] exemption applies to tools or apparatus fairly belonging to or usable in a trade and does not extend to articles such as furniture, fixtures, and other equipment which have a merely general value and use in setting up a business. [¶] [W]e believe the restrictive view prevails in Texas." *See also* ***Holland v. Alker***, No. 01-05-00666-CV (Tex.App.—Houston [1st Dist.] 2006, pet. denied) (memo op.; 4-20-06) (property owned by professional corporation was not exempt as attorney's personal property). *Compare* ***Commercial Credit Corp. v. Patterson***, 248 S.W.2d 965, 968-69 (Tex.App.—Austin 1952, writ ref'd n.r.e.) (liberal view), *with* ***McMillan v. Dean***, 174 S.W.2d 737, 739-40 (Tex.App.—Austin 1943, writ ref'd w.o.m.) (restrictive view).

PROP §42.0021. ADDITIONAL EXEMPTION FOR CERTAIN SAVINGS PLANS

(a) In addition to the exemption prescribed by Section 42.001, a person's right to the assets held in or to receive payments, whether vested or not, under any stock bonus, pension, annuity, deferred compensation, profit-sharing, or similar plan, including a retirement plan for self-employed individuals, or a simplified employee pension plan, an individual retirement account or individual retirement annuity, including an inherited individual retirement account, individual retirement annuity, Roth IRA, or inherited Roth IRA, or a health savings account, and under any annuity or similar contract purchased with assets distributed from that type of plan or

account, is exempt from attachment, execution, and seizure for the satisfaction of debts to the extent the plan, contract, annuity, or account is exempt from federal income tax, or to the extent federal income tax on the person's interest is deferred until actual payment of benefits to the person under Section 223, 401(a), 403(a), 403(b), 408(a), 408A, 457(b), or 501(a), Internal Revenue Code of 1986, including a government plan or church plan described by Section 414(d) or (e), Internal Revenue Code of 1986. For purposes of this subsection, the interest of a person in a plan, annuity, account, or contract acquired by reason of the death of another person, whether as an owner, participant, beneficiary, survivor, coannuitant, heir, or legatee, is exempt to the same extent that the interest of the person from whom the plan, annuity, account, or contract was acquired was exempt on the date of the person's death. If this subsection is held invalid or preempted by federal law in whole or in part or in certain circumstances, the subsection remains in effect in all other respects to the maximum extent permitted by law.

(b) Contributions to an individual retirement account that exceed the amounts permitted under the applicable provisions of the Internal Revenue Code of 1986 and any accrued earnings on such contributions are not exempt under this section unless otherwise exempt by law. Amounts qualifying as nontaxable rollover contributions under Section 402(a)(5), 403(a)(4), 403(b)(8), or 408(d)(3) of the Internal Revenue Code of 1986 before January 1, 1993, are treated as exempt amounts under Subsection (a). Amounts treated as qualified rollover contributions under Section 408A, Internal Revenue Code of 1986, are treated as exempt amounts under Subsection (a). In addition, amounts qualifying as nontaxable rollover contributions under Section 402(c), 402(e)(6), 402(f), 403(a)(4), 403(a)(5), 403(b)(8), 403(b)(10), 408(d)(3), or 408A of the Internal Revenue Code of 1986 on or after January 1, 1993, are treated as exempt amounts under Subsection (a). Amounts qualifying as nontaxable rollover contributions under Section 223(f)(5) of the Internal Revenue Code of 1986 on or after January 1, 2004, are treated as exempt amounts under Subsection (a).

(c) Amounts distributed from a plan, annuity, account, or contract entitled to an exemption under Subsection (a) are not subject to seizure for a creditor's claim for 60 days after the date of distribution if the amounts qualify as a nontaxable rollover contribution under Subsection (b).

(d) A participant or beneficiary of a plan, annuity, account, or contract entitled to an exemption under Subsection (a), other than an individual retirement account or individual retirement annuity, is not prohibited from granting a valid and enforceable security interest in the participant's or beneficiary's right to the assets held in or to receive payments under the exempt plan, annuity, account, or contract to secure a loan to the participant or beneficiary from the exempt plan, annuity, account, or contract, and the right to the assets held in or to receive payments from the plan, annuity, account, or contract is subject to attachment, execution, and seizure for the satisfaction of the security interest or lien granted by the participant or beneficiary to secure the loan.

(e) If Subsection (a) is declared invalid or preempted by federal law, in whole or in part or in certain circumstances, as applied to a person who has not brought a proceeding under Title 11, United States Code, the subsection remains in effect, to the maximum extent permitted by law, as to any person who has filed that type of proceeding.

(f) A reference in this section to a specific provision of the Internal Revenue Code of 1986 includes a subsequent amendment of the substance of that provision.

History of Prop. Code §42.0021: Acts 1987, 70th Leg., ch. 376, §1, eff. Sept. 1, 1987. Amended by Acts 1989, 71st Leg., ch. 1122, §1, eff. Sept. 1, 1989; Acts 1995, 74th Leg., ch. 963, §1, eff. Aug. 28, 1995; Acts 1999, 76th Leg., ch. 106, §1, eff. Sept. 1, 1999; Acts 2005, 79th Leg., ch. 130, §§1, 2, eff. May 24, 2005; Acts 2011, 82nd Leg., ch. 933, §1, eff. June 17, 2011; Acts 2013, 83rd Leg., ch. 91, §2, eff. Sept. 1, 2013.

See also CPRC §31.002(f).

ANNOTATIONS

Jones v. American Airlines, Inc., 131 S.W.3d 261, 266 (Tex.App.—Fort Worth 2004, no pet.). "The legislature enacted §42.0021 in 1987 in response to federal decisions holding that the benefits of retirement plans held by debtors in bankruptcy proceedings were not protected from the claims of creditors in Texas. [¶] [S]ection 42.0021 'is designed to protect retirement benefits from the claims of creditors,' including judgment creditors. However, this protection is not without limits. While §42.0021 was enacted 'to protect the unwary debtor from having his [or her] retirement funds seized for payment of past debts,' it was not intended to

'become a safe-haven for sham retirement plans created to defraud creditors.' Thus, if a debtor places funds in a retirement plan in an attempt to defraud his or her creditors, those creditors 'can still exercise their rights [concerning those funds] regardless of the type of retirement plan or the amount of deductible or excess contribution involved.'"

Leibman v. Grand, 981 S.W.2d 426, 435-36 (Tex. App.—El Paso 1998, no pet.). Section 42.0021 "provides an exemption for the assets held in, and payments from, qualified retirement plans. It is undisputed that [debtor's] employee savings plan is a qualified plan. [T]he Plan … provides that the loan amount is actually debited against the participant's various subaccounts." Held: Loan proceeds from qualified plan are exempt.

PROP §42.0022. EXEMPTION FOR COLLEGE SAVINGS PLANS

(a) In addition to the exemption prescribed by Section 42.001, a person's right to the assets held in or to receive payments or benefits under any of the following is exempt from attachment, execution, and seizure for the satisfaction of debts:

(1) any fund or plan established under Subchapter F, Chapter 54, Education Code, including the person's interest in a prepaid tuition contract;

(2) any fund or plan established under Subchapter G, Chapter 54, Education Code, including the person's interest in a savings trust account; or

(3) any qualified tuition program of any state that meets the requirements of Section 529, Internal Revenue Code of 1986, as amended.

(b) If any portion of this section is held to be invalid or preempted by federal law in whole or in part or in certain circumstances, this section remains in effect in all other respects to the maximum extent permitted by law.

History of Prop. Code §42.0022: Acts 2003, 78th Leg., ch. 113, §1, eff. Sept. 1, 2003.

See also Educ. Code §§54.6001-54.644, 54.701-54.809.

PROP §42.003. DESIGNATION OF EXEMPT PROPERTY

(a) If the number or amount of a type of personal property owned by a debtor exceeds the exemption allowed by Section 42.002 and the debtor can be found in the county where the property is located, the officer making a levy on the property shall ask the debtor to designate the personal property to be levied on. If the debtor cannot be found in the county or the debtor fails to make a designation within a reasonable time after the officer's request, the officer shall make the designation.

(b) If the aggregate value of a debtor's personal property exceeds the amount exempt from seizure under Section 42.001(a), the debtor may designate the portion of the property to be levied on. If, after a court's request, the debtor fails to make a designation within a reasonable time or if for any reason a creditor contests that the property is exempt, the court shall make the designation.

History of Prop. Code §42.003: Acts 1983, 68th Leg., ch. 576, §1, eff. Jan. 1, 1984. Amended by Acts 1991, 72nd Leg., ch. 175, §1, eff. May 24, 1991. Source: TRCS 1879 art. 2367.

See also TRCP 637.

ANNOTATIONS

Keathley v. J.J. Inv. Co., No. 06-14-00036-CV (Tex. App.—Texarkana 2015, no pet.) (memo op.; 6-26-15). Judgment debtor "complains that the trial court erred because the levy on the funds did not follow the requirements of … §42.003…. [¶] [Judgment creditor] responds … that the officer was not required to notify [judgment debtor] since he was not found in the county, and that any irregularity related to failing to notify [judgment debtor] was not sufficient to set aside the levy. [¶] The failure of an officer to make any attempt to contact the debtor and give him or her an opportunity to designate property to be levied on is an irregularity. An irregularity, however, standing alone, will not invalidate an execution sale. … This rule supports the policy in this state to uphold execution sales, and not set them aside merely for irregularities in the sale."

PROP §42.004. TRANSFER OF NONEXEMPT PROPERTY

(a) If a person uses the property not exempt under this chapter to acquire, obtain an interest in, make improvement to, or pay an indebtedness on personal property which would be exempt under this chapter with the intent to defraud, delay, or hinder an interested person from obtaining that to which the interested person is or may be entitled, the property, interest, or improvement acquired is not exempt from seizure for the satisfaction of liabilities. If the property, interest, or improvement is acquired by discharging an encumbrance held by a third person, a person defrauded, delayed, or hindered is subrogated to the rights of the third person.

(b) A creditor may not assert a claim under this section more than two years after the transaction from which the claim arises. A person with a claim that is unliquidated or contingent at the time of the transaction may not assert a claim under this section more than one year after the claim is reduced to judgment.

(c) It is a defense to a claim under this section that the transfer was made in the ordinary course of business by the person making the transfer.

History of Prop. Code §42.004: Acts 1983, 68th Leg., ch. 576, §1, eff. Jan. 1, 1984. Amended by Acts 1991, 72nd Leg., ch. 175, §1, eff. May 24, 1991. Source: TRCS art. 3836(b)-(d).

PROP §42.005. CHILD SUPPORT LIENS

Sections 42.001, 42.002, and 42.0021 of this code do not apply to a child support lien established under Subchapter G, Chapter 157, Family Code.

History of Prop. Code §42.005: Acts 1991, 72nd Leg., 1st C.S., ch. 15, §4.07, eff. Sept. 1, 1991. Amended by Acts 1997, 75th Leg., ch. 165, §7.56, eff. Sept. 1, 1997.

See also Fam. Code §§157.311-157.331.

ANNOTATIONS

Dryden v. Dryden, 97 S.W.3d 863, 866 (Tex.App.—Corpus Christi 2003, pet. denied). "[T]he obligation to support one's child is not a debt, but a natural and legal duty. Moreover, the child support obligation does not become a debt merely because arrearages have been reduced to a judgment that is enforceable in the same way as a judgment for a debt. Thus, because [the] obligation for child support is not a debt, we conclude [Prop. Code] §42.005 ... does not violate [Tex. Const. art. 49, §16]."

CHAPTER 43. EXEMPT PUBLIC PROPERTY

PROP §43.001. EXEMPT PUBLIC LIBRARY

A public library is exempt from attachment, execution, and forced sale.

History of Prop. Code §43.001: Acts 1983, 68th Leg., ch. 576, §1, eff. Jan. 1, 1984. Source: TRCS art. 3838.

PROP §43.002. EXEMPT PROPERTY

The real property of the state, including the real property held in the name of state agencies and funds, and the real property of a political subdivision of the state are exempt from attachment, execution, and forced sale. A judgment lien or abstract of judgment may not be filed or perfected against the state, a unit of state government, or a political subdivision of the state on property owned by the state, a unit of state government, or a political subdivision of the state; any such judgment lien or abstract of judgment is void and unenforceable.

History of Prop. Code §43.002: Acts 1997, 75th Leg., ch. 159, §1, eff. May 20, 1997.

ANNOTATIONS

Texas S. Univ. v. Cape Conroe Prop. Owners Ass'n, 245 S.W.3d 626, 634 (Tex.App.—Beaumont 2008, no pet.). "Although [§43.002] invalidates a lien and voids a judgment, its terms do not divest the trial court of jurisdiction over the creditor's claims. While the State's property may be exempt from execution on a claim, the statute does not make the State immune from suit. [Section 43.002] does not create immunity from a takings claim even if it voids judgments imposing a remedy of foreclosing on State-owned property. [¶] We conclude that §43.002 ... is a defense to foreclosure, but does not divest the courts of jurisdiction to hear a takings claim."

CHAPTER 44. TAXATION OF RETIREMENT BENEFITS BY ANOTHER STATE

PROP §44.001. DEFINITION

In this chapter, "pension or other retirement plan" includes:

(1) an annuity, pension, or profit-sharing or stock bonus or similar plan established to provide retirement benefits for an officer or employee of a public or private employer or for a self-employed individual;

(2) an annuity, pension, or military retirement pay plan or other retirement plan administered by the United States; and

(3) an individual retirement account.

History of Prop. Code §44.001: Acts 1993, 73rd Leg., ch. 95, §1, eff. May 7, 1993.

PROP §44.002. PROPERTY EXEMPT

All property in this state is exempt from attachment, execution, and seizure for the satisfaction of a judgment or claim in favor of another state or political subdivision of another state for failure to pay that state's or that political subdivision's income tax on benefits received from a pension or other retirement plan.

History of Prop. Code §44.002: Acts 1993, 73rd Leg., ch. 95, §1, eff. May 7, 1993.

PROP §44.003. LIEN NOT CREATED

A claim or judgment in favor of another state or political subdivision of another state for failure to pay that state's or that political subdivision's income tax on ben-

efits received from a pension or other retirement plan may not be a lien on any property in this state owned by a resident of this state.

History of Prop. Code §44.003: Acts 1993, 73rd Leg., ch. 95, §1, eff. May 7, 1993.

Chapters 45-50 blank

SUBTITLE B. LIENS

CHAPTER 51. PROVISIONS GENERALLY APPLICABLE TO LIENS

PROP §51.0001. DEFINITIONS

In this chapter:

(1) "Book entry system" means a national book entry system for registering a beneficial interest in a security instrument that acts as a nominee for the grantee, beneficiary, owner, or holder of the security instrument and its successors and assigns.

(2) "Debtor's last known address" means:

(A) for a debt secured by the debtor's residence, the debtor's residence address unless the debtor provided the mortgage servicer a written change of address before the date the mortgage servicer mailed a notice required by Section 51.002; or

(B) for a debt other than a debt described by Paragraph (A), the debtor's last known address as shown by the records of the mortgage servicer of the security instrument unless the debtor provided the current mortgage servicer a written change of address before the date the mortgage servicer mailed a notice required by Section 51.002.

(3) "Mortgage servicer" means the last person to whom a mortgagor has been instructed by the current mortgagee to send payments for the debt secured by a security instrument. A mortgagee may be the mortgage servicer.

(4) "Mortgagee" means:

(A) the grantee, beneficiary, owner, or holder of a security instrument;

(B) a book entry system; or

(C) if the security interest has been assigned of record, the last person to whom the security interest has been assigned of record.

(5) "Mortgagor" means the grantor of a security instrument.

(6) "Security instrument" means a deed of trust, mortgage, or other contract lien on an interest in real property.

(7) "Substitute trustee" means a person appointed by the current mortgagee or mortgage servicer under the terms of the security instrument to exercise the power of sale.

(8) "Trustee" means a person or persons authorized to exercise the power of sale under the terms of a security instrument in accordance with Section 51.0074.

History of Prop. Code §51.0001: Acts 2003, 78th Leg., ch. 554, §1, eff. Jan. 1, 2004. Amended by Acts 2007, 80th Leg., ch. 903, §1, eff. June 15, 2007.

PROP §51.001. EFFECT ON OTHER LIENS

Except as provided by Chapter 59, this subtitle does not affect:

(1) the right to create a lien by special contract or agreement; or

(2) a lien that is not treated in this subtitle, including a lien arising under common law, in equity, or under another statute of this state.

History of Prop. Code §51.001: Acts 1983, 68th Leg., ch. 576, §1, eff. Jan. 1, 1984. Source: TRCS art. 5506.

PROP §51.0011. DEFAULT ARISING FROM DELINQUENT AD VALOREM TAXES: INSTALLMENT AGREEMENTS

(a) Notwithstanding any agreement to the contrary, a debtor is not in default under a deed of trust or

other contract lien on real property used as the debtor's residence for the delinquent payment of ad valorem taxes if:

(1) the debtor gave notice to the mortgage servicer of the intent to enter into an installment agreement with the taxing unit under Section 33.02, Tax Code, for the payment of the taxes at least 10 days before the date the debtor entered into the agreement; and

(2) the property is protected from seizure and sale and a suit may not be filed to collect a delinquent tax on the property as provided by Section 33.02(d), Tax Code.

(b) A mortgage servicer who receives a notice described by Subsection (a)(1) may pay the taxes subject to the installment agreement at any time.

(c) A mortgage servicer who receives a notice described by Subsection (a)(1) and gives the debtor notice that the mortgage servicer intends to accelerate the note securing the deed of trust or other contract lien as a result of the delinquency of the taxes that are subject to the installment agreement must rescind the notice if the debtor enters into the agreement not later than the 30th day after the date the debtor delivers the notice.

History of Prop. Code §51.0011: Acts 2013, 83rd Leg., ch. 935, §4, eff. Sept. 1, 2013.

A PROP §51.002. SALE OF REAL PROPERTY UNDER CONTRACT LIEN

(a) Except as provided by Subsection (a-1), a [A] sale of real property under a power of sale conferred by a deed of trust or other contract lien must be a public sale at auction held between 10 a.m. and 4 p.m. of the first Tuesday of a month. Except as provided by Subsection (h), the sale must take place at the county courthouse in the county in which the land is located, or if the property is located in more than one county, the sale may be made at the courthouse in any county in which the property is located. The commissioners court shall designate the area at the courthouse where the sales are to take place and shall record the designation in the real property records of the county. The sale must occur in the designated area. If no area is designated by the commissioners court, the notice of sale must designate the area where the sale covered by that notice is to take place, and the sale must occur in that area.

(a-1) If the first Tuesday of a month occurs on January 1 or July 4, a public sale under Subsection (a) must be held between 10 a.m. and 4 p.m. on the first Wednesday of the month.

(b) Except as provided by Subsection (b-1), notice of the sale, which must include a statement of the earliest time at which the sale will begin, must be given at least 21 days before the date of the sale by:

(1) posting at the courthouse door of each county in which the property is located a written notice designating the county in which the property will be sold;

(2) filing in the office of the county clerk of each county in which the property is located a copy of the notice posted under Subdivision (1); and

(3) serving written notice of the sale by certified mail on each debtor who, according to the records of the mortgage servicer of the debt, is obligated to pay the debt.

(b-1) If the courthouse or county clerk's office is closed because of inclement weather, natural disaster, or other act of God, a notice required to be posted at the courthouse under Subsection (b)(1) or filed with the county clerk under Subsection (b)(2) may be posted or filed, as appropriate, up to 48 hours after the courthouse or county clerk's office reopens for business, as applicable.

(c) The sale must begin at the time stated in the notice of sale or not later than three hours after that time.

(d) Notwithstanding any agreement to the contrary, the mortgage servicer of the debt shall serve a debtor in default under a deed of trust or other contract lien on real property used as the debtor's residence with written notice by certified mail stating that the debtor is in default under the deed of trust or other contract lien and giving the debtor at least 20 days to cure the default before notice of sale can be given under Subsection (b). The entire calendar day on which the notice required by this subsection is given, regardless of the time of day at which the notice is given, is included in computing the 20-day notice period required by this subsection, and the entire calendar day on which notice of sale is given under Subsection (b) is excluded in computing the 20-day notice period.

(e) Service of a notice under this section by certified mail is complete when the notice is deposited in the United States mail, postage prepaid and addressed to the debtor at the debtor's last known address. The affidavit of a person knowledgeable of the facts to the effect that service was completed is prima facie evidence of service.

(f) Each county clerk shall keep all notices filed under Subdivision (2) of Subsection (b) in a convenient file that is available to the public for examination during normal business hours. The clerk may dispose of the notices after the date of sale specified in the notice has passed. The clerk shall receive a fee of $2 for each notice filed.

(f-1) If a county maintains an Internet website, the county must post a notice of sale filed with the county clerk under Subsection (b)(2) on the website on a page that is publicly available for viewing without charge or registration.

(g) The entire calendar day on which the notice of sale is given, regardless of the time of day at which the notice is given, is included in computing the 21-day notice period required by Subsection (b), and the entire calendar day of the foreclosure sale is excluded.

(h) For the purposes of Subsection (a), the commissioners court of a county may designate an area other than an area at the county courthouse where public sales of real property under this section will take place that is in a public place within a reasonable proximity of the county courthouse as determined by the commissioners court and in a location as accessible to the public as the courthouse door. The commissioners court shall record that designation in the real property records of the county. A designation by a commissioners court under this section is not a ground for challenging or invalidating any sale. A sale must be held at an area designated under this subsection if the sale is held on or after the 90th day after the date the designation is recorded. The posting of the notice required by Subsection (b)(1) of a sale designated under this subsection to take place at an area other than an area of the courthouse remains at the courthouse door of the appropriate county.

(i) Notice served on a debtor under this section must state the name and address of the sender of the notice and contain, in addition to any other statements required under this section, a statement that is conspicuous, printed in boldface or underlined type, and substantially similar to the following: "Assert and protect your rights as a member of the armed forces of the United States. If you are or your spouse is serving on active military duty, including active military duty as a member of the Texas National Guard or the National Guard of another state or as a member of a reserve component of the armed forces of the United States, please send written notice of the active duty military service to the sender of this notice immediately."

History of Prop. Code §51.002: Acts 1983, 68th Leg., ch. 576, §1, eff. Jan. 1, 1984. Amended by Acts 1984, 68th Leg., 2nd C.S., ch. 18, §3(b), eff. Oct. 2, 1984; Acts 1987, 70th Leg., ch. 540, §1, eff. Jan. 1, 1988; Acts 1993, 73rd Leg., ch. 48, §5, eff. Sept. 1, 1993; Acts 2003, 78th Leg., ch. 554, §2, eff. Jan. 1, 2004; Acts 2005, 79th Leg., ch. 533, §1 (eff. June 17, 2005), ch. 555, §1 (eff. Sept. 1, 2005); Acts 2007, 80th Leg., ch. 903, §2, eff. June 15, 2007; Acts 2011, 82nd Leg., ch. 252, §2 (eff. Jan. 1, 2012), ch. 592, §1 (eff. Sept. 1, 2011); Acts 2013, 83rd Leg., ch. 52, §1 (eff. Sept. 1, 2013), ch. 161, §17.001 (eff. Sept. 1, 2013), ch. 642, §2 (eff. Oct. 1, 2013); H.B. 1128, §3, 85th Leg., eff. Sept. 1, 2017. Source: TRCS art. 3810.

See also Prop. Code §51.0025; TRCP 309, 735, 736; ***Real Estate Forms***, FORMS 4A:3-4A:13.

ANNOTATIONS

Generally

Mercer v. Bludworth, 715 S.W.2d 693, 697 (Tex. App.—Houston [1st Dist.] 1986, writ ref'd n.r.e.), *disapproved on other grounds*, ***Shumway v. Horizon Credit Corp.***, 801 S.W.2d 890 (Tex.1991). "It is fundamental that a judgment lien on the land of a debtor is subject to every equity that existed against the land at the time of judgment. [¶] It is undisputed that [purchaser] acquired his judgment lien when [creditor's] deed of trust lien of record was not barred by limitations. Therefore, [purchaser] is not a bona fide third person entitled to the presumption that the debt was paid and that the lien became void and ceased to exist. *At 698:* [Purchaser] acquired his interest with knowledge that his rights were subject to the rights of a senior lienholder, and therefore took title subject to the rights and the lien of [creditor]. [¶] [Creditor's successor] introduced deeds and deeds of trust into evidence which proved his chain of title out of ... the common source of title. [¶] We hold that, as a matter of law, [successor's] title is superior to that of [purchaser]."

Bateman v. Carter-Jones Drilling Co., 290 S.W.2d 366, 370 (Tex.App.—Texarkana 1956, writ ref'd n.r.e.). "It is the contention of [Ps] that [TRCS art. 3759, now Prop. Code §51.002(a),] provides for the sale of lands in a different county from that in which it is situated only in case the land is contiguous to the tract or tracts of land in the county in which the sale is held. [W]e do not believe that to be a proper construction. Surely the Legislature, when [it] made the provision for the sale of land where the greater portion thereof is situated and if in equal quantities the notice shall designate in which of said counties the sale is to be made, did not anticipate that land could be situated in a half-dozen or more counties and likely to be contiguous, one tract to the other, making a complete chain back to the county in which the sale was to be held." *See also* ***Segal v.***

Emmes Capital, L.L.C., 155 S.W.3d 267, 295 (Tex. App.—Houston [1st Dist.] 2004, pet. dism'd) (Legislature intended to adopt ***Bateman*** interpretation).

Foreclosure Sale

Holy Cross Ch. of God in Christ v. Wolf, 44 S.W.3d 562, 569 (Tex.2001). Property Code §51.002 "establishes the procedures for conducting a foreclosure sale. ... However, §51.002 has nothing to do with accrual or limitations; it only governs the procedures noteholders must follow *if* they choose to exercise their power of sale. Rather, [CPRC] §16.035 ... governs accrual, and it provides that a cause of action accrues and limitations begins to run from an installment note's maturity date."

Wells Fargo Bank v. Robinson, 391 S.W.3d 590, 594 (Tex.App.—Dallas 2012, no pet.). "For a party to recover damages for wrongful foreclosure and breach of the deed of trust, he must show that he has suffered a loss or material injury as the result of an irregularity in the foreclosure sale. In general, this is shown where the actions of the lender or note holder have caused the property to be sold for a grossly inadequate price. In such a case, the damages are measured by the difference between the market value of the land and the remaining balance on the outstanding mortgage debt. [¶] The recovery of damages is not appropriate, however, where title to the property has not passed to a third party and the borrower's possession of the property has not been materially disturbed. Where the note holder obtains title to the property at the foreclosure sale and the borrower retains possession, the proper remedy is to set aside the trustee's deed and to restore the borrower's title, subject to the note holder's right to establish the debt owed and foreclose its lien."

Brown v. EMC Mortg. Corp., 326 S.W.3d 648, 654 (Tex.App.—Dallas 2010, pet. denied). "Because nothing in [Prop. Code] ch. 51 conflicts with [TRCP] 309, we must assume that the legislature intended for judicial foreclosures to continue to be conducted by sheriffs or constables even after the enactment of ch. 51."

Myrad Props., Inc. v. LaSalle Bank Nat'l Ass'n, 252 S.W.3d 605, 615 (Tex.App.—Austin 2008), *rev'd on other grounds*, 300 S.W.3d 746 (Tex.2009). See annotation under *Notice*, p. 212.

Capital Reserve Corp. v. Day, No. 2-03-264-CV (Tex.App.—Fort Worth 2004, pet. denied) (memo op.; 12-2-04). Held: The statute of frauds applies to nonjudicial foreclosure-sale auctions.

Dykes v. Cendant Mortg. Corp., No. 04-02-00383-CV (Tex.App.—San Antonio 2003, no pet.) (memo op.; 4-30-03). "A non-judicial foreclosure transfers title from the debtor to another party, but it does not put the new owner in possession; it gives him a right to possession. If a debtor remains on the property, most deeds of trust treat him as a tenant by sufferance. [¶] To remove a tenant by sufferance, the new owner must file a forcible detainer suit."

Notice

Bauder v. Alegria, 480 S.W.3d 92, 97 (Tex.App.—Houston [14th Dist.] 2015, no pet.). Mortgagee "asserts that because [debtor's] residence was [address 1] at the time the deed of trust was executed, she was required to give him written notice of a change in address to make [address 2] her last known address under [Prop. Code] §51.002. The deed of trust is silent with respect to whether and how the debtor should provide notice of a change of address. [¶] For the purpose of sending notices under [§51.002(b) and (d)], the debtor's last known address is defined under [Prop. Code §51.0001(2)(A) or (B)]. If part (A) applied in the case under review, then [§51.002(b) and (d)] required the trustee to send the Notice to Cure and the Foreclosure Notice to [debtor's] residence address[, which was address 2]. [¶] [I]f part (B) ... applied, then the notices should have been sent to [debtor's] last known address as shown by [mortgage servicer's] records[, which was address 2]. *At 98:* [Thus, regardless] of whether Part (A) or Part (B) ... applied, [debtor] was not required to give written notice that her address had changed...."

Kaldis v. Aurora Loan Servs., 424 S.W.3d 729, 732 (Tex.App.—Houston [14th Dist.] 2014, no pet.). "[T]o have given proper notice of the foreclosure sale, [mortgage servicer] was required to have served written notice on [debtors] by certified mail on or before October 13, 2008. [Mortgage servicer] asserts that notice of foreclosure was properly served on [debtors] by employees of the law firm ... on October 13, 2008. *At 735-36:* Even presuming that [law firm's] customary mailing routine ... satisfied all the requirements of ... §51.002, there is no summary-judgment evidence showing that this mailing routine was actually carried out as to the foreclosure notices at issue. The business records of [law firm] contained in the summary-judgment evidence do not reflect or recite that either foreclosure notice was mailed on October 13, 2008 or on

any other date. In addition, [debtors] have testified that they did not receive these notices. ... Therefore, the trial court erred in granting summary judgment as to [debtors'] wrongful-foreclosure claims and related claims for declaratory relief."

Montenegro v. Ocwen Loan Servicing, LLC, 419 S.W.3d 561, 570 (Tex.App.—Amarillo 2013, pet. denied). "The only defect in the foreclosure proceeding that [P] claimed in his live pleading was that [D] failed to give him notice of default and an opportunity to cure under ... §51.002(d). ... The summary judgment evidence conclusively establishes that [P] did not use the subject property as his residence. Rather, the evidence established that [P's] mother, father, sister, and nephew lived in the subject property. As such, §51.002(d) did not require [D] to give written notice of default and opportunity to cure to [P]."

Montgomery v. Aurora Loan Servs., 375 S.W.3d 617, 620 (Tex.App.—Dallas 2012, pet. denied). "[P] contends that [§51.002(b)(2)'s] filing requirement is actually a recording requirement. [P] contends that the notice of foreclosure sale must be recorded in the deed records and because [D] did not record the notice of foreclosure sale, the sale is void. *At 621:* The plain language of §51.002(b)(2) requires a party to file the notice of sale with the county clerk in which the property is located. It does not require the notice of sale to be recorded in the permanent deed records. This construction of subsection (b)(2) is supported by subsection (f), which states that the county clerk must keep the notices filed under subsection (b)(2) 'in a convenient file that is available to the public for examination during normal business hours.' Subsection (f) also allows the clerk to 'dispose of the notices after the date of sale specified in the notice has passed.' Based on the statute's plain language, we conclude that the legislature did not intend subsection (b)(2) of §51.002 to require a party to record a notice of foreclosure sale in the permanent deed records of the county in which the property is located." *See also* ***Givens v. Midland Mortg. Co.***, 393 S.W.3d 876, 882 (Tex.App.—Dallas 2012, no pet.).

Myrad Props., Inc. v. LaSalle Bank Nat'l Ass'n, 252 S.W.3d 605, 615 (Tex.App.—Austin 2008), *rev'd on other grounds*, 300 S.W.3d 746 (Tex.2009). "'The statutory notice provisions of §51.002 seek to not only protect the debtor by affording him a lengthy notice period in which he may cure, but also adequately inform the third party public in order to maximize the likelihood of a profitable public sale at market value in which the debtor may recover his equity in his property.' [N]oncompliance with these requirements can render a foreclosure sale void. [¶] The notice of the foreclosure sale must provide a description or other identification of the property to be sold."

Stanley v. CitiFinancial Mortg. Co., 121 S.W.3d 811, 817-18 (Tex.App.—Beaumont 2003, pet. denied). Section 51.002(e) "requires constructive notice; there is no requirement of actual notice. ... The affidavit does not state facts pertaining to the statutory requirements, i.e., whether the debt holder's records contain the last-known address of the debtor, and whether such notice was deposited in the U.S. Mail, certified mail, return receipt requested. Non-compliance with these two requirements must be shown to establish lack of notice." *See also* ***WTFO, Inc. v. Braithwaite***, 899 S.W.2d 709, 719-20 (Tex.App.—Dallas 1995, no writ); ***Onwuteaka v. Cohen***, 846 S.W.2d 889, 892 (Tex.App.—Houston [1st Dist.] 1993, writ denied). *Compare* ***First Gibraltar Bank v. Farley***, 895 S.W.2d 425, 429-30 (Tex.App.—San Antonio 1995, writ denied) ("forwarding address expired" notice shows good-faith effort to comply), *and* ***Johnson v. First S. Props., Inc.***, 687 S.W.2d 399, 402 (Tex.App.—Houston [14th Dist.] 1985, writ ref'd n.r.e.) (notice was sufficient because it was proper in all respects except for wrong address), *with* ***Mitchell v. Texas Commerce Bank***, 680 S.W.2d 681, 682-83 (Tex.App.—Fort Worth 1984, writ ref'd n.r.e.) (harm even if actual notice received and present at sale).

Mills v. Haggard, 58 S.W.3d 164, 167 (Tex.App.—Waco 2001, no pet.). "[A] notice-of-foreclosure on real property used as the debtor's residence is useless to the creditor unless a proper notice-to-cure has been sent pursuant to §51.002(d). [¶] 'An execution sale will be set aside upon proof that it was made for a grossly inadequate price and was accompanied by irregularities which tended to contribute to the inadequacy of price.' [¶] [T]he failure to send a notice-to-cure to the address in the holder's file is an irregularity and defeats the effect of sending the notice-of-foreclosure. Further, the failure to send any notice-to-cure to [co-debtor] is another irregularity that would justify the trial court's judgment setting aside the foreclosure." *See also Her-*

rington v. Sandcastle Condo. Ass'n, 222 S.W.3d 99, 102 (Tex.App.—Houston [14th Dist.] 2006, no pet.); ***Powell v. Stacy***, 117 S.W.3d 70, 73 (Tex.App.—Fort Worth 2003, no pet.).

Bishop v. National Loan Investors, L.P., 915 S.W.2d 241, 245 (Tex.App.—Fort Worth 1995, writ denied). "Guarantors, as opposed to the maker, of a note secured by realty do not enjoy the right to notice of the foreclosure sale under the Property Code's notice provisions. This case ... does not involve the intermingled rights of guarantors and note makers nor a guarantor who signed the note and therefore partakes in the nature and rights of a note maker; therefore, [guarantor] was not entitled to notice of the sale." *See also* ***Long v. NCNB-Tex. Nat'l Bank***, 882 S.W.2d 861, 865-66 (Tex. App.—Corpus Christi 1994, no writ) (guarantors' rights are distinct from note maker's right to notice of foreclosure sale).

Newman v. Woodhaven Nat'l Bank, Inc., 762 S.W.2d 374, 375-76 (Tex.App.—Fort Worth 1988, no writ). "The crux of [P's] argument is that excluding the day of notice and the day of sale, 21 days must fall between the two days. [P's] contention is incorrect. [F]or purposes of computing the 21 day notice period, the depositing of the notice in the mail starts the calendar running." *See also* ***Parker v. Frost Nat'l Bank***, 852 S.W.2d 741, 743 (Tex.App.—Austin 1993, writ dism'd); ***Bryant v. Texas Am. Bank***, 795 S.W.2d 915, 916 (Tex. App.—Amarillo 1990, writ dism'd).

PROP §51.0021. NOTICE OF CHANGE OF ADDRESS REQUIRED

A debtor shall inform the mortgage servicer of the debt in a reasonable manner of any change of address of the debtor for purposes of providing notice to the debtor under Section 51.002.

History of Prop. Code §51.0021: Acts 2003, 78th Leg., ch. 554, §1, eff. Jan. 1, 2004.

ANNOTATIONS

Houston Omni USA Co. v. Southtrust Bank Corp., No. 01-07-00433-CV (Tex.App.—Houston [1st Dist.] 2009, no pet.) (memo op.; 4-30-09). "Because the purpose of the statute is to provide a minimum level of protection for the debtor, only constructive notice of foreclosure is required."

PROP §51.0022. REPEALED

Repealed by Acts 2013, 83rd Leg., ch. 389, §3, eff. June 14, 2013.

PROP §51.0025. ADMINISTRATION OF FORECLOSURE BY MORTGAGE SERVICER

A mortgage servicer may administer the foreclosure of property under Section 51.002 on behalf of a mortgagee if:

(1) the mortgage servicer and the mortgagee have entered into an agreement granting the current mortgage servicer authority to service the mortgage; and

(2) the notices required under Section 51.002(b) disclose that the mortgage servicer is representing the mortgagee under a servicing agreement with the mortgagee and the name of the mortgagee and:

(A) the address of the mortgagee; or

(B) the address of the mortgage servicer, if there is an agreement granting a mortgage servicer the authority to service the mortgage.

History of Prop. Code §51.0025: Acts 2003, 78th Leg., ch. 554, §1, eff. Jan. 1, 2004. Amended by Acts 2005, 79th Leg., ch. 555, §2, eff. Sept. 1, 2005.

ANNOTATIONS

Morlock, L.L.C. v. Nationstar Mortg., L.L.C., 447 S.W.3d 42, 47 (Tex.App.—Houston [14th Dist.] 2014, pet. denied). "[P] asserts that there is no evidence that [D] is the owner and holder of the Note and therefore [D] has no right to enforce the Deed of Trust [through non judicial foreclosure]. [¶] [P's] allegation that [D] is not the owner or holder of the Note is irrelevant with respect to [D's] right to enforce the Deed of Trust through non judicial foreclosure under Texas law. Non judicial foreclosure sales of real property under contract liens are governed by Ch. 51.... No provision in Ch. 51 ... requires a foreclosing party to prove its status as 'holder' or 'owner' of the Note or the original of the Note prior to foreclosure. [D] may enforce the Deed of Trust even if it is not the owner and holder of the Note or of the original of the Note. Based upon the assignment of the Deed of Trust from [third party], [D] is entitled to enforce the Deed of Trust, and because [D] is a mortgagee ..., [D] may conduct foreclosure proceedings under the Deed of Trust."

Givens v. Midland Mortg. Co., 393 S.W.3d 876, 880 (Tex.App.—Dallas 2012, no pet.). "[A]ttorneys were retained by [mortgage servicer] as foreclosure counsel 'to commence foreclosure proceedings to enforce [mortgagee's] lien against the Property secured by the Loan Agreement' and to provide [mortgage servicer] with legal representation in protecting its interests against those of [mortgagor]. *At 881:* We are unper-

suaded by [mortgagor's] argument that a genuine issue of material fact exists as to whether [mortgage servicer's attorneys were] serving as the substitute trustee in providing the notice of the foreclosure sale. The summary judgment evidence established [mortgage servicer's attorneys were] serving as legal counsel for the mortgage servicer ... in providing the foreclosure notice on behalf of the lender, [mortgagee]. We are, therefore, also unpersuaded by [mortgagor's] argument that if the trial court was correct in granting summary judgment in favor of [mortgage servicer's attorneys] on [mortgagor's] claims that [mortgage servicer's attorneys were] the substitute trustee, then summary judgment in favor of [mortgage servicer] and [mortgagee] was error because the notice of sale was not delivered by the lender or trustee as required by the Deed of Trust."

PROP §51.003. DEFICIENCY JUDGMENT

(a) If the price at which real property is sold at a foreclosure sale under Section 51.002 is less than the unpaid balance of the indebtedness secured by the real property, resulting in a deficiency, any action brought to recover the deficiency must be brought within two years of the foreclosure sale and is governed by this section.

(b) Any person against whom such a recovery is sought by motion may request that the court in which the action is pending determine the fair market value of the real property as of the date of the foreclosure sale. The fair market value shall be determined by the finder of fact after the introduction by the parties of competent evidence of the value. Competent evidence of value may include, but is not limited to, the following: (1) expert opinion testimony; (2) comparable sales; (3) anticipated marketing time and holding costs; (4) cost of sale; and (5) the necessity and amount of any discount to be applied to the future sales price or the cashflow generated by the property to arrive at a current fair market value.

(c) If the court determines that the fair market value is greater than the sale price of the real property at the foreclosure sale, the persons against whom recovery of the deficiency is sought are entitled to an offset against the deficiency in the amount by which the fair market value, less the amount of any claim, indebtedness, or obligation of any kind that is secured by a lien or encumbrance on the real property that was not extinguished by the foreclosure, exceeds the sale price. If no party requests the determination of fair market value or if such a request is made and no competent evidence of fair market value is introduced, the sale price at the foreclosure sale shall be used to compute the deficiency.

(d) Any money received by a lender from a private mortgage guaranty insurer shall be credited to the account of the borrower prior to the lender bringing an action at law for any deficiency owed by the borrower. Notwithstanding the foregoing, the credit required by this subsection shall not apply to the exercise by a private mortgage guaranty insurer of its subrogation rights against a borrower or other person liable for any deficiency.

History of Prop. Code §51.003: Acts 1991, 72nd Leg., ch. 12, §1, eff. Apr. 1, 1991.

ANNOTATIONS

PlainsCapital Bank v. Martin, 459 S.W.3d 550, 555-57 (Tex.2015). "[D] contends that even if §51.003 applies to its claim, the court of appeals erred because it equated 'fair market value' as that term is used in §51.003 with the historic measure of fair market value.... [¶] The Legislature used the phrase 'fair market value' in §51.003 without defining it, so we would ordinarily presume the common meaning of the term applies.... However, the statute enumerates categories of evidence and clearly specifies that they may be considered by trial courts in determining fair market value. [Section 51.003(b)(5)] is forward looking, allowing the trial court to consider the price for which the lender eventually sells the property and to apply a discount, if appropriate, to determine a value as of the foreclosure sale date. It may seem odd to make the price for which the property sold *after* foreclosure an integral component of competent evidence of the property's fair market value on the foreclosure sale date, but that is clearly what the Legislature intended. If it were not, then the relevant part of §51.003(b)(5) would be nonsensical because an unknown fair market value, which is the value being sought, cannot mathematically be determined by applying a discount to an unknown future sales price, nor could either a prospective buyer or the seller know what the future sales price will be in order to factor it into their decision to buy or sell, regardless of whether a discount factor is applied. [¶] Therefore, the enumerated factors in §51.003(b) will support a fair market value finding under the statute even though

that type of evidence might not otherwise be competent in the common or historical fair market value construct." *See also* ***Calhoun/Holiday Place, Inc. v. Wells Fargo Bank***, No. 01-14-00872-CV (Tex.App.—Houston [1st Dist.] 2016, pet. filed 5-2-17) (memo op.; 12-22-16) (applying holding in ***PlainsCapital*** retroactively).

Moayedi v. Interstate 35/Chisam Rd., L.P., 438 S.W.3d 1, 2 (Tex.2014). "This dispute asks whether a party waives the statutory right of offset under §51.003(c) ... by agreeing to a general waiver of defenses in a guaranty agreement. *At 6:* We agree with the court of appeals that the general waiver in ... the guaranty agreement waives the application of §51.003. *At 7:* Until now, this Court has not addressed the level of specificity required to waive §51.003. Most cases in which courts have concluded §51.003 was waived involved language with more specificity than the language at issue here. *At 8:* Just because the waiver is all encompassing does not mean that it is unclear or vague. To waive all possible defenses seems to very clearly indicate what defenses are included: all of them." *See also* ***Holmes v. Graham Mortg. Corp.***, 449 S.W.3d 257, 265 (Tex.App.—Dallas 2014, pet. denied).

Provident Nat'l Assur. Co. v. Stephens, 910 S.W.2d 926, 929 (Tex.1995). "An allocation based on fair market value ... need not be completed prior to a foreclosure sale. [T]he allocation need only be based on the fair market value of the properties at the time of the sale. [Section 51.003] authorize[s] the use of postforeclosure appraisals to determine the fair market value of property in deficiency actions."

LSREF2 Cobalt (TX), LLC v. 410 Ctr. LLC, 501 S.W.3d 626, 631 (Tex.App.—San Antonio 2016, pet. denied). "[Ds] do not dispute that they waived the fair market value offset under §51.003 in the note and the guaranty. The real controversy here involves the construction of the pre-negotiation agreement, which was executed after the note and the guaranty[, and whether] it has [any] effect on [Ds'] prior waivers of §51.003. *At 632:* Paragraphs 2 and 5 [of the pre-negotiation agreement] demonstrate the parties' intention to maintain the status quo under the [original] loan documents, not to alter it. When Paragraph 3 is construed as the trial court construed it—to modify [Ds'] waiver of the statutory offset in the loan documents and the guaranty—Paragraphs 2 and 5 are rendered meaningless. *At 634:* We conclude that the pre-negotiation agreement, when construed as a whole and in light of the surrounding circumstances, did not modify the note or the guaranty[, and it] had no effect on [Ds'] previous waivers...."

Silberstein v. Trustmark Nat'l Bank, ___ S.W.3d ___ n.14 (Tex.App.—Houston [14th Dist.] 2016, pet. denied) (No. 14-14-00660-CV; 1-7-16). "[D] urges that, because ... §51.003 'does not limit the type of evidence the [factfinder] can consider in determining fair market value, it is not clear whether evidence of bid amounts or foreclosure sale prices would not be competent evidence under the statute.' But §51.003 is designed to permit a party who has been non-judicially foreclosed upon to seek a fair market determination in an effort to offset any deficiency between the foreclosure sale price of the property and the unpaid balance of the indebtedness secured by the property. Thus, it strains credulity to posit that the legislature intended a foreclosure bid or foreclosure sale[] price to be competent evidence of fair market value under this statute."

Marhaba Partners v. Kindron Holdings, LLC, 457 S.W.3d 208, 214 (Tex.App.—Houston [14th Dist.] 2015, pet. denied). "[D] argues that §51.003(a) applies here because [P's] declaratory judgment is an 'action brought to recover the deficiency.' *At 215:* The Property Code does not define the term 'deficiency.' Section 51.003 does not explicitly address how courts should address deficiencies when multiple sources of collateral secure the same loan. The statute does not state whether the existence of a 'deficiency' within the meaning of §51.003 should be determined after each foreclosure sale or after all sales. Additionally, the statute does not state whether §51.003 applies to situations involving mixed collateral encompassing real estate and personal property. *At 216:* In cases involving multiple sources of collateral, personal liability may not be at issue; the lender may be able to collect through a series of non-judicial foreclosure sales. In cases where multiple pieces of collateral are foreclosed upon in a series of non-judicial proceedings, the foreclosure sale price for each piece of collateral—not the collateral's fair market value—is applied to the loan balance after each sale. [S]ection 51.003 does not apply to prevent the sales or to require the lender to offset the debt in the manner stated in §51.003 before proceeding with additional sales. [¶] The inapplicability of the fair market value offset mechanism in cases involving serial foreclosure on multiple sources of collateral suggests that a 'deficiency' under §51.003 should be calculated

(1) after all collateral has been sold; or (2) when the lender seeks to impose personal liability against the debtor through judicial action."

Bagwell v. Ridge at Alta Vista Invs. I, LLC, 440 S.W.3d 287, 291-92 (Tex.App.—Dallas 2014, pet. denied). "[T]he evidence required to support an accord and satisfaction affirmative defense is markedly different than that required for a §51.003 defense. Namely, accord and satisfaction does not require any evidence of fair market value of the property subject to the contract; in contrast, fair market value is essential to the §51.003 affirmative defense. Additionally, whether any agreement to discharge the debt has been reached is irrelevant to the §51.003 affirmative defense, but is central to the accord and satisfaction defense. [¶] We conclude [Ds'] pleading of accord and satisfaction did not provide fair notice of the affirmative defense of offset under §51.003…."

Sowell v. International Interests, LP, 416 S.W.3d 593, 600 (Tex.App.—Houston [14th Dist.] 2013, pet. denied). "[G]uarantors … may be sued for breach of their guaranty obligations within four years after the claim accrues[,] and … this limitations period may be extended to two years after the date of foreclosure if a deficiency remains after a nonjudicial foreclosure sale under [Prop. Code] §51.002."

Thomas v. Graham Mortg. Corp., 408 S.W.3d 581, 592 (Tex.App.—Austin 2013, pet. denied). "A request for an offset against a deficiency claim under §51.003 is an affirmative defense that must be pleaded. This pleading requirement, however, is met when the offset is requested by motion. [F]or an offset defense under §51.003 to be considered in response to a motion for summary judgment on a deficiency claim, the request must be on file at the time of the summary-judgment hearing."

Preston Reserve, L.L.C. v. Compass Bank, 373 S.W.3d 652, 659-61 (Tex.App.—Houston [14th Dist.] 2012, no pet.). "A property owner generally is qualified to testify about the value of his own property even if he is not an expert and would not be qualified to testify about the value of property owned by others. This rule is based on the presumption that an owner will be familiar with his own property and know its value. [¶] The Property Owner Rule applies to corporate entities; organizations are treated 'the same as natural persons for purposes of the Property Owner Rule, with certain restrictions on whose testimony can be considered as that of the property owner.' The 'Property Owner Rule is limited to those witnesses who are officers of the entity in managerial positions with duties related to the property, or employees of the entity with substantially equivalent positions and duties.' [¶] The supreme court's extension of the Property Owner Rule to entities does not dispense with the requirement that 'a witness must be personally familiar with the property and its fair market value.' Thus, an officer or employee who lacks personal knowledge of the property in question and its fair market value is not a proper source of valuation testimony regardless of his job title."

Trunkhill Capital, Inc. v. Jansma, 905 S.W.2d 464, 468 (Tex.App.—Waco 1995, writ denied). "From the date that §51.003(a) requires the two-year period to begin, *i.e.*, the date of foreclosure, a creditor possesses all facts that authorize him to seek a judicial remedy. The creditor's cause of action for any deficiency exists on the date of foreclosure. Because he possesses a cause of action at that time for the deficient amount, and the beginning of the running of the statute is tied to that date, the legislature could have only intended that the two-year period in §51.003(a) operate as a statute of limitations."

PROP §51.004. JUDICIAL FORECLOSURE—DEFICIENCY

(a) This section applies if:

(1) real property subject to a deed of trust or other contract lien is sold at a foreclosure sale under a court judgment foreclosing the lien and ordering the sale; and

(2) the price at which the real property is sold is less than the unpaid balance of the indebtedness secured by the real property, resulting in a deficiency.

(b) Any person obligated on the indebtedness, including a guarantor, may bring an action in the district court in the county in which the real property is located for a determination of the fair market value of the real property as of the date of the foreclosure sale. The suit must be brought not later than the 90th day after the date of the foreclosure sale unless the suit is brought by a guarantor who did not receive actual notice of the sale before the date of sale, in which case the suit must be brought by the guarantor not later than the 90th day after the date the guarantor received actual notice of the sale. The fair market value shall be determined by the finder of fact after the introduction by the parties of competent evidence of the value. Competent evidence of value may include:

(1) expert opinion testimony;

(2) comparable sales;

(3) anticipated marketing time and holding costs;

(4) cost of sale; and

(5) the necessity and amount of any discount to be applied to the future sales price or the cash flow generated by the property to arrive at a fair market value as of the date of the foreclosure sale.

(c) If the finder of fact determines that the fair market value is greater than the sale price of the real property at the foreclosure sale, the persons obligated on the indebtedness, including guarantors, are entitled to an offset against the deficiency in the amount by which the fair market value, less the amount of any claim, indebtedness, or obligation of any kind that is secured by a lien or encumbrance on the real property that was not extinguished by the foreclosure, exceeds the sale price. If no competent evidence of fair market value is introduced, the sale price at the foreclosure sale shall be used to compute the deficiency.

(d) Any money received by a lender from a private mortgage guaranty insurer shall be credited to the account of the borrower before the lender brings an action at law for any deficiency owed by the borrower. However, the credit required by this subsection does not apply to the exercise by a private mortgage guaranty insurer of its subrogation rights against a borrower or other person liable for any deficiency.

History of Prop. Code §51.004: Acts 1991, 72nd Leg., ch. 361, §1, eff. June 5, 1991.

PROP §51.005. JUDICIAL OR NONJUDICIAL FORECLOSURE AFTER JUDGMENT AGAINST GUARANTOR—DEFICIENCY

(a) This section applies if:

(1) the holder of a debt obtains a court judgment against a guarantor of the debt;

(2) real property subject to a deed of trust or other contract lien securing the guaranteed debt is sold at a foreclosure sale under Section 51.002 or under a court judgment foreclosing the lien and ordering the sale;

(3) the price at which the real property is sold is less than the unpaid balance of the indebtedness secured by the real property, resulting in a deficiency; and

(4) a motion or suit to determine the fair market value of the real property as of the date of the foreclosure sale has not been filed under Section 51.003 or 51.004.

(b) The guarantor may bring an action in the district court in the county in which the real property is located for a determination of the fair market value of the real property as of the date of the foreclosure sale. The suit must be brought not later than the 90th day after the date of the foreclosure sale or the date the guarantor receives actual notice of the foreclosure sale, whichever is later. The fair market value shall be determined by the finder of fact after the introduction by the parties of competent evidence of the value. Competent evidence of value may include:

(1) expert opinion testimony;

(2) comparable sales;

(3) anticipated marketing time and holding costs;

(4) cost of sale; and

(5) the necessity and amount of any discount to be applied to the future sales price or the cash flow generated by the property to arrive at a fair market value as of the date of the foreclosure sale.

(c) If the finder of fact determines that the fair market value is greater than the sale price of the real property at the foreclosure sale, the persons obligated on the indebtedness, including guarantors, are entitled to an offset against the deficiency in the amount by which the fair market value, less the amount of any claim, indebtedness, or obligation of any kind that is secured by a lien or encumbrance on the real property that was not extinguished by the foreclosure, exceeds the sale price. If no competent evidence of fair market value is introduced, the sale price at the foreclosure sale shall be used to compute the deficiency.

(d) Any money received by a lender from a private mortgage guaranty insurer shall be credited to the account of the borrower before the lender brings an action at law for any deficiency owed by the borrower. However, the credit required by this subsection does not apply to the exercise by a private mortgage guaranty insurer of its subrogation rights against a borrower or other person liable for any deficiency.

History of Prop. Code §51.005: Acts 1991, 72nd Leg., ch. 361, §1, eff. June 5, 1991.

ANNOTATIONS

U.S. Bank v. Kobernick, 402 S.W.3d 748, 753 (Tex. App.—Houston [1st Dist.] 2012, pet. dism'd). "The requirement for the application of [Prop. Code] §51.005 that is at issue here is the requirement that 'a motion or suit to determine the fair market value of the real property as of the date of the foreclosure sale has not

been filed under [Prop. Code] §51.003 or 51.004.' This requirement ... only prohibits bringing an action under §51.005 when a party in the other suit has filed 'a motion or suit to determine the fair market value of the real property' under §51.003 or 51.004. *At 754:* Regardless of whether the trial court's application of a credit for the foreclosure in the federal suit was applied under the authority of §51.003, it is undisputed that neither [Ds] nor any other party to the federal suit filed a motion or suit to determine the fair market value of the real property. In fact, the trial court in the federal suit repeatedly emphasized in its orders that the fair market value of the real property *was not* an issue in that suit. Because no party in the federal suit filed such a motion or suit, any other application of §51.003 to the federal suit is immaterial. Accordingly, we hold that [Ds] satisfied this requirement to bring suit under §51.005."

Segal v. Emmes Capital, L.L.C., 155 S.W.3d 267, 278 (Tex.App.—Houston [1st Dist.] 2004, pet. dism'd). "[S]ection 51.005(b)'s purpose is to prevent mortgagees from recovering more than their due at the guarantor's expense. That purpose does not necessarily translate into a policy so fundamental to Texas jurisprudence that it cannot be waived contractually."

Mays v. Bank One, 150 S.W.3d 897, 898 (Tex. App.—Dallas 2004, no pet.). Junior lienholder's "note matured and was not paid. [First lienholder's] note was also in default, and it proceeded with foreclosure of its first lien. The foreclosure satisfied only [first lienholder's] debt. No proceeds were left for [junior lienholder]. Accordingly, [junior lienholder] filed suit on the promissory note.... *At 900-01:* The language of §51.005(c) makes it clear that the calculation of a 'deficiency' includes only a lien or encumbrance on the real property 'that *was not extinguished* by the foreclosure.' It is without question that [junior lienholder's] debt, which was secured by a second lien to that of [first lienholder], remained wholly unsatisfied from the proceeds of the foreclosure sale conducted by [first lienholder]. By operation of law, [junior lienholder's] second lien was extinguished when [first lienholder] foreclosed on its senior lien. [¶] [Section] 51.005 is inapplicable to this claim brought by [junior lienholder] against [debtor]."

Bishop v. National Loan Investors, L.P., 915 S.W.2d 241, 245 (Tex.App.—Fort Worth 1995, writ denied). See annotation under Property Code §51.002, *Notice*, p. 213.

PROP §51.006. DEED-OF-TRUST FORECLOSURE AFTER DEED IN LIEU OF FORECLOSURE

(a) This section applies to a holder of a debt under a deed of trust who accepts from the debtor a deed conveying real property subject to the deed of trust in satisfaction of the debt.

(b) The holder of a debt may void a deed conveying real property in satisfaction of the debt before the fourth anniversary of the date the deed is executed and foreclosed under the original deed of trust if:

(1) the debtor fails to disclose to the holder of the debt a lien or other encumbrance on the property before executing the deed conveying the property to the holder of the debt in satisfaction of the debt; and

(2) the holder of the debt has no personal knowledge of the undisclosed lien or encumbrance on the property.

(c) A third party may conclusively rely upon the affidavit of the holder of a debt stating that the holder has voided the deed as provided in this section.

(d) If the holder elects to void a deed in lieu of foreclosure as provided in this section, the priority of its deed of trust shall not be affected or impaired by the execution of the deed in lieu of foreclosure.

(e) If a holder accepts a deed in lieu of foreclosure, the holder may foreclose its deed of trust as provided in said deed of trust without electing to void the deed. The priority of such deed of trust shall not be affected or impaired by the deed in lieu of foreclosure.

History of Prop. Code §51.006: Acts 1995, 74th Leg., ch. 1020, §1, eff. Aug. 28, 1995.

ANNOTATIONS

Joiner v. Pactiv Corp., No. 13-04-00580-CV (Tex. App.—Corpus Christi 2005, pet. denied) (memo op.; 8-11-05). "[P] asserted that its perfected judgment lien was superior to any subsequent lien, including any lien [D] claimed. As an additional ground, [P] asserted that [D's] §51.006 defense failed as a matter of law because [D] could not prove he had no personal knowledge of the judgment lien, an essential element of his statutory defense. ... Implicit in the trial court's grant of summary judgment is its rejection of [D's] §51.006 defense based on lack of personal knowledge and, thus, its rejection of [D's] contention that his lien was superior to [P's] judgment lien. We conclude that [P's] summary-judgment evidence negated an essential element of [D's] statutory defense. Thus, the trial court could have

properly granted summary judgment on the theory that [D] did not prove either absence of 'personal knowledge' or a lien superior to [P's] lien."

PROP §51.007. TRUSTEE UNDER DEED OF TRUST, CONTRACT LIEN OR SECURITY INSTRUMENT

(a) The trustee named in a suit or proceeding may plead in the answer that the trustee is not a necessary party by a verified denial stating the basis for the trustee's reasonable belief that the trustee was named as a party solely in the capacity as a trustee under a deed of trust, contract lien, or security instrument.

(b) Within 30 days after the filing of the trustee's verified denial, a verified response is due from all parties to the suit or proceeding setting forth all matters, whether in law or fact, that rebut the trustee's verified denial.

(c) If a party has no objection or fails to file a timely verified response to the trustee's verified denial, the trustee shall be dismissed from the suit or proceeding without prejudice.

(d) If a respondent files a timely verified response to the trustee's verified denial, the matter shall be set for hearing. The court shall dismiss the trustee from the suit or proceeding without prejudice if the court determines that the trustee is not a necessary party.

(e) A dismissal of the trustee pursuant to Subsections (c) and (d) shall not prejudice a party's right to seek injunctive relief to prevent the trustee from proceeding with a foreclosure sale.

(f) A trustee shall not be liable for any good faith error resulting from reliance on any information in law or fact provided by the mortgagor or mortgagee or their respective attorney, agent, or representative or other third party.

History of Prop. Code §51.007: Acts 1999, 76th Leg., ch. 1304, §1, eff. Sept. 1, 1999.

PROP §51.0074. DUTIES OF TRUSTEE

(a) One or more persons may be authorized to exercise the power of sale under a security instrument.

(b) A trustee may not be:

(1) assigned a duty under a security instrument other than to exercise the power of sale in accordance with the terms of the security instrument; or

(2) held to the obligations of a fiduciary of the mortgagor or mortgagee.

History of Prop. Code §51.0074: Acts 2007, 80th Leg., ch. 903, §3, eff. June 15, 2007.

PROP §51.0075. AUTHORITY OF TRUSTEE OR SUBSTITUTE TRUSTEE

(a) A trustee or substitute trustee may set reasonable conditions for conducting the public sale if the conditions are announced before bidding is opened for the first sale of the day held by the trustee or substitute trustee.

(b) A trustee or substitute trustee is not a debt collector.

(c) Notwithstanding any agreement to the contrary, a mortgagee may appoint or may authorize a mortgage servicer to appoint a substitute trustee or substitute trustees to succeed to all title, powers, and duties of the original trustee. A mortgagee or mortgage servicer may make an appointment or authorization under this subsection by power of attorney, corporate resolution, or other written instrument.

(d) A mortgage servicer may authorize an attorney to appoint a substitute trustee or substitute trustees on behalf of a mortgagee under Subsection (c).

(e) The name and a street address for a trustee or substitute trustees shall be disclosed on the notice required by Section 51.002(b).

(f) The purchase price in a sale held by a trustee or substitute trustee under this section is due and payable without delay on acceptance of the bid or within such reasonable time as may be agreed upon by the purchaser and the trustee or substitute trustee if the purchaser makes such request for additional time to deliver the purchase price. The trustee or substitute trustee shall disburse the proceeds of the sale as provided by law.

History of Prop. Code §51.0075: Acts 2003, 78th Leg., ch. 554, §1, eff. Jan. 1, 2004. Amended by Acts 2005, 79th Leg., ch. 1231, §1, eff. Sept. 1, 2005; Acts 2007, 80th Leg., ch. 903, §4, eff. June 15, 2007; Acts 2009, 81st Leg., ch. 323, §1, eff. Sept. 1, 2009.

PROP §51.0076. EFFECTIVE DATE OF APPOINTMENT

The appointment or authorization of a trustee or substitute trustee made in a notice of sale is effective as of the date of the notice if the notice:

(1) complies with Sections 51.002 and 51.0075(e);

(2) is signed by an attorney or agent of the mortgagee or mortgage servicer; and

(3) contains a statement in all capital letters, boldface type, to read as follows:

THIS INSTRUMENT APPOINTS THE SUBSTITUTE TRUSTEE(S) IDENTIFIED TO SELL THE PROPERTY

DESCRIBED IN THE SECURITY INSTRUMENT IDENTIFIED IN THIS NOTICE OF SALE THE PERSON SIGNING THIS NOTICE IS THE ATTORNEY OR AUTHORIZED AGENT OF THE MORTGAGEE OR MORTGAGE SERVICER.

History of Prop. Code §51.0076: Acts 2015, 84th Leg., ch. 653, §2, eff. Sept. 1, 2015.

See also *Real Estate Forms*, FORM 4A:7.

PROP §51.008. CERTAIN LIENS ON REAL PROPERTY

(a) A lien on real property created under this code or another law of this state in favor of a governmental entity must be recorded as provided by Chapters 11 and 12 in the real property records of the county in which the property or a portion of the property is located unless:

(1) the lien is imposed as a result of failure to pay:

(A) ad valorem taxes; or

(B) a penalty or interest owed in connection with those taxes; or

(2) the law establishing the lien expressly states that recording the lien is not required.

(b) Any notice of the lien required by law must contain a legal description of the property.

(c) This section does not apply to:

(1) a lien created under Section 89.083, Natural Resources Code;

(2) a state tax lien under Chapter 113, Tax Code; or

(3) a lien established under Chapter 61 or 213, Labor Code.

History of Prop. Code §51.008: Acts 2001, 77th Leg., ch. 827, §1, eff. Sept. 1, 2001.

PROP §51.009. FORECLOSED PROPERTY SOLD "AS IS"

A purchaser at a sale of real property under Section 51.002:

(1) acquires the foreclosed property "as is" without any expressed or implied warranties, except as to warranties of title, and at the purchaser's own risk; and

(2) is not a consumer.

History of Prop. Code §51.009: Acts 2003, 78th Leg., ch. 554, §1, eff. Jan. 1, 2004.

Sections 51.010-51.014 blank

PROP §51.015. SALE OF CERTAIN PROPERTY OWNED BY MEMBER OF THE MILITARY

(a) In this section:

(1) "Active duty military service" means:

(A) service as a member of the armed forces of the United States; and

(B) with respect to a member of the Texas National Guard or the National Guard of another state or a member of a reserve component of the armed forces of the United States, active duty under an order of the president of the United States.

(1-a) "Assessment" and "assessments" have the meanings assigned by Sections 82.113(a) and 209.002, as applicable.

(2) "Dwelling" means a residential structure or manufactured home that contains one to four family housing units.

(3) "Military servicemember" means:

(A) a member of the armed forces of the United States;

(B) a member of the Texas National Guard or the National Guard of another state serving on active duty under an order of the president of the United States; or

(C) a member of a reserve component of the armed forces of the United States who is on active duty under an order of the president of the United States.

(4) "Person" has the meaning assigned by Section 311.005, Government Code.

(b) This section applies only to an obligation:

(1) that is secured by a mortgage, deed of trust, or other contract lien, including a lien securing payment of an assessment or assessments, as applicable, on real property or personal property that is a dwelling owned by a military servicemember;

(2) that originates before the date on which the servicemember's active duty military service commences; and

(3) for which the servicemember is still obligated.

(c) In an action filed during a military servicemember's period of active duty military service or during the nine months after the date on which that service period concludes to foreclose a lien or otherwise enforce an obligation described by Subsection (b), the court may after a hearing and on the court's own motion, and shall on the application by a servicemember whose ability to comply with the obligations of the contract secured by the lien is materially affected by the servicemember's military service:

(1) stay the proceedings for a period of time as justice and equity require; or

(2) adjust the obligations of the contract secured by the lien to preserve the interests of all parties.

(d) A sale, foreclosure, or seizure of property under a mortgage, deed of trust, or other contract lien described by Subsection (b) may not be conducted during the military servicemember's period of active duty military service or during the nine months after the date on which that service period concludes unless the sale, foreclosure, or seizure is conducted under:

(1) a court order issued before the sale, foreclosure, or seizure; or

(2) an agreement that complies with Subsection (e).

(e) A military servicemember may waive the servicemember's rights under this section only as provided by this subsection. The waiver must be:

(1) in writing in at least 12-point type;

(2) executed as an instrument separate from the obligation to which the waiver applies; and

(3) made under a written agreement:

(A) executed during or after the servicemember's period of active duty military service; and

(B) specifying the legal instrument to which the waiver applies and, if the servicemember is not a party to the instrument, the servicemember concerned.

(f) A person commits an offense if the person knowingly makes or causes to be made a sale, foreclosure, or seizure of property that is prohibited by Subsection (d). An offense under this subsection is a Class A misdemeanor.

(g) On application to a court, a dependent of a military servicemember is entitled to the protections of this section if the dependent's ability to comply with an obligation that is secured by a mortgage, deed of trust, or other contract lien on real property or personal property that is a dwelling is materially affected by the servicemember's military service.

(h) A court that issues a stay or takes any other action under this section regarding the enforcement of an obligation that is subject to this section may grant a similar stay or take similar action with respect to a surety, guarantor, endorser, accommodation maker, comaker, or other person who is or may be primarily or secondarily subject to the obligation.

(i) If a judgment or decree is vacated or set aside wholly or partly under this section, the court may also set aside or vacate, as applicable, the judgment or decree with respect to a surety, guarantor, endorser, accommodation maker, comaker, or other person who is or may be primarily or secondarily subject to the obligation that is subject to the judgment or decree.

(j) This section does not prevent a waiver in writing by a surety, guarantor, endorser, accommodation maker, comaker, or other person, whether primarily or secondarily liable on an obligation, of the protections provided under Subsections (h) and (i). A waiver described by this subsection is effective only if it is executed as an instrument separate from the obligation with respect to which it applies. If a waiver under this subsection is executed by an individual who after the execution of the waiver enters active duty military service, or by a dependent of an individual who after the execution of the waiver enters active duty military service, the waiver is not valid after the beginning of the period of the active duty military service unless the waiver was executed by the individual or dependent during the applicable period described by 50 U.S.C. App. Section 516, as that section existed on January 1, 2009.

History of Prop. Code §51.015: Acts 2009, 81st Leg., ch. 992, §1, eff. June 19, 2009. Amended by Acts 2011, 82nd Leg., ch. 592, §§2, 3, eff. Sept. 1, 2011.

PROP §51.016. RESCISSION OF NONJUDICIAL FORECLOSURE SALES

(a) This section applies only to a nonjudicial foreclosure sale of residential real property conducted under Section 51.002. In this subsection, "residential real property" means:

(1) a single family home, duplex, triplex, or quadraplex; or

(2) a unit in a multiunit residential structure in which title to an individual unit is transferred to the owner of the unit under a condominium or cooperative system.

(b) Not later than the 15th calendar day after the date of a foreclosure sale, a mortgagee, trustee, or substitute trustee may rescind the sale under this section if:

(1) the statutory requirements for the sale were not satisfied;

(2) the default leading to the sale was cured before the sale;

(3) a receivership or dependent probate administration involving the property was pending at the time of sale;

(4) a condition specified in the conditions of sale prescribed by the trustee or substitute trustee before the sale and made available in writing to prospective bidders at the sale was not met;

(5) the mortgagee or mortgage servicer and the debtor agreed before the sale to cancel the sale based on an enforceable written agreement by the debtor to cure the default; or

(6) at the time of the sale, a court-ordered or automatic stay of the sale imposed in a bankruptcy case filed by a person with an interest in the property was in effect.

(c) On or before the 15th calendar day after the date of the sale, the party rescinding the sale shall:

(1) serve a written notice of rescission that describes the reason for the rescission and includes recording information for any affected trustee's or substitute trustee's deed that was recorded on:

(A) the purchaser, if the mortgagee is not the purchaser; and

(B) each debtor who, according to the records of the mortgage servicer of the debt, is obligated to pay the debt; and

(2) file each notice for recording in the real property records of the county in which all or a part of the property is located.

(d) A notice required by Subsection (c) must be served by certified mail. Service of the notice is complete when the notice is deposited in the United States mail, postage prepaid and addressed to the purchaser or debtor, as applicable, at the purchaser's or debtor's last known address, as applicable. The affidavit of a person knowledgeable of the facts to the effect that service was completed is prima facie evidence of service.

(e) Not later than the fifth calendar day after the date a foreclosure sale is rescinded under this section, the mortgagee shall return to the purchaser by certified mail, electronic or wire transfer, or courier service with delivery tracking the amount of the bid paid by the purchaser for the property at the sale. The debtor shall return to the trustee the amount of any excess proceeds received by the debtor from the sale. The return of the bid amount is considered made on the date:

(1) the bid amount is deposited postage prepaid in the United States mail or with the courier service addressed to the purchaser at the purchaser's last known address; or

(2) the electronic or wire transfer is ordered.

(f) The rescinding mortgagee, trustee, or substitute trustee shall cause to be filed for recording in the real property records of the county where the notice required under Subsection (c) was recorded an affidavit stating the date the bid amount was returned together with the certified mail, electronic or wire transfer, or courier service delivery tracking information.

(g) An affidavit executed and filed in accordance with Subsection (f) is prima facie evidence of the return of the bid amount and of the authority of the maker of the affidavit. A bona fide purchaser, lender, or other person acquiring an interest in the property or an insurer of title is entitled to rely conclusively on the record of the filed affidavit and notice, and any subsequent purchaser in good faith and for value is entitled to bona fide purchaser protection.

(h) The rescission of a foreclosure sale under this section restores the mortgagee and the debtor to their respective title, rights, and obligations under any instrument relating to the foreclosed property that existed immediately prior to the sale.

(i) A rescission of a foreclosure sale under this section is void as to a creditor or to a subsequent purchaser for a valuable consideration without notice unless notice of the rescission has been acknowledged, sworn to, or proved and filed for recording as required by law. A rescission of a foreclosure sale under this section evidenced by an unrecorded instrument is binding on a party to the instrument, on the party's heirs, and on a subsequent purchaser who does not pay a valuable consideration or who has notice of the instrument.

(j) No action challenging the effectiveness of a rescission under this section may be commenced unless the action is filed on or before the 30th calendar day after the date the notices of rescission required by Subsection (c) are filed for recording. A lis pendens notice based on the rescission not recorded within that period has no effect. This subsection does not affect the limitations period for an action claiming damages resulting from the rescission.

(k) If the foreclosure sale is rescinded under this section for a reason listed in Subsection (b), other than a stay described by Subsection (b)(6), the court in a civil action filed by the purchaser challenging the effectiveness of the rescission or claiming damages resulting from the rescission may only award as damages to the purchaser the amount of the bid paid for the property by the purchaser at the sale that has not been refunded to the purchaser, plus interest on that amount

at the rate of 10 percent per year. Notwithstanding any other law, the court may not order specific performance of the sale as a remedy for the purchaser. Interest awarded under this subsection ceases to accrue on the fourth day after the date the mortgagee deposits the amount of the damages awarded in the United States mail or with a courier for delivery to the purchaser.

(*l*) If a foreclosure sale is rescinded under this section for a reason provided by Subsection (b)(6), the court in a civil action filed by the purchaser challenging the effectiveness of the rescission or claiming damages resulting from the rescission may only award as damages to the purchaser the amount of the bid paid for the property by the purchaser at the sale that has not been refunded to the purchaser.

(m) Nothing in this section prohibits the rescission of a sale by agreement of the affected parties on other terms or a suit to rescind a sale not rescinded under this section.

History of Prop. Code §51.016: Acts 2015, 84th Leg., ch. 551, §1, eff. Sept. 1, 2015.

See also ***Real Estate Forms***, FORMS 4A:16, 4A:17.

CHAPTER 52. JUDGMENT LIEN

SUBCHAPTER A. GENERAL PROVISIONS

PROP §52.001. ESTABLISHMENT OF LIEN

Except as provided by Section 52.0011 or 52.0012, a first or subsequent abstract of judgment, when it is recorded and indexed in accordance with this chapter, if the judgment is not then dormant, constitutes a lien on and attaches to any real property of the defendant, other than real property exempt from seizure or forced sale under Chapter 41, the Texas Constitution, or any other law, that is located in the county in which the abstract is recorded and indexed, including real property acquired after such recording and indexing.

History of Prop. Code §52.001: Acts 1983, 68th Leg., ch. 576, §1, eff. Jan. 1, 1984. Amended by Acts 1989, 71st Leg., ch. 1178, §2, eff. Sept. 1, 1989; Acts 1993, 73rd Leg., ch. 48, §6, eff. Sept. 1, 1993; Acts 2007, 80th Leg., ch. 374, §1, eff. Sept. 1, 2007. Source: TRCS art. 5449.

See also CPRC ch. 35; TRCP 300-314, 592-693a.

ANNOTATIONS

Generally

Drake Interiors, L.L.C. v. Thomas, 433 S.W.3d 841, 852 (Tex.App.—Houston [14th Dist.] 2014, pet. denied). Generally, "'[a]n abstracted judgment creates a lien only on the property of the judgment debtor and does not extend to land owned by those who are not parties to the judgment. ...' [However, if] a judgment is obtained during marriage against [debtor-spouse] alone, his joint management community property becomes subject to execution, even though [nondebtor-spouse] owns a community interest. [Nondebtor-spouse] does not have to be joined in the lawsuit for the community property to be subject to [debtor-spouse's] liabilities." *See also* ***Stewart Title Co. v. Huddleston***, 598 S.W.2d 321, 322-23 (Tex.App.—San Antonio 1980), *writ ref'd n.r.e.*, 608 S.W.2d 611 (Tex.1980) (judgments taken against husband for community debts did not impose liability on wife because creditors obtained judgments after spouses divorced and wife was not party to suits).

Martin v. Cadle Co., 133 S.W.3d 897, 906 (Tex. App.—Dallas 2004, pet. denied). "[J]udgment liens of different dates attach simultaneously to property acquired after the liens were recorded. The judgment holders are entitled to a pro rata portion of the proceeds from the sale of the after-acquired property regardless of the order in which the liens were recorded."

Schumann v. Breedlove & Bensey, 983 S.W.2d 333, 334 (Tex.App.—Houston [1st Dist.] 1998, no pet.).

"A rendition of judgment, standing alone, does not create a judgment lien. That is done by recording the lien. … 'A money judgment, unsecured by any lien, is simply an adjudication, between plaintiff and defendant, that defendant owes plaintiff $X. Such a judgment plaintiff has no rank, superior or inferior, to other claimants. His only superior position is against his judgment debtor, against whom he has litigated. The law allows him to fix or establish liens by attachment or execution which require affirmative action by plaintiff….'"

Woodward v. Jaster, 933 S.W.2d 777, 781 (Tex. App.—Austin 1996, no writ). "[A]n abstract of judgment against a devisee attaches to the devisee's vested interest in real property during the administration of the estate. [¶] [W]hen an independent administrator sells property pursuant to his authority to satisfy his claims against the estate, the sale divests a beneficiary of her interests and thus extinguishes a lien on the property held by the beneficiary's creditor."

Adverse Possession

Walker v. Geer, 99 S.W.3d 244, 246-47 (Tex.App.—Eastland 2003, no pet.). "A suit to recover property from any person in peaceable adverse possession under title or color of title shall be instituted within three years of the accrual of the cause of action. A judgment lien will be barred when a purchaser of land from a judgment debtor shows that they have maintained possession under title or color of title for more than three years. … A judgment creditor will be charged with notice and the cause of action will accrue when the judgment creditor knew or, with the exercise of ordinary care, should have known about the sale of the property." *See also* ***Jones v. Harrison***, 773 S.W.2d 759, 760 (Tex.App.—San Antonio 1989, writ denied).

Equitable Title

Cadle Co. v. Harvey, 46 S.W.3d 282, 287 (Tex. App.—Fort Worth 2001, pet. denied). "It is well-settled that a purchaser under a contract of sale for real property acquires an equitable interest in the property. It is equally well-settled that in considering a creditor's judgment lien, the equitable rights of third persons will be protected against the legal lien, with the legal lien being limited to the actual interest that the judgment debtor has in the estate. A purchaser under an executory contract to convey real property who goes into possession of the property, obtaining all rights and obligations of ownership in the property, is vested with equitable title from the date of the contract, or in any event, from the date he takes possession. An equitable title is superior to legal title to the property and may be asserted as a complete defense against the lien of a debtor's judgment creditor." *See also* ***West Trinity Props., Ltd. v. Chase Manhattan Mortg. Corp.***, 92 S.W.3d 866, 869 (Tex.App.—Texarkana 2002, no pet.); ***Gaona v. Gonzales***, 997 S.W.2d 784, 787 (Tex.App.—Austin 1999, no pet.).

Execution Lien

Won v. Fernandez, 324 S.W.3d 833, 835 n.3 (Tex. App.—Houston [14th Dist.] 2010, no pet.). "A judgment lien and execution lien work together. If a judgment creditor obtains a judgment lien and then executes on the judgment, the date of the execution lien relates back to the date of the judgment lien, thereby giving the judgment creditor priority over other creditors with claims arising after the date of the judgment lien."

Homesteads

Inwood N. Homeowners' Ass'n v. Harris, 736 S.W.2d 632, 634 (Tex.1987). "As a general rule, a homestead is protected against all debts of those who live in that homestead. *At 635-36:* Homestead rights … may not be construed so as to avoid or destroy pre-existing rights. [¶] Because the restrictions were placed on the land before it became the homestead of the parties, and because the restrictions contain valid contractual liens which run with the land, the homeowners were subject to the liens in question and an order of foreclosure would have been proper. *At 641:* When a lien arises simultaneously in time to the impression of homestead character on the land, then the homestead character of the property is superior. Further, even when an abstract of judgment has been filed, recorded and indexed, the purchaser's intent, formed at the time the property was acquired, to use it as homestead, 'render[s] the property exempt from the judgment lien.' Even if a lien to pay assessments runs with the land, the *judgment* ordering foreclosure arises *after* the property has acquired homestead status. Thus, a *judgment lien* attaching after the property has been designated homestead is invalid." *See also* ***Tarrant Bank v. Miller***, 833 S.W.2d 666, 667-68 (Tex.App.—Eastland 1992, writ denied) (unenforceable lien can still cast cloud on title).

Hankins v. Harris, 500 S.W.3d 140, 144-45 (Tex. App.—Houston [1st Dist.] 2016, pet. denied). "When an abstract of judgment is recorded and indexed it constitutes a lien and attaches to any real property owned

by the defendant that is not exempt. Generally, a lien may not attach to property that is held as the debtor's homestead, because the Texas Constitution provides that homestead property is exempt from forced sale to pay debts, except for certain specified categories of debts. … The forced sale of a homestead property for a debt not specifically allowed by the Texas Constitution is void, and the purchaser receives no rights in the property. [¶] Once a property has been established as a homestead, the property remains exempt unless it ceases to be a homestead due to abandonment, alienation, or death. [¶] If a property is exempt because it is the debtor's homestead, a lien will attach only if the property interest loses its homestead character. A judgment debtor may sell a homestead 'and pass title free of any judgment lien, and the purchaser may assert that title against the judgment creditor.' If the lien attaches, the lienholder may acquire an interest no greater than that held by the judgment debtor." *See also* ***Fairfield Fin. Grp. v. Synnott***, 300 S.W.3d 316, 320 (Tex.App.—Austin 2009, no pet.).

Prior Unrecorded Deed

Hahn v. Love, 394 S.W.3d 14, 27 (Tex.App.—Houston [1st Dist.] 2012, pet. denied). "When the second [judgment] lien was created—on March 1, 2004—the Property had already passed out of [third party's] hands by virtue of the 2002 Deed. That second lien based on the revived judgment never attached to the Property. Therefore, the Property passed to [purchaser from third party] unencumbered by the first [judgment] lien against [third party], which had expired, or the second [judgment] lien, which only attached to real property owned by [third party], the judgment debtor, at the time the lien attached. *At 28:* A purchaser of property is not charged with notice of deeds involving the same property which are recorded outside of his chain of title. [¶] Thus, [purchaser] is not charged with notice of the 2004 Correction Deed, because it was recorded outside his chain of title. Furthermore, just as a party has no obligation to search for subsequent deeds from the original grantor of the property, a purchaser has no obligation to search for subsequent liens entered against the original grantor after the Property has been transferred."

Gibraltar Sav. Ass'n v. Martin, 784 S.W.2d 555, 558 (Tex.App.—Amarillo 1990, writ denied). "[T]he lien of a judgment creditor takes precedence over a prior unrecorded deed executed by the judgment debtor, unless the creditor has notice of the unrecorded deed at or before the time the lien was fixed on the land. The creditor has no duty to examine the records as to the title of his debtor, since the debtor's deed is void as to him, and he is not, therefore, charged with notice of unadjudicated equitable rights existing between the debtor and the grantee in the unrecorded deed. Possession of the premises may be sufficient to defeat the lien but such possession … 'must be open and visible and unequivocal, meaning that it must be openly, visibly and unequivocally that of the claimant under the unrecorded instrument.'"

PROP §52.0011. ESTABLISHMENT OF LIEN PENDING APPEAL OF JUDGMENT

(a) A first or subsequent abstract of a judgment rendered by a court against a defendant, when it is recorded and indexed under this chapter, does not constitute a lien on the real property of the defendant if:

(1) the defendant has posted security as provided by law or is excused by law from posting security; and

(2) the court finds that the creation of the lien would not substantially increase the degree to which a judgment creditor's recovery under the judgment would be secured when balanced against the costs to the defendant after the exhaustion of all appellate remedies. A certified copy of the finding of the court must be recorded in the real property records in each county in which the abstract of judgment or a certified copy of the judgment is filed in the abstract of judgment records.

(b) The court may withdraw its finding under Subsection (a)(2) at any time the court determines, from evidence presented to it, that the finding should be withdrawn. The lien exists on withdrawal of the finding and on the filing of a certified copy of the withdrawal of the finding of the court in the real property records in each county in which the abstract of judgment or a certified copy of the judgment is filed in the abstract of judgment records.

History of Prop. Code §52.0011: Acts 1989, 71st Leg., ch. 1178, §3, eff. Sept. 1, 1989.

See also CPRC §§52.001, 52.005, 52.006; TRAP 24; TRCP 634; ***O'Connor's Texas Appeals***, "Should appellant file appellate security?," ch. 4-B, §2.3, p. 176.

ANNOTATIONS

Transcontinental Rlty. Investors, Inc. v. Orix Capital Mkts. LLC, 470 S.W.3d 844, 846-47 (Tex. App.—Dallas 2015, no pet.). "Ordinarily, … we may entertain appeals only from final judgments or interlocu-

tory orders whose appeal is authorized by statute. [D] characterizes the trial court's order denying relief under §52.0011 … as an appealable, final post-judgment order. [¶] Post-judgment orders are appealable only if the appeal is statutorily authorized or if the trial court's order operates as a mandatory injunction resolving property rights and imposing obligations on the judgment debtor or third party to transfer property to the judgment creditor. For that reason, Texas courts have concluded that turnover orders … are final, appealable orders because they are analogous to mandatory injunctions requiring a judgment debtor to turn over property. An order under §52.0011 …, whether granted or denied, does not have similar effect. [¶] [A]n order under §52.0011 … is simply ancillary to the filing of an abstract of the trial court's judgment. [¶] [Thus, an] order under §52.0011 … is not a final, appealable post-judgment order."

Chrysler First Fin. Servs. v. Kimbrough, Carson & Woods, 801 S.W.2d 213, 214 (Tex.App.—Houston [1st Dist.] 1990, no writ). Section 52.0011 "authorizes 'a court' that renders judgment to make a finding when 'the court' determines the benefits a judgment lien provides a judgment creditor are outweighed by the costs to the judgment debtor. The plain language of the statute designates the court rendering judgment, not the appellate court, as the court empowered to make such a finding."

PROP §52.0012. RELEASE OF RECORD OF LIEN ON HOMESTEAD PROPERTY

(a) In this section:

(1) "Homestead" has the meaning assigned by Section 41.002.

(2) "Judgment debtor" and "judgment creditor" have the meanings assigned by Section 31.008(h), Civil Practice and Remedies Code.

(b) A judgment debtor may, at any time, file an affidavit in the real property records of the county in which the judgment debtor's homestead is located that substantially complies with Subsection (f).

(c) Subject to Subsection (d) and except as provided by Subsection (e), an affidavit filed under Subsection (b) serves as a release of record of a judgment lien established under this chapter.

(d) A bona fide purchaser or a mortgagee for value or a successor or assign of a bona fide purchaser or mortgagee for value may rely conclusively on an affidavit filed under Subsection (b) if included with the affidavit is evidence that:

(1) the judgment debtor sent a letter and a copy of the affidavit, without attachments and before execution of the affidavit, notifying the judgment creditor of the affidavit and the judgment debtor's intent to file the affidavit; and

(2) the letter and the affidavit were sent by registered or certified mail, return receipt requested, 30 or more days before the affidavit was filed to:

(A) the judgment creditor's last known address;

(B) the address appearing in the judgment creditor's pleadings in the action in which the judgment was rendered or another court record, if that address is different from the judgment creditor's last known address;

(C) the address of the judgment creditor's last known attorney as shown in those pleadings or another court record; and

(D) the address of the judgment creditor's last known attorney as shown in the records of the State Bar of Texas, if that address is different from the address of the attorney as shown in those pleadings or another court record.

(e) An affidavit filed under Subsection (b) does not serve as release of record of a judgment lien established under this chapter with respect to a purchaser or mortgagee of real property that acquires the purchaser's or mortgagee's interest from the judgment debtor after the judgment creditor files a contradicting affidavit in the real property records of the county in which the real property is located asserting that:

(1) the affidavit filed by the judgment debtor under Subsection (b) is untrue; or

(2) another reason exists as to why the judgment lien attaches to the judgment debtor's property.

(f) An affidavit filed under Subsection (b) must be in substantially the following form:

HOMESTEAD AFFIDAVIT AS RELEASE OF JUDGMENT LIEN

Before me, the undersigned authority, on this day personally appeared ____________ ("Affiant(s)") (insert name of one or more affiants) who, being first duly sworn, upon oath states:

(1) My/our name is/are ____________ (insert name of Affiant(s)). I/we own the following described land ("Land"):

(describe the property claimed as homestead)

(2) This affidavit is made for the purpose of effecting a release of that judgment lien recorded in __________ (refer to recording information of judgment lien) ("Judgment Lien") as to the Land.

(3) The Land includes as its purpose use for a home for Affiant(s) and is the homestead of Affiant(s), as homestead is defined in Section 41.002, Property Code. The Land does not exceed:

(A) 10 acres of land, if used for the purposes of an urban home or as both an urban home and a place to exercise a calling or business; or

(B) 200 acres for a family or 100 acres for a single, adult person not otherwise entitled to a homestead, if used for the purposes of a rural home.

(4) Attached to this affidavit is evidence that:

(A) Affiant(s) sent a letter and a copy of this affidavit, without attachments and before execution of the affidavit, notifying the judgment creditor in the Judgment Lien of this affidavit and the Affiant(s)' intent to file for record this affidavit; and

(B) the letter and this affidavit were sent by registered or certified mail, return receipt requested, 30 or more days before this affidavit was filed to:

(i) the judgment creditor's last known address;

(ii) the address appearing in the judgment creditor's pleadings in the action in which the judgment was rendered or another court record, if that address is different from the judgment creditor's last known address;

(iii) the address of the judgment creditor's last known attorney as shown in those pleadings or another court record; and

(iv) the address of the judgment creditor's last known attorney as shown in the records of the State Bar of Texas, if that address is different from the address of the attorney as shown in those pleadings or another court record.

(5) This affidavit serves as a release of the Judgment Lien as to the Land in accordance with Section 52.0012, Property Code.

Signed on this _____ day of __________, _____.

____

____

(Signature of Affiant(s))

State of __________

County of __________

SWORN TO AND SUBSCRIBED before me on the __________ day of __________, 20___.

My commission expires:

____

____

Notary Public, State of Texas

Notary's printed name:

____

History of Prop. Code §52.0012: Acts 2007, 80th Leg., ch. 374, §2, eff. Sept. 1, 2007.

See also *O'Connor's Family Forms*, FORM 16F:4.

PROP §52.002. ISSUANCE OF ABSTRACT

(a) On application of a person in whose favor a judgment is rendered or on application of that person's agent, attorney, or assignee, the judge or justice of the peace who rendered the judgment or the clerk of the court in which the judgment is rendered shall prepare, certify, and deliver to the applicant an abstract of the judgment. The applicant for the abstract must pay the fee authorized by law for providing the abstract.

(b) The attorney of a person in whose favor a judgment is rendered in a small claims court[1] or a justice court or a person in whose favor a judgment is rendered in a court other than a small claims court[1] or a justice court or that person's agent, attorney, or assignee may prepare the abstract of judgment. An abstract of judgment prepared under this subsection must be verified by the person preparing the abstract.

1. **Editor's note:** Effective August 31, 2013, the Texas Legislature abolished small-claims courts by repealing Gov't Code ch. 28. *See* Acts 2013, 83rd Leg., R.S., ch. 2, §2, eff. Apr. 10, 2013; Acts 2011, 82nd Leg., 1st C.S., ch. 3, §§5.06, 5.09, eff. May 1, 2013. Now small-claims proceedings must be conducted by justice courts. Gov't Code §27.060(a); *see* TRCP 500.3(a).

History of Prop. Code §52.002: Acts 1983, 68th Leg., ch. 576, §1, eff. Jan. 1, 1984. Amended by Acts 1987, 70th Leg., ch. 663, §2, eff. Sept. 1, 1987; Acts 1999, 76th Leg., ch. 176, §1, eff. Sept. 1, 1999; Acts 2001, 77th Leg., ch. 668, §2, eff. Sept. 1, 2001. Source: TRCS art. 5447.

ANNOTATIONS

Askey v. Power, 36 S.W.2d 446, 447 (Tex.Comm'n App.1931) (holding approved). "The right to a judgment lien is purely statutory, and the statute must be substantially complied with before the lien will attach." *See also* ***McGlothlin v. Coody***, 59 S.W.2d 819, 821 (Tex. Comm'n App.1933) (holding approved).

Rogers v. Peeler, 271 S.W.3d 372, 375 (Tex.App.—Texarkana 2008, pet. denied) (memo op.). "'The judgment creditor's first step in creating a judicial lien is to obtain an abstract of the judgment.' When properly recorded and indexed, an abstract of judgment creates a judgment lien on nonexempt real property that is superior to the rights of subsequent purchasers and lien-

holders. The purpose of an abstract of judgment is to create a lien against the judgment debtor's real property and to provide notice to subsequent purchasers and encumbrancers of the existence of the judgment and lien." *See also* ***Wilson v. Dvorak***, 228 S.W.3d 228, 233 (Tex.App.—San Antonio 2007, pet. denied); ***Citicorp Real Estate, Inc. v. Banque Arabe Internationale D'Investissement***, 747 S.W.2d 926, 929 (Tex. App.—Dallas 1988, writ denied).

PROP §52.003. CONTENTS OF ABSTRACT

(a) An abstract of a judgment must show:

(1) the names of the plaintiff and defendant;

(2) the birthdate of the defendant, if available to the clerk or justice;

(3) the last three numbers of the driver's license of the defendant, if available;

(4) the last three numbers of the social security number of the defendant, if available;

(5) the number of the suit in which the judgment was rendered;

(6) the defendant's address, or if the address is not shown in the suit, the nature of citation and the date and place of service of citation;

(7) the date on which the judgment was rendered;

(8) the amount for which the judgment was rendered and the balance due;

(9) the amount of the balance due, if any, for child support arrearage; and

(10) the rate of interest specified in the judgment.

(b) An abstract of a judgment may show a mailing address for each plaintiff or judgment creditor.

History of Prop. Code §52.003: Acts 1983, 68th Leg., ch. 576, §1, eff. Jan. 1, 1984. Amended by Acts 1991, 72nd Leg., 1st C.S., ch. 15, §4.08, eff. Sept. 1, 1991; Acts 1993, 73rd Leg., ch. 134, §2, eff. May 12, 1993; Acts 2007, 80th Leg., ch. 143, §2, eff. Sept. 1, 2007. Source: TRCS art. 5447.

ANNOTATIONS

Austin v. Coface Seguro de Credito Mexico, S.A. de C.V., 506 S.W.3d 707, 712 (Tex.App.—Houston [1st Dist.] 2016, pet. filed 1-26-17). "[T]o create an enforceable lien, a judgment creditor must abstract the judgment and comply with Ch. 52's requirements. Substantial compliance is mandatory before the judgment creditor's lien will encumber any real property in Texas. An abstract with a minor deficiency as to one element, however, may substantially comply with the statute, so long as a statutorily required element is not omitted altogether. It is the judgment creditor's responsibility to ensure that the county clerk properly abstracts the judgment. *At 713:* [Creditor's] abstract complies with Ch. 52's name requirement by listing the full name of the judgment debtor.... [Purchaser] points to no deficiency in the abstract itself, but rather challenges [creditor's] failure to alternatively list [debtor's] name without the maternal surname; such a listing, [purchaser] argues, is essential to perfecting the lien against the [real property] because the warranty deed lists only [debtor's] paternal surname. [¶] We need not decide ... whether an abstract of judgment must alternatively individually list the paternal surname without the maternal surname to effectively index the judgment because the abstract does not stand alone in identifying [debtor] in the chain of title. [¶] We hold that [purchaser] and her title insurer had constructive knowledge of [debtor's] full name because it is contained both in the abstract of judgment and in the chain of title for the property as indexed under either surname."

Olivares v. Birdie L. Nix Trust, 126 S.W.3d 242, 249 (Tex.App.—San Antonio 2003, pet. denied). "An abstract should be treated no differently where a defendant's address is not readily ascertainable from the underlying suit. Under such circumstances, citation information is sufficient to provide the requisite notice to third parties, thereby fulfilling the abstract's purpose in providing notice. [¶] A creditor should not be left to decipher which address or how many addresses to include in the abstract of judgment, but should simply ensure that proper service is carried out and that the citation is sufficient to provide notice. Therefore, where the defendant's *definitive* address is not shown in the suit, the nature of citation and the date and place of service of citation provide substantial compliance with §52.003." *See also* ***Texas Am. Bank v. Southern Un. Expl. Co.***, 714 S.W.2d 105, 107 (Tex.App.—Eastland 1986, writ ref'd n.r.e.).

Hoffman, McBryde & Co. v. Heyland, 74 S.W.3d 906, 907 (Tex.App.—Dallas 2002, pet. denied). "[A]n otherwise properly issued, recorded, and indexed abstract of judgment that correctly reflects the balance due when it was issued creates a judgment lien under Texas law, even if the abstract does not reflect credits toward the satisfaction of the judgment arising after the abstract was issued and before it was filed." *See also* ***Rogers v. Peeler***, 271 S.W.3d 372, 378-79 (Tex. App.—Texarkana 2008, pet. denied) (memo op.).

Allied First Nat'l Bank v. Jones, 766 S.W.2d 800, 803 (Tex.App.—Dallas 1988, no writ). "[W]e conclude that if a counterplaintiff wants to obtain a judgment lien in the event he is successful, he must take the preliminary steps necessary to comply with the statutes governing the creation of a judgment lien. Thus, it is a counterplaintiff's responsibility to include the counterdefendant's address in his counterclaim if it does not already appear in the suit or, in the alternative, to serve the counterdefendant with citation so that the person preparing the abstract can comply with §52.003(4)." *See also* ***Houston Inv. Bankers Corp. v. First City Bank***, 640 S.W.2d 660, 662 (Tex.App.—Houston [14th Dist.] 1982, no writ) (clerk's abbreviation of city in D's name considered substantial compliance).

Reynolds v. Kessler, 669 S.W.2d 801, 806 (Tex. App.—El Paso 1984, no writ). "When the abstract is so improperly recorded and indexed that it creates no lien, even actual notice of the defective record cannot take the place of a proper record as to the purchaser of the land."

Chamlee v. Chamlee, 113 S.W.2d 290, 291 (Tex. App.—Waco 1938, no writ). "Any presumption of regularity will not be sufficient to dispense with affirmative proof of ... compliance [with §52.003]." *But see* ***Texas Bldg. & Mortg. Co. v. Morris***, 123 S.W.2d 365, 370 (Tex.App.—Beaumont 1938, writ dism'd) (presumption of clerk's seal enough for compliance with required proof).

PROP §52.004. RECORDING & INDEXING OF ABSTRACT

(a) The county clerk shall immediately record in the county real property records each properly authenticated abstract of judgment that is presented for recording. The clerk shall note in the records the date and hour an abstract of judgment is received.

(b) At the same time an abstract is recorded, the county clerk shall enter the abstract on the alphabetical index to the real property records, showing:

(1) the name of each plaintiff in the judgment;

(2) the name of each defendant in the judgment; and

(3) the volume and page or instrument number in the records in which the abstract is recorded.

History of Prop. Code §52.004: Acts 1983, 68th Leg., ch. 576, §1, eff. Jan. 1, 1984. Amended by Acts 2001, 77th Leg., ch. 668, §2, eff. Sept. 1, 2001. Source: TRCS art. 5448.

ANNOTATIONS

Austin v. Coface Seguro de Credito Mexico, S.A. de C.V., 506 S.W.3d 707, 712 (Tex.App.—Houston [1st Dist.] 2016, pet. filed 1-26-17). See annotation under Property Code §52.003, p. 228.

Murray v. Cadle Co., 257 S.W.3d 291, 296-97 (Tex. App.—Dallas 2008, pet. denied). "The purpose of the index is to provide notice to subsequent purchasers of the existence of the judgment and to indicate the source from which the full information about the judgment may be obtained. [¶] [Purchasers] argue that [§52.004] requires the abstract of judgment to be indexed by plaintiff and defendant and that [clerk's] affidavit establishes as a matter of law that the abstract of judgment was not properly recorded and indexed because it was indexed by grantor and grantee. [Purchasers] do not cite any authority to support their argument that the property code requires indexing by plaintiff and defendant. It requires *indexing* by 'the name of each plaintiff' and 'the name of each defendant.' But the language of [§52.004] does not mandate, or prohibit, particular headings for the alphabetical index to the real property records." *See also* ***Gordon v. West Houston Trees, Ltd.***, 352 S.W.3d 32, 41 (Tex.App.—Houston [1st Dist.] 2011, no pet.) (typographical error in cause number does not affect abstract of judgment's ability to put subsequent purchasers on notice); ***Womack v. Paris Grocer Co.***, 166 S.W.2d 366, 368-69 (Tex.App.—Galveston 1942), *writ ref'd*, 168 S.W.2d 645 (Tex.1943) (index is designed merely to indicate source from which full information may be obtained).

Wilson v. Dvorak, 228 S.W.3d 228, 233 (Tex. App.—San Antonio 2007, pet. denied). "'It is well settled in Texas that it is the judgment creditor's responsibility to ensure that the clerk abstracts the judgment properly.' [¶] When properly recorded and indexed, an abstract of judgment creates a judgment lien that is superior to the rights of subsequent purchasers and lien holders."

Gensheimer v. Kneisley, 778 S.W.2d 138, 140 (Tex. App.—Texarkana 1989, no writ). Section 52.004(b)(2) "provides that an abstract of judgment must be recorded and indexed alphabetically showing the name of each defendant in the *judgment*. No requirement exists that an abstract show the names of the parties to the suit or the names of the defendants in the suit; the only requirement is that the defendants against whom a judgment was taken be listed. Although [third party's

wife] was named as a party, the judgment was taken only against [third party]. The abstract of the judgment shows the name of the party against whom the judgment was taken—[third party]—as required by §52.004(b)(2)." *See also* ***Sarny Holdings, Ltd. v. Letsos***, 896 S.W.2d 274, 275-76 (Tex.App.—Houston [1st Dist.] 1995, writ denied).

PROP §52.0041. ADDRESS REQUIREMENT FOR RECORDING ABSTRACT

(a) A judgment abstracted after September 1, 1993, may not be recorded unless:

(1) a mailing address for each plaintiff or judgment creditor appears on the abstract of judgment; or

(2) a penalty filing fee equal to the greater of $25 or twice the statutory recording fee for the abstract is paid.

(b) The validity of an abstracted judgment as between the parties is not affected by a failure to include an address for each plaintiff or judgment creditor in the abstracted judgment.

(c) Payment of a filing fee and acceptance of the abstract of judgment by a county clerk for recording creates a conclusive presumption that the requirements of this section have been met.

History of Prop. Code §52.0041: Acts 1993, 73rd Leg., ch. 134, §1, eff. May 12, 1993.

PROP §52.005. SATISFACTION OF JUDGMENT

Satisfaction of a judgment in whole or in part may be shown by recordation of:

(1) a return on an execution issued on the judgment, or a copy of the return, certified by the officer making the return and showing:

(A) the names of the parties to the judgment;

(B) the number and style of the suit;

(C) the court in which the judgment was rendered;

(D) the date and amount of the judgment; and

(E) the dates of issuance and return of the execution; or

(2) a receipt, acknowledgement, or release that is signed by the party entitled to receive payment of the judgment or by that person's agent or attorney of record and that is acknowledged or proven for record in the manner required for deeds.

History of Prop. Code §52.005: Acts 1983, 68th Leg., ch. 576, §1, eff. Jan. 1, 1984. Amended by Acts 2001, 77th Leg., ch. 668, §2, eff. Sept. 1, 2001. Source: TRCS art. 5450.

See also *Real Estate Forms*, FORMS 11:1, 11:2.

ANNOTATIONS

Rushing v. Thomas, 63 S.W.2d 323, 324 (Tex. App.—Amarillo 1933, no writ). "[A] clerk has no authority to collect or receive money due upon a judgment, and payment to the clerk in the absence of such authority is not a satisfaction unless he was the agent of the judgment creditor."

PROP §52.006. DURATION OF LIEN

(a) Except as provided by Subsection (b), a judgment lien continues for 10 years following the date of recording and indexing the abstract, except that if the judgment becomes dormant during that period the lien ceases to exist.

(b) Notwithstanding Section 34.001, Civil Practice and Remedies Code, a judgment in favor of the state or a state agency, as that term is defined by Section 403.055, Government Code, does not become dormant. A properly filed abstract of the judgment continues to constitute a lien under Section 52.001 until the earlier of the 20th anniversary of the date the abstract is recorded and indexed or the date the judgment is satisfied or the lien is released. The judgment lien may be renewed for one additional 20-year period by filing, before the expiration of the initial 20-year period, a renewed abstract of judgment in the same manner as the original abstract of judgment is filed. The renewed judgment lien relates back to the date the original abstract of judgment was filed.

History of Prop. Code §52.006: Acts 1983, 68th Leg., ch. 576, §1, eff. Jan. 1, 1984. Amended by Acts 2007, 80th Leg., ch. 11, §1, eff. Apr. 23, 2007. Source: TRCS art. 5449.

ANNOTATIONS

Burton Lingo Co. v. Warren, 45 S.W.2d 750, 752 (Tex.App.—Eastland 1931, writ ref'd). "There can be no doubt ... that as to the particular lien which comes into existence by the recording and indexing of an abstract of judgment, that lien, when once it terminates by the expiration of the ten-year period, can never be extended. ... 'The mere judgment does not of itself operate as a lien.' If it did, there being one judgment, there could be but one lien. But nothing is more certain than that under some conditions there may be more than one lien authorized by the present statutes. Clearly the law contemplates that abstracts of a judgment may be recorded in different counties. If such abstracts be recorded in a number of different counties, each is an independent lien. When filed, recorded, and indexed at

different times, as they naturally would be, the term of the duration of the liens created thereby are different. This could not be true if there was only one lien. So it is thus seen that one or more liens may exist to secure the same judgment. The question arises: Why may they not exist in the same county? There is certainly no express restriction of the right to a single lien in any one county. If, therefore, any such restriction exists, it must arise from implication. [N]o such restriction is to be implied."

PROP §52.007. FEDERAL COURT JUDGMENT

An abstract of a judgment rendered in this state by a federal court may be recorded and indexed under this chapter on the certificate of the clerk of the court.

History of Prop. Code §52.007: Acts 1983, 68th Leg., ch. 576, §1, eff. Jan. 1, 1984. Source: TRCS art. 5451.

ANNOTATIONS

Tanner v. McCarthy, 274 S.W.3d 311, 319 (Tex. App.—Houston [1st Dist.] 2008, no pet.). "There is no language in §52.007 that can be read as establishing it as the exclusive means under state law for enforcing a judgment issued from a federal court 'situated' in Texas. *At 320:* [T]he availability under Texas law of one specific means of enforcement of judgments issued in Texas by a federal court—under ... §52.007—does not override the clear intent of the Texas Legislature to provide a more comprehensive remedy under the [Uniform Enforcement of Foreign Judgments Act] for the enforcement of judgments of 'court[s] of the U.S.' in this state."

Reynolds v. Kessler, 669 S.W.2d 801, 805 (Tex. App.—El Paso 1984, no writ). The question is whether "a federal judgment abstract and the indexation thereof ... should be considered differently. The answer to that question depends on whether the Texas statutes comport with federal law and provide uniformity of treatment of state judgment liens and federal judgment liens. We believe that they do. Although it is true that [TRCS art. 5451, now Prop. Code §52.001,] does not expressly provide for federal judgments 'registered' in this state and refers only to such judgments 'rendered' in this state, Art. 5451 must be read in conjunction with 28 U.S.C. §1963. That section of the [U.S.C.] provides that a federal judgment rendered in one federal district can be registered in another federal district and when so registered has the same effect as a judgment of the district court where newly registered and may be enforced in like manner. We conclude, therefore, that Art. 5451 when read in conjunction with ... §1963 provides uniformity of treatment of state and federal judgments...."

Sections 52.008-52.020 reserved for expansion

SUBCHAPTER B. CANCELLATION OF JUDGMENTS & JUDGMENT LIENS AGAINST BANKRUPTS—ABSTRACT RECORDED BEFORE SEPTEMBER 1, 1993

PROP §52.021. DISCHARGE & CANCELLATION

(a) In accordance with this subchapter, a judgment and judgment lien may be discharged and canceled if the person against whom the judgment was rendered is discharged from his debts under federal bankruptcy law.

(b) This subchapter applies to judgments against persons whose debts are discharged in bankruptcy and for which the abstracts of judgment are recorded before September 1, 1993, as provided by Subchapter A, regardless of the fact that the discharge in bankruptcy occurred before this law took effect.

History of Prop. Code §52.021: Acts 1983, 68th Leg., ch. 576, §1, eff. Jan. 1, 1984. Amended by Acts 1993, 73rd Leg., ch. 313, §2, eff. Sept. 1, 1993. Source: TRCS art. 5449(a), §1.

PROP §52.022. APPLICATION FOR COURT ORDER

(a) The person who has been discharged from his debts, that person's receiver or trustee, or any other interested person may apply, on proof of the discharge, to the court in which the judgment was rendered for an order discharging and canceling the judgment and judgment lien.

(b) A person may not apply for the order before a year has elapsed since the bankruptcy discharge.

History of Prop. Code §52.022: Acts 1983, 68th Leg., ch. 576, §1, eff. Jan. 1, 1984. Source: TRCS art. 5449(a), §1.

PROP §52.023. NOTICE OF APPLICATION

(a) Notice of the application for the order and copies of the papers on which application is made must be served on the judgment creditor or his attorney of record in the action in which the judgment was rendered.

(b) If the residence or place of business of the judgment creditor or his attorney is known, notice must be served in the manner prescribed for service of notice in an action.

(c) As an alternative to service under Subsection (b), the court may order that notice of the application be published in a newspaper designated in the order once a week for not more than three consecutive weeks if the applicant proves by affidavit that:

(1) the address of neither the judgment creditor nor his attorney is known and the address of neither can be ascertained by due diligence; or

(2) the judgment creditor is not a resident of this state and his attorney is dead, removed from the state, or unknown.

History of Prop. Code §52.023: Acts 1983, 68th Leg., ch. 576, §1, eff. Jan. 1, 1984. Source: TRCS art. 5449(a), §3.

PROP §52.024. COURT ORDER

(a) The court shall conduct a hearing on the application and shall enter an order of discharge and cancellation of the judgment and any abstracts of the judgment if the debtor or bankrupt has been discharged in bankruptcy from the payment of the obligation or debt represented by the judgment.

(b) In each county in which the court's order is recorded in the judgment lien records, the order constitutes a release, discharge, and cancellation of the judgment and of any unsatisfied judgment lien represented by an abstract that is of record in the county on the date of the order or is recorded in the county on or after the date of the order.

History of Prop. Code §52.024: Acts 1983, 68th Leg., ch. 576, §1, eff. Jan. 1, 1984. Source: TRCS art. 5449(a), §2.

PROP §52.025. EFFECT ON LIEN OF DISCHARGE OF DEBT IN BANKRUPTCY

(a) A judgment lien is not affected by the order of discharge and cancellation and may be enforced, if the lien is against real property owned by the bankrupt or debtor before the debtor was adjudged bankrupt or a petition for debtor relief was filed under federal bankruptcy law, and:

(1) the debt or obligation evidenced by the judgment is not discharged in bankruptcy; or

(2) the property is nonexempt and is abandoned during the course of the proceeding.

(b) Except as provided by Subsection (a), the judgment is of no force or validity and may not be a lien on real property acquired by the bankrupt or debtor after the discharge in bankruptcy.

History of Prop. Code §52.025: Acts 1983, 68th Leg., ch. 576, §1, eff. Jan. 1, 1984. Source: TRCS art. 5449(a), §§4, 5.

Sections 52.026-52.040 blank

SUBCHAPTER C. CANCELLATION OF JUDGMENTS & JUDGMENT LIENS AGAINST DEBTORS—ABSTRACT RECORDED ON OR AFTER SEPTEMBER 1, 1993

PROP §52.041. APPLICATION OF SUBCHAPTER

This subchapter applies to a judgment and judgment lien for which an abstract of judgment or judgment lien is recorded on or after September 1, 1993.

History of Prop. Code §52.041: Acts 1993, 73rd Leg., ch. 313, §3, eff. Sept. 1, 1993.

PROP §52.042. DISCHARGE & CANCELLATION

(a) A judgment is discharged and any abstract of judgment or judgment lien is canceled and released without further action in any court and may not be enforced if:

(1) the lien is against real property owned by the debtor before a petition for debtor relief was filed under federal bankruptcy law; and

(2) the debt or obligation evidenced by the judgment is discharged in the bankruptcy.

(b) A judgment evidencing a debt or obligation discharged in bankruptcy does not have force or validity and may not be a lien on real property acquired by the debtor after the petition for debtor relief was filed.

History of Prop. Code §52.042: Acts 1993, 73rd Leg., ch. 313, §3, eff. Sept. 1, 1993.

ANNOTATIONS

Hageman v. Luth, 150 S.W.3d 617, 625 (Tex.App.—Austin 2004, no pet.). "Under federal bankruptcy law, a discharge voids any judgment at any time obtained. However, a discharge in bankruptcy is neither a payment nor an extinguishment of a debt. The discharge simply bars future legal proceedings to enforce the discharged debt against the debtor. *At 626:* When we consider the guidance from Texas law in light of the federal approach to the discharge of debts in bankruptcy, we are convinced that §52.042(a)(2) … mirrors the federal approach to the proper characterization of a discharge in bankruptcy. … Because we find that the extinguishment rule maintains viability in Texas, and because [joint debtor's] obligation on [original] judgment continued after his bankruptcy discharge, the assignment of [original] judgment to [joint debtor] effectively extinguished the judgment, which is now satisfied in whole." (Internal quotes omitted.)

PROP §52.043. EXCEPTIONS TO DISCHARGE & CANCELLATION

A judgment lien is not affected by this subchapter and may be enforced if the lien is against real property owned by the debtor before a petition for debtor relief was filed under federal bankruptcy law and:

(1) the debt or obligation evidenced by the judgment is not discharged in bankruptcy; or

(2) the property is not exempted in the bankruptcy and is abandoned during the bankruptcy.

History of Prop. Code §52.043: Acts 1993, 73rd Leg., ch. 313, §3, eff. Sept. 1, 1993.

CHAPTER 53. MECHANIC'S, CONTRACTOR'S, OR MATERIALMAN'S LIEN

SUBCHAPTER A. GENERAL PROVISIONS

PROP §53.001. DEFINITIONS

In this chapter:

(1) "Contract price" means the cost to the owner for any part of construction or repair performed under an original contract.

(2) "Improvement" includes:

(A) abutting sidewalks and streets and utilities in or on those sidewalks and streets;

(B) clearing, grubbing, draining, or fencing of land;

(C) wells, cisterns, tanks, reservoirs, or artificial lakes or pools made for supplying or storing water;

(D) pumps, siphons, and windmills or other machinery or apparatuses used for raising water for stock, domestic use, or irrigation; and

(E) planting orchard trees, grubbing out orchards and replacing trees, and pruning of orchard trees.

(3) "Labor" means labor used in the direct prosecution of the work.

(4) "Material" means all or part of:

(A) the material, machinery, fixtures, or tools incorporated into the work, consumed in the direct prosecution of the work, or ordered and delivered for incorporation or consumption;

(B) rent at a reasonable rate and actual running repairs at a reasonable cost for construction equipment used or reasonably required and delivered for use in the direct prosecution of the work at the site of the construction or repair; or

(C) power, water, fuel, and lubricants consumed or ordered and delivered for consumption in the direct prosecution of the work.

(5) "Mechanic's lien" means the lien provided by this chapter.

(6) "Original contract" means an agreement to which an owner is a party either directly or by implication of law.

(7) "Original contractor" means a person contracting with an owner either directly or through the owner's agent.

(8) "Residence" means a single-family house, duplex, triplex, or quadruplex or a unit in a multiunit structure used for residential purposes that is:

(A) owned by one or more adult persons; and

(B) used or intended to be used as a dwelling by one of the owners.

(9) "Residential construction contract" means a contract between an owner and a contractor in which the contractor agrees to construct or repair the owner's residence, including improvements appurtenant to the residence.

(10) "Residential construction project" means a project for the construction or repair of a new or existing residence, including improvements appurtenant to the residence, as provided by a residential construction contract.

(11) "Retainage" means an amount representing part of a contract payment that is not required to be paid to the claimant within the month following the month in which labor is performed, material is furnished, or specially fabricated material is delivered. The term does not include retainage under Subchapter E.

(12) "Specially fabricated material" means material fabricated for use as a component of the construction or repair so as to be reasonably unsuitable for use elsewhere.

(13) "Subcontractor" means a person who has furnished labor or materials to fulfill an obligation to an

original contractor or to a subcontractor to perform all or part of the work required by an original contract.

(14) "Work" means any part of construction or repair performed under an original contract.

(15) "Completion" of an original contract means the actual completion of the work, including any extras or change orders reasonably required or contemplated under the original contract, other than warranty work or replacement or repair of the work performed under the contract.

History of Prop. Code §53.001: Acts 1983, 68th Leg., ch. 576, §1, eff. Jan. 1, 1984. Amended by Acts 1997, 75th Leg., ch. 526, §2, eff. Sept. 1, 1997; Acts 1999, 76th Leg., ch. 889, §1, eff. Sept. 1, 1999. Source: TRCS art. 5452, §§1, 2.

ANNOTATIONS

Labor

American Surety Co. v. Stuart, 151 S.W.2d 886, 887 (Tex.App.—Fort Worth 1941, no writ). "[P]rofessional services rendered by an attorney would not be classed as 'labor' within the meaning of that term as used in the mechanic's lien statutes of this state."

Materials

Lyda Swinerton Builders, Inc. v. Cathay Bank, 409 S.W.3d 221, 241 (Tex.App.—Houston [14th Dist.] 2013, pet. denied). "The [intervenor] contends that none of [the] post-work expenses are 'materials' because, once work ceased, nothing was 'used' or 'consumed' in the 'direct prosecution of the work.' We disagree because the definition of materials does not always require actual use or consumption in the direct prosecution of the work. Instead, mechanic's liens are also available when items are 'delivered for' use or consumption. [T]he availability of a mechanic's lien becomes a question of how the parties *intended* to use equipment and services delivered to the project.... [¶] [T]o obtain a mechanic's lien for rental expenses, the equipment must be not only 'delivered for use,' but also 'reasonably required' for use in the direct prosecution of the work. ... At some point, continuing to incur these expenses may ... become unreasonable, regardless of the parties' intent."

Original Contractor

Fidelity & Deposit Co. v. Felker, 469 S.W.2d 389, 394 (Tex.1971). Contractor 1 "does not now dispute that he, at one time, had a contract for the electrical work with [owner]. He argues, however, that his contract with [owner] was abandoned when an agreement was reached that [contractor 2] would be the general contractor and that one bond would cover the entire project. [Contractor 1] says the whole scheme changed from [owner] acting as its own general contractor to [contractor 2] assuming an obligation for all the construction project. He submits that [contractor 2], by later adding his signature to the contract between [contractor 1] and [owner], created a contract between [contractor 1] and [contractor 2]. We do not agree with this argument because there is no evidence that the contract between [contractor 1] and [owner] was abandoned; and upon the trial, [contractor 1] reaffirmed that he performed under his ... contract with [owner]. [Contractor 1] was not a subcontractor under [contractor 2]. He was an original contractor with [owner] just as [D] was in [***Trinity Univ'l Ins. v. Barlite***, 435 S.W.2d 849 (Tex.1968)]."

Truss World, Inc. v. ERJS, Inc., 284 S.W.3d 393, 395 (Tex.App.—Beaumont 2009, pet. denied). Owner "and [surety] argue ... that [contractor's] statement in the lien affidavits filed with the county clerk, identifying [contractor] as a subcontractor, constitutes a judicial admission that [contractor] was in fact [owner's] subcontractor. ... We decline to treat the statement in the lien affidavits as a binding judicial admission, but instead look at the actual relationship of the parties and the purpose of the statute. [¶] [Contractor] contracted directly with [owner] and was an original contractor, not a subcontractor or derivative claimant. As an original contractor, [contractor] was not required to serve additional notices required of a subcontractor or derivative claimant to perfect a lien claim."

Texas Wood Mill Cabinets, Inc. v. Butter, 117 S.W.3d 98, 105 (Tex.App.—Tyler 2003, no pet.). "For a contractor who has a constitutional lien to be protected against the rights of third parties, he must either comply with the statutes relating to affidavits for fixing mechanic's and materialmen's liens, thus giving constructive notice to third parties, or he must give actual notice to third parties within the time prescribed by statute. Once the lien affidavit has been properly filed, the lien relates back to the inception of the contract. When a lien affidavit is filed after the property is sold by the owner who contracted for the improvements, the purchaser is deemed to have constructive notice of a contractor's right to assert a lien for the statutory period, even where the filing period commenced prior to the purchase. Additionally, personal knowledge of im-

provements being made on the property at or shortly before the time the subsequent purchaser took possession of the property provides sufficient notice of a contractor's right to assert a lien claim." *See also* ***Apex Fin. Corp. v. Brown***, 7 S.W.3d 820, 830-31 (Tex.App.—Texarkana 1999, no pet.).

Subcontractor

First Nat'l Bank v. Sledge, 653 S.W.2d 283, 285 (Tex.1983). "Because a subcontractor is a derivative claimant and, unlike a general contractor, has no constitutional, common law, or contractual lien on the property of the owner, a subcontractor's lien rights are totally dependent on compliance with the statutes authorizing the lien. However, substantial compliance with the statutes is sufficient to perfect a lien under the Act."

Stolz v. Honeycutt, 42 S.W.3d 305, 310 (Tex. App.—Houston [14th Dist.] 2001, no pet.). "The two main statutory schemes providing [derivative] rights to spurned subcontractors are: (1) the 'Trapping Statute,' and (2) the 'Retainage Statute.' *At 311:* Under the Trapping Statute, when an owner receives proper notice that the original contractor has failed to pay funds owed on work done on the property, the owner may withhold payments to the contractor in an amount sufficient to cover the claim for which he received notice. If the owner pays any of the 'trapped' funds to the contractor after receiving notice, the claimant may obtain a lien on the property to the extent of the money paid. [¶] The Retainage Statute provides protection that is in some ways broader in application but also potentially more limited in monetary terms than the Trapping Statute. Under [Prop. Code] §53.101, an owner under an original contract on which a mechanic's lien may be claimed is required to retain in his possession ten percent of the contract price, or ten percent of the value of the work, for 30 days after the work is completed. A claimant may then secure a lien on the retained funds if he provides the owner with proper notice under the statute and files an affidavit claiming a lien no later than the 30th day after the work was completed. The amount trapped under the Trapping Statute (as big as the claim is big) may be more than the required retainage under the Retainage Statute (a flat ten percent of contract price or value)." *See also* ***Bond v. Kagan-Edelman Enters.***, 985 S.W.2d 253, 259-60 (Tex.App.—Houston [1st Dist.] 1999), *rev'd in part on other grounds*, 20 S.W.3d 706 (Tex.2000).

PROP §53.002. MORE THAN ONE ORIGINAL CONTRACTOR

On any work there may be more than one original contractor for purposes of this chapter.

History of Prop. Code §53.002: Acts 1983, 68th Leg., ch. 576, §1, eff. Jan. 1, 1984. Source: TRCS art. 5452, §2.

PROP §53.003. NOTICES

(a) This section applies to notices required by Subchapters B through G and K.

(b) Any notice or other written communication may be delivered in person to the party entitled to the notice or to that party's agent, regardless of the manner prescribed by law.

(c) If notice is sent by registered or certified mail, deposit or mailing of the notice in the United States mail in the form required constitutes compliance with the notice requirement. This subsection does not apply if the law requires receipt of the notice by the person to whom it is directed.

(d) If a written notice is received by the person entitled to receive it, the method by which the notice was delivered is immaterial.

History of Prop. Code §53.003: Acts 1983, 68th Leg., ch. 576, §1, eff. Jan. 1, 1984. Amended by Acts 1997, 75th Leg., ch. 526, §3, eff. Sept. 1, 1997. Source: TRCS art. 5456.

ANNOTATIONS

Wesco Distrib. v. Westport Grp., 150 S.W.3d 553, 556 (Tex.App.—Austin 2004, no pet.). General contractor argues "that notice mailed with insufficient postage does not comply with statutory requirements because 'sending' notice by mail necessarily includes attaching sufficient postage. Because [claimant] failed to timely notify [general contractor] of its lien claim, [general contractor] argues, the lien it claims is invalid. We agree. *At 561:* The district court's decision that [claimant's] lien is invalid because its attempt to timely notify [general contractor] failed for lack of sufficient postage is consistent with the statute. The effort [claimant] made did not satisfy the notice requirements mandated by the materialman's lien statute."

Occidental Neb. Fed. Sav. Bank v. East End Glass Co., 773 S.W.2d 687, 688 (Tex.App.—San Antonio 1989, no writ). "The common sense reason for requiring a materialman to give notice to the owner is to let the owner know that the contractor has not paid the materialman out of the construction draws. This gives the owner an opportunity to retain funds still under owner's control and to avoid the imposition of a statutory lien."

Sections 53.004-53.020 reserved for expansion

SUBCHAPTER B. PERSONS ENTITLED TO LIEN; SUBJECT PROPERTY

PROP §53.021. PERSONS ENTITLED TO LIEN

(a) A person has a lien if:

(1) the person labors, specially fabricates material, or furnishes labor or materials for construction or repair in this state of:

(A) a house, building, or improvement;

(B) a levee or embankment to be erected for the reclamation of overflow land along a river or creek; or

(C) a railroad; and

(2) the person labors, specially fabricates the material, or furnishes the labor or materials under or by virtue of a contract with the owner or the owner's agent, trustee, receiver, contractor, or subcontractor.

(b) A person who specially fabricates material has a lien even if the material is not delivered.

(c) An architect, engineer, or surveyor who prepares a plan or plat under or by virtue of a written contract with the owner or the owner's agent, trustee, or receiver in connection with the actual or proposed design, construction, or repair of improvements on real property or the location of the boundaries of real property has a lien on the property.

(d) A person who provides labor, plant material, or other supplies for the installation of landscaping for a house, building, or improvement, including the construction of a retention pond, retaining wall, berm, irrigation system, fountain, or other similar installation, under or by virtue of a written contract with the owner or the owner's agent, contractor, subcontractor, trustee, or receiver has a lien on the property.

(e) A person who performs labor as part of, or who furnishes labor or materials for, the demolition of a structure on real property under or by virtue of a written contract with the owner of the property or the owner's agent, trustee, receiver, contractor, or subcontractor has a lien on the property.

History of Prop. Code §53.021: Acts 1983, 68th Leg., ch. 576, §1, eff. Jan. 1, 1984. Amended by Acts 1989, 71st Leg., ch. 395, §1 (eff. Sept. 1, 1989), ch. 1138, §1 (eff. Sept. 1, 1989); Acts 1991, 72nd Leg., ch. 16, §16.01, eff. Aug. 26, 1991; Acts 1995, 74th Leg., ch. 851, §§1, 6, eff. Sept. 1, 1995; Acts 1999, 76th Leg., ch. 896, §1, eff. Sept. 1, 1999; Acts 2003, 78th Leg., ch. 410, §1, eff. Sept. 1, 2003; Acts 2011, 82nd Leg., ch. 271, §1, eff. Jan. 1, 2012. Source: TRCS art. 5452, §§1, 2.

See also *Real Estate Forms*, FORMS 5:1, 5:2.

ANNOTATIONS

Reliance Nat'l Indem. Co. v. Advanced Temporaries, Inc., 227 S.W.3d 46, 47 (Tex.2007). "[W]e decide whether a temporary employment agency, which places workers at a construction project under a contract with a subcontractor, 'furnishes labor' within the meaning of Ch. 53 ..., thus qualifying for a mechanic's lien. *At 49:* [P] hired construction workers as its employees, who then labored on a construction of an improvement in this state, by virtue of a contract with an owner, contractor, or subcontractor, thus satisfying the statutory requirement of the mechanic's lien statute. Under these circumstances, [P] is no different from a supplier who furnishes lumber, pipe, or shingles. Instead of materials, however, [P] furnished labor, paying the workers for their services, just as a hardware supplier might pay for the hinges, doorknobs, and fixtures it provides to a construction project. We therefore conclude that, because the temporary workers here were [P's] employees, [P] furnished labor by providing these workers to [subcontractor] for work at the ... construction project."

CVN Grp. v. Delgado, 95 S.W.3d 234, 247 (Tex. 2002). "[U]nlike the constitution, the statutory lien protects subcontractors as well as original contractors. Because of this difference, the statutory lien has become the primary vehicle for contract or protection. [¶] [W]hile [Prop. Code] ch. 53 provides greater protection for contractors [than the constitutional lien], it also sets out a number of specific requirements for perfecting and enforcing mechanic's liens. ... The lien statute reflects an attempt to create a workable balance among various and often antagonistic interests, protecting not only contractors and suppliers, but also lenders and property owners."

Diversified Mortg. Investors v. Lloyd D. Blaylock Gen. Contractor, Inc., 576 S.W.2d 794, 805 (Tex.1978). "[I]f a lessee contracts for construction, the mechanic's lien attaches only to the leasehold interest, not to the fee interest of the lessor." *See also* ***Denco CS Corp. v. Body Bar, LLC***, 445 S.W.3d 863, 871 (Tex.App.—Texarkana 2014, no pet.); ***2811 Assocs. v. Metroplex Lighting & Elec.***, 765 S.W.2d 851, 853 (Tex.App.—Dallas 1989, writ denied).

Big Three Welding Equip. Co. v. Crutcher, Rolfs, Cummings, Inc., 229 S.W.2d 600, 603 (Tex.1950). "The giving of liens to those who furnish materials and labor for works of improvement or construction, with the ac-

cording of priorities to those liens, is 'based upon the very just consideration that a person who by his labor or material expended on improvements made on the land of another, under contract, express or implied, that this shall be paid for, thereby increases its value, and ought to the extent of the contract price or value of the thing furnished, to have a lien on the land, of which the improvement becomes a part, to secure payment.' In accord with this principle, the prevailing view is that mechanics' lien statutes confer no right to assert a lien for performing labor or furnishing materials in the removal or demolition of structures or improvements, unless they expressly so provide." *See also* ***J&J Equip., Inc. v. Pilkinton***, 850 S.W.2d 804, 805-06 (Tex.App.—Corpus Christi 1993, writ denied).

Addison Urban Dev. Partners v. Alan Ritchey Materials Co., LC, 437 S.W.3d 597, 603 (Tex.App.—Dallas 2014, no pet.). "The parties differ on whether [the] delivery of excess materials defeats the conclusion that the materials were 'furnished' for the Project. *At 604:* [P] advances an application of the statute requiring proof that the materials were actually used for the Project. *At 606:* [T]here is nothing to suggest the legislature intended the additional burden on materialmen that [P] seeks to impose. [T]he legislature did not define the word 'furnish' as it pertains to §53.021. [¶] According to Black's Law Dictionary, the word 'furnish' means 'to supply, provide, or equip, for accomplishment of a particular purpose.' Webster's defines 'furnish' as to 'supply or give.' It seems clear through these definitions that the plain meaning of the word 'furnish,' in the context of furnishing materials for a specific job, involves supplying the materials and nothing more. The definitions in no way suggest that furnishing or supplying materials for a project equates to or entails actual use of such materials." *See also* ***Lexcon, Inc. v. Gray***, 740 S.W.2d 83, 85 (Tex.App.—Dallas 1987, no writ) (materialman furnishes goods if it proves delivery to construction site or to builder for specific job).

Gibson v. Bostick Roofing & Sheet Metal Co., 148 S.W.3d 482, 494-95 (Tex.App.—El Paso 2004, no pet.). "[W]here a contract for materials, labor and construction is not made with the owner or his duly-authorized agent, the owner of land may not be held liable personally, nor may a lien be fixed on his land. One merely in possession under a contract to purchase is not the owner of the land and cannot create a mechanic's lien on it; only the owner or his agent may make contracts fixing liens on lands and buildings. A contractor's and materialman's lien relates back to the inception of the contract, and the time when the first material was furnished, as against the immediate parties to, or those having prior notice of, the contract, but cannot be established against the landowner without his knowledge or consent, nor predicated on a mere executory contract of purchase between others."

Stolz v. Honeycutt, 42 S.W.3d 305, 310 (Tex.App.—Houston [14th Dist.] 2001, no pet.). See annotation under Property Code §53.001, *Subcontractor*, p. 236.

PROP §53.022. PROPERTY TO WHICH LIEN EXTENDS

(a) The lien extends to the house, building, fixtures, or improvements, the land reclaimed from overflow, or the railroad and all of its properties, and to each lot of land necessarily connected or reclaimed.

(b) The lien does not extend to abutting sidewalks, streets, and utilities that are public property.

(c) A lien against land in a city, town, or village extends to each lot on which the house, building, or improvement is situated or on which the labor was performed.

(d) A lien against land not in a city, town, or village extends to not more than 50 acres on which the house, building, or improvement is situated or on which the labor was performed.

History of Prop. Code §53.022: Acts 1983, 68th Leg., ch. 576, §1, eff. Jan. 1, 1984. Source: TRCS arts. 5452, §1, 5458.

See also *Real Estate Forms*, FORMS 5:1, 5:2.

ANNOTATIONS

Valdez v. Diamond Shamrock Ref. & Mktg. Co., 842 S.W.2d 273, 275 (Tex.1992). "[A] mechanic's lien extends to the entire 'lot' on which work is being performed. [Respondent] asserts that ... a 'lot' refers merely to the improvement and the land immediately surrounding the improvement. We disagree. [¶] [W]e believe the plain language of the statute indicates that an entire undivided tract is a single lot. [¶] The most reasonable and pragmatic interpretation of the term 'lot,' for purposes of §53.022, is that it refers to a single tract of land as recorded in the county deed records." *See also* ***Houston Elec. Distrib. Co. v. MBB Enters.***, 703 S.W.2d 206, 208 (Tex.App.—Houston [14th Dist.] 1985, no writ).

Exchange S&L Ass'n v. Monocrete Pty. Ltd., 629 S.W.2d 34, 37 (Tex.1982). To determine whether an improvement is removable, courts should consider the "nature of the improvements sought to be removed and the probabilities of post-removal damage to the existing structure. Some factors that may be considered are: the manner and extent of attachment to the land or existing improvements; the extent to which removal would necessitate repairs, modification and/or protection of the land or existing improvements; the stage of completion of improvements under construction at the time removal is sought; and the function of the improvements sought to be removed." *Compare* ***Occidental Neb. Fed. Sav. Bank v. East End Glass Co.***, 773 S.W.2d 687, 689 (Tex.App.—San Antonio 1989, no writ) (glass mirrors are removable), *with* ***McCallen v. Mogul Prod. & Ref. Co.***, 257 S.W. 918, 923 (Tex. App.—Galveston 1923, writ dism'd) (garage building is not removable).

First Nat'l Bank v. Whirlpool Corp., 517 S.W.2d 262, 269 (Tex.1974). "[A] mechanic's and materialman's statutory lien upon improvements made is superior to a prior recorded deed of trust lien where the improvements made can be removed without material injury to the land and pre-existing improvements, or to the improvements removed."

Moore v. Brenham Ready Mix, Inc., 463 S.W.3d 109, 119-20 (Tex.App.—Houston [1st Dist.] 2015, no pet.). Materialman "contends that because the lots ... were contiguous, because it delivered the materials to the project pursuant to a single contract, and because the contract did not specify the amount of materials to be used on each specific lot, the entire amount of the ... lien can be enforced against any given individual lot. We agree that the lien *attached* to all the properties. ... The issue is whether the lien may be *enforced* in its entirety against the subsequent purchasers of individual lots of the property. *At 122:* We now hold that [o]nce the owner no longer treats the lots encumbered by a materialman's lien as one piece of property by retaining ownership of the whole, then, although the lien is fixed upon the entire property and its scope extends to future purchasers, the value of the debt secured by any individual lot, or individual portion of the property divided and sold to another owner, must be proportioned to the percentage of the individual property or lot purchased relative to the entire property subject to the lien."

Dorsett Bros. Concrete Sup. v. Safeco Title Ins., 880 S.W.2d 417, 423 (Tex.App.—Houston [14th Dist.] 1993, writ denied). "Materialmen [argue] that mechanic's liens actually attach to *all* improvements, including improvements furnished by others. Therefore, even if their individually-supplied improvements might not be removable, their liens attach to removable improvements supplied by others. [¶] We [disagree]. [A] mechanic's lien extends to all improvements *supplied by the lien holder* regardless of who actually placed the improvements on the property. [¶] However, ... a contractor need not supply all of the materials for an improvement to be able to execute a lien on that improvement."

PROP §53.023. PAYMENT SECURED BY LIEN

The lien secures payment for:

(1) the labor done or material furnished for the construction or repair;

(2) the specially fabricated material, even if the material has not been delivered or incorporated into the construction or repair, less its fair salvage value; or

(3) the preparation of a plan or plat by an architect, engineer, or surveyor in accordance with Section 53.021(c).

History of Prop. Code §53.023: Acts 1983, 68th Leg., ch. 576, §1, eff. Jan. 1, 1984. Amended by Acts 1995, 74th Leg., ch. 851, §2, eff. Sept. 1, 1995. Source: TRCS art. 5452, §1.

See also *Real Estate Forms*, FORMS 5:1, 5:2.

ANNOTATIONS

Ambassador Dev. Corp. v. Valdez, 791 S.W.2d 612, 624 (Tex.App.—Fort Worth 1990, no writ). "[N]owhere is there any indication in the statutes that the lien should include prejudgment interest on a subcontractor's claim." *See also* ***Nixon Constr. Co. v. Downs***, 441 S.W.2d 284, 286 (Tex.App.—Houston [1st Dist.] 1969, no writ) (unearned or lost profits not covered by mechanic's lien).

PROP §53.024. LIMITATION ON SUBCONTRACTOR'S LIEN

The amount of a lien claimed by a subcontractor may not exceed:

(1) an amount equal to the proportion of the total subcontract price that the sum of the labor performed, materials furnished, materials specially fabricated, reasonable overhead costs incurred, and proportionate profit margin bears to the total subcontract price; minus

(2) the sum of previous payments received by the claimant on the subcontract.

History of Prop. Code §53.024: Acts 1983, 68th Leg., ch. 576, §1, eff. Jan. 1, 1984. Source: TRCS art. 5452, §2.

See also *Real Estate Forms*, FORMS 5:1, 5:2.

ANNOTATIONS

Lyon v. Building Galveston, Inc., No. 01-15-00664-CV (Tex.App.—Houston [1st Dist.] 2016, n.p.h.) (memo op.; 11-3-16). "[P] argues that there is legally insufficient evidence to support the jury's implicit finding that his ... lien is invalid because there is no evidence applying the statutory formula to the facts of this case, thereby, identifying the amount of §53.024's statutory cap. [¶] [Intervenor] responds that there is some evidence to support the jury's implicit finding that [P's] lien is invalid because the evidence establishes that [P] did not calculate his lien pursuant to ... §53.024's formula. It is undisputed that [P] did not calculate his lien based on the statutory formula. The plain language of the statute, however, does not require subcontractors to calculate their lien using a specific method. Thus, the fact that [P] used a different method to calculate his lien does not mean that his lien is per se invalid."

Ambassador Dev. Corp. v. Valdez, 791 S.W.2d 612, 624 (Tex.App.—Fort Worth 1990, no writ). "[W]e hold the trial court ... properly allowed [subcontractor] to recover prejudgment interest on his claim. However, although we are reluctant to follow our sister court and use ***Ingham*** [***v. Harrison***, 224 S.W.2d 1019 (Tex. 1949),] as authority for the proposition that prejudgment interest is not properly includable in the amount of the statutory lien, we do agree the ... Property Code does not make any provision for the inclusion of prejudgment interest in the statutory lien. [¶] [N]owhere is there any indication in the statutes that the lien should include prejudgment interest on a subcontractor's claim. In §53.024 the Texas legislature specifically delineated the items which could be included in a mechanic's and materialman's lien. The legislature could have provided for the inclusion of prejudgment interest in the lien, but did not do so."

PROP §53.025. LIMITATION ON ORDINARY RETAINAGE LIEN

A lien for retainage is valid only for the amount specified to be retained in the contract, including any amendments to the contract, between the claimant and the original contractor or between the claimant and a subcontractor.

History of Prop. Code §53.025: Acts 1983, 68th Leg., ch. 576, §1, eff. Jan. 1, 1984. Amended by Acts 1989, 71st Leg., ch. 1138, §2, eff. Sept. 1, 1989. Source: TRCS art. 5452, §2.

See also *Real Estate Forms*, FORMS 5:1, 5:2.

PROP §53.026. SHAM CONTRACT

(a) A person who labors, specially fabricates materials, or furnishes labor or materials under a direct contractual relationship with another person is considered to be in direct contractual relationship with the owner and has a lien as an original contractor, if:

(1) the owner contracted with the other person for the construction or repair of a house, building, or improvements and the owner can effectively control that person through ownership of voting stock, interlocking directorships, or otherwise;

(2) the owner contracted with the other person for the construction or repair of a house, building, or improvements and that other person can effectively control the owner through ownership of voting stock, interlocking directorships, or otherwise; or

(3) the owner contracted with the other person for the construction or repair of a house, building, or improvements and the contract was made without good faith intention of the parties that the other person was to perform the contract.

(b) In this section, "owner" does not include a person who has or claims a security interest only.

History of Prop. Code §53.026: Acts 1983, 68th Leg., ch. 576, §1, eff. Jan. 1, 1984. Amended by Acts 1989, 71st Leg., ch. 1138, §3, eff. Sept. 1, 1989; Acts 1997, 75th Leg., ch. 526, §4, eff. Sept. 1, 1997. Source: TRCS art. 5452-1.

See also *Real Estate Forms*, FORMS 5:1, 5:2.

ANNOTATIONS

Da-Col Paint Mfg. v. American Indem. Co., 517 S.W.2d 270, 272 (Tex.1974). "We hold that where [TRCS art. 5452-1, now Prop. Code §53.026,] applies, notice to the owner is also notice to the sham original contractor. *At 273-74:* At the time of contracting with the sham original contractor, parties ... may not be aware of the sham relationship between the owner and original contractor. They then assume their position to be that of subcontractor or materialmen and, as such, will not execute a bond. ... When the sham relationship is discovered, however, the sham contractor could invoke Art. 5452-1 to deny its liability on its bond by saying that another original contractor has been created by the statute, and any remedy is now against the new original contractor. ... This cannot be the intent of the Legislature, which adopted the sham contractor statute to protect subcontractors and materialmen, not to en-

courage sham relationships." *See also* ***Trinity Drywall Sys. v. TOKA Gen. Contractors, Ltd.***, 416 S.W.3d 201, 211-12 (Tex.App.—El Paso 2013, pet. denied) (under sham contracts provision, subcontractor is placed in direct privity with property owner for purposes of mechanic's and materialman's lien statutes).

Southwest Props., L.P. v. Lite-Dec, Inc., 989 S.W.2d 69, 72 (Tex.App.—San Antonio 1998, pet. denied). "[T]he only reasonable and just interpretation of §53.026 is to construe 'in a direct contractual relationship' as an effort to effectuate the timetables for filing liens and not an effort to control liability of an owner."

Sections 53.027-53.050 reserved for expansion

SUBCHAPTER C. PROCEDURE FOR PERFECTING LIEN

PROP §53.051. NECESSARY PROCEDURES

To perfect the lien, a person must comply with this subchapter.

History of Prop. Code §53.051: Acts 1983, 68th Leg., ch. 576, §1, eff. Jan. 1, 1984. Source: TRCS art. 5452, §1.

ANNOTATIONS

Interstate Contracting Corp. v. City of Dallas, 135 S.W.3d 605, 618-19 (Tex.2004). "[R]ecognition of pass-through claims does not ... affect the procedures for perfecting statutory mechanic's and materialman's liens in private contracts or for asserting claims on payment bonds in public contracts. [P]ass-through claims provide protections not afforded by the lien and payment bond statutes, and our recognition of pass-through claims does not disturb the existing statutory procedures and requirements."

PROP §53.052. FILING OF AFFIDAVIT

(a) Except as provided by Subsection (b), the person claiming the lien must file an affidavit with the county clerk of the county in which the property is located or into which the railroad extends not later than the 15th day of the fourth calendar month after the day on which the indebtedness accrues.

(b) A person claiming a lien arising from a residential construction project must file an affidavit with the county clerk of the county in which the property is located not later than the 15th day of the third calendar month after the day on which the indebtedness accrues.

(c) The county clerk shall record the affidavit in records kept for that purpose and shall index and cross-index the affidavit in the names of the claimant, the original contractor, and the owner. Failure of the county clerk to properly record or index a filed affidavit does not invalidate the lien.

History of Prop. Code §53.052: Acts 1983, 68th Leg., ch. 576, §1, eff. Jan. 1, 1984. Amended by Acts 1989, 71st Leg., ch. 1138, §4, eff. Sept. 1, 1989; Acts 1997, 75th Leg., ch. 526, §5, eff. Sept. 1, 1997. Source: TRCS art. 5453.

ANNOTATIONS

Ready Cable, Inc. v. RJP S. Comfort Homes, Inc., 295 S.W.3d 763, 763-64 (Tex.App.—Austin 2009, no pet.). "This suit involves whether a subcontractor may enforce a statutory materialman's lien against a property owner when the county clerk refused to accept the subcontractor's timely delivered lien affidavit for filing. We hold that where there is no legitimate basis for the clerk's refusal to file the lien affidavit, the affidavit should be deemed to have been filed on the date it was delivered for filing."

Detering Co. v. Green, 989 S.W.2d 479, 481 (Tex. App.—Houston [1st Dist.] 1999, pet. denied). "A lien affidavit that does not meet the requirements called for by statute does not provide the protection of constructive notice."

PROP §53.053. ACCRUAL OF INDEBTEDNESS

(a) For purposes of Section 53.052, indebtedness accrues on a contract under which a plan or plat is prepared, labor was performed, materials furnished, or specially fabricated materials are to be furnished in accordance with this section.

(b) Indebtedness to an original contractor accrues:

(1) on the last day of the month in which a written declaration by the original contractor or the owner is received by the other party to the original contract stating that the original contract has been terminated; or

(2) on the last day of the month in which the original contract has been completed, finally settled, or abandoned.

(c) Indebtedness to a subcontractor, or to any person not covered by Subsection (b) or (d), who has furnished labor or material to an original contractor or to another subcontractor accrues on the last day of the last month in which the labor was performed or the material furnished.

(d) Indebtedness for specially fabricated material accrues:

(1) on the last day of the last month in which materials were delivered;

(2) on the last day of the last month in which delivery of the last of the material would normally have been required at the job site; or

(3) on the last day of the month of any material breach or termination of the original contract by the owner or contractor or of the subcontract under which the specially fabricated material was furnished.

(e) A claim for retainage accrues on the earliest of the last day of the month in which all work called for by the contract between the owner and the original contractor has been completed, finally settled, terminated, or abandoned.

History of Prop. Code §53.053: Acts 1983, 68th Leg., ch. 576, §1, eff. Jan. 1, 1984. Amended by Acts 1989, 71st Leg., ch. 1138, §5, eff. Sept. 1, 1989; Acts 1995, 74th Leg., ch. 851, §3, eff. Sept. 1, 1995; Acts 2011, 82nd Leg., ch. 499, §1, eff. Sept. 1, 2011. Source: TRCS art. 5467.

ANNOTATIONS

Gibson v. Bostick Roofing & Sheet Metal Co., 148 S.W.3d 482, 495 (Tex.App.—El Paso 2004, no pet.). "[R]epairs were completed around July 23, 1993, so that the indebtedness accrued the last day of July 1993. [Contractor] filed its affidavit of lien on March 4, 1994. It had until the 15th day of the fourth calendar month after the day on which the indebtedness accrued to file its affidavit—November 15, 1993. Because [contractor] failed to comply with the statutory requirements, the statutory lien was invalid."

Raymond v. Rahme, 78 S.W.3d 552, 560 n.2 (Tex.App.—Austin 2002, no pet.). "'[R]etainage' as defined by [Prop. Code] ch. 53 'does not include retainage under Subch. E' (the retainage statute). [Subcontractor] agrees that the definition of 'retainage' refers to contractual retainage agreements, not to statutorily-required retainage, and admits that [Prop. Code] §§53.025 … and 53.057 … apply only to contractual retainage and not to his claims. We believe [Prop. Code] §53.053(e) also applies to contractual retainage, and [subcontractor] gives no explanation or authority to support his contrary assertion. We hold that [subcontractor's] debt accrued according to §53.053(c)."

PROP §53.054. CONTENTS OF AFFIDAVIT

(a) The affidavit must be signed by the person claiming the lien or by another person on the claimant's behalf and must contain substantially:

(1) a sworn statement of the amount of the claim;

(2) the name and last known address of the owner or reputed owner;

(3) a general statement of the kind of work done and materials furnished by the claimant and, for a claimant other than an original contractor, a statement of each month in which the work was done and materials furnished for which payment is requested;

(4) the name and last known address of the person by whom the claimant was employed or to whom the claimant furnished the materials or labor;

(5) the name and last known address of the original contractor;

(6) a description, legally sufficient for identification, of the property sought to be charged with the lien;

(7) the claimant's name, mailing address, and, if different, physical address; and

(8) for a claimant other than an original contractor, a statement identifying the date each notice of the claim was sent to the owner and the method by which the notice was sent.

(b) The claimant may attach to the affidavit a copy of any applicable written agreement or contract and a copy of each notice sent to the owner.

(c) The affidavit is not required to set forth individual items of work done or material furnished or specially fabricated. The affidavit may use any abbreviations or symbols customary in the trade.

History of Prop. Code §53.054: Acts 1983, 68th Leg., ch. 576, §1, eff. Jan. 1, 1984. Amended by Acts 1989, 71st Leg., ch. 1138, §6, eff. Sept. 1, 1989; Acts 1997, 75th Leg., ch. 526, §6, eff. Sept. 1, 1997. Source: TRCS art. 5455.

ANNOTATIONS

Lyda Swinerton Builders, Inc. v. Cathay Bank, 409 S.W.3d 221, 239-40 (Tex.App.—Houston [14th Dist.] 2013, pet. denied). "[P] contends that any late affidavits 'relat[e] back' to [the] timely [first amended affidavit]. [¶] [P's] first amended affidavit satisfied *both* the timeliness requirement and the amount-of-the-claim requirement only to the extent of the $2.9 million claim it substantially recited. We … reject [P's] argument that its first amended affidavit satisfied the timeliness requirement as to all subsequent affidavits."

Mustang Tractor & Equip. Co. v. Hartford Acc. & Indem. Co., 263 S.W.3d 437, 440 (Tex.App.—Austin 2008, pet. denied). "[A] lien affidavit should not be judged by a strict standard but by whether the claimant substantially complied with the statutory requirements. *At 441:* [Claimant] argues that because omission of the information described in [§53.054(a)(8)] was merely

a technical defect that did not prejudice the contractor or owner, the lien affidavits substantially complied with the statutory requirements. [¶] Courts have been more willing to excuse a mistake or omission in cases where no party is prejudiced by the defect. *At 443-44:* Because the document provides all other required information in the sworn section, and because the mailing address contained on the document accurately provides a means of contact with the claimant ..., we find it substantially complies with the statute." *Compare* ***Lyda Swinerton Builders, Inc. v. Cathay Bank***, 409 S.W.3d 221, 234-35 (Tex.App.—Houston [14th Dist.] 2013, pet. denied) (amended affidavit substantially complied even though it purported to amend original affidavit of lien that had already been released), *and* ***Gill Sav. Ass'n v. International Sup. Co.***, 759 S.W.2d 697, 700 (Tex.App.—Dallas 1988, writ denied) (affidavit in substantial compliance when lien filed for amount greater than actual amount reconciled), *with* ***Wesco Distrib. v. Westport Grp.***, 150 S.W.3d 553, 561 (Tex.App.—Austin 2004, no pet.) (lien invalid because no pre-lien notice before deadline could mislead owner to his prejudice), *and* ***Tribble & Stephens Co. v. Consolidated Servs.***, 744 S.W.2d 945, 951 (Tex.App.—San Antonio 1987, writ denied) (lien invalid because potential for misleading owner to his prejudice when no copies of affidavit were sent).

Stolz v. Honeycutt, 42 S.W.3d 305, 313 (Tex. App.—Houston [14th Dist.] 2001, no pet.). The ability "to 'trap' funds is extinguished if the 'claim is otherwise paid or settled.' [I]t is clear that [subcontractor's wife's] accepting of the post-dated check from [prime contractor] and signing of the mutual release operates as a payment and settlement of the underlying claim. If the underlying claim ceases to exist the derivative claims also cease to exist. [¶] [T]he release signed ... was a mutual release wherein [subcontractor] and [prime contractor] each purported to release the other for all claims which either of them may have had against the other, and the four corners of the document do not reference any payment as a part of consideration or performance. The return of the check [for insufficient funds] would not then invalidate the agreement on its face."

PROP §53.055. NOTICE OF FILED AFFIDAVIT

(a) A person who files an affidavit must send a copy of the affidavit by registered or certified mail to the owner or reputed owner at the owner's last known business or residence address not later than the fifth day after the date the affidavit is filed with the county clerk.

(b) If the person is not an original contractor, the person must also send a copy of the affidavit to the original contractor at the original contractor's last known business or residence address within the same period.

History of Prop. Code §53.055: Acts 1983, 68th Leg., ch. 576, §1, eff. Jan. 1, 1984. Amended by Acts 1989, 71st Leg., ch. 1138, §7, eff. Sept. 1, 1989; Acts 1993, 73rd Leg., ch. 48, §7, eff. Sept. 1, 1993; Acts 1997, 75th Leg., ch. 526, §7, eff. Sept. 1, 1997; Acts 1999, 76th Leg., ch. 889, §2, eff. Sept. 1, 1999. Source: TRCS art. 5453.

ANNOTATIONS

Denco CS Corp. v. Body Bar, LLC, 445 S.W.3d 863, 871 n.12 (Tex.App.—Texarkana 2014, no pet.). Lessee "argues that [contractor] failed to meet statutory requirements to perfect the lien. [Contractor] admitted that it failed to comply with [Prop. Code] §53.055(a). However, substantial compliance with [Prop. Code] Ch. 53 is sufficient, and '[c]ases interpreting the mechanic's and materialman's lien statutes counsel against invalidating a lien on a purely technical basis.'" *See also* ***Truss World, Inc. v. ERJS, Inc.***, 284 S.W.3d 393, 396 (Tex.App.—Beaumont 2009, pet. denied).

Wade & Sons, Inc. v. American Std., Inc., 127 S.W.3d 814, 825 (Tex.App.—San Antonio 2003, pet. denied). "According to [mechanical contractor], there is no evidence that copies of the affidavit were sent to [purchaser] and [general contractor] or such copies were sent by registered or certified mail. [¶] According to [vendor], however, it was not required to prove that it complied with [Prop. Code] §53.055, because pursuant to [TRCP] 54, it pled that all conditions precedent have been performed or have occurred. [Mechanical contractor], however, claims that [vendor] did not sufficiently plead that all conditions to enforceability of the lien had occurred. ... On page two of its first amended cross claim, [vendor] states that '[t]his is a suit to foreclose on a Bond to Indemnify Against *Lien* and a suit on sworn account. All conditions precedent have been performed or have occurred.' This language sufficiently placed [mechanical contractor] on notice of [vendor's] suit and of [vendor's] performance or occurrence of all conditions precedent. We hold that pursuant to [TRCP] 54, [vendor's] petition was sufficient."

PROP §53.056. DERIVATIVE CLAIMANT: NOTICE TO OWNER OR ORIGINAL CONTRACTOR

(a) Except as provided by Subchapter K, a claimant other than an original contractor must give the notice prescribed by this section for the lien to be valid.

(b) If the lien claim arises from a debt incurred by a subcontractor, the claimant must give to the original contractor written notice of the unpaid balance. The claimant must give the notice not later than the 15th day of the second month following each month in which all or part of the claimant's labor was performed or material delivered. The claimant must give the same notice to the owner or reputed owner and the original contractor not later than the 15th day of the third month following each month in which all or part of the claimant's labor was performed or material or specially fabricated material was delivered.

(c) If the lien claim arises from a debt incurred by the original contractor, the claimant must give notice to the owner or reputed owner, with a copy to the original contractor, in accordance with Subsection (b).

(d) To authorize the owner to withhold funds under Subchapter D, the notice to the owner must state that if the claim remains unpaid, the owner may be personally liable and the owner's property may be subjected to a lien unless:

(1) the owner withholds payments from the contractor for payment of the claim; or

(2) the claim is otherwise paid or settled.

(e) The notice must be sent by registered or certified mail and must be addressed to the owner or reputed owner or the original contractor, as applicable, at his last known business or residence address.

(f) A copy of the statement or billing in the usual and customary form is sufficient as notice under this section.

History of Prop. Code §53.056: Acts 1983, 68th Leg., ch. 576, §1, eff. Jan. 1, 1984. Amended by Acts 1989, 71st Leg., ch. 1138, §8, eff. Sept. 1, 1989; Acts 1997, 75th Leg., ch. 526, §8, eff. Sept. 1, 1997. Source: TRCS art. 5453.

ANNOTATIONS

Valdez v. Diamond Shamrock Ref. & Mktg. Co., 842 S.W.2d 273, 276 (Tex.1992). "[W]e hold that as a matter of law, a purchaser's knowledge that improvements have been recently made on a single piece of property is sufficient to impose constructive notice of a worker's right to assert a mechanic's lien within the statutory period. [Purchaser] cannot now claim that it had no indication that a lien might have been in force covering the entire [lot]. We do not see the need to impose an additional burden on subcontractors to recheck deed records for a purchase that occurs after construction has started." *See also* ***Industrial Structure & Fabrication, Inc. v. Arrowhead Indus. Water, Inc.***, 888 S.W.2d 840, 843-44 (Tex.App.—Houston [1st Dist.] 1994, no writ).

Industrial Indem. Co. v. Zack Burkett Co., 677 S.W.2d 493, 495 (Tex.1984). "To require that an owner be warned that 'he may be personally liable and his property subjected to a lien' when, because of the presence of the payment bond, the owner is relieved of liability, would be to require subcontractors to perform a meaningless exercise. [¶] The 'statutory warning' is not an essential element of a subcontractor's notice when perfecting a claim against a payment bond."

Morrell Masonry Sup. v. Lupe's Shenandoah Reserve, LLC, 363 S.W.3d 901, 903 (Tex.App.—Beaumont 2012, no pet.). "This case requires us to decide whether a materialman to a subcontractor must give notice to the original contractor to perfect a lien and to recover on fund-trapping and retainage claims against the landowner. Because the statute that creates the rights of derivative suppliers requires timely notice to perfect a lien, we hold that a failure to provide notice in accordance with the statute precludes recovery." *See also* ***Morrell Masonry Sup. v. Loeb***, 349 S.W.3d 664, 669-70 (Tex.App.—Houston [14th Dist.] 2011, no pet.).

Wesco Distrib. v. Westport Grp., 150 S.W.3d 553, 561 (Tex.App.—Austin 2004, no pet.). "When a sender has done everything necessary for notice to arrive, notice is considered effective as to the intended recipient. ... Correspondence without postage will not and cannot ever reach the party entitled to notice. Imputing notice to the intended recipient when the sender had not done everything necessary for notice to arrive would be nonsensical and unfair, and would render the notice provisions of the statute a meaningless ritual."

PROP §53.057. DERIVATIVE CLAIMANT: NOTICE FOR CONTRACTUAL RETAINAGE CLAIM

(a) A claimant may give notice under this section instead of or in addition to notice under Section 53.056 or 53.252 if the claimant is to labor, furnish labor or materials, or specially fabricate materials, or has labored, furnished labor or materials, or specially fabricated ma-

terials, under an agreement with an original contractor or a subcontractor providing for retainage.

(b) The claimant must give the owner or reputed owner notice of contractual retainage not later than the earlier of:

(1) the 30th day after the date the claimant's agreement providing for retainage is completed, terminated, or abandoned; or

(2) the 30th day after the date the original contract is terminated or abandoned.

(b-1) If an agreement for contractual retainage is with a subcontractor, the claimant must also give the notice of contractual retainage to the original contractor within the period prescribed by Subsection (b).

(c) The notice must generally state the existence of a requirement for retainage and contain:

(1) the name and address of the claimant; and

(2) if the agreement is with a subcontractor, the name and address of the subcontractor.

(d) The notice must be sent to the last known business or residence address of the owner or reputed owner or the original contractor, as applicable.

(e) If a claimant gives notice under this section and Section 53.055 or, if the claim relates to a residential construction project, under this section and Section 53.252, the claimant is not required to give any other notice as to the retainage.

(f) A claimant has a lien on, and the owner is personally liable to the claimant for, the retained funds under Subchapter E if the claimant:

(1) gives notice in accordance with this section and:

(A) complies with Subchapter E; or

(B) files an affidavit claiming a lien not later than the earliest of:

(i) the date required for filing an affidavit under Section 53.052;

(ii) the 40th day after the date stated in an affidavit of completion as the date of completion of the work under the original contract, if the owner sent the claimant notice of an affidavit of completion in the time and manner required;

(iii) the 40th day after the date of termination or abandonment of the original contract, if the owner sent the claimant a notice of such termination or abandonment in the time and manner required; or

(iv) the 30th day after the date the owner sent to the claimant to the claimant's address provided in the notice for contractual retainage, as required under Subsection (c), a written notice of demand for the claimant to file the affidavit claiming a lien; and

(2) gives the notice of the filed affidavit as required by Section 53.055.

(g) The written demand under Subsection (f)(1)(B)(iv):

(1) must contain the owner's name and address and a description, legally sufficient for identification, of the real property on which the improvement is located;

(2) must state that the claimant must file the lien affidavit not later than the 30th day after the date the demand is sent; and

(3) is effective only for the amount of contractual retainage earned by the claimant as of the day the demand was sent.

History of Prop. Code §53.057: Acts 1983, 68th Leg., ch. 576, §1, eff. Jan. 1, 1984. Amended by Acts 1989, 71st Leg., ch. 1138, §9, eff. Sept. 1, 1989; Acts 1997, 75th Leg., ch. 526, §9, eff. Sept. 1, 1997; Acts 1999, 76th Leg., ch. 889, §3, eff. Sept. 1, 1999; Acts 2011, 82nd Leg., ch. 499, §2, eff. Sept. 1, 2011. Source: TRCS art. 5453.

ANNOTATIONS

Page v. Structural Wood Components, Inc., 102 S.W.3d 720, 730-31 (Tex.2003). "The Texas mechanic's and materialman's lien statutes do not focus on *who* does the work; they focus on whether and when the work is actually completed. [T]he mechanic's and materialman's lien statutes are meant to protect the *subcontractor*, not the general contractor. The subcontractor is a derivative claimant, and the provisions governing the claims of derivative claimants, including the retainage lien provisions, are specifically distinguished from the provisions governing the rights and remedies of original contractors. There is a reason for this. '[P]roperly characterizing the claimant as an original contractor or subcontractor is important because a subcontractor is not entitled to a constitutional lien, and it is relatively difficult for him to perfect a statutory lien.' There are other provisions in place to protect the general contractor. 'An original contractor often has a constitutional lien automatically, and the manner of perfecting his statutory lien is relatively simple.'"

PROP §53.058. DERIVATIVE CLAIMANT: NOTICE FOR SPECIALLY FABRICATED ITEMS

(a) Except as provided by Subchapter K, a claimant who specially fabricates material must give notice under this section for the lien to be valid.

(b) The claimant must give the owner or reputed owner notice not later than the 15th day of the second month after the month in which the claimant receives and accepts the order for the material. If the indebtedness is incurred by a person other than the original contractor, the claimant must also give notice within that time to the original contractor.

(c) The notice must contain:

(1) a statement that the order has been received and accepted; and

(2) the price of the order.

(d) The notice must be sent by registered or certified mail to the last known business or residence address of the owner or the reputed owner or the original contractor, as applicable.

(e) In addition to notice under this section, the claimant must give notice under Section 53.056 if delivery has been made or if the normal delivery time for the job has passed.

(f) The lien of a claimant who accepts an order but fails to give notice under this section is valid as to delivered items if the claimant has given notice under Section 53.056.

(g) If a retainage agreement consists in whole or part of an obligation to furnish specially fabricated materials and the claimant has given notice under Section 53.057, the claimant is not required to give notice under this section.

History of Prop. Code §53.058: Acts 1983, 68th Leg., ch. 576, §1, eff. Jan. 1, 1984. Amended by Acts 1989, 71st Leg., ch. 1138, §10, eff. Sept. 1, 1989; Acts 1997, 75th Leg., ch. 526, §10, eff. Sept. 1, 1997. Source: TRCS art. 5453.

ANNOTATIONS

Truss World, Inc. v. ERJS, Inc., 284 S.W.3d 393, 396 (Tex.App.—Beaumont 2009, pet. denied). "Contrary to the trial court's finding, however, the Property Code provisions dealing with 'specially fabricated items' are inapplicable here, because the Property Code notice requirements for 'specially fabricated items' apply to derivative claimants, not original contractors."

PROP §53.059. REPEALED

Repealed by Acts 1997, 75th Leg., ch. 526, §24, eff. Sept. 1, 1997.

Sections 53.060-53.080 reserved for expansion

SUBCHAPTER D. FUNDS WITHHELD BY OWNER FOLLOWING NOTICE

PROP §53.081. AUTHORITY TO WITHHOLD FUNDS FOR BENEFIT OF CLAIMANTS

(a) If an owner receives notice under Section 53.056, 53.057, 53.058, 53.252, or 53.253, the owner may withhold from payments to the original contractor an amount necessary to pay the claim for which he receives notice.

(b) If notice is sent in a form that substantially complies with Section 53.056 or 53.252, the owner may withhold the funds immediately on receipt of the notice.

(c) If notice is sent under Section 53.057, the owner may withhold funds immediately on receipt of a copy of the claimant's affidavit prepared in accordance with Sections 53.052 through 53.055.

(d) If notice is sent under Section 53.058, the owner may withhold funds immediately on receipt of the notices sent under Subsection (e) of that section. If notice is sent as provided by Section 53.253(b), the owner may withhold funds immediately on receipt of the notice sent as required by Section 53.252.

History of Prop. Code §53.081: Acts 1983, 68th Leg., ch. 576, §1, eff. Jan. 1, 1984. Amended by Acts 1989, 71st Leg., ch. 1138, §12, eff. Sept. 1, 1989; Acts 1997, 75th Leg., ch. 526, §11, eff. Sept. 1, 1997. Source: TRCS art. 5463, §1.

ANNOTATIONS

Page v. Marton Roofing, Inc., 102 S.W.3d 733, 735 (Tex.2003). See annotation under Property Code §53.084, p. 247.

First Nat'l Bank v. Sledge, 653 S.W.2d 283, 286 (Tex.1983). The statutory fund-trapping provision provides that "subcontractors can trap, in the owner's hands, funds payable to the general contractor if the owner receives notice from the subcontractors that they are not being paid. If the owner pays any money to the general contractor after receiving notice from the subcontractors, the owner's property will be subject to a lien to the extent of the money paid." *See also* ***Raymond v. Rahme***, 78 S.W.3d 552, 559 (Tex.App.—Austin 2002, no pet.); ***Stolz v. Honeycutt***, 42 S.W.3d 305, 311 (Tex.App.—Houston [14th Dist.] 2001, no pet.); ***Bond v. Kagan-Edelman Enters.***, 985 S.W.2d 253, 259 (Tex.App.—Houston [1st Dist.] 1999), *rev'd in part on other grounds*, 20 S.W.3d 706 (Tex.2000).

PROP §53.082. TIME FOR WHICH FUNDS ARE WITHHELD

Unless payment is made under Section 53.083 or the claim is otherwise settled, discharged, indemnified against under Subchapter H or I, or determined to be invalid by a final judgment of a court, the owner shall retain the funds withheld until:

(1) the time for filing the affidavit of mechanic's lien has passed; or

(2) if a lien affidavit has been filed, until the lien claim has been satisfied or released.

History of Prop. Code §53.082: Acts 1983, 68th Leg., ch. 576, §1, eff. Jan. 1, 1984. Amended by Acts 1989, 71st Leg., ch. 1138, §13, eff. Sept. 1, 1989. Source: TRCS art. 5463, §1.

ANNOTATIONS

Stolz v. Honeycutt, 42 S.W.3d 305, 313 (Tex. App.—Houston [14th Dist.] 2001, no pet.). "[T]he ability to 'trap' funds is extinguished if the 'claim is otherwise paid or settled.' Here, it is clear that [subcontractor's wife's] accepting of the post-dated check from [prime contractor] and signing of the mutual release operates as a payment and settlement of the underlying claim. If the underlying claim ceases to exist the derivative claims also cease to exist."

PROP §53.083. PAYMENT TO CLAIMANT ON DEMAND

(a) The claimant may make written demand for payment of the claim to an owner authorized to withhold funds under this subchapter. The demand must give notice to the owner that all or part of the claim has accrued under Section 53.053 or is past due according to the agreement between the parties.

(b) The claimant must send a copy of the demand to the original contractor. The original contractor may give the owner written notice that the contractor intends to dispute the claim. The original contractor must give the notice not later than the 30th day after the day he receives the copy of the demand. If the original contractor does not give the owner timely notice, he is considered to have assented to the demand and the owner shall pay the claim.

(c) The claimant's demand may accompany the original notice of nonpayment or of a past-due claim and may be stamped or written in legible form on the face of the notice.

(d) Unless the lien has been secured, the demand may not be made after expiration of the time within which the claimant may secure the lien for the claim.

History of Prop. Code §53.083: Acts 1983, 68th Leg., ch. 576, §1, eff. Jan. 1, 1984. Source: TRCS arts. 5453, 5454.

PROP §53.084. OWNER'S LIABILITY

(a) Except for the amount required to be retained under Subchapter E, the owner is not liable for any amount paid to the original contractor before the owner is authorized to withhold funds under this subchapter.

(b) If the owner has received the notices required by Subchapter C or K, if the lien has been secured, and if the claim has been reduced to final judgment, the owner is liable and the owner's property is subject to a claim for any money paid to the original contractor after the owner was authorized to withhold funds under this subchapter. The owner is liable for that amount in addition to any amount for which he is liable under Subchapter E.

History of Prop. Code §53.084: Acts 1983, 68th Leg., ch. 576, §1, eff. Jan. 1, 1984. Amended by Acts 1997, 75th Leg., ch. 526, §12, eff. Sept. 1, 1997. Source: TRCS art. 5463, §2.

ANNOTATIONS

Page v. Marton Roofing, Inc., 102 S.W.3d 733, 735 (Tex.2003). Subcontractor "argues that it is entitled to a lien on [owner's] property because [owner] paid money to the replacement contractors after receiving notice that [prime contractor] had failed to pay [subcontractor]. It is undisputed, however, that [owner] neither made nor owed any further payments to [prime contractor] at any time after [owner] received notice of [subcontractor's] claims. As with retainage liens, fund-trapping liens must be judged in relation to individual original contracts. [Subcontractor's] notice authorized [owner] to withhold funds from [prime contractor], because [prime contractor] was the original contractor that hired [subcontractor]. [Owner] was not authorized to withhold funds from the replacement contractors who had no relationship to [subcontractor]. Consequently, [owner] cannot be liable under the fund-trapping statute for any funds paid to the replacement contractors."

Jewelry Mfr.'s Exch., Inc. v. Tafoya, 374 S.W.3d 639, 643 (Tex.App.—Dallas 2012, pet. denied). "[D] asserts the trial court improperly awarded … $5,611.23 to [replacement contractor]. [P] claims the amounts were all paid 'for or on behalf of [general contractor],' were all paid after [D] received [P's] notice … and are therefore, amounts for which [D] became personally liable. [P] contends the amounts were all paid after [D] received [P's] notice and now [D] is liable to [P] for these amounts under the trapping statute. [¶] [T]he record is clear that [replacement contractor]

was hired after [P] stopped working on the project. [P's] affidavit states he personally walked through the job site with [replacement contractor] employees and explained what work he had done as well as what work was left incomplete. The Texas Supreme Court has made it clear that 'work must be defined in relation to a particular contract' thus, [D] was not authorized to withhold funds from replacement contractors who had no relationship to [P]. Consequently, we conclude the $5,611.2[3] should not have been included in the summary judgment award to [P] under the fund trapping statute."

Bond v. Kagan-Edelman Enters., 985 S.W.2d 253, 259 (Tex.App.—Houston [1st Dist.] 1999), *rev'd in part on other grounds*, 20 S.W.3d 706 (Tex.2000). Subcontractor "perfected his lien according to the procedures in Subch. D for fund-trapping. [Prime contractor] did not give written notice to [owner] of any intent to dispute the claim; therefore, [owner] was required to withhold the funds and pay [subcontractor's] claim. *At 260:* We find that [owner] is liable to [subcontractor] for trapped funds to the extent of the amount it paid [prime contractor] after receiving notice from [subcontractor]." *See also* ***Weaver v. King Ready Mix Concrete, Inc.***, 750 S.W.2d 913, 915 (Tex.App.—Waco 1988, no writ).

PROP §53.085. AFFIDAVIT REQUIRED

(a) Any person who furnishes labor or materials for the construction of improvements on real property shall, if requested and as a condition of payment for such labor or materials, provide to the requesting party, or the party's agent, an affidavit stating that the person has paid each of the person's subcontractors, laborers, or materialmen in full for all labor and materials provided to the person for the construction. In the event, however, that the person has not paid each of the person's subcontractors, laborers, or materialmen in full, the person shall state in the affidavit the amount owed and the name and, if known, the address and telephone number of each subcontractor, laborer, or materialman to whom the payment is owed.

(b) The seller of any real property shall, upon request by the purchaser or the purchaser's agent prior to closing of the purchase of the real property, provide to the purchaser or the purchaser's agent, a written affidavit stating that the seller has paid each of the seller's contractors, laborers, or materialmen in full for all labor and materials provided to the seller through the date specified in the affidavit for any construction of improvements on the real property and that the seller is not indebted to any person, firm, or corporation by reason of any such construction through the date specified in the affidavit. In the event that the seller has not paid each of the seller's contractors, laborers, or materialmen in full for labor and material provided through the date specified in the affidavit, the seller shall state in the affidavit the amount owed and the name and, if known, the address and telephone number of each contractor, laborer, or materialman to whom the payment is owed.

(c) The affidavit may include:

(1) a waiver or release of lien rights or payment bond claims by the affiant that is conditioned on the receipt of actual payment or collection of funds when payment is made by check or draft, as provided by Subchapter L;

(2) a warranty or representation that certain bills or classes of bills will be paid by the affiant from funds paid in reliance on the affidavit; and

(3) an indemnification by the affiant for any loss or expense resulting from false or incorrect information in the affidavit.

(d) A person, including a seller, commits an offense if the person intentionally, knowingly, or recklessly makes a false or misleading statement in an affidavit under this section. An offense under this section is a misdemeanor. A person adjudged guilty of an offense under this section shall be punished by a fine not to exceed $4,000 or confinement in jail for a term not to exceed one year or both a fine and confinement. A person may not receive community supervision for the offense.

(e) A person signing an affidavit under this section is personally liable for any loss or damage resulting from any false or incorrect information in the affidavit.

History of Prop. Code §53.085: Acts 1987, 70th Leg., ch. 578, §1, eff. Aug. 31, 1987. Amended by Acts 1989, 71st Leg., ch. 1138, §14, eff. Sept. 1, 1989; Acts 1997, 75th Leg., ch. 526, §13, eff. Sept. 1, 1997; Acts 2011, 82nd Leg., ch. 271, §2, eff. Jan. 1, 2012.

ANNOTATIONS

Solar Applications Eng'g v. T.A. Oper. Corp., 327 S.W.3d 104, 108 (Tex.2010). "Whether [general contractor] is barred from receiving the contract balance depends on whether the lien-release provision is a condition precedent to [general contractor's] recovery for

breach of contract. *At 109-10:* The operative language [in the contract], that [general contractor] will provide 'complete and legally effective releases or waivers ... of all Lien rights' does not contain language that is traditionally associated with a condition precedent. The language preceding the lien-release provision does not make performance conditional. In the absence of any conditional language, a reasonable reading of the lien-release provision is that it is a promise or covenant by [general contractor] to provide a lien-release affidavit in exchange for receiving final payment. This interpretation avoids forfeiture and completes the contract: [general contractor] is paid for the work it completed, and [owner] receives an unencumbered building."

Author's comment: Acts 2011, 82nd Leg., ch. 271, §3, eff. Jan. 1, 2012, enacted Subch. L, entitled "Waiver & Release of Lien or Payment Bond Claim," p. 273, to make contractual requirements like those in ***Solar Applications Eng'g*** unenforceable. ***Solar Applications Eng'g*** will remain relevant for contracts entered before January 1, 2012.

Wasserberg v. Flooring Servs., 376 S.W.3d 202, 204-05 (Tex.App.—Houston [14th Dist.] 2012, no pet.). Underwriter "settled the claims related to the liens on behalf of the home-buyers, then intervened in [P's] lawsuit to seek indemnity from [Ds] for the settlement amounts. [Underwriter] argued that, under ... §53.085(e), the 'all bills paid' affidavits signed by [D] rendered him personally liable for any damages resulting from the false or incorrect information in the affidavits. *At 208-09:* [D] claims he was prevented from arguing that 'some other person or entity was responsible' for listing exceptions to this statement for amounts owed to certain vendors without also listing the amounts owed to [P]. [D] argues that because this argument is not an affirmative defense, his general denial 'was sufficient to put the existence of any misrepresentation ... at issue, including any showing that some other person or entity was responsible.' [¶] Regardless of whether the trial court properly ruled that [D's] argument constituted an unpleaded affirmative defense for which no evidence was permitted, [D] was allowed to testify that when he signed the affidavits, the document did not contain any information regarding outstanding amounts owed for labor and materials to [P] or any other vendor. [¶] [D] fails to specify on appeal what additional testimony he was prevented from giving. We therefore reject [D's] contention that the trial court 'prevented him from contesting his personal liability' pursuant to this argument...."

Beard Family Prtshp. v. Commercial Indem. Ins., 116 S.W.3d 839, 845 (Tex.App.—Austin 2003, no pet.). Owner urges that "an all-bills-paid affidavit is required by §53.085 [as a condition precedent for contract payment]. Because [owner] requested the affidavit and [surety] did not provide it, [owner] contends it is not liable for the retained contract balance. *At 846:* [However,] the affidavit is not a requirement also imposed upon the surety. In addition to the affidavit, [the contract] also requires the 'consent of surety, if any, to final payment.' Because the surety is the assurance of payment—and continues to be liable on the bond until the expiration of a specified time period—the affidavit would under these circumstances perform no function."

Sections 53.086-53.100 reserved for expansion

SUBCHAPTER E. REQUIRED RETAINAGE FOR BENEFIT OF LIEN CLAIMANTS

PROP §53.101. REQUIRED RETAINAGE

(a) During the progress of work under an original contract for which a mechanic's lien may be claimed and for 30 days after the work is completed, the owner shall retain:

(1) 10 percent of the contract price of the work to the owner; or

(2) 10 percent of the value of the work, measured by the proportion that the work done bears to the work to be done, using the contract price or, if there is no contract price, using the reasonable value of the completed work.

(b) In this section, "owner" includes the owner's agent, trustee, or receiver.

History of Prop. Code §53.101: Acts 1983, 68th Leg., ch. 576, §1, eff. Jan. 1, 1984. Amended by Acts 1989, 71st Leg., ch. 1138, §15, eff. Sept. 1, 1989. Source: TRCS art. 5469.

See also ***Real Estate Forms***, FORM 5:1.

ANNOTATIONS

Page v. Marton Roofing, Inc., 102 S.W.3d 733, 734 (Tex.2003). "Our decision today in ***Page v. Structural Wood Components, Inc.***, [below], rejects [***Page v. Marton Roofing, Inc.***, 102 S.W.3d 750 (Tex.App.—Houston [1st Dist.] 2002)]. In ***Structural Wood***, we held that 'work must be defined in relation to a particular contract.' In order to perfect a statutory retainage lien, therefore, a subcontractor must file its lien affidavit within 30 days of the time that the original contract is completed, terminated, or abandoned. Here, [sub-

contractor] filed its affidavit two months after the original contract was terminated, and consequently failed to perfect a lien on the statutory retainage."

Page v. Structural Wood Components, Inc., 102 S.W.3d 720, 722 (Tex.2003). "To determine when the 30-day period ends, we look to the statutory definitions of work and completion of an original contract. The Property Code provides that completion of an original contract means the actual completion of the work, including any extras or change orders reasonably required or contemplated under the original contract.... The Code defines work as any part of construction of repair performed under an original contract. *At 723:* [W]e conclude that ... work ends when a contract is terminated. The history of the mechanic's lien statute demonstrates the Legislature's intent to make retainage requirements dependent on individual contracts. *At 724:* Focusing on the work initially contemplated may give a subcontractor more time to perfect a lien, but it may also greatly delay payment for contractors in general." (Internal quotes omitted.)

Stolz v. Honeycutt, 42 S.W.3d 305, 313 (Tex. App.—Houston [14th Dist.] 2001, no pet.). "The 30 day retention provisions ... appear to create a strict requirement that is not waivable by a subcontractor's action or inaction."

Hadnot v. Wenco Distribs., 961 S.W.2d 232, 235 (Tex.App.—Houston [1st Dist.] 1997, no pet.). "When the owner does not retain the 10% fund, the 30-day period for claiming liens is inapplicable. The owner becomes personally liable to the claimant if the owner does not retain the 10% fund." *See also* ***Bond v. Kagan-Edelman Enters.***, 985 S.W.2d 253, 260 (Tex.App.—Houston [1st Dist.] 1999), *rev'd in part on other grounds*, 20 S.W.3d 706 (Tex.2000); ***Hunt Cty. Lumber, Inc. v. Hunt-Collin Elec. Coop.***, 749 S.W.2d 179, 182 (Tex.App.—Dallas 1988, writ denied).

PROP §53.102. PAYMENT SECURED BY RETAINAGE

The retained funds secure the payment of artisans and mechanics who perform labor or service and the payment of other persons who furnish material, material and labor, or specially fabricated material for any contractor, subcontractor, agent, or receiver in the performance of the work.

History of Prop. Code §53.102: Acts 1983, 68th Leg., ch. 576, §1, eff. Jan. 1, 1984. Source: TRCS art. 5469.

ANNOTATIONS

Page v. Structural Wood Components, Inc., 102 S.W.3d 720, 722 (Tex.2003). "A subcontractor or other claimant who wants to make a claim on that retainage must properly give notice and file 'an affidavit claiming a lien not later than the 30th day after the work is completed.' The period during which a claimant can and must file a lien affidavit under [Prop. Code] §53.103 is therefore the same period that an owner can and must hold retainage under [Prop. Code] §53.101—30 days after the completion of work. It is consequently in the best interest of all construction participants to know when the 30-day period terminates—the owner so that it can release the remaining funds, the original contractor so that it can budget for its final payment, and the claimant so that it can file the lien affidavit before that date." *See also* ***Bond v. Kagan-Edelman Enters.***, 985 S.W.2d 253, 260 (Tex.App.—Houston [1st Dist.] 1999), *rev'd in part on other grounds*, 20 S.W.3d 706 (Tex.2000).

PROP §53.103. LIEN ON RETAINED FUNDS

A claimant has a lien on the retained funds if the claimant:

(1) sends the notices required by this chapter in the time and manner required; and

(2) except as allowed by Section 53.057(f), files an affidavit claiming a lien not later than the 30th day after the earliest of the date:

(A) the work is completed;

(B) the original contract is terminated; or

(C) the original contractor abandons performance under the original contract.

History of Prop. Code §53.103: Acts 1983, 68th Leg., ch. 576, §1, eff. Jan. 1, 1984. Amended by Acts 2005, 79th Leg., ch. 1033, §1, eff. Sept. 1, 2005; Acts 2011, 82nd Leg., ch. 499, §3, eff. Sept. 1, 2011. Source: TRCS art. 5469.

ANNOTATIONS

Solar Applications Eng'g v. T.A. Oper. Corp., 327 S.W.3d 104, 111 (Tex.2010). Under Tex. Const. art. 16, §37 and Prop. Code §§53.001-53.260, "if the owner becomes insolvent or refuses to pay, the contractor has recourse to recover the sums owed by foreclosing on the liens on the property. However, the contractor's lien gives contractors unequal leverage over owners and leaves owners vulnerable to insolvent contractors. [¶] The unequal bargaining positions created by the con-

tractor's lien rights is addressed through the mechanism of 'retainage.' ... This retainage secures the payment of any contractor or subcontractor[, under Prop. Code §53.102,] who may assert a lien on the property in the event that the general fails to pay them. [R]etainage gives the owner offsetting leverage against the general contractor, whose receipt of the final ten percent of the contract balance is subject to its payment of the subcontractors in full. [¶] Finally, [Prop. Code §53.085] allows the parties to contract for payment of the retainage to the contractor upon the owner's receipt of a lien-release affidavit. [T]he owner trades the retainage for the contractor's sworn assurance that property is lien-free. *At 112:* Parties are free, of course, to contract out of statutory default rules such as those established by the lien statutes and may even contractually waive constitutional rights."

Page v. Structural Wood Components, Inc., 102 S.W.3d 720, 721 (Tex.2003). "[T]he owner terminated the general contractor and hired other contractors to complete the project. The question before us is when, in fulfilling the affidavit requirement of the statute, 'work' is completed. The subcontractor here filed its affidavit 31 days after the original contract was terminated but well before subsequent contractors finished the project. ... Because we conclude that work must be defined in relation to a particular contract, and that the work under that contract was completed when the contract was terminated, we hold that the affidavit was not timely filed."

General Air Conditioning Co. v. Third Ward Ch. of Christ, 426 S.W.2d 541, 544 (Tex.1968). "We do not construe the 30-day period for claiming liens contained in [TRCS art. 5469, now Prop. Code §53.103,] as being applicable when the owner fails or refuses to retain the ten per cent fund, because, under these circumstances, Art. 5469 grants a lien against the owner's property to 'all claimants complying with the provisions of this Act'; and [TRCS art. 5463, now Prop. Code §53.084,] authorizes recovery from the owner of the amount that should have been retained '[i]f the notices prescribed by [TRCS art. 5453, now Prop. Code §§53.055-53.058,] have been received by the owner and claimant's lien has been secured in accordance with Art. 5453.'" *See also* ***Stolz v. Honeycutt***, 42 S.W.3d 305, 314 (Tex. App.—Houston [14th Dist.] 2001, no pet.) (if no money to which lien could attach, unreasonable to require claimant to file affidavit claiming lien).

PROP §53.104. PREFERENCES

(a) Individual artisans and mechanics are entitled to a preference to the retained funds and shall share proportionately to the extent of their claims for wages and fringe benefits earned.

(b) After payment of artisans and mechanics who are entitled to a preference under Subsection (a), other participating claimants share proportionately in the balance of the retained funds.

History of Prop. Code §53.104: Acts 1983, 68th Leg., ch. 576, §1, eff. Jan. 1, 1984. Amended by Acts 1989, 71st Leg., ch. 1138, §16, eff. Sept. 1, 1989. Source: TRCS art. 5469.

PROP §53.105. OWNER'S LIABILITY FOR FAILURE TO RETAIN

(a) If the owner fails or refuses to comply with this subchapter, the claimants complying with Subchapter C or this subchapter have a lien, at least to the extent of the amount that should have been retained from the original contract under which they are claiming, against the house, building, structure, fixture, or improvement and all of its properties and against the lot or lots of land necessarily connected.

(b) The claimants share the lien proportionately in accordance with the preference provided by Section 53.104.

History of Prop. Code §53.105: Acts 1983, 68th Leg., ch. 576, §1, eff. Jan. 1, 1984. Amended by Acts 1989, 71st Leg., ch. 2, §13.02 (eff. Aug. 28, 1989), ch. 1138, §17 (eff. Sept. 1, 1989); Acts 2011, 82nd Leg., ch. 499, §4, eff. Sept. 1, 2011. Source: TRCS art. 5469.

PROP §53.106. AFFIDAVIT OF COMPLETION

(a) An owner may file with the county clerk of the county in which the property is located an affidavit of completion. The affidavit must contain:

(1) the name and address of the owner;

(2) the name and address of the original contractor;

(3) a description, legally sufficient for identification, of the real property on which the improvements are located;

(4) a description of the improvements furnished under the original contract;

(5) a statement that the improvements under the original contract have been completed and the date of completion; and

(6) a conspicuous statement that a claimant may not have a lien on retained funds unless the claimant files an affidavit claiming a lien not later than the 40th day after the date the work under the original contract is completed.

(b) A copy of the affidavit must be sent by certified or registered mail to the original contractor not later than the date the affidavit is filed and to each claimant who sends a notice of lien liability to the owner under Section 53.056, 53.057, 53.058, 53.252, or 53.253 not later than the date the affidavit is filed or the 10th day after the date the owner receives the notice of lien liability, whichever is later.

(c) A copy of the affidavit must also be sent to each person who furnishes labor or materials for the property and who furnishes the owner with a written request for the copy. The owner must furnish the copy to the person not later than the date the affidavit is filed or the 10th day after the date the request is received, whichever is later.

(d) Except as provided by this subsection, an affidavit filed under this section on or before the 10th day after the date of completion of the improvements is prima facie evidence of the date the work under the original contract is completed for purposes of this subchapter and Section 53.057. If the affidavit is filed after the 10th day after the date of completion, the date of completion for purposes of this subchapter and Section 53.057 is the date the affidavit is filed. This subsection does not apply to a person to whom the affidavit was not sent as required by this section.

(e) Repealed by Acts 1999, 76th Leg., ch. 889, §12, eff. Sept. 1, 1999.

History of Prop. Code §53.106: Acts 1989, 71st Leg., ch. 1138, §18, eff. Sept. 1, 1989. Amended by Acts 1997, 75th Leg., ch. 526, §14, eff. Sept. 1, 1997; Acts 1999, 76th Leg., ch. 889, §12, eff. Sept. 1, 1999; Acts 2011, 82nd Leg., ch. 499, §5, eff. Sept. 1, 2011.

PROP §53.107. NOTICE RELATING TO TERMINATION OF WORK OR ABANDONMENT OF PERFORMANCE BY ORIGINAL CONTRACTOR OR OWNER

(a) Not later than the 10th day after the date an original contract is terminated or the original contractor abandons performance under the original contract, the owner shall give notice to each subcontractor who, before the date of termination or abandonment, has:

(1) given notice to the owner as provided by Section 53.056, 53.057, or 53.058; or

(2) sent to the owner by certified or registered mail a written request for notice of termination or abandonment.

(b) The notice must contain:

(1) the name and address of the owner;

(2) the name and address of the original contractor;

(3) a description, legally sufficient for identification, of the real property on which the improvements are located;

(4) a general description of the improvements agreed to be furnished under the original contract;

(5) a statement that the original contract has been terminated or that performance under the contract has been abandoned;

(6) the date of the termination or abandonment; and

(7) a conspicuous statement that a claimant may not have a lien on the retained funds unless the claimant files an affidavit claiming a lien not later than the 40th day after the date of the termination or abandonment.

(c) A notice sent in compliance with this section on or before the 10th day after the date of termination or abandonment is prima facie evidence of the date the original contract was terminated or work was abandoned for purposes of this subchapter.

(d) If an owner is required to send a notice to a subcontractor under this section and fails to send the notice, the subcontractor is not required to comply with Section 53.057 to claim retainage and may claim a lien by filing a lien affidavit as prescribed by Section 53.052.

(e) This section does not apply to a residential construction project.

History of Prop. Code §53.107: Acts 2005, 79th Leg., ch. 1003, §2, eff. Sept. 1, 2005. Amended by Acts 2011, 82nd Leg., ch. 499, §6, eff. Sept. 1, 2011.

Sections 53.108-53.120 reserved for expansion

SUBCHAPTER F. PRIORITIES & PREFERENCES

PROP §53.121. PREFERENCE OVER OTHER CREDITORS

All subcontractors, laborers, and materialmen who have a mechanic's lien have preference over other creditors of the original contractor.

History of Prop. Code §53.121: Acts 1983, 68th Leg., ch. 576, §1, eff. Jan. 1, 1984. Source: TRCS art. 5464.

PROP §53.122. EQUALITY OF MECHANIC'S LIENS

(a) Except as provided by Subchapter E and Section 53.124(e), perfected mechanic's liens are on equal footing without reference to the date of filing the affidavit claiming the lien.

(b) If the proceeds of a foreclosure sale of property are insufficient to discharge all mechanic's liens against the property, the proceeds shall be paid pro rata on the perfected mechanic's liens on which suit is brought.

(c) This chapter does not affect the contract between the owner and the original contractor as to the amount, manner, or time of payment of the contract price.

History of Prop. Code §53.122: Acts 1983, 68th Leg., ch. 576, §1, eff. Jan. 1, 1984. Amended by Acts 1995, 74th Leg., ch. 851, §4, eff. Sept. 1, 1995. Source: TRCS art. 5468.

PROP §53.123. PRIORITY OF MECHANIC'S LIEN OVER OTHER LIENS

(a) Except as provided by this section, a mechanic's lien attaches to the house, building, improvements, or railroad property in preference to any prior lien, encumbrance, or mortgage on the land on which it is located, and the person enforcing the lien may have the house, building, improvement, or any piece of the railroad property sold separately.

(b) The mechanic's lien does not affect any lien, encumbrance, or mortgage on the land or improvement at the time of the inception of the mechanic's lien, and the holder of the lien, encumbrance, or mortgage need not be made a party to a suit to foreclose the mechanic's lien.

History of Prop. Code §53.123: Acts 1983, 68th Leg., ch. 576, §1, eff. Jan. 1, 1984. Source: TRCS art. 5459, §1.

ANNOTATIONS

First Nat'l Bank v. Whirlpool Corp., 517 S.W.2d 262, 269 (Tex.1974). "[A] mechanic's and materialman's statutory lien upon improvements made is superior to a prior recorded deed of trust lien where the improvements made can be removed without material injury to the land and pre-existing improvements, or to the improvements removed." *See also* ***Exchange S&L Ass'n v. Monocrete Pty. Ltd.***, 629 S.W.2d 34, 37 (Tex. 1982) (includes factors for determining whether an improvement is removable).

Dorsett Bros. Concrete Sup. v. Safeco Title Ins., 880 S.W.2d 417, 423 (Tex.App.—Houston [14th Dist.] 1993, writ denied). See annotation under Property Code §53.022, p. 239.

MBank El Paso v. Featherlite Corp., 792 S.W.2d 472, 475 (Tex.App.—El Paso 1990, writ denied). Generally, "the lien of a materialman, properly perfected, is superior and has priority over any other lien against the land or a security interest in goods or accounts that has not actually attached prior to the inception of the materialman's lien. Inception of the lien takes place when there first is a delivery of construction materials to the construction site and a properly filed lien relates back to that time. [Lender's] security interest could not attach to an account receivable until it had come into existence and therefore would not be a perfected security interest under [B&CC] §9.303.... [¶] At the time of its creation by the delivery of materials to [subcontractor], the account receivable immediately became subject to the materialman's lien and [lender's] security interest, while it would have attached while that lien remained an outstanding charge against the owner's property, was inferior to the lien except as to any amount owed by the contractor or subcontractor to the lienholder in excess of the latter's claim."

PROP §53.124. INCEPTION OF MECHANIC'S LIEN

(a) Except as provided by Subsection (e), for purposes of Section 53.123, the time of inception of a mechanic's lien is the commencement of construction of improvements or delivery of materials to the land on which the improvements are to be located and on which the materials are to be used.

(b) The construction or materials under Subsection (a) must be visible from inspection of the land on which the improvements are being made.

(c) An owner and original contractor may jointly file an affidavit of commencement with the county clerk of the county in which the land is located not later than the 30th day after the date of actual commencement of construction of the improvements or delivery of materials to the land. The affidavit must contain:

(1) the name and address of the owner;

(2) the name and address of each original contractor, known at the time to the owner, that is furnishing labor, service, or materials for the construction of the improvements;

(3) a description, legally sufficient for identification, of the property being improved;

(4) the date the work actually commenced; and

(5) a general description of the improvement.

(d) An affidavit filed in compliance with this section is prima facie evidence of the date of the commencement of the improvement described in the affidavit. The time of inception of a mechanic's lien arising

from work described in an affidavit of commencement is the date of commencement of the work stated in the affidavit.

(e) The time of inception of a lien that is created under Section 53.021(c), (d), or (e) is the date of recording of an affidavit of lien under Section 53.052. The priority of a lien claimed by a person entitled to a lien under Section 53.021(c), (d), or (e) with respect to other mechanic's liens is determined by the date of recording. A lien created under Section 53.021(c), (d), or (e) is not valid or enforceable against a grantee or purchaser who acquires an interest in the real property before the time of inception of the lien.

History of Prop. Code §53.124: Acts 1983, 68th Leg., ch. 576, §1, eff. Jan. 1, 1984. Amended by Acts 1989, 71st Leg., ch. 1138, §19, eff. Sept. 1, 1989; Acts 1995, 74th Leg., ch. 851, §5, eff. Sept. 1, 1995; Acts 1999, 76th Leg., ch. 896, §2, eff. Sept. 1, 1999; Acts 2003, 78th Leg., ch. 410, §2, eff. Sept. 1, 2003. Source: TRCS art. 5459, §2.

ANNOTATIONS

Valdez v. Diamond Shamrock Ref. & Mktg. Co., 842 S.W.2d 273, 276 (Tex.1992). Section 53.124 "fixes the protections and obligations of the lien statutes in general as having arisen on the inception date, and taking priority over the subsequent transfer of interest. Consequently, because [purchaser's] deed was not filed until after the date visible construction began—whereby [subcontractor's] lien took effect—[subcontractor] has a superior claim to the property covered by his lien."

Diversified Mortg. Investors v. Lloyd D. Blaylock Gen. Contractor, Inc., 576 S.W.2d 794, 803 (Tex.1978). Under the definition of "material" under Prop. Code §53.001, "only the delivery of certain types of material will constitute the inception of a mechanic's lien: specifically, either material which will be incorporated into the permanent structure or material which will be consumed or used up during the construction of the permanent structure. Therefore, in order for the delivery of material to constitute the inception of a lien, the court must find: (1) that there has been a delivery of material to the site of construction; (2) that such material is visible upon inspection of the land; and (3) that such material constitutes either (a) material which will be consumed during construction or (b) material which will be incorporated in the permanent structure."

Sections 53.125-53.150 reserved for expansion

SUBCHAPTER G. RELEASE & FORECLOSURE; ACTION ON CLAIM

PROP §53.151. ENFORCEMENT OF REMEDIES AGAINST MONEY DUE ORIGINAL CONTRACTOR OR SUBCONTRACTOR

(a) A creditor of an original contractor may not collect, enforce a security interest against, garnish, or levy execution on the money due the original contractor or the contractor's surety from the owner, and a creditor of a subcontractor may not collect, enforce a security interest against, garnish, or levy execution on the money due the subcontractor, to the prejudice of the subcontractors, mechanics, laborers, materialmen, or their sureties.

(b) A surety issuing a payment bond or performance bond in connection with the improvements has a priority claim over other creditors of its principal to contract funds to the extent of any loss it suffers or incurs. That priority does not excuse the surety from paying any obligations that it may have under its payment bonds.

History of Prop. Code §53.151: Acts 1983, 68th Leg., ch. 576, §1, eff. Jan. 1, 1984. Amended by Acts 1989, 71st Leg., ch. 1138, §20, eff. Sept. 1, 1989. Source: TRCS art. 5466.

ANNOTATIONS

In re Waterpoint Int'l, 330 F.3d 339, 347-48 (5th Cir.2003). "To accept [subcontractor's] argument that [Prop. Code] §53.151 was meant to address funds held in trust for the benefit of subcontractors, we must creatively (and, we think, incorrectly) bridge [Prop. Code chs. 53 and 162]. ... The chapters address different situations. [¶] The upshot of [subcontractor's] argument is that §53.151 precludes a creditor of a contractor from ever collecting the proceeds of an account receivable in which the creditor has a security interest when the owner has not first ensured that all derivative claimants ... have been paid by the contractor. However, if it were this easy for a subcontractor to trap a general contractor's receivable, there would be no need for the elaborate trapping and retention schemes found in Ch. 53. These provisions are designed to protect those subcontractors and materialmen who provide adequate notice to the owner of their presence and their rights to funds owed the contractor."

PROP §53.152. RELEASE OF CLAIM OR LIEN

(a) When a debt for labor or materials is satisfied or paid by collected funds, the person who furnished the labor or materials shall, not later than the 10th day

after the date of receipt of a written request, furnish to the requesting person a release of the indebtedness and any lien claimed, to the extent of the indebtedness paid. An owner, the original contractor, or any person making the payment may request the release.

(b) A release of lien must be in a form that would permit it to be filed of record.

History of Prop. Code §53.152: Acts 1983, 68th Leg., ch. 576, §1, eff. Jan. 1, 1984. Amended by Acts 1989, 71st Leg., ch. 1138, §21, eff. Sept. 1, 1989. Source: TRCS art. 5470.

ANNOTATIONS

Lyda Swinerton Builders, Inc. v. Cathay Bank, 409 S.W.3d 221, 231-32 (Tex.App.—Houston [14th Dist.] 2013, pet. denied). "Here, in exchange for immediate payment, [P] executed a broader release and thereby fully released its initial lien. [¶] But the release itself does not forgive the unpaid portion of [D's] underlying debt. Thus, although the release extinguished the lien, nothing in the document suggests [P] intended to forgive the remaining $1.7 million debt that had not been paid. To the contrary, the release distinguishes the 'indebtedness' from the 'lien' and releases only the lien. [¶] In this way, [P] unambiguously demonstrated its intent to release only 'the lien' without forgiving the unpaid portion of the separately defined 'indebtedness.'"

PROP §53.153. DEFENSE OF ACTIONS

(a) If an affidavit claiming a mechanic's lien is filed by a person other than the original contractor, the original contractor shall defend at his own expense a suit brought on the claim.

(b) If the suit results in judgment on the lien against the owner or the owner's property, the owner is entitled to deduct the amount of the judgment and costs from any amount due the original contractor. If the owner has settled with the original contractor in full, the owner is entitled to recover from the original contractor any amount paid for which the original contractor was originally liable.

History of Prop. Code §53.153: Acts 1983, 68th Leg., ch. 576, §1, eff. Jan. 1, 1984. Source: TRCS art. 5463, §2.

ANNOTATIONS

Weaver v. Jock, 717 S.W.2d 654, 659 (Tex.App.—Waco 1986, writ ref'd n.r.e.). Property Code §53.153(b) allowed motel owners "to deduct the $66,322.86 judgment obtained by [subcontractor] from whatever amount they still owed … general contractor or, if they had already paid him in full, to recover from [general contractor] any amount of the judgment for which he had been originally liable to [subcontractor]. Therefore, [subcontractor's] claim against [motel owners] was contingent and unliquidated when [general contractor] filed the bankruptcy petition under Ch. 11, and [motel owners'] claim for indemnity against [general contractors] under §53.153(b) was likewise contingent and unliquidated at that time. … The automatic stay under [11 U.S.C.] §362(a) … did not preclude [subcontractor] from obtaining a judgment against [motel owners], thereby maturing and liquidating his claim, which automatically matured and liquidated [motel owners'] claim for indemnity against [general contractors] under §53.153(b)…."

PROP §53.154. FORECLOSURE

A mechanic's lien may be foreclosed only on judgment of a court of competent jurisdiction foreclosing the lien and ordering the sale of the property subject to the lien.

History of Prop. Code §53.154: Acts 1983, 68th Leg., ch. 576, §1, eff. Jan. 1, 1984. Source: TRCS art. 5472.

ANNOTATIONS

CVN Grp. v. Delgado, 95 S.W.3d 234, 239 (Tex. 2002). "The dissent extrapolates from [§53.154's] requirement of judicial foreclosure that courts are the exclusive arbiters of whether the technical requirements for perfecting a mechanic's lien have been satisfied. [¶] Nothing in the language or history of §53.154 supports the dissent's position. *At 242-43:* [T]he parties affected by a mechanic's lien can agree to arbitrate its existence."

Crawford Servs. v. Skillman Int'l Firm, LLC, 444 S.W.3d 265, 268-69 (Tex.App.—Dallas 2014, pet. dism'd). "[P] argues … that [§53.154] does not give the court discretion to deny foreclosure of a perfected mechanic's lien. It contends that the word 'may' must be understood as part of the phrase 'may only' and when read in that context means that the only way to foreclose a mechanic's lien is through court order. [¶] [D] contends that 'may' connotes discretion and that [P's] interpretation of the statute changes the word 'may' to 'shall.' *At 271:* [We agree with P and] conclude that once the trial court determined that the lienholder had a valid debt and a perfected mechanic's lien, it did not have discretion under §53.154 to deny a judgment of foreclosure and order of sale of the property subject to the lien. An interpretation that the statute affords

the trial court unlimited discretion would introduce uncertainty into the mechanic's lien enforcement process and defeat the purpose for enacting the mechanic's lien statutes: to provide security to those who supply labor and materials for improving the value of another's land."

Cadle Co. v. Ortiz, 227 S.W.3d 831, 835 (Tex. App.—Corpus Christi 2007, pet. denied). "Under the existing homestead law, [D's] lien on [Ps'] home must be found invalid because it depends upon three documents—the assumption deed, the note, and the trust deed—that are not signed by both [spouses] as the Texas Constitution explicitly requires. [D] attempts to overcome the two-spouse signature requirement with an affirmative defense: [D] argues that [wife] misrepresented her marital status by omitting [husband's] name from the lien documents, and thus a finding that [Ps] did not waive their homestead rights by deliberately misrepresenting creditors is against the great weight and preponderance of the evidence. We disagree. *At 836:* We hold … that [D] has not demonstrated that the great weight and preponderance of the evidence favors a reversal of the trial court's implied finding that [Ps] did not waive their homestead rights. The mechanic's lien asserted by [D] against [Ps'] homestead is invalid because the relevant documents do not meet the statutory requirement of having been signed by both spouses. [D's] asserted lien does not supersede [Ps'] homestead exemption, and thus the foreclosure on the home was wrongful."

PROP §53.155. TRANSFER OF PROPERTY SOLD

If the house, building, improvement, or any piece of railroad property is sold separately, the officer making the sale shall place the purchaser in possession. The purchaser is entitled to a reasonable time after the date of purchase within which to remove the purchased property.

History of Prop. Code §53.155: Acts 1983, 68th Leg., ch. 576, §1, eff. Jan. 1, 1984. Source: TRCS art. 5471.

PROP §53.156. COSTS & ATTORNEY'S FEES

In any proceeding to foreclose a lien or to enforce a claim against a bond issued under Subchapter H, I, or J or in any proceeding to declare that any lien or claim is invalid or unenforceable in whole or in part, the court shall award costs and reasonable attorney's fees as are equitable and just. With respect to a lien or claim arising out of a residential construction contract, the court is not required to order the property owner to pay costs and attorney's fees under this section.

History of Prop. Code §53.156: Acts 1984, 68th Leg., 2nd C.S., ch. 18, §4(a), eff. Oct. 2, 1984. Amended by Acts 1989, 71st Leg., ch. 1138, §22, eff. Sept. 1, 1989; Acts 2011, 82nd Leg., ch. 51, §1, eff. Sept. 1, 2011. Source: TRCS arts. 5453, subdivs. 4, 5; 5472b-1, §2; 5472c, §§4a, 6; 5472d, §6.

ANNOTATIONS

Bluelinx Corp. v. Texas Constr. Sys., 363 S.W.3d 623, 631 (Tex.App.—Houston [14th Dist.] 2011, no pet.). "[D] argues that the trial court erred in awarding costs to [P] because [P] was not the successful party and because [P] did not present an itemized list of all costs. Section 53.156 … authorizes the court to award not only attorney's fees in a proceeding to foreclose a lien but costs as well. [P] was successful in its proceeding to foreclose on its lien, and the trial court did not abuse its discretion in awarding [P] costs. Further, the judgment does not recite a specific amount of costs but merely states that '[a]ll costs of court are assessed against' [D]. The clerk's record contains an itemization of costs, and [P] is entitled under the court's order to recover those costs of record."

Chubb Lloyds Ins. v. Andrew's Restoration, Inc., 323 S.W.3d 564, 583 (Tex.App.—Dallas 2010), *rev'd in part on other grounds sub nom.* ***Cruz v. Andrews Restoration, Inc.***, 364 S.W.3d 817 (Tex.2012). "Any fee award had to be both reasonable and just. The reasonableness of a particular amount of attorneys' fees 'is a question of fact for the jury's determination.' Whether an award of fees would be equitable and just is a matter addressed to the court's discretion. 'Unreasonable fees cannot be awarded, even if the court believed them just, but the court may conclude that it is not equitable or just to award even reasonable and necessary fees.' … Although the attorney testified about his background and experience, he did not testify about the number of hours spent on the lien-removal claim, nor did he offer any details about the work performed specifically on that part of the case. The court could reasonably have decided it would not be equitable and just to award any fee based on the quality of [D's] evidence of the reasonableness of the amount sought, particularly without a jury finding of reasonableness in support. Its denial of fees was not an abuse of discretion."

West v. Triple B Servs., 264 S.W.3d 440, 455 (Tex. App.—Houston [14th Dist.] 2008, no pet.). Contractor "contends that, because costs and attorney's fees can

often exceed the difference between the face value of the bond and actual damages, public policy weighs against such a result because it would be neither equitable nor just. We acknowledge that limiting the recovery of costs and attorney's fees to the face amount of the bond could limit a contractor's potential recovery of costs and attorney's fees, but that is always a potential outcome when a party sues on a bond, unless there is some other statutory or contractual basis for a full recovery of costs and attorney's fees against the surety. [¶] Therefore, ... we hold that the Legislature did not intend ... §53.156 to alter the general rule that the surety's liability is limited to the face amount of the bond."

PROP §53.157. DISCHARGE OF LIEN

A mechanic's lien or affidavit claiming a mechanic's lien filed under Section 53.052 may be discharged of record by:

(1) recording a lien release signed by the claimant under Section 53.152;

(2) failing to institute suit to foreclose the lien in the county in which the property is located within the period prescribed by Section 53.158, 53.175, or 53.208;

(3) recording the original or certified copy of a final judgment or decree of a court of competent jurisdiction providing for the discharge;

(4) filing the bond and notice in compliance with Subchapter H;

(5) filing the bond in compliance with Subchapter I; or

(6) recording a certified copy of the order removing the lien under Section 53.160 and a certificate from the clerk of the court that states that no bond or deposit as described by Section 53.161 was filed by the claimant within 30 days after the date the order was entered.

History of Prop. Code §53.157: Acts 1989, 71st Leg., ch. 1138, §23, eff. Sept. 1, 1989. Amended by Acts 1997, 75th Leg., ch. 526, §15, eff. Sept. 1, 1997.

ANNOTATIONS

Pineridge Assocs. v. Ridgepine, LLC, 337 S.W.3d 461, 466-67 (Tex.App.—Fort Worth 2011, no pet.). "[Ds] argue that the mechanic's liens were released of record when they were extinguished by the ... foreclosure sale.... [Ds] assume that 'extinguished' and 'released of record' are synonymous. We disagree.... [¶] [The only] way a mechanic's lien may be discharged of record ... under §53.157 without filing a document in the county deed records ... is by failing to initiate suit to foreclose the lien within the applicable statute of limitations. [Ds] argue that the extinguishment of the mechanic's liens by foreclosure sale is analogous to this ... provision. But while neither the extinguishment of a junior lien through foreclosure nor the failure to file suit within the statute of limitations requires the filing of a document reflecting the unenforceability of the lien, the legislature chose not to include extinguishment through foreclosure in §53.157. [T]he rule that foreclosure extinguishes junior liens has been part of Texas law since at least 1890. ... Thus, we are not persuaded that the extinguishment of a mechanic's lien through foreclosure is equivalent to a lien that has been 'discharged of record' by failing to file suit within the applicable statute of limitations. *At 468:* We hold that the mechanic's liens were not automatically released of record when they were extinguished through the foreclosure sale."

Stolz v. Honeycutt, 42 S.W.3d 305, 311 (Tex. App.—Houston [14th Dist.] 2001, no pet.). See annotation under Property Code §53.175, p. 262.

Apex Fin. Corp. v. Brown, 7 S.W.3d 820, 830 (Tex. App.—Texarkana 1999, no pet.). "[A] statutory mechanic's lien will not be enforceable if it has been discharged by recording a lien release signed by the lienholder. [¶] [Contractor] contends ... that a new statutory lien arose when he refiled the original contract with the original acknowledgment in the county records. [¶] Once waived, a statutory lien cannot be revived. *At 830 n.5:* Even if a previously waived lien could be revived in some manner, refiling the original lien contract without new signatures or a new acknowledgment will not be sufficient."

PROP §53.158. PERIOD FOR BRINGING SUIT TO FORECLOSE LIEN

(a) Except as provided by Subsection (b), suit must be brought to foreclose the lien within two years after the last day a claimant may file the lien affidavit under Section 53.052 or within one year after completion, termination, or abandonment of the work under the original contract under which the lien is claimed, whichever is later.

(b) For a claim arising from a residential construction project, suit must be brought to foreclose the lien within one year after the last day a claimant may file a lien affidavit under Section 53.052 or within one year after completion, termination, or abandonment of the

work under the original contract under which the lien is claimed, whichever is later.

History of Prop. Code §53.158: Acts 1989, 71st Leg., ch. 1138, §23, eff. Sept. 1, 1989. Amended by Acts 1997, 75th Leg., ch. 526, §16, eff. Sept. 1, 1997; Acts 1999, 76th Leg., ch. 889, §4, eff. Sept. 1, 1999.

PROP §53.159. OBLIGATION TO FURNISH INFORMATION

(a) An owner, on written request, shall furnish the following information within a reasonable time, but not later than the 10th day after the date the request is received, to any person furnishing labor or materials for the project:

(1) a description of the real property being improved legally sufficient to identify it;

(2) whether there is a surety bond and if so, the name and last known address of the surety and a copy of the bond;

(3) whether there are any prior recorded liens or security interests on the real property being improved and if so, the name and address of the person having the lien or security interest; and

(4) the date on which the original contract for the project was executed.

(b) An original contractor, on written request by a person who furnished work under the original contract, shall furnish to the person the following information within a reasonable time, but not later than the 10th day after the date the request is received:

(1) the name and last known address of the person to whom the original contractor furnished labor or materials for the construction project;

(2) whether the original contractor has furnished or has been furnished a payment bond for any of the work on the construction project and if so, the name and last known address of the surety and a copy of the bond; and

(3) the date on which the original contract for the project was executed.

(c) A subcontractor, on written request by an owner of the property being improved, the original contractor, a surety on a bond covering the original contract, or any person furnishing work under the subcontract, shall furnish to the person the following information within a reasonable time, but not later than the 10th day after the date the request is received:

(1) the name and last known address of each person from whom the subcontractor purchased labor or materials for the construction project, other than those materials that were furnished to the project from the subcontractor's inventory;

(2) the name and last known address of each person to whom the subcontractor furnished labor or materials for the construction project; and

(3) whether the subcontractor has furnished or has been furnished a payment bond for any of the work on the construction project and if so, the name and last known address of the surety and a copy of the bond.

(d) Not later than the 30th day after the date a written request is received from the owner, the contractor under whom a claim of lien or under whom a bond is made, or a surety on a bond on which a claim is made, a claimant for a lien or under a bond shall furnish to the requesting person a copy of any applicable written agreement, purchase order, or contract and any billing, statement, or payment request of the claimant reflecting the amount claimed and the work performed by the claimant for which the claim is made. If requested, the claimant shall provide the estimated amount due for each calendar month in which the claimant has performed labor or furnished materials.

(e) If a person from whom information is requested does not have a direct contractual relationship on the project with the person requesting the information, the person from whom information is requested, other than a claimant requested to furnish information under Subsection (d), may require payment of the actual costs, not to exceed $25, in furnishing the requested information.

(f) A person, other than a claimant requested to furnish information under Subsection (d), who fails to furnish information as required by this section is liable to the requesting person for that person's reasonable and necessary costs incurred in procuring the requested information.

(g) Expired.

History of Prop. Code §53.159: Acts 1989, 71st Leg., ch. 1138, §23, eff. Sept. 1, 1989. Amended by Acts 2011, 82nd Leg., ch. 499, §7, eff. Sept. 1, 2011.

PROP §53.160. SUMMARY MOTION TO REMOVE INVALID OR UNENFORCEABLE LIEN

(a) In a suit brought to foreclose a lien or to declare a claim or lien invalid or unenforceable, a party objecting to the validity or enforceability of the claim or lien may file a motion to remove the claim or lien. The motion must be verified and state the legal and factual

basis for objecting to the validity or enforceability of the claim or lien. The motion may be accompanied by supporting affidavits.

(b) The grounds for objecting to the validity or enforceability of the claim or lien for purposes of the motion are limited to the following:

(1) notice of claim was not furnished to the owner or original contractor as required by Section 53.056, 53.057, 53.058, 53.252, or 53.253;

(2) an affidavit claiming a lien failed to comply with Section 53.054 or was not filed as required by Section 53.052;

(3) notice of the filed affidavit was not furnished to the owner or original contractor as required by Section 53.055;

(4) the deadlines for perfecting a lien claim for retainage under this chapter have expired and the owner complied with the requirements of Section 53.101 and paid the retainage and all other funds owed to the original contractor before:

(A) the claimant perfected the lien claim; and

(B) the owner received a notice of the claim as required by this chapter;

(5) all funds subject to the notice of a claim to the owner and a notice regarding the retainage have been deposited in the registry of the court and the owner has no additional liability to the claimant;

(6) when the lien affidavit was filed on homestead property:

(A) no contract was executed or filed as required by Section 53.254;

(B) the affidavit claiming a lien failed to contain the notice as required by Section 53.254; or

(C) the notice of the claim failed to include the statement required by Section 53.254; and

(7) the claimant executed a valid and enforceable waiver or release of the claim or lien claimed in the affidavit.

(c) The claimant is not required to file a response. The claimant and any other party that has appeared in the proceeding must be notified by at least 21 days before the date of the hearing on the motion. A motion may not be heard before the 21st day after the date the claimant answers or appears in the proceeding.

(d) At the hearing on the motion, the burden is on:

(1) the claimant to prove that the notice of claim and affidavit of lien were furnished to the owner and original contractor as required by this chapter; and

(2) the movant to establish that the lien should be removed for any other ground authorized by this section.

(e) The court shall promptly determine a motion to remove a claim or lien under this section. If the court determines that the movant is not entitled to remove the lien, the court shall enter an order denying the motion. If the court determines that the movant is entitled to remove the lien, the court shall enter an order removing the lien claimed in the lien affidavit. A party to the proceeding may not file an interlocutory appeal from the court's order.

(f) Any admissible evidence offered at the hearing may be admitted in the trial of the case. The court's order under Subsection (e) is not admissible as evidence in determining the validity and enforceability of the claim or lien.

History of Prop. Code §53.160: Acts 1997, 75th Leg., ch. 526, §17, eff. Sept. 1, 1997. Amended by Acts 2011, 82nd Leg., ch. 499, §8, eff. Sept. 1, 2011.

ANNOTATIONS

In re M&O Homebuilders, Inc., 516 S.W.3d 101, 106 (Tex.App.—Houston [1st Dist.] 2017, orig. proceeding). "[P] argues that [D's] motion sought only to remove a lien and did not seek a judgment. [P] maintains that the ... order cannot be a judgment because it grants a motion that did not seek a partial summary judgment. *At 107:* The motion sought a declaration by the trial court that the lien filed by [P] on [D's] property was defective and should be removed. [¶] [A] summary motion that seeks a declaration that a lien is invalid ... seeks a summary adjudication of that claim and operates, in effect, as a motion for partial summary judgment."

Big H Constr., Inc. v. Hensley, No. 01-10-00379-CV (Tex.App.—Houston [1st Dist.] 2011, no pet.) (memo op.; 3-31-11). "[D] moved to strike the summary motion because [Ps] failed to give 21-days' notice of a hearing on the motion, as §53.160(c) ... requires. [¶] [Ps] did not comply with the notice requirement of the statute. [¶] [Ps] maintain that [D] did not preserve error on this issue. ... To preserve error for a complaint regarding late notice of a summary judgment hearing, a nonmovant who receives notice that is untimely but sufficient to enable the nonmovant to attend the hearing must move for continuance or raise the late-notice complaint in writing. [D] presented a written objection to the trial court.... We hold that the trial court erred in

granting [Ps'] summary motion because [D] did not receive the required 21-days' notice of the hearing."

Dalton Contractors, Inc. v. Bryan Autumn Woods, Ltd., 60 S.W.3d 351, 354 (Tex.App.—Houston [1st Dist.] 2001, no pet.). "While the property code provides a mechanism for determining the validity of a lien, there is nothing to indicate that the issue may not also be resolved by an arbitrator, if the parties have agreed to arbitration.... ***Hearthshire [Braeswood Plaza, Ltd. v. Bill Kelly Co.***, 849 S.W.2d 380 (Tex.App.—Houston [14th Dist.] 1993, writ denied),] is a clear indication that arbitration is an appropriate mechanism for resolving the validity of liens, despite the existence of other avenues of legal recourse."

PROP §53.161. BOND REQUIREMENTS AFTER ORDER TO REMOVE

(a) In the order removing a lien, the court shall set the amount of security that the claimant may provide in order to stay the removal of the claim or lien. The sum must be an amount that the court determines is a reasonable estimate of the costs and attorney's fees the movant is likely to incur in the proceeding to determine the validity or enforceability of the lien. The sum may not exceed the amount of the lien claim.

(b) The court shall stay the order removing the lien if the claimant files a bond or a deposit in lieu of a bond in the amount set in the order with the clerk of the court not later than the 30th day after the date the order is entered by the court unless, for good cause, the court orders a later date for filing the bond or the deposit in lieu of a bond. If the court fails to set the amount of the security required, the amount required is the amount of the lien claim.

(c) The bond must be:

(1) executed by a corporate surety authorized to do business in this state and licensed by this state to execute bonds as surety; and

(2) conditioned on the claimant's payment of any final judgment rendered against the claimant in the proceeding for attorney's fees and costs to the movant under Section 53.156.

(d) In lieu of filing a bond, the claimant may deposit in the amount set by the court for the surety bond:

(1) cash;

(2) a negotiable obligation of the federal government or a federal agency; or

(3) a negotiable obligation of a financial institution chartered by the federal or state government that is insured by the federal government or a federal agency.

(e) A deposit made under Subsection (d) must be conditioned in the same manner as a surety bond. Any interest accrued on the deposit amount is a part of the deposit.

(f) If the claimant fails to file the bond or the deposit in lieu of the bond in compliance with this section, the owner may file:

(1) a certified copy of the order; and

(2) a certificate from the clerk of the court stating that:

(A) no bond or deposit in lieu of the bond was filed within 30 days after the date the order was entered by the court; and

(B) no order staying the order to remove the lien was entered by the court.

(g) The claim or lien is removed and extinguished as to a creditor or subsequent purchaser for valuable consideration who obtains an interest in the property after the certified copy of the order and certificate of the clerk of the court are filed with the county clerk. The removal of the lien does not constitute a release of the liability of the owner, if any, to the claimant.

History of Prop. Code §53.161: Acts 1997, 75th Leg., ch. 526, §17, eff. Sept. 1, 1997.

PROP §53.162. REVIVAL OF REMOVED LIEN

(a) If an order removing the lien is not stayed as provided by Section 53.161 and the claimant later obtains a final judgment in the suit establishing the validity and ordering the foreclosure of the lien, the claimant may file a certified copy of the final judgment with the county clerk.

(b) The filed judgment revives the lien, and the claimant may foreclose the lien.

(c) A lien revived under this section is void as to a creditor or subsequent purchaser for valuable consideration who obtained an interest in the property:

(1) after the order removing the lien and the certificate from the clerk of the court was filed with the county clerk; and

(2) before the final judgment reviving the lien was filed with the county clerk.

History of Prop. Code §53.162: Acts 1997, 75th Leg., ch. 526, §17, eff. Sept. 1, 1997.

Sections 53.163-53.170 reserved for expansion

SUBCHAPTER H. BOND TO INDEMNIFY AGAINST LIEN

PROP §53.171. BOND

(a) If a lien, other than a lien granted by the owner in a written contract, is fixed or is attempted to be fixed by a recorded instrument under this chapter, any person may file a bond to indemnify against the lien.

(b) The bond shall be filed with the county clerk of the county in which the property subject to the lien is located.

(c) A mechanic's lien claim against an owner's property is discharged after:

(1) a bond that complies with Section 53.172 is filed;

(2) the notice of the bond is issued as provided by Section 53.173; and

(3) the bond and notice are recorded as provided by Section 53.174.

History of Prop. Code §53.171: Acts 1983, 68th Leg., ch. 576, §1, eff. Jan. 1, 1984. Amended by Acts 1989, 71st Leg., ch. 1138, §§24, 39(1), eff. Sept. 1, 1989; Acts 1997, 75th Leg., ch. 526, §18, eff. Sept. 1, 1997. Source: TRCS art. 5472c, §§1, 4.

ANNOTATIONS

Stolz v. Honeycutt, 42 S.W.3d 305, 311 (Tex. App.—Houston [14th Dist.] 2001, no pet.). See annotation under Property Code §53.175, p. 262.

PROP §53.172. BOND REQUIREMENTS

The bond must:

(1) describe the property on which the liens are claimed;

(2) refer to each lien claimed in a manner sufficient to identify it;

(3) be in an amount that is double the amount of the liens referred to in the bond unless the total amount claimed in the liens exceeds $40,000, in which case the bond must be in an amount that is the greater of 1-½ times the amount of the liens or the sum of $40,000 and the amount of the liens;

(4) be payable to the parties claiming the liens;

(5) be executed by:

(A) the party filing the bond as principal; and

(B) a corporate surety authorized and admitted to do business under the law in this state and licensed by this state to execute the bond as surety, subject to Section 1, Chapter 87, Acts of the 56th Legislature, Regular Session, 1959 (Article 7.19-1, Vernon's Texas Insurance Code); and

(6) be conditioned substantially that the principal and sureties will pay to the named obligees or to their assignees the amount that the named obligees would have been entitled to recover if their claims had been proved to be valid and enforceable liens on the property.

History of Prop. Code §53.172: Acts 1983, 68th Leg., ch. 576, §1, eff. Jan. 1, 1984. Amended by Acts 1989, 71st Leg., ch. 1138, §25, eff. Sept. 1, 1989; Acts 1997, 75th Leg., ch. 1132, §2, eff. Sept. 1, 1997. Source: TRCS art. 5472c, §1.

ANNOTATIONS

Sheldon Pollack Corp. v. Pioneer Concrete, Inc., 765 S.W.2d 843, 846 (Tex.App.—Dallas 1989, writ denied). "[P] concedes that its sole cause of action against [D] is based upon [D's] liability under the indemnity bond. [P] asserts that it complied with all of the statutory requirements to proceed against the bond and that the only arguable reason for absolving [D] from liability is the imposition of the rider condition against it. [P] argues that the rider provision is unenforceable and void because it conflicts with the provisions of §53.172 … and the public policy of the lien and bond laws. We agree with [P]. [¶] Where a bond is executed with the intention of the parties to comply with the requirements of a statute, the terms of such statute will become a part of such obligation, by incorporation, even though the bond itself is otherwise silent as to the statutory obligations. [Section 53.172] contains no limitation of liability such as that made a part of this bond by the rider…."

PROP §53.173. NOTICE OF BOND

(a) After the bond is filed, the county clerk shall issue notice of the bond to all named obligees.

(b) A copy of the bond must be attached to the notice.

(c) The notice must be served on each obligee by mailing a copy of the notice and the bond to the obligee by certified United States mail, return receipt requested, addressed to the claimant at the address stated in the lien affidavit for the obligee.

(d) If the claimant's lien affidavit does not state the claimant's address, the notice is not required to be mailed to the claimant.

History of Prop. Code §53.173: Acts 1983, 68th Leg., ch. 576, §1, eff. Jan. 1, 1984. Amended by Acts 1989, 71st Leg., ch. 1138, §26, eff. Sept. 1, 1989; Acts 1997, 75th Leg., ch. 526, §19, eff. Sept. 1, 1997. Source: TRCS art. 5472c, §2.

PROP §53.174. RECORDING OF BOND & NOTICE

(a) The county clerk shall record the bond, the notice, and a certificate of mailing in the real property records.

(b) In acquiring an interest in or insuring title to real property, a purchaser, insurer of title, or lender may rely on and is absolutely protected by the record of the bond and the notice to the same extent as if the lien claimant had filed a release of lien in the real property records.

History of Prop. Code §53.174: Acts 1983, 68th Leg., ch. 576, §1, eff. Jan. 1, 1984. Amended by Acts 1989, 71st Leg., ch. 1138, §27, eff. Sept. 1, 1989; Acts 1997, 75th Leg., ch. 526, §20, eff. Sept. 1, 1997. Source: TRCS art. 5472c, §3.

PROP §53.175. ACTION ON BOND

(a) A party making or holding a lien claim may not sue on the bond later than one year after the date on which the notice is served or after the date on which the underlying lien claim becomes unenforceable under Section 53.158.

(b) The bond is not exhausted by one action against it. Each named obligee or assignee of an obligee may maintain a separate suit on the bond in any court of jurisdiction in the county in which the real property is located.

History of Prop. Code §53.175: Acts 1983, 68th Leg., ch. 576, §1, eff. Jan. 1, 1984. Amended by Acts 1989, 71st Leg., ch. 1138, §28, eff. Sept. 1, 1989; Acts 1997, 75th Leg., ch. 526, §21, eff. Sept. 1, 1997. Source: TRCS art. 5472c, §4.

ANNOTATIONS

Stolz v. Honeycutt, 42 S.W.3d 305, 311 (Tex. App.—Houston [14th Dist.] 2001, no pet.). "[P] obtained an indemnity bond from [insurance company] and gave notice to [D]. [D's] failure to timely sue on the bond precludes recovery against the surety of the bond."

PROP §53.176. REPEALED

Repealed by Acts 1989, 71st Leg., ch. 1138, §39(2), eff. Sept. 1, 1989.

Sections 53.177-53.200 reserved for expansion

SUBCHAPTER I. BOND TO PAY LIENS OR CLAIMS

PROP §53.201. BOND

(a) An original contractor who has a written contract with the owner may furnish at any time a bond for the benefit of claimants.

(b) If a valid bond is filed, a claimant may not file suit against the owner or the owner's property and the owner is relieved of obligations under Subchapter D or E.

History of Prop. Code §53.201: Acts 1983, 68th Leg., ch. 576, §1, eff. Jan. 1, 1984. Amended by Acts 1997, 75th Leg., ch. 526, §22, eff. Sept. 1, 1997. Source: TRCS art. 5472d, §§1, 7.

ANNOTATIONS

Laughlin Envtl., Inc. v. Premier Towers, L.P., 126 S.W.3d 668, 675 (Tex.App.—Houston [14th Dist.] 2004, no pet.). See annotation under Property Code §53.202, p. 263.

Staff Indus. v. Hallmark Contracting, Inc., 846 S.W.2d 542, 550 (Tex.App.—Corpus Christi 1993, no writ). Section 53.201 "provides a procedure, by way of a bond furnished by the original contractor for the benefit of claimants, for the owner of a construction project to escape liability to subcontractors, laborers and materialmen who would otherwise have a claim against the owner for labor and materials and a lien against his property."

Sentry Ins. v. Radcliff Materials, Inc., 687 S.W.2d 437, 440 (Tex.App.—Houston [14th Dist.] 1985, no writ). The bond "before us states only that [materialman] will reimburse the Obligee ... for all loss and damages sustained *if [materialman] fails to perform its obligations*. There is no language contained in the bond to show it was intended for the protection of subcontractors or materialmen who are not paid for services or materials provided to the general contractor. Thus, it is clear that the requirements of [Prop. Code] §53.202 ... were not complied with, and the bond in question is not a Hardeman Act bond on its face." *See also* ***Sherwin-Williams Co. v. American Indem. Co.***, 504 S.W.2d 400, 402 (Tex.1973).

PROP §53.202. BOND REQUIREMENTS

The bond must:

(1) be in a penal sum at least equal to the total of the original contract amount;

(2) be in favor of the owner;

(3) have the written approval of the owner endorsed on it;

(4) be executed by:

(A) the original contractor as principal; and

(B) a corporate surety authorized and admitted to do business in this state and licensed by this state to execute bonds as surety, subject to Section 1, Chapter 87, Acts of the 56th Legislature, Regular Session, 1959 (Article 7.19-1, Vernon's Texas Insurance Code);

(5) be conditioned on prompt payment for all labor, subcontracts, materials, specially fabricated materials,

and normal and usual extras not exceeding 15 percent of the contract price; and

(6) clearly and prominently display on the bond or on an attachment to the bond:

(A) the name, mailing address, physical address, and telephone number, including the area code, of the surety company to which any notice of claim should be sent; or

(B) the toll-free telephone number maintained by the Texas Department of Insurance under Subchapter B, Chapter 521, Insurance Code, and a statement that the address of the surety company to which any notice of claim should be sent may be obtained from the Texas Department of Insurance by calling the toll-free telephone number.

History of Prop. Code §53.202: Acts 1983, 68th Leg., ch. 576, §1, eff. Jan. 1, 1984. Amended by Acts 1989, 71st Leg., ch. 1138, §29, eff. Sept. 1, 1989; Acts 1997, 75th Leg., ch. 1132, §2, eff. Sept. 1, 1997; Acts 2001, 77th Leg., ch. 380, §5, eff. Sept. 1, 2001; Acts 2005, 79th Leg., ch. 728, §11.158, eff. Sept. 1, 2005. Source: TRCS art. 5472d, §§1, 2.

ANNOTATIONS

Fondren Constr. Co. v. Briarcliff Hous. Dev. Assocs., 196 S.W.3d 210, 213 (Tex.App.—Houston [1st Dist.] 2006, no pet.). "[P] relies on §53.202(1) ..., which requires that the penal sum of the bond be at least equal to the original contract amount. Because the penal sum sets the financial limits of the surety's obligations, it is the most material aspect of a payment bond. ... The original amount of the contract ... is $4,224,485.00, and the amount of the payment bond issued by [surety] is $4,224,485.00—exactly equal to the amount of the contract. The contract and the bond are evidence that the bond is in a penal sum equal to the total of the original contract, and [P] did not offer any controverting evidence. ... We hold that the payment bond complied with ... §53.202(1)."

Laughlin Envtl., Inc. v. Premier Towers, L.P., 126 S.W.3d 668, 675 (Tex.App.—Houston [14th Dist.] 2004, no pet.). "[T]he property owner seeking protection under [§53.202] is required to give written approval of the payment bond before it is filed. In placing this burden on the property owner, the legislature clearly assigned the risk of noncompliance to the owner. [¶] Based on the noted defects, the Bond does not have the legal effect of a statutory payment bond, and is nothing more than a common-law payment bond. [T]he requirements for making a claim and filing suit on the Bond are governed by the terms of the Bond itself, as well as applicable common-law principles. More importantly, because [the Hardeman Act] does not apply, the Bond does not operate to preclude the Lien claim against the Property."

Sentry Ins. v. Radcliff Materials, Inc., 687 S.W.2d 437, 440 (Tex.App.—Houston [14th Dist.] 1985, no writ). "The Hardeman Act provisions set out a general statutory scheme whereby a payment bond, executed by an original contractor, is substituted for whatever other relief might be obtained by subcontractors and those furnishing materials and labor against the owner and his property. When the bond is properly executed and recorded, the owner is not liable to derivative claimants."

PROP §53.203. RECORDING OF BOND & CONTRACT

(a) The bond and the contract between the original contractor and the owner shall be filed with the county clerk of the county in which is located all or part of the owner's property on which the construction or repair is being performed or is to be performed. A memorandum of the contract or a copy of the contract may be substituted for the original.

(b) The plans, specifications, and general conditions of the contract are not required to be filed.

(c) The county clerk shall record the bond and place the contract on file in the clerk's office and shall index and cross-index both in the names of the original contractor and the owner in records kept for that purpose.

(d) On request and payment of a reasonable fee, the county clerk shall furnish a copy of the bond and contract to any person.

(e) In any court of this state or in the United States, a copy of the bond and contract certified by the county clerk constitutes prima facie evidence of the contents, execution, delivery, and filing of the originals.

History of Prop. Code §53.203: Acts 1983, 68th Leg., ch. 576, §1, eff. Jan. 1, 1984. Amended by Acts 1987, 70th Leg., ch. 683, §1, eff. Aug. 31, 1987; Acts 1989, 71st Leg., ch. 1138, §30, eff. Sept. 1, 1989. Source: TRCS art. 5472d, §§1-3.

PROP §53.204. RELIANCE ON RECORD

A purchaser, lender, or other person acquiring an interest in the owner's property or an insurer of title is entitled to rely on the record of the bond and contract as constituting payment of all claims and liens for labor, subcontracts, materials, or specially fabricated materials incurred by the original contractor as if the purchaser, lender, or other person acquiring an interest in

the owner's property or an insurer of title were the owner who approved, accepted, and endorsed the bond and as if each person furnishing labor or materials for the work performed under the original contract, other than the original contractor, had filed a complete release and relinquishment of lien of record.

History of Prop. Code §53.204: Acts 1983, 68th Leg., ch. 576, §1, eff. Jan. 1, 1984. Amended by Acts 1989, 71st Leg., ch. 1138, §31, eff. Sept. 1, 1989. Source: TRCS art. 5472d, §7.

PROP §53.205. ENFORCEABLE CLAIMS

(a) The bond protects all persons with a claim that is:

(1) perfected in the manner prescribed for fixing a lien under Subchapter C or, if the claim relates to a residential construction project, under Subchapter K; or

(2) perfected in the manner prescribed by Section 53.206.

(b) A claim or the rights to a claim under the bond may be assigned.

History of Prop. Code §53.205: Acts 1983, 68th Leg., ch. 576, §1, eff. Jan. 1, 1984. Amended by Acts 1999, 76th Leg., ch. 889, §5, eff. Sept. 1, 1999. Source: TRCS art. 5472d, §1.

ANNOTATIONS

Pavecon, Inc. v. R-Com, Inc., 159 S.W.3d 219, 223-24 (Tex.App.—Fort Worth 2005, no pet.). See annotation under Property Code §53.206, this page.

PROP §53.206. PERFECTION OF CLAIM

(a) To perfect a claim against a bond in a manner other than that prescribed by Subchapter C or K for fixing a lien, a person must:

(1) give to the original contractor all applicable notices under the appropriate subchapter; and

(2) give to the surety on the bond, instead of the owner, all notices under the appropriate subchapter required to be given to the owner.

(b) To perfect a claim under this section, a person is not required to:

(1) give notice to the surety under Section 53.057, unless the claimant has a direct contractual relationship with the original contractor and the agreed retainage is in excess of 10 percent of the contract;

(2) give notice to the surety under Section 53.058(b) or, if the claim relates to a residential construction project, under Section 53.253(c); or

(3) file any affidavit with the county clerk.

(c) For the claim to be valid, a person must give notice in the time and manner required by this section, but the content of the notices need only provide fair notice of the amount and the nature of the claim asserted.

(d) A person satisfies the requirements of this section relating to providing notice to the surety if the person mails the notice by certified or registered mail to the surety:

(1) at the address stated on the bond or on an attachment to the bond;

(2) at the address on file with the Texas Department of Insurance; or

(3) at any other address allowed by law.

History of Prop. Code §53.206: Acts 1983, 68th Leg., ch. 576, §1, eff. Jan. 1, 1984. Amended by Acts 1989, 71st Leg., ch. 1138, §32, eff. Sept. 1, 1989; Acts 1999, 76th Leg., ch. 889, §6, eff. Sept. 1, 1999; Acts 2001, 77th Leg., ch. 380, §6, eff. Sept. 1, 2001. Source: TRCS art. 5472d, §4.

ANNOTATIONS

Pavecon, Inc. v. R-Com, Inc., 159 S.W.3d 219, 223-24 (Tex.App.—Fort Worth 2005, no pet.). "The parties agree that [D's] bond is not a statutory bond covered by the property code. [P] asserts that, because [D's] bond is not a statutory bond, there is no 'appropriate subchapter' of the property code covering the bond and that the express terms of the bond therefore required no notice from [P] to [D] in order for [P] to perfect its claims against the bond. [¶] [D] asserts that the 'appropriate subchapter' in [Prop. Code] §53.206 refers to subch. C or K, and in this case, subch. C. We agree. [¶] [D] further contends that §53.206(a) applies subch. C's notice provision, which is found in [Prop. Code] §53.056(b), to a subcontractor's claims against a surety bond. Section 53.056(b) requires a subcontractor to give the owner written notice of the unpaid balance of a claim by the 15th day of the third month after the month in which the materials or services were provided. Section 53.206(a)(2) requires the subcontractor desiring to perfect a claim against a surety bond to give this notice to the surety instead of the owner. [D] asserts that the bond, which incorporates these statutory provisions, required [P] to give this notice to [D] and that, because [P] failed to do so, [P] cannot recover on its claims against [D's] bond. This construction gives effect to the bond provision and is also in accordance with the plain meaning of §§53.206(a) and 53.056(b). [¶] [W]e conclude that [D's] construction of 'the appropriate subchapter' is correct."

PROP §53.207. OWNER'S NOTICE OF CLAIM TO SURETY

(a) If the owner receives any of the notices or a lien is fixed under Subchapter C or K, the owner shall mail to the surety on the bond a copy of all notices received.

(b) Failure of the owner to send copies of notices to the surety does not relieve the surety of any liability under the bond if the claimant has complied with the requirements of this subchapter, nor does that failure impose any liability on the owner.

History of Prop. Code §53.207: Acts 1983, 68th Leg., ch. 576, §1, eff. Jan. 1, 1984. Amended by Acts 1999, 76th Leg., ch. 889, §7, eff. Sept. 1, 1999. Source: TRCS art. 5472d, §5.

PROP §53.208. ACTION ON BOND

(a) A claimant may sue the principal and surety on the bond either jointly or severally, if his claim remains unpaid for 60 days after the claimant perfects the claim.

(b) The claimant may sue for the amount of the claim and court costs.

(c) The suit must be brought in the county in which the property being improved is located.

(d) If the bond is recorded at the time the lien is filed, the claimant must sue on the bond within one year following perfection of his claim. If the bond is not recorded at the time the lien is filed, the claimant must sue on the bond within two years following perfection of his claim.

History of Prop. Code §53.208: Acts 1983, 68th Leg., ch. 576, §1, eff. Jan. 1, 1984. Amended by Acts 1989, 71st Leg., ch. 1138, §33, eff. Sept. 1, 1989. Source: TRCS art. 5472d, §6.

PROP §53.209. REPEALED

Repealed by Acts 1989, 71st Leg., ch. 1138, §39(3), eff. Sept. 1, 1989.

PROP §53.210. CLAIMS IN EXCESS OF BOND AMOUNT

If valid claims against the bond exceed the penal sum of the bond, each claimant is entitled to a pro rata share of the penal sum.

History of Prop. Code §53.210: Acts 1983, 68th Leg., ch. 576, §1, eff. Jan. 1, 1984. Source: TRCS art. 5472d, §7.

PROP §53.211. ATTEMPTED COMPLIANCE

(a) A bond shall be construed to comply with this subchapter, and the rights and remedies on the bond are enforceable in the same manner as on other bonds under this subchapter, if the bond:

(1) is furnished and filed in attempted compliance with this subchapter; or

(2) evidences by its terms intent to comply with this subchapter.

(b) Any provision in any payment bond furnished or filed in attempted compliance with this subchapter that expands or restricts the rights or liabilities provided under this chapter shall be disregarded and the provisions of this subchapter shall be read into that bond.

History of Prop. Code §53.211: Acts 1983, 68th Leg., ch. 576, §1, eff. Jan. 1, 1984. Amended by Acts 1989, 71st Leg., ch. 1138, §34, eff. Sept. 1, 1989. Source: TRCS art. 5472d, §8.

ANNOTATIONS

Laughlin Envtl., Inc. v. Premier Towers, L.P., 126 S.W.3d 668, 671-72 (Tex.App.—Houston [14th Dist.] 2004, no pet.). "[A]lthough [Prop. Code] §53.202 speaks in terms of mandatory requirements for statutory payment bonds, the Texas Property Code does not require perfect compliance with these requirements. The legislature included a savings provision in [Prop. Code] §53.211(a), which allows a nonconforming payment bond to be treated as a conforming one as long as there is 'attempted compliance with [Prop. Code ch. 53, subch. I,]' or the bond evidences by its terms an 'intent to comply with [subch. I].' ... In the absence of compliance or attempted compliance, the bond will not qualify for treatment as a statutory payment bond and thus will not protect the owner from suit or the property from liens. [¶] For a property owner to reap the benefits of §53.211 and thereby enjoy the protections it affords, there must be a bona fide attempt to comply with the statute's requirements." *See also* ***New AAA Apt. Plumbers, Inc. v. DPMC-Briarcliff, L.P.***, No. 14-05-00485-CV (Tex.App.—Houston [14th Dist.] 2006, no pet.) (memo op.; 10-5-06); ***Staff Indus. v. Hallmark Contracting, Inc.***, 846 S.W.2d 542, 550-51 (Tex.App.—Corpus Christi 1993, no writ).

Sections 53.212-53.230 reserved for expansion

SUBCHAPTER J. LIEN ON MONEY DUE PUBLIC WORKS CONTRACTOR

PROP §53.231. LIEN

(a) A person who furnishes material or labor to a contractor under a prime contract with a governmental entity other than a municipality or a joint board created under Subchapter D, Chapter 22, Transportation Code, that does not exceed $25,000 and that is for public improvements in this state and who gives notice required by this subchapter has a lien on the money, bonds, or warrants due the contractor for the improvements.

(b) A person who furnishes material or labor to a contractor under a prime contract with a municipality or a joint board created under Subchapter D, Chapter 22, Transportation Code, that does not exceed $50,000 and that is for public improvements in this state and who gives notice required by this subchapter has a lien on the money, bonds, or warrants due the contractor for the improvements.

History of Prop. Code §53.231: Acts 1983, 68th Leg., ch. 576, §1, eff. Jan. 1, 1984. Amended by Acts 2009, 81st Leg., ch. 1304, §2, eff. Sept. 1, 2009. Source: TRCS art. 5472a.

ANNOTATIONS

City of La Porte v. Taylor, 836 S.W.2d 829, 831 (Tex.App.—Houston [1st Dist.] 1992, no writ). "Mechanic's liens can only be created against public buildings and grounds when the right is *expressly* conferred by the statutes. As a matter of public policy, liens are not permitted on public improvements where payment and performance bonds are required. *At 832:* A subcontractor on a public building is prohibited from asserting a mechanic's lien, the normal remedy available to him on private construction projects. Under §53.231, a subcontractor may claim a statutory lien on money due the general contractor for public improvements where the prime contract does not exceed $25,000, but where the contract exceeds $25,000, no such statutory lien attaches to retained funds."

Editor's note: Acts 2009, 81st Leg., ch. 1304, §2, eff. Sept. 1, 2009, revised the $25,000 amount to $50,000 for prime contracts with a municipality.

PROP §53.232. TO WHOM NOTICE GIVEN; MANNER

The lien claimant must send written notice of his claim by registered or certified mail to:

(1) the officials of the state, county, town, or municipality whose duty it is to pay the contractor; and

(2) the contractor at the contractor's last known business or residence address.

History of Prop. Code §53.232: Acts 1983, 68th Leg., ch. 576, §1, eff. Jan. 1, 1984. Source: TRCS art. 5472a.

See also Gov't Code §§2253.041-2253.048.

PROP §53.233. CONTENTS OF NOTICE

(a) Whether based on written or oral agreement, the notice must contain:

(1) the amount claimed;

(2) the name of the party to whom the materials were delivered or for whom the labor was performed;

(3) the dates and place of delivery or performance;

(4) a description reasonably sufficient to identify the materials delivered or labor performed and the amount due;

(5) a description reasonably sufficient to identify the project for which the material was delivered or the labor performed; and

(6) the claimant's business address.

(b) The notice must be accompanied by a statement under oath that the amount claimed is just and correct and that all payments, lawful offsets, and credits known to the affiant have been allowed.

History of Prop. Code §53.233: Acts 1983, 68th Leg., ch. 576, §1, eff. Jan. 1, 1984. Amended by Acts 1989, 71st Leg., ch. 1138, §35, eff. Sept. 1, 1989. Source: TRCS art. 5472a.

PROP §53.234. TIME FOR NOTICE

The lien claimant must give notice not later than the 15th day of the second month following the month in which the labor was performed or the material furnished.

History of Prop. Code §53.234: Acts 1983, 68th Leg., ch. 576, §1, eff. Jan. 1, 1984. Amended by Acts 1989, 71st Leg., ch. 1138, §36, eff. Sept. 1, 1989; Acts 2009, 81st Leg., ch. 1304, §3, eff. Sept. 1, 2009. Source: TRCS art. 5472a.

PROP §53.235. OFFICIAL TO RETAIN FUNDS

A public official who receives the notice may not pay all of the money, bonds, or warrants due the contractor, but shall retain enough to pay the claim for which notice is given.

History of Prop. Code §53.235: Acts 1983, 68th Leg., ch. 576, §1, eff. Jan. 1, 1984. Source: TRCS art. 5472b.

PROP §53.236. BOND FOR RELEASE OF LIEN

(a) If a claim is filed attempting to fix a lien under this subchapter, the contractor against whom the claim is made may file a bond with the officials of the state, county, town, or municipality whose duty it is to pay the money, bonds, or warrants to the contractor.

(b) If the bond is approved by the proper official, its filing releases and discharges all liens fixed or attempted to be fixed by the filing of a claim, and the appropriate officials shall pay the money, bonds, or warrants to the contractor or the contractor's assignee.

History of Prop. Code §53.236: Acts 1983, 68th Leg., ch. 576, §1, eff. Jan. 1, 1984. Source: TRCS art. 5472b-1, §1.

See also Gov't Code §2253.021.

PROP §53.237. BOND REQUIREMENTS

The bond must be:

(1) in an amount double the amount of the claims filed;

(2) payable to the claimants;

(3) executed by:

(A) the party filing the bond as principal; and

(B) a corporate surety authorized, admitted to do business, and licensed by the law of this state to execute the bond as surety; and

(4) conditioned that:

(A) the principal and surety will pay to the obligees named or to their assignees the amount of the claims or the portions of the claims proved to be liens under this subchapter; and

(B) the principal and surety will pay all court costs adjudged against the principal in actions brought by a claimant on the bond.

History of Prop. Code §53.237: Acts 1983, 68th Leg., ch. 576, §1, eff. Jan. 1, 1984. Amended by Acts 1989, 71st Leg., ch. 1138, §37, eff. Sept. 1, 1989. Source: TRCS art. 5472b-1, §§1, 2.

See also Gov't Code §2253.021.

PROP §53.238. NOTICE OF BOND

The official with whom the bond is filed shall send an exact copy of the bond by registered mail or certified mail, return receipt requested, to all claimants.

History of Prop. Code §53.238: Acts 1983, 68th Leg., ch. 576, §1, eff. Jan. 1, 1984. Source: TRCS art. 5472b-1, §1.

PROP §53.239. ACTION ON BOND

(a) A claimant must sue on the bond within six months after the bond is filed.

(b) The bond is not exhausted by one action on it. Each obligee or his assignee may maintain a separate suit on the bond in any court of jurisdiction.

History of Prop. Code §53.239: Acts 1983, 68th Leg., ch. 576, §1, eff. Jan. 1, 1984. Source: TRCS art. 5472b-1, §2.

PROP §53.240. REPEALED

Repealed by Acts 1989, 71st Leg., ch. 1138, §39(4), eff. Sept. 1, 1989.

Sections 53.241-53.250 blank

SUBCHAPTER K. RESIDENTIAL CONSTRUCTION PROJECTS

PROP §53.251. PROCEDURES FOR RESIDENTIAL CONSTRUCTION PROJECTS

(a) This subchapter applies only to residential construction projects.

(b) A person must comply with this subchapter in addition to the other applicable provisions of this chapter to perfect a lien that arises from a claim resulting from a residential construction project.

History of Prop. Code §53.251: Acts 1997, 75th Leg., ch. 526, §23, eff. Sept. 1, 1997.

PROP §53.252. DERIVATIVE CLAIMANT: NOTICE TO OWNER OR ORIGINAL CONTRACTOR

(a) A claimant other than an original contractor must give the notice prescribed by this section for the lien to be valid. If the property that is the subject of the lien is a homestead, the notice must also comply with Section 53.254.

(b) The claimant must give to the owner or reputed owner and the original contractor written notice of the unpaid balance. The claimant must give the notice not later than the 15th day of the second month following each month in which all or part of the claimant's labor was performed or material or specially fabricated material was delivered.

(c) To authorize the owner to withhold funds under Subchapter D, the notice to the owner must state that if the claim remains unpaid, the owner may be personally liable and the owner's property may be subjected to a lien unless:

(1) the owner withholds payments from the contractor for payment of the claim; or

(2) the claim is otherwise paid or settled.

(d) The notice must be sent by registered or certified mail and must be addressed to the owner or reputed owner and the original contractor, as applicable, at the person's last known business or residence address.

(e) A copy of the statement or billing in the usual and customary form is sufficient as notice under this section.

History of Prop. Code §53.252: Acts 1997, 75th Leg., ch. 526, §23, eff. Sept. 1, 1997.

ANNOTATIONS

Morrell Masonry Sup. v. Loeb, 349 S.W.3d 664, 670 (Tex.App.—Houston [14th Dist.] 2011, no pet.). "The statement [required by Prop. Code §53.254(g)] is an explanation to the property owner of the possibility that a lien may be filed on his property and his potential liability to the derivative claimant. [W]e decline to hold it is a mere technical requirement that may be excused by substantial compliance."

PROP §53.253. DERIVATIVE CLAIMANT: NOTICE FOR SPECIALLY FABRICATED ITEMS

(a) If specially fabricated materials have not been delivered to the property or incorporated in the residential construction project, the claimant who specially

fabricates material for incorporation in the residential construction project must give notice under this section for the lien to be valid.

(b) Once the specially fabricated materials have been delivered, the claimant must give notice under Section 53.252.

(c) The claimant must give the owner or reputed owner notice not later than the 15th day of the second month after the month in which the claimant receives and accepts the order for the material. If the indebtedness is incurred by a person other than the original contractor, the claimant must also give notice within that time to the original contractor.

(d) The notice must contain:

(1) a statement that the order has been received and accepted; and

(2) the price of the order.

(e) The notice must be sent by registered or certified mail to the last known business or residence address of the owner or the reputed owner or the original contractor, as applicable.

(f) The lien of a claimant who accepts an order but fails to give notice under this section is valid as to delivered items if the claimant has given notice under Section 53.252.

History of Prop. Code §53.253: Acts 1997, 75th Leg., ch. 526, §23, eff. Sept. 1, 1997.

PROP §53.254. HOMESTEAD

(a) To fix a lien on a homestead, the person who is to furnish material or perform labor and the owner must execute a written contract setting forth the terms of the agreement.

(b) The contract must be executed before the material is furnished or the labor is performed.

(c) If the owner is married, the contract must be signed by both spouses.

(d) If the contract is made by an original contractor, the contract inures to the benefit of all persons who labor or furnish material for the original contractor.

(e) The contract must be filed with the county clerk of the county in which the homestead is located. The county clerk shall record the contract in records kept for that purpose.

(f) An affidavit for lien filed under this subchapter that relates to a homestead must contain the following notice conspicuously printed, stamped, or typed in a size equal to at least 10-point boldface or the computer equivalent, at the top of the page:

"NOTICE: THIS IS NOT A LIEN. THIS IS ONLY AN AFFIDAVIT CLAIMING A LIEN."

(g) For the lien on a homestead to be valid, the notice required to be given to the owner under Section 53.252 must include or have attached the following statement:

"If a subcontractor or supplier who furnishes materials or performs labor for construction of improvements on your property is not paid, your property may be subject to a lien for the unpaid amount if:

(1) after receiving notice of the unpaid claim from the claimant, you fail to withhold payment to your contractor that is sufficient to cover the unpaid claim until the dispute is resolved; or

(2) during construction and for 30 days after completion of construction, you fail to retain 10 percent of the contract price or 10 percent of the value of the work performed by your contractor.

"If you have complied with the law regarding the 10 percent retainage and you have withheld payment to the contractor sufficient to cover any written notice of claim and have paid that amount, if any, to the claimant, any lien claim filed on your property by a subcontractor or supplier, other than a person who contracted directly with you, will not be a valid lien on your property. In addition, except for the required 10 percent retainage, you are not liable to a subcontractor or supplier for any amount paid to your contractor before you received written notice of the claim."

History of Prop. Code §53.254: Acts 1997, 75th Leg., ch. 526, §23, eff. Sept. 1, 1997.

See also Tex. Const. art. 16, §50; Prop. Code ch. 41.

ANNOTATIONS

Morrell Masonry Sup. v. Loeb, 349 S.W.3d 664, 670 (Tex.App.—Houston [14th Dist.] 2011, no pet.). "While conceding it omitted part of the required statutory statement from its pre-lien claim notice, [supplier] argues it nonetheless substantially complied with [Prop. Code] §53.254(g). [¶] In the introduction to the body of the required statement, §53.254(g) … states: 'For the lien on a homestead to be valid, the notice required to be given to the owner under [Prop. Code] §53.252 *must* include or have attached the following statement.' The statement that follows is an explanation to the property owner of the possibility that a lien may be filed on his property and his potential liability to the derivative claimant. Without any additional argument from [supplier], we decline to hold it is a

mere technical requirement that may be excused by substantial compliance."

Denmon v. Atlas Leasing, L.L.C., 285 S.W.3d 591, 594-95 (Tex.App.—Dallas 2009, no pet.). "To fix a lien on a homestead, the person who is to furnish material or perform labor and the owner must execute a written contract setting forth the terms of the agreement. If the owner is married, the contract must be signed by both spouses. Because it is undisputed they were married, [Prop. Code] §53.254 applies if [wife's] property was in fact their family homestead. *At 596:* [W]e conclude because [wife] and [husband] were married at the time she purchased [her] property, she intended it to be the family homestead, and [lienholders] never pleaded and proved abandonment, [wife's] property was also [husband's] family homestead. Therefore, the trial court erred in concluding the lien did not violate the homestead protection of [Tex. Const. art. 16, §50]. As the family homestead, … §53.254 required his signature on the loan documents before a lien could attach that resulted in foreclosure. It is undisputed he did not sign the documents. As such, the lien on [wife's] property and the resulting foreclosure is void."

Jordan v. Hagler, 179 S.W.3d 217, 220 (Tex.App.—Fort Worth 2005, no pet.). "Read together, [Prop. Code §§41.001(a), (b) and 53.254] provide that a lien, not a constructive trust, is the encumbrance that may be placed on a homestead for labor and materials used so long as the person furnishing the material or performing labor executes a written contract with the owner."

Skelton v. Washington Mut. Bank, F.A., 61 S.W.3d 56, 60 (Tex.App.—Amarillo 2001, no pet.). "[T]o fix a lien on a homestead for materials and labor, among other documentation, the owner and his or her spouse must execute a written contract signed by both spouses, but the statute does not require the documentation for a purchase money lien." *See also* ***Spradlin v. Jim Walter Homes, Inc.***, 9 S.W.3d 473, 476 (Tex. App.—Dallas 2000), *aff'd*, 34 S.W.3d 578 (Tex.2000).

PROP §53.255. DISCLOSURE STATEMENT REQUIRED FOR RESIDENTIAL CONSTRUCTION CONTRACT

(a) Before a residential construction contract is executed by the owner, the original contractor shall deliver to the owner a disclosure statement described by this section.

(b) The disclosure statement must read substantially similar to the following:

"KNOW YOUR RIGHTS AND RESPONSIBILITIES UNDER THE LAW. You are about to enter into a transaction to build a new home or remodel existing residential property. Texas law requires your contractor to provide you with this brief overview of some of your rights, responsibilities, and risks in this transaction.

"CONVEYANCE TO CONTRACTOR NOT REQUIRED. Your contractor may not require you to convey your real property to your contractor as a condition to the agreement for the construction of improvements on your property.

"KNOW YOUR CONTRACTOR. Before you enter into your agreement for the construction of improvements to your real property, make sure that you have investigated your contractor. Obtain and verify references from other people who have used the contractor for the type and size of construction project on your property.

"GET IT IN WRITING. Make sure that you have a written agreement with your contractor that includes: (1) a description of the work the contractor is to perform; (2) the required or estimated time for completion of the work; (3) the cost of the work or how the cost will be determined; and (4) the procedure and method of payment, including provisions for statutory retainage and conditions for final payment. If your contractor made a promise, warranty, or representation to you concerning the work the contractor is to perform, make sure that promise, warranty, or representation is specified in the written agreement. An oral promise that is not included in the written agreement may not be enforceable under Texas law.

"READ BEFORE YOU SIGN. Do not sign any document before you have read and understood it. NEVER SIGN A DOCUMENT THAT INCLUDES AN UNTRUE STATEMENT. Take your time in reviewing documents. If you borrow money from a lender to pay for the improvements, you are entitled to have the loan closing documents furnished to you for review at least one business day before the closing. Do not waive this requirement unless a bona fide emergency or another good cause exists, and make sure you understand the documents before you sign them. If you fail to comply with the terms of the documents, you could lose your property. You are entitled to have your own attorney review any documents. If you have any question about the meaning of a document, consult an attorney.

"GET A LIST OF SUBCONTRACTORS AND SUPPLIERS. Before construction commences, your contractor

is required to provide you with a list of the subcontractors and suppliers the contractor intends to use on your project. Your contractor is required to supply updated information on any subcontractors and suppliers added after the list is provided. Your contractor is not required to supply this information if you sign a written waiver of your rights to receive this information.

"MONITOR THE WORK. Lenders and governmental authorities may inspect the work in progress from time to time for their own purposes. These inspections are not intended as quality control inspections. Quality control is a matter for you and your contractor. To ensure that your home is being constructed in accordance with your wishes and specifications, you should inspect the work yourself or have your own independent inspector review the work in progress.

"MONITOR PAYMENTS. If you use a lender, your lender is required to provide you with a periodic statement showing the money disbursed by the lender from the proceeds of your loan. Each time your contractor requests payment from you or your lender for work performed, your contractor is also required to furnish you with a disbursement statement that lists the name and address of each subcontractor or supplier that the contractor intends to pay from the requested funds. Review these statements and make sure that the money is being properly disbursed.

"CLAIMS BY SUBCONTRACTORS AND SUPPLIERS. Under Texas law, if a subcontractor or supplier who furnishes labor or materials for the construction of improvements on your property is not paid, you may become liable and your property may be subject to a lien for the unpaid amount, even if you have not contracted directly with the subcontractor or supplier. To avoid liability, you should take the following actions:

(1) If you receive a written notice from a subcontractor or supplier, you should withhold payment from your contractor for the amount of the claim stated in the notice until the dispute between your contractor and the subcontractor or supplier is resolved. If your lender is disbursing money directly to your contractor, you should immediately provide a copy of the notice to your lender and instruct the lender to withhold payment in the amount of the claim stated in the notice. If you continue to pay the contractor after receiving the written notice without withholding the amount of the claim, you may be liable and your property may be subject to a lien for the amount you failed to withhold.

(2) During construction and for 30 days after final completion, termination, or abandonment of the contract by the contractor, you should withhold or cause your lender to withhold 10 percent of the amount of payments made for the work performed by your contractor. This is sometimes referred to as 'statutory retainage.' If you choose not to withhold the 10 percent for at least 30 days after final completion, termination, or abandonment of the contract by the contractor and if a valid claim is timely made by a claimant and your contractor fails to pay the claim, you may be personally liable and your property may be subject to a lien up to the amount that you failed to withhold.

"If a claim is not paid within a certain time period, the claimant is required to file a mechanic's lien affidavit in the real property records in the county where the property is located. A mechanic's lien affidavit is not a lien on your property, but the filing of the affidavit could result in a court imposing a lien on your property if the claimant is successful in litigation to enforce the lien claim.

"SOME CLAIMS MAY NOT BE VALID. When you receive a written notice of a claim or when a mechanic's lien affidavit is filed on your property, you should know your legal rights and responsibilities regarding the claim. Not all claims are valid. A notice of a claim by a subcontractor or supplier is required to be sent, and the mechanic's lien affidavit is required to be filed, within strict time periods. The notice and the affidavit must contain certain information. All claimants may not fully comply with the legal requirements to collect on a claim. If you have paid the contractor in full before receiving a notice of a claim and have fully complied with the law regarding statutory retainage, you may not be liable for that claim. Accordingly, you should consult your attorney when you receive a written notice of a claim to determine the true extent of your liability or potential liability for that claim.

"OBTAIN A LIEN RELEASE AND A BILLS-PAID AFFIDAVIT. When you receive a notice of claim, do not release withheld funds without obtaining a signed and notarized release of lien and claim from the claimant. You can also reduce the risk of having a claim filed by a subcontractor or supplier by requiring as a condition of each payment made by you or your lender that your contractor furnish you with an affidavit stating that all bills have been paid. Under Texas law, on final completion of the work and before final payment, the contractor is re-

quired to furnish you with an affidavit stating that all bills have been paid. If the contractor discloses any unpaid bill in the affidavit, you should withhold payment in the amount of the unpaid bill until you receive a waiver of lien or release from that subcontractor or supplier.

"OBTAIN TITLE INSURANCE PROTECTION. You may be able to obtain a title insurance policy to insure that the title to your property and the existing improvements on your property are free from liens claimed by subcontractors and suppliers. If your policy is issued before the improvements are completed and covers the value of the improvements to be completed, you should obtain, on the completion of the improvements and as a condition of your final payment, a 'completion of improvements' policy endorsement. This endorsement will protect your property from liens claimed by subcontractors and suppliers that may arise from the date the original title policy is issued to the date of the endorsement."

(c) The failure of a contractor to comply with this section does not invalidate a lien under this chapter, a contract lien, or a deed of trust.

History of Prop. Code §53.255: Acts 1997, 75th Leg., ch. 526, §23, eff. Sept. 1, 1997. Amended by Acts 1999, 76th Leg., ch. 889, §8, eff. Sept. 1, 1999.

ANNOTATIONS

Page v. Structural Wood Components, Inc., 102 S.W.3d 720, 726 (Tex.2003). "[W]e note that the Legislature has recently mandated that contractors provide a disclosure statement to homeowners engaging in residential construction projects. The disclosure statement is not applicable in this case, as [owner] hired [prime contractor] for a commercial, not a residential, project. Nevertheless, the disclosure statement offers guidance because it provides a plain-English description of an owner's retainage duties under the mechanic's lien statute, and these duties are the same in both residential projects and commercial projects. The disclosure statement informs the owner that: During construction and for 30 days after final completion, termination, or abandonment of the contract you should withhold or cause your lender to withhold 10% of the amount of payments made for the work performed by your contractor. This is sometimes referred to as statutory retainage. The Legislature's description of the statutory retainage requirement indicates that the Legislature did not intend to require an owner to hold on to the statutory retainage for more than 30 days after the contract's termination." (Internal quotes omitted.)

PROP §53.256. LIST OF SUBCONTRACTORS & SUPPLIERS

(a) Except as provided by Subsection (d), for the construction of improvements under a residential construction contract, the original contractor shall:

(1) furnish to the owner before the commencement of construction a written list that identifies by name, address, and telephone number each subcontractor and supplier the contractor intends to use in the work to be performed; and

(2) provide the owner with an updated list of subcontractors and suppliers not later than the 15th day after the date a subcontractor or supplier is added or deleted.

(b) The list must contain the following notice conspicuously printed, stamped, or typed in a size equal to at least 10-point boldface or the computer equivalent:

"NOTICE: THIS LIST OF SUBCONTRACTORS AND SUPPLIERS MAY NOT BE A FINAL LISTING. UNLESS YOU SIGN A WAIVER OF YOUR RIGHT TO RECEIVE UPDATED INFORMATION, THE CONTRACTOR IS REQUIRED BY LAW TO SUPPLY UPDATED INFORMATION, AS THE INFORMATION BECOMES AVAILABLE, FOR EACH SUBCONTRACTOR OR SUPPLIER USED IN THE WORK PERFORMED ON YOUR RESIDENCE."

(c) The failure of a contractor to comply with this section does not invalidate a lien under this chapter, a contract lien, or a deed of trust.

(d) An owner may waive the right to receive the list of subcontractors and suppliers or any updated information required by this section only as provided by this subsection. The waiver must be in writing and may be included in the residential construction contract. If the waiver is not included as a provision of the residential construction contract, the separate waiver statement must be signed by the owner. The waiver must be conspicuously printed in at least 10-point boldfaced type and read substantially similar to the following:

"WAIVER OF THE LIST OF SUBCONTRACTORS AND SUPPLIERS. AN OWNER IS NOT REQUIRED TO WAIVE THE RIGHT GRANTED BY SECTION 53.256, PROPERTY CODE, TO RECEIVE FROM THE CONTRACTOR AN ORIGINAL OR UPDATED LIST OF SUBCONTRACTORS AND SUPPLIERS.

"BY SIGNING THIS DOCUMENT, I AGREE TO WAIVE MY RIGHT TO RECEIVE FROM THE CONTRAC-

TOR AN ORIGINAL OR UPDATED LIST OF SUBCONTRACTORS AND SUPPLIERS.

"I UNDERSTAND AND ACKNOWLEDGE THAT, AFTER SIGNING THIS DOCUMENT, THIS WAIVER MAY NOT BE CANCELED AT A LATER DATE.

"I HAVE VOLUNTARILY CONSENTED TO THIS WAIVER."

History of Prop. Code §53.256: Acts 1997, 75th Leg., ch. 526, §23, eff. Sept. 1, 1997. Amended by Acts 1999, 76th Leg., ch. 889, §9, eff. Sept. 1, 1999.

PROP §53.257. PROVISIONS RELATED TO CLOSING OF LOAN FOR CONSTRUCTION OF IMPROVEMENTS

(a) If the owner is obtaining third-party financing for the construction of improvements under a residential construction contract, the lender shall deliver to the owner all documentation relating to the closing of the loan not later than one business day before the date of the closing. If a bona fide emergency or another good cause exists and the lender obtains the written consent of the owner, the lender may provide the documentation to the owner or the lender may modify previously provided documentation on the date of closing.

(b) The lender shall provide to the owner the disclosure statement described by Section 53.255(b). The disclosure statement must be provided to the owner before the date of closing. If a bona fide emergency or another good cause exists and the lender obtains the written consent of the owner, the lender may provide the disclosure statement at the closing. The lender shall retain a signed and dated copy of the disclosure statement with the closing documents.

(c) The failure of a lender to comply with this section does not invalidate a lien under this chapter, a contract lien, or a deed of trust.

History of Prop. Code §53.257: Acts 1997, 75th Leg., ch. 526, §23, eff. Sept. 1, 1997.

PROP §53.258. DISBURSEMENTS OF FUNDS

(a) At the time the original contractor requests payment from the owner or the owner's lender for the construction of improvements under a residential construction contract, the original contractor shall provide to the owner a disbursement statement. The statement may include any information agreed to by the owner and the original contractor and must include at least the name and address of each person who subcontracted directly with the original contractor and who the original contractor intends to pay from the requested funds. The original contractor shall provide the disbursement statement:

(1) in the manner agreed to in writing by the owner and original contractor; or

(2) if no agreement exists, by depositing the statement in the United States mail, first class, postage paid, and properly addressed to the owner or by hand delivering the statement to the owner before the original contractor receives the requested funds.

(b) If the owner finances the construction of improvements through a third party that advances loan proceeds directly to the original contractor, the lender shall:

(1) obtain from the original contractor the signed disbursement statement required by Subsection (a) that covers the funds for which the original contractor is requesting payment; and

(2) provide to the owner a statement of funds disbursed by the lender since the last statement was provided to the owner.

(c) The lender shall provide to the owner the lender's disbursement statement and the disbursement statement the lender obtained from the contractor before the lender disburses the funds to the original contractor. The disbursement statements may be provided in any manner agreed to by the lender and the owner.

(d) The lender is not responsible for the accuracy of the information contained in the disbursement statement obtained from the original contractor.

(e) The failure of a lender or an original contractor to comply with this section does not invalidate a lien under this chapter, a contract lien, or a deed of trust.

(f) A person commits an offense if the person intentionally, knowingly, or recklessly provides false or misleading information in a disbursement statement required under this section. An offense under this section is a misdemeanor. A person adjudged guilty of an offense under this section shall be punished by a fine not to exceed $4,000 or confinement in jail for a term not to exceed one year or both a fine and confinement. A person may not receive community supervision for the offense.

History of Prop. Code §53.258: Acts 1997, 75th Leg., ch. 526, §23, eff. Sept. 1, 1997. Amended by Acts 1999, 76th Leg., ch. 889, §10, eff. Sept. 1, 1999.

PROP §53.259. FINAL BILLS-PAID AFFIDAVIT REQUIRED

(a) As a condition of final payment under a residential construction contract, the original contractor

shall, at the time the final payment is tendered, execute and deliver to the owner, or the owner's agent, an affidavit stating that the original contractor has paid each person in full for all labor and materials used in the construction of improvements on the real property. If the original contractor has not paid each person in full, the original contractor shall state in the affidavit the amount owed and the name and, if known, the address and telephone number of each person to whom a payment is owed.

(b) The seller of any real property on which a structure of not more than four units is constructed and that is intended as the principal place of residence for the purchaser shall, at the closing of the purchase of the real property, execute and deliver to the purchaser, or the purchaser's agent, an affidavit stating that the seller has paid each person in full for all labor and materials used in the construction of improvements on the real property and that the seller is not indebted to any person by reason of any construction. In the event that the seller has not paid each person in full, the seller shall state in the affidavit the amount owed and the name and, if known, the address and telephone number of each person to whom a payment is owed.

(c) A person commits an offense if the person intentionally, knowingly, or recklessly makes a false or misleading statement in an affidavit under this section. An offense under this section is a misdemeanor. A person adjudged guilty of an offense under this section shall be punished by a fine not to exceed $4,000 or confinement in jail for a term not to exceed one year or both a fine and confinement. A person may not receive community supervision for the offense.

(d) A person signing an affidavit under this section is personally liable for any loss or damage resulting from any false or incorrect information in the affidavit.

History of Prop. Code §53.259: Acts 1997, 75th Leg., ch. 526, §23, eff. Sept. 1, 1997.

PROP §53.260. CONVEYANCE TO CONTRACTOR NOT REQUIRED

An original contractor may not require an owner of real property to convey the real property to the original contractor or an entity controlled by the original contractor as a condition to the performance of the residential construction contract for improvements to the real property.

History of Prop. Code §53.260: Acts 1997, 75th Leg., ch. 526, §23, eff. Sept. 1, 1997. Amended by Acts 1999, 76th Leg., ch. 889, §11, eff. Sept. 1, 1999.

Sections 53.261-53.280 blank

SUBCHAPTER L. WAIVER & RELEASE OF LIEN OR PAYMENT BOND CLAIM

PROP §53.281. WAIVER & RELEASE OF LIEN OR PAYMENT BOND CLAIM

(a) Any waiver and release of a lien or payment bond claim under this chapter is unenforceable unless a waiver and release is executed and delivered in accordance with this subchapter.

(b) A waiver and release is effective to release the owner, the owner's property, the contractor, and the surety on a payment bond from claims and liens only if:

(1) the waiver and release substantially complies with one of the forms prescribed by Section 53.284;

(2) the waiver and release is signed by the claimant or the claimant's authorized agent and notarized; and

(3) in the case of a conditional release, evidence of payment to the claimant exists.

History of Prop. Code §53.281: Acts 2011, 82nd Leg., ch. 271, §3, eff. Jan. 1, 2012.

PROP §53.282. CONDITIONS FOR WAIVER, RELEASE, OR IMPAIRMENT OF LIEN OR PAYMENT BOND CLAIM

(a) A statement purporting to waive, release, or otherwise adversely affect a lien or payment bond claim is not enforceable and does not create an estoppel or impairment of a lien or payment bond claim unless:

(1) the statement is in writing and substantially complies with a form prescribed by Section 53.284;

(2) the claimant has actually received payment in good and sufficient funds in full for the lien or payment bond claim; or

(3) the statement is:

(A) in a written original contract or subcontract for the construction, remodel, or repair of a single-family house, townhouse, or duplex or for land development related to a single-family house, townhouse, or duplex; and

(B) made before labor or materials are provided under the original contract or subcontract.

(b) The filing of a lien rendered unenforceable by a lien waiver under Subsection (a)(3) does not violate Section 12.002, Civil Practice and Remedies Code, unless:

(1) an owner or original contractor sends a written explanation of the basis for nonpayment, evidence of the contractual waiver of lien rights, and a notice of request for release of the lien to the claimant at the claimant's address stated in the lien affidavit; and

(2) the lien claimant does not release the filed lien affidavit on or before the 14th day after the date the owner or the original contractor sends the items required by Subdivision (1).

(c) Subsection (a)(3) does not apply to a person who supplies only material, and not labor, for the construction, remodel, or repair of a single-family house, townhouse, or duplex or for land development related to a single-family house, townhouse, or duplex.

History of Prop. Code §53.282: Acts 2011, 82nd Leg., ch. 271, §3, eff. Jan. 1, 2012.

PROP §53.283. UNCONDITIONAL WAIVER & RELEASE: PAYMENT REQUIRED

A person may not require a claimant or potential claimant to execute an unconditional waiver and release for a progress payment or final payment amount unless the claimant or potential claimant received payment in that amount in good and sufficient funds.

History of Prop. Code §53.283: Acts 2011, 82nd Leg., ch. 271, §3, eff. Jan. 1, 2012.

PROP §53.284. FORMS FOR WAIVER & RELEASE OF LIEN OR PAYMENT BOND CLAIM

(a) A waiver and release given by a claimant or potential claimant is unenforceable unless it substantially complies with the applicable form described by Subsections (b)-(e).

(b) If a claimant or potential claimant is required to execute a waiver and release in exchange for or to induce the payment of a progress payment and is not paid in exchange for the waiver and release or if a single payee check or joint payee check is given in exchange for the waiver and release, the waiver and release must read:

"CONDITIONAL WAIVER AND RELEASE ON PROGRESS PAYMENT

"Project ______________

"Job No. ______________

"On receipt by the signer of this document of a check from ______________ (maker of check) in the sum of $______ payable to ______________ (payee or payees of check) and when the check has been properly endorsed and has been paid by the bank on which it is drawn, this document becomes effective to release any mechanic's lien right, any right arising from a payment bond that complies with a state or federal statute, any common law payment bond right, any claim for payment, and any rights under any similar ordinance, rule, or statute related to claim or payment rights for persons in the signer's position that the signer has on the property of ______________ (owner) located at ______________ (location) to the following extent: ______________ (job description).

"This release covers a progress payment for all labor, services, equipment, or materials furnished to the property or to ______________ (person with whom signer contracted) as indicated in the attached statement(s) or progress payment request(s), except for unpaid retention, pending modifications and changes, or other items furnished.

"Before any recipient of this document relies on this document, the recipient should verify evidence of payment to the signer.

"The signer warrants that the signer has already paid or will use the funds received from this progress payment to promptly pay in full all of the signer's laborers, subcontractors, materialmen, and suppliers for all work, materials, equipment, or services provided for or to the above referenced project in regard to the attached statement(s) or progress payment request(s).

"Date ______________

"______________ (Company name)

"By ______________ (Signature)

"______________ (Title)"

(c) If a claimant or potential claimant is required to execute an unconditional waiver and release to prove the receipt of good and sufficient funds for a progress payment and the claimant or potential claimant asserts in the waiver and release that the claimant or potential claimant has been paid the progress payment, the waiver and release must:

(1) contain a notice at the top of the document, printed in bold type at least as large as the largest type used in the document, but not smaller than 10-point type, that reads:

"NOTICE:

"This document waives rights unconditionally and states that you have been paid for giving up those rights. It is prohibited for a person to require you to sign this document if you have not been paid the payment amount set forth below. If you have not been paid, use a conditional release form."; and

(2) below the notice, read:

"UNCONDITIONAL WAIVER AND RELEASE ON PROGRESS PAYMENT

"Project ____________

"Job No. ____________

"The signer of this document has been paid and has received a progress payment in the sum of $______ for all labor, services, equipment, or materials furnished to the property or to ____________ (person with whom signer contracted) on the property of ____________ (owner) located at ____________ (location) to the following extent: ____________ (job description). The signer therefore waives and releases any mechanic's lien right, any right arising from a payment bond that complies with a state or federal statute, any common law payment bond right, any claim for payment, and any rights under any similar ordinance, rule, or statute related to claim or payment rights for persons in the signer's position that the signer has on the above referenced project to the following extent:

"This release covers a progress payment for all labor, services, equipment, or materials furnished to the property or to ____________ (person with whom signer contracted) as indicated in the attached statement(s) or progress payment request(s), except for unpaid retention, pending modifications and changes, or other items furnished.

"The signer warrants that the signer has already paid or will use the funds received from this progress payment to promptly pay in full all of the signer's laborers, subcontractors, materialmen, and suppliers for all work, materials, equipment, or services provided for or to the above referenced project in regard to the attached statement(s) or progress payment request(s).

"Date ____________

"____________ (Company name)

"By ____________ (Signature)

"____________ (Title)"

(d) If a claimant or potential claimant is required to execute a waiver and release in exchange for or to induce the payment of a final payment and is not paid in good and sufficient funds in exchange for the waiver and release or if a single payee check or joint payee check is given in exchange for the waiver and release, the waiver and release must read:

"CONDITIONAL WAIVER AND RELEASE ON FINAL PAYMENT

"Project ____________

"Job No. ____________

"On receipt by the signer of this document of a check from ____________ (maker of check) in the sum of $______ payable to ____________ (payee or payees of check) and when the check has been properly endorsed and has been paid by the bank on which it is drawn, this document becomes effective to release any mechanic's lien right, any right arising from a payment bond that complies with a state or federal statute, any common law payment bond right, any claim for payment, and any rights under any similar ordinance, rule, or statute related to claim or payment rights for persons in the signer's position that the signer has on the property of ____________ (owner) located at ____________ (location) to the following extent: ____________ (job description).

"This release covers the final payment to the signer for all labor, services, equipment, or materials furnished to the property or to ____________ (person with whom signer contracted).

"Before any recipient of this document relies on this document, the recipient should verify evidence of payment to the signer.

"The signer warrants that the signer has already paid or will use the funds received from this final payment to promptly pay in full all of the signer's laborers, subcontractors, materialmen, and suppliers for all work, materials, equipment, or services provided for or to the above referenced project up to the date of this waiver and release.

"Date ____________

"____________ (Company name)

"By ____________ (Signature)

"____________ (Title)"

(e) If a claimant or potential claimant is required to execute an unconditional waiver and release to prove the receipt of good and sufficient funds for a final payment and the claimant or potential claimant asserts in the waiver and release that the claimant or potential claimant has been paid the final payment, the waiver and release must:

(1) contain a notice at the top of the document, printed in bold type at least as large as the largest type used in the document, but not smaller than 10-point type, that reads:

"NOTICE:

"This document waives rights unconditionally and states that you have been paid for giving up those rights. It is prohibited for a person to require you to sign this document if you have not been paid the payment amount set forth below. If you have not been paid, use a conditional release form."; and

(2) below the notice, read:

"UNCONDITIONAL WAIVER AND RELEASE ON FINAL PAYMENT

"Project ______________

"Job No. ______________

"The signer of this document has been paid in full for all labor, services, equipment, or materials furnished to the property or to ______________ (person with whom signer contracted) on the property of ______________ (owner) located at ______________ (location) to the following extent: ______________ (job description). The signer therefore waives and releases any mechanic's lien right, any right arising from a payment bond that complies with a state or federal statute, any common law payment bond right, any claim for payment, and any rights under any similar ordinance, rule, or statute related to claim or payment rights for persons in the signer's position.

"The signer warrants that the signer has already paid or will use the funds received from this final payment to promptly pay in full all of the signer's laborers, subcontractors, materialmen, and suppliers for all work, materials, equipment, or services provided for or to the above referenced project up to the date of this waiver and release.

"Date ______________

" ______________ (Company name)

"By ______________ (Signature)

" ______________ (Title)"

History of Prop. Code §53.284: Acts 2011, 82nd Leg., ch. 271, §3, eff. Jan. 1, 2012.

PROP §53.285. EXPIRED

PROP §53.286. PUBLIC POLICY

Notwithstanding any other law and except as provided by Section 53.282, any contract, agreement, or understanding purporting to waive the right to file or enforce any lien or claim created under this chapter is void as against public policy.

History of Prop. Code §53.286: Acts 2011, 82nd Leg., ch. 271, §3, eff. Jan. 1, 2012.

PROP §53.287. CERTAIN AGREEMENTS EXEMPT

This subchapter does not apply to a written agreement to subordinate, release, waive, or satisfy all or part of a lien or bond claim in:

(1) an accord and satisfaction of an identified dispute;

(2) an agreement concerning an action pending in any court or arbitration proceeding; or

(3) an agreement that is executed after an affidavit claiming the lien has been filed or the bond claim has been made.

History of Prop. Code §53.287: Acts 2011, 82nd Leg., ch. 271, §3, eff. Jan. 1, 2012.

CHAPTER 54. LANDLORD'S LIENS

SUBCHAPTER A. AGRICULTURAL LANDLORD'S LIEN

PROP §54.001. LIEN

A person who leases land or tenements at will or for a term of years has a preference lien for rent that becomes due and for the money and the value of property that the landlord furnishes or causes to be furnished to the tenant to grow a crop on the leased premises and to gather, store, and prepare the crop for marketing.

History of Prop. Code §54.001: Acts 1983, 68th Leg., ch. 576, §1, eff. Jan. 1, 1984. Source: TRCS art. 5222.

ANNOTATIONS

Dill v. Graham, 530 S.W.2d 157, 160 (Tex.App.—Amarillo 1975, writ ref'd n.r.e.). "Unless their agreement provides otherwise, the tenant owns the entire crop prior to harvest. Nevertheless, the landlord has the fixed right to become owner of his share when the time for segregation and delivery arrives. To secure this right, he holds a landlord's lien. [TRCS] art. 5222 [now Prop. Code §54.001] provides a preference lien on the crop regardless of actual notice or lack of notice to the purchaser. The statute is notice to all persons. The landlord may enforce his lien either by following the cotton and foreclosing the lien, or by suing the purchaser for conversion. The landlord waives his lien by authorizing the tenant to sell the crop. If a purchaser buys the crop or a part of it on which the landlord has a lien, without the landlord's consent or authorization to sell, the purchaser is liable in conversion to the landlord to the extent of the lesser of the value of the crop converted or the amount of rent due. Since one may convert personal property by receiving it pursuant to a transfer made without authority, it is thus incumbent upon the purchaser to ascertain the seller's authority to sell, if he would protect himself from potential liability. The exercise of dominion or control over another's property in denial of or inconsistent with his rights is a conversion."

Associates Fin. Servs. v. Solomon, 523 S.W.2d 722, 724 (Tex.App.—Waco 1975, no writ). "When property is placed in a rented building by the tenant prior to recording a chattel mortgage thereon, the landlord's lien has preference. [¶] And a landlord's lien is also superior to any unrecorded chattel mortgage, even if the mortgage is older than the landlord's lien. [¶] As to the priority between a landlord's lien and a security interest, … 'it would seem that the likely future rule as to the priority of a landlord's lien over a security interest is that if the security interest is perfected at the time the personal property is placed on the leased premises, the security interest should be paramount; on the other hand, if the security interest is perfected with respect to the property after it is on the premises, the landlord's lien should be superior.'"

PROP §54.002. PROPERTY TO WHICH LIEN ATTACHES

(a) Except as provided by Subsections (b) and (c), the lien attaches to:

(1) the property on the leased premises that the landlord furnishes or causes to be furnished to the tenant to grow a crop on the leased premises; and

(2) the crop grown on the leased premises in the year that the rent accrues or the property is furnished.

(b) If the landlord provides everything except labor, the lien attaches only to the crop grown in the year that the property is furnished.

(c) The lien does not attach to the goods of a merchant, trader, or mechanic if the tenant sells and delivers the goods in good faith in the regular course of business.

(d) A law exempting property from forced sale does not apply to a lien under this subchapter on agricultural products, animals, or tools.

History of Prop. Code §54.002: Acts 1983, 68th Leg., ch. 576, §1, eff. Jan. 1, 1984. Source: TRCS arts. 5222-5224.

See also Prop. Code §§70.402, 70.403, 70.405.

PROP §54.003. EXCEPTIONS

The lien does not arise if:

(1) a tenant provides everything necessary to cultivate the leased premises and the landlord charges rent of more than one-third of the value of the grain and one-fourth of the value of the cotton grown on the premises; or

(2) a landlord provides everything except the labor and directly or indirectly charges rent of more than one-half of the value of the grain and cotton grown on the premises.

History of Prop. Code §54.003: Acts 1983, 68th Leg., ch. 576, §1, eff. Jan. 1, 1984. Source: TRCS art. 5222.

ANNOTATIONS

Tigner v. First Nat'l Bank, 264 S.W.2d 85, 89 (Tex. 1954). "The use of the word 'value' indicates that the Legislature more specifically referred to contracts for money rent than to contracts for rents payable in kind. This [is] for the reason that the value cannot be ascer-

tained until after the crops are harvested. The word 'value' has no place in measuring rent payable in kind."

PROP §54.004. DURATION OF LIEN

The lien exists while the property to which it is attached remains on the leased premises and until one month after the day that the property is removed from the premises. If agricultural products to which the lien is attached are placed in a public or bonded warehouse regulated by state law before the 31st day after the day that they are removed from the leased premises, the lien exists while they remain in the warehouse.

History of Prop. Code §54.004: Acts 1983, 68th Leg., ch. 576, §1, eff. Jan. 1, 1984. Source: TRCS art. 5223.

See also Prop. Code §70.405.

PROP §54.005. REMOVAL OF PROPERTY

(a) If an advance or rent is unpaid, a tenant may not without the landlord's consent remove or permit the removal of agricultural products or other property to which the lien is attached from the leased premises.

(b) If agricultural products subject to the lien are removed with the landlord's consent from the leased premises for preparation for market, the lien continues to exist as if the products had not been removed.

History of Prop. Code §54.005: Acts 1983, 68th Leg., ch. 576, §1, eff. Jan. 1, 1984. Source: TRCS arts. 5225, 5226.

PROP §54.006. DISTRESS WARRANT

(a) The person to whom rent or an advance is payable under the lease or the person's agent, attorney, assign, or other legal representative may apply to an appropriate justice of the peace for a distress warrant if the tenant:

(1) owes any rent or an advance;

(2) is about to abandon the premises; or

(3) is about to remove the tenant's property from the premises.

(b) The application for a warrant must be filed with a justice of the peace:

(1) in the precinct in which the leasehold is located or in which the property subject to the landlord's lien is located; or

(2) who has jurisdiction of the cause of action.

History of Prop. Code §54.006: Acts 1983, 68th Leg., ch. 576, §1, eff. Jan. 1, 1984. Amended by Acts 1993, 73rd Leg., ch. 48, §9, eff. Sept. 1, 1993. Source: TRCS art. 5227.

PROP §54.007. JUDGMENT ON REPLEVIN BOND

If a final judgment is rendered against a defendant who has replevied property seized under a distress warrant, the sureties on the defendant's replevy bond are also liable under the judgment, according to the terms of the bond.

History of Prop. Code §54.007: Acts 1983, 68th Leg., ch. 576, §1, eff. Jan. 1, 1984. Source: TRCS art. 5232.

Sections 54.008-54.020 reserved for expansion

SUBCHAPTER B. BUILDING LANDLORD'S LIEN

PROP §54.021. LIEN

A person who leases or rents all or part of a building for nonresidential use has a preference lien on the property of the tenant or subtenant in the building for rent that is due and for rent that is to become due during the current 12-month period succeeding the date of the beginning of the rental agreement or an anniversary of that date.

History of Prop. Code §54.021: Acts 1983, 68th Leg., ch. 576, §1, eff. Jan. 1, 1984. Amended by Acts 1985, 69th Leg., ch. 200, §2, eff. Aug. 26, 1985. Source: TRCS art. 5238.

ANNOTATIONS

FDIC v. Sears, Roebuck & Co., 743 S.W.2d 772, 773 (Tex.App.—El Paso 1988, no writ). Section 54.021 "has been interpreted to provide a preference lien to a landlord for rent that is due and for rent that is to become due during the current 12-month period succeeding the date of the beginning of the lease or an anniversary of that date. The statute effectively divides a lease contract 'as far as the lien is concerned, into a series of yearly contracts….' Each year of the contract is viewed separately. At the beginning of each contract year, if a [Uniform Commercial Code] financing statement has been filed during the previous year, it then becomes superior to the landlord's lien."

Bank of N. Am. v. Kruger, 551 S.W.2d 63, 66 (Tex. App.—Houston [1st Dist.] 1977, writ ref'd n.r.e.). The bank "first perfected its security interest in the collateral on November 27, 1970. At that time, and also in August 1971, when it made the additional loan to [tenant], its security interest was subordinate to the landlord's statutory lien for the contract year beginning September 1, 1970, and ending August 31, 1971. However, at the beginning of the next contract year, September 1, 1971, the Bank's prior perfected security in-

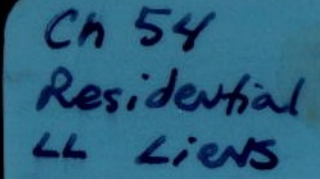

terest became superior to the landlord's statutory lien in the same property. [¶] It is, therefore, this court's ruling that at the time of the lessee's default in the payment of lease rentals, December 1, 1971, the Bank held a perfected security interest in the chattels which was entitled to priority over the statutory lien asserted by the landlord in the same property."

PROP §54.022. COMMERCIAL BUILDING

(a) The lien is unenforceable for rent on a commercial building that is more than six months past due unless the landlord files a lien statement with the county clerk of the county in which the building is located.

(b) The lien statement must be verified by the landlord or the landlord's agent or attorney and must contain:

(1) an account, itemized by month, of the rent for which the lien is claimed;

(2) the name and address of the tenant or subtenant, if any;

(3) a description of the leased premises; and

(4) the beginning and termination dates of the lease.

(c) Each county clerk shall index alphabetically and record the rental lien statements filed in the clerk's office.

History of Prop. Code §54.022: Acts 1983, 68th Leg., ch. 576, §1, eff. Jan. 1, 1984. Source: TRCS art. 5238.

ANNOTATIONS

Lincoln Ten, Ltd. v. White, 706 S.W.2d 125, 129 (Tex.App.—Houston [14th Dist.] 1986, orig. proceeding). Section 54.022's "purpose is to ensure the priority of the landlord lien over other creditors of the debtor tenant."

PROP §54.023. EXEMPTIONS

This subchapter does not affect a statute exempting property from forced sale.

History of Prop. Code §54.023: Acts 1983, 68th Leg., ch. 576, §1, eff. Jan. 1, 1984. Source: TRCS art. 5238.

PROP §54.024. DURATION OF LIEN

The lien exists while the tenant occupies the building and until one month after the day that the tenant abandons the building.

History of Prop. Code §54.024: Acts 1983, 68th Leg., ch. 576, §1, eff. Jan. 1, 1984. Source: TRCS art. 5238.

PROP §54.025. DISTRESS WARRANT

The person to whom rent is payable under a building lease or the person's agent, attorney, assign, or other legal representative may apply to the justice of the peace in the precinct in which the building is located for a distress warrant if the tenant:

(1) owes rent;

(2) is about to abandon the building; or

(3) is about to remove the tenant's property from the building.

Sections 54.026-54.040 reserved for expansion

SUBCHAPTER C. RESIDENTIAL LANDLORD'S LIEN

PROP §54.041. LIEN

A landlord of a single or multifamily residence has a lien for unpaid rent that is due. The lien attaches to nonexempt property that is in the residence or that the tenant has stored in a storage room.

History of Prop. Code §54.041: Acts 1983, 68th Leg., ch. 576, §1, eff. Jan. 1, 1984. Source: TRCS art. 5236d, §1.

PROP §54.042. EXEMPTIONS

A lien under this subchapter does not attach to:

(1) wearing apparel;

(2) tools, apparatus, and books of a trade or profession;

(3) schoolbooks;

(4) a family library;

(5) family portraits and pictures;

(6) one couch, two living room chairs, and a dining table and chairs;

(7) beds and bedding;

(8) kitchen furniture and utensils;

(9) food and foodstuffs;

(10) medicine and medical supplies;

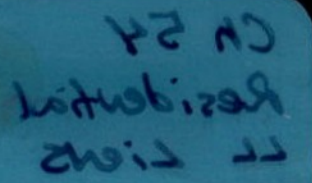

(11) one automobile and one truck;

(12) agricultural implements;

(13) children's toys not commonly used by adults;

(14) goods that the landlord or the landlord's agent knows are owned by a person other than the tenant or an occupant of the residence; and

(15) goods that the landlord or the landlord's agent knows are subject to a recorded chattel mortgage or financing agreement.

History of Prop. Code §54.042: Acts 1983, 68th Leg., ch. 576, §1, eff. Jan. 1, 1984. Amended by Acts 1985, 69th Leg., ch. 305, §1, eff. Aug. 26, 1985. Source: TRCS art. 5236d, §2.

PROP §54.043. ENFORCEABILITY OF CONTRACTUAL PROVISIONS

(a) A contractual landlord's lien is not enforceable unless it is underlined or printed in conspicuous bold print in the lease agreement.

(b) A provision of a lease that purports to waive or diminish a right, liability, or exemption of this subchapter is void to the extent limited by this subchapter.

History of Prop. Code §54.043: Acts 1983, 68th Leg., ch. 576, §1, eff. Jan. 1, 1984. Source: TRCS art. 5236d, §§3, 4.

PROP §54.044. SEIZURE OF PROPERTY

(a) The landlord or the landlord's agent may not seize exempt property and may seize nonexempt property only if it is authorized by a written lease and can be accomplished without a breach of the peace.

(b) Immediately after seizing property under Subsection (a) of this section, the landlord or the landlord's agent shall leave written notice of entry and an itemized list of the items removed. The notice and list shall be left in a conspicuous place within the dwelling. The notice must state the amount of delinquent rent and the name, address, and telephone number of the person the tenant may contact regarding the amount owed. The notice must also state that the property will be promptly returned on full payment of the delinquent rent.

(c) Unless authorized in a written lease, the landlord is not entitled to collect a charge for packing, removing, or storing property seized under this section.

(d) If the tenant has abandoned the premises, the landlord or the landlord's agent may remove its contents.

History of Prop. Code §54.044: Acts 1983, 68th Leg., ch. 576, §1, eff. Jan. 1, 1984. Amended by Acts 1985, 69th Leg., ch. 305, §1, eff. Aug. 26, 1985. Source: TRCS art. 5236d, §§5, 6.

See also Prop. Code §54.042.

ANNOTATIONS

Levine v. Smith, 625 S.W.2d 777, 779 (Tex.App.—Fort Worth 1981, writ ref'd n.r.e.). Landlords "appear to reason that (1) there was some question as to when, or if, [tenant] vacated the apartment; (2) anytime she ceased to reside in the apartment, she *ipso facto* ceased to be a 'tenant'; and (3) *ipso jure* ceased to be eligible under [TRCS art. 5236d, now Prop. Code §§54.041-54.045,] to bring this action against [landlords]. [¶] However, if [tenant] thereby ceased to be a 'tenant' and so lost her rights under the statute, [landlords] likewise ceased to be her 'landlord' and so lost their own statutory rights. [¶] We do not construe the statute to that effect. [¶] We conclude that art. 5236d does not depend for its application upon the existence of a continuing tenancy on the day the landlord seizes property from the premises. [TRCS art. 5326, §6, now Prop. Code §54.044,] makes clear that a landlord's lien born when the tenancy began does not die when tenancy ceases and the premises are abandoned. [¶] Section 6 is authority for enforcing the landlords' lien after tenancy has ceased.... [¶] If the landlord's rights under art. 5236d survive the tenancy, so must the tenant's statutory remedies for any willful violation of the statute by the landlord."

PROP §54.045. SALE OF PROPERTY

(a) Property seized under Section 54.044 may not be sold or otherwise disposed of unless the sale or disposition is authorized in a written lease.

(b) Before selling seized property, the landlord or the landlord's agent must give notice to the tenant not later than the 30th day before the date of the sale. The notice must be sent to the tenant by both first class mail and certified mail, return receipt requested, at the tenant's last known address. The notice must contain:

(1) the date, time, and place of the sale;

(2) an itemized account of the amount owed by the tenant to the landlord; and

(3) the name, address, and telephone number of the person the tenant may contact regarding the sale, the amount owed, and the right of the tenant to redeem the property under Subsection (e) of this section.

(c) A sale under this section is subject to a recorded chattel mortgage or financing statement. The property shall be sold to the highest cash bidder. Proceeds from the sale shall be applied first to delinquent

rents and, if authorized by the written lease, reasonable packing, moving, storage, and sale costs.

(d) Any sale proceeds remaining after payment of the amounts authorized in Subsection (c) of this section shall be mailed to the tenant at the tenant's last known address not later than the 30th day after the date of the sale. The landlord shall provide the tenant with an accounting of all proceeds of the sale not later than the 30th day after the date on which the tenant makes a written request for the accounting.

(e) The tenant may redeem the property at any time before the property is sold by paying to the landlord or the landlord's agent all delinquent rents and, if authorized in the written lease, all reasonable packing, moving, storage, and sale costs.

History of Prop. Code §54.045: Acts 1985, 69th Leg., ch. 305, §1, eff. Aug. 26, 1985. Source: TRCS art. 5236d, §7.

PROP §54.046. VIOLATION BY LANDLORD

If a landlord or the landlord's agent wilfully violates this subchapter, the tenant is entitled to:

(1) actual damages, return of any property seized that has not been sold, return of the proceeds of any sale of seized property, and the sum of one month's rent and $1,000, less any amount for which the tenant is liable; and

(2) reasonable attorney's fees.

History of Prop. Code §54.046: Acts 1983, 68th Leg., ch. 5761, §1, eff. Jan. 1, 1984. Renumbered from §54.045 and amended by Acts 1985, 69th Leg., ch. 305, §1, eff. Aug. 26, 1985. Amended by Acts 2015, 84th Leg., ch. 1198, §2, eff. Jan. 1, 2016. Source: TRCS art. 5236d, §7.

ANNOTATIONS

Causey v. Catlett, 605 S.W.2d 719, 720 (Tex.App.—Dallas 1980, no writ). "[P] maintains that the trial court's finding ... that if [D] violated [TRCS art. 5236d, now Prop. Code §54.046,] such violation was not willful, is against the great weight and preponderance of the evidence. *At 721:* [D's] agent, the apartment manager, admitted that she had 'a copy of a statute' showing her 'what could be confiscated under the landlord's lien law and what should be not.' She agreed that there are certain items that are exempt from a landlord's lien, and admitted making the statement, 'Will remove all if not taken out in three days.' [D] admitted that he is familiar with the landlord's lien statute in Texas and that the apartment manager had been trained 'as to what she may do and may not do....' [W]e conclude that finding [that D did not violate art. 5236d] is so against the great weight and preponderance of the evidence as to be manifestly unjust."

PROP §54.047. OTHER RIGHTS NOT AFFECTED

This subchapter does not affect or diminish any other rights or obligations arising under common law or any statute.

History of Prop. Code §54.047: Acts 1985, 69th Leg., ch. 305, §1, eff. Aug. 26, 1985.

PROP §54.048. TENANT MAY REPLEVY

At any time before judgment in a suit for unpaid rent, the tenant may replevy any of the property that has been seized, if the property has not been claimed or sold, by posting a bond in an amount approved by the court, payable to the landlord, and conditioned that if the landlord prevails in the suit, the amount of the judgment rendered and any costs assessed against the tenant shall be first satisfied, to the extent possible, out of the bond.

History of Prop. Code §54.048: Acts 1987, 70th Leg., ch. 266, §1, eff. Sept. 1, 1987.

Subchapters D-Y blank

E SUBCHAPTER Z. MISCELLANEOUS PROVISIONS

PROP §54.901. DISPOSAL OF CERTAIN MOTOR VEHICLES SUBJECT TO LIEN

(a) Notwithstanding any other law, a person authorized to dispose of property for which a lien under this chapter is attached may dispose of the property in accordance with Subchapter D, Chapter 683, Transportation Code, if:

(1) the property is a motor vehicle; and

(2) the person determines that:

(A) the vehicle's only residual value is as a source of parts or scrap metal; or

(B) it is not economical to dispose of the vehicle at a public sale.

(b) If a person disposes of the property under Subsection (a), the person shall apply the fair market value of the motor vehicle to the charges due to the person.

History of Prop. Code §54.901: Enacted by H.B. 3131, §3, 85th Leg., eff. Sept. 1, 2017.

CHAPTER 55. HOSPITAL & EMERGENCY MEDICAL SERVICES LIENS

PROP §55.001. DEFINITIONS

In this chapter:

(1) "Emergency medical services" has the meaning assigned by Section 773.003, Health and Safety Code.

(2) "Emergency medical services provider" has the meaning assigned by Section 773.003, Health and Safety Code.

(3) "Hospital" means a person or institution maintaining a facility that provides hospital services in this state.

(4) "Person" does not include a county, common, or independent school district.

History of Prop. Code §55.001: Acts 1983, 68th Leg., ch. 576, §1, eff. Jan. 1, 1984. Amended by Acts 2003, 78th Leg., ch. 337, §1, eff. Sept. 1, 2003. Source: TRCS art. 5506a, §§1, 4.

PROP §55.002. LIEN

(a) A hospital has a lien on a cause of action or claim of an individual who receives hospital services for injuries caused by an accident that is attributed to the negligence of another person. For the lien to attach, the individual must be admitted to a hospital not later than 72 hours after the accident.

(b) The lien extends to both the admitting hospital and a hospital to which the individual is transferred for treatment of the same injury.

(c) An emergency medical services provider has a lien on a cause of action or claim of an individual who receives emergency medical services in a county with a population of 800,000 or less for injuries caused by an accident that is attributed to the negligence of another person. For the lien to attach, the individual must receive the emergency medical services not later than 72 hours after the accident.

History of Prop. Code §55.002: Acts 1983, 68th Leg., ch. 576, §1, eff. Jan. 1, 1984. Amended by Acts 2003, 78th Leg., ch. 337, §1, eff. Sept. 1, 2003; Acts 2011, 82nd Leg., ch. 576, §1, eff. Sept. 1, 2011. Source: TRCS art. 5506a, §1.

ANNOTATIONS

Daughters of Charity Health Servs. v. Linnstaedter, 226 S.W.3d 409, 410 (Tex.2007). "The question presented here is whether a hospital paid by a workers' compensation carrier can recover the discount from its full charges by filing a lien against a patient's tort recovery. Because hospitals cannot sue such patients for the discount, we hold they cannot accomplish indirectly (by filing a lien) what they could not do directly (by filing suit). *At 411:* [Because] a hospital has neither tort nor contract rights against a tortfeasor who has injured a patient, the only support for a hospital lien is its claim for reimbursement from the patient. Thus, a lien against a patient's tort recovery is just as much a claim against the patient as if it were filed against the patient's house, car, or bank account. [¶] So while the Property Code grants hospitals a lien to secure their fees, the Labor Code prohibits liens against compensation patients. We think both can be given effect by limiting hospital liens involving compensation patients to amounts due under the workers' compensation system. *At 412:* [W]e hold the hospital's lien violated [Lab. Code §413.042(a)'s] prohibition of private claims against compensation patients."

Members Mut. Ins. v. Hermann Hosp., 664 S.W.2d 325, 326 (Tex.1984). "The issue … is whether the insurance proceeds from uninsured/underinsured motorists coverage are subject to a statutory hospital lien. *At 328:* Here, the uninsured motorists coverage did not protect the insured from liability for damages caused to others, thus it does not fit within the definition of liability insurance or public liability insurance. We therefore hold that the proceeds of uninsured motorists coverage are not subject to a hospital lien under [TRCS art. 5506a, now Prop. Code §55.002]."

Columbia Rio Grande Reg'l Hosp. v. Stover, 17 S.W.3d 387, 389 n.2 (Tex.App.—Corpus Christi 2000, no pet.). "A hospital lien attaches to a cause of action for damages arising from an injury for which the hospital provided treatment, as well as to any proceeds from settlement of that action or the underlying claim brought by the injured individual or another person entitled to make the claim." *See also* ***Nacogdoches Cty. Hosp. Dist. v. Newman***, No. 12-06-00375-CV (Tex. App.—Tyler 2007, pet. denied) (memo op.; 5-23-07) (hospital cannot directly sue third party if injured individual does not sue; no fund to which lien can attach).

Hermann Hosp. v. Martinez, 990 S.W.2d 476, 481 (Tex.App.—Houston [14th Dist.] 1999, pet. denied). "'The purpose of a hospital lien statute is to provide hospitals an additional method of securing payment for medical services, thus encouraging the prompt and ad-

equate treatment of accident victims.' Nowhere in the language of the hospital lien statute does it distinguish between recovery for 'medical expenses' and any other kind of monetary recovery awarded for injuries caused by an accident that is attributed to the negligence of another person. [¶] The clear language of the statute compels this court to conclude that a hospital lien attaches to *any* claim brought by the injured person which is attributed to the negligence of another." *See also* ***Tarrant Cty. Hosp. Dist. v. Jones***, 664 S.W.2d 191, 195 (Tex.App.—Fort Worth 1984, no writ) (hospital lien will not attach to wrongful-death award).

Baylor Univ. Med. Ctr. v. Travelers Ins., 587 S.W.2d 501, 504 (Tex.App.—Dallas 1979, writ ref'd n.r.e.). "The overriding purpose of [TRCS art. 5506a, now Prop. Code §55.002,] is to *induce* hospitals to receive a patient, injured by the negligence of others, by giving the hospital a lien on the claims, suit or settlement of the patient. The inducement is for 'immediate' (within 72 hours) reception of the patient. ... The inducement extends alike to the 'admitting hospital and to any hospital to which injured persons may be transferred.' The inducement secures the first administered treatment and 'subsequent treatments of the same injuries for which he was originally admitted.' ... We hold, therefore, that the 72 hour requirement concerns the initial hospital admission and not subsequent admissions for treatment of injuries received in the same accident. To hold to the contrary would thwart the overriding purpose of the statute."

PROP §55.003. PROPERTY TO WHICH LIEN ATTACHES

(a) A lien under this chapter attaches to:

(1) a cause of action for damages arising from an injury for which the injured individual is admitted to the hospital or receives emergency medical services;

(2) a judgment of a court in this state or the decision of a public agency in a proceeding brought by the injured individual or by another person entitled to bring the suit in case of the death of the individual to recover damages arising from an injury for which the injured individual is admitted to the hospital or receives emergency medical services; and

(3) the proceeds of a settlement of a cause of action or a claim by the injured individual or another person entitled to make the claim, arising from an injury for which the injured individual is admitted to the hospital or receives emergency medical services.

(b) The lien does not attach to:

(1) a claim under the workers' compensation law of this state, the Federal Employees Liability Act, or the Federal Longshore and Harbor Workers' Compensation Act; or

(2) the proceeds of an insurance policy in favor of the injured individual or the injured individual's beneficiary or legal representative, except public liability insurance carried by the insured that protects the insured against loss caused by an accident or collision.

(c) A hospital lien described by Section 55.002(a) does not attach to a claim against the owner or operator of a railroad company that maintains or whose employees maintain a hospital in which the injured individual is receiving hospital services.

History of Prop. Code §55.003: Acts 1983, 68th Leg., ch. 576, §1, eff. Jan. 1, 1984. Amended by Acts 2003, 78th Leg., ch. 337, §1, eff. Sept. 1, 2003. Source: TRCS art. 5506a, §§1-3, 4c.

ANNOTATIONS

Members Mut. Ins. v. Hermann Hosp., 664 S.W.2d 325, 328 (Tex.1984). "[T]he proceeds of uninsured motorists coverage are not subject to a hospital lien under [TRCS art. 5506a, now Prop. Code ch. 55]." *See also* ***Tarrant Cty. Hosp. Dist. v. Jones***, 664 S.W.2d 191, 195 (Tex.App.—Fort Worth 1984, no writ) (hospital lien will not attach to wrongful-death award).

Hermann Hosp. v. Martinez, 990 S.W.2d 476, 477-78 (Tex.App.—Houston [14th Dist.] 1999, pet. denied). "[A] hospital lien may be enforced against a child's monetary judgment. *At 481:* The only statutory limitations placed upon a hospital lien are procedural filing requirements and reasonableness of the amount charged."

McCollum v. Baylor Univ. Med. Ctr., 697 S.W.2d 22, 25 (Tex.App.—Dallas 1985, no writ). "Regardless of its rights against [patient], [hospital] has a cause of action against [tortfeasor] for settling with [patient] without paying [hospital's] bill. [¶] We hold that if the trial court finds that [patient] did not suffer a compensable injury, then his relationship with [hospital] is not governed by the Workers' Compensation Act, and in addition to owing the bill, he owes [hospital] contractual interest and attorney's fees. If, however, [patient] is found to have suffered a compensable injury, then the rights and obligations of [hospital] and [patient] are governed entirely by the Workers' Compensation Act."

PROP §55.004. AMOUNT OF LIEN

(a) In this section, "emergency hospital care" means health care services provided in a hospital to evaluate, stabilize, and treat a serious medical problem of recent onset or severity, including severe pain that would lead a prudent layperson possessing an average knowledge of medicine and health to believe that the condition, illness, or injury is of such a nature that failure to obtain immediate medical care would in all reasonable probability:

(1) seriously jeopardize the patient's health;

(2) seriously impair one or more bodily functions;

(3) seriously harm an organ or other part of the body;

(4) cause serious disfigurement; or

(5) in the case of a pregnant woman, seriously jeopardize the health of the fetus.

(b) A hospital lien described by Section 55.002(a) is for the amount of the hospital's charges for services provided to the injured individual during the first 100 days of the injured individual's hospitalization.

(c) A hospital lien described by Section 55.002(a) may also include the amount of a physician's reasonable and necessary charges for emergency hospital care services provided to the injured individual during the first seven days of the injured individual's hospitalization. At the request of the physician, the hospital may act on the physician's behalf in securing and discharging the lien.

(d) A hospital lien described by Section 55.002(a) does not cover:

(1) charges for other services that exceed a reasonable and regular rate for the services;

(2) charges by the physician related to any services provided under Subsection (c) for which the physician has accepted insurance benefits or payment under a private medical indemnity plan or program, regardless of whether the benefits or payment equals the full amount of the physician's charges for those services;

(3) charges by the physician for services provided under Subsection (c) if the injured individual has coverage under a private medical indemnity plan or program from which the physician is entitled to recover payment for the physician's services under an assignment of benefits or similar rights; or

(4) charges by the physician related to any services provided under Subsection (c) if the physician is a member of the legislature.

(e) A hospital lien described by Section 55.002(a) is not affected by a hospital's use of a method of classifying patients according to their ability to pay that is solely intended to obtain a lien for services provided to an indigent injured individual.

(f) An emergency medical services lien described by Section 55.002(c) is for the amount charged by the emergency medical services provider, not to exceed $1,000, for emergency medical services provided to the injured individual during the 72 hours following the accident that caused the individual's injuries.

(g) An emergency medical services lien described by Section 55.002(c) does not cover:

(1) charges for services that exceed a reasonable and regular rate for the services;

(2) charges by the emergency medical services provider related to any services for which the emergency medical services provider has accepted insurance benefits or payment under a private medical indemnity plan or program, regardless of whether the benefits or payments equal the full amount of the charges for those services; or

(3) charges by the emergency medical services provider for services provided if the injured individual has coverage under a private medical indemnity plan or program from which the provider is entitled to recover payment for the provider's services under an assignment of benefits or similar right.

(h) If the physician is employed in that capacity by an institution of higher education, as defined by Section 61.003, Education Code, and the lien does not include the amount of the physician's reasonable and necessary charges described by Subsection (c), the physician has a lien on the cause of action in the same manner as a hospital under this chapter. The lien is subject to provisions of this chapter applicable to a hospital lien, and the physician or the physician's employing institution may secure and enforce the lien in the manner provided by this chapter.

History of Prop. Code §55.004: Acts 1983, 68th Leg., ch. 576, §1, eff. Jan. 1, 1984. Amended by Acts 2001, 77th Leg., ch. 930, §1, eff. Sept. 1, 2001; Acts 2003, 78th Leg., ch. 337, §1 (eff. Sept. 1, 2003), ch. 1266, §1.16 (eff. June 21, 2003); Acts 2005, 79th Leg., ch. 728, §23.001(79), eff. Sept. 1, 2005. Source: TRCS art. 5506a, §§1, 3.

ANNOTATIONS

Hermann Hosp. v. Vardeman, 775 S.W.2d 866, 868 (Tex.App.—Houston [1st Dist.] 1989, no writ). Held: The hospital-lien statute does not provide for prejudgment interest or attorney fees. *See also* ***Bashara v.***

Baptist Mem'l Hosp. Sys., 685 S.W.2d 307, 309-10 (Tex.1985) (attorney fees).

Dallas Cty. Hosp. Dist. v. Perrin, 694 S.W.2d 257, 260 (Tex.App.—Dallas 1985, writ ref'd n.r.e.). Hospital "had the burden of proving that its charge was not more than a reasonable and regular rate for the services billed to [patient]." *See also* ***Garner v. City of Houston***, 323 S.W.2d 659, 662 (Tex.App.—Houston 1959, no writ) (by "regular," Legislature meant charges that are usually and customarily made).

PROP §55.005. SECURING LIEN

(a) To secure the lien, a hospital or emergency medical services provider must:

(1) provide notice to the injured individual in accordance with Subsection (d); and

(2) file written notice of the lien with the county clerk of the county in which the services were provided before money is paid to an entitled person because of the injury.

(b) The notice must contain:

(1) the injured individual's name and address;

(2) the date of the accident;

(3) the name and location of the hospital or emergency medical services provider claiming the lien; and

(4) the name of the person alleged to be liable for damages arising from the injury, if known.

(c) The county clerk shall record the name of the injured individual, the date of the accident, and the name and address of the hospital or emergency medical services provider and shall index the record in the name of the injured individual.

(d) Except as provided by Subsection (e), not later than the fifth business day after the date a hospital or emergency medical services provider receives notice from the county clerk that a notice of lien filed under Subsection (a)(2) has been recorded in the county records, the hospital or emergency medical services provider must send a written notice to the injured individual or the injured individual's legal representative, by regular mail, to the individual's last known address, informing the individual that:

(1) the lien will attach to any cause of action or claim the individual may have against another person for the individual's injuries; and

(2) the lien does not attach to real property owned by the individual.

(e) An emergency medical services provider is not required to provide notice by mail if the emergency medical services provider provides the notice required by Subsection (d) to the injured individual or the injured individual's representative at the time emergency medical services are provided and if:

(1) the required notice is included on the emergency medical services authorization form in a paper or electronic version in a separate paragraph that is bolded and in at least 14-point type; and

(2) except as provided by Subsection (f), the notice is signed by the injured individual or the injured individual's representative.

(f) For the purposes of Subsection (e), if consent for emergency care of an individual is not required under Section 773.008, Health and Safety Code, notice provided on an emergency medical services authorization form to the injured individual is not required to be signed.

(g) The failure of an individual to receive a notice mailed in accordance with Subsection (d) does not affect the validity of a lien under this chapter.

History of Prop. Code §55.005: Acts 1983, 68th Leg., ch. 576, §1, eff. Jan. 1, 1984. Amended by Acts 1995, 74th Leg., ch. 1031, §1, eff. Aug. 28, 1995; Acts 2003, 78th Leg., ch. 337, §1, eff. Sept. 1, 2003; Acts 2011, 82nd Leg., ch. 169, §1, eff. Sept. 1, 2011. Source: TRCS art. 5506a, §§3, 4.

ANNOTATIONS

Methodist Hosps. v. Mid-Century Ins., 259 S.W.3d 358, 361 (Tex.App.—Dallas 2008, no pet.). "There is nothing on [hospital's] notice to indicate the time of the accident.... Because the lien attaches only to a cause of action, judgment, or settlement based on the accident giving rise to the injuries treated by the hospital, the date of the accident listed on the notice is crucial. It is by comparing the date and the name of the responsible party, if known, that one can determine whether the accident made the subject of the legal claims is the same as the accident made the subject of the lien. There is nothing on [hospital's] notice of lien that would enable someone searching the record to determine that the lien was intended to attach to the accident occurring on an earlier date. [¶] We conclude the trial court properly ruled [hospital's] lien was unenforceable under §55.005."

Ohio Med. Prods. v. Suber, 758 S.W.2d 870, 873 (Tex.App.—Houston [14th Dist.] 1988, writ denied). "The right to assert [the hospital] lien belongs to the hospital which must file written notice before money is paid to one entitled to it because of the injury. ...

Whether the judgment provides for the lien is irrelevant to this appeal, and its absence in no way affects the validity of the judgment."

PROP §55.006. DISCHARGE OF LIEN

(a) To discharge a lien under this chapter, the authorities of the hospital or emergency medical services provider claiming the lien or the person in charge of the finances of the hospital or emergency medical services provider must execute and file with the county clerk of the county in which the lien notice was filed a certificate stating that the debt covered by the lien has been paid or released and authorizing the clerk to discharge the lien.

(b) The county clerk shall record a memorandum of the certificate and the date it was filed.

(c) The filing of the certificate and recording of the memorandum discharge the lien.

History of Prop. Code §55.006: Acts 1983, 68th Leg., ch. 576, §1, eff. Jan. 1, 1984. Amended by Acts 2003, 78th Leg., ch. 337, §1, eff. Sept. 1, 2003. Source: TRCS art. 5506a, §4b.

PROP §55.007. VALIDITY OF RELEASE

(a) A release of a cause of action or judgment to which a lien under this chapter may attach is not valid unless:

(1) the charges of the hospital or emergency medical services provider claiming the lien were paid in full before the execution and delivery of the release;

(2) the charges of the hospital or emergency medical services provider claiming the lien were paid before the execution and delivery of the release to the extent of any full and true consideration paid to the injured individual by or on behalf of the other parties to the release; or

(3) the hospital or emergency medical services provider claiming the lien is a party to the release.

(b) A judgment to which a lien under this chapter has attached remains in effect until the charges of the hospital or emergency medical services provider claiming the lien are paid in full or to the extent set out in the judgment.

History of Prop. Code §55.007: Acts 1983, 68th Leg., ch. 576, §1, eff. Jan. 1, 1984. Amended by Acts 2003, 78th Leg., ch. 337, §1, eff. Sept. 1, 2003. Source: TRCS art. 5506a, §3.

ANNOTATIONS

McAllen Hosps., L.P. v. State Farm Cty. Mut. Ins., 433 S.W.3d 535, 536 (Tex.2014). "In this case, two patients treated at the ... hospital settled with the negligent third party. That party's liability insurer made the settlement checks jointly payable to the patients and the hospital and delivered the checks to the patients, who deposited them without the hospital's endorsement. The issue presented is whether the hospital's charges were 'paid' under the Hospital Lien Statute and the Uniform Commercial Code even though the hospital never received notice that the settlement funds had been delivered to the patients and were never reimbursed for the treatment costs. We hold that they were not."

Trinity Univ'l Ins. v. Bleeker, 966 S.W.2d 489, 491 (Tex.1998). "As a threshold matter, 'a settlement demand must propose to release the insured fully in exchange for a stated sum of money.' [¶] When a hospital lien exists, a release is not valid unless: (1) the hospital's charges were paid in full before the execution and delivery of the release; (2) the hospital's charges were paid before the execution and delivery of the release to the extent of any full and true consideration paid to the injured individual by or on behalf of the other parties to the release; or (3) the hospital is a party to the release. [¶] [Tort claimants] made one written and several oral offers to settle. None of the offers included the hospital liens. ... Any implied release that [tort claimants] offered to [insurer] was not a full one under §55.007(a)."

Bashara v. Baptist Mem'l Hosp. Sys., 685 S.W.2d 307, 308 (Tex.1985). "This is a case of first impression in Texas, presenting the question whether a plaintiff's attorney can enforce a quantum meruit claim against a health care provider, thereby reducing the amount otherwise recoverable by virtue of a hospital lien. We hold that such a claim is precluded as a matter of law.... *At 309:* [T]he language and intent of [§55.007] militate strongly against permitting recovery of a patient's attorney's fees from the corpus of the hospital lien."

PROP §55.008. RECORDS

(a) On request by an attorney for a party by, for, or against whom a claim is asserted for damages arising from an injury, a hospital or emergency medical services provider shall as promptly as possible make available for the attorney's examination its records concerning the services provided to the injured individual.

(b) The hospital or emergency medical services provider may issue reasonable rules for granting access to its records under this section, but it may not deny access because a record is incomplete.

(c) The records are admissible, subject to applicable rules of evidence, in a civil suit arising from the injury.

History of Prop. Code §55.008: Acts 1983, 68th Leg., ch. 576, §1, eff. Jan. 1, 1984. Amended by Acts 2003, 78th Leg., ch. 337, §1, eff. Sept. 1, 2003. Source: TRCS art. 5506a, §4a.

CHAPTER 56. LIENS AGAINST MINERAL PROPERTY

SUBCHAPTER A. GENERAL PROVISIONS

PROP §56.001. DEFINITIONS

In this chapter:

(1) "Mineral activities" means digging, drilling, torpedoing, operating, completing, maintaining, or repairing an oil, gas, or water well, an oil or gas pipeline, or a mine or quarry.

(2) "Mineral contractor" means a person who performs labor or furnishes or hauls material, machinery, or supplies used in mineral activities under an express or implied contract with a mineral property owner or with a trustee, agent, or receiver of a mineral property owner.

(3) "Mineral property owner" means an owner of land, an oil, gas, or other mineral leasehold, an oil or gas pipeline, or an oil or gas pipeline right-of-way.

(4) "Mineral subcontractor" means a person who:

(A) furnishes or hauls material, machinery, or supplies used in mineral activities under contract with a mineral contractor or with a subcontractor;

(B) performs labor used in mineral activities under contract with a mineral contractor; or

(C) performs labor used in mineral activities as an artisan or day laborer employed by a subcontractor.

History of Prop. Code §56.001: Acts 1983, 68th Leg., ch. 576, §1, eff. Jan. 1, 1984. Source: TRCS arts. 5473, 5474.

ANNOTATIONS

Bandera Drilling Co. v. Lavino, 824 S.W.2d 782, 784 (Tex.App.—Eastland 1992, no writ). "A 'mineral subcontractor' is, by definition, a person who is employed by a 'mineral contractor.' ... Merely because an additional party ... exists between the laborer and some of the mineral property owners does not make [P] a 'mineral subcontractor' in relation to [Ds]."

Rees-Jones (Atkins Pet. Corp.) v. Rees-Jones (Apache Servs.), 799 S.W.2d 463, 465-66 (Tex.App.—El Paso 1990, writ denied). "Can the issue of whether those who provide services and materials are contractors or subcontractors be dependent upon events that occur after the contract for such services and materials is made? We believe the answer should be 'No.' ... If we are to say that the lien claimants did not 'contract with a mineral property owner' who did they contract with? Certainly [owner of the working interest] comes within the definition of a 'Mineral property owner' as that term is defined in §56.001(3).... Without dispute, [owner] was the owner of the mineral leasehold. [¶] [Assignees] argue that because their letter agreements and the Operating Agreement with [owner] defined their relationship as independent contractors, [owner] had to be a mineral contractor acting in their behalf, and therefore the lien claimants were mineral subcontractors. Whatever that relationship was does not define the relationship between [owner] and the lien claimants. The lien claimants' status as contractors cannot be converted to that of subcontractors by another contract to which they are not privy. Most likely [assignees] wanted their relationship with [owner] to be that of independent contractors so as to avoid personal liability that could arise from a partnership, agency relationship or joint venture."

PROP §56.002. LIEN

A mineral contractor or subcontractor has a lien to secure payment for labor or services related to the mineral activities.

History of Prop. Code §56.002: Acts 1983, 68th Leg., ch. 576, §1, eff. Jan. 1, 1984. Source: TRCS arts. 5473, 5474.

ANNOTATIONS

Noble Expl., Inc. v. Nixon Drilling Co., 794 S.W.2d 589, 591 (Tex.App.—Austin 1990, no writ). "Chapter 56

is the exclusive statute governing liens against mineral property to secure payment for labor or services related to mineral activities. Persons entitled to liens under this statute are not entitled to liens provided by other statutes."

PROP §56.003. PROPERTY SUBJECT TO LIEN

(a) The following property is subject to the lien:

(1) the material, machinery, and supplies furnished or hauled by the lien claimant;

(2) the land, leasehold, oil or gas well, water well, oil or gas pipeline and its right-of-way, and lease for oil and gas purposes for which the labor was performed or material, machinery, or supplies were furnished or hauled, and the buildings and appurtenances on this property;

(3) other material, machinery, and supplies used for mineral activities and owned by the owner of the property listed in Subdivision (2); and

(4) other wells and pipelines used in operations related to oil, gas, and minerals and located on property listed in Subdivision (2).

(b) A lien created by performing labor or furnishing or hauling material, machinery, or supplies for a leaseholder does not attach to the fee title to the property.

History of Prop. Code §56.003: Acts 1983, 68th Leg., ch. 576, §1, eff. Jan. 1, 1984. Source: TRCS art. 5473.

ANNOTATIONS

Abella v. Knight Oil Tools, 945 S.W.2d 847, 851 (Tex.App.—Houston [1st Dist.] 1997, no writ). "[Ps'] recorded lien affidavits state that [Ps] provided labor and materials to [production company], and that [production company] was the owner of the 'oil and gas leasehold estate and of the oil and gas wells.' Therefore, [Ps'] liens attached not only to the materials they supplied, but also to the oil and gas leaseholds and the oil and gas wells. The oil and gas leases grant the right to extract and produce the oil and gas from the land. [¶] There is no dispute that the value of [Ps'] liens diminish as the wells are produced, and it is clear that the action to foreclose on [Ps'] liens is an 'action by creditors to subject the oil and gas leases to the creditors' claims,' as contemplated by [CPRC] §64.001(a) governing the appointment of receivers. Under the facts of this case, we cannot say that [Ps] are not entitled to the appointment of a receiver as a matter of law…."

Dunigan Tool & Sup. v. Burris, 427 S.W.2d 341, 344 (Tex.App.—Eastland, 1968, writ ref'd n.r.e.). "[U]nder [§56.003,] a lien exists upon an entire tract of land or leasehold interest upon which materials were delivered to or used and if such material was furnished or used on one of two or more tracts which tracts were treated as a unit, the lien exists as to the entire unit. The lien exists, however, only upon the tract, leasehold interest or unit upon which the material was furnished or used."

PROP §56.004. PRIORITY

(a) The lien does not affect an encumbrance that attached to land or a leasehold before the lien's inception.

(b) The lien on material, machinery, supplies, or a specific improvement takes priority over an earlier encumbrance on the land or leasehold on which the material, machinery, supplies, or improvement is placed or located.

History of Prop. Code §56.004: Acts 1983, 68th Leg., ch. 576, §1, eff. Jan. 1, 1984. Source: TRCS art. 5475.

PROP §56.005. ACCRUAL OF INDEBTEDNESS

(a) The indebtedness for labor performed by the day or week accrues at the end of each week during which the labor is performed.

(b) The indebtedness for material or services accrues on the date the material or services were last furnished. All material or services that a person furnishes for the same land, leasehold interest, oil or gas pipeline, or oil or gas pipeline right-of-way are considered to be furnished under a single contract unless more than six months elapse between the dates the material or services are furnished.

History of Prop. Code §56.005: Acts 1983, 68th Leg., ch. 576, §1, eff. Jan. 1, 1984. Source: TRCS art. 5476b.

ANNOTATIONS

Shell W. E&P, Inc. v. Pel-State Bulk Plant, LLC, 509 S.W.3d 581, 589 (Tex.App.—San Antonio 2016, no pet.). See annotation under Property Code §56.006, p. 289.

PROP §56.006. LIABILITY OF OWNER

An owner of land or a leasehold may not be subjected to liability under this chapter greater than the amount agreed to be paid in the contract for furnishing material or performing labor.

History of Prop. Code §56.006: Acts 1983, 68th Leg., ch. 576, §1, eff. Jan. 1, 1984. Source: TRCS art. 5478.

ANNOTATIONS

Shell W. E&P, Inc. v. Pel-State Bulk Plant, LLC, 509 S.W.3d 581, 589 (Tex.App.—San Antonio 2016, no pet.). "[D1] argues the trial court erred by calculating the amount of [P's] lien by using the cumulative sum of multiple contracts between [Ds] rather than the amount of each specific contract for which [P] provided labor and materials. [D1] emphasizes the use of the word 'contract' [in Prop. Code §56.006] in the singular, and argues that because it had multiple contracts with [D2], the trial court erred in construing §56.006. [¶] We decline to construe §56.006 in the narrow manner advocated by [D1]. As we have already determined, [Ds] had a single contract. However, even if [Ds] had entered into multiple contracts, the trial court did not err in construing §56.006. The Legislature has instructed that number-specific references in statutes are not dispositive. Therefore, the word 'contract' as used in §56.006 is not restricted to the singular. [¶] Additionally, [Prop. Code §56.005(b)] assigns a particular meaning to the word 'contract.' ... Thus, under the guidance provided by §56.005(b), it is presumed that materials or services furnished within a six-month period are furnished under a single contract."

Energy-Agri Prods. v. Eisenman Chem. Co., 717 S.W.2d 651, 653 (Tex.App.—Amarillo 1986, no writ). "[T]he right to the enforcement of the lien depends upon the state of the account between the owner and his contractor, and not upon the condition of the account between the contractor and his subcontractor, when the owner receives notice of the claim. It follows, as a necessary corollary, that if the owner has paid his contractor in full before notice of the subcontractor's claim is received, then the owner is not liable, and his property is not subject to the lien afforded by ch. 56, for payment of the subcontractor's claim."

Sections 56.007-56.020 reserved for expansion

SUBCHAPTER B. SECURING LIEN

PROP §56.021. SECURING LIEN

(a) Not later than six months after the day the indebtedness accrues, a person claiming the lien must file an affidavit with the county clerk of the county in which the property is located.

(b) Not later than the 10th day before the day the affidavit is filed, a mineral subcontractor claiming the lien must serve on the property owner written notice that the lien is claimed.

History of Prop. Code §56.021: Acts 1983, 68th Leg., ch. 576, §1, eff. Jan. 1, 1984. Source: TRCS arts. 5476a, 5476c.

ANNOTATIONS

Seven N. Holdings, L.P. v. Mathis & Sons, Inc., No. 11-12-00008-CV (Tex.App.—Eastland 2014, no pet.) (memo op.; 1-24-14). "A 'mineral contractor' is not required to give notice to the mineral property owner to secure a Ch. 56 lien. Had the legislature intended for all mineral property owners of record to be notified by a 'mineral contractor' in order to secure the lien, then it would have so provided. Chapter 56 should be liberally construed for the protection of laborers and materialmen." (Internal quotes omitted.)

Flournoy Drilling Co. v. Walker, 750 S.W.2d 911, 913 (Tex.App.—Corpus Christi 1988, writ denied). "Under §56.021 ..., the legislature has provided six months from the date the indebtedness accrues in which the mineral contractor or subcontractor may file the lien in order to perfect it. Undoubtedly, the legislature intended the statute to promote and encourage the important oil and gas industry and facilitate the development of our mineral resources by providing contractors and subcontractors a lien, should they choose to perfect it, in the oilfield equipment they have installed and in the land itself. To permit the debtor's death to terminate the six-month time period would defeat that purpose."

PROP §56.022. CONTENTS OF AFFIDAVIT

(a) A lien claimant's affidavit must include:

(1) the name of the mineral property owner involved, if known;

(2) the name and mailing address of the claimant;

(3) the dates of performance or furnishing;

(4) a description of the land, leasehold interest, pipeline, or pipeline right-of-way involved; and

(5) an itemized list of amounts claimed.

(b) A mineral subcontractor's affidavit must in addition include:

(1) the name of the person for whom labor was performed or material was furnished or hauled; and

(2) a statement that the subcontractor timely served written notice that the lien is claimed on the property owner or the owner's agent, representative, or receiver.

History of Prop. Code §56.022: Acts 1983, 68th Leg., ch. 576, §1, eff. Jan. 1, 1984. Source: TRCS art. 5476a.

ANNOTATIONS

Bandera Drilling Co. v. Lavino, 824 S.W.2d 782, 785 (Tex.App.—Eastland 1992, no writ). While §56.022(a)(1) "provides that the lien affidavit must include the name of the mineral property owner if known, Texas applies a 'substantial compliance' rule. Had the legislature intended for all mineral property owners of record to be notified by a 'mineral contractor' in order to secure the lien, then it would have so provided. Chapter 56 should be liberally construed for the protection of laborers and materialmen."

PROP §56.023. CONTENTS OF MINERAL SUBCONTRACTOR'S NOTICE

A mineral subcontractor's notice to the property owner must include the amount of the lien, the name of the person indebted to the subcontractor, and a description of the land, leasehold interest, pipeline, or pipeline right-of-way involved.

History of Prop. Code §56.023: Acts 1983, 68th Leg., ch. 576, §1, eff. Jan. 1, 1984. Source: TRCS art. 5476c.

PROP §56.024. FILING IN NEW COUNTY

(a) Not later than the 90th day after the day that property to which the lien has attached is removed from a county in which the lien affidavit covering the property has been filed, the lienholder may file with the clerk of the county to which the property has been moved an itemized inventory of the property showing the unpaid amount due.

(b) The lien attaches to all property subject to the lien located in a county in which an inventory is filed under this section.

(c) An inventory filed under this section is notice of the lien's existence.

History of Prop. Code §56.024: Acts 1983, 68th Leg., ch. 576, §1, eff. Jan. 1, 1984. Source: TRCS art. 5476.

Sections 56.025-56.040 reserved for expansion

SUBCHAPTER C. ENFORCEMENT

PROP §56.041. ENFORCEMENT

(a) A claimant must enforce the lien within the same time and in the same manner as a mechanic's, contractor's, or materialman's lien under Chapter 53.

(b) A holder of a prior encumbrance on land or a leasehold is not a necessary party to a suit to foreclose the lien.

History of Prop. Code §56.041: Acts 1983, 68th Leg., ch. 576, §1, eff. Jan. 1, 1984. Source: TRCS arts. 5475, 5476.

PROP §56.042. SALE OR REMOVAL OF PROPERTY

(a) A mineral property owner, contractor, subcontractor, or purchaser or an agent, trustee, or receiver of one of those persons may not sell property to which the lien has attached or remove it from the land on which it was to be used, unless the lienholder consents in writing.

(b) On a violation of this section, a lienholder is entitled to possession of the property regardless of where it is found, and the lienholder may have the property sold to satisfy the debt on which the lien is based regardless of whether the debt is due.

History of Prop. Code §56.042: Acts 1983, 68th Leg., ch. 576, §1, eff. Jan. 1, 1984. Source: TRCS art. 5477.

PROP §56.043. RETENTION OF PAYMENT

A property owner who is served with a mineral subcontractor's notice may withhold payment to the contractor in the amount claimed until the debt on which the lien is based is settled or determined to be not owed. The owner is not liable to the subcontractor for more than the amount that the owner owes the original contractor when the notice is received.

History of Prop. Code §56.043: Acts 1983, 68th Leg., ch. 576, §1, eff. Jan. 1, 1984. Source: TRCS art. 5476c.

ANNOTATIONS

Shell W. E&P, Inc. v. Pel-State Bulk Plant, LLC, 509 S.W.3d 581, 590 (Tex.App.—San Antonio 2016, no pet.). D1, a mineral lease owner, "argues the trial court erred in construing §56.043 by not limiting [D1's] liability to the amount [D1] owed [D2, a general contractor,] on the lien notice date for each specific well on which [P-subcontractor's] claim was based. [¶] Examining the plain language of the statute, we note that the word 'contract' does not appear in §56.043. … Thus, under §56.043, any limitation on the amount of [P's] lien must be determined by the state of the account between [D1] and [D2] at the time [D1] received the lien notice, not by amounts [D1] owed [D2] on particular wells. [D1's] argument that the trial court was required to consider the status of the invoices on individual wells is not supported by the plain language of the statute."

PROP §56.044. FORFEITURE OF LEASEHOLD

Forfeiture of a leasehold does not impair a lien on material, machinery, supplies, or an improvement located on the leasehold if:

(1) the lien attached to the property before the leasehold was forfeited;

(2) the property is not permanently attached to the land; and

(3) the lienholder pays the owner of the land the damages caused to the land by removal of the property.

History of Prop. Code §56.044: Acts 1983, 68th Leg., ch. 576, §1, eff. Jan. 1, 1984. Source: TRCS art. 5476d.

PROP §56.045. EQUITABLE OR CONTINGENT INTEREST

Failure of an equitable interest to become legal title or nonfulfillment of a condition subsequent on which a legal interest is contingent does not impair a lien on material, machinery, supplies, or an improvement located on the land covered by the equitable interest if the lien attached to the material, machinery, supplies, or improvement before the failure.

History of Prop. Code §56.045: Acts 1983, 68th Leg., ch. 576, §1, eff. Jan. 1, 1984. Source: TRCS art. 5476d.

CHAPTER 57. RAILROAD LABORER'S LIEN

PROP §57.001. RAILROAD LABORER'S LIEN

A mechanic, laborer, or other person who works or uses tools or a team in the construction, operation, or repair of a railroad or railroad equipment has a lien on the railroad and equipment for the amount owed for the labor or the use of the tools or team.

History of Prop. Code §57.001: Acts 1983, 68th Leg., ch. 576, §1, eff. Jan. 1, 1984. Source: TRCS art. 5480.

PROP §57.002. PRIORITY

A lien under this chapter takes priority over all other liens on the same property.

History of Prop. Code §57.002: Acts 1983, 68th Leg., ch. 576, §1, eff. Jan. 1, 1984. Source: TRCS art. 5480.

PROP §57.003. DURATION OF LIEN

A lien under this chapter ceases to exist 12 months after the day that it is created, unless the lien claimant has sued to foreclose the lien.

History of Prop. Code §57.003: Acts 1983, 68th Leg., ch. 576, §1, eff. Jan. 1, 1984. Source: TRCS art. 5480.

PROP §57.004. ENFORCEMENT

A court in a suit to foreclose the lien shall render judgment for the amount due and order to be sold as much of the railroad right-of-way and equipment as is necessary to satisfy the judgment only if:

(1) the work was performed at the instance of the railroad company or the company's agent, contractor, or subcontractor; and

(2) the amount claimed is due.

History of Prop. Code §57.004: Acts 1983, 68th Leg., ch. 576, §1, eff. Jan. 1, 1984. Source: TRCS art. 5481.

PROP §57.005. VENUE

A suit to foreclose a lien under this chapter may be brought in a county in which:

(1) the work was performed or any part of the cause of action accrued; or

(2) the principal office of the railroad company is located.

History of Prop. Code §57.005: Acts 1983, 68th Leg., ch. 576, §1, eff. Jan. 1, 1984. Source: TRCS art. 5482.

PROP §57.006. PARTIES

Holders of other liens on the same property are not necessary parties to a suit to foreclose a lien under this chapter but may intervene in the suit.

History of Prop. Code §57.006: Acts 1983, 68th Leg., ch. 576, §1, eff. Jan. 1, 1984. Source: TRCS art. 5481.

CHAPTER 58. FARM, FACTORY, & STORE WORKER'S LIENS

PROP §58.001. DEFINITIONS

In this chapter:

(1) "Employer" means a person with whom a worker contracts, directly or through an agent, receiver, or trustee of the person, for the performance of labor or a service by the worker. The contract may be oral or in writing.

(2) "Worker" means a clerk, accountant, bookkeeper, waiter, waitress, cook, maid, porter, servant,

employee, artisan, craftsman, factory operator, mill operator, mechanic, quarry worker, common laborer, or farmhand.

History of Prop. Code §58.001: Acts 1983, 68th Leg., ch. 576, §1, eff. Jan. 1, 1984. Source: TRCS art. 5483.

PROP §58.002. LIEN

(a) A worker has a lien as provided by this chapter if, under the contract with the employer, the worker:

(1) labors or performs a service in an office, store, hotel, rooming house or boardinghouse, restaurant, shop, factory, mine, quarry, or mill or on a farm; or

(2) performs a service:

(A) in cutting, preparing, hauling, or transporting logs or timber to a place of disposition;

(B) on a means of transportation of logs or timber; or

(C) in constructing or maintaining a tram or railroad constructed or used for transporting logs or timber to their owner or a point of disposition.

(b) The amount of the lien is the amount owed under the contract.

History of Prop. Code §58.002: Acts 1983, 68th Leg., ch. 576, §1, eff. Jan. 1, 1984. Source: TRCS art. 5483.

PROP §58.003. PROPERTY SUBJECT TO LIEN

Each thing of value owned by or in the possession or control of the employer or the employer's agent, receiver, or trustee is subject to the lien if:

(1) created in whole or part by the lien claimant's work;

(2) used by or useful to the lien claimant in the performance of the work; or

(3) necessarily connected with the performance of the work.

History of Prop. Code §58.003: Acts 1983, 68th Leg., ch. 576, §1, eff. Jan. 1, 1984. Source: TRCS art. 5483.

PROP §58.004. SECURING LIEN

(a) Not later than the 30th day after the day that the indebtedness accrues, a worker who has not received payment for work performed and who wishes to claim the lien must:

(1) serve a copy of an account of the services, stating the amount due, on the employer or the employer's agent, receiver, or trustee; and

(2) file a copy of the account with the county clerk of the county in which the services were performed.

(b) The party making an account must execute an affidavit verifying the contents of the account.

(c) Substantial compliance with this section secures the lien.

History of Prop. Code §58.004: Acts 1983, 68th Leg., ch. 576, §1, eff. Jan. 1, 1984. Source: TRCS art. 5486.

PROP §58.005. PRIORITY

(a) A lien under this chapter is a first lien, except that a farmhand's lien is subordinate to a landlord's lien provided by law.

(b) Liens under this chapter take priority in the order that the accounts are filed with the county clerk.

History of Prop. Code §58.005: Acts 1983, 68th Leg., ch. 576, §1, eff. Jan. 1, 1984. Source: TRCS arts. 5483, 5486.

PROP §58.006. DURATION OF LIEN

The lien ceases to exist six months after the day that it is secured unless the lien claimant has sued to foreclose the lien.

History of Prop. Code §58.006: Acts 1983, 68th Leg., ch. 576, §1, eff. Jan. 1, 1984. Source: TRCS arts. 5486, 5488.

PROP §58.007. PURCHASE OF PROPERTY TO WHICH LIEN HAS ATTACHED

(a) A person who purchases from its owner property to which the lien has attached and who has no actual or constructive notice of the lien takes the property free from the lien.

(b) An account filed with the county clerk under this chapter or a suit to foreclose a lien is constructive notice of the lien's existence.

History of Prop. Code §58.007: Acts 1983, 68th Leg., ch. 576, §1, eff. Jan. 1, 1984. Source: TRCS art. 5486.

PROP §58.008. ASSIGNMENT OF LIEN

The lien may be assigned. An assignee receives the rights and privileges held by the assignor under the lien.

History of Prop. Code §58.008: Acts 1983, 68th Leg., ch. 576, §1, eff. Jan. 1, 1984. Source: TRCS art. 5487.

PROP §58.009. PAYMENT OF WAGES

For purposes of this chapter, wages are due weekly for work performed by the day or week and monthly for work performed by the month, and an employer shall pay wages in United States legal tender.

History of Prop. Code §58.009: Acts 1983, 68th Leg., ch. 576, §1, eff. Jan. 1, 1984. Source: TRCS art. 5485.

CHAPTER 59. SELF-SERVICE STORAGE FACILITY LIENS

Subchapter A. General Provisions

SUBCHAPTER A. GENERAL PROVISIONS

PROP §59.001. DEFINITIONS

In this chapter:

(1) "Lessor" means an owner, lessor, sublessor, or managing agent of a self-service storage facility.

(1-a) "Military service" means:

(A) military service as defined by Section 101, Servicemembers Civil Relief Act (50 U.S.C. App. Section 511); and

(B) active duty service for a period of more than 30 consecutive days as a member of the Texas State Guard or Texas National Guard under the call of the governor.

(2) "Rental agreement" means a written or oral agreement that establishes or modifies the terms of use of a self-service storage facility.

(3) "Self-service storage facility" means real property that is rented to be used exclusively for storage of property and is cared for and controlled by the tenant.

(4) "Tenant" means a person entitled under a rental agreement to the exclusive use of storage space at a self-service storage facility.

(5) "Verified mail" means any method of mailing that provides evidence of mailing.

History of Prop. Code §59.001: Acts 1983, 68th Leg., ch. 576, §1, eff. Jan. 1, 1984. Amended by Acts 2011, 82nd Leg., ch. 405, §1, eff. Jan. 1, 2012. Source: TRCS art. 5238b, §3.

PROP §59.002. APPLICABILITY

This chapter applies to a self-service storage facility rental agreement that is entered into, extended, or renewed after September 1, 1981.

History of Prop. Code §59.002: Acts 1983, 68th Leg., ch. 576, §1, eff. Jan. 1, 1984. Source: TRCS art. 5238b, §3.

PROP §59.003. APPLICABILITY OF OTHER STATUTES

(a) The following provisions do not apply to a self-service storage facility:

(1) Subchapter B, Chapter 54;

(2) Chapter 70; and

(3) Chapter 181, Health and Safety Code.

(b) Unless a lessor issues a warehouse receipt, bill of lading, or other document of title relating to property stored at the facility, the following statutes do not apply to a self-service storage facility:

(1) Chapter 7, Business & Commerce Code, as amended; and

(2) Chapter 14, Agriculture Code.

History of Prop. Code §59.003: Acts 1983, 68th Leg., ch. 576, §1, eff. Jan. 1, 1984. Amended by Acts 2001, 77th Leg., ch. 1124, §3, eff. Sept. 1, 2001; Acts 2011, 82nd Leg., ch. 405, §2, eff. Jan. 1, 2012. Source: TRCS art. 5238b, §2.

PROP §59.004. VARIATION BY AGREEMENT & WAIVER

Except as expressly provided by this chapter, a lessor or tenant may not vary the provisions of this chapter by agreement or waive rights conferred by this chapter.

History of Prop. Code §59.004: Acts 1983, 68th Leg., ch. 576, §1, eff. Jan. 1, 1984. Source: TRCS art. 5238b, §12.

PROP §59.005. DAMAGES FOR VIOLATION

A person injured by a violation of this chapter may sue for damages under the Deceptive Trade Practices—Consumer Protection Act (Subchapter E, Chapter 17, Business & Commerce Code).

History of Prop. Code §59.005: Acts 1983, 68th Leg., ch. 576, §1, eff. Jan. 1, 1984. Source: TRCS art. 5238b, §14.

See also B&CC §§17.46, 17.50; *O'Connor's Texas Bus. & Com. Code*, "DTPA Tie-In Statutes Chart," chart 3, p. 998.

PROP §59.006. ATTACHMENT & PRIORITY OF LIEN

A lien under this chapter attaches on the date the tenant places the property at the self-service storage facility. The lien takes priority over all other liens on the same property.

History of Prop. Code §59.006: Acts 1983, 68th Leg., ch. 576, §1, eff. Jan. 1, 1984. Source: TRCS art. 5238b, §10.

PROP §59.007. PURCHASE OF PROPERTY

A good faith purchaser of property sold to satisfy a lien under this chapter takes the property free of a claim by a person against whom the lien was valid, regardless of whether the lessor has complied with this chapter.

History of Prop. Code §59.007: Acts 1983, 68th Leg., ch. 576, §1, eff. Jan. 1, 1984. Source: TRCS art. 5238b, §13.

PROP §59.008. REDEMPTION

A tenant may redeem property seized under a judicial order or a contractual landlord's lien prior to its sale or other disposition by paying the lessor the amount of the lien and the lessor's reasonable expenses incurred under this chapter.

History of Prop. Code §59.008: Acts 1983, 68th Leg., ch. 576, §1, eff. Jan. 1, 1984. Source: TRCS art. 5238b, §9.

PROP §59.009. RESIDENTIAL USE

A tenant may not use or allow the use of a self-service storage facility as a residence.

History of Prop. Code §59.009: Acts 1983, 68th Leg., ch. 576, §1, eff. Jan. 1, 1984. Source: TRCS art. 5238b, §11.

PROP §59.010. RIGHTS OF CERTAIN MILITARY MEMBERS

(a) In this section, "servicemember" has the meaning assigned by Section 101, Servicemembers Civil Relief Act (50 U.S.C. App. Section 511).

(b) A member of the Texas State Guard or Texas National Guard who is in military service is entitled to the same protections and rights relating to the enforcement of storage liens under the Servicemembers Civil Relief Act (50 U.S.C. App. Section 501 et seq.) to which a servicemember is entitled.

History of Prop. Code §59.010: Acts 2011, 82nd Leg., ch. 405, §3, eff. Jan. 1, 2012.

Sections 59.011-59.020 reserved for expansion

SUBCHAPTER B. LIEN

PROP §59.021. LIEN; PROPERTY ATTACHED

A lessor has a lien on all property in a self-service storage facility for the payment of charges that are due and unpaid by the tenant.

History of Prop. Code §59.021: Acts 1983, 68th Leg., ch. 576, §1, eff. Jan. 1, 1984. Amended by Acts 1985, 69th Leg., ch. 117, §12(a), eff. Sept. 1, 1985. Source: TRCS art. 5238b, §4.

PROP §59.022. TRANSFERRED

Transferred to §59.041(a) by Acts 1985, 69th Leg., ch. 117, §12(c), eff. Sept. 1, 1985.

Sections 59.023-59.040 reserved for expansion

SUBCHAPTER C. ENFORCEMENT OF LIEN

PROP §59.041. ENFORCEMENT OF LIEN

(a) Except as provided by Subsection (b) of this section, a lessor may enforce a lien under this chapter only under a judgment by a court of competent jurisdiction that forecloses the lien and orders the sale of the property to which it is attached.

(b) A lessor may enforce a lien under this chapter by seizing and selling the property to which the lien is attached if:

(1) the seizure and sale are made under the terms of a contractual landlord's lien as underlined or printed in conspicuous bold print in a written rental agreement between the lessor and tenant; and

(2) the seizure and sale are made in accordance with this chapter.

History of Prop. Code §59.041: Acts 1983, 68th Leg., ch. 576, §1, eff. Jan. 1, 1984. Amended by Acts 1985, 69th Leg., ch. 117, §12(c), eff. Sept. 1, 1985. Source: TRCS art. 5238b, §5(a), (b).

PROP §59.042. PROCEDURE FOR SEIZURE & SALE

(a) A lessor who wishes to enforce a contractual landlord's lien by seizing and selling or otherwise disposing of the property to which it is attached must deliver written notice of the claim to the tenant.

(b) If the tenant fails to satisfy the claim on or before the 14th day after the date the notice is delivered, the lessor must publish or post notices advertising the sale as provided by this subchapter.

(c) If notice is by publication, the lessor may not sell the property until the 15th day after the date the notice is first published. If notice is by posting, the lessor may sell the property after the 10th day after the date the notices are posted.

History of Prop. Code §59.042: Acts 1983, 68th Leg., ch. 576, §1, eff. Jan. 1, 1984. Amended by Acts 1984, 68th Leg., 2nd C.S., ch. 18, §5, eff. Oct. 2, 1984; Acts 1985, 69th Leg., ch. 117, §12(d), eff. Sept. 1, 1985; Acts 2011, 82nd Leg., ch. 405, §4, eff. Jan. 1, 2012. Source: TRCS art. 5238b, §§6(a), 7, 8(a), (b), (d).

PROP §59.043. CONTENTS & DELIVERY OF NOTICE OF CLAIM; INFORMATION REGARDING TENANT'S MILITARY SERVICE

(a) The lessor's notice to the tenant of the claim must contain:

(1) an itemized account of the claim;

(2) the name, address, and telephone number of the lessor or the lessor's agent;

(3) a statement that the contents of the self-service storage facility have been seized under the contractual landlord's lien;

(4) a statement that if the tenant fails to satisfy the claim on or before the 14th day after the date the notice is delivered, the property may be sold at public auction; and

(5) a statement underlined or printed in conspicuous bold print requesting a tenant who is in military service to notify the lessor of the status of the tenant's current military service immediately.

(b) A lessor may require written proof of a tenant's military service in the form of documentation from the United States Department of Defense or other documentation reasonably acceptable to the lessor.

(c) Subject to Subsection (d), the lessor must deliver the notice in person or by e-mail or verified mail to the tenant's last known e-mail or postal address as stated in the rental agreement or in a written notice from the tenant to the lessor furnished after the execution of the rental agreement. Notice by verified mail is considered delivered when the notice, properly addressed with postage prepaid, is deposited with the United States Postal Service or a common carrier. Notice by e-mail is considered delivered when sent to the last known e-mail address of the tenant.

(d) The notice may not be sent by e-mail unless a written rental agreement between the lessor and the tenant contains language underlined or in conspicuous bold print that notice may be given by e-mail if the tenant elects to provide an e-mail address.

History of Prop. Code §59.043: Acts 1983, 68th Leg., ch. 576, §1, eff. Jan. 1, 1984. Amended by Acts 2011, 82nd Leg., ch. 405, §5, eff. Jan. 1, 2012. Source: TRCS art. 5238b, §§3, 7.

A PROP §59.044. NOTICE OF SALE

(a) The notice advertising the sale must contain:

(1) a general description of the property;

(2) a statement that the property is being sold to satisfy a landlord's lien;

(3) the tenant's name;

(4) the address of the self-service storage facility; and

(5) the time, place, and terms of the sale.

(a-1) For the purposes of Subsection (a)(5), the place of a sale is:

(1) the physical address of the location of the sale if the sale is conducted at the self-service storage facility or a reasonably near public place; or

(2) the address of the Internet website if the sale is conducted through an Internet website.

(b) The lessor must publish the notice once in each of two consecutive weeks in a newspaper of general circulation in the county in which the self-service storage facility is located. If there is not a newspaper of general circulation in the county, the lessor may instead post a copy of the notice at the self-service storage facility and at least five other conspicuous locations near the facility.

History of Prop. Code §59.044: Acts 1983, 68th Leg., ch. 576, §1, eff. Jan. 1, 1984. Amended by S.B. 952, §1, 85th Leg., eff. Sept. 1, 2017. Source: TRCS art. 5238b, §8(a), (c), (d).

A PROP §59.0445. NOTICE TO OWNER & LIENHOLDERS

(a) This section applies to the enforcement of a lien under this chapter on:

(1) a motor vehicle subject to Chapter 501, Transportation Code;

(2) a motorboat, vessel, or outboard motor for which a certificate of title is required under Subchapter B, Chapter 31, Parks and Wildlife Code; or

(3) a motor vehicle, motorboat, vessel, or outboard motor registered or titled outside this state.

(b) In addition to the notices required by Sections 59.042 and 59.044, not later than the 30th day after the date the lessor takes possession of the motor vehicle, motorboat, vessel, or outboard motor to enforce a lien under this chapter, the lessor shall give written notice of sale to the last known owner and each holder of a lien recorded on the registration or certificate of title of the motor vehicle, motorboat, vessel, or outboard motor or, if the registration or title is outside this state, the owner and each lienholder of record in the location in which the motor vehicle, motorboat, vessel, or outboard motor is registered or titled.

(c) Except as provided by Subsection (d), the notice required by this section must be sent by verified mail. Notice by verified mail is considered mailed when the notice, properly addressed with postage prepaid, is deposited with the United States Postal Service or a common carrier. The notice must include:

(1) the amount of the charges secured by the lien;

(2) a request for payment; and

(3) a statement that if the charges are not paid in full before the 31st day after the date the notice is mailed or published, as applicable, the property may be sold at public auction.

(d) The notice required by this section may be given by publishing the notice once in a print or electronic version of a newspaper of general circulation in the county in which the motor vehicle, motorboat, vessel, or outboard motor is stored if:

(1) the lessor submits a written request by verified mail to the governmental entity with which the motor vehicle, motorboat, vessel, or outboard motor is registered or titled requesting information relating to the identity of the last known owner of record and any lienholder of record;

(2) the lessor:

(A) is advised in writing by the governmental entity with which the motor vehicle, motorboat, vessel, or outboard motor is registered or titled that the entity is unwilling or unable to provide information on the last known owner of record or any lienholder of record; or

(B) does not receive a response from the governmental entity with which the motor vehicle, motorboat, vessel, or outboard motor is registered or titled on or before the 21st day after the date the lessor submits the request;

(3) the identity of the last known owner of record cannot be determined;

(4) the registration or title does not contain an address for the last known owner of record; and

(5) the lessor cannot determine the identities and addresses of the lienholders of record.

(e) The lessor is not required to publish notice under Subsection (d) if a correctly addressed notice is sent with sufficient postage in accordance with Subsections (b) and (c) and is returned as unclaimed or refused or with a notation that the addressee is unknown or has moved without leaving a forwarding address or the forwarding order has expired.

(f) After notice is given under this section to the owner of or the holder of a lien on the motor vehicle, motorboat, vessel, or outboard motor, the owner or lienholder may take possession of the motor vehicle, motorboat, vessel, or outboard motor by paying all charges due to the lessor before the 31st day after the date the notice is mailed or published as provided by this section.

(g) If the charges are not paid before the 31st day after the date the notice is mailed or published, as applicable, the lessor may:

(1) sell the motor vehicle, motorboat, vessel, or outboard motor at a public sale and apply the proceeds to the charges; or

(2) if the property that is the subject of the notice is a motor vehicle, dispose of the motor vehicle in accordance with Subchapter D, Chapter 683, Transportation Code, if the lessor determines that:

(A) the vehicle's only residual value is as a source of parts or scrap metal; or

(B) it is not economical to dispose of the vehicle at a public sale.

(g-1) If the lessor disposes of the property under Subsection (g)(2), the lessor shall apply the fair market value of the motor vehicle to the charges due to the lessor.

(h) A person commits an offense if the person knowingly provides false or misleading information in a notice required by this section. An offense under this subsection is a Class B misdemeanor.

History of Prop. Code §59.0445: Acts 2011, 82nd Leg., ch. 405, §6, eff. Jan. 1, 2012. Amended by H.B. 3131, §4, 85th Leg., eff. Sept. 1, 2017.

A PROP §59.045. CONDUCT OF SALE

(a) A sale under this subchapter must be a public sale:

(1) conducted at the self-service storage facility or a reasonably near public place; or

(2) conducted through an Internet website accessible to the public.

(b) The lessor must conduct the sale according to the terms specified in the notice advertising the sale and sell the property to the highest bidder.

History of Prop. Code §59.045: Acts 1983, 68th Leg., ch. 576, §1, eff. Jan. 1, 1984. Amended by S.B. 952, §2, 85th Leg., eff. Sept. 1, 2017. Source: TRCS art. 5238b, §6(b), (c).

ANNOTATIONS

McDonald v. Boat Barn, 994 S.W.2d 763, 764-65 (Tex.App.—Houston [1st Dist.] 1999, no pet.). Purchasers "argue that [§59.045] required [lessor] to accept their high bid. [¶] [L]essor must follow the dictates of [§59.045], but the critical issue is whether the sale had been completed. [T]he sale had not been completed. [Lessor] was not required by [§59.045] to accept [purchaser's] bid. [¶] The [Uniform Commercial Code (UCC)] presumes an auction is with reserve and allows the auctioneer to withdraw the goods up until the time [of] sale's completion. [T]he UCC allows the lessor to withdraw an item from sale, while §59.045 requires the lessor to sell to the highest bidder if there is a sale."

PROP §59.046. EXCESS PROCEEDS OF SALE

If the proceeds of a sale under this subchapter are greater than the amount of the lien and the reasonable expenses of the sale, the lessor shall deliver written notice of the excess to the tenant's last known address as

stated in the rental agreement or in a written notice from the tenant to the lessor furnished after the execution of the rental agreement. The lessor shall retain the excess and deliver it to the tenant if the tenant requests it before two years after the date of the sale. If the tenant does not request the excess before two years after the date of the sale, the lessor owns the excess.

History of Prop. Code §59.046: Acts 1983, 68th Leg., ch. 576, §1, eff. Jan. 1, 1984. Source: TRCS art. 5238b, §§3, 6(d).

PROP §59.047. REPEALED

Repealed by Acts 2011, 82nd Leg., ch. 405, §9, eff. Jan. 1, 2012.

CHAPTER 60. NEWSPAPER EMPLOYEE'S LIEN

PROP §60.001. LIEN

A worker in the editorial, reportorial, advertising, or business department of a newspaper, periodical, or other publication who labors or performs a service for the publication under a written or an oral contract with any person has a first lien under this chapter for the amount due under the contract.

History of Prop. Code §60.001: Acts 1983, 68th Leg., ch. 576, §1, eff. Jan. 1, 1984. Source: TRCS art. 5484.

PROP §60.002. PROPERTY SUBJECT TO LIEN

The lien attaches to all products, papers, machinery, tools, fixtures, appurtenances, goods, wares, merchandise, subscription contracts, chattels, or other things of value that are created wholly or partly by the labor of the workers or that are necessarily connected with the performance of their labor or service and that are owned by or in possession of the person with whom the workers contracted.

History of Prop. Code §60.002: Acts 1983, 68th Leg., ch. 576, §1, eff. Jan. 1, 1984. Source: TRCS art. 5484.

CHAPTER 61. MOTOR VEHICLE MORTGAGEE'S LIEN

PROP §61.001. DEFINITIONS

In this chapter:

(1) "Motor vehicle" means any motor-driven or propelled vehicle required to be registered or licensed under the laws of this state.

(2) "Mortgagee" means a secured party, as defined by Section 9.102, Business & Commerce Code, holding a lien on a motor vehicle that has been perfected pursuant to Subchapter F, Chapter 501, Transportation Code.

(3) "Mortgagor" means a debtor, as defined by Section 9.102, Business & Commerce Code, giving a lien or agreeing that a lien may be retained on a motor vehicle.

History of Prop. Code §61.001: Acts 1989, 71st Leg., ch. 171, §1, eff. Sept. 1, 1989. Amended by Acts 1997, 75th Leg., ch. 165, §30.246, eff. Sept. 1, 1997; Acts 1999, 76th Leg., ch. 414, §2.37, eff. July 1, 2001.

PROP §61.002. LIEN

A mortgagee has a lien on a cause of action or other claim of a mortgagor in connection with an accident that involves a motor vehicle on which the mortgagee has perfected a lien and that is attributable to the negligence of another person.

History of Prop. Code §61.002: Acts 1989, 71st Leg., ch. 171, §1, eff. Sept. 1, 1989.

See also Transp. Code ch. 501.

PROP §61.003. PROPERTY TO WHICH LIEN ATTACHES

The lien attaches to:

(1) a cause of action for damages arising from property damage to a motor vehicle on which the mortgagee has perfected a lien caused by an accident that is attributable to the negligence of another person;

(2) a judgment of a court in favor of a mortgagor arising from property damage to a motor vehicle on which the mortgagee has perfected a lien caused by an accident that is attributable to the negligence of another person;

(3) the proceeds of a settlement of a cause of action or a claim by the mortgagor for property damage to a motor vehicle on which the mortgagee has perfected a lien caused by an accident that is attributable to the negligence of another person; and

(4) the proceeds of a property damage liability insurance policy carried by another person that protects the other person against property damage loss caused by accident or collision.

History of Prop. Code §61.003: Acts 1989, 71st Leg., ch. 171, §1, eff. Sept. 1, 1989.

PROP §61.004. AMOUNT OF LIEN

The amount of the lien is the lesser of:

(1) the fair market value of the motor vehicle before the accident;

(2) the reasonable cost of repair to the motor vehicle; or

(3) the balance owed to the mortgagee by the mortgagor.

History of Prop. Code §61.004: Acts 1989, 71st Leg., ch. 171, §1, eff. Sept. 1, 1989. Amended by Acts 1993, 73rd Leg., ch. 48, §11, eff. Sept. 1, 1993.

PROP §61.005. DISCHARGE OF LIEN

If the property to which a lien created under this chapter attaches is paid jointly to the mortgagee and the mortgagor, the lien is discharged.

History of Prop. Code §61.005: Acts 1989, 71st Leg., ch. 171, §1, eff. Sept. 1, 1989.

CHAPTER 62. BROKER'S & APPRAISER'S LIEN ON COMMERCIAL REAL ESTATE

SUBCHAPTER A. GENERAL PROVISIONS

PROP §62.001. SHORT TITLE

This chapter may be cited as the Broker's and Appraiser's Lien on Commercial Real Estate Act.

History of Prop. Code §62.001: Acts 1999, 76th Leg., ch. 1571, §1, eff. Aug. 30, 1999.

PROP §62.002. APPLICABILITY

(a) This chapter applies only to real estate that is commercial real estate on the date the notice of lien is filed under this chapter.

(b) This chapter does not apply to:

(1) a transaction involving a claim for a commission of $2,500 or less in the aggregate; or

(2) a transaction for the sale of commercial real estate involving a claim for a commission of $5,000 or less in the aggregate if the commercial real estate:

(A) is the principal place of business of the record title owner;

(B) is occupied by more than one and fewer than five tenants; and

(C) is improved with 7,500 square feet or less of total gross building area.

History of Prop. Code §62.002: Acts 1999, 76th Leg., ch. 1571, §1, eff. Aug. 30, 1999.

PROP §62.003. DEFINITIONS

In this chapter:

(1) "Broker" means a person who:

(A) is licensed as a broker under Chapter 1101, Occupations Code, and is not acting as a residential rental locator as defined by Section 1101.002, Occupations Code; or

(B) is licensed or certified as a real estate appraiser under Chapter 1103, Occupations Code.

(2) "Commercial real estate" means all real estate except:

(A) real estate improved with one to four residential units;

(B) a single-family residential unit, including a condominium, townhouse, or home in a subdivision, if the unit is sold, leased, or otherwise conveyed on a unit-by-unit basis and regardless of whether the unit is part of a larger building or located on real estate containing more than four residential units;

(C) real estate that is or includes on the real estate a person's homestead;

(D) real estate that is not improved with a structure and is:

(i) zoned for single-family residential use; or

(ii) restricted for single-family use under restrictive covenants that will remain in effect for at least the next two years; or

(E) real estate that:

(i) is primarily used for farming and ranching purposes;

(ii) will continue to be used primarily for farming and ranching purposes; and

(iii) is located more than three miles from the corporate boundaries of any municipality.

(3) "Commission" includes a fee or other valuable consideration.

(4) "Commission agreement" means a written instrument that:

(A) entitles a broker to a commission;

(B) is signed by the person obligated to pay the commission or that person's authorized agent;

(C) references the commission amount or describes the formula used to determine the commission amount; and

(D) contains a description legally sufficient for identification of the real estate interest that is the subject of the agreement if the person obligated to pay the commission is a seller or lessor.

(5) "Deferred commission" means a commission that is earned and is not yet payable.

(6) "Real estate" has the meaning assigned by Section 1101.002, Occupations Code.

History of Prop. Code §62.003: Acts 1999, 76th Leg., ch. 1571, §1, eff. Aug. 30, 1999. Amended by Acts 2003, 78th Leg., ch. 1276, §14A.803, eff. Sept. 1, 2003.

PROP §62.004. PAYABLE COMMISSION & EARNED COMMISSION

(a) A commission is payable at the time provided in the commission agreement. If payment of the commission is conditioned on the occurrence of an event and that event does not occur, the person obligated to pay the commission is not required to pay the commission.

(b) Except as provided by Subsection (c), a commission is earned on the earlier of the date that:

(1) an event occurs that, under the commission agreement, defines when the commission is earned; or

(2) the person obligated to pay the commission enters into a purchase contract or a lease during the period prescribed by the commission agreement for all or part of the commercial real estate if the purchase contract or lease is contemplated by the commission agreement and if the parties to the purchase contract or lease are contemplated by the commission agreement.

(c) If a broker has earned a commission under a commission agreement relating to a lease transaction and the commission agreement provides that the broker may receive an additional commission when the lease is modified to expand the lease space or renewed, the additional commission is earned when:

(1) the broker performs all the additional services relating to the lease modification or renewal expressly prescribed by the commission agreement; or

(2) the broker first earned a commission under the commission agreement if the commission agreement does not expressly require the broker to perform additional services relating to a lease modification or renewal.

History of Prop. Code §62.004: Acts 1999, 76th Leg., ch. 1571, §1, eff. Aug. 30, 1999.

PROP §62.005. BROKER'S ADDRESS FOR RECEIPT OF NOTICE

A seller, lessor, buyer, or tenant shall send any notice required to be sent to the broker under this chapter to the broker:

(1) at the broker's address as reflected in the records of the Texas Real Estate Commission; and

(2) at the broker's last address that the broker furnished the seller, lessor, buyer, or tenant by certified mail, return receipt requested, if the broker's license is expired.

History of Prop. Code §62.005: Acts 1999, 76th Leg., ch. 1571, §1, eff. Aug. 30, 1999.

Sections 62.006-62.020 reserved for expansion

SUBCHAPTER B. BROKER'S LIEN

PROP §62.021. PERSON ENTITLED TO LIEN

(a) A broker has a lien on a seller's or lessor's commercial real estate interest in the amount specified by the commission agreement if:

(1) the broker has earned a commission under a commission agreement signed by the seller or lessor of the commercial real estate interest or the seller's or lessor's authorized agent; and

(2) a notice of lien is recorded and indexed as provided by Section 62.024.

(b) A broker has a lien on the commercial real estate interest purchased by a prospective buyer in the amount specified by the commission agreement if:

(1) the broker has earned a commission under a commission agreement signed by the prospective buyer of the commercial real estate interest or the prospective buyer's authorized agent; and

(2) a notice of lien is recorded and indexed as provided by Section 62.024.

(c) A broker has a lien on the leasehold interest in the commercial real estate that a prospective tenant leases in the amount specified by the commission agreement if:

(1) the broker has earned a commission under a commission agreement signed by the prospective tenant of the commercial real estate interest or the prospective tenant's authorized agent; and

(2) a notice of lien is recorded and indexed as provided by Section 62.024.

(d) A lien described by this section is available only to the broker named in the commission agreement. The lien is not available to an employee or independent contractor of the broker.

(e) The broker's right to claim a lien based on the commission agreement must be disclosed in the commission agreement.

History of Prop. Code §62.021: Acts 1999, 76th Leg., ch. 1571, §1, eff. Aug. 30, 1999.

PROP §62.022. WAIVER, RELEASE, OR DISCHARGE OF LIEN; ASSUMPTION OF COMMISSION OBLIGATION

(a) Except as provided by Subsection (b), the waiver of a broker's right to a lien under this chapter, or a release given for the purpose of releasing the broker's lien before the commission is satisfied or forgiven, is void.

(b) A broker's entitlement to a lien on the interest of an owner or tenant in commercial real estate shall be automatically waived if:

(1) the commission is earned and payable for services provided relating to a lease transaction; and

(2) the commission agreement is included as a provision of the lease agreement.

(c) A lien under this chapter is discharged by:

(1) a court order discharging the lien;

(2) paying the commission to the broker named in the commission agreement; or

(3) establishing an escrow account described by Subchapter F.

(d) A person who assumes an owner's or tenant's commercial real estate interest is bound by a commission agreement included in a lease agreement unless an escrow account is established under Subchapter F or a bond is provided under Subchapter G.

(e) This section does not affect the rights of a mortgagee who forecloses on commercial real estate and does not assume the lease on which a commission agreement is based.

History of Prop. Code §62.022: Acts 1999, 76th Leg., ch. 1571, §1, eff. Aug. 30, 1999.

PROP §62.023. AFFIDAVIT IDENTIFYING BROKER

If requested by the buyer, the buyer's authorized agent, or the escrow agent for the commercial real estate transaction, the seller of commercial real estate and the broker representing the seller shall provide to the requesting party before the closing of the transaction a written affidavit identifying each broker with whom the affiant knows or believes the seller or the seller's authorized agent has signed a commission agreement under which a commission is claimed or earned and has not been paid.

History of Prop. Code §62.023: Acts 1999, 76th Leg., ch. 1571, §1, eff. Aug. 30, 1999.

PROP §62.024. FILING OF NOTICE OF LIEN

(a) A broker claiming a lien under this chapter may not file a notice of lien unless the commission on which the lien is based is earned.

(b) A broker claiming a lien under this chapter must file a notice of lien as provided by Subchapter C with the county clerk of the county in which the commercial real estate is located.

(c) The county clerk shall record the notice of lien in records kept for that purpose and shall index and cross-index the notice of lien in the names of the broker, each person obligated to pay the commission under the commission agreement, and each person who owns an interest in the commercial real estate if the broker claims a lien on that interest.

History of Prop. Code §62.024: Acts 1999, 76th Leg., ch. 1571, §1, eff. Aug. 30, 1999.

PROP §62.025. CONTENTS OF NOTICE OF LIEN

The notice of lien must be signed by the broker or by a person authorized to sign on behalf of the broker and must contain the following:

(1) a sworn statement of the nature and amount of the claim, including:

(A) the commission amount or the formula used to determine the commission;

(B) the type of commission at issue, including a deferred commission; and

(C) the month and year in which the commission was earned;

(2) the name of the broker and the real estate license number of the broker;

(3) the name as reflected in the broker's records of any person who the broker believes is obligated to pay the commission under the commission agreement;

(4) the name as reflected in the broker's records of any person the broker believes to be an owner of the commercial real estate interest on which the lien is claimed;

(5) a description legally sufficient for identification of the commercial real estate interest sought to be charged with the lien;

(6) the name of any cooperating broker or principal in the transaction with whom the broker intends to share the commission and the dollar or percentage amount to be shared; and

(7) a copy of the commission agreement on which the lien is based.

History of Prop. Code §62.025: Acts 1999, 76th Leg., ch. 1571, §1, eff. Aug. 30, 1999.

PROP §62.026. NOTICE OF FILING

(a) In this section, "business day" means a day other than a Saturday, Sunday, or holiday recognized by this state.

(b) Not later than one business day after the date the broker files a notice of lien, the broker shall mail a copy of the notice of lien by certified mail, return receipt requested, or registered mail to:

(1) the owner of record of the commercial real estate interest on which the lien is claimed or the owner's authorized agent; and

(2) the prospective buyer or tenant and any escrow agent named in a contract for the sale or lease of the commercial real estate interest on which the lien is claimed if:

(A) a binding written contract for the sale or lease of the commercial real estate interest is in effect between the owner and the prospective buyer or tenant in a transaction that is the basis for the commission; and

(B) the binding written contract was executed by the owner and the prospective buyer or tenant before the date the notice of lien is filed.

(c) Service of the notice under Subsection (b) is complete when the notice is deposited in the United States mail, postage prepaid, and addressed to the persons entitled to receive the notice under this section.

(d) If the broker has actual knowledge of the identity of the escrow agent named in the contract for the sale or lease of the commercial real estate interest on which the broker claims a lien or of the escrow agent otherwise closing the sale or lease of the commercial real estate interest, the broker, before the first business day before the date that the sale or lease is closed on commercial real estate for which a notice of lien is filed, shall deliver a file-stamped copy or transmit a facsimile of a file-stamped copy of the notice of lien to each escrow agent at the office in which the closing of the sale or lease will occur for use during the closing of the sale or lease. The broker shall deliver the copy or transmit the facsimile directly to the individual escrow agent responsible for closing the sale or lease if the broker knows that person's name.

(e) If the escrow agent receives the notice of lien, the escrow agent and other parties to the sale or lease may not close the transaction unless the lien is released, the prospective buyer or tenant purchases or leases the property subject to the lien, the funds are held in escrow as provided by Subchapter F, or a bond is filed as provided by Subchapter G.

(f) If the broker fails to comply with this section, the notice of lien is void.

History of Prop. Code §62.026: Acts 1999, 76th Leg., ch. 1571, §1, eff. Aug. 30, 1999.

PROP §62.027. INCEPTION OF BROKER'S LIEN

(a) A broker's lien attaches to the commercial real estate interest owned by the person obligated to pay the commission on the date the notice of lien is recorded as provided by this chapter. The lien does not relate back to the date of the commission agreement.

(b) A notice of lien for amounts earned by the broker under an installment contract or under a commis-

sion agreement for a deferred commission is enforceable only to the extent that the installment or commission has become payable.

History of Prop. Code §62.027: Acts 1999, 76th Leg., ch. 1571, §1, eff. Aug. 30, 1999.

PROP §62.028. PRIORITY

(a) A recorded lien, mortgage, or other encumbrance on commercial real estate, including a recorded lien securing revolving credit and future advances for a loan, recorded before the date a broker's lien is recorded has priority over the broker's lien.

(b) A broker's lien on the commercial real estate interest of a person obligated to pay a commission is not valid or enforceable against a grantee, buyer, lessee, or transferee of the interest of the person obligated to pay the commission if the deed, lease, or instrument transferring the interest is recorded before the notice of the broker's lien is recorded.

(c) A purchase-money mortgage lien executed by the buyer of the commercial real estate interest has priority over a broker's lien claimed for the commission owed by the buyer against the commercial real estate interest purchased by the buyer.

(d) A mechanic's lien that is recorded after a broker's lien and that relates back to a date before the date the broker's lien is recorded has priority over the broker's lien.

History of Prop. Code §62.028: Acts 1999, 76th Leg., ch. 1571, §1, eff. Aug. 30, 1999.

PROP §62.029. SUBORDINATION

(a) If the person obligated to pay the commission sells that person's commercial real estate interest, the broker's lien is subordinate to a recorded purchase-money first lien authorized by the buyer if the buyer:

(1) executes and files with the county clerk of the county in which the broker's lien is filed a memorandum that evidences the buyer's acknowledgment of the existence of the broker's lien; and

(2) sends the broker, by certified mail, return receipt requested, or registered mail, a copy of the recorded memorandum required by this subsection.

(b) If the person obligated to pay the commission refinances a recorded first lien secured by that person's commercial real estate interest, the broker's lien is subordinate to the recorded refinanced first lien, regardless of the amount of the first lien after refinancing, if the person obligated to pay the commission:

(1) executes and files with the county clerk of the county in which the broker's lien is filed a memorandum that evidences the person's acknowledgment of the existence of the broker's lien; and

(2) sends the broker, by certified mail, return receipt requested, or registered mail, a copy of the recorded memorandum required by this subsection.

(c) If the person obligated to pay the commission obtains an extension of credit secured by that person's commercial real estate interest, the broker's lien is subordinate to the lien securing the extension of credit if, according to the loan documents, the extension of credit is made only for the purpose of:

(1) repairing or renovating the commercial real estate; or

(2) completing construction or providing additional improvements on the commercial real estate.

(d) If the person obligated to pay the commission furnishes a subordination agreement as provided by this section to be executed by the broker, the broker must:

(1) execute and acknowledge the subordination agreement before a notary public; and

(2) return the subordination agreement to the person not later than the seventh day after the date the broker receives the subordination agreement and other documents the broker reasonably requests in order to determine that the subordination agreement complies with this section.

History of Prop. Code §62.029: Acts 1999, 76th Leg., ch. 1571, §1, eff. Aug. 30, 1999.

See also *Real Estate Forms*, FORMS 11:1, 11:2.

PROP §62.030. MIXED-USE REAL ESTATE

If real estate is zoned or restricted for more than one use, the broker's lien attaches only to the portions of the real estate that constitute commercial real estate.

History of Prop. Code §62.030: Acts 1999, 76th Leg., ch. 1571, §1, eff. Aug. 30, 1999.

PROP §62.031. CHANGE IN USE OF REAL ESTATE

(a) Except as provided by Subsection (b), any change in the use of the real estate does not affect a broker's lien if the notice of the lien was filed when the real estate was commercial real estate.

(b) The broker's lien is extinguished if:

(1) not later than the 360th day after the date on which the broker's commission is payable, the commercial real estate interest on which a broker claims a lien is zoned for single-family use or restricted for single-family use under recorded restrictive covenants; and

(2) the zoning ordinances or restrictive covenants for single-family use are in effect until at least the second anniversary of the date the commission is payable.

History of Prop. Code §62.031: Acts 1999, 76th Leg., ch. 1571, §1, eff. Aug. 30, 1999.

Sections 62.032-62.040 reserved for expansion

SUBCHAPTER C. TIME FOR FILING NOTICE OF LIEN

PROP §62.041. TIME TO FILE

(a) If a broker has earned a commission under a commission agreement signed by a seller or the seller's authorized agent, a broker must record a notice of lien:

(1) after the commission is earned; and

(2) before the conveyance of the commercial real estate interest on which the broker is claiming a lien.

(b) If a broker has earned a commission under a commission agreement signed by a prospective buyer or a prospective buyer's authorized agent, the broker must record a notice of lien:

(1) after the buyer acquires legal title to the commercial real estate interest on which the broker is claiming a lien; and

(2) before the buyer conveys the buyer's commercial real estate interest on which the broker is claiming a lien.

(c) If the lien is based on a lease transaction, the broker must record a notice of lien after the commission is earned and before the earlier of:

(1) the 91st day after the date the event for which the commission becomes payable occurs; or

(2) the date the person obligated to pay the commission records a subsequent conveyance of that person's commercial real estate interest after executing the lease agreement relating to the lease transaction for which the lien is claimed.

(d) If a notice of lien is not filed within the time required by this section, the lien is void.

History of Prop. Code §62.041: Acts 1999, 76th Leg., ch. 1571, §1, eff. Aug. 30, 1999.

Sections 62.042-62.060 reserved for expansion

SUBCHAPTER D. ENFORCEMENT OF LIEN

PROP §62.061. SUIT TO FORECLOSE LIEN

(a) A broker may not bring a suit to foreclose a lien under this chapter unless the commission is earned and payable. A broker may bring a suit to foreclose a lien in any district court for the county in which the commercial real estate is located by filing a sworn complaint stating that the notice of lien has been recorded.

(b) A complaint in a suit filed under this section must contain:

(1) a brief description of the commission agreement that is the basis for the lien, including:

(A) a description of the disclosure of the broker's right to the lien contained in the commission agreement;

(B) the date on which the commission agreement was executed;

(C) the event for which a commission is considered to be earned; and

(D) the event for which a commission is considered to be payable;

(2) a description of the services performed by the broker;

(3) the amount of the payable commission that is unpaid;

(4) a description of the commercial real estate to which the lien attaches; and

(5) other facts necessary for a full understanding of the rights of the parties.

(c) The broker must include as a defendant in a suit brought under this subchapter each person the broker believes to have an interest in the commercial real estate that is subordinate to or encumbered by the broker's lien.

(d) If the broker and a person against whom the broker claims a commission use alternative dispute resolution procedures to resolve a dispute concerning entitlement to the broker's commission, the broker's lien remains valid, and any suit to foreclose the lien is stayed until the alternative dispute resolution process is completed.

History of Prop. Code §62.061: Acts 1999, 76th Leg., ch. 1571, §1, eff. Aug. 30, 1999.

PROP §62.062. STATUTE OF LIMITATIONS

(a) Except as provided by this section, a broker claiming a lien under this chapter must bring a suit to foreclose the lien on or before the second anniversary of the date the notice of lien is recorded.

(b) A broker claiming a lien to collect a deferred commission must bring a suit to foreclose the lien on or before the earlier of:

(1) the second anniversary of the date on which the commission is payable; or

(2) the 10th anniversary of the date the lien is recorded or the 10th anniversary of the date the broker records a subsequent notice of the lien as a renewal of the broker's right to the lien, whichever date is later.

(c) A renewal of a notice of lien must state that it is a renewal of the broker's lien and must be recorded after the ninth anniversary after the date the original notice of lien or last renewal notice is recorded and on or before the 10th anniversary of the date the original notice of lien or last renewal notice is recorded.

(d) A broker claiming a lien for a commission that is payable must bring a suit to foreclose the lien not later than the 30th day after the date the broker receives a written demand to bring a suit to foreclose the lien from the owner of the commercial real estate interest on which the lien is claimed.

(e) If a suit to foreclose the lien is not brought within the period prescribed by this section, the lien is void.

History of Prop. Code §62.062: Acts 1999, 76th Leg., ch. 1571, §1, eff. Aug. 30, 1999.

PROP §62.063. ASSESSMENT OF COSTS, FEES, & INTEREST

The prevailing party in a suit brought under this subchapter is entitled to court costs, reasonable attorney's fees, and prejudgment interest from the date the commission becomes payable or the date the damage accrues.

History of Prop. Code §62.063: Acts 1999, 76th Leg., ch. 1571, §1, eff. Aug. 30, 1999.

Sections 62.064-62.080 reserved for expansion

SUBCHAPTER E. RELEASE OF LIEN

PROP §62.081. RELEASE OF LIEN

(a) Not later than the fifth day after the date a broker receives a written request from the owner of a commercial real estate interest on which a lien is claimed, the broker shall furnish to the owner a release of indebtedness and any lien claimed if:

(1) the debt that is the basis for the lien is satisfied; or

(2) the lien is discharged under Section 62.022, rendered void under Section 62.026 or 62.062, or extinguished under Section 62.031.

(b) When a condition occurs that would preclude the broker from receiving a commission under the terms of the commission agreement that is the basis for the lien, the broker shall, not later than the 10th day after the date the broker receives a written request from the owner of the commercial real estate interest on which the lien is claimed, furnish to the owner a release of indebtedness and any lien claimed.

(c) Not later than the 10th day after the date a broker receives a written request for the release of the broker's lien from the escrow agent responsible for closing the purchase and sale of a commercial real estate interest on which the lien is claimed, the broker shall furnish to the escrow agent a release of indebtedness and any lien claimed if:

(1) the commercial real estate interest to which the lien attaches is subject to a contract for purchase and sale;

(2) the release of indebtedness and any lien claimed is conditioned on the closing of the transaction; and

(3) the broker would otherwise be obligated to release the indebtedness and any lien claimed under Subsection (a) or (b) on the closing of the transaction.

(d) A release of lien must be in a form that permits the instrument to be filed of record.

History of Prop. Code §62.081: Acts 1999, 76th Leg., ch. 1571, §1, eff. Aug. 30, 1999.

Sections 62.082-62.100 reserved for expansion

SUBCHAPTER F. ESCROW OF DISPUTED AMOUNTS

PROP §62.101. ESCROW ACCOUNT

If a claim for a lien under a recorded notice of lien is not paid or assumed at the closing of a sale, lease, or mortgage of the commercial real estate interest subject to the lien and would prevent the closing of the transaction or conveyance or if a claim for a lien under a re-

corded notice of lien does not survive the closing, any person named in the notice of lien as obligated to pay the commission shall, on the date of the closing:

(1) establish an escrow account from any net proceeds of the transaction or conveyance in an amount equal to the amount sufficient to satisfy the lien plus 15 percent of that amount; or

(2) file a bond to indemnify against the lien as provided by Subchapter G.

History of Prop. Code §62.101: Acts 1999, 76th Leg., ch. 1571, §1, eff. Aug. 30, 1999.

PROP §62.102. NAMED ESCROW AGENT

If an escrow agent is named in the contract on which the transaction or conveyance is based, the escrow account shall be established with the named escrow agent.

History of Prop. Code §62.102: Acts 1999, 76th Leg., ch. 1571, §1, eff. Aug. 30, 1999.

PROP §62.103. COSTS OF INTERPLEADER

Related costs for any interpleader action may be deducted from the escrow account by the person maintaining the escrow account.

History of Prop. Code §62.103: Acts 1999, 76th Leg., ch. 1571, §1, eff. Aug. 30, 1999.

PROP §62.104. REFUSAL TO ESTABLISH ESCROW ACCOUNT OR BOND

(a) A party may not refuse to close a transaction because of the requirement to establish an escrow account or bond as provided by Section 62.101 if:

(1) the broker provides a copy of the notice of lien that complies with Sections 62.025 and 62.026;

(2) sufficient proceeds will result from the proposed transaction for the payment of the commission and costs of the interpleader; and

(3) the broker executes and delivers a full release of the broker's lien in a recordable form.

(b) A prospective buyer of a commercial real estate interest may not refuse to close the purchase solely because a broker's lien is filed after the date a title commitment or abstract of title relating to the interest is issued if an escrow account is established as provided by this subchapter or a bond is filed as provided by Subchapter G.

History of Prop. Code §62.104: Acts 1999, 76th Leg., ch. 1571, §1, eff. Aug. 30, 1999.

PROP §62.105. TERM OF ESCROW ACCOUNT

The amount held in escrow shall be held in escrow until:

(1) the rights of the parties claiming the amount in escrow are determined by a written agreement of the parties, a court order, or an alternative dispute resolution process agreed to by the parties;

(2) the broker's lien is no longer enforceable; or

(3) the funds are interpled into a district court for the county in which the commercial real estate is located.

History of Prop. Code §62.105: Acts 1999, 76th Leg., ch. 1571, §1, eff. Aug. 30, 1999.

PROP §62.106. EXTINGUISHMENT OF LIEN UPON ESCROW

When the escrow account is established under this subchapter, the broker's lien against the commercial real estate is extinguished and becomes a lien on the proceeds in the escrow account.

History of Prop. Code §62.106: Acts 1999, 76th Leg., ch. 1571, §1, eff. Aug. 30, 1999.

Sections 62.107-62.120 reserved for expansion

SUBCHAPTER G. BOND TO INDEMNIFY AGAINST LIEN

PROP §62.121. BOND

(a) If a lien is fixed or is attempted to be fixed by a recorded instrument under this chapter, any person may file a bond to indemnify against the lien.

(b) The bond shall be filed with the county clerk of the county in which the commercial real estate subject to the lien is located.

History of Prop. Code §62.121: Acts 1999, 76th Leg., ch. 1571, §1, eff. Aug. 30, 1999.

PROP §62.122. BOND REQUIREMENTS

The bond must:

(1) describe the commercial real estate on which the lien is claimed;

(2) refer to the lien claimed in a manner sufficient to identify it;

(3) be in an amount that is double the amount of the lien referred to in the bond as of the date of execution of the bond by the surety, unless the total amount claimed in the lien exceeds $40,000, in which case the bond must be in an amount that is 1-½ times the amount of the lien;

(4) be payable to the party claiming the lien;

(5) be executed by:

(A) the party filing the bond as principal; and

(B) a corporate surety licensed by this state to execute the bond as surety;

(6) be conditioned substantially that the principal and sureties will pay the named obligees or their assignees the amount that the named obligees would have been entitled to recover if their claim had been proved to be valid and enforceable liens on the commercial real estate; and

(7) identify the last known mailing address of the person claiming the lien.

History of Prop. Code §62.122: Acts 1999, 76th Leg., ch. 1571, §1, eff. Aug. 30, 1999.

PROP §62.123. NOTICE OF BOND

(a) After the bond is filed, the county clerk shall issue notice of the bond to all named obligees.

(b) A copy of the bond must be attached to the notice.

(c) The notice must be served on each obligee by mailing a copy of the notice and the bond to the obligee by certified mail, return receipt requested, addressed to the claimant at the address stated in the bond for the obligee.

History of Prop. Code §62.123: Acts 1999, 76th Leg., ch. 1571, §1, eff. Aug. 30, 1999.

PROP §62.124. RECORDING OF BOND & NOTICE

(a) The county clerk shall record the bond, the notice, and a certificate of mailing in the real property records.

(b) In acquiring an interest in or insuring title to the commercial real estate, a buyer, insurer of title, or lender may rely on and is absolutely protected by the record of the bond and the notice to the same extent as if the lien claimant had filed a release of lien in the real property records.

History of Prop. Code §62.124: Acts 1999, 76th Leg., ch. 1571, §1, eff. Aug. 30, 1999.

PROP §62.125. ACTION ON BOND

(a) A party making or holding a lien claim may not sue on the bond later than the last date on which a person may bring a suit to foreclose the lien under Section 62.062.

(b) The bond is not exhausted by one action against it. Each named obligee or assignee of an obligee may maintain a separate suit on the bond in any district court for the county in which the commercial real estate is located.

History of Prop. Code §62.125: Acts 1999, 76th Leg., ch. 1571, §1, eff. Aug. 30, 1999.

Sections 62.126-62.140 reserved for expansion

SUBCHAPTER H. REMEDIES

PROP §62.141. OWNER'S OR TENANT'S REMEDIES

(a) An owner or tenant may file suit against a broker under this chapter.

(b) In an action filed under this section, the court shall discharge a broker's lien if the broker:

(1) failed to mail a copy of the notice of lien within the period prescribed by Section 62.026;

(2) failed to execute, acknowledge, and return a subordination agreement within the period prescribed by Section 62.029(d);

(3) failed to record the notice of lien within the period prescribed by Section 62.041; or

(4) failed to release a lien within the period prescribed by Section 62.081.

(c) A broker is liable to an owner or tenant for damages as provided by Subsection (d) if:

(1) the broker recorded a lien on the commercial real estate interest of the owner or tenant;

(2) the broker failed to:

(A) execute, acknowledge, and return a subordination agreement within the period prescribed by Section 62.029(d); or

(B) release a lien within the period prescribed by Section 62.081;

(3) the owner, tenant, or escrow agent mailed to the broker by certified mail, return receipt requested, a copy of this section and a notice requesting the broker to execute, acknowledge, and return the subordination agreement or release the lien not later than the 10th day after the date the broker receives the notice; and

(4) the broker failed to comply with the owner's, tenant's, or escrow agent's written notice within the prescribed period.

(d) If the court finds that a broker is liable to an owner or tenant under Subsection (c), the court may award the owner or tenant:

(1) actual damages, including attorney's fees and court costs, incurred by the owner or tenant that are

proximately caused by the broker's failure to execute, acknowledge, and return the subordination agreement or release the lien; and

(2) a civil penalty in an amount not to exceed three times the amount of the claimed commission if the court finds that the broker acted with gross negligence or acted in bad faith in violation of Chapter 1101, Occupations Code.

(e) This section does not prevent:

(1) a person from filing a complaint with the Texas Real Estate Commission against a broker who fails to comply with this chapter; or

(2) the Texas Real Estate Commission at any time from investigating or initiating a disciplinary proceeding against a broker who fails to comply with this chapter.

History of Prop. Code §62.141: Acts 1999, 76th Leg., ch. 1571, §1, eff. Aug. 30, 1999. Amended by Acts 2003, 78th Leg., ch. 1276, §14A.804, eff. Sept. 1, 2003.

PROP §62.142. BROKER'S REMEDIES

(a) A broker may file suit against an owner or tenant to enforce a commission agreement.

(b) If the court finds that the broker waived the right to file a lien under Section 62.022 and that the owner or tenant violated the commission agreement, the court may award to the broker:

(1) actual damages, including attorney's fees and court costs, that are proximately caused by the owner's or tenant's failure to comply with the commission agreement; and

(2) a civil penalty in an amount not to exceed three times the amount of the claimed commission if the court finds that the owner or tenant acted with gross negligence or in bad faith.

History of Prop. Code §62.142: Acts 1999, 76th Leg., ch. 1571, §1, eff. Aug. 30, 1999.

CHAPTER 63. MANUFACTURED HOME LIEN

PROP §63.001. MANUFACTURED HOMES

In this chapter, "manufactured home" has the meaning assigned by Chapter 1201, Occupations Code.

History of Prop. Code §63.001: Acts 1999, 76th Leg., ch. 742, §1, eff. Sept. 1, 1999. Renumbered from §62.001 by Acts 2001, 77th Leg., ch. 1420, §21.001(96), eff. Sept. 1, 2001. Amended by Acts 2003, 78th Leg., ch. 1276, §14A.805, eff. Sept. 1, 2003.

PROP §63.002. APPLICABILITY

This chapter applies only to a lien on a manufactured home if the loan or credit advance documents state or indicate that the lien:

(1) is or is in the nature of a vendor's lien;

(2) is or is in the nature of a purchase money lien; or

(3) is or is in the nature of a retail installment lien.

History of Prop. Code §63.002: Acts 1999, 76th Leg., ch. 742, §1, eff. Sept. 1, 1999. Renumbered from §62.002 by Acts 2001, 77th Leg., ch. 1420, §21.001(96), eff. Sept. 1, 2001.

PROP §63.003. CONVERSION OF LIEN FROM PERSONAL PROPERTY LIEN TO REAL PROPERTY LIEN

When the manufactured home converts to real property as provided by Section 2.001(b), the lien on the property:

(1) is converted to a purchase money lien on real property by operation of law; and

(2) exists independently of any existing lien on the real property to which the home is permanently attached.

History of Prop. Code §63.003: Acts 1999, 76th Leg., ch. 742, §1, eff. Sept. 1, 1999. Renumbered from §62.003 by Acts 2001, 77th Leg., ch. 1420, §21.001(96), eff. Sept. 1, 2001.

PROP §63.004. REFINANCING OF LIEN

(a) A person who provides funds to refinance a lien secured by a manufactured home is subrogated to the lien position of the previous lienholder.

(b) If the holder of a lien secured by a manufactured home transfers loan or credit advance documents to a lender refinancing the lien, that lender and a title insurance company, title insurance agent or direct operation, or attorney to whom the loan or credit advance documents are delivered holds the loan or credit advance documents in trust for that lienholder. In this subsection, "direct operation" has the meaning assigned by Section 2501.003, Insurance Code.

(c) A lien that is converted to a purchase money lien on real property under Section 63.003, or a lien for the debt for new improvements thereon under Section 63.005, may be refinanced with another lien on the real property to which the manufactured home is permanently attached as provided by Section 2.001.

History of Prop. Code §63.004: Acts 1999, 76th Leg., ch. 742, §1, eff. Sept. 1, 1999. Renumbered from §62.004 and amended by Acts 2001, 77th Leg., ch. 1420, §§21.001(96), 21.002(16), eff. Sept. 1, 2001. Amended by Acts 2001, 77th Leg., ch. 1055, §6, eff. Jan. 1, 2002; Acts 2003, 78th Leg., ch. 1275, §3(38), eff. Sept. 1, 2003; Acts 2005, 79th Leg., ch. 728, §11.159, eff. Sept. 1, 2005.

A PROP §63.005. CONVERSION OF LIEN FROM A PERSONAL PROPERTY LIEN TO A REAL PROPERTY LIEN FOR THE DEBT FOR THE NEW IMPROVEMENTS THEREON

(a) A manufactured home becomes a new improvement to the homestead of a family or of a single adult person upon the filing of the appropriate statement of ownership [~~certificate of attachment~~] as provided in Chapter 1201, Occupations Code. As such, if the debt for the manufactured home was contracted for in writing, that debt is considered to be for work and materials used in constructing new improvements thereon and thus constitutes a valid lien on the homestead when the appropriate statement of ownership [~~certificate of attachment~~] is filed in the Official Public Records of Real Property in the county in which the land is located.

(b) When the manufactured home converts to real property as provided by Section 2.001 of this code, the lien on the property exists independently of any existing lien on the real property to which the home is permanently attached.

History of Prop. Code §63.005: Acts 2001, 77th Leg., ch. 1055, §7, eff. Jan. 1, 2002. Renumbered from §62.005 by Acts 2003, 78th Leg., ch. 1275, §2(118), eff. Sept. 1, 2003. Amended by Acts 2003, 78th Leg., ch. 1276, §14A.806, eff. Sept. 1, 2003; H.B. 2019, §78, 85th Leg., eff. Sept. 1, 2017.

CHAPTER 64. ASSIGNMENT OF RENTS TO LIENHOLDER

SUBCHAPTER A. GENERAL PROVISIONS

PROP §64.001. DEFINITIONS

In this chapter:

(1) "Assignee" means a person entitled to enforce a security instrument.

(2) "Assignment of rents" means a transfer of an interest in rents in connection with an obligation secured by real property from which the rents arise. The term does not include a contract for a charge authorized by Section 306.101, Finance Code, or a true sale of rents.

(3) "Assignor" means a person who makes a security instrument that creates an assignment of rents arising from real property or that person's successor in interest with respect to the real property.

(4) "Cash proceeds" means proceeds that are money, checks, deposit accounts, or the like.

(5) "Day" means a calendar day.

(6) "Deposit account" means a demand, time, savings, passbook, escrow, or similar account maintained with a bank, savings bank, savings and loan association, credit union, trust company, or other person.

(7) "Document" means information that is inscribed on a tangible medium or that is stored on an electronic or other medium and is retrievable in perceivable form.

(8) "Proceeds" means personal property that is received, collected, or distributed on account of an obligation to pay rents.

(9) "Rents" means consideration payable for the right to possess or occupy, or for possessing or occupying, real property, consideration payable to an assignor under a policy of rental interruption insurance covering real property, claims arising out of a default in the payment of consideration payable for the right to possess or occupy real property, consideration payable to terminate an agreement to possess or occupy real property, consideration payable to an assignor for payment or reimbursement of expenses incurred in owning, operating, and maintaining, or constructing or installing improvements on, real property, or any other consideration payable under an agreement relating to the real property that constitutes rents under a law of this state other than this chapter. The term does not include con-

sideration payable under an oil and gas lease, mineral lease, or other conveyance of a mineral estate.

(10) "Secured obligation" means an obligation secured by an assignment of rents.

(11) "Security instrument" means:

(A) a security instrument, as that term is defined by Section 51.0001; or

(B) an agreement containing an assignment of rents.

(12) "Security interest" means an interest in property that arises by agreement and secures an obligation.

(13) "Sign" includes to sign by an electronic signature, as defined by Section 15.002.

(14) "Tenant" means a person who has an obligation to pay for the right to possess or occupy, or for possessing or occupying, real property.

History of Prop. Code §64.001: Acts 2011, 82nd Leg., ch. 636, §2, eff. June 17, 2011. Amended by Acts 2013, 83rd Leg., ch. 453, §1, eff. June 14, 2013.

PROP §64.002. MANNER OF GIVING NOTICE

(a) A person may give notice under this chapter:

(1) by transmitting the notice in the manner described by Section 51.002(e);

(2) by depositing the notice with the United States Postal Service or a commercially reasonable delivery service, properly addressed to the intended recipient's address in accordance with this section, with first class postage or other cost of delivery paid; or

(3) by transmitting the notice to the intended recipient by any means agreed to by the intended recipient.

(b) The following rules determine the address for notices under Subsection (a):

(1) the address for notices to an assignee is the address of the assignee agreed in the security instrument or other document between the parties as the address for notices to the assignee, unless a more recent address for notices has been given by the assignee to the person giving the notice in accordance with Subsection (a) or as agreed in a security instrument or other document signed by the assignee;

(2) the address for notices to an assignor is the address of the assignor agreed in the security instrument or other document between the parties as the address for notices to the assignor or as provided in Section 51.002, unless a more recent address for notices has been given by the assignor to the person giving the notice in accordance with Subsection (a) or as agreed in a security instrument or other document signed by the assignor; and

(3) for notices to a tenant:

(A) if there is an address for notices to the tenant in a signed document between the tenant and the person giving the notice, the person giving the notice shall use that address unless a more recent address for notices has been given by the tenant in accordance with that document;

(B) if an address for notices described by Paragraph (A) does not exist, but the tenant's agreement with the assignor has an address for notices to the tenant and the person giving the notice has received a copy of that document or has actual knowledge of the address for notices specified in that document, the person giving the notice shall use that address; or

(C) if an address for notices described by Paragraphs (A) and (B) does not exist, the person giving the notice shall use the tenant's address at the real property covered by the security instrument.

(c) Notice given in accordance with this chapter is deemed received on the earliest of:

(1) the date the notice is received by the person to whom the notice is given;

(2) the fifth day after the date the notice is given in accordance with Subsection (a)(2); or

(3) the date on which notice is deemed received in accordance with an agreement made by the person to whom the notice is given.

(d) A notice under this chapter must be a document.

History of Prop. Code §64.002: Acts 2011, 82nd Leg., ch. 636, §2, eff. June 17, 2011. Amended by Acts 2013, 83rd Leg., ch. 453, §2, eff. June 14, 2013.

Sections 64.003-64.050 reserved for expansion

SUBCHAPTER B. ASSIGNMENT OF RENTS

PROP §64.051. SECURITY INSTRUMENT CREATES ASSIGNMENT OF RENTS; ASSIGNMENT OF RENTS CREATES SECURITY INTEREST

(a) An enforceable security instrument creates an assignment of rents arising from real property described in that security instrument, unless the security instrument provides otherwise or the security instrument is governed by Section 50(a)(6), (7), or (8), Article XVI, Texas Constitution.

(b) An assignment of rents creates a presently effective security interest in all accrued and unaccrued rents arising from the real property described in the security instrument creating the assignment, regardless of whether the security instrument is in the form of an absolute assignment, an absolute assignment conditioned on default or other event, an assignment as additional security, or any other form. The security interest in rents is separate and distinct from any security interest held by the assignee in the real property from which the rents arise.

(c) An assignment of rents does not reduce the secured obligation except to the extent the assignee collects rents and applies, or is obligated to apply, the collected rents to payment of the secured obligation.

History of Prop. Code §64.051: Acts 2011, 82nd Leg., ch. 636, §2, eff. June 17, 2011. Amended by Acts 2013, 83rd Leg., ch. 453, §3, eff. June 14, 2013.

PROP §64.052. RECORDATION & PERFECTION OF SECURITY INTEREST IN RENTS; PRIORITY OF INTERESTS IN RENTS

(a) A security instrument creating an assignment of rents may be recorded in the county in which any part of the real property is located in accordance with this code.

(b) On recordation of a security instrument creating an assignment of rents, the security interest in the rents is perfected. This subsection prevails over a conflicting provision in the security instrument creating the assignment of rents or a law of this state other than this chapter that prohibits or defers enforcement of the security interest until the occurrence of a subsequent event, including a subsequent default of the assignor, the assignee's obtaining possession of the real property, or the appointment of a receiver.

(c) Except as provided by Subsection (d), a perfected security interest in rents has priority over the rights of a person who, after the security interest is perfected, acquires:

(1) a lien on or other security interest in the rents or the real property from which the rents arise; or

(2) an interest in the rents or the real property from which the rents arise.

(d) An assignee with a perfected security interest in rents has the same priority over the rights of a person described by Subsection (c) with respect to future advances as the assignee has with respect to the assignee's security interest in the real property from which the rents arise.

History of Prop. Code §64.052: Acts 2011, 82nd Leg., ch. 636, §2, eff. June 17, 2011. Amended by Acts 2013, 83rd Leg., ch. 453, §4, eff. June 14, 2013.

PROP §64.053. ENFORCEMENT OF SECURITY INTEREST IN RENTS GENERALLY

(a) An assignee may enforce an assignment of rents using one or more of the methods provided by Section 64.054 or 64.055 or any other method sufficient to enforce an assignment of rents under a law of this state other than this chapter.

(b) On and after the date on which an assignee begins to enforce an assignment of rents, the assignee is entitled to collect all rents that:

(1) have accrued but remain unpaid on that date; and

(2) accrue on or after that date.

History of Prop. Code §64.053: Acts 2011, 82nd Leg., ch. 636, §2, eff. June 17, 2011. Amended by Acts 2013, 83rd Leg., ch. 453, §5, eff. June 14, 2013.

PROP §64.054. ENFORCEMENT BY NOTICE TO ASSIGNOR

(a) After default, or as otherwise agreed by the assignor, the assignee may give the assignor a notice demanding that the assignor pay the assignee the proceeds of any rents that the assignee is entitled to collect under Section 64.053.

(b) For the purposes of Section 64.053, the assignee begins enforcement under this section on the date on which the assignee gives notice to the assignor in accordance with Section 64.002.

(c) An assignee may not enforce an assignment of rents under this section if, on the date the security instrument was signed and the date of prospective enforcement, the real property constitutes the assignor's homestead on which is located a one-family to four-family dwelling.

History of Prop. Code §64.054: Acts 2011, 82nd Leg., ch. 636, §2, eff. June 17, 2011. Amended by Acts 2013, 83rd Leg., ch. 453, §6, eff. June 14, 2013.

PROP §64.055. ENFORCEMENT BY NOTICE TO TENANT

(a) After default, or as otherwise agreed by the assignor, the assignee may give to a tenant of real property that is subject to an assignment of rents a notice demanding that the tenant pay to the assignee all unpaid accrued rents and all unaccrued rents as they accrue. The assignee shall give a copy of the notice to the assignor in accordance with Section 64.002. The notice must substantially comply with the form prescribed by Section 64.056 and be signed by the assignee or the assignee's authorized agent or representative.

(b) For the purposes of Section 64.053(b), the assignee begins enforcement under this section on the date on which the tenant receives a notice complying with Subsection (a).

(c) Subject to Subsection (d) and any other claim or defense that a tenant has under a law of this state other than this chapter, after a tenant receives a notice under Subsection (a):

(1) the tenant is obligated to pay to the assignee all unpaid accrued rents and all unaccrued rents as they accrue, unless the tenant has previously received a notice under this section from another assignee of rents given by that assignee in accordance with this section and the other assignee has not canceled that notice;

(2) except as otherwise agreed in a document signed by the tenant, the tenant is not obligated to pay to an assignee rent that was prepaid to the assignor before the tenant received the notice under Subsection (a);

(3) unless the tenant occupies the premises as the tenant's primary residence, the tenant is not discharged from the obligation to pay rents to the assignee if the tenant pays rents to the assignor;

(4) the tenant's payment to the assignee of rents then due satisfies the tenant's obligation under the tenant's agreement with the assignor to the extent of the payment made; and

(5) the tenant's obligation to pay rents to the assignee continues until the earliest date on which the tenant receives:

(A) a court order directing the tenant to pay the rents in a different manner;

(B) a signed notice that a perfected security instrument that has priority over the assignee's security interest has been foreclosed; or

(C) a signed document from the assignee canceling the assignee's notice.

(d) Except as otherwise agreed in a document signed by the tenant, a tenant who has received a notice under Subsection (a) is not in default for nonpayment of rents that accrue during the 30 days after the date the tenant receives the notice until the earlier of:

(1) the 10th day after the date the next regularly scheduled rental payment would be due; or

(2) the 30th day after the date the tenant receives the notice.

(e) On receiving a notice from another assignee who has priority under Section 64.052(c) that the assignee with priority has conducted a foreclosure sale of the real property from which the rents arise or is enforcing the interest in rents of the assignee with priority by notice to the tenant, an assignee that has given a notice to a tenant under Subsection (a) shall immediately give another notice to the tenant canceling the earlier notice.

History of Prop. Code §64.055: Acts 2011, 82nd Leg., ch. 636, §2, eff. June 17, 2011. Amended by Acts 2013, 83rd Leg., ch. 453, §7, eff. June 14, 2013.

PROP §64.056. FORM OF NOTICE TO TENANT

The following form of notice, when properly completed, satisfies the requirements of Section 64.055(a):

NOTICE TO PAY RENTS TO PERSON OTHER THAN LANDLORD

Tenant: [Name of tenant]

Property Occupied by Tenant (the "Premises"): [Address]

Landlord: [Name of landlord]

Assignee: [Name of assignee]

Address of Assignee and Telephone Number of Contact Person: [Address of assignee] [Telephone number of person to contact]

1. Assignee is entitled to collect rents on the Premises under [Name of Document] (the "Assignment of Rents") dated [Date of Assignment of Rents], and recorded at [Recording Data] of [Name of County] County, Texas. You may obtain additional information about the Assignment of Rents and the Assignee's right to enforce it at the address of the Assignee.

2. A default exists under the Assignment of Rents or related documents between the Landlord and the Assignee. The Assignee is entitled to collect rents from the Premises.

3. This notice affects your rights and obligations under the agreement under which you occupy the Premises (your "Lease Agreement"). Unless you have otherwise agreed in a document signed by you, if your next scheduled rental payment is due within 30 days after you receive this notice, you will not be in default under your Lease Agreement for nonpayment of that rental payment until the 10th day after the due date of that payment or the 30th day following the date you receive this notice, whichever occurs first.

4. You may consult a lawyer at your expense concerning your rights and obligations under your Lease Agreement and the effect of this notice.

5. You must pay to the Assignee at the Address of the Assignee all rents under your Lease Agreement that are due and payable on the date you receive this notice and all rents accruing under your Lease Agreement after you receive this notice.

6. If you pay rents to the Assignee after receiving this notice, the payment will satisfy your rental obligation to the extent of that payment.

7. If you pay any rents to the Landlord after receiving this notice, your payment to the Landlord will not discharge your rental obligation, and the Assignee may hold you liable for that rental obligation notwithstanding your payment to the Landlord unless you occupy the Premises as your primary residence.

8. If you have previously received a notice from another person who also holds an assignment of the rents due under your Lease Agreement, you should continue paying your rents to the person that sent that notice until that person cancels that notice. Once that notice is canceled, you must begin paying rents to the Assignee in accordance with this notice.

Name of assignee: ______

By: [Officer/authorized agent of assignee]

History of Prop. Code §64.056: Acts 2011, 82nd Leg., ch. 636, §2, eff. June 17, 2011.

PROP §64.057. EFFECT OF ENFORCEMENT

The enforcement of an assignment of rents by a method provided by Section 64.054 or 64.055, the application of proceeds by the assignee under Section 64.059 after enforcement, the payment of expenses under Section 64.058, or an action under Section 64.060 does not:

(1) make the assignee a mortgagee in possession of the real property from which the rents arise;

(2) make the assignee an agent of the assignor;

(3) constitute an election of remedies that precludes a later action to enforce the secured obligation;

(4) make the secured obligation unenforceable;

(5) limit any right available to the assignee with respect to the secured obligation; or

(6) bar a deficiency judgment under any law of this state governing or relating to deficiency judgments following the enforcement of any encumbrance, lien, or security interest.

History of Prop. Code §64.057: Acts 2011, 82nd Leg., ch. 636, §2, eff. June 17, 2011.

PROP §64.058. APPLICATION OF PROCEEDS GENERALLY

Unless otherwise agreed, an assignee who collects rents under this chapter or collects on a judgment in an action under Section 64.060 shall apply the sums collected in the following order to:

(1) reimbursement of the assignee's expenses of enforcing the assignee's assignment of rents, including, to the extent provided for by agreement by the assignor and not prohibited by a law of this state other than this chapter, reasonable attorney's fees and costs incurred by the assignee;

(2) reimbursement of any expenses incurred by the assignee to protect or maintain the real property that is subject to the assignment of rents;

(3) payment of the secured obligation;

(4) payment of any obligation secured by a subordinate security interest or other lien on the rents if, before distribution of the proceeds, the assignee receives a signed notice from the holder of the interest or lien demanding payment of the proceeds; and

(5) payment of any excess proceeds to the assignor.

History of Prop. Code §64.058: Acts 2011, 82nd Leg., ch. 636, §2, eff. June 17, 2011. Amended by Acts 2013, 83rd Leg., ch. 453, §8, eff. June 14, 2013.

PROP §64.059. APPLICATION OF PROCEEDS TO EXPENSES OF PROTECTING REAL PROPERTY; CLAIMS & DEFENSES OF TENANT

(a) Unless otherwise agreed by the assignee, an assignee that collects rents following enforcement under Section 64.054 or 64.055 is not obligated to apply the collected rents to the payment of expenses of protecting or maintaining the real property subject to an assignment of rents.

(b) Unless otherwise agreed by a tenant, the right of the assignee to collect rents from the tenant is subject to the terms of any agreement between the assignor and tenant or any claim or defense of the tenant arising from the assignor's nonperformance of that agreement.

History of Prop. Code §64.059: Acts 2011, 82nd Leg., ch. 636, §2, eff. June 17, 2011. Amended by Acts 2013, 83rd Leg., ch. 453, §9, eff. June 14, 2013.

PROP §64.060. TURNOVER OF RENTS; LIABILITY OF ASSIGNOR

(a) If an assignor collects rents that the assignee is entitled to collect under this chapter, the assignor shall turn over the proceeds to the assignee not later than the 30th day after the date the assignor receives

notice from the assignee under Section 64.054 or within such other period agreed by the assignor and assignee in a security instrument or other document, less any amount representing payment of expenses agreed in that security instrument or other document.

(b) In addition to any other remedy available to the assignee under a law of this state other than this chapter, if an assignor does not turn over proceeds to the assignee as required by Subsection (a), the assignee may recover from the assignor in a civil action:

(1) the proceeds, or an amount equal to the proceeds, that the assignor was obligated to turn over under Subsection (a); and

(2) reasonable attorney's fees and costs incurred by the assignee to the extent provided for by an agreement between the assignor and assignee and not prohibited by a law of this state other than this chapter.

(c) The assignee may maintain an action under Subsection (b) with or without taking action to foreclose any security interest that the assignee has in the real property.

(d) Unless otherwise agreed, if an assignee who has a security interest in rents that is subordinate to the security interest of another assignee under Section 64.052 enforces the subordinate assignee's interest under Section 64.054 or 64.055 before the assignee with priority enforces the interests in rents of the assignee with priority, the subordinate assignee is not obligated to turn over any proceeds that the subordinate assignee collects before the subordinate assignee receives a signed notice from the assignee with priority informing the subordinate assignee that the assignee with priority is enforcing the interest in rents of the assignee with priority. The subordinate assignee shall turn over to the assignee with priority any proceeds that the subordinate assignee collects after the subordinate assignee receives the notice from the assignee with priority that the assignee with priority is enforcing the interest in rents of the assignee with priority not later than the 30th day after the date the subordinate assignee receives the notice or as otherwise agreed between the assignee with priority and the subordinate assignee. Any proceeds subsequently collected by the subordinate assignee shall be turned over to the assignee with priority not later than the 10th day after the date the proceeds are collected or as otherwise agreed between the assignee with priority and the subordinate assignee.

History of Prop. Code §64.060: Acts 2011, 82nd Leg., ch. 636, §2, eff. June 17, 2011. Amended by Acts 2013, 83rd Leg., ch. 453, §10, eff. June 14, 2013.

PROP §64.061. ATTACHMENT, PERFECTION, & PRIORITY OF ASSIGNEE'S SECURITY INTEREST IN PROCEEDS

(a) An assignee's security interest in rents attaches to identifiable proceeds.

(b) If an assignee's security interest in rents is perfected, the assignee's security interest in identifiable cash proceeds is perfected.

(c) Except as provided by Subsection (b), the provisions of Chapter 9, Business & Commerce Code, or the comparable Uniform Commercial Code provisions of another applicable jurisdiction, determine:

(1) whether an assignee's security interest in proceeds is perfected;

(2) the effect of perfection or nonperfection;

(3) the priority of an interest in proceeds; and

(4) the law governing perfection, the effect of perfection or nonperfection, and the priority of an interest in proceeds.

(d) For purposes of this chapter, cash proceeds are identifiable if they are maintained in a segregated deposit account or, if commingled with other funds, to the extent they can be identified by a method of tracing, including application of equitable principles, that is permitted under a law of this state other than this chapter with respect to commingled funds.

History of Prop. Code §64.061: Acts 2011, 82nd Leg., ch. 636, §2, eff. June 17, 2011.

PROP §64.062. PRIORITY SUBJECT TO SUBORDINATION

This chapter does not preclude subordination by agreement by a person entitled to priority.

History of Prop. Code §64.062: Acts 2011, 82nd Leg., ch. 636, §2, eff. June 17, 2011.

CHAPTER 65. AUTHORITY OF CO-OWNER TO ENCUMBER RESIDENTIAL PROPERTY

PROP §65.001. APPLICATION OF CHAPTER

This chapter applies only to residential property:

(1) that has residential improvements primarily designed for not more than four families;

(2) that is not more than 10 acres of land;

(3) that is owned by more than one person; and

(4) for which at least one co-owner has received a residence homestead exemption under Section 11.13, Tax Code.

History of Prop. Code §65.001: Acts 2011, 82nd Leg., ch. 918, §1, eff. Sept. 1, 2011. Renumbered from §64.001 by Acts 2013, 83rd Leg., ch. 161, §22.001(39), eff. Sept. 1, 2013.

PROP §65.0011.[1] APPLICATION TO INSTITUTIONS OF HIGHER EDUCATION

This chapter does not apply to residential property for which an institution of higher education is a co-owner.

1. **Editor's note:** Section 64.0011 was enacted by Acts 2013, 83rd Leg., ch. 1366, §2, effective June 14, 2013, without reference to the renumbering of Property Code ch. 64, as enacted by Acts 2011, 82nd Leg., ch. 918, §1, effective Sept. 1, 2011, to ch. 65 made by Acts 2013, 83rd Leg., ch. 161, §22.001(39), effective Sept. 1, 2013. Numbering has been corrected in this book to reflect the Legislature's probable intent.

History of Prop. Code §64.0011: Acts 2013, 83rd Leg., ch. 1366, §2, eff. June 14, 2013.

PROP §65.002. CONDITIONS FOR AUTHORITY TO ACT AS AGENT FOR CO-OWNER

A co-owner of residential property may act in the name of and on behalf of another co-owner, whether known or unknown, as the co-owner's statutory agent and attorney-in-fact for the purposes described by Section 65.004 if:

(1) the co-owner has occupied the property for more than five years;

(2) the co-owner has a residence homestead exemption for the property under Section 11.13, Tax Code;

(3) for the five years preceding the date the documents required by Section 65.003 are filed, the occupying co-owner has paid all assessed ad valorem taxes without delinquency and without contribution from the other co-owner; and

(4) the occupying co-owner files the documents required by Section 65.003.

History of Prop. Code §65.002: Acts 2011, 82nd Leg., ch. 918, §1, eff. Sept. 1, 2011. Renumbered from §64.002 by Acts 2013, 83rd Leg., ch. 161, §22.001(39), eff. Sept. 1, 2013. Amended by Acts 2013, 83rd Leg., ch. 161, §22.002(29), eff. Sept. 1, 2013.

PROP §65.003. REQUIRED DOCUMENTATION

The occupying co-owner may establish the authority to act as an agent and attorney-in-fact for another co-owner by filing in the office of the county clerk of the county in which the real property is located:

(1) an affidavit of the occupying co-owner affirming the facts described by Sections 65.002(1)-(3);

(2) the affidavits of two additional affiants personally familiar with the co-owner's occupancy of the real property corroborating the occupancy during the preceding five years; and

(3) a certificate of the tax assessor-collector for the county in which the real property is located affirming that the co-owner has paid all taxes assessed against the real property for the preceding five years without delinquency.

History of Prop. Code §65.003: Acts 2011, 82nd Leg., ch. 918, §1, eff. Sept. 1, 2011. Renumbered from §64.003 by Acts 2013, 83rd Leg., ch. 161, §22.001(39), eff. Sept. 1, 2013. Amended by Acts 2013, 83rd Leg., ch. 161, §22.002(30), eff. Sept. 1, 2013.

PROP §65.004. SCOPE OF AUTHORITY

(a) The authority of the occupying co-owner to act as an agent and attorney-in-fact is limited to the authority to enter into a contract giving rise to a mechanic's and materialman's lien and to execute a deed of trust for the purpose of preserving or improving the residential property. The occupying co-owner is the sole obligor of the debt incurred under the contract and secured by the deed of trust.

(b) A lien that arises under a contract entered into by an occupying co-owner under this section is not subject to repudiation or disaffirmance by another co-owner.

History of Prop. Code §65.004: Acts 2011, 82nd Leg., ch. 918, §1, eff. Sept. 1, 2011. Renumbered from §64.004 by Acts 2013, 83rd Leg., ch. 161, §22.001(39), eff. Sept. 1, 2013.

CHAPTER 66. SALE OF PROPERTY SUBJECT TO OIL OR GAS LEASE

PROP §66.001. SALE OF PROPERTY SUBJECT TO OIL OR GAS LEASE

(a) In this section:

(1) "Mortgagee," "mortgagor," and "security instrument" have the meanings assigned by Section 51.0001.

(2) "Oil or gas lease" means an instrument conveying a fee simple determinable interest in a mineral estate covering oil, gas, or other hydrocarbons or a recorded memorandum of such an instrument.

(3) "Real property" means an estate covering the mineral interest in hydrocarbons or the mineral interest in hydrocarbons together with the surface overlying

such mineral interest. The term does not include a surface interest or other interest that excludes a mineral interest in hydrocarbons.

(b) Notwithstanding any other law, an oil or gas lease covering real property subject to a security instrument that has been foreclosed remains in effect after the foreclosure sale if the oil or gas lease has not terminated or expired on its own terms and was executed and recorded in the real property records of the county before the foreclosure sale. An interest of the mortgagor or the mortgagor's assigns in the oil or gas lease, including a right to receive royalties or other payments that become due and payable after the date of the foreclosure, passes to the purchaser of the foreclosed property to the extent that the security instrument under which the real property was foreclosed had priority over the interest in the oil or gas lease of the mortgagor or the mortgagor's assigns.

(c) Notwithstanding Subsection (b), if real property that includes the mineral interest in hydrocarbons together with the surface overlying such mineral interest is subject to both an oil or gas lease and a security instrument and the security interest is foreclosed, the foreclosure sale terminates and extinguishes any right granted under the oil or gas lease for the lessee to use the surface of the real property to the extent that the security instrument under which the real property was foreclosed had priority over the rights of the lessee under the oil or gas lease.

(d) An agreement, including a subordination agreement, between a lessee of an oil or gas lease and a mortgagee of real property or the lessee of an oil or gas lease and the purchaser of foreclosed real property controls over any conflicting provision of this section. An agreement between a mortgagor and mortgagee may not modify the application of this section unless the affected lessee agrees to the modification.

(e) This section does not apply to a security instrument that does not attach to a mineral interest in hydrocarbons in the mortgaged real property.

History of Prop. Code §66.001: Acts 2015, 84th Leg., ch. 461, §1, eff. Jan. 1, 2016.

Chapters 67-69 blank

CHAPTER 70. MISCELLANEOUS LIENS

SUBCHAPTER A. POSSESSORY LIENS

PROP §70.001. WORKER'S LIEN

(a) A worker in this state who by labor repairs an article, including a vehicle, motorboat, vessel, or outboard motor, may retain possession of the article until:

(1) the amount due under the contract for the repairs is paid; or

(2) if no amount is specified by contract, the reasonable and usual compensation is paid.

(b) If a worker relinquishes possession of a motor vehicle, motorboat, vessel, or outboard motor in return for a check, money order, or a credit card transaction on which payment is stopped, has been dishonored because of insufficient funds, no funds or because the drawer or maker of the order or the credit card holder has no account or the account upon which it was drawn or the credit card account has been closed, the lien provided by this section continues to exist and the worker is entitled to possession of the vehicle, motorboat, vessel, or outboard motor until the amount due is paid, unless the vehicle, motorboat, vessel, or outboard motor is possessed by a person who became a bona fide purchaser of the vehicle after a stop payment order was made. A person entitled to possession of property under this subsection is entitled to take possession thereof in accordance with the provisions of Section 9.609, Business & Commerce Code.

(b-1) Except as provided by Subsection (b), a lien provided by this section on a motor vehicle, motorboat, vessel, or outboard motor is released when a worker:

(1) receives good and sufficient payment of the amounts due under Subsection (a) and, if applicable, Subsection (d); or

(2) relinquishes possession of the motor vehicle, motorboat, vessel, or outboard motor.

(b-2) A worker's right to possession under this section may not be assigned to a third party in return for payment of any amount due under Subsection (a) or (d).

(c) A worker may take possession of an article under Subsection (b) only if the person obligated under the repair contract has signed a notice stating that the article may be subject to repossession under this section. A notice under this subsection must be:

(1) separate from the written repair contract; or

(2) printed on the written repair contract, credit agreement, or other document in type that is boldfaced, capitalized, underlined, or otherwise set out from surrounding written material so as to be conspicuous with a separate signature line.

(d) A worker who takes possession of an article under Subsection (b) may require a person obligated under the repair contract to pay the costs of repossession as a condition of reclaiming the article only to the extent of the reasonable fair market value of the services required to take possession of the article. For the purpose of this subsection, charges represent the fair market value of the services required to take possession of an article if the charges represent the actual cost incurred by the worker in taking possession of the article.

(e) A worker may not transfer to a third party, and a person who performs repossession services may not accept, a check, money order, or credit card transaction that is received as payment for repair of an article and that is returned to the worker because of insufficient funds or no funds, because the drawer or maker of the check or money order or the credit card holder has no account, or because the account on which the check or money order is drawn or the credit card account has been closed.

(f) A person commits an offense if the person transfers or accepts a check, money order, or credit card transaction in violation of Subsection (e). An offense under this subsection is a Class B misdemeanor.

(g) A motor vehicle that is repossessed under this section shall be promptly delivered to the location where the repair was performed or a vehicle storage facility licensed under Chapter 2303, Occupations Code. The motor vehicle must remain at the repair location or a licensed vehicle storage facility at all times until the motor vehicle is lawfully returned to the motor vehicle's owner or a lienholder or is disposed of as provided by this subchapter.

History of Prop. Code §70.001: Acts 1983, 68th Leg., ch. 576, §1, eff. Jan. 1, 1984. Amended by Acts 1984, 68th Leg., 2nd C.S., ch. 18, §6(b), eff. Oct. 2, 1984; Acts 1985, 69th Leg., ch. 275, §1, eff. June 5, 1985; Acts 1993, 73rd Leg., ch. 754, §§1, 2, eff. Sept. 1, 1993; Acts 1995, 74th Leg., ch. 375, §1, eff. Sept. 1, 1995; Acts 1999, 76th Leg., ch. 414, §2.38 (eff. July 1, 2001), ch. 978, §1 (eff. Sept. 1, 1999); Acts 2003, 78th Leg., ch. 1276, §14A.807, eff. Sept. 1, 2003; Acts 2015, 84th Leg., ch. 1058, §1, eff. June 19, 2015. Source: TRCS art. 5503(a), (b).

See also Tex. Const. art. 16, §37; B&CC §§9.310, 9.609; ***O'Connor's Texas COA***, "Possession after repair," ch. 6, §5.8, p. 171.

ANNOTATIONS

Drake Ins. v. King, 606 S.W.2d 812, 818 (Tex.1980). "Only work on the automobile authorized by the owner will give rise to an artisan's lien. One without title cannot be permitted to make repairs and accessions to a

stolen vehicle and then demand payment for them upon recovery by the true owner." *See also* ***Southwestern Inv. v. Gilbreath***, 380 S.W.2d 196, 197 (Tex.App.—Amarillo 1964, no writ).

Gulf Coast State Bank v. Nelms, 525 S.W.2d 866, 870 (Tex.1975). "Although [TRCS art. 5506, now Prop. Code §70.001,] has been interpreted as preserving 'the general rule of sanctity of contract' that subsequently acquired liens are inferior to prior existing liens, to hold that the phrase, 'nor shall it in any manner affect or impair other liens,' expressly provides that artisan's and mechanic's liens are inferior, would defeat the clear intent of [B&CC §9.310]. [¶] [W]e hold that [TRCS arts.] 5503 & 5506 do not 'expressly provide' that an artisan's or mechanic's lien is subordinate to a prior perfected security interest. Therefore, by the express terms of §9.310, [artisan's] possessory mechanic's lien is entitled to priority over [bank's] security interest." *See also* ***Miller & Freeman Ford, Inc. v. Greater Houston Bank***, 544 S.W.2d 925, 926 (Tex. 1976); ***Krueger v. Texas State Bank***, 528 S.W.2d 121, 122-23 (Tex.App.—Austin 1975, no writ).

Mossman v. Banatex, LLC, 479 S.W.3d 854, 857-58 (Tex.App.—El Paso 2015, no pet.). Tax Assessor-Collector (TAC) "complains that there was legally insufficient evidence to support the trial court[']s 'finding' that [finance company] presented TAC with a worker's lien notice as defined by [Prop. Code] §70.001.... Specifically, TAC argues that there is no evidence that [finance company] was a 'worker' as that term is used in §70.001; a predicate of this argument is that a worker's lien cannot be assigned. *At 862:* [T]he TAC offers no compelling reason why Texas law would not permit an assignment of [repair shop's] lien rights. Its argument that a worker's lien cannot be assigned is based exclusively on the wording of §70.001 which consistently identifies a 'worker' as one who holds the lien. But simply because a statute creates a lien in the name of one person does not mean it could not be assigned to another. *At 863:* We also find it instructive that while §70.001(e) creates a lien in favor of a 'worker,' [Prop. Code] §70.006 allows enforcement by the 'holder of a lien.' Were the term 'worker,' which is nowhere defined in the statute, meant to have some exclusive meaning preventing the assignment of any rights, then §70.006 which governs sale of the item would not use a different, and arguably broader term. [W]hether an assignment of [repair shop's] lien is proper, or even occurred in this case, is a matter between [customer], the first lien holder, [finance company], and [repair shop]. The TAC's role in this transaction is only to file and serve any notices which facially comply with ... §70.006."

Jones v. Boswell, 250 S.W.3d 140, 143-44 (Tex. App.—Eastland 2008, no pet.). "Unquestionably, [D] paid for towing the dozer out of the tank, and he performed repair services on it. This would suggest that a valid possessory lien existed, but Texas courts have consistently held that, before a statutory or constitutional lien can be created to secure payment for repairs, the owner must consent to the repair. [D] testified that [contractor who rented dozer from Ps' employee] authorized him to hire a wrecker and repair the dozer. But, he agreed that neither [Ps' employee] nor [Ps] authorized any charges. The trial court found that as a matter of law there was no agency relationship between [contractor] and [Ps]. [D] does not challenge that finding. Consequently, because there was no evidence that [Ps] authorized [D] to hire a wrecker or repair the dozer, he had no right to refuse to release the dozer to them, and he committed a trespass as a matter of law."

Ryan v. Abdel-Salam, 39 S.W.3d 332, 336 (Tex. App.—Houston [1st Dist.] 2001, pet. denied). "The record reflects a repair order containing a clause that states, '[A]n express mechanics lien is acknowledged on above vehicle to secure the amount of repairs thereto.' The clause appears in a separate box near the bottom of the repair order next to the 'total,' and contains a signature line that [owner] signed. In addition, [worker] stamped a notice pursuant to §70.001 ... over the signature and posted notice signs in his store explaining that failure to pay for repair services could result in repossession. [Worker] also called [owner] numerous times asking him to pay the balance owed on the repairs or it would be repossessed. [¶] [W]e find the trial court properly denied [owner] relief on the illegal seizure claim."

Thompson v. Apollo Paint & Body Shop, 768 S.W.2d 373, 376 (Tex.App.—Houston [14th Dist.] 1989, writ denied). "The concept of constructive possession is inappropriate in this context dealing with worker's liens. ... While the constitutional lien does not authorize a repairman to take possession of the article repaired and hold it until his charges are paid, the lien statutes do give the repairman the right to retain possession. Subsequent statutory amendments have provided for repossession. ... Recording laws do not em-

brace liens that are not evidenced by a writing. There is no recordation scheme upon which prospective purchasers could rely for disclosure of liens which are not evidenced by a writing, nor is such a system feasible. It is for this reason that possession of the vehicle is indispensable to the rights of the one claiming the lien."

PROP §70.002. LIENS ON GARMENTS

A person with whom a garment is left for repair, alteration, dyeing, cleaning, laundering, or pressing may retain possession of the garment until:

(1) the amount due the person under the contract for the work is paid; or

(2) if no amount is specified by contract, the reasonable and usual compensation is paid.

History of Prop. Code §70.002: Acts 1983, 68th Leg., ch. 576, §1, eff. Jan. 1, 1984. Source: TRCS art. 5506b, §1.

ANNOTATIONS

W.E. Stephens Mfg. v. Goldberg, 225 S.W.3d 75, 81-82 (Tex.App.—El Paso 2005, pet. denied). "[D] acknowledges the general rule that a possessory lien, such as the one provided by §70.002, is extinguished when an artisan gives up possession of the goods, but it argues that this rule should not apply when an artisan works on incremental lots under a single long-term contract. *At 83:* [D] asserts that since §70.002 permits a laundry to retain possession of a garment until the amount due under 'the contract' is paid, it essentially codifies the 'single contract' rule.... [¶] The summary judgment evidence revealed that [D] returned multiple lots of garments to [debtor independent contractor] between August 21, 2000 and October 13, 2000. [Debtor independent contractor] was not obligated to pay [D] immediately on receipt of the goods because [D] provided [debtor independent contractor] with invoices setting forth the work done and the amount due 'net 15.' Thus, the contract set forth a future time of payment and the 'single contract' rule would not apply."

PROP §70.003. STABLE KEEPER'S, GARAGEMAN'S, PASTURER'S, & COTTON GINNER'S LIEN'S

(a) A stable keeper with whom an animal is left for care has a lien on the animal for the amount of the charges for the care.

(b) An owner or lessee of a pasture with whom an animal is left for grazing has a lien on the animal for the amount of charges for the grazing.

(c) A garageman with whom a motor vehicle, motorboat, vessel, or outboard motor is left for care has a lien on the motor vehicle, motorboat, vessel, or outboard motor for the amount of the charges for the care, including reasonable charges for towing the motor vehicle, motorboat, vessel, or outboard motor to the garageman's place of business and excluding charges for repairs.

(d)(1) A cotton ginner to whom a cotton crop has been delivered for processing or who, under an agreement, is to be paid for harvesting a cotton crop has a lien on the cotton processed or harvested for the amount of the charges for the processing or harvesting. The lienholder is entitled to retain possession of the cotton until the amount of the charge due under an agreement is paid or, if an amount is not specified by agreement, the reasonable and usual compensation is paid. If the cotton owner's address is known and the amount of the charge is not paid before the 31st day after the date the cotton ginner's work is completed or the date payment is due under a written agreement, whichever is later, the lienholder shall request the owner to pay the unpaid charge due and shall notify the owner and any other person having a lien on the cotton which is properly recorded under applicable law with the secretary of state of the fact that unless payment is made not later than the 15th day after the date the notice is received, the lienholder is entitled to sell the cotton under any procedure authorized by Section 9.610, Business & Commerce Code. If the cotton owner's address is not known and the amount of the charge is not paid before the 61st day after the date the cotton ginner's work is completed or the date payment is due under a written agreement, whichever is later, the lienholder is entitled to sell the cotton without notice at a commercially reasonable sale. The proceeds of a sale under this subsection shall be applied first to charges due under this subsection, and any remainder shall be paid in appropriate proportion to:

(A) any other person having a lien on the cotton which is properly recorded under applicable law with the secretary of state; and

(B) the cotton owner.

(2) Nothing in this subsection shall be construed to place an affirmative burden on the cotton ginner to perform any lien searches except as may be appropriate to provide notices required by this section.

History of Prop. Code §70.003: Acts 1983, 68th Leg., ch. 576, §1, eff. Jan. 1, 1984. Amended by Acts 1989, 71st Leg., ch. 629, §1, eff. June 14, 1989; Acts 1997, 75th Leg., ch. 462, §§1, 2, eff. Sept. 1, 1997; Acts 1999, 76th Leg., ch. 414, §2.39, eff. July 1, 2001; Acts 2009, 81st Leg., ch. 80, §1, eff. Sept. 1, 2009. Source: TRCS art. 5502.

See also B&CC §9.610.

ANNOTATIONS

Thoroughbred Horsemen's Ass'n v. Dyer, 905 S.W.2d 752, 755 (Tex.App.—Houston [14th Dist.] 1995, no writ). Boarder's "contention that the lien is not enforceable *against him* assumes that he has some right of possession to the certificates. However, the facts are clear that only the horses, and not the certificates, were placed with him. Moreover, under the Property Code, the lien for the amount of his charges was on the animals left with him for care. Therefore, the only property which he was entitled to sell in satisfaction of that lien, or to buy at the resulting public sale, was the horses. The fact that the certificates may have no use apart from the horses, or that the registration may effectively be lost if the certificates are not redeemed, does not create a legal entitlement to their transfer. If, for example, it had been [owner] who boarded the horses with [boarder], we believe that [boarder] would have had no right to claim possession of the certificates from [owner]. The result is no different because the Association happened to be an intermediate party." Held: Common-law lien existed.

Bosworth v. Gulf Coast Dodge, Inc., 879 S.W.2d 152, 158 (Tex.App.—Houston [14th Dist.] 1994, no writ). "The provisions in the Property Code relied on by [Ds] deal with situations in which an owner has left a vehicle with a garageman and does not return to pick it up. In that instance, the garageman does have a choice, he can exercise his rights under the Property Code ... or call the police and report the car as an abandoned vehicle and let them deal with it. Here, [Ds] had no choice because the [car] was an abandoned vehicle taken into custody by, and under the control of, the ... Police Department. [¶] Because the [car] was an abandoned vehicle rather than a vehicle left by an owner in the care of a garageman, the provisions of the Texas Abandoned Motor Vehicle Act [Transp. Code ch. 683] controlled the disposition of the [car] and [Ds'] attempt to foreclose under the provisions of the ... Property Code was unlawful and invalid."

Davis v. Sewell, 696 S.W.2d 247, 248 (Tex.App.—Texarkana 1985, no writ). Stableman's "lien arises by virtue of possession of the animals when money is owed for their care. [¶] [D] argues, however, that the lien was defeated because two of the horses left [P's] possession. The horses were in [P's] pasture. [D] leased one-half of the pasture which was divided by a barbed wire fence. The fence was torn down and the horses got into the area leased by [D]. The horses were returned as soon as [P] became aware of the problem. This temporary absence, without [P's] consent, is not the kind of loss of possession which will defeat the lien."

PROP §70.004. POSSESSION OF MOTOR VEHICLE, MOTORBOAT, VESSEL, OR OUTBOARD MOTOR

(a) A holder of a lien under Section 70.003 on a motor vehicle, motorboat, vessel, or outboard motor who obtains possession of the motor vehicle, motorboat, vessel, or outboard motor under a state law or city ordinance shall give notice for a motor vehicle, motorboat, vessel, or outboard motor registered in this state to the last known registered owner and each lienholder of record not later than the fifth day after the day possession is obtained. If the motor vehicle, motorboat, vessel, or outboard motor is registered outside this state, the notice shall be given to the last known registered owner and each lienholder of record not later than the 14th day after the day possession is obtained.

(b) Except as provided by Subsection (c), the notice must be sent by certified mail with return receipt requested and must contain:

(1) a request to remove the motor vehicle, motorboat, vessel, or outboard motor;

(2) a request for payment;

(3) the location of the motor vehicle, motorboat, vessel, or outboard motor; and

(4) the amount of accrued charges.

(c) The notice may be given by publishing the notice once in a newspaper of general circulation in the county in which the motor vehicle, motorboat, vessel, or outboard motor is stored if:

(1) the motor vehicle, motorboat, vessel, or outboard motor is registered in another state;

(2) the holder of the lien submits a written request by certified mail, return receipt requested, to the governmental entity with which the motor vehicle, motorboat, vessel, or outboard motor is registered requesting information relating to the identity of the last known registered owner and any lienholder of record;

(3) the holder of the lien:

(A) is advised in writing by the governmental entity with which the motor vehicle, motorboat, vessel, or outboard motor is registered that the entity is unwilling or unable to provide information on the last known registered owner or any lienholder of record; or

(B) does not receive a response from the governmental entity with which the motor vehicle, motorboat, vessel, or outboard motor is registered on or before the 21st day after the date the holder of the lien submits a request under Subdivision (2);

(4) the identity of the last known registered owner cannot be determined;

(5) the registration does not contain an address for the last known registered owner; and

(6) the holder of the lien cannot determine the identities and addresses of the lienholders of record.

(d) The holder of the lien is not required to publish notice under Subsection (c) if a correctly addressed notice is sent with sufficient postage under Subsection (b) and is returned as unclaimed or refused or with a notation that the addressee is unknown or has moved without leaving a forwarding address.

(e) A person is entitled to fees for towing, impoundment, preservation, and notification and to reasonable storage fees for up to five days before the day that the notice is mailed or published, as applicable. After the day that the notice is mailed or published, the person is entitled to reasonable storage, impoundment, and preservation fees until the motor vehicle, motorboat, vessel, or outboard motor is removed and accrued charges are paid.

(f) A person charging fees under Subsection (e) commits an offense if the person charges a storage fee for a period of time not authorized by that subsection. An offense under this subsection is punishable by a fine of not less than $200 nor more than $1,000.

History of Prop. Code §70.004: Acts 1983, 68th Leg., ch. 576, §1, eff. Jan. 1, 1984. Amended by Acts 1984, 68th Leg., 2nd C.S., ch. 18, §6(c), eff. Oct. 2, 1984; Acts 1985, 69th Leg., ch. 308, §1, eff. Sept. 1, 1985; Acts 1989, 71st Leg., ch. 629, §2, eff. June 14, 1989; Acts 1999, 76th Leg., ch. 70, §2, eff. Sept. 1, 1999. Source: TRCS art. 5504a(c).

See also Transp. Code ch. 501.

PROP §70.005. SALE OF PROPERTY

(a) Except as provided by Subsection (c), a person holding a lien under this subchapter on property other than a motor vehicle subject to Chapter 501, Transportation Code, or cotton under Section 70.003(d), who retains possession of the property for 60 days after the day that the charges accrue shall request the owner to pay the unpaid charges due if the owner's residence is in this state and known. If the charges are not paid before the 11th day after the day of the request, the lienholder may, after 20 days' notice, sell the property at a public sale, or if the lien is on a garment, at a public or private sale.

(b) Except as provided by Subsection (c), if the residence of the owner of property subject to sale under this section is not in this state or not known, the lienholder may sell the property without notice at a public sale after the 60th day after the day that the unpaid charges accrued.

(c) A person holding a lien under Section 70.003(a) on an animal fed in confinement for slaughter may enforce that lien in any manner authorized by Sections 9.610-9.619, Business & Commerce Code.

(d) The lienholder shall apply the proceeds of a sale under this section to the charges. If the lien is on a garment, the lienholder shall apply the proceeds to the charges and the reasonable costs of holding the sale. The lienholder shall pay excess proceeds to the person entitled to them.

History of Prop. Code §70.005: Acts 1983, 68th Leg., ch. 576, §1, eff. Jan. 1, 1984. Amended by Acts 1997, 75th Leg., ch. 165, §30.247 (eff. Sept. 1, 1997), ch. 249, §1 (eff. Sept. 1, 1997), ch. 462, §§3, 4 (eff. Sept. 1, 1997); Acts 1999, 76th Leg., ch. 414, §2.40, eff. July 1, 2001. Source: TRCS arts. 5504, 5506b, §2.

See also B&CC §§9.610-9.619; Transp. Code ch. 501.

ANNOTATIONS

Cranetex, Inc. v. Precision Crane & Rigging, Inc., 760 S.W.2d 298, 305 (Tex.App.—Texarkana 1988, writ denied). Under §70.005, "if the charges are not paid before the 11th day after the demand, the lienholder is required to give notice of the sale. The notice of sale letter went out August 21, which was more than 11 days after the making of the demand letter. That statute requires that the lienholder may sell the property at a public sale after 20 days' notice. The property was not sold until September 19, which gave [owner] more than 20 days. [Owner] did not seek to enjoin the sale, or contest it in any fashion until this suit was brought to recover the remainder of the repair costs. The time errors consisted of prematurity of the demand and the notice of sale; however, the sale was not conducted until the 91st day after the charges accrued. The prematurity of these two notices could only work to the benefit of [owner] by giving more notice time than required by statute. Substantial compliance as found by

the trial court in this case satisfies §70.005, so long as the time of sale is not shortened."

A PROP §70.006. SALE OR DISPOSAL OF MOTOR VEHICLE, MOTORBOAT, VESSEL, OR OUTBOARD MOTOR

(a) A holder of a lien under this subchapter on a motor vehicle subject to Chapter 501, Transportation Code, or on a motorboat, vessel, or outboard motor for which a certificate of title is required under Subchapter B, Chapter 31, Parks and Wildlife Code, as amended, who retains possession of the motor vehicle, motorboat, vessel, or outboard motor shall give written notice to the owner and each holder of a lien recorded on the certificate of title. Not later than the 30th day after the date on which the charges accrue, a holder of a possessory lien on a motor vehicle under Section 70.001, other than a person licensed as a franchised dealer under Chapter 2301, Occupations Code, shall file a copy of the notice and all information required by this section with the county tax assessor-collector's office in the county in which the repairs were made with an administrative fee of $25 payable to the county tax assessor-collector. If the motor vehicle, motorboat, vessel, or outboard motor is registered outside this state, the holder of a lien under this subchapter who retains possession during that period shall give notice to the last known registered owner and each lienholder of record.

(b) Except as provided by Subsection (c), the notice must be sent by certified mail with return receipt requested and must include the amount of the charges and a request for payment.

(b-1) A holder of a possessory lien on a motor vehicle under Section 70.001, other than a person licensed as a franchised dealer under Chapter 2301, Occupations Code, who is required to give notice to a lienholder of record under this section must include in the notice:

(1) the physical address of the real property at which the repairs to the motor vehicle were made;

(2) the legal name of the person that holds the possessory lien for which the notice is required;

(3) the taxpayer identification number or employer identification number, as applicable, of the person that holds the possessory lien for which the notice is required; and

(4) a signed copy of the work order authorizing the repairs on the motor vehicle.

(b-2) If the holder of a possessory lien required to give notice in accordance with Subsection (b-1) does not comply with that subsection, a lien recorded on the certificate of title of the motor vehicle is superior to the possessory lienholder's lien.

(b-3) A person commits an offense if the person knowingly provides false or misleading information in a notice required by this section. An offense under this subsection is a Class B misdemeanor.

(c) The notice may be given by publishing the notice once in a newspaper of general circulation in the county in which the motor vehicle, motorboat, vessel, or outboard motor is stored if:

(1) the holder of the lien submits a written request by certified mail, return receipt requested, to the governmental entity with which the motor vehicle, motorboat, vessel, or outboard motor is registered requesting information relating to the identity of the last known registered owner and any lienholder of record;

(2) the holder of the lien:

(A) is advised in writing by the governmental entity with which the motor vehicle, motorboat, vessel, or outboard motor is registered that the entity is unwilling or unable to provide information on the last known registered owner or any lienholder of record; or

(B) does not receive a response from the governmental entity with which the motor vehicle, motorboat, vessel, or outboard motor is registered on or before the 21st day after the date the holder of the lien submits a request under Subdivision (1);

(3) the identity of the last known registered owner cannot be determined;

(4) the registration does not contain an address for the last known registered owner; and

(5) the holder of the lien cannot determine the identities and addresses of the lienholders of record.

(d) The holder of the lien is not required to publish notice under Subsection (c) if a correctly addressed notice is sent with sufficient postage under Subsection (b) and is returned as unclaimed or refused or with a notation that the addressee is unknown or has moved without leaving a forwarding address.

(e) After notice is given under this section to the owner of or the holder of a lien on the motor vehicle, motorboat, vessel, or outboard motor, the owner or holder of the lien may obtain possession of the motor vehicle, motorboat, vessel, or outboard motor by paying

all charges due to the holder of a lien under this subchapter before the 31st day after the date a copy of the notice is filed with the county tax assessor-collector's office.

(f) If the charges are not paid before the 31st day after the date that a copy of the notice required by Subsection (a) is filed with the county tax assessor-collector's office, the lienholder may sell the motor vehicle, motorboat, vessel, or outboard motor at a public sale and apply the proceeds to the charges. The lienholder shall pay excess proceeds to the person entitled to them. The public sale may not take place before the 31st day after the date a copy of the notice is filed with the county tax assessor-collector's office.

(f-1) If the charges are not paid before the 31st day after the date that a copy of the notice required by Subsection (a) is filed with the county tax assessor-collector's office and the property that is the subject of the notice is a motor vehicle, the lienholder may, in lieu of selling the vehicle under Subsection (f), dispose of the vehicle in accordance with Subchapter D, Chapter 683, Transportation Code, if the lienholder determines that:

(1) the vehicle's only residual value is as a source of parts or scrap metal; or

(2) it is not economical to dispose of the vehicle at a public sale.

(f-2) If the lienholder disposes of the property under Subsection (f-1), the lienholder shall apply the fair market value of the motor vehicle to the charges due to the lienholder.

(g) After providing notice in accordance with this section, a holder of a possessory lien on a motor vehicle under Section 70.001, other than a person licensed as a franchised dealer under Chapter 2301, Occupations Code, shall, on request, allow an owner and each lienholder of record to inspect or arrange an inspection of the motor vehicle by a qualified professional to verify that the repairs were made. The inspection must be completed before the date of the public sale authorized by Subsection (f).

(h) Not later than the 15th business day after the date the county tax assessor-collector receives notice under this section, the county tax assessor-collector shall provide a copy of the notice that indicates the date the notice was filed with the county tax assessor-collector to the owner of the motor vehicle and each holder of a lien recorded on the certificate of title of the motor vehicle. Except as provided by this subsection, the county tax assessor-collector shall provide the notice required by this section in the same manner as a holder of a lien is required to provide a notice under this section, except that the county tax assessor-collector is not required to use certified mail. Notice under this section is required regardless of the date on which the charges on which the possessory lien is based accrued.

History of Prop. Code §70.006: Acts 1983, 68th Leg., ch. 576, §1, eff. Jan. 1, 1984. Amended by Acts 1984, 68th Leg., 2nd C.S., ch. 18, §6(d), eff. Oct. 2, 1984; Acts 1997, 75th Leg., ch. 165, §30.248, eff. Sept. 1, 1997; Acts 1999, 76th Leg., ch. 70, §3, eff. Sept. 1, 1999; Acts 2009, 81st Leg., ch. 80, §2, eff. Sept. 1, 2009; Acts 2011, 82nd Leg., ch. 405, §7 (eff. Jan. 1, 2012), ch. 1204, §1 (eff. Sept. 1, 2011); Acts 2015, 84th Leg., ch. 1058, §2, eff. Sept. 1, 2015; H.B. 3131, §§5, 6, 85th Leg., eff. Sept. 1, 2017. Source: TRCS art. 5504a(a), (b).

See also Transp. Code ch. 683.

ANNOTATIONS

Mossman v. Banatex, LLC, 479 S.W.3d 854, 857-58 (Tex.App.—El Paso 2015, no pet.). See annotation under Property Code §70.001, p. 317.

Dob's Tire & Auto Ctr. v. Safeway Ins. Agency, 923 S.W.2d 715, 720 (Tex.App.—Houston [1st Dist.] 1996, writ dism'd). "We read [Prop. Code §70.006] as requiring the lienholder to send an additional notice to the owner separate and apart from any previous notice sent under [Prop. Code] §70.004." *See also* ***Elite Towing, Inc. v. LSI Fin. Grp.***, 985 S.W.2d 635, 640 (Tex.App.—Austin 1999, no pet.) (sale of vehicle without proper notice under §70.006 constitutes conversion).

Bosworth v. Gulf Coast Dodge, Inc., 879 S.W.2d 152, 158 (Tex.App.—Houston [14th Dist.] 1994, no writ). "Because [vehicle] was an abandoned vehicle rather than a vehicle left by an owner in the care of a garageman, the provisions of the Texas Abandoned Motor Vehicle Act controlled the disposition of [vehicle] and [garageman's] attempt to foreclose under the provisions of the … Property Code was unlawful and invalid."

First State Bank v. Arsiaga, 804 S.W.2d 343, 345 (Tex.App.—Eastland 1991, writ denied). "The notice requirement contained in §70.006 is not required to perfect a possessory lien. Section 70.006 notice is required before a possessory lienholder can nonjudicially foreclose on the collateral. [¶] A lender has recourse against the borrower as well as its collateral. [Lender] had the opportunity to attack the reasonableness and necessity of the storage and repair charges at trial. If the facts show that a mechanic secretly stored the ve-

hicle until such time as the storage charges exceeded the value of the collateral, then these charges would not be reasonable."

Collision Ctr. Paint & Body, Inc. v. Campbell, 773 S.W.2d 354, 357 (Tex.App.—Dallas 1989, no writ). "[W]e hold that a proper tender of the amount claimed in the notice is sufficient; the possessory lien expires upon tender the same as if the tendered amount had been retained; the subsequent refusal to surrender the car to the lienholder constitutes conversion. [¶] 'Tender' is an unconditional offer by a debtor to pay a sum of money not less than the amount due on the obligation. As a general rule, a tender of payment must include everything to which the creditor is entitled; any less sum is ineffectual."

PROP §70.007. UNCLAIMED EXCESS

(a) If a person entitled to excess proceeds under this subchapter is not known or has moved from this state or the county in which the lien accrued, the person holding the excess shall pay it to the county treasurer of the county in which the lien accrued. The treasurer shall issue the person a receipt for the payment.

(b) If the person entitled to the excess does not claim it before two years after the day it is paid to the treasurer, the excess becomes a part of the county's general fund.

History of Prop. Code §70.007: Acts 1983, 68th Leg., ch. 576, §1, eff. Jan. 1, 1984. Source: TRCS arts. 5505, 5506b, §3.

PROP §70.008. ATTORNEY'S FEES

The court in a suit concerning possession of a motor vehicle, motorboat, vessel, or outboard motor and a debt due on it may award reasonable attorney's fees to the prevailing party.

History of Prop. Code §70.008: Acts 1983, 68th Leg., ch. 576, §1, eff. Jan. 1, 1984. Amended by Acts 1984, 68th Leg., 2nd C.S., ch. 18, §6(e), eff. Oct. 2, 1984. Source: TRCS art. 5503(c).

ANNOTATIONS

Kollision King, Inc. v. Calderon, 968 S.W.2d 20, 24 (Tex.App.—Corpus Christi 1998, no pet.). Section 70.008 "does not restrict the award of attorney's fees to one suing on a debt who wishes to retain possession of a vehicle. [P] sued in conversion and not for possession of the vehicle, because the vehicle could not be returned to him by [Ds]. [A]t issue was the right of possession of the vehicle and the debt claimed secured by the possessory lien. [P], ... being the prevailing party, was entitled to attorney's fees under the statute." *See also* ***Elite Towing, Inc. v. LSI Fin. Grp.***, 985 S.W.2d 635, 645 (Tex.App.—Austin 1999, no pet.).

PROP §70.009. PLASTIC FABRICATOR LIENS

(a) A plastic fabricator has a lien on any die, mold, form, or pattern in his possession that belongs to a customer for the amount due from the customer for plastic fabrication work performed with the die, mold, form, or pattern. The plastic fabricator may retain possession of the die, mold, form, or pattern until the amount due is paid.

(b) In this section:

(1) "Customer" means a person who contracts with or causes a plastic fabricator to use a die, mold, form, or pattern to manufacture, assemble, or otherwise make a plastic product or products.

(2) "Plastic fabricator" means a person, including a tool or die maker, who manufactures or causes to be manufactured, or who assembles or improves, a die, form, mold, or pattern for a customer, or who uses or contracts to use a die, mold, form, or pattern to manufacture, assemble, or otherwise make a plastic product or products for a customer.

History of Prop. Code §70.009: Acts 1985, 69th Leg., ch. 357, §1, eff. Sept. 1, 1985.

PROP §70.010. LIENS FOR VETERINARY CARE CHARGES FOR LARGE ANIMALS

(a) In this section, "large animal" means exotic livestock or a cow, horse, mule, ass, sheep, goat, llama, alpaca, farm elk, or hog. The term does not include a common household pet such as a cat or dog.

(b) A veterinarian licensed under Chapter 801, Occupations Code, has a lien on a large animal and the proceeds from the disposition of the large animal to secure the cost of veterinary care the veterinarian provided to the large animal.

(c) A lien under this section:

(1) attaches on the 20th day after the date the veterinarian first provides care to the large animal;

(2) attaches regardless of whether the veterinarian retains possession of the large animal;

(3) takes priority over all other liens on the large animal for the period during which the veterinarian retains possession of the large animal, regardless of whether the lien under this section was created or perfected after the date on which another lien was created or perfected, if the veterinarian retains possession; and

(4) has the priority with respect to other liens as provided by Subchapter C, Chapter 9, Business & Commerce Code, if the veterinarian does not retain possession.

(d) The veterinarian may retain possession of a large animal under this section and enforce a lien under this section as provided by Section 70.005(c).

(e) A veterinarian who does not retain possession of a large animal under this section may enforce a lien under this section in the same manner as a statutory residential landlord's lien.

History of Prop. Code §70.010: Acts 2009, 81st Leg., ch. 1387, §1, eff. Sept. 1, 2009.

Sections 70.011-70.100 reserved for expansion

SUBCHAPTER B. LIENS ON VESSELS

PROP §70.101. GENERAL LIEN ON VESSELS

A person who furnishes supplies or materials or who performs repairs or labor for or on account of a domestic vessel that is owned in whole or part in this state has a lien for the person's charges.

History of Prop. Code §70.101: Acts 1983, 68th Leg., ch. 576, §1, eff. Jan. 1, 1984. Source: TRCS art. 5500, §1.

PROP §70.102. LIEN OF NAVIGATION DISTRICT OR PORT

(a) A navigation district or port within the territorial limits of this state that furnishes supplies or materials, performs repairs or labor, or provides a facility or service for which charges are specified in its official published port tariff for or on account of a domestic vessel that is owned in whole or part in this state has a maritime lien for the amount of its charges.

(b) A lien under this section may be enforced in rem. A plaintiff in an action to enforce the lien need not allege or prove that credit was given to the vessel.

History of Prop. Code §70.102: Acts 1983, 68th Leg., ch. 576, §1, eff. Jan. 1, 1984. Source: TRCS art. 5500, §2.

PROP §70.103. PROPERTY SUBJECT TO LIEN

A lien under this subchapter attaches to the vessel and its tackle, apparel, furniture, and freight money.

History of Prop. Code §70.103: Acts 1983, 68th Leg., ch. 576, §1, eff. Jan. 1, 1984. Source: TRCS art. 5500, §§1, 2.

PROP §70.104. PERSONS WHO MAY BIND VESSEL

(a) The following persons are presumed to be authorized by the owner of a vessel to incur charges that give rise to a lien under this subchapter:

(1) the managing owner;

(2) the ship's husband;

(3) the master;

(4) the local agent; and

(5) a person entrusted with management of the vessel at the port of supply.

(b) A person tortiously or unlawfully in possession or charge of a vessel may not bind the vessel.

History of Prop. Code §70.104: Acts 1983, 68th Leg., ch. 576, §1, eff. Jan. 1, 1984. Source: TRCS art. 5500, §3.

Sections 70.105-70.200 reserved for expansion

SUBCHAPTER C. STOCK BREEDER'S LIEN

PROP §70.201. STOCK BREEDER'S LIEN

An owner or keeper of a stallion, jack, bull, or boar confined to be bred for profit has a preference lien on the offspring of the animal for the amount of the charges for the breeding services, unless the owner or keeper misrepresents the animal by false pedigree.

History of Prop. Code §70.201: Acts 1983, 68th Leg., ch. 576, §1, eff. Jan. 1, 1984. Source: TRCS art. 5501.

PROP §70.202. ENFORCEMENT OF LIEN

The lien may be enforced in the same manner as a statutory landlord's lien. The lien remains in force for 10 months from the day that the offspring is born, but the lien may not be enforced until five months after the date of birth of the offspring.

History of Prop. Code §70.202: Acts 1983, 68th Leg., ch. 576, §1, eff. Jan. 1, 1984. Source: TRCS art. 5501.

Sections 70.203-70.300 reserved for expansion

SUBCHAPTER D. AIRCRAFT REPAIR & MAINTENANCE LIEN

PROP §70.301. LIEN

(a) A person who stores, fuels, repairs, or performs maintenance work on an aircraft has a lien on the aircraft for:

(1) the amount due under a contract for the storage, fuel, repairs, or maintenance work; or

(2) if no amount is specified by contract, the reasonable and usual compensation for the storage, fuel, repairs, or maintenance work.

(b) This subchapter applies to a contract for storage only if it is:

(1) written; or

(2) oral and provides for a storage period of at least 30 days.

History of Prop. Code §70.301: Acts 1989, 71st Leg., ch. 250, §1, eff. Sept. 1, 1989. Amended by Acts 1995, 74th Leg., ch. 946, §1, eff. Aug. 28, 1995; Acts 2001, 77th Leg., ch. 1171, §1, eff. Sept. 1, 2001.

ANNOTATIONS

Roach v. Dickenson, 50 S.W.3d 709, 714 (Tex. App.—Eastland 2001, no pet.). "The fact that [P] acquired ownership of the entire plane did not automatically merge the lesser lien interest into the greater ownership interest. Even though [D] pleaded merger, the evidence must show that the parties intended the sale of the entire plane to extinguish the debt obligation represented by the first lien. [P's] testimony that he forgave the first lien debt as part payment on the plane is sufficient to establish conclusively the defense of merger as to the first lien. The trial court erred in granting [P] judgment on the first lien and in foreclosing the first lien. [¶] The second lien arose when [P] performed the second round of repairs on the plane. Even if [D] had pleaded merger as to the second lien, the record does not show that [P] intended to release the lien or to extinguish the underlying debt when he purchased the plane. [P] testified that he offered to offset the second lien against the purchase price as well but that [D's agent] and [D] wanted to receive some money from the sale. ... The evidence is insufficient to support the trial court's enforcement of the entire second lien. Further evidence is required to determine how much of the second lien arose prior to [P's] purchase of the plane."

PROP §70.302. POSSESSION

(a) A holder of a lien under this subchapter may retain possession of the aircraft subject to the lien until the amount due is paid.

(b) Except as provided by Subsection (c), if the holder of a lien under this subchapter relinquishes possession of the aircraft before the amount due is paid, the person may retake possession of the aircraft as provided by Section 9.609, Business & Commerce Code.

(c) The holder of a lien under this subchapter may not retake possession of the aircraft from a bona fide purchaser for value who purchases the aircraft without knowledge of the lien before the date the lien is recorded under Section 70.303.

History of Prop. Code §70.302: Acts 1989, 71st Leg., ch. 250, §1, eff. Sept. 1, 1989. Amended by Acts 1999, 76th Leg., ch. 414, §2.41, eff. July 1, 2001.

See also B&CC §9.609.

ANNOTATIONS

In re Curry, 407 S.W.3d 376, 380 (Tex.App.—Dallas 2013, orig. proceeding). "While [Prop. Code] §70.302(b) authorizes a holder of a lien that has relinquished possession of the aircraft before the amount due is paid to retake possession of the aircraft *as provided* by [B&CC] §9.609 ..., the reference to §9.609 is not in limitation of the type of lienholder who may enforce a lien, but rather a reference to a *process* that must be used for repossession; repossession may occur either pursuant to judicial process or without judicial process if the repossession can occur without breach of the peace. *At 381:* [W]e conclude §70.302(b) provides a remedy for a lienholder who is not a secured party under [B&CC] ch. 9.... We further conclude the purpose of §70.302(b)'s reference to §9.609 ... was not, as relators claim, to limit application of §70.302(b) to retaking of an aircraft by a secured party, but rather to provide by simple reference a process by which repossession may occur."

PROP §70.303. RECORDING OF LIEN: AIRCRAFT REGISTERED IN UNITED STATES

A holder of a lien under this subchapter may record the lien on the aircraft by filing with the Federal Aviation Administration Aircraft Registry not later than the 180th day after the date of the completion of the contractual storage period or the performance of the last repair or maintenance a verified document in the form and manner required by applicable federal laws and regulations that states:

(1) the name, address, and telephone number of the holder of the lien under this subchapter;

(2) the amount due for storage, fuel, repairs, or maintenance;

(3) a complete description of the aircraft; and

(4) the name and address of the owner of the aircraft and the number assigned the aircraft by the Federal Aviation Administration, if known.

History of Prop. Code §70.303: Acts 1989, 71st Leg., ch. 250, §1, eff. Sept. 1, 1989. Amended by Acts 1995, 74th Leg., ch. 946, §1, eff. Aug. 28, 1995; Acts 2001, 77th Leg., ch. 1171, §2, eff. Sept. 1, 2001; Acts 2005, 79th Leg., ch. 677, §1, eff. June 17, 2005.

PROP §70.3031. RECORDING OF LIEN: AIRCRAFT NOT REGISTERED IN UNITED STATES

(a) A holder of a lien under this subchapter on an aircraft that is registered in a nation other than

the United States or that is not registered in any national jurisdiction may record the lien on the aircraft by filing with the secretary of state not later than the 180th day after the date of the completion of the contractual storage period or the performance of the last repair, fueling, or maintenance an affidavit that states:

(1) the name, address, and telephone number of the holder of the lien under this subchapter;

(2) the amount due for storage, repairs, fuel, or maintenance;

(3) a complete description of the aircraft; and

(4) the name and last known address of the owner of the aircraft and the number assigned the aircraft by the applicable jurisdiction, if known.

(b) An inaccurate address stated under Subsection (a)(4) does not invalidate the affidavit.

(c) The secretary of state shall maintain a record of information filed with the secretary of state under this section and index the records in the name of the owner of the aircraft.

(d) The fee for filing information with the secretary of state under this section is:

(1) $15 if the information is communicated in writing and consists of one or two pages;

(2) $30 if the information is communicated in writing and consists of more than two pages; and

(3) $5 if the information is communicated by another medium authorized by the secretary of state by rule.

History of Prop. Code §70.3031: Acts 2005, 79th Leg., ch. 677, §2, eff. June 17, 2005.

PROP §70.304. NOTICE TO OWNER & LIENHOLDERS

(a) Not later than the 60th day after the date of the completion of the contractual storage period or the performance of the last fueling, repair, or maintenance, a holder of a lien under this subchapter who retains possession of the aircraft shall notify the owner shown on the certificate of registration and each holder of a lien on the aircraft as shown by the records maintained for that purpose by the Federal Aviation Administration Aircraft Registry or the secretary of state. The notice must state:

(1) the name, address, and telephone number of the holder of the lien under this subchapter;

(2) the amount due for storage, fuel, repairs, or maintenance;

(3) a complete description of the aircraft; and

(4) the legal right of the holder of the lien under this subchapter to sell the aircraft at public auction and apply the proceeds to the amount due.

(b) The notice must be delivered by certified or registered mail, return receipt requested.

History of Prop. Code §70.304: Acts 1989, 71st Leg., ch. 250, §1, eff. Sept. 1, 1989. Amended by Acts 1991, 72nd Leg., ch. 538, §1, eff. June 15, 1991; Acts 1995, 74th Leg., ch. 946, §1, eff. Aug. 28, 1995; Acts 2001, 77th Leg., ch. 1171, §3, eff. Sept. 1, 2001; Acts 2005, 79th Leg., ch. 677, §3, eff. June 17, 2005.

PROP §70.305. SALE OF AIRCRAFT

If the holder of a lien under this subchapter provides the notice required by Section 70.304 and the amount due remains unpaid after the 90th day after the date of the completion of the contractual storage period or the performance of the last fueling, repair, or maintenance, the holder of the lien may sell the aircraft at a public sale and apply the proceeds to the amount due. The lienholder shall pay any excess proceeds to the person entitled to them.

History of Prop. Code §70.305: Acts 1989, 71st Leg., ch. 250, §1, eff. Sept. 1, 1989. Amended by Acts 1995, 74th Leg., ch. 946, §1, eff. Aug. 28, 1995; Acts 2001, 77th Leg., ch. 1171, §4, eff. Sept. 1, 2001; Acts 2005, 79th Leg., ch. 677, §4, eff. June 17, 2005.

PROP §70.306. ATTORNEY'S FEES

The court in a suit brought under this subchapter may award reasonable attorney's fees to the prevailing party.

History of Prop. Code §70.306: Acts 1989, 71st Leg., ch. 250, §1, eff. Sept. 1, 1989.

PROP §70.307. CRIMINAL OFFENSE: IMPROPERLY OBTAINING POSSESSION OF AIRCRAFT SUBJECT TO LIEN

(a) A person commits an offense if the person, through surreptitious removal or by trick, fraud, or device perpetrated on the holder of the lien, obtains possession of all or part of an aircraft that is subject to a lien under this subchapter.

(b) An offense under this section is a Class B misdemeanor.

(c) If conduct that constitutes an offense under this section also constitutes an offense under any other law, the actor may be prosecuted under this section or the other law.

History of Prop. Code §70.307: Acts 2005, 79th Leg., ch. 677, §5, eff. June 17, 2005.

Sections 70.308-70.400 reserved for expansion

SUBCHAPTER E. AGRICULTURAL LIENS

A PROP §70.401. DEFINITIONS

The amended text in §70.401 is effective for agricultural producers who deliver or transfer an agricultural crop grown, produced, or harvested by the producer to a warehouse or a contract purchaser on or after Sept. 1, 2017. Agricultural producers who deliver or transfer an agricultural crop to a warehouse or a contract purchaser before Sept. 1, 2017, are governed by the former law in effect at that time.

In this subchapter:

(1) "Agricultural crop" means a plant product that is grown, produced, or harvested as a result of an agricultural producer's farm operation.

(2) "Agricultural producer" means a person who is engaged in the business of growing, producing, or harvesting an agricultural crop.

(3) "Buyer in ordinary course of business" has the meaning assigned by Section 1.201, Business & Commerce Code.

(4) "Company-owned crop" means an agricultural crop:

(A) that is in the possession of a warehouse or contract purchaser located in this state and for which the agricultural producer has received full payment;

(B) that is not an open storage crop; or

(C) for which the warehouse or the contract purchaser tenders payment and the agricultural producer, without coercion, defers payment.

(5) "Contract purchaser" means a person who has agreed under a contract to purchase an agricultural crop or otherwise pay the agricultural producer for growing, producing, or harvesting the agricultural crop. The term includes [does not include] a person who, as to the transaction in question, is licensed and bonded under Chapter 14, Agriculture Code, or the United States Warehouse Act (7 U.S.C. Section 241 et seq.).

(6) "Open storage crop" means an agricultural crop that:

(A) an agricultural producer delivers or transfers to:

(i) a warehouse for storage; or

(ii) a contract purchaser located in this state;

(B) is not covered by a warehouse receipt; and

(C) is not owned by the lessee, owner, or operator of the warehouse in which the crop is stored or the contract purchaser to which the crop is delivered or transferred.

(7) "Secured lender" means a person that:

(A) has loaned money to a warehouse or a contract purchaser; and

(B) holds a perfected secured lien against a company-owned crop.

(8) "Warehouse" means a facility that stores or handles any agricultural crop after the crop is harvested, including a facility operated by a person who, as to the transaction in question, is licensed and bonded under Chapter 14, Agriculture Code, or the United States Warehouse Act (7 U.S.C. Section 241 et seq.). The term includes a person engaged in the business of operating a warehouse.

History of Prop. Code §70.401: Acts 2001, 77th Leg., ch. 732, §1, eff. Sept. 1, 2001. Amended by Acts 2015, 84th Leg., ch. 628, §1, eff. Sept. 1, 2015; H.B. 3063, §1, 85th Leg., eff. Sept. 1, 2017.

A PROP §70.402. LIEN CREATED

The amended text in §70.402 is effective for agricultural producers who deliver or transfer an agricultural crop grown, produced, or harvested by the producer to a warehouse or a contract purchaser on or after Sept. 1, 2017. Agricultural producers who deliver or transfer an agricultural crop to a warehouse or a contract purchaser before Sept. 1, 2017, are governed by the former law in effect at that time.

(a) An agricultural producer who, under a contract with a contract purchaser, is to receive consideration for selling an agricultural crop grown, produced, or harvested by the producer has a lien against that crop for the amount owed under the contract, or for the market [reasonable] value of the crop on the date of transfer or delivery if there is no agreement concerning the amount owed under the contract.

(b) An agricultural producer who delivers or transfers an agricultural crop grown, produced, or harvested by the producer to a warehouse has a lien against that agricultural crop for the market value of the agricultural crop:

(1) on the date of delivery or transfer; or

(2) if there is to be a series of deliveries to the warehouse, on the date of the first delivery of the agricultural crop to the warehouse.

(c) A lien created under this subchapter is on every agricultural crop, either in raw or processed form, that has been transferred or delivered by the agricultural producer and is in the possession of the warehouse or the contract purchaser, and if the warehouse or the contract purchaser sells all or part of the crop, on the proceeds of the sale. If an open storage [~~the agricultural~~] crop is commingled with a company-owned crop by a warehouse or a contract purchaser after the crop has been transferred or delivered, a lien created under this subchapter applies only to that portion of the agricultural crop in the possession of the warehouse or the contract purchaser [~~purchaser's inventory~~] in an amount that is equal to the amount of the crop transferred or delivered by the agricultural producer.

(d) [~~(c)~~] For purposes of this subchapter, an agricultural crop or processed form of an agricultural crop deposited by a contract purchaser with a warehouse, whether or not a warehouse receipt is given as security, is considered to be in the possession of the contract purchaser and subject to the lien created by this subchapter.

History of Prop. Code §70.402: Acts 2001, 77th Leg., ch. 732, §1, eff. Sept. 1, 2001. Amended by Acts 2015, 84th Leg., ch. 628, §2, eff. Sept. 1, 2015; H.B. 3063, §2, 85th Leg., eff. Sept. 1, 2017.

See also Prop. Code §§54.002, 70.403, 70.405.

A PROP §70.403. WHEN LIEN ATTACHES

The amended text in §70.403 is effective for agricultural producers who deliver or transfer an agricultural crop grown, produced, or harvested by the producer to a warehouse or a contract purchaser on or after Sept. 1, 2017. Agricultural producers who deliver or transfer an agricultural crop to a warehouse or a contract purchaser before Sept. 1, 2017, are governed by the former law in effect at that time.

A lien created under this subchapter attaches on the date on which physical possession of the agricultural crop is delivered or transferred by the agricultural producer to the warehouse or to the contract purchaser or the purchaser's agent, or if there is to be a series of deliveries [~~to the contract purchaser or purchaser's agent~~], on the date of the first delivery of the agricultural crop [~~to the contract purchaser or purchaser's agent~~].

History of Prop. Code §70.403: Acts 2001, 77th Leg., ch. 732, §1, eff. Sept. 1, 2001. Amended by Acts 2015, 84th Leg., ch. 628, §3, eff. Sept. 1, 2015; H.B. 3063, §3, 85th Leg., eff. Sept. 1, 2017.

See also Prop. Code §§54.002, 70.402, 70.405.

A PROP §70.404. APPLICABILITY OF OTHER LAW; EFFECT ON OTHER LAW

The amended text in §70.404 is effective for agricultural producers who deliver or transfer an agricultural crop grown, produced, or harvested by the producer to a warehouse or a contract purchaser on or after Sept. 1, 2017. Agricultural producers who deliver or transfer an agricultural crop to a warehouse or a contract purchaser before Sept. 1, 2017, are governed by the former law in effect at that time.

(a) Except as provided by Section 70.4045 of this code, Chapter 9, Business & Commerce Code, including applicable filing and perfection requirements, applies to a lien created under this subchapter.

(b) Except as provided by Subsection (c), to the extent of a conflict, this subchapter controls over any other law.

(c) This subchapter does not abridge the protections afforded by any applicable law, including:

(1) Chapter 14, Agriculture Code;

(2) Chapter 7, Business & Commerce Code;

(3) the United States Warehouse Act (7 U.S.C. Section 241 et seq.); or

(4) common law, including the law of bailment.

History of Prop. Code §70.404: Acts 2001, 77th Leg., ch. 732, §1, eff. Sept. 1, 2001. Amended by Acts 2015, 84th Leg., ch. 628, §4, eff. Sept. 1, 2015; H.B. 3063, §4, 85th Leg., eff. Sept. 1, 2017.

See also B&CC §§9.302, 9.322.

A PROP §70.4045. PERFECTION & PRIORITY OF AGRICULTURAL LIEN ON CROPS

The amended text in §70.4045 is effective for agricultural producers who deliver or transfer an agricultural crop grown, produced, or harvested by the producer to a warehouse or a contract purchaser on or after Sept. 1, 2017. Agricultural producers who deliver or transfer an agricultural crop to a warehouse or a contract purchaser before Sept. 1, 2017, are governed by the former law in effect at that time.

(a) Notwithstanding Chapter 9, Business & Commerce Code, a lien created under this subchapter is perfected at the time the lien attaches under Section 70.403 and continues to be perfected if a financing statement covering the agricultural crop is filed on or before the 90th day after the date:

(1) the physical possession of the crop is delivered or transferred by the agricultural producer to the ware-

house or the contract purchaser or the purchaser's agent, if there is only one delivery [under the contract]; or

(2) of the last delivery of the crop to the warehouse or the contract purchaser or the purchaser's agent, if there is a series of deliveries [under the contract].

(b) If a financing statement covering the agricultural crop is not filed within the time prescribed by Subsection (a)(1) or (2), as applicable, the lien is considered unperfected [on the date the lien attached until the date the financing statement is filed or the lien is perfected under Chapter 9, Business & Commerce Code].

(c) Notwithstanding Chapter 9, Business & Commerce Code, and except as provided by Subsection (d), a lien created and perfected under this subchapter has priority over a conflicting security interest in or lien on the agricultural crop or the proceeds from the sale of the crop created by the warehouse or the contract purchaser in favor of a third party, [other than a cotton ginner's lien created under Section 70.003(d),] regardless of the date the security interest or lien created by the warehouse or the contract purchaser attached. This subsection does not affect:

(1) the validity or priority of a security interest or lien:

(A) created and perfected to secure a loan directly to the agricultural producer; or

(B) created and perfected under Chapter 9, Business & Commerce Code, to secure a loan to a warehouse or a contract purchaser on a company-owned crop in favor of a secured lender;

(2) the validity or priority of a cotton ginner's lien created under Section 70.003(d); or

(3) the rights of a holder of a negotiable warehouse receipt.

(d) Subsection (c) does not apply to a contract purchaser who purchases an agricultural crop from an agricultural producer under a marketing contract created under:

(1) Section 52.016, Agriculture Code; or

(2) regulations adopted by the United States Department of Agriculture under Title 7 of the United States Code.

History of Prop. Code §70.4045: Acts 2015, 84th Leg., ch. 628, §5, eff. Sept. 1, 2015. Amended by H.B. 3063, §5, 85th Leg., eff. Sept. 1, 2017.

PROP §70.405. DURATION OF LIEN

A lien created under this subchapter expires on the first anniversary of the date of attachment.

History of Prop. Code §70.405: Acts 2001, 77th Leg., ch. 732, §1, eff. Sept. 1, 2001.

See also Prop. Code §§54.002, 54.004, 70.402, 70.403.

A PROP §70.406. EFFECT OF LIEN; RECOVERY

The amended text in §70.406 is effective for agricultural producers who deliver or transfer an agricultural crop grown, produced, or harvested by the producer to a warehouse or a contract purchaser on or after Sept. 1, 2017. Agricultural producers who deliver or transfer an agricultural crop to a warehouse or a contract purchaser before Sept. 1, 2017, are governed by the former law in effect at that time.

(a) A buyer in ordinary course of business of an agricultural crop, including a person who buys any portion of an agricultural crop from a warehouse or a contract purchaser, whether or not the agricultural crop has been commingled, takes the agricultural crop free of a lien created under this subchapter, and the lien created by this subchapter does not pass to any subsequent claimant of the agricultural crop.

(b) An unequal pro rata recovery between agricultural producers is not prohibited under this subchapter if the inequality results from a lien on accounts receivable.

History of Prop. Code §70.406: Acts 2001, 77th Leg., ch. 732, §1, eff. Sept. 1, 2001. Amended by H.B. 3063, §6, 85th Leg., eff. Sept. 1, 2017.

A PROP §70.407. DISCHARGE OF LIEN

The amended text in §70.407 is effective for agricultural producers who deliver or transfer an agricultural crop grown, produced, or harvested by the producer to a warehouse or a contract purchaser on or after Sept. 1, 2017. Agricultural producers who deliver or transfer an agricultural crop to a warehouse or a contract purchaser before Sept. 1, 2017, are governed by the former law in effect at that time.

(a) A lien created under this subchapter is discharged when:

(1) the lienholder receives full payment for the agricultural crop; or

(2) payment is tendered by the warehouse or the contract purchaser, as applicable, and the lienholder, without coercion, defers payment.

(b) If payment for the agricultural crop is received in the form of a negotiable instrument, full payment is

received when the negotiable instrument clears all financial institutions.

History of Prop. Code §70.407: Acts 2001, 77th Leg., ch. 732, §1, eff. Sept. 1, 2001. Amended by H.B. 3063, §7, 85th Leg., eff. Sept. 1, 2017.

PROP §70.408. JOINDER OF ACTIONS

Persons claiming a lien against the same agricultural crop under this subchapter may join in the same action, and if separate actions are commenced, the court may consolidate them.

History of Prop. Code §70.408: Acts 2001, 77th Leg., ch. 732, §1, eff. Sept. 1, 2001.

PROP §70.409. RECOVERY OF COSTS

An agricultural producer who prevails in an action brought to enforce a lien created under this subchapter is entitled to recover:

(1) reasonable and necessary attorney's fees and court costs; and

(2) interest on funds subject to the lien at the judgment interest rate as provided by Chapter 304, Finance Code.

History of Prop. Code §70.409: Acts 2001, 77th Leg., ch. 732, §1, eff. Sept. 1, 2001.

See also Fin. Code chs. 302, 304.

A PROP §70.410. WAIVER OF CERTAIN RIGHTS PROHIBITED

The amended text in §70.410 is effective for agricultural producers who deliver or transfer an agricultural crop grown, produced, or harvested by the producer to a warehouse or a contract purchaser on or after Sept. 1, 2017. Agricultural producers who deliver or transfer an agricultural crop to a warehouse or a contract purchaser before Sept. 1, 2017, are governed by the former law in effect at that time.

An agricultural producer's agreement with a warehouse or a contract purchaser to waive the producer's right to seek a remedy provided by this subchapter is void.

History of Prop. Code §70.410: Acts 2001, 77th Leg., ch. 732, §1, eff. Sept. 1, 2001. Amended by H.B. 3063, §8, 85th Leg., eff. Sept. 1, 2017.

Sections 70.411-70.500 blank

SUBCHAPTER F. LIEN RELATED TO DAMAGED FENCE

PROP §70.501. LANDOWNER'S LIEN

A person who owns real property in this state that is enclosed by a fence or other structure obviously designed to exclude intruders or to contain livestock or other animals may obtain from a court in this state a judgment entitling the person to a lien against the motor vehicle of a person who damages the landowner's fence with the motor vehicle if the person who damages the landowner's fence:

(1) owns the motor vehicle; or

(2) has the consent of the owner of the motor vehicle to drive the vehicle at the time the person damages the landowner's fence.

History of Prop. Code §70.501: Acts 2007, 80th Leg., ch. 330, §1, eff. Sept. 1, 2007.

PROP §70.502. AMOUNT OF LIEN

The amount of a landowner's lien under this subchapter is equal to the lesser of:

(1) the fair market value of the motor vehicle on the date the landowner's fence is damaged; or

(2) the actual cost incurred by the landowner to:

(A) repair the fence;

(B) recapture any livestock or other animals that escaped as a direct result of the damage to the fence; and

(C) have the vehicle towed from the property and stored.

History of Prop. Code §70.502: Acts 2007, 80th Leg., ch. 330, §1, eff. Sept. 1, 2007.

PROP §70.503. PROPERTY TO WHICH LIEN ATTACHES

A landowner's lien under this chapter attaches only to a motor vehicle that causes damage to a fence as described by Section 70.501.

History of Prop. Code §70.503: Acts 2007, 80th Leg., ch. 330, §1, eff. Sept. 1, 2007.

PROP §70.504. PERFECTING LIEN

A landowner may perfect a lien under this subchapter in the manner provided by Subchapter F, Chapter 501, Transportation Code.

History of Prop. Code §70.504: Acts 2007, 80th Leg., ch. 330, §1, eff. Sept. 1, 2007.

PROP §70.505. EXPIRATION & DISCHARGE OF LIEN

A lien under this subchapter does not expire and is discharged only when the landowner receives payment of the lien.

History of Prop. Code §70.505: Acts 2007, 80th Leg., ch. 330, §1, eff. Sept. 1, 2007.

PROP §70.506. REMOVAL OF VEHICLE FROM LANDOWNER'S PROPERTY

A landowner whose fence is damaged by a motor vehicle that is then abandoned on the owner's property, or the landowner's agent, may:

(1) select a towing service to remove the vehicle from the landowner's property; and

(2) designate the time at which the towing service may enter the property to remove the vehicle.

History of Prop. Code §70.506: Acts 2007, 80th Leg., ch. 330, §1, eff. Sept. 1, 2007.

TITLE 6. UNCLAIMED PROPERTY

CHAPTER 71. ESCHEAT OF PROPERTY

SUBCHAPTER A. GENERAL PROVISIONS

PROP §71.001. ESCHEAT

(a) If an individual dies intestate and without heirs, the real and personal property of that individual is subject to escheat.

(b) "Escheat" means the vesting of title to property in the state in an escheat proceeding under Subchapter B.

History of Prop. Code §71.001: Acts 1983, 68th Leg., ch. 576, §1, eff. Jan. 1, 1984. Amended by Acts 1985, 69th Leg., ch. 230, §2, eff. Sept. 1, 1985. Source: TRCS art. 3272, §1.

ANNOTATIONS

Texas Mun. League Intergov'tal Risk Pool v. TWCC, 74 S.W.3d 377, 382 (Tex.2002). "Under absolute-escheat statutes, the state acquires title to property through operation of law or a judicial proceeding. ... Escheat statutes, whether absolute or custodial, are constitutional if they give potential claimants notice after the state acquires the funds and an administrative and judicial hearing to adjudicate claims. A state must also use reasonable diligence to discover the potential claimants to the property."

PROP §71.002. PRESUMPTION OF DEATH

An individual is presumed dead for the purpose of determining if the individual's real or personal property is subject to escheat if the individual:

(1) is absent from the individual's place of residence for seven years or longer; and

(2) is not known to exist.

History of Prop. Code §71.002: Acts 1983, 68th Leg., ch. 576, §1, eff. Jan. 1, 1984. Amended by Acts 1985, 69th Leg., ch. 230, §3, eff. Sept. 1, 1985. Source: TRCS art. 3272, §§1, 2.

See also CPRC §§133.001-133.003; Est. Code ch. 454.

ANNOTATIONS

Latham v. Tombs, 73 S.W. 1060, 1060 (Tex.App.—Austin 1903, no writ). "[T]he person referred to must absent himself from his home, and proof of change of residence from one State to another, and the party not having been heard of in the former State for a period of seven years, does not make a case within the purview of the statute."

PROP §71.003. PRESUMPTION OF INTESTACY

An individual is presumed to have died intestate if, on or before the seventh anniversary of the date of the individual's death, the individual's will has not been recorded or probated in the county where the individual's property is located.

History of Prop. Code §71.003: Acts 1983, 68th Leg., ch. 576, §1, eff. Jan. 1, 1984. Source: TRCS art. 3272, §1.

See also Est. Code §§201.001, 201.002.

PROP §71.004. PRESUMPTION OF DEATH WITHOUT HEIRS

An individual is presumed to have died leaving no heirs if for the seven-year period preceding the court's determination:

(1) a lawful claim to the individual's property has not been asserted; and

(2) a lawful act of ownership of the individual's property has not been exercised.

History of Prop. Code §71.004: Acts 1983, 68th Leg., ch. 576, §1, eff. Jan. 1, 1984. Source: TRCS art. 3272, §1.

PROP §71.005. ACT OF OWNERSHIP

For the purposes of this chapter, an individual exercises a lawful act of ownership in property by, personally or through an agent, paying taxes to this state on the property.

History of Prop. Code §71.005: Acts 1983, 68th Leg., ch. 576, §1, eff. Jan. 1, 1984. Source: TRCS art. 3272, §1.

PROP §71.006. REVIEW OF PROBATE DECREE

(a) If the state claims that an estate that has been administered in probate court in this state is subject to escheat, the state may have the judgment of the probate court reviewed by filing a petition in district court alleging that the administration of the estate was obtained by fraud or mistake of fact.

(b) The case shall be tried in accordance with the law for the revision and correction of a decree of the probate court.

History of Prop. Code §71.006: Acts 1983, 68th Leg., ch. 576, §1, eff. Jan. 1, 1984. Source: TRCS art. 3288.

PROP §71.007. IDENTIFICATION OF REAL PROPERTY SUBJECT TO ESCHEAT

The tax assessor-collector of each county shall:

(1) take all steps necessary to identify real property that may be subject to escheat; and

(2) notify the commissioner of the General Land Office and the attorney general so that they may take appropriate action.

History of Prop. Code §71.007: Acts 2003, 78th Leg., ch. 1276, §13.002(d), eff. Sept. 1, 2003.

Sections 71.008-71.100 reserved for expansion

SUBCHAPTER B. ESCHEAT PROCEEDINGS

PROP §71.101. PETITION FOR ESCHEAT

(a) If any person, including the attorney general, the comptroller, or a district attorney, criminal district attorney, county attorney, county clerk, district clerk, or attorney ad litem is informed or has reason to believe that real or personal property is subject to escheat under this chapter, the person may file a sworn petition requesting the escheat of the property and requesting a writ of possession for the property.

(b) The petition must contain:

(1) a description of the property;

(2) the name of the deceased owner of the property;

(3) the name of the tenants or persons claiming the estate, if known; and

(4) the facts supporting the escheat of the estate.

(c) If the petition is filed by a person other than the attorney general, the person shall send to the attorney general written notice of the filing and a copy of the petition to permit the attorney general to elect to participate on behalf of the state.

(d) An action brought under this section is governed by the procedure relating to class actions provided by the Texas Rules of Civil Procedure.

(e) A petition filed under this section is not subject to an objection relating to misjoinder of parties or causes of action.

History of Prop. Code §71.101: Acts 1983, 68th Leg., ch. 576, §1, eff. Jan. 1, 1984. Amended by Acts 1985, 69th Leg., ch. 230, §4, eff. Sept. 1, 1985; Acts 1991, 72nd Leg., ch. 153, §1, eff. Sept. 1, 1991; Acts 1997, 75th Leg., ch. 1037, §4 (eff. Sept. 1, 1997), ch. 1423, §16.01 (eff. Sept. 1, 1997). Source: TRCS art. 3273.

See also TRCP 42.

ANNOTATIONS

Branham v. Minear, 199 S.W.2d 841, 845 (Tex. App.—Eastland 1947, writ ref'd n.r.e.). "'The proceeding to enforce an escheat is in the nature of an inquest of office. [T]he escheat must be established in the manner prescribed and all the requirements of the statute substantially complied with.'"

Robinson v. State, 87 S.W.2d 297, 298 (Tex. App.—El Paso 1935, writ dism'd). "If in truth the circumstances exist which escheat the property to the state, the title vests in the state by operation of law upon the death of the owner. And the only purpose of the proceedings provided by the statutes is to secure a judicial declaration that the facts exist which, under the law, cast title upon the state. [¶] [T]he Legislature very properly placed upon the state the burden of using ordinary diligence to discover claimants of the estate before bringing its action to establish its title thereto. [¶] We are further of the opinion that the Legislature, by requiring that the diligence used be alleged, also intended that proof be made of the facts as alleged, and that the state is not entitled to a judgment until it has made such proof."

PROP §71.102. CITATION

(a) If a petition is filed under this subchapter, the district clerk shall issue citation as in other civil suits to:

(1) each defendant alleged by the petition to possess or claim the property that is the subject of the petition;

(2) any person required by this chapter to be cited; and

(3) persons interested in the estate, including lienholders of record.

(b) The citation required by Subdivision (3) of Subsection (a) must be published as required for other civil suits and must:

(1) briefly state the contents of the petition; and

(2) request all persons interested in the estate to appear and answer at the next term of the court.

History of Prop. Code §71.102: Acts 1983, 68th Leg., ch. 576, §1, eff. Jan. 1, 1984. Amended by Acts 1985, 69th Leg., ch. 923, §21, eff. Aug. 26, 1985. Source: TRCS arts. 3274, 3275.

PROP §71.103. PARTY TO PROCEEDING

(a) A person who exercises a lawful act of ownership in property that is the subject of an escheat proceeding must be made a party to the proceeding by:

(1) personal service of citation if the person is a resident of this state and the person's address can be obtained by reasonable diligence; or

(2) service of citation on a person's agent if the person is a nonresident or a resident who cannot be found and the agent can be found by the use of reasonable diligence.

(b) For the purposes of this section, reasonable diligence includes an inquiry and investigation of the records of the office of the tax assessor-collector of the county in which the property sought to be escheated is located.

(c) The comptroller is an indispensable party to any judicial or administrative proceeding concerning the disposition and handling of property that is the subject of an escheat proceeding and must be made a party to the proceeding by personal service of citation.

History of Prop. Code §71.103: Acts 1983, 68th Leg., ch. 576, §1, eff. Jan. 1, 1984. Amended by Acts 1991, 72nd Leg., ch. 153, §2, eff. Sept. 1, 1991; Acts 1997, 75th Leg., ch. 1037, §5 (eff. Sept. 1, 1997), ch. 1423, §16.02 (eff. Sept. 1, 1997). Source: TRCS art. 3272, §1.

ANNOTATIONS

Robinson v. State, 87 S.W.2d 297, 298 (Tex. App.—El Paso 1935, writ dism'd). See annotation under Property Code §71.101, p. 332.

PROP §71.104. APPEARANCE OF CLAIMANTS

Any person, whether named in the escheat petition or not, who claims an interest in property that is the subject of an escheat proceeding may appear, enter a pleading, and oppose the facts stated in the petition.

History of Prop. Code §71.104: Acts 1983, 68th Leg., ch. 576, §1, eff. Jan. 1, 1984. Source: TRCS art. 3276.

PROP §71.105. TRIAL

(a) If a person appears and denies the state's right to the property or opposes a material fact of the petition, the court shall try the issue as any other issue of fact.

(b) The court may order a survey as in other cases in which the title or the boundary of the land is in question.

History of Prop. Code §71.105: Acts 1983, 68th Leg., ch. 576, §1, eff. Jan. 1, 1984. Source: TRCS art. 3278.

PROP §71.106. DEFAULT JUDGMENT

If citation is issued in accordance with Section 71.102 and no person answers within the period provided by the Texas Rules of Civil Procedure, the court shall render a default judgment in favor of the state.

History of Prop. Code §71.106: Acts 1983, 68th Leg., ch. 576, §1, eff. Jan. 1, 1984. Source: TRCS art. 3277.

See also TRCP 99(b), 239, 239a, 240; *O'Connor's Texas Rules*, "Deadline to Answer," ch. 3-E, §2, p. 263; "Default Judgment," ch. 7-A, p. 671.

PROP §71.107. JUDGMENT FOR STATE

(a) If the court renders a judgment for the state finding that an intestate died without heirs, the property escheats to the state and title to the property is considered to pass to the state on the date of death of the owner as established by the escheat proceeding. The court may award court costs to the state.

(b) If the judgment involves real property, the state may sell the property under the general laws governing the sale of Permanent School Fund lands, and, after the second anniversary of the date of the final judgment, the court shall issue a writ of possession for the property.

(c) If the judgment involves personal property, the court shall issue a writ of possession that contains an adequate description of the property as in other cases for recovery of personal property.

(d) When the record of an escheat proceeding reflects that a lienholder or his predecessor received actual or constructive notice of the escheat proceeding, the entry of the judgment in the escheat proceeding

will either satisfy or extinguish any lien which the lienholder or his predecessor claimed or could have claimed on the escheated property at the escheat proceeding.

(e) The sheriff, constable, court clerk, or other officer appointed by the judge in an escheat proceeding shall execute a writ of possession by filing the writ with the deed or map records of the county when the escheated property relates to realty and by serving the writ on any holder, tenant, or occupant of any escheated property. Additionally, the person who executes a writ of possession shall either:

(1) post the writ for at least three consecutive weeks on the door or posting board of the county courthouse in the county where the proceeding was conducted or in the county where the property is located; or

(2) in the case of real property, post the writ for at least two consecutive weeks at a reasonably conspicuous place on the realty; or

(3) publicize the writ in any other fashion ordered by the court.

(f) After validly executing a writ of possession, the sheriff, constable, court clerk, or other appointed officer shall note the method of the execution of the writ on the writ return and shall return the writ to the clerk to be filed in the court records of the escheat proceeding.

History of Prop. Code §71.107: Acts 1983, 68th Leg., ch. 576, §1, eff. Jan. 1, 1984. Amended by Acts 1985, 69th Leg., ch. 230, §5 (eff. Sept. 1, 1985), ch. 923, §22 (eff. Aug. 26, 1985). Source: TRCS art. 3279.

PROP §71.108. COSTS PAID BY STATE

If the property does not escheat, the state shall pay court costs. The clerk of the court shall certify the amount of the costs, and when the certificate is filed in the office of the comptroller of public accounts, the comptroller shall issue a warrant for the amount of the costs.

History of Prop. Code §71.108: Acts 1983, 68th Leg., ch. 576, §1, eff. Jan. 1, 1984. Source: TRCS art. 3280.

PROP §71.109. APPEAL; WRIT OF ERROR

A party who appeared at an escheat proceeding may appeal the judgment rendered or may file an application for a writ of error on the judgment. The attorney general or the other person acting on behalf of the state in the escheat proceeding may make an appeal or file the writ.

History of Prop. Code §71.109: Acts 1983, 68th Leg., ch. 576, §1, eff. Jan. 1, 1984. Source: TRCS art. 3284.

Sections 71.110-71.200 reserved for expansion

SUBCHAPTER C. DISPOSITION OF ESCHEATED PROPERTY

PROP §71.201. SEIZURE & SALE OF PERSONAL PROPERTY

(a) If personal property escheated to the state, the court shall issue to the sheriff a writ that commands the sheriff to seize the escheated property.

(b) The sheriff shall:

(1) dispose of the personal property at public auction in accordance with the law regarding the sale of personal property under execution; and

(2) deposit into the State Treasury the proceeds of the sale, less court costs.

History of Prop. Code §71.201: Acts 1983, 68th Leg., ch. 576, §1, eff. Jan. 1, 1984. Source: TRCS art. 3282.

See also TRCP 631, 633.

PROP §71.202. DISPOSITION OF REAL PROPERTY

(a) Real property that escheats to the state under this title before January 1, 1985, becomes a part of the permanent school fund. Real property that escheats to the state on or after January 1, 1985, is held in trust by the Commissioner of the General Land Office for the use and benefit of the foundation school fund. The revenue from all leases, sales, and use of land held for the foundation school fund shall be deposited to the credit of the foundation school fund.

(b) Before the 91st day after the day on which a judgment that provides for the recovery of real property is rendered, the clerk of the district court rendering the judgment shall send to the Commissioner of the General Land Office:

(1) a certified copy of the judgment; and

(2) notice of any appeal of that judgment.

(c) The commissioner shall list real property as escheated foundation school fund land or permanent school land as appropriate when the commissioner receives:

(1) a certified copy of a judgment under which the property escheats to the state and from which appeal is not taken; or

(2) a certified copy of notice of the affirmance on appeal of a judgment under which the property escheats to the state.

History of Prop. Code §71.202: Acts 1983, 68th Leg., ch. 576, §1, eff. Jan. 1, 1984. Amended by Acts 1984, 68th Leg., 2nd C.S., ch. 28, art. II, part B, §13, eff. Sept. 1, 1984. Source: TRCS art. 3281.

PROP §71.203. ACCOUNT OF ESCHEATED PROPERTY

The comptroller shall keep an account of the money paid to and real property vested in this state under this chapter.

History of Prop. Code §71.203: Acts 1983, 68th Leg., ch. 576, §1, eff. Jan. 1, 1984. Source: TRCS art. 3285.

Sections 71.204-71.300 reserved for expansion

SUBCHAPTER D. RECOVERY OF ESCHEATED PROPERTY

PROP §71.301. SUIT FOR ESCHEATED PERSONAL PROPERTY

(a) If personal property of a deceased owner escheats to the state under this chapter and is delivered to the state, a person who claims the property as an heir, devisee, or legatee of the deceased may file suit against the state in a district court of Travis County, Texas. The suit must be filed on or before the fourth anniversary of the date of the final judgment of the escheat proceeding.

(b) The petition must state the nature of the claim and request that the money be paid to the claimant.

(c) A copy of the petition shall be served on the comptroller, who shall represent the interests of the state. As the comptroller elects and with the approval of the attorney general, the attorney general, the county attorney or criminal district attorney for the county, or the district attorney for the district shall represent the comptroller.

History of Prop. Code §71.301: Acts 1983, 68th Leg., ch. 576, §1, eff. Jan. 1, 1984. Amended by Acts 1991, 72nd Leg., ch. 153, §3, eff. Sept. 1, 1991; Acts 1997, 75th Leg., ch. 1037, §6 (eff. Sept. 1, 1997), ch. 1423, §16.03 (eff. Sept. 1, 1997). Source: TRCS art. 3286.

PROP §71.302. RECOVERY OF PERSONAL PROPERTY

(a) If in a suit filed under Section 71.301 the court finds that a claimant is entitled to recover personal property, the court shall order the comptroller to issue a warrant for payment of the claim without interest or costs.

(b) A copy of the order under seal of the court is sufficient voucher for issuing the warrant.

History of Prop. Code §71.302: Acts 1983, 68th Leg., ch. 576, §1, eff. Jan. 1, 1984. Source: TRCS art. 3287.

PROP §71.303. SUIT FOR ESCHEATED REAL PROPERTY

(a) If real property escheats to the state under this chapter, a person who was not personally served with citation in the escheat proceedings may file suit in the district court of Travis County for all or a part of the property. The suit must be filed not later than the second anniversary of the date of the final judgment in the escheat proceedings.

(b) A copy of the petition must be served on the attorney general, who shall represent the interests of the state.

(c) To the extent the claimant is adjudged to be the owner of all or a part of the property, the state is divested of the property.

History of Prop. Code §71.303: Acts 1983, 68th Leg., ch. 576, §1, eff. Jan. 1, 1984. Amended by Acts 1991, 72nd Leg., ch. 153, §4, eff. Sept. 1, 1991. Source: TRCS art. 3283.

PROP §71.304. STATE AS PARTY IN SUIT FOR ASSETS

(a) A suit brought for the collection of personal property delivered to the comptroller under this chapter must be brought in the name of this state.

(b) A suit brought for the possession of real property held in trust by the Commissioner of the General Land Office under this chapter must be brought in the name of this state.

History of Prop. Code §71.304: Acts 1983, 68th Leg., ch. 576, §1, eff. Jan. 1, 1984. Amended by Acts 1991, 72nd Leg., ch. 153, §4, eff. Sept. 1, 1991; Acts 1997, 75th Leg., ch. 1037, §7 (eff. Sept. 1, 1997), ch. 1423, §16.04 (eff. Sept. 1, 1997). Source: TRCS art. 3289.

CHAPTER 72. ABANDONMENT OF PERSONAL PROPERTY

SUBCHAPTER A. GENERAL PROVISIONS

PROP §72.001. APPLICATION OF CHAPTER

(a) Tangible or intangible personal property is subject to this chapter if it is covered by Section 72.101 and:

(1) the last known address of the apparent owner, as shown on the records of the holder, is in this state;

(2) the records of the holder do not disclose the identity of the person entitled to the property, and it is

established that the last known address of the person entitled to the property is in this state;

(3) the records of the holder do not disclose the last known address of the apparent owner, and it is established that:

(A) the last known address of the person entitled to the property is in this state; or

(B) the holder is a domiciliary or a government or governmental subdivision or agency of this state and has not previously paid or delivered the property to the state of the last known address of the apparent owner or other person entitled to the property;

(4) the last known address of the apparent owner, as shown on the records of the holder, is in a state that does not provide by law for the escheat or custodial taking of the property or is in a state in which the state's escheat or unclaimed property law is not applicable to the property, and the holder is a domiciliary or a government or governmental subdivision or agency of this state;

(5) the last known address of the apparent owner, as shown on the records of the holder, is in a foreign nation and the holder is a domiciliary or a government or governmental subdivision or agency of this state; or

(6) the transaction out of which the property arose occurred in this state and:

(A) the last known address of the apparent owner or other person entitled to the property is:

(i) unknown; or

(ii) in a state that does not provide by law for the escheat or custodial taking of the property or in a state in which the state's escheat or unclaimed property law is not applicable to the property; and

(B) the holder is a domiciliary of a state that does not provide by law for the escheat or custodial taking of the property or a state in which the state's escheat or unclaimed property law is not applicable to the property.

(b) This chapter supplements other chapters in this title, and each chapter shall be followed to the extent applicable.

(c) This chapter applies to property held by life insurance companies with the exception of unclaimed proceeds to which Chapter 1109, Insurance Code, applies and that are held by those companies that are subject to Chapter 1109, Insurance Code.

(d) A holder of property presumed abandoned under this chapter is subject to the procedures of Chapter 74.

(e) In this chapter, a holder is a person, wherever organized or domiciled, who is:

(1) in possession of property that belongs to another;

(2) a trustee; or

(3) indebted to another on an obligation.

(f) In this chapter, a corporation shall be deemed to be a domiciliary of the state of its incorporation.

History of Prop. Code §72.001: Acts 1983, 68th Leg., ch. 576, §1, eff. Jan. 1, 1984. Amended by Acts 1985, 69th Leg., ch. 230, §7, eff. Sept. 1, 1985; Acts 1987, 70th Leg., ch. 426, §2, eff. Sept. 1, 1987; Acts 1991, 72nd Leg., ch. 153, §5, eff. Sept. 1, 1991; Acts 2001, 77th Leg., ch. 1419, §30, eff. June 1, 2003. Source: TRCS arts. 3272a, §§1, 10, 10a, 14; 3273.

ANNOTATIONS

Melton v. State, 993 S.W.2d 95, 100 (Tex.1999). "A 'holder' is a person who is (1) in possession of property that belongs to another, (2) a trustee, or (3) indebted to another on an obligation. *At 101:* We hold that the county clerk's statutory custody and control over cash bail bonds confers holder status on the clerk."

Sections 72.002-72.100 reserved for expansion

SUBCHAPTER B. PRESUMPTION OF ABANDONMENT

PROP §72.101. PERSONAL PROPERTY PRESUMED ABANDONED

(a) Except as provided by this section and Sections 72.1015, 72.1016, 72.1017, 72.102, and 72.104, personal property is presumed abandoned if, for longer than three years:

(1) the existence and location of the owner of the property is unknown to the holder of the property; and

(2) according to the knowledge and records of the holder of the property, a claim to the property has not been asserted or an act of ownership of the property has not been exercised.

(b)(1) The three-year period leading to a presumption of abandonment of stock or another intangible ownership interest in a business association, the existence of which is evidenced by records available to the association, commences on the first date that either a sum payable as a result of the ownership interest is unclaimed by the owner or a communication to the owner is returned undelivered by the United States Postal Service.

(2) The running of the three-year period of abandonment ceases immediately on the exercise of an act of ownership interest or sum payable or a commu-

nication with the association as evidenced by a memorandum or other record on file with the association or its agents.

(3) At the time an ownership is presumed abandoned under this section, any sum then held for interest or owing to the owner as a result of the interest and not previously presumed abandoned is presumed abandoned.

(4) Any stock or other intangible ownership interest enrolled in a plan that provides for the automatic reinvestment of dividends, distributions, or other sums payable as a result of the ownership interest is subject to the presumption of abandonment as provided by this section.

(c) Property distributable in the course of a demutualization or related reorganization of an insurance company is presumed abandoned on the first anniversary of the date the property becomes distributable if, at the time of the first distribution, the last known address of the owner according to the records of the holder of the property is known to be incorrect or the distribution or statements related to the distribution are returned by the post office as undeliverable and the owner has not:

(1) communicated in writing with the holder of the property or the holder's agent regarding the interest; or

(2) otherwise communicated with the holder regarding the interest as evidenced by a memorandum or other record on file with the holder or its agents.

(d) Property distributable in the course of a demutualization or related reorganization of an insurance company that is not subject to Subsection (c) is presumed abandoned as otherwise provided by this section.

(e) This section does not apply to money collected as child support that:

(1) is being held for disbursement by the state disbursement unit under Chapter 234, Family Code, or a local registry, as defined by Section 101.018, Family Code, pending identification and location of the person to whom the money is owed; or

(2) has been disbursed by the state disbursement unit under Chapter 234, Family Code, by electronic funds transfer into a child support debit card account established for an individual under Section 234.010, Family Code, but not activated by the individual.

History of Prop. Code §72.101: Acts 1983, 68th Leg., ch. 576, §1, eff. Jan. 1, 1984. Amended by Acts 1985, 69th Leg., ch. 230, §9, eff. Sept. 1, 1985; Acts 1987, 70th Leg., ch. 426, §3, eff. Sept. 1, 1987; Acts 1991, 72nd Leg., ch. 153, §6, eff. Sept. 1, 1991; Acts 1993, 73rd Leg., ch. 36, §3.01, eff. Sept. 1, 1993; Acts 2003, 78th Leg., 3rd C.S., ch. 3, §§2.01, 3.01, eff. Jan. 11, 2004; Acts 2005, 79th Leg., ch. 81, §2, eff. Sept. 1, 2005; Acts 2009, 81st Leg., ch. 550, §2 (eff. June 19, 2009), ch. 767, §34 (eff. June 19, 2009); Acts 2011, 82nd Leg., ch. 685, §1, eff. Sept. 1, 2011; Acts 2015, 84th Leg., ch. 606, §1, eff. Sept. 1, 2015.

ANNOTATIONS

Melton v. State, 993 S.W.2d 95, 98-99 (Tex.1999). "The fact that [D's] 'existence and location' may have been 'known' when the bond was filed does not mean that it is 'known' after the passage of more than three years with no request from [D] for the bond's release. We conclude that knowledge of [D's] name and last known address at the time the bond was filed does not preclude the application of §72.101(a)."

Texas Dept. of Banking v. Mount Olivet Cemetery Ass'n, 27 S.W.3d 276, 284 (Tex.App.—Austin 2000, pet. denied). "Once property is presumed abandoned, the Comptroller assumes responsibility for it and essentially steps into the shoes of the absent owner."

Tex. Atty. Gen. Op. No. GA-0061 (2003). Section 72.101(a) "establishes the general parameters of the presumption. [¶] There is no provision that establishes the beginning of the dormancy period for property such as unauthorized fees collected by a county or municipality and there is no case law on the issue. [¶] We conclude that the dormancy period for these unauthorized fees begins on the date a fee, or partial payment of a fee, is paid. [¶] If an individual was allowed to make multiple payments, the dormancy period for each payment starts to run on the date of the payment." *See also* ***Tex. Atty. Gen. Op.*** No. JC-0195 (2000).

PROP §72.1015. UNCLAIMED WAGES

(a) In this section, "wages" has the meaning assigned by Section 61.001, Labor Code.

(b) An amount of unclaimed wages is presumed abandoned if, for longer than one year:

(1) the existence and location of the person to whom the wages are owed is unknown to the holder of the wages; and

(2) according to the knowledge and records of the holder of the wages, a claim to the wages has not been asserted or an act of ownership of the wages has not been exercised.

History of Prop. Code §72.1015: Acts 2003, 78th Leg., 3rd C.S., ch. 3, §2.02, eff. Jan. 11, 2004. Source: TRCS art. 3272a, §1.

PROP §72.1016. STORED VALUE CARD

(a) This section applies to a stored value card, as defined by Section 604.001, Business & Commerce Code, other than a card:

(1) to which Chapter 604, Business & Commerce Code, does not apply by operation of Sections 604.002(1)(A) and (C) and 604.002(2)-(5) of that code; or

(2) that is linked to and draws its value solely from a deposit account subject to Chapter 73.

(b) If the existence and location of the owner of a stored value card is unknown to the holder of the property, the stored value card is presumed abandoned to the extent of its unredeemed and uncharged value on the earlier of:

(1) the card's expiration date;

(2) the third anniversary of the date the card was issued, if the card is not used after it is issued, or the date the card was last used or value was last added to the card; or

(3) the first anniversary of the date the card was issued, if the card is not used after it is issued, or the date the card was last used or value was last added to the card, if the card's value represents wages, as defined by Section 61.001, Labor Code.

(c) If the person who sells or issues a stored value card in this state does not obtain the name and address of the apparent owner of the card and maintain a record of the owner's name and address and the identification number of the card, the address of the apparent owner is considered to be the Austin, Texas, address of the comptroller.

(d) A person may charge a fee against a stored value card as provided by Chapter 604, Business & Commerce Code. A fee may not be charged against a stored value card after the card is presumed abandoned under this section.

(e) The comptroller shall transfer five percent of the money collected from cards presumed to be abandoned for use as grants under Subchapter M, Chapter 56, Education Code.

(f) This section does not create a cause of action against a person who issues or sells a stored value card.

History of Prop. Code §72.1016: Acts 2005, 79th Leg., ch. 81, §3, eff. Sept. 1, 2005. Amended by Acts 2007, 80th Leg., ch. 885, §2.33, eff. Apr. 1, 2009.

PROP §72.1017. UTILITY DEPOSITS

(a) In this section:

(1) "Utility" has the meaning assigned by Section 183.001, Utilities Code.

(2) "Utility deposit" is a refundable money deposit a utility requires a user of the utility service to pay as a condition of initiating the service.

(b) Notwithstanding Section 73.102, a utility deposit is presumed abandoned on the latest of:

(1) the first anniversary of the date a refund check for the utility deposit was payable to the owner of the deposit;

(2) the first anniversary of the date the utility last received documented communication from the owner of the utility deposit; or

(3) the first anniversary of the date the utility issued a refund check for the deposit payable to the owner of the deposit if, according to the knowledge and records of the utility or payor of the check, during that period, a claim to the check has not been asserted or an act of ownership by the payee has not been exercised.

(c) A utility deposit is not presumed abandoned for two years from the time the depositor provides documentation to the utility of being called to active military service in any branch of the United States armed forces during any part of the period described by Subsection (b).

History of Prop. Code §72.1017: Acts 2011, 82nd Leg., ch. 685, §2, eff. Sept. 1, 2011. Amended by Acts 2011, 82nd Leg., 1st C.S., ch. 4, §5.01, eff. Sept. 28, 2011.

PROP §72.102. TRAVELER'S CHECK & MONEY ORDER

(a) A traveler's check or money order is not presumed to be abandoned under this chapter unless:

(1) the records of the issuer of the check or money order indicate that it was purchased in this state;

(2) the issuer's principal place of business is in this state and the issuer's records do not indicate the state in which the check or money order was purchased; or

(3) the issuer's principal place of business is in this state, the issuer's records indicate that the check or money order was purchased in another state, and the laws of that state do not provide for the escheat or custodial taking of the check or money order.

(b) A traveler's check to which Subsection (a) applies is presumed to be abandoned on the latest of:

(1) the 15th anniversary of the date on which the check was issued;

(2) the 15th anniversary of the date on which the issuer of the check last received from the owner of the check communication concerning the check; or

(3) the 15th anniversary of the date of the last writing, on file with the issuer, that indicates the owner's interest in the check.

(c) A money order to which Subsection (a) applies is presumed to be abandoned on the latest of:

(1) the third anniversary of the date on which the money order was issued;

(2) the third anniversary of the date on which the issuer of the money order last received from the owner of the money order communication concerning the money order; or

(3) the third anniversary of the date of the last writing, on file with the issuer, that indicates the owner's interest in the money order.

History of Prop. Code §72.102: Acts 1983, 68th Leg., ch. 576, §1, eff. Jan. 1, 1984. Amended by Acts 1985, 69th Leg., ch. 230, §10, eff. Sept. 1, 1985; Acts 1997, 75th Leg., ch. 1037, §8, eff. Sept. 1, 1997; Acts 2001, 77th Leg., ch. 179, §1, eff. June 1, 2004; Acts 2011, 82nd Leg., ch. 685, §3, eff. Sept. 1, 2011. Source: TRCS art. 3272a, §2.

E PROP §72.1021. SHARES OF MUTUAL FUND; DESIGNATION OF REPRESENTATIVE FOR NOTICE

(a) The owner of shares of a mutual fund may designate the name and a mailing or e-mail address of a representative of the owner only for the purpose of receiving the notice required by Section 74.1011. The owner is not required to designate a representative under this subsection.

(a-1) A holder of shares of a mutual fund shall notify the owner of the shares when the owner makes the initial purchase of shares in the fund that the owner may designate a representative under Subsection (a).

(b) The comptroller shall prescribe a form that a holder of shares of a mutual fund may make available to an owner of the shares to designate a representative for notice under this section.

(c) A representative for notice designated under this section does not have any rights to the mutual fund shares and may not access the shares.

(d) The running of the three-year period of abandonment under Section 72.101 ceases immediately if a representative designated under this section communicates to the holder that the representative knows:

(1) the owner's location; and

(2) that the owner exists and has not abandoned the shares of the mutual fund.

History of Prop. Code §72.1021: Acts 2015, 84th Leg., ch. 925, §1, eff. Sept. 1, 2017. Amended by H.B. 2964, §1, 85th Leg., eff. Sept. 1, 2017.

PROP §72.103. PRESERVATION OF PROPERTY

Notwithstanding any other provision of this title except a provision of this section or Section 72.1016 relating to a money order or a stored value card, a holder of abandoned property shall preserve the property and may not at any time, by any procedure, including a deduction for service, maintenance, or other charge, transfer or convert to the profits or assets of the holder or otherwise reduce the value of the property. For purposes of this section, value is determined as of the date of the last transaction or contact concerning the property, except that in the case of a money order, value is determined as of the date the property is presumed abandoned under Section 72.102(c). If a holder imposes service, maintenance, or other charges on a money order prior to the time of presumed abandonment, such charges may not exceed the amount of $1 per month for each month the money order remains uncashed prior to the month in which the money order is presumed abandoned.

History of Prop. Code §72.103: Acts 1983, 68th Leg., ch. 576, §1, eff. Jan. 1, 1984. Amended by Acts 1985, 69th Leg., ch. 230, §11, eff. Sept. 1, 1985; Acts 1997, 75th Leg., ch. 1037, §9, eff. Sept. 1, 1997; Acts 2001, 77th Leg., ch. 179, §2, eff. June 1, 2002; Acts 2005, 79th Leg., ch. 81, §4, eff. Sept. 1, 2005; Acts 2011, 82nd Leg., ch. 685, §4, eff. Sept. 1, 2011. Source: TRCS art. 3272a, §2.

ANNOTATIONS

GSC Enters. v. Rylander, 85 S.W.3d 469, 474 (Tex. App.—Austin 2002, no pet.). "Typically, the last contact or transaction between the purchaser of the money order and the holder is the moment when the money order is issued. According to the language of the statute then, the value of the property to be preserved will almost always be the face value of the money order. [¶] [S]ection 72.103 unambiguously provides that a holder of a money order may not deduct a contracted-for service charge from the money order that is eventually deemed abandoned property. After five years, the holder of the money order is to submit the entire face value to the Comptroller."

PROP §72.104. TANGIBLE PERSONAL PROPERTY HELD BY COUNTY

Tangible personal property that is found on county land or in a county park, facility, or right-of-way is presumed abandoned if, for longer than 120 days:

(1) the personal property is held by the county;

(2) the existence and location of the owner of the personal property is unknown to the county; and

(3) according to the knowledge and records of the county, a claim to the personal property has not been asserted or an act of ownership of the personal property has not been exercised.

History of Prop. Code §72.104: Acts 2015, 84th Leg., ch. 606, §2, eff. Sept. 1, 2015.

History of Former Prop. Code §72.104: Repealed by Acts 1985, 69th Leg., ch. 230, §20(b), eff. Sept. 1, 1985.

PROP §72.105. REPEALED

Repealed by Acts 1985, 69th Leg., ch. 230, §20(b), eff. Sept. 1, 1985.

Sections 72.106-72.200 reserved for expansion

SUBCHAPTERS C TO H. REPEALED

Repealed by Acts 1985, 69th Leg., ch. 230, §20(b), eff. Sept. 1, 1985.

CHAPTER 73. PROPERTY HELD BY FINANCIAL INSTITUTIONS

SUBCHAPTER A. GENERAL PROVISIONS

PROP §73.001. DEFINITIONS & APPLICATION OF CHAPTER

(a) In this chapter:

(1) "Account" means funds deposited with a depository in an interest-bearing account, a checking or savings account, or a child support debit card account established under Section 234.010, Family Code, or funds received by a depository in exchange for the purchase of a stored value card.

(2) "Depositor" means a person who has an ownership interest in an account.

(3) "Owner" means a person who has an ownership interest in a safe deposit box.

(4) "Holder" means a depository.

(5) "Check" includes a draft, cashier's check, certified check, registered check, or similar instrument.

(b) This chapter supplements other chapters in this title, and each chapter shall be followed to the extent applicable.

(c) Any property, other than an account, check, or safe deposit box, held by a depository is subject to the abandonment provisions of Chapter 72.

(d) A holder of accounts, checks, or safe deposit boxes presumed abandoned under this chapter is subject to the procedures of Chapter 74.

History of Prop. Code §73.001: Acts 1983, 68th Leg., ch. 576, §1, eff. Jan. 1, 1984. Amended by Acts 1985, 69th Leg., ch. 230, §13, eff. Sept. 1, 1985; Acts 1991, 72nd Leg., ch. 153, §§7, 8, eff. Sept. 1, 1991; Acts 1997, 75th Leg., ch. 1037, §§11, 12, eff. Sept. 1, 1997; Acts 2005, 79th Leg., ch. 81, §5, eff. Sept. 1, 2005; Acts 2009, 81st Leg., ch. 551, §3 (eff. June 19, 2009), ch. 767, §35 (eff. June 19, 2009). Source: TRCS art. 3272b, §1.

PROP §73.002. DEPOSITORY

For the purposes of this chapter, a depository is a bank, savings and loan association, credit union, or other banking organization that:

(1) receives and holds a deposit of money or the equivalent of money in banking practice or other personal property in this state; or

(2) receives and holds such a deposit or other personal property in another state for a person whose last known residence is in this state.

History of Prop. Code §73.002: Acts 1983, 68th Leg., ch. 576, §1, eff. Jan. 1, 1984. Amended by Acts 1997, 75th Leg., ch. 1037, §13, eff. Sept. 1, 1997. Source: TRCS art. 3272b, §1.

PROP §73.003. PRESERVATION OF INACTIVE ACCOUNT OR SAFE DEPOSIT BOX

(a) A depository shall preserve an account that is inactive and the contents of a safe deposit box that is inactive. The depository may not, at any time, by any procedure, including the imposition of a service charge, transfer or convert to the profits or assets of the depository or otherwise reduce the value of the account or the contents of such a box. For purposes of this subsection, value is determined as of the date the account or safe deposit box becomes inactive.

(b) An account is inactive if for more than one year there has not been a debit or credit to the account because of an act by the depositor or an agent of the depositor, other than the depository, and the depositor has not communicated with the depository. A safe deposit box is inactive if the rental on the box is delinquent.

(c) This section does not affect the provisions of Subchapter B, Chapter 59, Finance Code.

History of Prop. Code §73.003: Acts 1983, 68th Leg., ch. 576, §1, eff. Jan. 1, 1984. Amended by Acts 1984, 68th Leg., 2nd C.S., ch. 18, §8(b), eff. Oct. 2, 1984; Acts 1985, 69th Leg., ch. 230, §14, eff. Sept. 1, 1985; Acts 1991, 72nd Leg., ch. 153, §9, eff. Sept. 1, 1991; Acts 1993, 73rd Leg., ch. 36, §3.02, eff. Sept. 1, 1993; Acts 1995, 74th Leg., ch. 914, §11, eff. Sept. 1, 1995; Acts 1997, 75th Leg., ch. 1037, §13, eff. Sept. 1, 1997; Acts 1999, 76th Leg., ch. 62, §7.85, eff. Sept. 1, 1999. Source: TRCS art. 3272b, §1.

PROP §73.004. REPEALED

Repealed by Acts 1997, 75th Leg., ch. 1037, §40, eff. Sept. 1, 1997.

Sections 73.005-73.100 reserved for expansion

SUBCHAPTER B. PRESUMPTION OF ABANDONMENT

PROP §73.101. INACTIVE ACCOUNT OR SAFE DEPOSIT BOX PRESUMED ABANDONED

(a) An account or safe deposit box is presumed abandoned if:

(1) except as provided by Subsection (c), the account or safe deposit box has been inactive for at least five years as determined under Subsection (b);

(2) the location of the depositor of the account or owner of the safe deposit box is unknown to the depository; and

(3) the amount of the account or the contents of the box have not been delivered to the comptroller in accordance with Chapter 74.

(b) For purposes of Subsection (a)(1):

(1) an account becomes inactive beginning on the date of the depositor's last transaction or correspondence concerning the account; and

(2) a safe deposit box becomes inactive beginning on the date a rental was due but not paid.

(c) If the account is a checking or savings account or is a matured certificate of deposit, the account is presumed abandoned if the account has been inactive for at least three years as determined under Subsection (b)(1).

History of Prop. Code §73.101: Acts 1983, 68th Leg., ch. 576, §1, eff. Jan. 1, 1984. Amended by Acts 1984, 68th Leg., 2nd C.S., ch. 18, §8(d), eff. Oct. 2, 1984; Acts 1985, 69th Leg., ch. 230, §16, eff. Sept. 1, 1985; Acts 1991, 72nd Leg., ch. 153, §§11, 12, eff. Sept. 1, 1991; Acts 1997, 75th Leg., ch. 1037, §14 (eff. Sept. 1, 1997), ch. 1423, §16.05 (eff. Sept. 1, 1997); Acts 2011, 82nd Leg., ch. 685, §5, eff. Sept. 1, 2011. Source: TRCS art. 3272b, §3.

PROP §73.102. CHECKS

A check is presumed to be abandoned on the latest of:

(1) the third anniversary of the date the check was payable;

(2) the third anniversary of the date the issuer or payor of the check last received documented communication from the payee of the check; or

(3) the third anniversary of the date the check was issued if, according to the knowledge and records of the issuer or payor of the check, during that period, a claim to the check has not been asserted or an act of ownership by the payee has not been exercised.

History of Prop. Code §73.102: Acts 1997, 75th Leg., ch. 1037, §15, eff. Sept. 1, 1997.

E PROP §73.103. DESIGNATION OF REPRESENTATIVE FOR NOTICE

(a) The depositor of an account or the owner of the contents of a safe deposit box may designate the name and a mailing or e-mail address of a representative of the depositor or the owner only for the purpose of receiving the notice required by Section 74.1011. The depositor or owner is not required to designate a representative under this subsection.

(b) The comptroller shall prescribe a form that a holder of an account or the contents of a safe deposit box may make available to a depositor of the account or owner of the contents of the box to designate a representative for notice under this section.

(c) A representative for notice designated under this section does not have any rights to the account or safe deposit box and may not access the account or box.

(d) The running of a period of abandonment under Section 73.101 ceases immediately if a representative designated under this section communicates to the holder that the representative knows:

(1) the depositor's or owner's location; and

(2) that the depositor or owner exists and has not abandoned the account or the contents of a safe deposit box.

History of Prop. Code §73.103: Acts 2015, 84th Leg., ch. 925, §2, eff. Sept. 1, 2017.

History of Former Prop. Code §73.103: Repealed by Acts 1985, 69th Leg., ch. 230, §20(c), eff. Sept. 1, 1985.

PROP §73.104. REPEALED

Repealed by Acts 1985, 69th Leg., ch. 230, §20(c), eff. Sept. 1, 1985.

Sections 73.105-73.200 reserved for expansion

SUBCHAPTERS C TO F. REPEALED

Repealed by Acts 1985, 69th Leg., ch. 230, §20(c), eff. Sept. 1, 1985.

CHAPTER 74. REPORT, DELIVERY, & CLAIMS PROCESS

PROPERTY CODE
CHAPTER 74. REPORT, DELIVERY, & CLAIMS PROCESS
§§74.001 - 74.101

SUBCHAPTER A. APPLICABILITY

PROP §74.001. APPLICABILITY

(a) Except as provided by Subsection (b), this chapter applies to a holder of property that is presumed abandoned under Chapter 72, Chapter 73, or Chapter 75.

(b) This chapter does not apply to a holder of property subject to Chapter 76.

(c) This chapter does not apply to small credit balances held by an institution of higher education in an unclaimed money fund under Section 51.011, Education Code.

History of Prop. Code §74.001: Acts 1985, 69th Leg., ch. 230, §17, eff. Sept. 1, 1985. Amended by Acts 1991, 72nd Leg., ch. 153, §13, eff. Sept. 1, 1991; Acts 1997, 75th Leg., ch. 1037, §16, eff. Sept. 1, 1997; Acts 2003, 78th Leg., ch. 465, §2 (eff. Sept. 1, 2003), 3rd C.S., ch. 3, §2.03 (eff. Jan. 11, 2004); Acts 2011, 82nd Leg., ch. 1049, §1.07, eff. June 17, 2011.

ANNOTATIONS

Highland Homes Ltd. v. State, 448 S.W.3d 403, 411 (Tex.2014). "Chapter 74 does not apply when a claim to property has been asserted or an act of ownership exercised. It is of no consequence that several owners have not *collected* their property within the time period to which they agreed through class representatives. An owner need not actually *collect* his property to rebut the presumption of abandonment and render the [Unclaimed Property] Act inapplicable; he need only *claim* it. Nor is the settlement's labeling of undistributed refunds as 'unclaimed funds' determinative; the refunds were, in fact, claimed."

Sections 74.002-74.100 reserved for expansion

SUBCHAPTER B. PROPERTY REPORT

Ⓐ PROP §74.101. PROPERTY REPORT

(a) Each holder who on March 1 holds property that is presumed abandoned under Chapter 72, 73, or 75 of this code or under Chapter 154, Finance Code, shall file a report of that property on or before the following July 1. The comptroller may require the report to be in a particular format, including a format that can be read by a computer.

(b) Repealed by Acts 1999, 76th Leg., ch. 1208, §5, eff. Sept. 1, 1999.

(c) The property report must include, if known by the holder:

(1) the name, social security number, driver's license or state identification number, e-mail address, and [the] last known address of:

(A) each person who, from the records of the holder of the property, appears to be the owner of the property; or

(B) any person who is entitled to the property;

(2) the name and last known mailing or e-mail address of any person designated as a representative for notice under Section 72.1021 or 73.103;

(3) a description of the property, the identification number, if any, and, if appropriate, a balance of each account, except as provided by Subsection (d);

(4) [(3)] the date that the property became payable, demandable, or returnable;

(5) [(4)] the date of the last transaction with the owner concerning the property; and

(6) [(5)] other information that the comptroller by rule requires to be disclosed as necessary for the administration of this chapter.

(d) Amounts due that individually are less than $25 may be reported in the aggregate without furnishing any of the information required by Subsection (c).

(e) A holder of mineral proceeds under Chapter 75 that is regulated by the Railroad Commission of Texas under Chapter 91, Natural Resources Code, shall include in the property report for the proceeds, in addition to the information listed in Subsection (c), the following information with respect to each well the production from which resulted in the proceeds:

(1) the lease, property, or well name;

(2) any lease, property, or well identification number used to identify the lease, property, or well; and

(3) the county in which the lease, property, or well is located.

History of Prop. Code §74.101: Acts 1985, 69th Leg., ch. 230, §17, eff. Sept. 1, 1985. Amended by Acts 1987, 70th Leg., ch. 426, §4, eff. Sept. 1, 1987; Acts 1991, 72nd Leg., ch. 153, §14 (eff. Sept. 1, 1991), 1st C.S., ch. 1, §2 (eff. Sept. 1, 1991); Acts 1997, 75th Leg., ch. 1037, §17 (eff. Sept. 1, 1997), ch. 1423, §16.06 (eff. Sept. 1, 1997); Acts 1999, 76th Leg., ch. 62, §7.86 (eff. Sept. 1, 1999), ch. 1208, §5 (eff. Sept. 1, 1999); Acts 2003, 78th Leg., ch. 465, §3 (eff. Sept. 1, 2003), 3rd C.S., ch. 3, §2.04 (eff. Jan. 11, 2004); Acts 2009, 81st Leg., ch. 232, §1, eff. Sept. 1, 2009; Acts 2011, 82nd Leg., ch. 685, §6, eff. Jan. 1, 2013; Acts 2015, 84th Leg., ch. 118, §2 (eff. Sept. 1, 2015), ch. 480, §1 (eff. Jan. 1, 2016), ch. 925, §3 (eff. Sept. 1, 2017). Source: TRCS ch. 465, §3, art. 3272a, §§1, 2.

See also Fin. Code ch. 154; Prop. Code chs. 72, 73, 75.

A PROP §74.1011. NOTICE BY PROPERTY HOLDER REQUIRED

(a) Except as provided by Subsection (b), a holder who on March 1 holds property valued at more than $250 that is presumed abandoned under Chapter 72, 73, or 75 of this code or Chapter 154, Finance Code, shall, on or before the following May 1, mail to the last known address of the known owner written notice stating that:

(1) the holder is holding the property; and

(2) the holder may be required to deliver the property to the comptroller on or before July 1 if the property is not claimed.

(b) The notice required under Subsection (a) does not apply to a holder who:

(1) has already provided such notice to the owner of the property or a person entitled to the property under existing federal law, rules, and regulations or state law within the time specified under Subsection (a); or

(2) does not have a record of an address for the property owner or any other person entitled to the property.

(b-1) If an owner has designated a representative for notice under Section 72.1021 or 73.103, the holder shall mail or e-mail the written notice required under Subsection (a) to the representative in addition to mailing the notice to the owner.

(c) A holder that provides notice under this section may charge the cost of the postage as a service charge against the property.

History of Prop. Code §74.1011: Acts 2009, 81st Leg., ch. 232, §2, eff. Sept. 1, 2009. Amended by Acts 2011, 82nd Leg., ch. 685, §7, eff. Jan. 1, 2013; Acts 2015, 84th Leg., ch. 925, §4, eff. Sept. 1, 2017.

PROP §74.102. SIGNED STATEMENT

(a) The person preparing a property report shall provide with each copy of the report a statement signed by:

(1) the individual holding the reported property;

(2) a partner, if the holder is a partnership;

(3) an officer, if the holder is an unincorporated association or a private corporation; or

(4) the chief fiscal officer, if the holder is a public corporation.

(b) The statement must include the following sentence:

"This report contains a full and complete list of all property held by the undersigned that, from the knowledge and records of the undersigned, is abandoned under the laws of the State of Texas."

(c) The comptroller may adopt rules or policies relating to the signature requirement, as the comptroller determines appropriate, to maximize the use of future developments in electronic filing technology.

History of Prop. Code §74.102: Acts 1985, 69th Leg., ch. 230, §17, eff. Sept. 1, 1985. Amended by Acts 1997, 75th Leg., ch. 1037, §18, eff. Sept. 1, 1997; Acts 1999, 76th Leg., ch. 1208, §1, eff. Sept. 1, 1999. Source: TRCS art. 3272a, §2.

A

PROP §74.103. RETENTION OF RECORDS

(a) A holder required to file a property report under Section 74.101 shall keep a record of:

(1) the name, the social security number, if known, and the last known address of each person who, from the records of the holder of the property, appears to be the owner of the property;

(2) the name and last known mailing or e-mail address of any representative for notice designated under Section 72.1021 or 73.103;

(3) a brief description of the property, including the identification number, if any; and

(4) [~~(3)~~] the balance of each account, if appropriate.

(b) The record must be kept for 10 years from the date on which the property is reportable, regardless of whether the property is reported in the aggregate under Section 74.101.

(c) The comptroller may by rule provide for a shorter period for keeping a record required by this section.

(d) The comptroller may determine the liability of a holder required to file a property report under Section 74.101 using the best information available to the comptroller if the records of the holder are unavailable or incomplete for any portion of the required retention period.

History of Prop. Code §74.103: Acts 1985, 69th Leg., ch. 230, §17, eff. Sept. 1, 1985. Amended by Acts 1997, 75th Leg., ch. 1037, §19 (eff. Sept. 1, 1997), ch. 1423, §16.07 (eff. Sept. 1, 1997); Acts 2003, 78th Leg., ch. 1310, §84, eff. Sept. 1, 2003; Acts 2015, 84th Leg., ch. 925, §5, eff. Sept. 1, 2017.

PROP §74.104. CONFIDENTIALITY OF PROPERTY REPORT; EXCEPTIONS

(a) Except as provided by Subsection (c) and Section 74.201, 74.203, or 74.307, a property report filed with the comptroller under Section 74.101 is confidential until the second anniversary of the date the report is filed.

(b) The social security number of an owner that is provided to the comptroller is confidential.

(c) The information reported under Section 74.101(e) is confidential and not subject to disclosure under Chapter 552, Government Code.

(d) Notwithstanding Subsection (c), the comptroller may release the information about a well reported under Section 74.101(e) to a claimant of mineral proceeds from the well if the claim is approved by the comptroller under Section 74.501.

(e) Notwithstanding Subsection (c), the information compiled under Section 74.307(a)(2) is subject to disclosure under Chapter 552, Government Code.

History of Prop. Code §74.104: Acts 1991, 72nd Leg., ch. 153, §15, eff. Sept. 1, 1991. Amended by Acts 1997, 75th Leg., ch. 1037, §20 (eff. Sept. 1, 1997), ch. 1423, §16.08 (eff. Sept. 1, 1997); Acts 2015, 84th Leg., ch. 480, §§2, 3, eff. Jan. 1, 2016.

ANNOTATIONS

Tex. Atty. Gen. Op. No. OR-00399 (2006). Government Code §552.101 "excepts from disclosure 'information considered to be confidential by law, either constitutional, statutory, or by judicial decision….' Section 552.101 encompasses [Prop. Code] §74.104…. Under [Prop. Code] ch. 74 …, a holder of property presumed abandoned … must file a report of the property with the Comptroller of Public Accounts. … Under [Prop. Code] §76.101 …, a municipality holding property that is presumed abandoned and is subject to [Prop. Code] ch. 76 must file a report of the property with the treasurer of the municipality. [¶] The public availability of the property reports required under [Prop. Code] §74.101 is governed by [Prop. Code] §§74.104 and 76.104…."

Sections 74.105-74.200 reserved for expansion

SUBCHAPTER C. NOTICE BY COMPTROLLER

PROP §74.201. REQUIRED NOTICE

(a) Except as provided by Section 74.202, the comptroller may use one or more methods as necessary to provide the most efficient and effective notice to each reported owner in the calendar year immediately following the year in which the report required by Section 74.101 is filed. The notice must be provided:

(1) in the county of the property owner's last known address; or

(2) in the county in which the holder has its principal place of business or its registered office for service in this state, if the property owner's last address is unknown.

(b) The notice must state that the reported property is presumed abandoned and subject to this chapter and must contain:

(1) the name and city of last known address of the reported owner;

(2) a statement that, by inquiry, any person possessing a legal or beneficial interest in the reported property may obtain information concerning the amount and description of the property; and

(3) a statement that the person may present proof of the claim and establish the person's right to receive the property.

(c) Deleted by Acts 1997, 75th Leg., ch. 1037, §21, eff. Sept. 1, 1997.

(d) The comptroller may offer for sale space for suitable advertisements in a notice published under this section.

History of Prop. Code §74.201: Acts 1985, 69th Leg., ch. 230, §17, eff. Sept. 1, 1985. Amended by Acts 1987, 70th Leg., ch. 426, §5, eff. Sept. 1, 1987; Acts 1991, 72nd Leg., ch. 153, §16, eff. Sept. 1, 1991; Acts 1993, 73rd Leg., ch. 36, §3.03, eff. Sept. 1, 1993; Acts 1997, 75th Leg., ch. 1037, §21 (eff. Sept. 1, 1997), ch. 1423, §16.09 (eff. Sept. 1, 1997). Source: TRCS art. 3272a, §3(b), (c).

PROP §74.202. NOTICE FOR ITEM WITH VALUE OF LESS THAN $100

In the notice required by Section 74.201, the comptroller is not required to publish information regarding an item having a value that is less than $100 unless the comptroller determines that publication of that information is in the public interest.

History of Prop. Code §74.202: Acts 1985, 69th Leg., ch. 230, §17, eff. Sept. 1, 1985. Amended by Acts 1997, 75th Leg., ch. 571, §1 (eff. Sept. 1, 1997), ch. 1037, §21 (eff. Sept. 1, 1997), ch. 1423, §16.10 (eff. Sept. 1, 1997). Source: TRCS art. 3272a, §3(d).

PROP §74.203. AUTHORIZED NOTICE

(a) During the calendar year immediately following the year in which the report required by Section 74.101 is filed, notice may be mailed to each person who has been reported with a Texas address and appears to be entitled to the reported property.

(b) The notice under Subsection (a) must conform to the requirements for notice under Section 74.201(b).

History of Prop. Code §74.203: Acts 1985, 69th Leg., ch. 230, §17, eff. Sept. 1, 1985. Amended by Acts 1991, 72nd Leg., ch. 153, §17, eff. Sept. 1, 1991; Acts 1997, 75th Leg., ch. 1037, §21 (eff. Sept. 1, 1997), ch. 1423, §16.11 (eff. Sept. 1, 1997). Source: TRCS art. 3272a, §3(e), (f).

PROP §74.204. REPEALED

Repealed by Acts 1997, 75th Leg., ch. 1097, §40, eff. Sept. 1, 1997.

PROP §74.205. CHARGE FOR NOTICE

The comptroller may charge the following against the property delivered under this chapter:

(1) expenses incurred for the publication of notice required by Section 74.201; and

(2) the amount paid in postage for the notice to the owner required by Section 74.203.

History of Prop. Code §74.205: Acts 1985, 69th Leg., ch. 230, §17, eff. Sept. 1, 1985. Amended by Acts 1997, 75th Leg., ch. 1037, §22 (eff. Sept. 1, 1997), ch. 1423, §16.12 (eff. Sept. 1, 1997). Source: TRCS art. 3272b, §3.

Sections 74.206-74.300 reserved for expansion

SUBCHAPTER D. DELIVERY

PROP §74.301. DELIVERY OF PROPERTY TO COMPTROLLER

(a) Except as provided by Subsection (c), each holder who on March 1 holds property that is presumed abandoned under Chapter 72, 73, or 75 shall deliver the property to the comptroller on or before the following July 1 accompanied by the report required to be filed under Section 74.101.

(b) If the property subject to delivery under Subsection (a) is stock or some other intangible ownership interest in a business association for which there is no evidence of ownership, the holder shall issue a duplicate certificate or other evidence of ownership to the comptroller at the time delivery is required under this section.

(c) If the property subject to delivery under Subsection (a) is the contents of a safe deposit box, the comptroller may instruct a holder to deliver the property on a specified date before July 1 of the following year.

History of Prop. Code §74.301: Acts 1985, 69th Leg., ch. 230, §17, eff. Sept. 1, 1985. Amended by Acts 1991, 72nd Leg., ch. 153, §§19, 30(2), eff. Sept. 1, 1991; Acts 1997, 75th Leg., ch. 1037, §22 (eff. Sept. 1, 1997), ch. 1423, §16.13 (eff. Sept. 1, 1997); Acts 1999, 76th Leg., ch. 1208, §2, eff. Sept. 1, 1999; Acts 2003, 78th Leg., ch. 465, §4 (eff. Sept. 1, 2003), 3rd C.S., ch. 3, §2.05 (eff. Jan. 11, 2004); Acts 2011, 82nd Leg., ch. 685, §8, eff. Jan. 1, 2013. Source: TRCS art. 3272a, §§3(c), 4(b).

ANNOTATIONS

Melton v. State, 993 S.W.2d 95, 102 (Tex.1999). "Because [CCP art. 17.02] speaks specifically to the release of cash bail bonds, it controls over the more general Property Code provisions [§74.301] regarding delivery of abandoned property. Accordingly, we hold that the clerk has no duty to deliver abandoned cash bail bonds until the court in the underlying criminal prosecution has ordered their release."

PROP §74.3011. DELIVERY OF MONEY TO RURAL SCHOLARSHIP FUND

(a) Notwithstanding and in addition to any other provision of this chapter or other law, a local telephone exchange company may deliver reported money to a scholarship fund for rural students instead of delivering the money to the comptroller as prescribed by Section 74.301.

(b) A local telephone exchange company may deliver the money under this section only to a scholarship fund established by one or more local telephone exchange companies in this state to enable needy students from rural areas to attend college, technical school, or another postsecondary educational institution.

(c) A local telephone exchange company shall file with the comptroller a verification of money delivered under this section that complies with Section 74.302.

(d) A claim for money delivered to a scholarship fund under this section must be filed with the local telephone exchange company that delivered the money. The local telephone exchange company shall forward the claim to the administrator of the scholarship fund to which the money was delivered. The scholarship fund shall pay the claim if the fund determines in good faith that the claim is valid. A person aggrieved by a claim decision may file a suit against the fund in a district court in the county in which the administrator of the scholarship fund is located in accordance with Section 74.506.

(e) The comptroller shall prescribe forms and procedures governing this section, including forms and procedures relating to:

(1) notice of presumed abandoned property;

(2) delivery of reported money to a scholarship fund; and

(3) filing of a claim.

(f) In this section, "local telephone exchange company" means a telecommunications utility certificated to provide local exchange service within the state and that is a telephone cooperative or has fewer than 50,000 access lines in service in this state.

(g) During a state fiscal year, the total amount of money that may be transferred by all local telephone exchange companies under this section may not exceed $800,000. The comptroller shall keep a record of the total amount of money transferred annually. When the total amount of money transferred during a state fiscal year equals the amount allowed by this subsection, the comptroller shall notify each local telephone exchange company that the company may not transfer any additional money to the company's scholarship fund during the remainder of that state fiscal year.

History of Prop. Code §74.3011: Acts 1995, 74th Leg., ch. 231, §50(a), eff. Sept. 1, 1995. Amended by Acts 1997, 75th Leg., ch. 1037, §23 (eff. Sept. 1, 1997), ch. 1423, §16.14 (eff. Sept. 1, 1997); Acts 2007, 80th Leg., ch. 163, §1, eff. Sept. 1, 2007.

PROP §74.3012. DELIVERY OF MONEY TO URBAN SCHOLARSHIP FUND

(a) Notwithstanding and in addition to any other provision of this chapter or other law, a local exchange company may deliver reported money to a scholarship fund for urban students instead of delivering the money to the comptroller as prescribed by Section 74.301.

(b) A local exchange company may deliver the money under this section only to a scholarship fund established by one or more local exchange companies in this state to enable needy students from urban areas to attend college, technical school, or another postsecondary educational institution.

(c) A local exchange company shall file with the comptroller a verification of money delivered under this section that complies with Section 74.302.

(d) A claim for money delivered to a scholarship fund under this section must be filed with the local exchange company that delivered the money. The local exchange company shall forward the claim to the administrator of the scholarship fund to which the money was delivered. The scholarship fund shall pay the claim if the fund determines in good faith that the claim is valid. A person aggrieved by a claim decision may file a suit against the fund in a district court in the county in which the administrator of the scholarship fund is located in accordance with Section 74.506.

(e) The comptroller shall prescribe forms and procedures governing this section, including forms and procedures relating to:

(1) notice of presumed abandoned property;

(2) delivery of reported money to a scholarship fund; and

(3) filing of a claim.

(f) In this section, "local exchange company" means a telecommunications utility certificated to provide local exchange telephone service within the state and that has 50,000 or more access lines in service in this state and is not a telephone cooperative.

(g) During each state fiscal year, the total amount of money that may be transferred by all local exchange companies under this section may not exceed the total amount of money transferred to rural scholarship funds under Section 74.3011 during the previous state fiscal year. The comptroller shall keep a record of the total amount of money transferred annually. If the total amount of money transferred during a state fiscal year

equals the amount allowed by this subsection, the comptroller shall notify each local exchange company that the company may not transfer any additional money to the company's scholarship fund during the remainder of that state fiscal year.

History of Prop. Code §74.3012: Acts 1995, 74th Leg., ch. 231, §51(a), eff. Sept. 1, 1995. Amended by Acts 1997, 75th Leg., ch. 1037, §24 (eff. Sept. 1, 1997), ch. 1423, §16.15 (eff. Sept. 1, 1997).

PROP §74.3013. DELIVERY OF MONEY FOR RURAL SCHOLARSHIP, ECONOMIC DEVELOPMENT, & ENERGY EFFICIENCY ASSISTANCE

(a) Notwithstanding and in addition to any other provision of this chapter or other law, a nonprofit cooperative corporation may deliver reported money to a scholarship fund for rural students, to stimulate rural economic development, or to provide energy efficiency assistance to members of electric cooperatives, instead of delivering the money to the comptroller as prescribed in Section 74.301.

(b) A nonprofit cooperative corporation may deliver the money under this section only:

(1) to a scholarship fund established by one or more nonprofit cooperative corporations in this state to enable students from rural areas to attend college, technical school, or other postsecondary educational institution;

(2) to an economic development fund for the stimulation and improvement of business and commercial activity for economic development in rural communities; and

(3) to an energy efficiency assistance fund to assist members of an electric cooperative in reducing their energy consumption and electricity bills.

(c) A nonprofit cooperative corporation shall file with the comptroller a verification of money delivered under this section that complies with Section 74.302.

(d) A claim for money delivered under this section must be filed with the nonprofit cooperative corporation that delivered the money. A nonprofit cooperative corporation shall forward the claim to the administrator of the fund to which the money was delivered. The fund shall pay the claim if the fund determines in good faith that the claim is valid. A person aggrieved by a claim decision may file a suit against the fund in a district court in the county in which the administrator of the fund is located in accordance with Section 74.506.

(e) The comptroller shall prescribe forms and procedures governing this section, including forms and procedures relating to:

(1) notice of presumed abandoned property;

(2) delivery of reported money to a scholarship, economic development fund, or energy efficiency assistance fund;

(3) filing of a claim; and

(4) procedures to allow equitable opportunity for participation by each nonprofit cooperative corporation in the state.

(f) During a state fiscal year the total amount of money that may be transferred by all nonprofit cooperative corporations under this section may not exceed $2 million. No more than 20 percent of each nonprofit cooperative's funds eligible for delivery under this section shall be used for economic development. The comptroller shall adopt procedures to record the total amount of money transferred annually.

(g) Nonprofit cooperative corporations may combine funds from other sources with any funds delivered under this section. In addition, such cooperatives may engage in other business and commercial activities, in their own behalf or through such subsidiaries and affiliates as deemed necessary, in order to provide and promote educational opportunities and to stimulate rural economic development.

(h) In this section, a nonprofit cooperative corporation means a cooperative corporation organized under Chapters 51 and 52, Agriculture Code, the Texas Non-Profit Corporation Act (Article 1396-1.01 et seq., Vernon's Texas Civil Statutes), the Cooperative Association Act (Article 1396-50.01, Vernon's Texas Civil Statutes), and Chapter 161, Utilities Code.

History of Prop. Code §74.3013: Acts 1997, 75th Leg., ch. 904, §1, eff. Sept. 1, 1997. Amended by Acts 1999, 76th Leg., ch. 62, §18.45, eff. Sept. 1, 1999; Acts 2007, 80th Leg., ch. 939, §§14, 15, eff. Sept. 1, 2007.

PROP §74.302. STATEMENT OF DELIVERED PROPERTY

(a) Property delivered under Section 74.301 must be accompanied by a statement that:

(1) the property delivered is a complete and correct remittance of all accounts subject to this chapter in the holder's possession;

(2) the existence and location of the listed owners are unknown to the holder; and

(3) the listed owners have not asserted a claim or exercised an act of ownership with respect to the owner's reported property.

(b) The statement required by Subsection (a) shall be signed by:

(1) the individual holding the reported property;

(2) a partner, if the holder is a partnership;

(3) an officer, if the holder is an unincorporated association or a private corporation; or

(4) the chief fiscal officer, if the holder is a public corporation.

History of Prop. Code §74.302: Acts 1985, 69th Leg., ch. 230, §17, eff. Sept. 1, 1985. Amended by Acts 1991, 72nd Leg., ch. 153, §20, eff. Sept. 1, 1991; Acts 1999, 76th Leg., ch. 1208, §3, eff. Sept. 1, 1999.

PROP §74.303. REPEALED

Repealed by Acts 1991, 72nd Leg., ch. 153, §30, eff. Sept. 1, 1991.

PROP §74.304. RESPONSIBILITY AFTER DELIVERY

(a) If reported property is delivered to the comptroller, the state shall assume custody of the property and responsibility for its safekeeping.

(b) A holder who delivers property to the comptroller in good faith is relieved of all liability to the extent of the value of the property delivered for any claim then existing, that may arise after delivery to the comptroller, or that may be made with respect to the property.

(c) If the holder delivers property to the comptroller in good faith and, after delivery, a person claims the property from the holder or another state claims the property under its laws relating to escheat or unclaimed property, the attorney general shall, on written notice of the claim, defend the holder against the claim, and the holder shall be indemnified from the unclaimed money received under this chapter or any other statute requiring delivery of unclaimed property to the comptroller against any liability on the claim.

(d) The comptroller is not, in the absence of negligence or mishandling of the property, liable to the person who claims the property for damages incurred while the property or the proceeds from the sale of the property are in the comptroller's possession. But in any event the liability of the state is limited to the extent of the property delivered under this chapter and remaining in the possession of the comptroller at the time a suit is filed.

(e) For the purposes of this section, payment or delivery is made in good faith if:

(1) payment or delivery was made in a reasonable attempt to comply with this chapter;

(2) the holder delivering the property was not a fiduciary then in breach of trust with respect to the property and had a reasonable basis for believing based on the facts then known to the holder that the property was abandoned or inactive for purposes of this chapter; and

(3) there is no showing that the records under which the delivery was made did not meet reasonable commercial standards of practice in the industry.

(f) On delivery of a duplicate certificate or other evidence of ownership to the comptroller under Subsection (b) of Section 74.301, the holder and any transfer agent, registrar, or other person acting for or on behalf of a holder in executing or delivering the duplicate certificate are relieved of all liability of every kind in accordance with this section to any person, including any person acquiring the original certificate or the duplicate of the certificate issued to the comptroller, for any losses or damages resulting to any person by the issuance and delivery to the comptroller of the duplicate certificate.

History of Prop. Code §74.304: Acts 1985, 69th Leg., ch. 230, §17, eff. Sept. 1, 1985. Amended by Acts 1997, 75th Leg., ch. 1037, §25 (eff. Sept. 1, 1997), ch. 1423, §16.16 (eff. Sept. 1, 1997). Source: TRCS art. 3272a, §4(c).

ANNOTATIONS

Combs v. B.A.R.D. Indus., 299 S.W.3d 463, 469 (Tex.App.—Austin 2009, no pet.). "[P] sought to recover damages for 'the Comptroller's failure to return [P's] property and to promptly tender funds received from its unlawful sale,' which 'deprived [P] of the increased value of the securities and the interest earned while in the wrongful possession of the Comptroller.' According to [P's] pleadings, the property that was delivered under [Prop. Code] ch. 74 is the ... stock certificates, while the property that the Comptroller 'is still, at the time of filing suit, in possession of' is '[P's] interest that was earned while the Comptroller possessed [P's] property and after [P] asserted ownership.' [Property Code §74.304], by its plain language, does not waive immunity unless the property giving rise to damages is *both* 'delivered under this chapter' *and* 'remaining in the possession' of the Comptroller when suit is filed."

Clark v. Strayhorn, 184 S.W.3d 906, 911 (Tex. App.—Austin 2006, pet. denied). Claimant's "contention that unclaimed property is held in trust for owners and that interest must be paid rests primarily on [Prop.

Code §§74.304 and 74.601]. ... We ... conclude that the Comptroller is directed to invest the unclaimed property for the benefit of the State, not the owners. *At 915:* We hold that the unclaimed property act does not require the State to hold unclaimed property in trust or otherwise require payment of interest to owners. Moreover, the State's use of unclaimed property and retention of any interest earned before the owner asserts a claim is not an unconstitutional taking."

Texas Dept. of Banking v. Mount Olivet Cemetery Ass'n, 27 S.W.3d 276, 284 (Tex.App.—Austin 2000, pet. denied). "The purpose of removing abandoned property from the possession of the holder is to relieve that holder of any further liability with regard to such property and place it in the hands of the State, thereby providing a means for the absent owner to reclaim the abandoned property."

PROP §74.305. REPEALED

Repealed by Acts 1997, 75th Leg., ch. 1037, §40, eff. Sept. 1, 1997.

PROP §74.306. UNCLAIMED PROPERTY HELD BY FEDERAL GOVERNMENT

(a) If the federal government enacts a law that provides for the discovery of unclaimed property held by the federal government and that provides or makes that information available to the states, the comptroller may pay to the federal government from the unclaimed money received under this chapter or any other statute requiring the delivery of unclaimed property to the comptroller the proportional share of the necessary cost of examining records.

(b) If the federal government delivers unclaimed property to the comptroller, this state shall hold the federal government harmless from claims made by owners of the property after the delivery.

History of Prop. Code §74.306: Acts 1985, 69th Leg., ch. 230, §17, eff. Sept. 1, 1985. Amended by Acts 1997, 75th Leg., ch. 1037, §25 (eff. Sept. 1, 1997), ch. 1423, §16.18 (eff. Sept. 1, 1997). Source: TRCS art. 3272a, §11.

PROP §74.3061. ESCHEAT OF FUNDS IN THE POSSESSION OF THE UNITED STATES

(a) In the event any money is due to a resident of this state in the nature of a refund, rebate, or other overpayment of taxes or fees to the United States with respect to which the resident is likely to have his rights to secure such refund or rebate barred by a statute of limitations, or if for any reason at least three years has elapsed after the date on which the resident could have filed a timely claim for said refund or rebate, the comptroller is appointed agent of such resident to apply for said refund or rebate and is authorized to do any act which a natural person could do to recover said money. When the comptroller files an application or initiates any other proceeding to secure said refund or rebate, the comptroller is coupled with an interest in the money sought and money recovered. All property within this provision, including all principal and interest accruing thereon, is declared to have escheated and to have become the property of the state.

(b) The funds escheated by the state pursuant to this provision shall be given notice as provided by Section 74.201. Title to any such property shall be transferred by the state to any persons who in accordance with Subchapter F can show that the property belonged to them immediately prior to the escheat or that they were heirs to those funds immediately prior to the escheat.

History of Prop. Code §74.3061: Acts 1997, 75th Leg., ch. 1037, §25, eff. Sept. 1, 1997.

PROP §74.307. LIST OF OWNERS; OTHER PUBLIC INFORMATION

(a) The comptroller shall compile and revise each year:

(1) except as to amounts reported in the aggregate, an alphabetical list of the names and last known addresses of the owners listed in the reports and the amount credited to each account; and

(2) an alphabetical list by county of:

(A) the number of reports filed under Section 74.101 for mineral proceeds attributable to all wells located in each respective county; and

(B) the aggregate amount of mineral proceeds reported under Section 74.101 attributable to all wells, if any, located in each respective county.

(b) The comptroller shall make the lists available for public inspection during all reasonable business hours.

History of Prop. Code §74.307: Acts 1985, 69th Leg., ch. 230, §17, eff. Sept. 1, 1985. Amended by Acts 1997, 75th Leg., ch. 1037, §25 (eff. Sept. 1, 1997), ch. 1423, §16.19 (eff. Sept. 1, 1997); Acts 2015, 84th Leg., ch. 480, §4, eff. Jan. 1, 2016.

PROP §74.308. PERIOD OF LIMITATION NOT A BAR

The expiration, on or after September 1, 1987, of any period specified by contract, statute, or court order, during which an action or proceeding may be initiated or enforced to obtain payment of a claim for money or recovery of property, does not prevent the money or

property from being presumed abandoned property and does not affect any duty to file a report required by this chapter or to pay or deliver abandoned property to the comptroller.

History of Prop. Code §74.308: Acts 1987, 70th Leg., ch. 426, §5, eff. Sept. 1, 1987. Amended by Acts 1997, 75th Leg., ch. 1037, §25 (eff. Sept. 1, 1997), ch. 1423, §16.20 (eff. Sept. 1, 1997).

ANNOTATIONS

Highland Homes Ltd. v. State, 448 S.W.3d 403, 409 (Tex.2014). "The State argues that [Prop. Code §§74.308 and 74.309] prohibit the *cy pres* award in this case. Specifically, under §74.308, the 90-day period for negotiating settlement checks does not preclude a presumption that amounts not paid to class members are abandoned, and §74.309 prohibits the diversion of settlement funds.... *At 410-11:* The State's argument assumes that absent class members have neither asserted claims nor exercised acts of ownership in the litigation. But they have—through the class representatives. ... Class representatives' actions are those of class members, and are therefore binding on class members, including absent class members, so long as the requirements of due process are met. [¶] The property—settlement payments on refund claims—cannot be presumed abandoned, not because of the 90-day limitation on negotiating settlement checks, but because the property was not unclaimed. To the contrary, this property was claimed by the owners—all settlement class members—through their representatives. For the same reason, §74.309 does not apply in these circumstances."

PROP §74.309. PRIVATE ESCHEAT AGREEMENTS PROHIBITED

An individual, corporation, business association, or other organization may not act through amendment of articles of incorporation, amendment of bylaws, private agreement, or any other means to take or divert funds or personal property into income, divide funds or personal property among locatable patrons or stockholders, or divert funds or personal property by any other method for the purpose of circumventing the unclaimed property process.

History of Prop. Code §74.309: Acts 1987, 70th Leg., ch. 426, §5, eff. Sept. 1, 1987.

ANNOTATIONS

Highland Homes Ltd. v. State, 448 S.W.3d 403, 409 (Tex.2014). See annotation under Property Code §74.308, this page.

Sections 74.310-74.400 reserved for expansion

SUBCHAPTER E. DISPOSITION OF DELIVERED PROPERTY

PROP §74.401. SALE OF PROPERTY

(a) Except as provided by Subsection (c) or Section 74.404, the comptroller shall sell at public sale all personal property, other than money and marketable securities, delivered to the comptroller in accordance with Section 74.301. The comptroller shall conduct the sale in the city in this state that the comptroller determines affords the most favorable market for the particular property.

(b) The comptroller shall sell the property to the highest bidder. If the comptroller determines that the highest bid is insufficient, the comptroller may decline that bid and offer the property for public or private sale.

(c) The comptroller is not required to offer property for sale if the property belongs to a person with an address outside this state or the comptroller determines that the probable cost of the sale of the property exceeds its value.

(d) If after investigation the comptroller determines that property delivered from a safe deposit box or other repository has insubstantial commercial value, the comptroller may destroy or otherwise dispose of the property at any time.

(e) A person may not maintain any action or proceeding against the state, an officer of the state, or the holder of property because of an action taken by the comptroller under this section.

History of Prop. Code §74.401: Acts 1985, 69th Leg., ch. 230, §17, eff. Sept. 1, 1985. Amended by Acts 1993, 73rd Leg., ch. 36, §3.04, eff. Sept. 1, 1993; Acts 1997, 75th Leg., ch. 1037, §26 (eff. Sept. 1, 1997), ch. 1423, §16.21 (eff. Sept. 1, 1997); Acts 2001, 77th Leg., ch. 800, §1, eff. Sept. 1, 2001. Source: TRCS art. 3272a, §5(a).

ANNOTATIONS

Tex. Atty. Gen. Op. No. GA-0309 (2005). "With respect to disposing of unclaimed, unmarketable securities that have escheated to the state, which the comptroller must sell under [Prop. Code] §74.401(a), the comptroller generally is not an underwriter for purposes of 15 U.S.C. §77e(a) [, which regulates the sale of unregistered securities]. Accordingly, she must sell the securities at public sale in compliance with ... §74.401(a)."

PROP §74.402. NOTICE OF SALE

Before the 21st day preceding the day on which a public sale is held under Section 74.401, the comptroller shall publish notice of the sale in a newspaper of general circulation in Travis County or in the county where the sale is to be held. If the public sale is to be held on the Internet or by an online auction, the comptroller may post the notice on the comptroller's own website before the seventh day preceding the date on which the sale or auction is held.

History of Prop. Code §74.402: Acts 1985, 69th Leg., ch. 230, §17, eff. Sept. 1, 1985. Amended by Acts 1993, 73rd Leg., ch. 36, §3.05, eff. Sept. 1, 1993; Acts 1997, 75th Leg., ch. 1037, §26 (eff. Sept. 1, 1997), ch. 1423, §16.22 (eff. Sept. 1, 1997); Acts 2001, 77th Leg., ch. 1263, §80, eff. Sept. 1, 2001. Source: TRCS art. 3272a, §5(b).

PROP §74.403. PURCHASER'S TITLE

(a) At a sale, public or private, of property that is held under this subchapter, the purchaser receives title to the purchased property free from all claims of the prior owner and prior holder of the property and all persons claiming through or under the owner or holder.

(b) The comptroller shall execute all documents necessary to complete the transfer of title.

History of Prop. Code §74.403: Acts 1985, 69th Leg., ch. 230, §17, eff. Sept. 1, 1985. Amended by Acts 1997, 75th Leg., ch. 1037, §27 (eff. Sept. 1, 1997), ch. 1423, §16.23 (eff. Sept. 1, 1997). Source: TRCS art. 3272a, §5(c).

PROP §74.404. SALE OF MILITARY AWARDS & DECORATIONS PROHIBITED

(a) In this section, "military award or decoration" means a military decoration for an act of valor, heroism, or exceptional service, a good conduct medal, a service medal, a service ribbon, or a badge, tab, certificate, or letter awarded in connection with military service.

(b) A military award or decoration delivered to the comptroller under this chapter:

(1) may not be sold under Section 74.401 or destroyed; and

(2) shall be delivered by the comptroller to the Texas military forces.

(c) The Texas military forces shall conduct a reasonable search of public records to locate the person to whom the military award or decoration was awarded. If the department cannot locate the person, the department shall attempt to locate the person's next of kin. If the department locates the person or the person's next of kin, the department shall deliver the award or decoration to the person or the person's next of kin, as applicable.

(d) If the Texas military forces cannot locate the person to whom a military award or decoration was awarded or the person's next of kin, the award or decoration shall be held in trust for the comptroller at:

(1) a museum established by the department; or

(2) if no museum exists, any other public facility designated by the department.

(e) Except as provided by this subsection, a military award or decoration held in trust by a museum or facility designated under Subsection (d) shall be used in a display or exhibit that honors persons who have served the state or nation in military service. If the museum or facility cannot practically incorporate the award or decoration into an established display or exhibit of the museum or facility, the award or decoration shall be kept in a secure storage area or loaned to another museum for use in a display or exhibit that honors persons who have served the state or nation in military service.

(f) This section does not affect a person's right to claim a military award or decoration under Subchapter F.

History of Prop. Code §74.404: Acts 2001, 77th Leg., ch. 800, §2, eff. Sept. 1, 2001. Amended by Acts 2013, 83rd Leg., ch. 1217, §2.14, eff. Sept. 1, 2013.

Sections 74.405-74.500 reserved for expansion

SUBCHAPTER F. CLAIM FOR DELIVERED PROPERTY

A PROP §74.501. CLAIM FILED WITH COMPTROLLER

(a) The comptroller shall review the validity of each claim filed under this section.

(b) If the comptroller determines that a claim is valid, the comptroller or the comptroller's authorized agent shall approve the claim. If the claim is for money and has been approved under this section, the comptroller shall pay the claim. If a claim is for personal property other than money and has been approved under this section, the comptroller shall deliver the property to the claimant unless the comptroller has sold the property. If the property has been sold under Section 74.401, the comptroller shall pay to the claimant the proceeds from the sale.

(c) All claims to which this section applies must be filed in accordance with procedures, contain the information, and be on forms prescribed by the comptroller.

(d) On receipt of a claim form and all necessary documentation and as may be appropriate under the circumstances, the comptroller may approve the claim of:

(1) the reported owner of the property;

(2) if the reported owner died testate:

(A) the appropriate legal beneficiaries of the owner as provided by the last will and testament of the owner that has been accepted into probate or filed as a muniment of title; or

(B) the executor of the owner's last will and testament who holds current letters testamentary;

(3) if the reported owner died intestate:

(A) the legal heirs of the owner as provided by Sections 201.001 and 201.002, Estates [~~Section 38, Texas Probate~~] Code; or

(B) the court-appointed administrator of the owner's estate;

(4) the legal heirs of the reported owner as established by an affidavit of heirship order signed by a judge of the county probate court or by a county judge;

(5) if the reported owner is a minor child or an adult who has been adjudged incompetent by a court of law, the parent or legal guardian of the child or adult;

(6) if the reported owner is a corporation:

(A) the president or chair of the board of directors of the corporation, on behalf of the corporation; or

(B) any person who has legal authority to act on behalf of the corporation;

(7) if the reported owner is a corporation that has been dissolved or liquidated:

(A) the sole surviving shareholder of the corporation, if there is only one surviving shareholder;

(B) the surviving shareholders of the corporation in proportion to their ownership of the corporation, if there is more than one surviving shareholder;

(C) the corporation's bankruptcy trustee; or

(D) the court-ordered receiver for the corporation; or

(8) any other person that is entitled to receive the unclaimed property under other law or comptroller policy.

(e) Except as provided by Subsection (f), the comptroller may not pay to the following persons a claim to which this section applies:

(1) a creditor, a judgment creditor, a lienholder, or an assignee of the reported owner or of the owner's heirs; or

(2) a person holding a power of attorney from the reported owner or the owner's heirs.

(f) The comptroller may approve a claim for child support arrearages owed by the reported owner of the property and reflected in a child support lien notice that complies with Section 157.313, Family Code. A claim under this subsection may be submitted by the lienholder or the attorney general on behalf of the lienholder.

History of Prop. Code §74.501: Acts 1985, 69th Leg., ch. 230, §17, eff. Sept. 1, 1985. Amended by Acts 1997, 75th Leg., ch. 1037, §28 (eff. Sept. 1, 1997), ch. 1423, §16.24 (eff. Sept. 1, 1997); Acts 2003, 78th Leg., ch. 1310, §85, eff. Sept. 1, 2003; Acts 2005, 79th Leg., ch. 165, §1, eff. May 27, 2005; S.B. 1488, §22.059, 85th Leg., eff. Sept. 1, 2017. Source: TRCS art. 3272a, §6(a).

PROP §74.502. CLAIM FILED WITH HOLDER

(a) If a claim is filed with a holder under this section and the holder determines in good faith that the claim is valid, the holder may pay the amount of the claim.

(b) The comptroller shall reimburse the holder for a valid claim paid under this section.

(c) The request from a holder for reimbursement must be filed in accordance with procedures and on forms prescribed by the comptroller.

History of Prop. Code §74.502: Acts 1985, 69th Leg., ch. 230, §17, eff. Sept. 1, 1985. Amended by Acts 1993, 73rd Leg., ch. 851, §1, eff. Sept. 1, 1993; Acts 1997, 75th Leg., ch. 1037, §28 (eff. Sept. 1, 1997), ch. 1423, §16.25 (eff. Sept. 1, 1997). Source: TRCS art. 3272a, §7(a).

PROP §74.503. REPEALED

Repealed by Acts 1997, 75th Leg., ch. 1037, §40, eff. Sept. 1, 1997.

PROP §74.504. HEARING

(a) The comptroller may hold a hearing and receive evidence concerning a claim filed under this subchapter.

(b) If the comptroller considers that a hearing is necessary to determine the validity of a claim, the comptroller shall sign the statement of the findings and the decision on the claim. The statement shall report the substance of the evidence heard and the reasons for the decision. The statement is a public record.

(c) If the comptroller determines that a claim is valid, the comptroller shall approve and sign the claim.

History of Prop. Code §74.504: Acts 1985, 69th Leg., ch. 230, §17, eff. Sept. 1, 1985. Amended by Acts 1993, 73rd Leg., ch. 36, §3.07 (eff. Sept. 1, 1993), ch. 851, §3 (eff. Sept. 1, 1993); Acts 1997, 75th Leg., ch. 1037, §29 (eff. Sept. 1, 1997), ch. 1423, §16.27 (eff. Sept. 1, 1997). Source: TRCS art. 3272a, §7(b).

PROP §74.505. REPEALED

Repealed by Acts 1997, 75th Leg., ch. 1037, §40, eff. Sept. 1, 1997.

PROP §74.506. APPEAL

(a) A person aggrieved by the decision of a claim filed under this subchapter may appeal the decision before the 61st day after the day on which it was rendered.

(b) If a claim has not been decided before the 91st day after the day on which it was filed, the claimant may appeal within the 60-day period beginning on the 91st day after the day of filing.

(c) An appeal under this section must be made by filing suit against the state in a district court in Travis County, Texas. The state's immunity from suit without consent is abolished with respect to suits brought under this section.

(d) A court shall try an action filed under this section de novo and shall apply the rules of practice of the court.

History of Prop. Code §74.506: Acts 1985, 69th Leg., ch. 230, §17, eff. Sept. 1, 1985. Amended by Acts 1997, 75th Leg., ch. 1037, §30, eff. Sept. 1, 1997. Source: TRCS art. 3272a, §6(b).

PROP §74.507. FEE FOR RECOVERY

(a) A person who informs a potential claimant that the claimant may be entitled to claim property that is reportable to the comptroller under this chapter, that has been reported to the comptroller, or that is in the possession of the comptroller may not contract for or receive from the claimant for services an amount that exceeds 10 percent of the value of the property recovered. If the property involved is mineral proceeds, the amount for services may not include a portion of the underlying minerals or any production payment, overriding royalty, or similar payment.

(b) The person who informs a potential claimant and by contract or other written agreement is to receive a percentage of the value of the property may not file or receive a form to claim on behalf of a claimant.

History of Prop. Code §74.507: Acts 1985, 69th Leg., ch. 230, §17, eff. Sept. 1, 1985. Amended by Acts 1987, 70th Leg., ch. 426, §5, eff. Sept. 1, 1987; Acts 1993, 73rd Leg., ch. 36, §3.09, eff. Sept. 1, 1993; Acts 1997, 75th Leg., ch. 1037, §31 (eff. Sept. 1, 1997), ch. 1423, §16.29 (eff. Sept. 1, 1997); Acts 1999, 76th Leg., ch. 1208, §4, eff. Sept. 1, 1999. Source: TRCS art. 3272a, §6(b).

PROP §74.508. CLAIM OF ANOTHER STATE TO RECOVER PROPERTY; PROCEDURE

(a) At any time after property has been paid or delivered to the comptroller under this chapter, another state may recover the property if:

(1) the property was subjected to custody by this state because the records of the holder did not reflect the last known address of the apparent owner when the property was presumed abandoned under this chapter, and the other state establishes that the last known address of the apparent owner or other person entitled to the property was in that state and under the laws of that state the property escheated to or was subject to a claim of abandonment by that state;

(2) the last known address of the apparent owner or other person entitled to the property, as reflected by the records of the holder are in the other state and under the laws of that state the property has escheated to or become subject to a claim of abandonment by that state;

(3) the records of the holder were erroneous in that they did not accurately reflect the actual owner of the property and the last known address of the actual owner is in the other state and under the laws of that state the property escheated to or was subject to a claim of abandonment by that state;

(4) the property was subjected to custody by this state under Subdivision (6) of Subsection (a) of Section 72.001 and under the laws of the state of domicile of the holder the property has escheated to or become subject to a claim of abandonment by that state; or

(5) the property is the sum payable on a traveler's check, money order, or other similar instrument that was subjected to custody by this state under Subdivision (4) and the instrument was purchased in the other state and under the laws of that state the property escheated to or became subject to a claim of abandonment by that state.

(b) The claim of another state to recover escheated or abandoned property must be presented in a form prescribed by the comptroller, who shall decide the claim within 90 days after it is presented. The comptroller shall allow the claim if he determines that the other state is entitled to the abandoned property under Subsection (a).

History of Prop. Code §74.508: Acts 1987, 70th Leg., ch. 426, §5, eff. Sept. 1, 1987. Amended by Acts 1997, 75th Leg., ch. 1037, §31 (eff. Sept. 1, 1997), ch. 1423, §16.30 (eff. Sept. 1, 1997).

PROP §74.509. HANDLING FEE FOR PROCESSING UNCLAIMED PROPERTY

A handling fee may be deducted from the amount of the claim payment if the payment is at least $100.

History of Prop. Code §74.509: Acts 1993, 73rd Leg., ch. 36, §3.10, eff. Sept. 1, 1993. Amended by Acts 1997, 75th Leg., ch. 1037, §31 (eff. Sept. 1, 1997), ch. 1423, §16.31 (eff. Sept. 1, 1997).

Sections 74.510-74.600 reserved for expansion

SUBCHAPTER G. UNCLAIMED MONEY

PROP §74.601. UNCLAIMED MONEY

(a) The comptroller shall maintain a record that documents unclaimed money received under this chap-

ter or any other statute requiring the delivery of unclaimed property to the comptroller.

(b) The comptroller shall deposit to the credit of the general revenue fund:

(1) all funds, including marketable securities, delivered to the comptroller under this chapter or any other statute requiring the delivery of unclaimed property to the comptroller;

(2) all proceeds from the sale of any property, including marketable securities, under this chapter;

(3) all funds that have escheated to the state under Chapter 71, except that funds relating to escheated real property shall be deposited according to Section 71.202; and

(4) any income derived from investments of the unclaimed money.

(c) The comptroller shall keep a separate record and accounting for delivered unclaimed property, other than money, before its sale.

(d) Except as provided by Subsection (e), the comptroller shall from time to time invest the amount of unclaimed money in investments approved by law for the investment of state funds.

(e) The comptroller on receipt or from time to time may sell securities, including stocks, bonds, and mutual funds, received under this chapter or any other statute requiring the delivery of unclaimed property to the comptroller and use the proceeds to buy, exchange, invest, or reinvest in marketable securities. When making or selling the investments, the comptroller shall exercise the judgment and care of a prudent person.

(f) The comptroller shall keep a separate record and accounting for securities delivered, sold, purchased, or exchanged and the proceeds and earnings from the securities.

(g) If an owner does not assert a claim for unclaimed money and the owner is reported to be the state or a state agency, the comptroller may deposit the unclaimed money to the credit of the general revenue fund. The comptroller may establish procedures and adopt rules as necessary to implement this subsection.

History of Prop. Code §74.601: Acts 1985, 69th Leg., ch. 230, §17, eff. Sept. 1, 1985. Amended by Acts 1993, 73rd Leg., ch. 36, §3.11, eff. Sept. 1, 1993; Acts 1997, 75th Leg., ch. 1037, §32 (eff. Sept. 1, 1997), ch. 1423, §16.32 (eff. Sept. 1, 1997); Acts 2009, 81st Leg., ch. 232, §4, eff. Sept. 1, 2009; Acts 2011, 82nd Leg., ch. 685, §9, eff. Sept. 1, 2011. Source: TRCS art. 3272a, §15.

ANNOTATIONS

Clark v. Strayhorn, 184 S.W.3d 906, 911 (Tex. App.—Austin 2006, pet. denied). See annotation under Property Code §74.304, p. 348.

Robinson v. Strayhorn, No. 03-05-00855-CV (Tex. App.—Austin 2006, no pet.) (memo op.; 9-26-06). "Section 74.601(b)(2) of the unclaimed property act implicitly recognizes that the Comptroller has authority to sell securities. … The act also directs the Comptroller to invest unclaimed property for the benefit of the State and explicitly permits selling and buying securities. [¶] [I]t is clear from the statutory framework that [§74.601(e)] was meant to provide investing flexibility rather than to limit the Comptroller's actions. [T]he Comptroller *may* reinvest proceeds from marketable securities rather than deposit them in the general revenue fund as required by subsection (b); it does not, however, prevent the Comptroller from simply depositing the proceeds in the fund."

PROP §74.602. USE OF MONEY

Except as provided by Section 381.004, Local Government Code, the comptroller shall use the unclaimed money received under this chapter or any other statute requiring the delivery of unclaimed property to the comptroller to pay the claims of persons or states establishing ownership of property in the possession of the comptroller under this chapter or under any other unclaimed property or escheat statute.

History of Prop. Code §74.602: Acts 1985, 69th Leg., ch. 230, §17, eff. Sept. 1, 1985. Amended by Acts 1991, 72nd Leg., ch. 304, §1.40, eff. Jan. 1, 1992; Acts 1993, 73rd Leg., ch. 27, §3 (eff. Apr. 13, 1993), ch. 36, §3.13 (eff. Sept. 1, 1993), ch. 506, §1 (eff. Sept. 1, 1995); Acts 1997, 75th Leg., ch. 1037, §32 (eff. Sept. 1, 1997), ch. 1423, §16.33 (eff. Sept. 1, 1997). Source: TRCS art. 3272a, §15.

PROP §74.603. AUDIT; APPROPRIATION

The unclaimed money received under this chapter or any other statute requiring the delivery of unclaimed property to the comptroller is subject to audit by the State Auditor and to appropriation by the legislature for enforcing and administering this title.

History of Prop. Code §74.603: Acts 1985, 69th Leg., ch. 230, §17, eff. Sept. 1, 1985. Amended by Acts 1997, 75th Leg., ch. 1037, §32, eff. Sept. 1, 1997. Source: TRCS art. 3272a, §15.

Sections 74.604-74.700 reserved for expansion

SUBCHAPTER H. ENFORCEMENT

PROP §74.701. RULES

The comptroller may adopt rules necessary to carry out this title.

History of Prop. Code §74.701: Acts 1985, 69th Leg., ch. 230, §17, eff. Sept. 1, 1985. Amended by Acts 1997, 75th Leg., ch. 1037, §33 (eff. Sept. 1, 1997), ch. 1423, §16.34 (eff. Sept. 1, 1997). Source: TRCS art. 3272a, §12.

PROP §74.702. EXAMINATION OF RECORDS

(a) To enforce this chapter and to determine whether reports have been made as required by this chapter, the comptroller, the attorney general, or an authorized agent of either, at any reasonable time, may examine the books and records of any holder.

(b) The comptroller, the attorney general, or an agent of either may not make public any information obtained by an examination made under this section and may not disclose that information except in the course of a judicial proceeding, authorized by this chapter, in which the state is a party or pursuant to an agreement with another state allowing joint audits or the exchange of information obtained under this section.

History of Prop. Code §74.702: Acts 1985, 69th Leg., ch. 230, §17, eff. Sept. 1, 1985. Amended by Acts 1991, 72nd Leg., ch. 153, §21, eff. Sept. 1, 1991; Acts 1993, 73rd Leg., ch. 36, §3.12, eff. Sept. 1, 1993; Acts 1997, 75th Leg., ch. 1037, §33 (eff. Sept. 1, 1997), ch. 1423, §16.35 (eff. Sept. 1, 1997). Source: TRCS art. 3272a, §9.

PROP §74.703. ADDITIONAL PERSONNEL

(a) The comptroller and the attorney general may employ, in the office of either official, additional personnel necessary to enforce this title.

(b) The salary rate of additional personnel may not exceed the rate paid to other state employees for similar services.

(c) The salaries of additional personnel shall be paid in accordance with Section 74.602.

History of Prop. Code §74.703: Acts 1985, 69th Leg., ch. 230, §17, eff. Sept. 1, 1985. Amended by Acts 1997, 75th Leg., ch. 1037, §34 (eff. Sept. 1, 1997), ch. 1423, §16.36 (eff. Sept. 1, 1997). Source: TRCS art. 3272a, §15.

PROP §74.704. ASSISTANCE IN ENFORCEMENT

If the comptroller or the attorney general requests, the State Auditor, Banking Commissioner of Texas, securities commissioner, commissioner of insurance, savings and mortgage lending commissioner, Credit Union Commission, Department of Public Safety of the State of Texas, or any district or county attorney shall assist the comptroller or attorney general in enforcing this title.

History of Prop. Code §74.704: Acts 1985, 69th Leg., ch. 230, §17, eff. Sept. 1, 1985. Amended by Acts 1997, 75th Leg., ch. 1037, §35 (eff. Sept. 1, 1997), ch. 1423, §16.37 (eff. Sept. 1, 1997); Acts 2007, 80th Leg., ch. 921, §6.065, eff. Sept. 1, 2007. Source: TRCS art. 3272a, §9.

PROP §74.705. INTEREST

A holder who fails to pay or deliver property within the time prescribed by this chapter shall pay to the comptroller interest, at an annual rate of 10 percent, on the property from the date the property should have been paid or delivered until the date the property is actually paid or delivered.

(b) to **(e)** Deleted by Acts 1997, 75th Leg., ch. 1037, §35, eff. Sept. 1, 1997.

(f) A person is exempt from payment of interest under Subsection (a)[1] if the person's action or omission is in connection with the person's official duties as an officer or employee of a political subdivision of this state.

(g) In this section, "person" does not include a local governmental entity or an officer or employee of a local governmental entity who is performing the officer's or employee's official duties for the local governmental entity.

1. **Editor's note:** The subsection (a) designator was removed by Acts 1997, 75th Leg., ch. 1037, §35, eff. Sept. 1, 1997.

History of Prop. Code §74.705: Acts 1985, 69th Leg., ch. 230, §17, eff. Sept. 1, 1985. Amended by Acts 1987, 70th Leg., ch. 426, §5, eff. Sept. 1, 1987; Acts 1997, 75th Leg., ch. 483, §1 (eff. Sept. 1, 1997), ch. 888, §1 (eff. Sept. 1, 1997), ch. 1037, §35 (eff. Sept. 1, 1997), ch. 1423, §16.38 (eff. Sept. 1, 1997); Acts 1999, 76th Leg., ch. 62, §19.01(90), eff. Sept. 1, 1999. Source: TRCS art. 3272a, §30.

PROP §74.706. PENALTY

(a) A penalty equal to five percent of the value of the property due shall be imposed on a holder who fails to pay or deliver property within the time prescribed by this chapter. If a holder fails to pay or deliver property before the 31st day after the date the property is due, an additional penalty equal to five percent of the value of the property due shall be imposed.

(b) For purposes of Subsection (a), "holder" does not include a local governmental entity or an officer or employee of a local governmental entity who is performing the officer's or employee's official duties for the local governmental entity.

History of Prop. Code §74.706: Acts 1997, 75th Leg., ch. 1037, §36, eff. Sept. 1, 1997. Amended by Acts 1999, 76th Leg., ch. 748, §1, eff. Sept. 1, 1999.

PROP §74.707. WAIVER OR ABATEMENT OF PENALTY OR INTEREST

(a) The comptroller may waive penalty or interest imposed on delinquent property if the comptroller determines that the holder has made a good faith effort to comply with Chapters 72-75.

(b) The comptroller may provide for periods during which a holder of delinquent property may report and remit the unclaimed property without paying a penalty or interest.

(c) The comptroller may waive penalty and interest imposed on delinquent property if the holder delivering the property was required to deliver the property on or before November 1, 1997.

History of Prop. Code §74.707: Acts 1997, 75th Leg., ch. 1037, §36, eff. Sept. 1, 1997. Amended by Acts 2001, 77th Leg., ch. 137, §1, eff. May 16, 2001.

PROP §74.708. PROPERTY HELD IN TRUST

A holder who on March 1 holds property presumed abandoned under Chapters 72-75 holds the property in trust for the benefit of the state on behalf of the missing owner and is liable to the state for the full value of the property, plus any accrued interest and penalty. A holder is not required by this section to segregate or establish trust accounts for the property provided the property is timely delivered to the comptroller in accordance with Section 74.301.

History of Prop. Code §74.708: Acts 1997, 75th Leg., ch. 1037, §36, eff. Sept. 1, 1997. Amended by Acts 2011, 82nd Leg., ch. 685, §10, eff. Jan. 1, 2013.

PROP §74.709. SUIT TO COMPEL DELIVERY OF PROPERTY & CIVIL PENALTIES

(a) On request of the comptroller, the attorney general shall bring an action in district court, in the name of the state, to compel a holder to deliver property or to file a property report.

(b) Venue for a suit brought under this section is in Travis County.

(c) The fact that a suit seeks enforcement of this section from more than one holder is not grounds for an objection concerning misjoinder of parties or causes of action.

(d) When introduced into evidence, the verified property report, unless rebutted, is sufficient evidence that the property is abandoned and subject to delivery under this chapter and for entry of a judgment transferring custody of the property to the comptroller.

(e) The attorney general, on behalf of the comptroller, may recover reasonable attorney's fees from the holder in addition to recovery of any unclaimed property accrued or a penalty or interest due.

(f) In addition to a penalty or interest assessed on delinquent property, a holder who fails to pay or deliver property or who fails to file a property report within the time prescribed by this chapter is subject to a civil penalty not to exceed $100 for each day of violation.

History of Prop. Code §74.709: Acts 1997, 75th Leg., ch. 1037, §36, eff. Sept. 1, 1997.

PROP §74.710. CRIMINAL OFFENSE

(a) A holder commits an offense if the holder wilfully violates this chapter, including:

(1) failing to file a report in accordance with this chapter;

(2) failing to pay or deliver property in accordance with this chapter; or

(3) refusing to permit examination of records in accordance with this chapter.

(b) An offense under this section is a Class B misdemeanor.

History of Prop. Code §74.710: Acts 1997, 75th Leg., ch. 1037, §36, eff. Sept. 1, 1997.

CHAPTER 75. TEXAS MINERALS

SUBCHAPTER A. APPLICABILITY

PROP §75.001. DEFINITIONS; APPLICATION OF CHAPTER

(a) In this chapter:

(1) "Mineral" means oil, gas, uranium, sulphur, lignite, coal, and any other substance that is ordinarily and naturally considered a mineral in this state, regardless of the depth at which the oil, gas, uranium, sulphur, lignite, coal, or other substance is found.

(2) "Mineral proceeds" includes:

(A) all obligations to pay resulting from the production and sale of minerals, including net revenue interests, royalties, overriding royalties, production payments, and joint operating agreements; and

(B) all obligations for the acquisition and retention of a mineral lease, including bonuses, delay rentals, shut-in royalties, and minimum royalties.

(3) "Holder" means a person, wherever organized or domiciled, who is:

(A) in possession of property that belongs to another;

(B) a trustee; or

(C) indebted to another on an obligation.

(b) This chapter applies to mineral proceeds and the owner's underlying right to receive those mineral proceeds if:

(1) the owner's underlying right to receive mineral proceeds is related to land located in this state;

(2) the mineral proceeds result from the production of minerals located in this state; or

(3) the mineral proceeds are an obligation for the acquisition or retention of a mineral lease to produce minerals located in this state.

(c) A holder of property presumed abandoned under this chapter is subject to the procedures of Chapter 74.

(d) This chapter supplements other chapters in this title, and each chapter shall be followed to the extent applicable.

History of Prop. Code §75.001: Acts 1985, 69th Leg., ch. 230, §17, eff. Sept. 1, 1985. Amended by Acts 1987, 70th Leg., ch. 426, §6, eff. Sept. 1, 1987.

ANNOTATIONS

Dyegard Land Prtshp. v. Hoover, 39 S.W.3d 300, 311 (Tex.App.—Fort Worth 2001, no pet.). "The property code definition of 'minerals' is not limited to conveyances in the context of oil and gas nor to cases involving severance of the surface ownership from the minerals."

PROP §75.002. TRANSFER & PURCHASE OF MINERAL INTEREST ON MINERAL PROCEEDS

A person purchasing mineral proceeds of an owner whose name has been reported or is reportable to the comptroller shall provide documentation required by the comptroller to substantiate that the transfer is executed by the reported owner or the reported owner's legal agent.

History of Prop. Code §75.002: Acts 1997, 75th Leg., ch. 1037, §37, eff. Sept. 1, 1997.

Sections 75.003-75.100 reserved for expansion

SUBCHAPTER B. PRESUMPTION OF ABANDONMENT

PROP §75.101. PRESUMPTION OF ABANDONMENT

(a) All mineral proceeds that are held or owing by the holder and that have remained unclaimed by the owner for longer than three years after they became payable or distributable and the owner's underlying right to receive those mineral proceeds are presumed abandoned.

(b) At the time any owner's underlying right to receive mineral proceeds is presumed abandoned under this section, any mineral proceeds then held for or owing to the owner as a result of the underlying right and any mineral proceeds accruing after that time as a result of the underlying right and not previously presumed abandoned are presumed abandoned.

History of Prop. Code §75.101: Acts 1985, 69th Leg., ch. 230, §17, eff. Sept. 1, 1985. Amended by Acts 1987, 70th Leg., ch. 426, §7, eff. Sept. 1, 1987.

PROP §75.102. PRESERVATION OF PROPERTY

A holder of abandoned property shall preserve that property and may not by any procedure, including a deduction for service, maintenance, or other charge, transfer, convert, or reduce the property to the profits or assets of the holder.

History of Prop. Code §75.102: Acts 1985, 69th Leg., ch. 230, §17, eff. Sept. 1, 1985.

CHAPTER 76. REPORT, DELIVERY, & CLAIMS PROCESS FOR CERTAIN PROPERTY

SUBCHAPTER A. GENERAL PROVISIONS

PROP §76.001. APPLICABILITY

(a) This chapter applies only to the holder of property if:

(1) the holder is a:

(A) school district;

(B) municipality;

(C) county; or

(D) junior college that has, in the manner described by Subsection (b), opted to handle property described by Subdivision (2) in accordance with this chapter; and

(2) the property is:

(A) presumed abandoned under Chapter 72 or 75; and

(B) valued at $100 or less.

(b) This chapter applies to a junior college only if the governing board of the junior college takes formal action to opt to handle property described by Subsection (a)(2) in accordance with this chapter.

History of Prop. Code §76.001: Acts 1997, 75th Leg., ch. 1037, §38, eff. Sept. 1, 1997. Amended by Acts 1999, 76th Leg., ch. 1015, §1, eff. Sept. 1, 2000; Acts 2011, 82nd Leg., ch. 478, §1, eff. June 17, 2011.

PROP §76.002. OFFICERS & REPRESENTATIVES

In this chapter:

(1) a reference to the treasurer of a holder includes a person performing the duties of the treasurer of a holder in a school district, municipality, or county in which the office of treasurer does not exist;

(2) a reference to the chief fiscal officer of a holder includes a person performing the duties of the chief fiscal officer of a holder in a school district, municipality, or county in which the office of chief fiscal officer does not exist; and

(3) a reference to the attorney for a holder includes an attorney designated by the governing body of the holder to represent the holder.

History of Prop. Code §76.002: Acts 1997, 75th Leg., ch. 1037, §38, eff. Sept. 1, 1997. Amended by Acts 1999, 76th Leg., ch. 1015, §2, eff. Sept. 1, 2000.

Sections 76.003-76.100 reserved for expansion

SUBCHAPTER B. PROPERTY REPORT

PROP §76.101. PROPERTY REPORT

(a) Each holder who on June 30 holds property subject to this chapter shall file a report of that property on or before the following November 1. Each report shall be filed with the treasurer of the holder as provided by this section and on forms prescribed by the treasurer of the holder.

(b) A holder required by Subsection (a) to file a report shall file a report each successive year regardless of whether the holder has any reportable property on June 30 of the year in which the report is filed.

History of Prop. Code §76.101: Acts 1997, 75th Leg., ch. 1037, §38, eff. Sept. 1, 1997.

PROP §76.102. VERIFICATION

(a) The person preparing a property report shall place at the end of each copy of the report a verification made under oath and executed by the chief fiscal officer of the holder, as designated by the holder.

(b) The verification must include the following sentence: "This report contains a full and complete list of all property held by the undersigned that, from the knowledge and records of the undersigned, is abandoned under the laws of the State of Texas."

History of Prop. Code §76.102: Acts 1997, 75th Leg., ch. 1037, §38, eff. Sept. 1, 1997.

PROP §76.103. RETENTION OF RECORDS

(a) The holder required to file a property report shall keep a record of:

(1) the name and last known address of each person who, from the records of the holder, appears to be the owner of the property;

(2) a brief description of the property, including the identification number of the account, if any; and

(3) the balance of each account, if appropriate.

(b) The record must be kept until the 10th anniversary of the date on which the property is reportable.

(c) The treasurer of the holder may provide for a shorter period for keeping a record required by this section.

History of Prop. Code §76.103: Acts 1997, 75th Leg., ch. 1037, §38, eff. Sept. 1, 1997.

PROP §76.104. CONFIDENTIALITY OF PROPERTY REPORT

(a) Except as provided by this chapter, a property report filed with the treasurer of the holder is confidential until the second anniversary of the date the report is filed.

(b) Notwithstanding other law, the social security number of an owner that is reported to the treasurer of the holder is confidential.

History of Prop. Code §76.104: Acts 1997, 75th Leg., ch. 1037, §38, eff. Sept. 1, 1997.

ANNOTATIONS

Tex. Atty. Gen. Op. No. OR-00399 (2006). See annotation under Property Code §74.104, p. 344.

Sections 76.105-76.200 reserved for expansion

SUBCHAPTER C. NOTICE

PROP §76.201. PUBLISHED NOTICE

(a) Except as provided by Subsections (b) and (e), the treasurer of a holder shall publish a notice in a newspaper in the calendar year immediately following the year in which the property report is filed. The newspaper must be a newspaper of general circulation in the jurisdiction of the holder.

(b) The treasurer of the holder may use a method of publishing notice that is different from that prescribed by Subsection (a) if the treasurer determines that the different method would be as likely as the prescribed method to give actual notice to the person required to be named in the notice.

(c) The published notice must state that the reported property is presumed abandoned and subject to this chapter and must contain:

(1) a statement that, by addressing an inquiry to the treasurer of the holder, any person possessing a legal or beneficial interest in the reported property may obtain information concerning the amount of the property; and

(2) a statement that the owner may present proof of the claim to the treasurer of the holder and establish the owner's right to receive the property.

(d) The treasurer of a holder may offer for sale space for suitable advertisements in a notice published under this section. Proceeds from the sale of the advertising space shall be used to defray the cost of publishing the notices, with the remaining amount, if any, to be deposited to the credit of the unclaimed money fund.

(e) In the notice required by this section, the treasurer of the holder may publish other information regarding property if the treasurer determines that publication of that information is in the public interest.

History of Prop. Code §76.201: Acts 1997, 75th Leg., ch. 1037, §38, eff. Sept. 1, 1997.

PROP §76.202. NOTICE TO OWNER

(a) During the calendar year immediately following the year in which the property report is filed, the treasurer of the holder may mail a notice to each person who has an address in this state and appears to be entitled to the reported property.

(b) The notice must contain:

(1) a statement that property is being held by the treasurer of the holder to which the addressee appears to be entitled; and

(2) a statement that the owner may present proof of the claim to the treasurer of the holder and establish the owner's right to receive the property.

History of Prop. Code §76.202: Acts 1997, 75th Leg., ch. 1037, §38, eff. Sept. 1, 1997.

PROP §76.203. NOTICE THAT ACCOUNTS ARE SUBJECT TO THIS CHAPTER

Publication of notice in accordance with Section 76.201 is notice to the owner by the holder that the reported property is subject to this chapter.

History of Prop. Code §76.203: Acts 1997, 75th Leg., ch. 1037, §38, eff. Sept. 1, 1997.

PROP §76.204. CHARGE FOR NOTICE

The treasurer of the holder may charge the following against the property delivered under this chapter:

(1) expenses incurred for the publication of notice required by Section 76.201; and

(2) the amount paid in postage for the notice to the owner required by Section 76.202.

History of Prop. Code §76.204: Acts 1997, 75th Leg., ch. 1037, §38, eff. Sept. 1, 1997.

Sections 76.205-76.300 reserved for expansion

SUBCHAPTER D. DELIVERY

PROP §76.301. DELIVERY OF PROPERTY TO TREASURER

(a) Each holder who on June 30 holds property that is subject to this chapter shall deliver the property to the treasurer of the holder on or before the following November 1 accompanied by the property report.

(b) If the property subject to delivery under Subsection (a) is stock or some other intangible ownership interest in a business association for which there is no evidence of ownership, the holder shall issue a duplicate certificate or other evidence of ownership to the treasurer of the holder at the time delivery is required under this section.

History of Prop. Code §76.301: Acts 1997, 75th Leg., ch. 1037, §38, eff. Sept. 1, 1997.

PROP §76.302. VERIFICATION OF DELIVERED PROPERTY

(a) Property delivered under Section 76.301 must be accompanied by a verification under oath that:

(1) the property delivered is a complete and correct remittance of all accounts subject to this chapter in the holder's possession;

(2) the existence and location of the listed owners are unknown to the holder; and

(3) the listed owners have not asserted a claim or exercised an act of ownership with respect to the owner's reported property.

(b) The verification required by Subsection (a) shall be signed by the chief fiscal officer of the holder, as designated by the holder.

History of Prop. Code §76.302: Acts 1997, 75th Leg., ch. 1037, §38, eff. Sept. 1, 1997.

PROP §76.303. LIST OF OWNERS

(a) The treasurer of the holder shall compile and revise each year an alphabetical list of names and last known addresses of the owners listed in the reports and the amount credited to each account.

(b) The treasurer of the holder shall make the list available for public inspection during all reasonable business hours.

History of Prop. Code §76.303: Acts 1997, 75th Leg., ch. 1037, §38, eff. Sept. 1, 1997.

PROP §76.304. PERIOD OF LIMITATION NOT A BAR

The expiration of any period specified by statute or court order, during which an action or proceeding may be initiated or entered to obtain payment of a claim for money, does not prevent the money from being presumed abandoned property and does not affect any duty to file a report required by this chapter or to deliver abandoned property to the treasurer of the holder.

History of Prop. Code §76.304: Acts 1997, 75th Leg., ch. 1037, §38, eff. Sept. 1, 1997.

Sections 76.305-76.400 reserved for expansion

SUBCHAPTER E. DISPOSITION OF DELIVERED PROPERTY

PROP §76.401. SALE OF PROPERTY

(a) Except as provided by Subsection (c), the treasurer of the holder shall sell at public sale all personal property, other than money and marketable securities, delivered to the treasurer of the holder in accordance with Section 76.301. The treasurer of the holder shall conduct the sale in the holder's jurisdiction.

(b) The treasurer of the holder shall sell the property to the highest bidder. If the treasurer of the holder determines that the highest bid is insufficient, the treasurer of the holder may decline that bid and offer the property for public or private sale.

(c) The treasurer of the holder is not required to offer property for sale if the property belongs to a person with an address outside this state or the treasurer of the holder determines that the probable cost of the sale of the property exceeds its value.

(d) If after investigation the treasurer of the holder determines that property delivered has insubstantial commercial value, the treasurer of the holder may destroy or otherwise dispose of the property at any time.

(e) A person may not maintain any action or proceeding against the state, an officer of the state, or the holder of property because of an action taken by the treasurer of the holder under this section.

History of Prop. Code §76.401: Acts 1997, 75th Leg., ch. 1037, §38, eff. Sept. 1, 1997.

PROP §76.402. NOTICE OF SALE

Before the 21st day before the day on which a public sale is held under Section 76.401, the treasurer of the holder shall publish notice of the sale in a newspaper of general circulation in the county where the sale is to be held.

History of Prop. Code §76.402: Acts 1997, 75th Leg., ch. 1037, §38, eff. Sept. 1, 1997.

PROP §76.403. PURCHASER'S TITLE

(a) At a sale, public or private, of property that is held under this subchapter, the purchaser receives title to the purchased property free from all claims of the prior owner and prior holder of the property and all persons claiming through or under the owner or holder.

(b) The treasurer of the holder shall execute all documents necessary to complete the transfer of title.

History of Prop. Code §76.403: Acts 1997, 75th Leg., ch. 1037, §38, eff. Sept. 1, 1997.

Sections 76.404-76.500 reserved for expansion

SUBCHAPTER F. CLAIM FOR DELIVERED PROPERTY

PROP §76.501. FILING OF CLAIM

(a) A claim for property delivered to the treasurer of the holder under this chapter must be filed with the treasurer of the holder.

(b) All claims to which this section applies must be filed in accordance with procedures and on forms prescribed by the treasurer of the holder.

History of Prop. Code §76.501: Acts 1997, 75th Leg., ch. 1037, §38, eff. Sept. 1, 1997.

PROP §76.502. CONSIDERATION OF CLAIM

The treasurer of the holder shall consider the validity of each claim filed under this subchapter.

History of Prop. Code §76.502: Acts 1997, 75th Leg., ch. 1037, §38, eff. Sept. 1, 1997.

PROP §76.503. HEARING

(a) The treasurer of the holder may hold a hearing and receive evidence concerning a claim filed under this subchapter.

(b) If the treasurer of the holder considers that a hearing is necessary to determine the validity of a claim, the treasurer of the holder shall sign the statement of the findings and the decision on the claim. The statement shall report the substance of the evidence heard and the reasons for the decision. The statement is a public record.

(c) If the treasurer of the holder determines that a claim is valid, the treasurer of the holder shall approve and sign the claim.

History of Prop. Code §76.503: Acts 1997, 75th Leg., ch. 1037, §38, eff. Sept. 1, 1997.

PROP §76.504. PAYMENT OF CLAIM

(a) If a claim has been approved under this subchapter, the treasurer of the holder shall pay the claim.

(b) If a claim is for personal property other than money and has been approved under this subchapter, the treasurer of the holder promptly shall deliver the property to the claimant unless the treasurer of the holder has sold the property. If the property has been sold under Section 76.401, the treasurer of the holder shall pay to the claimant the proceeds from the sale.

(c) Costs of publication and postage shall be deducted from the amounts paid under this section, but deductions for any costs of administration or service charges may not be made.

History of Prop. Code §76.504: Acts 1997, 75th Leg., ch. 1037, §38, eff. Sept. 1, 1997.

PROP §76.505. APPEAL

(a) A person aggrieved by the decision on a claim filed under this subchapter may appeal the decision before the 61st day after the date the decision was rendered.

(b) If a claim has not been decided before the 91st day after the date the claim was filed, the claimant may appeal within the 60-day period beginning on the 91st day after the date of filing.

(c) An appeal under this section must be made by filing suit against the holder in a district court in the county in which the claimed property is located. The holder's immunity from suit without consent is waived with respect to a suit under this section.

(d) A court shall try an action filed under this section de novo and shall apply the rules of practice of the court.

History of Prop. Code §76.505: Acts 1997, 75th Leg., ch. 1037, §38, eff. Sept. 1, 1997.

PROP §76.506. FEE FOR RECOVERY

A person who informs a potential claimant that the claimant may be entitled to claim property that is reportable to the treasurer of the holder under this chapter, that has been reported to the treasurer of the holder, or that is in the possession of the treasurer of the holder may not contract for or receive from the claimant for services an amount that exceeds 10 percent of the value of the property recovered. If the property involved is mineral proceeds, the amount for services may not include a portion of the underlying minerals or any production payment, overriding royalty, or similar payment.

History of Prop. Code §76.506: Acts 1997, 75th Leg., ch. 1037, §38, eff. Sept. 1, 1997.

PROP §76.507. CLAIM OF ANOTHER STATE TO RECOVER PROPERTY; PROCEDURE

(a) At any time after property has been paid or delivered to the treasurer of the holder under this chapter, another state may recover the property if:

(1) the property was subjected to custody by the holder because the records of the holder did not reflect the last known address of the apparent owner when the property was presumed abandoned under this chapter, and the other state establishes that the last known address of the apparent owner or other person entitled to the property was in that state and under the laws of that state the property escheated to or was subject to a claim of abandonment by that state;

(2) the last known address of the apparent owner or other person entitled to the property, as reflected by the records of the holder, is in the other state and under the laws of that state the property has escheated to or become subject to a claim of abandonment by that state; or

(3) the records of the holder were erroneous in that the records did not accurately reflect the actual owner of the property and the last known address of the actual owner is in the other state and under the laws of that state the property escheated to or was subject to a claim of abandonment by that state.

(b) The claim of another state to recover escheated or abandoned property must be presented in a form prescribed by the treasurer of the holder, who shall decide the claim within 90 days after the date it is presented. The treasurer of the holder shall allow the claim if the treasurer of the holder determines that the other state is entitled to the abandoned property under Subsection (a).

History of Prop. Code §76.507: Acts 1997, 75th Leg., ch. 1037, §38, eff. Sept. 1, 1997.

Sections 76.508-76.600 reserved for expansion

SUBCHAPTER G. UNCLAIMED MONEY FUND

PROP §76.601. FUND

(a) The treasurer of the holder shall maintain a fund known as the unclaimed money fund.

(b) The treasurer of the holder shall deposit to the credit of the fund:

(1) all funds, including marketable securities, delivered to the treasurer of the holder under this chapter or any other statute requiring the delivery of unclaimed property to the treasurer of the holder;

(2) all proceeds from the sale of any property, including marketable securities, under this chapter; and

(3) any income derived from investments of the fund.

(c) The treasurer of the holder shall keep a separate record and accounting for delivered unclaimed property, other than money, before its sale.

(d) The treasurer of the holder shall from time to time invest the amount in the unclaimed money fund in investments approved by law for the investment of funds by the holder.

(e) The treasurer of the holder may from time to time sell securities in the fund, including stocks, bonds, and mutual funds, and use the proceeds to buy, exchange, invest, or reinvest in marketable securities. When making the investments, the treasurer of the holder shall exercise the judgment and care of a prudent person.

(f) The treasurer of the holder shall keep a separate record and accounting for securities delivered, sold, purchased, or exchanged and the proceeds and earnings from the securities.

History of Prop. Code §76.601: Acts 1997, 75th Leg., ch. 1037, §38, eff. Sept. 1, 1997.

PROP §76.602. USE OF FUND

(a) The treasurer of the holder shall use the unclaimed money fund to pay the claims of persons establishing ownership of property in the possession of the treasurer of the holder under this chapter or under any other unclaimed property or escheat statute.

(b) Each fiscal year after deducting funds sufficient to pay anticipated expenses and claims of the unclaimed money fund, the treasurer of the holder shall transfer the remainder to the general fund of the holder.

(c) The treasurer of the holder and the attorney for the holder may use the unclaimed money fund generally for the enforcement and administration of this chapter, including the expenses of forms, notices, examinations, travel, court costs, supplies, equipment, and employment of necessary personnel and other necessary expenses.

History of Prop. Code §76.602: Acts 1997, 75th Leg., ch. 1037, §38, eff. Sept. 1, 1997.

PROP §76.603. AUDIT; BUDGET

The unclaimed money fund is subject to:

(1) audit by the auditor of the holder or an independent auditor if the holder does not have an auditor; and

(2) budgetary procedures adopted by the governing body of the holder.

History of Prop. Code §76.603: Acts 1997, 75th Leg., ch. 1037, §38, eff. Sept. 1, 1997.

Sections 76.604-76.700 reserved for expansion

SUBCHAPTER H. ENFORCEMENT

PROP §76.701. RULES

The treasurer of the holder may adopt rules necessary to carry out this chapter.

History of Prop. Code §76.701: Acts 1997, 75th Leg., ch. 1037, §38, eff. Sept. 1, 1997.

PROP §76.702. EXAMINATION OF RECORDS

(a) To enforce this chapter and to determine whether reports have been made as required by this

chapter, the treasurer of the holder, at any reasonable time, may examine the books and records of the holder.

(b) The treasurer of the holder, attorney for the holder, or an agent of either person may not make public any information obtained by an examination made under this section and may not disclose that information except:

(1) in the course of a judicial proceeding authorized by this chapter in which the holder is a party; or

(2) under an agreement with another state allowing joint audits or the exchange of information obtained under this section.

History of Prop. Code §76.702: Acts 1997, 75th Leg., ch. 1037, §38, eff. Sept. 1, 1997.

PROP §76.703. ADDITIONAL PERSONNEL

(a) The treasurer of the holder and the attorney for the holder may employ, in the office of either person, additional personnel necessary to enforce this chapter.

(b) The salary rate of additional personnel may not exceed the rate paid to other employees of the holder for similar services.

(c) The salaries of additional personnel shall be paid in accordance with Section 76.602.

(d) The provisions of this section are subject to the budgetary procedures adopted by the governing body of the holder.

History of Prop. Code §76.703: Acts 1997, 75th Leg., ch. 1037, §38, eff. Sept. 1, 1997.

PROP §76.704. OFFENSE

(a) A person commits an offense if the person:

(1) wilfully fails to file a report required by this chapter;

(2) refuses to permit examination of records in accordance with this chapter;

(3) makes a deduction from or a service charge against a dormant account or dormant deposit of funds; or

(4) violates any other provision of this chapter.

(b) An offense under this section is punishable by:

(1) a fine of not less than $500 or more than $1,000;

(2) confinement in jail for a term not to exceed six months; or

(3) both the fine and confinement.

(c) In addition to a criminal penalty, a person who commits an offense under Subsection (a) is subject to a civil penalty not to exceed $100 for each day of the violation. The attorney for the holder shall collect the civil penalty by bringing suit in a district court of the county in which the holder is located.

History of Prop. Code §76.704: Acts 1997, 75th Leg., ch. 1037, §38, eff. Sept. 1, 1997.

E CHAPTER 77. REPORT, DELIVERY, & CLAIMS PROCESS FOR UNCLAIMED RESTITUTION PAYMENTS

SUBCHAPTER A. APPLICABILITY

PROP §77.001. APPLICABILITY

This chapter applies to unclaimed restitution payments that are presumed abandoned under Section 76.013 or 508.322, Government Code.

History of Prop. Code §77.001: Enacted by H.B. 1866, §4, 85th Leg., eff. Sept. 1, 2017.

PROPERTY CODE

CHAPTER 77. PROCESS FOR UNCLAIMED RESTITUTION PAYMENTS §§77.051 - 77.055

Sections 77.002-77.050 blank

SUBCHAPTER B. PROPERTY REPORT

PROP §77.051. PROPERTY REPORT

(a) Notwithstanding the confidentiality provisions of Chapters 57, 57A, 57B, and 57D, Code of Criminal Procedure, each holder who on March 1 holds an unclaimed restitution payment that is presumed abandoned under Section 76.013 or 508.322, Government Code, shall file a property report with the comptroller on or before the following July 1. The comptroller may prescribe the form to be used for the report required by this section and may require the report to be filed electronically.

(b) The property report must include, if known by the holder:

(1) the name, social security number, driver's license or state identification number, e-mail address, and last known address of the victim who, from the records of the holder, is entitled to the unclaimed restitution payment;

(2) the cause number of the case in which a judge ordered a defendant to pay restitution to the victim, the amount of restitution ordered, and the balance owed to the victim;

(3) the date of the last transaction with the victim concerning the restitution payments; and

(4) other information that the comptroller requires to be disclosed as necessary for the administration of this chapter.

(c) A holder who is required by Subsection (a) to file a report in any year shall file a report each successive year thereafter. If a person required to file a report under this subsection is not holding any restitution payments that are presumed abandoned under Section 76.013 or 508.322, Government Code, the person shall certify that the person is not holding any restitution payments that are presumed abandoned under those sections.

History of Prop. Code §77.051: Enacted by H.B. 1866, §4, 85th Leg., eff. Sept. 1, 2017.

PROP §77.052. NOTICE BY HOLDER REQUIRED

A holder who on March 1 holds an unclaimed restitution payment that is presumed abandoned under Section 76.013 or 508.322, Government Code, shall, on or before the following May 1, mail to the last known address of the victim entitled to the unclaimed restitution payment written notice stating that:

(1) the holder is holding the restitution payment to which the victim is entitled; and

(2) the holder may be required to deliver the restitution payment to the comptroller on or before July 1 if the victim does not claim the restitution payment.

History of Prop. Code §77.052: Enacted by H.B. 1866, §4, 85th Leg., eff. Sept. 1, 2017.

PROP §77.053. SIGNED STATEMENT

(a) The person preparing a property report required by this chapter shall provide with each copy of the report a statement signed by the holder's chief fiscal officer, as designated by the holder. The signature required by this section may be in an electronic or other form prescribed by the comptroller and shall have the same effect as an original signature.

(b) The statement must include the following sentence:

"This report contains a full and complete list of all restitution payments held by the undersigned that, from the knowledge and records of the undersigned, are abandoned under the laws of the State of Texas."

History of Prop. Code §77.053: Enacted by H.B. 1866, §4, 85th Leg., eff. Sept. 1, 2017.

PROP §77.054. CONFIDENTIALITY OF PROPERTY REPORT

(a) The property report filed with the comptroller under Section 77.051 is confidential and is not subject to disclosure under Chapter 552, Government Code.

(b) The social security number, driver's license or state identification number, and address of a victim are confidential and are not subject to disclosure under Chapter 552, Government Code. For the purposes of this subsection, the victim's address includes information that identifies a victim's place of residence or post office box but does not include the city or county in which the victim resides.

History of Prop. Code §77.054: Enacted by H.B. 1866, §4, 85th Leg., eff. Sept. 1, 2017.

PROP §77.055. EXCEPTION TO LIABILITY

(a) It is an exception to the application of Section 552.352, Government Code, that the comptroller or an officer or employee of the comptroller's office published or disclosed information in reliance on the report filed with the comptroller under Section 77.051.

(b) The comptroller or an officer or employee of the comptroller's office is immune from any civil liability for publishing or disclosing confidential information

under this section if the comptroller, officer, or employee published or disclosed the information in reliance on the report filed with the comptroller under Section 77.051.

History of Prop. Code §77.055: Enacted by H.B. 1866, §4, 85th Leg., eff. Sept. 1, 2017.

Sections 77.056-77.100 blank

SUBCHAPTER C. NOTICE BY COMPTROLLER

PROP §77.101. NOTICE

The comptroller may use one or more methods as necessary to provide the most efficient and effective notice to victims that the comptroller is holding unclaimed restitution payments that are subject to this chapter.

History of Prop. Code §77.101: Enacted by H.B. 1866, §4, 85th Leg., eff. Sept. 1, 2017.

PROP §77.102. PUBLICATION

Notwithstanding Section 77.054, the comptroller may publish on the Internet information regarding unclaimed restitution payments received by the comptroller, except that the comptroller may not publish information that identifies a person as a victim or information that identifies a victim's address. For the purposes of this subsection, the victim's address includes information that identifies a victim's place of residence or post office box but does not include the city or county in which the victim resides.

History of Prop. Code §77.102: Enacted by H.B. 1866, §4, 85th Leg., eff. Sept. 1, 2017.

Sections 77.103-77.150 blank

SUBCHAPTER D. DELIVERY

PROP §77.151. DELIVERY OF PROPERTY TO COMPTROLLER

Each holder who on March 1 holds an unclaimed restitution payment that is presumed abandoned under Section 76.013 or 508.322, Government Code, shall deliver the property to the comptroller on or before the following July 1 accompanied by the report required to be filed under Section 77.051.

History of Prop. Code §77.151: Enacted by H.B. 1866, §4, 85th Leg., eff. Sept. 1, 2017.

PROP §77.152. RESPONSIBILITY AFTER DELIVERY

(a) If an unclaimed restitution payment that is presumed abandoned under Section 76.013 or 508.322, Government Code, is reported and delivered to the comptroller, the state shall assume custody of the payment and responsibility for its safekeeping.

(b) A holder who delivers an unclaimed restitution payment to the comptroller in compliance with this chapter is relieved of all liability to the extent of the value of the payment delivered for any claim then existing, that may arise after delivery to the comptroller, or that may be made with respect to the payment.

(c) If the holder delivers an unclaimed restitution payment to the comptroller in good faith and, after delivery, a person claims the property from the holder, the attorney general shall, on written notice of the claim, defend the holder against the claim, and the holder shall be indemnified against any liability on the claim.

History of Prop. Code §77.152: Enacted by H.B. 1866, §4, 85th Leg., eff. Sept. 1, 2017.

Sections 77.153-77.200 blank

SUBCHAPTER E. CLAIM FOR DELIVERED PROPERTY

PROP §77.201. CLAIM FILED WITH COMPTROLLER

(a) The comptroller shall review the validity of each claim for an unclaimed restitution payment filed under this section.

(b) If the comptroller determines a claim for an unclaimed restitution payment is valid, the comptroller shall approve the claim. If a claim is approved under this section, the comptroller shall pay the claim.

(c) All claims to which this section applies must be filed in accordance with the procedures, contain the information, and be on forms prescribed by the comptroller.

(d) On receipt of a claim form and all necessary documentation as may be appropriate under the circumstances, the comptroller may approve the claim of:

(1) the victim;

(2) if the victim died testate:

(A) the appropriate legal beneficiaries of the victim as provided by the last will and testament of the victim that has been accepted into probate or filed as a muniment of title; or

(B) the executor of the victim's last will and testament who holds current letters testamentary;

(3) if the victim died intestate or is deceased and presumed intestate:

(A) the legal heirs of the victim as provided by Chapter 201, Estates Code; or

(B) the court-appointed administrator of the victim's estate, on behalf of the legal heirs of the victim;

(4) the legal heirs of the victim as established by an affidavit of heirship order signed by a judge of the county probate court or by a county judge;

(5) if the victim is a minor child or an adult who has been adjudged incompetent by a court of law, the parent or legal guardian of the child or adult;

(6) if the victim is a trust:

(A) the trustee, on behalf of the trust; or

(B) the beneficiaries of the trust, if the trust is dissolved;

(7) if the victim is a corporation:

(A) the president or chair of the board of directors of the corporation, on behalf of the corporation;

(B) any person who has been delegated legal authority to act on behalf of the corporation by the president or board of directors of the corporation; or

(C) a receiver appointed for the corporation;

(8) if the victim is a corporation that has been dissolved, liquidated, or otherwise terminated:

(A) the surviving shareholders of the corporation in proportion to their ownership of the corporation at the time of dissolution, liquidation, or termination;

(B) the corporation's bankruptcy trustee; or

(C) a receiver appointed for the corporation;

(9) if the victim is a state agency, the comptroller; or

(10) any other person that is entitled to receive the unclaimed restitution payment under other law or comptroller policy.

(e) Except as provided by Subsections (f) and (g), the comptroller may not approve the claim of or pay a claim to the following persons:

(1) a creditor, a judgment creditor, a lienholder, or an assignee of the victim or of any other person entitled to receive an unclaimed restitution payment under this section;

(2) a receiver, if the receiver is appointed at the request of a person the comptroller may not pay under Subdivision (1);

(3) a person attempting to make a claim on behalf of a trust or corporation that has previously been dissolved or terminated, if it appears the trust or corporation was revived for the purpose of making a claim under this section and the person submitting the claim was not an authorized representative of the corporation or trust at the time of the dissolution or termination; or

(4) a person holding a power of attorney, if the person holding a power of attorney is a person the comptroller may not pay under this subsection.

(f) The comptroller may approve a claim for child support arrearages owed by the victim and reflected in a child support lien notice that complies with Section 157.313, Family Code. A claim under this subsection may be submitted by the lienholder.

(g) The comptroller may approve a claim for debts owed by the victim to the state or any state agency. A claim under this subsection may be submitted by the attorney general or the comptroller on behalf of the state or state agency.

History of Prop. Code §77.201: Enacted by H.B. 1866, §4, 85th Leg., eff. Sept. 1, 2017.

PROP §77.202. CLAIMS NOT ASSIGNABLE

Notwithstanding Section 9.406(f), Business & Commerce Code, an interest in a claim under this chapter may not be assigned.

History of Prop. Code §77.202: Enacted by H.B. 1866, §4, 85th Leg., eff. Sept. 1, 2017.

PROP §77.203. CLAIM FILED WITH HOLDER

(a) If a claim for an unclaimed restitution payment is filed with a holder under this section and the holder determines in good faith that the claim is valid, the holder may pay the amount of the claim.

(b) The comptroller may reimburse the holder for a valid claim paid under this section.

(c) The request from a holder for reimbursement must be filed in accordance with procedures and on forms prescribed by the comptroller and may not exceed the amount previously reported and delivered by the holder to the comptroller.

(d) The comptroller may not reimburse a holder for a claim paid to a person the comptroller is not permitted to pay under Section 77.201(e).

(e) The liability of the comptroller to reimburse a holder under this section is limited to the extent of the property delivered under this chapter and remaining in the possession of the comptroller at the time a holder requests reimbursement.

History of Prop. Code §77.203: Enacted by H.B. 1866, §4, 85th Leg., eff. Sept. 1, 2017.

PROP §77.204. APPEAL

(a) A person aggrieved by the decision of a claim filed under this chapter may appeal the decision before the 61st day after the day on which it was rendered.

(b) If a claim has not been decided before the 91st day after the day on which it was filed, the claimant may appeal within the 60-day period beginning on the 91st day after the day of filing.

(c) An appeal under this section must be made by filing suit against the state in a district court in Travis County.

(d) A court shall try an action filed under this section de novo and shall apply the rules of practice of the court.

History of Prop. Code §77.204: Enacted by H.B. 1866, §4, 85th Leg., eff. Sept. 1, 2017.

PROP §77.205. LIMITATION OF LIABILITY

The liability of the state is limited to the extent of the property delivered under this chapter and remaining in the possession of the comptroller at the time a suit is filed.

History of Prop. Code §77.205: Enacted by H.B. 1866, §4, 85th Leg., eff. Sept. 1, 2017.

PROP §77.206. FEE FOR RECOVERY

(a) A person who informs a potential claimant that the claimant may be entitled to claim property under this chapter may not contract for or receive from the claimant for services an amount that exceeds 10 percent of the value of the property recovered.

(b) A person who receives a fee for recovery from a claimant that exceeds 10 percent of the value of the property recovered is liable to the claimant for the amount of the fee plus attorney's fees and expenses.

History of Prop. Code §77.206: Enacted by H.B. 1866, §4, 85th Leg., eff. Sept. 1, 2017.

Sections 77.207-77.250 blank

SUBCHAPTER F. UNCLAIMED PAYMENTS

PROP §77.251. UNCLAIMED RESTITUTION PAYMENTS

(a) The comptroller shall maintain a record that documents unclaimed restitution payments received under this chapter.

(b) The comptroller shall deposit all unclaimed restitution payments to the credit of the compensation to victims of crime auxiliary fund in the state treasury.

(c) Income or interest derived from unclaimed restitution payments deposited in the fund shall remain in the compensation to victims of crime auxiliary fund.

History of Prop. Code §77.251: Enacted by H.B. 1866, §4, 85th Leg., eff. Sept. 1, 2017.

PROP §77.252. USE OF MONEY

(a) Except as provided by Subsection (b) and Chapter 56, Code of Criminal Procedure, money in the compensation to victims of crime auxiliary fund may only be used to pay claims as provided by this chapter and is not available for any other purpose. Section 403.095, Government Code, does not apply to the fund.

(b) The legislature may appropriate money in the compensation to victims of crime auxiliary fund to cover costs incurred by the comptroller in administering this chapter.

History of Prop. Code §77.252: Enacted by H.B. 1866, §4, 85th Leg., eff. Sept. 1, 2017.

PROP §77.253. EXCESS CLAIMS

The comptroller may pay a claim under this chapter that is more than the money available in the compensation to victims of crime auxiliary fund using funds appropriated by the legislature for paying claims under this title.

History of Prop. Code §77.253: Enacted by H.B. 1866, §4, 85th Leg., eff. Sept. 1, 2017.

Sections 77.254-77.300 blank

SUBCHAPTER G. ENFORCEMENT

PROP §77.301. RULES

The comptroller may adopt rules necessary to carry out this chapter.

History of Prop. Code §77.301: Enacted by H.B. 1866, §4, 85th Leg., eff. Sept. 1, 2017.

PROP §77.302. EXAMINATION OF RECORDS

(a) To enforce this chapter and to determine whether reports have been made as required by this chapter, the comptroller, the attorney general, or an authorized agent of either, may, at any reasonable time and place, examine the books and records of any holder.

(b) The comptroller, the attorney general, or an agent of either may not make public any information obtained by an examination made under this section and may not disclose that information except in the course of a judicial proceeding, authorized by this chapter, in which the state is a party or under an agreement

with another state allowing joint audits or the exchange of information obtained under this section.

History of Prop. Code §77.302: Enacted by H.B. 1866, §4, 85th Leg., eff. Sept. 1, 2017.

PROP §77.303. AUTHORITY TO TAKE TESTIMONY & ISSUE ADMINISTRATIVE SUBPOENAS

(a) In addition to the authority to examine granted by Section 77.302, to enforce this chapter and to determine whether reports have been made as required by this chapter, the comptroller, or the comptroller's designee, may take testimony, administer oaths, and issue subpoenas to compel any person, at a time and place reasonable under the circumstances, to appear and give testimony, and to produce relevant books, records, documents, or other data, in whatever form, for audit, inspection, and copying.

(b) A person authorized to serve process under the Texas Rules of Civil Procedure may serve a subpoena issued under Subsection (a). The person shall serve the subpoena in accordance with the Texas Rules of Civil Procedure.

History of Prop. Code §77.303: Enacted by H.B. 1866, §4, 85th Leg., eff. Sept. 1, 2017.

PROP §77.304. ENFORCEMENT OF SUBPOENAS

(a) If the person to whom a subpoena is directed under Section 77.303 fails to comply with the subpoena, or fails to file a motion to quash or otherwise demand a pre-compliance review of the subpoena, within the return date specified in the subpoena, the attorney general shall, on the request of the comptroller, bring suit to enforce the subpoena. The suit may be brought in a state district court where service may be obtained on the person refusing to testify or produce records.

(b) A court that determines that the subpoena was issued in good faith shall order compliance with the subpoena. The court may apply penalties for civil and criminal contempt otherwise available at law where a person refuses to comply with the court's order.

History of Prop. Code §77.304: Enacted by H.B. 1866, §4, 85th Leg., eff. Sept. 1, 2017.

PROP §77.305. VENUE FOR PRE-COMPLIANCE REVIEW

A person receiving a subpoena under this chapter may, before the return date specified in the subpoena, petition a district court in Travis County for an order to modify or quash the subpoena.

History of Prop. Code §77.305: Enacted by H.B. 1866, §4, 85th Leg., eff. Sept. 1, 2017.

PROP §77.306. ASSISTANCE IN ENFORCEMENT

If the comptroller or attorney general requests, any state agency, county clerk, district clerk, county attorney, or district attorney shall assist the comptroller or attorney general in enforcing this chapter.

History of Prop. Code §77.306: Enacted by H.B. 1866, §4, 85th Leg., eff. Sept. 1, 2017.

PROP §77.307. PENALTY

A penalty equal to five percent of the value of the unclaimed restitution payment due shall be imposed on a holder who fails to pay or deliver the payment within the time prescribed by this chapter. If a holder fails to pay or deliver an unclaimed restitution payment before the 121st day after the date the payment is due, an additional penalty equal to five percent of the value of the payment due shall be imposed.

History of Prop. Code §77.307: Enacted by H.B. 1866, §4, 85th Leg., eff. Sept. 1, 2017.

PROP §77.308. WAIVER OR ABATEMENT OF PENALTY

The comptroller may waive any penalty or interest imposed under this chapter.

History of Prop. Code §77.308: Enacted by H.B. 1866, §4, 85th Leg., eff. Sept. 1, 2017.

Chapters 78 & 79 blank

TITLE 6A. PROPERTY LOANED TO MUSEUMS

CHAPTER 80. OWNERSHIP, CONSERVATION, & DISPOSITION OF PROPERTY LOANED TO MUSEUM

PROP §80.001. PURPOSES

The purposes of this chapter are to establish the ownership of loaned cultural property that has been abandoned by the lender, to establish uniform procedures for the termination of loans of property to muse-

ums, to allow museums to conserve loaned property under certain conditions, and to limit actions to recover loaned property.

History of Prop. Code §80.001: Acts 1987, 70th Leg., ch. 1076, §1, eff. Sept. 1, 1987.

PROP §80.002. DEFINITIONS

In this chapter:

(1) "Museum" means an institution located in this state and operated by a nonprofit corporation or public agency, primarily educational, scientific, or aesthetic in purpose, that owns, borrows, or cares for and studies, archives, or exhibits property.

(2) "Lender" means a person whose name appears on the records of a museum as the person entitled to property held or owed by the museum.

(3) "Loan," "loaned," and "on loan" include all deposits of property with a museum that are not accompanied by a transfer of title to the property.

(4) "Property" or "cultural property" means all tangible objects, animate and inanimate, under a museum's care that have intrinsic, scientific, historic, artistic, or cultural value.

History of Prop. Code §80.002: Acts 1987, 70th Leg., ch. 1076, §1, eff. Sept. 1, 1987.

PROP §80.003. NOTICE TO LENDER

(a) If a museum is required to give a lender notice under this chapter, the museum is considered to have given the lender notice if the museum mails the notice to the lender at the lender's address and proof of receipt is received by the museum within 30 days after the date the notice is mailed.

(b) If the museum does not have an address for the lender or if proof of receipt is not received by the museum, the notice is considered to be given if the museum publishes notice at least once a week for two consecutive weeks in a newspaper of general circulation in both the county in which the museum is located and the county of the lender's address, if known.

(c) In addition to any other information prescribed by this chapter, notices given under this chapter must contain, if known, the lender's name, the lender's address, the date of the loan, and the name, address, and telephone number of the appropriate office or official to be contacted at the museum for information regarding the loan.

History of Prop. Code §80.003: Acts 1987, 70th Leg., ch. 1076, §1, eff. Sept. 1, 1987.

PROP §80.004. ABANDONED PROPERTY; NOTICE; TITLE TO PROPERTY

(a) Unless there is a written unexpired loan agreement to the contrary, any property on loan to a museum for 15 years or more and to which no person has made claim according to the records of the museum is considered abandoned and, notwithstanding Chapter 72, becomes the property of the museum if the museum has given the lender notice in accordance with Section 80.003.

(b) If no valid claim has been made to the property within 65 days after the date of the last notice given under Section 80.003, title to the property vests in the museum free from all claims of the owner and all persons claiming through or under the owner.

History of Prop. Code §80.004: Acts 1987, 70th Leg., ch. 1076, §1, eff. Sept. 1, 1987.

See also Prop. Code §§72.101, 72.103.

PROP §80.005. INTENT TO TERMINATE LOAN; FORM; TRANSFORMATION OF SPECIFIED TERM TO INDEFINITE TERM

(a) A museum may give the lender notice of the museum's intent to terminate a loan that was made for an indefinite term or for a term in excess of seven years. A notice of intent to terminate a loan given under this section must comply with Section 80.003 and must include a statement containing substantially the following information:

The records of (name of museum) indicate that you have property on loan to it. The museum wishes to terminate the loan. You must contact the museum, establish your ownership of the property, and make arrangements to collect the property. If you fail to do so within 65 days after the date of this notice, you will be deemed to have donated the property to the museum. See Chapter 80, Property Code.

(b) If, within 65 days after the date of the notice given under Subsection (a), the lender fails to contact the museum, establish ownership of the property, and make arrangements to collect the property, the property is considered to be donated to the museum.

(c) For the purposes of this chapter, a loan for a specified term becomes a loan for an indefinite term if the property remains in the custody of the museum when the specified term expires.

History of Prop. Code §80.005: Acts 1987, 70th Leg., ch. 1076, §1, eff. Sept. 1, 1987.

PROP §80.006. CONSERVATION OR DISPOSAL OF LOANED PROPERTY; CONDITIONS; LIEN; LIABILITY OF MUSEUM

(a) Unless there is a written loan agreement to the contrary, a museum may apply conservation measures to or dispose of property on loan to the museum without a lender's permission if immediate action is required to protect the property on loan or to protect other property in the custody of the museum, or the property on loan has become a hazard to the health and safety of the public or of the museum's staff, and:

(1) the museum cannot reach the lender at the lender's last address of record so that the museum and the lender can promptly agree on a solution; or

(2) the lender will not agree to the protective measures the museum recommends, yet is unwilling or unable to terminate the loan and retrieve the property.

(b) If a museum applies conservation measures to or disposes of property under Subsection (a), the museum:

(1) has a lien on the property and on the proceeds from any disposition of the property for the costs incurred by the museum; and

(2) is not liable for injury to or loss of the property if the museum:

(A) had a reasonable belief at the time the action was taken that the action was necessary to protect the property on loan or other property in the custody of the museum, or that the property on loan constituted a hazard to the health and safety of the public or the museum's staff; and

(B) exercised reasonable care in the choice and application of the conservation measures.

History of Prop. Code §80.006: Acts 1987, 70th Leg., ch. 1076, §1, eff. Sept. 1, 1987.

PROP §80.007. ACTION TO RECOVER PROPERTY; LIMITATIONS

(a) The two-year limitation on actions to recover personal property prescribed by Section 16.003, Civil Practice and Remedies Code, runs from the date the museum gives the lender notice of its intent to terminate the loan under Section 80.005.

(b) No action may be brought against a museum to recover property on loan to a museum for 15 years or more and to which no person has made claim if the museum has complied with Section 80.004.

(c) A lender is considered to have donated loaned property to a museum if the lender fails to file an action to recover the property on loan to the museum within the period specified by Subsection (a).

(d) A person who purchases property from a museum acquires valid title to the property if the museum represents that it has acquired title to the property under Subsection (b) or (c).

History of Prop. Code §80.007: Acts 1987, 70th Leg., ch. 1076, §1, eff. Sept. 1, 1987.

PROP §80.008. NOTICE OF PROVISIONS OF CHAPTER; LENDER'S NOTICES

(a) If, after August 31, 1987, a museum accepts a loan of property for an indefinite term or for a term in excess of seven years, the museum shall inform the lender in writing at the time of the loan of the provisions of this chapter.

(b) The lender of property to a museum shall notify the museum promptly in writing of any changes of address or change in ownership of the property.

History of Prop. Code §80.008: Acts 1987, 70th Leg., ch. 1076, §1, eff. Sept. 1, 1987.

TITLE 7. CONDOMINIUMS

CHAPTER 81. CONDOMINIUMS CREATED BEFORE ADOPTION OF UNIFORM CONDOMINIUM ACT

SUBCHAPTER A. PROVISIONS GENERALLY APPLICABLE TO CONDOMINIUMS

PROP §81.001. SHORT TITLE

This chapter may be cited as the Condominium Act.

History of Prop. Code §81.001: Acts 1983, 68th Leg., ch. 576, §1, eff. Jan. 1, 1984. Source: TRCS art. 1301a, §1.

PROP §81.0011. APPLICABILITY

(a) This chapter applies only to a condominium regime created before January 1, 1994. A condominium regime created on or after January 1, 1994, is governed by Chapter 82.

(b) A condominium regime created before January 1, 1994, to which this chapter applies is also governed by Chapter 82 as provided by Section 82.002.

History of Prop. Code §81.0011: Acts 1993, 73rd Leg., ch. 244, §3, eff. Jan. 1, 1994.

PROP §81.002. DEFINITIONS

In this chapter:

(1) "Apartment" means an enclosed space, regardless of whether it is designed for residential or other use, that consists of one or more rooms in a building and that has a direct exit to a thoroughfare or to a common space that leads to a thoroughfare.

(2) "Building" includes each principal structure on or to be erected on real property dedicated in a declaration to a condominium regime.

(3) "Condominium" means a form of real property ownership that combines separate ownership of individual apartments or units with common ownership of other elements.

(4) "Council of owners" means all the apartment owners in a condominium project.

(5) "Declaration" means the instrument that establishes property under a condominium regime.

(6) "General common elements" means the property that is part of a condominium regime other than property that is part of or belongs to an apartment in the regime, including:

(A) land on which the building is erected;

(B) foundations, bearing walls and columns, roofs, halls, lobbies, stairways, and entrance, exit, and communication ways;

(C) basements, flat roofs, yards, and gardens, except as otherwise provided;

(D) premises for the lodging of janitors or persons in charge of the building, except as otherwise provided;

(E) compartments or installation of central services such as power, light, gas, water, refrigeration, central heat and air, reservoirs, water tanks and pumps, and swimming pools; and

(F) elevators and elevator shafts, garbage incinerators, and all other devices and installations generally existing for common use.

(7) "Limited common elements" means a portion of the common elements allocated by unanimous agreement of a council of owners for the use of one or more but less than all of the apartments, such as special corridors, stairways and elevators, sanitary services common to the apartments of a particular floor, and similar areas or facilities.

(8) "Master deed" means a deed that establishes property under a condominium regime.

(9) "Master lease" means a lease that establishes property under a condominium regime.

(10) "Project" means a plan to offer for sale or to sell real property consisting of four or more apartments, rooms, office spaces, or other units in an existing or proposed building as a condominium.

(11) "Property" means real property, whether leased or owned, the improvements on the property, and the incorporeal rights that are appurtenant to the property.

History of Prop. Code §81.002: Acts 1983, 68th Leg., ch. 576, §1, eff. Jan. 1, 1984. Source: TRCS art. 1301a, §2.

See also Prop. Code §82.003.

ANNOTATIONS

Dutcher v. Owens, 647 S.W.2d 948, 949 (Tex.1983). "A condominium is an estate in real property consisting of an undivided interest in a portion of a parcel of real property together with a separate fee simple interest in another portion of the same parcel. In essence, condominium ownership is the merger of two estates in land into one: the fee simple ownership of an apartment or

unit in a condominium project and a tenancy in common with other co-owners in the common elements." *See also* ***Pooser v. Lovett Square Townhomes Owners' Ass'n***, 702 S.W.2d 226, 231 (Tex.App.—Houston [1st Dist.] 1985, writ ref'd n.r.e.).

Board of Dirs. of By the Sea Council of Co-owners, Inc. v. Sondock, 644 S.W.2d 774, 777 (Tex.App.—Corpus Christi 1982, writ ref'd n.r.e.). "The Board contends that the nature and use of the common elements may be modified from time to time, provided the Condominium Declaration is properly amended in accordance with the Declaration. We agree."

PROP §81.003. APPLICABILITY OF LOCAL ORDINANCES & REGULATIONS

(a) A planning or zoning commission of a county or municipality may adopt regulations governing condominium regimes that supplement this chapter.

(b) A local zoning ordinance must be construed to treat similar structures, lots, or parcels in a similar manner regardless of whether the property is a condominium or is leased.

History of Prop. Code §81.003: Acts 1983, 68th Leg., ch. 576, §1, eff. Jan. 1, 1984. Source: TRCS art. 1301a, §23.

ANNOTATIONS

Myer v. Cuevas, 119 S.W.3d 830, 832 (Tex. App.—San Antonio 2003, no pet.). "Condominium ownership combines separate ownership of individual units with joint ownership of common elements. *At 832 n.1:* Common elements consist of the property that is part of the condominium regime other than that which belongs to an apartment in the regime, including land, foundations, walls, roofs, halls, and other parts of the realty."

Sections 81.004-81.100 reserved for expansion

SUBCHAPTER B. CREATION, ALTERATION, & TERMINATION OF CONDOMINIUMS

PROP §81.101. CREATION OF CONDOMINIUM

An owner or developer of an existing or a planned building establishes a condominium regime by recording a master deed, master lease, or declaration under Section 81.102.

History of Prop. Code §81.101: Acts 1983, 68th Leg., ch. 576, §1, eff. Jan. 1, 1984. Source: TRCS art. 1301a, §3.

ANNOTATIONS

Pooser v. Lovett Square Townhomes Owners' Ass'n, 702 S.W.2d 226, 231 (Tex.App.—Houston [1st Dist.] 1985, writ ref'd n.r.e.). "'Condominium unit owners constitute a democratic subsociety, of necessity more restrictive in the use of condominium property than might be acceptable given traditional forms of property ownership. Therefore, each constituent must relinquish some degree of freedom of choice and agree to subordinate some of his traditional ownership rights when he elects this type of ownership experience.' The relinquishment of certain ownership rights is consistent with the condominium concept in Texas…."

PROP §81.102. CONTENTS OF DECLARATION, MASTER DEED, OR MASTER LEASE

(a) A declaration, master deed, or master lease for a condominium must contain:

(1) the legal description of the real property dedicated to the condominium regime, depicted by a plat of the property that locates and identifies by letter each existing or proposed building;

(2) a general description of each apartment, including the square footage, location, number, and other information necessary for identification of the apartment, depicted by a plat of the floor of the building in which the apartment is located that identifies the building by letter and the floor and the apartment by number;

(3) a general description of each area not already described that is subject to individual ownership and exclusive control, such as a garage or carport, depicted by a plat that shows the area and appropriately identifies it by letter or number;

(4) a description of the general common elements that are not described under Subdivision 1;

(5) a description of the limited common elements;

(6) each apartment's fractional or percentage interest in the entire condominium regime;

(7) a provision that the declaration may only be amended at a meeting of the apartment owners at which the amendment is approved by the holders of at least 67 percent of the ownership interests in the condominium; and

(8) a provision that an amendment of the declaration may not alter or destroy a unit or a limited common

element without the consent of the owners affected and the owners' first lien mortgagees.

(b) A declaration, master deed, or master lease for a condominium may contain any covenants or other matters the declarant considers appropriate.

History of Prop. Code §81.102: Acts 1983, 68th Leg., ch. 576, §1, eff. Jan. 1, 1984. Amended by Acts 1984, 68th Leg., 2nd C.S., ch. 18, §9(b), eff. Oct. 2, 1984. Source: TRCS art. 1301a, §7(B).

See also Prop. Code §§81.104, 81.111, 82.052, 82.055, 82.059, 82.061, 82.067, 82.070.

ANNOTATIONS

Cavazos v. Board of Govs. of the Council of Co-owners of the Summit Condos., No. 13-12-00524-CV (Tex.App.—Corpus Christi 2013, no pet.) (memo op.; 9-19-13). "[A]ccording to [Ps], [the] restriction on their ability to rent 'alters or destroys' an ownership interest without their consent. [¶] [D], on the other hand, contends that [Prop. Code] §81.102(a)(8) refers to the 'alteration' or 'destruction' of a physical aspect of the unit, such as removing a wall. [¶] We note that [Prop. Code] ch. 82 ... defines a condominium unit as 'a *physical* portion of the condominium designated for separate ownership or occupancy.' [¶] Here, the facts and supporting case law support the conclusion that §81.102(a)(8) refers to the 'alteration' or 'destruction' of a physical aspect of a condominium unit, not the 'alteration or destruction' of ownership rights like leasing or renting."

Nottingham Manor Owners Ass'n v. El Paso Elec. Co., 260 S.W.3d 186, 193 (Tex.App.—El Paso 2008, no pet.). P argues "when [developer] sold the condominium units to the individual buyers, it no longer had any ownership or management interest in the project or any interest in the lease. As a result, the lease was transferred to [P], and it formed part of the common elements conveyed to the buyer of each unit. [¶] [D] responds that the Declaration did not meet the statutory requirements for the creation of a condominium regime. Consequently, [P] did not obtain the lease. *At 194:* [D's] most significant argument ... is that, because only 19 of the 50 units contemplated by the Declaration were built, the condominium regime was never formed. The implication is that full ownership of the common elements, including the lease, was never conveyed to [P]." Held: P did not establish that it was owner of lease and that developer was without authority to terminate it.

PROP §81.103. PUBLIC RECORDS

(a) Each county clerk shall maintain suitable records called "Condominium Records" in which the clerk shall record master deeds, master leases, and declarations for condominiums.

(b) A county clerk shall record plats and other instruments in a declaration without prior approval from any other authority.

(c) A document required or authorized by this chapter to be recorded must be recorded according to law in the real property records of the county in which the property to which the document relates is located.

History of Prop. Code §81.103: Acts 1983, 68th Leg., ch. 576, §1, eff. Jan. 1, 1984. Source: TRCS art. 1301a, §§2, 7(A).

PROP §81.104. APARTMENT OWNERSHIP

(a) An owner of an apartment in a condominium regime owns it exclusively, and the owner may possess, convey, or encumber the apartment, or subject it to judicial acts, independently of the other apartments in the condominium regime.

(b) An individual title or interest in an apartment in a condominium regime is recordable.

(c) The entire interest in the condominium regime shall be divided among the apartments.

(d) A person may own an apartment in a condominium regime jointly or in common with others.

(e) A condominium association may not alter or destroy an apartment or a limited common element without the consent of all owners affected and the first lien mortgagees of all affected owners.

History of Prop. Code §81.104: Acts 1983, 68th Leg., ch. 576, §1, eff. Jan. 1, 1984. Amended by Acts 1984, 68th Leg., 2nd C.S., ch. 18, §9(c), eff. Oct. 2, 1984. Source: TRCS art. 1301a, §§4-6, 7(B).

See also Prop. Code §§81.102, 82.061.

ANNOTATIONS

Fairway Villas Venture v. Fairway Villas Condo. Ass'n, 815 S.W.2d 912, 914 (Tex.App.—Austin 1991, no writ). See annotation under Property Code §81.204, p. 376.

PROP §81.105. APARTMENT BOUNDARIES

(a) The boundaries of an apartment in a condominium regime are the interior surfaces of the apartment's perimeter walls, floors, and ceilings, and the exterior surfaces of the apartment's balconies and terraces.

(b) Except for common elements, the portions of a building on the boundaries of an apartment in a condominium regime and the airspace within those boundaries are part of the apartment.

(c) In interpreting a legal instrument relating to an apartment or to an apartment that has been reconstructed substantially according to the original plans of the apartment, the physical boundaries of the apartment are conclusively presumed to be the proper boundaries of the apartment regardless of settling, rising, or lateral movement of the building containing the apartment and regardless of variances between boundaries shown on the plat of the building and the actual boundaries of the building.

History of Prop. Code §81.105: Acts 1983, 68th Leg., ch. 576, §1, eff. Jan. 1, 1984. Source: TRCS art. 1301a, §9.

See also Prop. Code §§82.052, 82.059, 82.062.

PROP §81.106. APARTMENT DEEDS

A deed to an apartment in a condominium regime must:

(1) include by reference the plats in the declaration;

(2) state the encumbrances against the apartment;

(3) describe the apartment according to the plat; and

(4) state the apartment's fractional or percentage interest in the condominium regime.

History of Prop. Code §81.106: Acts 1983, 68th Leg., ch. 576, §1, eff. Jan. 1, 1984. Source: TRCS art. 1301a, §9.

PROP §81.107. INTERESTS IN COMMON ELEMENTS

An owner of an apartment in a condominium regime shares ownership of the regime's common elements with the other apartment owners. An apartment owner may use the common elements according to their intended purposes, as expressed in the plat, declaration, or bylaws of the condominium regime, without interfering with the rights of the other apartment owners.

History of Prop. Code §81.107: Acts 1983, 68th Leg., ch. 576, §1, eff. Jan. 1, 1984. Source: TRCS art. 1301a, §6.

ANNOTATIONS

Dutcher v. Owens, 647 S.W.2d 948, 951 (Tex.1983). "[B]ecause of the limited control afforded a unit owner by the statutory condominium regime, the creation of the regime effects a reallocation of tort liability. The liability of a condominium co-owner is limited to his *pro rata* interest in the regime as a whole, where such liability arises from those areas held in tenancy-in-common."

Celotex Corp. v. Gracy Meadow Owners Ass'n, 847 S.W.2d 384, 389-90 (Tex.App.—Austin 1993, writ denied). "[E]ach owner has an undivided ownership interest in all common elements."

PROP §81.108. PARTITION OF COMMON ELEMENTS

(a) The ownership of the general and the limited common elements of a condominium regime may not be judicially partitioned or divided while they are suitable for a condominium regime.

(b) A person may not initiate an action for partition of the limited or general common elements of a condominium regime unless the mortgages on the property are paid or the consent of the mortgagees is obtained.

(c) An agreement contrary to this section is void.

History of Prop. Code §81.108: Acts 1983, 68th Leg., ch. 576, §1, eff. Jan. 1, 1984. Source: TRCS art. 1301a, §8.

See also Prop. Code §82.057.

PROP §81.109. CONVEYANCE OF COMMON ELEMENTS

An apartment in a condominium regime and the undivided interest of an apartment owner in the common elements of the regime that are attributable to the apartment may not be conveyed separately. If a conveyance of an apartment does not refer to the common elements, the undivided interest of the apartment owner in the general and the limited common elements of the regime attributable to the apartment is conveyed with the apartment.

History of Prop. Code §81.109: Acts 1983, 68th Leg., ch. 576, §1, eff. Jan. 1, 1984. Source: TRCS art. 1301a, §9.

See also Prop. Code §82.057.

PROP §81.110. TERMINATION OF CONDOMINIUM REGIME

(a) By unanimous agreement, or if the declaration provides for termination by agreement of the owners, by agreement of the holders of at least 67 percent or a stated percentage in the declaration, whichever is greater, of the ownership interests in the condominium, the owners of a building in a condominium regime may terminate the regime and request the county clerk of the county in which the regime is located to merge the records of the estates that comprise the condominium regime, if any creditors in whose behalf en-

cumbrances against the building are recorded agree to accept the undivided portions of the property owned by the debtors as security, provided no amendment may be made to a declaration to reduce the vote required for termination of the condominium regime.

(b) If a condominium regime is terminated, each apartment owner owns an undivided interest in the common property that corresponds to the undivided interest previously owned by the apartment owner in the common elements.

(c) Property that has been removed from a condominium regime may be dedicated to another condominium regime at any time.

History of Prop. Code §81.110: Acts 1983, 68th Leg., ch. 576, §1, eff. Jan. 1, 1984. Amended by Acts 1989, 71st Leg., ch. 157, §1, eff. May 25, 1989. Source: TRCS art. 1301a, §§11, 12.

See also Prop. Code §§82.068, 82.101.

PROP §81.111. AMENDMENT OF CONDOMINIUM DECLARATION

After a condominium declaration is recorded with a county clerk, the declaration may not be amended except at a meeting of the apartment owners at which the amendment is approved by the holders of at least 67 percent of the ownership interests in the condominium.

History of Prop. Code §81.111: Acts 1984, 68th Leg., 2nd C.S., ch. 18, §9(d), eff. Oct. 2, 1984. Source: TRCS art. 1301a, §7(D).

See also Prop. Code §§81.102, 82.055, 82.067, 82.070.

PROP §81.112. RESTRICTION RELATING TO CLUB MEMBERSHIP

(a) A provision of a declaration, master deed, master lease, or other recorded contract that requires owners of apartments in a condominium regime to maintain a membership in a specified private club is not valid after the 10th anniversary of the date the provision is recorded or renewed unless renewed after the ninth anniversary of that date at a meeting of the apartment owners at which the renewal is approved by the holders of at least 67 percent of the ownership interests in the condominium and the text of the renewed provision is recorded in the real property records of each county in which the condominium is located.

(b) A provision described by this section may not be enacted or renewed as a bylaw by a council of owners.

History of Prop. Code §81.112: Acts 2003, 78th Leg., ch. 1101, §1, eff. Sept. 1, 2003.

See also Prop. Code §82.0675.

Sections 81.113-81.200 reserved for expansion

SUBCHAPTER C. CONDOMINIUM MANAGEMENT

PROP §81.201. AUTHORITY OF COUNCIL OF OWNERS

(a) The council of owners of a condominium regime may adopt and amend bylaws.

(b) A council of owners of a condominium regime may institute litigation on behalf of two or more apartment owners concerning a matter related to the common elements of two or more apartments. The council of owners may delegate its authority under this subsection by designating in the bylaws a person who may exercise the authority. This subsection does not limit the right of an apartment owner to bring an action in the apartment owner's own behalf.

History of Prop. Code §81.201: Acts 1983, 68th Leg., ch. 576, §1, eff. Jan. 1, 1984. Source: TRCS art. 1301a, §§13, 16.

ANNOTATIONS

Myer v. Cuevas, 119 S.W.3d 830, 835 (Tex. App.—San Antonio 2003, no pet.). Section 81.201 "does not establish standing for individual owners or exempt a plaintiff from the requirement of invoking the trial court's jurisdiction by establishing subject matter jurisdiction. [¶] [R]ecovery for damages done to common areas by a townhome association's failure to maintain the common areas belongs solely to the townhome association; the unit owners have no individual property right in the common areas for which they can sue for damages. We believe this rule is necessary because it prevents duplicate litigation arising from the same injury."

Riddick v. Quail Harbor Condo. Ass'n, 7 S.W.3d 663, 672 (Tex.App.—Houston [14th Dist.] 1999, no pet.). "[W]here the action was not brought as a class action, [Ps] were not contractually authorized to sue for the absent owners, and the provisions of [§81.201(b)] were not followed."

Augusta Court Co-owners' Ass'n v. Levin, Roth & Kasner, P.C., 971 S.W.2d 119, 126 n.5 (Tex.App.—Houston [14th Dist.] 1998, pet. denied). "The fact the Association may represent individual homeowners in litigation ... does not mean ... that it has assumed their burdens of ownership."

Celotex Corp. v. Gracy Meadow Owners Ass'n, 847 S.W.2d 384, 390 (Tex.App.—Austin 1993, writ denied). "Although the last sentence of §81.201(b) ... entitles an individual owner to bring an action in his own behalf, we interpret this provision as allowing the

owner to sue individually to recover his proportionate share of damages for injury done to a common element. An owner who suffers harm specific to his own property may, of course, always sue in his own behalf, even if the harm is somehow 'related' to common elements. For example, an owner who incurred water damage as a result of a defective roof that leaked would be entitled to bring an individual claim, recover individual damages, and receive treble damages on the basis of his individual damage award."

PROP §81.202. BYLAWS

The bylaws of a condominium regime govern the administration of the buildings that comprise the regime.

History of Prop. Code §81.202: Acts 1983, 68th Leg., ch. 576, §1, eff. Jan. 1, 1984. Source: TRCS art. 1301a, §13.

See also Prop. Code §82.106.

PROP §81.203. VOTING MAJORITY

For the purposes of this chapter, the apartment owners who own at least 51 percent of the interests in a condominium regime, as determined under the declaration, are a majority of the apartment owners.

History of Prop. Code §81.203: Acts 1983, 68th Leg., ch. 576, §1, eff. Jan. 1, 1984. Source: TRCS art. 1301a, §2.

PROP §81.204. MAINTENANCE OF CONDOMINIUM

(a) An apartment owner in a condominium regime is responsible for the apartment owner's pro rata share of:

(1) the expenses to administer the condominium regime and to maintain and repair the general common elements;

(2) in proper cases, the expenses to administer the limited common elements of the buildings in the condominium regime; and

(3) other expenses approved by the council of owners.

(b) An apartment owner in a condominium regime is not exempted from the obligation under this section to contribute toward the expenses of the condominium regime by waiving the use of the common elements or abandoning the apartment.

History of Prop. Code §81.204: Acts 1983, 68th Leg., ch. 576, §1, eff. Jan. 1, 1984. Source: TRCS art. 1301a, §15.

ANNOTATIONS

Alma Invs. v. Bahia Mar Co-owners Ass'n, 999 S.W.2d 820, 825 (Tex.App.—Corpus Christi 1999, pet. denied). "The purpose for the maintenance charges is to provide for the general benefit of the [condominium] through the maintenance, improvement, and construction of recreational and other facilities in and for the [condominium]. Section 81.204 … explicitly states that each apartment owner shall pay his *pro rata* share. *At 826:* We hold … that the [provisions of a maintenance agreement allowing the developer to exempt units from maintenance fees] are against public policy, void, and unenforceable."

Richardson Lifestyle Ass'n v. Houston, 853 S.W.2d 796, 801 (Tex.App.—Dallas 1993, writ denied). "According to the plain language of §2.02(b) [of the bylaws], replacements, being included in §2.02(a) and §2.02(c)(vii), are excluded from §2.02(b) and its approval requirement. [¶] The roof work was a replacement under §§2.02(a) and 2.02(c)(vii). The contract itself provided for removal and replacement of the roofs. [¶] Therefore, it is immaterial whether the roof work was a capital improvement because the work was a replacement under §§2.02(a) and 2.02(c)(vii).… Since the work to the roofs was a replacement, the board of directors was not required to seek approval to authorize the assessment."

Fairway Villas Venture v. Fairway Villas Condo. Ass'n, 815 S.W.2d 912, 914 (Tex.App.—Austin 1991, no writ). "An individual's exclusive ownership of an apartment does *not* include the land or land surface underlying the building in which an apartment is located, for these are part of the 'general common elements.' [¶] When §81.204 employs the term 'apartment owner,' it necessarily refers to and incorporates the foregoing propositions, and these indicate the meaning intended for that term by the legislature. *At 915:* The [Condominium] Act contemplates both existing and proposed buildings in a condominium regime, and the word 'apartment' must therefore accommodate both because that word is defined solely in terms of a 'building' in which the 'apartment' is enclosed. We hold, therefore, that §81.204 applies to the owners of apartments in both existing and proposed buildings."

Richard Gill Co. v. Jackson's Landing Owners' Ass'n, 758 S.W.2d 921, 924 (Tex.App.—Corpus Christi 1988, writ denied). "[P] points out that it is not inconsistent for [developer] to be considered an apartment owner and at the same time exercise powers specifically denied to individual owners in the declaration. The board of directors itself, though merely a group of individual owners, would eventually gain these same powers. The distinction is that [developer] was not act-

ing in its capacity as an owner of individual apartments when it undertook maintenance or advertising, but in its capacity as an interim manager. This did not detract from [developer's] status under either capacity, nor does it make the declaration ambiguous. The trial court correctly concluded that [developer] was an apartment owner under the declaration for the purpose of assessments."

Pooser v. Lovett Square Townhomes Owners' Ass'n, 702 S.W.2d 226, 231-32 (Tex.App.—Houston [1st Dist.] 1985, writ ref'd n.r.e.). "The record reflects that numerous repairs and steps were made to resolve the leakage problem. The majority of homeowners had rejected the proposal of levying special assessments to immediately cure the problem. Homeowners with particularly serious leakage problems, however, were allowed to immediately repair their roofs at their own expense and receive reimbursement later. [¶] By purchasing a condominium unit, [Ps] delegated decision making authority concerning the common areas to [D]. [Ps] then chose not to participate in their Association or to vote or run for office. [¶] We ... apply a standard of reasonableness in evaluating [D's] conduct. The delegation of authority to the condominium association is implicit in the condominium scheme, and the record shows reasonable efforts of [D] to solve the leakage problem."

PROP §81.205. INSURANCE

(a) By resolution of a majority of the council of owners or in the manner provided or required by the declaration or bylaws, the council of owners may acquire the insurance it deems appropriate for the protection of the buildings and the apartment owners.

(b) Insurance may be written in the name of the council of owners, or in the name of a person designated in the declaration or bylaws, as trustee for the apartment owners and their mortgagees. Each apartment owner and mortgagee of an apartment owner is a beneficiary of the policy, whether named as a beneficiary or not, in proportion to the interest of an apartment owner in the condominium regime as established by the declaration.

(c) The acquisition of insurance by the council of owners does not prejudice the right of an apartment owner in a condominium regime to obtain insurance for the apartment owner's own benefit.

History of Prop. Code §81.205: Acts 1983, 68th Leg., ch. 576, §1, eff. Jan. 1, 1984. Source: TRCS art. 1301a, §19.

PROP §81.206. DISPOSITION OF INSURANCE PROCEEDS

(a) Except as provided by Subsection (b), if a building in a condominium regime is damaged by a casualty against which it is insured, the proceeds of the insurance policy shall be used to reconstruct the building. The council of owners or the bylaws of the condominium regime govern the conduct of the reconstruction.

(b) If more than two-thirds of a building in a condominium regime requires reconstruction because of a casualty against which it is insured, the council of owners may elect not to reconstruct the building. Unless the council of owners unanimously agrees otherwise, the insurance proceeds shall be paid to the individual apartment owners or their mortgagees, as their interest may appear, in proportion to the interest of an apartment owner in the condominium regime as established by the declaration.

History of Prop. Code §81.206: Acts 1983, 68th Leg., ch. 576, §1, eff. Jan. 1, 1984. Source: TRCS art. 1301a, §20.

PROP §81.207. INSUFFICIENT INSURANCE

(a) If under Section 81.206 a damaged building in a condominium regime must be reconstructed but insurance proceeds are insufficient to pay for the cost of reconstruction, the apartment owners directly affected by the damage shall pay the difference between the cost of reconstruction and the insurance proceeds, unless the bylaws provide otherwise. Each affected apartment owner shall contribute an amount for reconstruction that is proportionate to the interest of the apartment owner in the condominium regime.

(b) If one or more but less than a majority of the affected apartment owners refuse to make a payment required under this section, after a resolution by the majority of the affected apartment owners stating the circumstances of the case and the cost of the work, the majority may repair the damage at the expense of all apartment owners benefited by the reconstruction.

(c) By a unanimous resolution subsequent to the date of a casualty, the apartment owners in a condominium regime who are concerned with the application of this section may elect to modify its effects.

History of Prop. Code §81.207: Acts 1983, 68th Leg., ch. 576, §1, eff. Jan. 1, 1984. Source: TRCS art. 1301a, §21.

PROP §81.208. ASSESSMENTS DUE ON CONVEYANCE

If an apartment owner conveys the apartment and assessments against the apartment are unpaid, the apartment owner shall pay the past due assessments out of the sale price of the apartment, or the purchaser shall pay the assessments, in preference to any other charges against the property except:

(1) assessments, liens, and charges in favor of this state or a political subdivision of this state for taxes on the apartment that are due and unpaid; or

(2) an obligation due under a validly recorded mortgage.

History of Prop. Code §81.208: Acts 1983, 68th Leg., ch. 576, §1, eff. Jan. 1, 1984. Source: TRCS art. 1301a, §18.

See also Prop. Code §82.113.

ANNOTATIONS

Bundren v. Holly Oaks Townhomes Ass'n, 347 S.W.3d 421, 434 (Tex.App.—Dallas 2011, pet. denied). "The only purchase or sale of [condominium unit] after the disputed [homeowners' association (HOA)] dues became due and that involved [property investors] was [their] purchase of the unit at the foreclosure sale.... [Property investors] argue that (1) [Prop. Code] §81.208 does not apply to a foreclosure sale, and (2) [Prop. Code ch. 82] applies to this case and defines a 'purchaser' to be a person who acquires title to the property by means of a voluntary transfer, which would not include a foreclosure sale. *At 435:* [R]egardless of whether §81.208 generally applies to the purchase of a condominium unit at a foreclosure sale, [HOA] agreed [in the declaration] that it would not seek to hold the purchaser of a unit at a foreclosure sale personally liable for all the outstanding HOA dues. Accordingly, [HOA] cannot seek to hold [property investors] liable under §81.208 ... for all HOA dues that were outstanding when [property investors] acquired the property at the foreclosure sale...."

Johnson v. First S. Props., Inc., 687 S.W.2d 399, 402 (Tex.App.—Houston [14th Dist.] 1985, writ ref'd n.r.e.). "[D] suggests that the [Condominium] Act did not authorize non-judicial foreclosure, and in fact provided that the sole remedy was to be a preferential payment upon sale of the unit. Consequently, he argues that the declaration providing for non-judicial foreclosure is invalid. [¶] Neither the Act nor the declaration state that the remedies found in the Act are exclusive. The Act provides a framework to be utilized, if desired, but co-owners may certainly establish remedies in addition to those in the Act. [D's] points contesting the substantial validity of the foreclosure are overruled."

PROP §81.209. CONDOMINIUM RECORDS

(a) The administrator or board of administration of a condominium regime or a person appointed by the bylaws of the regime shall keep a detailed written account of the receipts and expenditures related to the building and its administration that specifies the expenses incurred by the regime.

(b) The accounts and supporting vouchers of a condominium regime shall be made available to the apartment owners for examination on working days at convenient, established, and publicly announced hours.

(c) The books and records of a condominium regime must comply with good accounting procedures and must be audited at least once each year by an auditor who is not associated with the condominium regime.

History of Prop. Code §81.209: Acts 1983, 68th Leg., ch. 576, §1, eff. Jan. 1, 1984. Source: TRCS art. 1301a, §14.

See also Prop. Code §82.114.

ANNOTATIONS

Board of Dirs. of By the Sea Council of Co-owners, Inc. v. Sondock, 644 S.W.2d 774, 782 (Tex.App.—Corpus Christi 1982, writ ref'd n.r.e.). "It is inconvenient and not very practical for an owner to go to somebody's home in a different city to avail himself of his right to inspect the books and records of the condominium. ... Clearly, the legislative intent was to provide owners with ready access to the books and records of their condominium and the most logical place for keeping these records is on the premises."

PROP §81.210. LOANS AS ELIGIBLE INVESTMENTS

(a) If a fiduciary or a bank, savings and loan association, trust company, life insurance company, or other lending institution is authorized to make real estate loans, a loan on an apartment in a condominium regime and the undivided interest in the common elements of the regime that is appurtenant to the apartment is an eligible investment for the fiduciary or lending institution.

(b) A lender may not consider the existence of a prior lien for taxes, assessments, or other similar charges that are not delinquent in determining whether a mortgage or deed of trust is a first lien on the security for a loan under this section.

(c) For the purposes of this section, an apartment in a condominium regime and the undivided interest in the common elements appurtenant to the apartment are a single unit independent of the other units in the regime.

(d) This section does not affect any otherwise applicable provision of law that limits mortgage investments based on a special fraction or percentage of the value of the mortgaged property.

History of Prop. Code §81.210: Acts 1983, 68th Leg., ch. 576, §1, eff. Jan. 1, 1984. Source: TRCS art. 1301a, §10.

CHAPTER 82. UNIFORM CONDOMINIUM ACT

NCCUSL Prefatory Comment*

This Chapter contains comprehensive provisions designed to unify and modernize the law of condominiums, which has undergone great change in the last 16 years. As a result of the increasing usefulness and flexibility of the condominium concept, condominiums have become one of the most common forms of community ownership of property in the United States.

All states have statutes which provide for the creation of condominiums and establish some rules concerning their governance. The first statute in the United States was adopted in 1958 in Puerto Rico, and most of the present state statutes are patterned after that 1958 statute, or after the 1962 Federal Housing Administration model condominium statute. As the condominium form of ownership became widespread, however, many states realized that these early statutes were inadequate to deal with the growing condominium industry. In particular, many states perceived a need for additional consumer protection, as

* **Editor's note:**

The NCCUSL comments have been edited to reflect the Texas Legislature's omission of sections and changing of section numbers from the original uniform act. The Texas Legislature did not adopt the NCCUSL comments when it adopted the Uniform Condominium Act. The full uniform act and comments can be found at www.uniformlaws.org.

well as a need for more flexibility in the creation and use of condominiums. As a result, some states have recently enacted more detailed and comprehensive "second generation" statutes.

The statutes governing condominiums in the various states use varying and sometimes inappropriate terminology, and differ in numerous details, all of which make it difficult for a national lender to assess the appropriateness of condominium documents and of condominium financing arrangements in those states. Moreover, the varying statutes, creating different "bundles of rights" for purchasers of condominiums in the various states, also make it difficult for the increasingly mobile consumer to become educated in this very complex area. Finally, many actual or potential problems involving such matters as termination of condominiums, eminent domain, insurance, and the rights and obligations of lenders upon foreclosure of a condominium project, have not been satisfactorily addressed by any existing statute. It is primarily to resolve these various problems that the Uniform Condominium Act was drafted.

Subchapter A contains definitions and general provisions applicable throughout the Chapter. The subchapter deals with such matters as applicability, separate titles and taxation, eminent domain, applicability of other statutes, and other general matters.

Subchapter B provides for the creation, alteration, and termination of the condominium. The subchapter provides great flexibility to a developer in creating a condominium project designed to meet the needs of a modern real estate market, while imposing reasonable restrictions on developers' practices which have a potential for harm to unit purchasers.

Subchapter C concerns the administration of the unit owners' association, a matter which has received very limited attention in the statutes of the various states. This subchapter provides broad-ranging powers to the association, and covers such matters as insurance, tort and contract liability of the association, and other matters often not dealt with in current statutes.

Subchapter D deals with consumer protection for condominium unit purchasers. In addition to treating specific abuses which have developed in the condominium industry in the past, the subchapter requires very substantial disclosure by developers, which must be made available to consumers before conveyance of a unit. To further promote disclosure, the subchapter also requires that all owners of units in residential condominiums provide resale certificates to subsequent purchasers, regardless of when the condominium was created.

...

The Uniform Condominium Act was originally a part of the Uniform Land Transactions Act, but was separated from that Act for further consideration at the 1975 annual meeting of the National Conference of Commissioners on Uniform State Laws. This Chapter was approved at the annual meeting of the Conference in Vail, Colorado in August 1977.

Since promulgation of the Chapter in 1977, and approval by the American Bar Association in 1978, the Chapter has received widespread legislative attention. The Chapter was enacted in its uniform version in Minnesota, Pennsylvania, and West Virginia during the 1979-80 legislative year, and was enacted with substantial amendments in Louisiana in 1978-79. By 1980, it had also been introduced in the legislatures of Arizona, Colorado, Connecticut, Idaho, Illinois, Massachusetts, Missouri, Tennessee, Vermont, and Wyoming.

During this same period, the National Conference appointed a Drafting Committee to draft a Uniform Planned Community Act (UPCA), and that Act was promulgated by the Conference at its 1980 annual meeting. UPCA applies to a wide variety of other forms of multiple ownership real estate regimes which are similar in legal structure to condominiums, but do not meet the definition of "condominium" either, under present state law or the Uniform Condominium Act.

As a result of the legislative process in the various states considering the Chapter, and review of the Chapter by the Drafting Committee on UPCA, a large number of amendments to the 1977 Act were proposed to the Conference.

Many of the amendments were adopted at the 1980 annual meeting of the Conference, and have been included in this edition of the Chapter. Most of them are of a minor non-substantial nature; they are intended to resolve insignificant technical questions, or to clarify the meaning of provisions susceptible to misinterpretation. A few amendments were adopted which result in more significant changes, either on particular matters of substance, or in the use of terms throughout the Chapter which simplify the structure and readability of the Chapter. A summary of the more significant amendments can be obtained from the Headquarters Office of the NCCUSL, Suite 510, 645 N. Michigan Ave., Chicago, IL 60611.

A second category of changes results from a decision of the Conference at its 1978 annual meeting that the Condominium and Planned Community Acts should contain identical provisions wherever possible, in order to facilitate the consolidation of the two Acts in those states desiring a single Uniform Act covering both forms of multiple ownership developments. This required a large number of textual changes with no substantive effect. As a result, however, there are very few differences between the two Acts, and consolidation would be a simple and desirable approach in states desiring uniform coverage of both forms of ownership. An analysis of the differences between the Chapters, and a general description of how the Chapters might be consolidated, appear in the Prefatory Note to UPCA. However, at this time, the Conference has not prepared a consolidated text, because of its continuing consideration of the co-operative form of ownership, and the possibility that a consolidated Act might be applicable to co-operatives as well.

SUBCHAPTER A. GENERAL PROVISIONS

PROP §82.001. SHORT TITLE

This chapter may be cited as the Uniform Condominium Act.

History of Prop. Code §82.001: Acts 1993, 73rd Leg., ch. 244, §1, eff. Jan. 1, 1994.

PROP §82.002. APPLICABILITY

(a) This chapter applies to all commercial, industrial, residential, and other types of condominiums in this state for which the declaration is recorded on or after January 1, 1994. A condominium for which the declaration was recorded before January 1, 1994, may be governed exclusively under this chapter if either:

(1) the owners of units vote to amend the declaration, in accordance with the amendment process authorized by the declaration, to have this chapter apply and that amendment is filed for record in the condominium records in each county in which the condominium is located; or

(2) a declaration or amendment of declaration was recorded before January 1, 1994, and the declaration or amendment states that this chapter will apply in its entirety on January 1, 1994.

(b) An amendment to a declaration under Subsection (a)(1) that implements a vote of the unit owners to be governed by this chapter may not affect the rights of a declarant or impose duties on a declarant that are greater than or in addition to the declarant's duties immediately before the date of the vote or amendment.

(c) This section and the following sections apply to a condominium in this state for which the declaration was recorded before January 1, 1994: Sections 82.005, 82.006, 82.007, 82.053, 82.054, 82.102(a)(1)-(7), (a)(12)-(21), (f), and (g), 82.108, 82.111, 82.113, 82.114, 82.116, 82.118, 82.157, and 82.161. The definitions prescribed by Section 82.003 apply to a condominium in this state for which the declaration was recorded before January 1, 1994, to the extent the defini-

tions do not conflict with the declaration. The sections listed in this subsection apply only with respect to events and circumstances occurring on or after January 1, 1994, and do not invalidate existing provisions of the declaration, bylaws, or plats or plans of a condominium for which the declaration was recorded before January 1, 1994.

(d) Chapter 81 does not apply to a condominium for which the declaration was recorded on or after January 1, 1994, and does not invalidate any amendment to the declaration, bylaws, or plats and plans of any condominium for which the declaration was recorded before January 1, 1994, if the amendment would be permitted by this chapter. The amendment must be adopted in conformity with the procedures and requirements specified by those instruments and by Chapter 81. If the amendment grants to a person a right, power, or privilege permitted by this chapter, all correlative obligations, liabilities, and restrictions prescribed by this chapter also apply to that person.

History of Prop. Code §82.002: Acts 1993, 73rd Leg., ch. 244, §1, eff. Jan. 1, 1994. Amended by Acts 1997, 75th Leg., ch. 956, §1, eff. Jan. 1, 1998; Acts 2009, 81st Leg., ch. 1323, §1, eff. Sept. 1, 2009; Acts 2013, 83rd Leg., ch. 678, §1, eff. Sept. 1, 2013.

NCCUSL Comment*

1. The question of the extent to which a state statute should apply to particular condominiums involves two problems: first, the extent to which the statute should require or permit different results for condominiums created before and after the statute becomes effective; and second, whether the statute should impose any or all of its substantive requirements on condominiums located outside the state.

Two conflicting policies are proposed when considering the applicability of this Chapter to "old" and "new" condominiums located in the enacting state. On the one hand, it is desirable, for reasons of uniformity, for the Chapter to apply to all condominiums located in a particular state, regardless of whether the condominium was created before or after adoption of the Chapter in that state. To the extent that different laws apply within the same state to different condominiums, confusion results in the minds of both lenders and consumers. Moreover, because of the inadequacies and uncertainties of condominiums created under old law, and because of the requirements placed on declarants' and unit owners' associations by this Chapter which might increase the costs of new condominiums, different markets might tend to develop for condominiums created before and after adoption of the Chapter.

On the other hand, to make all provisions of this Chapter automatically apply to "old" condominiums might violate the constitutional prohibition of impairment of contracts. In addition, aside from the constitutional issue, automatic applicability of the entire Chapter almost certainly would unduly alter the legitimate expectations of some present unit owners and declarants.

Accordingly, the philosophy of this section reflects a desire to maximize the uniform applicability of the Chapter to all condominiums in the enacting state, while avoiding the difficulties raised by automatic application of the entire Chapter to pre-existing condominiums.

2. In carrying out this philosophy with respect to "new" condominiums, the Chapter applies to all condominiums "created" within the state after the Chapter's effective date. This is the effect of the first sentence of subsection (a). The first sentence of subsection (b) makes clear that the provisions of old statutes expressly applicable to condominiums do not apply to condominiums created after the effective date of this Chapter.

"Creation" of a condominium pursuant to this Chapter occurs upon recordation of a declaration pursuant to Section 82.051; however, the definition of "condominium" in Section 82.003(8) contemplates that *de facto* condominiums may exist, if the nature of the ownership interest fits the definition, and the Chapter would apply to such a condominium. Any real estate project which includes individually owned units and common elements owned by the unit owners as tenants in common is therefore subject to the Chapter if created within the state after the Chapter's effective date. No intent to subject the condominium to the Chapter is required, and an express intention to the contrary would be invalid and ineffective.

3. The section adopts a novel three-step approach to condominiums created before the effective date of the Chapter. First, certain provisions of the Chapter automatically apply to "old" condominiums, but only prospectively, and only in a manner which does not invalidate provisions of condominium declarations and bylaws valid under "old" law. Second, "old" law remains applicable to previously created condominiums where not automatically displaced by the Chapter. Third, owners of "old" condominiums may amend any provisions of their declaration or bylaws, even if the amendment would not be permitted by "old" law, so long as (a) the amendment is adopted in accordance with the procedure required by "old" law and the existing declaration and bylaws, and (b) the substance of the amendment does not violate this Chapter.

4. Elaboration of the principles described in Comment 3 may be helpful.

First, the second sentence of subsection (a) provides that the enumerated provisions automatically apply to condominiums created under pre-existing law, even though no action is taken by the unit owners. Many of the sections which do apply should measurably increase the ability of the unit owners to effectively manage the association, and should help to encourage the marketability of condominiums created under early condominium statutes. To avoid possible constitutional challenges, these provisions, as applied to "old" condominiums, apply only to "events and circumstances occurring after the effective date of this Chapter"; moreover, the provisions of this Chapter are subject to the provisions of the instruments creating the condominium, and this Chapter does not invalidate those instruments.

EXAMPLE 1:

Under subsection (a), Section 82.157 (Resale of Unit) automatically applies to "old" condominiums. Accordingly, unit owners in condominiums established prior to adoption of the Chapter would be obligated after the Chapter's effective date to provide resale certificates to future purchasers of units in "old" condominiums. However, the failure of a unit owner to provide such a certificate to a purchaser who acquired the unit before the effective date of the Chapter would not create a cause of action in the purchaser, because the conveyance was an event occurring before the effective date of the Chapter.

EXAMPLE 2:

Under subsection (a), Section 82.114 (Association Records) automatically applies to "old" condominiums. As a result, a unit owners' association of an "old" condominium must maintain certain financial records, and all the records of the association "shall be made reasonably available for examination by any unit owner and his authorized agents," even if the "old" law did not require that records be kept, or access provided. If the declaration or bylaws, however, provided that unit owners could not inspect the records of the association without permission of the president of the association, the restriction in the declaration would continue to be valid and enforceable.

Second, the prior laws of the state relating to condominiums are not repealed by this Chapter because those laws will still apply to previously-created condominiums, except when displaced. Some states, such as Connecticut and Florida, have made certain provisions of their condominium statutes automatically applicable to pre-existing condominiums. In certain instances, this attempted retroactive application has raised serious constitutional questions, has caused doubts to arise as to the continued validity of those condominiums, and has created general confusion as to what statutory rules should be applied.

Third, the Chapter seeks to alleviate any undesirable consequences of "old" law, by a limited "opt-in" provision. More specifically, subsection (b) permits the owners of a pre-existing condominium to take advantage of the salutary provisions of this statute to the extent that can be accomplished consistent with the procedures for amending the condominium instruments as specified in those instruments and in the pre-existing statute.

EXAMPLE 3:

Under most "first generation" condominium statutes, unit owners have no power to relocate boundaries between adjoining units. Under Section 82.062 of this Chapter, unit owners have such power, unless limited by the declaration.

* See footnote on p. 379.

While Section 82.062 does not automatically apply to "old" condominiums, if the unit owners of a pre-existing condominium amend their condominium instruments in the manner permitted by the old statute and their existing instruments to permit unit owners to relocate boundaries, this section would validate that amendment, even if it were invalid under old law.

5. In considering the permissible amendments under subsection (b), it is important to distinguish between the law governing the procedure for amending declarations, and the substance of the amendments themselves. An amendment to the declaration of the condominium created under "old" law, even if permissible under this Chapter, must nevertheless be adopted "in conformity with the procedures and requirements specified" by the original condominium instruments, and in compliance with the old law.

EXAMPLE:

Suppose an "old" condominium declaration and "old" state law both provide that approval by 100% of the unit owners is required to amend the declaration, but the unit owners wish to amend the declaration to provide for only 67% of the unit owners' approval of future amendments, as permitted by Section 82.067 of this Chapter. The amendment would not be valid unless 100% of the unit owners approved it, because of the procedural requirement of the declaration and "old" law. Once approved, however, only 67% would be required for subsequent amendments.

6. The last sentence of subsection (b) addresses the potential problem of a declarant seeking to take undue advantage of the amendment provisions to assume a power granted by the Chapter without being subject to the Chapter's limitations on the power. The last sentence insures that, if declarants or other persons assume any of the powers and rights which the Chapter grants, the correlative obligations, liabilities, and restrictions of the Chapter also apply to that person, even if the amendment itself does not require that result.

EXAMPLE:

Assume that, pursuant to the provisions of the "old" law, the declarant may exercise control over the association for only 3 years from the date the condominium is created, but the control may be maintained during that period for so long as declarant owns any units. In the absence of any amendment, a provision in the declaration taking full advantage of the "old" law would be valid and enforceable. Assume further that, in the second year following creation of the condominium in question, this Chapter is adopted. The declarant then properly amends the declaration pursuant to subsection (b) to extend the period of declarant control for 5 years from the date of creation. The amendment would effectively extend control for 2 additional years, because Section 82.103(c) does not limit the number of the years the declarant may specify as a control period.

Nevertheless, if the declarant, before that extended time limit has expired, conveys 75 percent of the units that may ever be a part of the condominium, or fails for 2 years to exercise development rights or offer units for sale in the ordinary course of business, the period of declarant control would terminate by virtue of the limitations in Section 82.103(c). That limitation is imposed on the declarant even if the amendment called for retaining control for so long as any units were owned by declarant, and despite the provision in the "old" law permitting such a restriction.

7. The reference in subsection (b) to Chapter 81 is intended to distinguish between a state's condominium enabling statutes and those statutes which apply not only to condominiums but to other forms of real estate, such as taxation statutes or subdivision statutes. Thus, reference to the state's condominium or horizontal property regime enabling statutes should be included here, while references to taxation, subdivision, or other statutes which are not restricted solely to condominiums should not be included.

8. This section does not permit a pre-existing condominium to elect to come entirely within the provisions of the Chapter, disregarding old law. However, the owners of a pre-existing condominium may elect to terminate the condominium under pre-existing law and create a new condominium which would be subject to all the provisions of this Chapter.

9. Subsection (c) reflects the fact that there are practical as well as constitutional limits regarding the extent to which a state should or may extend its jurisdiction to out-of-state transactions. A state may, of course, properly exercise its authority to protect its citizens from false or misleading information relating to condominiums located in other states but sold in that state. However, where sales contracts are executed wholly outside the enacting state and relate to condominiums located outside the state, it seems more appropriate for the courts of the jurisdiction(s) in which the condominium is located and where the transaction occurs to have jurisdiction over the transaction.

PROP §82.003. DEFINITIONS

(a) In this chapter:

(1) "Affiliate of a declarant" means any person who controls, is controlled by, or is under common control with a declarant. A person "controls" a declarant if the person is a general partner, officer, director, or employer of the declarant; directly or indirectly or acting in concert with one or more other persons, or through one or more subsidiaries, owns, controls, holds with power to vote or holds proxies representing more than 20 percent of the voting interests in the declarant; determines in any manner the election of a majority of the directors of the declarant; or has contributed more than 20 percent of the capital of the declarant. A person "is controlled by" a declarant if the declarant is a general partner, officer, director, or employer of the person; directly or indirectly or acting in concert with one or more other persons, or through one or more subsidiaries, owns, controls, holds with power to vote, or holds proxies representing more than 20 percent of the voting interests in the person; determines in any manner the election of a majority of the directors of the person; or has contributed more than 20 percent of the capital of the person.

(2) "Allocated interests" means the undivided interest in the common elements, the common expense liability, and votes in the association allocated to each unit.

(3) "Association" means the unit owners' association organized under Section 82.101.

(4) "Board" means the board of directors or the body, regardless of name, designated to act on behalf of the association.

(5) "Common elements" means all portions of a condominium other than the units and includes both general and limited common elements.

(6) "Common expense liability" means the liability for common expenses allocated to each unit.

(7) "Common expenses" means expenditures made by or financial liabilities of the association, together with any allocations to reserves.

(8) "Condominium" means a form of real property with portions of the real property designated for separate ownership or occupancy, and the remainder of the real property designated for common ownership or occupancy solely by the owners of those portions. Real property is a condominium only if one or more of the

common elements are directly owned in undivided interests by the unit owners. Real property is not a condominium if all of the common elements are owned by a legal entity separate from the unit owners, such as a corporation, even if the separate legal entity is owned by the unit owners.

(9) "Conversion building" means a building that at any time before creation of the condominium was occupied wholly or partially by persons other than purchasers and persons who occupy with the consent of purchasers.

(10) "Declarant" means a person, or group of persons acting in concert, who:

(A) as part of a common promotional plan, offers to dispose of the person's interest in a unit not previously disposed of; or

(B) reserves or succeeds to any special declarant right.

(11) "Declaration" means an instrument, however denominated, that creates a condominium, and any amendment to that instrument.

(11-a) "Dedicatory instrument" means each document governing the establishment, maintenance, or operation of a condominium regime. The term includes a declaration or similar instrument subjecting real property to:

(A) restrictive covenants, bylaws, or similar instruments governing the administration or operation of a unit owners' association;

(B) properly adopted rules and regulations of the unit owners' association; or

(C) all lawful amendments to the covenants, bylaws, instruments, rules, or regulations.

(12) "Development rights" means a right or combination of rights reserved by a declarant in the declaration to:

(A) add real property to a condominium;

(B) create units, common elements, or limited common elements within a condominium;

(C) subdivide units or convert units into common elements; or

(D) withdraw real property from a condominium.

(13) "Disposition" means a voluntary transfer to a purchaser of any legal or equitable interest in a unit but does not include the transfer or release of a security interest.

(14) "General common elements" means common elements that are not limited common elements.

(15) "Identifying number" means a symbol or address that identifies only one unit in a condominium.

(16) "Leasehold condominium" means a condominium in which all or a portion of the real property is subject to a lease the expiration or termination of which will terminate the condominium or reduce its size.

(17) "Limited common element" means a portion of the common elements allocated by the declaration or by operation of Section 82.052 for the exclusive use of one or more but less than all of the units.

(18) "Plan" means a dimensional drawing that is recordable in the real property records or the condominium plat records and that horizontally and vertically identifies or describes units and common elements that are contained in buildings.

(19) "Plat" means a survey recordable in the real property records or the condominium plat records and containing the information required by Section 82.059. As used in this chapter, "plat" does not have the same meaning as "plat" in Chapter 212 or 232, Local Government Code, or other statutes dealing with municipal or county regulation of property development.

(20) "Purchaser" means a person, other than a declarant, who by means of a voluntary transfer acquires a legal or equitable interest in a unit other than a leasehold interest or as security for an obligation.

(21) "Residential purposes" means recreational or dwelling purposes, or both.

(22) "Special declarant rights" means rights reserved for the benefit of a declarant to:

(A) complete improvements indicated on plats and plans filed with the declaration;

(B) exercise any development right;

(C) make the condominium part of a larger condominium or a planned community;

(D) maintain sales, management, and leasing offices, signs advertising the condominium, and models;

(E) use easements through the common elements for the purpose of making improvements within the condominium or within real property that may be added to the condominium; or

(F) appoint or remove any officer or board member of the association during any period of declarant control.

(23) "Unit" means a physical portion of the condominium designated for separate ownership or occupancy, the boundaries of which are described by the declaration.

(24) "Unit owner" means a declarant or other person who owns a unit, or a lessee of a unit in a leasehold condominium whose lease expires simultaneously with any lease the expiration or termination of which will remove the unit from the condominium, but does not include a person having an interest in a unit solely as security for an obligation.

(b) Unless otherwise provided by the declaration or bylaws, a term defined by Subsection (a) has the same meaning if used in a declaration or bylaws.

History of Prop. Code §82.003: Acts 1993, 73rd Leg., ch. 244, §1, eff. Jan. 1, 1994. Amended by Acts 2013, 83rd Leg., ch. 678, §2, eff. Sept. 1, 2013.

ANNOTATIONS

Bankler v. Vale, 75 S.W.3d 29, 34 (Tex.App.—San Antonio 2001, no pet.). "The Board attacks the language 'prospective purchaser,' [in the injunction preventing the Board from building a reserve account from a special assessment and from funding 'emergency' improvements to the townhomes] asserting it is overly broad and may include an unlimited and unidentifiable class of persons. [¶] By definition, a 'purchaser' is actually an owner. A 'prospective purchaser,' in laymen's terms, would be someone 'likely to be or become' a purchaser of a [townhome] unit. Accordingly, a 'prospective purchaser' does not include an unidentifiable group of people. Furthermore, by including the term 'prospective purchaser,' the trial court precluded the Board from circumventing the injunction by simply labeling a person as a 'prospective purchaser,' someone who has not yet acquired an interest in a condominium unit, rather than a 'purchaser.'"

NCCUSL Comment*

1. The definition of "affiliate of a declarant" (Section 82.003(1)) is similar to the definitions in 12 U.S.C. §1730(a), which prescribes the authority of the Federal Savings and Loan Insurance Corporation to regulate the activities of savings and loan holding companies, and in 15 U.S.C. §78(c)(18), which defines persons deemed to be associated with a broker or dealer for purposes of the federal securities laws.

The objective standards of the definition permit a ready determination of the existence of affiliate status to be made. Unlike 12 U.S.C. §1730(a)(2)B, no power is vested in an agency to subjectively determine the existence of "control" necessary to establish affiliate status. Thus, affiliate status does not exist under the Chapter unless these objective criteria are met.

2. Definition (2), "allocated interests," refers to all of the interests which this Chapter requires the declaration to allocate. *See* Section 82.057.

3. Definitions (5) and (23), treating "common elements" and "units," should be examined in light of Section 82.052, which specifies in detail how the precise differentiation between units and common elements is to be determined in any given condominium to the extent that the declaration does not provide a different scheme. No exhaustive list of items comprising the common elements is necessary in this Chapter or in the declaration; as long as the boundaries between units and common elements can be ascertained with certainty, the common elements include by definition all of the real estate in the condominium not designated as part of the units.

4. Definition (8), "condominium," makes clear that, unless the ownership interest in the common elements is vested in the owners of the units, the project is not a condominium. Thus, for example, if the common elements were owned by an association in which each unit owner was a member, the project would not be a condominium. Similarly, if a declarant sold units in a building but retained title to the common areas, granting easements over them to unit owners, no condominium would have been created. Such projects have many of the attributes of condominiums, but they are not covered by this Chapter.

5. Definition (9), "conversion building," distinguishes between buildings which have never been occupied by any person before the time that the building is submitted to the condominium form of ownership, and buildings, whether new or old, which have been previously occupied by tenants.

6. Definition (10), "declarant," is designed to exclude persons who may be called upon to execute the declaration in order to ratify the creation of the condominium, but who are not intended to be charged with the responsibilities imposed on declarants by this Chapter if that is all they do. Examples of such persons include holders of pre-existing liens and, in the case of leasehold condominiums, ground lessors. (Of course, such a person could become a declarant by subsequently succeeding to a special declarant right.) Other persons similarly protected by the narrow wording of this definition include real estate brokers, because they do not offer to dispose of their own interest in a unit. Similarly, unit owners reselling their units are not declarants because their units were "previously disposed of" when originally conveyed.

7. Definition (12), "development rights," includes a panoply of sophisticated development techniques that have evolved over time throughout the United States and which have been expressly recognized (and regulated) in an increasing number of jurisdictions, beginning with Virginia in 1974.

Some of these techniques relate to the phased (or incremental) development of condominiums which the declarant hopes, but cannot be sure, will be successful enough to grow to include more land than he is initially willing to commit to the condominium. For example, a declarant may be building (or converting) a 50-unit building on Parcel A with the intention, if all goes well, to "expand" the condominium by adding an additional building on Parcel B, containing additional units, as part of the same condominium. If he reserves the right to do so, *i.e.*, to "add real property to a condominium," he has reserved a "development right."

In certain cases, however, the declarant may desire, for a variety of reasons, to include both parcels in the condominium from the outset, even though he may subsequently be obliged to withdraw all or part of one parcel. Assume, for example, that in the example just given the declarant intends to build an underground parking garage that will extend into both parcels. If the project is a success, his documentation will be simpler if both parcels were included in the condominium from the beginning. If his hopes are not realized, however, and it becomes necessary to withdraw all or part of Parcel B from the condominium and devote it to some other use, he may do so if he has reserved such a development right "to withdraw real property from a condominium." The portion of the garage which extends into Parcel B may be left in the condominium (separated from the remainder of Parcel B by a horizontal boundary), or the garage may be divided between Parcels A and B with appropriate cross-easement agreements.

The right "to create units, common elements, or limited common elements" is frequently useful in commercial or mixed-use condominiums where the declarant needs to retain a high degree of flexibility to meet the space requirements of prospective purchasers who may not approach him until the condominium has already been created. For example, an entire floor of a high-rise building may be intended for commercial buyers, but the declarant may not know in advance whether one purchaser will want to buy the whole floor as a single units or whether several purchasers will want the floor divided into several units, separated by common element walls and served by a limited common element corridor. This development right is sometimes useful even in purely residential condominiums, especially those designed to appeal to affluent buyers. Similarly, the development rights "to subdivide units or convert units into

* See footnote on p. 379.

common elements" is most often of value in commercial condominiums, but can occasionally be useful in certain kinds of residential condominiums as well.

8. Definition (13), "disposition," includes voluntary transfers to purchasers of any interest in a unit, other than as security for an obligation. Consequently, the grant of a mortgage or other security interest is not a "disposition," nor is any transfer of any interest to a person who is excluded from the definition of "purchaser," *infra*. However, the term includes more than conveyances and would, for example, cover contracts of sale.

9. Definition (16), "leasehold condominium," should be distinguished from land which is leased to a condominium but not subjected to the condominium regime. A leasehold condominium means, by definition, real estate which has been subjected to the condominium form of ownership. In such a case, units located on the leasehold real estate are typically leased for long terms. At the expiration of such a lease, the condominium unit or the real estate underlying the unit would be removed from the condominium if the lease were not extended or renewed. On the other hand, real estate may not be subjected to condominium ownership, but may be leased directly to the association or to one or more unit owners for a term of years.

This distinction is very significant. Under Section 82.105, the unit owners' association is empowered, following expiration of the period of declarant control, to cancel any lease of recreational or parking areas or facilities to which it is a party, regardless of who the lessor is. The association also has the power to cancel any lease for any land if the declarant or an affiliate of the declarant is a party to that lease. If the leased real estate, however, is subjected by the declarant to condominium form of ownership, that lease may not be cancelled unless it is unconscionable or unless the real estate was submitted to the condominium regime for the purpose of avoiding the right to terminate the lease. *See* Section 82.105.

While the subjective test of declarant's "purpose" may not always be clear, the rights of the association to cancel a lease depend upon the test. Thus, for example, a declarant who wishes to lease a swimming pool to the unit owners would have a choice of subjecting the pool for, say, a term of 20 years to the condominium form of ownership as a common element. At the end of the term, the lease would terminate and the real estate containing the pool would be automatically removed from the condominium unless there were a right to renew the lease. During the 20-year term, the lease would not be cancellable, regardless of the terms, or cancellable because submitted for the purpose of avoiding the right to cancel. On the other hand, if the pool were not submitted to the condominium form of ownership and was leased directly to the association for a 20-year term, the association could cancel that lease 90 days after the period of declarant control expired, even if, for example, 18 years remained of the term.

In either case, the terms of the lease would have to be disclosed in the condominium information statement.

10. Definition (20), "purchaser," includes a person who acquires any interest in a unit, even as a tenant, if his tenancy entitles him to occupy the premises for more than 20 years. This would include a tenant who holds a lease of a unit in a fee simple condominium for one year, if the lease entitles the tenant to renew the lease for more than 4 additional years. Excluded from the definition, however, are mortgagees, declarants, and people in the business of selling real estate for their account. Persons excluded from the definition of "purchaser" do not receive certain benefits under Subchapter D, such as the right to a condominium information statement (Section 82.152(c)) and the right to rescind (Section 82.156).

...

11. Definition (22), "special declarant rights," seeks to isolate those rights reserved for the benefit of a declarant which are unique to the declarant and not shared in common with other unit owners. The list, while short, encompasses virtually every significant right which a declarant might seek in the course of creating or expanding a condominium.

Any person who possesses a special declarant right would be a "declarant," including any who succeed under Section 82.104 to any of those rights. Thus, the concept of special declarant rights triggers the imposition of obligations on those who possess the rights. Under Section 82.104, those obligations vary significantly, depending upon the particular special declarant rights possessed by a particular declarant. These circumstances are described more fully in the comments to Section 82.104.

12. Definition (23), "unit," describes a tangible, physical part of the project, rather than a right in, or claim to, a tangible physical part of the property. Therefore, for example, a "time-share" arrangement in which a unit is sold to 12 different persons each of whom has the right to occupy the unit for one month does not create 12 new units-there are, rather, 12 owners of the unit. (Under the section on voting (Section 82.060), a majority of the time-share owners of a unit are entitled to cast the votes assigned to that unit.)

While a separately described part of the project is not a unit unless it is designed for, and is subject to, separate ownership by persons other than the association, the association developer can hold or acquire units unless otherwise provided in the declaration. *See*, also, Comment 4.

13. Definition (24), "unit owner," contemplates that a seller under a land installment contract would remain the unit owner until the contract is fulfilled. As between the seller and the buyer, various rights and responsibilities might be assigned to the buyer by the contract itself, but the association would continue to look to the seller (for payment of any arrears in common expense assessments, for example) as long as the seller holds title.

The definition makes it clear that declarants, so long as they own units in the condominium, are unit owners and are therefore subject to all of the obligations imposed on other unit owners, including the obligation to pay common expense assessments against those units. This provision is designed to resolve ambiguities on this point which have arisen under several existing state statutes.

PROP §82.004. VARIATION BY AGREEMENT

Except as expressly provided by this chapter, provisions of this chapter may not be varied by agreement, and rights conferred by this chapter may not be waived. A person may not act under a power of attorney or use any other device to evade the limitations or prohibitions of this chapter or the declaration.

History of Prop. Code §82.004: Acts 1993, 73rd Leg., ch. 244, §1, eff. Jan. 1, 1994.

ANNOTATIONS

Jistel v. Tiffany Trail Owners Ass'n, 215 S.W.3d 474, 482 (Tex.App.—Eastland 2006, no pet.). "Nothing in the language of §82.004 ... prohibits parties from settling existing, disputed claims in any manner they wish to settle them. Construing §82.004 otherwise would violate this State's policy of encouraging 'the peaceable resolution of disputes' and 'the early settlement of pending litigation through voluntary settlement procedures.' It would also lead to great uncertainty in the finality of settlement agreements and judgments. [S]uch a construction would lead to unfair results...."

NCCUSL Comment*

1. The Chapter is generally designed to provide great flexibility in the creation of condominiums and, to that end, the Chapter permits the parties to vary many of its provisions. In many instances, however, provisions of the Chapter may not be varied, because of the need to protect purchasers, lenders, and declarants. Accordingly, this section adopts the approach of prohibiting variation by agreement except in those cases where it is expressly permitted by the terms of the Chapter itself.

2. One of the consumer protections in this Chapter is the requirement for consent by specified percentages of unit owners to particular actions or changes in the declaration. In order to prevent declarants from evading these requirements by obtaining powers of attorney from all unit owners, or in some

* See footnote on p. 379.

other fashion controlling the votes of unit owners, this section forbids the use by a declarant of any device to evade the limitations or prohibitions of the Chapter or of the declaration.

3. The following sections permit variation:

Section 82.002. Preexisting condominiums may elect to conform to the Chapter.

Section 82.003. All definitions used in the declaration and bylaws may be varied in the declaration, but not in interpretation of the Chapter.

Section 82.007. The formulas for reallocation upon taking a part of a unit, and for allocation of proceeds attributable to limited common elements, may be varied.

Section 82.052. The declaration may vary the distinctions as to what constitutes the units and common elements.

Section 82.055. A declarant may add any information he desires to the required content of the declaration.

Section 82.057. A declarant may allocate the interests in any way desired, subject to certain limitations.

Section 82.058. The Chapter permits reallocation of limited common elements unless prohibited by the declaration.

Section 82.059. There is a presumption regarding horizontal boundaries of units, unless the declaration provides otherwise.

Section 82.061. Subject to the provisions of the declaration, unit owners may make alterations and improvements to units.

Section 82.062. Subject to the provisions of the declaration, boundaries between adjoining units may be relocated by affected unit owners.

Section 82.063. If the declaration expressly so permits, a unit may be subdivided into two or more units.

Section 82.065. The declarant may maintain sales offices, management offices, and model units only if the declaration so provides. Unless the declaration provides otherwise, the declarant may maintain advertising on the common elements.

Section 82.066. Subject to the provisions of the declaration, the declarant has an easement for these purposes.

Section 82.067. The declaration of a non-residential condominium may specify less than a two-thirds vote to amend the declaration. Any declaration may require a larger majority.

Section 82.068. The declaration may specify a majority larger than 80 percent to terminate and, in a non-residential condominium, a smaller majority. The declarant may require that the units be sold following termination even though none of them have horizontal boundaries.

Section 82.102. The declaration may limit the right of the association to exercise any of the listed powers, except in a manner which discriminates in favor of a declarant. The declaration may authorize the association to assign its rights to future income.

Section 82.103. Except as limited by the declaration or bylaws, the Executive Board may act for the association.

Section 82.106. Subject to the provisions of the declaration, the bylaws may contain any matter in addition to that required by the Chapter.

Section 82.107. Except to the extent otherwise provided by the declaration, maintenance responsibilities are set forth in this section, and income from real estate subject to development rights inures to the declarant.

Section 82.108. The bylaws may provide for special meetings at the call of less than 20 percent of the Executive Board or the unit owners.

Section 82.109. This section permits statutory quorum requirements to be varied by the bylaws.

Section 82.110. A majority in interest of the multiple owners of a single unit determine how that unit's vote is to be cast unless the declaration provides otherwise. The declaration may require that lessees vote on specified matters.

Section 82.111. The declaration may vary the provisions of this section in non-residential condominiums, and may require additional insurance in any condominium.

Section 82.112. To the extent otherwise provided in the declaration, common expenses for limited common elements must be assessed against the units to which they are assigned, common expenses benefiting fewer than all the units must be assessed only against the units benefited, insurance costs must be assessed in proportion to risk, and utility costs must be assessed in proportion to usage.

Section 82.151. All of Subchapter D is modifiable or waivable by agreement in a condominium restricted to non-residential use.

4. The second sentence of the section is an important limitation upon the rights of a declarant. It is the practice in many jurisdiction today, particularly jurisdictions which do not permit expansion of a condominium by statute, for a declarant to secure powers of attorney from all unit purchasers permitting the declarant unilaterally to expand the condominium by "unanimous consent" to include new units and to reallocate common element interests, common expense liability, and votes. With such powers of attorney, many declarants have purported to comply with the typical provision of "first generation" condominium statutes requiring unanimous consent for amendments of the declaration concerning such matters.

Section 82.067 requires unanimous consent to make certain amendments to the declaration and bylaws. If a declarant were permitted to use powers of attorney to accomplish such changes, the substantial protection which Section 82.067(e) provides to unit owners would be illusory. Section 82.004 prohibits the declarant from using powers of attorney for such purposes.

PROP §82.005. SEPARATE TITLES & TAXATION

(a) If there is a unit owner other than a declarant, each unit that has been created, together with its interest in the common elements, constitutes for all purposes a separate parcel of real property.

(b) If there is a unit owner other than a declarant, each unit must be separately taxed and assessed, and no separate tax or assessment may be rendered against common elements for which a declarant has not reserved development rights. Any portion of the common elements for which a declarant has reserved any development right must be separately taxed and assessed against the declarant, and the declarant alone is liable for payment of those taxes.

(c) If there is no unit owner other than a declarant, the real property constituting the condominium may be taxed and assessed in any manner provided by law.

(d) The laws relating to homestead exemptions from property taxes apply to condominium units, which are entitled to homestead exemptions in those cases in which the owner of a single family dwelling would qualify.

History of Prop. Code §82.005: Acts 1993, 73rd Leg., ch. 244, §1, eff. Jan. 1, 1994.

NCCUSL Comment*

1. A condominium may be created, by the recordation of a declaration, long before the first unit is conveyed. This happens frequently with existing rental apartment projects which are converted into condominiums. Subsection (c) spares the local taxing authorities from having to assess each unit separately until such time as the declarant begins conveying units, although separate assessment from the date the condominium is created may be permitted under other law. *See* subsection (c). When separate tax assessments become mandatory under this section, the assessment for each unit must include the value of that unit's common element interest, and no separate tax bill on the common elements is to be rendered to the association or the unit owners collectively. Any common elements subject to development rights, however, are separately taxed to the declarant.

2. Even if real estate subject to development rights is a part of the condominium and lawfully "owned" by the unit owners in common, it is in fact an as-

* See footnote on p. 379.

set of the declarant, and must not be taxed and assessed against unit owners. Under subsection (b), the declarant is exclusively liable for those taxes.

3. Unlike the law of New York and perhaps other states, this section imposes no limitation on the power of a jurisdiction to tax the condominium unit based on its fair market value. In most jurisdictions, experience has shown that the conversion of an apartment building to the condominium form of ownership greatly increases the fair market value of that building. Accordingly, a jurisdiction under this Chapter may impose real estate taxes on condominium units which reflect the fair market value of those units in the same way that the jurisdiction taxes other forms of real estate.

PROP §82.006. APPLICABILITY OF LOCAL ORDINANCES, REGULATIONS, & BUILDING CODES

A zoning, subdivision, building code, or other real property use law, ordinance, or regulation may not prohibit the condominium form of ownership or impose any requirement on a condominium that it would not impose on a physically identical development under a different form of ownership. Otherwise, this chapter does not invalidate or modify any provision of any zoning, subdivision, building code, or other real property use law, ordinance, or regulation.

History of Prop. Code §82.006: Acts 1993, 73rd Leg., ch. 244, §1, eff. Jan. 1, 1994.

NCCUSL Comment*

1. The first sentence of this section prohibits discrimination against condominiums by local law-making authorities. Thus, if a local law, ordinance, or regulation imposes a requirement which cannot be met if property is subdivided as a condominium but which would not be violated if all of the property constituting the condominium were owned by a single owner, this section makes it unlawful to apply that requirement or restriction to the condominium. For example, in the case of a high-rise apartment building, if a local requirement imposing a minimum number of parking spaces per apartment would not prevent a rental apartment building from being built, this Chapter would override any requirement that might impose a higher number of spaces per apartment merely by virtue of the same building being owned as a condominium.

2. The second sentence makes clear that, except for the prohibition on discrimination against condominiums, the Chapter has no effect on real estate use laws. For example, a particular piece of real estate submitted to the condominium form of ownership might be of such size that all of the real estate is required to support a proposed density of units or to satisfy minimum setback requirements. Under this Chapter, part of the submitted real estate might be subject to a development right entitling the declarant to withdraw it from the condominium but the mere reservation of this right would not constitute a subdivision of the parcel into separate ownership. If a declarant or foreclosing lender at a later time sought to exercise the option to withdraw the real estate, however, withdrawal would constitute a subdivision and would be illegal if the effect of withdrawal would be to violate setback requirements, or to exceed the density of units permitted on the remaining parcel.

PROP §82.007. CONDEMNATION

(a) If a unit is acquired by condemnation, or if part of a unit is acquired by condemnation leaving the unit owner with a remnant that may not practically or lawfully be used for any purpose permitted by the declaration, the condemnation award must compensate the unit owner for the unit and its common element interest, whether or not any common element interest is acquired. On acquisition, unless the decree provides otherwise, the condemned unit's entire allocated interests are automatically reallocated to the remaining units in proportion to the respective allocated interests of those units before the taking, and the association shall promptly prepare, execute, and record an amendment to the declaration reflecting the reallocations. A remnant of a unit remaining after part of a unit is taken under this subsection is a common element.

(b) Except as provided by Subsection (a), if part of a unit is acquired by condemnation, the award must compensate the unit owner for the reduction in value of the unit and its common element interest. On acquisition, the condemned unit's allocated interests are reduced in proportion to the reduction in the size of the unit, or on any other basis specified by the declaration, and the portion of the allocated interests divested from the partially acquired unit are automatically reallocated to that unit and the remaining units in proportion to the respective allocated interests of those units before the taking, with the partially acquired unit participating in the reallocation on the basis of its reduced allocated interests.

(c) If part of the common elements is acquired by condemnation, the award must be paid to the association, as trustee for the unit owners, and to persons holding liens on the condemned property, as their interests may appear. The association shall divide any portion of the award not used for any restoration or repair of the remaining common elements among the unit owners in proportion to their respective common element interests before the taking, but the portion of the award attributable to the acquisition of a limited common element must be equally divided among the owners of the units to which that limited common element was allocated at the time of acquisition, or in any manner the declaration provides.

(d) The court decree shall be recorded in each county in which any portion of the condominium is located.

History of Prop. Code §82.007: Acts 1993, 73rd Leg., ch. 244, §1, eff. Jan. 1, 1994.

NCCUSL Comment*

1. The provisions of this statute are not intended to supplant the usual rules of condemnation but merely to supplement the rules to address the unique problems which condemnation raises in the context of a condominium.

2. When a unit is taken or partially taken by condemnation, this section provides for a recalculation of the allocated interests of all units.

EXAMPLE 1:

Suppose that all allocated interests in a 9-unit condominium were originally allocated to the units on the basis of size. If eight of the units are equal in

* See footnote on p. 379.

size and one is twice as large as the others, the allocated interests would be 20% for the largest unit and 10% for each of the other eight units.

Suppose that one of the smaller units is taken out of the condominium by a condemning authority. Subsection (a) provides that the allocated interests would automatically shift, at the time of the taking, so that the larger unit would have 22 2/9% while each of the small units would have 11 1/9%.

EXAMPLE 2:

Suppose, in Example 1, that the condemnation only reduced the size of one of the smaller units by 50%, leaving the remaining half of the unit usable. Subsection (b) provides that the allocated interests would automatically shift to 5 5/19% for the partially taken unit, 21 1/19% for the largest unit, and 10 10/19% for each of the other units. Note that the fact that the partially taken unit was reduced to half its former size does not mean that its allocated interests are only half as large as before the taking. Rather, that unit participates in the reallocation in proportion to its reduced size. That is why the partially taken unit's reallocated interests are 5 5/19% rather than 5%.

3. An important issue raised by this section is whether or not a governmental body acquiring a unit by condemnation has a right to also take that unit's allocated interests and thereby assume membership in the association by virtue of its power of condemnation. While there is no question that a governmental body may acquire any real property by condemnation, there is no case law on the question of whether or not the governmental body may take a condominium unit as a part of the condominium or must take the unit and have the unit excluded from the condominium.

Subsection (a) merely requires that the taking body compensate the unit owner for all of his unit and its interest in the common element, whether or not the common element interest is acquired. The Chapter also requires that the allocated interests are automatically reallocated upon taking to the remaining units unless the decree provides otherwise. Whether or not the decree may constitutionally provide otherwise in the case of a particular taking (for example, by allocating the common element interest, votes, and common expense liability to the government) is an unanswered question.

4. In the circumstances of a taking of part of a unit, it is important to have some objective test by which to measure the portion of allocated interest to be reallocated. Subsection (b) sets forth a formula based on relative size, but permits the declaration to vary that formula to some other more appropriate formula in a particular circumstance. This right to vary the formula in the declaration is important, since it is clear that the formula set forth in the statute may in some instances result in gross inequities.

EXAMPLE 1:

Suppose, in a commercial condominium consisting of four units, each unit consists of a factory and parking lot, and that the declaration provides that each unit's common expense liability, including utilities, is equal. Suppose further that the area of the factory building and parking lot in unit #1 are equal, and that ½ the parking lot is taken by condemnation, leaving the factory and ½ the lot intact. Under the formula set out in the statute, unit #1's common expense liability would be reduced even though its utilities might not be reduced at all, thus resulting in a windfall for the unit owner.

EXAMPLE 2:

Suppose that a condominium contains ten units, each of which is allocated at 1/10 undivided interest in the common elements. Suppose further that a taking by condemnation reduces the size of one of the units by 50%. In such case, the common element interest of all the units will be reallocated so that the partially-taken unit has a 1/19 undivided interest in the common elements and the remaining 9 units each a 2/19 undivided interest in the common elements. Thus, the partially-taken unit has a common element interest equal to ½ of the common element interest allocated to each of the other units. Note that this is not equivalent to the partially-taken unit having a 5% undivided interest and the remaining 9 units each having a 10% undivided interest.

5. Even before the amendment formally acknowledging the reallocation of percentages required by this section is recorded, the reallocation is deemed to have occurred simultaneously with the taking. This rule is necessary to avoid the hiatus that otherwise could occur between the taking and reallocation of interests, votes, and liabilities.

6. Subsection (c) provides that, if part of the common elements is acquired, the award is paid to the association. This would not normally be the rule in the absence of such a provision.

PROP §82.008. VENUE

Venue for an action to enforce a right or obligation arising under the declaration, bylaws, or rules of the association is in each county in which any part of the condominium is located.

History of Prop. Code §82.008: Acts 1993, 73rd Leg., ch. 244, §1, eff. Jan. 1, 1994.

Sections 82.009-82.050 reserved for expansion

SUBCHAPTER B. CREATION, ALTERATION, & TERMINATION OF CONDOMINIUMS

PROP §82.051. CREATION OF CONDOMINIUM

(a) A condominium may be created under this chapter only by recording a declaration executed in the same manner as a deed by all persons who have an interest in the real property that will be conveyed to unit owners and by every lessor of a lease the expiration or termination of which will terminate the condominium or reduce its size. The declaration shall be recorded in each county in which any portion of the condominium is located.

(b) A declarant may not convey an interest in a unit until each holder of a mortgage on the unit immediately before conveyance has executed a consent to declaration, and the consent has been recorded, or is recorded concurrently with the conveyance, as part of the declaration or an amendment to the declaration.

(c) If a recorded declaration is not properly executed, that defect may be cured by a subsequent execution conforming to Subsection (a). After an execution defect is cured by authority of this subsection, the declaration is retroactively effective on the date it was first recorded.

(d) A county clerk shall, without prior approval from any other authority, record declarations and amendments to declarations in the real property records and record condominium plats or plans in the real property records or in books maintained for that purpose. If a county clerk maintains a book for the condominium plat records, the book shall be the same size and type as the book for recording subdivision plats.

(e) This chapter does not affect or diminish the rights of municipalities and counties to approve plats of subdivisions and enforce building codes as may be authorized or required by law.

(f) A person may not file for record or have recorded in the county clerk's office a plat, replat, or

amended plat or replat of a condominium unless the plat, replat, or amended plat or replat has attached to it an original tax certificate from each taxing unit with jurisdiction of the real property indicating that no delinquent ad valorem taxes are owed on the real property. If the plat, replat, or amended plat or replat is filed after September 1 of a year, the plat, replat, or amended plat or replat must also have attached to it a tax receipt issued by the collector for each taxing unit with jurisdiction of the property indicating that the taxes imposed by the taxing unit for the current year have been paid or, if the taxes for the current year have not been calculated, a statement from the collector for the taxing unit indicating that the taxes to be imposed by that taxing unit for the current year have not been calculated. If the tax certificate for a taxing unit does not cover the preceding year, the plat, replat, or amended plat or replat must also have attached to it a tax receipt issued by the collector for the taxing unit indicating that the taxes imposed by the taxing unit for the preceding year have been paid. This subsection does not apply if a taxing unit acquired the condominium for public use through eminent domain proceedings or voluntary sale.

(g) This chapter does not permit development of a subdivision golf course, as defined by Section 212.0155(b), Local Government Code, without a plat if the plat is otherwise required by applicable law. A municipality may require as a condition to the development of a previously platted or unplatted subdivision golf course that the subdivision golf course be platted or replatted.

History of Prop. Code §82.051: Acts 1993, 73rd Leg., ch. 244, §1, eff. Jan. 1, 1994. Amended by Acts 2007, 80th Leg., ch. 289, §2 (eff. Sept. 1, 2007), ch. 1092, §2 (eff. June 15, 2007); Acts 2009, 81st Leg., ch. 87, §27.001(77), eff. Sept. 1, 2009.

See also Loc. Gov't Code ch. 232.

ANNOTATIONS

Tex. Atty. Gen. Op. No. GA-0223 (2004). "[W]hile a commissioners court lacks the authority to approve a *condominium plat*, [Prop. Code] ch. 82 does not affect county authority to require or approve a *subdivision plat* for a condominium for which a subdivision plat is required under [Loc. Gov't Code] ch. 232.... [¶] For these reasons, we conclude that ch. 82 does not prohibit a county from requiring a condominium development to file a plat under ch. 232, subch. A."

NCCUSL Comment*

1. A condominium is created pursuant to this Chapter only by recording a declaration. As with any instrument affecting real estate, the declaration must be recorded in every recording district in which any portion of the condominium is located, in the manner described in subsection (a).

...

2. In Section 82.003, the Chapter defines the term "Declaration" as any instruments, however denominated, which create a condominium, and any amendments to those instruments. "Condominium," in turn, is defined as "real estate, portions of which are designated for separate ownership and the remainder of which is designated for common ownership solely by the owners of those portions." It is important to emphasize that other covenants, conditions or restrictions applicable to the real estate in the condominium might be recorded before or after the instruments are recorded which divide the real estate into units and common elements, thereby creating the condominium.

Until the actual recordation of the document which accomplished that result, however, the condominium has not been created.

3. A condominium has not been lawfully created unless the requirements of this section have been complied with. Nevertheless, a project which meets the definition of "condominium" in Section 82.003(8) is subject to this Chapter even if this or other sections of the Chapter have not been complied with.

4. Mortgagees and other lienholders need not execute the declaration, and foreclosure of a mortgage or other lien will not, of itself, terminate the condominium. However, if that lien is prior to the declaration itself, the lienholder may exclude that real estate from the condominium. *See* Sections 82.068(h) and (i). Moreover, the declarant may wish to obtain agreements from mortgagees or other lienholders that they will give partial releases permitting lien-free conveyance of the condominium units. *See* Section 82.159.

...

PROP §82.052. UNIT BOUNDARIES

Except as otherwise provided by the declaration or plat:

(1) if walls, floors, or ceilings are designated as boundaries of a unit, then all lath, furring, wallboard, plasterboard, plaster, paneling, tiles, wallpaper, paint, finished flooring, and any other materials constituting part of the finished surfaces are a part of the unit, and all other portions of the walls, floors, or ceilings are a part of the common elements;

(2) if any chute, flue, duct, wire, conduit, bearing wall, bearing column, or any other fixture is partially within and partially outside the designated boundaries of a unit, then the portion serving only that unit is a limited common element allocated solely to that unit, and the portion serving more than one unit or the common elements is a part of the general common elements;

(3) subject to Subdivision (2), the spaces, interior partitions, and other fixtures and improvements within the boundaries of a unit are a part of the unit; and

(4) shutters, awnings, window boxes, doorsteps, stoops, porches, balconies, patios, and exterior doors and windows or other fixtures designed to serve a single unit, but located outside the unit's boundaries, are limited common elements allocated exclusively to that unit.

History of Prop. Code §82.052: Acts 1993, 73rd Leg., ch. 244, §1, eff. Jan. 1, 1994.

* See footnote on p. 379.

NCCUSL Comment*

1. It is important for title purposes and other reasons to have a clear guide as to precisely which parts of a condominium constitute the units and which parts constitute the common elements. This section fills the gap left when the declaration merely defines unit boundaries in terms of floor, ceilings, and perimetric walls.

The provisions of this section may be varied, of course, to the extent that the declarant wishes to modify the details for a particular condominium.

For example, in a townhouse project structured as a condominium, it may be desirable that the boundaries of the unit constitute the exterior surfaces of the roof and exterior walls, with the center line of the party walls constituting the perimetric boundaries of the units in that plane, and the undersurface of the bottom slab dividing the unit itself from the underlying land. Alternatively, the boundaries of the units at the party walls might be extended to include actual division of underlying land itself. In those cases it would not be appropriate for walls, floors and ceilings to be designated as boundaries, and the declaration would describe the boundaries in the above manner. The differentiations made clear here, in conjunction with the provisions of Section 82.107, will assist in minimizing disputes which have historically arisen in association administration with respect to liability for repair of such things as pipes, porches and other components of a building which unit owners may expect the association to pay for and which the association may wish to have repaired by unit owners. Problems which may arise as a result of negligence in the use of components—such as stoops and pipes—are resolved by Section 82.107.

2. The differentiation between components constituting common elements and components which are part of the units is particularly important in light of Section 82.107(a), which (subject to the exceptions therein mentioned) makes the association responsible for upkeep of common elements and each unit owner individually responsible for upkeep of his unit.

3. The differentiation between unit components and common element components may or may not be important for insurance purposes under this Chapter. While the common elements in a project must always be insured, the units themselves need not be insured by the association unless the project contains units divided by horizontal boundaries; *see* Section 82.111(b). In a "high rise" configuration, however, Section 82.111(a) contemplates that both will normally be insured by the association (exclusive of improvements and betterments in individual units) and that the cost of such insurance will be a common expense.

PROP §82.053. CONSTRUCTION & VALIDITY OF DECLARATION & BYLAWS

(a) The provisions of the declaration and bylaws are severable.

(b) The rule against perpetuities may not be applied to defeat any provision of the declaration, bylaws, or rules of the association.

(c) If there is a conflict between the provisions of the declaration and the bylaws, the declaration prevails except to the extent the declaration is inconsistent with this chapter.

(d) Title to a unit and common elements is not made unmarketable or otherwise affected by a provision of unrecorded bylaws or by reason of an insubstantial failure of the declaration to comply with this chapter. Whether a substantial failure impairs marketability is not affected by this chapter.

History of Prop. Code §82.053: Acts 1993, 73rd Leg., ch. 244, §1, eff. Jan. 1, 1994.

NCCUSL Comment*

1. Subsection (b) does not totally invalidate the rule against perpetuities as applied to condominiums. The language does provide that the rule against perpetuities is ineffective as to documents which would govern the condominium during the entire life of the project, regardless of how long that should be. With respect to deeds or devises of units, however, the policies underlying the rule against perpetuities continue to have validity and remain applicable under this Chapter.

2. In considering the effect of failures to comply with this Chapter on title matters, subsection (d) refers only to defects in the declaration—which includes the plats and plans—because the declaration is the instrument which creates and defines the units and common elements. No reference is made to other instruments, such as bylaws, because these instruments have no impact on title, whether or not recorded. However, in all cases of violations of the Chapter, a failure of the bylaws—or any other instrument—to comply with the Chapter, would entitle any affected persons to appropriate relief under Section 82.161.

3. No special prohibition against racial or other forms of discrimination is included in this Chapter because the provisions of generally applicable federal and state law apply as much to condominiums as to other forms of real estate.

4. Some examples may help to clarify what sorts of defects in the declaration are to be regarded as "insubstantial" within the meaning of the first sentence of subsection (d).

Suppose the declaration allocates common element interests to all the units, but fails to indicate the formula for the allocation as required by Section 82.057. This would be a substantial defect if the assigned interests were unequal, but if all units were assigned identical interests it would be possible to infer that the basis of allocation was equality—and the failure of the declaration to say so would be an insubstantial defect. Were this to happen in a condominium where the right to add new units is reserved, however, it should be noted that a subsequent amendment to the declaration adding new units could not use any formula other than equality for reallocating the common element interests unless a different formula were specified pursuant to Section 82.057(b).

Other examples of insubstantial defects that might occur include failure of the declaration to include the word "condominium" in the name of the project, as required by Section 82.055(1), or failure of the plats and plans to comply satisfactorily with the requirement of Section 82.059(a) that they be "legible," so long as they can at least be deciphered by persons with proper expertise. Failure to organize the unit owners' association at the time specified in Section 82.101 would not be a defect in the declaration at all, and would not affect the validity or marketability of titles in the condominium. It would, however, be a violation of this Chapter, and create a claim for relief under Section 82.161.

5. Each state has case or statutory law dealing with marketability of titles, and the question of whether substantial failures of the declaration to comply with the Chapter affect marketability of title should be determined by that law and not by this Chapter.

PROP §82.054. DESCRIPTION OF UNITS

A description of a unit is a sufficient legal description of the unit and all rights, obligations, and interests appurtenant to the unit that were created by the declaration or bylaws if the description contains:

(1) the name of the condominium;

(2) the recording data for the declaration, including any amendments, plats, and plans;

(3) the county in which the condominium is located; and

(4) the identifying number of the unit.

History of Prop. Code §82.054: Acts 1993, 73rd Leg., ch. 244, §1, eff. Jan. 1, 1994.

NCCUSL Comment*

1. The intent of this section is that no description of a unit in a deed, lease, deed of trust, mortgage, or any other instrument or document shall be subject to

* See footnote on p. 379.

challenge for failure to meet any common law or other requirements so long as the requirements of this section are satisfied, and so long as the declaration itself, together with the plats and plans which are a part of the declaration, provides a legally sufficient description.

2. The last sentence makes clear that an instrument which does meet those requirements includes all interest appurtenant to the unit. As a result, it will not be necessary under this Chapter to continue the practice, common in some jurisdictions, of describing the common element interests, or limited common elements, that are appurtenant to a unit in the instrument conveying title to that unit.

PROP §82.055. CONTENTS OF DECLARATION FOR ALL CONDOMINIUMS

The declaration for a condominium must contain:

(1) the name of the condominium, which must include the word "condominium" or be followed by the words "a condominium" or a phrase that includes the word "condominium," and the name of the association;

(2) the name of each county in which any part of the condominium is located;

(3) a legally sufficient description of the real property included in the condominium;

(4) a description of the boundaries of each unit created by the declaration, including the unit's identifying number;

(5) a statement of the maximum number of units that the declarant reserves the right to create;

(6) a description of the limited common elements other than those listed in Sections 82.052(2) and (4);

(7) a description of any real property, except real property subject to development rights, that may be allocated subsequently as limited common elements, together with a statement that the property may be so allocated;

(8) an allocation to each unit of its allocated interests;

(9) any restrictions on use, occupancy, or alienation of the units;

(10) a description of and the recording data for recorded easements and licenses appurtenant to or included in the condominium or to which any portion of the condominium is or may become subject by reservation in the declaration;

(11) the method of amending the declaration;

(12) a plat or plan or the recording data of a plat or plan that has been recorded in the real property or condominium plat records;

(13) a statement of the association's obligation under Section 82.111(i) to rebuild or repair any part of the condominium after a casualty or any other disposition of the proceeds of a casualty insurance policy;

(14) a description of any development rights and other special declarant rights reserved by the declarant, together with a legally sufficient description of the real property to which each of those rights applies, and a time limit within which each of those rights must be exercised;

(15) if any development right may be exercised with respect to different parcels of real property at different times, a statement to that effect, together with:

(A) either a statement fixing the boundaries of those portions and regulating the order in which those portions may be subjected to the exercise of each development right, or a statement that no assurances are made in those regards; and

(B) a statement as to whether, if any development right is exercised in any portion of the real property subject to that development right, that development right must be exercised in all or in any other portion of the remainder of that real property;

(16) all matters required by this chapter to be stated in the declaration; and

(17) any other matters the declarant considers appropriate.

History of Prop. Code §82.055: Acts 1993, 73rd Leg., ch. 244, §1, eff. Jan. 1, 1994.

See also Prop. Code §§81.102, 81.111, 82.067.

NCCUSL Comment*

1. Many statutes and other regulatory schemes in the multi-owner project field do not separate the functions of a recorded declaration and unrecorded condominium information statements or disclosure documents. As a result, many of the developer's representations and assurances concerning his future plans must appear in the declaration as well as the condominium information statement, even though they may have nothing to do with the legal structure or title of the project. *See* e.g., Section 47-70, Conn.Gen.Stat. (1980). This results in duplicative requirements and unnecessarily complex declarations.

This Chapter seeks functionally to distinguish between the declaration and the condominium information statement. It requires the declaration to contain only those matters which affect the legal structure or title of the condominium. This includes the reserved powers of the declarant to exercise development rights within the condominium. A narrative description of those rights, however, and the possible consequences flowing from their exercise, are required to be disclosed only in the condominium information statement and not in the declaration.

...

2. Paragraph (5) requires the declarant to state the largest number of units he reserves the right to build. Unlike many current condominium statutes, this Chapter imposes no time limit, measured by an absolute number of years, at the expiration of which the declarant must relinquish control of the association. Instead, declarant control ends when 75% of the maximum number of units which may be created by the declarant have been sold, or at the end of a 2-year period during which development is not proceeding. *See* Section 82.103(c). The flexibility afforded by this section may be important to a declarant as he responds to unanticipated future changes in his market.

In theory, a declarant might overstate the maximum number of units in an attempt to artificially extend the period of declarant control, since the time

* See footnote on p. 379.

might never come when a declarant had sold 75% of that number of units. As a practical matter, however, such a practice would not likely achieve long-term control.

EXAMPLE:

A declarant reserves the right to build 100 units, even though zoning would permit only 75 units on the site, and the declarant actually plans on building only 50 units. As a result of the reservation, the declarant would not lose control of the association under the 75% rule stated in Section 82.103(c) even when all 50 units had been built and sold, because that percentage applies to all potential units, not units actually built. *See* Section 82.103(c).

However, there are practical constraints on the declarant's decision in this matter. Substantial exaggeration of the future density of the development might tend to impede sales of units in that project. Moreover, such a statement might also produce negative governmental reaction to proposals which might require local approval.

...

3. Paragraph (4) requires that the boundaries of each unit created by the declaration be identified. The words "created by the declaration" emphasize that in an expandable project, new units may be created in the future by amendments to the declaration. Until those new units are actually added to the project by amending the declaration, however, they are not units within the meaning of that defined term, and they need not be described.

4. Section 82.052 makes it possible in many projects to satisfy paragraph (4) of this section by merely providing the identifying number of the units and stating that each unit is bounded by its ceiling, floor, and walls. The plats and plans will show where those ceilings, floors, and perimetric walls are located, and Section 82.052 provides all other details, except to the extent the declaration may make additional or contradictory specifications because of the unique nature of the project.

5. Paragraph (6) makes clear that the limited common elements described in Section 82.052(2) and (4) need not be described in the declaration. These limited common elements are typically porches, balconies, patios, or other amenities which may be included in a project. Such improvements are treated by the Chapter as limited common elements, rather than either common elements or parts of units, in order to minimize the attention which the documents need to give them, and to secure the result that would be desired in the usual case. Thus, if these improvements remain limited common elements, and no special provisions concerning them are included in the declaration, they may be used only by the units to which they are physically attached; maintenance of those improvements must be paid for by the association; and such improvements need not be specially referred to in the declaration. Porches, balconies and patios must be shown on the plats and plans (*see* Section 82.059(b)(10)), but other limited common elements described in Section 82.052(2) and (4) need not be shown.

6. Paragraph (7) contemplates that the common elements in the project may be allocated as limited common elements at some future time, either by the declarant or the association. For example, a swimming pool might serve an entire project during early phases of development. At the outset, that pool might be a common element which all the unit owners may use. At a later time, with more units and additional pools built in subsequent phases, either the declarant or the association might determine that the first pool should become a limited common element reserved for the use only of units in the first phase, while the other pools should be reserved exclusively for units in the subsequent phases. Such a potential allocation should be described in the declaration pursuant to this section.

7. Paragraph (14) requires the declaration to describe all development rights and other special declarant rights which the declarant reserves. The declaration must describe the real estate to which each right applies, and state the time limit within which each of those rights must be exercised. The Chapter imposes no maximum time limit for the exercise of those rights, and the particular language of a declaration will vary from project to project depending on the requirements of each project. This Chapter contemplates that those rights may be exercised after the period of declarant control terminates.

8. Plats and plans are made a part of the declaration for legal purposes by Section 82.060, and their content may in part provide some of the information required by this section.

9. Paragraph (16) is a cross-reference to other sections of the Chapter which require the declaration to contain particular matters. Some of these sections, such as 82.057 on the allocations of allocated interests or 82.059 on plats and plans, will affect all projects. Others, such as 82.056 on leasehold condominiums, will apply only to particular kinds of projects.

10. Subsection (17) contemplates that, in addition to the content required by subsections (1) through (16), other matters may also be included in the declaration if the declarant or lender feel they are appropriate to the particular project. In particular, the draftsman should carefully consider any desired provisions which would vary any of the many sections of the Chapter where variation is permitted, including such matters as expanding or restricting the association's powers. A list of sections which may be varied appears in the comment to Section 82.004.

PROP §82.056. LEASEHOLD CONDOMINIUMS

(a) Any lease the expiration or termination of which may terminate the condominium or reduce its size must be recorded. The lessor shall sign the declaration, and the declaration must state:

(1) the recording data for the lease;

(2) the date on which the lease is scheduled to expire;

(3) a legally sufficient description of the real property subject to the lease;

(4) any right of the unit owners to redeem the reversion and the manner in which the unit owners may exercise that right, or a statement that the unit owners do not have that right;

(5) any right of the unit owners to remove improvements within a reasonable time after the expiration or termination of the lease, or a statement that the unit owners do not have that right; and

(6) any right of the unit owners to renew the lease and the conditions of renewal, or a statement that the unit owners do not have that right.

(b) After the declaration for a leasehold condominium is recorded, neither the lessor nor the lessor's successor in interest may terminate the leasehold interest of a unit owner who makes timely payment of the unit owner's share of the rent and otherwise complies with all covenants that, if violated, would entitle the lessor to terminate the lease. A unit owner's leasehold interest is not affected by failure of any other person to pay rent or fulfill any other covenant.

(c) Acquisition of the leasehold interest of a unit owner by the owner of the reversion or remainder does not merge the leasehold and fee simple interests unless the leasehold interests of all unit owners subject to that reversion or remainder are acquired.

(d) If the expiration or termination of a lease decreases the number of units in a condominium, the allocated interests shall be reallocated as though those units had been taken by condemnation unless other-

wise provided by the declaration. Reallocation shall be confirmed by an amendment to the declaration prepared, executed, and recorded by the association.

History of Prop. Code §82.056: Acts 1993, 73rd Leg., ch. 244, §1, eff. Jan. 1, 1994.

NCCUSL Comment*

1. Subsection (a) requires that the lessor of any lease, which upon termination will terminate the condominium or reduce its size, must sign the declaration. This requirement insures that the lessor has consented to use of his land as a condominium.

...

2. This section sets out requirements concerning leasehold condominiums which are not typically contained in the statutes of most states. In particular, it requires that the declaration describe the rights of the unit owners, or state that they have no rights concerning a variety of significant matters. The section also contains a number of other consumer protection provisions. However, in contrast to the result under some states' laws, unit owners have no statutory right to renewal of a lease upon termination.

3. The most significant matter of consumer protection in this section is subsection (b), which provides that unit owners who pay their share of the rent of the underlying lease may not be deprived of their enjoyment of the leasehold premises.

Subsection (b) is intended to protect the "unit owner" regardless of whether he is a lessee, sublessee, or even further down in a chain of transfer of leasehold interests. Thus, for example, if the "unit owner" is a sublessee, the term "lessor (or) his successor in interest" includes not only the lessor, but also the lessee.

Subsection (b) further protects the unit owner by assuring that he will not share with his fellow unit owners any collective obligations toward their common lessor. All obligations are instead fractionalized so that no unit owner can be made liable or otherwise penalized for a default by any of his fellows. Thus, a default by the association in payment of the rent due the lessor, in a case where the lease of common elements ran to the association, would not permit the lessor to terminate continued use of those common elements by those unit owners who then pay their share of the rent.

4. Subsection (d) considers the problems created when termination of a lease reduces the size of a condominium. In the event that some units are thereby withdrawn from the condominium, reallocation of the allocated interests would be required; the section describes how that reallocation would occur.

PROP §82.057. ALLOCATION OF COMMON ELEMENT INTERESTS, VOTES, & COMMON EXPENSE LIABILITIES

(a) The declaration shall allocate a fraction or percentage of undivided interests in the common elements and in the common expenses of the association, and a portion of the votes in the association, to each unit and state the formulas used to establish those allocations. These allocations may not discriminate in favor of units owned by a declarant.

(b) If units may be added to or withdrawn from the condominium, the declaration must state the formulas to be used to reallocate the allocated interests among all units included in the condominium after the addition or withdrawal.

(c) The declaration may provide:

(1) that different allocations of votes must be made to the units on particular matters specified in the declaration; and

(2) for class voting on specified issues affecting the class if necessary to protect valid interests of the class.

(d) A declarant may not use cumulative or class voting to evade any limitation imposed on declarants by this chapter. Units may not constitute a class because the units are owned by a declarant.

(e) Except for minor variations due to rounding, the sums of the undivided interests in the common elements and of the common expense liabilities allocated at any time to all the units shall each equal one if stated as fractions or 100 percent if stated as percentages. If a discrepancy exists between an allocated interest and the result derived from application of the pertinent formula, the allocated interest prevails.

(f) The common elements are not subject to partition. Any purported conveyance, judicial sale, or other voluntary or involuntary transfer of an undivided interest in the common elements without the unit to which that interest is allocated is void.

History of Prop. Code §82.057: Acts 1993, 73rd Leg., ch. 244, §1, eff. Jan. 1, 1994.

See also Prop. Code §§81.108, 81.109.

NCCUSL Comment*

1. Most existing condominium statutes require a single common basis, usually related to the "value" of the units, to be used in the allocation of common element interests, votes in the association, and common expense liabilities. This Chapter departs radically from such requirements by permitting each of these allocations to be made on different bases, and by permitting allocations which are unrelated to value.

Thus, all three allocations might be made equally among all units, or in proportion to the relative size of each unit, or on the basis of any other formula the declarant may select, regardless of the values of those units. Moreover, "size" might be used, for example, in allocating common expenses and common element interests, while equality is used in allocating votes in the association. This section does not require that the formulas used by the declarant be justified, but it does require that the formulas be explained. The sole restriction on the formulas to be used in these allocations is that they not discriminate in favor of the units owned by the declarant. Otherwise, each of the separate allocations may be made on any basis which the declarant chooses, and none of the allocations need be tied to any other allocation.

2. While the flexibility permitted in allocations is broader than that permitted by any present statutes, it is likely that the traditional bases for allocation will continue to be used, and that the allocations for all allocated interests will often be based on the same formulas. Most commonly, those bases include size, equality, or value of units. Each of these is discussed below.

3. If size is chosen as a basis of allocation, the declarant must choose between reliance on area or volume, and the choice must be indicated in the declaration. The declarant might further refine the formula by, for example, excluding unheated areas from the calculation or by partially discounting such areas by means of a ratio. Again, the declarant must indicate the choices he has made and explain the formulas he has chosen.

4. Most existing condominium statutes require that "value" be used as the basis of all allocations. Under this Chapter a declarant is free to select such a

* See footnote on p. 379.

basis if he wishes to do so. For example, he might designate the "par value" of each unit as a stated number of dollars or points. However, the formula used to develop the par values of the various units would have to be explained in the declaration. For example, the declaration for a high-rise condominium might disclose that the par value of each unit is based on the relative area of each unit on the lower floors, but increases by specified percentages at designated higher levels. The formula for determining area in this example could be further refined in the manner suggested in Comment 2, above, and any other factors (such as the direction in which a unit faces) could also be given weight so long as the weight given to each factor is explained in the declaration.

5. The purpose of subsection (b) is to afford some advance disclosure to purchasers of units in the first phase of a flexible condominium of how common element interests, votes and common expense liabilities will be reallocated if additional units are added.

6. Subsection (f) means what it says when it states that a lien or encumbrance on a common element interest without the unit to which that common element interest is allocated is void. Thus, consider the case of a flexible condominium in which there are 50 units in the first phase, each of which initially has a 2 percent undivided interest in the common elements. The declarant borrows money by mortgaging additional real estate. When the declarant expands the condominium by adding phase 2 containing an additional 50 units, he reallocates the common element interests in the manner described in his original declaration, to give each of the 100 units a 1 percent undivided interest in the common elements in both phases of the condominium. At this point, the construction lender cannot have a lien on the undivided interest of phase 1 owners in the common elements of phase 2 because of the wording of the statute. Thus, the most that the construction lender can have is a lien on the phase 2 units together with their common element interests. The mortgage documents may be written to reflect the fact that upon the addition of phase 2 of the condominium, the lien on the additional real estate will be converted into a lien on the phase 2 units and on the common element interest as they pertain to those units in both phase 1 and phase 2; however, *see* Comment to Section 82.060.

Unless the lender also requires phase 2 to be designated as withdrawable real estate, the phase 2 portion may not be foreclosed upon other than as condominium units and the construction lender may not dispose of phase 2 other than as units which are a part of the condominium. In the event that phase 2 is designated as withdrawable land, then the construction lender may force withdrawal of phase 2 and dispose of it as he wishes, subject to the provisions of the declaration. If one unit in phase 2, however, has been sold to anyone other than the declarant, then phase 2 ceases to be withdrawable land by operation of Section 82.060(d)(2).

7. If a unit owned only by the declarant—as opposed to the same unit if owned by another person—may be subdivided into 2 or more units but cannot be converted in whole or in part into common elements, it is still a unit that may be subdivided or converted into 2 or more units or common elements, within the meaning of the definition of development rights, and is not governed by Section 82.063 (Subdivision of Units).

8. Subsection (c) represents a significant departure from practice in most states concerning the allocation of votes. The usual rule is that a single allocation of votes is made to each unit, and that allocation applies to all matters on which those votes may be cast. This section recognizes that the increasingly complex nature of some projects requires different allocation on particular questions. It may be appropriate, for example, in a project where common expense liabilities, or questions concerning rules and regulations, affect different units differently.

EXAMPLE:

In a mixed commercial and residential project, the declaration might provide that each unit owner would have an equal vote for the election of the Board of Directors. However, on matters concerning ratification of the common expense budget, where the commercial unit owners paid a much larger share than their proportion of the total units, the vote of commercial unit owners would be increased to 3 times the number of votes the residential owners held. Alternatively, of course, it might be possible to treat this question as a class voting matter, but the draftsman is provided flexibility in this section to choose the most appropriate solution.

9. This section recognizes that there may be certain instances in which class voting in the association would be desirable. For example, in a mixed-use condominium consisting of both residential and commercial units, there may be certain kinds of issues upon which the residential or commercial unit owners should have a special voice, and the device described in Comment 9 was not desired. To prevent abuse of class voting by the declarant, subsection (c) permits class voting only with respect to specified issues directly affecting the designated class and only insofar as necessary to protect valid interests of the designated class.

EXAMPLE:

Owners of town house units, in a single project consisting of both town house and high-rise buildings, might properly constitute a separate class for purposes of voting on expenditures affecting just the town house units, but they might not be permitted to vote by class on rules for the use of facilities used by all the units.

10. Subsection (d) provides that the declarant may not use the class voting device for the purpose of evading any limitation imposed on declarants by this Chapter (e.g., to maintain declarant control beyond the period permitted by Section 82.103).

The last clause of subsection (d) prohibits a practice common in the planned community or other non-condominium multi-ownership projects, where units owned by declarant constitute a separate class of units for voting and other purposes. Upon transfer of title, those units lose these more favorable voting rights. This section makes clear that the votes and other attributes of ownership of a unit may not change by virtue of the identity of the owner. In those circumstances which such classes were legitimately intended to address, principally control of the association, the Chapter provides other, more balanced devices for declarant control. *See* Section 82.103(c).

PROP §82.058. LIMITED COMMON ELEMENTS

(a) The limited common elements and the provisions of the declaration relating to the right to use the limited common elements may not be altered without the consent of each affected unit owner and the owner's first lien mortgagee.

(b) Except as otherwise provided by the declaration, a limited common element may be reallocated by an amendment to the declaration, executed by the unit owners between or among whose units the reallocation is made. The persons executing the amendment shall deliver it to the association, which shall record it at the expense of the reallocating unit owners.

(c) A common element not previously allocated as a limited common element may not be allocated except pursuant to the declaration made in accordance with Section 82.055(7). The allocation shall be made by amendment to the declaration.

History of Prop. Code §82.058: Acts 1993, 73rd Leg., ch. 244, §1, eff. Jan. 1, 1994.

NCCUSL Comment*

1. Like all other common elements, limited common elements are owned in common by all unit owners. The use of a limited common element, however, is reserved to less than all of the unit owners. Unless the declaration provides otherwise, the association is responsible for the upkeep of a limited common element and the cost of such upkeep is assessed against all the units. *See* Sections 82.107(a) and 82.112(d). This might include the costs of repainting all shutters, or balconies, for example, which are limited common elements pursuant to Section 82.102(4). Accordingly, there may be occasions where, to meet the expectations of owners and to have costs borne directly by those who benefit from those amenities, the declaration might provide that the costs will be borne, not by all unit owners as part of their common expense assessments, but only by the owners to which the limited common elements are assigned.

---

* See footnote on p. 379.

2. Even common elements which are not "limited" within the meaning of this Chapter may nevertheless be restricted by the unit owners' association pursuant to the powers set forth in Section 82.102(6) and (11), unless that power is limited in the declaration. For example, the association might assign reserved parking spaces to designated unit owners, or even to persons who are not unit owners. Such a parking space would differ from a limited common element in that its use would be merely a personal right of the person to whom it is assigned and this section would not have to be complied with to allocate it or to reallocate it.

3. Because a mortgage or deed of trust may restrict the borrower's right to transfer the use of a limited common element without the lender's consent, the terms of the encumbrance should be examined to determine whether the lender's consent or release is needed to transfer that right of use to another person.

PROP §82.059. PLATS & PLANS

(a) Plats and plans are a part of the declaration and may be recorded as a part of the declaration or separately. Each plat or plan must be legible and contain a certification that the plat or plan contains all information required by this section.

(b) Each plat must show:

(1) the name and a survey or general schematic map of the entire condominium;

(2) the location and dimensions of all real property not subject to development rights, or subject only to the development right to withdraw, and the location and dimensions of all existing improvements within that real property;

(3) a legally sufficient description of any real property subject to development rights, labeled to identify the rights applicable to each parcel;

(4) the extent of any encroachments by or on any portion of the condominium;

(5) to the extent feasible, a legally sufficient description of all easements serving or burdening any portion of the condominium, and the location of any underground utility line that is actually known by the declarant at the time of filing the declaration to have been constructed outside a recorded easement;

(6) the location and dimensions of any vertical unit boundaries not shown or projected on recorded plans and the unit's identifying number;

(7) the location, with reference to established data, of any horizontal unit boundaries not shown or projected on recorded plans and the unit's identifying number;

(8) a legally sufficient description of any real property in which the unit owners will own only an estate for years, labeled as "leasehold real property";

(9) the distance between noncontiguous parcels of real property constituting the condominium;

(10) the location and dimensions of limited common elements, other than those described by Sections 82.052(2) and (4);

(11) in the case of real property not subject to development rights, all other matters required by law on land surveys; and

(12) the distance and bearings locating each building from all other buildings and from at least one boundary line of the real property constituting the condominium.

(c) A plat may also show the intended location and dimensions of a contemplated improvement to be constructed anywhere within the condominium, which must be labeled either "MUST BE BUILT" or "NEED NOT BE BUILT."

(d) To the extent not shown on the plats, plans must show:

(1) the location and dimensions of the vertical boundaries of each unit, and the unit's identifying number;

(2) the horizontal unit boundaries, with reference to established data, and the unit's identifying number; and

(3) any units, appropriately identified, in which the declarant has reserved the right to create additional units or common elements.

(e) Unless the declaration provides otherwise, the horizontal boundaries of part of a unit located outside a building have the same elevation as the horizontal boundaries of the inside part and need not be depicted on the plats and plans. Interior walls and partitions within a unit need not be included in the plats or plans.

(f) On exercising any development right, the declarant shall record either new plats and plans necessary to conform to the requirements of this section or new certifications of plats and plans previously recorded if those plats and plans otherwise conform to the requirements of this section.

(g) An independent licensed surveyor or engineer shall certify at least one plat, whether contained in one or more pages, showing all perimeter land boundaries of the condominium, except for additional real property, and showing the locations on the ground of all buildings labeled "MUST BE BUILT" in relation to land boundaries. Certification of any other plat or plan required by this chapter shall be made by an independent licensed architect, surveyor, or engineer.

History of Prop. Code §82.059: Acts 1993, 73rd Leg., ch. 244, §1, eff. Jan. 1, 1994.

See also Prop. Code §§81.102, 81.105, 82.052, 82.062.

NCCUSL Comment*

1. The terms "plat" or "plan" have been given a variety of meanings by custom and usage in the various jurisdictions. Under this Chapter, it is important to recognize that a "plat" need not mean a "survey" of the entire real estate constituting a project at the time the initial plat is recorded, although, through amendments to the plat as development proceeds, it ultimately becomes a survey of the entire project.

As to "plan," the Chapter does not use that term to mean the actual building plans used for construction of the project. Instead, the required content of the plans in this Chapter is described in subsection (d). Essentially, the plans constitute a boundary survey of each unit. Typically, the walls will be the vertical ("up and down" or "perimetric") boundaries, and the floors and ceilings will be the horizontal boundaries. Importantly, these boundaries need not be physically measured, but may instead be projected from the plat or from actual building construction plans. Thus, the plans under this Chapter are not conceived to be "as built" plans.

2. Subsection (c) permits, but does not require, the plats to show the location of contemplated improvements. Since construction of contemplated improvements by a declarant involves the exercise of development rights, a declarant may not create any improvement within real estate where no development rights have been reserved, unless the plats actually show that proposed improvement or unless the association (which the declarant may control) makes the improvement pursuant to Section 82.102(a)(8). Should the association attempt that improvement, in the face of unit owner's objections, it may involve risk of challenge. Within land subject to development rights, of course, construction may take place in accordance with the reserved rights, even if no contemplated improvements are shown on the plats. As to the declarant's obligation to complete an improvement that is shown, *see* Section 82.162.

3. In detailing the required contents of the plats, two different types of legal description are contemplated. First, in subsection (b)(1), the plat must show at least a general schematic map of the entire project. While this may be by survey, the Chapter recognizes that a survey may be unduly expensive or impractical in a large project, and accordingly permits a general schematic map of the entire project at the commencement of development. With respect to those portions of the project, however, where no future development may take place, the flexibility of a general schematic map is not necessary. At the same time, it becomes important for title purposes to be able to identify precisely that portion of the project which is essentially completed. Accordingly, as development ceases in particular phases, subsection (b)(2) contemplates that the locations and dimensions of that real estate will be identified. As this process continues, all of the real estate originally shown in a general schematic map will have been surveyed, and the location and dimensions of that real estate identified, at the expiration of development rights. In addition, subsection (b)(2) contemplates that existing improvements must be shown within real estate where no further development will take place. This does not mean the units which may be within each building, but it does mean the external physical dimensions of the buildings themselves. As implied by subsection (b)(11), the nature of "existing improvements" required to be surveyed under subsection (b)(2) should be determined by local practices in the particular state.

4. Subsection (b)(3) requires that the real estate which is subject to development rights must be identified with a legally sufficient description, that is, either a metes and bounds description, or reference to the deeds of that real estate. Since different portions of the real estate may be subject to differing development rights—for example, only a portion of the total real estate may be added as well as withdrawn from the project—the plat must identify the rights applicable to each portion of that real estate. The same reasoning applies to the legally sufficient description of easements affecting the condominium and any leasehold real estate.

5. Subsection (f) describes the amendments to the plats and plans which must be made as development rights are exercised. This section requires that the plats and plans be amended at each stage of development to reflect actual progress to date. If an original schematic map was initially recorded as required by subsection (b)(1), the survey required by (b)(2) would also constitute the amendments required by subsection (f).

6. The terms "horizontal" and "vertical" are now commonly understood in condominium parlance to refer, respectively, to "upper and lower" and "lateral or perimetric." Thus, Section 82.052 contemplates that the perimetric walls may be designated as the "vertical" boundaries of a unit and the floor and ceiling as its "horizontal" boundaries. That is the sense in which the words "horizontal" and "vertical" are to be understood in this section and throughout this Chapter.

7. Sections 82.162 and 82.163 reveal the effect of labeling an improvement "MUST BE BUILT" or "NEED NOT BE BUILT," as required by subsection (b)(3).

* See footnote on p. 379.

PROP §82.060. EXERCISE OF DEVELOPMENT RIGHT

(a) To exercise a development right, the declarant must prepare, execute, and record an amendment to the declaration and record new plats and plans for that real property. The declarant is the unit owner of any units created. The amendment to the declaration must assign an identifying number to each new unit created and, except for subdivision or conversion of units described by Subsection (b), reallocate the allocated interest among all units. The amendment must describe any limited common elements created, designating the unit to which each is allocated.

(b) Development rights may be reserved within any real property added to the condominium if the amendment adding the real property includes the information required by Section 82.055 or 82.056, as appropriate, and the plats and plans include the information required by Section 82.059(b). This provision does not extend the time limit on the exercise of development rights imposed by the declaration. Real property to be added is not part of a condominium or subject to a declaration until the declaration is amended to make the additional real property part of the condominium.

(c) Whenever a declarant exercises a development right to subdivide or convert a unit previously created into additional units, common elements, or both:

(1) if the declarant converts the unit entirely to common elements, the amendment to the declaration must reallocate all the allocated interests of the unit among the other units as if the unit had been taken by condemnation; and

(2) if the declarant subdivides the unit into two or more units, whether or not any part of the unit is converted into common elements, the amendment to the declaration must reallocate all the allocated interests of the unit among the units created by the subdivision in any reasonable manner prescribed by the declarant.

(d) If the declaration provides that all or a portion of the real property is subject to the development right of withdrawal:

(1) if all the real property is subject to withdrawal, and the declaration does not describe separate portions of real property subject to that right, none of the real property may be withdrawn after a unit has been conveyed to a purchaser; and

(2) if a portion or portions are subject to withdrawal, no portion may be withdrawn after a unit in that portion has been conveyed to a purchaser.

History of Prop. Code §82.060: Acts 1993, 73rd Leg., ch. 244, §1, eff. Jan. 1, 1994.

NCCUSL Comment*

1. This section generally describes the method by which any development right may be exercised. Importantly, while new development rights may be reserved within new real estate which is added to the condominium, the original time limits on the exercise of these rights which the declarant must include in the original declaration may not be extended. Thus, the development process may continue only within the self-determined constraints originally described by the declarant.

2. The reservation and exercise of development rights is and must be closely co-ordinated with financing for the project. As a result, lender review and control of that process is common, and the financing documents should reflect the proposed development process.

A typical construction loan mortgage on a portion of a phased condominium might provide that as soon as new units are built on new land to be added (or, if the portion is also designated withdrawable land, as soon thereafter as anyone other than the declarant becomes the unit owner of a unit in the withdrawable land) the mortgage on that land converts into a mortgage on all of the units located within that portion, together with their respective common element interests. The common element interest of those units will, of course, extend to the common elements in other sections of the condominium. However, failure of a construction loan mortgage to so provide is inconsequential, because conveyance of the units in that phase to the lender or to a purchaser at a foreclosure sale would automatically transfer all of those units' common element interests, as a result of the requirements of Sections 82.058 and 82.061.

3. A lender who holds a mortgage lien on one portion of a condominium may not cause that portion to be withdrawn from the condominium unless the portion constitutes withdrawable real estate in which there is no unit owner other than the declarant. Even then, the amendment effectuating the withdrawal must be executed by the declarant. Consequently, unless the lender wishes to become a declarant subsequent to foreclosure or a deed in lieu of foreclosure in order to execute the amendment, or forecloses in order to require an amendment from the association under Section 82.068(h), a lender might require that the signed amendment be deposited in escrow at the time the loan is made in order to protect against a recalcitrant borrower.

4. As indicated in the Comment to Section 82.006, the withdrawal of real estate from a condominium may constitute a subdivision of land under the applicable subdivision ordinance. Under most subdivision ordinances, the owner of the real estate is regarded as the "subdivider." In the event of a withdrawal under this section, however, the declarant is in fact the subdivider because of his unique interest in and control over the real estate, even though the real estate, for title purposes, is a common element until withdrawn. Accordingly, he would bear the cost of compliance with any subdivision ordinance required to withdraw a part of the real estate from the condominium.

5. Subsection (c) deals with special problems surrounding allocated interests when the declarant subdivides or converts units which were originally created in the declaration into additional units, common elements or both. This development right permits the declarant to defer a final decision as to the size of certain units by permitting the subdivision of larger interior spaces into smaller units. The declarant may thus "build to suit" for purchasers' needs or to meet changing market demand. The concept is called "convertible space" in several existing state statutes.

For example, a declarant of a 5-story office building condominium may have purchasers committed at the time of the filing of the condominium declaration but a lack of purchasers for the upper 2 floors. In such a circumstance, the declarant could designate the upper 2 floors as a unit, reserving to himself the right to subdivide or convert that unit into additional units, common elements or a combination of units and common elements as needed to suit the requirements of ultimate purchasers.

If, at a later time, a purchaser wishes to purchase half of one floor as a unit, the declarant could exercise the development right to subdivide his 2-floor unit into 2 or more units. He may also wish to reserve a portion of the divided floor as a corridor which will constitute common elements. In that case, he would proceed pursuant to this subsection to reallocate the allocated interests among the units in the manner described in this section.

Alternatively, the declarant may ultimately decide that the entire 2 floors should be turned over to the unit owners' association not as a unit but as common elements to be used perhaps as a cafeteria serving the balance of the building, or for retail space to be rented by the association. In that case, should he choose to make the entire 2 floors common elements, the provisions of paragraph (c)(1) would apply.

PROP §82.061. ALTERATIONS OF UNITS

(a) Subject to the provisions of the declaration and other provisions of law, a unit owner:

(1) may make improvements or alterations to the owner's unit that do not impair the structural integrity or mechanical systems or lessen the support of any portion of the condominium;

(2) may not change the appearance of the common elements or the exterior appearance of a unit or any other portion of the condominium without prior written permission of the association; and

(3) after acquiring an adjoining unit or an adjoining part of an adjoining unit, with the prior written approval of the association, may remove, alter, and create apertures in an intervening partition, even if the partition in whole or in part is a common element, if those acts do not impair the structural integrity or mechanical systems or lessen the support of any portion of the condominium.

(b) Removal of partitions or creation of apertures under Subsection (a)(3) is not an alteration of boundaries.

History of Prop. Code §82.061: Acts 1993, 73rd Leg., ch. 244, §1, eff. Jan. 1, 1994.

See also Prop. Code §§81.102, 81.104.

NCCUSL Comment*

1. This section deals with permissible alterations of the interior of a unit, and impermissible alterations of the exterior of a unit and the common elements, in ways which reflect common practice. The stated rules, of course, may be varied by the declaration where desired.

2. Subsection (a)(3) deals in a unique manner with the problem of creating access between adjoining units owned by the same person. The subsection provides a specific rule which would permit a door, stairwell, or removal of a partition wall between those units, so long as structural integrity is not impaired. That alteration would not be an alteration of boundaries, but would be an exception to the basic rule stated in subsection (a)(2).

3. In considering permissible alteration of the interior of a unit, an example may be useful. A nail driven by a unit owner to hang a picture might enter a portion of the wall designated as part of the common elements, but this section would not be violated because structural integrity would not be im-

* See footnote on p. 379.

paired. Moreover, no trespass would be committed because each unit owner, as a part owner of the common elements, has a right to utilize them subject only to such restrictions as may be created by the Chapter, the declaration, bylaws, and the unit owners' association pursuant to Section 82.102.

4. Removal of a partition or the creation of an aperture between adjoining units would permit the units to be used as one, but they would not become one unit. They would continue to be separate units within the meaning of Section 82.003 and would continue to be treated separately for the purposes of this Chapter.

5. In addition to the restrictions placed on unit owners by this section, the declaration or bylaws may restrict a unit owner from altering the interior appearance of his unit. Although this might be an undue restriction if imposed upon the primary residence of a unit owner, it may be appropriate in the case of time-share or other condominiums.

PROP §82.062. RELOCATION OF BOUNDARIES BETWEEN ADJOINING UNITS

Subject to the declaration, the boundaries between adjoining units may be relocated by an amendment to the declaration on written application to the association by the owners of those units. If the owners of the adjoining units have specified a reallocation between their units of their allocated interests, the application must state the proposed reallocations. Unless the board determines not later than the 30th day after the date the application is received that the reallocation is unreasonable, the association shall prepare an amendment that identifies the units involved, states the reallocation, is executed by the applying unit owners, and contains words of conveyance between them. At the expense of the applying unit owners, the association shall prepare and record the amendment and plats or plans necessary to show the altered boundaries between adjoining units, and the units' dimensions and identifying numbers.

History of Prop. Code §82.062: Acts 1993, 73rd Leg., ch. 244, §1, eff. Jan. 1, 1994.

See also Prop. Code §§81.105, 82.052, 82.059.

NCCUSL Comment*

1. This section changes the effect of most current condominium statutes, under which the boundaries between units may not be altered without unanimous or nearly unanimous consent of the unit owners. As the section makes clear, this result may be varied by restrictions in the declaration.

2. This section contemplates that, upon relocation of the unit boundaries, no reallocation of allocated interests will occur if none is specified in the application. If a reallocation is specified but the executive board deems it unreasonable, then the applicants have the choice of resubmitting the application with a reallocation more acceptable to the board, or going to court to challenge the board's finding as unreasonable.

PROP §82.063. SUBDIVISION OF UNITS

(a) If the declaration expressly permits, a unit may be subdivided into two or more units. Subject to the declaration, on written application of a unit owner to subdivide a unit and after payment by the unit owner of the cost of preparing and recording amendments and plats, the association shall prepare, execute, and record an amendment to the declaration, including the plats and plans, subdividing the unit.

(b) The amendment to the declaration must be executed by the owner of the unit to be subdivided, assign an identifying number to each unit created, and reallocate the allocated interests formerly allocated to the subdivided unit to the new units in any reasonable manner prescribed by the owner of the subdivided unit.

History of Prop. Code §82.063: Acts 1993, 73rd Leg., ch. 244, §1, eff. Jan. 1, 1994.

NCCUSL Comment*

1. This section provides for subdivision of units by unit owners, thereby creating more and smaller units than were originally created. The underlying policy of this section is that the original development plan of the project must be followed, and the expectations of unit owners realized. Accordingly, unless subdivision of the units is expressly permitted by the original declaration, a unit may not be subdivided into 2 or more units unless the declaration is amended to permit it. A subdivision itself is accomplished by an amendment to the declaration.

2. At the same time, situations will often occur where future subdivision is appropriate, and this section permits the declaration to provide for it. Most state statutes do not presently provide for subdivision of units.

An analogous concept in the context of development rights is subdivision of units by a declarant. The development right is described in Section 82.060.

PROP §82.064. EASEMENT FOR ENCROACHMENTS

To the extent that a unit or common element encroaches on another unit or common element, a valid easement for the encroachment exists. The easement does not relieve a unit owner of liability in case of the owner's wilful misconduct nor relieve a declarant or any other person of liability for failure to adhere to the plats and plans.

History of Prop. Code §82.064: Acts 1993, 73rd Leg., ch. 244, §1, eff. Jan. 1, 1994.

PROP §82.065. USE FOR SALES PURPOSES

The declaration may permit a declarant to maintain sales, leasing, or management offices and models in units or on common elements in the condominium if the declaration specifies the rights of a declarant with regard to the number, size, location, and relocation of the offices and models. If the declaration fails to expressly permit an office or model, a declarant may maintain no more than one unit as a model and no more than one unit as an office for sales, leasing, and management purposes at any one time. A sales, leasing, or management office or model not designated as a unit by the declaration is a common element and is subject to the exclusive use of a declarant until the declarant ceases to be a unit owner or until the declarant no longer uses the

* See footnote on p. 379.

office or model for such purposes, whichever occurs earlier. A declarant may modify the exterior of a sales, leasing, or management office to conform to the aesthetic exterior plan of the condominium. A declarant who ceases to be a unit owner ceases to have any rights with regard to an office or model unless it is removed within a reasonable time from the condominium in accordance with a right to remove reserved in the declaration. Subject to limitations in the declaration, a declarant may maintain signs on the common elements that advertise the condominium for sale or lease. This section is subject to local ordinances and other state law.

History of Prop. Code §82.065: Acts 1993, 73rd Leg., ch. 244, §1, eff. Jan. 1, 1994.

NCCUSL Comment*

1. This section prescribes the circumstances under which portions of the condominium—either units or common elements—may be used for sales offices, management offices, or models. The basic requirement is that the declarant must describe his rights to maintain such offices in the declaration. There are no limitations on that right, so that either units owned by the declarant or other persons, or the common elements themselves, may be used for that purpose. Typical common element uses might include a sales booth in the lobby of the building, or a trailer or temporary building located outside the buildings on the grounds of the property.

2. In addition, this section contains a permissive provision permitting advertising on the common elements. The declarant may choose to limit his rights in terms of the size, location, or other matters affecting the advertising. The Chapter, however, imposes no limitation. At the same time, the last sentence of the section recognizes that state or local zoning or other laws may limit advertising, both in terms of size and content of the advertising, or the use of the units or common elements for such purposes. This section makes it clear that local law would apply in those cases.

PROP §82.066. EASEMENT RIGHTS

Subject to the declaration, a declarant has an easement through the common elements as may be reasonably necessary for discharging the declarant's obligations or exercising special declarant rights whether arising under this chapter or reserved by the declaration.

History of Prop. Code §82.066: Acts 1993, 73rd Leg., ch. 244, §1, eff. Jan. 1, 1994.

NCCUSL Comment*

1. This section grants to declarant an easement across the common elements, subject to any self-imposed restrictions on that easement contained in the declaration. At the same time, the easement is not an easement for all purposes and under all circumstances, but only a grant of such rights as may be reasonably necessary for the purpose of exercising the declarant's rights. Thus, for example, if other access were equally available to the land where new units are being created, which did not require the declarant's construction equipment to pass and repass over the common elements in a manner which significantly inconvenienced the unit owners, a court might apply the "reasonably necessary" test contained in this section to consider limitations on the declarant's easement. The rights granted by this section may be enlarged by a specific reservation in the declaration.

2. The declarant is also required to repair and restore any portion of the condominium used for the easement granted under this section. *See* Section 82.163.

* See footnote on p. 379.

PROP §82.067. AMENDMENT OF DECLARATION

(a) Except as provided by Subsection (b), a declaration, including the plats and plans, may be amended only by vote or agreement of unit owners to which at least 67 percent of the votes in the association are allocated, or any larger majority the declaration specifies. A declaration may specify a smaller number only if all of the units are restricted exclusively to nonresidential use. An amendment to a declaration may be adopted:

(1) by written ballot that states the exact wording or substance of the amendment and that specifies the date by which a ballot must be received to be counted;

(2) at a meeting of the members of the association after written notice of the meeting has been delivered to an owner of each unit stating that a purpose of the meeting is to consider an amendment to the declaration; or

(3) by any method permitted by the declaration.

(b) The amendment procedures of this section do not apply to amendments that may be executed by:

(1) a declarant under Section 82.051(c), 82.059(f), or 82.060 or Subsection (f);

(2) the association under Section 82.007, 82.056(d), 82.058(c), 82.062, or 82.063 or Subsection (f); or

(3) certain unit owners under Section 82.058(b), 82.062, 82.063(b), or 82.068(b).

(c) An action to challenge the validity of an amendment adopted by the association under this section must be brought before the first anniversary of the date the amendment is recorded.

(d) To be effective, an amendment to the declaration must be recorded in each county in which any portion of the condominium is located.

(e) Except as permitted or required by this chapter, an amendment may not create or increase special declarant rights, increase the number of units, change the boundaries of a unit, alter or destroy a unit or limited common element, change a unit's allocated interest, or change the use restrictions on a unit unless the amendment is approved by 100 percent of the votes in the association. Except as agreed to by the declarant, an amendment may not increase or otherwise modify the obligations imposed by a declaration on a declarant, or reduce or otherwise modify the rights granted by a declaration to a declarant, including special declarant rights.

(f) If permitted by the declaration, the board or the declarant, if the declarant owns a unit that has never been occupied, may without a vote of the unit owners or approval of the association amend the declaration in any manner necessary to meet the requirements of the Federal National Mortgage Association, the Federal Home Loan Mortgage Corporation, the Federal Housing Administration, or the Veterans Administration.

(g) Amendments to the declaration required by this chapter to be recorded by the association must be prepared, executed, recorded, and certified by an officer of the association designated for that purpose or, in the absence of designation, by the president of the association.

(h) An association may amend the declaration to authorize the board:

(1) to bring an action to evict a tenant of a unit owner for the tenant's violation of the declaration, bylaws, or rules of the association;

(2) to bring an action to evict a tenant of a unit owner who fails to pay the association for the cost of repairs to common elements damaged substantially by the owner's tenant; or

(3) to collect rents from a tenant of a unit owner who is at least 60 days' delinquent in the payment of any amount due to the association.

History of Prop. Code §82.067: Acts 1993, 73rd Leg., ch. 244, §1, eff. Jan. 1, 1994.

See also Prop. Code §§81.111, 82.055.

NCCUSL Comment*

1. This section recognizes that the declaration, as the perpetual governing instrument for the condominium, may be amended by various parties at various times in the life of the project. The basic rule, stated in subsection (a), is that the declaration, including the plats and plans, may only be amended by vote of 67% of the unit owners. The section permits a larger percentage to be required by the declaration, and also recognizes that, in an entirely non-residential condominium, a smaller percentage might be appropriate.

In addition to that basic rule, subsection (a) lists those other instances where the declaration may be amended by the declarant alone without association approval, or by the association acting through its board of directors.

2. Section 82.004 does not permit the declarant to use any device, such as powers of attorney executed by purchasers at closings, to circumvent subsection (e)'s requirement of unanimous consent. This section does not supplant any requirements of common law or of other statutes with respect to conveyancing if title to real property is to be affected.

3. Subsection (g) describes the mechanics by which amendments recorded by the association are filed, and resolves a number of matters often neglected by bylaws.

PROP §82.0675. RESTRICTION RELATING TO CLUB MEMBERSHIP

(a) A provision of a declaration or recorded contract that requires owners of units in a condominium to maintain a membership in a specified private club is not valid after the 10th anniversary of the date the provision is recorded or renewed unless renewed after the ninth anniversary of that date in the manner provided by the declaration or recorded contract for amending the declaration or recorded contract and the text of the renewed provision is filed in the real property records of each county in which the condominium is located.

(b) A provision described by this section may not be enacted or renewed as a bylaw by the unit owners' association.

History of Prop. Code §82.0675: Acts 2003, 78th Leg., ch. 1101, §2, eff. Sept. 1, 2003.

See also Prop. Code §81.112.

PROP §82.068. TERMINATION OF CONDOMINIUM

(a) Unless the declaration provides otherwise and except for a taking of all the units by condemnation, a condominium may be terminated only by the agreement of 100 percent of the votes in the association and each holder of a deed of trust or vendor's lien on a unit. The declaration may not allow a termination by less than 80 percent of the votes in the association if any unit is restricted exclusively to residential uses.

(b) An agreement of unit owners to terminate a condominium must be evidenced by the execution or ratification of a termination agreement by the requisite number of unit owners. If, pursuant to a termination agreement, the real property constituting the condominium is to be sold following termination, the termination agreement must set forth the terms of the sale. To be effective, a termination agreement and all ratifications of the agreement must be recorded in each county in which a portion of the condominium is located.

(c) The association, on behalf of the unit owners, may contract for the sale of real property in the condominium, but the contract is not binding on the unit owners until it is approved under Subsections (a) and (b). If the real property constituting the condominium is to be sold following termination, on termination title to that real property vests in the association as trustee for the holders of all interests in the units, and the association has all powers necessary and appropriate to effect the sale, including the power to convey the interests of nonconsenting owners. Until the sale has been concluded and the proceeds distributed, the association shall continue to exist and retains the powers it had before termination. Proceeds of the sale must be distrib-

* See footnote on p. 379.

uted to unit owners and lienholders as their interests may appear, in proportion to the respective interests of unit owners as provided by Subsection (f). Unless the termination agreement specifies differently, as long as the association holds title to the real property, each unit owner and the owner's successors in interest have an exclusive right to occupy the portion of the real property that formerly constituted the owner's unit. During that period of occupancy a unit owner and the owner's successors in interest remain liable for all assessments and other obligations imposed on unit owners by this chapter or the declaration.

(d) If the real property constituting the condominium is not to be sold following termination, on termination title to the real property vests in the unit owners as tenants in common in proportion to their respective interests, and liens on the units shift accordingly. While the tenancy in common exists, a unit owner and the owner's successors in interest have an exclusive right to occupy the portion of the real property that formerly constituted the owner's unit.

(e) Following termination of the condominium, and after payment of or provision for the claims of the association's creditors, the assets of the association shall be distributed to unit owners in proportion to their respective interests. The proceeds of sale described by Subsection (c) and held by the association as trustee are not assets of the association.

(f) The interest of a unit owner referred to in Subsections (c), (d), and (e) is, except as provided by Subsection (g), the fair market value of the owner's unit, limited common elements, and common element interest immediately before the termination, as determined by one or more independent appraisers selected by the association. The decision of the independent appraisers shall be distributed to the unit owners and becomes final unless disapproved by unit owners of units to which 25 percent of the votes in the association are allocated not later than the 30th day after the date of distribution. The proportion of a unit owner's interest to that of all unit owners is determined by dividing the fair market value of the unit owner's unit and common element interest by the total fair market values of all the units and common elements.

(g) If a unit or a limited common element is destroyed to the extent that an appraisal of the fair market value before the destruction cannot be made, the interest of a unit owner is the owner's common element interest immediately before the termination.

(h) Foreclosure or enforcement of a lien or encumbrance against the entire condominium does not of itself terminate the condominium, and foreclosure or enforcement of a lien or encumbrance against a portion of the condominium does not withdraw that portion from the condominium, unless the portion is withdrawable real property or unless the mortgage being foreclosed was recorded before the date the declaration was recorded and the mortgagee did not consent in writing to the declaration.

(i) By agreement of the same percentage of unit owners that is required to terminate the condominium, the unit owners may rescind a termination agreement and reinstate the declaration in effect immediately before the election to terminate. To be effective, the rescission agreement must be in writing, executed by the unit owners who desire to rescind, and recorded in each county in which any portion of the condominium is located.

History of Prop. Code §82.068: Acts 1993, 73rd Leg., ch. 244, §1, eff. Jan. 1, 1994.

See also Prop. Code §§81.110, 82.101.

NCCUSL Comment*

1. While few condominiums have yet been terminated under present state law, a number of problems are certain to arise upon termination which have not been adequately addressed by most of those statutes. These include such matters as the percentage of unit owners which should be required for termination; the time frame within which written consents from all unit owners must be secured; the manner in which common elements and units should be disposed of following termination, both in the case of sale and non-sale of all of the real estate; the circumstances under which sale of units may be imposed on dissenting owners; the powers held by the Board of Directors on behalf of the association to negotiate a sales agreement; the practical consequences to the project from the time the unit owners approve the termination until the transfer of title and occupancy actually occurs; the impact of termination on liens on the units and common elements; distribution of sales proceeds; the effect of foreclosure or enforcement of liens against the entire condominium with respect to the validity of the project; and other matters.

2. Recognizing that unanimous consent from all unit owners would be impossible to secure as a practical matter on a project of any size, subsection (a) states a general rule that 80% consent of the unit owners would be required for termination of a project. The declaration may require a larger percentage of the unit owners and, in a non-residential project, it may also require a smaller percentage. Pursuant to Section 82.069 (Rights of Secured Lenders), lenders may require that the declaration specify a larger percentage of unit owner consent or, more typically, will require the consent of a percentage of the lenders before the project may be terminated.

...

3. Subsection (a) describes the procedure for execution of the termination agreement. It recognizes that not all unit owners will be able to execute the same instrument, and permits execution or ratification of the master termination agreement. Since the transfer of an interest in real estate is being accomplished by the agreements, each of the ratifications must be executed in the same manner as a deed. Importantly, the agreement must specify the time within which it will be effective; otherwise, the project might be indefinitely in

* See footnote on p. 379.

"limbo" if ratifications had been signed by some, but not all, required unit owners, and the signing unit owners fail to revoke their agreements. Importantly, the agreement becomes effective only when it is recorded.

...

4. Subsection (c) describes the powers of the association during the pendency of the termination proceedings. It empowers the association to negotiate for the sale, but makes the validity of any contract dependent on unit owner approval. This section also makes clear that, upon termination, title to the real estate shall be held by the association, so that the association may convey title without the necessity of each unit owner signing the deed. Finally, this section makes clear that, until the association delivers title to the condominium property, the project will continue to operate as it had prior to the termination, thus insuring that the practical necessities of operation of the real estate will not be impaired.

5. Subsection (d) contemplates the possibility that a condominium might be terminated but the real estate not sold. While this is not likely to be the usual case, it is important to provide for the possibility.

6. A complex series of creditors' rights questions may arise upon termination. Those questions involve competing claims of first mortgage holders on individual units, other secured and unsecured creditors of individual unit owners, judgment creditors of the association, creditors of the association to whom a security interest in the common elements has been granted, and unsecured creditors of the association. Subsection (e) attempts to establish general rules with respect to these competing claims, but leaves to state law the resolution of the priorities of those competing claims.

The examples which follow illustrate the relative effects of several provisions set out in the Chapter, based on application of an assumed state lien priority rule of "first in time, first in right." In those instances, particularly involving mechanics' liens, where state law often establishes priorities at variance with that rule, that result is also indicated.

EXAMPLE 1:

HYPOTHETICAL FOR EXAMPLES 1A-1H: A condominium consists of 5 detached single family homes on 5 individually owned lots, together with a 6th lot which is undeveloped but intended for future construction of a swimming pool serving all units. The development is served by a private road. Lot 6 and the private road are common elements owned on an undivided interest basis by the unit owners.

The declaration provides that: (1) upon termination, all units and the common elements must be sold; (2) the association is permitted to encumber Lot 6, and to grant a security interest in that lot for any purpose; and (3) common element interest votes and common expense liabilities are allocated equally among the units. For purposes of the example, we have assumed that the documents do not require the consent of first mortgage holders before the unit owners may vote to terminate.

The 5 units were originally sold at equal prices of $50,000. Common expenses in the project are $100 per unit, per month, and are used for a variety of purposes, including insurance and upkeep of the units and common elements. At the time the units were conveyed, each of them was released from all liens affecting the condominium which were senior to the declaration.

A shopping center developer has offered $380,000 for the purchase of the entire condominium. The association's members unanimously vote in favor of termination, and otherwise comply with Section 82.068. The appraisal required by Section 2-118(h) shows that the units are still of equal value.

EXAMPLE 1A:

At the time of termination, the 5 units were financed as follows:

Unit 1: The owner's first mortgage had an unpaid balance of $50,000.

Unit 2: The owner's first mortgage had an unpaid balance of $40,000.

Unit 3: The owner's first mortgage had an unpaid balance of $25,000.

Units 4 and 5: The owners paid cash, and there is no mortgage on either unit.

In addition, all common expenses had been paid when due. The other assets of the association, including reserves, bank account, and all other personal property, total $20,000.

Under the Chapter (Section 82.068(c)), the association, following sale, holds the proceeds of sale together with the assets of the association, "as trustee for the holders of all interests in the units." In these circumstances, the interests of each party in the total value of $400,000 would be as follows:

UNIT #	1	2	3	4	5
Share of Proceeds	80,000	80,000	80,000	80,000	80,000
Due 1st Mortgage Holders	50,000	40,000	25,000	-0-	-0-
Due Owners	30,000	40,000	55,000	80,000	80,000

EXAMPLE 1B:

The facts stated in Example 1A remain true. However, at termination, Unit 1 has failed to pay its common expenses for 12 months. In these circumstances, the interests of each party would be as follows:

UNIT #	1	2	3	4	5
Share of Proceeds	80,000	80,000	80,000	80,000	80,000
Due Association (Priming 1st Mortgage)	600	-0-	-0-	-0-	-0-
Due 1st Mortgage Holders	50,000	40,000	25,000	-0-	-0-
Due Association (Not Priming 1st Mortgage)	600	-0-	-0-	-0-	-0-
Due Owners	28,000	40,000	55,000	80,000	80,000

In this example, both the lenders and the association are fully paid because the sales proceeds exceed the liens on the units. Note, however, that 6 months of the unpaid assessments prime the first mortgage pursuant to Section 82.113(b). Thus, if the sales proceeds had been only $50,000 per unit, rather than $80,000, the results with respect to Unit 1 would have been as follows:

Sales Proceeds	$50,000
6-Month Assessment Due Association	600
Balance	$49,400
Paid to 1st Mortgage Holder	$49,400
Loss to 1st Mortgage Lender	(600)
Loss to Association	(600)

Of course, the association has, and the lender may have, a claim against the unit owner, personally, for the unpaid sums due them. Importantly, however, neither the other unit owners nor their units are subject to any liability for those claims.

Because the lien of the first mortgage holder, at termination or foreclosure, is junior to the first 6 months of unpaid assessments due the association, lenders may protect themselves under the Chapter by requiring the escrow of 6 months' common expense assessments, as they often do for real property taxes.

...

7. Subsection (f) departs significantly from the usual result under most condominium acts. Under those acts the proceeds of the sale of the entire project are distributed upon termination to each unit owner in accordance with the common element interest which was allocated at the outset of the project. Of course, in an older development, those original allocations will bear little resemblance to the actual value of the units. For that reason, the Chapter adopts an appraisal procedure for distribution of the sales proceeds. As suggested in the examples on the distribution of proceeds, this appraisal may dramatically affect the amount of dollars actually received by unit owners. Accordingly, it is likely the appraisal will be required to be distributed prior to the time the termination agreement is approved, so that unit owners may understand the likely financial consequences of the termination.

8. Subsection (g) is an exception to the "fair market value" rule. It provides that, if appraisal of any unit cannot be made, either through pictures or comparison with other units, so that any unit's appropriate share in the overall proceeds cannot be calculated, then the distribution will fall back on the only objective, albeit artificial, standard available, which is the common element interest allocated to each unit.

9. Foreclosure of a mortgage or other lien or encumbrance does not automatically terminate the condominium, but, if a mortgagee or other lienholder (or any other party) acquires units with a sufficient number of votes, that party can cause the condominium to be terminated pursuant to subsection (a) of this section.

10. A mortgage or deed of trust on a condominium unit may provide for the lien to shift, upon termination, to become a lien on what will then be the borrower's undivided interest in the whole property.

11. If an initial appraisal made pursuant to subsection (f) were rejected by vote of the unit owners, the association would be obligated to secure a new appraisal.

12. "Foreclosure" in subsection (h) includes deeds in lieu of foreclosure, and "liens" includes tax and other liens on real estate which may be converted or withdrawn from the project.

13. The termination agreement should adopt or contain any restrictions, covenants and other provisions for the governance and operation of the property formerly constituting the condominium which the owners deem appropriate. These might closely parallel the provisions of the declaration and bylaws. This is particularly important in the case of a condominium which is not to be sold pursuant to the terms of the termination agreement. In the absence of such provisions, the general law of the state governing tenancies in common would apply.

...

PROP §82.069. RIGHTS OF SECURED LENDERS

The declaration may require that all or a specified number or percentage of the mortgagees or beneficiaries of deeds of trust encumbering the units approve specified actions of the unit owners or the association as a condition to the effectiveness of those actions, but a requirement for approval may not operate to:

(1) deny or delegate control over the general administrative affairs of the association by the unit owners or the board; or

(2) prevent the association or the board from:

(A) commencing, intervening in, or settling any litigation or proceeding; or

(B) receiving and distributing insurance proceeds under Section 82.111.

History of Prop. Code §82.069: Acts 1993, 73rd Leg., ch. 244, §1, eff. Jan. 1, 1994.

NCCUSL Comment*

1. In a number of instances, particularly sale or encumbrance of common elements, or termination of a condominium, a lender's security may be dramatically affected by acts of the association. For that reason, this section permits ratification of those acts of the association which are specified in that declaration as a condition of their effectiveness.

2. There are three important limitations on the rights of lender consent. They are: (1) a prohibition on control over the general administrative affairs of the association; (2) restrictions on control over the association's powers during litigation or other proceedings; and (3) prohibition of receipt or distribution of insurance proceeds prior to application of those proceeds for rebuilding.

3. It is important that lenders not be able to step in and unilaterally act as receiver or trustee of the association. There may, of course, be occasions when a court of competent jurisdiction would order appointment of a receiver for an association. While this would be possible in a court proceeding, the Chapter prohibits private contractual granting of such a power.

4. Since it may well be that the association might find itself involved in litigation which would be adverse to the interests of the lender or the declarant, it is inappropriate for a secured party to be able to control the course of litigation in the absence of the consent of the other parties. In an appropriate case, of course, where the lenders' interests are affected, a lender might seek to intervene as a party in that proceeding.

5. Section 82.111 provides for the distribution of insurance proceeds in a particular manner. In particular, it prevents distribution of those proceeds to lenders until the intended purpose of the insurance has been met. For that reason, under this section the declaration may not provide the lender a right to receive insurance proceeds in any manner except the manner provided in Section 82.111.

6. In addition to the provision of the declaration, the provisions of individual deeds to units may require that unit owner to secure his lender's consent before taking particular actions.

PROP §82.070. MEETING AT WHICH AMENDMENTS MAY BE ADOPTED

(a) An association or a board may not meet to adopt an amendment or other change to the declaration, articles of incorporation, bylaws, or rules of the association unless the association or board has given to each unit owner a document showing the specific amendment or other change that would be made to the declaration, articles of incorporation, bylaws, or rules.

(b) The information described by Subsection (a) must be given to each unit owner after the 20th day but before the 10th day preceding the date of the meeting. The information is considered to have been given to a unit owner on the date the information is personally delivered to the unit owner, as shown by a receipt signed by the unit owner, or on the date shown by the postmark on the information after it is deposited in the United States mail with a proper address and postage paid.

History of Prop. Code §82.070: Acts 1997, 75th Leg., ch. 956, §2, eff. Jan. 1, 1998.

Sections 82.071-82.100 reserved for expansion

SUBCHAPTER C. CONDOMINIUM MANAGEMENT

PROP §82.101. ORGANIZATION OF UNIT OWNERS' ASSOCIATION

A unit owners' association must be organized as a profit or nonprofit corporation. The declarant may not convey a unit until the secretary of state has issued a certificate of incorporation under Article 3.03, Texas Business Corporation Act, or Article 3.03, Texas Non-Profit Corporation Act (Article 1396-3.03, Vernon's Texas Civil Statutes). The membership of the association at all times consists exclusively of all the unit own-

* See footnote on p. 379.

ers or, following termination of the condominium, all former unit owners entitled to distribution of proceeds, or the owners' heirs, successors, or assigns.

History of Prop. Code §82.101: Acts 1993, 73rd Leg., ch. 244, §1, eff. Jan. 1, 1994.

See also Prop. Code §§81.110, 82.068.

ANNOTATIONS

Plano Parkway Office Condos. v. Bever Props. LLC, 246 S.W.3d 188, 193 (Tex.App.—Dallas 2007, pet. denied). "To determine whether the unit owners are excused from the condominium regime we must determine whether the language of [Prop. Code] §82.101 stating 'declarant may not convey a unit until the secretary of state has issued a certificate of incorporation' is mandatory or directory. *At 195:* [T]he defining event in the creation of a condominium regime is the filing of a declaration ..., not the incorporation of the unit owners' association. [W]e conclude that the language in §82.101 concerning the timing of incorporating the unit owners' association is directory. *At 196:* The language used in §82.101 makes clear that all unit owners—and only unit owners—are members of the owners' association. And incorporating an association with no members, with less than all unit owners as members, or with non-unit-owners as members would not comply with §82.101. [¶] [W]e conclude that the legislature's intent was that the consequence of a defect in the articles of incorporation is to allow the owner to pursue 'appropriate relief' under [Prop. Code] §82.161 (e.g., suing to force the developer/declarant to incorporate), not to defeat the entire condominium regime."

NCCUSL Comment*

The first purchaser of a unit is entitled to have in place the legal structure of the unit owners' association. The existence of the structure clarifies the relationship between the developer and other unit owners and makes it easy for the developer to involve unit owners in the governance of the condominium even during a period of declarant control reserved pursuant to Section 82.103(c).

PROP §82.102. POWERS OF UNIT OWNERS' ASSOCIATION

(a) Unless otherwise provided by the declaration, the association, acting through its board, may:

(1) adopt and amend bylaws;

(2) adopt and amend budgets for revenues, expenditures, and reserves, and collect assessments for common expenses from unit owners;

(3) hire and terminate managing agents and other employees, agents, and independent contractors;

(4) institute, defend, intervene in, settle, or compromise litigation or administrative proceedings in its own name on behalf of itself or two or more unit owners on matters affecting the condominium;

(5) make contracts and incur liabilities relating to the operation of the condominium;

(6) regulate the use, maintenance, repair, replacement, modification, and appearance of the condominium;

(7) adopt and amend rules regulating the use, occupancy, leasing or sale, maintenance, repair, modification, and appearance of units and common elements, to the extent the regulated actions affect common elements or other units;

(8) cause additional improvements to be made as a part of the common elements;

(9) acquire, hold, encumber, and convey in its own name any right, title, or interest to real or personal property, except common elements of the condominium;

(10) grant easements, leases, licenses, and concessions through or over the common elements;

(11) impose and receive payments, fees, or charges for the use, rental, or operation of the common elements and for services provided to unit owners;

(12) impose interest and late charges for late payments of assessments, returned check charges, and, if notice and an opportunity to be heard are given in accordance with Subsection (d), reasonable fines for violations of the declaration, bylaws, and rules of the association;

(13) adopt and amend rules regulating the collection of delinquent assessments and the application of payments;

(14) adopt and amend rules regulating the termination of utility service to a unit, the owner of which is delinquent in the payment of an assessment that is used, in whole or in part, to pay the cost of that utility;

(15) impose reasonable charges for preparing, recording, or copying declaration amendments, resale certificates, or statements of unpaid assessments;

(16) enter a unit for bona fide emergency purposes when conditions present an imminent risk of harm or damage to the common elements, another unit, or the occupants;

* See footnote on p. 379.

(17) suspend the voting privileges of or the use of certain general common elements by an owner delinquent for more than 30 days in the payment of assessments;

(18) purchase insurance and fidelity bonds it considers appropriate or necessary;

(19) exercise any other powers conferred by the declaration or bylaws;

(20) exercise any other powers that may be exercised in this state by a corporation of the same type as the association; and

(21) exercise any other powers necessary and proper for the government and operation of the association.

(b) The declaration may not impose limitations on the power of the association to deal with the declarant that are more restrictive than the limitations imposed on the power of the association to deal with other persons.

(c) To be enforceable, a bylaw or rule of the association must not be arbitrary or capricious.

(d) Before an association may charge the unit owner for property damage for which the unit owner is liable or levy a fine for violation of the declaration, bylaws, or rules, the association shall give to the unit owner a written notice that:

(1) describes the violation or property damage and states the amount of the proposed fine or damage charge;

(2) states that not later than the 30th day after the date of the notice, the unit owner may request a hearing before the board to contest the fine or damage charge; and

(3) allows the unit owner a reasonable time, by a specified date, to cure the violation and avoid the fine unless the unit owner was given notice and a reasonable opportunity to cure a similar violation within the preceding 12 months.

(e) The association may give a copy of the notice required by Subsection (d) to an occupant of the unit. The association must give notice of a levied fine or damage charge to the unit owner not later than the 30th day after the date of levy.

(f) Except as provided by Subsection (g), the association by resolution of the board of directors may:

(1) borrow money; and

(2) assign as collateral for the loan authorized by the resolution:

(A) the association's right to future income, including the right to receive assessments; and

(B) the association's lien rights.

(g) If a dedicatory instrument requires a vote of members of the association to borrow money or assign the association's right to future income or the association's lien rights, the loan or assignment must be approved as provided by the dedicatory instrument. The board may determine whether a vote for that purpose may be cast electronically, by absentee ballot, in person or by proxy at a meeting called for that purpose, or by written consent. If a lower approval threshold is not provided by the dedicatory instrument, approval requires the consent of owners holding 67 percent of all voting interests.

History of Prop. Code §82.102: Acts 1993, 73rd Leg., ch. 244, §1, eff. Jan. 1, 1994. Amended by Acts 2013, 83rd Leg., ch. 678, §3, eff. Sept. 1, 2013.

ANNOTATIONS

Stanford Dev. Corp. v. Stanford Condo. Owners Ass'n, 285 S.W.3d 45, 50 (Tex.App.—Houston [1st Dist.] 2009, no pet.). "The Association purchased nothing from [developer] and serves only to represent the interests of the individual homeowners. [¶] [T]he individual owners bound themselves to arbitrate their claims with [developer]. Thus, the Association, when suing *on the owners' behalf*, is also bound to arbitrate.... [¶] The Association does not own the property that is the subject of the dispute. Each individual homeowner owns an undivided interest in the common areas that are the subject of this dispute. Although the Association has standing to bring the suit, its rights are limited to those possessed by the people it represents. Because the homeowners are bound by arbitration agreements, and the Association has sued on their behalf, it, too, is bound by the agreements."

Phan v. Addison Spectrum, L.P., 244 S.W.3d 892, 897 (Tex.App.—Dallas 2008, no pet.). Held: Individual homeowners are bound by consequences of suit that was brought by their homeowners' association on their behalf and to which they have consented by virtue of their membership in the association.

NCCUSL Comment*

1. Required provisions of the bylaws of the association, referenced in paragraph (a)(1), are set forth in Section 82.106.

---

* See footnote on p. 379.

2. Many state condominium statutes give the association the power to sue and be sued in its own name. In the absence of a statutory grant of standing such as that set forth in paragraph (a)(4), some courts have held that the association, because it has no ownership interest in the condominium, has no standing to bring, defend, or to intervene in litigation or administrative proceedings in its own name.

...

3. The powers granted the association in paragraph (a)(12) to impose charges for late payment of assessments and to levy reasonable fines for violations of the association's rules reflect the need to provide the association with sufficient powers to exercise its "governmental" functions as the ruling body of the condominium community. These powers are intended to be in addition to any rights which the association may have under other law.

4. If the association is incorporated, it may, pursuant to paragraph (a)(20), exercise all other powers of a corporation. Similarly, if the association is unincorporated, the association may, by virtue of paragraph (a)(20), exercise all other powers of an unincorporated association.

5. Under subsections (f) and (g), the declaration may provide for the assignment of income of the association, including common expense assessment income, as security for, or payment of, debts of the association. The power may be limited in any manner specified in the declaration—for example, the power might be limited to specified purposes such as repair of existing structures, or to income from particular sources such as income from tenants, or to a specified percentage of common expense assessments. The power, in many instances, should help materially in securing credit for the association at favorable interest rates. The inability of associations to borrow because of a lack of assets, in spite of its income stream, has been a significant problem.

PROP §82.103. BOARD MEMBERS & OFFICERS

(a) Except as provided by the declaration, bylaws, or this chapter, the board shall act in all instances on behalf of the association if in the good-faith judgment of the board the action is reasonable. Each officer or member of the board is liable as a fiduciary of the unit owners for the officer's or member's acts or omissions. All acts of the association must be by and through the board unless otherwise provided by the declaration or bylaws or by law.

(b) The board may not act on behalf of the association to amend the declaration except as permitted by this chapter, to terminate the condominium, to elect members of the board, or to determine the qualifications, powers and duties, or terms of office of board members. The board may fill a vacancy in its membership for the unexpired portion of a term.

(c) Subject to Subsection (d), the declaration may provide for a period of declarant control of the association during which a declarant, or persons designated by the declarant, may appoint and remove the officers and members of the board. Regardless of the period provided by the declaration, a period of declarant control terminates not later than the 120th day after conveyance of 75 percent of the units that may be created to unit owners other than a declarant. Transfer of special declarant rights does not terminate the period of declarant control. A declarant may voluntarily surrender the right to appoint and remove officers and members of the board before termination of the period, but in that event the declarant may require, for the duration of the period that the declarant would otherwise control, that specified actions of the association or board be approved by the declarant before they become effective.

(d) Not later than the 120th day after conveyance of 50 percent of the units that may be created to unit owners other than a declarant, not less than one-third of the members of the board must be elected by unit owners other than the declarant.

(e) Not later than the termination of a period of declarant control, the unit owners shall elect a board of at least three members who need not be unit owners. The board shall elect the officers before the 31st day after the date declarant control terminates. The persons elected shall take office on election.

(f) An officer or director of the association is not liable to the association or any unit owner for monetary damages for an act or omission occurring in the person's capacity as an officer or director unless:

(1) the officer or director breached a fiduciary duty to the association or a unit owner;

(2) the officer or director received an improper benefit; or

(3) the act or omission was in bad faith, involved intentional misconduct, or was one for which liability is expressly provided by statute.

(g) Subsection (f) does not diminish a limitation of liability provided an officer or director of the association by the declaration, bylaws, articles of incorporation of the association, or other laws.

History of Prop. Code §82.103: Acts 1993, 73rd Leg., ch. 244, §1, eff. Jan. 1, 1994.

ANNOTATIONS

Bever Props., L.L.C. v. Jerry Huffman Custom Builder, L.L.C., 355 S.W.3d 878, 891 (Tex.App.—Dallas 2011, no pet.). "[Ps'] pleading alleges numerous instances in which condominium association officers … acted in disregard of provisions of the Declaration, including allowing subtenants in violation of the Declaration, permitting [D's] delinquency in payment of condominium assessments, entering into contractual arrangements with other entities in contravention of the Declaration, and 'self-serving and illegal actions of [Ds] (acting to cover up the wrongdoings of [other D]).' [Ds] failed to address these factual allegations in

their motions for summary judgment, relying solely on the statement in ... their motions that [Ps] knew what their rights and liabilities were pursuant to the Declaration and understood 'that the ultimate control of the complex was in the hands of the association.' This statement alone does not satisfy [Ds'] burden to disprove an essential element of [Ps'] cause of action for breach of fiduciary duties. [¶] We conclude the trial court erred in granting summary judgment in favor of [Ds] on [Ps'] claim of breach of fiduciary duties."

Harris v. Spires Council of Co-owners, 981 S.W.2d 892, 897 (Tex.App.—Houston [1st Dist.] 1998, no pet.). "The Property Code recognizes that each officer or member of a condominium board is liable as a fiduciary of the unit owners for the officers' or members' acts or omissions. The officers and members must fulfill the duties owed to the unit owners with reasonable care, diligence, good faith, and judgment. A fiduciary duty may also arise by contract or in the context of an informal moral, social, domestic, or personal relationship in which one person trusts or relies on another."

NCCUSL Comment*

1. Subsection (a) makes members of the executive board appointed by the declarant liable as fiduciaries of the unit owners with respect to their actions or omissions as members of the board. This provision imposes a very high standard of duty because the board is vested with great power over the property interests of unit owners, and because there is a great potential for conflicts of interest between the unit owners and the declarant.

Officers and board members elected by the unit owners are required only to exercise ordinary and reasonable care. This lower standard of care should increase the willingness of unit owners to serve as officers and members of the board.

...

2. Subsections (c) and (d) recognize the practical necessity for the declarant to control the association during the developmental phases of a condominium project. However, any executive board member appointed by the declarant pursuant to subsection (d) is liable as a fiduciary to any unit owner for his acts or omissions in such capacity.

3. Subsection (c) permits a declarant to surrender his right to appoint and remove officers and executive board members prior to the termination of the period of declarant control in exchange for a veto right over certain actions of the association or its executive board. This provision is designed to encourage transfer of control by declarants to unit owners as early as possible, without impinging upon the declarant's rights (for the duration of the period of declarant control) to maintain ultimate control of those matters which he may deem particularly important to him. It might be noted that the declarant at all times (even after the expiration of the period of declarant control) is entitled to cast the votes allocated to his units in the same manner as any other unit owner.

4. Subsection (d), in combination with subsection (c), provides for a gradual transfer of control of the association to the unit owners from the declarant. Such a gradual transfer is preferable to a one-time turnover of control since it assures that the unit owners will be involved, to some extent, in the affairs of the association from a relatively early date and that some unit owners will acquire experience in dealing with association matters.

* See footnote on p. 379.

PROP §82.104. TRANSFER OF SPECIAL DECLARANT RIGHTS

(a) Special declarant rights created or reserved under this chapter may not be transferred except by an instrument evidencing the transfer recorded in each county in which any portion of the condominium is located. The instrument is not effective unless executed by the transferee.

(b) On transfer of any special declarant right, a transferor is not relieved of an obligation or liability arising before the transfer. A transferor is not liable for an act or omission or a breach of an obligation arising from the exercise of a special declarant right by a successor declarant who is not an affiliate of the transferor.

(c) Unless otherwise provided by a mortgage instrument or deed of trust, in case of foreclosure of a mortgage, tax sale, judicial sale, sale by a trustee under a deed of trust, or sale under Bankruptcy Code or receivership proceedings, of a unit owned by a declarant or of real property in a condominium subject to development rights, a person acquiring title to all the real property being foreclosed or sold may request to succeed to all special declarant rights or only to rights reserved by the declaration to maintain models, offices, and signs. The judgment or instrument conveying title may provide for transfer of only the special declarant rights requested.

(d) On foreclosure, tax sale, judicial sale, sale by a trustee under a deed of trust, or sale under Bankruptcy Code or receivership proceedings of all units and other real property in a condominium owned by a declarant:

(1) the declarant ceases to have any special declarant rights; and

(2) the period of declarant control terminates unless the judgment or instrument conveying title provides for transfer of all special declarant rights held by that declarant to a successor declarant.

(e) The liabilities and obligations of a person who succeeds to special declarant rights are as follows:

(1) a successor to a special declarant right who is an affiliate of a declarant is subject to all obligations and liabilities imposed on the transferor by this chapter or by the declaration;

(2) a successor to a special declarant right, other than a successor described by Subdivision (3) or (4), who is not an affiliate of a declarant, is subject to all ob-

ligations and liabilities imposed on the transferor by this chapter or by the declaration;

(3) a successor to only a right reserved by the declaration to maintain models, offices, and signs, who is not an affiliate of a declarant, may not exercise any other special declarant right, and is not subject to any liability or obligation as a declarant, except the obligation to provide a condominium information statement and any liability arising as a result; and

(4) a successor to all special declarant rights held by the successor's transferor who is not an affiliate of that declarant and who succeeded to those rights pursuant to a deed in lieu of foreclosure or a judgment or instrument conveying title to units under Subsection (c) may declare the person's intention in a recorded instrument to hold those rights solely for transfer to another person; thereafter, until all special declarant rights are transferred to a person acquiring title to any unit owned by the successor, or until an instrument permitting exercise of all those rights is recorded, the successor may not exercise any of those rights other than any right held by the successor's transferor to control the board as provided by Section 82.103(c) for the duration of the period of declarant control, and an attempt to exercise those rights is void; so long as a successor declarant may not exercise special declarant rights under this subdivision, the successor is not subject to any liability or obligation as a declarant other than liability for acts and omissions under Section 82.103(a).

(f) This section does not subject a successor to a special declarant right to any claims against or other obligations of a transferor declarant, other than claims and obligations arising under this chapter or the declaration.

History of Prop. Code §82.104: Acts 1993, 73rd Leg., ch. 244, §1, eff. Jan. 1, 1994.

NCCUSL Comment*

1. This section deals with the issue of the extent to which obligations and liabilities imposed upon a declarant by this Chapter are transferred to a third party by a transfer of the declarant's interest in a condominium. There are two parts to the problem. First, what obligations and liabilities to unit owners (both existing unit owners and persons who become unit owners in the future) should a declarant retain, notwithstanding his transfer of interests. Second, what obligations and liabilities may fairly be imposed upon the declarant's successor in interest. No present condominium state adequately addresses these issues.

2. This section strikes a balance between the obvious need to protect the interests of unit owners and the equally important need to protect innocent successors to a declarant's rights, especially persons such as mortgagees whose only interest in the condominium project is to protect their debt security. The general scheme of the section is to impose upon a declarant continuing obligations and liabilities for promises, acts, or omissions undertaken during the period that he was in control of the condominium, while relieving a declarant who transfers all or part of his special declarant rights in a project of such responsibilities with respect to the promises, acts, or omissions of a successor over whom he has no control. Similarly, the section imposes obligations and liabilities arising after the transfer upon a non-affiliated successor to a declarant's interests, but absolves such a transferee of responsibility for the promises, acts, or omissions of a transferor declarant over which he had no control. Finally, the section makes special provision for the interests of certain successor declarants (*e.g.*, a mortgagee who succeeds to the rights of the declarant pursuant to a "deed in lieu of foreclosure" and who holds the project solely for transfer to another person) by relieving such persons of virtually all of the obligations and liabilities imposed upon declarants by this Chapter.

3. Subsection (a) provides that a successor in interest to a declarant may acquire the special rights of the declarant only by recording an instrument which reflects a transfer of those rights. This recordation requirement is important to determine the duration of the period of declarant control pursuant to Section 82.103(c) and (d), as well as to place unit owners on notice of all persons entitled to exercise the special rights of a declarant under this Chapter. The transfer by a declarant of all of his interest in a condominium project to a successor, without a concomitant transfer of the special rights of a declarant pursuant to this subsection, results in the automatic termination of such special declarant rights and of any period of declarant control.

4. Under subsection (b), a transferor declarant remains liable to unit owners (both existing unit owners and persons who subsequently become unit owners) for all obligations and liabilities, including warranty obligations on all improvements made by him, arising prior to the transfer. If a declarant transfers any special declarant right to an affiliate (as defined in Section 82.003(1)), the transferor remains subject to all liabilities specified in subsection (b) and, in addition, is jointly and severally liable with his successor in interest for all obligations and liabilities of the successor.

5. The obligations and liabilities imposed upon transferee declarants under the Chapter are set forth in subsection (e). In general, a transferee declarant (other than an affiliate of the original declarant and other than a successor whose interest in the project is solely for the protection of debt security) becomes subject to all obligations and liabilities imposed upon a declarant by the Chapter or by the declaration with respect to any promises, acts, or omissions undertaken subsequent to the transfer which relate to the rights he holds. Such a transferee is liable for the promises, acts, or omissions of the original declarant undertaken prior to the transfer.

6. To preclude declarants from evading their obligations and liabilities under this Chapter by transferring their interests to affiliated companies, paragraph (1) of subsection (e) makes clear that any successor declarant who is an affiliate of the original declarant is subject to all obligations and liabilities imposed upon the original declarant by the Chapter or by the declaration. Similarly, as previously noted, paragraph (2) of subsection (b) provides that an original declarant who transfers his rights to an affiliate remains jointly and severally liable with his successor for all obligations and liabilities imposed upon declarants by the Chapter or by the declaration.

7. The section handles the problem of certain successor declarants (*i.e.*, persons whose sole interest in the condominium project is the protection of debt security) in three ways. First, subsection (c) provides that, in the case of a foreclosure of a mortgage, a sale by a trustee under a deed of trust, or a sale by a trustee in bankruptcy of any units owned by a declarant, any person acquiring title to all of the units being foreclosed or sold may request the transfer of special declarant rights. In that event, and only upon such request, such rights will be transferred in the instrument conveying title to the units and such transferee will thereafter become a successor declarant subject to the other provisions of this section. In the event of a foreclosure, sale by a trustee under a deed of trust, or sale by a trustee in bankruptcy of all units owned by a declarant, if the transferee of such units does not request the transfer of special declarant rights, then, under subsection (d), such special declarant rights cease to exist and any period of declarant control terminates.

Second, any person who succeeds to special declarant rights as a result of the transfers just described or by deed in lieu of foreclosure, may, pursuant to paragraph (4) of subsection (e), declare his intention (in a recorded instrument) to hold those rights solely for transfer to another person. Thereafter, such a successor may transfer all special declarant rights to a third party acquiring title to any units owned by the successor but may not, prior to such transfer, exercise any special declarant rights. A successor declarant who exercises such

* See footnote on p. 379.

a right is relieved of any liability under the Chapter except liability for any acts or omissions related to his control of the executive board of the association. This provision is designed to deal with the typical problem of a foreclosing mortgage lender who opts to bid in and obtain the project at the foreclosure sale solely for the purpose of subsequent resale. It permits such a foreclosing lender to undertake such a transaction without incurring the full burden of declarant obligations and liabilities. At the same time, the provision recognizes the need for continuing operation of the association and, to that end, permits a foreclosing lender to assume control of the association for the purpose of ensuring a smooth transition.

Third, paragraph (3) of subsection (e) provides that a successor who has only the right to maintain model units, sales offices, and signs does not thereby become subject to any obligations or liabilities as a declarant except for the obligation to provide a condominium information statement and any liability resulting therefrom. This provision also is designed to protect mortgage lenders and contemplates the situation where a lender takes over a condominium project and desires to sell out existing units without making any additional improvements to the project. This provision facilitates such a transaction by relieving the mortgage lender, in that instance, from the full burden of obligations and liabilities ordinarily imposed upon a declarant under the Chapter.

Under Section 82.060, a declarant may reserve the right to create additional units in portions of the condominium which were originally designated as common elements. The declarant becomes the owner of any units created, but, prior to creation of units, the title to those portions of the condominium is in the unit owners. The right to create the units is an interest in land in which a security interest might be granted. If the mortgagee of that interest forecloses, the purchaser at the foreclosure sale has the choices concerning development rights and resulting liability which are described in the preceding paragraph. That is, under subsections (c) and (d), the purchaser may limit his liability by agreeing to hold the developments only for the purpose of transfer as provided by paragraph (e)(4) or may buy the rights under paragraph (c).

PROP §82.105. TERMINATION OF CONTRACTS & LEASES OF DECLARANT

An association in a residential or recreational condominium may terminate, without penalty, contracts or leases between the association and a declarant or an affiliate of a declarant if:

(1) the contract is entered into by the association while controlled by the declarant;

(2) the association terminates the contract or lease before the first anniversary of the date a board elected by the unit owners takes office; and

(3) the association gives at least 90 days' notice of its intent to terminate the contract or lease to the other party.

History of Prop. Code §82.105: Acts 1993, 73rd Leg., ch. 244, §1, eff. Jan. 1, 1994.

NCCUSL Comment*

1. This section deals with a common problem in the development of condominium projects: the temptation on the part of the developer, while in control of the association, to enter into, on behalf of the association, long-term contracts and leases with himself or with an affiliated entity.

The Chapter deals with this problem is two ways. First, Section 82.103(a) imposes upon all executive board members appointed by the declarant liability as fiduciaries of the unit owners for all of their acts or omissions as members of the board. Second, Section 82.105 provides for the termination of certain contracts and leases made during a period of declarant control.

2. In addition to contracts or leases made by a declarant with himself or with an affiliated entity, there are also certain contracts and leases so critical to the operation of the condominium and to the unit owners' full enjoyment of their rights of ownership that they too should be voidable by the unit owners upon the expiration of any period of declarant control. At the same time, a statutorily-sanctioned right of cancellation should not be applicable to all contracts or leases which a declarant may enter into in the course of developing a condominium project. For example, a commercial tenant would not be willing to invest substantial amounts in equipment and other improvements for the operation of his business if the lease could unilaterally be cancelled by the association. Accordingly, this section provides that (subject to the exception set forth in the last sentence thereof), upon the expiration of any period of declarant control, the association may terminate without penalty, any "critical" contract (*i.e.*, any management contract, employment contract, or lease of recreational or parking areas or facilities) entered into during a period of declarant control, any contract or lease to which the declarant or an affiliate of the declarant is a party, or any contract or lease previously entered into by the declarant which is not *bona fide* or which was unconscionable to the unit owners at the time entered into under the circumstances then prevailing.

...

* See footnote on p. 379.

PROP §82.106. BYLAWS

(a) The administration and operation of the condominium are governed by the bylaws, which must provide for:

(1) the number of members on the board and the titles of the officers of the association;

(2) election by the board of a president, treasurer, secretary, and any other officers the bylaws specify;

(3) the qualifications, powers and duties, terms of office, and the manner of electing and removing a board member or officer and filling vacancies;

(4) the powers, if any, that the board or an officer may delegate to other persons or to a managing agent;

(5) the designation of officers who are authorized to prepare, execute, certify, and record amendments to the declaration on behalf of the association;

(6) the method of amending the bylaws; and

(7) the manner of notice of meetings of the association.

(b) Subject to the declaration, the bylaws may provide for other matters the association considers desirable, necessary, or appropriate.

History of Prop. Code §82.106: Acts 1993, 73rd Leg., ch. 244, §1, eff. Jan. 1, 1994.

See also Prop. Code §81.202.

NCCUSL Comment*

1. Because the Chapter does not require the recordation of bylaws, it is contemplated that unrecorded bylaws will set forth only matters relating to the internal operations of the association and various "housekeeping" matters with respect to the condominium. The Chapter requires specific matters to be set forth in the recorded declaration and not in the bylaws, unless the bylaws are to be recorded as an exhibit to the declaration.

2. The requirement, set forth in subsection (a)(5), that the bylaws designate which of the officers of the association has the responsibility to prepare, execute, certify, and record amendments to the declaration reflects the obligation imposed upon the association by several provisions of this Chapter to record such amendments in certain circumstances. These provisions include Section 82.007 (Condemnation), Section 82.056 (Leasehold Condominiums), Section 82.062 (Relocation of Boundaries Between Adjoining Units), and Sec-

tion 82.063 (Subdivision of Units). Section 82.067(g) provides that, if no officer is designated for this purpose, it shall be the duty of the president.

PROP §82.107. UPKEEP OF CONDOMINIUM

(a) Except as provided by the declaration or Subsections (b) and (c), the association is responsible for maintenance, repair, and replacement of the common elements, and each unit owner is responsible for maintenance, repair, and replacement of the owner's unit. Each unit owner shall afford to the association and the other unit owners, and to their agents or employees, access through the owner's unit reasonably necessary for those purposes. If damage is inflicted on the common elements or on any unit through which access is taken, the unit owner responsible for the damage, or the association if it is responsible, is liable for the prompt repair of the damage.

(b) Except as provided by the declaration, each unit owner is responsible for the cost of maintenance, repair, and replacement of any utility installation or equipment serving only the owner's unit, without regard to whether the installation or equipment is located wholly or partially outside the designated boundaries of the unit. For purposes of this subsection, utility installations and equipment include electricity, water, sewage, gas, water heaters, heating and air conditioning equipment, and television antennas.

(c) Except as provided by the declaration, each unit owner is responsible for the cost of maintenance, repair, and replacement of windows and doors serving only the owner's unit.

(d) Unless otherwise provided by the declaration, the association may enter a unit, after giving notice to the owner and occupant of the unit, to:

(1) prevent or terminate waste of water purchased by the association as a common expense; or

(2) perform maintenance and repairs of the condominium that, if not performed, may result in increased damage by water to components of the condominium that the association maintains.

History of Prop. Code §82.107: Acts 1993, 73rd Leg., ch. 244, §1, eff. Jan. 1, 1994.

NCCUSL Comment*

1. The Chapter permits the declaration to separate maintenance responsibility from ownership. This is commonly done in practice. In the absence of any provision in the declaration, maintenance responsibility follows ownership of the unit or rests with the association in the case of common elements. Under this Chapter, limited common elements (which might include, for example, patios, balconies, and parking spaces) are common elements. *See* Section 82.003(17). As a result, under subsection (a), unless the declaration requires that unit owners are responsible for the upkeep of such limited common elements, the association will be responsible for their maintenance. Under Section 82.112(d), the cost of maintenance, repair, and replacement for such limited common elements is assessed against all the units in the condominium, unless the declaration provides for such expenses to be paid only by the units benefited. *See* Comment 1 to Section 82.058.

2. Under Section 82.060, a declarant may reserve the right to create units in portions of the condominium originally designated as common elements. Prior to creation of the units, title to those portions of the condominium is in the unit owners.

* See footnote on p. 379.

PROP §82.108. MEETINGS

(a) Meetings of the association must be held at least once each year. Unless the declaration provides otherwise, special meetings of the association may be called by the president, a majority of the board, or unit owners having at least 20 percent of the votes in the association.

(b) Meetings of the association and board must be open to unit owners, subject to the right of the board to adjourn a meeting of the board and reconvene in closed executive session to consider actions involving personnel, pending litigation, contract negotiations, enforcement actions, matters involving the invasion of privacy of individual unit owners, or matters that are to remain confidential by request of the affected parties and agreement of the board. The general nature of any business to be considered in executive session must first be announced at the open meeting.

(c) Unless the declaration, bylaws, or articles of incorporation of the association provide otherwise:

(1) a meeting of the board may be held by any method of communication, including electronic and telephonic, if:

(A) notice of the meeting has been given in accordance with Subsection (e);

(B) each director may hear and be heard by every other director; and

(C) the meeting does not involve voting on a fine, damage assessment, appeal from a denial of architectural control approval, or suspension of a right of a particular association member before the member has an opportunity to attend a board meeting to present the member's position, including any defense, on the issue; and

(2) the board may act by unanimous written consent of all the directors, without a meeting, if:

(A) the board action does not involve voting on a fine, damage assessment, appeal from a denial of architectural control approval, or suspension of a right of a

particular association member before the member has an opportunity to attend a board meeting to present the member's position, including any defense, on the issue; and

(B) a record of the board action is filed with the minutes of board meetings.

(d) Notice of a meeting of the association must be given as provided by the bylaws, or, if the bylaws do not provide for notice, notice must be given to each unit owner in the same manner in which notice is given to members of a nonprofit corporation under Section A, Article 2.11, Texas Non-Profit Corporation Act (Article 1396-2.11, Vernon's Texas Civil Statutes).

(e) Notice of a meeting of the board must be given as provided by the bylaws, or, if the bylaws do not provide for notice, notice must be given to each board member in the same manner in which notice is given to members of the board of a nonprofit corporation under Section B, Article 2.19, Texas Non-Profit Corporation Act (Article 1396-2.19, Vernon's Texas Civil Statutes).

(f) An association, on the written request of a unit owner, shall inform the unit owner of the time and place of the next regular or special meeting of the board. If the association representative to whom the request is made does not know the time and place of the meeting, the association promptly shall obtain the information and disclose it to the unit owner or inform the unit owner where the information may be obtained.

History of Prop. Code §82.108: Acts 1993, 73rd Leg., ch. 244, §1, eff. Jan. 1, 1994. Amended by Acts 1997, 75th Leg., ch. 956, §3, eff. Jan. 1, 1998.

PROP §82.109. QUORUMS

(a) Unless the bylaws provide otherwise, a quorum is present throughout any meeting of the association if persons entitled to cast at least 20 percent of the votes that may be cast for election of the board are present in person or by proxy at the beginning of the meeting. The bylaws may not reduce the standard for a quorum to less than 10 percent.

(b) Unless the bylaws specify a larger percentage, a quorum is present throughout a meeting of the board if persons entitled to cast at least 50 percent of the votes on the board are present at the beginning of the meeting.

History of Prop. Code §82.109: Acts 1993, 73rd Leg., ch. 244, §1, eff. Jan. 1, 1994.

NCCUSL Comment*

Mandatory quorum requirements lower than 50 percent for meetings of the association are often justified because of the common difficulty of inducing unit owners to attend meetings. The problem is particularly acute in the case of resort condominiums where many owners may reside elsewhere, often at considerable distances, for most of the year.

PROP §82.110. VOTING & PROXIES

(a) If only one of the multiple owners of a unit is present at a meeting of the association, that person may cast the vote or votes allocated to that unit. If more than one of the multiple owners is present, the vote or votes allocated to that unit may be cast only in accordance with the owners' unanimous agreement unless the declaration provides otherwise. Multiple owners are in unanimous agreement if one of the multiple owners casts the votes allocated to a unit and none of the other owners makes prompt protest to the person presiding over the meeting.

(b) Votes allocated to a unit may be cast under a written proxy duly executed by a unit owner. If a unit is owned by more than one person, each owner of the unit may vote or register protest to the casting of votes by the other owners of the unit through a proxy duly executed by the unit owner. A unit owner may not revoke a proxy given under this section except by giving actual notice of revocation to the person presiding over a meeting of the association. A proxy is void if it is not dated or if it purports to be revocable without notice. A proxy terminates one year after its date unless it specifies a shorter or longer time.

(c) Cumulative voting is not allowed.

History of Prop. Code §82.110: Acts 1993, 73rd Leg., ch. 244, §1, eff. Jan. 1, 1994.

PROP §82.111. INSURANCE

(a) Beginning not later than the time of the first conveyance of a unit to a person other than a declarant, the association shall maintain, to the extent reasonably available:

(1) property insurance on the insurable common elements insuring against all risks of direct physical loss commonly insured against, including fire and extended coverage, in a total amount of at least 80 percent of the replacement cost or actual cash value of the insured property as of the effective date and at each renewal date of the policy; and

(2) commercial general liability insurance, including medical payments insurance, in an amount deter-

* See footnote on p. 379.

mined by the board but not less than any amount specified by the declaration covering all occurrences commonly insured against for death, bodily injury, and property damage arising out of or in connection with the use, ownership, or maintenance of the common elements.

(b) If a building contains units having horizontal boundaries described in the declaration, the insurance maintained under Subsection (a)(1), to the extent reasonably available, must include the units, but need not include improvements and betterments installed by unit owners.

(c) If the insurance described by Subsections (a) and (b) is not reasonably available, the association shall cause notice of that fact to be delivered or mailed to all unit owners and lienholders. The declaration may require the association to carry any other insurance, and the association in any event may carry any other insurance the board considers appropriate to protect the condominium, the association, or the unit owners. Insurance policies maintained under Subsection (a) may provide for commercially reasonable deductibles as the board determines appropriate or necessary. This section does not affect the right of a holder of a mortgage on a unit to require a unit owner to acquire insurance in addition to that provided by the association.

(d) Insurance policies carried under Subsection (a) must provide that:

(1) each unit owner is an insured person under the policy with respect to liability arising out of the person's ownership of an undivided interest in the common elements or membership in the association;

(2) the insurer waives its right to subrogation under the policy against a unit owner;

(3) no action or omission of a unit owner, unless within the scope of the unit owner's authority on behalf of the association, will void the policy or be a condition to recovery under the policy; and

(4) if, at the time of a loss under the policy, there is other insurance in the name of a unit owner covering the same property covered by the policy, the association's policy provides primary insurance.

(e) A claim for any loss covered by the policy under Subsection (a)(1) must be submitted by and adjusted with the association. The insurance proceeds for that loss shall be payable to an insurance trustee designated by the association for that purpose, if the designation of an insurance trustee is considered by the board to be necessary or desirable, or otherwise to the association, and not to any unit owner or lienholder.

(f) The insurance trustee or the association shall hold insurance proceeds in trust for unit owners and lienholders as their interests may appear. Subject to Subsection (i), the proceeds paid under a policy must be disbursed first for the repair or restoration of the damaged common elements and units, and unit owners and lienholders are not entitled to receive payment of any portion of the proceeds unless there is a surplus of proceeds after the property has been completely repaired or restored, or the condominium is terminated.

(g) An insurance policy issued to the association does not prevent a unit owner from obtaining insurance for the owner's own benefit.

(h) The insurer issuing the policy may not cancel or refuse to renew it less than 30 days after written notice of the proposed cancellation or nonrenewal has been mailed to the association.

(i) Except as provided by this section, any portion of the condominium for which insurance is required that is damaged or destroyed shall be promptly repaired or replaced by the association unless the condominium is terminated, repair or replacement would be illegal under any state or local health or safety statute or ordinance, or at least 80 percent of the unit owners vote to not rebuild. Each owner of a unit may vote, regardless of whether the owner's unit or limited common element has been damaged or destroyed. A vote may be cast electronically or by written ballot if a meeting is not held for that purpose or in person or by proxy at a meeting called for that purpose. A vote to not rebuild does not increase an insurer's liability to loss payment obligation under a policy, and the vote does not cause a presumption of total loss. Except as provided by this section, the cost of repair or replacement in excess of the insurance proceeds is a common expense, and the board may levy an assessment to pay the expenses in accordance with each owner's common expense liability. If the entire condominium is not repaired or replaced, any insurance proceeds attributable to the damaged common elements shall be used to restore the damaged area to a condition compatible with the remainder of the condominium, the insurance proceeds attributable to units and limited common elements that are not rebuilt shall be distributed to the owners of those units and the owners of the units to which those limited common elements were assigned, or to their

mortgagees, as their interests may appear, and the remainder of the proceeds shall be distributed to all the unit owners in accordance with each owner's undivided interest in the common elements unless otherwise provided in the declaration. If the unit owners vote to not rebuild any unit, that unit's allocated interests shall be automatically reallocated on the vote as if the unit had been condemned, and the association shall prepare, execute, and record an amendment to the declaration reflecting the reallocation. Section 82.068 governs the distribution of insurance proceeds if the condominium is terminated.

(j) If the cost to repair damage to a unit or common element covered by the association's insurance is less than the amount of the applicable insurance deductible, the party who would be responsible for the repair in the absence of insurance shall pay the cost for the repair of the unit or common element.

(k) If the association's insurance provides coverage for the loss and the cost to repair the damage to a unit or common element is more than the amount of the applicable insurance deductible, the dedicatory instruments determine payment for the cost of the association's deductible and costs incurred before insurance proceeds are available. If the dedicatory instruments are silent, the board of directors of the association by resolution shall determine the payment of those costs, or if the board does not approve a resolution, the costs are a common expense. A resolution under this subsection is considered a dedicatory instrument and must be recorded in each location in which the declaration is recorded.

(*l*) If damage to a unit or the common elements is due wholly or partly to an act or omission of any unit owner or a guest or invitee of the unit owner, the association may assess the deductible expense and any other expense in excess of insurance proceeds against the owner and the owner's unit.

(m) The provisions of this section may be varied or waived if all the units in a condominium are restricted to nonresidential use.

History of Prop. Code §82.111: Acts 1993, 73rd Leg., ch. 244, §1, eff. Jan. 1, 1994. Amended by Acts 2013, 83rd Leg., ch. 678, §4, eff. Sept. 1, 2013.

NCCUSL Comment*

1. Subsections (a) and (b) provide that the required insurance must be maintained only to the extent reasonably available. This permits the association to comply with the insurance requirements even if certain coverages are unavailable or unreasonably expensive.

2. Subsection (b) represents a significant departure from the present law in virtually all states by requiring that the association obtain and maintain property insurance on both the common elements and the units within buildings with "stacked" units. *See* Comment 3. While it has been common practice in many parts of the country (either by custom or as mandated by statute) for associations to maintain property insurance on the common elements, it has generally not been the practice for the property insurance policy to cover individual units as well. However, given the great interdependence of the unit owners in the stacked unit condominium situation, mandating property insurance for the entire building is the preferable approach. Moreover, such an approach will greatly simplify claims procedures, particularly where both common elements and portions of a unit have been destroyed. If common elements and units are insured separately, the insurers could be involved in disputes as to the coverage provided by each policy.

The Chapter does not mandate association insurance on units in town house or other arrangements in which there are no stacked units. However, if the developer wishes, the declaration may require association insurance as to units having shared walls or as to all units in the development. Many developments will have some units with horizontal boundaries and other units with no horizontal boundaries. In that case, association insurance as to the units having horizontal boundaries is required, but it is not necessary as to other units.

3. The distinction between what is a common element and what is a unit with respect to the insurance coverage required by this section is complex. The definitions of common elements and a unit in Section 82.003(5) and (23) are not sufficient for this purpose. To determine the distinction between the common elements and units, one must refer first to the declaration's section on unit boundaries. That section will define the unit boundaries. If the declaration fails to do so, the provisions of Section 82.052 apply.

In summary, Section 82.052 provides that, if the declaration is silent, all non-loadbearing and non-structural portions of the walls, floors and ceilings are part of the unit, while all loadbearing and structural portions of the walls, floors and ceilings are common elements. Further, with respect to any structure partially within and partially outside of the boundaries of a unit, any portion thereof serving only that unit is a limited common element (*see* definition in Section 82.003(17)), and any portion thereof serving more than one unit or any portion of the common elements is a part of the common elements. This treats and defines ownership of all portions of the electrical, plumbing and mechanical systems serving the building not entirely within the boundaries of a unit.

All spaces, interior partitions, electrical, plumbing and mechanical systems, and all other items within the boundaries of the unit which are attached to the unit boundaries, whether or not deemed fixtures under state law, are part of the unit.

Put simply, if any item is installed, constructed, repaired or replaced by the declarant or his successor in connection with the original sale of a stacked unit, the item is insured by the association. Clearly, this does not include items of personal property easily movable within the unit or easily removable from the unit (whether or not deemed a fixture under state law), such as a vase, table or other furnishings. If installed by the unit owner, the item should be insured by the unit owner. Those items, installed by the unit owner and not covered by the association policy, are called "improvements and betterments."

4. Although "all risk" coverage is not required as to conversion buildings, but merely fire and extended coverage, this is not intended to imply that such coverage is unnecessary. "All risk" coverage is not required because it may not be appropriate in the case of an unrenovated conversion where cost is a critical factor.

5. The minimum requirement as to the amount of insurance, which is 80% of the actual cash value, should not be viewed as a recommendation; rather, the 80% is a floor. Typically, many condominium documents require insurance in an amount equal to 100% of the replacement cost of the insured property. The Chapter permits greater flexibility, however, inasmuch as different types of construction and varieties of projects may not require such total coverage with its attendant higher premium cost.

6. Subsection (a)(2) covers only the liability of the association, and unit owners as members, but does not cover the unit owner's individual liability for his acts or omissions or liability for occurrences within his unit.

7. Restoration as described in the sixth sentence of subsection (i) would operate as follows: (1) if the condominium consists of campsites, restoration after fire damage might consist of merely resodding the area damaged; (2) if the condominium consists of separate gardentype buildings, restoration after fire damage might consist of demolishing the remaining structure and paving

* See footnote on p. 379.

or landscaping the area; and (3) if the condominium consists of a single high-rise building, restoration may not be required (if the building is substantially destroyed) inasmuch as "a condition compatible with the remainder of the condominium" would be damaged and unrestored.

8. The scheme of this section, as set forth in subsection (i), is that any damage or destruction to any portion of the condominium must be repaired (if repairs can be made consistent with applicable safety and health laws) absent a decision to terminate the condominium or a decision by 80% of the unit owners (including the owners of any damaged units) not to rebuild. Unless a decision is made not to rebuild, any available insurance proceeds must be used to effectuate such repairs. For this reason, subsection (e) provides that any loss covered by the association's property insurance policy shall be adjusted with the association and that the proceeds for any loss shall be payable to the association or to any insurance trustee that may be designated for such purpose. Significantly, such insurance proceeds may not be paid to any mortgagee or other outside party. This provision is necessary to insure that insurance proceeds are available to effectuate any repairs or restoration to the condominium that may be required.

9. In the case of commercial or industrial condominiums, unit owners may prefer to act as self-insurers or make other arrangements with respect to property insurance. Accordingly, subsection (m) provides that the insurance requirements of this section may be varied or waived in the case of a condominium all of the units of which are reserved exclusively for non-residential use. Such waiver or modification is not possible in the case of a mixed-use condominium, some of the units of which are used for residential purposes.

PROP §82.112. ASSESSMENTS FOR COMMON EXPENSES

(a) Until an association makes a common expense assessment, a declarant shall pay all the expenses of the condominium as the expenses accrue. After an initial assessment by an association, assessments must be made at least annually and must be based on a budget adopted at least annually by the association. The association's reserves and the unit owners' working capital contributions may not be used to pay operational expenses until the declarant control terminates.

(b) From the date of the initial assessment until declarant control terminates, or three years from a declarant's first conveyance of a unit, whichever is earlier, the declarant shall periodically pay to the association:

(1) an amount equal to all operational expenses of the association, less the operational expense portion of the assessments paid by unit owners other than declarant; or

(2) the common expense liability allocated to each unit owned by the declarant.

(c) Common expenses shall be assessed against all units conveyed, rented, or used as models or offices by the declarant and against all units owned by a declarant after termination of a declarant's control or three years from a declarant's first conveyance of a unit, whichever is earlier, in accordance with the common expense liability allocated to each unit. A past due assessment or installment of an assessment may bear interest at a lawful rate established by the association.

(d) Except as provided by the declaration and Section 82.107, a common expense for the maintenance, repair, or replacement of a limited common element shall be assessed against all the units as if it were for a general common element.

(e) If common expense liabilities are reallocated, common expense assessments and an assessment installment not yet due shall be recomputed in accordance with the reallocated common expense liabilities.

(f) A declaration may allow the accumulation of reserve funds for an unspecified period to provide for any anticipated expense of the condominium.

(g) This section does not prevent a declarant from collecting from a purchaser at closing the prorated amount of any expenses, such as insurance or taxes, that the declarant has prepaid to the association or directly to others on behalf of the unit that is being purchased.

History of Prop. Code §82.112: Acts 1993, 73rd Leg., ch. 244, §1, eff. Jan. 1, 1994.

NCCUSL Comment*

1. This section contemplates that a declarant might find it advantageous, particularly in the early stages of condominium development, to pay all of the expenses of the condominium himself rather than assessing each unit individually. Such a situation might arise, for example, where a declarant owns most of the units in the condominium and wishes to avoid building the costs of each unit separately and crediting payment to each unit. It might also arise in the case of a declarant who, although willing to assume all expenses of the condominium, is unwilling to make payments for replacement reserves or for other expenses which he expects will ultimately be part of the association's budget. Subsection (a) grants the declarant such flexibility while at the same time providing that once an assessment is made against any unit, all units, including those owned by the declarant, must be assessed for their full portion of the common expense liability.

2. Under subsection (c), the declaration may provide for assessment on a basis other than the allocation made in Section 82.057 as to limited common elements, other expenses benefiting less than all units, insurance costs, and utility costs.

3. If additional units are added to a condominium after a judgment has been entered against the association, the new units are not assessed any part of the judgment debt. Since unit owners will know the assessment, and since such unpaid judgment assessments would affect the price paid by purchasers of units, it would be complicated and unnecessary to fairness to reallocate judgment assessments when new units are added.

4. Subsection (e) refers to those instances in which various provisions of this Chapter require that common expense liabilities be reallocated among the units of a condominium by amendment to the declaration. These provisions include Section 82.007 (Condemnation), Section 82.056(d) (Leasehold Condominiums), Section 82.060 (Exercise of Development Rights) and Section 82.063(b) (Subdivision of Units).

PROP §82.113. ASSOCIATION'S LIEN FOR ASSESSMENTS

(a) An assessment levied by the association against a unit or unit owner is a personal obligation of the unit owner and is secured by a continuing lien on

* See footnote on p. 379.

the unit and on rents and insurance proceeds received by the unit owner and relating to the owner's unit. In this section, "assessments" means regular and special assessments, dues, fees, charges, interest, late fees, fines, collection costs, attorney's fees, and any other amount due to the association by the unit owner or levied against the unit by the association, all of which are enforceable as assessments under this section unless the declaration provides otherwise.

(b) The association's lien for assessments has priority over any other lien except:

(1) a lien for real property taxes and other governmental assessments or charges against the unit unless otherwise provided by Section 32.05, Tax Code;

(2) a lien or encumbrance recorded before the declaration is recorded;

(3) a first vendor's lien or first deed of trust lien recorded before the date on which the assessment sought to be enforced becomes delinquent under the declaration, bylaws, or rules; and

(4) unless the declaration provides otherwise, a lien for construction of improvements to the unit or an assignment of the right to insurance proceeds on the unit if the lien or assignment is recorded or duly perfected before the date on which the assessment sought to be enforced becomes delinquent under the declaration, bylaws, or rules.

(c) The association's lien for assessments is created by recordation of the declaration, which constitutes record notice and perfection of the lien. Unless the declaration provides otherwise, no other recordation of a lien or notice of lien is required.

(d) By acquiring a unit, a unit owner grants to the association a power of sale in connection with the association's lien. By written resolution, a board may appoint, from time to time, an officer, agent, trustee, or attorney of the association to exercise the power of sale on behalf of the association. Except as provided by the declaration, an association shall exercise its power of sale pursuant to Section 51.002.

(e) The association has the right to foreclose its lien judicially or by nonjudicial foreclosure pursuant to the power of sale created by this chapter or the declaration, except that the association may not foreclose a lien for assessments consisting solely of fines. Costs of foreclosure may be added to the amount owed by the unit owner to the association. A unit owner may not petition a court to set aside a sale solely because the purchase price at the foreclosure sale was insufficient to fully satisfy the owner's debt.

(f) The association may bid for and purchase the unit at foreclosure sale as a common expense. The association may own, lease, encumber, exchange, sell, or convey a unit.

(g) The owner of a unit purchased at a foreclosure sale of the association's lien for assessments may redeem the unit not later than the 90th day after the date of the foreclosure sale. If the association is the purchaser, the owner must pay to the association to redeem the unit all amounts due the association at the time of the foreclosure sale, interest from the date of foreclosure sale to the date of redemption at the rate provided by the declaration for delinquent assessments, reasonable attorney's fees and costs incurred by the association in foreclosing the lien, any assessment levied against the unit by the association after the foreclosure sale, and any reasonable cost incurred by the association as owner of the unit, including costs of maintenance and leasing. If a party other than the association is the purchaser, the redeeming owner must pay to the purchaser of the unit at the foreclosure sale an amount equal to the amount bid at the sale, interest on the bid amount computed from the date of the foreclosure sale to the date of redemption at the rate of six percent, any assessment paid by the purchaser after the date of foreclosure, and any reasonable costs incurred by the purchaser as the owner of the unit, including costs of maintenance and leasing. The redeeming owner must also pay to the association all assessments that are due as of the date of the redemption and reasonable attorney's fees and costs incurred by the association in foreclosing the lien. On redemption, the purchaser of the unit at the foreclosure sale shall execute a deed with no warranty to the redeeming unit owner. The exercise of the right of redemption is not effective against a subsequent purchaser or lender for value without notice of the redemption after the redemption period expires unless the redeeming unit owner records the deed from the purchaser of the unit at the foreclosure sale or an affidavit stating that the owner has exercised the right of redemption. A unit that has been redeemed remains subject to all liens and encumbrances on the unit before foreclosure. All rents and other income collected from the unit by the purchaser of the unit at the foreclosure sale from the date of foreclosure sale to the date of redemption belong to the pur-

chaser of the unit at the foreclosure sale, but the rents and income shall be credited against the redemption amount. The purchaser of a unit at a sale foreclosing an association's assessment lien may not transfer ownership of the unit during the redemption period to a person other than a redeeming owner.

(h) If a unit owner defaults in the owner's monetary obligations to the association, the association may notify other lien holders of the default and the association's intent to foreclose its lien. The association shall notify any holder of a recorded lien or duly perfected mechanic's lien against a unit who has given the association a written request for notification of the unit owner's monetary default or the association's intent to foreclose its lien.

(i) This section does not prohibit the association from taking a deed in lieu of foreclosure or from filing suit to recover a money judgment for sums that may be secured by the lien.

(j) At any time before a nonjudicial foreclosure sale, a unit owner may avoid foreclosure by paying all amounts due the association.

(k) If, on January 1, 1994, a unit is the homestead of the unit owner and is subject to a declaration that does not contain a valid assessment lien against the unit, the lien provided by this section does not attach against the unit until the unit ceases to be the homestead of the person owning it on January 1, 1994.

(*l*) Foreclosure of a tax lien attaching against a unit under Chapter 32, Tax Code, does not discharge the association's lien for assessments under this section or under a declaration for amounts becoming due to the association after the date of foreclosure of the tax lien.

(m) If a unit owner is delinquent in payment of assessments to an association, at the request of the association a holder of a recorded lien against the unit may provide the association with information about the unit owner's debt secured by the holder's lien against the unit and other relevant information. At the request of a lien holder, the association may furnish the lien holder with information about the condominium and the unit owner's obligations to the association.

History of Prop. Code §82.113: Acts 1993, 73rd Leg., ch. 244, §1, eff. Jan. 1, 1994. Amended by Acts 2013, 83rd Leg., ch. 678, §5, eff. Sept. 1, 2013.

See also Prop. Code §81.208; Tax Code §32.05.

NCCUSL Comment*

1. To ensure prompt and efficient enforcement of the association's lien for unpaid assessments, such liens should enjoy statutory priority over most other liens. Accordingly, subsection (b) provides that the association's lien takes priority over all other liens and encumbrances except those recorded prior to the recordation of the declaration, those imposed for real estate taxes or other governmental assessments or charges against the unit, and first mortgages recorded before the date the assessment became delinquent. However, as to prior first mortgages, the association's lien does have priority for 6 months' assessments based on the periodic budget. A significant departure from existing practice, the 6 months' priority for the assessment lien strikes an equitable balance between the need to enforce collection of unpaid assessments and the obvious necessity for protecting the priority of the security interests of mortgage lenders. As a practical matter, mortgage lenders will most likely pay the 6 months' assessments demanded by the association rather than having the association foreclose on the unit. If the mortgage lender wishes, an escrow for assessments can be required.

...

2. In view of the association's powers to enforce its lien for unpaid assessments, subsection (i) provides unit owners with a method to determine the amount presently due and owing. A unit owner may obtain a statement of any unpaid assessment, including fines and other charges enforceable as assessments under subsection (a), currently levied against his unit. The statement is binding on the association, the executive board, and every unit owner in any subsequent action to collect such unpaid assessments.

3. Units may be part of a condominium and of a larger real estate regime (*see* the Uniform Planned Community Act, promulgated by the National Conference of Commissioners on Uniform State Laws in 1980, which would govern most associations with assessment powers). For example, a large real estate development may consist of a larger planned community which contains detached single family dwellings and town houses which are not part of any condominium and a highrise building which is organized as a condominium within the planned community. In that case, the planned community association might assess the condominium units for the general maintenance expenses of the planned community and the condominium association would assess for the direct maintenance expenses of the building itself.

ANNOTATIONS

Riner v. Neumann, 353 S.W.3d 312, 317 (Tex. App.—Dallas 2011, no pet.). Lender's "lien was recorded on February 20, 2004. The question presented is whether [landowner's] assessment lien attached before or after that date. [¶] The evidence shows that ... the prior owner of the unit[] was current in paying his assessments both at the time he borrowed the money from [lender] and at the time [lender] recorded its lien instrument. [Prior unit owner] also established by affidavit that he was current on all of his obligations to [landowners] as late as April 14, 2005. Other evidence shows that [prior unit owner] started to fall behind on his assessments in May 2005. Thus, under ... the declaration, [landowner's] assessment lien attached no earlier than May 2005. By comparison, [lender's] lien was a 'prior recorded' lien. [¶] [D] argues that [landowner's] assessment lien was first in time under [Prop. Code] §82.113(c).... [H]e contends the assessment lien attached on December 20, 1983—when the condominium declaration was recorded, and long before [lender] recorded its lien instrument. But even assuming [D's] interpretation of §82.113(c) is correct, applying that interpretation in this case would invalidate the declaration's contrary provision that assess-

* See footnote on p. 379.

ment liens attach only when assessments become delinquent. Under [Prop. Code] §82.002(c), we do not apply §82.113 to invalidate any existing provisions of the declaration. Accordingly, we conclude that [lender's] lien was a 'prior recorded' lien as compared to [landowner's] assessment lien."

Bundren v. Holly Oaks Townhomes Ass'n, 347 S.W.3d 421, 440-41 (Tex.App.—Dallas 2011, pet. denied). Homeowners' association (HOA) argues that, "under [Prop. Code] §82.113 ..., they were entitled to recover as an assessment all attorney's fees incurred in collecting unpaid [HOA] dues from [property investors]. However, [HOA's] declaration defines an assessment to include 'costs incurred in their collection, including reasonable attorney's fees.' Further, [Prop. Code] §82.161 ... specifically allows for the recovery of 'reasonable' fees by the prevailing party in a suit to enforce a violation of the declaration. We conclude, that under the facts of this case, [HOA] could recover only reasonable attorney's fees incurred in recovering unpaid HOA dues from [property investors]."

Holly Park Condo. Homeowners' Ass'n v. Lowery, 310 S.W.3d 144, 147-48 (Tex.App.—Dallas 2010, pet. denied). "[P] argues that [Prop. Code §82.113](e)'s grant of the right to foreclose judicially or nonjudicially is limited by the language immediately preceding it [in §82.113(d)]: 'Except as provided by the declaration, an association shall exercise its power of sale pursuant to [Prop. Code] §51.002.' According to [P], this sentence means the subsection (e) authority to foreclose judicially or nonjudicially operates '[e]xcept as provided by the declaration.' We cannot agree. Subsection (d) deals with the power of sale, not with the foreclosure process that precedes sale of the property. The plain language of the quoted sentence—as well as its placement in subsection (d)—indicates the sentence speaks only to the issue of sale, not to the method of foreclosure. [¶] Nor does the reference to §51.002, governing sale of property pursuant to a contract lien (i.e., a nonjudicial foreclosure), limit the applicability of subsection (d). The sentence concerns the manner in which the newly granted power of sale is to be exercised. ... Section 51.002 safeguards the integrity of the sale of property. Subsection (e)'s final sentence, likewise, provides safeguards for the sale of property.... Although the provision means an owner cannot be faced with a sale of her condominium at an undisclosed location at an unknown time, it does not limit an association's right to choose its method of foreclosure. [¶] However, the application of §82.113(e) is not completely unlimited. [S]ection 82.113 can be applied only to the extent that it does not invalidate existing provisions of [P's] declaration or bylaws. *At 149:* [P's] declaration allows only judicial foreclosure of assessment liens. Thus, §82.113(d)'s provision allowing nonjudicial foreclosure does not apply in her case."

PROP §82.114. ASSOCIATION RECORDS

(a) The association shall keep:

(1) detailed financial records that comply with generally accepted accounting principles and that are sufficiently detailed to enable the association to prepare a resale certificate under Section 82.157;

(2) the plans and specifications used to construct the condominium except for buildings originally constructed before January 1, 1994;

(3) the condominium information statement prepared under Section 82.152 and any amendments;

(4) the name and mailing address of each unit owner;

(5) voting records, proxies, and correspondence relating to amendments to the declaration; and

(6) minutes of meetings of the association and board.

(b) All financial and other records of the association shall be reasonably available at its registered office or its principal office in this state for examination by a unit owner and the owner's agents. An attorney's files and records relating to the association are not records of the association and are not subject to inspection by unit owners or production in a legal proceeding.

(c) The association shall, as a common expense, annually obtain an independent audit of the records. Copies of the audit must be made available to the unit owners. An audit required by this subsection shall be performed by a certified public accountant if required by the bylaws or a vote of the board of directors or a majority vote of the members of the association voting at a meeting of the association.

(d) A declarant shall furnish copies to the association of the information required by Subsection (a) on the date the first unit is sold.

(e) Not later than the 30th day after the date of acquiring an interest in a unit, the unit owner shall provide the association with:

(1) the unit owner's mailing address, telephone number, and driver's license number, if any;

(2) the name and address of the holder of any lien against the unit, and any loan number;

(3) the name and telephone number of any person occupying the unit other than the unit owner; and

(4) the name, address, and telephone number of any person managing the unit as agent of the unit owner.

(f) A unit owner shall notify the association not later than the 30th day after the date the owner has notice of a change in any information required by Subsection (e), and shall provide the information on request by the association from time to time.

History of Prop. Code §82.114: Acts 1993, 73rd Leg., ch. 244, §1, eff. Jan. 1, 1994.

See also Prop. Code §81.209.

PROP §82.115. ASSOCIATION AS TRUSTEE

A third person dealing with an association in the association's capacity as a trustee may assume without inquiry the existence of trust powers and their proper exercise by the association. A third person who lacks actual knowledge that an association is exceeding or improperly exercising its powers is fully protected in dealing with the association as if the association possessed and properly exercised the powers it purports to exercise. A third person is not bound to ensure the proper application of trust assets paid or delivered to an association in its capacity as trustee.

History of Prop. Code §82.115: Acts 1993, 73rd Leg., ch. 244, §1, eff. Jan. 1, 1994.

NCCUSL Comment*

Based on Section 7 of the Uniform Trustees' Powers Act, this section is intended to protect an innocent third party in its dealings with the association only when the association is acting as a trustee for the unit owners, either under Section 82.111 for insurance proceeds, or Section 82.068 following termination.

PROP §82.116. MANAGEMENT CERTIFICATE

(a) An association shall record in each county in which any portion of the condominium is located a certificate, signed and acknowledged by an officer of the association, stating:

(1) the name of the condominium;

(2) the name of the association;

(3) the location of the condominium;

(4) the recording data for the declaration;

(5) the mailing address of the association, or the name and mailing address of the person or entity managing the association; and

(6) other information the association considers appropriate.

(a-1) The county clerk of each county in which a management certificate is filed as required by this section shall record the management certificate in the real property records of the county and index the document as a "Condominium Association Management Certificate."

(a-2) Expired.

(b) The association shall record a management certificate not later than the 30th day after the date the association has notice of a change in any information in a recorded certificate required by Subdivisions (a)(1)-(5).

(c) The association and its officers, directors, employees, and agents are not subject to liability to any person for delay or failure to record a management certificate, unless the delay or failure is wilful or caused by gross negligence.

History of Prop. Code §82.116: Acts 1993, 73rd Leg., ch. 244, §1, eff. Jan. 1, 1994. Amended by Acts 2013, 83rd Leg., ch. 678, §6, eff. Sept. 1, 2013.

See also *Real Estate Forms*, FORMS 11:1, 11:2.

PROP §82.117. OBLIGATIONS OF UNIT OWNERS

Without limiting the obligations of the unit owners and except as provided by the declaration, bylaws, rules of the association, or this chapter, the unit owner:

(1) shall pay assessments, interest, and other charges properly levied by the association against the owner or the owner's unit, and shall pay regular periodic assessments without demand by the association;

(2) shall comply with the declaration, bylaws, and rules of the association, including any amendments;

(3) shall pay for damage to the condominium caused by the negligence or wilful misconduct of the owner, an occupant of the owner's unit, or the owner or occupant's family, guests, employees, contractors, agents, or invitees; and

(4) is liable to the association for violations of the declaration, bylaws, or rules of the association, including any amendments, by the owner, an occupant of the owner's unit, or the owner or occupant's family, guests, employees, agents, or invitees, and for costs incurred by the association to obtain compliance, including attorney's fees whether or not suit is filed.

* See footnote on p. 379.

History of Prop. Code §82.117: Acts 1993, 73rd Leg., ch. 244, §1, eff. Jan. 1, 1994.

ANNOTATIONS

Daly v. River Oaks Place Council of Co-owners, 59 S.W.3d 416, 418 (Tex.App.—Houston [1st Dist.] 2001, no pet.). "Owners of condominium units accept the terms, conditions, and restrictions in the condominium's declaration by accepting deeds to individual units."

PROP §82.118. SERVICE OF PROCESS ON UNIT OWNERS IN CERTAIN MUNICIPALITIES; CHANGE OF ADDRESS REQUIRED

(a) A unit owner of a condominium located wholly or partly in a municipality with a population of more than 1.9 million may be served with process by the municipality or the municipality's agent for a judicial or administrative proceeding initiated by the municipality and directly related to the unit owner's property interest in the condominium by serving the unit owner at the unit owner's last known address, according to the records of the appraisal district in which the condominium is located, by any means permitted by Rule 21a, Texas Rules of Civil Procedure.

(b) Notwithstanding Subsection (a), a unit owner may not offer proof in the judicial or administrative proceeding, or in a subsequent related proceeding, that otherwise proper service by mail of the notice was not received not later than three days after the date the notice was deposited in a post office or official depository under the care and custody of the United States Postal Service.

(c) Not later than the 90th day after the date a unit owner changes the unit owner's mailing address, the owner must provide written notice of the owner's new address to the appraisal district in which the condominium is located.

History of Prop. Code §82.118: Acts 2009, 81st Leg., ch. 1323, §2, eff. Sept. 1, 2009. Amended by Acts 2011, 82nd Leg., ch. 693, §§2, 3, eff. Sept. 1, 2011.

PROP §82.119. PROCEDURES FOR FILING SUIT OR INITIATING ARBITRATION PROCEEDINGS FOR DEFECT OR DESIGN CLAIMS FOR CERTAIN ASSOCIATIONS

(a) This section does not apply to an association with less than eight units.

(b) In addition to any preconditions to filing suit or initiating an arbitration proceeding included in the declaration, an association, before filing suit or initiating an arbitration proceeding to resolve a claim pertaining to the construction or design of a unit or the common elements, must:

(1) obtain an inspection and a written independent third-party report from a licensed professional engineer that:

(A) identifies the specific units or common elements subject to the claim;

(B) describes the present physical condition of the units or common elements subject to the claim; and

(C) describes any modifications, maintenance, or repairs to the units or common elements performed by the unit owners or the association; and

(2) obtain approval from unit owners holding more than 50 percent of the total votes allocated under the declaration, voting in person or by proxy as provided by Section 82.110, at a regular, annual, or special meeting called in accordance with the declaration or bylaws, as applicable.

(c) The association must provide written notice of the inspection to be conducted by the engineer to each party subject to a claim not later than the 10th day before the date the inspection occurs. The notice must:

(1) identify the party engaged to prepare the report required by Subsection (b)(1);

(2) identify the specific units or common elements to be inspected; and

(3) include the date and time the inspection will occur.

(d) Each party subject to a claim may attend the inspection conducted by the engineer, either personally or through an agent.

(e) Before providing the notice of the meeting under Subsection (f), an association must:

(1) on completion of the independent third-party report, provide the report to each unit owner and each party subject to a claim; and

(2) allow each party subject to a claim at least 90 days after the date of completion of the report to inspect and correct any condition identified in the report.

(f) Not later than the 30th day before the date the meeting described by Subsection (b)(2) is held, the association must provide each unit owner with written notice of the date, time, and location of the meeting. The notice must also include:

(1) a description of the nature of the claim, the relief sought, the anticipated duration of prosecuting the claim, and the likelihood of success;

(2) a copy of the report required by Subsection (b)(1);

(3) a copy of the contract or proposed contract between the association and the attorney selected by the board to assert or provide assistance with the claim;

(4) a description of the attorney's fees, consultant fees, expert witness fees, and court costs, whether incurred by the association directly or for which the association may be liable as a result of prosecuting the claim;

(5) a summary of the steps previously taken by the association to resolve the claim;

(6) a statement that initiating a lawsuit or arbitration proceeding to resolve a claim may affect the market value, marketability, or refinancing of a unit while the claim is prosecuted; and

(7) a description of the manner in which the association proposes to fund the cost of prosecuting the claim.

(g) The notice required by Subsection (f) must be prepared and signed by a person who is not:

(1) the attorney who represents or will represent the association in the claim;

(2) a member of the law firm of the attorney who represents or will represent the association in the claim; or

(3) employed by or otherwise affiliated with the law firm of the attorney who represents or will represent the association in the claim.

(h) The period of limitations for filing a suit or initiating an arbitration proceeding for a claim described by Subsection (b) is tolled until the first anniversary of the date the procedures are initiated by the association under that subsection if the procedures are initiated during the final year of the applicable period of limitation.

History of Prop. Code §82.119: Acts 2015, 84th Leg., ch. 730, §1, eff. Sept. 1, 2015.

PROP §82.120. BINDING ARBITRATION FOR CERTAIN CLAIMS

(a) A declaration may provide that a claim pertaining to the construction or design of a unit or the common elements must be resolved by binding arbitration and may provide for a process by which the claim is resolved.

(b) An amendment to the declaration that modifies or removes the arbitration requirement or the process associated with resolution of a claim may not apply retroactively to a claim regarding the construction or design of units or common elements based on an alleged act or omission that occurred before the date of the amendment.

History of Prop. Code §82.120: Acts 2015, 84th Leg., ch. 730, §1, eff. Sept. 1, 2015.

Sections 82.121-82.150 reserved for expansion

SUBCHAPTER D. PROTECTION OF PURCHASERS

PROP §82.151. APPLICABILITY

(a) This subchapter applies to each unit subject to this chapter, except as provided by Subsection (b) or as modified or waived by the agreement of a purchaser of a unit in a condominium in which all units are restricted to nonresidential use.

(b) A condominium information statement or resale certificate need not be prepared or delivered in the case of:

(1) a gratuitous disposition of a unit;

(2) a disposition pursuant to court order;

(3) a disposition by a government or governmental agency;

(4) a disposition by foreclosure or deed in lieu of foreclosure; or

(5) a disposition that may be canceled at any time, for any reason, and without penalty.

History of Prop. Code §82.151: Acts 1993, 73rd Leg., ch. 244, §1, eff. Jan. 1, 1994.

NCCUSL Comment*

In the case of commercial and industrial condominiums, the purchaser is often more sophisticated than the purchaser of residential units and thus better able to bargain for the protections he believes necessary. While this may not always be true, no objective test can be developed which easily distinguishes those commercial purchasers who are able to protect themselves from those who, in the ordinary course of business, have not developed such sophistication. At the same time, the cost of protection imposed by Subchapter D may be substantial. Accordingly, subsection (a) permits waiver or modification of Subchapter D protection in condominiums where all units are restricted to nonresidential use, *e.g.*, in the case of most commercial and industrial condominiums. However, except for certain exemptions from condominium information statement and resale certificate requirements (*see* subsection (b)), no express waiver of the protections of this Subchapter with respect to the purchasers of residential units is permitted by this subsection. Accordingly, by operation of Section 82.004, the rights provided by this Subchapter may not be waived in the case of residential purchasers. Moreover, because of the interrelated rights of residential and commercial owners in mixed-use condominiums, waiver or modification of rights conferred by this Subchapter is restricted to purchasers in wholly non-residential condominiums.

* See footnote on p. 379.

PROP §82.152. LIABILITY FOR CONDOMINIUM INFORMATION STATEMENT

(a) Except as provided by Subsection (b), a declarant shall prepare a condominium information statement before offering to the public any interest in a unit.

(b) A declarant may transfer responsibility for preparation of all or a part of the condominium information statement to a successor declarant or to a person in the business of selling real property who intends to offer units in the condominium for the person's own account. On such transfer, the transferor shall provide the transferee with any information necessary to enable the transferee to prepare a condominium information statement.

(c) A declarant or other person in the business of selling real property who offers a unit for the person's own account to a purchaser shall provide a purchaser of a unit with a copy of the condominium information statement, as amended, before conveyance of the unit or the date of a contract of sale, whichever is earlier.

(d) The person preparing all or part of the condominium information statement is liable for any false or misleading statement or for any omission of material fact in the portion of the condominium information statement that the person prepared. If a declarant did not prepare any part of a condominium information statement that the declarant delivers, the declarant is not liable for any false or misleading statement or any omission of material fact unless the declarant actually knew or should have known of the statement or omission.

History of Prop. Code §82.152: Acts 1993, 73rd Leg., ch. 244, §1, eff. Jan. 1, 1994.

NCCUSL Comment*

This section permits declarants to transfer responsibility for preparation of a condominium information statement to successor declarants or dealers, provided the declarant furnishes the information needed by the successor or dealer to complete the statement. The person who prepares the condominium information statement is liable for his own misrepresentations and material omissions. A person who delivers a condominium information statement prepared by others is responsible for any such deficiencies only to the extent he knows or reasonably should have known of them.

PROP §82.153. CONDOMINIUM INFORMATION STATEMENTS IN GENERAL

(a) A condominium information statement must contain or accurately disclose:

(1) the name and principal address of the declarant and of the condominium;

(2) a general description of the condominium that includes the types of units and the maximum number of units;

(3) the minimum and maximum number of additional units, if any, that may be included in the condominium;

(4) a brief narrative description of any development rights reserved by a declarant and of any conditions relating to or limitations upon the exercise of development rights;

(5) copies of the declaration, articles of incorporation of the association, the bylaws, any rules of the association, and amendments to any of them, and copies of leases and contracts, other than loan documents, that are required by the declarant to be signed by purchasers at closing;

(6) a projected or pro forma budget for the association that complies with Subsection (b) for the first fiscal year of the association following the date of the first conveyance to a purchaser, identification of the person who prepared the budget, and a statement of the budget's assumptions concerning occupancy and inflation factors;

(7) a general description of each lien, lease, or encumbrance on or affecting the title to the condominium after conveyance by the declarant;

(8) a copy of each written warranty provided by the declarant;

(9) a description of any unsatisfied judgments against the association and any pending suits to which the association is a party or which are material to the land title and construction of the condominium of which a declarant has actual knowledge;

(10) a general description of the insurance coverage provided for the benefit of unit owners;

(11) current or expected fees or charges to be paid by unit owners for the use of the common elements and other facilities related to the condominium; and

(12) for a condominium located wholly or partly in a municipality with a population of more than 1.9 million a statement that a unit owner:

(A) as an alternative to personal service, may be served with process by the municipality or the municipality's agent for a judicial or administrative proceeding initiated by the municipality and directly related to the unit owner's property interest in the condominium by serving the unit owner at the unit owner's last

* See footnote on p. 379.

known address, according to the records of the appraisal district in which the condominium is located, by any means permitted by Rule 21a, Texas Rules of Civil Procedure;

(B) shall notify the appraisal district in writing of a change in the unit owner's mailing address not later than the 90th day after the date the unit owner changes the address; and

(C) may not offer proof in the judicial or administrative proceeding, or in a subsequent related proceeding, that otherwise proper service by mail of the notice was not received not later than three days after the date the notice was deposited in a post office or official depository under the care and custody of the United States Postal Service.

(b) A budget under Subsection (a)(6) must be prepared in accordance with generally accepted accounting principles and a consideration of the physical condition of the condominium and be based on assumptions that, to the best of the declarant's knowledge and belief, are reasonable. The budget must include:

(1) a statement of the amount included, or a statement that no amount is included, in the budget as a reserve; and

(2) the projected monthly common expense assessment for each type of unit.

(c) A declarant shall promptly amend the condominium information statement to reflect a material and substantial change in its contents. If the change may adversely affect a prospective purchaser who has received a condominium information statement, the declarant shall furnish a copy of the amendment to the prospective purchaser before closing.

History of Prop. Code §82.153: Acts 1993, 73rd Leg., ch. 244, §1, eff. Jan. 1, 1994. Amended by Acts 2009, 81st Leg., ch. 1323, §3, eff. Sept. 1, 2009; Acts 2011, 82nd Leg., ch. 693, §4, eff. Sept. 1, 2011.

NCCUSL Comment*

1. The best "consumer protection" that the law can provide to any purchaser is to insure that he has an opportunity to acquire an understanding of the nature of the products which he is purchasing. Such a result is difficult to achieve, however, in the case of the condominium purchaser because of the complex nature of the bundle of rights and obligations which each unit owner obtains. For this reason, the Chapter, adopting the approach of many so-called "second generation" condominium statutes, sets forth a lengthy list of information which must be provided to each purchaser before he contracts for a unit. This list includes a number of important matters not typically required in condominium information statements under existing law. The requirement for providing the condominium information statement appears in Section 82.152(c), and Section 82.156 provides purchasers with cancellation rights and imposes civil penalties upon declarants not complying with the condominium information statement requirements of the Chapter.

2. Paragraph (a)(2) requires a general description of the condominium and, to the extent possible, the declarant's schedule for commencement and completion of construction for all building amenities that will comprise portions of the condominium. Under Section 82.059, the declarant is obligated to label all improvements which may be made in the condominium as either "MUST BE BUILT" or "NEED NOT BE BUILT." Under Section 82.163, the declarant is obligated to complete all improvements labeled "MUST BE BUILT." The estimated schedule of commencement and completion of construction dates provides a standard for judging whether a declarant has complied with the requirements of Section 82.163.

3. Paragraph (a)(5) requires the condominium information statement to include copies of the declaration, bylaws, and any rules and regulations of the condominium, as well as copies of any contracts or leases to be executed by the purchaser.

4. The disclosure requirement of paragraph (a)(11) is intended to eliminate the common deceptive sales practice known as "lowballing," a practice by which a declarant intentionally underestimates the budget for the association by providing many of the services himself during the initial sales period. In such a circumstance, the declarant commonly intends that, after a certain time, these services (which might include lawn maintenance, painting, security, bookkeeping, or other services) will become expenses of the association, thereby substantially increasing the periodic common expense assessments which association members must ultimately bear. By requiring the disclosure of these services (including the projected common expense assessment attributable to each) in paragraph (a)(11), the Chapter seeks to minimize "lowballing." In order to comply fully with the provisions of paragraph (a)(6), the declarant must calculate the budget on the basis of his best estimate of the number of units which will be part of the condominium during that budget year. This requirement as well operates to negate the effects of any attempted "lowballing."

...

5. Paragraph (10) corrects a defect common to many condominium statutes by requiring the declarant to describe the insurance coverage provided for the benefit of unit owners. *See* Section 82.111.

...

PROP §82.154. CONDOMINIUMS WITH CONVERSION BUILDINGS

If a building contains units that may be occupied for residential use, the condominium information statement of a condominium containing any conversion building must additionally contain:

(1) a dated statement by the declarant, based on a report by an independent architect or engineer, describing the present condition of all structural components and mechanical and electrical installations material to the use and enjoyment of the building;

(2) a dated statement by the declarant of the expected useful life of each item reported in Subdivision (1) or a statement that no representations are made in that regard; and

(3) a list of violations of building code or other governmental regulations of which the declarant has received notice and that have not been cured, together with the estimated cost of curing those violations.

History of Prop. Code §82.154: Acts 1993, 73rd Leg., ch. 244, §1, eff. Jan. 1, 1994.

NCCUSL Comment*

1. In the case of a condominium containing one or more conversion buildings, the disclosure of additional information relating to the condition of those buildings is required in the condominium information statement because of

* See footnote on p. 379.

the difficulty inherent in a single purchaser attempting to determine the condition of what is likely to be an older building being renovated for the purpose of condominium sales.

2. Paragraph (1) requires the person who gives the condominium information statement to retain an independent architect or engineer to report on the present condition of all structural components and fixed mechanical and electrical installations in the conversion building.

...

3. Under paragraph (3), the person required to give the condominium information statement is required to provide purchasers with a list of all outstanding notices of uncured violations of building codes or other municipal regulations. The literal wording of this provision does not require disclosure of known violations of such building codes or municipal regulations (at least violations having no effect upon the structural components or fixed mechanical and electrical installations of the condominium) unless actual "notices" of such violations have been received. To the extent that outstanding notices of uncured violations do exist, the cost of curing such violations would become a liability of the unit owners or the association following transfer of the unit to a purchaser. For that reason, the estimated cost of curing any outstanding violations must also be disclosed.

4. For the same reasons set forth in the Comment to Section 82.151(a), this section does not apply to units which are restricted exclusively to nonresidential use.

PROP §82.155. CONDOMINIUM SECURITIES

A declarant satisfies all requirements relating to preparation of a condominium information statement if an interest in the condominium is currently registered with the Securities and Exchange Commission of the United States and if the declarant delivers to the purchaser a copy of the public offering statement filed with the commission.

History of Prop. Code §82.155: Acts 1993, 73rd Leg., ch. 244, §1, eff. Jan. 1, 1994.

NCCUSL Comment*

Some condominiums are regarded as "investment contracts" or other "securities" under federal law because they exhibit certain investment features such as mandatory rental pools. *See* SEC Securities Act Release No. 5347 (January 1973). The purpose of this section is to permit the declarant to file or deliver, in lieu of a condominium information statement specifically prepared to comply with the provisions of this Chapter, the prospectus filed with and distributed pursuant to the regulations of the United States Securities and Exchange Commission. Absent this provision, prospective purchasers of condominiums classified by the SEC as "securities" would have to be given two condominium information statements, one prepared pursuant to this Chapter and the other prepared pursuant to the Securities Act of 1933. Not only would this result increase the declarant's costs (and thus the price) of units, it might also reduce the likelihood of either condominium information statement actually being read by prospective purchasers.

PROP §82.156. PURCHASER'S RIGHT TO CANCEL

(a) If a purchaser of a unit from a unit owner other than a declarant has not received from the seller the declaration, bylaws, and association rules required by Section 82.157 before the purchaser executes a contract of sale or if the contract does not contain an underlined or bold-print provision acknowledging the purchaser's receipt of those documents and recommending that the purchaser read those documents before executing the contract, the purchaser may cancel the contract before the sixth day after the date the purchaser receives those documents. If a purchaser has not received a resale certificate before executing a contract of sale, the purchaser may cancel the contract before the sixth day after the date the purchaser receives the resale certificate or executes a waiver under Section 82.157, whichever occurs first.

(b) If a purchaser from a declarant has not received the condominium information statement before the purchaser executes a contract of sale or if a contract does not contain an underlined or bold-print provision acknowledging the purchaser's receipt of the condominium information statement and recommending that the purchaser read the condominium information statement before executing the contract, the purchaser may cancel the contract before the sixth day after the date the purchaser receives the condominium information statement.

(c) If a purchaser elects to cancel a contract under Subsection (a) or (b), the cancellation must be by hand-delivering written notice of cancellation to the declarant or selling unit owner or by mailing notice of cancellation by certified United States mail, return receipt requested, to the offeror or the offeror's agent for service of process within the five-day cancellation period. Cancellation is without penalty, and all payments made by the purchaser before cancellation must be refunded.

(d) A selling unit owner may not require a purchaser to close until the purchaser is given the declaration, bylaws, and any association rules. A declarant may not require a purchaser to close until a condominium information statement has been furnished to the purchaser.

History of Prop. Code §82.156: Acts 1993, 73rd Leg., ch. 244, §1, eff. Jan. 1, 1994.

NCCUSL Comment*

1. The "cooling off" period provided to a purchaser in this section is similar to provisions in many current state condominium statutes.

2. Subsection (a) requires that each purchaser be provided with the condominium information statement prior to the time that the unit is conveyed. If there is a contract for the sale of the unit, these documents must be provided not later than the date of the contract.

3. This section does not require the delivery of a condominium information statement prior to the execution by the purchaser of an agreement pursuant to which the purchaser reserves the right to buy a unit but is not contractually bound to do so. Because such agreements (frequently referred to as "nonbinding reservation agreements") may be unilaterally cancelled at any time by a prospective purchaser without penalty, they do not constitute "contract[s] of sale" within the meaning of the section.

...

* See footnote on p. 379.

4. Under the scheme set forth in this section, it is at least theoretically possible that there will be a contract for sale of the unit, and that a condominium information statement will be given to the purchaser at closing just prior to conveyance. However, the available evidence suggests that such practice would be rare, and that the provision of a condominium information statement moments prior to conveyance would, in itself, tend to dampen the enthusiasm of the purchaser for immediate closing. In such circumstances, under subsection (a), the purchaser would, as a matter of right, be able to extend the date of closing for six days from the time the condominium information statement was provided. This fact, together with the generally unsatisfactory experience with mandatory "cooling off" periods such as that imposed under the federal Real Estate Settlement Procedures Act, supports the conclusion that it is inappropriate to require a minimum period of delay between delivery of a condominium information statement and conveyance.

5. Under subsection (a), the failure to deliver a condominium information statement before conveyance does not result in a statutory right by the purchaser to cancel the conveyance or to reconvey the unit once conveyance has occurred. Any such cancellation or reconveyance right following an actual conveyance could create serious mechanical and title problems that could not be easily resolved. The failure of the Chapter to provide for such cancellation or reconveyance is not, however, intended to diminish any right which a purchaser may otherwise have under general state law. For example, where it appears that a seller, by deliberately failing to disclose certain material information with respect to a transaction, substantially changed the bargain which he and the purchaser entered into, it is possible under the common law in some states that reconveyance would be an available remedy.

...

PROP §82.157. RESALE OF UNIT

(a) Except as provided by Subsection (c), if a unit owner other than a declarant intends to sell a unit, before executing a contract or conveying the unit, the unit owner must furnish to the purchaser a current copy of the declaration, bylaws, any association rules, and a resale certificate that must have been prepared not earlier than three months before the date it is delivered to the purchaser. The resale certificate must be issued by the association and must contain the current operating budget of the association and statements of:

(1) any right of first refusal or other restraint contained in the declaration that restricts the right to transfer a unit;

(2) the amount of the periodic common expense assessment and the unpaid common expenses or special assessments currently due and payable from the selling unit owner;

(3) other unpaid fees or amounts payable to the association by the selling unit owner;

(4) capital expenditures, if any, approved by the association for the next 12 months;

(5) the amount of reserves, if any, for capital expenditures and of portions of those reserves designated by the association for a specified project;

(6) any unsatisfied judgments against the association;

(7) the nature of any pending suits against the association;

(8) insurance coverage provided for the benefit of unit owners;

(9) whether the board has knowledge that any alterations or improvements to the unit or to the limited common elements assigned to that unit violate the declaration, bylaws, or association rules;

(10) whether the board has received notice from a governmental authority concerning violations of health or building codes with respect to the unit, the limited common elements assigned to that unit, or any other portion of the condominium;

(11) the remaining term of any leasehold estate that affects the condominium and the provisions governing an extension or renewal of the lease;

(12) the name, mailing address, and telephone number of the association's managing agent, if any;

(13) the association's current operating budget and balance sheet; and

(14) all fees payable to the association or an agent of the association that are associated with the transfer of ownership, including a description of each fee, to whom the fee is paid, and the amount of the fee.

(b) Not later than the 10th day after the date of receiving a written request by a unit owner, an association shall furnish to the selling unit owner or the owner's agent a resale certificate signed and dated by an officer or authorized agent of the association containing the information required by Subsection (a). A selling unit owner or the owner's agent is not liable to the purchaser for erroneous information provided by the association in the certificate. If an association does not furnish a resale certificate or any information required in the certificate within the 10-day period, the unit owner may provide the purchaser with a sworn affidavit signed by the unit owner in lieu of the certificate. An affidavit must state that the unit owner requested information from the association concerning its financial condition, as required by this section, and that the association did not timely provide a resale certificate or the information required in the certificate. If a unit owner has furnished an affidavit to a purchaser, the unit owner and the purchaser may agree in writing to waive the requirement to furnish a resale certificate. The association is not liable to a selling unit owner for delay or failure to furnish a resale certificate, and an officer or agent of the association is not liable for a delay or failure to furnish a certificate unless the officer or agent wilfully refuses to furnish the certificate or is

grossly negligent in not furnishing the resale certificate. Failure to provide a resale certificate does not void a deed to a purchaser.

(c) If a properly executed resale certificate incorrectly states the total of delinquent sums owed by the selling unit owner to the association, the purchaser is not liable for payment of additional delinquencies that are unpaid on the date the certificate is prepared and that exceed the total sum stated in the certificate. A unit owner or the owner's agent is not liable to a purchaser for the failure or delay of the association to provide the certificate in a timely manner.

(d) A resale certificate does not affect:

(1) an association's right to recover debts or claims that arise or become due after the date the certificate is prepared; or

(2) an association's lien on a unit securing payment of future assessments.

(e) A purchaser, lender, or title insurer who relies on a resale certificate is not liable for any debt or claim that is not disclosed in the certificate. An association may not deny the validity of any statement in the certificate.

History of Prop. Code §82.157: Acts 1993, 73rd Leg., ch. 244, §1, eff. Jan. 1, 1994. Amended by Acts 2015, 84th Leg., ch. 1183, §1, eff. Sept. 1, 2015.

NCCUSL Comment*

1. In the case of the resale of a unit by a private unit owner who is not a declarant or a person in the business of selling real estate for his own account, a condominium information statement need not be provided. *See* Section 82.152(c). Nevertheless, there are important facts which a purchaser should have in order to make a rational judgment about the advisability of purchasing the particular condominium unit. Accordingly, each unit owner not required to furnish a condominium information statement under Section 82.152(c) and not exempt under Section 82.151(b) is required to furnish to a resale purchaser, before the execution of any contract of sale, a copy of the declaration, bylaws, and rules and regulations of the association and a variety of fiscal, insurance, and other information concerning the condominium and the unit.

2. While the obligation to provide the information required by this section rests upon each unit owner (since the purchaser is in privity only with that unit owner), the association has an obligation to provide the information to the unit owner within 10 days after a request for such information. Under Section 82.102(a)(15), the association is entitled to charge the unit owner a reasonable fee for the preparation of the certificate. Should the association fail to provide the certificate as required, the unit owner would have a right to action against the association pursuant to Section 82.161.

3. Under subsection (e), if a purchaser receives a resale certificate which fails to state the proper amount of the unpaid assessments due from the purchased unit, the purchaser is not liable for any amount greater than that disclosed in the resale certificate. Because a resale purchaser is dependent upon the association for information with respect to the outstanding assessments against the unit which he contemplates buying, it is altogether appropriate that the association should be prohibited from later collecting greater assessments than those disclosed prior to the time of the resale purchase.

* See footnote on p. 379.

PROP §82.158. ESCROW OF DEPOSITS

A deposit made in connection with the purchase or reservation of a unit from a declarant shall be placed in escrow and held in this state in an account designated for that purpose by a real estate broker, an attorney, a title insurance company licensed in this state, an independent bonded escrow company, or an institution whose accounts are insured by a governmental agency or instrumentality until delivered to the declarant at closing, delivered to the declarant because of the purchaser's default under a contract to purchase the unit, or refunded to the purchaser. Escrow deposits may be placed in interest-bearing accounts, and the interest is payable as may be agreed in writing between the declarant and the purchaser.

History of Prop. Code §82.158: Acts 1993, 73rd Leg., ch. 244, §1, eff. Jan. 1, 1994.

NCCUSL Comment*

1. This section applies to the sale by persons required to furnish condominium information statements of residential units and of non-residential units unless waived pursuant to the provisions of Section 82.151. It does not apply, however, to resales of units between private parties. Escrow provisions are not part of the law in several jurisdictions.

2. This section provides a declarant a number of choices as to the appropriate escrow agent. Whether the escrow agent must deposit the funds in an insured institutional depository, or in a particular type of account, depends on state law, or the agreement of the parties. To minimize record keeping, of course, the institutional depository could itself be the escrow agent. The section does not require a separate account for each unit, so that mingling of funds in a single escrow account would be permitted. The account may be held whether in the state where the unit is located, or in the enacting state, in recognition that buyers are often from outside the state where the unit is located.

3. The escrow requirements of this section apply in connection with any deposit made by a purchaser, whether such deposit is made pursuant to a binding contract or pursuant to a nonbinding reservation agreement (with respect to which no condominium information statement is required under Section 82.151(b)(5)).

...

4. Under this section, any interest earned on an escrow deposit may, but need not, be credited to the purchaser at closing, added to any deposit forfeited to the seller, or added to any deposit refunded to the purchaser. In short, disposition of any interest is left to agreement of the parties.

5. The evidence indicates, however, that in many instances the use of the bonding device has forced purchasers to incur substantial costs and delay prior to obtaining refunds to which they are entitled. For this reason, this Chapter does not include bonding as an alternative to the required escrow of deposits.

PROP §82.159. RELEASE OF LIENS

Before conveying real property to an association, a declarant shall have that real property released from all liens the foreclosure of which would deprive unit owners of any right of access to or easement of support of the owners' units, and all other liens on that real property unless the condominium information statement describes certain real property that may be conveyed subject to liens in specified amounts.

History of Prop. Code §82.159: Acts 1993, 73rd Leg., ch. 244, §1, eff. Jan. 1, 1994.

NCCUSL Comment*

The exemption for withdrawable real estate set forth in this section is designed to preserve flexibility for the declarant in terms of financing arrangements. Theoretically, a developer might partially avoid the lien release requirement by placing part of the common element improvements such as a swimming pool or tennis court on withdrawable real estate. By doing so, it could separately mortgage that part of the common elements without being obligated to discharge the mortgage or secure partial releases when individual units are sold. (However, even if there were no withdrawable real estate exemption from the release of lien requirement, developers could still separately mortgage such improvements as pools and tennis courts without having to discharge the mortgage on sale of units. All they would have to do is leave the particular real estate out of the condominium and then convey it directly to the association subject to the mortgage.)

If a mortgage or other lien created by or arising against the developer attaches to withdrawable real estate after the declaration has been recorded, a lapse of the developer's right to withdraw the real estate would also terminate the rights of the lienor, since the lien would attach only to the developer's interest (the right to withdraw). However, an alert lienor would not permit the right to withdraw to lapse without taking steps to see that the right to withdraw is exercised. If the mortgage or other lien attached to the real estate and was perfected before the condominium declaration was recorded, lapse of the right to withdraw would not affect the lienor's rights and it could foreclose on the real estate whether or not the developer had lost the right to withdraw. As a practical matter, whether the mortgage or other lien against withdrawable real estate arises before or after the declaration is recorded, unit owners may find that, if the association does not release liens on withdrawable real estate containing common elements, the lienor will be able to withdraw the land and deprive the unit owners of its use. Therefore, unit purchasers and their counsel should be alert to that possibility.

If units are created in withdrawable real estate, the units, when sold, are subject to the release-of-lien rule of this section and after a unit in a particular withdrawable parcel is sold, that parcel can no longer be withdrawn. In that case, any lien created by or arising against the developer which attached to the real estate and is subordinate to the condominium declaration would automatically expire.

PROP §82.160. CONVERSION BUILDINGS

(a) A declarant of a condominium containing a conversion building shall give each residential tenant or subtenant in possession of a portion of a conversion building notice of the conversion at least 60 days before the date the declarant will require the tenant or subtenant in possession to vacate. The notice must state generally the rights of tenants and subtenants under this section and shall be hand-delivered to the unit or mailed by certified United States mail, return receipt requested, to the tenant or subtenant at the address of the unit or any other mailing address provided by the tenant or subtenant. The declarant may not require a tenant or subtenant to vacate on less than 60 days' notice, except for nonpayment of rent, waste, or conduct that violates the rental agreement or is illegal, and the terms of a tenancy may not be altered during that period. Failure of a declarant to give notice as required by this section is a defense to an action for possession.

(b) If a notice of conversion specifies a date by which a unit or proposed unit must be vacated and otherwise complies with Section 24.005, the notice also constitutes legal notice to vacate on that date for purposes of Section 24.005. A declarant may not terminate a lease in violation of its terms.

(c) Unless expressly authorized by a rental agreement, a declarant may not make substantial alterations to the interior of a leased premises for purposes of a condominium conversion.

History of Prop. Code §82.160: Acts 1993, 73rd Leg., ch. 244, §1, eff. Jan. 1, 1994.

NCCUSL Comment*

1. One of the most controversial issues in the field of condominium development relates to conversion of rental buildings to condominiums. Opponents of conversions point out that the frequent result of conversions, which occur principally in large urban areas, is to displace low- and moderate-income tenants and provide homes for more affluent persons able to afford the higher prices which the converted apartments command. Indeed, studies indicate that the burden of conversion displacement falls most frequently on low- and moderate-income and elderly persons. At the same time, the conversion of a building to condominium ownership can lead to a substantial increase in property value, a result which proponents believe can be an important factor in curtailing the problem of declining urban tax bases. Proponents also point out that the conversion of rental units in inner-city areas to individual ownership frequently results in the stabilization of the buildings concerned, thus providing an important technique for use in neighborhood preservation and revitalization. This section, which seeks to balance these competing interests, is based principally on similar provisions set forth in the condominium statutes of Virginia and the District of Columbia.

...

2. Jurisdictions with rent control statutes should consider whether amendments to this section are necessary to conform to the procedures or substantive requirements set out in the rent control laws or whether modifications to the rent control laws may be required as a result of the enactment of this section.

3. Except for the restrictions on permissible evictions stated in subsection (a), this Chapter does not change the law of summary process of the state. As a result, if a tenant refuses to vacate the premises following the 60-day notice, the usual provisions of the state's summary process statutes would apply, while any defenses available to a tenant would also be available.

PROP §82.161. EFFECT OF VIOLATIONS ON RIGHTS OF ACTION & ATTORNEY'S FEES

(a) If a declarant or any other person subject to this chapter violates this chapter, the declaration, or the bylaws, any person or class of persons adversely affected by the violation has a claim for appropriate relief.

(b) The prevailing party in an action to enforce the declaration, bylaws, or rules is entitled to reasonable attorney's fees and costs of litigation from the nonprevailing party.

History of Prop. Code §82.161: Acts 1993, 73rd Leg., ch. 244, §1, eff. Jan. 1, 1994.

ANNOTATIONS

Wheelbarger v. Landing Council of Co-Owners, 471 S.W.3d 875, 896-97 (Tex.App.—Houston [1st Dist.] 2015, pet. denied). "[P] contends that the trial court should have awarded her attorney's fees because the jury found that she was 'adversely affected' by [D's]

* See footnote on p. 379.

failure to comply with the ... Property Code. [¶] It is well-settled under Texas law that 'to prevail, a claimant must obtain actual and meaningful relief, something that materially alters the parties' legal relationship.' This rule applies in the context of §82.161: to qualify as a 'prevailing party,' [P] must show not only that she was 'adversely affected' but also that she suffered damages or otherwise obtained affirmative relief from the trial court. She obtained no relief from the trial court, however, and therefore she is not a prevailing party within the meaning of §82.161."

Bever Props., L.L.C. v. Jerry Huffman Custom Builder, L.L.C., 355 S.W.3d 878, 897 (Tex.App.—Dallas 2011, no pet.). "[D] was not a 'prevailing party' with regard to its application for an injunction; [D's] application for injunction was denied by the trial court in its ... order and [D] has not appealed that trial court determination. In light of our reversal of the summary judgments in favor of [Ds] on a number of [Ps'] claims, we conclude the issue of [Ds'] attorney's fees must be reversed and remanded to the trial court for reconsideration." *See also* ***River Oaks Place Council of Co-owners v. Daly***, 172 S.W.3d 314, 325-26 (Tex. App.—Corpus Christi 2005, no pet.).

Myer v. Cuevas, 119 S.W.3d 830, 837 (Tex. App.—San Antonio 2003, no pet.). "To have standing to sue for violation of the Uniform Condominium Act, the declaration, or the bylaws, [P] must allege that he was adversely affected. Because [P's] petition failed to allege how he was adversely affected, he did not establish his standing to pursue this claim. We are aware that the act of preventing an owner from viewing the books of the condominium may be considered a harm in and of itself. However, the Act expressly requires one complaining of a violation of the Condominium Act to allege that they were 'adversely affected.' We are unable to read [P's] naked assertion that he was denied access to corporate records as fulfilling the requirement of showing that he was adversely affected."

NCCUSL Comment*

This section provides a general clause of action or claim for relief for failure to comply with the Chapter by either a declarant or any other person subject to the Chapter's provisions. Such persons might include unit owners, persons exercising a declarant's rights of appointment pursuant to Section 82.103(c), or the association itself. A claim for appropriate relief might include damages, injunctive relief, specific performance, rescission or reconveyance, or any other remedy normally available under state law. The section specifically refers to "any person or class of persons" to indicate that any relief available under the state class action statute would be available in circumstances where a failure to comply with this Chapter has occurred. This section specifically permits punitive damages to be awarded in the case of willful failure to comply with the Chapter and also permits attorney's fees to be awarded in the discretion of the court to any party that prevails in an action.

PROP §82.162. LABELING OF PROMOTIONAL MATERIAL

If any improvement contemplated in a condominium is labeled "NEED NOT BE BUILT" on a plat or plan or is to be located within a portion of a condominium with respect to which the declarant has reserved a development right, no promotional material that describes or depicts the improvement may be displayed or delivered to prospective purchasers unless the description or depiction of the improvement is conspicuously labeled or identified as "NEED NOT BE BUILT."

History of Prop. Code §82.162: Acts 1993, 73rd Leg., ch. 244, §1, eff. Jan. 1, 1994.

NCCUSL Comment*

1. Section 82.059(c) requires that the plats and plans for every condominium indicate whether or not any improvement that might be built in the condominium must be built. However, Section 82.153 does not require that copies of the plats and plans be provided to purchasers as part of the condominium information statement. Consequently, this section requiring the labeling of improvements depicted on promotional material is necessary to assure that purchasers are not deceived with respect to which improvements the declarant is obligated to make in a particular condominium project.

2. Since no contemplated improvements on real estate subject to development rights need be shown on plats and plans, additional labeling is required by this section to insure that, if the declarant shows any contemplated improvements in his promotional material which are not shown on the plats and plans, those improvements must also be appropriately labeled.

PROP §82.163. DECLARANT'S OBLIGATION TO COMPLETE & RESTORE

The declarant shall complete all improvements labeled "MUST BE BUILT" on plats or plans. The declarant is subject to liability for the prompt repair and restoration, to a condition compatible with the remainder of the condominium, of any portion of the condominium affected by the exercise of rights reserved pursuant to or created under this chapter.

History of Prop. Code §82.163: Acts 1993, 73rd Leg., ch. 244, §1, eff. Jan. 1, 1994.

NCCUSL Comment*

1. This section requires the declarant to complete any improvement which the plats or plans indicate, pursuant to the requirements of Section 82.059(c), "MUST BE BUILT." This is a fundamental obligation of the declarant and is one with which a successor declarant is obligated to comply under Section 82.104.

2. In the event that a declarant exercises the right to use an easement which is created by Section 82.066, or in the event the declarant maintains model units or signs on the condominium, the declarant is obligated to restore the portions of the condominiums used to a condition compatible with the remainder of the condominium.

PROP §82.164. LOANS AS ELIGIBLE INVESTMENTS

(a) A loan on a condominium unit and the undivided interest in the common elements is an eligible

* See footnote on p. 379.

investment for a bank, savings and loan association, trust company, life insurance company, or other lending institution that is authorized to make real property loans, and for an administrator, guardian, executor, trustee, individual, partnership, corporation, or other fiduciary that is authorized to make real property loans. In determining eligibility, the existence of a prior lien for taxes, assessments, or other similar charges not yet delinquent may not be considered in determining whether a mortgage or deed of trust on the security is a first lien. This section does not change any provision of law that would otherwise be applicable that limits mortgage investments based on a special fraction or percentage of the value of the mortgaged property.

(b) An association's lien for assessments does not make a condominium unit ineligible for loans for which the unit would otherwise qualify.

History of Prop. Code §82.164: Acts 1993, 73rd Leg., ch. 244, §1, eff. Jan. 1, 1994.

Chapters 83-90 blank

TITLE 8. LANDLORD & TENANT

CHAPTER 91. PROVISIONS GENERALLY APPLICABLE TO LANDLORDS & TENANTS

PROP §91.001. NOTICE FOR TERMINATING CERTAIN TENANCIES

(a) A monthly tenancy or a tenancy from month to month may be terminated by the tenant or the landlord giving notice of termination to the other.

(b) If a notice of termination is given under Subsection (a) and if the rent-paying period is at least one month, the tenancy terminates on whichever of the following days is the later:

(1) the day given in the notice for termination; or

(2) one month after the day on which the notice is given.

(c) If a notice of termination is given under Subsection (a) and if the rent-paying period is less than a month, the tenancy terminates on whichever of the following days is the later:

(1) the day given in the notice for termination; or

(2) the day following the expiration of the period beginning on the day on which notice is given and extending for a number of days equal to the number of days in the rent-paying period.

(d) If a tenancy terminates on a day that does not correspond to the beginning or end of a rent-paying period, the tenant is liable for rent only up to the date of termination.

(e) Subsections (a), (b), (c), and (d) do not apply if:

(1) a landlord and a tenant have agreed in an instrument signed by both parties on a different period of notice to terminate the tenancy or that no notice is required; or

(2) there is a breach of contract recognized by law.

History of Prop. Code §91.001: Acts 1983, 68th Leg., ch. 576, §1, eff. Jan. 1, 1984. Amended by Acts 1985, 69th Leg., ch. 200, §3, eff. Aug. 26, 1985. Source: TRCS art. 5236a.

See also *Real Estate Forms*, FORM 2:31.

CHARTS

See timetable, "Eviction," p. 1541.

ANNOTATIONS

Fidelity Mgmt. v. Herod, 600 S.W.2d 380, 382 (Tex. App.—Corpus Christi 1980, no writ). "We hold that the lease was terminated by the letter written by the landlord, followed by the institution of forceable detainer action which proceeded to judgment, which was not appealed, and became final. The landlord's conduct amounted to a termination of the existing lease and the tenant's removal from the lease premises in obedience to the Justice Court's judgment amounts to an acceptance of the termination by the tenant. [¶] The trial court was correct in finding that the tenant did not abandon the premises, but was forced to vacate the same by the landlord."

J.R. Skillern, Inc. v. leVison, 591 S.W.2d 598, 599 (Tex.App.—Eastland 1979, writ ref'd n.r.e.). "Under Texas law, parties have a right to contract for termination of a lease in the event of condemnation. [¶] 'A tenant whose lease provides for its termination upon the taking of the leased premises for a public use, is entitled to no compensation when it is condemned.' [¶] We must determine whether the lease terminated automatically upon the total taking of the leasehold estate. The lease provides in the event of condemnation that the lease 'shall, at the option of the landlord, terminate.' [P] argues that this clause requires the landlord

to give the lessee notice that he intends to exercise his option and terminate the lease. We disagree."

PROP §91.002. RENUMBERED

Renumbered as §92.008 by Acts 1987, 70th Leg., ch. 683, §2, eff. Aug. 31, 1987; Acts 1989, 71st Leg., ch. 689, §1, eff. Sept. 1, 1989.

PROP §91.003. TERMINATION OF LEASE BECAUSE OF PUBLIC INDECENCY CONVICTION

(a) A landlord may terminate a lease executed or renewed after June 15, 1981, if:

(1) the tenant or occupant of the leasehold uses the property for an activity for which the tenant or occupant or for which an agent or employee of the tenant or occupant is convicted under Chapter 43, Penal Code, as amended; and

(2) the convicted person has exhausted or abandoned all avenues of direct appeal from the conviction.

(b) The fee owner or an intermediate lessor terminates the lease by giving written notice of termination to the tenant or occupant within six months after the right to terminate arises under this section. The right to possess the property reverts to the landlord on the 10th day after the date the notice is given.

(c) This section applies regardless of a term of the lease to the contrary.

History of Prop. Code §91.003: Acts 1983, 68th Leg., ch. 576, §1, eff. Jan. 1, 1984. Source: TRCS art. 5236g.

PROP §91.004. LANDLORD'S BREACH OF LEASE; LIEN

(a) If the landlord of a tenant who is not in default under a lease fails to comply in any respect with the lease agreement, the landlord is liable to the tenant for damages resulting from the failure.

(b) To secure payment of the damages, the tenant has a lien on the landlord's nonexempt property in the tenant's possession and on the rent due to the landlord under the lease.

History of Prop. Code §91.004: Acts 1983, 68th Leg., ch. 576, §1, eff. Jan. 1, 1984. Source: TRCS art. 5236.

See also Prop. Code §92.104; *Real Estate Forms*, FORM 2:21.

ANNOTATIONS

Weber v. Domel, 48 S.W.3d 435, 437 (Tex.App.—Waco 2001, no pet.). "Although there was no express covenant in the lease for the landowner to preserve the grass, because the express purpose of the lease was for grazing, destruction of the subject of the contract by the landowner would be a breach of the lease."

Charalambous v. Jean Lafitte Corp., 652 S.W.2d 521, 526 (Tex.App.—El Paso 1983, writ ref'd n.r.e.). "The general requirements for constructive eviction are (1) an intention on the part of the landlord that the tenant shall no longer enjoy the premises which intention may be inferred from the circumstances proven; (2) a material act by the landlord or those acting for him that substantially interferes with the use and enjoyment of the premises for the purpose for which they are let; (3) the act must permanently deprive the tenant of the use and enjoyment of the premises; and (4) the tenant must abandon the premises within a reasonable time after the commission of the act. [¶] The general rule has been stated that a tenant who, being lawfully in possession, is wrongfully evicted by his landlord before the expiration of his term may bring an action for the resulting damages. He is not confined to an action of forceful entry and detainer to regain possession or to an action for breach of covenant. He has a cause of action and may sue in tort by resorting to the ordinary action of trespass where the eviction was forcible." *See also* ***2616 S. Loop L.L.C. v. Health Source Home Care, Inc.***, 201 S.W.3d 349, 358 n.7 (Tex.App.—Houston [14th Dist.] 2006, no pet.) (breach of covenant of quiet enjoyment).

McKenzie v. Carte, 385 S.W.2d 520, 528 (Tex. App.—Corpus Christi 1964, writ ref'd n.r.e.). "When the landlord wrongfully evicts the tenant, the latter shows a cause of action for damages by averring and proving the following facts: (1) The existence of an unexpired contract of renting; (2) occupancy of the premises in question by the tenant; (3) eviction or dispossession by the landlord; (4) damages attributable to such eviction. It has been held that the measure of damages for the breach of a contract of lease by the lessor is such damages as naturally and proximately result from the breach. [¶] Why should not [tenant] be entitled to damages for the loss sustained by him during the period of time he was evicted from the premises?" Held: Tenant entitled to damages sustained during eviction.

PROP §91.005. SUBLETTING PROHIBITED

During the term of a lease, the tenant may not rent the leasehold to any other person without the prior consent of the landlord.

History of Prop. Code §91.005: Acts 1983, 68th Leg., ch. 576, §1, eff. Jan. 1, 1984. Source: TRCS art. 5237.

See also *O'Connor's Texas COA*, "Ability to lease," ch. 16-A, §3.2, p. 422; *Real Estate Forms*, FORMS 2:19, 2:20.

ANNOTATIONS

Regency Advantage L.P. v. Bingo Idea-Watauga, Inc., 936 S.W.2d 275, 276 (Tex.1996). "This case presents the question of an assignee's liability for its predecessor-in-interest's alleged breach of a lease and a contract to pay a real estate commission. Because any breach of the lease occurred before the original lessor transferred its interest in the lease to the assignee and the lease obligation was not capable of successive independent breaches, [assignee is not liable for a breach of the lease]."

Tenet Health Sys. Hosps. Dallas, Inc. v. North Tex. Hosp. Physicians Grp., 438 S.W.3d 190, 196 (Tex. App.—Dallas 2014, no pet.). Sublessee argued in the trial court that "the Sublease [was] unenforceable because it was not approved by the Landlord, and it therefore create[d] no indebtedness from [sublessee] to [lessee]. *At 197:* Underlying the question of whether the Sublease created an indebtedness is the question of the enforceability of the Sublease. *At 198:* The prohibition against subleasing without a landlord's consent arises by statute and may also be included in the lease itself. [T]his limitation is for the benefit of the landlord, and an assignment of a lease in violation of this limitation 'does not invalidate the lease, nor relieve the lessee from the obligations imposed by such lease or the assignee who assumes them.' ... Because any objection to a sublease belongs to the landlord, courts have rejected sublessees' attempts to invoke this prohibition to their advantage. ... Applying these principles here, we conclude that [sublessee] cannot enter into the Sublease, enjoy occupancy of the premises, and then complain that the Sublease is unenforceable. The fact that the Landlord did not consent to the Sublease is of no consequence.... Therefore, having determined that the Sublease is not void, we consider whether the Sublease created an indebtedness from [sublessee] to [lessee]." Held: Sublessee created an indebtedness.

718 Assocs. v. Sunwest N.O.P., Inc., 1 S.W.3d 355, 362 (Tex.App.—Waco 1999, pet. denied). Section 91.005 "applies to both assignments and subleases. As a matter of public policy, the provision is incorporated into all leases by operation of law. [¶] The parties agree that this statutory provision can be avoided if the lease 'clearly expresses such an intent.' *At 363:* [Lease provision] states that the lessee has the right to assign the lease. [It] further states that if the lessee assigns the lease, it would nevertheless remain liable on its obligations. [T]his expresses a clear intent to allow the lessee to assign without prior consent." *See also* ***Trinity Prof'l Plaza Assocs. v. Metrocrest Hosp. Auth.***, 987 S.W.2d 621, 624 (Tex.App.—Eastland 1999, pet. denied); ***Lawther v. Super X Drugs***, this page.

Lampasas v. Spring Ctr., Inc., 988 S.W.2d 428, 433 (Tex.App.—Houston [14th Dist.] 1999, no pet.). "A subtenant without consent of the landlord is merely a trespasser."

Twelve Oaks Tower I, Ltd. v. Premier Allergy, Inc., 938 S.W.2d 102, 112 (Tex.App.—Houston [14th Dist.] 1996, no writ). "[A] tenant's failure to obtain the required consent does not render the assignment void, rather, it is voidable at the option of the lessor. The lease does not terminate unless the landlord undertakes to terminate it or declare a forfeiture or reenter. Furthermore, because the provision is for the landlord's benefit, only he may complain of the wrong done by such assignment. [¶] A lessor waives its right to forfeit a lease for a tenant's failure to obtain consent before assigning or subleasing if it accepts rents after the assignment or sublease."

Fabrique, Inc. v. Corman, 796 S.W.2d 790, 793 (Tex.App.—Dallas 1990), *writ denied*, 806 S.W.2d 801 (Tex.1991). "[T]he landlord impliedly covenants that it will put the tenant into peaceful possession. The rule is that when the terms of a lease contract have expressly or impliedly conferred on the tenant the right to assign the lease the landlord impliedly covenants that it will not unjustly hinder an assignee's future possession if there has been a valid assignment under the law or terms of the lease."

Reynolds v. McCullough, 739 S.W.2d 424, 429 (Tex.App.—San Antonio 1987, writ denied). "A lessor may contract, by provision in the lease, not to unreasonably withhold his consent to an assignment or sublease of the premises. This type of provision is in the nature of a promise or covenant which, if breached, could be grounds for an action for damages. Absent this promise, we hold that there is no implied covenant by the lessor to act reasonably in withholding his consent."

Lawther v. Super X Drugs, 671 S.W.2d 591, 593-94 (Tex.App.—Houston [1st Dist.] 1984, no writ). "The issue presented is whether the parties clearly expressed an intent to avoid the prohibition of [TRCS art. 5237, now Prop. Code §91.005,] against assignments without consent. It is evident from the face of the lease,

especially from paragraphs 25 and 28, that no such intent was expressed. Paragraph 25 is entirely consistent with art. 5237. It gives the lessor the right to refuse an assignment and hold the lessee to the terms of the lease, if the assignment would violate the exclusive rights of another tenant. It further provides that if the lessor refuses an assignment 'for any other reason,' the lessee may terminate the lease. The landlord's right to refuse assignment 'for any other reason' is thus expressly retained. Termination is the tenant's sole remedy. The lease does not grant to the tenant the additional right to assign in the absence of consent. Paragraph 28, construed along with paragraph 25, merely provides that, if the landlord consents to an assignment, then both parties are bound by the terms of the original lease." *See also* ***Cedar Contracting, Inc. v. Hernandez***, No. 03-11-00327-CV (Tex.App.—Austin 2014, pet. denied) (memo op.; 2-21-14); ***718 Assocs. v. Sunwest N.O.P., Inc.***, p. 430. *But see* ***Houck v. Kroger Co.***, 555 S.W.2d 803, 805-06 (Tex.App.—Houston [14th Dist.] 1977, writ ref'd n.r.e.) (determining equitable rights, court held that clauses identical to those in ***Lawther*** allowed tenant to sublease).

Heflin v. Stiles, 663 S.W.2d 131, 134 (Tex.App.—Fort Worth 1983, no writ). "Neither [TRCS art. 5237, now Prop. Code §91.005,] nor [the] lease provides an exception for a subletting or assignment between co-lessees or business partners."

American Nat'l Bank & Trust Co. v. First Wis. Mortg. Trust, 577 S.W.2d 312, 316 (Tex.App.—Beaumont 1979, writ ref'd n.r.e.), *disapproved on other grounds*, ***Stewart Title Guar. Co. v. Sterling***, 822 S.W.2d 1 (Tex.1991). "[D's] sole claim of title is through the tenant who mortgaged the property without the consent of the lessor. 'Without this consent one holding premises under a subletting is a trespasser and occupies the attitude of a stranger to the landlord.' [¶] At the time [D] negotiated the deed of trust lien it was charged that it was dealing not with an owner, but with a lessee who had no right to assign his lease without the consent of the lessor. At the time [D] foreclosed on its invalid deed of trust, it knew that the trustee's deed was invalid because it was a stranger to [P's] title. Nevertheless, and with knowledge of [P's pending third-party] negotiation, and in an effort to frustrate such transaction, it filed its trustee's deed for record. It cannot now be heard to say that it was only litigating its 'bona fide' claim to the property." *See also* ***Digby v. Hatley***, 574 S.W.2d 186, 189-90 (Tex. App.—San Antonio 1978, no writ).

PROP §91.006. LANDLORD'S DUTY TO MITIGATE DAMAGES

(a) A landlord has a duty to mitigate damages if a tenant abandons the leased premises in violation of the lease.

(b) A provision of a lease that purports to waive a right or to exempt a landlord from a liability or duty under this section is void.

History of Prop. Code §91.006: Acts 1997, 75th Leg., ch. 1205, §8, eff. Sept. 1, 1997.

ANNOTATIONS

White v. Harrison, 390 S.W.3d 666, 675 (Tex. App.—Dallas 2012, no pet.). "The landlord's duty to mitigate requires him to use 'objectively reasonable efforts' to release the premises to a tenant 'suitable under the circumstances.' If the landlord fails to use reasonable efforts to mitigate damages, his recovery from the tenant is barred to the extent that damages reasonably could have been avoided. The reasonableness of the landlord's efforts to avoid damages is an issue for the fact finder. The tenant bears the burden of proof to demonstrate that the landlord has failed to mitigate damages and the amount by which the landlord could have reduced his damages." *See also* ***Levertov v. Hold Props., Ltd.***, No. 11-11-00284-CV (Tex.App.—Eastland 2014, no pet.) (memo op.; 2-27-14); ***Hoppenstein Props., Inc. v. Schober***, 329 S.W.3d 846, 849-50 (Tex. App.—Fort Worth 2010, no pet.).

CHAPTER 92. RESIDENTIAL TENANCIES

Subchapter A. General Provisions

PROPERTY CODE
CHAPTER 92. RESIDENTIAL TENANCIES

SUBCHAPTER A. GENERAL PROVISIONS

PROP §92.001. DEFINITIONS

Except as otherwise provided by this chapter, in this chapter:

(1) "Dwelling" means one or more rooms rented for use as a permanent residence under a single lease to one or more tenants.

(2) "Landlord" means the owner, lessor, or sublessor of a dwelling, but does not include a manager or agent of the landlord unless the manager or agent purports to be the owner, lessor, or sublessor in an oral or written lease.

(3) "Lease" means any written or oral agreement between a landlord and tenant that establishes or modifies the terms, conditions, rules, or other provisions regarding the use and occupancy of a dwelling.

(4) "Normal wear and tear" means deterioration that results from the intended use of a dwelling, including, for the purposes of Subchapters B and D, breakage or malfunction due to age or deteriorated condition, but the term does not include deterioration that results from negligence, carelessness, accident, or abuse of the premises, equipment, or chattels by the tenant, by a member of the tenant's household, or by a guest or invitee of the tenant.

(5) "Premises" means a tenant's rental unit, any area or facility the lease authorizes the tenant to use, and the appurtenances, grounds, and facilities held out for the use of tenants generally.

(6) "Tenant" means a person who is authorized by a lease to occupy a dwelling to the exclusion of others and, for the purposes of Subchapters D, E, and F, who is obligated under the lease to pay rent.

History of Prop. Code §92.001: Acts 1983, 68th Leg., ch. 576, §1, eff. Jan. 1, 1984. Amended by Acts 1993, 73rd Leg., ch. 48, §12 (eff. Sept. 1, 1993), ch. 357, §1 (eff. Sept. 1, 1993). Source: TRCS arts. 5236e, §1(2)-(6); 5236f, §1; 5236h, §1(3), (5), (10); 5236i, §1(4), (6).

See also *O'Connor's Texas COA*, "Residential or commercial," ch. 16-A, §2.2, p. 420.

ANNOTATIONS

Munson v. Milton, 948 S.W.2d 813, 817 (Tex. App.—San Antonio 1997, pet. denied). "The Texas Property Code draws a distinction between a permanent residence and transient housing, which includes rooms at hotels, motels, inns and the like."

Warehouse Partners v. Gardner, 910 S.W.2d 19, 23 (Tex.App.—Dallas 1995, writ denied). "[T]he record shows that for nearly two years prior to the lockout, [tenant's agent] had used the Lease Space as his residence. We conclude that this evidence constitutes some evidence that the Lease Space constituted [tenant's agent's] 'permanent residence' and therefore his 'dwelling.' Thus, the express and presumed findings support the trial court's judgment applying the lockout provisions of [Prop. Code] §92.008 to [tenant's agent] and [lease-space owners]."

Virani v. Syal, 836 S.W.2d 749, 751 (Tex.App.—Houston [1st Dist.] 1992, writ denied). "A lease is a grant of an estate in land for a limited term, with conditions attached. A lease contract must state its duration or refer to a certain date of expiration. If a tenant is holding premises for no certain time as provided by a contract, he is merely a tenant at will."

PROP §92.002. APPLICATION

This chapter applies only to the relationship between landlords and tenants of residential rental property.

History of Prop. Code §92.002: Acts 1983, 68th Leg., ch. 576, §1, eff. Jan. 1, 1984. Source: TRCS arts. 5236e, §11; 5236f, §17.

ANNOTATIONS

Brown v. Hearthwood II Owners Ass'n, 201 S.W.3d 153, 160 (Tex.App.—Houston [14th Dist.] 2006, pet. denied). Landlord "bore the burden to prove that appellants were its tenants. Having submitted no evidence on this issue, [landlord] has failed to meet its burden of proof." *See also* ***Gilstrap v. Park Lane Town Home Ass'n***, 885 S.W.2d 589, 591 (Tex.App.—Amarillo 1994, no writ) (reversing summary judgment in favor of condominium owners' association when Ps were not shown to be the association's tenants).

PROP §92.003. LANDLORD'S AGENT FOR SERVICE OF PROCESS

(a) In a lawsuit by a tenant under either a written or oral lease for a dwelling or in a suit to enforce a legal obligation of the owner as landlord of the dwelling, the owner's agent for service of process is determined according to this section.

(b) If written notice of the name and business street address of the company that manages the dwelling has been given to the tenant, the management company is the owner's sole agent for service of process.

(c) If Subsection (b) does not apply, the owner's management company, on-premise manager, or rent collector serving the dwelling is the owner's authorized agent for service of process unless the owner's name and business street address have been furnished in writing to the tenant.

History of Prop. Code §92.003: Acts 1983, 68th Leg., ch. 576, §1, eff. Jan. 1, 1984. Source: TRCS art. 5236b.

ANNOTATIONS

Renaissance Park v. Davila, 27 S.W.3d 252, 257 (Tex.App.—Austin 2000, no pet.). "[W]e hold that [P] was required to plead that she did not receive either notice mentioned in the property code. She did not do so. [¶] We are further persuaded that service was ineffective because [P] does not allege that a landlord-tenant relationship ever existed between herself and [D]. … We hold that in order for a tenant to serve a landlord under §92.003 …, the tenant must allege that she had a landlord-tenant relationship with that particular landlord at some point in time."

Exposition Apts. Co. v. Barba, 630 S.W.2d 462, 465 (Tex.App.—Austin 1982, no writ). "[W]e believe strict compliance requires *a fortiori* another identifying name to accompany the surname of the agent. We hold, therefore, that delivery of citation to Mr. Tommy Thompson, petitioner's on-premise manager, may not be inferred from the face of the return which states citation was delivered to 'Mr. Thompson.' [¶] We hold, in addition, that the simple description of 'manager' following the name of 'Mr. Thompson,' does not constitute strict compliance with the statute, which allows for delivery of citation only to the owner's 'management company, on-premise manager, or rent collector.'"

PROP §92.004. HARASSMENT

A party who files or prosecutes a suit under Subchapter B, D, E, or F in bad faith or for purposes of harassment is liable to the defendant for one month's rent plus $100 and for attorney's fees.

History of Prop. Code §92.004: Acts 1983, 68th Leg., ch. 576, §1, eff. Jan. 1, 1984. Source: TRCS arts. 5236f, §11; 5236h, §9; 5236j, §10.

See also Prop. Code §94.302.

PROP §92.005. ATTORNEY'S FEES

(a) A party who prevails in a suit brought under this subchapter or Subchapter B, E, or F may recover the party's costs of court and reasonable attorney's fees in relation to work reasonably expended.

(b) This section does not authorize a recovery of attorney's fees in an action brought under Subchapter E or F for damages that relate to or arise from property damage, personal injury, or a criminal act.

History of Prop. Code §92.005: Acts 1983, 68th Leg., ch. 576, §1, eff. Jan. 1, 1984. Amended by Acts 1993, 73rd Leg., ch. 357, §2, eff. Sept. 1, 1993; Acts 1999, 76th Leg., ch. 1439, §2, eff. Sept. 1, 1999. Source: TRCS arts. 5236f, §10; 5236h, §10; 5236i, §10; 5236j, §11.

ANNOTATIONS

Stroman v. Tautenhahn, 465 S.W.3d 715, 718 (Tex.App.—Houston [14th Dist.] 2015, pet. dism'd). "[D] asserts that he had a request for affirmative relief pending in the trial court because he is entitled to attorney's fees as a matter of law under … §92.005. *At 719:* Presuming for the sake of argument that [D] could recover fees under §92.005, the statute does not require that the trial court automatically award a prevailing party fees *sua sponte*. Nor does the statute otherwise vitiate [D's] obligation to request attorney's fees under this section. Because a request for attorney's fees is neither implied nor presumed under the statute, in the absence of an actual request for attorneys' fees, none will be considered 'pending.'"

PROP §92.006. WAIVER OR EXPANSION OF DUTIES & REMEDIES

(a) A landlord's duty or a tenant's remedy concerning security deposits, security devices, the landlord's disclosure of ownership and management, or utility cutoffs, as provided by Subchapter C, D, E, or G, respectively, may not be waived. A landlord's duty to install a smoke alarm under Subchapter F may not be waived, nor may a tenant waive a remedy for the landlord's noninstallation or waive the tenant's limited right of installation and removal. The landlord's duty of inspection and repair of smoke alarms under Subchapter F may be waived only by written agreement.

(b) A landlord's duties and the tenant's remedies concerning security devices, the landlord's disclosure

of ownership and management, or smoke alarms, as provided by Subchapter D, E, or F, respectively, may be enlarged only by specific written agreement.

(c) A landlord's duties and the tenant's remedies under Subchapter B, which covers conditions materially affecting the physical health or safety of the ordinary tenant, may not be waived except as provided in Subsections (d), (e), and (f) of this section.

(d) A landlord and a tenant may agree for the tenant to repair or remedy, at the landlord's expense, any condition covered by Subchapter B.

(e) A landlord and a tenant may agree for the tenant to repair or remedy, at the tenant's expense, any condition covered by Subchapter B if all of the following conditions are met:

(1) at the beginning of the lease term the landlord owns only one rental dwelling;

(2) at the beginning of the lease term the dwelling is free from any condition which would materially affect the physical health or safety of an ordinary tenant;

(3) at the beginning of the lease term the landlord has no reason to believe that any condition described in Subdivision (2) of this subsection is likely to occur or recur during the tenant's lease term or during a renewal or extension; and

(4)(A) the lease is in writing;

(B) the agreement for repairs by the tenant is either underlined or printed in boldface in the lease or in a separate written addendum;

(C) the agreement is specific and clear; and

(D) the agreement is made knowingly, voluntarily, and for consideration.

(f) A landlord and tenant may agree that, except for those conditions caused by the negligence of the landlord, the tenant has the duty to pay for repair of the following conditions that may occur during the lease term or a renewal or extension:

(1) damage from wastewater stoppages caused by foreign or improper objects in lines that exclusively serve the tenant's dwelling;

(2) damage to doors, windows, or screens; and

(3) damage from windows or doors left open.

This subsection shall not affect the landlord's duty under Subchapter B to repair or remedy, at the landlord's expense, wastewater stoppages or backups caused by deterioration, breakage, roots, ground conditions, faulty construction, or malfunctioning equipment. A landlord and tenant may agree to the provisions of this subsection only if the agreement meets the requirements of Subdivision (4) of Subsection (e) of this section.

(g) A tenant's right to vacate a dwelling and avoid liability under Section 92.016 or 92.017 may not be waived by a tenant or a landlord, except as provided by those sections.

(h) A tenant's right to a jury trial in an action brought under this chapter may not be waived in a lease or other written agreement.

History of Prop. Code §92.006: Acts 1983, 68th Leg., ch. 576, §1, eff. Jan. 1, 1984. Amended by Acts 1989, 71st Leg., ch. 650, §1, eff. Aug. 28, 1989; Acts 2005, 79th Leg., ch. 348, §2, eff. Jan. 1, 2006; Acts 2011, 82nd Leg., ch. 257, §1, eff. Sept. 1, 2011; Acts 2015, 84th Leg., ch. 1198, §3, eff. Jan. 1, 2016. Source: TRCS arts. 5236e, §7; 5236f, §13; 5236h, §11; 5236i, §11; 5236j, §14.

See also *O'Connor's Texas COA*, "Counterclaim – damage caused by tenant," ch. 23-B, §5.2, p. 810.

ANNOTATIONS

has no duty to repair [under Prop. Code §92.052] in the first instance. Landlords have no obligation to repair premises conditions that are tenant-caused and therefore are not restrained from contracting with tenants for reimbursement of associated repair costs."

Churchill Forge, Inc. v. Brown, 61 S.W.3d 368, 372-73 (Tex.2001). The Property Code "not only permits the parties to contract over who will pay for repairs when the tenant causes damage, it specifically authorizes the parties to shift by contract costs of repairs for certain damages from the landlord to the tenant irrespective of whether the damage was caused by the tenant. [¶] The agreement must be conspicuous, clear,

and voluntary, but the responsibility shifting can occur, regardless of whether the damages were caused by the tenant. And not covered by that dictate are those agreements between the parties concerning damages for which the landlord has no duty to repair, i.e., tenant-caused damages. Nothing in the Property Code restricts the parties' freedom to negotiate over who will pay for repair of damages negligently or intentionally caused by the tenant, the tenant's occupant, or guest."

make a landlord invariably liable to his tenant for failing to install, inspect, or repair a smoke detector even though the tenant never notified the landlord of the malfunction or requested repair. As such, we hold that §92.006 does not establish, or even address for that matter, any basis of landlord liability beyond that established by the Texas Smoke Detector Statute."

PROP §92.007. VENUE

Venue for an action under this chapter is governed by Section 15.0115, Civil Practice and Remedies Code.

History of Prop. Code §92.007: Acts 1983, 68th Leg., ch. 576, §1, eff. Jan. 1, 1984. Amended by Acts 1989, 71st Leg., ch. 332, §1 (eff. Sept. 1, 1989), ch. 650, §2 (eff. Aug. 28, 1989); Acts 1993, 73rd Leg., ch. 48, §13, eff. Sept. 1, 1993; Acts 1995, 74th Leg., ch. 138, §9, eff. Aug. 28, 1995. Source: TRCS arts. 5236f, §16; 5236h, §13; 5236i, §14; 5236j, §16.

PROP §92.008. INTERRUPTION OF UTILITIES

(a) A landlord or a landlord's agent may not interrupt or cause the interruption of utility service paid for directly to the utility company by a tenant unless the interruption results from bona fide repairs, construction, or an emergency.

(b) Except as provided by this section, a landlord may not interrupt or cause the interruption of water, wastewater, gas, or electric service furnished to a tenant by the landlord as an incident of the tenancy or by other agreement unless the interruption results from bona fide repairs, construction, or an emergency.

(c) to **(e)** Repealed by Acts 2009, 81st Leg., ch. 1112, §3, eff. Jan. 1, 2010.

(f) If a landlord or a landlord's agent violates this section, the tenant may:

(1) either recover possession of the premises or terminate the lease; and

(2) in addition to other remedies available under law, recover from the landlord an amount equal to the sum of the tenant's actual damages, one month's rent plus $1,000, reasonable attorney's fees, and court costs, less any delinquent rents or other sums for which the tenant is liable to the landlord.

(g) A provision of a lease that purports to waive a right or to exempt a party from a liability or duty under this section is void.

(h) Subject to Subsections (i), (j), (k), (m), and (o), a landlord who submeters electricity or allocates or prorates nonsubmetered master metered electricity may interrupt or cause the interruption of electric service for nonpayment by the tenant of an electric bill issued to the tenant if:

(1) the landlord's right to interrupt electric service is provided by a written lease entered into by the tenant;

(2) the tenant's electric bill is not paid on or before the 12th day after the date the electric bill is issued;

(3) advance written notice of the proposed interruption is delivered to the tenant by mail or hand delivery separately from any other written content that:

(A) prominently displays the words "electricity termination notice" or similar language underlined or in bold;

(B) includes:

(i) the date on which the electric service will be interrupted;

(ii) a location where the tenant may go during the landlord's normal business hours to make arrangements to pay the bill to avoid interruption of electric service;

(iii) the amount that must be paid to avoid interruption of electric service;

(iv) a statement providing that when the tenant makes a payment to avoid interruption of electric service, the landlord may not apply that payment to rent or other amounts owed under the lease;

(v) a statement providing that the landlord may not evict a tenant for failure to pay an electric bill when the landlord has interrupted the tenant's electric service unless the tenant fails to pay for the electric service after the electric service has been interrupted for at least two days, not including weekends or state or federal holidays; and

(vi) a description of the tenant's rights under Subsection (j) to avoid interruption of electric service if the interruption will cause a person residing in the tenant's dwelling to become seriously ill or more seriously ill; and

(C) is delivered not earlier than the first day after the bill is past due or later than the fifth day before the interruption date stated in the notice; and

(4) the landlord, at the same time the service is interrupted, hand delivers or places on the tenant's front door a written notice that:

(A) prominently displays the words "electricity termination notice" or similar language underlined or in bold; and

(B) includes:

(i) the date the electric service has been interrupted;

(ii) a location where the tenant may go during the landlord's normal business hours to make arrangements to pay the bill to reestablish interrupted electric service;

(iii) the amount that must be paid to reestablish electric service;

(iv) a statement providing that when the tenant makes a payment to reestablish electric service, a landlord may not apply that payment to rent or other amounts owed under the lease;

(v) a statement providing that the landlord may not evict a tenant for failure to pay an electric bill when the landlord has interrupted the tenant's electric service unless the tenant fails to pay for the electric service after the electric service has been interrupted for at least two days, not including weekends or state or federal holidays; and

(vi) a description of the tenant's rights under Subsection (j) to avoid interruption of electric service if the interruption will cause a person residing in the tenant's dwelling to become seriously ill or more seriously ill.

(i) Unless a dangerous condition exists or the tenant requests disconnection, a landlord may not interrupt or cause the interruption of electric service under Subsection (h) on a day:

(1) on which the landlord or a representative of the landlord is not available to collect electric bill payments and reestablish electric service;

(2) that immediately precedes a day described by Subdivision (1); or

(3) on which:

(A) the previous day's highest temperature did not exceed 32 degrees Fahrenheit and the temperature is predicted to remain at or below that level for the next 24 hours according to the nearest National Weather Service reports; or

(B) the National Weather Service issues a heat advisory for a county in which the premises is located or has issued such an advisory on one of the two preceding days.

(j) A landlord may not interrupt or cause the interruption of electric service under Subsection (h) of a tenant who, before the interruption date specified in the notice required by Subsection (h)(3), has:

(1) established that the interruption will cause a person residing in the tenant's dwelling to become seriously ill or more seriously ill by having a physician, nurse, nurse practitioner, or other similar licensed health care practitioner attending to the person who is or may become ill provide a written statement to the landlord or a representative of the landlord stating that the person will become seriously ill or more seriously ill if the electric service is interrupted; and

(2) entered into a deferred payment plan that complies with Subsection (*l*).

(k) If a tenant has established, in accordance with Subsection (j), the circumstances necessary to avoid electric service interruption under that subsection, the landlord may not interrupt or cause the interruption of the tenant's electric service under Subsection (h) before:

(1) the 63rd day after the date those circumstances are established; or

(2) an earlier date agreed to by the landlord and the tenant.

(*l*) A deferred payment plan for the purposes of this section must be in writing. The deferred payment plan must allow the tenant to pay the outstanding electric bill

in installments that extend beyond the due date of the next electric bill and must provide that the delinquent amount may be paid in equal installments over a period equal to at least three electric service billing cycles.

(m) A landlord may not interrupt or cause the interruption of electric service under Subsection (h) to a tenant who receives energy assistance for a billing period during which the landlord receives a pledge, letter of intent, purchase order, or other notification that the energy assistance provider is forwarding sufficient payment to continue the electric service.

(n) If a delinquent electric bill is paid, or a deferred payment plan is entered into, during normal business hours, the landlord shall reconnect the tenant's electric service within two hours of payment or entry into the deferred payment plan.

(o) A landlord may not interrupt or cause the interruption of electric service under Subsection (h) for any of the following reasons:

(1) a delinquency in payment for electric service furnished to a previous tenant;

(2) failure to pay non-electric bills, rent, or other fees;

(3) failure to pay electric bills that are six or more months delinquent; or

(4) failure to pay an electric bill disputed by the tenant, unless the landlord has conducted an investigation as required by the particular case and reported the results in writing to the tenant.

(p) A landlord who provides notice in accordance with Subsection (h) may not apply a payment made by a tenant to avoid interruption of electric service or reestablish electric service to rent or any other amounts owed under the lease.

(q) The landlord may not evict a tenant for failure to pay an electric bill when the landlord has interrupted the tenant's electric service under Subsection (h) unless the tenant fails to pay for the electric service after the electric service has been interrupted for at least two days, not including weekends or state or federal holidays.

(r) Subject to this subsection, a reconnection fee may be applied if electric service to the tenant is disconnected for nonpayment of bills under Subsection (h). The reconnection fee must be computed based on the average cost to the landlord for the expenses associated with the reconnection, but may not exceed $10. A reconnection fee may not be applied unless agreed to by the tenant in a written lease that states the exact dollar amount of the reconnection fee. A fee may not be applied to a deferred payment plan entered into under this section.

History of Prop. Code §92.008: Acts 1983, 68th Leg., ch. 576, §1, eff. Jan. 1, 1984. Amended by Acts 1985, 69th Leg., ch. 200, §4, eff. Aug. 26, 1985. Renumbered from §91.002 by Acts 1987, 70th Leg., ch. 683, §2, eff. Aug. 31, 1987. Amended by Acts 1987, 70th Leg., ch. 826, §1, eff. Aug. 31, 1987. Renumbered from §91.002 and amended by Acts 1989, 71st Leg., ch. 689, §§1, 3, eff. Sept. 1, 1989. Amended by Acts 1995, 74th Leg., ch. 869, §1 (eff. Jan. 1, 1996), ch. 952, §1 (eff. Sept. 1, 1995); Acts 2009, 81st Leg., ch. 1112, §§1, 3, eff. Jan. 1, 2010; Acts 2013, 83rd Leg., ch. 899, §1, eff. Sept. 1, 2013. Source: TRCS art. 5236c.

See also Prop. Code §93.002; *O'Connor's Texas COA*, "Unlawful Interruption of Utility Service," ch. 16-E, p. 453.

PROP §92.0081. REMOVAL OF PROPERTY & EXCLUSION OF RESIDENTIAL TENANT

(a) A landlord may not remove a door, window, or attic hatchway cover or a lock, latch, hinge, hinge pin, doorknob, or other mechanism connected to a door, window, or attic hatchway cover from premises leased to a tenant or remove furniture, fixtures, or appliances furnished by the landlord from premises leased to a tenant unless the landlord removes the item for a bona fide repair or replacement. If a landlord removes any of the items listed in this subsection for a bona fide repair or replacement, the repair or replacement must be promptly performed.

(b) A landlord may not intentionally prevent a tenant from entering the leased premises except by judicial process unless the exclusion results from:

(1) bona fide repairs, construction, or an emergency;

(2) removing the contents of premises abandoned by a tenant; or

(3) changing the door locks on the door to the tenant's individual unit of a tenant who is delinquent in paying at least part of the rent.

(c) If a landlord or a landlord's agent changes the door lock of a tenant who is delinquent in paying rent, the landlord or the landlord's agent must place a written notice on the tenant's front door stating:

(1) an on-site location where the tenant may go 24 hours a day to obtain the new key or a telephone number that is answered 24 hours a day that the tenant may call to have a key delivered within two hours after calling the number;

(2) the fact that the landlord must provide the new key to the tenant at any hour, regardless of whether or not the tenant pays any of the delinquent rent; and

(3) the amount of rent and other charges for which the tenant is delinquent.

(d) A landlord may not intentionally prevent a tenant from entering the leased premises under Subsection (b)(3) unless:

(1) the landlord's right to change the locks because of a tenant's failure to timely pay rent is placed in the lease;

(2) the tenant is delinquent in paying all or part of the rent; and

(3) the landlord has locally mailed not later than the fifth calendar day before the date on which the door locks are changed or hand-delivered to the tenant or posted on the inside of the main entry door of the tenant's dwelling not later than the third calendar day before the date on which the door locks are changed a written notice stating:

(A) the earliest date that the landlord proposes to change the door locks;

(B) the amount of rent the tenant must pay to prevent changing of the door locks;

(C) the name and street address of the individual to whom, or the location of the on-site management office at which, the delinquent rent may be discussed or paid during the landlord's normal business hours; and

(D) in underlined or bold print, the tenant's right to receive a key to the new lock at any hour, regardless of whether the tenant pays the delinquent rent.

(e) A landlord may not change the locks on the door of a tenant's dwelling under Subsection (b)(3) on a day, or on a day immediately before a day, on which the landlord or other designated individual is not available, or on which any on-site management office is not open, for the tenant to tender the delinquent rent.

(e-1) A landlord who changes the locks or otherwise prevents a tenant from entering the tenant's individual rental unit may not change the locks or otherwise prevent a tenant from entering a common area of residential rental property.

(f) A landlord who intentionally prevents a tenant from entering the tenant's dwelling under Subsection (b)(3) must provide the tenant with a key to the changed lock on the dwelling without regard to whether the tenant pays the delinquent rent.

(g) If a landlord arrives at the dwelling in a timely manner in response to a tenant's telephone call to the number contained in the notice as described by Subsection (c)(1) and the tenant is not present to receive the key to the changed lock, the landlord shall leave a notice on the front door of the dwelling stating the time the landlord arrived with the key and the street address to which the tenant may go to obtain the key during the landlord's normal office hours.

(h) If a landlord violates this section, the tenant may:

(1) either recover possession of the premises or terminate the lease; and

(2) recover from the landlord a civil penalty of one month's rent plus $1,000, actual damages, court costs, and reasonable attorney's fees in an action to recover property damages, actual expenses, or civil penalties, less any delinquent rent or other sums for which the tenant is liable to the landlord.

(i) If a landlord violates Subsection (f), the tenant may recover, in addition to the remedies provided by Subsection (h), an additional civil penalty of one month's rent.

(j) A provision of a lease that purports to waive a right or to exempt a party from a liability or duty under this section is void.

(k) A landlord may not change the locks on the door of a tenant's dwelling under Subsection (b)(3):

(1) when the tenant or any other legal occupant is in the dwelling; or

(2) more than once during a rental payment period.

(*l*) This section does not affect the ability of a landlord to pursue other available remedies, including the remedies provided by Chapter 24.

History of Prop. Code §92.0081: Acts 1983, 68th Leg., ch. 576, §1, eff. Jan. 1, 1984. Amended by Acts 1985, 69th Leg., ch. 200, §4, eff. Aug. 26, 1985. Renumbered from §91.002 by Acts 1987, 70th Leg., ch. 683, §2, eff. Aug. 31, 1987. Amended by Acts 1987, 70th Leg., ch. 826, §1, eff. Aug. 31, 1987. Renumbered from §91.002 and amended by Acts 1989, 71st Leg., ch. 689, §§1, 3, eff. Sept. 1, 1989. Renumbered from §92.008(b)-(f) and amended by Acts 1995, 74th Leg., ch. 869, §1 (eff. Jan. 1, 1996), ch. 952, §1 (eff. Sept. 1, 1995). Amended by Acts 2007, 80th Leg., ch. 917, §1, eff. Jan. 1, 2008.

See also Prop. Code §93.002; ***O'Connor's Texas COA***, "Reentry," ch. 16-C, p. 441; "Unlawful Lockout," ch. 16-D, p. 450; ***Real Estate Forms***, FORM 2:25.

ANNOTATIONS

Jespersen v. Sweetwater Ranch Apts., 390 S.W.3d 644, 657-58 (Tex.App.—Dallas 2012, no pet.). "The evidence conclusively established [manager] saw [tenant] moving her belongings out of the apartment on July 11, 2008. [Tenant] does not dispute most of her belongings were moved out of the apartment prior to July 24, 2008. … The lease required [apartment complex]

to post a notice on the inside of any apartment that it believed had been abandoned by the tenant. [Manager] posted this notice. Pursuant to the lease, [tenant] had two days to dispute whether she had abandoned the apartment. [Tenant] failed to do so. Accordingly, under the lease, [tenant] abandoned the apartment prior to July 24, 2008 and no longer had any right of possession to the apartment. On July 24, 2008, [tenant] was told she could not return to the apartment. [Apartment complex] then changed the locks to the apartment. [¶] As relevant to this case, a tenant under §92.0081 is a 'person who is authorized by a lease to occupy a dwelling to the exclusion of all others.' On July 24, 2008, [tenant] was not authorized by a lease to occupy her apartment and, therefore, was not a tenant for purposes of §92.0081."

Charette v. Fitzgerald, 213 S.W.3d 505, 511 (Tex. App.—Houston [14th Dist.] 2006, no pet.). Landlord argues "that if a landlord can lock out a tenant who retains personal property on the leased premises under §92.0081(b)(3) for failure to pay rent, then a landlord should be able to do the same under §92.0081(b)(2) in situations in which the tenant, though having fully paid all rent, has moved into another dwelling, thereby 'abandoning' the leased premises. ... We find no merit in [landlord's] argument. [¶] [Tenant] did not abandon the Rental Property within the meaning of the Texas Property Code. [¶] [Landlord] locked [tenant] out of the Rental Property for reasons other than [those authorized by §92.0081(b)]. We cannot expand the language in §92.0081(b) to allow a landlord to prevent a tenant from entering the leased property even though the landlord does not do so to remove the contents of the tenant's personal property."

PROP §92.009. RESIDENTIAL TENANT'S RIGHT OF REENTRY AFTER UNLAWFUL LOCKOUT

(a) If a landlord has locked a tenant out of leased premises in violation of Section 92.0081, the tenant may recover possession of the premises as provided by this section.

(b) The tenant must file with the justice court in the precinct in which the rental premises are located a sworn complaint for reentry, specifying the facts of the alleged unlawful lockout by the landlord or the landlord's agent. The tenant must also state orally under oath to the justice the facts of the alleged unlawful lockout.

(c) If the tenant has complied with Subsection (b) and if the justice reasonably believes an unlawful lockout has likely occurred, the justice may issue, ex parte, a writ of reentry that entitles the tenant to immediate and temporary possession of the premises, pending a final hearing on the tenant's sworn complaint for reentry.

(d) The writ of reentry must be served on either the landlord or the landlord's management company, on-premises manager, or rent collector in the same manner as a writ of possession in a forcible detainer action. A sheriff or constable may use reasonable force in executing a writ of reentry under this section.

(e) The landlord is entitled to a hearing on the tenant's sworn complaint for reentry. The writ of reentry must notify the landlord of the right to a hearing. The hearing shall be held not earlier than the first day and not later than the seventh day after the date the landlord requests a hearing.

(f) If the landlord fails to request a hearing on the tenant's sworn complaint for reentry before the eighth day after the date of service of the writ of reentry on the landlord under Subsection (d), a judgment for court costs may be rendered against the landlord.

(g) A party may appeal from the court's judgment at the hearing on the sworn complaint for reentry in the same manner as a party may appeal a judgment in a forcible detainer suit.

(h) If a writ of possession is issued, it supersedes a writ of reentry.

(i) If the landlord or the person on whom a writ of reentry is served fails to immediately comply with the writ or later disobeys the writ, the failure is grounds for contempt of court against the landlord or the person on whom the writ was served, under Section 21.002, Government Code. If the writ is disobeyed, the tenant or the tenant's attorney may file in the court in which the reentry action is pending an affidavit stating the name of the person who has disobeyed the writ and describing the acts or omissions constituting the disobedience. On receipt of an affidavit, the justice shall issue a show cause order, directing the person to appear on a designated date and show cause why he should not be adjudged in contempt of court. If the justice finds, after considering the evidence at the hearing, that the person has directly or indirectly disobeyed the writ, the justice may commit the person to jail without bail until the person purges himself of the contempt in a manner and form as the justice may direct. If the person disobeyed

the writ before receiving the show cause order but has complied with the writ after receiving the order, the justice may find the person in contempt and assess punishment under Section 21.002(c), Government Code.

(j) This section does not affect a tenant's right to pursue a separate cause of action under Section 92.0081.

(k) If a tenant in bad faith files a sworn complaint for reentry resulting in a writ of reentry being served on the landlord or landlord's agent, the landlord may in a separate cause of action recover from the tenant an amount equal to actual damages, one month's rent or $500, whichever is greater, reasonable attorney's fees, and costs of court, less any sums for which the landlord is liable to the tenant.

(*l*) The fee for filing a sworn complaint for reentry is the same as that for filing a civil action in justice court. The fee for service of a writ of reentry is the same as that for service of a writ of possession. The fee for service of a show cause order is the same as that for service of a civil citation. The justice may defer payment of the tenant's filing fees and service costs for the sworn complaint for reentry and writ of reentry. Court costs may be waived only if the tenant executes a pauper's affidavit.

(m) This section does not affect the rights of a landlord or tenant in a forcible detainer or forcible entry and detainer action.

History of Prop. Code §92.009: Acts 1989, 71st Leg., ch. 687, §1, eff. Sept. 1, 1989. Amended by Acts 1997, 75th Leg., ch. 1205, §9, eff. Sept. 1, 1997; Acts 2011, 82nd Leg., ch. 91, §21.001, eff. Sept. 1, 2011.

See also Prop. Code §§93.003, 94.203; *O'Connor's Texas COA*, "Reentry," ch. 16-C, p. 441.

ANNOTATIONS

Warehouse Partners v. Gardner, 910 S.W.2d 19, 27 (Tex.App.—Dallas 1995, writ denied). Property Code §92.009 "provides the procedure for obtaining a writ of reentry due to a landlord's violation of [Prop. Code §92.008, now §92.0081]. ... We construe [§§92.0081 and 92.009] as permitting a tenant to seek a writ of reentry in one suit and bring a cause of action for actual damages, attorney's fees, and court costs in a second suit."

PROP §92.0091. RESIDENTIAL TENANT'S RIGHT OF RESTORATION AFTER UNLAWFUL UTILITY DISCONNECTION

(a) If a landlord has interrupted utility service in violation of Section 92.008, the tenant may obtain relief as provided by this section.

(b) The tenant must file with the justice court in the precinct in which the rental premises are located a sworn complaint specifying the facts of the alleged unlawful utility disconnection by the landlord or the landlord's agent. The tenant must also state orally under oath to the justice the facts of the alleged unlawful utility disconnection.

(c) If the tenant has complied with Subsection (b) and if the justice reasonably believes an unlawful utility disconnection has likely occurred, the justice may issue, ex parte, a writ of restoration of utility service that entitles the tenant to immediate and temporary restoration of the disconnected utility service, pending a final hearing on the tenant's sworn complaint.

(d) The writ of restoration of utility service must be served on either the landlord or the landlord's management company, on-premises manager, or rent collector in the same manner as a writ of possession in a forcible detainer suit.

(e) The landlord is entitled to a hearing on the tenant's sworn complaint for restoration of utility service. The writ of restoration of utility service must notify the landlord of the right to a hearing. The hearing shall be held not earlier than the first day and not later than the seventh day after the date the landlord requests a hearing.

(f) If the landlord fails to request a hearing on the tenant's sworn complaint for restoration of utility service before the eighth day after the date of service of the writ of restoration of utility service on the landlord under Subsection (d), a judgment for court costs may be rendered against the landlord.

(g) A party may appeal from the court's judgment at the hearing on the sworn complaint for restoration of utility service in the same manner as a party may appeal a judgment in a forcible detainer suit.

(h) If a writ of possession is issued, it supersedes a writ of restoration of utility service.

(i) If the landlord or the person on whom a writ of restoration of utility service is served fails to immediately comply with the writ or later disobeys the writ, the failure is grounds for contempt of court against the landlord or the person on whom the writ was served under Section 21.002, Government Code. If the writ is disobeyed, the tenant or the tenant's attorney may file in the court in which the action is pending an affidavit stating the name of the person who has disobeyed the writ and describing the acts or omissions constituting

the disobedience. On receipt of an affidavit, the justice shall issue a show cause order, directing the person to appear on a designated date and show cause why the person should not be adjudged in contempt of court. If the justice finds, after considering the evidence at the hearing, that the person has directly or indirectly disobeyed the writ, the justice may commit the person to jail without bail until the person purges the contempt action or omission in a manner and form as the justice may direct. If the person disobeyed the writ before receiving the show cause order but has complied with the writ after receiving the order, the justice may find the person in contempt and assess punishment under Section 21.002(c), Government Code.

(j) If a tenant in bad faith files a sworn complaint for restoration of utility service resulting in a writ being served on the landlord or landlord's agent, the landlord may in a separate cause of action recover from the tenant an amount equal to actual damages, one month's rent or $500, whichever is greater, reasonable attorney's fees, and costs of court, less any sums for which the landlord is liable to the tenant.

(k) The fee for filing a sworn complaint for restoration of utility service is the same as that for filing a civil action in justice court. The fee for service of a writ of restoration of utility service is the same as that for service of a writ of possession. The fee for service of a show cause order is the same as that for service of a civil citation. The justice may defer payment of the tenant's filing fees and service costs for the sworn complaint for restoration of utility service and writ of restoration of utility service. Court costs may be waived only if the tenant executes a pauper's affidavit.

History of Prop. Code §92.0091: Acts 2009, 81st Leg., ch. 1112, §2, eff. Jan. 1, 2010.

PROP §92.010. OCCUPANCY LIMITS

(a) Except as provided by Subsection (b), the maximum number of adults that a landlord may allow to occupy a dwelling is three times the number of bedrooms in the dwelling.

(b) A landlord may allow an occupancy rate of more than three adult tenants per bedroom:

(1) to the extent that the landlord is required by a state or federal fair housing law to allow a higher occupancy rate; or

(2) if an adult whose occupancy causes a violation of Subsection (a) is seeking temporary sanctuary from family violence, as defined by Section 71.004, Family Code, for a period that does not exceed one month.

(c) An individual who owns or leases a dwelling within 3,000 feet of a dwelling as to which a landlord has violated this section, or a governmental entity or civic association acting on behalf of the individual, may file suit against a landlord to enjoin the violation. A party who prevails in a suit under this subsection may recover court costs and reasonable attorney's fees from the other party. In addition to court costs and reasonable attorney's fees, a plaintiff who prevails under this subsection may recover from the landlord $500 for each violation of this section.

(d) In this section:

(1) "Adult" means an individual 18 years of age or older.

(2) "Bedroom" means an area of a dwelling intended as sleeping quarters. The term does not include a kitchen, dining room, bathroom, living room, utility room, or closet or storage area of a dwelling.

History of Prop. Code §92.010: Acts 1993, 73rd Leg., ch. 937, §1, eff. Sept. 1, 1993. Amended by Acts 2003, 78th Leg., ch. 1276, §7.002(o), eff. Sept. 1, 2003.

PROP §92.011. CASH RENTAL PAYMENTS

(a) A landlord shall accept a tenant's timely cash rental payment unless a written lease between the landlord and tenant requires the tenant to make rental payments by check, money order, or other traceable or negotiable instrument.

(b) A landlord who receives a cash rental payment shall:

(1) provide the tenant with a written receipt; and

(2) enter the payment date and amount in a record book maintained by the landlord.

(c) A tenant or a governmental entity or civic association acting on the tenant's behalf may file suit against a landlord to enjoin a violation of this section. A party who prevails in a suit brought under this subsection may recover court costs and reasonable attorney's fees from the other party. In addition to court costs and reasonable attorney's fees, a tenant who prevails under this subsection may recover from the landlord the greater of one month's rent or $500 for each violation of this section.

History of Prop. Code §92.011: Acts 1993, 73rd Leg., ch. 938, §1, eff. Sept. 1, 1993. Renumbered from §92.010 by Acts 1995, 74th Leg., ch. 76, §17.01(44), eff. Sept. 1, 1995.

PROP §92.012. NOTICE TO TENANT AT PRIMARY RESIDENCE

(a) If, at the time of signing a lease or lease renewal, a tenant gives written notice to the tenant's landlord that the tenant does not occupy the leased premises as a primary residence and requests in writing that the landlord send notices to the tenant at the tenant's primary residence and provides to the landlord the address of the tenant's primary residence, the landlord shall mail to the tenant's primary residence:

(1) all notices of lease violations;

(2) all notices of lease termination;

(3) all notices of rental increases at the end of the lease term; and

(4) all notices to vacate.

(b) The tenant shall notify the landlord in writing of any change in the tenant's primary residence address. Oral notices of change are insufficient.

(c) A notice to a tenant's primary residence under Subsection (a) may be sent by regular United States mail and shall be considered as having been given on the date of postmark of the notice.

(d) If there is more than one tenant on a lease, the landlord is not required under this section to send notices to the primary residence of more than one tenant.

(e) This section does not apply if notice is actually hand delivered to and received by a person occupying the leased premises.

History of Prop. Code §92.012: Acts 1997, 75th Leg., ch. 1205, §10, eff. Sept. 1, 1997.

PROP §92.013. NOTICE OF RULE OR POLICY CHANGE AFFECTING TENANT'S PERSONAL PROPERTY

(a) A landlord shall give prior written notice to a tenant regarding a landlord rule or policy change that is not included in the lease agreement and that will affect any personal property owned by the tenant that is located outside the tenant's dwelling. A landlord shall provide to the tenant in a multiunit complex, as that term is defined by Section 92.151, a copy of any applicable vehicle towing or parking rules or policies of the landlord and any changes to those rules or policies as provided by Section 92.0131.

(b) The notice must be given in person or by mail to the affected tenant. Notice in person may be by personal delivery to the tenant or any person residing at the tenant's dwelling who is 16 years of age or older or by personal delivery to the tenant's dwelling and affixing the notice to the inside of the main entry door. Notice by mail may be by regular mail, by registered mail, or by certified mail, return receipt requested. If the dwelling has no mailbox and has a keyless bolting device, alarm system, or dangerous animal that prevents the landlord from entering the premises to leave the notice on the inside of the main entry door, the landlord may securely affix the notice on the outside of the main entry door.

(c) A landlord who fails to give notice as required by this section is liable to the tenant for any expense incurred by the tenant as a result of the landlord's failure to give the notice.

History of Prop. Code §92.013: Acts 1999, 76th Leg., ch. 942, §1, eff. Sept. 1, 1999. Amended by Acts 2005, 79th Leg., ch. 1060, §1, eff. Jan. 1, 2006.

PROP §92.0131. NOTICE REGARDING VEHICLE TOWING OR PARKING RULES OR POLICIES

(a) This section applies only to a tenant in a multiunit complex, as that term is defined by Section 92.151.

(b) If at the time a lease agreement is executed a landlord has vehicle towing or parking rules or policies that apply to the tenant, the landlord shall provide to the tenant a copy of the rules or policies before the lease agreement is executed. The copy of the rules or policies must be:

(1) signed by the tenant;

(2) included in a lease agreement signed by the tenant; or

(3) included in an attachment to the lease agreement that is signed by the tenant, but only if the attachment is expressly referred to in the lease agreement.

(c) If the rules or policies are contained in the lease agreement or an attachment to the lease agreement, the title to the paragraph containing the rules or policies must read "Parking" or "Parking Rules" and be capitalized, underlined, or printed in bold print.

(c-1) As a precondition for allowing a tenant to park in a specific parking space or a common parking area that the landlord has made available for tenant use, the landlord may require a tenant to provide only the make, model, color, year, license number, and state of registration of the vehicle to be parked.

(c-2) Notwithstanding Subsection (c-1), a municipal housing authority located in a municipality that has a population of more than 500,000 and is not more than 50 miles from an international border, or a public facility corporation, affiliate, or subsidiary of the authority,

may require that vehicles parked in a community of the authority, corporation, affiliate, or subsidiary be registered with the housing authority.

(d) If a landlord changes the vehicle towing or parking rules or policies during the term of the lease agreement, the landlord shall provide written notice of the change to the tenant before the tenant is required to comply with the rule or policy change. The landlord has the burden of proving that the tenant received a copy of the rule or policy change. The landlord may satisfy that burden of proof by providing evidence that the landlord:

(1) delivered the notice by certified mail, return receipt requested, addressed to the tenant at the tenant's dwelling; or

(2) made a notation in the landlord's files of the time, place, and method of providing the notice and the name of the person who delivered the notice by:

(A) hand delivery to the tenant or any occupant of the tenant's dwelling over the age of 16 years at the tenant's dwelling;

(B) facsimile to a facsimile number the tenant provided to the landlord for the purpose of receiving notices; or

(C) taping the notice to the inside of the main entry door of the tenant's dwelling.

(e) If a rule or policy change is made during the term of the lease agreement, the change:

(1) must:

(A) apply to all of the landlord's tenants in the same multiunit complex and be based on necessity, safety or security of tenants, reasonable requirements for construction on the premises, or respect for other tenants' parking rights; or

(B) be adopted based on the tenant's written consent; and

(2) may not be effective before the 14th day after the date notice of the change is delivered to the tenant, unless the change is the result of a construction or utility emergency.

(f) A landlord who violates Subsection (b), (c), (d), or (e) is liable for a civil penalty in the amount of $100 plus any towing or storage costs that the tenant incurs as a result of the towing of the tenant's vehicle. The nonprevailing party in a suit under this section is liable to the prevailing party for reasonable attorney's fees and court costs.

(g) A landlord is liable for any damage to a tenant's vehicle resulting from the negligence of a towing service that contracts with the landlord or the landlord's agent to remove vehicles that are parked in violation of the landlord's rules and policies if the towing company that caused the damage does not carry insurance that covers the damage.

History of Prop. Code §92.0131: Acts 2005, 79th Leg., ch. 1060, §2, eff. Jan. 1, 2006. Amended by Acts 2007, 80th Leg., ch. 917, §2, eff. Jan. 1, 2008; Acts 2011, 82nd Leg., ch. 969, §1, eff. Sept. 1, 2011.

PROP §92.014. PERSONAL PROPERTY & SECURITY DEPOSIT OF DECEASED TENANT

(a) Upon written request of a landlord, the landlord's tenant shall:

(1) provide the landlord with the name, address, and telephone number of a person to contact in the event of the tenant's death; and

(2) sign a statement authorizing the landlord in the event of the tenant's death to:

(A) grant to the person designated under Subdivision (1) access to the premises at a reasonable time and in the presence of the landlord or the landlord's agent;

(B) allow the person designated under Subdivision (1) to remove any of the tenant's property found at the leased premises; and

(C) refund the tenant's security deposit, less lawful deductions, to the person designated under Subdivision (1).

(b) A tenant may, without request from the landlord, provide the landlord with the information in Subsection (a).

(c) Except as provided in Subsection (d), in the event of the death of a tenant who is the sole occupant of a rental dwelling:

(1) the landlord may remove and store all property found in the tenant's leased premises;

(2) the landlord shall turn over possession of the property to the person who was designated by the tenant under Subsection (a) or (b) or to any other person lawfully entitled to the property if the request is made prior to the property being discarded under Subdivision (5);

(3) the landlord shall refund the tenant's security deposit, less lawful deductions, including the cost of removing and storing the property, to the person designated under Subsection (a) or (b) or to any other person lawfully entitled to the refund;

(4) the landlord may require any person who removes the property from the tenant's leased premises to sign an inventory of the property being removed; and

(5) the landlord may discard the property removed by the landlord from the tenant's leased premises if:

(A) the landlord has mailed a written request by certified mail, return receipt requested, to the person designated under Subsection (a) or (b), requesting that the property be removed;

(B) the person failed to remove the property by the 30th day after the postmark date of the notice; and

(C) the landlord, prior to the date of discarding the property, has not been contacted by anyone claiming the property.

(d) In a written lease or other agreement, a landlord and a tenant may agree to a procedure different than the procedure in this section for removing, storing, or disposing of property in the leased premises of a deceased tenant.

(e) If a tenant, after being furnished with a copy of this subchapter, knowingly violates Subsection (a), the landlord shall have no responsibility after the tenant's death for removal, storage, disappearance, damage, or disposition of property in the tenant's leased premises.

(f) If a landlord, after being furnished with a copy of this subchapter, knowingly violates Subsection (c), the landlord shall be liable to the estate of the deceased tenant for actual damages.

History of Prop. Code §92.014: Acts 1999, 76th Leg., ch. 1439, §1, eff. Sept. 1, 1999. Renumbered from §92.013 by Acts 2001, 77th Leg., ch. 1420, §21.001(97), eff. Sept. 1, 2001.

A PROP §92.015. TENANT'S RIGHT TO SUMMON POLICE OR EMERGENCY ASSISTANCE

The amended text in §92.015 is effective for leases entered into or renewed on or after Sept. 1, 2017. Leases entered into or renewed before Sept. 1, 2017, are governed by the former law in effect at that time.

(a) A landlord may not:

(1) prohibit or limit a residential tenant's right to summon police or other emergency assistance based on the tenant's reasonable belief that an individual is in need of intervention or emergency assistance [~~in response to family violence~~]; or

(2) impose monetary or other penalties on a tenant who summons police or emergency assistance if the assistance was requested or dispatched based on the tenant's reasonable belief that an individual was in need of intervention or emergency assistance [~~in response to family violence~~].

(b) A provision in a lease is void if the provision purports to:

(1) waive a tenant's right to summon police or other emergency assistance based on the tenant's reasonable belief that an individual is in need of intervention or emergency assistance [~~in response to family violence~~]; or

(2) exempt any party from a liability or a duty under this section.

(c) In addition to other remedies provided by law, if a landlord violates this section, a tenant is entitled to recover from or against the landlord:

(1) a civil penalty in an amount equal to one month's rent;

(2) actual damages suffered by the tenant as a result of the landlord's violation of this section;

(3) court costs;

(4) injunctive relief; and

(5) reasonable attorney's fees incurred by the tenant in seeking enforcement of this section.

(d) For purposes of this section, if a tenant's rent is subsidized in whole or in part by a governmental entity, "one month's rent" means one month's fair market rent.

(e) Repealed by H.B. 1099, §2, 85th Leg., eff. Sept. 1, 2017.

[~~(e)~~] [~~For purposes of this section, "family violence" has the meaning assigned by Section 71.004, Family Code.~~]

History of Prop. Code §92.015: Acts 2003, 78th Leg., ch. 794, §1, eff. June 20, 2003. Amended by H.B. 1099, §§1, 2, 85th Leg., eff. Sept. 1, 2017.

PROP §92.016. RIGHT TO VACATE & AVOID LIABILITY FOLLOWING FAMILY VIOLENCE

(a) For purposes of this section:

(1) "Family violence" has the meaning assigned by Section 71.004, Family Code.

(2) "Occupant" means a person who has the landlord's consent to occupy a dwelling but has no obligation to pay the rent for the dwelling.

(b) A tenant may terminate the tenant's rights and obligations under a lease and may vacate the dwelling and avoid liability for future rent and any other sums due under the lease for terminating the lease and va-

cating the dwelling before the end of the lease term if the tenant complies with Subsection (c) and provides the landlord or the landlord's agent a copy of one or more of the following orders protecting the tenant or an occupant from family violence:

(1) a temporary injunction issued under Subchapter F, Chapter 6, Family Code;

(2) a temporary ex parte order issued under Chapter 83, Family Code; or

(3) a protective order issued under Chapter 85, Family Code.

(c) A tenant may exercise the rights to terminate the lease under Subsection (b), vacate the dwelling before the end of the lease term, and avoid liability beginning on the date after all of the following events have occurred:

(1) a judge signs an order described by Subsection (b);

(2) the tenant provides a copy of the relevant documentation described by Subsection (b) to the landlord;

(3) the tenant provides written notice of termination of the lease to the landlord on or before the 30th day before the date the lease terminates;

(4) the 30th day after the date the tenant provided notice under Subdivision (3) expires; and

(5) the tenant vacates the dwelling.

(c-1) If the family violence is committed by a cotenant or occupant of the dwelling, a tenant may exercise the right to terminate the lease under the procedures provided by Subsection (b)(1) or (3) and Subsection (c), except that the tenant is not required to provide the notice described by Subsection (c)(3).

(d) Except as provided by Subsection (f), this section does not affect a tenant's liability for delinquent, unpaid rent or other sums owed to the landlord before the lease was terminated by the tenant under this section.

(e) A landlord who violates this section is liable to the tenant for actual damages, a civil penalty equal in amount to the amount of one month's rent plus $500, and attorney's fees.

(f) A tenant who terminates a lease under Subsection (b) is released from all liability for any delinquent, unpaid rent owed to the landlord by the tenant on the effective date of the lease termination if the lease does not contain language substantially equivalent to the following:

"Tenants may have special statutory rights to terminate the lease early in certain situations involving family violence or a military deployment or transfer."

(g) A tenant's right to terminate a lease before the end of the lease term, vacate the dwelling, and avoid liability under this section may not be waived by a tenant.

History of Prop. Code §92.016: Acts 2005, 79th Leg., ch. 348, §1, eff. Jan. 1, 2006. Amended by Acts 2009, 81st Leg., ch. 18, §1, eff. Jan. 1, 2010.

PROP §92.0161. RIGHT TO VACATE & AVOID LIABILITY FOLLOWING CERTAIN SEX OFFENSES OR STALKING

(a) In this section, "occupant" has the meaning assigned by Section 92.016.

(b) A tenant may terminate the tenant's rights and obligations under a lease and may vacate the dwelling and avoid liability for future rent and any other sums due under the lease for terminating the lease and vacating the dwelling before the end of the lease term after the tenant complies with Subsection (c) or (c-1).

(c) If the tenant is a victim or a parent or guardian of a victim of sexual assault under Section 22.011, Penal Code, aggravated sexual assault under Section 22.021, Penal Code, indecency with a child under Section 21.11, Penal Code, sexual performance by a child under Section 43.25, Penal Code, continuous sexual abuse of a child under Section 21.02, Penal Code, or an attempt to commit any of the foregoing offenses under Section 15.01, Penal Code, that takes place during the preceding six-month period on the premises or at any dwelling on the premises, the tenant shall provide to the landlord or the landlord's agent a copy of:

(1) documentation of the assault or abuse, or attempted assault or abuse, of the victim from a licensed health care services provider who examined the victim;

(2) documentation of the assault or abuse, or attempted assault or abuse, of the victim from a licensed mental health services provider who examined or evaluated the victim;

(3) documentation of the assault or abuse, or attempted assault or abuse, of the victim from an individual authorized under Chapter 420, Government Code, who provided services to the victim; or

(4) documentation of a protective order issued under Chapter 7A, Code of Criminal Procedure, except for a temporary ex parte order.

(c-1) If the tenant is a victim or a parent or guardian of a victim of stalking under Section 42.072, Penal

Code, that takes place during the preceding six-month period on the premises or at any dwelling on the premises, the tenant shall provide to the landlord or the landlord's agent a copy of:

(1) documentation of a protective order issued under Chapter 7A or Article 6.09, Code of Criminal Procedure, except for a temporary ex parte order; or

(2) documentation of the stalking from a provider of services described by Subsection (c)(1), (2), or (3) and:

(A) a law enforcement incident report or, if a law enforcement incident report is unavailable, another record maintained in the ordinary course of business by a law enforcement agency; and

(B) if the report or record described by Paragraph (A) identifies the victim by means of a pseudonym, as defined by Article 57A.01, Code of Criminal Procedure, a copy of a pseudonym form completed and returned under Article 57A.02 of that code.

(d) A tenant may exercise the rights to terminate the lease under Subsection (b), vacate the dwelling before the end of the lease term, and avoid liability beginning on the date after all of the following events have occurred:

(1) the tenant provides a copy of the relevant documentation described by Subsection (c) or (c-1) to the landlord;

(2) the tenant provides written notice of termination of the lease to the landlord on or before the 30th day before the date the lease terminates;

(3) the 30th day after the date the tenant provided notice under Subdivision (2) expires; and

(4) the tenant vacates the dwelling.

(e) Except as provided by Subsection (g), this section does not affect a tenant's liability for delinquent, unpaid rent or other sums owed to the landlord before the lease was terminated by the tenant under this section.

(f) A landlord who violates this section is liable to the tenant for actual damages, a civil penalty equal to the amount of one month's rent plus $500, and attorney's fees.

(g) A tenant who terminates a lease under Subsection (b) is released from all liability for any delinquent, unpaid rent owed to the landlord by the tenant on the effective date of the lease termination if the lease does not contain language substantially equivalent to the following:

"Tenants may have special statutory rights to terminate the lease early in certain situations involving certain sexual offenses or stalking."

(h) A tenant may not waive a tenant's right to terminate a lease before the end of the lease term, vacate the dwelling, and avoid liability under this chapter.

(i) For purposes of Subsections (c) and (c-1), a tenant who is a parent or guardian of a victim described by those subsections must reside with the victim to exercise the rights established by this section.

(j) A person who receives information under Subsection (c), (c-1), or (d) may not disclose the information to any other person except for a legitimate or customary business purpose or as otherwise required by law.

History of Prop. Code §92.0161: Acts 2009, 81st Leg., ch. 18, §2, eff. Jan. 1, 2010. Amended by Acts 2013, 83rd Leg., ch. 593, §§1, 2, eff. Jan. 1, 2014; Acts 2015, 84th Leg., ch. 394, §2, eff. Sept. 1, 2015.

PROP §92.017. RIGHT TO VACATE & AVOID LIABILITY FOLLOWING CERTAIN DECISIONS RELATED TO MILITARY SERVICE

(a) For purposes of this section, "dependent," "military service," and "servicemember" have the meanings assigned by 50 App. U.S.C. Section 511.

(b) A tenant who is a servicemember or a dependent of a servicemember may vacate the dwelling leased by the tenant and avoid liability for future rent and all other sums due under the lease for terminating the lease and vacating the dwelling before the end of the lease term if:

(1) the lease was executed by or on behalf of a person who, after executing the lease or during the term of the lease, enters military service; or

(2) a servicemember, while in military service, executes the lease and after executing the lease receives military orders:

(A) for a permanent change of station; or

(B) to deploy with a military unit for a period of 90 days or more.

(c) A tenant who terminates a lease under Subsection (b) shall deliver to the landlord or landlord's agent:

(1) a written notice of termination of the lease; and

(2) a copy of an appropriate government document providing evidence of the tenant's entrance into military service if Subsection (b)(1) applies or a copy of the servicemember's military orders if Subsection (b)(2) applies.

(d) Termination of a lease under this section is effective:

(1) in the case of a lease that provides for monthly payment of rent, on the 30th day after the first date on which the next rental payment is due after the date on which the notice under Subsection (c)(1) is delivered; or

(2) in the case of a lease other than a lease described by Subdivision (1), on the last day of the month following the month in which the notice under Subsection (c)(1) is delivered.

(e) A landlord, not later than the 30th day after the effective date of the termination of a lease under this section, shall refund to the residential tenant terminating the lease under Subsection (b) all rent or other amounts paid in advance under the lease for any period after the effective date of the termination of the lease.

(f) Except as provided by Subsection (g), this section does not affect a tenant's liability for delinquent, unpaid rent or other sums owed to the landlord before the lease was terminated by the tenant under this section.

(g) A tenant who terminates a lease under Subsection (b) is released from all liability for any delinquent, unpaid rent owed to the landlord by the tenant on the effective date of the lease termination if the lease does not contain language substantially equivalent to the following:

"Tenants may have special statutory rights to terminate the lease early in certain situations involving family violence or a military deployment or transfer."

(h) A landlord who violates this section is liable to the tenant for actual damages, a civil penalty in an amount equal to the amount of one month's rent plus $500, and attorney's fees.

(i) Except as provided by Subsection (j), a tenant's right to terminate a lease before the end of the lease term, vacate the dwelling, and avoid liability under this section may not be waived by a tenant.

(j) A tenant and a landlord may agree that the tenant waives a tenant's rights under this section if the tenant or any dependent living with the tenant moves into base housing or other housing within 30 miles of the dwelling. A waiver under this section must be signed and in writing in a document separate from the lease and must comply with federal law. A waiver under this section does not apply if:

(1) the tenant or the tenant's dependent moves into housing owned or occupied by family or relatives of the tenant or the tenant's dependent; or

(2) the tenant and the tenant's dependent move, wholly or partly, because of a significant financial loss of income caused by the tenant's military service.

(k) For purposes of Subsection (j), "significant financial loss of income" means a reduction of 10 percent or more of the tenant's household income caused by the tenant's military service. A landlord is entitled to verify the significant financial loss of income in order to determine whether a tenant is entitled to terminate a lease if the tenant has signed a waiver under this section and moves within 30 miles of the dwelling into housing that is not owned or occupied by family or relatives of the tenant or the tenant's dependent. For purposes of this subsection, a pay stub or other statement of earnings issued by the tenant's employer is sufficient verification.

History of Prop. Code §92.017: Acts 2005, 79th Leg., ch. 348, §1, eff. Jan. 1, 2006.

PROP §92.018. LIABILITY OF TENANT FOR GOVERNMENTAL FINES

(a) In this section, "governmental entity" means the state, an agency of the state, or a political subdivision of the state.

(b) A landlord or a landlord's manager or agent may not charge or seek reimbursement from the landlord's tenant for the amount of a fine imposed on the landlord by a governmental entity unless the tenant or another occupant of the tenant's dwelling actually caused the damage or other condition on which the fine is based.

History of Prop. Code §92.018: Acts 2005, 79th Leg., ch. 1344, §1, eff. June 18, 2005. Renumbered from §92.016 by Acts 2007, 80th Leg., ch. 921, §17.001(64), eff. Sept. 1, 2007.

PROP §92.019. LATE PAYMENT OF RENT; FEES

(a) A landlord may not charge a tenant a late fee for failing to pay rent unless:

(1) notice of the fee is included in a written lease;

(2) the fee is a reasonable estimate of uncertain damages to the landlord that are incapable of precise calculation and result from late payment of rent; and

(3) the rent has remained unpaid one full day after the date the rent was originally due.

(b) A late fee under this section may include an initial fee and a daily fee for each day the rent continues to remain unpaid.

WAIVER

(c) A landlord who violates this section is liable to the tenant for an amount equal to the sum of $100, three times the amount of the late fee charged in violation of this section, and the tenant's reasonable attorney's fees.

(d) A provision of a lease that purports to waive a right or exempt a party from a liability or duty under this section is void.

(e) This section relates only to a fee, charge, or other sum of money required to be paid under the lease if rent is not paid as provided by Subsection (a)(3), and does not affect the landlord's right to terminate the lease or take other action permitted by the lease or other law. Payment of the fee, charge, or other sum of money by a tenant does not waive the right or remedies provided by this section.

History of Prop. Code §92.019: Acts 2007, 80th Leg., ch. 917, §3, eff. Jan. 1, 2008. Amended by Acts 2009, 81st Leg., ch. 1268, §1, eff. June 19, 2009.

PROP §92.020. EMERGENCY PHONE NUMBER

(a) A landlord that has an on-site management or superintendent's office for a residential rental property must provide to a tenant a telephone number that will be answered 24 hours a day for the purpose of reporting emergencies related to a condition of the leased premises that materially affects the physical health or safety of an ordinary tenant.

(b) The landlord must post the phone number required by Subsection (a) prominently outside the management or superintendent's office.

(c) This section does not apply to or affect a local ordinance governing a landlord's obligation to provide a 24-hour emergency contact number to a tenant that is adopted before January 1, 2008, if the ordinance conforms with or is amended to conform with this section.

(d) A landlord to whom Subsection (a) does not apply must provide to a tenant a telephone number for the purpose of reporting emergencies described by that subsection.

History of Prop. Code §92.020: Acts 2007, 80th Leg., ch. 917, §4, eff. Jan. 1, 2008.

PROP §92.021. LIABILITY OF CERTAIN GUARANTORS UNDER LEASE

(a) A person other than a tenant who guarantees a lease is liable only for the original lease term except that a person may specify that the person agrees to guarantee a renewal of the lease as provided by Subsection (b).

(b) A person may specify in writing in an original lease that the person will guarantee a renewal of the lease only if the original lease states:

(1) the last date, as specified by the guarantor, on which the renewal of the lease will renew the obligation of the guarantor;

(2) that the guarantor is liable under a renewal of the lease that occurs on or before that date; and

(3) that the guarantor is liable under a renewal of the lease only if the renewal:

(A) involves the same parties as the original lease; and

(B) does not increase the guarantor's potential financial obligation for rent that existed under the original lease.

(c) Subsection (b) does not prohibit a guarantor from voluntarily entering into an agreement at the time of the renewal of a lease, in a separate written document, to guarantee an increased amount of rent.

(d) This section does not release a guarantor from the obligations of the guarantor under the terms of the original lease or a valid renewal for costs and damages owed to the lessor that arise after the date specified by the guarantor in the original lease in accordance with Subsection (b), if the costs or damages relate to actions of the tenant before that date or arise as a result of the tenant refusing to vacate the leased premises.

History of Prop. Code §92.021: Acts 2009, 81st Leg., ch. 601, §1, eff. Jan. 1, 2010.

See also *Real Estate Forms*, FORM 2:18.

Section 92.022 blank

PROP §92.023. TENANT'S REMEDIES REGARDING REVOCATION OF CERTIFICATE OF OCCUPANCY

If a municipality or a county revokes a certificate of occupancy for a leased premises because of the landlord's failure to maintain the premises, the landlord is liable to a tenant who is not in default under the lease for:

(1) the full amount of the tenant's security deposit;

(2) the pro rata portion of any rental payment the tenant has paid in advance;

(3) the tenant's actual damages, including any moving costs, utility connection fees, storage fees, and lost wages; and

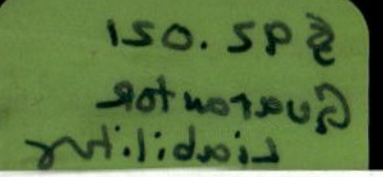

(4) court costs and attorney's fees arising from any related cause of action by the tenant against the landlord.

History of Prop. Code §92.023: Acts 2011, 82nd Leg., ch. 512, §1, eff. Sept. 1, 2011.

PROP §92.024. LANDLORD'S DUTY TO PROVIDE COPY OF LEASE

(a) Not later than the third business day after the date the lease is signed by each party to the lease, a landlord shall provide at least one complete copy of the lease to at least one tenant who is a party to the lease.

(b) If more than one tenant is a party to the lease, not later than the third business day after the date a landlord receives a written request for a copy of a lease from a tenant who has not received a copy of the lease under Subsection (a), the landlord shall provide one complete copy of the lease to the requesting tenant.

(c) A landlord's failure to provide a complete copy of the lease as described by Subsection (a) or (b) does not invalidate the lease or, subject to Subsection (d), prevent the landlord from prosecuting or defending a legal action or proceeding to enforce the lease.

(d) A landlord may not continue to prosecute and a court shall abate an action to enforce the lease, other than an action for nonpayment of rent, only until the landlord provides to a tenant a complete copy of the lease if the tenant submits to the court evidence in a plea in abatement or otherwise that the landlord failed to comply with Subsection (a) or (b).

(e) A landlord may comply with this section by providing to a tenant a complete copy of the lease:

(1) in a paper format;

(2) in an electronic format if requested by the tenant; or

(3) by e-mail if the parties have communicated by e-mail regarding the lease.

History of Prop. Code §92.024: Acts 2013, 83rd Leg., ch. 588, §1, eff. Jan. 1, 2014.

A PROP §92.025. LIABILITY FOR LEASING TO PERSON WITH CRIMINAL RECORD

(a) A cause of action does not accrue against a landlord or a landlord's manager or agent solely for leasing a dwelling to a tenant convicted of, or arrested or placed on deferred adjudication for, an offense.

(b) This section does not preclude a cause of action for negligence in leasing of a dwelling by a landlord or a landlord's manager or agent to a tenant, if:

(1) the tenant:

(A) was convicted of an offense listed in [~~Section 3g,~~] Article 42A.054 [~~42.12~~], Code of Criminal Procedure; or

(B) has a reportable conviction or adjudication, as defined by Article 62.001, Code of Criminal Procedure; and

(2) the person against whom the action is filed knew or should have known of the conviction or adjudication.

(c) This section does not create a cause of action or expand an existing cause of action.

History of Prop. Code §92.025: Acts 2015, 84th Leg., ch. 651, §1, eff. Jan. 1, 2016. Amended by S.B. 1488, §23.011, 85th Leg., eff. Sept. 1, 2017.

Sections 92.026-92.050 reserved for expansion

SUBCHAPTER B. REPAIR OR CLOSING OF LEASEHOLD

PROP §92.051. APPLICATION

This subchapter applies to a lease executed, entered into, renewed, or extended on or after September 1, 1979.

History of Prop. Code §92.051: Acts 1983, 68th Leg., ch. 576, §1, eff. Jan. 1, 1984. Source: TRCS art. 5236f, §17.

PROP §92.052. LANDLORD'S DUTY TO REPAIR OR REMEDY

(a) A landlord shall make a diligent effort to repair or remedy a condition if:

(1) the tenant specifies the condition in a notice to the person to whom or to the place where rent is normally paid;

(2) the tenant is not delinquent in the payment of rent at the time notice is given; and

(3) the condition:

(A) materially affects the physical health or safety of an ordinary tenant; or

(B) arises from the landlord's failure to provide and maintain in good operating condition a device to supply hot water of a minimum temperature of 120 degrees Fahrenheit.

(b) Unless the condition was caused by normal wear and tear, the landlord does not have a duty during the lease term or a renewal or extension to repair or remedy a condition caused by:

(1) the tenant;

(2) a lawful occupant in the tenant's dwelling;

(3) a member of the tenant's family; or

(4) the landlord has had a reasonable time to repair or remedy the condition after the landlord received the tenant's notice under Subdivision (1) and, if applicable, the tenant's subsequent notice under Subdivision (3);

(5) the landlord has not made a diligent effort to repair or remedy the condition after the landlord received the tenant's notice under Subdivision (1) and, if applicable, the tenant's notice under Subdivision (3); and

(6) the tenant was not delinquent in the payment of rent at the time any notice required by this subsection was given.

(c) For purposes of Subsection (b)(4) or (5), a landlord is considered to have received the tenant's notice when the landlord or the landlord's agent or employee has actually received the notice or when the United States Postal Service has attempted to deliver the notice to the landlord.

(d) For purposes of Subsection (b)(3) or (4), in determining whether a period of time is a reasonable time to repair or remedy a condition, there is a rebuttable presumption that seven days is a reasonable time. To rebut that presumption, the date on which the landlord received the tenant's notice, the severity and nature of the condition, and the reasonable availability of materials and labor and of utilities from a utility company must be considered.

(e) Except as provided in Subsection (f), a tenant to whom a landlord is liable under Subsection (b) of this section may:

(1) terminate the lease;

(2) have the condition repaired or remedied according to Section 92.0561;

(3) deduct from the tenant's rent, without necessity of judicial action, the cost of the repair or remedy according to Section 92.0561; and

(4) obtain judicial remedies according to Section 92.0563.

(f) A tenant who elects to terminate the lease under Subsection (e) is:

(1) entitled to a pro rata refund of rent from the date of termination or the date the tenant moves out, whichever is later;

(2) entitled to deduct the tenant's security deposit from the tenant's rent without necessity of lawsuit or obtain a refund of the tenant's security deposit according to law; and

(3) not entitled to the other repair and deduct remedies under Section 92.0561 or the judicial remedies under Subdivisions (1) and (2) of Subsection (a) of Section 92.0563.

(g) A lease must contain language in underlined or bold print that informs the tenant of the remedies available under this section and Section 92.0561.

History of Prop. Code §92.056: Acts 1983, 68th Leg., ch. 576, §1, eff. Jan. 1, 1984. Amended by Acts 1989, 71st Leg., ch. 650, §5, eff. Aug. 28, 1989; Acts 1997, 75th Leg., ch. 1205, §11, eff. Jan. 1, 1998; Acts 2007, 80th Leg., ch. 917, §5, eff. Jan. 1, 2008; Acts 2015, 84th Leg., ch. 1198, §4, eff. Jan. 1, 2016. Source: TRCS art. 5236f, §§3, 5, 6, 10.

See also Prop. Code §92.166; *O'Connor's Texas COA*, "Tenant's Elements," ch. 16-F, §2, p. 461.

PROP §92.0561. TENANT'S REPAIR & DEDUCT REMEDIES

(a) If the landlord is liable to the tenant under Section 92.056(b), the tenant may have the condition repaired or remedied and may deduct the cost from a subsequent rent payment as provided in this section.

(b) The tenant's deduction for the cost of the repair or remedy may not exceed the amount of one month's rent under the lease or $500, whichever is greater. However, if the tenant's rent is subsidized in whole or in part by a governmental agency, the deduction limitation of one month's rent shall mean the fair market rent for the dwelling and not the rent that the tenant pays. The fair market rent shall be determined by the governmental agency subsidizing the rent, or in the absence of such a determination, it shall be a reasonable amount of rent under the circumstances.

(c) Repairs and deductions under this section may be made as often as necessary so long as the total repairs and deductions in any one month do not exceed one month's rent or $500, whichever is greater.

Repairs if:

(d) Repairs under this section may be made only if all of the following requirements are met:

(1) The landlord has a duty to repair or remedy the condition under Section 92.052, and the duty has not been waived in a written lease by the tenant under Subsection (e) or (f) of Section 92.006.

(2) The tenant has given notice to the landlord as required by Section 92.056(b)(1), and, if required, a subsequent notice under Section 92.056(b)(3), and at least one of those notices states that the tenant intends to repair or remedy the condition. The notice shall also contain a reasonable description of the intended repair or remedy.

(3) Any one of the following events has occurred:

(A) The landlord has failed to remedy the backup or overflow of raw sewage inside the tenant's dwelling or the flooding from broken pipes or natural drainage inside the dwelling.

(B) The landlord has expressly or impliedly agreed in the lease to furnish potable water to the tenant's dwelling and the water service to the dwelling has totally ceased.

(C) The landlord has expressly or impliedly agreed in the lease to furnish heating or cooling equipment; the equipment is producing inadequate heat or cooled air; and the landlord has been notified in writing by the appropriate local housing, building, or health official or other official having jurisdiction that the lack of heat or cooling materially affects the health or safety of an ordinary tenant.

(D) The landlord has been notified in writing by the appropriate local housing, building, or health official or other official having jurisdiction that the condition materially affects the health or safety of an ordinary tenant.

T may...

(e) If the requirements of Subsection (d) of this section are met, a tenant may:

(1) have the condition repaired or remedied immediately following the tenant's notice of intent to repair if the condition involves sewage or flooding as referred to in Paragraph (A) of Subdivision (3) of Subsection (d) of this section;

(2) have the condition repaired or remedied if the condition involves a cessation of potable water as referred to in Paragraph (A) of Subdivision (3) of Subsection (d) of this section and if the landlord has failed to repair or remedy the condition within three days following the tenant's delivery of notice of intent to repair;

(3) have the condition repaired or remedied if the condition involves inadequate heat or cooled air as referred to in Paragraph (C) of Subdivision (3) of Subsection (d) of this section and if the landlord has failed to repair the condition within three days after delivery of the tenant's notice of intent to repair; or

(4) have the condition repaired or remedied if the condition is not covered by Paragraph (A), (B), or (C) of Subdivision (3) of Subsection (d) of this section and involves a condition affecting the physical health or safety of the ordinary tenant as referred to in Paragraph (D) of Subdivision (3) of Subsection (d) of this section and if the landlord has failed to repair or remedy the condition within seven days after delivery of the tenant's notice of intent to repair.

(f) Repairs made pursuant to the tenant's notice must be made by a company, contractor, or repairman listed in the yellow or business pages of the telephone directory or in the classified advertising section of a newspaper of the local city, county, or adjacent county at the time of the tenant's notice of intent to repair. Unless the landlord and tenant agree otherwise under Subsection (g) of this section, repairs may not be made by the tenant, the tenant's immediate family, the tenant's employer or employees, or a company in which the tenant has an ownership interest. Repairs may not be made to the foundation or load-bearing structural elements of the building if it contains two or more dwelling units.

(g) A landlord and a tenant may mutually agree for the tenant to repair or remedy, at the landlord's expense, any condition of the dwelling regardless of whether it materially affects the health or safety of an ordinary tenant. However, the landlord's duty to repair or remedy conditions covered by this subchapter may not be waived except as provided by Subsection (e) or (f) of Section 92.006.

(h) Repairs made pursuant to the tenant's notice must be made in compliance with applicable building codes, including a building permit when required.

(i) The tenant shall not have authority to contract for labor or materials in excess of what the tenant may deduct under this section. The landlord is not liable to repairmen, contractors, or material suppliers who fur-

nish labor or materials to repair or remedy the condition. A repairman or supplier shall not have a lien for materials or services arising out of repairs contracted for by the tenant under this section.

(j) When deducting the cost of repairs from the rent payment, the tenant shall furnish the landlord, along with payment of the balance of the rent, a copy of the repair bill and the receipt for its payment. A repair bill and receipt may be the same document.

(k) If the landlord repairs or remedies the condition or delivers an affidavit for delay under Section 92.0562 to the tenant after the tenant has contacted a repairman but before the repairman commences work, the landlord shall be liable for the cost incurred by the tenant for the repairman's trip charge, and the tenant may deduct the charge from the tenant's rent as if it were a repair cost.

History of Prop. Code §92.0561: Acts 1989, 71st Leg., ch. 650, §6, eff. Aug. 28, 1989. Amended by Acts 1997, 75th Leg., ch. 1205, §12, eff. Jan. 1, 1998.

ANNOTATIONS

Bockelmann v. Marynick, 788 S.W.2d 569, 570 (Tex.1990). "The issue in this appeal of a landlord-tenant dispute is whether a tenant who has vacated the leased premises before the end of the term is liable for rent and repairs accruing during a cotenant's holdover tenancy. [We hold] one tenant is not jointly liable for the holding over of another." *But see* ***Clark v. Whitehead***, 874 S.W.2d 282, 283-84 (Tex.App.—Houston [1st Dist.] 1994, writ denied) (guarantor liable for unpaid property taxes).

PROP §92.0562. LANDLORD AFFIDAVIT FOR DELAY

(a) The tenant must delay contracting for repairs under Section 92.0561 if, before the tenant contracts for the repairs, the landlord delivers to the tenant an affidavit, signed and sworn to under oath by the landlord or his authorized agent and complying with this section.

(b) The affidavit must summarize the reasons for the delay and the diligent efforts made by the landlord up to the date of the affidavit to get the repairs done. The affidavit must state facts showing that the landlord has made and is making diligent efforts to repair the condition, and it must contain dates, names, addresses, and telephone numbers of contractors, suppliers, and repairmen contacted by the owner.

(c) Affidavits under this section may delay repair by the tenant for:

(1) 15 days if the landlord's failure to repair is caused by a delay in obtaining necessary parts for which the landlord is not at fault; or

(2) 30 days if the landlord's failure to repair is caused by a general shortage of labor or materials for repair following a natural disaster such as a hurricane, tornado, flood, extended freeze, or widespread windstorm.

(d) Affidavits for delay based on grounds other than those listed in Subsection (c) of this section are unlawful, and if used, they are of no effect. The landlord may file subsequent affidavits, provided that the total delay of the repair or remedy extends no longer than six months from the date the landlord delivers the first affidavit to the tenant.

(e) The affidavit must be delivered to the tenant by any of the following methods:

(1) personal delivery to the tenant;

(2) certified mail, return receipt requested, to the tenant; or

(3) leaving the notice inside the dwelling in a conspicuous place if notice in that manner is authorized in a written lease.

(f) Affidavits for delay by a landlord under this section must be submitted in good faith. Following delivery of the affidavit, the landlord must continue diligent efforts to repair or remedy the condition. There shall be a rebuttable presumption that the landlord acted in good faith and with continued diligence for the first affidavit for delay the landlord delivers to the tenant. The landlord shall have the burden of pleading and proving good faith and continued diligence for subsequent affidavits for delay. A landlord who violates this section shall be liable to the tenant for all judicial remedies under Section 92.0563 except that the civil penalty under Subdivision (3) of Subsection (a) of Section 92.0563 shall be one month's rent plus $1,000.

(g) If the landlord is liable to the tenant under Section 92.056 and if a new landlord, in good faith and without knowledge of the tenant's notice of intent to repair, has acquired title to the tenant's dwelling by foreclosure, deed in lieu of foreclosure, or general warranty deed in a bona fide purchase, then the following shall apply:

(1) The tenant's right to terminate the lease under this subchapter shall not be affected, and the tenant shall have no duty to give additional notice to the new landlord.

(2) The tenant's right to repair and deduct for conditions involving sewage backup or overflow, flooding inside the dwelling, or a cutoff of potable water under Subsection (e) of Section 92.0561 shall not be affected, and the tenant shall have no duty to give additional notice to the new landlord.

(3) For conditions other than those specified in Subdivision (2) of this subsection, if the new landlord acquires title as described in this subsection and has notified the tenant of the name and address of the new landlord or the new landlord's authorized agent and if the tenant has not already contracted for the repair or remedy at the time the tenant is so notified, the tenant must deliver to the new landlord a written notice of intent to repair or remedy the condition, and the new landlord shall have a reasonable time to complete the repair before the tenant may repair or remedy the condition. No further notice from the tenant is necessary in order for the tenant to repair or remedy the condition after a reasonable time has elapsed.

(4) The tenant's judicial remedies under Section 92.0563 shall be limited to recovery against the landlord to whom the tenant gave the required notices until the tenant has given the new landlord the notices required by this section and otherwise complied with Section 92.056 as to the new landlord.

(5) If the new landlord violates this subsection, the new landlord is liable to the tenant for a civil penalty of one month's rent plus $2,000, actual damages, and attorney's fees.

(6) No provision of this section shall affect any right of a foreclosing superior lienholder to terminate, according to law, any interest in the premises held by the holders of subordinate liens, encumbrances, leases, or other interests and shall not affect any right of the tenant to terminate the lease according to law.

History of Prop. Code §92.0562: Acts 1989, 71st Leg., ch. 650, §7, eff. Aug. 28, 1989.

PROP §92.0563. TENANT'S JUDICIAL REMEDIES

(a) A tenant's judicial remedies under Section 92.056 shall include:

(1) an order directing the landlord to take reasonable action to repair or remedy the condition;

(2) an order reducing the tenant's rent, from the date of the first repair notice, in proportion to the reduced rental value resulting from the condition until the condition is repaired or remedied;

(3) a judgment against the landlord for a civil penalty of one month's rent plus $500;

(4) a judgment against the landlord for the amount of the tenant's actual damages; and

(5) court costs and attorney's fees, excluding any attorney's fees for a cause of action for damages relating to a personal injury.

(b) A landlord who knowingly violates Section 92.006 by contracting orally or in writing with a tenant to waive the landlord's duty to repair under this subchapter shall be liable to the tenant for actual damages, a civil penalty of one month's rent plus $2,000, and reasonable attorney's fees. For purposes of this subsection, there shall be a rebuttable presumption that the landlord acted without knowledge of the violation. The tenant shall have the burden of pleading and proving a knowing violation. If the lease is in writing and is not in violation of Section 92.006, the tenant's proof of a knowing violation must be clear and convincing. A mutual agreement for tenant repair under Subsection (g) of Section 92.0561 is not a violation of Section 92.006.

(c) The justice, county, and district courts have concurrent jurisdiction in an action under Subsection (a).

(d) Repealed by Tex.Sup.Ct. Order, Misc. Docket No. 13-9049 (eff. Aug. 31, 2013).

(e) A justice court may not award a judgment under this section, including an order of repair, that exceeds $10,000, excluding interest and costs of court.

(f) An appeal of a judgment of a justice court under this section takes precedence in county court and may be held at any time after the eighth day after the date the transcript is filed in the county court. An owner of real property who files a notice of appeal of a judgment of a justice court to the county court perfects the owner's appeal and stays the effect of the judgment without the necessity of posting an appeal bond.

History of Prop. Code §92.0563: Acts 1989, 71st Leg., ch. 650, §8, eff. Aug. 28, 1989. Amended by Acts 2009, 81st Leg., ch. 225, §1, eff. Jan. 1, 2010.

See also Prop. Code §§92.260, 94.159; TRCP 500-507, 509; *O'Connor's Texas COA*, "Judicial remedies," ch. 16-F, §3.1, p. 464.

PROP §92.057. RENUMBERED

Renumbered as §§92.331-92.334 by Acts 1995, 74th Leg., ch. 869, §5, eff. Jan. 1, 1996.

PROP §92.058. LANDLORD REMEDY FOR TENANT VIOLATION

(a) If the tenant withholds rents, causes repairs to be performed, or makes rent deductions for repairs in

violation of this subchapter, the landlord may recover actual damages from the tenant. If, after a landlord has notified a tenant in writing of (1) the illegality of the tenant's rent withholding or the tenant's proposed repair and (2) the penalties of this subchapter, the tenant withholds rent, causes repairs to be performed, or makes rent deductions for repairs in bad faith violation of this subchapter, the landlord may recover from the tenant a civil penalty of one month's rent plus $500.

(b) Notice under this section must be in writing and may be given in person, by mail, or by delivery to the premises.

(c) The landlord has the burden of pleading and proving, by clear and convincing evidence, that the landlord gave the tenant the required notice of the illegality and the penalties and that the tenant's violation was done in bad faith. In any litigation under this subsection, the prevailing party shall recover reasonable attorney's fees from the nonprevailing party.

History of Prop. Code §92.058: Acts 1983, 68th Leg., ch. 576, §1, eff. Jan. 1, 1984. Amended by Acts 1989, 71st Leg., ch. 650, §10, eff. Aug. 28, 1989. Source: TRCS art. 5236f, §8.

See also *O'Connor's Texas COA*, "Tenant violated subchapter B," ch. 16-F, §5.2.1, p. 467.

PROP §92.059. RENUMBERED

Renumbered as §92.335 by Acts 1995, 74th Leg., ch. 869, §5, eff. Jan. 1, 1996.

PROP §92.060. AGENTS FOR DELIVERY OF NOTICE

A managing agent, leasing agent, or resident manager is the agent of the landlord for purposes of notice and other communications required or permitted by this subchapter.

History of Prop. Code §92.060: Acts 1983, 68th Leg., ch. 576, §1, eff. Jan. 1, 1984. Source: TRCS art. 5236f, §1.

PROP §92.061. EFFECT ON OTHER RIGHTS

The duties of a landlord and the remedies of a tenant under this subchapter are in lieu of existing common law and other statutory law warranties and duties of landlords for maintenance, repair, security, habitability, and nonretaliation, and remedies of tenants for a violation of those warranties and duties. Otherwise, this subchapter does not affect any other right of a landlord or tenant under contract, statutory law, or common law that is consistent with the purposes of this subchapter or any right a landlord or tenant may have to bring an action for personal injury or property damage under the law of this state. This subchapter does not impose obligations on a landlord or tenant other than those expressly stated in this subchapter.

History of Prop. Code §92.061: Acts 1983, 68th Leg., ch. 576, §1, eff. Jan. 1, 1984. Amended by Acts 1985, 69th Leg., ch. 200, §5, eff. Aug. 26, 1985. Source: TRCS art. 5236f, §14.

ANNOTATIONS

Churchill Forge, Inc. v. Brown, 61 S.W.3d 368, 372 (Tex.2001). "[B]ecause under Subch. B landlords have no duty to repair or pay to repair tenant-caused damage, and tenants have no remedy for such damage, §92.061 makes clear that the Legislature did not intend the Subchapter to otherwise affect the parties' presumptive right to contract over who would be responsible for conditions caused by the tenant, the tenant's occupant, or guest."

Timberwalk Apts., Partners v. Cain, 972 S.W.2d 749, 754 (Tex.1998). "Hardly a model of clarity, §92.061 appears self-contradictory. The first sentence preempts landlords' common law duties 'for maintenance, repair, security, habitability, and nonretaliation,' while the second sentence 'otherwise' preserves tenants' rights to sue for personal injuries under the common law. The first sentence read literally makes the second sentence entirely superfluous. The only actions not preempted would be those not covered by the first sentence. But the second sentence appears to suggest that the preemptive effect of the first sentence is limited. *At 755:* It ... appears that subch. B was intended to govern disputes between a landlord and a tenant over repairs and not liability for personal injuries resulting from premises defects actionable under the common law. Viewed in light of the statute's purpose, the first two sentences of §92.061 are reconciled by limiting their preemptive effect to such matters comprehended within the implied warranty of habitability ***Kamarath*** [***v. Bennett***, 568 S.W.2d 658 (Tex.1978),] recognized." *See also* ***Moreno v. Brittany Square Assocs.***, 899 S.W.2d 261, 263 (Tex.App.—Houston [14th Dist.] 1995, writ denied).

Richardson v. Bigelow Mgmt., No. 05-06-00213-CV (Tex.App.—Dallas 2007, no pet.) (memo op.; 4-18-07). Held: Section 92.061 does not apply to a hotel or motel guest.

Bolin Dev. Corp. v. Indart, 803 S.W.2d 817, 820 (Tex.App.—Houston [14th Dist.] 1991), *writ denied*, 814 S.W.2d 750 (Tex.1991). "[T]enants seeking property damages may bring a negligence cause of action

against the landlord. Accordingly, no action for breach of the common law implied warranty of habitability exists for recovery of property damages."

PROP §92.062. LEASE TERM AFTER NATURAL DISASTER

If a rental premises is, as a practical matter, totally unusable for residential purposes as a result of a natural disaster such as a hurricane, tornado, flood, extended freeze, or widespread windstorm, a landlord that allows a tenant to move to another rental unit owned by the landlord may not require the tenant to execute a lease for a term longer than the term remaining on the tenant's lease on the date the premises was rendered unusable as a result of the natural disaster.

History of Prop. Code §92.062: Acts 2013, 83rd Leg., ch. 475, §1, eff. Jan. 1, 2014.

Sections 92.063-92.100 reserved for expansion

SUBCHAPTER C. SECURITY DEPOSITS

PROP §92.101. APPLICATION

This subchapter applies to all residential leases.

History of Prop. Code §92.101: Acts 1983, 68th Leg., ch. 576, §1, eff. Jan. 1, 1984. Amended by Acts 1995, 74th Leg., ch. 744, §1, eff. Jan. 1, 1996. Source: TRCS art. 5236e, §11.

PROP §92.102. SECURITY DEPOSIT

A security deposit is any advance of money, other than a rental application deposit or an advance payment of rent, that is intended primarily to secure performance under a lease of a dwelling that has been entered into by a landlord and a tenant.

History of Prop. Code §92.102: Acts 1983, 68th Leg., ch. 576, §1, eff. Jan. 1, 1984. Amended by Acts 1995, 74th Leg., ch. 744, §2, eff. Jan. 1, 1996. Source: TRCS art. 5236e, §1.

PROP §92.103. OBLIGATION TO REFUND

(a) Except as provided by Section 92.107, the landlord shall refund a security deposit to the tenant on or before the 30th day after the date the tenant surrenders the premises.

(b) A requirement that a tenant give advance notice of surrender as a condition for refunding the security deposit is effective only if the requirement is underlined or is printed in conspicuous bold print in the lease.

(c) The tenant's claim to the security deposit takes priority over the claim of any creditor of the landlord, including a trustee in bankruptcy.

History of Prop. Code §92.103: Acts 1983, 68th Leg., ch. 576, §1, eff. Jan. 1, 1984. Amended by Acts 1995, 74th Leg., ch. 744, §3, eff. Jan. 1, 1996. Source: TRCS art. 5236e, §2(a), (b).

ANNOTATIONS

Marino v. Hartfield, 877 S.W.2d 508, 510 (Tex. App.—Beaumont 1994, writ denied). "On August 1, 1989, [tenant] delivered to [landlord] a notice of his intent to vacate the house as of August 31, 1989. ... On Monday, September 4, 1989, [landlord], having become impatient with [tenants'] failure to vacate the premises and return the keys, hired a locksmith to change the locks and then had [tenants'] possessions removed. Following [tenants'] involuntary surrender of the premises on September 4, 1989, [landlord] spent in excess of the amount of the security deposit in repairing the damage done to her house by [tenants] and their children. On October 4, 1989, [landlord] provided appellants an itemization of the deductions to the security deposit. *At 512:* The record supports that fact that [landlord] regained possession of the premises on September 4, 1989. A finding that [landlord] supplied the required itemization of charges to the security deposit within 30 days following surrender of possession should have and apparently was deemed by the trial court." *See also* ***Minor v. Adams***, this page.

Reed v. Ford, 760 S.W.2d 26, 28 (Tex.App.—Dallas 1988, no writ). "Tenant did not give written notice of intent to vacate on or before May 14, 1986, being the 30th day before expiration of the initial term. Neither did Owner notify Tenant of any intent not to renew. However, after May 14, the parties began negotiating a possible renewal of the lease for another year. Although they had not agreed on a new lease before the termination date, June 14, 1986, Tenant remained in the house, and Owner accepted from him a check for rent through June 30, 1986. *At 29:* [T]enant's failure to give notice on May 14th did not authorize Owner to retain Tenant's deposit. Instead, the lease was automatically renewed, and Tenant was entitled to a refund of the entire deposit so long as he gave 30 days' written notice before terminating the resultant month-to-month tenancy. Because Owner's subsequent demand prevented Tenant from fulfilling his 30-day notice requirement, we treat the notice requirement as fulfilled. Owner does not dispute that Tenant fulfilled the other requirements for a refund of his entire deposit. We hold that after complying with a demand that he vacate, Tenant was entitled to a refund of his security deposit."

Minor v. Adams, 694 S.W.2d 148, 151 (Tex.App.—Houston [14th Dist.] 1985, no writ). The court con-

strued the 30-day requirement of Prop. Code §92.103 and the forwarding-address requirement in Prop. Code §92.107 together "to mean that the landlord has no more than 30 days after receiving the forwarding address to refund the deposit." *See also* ***Marino v. Hartfield***, p. 458.

PROP §92.1031. CONDITIONS FOR RETENTION OF SECURITY DEPOSIT OR RENT PREPAYMENT

(a) Except as provided in Subsection (b), a landlord who receives a security deposit or rent prepayment for a dwelling from a tenant who fails to occupy the dwelling according to a lease between the landlord and the tenant may not retain the security deposit or rent prepayment if:

(1) the tenant secures a replacement tenant satisfactory to the landlord and the replacement tenant occupies the dwelling on or before the commencement date of the lease; or

(2) the landlord secures a replacement tenant satisfactory to the landlord and the replacement tenant occupies the dwelling on or before the commencement date of the lease.

(b) If the landlord secures the replacement tenant, the landlord may retain and deduct from the security deposit or rent prepayment either:

(1) a sum agreed to in the lease as a lease cancellation fee; or

(2) actual expenses incurred by the landlord in securing the replacement, including a reasonable amount for the time of the landlord in securing the replacement tenant.

History of Prop. Code §92.1031: Acts 1995, 74th Leg., ch. 869, §13, eff. Jan. 1, 1996.

PROP §92.104. RETENTION OF SECURITY DEPOSIT; ACCOUNTING

(a) Before returning a security deposit, the landlord may deduct from the deposit damages and charges for which the tenant is legally liable under the lease or as a result of breaching the lease.

(b) The landlord may not retain any portion of a security deposit to cover normal wear and tear.

(c) If the landlord retains all or part of a security deposit under this section, the landlord shall give to the tenant the balance of the security deposit, if any, together with a written description and itemized list of all deductions. The landlord is not required to give the tenant a description and itemized list of deductions if:

(1) the tenant owes rent when he surrenders possession of the premises; and

(2) there is no controversy concerning the amount of rent owed.

History of Prop. Code §92.104: Acts 1983, 68th Leg., ch. 576, §1, eff. Jan. 1, 1984. Source: TRCS art. 5236e, §3(a), (b).

See also Prop. Code §§91.004, 92.109, 93.006, 93.011.

ANNOTATIONS

Southmark Mgmt. v. Vick, 692 S.W.2d 157, 160 (Tex.App.—Houston [1st Dist.] 1985, writ ref'd n.r.e.). Property manager induced tenant "to return to the apartment and thoroughly clean it, 'so that they didn't have to go in and clean it up and have their maids work there,' by promising to return his security deposit if he did so. By statute, [landlord] could not retain any portion of the security deposit to cover normal wear and tear. [Tenant] could have vacated the apartment, leaving the normal amount of wear and soil, without forfeiting any portion of his security. Instead, [tenant] agreed to clean the apartment to such an the extent that [landlord] actually received the benefit of his labor. If [tenant] had not cleaned the apartment as he testified, [landlord] was in a position to rebut his testimony. This it did not do. We find that there was sufficient evidence for the jury to find that [landlord], by retaining the security deposit, acted in dishonest disregard of [tenant's] rights and intentionally deprived him of the refund lawfully due to him."

PROP §92.1041. PRESUMPTION OF REFUND OR ACCOUNTING

A landlord is presumed to have refunded a security deposit or made an accounting of security deposit deductions if, on or before the date required under this subchapter, the refund or accounting is placed in the United States mail and postmarked on or before the required date.

History of Prop. Code §92.1041: Acts 1995, 74th Leg., ch. 744, §4, eff. Jan. 1, 1996.

PROP §92.105. CESSATION OF OWNER'S INTEREST

(a) If the owner's interest in the premises is terminated by sale, assignment, death, appointment of a receiver, bankruptcy, or otherwise, the new owner is liable for the return of security deposits according to this subchapter from the date title to the premises is acquired.

(b) The new owner shall deliver to the tenant a signed statement acknowledging that the new owner

has acquired the property and is responsible for the tenant's security deposit and specifying the exact dollar amount of the deposit.

(b-1) The person who no longer owns an interest in the rental premises is liable for a security deposit received while the person was the owner until the new owner has received the deposit or has assumed the liability for the deposit, unless otherwise specified by the parties in a written contract.

(c) Subsection (a) does not apply to a real estate mortgage lienholder who acquires title by foreclosure.

History of Prop. Code §92.105: Acts 1983, 68th Leg., ch. 576, §1, eff. Jan. 1, 1984. Amended by Acts 1985, 69th Leg., ch. 305, §2, eff. Aug. 26, 1985; Acts 2015, 84th Leg., ch. 1198, §5, eff. Jan. 1, 2016. Source: TRCS art. 5236e, §5.

See also Prop. Code §93.007.

ANNOTATIONS

E&E Invs. v. Strong, 593 S.W.2d 412, 413 (Tex. App.—Fort Worth 1980, no writ). "[D] asserts that its answer merely admits ownership at the time of service of process, and that the trial court improperly assumed it was the owner at the time the cause of action arose. *At 414:* [T]here is an admission by [D] that it owned the apartment complex which infers liability. … This admission coupled with the letter notifying [P] of the change in ownership is sufficient to establish that [D] was the owner at the time [P's] cause of action accrued. We do not find that the trial court merely assumed ownership. It was proper for the trial court to infer ownership from the letter coupled with the admission of ownership."

Johnson v. Huie Props., 594 S.W.2d 488, 490 (Tex. App.—Dallas 1979, no writ). Owner of apartment complex posted a notice that the apartments were being sold. The notice stated that the next month's rent and all succeeding rent payments should be made payable to the apartment complex for the credit of the new owners, that the rent deposit and pet deposit were being transferred to the new owner along with the lease agreement, and that the same lease terms will prevail and it will be necessary for tenants to live up to the terms of the lease to qualify for any deposit refund if and when they vacate the apartment. "[L]andlord contends this notice is sufficient to comply with [TRCS art. 5236e, §5(b), now Prop. Code §92.105]. [¶] While the notice may be sufficient to advise a tenant of the party to whom future rents should be paid, it falls short of the requirement of §5(b) that the new owner or his agent acknowledge *receipt of as well as responsibility for* the security deposit. In the absence of an acknowledgment of responsibility, the tenant has no cause of action against the new owner because the deposit was not paid to him. … We hold that the notice was insufficient to comply with the statute."

PROP §92.106. RECORDS

The landlord shall keep accurate records of all security deposits.

History of Prop. Code §92.106: Acts 1983, 68th Leg., ch. 576, §1, eff. Jan. 1, 1984. Source: TRCS art. 5236e, §2(b).

PROP §92.107. TENANT'S FORWARDING ADDRESS

(a) The landlord is not obligated to return a tenant's security deposit or give the tenant a written description of damages and charges until the tenant gives the landlord a written statement of the tenant's forwarding address for the purpose of refunding the security deposit.

(b) The tenant does not forfeit the right to a refund of the security deposit or the right to receive a description of damages and charges merely for failing to give a forwarding address to the landlord.

History of Prop. Code §92.107: Acts 1983, 68th Leg., ch. 576, §1, eff. Jan. 1, 1984. Source: TRCS art. 5236e, §6(a).

See also Prop. Code §§93.005, 93.009; ***Real Estate Forms***, FORM 2:6.

ANNOTATIONS

Minor v. Adams, 694 S.W.2d 148, 151 (Tex.App.—Houston [14th Dist.] 1985, no writ). See annotation under Property Code §92.103, p. 458.

Ackerman v. Little, 679 S.W.2d 70, 75 (Tex.App.—Dallas 1984, no writ). Section 92.107 "does not require the tenant to furnish … a forwarding address within 30 days of his surrender, and failure to do so does not waive any rights the tenant may have. [A] landlord shall have 30 days from the tenant's furnishing of a forwarding address to refund the deposit or provide an itemization of damages before the presumption of bad faith will arise."

Tammen v. Page, 584 S.W.2d 914, 917 (Tex.App.—Eastland 1979, writ dism'd). "We hold that a tenant may furnish the written notice through an agent or attorney and that the 'tenant's forwarding address for purposes of security deposit refunding' can be the address of the tenant's agent or attorney." *See also* ***Johnson v. Huie Props.***, 594 S.W.2d 488, 492 (Tex.App.—Dallas 1979, no writ) (letter failed as notice because no forwarding address was given); ***Michaux v. Koebig***, 555 S.W.2d 171, 175 (Tex.App.—Austin 1977, no writ) (printed ad-

dress on check given for rent is not sufficient compliance to discharge tenant's initial obligation).

PROP §92.108. LIABILITY FOR WITHHOLDING LAST MONTH'S RENT

(a) The tenant may not withhold payment of any portion of the last month's rent on grounds that the security deposit is security for unpaid rent.

(b) A tenant who violates this section is presumed to have acted in bad faith. A tenant who in bad faith violates this section is liable to the landlord for an amount equal to three times the rent wrongfully withheld and the landlord's reasonable attorney's fees in a suit to recover the rent.

History of Prop. Code §92.108: Acts 1983, 68th Leg., ch. 576, §1, eff. Jan. 1, 1984. Source: TRCS art. 5236e, §6(b).

See also CPRC §15.091; Prop. Code §93.010; ***Real Estate Forms***, FORM 2:6.

ANNOTATIONS

Shamoun v. Shough, 377 S.W.3d 63, 73 (Tex. App.—Dallas 2012, pet. denied). "The evidence was uncontroverted that Tenant did not pay the last month's rent under the lease. Tenant's own testimony provided evidence from which the jury could have found that Tenant withheld the last month's rent on grounds that the security deposit was security for unpaid rent. [¶] This evidence would also support a presumption that the statutory violation was in bad faith. *At 77:* The lease itself, on which both parties relied, showed that the amount of the monthly rent was $4,800, and the jury found that $4,800 was the amount of rent withheld by Tenant in bad faith. Therefore, under §92.108(b), the amount of damages to be awarded Landlord for Tenant's violation would be 'three times the rent wrongfully withheld,' or $14,400, plus attorney's fees."

PROP §92.109. LIABILITY OF LANDLORD

(a) A landlord who in bad faith retains a security deposit in violation of this subchapter is liable for an amount equal to the sum of $100, three times the portion of the deposit wrongfully withheld, and the tenant's reasonable attorney's fees in a suit to recover the deposit.

(b) A landlord who in bad faith does not provide a written description and itemized list of damages and charges in violation of this subchapter:

(1) forfeits the right to withhold any portion of the security deposit or to bring suit against the tenant for damages to the premises; and

(2) is liable for the tenant's reasonable attorney's fees in a suit to recover the deposit.

(c) In an action brought by a tenant under this subchapter, the landlord has the burden of proving that the retention of any portion of the security deposit was reasonable.

(d) A landlord who fails either to return a security deposit or to provide a written description and itemization of deductions on or before the 30th day after the date the tenant surrenders possession is presumed to have acted in bad faith.

History of Prop. Code §92.109: Acts 1983, 68th Leg., ch. 576, §1, eff. Jan. 1, 1984. Source: TRCS art. 5236e, §§3(a), 4.

See also Prop. Code §§92.104, 93.006, 93.011, 94.109; ***O'Connor's Texas COA***, "Security-deposit statute," ch. 6, §7.6, p. 172.

ANNOTATIONS

Johnson v. Waters at Elm Creek L.L.C., 416 S.W.3d 42, 47-48 (Tex.App.—San Antonio 2013, pet. denied). "A landlord acts in bad faith if the landlord acts in dishonest disregard of the tenant's rights or intends to deprive the tenant of a lawfully due refund. Good faith is established by showing 'honesty in fact in the conduct or transaction concerned.' 'Evidence that a landlord had reason to believe he was entitled to retain a security deposit to recover reasonable damages is sufficient to rebut the presumption of bad faith created by the Texas Property Code.' 'Other evidence may include: (1) the landlord is an amateur lessor because the residence is his only rental property; (2) the landlord had no knowledge of the requirement to submit an itemized list of all deductions from the security deposit; (3) extensive damage was done to the residence; (4) the landlord attempted to do some of the repairs himself to save money; or (5) the landlord had a reasonable excuse for the delay, e.g., he was on vacation.' [¶] If the landlord is able to defeat the presumption of bad faith with regard to the retention of a security deposit, the landlord also is required to prove that his retention of any portion of the security deposit was reasonable. 'A landlord's retention of the security deposit may be reasonable if: (1) the tenant is legally liable under the lease or as a result of breaching the lease; (2) the damages did not exist before the tenant leased the premises; or (3) the damages or charges are equal to or in excess of the security deposit or the amount deducted from the security deposit.' If the lease imposes an obligation on the tenant to pay for damage to the premises, the landlord is entitled to recover the reasonable cost of repairs. The landlord is not required to establish the

amount of damages with 'mathematical precision' but 'needs only to present sufficient evidence to justify a finding [by the trier of fact] that the costs were reasonable and the repairs were necessary.'" *See also* ***Pulley v. Milberger***, 198 S.W.3d 418, 430-31 (Tex.App.—Dallas 2006, pet. denied) (no bad faith in providing tenants written description and offering photographs as proof); ***Miro v. Garner***, 52 S.W.3d 407, 411 (Tex. App.—Corpus Christi 2001, pet. denied) (not providing sufficient evidence of damages to premises as basis for withholding deposit is bad faith).

Jones v. Falcon, 875 S.W.2d 29, 31-32 (Tex.App.—Houston [14th Dist.] 1994, writ denied). "The Property Code provides that a landlord who in bad faith retains a security deposit is liable for reasonable attorney's fees in a suit to recover the deposit. Therefore, [tenant] was not required to plead for attorney's fees in the justice court in order to plead for them on a de novo appeal to the county court." *See also* ***Crumpton v. Stevens***, 936 S.W.2d 473, 476 (Tex.App.—Fort Worth 1996, no writ). *But see* ***Kramek v. Stewart***, 648 S.W.2d 399, 401-02 (Tex.App.—San Antonio 1983, no writ) (if attorney fees not pleaded for in justice court, cannot request in county court).

Minor v. Adams, 694 S.W.2d 148, 152 (Tex.App.—Houston [14th Dist.] 1985, no writ). "The lease contained an advance notice provision, even though technically the provision did not meet the statutory requirements of being underlined or in conspicuous bold print. The tenants failed to comply with this provision despite the fact that they admittedly were aware of it and understood its meaning. Consequently, the landlords apparently felt they rightfully retained the security deposit. This behavior does not constitute a 'dishonest disregard' of the tenants' rights. [¶] [E]ven though the landlords in the instant case have *never* refunded the deposit, we find in the record evidence of a legitimate legal dispute sufficient to rebut the §92.109(d) presumption." *See also* ***Wilson v. O'Connor***, 555 S.W.2d 776, 780 (Tex.App.—Dallas 1977, writ dism'd).

PROP §92.110. LEASE WITHOUT SECURITY DEPOSIT; REQUIRED NOTICE

(a) If a security deposit was not required by a residential lease and the tenant is liable for damages and charges on surrender of the premises, the landlord shall notify the tenant in writing of the landlord's claim for damages and charges on or before the date the landlord reports the claim to a consumer reporting agency or third-party debt collector.

(b) A landlord is not required to provide the notice under Subsection (a) if the tenant has not given the landlord the tenant's forwarding address as provided by Section 92.107.

(c) If a landlord does not provide the tenant the notice as required by this section, the landlord forfeits the right to collect damages and charges from the tenant. Forfeiture of the right to collect damages and charges from the tenant is the exclusive remedy for the failure to provide the proper notice to the tenant.

History of Prop. Code §92.110: Acts 2015, 84th Leg., ch. 1198, §6, eff. Jan. 1, 2016.

Sections 92.111-92.150 reserved for expansion

SUBCHAPTER D. SECURITY DEVICES

PROP §92.151. DEFINITIONS

In this subchapter:

(1) "Doorknob lock" means a lock in a doorknob, with the lock operated from the exterior by a key, card, or combination and from the interior without a key, card, or combination.

(2) "Door viewer" means a permanently installed device in an exterior door that allows a person inside the dwelling to view a person outside the door. The device must be:

(A) a clear glass pane or one-way mirror; or

(B) a peephole having a barrel with a one-way lens of glass or other substance providing an angle view of not less than 160 degrees.

(3) "Exterior door" means a door providing access from a dwelling interior to the exterior. The term includes a door between a living area and a garage but does not include a sliding glass door or a screen door.

(4) "French doors" means a set of two exterior doors in which each door is hinged and abuts the other door when closed. The term includes double-hinged patio doors.

(5) "Keyed dead bolt" means:

(A) a door lock not in the doorknob that:

(i) locks with a bolt into the doorjamb; and

(ii) is operated from the exterior by a key, card, or combination and from the interior by a knob or lever without a key, card, or combination; or

(B) a doorknob lock that contains a bolt with at least a one-inch throw.

(6) "Keyless bolting device" means a door lock not in the doorknob that locks:

(A) with a bolt into a strike plate screwed into the portion of the doorjamb surface that faces the edge of the door when the door is closed or into a metal doorjamb that serves as the strike plate, operable only by knob or lever from the door's interior and not in any manner from the door's exterior, and that is commonly known as a keyless dead bolt;

(B) by a drop bolt system operated by placing a central metal plate over a metal doorjamb restraint that protrudes from the doorjamb and that is affixed to the doorjamb frame by means of three case-hardened screws at least three inches in length. One-half of the central plate must overlap the interior surface of the door and the other half of the central plate must overlap the doorjamb when the plate is placed over the doorjamb restraint. The drop bolt system must prevent the door from being opened unless the central plate is lifted off of the doorjamb restraint by a person who is on the interior side of the door.

The term "keyless bolting device" does not include a chain latch, flip latch, surface-mounted slide bolt, mortise door bolt, surface-mounted barrel bolt, surface-mounted swing bar door guard, spring-loaded nightlatch, foot bolt, or other lock or latch; or

(C) by a metal bar or metal tube that is placed across the entire interior side of the door and secured in place at each end of the bar or tube by heavy-duty metal screw hooks. The screw hooks must be at least three inches in length and must be screwed into the door frame stud or wall stud on each side of the door. The bar or tube must be capable of being secured to both of the screw hooks and must be permanently attached in some way to the door frame stud or wall stud. When secured to the screw hooks, the bar or tube must prevent the door from being opened unless the bar or tube is removed by a person who is on the interior side of the door.

(7) "Landlord" means a dwelling owner, lessor, sublessor, management company, or managing agent, including an on-site manager.

(8) "Multiunit complex" means two or more dwellings in one or more buildings that are:

(A) under common ownership;

(B) managed by the same owner, agent, or management company; and

(C) located on the same lot or tract or adjacent lots or tracts of land.

(9) "Possession of a dwelling" means occupancy by a tenant under a lease, including occupancy until the time the tenant moves out or a writ of possession is issued by a court. The term does not include occupancy before the initial occupancy date authorized under a lease.

(10) "Rekey" means to change or alter a security device that is operated by a key, card, or combination so that a different key, card, or combination is necessary to operate the security device.

(11) "Security device" means a doorknob lock, door viewer, keyed dead bolt, keyless bolting device, sliding door handle latch, sliding door pin lock, sliding door security bar, or window latch in a dwelling.

(12) "Sliding door handle latch" means a latch or lock:

(A) located near the handle on a sliding glass door;

(B) operated with or without a key; and

(C) designed to prevent the door from being opened.

(13) "Sliding door pin lock" means a lock on a sliding glass door that consists of a pin or nail inserted from the interior side of the door at the side opposite the door's handle and that is designed to prevent the door from being opened or lifted.

(14) "Sliding door security bar" means a bar or rod that can be placed at the bottom of or across the interior side of the fixed panel of a sliding glass door and that is designed to prevent the door from being opened.

(15) "Tenant turnover date" means the date a tenant moves into a dwelling under a lease after all previous occupants have moved out. The term does not include dates of entry or occupation not authorized by the landlord.

(16) "Window latch" means a device on a window that prevents the window from being opened and that is operated without a key and only from the interior.

History of Prop. Code §92.151: Acts 1983, 68th Leg., ch. 576, §1, eff. Jan. 1, 1984. Amended by Acts 1993, 73rd Leg., ch. 357, §3, eff. Sept. 1, 1993; Acts 1999, 76th Leg., ch. 16, §1, eff. Sept. 1, 1999. Source: TRCS art. 5236h, §1(1), (2), (6), (7), (11); former Prop. Code §92.151.

PROP §92.152. APPLICATION OF SUBCHAPTER

(a) This subchapter does not apply to:

(1) a room in a hotel, motel, or inn or to similar transient housing;

(2) residential housing owned or operated by a public or private college or university accredited by a recognized accrediting agency as defined under Section 61.003, Education Code;

(3) residential housing operated by preparatory schools accredited by the Texas Education Agency, a regional accrediting agency, or any accrediting agency recognized by the commissioner of education; or

(4) a temporary residential tenancy created by a contract for sale in which the buyer occupies the property before closing or the seller occupies the property after closing for a specific term not to exceed 90 days.

(b) Except as provided by Subsection (a), a dwelling to which this subchapter applies includes:

(1) a room in a dormitory or rooming house;

(2) a mobile home;

(3) a single family house, duplex, or triplex; and

(4) a living unit in an apartment, condominium, cooperative, or townhome project.

History of Prop. Code §92.152: Acts 1983, 68th Leg., ch. 576, §1, eff. Jan. 1, 1984. Amended by Acts 1993, 73rd Leg., ch. 357, §3, eff. Sept. 1, 1993; Acts 1995, 74th Leg., ch. 126, §1 (eff. Aug. 28, 1995), ch. 869, §2 (eff. Jan. 1, 1996).

PROP §92.153. SECURITY DEVICES REQUIRED WITHOUT NECESSITY OF TENANT REQUEST

(a) Except as provided by Subsections (b), (e), (f), (g), and (h) and without necessity of request by the tenant, a dwelling must be equipped with:

(1) a window latch on each exterior window of the dwelling;

(2) a doorknob lock or keyed dead bolt on each exterior door;

(3) a sliding door pin lock on each exterior sliding glass door of the dwelling;

(4) a sliding door handle latch or a sliding door security bar on each exterior sliding glass door of the dwelling; and

(5) a keyless bolting device and a door viewer on each exterior door of the dwelling.

(b) If the dwelling has French doors, one door of each pair of French doors must meet the requirements of Subsection (a) and the other door must have:

(1) a keyed dead bolt or keyless bolting device capable of insertion into the doorjamb above the door and a keyless bolting device capable of insertion into the floor or threshold, each with a bolt having a throw of one inch or more; or

(2) a bolt installed inside the door and operated from the edge of the door, capable of insertion into the doorjamb above the door, and another bolt installed inside the door and operated from the edge of the door capable of insertion into the floor or threshold, each bolt having a throw of three-fourths inch or more.

(c) A security device required by Subsection (a) or (b) must be installed at the landlord's expense.

(d) Subsections (a) and (b) apply only when a tenant is in possession of a dwelling.

(e) A keyless bolting device is not required to be installed at the landlord's expense on an exterior door if:

(1) the dwelling is part of a multiunit complex in which the majority of dwelling units are leased to tenants who are over 55 years of age or who have a physical or mental disability;

(2) a tenant or occupant in the dwelling is over 55 years of age or has a physical or mental disability; and

(3) the landlord is expressly required or permitted to periodically check on the well-being or health of the tenant as a part of a written lease or other written agreement.

(f) A keyless bolting device is not required to be installed at the landlord's expense if a tenant or occupant in the dwelling is over 55 years of age or has a physical or mental disability, the tenant requests, in writing, that the landlord deactivate or not install the keyless bolting device, and the tenant certifies in the request that the tenant or occupant is over 55 years of age or has a physical or mental disability. The request must be a separate document and may not be included as part of a lease agreement. A landlord is not exempt as provided by this subsection if the landlord knows or has reason to know that the requirements of this subsection are not fulfilled.

(g) A keyed dead bolt or a doorknob lock is not required to be installed at the landlord's expense on an exterior door if at the time the tenant agrees to lease the dwelling:

(1) at least one exterior door usable for normal entry into the dwelling has both a keyed dead bolt and a keyless bolting device, installed in accordance with the height, strike plate, and throw requirements of Section 92.154; and

(2) all other exterior doors have a keyless bolting device installed in accordance with the height, strike plate, and throw requirements of Section 92.154.

(h) A security device required by this section must be operable throughout the time a tenant is in possession of a dwelling. However, a landlord may deactivate or remove the locking mechanism of a doorknob lock or remove any device not qualifying as a keyless bolting device if a keyed dead bolt has been installed on the same door.

(i) A landlord is subject to the tenant remedies provided by Section 92.164(a)(4) if the landlord:

(1) deactivates or does not install a keyless bolting device, claiming an exemption under Subsection (e), (f), or (g); and

(2) knows or has reason to know that the requirements of the subsection granting the exemption are not fulfilled.

History of Prop. Code §92.153: Acts 1983, 68th Leg., ch. 576, §1, eff. Jan. 1, 1984. Amended by Acts 1993, 73rd Leg., ch. 357, §3, eff. Sept. 1, 1993; Acts 1995, 74th Leg., ch. 869, §3, eff. Jan. 1, 1996.

See also CPRC §41.005; *O'Connor's Texas COA*, "Giving notice to repair or exercising remedy," ch. 16-G, §2.2.1, p. 474.

PROP §92.154. HEIGHT, STRIKE PLATE, & THROW REQUIREMENTS—KEYED DEAD BOLT OR KEYLESS BOLTING DEVICE

(a) A keyed dead bolt or a keyless bolting device required by this subchapter must be installed at a height:

(1) not lower than 36 inches from the floor; and

(2) not higher than:

(A) 54 inches from the floor, if installed before September 1, 1993; or

(B) 48 inches from the floor, if installed on or after September 1, 1993.

(b) A keyed dead bolt or a keyless bolting device described in Section 92.151(6)(A) or (B) in a dwelling must:

(1) have a strike plate screwed into the portion of the doorjamb surface that faces the edge of the door when the door is closed; or

(2) be installed in a door with a metal doorjamb that serves as the strike plate.

(c) A keyed dead bolt or keyless dead bolt, as described by Section 92.151(6)(A), installed in a dwelling on or after September 1, 1993, must have a bolt with a throw of not less than one inch.

(d) The requirements of this section do not apply to a keyed dead bolt or a keyless bolting device in one door of a pair of French doors that is installed in accordance with the requirements of Section 92.153(b)(1) or (2).

History of Prop. Code §92.154: Acts 1983, 68th Leg., ch. 576, §1, eff. Jan. 1, 1984. Amended by Acts 1993, 73rd Leg., ch. 357, §3, eff. Sept. 1, 1993.

PROP §92.155. HEIGHT REQUIREMENTS—SLIDING DOOR SECURITY DEVICES

A sliding door pin lock or sliding door security bar required by this subchapter must be installed at a height not higher than:

(1) 54 inches from the floor, if installed before September 1, 1993; or

(2) 48 inches from the floor, if installed on or after September 1, 1993.

History of Prop. Code §92.155: Acts 1983, 68th Leg., ch. 576, §1, eff. Jan. 1, 1984. Amended by Acts 1993, 73rd Leg., ch. 357, §3, eff. Sept. 1, 1993.

PROP §92.156. REKEYING OR CHANGE OF SECURITY DEVICES

(a) Except as otherwise provided by Subsection (e), a security device operated by a key, card, or combination shall be rekeyed by the landlord at the landlord's expense not later than the seventh day after each tenant turnover date.

(b) A landlord shall perform additional rekeying or change a security device at the tenant's expense if requested by the tenant. A tenant may make an unlimited number of requests under this subsection.

(c) The expense of rekeying security devices for purposes of the use or change of the landlord's master key must be paid by the landlord.

(d) This section does not apply to locks on closet doors or other interior doors.

(e) If a tenant vacates the premises in breach of a written lease, the landlord may deduct from the tenant's security deposit the reasonable cost incurred by the landlord to rekey a security device as required by this section only if the lease includes a provision that is underlined or printed in boldface type authorizing the deduction.

History of Prop. Code §92.156: Acts 1983, 68th Leg., ch. 576, §1, eff. Jan. 1, 1984. Amended by Acts 1993, 73rd Leg., ch. 357, §3, eff. Sept. 1, 1993; Acts 2015, 84th Leg., ch. 1072, §1, eff. Jan. 1, 2016. Source: TRCS art. 5236h, §§1-3, 6(b); former Prop. Code §92.153.

See also *O'Connor's Texas COA*, "Giving notice to repair or exercising remedy," ch. 16-G, §2.2.1, p. 474.

PROP §92.157. SECURITY DEVICES REQUESTED BY TENANT

(a) At a tenant's request made at any time, a landlord, at the tenant's expense, shall install:

(1) a keyed dead bolt on an exterior door if the door has:

(A) a doorknob lock but not a keyed dead bolt; or

(B) a keyless bolting device but not a keyed dead bolt or doorknob lock; and

(2) a sliding door handle latch or sliding door security bar if the door is an exterior sliding glass door without a sliding door handle latch or sliding door security bar.

(b) At a tenant's request made before January 1, 1995, a landlord, at the tenant's expense, shall install on an exterior door of a dwelling constructed before September 1, 1993:

(1) a keyless bolting device if the door does not have a keyless bolting device; and

(2) a door viewer if the door does not have a door viewer.

(c) If a security device required by Section 92.153 to be installed on or after January 1, 1995, without necessity of a tenant's request has not been installed by the landlord, the tenant may request the landlord to immediately install it, and the landlord shall immediately install it at the landlord's expense.

History of Prop. Code §92.157: Acts 1983, 68th Leg., ch. 576, §1, eff. Jan. 1, 1984. Amended by Acts 1993, 73rd Leg., ch. 357, §3, eff. Sept. 1, 1993; Acts 2015, 84th Leg., ch. 1072, §2 (eff. Jan. 1, 2016), ch. 1198, §7 (eff. Jan. 1, 2016). Source: TRCS art. 5236h, §§1-3, 6(b).

See also *O'Connor's Texas COA*, "Giving notice to repair or exercising remedy," ch. 16-G, §2.2.1, p. 474.

PROP §92.158. LANDLORD'S DUTY TO REPAIR OR REPLACE SECURITY DEVICE

During the lease term and any renewal period, a landlord shall repair or replace a security device on request or notification by the tenant that the security device is inoperable or in need of repair or replacement.

History of Prop. Code §92.158: Acts 1983, 68th Leg., ch. 576, §1, eff. Jan. 1, 1984. Amended by Acts 1993, 73rd Leg., ch. 357, §3, eff. Sept. 1, 1993. Source: TRCS art. 5236h, §§1-3, 6(b).

See also *O'Connor's Texas COA*, "Giving notice to repair or exercising remedy," ch. 16-G, §2.2.1, p. 474.

PROP §92.159. WHEN TENANT'S REQUEST OR NOTICE MUST BE IN WRITING

A tenant's request or notice under this subchapter may be given orally unless the tenant has a written lease that requires the request or notice to be in writing and that requirement is underlined or in boldfaced print in the lease.

History of Prop. Code §92.159: Acts 1983, 68th Leg., ch. 576, §1, eff. Jan. 1, 1984. Amended by Acts 1993, 73rd Leg., ch. 357, §3, eff. Sept. 1, 1993. Source: TRCS art. 5236h, §§1-3, 6(b).

PROP §92.160. TYPE, BRAND, & MANNER OF INSTALLATION

Except as otherwise required by this subchapter, a landlord may select the type, brand, and manner of installation, including placement, of a security device installed under this subchapter. This section does not apply to a security device installed, repaired, changed, replaced, or rekeyed by a tenant under Section 92.164(a)(1) or 92.165(1).

History of Prop. Code §92.160: Acts 1983, 68th Leg., ch. 576, §1, eff. Jan. 1, 1984. Amended by Acts 1993, 73rd Leg., ch. 357, §3, eff. Sept. 1, 1993. Source: TRCS art. 5236h, §§1(9), 12; former Prop. Code §92.152.

PROP §92.161. COMPLIANCE WITH TENANT REQUEST REQUIRED WITHIN REASONABLE TIME

(a) Except as provided by Subsections (b) and (c), a landlord must comply with a tenant's request for rekeying, changing, installing, repairing, or replacing a security device under Section 92.156, 92.157, or 92.158 within a reasonable time. A reasonable time for purposes of this subsection is presumed to be not later than the seventh day after the date the request is received by the landlord.

(b) If within the time allowed under Section 92.162(c) a landlord requests advance payment of charges that the landlord is entitled to collect under that section, the landlord shall comply with a tenant's request under Section 92.156(b), 92.157(a), or 92.157(b) within a reasonable time. A reasonable time for purposes of this subsection is presumed to be not later than the seventh day after the date a tenant's advance payment is received by the landlord, except as provided by Subsection (c).

(c) A reasonable time for purposes of Subsections (a) and (b) is presumed to be not later than 72 hours after the time of receipt of the tenant's request and any required advance payment if at the time of making the request the tenant informed the landlord that:

(1) an unauthorized entry occurred or was attempted in the tenant's dwelling;

(2) an unauthorized entry occurred or was attempted in another unit in the multiunit complex in which the tenant's dwelling is located during the two months preceding the date of the request; or

(3) a crime of personal violence occurred in the multiunit complex in which the tenant's dwelling is located during the two months preceding the date of the request.

(d) A landlord may rebut the presumption provided by Subsection (a) or (b) if despite the diligence of the landlord:

(1) the landlord did not know of the tenant's request, without the fault of the landlord;

(2) materials, labor, or utilities were unavailable; or

(3) a delay was caused by circumstances beyond the landlord's control, including the illness or death of the landlord or a member of the landlord's immediate family.

(e) This section does not apply to a landlord's duty to install or rekey, without necessity of a tenant's request, a security device under Section 92.153 or 92.156(a).

History of Prop. Code §92.161: Acts 1993, 73rd Leg., ch. 357, §3, eff. Sept. 1, 1993. Source: TRCS art. 5236h, §§1-3, 6(b).

PROP §92.162. PAYMENT OF CHARGES; LIMITS ON AMOUNT CHARGED

(a) A landlord may not require a tenant to pay for repair or replacement of a security device due to normal wear and tear. A landlord may not require a tenant to pay for other repairs or replacements of a security device except as provided by Subsections (b), (c), and (d).

(b) A landlord may require a tenant to pay for repair or replacement of a security device if an underlined provision in a written lease authorizes the landlord to do so and the repair or replacement is necessitated by misuse or damage by the tenant, a member of the tenant's family, an occupant, or a guest, and not by normal wear and tear. Misuse of or damage to a security device that occurs during the tenant's occupancy is presumed to be caused by the tenant, a family member, an occupant, or a guest. The tenant has the burden of proving that the misuse or damage was caused by another party.

(c) A landlord may require a tenant to pay in advance charges for which the tenant is liable under this subchapter if a written lease authorizes the landlord to require advance payment, and the landlord notifies the tenant within a reasonable time after the tenant's request that advance payment is required, and:

(1) the tenant is more than 30 days delinquent in reimbursing the landlord for charges to which the landlord is entitled under Subsection (b); or

(2) the tenant requested that the landlord repair, install, change, or rekey the same security device during the 30 days preceding the tenant's request, and the landlord complied with the request.

(d) A landlord authorized by this subchapter to charge a tenant for repairing, installing, changing, or rekeying a security device under this subchapter may not require the tenant to pay more than the total cost charged by a third-party contractor for material, labor, taxes, and extra keys. If the landlord's employees perform the work, the charge may include a reasonable amount for overhead but may not include a profit to the landlord. If management company employees perform the work, the charge may include reasonable overhead and profit but may not exceed the cost charged to the owner by the management company for comparable security devices installed by management company employees at the owner's request and expense.

(e) The owner of a dwelling shall reimburse a management company, managing agent, or on-site manager for costs expended by that person in complying with this subchapter. A management company, managing agent, or on-site manager may reimburse itself for the costs from the owner's funds in its possession or control.

History of Prop. Code §92.162: Acts 1993, 73rd Leg., ch. 357, §3, eff. Sept. 1, 1993. Source: TRCS art. 5236h, §4; former Prop. Code §92.154.

PROP §92.163. REMOVAL OR ALTERATION OF SECURITY DEVICE BY TENANT

A security device that is installed, changed, or rekeyed under this subchapter becomes a fixture of the dwelling. Except as provided by Section 92.164(a)(1) or 92.165(1) regarding the remedy of repair-and-deduct, a tenant may not remove, change, rekey, replace, or alter a security device or have it removed, changed, rekeyed, replaced, or altered without permission of the landlord.

History of Prop. Code §92.163: Acts 1993, 73rd Leg., ch. 357, §3, eff. Sept. 1, 1993. Source: TRCS art. 5236h, §5; former Prop. Code §92.155.

PROP §92.164. TENANT REMEDIES FOR LANDLORD'S FAILURE TO INSTALL OR REKEY CERTAIN SECURITY DEVICES

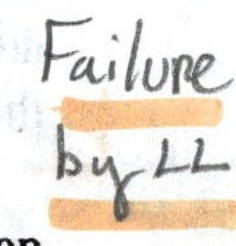

(a) If a landlord does not comply with Section 92.153 or 92.156(a) regarding installation or rekeying of a security device, the tenant may:

(1) install or rekey the security device as required by this subchapter and deduct the reasonable cost of material, labor, taxes, and extra keys from the tenant's next rent payment, in accordance with Section 92.166;

(2) serve a written request for compliance on the landlord, and, except as provided by Subsections (b) and (c), if the landlord does not comply on or before the third day after the date the notice is received, unilaterally terminate the lease without court proceedings;

(3) file suit against the landlord without serving a request for compliance and obtain a judgment for:

(A) a court order directing the landlord to comply, if the tenant is in possession of the dwelling;

(B) the tenant's actual damages;

(C) court costs; and

(D) attorney's fees except in suits for recovery of property damages, personal injuries, or wrongful death; and

(4) serve a written request for compliance on the landlord, and, except as provided by Subsections (b) and (c), if the landlord does not comply on or before the third day after the date the notice is received, file suit against the landlord and obtain a judgment for:

(A) a court order directing the landlord to comply and bring all dwellings owned by the landlord into compliance, if the tenant serving the written request is in possession of the dwelling;

(B) the tenant's actual damages;

(C) punitive damages if the tenant suffers actual damages;

(D) a civil penalty of one month's rent plus $500;

(E) court costs; and

(F) attorney's fees except in suits for recovery of property damages, personal injuries, or wrongful death.

(b) A tenant may not unilaterally terminate the lease under Subsection (a)(2) or file suit against the landlord to obtain a judgment under Subsection (a)(4) unless the landlord does not comply on or before the seventh day after the date the written request for compliance is received if the lease includes language underlined or in boldface print that in substance provides the tenant with notice that:

(1) the landlord at the landlord's expense is required to equip the dwelling, when the tenant takes possession, with the security devices described by Sections 92.153(a)(1)-(4) and (6);

(2) the landlord is not required to install a doorknob lock or keyed dead bolt at the landlord's expense if the exterior doors meet the requirements of Section 92.153(f);

(3) the landlord is not required to install a keyless bolting device at the landlord's expense on an exterior door if the landlord is expressly required or permitted to periodically check on the well-being or health of the tenant as provided by Section 92.153(e)(3); and

(4) the tenant has the right to install or rekey a security device required by this subchapter and deduct the reasonable cost from the tenant's next rent payment, as provided by Subsection (a)(1).

(c) Regardless of whether the lease contains language complying with the requirements of Subsection (b), the additional time for landlord compliance provided by Subsection (b) does not apply if at the time the tenant served the written request for compliance on the landlord the tenant informed the landlord that an unauthorized entry occurred or was attempted in the tenant's dwelling, an unauthorized entry occurred or was attempted in another unit in the multiunit complex in which the tenant's dwelling is located during the two months preceding the date of the request, or a crime of personal violence occurred in the multiunit complex in which the tenant's dwelling is located during the two months preceding the date of the request, unless despite the diligence of the landlord:

(1) the landlord did not know of the tenant's request, without the fault of the landlord;

(2) materials, labor, or utilities were unavailable; or

(3) a delay was caused by circumstances beyond the landlord's control, including the illness or death of the landlord or a member of the landlord's immediate family.

History of Prop. Code §92.164: Acts 1993, 73rd Leg., ch. 357, §3, eff. Sept. 1, 1993. Source: TRCS art. 5236h, §8; former Prop. Code §§92.156, 92.157.

See also *O'Connor's Texas COA*, "Exercising right or remedy," ch. 16-G, §2.2.2, p. 475.

PROP §92.1641. LANDLORD'S DEFENSES RELATING TO INSTALLING OR REKEYING CERTAIN SECURITY DEVICES

The landlord has a defense to liability under Section 92.164 if:

(1) the tenant has not fully paid all rent then due from the tenant on the date the tenant gives a request under Section 92.157(c) or the notice required by Section 92.164; or

(2) on the date the tenant terminates the lease or files suit the tenant has not fully paid costs requested by the landlord and authorized by Section 92.162.

History of Prop. Code §92.1641: Acts 1983, 68th Leg., ch. 576, §1, eff. Jan. 1, 1984. Amended by Acts 1993, 73rd Leg., ch. 48, §17, eff. Sept. 1, 1993. Renumbered from §92.158 and amended by Acts 2001, 77th Leg., ch. 1420, §17.001(a), eff. Sept. 1, 2001. Amended by Acts 2015, 84th Leg., ch. 1072, §3 (eff. Jan. 1, 2016), ch. 1198, §8 (eff. Jan. 1, 2016).

PROP §92.165. TENANT REMEDIES FOR OTHER LANDLORD VIOLATIONS

If a landlord does not comply with a tenant's request regarding rekeying, changing, adding, repairing, or replacing a security device under Section 92.156(b), 92.157, or 92.158 in accordance with the time limits and other requirements of this subchapter, the tenant may:

(1) install, repair, change, replace, or rekey the security devices as required by this subchapter and deduct the reasonable cost of material, labor, taxes, and extra keys from the tenant's next rent payment in accordance with Section 92.166;

(2) unilaterally terminate the lease without court proceedings; and

(3) file suit against the landlord and obtain a judgment for:

(A) a court order directing the landlord to comply, if the tenant is in possession of the dwelling;

(B) the tenant's actual damages;

(C) punitive damages if the tenant suffers actual damages and the landlord's failure to comply is intentional, malicious, or grossly negligent;

(D) a civil penalty of one month's rent plus $500;

(E) court costs; and

(F) attorney's fees except in suits for recovery of property damages, personal injuries, or wrongful death.

History of Prop. Code §92.165: Acts 1993, 73rd Leg., ch. 357, §3, eff. Sept. 1, 1993. Source: TRCS art. 5236h, §§8, 10.

See also *O'Connor's Texas COA*, "Exercising right or remedy," ch. 16-G, §2.2.2, p. 475.

PROP §92.166. NOTICE OF TENANT'S DEDUCTION OF REPAIR COSTS FROM RENT

(a) A tenant shall notify the landlord of a rent deduction attributable to the tenant's installing, repairing, changing, replacing, or rekeying of a security device under Section 92.164(a)(1) or 92.165(1) after the landlord's failure to comply with this subchapter. The notice must be given at the time of the reduced rent payment.

(b) Unless otherwise provided in a written lease, a tenant shall provide one duplicate of the key to any key-operated security device installed or rekeyed by the tenant under Section 92.164(a)(1) or 92.165(1) within a reasonable time after the landlord's written request for the key.

History of Prop. Code §92.166: Acts 1993, 73rd Leg., ch. 357, §3, eff. Sept. 1, 1993.

See also Prop. Code §92.056; *O'Connor's Texas COA*, "Exercising right or remedy," ch. 16-G, §2.2.2, p. 475.

PROP §92.167. LANDLORD'S DEFENSES RELATING TO COMPLIANCE WITH TENANT'S REQUEST

(a) A landlord has a defense to liability under Section 92.165 if on the date the tenant terminates the lease or files suit the tenant has not fully paid costs requested by the landlord and authorized by this subchapter.

(b) A management company or managing agent who is not the owner of a dwelling and who has not purported to be the owner in the lease has a defense to liability under Sections 92.164 and 92.165 if before the date the tenant is in possession of the dwelling or the date of the tenant's request for installation, repair, replacement, change, or rekeying and before any property damage or personal injury to the tenant, the management company or managing agent:

(1) did not have funds of the dwelling owner in its possession or control with which to comply with this subchapter;

(2) made written request to the dwelling owner that the owner fund and allow installation, repair, change, replacement, or rekeying of security devices as required under this subchapter and mailed the request, certified mail return receipt requested, to the dwelling owner; and

(3) not later than the third day after the date of receipt of the tenant's request, provided the tenant with a written notice:

(A) stating that the management company or managing agent has taken the actions in Subdivisions (1) and (2);

(B) stating that the owner has not provided or will not provide the necessary funds; and

(C) explaining the remedies available to the tenant for the landlord's failure to comply.

History of Prop. Code §92.167: Acts 1993, 73rd Leg., ch. 357, §3, eff. Sept. 1, 1993. Amended by Acts 2001, 77th Leg., ch. 1420, §17.00(b), eff. Sept. 1, 2001. Source: TRCS art. 5236h, §7; former Prop. Code §92.158.

PROP §92.168. TENANT'S REMEDY ON NOTICE FROM MANAGEMENT COMPANY

The tenant may unilaterally terminate the lease or exercise other remedies under Sections 92.164 and 92.165 after receiving written notice from a management company that the owner of the dwelling has not provided or will not provide funds to repair, install, change, replace, or rekey a security device as required by this subchapter.

History of Prop. Code §92.168: Acts 1993, 73rd Leg., ch. 357, §3, eff. Sept. 1, 1993. Source: TRCS art. 5236h, §8.

PROP §92.169. AGENT FOR DELIVERY OF NOTICE

A managing agent or an agent to whom rent is regularly paid, whether residing or maintaining an office on-site or off-site, is the agent of the landlord for purposes of notice and other communications required or permitted by this subchapter.

History of Prop. Code §92.169: Acts 1993, 73rd Leg., ch. 357, §3, eff. Sept. 1, 1993. Source: TRCS art. 5236h, §1; former Prop. Code §92.150.

PROP §92.170. EFFECT ON OTHER LANDLORD DUTIES & TENANT REMEDIES

The duties of a landlord and the remedies of a tenant under this subchapter are in lieu of common law, other statutory law, and local ordinances relating to a residential landlord's duty to install, change, rekey, repair, or replace security devices and a tenant's remedies for the landlord's failure to install, change, rekey, repair, or replace security devices, except that a municipal ordinance adopted before January 1, 1993, may require installation of security devices at the landlord's expense by an earlier date than a date required by this subchapter. This subchapter does not affect a duty of a landlord or a remedy of a tenant under Subchapter B regarding habitability.

History of Prop. Code §92.170: Acts 1993, 73rd Leg., ch. 357, §3, eff. Sept. 1, 1993. Source: TRCS art. 5236h, §12; former Prop. Code §92.160.

Sections 92.171-92.200 reserved for expansion

SUBCHAPTER E. DISCLOSURE OF OWNERSHIP & MANAGEMENT

PROP §92.201. DISCLOSURE OF OWNERSHIP & MANAGEMENT

(a) A landlord shall disclose to a tenant, or to any government official or employee acting in an official capacity, according to this subchapter:

(1) the name and either a street or post office box address of the holder of record title, according to the deed records in the county clerk's office, of the dwelling rented by the tenant or inquired about by the government official or employee acting in an official capacity; and

(2) if an entity located off-site from the dwelling is primarily responsible for managing the dwelling, the name and street address of the management company.

(b) Disclosure to a tenant under Subsection (a) must be made by:

(1) giving the information in writing to the tenant on or before the seventh day after the day the landlord receives the tenant's request for the information;

(2) continuously posting the information in a conspicuous place in the dwelling or the office of the on-site manager or on the outside of the entry door to the office of the on-site manager on or before the seventh day after the date the landlord receives the tenant's request for the information; or

(3) including the information in a copy of the tenant's lease or in written rules given to the tenant before the tenant requests the information.

(c) Disclosure of information to a tenant may be made under Subdivision (1) or (2) of Subsection (b) before the tenant requests the information.

(d) Disclosure of information to a government official or employee must be made by giving the information in writing to the official or employee on or before the seventh day after the date the landlord receives the request from the official or employee for the information.

(e) A correction to the information may be made by any of the methods authorized for providing the information.

(f) For the purposes of this section, an owner or property manager may disclose either an actual name or names or an assumed name if an assumed name certificate has been recorded with the county clerk.

History of Prop. Code §92.201: Acts 1983, 68th Leg., ch. 576, §1, eff. Jan. 1, 1984. Amended by Acts 1995, 74th Leg., ch. 869, §4, eff. Jan. 1, 1996. Source: TRCS art. 5236i, §§1(c), 2, 3.

PROP §92.202. LANDLORD'S FAILURE TO DISCLOSE INFORMATION

(a) A landlord is liable to a tenant or a governmental body according to this subchapter if:

(1) after the tenant or government official or employee makes a request for information under Section 92.201, the landlord does not provide the information; and

(2) the landlord does not give the information to the tenant or government official or employee before the eighth day after the date the tenant, official, or employee gives the landlord written notice that the tenant, official, or employee may exercise remedies under this subchapter if the landlord does not comply with the request by the tenant, official, or employee for the information within seven days.

(b) If the tenant's lease is in writing, the lease may require the tenant's initial request for information to be written. A request by a government official or employee for information must be in writing.

History of Prop. Code §92.202: Acts 1983, 68th Leg., ch. 576, §1, eff. Jan. 1, 1984. Amended by Acts 1995, 74th Leg., ch. 869, §4, eff. Jan. 1, 1996. Source: TRCS art. 5236i, §4.

See also *O'Connor's Texas COA*, "Giving notice to repair or exercising remedy," ch. 16-G, §2.2.1, p. 474.

ANNOTATIONS

McBeath v. Estrada Oaks Apts., 135 S.W.3d 694, 697 (Tex.App.—Dallas 2003, no pet.). "[P] sent [D] letters on January 19, 2002 and January 25, 2002, and in both letters she requested the name and address of the owner of her rental unit. Also in these letters, [P] stated that if she did not receive the information within seven days, she 'may take legal action.' Because her letter notified [D] the consequence of its failure to respond would be 'legal action,' we conclude [P] substantially complied with §92.202(a)(2)."

PROP §92.203. LANDLORD'S FAILURE TO CORRECT INFORMATION

A landlord who has provided information under Subdivision (2) or (3) of Subsection (b) of Section 92.201 is liable to a tenant according to this subchapter if:

(1) the information becomes incorrect because a name or address changes; and

(2) the landlord fails to correct the information on or before the seventh day after the date the tenant gives the landlord written notice that the tenant may exercise the remedies under this subchapter if the corrected information is not provided within seven days.

History of Prop. Code §92.203: Acts 1983, 68th Leg., ch. 576, §1, eff. Jan. 1, 1984. Amended by Acts 1995, 74th Leg., ch. 869, §4, eff. Jan. 1, 1996. Source: TRCS art. 5236i, §5.

PROP §92.204. BAD FAITH VIOLATION

A landlord acts in bad faith and is liable according to this subchapter if the landlord gives an incorrect name or address under Subsection (a) of Section 92.201 by wilfully:

(1) disclosing incorrect information under Section 92.201(b)(1) or (2) or Section 92.201(d); or

(2) failing to correct information given under Section 92.201(b)(1) or (2) or Section 92.201(d) that the landlord knows is incorrect.

History of Prop. Code §92.204: Acts 1983, 68th Leg., ch. 576, §1, eff. Jan. 1, 1984. Amended by Acts 1993, 73rd Leg., ch. 48, §18, eff. Sept. 1, 1993; Acts 1995, 74th Leg., ch. 869, §4, eff. Jan. 1, 1996. Source: TRCS art. 5236i, §6.

PROP §92.205. REMEDIES

(a) A tenant of a landlord who is liable under Section 92.202, 92.203, or 92.204 may obtain or exercise one or more of the following remedies:

(1) a court order directing the landlord to make a disclosure required by this subchapter;

(2) a judgment against the landlord for an amount equal to the tenant's actual costs in discovering the information required to be disclosed by this subchapter;

(3) a judgment against the landlord for one month's rent plus $100;

(4) a judgment against the landlord for court costs and attorney's fees; and

(5) unilateral termination of the lease without a court proceeding.

(b) A governmental body whose official or employee has requested information from a landlord who is liable under Section 92.202 or 92.204 may obtain or exercise one or more of the following remedies:

(1) a court order directing the landlord to make a disclosure required by this subchapter;

(2) a judgment against the landlord for an amount equal to the governmental body's actual costs in discovering the information required to be disclosed by this subchapter;

(3) a judgment against the landlord for $500; and

(4) a judgment against the landlord for court costs and attorney's fees.

History of Prop. Code §92.205: Acts 1983, 68th Leg., ch. 576, §1, eff. Jan. 1, 1984. Amended by Acts 1995, 74th Leg., ch. 869, §4, eff. Jan. 1, 1996. Source: TRCS art. 5236i, §8.

See also *O'Connor's Texas COA*, "Exercising right or remedy," ch. 16-G, §2.2.2, p. 475.

PROP §92.206. LANDLORD'S DEFENSE

A landlord has a defense to liability under Section 92.202 or 92.203 if the tenant owes rent on the date the tenant gives a notice required by either of those sections. Rent delinquency is not a defense for a violation of Section 92.204.

History of Prop. Code §92.206: Acts 1983, 68th Leg., ch. 576, §1, eff. Jan. 1, 1984. Source: TRCS art. 5236i, §7.

PROP §92.207. AGENTS FOR DELIVERY OF NOTICE

(a) A managing or leasing agent, whether residing or maintaining an office on-site or off-site, is the agent of the landlord for purposes of:

(1) notice and other communications required or permitted by this subchapter;

(2) notice and other communications from a governmental body relating to a violation of health, sanitation, safety, or nuisance laws on the landlord's property where the dwelling is located, including notices of:

(A) demands for abatement of nuisances;

(B) repair of a substandard dwelling;

(C) remedy of dangerous conditions;

(D) reimbursement of costs incurred by the governmental body in curing the violation;

(E) fines; and

(F) service of process.

(b) If the landlord's name and business street address in this state have not been furnished in writing to the tenant or government official or employee, the person who collects the rent from a tenant is the landlord's authorized agent for purposes of Subsection (a).

History of Prop. Code §92.207: Acts 1983, 68th Leg., ch. 576, §1, eff. Jan. 1, 1984. Amended by Acts 1995, 74th Leg., ch. 869, §4, eff. Jan. 1, 1996. Source: TRCS art. 5236i, §1(d).

PROP §92.208. ADDITIONAL ENFORCEMENT BY LOCAL ORDINANCE

The duties of a landlord and the remedies of a tenant under this subchapter are in lieu of the common law, other statutory law, and local ordinances relating to the disclosure of ownership and management of a dwelling by a landlord to a tenant. However, this subchapter does not prohibit the adoption of a local ordinance that conforms to this subchapter but which contains additional enforcement provisions.

History of Prop. Code §92.208: Acts 1983, 68th Leg., ch. 576, §1, eff. Jan. 1, 1984. Source: TRCS art. 5236i, §12.

Sections 92.209-92.250 reserved for expansion

SUBCHAPTER F. SMOKE ALARMS & FIRE EXTINGUISHERS

PROP §92.251. DEFINITIONS

In this subchapter:

(1) "Bedroom" means a room designed with the intent that it be used for sleeping purposes.

(2) "Dwelling unit" means a home, mobile home, duplex unit, apartment unit, condominium unit, or any dwelling unit in a multiunit residential structure. It also means a "dwelling" as defined by Section 92.001.

(3) "Smoke alarm" means a device designed to detect and to alert occupants of a dwelling unit to the visible and invisible products of combustion by means of an audible alarm.

History of Prop. Code §92.251: Acts 1983, 68th Leg., ch. 576, §1, eff. Jan. 1, 1984. Amended by Acts 2011, 82nd Leg., ch. 257, §§2, 3, eff. Sept. 1, 2011. Source: TRCS art. 5236j, §1(3).

PROP §92.252. APPLICATION OF OTHER LAW; MUNICIPAL REGULATION

(a) The duties of a landlord and the remedies of a tenant under this subchapter are in lieu of common law, other statutory law, and local ordinances regarding a residential landlord's duty to install, inspect, or repair a fire extinguisher or smoke alarm in a dwelling unit. However, this subchapter does not:

(1) affect a local ordinance adopted before September 1, 1981, that requires landlords to install smoke alarms in new or remodeled dwelling units before September 1, 1981, if the ordinance conforms with or is amended to conform with this subchapter;

(2) limit or prevent adoption or enforcement of a local ordinance relating to fire safety as a part of a building, fire, or housing code, including any requirements relating to the installation of smoke alarms or the type of smoke alarms;

(3) otherwise limit or prevent the adoption of a local ordinance that conforms to this subchapter but which contains additional enforcement provisions, except as provided by Subsection (b); or

(4) affect a local ordinance that requires regular inspections by local officials of smoke alarms in dwelling units and that requires smoke alarms to be operational at the time of inspection.

(b) If a smoke alarm powered by battery has been installed in a dwelling unit built before September 1, 1987, in compliance with this subchapter and local ordi-

nances, a local ordinance may not require that a smoke alarm powered by alternating current be installed in the unit unless:

(1) the interior of the unit is repaired, remodeled, or rebuilt at a projected cost of more than $5,000 and:

(A) the repair, remodeling, or rebuilding requires a municipal building permit; and

(B) either:

(i) the repair, remodeling, or rebuilding results in the removal of interior walls or ceiling finishes exposing the structure; or

(ii) the interior of the unit provides access for building wiring through an attic, crawl space, or basement without the removal of interior walls or ceiling finishes;

(2) an addition occurs to the unit at a projected cost of more than $5,000;

(3) a smoke alarm powered by alternating current was actually installed in the unit at any time prior to September 1, 1987; or

(4) a smoke alarm powered by alternating current was required by lawful city ordinance at the time of initial construction of the unit.

History of Prop. Code §92.252: Acts 1983, 68th Leg., ch. 576, §1, eff. Jan. 1, 1984. Amended by Acts 1987, 70th Leg., ch. 475, §1, eff. Sept. 1, 1987; Acts 1997, 75th Leg., ch. 1205, §13, eff. Sept. 1, 1997; Acts 2011, 82nd Leg., ch. 257, §3, eff. Sept. 1, 2011. Source: TRCS art. 5236j, §15.

ANNOTATIONS

Rao v. Rodriguez, 923 S.W.2d 176, 180 (Tex.App.—Beaumont 1996, no writ). Section 92.252(a) "provides the duties of a landlord and the remedies of a tenant under the smoke detector [now 'alarm'] statute are in lieu of common law. Therefore, the liability provisions of the smoke detector statute provide an exclusive remedy as between a tenant and landlord, as defined, and expressly preempts any common law basis of liability." *See also* ***Epps v. Ayer***, 859 S.W.2d 107, 109 (Tex.App.—Eastland 1993, writ denied); ***Garza-Vale v. Kwiecien***, 796 S.W.2d 500, 504 (Tex.App.—San Antonio 1990, writ denied).

Gilstrap v. Park Lane Town Home Ass'n, 885 S.W.2d 589, 591 (Tex.App.—Amarillo 1994, no writ). "[D] asserts that [P's] contention that the smoke detector [now 'alarm'] statute is limited to the landlord-tenant relationship must be rejected. [D] concludes, it is inconceivable that the legislature would desire to preempt smoke detector [now 'alarm'] claims against landlords, while intending the same claims to be maintained against town home owners associations, which do not own, occupy, control, or make repairs to the condominiums. We do not agree. [¶] [Because D] was not a landlord, it was not entitled to claim the preexemption applicable to landlords in §92.252(a)."

PROP §92.253. EXEMPTIONS

(a) This subchapter does not apply to:

(1) a dwelling unit that is occupied by its owner, no part of which is leased to a tenant;

(2) a dwelling unit in a building five or more stories in height in which smoke alarms are required or regulated by local ordinance; or

(3) a nursing or convalescent home licensed by the Department of State Health Services and certified to meet the Life Safety Code under federal law and regulations.

(b) Notwithstanding this subchapter, a person licensed to install fire alarms or fire detection devices under Chapter 6002, Insurance Code, shall comply with that chapter when installing smoke alarms.

History of Prop. Code §92.253: Acts 1983, 68th Leg., ch. 576, §1, eff. Jan. 1, 1984. Amended by Acts 2011, 82nd Leg., ch. 257, §3, eff. Sept. 1, 2011. Source: TRCS art. 5236j, §§12, 13.

PROP §92.254. SMOKE ALARM

(a) A smoke alarm must be:

(1) designed to detect both the visible and invisible products of combustion;

(2) designed with an alarm audible to a person in the bedrooms it serves; and

(3) tested and listed for use as a smoke alarm by Underwriters Laboratories, Inc., Factory Mutual Research Corporation, or United States Testing Company, Inc.

(a-1) If requested by a tenant as an accommodation for a person with a hearing-impairment disability or as required by law as a reasonable accommodation for a person with a hearing-impairment disability, a smoke alarm must, in addition to complying with Subsection (a), be capable of alerting a hearing-impaired person in the bedrooms it serves.

(b) Except as provided by Section 92.255(b), a smoke alarm may be powered by battery, alternating current, or other power source as required by local ordinance. The power system and installation procedure of a security device that is electrically operated rather than battery operated must comply with applicable local ordinances.

History of Prop. Code §92.254: Acts 1983, 68th Leg., ch. 576, §1, eff. Jan. 1, 1984. Amended by Acts 1987, 70th Leg., ch. 475, §2, eff. Sept. 1, 1987; Acts 2009, 81st Leg., ch. 824, §2, eff. Jan. 1, 2010; Acts 2011, 82nd Leg., ch. 257, §3, eff. Sept. 1, 2011. Source: TRCS art. 5236j, §§1(5), 2(b).

PROP §92.255. INSTALLATION & LOCATION

(a) A landlord shall install at least one smoke alarm in each separate bedroom in a dwelling unit. In addition:

(1) if the dwelling unit is designed to use a single room for dining, living, and sleeping, the smoke alarm must be located inside the room;

(2) if multiple bedrooms are served by the same corridor, at least one smoke alarm must be installed in the corridor in the immediate vicinity of the bedrooms; and

(3) if the dwelling unit has multiple levels, at least one smoke alarm must be located on each level.

(b) If a dwelling unit was occupied as a residence before September 1, 2011, or a certificate of occupancy was issued for the dwelling unit before that date, a smoke alarm installed in accordance with Subsection (a) may be powered by battery and is not required to be interconnected with other smoke alarms, except that a smoke alarm that is installed to replace a smoke alarm that was in place on the date the dwelling unit was first occupied as a residence must comply with residential building code standards that applied to the dwelling unit on that date or Section 92.252(b).

History of Prop. Code §92.255: Acts 1983, 68th Leg., ch. 576, §1, eff. Jan. 1, 1984. Amended by Acts 2011, 82nd Leg., ch. 257, §3, eff. Sept. 1, 2011. Source: TRCS art. 5236j, §§1(1), 2.

See also *Real Estate Forms*, FORM 2:6.

PROP §92.256. REPEALED

Repealed by Acts 2011, 82nd Leg., ch. 257, §7, eff. Sept. 1, 2011.

PROP §92.257. INSTALLATION PROCEDURE

(a) Subject to Subsections (b) and (c), a smoke alarm must be installed according to the manufacturer's recommended procedures.

(b) A smoke alarm must be installed on a ceiling or wall. If on a ceiling, it must be no closer than six inches to a wall or otherwise located in accordance with the manufacturer's installation instructions. If on a wall, it must be no closer than six inches and no farther than 12 inches from the ceiling or otherwise located in accordance with the manufacturer's installation instructions.

(c) A smoke alarm may be located other than as required by Subsection (a) or (b) if a local ordinance or a local or state fire marshal approves.

History of Prop. Code §92.257: Acts 1983, 68th Leg., ch. 576, §1, eff. Jan. 1, 1984. Amended by Acts 2011, 82nd Leg., ch. 257, §3, eff. Sept. 1, 2011. Source: TRCS art. 5236j, §2(b).

PROP §92.2571. ALTERNATIVE COMPLIANCE

A landlord complies with the requirements of this subchapter relating to the provision of smoke alarms in the dwelling unit if the landlord:

(1) has a fire detection device, as defined by Section 6002.002, Insurance Code, that includes a fire alarm device, as defined by Section 6002.002, Insurance Code, installed in a dwelling unit; or

(2) for a dwelling unit that is a one-family or two-family dwelling unit, installs smoke detectors in compliance with Chapter 766, Health and Safety Code.

History of Prop. Code §92.2571: Acts 2007, 80th Leg., ch. 1051, §12, eff. Sept. 1, 2007. Amended by Acts 2011, 82nd Leg., ch. 257, §3, eff. Sept. 1, 2011.

PROP §92.258. INSPECTION & REPAIR

(a) The landlord shall inspect and repair a smoke alarm according to this section.

(b) The landlord shall determine that the smoke alarm is in good working order at the beginning of the tenant's possession by testing the smoke alarm with smoke, by operating the testing button on the smoke alarm, or by following other recommended test procedures of the manufacturer for the particular model.

(c) During the term of a lease or during a renewal or extension, the landlord has a duty to inspect and repair a smoke alarm, but only if the tenant gives the landlord notice of a malfunction or requests to the landlord that the smoke alarm be inspected or repaired. This duty does not exist with respect to damage or a malfunction caused by the tenant, the tenant's family, or the tenant's guests or invitees during the term of the lease or a renewal or extension, except that the landlord has a duty to repair or replace the smoke alarm if the tenant pays in advance the reasonable repair or replacement cost, including labor, materials, taxes, and overhead.

(d) The landlord must comply with the tenant's request for inspection or repair of a smoke alarm within a reasonable time, considering the availability of material, labor, and utilities.

(e) The landlord has met the duty to inspect and repair if the smoke alarm is in good working order after

the landlord tests the smoke alarm with smoke, operates the testing button on the smoke alarm, or follows other recommended test procedures of the manufacturer for the particular model.

(f) The landlord is not obligated to provide batteries for a battery-operated smoke alarm after a tenant takes possession if the smoke alarm was in good working order at the time the tenant took possession.

(g) A smoke alarm that is in good working order at the beginning of a tenant's possession is presumed to be in good working order until the tenant requests repair of the smoke alarm as provided by this subchapter.

History of Prop. Code §92.258: Acts 1983, 68th Leg., ch. 576, §1, eff. Jan. 1, 1984. Amended by Acts 1993, 73rd Leg., ch. 48, §19, eff. Sept. 1, 1993; Acts 1995, 74th Leg., ch. 869, §7 (eff. Sept. 1, 1995), ch. 918, §1 (eff. Sept. 1, 1995); Acts 2011, 82nd Leg., ch. 257, §3, eff. Sept. 1, 2011. Source: TRCS art. 5236j, §§1(7), 4, 5.

See also *O'Connor's Texas COA*, "Giving notice to repair or exercising remedy," ch. 16-G, §2.2.1, p. 474.

PROP §92.259. LANDLORD'S FAILURE TO INSTALL, INSPECT, OR REPAIR

(a) A landlord is liable according to this subchapter if:

(1) the landlord did not install a smoke alarm at the time of initial occupancy by the tenant as required by this subchapter or a municipal ordinance permitted by this subchapter; or

(2) the landlord does not install, inspect, or repair the smoke alarm on or before the seventh day after the date the tenant gives the landlord written notice that the tenant may exercise his remedies under this subchapter if the landlord does not comply with the request within seven days.

(b) If the tenant gives notice under Subsection (a)(2) and the tenant's lease is in writing, the lease may require the tenant to make the initial request for installation, inspection, or repair of a smoke alarm in writing.

History of Prop. Code §92.259: Acts 1983, 68th Leg., ch. 576, §1, eff. Jan. 1, 1984. Amended by Acts 1995, 74th Leg., ch. 869, §8 (eff. Sept. 1, 1995), ch. 918, §2 (eff. Sept. 1, 1995); Acts 2011, 82nd Leg., ch. 257, §3, eff. Sept. 1, 2011. Source: TRCS art. 5236j, §§6, 7.

See also H&SC §§791.001-791.016; *O'Connor's Texas COA*, "Giving notice to repair or exercising remedy," ch. 16-G, §2.2.1, p. 474.

ANNOTATIONS

Zuniga v. Salazar, 69 S.W.3d 586, 589 (Tex.App.—Corpus Christi 2001, no pet.). Property Code §92.259 "does not contain an express requirement that the tenant request the installation of the smoke detector [now 'alarm'] at the tenant's initial occupancy, and we decline to interpret this section so as to impose such a requirement. We hold, therefore, that the defense set forth in [Prop. Code] §92.261 may only be raised by a landlord in a situation where the tenant makes a request that the landlord install, inspect, or repair a smoke detector in accordance with §92.259(a)(2). We further hold that the defense set forth in §92.261 is not applicable to situations where the landlord fails to install a smoke detector [now 'alarm'] at the time of the tenant's initial occupancy."

PROP §92.260. TENANT REMEDIES

A tenant of a landlord who is liable under Section 92.259 may obtain or exercise one or more of the following remedies:

(1) a court order directing the landlord to comply with the tenant's request if the tenant is in possession of the dwelling unit;

(2) a judgment against the landlord for damages suffered by the tenant because of the landlord's violation;

(3) a judgment against the landlord for a civil penalty of one month's rent plus $100 if the landlord violates Section 92.259(a)(2);

(4) a judgment against the landlord for court costs;

(5) a judgment against the landlord for attorney's fees in an action under Subdivision (1) or (3); and

(6) unilateral termination of the lease without a court proceeding if the landlord violates Section 92.259(a)(2).

History of Prop. Code §92.260: Acts 1983, 68th Leg., ch. 576, §1, eff. Jan. 1, 1984. Amended by Acts 1995, 74th Leg., ch. 869, §9 (eff. Sept. 1, 1995), ch. 918, §3 (eff. Sept. 1, 1995). Source: TRCS art. 5236j, §9.

See also *O'Connor's Texas COA*, "Exercising right or remedy," ch. 16-G, §2.2.2, p. 475.

PROP §92.261. LANDLORD'S DEFENSES

The landlord has a defense to liability under Section 92.259 if:

(1) on the date the tenant gives the notice required by Section 92.259 the tenant has not paid all rent due from the tenant; or

(2) on the date the tenant terminates the lease or files suit the tenant has not fully paid costs requested by the landlord and authorized by Section 92.258.

History of Prop. Code §92.261: Acts 1983, 68th Leg., ch. 576, §1, eff. Jan. 1, 1984. Source: TRCS art. 5236j, §8.

ANNOTATIONS

Zuniga v. Salazar, 69 S.W.3d 586, 589 (Tex.App.—Corpus Christi 2001, no pet.). See annotation under Property Code §92.259, p. 475.

PROP §92.2611. TENANT'S DISABLING OF A SMOKE ALARM

(a) A tenant is liable according to this subchapter if the tenant removes a battery from a smoke alarm without immediately replacing it with a working battery or knowingly disconnects or intentionally damages a smoke alarm, causing it to malfunction.

(b) Except as provided in Subsection (c), a landlord of a tenant who is liable under Subsection (a) may obtain a judgment against the tenant for damages suffered by the landlord because the tenant removed a battery from a smoke alarm without immediately replacing it with a working battery or knowingly disconnected or intentionally damaged the smoke alarm, causing it to malfunction.

(c) A tenant is not liable for damages suffered by the landlord if the damage is caused by the landlord's failure to repair the smoke alarm within a reasonable time after the tenant requests it to be repaired, considering the availability of material, labor, and utilities.

(d) A landlord of a tenant who is liable under Subsection (a) may obtain or exercise one or more of the remedies in Subsection (e) if:

(1) a lease between the landlord and tenant contains a notice, in underlined or boldfaced print, which states in substance that the tenant must not disconnect or intentionally damage a smoke alarm or remove the battery without immediately replacing it with a working battery and that the tenant may be subject to damages, civil penalties, and attorney's fees under Section 92.2611 of the Property Code for not complying with the notice; and

(2) the landlord has given notice to the tenant that the landlord intends to exercise the landlord's remedies under this subchapter if the tenant does not reconnect, repair, or replace the smoke alarm or replace the removed battery within seven days after being notified by the landlord to do so.

(d-1) The notice in Subsection (d)(2) must be in a separate document furnished to the tenant after the landlord has discovered that the tenant has disconnected or damaged the smoke alarm or removed a battery from it.

(e) If a tenant is liable under Subsection (a) and the tenant does not comply with the landlord's notice under Subsection (d), the landlord shall have the following remedies against the tenant:

(1) a court order directing the tenant to comply with the landlord's notice;

(2) a judgment against the tenant for a civil penalty of one month's rent plus $100;

(3) a judgment against the tenant for court costs; and

(4) a judgment against the tenant for reasonable attorney's fees.

(f) A tenant's guest or invitee who suffers damage because of a landlord's failure to install, inspect, or repair a smoke alarm as required by this subchapter may recover a judgment against the landlord for the damage. A tenant's guest or invitee who suffers damage because the tenant removed a battery without immediately replacing it with a working battery or because the tenant knowingly disconnected or intentionally damaged the smoke alarm, causing it to malfunction, may recover a judgment against the tenant for the damage.

History of Prop. Code §92.2611: Acts 1995, 74th Leg., ch. 869, §10 (eff. Sept. 1, 1995), ch. 918, §4 (eff. Sept. 1, 1995). Amended by Acts 1997, 75th Leg., ch. 165, §28.01, eff. Sept. 1, 1997; Acts 2011, 82nd Leg., ch. 257, §§4, 5, eff. Sept. 1, 2011.

PROP §92.262. AGENTS FOR DELIVERY OF NOTICE

A managing or leasing agent, whether residing or maintaining an office on-site or off-site, is the agent of the landlord for purposes of notice and other communications required or permitted by this subchapter.

History of Prop. Code §92.262: Acts 1983, 68th Leg., ch. 576, §1, eff. Jan. 1, 1984. Source: TRCS art. 5236j, §1(4).

PROP §92.263. INSPECTION OF RESIDENTIAL FIRE EXTINGUISHER

(a) If a landlord has installed a 1A10BC residential fire extinguisher as defined by the National Fire Protection Association or other non-rechargeable fire extinguisher in accordance with a local ordinance or other law, the landlord or the landlord's agent shall inspect the fire extinguisher:

(1) at the beginning of a tenant's possession; and

(2) within a reasonable time after receiving a written request by a tenant.

(b) At a minimum, an inspection under this section must include:

(1) checking to ensure the fire extinguisher is present; and

(2) checking to ensure the fire extinguisher gauge or pressure indicator indicates the correct pressure as recommended by the manufacturer of the fire extinguisher.

(c) A fire extinguisher that satisfies the inspection requirements of Subsection (b) at the beginning of a tenant's possession is presumed to be in good working order until the tenant requests an inspection in writing.

History of Prop. Code §92.263: Acts 2011, 82nd Leg., ch. 257, §6, eff. Sept. 1, 2011.

PROP §92.264. DUTY TO REPAIR OR REPLACE

(a) The landlord shall repair or replace a fire extinguisher at the landlord's expense if:

(1) on inspection, the fire extinguisher is found:

(A) not to be functioning; or

(B) not to have the correct pressure indicated on the gauge or pressure indicator as recommended by the manufacturer of the fire extinguisher; or

(2) a tenant has notified the landlord that the tenant has used the fire extinguisher for a legitimate purpose.

(b) If the tenant or the tenant's invited guest removes, misuses, damages, or otherwise disables a fire extinguisher:

(1) the landlord is not required to repair or replace the fire extinguisher at the landlord's expense; and

(2) the landlord is required to repair or replace the fire extinguisher within a reasonable time if the tenant pays in advance the reasonable repair or replacement cost, including labor, materials, taxes, and overhead.

History of Prop. Code §92.264: Acts 2011, 82nd Leg., ch. 257, §6, eff. Sept. 1, 2011.

Sections 92.265-92.300 blank

SUBCHAPTER G. UTILITY CUTOFF

PROP §92.301. LANDLORD LIABILITY TO TENANT FOR UTILITY CUTOFF

(a) A landlord who has expressly or impliedly agreed in the lease to furnish and pay for water, gas, or electric service to the tenant's dwelling is liable to the tenant if the utility company has cut off utility service to the tenant's dwelling or has given written notice to the tenant that such utility service is about to be cut off because of the landlord's nonpayment of the utility bill.

(b) If a landlord is liable to the tenant under Subsection (a) of this section, the tenant may:

(1) pay the utility company money to reconnect or avert the cutoff of utilities according to this section;

(2) terminate the lease if the termination notice is in writing and move-out is to be within 30 days from the date the tenant has notice from the utility company of a future cutoff or notice of an actual cutoff, whichever is sooner;

(3) deduct from the tenant's rent, without necessity of judicial action, the amounts paid to the utility company to reconnect or avert a cutoff;

(4) if the lease is terminated by the tenant, deduct the tenant's security deposit from the tenant's rent without necessity of lawsuit or obtain a refund of the tenant's security deposit pursuant to law;

(5) if the lease is terminated by the tenant, recover a pro rata refund of any advance rentals paid from the date of termination or the date the tenant moves out, whichever is later;

(6) recover actual damages, including but not limited to moving costs, utility connection fees, storage fees, and lost wages from work; and

(7) recover court costs and attorney's fees, excluding any attorney's fees for a cause of action for damages relating to a personal injury.

(c) When deducting for the tenant's payment of the landlord's utility bill under this section, the tenant shall submit to the landlord a copy of a receipt from the utility company which evidences the amount of payment made by the tenant to reconnect or avert cutoff of utilities.

(d) The tenant remedies under this section are effective on the date the tenant has notice from the utility company of a future cutoff or notice of an actual cutoff, whichever is sooner. However, the tenant's remedies under this section shall cease if:

(1) the landlord provides the tenant with written evidence from the utility that all delinquent sums due the utility have been paid in full; and

(2) at the time the tenant receives such evidence, the tenant has not yet terminated the lease or filed suit under this section.

History of Prop. Code §92.301: Acts 1989, 71st Leg., ch. 650, §12, eff. Aug. 28, 1989.

See also *O'Connor's Texas COA*, "Exercising right or remedy," ch. 16-G, §2.2.2, p. 475.

PROP §92.302. NOTICE OF UTILITY DISCONNECTION OF NONSUBMETERED MASTER METERED MULTIFAMILY PROPERTY TO MUNICIPALITIES, OWNERS, & TENANTS

[illegible] must provide the notice by mail to the [illegible] owner's preferred mailing address or hand deliver the notice to the tenant or owner. The written notice must include the customer's contact information and the tenant's remedies under Section 92.301. The notice must include the following text in both English and Spanish:

"Notice to residents of (name and address of nonsubmetered master metered multifamily property): Electric (or gas) service to this property is scheduled for disconnection on (date) because (reason for disconnection)."

(c) If the property is located in a municipality, the customer shall provide the same notice described by Subsection (b) to the governing body of that municipality by certified mail. The governing body of the municipality may provide additional notice to the property's tenants and owners after receipt of the service disconnection notice under this subsection.

(d) A customer is not required to provide the notices described by this section if the customer avoids the disconnection by paying the bill.

History of Prop. Code §92.302: Acts 2013, 83rd Leg., ch. 322, §1, eff. Jan. 1, 2014.

Sections 92.303-92.330 blank

SUBCHAPTER H. RETALIATION

PROP §92.331. RETALIATION BY LANDLORD

(a) A landlord may not retaliate against a tenant by taking an action described by Subsection (b) because the tenant:

(1) in good faith exercises or attempts to exercise against a landlord a right or remedy granted to the tenant by lease, municipal ordinance, or federal or state statute;

(2) gives a landlord a notice to repair or exercise a remedy under this chapter;

(3) complains to a governmental entity responsible for enforcing building or housing codes, a public utility, or a civic or nonprofit agency, and the tenant:

(A) claims a building or housing code violation or utility problem; and

(B) believes in good faith that the complaint is valid and that the violation or problem occurred; or

(4) establishes, attempts to establish, or participates in a tenant organization.

(b) A landlord may not, within six months after the date of the tenant's action under Subsection (a), retaliate against the tenant by:

(1) filing an eviction proceeding, except for the grounds stated by Section 92.332;

(2) depriving the tenant of the use of the premises, except for reasons authorized by law;

(3) decreasing services to the tenant;

(4) increasing the tenant's rent or terminating the tenant's lease; or

(5) engaging, in bad faith, in a course of conduct that materially interferes with the tenant's rights under the tenant's lease.

History of Prop. Code §92.331: Acts 1983, 68th Leg., ch. 576, §1, eff. Jan. 1, 1984. Amended by Acts 1989, 71st Leg., ch. 650, §9, eff. Aug. 28, 1989; Acts 1993, 73rd Leg., ch. 48, §16, eff. Sept. 1, 1993. Renumbered from §92.057(a) and amended by Acts 1995, 74th Leg., ch. 869, §5, eff. Jan. 1, 1996. Amended by Acts 2013, 83rd Leg., ch. 588, §2, eff. Jan. 1, 2014. Source: TRCS art. 5236f, §7.

See also Prop. Code §§92.334, 92.335, 93.011, 94.251, 94.255; ***O'Connor's Texas COA***, "Landlord's retaliatory action," ch. 16-G, §2.3, p. 476.

ANNOTATIONS

Sims v. Century Kiest Apts., 567 S.W.2d 526, 532 (Tex.App.—Dallas 1978, no writ). "[W]e hold that retaliatory eviction is a legal wrong for which an action for damages will lie."

PROP §92.332. NONRETALIATION

(a) The landlord is not liable for retaliation under this subchapter if the landlord proves that the action was not made for purposes of retaliation, nor is the landlord liable, unless the action violates a prior court order under Section 92.0563, for:

(1) increasing rent under an escalation clause in a written lease for utilities, taxes, or insurance; or

(2) increasing rent or reducing services as part of a pattern of rent increases or service reductions for an entire multidwelling project.

(b) An eviction or lease termination based on the following circumstances, which are valid grounds for eviction or lease termination in any event, does not constitute retaliation:

(1) the tenant is delinquent in rent when the landlord gives notice to vacate or files an eviction action;

(2) the tenant, a member of the tenant's family, or a guest or invitee of the tenant intentionally damages property on the premises or by word or conduct threatens the personal safety of the landlord, the landlord's employees, or another tenant;

(3) the tenant has materially breached the lease, other than by holding over, by an action such as violating written lease provisions prohibiting serious misconduct or criminal acts, except as provided by this section;

(4) the tenant holds over after giving notice of termination or intent to vacate;

(5) the tenant holds over after the landlord gives notice of termination at the end of the rental term and the tenant does not take action under Section 92.331 until after the landlord gives notice of termination; or

(6) the tenant holds over and the landlord's notice of termination is motivated by a good faith belief that the tenant, a member of the tenant's family, or a guest or invitee of the tenant might:

(A) adversely affect the quiet enjoyment by other tenants or neighbors;

(B) materially affect the health or safety of the landlord, other tenants, or neighbors; or

(C) damage the property of the landlord, other tenants, or neighbors.

History of Prop. Code §92.332: Acts 1983, 68th Leg., ch. 576, §1, eff. Jan. 1, 1984. Amended by Acts 1989, 71st Leg., ch. 650, §9, eff. Aug. 28, 1989; Acts 1993, 73rd Leg., ch. 48, §16, eff. Sept. 1, 1993. Renumbered from §92.057(b), (c) and amended by Acts 1995, 74th Leg., ch. 869, §5, eff. Jan. 1, 1996.

See also *O'Connor's Texas COA*, "Landlord's retaliatory action," ch. 16-G, §2.3, p. 476.

PROP §92.333. TENANT REMEDIES

In addition to other remedies provided by law, if a landlord retaliates against a tenant under this subchapter, the tenant may recover from the landlord a civil penalty of one month's rent plus $500, actual damages, court costs, and reasonable attorney's fees in an action for recovery of property damages, moving costs, actual expenses, civil penalties, or declaratory or injunctive relief, less any delinquent rents or other sums for which the tenant is liable to the landlord. If the tenant's rent payment to the landlord is subsidized in whole or in part by a governmental entity, the civil penalty granted under this section shall reflect the fair market rent of the dwelling plus $500.

History of Prop. Code §92.333: Acts 1983, 68th Leg., ch. 576, §1, eff. Jan. 1, 1984. Amended by Acts 1989, 71st Leg., ch. 650, §9, eff. Aug. 28, 1989; Acts 1993, 73rd Leg., ch. 48, §16, eff. Sept. 1, 1993. Renumbered from §92.057(d) and amended by Acts 1995, 74th Leg., ch. 869, §5, eff. Jan. 1, 1996.

See also *O'Connor's Texas COA*, "Remedies," ch. 16-G, §3, p. 478.

PROP §92.334. INVALID COMPLAINTS

(a) If a tenant files or prosecutes a suit for retaliatory action based on a complaint asserted under Section 92.331(a)(3), and the government building or housing inspector or utility company representative visits the premises and determines in writing that a violation of a building or housing code does not exist or that a utility problem does not exist, there is a rebuttable presumption that the tenant acted in bad faith.

(b) If a tenant files or prosecutes a suit under this subchapter in bad faith, the landlord may recover possession of the dwelling unit and may recover from the tenant a civil penalty of one month's rent plus $500, court costs, and reasonable attorney's fees. If the tenant's rent payment to the landlord is subsidized in whole or in part by a governmental entity, the civil penalty granted under this section shall reflect the fair market rent of the dwelling plus $500.

History of Prop. Code §92.334: Acts 1995, 74th Leg., ch. 869, §5, eff. Jan. 1, 1996.

See also Prop. Code §§92.331, 94.251, 94.255; *O'Connor's Texas COA*, "Bad-faith complaint," ch. 16-G, §6.1, p. 479.

PROP §92.335. EVICTION SUITS

In an eviction suit, retaliation by the landlord under Section 92.331 is a defense and a rent deduction lawfully made by the tenant under this chapter is a defense for nonpayment of the rent to the extent allowed by this chapter. Other judicial actions under this chapter may not be joined with an eviction suit or asserted as a defense or crossclaim in an eviction suit.

History of Prop. Code §92.335: Acts 1983, 68th Leg., ch. 576, §1, eff. Jan. 1, 1984. Amended by Acts 1989, 71st Leg., ch. 650, §11, eff. Aug. 28, 1989. Renumbered from §92.059 and amended by Acts 1995, 74th Leg., ch. 869, §5, eff. Jan. 1, 1996.

See also *O'Connor's Texas COA*, "Landlord's retaliatory action," ch. 16-G, §2.3, p. 476.

ANNOTATIONS

Colbert v. Langwick Senior Residences, No. 14-10-01163-CV (Tex.App.—Houston [14th Dist.] 2011, no pet.) (memo op.; 12-13-11). Tenant "asserted retaliation as a defense to the forcible detainer action.... [Landlord] argued that (1) it did not move to evict [tenant] because of any complaints she may have filed with governmental entities, and (2) it instead moved to evict her based on her conduct toward other residents in violation of the lease agreement. [T]he trial court was within its authority as trier-of-fact to accept the testimony of the manager and other residents and discount that of [tenant]. [¶] The evidence is sufficient to support the trial court's implied finding that [landlord] did not file its forcible detainer action in retaliation for [tenant] having filed a complaint with a governmental entity."

Sections 92.336-92.350 blank

SUBCHAPTER I. RENTAL APPLICATION

PROP §92.351. DEFINITIONS

For purposes of this subchapter:

(1) "Application deposit" means a sum of money that is given to the landlord in connection with a rental application and that is refundable to the applicant if the applicant is rejected as a tenant.

(1-a) "Application fee" means a nonrefundable sum of money that is given to the landlord to offset the costs of screening an applicant for acceptance as a tenant.

(2) "Applicant" or "rental applicant" means a person who makes an application to a landlord for rental of a dwelling.

(3) "Co-applicant" means a person who makes an application for rental of a dwelling with other applicants and who plans to live in the dwelling with other applicants.

(4) "Deposited" means deposited in an account of the landlord or the landlord's agent in a bank or other financial institution.

(5) "Landlord" means a prospective landlord to whom a person makes application for rental of a dwelling.

(5-a) "Rental application" means a written request made by an applicant to a landlord to lease premises from the landlord.

(6) "Required date" means the required date for any acceptance of the applicant under Section 92.352.

History of Prop. Code §92.351: Acts 1995, 74th Leg., ch. 744, §5, eff. Jan. 1, 1996. Renumbered from §92.331 by Acts 1997, 75th Leg., ch. 165, §31.01(71), eff. Sept. 1, 1997. Amended by Acts 2007, 80th Leg., ch. 917, §§6, 7, eff. Jan. 1, 2008.

PROP §92.3515. NOTICE OF ELIGIBILITY REQUIREMENTS

(a) At the time an applicant is provided with a rental application, the landlord shall make available to the applicant printed notice of the landlord's tenant selection criteria and the grounds for which the rental application may be denied, including the applicant's:

(1) criminal history;

(2) previous rental history;

(3) current income;

(4) credit history; or

(5) failure to provide accurate or complete information on the application form.

(b) If the landlord makes the notice available under Subsection (a), the applicant shall sign an acknowledgment indicating the notice was made available. If the acknowledgment is not signed, there is a rebuttable presumption that the notice was not made available to the applicant.

(c) The acknowledgment required by Subsection (b) must include a statement substantively equivalent to the following: "Signing this acknowledgment indicates that you have had the opportunity to review the landlord's tenant selection criteria. The tenant selection criteria may include factors such as criminal history, credit history, current income, and rental history. If you do not meet the selection criteria, or if you provide inaccurate or incomplete information, your application may be rejected and your application fee will not be refunded."

(d) The acknowledgment may be part of the rental application if the notice is underlined or in bold print.

(e) If the landlord rejects an applicant and the landlord has not made the notice required by Subsection (a) available, the landlord shall return the application fee and any application deposit.

(f) If an applicant requests a landlord to mail a refund of the applicant's application fee to the applicant,

the landlord shall mail the refund check to the applicant at the address furnished by the applicant.

History of Prop. Code §92.3515: Acts 2007, 80th Leg., ch. 917, §8, eff. Jan. 1, 2008.

PROP §92.352. REJECTION OF APPLICANT

(a) The applicant is deemed rejected by the landlord if the landlord does not give notice of acceptance of the applicant on or before the seventh day after the:

(1) date the applicant submits a completed rental application to the landlord on an application form furnished by the landlord; or

(2) date the landlord accepts an application deposit if the landlord does not furnish the applicant an application form.

(b) A landlord's rejection of one co-applicant shall be deemed as a rejection of all co-applicants.

History of Prop. Code §92.352: Acts 1995, 74th Leg., ch. 744, §5, eff. Jan. 1, 1996. Renumbered from §92.332 by Acts 1997, 75th Leg., ch. 165, §31.01(71), eff. Sept. 1, 1997.

PROP §92.353. PROCEDURES FOR NOTICE OR REFUND

(a) Except as provided in Subsection (b), a landlord is presumed to have given notice of an applicant's acceptance or rejection if the notice is by:

(1) telephone to the applicant, co-applicant, or a person living with the applicant or co-applicant on or before the required date; or

(2) United States mail, addressed to the applicant and postmarked on or before the required date.

(b) If a rental applicant requests that any acceptance of the applicant or any refund of the applicant's application deposit be mailed to the applicant, the landlord must mail the refund check to the applicant at the address furnished by the applicant.

(c) If the date of required notice of acceptance or required refund of an application deposit is a Saturday, Sunday, or state or federal holiday, the required date shall be extended to the end of the next day following the Saturday, Sunday, or holiday.

History of Prop. Code §92.353: Acts 1995, 74th Leg., ch. 744, §5, eff. Jan. 1, 1996. Renumbered from §92.333 by Acts 1997, 75th Leg., ch. 165, §31.01(71), eff. Sept. 1, 1997.

PROP §92.354. LIABILITY OF LANDLORD

A landlord who in bad faith fails to refund an application fee or deposit in violation of this subchapter is liable for an amount equal to the sum of $100, three times the amount wrongfully retained, and the applicant's reasonable attorney's fees.

History of Prop. Code §92.354: Acts 1995, 74th Leg., ch. 744, §5, eff. Jan. 1, 1996. Renumbered from §92.334 by Acts 1997, 75th Leg., ch. 165, §31.01(71), eff. Sept. 1, 1997. Amended by Acts 2007, 80th Leg., ch. 917, §9, eff. Jan. 1, 2008.

ANNOTATIONS

Chen v. Johnson, No. 02-12-00428-CV (Tex.App.—Fort Worth 2013, no pet.) (memo op.; 5-30-13). "The documentary evidence establishes that [Ps] paid the application deposit on August 10 and that a refund was requested on August 14. … The evidence reflects that [Ps] were given two contradictory explanations for [Ds'] failure to refund the application deposit. First, they were told in [realtor's] August 24 letter that the application deposit was not refundable because [Ds] had accepted [Ps'] application and had taken the house off the market to lease to [Ps]. But the application itself states that 'unless Landlord and Applicant enter into a separate written agreement otherwise, the Property remains on the market until a lease is signed by all parties.' [P's] affidavit attests that no such separate agreement exists. Second, [Ps] were told verbally that the application they had completed was not a form furnished by [Ds]. But [Ps] were never provided with a different application. Finally, the September 9, 2011 letter from [Ps'] attorney expressly sets forth a demand for a refund of [Ps'] $1,500 application deposit and details why a refund is mandated pursuant to the terms of the property code. Yet, [Ps'] $1,500 application deposit was not refunded. [¶] Viewing the facts in the light most favorable to [Ps], more than a scintilla of evidence [exists] that a reasonable factfinder could have credited as constituting a bad faith failure by [co-D landlord] to refund [Ps'] application deposit."

PROP §92.355. WAIVER

A provision of a rental application that purports to waive a right or exempt a party from a liability or duty under this subchapter is void.

History of Prop. Code §92.355: Acts 2007, 80th Leg., ch. 917, §10, eff. Jan. 1, 2008.

CHAPTER 93. COMMERCIAL TENANCIES

PROP §93.001. APPLICABILITY OF CHAPTER

(a) This chapter applies only to the relationship between landlords and tenants of commercial rental property.

(b) For purposes of this chapter, "commercial rental property" means rental property that is not covered by Chapter 92.

History of Prop. Code §93.001: Acts 1989, 71st Leg., ch. 687, §2 (eff. Sept. 1, 1989), ch. 689, §2 (eff. Sept. 1, 1989).

See also *O'Connor's Texas COA*, "Residential or commercial," ch. 16-A, §2.2, p. 420.

ANNOTATIONS

Gym-N-I Playgrounds, Inc. v. Snider, 220 S.W.3d 905, 912 (Tex.2007). "[W]e squarely address whether an express disclaimer may waive the implied warranty of suitability in a commercial lease. ***Davidow [v. Inwood N. Prof'l Grp.***, 747 S.W.2d 373 (Tex.1988),] noted that the provisions of the lease would control if the parties expressly agreed that the tenant would repair certain defects. ***Prudential [Ins. v. Jefferson Assocs.***, 896 S.W.2d 156 (Tex.1995),] stands for the proposition that—absent fraud in the inducement—an 'as is' provision can waive claims based on a condition of the property. Taken together, these cases lead to one logical conclusion: the implied warranty of suitability is waived when … the lease expressly disclaims that warranty. *At 913-14:* We recognize that our holding today stands in contrast to the implied warranty of habitability, which 'can be waived only to the extent that defects are adequately disclosed.' … The fact that the lessor impliedly warrants suitability … ensures that, when the warranty is waived, the parties focus their attention on who is responsible for discovering and repairing latent defects, and they may allocate the risk accordingly. We see no compelling reason to disturb that market transaction here."

PROP §93.002. INTERRUPTION OF UTILITIES, REMOVAL OF PROPERTY, & EXCLUSION OF COMMERCIAL TENANT

(a) A landlord or a landlord's agent may not interrupt or cause the interruption of utility service paid for directly to the utility company by a tenant unless the interruption results from bona fide repairs, construction, or an emergency.

(b) A landlord may not remove a door, window, or attic hatchway cover or a lock, latch, hinge, hinge pin, doorknob, or other mechanism connected to a door, window, or attic hatchway cover from premises leased to a tenant or remove furniture, fixtures, or appliances furnished by the landlord from premises leased to a tenant unless the landlord removes the item for a bona fide repair or replacement. If a landlord removes any of the items listed in this subsection for a bona fide repair or replacement, the repair or replacement must be promptly performed.

(c) A landlord may not intentionally prevent a tenant from entering the leased premises except by judicial process unless the exclusion results from:

(1) bona fide repairs, construction, or an emergency;

(2) removing the contents of premises abandoned by a tenant; or

(3) changing the door locks of a tenant who is delinquent in paying at least part of the rent.

(d) A tenant is presumed to have abandoned the premises if goods, equipment, or other property, in an amount substantial enough to indicate a probable intent to abandon the premises, is being or has been removed from the premises and the removal is not within the normal course of the tenant's business.

(e) A landlord may remove and store any property of a tenant that remains on premises that are abandoned. In addition to the landlord's other rights, the landlord may dispose of the stored property if the tenant does not claim the property within 60 days after the date the property is stored. The landlord shall deliver by certified mail to the tenant at the tenant's last known address a notice stating that the landlord may dispose of the tenant's property if the tenant does not claim the property within 60 days after the date the property is stored.

(f) If a landlord or a landlord's agent changes the door lock of a tenant who is delinquent in paying rent, the landlord or agent must place a written notice on the tenant's front door stating the name and the address or telephone number of the individual or company from which the new key may be obtained. The new key is required to be provided only during the tenant's regular business hours and only if the tenant pays the delinquent rent.

(g) If a landlord or a landlord's agent violates this section, the tenant may:

(1) either recover possession of the premises or terminate the lease; and

(2) recover from the landlord an amount equal to the sum of the tenant's actual damages, one month's rent or $500, whichever is greater, reasonable attorney's fees, and court costs, less any delinquent rents or other sums for which the tenant is liable to the landlord.

(h) A lease supersedes this section to the extent of any conflict.

History of Prop. Code §93.002: Acts 1989, 71st Leg., ch. 689, §2, eff. Sept. 1, 1989. Amended by Acts 1993, 73rd Leg., ch. 44, §1, eff. Sept. 1, 1993.

See also Prop. Code §§92.008, 92.0081; *O'Connor's Texas COA*, "Reentry," ch. 16-C, p. 441; "Unlawful Lockout," ch. 16-D, p. 450; "Defenses," ch. 16-H, §5, p. 484; ***Real Estate Forms***, FORMS 2:2, 2:22, 2:23.

ANNOTATIONS

Lee v. Lee, 411 S.W.3d 95, 108 (Tex.App.—Houston [1st Dist.] 2013, no pet.). "The tenant's recovery for both rent and actual damages is not a double recovery, but instead it is expressly authorized by statute."

CenterPlace Props., Ltd. v. Columbia Med. Ctr. of Lewisville Subsidiary, L.P., 406 S.W.3d 674, 683-84 (Tex.App.—Fort Worth 2013, pet. granted, judgm't vacated w.r.m.). "[W]e hold that some level of landlord self-help beyond a notice of default or to vacate is required to create liability under §93.002(c). [Landlord] did not take any action—such as changing the locks, cutting off the utilities, reletting the premises to another tenant, or denying a request from [tenant] for access to the premises—that actually prevented [tenant] from entering the premises. The demand letters were legally incorrect and used sharp language, but notices alone are legally insufficient evidence of a §93.002(c) violation."

Zinda v. McCann St., Ltd., 178 S.W.3d 883, 890 (Tex.App.—Texarkana 2005, pet. denied). Tenant "contends the partnership did not comply with ... §93.002(f) because it did not put a written notice on the restaurant's front door stating where [tenant] could obtain a new key, and that this constitutes a breach, as a matter of law, that would prevent the partnership from executing the eviction under the terms of the agreement. The evidence does show that no notice was posted on the restaurant's front door. [Tenant] testified, however, that he already had all the information such a notice would have provided. There is evidence that [tenant] was present when the locks were being changed and that he and [his partners] had a meeting immediately thereafter to consider their options. Thus, unlike the absentee landlord situation that would be remedied by the posting of a formal notice on the door, there is no evidence [tenant] was harmed by the failure to so post a notice where all parties were fully involved in the proceedings leading up to the changing of the locks." *See also* ***Zouzalik v. Wells Fargo Bank***, No. 07-08-00411-CV (Tex.App.—Amarillo 2010, no pet.) (memo op.; 4-29-10).

Myers v. Ginsburg, 735 S.W.2d 600, 605 (Tex. App.—Dallas 1987, no writ). "[T]he fact that the lease authorized [landlord] to re-enter the premises and take possession of the equipment did not confer on him the right to take the equipment and hold it indefinitely without sale, credit, or payment of any surplus by which the value of the equipment exceeded the amount due for rent. Where a landlord's lien is foreclosed through sale of the property attached under said lien, or through a judgment of court, the tenant is entitled to have the sale proceeds, or the value of the property, credited against his arrearage for rent and to have any surplus paid to him."

PROP §93.003. COMMERCIAL TENANT'S RIGHT OF REENTRY AFTER UNLAWFUL LOCKOUT

(a) If a landlord has locked a tenant out of leased premises in violation of Section 93.002, the tenant may recover possession of the premises as provided by this section.

(b) The tenant must file with the justice court in the precinct in which the rental premises are located a sworn complaint for reentry, specifying the facts of the alleged unlawful lockout by the landlord or the landlord's agent. The tenant must also state orally under oath to the justice the facts of the alleged unlawful lockout.

(c) If the tenant has complied with Subsection (b) and if the justice reasonably believes an unlawful lockout has likely occurred, the justice may issue, ex parte, a writ of reentry that entitles the tenant to immediate and temporary possession of the premises, pending a final hearing on the tenant's sworn complaint for reentry.

(d) The writ of reentry must be served on either the landlord or the landlord's management company, on-premises manager, or rent collector in the same manner as a writ of possession in a forcible detainer action. A sheriff or constable may use reasonable force in executing a writ of reentry under this section.

(e) The landlord is entitled to a hearing on the tenant's sworn complaint for reentry. The writ of reentry must notify the landlord of the right to a hearing. The hearing shall be held not earlier than the first day and not later than the seventh day after the date the landlord requests a hearing.

(f) If the landlord fails to request a hearing on the tenant's sworn complaint for reentry before the eighth day after the date of service of the writ of reentry on the landlord under Subsection (d), a judgment for court costs may be rendered against the landlord.

(g) A party may appeal from the court's judgment at the hearing on the sworn complaint for reentry in the same manner as a party may appeal a judgment in a forcible detainer suit.

(h) If a writ of possession is issued, it supersedes a writ of reentry.

(i) If the landlord or the person on whom a writ of reentry is served fails to immediately comply with the writ or later disobeys the writ, the failure is grounds for contempt of court against the landlord or the person on whom the writ was served, under Section 21.002, Government Code. If the writ is disobeyed, the tenant or the tenant's attorney may file in the court in which the reentry action is pending an affidavit stating the name of the person who has disobeyed the writ and describing the acts or omissions constituting the disobedience. On receipt of an affidavit, the justice shall issue a show cause order, directing the person to appear on a designated date and show cause why he should not be adjudged in contempt of court. If the justice finds, after considering the evidence at the hearing, that the person has directly or indirectly disobeyed the writ, the justice may commit the person to jail without bail until the person purges himself of the contempt in a manner and form as the justice may direct. If the person disobeyed the writ before receiving the show cause order but has complied with the writ after receiving the order, the justice may find the person in contempt and assess punishment under Section 21.002(c), Government Code.

(j) This section does not affect a tenant's right to pursue a separate cause of action under Section 93.002.

(k) If a tenant in bad faith files a sworn complaint for reentry resulting in a writ of reentry being served on the landlord or landlord's agent, the landlord may in a separate cause of action recover from the tenant an amount equal to actual damages, one month's rent or $500, whichever is greater, reasonable attorney's fees, and costs of court, less any sums for which the landlord is liable to the tenant.

(*l*) The fee for filing a sworn complaint for reentry is the same as that for filing a civil action in justice court. The fee for service of a writ of reentry is the same as that for service of a writ of possession. The fee for service of a show cause order is the same as that for service of a civil citation. The justice may defer payment of the tenant's filing fees and service costs for the sworn complaint for reentry and writ of reentry. Court costs may be waived only if the tenant executes a pauper's affidavit.

(m) This section does not affect the rights of a landlord or tenant in a forcible detainer or forcible entry and detainer action.

History of Prop. Code §93.003: Acts 1989, 71st Leg., ch. 687, §2, eff. Sept. 1, 1989. Amended by Acts 2001, 77th Leg., ch. 595, §1, eff. June 11, 2001.

See also Prop. Code §§92.0081, 92.009; ***O'Connor's Texas COA***, "Reentry," ch. 16-C, p. 441.

ANNOTATIONS

Big State Pawn & Bargain Ctr. v. Garton, 833 S.W.2d 669, 671 (Tex.App.—Eastland 1992, writ denied). "We hold that [CPRC] §51.002 … does not exclude suits for reentry under [Prop. Code] §93.003…. [A] party in a suit for reentry under §93.003 may either appeal 'in the same manner as a party may appeal a judgment in a forcible detainer suit' or file a writ of certiorari under §51.002."

PROP §93.004. SECURITY DEPOSIT

A security deposit is any advance of money, other than a rental application deposit or an advance payment of rent, that is intended primarily to secure performance under a lease of commercial rental property.

History of Prop. Code §93.004: Acts 2001, 77th Leg., ch. 1460, §1, eff. Sept. 1, 2001.

PROP §93.005. OBLIGATION TO REFUND SECURITY DEPOSIT

(a) The landlord shall refund the security deposit to the tenant not later than the 60th day after the date the tenant surrenders the premises and provides notice to the landlord or the landlord's agent of the tenant's forwarding address under Section 93.009.

(b) The tenant's claim to the security deposit takes priority over the claim of any creditor of the landlord, including a trustee in bankruptcy.

History of Prop. Code §93.005: Acts 2001, 77th Leg., ch. 1460, §1, eff. Sept. 1, 2001. Amended by Acts 2003, 78th Leg., ch. 1143, §1, eff. Sept. 1, 2003.

See also Prop. Code §§92.107, 93.009.

ANNOTATIONS

Jones & Gonzalez, P.C. v. Trinh, 340 S.W.3d 830, 837 (Tex.App.—San Antonio 2011, no pet.). "To be liable for bad faith retention of a security deposit, a landlord must have failed to return the tenant's security deposit and a written list of itemized deductions, if any, for any portion of the security deposit that the landlord retains. The landlord must send to the tenant the remaining security deposit and the list of itemized deductions within 60 days of the tenant's surrendering possession of the premises. However, the 60-day period does not start until after the tenant provides the landlord with a written statement of a forwarding address for the purpose of returning the security deposit. Given the penal nature of the statutory remedy, this requirement is strictly construed. [¶] Because this requirement is strictly construed, it does not matter whether or not [lessor] had actual knowledge of an address where [lessee] could be contacted."

PROP §93.006. RETENTION OF SECURITY DEPOSIT; ACCOUNTING

(a) Before returning a security deposit, the landlord may deduct from the deposit damages and charges for which the tenant is legally liable under the lease or damages and charges that result from a breach of the lease.

(b) The landlord may not retain any portion of a security deposit to cover normal wear and tear. In this subsection, "normal wear and tear" means deterioration that results from the intended use of the commercial premises, including breakage or malfunction due to age or deteriorated condition, but the term does not include deterioration that results from negligence, carelessness, accident, or abuse of the premises, equipment, or chattels by the tenant or by a guest or invitee of the tenant.

(c) If the landlord retains all or part of a security deposit under this section, the landlord shall give to the tenant the balance of the security deposit, if any, together with a written description and itemized list of all deductions. The landlord is not required to give the tenant a description and itemized list of deductions if:

(1) the tenant owes rent when the tenant surrenders possession of the premises; and

(2) no controversy exists concerning the amount of rent owed.

History of Prop. Code §93.006: Acts 2001, 77th Leg., ch. 1460, §1, eff. Sept. 1, 2001.

See also Prop. Code §§92.104, 92.109, 93.011.

ANNOTATIONS

Lone Starr Multi-Theatres, Ltd. v. Max Interests, Ltd., 365 S.W.3d 688, 701 (Tex.App.—Houston [1st Dist.] 2011, no pet.). Landlord "sent to [tenant] a letter with an attached [construction schedule] and setting forth an itemized list of repairs. [¶] [Tenant] asserts that, 'as a matter of law,' the construction schedule is not sufficiently detailed and '[m]erely naming a thing does not describe it.' [W]e conclude that the jury could have reasonably found that the schedule provided by [landlord] sufficiently described each item within the property that was not in 'good condition' and the photographs attached to the original e-mail provided further detail. [Tenant] did not agree with [landlord] that the items listed in the schedule were in poor condition, and it asserted that many of the photographs depicted only 'normal wear and tear.' However, the jury could have reasonably found that [landlord], by providing the written and itemized schedule, furnished the necessary information in compliance with §93.006(c). [¶] [Tenant], at trial, ... only argued that [landlord] had forfeited its right to withhold any portion of the security deposit or to bring suit against it for damages to the premises."

PROP §93.007. CESSATION OF OWNER'S INTEREST

(a) If the owner's interest in the premises is terminated by sale, assignment, death, appointment of a receiver, bankruptcy, or otherwise, the new owner is liable for the return of the security deposit according to this chapter from the date title to the premises is acquired, regardless of whether an acknowledgement is given to the tenant under Subsection (b).

(b) The person who no longer owns an interest in the rental premises remains liable for a security deposit received while the person was the owner until the new owner delivers to the tenant a signed statement acknowledging that the new owner has received and is responsible for the tenant's security deposit and specifying the exact dollar amount of the deposit. The amount of the security deposit is the greater of:

(1) the amount provided in the tenant's lease; or

(2) the amount provided in an estoppel certificate prepared by the owner at the time the lease was ex-

ecuted or prepared by the new owner at the time the commercial property is transferred.

(c) Subsection (a) does not apply to a real estate mortgage lienholder who acquires title by foreclosure.

History of Prop. Code §93.007: Acts 2001, 77th Leg., ch. 1460, §1, eff. Sept. 1, 2001.

See also Prop. Code §92.105; *Real Estate Forms*, FORM 1:19.

PROP §93.008. RECORDS

The landlord shall keep accurate records of all security deposits.

History of Prop. Code §93.008: Acts 2001, 77th Leg., ch. 1460, §1, eff. Sept. 1, 2001.

PROP §93.009. TENANT'S FORWARDING ADDRESS

(a) The landlord is not obligated to return a tenant's security deposit or give the tenant a written description of damages and charges until the tenant gives the landlord a written statement of the tenant's forwarding address for the purpose of refunding the security deposit.

(b) The tenant does not forfeit the right to a refund of the security deposit or the right to receive a description of damages and charges for failing to give a forwarding address to the landlord.

History of Prop. Code §93.009: Acts 2001, 77th Leg., ch. 1460, §1, eff. Sept. 1, 2001.

ANNOTATIONS

Jones & Gonzalez, P.C. v. Trinh, 340 S.W.3d 830, 837 (Tex.App.—San Antonio 2011, no pet.). See annotation under Property Code §93.005, p. 485.

PROP §93.010. LIABILITY FOR WITHHOLDING LAST MONTH'S RENT

(a) The tenant may not withhold payment of any portion of the last month's rent on grounds that the security deposit is security for unpaid rent.

(b) A tenant who violates this section is presumed to have acted in bad faith. A tenant who in bad faith violates this section is liable to the landlord for an amount equal to three times the rent wrongfully withheld and the landlord's reasonable attorney's fees in a suit to recover the rent.

History of Prop. Code §93.010: Acts 2001, 77th Leg., ch. 1460, §1, eff. Sept. 1, 2001.

ANNOTATIONS

S.T.N. Props., Ltd. v. Rio Grande Valley All Tune & Lube, Inc., No. 13-13-00706-CV (Tex.App.—Corpus Christi 2015, no pet.) (memo op.; 9-1-15). "[P] asserts that [D] breached §93.010 … when [D] attempted to apply the security deposit to the outstanding [Common Area Maintenance (CAM)] fee. [D] responds that §93.010 applies specifically to the withholding of the 'last month's rent' and is inapplicable to the quarterly CAM fee at issue. [¶] Section 93.010 is titled 'Liability for Withholding *Last Month's* Rent' and in subsection (a) specifically references that it prohibits the withholding of any portion of the *last month's* rent. [W]e cannot disregard the Legislature's deliberate use of the words 'last month's rent' in the statute. Had the Legislature intended to create statutory liability for the withholding of fees or other rental amounts, it could have written the statute to apply more broadly. [¶] Though the commercial lease agreement identifies the quarterly CAM fees as 'additional rents,' it is clear from the record that the CAM fees were not a portion of the last month's rent that [D] owed [P]. … Therefore, … we conclude that [D] did not violate §93.010…."

PROP §93.011. LIABILITY OF LANDLORD

(a) A landlord who in bad faith retains a security deposit in violation of this chapter is liable for an amount equal to the sum of $100, three times the portion of the deposit wrongfully withheld, and the tenant's reasonable attorney's fees incurred in a suit to recover the deposit after the period prescribed for returning the deposit expires.

(b) A landlord who in bad faith does not provide a written description and itemized list of damages and charges in violation of this chapter:

(1) forfeits the right to withhold any portion of the security deposit or to bring suit against the tenant for damages to the premises; and

(2) is liable for the tenant's reasonable attorney's fees in a suit to recover the deposit.

(c) In a suit brought by a tenant under this chapter, the landlord has the burden of proving that the retention of any portion of the security deposit was reasonable.

(d) A landlord who fails to return a security deposit or to provide a written description and itemized list of deductions on or before the 60th day after the date the tenant surrenders possession is presumed to have acted in bad faith.

History of Prop. Code §93.011: Acts 2001, 77th Leg., ch. 1460, §1, eff. Sept. 1, 2001. Amended by Acts 2003, 78th Leg., ch. 1143, §2, eff. Sept. 1, 2003.

See also Prop. Code §§92.104, 92.109, 92.331, 93.006, 94.251.

ANNOTATIONS

FP Stores v. Tramontina US, Inc., 513 S.W.3d 684, 692-93 (Tex.App.—Houston [1st Dist.] 2016, pet. filed 3-31-17). "There is a dearth of case law construing and applying [Prop. Code] §93.011. For guidance, then, we look to the more developed body of case law construing and applying [Prop.] Code §92.109—a parallel statute that applies to residential tenancies. [¶] The §92.109 case law is instructive here. Accordingly, we hold that, under ... §93.011, a commercial landlord retains a tenant's security deposit in bad faith if it retains the security deposit in dishonest disregard of the tenant's rights or with the intent to deprive the tenant of a lawfully due refund. [¶] To rebut the presumption to defeat a tenant's motion for summary judgment, ... the landlord must present more than a scintilla of evidence of 'honesty in fact in the conduct or transaction involved'—that it acted with an honest regard for the tenant's rights and the intent to provide the tenant with a refund and an accounting."

Lee v. Lee, 411 S.W.3d 95, 106 (Tex.App.—Houston [1st Dist.] 2013, no pet.). "[T]he issue of §93.011 statutory damages for wrongful retention of the security deposit in bad faith was not raised in either party's pleadings. Thus, we must determine whether the issue was tried by consent. *At 107:* [T]here is a dearth of evidence that the parties tried the issue.... No testimony was elicited on whether his actions were in bad faith, as opposed to a good-faith disagreement about the interpretation of the parties' agreements. The landlord also did not present evidence to attempt to rebut the presumption of bad faith." Held: Unpleaded issue was not tried by consent.

PROP §93.012. ASSESSMENT OF CHARGES

(a) A landlord may not assess a charge, excluding a charge for rent or physical damage to the leased premises, to a tenant unless the amount of the charge or the method by which the charge is to be computed is stated in the lease, an exhibit or attachment that is part of the lease, or an amendment to the lease.

(b) This section does not affect a landlord's right to assess a charge or obtain a remedy allowed under a statute or common law.

(c) This section does not affect the contractual right of a landlord that is a governmental entity created under Subchapter D, Chapter 22, Transportation Code, whose constituent municipalities are populous home-rule municipalities to assess charges under a lease to fully compensate the governmental entity for the governmental entity's operating costs.

History of Prop. Code §93.012: Acts 2001, 77th Leg., ch. 1397, §1, eff. Sept. 1, 2001. Renumbered from §93.004 by Acts 2003, 78th Leg., ch. 1275, §2(119), eff. Sept. 1, 2003. Amended by Acts 2009, 81st Leg., ch. 71, §1, eff. May 20, 2009.

See also *Real Estate Forms*, FORMS 2:2, 2:3.

Ⓔ PROP §93.013. CERTAIN UNLAWFUL USES OF PREMISES; TERMINATION OF TENANT'S RIGHT OF POSSESSION

(a) Notwithstanding a provision in a lease to the contrary, a tenant's right of possession terminates and the landlord has a right to recover possession of the leased premises if the tenant is using the premises or allowing the premises to be used for the purposes of prostitution, promotion of prostitution, aggravated promotion of prostitution, or compelling prostitution, as prohibited by the Penal Code, or trafficking of persons as described by Section 20A.02, Penal Code.

(b) A landlord who reasonably believes a tenant is using the leased premises or allowing the leased premises to be used for a purpose described by Subsection (a) may file a forcible detainer suit under Chapter 24 seeking possession of the premises and unpaid rent, including rent for any period of occupancy after the tenant's right of possession terminates.

(c) Notwithstanding Section 24.005 or 91.001 or any other law or a provision in the lease to the contrary, the landlord is not required for purposes of a forcible detainer suit authorized by this section:

(1) to give a notice of proposed eviction or a notice of termination before giving notice to vacate; or

(2) to give the tenant more than three days' notice to vacate before filing the suit.

(d) A pending suit brought by the attorney general or a district, county, or city attorney under Chapter 125, Civil Practice and Remedies Code, alleging that a common nuisance is being maintained on the leased premises with respect to an activity described by Subsection (a) is prima facie evidence that the tenant's right of possession has terminated and the landlord has a right to recover possession of the premises under Subsection (a).

(e) A final, nonappealable determination by a court under Chapter 125, Civil Practice and Remedies Code, that a common nuisance is being maintained on the leased premises with respect to an activity described by

Subsection (a) creates an irrebuttable presumption that the tenant's right of possession has terminated and the landlord has a right to recover possession of the premises under Subsection (a).

History of Prop. Code §93.013: Enacted by H.B. 2552, §19, 85th Leg., eff. Sept. 1, 2017.

CHAPTER 94. MANUFACTURED HOME TENANCIES

SUBCHAPTER A. GENERAL PROVISIONS

PROP §94.001. DEFINITIONS

In this chapter:

(1) "Landlord" means the owner or manager of a manufactured home community and includes an employee or agent of the landlord.

(2) "Lease agreement" means a written agreement between a landlord and a tenant that establishes the terms, conditions, and other provisions for placing a manufactured home on the premises of a manufactured home community.

(3) "Manufactured home" has the meaning assigned by Section 1201.003, Occupations Code.

(4) "Manufactured home community" means a parcel of land on which four or more lots are offered for lease for installing and occupying manufactured homes.

(5) "Manufactured home community rules" means the rules provided in a written document that establish the policies and regulations of the manufactured home community, including regulations relating to the use, occupancy, and quiet enjoyment of and the health, safety, and welfare of tenants of the manufactured home community.

(6) "Manufactured home lot" means the space allocated in the lease agreement for the placement of the tenant's manufactured home and the area adjacent to that space designated in the lease agreement for the tenant's exclusive use.

(7) "Normal wear and tear" means deterioration that results from intended use of the premises, includ-

ing breakage or malfunction due to age or deteriorated condition, but the term does not include deterioration that results from negligence, carelessness, accident, or abuse of the premises, equipment, or chattels by the tenant, a member of the tenant's household, or a guest or invitee of the tenant.

(8) Repealed by Acts 2013, 83rd Leg., ch. 613, §8, eff. Sept. 1, 2013.

(9) "Premises" means a tenant's manufactured home lot, any area or facility the lease authorizes the tenant to use, and the appurtenances, grounds, and facilities held out for the use of tenants generally.

(10) Repealed by Acts 2013, 83rd Leg., ch. 613, §8, eff. Sept. 1, 2013.

(11) "Tenant" means a person who is:

(A) authorized by a lease agreement to occupy a lot to the exclusion of others in a manufactured home community; and

(B) obligated under the lease agreement to pay rent, fees, and other charges.

History of Prop. Code §94.001: Acts 2001, 77th Leg., ch. 801, §1, eff. Apr. 1, 2002. Amended by Acts 2003, 78th Leg., ch. 75, §1 (eff. May 16, 2003), ch. 1276, §14A.808 (eff. Sept. 1, 2003); Acts 2013, 83rd Leg., ch. 613, §§2, 8, eff. Sept. 1, 2013.

PROP §94.002. APPLICABILITY

(a) This chapter applies only to the relationship between a landlord who leases property in a manufactured home community and a tenant leasing property in the manufactured home community for the purpose of situating a manufactured home on the property.

(b) This chapter does not apply to the relationship between:

(1) a landlord who owns a manufactured home and a tenant who leases the manufactured home from the landlord;

(2) a landlord who leases property in a manufactured home community and a tenant leasing property in the manufactured home community for the placement of personal property to be used for human habitation, excluding a manufactured home; or

(3) a landlord and an employee or an agent of the landlord.

History of Prop. Code §94.002: Acts 2001, 77th Leg., ch. 801, §1, eff. Apr. 1, 2002. Amended by Acts 2013, 83rd Leg., ch. 613, §3, eff. Sept. 1, 2013.

PROP §94.003. WAIVER OF RIGHTS & DUTIES

A provision in a lease agreement or a manufactured home community rule that purports to waive a right or to exempt a landlord or a tenant from a duty or from liability under this chapter is void.

History of Prop. Code §94.003: Acts 2001, 77th Leg., ch. 801, §1, eff. Apr. 1, 2002.

PROP §94.004. LANDLORD'S RIGHT OF ENTRY

(a) Except as provided by this chapter, the landlord may not enter a tenant's manufactured home unless:

(1) the tenant is present and gives consent; or

(2) the tenant has previously given written consent.

(b) The written consent under Subsection (a)(2) must specify the date and time entry is permitted and is valid only for the date and time specified. The tenant may revoke the consent without penalty at any time by notifying the landlord in writing that the consent has been revoked.

(c) The landlord may enter the tenant's manufactured home in a reasonable manner and at a reasonable time if:

(1) an emergency exists; or

(2) the tenant abandons the manufactured home.

History of Prop. Code §94.004: Acts 2001, 77th Leg., ch. 801, §1, eff. Apr. 1, 2002.

PROP §94.005. COMMON AREA FACILITIES

Each common area facility, if any, must be open or available to tenants. The landlord shall post the hours of operation or availability of the facility in a conspicuous place at the facility.

History of Prop. Code §94.005: Acts 2001, 77th Leg., ch. 801, §1, eff. Apr. 1, 2002.

PROP §94.006. TENANT MEETINGS

(a) Except as provided by Subsection (b), a landlord may not interfere with meetings by tenants of the manufactured home community related to manufactured home living.

(b) Any limitations on meetings by tenants in the common area facilities must be included in the manufactured home community rules.

History of Prop. Code §94.006: Acts 2001, 77th Leg., ch. 801, §1, eff. Apr. 1, 2002.

PROP §94.007. CASH RENTAL PAYMENTS

(a) A landlord shall accept a tenant's cash rental payment unless the lease agreement requires the tenant to make rental payments by check, money order, or other traceable or negotiable instrument.

(b) A landlord who receives a cash rental payment shall:

(1) provide the tenant with a written receipt; and

(2) enter the payment date and amount in a record book maintained by the landlord.

(c) A tenant or a governmental entity or civic association acting on the tenant's behalf may file suit against a landlord to enjoin a violation of this section.

History of Prop. Code §94.007: Acts 2001, 77th Leg., ch. 801, §1, eff. Apr. 1, 2002.

See also *Real Estate Forms*, FORM 2:6.

PROP §94.008. MANUFACTURED HOME COMMUNITY RULES

(a) A landlord may adopt manufactured home community rules that are not arbitrary or capricious.

(b) Manufactured home community rules are considered part of the lease agreement.

(c) The landlord may add to or amend manufactured home community rules. If the landlord adds or amends a rule:

(1) the rule is not effective until the 30th day after the date each tenant is provided with a written copy of the added or amended rule; and

(2) if a tenant is required to take any action that requires the expenditure of funds in excess of $25 to comply with the rule, the landlord shall give the tenant at least 90 days after the date each tenant is provided with a written copy of the added or amended rule to comply with the rule.

History of Prop. Code §94.008: Acts 2001, 77th Leg., ch. 801, §1, eff. Apr. 1, 2002.

PROP §94.009. NOTICE TO TENANT AT PRIMARY RESIDENCE

(a) If, at the time of signing a lease agreement or lease renewal, a tenant gives written notice to the tenant's landlord that the tenant does not occupy the manufactured home lot as a primary residence and requests in writing that the landlord send notices to the tenant at the tenant's primary residence and provides to the landlord the address of the tenant's primary residence, the landlord shall mail to the tenant's primary residence all notices required by the lease agreement, by this chapter, or by Chapter 24.

(b) The tenant shall notify the landlord in writing of any change in the tenant's primary residence address. Oral notices of change are insufficient.

(c) A notice to a tenant's primary residence under Subsection (a) may be sent by regular United States mail and is considered as having been given on the date of postmark of the notice.

(d) If there is more than one tenant on a lease agreement, the landlord is not required under this section to send notices to the primary residence of more than one tenant.

(e) This section does not apply if notice is actually hand delivered to and received by a person 16 years of age or older occupying the leased premises.

History of Prop. Code §94.009: Acts 2001, 77th Leg., ch. 801, §1, eff. Apr. 1, 2002.

PROP §94.010. DISCLOSURE OF OWNERSHIP & MANAGEMENT

(a) A landlord shall disclose to a tenant, or to any governmental official or employee acting in an official capacity, according to this section:

(1) the name and either a street or post office box address of the holder of record title, according to the deed records in the county clerk's office, of the premises leased by the tenant or inquired about by the governmental official or employee acting in an official capacity; and

(2) if an entity located off-site from the manufactured home community is primarily responsible for managing the leased premises, the name and street address of that entity.

(b) Disclosure to a tenant under Subsection (a) must be made by:

(1) giving the information in writing to the tenant on or before the seventh day after the date the landlord receives the tenant's written request for the information;

(2) continuously posting the information in a conspicuous place in the manufactured home community or the office of the on-site manager or on the outside of the entry door to the office of the on-site manager on or before the seventh day after the date the landlord receives the tenant's written request for the information; or

(3) including the information in a copy of the tenant's lease or in written manufactured home community rules given to the tenant before the tenant requests the information.

(c) Disclosure of information to a tenant may be made under Subsection (b)(1) or (2) before the tenant requests the information.

(d) Disclosure of information to a governmental official or employee must be made by giving the infor-

mation in writing to the official or employee on or before the seventh day after the date the landlord receives a written request for the information from the official or employee.

(e) A correction to the information may be made by any of the methods authorized and must be made within the period prescribed by this section for providing the information.

(f) For the purposes of this section, an owner or property manager may disclose either an actual name or an assumed name if an assumed name certificate has been recorded with the county clerk.

(g) A landlord who provides information under this section violates this section if:

(1) the information becomes incorrect because a name or address changes; and

(2) the landlord fails to correct the information given to a tenant on or before the 15th day after the date the information becomes incorrect.

History of Prop. Code §94.010: Acts 2001, 77th Leg., ch. 801, §1, eff. Apr. 1, 2002.

PROP §94.011. LANDLORD'S AGENT FOR SERVICE OF PROCESS

(a) In a lawsuit by a tenant to enforce a legal obligation of the owner as landlord of the manufactured home community, the owner's agent for service of process is determined according to this section.

(b) The owner's management company, on-site manager, or rent collector for the manufactured home community is the owner's authorized agent for service of process unless the owner's name and business street address have been furnished in writing to the tenant.

History of Prop. Code §94.011: Acts 2001, 77th Leg., ch. 801, §1, eff. Apr. 1, 2002.

PROP §94.012. VENUE

Venue for an action under this chapter is governed by Section 15.0115, Civil Practice and Remedies Code.

History of Prop. Code §94.012: Acts 2001, 77th Leg., ch. 801, §1, eff. Apr. 1, 2002.

Sections 94.013-94.050 reserved for expansion

SUBCHAPTER B. LEASE AGREEMENT

PROP §94.051. INFORMATION TO BE PROVIDED TO PROSPECTIVE TENANT

At the time the landlord receives an application from a prospective tenant, the landlord shall give the tenant a copy of:

(1) the proposed lease agreement for the manufactured home community;

(2) any manufactured home community rules; and

(3) a separate disclosure statement with the following prominently printed in at least 10-point type:

"You have the legal right to an initial lease term of six months. If you prefer a different lease period, you and your landlord may negotiate a shorter or longer lease period. After the initial lease period expires, you and your landlord may negotiate a new lease term by mutual agreement. Regardless of the term of the lease, the landlord must give you at least 60 days' notice of a nonrenewal of the lease, except that if the manufactured home community's land use will change, the landlord must give you at least 180 days' notice. During the applicable period, you must continue to pay all rent and other amounts due under the lease agreement, including late charges, if any, after receiving notice of the nonrenewal."

History of Prop. Code §94.051: Acts 2001, 77th Leg., ch. 801, §1, eff. Apr. 1, 2002. Amended by Acts 2003, 78th Leg., ch. 75, §2, eff. May 16, 2003; Acts 2007, 80th Leg., ch. 863, §65, eff. Jan. 1, 2008.

PROP §94.052. TERM OF LEASE

(a) A landlord shall offer the tenant a lease agreement with an initial lease term of at least six months. If the tenant requests a lease agreement with a different lease period, the landlord and the tenant may mutually agree to a shorter or longer lease period. The landlord and the tenant may mutually agree to subsequent lease periods of any length for each renewal of the lease agreement.

(b) Except as provided by Section 94.204, regardless of the term of the lease, the landlord must provide notice to the tenant not later than the 60th day before the date of the expiration of the lease if the landlord chooses not to renew the lease. During the applicable period, the tenant must pay all rent and other amounts due under the lease agreement, including late charges, if any, after receiving notice of the nonrenewal.

History of Prop. Code §94.052: Acts 2001, 77th Leg., ch. 801, §1, eff. Apr. 1, 2002. Amended by Acts 2007, 80th Leg., ch. 863, §66, eff. Jan. 1, 2008.

PROP §94.053. LEASE REQUIREMENTS & DISCLOSURES

(a) A lease agreement must be:

(1) typed or printed in legible handwriting; and

(2) signed by the landlord and the tenant.

(b) The landlord shall provide the tenant with a copy of the lease agreement and a current copy of the manufactured home community rules after the lease has been signed.

(c) A lease agreement must contain the following information:

(1) the address or number of the manufactured home lot and the number and location of any accompanying parking spaces;

(2) the lease term;

(3) the rental amount;

(4) the interval at which rent must be paid and the date on which periodic rental payments are due;

(5) any late charge or fee or charge for any service or facility;

(6) the amount of any security deposit;

(7) a description of the landlord's maintenance responsibilities;

(8) the telephone number of the person who may be contacted for emergency maintenance;

(9) the name and address of the person designated to accept official notices for the landlord;

(10) the penalty the landlord may impose for the tenant's early termination as provided by Section 94.201;

(11) the grounds for eviction as provided by Subchapter E;

(12) a disclosure of the landlord's right to choose not to renew the lease agreement if there is a change in the land use of the manufactured home community during the lease term as provided by Section 94.204;

(13) a disclosure of any incorporation by reference of an addendum relating to submetering of utility services;

(14) a prominent disclosure informing the tenant that Chapter 94, Property Code, governs certain rights granted to the tenant and obligations imposed on the landlord by law;

(15) if there is a temporary zoning permit for the land use of the manufactured home community, the date the zoning permit expires; and

(16) any other terms or conditions of occupancy not expressly included in the manufactured home community rules.

(d) A lease provision requiring an increase in rent or in fees or charges during the lease term must be initialed by the tenant or the provision is void.

(e) Any illegal or unconscionable provision in a lease is void. If a lease provision is determined void, the invalidity of the provision does not affect other provisions of the lease that can be given effect without reference to the invalid provision.

History of Prop. Code §94.053: Acts 2001, 77th Leg., ch. 801, §1, eff. Apr. 1, 2002. Amended by Acts 2007, 80th Leg., ch. 863, §67, eff. Jan. 1, 2008.

PROP §94.054. DISCLOSURE BY TENANT REQUIRED

A tenant shall disclose to the landlord before the lease agreement is signed the name and address of any person who holds a lien on the tenant's manufactured home.

History of Prop. Code §94.054: Acts 2001, 77th Leg., ch. 801, §1, eff. Apr. 1, 2002.

PROP §94.055. NOTICE OF LEASE RENEWAL

(a) The landlord shall provide a tenant a notice to vacate the leased premises or an offer of lease renewal:

(1) not later than the 60th day before the date the current lease term expires; or

(2) if the lease is a month-to-month lease, not later than the 60th day before the date the landlord intends to terminate the current term of the lease.

(b) If the landlord offers to renew the lease, the landlord shall notify the tenant of the proposed rent amount and any change in the lease terms. The notice must also include a statement informing the tenant that the tenant's failure to reject the landlord's offer to renew the lease within the 30-day period prescribed by Subsection (c) will result in the renewal of the lease under the modified terms as provided by Subsection (c).

(c) If the landlord offers to renew the lease, the tenant must notify the landlord not later than the 30th day before the date the current lease expires whether the tenant rejects the terms of the offer and intends to vacate the leased premises on the date the current lease term expires. If the tenant fails to provide the notice within the period prescribed by this subsection, the lease is renewed under the modified terms beginning on the first day after the date of the expiration of the current lease term.

(d) Notwithstanding Subsection (a), the landlord may request a tenant to vacate the leased premises before the end of the notice period prescribed by Subsection (a) only if the landlord compensates the tenant in advance for relocation expenses, including the cost of moving and installing the manufactured home at a new location.

History of Prop. Code §94.055: Acts 2001, 77th Leg., ch. 801, §1, eff. Apr. 1, 2002.

PROP §94.056. PENALTY FOR LATE PAYMENT

A landlord may assess a penalty for late payment of rent or another fee or charge if the payment is not remitted on or before the date stipulated in the lease agreement.

History of Prop. Code §94.056: Acts 2001, 77th Leg., ch. 801, §1, eff. Apr. 1, 2002.

PROP §94.057. ASSIGNMENT OF LEASE & SUBLEASE

(a) A landlord may prohibit a tenant from assigning a lease agreement or subleasing the leased premises if the prohibition is included in the lease agreement.

(b) If the landlord permits a tenant to assign a lease agreement or sublease the leased premises, the lease agreement must specify the conditions under which the tenant may enter into an assignment or sublease agreement.

History of Prop. Code §94.057: Acts 2001, 77th Leg., ch. 801, §1, eff. Apr. 1, 2002.

Sections 94.058-94.100 reserved for expansion

SUBCHAPTER C. SECURITY DEPOSIT

PROP §94.101. SECURITY DEPOSIT

In this chapter, "security deposit" means any advance of money, other than a rental application deposit or an advance payment of rent, that is intended primarily to secure performance under a lease of a lot in a manufactured home community that has been entered into by a landlord and a tenant.

History of Prop. Code §94.101: Acts 2001, 77th Leg., ch. 801, §1, eff. Apr. 1, 2002.

PROP §94.102. SECURITY DEPOSIT PERMITTED

(a) At the time the tenant executes the initial lease agreement, the landlord may require a security deposit.

(b) The landlord shall keep accurate records relating to security deposits.

History of Prop. Code §94.102: Acts 2001, 77th Leg., ch. 801, §1, eff. Apr. 1, 2002.

PROP §94.103. OBLIGATION TO REFUND

(a) Except as provided by this subchapter, the landlord shall refund the security deposit not later than the 30th day after the date the tenant surrenders the manufactured home lot.

(b) A requirement that a tenant give advance notice of surrender as a condition for refunding the security deposit is effective only if the requirement is underlined or is printed in conspicuous bold print in the lease.

(c) The tenant's claim to the security deposit takes priority over the claim of any creditor of the landlord, including a trustee in bankruptcy.

History of Prop. Code §94.103: Acts 2001, 77th Leg., ch. 801, §1, eff. Apr. 1, 2002.

PROP §94.104. CONDITIONS FOR RETENTION OF SECURITY DEPOSIT OR RENT PREPAYMENT

(a) Except as provided by Subsection (b), a landlord who receives a security deposit or rent prepayment for a manufactured home lot from a tenant who fails to occupy the lot according to a lease agreement between the landlord and the tenant may not retain the security deposit or rent prepayment if:

(1) the tenant secures a replacement tenant satisfactory to the landlord and the replacement tenant occupies the lot on or before the commencement date of the lease; or

(2) the landlord secures a replacement tenant satisfactory to the landlord and the replacement tenant occupies the lot on or before the commencement date of the lease.

(b) If the landlord secures the replacement tenant, the landlord may retain and deduct from the security deposit or rent prepayment either:

(1) an amount agreed to in the lease agreement as a lease cancellation fee; or

(2) actual expenses incurred by the landlord in securing the replacement tenant, including a reasonable amount for the time spent by the landlord in securing the replacement tenant.

History of Prop. Code §94.104: Acts 2001, 77th Leg., ch. 801, §1, eff. Apr. 1, 2002.

PROP §94.105. RETENTION OF SECURITY DEPOSIT; ACCOUNTING

(a) Before returning a security deposit, the landlord may deduct from the deposit damages and charges for which the tenant is legally liable under the lease agreement or as a result of breaching the lease.

(b) The landlord may not retain any portion of a security deposit to cover normal wear and tear.

(c) If the landlord retains all or part of a security deposit under this section, the landlord shall give to the

tenant the balance of the security deposit, if any, together with a written description and itemized list of all deductions. The landlord is not required to give the tenant a description and itemized list of deductions if:

(1) the tenant owes rent when the tenant surrenders possession of the manufactured home lot; and

(2) no controversy exists concerning the amount of rent owed.

History of Prop. Code §94.105: Acts 2001, 77th Leg., ch. 801, §1, eff. Apr. 1, 2002.

PROP §94.106. CESSATION OF OWNER'S INTEREST

(a) If the owner's interest in the premises is terminated by sale, assignment, death, appointment of a receiver, bankruptcy, or otherwise, the new owner is liable for the return of security deposits according to this subchapter from the date title to the premises is acquired, regardless of whether notice is given to the tenant under Subsection (b).

(b) The person who no longer owns an interest in the leased premises remains liable for a security deposit received while the person was the owner until the new owner delivers to the tenant a signed statement acknowledging that the new owner has received and is responsible for the tenant's security deposit and specifying the exact dollar amount of the deposit.

(c) Subsection (a) does not apply to a real estate mortgage lienholder who acquires title by foreclosure.

History of Prop. Code §94.106: Acts 2001, 77th Leg., ch. 801, §1, eff. Apr. 1, 2002.

PROP §94.107. TENANT'S FORWARDING ADDRESS

(a) A landlord is not obligated to return a tenant's security deposit or give the tenant a written description of damages and charges until the tenant gives the landlord a written statement of the tenant's forwarding address for the purpose of refunding the security deposit.

(b) The tenant does not forfeit the right to a refund of the security deposit or the right to receive a description of damages and charges merely for failing to give a forwarding address to the landlord.

History of Prop. Code §94.107: Acts 2001, 77th Leg., ch. 801, §1, eff. Apr. 1, 2002.

PROP §94.108. LIABILITY FOR WITHHOLDING LAST MONTH'S RENT

(a) A tenant may not withhold payment of any portion of the last month's rent on grounds that the security deposit is security for unpaid rent.

(b) A tenant who violates this section is presumed to have acted in bad faith. A tenant who in bad faith violates this section is liable to the landlord for an amount equal to three times the rent wrongfully withheld and the landlord's reasonable attorney's fees in a suit to recover the rent.

History of Prop. Code §94.108: Acts 2001, 77th Leg., ch. 801, §1, eff. Apr. 1, 2002.

PROP §94.109. LIABILITY OF LANDLORD

(a) A landlord who in bad faith retains a security deposit in violation of this subchapter is liable for an amount equal to the sum of $100, three times the portion of the deposit wrongfully withheld, and the tenant's reasonable attorney's fees in a suit to recover the deposit.

(b) A landlord who in bad faith does not provide a written description and itemized list of damages and charges in violation of this subchapter:

(1) forfeits the right to withhold any portion of the security deposit or to bring suit against the tenant for damages to the premises; and

(2) is liable for the tenant's reasonable attorney's fees in a suit to recover the deposit.

(c) In an action brought by a tenant under this subchapter, the landlord has the burden of proving that the retention of any portion of the security deposit was reasonable.

(d) A landlord who fails either to return a security deposit or to provide a written description and itemization of deductions on or before the 30th day after the date the tenant surrenders possession is presumed to have acted in bad faith.

History of Prop. Code §94.109: Acts 2001, 77th Leg., ch. 801, §1, eff. Apr. 1, 2002.

Sections 94.110-94.150 reserved for expansion

SUBCHAPTER D. PREMISES CONDITION, MAINTENANCE, & REPAIRS

PROP §94.151. WARRANTY OF SUITABILITY

By executing a lease agreement, the landlord warrants that the manufactured home lot is suitable for the installation of a manufactured home during the term of the lease agreement.

History of Prop. Code §94.151: Acts 2001, 77th Leg., ch. 801, §1, eff. Apr. 1, 2002.

PROP §94.152. LANDLORD'S MAINTENANCE OBLIGATIONS

The landlord shall:

(1) comply with any code, statute, ordinance, and administrative rule applicable to the manufactured home community;

(2) maintain all common areas, if any, of the manufactured home community in a clean and useable condition;

(3) maintain all utility lines installed in the manufactured home community by the landlord unless the utility lines are maintained by a public utility or political subdivision, including a municipality;

(4) maintain individual mailboxes for the tenants in accordance with United States Postal Service regulations unless mailboxes are permitted to be located on the tenant's manufactured home lot;

(5) maintain roads in the manufactured home community to the extent necessary to provide access to each tenant's manufactured home lot;

(6) provide services for the common collection and removal of garbage and solid waste from within the manufactured home community; and

(7) repair or remedy conditions on the premises that materially affect the physical health or safety of an ordinary tenant of the manufactured home community.

History of Prop. Code §94.152: Acts 2001, 77th Leg., ch. 801, §1, eff. Apr. 1, 2002.

PROP §94.153. LANDLORD'S REPAIR OBLIGATIONS

(a) This section does not apply to a condition present in or on a tenant's manufactured home.

(b) A landlord shall make a diligent effort to repair or remedy a condition if:

(1) the tenant specifies the condition in a notice to the person to whom or to the place at which rent is normally paid;

(2) the tenant is not delinquent in the payment of rent at the time notice is given; and

(3) the condition materially affects the physical health or safety of an ordinary tenant.

(c) Unless the condition was caused by normal wear and tear, the landlord does not have a duty during the lease term or a renewal or extension to repair or remedy a condition caused by:

(1) the tenant;

(2) a lawful occupant of the tenant's manufactured home lot;

(3) a member of the tenant's family; or

(4) a guest or invitee of the tenant.

(d) This subchapter does not require the landlord:

(1) to furnish utilities from a utility company if as a practical matter the utility lines of the company are not reasonably available; or

(2) to furnish security guards.

History of Prop. Code §94.153: Acts 2001, 77th Leg., ch. 801, §1, eff. Apr. 1, 2002.

PROP §94.154. BURDEN OF PROOF

(a) Except as provided by this section, the tenant has the burden of proof in a judicial action to enforce a right resulting from the landlord's failure to repair or remedy a condition under Section 94.153.

(b) If the landlord does not provide a written explanation for delay in performing a duty to repair or remedy on or before the fifth day after receiving from the tenant a written demand for an explanation, the landlord has the burden of proving that the landlord made a diligent effort to repair and that a reasonable time for repair did not elapse.

History of Prop. Code §94.154: Acts 2001, 77th Leg., ch. 801, §1, eff. Apr. 1, 2002.

PROP §94.155. CASUALTY LOSS

(a) If a condition results from an insured casualty loss, such as fire, smoke, hail, explosion, or a similar cause, the period for repair does not begin until the landlord receives the insurance proceeds.

(b) If after a casualty loss the leased premises are as a practical matter totally unusable for the purposes for which the premises were leased and if the casualty loss is not caused by the negligence or fault of the tenant, a member of the tenant's family, or a guest or invitee of the tenant, either the landlord or the tenant may terminate the lease by giving written notice to the other any time before repairs are completed. If the lease is terminated, the tenant is entitled only to a pro rata refund of rent from the date the tenant moves out and to a refund of any security deposit otherwise required by law.

(c) If after a casualty loss the leased premises are partially unusable for the purposes for which the premises were leased and if the casualty loss is not caused by the negligence or fault of the tenant, a member of the tenant's family, or a guest or invitee of the tenant, the tenant is entitled to reduction in the rent in an amount proportionate to the extent the premises are unusable because of the casualty, but only on judgment

of a county or district court. A landlord and tenant may agree otherwise in a written lease.

History of Prop. Code §94.155: Acts 2001, 77th Leg., ch. 801, §1, eff. Apr. 1, 2002.

PROP §94.156. LANDLORD LIABILITY & TENANT REMEDIES; NOTICE & TIME FOR REPAIR

(a) A landlord's liability under this section is subject to Section 94.153(c) regarding conditions that are caused by a tenant.

(b) A landlord is liable to a tenant as provided by this subchapter if:

(1) the tenant has given the landlord notice to repair or remedy a condition by giving that notice to the person to whom or to the place where the tenant's rent is normally paid;

(2) the condition materially affects the physical health or safety of an ordinary tenant;

(3) the tenant has given the landlord a subsequent written notice to repair or remedy the condition after a reasonable time to repair or remedy the condition following the notice given under Subdivision (1) or the tenant has given the notice under Subdivision (1) by sending that notice by certified mail, return receipt requested, or by registered mail;

(4) the landlord has had a reasonable time to repair or remedy the condition after the landlord received the tenant's notice under Subdivision (1) and, if applicable, the tenant's subsequent notice under Subdivision (3);

(5) the landlord has not made a diligent effort to repair or remedy the condition after the landlord received the tenant's notice under Subdivision (1) and, if applicable, the tenant's notice under Subdivision (3); and

(6) the tenant was not delinquent in the payment of rent at the time any notice required by this subsection was given.

(c) For purposes of Subsection (b)(4) or (5), a landlord is considered to have received the tenant's notice when the landlord or the landlord's agent or employee has actually received the notice or when the United States Postal Service has attempted to deliver the notice to the landlord.

(d) For purposes of Subsection (b)(3) or (4), in determining whether a period of time is a reasonable time to repair or remedy a condition, there is a rebuttable presumption that seven days is a reasonable time. To rebut that presumption, the date on which the landlord received the tenant's notice, the severity and nature of the condition, and the reasonable availability of materials and labor and of utilities from a utility company must be considered.

(e) Except as provided by Subsection (f), a tenant to whom a landlord is liable under Subsection (b) may:

(1) terminate the lease;

(2) have the condition repaired or remedied according to Section 94.157;

(3) deduct from the tenant's rent, without necessity of judicial action, the cost of the repair or remedy according to Section 94.157; and

(4) obtain judicial remedies according to Section 94.159.

(f) A tenant who elects to terminate the lease under Subsection (e) is:

(1) entitled to a pro rata refund of rent from the date of termination or the date the tenant moves out, whichever is later;

(2) entitled to deduct the tenant's security deposit from the tenant's rent without necessity of lawsuit or to obtain a refund of the tenant's security deposit according to law; and

(3) not entitled to the other repair and deduct remedies under Section 94.157 or the judicial remedies under Sections 94.159(a)(1) and (2).

History of Prop. Code §94.156: Acts 2001, 77th Leg., ch. 801, §1, eff. Apr. 1, 2002.

PROP §94.157. TENANT'S REPAIR & DEDUCT REMEDIES

(a) If the landlord is liable to the tenant under Section 94.156(b), the tenant may have the condition repaired or remedied and may deduct the cost from a subsequent rent payment as provided by this section.

(b) Except as provided by this subsection, the tenant's deduction for the cost of the repair or remedy may not exceed the amount of one month's rent under the lease agreement or $500, whichever is greater. If the tenant's rent is subsidized in whole or in part by a governmental agency, the deduction limitation of one month's rent means the fair market rent for the manufactured home lot and not the rent that the tenant pays. The governmental agency subsidizing the rent shall determine the fair market rent. If the governmental agency does not make a determination, the fair market rent means a reasonable amount of rent under the circumstances.

(c) Repairs and deductions under this section may be made as often as necessary provided that the total repairs and deductions in any one month may not exceed one month's rent or $500, whichever is greater.

(d) Repairs under this section may be made only if all of the following requirements are met:

(1) the landlord has a duty to repair or remedy the condition under Section 94.153;

(2) the tenant has given notice to the landlord in the same manner as prescribed by Section 92.056(b)(1) and, if required under Section 92.056(b)(3), a subsequent notice in the same manner as prescribed by that subsection; and

(3) any one of the following events has occurred:

(A) the landlord has failed to remedy the backup or overflow of raw sewage inside the tenant's manufactured home that results from a condition in the utility lines installed in the manufactured home community by the landlord;

(B) the landlord has expressly or impliedly agreed in the lease agreement to furnish potable water to the tenant's manufactured home lot and the water service to the lot has totally ceased; or

(C) the landlord has been notified in writing by the appropriate local housing, building, or health official or other official having jurisdiction that a condition existing on the manufactured home lot materially affects the health or safety of an ordinary tenant.

(e) At least one of the notices given under Subsection (d)(2) must state that the tenant intends to repair or remedy the condition. The notice must also contain a reasonable description of the intended repair or remedy.

(f) If the requirements prescribed by Subsections (d) and (e) are met, a tenant may:

(1) have the condition repaired or remedied immediately following the tenant's notice of intent to repair if the condition involves the backup or overflow of sewage;

(2) have the condition repaired or remedied if the condition involves a cessation of potable water if the landlord has failed to repair or remedy the condition before the fourth day after the date the tenant delivers a notice of intent to repair; or

(3) have the condition repaired or remedied if the condition is not covered by Subsection (d)(3)(A) or (B) and involves a condition affecting the physical health or safety of the ordinary tenant if the landlord has failed to repair or remedy the condition before the eighth day after the date the tenant delivers a notice of intent to repair.

(g) Repairs made based on a tenant's notice must be made by a company, contractor, or repairman listed at the time of the tenant's notice of intent to repair in the yellow or business pages of the telephone directory or in the classified advertising section of a newspaper of the municipality or county in which the manufactured home community is located or in an adjacent county. Unless the landlord and tenant agree otherwise under Subsection (i), repairs may not be made by the tenant, the tenant's immediate family, the tenant's employer or employees, or a company in which the tenant has an ownership interest. Repairs may not be made to the foundation or load-bearing structural elements of the manufactured home lot.

(h) Repairs made based on a tenant's notice must comply with applicable building codes, including any required building permit.

(i) A landlord and a tenant may mutually agree for the tenant to repair or remedy, at the landlord's expense, any condition on the manufactured home lot regardless of whether it materially affects the health or safety of an ordinary tenant.

(j) The tenant may not contract for labor or materials in excess of the amount the tenant may deduct under this section. The landlord is not liable to repairmen, contractors, or material suppliers who furnish labor or materials to repair or remedy the condition. A repairman or supplier does not have a lien for materials or services arising out of repairs contracted for by the tenant under this section.

(k) When deducting the cost of repairs from the rent payment, the tenant shall furnish the landlord, along with payment of the balance of the rent, a copy of the repair bill and the receipt for its payment. A repair bill and receipt may be the same document.

(*l*) If the landlord repairs or remedies the condition after the tenant has contacted a repairman but before the repairman commences work, the landlord is liable for the cost incurred by the tenant for the repairman's charge for traveling to the premises, and the tenant may deduct the charge from the tenant's rent as if it were a repair cost.

History of Prop. Code §94.157: Acts 2001, 77th Leg., ch. 801, §1, eff. Apr. 1, 2002.

PROP §94.158. LANDLORD AFFIDAVIT FOR DELAY

(a) The tenant must delay contracting for repairs under Section 94.157 if, before the tenant contracts for the repairs, the landlord delivers to the tenant an affidavit signed and sworn to under oath by the landlord or the landlord's authorized agent and complying with this section.

(b) The affidavit must summarize the reasons for the delay and the diligent efforts made by the landlord up to the date of the affidavit to get the repairs done. The affidavit must state facts showing that the landlord has made and is making diligent efforts to repair the condition, and it must contain dates, names, addresses, and telephone numbers of contractors, suppliers, and repairers contacted by the owner.

(c) Affidavits under this section may delay repair by the tenant for:

(1) 15 days if the landlord's failure to repair is caused by a delay in obtaining necessary parts for which the landlord is not at fault; or

(2) 30 days if the landlord's failure to repair is caused by a general shortage of labor or materials for repair following a natural disaster such as a hurricane, tornado, flood, extended freeze, or widespread windstorm.

(d) Affidavits for delay based on grounds other than those listed in Subsection (c) are unlawful and, if used, are of no effect. The landlord may file subsequent affidavits, provided that the total delay of the repair or remedy extends no longer than six months from the date the landlord delivers the first affidavit to the tenant.

(e) The affidavit must be delivered to the tenant by any of the following methods:

(1) personal delivery to the tenant;

(2) certified mail, return receipt requested, to the tenant; or

(3) leaving the notice securely fixed on the outside of the main entry door of the manufactured home if notice in that manner is authorized in a written lease.

(f) Affidavits for delay by a landlord under this section must be submitted in good faith. Following delivery of the affidavit, the landlord must continue diligent efforts to repair or remedy the condition. There shall be a rebuttable presumption that the landlord acted in good faith and with continued diligence for the first affidavit for delay the landlord delivers to the tenant. The landlord shall have the burden of pleading and proving good faith and continued diligence for subsequent affidavits for delay. A landlord who violates this section shall be liable to the tenant for all judicial remedies under Section 94.159, except that the civil penalty under Section 94.159(a)(3) shall be one month's rent plus $1,000.

(g) If the landlord is liable to the tenant under Section 94.156 and if a new landlord, in good faith and without knowledge of the tenant's notice of intent to repair, has acquired title to the tenant's dwelling by foreclosure, deed in lieu of foreclosure, or general warranty deed in a bona fide purchase, then the following shall apply:

(1) The tenant's right to terminate the lease under this subchapter shall not be affected, and the tenant shall have no duty to give additional notice to the new landlord.

(2) The tenant's right to repair and deduct for conditions involving sewage backup or overflow or a cutoff of potable water under Section 94.157(f) shall not be affected, and the tenant shall have no duty to give additional notice to the new landlord.

(3) For conditions other than those specified in Subdivision (2), if the new landlord acquires title as described by this subsection and has notified the tenant of the name and address of the new landlord or the new landlord's authorized agent and if the tenant has not already contracted for the repair or remedy at the time the tenant is so notified, the tenant must deliver to the new landlord a written notice of intent to repair or remedy the condition, and the new landlord shall have a reasonable time to complete the repair before the tenant may repair or remedy the condition. No further notice from the tenant is necessary in order for the tenant to repair or remedy the condition after a reasonable time has elapsed.

(4) The tenant's judicial remedies under Section 94.159 shall be limited to recovery against the landlord to whom the tenant gave the required notices until the tenant has given the new landlord the notices required by this section and otherwise complied with Section 94.156 as to the new landlord.

(5) If the new landlord violates this subsection, the new landlord is liable to the tenant for a civil penalty of one month's rent plus $2,000, actual damages, and attorney's fees.

(6) No provision of this section shall affect any right of a foreclosing superior lienholder to terminate,

according to law, any interest in the premises held by the holders of subordinate liens, encumbrances, leases, or other interests and shall not affect any right of the tenant to terminate the lease according to law.

History of Prop. Code §94.158: Acts 2001, 77th Leg., ch. 801, §1, eff. Apr. 1, 2002.

PROP §94.159. TENANT'S JUDICIAL REMEDIES

(a) A tenant's judicial remedies under Section 94.156 shall include:

(1) an order directing the landlord to take reasonable action to repair or remedy the condition;

(2) an order reducing the tenant's rent, from the date of the first repair notice, in proportion to the reduced rental value resulting from the condition until the condition is repaired or remedied;

(3) a judgment against the landlord for a civil penalty of one month's rent plus $500;

(4) a judgment against the landlord for the amount of the tenant's actual damages; and

(5) court costs and attorney's fees, excluding any attorney's fees for a cause of action for damages relating to a personal injury.

(b) A landlord who knowingly violates Section 94.003 by contracting with a tenant to waive the landlord's duty to repair under this subchapter shall be liable to the tenant for actual damages, a civil penalty of one month's rent plus $2,000, and reasonable attorney's fees. For purposes of this subsection, there shall be a rebuttable presumption that the landlord acted without knowledge of the violation. The tenant shall have the burden of pleading and proving a knowing violation. If the lease is not in violation of Section 94.003, the tenant's proof of a knowing violation must be clear and convincing. A mutual agreement for tenant repair under Section 94.157(i) is not a violation of Section 94.003.

(c) The justice, county, and district courts have concurrent jurisdiction of an action under Subsection (a), except that the justice court may not order repairs under Subsection (a)(1).

History of Prop. Code §94.159: Acts 2001, 77th Leg., ch. 801, §1, eff. Apr. 1, 2002.

See also Prop. Code §92.0563.

PROP §94.160. LANDLORD REMEDY FOR TENANT VIOLATION

(a) If a tenant withholds rent, causes repairs to be performed, or makes rent deductions for repairs in violation of this subchapter, the landlord may recover actual damages from the tenant. If, after a landlord has notified a tenant in writing of the illegality of the tenant's rent withholding or the tenant's proposed repair and the penalties of this subchapter, the tenant withholds rent, causes repairs to be performed, or makes rent deductions for repairs in bad faith violation of this subchapter, the landlord may recover from the tenant a civil penalty of one month's rent plus $500.

(b) Notice under this section must be in writing and may be given in person, by mail, or by delivery to the premises.

(c) The landlord has the burden of pleading and proving, by clear and convincing evidence, that the landlord gave the tenant the required notice of the illegality and the penalties and that the tenant's violation was done in bad faith. In any litigation under this subsection, the prevailing party shall recover reasonable attorney's fees from the nonprevailing party.

History of Prop. Code §94.160: Acts 2001, 77th Leg., ch. 801, §1, eff. Apr. 1, 2002.

See also Prop. Code §92.058.

PROP §94.161. AGENTS FOR DELIVERY OF NOTICE

A managing agent, leasing agent, or resident manager is the agent of the landlord for purposes of notice and other communications required or permitted by this subchapter.

History of Prop. Code §94.161: Acts 2001, 77th Leg., ch. 801, §1, eff. Apr. 1, 2002.

PROP §94.162. EFFECT ON OTHER RIGHTS

The duties of a landlord and the remedies of a tenant under this subchapter are in lieu of existing common law and other statutory law warranties and duties of landlords for maintenance, repair, security, suitability, and nonretaliation, and remedies of tenants for a violation of those warranties and duties. Otherwise, this subchapter does not affect any other right of a landlord or tenant under contract, statutory law, or common law that is consistent with the purposes of this subchapter or any right a landlord or tenant may have to bring an action for personal injury or property damage under the law of this state. This subchapter does not impose obligations on a landlord or tenant other than those expressly stated in this subchapter.

History of Prop. Code §94.162: Acts 2001, 77th Leg., ch. 801, §1, eff. Apr. 1, 2002.

Sections 94.163-94.200 reserved for expansion

SUBCHAPTER E. TERMINATION, EVICTION, & FORECLOSURE

PROP §94.201. LANDLORD'S REMEDY FOR EARLY TERMINATION

(a) Except as provided by Subsection (b), the maximum amount a landlord may recover as damages for a tenant's early termination of a lease agreement is an amount equal to the amount of rent that remains outstanding for the term of the lease and any other amounts owed for the remainder of the lease under the terms of the lease.

(b) If the tenant's manufactured home lot is reoccupied before the 21st day after the date the tenant surrenders the lot, the maximum amount the landlord may obtain as damages is an amount equal to one month's rent.

History of Prop. Code §94.201: Acts 2001, 77th Leg., ch. 801, §1, eff. Apr. 1, 2002.

PROP §94.202. LANDLORD'S DUTY TO MITIGATE DAMAGES

(a) A landlord has a duty to mitigate damages if a tenant vacates the manufactured home lot before the end of the lease term.

(b) A provision of a lease agreement that purports to waive a right or to exempt a landlord from a liability or duty under this section is void.

History of Prop. Code §94.202: Acts 2001, 77th Leg., ch. 801, §1, eff. Apr. 1, 2002.

PROP §94.203. EVICTION PROCEDURES GENERALLY

(a) A landlord may prevent a tenant from entering the manufactured home lot, evict a tenant, or require the removal of a manufactured home from the manufactured home lot only after obtaining a writ of possession under Chapter 24.

(b) If the tenant has disclosed the name of a lienholder as provided by Section 94.054, the landlord shall give written notice of eviction proceedings to the lienholder of the manufactured home not later than the third day after the date the landlord files an application or petition for a judgment for possession.

(c) If the court finds that the landlord initiated the eviction proceeding to retaliate against the tenant in violation of Section 94.251, the court may not approve the eviction of the tenant.

(d) Notwithstanding other law, a court may not issue a writ of possession in favor of a landlord before the 30th day after the date the judgment for possession is rendered if the tenant has paid the rent amount due under the lease for that 30-day period.

(e) The court shall notify a tenant in writing of a default judgment for possession by sending a copy of the judgment to the leased premises by first class mail not later than 48 hours after the entry of the judgment. In addition, the court shall send a copy of the judgment to the owner of the manufactured home if the tenant is not the owner and to any person who holds a lien on the manufactured home if the court has been notified in writing of the name and address of the owner and lienholder.

(f) If, after executing a writ of possession for the manufactured home lot, the landlord removes the manufactured home from the lot, the landlord not later than the 10th day after the date the manufactured home is removed shall send a written notice regarding the location of the manufactured home to the tenant at the tenant's most recent mailing address as reflected in the landlord's records and, if different, to the owner if the landlord is given written notice of the owner's name and address.

History of Prop. Code §94.203: Acts 2001, 77th Leg., ch. 801, §1, eff. Apr. 1, 2002.

See also Prop. Code §§92.009, 93.003.

PROP §94.204. NONRENEWAL OF LEASE FOR CHANGE IN LAND USE

(a) A landlord may choose not to renew a lease agreement to change the manufactured home community's land use only if not later than the 180th day before the date the land use will change:

(1) the landlord sends notice to the tenant, to the owner of the manufactured home if the owner is not the tenant, and to the holder of any lien on the manufactured home:

(A) specifying the date that the land use will change; and

(B) informing the tenant, owner, and lienholder, if any, that the owner must relocate the manufactured home; and

(2) the landlord posts in a conspicuous place in the manufactured home community a notice stating that the land use will change and specifying the date that the land use will change.

(b) The landlord is required to give the owner and lienholder, if any, of the manufactured home notice under Subsection (a)(1) only if the landlord is given written notice of the name and address of the owner and lienholder.

History of Prop. Code §94.204: Acts 2001, 77th Leg., ch. 801, §1, eff. Apr. 1, 2002. Amended by Acts 2007, 80th Leg., ch. 863, §§68, 69, eff. Jan. 1, 2008.

PROP §94.205. TERMINATION & EVICTION FOR VIOLATION OF LEASE

A landlord may terminate the lease agreement and evict a tenant for a violation of a lease provision, including a manufactured home community rule incorporated in the lease.

History of Prop. Code §94.205: Acts 2001, 77th Leg., ch. 801, §1, eff. Apr. 1, 2002.

PROP §94.206. TERMINATION & EVICTION FOR NONPAYMENT OF RENT

A landlord may terminate the lease agreement and evict a tenant if:

(1) the tenant fails to timely pay rent or other amounts due under the lease that in the aggregate equal the amount of at least one month's rent;

(2) the landlord notifies the tenant in writing that the payment is delinquent; and

(3) the tenant has not tendered the delinquent payment in full to the landlord before the 10th day after the date the tenant receives the notice.

History of Prop. Code §94.206: Acts 2001, 77th Leg., ch. 801, §1, eff. Apr. 1, 2002.

Sections 94.207-94.250 reserved for expansion

SUBCHAPTER F. PROHIBITED ACTS

PROP §94.251. RETALIATION BY LANDLORD

(a) A landlord may not retaliate against a tenant by taking an action described by Subsection (b) because the tenant:

(1) in good faith exercises or attempts to exercise against a landlord a right or remedy granted to the tenant by the lease agreement, a municipal ordinance, or a federal or state statute;

(2) gives the landlord a notice to repair or exercise a remedy under this chapter; or

(3) complains to a governmental entity responsible for enforcing building or housing codes, a public utility, or a civic or nonprofit agency, and the tenant:

(A) claims a building or housing code violation or utility problem; and

(B) believes in good faith that the complaint is valid and that the violation or problem occurred.

(b) A landlord may not, within six months after the date of the tenant's action under Subsection (a), retaliate against the tenant by:

(1) filing an eviction proceeding, except for the grounds stated by Subchapter E;

(2) depriving the tenant of the use of the premises, except for reasons authorized by law;

(3) decreasing services to the tenant;

(4) increasing the tenant's rent;

(5) terminating the tenant's lease agreement; or

(6) engaging, in bad faith, in a course of conduct that materially interferes with the tenant's rights under the tenant's lease agreement.

History of Prop. Code §94.251: Acts 2001, 77th Leg., ch. 801, §1, eff. Apr. 1, 2002.

See also Prop. Code §§92.331, 92.334, 93.011, 94.255.

PROP §94.252. RESTRICTION ON SALE OF MANUFACTURED HOME

(a) The owner of a manufactured home may sell a home located on the leased premises if:

(1) the purchaser is approved in writing by the landlord; and

(2) a lease agreement is signed by the purchaser.

(b) Unless the owner of a manufactured home has agreed in writing, the landlord may not:

(1) require the owner to contract with the landlord to act as an agent or broker in selling the home; or

(2) require the owner to pay a commission or fee from the sale of the home.

History of Prop. Code §94.252: Acts 2001, 77th Leg., ch. 801, §1, eff. Apr. 1, 2002.

PROP §94.253. NONRETALIATION

(a) A landlord is not liable for retaliation under this subchapter if the landlord proves that the action was not made for purposes of retaliation, nor is the landlord liable, unless the action violates a prior court order under Section 94.159, for:

(1) increasing rent under an escalation clause in a written lease for utilities, taxes, or insurance; or

(2) increasing rent or reducing services as part of a pattern of rent increases or service reductions for an entire manufactured home community.

(b) An eviction or lease termination based on the following circumstances, which are valid grounds for eviction or lease termination in any event, does not constitute retaliation:

(1) the tenant is delinquent in rent or other amounts due under the lease that in the aggregate equal the amount of at least one month's rent when the landlord gives notice to vacate or files an eviction action;

(2) the tenant, a member of the tenant's family, or a guest or invitee of the tenant intentionally damages property on the premises or by word or conduct threatens the personal safety of the landlord, the landlord's employees, or another tenant;

(3) the tenant has materially breached the lease, other than by holding over, by an action such as violating written lease provisions prohibiting serious misconduct or criminal acts, except as provided by this section;

(4) the tenant holds over after giving notice of termination or intent to vacate;

(5) the tenant holds over after the landlord gives notice of termination at the end of the rental term and the tenant does not take action under Section 94.251 until after the landlord gives notice of termination; or

(6) the tenant holds over and the landlord's notice of termination is motivated by a good faith belief that the tenant, a member of the tenant's family, or a guest or invitee of the tenant might:

(A) adversely affect the quiet enjoyment by other tenants or neighbors;

(B) materially affect the health or safety of the landlord, other tenants, or neighbors; or

(C) damage the property of the landlord, other tenants, or neighbors.

History of Prop. Code §94.253: Acts 2001, 77th Leg., ch. 801, §1, eff. Apr. 1, 2002.

PROP §94.254. TENANT REMEDIES

In addition to other remedies provided by law, if a landlord retaliates against a tenant under this subchapter, the tenant may recover from the landlord a civil penalty of one month's rent plus $500, actual damages, court costs, and reasonable attorney's fees in an action for recovery of property damages, moving costs, actual expenses, civil penalties, or declaratory or injunctive relief, less any delinquent rents or other sums for which the tenant is liable to the landlord. If the tenant's rent payment to the landlord is subsidized in whole or in part by a governmental entity, the civil penalty granted under this section shall reflect the fair market rent of the leased premises plus $500.

History of Prop. Code §94.254: Acts 2001, 77th Leg., ch. 801, §1, eff. Apr. 1, 2002.

PROP §94.255. INVALID COMPLAINTS

(a) If a tenant files or prosecutes a suit for retaliatory action based on a complaint asserted under Section 94.251(a)(3), and a government building or housing inspector or utility company representative visits the manufactured home community and determines in writing that a violation of a building or housing code does not exist or that a utility problem does not exist, there is a rebuttable presumption that the tenant acted in bad faith.

(b) If a tenant files or prosecutes a suit under this subchapter in bad faith, the landlord may recover possession of the leased premises and may recover from the tenant a civil penalty of one month's rent plus $500, court costs, and reasonable attorney's fees. If the tenant's rent payment to the landlord is subsidized in whole or in part by a governmental entity, the civil penalty granted under this subsection shall reflect the fair market rent of the leased premises plus $500.

History of Prop. Code §94.255: Acts 2001, 77th Leg., ch. 801, §1, eff. Apr. 1, 2002.

See also Prop. Code §§92.331, 92.334, 94.251.

PROP §94.256. EVICTION SUITS

In an eviction suit, retaliation by the landlord under Section 94.251 is a defense and a rent deduction lawfully made by the tenant under this chapter is a defense for nonpayment of the rent to the extent allowed by this chapter. Other judicial actions under this chapter, excluding an action that would be permitted under Chapter 24, may not be joined with an eviction suit or asserted as a defense or cross-claim in an eviction suit.

History of Prop. Code §94.256: Acts 2001, 77th Leg., ch. 801, §1, eff. Apr. 1, 2002.

Sections 94.257-94.300 reserved for expansion

SUBCHAPTER G. REMEDIES

PROP §94.301. TENANT'S REMEDIES

A person may recover from a landlord who violates this chapter:

(1) actual damages;

(2) a civil penalty in an amount equal to two months' rent and $500; and

(3) reasonable attorney's fees and costs.

History of Prop. Code §94.301: Acts 2001, 77th Leg., ch. 801, §1, eff. Apr. 1, 2002.

PROP §94.302. LANDLORD'S REMEDIES

If the court finds that a tenant filed or prosecuted a suit under this chapter in bad faith or for purposes of harassment, the court shall award the landlord:

(1) an amount equal to two months' rent and $500; and

(2) reasonable attorney's fees and costs.

History of Prop. Code §94.302: Acts 2001, 77th Leg., ch. 801, §1, eff. Apr. 1, 2002.

See also Prop. Code §92.004.

PROP §94.303. CUMULATIVE REMEDIES

(a) The provisions of this chapter are not exclusive and are in addition to any other remedy provided by other law.

(b) A specific remedy provided by this chapter supersedes the general remedy provided by this subchapter and is in addition to any other remedy provided by other law.

History of Prop. Code §94.303: Acts 2001, 77th Leg., ch. 801, §1, eff. Apr. 1, 2002.

Chapters 95-100 reserved for expansion

TITLE 9. TRUSTS

Editor's note: *For an annotated version of the Trust Code, see the current edition of* ***O'Connor's Texas Estates Code Plus***. To order, call 1-800-OCONNOR (1-800-626-6667) or visit www.oconnors.com.

SUBTITLE A. PROVISIONS GENERALLY APPLICABLE TO TRUSTS

CHAPTER 101. PROVISIONS GENERALLY APPLICABLE TO TRUSTS

PROP §101.001. CONVEYANCE BY PERSON DESIGNATED AS TRUSTEE

If property is conveyed or transferred to a person designated as a trustee but the conveyance or transfer does not identify a trust or disclose the name of any beneficiary, the person designated as trustee may convey, transfer, or encumber the title of the property without subsequent question by a person who claims to be a beneficiary under a trust or who claims by, through, or under any undisclosed beneficiary or by, through, or under the person designated as trustee in that person's individual capacity.

History of Prop. Code §101.001: Acts 1983, 68th Leg., ch. 576, §1, eff. Jan. 1, 1984. Amended by Acts 1987, 70th Leg., ch. 683, §3, eff. Aug. 31, 1987. Source: TRCS art. 7435b-8.

PROP §101.002. LIABILITY OF TRUST PROPERTY

Although trust property is held by the trustee without identifying the trust or its beneficiaries, the trust property is not liable to satisfy the personal obligations of the trustee.

History of Prop. Code §101.002: Acts 1983, 68th Leg., ch. 576, §1, eff. Jan. 1, 1984. Renumbered from §101.001(b) by Acts 1987, 70th Leg., ch. 683, §3, eff. Aug. 31, 1987.

Chapters 102-110 reserved for expansion

SUBTITLE B. TEXAS TRUST CODE: CREATION, OPERATION, & TERMINATION OF TRUSTS

CHAPTER 111. GENERAL PROVISIONS

PROP §111.001. SHORT TITLE

This subtitle may be cited as the Texas Trust Code.

History of Prop. Code §111.001: Acts 1983, 68th Leg., ch. 576, §1, eff. Jan. 1, 1984. Amended by Acts 1983, 68th Leg., ch. 576, §1, eff. Jan. 1, 1984. Source: TRCS art. 7425b-1.

See also H&SC §712.020.

PROP §111.002. CONSTRUCTION OF SUBTITLE

This subtitle and the Texas Trust Act, as amended (Articles 7425b-1 through 7425b-48, Vernon's Texas Civil Statutes),[1] shall be considered one continuous statute, and for the purposes of any statute or of any instrument creating a trust that refers to the Texas Trust Act, this subtitle shall be considered an amendment to the Texas Trust Act.

1. **Editor's note:** Codified as Property Code chs. 111-117.

History of Prop. Code §111.002: Acts 1983, 68th Leg., ch. 576, §1, eff. Jan. 1, 1984. Amended by Acts 1983, 68th Leg., ch. 576, §1, eff. Jan. 1, 1984; Acts 2005, 79th Leg., ch. 148, §1, eff. Jan. 1, 2006.

PROP §111.003. TRUSTS SUBJECT TO THIS SUBTITLE

For the purposes of this subtitle, a "trust" is an express trust only and does not include:

(1) a resulting trust;

(2) a constructive trust;

(3) a business trust; or

(4) a security instrument such as a deed of trust, mortgage, or security interest as defined by the Business & Commerce Code.

History of Prop. Code §111.003: Acts 1983, 68th Leg., ch. 576, §1, eff. Jan. 1, 1984. Source: TRCS art. 7425b-2.

A PROP §111.0035. DEFAULT & MANDATORY RULES; CONFLICT BETWEEN TERMS & STATUTE

(a) Except as provided by the terms of a trust and Subsection (b), this subtitle governs:

(1) the duties and powers of a trustee;

(2) relations among trustees; and

(3) the rights and interests of a beneficiary.

(b) The terms of a trust prevail over any provision of this subtitle, except that the terms of a trust may not limit:

(1) the requirements imposed under Section 112.031;

(2) the applicability of Section 114.007 to an exculpation term of a trust;

(3) the periods of limitation for commencing a judicial proceeding regarding a trust;

(4) a trustee's duty:

(A) with regard to an irrevocable trust, to respond to a demand for accounting made under Section 113.151 if the demand is from a beneficiary who, at the time of the demand:

(i) is entitled or permitted to receive distributions from the trust; or

(ii) would receive a distribution from the trust if the trust terminated at the time of the demand; and

(B) to act in good faith and in accordance with the purposes of the trust;

(5) the power of a court, in the interest of justice, to take action or exercise jurisdiction, including the power to:

(A) modify, reform, or terminate a trust or take other action under Section 112.054;

(B) remove a trustee under Section 113.082;

(C) exercise jurisdiction under Section 115.001;

(D) require, dispense with, modify, or terminate a trustee's bond; or

(E) adjust or deny a trustee's compensation if the trustee commits a breach of trust; or

(6) the applicability of Section 112.038.

(c) The terms of a trust may not limit any common-law duty to keep a beneficiary of an irrevocable trust who is 25 years of age or older informed at any time during which the beneficiary:

(1) is entitled or permitted to receive distributions from the trust; or

(2) would receive a distribution from the trust if the trust were terminated.

History of Prop. Code §111.0035: Acts 2005, 79th Leg., ch. 148, §2, eff. Jan. 1, 2006. Amended by Acts 2007, 80th Leg., ch. 451, §2, eff. June 16, 2007; Acts 2009, 81st Leg., ch. 414, §2, eff. June 19, 2009; S.B. 617, §1, 85th Leg., eff. Sept. 1, 2017.

PROP §111.004. DEFINITIONS

In this subtitle:

(1) "Affiliate" includes:

(A) a person who directly or indirectly, through one or more intermediaries, controls, is controlled by, or is under common control with another person; or

(B) any officer, director, partner, employee, or relative of a person, and any corporation or partnership of which a person is an officer, director, or partner.

(2) "Beneficiary" means a person for whose benefit property is held in trust, regardless of the nature of the interest.

(3) "Court" means a court of appropriate jurisdiction.

(4) "Express trust" means a fiduciary relationship with respect to property which arises as a manifestation by the settlor of an intention to create the relationship and which subjects the person holding title to the property to equitable duties to deal with the property for the benefit of another person.

(5) "Income" is defined in Section 116.002.

(6) "Interest" means any interest, whether legal or equitable or both, present or future, vested or contingent, defeasible or indefeasible.

(7) "Interested person" means a trustee, beneficiary, or any other person having an interest in or a claim against the trust or any person who is affected by the administration of the trust. Whether a person, excluding a trustee or named beneficiary, is an interested person may vary from time to time and must be determined according to the particular purposes of and matter involved in any proceeding.

(8) "Internal Revenue Code" means the Internal Revenue Code of 1954, as amended, or any corresponding statute subsequently in effect.

(9) "Inventory value" means the cost of property purchased by a trustee, the market value of property at

the time it became subject to the trust, or, in the case of a testamentary trust, any value used by the trustee that is finally determined for the purposes of an estate or inheritance tax.

(10) "Person" means:

(A) an individual;

(B) a corporation;

(C) a limited liability company;

(D) a partnership;

(E) a joint venture;

(F) an association;

(G) a joint-stock company;

(H) a business trust;

(I) an unincorporated organization;

(J) two or more persons having a joint or common interest, including an individual or a corporation acting as a personal representative or in any other fiduciary capacity;

(K) a government;

(L) a governmental subdivision, agency, or instrumentality;

(M) a public corporation; or

(N) any other legal or commercial entity.

(11) "Principal" is defined in Section 116.002.

(12) "Property" means any type of property, whether real, tangible or intangible, legal, or equitable, including property held in any digital or electronic medium. The term also includes choses in action, claims, and contract rights, including a contractual right to receive death benefits as designated beneficiary under a policy of insurance, contract, employees' trust, retirement account, or other arrangement.

(13) "Relative" means a spouse or, whether by blood or adoption, an ancestor, descendant, brother, sister, or spouse of any of them.

(14) "Settlor" means a person who creates a trust or contributes property to a trustee of a trust. If more than one person contributes property to a trustee of a trust, each person is a settlor of the portion of the property in the trust attributable to that person's contribution to the trust. The terms "grantor" and "trustor" mean the same as "settlor."

(15) "Terms of the trust" means the manifestation of intention of the settlor with respect to the trust expressed in a manner that admits of its proof in judicial proceedings.

(16) "Transaction" means any act performed by a settlor, trustee, or beneficiary in relation to a trust, including the creation or termination of a trust, the investment of trust property, a breach of duty, the receipt of trust property, the receipt of income or the incurring of expense, a distribution of trust property, an entry in the books and records of the trust, and an accounting by a trustee to any person entitled to receive an accounting.

(17) "Trust property" means property placed in trust by one of the methods specified in Section 112.001 or property otherwise transferred to or acquired or retained by the trustee for the trust.

(18) "Trustee" means the person holding the property in trust, including an original, additional, or successor trustee, whether or not the person is appointed or confirmed by a court.

(19) "Employees' trust" means:

(A) a trust that forms a part of a stock-bonus, pension, or profit-sharing plan under Section 401, Internal Revenue Code of 1954 (26 U.S.C.A. Sec. 401 (1986));

(B) a pension trust under Chapter 111; and

(C) an employer-sponsored benefit plan or program, or any other retirement savings arrangement, including a pension plan created under Section 3, Employee Retirement Income Security Act of 1974 (29 U.S.C.A. Sec. 1002 (1986)), regardless of whether the plan, program, or arrangement is funded through a trust.

(20) "Individual retirement account" means a trust, custodial arrangement, or annuity under Section 408(a) or (b), Internal Revenue Code of 1954 (26 U.S.C.A. Sec. 408 (1986)).

(21) "Retirement account" means a retirement-annuity contract, an individual retirement account, a simplified employee pension, or any other retirement savings arrangement.

(22) "Retirement-annuity contract" means an annuity contract under Section 403, Internal Revenue Code of 1954 (26 U.S.C.A. Sec. 403 (1986)).

(23) "Simplified employee pension" means a trust, custodial arrangement, or annuity under Section 408, Internal Revenue Code of 1954 (26 U.S.C.A. Sec. 408 (1986)).

(24) "Environmental law" means any federal, state, or local law, rule, regulation, or ordinance relating to protection of the environment.

(25) "Breach of trust" means a violation by a trustee of a duty the trustee owes to a beneficiary.

History of Prop. Code §111.004: Acts 1983, 68th Leg., ch. 576, §1, eff. Jan. 1, 1984. Amended by Acts 1987, 70th Leg., ch. 741, §§1, 2, eff. Aug. 31, 1987; Acts 1993, 73rd Leg., ch. 846, §28, eff. Sept. 1, 1993; Acts 1995, 74th Leg., ch. 642, §14, eff. Sept. 1, 1995; Acts 2003, 78th Leg., ch. 659, §2 (eff. Jan. 1, 2004), ch. 1103, §2 (eff. Jan. 1, 2004); Acts 2005, 79th Leg., ch. 148, §3, eff. Jan. 1, 2006; Acts 2007, 80th Leg., ch. 451, §3, eff. Sept. 1, 2007; Acts 2013, 83rd Leg., ch. 699, §1, eff. Sept. 1, 2013. Source: TRCS art. 7425b-4.

PROP §111.005. REENACTMENT OF COMMON LAW

If the law codified in this subtitle repealed a statute that abrogated or restated a common law rule, that common law rule is reestablished, except as the contents of the rule are changed by this subtitle.

History of Prop. Code §111.005: Acts 1983, 68th Leg., ch. 576, §1, eff. Jan. 1, 1984. Source: TRCS art. 7425 9-45.

PROP §111.006. APPLICATION

This subtitle applies:

(1) to all trusts created on or after January 1, 1984, and to all transactions relating to such trusts; and

(2) to all transactions occurring on or after January 1, 1984, relating to trusts created before January 1, 1984; provided that transactions entered into before January 1, 1984, and which were subject to the Texas Trust Act, as amended (Articles 7425b-1 through 7425b-48, Vernon's Texas Civil Statutes),[1] and the rights, duties, and interests flowing from such transactions remain valid on and after January 1, 1984, and must be terminated, consummated, or enforced as required or permitted by this subtitle.

1. **Editor's note:** Codified as Property Code chs. 111-117.

History of Prop. Code §111.006: Acts 1983, 68th Leg., ch. 576, §1, eff. Jan. 1, 1984.

CHAPTER 112. CREATION, VALIDITY, MODIFICATION, & TERMINATION OF TRUSTS

SUBCHAPTER A. CREATION

PROP §112.001. METHODS OF CREATING TRUST

A trust may be created by:

(1) a property owner's declaration that the owner holds the property as trustee for another person;

(2) a property owner's inter vivos transfer of the property to another person as trustee for the transferor or a third person;

(3) a property owner's testamentary transfer to another person as trustee for a third person;

(4) an appointment under a power of appointment to another person as trustee for the donee of the power or for a third person; or

(5) a promise to another person whose rights under the promise are to be held in trust for a third person.

History of Prop. Code §112.001: Acts 1983, 68th Leg., ch. 576, §1, eff. Jan. 1, 1984. Source: TRCS art. 7425b-7.

PROP §112.002. INTENTION TO CREATE TRUST

A trust is created only if the settlor manifests an intention to create a trust.

History of Prop. Code §112.002: Acts 1983, 68th Leg., ch. 576, §1, eff. Jan. 1, 1984.

PROP §112.003. CONSIDERATION

Consideration is not required for the creation of a trust. A promise to create a trust in the future is enforceable only if the requirements for an enforceable contract are present.

History of Prop. Code §112.003: Acts 1983, 68th Leg., ch. 576, §1, eff. Jan. 1, 1984.

PROP §112.004. STATUTE OF FRAUDS

A trust in either real or personal property is enforceable only if there is written evidence of the trust's terms bearing the signature of the settlor or the settlor's authorized agent. A trust consisting of personal property, however, is enforceable if created by:

(1) a transfer of the trust property to a trustee who is neither settlor nor beneficiary if the transferor expresses simultaneously with or prior to the transfer the intention to create a trust; or

(2) a declaration in writing by the owner of property that the owner holds the property as trustee for another person or for the owner and another person as a beneficiary.

History of Prop. Code §112.004: Acts 1983, 68th Leg., ch. 576, §1, eff. Jan. 1, 1984. Source: TRCS art. 7425b-7.

PROP §112.005. TRUST PROPERTY

A trust cannot be created unless there is trust property.

History of Prop. Code §112.005: Acts 1983, 68th Leg., ch. 576, §1, eff. Jan. 1, 1984.

PROP §112.006. ADDITIONS TO TRUST PROPERTY

Property may be added to an existing trust from any source in any manner unless the addition is prohibited by the terms of the trust or the property is unacceptable to the trustee.

History of Prop. Code §112.006: Acts 1983, 68th Leg., ch. 576, §1, eff. Jan. 1, 1984.

PROP §112.007. CAPACITY OF SETTLOR

A person has the same capacity to create a trust by declaration, inter vivos or testamentary transfer, or appointment that the person has to transfer, will, or appoint free of trust.

History of Prop. Code §112.007: Acts 1983, 68th Leg., ch. 576, §1, eff. Jan. 1, 1984. Source: TRCS art. 7425b-3.

PROP §112.008. CAPACITY OF TRUSTEE

(a) The trustee must have the legal capacity to take, hold, and transfer the trust property. If the trustee is a corporation, it must have the power to act as a trustee in this state.

(b) Except as provided by Section 112.034, the fact that the person named as trustee is also a beneficiary does not disqualify the person from acting as trustee if he is otherwise qualified.

(c) The settlor of a trust may be the trustee of the trust.

History of Prop. Code §112.008: Acts 1983, 68th Leg., ch. 576, §1, eff. Jan. 1, 1984.

PROP §112.009. ACCEPTANCE BY TRUSTEE

(a) The signature of the person named as trustee on the writing evidencing the trust or on a separate written acceptance is conclusive evidence that the person accepted the trust. A person named as trustee who exercises power or performs duties under the trust is presumed to have accepted the trust, except that a person named as trustee may engage in the following conduct without accepting the trust:

(1) acting to preserve the trust property if, within a reasonable time after acting, the person gives notice of the rejection of the trust to:

(A) the settlor; or

(B) if the settlor is deceased or incapacitated, all beneficiaries then entitled to receive trust distributions from the trust; and

(2) inspecting or investigating trust property for any purpose, including determining the potential liability of the trust under environmental or other law.

(b) A person named as trustee who does not accept the trust incurs no liability with respect to the trust.

(c) If the person named as the original trustee does not accept the trust or if the person is dead or does

not have capacity to act as trustee, the person named as the alternate trustee under the terms of the trust or the person selected as alternate trustee according to a method prescribed in the terms of the trust may accept the trust. If a trustee is not named or if there is no alternate trustee designated or selected in the manner prescribed in the terms of the trust, the court shall appoint a trustee on a petition of any interested person.

History of Prop. Code §112.009: Acts 1983, 68th Leg., ch. 576, §1, eff. Jan. 1, 1984. Amended by Acts 2005, 79th Leg., ch. 148, §4, eff. Jan. 1, 2006.

PROP §112.010. PRESUMED ACCEPTANCE BY BENEFICIARY; DISCLAIMER

(a) Acceptance by a beneficiary of an interest in a trust is presumed.

(b) A disclaimer of an interest in or power over trust property is governed by Chapter 240.

(c) to **(c-2)** Repealed by Acts 2015, 84th Leg., ch. 562, §16(4), eff. Sept. 1, 2015.

(c-3) Expired.

(d), **(e)** Repealed by Acts 2015, 84th Leg., ch. 562, §16(4), eff. Sept. 1, 2015.

History of Prop. Code §112.010: Acts 1983, 68th Leg., ch. 576, §1, eff. Jan. 1, 1984. Amended by Acts 1987, 70th Leg., ch. 467, §3, eff. Sept. 1, 1987; Acts 1993, 73rd Leg., ch. 846, §3, eff. Sept. 1, 1993; Acts 2009, 81st Leg., ch. 672, §2, eff. Sept. 1, 2009; Acts 2011, 82nd Leg., ch. 657, §1, eff. Sept. 1, 2011; Acts 2015, 84th Leg., ch. 562, §§13, 14, 16(4), eff. Sept. 1, 2015.

E PROP §112.011. POSTHUMOUS CLASS GIFTS MEMBERSHIP

(a) A right to take as a member under a class gift does not accrue to any person unless the person is born before, or is in gestation at, the time of death of the person by which the class is measured and survives that person by at least 120 hours.

(b) For purposes of Subsection (a), a person is:

(1) considered to be in gestation if insemination or implantation occurs at or before the time of death of the person by which the class is measured; and

(2) presumed to be in gestation at the time of death of the person by which the class is measured if the person was born before the 301st day after the date of the person's death.

(c) A provision in the trust instrument that is contrary to this section prevails over this section.

History of Prop. Code §112.011: Enacted by H.B. 2271, §37, 85th Leg., eff. Sept. 1, 2017.

Sections 112.012-112.030 reserved for expansion

SUBCHAPTER B. VALIDITY

PROP §112.031. TRUST PURPOSES

A trust may be created for any purpose that is not illegal. The terms of the trust may not require the trustee to commit a criminal or tortious act or an act that is contrary to public policy.

History of Prop. Code §112.031: Acts 1983, 68th Leg., ch. 576, §1, eff. Jan. 1, 1984. Source: TRCS art. 7425b-2.

PROP §112.032. ACTIVE & PASSIVE TRUSTS; STATUTE OF USES

(a) Except as provided by Subsection (b), title to real property held in trust vests directly in the beneficiary if the trustee has neither a power nor a duty related to the administration of the trust.

(b) The title of a trustee in real property is not divested if the trustee's title is not merely nominal but is subject to a power or duty in relation to the property.

History of Prop. Code §112.032: Acts 1983, 68th Leg., ch. 576, §1, eff. Jan. 1, 1984. Source: TRCS arts. 7425b-5, 7425b-6.

PROP §112.033. RESERVATION OF INTERESTS & POWERS BY SETTLOR

If during the life of the settlor an interest in a trust or the trust property is created in a beneficiary other than the settlor, the disposition is not invalid as an attempted testamentary disposition merely because the settlor reserves or retains, either in himself or another person who is not the trustee, any or all of the other interests in or powers over the trust or trust property, such as:

(1) a beneficial life interest for himself;

(2) the power to revoke, modify, or terminate the trust in whole or in part;

(3) the power to designate the person to whom or on whose behalf the income or principal is to be paid or applied;

(4) the power to control the administration of the trust in whole or in part;

(5) the right to exercise a power or option over property in the trust or over interests made payable to the trust under an employee benefit plan, life insurance policy, or otherwise; or

(6) the power to add property or cause additional employee benefits, life insurance, or other interests to be made payable to the trust at any time.

History of Prop. Code §112.033: Acts 1983, 68th Leg., ch. 576, §2, eff. Jan. 1, 1984.

PROP §112.034. MERGER

(a) If a settlor transfers both the legal title and all equitable interests in property to the same person or

retains both the legal title and all equitable interests in property in himself as both the sole trustee and the sole beneficiary, a trust is not created and the transferee holds the property as his own. This subtitle does not invalidate a trust account validly created and in effect under Chapter XI, Texas Probate Code.[1]

(b) Except as provided by Subsection (c) of this section, a trust terminates if the legal title to the trust property and all equitable interests in the trust become united in one person.

(c) The title to trust property and all equitable interests in the trust property may not become united in a beneficiary, other than the settlor, whose interest is protected under a spendthrift trust, and in that case the court shall appoint a new trustee or cotrustee to administer the trust for the benefit of the beneficiary.

1. **Editor's note:** Now Estates Code chs. 112, 113.

History of Prop. Code §112.034: Acts 1983, 68th Leg., ch. 576, §2, eff. Jan. 1, 1984.

A PROP §112.035. SPENDTHRIFT TRUSTS

(a) A settlor may provide in the terms of the trust that the interest of a beneficiary in the income or in the principal or in both may not be voluntarily or involuntarily transferred before payment or delivery of the interest to the beneficiary by the trustee.

(b) A declaration in a trust instrument that the interest of a beneficiary shall be held subject to a "spendthrift trust" is sufficient to restrain voluntary or involuntary alienation of the interest by a beneficiary to the maximum extent permitted by this subtitle.

(c) A trust containing terms authorized under Subsection (a) or (b) of this section may be referred to as a spendthrift trust.

(d) If the settlor is also a beneficiary of the trust, a provision restraining the voluntary or involuntary transfer of the settlor's beneficial interest does not prevent the settlor's creditors from satisfying claims from the settlor's interest in the trust estate. A settlor is not considered a beneficiary of a trust solely because:

(1) a trustee who is not the settlor is authorized under the trust instrument to pay or reimburse the settlor for, or pay directly to the taxing authorities, any tax on trust income or principal that is payable by the settlor under the law imposing the tax; or

(2) the settlor's interest in the trust was created by the exercise of a power of appointment by a third party.

(e) A beneficiary of the trust may not be considered a settlor merely because of a lapse, waiver, or release of:

(1) a power described by Subsection (f); or

(2) the beneficiary's right to withdraw a part of the trust property to the extent that the value of the property affected by the lapse, waiver, or release in any calendar year does not exceed the greater of [~~the amount specified in~~]:

(A) the amount specified in Section 2041(b)(2) or 2514(e), Internal Revenue Code of 1986; or

(B) the amount specified in Section 2503(b), Internal Revenue Code of 1986, with respect to the contributions by each donor.

(f) A beneficiary of the trust may not be considered to be a settlor, to have made a voluntary or involuntary transfer of the beneficiary's interest in the trust, or to have the power to make a voluntary or involuntary transfer of the beneficiary's interest in the trust, merely because the beneficiary, in any capacity, holds or exercises:

(1) a presently exercisable power to:

(A) consume, invade, appropriate, or distribute property to or for the benefit of the beneficiary, if the power is:

(i) exercisable only on consent of another person holding an interest adverse to the beneficiary's interest; or

(ii) limited by an ascertainable standard, including health, education, support, or maintenance of the beneficiary; or

(B) appoint any property of the trust to or for the benefit of a person other than the beneficiary, a creditor of the beneficiary, the beneficiary's estate, or a creditor of the beneficiary's estate;

(2) a testamentary power of appointment; or

(3) a presently exercisable right described by Subsection (e)(2).

(g) For the purposes of this section, property contributed to the following trusts is not considered to have been contributed by the settlor, and a person who would otherwise be treated as a settlor or a deemed settlor of the following trusts may not be treated as a settlor:

(1) an irrevocable inter vivos marital trust if:

(A) the settlor is a beneficiary of the trust after the death of the settlor's spouse; and

(B) the trust is treated as:

(i) qualified terminable interest property under Section 2523(f), Internal Revenue Code of 1986; or

(ii) a general power of appointment trust under Section 2523(e), Internal Revenue Code of 1986;

(2) an irrevocable inter vivos trust for the settlor's spouse if the settlor is a beneficiary of the trust after the death of the settlor's spouse; or

(3) an irrevocable trust for the benefit of a person:

(A) if the settlor is the person's spouse, regardless of whether or when the person was the settlor of an irrevocable trust for the benefit of that spouse; or

(B) to the extent that the property of the trust was subject to a general power of appointment in another person.

(h) For the purposes of Subsection (g), a person is a beneficiary whether named a beneficiary:

(1) under the initial trust instrument; or

(2) through the exercise of a limited or general power of appointment by:

(A) that person's spouse; or

(B) another person.

History of Prop. Code §112.035: Acts 1983, 68th Leg., ch. 576, §1, eff. Jan. 1, 1984. Amended by Acts 1997, 75th Leg., ch. 109, §1, eff. Sept. 1, 1997; Acts 2005, 79th Leg., ch. 148, §5, eff. Jan. 1, 2006; Acts 2007, 80th Leg., ch. 451, §4, eff. Sept. 1, 2007; Acts 2013, 83rd Leg., ch. 699, §2, eff. Sept. 1, 2013; S.B. 617, §2, 85th Leg., eff. Sept. 1, 2017.

PROP §112.036. RULE AGAINST PERPETUITIES

The rule against perpetuities applies to trusts other than charitable trusts. Accordingly, an interest is not good unless it must vest, if at all, not later than 21 years after some life in being at the time of the creation of the interest, plus a period of gestation. Any interest in a trust may, however, be reformed or construed to the extent and as provided by Section 5.043.

History of Prop. Code §112.036: Acts 1983, 68th Leg., ch. 576, §1, eff. Jan. 1, 1984. Amended by Acts 1984, 68th Leg., 2nd C.S., ch. 18, §10, eff. Oct. 2, 1984.

PROP §112.037. TRUST FOR CARE OF ANIMAL

(a) A trust may be created to provide for the care of an animal alive during the settlor's lifetime. The trust terminates on the death of the animal or, if the trust is created to provide for the care of more than one animal alive during the settlor's lifetime, on the death of the last surviving animal.

(b) A trust authorized by this section may be enforced by a person appointed in the terms of the trust or, if a person is not appointed in the terms of the trust, by a person appointed by the court. A person having an interest in the welfare of an animal that is the subject of a trust authorized by this section may request the court to appoint a person to enforce the trust or to remove a person appointed to enforce the trust.

(c) Except as provided by Subsections (d) and (e), property of a trust authorized by this section may be applied only to the property's intended use under the trust.

(d) Property of a trust authorized by this section may be applied to a use other than the property's intended use under the trust to the extent the court determines that the value of the trust property exceeds the amount required for the intended use.

(e) Except as otherwise provided by the terms of the trust, property not required for the trust's intended use must be distributed to:

(1) if the settlor is living at the time the trust property is distributed, the settlor; or

(2) if the settlor is not living at the time the trust property is distributed:

(A) if the settlor has a will, beneficiaries under the settlor's will; or

(B) in the absence of an effective provision in a will, the settlor's heirs.

(f) For purposes of Section 112.036, the lives in being used to determine the maximum duration of a trust authorized by this section are:

(1) the individual beneficiaries of the trust;

(2) the individuals named in the instrument creating the trust; and

(3) if the settlor or settlors are living at the time the trust becomes irrevocable, the settlor or settlors of the trust or, if the settlor or settlors are not living at the time the trust becomes irrevocable, the individuals who would inherit the settlor[1] or settlors' property under the law of this state had the settlor or settlors died intestate at the time the trust becomes irrevocable.

1. Editor's note: Probably should be "settlor's."

History of Prop. Code §112.037: Acts 2005, 79th Leg., ch. 148, §6, eff. Jan. 1, 2006.

A PROP §112.038. FORFEITURE CLAUSE

(a) A provision in a trust that would cause a forfeiture of or void an interest for bringing any court action, including contesting a trust, is enforceable unless in a court action determining whether the forfeiture clause

should be enforced, the person who brought the action contrary to the forfeiture clause establishes by a preponderance of the evidence that:

(1) just cause existed for bringing the action; and

(2) the action was brought and maintained in good faith.

(b) This section is not intended to and does not repeal any law, recognizing that forfeiture clauses generally will not be construed to prevent a beneficiary from seeking to compel a fiduciary to perform the fiduciary's duties, seeking redress against a fiduciary for a breach of the fiduciary's duties, or seeking a judicial construction of a will or trust.

History of Prop. Code §112.038: Acts 2009, 81st Leg., ch. 414, §3, eff. June 19, 2009. Amended by Acts 2011, 82nd Leg., ch. 657, §2, eff. Sept. 1, 2011; Acts 2013, 83rd Leg., ch. 351, §3.01, eff. Sept. 1, 2013; S.B. 617, §3, 85th Leg., eff. Sept. 1, 2017.

Sections 112.039-112.050 reserved for expansion

SUBCHAPTER C. REVOCATION, MODIFICATION, & TERMINATION OF TRUSTS

PROP §112.051. REVOCATION, MODIFICATION, OR AMENDMENT BY SETTLOR

(a) A settlor may revoke the trust unless it is irrevocable by the express terms of the instrument creating it or of an instrument modifying it.

(b) The settlor may modify or amend a trust that is revocable, but the settlor may not enlarge the duties of the trustee without the trustee's express consent.

(c) If the trust was created by a written instrument, a revocation, modification, or amendment of the trust must be in writing.

History of Prop. Code §112.051: Acts 1983, 68th Leg., ch. 576, §1, eff. Jan. 1, 1984. Source: TRCS art. 7425b-41.

PROP §112.052. TERMINATION

A trust terminates if by its terms the trust is to continue only until the expiration of a certain period or until the happening of a certain event and the period of time has elapsed or the event has occurred. If an event of termination occurs, the trustee may continue to exercise the powers of the trustee for the reasonable period of time required to wind up the affairs of the trust and to make distribution of its assets to the appropriate beneficiaries. The continued exercise of the trustee's powers after an event of termination does not affect the vested rights of beneficiaries of the trust.

History of Prop. Code §112.052: Acts 1983, 68th Leg., ch. 576, §1, eff. Jan. 1, 1984.

PROP §112.053. DISPOSITION OF TRUST PROPERTY ON FAILURE OF TRUST

The settlor may provide in the trust instrument how property may or may not be disposed of in the event of failure, termination, or revocation of the trust.

History of Prop. Code §112.053: Acts 1983, 68th Leg., ch. 576, §1, eff. Jan. 1, 1984. Amended by Acts 1991, 72nd Leg., ch. 895, §17, eff. Sept. 1, 1991. Source: TRCS arts. 7425b-39, 7425b-42.

Ⓐ PROP §112.054. JUDICIAL MODIFICATION, REFORMATION, OR TERMINATION OF TRUSTS

(a) On the petition of a trustee or a beneficiary, a court may order that the trustee be changed, that the terms of the trust be modified, that the trustee be directed or permitted to do acts that are not authorized or that are forbidden by the terms of the trust, that the trustee be prohibited from performing acts required by the terms of the trust, or that the trust be terminated in whole or in part, if:

(1) the purposes of the trust have been fulfilled or have become illegal or impossible to fulfill;

(2) because of circumstances not known to or anticipated by the settlor, the order will further the purposes of the trust;

(3) modification of administrative, nondispositive terms of the trust is necessary or appropriate to prevent waste or [~~avoid~~] impairment of the trust's administration;

(4) the order is necessary or appropriate to achieve the settlor's tax objectives or to qualify a distributee for governmental benefits and is not contrary to the settlor's intentions; or

(5) subject to Subsection (d):

(A) continuance of the trust is not necessary to achieve any material purpose of the trust; or

(B) the order is not inconsistent with a material purpose of the trust.

(b) The court shall exercise its discretion to order a modification or termination under Subsection (a) or reformation under Subsection (b-1) in the manner that conforms as nearly as possible to the probable intention of the settlor. The court shall consider spendthrift provisions as a factor in making its decision whether to modify, [~~or~~] terminate, or reform, but the court is not precluded from exercising its discretion to modify, [~~or~~] terminate, or reform solely because the trust is a spendthrift trust.

(b-1) On the petition of a trustee or a beneficiary, a court may order that the terms of the trust be reformed if:

(1) reformation of administrative, nondispositive terms of the trust is necessary or appropriate to prevent waste or impairment of the trust's administration;

(2) reformation is necessary or appropriate to achieve the settlor's tax objectives or to qualify a distributee for governmental benefits and is not contrary to the settlor's intentions; or

(3) reformation is necessary to correct a scrivener's error in the governing document, even if unambiguous, to conform the terms to the settlor's intent.

(c) The court may direct that an order described by Subsection (a)(4) or (b-1) has retroactive effect.

(d) The court may not take the action permitted by Subsection (a)(5) unless all beneficiaries of the trust have consented to the order or are deemed to have consented to the order. A minor, incapacitated, unborn, or unascertained beneficiary is deemed to have consented if a person representing the beneficiary's interest under Section 115.013(c) has consented or if a guardian ad litem appointed to represent the beneficiary's interest under Section 115.014 consents on the beneficiary's behalf.

(e) An order described by Subsection (b-1)(3) may be issued only if the settlor's intent is established by clear and convincing evidence.

(f) Subsection (b-1) is not intended to state the exclusive basis for reformation of trusts, and the bases for reformation of trusts in equity or common law are not affected by this section.

History of Prop. Code §112.054: Acts 1983, 68th Leg., ch. 576, §1, eff. Jan. 1, 1984. Amended by Acts 1985, 69th Leg., ch. 149, §1, eff. May 24, 1985; Acts 2005, 79th Leg., ch. 148, §7, eff. Jan. 1, 2006; S.B. 617, §§4, 5, 85th Leg., eff. Sept. 1, 2017.

PROP §112.055. AMENDMENT OF CHARITABLE TRUSTS BY OPERATION OF LAW

(a) Except as provided by Section 112.056 and Subsection (b) of this section, the governing instrument of a trust that is a private foundation under Section 509, Internal Revenue Code, as amended, a nonexempt charitable trust that is treated as a private foundation under Section 4947(a)(1), Internal Revenue Code, as amended, or, to the extent that Section 508(e), Internal Revenue Code, is applicable to it, a nonexempt split-interest trust under Section 4947(a)(2), Internal Revenue Code, as amended, is considered to contain provisions stating that the trust:

(1) shall make distributions at times and in a manner as not to subject the trust to tax under Section 4942, Internal Revenue Code;

(2) may not engage in an act of self-dealing that would be subject to tax under Section 4941, Internal Revenue Code;

(3) may not retain excess business holdings that would subject it to tax under Section 4943, Internal Revenue Code;

(4) may not make an investment that would subject it to tax under Section 4944, Internal Revenue Code; and

(5) may not make a taxable expenditure that would subject it to tax under Section 4945, Internal Revenue Code.

(b) If a trust was created before January 1, 1970, this section applies to it only for its taxable years that begin on or after January 1, 1972.

(c) This section applies regardless of any provision in a trust's governing instrument and regardless of any other law of this state, including the provisions of this title.

History of Prop. Code §112.055: Acts 1983, 68th Leg., ch. 576, §1, eff. Jan. 1, 1984.

PROP §112.056. PERMISSIVE AMENDMENT BY TRUSTEE OF CHARITABLE TRUST

(a) If the settlor of a trust that is described under Subsection (a) of Section 112.055 of this Act is living and competent and consents, the trustee may, without judicial proceedings, amend the trust to expressly include or exclude the provisions required by Subsection (a) of Section 112.055 of this Act.

(b) The amendment must be in writing, and it is effective when a duplicate original is filed with the attorney general's office.

History of Prop. Code §112.056: Acts 1983, 68th Leg., ch. 576, §1, eff. Jan. 1, 1984.

PROP §112.057. DIVISION & COMBINATION OF TRUSTS

(a) The trustee may, unless expressly prohibited by the terms of the instrument establishing the trust, divide a trust into two or more separate trusts without a judicial proceeding if the result does not impair the rights of any beneficiary or adversely affect achievement of the purposes of the original trust. The trustee may make a division under this subsection by:

(1) giving written notice of the division, not later than the 30th day before the date of a division under this subsection, to each beneficiary who might then be entitled to receive distributions from the trust or may be entitled to receive distributions from the trust once it is funded; and

(2) executing a written instrument, acknowledged before a notary public or other person authorized to take acknowledgements of conveyances of real estate stating that the trust has been divided pursuant to this section and that the notice requirements of this subsection have been satisfied.

(b) A trustee, in the written instrument dividing a trust, shall allocate trust property among the separate trusts on a fractional basis, by identifying the assets and liabilities passing to each separate trust, or in any other reasonable manner. The trustee shall allocate undesignated trust property received after the trustee has divided the trust into separate trusts in the manner provided by the written instrument dividing the trust or, in the absence of a provision in the written instrument, in a manner determined by the trustee.

(c) The trustee may, unless expressly prohibited by the terms of the instrument establishing a trust, combine two or more trusts into a single trust without a judicial proceeding if the result does not impair the rights of any beneficiary or adversely affect achievement of the purposes of one of the separate trusts. The trustee shall complete the trust combination by:

(1) giving a written notice of the combination, not later than the 30th day before the effective date of the combination, to each beneficiary who might then be entitled to receive distributions from the separate trusts being combined or to each beneficiary who might be entitled to receive distributions from the separate trusts once the trusts are funded; and

(2) executing a written instrument, acknowledged before a notary public or other person authorized to take acknowledgments of conveyances of real estate stating that the trust has been combined pursuant to this section and that the notice requirements of this subsection have been satisfied.

(d) The trustee may divide or combine a testamentary trust after the will establishing the trust has been admitted to probate, even if the trust will not be funded until a later date. The trustee may divide or combine any other trust before it is funded.

(e) A beneficiary to whom written notice is required to be given under this section may waive the notice requirement in a writing delivered to the trustee. If all beneficiaries to whom notice would otherwise be required to be given under this section waive the notice requirement, notice is not required.

(f) Notice required under this section shall be given to a guardian of the estate, guardian ad litem, or parent of a minor or incapacitated beneficiary. A guardian of the estate, guardian ad litem, or parent of a minor or incapacitated beneficiary may waive the notice requirement in accordance with this section on behalf of the minor or incapacitated beneficiary.

History of Prop. Code §112.057: Acts 1991, 72nd Leg., ch. 895, §18, eff. Sept. 1, 1991. Amended by Acts 2005, 79th Leg., ch. 148, §§8, 9, eff. Jan. 1, 2006; Acts 2011, 82nd Leg., ch. 657, §3, eff. Sept. 1, 2011.

See also *Real Estate Forms*, FORMS 11:1, 11:2.

(A) PROP §112.058. CONVERSION OF COMMUNITY TRUST TO NONPROFIT CORPORATION

(a) In this section:

(1) "Assets" means the assets of the component trust funds of a community trust.

(2) "Community trust" means a community trust as described by 26 C.F.R. Section 1.170A-9 (2008) [~~1.170A-9(e)(11) (1999)~~], including subsequent amendments.

(b) A community trust with court approval may transfer the assets of the trust to a nonprofit corporation and terminate the trust as provided by this section.

(c) The community trust may transfer assets of the trust to a nonprofit corporation only if the nonprofit corporation is organized under the Texas Non-Profit Corporation Act (Article 1396-1.01 et seq., Vernon's Texas Civil Statutes) and organized for the same purpose as the community trust. The charter of the nonprofit corporation must describe the purpose of the corporation and the proposed use of the assets transferred using language substantially similar to the language used in the instrument creating the community trust.

(d) To transfer the assets of and terminate a community trust under this section, the governing body of the community trust must:

(1) file a petition in a probate court, county court, or district court requesting:

(A) the transfer of the assets of the trust to a nonprofit corporation established for the purpose of receiving and administering the assets of the trust; and

(B) the termination of the trust;

(2) send by first class mail to each trust settlor and each trustee of each component trust of the community trust who can be located by the exercise of reasonable diligence a copy of the governing body's petition and a notice specifying the time and place of the court-scheduled hearing on the petition; and

(3) publish once in a newspaper of general circulation in the county in which the proceeding is pending a notice that reads substantially similar to the following:

TO ALL INTERESTED PERSONS:

(NAME OF COMMUNITY TRUST) HAS FILED A PETITION IN (NAME OF COURT) OF (NAME OF COUNTY), TEXAS, REQUESTING PERMISSION TO CONVERT TO A NONPROFIT CORPORATION. IF PERMITTED TO CONVERT:

(1) THE (NAME OF COMMUNITY TRUST) WILL BE TERMINATED; AND

(2) THE ASSETS OF THE TRUST WILL BE:

(A) TRANSFERRED TO A NONPROFIT CORPORATION WITH THE SAME NAME AND CREATED FOR THE SAME PURPOSE AS THE (NAME OF COMMUNITY TRUST); AND

(B) HELD AND ADMINISTERED BY THE CORPORATION AS PROVIDED BY THE TEXAS NON-PROFIT CORPORATION ACT (ARTICLE 1396-1.01 ET SEQ., VERNON'S TEXAS CIVIL STATUTES).

THE PURPOSE OF THE CONVERSION IS TO ACHIEVE SAVINGS AND USE THE MONEY SAVED TO FURTHER THE PURPOSES FOR WHICH THE (NAME OF COMMUNITY TRUST) WAS CREATED.

A HEARING ON THE PETITION IS SCHEDULED ON (DATE AND TIME) AT (LOCATION OF COURT).

FOR ADDITIONAL INFORMATION, YOU MAY CONTACT THE GOVERNING BODY OF THE (NAME OF COMMUNITY TRUST) AT (ADDRESS AND TELEPHONE NUMBER) OR THE COURT.

(e) The court shall schedule a hearing on the petition to be held after the 10th day after the date the notices required by Subsection (d)(2) are deposited in the mail or the date the notice required by Subsection (d)(3) is published, whichever is later. The hearing must be held at the time and place stated in the notices unless the court, for good cause, postpones the hearing. If the hearing is postponed, a notice of the rescheduled hearing date and time must be posted at the courthouse of the county in which the proceeding is pending or at the place in or near the courthouse where public notices are customarily posted.

(f) The court, on a request from the governing body of the community trust, may by order require approval from the Internal Revenue Service for an asset transfer under this section. If the court orders approval from the Internal Revenue Service, the asset transfer may occur on the date the governing body of the community trust files a notice with the court indicating that the Internal Revenue Service has approved the asset transfer. The notice required by this subsection must be filed on or before the first anniversary of the date the court's order approving the asset transfer is signed. If the notice is not filed within the period prescribed by this subsection, the court's order is dissolved.

(g) A court order transferring the assets of and terminating a community trust must provide that the duties of each trustee of each component trust fund of the community trust are terminated on the date the assets are transferred. This subsection does not affect the liability of a trustee for acts or omissions that occurred before the duties of the trustee are terminated.

History of Prop. Code §112.058: Acts 1999, 76th Leg., ch. 1035, §1, eff. Sept. 1, 1999. Amended by S.B. 617, §6, 85th Leg., eff. Sept. 1, 2017.

PROP §112.059. TERMINATION OF UNECONOMIC TRUST

(a) After notice to beneficiaries who are distributees or permissible distributees of trust income or principal or who would be distributees or permissible distributees if the interests of the distributees or the trust were to terminate and no powers of appointment were exercised, the trustee of a trust consisting of trust property having a total value of less than $50,000 may terminate the trust if the trustee concludes after considering the purpose of the trust and the nature of the trust assets that the value of the trust property is insufficient to justify the continued cost of administration.

(b) On termination of a trust under this section, the trustee shall distribute the trust property in a manner consistent with the purposes of the trust.

(c) A trustee may not exercise a power described by Subsection (a) if the trustee's possession of the power would cause the assets of the trust to be included in the trustee's estate for federal estate tax purposes.

(d) This section does not apply to an easement for conservation or preservation.

History of Prop. Code §112.059: Acts 2007, 80th Leg., ch. 451, §5, eff. Sept. 1, 2007.

Sections 112.060-112.070 blank

SUBCHAPTER D. DISTRIBUTION OF TRUST PRINCIPAL IN FURTHER TRUST

A PROP §112.071. DEFINITIONS

In this subchapter:

(1) "Authorized trustee" means a person, other than the settlor, who has authority under the terms of a first trust to distribute the principal of the trust to or for the benefit of one or more current beneficiaries.

(2) "Charity" means a charitable entity or a charitable trust, as those terms are defined by Section 123.001.

(3) "Current beneficiary," with respect to a particular date, means a person who is receiving or is eligible to receive a distribution of income or principal from a trust on that date.

(4) "First trust" means an existing irrevocable inter vivos or testamentary trust all or part of the principal of which is distributed in further trust under Section 112.072 or 112.073.

(5) "Full discretion" means a [the] power to distribute principal to or for the benefit of one or more of the beneficiaries of a trust that is not a trust with limited discretion [limited or modified by the terms of the trust in any way, including by restrictions that limit distributions to purposes such as the best interests, welfare, or happiness of the beneficiaries].

(6) "Limited discretion" means:

(A) a power to distribute principal according to mandatory distribution provisions under which the trustee has no discretion; or

(B) a [limited or modified] power to distribute principal to or for the benefit of one or more beneficiaries of a trust that is limited by an ascertainable standard, including the health, education, support, or maintenance of the beneficiary.

(7) "Presumptive remainder beneficiary," with respect to a particular date, means a beneficiary of a trust on that date who, in the absence of notice to the trustee of the exercise of the power of appointment and assuming that any other powers of appointment under the trust are not exercised, would be eligible to receive a distribution from the trust if:

(A) the trust terminated on that date; or

(B) the interests of all current beneficiaries [currently eligible to receive income or principal from the trust] ended on that date without causing the trust to terminate.

(8) "Principal" means property held in trust for distribution to a remainder beneficiary when the trust terminates and includes income of the trust that, at the time of the exercise of a power of distribution under Section 112.072 or 112.073, is not currently required to be distributed.

(9) "Second trust" means any irrevocable trust to which principal is distributed under Section 112.072 or 112.073.

(10) "Successor beneficiary" means a beneficiary other than a current or presumptive remainder beneficiary. The term does not include a potential appointee under a power of appointment held by a beneficiary.

History of Prop. Code §112.071: Acts 2013, 83rd Leg., ch. 699, §3, eff. Sept. 1, 2013. Amended by S.B. 617, §7, 85th Leg., eff. Sept. 1, 2017.

A PROP §112.072. DISTRIBUTION TO SECOND TRUST: TRUSTEE WITH FULL DISCRETION

(a) An authorized trustee who has the full discretion to distribute the principal of a trust may distribute all or part of the principal of that trust in favor of a trustee of a second trust for the benefit of one, [or] more than one, or all of the current beneficiaries of the first trust [who are eligible to receive income or principal from the trust] and for the benefit of one, [or] more than one, or all of the successor or presumptive remainder beneficiaries of the first trust [who are eligible to receive income or principal from the trust].

(b) The authorized trustee may, in connection with the exercise of a power of distribution under this section, grant a power of appointment, including a currently exercisable power of appointment, in the second trust to one or more of the current beneficiaries of the first trust who, at the time the power of appointment is granted, is eligible to receive the principal outright under the terms of the first trust.

(c) If the authorized trustee grants a power of appointment to a beneficiary under Subsection (b), the class of permissible appointees in whose favor the beneficiary may appoint under that power may be broader or different than the current, successor, and presumptive remainder beneficiaries of the first trust.

(d) If the beneficiaries of the first trust are described as a class of persons, the beneficiaries of the second trust may include one or more persons who become members of that class after the distribution to the second trust.

(e) The authorized trustee shall exercise a power to distribute under this section in good faith, in accor-

dance with the terms and purposes of the trust, and in the interests of the beneficiaries.

History of Prop. Code §112.072: Acts 2013, 83rd Leg., ch. 699, §3, eff. Sept. 1, 2013. Amended by S.B. 617, §8, 85th Leg., eff. Sept. 1, 2017.

PROP §112.073. DISTRIBUTION TO SECOND TRUST: TRUSTEE WITH LIMITED DISCRETION

(a) An authorized trustee who has limited discretion to distribute the principal of a trust may distribute all or part of the principal of that trust in favor of a trustee of a second trust as provided by this section.

(b) The current beneficiaries of the second trust must be the same as the current beneficiaries of the first trust, and the successor and presumptive remainder beneficiaries of the second trust must be the same as the successor and presumptive remainder beneficiaries of the first trust.

(c) The second trust must include the same language authorizing the trustee to distribute the income or principal of the trust that was included in the first trust.

(d) If the beneficiaries of the first trust are described as a class of persons, the beneficiaries of the second trust must include all persons who become members of that class after the distribution to the second trust.

(e) If the first trust grants a power of appointment to a beneficiary of the trust, the second trust must grant the power of appointment to the beneficiary in the second trust, and the class of permissible appointees under that power must be the same as the class of permissible appointees under the power granted by the first trust.

(f) The authorized trustee shall exercise a power of distribution under this section in good faith, in accordance with the terms and purposes of the trust, and in the interests of the beneficiaries.

History of Prop. Code §112.073: Acts 2013, 83rd Leg., ch. 699, §3, eff. Sept. 1, 2013.

A PROP §112.074. NOTICE REQUIRED

(a) An authorized trustee may exercise a power of distribution under Section 112.072 or 112.073 without the consent of the settlor or beneficiaries of the first trust and without court approval if the trustee provides to all of the current beneficiaries and presumptive remainder beneficiaries written notice of the trustee's decision to exercise the power.

(b) For the purpose of determining who is a current beneficiary or presumptive remainder beneficiary entitled to the notice, a beneficiary is determined as of the date the notice is sent. A beneficiary includes a person entitled to receive property under the terms of the first trust.

(c) Except as provided by Subsection (e-1), in [~~In~~] addition to the notice required under Subsection (a), the authorized trustee shall give written notice of the trustee's decision to the attorney general if:

(1) a charity is entitled to notice;

(2) a charity entitled to notice is no longer in existence;

(3) the trustee has the authority to distribute trust assets to one or more charities that are not named in the trust instrument; or

(4) the trustee has the authority to make distributions for a charitable purpose described in the trust instrument, but no charity is named as a beneficiary for that purpose.

(d) If the beneficiary has a court-appointed guardian or conservator, the notice required to be given by this section must be given to that guardian or conservator. If the beneficiary is a minor for whom no guardian or conservator has been appointed, the notice required to be given by this section must be given to a parent of the minor.

(e) The authorized trustee is not required to provide the notice to a beneficiary who:

(1) is known to the trustee and cannot be located by the trustee after reasonable diligence;

(2) is not known to the trustee;

(3) waives the requirement of the notice under this section; or

(4) is a descendant of a beneficiary to whom the trustee has given notice if the beneficiary and the beneficiary's ancestor have similar interests in the trust and no apparent conflict of interest exists between them.

(e-1) The trustee is not required to give notice to the attorney general under Subsection (c) if the attorney general waives that requirement in writing.

(e-2) For purposes of Subsection (e)(3), a beneficiary is considered to have waived the requirement that notice be given under this section if a person to whom notice is required to be given with respect to that beneficiary under Subsection (d) waives the requirement that notice be given under this section.

(f) The notice required under Subsection (a) must:

(1) include a statement that:

(A) the authorized trustee intends to exercise the power of distribution;

(B) the beneficiary has the right to object to the exercise of the power; and

(C) the beneficiary may petition a court to approve, modify, or deny the exercise of the trustee's power to make a distribution under this subchapter;

(2) describe the manner in which the trustee intends to exercise the power;

(3) specify the date the trustee proposes to distribute the first trust to the second trust;

(4) include the name and mailing address of the trustee;

(5) include copies of the agreements of the first trust and the proposed second trust;

(6) be given not later than the 30th day before the proposed date of distribution to the second trust; and

(7) be sent by registered or certified mail, return receipt requested, or delivered in person, unless the notice is waived in writing by the person to whom notice is required to be given.

History of Prop. Code §112.074: Acts 2013, 83rd Leg., ch. 699, §3, eff. Sept. 1, 2013. Amended by S.B. 617, §9, 85th Leg., eff. Sept. 1, 2017.

PROP §112.075. WRITTEN INSTRUMENT REQUIRED

A distribution under Section 112.072 or 112.073 must be made by a written instrument that is signed and acknowledged by the authorized trustee and filed with the records of the first trust and the second trust.

History of Prop. Code §112.075: Acts 2013, 83rd Leg., ch. 699, §3, eff. Sept. 1, 2013.

PROP §112.076. REFERENCE TO TRUST TERMS

A reference to the governing instrument or terms of the governing instrument of a trust includes the terms of a second trust to which that trust's principal was distributed under this subchapter.

History of Prop. Code §112.076: Acts 2013, 83rd Leg., ch. 699, §3, eff. Sept. 1, 2013.

PROP §112.077. SETTLOR OF SECOND TRUST

(a) Except as provided by Subsection (b), the settlor of a first trust is considered to be the settlor of a second trust established under this subchapter.

(b) If a settlor of a first trust is not also the settlor of a second trust into which principal of that first trust is distributed, the settlor of the first trust is considered the settlor of the portion of the second trust distributed to the second trust from that first trust under this subchapter.

History of Prop. Code §112.077: Acts 2013, 83rd Leg., ch. 699, §3, eff. Sept. 1, 2013.

Ⓐ PROP §112.078. COURT-ORDERED DISTRIBUTION

(a) An authorized trustee may petition a court to order a distribution under this subchapter.

(b) If the authorized trustee receives a written objection to a distribution under this subchapter from a beneficiary before the proposed effective date of the distribution specified in the notice provided to the beneficiary under Section 112.074, the trustee or the beneficiary may petition a court to approve, modify, or deny the exercise of the trustee's power to make a distribution under this subchapter.

(c) If the authorized trustee receives a written objection to the distribution from the attorney general not later than the 30th day after the date the notice required by Section 112.074 was received by the attorney general, the trustee may not make a distribution under Section 112.072 or 112.073 without petitioning a court to approve or modify the exercise of the trustee's power to make a distribution under this subchapter.

(d) In a judicial proceeding under this section, the authorized trustee may present the trustee's reasons for supporting or opposing a proposed distribution, including whether the trustee believes the distribution would enable the trustee to better carry out the purposes of the trust.

(e) The authorized trustee has the burden of proving that the proposed distribution furthers the purposes of the trust, is in accordance with the terms of the trust, and is in the interests of the beneficiaries.

(f) This section does not limit a beneficiary's right to bring an action against a trustee for a breach of trust.

History of Prop. Code §112.078: Acts 2013, 83rd Leg., ch. 699, §3, eff. Sept. 1, 2013. Amended by S.B. 617, §10, 85th Leg., eff. Sept. 1, 2017.

PROP §112.079. DIVIDED DISCRETION

If an authorized trustee has full discretion to distribute the principal of a trust and another trustee has limited discretion to distribute principal under the trust

instrument, the authorized trustee having full discretion may exercise the power to distribute the trust's principal under Section 112.072.

History of Prop. Code §112.079: Acts 2013, 83rd Leg., ch. 699, §3, eff. Sept. 1, 2013.

PROP §112.080. LATER DISCOVERED ASSETS

To the extent the authorized trustee does not provide otherwise:

(1) the distribution of all of the principal of a first trust to a second trust includes subsequently discovered assets otherwise belonging to the first trust and principal paid to or acquired by the first trust after the distribution of the first trust's principal to the second trust; and

(2) the distribution of part of the principal of a first trust to a second trust does not include subsequently discovered assets belonging to the first trust or principal paid to or acquired by the first trust after the distribution of principal from the first trust to the second trust, and those assets or that principal remain the assets or principal of the first trust.

History of Prop. Code §112.080: Acts 2013, 83rd Leg., ch. 699, §3, eff. Sept. 1, 2013.

PROP §112.081. OTHER AUTHORITY TO DISTRIBUTE IN FURTHER TRUST NOT LIMITED

This subchapter may not be construed to limit the power of an authorized trustee to distribute property in further trust under the terms of the governing instrument of a trust, other law, or a court order.

History of Prop. Code §112.081: Acts 2013, 83rd Leg., ch. 699, §3, eff. Sept. 1, 2013.

PROP §112.082. NEED FOR DISTRIBUTION NOT REQUIRED

An authorized trustee may exercise the power to distribute principal to a second trust under Section 112.072 or 112.073 regardless of whether there is a current need to distribute principal under the terms of the first trust.

History of Prop. Code §112.082: Acts 2013, 83rd Leg., ch. 699, §3, eff. Sept. 1, 2013.

PROP §112.083. DUTIES NOT CREATED

(a) This subchapter does not create or imply a duty for an authorized trustee to exercise a power to distribute principal, and impropriety may not be inferred as a result of the trustee not exercising a power conferred by Section 112.072 or 112.073.

(b) An authorized trustee does not have a duty to inform beneficiaries about the availability of the authority provided by this subchapter or a duty to review the trust to determine whether any action should be taken under this subchapter.

History of Prop. Code §112.083: Acts 2013, 83rd Leg., ch. 699, §3, eff. Sept. 1, 2013.

PROP §112.084. CERTAIN DISTRIBUTIONS PROHIBITED

(a) Except as provided by Subsection (b), an authorized trustee may not exercise a power to distribute principal of a trust otherwise provided by Section 112.072 or 112.073 if the distribution is expressly prohibited by the terms of the governing instrument of the trust.

(b) A general prohibition of the amendment or revocation of a trust or a provision that constitutes a spendthrift clause does not preclude the exercise of a power to distribute principal of a trust under Section 112.072 or 112.073.

History of Prop. Code §112.084: Acts 2013, 83rd Leg., ch. 699, §3, eff. Sept. 1, 2013.

A PROP §112.085. EXCEPTIONS TO POWER OF DISTRIBUTION

An authorized trustee may not exercise a power to distribute principal of a trust under Section 112.072 or 112.073 to:

(1) reduce, limit, or modify a beneficiary's current, vested right to:

(A) receive a mandatory distribution of income or principal;

(B) receive a mandatory annuity or unitrust interest;

(C) withdraw a percentage of the value of the trust; or

(D) withdraw a specified dollar amount from the trust;

(2) [~~materially impair the rights of any beneficiary of the trust;~~]

[~~(3)~~] materially limit a trustee's fiduciary duty:

(A) under the terms of the trust; or

(B) in a manner that would be prohibited [~~as described~~] by Section 111.0035;

(3) [~~(4)~~] decrease or indemnify against a trustee's liability;

(4) add a provision exonerating [~~or exonerate~~] a trustee from liability for failure to exercise reasonable care, diligence, and prudence;

(5) eliminate a provision granting another person the right to remove or replace the authorized trustee exercising the distribution power under Section 112.072 or 112.073; or

(6) reduce, limit, or modify in the second trust a perpetuities provision included in the first trust, unless expressly permitted by the terms of the first trust.

History of Prop. Code §112.085: Acts 2013, 83rd Leg., ch. 699, §3, eff. Sept. 1, 2013. Amended by S.B. 617, §11, 85th Leg., eff. Sept. 1, 2017.

PROP §112.086. TAX-RELATED LIMITATIONS

(a) The authorized trustee may not distribute the principal of a trust under Section 112.072 or 112.073 in a manner that would prevent a contribution to that trust from qualifying for or that would reduce the exclusion, deduction, or other federal tax benefit that was originally claimed for that contribution, including:

(1) the annual exclusion under Section 2503(b), Internal Revenue Code of 1986;

(2) a marital deduction under Section 2056(a) or 2523(a), Internal Revenue Code of 1986;

(3) the charitable deduction under Section 170(a), 642(c), 2055(a), or 2522(a), Internal Revenue Code of 1986;

(4) direct skip treatment under Section 2642(c), Internal Revenue Code of 1986; or

(5) any other tax benefit for income, gift, estate, or generation-skipping transfer tax purposes under the Internal Revenue Code of 1986.

(b) Notwithstanding Subsection (a), an authorized trustee may distribute the principal of a first trust to a second trust regardless of whether the settlor is treated as the owner of either or both trusts under Sections 671-679, Internal Revenue Code of 1986.

(c) If S corporation stock is held in trust, an authorized trustee may not distribute all or part of that stock under Section 112.072 or 112.073 to a second trust that is not a permitted shareholder under Section 1361(c)(2), Internal Revenue Code of 1986.

(d) If an interest in property that is subject to the minimum distribution rules of Section 401(a)(9), Internal Revenue Code of 1986, is held in trust, an authorized trustee may not distribute the trust's interest in the property to a second trust under Section 112.072 or 112.073 if the distribution would shorten the minimum distribution period applicable to the property.

History of Prop. Code §112.086: Acts 2013, 83rd Leg., ch. 699, §3, eff. Sept. 1, 2013.

PROP §112.087. COMPENSATION OF TRUSTEE

(a) Except as provided by Subsection (b) and unless a court, on application of the authorized trustee, directs otherwise, the trustee may not exercise a power under Section 112.072 or 112.073 solely to change trust provisions regarding the determination of the compensation of any trustee.

(b) An authorized trustee, in connection with the exercise of a power under Section 112.072 or 112.073 for another valid and reasonable purpose, may bring the trustee's compensation into conformance with reasonable limits authorized by state law.

(c) The compensation payable to an authorized trustee of the first trust may continue to be paid to the trustee of the second trust during the term of the second trust and may be determined in the same manner as the compensation would have been determined in the first trust.

(d) An authorized trustee may not receive a commission or other compensation for the distribution of a particular asset from a first trust to a second trust under Section 112.072 or 112.073.

History of Prop. Code §112.087: Acts 2013, 83rd Leg., ch. 699, §3, eff. Sept. 1, 2013.

CHAPTER 113. ADMINISTRATION

Subchapter A. Powers of Trustee

PROPERTY CODE

CHAPTER 113. ADMINISTRATION
§§113.001 - 113.008

SUBCHAPTER A. POWERS OF TRUSTEE

PROP §113.001. LIMITATION OF POWERS

A power given to a trustee by this subchapter does not apply to a trust to the extent that the instrument creating the trust, a subsequent court order, or another provision of this subtitle conflicts with or limits the power.

History of Prop. Code §113.001: Acts 1983, 68th Leg., ch. 576, §1, eff. Jan. 1, 1984. Source: TRCS art. 7425b-25.

PROP §113.002. GENERAL POWERS

Except as provided by Section 113.001, a trustee may exercise any powers in addition to the powers authorized by this subchapter that are necessary or appropriate to carry out the purposes of the trust.

History of Prop. Code §113.002: Acts 1983, 68th Leg., ch. 576, §1, eff. Jan. 1, 1984. Source: TRCS art. 7425b-25.

PROP §113.003. OPTIONS

A trustee may:

(1) grant an option involving a sale, lease, or other disposition of trust property, including an option exercisable beyond the duration of the trust; or

(2) acquire and exercise an option for the acquisition of property, including an option exercisable beyond the duration of the trust.

History of Prop. Code §113.003: Acts 2005, 79th Leg., ch. 148, §10, eff. Jan. 1, 2006.

PROP §113.004. ADDITIONS TO TRUST ASSETS

A trustee may receive from any source additions to the assets of the trust.

History of Prop. Code §113.004: Acts 1983, 68th Leg., ch. 576, §1, eff. Jan. 1, 1984.

PROP §113.005. ACQUISITION OF UNDIVIDED INTERESTS

A trustee may acquire all or a portion of the remaining undivided interest in property in which the trust holds an undivided interest.

History of Prop. Code §113.005: Acts 1983, 68th Leg., ch. 576, §1, eff. Jan. 1, 1984.

PROP §113.006. GENERAL AUTHORITY TO MANAGE & INVEST TRUST PROPERTY

Subject to the requirements of Chapter 117, a trustee may manage the trust property and invest and reinvest in property of any character on the conditions and for the lengths of time as the trustee considers proper, notwithstanding that the time may extend beyond the term of the trust.

History of Prop. Code §113.006: Acts 1983, 68th Leg., ch. 576, §1, eff. Jan. 1, 1984. Amended by Acts 2003, 78th Leg., ch. 1103, §3, eff. Jan. 1, 2004.

PROP §113.007. TEMPORARY DEPOSITS OF FUNDS

A trustee may deposit trust funds that are being held pending investment, distribution, or the payment of debts in a bank that is subject to supervision by state or federal authorities. However, a corporate trustee depositing funds with itself is subject to the requirements of Section 113.057 of this code.

History of Prop. Code §113.007: Acts 1983, 68th Leg., ch. 576, §1, eff. Jan. 1, 1984. Amended by Acts 1984, 68th Leg., 2nd C.S., ch. 18, §11, eff. Oct. 2, 1984.

PROP §113.008. BUSINESS ENTITIES

A trustee may invest in, continue, or participate in the operation of any business or other investment enterprise in any form, including a sole proprietorship,

partnership, limited partnership, corporation, or association, and the trustee may effect any change in the organization of the business or enterprise.

History of Prop. Code §113.008: Acts 1983, 68th Leg., ch. 576, §1, eff. Jan. 1, 1984.

PROP §113.009. REAL PROPERTY MANAGEMENT

A trustee may:

(1) exchange, subdivide, develop, improve, or partition real property;

(2) make or vacate public plats;

(3) adjust boundaries;

(4) adjust differences in valuation by giving or receiving value;

(5) dedicate real property to public use or, if the trustee considers it in the best interest of the trust, dedicate easements to public use without consideration;

(6) raze existing walls or buildings;

(7) erect new party walls or buildings alone or jointly with an owner of adjacent property;

(8) make repairs; and

(9) make extraordinary alterations or additions in structures as necessary to make property more productive.

History of Prop. Code §113.009: Acts 1983, 68th Leg., ch. 576, §1, eff. Jan. 1, 1984. Source: TRCS art. 7425b-25.

PROP §113.010. SALE OF PROPERTY

A trustee may contract to sell, sell and convey, or grant an option to sell real or personal property at public auction or private sale for cash or for credit or for part cash and part credit, with or without security.

History of Prop. Code §113.010: Acts 1983, 68th Leg., ch. 576, §1, eff. Jan. 1, 1984. Source: TRCS art. 7425b-25.

PROP §113.011. LEASES

(a) A trustee may grant or take a lease of real or personal property for any term, with or without options to purchase and with or without covenants relating to erection of buildings or renewals, including the lease of a right or privilege above or below the surface of real property.

(b) A trustee may execute a lease containing terms or options that extend beyond the duration of the trust.

History of Prop. Code §113.011: Acts 1983, 68th Leg., ch. 576, §1, eff. Jan. 1, 1984. Source: TRCS art. 7425b-25.

PROP §113.012. MINERALS

(a) A trustee may enter into mineral transactions, including:

(1) negotiating and making oil, gas, and other mineral leases covering any land, mineral, or royalty interest at any time forming a part of a trust;

(2) pooling and unitizing part or all of the land, mineral leasehold, mineral, royalty, or other interest of a trust estate with land, mineral leasehold, mineral, royalty, or other interest of one or more persons or entities for the purpose of developing and producing oil, gas, or other minerals, and making leases or assignments granting the right to pool and unitize;

(3) entering into contracts and agreements concerning the installation and operation of plants or other facilities for the cycling, repressuring, processing, or other treating or handling of oil, gas, or other minerals;

(4) conducting or contracting for the conducting of seismic evaluation operations;

(5) drilling or contracting for the drilling of wells for oil, gas, or other minerals;

(6) contracting for and making "dry hole" and "bottom hole" contributions of cash, leasehold interests, or other interests towards the drilling of wells;

(7) using or contracting for the use of any method of secondary or tertiary recovery of any mineral, including the injection of water, gas, air, or other substances;

(8) purchasing oil, gas, or other mineral leases, leasehold interests, or other interests for any type of consideration, including farmout agreements requiring the drilling or reworking of wells or participation therein;

(9) entering into farmout contracts or agreements committing a trust estate to assign oil, gas, or other mineral leases or interests in consideration for the drilling of wells or other oil, gas, or mineral operations;

(10) negotiating the transfer of and transferring oil, gas, or other mineral leases or interests for any consideration, such as retained overriding royalty interests of any nature, drilling or reworking commitments, or production interests; and

(11) executing and entering into contracts, conveyances, and other agreements or transfers considered necessary or desirable to carry out the powers granted in this section, whether or not the action is now or subsequently recognized or considered as a common or proper practice by those engaged in the business of prospecting for, developing, producing, processing, transporting, or marketing minerals, including entering into and executing division orders, oil, gas, or

other mineral sales contracts, exploration agreements, processing agreements, and other contracts relating to the processing, handling, treating, transporting, and marketing of oil, gas, or other mineral production from or accruing to a trust and receiving and receipting for the proceeds thereof on behalf of a trust.

(b) A trustee may enter into mineral transactions that extend beyond the term of the trust.

History of Prop. Code §113.012: Acts 1983, 68th Leg., ch. 576, §2, eff. Jan. 1, 1984. Amended by Acts 1983, 68th Leg., ch. 576, §1, eff. Jan. 1, 1984.

PROP §113.013. INSURANCE

A trustee may purchase insurance of any nature, form, or amount to protect the trust property and the trustee.

History of Prop. Code §113.013: Acts 1983, 68th Leg., ch. 576, §1, eff. Jan. 1, 1984. Source: TRCS art. 7425b-25.

PROP §113.014. PAYMENT OF TAXES

A trustee may pay taxes and assessments levied or assessed against the trust estate or the trustee by governmental taxing or assessing authorities.

History of Prop. Code §113.014: Acts 1983, 68th Leg., ch. 576, §1, eff. Jan. 1, 1984. Source: TRCS art. 7425b-25.

PROP §113.015. AUTHORITY TO BORROW

A trustee may borrow money from any source, including a trustee, purchase property on credit, and mortgage, pledge, or in any other manner encumber all or any part of the assets of the trust as is advisable in the judgment of the trustee for the advantageous administration of the trust.

History of Prop. Code §113.015: Acts 1983, 68th Leg., ch. 576, §1, eff. Jan. 1, 1984. Source: TRCS art. 7425b-25.

PROP §113.016. MANAGEMENT OF SECURITIES

A trustee may:

(1) pay calls, assessments, or other charges against or because of securities or other investments held by the trust;

(2) sell or exercise stock subscription or conversion rights;

(3) vote corporate stock, general or limited partnership interests, or other securities in person or by general or limited proxy;

(4) consent directly or through a committee or other agent to the reorganization, consolidation, merger, dissolution, or liquidation of a corporation or other business enterprise; and

(5) participate in voting trusts and deposit stocks, bonds, or other securities with any protective or other committee formed by or at the instance of persons holding similar securities, under such terms and conditions respecting the deposit thereof as the trustee may approve; sell any stock or other securities obtained by conversion, reorganization, consolidation, merger, liquidation, or the exercise of subscription rights free of any restrictions upon sale otherwise contained in the trust instrument relative to the securities originally held; assent to corporate sales, leases, encumbrances, and other transactions.

History of Prop. Code §113.016: Acts 1983, 68th Leg., ch. 576, §1, eff. Jan. 1, 1984. Source: TRCS art. 7425b-25.

PROP §113.017. CORPORATE STOCK OR OTHER SECURITIES HELD IN NAME OF NOMINEE

A trustee may:

(1) hold corporate stock or other securities in the name of a nominee;

(2) under Subchapter B, Chapter 161, or other law, employ a bank incorporated in this state or a national bank located in this state as custodian of any corporate stock or other securities held in trust; and

(3) under Subchapter C, Chapter 161, or other law, deposit or arrange for the deposit of securities with a Federal Reserve Bank or in a clearing corporation.

History of Prop. Code §113.017: Acts 1983, 68th Leg., ch. 576, §1, eff. Jan. 1, 1984. Source: TRCS art. 7425b-16.

A PROP §113.018. EMPLOYMENT & APPOINTMENT OF AGENTS

(a) A trustee may employ attorneys, accountants, agents, including investment agents, and brokers reasonably necessary in the administration of the trust estate.

(b) Without limiting the trustee's discretion under Subsection (a), a trustee may grant an agent powers with respect to property of the trust to act for the trustee in any lawful manner for purposes of real property transactions.

(c) A trustee acting under Subsection (b) may delegate any or all of the duties and powers to:

(1) execute and deliver any legal instruments relating to the sale and conveyance of the property, including affidavits, notices, disclosures, waivers, or designations or general or special warranty deeds binding the trustee with vendor's liens retained or disclaimed, as applicable, or transferred to a third-party lender;

(2) accept notes, deeds of trust, or other legal instruments;

(3) approve closing statements authorizing deductions from the sale price;

(4) receive trustee's net sales proceeds by check payable to the trustee;

(5) indemnify and hold harmless any third party who accepts and acts under a power of attorney with respect to the sale;

(6) take any action, including signing any document, necessary or appropriate to sell the property and accomplish the delegated powers;

(7) contract to purchase the property for any price on any terms;

(8) execute, deliver, or accept any legal instruments relating to the purchase of the property or to any financing of the purchase, including deeds, notes, deeds of trust, guaranties, or closing statements;

(9) approve closing statements authorizing payment of prorations and expenses;

(10) pay the trustee's net purchase price from funds provided by the trustee;

(11) indemnify and hold harmless any third party who accepts and acts under a power of attorney with respect to the purchase; or

(12) take any action, including signing any document, necessary or appropriate to purchase the property and accomplish the delegated powers.

(d) A trustee who delegates a power under Subsection (b) is liable to the beneficiaries or to the trust for an action of the agent to whom the power was delegated.

(e) A delegation by the trustee under Subsection (b) must be documented in a written instrument acknowledged by the trustee before an officer authorized under the law of this state or another state to take acknowledgments to deeds of conveyance and administer oaths. A signature on a delegation by a trustee for purposes of this subsection is presumed to be genuine if the trustee acknowledges the signature in accordance with Chapter 121, Civil Practice and Remedies Code.

(f) A delegation to an agent under Subsection (b) terminates six months from the date of the acknowledgment of the written delegation unless terminated earlier by:

(1) the death or incapacity of the trustee;

(2) the resignation or removal of the trustee; or

(3) a date specified in the written delegation.

(g) A person who in good faith accepts a delegation under Subsection (b) without actual knowledge that the delegation is void, invalid, or terminated, that the purported agent's authority is void, invalid, or terminated, or that the agent is exceeding or improperly exercising the agent's authority may rely on the delegation as if:

(1) the delegation were genuine, valid, and still in effect;

(2) the agent's authority were genuine, valid, and still in effect; and

(3) the agent had not exceeded and had properly exercised the authority.

(h) A trustee may delegate powers under Subsection (b) if the governing instrument does not affirmatively permit the trustee to hire agents or expressly prohibit the trustee from hiring agents.

History of Prop. Code §113.018: Acts 1983, 68th Leg., ch. 576, §1, eff. Jan. 1, 1984. Amended by Acts 1999, 76th Leg., ch. 794, §1, eff. Sept. 1, 1999; S.B. 617, §12, 85th Leg., eff. Sept. 1, 2017. Source: TRCS art. 7425b-25.

PROP §113.019. CLAIMS

A trustee may compromise, contest, arbitrate, or settle claims of or against the trust estate or the trustee.

History of Prop. Code §113.019: Acts 1983, 68th Leg., ch. 576, §1, eff. Jan. 1, 1984. Source: TRCS art. 7425b-25.

PROP §113.020. BURDENSOME OR WORTHLESS PROPERTY

A trustee may abandon property the trustee considers burdensome or worthless.

History of Prop. Code §113.020: Acts 1983, 68th Leg., ch. 576, §1, eff. Jan. 1, 1984. Source: TRCS art. 7425b-25.

PROP §113.021. DISTRIBUTION TO MINOR OR INCAPACITATED BENEFICIARY

(a) A trustee may make a distribution required or permitted to be made to any beneficiary in any of the following ways when the beneficiary is a minor or a person who in the judgment of the trustee is incapacitated by reason of legal incapacity or physical or mental illness or infirmity:

(1) to the beneficiary directly;

(2) to the guardian of the beneficiary's person or estate;

(3) by utilizing the distribution, without the interposition of a guardian, for the health, support, maintenance, or education of the beneficiary;

(4) to a custodian for the minor beneficiary under the Texas Uniform Transfers to Minors Act (Chapter 141) or a uniform gifts or transfers to minors act of another state;

(5) by reimbursing the person who is actually taking care of the beneficiary, even though the person is not the legal guardian, for expenditures made by the person for the benefit of the beneficiary; or

(6) by managing the distribution as a separate fund on the beneficiary's behalf, subject to the beneficiary's continuing right to withdraw the distribution.

(b) The written receipts of persons receiving distributions under Subsection (a) of this section are full and complete acquittances to the trustee.

History of Prop. Code §113.021: Acts 1983, 68th Leg., ch. 576, §1, eff. Jan. 1, 1984. Amended by Acts 2005, 79th Leg., ch. 148, §11, eff. Jan. 1, 2006.

PROP §113.0211. ADJUSTMENT OF CHARITABLE TRUST

(a) In this section:

(1) "Charitable entity" has the meaning assigned by Section 123.001(1).

(2) "Charitable trust" means a trust:

(A) the stated purpose of which is to benefit only one or more charitable entities; and

(B) that qualifies as a charitable entity.

(b) The trustee of a charitable trust may acquire, exchange, sell, supervise, manage, or retain any type of investment, subject to restrictions and procedures established by the trustee and in an amount considered appropriate by the trustee, that a prudent investor, exercising reasonable skill, care, and caution, would acquire or retain in light of the purposes, terms, distribution requirements, and other circumstances of the trust. The prudence of a trustee's actions under this subsection is judged with reference to the investment of all of the trust assets rather than with reference to a single trust investment.

(c) The trustee of a charitable trust may make one or more adjustments between the principal and the income portions of a trust to the extent that the trustee considers the adjustments necessary:

(1) to comply with the terms of the trust, if any, that describe the amount that may or must be distributed to a charitable entity beneficiary by referring to the income portion of the trust; and

(2) to administer the trust in order to carry out the purposes of the charitable trust.

(d) The authority to make adjustments under Subsection (c) includes the authority to allocate all or part of a capital gain to trust income.

(e) In making adjustments under Subsection (c), the trustee shall consider:

(1) except to the extent that the terms of the trust clearly manifest an intention that the trustee shall or may favor one or more charitable entity beneficiaries, the needs of a charitable entity beneficiary, based on what is fair and reasonable to all other charitable entity beneficiaries of the trust, if any; and

(2) the need of the trust to maintain the purchasing power of the trust's investments over time.

History of Prop. Code §113.0211: Acts 2003, 78th Leg., ch. 550, §1, eff. Sept. 1, 2003.

PROP §113.022. POWER TO PROVIDE RESIDENCE & PAY FUNERAL EXPENSES

A trustee of a trust that is not a charitable remainder unitrust, annuity trust, or pooled income fund that is intended to qualify for a federal tax deduction under Section 664, Internal Revenue Code, after giving consideration to the probable intention of the settlor and finding that the trustee's action would be consistent with that probable intention, may:

(1) permit real estate held in trust to be occupied by a beneficiary who is currently eligible to receive distributions from the trust estate;

(2) if reasonably necessary for the maintenance of a beneficiary who is currently eligible to receive distributions from the trust estate, invest trust funds in real property to be used for a home by the beneficiary; and

(3) in the trustee's discretion, pay funeral expenses of a beneficiary who at the time of the beneficiary's death was eligible to receive distributions from the trust estate.

History of Prop. Code §113.022: Acts 1983, 68th Leg., ch. 576, §1, eff. Jan. 1, 1984. Amended by Acts 1985, 69th Leg., ch. 149, §2, eff. May 24, 1985. Source: TRCS art. 7425b-25.

PROP §113.023. ANCILLARY TRUSTEE

(a) If trust property is situated outside this state, a Texas trustee may name in writing an individual or corporation qualified to act in the foreign jurisdiction in connection with trust property as ancillary trustee.

(b) Within the limits of the authority of the Texas trustee, the ancillary trustee has the rights, powers, discretions, and duties the Texas trustee delegates,

subject to the limitations and directions of the Texas trustee specified in the instrument evidencing the appointment of the ancillary trustee.

(c) The Texas trustee may remove an ancillary trustee and appoint a successor at any time as to all or part of the trust assets.

(d) The Texas trustee may require security of the ancillary trustee, who is answerable to the Texas trustee for all trust property entrusted to or received by the ancillary trustee in connection with the administration of the trust.

(e) If the law of the foreign jurisdiction requires a certain procedure or a judicial order for the appointment of an ancillary trustee or to authorize an ancillary trustee to act, the Texas trustee and the ancillary trustee must satisfy the requirements.

History of Prop. Code §113.023: Acts 1983, 68th Leg., ch. 576, §1, eff. Jan. 1, 1984. Source: TRCS art. 7425b-25.

PROP §113.024. IMPLIED POWERS

The powers, duties, and responsibilities under this subtitle do not exclude other implied powers, duties, or responsibilities that are not inconsistent with this subtitle.

History of Prop. Code §113.024: Acts 1983, 68th Leg., ch. 576, §1, eff. Jan. 1, 1984. Source: TRCS art. 7425b-25.

PROP §113.025. POWERS OF TRUSTEE REGARDING ENVIRONMENTAL LAWS

(a) A trustee or a potential trustee may inspect, investigate, cause to be inspected, or cause to be investigated trust property, property that the trustee or potential trustee has been asked to hold, or property owned or operated by an entity in which the trustee or potential trustee holds or has been asked to hold any interest or for the purpose of determining the potential application of environmental law with respect to the property. This subsection does not grant any person the right of access to any property. The taking of any action under this subsection with respect to a trust or an addition to a trust is not evidence that a person has accepted the trust or the addition to the trust.

(b) A trustee may take on behalf of the trust any action before or after the initiation of an enforcement action or other legal proceeding that the trustee reasonably believes will help to prevent, abate, or otherwise remedy any actual or potential violation of any environmental law affecting property held directly or indirectly by the trustee.

History of Prop. Code §113.025: Acts 1993, 73rd Leg., ch. 846, §29, eff. Sept. 1, 1993.

PROP §113.026. AUTHORITY TO DESIGNATE NEW CHARITABLE BENEFICIARY

(a) In this section:

(1) "Charitable entity" has the meaning assigned by Section 123.001.

(2) "Failed charitable beneficiary" means a charitable entity that is named as a beneficiary of a trust and that:

(A) does not exist at the time the charitable entity's interest in the trust becomes vested;

(B) ceases to exist during the term of the trust; or

(C) ceases to be a charitable entity during the term of the trust.

(b) This section applies only to an express written trust created by an individual with a charitable entity as a beneficiary. If the trust instrument provides a means for replacing a failed charitable beneficiary, the trust instrument governs the replacement of a failed charitable beneficiary, and this section does not apply.

(c) The trustee of a trust may select one or more replacement charitable beneficiaries for a failed charitable beneficiary in accordance with this section.

(d) Each replacement charitable beneficiary selected under this section by any person must:

(1) be a charitable entity and an entity described under Sections 170(b)(1)(A), 170(c), 2055(a), and 2522(a) of the Internal Revenue Code of 1986, as amended; and

(2) have the same or similar charitable purpose as the failed charitable beneficiary.

(e) If the settlor of the trust is living and not incapacitated at the time a trustee is selecting a replacement charitable beneficiary, the trustee shall consult with the settlor concerning the selection of one or more replacement charitable beneficiaries.

(f) If the trustee and the settlor agree on the selection of one or more replacement charitable beneficiaries, the trustee shall send notice of the selection to the attorney general. If the attorney general determines that one or more replacement charitable beneficiaries do not have the same or similar charitable purpose as the failed charitable beneficiary, not later than the 21st day after the date the attorney general receives notice of the selection, the attorney general shall request in

writing that a district court in the county in which the trust was created review the selection. If the court agrees with the attorney general's determination, any remaining replacement charitable beneficiary agreed on by the trustee and the settlor is the replacement charitable beneficiary. If there is not a remaining replacement charitable beneficiary agreed on by the trustee and the settlor, the court shall select one or more replacement charitable beneficiaries. If the court finds that the attorney general's request for a review is unreasonable, the replacement charitable beneficiary is the charitable beneficiary agreed on by the trustee and the settlor, and the court may require the attorney general to pay all court costs of the parties involved. Not later than the 30th day after the date the selection is final, the trustee shall provide to each replacement charitable beneficiary selected notice of the selection by certified mail, return receipt requested.

(g) If the trustee and the settlor cannot agree on the selection of a replacement charitable beneficiary, the trustee shall send notice of that fact to the attorney general not later than the 21st day after the date the trustee determines that an agreement cannot be reached. The attorney general shall refer the matter to a district court in the county in which the trust was created. The trustee and the settlor may each recommend to the court one or more replacement charitable beneficiaries. The court shall select a replacement charitable beneficiary and, not later than the 30th day after the date of the selection, provide to each charitable beneficiary selected notice of the selection by certified mail, return receipt requested.

History of Prop. Code §113.026: Acts 1999, 76th Leg., ch. 63, §1, eff. Aug. 30, 1999.

PROP §113.027. DISTRIBUTIONS GENERALLY

When distributing trust property or dividing or terminating a trust, a trustee may:

(1) make distributions in divided or undivided interests;

(2) allocate particular assets in proportionate or disproportionate shares;

(3) value the trust property for the purposes of acting under Subdivision (1) or (2); and

(4) adjust the distribution, division, or termination for resulting differences in valuation.

History of Prop. Code §113.027: Acts 2005, 79th Leg., ch. 148, §12, eff. Jan. 1, 2006.

PROP §113.028. CERTAIN CLAIMS & CAUSES OF ACTION PROHIBITED

(a) A trustee may not prosecute or assert a claim for damages in a cause of action against a party who is not a beneficiary of the trust if each beneficiary of the trust provides written notice to the trustee of the beneficiary's opposition to the trustee's prosecuting or asserting the claim in the cause of action.

(b) This section does not apply to a cause of action that is prosecuted by a trustee in the trustee's individual capacity.

(c) The trustee is not liable for failing to prosecute or assert a claim in a cause of action if prohibited by the beneficiaries under Subsection (a).

History of Prop. Code §113.028: Acts 2005, 79th Leg., ch. 765, §3, eff. June 17, 2005.

PROP §113.029. DISCRETIONARY POWERS; TAX SAVINGS

(a) Notwithstanding the breadth of discretion granted to a trustee in the terms of the trust, including the use of terms such as "absolute," "sole," or "uncontrolled," the trustee shall exercise a discretionary power in good faith and in accordance with the terms and purposes of the trust and the interests of the beneficiaries.

(b) Subject to Subsection (d), and unless the terms of the trust expressly indicate that a requirement provided by this subsection does not apply:

(1) a person, other than a settlor, who is a beneficiary and trustee, trustee affiliate, or discretionary power holder of a trust that confers on the trustee a power to make discretionary distributions to or for the trustee's, the trustee affiliate's, or the discretionary power holder's personal benefit may exercise the power only in accordance with an ascertainable standard relating to the trustee's, the trustee affiliate's, or the discretionary power holder's individual health, education, support, or maintenance within the meaning of Section 2041(b)(1)(A) or 2514(c)(1), Internal Revenue Code of 1986; and

(2) a trustee may not exercise a power to make discretionary distributions to satisfy a legal obligation of support that the trustee personally owes another person.

(c) A power the exercise of which is limited or prohibited by Subsection (b) may be exercised by a majority of the remaining trustees whose exercise of the power is not limited or prohibited by Subsection (b). If

the power of all trustees is limited or prohibited by Subsection (b), the court may appoint a special fiduciary with authority to exercise the power.

(d) Subsection (b) does not apply to:

(1) a power held by the settlor's spouse who is the trustee of a trust for which a marital deduction, as defined by Section 2056(b)(5) or 2523(e), Internal Revenue Code of 1986, was previously allowed;

(2) any trust during any period that the trust may be revoked or amended by its settlor; or

(3) a trust if contributions to the trust qualify for the annual exclusion under Section 2503(c), Internal Revenue Code of 1986.

(e) In this section, "discretionary power holder" means a person who has the sole power or power shared with another person to make discretionary decisions on behalf of a trustee with respect to distributions from a trust.

History of Prop. Code §113.029: Acts 2009, 81st Leg., ch. 672, §3, eff. Sept. 1, 2009. Amended by Acts 2013, 83rd Leg., ch. 699, §4, eff. Sept. 1, 2013.

PROP §113.030. RELOCATION OF ADMINISTRATION OF CHARITABLE TRUST

(a) In this section:

(1) "Charitable entity" has the meaning assigned by Section 123.001.

(2) "Charitable trust" means a trust:

(A) the stated purpose of which is to benefit only one or more charitable entities; and

(B) that qualifies as a charitable entity.

(3) "Trust administration" means the grant-making function of the trust.

(b) Except as provided by this section or specifically authorized by the terms of a trust, the trustee of a charitable trust may not change the location in which the trust administration takes place from a location in this state to a location outside this state.

(c) If the trustee decides to change the location in which the trust is administered from a location in this state to a location outside this state, the trustee shall:

(1) if the settlor is living and not incapacitated:

(A) consult the settlor concerning the selection of a new location for the administration of the trust; and

(B) submit the selection to the attorney general; or

(2) if the settlor is not living or is incapacitated:

(A) propose a new location; and

(B) submit the proposal to the attorney general.

(d) The trustee may file an action in the district court or statutory probate court in which the trust was created seeking a court order authorizing the trustee to change the location in which the trust is administered to a location outside this state. The court may exercise its equitable powers to effectuate the original purpose of the trust.

(e) Except as provided by Subsection (b), the location in which the administration of the trust takes place may not be changed to a location outside this state unless:

(1) the charitable purposes of the trust would not be impaired if the trust administration is moved; and

(2) a district court or statutory probate court authorizes the relocation.

(f) The attorney general may bring an action to enforce the provisions of this section. If a trustee of a charitable trust fails to comply with the provisions of this section, the district court or statutory probate court in the county in which the trust administration was originally located may remove the trustee and appoint a new trustee. Costs of a proceeding to remove a trustee, including reasonable attorney's fees, may be assessed against the removed trustee. This provision is in addition to and does not supersede the provisions of Chapter 123.

(g) This section does not affect a trustee's authority to sell real estate owned by a charitable trust.

History of Prop. Code §113.030: Acts 2009, 81st Leg., ch. 754, §1, eff. Sept. 1, 2009. Renumbered from §113.029 by Acts 2011, 82nd Leg., ch. 91, §27.001(52), eff. Sept. 1, 2011.

E PROP §113.031. DIGITAL ASSETS

(a) In this section, "digital asset" has the meaning assigned by Section 2001.002, Estates Code.

(b) A trustee may access digital assets as provided by Chapter 2001, Estates Code.

History of Prop. Code §113.031: Enacted by S.B. 1193, §6, 85th Leg., eff. Sept. 1, 2017.

Sections 113.032-113.050 reserved for expansion

SUBCHAPTER B. DUTIES OF TRUSTEE

PROP §113.051. GENERAL DUTY

The trustee shall administer the trust in good faith according to its terms and this subtitle. In the absence of any contrary terms in the trust instrument or contrary provisions of this subtitle, in administering the trust the trustee shall perform all of the duties imposed on trustees by the common law.

History of Prop. Code §113.051: Acts 1983, 68th Leg., ch. 576, §1, eff. Jan. 1, 1984. Amended by Acts 2005, 79th Leg., ch. 148, §13, eff. Jan. 1, 2006.

PROP §113.052. LOAN OF TRUST FUNDS TO TRUSTEE

(a) Except as provided by Subsection (b) of this section, a trustee may not lend trust funds to:

(1) the trustee or an affiliate;

(2) a director, officer, or employee of the trustee or an affiliate;

(3) a relative of the trustee; or

(4) the trustee's employer, employee, partner, or other business associate.

(b) This section does not prohibit:

(1) a loan by a trustee to a beneficiary of the trust if the loan is expressly authorized or directed by the instrument or transaction establishing the trust; or

(2) a deposit by a corporate trustee with itself under Section 113.057 of this Act.

History of Prop. Code §113.052: Acts 1983, 68th Leg., ch. 576, §1, eff. Jan. 1, 1984. Source: TRCS art. 7425b-10.

PROP §113.053. PURCHASE OR SALE OF TRUST PROPERTY BY TRUSTEE

(a) Except as provided by Subsections (b), (c), (d), (e), (f), and (g), a trustee shall not directly or indirectly buy or sell trust property from or to:

(1) the trustee or an affiliate;

(2) a director, officer, or employee of the trustee or an affiliate;

(3) a relative of the trustee; or

(4) the trustee's employer, partner, or other business associate.

(b) A national banking association or a state-chartered corporation with the right to exercise trust powers that is serving as executor, administrator, guardian, trustee, or receiver may sell shares of its own capital stock held by it for an estate to one or more of its officers or directors if a court:

(1) finds that the sale is in the best interest of the estate that owns the shares;

(2) fixes or approves the sales price of the shares and the other terms of the sale; and

(3) enters an order authorizing and directing the sale.

(c) If a corporate trustee, executor, administrator, or guardian is legally authorized to retain its own capital stock in trust, the trustee may exercise rights to purchase its own stock if increases in the stock are offered pro rata to shareholders.

(d) If the exercise of rights or the receipt of a stock dividend results in a fractional share holding and the acquisition meets the investment standard required by this subchapter, the trustee may purchase additional fractional shares to round out the holding to a full share.

(e) A trustee may:

(1) comply with the terms of a written executory contract signed by the settlor, including a contract for deed, earnest money contract, buy/sell agreement, or stock purchase or redemption agreement; and

(2) sell the stock, bonds, obligations, or other securities of a corporation to the issuing corporation or to its corporate affiliate if the sale is made under an agreement described in Subdivision (1) or complies with the duties imposed by Chapter 117.

(f) A national banking association, a state-chartered corporation, including a state-chartered bank or trust company, a state or federal savings and loan association that has the right to exercise trust powers and that is serving as trustee, or such an institution that is serving as custodian with respect to an individual retirement account, as defined by Section 408, Internal Revenue Code, or an employee benefit plan, as defined by Section 3(3), Employee Retirement Income Security Act of 1974 (29 U.S.C. Section 1002(3)), regardless of whether the custodial account is, or would otherwise be, considered a trust for purposes of this subtitle, may, subject to its fiduciary duties:

(1) employ an affiliate or division within a financial institution to provide brokerage, investment, administrative, custodial, or other account services for the trust or custodial account and charge the trust or custodial account for the services;

(2) unless the instrument governing the fiduciary relationship expressly prohibits the purchase or charge, purchase insurance underwritten or otherwise distributed by an affiliate, a division within the financial institution, or a syndicate or selling group that includes the financial institution or an affiliate and charge the trust or custodial account for the insurance premium, provided that:

(A) the person conducting the insurance transaction is appropriately licensed if required by applicable licensing and regulatory requirements administered by a functional regulatory agency of this state; and

(B) the insurance product and premium are the same or similar to a product and premium offered by organizations that are not an affiliate, a division within the financial institution, or a syndicate or selling group that includes the financial institution or an affiliate; and

(3) receive a fee or compensation, directly or indirectly, on account of the services performed or the insurance product sold by the affiliate, division within the financial institution, or syndicate or selling group that includes the financial institution or an affiliate, whether in the form of shared commissions, fees, or otherwise, provided that any amount charged by the affiliate, division, or syndicate or selling group that includes the financial institution or an affiliate for the services or insurance product is disclosed and does not exceed the customary or prevailing amount that is charged by the affiliate, division, or syndicate or selling group that includes the financial institution or an affiliate, or a comparable entity, for comparable services rendered or insurance provided to a person other than the trust.

(g) In addition to other investments authorized by law for the investment of funds held by a fiduciary or by the instrument governing the fiduciary relationship, and notwithstanding any other provision of law and subject to the standard contained in Chapter 117, a bank or trust company acting as a fiduciary, agent, or otherwise, in the exercise of its investment discretion or at the direction of another person authorized to direct the investment of funds held by the bank or trust company as fiduciary, may invest and reinvest in the securities of an open-end or closed-end management investment company or investment trust registered under the Investment Company Act of 1940 (15 U.S.C. Sec. 80a-1 et seq.) if the portfolio of the investment company or investment trust consists substantially of investments that are not prohibited by the governing instrument. The fact that the bank or trust company or an affiliate of the bank or trust company provides services to the investment company or investment trust, such as those of an investment advisor, custodian, transfer agent, registrar, sponsor, distributor, manager, or otherwise, and receives compensation for those services does not preclude the bank or trust company from investing or reinvesting in the securities if the compensation is disclosed by prospectus, account statement, or otherwise. An executor or administrator of an estate under a dependent administration or a guardian of an estate shall not so invest or reinvest unless specifically authorized by the court in which such estate or guardianship is pending.

History of Prop. Code §113.053: Acts 1983, 68th Leg., ch. 576, §1, eff. Jan. 1, 1984. Amended by Acts 1985, 69th Leg., ch. 974, §§1, 2, eff. Aug. 26, 1985; Acts 1989, 71st Leg., ch. 341, §1, eff. Aug. 28, 1989; Acts 1993, 73rd Leg., ch. 933, §1, eff. Aug. 30, 1993; Acts 2003, 78th Leg., ch. 1103, §4, eff. Jan. 1, 2004; Acts 2013, 83rd Leg., ch. 1337, §1, eff. Sept. 1, 2013. Source: TRCS art. 7425b-12.

PROP §113.054. SALES FROM ONE TRUST TO ANOTHER

A trustee of one trust may not sell property to another trust of which it is also trustee unless the property is:

(1) a bond, note, bill, or other obligation issued or fully guaranteed as to principal and interest by the United States; and

(2) sold for its current market price.

History of Prop. Code §113.054: Acts 1983, 68th Leg., ch. 576, §1, eff. Jan. 1, 1984. Source: TRCS art. 7425b-13.

PROP §113.055. PURCHASE OF TRUSTEE'S SECURITIES

(a) Except as provided by Subsection (b) of this section, a corporate trustee may not purchase for the trust the stock, bonds, obligations, or other securities of the trustee or an affiliate, and a noncorporate trustee may not purchase for the trust the stock, bonds, obligations, or other securities of a corporation with which the trustee is connected as director, owner, manager, or any other executive capacity.

(b) A trustee may:

(1) retain stock already owned by the trust unless the retention does not satisfy the requirements prescribed by Chapter 117; and

(2) exercise stock rights or purchase fractional shares under Section 113.053 of this Act.

History of Prop. Code §113.055: Acts 1983, 68th Leg., ch. 576, §1, eff. Jan. 1, 1984. Amended by Acts 2003, 78th Leg., ch. 1103, §5, eff. Jan. 1, 2004. Source: TRCS art. 7425b-14.

PROP §113.056. AUTHORIZATION TO MAKE CERTAIN INVESTMENTS

(a) Unless the terms of the trust instrument provide otherwise, and subject to the investment standards provided by this subtitle and any investment standards provided by the trust instrument, the trustee may invest all or part of the trust assets in an investment vehicle authorized for the collective investment of trust funds pursuant to Part 9, Title 12, of the Code of Federal Regulations.

(b), (c) Repealed by Acts 2003, 78th Leg., ch. 1103, §17, eff. Jan. 1, 2004.

(d) Subject to any investment standards provided by this chapter, Chapter 117, or the trust instrument, whenever the instrument directs, requires, authorizes, or permits investment in obligations of the United States government, the trustee may invest in and hold such obligations either directly or in the form of interests in an open-end management type investment company or investment trust registered under the Investment Company Act of 1940, 15 U.S.C. 80a-1 et seq., or in an investment vehicle authorized for the collective investment of trust funds pursuant to Part 9, Title 12 of the Code of Federal Regulations, so long as the portfolio of such investment company, investment trust, or collective investment vehicle is limited to such obligations and to repurchase agreements fully collateralized by such obligations.

History of Prop. Code §113.056: Acts 1983, 68th Leg., ch. 576, §1, eff. Jan. 1, 1984. Amended by Acts 1985, 69th Leg., ch. 341, §1, eff. June 10, 1985; Acts 1991, 72nd Leg., ch. 876, §1, eff. June 16, 1991; Acts 2003, 78th Leg., ch. 1103, §§6, 7, 17, eff. Jan. 1, 2004. Source: TRCS art. 7425b-46.

PROP §113.057. DEPOSITS BY CORPORATE TRUSTEE WITH ITSELF

(a) A corporate trustee may deposit trust funds with itself as a permanent investment if authorized by the settlor in the instrument creating the trust or if authorized in a writing delivered to the trustee by a beneficiary currently eligible to receive distributions from a trust created before January 1, 1988.

(b) A corporate trustee may deposit with itself trust funds that are being held pending investment, distribution, or payment of debts if, except as provided by Subsection (d) of this section:

(1) it maintains under control of its trust department as security for the deposit a separate fund of securities legal for trust investments;

(2) the total market value of the security is at all times at least equal to the amount of the deposit; and

(3) the separate fund is marked as such.

(c) The trustee may make periodic withdrawals from or additions to the securities fund required by Subsection (b) of this section as long as the required value is maintained. Income from securities in the fund belongs to the trustee.

(d) Security for a deposit under this section is not required for a deposit under Subsection (a) or under Subsection (b) of this section to the extent the deposit is insured or otherwise secured under state or federal law.

History of Prop. Code §113.057: Acts 1983, 68th Leg., ch. 576, §1, eff. Jan. 1, 1984. Amended by Acts 1985, 69th Leg., ch. 149, §3, eff. May 24, 1985. Source: TRCS art. 7425b-11.

PROP §113.058. BOND

(a) A corporate trustee is not required to provide a bond to secure performance of its duties as trustee.

(b) Unless the instrument creating the trust provides otherwise, a noncorporate trustee must give bond:

(1) payable to the trust estate of the trust, the registry of the court, or each person interested in the trust, as their interests may appear; and

(2) conditioned on the faithful performance of the trustee's duties.

(c) The bond must be in an amount and with the sureties required by order of a court in a proceeding brought for this determination.

(d) Any interested person may bring an action to increase or decrease the amount of a bond, require a bond, or substitute or add sureties. Notwithstanding Subsection (b), for cause shown, a court may require a bond even if the instrument creating the trust provides otherwise.

(e) The trustee shall deposit the bond with the clerk of the court that issued the order requiring the bond. A suit on the bond may be maintained on a certified copy. Appropriate proof of a recovery on a bond reduces the liability of the sureties pro tanto.

(f) Failure to comply with this section does not make void or voidable or otherwise affect an act or transaction of a trustee with any third person.

History of Prop. Code §113.058: Acts 1983, 68th Leg., ch. 576, §1, eff. Jan. 1, 1984. Amended by Acts 2005, 79th Leg., ch. 148, §14, eff. Jan. 1, 2006; Acts 2007, 80th Leg., ch. 451, §6, eff. Sept. 1, 2007. Source: TRCS art. 7425b-25.

PROP §113.059. REPEALED

Repealed by Acts 2005, 79th Leg., ch. 148, §29, eff. Jan. 1, 2006.

PROP §113.060. REPEALED

Repealed by Acts 2007, 80th Leg., ch. 451, §21, eff. June 16, 2007.

Sections 113.061-113.080 reserved for expansion

SUBCHAPTER C. RESIGNATION OR REMOVAL OF TRUSTEE, & AUTHORITY OF MULTIPLE & SUCCESSOR TRUSTEES

PROP §113.081. RESIGNATION OF TRUSTEE

(a) A trustee may resign in accordance with the terms of the trust instrument, or a trustee may petition a court for permission to resign as trustee.

(b) The court may accept a trustee's resignation and discharge the trustee from the trust on the terms and conditions necessary to protect the rights of other interested persons.

History of Prop. Code §113.081: Acts 1983, 68th Leg., ch. 576, §1, eff. Jan. 1, 1984. Source: TRCS art. 7425b-38.

PROP §113.082. REMOVAL OF TRUSTEE

(a) A trustee may be removed in accordance with the terms of the trust instrument, or, on the petition of an interested person and after hearing, a court may, in its discretion, remove a trustee and deny part or all of the trustee's compensation if:

(1) the trustee materially violated or attempted to violate the terms of the trust and the violation or attempted violation results in a material financial loss to the trust;

(2) the trustee becomes incapacitated or insolvent;

(3) the trustee fails to make an accounting that is required by law or by the terms of the trust; or

(4) the court finds other cause for removal.

(b) A beneficiary, cotrustee, or successor trustee may treat a violation resulting in removal as a breach of trust.

(c) A trustee of a charitable trust may not be removed solely on the grounds that the trustee exercised the trustee's power to adjust between principal and income under Section 113.0211.

History of Prop. Code §113.082: Acts 1983, 68th Leg., ch. 576, §1, eff. Jan. 1, 1984. Amended by Acts 2003, 78th Leg., ch. 550, §2, eff. Sept. 1, 2003; Acts 2005, 79th Leg., ch. 148, §16, eff. Jan. 1, 2006. Source: TRCS art. 7425b-39.

PROP §113.083. APPOINTMENT OF SUCCESSOR TRUSTEE

(a) On the death, resignation, incapacity, or removal of a sole or surviving trustee, a successor trustee shall be selected according to the method, if any, prescribed in the trust instrument. If for any reason a successor is not selected under the terms of the trust instrument, a court may and on petition of any interested person shall appoint a successor in whom the trust shall vest.

(b) If a vacancy occurs in the number of trustees originally appointed under a valid charitable trust agreement and the trust agreement does not provide for filling the vacancy, the remaining trustees may fill the vacancy by majority vote.

History of Prop. Code §113.083: Acts 1983, 68th Leg., ch. 576, §1, eff. Jan. 1, 1984. Source: TRCS art. 7425b-37.

PROP §113.084. POWERS OF SUCCESSOR TRUSTEE

Unless otherwise provided in the trust instrument or by order of the court appointing a successor trustee, the successor trustee has the rights, powers, authority, discretion, and title to trust property conferred on the trustee.

History of Prop. Code §113.084: Acts 1983, 68th Leg., ch. 576, §1, eff. Jan. 1, 1984. Source: TRCS art. 7425b-40.

PROP §113.085. EXERCISE OF POWERS BY MULTIPLE TRUSTEES

(a) Cotrustees may act by majority decision.

(b) If a vacancy occurs in a cotrusteeship, the remaining cotrustees may act for the trust.

(c) A cotrustee shall participate in the performance of a trustee's function unless the cotrustee:

(1) is unavailable to perform the function because of absence, illness, suspension under this code or other law, disqualification, if any, under this code, disqualification under other law, or other temporary incapacity; or

(2) has delegated the performance of the function to another trustee in accordance with the terms of the trust or applicable law, has communicated the delegation to all other cotrustees, and has filed the delegation in the records of the trust.

(d) If a cotrustee is unavailable to participate in the performance of a trustee's function for a reason described by Subsection (c)(1) and prompt action is necessary to achieve the efficient administration or purposes of the trust or to avoid injury to the trust property or a beneficiary, the remaining cotrustee or a majority of the remaining cotrustees may act for the trust.

(e) A trustee may delegate to a cotrustee the performance of a trustee's function unless the settlor specifically directs that the function be performed jointly. Unless a cotrustee's delegation under this subsection is irrevocable, the cotrustee making the delegation may revoke the delegation.

History of Prop. Code §113.085: Acts 1983, 68th Leg., ch. 576, §1, eff. Jan. 1, 1984. Amended by Acts 2005, 79th Leg., ch. 148, §17, eff. Jan. 1, 2006; Acts 2007, 80th Leg., ch. 451, §7, eff. Sept. 1, 2007; Acts 2009, 81st Leg., ch. 973, §1, eff. Sept. 1, 2009. Source: TRCS art. 7425b-18.

Sections 113.086-113.100 reserved for expansion

PROP §§113.101 TO 113.111. REPEALED

Repealed by Acts 2003, 78th Leg., ch. 659, §4, eff. Jan. 1, 2004.

Sections 113.112-113.150 reserved for expansion

SUBCHAPTER E. ACCOUNTING BY TRUSTEE

PROP §113.151. DEMAND FOR ACCOUNTING

(a) A beneficiary by written demand may request the trustee to deliver to each beneficiary of the trust a written statement of accounts covering all transactions since the last accounting or since the creation of the trust, whichever is later. If the trustee fails or refuses to deliver the statement on or before the 90th day after the date the trustee receives the demand or after a longer period ordered by a court, any beneficiary of the trust may file suit to compel the trustee to deliver the statement to all beneficiaries of the trust. The court may require the trustee to deliver a written statement of account to all beneficiaries on finding that the nature of the beneficiary's interest in the trust or the effect of the administration of the trust on the beneficiary's interest is sufficient to require an accounting by the trustee. However, the trustee is not obligated or required to account to the beneficiaries of a trust more frequently than once every 12 months unless a more frequent accounting is required by the court. If a beneficiary is successful in the suit to compel a statement under this section, the court may, in its discretion, award all or part of the costs of court and all of the suing beneficiary's reasonable and necessary attorney's fees and costs against the trustee in the trustee's individual capacity or in the trustee's capacity as trustee.

(b) An interested person may file suit to compel the trustee to account to the interested person. The court may require the trustee to deliver a written statement of account to the interested person on finding that the nature of the interest in the trust of, the claim against the trust by, or the effect of the administration of the trust on the interested person is sufficient to require an accounting by the trustee.

History of Prop. Code §113.151: Acts 1983, 68th Leg., ch. 576, §1, eff. Jan. 1, 1984. Amended by Acts 2003, 78th Leg., ch. 550, §3, eff. Sept. 1, 2003. Source: TRCS art. 7425b-48.

PROP §113.152. CONTENTS OF ACCOUNTING

A written statement of accounts shall show:

(1) all trust property that has come to the trustee's knowledge or into the trustee's possession and that has not been previously listed or inventoried as property of the trust;

(2) a complete account of receipts, disbursements, and other transactions regarding the trust property for the period covered by the account, including their source and nature, with receipts of principal and income shown separately;

(3) a listing of all property being administered, with an adequate description of each asset;

(4) the cash balance on hand and the name and location of the depository where the balance is kept; and

(5) all known liabilities owed by the trust.

History of Prop. Code §113.152: Acts 1983, 68th Leg., ch. 576, §1, eff. Jan. 1, 1984.

Sections 113.153-113.170 reserved for expansion

SUBCHAPTER F. COMMON TRUST FUNDS

PROP §113.171. COMMON TRUST FUNDS

(a) A bank or trust company qualified to act as a fiduciary in this state may establish common trust funds to provide investments to itself as a fiduciary, including as a custodian under the Texas Uniform Transfers to Minors Act (Chapter 141) or a uniform gifts or transfers to minors act of another state or to itself and others as cofiduciaries.

(b) The fiduciary or cofiduciary may place investment funds in interests in common trust funds if:

(1) the investment is not prohibited by the instrument or order creating the fiduciary relationship; and

(2) if there are cofiduciaries, the cofiduciaries consent to the investment.

(c) A common trust fund includes a fund:

(1) qualified for exemption from federal income taxation as a common trust fund and maintained exclusively for eligible fiduciary accounts; and

(2) consisting solely of assets of retirement, pension, profit sharing, stock bonus, or other employees' trusts that are exempt from federal income taxation.

History of Prop. Code §113.171: Acts 1983, 68th Leg., ch. 576, §1, eff. Jan. 1, 1984. Amended by Acts 2005, 79th Leg., ch. 148, §18, eff. Jan. 1, 2006. Source: TRCS art. 7425b-48.

PROP §113.172. AFFILIATED INSTITUTIONS

A bank or trust company that is a member of an affiliated group under Section 1504, Internal Revenue Code of 1954 (26 U.S.C. 1504), with a bank or trust company maintaining common trust funds may participate in one or more of the funds.

History of Prop. Code §113.172: Acts 1983, 68th Leg., ch. 576, §1, eff. Jan. 1, 1984. Source: TRCS art. 7425b-48.

CHAPTER 114. LIABILITIES, RIGHTS, & REMEDIES OF TRUSTEES, BENEFICIARIES, & THIRD PERSONS

SUBCHAPTER A. LIABILITY OF TRUSTEE

PROP §114.001. LIABILITY OF TRUSTEE TO BENEFICIARY

(a) The trustee is accountable to a beneficiary for the trust property and for any profit made by the trustee through or arising out of the administration of the trust, even though the profit does not result from a breach of trust; provided, however, that the trustee is not required to return to a beneficiary the trustee's compensation as provided by this subtitle, by the terms of the trust instrument, or by a writing delivered to the trustee and signed by all beneficiaries of the trust who have full legal capacity.

(b) The trustee is not liable to the beneficiary for a loss or depreciation in value of the trust property or for a failure to make a profit that does not result from a failure to perform the duties set forth in this subtitle or from any other breach of trust.

(c) A trustee who commits a breach of trust is chargeable with any damages resulting from such breach of trust, including but not limited to:

(1) any loss or depreciation in value of the trust estate as a result of the breach of trust;

(2) any profit made by the trustee through the breach of trust; or

(3) any profit that would have accrued to the trust estate if there had been no breach of trust.

(d) The trustee is not liable to the beneficiary for a loss or depreciation in value of the trust property or for acting or failing to act under Section 113.025 or under any other provision of this subtitle if the action or failure to act relates to compliance with an environmental law and if there is no gross negligence or bad faith on the part of the trustee. The provision of any instrument governing trustee liability does not increase the liability of the trustee as provided by this section unless the settlor expressly makes reference to this subsection.

(e) The trustee has the same protection from liability provided for a fiduciary under 42 U.S.C. Section 9607(n).

History of Prop. Code §114.001: Acts 1983, 68th Leg., ch. 576, §1, eff. Jan. 1, 1984. Amended by Acts 1984, 68th Leg., 2nd C.S., ch. 18, §13, eff. Oct. 2, 1984; Acts 1989, 71st Leg., ch. 341, §2, eff. Aug. 28, 1989; Acts 1993, 73rd Leg., ch. 846, §30, eff. Sept. 1, 1993; Acts 1997, 75th Leg., ch. 263, §1, eff. Sept. 1, 1997; Acts 2003, 78th Leg., ch. 1103, §8, eff. Jan. 1, 2004. Source: TRCS arts. 7425b-15, 7425b-16.

PROP §114.002. LIABILITY OF SUCCESSOR TRUSTEE FOR BREACH OF TRUST BY PREDECESSOR

A successor trustee is liable for a breach of trust of a predecessor only if he knows or should know of a situation constituting a breach of trust committed by the predecessor and the successor trustee:

(1) improperly permits it to continue;

(2) fails to make a reasonable effort to compel the predecessor trustee to deliver the trust property; or

(3) fails to make a reasonable effort to compel a redress of a breach of trust committed by the predecessor trustee.

History of Prop. Code §114.002: Acts 1983, 68th Leg., ch. 576, §1, eff. Jan. 1, 1984. Amended by Acts 1983, 68th Leg., ch. 576, §1, eff. Jan. 1, 1984.

PROP §114.003. POWERS TO DIRECT: CHARITABLE TRUSTS

(a) In this section, "charitable trust" has the meaning assigned by Section 123.001.

(a-1) The terms of a charitable trust may give a trustee or other person a power to direct the modification or termination of the trust.

(b) If the terms of a charitable trust give a person the power to direct certain actions of the trustee, the trustee shall act in accordance with the person's direction unless:

(1) the direction is manifestly contrary to the terms of the trust; or

(2) the trustee knows the direction would constitute a serious breach of a fiduciary duty that the person holding the power to direct owes to the beneficiaries of the trust.

(c) A person, other than a beneficiary, who holds a power to direct with respect to a charitable trust is presumptively a fiduciary required to act in good faith with regard to the purposes of the trust and the interests of the beneficiaries. The holder of a power to direct with respect to a charitable trust is liable for any loss that results from a breach of the person's fiduciary duty.

History of Prop. Code §114.003: Acts 1983, 68th Leg., ch. 576, §1, eff. Jan. 1, 1984. Amended by Acts 2005, 79th Leg., ch. 148, §19, eff. Jan. 1, 2006; Acts 2015, 84th Leg., ch. 1108, §1, eff. June 19, 2015. Source: TRCS art. 7425b-25.

PROP §114.0031. DIRECTED TRUSTS; ADVISORS

(a) In this section:

(1) "Advisor" includes protector.

(2) "Investment decision" means, with respect to any investment, the retention, purchase, sale, exchange, tender, or other transaction affecting the ownership of the investment or rights in the investment and, with respect to a nonpublicly traded investment, the valuation of the investment.

(b) This section does not apply to a charitable trust as defined by Section 123.001.

(c) For purposes of this section, an advisor with authority with respect to investment decisions is an investment advisor.

(d) A protector has all the power and authority granted to the protector by the trust terms, which may include:

(1) the power to remove and appoint trustees, advisors, trust committee members, and other protectors;

(2) the power to modify or amend the trust terms to achieve favorable tax status or to facilitate the efficient administration of the trust; and

(3) the power to modify, expand, or restrict the terms of a power of appointment granted to a beneficiary by the trust terms.

(e) If the terms of a trust give a person the authority to direct, consent to, or disapprove a trustee's actual or proposed investment decisions, distribution decisions, or other decisions, the person is considered to be an advisor and a fiduciary when exercising that authority except that the trust terms may provide that an advisor acts in a nonfiduciary capacity.

(f) A trustee who acts in accordance with the direction of an advisor, as prescribed by the trust terms, is not liable, except in cases of wilful misconduct on the part of the trustee so directed, for any loss resulting directly or indirectly from that act.

(g) If the trust terms provide that a trustee must make decisions with the consent of an advisor, the trustee is not liable, except in cases of wilful misconduct or gross negligence on the part of the trustee, for any loss resulting directly or indirectly from any act taken or not taken as a result of the advisor's failure to provide the required consent after having been requested to do so by the trustee.

(h) If the trust terms provide that a trustee must act in accordance with the direction of an advisor with respect to investment decisions, distribution decisions, or other decisions of the trustee, the trustee does not, except to the extent the trust terms provide otherwise, have the duty to:

(1) monitor the conduct of the advisor;

(2) provide advice to the advisor or consult with the advisor; or

(3) communicate with or warn or apprise any beneficiary or third party concerning instances in which the trustee would or might have exercised the trustee's own discretion in a manner different from the manner directed by the advisor.

(i) Absent clear and convincing evidence to the contrary, the actions of a trustee pertaining to matters within the scope of the advisor's authority, such as confirming that the advisor's directions have been carried out and recording and reporting actions taken at the advisor's direction, are presumed to be administrative actions taken by the trustee solely to allow the trustee to perform those duties assigned to the trustee under the trust terms, and such administrative actions are not considered to constitute an undertaking by the trustee

to monitor the advisor or otherwise participate in actions within the scope of the advisor's authority.

History of Prop. Code §114.0031: Acts 2015, 84th Leg., ch. 1108, §2, eff. June 19, 2015.

PROP §114.004. ACTIONS TAKEN PRIOR TO KNOWLEDGE OR NOTICE OF FACTS

A trustee is not liable for a mistake of fact made before the trustee has actual knowledge or receives written notice of the happening of any event that determines or affects the distribution of the income or principal of the trust, including marriage, divorce, attainment of a certain age, performance of education requirements, or death.

History of Prop. Code §114.004: Acts 1983, 68th Leg., ch. 576, §1, eff. Jan. 1, 1984. Source: TRCS art. 7425b-25.

PROP §114.005. RELEASE OF LIABILITY BY BENEFICIARY

(a) A beneficiary who has full legal capacity and is acting on full information may relieve a trustee from any duty, responsibility, restriction, or liability as to the beneficiary that would otherwise be imposed on the trustee by this subtitle, including liability for past violations.

(b) The release must be in writing and delivered to the trustee.

History of Prop. Code §114.005: Acts 1983, 68th Leg., ch. 576, §1, eff. Jan. 1, 1984. Amended by Acts 2007, 80th Leg., ch. 451, §8, eff. Sept. 1, 2007. Source: TRCS art. 7425b-23.

PROP §114.006. LIABILITY OF COTRUSTEES FOR ACTS OF OTHER COTRUSTEES

(a) A trustee who does not join in an action of a cotrustee is not liable for the cotrustee's action, unless the trustee does not exercise reasonable care as provided by Subsection (b).

(b) Each trustee shall exercise reasonable care to:

(1) prevent a cotrustee from committing a serious breach of trust; and

(2) compel a cotrustee to redress a serious breach of trust.

(c) Subject to Subsection (b), a dissenting trustee who joins in an action at the direction of the majority of the trustees and who has notified any cotrustee of the dissent in writing at or before the time of the action is not liable for the action.

History of Prop. Code §114.006: Acts 1983, 68th Leg., ch. 576, §1, eff. Jan. 1, 1984. Amended by Acts 2005, 79th Leg., ch. 148, §20, eff. Jan. 1, 2006. Source: TRCS art. 7425b-18.

PROP §114.007. EXCULPATION OF TRUSTEE

(a) A term of a trust relieving a trustee of liability for breach of trust is unenforceable to the extent that the term relieves a trustee of liability for:

(1) a breach of trust committed:

(A) in bad faith;

(B) intentionally; or

(C) with reckless indifference to the interest of a beneficiary; or

(2) any profit derived by the trustee from a breach of trust.

(b) A term in a trust instrument relieving the trustee of liability for a breach of trust is ineffective to the extent that the term is inserted in the trust instrument as a result of an abuse by the trustee of a fiduciary duty to or confidential relationship with the settlor.

(c) This section applies only to a term of a trust that may otherwise relieve a trustee from liability for a breach of trust. Except as provided in Section 111.0035, this section does not prohibit the settlor, by the terms of the trust, from expressly:

(1) relieving the trustee from a duty or restriction imposed by this subtitle or by common law; or

(2) directing or permitting the trustee to do or not to do an action that would otherwise violate a duty or restriction imposed by this subtitle or by common law.

History of Prop. Code §114.007: Acts 2005, 79th Leg., ch. 148, §21, eff. Jan. 1, 2006.

PROP §114.008. REMEDIES FOR BREACH OF TRUST

(a) To remedy a breach of trust that has occurred or might occur, the court may:

(1) compel the trustee to perform the trustee's duty or duties;

(2) enjoin the trustee from committing a breach of trust;

(3) compel the trustee to redress a breach of trust, including compelling the trustee to pay money or to restore property;

(4) order a trustee to account;

(5) appoint a receiver to take possession of the trust property and administer the trust;

(6) suspend the trustee;

(7) remove the trustee as provided under Section 113.082;

(8) reduce or deny compensation to the trustee;

(9) subject to Subsection (b), void an act of the trustee, impose a lien or a constructive trust on trust property, or trace trust property of which the trustee wrongfully disposed and recover the property or the proceeds from the property; or

(10) order any other appropriate relief.

(b) Notwithstanding Subsection (a)(9), a person other than a beneficiary who, without knowledge that a trustee is exceeding or improperly exercising the trustee's powers, in good faith assists a trustee or in good faith and for value deals with a trustee is protected from liability as if the trustee had or properly exercised the power exercised by the trustee.

History of Prop. Code §114.008: Acts 2005, 79th Leg., ch. 148, §21, eff. Jan. 1, 2006.

Sections 114.009-114.030 reserved for expansion

SUBCHAPTER B. LIABILITY OF BENEFICIARY

PROP §114.031. LIABILITY OF BENEFICIARY TO TRUSTEE

(a) A beneficiary is liable for loss to the trust if the beneficiary has:

(1) misappropriated or otherwise wrongfully dealt with the trust property;

(2) expressly consented to, participated in, or agreed with the trustee to be liable for a breach of trust committed by the trustee;

(3) failed to repay an advance or loan of trust funds;

(4) failed to repay a distribution or disbursement from the trust in excess of that to which the beneficiary is entitled; or

(5) breached a contract to pay money or deliver property to the trustee to be held by the trustee as part of the trust.

(b) Unless the terms of the trust provide otherwise, the trustee is authorized to offset a liability of the beneficiary to the trust estate against the beneficiary's interest in the trust estate, regardless of a spendthrift provision in the trust.

History of Prop. Code §114.031: Acts 1983, 68th Leg., ch. 576, §1, eff. Jan. 1, 1984.

PROP §114.032. LIABILITY FOR WRITTEN AGREEMENTS

(a) A written agreement between a trustee and a beneficiary, including a release, consent, or other agreement relating to a trustee's duty, power, responsibility, restriction, or liability, is final and binding on the beneficiary and any person represented by a beneficiary as provided by this section if:

(1) the instrument is signed by the beneficiary;

(2) the beneficiary has legal capacity to sign the instrument; and

(3) the beneficiary has full knowledge of the circumstances surrounding the agreement.

(b) A written agreement signed by a beneficiary who has the power to revoke the trust or the power to appoint, including the power to appoint through a power of amendment, the income or principal of the trust to or for the benefit of the beneficiary, the beneficiary's creditors, the beneficiary's estate, or the creditors of the beneficiary's estate is final and binding on any person who takes under the power of appointment or who takes in default if the power of appointment is not executed.

(c) A written instrument is final and binding on a beneficiary who is a minor if:

(1) the minor's parent, including a parent who is also a trust beneficiary, signs the instrument on behalf of the minor;

(2) no conflict of interest exists; and

(3) no guardian, including a guardian ad litem, has been appointed to act on behalf of the minor.

(d) A written instrument is final and binding on an unborn or unascertained beneficiary if a beneficiary who has an interest substantially identical to the interest of the unborn or unascertained beneficiary signs the instrument. For purposes of this subsection, an unborn or unascertained beneficiary has a substantially identical interest only with a trust beneficiary from whom the unborn or unascertained beneficiary descends.

(e) This section does not apply to a written instrument that modifies or terminates a trust in whole or in part unless the instrument is otherwise permitted by law.

History of Prop. Code §114.032: Acts 1999, 76th Leg., ch. 794, §3, eff. Sept. 1, 1999.

Sections 114.033-114.060 reserved for expansion

SUBCHAPTER C. RIGHTS OF TRUSTEE

PROP §114.061. COMPENSATION

(a) Unless the terms of the trust provide otherwise and except as provided in Subsection (b) of this sec-

tion, the trustee is entitled to reasonable compensation from the trust for acting as trustee.

(b) If the trustee commits a breach of trust, the court may in its discretion deny him all or part of his compensation.

History of Prop. Code §114.061: Acts 1983, 68th Leg., ch. 576, §1, eff. Jan. 1, 1984.

PROP §114.062. EXONERATION OR REIMBURSEMENT FOR TORT

(a) Except as provided in Subsection (b) of this section, a trustee who incurs personal liability for a tort committed in the administration of the trust is entitled to exoneration from the trust property if the trustee has not paid the claim or to reimbursement from the trust property if the trustee has paid the claim, if:

(1) the trustee was properly engaged in a business activity for the trust and the tort is a common incident of that kind of activity;

(2) the trustee was properly engaged in a business activity for the trust and neither the trustee nor an officer or employee of the trustee is guilty of actionable negligence or intentional misconduct in incurring the liability; or

(3) the tort increased the value of the trust property.

(b) A trustee who is entitled to exoneration or reimbursement under Subdivision (3) of Subsection (a) is entitled to exoneration or reimbursement only to the extent of the increase in the value of the trust property.

History of Prop. Code §114.062: Acts 1983, 68th Leg., ch. 576, §1, eff. Jan. 1, 1984.

PROP §114.063. GENERAL RIGHT TO REIMBURSEMENT

(a) A trustee may discharge or reimburse himself from trust principal or income or partly from both for:

(1) advances made for the convenience, benefit, or protection of the trust or its property;

(2) expenses incurred while administering or protecting the trust or because of the trustee's holding or owning any of the trust property; and

(3) expenses incurred for any action taken under Section 113.025.

(b) The trustee has a lien against trust property to secure reimbursement under Subsection (a).

(c) A potential trustee is entitled to reimbursement from trust principal or income or partly from both for reasonable expenses incurred for any action taken under Section 113.025(a) if:

(1) a court orders reimbursement or the potential trustee has entered into a written agreement providing for reimbursement with the personal representative of the estate, the trustee of the trust, the settlor, the settlor's attorney-in-fact, the settlor's personal representative, or the person or entity designated in the trust instrument or will to appoint a trustee; and

(2) the potential trustee has been appointed trustee under the terms of the trust instrument or will or has received a written request to accept the trust from the settlor, the settlor's attorney-in-fact, the settlor's personal representative, or the person or entity designated in the trust instrument or will to appoint a trustee.

History of Prop. Code §114.063: Acts 1983, 68th Leg., ch. 576, §1, eff. Jan. 1, 1984. Amended by Acts 1993, 73rd Leg., ch. 846, §31, eff. Sept. 1, 1993. Source: TRCS art. 7425b-25.

PROP §114.064. COSTS

(a) In any proceeding under this code the court may make such award of costs and reasonable and necessary attorney's fees as may seem equitable and just.

History of Prop. Code §114.064: Acts 1985, 69th Leg., ch. 149, §4, eff. May 24, 1985.

Sections 114.065-114.080 reserved for expansion

SUBCHAPTER D. THIRD PERSONS

PROP §114.081. PROTECTION OF PERSON DEALING WITH TRUSTEE

(a) A person who deals with a trustee in good faith and for fair value actually received by the trust is not liable to the trustee or the beneficiaries of the trust if the trustee has exceeded the trustee's authority in dealing with the person.

(b) A person other than a beneficiary is not required to inquire into the extent of the trustee's powers or the propriety of the exercise of those powers if the person:

(1) deals with the trustee in good faith; and

(2) obtains:

(A) a certification of trust described by Section 114.086; or

(B) a copy of the trust instrument.

(c) A person who in good faith delivers money or other assets to a trustee is not required to ensure the proper application of the money or other assets.

(d) A person other than a beneficiary who in good faith assists a former trustee, or who in good faith and for value deals with a former trustee, without knowl-

edge that the trusteeship has terminated, is protected from liability as if the former trustee were still a trustee.

(e) Comparable protective provisions of other laws relating to commercial transactions or transfer of securities by fiduciaries prevail over the protection provided by this section.

History of Prop. Code §114.081: Acts 1983, 68th Leg., ch. 576, §1, eff. Jan. 1, 1984. Amended by Acts 2007, 80th Leg., ch. 451, §9, eff. Sept. 1, 2007. Source: TRCS art. 7425b-9.

PROP §114.082. CONVEYANCE BY TRUSTEE

If property is conveyed or transferred to a trustee in trust but the conveyance or transfer does not identify the trust or disclose the names of the beneficiaries, the trustee may convey, transfer, or encumber the title of the property without subsequent question by a person who claims to be a beneficiary under the trust or who claims by, through, or under an undisclosed beneficiary.

History of Prop. Code §114.082: Acts 1983, 68th Leg., ch. 576, §1, eff. Jan. 1, 1984. Amended by Acts 1987, 70th Leg., ch. 683, §4, eff. Aug. 31, 1987. Source: TRCS arts. 7425a, 7425b-8.

PROP §114.0821. LIABILITY OF TRUST PROPERTY

Although trust property is held by the trustee without identifying the trust or its beneficiaries, the trust property is not liable to satisfy the personal obligations of the trustee.

History of Prop. Code §114.0821: Acts 1983, 68th Leg., ch. 576, §1, eff. Jan. 1, 1984. Renumbered from §114.082(b) by Acts 1987, 70th Leg., ch. 683, §4, eff. Aug. 31, 1987. Source: TRCS art. 7425a.

PROP §114.083. RIGHTS & LIABILITIES FOR COMMITTING TORTS

(a) A personal liability of a trustee or a predecessor trustee for a tort committed in the course of the administration of the trust may be collected from the trust property if the trustee is sued in a representative capacity and the court finds that:

(1) the trustee was properly engaged in a business activity for the trust and the tort is a common incident of that kind of activity;

(2) the trustee was properly engaged in a business activity for the trust and neither the trustee nor an officer or employee of the trustee is guilty of actionable negligence or intentional misconduct in incurring the liability; or

(3) the tort increased the value of the trust property.

(b) A trust that is liable for the trustee's tort under Subdivision (3) of Subsection (a) is liable only to the extent of the permanent increase in value of the trust property.

(c) A plaintiff in an action against the trustee as the representative of the trust does not have to prove that the trustee could have been reimbursed by the trust if the trustee had paid the claim.

(d) Subject to the rights of exoneration or reimbursement under Section 114.062, the trustee is personally liable for a tort committed by the trustee or by the trustee's agents or employees in the course of their employment.

History of Prop. Code §114.083: Acts 1983, 68th Leg., ch. 576, §1, eff. Jan. 1, 1984. Source: TRCS art. 7425b-21.

PROP §114.084. CONTRACTS OF TRUSTEE

(a) If a trustee or a predecessor trustee makes a contract that is within his power as trustee and a cause of action arises on the contract, the plaintiff may sue the trustee in his representative capacity, and a judgment rendered in favor of the plaintiff is collectible by execution against the trust property. The plaintiff may sue the trustee individually if the trustee made the contract and the contract does not exclude the trustee's personal liability.

(b) The addition of "trustee" or "as trustee" after the signature of a trustee who is party to a contract is prima facie evidence of an intent to exclude the trustee from personal liability.

(c) In an action on a contract against a trustee in the trustee's representative capacity the plaintiff does not have to prove that the trustee could have been reimbursed by the trust if the trustee had paid the claim.

History of Prop. Code §114.084: Acts 1983, 68th Leg., ch. 576, §1, eff. Jan. 1, 1984. Source: TRCS art. 7425b-19.

PROP §114.085. PARTNERSHIPS

(a) To the extent allowed by law, a trustee who takes the place of a deceased partner in a general partnership in accordance with the articles of partnership is liable to third persons only to the extent of the:

(1) deceased partner's capital in the partnership; and

(2) trust funds held by the trustee.

(b) A trustee who contracts to enter a general partnership in its capacity as trustee shall limit, to the extent allowed by law, the trust's liability to:

(1) the trust assets contributed to the partnership; and

(2) other assets of the trust under the management of the contracting trustee.

(c) If another provision of this subtitle conflicts with this section, this section controls. This section does not exonerate a trustee from liability for negligence.

History of Prop. Code §114.085: Acts 1983, 68th Leg., ch. 576, §1, eff. Jan. 1, 1984. Source: TRCS art. 7425b-19.

PROP §114.086. CERTIFICATION OF TRUST

(a) As an alternative to providing a copy of the trust instrument to a person other than a beneficiary, the trustee may provide to the person a certification of trust containing the following information:

(1) a statement that the trust exists and the date the trust instrument was executed;

(2) the identity of the settlor;

(3) the identity and mailing address of the currently acting trustee;

(4) one or more powers of the trustee or a statement that the trust powers include at least all the powers granted a trustee by Subchapter A, Chapter 113;

(5) the revocability or irrevocability of the trust and the identity of any person holding a power to revoke the trust;

(6) the authority of cotrustees to sign or otherwise authenticate and whether all or less than all of the cotrustees are required in order to exercise powers of the trustee; and

(7) the manner in which title to trust property should be taken.

(b) A certification of trust may be signed or otherwise authenticated by any trustee.

(c) A certification of trust must state that the trust has not been revoked, modified, or amended in any manner that would cause the representations contained in the certification to be incorrect.

(d) A certification of trust:

(1) is not required to contain the dispositive terms of a trust; and

(2) may contain information in addition to the information required by Subsection (a).

(e) A recipient of a certification of trust may require the trustee to furnish copies of the excerpts from the original trust instrument and later amendments to the trust instrument that designate the trustee and confer on the trustee the power to act in the pending transaction.

(f) A person who acts in reliance on a certification of trust without knowledge that the representations contained in the certification are incorrect is not liable to any person for the action and may assume without inquiry the existence of the facts contained in the certification.

(g) If a person has actual knowledge that the trustee is acting outside the scope of the trust, and the actual knowledge was acquired by the person before the person entered into the transaction with the trustee or made a binding commitment to enter into the transaction, the transaction is not enforceable against the trust.

(h) A person who in good faith enters into a transaction relying on a certification of trust may enforce the transaction against the trust property as if the representations contained in the certification are correct. This section does not create an implication that a person is liable for acting in reliance on a certification of trust that fails to contain all the information required by Subsection (a). A person's failure to demand a certification of trust does not:

(1) affect the protection provided to the person by Section 114.081; or

(2) create an inference as to whether the person has acted in good faith.

(i) A person making a demand for the trust instrument in addition to a certification of trust or excerpts as described by Subsection (e) is liable for damages if the court determines that the person did not act in good faith in making the demand.

(j) This section does not limit the right of a person to obtain a copy of the trust instrument in a judicial proceeding concerning the trust.

(k) This section does not limit the rights of a beneficiary of the trust against the trustee.

History of Prop. Code §114.086: Acts 2007, 80th Leg., ch. 451, §10, eff. Sept. 1, 2007.

CHAPTER 115. JURISDICTION, VENUE, & PROCEEDINGS

Subchapter A. Jurisdiction & Venue

SUBCHAPTER A. JURISDICTION & VENUE

A PROP §115.001. JURISDICTION

(a) Except as provided by Subsection (d) of this section, a district court has original and exclusive jurisdiction over all proceedings by or against a trustee and all proceedings concerning trusts, including proceedings to:

(1) construe a trust instrument;

(2) determine the law applicable to a trust instrument;

(3) appoint or remove a trustee;

(4) determine the powers, responsibilities, duties, and liability of a trustee;

(5) ascertain beneficiaries;

(6) make determinations of fact affecting the administration, distribution, or duration of a trust;

(7) determine a question arising in the administration or distribution of a trust;

(8) relieve a trustee from any or all of the duties, limitations, and restrictions otherwise existing under the terms of the trust instrument or of this subtitle;

(9) require an accounting by a trustee, review trustee fees, and settle interim or final accounts; and

(10) surcharge a trustee.

(a-1) The list of proceedings described by Subsection (a) over which a district court has exclusive and original jurisdiction is not exhaustive. A district court has exclusive and original jurisdiction over a proceeding by or against a trustee or a proceeding concerning a trust under Subsection (a) whether or not the proceeding is listed in Subsection (a).

(b) The district court may exercise the powers of a court of equity in matters pertaining to trusts.

(c) The court may intervene in the administration of a trust to the extent that the court's jurisdiction is invoked by an interested person or as otherwise provided by law. A trust is not subject to continuing judicial supervision unless the court orders continuing judicial supervision.

(d) The jurisdiction of the district court is exclusive except for jurisdiction conferred by law on:

(1) a statutory probate court;

(2) a court that creates a trust under Subchapter B, Chapter 1301, Estates [~~Section 867, Texas Probate~~] Code;

(3) a court that creates a trust under Section 142.005;

(4) a justice court under Chapter 27, Government Code; or

(5) [~~a small claims court under Chapter 28, Government Code; or~~]

[~~(6)~~] a county court at law.

History of Prop. Code §115.001: Acts 1983, 68th Leg., ch. 576, §1, eff. Jan. 1, 1984. Amended by Acts 1997, 75th Leg., ch. 1375, §5, eff. Sept. 1, 1997; Acts 2005, 79th Leg., ch. 148, §22, eff. Jan. 1, 2006; Acts 2007, 80th Leg., ch. 451, §11, eff. Sept. 1, 2007; Acts 2011, 82nd Leg., ch. 657, §4, eff. Sept. 1, 2011; S.B. 1488, §22.060, 85th Leg., eff. Sept. 1, 2017. Source: TRCS art. 7425b-24.

A PROP §115.002. VENUE

(a) The venue of an action under Section 115.001 of this Act is determined according to this section.

(b) If there is a single, noncorporate trustee, an action shall be brought in the county in which:

(1) the trustee resides or has resided at any time during the four-year period preceding the date the action is filed; or

(2) the situs of administration of the trust is maintained or has been maintained at any time during the four-year period preceding the date the action is filed.

(b-1) If there are multiple [~~noncorporate~~] trustees none of whom is a corporate trustee and the trustees maintain a principal office in this state, an action shall be brought in the county in which:

(1) the situs of administration of the trust is maintained or has been maintained at any time during the four-year period preceding the date the action is filed; or

(2) the trustees maintain the principal office.

(b-2) If there are multiple [~~noncorporate~~] trustees none of whom is a corporate trustee and the trustees do not maintain a principal office in this state, an action shall be brought in the county in which:

(1) the situs of administration of the trust is maintained or has been maintained at any time during the four-year period preceding the date the action is filed; or

(2) any trustee resides or has resided at any time during the four-year period preceding the date the action is filed.

(c) If there are one or more corporate trustees, an action shall be brought in the county in which:

(1) the situs of administration of the trust is maintained or has been maintained at any time during the four-year period preceding the date the action is filed; or

(2) any corporate trustee maintains its principal office in this state.

(c-1) Notwithstanding Subsections (b), (b-1), (b-2), and (c), if the settlor is deceased and an administration of the settlor's estate is pending in this state, an action involving the interpretation and administration of an inter vivos trust created by the settlor or a testamentary trust created by the settlor's will may be brought:

(1) in a county in which venue is proper under Subsection (b), (b-1), (b-2), or (c); or

(2) in the county in which the administration of the settlor's estate is pending.

(d) For just and reasonable cause, including the location of the records and the convenience of the parties and witnesses, the court may transfer an action from a county of proper venue under this section to another county of proper venue:

(1) on motion of a defendant or joined party, filed concurrently with or before the filing of the answer or other initial responsive pleading, and served in accordance with law; or

(2) on motion of an intervening party, filed not later than the 20th day after the court signs the order allowing the intervention, and served in accordance with law.

(e) Notwithstanding any other provision of this section, on agreement by all parties the court may transfer an action from a county of proper venue under this section to any other county.

(f) For the purposes of this section:

(1) "Corporate trustee" means an entity organized as a financial institution or a corporation with the authority to act in a fiduciary capacity.

(2) "Principal office" means:

(A) if there are one or more corporate trustees, an office of a corporate trustee in this state where the decision makers for the corporate trustee within this state conduct the daily affairs of the corporate trustee; or

(B) if there are multiple trustees, none of which is a corporate trustee, an office in this state that is not maintained within the personal residence of any trustee, and in which one or more trustees conducts the daily affairs of the trustees.

(2-a) The mere presence of an agent or representative of a trustee does not establish a principal office as defined by Subdivision (2). The principal office of a corporate trustee or the principal office maintained by multiple noncorporate trustees may also be but is not necessarily the same as the situs of administration of the trust.

(3) "Situs of administration" means the location in this state where the trustee maintains the office that is primarily responsible for dealing with the settlor and beneficiaries of the trust. The situs of administration may also be but is not necessarily the same as the principal office of a corporate trustee or the principal office maintained by multiple noncorporate trustees.

History of Prop. Code §115.002: Acts 1983, 68th Leg., ch. 576, §1, eff. Jan. 1, 1984. Amended by Acts 1999, 76th Leg., ch. 344, §4.026 (eff. Sept. 1, 1999), ch. 933, §1 (eff. Sept. 1, 1999); Acts 2011, 82nd Leg., ch. 657, §5, eff. Sept. 1, 2011; Acts 2013, 83rd Leg., ch. 699, §5, eff. Sept. 1, 2013; S.B. 617, §13, 85th Leg., eff. Sept. 1, 2017. Source: TRCS art. 7425b-24.

Sections 115.003-115.010 reserved for expansion

SUBCHAPTER B. PARTIES, PROCEDURE, & JUDGMENTS

PROP §115.011. PARTIES

(a) Any interested person may bring an action under Section 115.001 of this Act.

(b) Contingent beneficiaries designated as a class are not necessary parties to an action under Section 115.001. The only necessary parties to such an action are:

(1) a beneficiary of the trust on whose act or obligation the action is predicated;

(2) a beneficiary of the trust designated by name, other than a beneficiary whose interest has been distributed, extinguished, terminated, or paid;

(3) a person who is actually receiving distributions from the trust estate at the time the action is filed; and

(4) the trustee, if a trustee is serving at the time the action is filed.

(c) The attorney general shall be given notice of any proceeding involving a charitable trust as provided by Chapter 123 of this code.

(d) A beneficiary of a trust may intervene and contest the right of the plaintiff to recover in an action

against the trustee as representative of the trust for a tort committed in the course of the trustee's administration or on a contract executed by the trustee.

History of Prop. Code §115.011: Acts 1983, 68th Leg., ch. 576, §1, eff. Jan. 1, 1984. Amended by Acts 1995, 74th Leg., ch. 172, §1, eff. Sept. 1, 1995; Acts 2005, 79th Leg., ch. 148, §23, eff. Jan. 1, 2006; Acts 2011, 82nd Leg., ch. 657, §6, eff. Sept. 1, 2011. Source: TRCS arts. 7425b-19, 7425b-21, 7425b-24.

PROP §115.012. RULES OF PROCEDURE

Except as otherwise provided, all actions instituted under this subtitle are governed by the Texas Rules of Civil Procedure and the other statutes and rules that are applicable to civil actions generally.

History of Prop. Code §115.012: Acts 1983, 68th Leg., ch. 576, §1, eff. Jan. 1, 1984. Source: TRCS art. 7425b-24.

PROP §115.013. PLEADINGS & JUDGMENTS

(a) Actions and proceedings involving trusts are governed by this section.

(b) An affected interest shall be described in pleadings that give reasonable information to an owner by name or class, by reference to the instrument creating the interest, or in other appropriate manner.

(c) A person is bound by an order binding another in the following cases:

(1) an order binding the sole holder or all coholders of a power of revocation or a presently exercisable general power of appointment, including one in the form of a power of amendment, binds other persons to the extent their interests, as objects, takers in default, or otherwise are subject to the power;

(2) to the extent there is no conflict of interest between them or among persons represented:

(A) an order binding a guardian of the estate or a guardian ad litem binds the ward; and

(B) an order binding a trustee binds beneficiaries of the trust in proceedings to review the acts or accounts of a prior fiduciary and in proceedings involving creditors or other third parties;

(3) if there is no conflict of interest and no guardian of the estate or guardian ad litem has been appointed, a parent may represent his minor child as guardian ad litem or as next friend; and

(4) an unborn or unascertained person who is not otherwise represented is bound by an order to the extent his interest is adequately represented by another party having a substantially identical interest in the proceeding.

(d) Notice under Section 115.015 shall be given either to a person who will be bound by the judgment or to one who can bind that person under this section, and notice may be given to both. Notice may be given to unborn or unascertained persons who are not represented under Subdivision (1) or (2) of Subsection (c) by giving notice to all known persons whose interests in the proceedings are substantially identical to those of the unborn or unascertained persons.

History of Prop. Code §115.013: Acts 1983, 68th Leg., ch. 576, §1, eff. Jan. 1, 1984. Amended by Acts 2009, 81st Leg., ch. 672, §4, eff. Sept. 1, 2009.

PROP §115.014. GUARDIAN OR ATTORNEY AD LITEM

(a) At any point in a proceeding a court may appoint a guardian ad litem to represent the interest of a minor, an incapacitated, unborn, or unascertained person, or person whose identity or address is unknown, if the court determines that representation of the interest otherwise would be inadequate. If there is not a conflict of interests, a guardian ad litem may be appointed to represent several persons or interests.

(b) At any point in a proceeding a court may appoint an attorney ad litem to represent any interest that the court considers necessary, including an attorney ad litem to defend an action under Section 114.083 for a beneficiary of the trust who is a minor or who has been adjudged incompetent.

(c) A guardian ad litem may consider general benefit accruing to the living members of a person's family.

(d) A guardian ad litem is entitled to reasonable compensation for services in the amount set by the court to be taxed as costs in the proceeding.

(e) An attorney ad litem is entitled to reasonable compensation for services in the amount set by the court in the manner provided by Section 114.064.

History of Prop. Code §115.014: Acts 1983, 68th Leg., ch. 576, §1, eff. Jan. 1, 1984. Amended by Acts 2005, 79th Leg., ch. 148, §24, eff. Jan. 1, 2006; Acts 2009, 81st Leg., ch. 672, §§5, 6, eff. Sept. 1, 2009.

PROP §115.015. NOTICE TO BENEFICIARIES OF TORT OR CONTRACT PROCEEDING

(a) A court may not render judgment in favor of a plantiff[1] in an action on a contract executed by the trustee or in an action against the trustee as representative of the trust for a tort committed in the course of the trustee's administration unless the plaintiff proves that before the 31st day after the date the action began or within any other period fixed by the court that is more than 30 days before the date of the

judgment, the plaintiff gave notice of the existence and nature of the action to:

(1) each beneficiary known to the trustee who then had a present or contingent interest; or

(2) in an action on a contract involving a charitable trust, the attorney general and any corporation that is a beneficiary or agency in the performance of the trust.

(b) The plaintiff shall give the notice required by Subsection (a) of this section by registered mail or by certified mail, return receipt requested, addressed to the party to be notified at the party's last known address. The trustee shall give the plaintiff a list of the beneficiaries or persons having an interest in the trust estate and their addresses, if known to the trustee, before the 11th day after the date the plaintiff makes a written request for the information.

(c) The plaintiff satisfies the notice requirements of this section by notifying the persons on the list provided by the trustee.

1. **Editor's note:** Probably should be "plaintiff."

History of Prop. Code §115.015: Acts 1983, 68th Leg., ch. 576, §1, eff. Jan. 1, 1984. Source: TRCS arts. 7425b-19, 7425b-21.

PROP §115.016. NOTICE

(a) If notice of hearing on a motion or other proceeding is required, the notice may be given in the manner prescribed by law or the Texas Rules of Civil Procedure, or, alternatively, notice may be given to any party or to his attorney if the party has appeared by attorney or requested that notice be sent to his attorney.

(b) If the address or identity of a party is not known and cannot be ascertained with reasonable diligence, on order of the court notice may be given by publishing a copy of the notice at least three times in a newspaper having general circulation in the county where the hearing is to be held. The first publication of the notice must be at least 10 days before the time set for the hearing. If there is no newspaper of general circulation in the county where the hearing is to be held, the publication shall be made in a newspaper of general circulation in an adjoining county.

History of Prop. Code §115.016: Acts 1983, 68th Leg., ch. 576, §1, eff. Jan. 1, 1984.

PROP §115.017. WAIVER OF NOTICE

A person, including a guardian of the estate, a guardian ad litem, or other fiduciary, may waive notice by a writing signed by the person or his attorney and filed in the proceedings.

History of Prop. Code §115.017: Acts 1983, 68th Leg., ch. 576, §1, eff. Jan. 1, 1984.

CHAPTER 116. UNIFORM PRINCIPAL & INCOME ACT

SUBCHAPTER A. DEFINITIONS, FIDUCIARY DUTIES, & OTHER MISCELLANEOUS PROVISIONS

PROP §116.001. SHORT TITLE

This chapter may be cited as the Uniform Principal and Income Act.

History of Prop. Code §116.001: Acts 2003, 78th Leg., ch. 659, §1, eff. Jan. 1, 2004.

PROP §116.002. DEFINITIONS

In this chapter:

(1) "Accounting period" means a calendar year unless another 12-month period is selected by a fiduciary. The term includes a portion of a calendar year or other 12-month period that begins when an income interest begins or ends when an income interest ends.

(2) "Beneficiary" includes, in the case of a decedent's estate, an heir, legatee, and devisee and, in the case of a trust, an income beneficiary and a remainder beneficiary.

(3) "Fiduciary" means a personal representative or a trustee. The term includes an executor, administrator, successor personal representative, special administrator, and a person performing substantially the same function.

(4) "Income" means money or property that a fiduciary receives as current return from a principal asset. The term includes a portion of receipts from a sale, exchange, or liquidation of a principal asset, to the extent provided in Subchapter D.

(5) "Income beneficiary" means a person to whom net income of a trust is or may be payable.

(6) "Income interest" means the right of an income beneficiary to receive all or part of net income, whether the terms of the trust require it to be distributed or authorize it to be distributed in the trustee's discretion.

(7) "Mandatory income interest" means the right of an income beneficiary to receive net income that the terms of the trust require the fiduciary to distribute.

(8) "Net income" means the total receipts allocated to income during an accounting period minus the disbursements made from income during the period, plus or minus transfers under this chapter to or from income during the period.

(9) "Person" has the meaning assigned by Section 111.004.

(10) "Principal" means property held in trust for distribution to a remainder beneficiary when the trust terminates.

(11) "Remainder beneficiary" means a person entitled to receive principal when an income interest ends.

(12) "Terms of a trust" means the manifestation of the intent of a settlor or decedent with respect to the trust, expressed in a manner that admits of its proof in a judicial proceeding, whether by written or spoken words or by conduct.

(13) "Trustee" has the meaning assigned by Section 111.004.

History of Prop. Code §116.002: Acts 2003, 78th Leg., ch. 659, §1, eff. Jan. 1, 2004. Amended by Acts 2007, 80th Leg., ch. 451, §12, eff. Sept. 1, 2007.

PROP §116.003. UNIFORMITY OF APPLICATION & CONSTRUCTION

In applying and construing this Uniform Act, consideration must be given to the need to promote uniformity of the law with respect to its subject matter among states that enact it.

History of Prop. Code §116.003: Acts 2003, 78th Leg., ch. 659, §1, eff. Jan. 1, 2004.

PROP §116.004. FIDUCIARY DUTIES; GENERAL PRINCIPLES

(a) In allocating receipts and disbursements to or between principal and income, and with respect to any matter within the scope of Subchapters B and C, a fiduciary:

(1) shall administer a trust or estate in accordance with the terms of the trust or the will, even if there is a different provision in this chapter;

(2) may administer a trust or estate by the exercise of a discretionary power of administration given to the fiduciary by the terms of the trust or the will, even if the exercise of the power produces a result different from a result required or permitted by this chapter;

(3) shall administer a trust or estate in accordance with this chapter if the terms of the trust or the will do not contain a different provision or do not give the fiduciary a discretionary power of administration; and

(4) shall add a receipt or charge a disbursement to principal to the extent that the terms of the trust and this chapter do not provide a rule for allocating the receipt or disbursement to or between principal and income.

(b) In exercising the power to adjust under Section 116.005(a) or a discretionary power of administration regarding a matter within the scope of this chapter, whether granted by the terms of a trust, a will, or this chapter, a fiduciary shall administer a trust or estate impartially, based on what is fair and reasonable to all of the beneficiaries, except to the extent that the terms of the trust or the will clearly manifest an intention that the fiduciary shall or may favor one or more of the beneficiaries. A determination in accordance with this chapter is presumed to be fair and reasonable to all of the beneficiaries.

History of Prop. Code §116.004: Acts 2003, 78th Leg., ch. 659, §1, eff. Jan. 1, 2004.

PROP §116.005. TRUSTEE'S POWER TO ADJUST

(a) A trustee may adjust between principal and income to the extent the trustee considers necessary if the trustee invests and manages trust assets as a prudent investor, the terms of the trust describe the amount that may or must be distributed to a beneficiary by referring to the trust's income, and the trustee determines, after applying the rules in Section 116.004(a), that the trustee is unable to comply with Section 116.004(b). The power to adjust conferred by this subsection includes the power to allocate all or part of a capital gain to trust income.

(b) In deciding whether and to what extent to exercise the power conferred by Subsection (a), a trustee shall consider all factors relevant to the trust and its beneficiaries, including the following factors to the extent they are relevant:

(1) the nature, purpose, and expected duration of the trust;

(2) the intent of the settlor;

(3) the identity and circumstances of the beneficiaries;

(4) the needs for liquidity, regularity of income, and preservation and appreciation of capital;

(5) the assets held in the trust; the extent to which they consist of financial assets, interests in closely held enterprises, tangible and intangible personal property, or real property; the extent to which an asset is used by a beneficiary; and whether an asset was purchased by the trustee or received from the settlor;

(6) the net amount allocated to income under the other sections of this chapter and the increase or decrease in the value of the principal assets, which the trustee may estimate as to assets for which market values are not readily available;

(7) whether and to what extent the terms of the trust give the trustee the power to invade principal or accumulate income or prohibit the trustee from invading principal or accumulating income, and the extent to which the trustee has exercised a power from time to time to invade principal or accumulate income;

(8) the actual and anticipated effect of economic conditions on principal and income and effects of inflation and deflation; and

(9) the anticipated tax consequences of an adjustment.

(c) A trustee may not make an adjustment:

(1) that reduces the actuarial value of the income interest in a trust to which a person transfers property with the intent to qualify for a gift tax exclusion;

(2) that changes the amount payable to a beneficiary as a fixed annuity or a fixed fraction of the value of the trust assets;

(3) from any amount that is permanently set aside for charitable purposes under a will or the terms of a trust unless both income and principal are so set aside;

(4) if possessing or exercising the power to make an adjustment causes an individual to be treated as the owner of all or part of the trust for income tax purposes, and the individual would not be treated as the owner if the trustee did not possess the power to make an adjustment;

(5) if possessing or exercising the power to make an adjustment causes all or part of the trust assets to be included for estate tax purposes in the estate of an individual who has the power to remove a trustee or appoint a trustee, or both, and the assets would not be included in the estate of the individual if the trustee did not possess the power to make an adjustment;

(6) if the trustee is a beneficiary of the trust; or

(7) if the trustee is not a beneficiary, but the adjustment would benefit the trustee directly or indirectly.

(d) If Subsection (c)(4), (5), (6), or (7) applies to a trustee and there is more than one trustee, a cotrustee to whom the provision does not apply may make the adjustment unless the exercise of the power by the remaining trustee or trustees is not permitted by the terms of the trust.

(e) A trustee may release the entire power conferred by Subsection (a) or may release only the power

to adjust from income to principal or the power to adjust from principal to income if the trustee is uncertain about whether possessing or exercising the power will cause a result described in Subsections (c)(1)-(5) or Subsection (c)(7) or if the trustee determines that possessing or exercising the power will or may deprive the trust of a tax benefit or impose a tax burden not described in Subsection (c). The release may be permanent or for a specified period, including a period measured by the life of an individual.

(f) Terms of a trust that limit the power of a trustee to make an adjustment between principal and income do not affect the application of this section unless it is clear from the terms of the trust that the terms are intended to deny the trustee the power of adjustment conferred by Subsection (a).

History of Prop. Code §116.005: Acts 2003, 78th Leg., ch. 659, §1, eff. Jan. 1, 2004. Amended by Acts 2005, 79th Leg., ch. 148, §25, eff. Jan. 1, 2006; Acts 2011, 82nd Leg., ch. 91, §21.002 (eff. Sept. 1, 2011), ch. 657, §7 (eff. Sept. 1, 2011).

PROP §116.006. JUDICIAL CONTROL OF DISCRETIONARY POWER

(a) The court may not order a trustee to change a decision to exercise or not to exercise a discretionary power conferred by Section 116.005 of this chapter unless the court determines that the decision was an abuse of the trustee's discretion. A trustee's decision is not an abuse of discretion merely because the court would have exercised the power in a different manner or would not have exercised the power.

(b) The decisions to which Subsection (a) applies include:

(1) a decision under Section 116.005(a) as to whether and to what extent an amount should be transferred from principal to income or from income to principal; and

(2) a decision regarding the factors that are relevant to the trust and its beneficiaries, the extent to which the factors are relevant, and the weight, if any, to be given to those factors in deciding whether and to what extent to exercise the discretionary power conferred by Section 116.005(a).

(c) If the court determines that a trustee has abused the trustee's discretion, the court may place the income and remainder beneficiaries in the positions they would have occupied if the discretion had not been abused, according to the following rules:

(1) to the extent that the abuse of discretion has resulted in no distribution to a beneficiary or in a distribution that is too small, the court shall order the trustee to distribute from the trust to the beneficiary an amount that the court determines will restore the beneficiary, in whole or in part, to the beneficiary's appropriate position;

(2) to the extent that the abuse of discretion has resulted in a distribution to a beneficiary which is too large, the court shall place the beneficiaries, the trust, or both, in whole or in part, in their appropriate positions by ordering the trustee to withhold an amount from one or more future distributions to the beneficiary who received the distribution that was too large or ordering that beneficiary to return some or all of the distribution to the trust; and

(3) to the extent that the court is unable, after applying Subdivisions (1) and (2), to place the beneficiaries, the trust, or both, in the positions they would have occupied if the discretion had not been abused, the court may order the trustee to pay an appropriate amount from its own funds to one or more of the beneficiaries or the trust or both.

(d) If the trustee of a trust reasonably believes that one or more beneficiaries of such trust will object to the manner in which the trustee intends to exercise or not exercise a discretionary power conferred by Section 116.005, the trustee may petition the court having jurisdiction over the trust, and the court shall determine whether the proposed exercise or nonexercise by the trustee of such discretionary power will result in an abuse of the trustee's discretion. The trustee shall state in such petition the basis for its belief that a beneficiary would object. The failure or refusal of a beneficiary to sign a waiver or release is not reasonable grounds for a trustee to believe the beneficiary will object. The court may appoint one or more guardians ad litem or attorneys ad litem pursuant to Section 115.014. If the petition describes the proposed exercise or nonexercise of the power and contains sufficient information to inform the beneficiaries of the reasons for the proposal, the facts upon which the trustee relies, and an explanation of how the income and remainder beneficiaries will be affected by the proposed exercise or nonexercise of the power, a beneficiary who challenges the proposed exercise or nonexercise has the burden of establishing that it will result in an abuse of discretion. The trustee shall advance from the trust principal all costs incident to the judicial determination, including the reasonable attorney's fees and costs of the trustee, any beneficiary or

beneficiaries who are parties to the action and who retain counsel, any guardian ad litem, and any attorney ad litem. At the conclusion of the proceeding, the court may award costs and reasonable and necessary attorney's fees as provided in Section 114.064, including, if the court considers it appropriate, awarding part or all of such costs against the trust principal or income, awarding part or all of such costs against one or more beneficiaries or such beneficiary's or beneficiaries' share of the trust, or awarding part or all of such costs against the trustee in the trustee's individual capacity, if the court determines that the trustee's exercise or nonexercise of discretionary power would have resulted in an abuse of discretion or that the trustee did not have reasonable grounds for believing one or more beneficiaries would object to the proposed exercise or nonexercise of the discretionary power.

History of Prop. Code §116.006: Acts 2003, 78th Leg., ch. 659, §1, eff. Jan. 1, 2004. Amended by Acts 2009, 81st Leg., ch. 672, §7, eff. Sept. 1, 2009.

PROP §116.007. PROVISIONS REGARDING NONCHARITABLE UNITRUSTS

(a) This section does not apply to a charitable remainder unitrust as defined by Section 664(d), Internal Revenue Code of 1986 (26 U.S.C. Section 664), as amended.

(b) In this section:

(1) "Unitrust" means a trust the terms of which require distribution of a unitrust amount.

(2) "Unitrust amount" means a distribution mandated by the terms of a trust in an amount equal to a fixed percentage of not less than three or more than five percent per year of the net fair market value of the trust's assets, valued at least annually. The unitrust amount may be determined by reference to the net fair market value of the trust's assets in one year or more than one year.

(c) Distribution of the unitrust amount is considered a distribution of all of the income of the unitrust and shall not be considered a fundamental departure from applicable state law. A distribution of the unitrust amount reasonably apportions the total return of a unitrust.

(d) Unless the terms of the trust specifically provide otherwise, a distribution of the unitrust amount shall be treated as first being made from the following sources in order of priority:

(1) from net accounting income determined as if the trust were not a unitrust;

(2) from ordinary accounting income not allocable to net accounting income;

(3) from net realized short-term capital gains;

(4) from net realized long-term capital gains; and

(5) from the principal of the trust estate.

History of Prop. Code §116.007: Acts 2003, 78th Leg., ch. 659, §1, eff. Jan. 1, 2004.

Sections 116.008-116.050 reserved for expansion

Subchapter B. Decedent's Estate or Terminating Income Interest

PROP §116.051. DETERMINATION & DISTRIBUTION OF NET INCOME

After a decedent dies, in the case of an estate, or after an income interest in a trust ends, the following rules apply:

(1) A fiduciary of an estate or of a terminating income interest shall determine the amount of net income and net principal receipts received from property specifically given to a beneficiary under the rules in Subchapters C, D, and E which apply to trustees and the rules in Subdivision (5). The fiduciary shall distribute the net income and net principal receipts to the beneficiary who is to receive the specific property.

(2) A fiduciary shall determine the remaining net income of a decedent's estate or a terminating income interest under the rules in Subchapters C, D, and E which apply to trustees and by:

(A) including in net income all income from property used to discharge liabilities;

(B) paying from income or principal, in the fiduciary's discretion, fees of attorneys, accountants, and fiduciaries; court costs and other expenses of administration; and interest on death taxes, but the fiduciary may pay those expenses from income of property passing to a trust for which the fiduciary claims an estate tax marital or charitable deduction only to the extent that the payment of those expenses from income will not cause the reduction or loss of the deduction; and

(C) paying from principal all other disbursements made or incurred in connection with the settlement of a decedent's estate or the winding up of a terminating income interest, including debts, funeral expenses, disposition of remains, family allowances, and death taxes and related penalties that are apportioned to the estate or terminating income interest by the will, the terms of the trust, or applicable law.

(3) A fiduciary shall distribute to a beneficiary who receives a pecuniary amount outright the interest or any other amount provided by the will, the terms of the trust, or applicable law from net income determined under Subdivision (2) or from principal to the extent that net income is insufficient. If a beneficiary is to receive a pecuniary amount outright from a trust after an income interest ends and no interest or other amount is provided for by the terms of the trust or applicable law, the fiduciary shall distribute the interest or other amount to which the beneficiary would be entitled under applicable law if the pecuniary amount were required to be paid under a will. Unless otherwise provided by the will or the terms of the trust, a beneficiary who receives a pecuniary amount, regardless of whether in trust, shall be paid interest on the pecuniary amount at the legal rate of interest as provided by Section 302.002, Finance Code. Interest on the pecuniary amount is payable:

(A) under a will, beginning on the first anniversary of the date of the decedent's death; or

(B) under a trust, beginning on the first anniversary of the date on which an income interest ends.

(4) A fiduciary shall distribute the net income remaining after distributions required by Subdivision (3) in the manner described in Section 116.052 to all other beneficiaries even if the beneficiary holds an unqualified power to withdraw assets from the trust or other presently exercisable general power of appointment over the trust.

(5) A fiduciary may not reduce principal or income receipts from property described in Subdivision (1) because of a payment described in Section 116.201 or 116.202 to the extent that the will, the terms of the trust, or applicable law requires the fiduciary to make the payment from assets other than the property or to the extent that the fiduciary recovers or expects to recover the payment from a third party. The net income and principal receipts from the property are determined by including all of the amounts the fiduciary receives or pays with respect to the property, whether those amounts accrued or became due before, on, or after the date of a decedent's death or an income interest's terminating event, and by making a reasonable provision for amounts that the fiduciary believes the estate or terminating income interest may become obligated to pay after the property is distributed.

(6) A fiduciary, without reduction for taxes, shall pay to a charitable organization that is entitled to receive income under Subdivision (4) any amount allowed as a tax deduction to the estate or trust for income payable to the charitable organization.

History of Prop. Code §116.051: Acts 2003, 78th Leg., ch. 659, §1, eff. Jan. 1, 2004.

PROP §116.052. DISTRIBUTION TO RESIDUARY & REMAINDER BENEFICIARIES

(a) Each beneficiary described in Section 116.051(4) is entitled to receive a portion of the net income equal to the beneficiary's fractional interest in undistributed principal assets, using values as of the distribution date. If a fiduciary makes more than one distribution of assets to beneficiaries to whom this section applies, each beneficiary, including one who does not receive part of the distribution, is entitled, as of each distribution date, to the net income the fiduciary has received after the date of death or terminating event or earlier distribution date but has not distributed as of the current distribution date.

(b) In determining a beneficiary's share of net income, the following rules apply:

(1) The beneficiary is entitled to receive a portion of the net income equal to the beneficiary's fractional interest in the undistributed principal assets immediately before the distribution date, including assets that later may be sold to meet principal obligations.

(2) The beneficiary's fractional interest in the undistributed principal assets must be calculated without regard to property specifically given to a beneficiary and property required to pay pecuniary amounts not in trust.

(3) The beneficiary's fractional interest in the undistributed principal assets must be calculated on the basis of the aggregate value of those assets as of the distribution date without reducing the value by any unpaid principal obligation.

(4) The distribution date for purposes of this section may be the date as of which the fiduciary calculates the value of the assets if that date is reasonably near the date on which assets are actually distributed.

(c) If a fiduciary does not distribute all of the collected but undistributed net income to each person as of a distribution date, the fiduciary shall maintain appropriate records showing the interest of each beneficiary in that net income.

(d) A fiduciary may apply the rules in this section, to the extent that the fiduciary considers it appropriate,

to net gain or loss realized after the date of death or terminating event or earlier distribution date from the disposition of a principal asset if this section applies to the income from the asset.

History of Prop. Code §116.052: Acts 2003, 78th Leg., ch. 659, §1, eff. Jan. 1, 2004.

Sections 116.053-116.100 reserved for expansion

SUBCHAPTER C. APPORTIONMENT AT BEGINNING & END OF INCOME INTEREST

PROP §116.101. WHEN RIGHT TO INCOME BEGINS & ENDS

(a) An income beneficiary is entitled to net income from the date on which the income interest begins. An income interest begins on the date specified in the terms of the trust or, if no date is specified, on the date an asset becomes subject to a trust or successive income interest.

(b) An asset becomes subject to a trust:

(1) on the date it is transferred to the trust in the case of an asset that is transferred to a trust during the transferor's life;

(2) on the date of a testator's death in the case of an asset that becomes subject to a trust by reason of a will, even if there is an intervening period of administration of the testator's estate; or

(3) on the date of an individual's death in the case of an asset that is transferred to a fiduciary by a third party because of the individual's death.

(c) An asset becomes subject to a successive income interest on the day after the preceding income interest ends, as determined under Subsection (d), even if there is an intervening period of administration to wind up the preceding income interest.

(d) An income interest ends on the day before an income beneficiary dies or another terminating event occurs, or on the last day of a period during which there is no beneficiary to whom a trustee may distribute income.

History of Prop. Code §116.101: Acts 2003, 78th Leg., ch. 659, §1, eff. Jan. 1, 2004.

PROP §116.102. APPORTIONMENT OF RECEIPTS & DISBURSEMENTS WHEN DECEDENT DIES OR INCOME INTEREST BEGINS

(a) A trustee shall allocate an income receipt or disbursement other than one to which Section 116.051(1) applies to principal if its due date occurs before a decedent dies in the case of an estate or before an income interest begins in the case of a trust or successive income interest.

(b) A trustee shall allocate an income receipt or disbursement to income if its due date occurs on or after the date on which a decedent dies or an income interest begins and it is a periodic due date. An income receipt or disbursement must be treated as accruing from day to day if its due date is not periodic or it has no due date. The portion of the receipt or disbursement accruing before the date on which a decedent dies or an income interest begins must be allocated to principal and the balance must be allocated to income.

(c) An item of income or an obligation is due on the date the payer is required to make a payment. If a payment date is not stated, there is no due date for the purposes of this chapter. Distributions to shareholders or other owners from an entity to which Section 116.151 applies are deemed to be due on the date fixed by the entity for determining who is entitled to receive the distribution or, if no date is fixed, on the declaration date for the distribution. A due date is periodic for receipts or disbursements that must be paid at regular intervals under a lease or an obligation to pay interest or if an entity customarily makes distributions at regular intervals.

History of Prop. Code §116.102: Acts 2003, 78th Leg., ch. 659, §1, eff. Jan. 1, 2004.

PROP §116.103. APPORTIONMENT WHEN INCOME INTEREST ENDS

(a) In this section, "undistributed income" means net income received before the date on which an income interest ends. The term does not include an item of income or expense that is due or accrued or net income that has been added or is required to be added to principal under the terms of the trust.

(b) When a mandatory income interest ends, the trustee shall pay to a mandatory income beneficiary who survives that date, or the estate of a deceased mandatory income beneficiary whose death causes the interest to end, the beneficiary's share of the undistributed income that is not disposed of under the terms of the trust unless the beneficiary has an unqualified power to revoke more than five percent of the trust immediately before the income interest ends. In the latter case, the undistributed income from the portion of the trust that may be revoked must be added to principal.

(c) When a trustee's obligation to pay a fixed annuity or a fixed fraction of the value of the trust's assets ends, the trustee shall prorate the final payment if and to the extent required by applicable law to accomplish a purpose of the trust or its settlor relating to income, gift, estate, or other tax requirements.

History of Prop. Code §116.103: Acts 2003, 78th Leg., ch. 659, §1, eff. Jan. 1, 2004.

Sections 116.104-116.150 reserved for expansion

SUBCHAPTER D. ALLOCATION OF RECEIPTS DURING ADMINISTRATION OF TRUST

PART 1. RECEIPTS FROM ENTITIES

PROP §116.151. CHARACTER OF RECEIPTS

(a) In this section, "entity" means a corporation, partnership, limited liability company, regulated investment company, real estate investment trust, common trust fund, or any other organization in which a trustee has an interest other than a trust or estate to which Section 116.152 applies, a business or activity to which Section 116.153 applies, or an asset-backed security to which Section 116.178 applies.

(b) Except as otherwise provided in this section, a trustee shall allocate to income money received from an entity.

(c) A trustee shall allocate the following receipts from an entity to principal:

(1) property other than money;

(2) money received in one distribution or a series of related distributions in exchange for part or all of a trust's interest in the entity;

(3) money received in total or partial liquidation of the entity; and

(4) money received from an entity that is a regulated investment company or a real estate investment trust if the money distributed is a capital gain dividend for federal income tax purposes.

(d) Money is received in partial liquidation:

(1) to the extent that the entity, at or near the time of a distribution, indicates that it is a distribution in partial liquidation; or

(2) if the total amount of money and property received in a distribution or series of related distributions is greater than 20 percent of the entity's gross assets, as shown by the entity's year-end financial statements immediately preceding the initial receipt.

(e) Money is not received in partial liquidation, nor may it be taken into account under Subsection (d)(2), to the extent that it does not exceed the amount of income tax that a trustee or beneficiary must pay on taxable income of the entity that distributes the money.

(f) A trustee may rely upon a statement made by an entity about the source or character of a distribution if the statement is made at or near the time of distribution by the entity's board of directors or other person or group of persons authorized to exercise powers to pay money or transfer property comparable to those of a corporation's board of directors.

History of Prop. Code §116.151: Acts 2003, 78th Leg., ch. 659, §1, eff. Jan. 1, 2004.

PROP §116.152. DISTRIBUTION FROM TRUST OR ESTATE

A trustee shall allocate to income an amount received as a distribution of income from a trust or an estate in which the trust has an interest other than a purchased interest, and shall allocate to principal an amount received as a distribution of principal from such a trust or estate. If a trustee purchases an interest in a trust that is an investment entity, or a decedent or donor transfers an interest in such a trust to a trustee, Section 116.151 or 116.178 applies to a receipt from the trust.

History of Prop. Code §116.152: Acts 2003, 78th Leg., ch. 659, §1, eff. Jan. 1, 2004.

PROP §116.153. BUSINESS & OTHER ACTIVITIES CONDUCTED BY TRUSTEE

(a) If a trustee who conducts a business or other activity determines that it is in the best interest of all the beneficiaries to account separately for the business or activity instead of accounting for it as part of the trust's general accounting records, the trustee may maintain separate accounting records for its transactions, whether or not its assets are segregated from other trust assets.

(b) A trustee who accounts separately for a business or other activity may determine the extent to which its net cash receipts must be retained for working capital, the acquisition or replacement of fixed assets, and other reasonably foreseeable needs of the business or activity, and the extent to which the remaining net cash receipts are accounted for as principal or income in the trust's general accounting records. If a trustee sells assets of the business or other activity, other than in the ordinary course of the business or ac-

tivity, the trustee shall account for the net amount received as principal in the trust's general accounting records to the extent the trustee determines that the amount received is no longer required in the conduct of the business.

(c) Activities for which a trustee may maintain separate accounting records include:

(1) retail, manufacturing, service, and other traditional business activities;

(2) farming;

(3) raising and selling livestock and other animals;

(4) management of rental properties;

(5) extraction of minerals and other natural resources;

(6) timber operations; and

(7) activities to which Section 116.177 applies.

History of Prop. Code §116.153: Acts 2003, 78th Leg., ch. 659, §1, eff. Jan. 1, 2004.

Sections 116.154-116.160 reserved for expansion

PART 2. RECEIPTS NOT NORMALLY APPORTIONED

PROP §116.161. PRINCIPAL RECEIPTS

A trustee shall allocate to principal:

(1) to the extent not allocated to income under this chapter, assets received from a transferor during the transferor's lifetime, a decedent's estate, a trust with a terminating income interest, or a payer under a contract naming the trust or its trustee as beneficiary;

(2) money or other property received from the sale, exchange, liquidation, or change in form of a principal asset, including realized profit, subject to this subchapter;

(3) amounts recovered from third parties to reimburse the trust because of disbursements described in Section 116.202(a)(7) or for other reasons to the extent not based on the loss of income;

(4) proceeds of property taken by eminent domain, but a separate award made for the loss of income with respect to an accounting period during which a current income beneficiary had a mandatory income interest is income;

(5) net income received in an accounting period during which there is no beneficiary to whom a trustee may or must distribute income; and

(6) other receipts as provided in Part 3.

History of Prop. Code §116.161: Acts 2003, 78th Leg., ch. 659, §1, eff. Jan. 1, 2004.

PROP §116.162. RENTAL PROPERTY

To the extent that a trustee accounts for receipts from rental property pursuant to this section, the trustee shall allocate to income an amount received as rent of real or personal property, including an amount received for cancellation or renewal of a lease. An amount received as a refundable deposit, including a security deposit or a deposit that is to be applied as rent for future periods, must be added to principal and held subject to the terms of the lease and is not available for distribution to a beneficiary until the trustee's contractual obligations have been satisfied with respect to that amount.

History of Prop. Code §116.162: Acts 2003, 78th Leg., ch. 659, §1, eff. Jan. 1, 2004.

PROP §116.163. OBLIGATION TO PAY MONEY

(a) An amount received as interest, whether determined at a fixed, variable, or floating rate, on an obligation to pay money to the trustee, including an amount received as consideration for prepaying principal, must be allocated to income without any provision for amortization of premium.

(b) A trustee shall allocate to principal an amount received from the sale, redemption, or other disposition of an obligation to pay money to the trustee more than one year after it is purchased or acquired by the trustee, including an obligation whose purchase price or value when it is acquired is less than its value at maturity. If the obligation matures within one year after it is purchased or acquired by the trustee, an amount received in excess of its purchase price or its value when acquired by the trust must be allocated to income.

(c) This section does not apply to an obligation to which Section 116.172, 116.173, 116.174, 116.175, 116.177, or 116.178 applies.

History of Prop. Code §116.163: Acts 2003, 78th Leg., ch. 659, §1, eff. Jan. 1, 2004.

PROP §116.164. INSURANCE POLICIES & SIMILAR CONTRACTS

(a) Except as otherwise provided in Subsection (b), a trustee shall allocate to principal the proceeds of a life insurance policy or other contract in which the trust or its trustee is named as beneficiary, including a contract that insures the trust or its trustee against loss for damage to, destruction of, or loss of title to a trust asset. The trustee shall allocate dividends on an insurance policy to income if the premiums on the policy are

paid from income, and to principal if the premiums are paid from principal.

(b) A trustee shall allocate to income proceeds of a contract that insures the trustee against loss of occupancy or other use by an income beneficiary, loss of income, or, subject to Section 116.153, loss of profits from a business.

(c) This section does not apply to a contract to which Section 116.172 applies.

History of Prop. Code §116.164: Acts 2003, 78th Leg., ch. 659, §1, eff. Jan. 1, 2004.

Sections 116.165-116.170 reserved for expansion

PART 3. RECEIPTS NORMALLY APPORTIONED

PROP §116.171. INSUBSTANTIAL ALLOCATIONS NOT REQUIRED

If a trustee determines that an allocation between principal and income required by Section 116.172, 116.173, 116.174, 116.175, or 116.178 is insubstantial, the trustee may allocate the entire amount to principal unless one of the circumstances described in Section 116.005(c) applies to the allocation. This power may be exercised by a cotrustee in the circumstances described in Section 116.005(d) and may be released for the reasons and in the manner described in Section 116.005(e).

History of Prop. Code §116.171: Acts 2003, 78th Leg., ch. 659, §1, eff. Jan. 1, 2004.

PROP §116.172. DEFERRED COMPENSATION, ANNUITIES, & SIMILAR PAYMENTS

(a) In this section:

(1) "Future payment asset" means the asset from which a payment is derived.

(2) "Payment" means a payment that a trustee may receive over a fixed number of years or during the life of one or more individuals because of services rendered or property transferred to the payer in exchange for future payments. The term includes a payment made in money or property from the payer's general assets or from a separate fund created by the payer.

(3) "Separate fund" includes a private or commercial annuity, an individual retirement account, and a pension, profit-sharing, stock-bonus, or stock-ownership plan.

(b) To the extent that the payer characterizes a payment as interest or a dividend or a payment made in lieu of interest or a dividend, a trustee shall allocate it to income. The trustee shall allocate to principal the balance of the payment and any other payment received in the same accounting period that is not characterized as interest, a dividend, or an equivalent payment.

(c) If no part of a payment is characterized as interest, a dividend, or an equivalent payment, and all or part of the payment is required to be made, a trustee shall allocate to income the part of the payment that does not exceed an amount equal to:

(1) four percent of the fair market value of the future payment asset on the date specified in Subsection (d); less

(2) the total amount that the trustee has allocated to income for all previous payments received from the future payment asset during the same accounting period in which the payment is received.

(d) For purposes of Subsection (c)(1), the determination of the fair market value of a future payment asset is made on the later of:

(1) the date on which the future payment asset first becomes subject to the trust; or

(2) the last day of the accounting period of the trust that immediately precedes the accounting period during which the payment is received.

(e) For each accounting period a payment is received, the amount determined under Subsection (c)(1) must be prorated on a daily basis unless the determination of the fair market value of a future payment asset is made under Subsection (d)(2) and is for an accounting period of 365 days or more.

(f) A trustee shall allocate to principal the part of the payment described by Subsection (c) that is not allocated to income.

(g) If no part of a payment is required to be made or the payment received is the entire amount to which the trustee is entitled, the trustee shall allocate the entire payment to principal. For purposes of Subsection (c) and this subsection, a payment is not "required to be made" to the extent that it is made only because the trustee exercises a right of withdrawal.

(h) Subsections (j) and (k) apply and Subsections (b) and (c) do not apply in determining the allocation of a payment made from a separate fund to:

(1) a trust to which an election to qualify for a marital deduction under Section 2056(b)(7), Internal Revenue Code of 1986, has been made; or

(2) a trust that qualifies for the marital deduction under Section 2056(b)(5), Internal Revenue Code of 1986.

(i) Subsections (h), (j), and (k) do not apply if and to the extent that a series of payments would, without the application of Subsection (h), qualify for the marital deduction under Section 2056(b)(7)(C), Internal Revenue Code of 1986.

(j) The trustee shall determine the internal income of the separate fund for the accounting period as if the separate fund were a trust subject to this code. On request of the surviving spouse, the trustee shall demand of the person administering the separate fund that this internal income be distributed to the trust. The trustee shall allocate a payment from the separate fund to income to the extent of the internal income of the separate fund, and the balance to the principal. On request of the surviving spouse, the trustee shall allocate principal to income to the extent the internal income of the separate fund exceeds payments made to the trust during the accounting period from the separate fund.

(k) If the trustee cannot determine the internal income of the separate fund but can determine the value of the separate fund, the internal income of the separate fund shall be four percent of the fund's value, according to the most recent statement of value preceding the beginning of the accounting period. If the trustee can determine neither the internal income of the separate fund nor the fund's value, the internal income of the fund shall be the product of the interest rate and the present value of the expected future payments, as determined under Section 7520, Internal Revenue Code of 1986, for the month preceding the accounting period for which the computation is made.

History of Prop. Code §116.172: Acts 2003, 78th Leg., ch. 659, §1, eff. Jan. 1, 2004. Amended by Acts 2005, 79th Leg., ch. 148, §26, eff. Jan. 1, 2006; Acts 2007, 80th Leg., ch. 451, §13, eff. Sept. 1, 2007; Acts 2009, 81st Leg., ch. 672, §§8, 9, eff. Sept. 1, 2009.

PROP §116.173. LIQUIDATING ASSET

(a) In this section, "liquidating asset" means an asset whose value will diminish or terminate because the asset is expected to produce receipts for a period of limited duration. The term includes a leasehold, patent, copyright, royalty right, and right to receive payments during a period of more than one year under an arrangement that does not provide for the payment of interest on the unpaid balance. The term does not include a payment subject to Section 116.172, resources subject to Section 116.174, timber subject to Section 116.175, an activity subject to Section 116.177, an asset subject to Section 116.178, or any asset for which the trustee establishes a reserve for depreciation under Section 116.203.

(b) A trustee shall allocate to income 10 percent of the receipts from a liquidating asset and the balance to principal.

(c) The trustee may allocate a receipt from any interest in a liquidating asset the trust owns on January 1, 2004, in the manner provided by this chapter or in any lawful manner used by the trustee before January 1, 2004, to make the same allocation.

History of Prop. Code §116.173: Acts 2003, 78th Leg., ch. 659, §1, eff. Jan. 1, 2004.

PROP §116.174. MINERALS, WATER, & OTHER NATURAL RESOURCES

(a) To the extent that a trustee accounts for receipts from an interest in minerals or other natural resources pursuant to this section, the trustee shall allocate them as follows:

(1) If received as delay rental or annual rent on a lease, a receipt must be allocated to income.

(2) If received from a production payment, a receipt must be allocated to income if and to the extent that the agreement creating the production payment provides a factor for interest or its equivalent. The balance must be allocated to principal.

(3) If received as a royalty, shut-in-well payment, take-or-pay payment, or bonus, the trustee shall allocate the receipt equitably.

(4) If an amount is received from a working interest or any other interest not provided for in Subdivision (1), (2), or (3), the trustee must allocate the receipt equitably.

(b) An amount received on account of an interest in water that is renewable must be allocated to income. If the water is not renewable, the trustee must allocate the receipt equitably.

(c) This chapter applies whether or not a decedent or donor was extracting minerals, water, or other natural resources before the interest became subject to the trust.

(d) The trustee may allocate a receipt from any interest in minerals, water, or other natural resources the trust owns on January 1, 2004, in the manner provided

by this chapter or in any lawful manner used by the trustee before January 1, 2004, to make the same allocation. The trustee shall allocate a receipt from any interest in minerals, water, or other natural resources acquired by the trust after January 1, 2004, in the manner provided by this chapter.

(e) An allocation of a receipt under this section is presumed to be equitable if the amount allocated to principal is equal to the amount allowed by the Internal Revenue Code of 1986 as a deduction for depletion of the interest.

History of Prop. Code §116.174: Acts 2003, 78th Leg., ch. 659, §1, eff. Jan. 1, 2004. Amended by Acts 2007, 80th Leg., ch. 451, §14, eff. Sept. 1, 2007.

PROP §116.175. TIMBER

(a) To the extent that a trustee accounts for receipts from the sale of timber and related products pursuant to this section, the trustee shall allocate the net receipts:

(1) to income to the extent that the amount of timber removed from the land does not exceed the rate of growth of the timber during the accounting periods in which a beneficiary has a mandatory income interest;

(2) to principal to the extent that the amount of timber removed from the land exceeds the rate of growth of the timber or the net receipts are from the sale of standing timber;

(3) to or between income and principal if the net receipts are from the lease of timberland or from a contract to cut timber from land owned by a trust, by determining the amount of timber removed from the land under the lease or contract and applying the rules in Subdivisions (1) and (2); or

(4) to principal to the extent that advance payments, bonuses, and other payments are not allocated pursuant to Subdivision (1), (2), or (3).

(b) In determining net receipts to be allocated pursuant to Subsection (a), a trustee shall deduct and transfer to principal a reasonable amount for depletion.

(c) This chapter applies whether or not a decedent or transferor was harvesting timber from the property before it became subject to the trust.

(d) If a trust owns an interest in timberland on January 1, 2004, the trustee may allocate a net receipt from the sale of timber and related products in the manner provided by this chapter or in any lawful manner used by the trustee before January 1, 2004, to make the same allocation. If the trust acquires an interest in timberland after January 1, 2004, the trustee shall allocate net receipts from the sale of timber and related products in the manner provided by this chapter.

History of Prop. Code §116.175: Acts 2003, 78th Leg., ch. 659, §1, eff. Jan. 1, 2004.

PROP §116.176. PROPERTY NOT PRODUCTIVE OF INCOME

(a) If a marital deduction is allowed for all or part of a trust whose assets consist substantially of property that does not provide the spouse with sufficient income from or use of the trust assets, and if the amounts that the trustee transfers from principal to income under Section 116.005 and distributes to the spouse from principal pursuant to the terms of the trust are insufficient to provide the spouse with the beneficial enjoyment required to obtain the marital deduction, the spouse may require the trustee to make property productive of income, convert property within a reasonable time, or exercise the power conferred by Section 116.005(a). The trustee may decide which action or combination of actions to take.

(b) In cases not governed by Subsection (a), proceeds from the sale or other disposition of an asset are principal without regard to the amount of income the asset produces during any accounting period.

History of Prop. Code §116.176: Acts 2003, 78th Leg., ch. 659, §1, eff. Jan. 1, 2004.

PROP §116.177. DERIVATIVES & OPTIONS

(a) In this section, "derivative" means a contract or financial instrument or a combination of contracts and financial instruments which gives a trust the right or obligation to participate in some or all changes in the price of a tangible or intangible asset or group of assets, or changes in a rate, an index of prices or rates, or other market indicator for an asset or a group of assets.

(b) To the extent that a trustee does not account under Section 116.153 for transactions in derivatives, the trustee shall allocate to principal receipts from and disbursements made in connection with those transactions.

(c) If a trustee grants an option to buy property from the trust, whether or not the trust owns the property when the option is granted, grants an option that permits another person to sell property to the trust, or acquires an option to buy property for the trust or an option to sell an asset owned by the trust, and the trustee or other owner of the asset is required to deliver the asset if the option is exercised, an amount received for

granting the option must be allocated to principal. An amount paid to acquire the option must be paid from principal. A gain or loss realized upon the exercise of an option, including an option granted to a settlor of the trust for services rendered, must be allocated to principal.

History of Prop. Code §116.177: Acts 2003, 78th Leg., ch. 659, §1, eff. Jan. 1, 2004.

PROP §116.178. ASSET-BACKED SECURITIES

(a) In this section, "asset-backed security" means an asset whose value is based upon the right it gives the owner to receive distributions from the proceeds of financial assets that provide collateral for the security. The term includes an asset that gives the owner the right to receive from the collateral financial assets only the interest or other current return or only the proceeds other than interest or current return. The term does not include an asset to which Section 116.151 or 116.172 applies.

(b) If a trust receives a payment from interest or other current return and from other proceeds of the collateral financial assets, the trustee shall allocate to income the portion of the payment which the payer identifies as being from interest or other current return and shall allocate the balance of the payment to principal.

(c) If a trust receives one or more payments in exchange for the trust's entire interest in an asset-backed security in one accounting period, the trustee shall allocate the payments to principal. If a payment is one of a series of payments that will result in the liquidation of the trust's interest in the security over more than one accounting period, the trustee shall allocate 10 percent of the payment to income and the balance to principal.

History of Prop. Code §116.178: Acts 2003, 78th Leg., ch. 659, §1, eff. Jan. 1, 2004.

Sections 116.179-116.200 reserved for expansion

SUBCHAPTER E. ALLOCATION OF DISBURSEMENTS DURING ADMINISTRATION OF TRUST

PROP §116.201. DISBURSEMENTS FROM INCOME

A trustee shall make the following disbursements from income to the extent that they are not disbursements to which Section 116.051(2)(B) or (C) applies:

(1) one-half of the regular compensation of the trustee and of any person providing investment advisory or custodial services to the trustee unless, consistent with the trustee's fiduciary duties, the trustee determines that a different portion, none, or all of the compensation should be allocated to income;

(2) one-half of all expenses for accountings, judicial proceedings, or other matters that involve both the income and remainder interests;

(3) all of the other ordinary expenses incurred in connection with the administration, management, or preservation of trust property and the distribution of income, including interest, ordinary repairs, regularly recurring taxes assessed against principal, and expenses of a proceeding or other matter that concerns primarily the income interest; and

(4) recurring premiums on insurance covering the loss of a principal asset or the loss of income from or use of the asset.

History of Prop. Code §116.201: Acts 2003, 78th Leg., ch. 659, §1, eff. Jan. 1, 2004. Amended by Acts 2013, 83rd Leg., ch. 1337, §2, eff. Sept. 1, 2013.

PROP §116.202. DISBURSEMENTS FROM PRINCIPAL

(a) A trustee shall make the following disbursements from principal:

(1) the remaining one-half of the disbursements described in Section 116.201(1) unless, consistent with the trustee's fiduciary duties, the trustee determines that a different portion, none, or all of those disbursements should be allocated to income, in which case that portion of the disbursements that are not allocated to income shall be allocated to principal;

(1-a) the remaining one-half of the disbursements described in Section 116.201(2);

(2) all of the trustee's compensation calculated on principal as a fee for acceptance, distribution, or termination, and disbursements made to prepare property for sale;

(3) payments on the principal of a trust debt;

(4) expenses of a proceeding that concerns primarily principal, including a proceeding to construe the trust or to protect the trust or its property;

(5) premiums paid on a policy of insurance not described in Section 116.201(4) of which the trust is the owner and beneficiary;

(6) estate, inheritance, and other transfer taxes, including penalties, apportioned to the trust; and

(7) disbursements related to environmental matters, including reclamation, assessing environmental conditions, remedying and removing environmental

contamination, monitoring remedial activities and the release of substances, preventing future releases of substances, collecting amounts from persons liable or potentially liable for the costs of those activities, penalties imposed under environmental laws or regulations and other payments made to comply with those laws or regulations, statutory or common law claims by third parties, and defending claims based on environmental matters.

(b) If a principal asset is encumbered with an obligation that requires income from that asset to be paid directly to the creditor, the trustee shall transfer from principal to income an amount equal to the income paid to the creditor in reduction of the principal balance of the obligation.

History of Prop. Code §116.202: Acts 2003, 78th Leg., ch. 659, §1, eff. Jan. 1, 2004. Amended by Acts 2013, 83rd Leg., ch. 1337, §3, eff. Sept. 1, 2013.

PROP §116.203. TRANSFERS FROM INCOME TO PRINCIPAL FOR DEPRECIATION

(a) In this section, "depreciation" means a reduction in value due to wear, tear, decay, corrosion, or gradual obsolescence of a fixed asset having a useful life of more than one year.

(b) A trustee may transfer to principal a reasonable amount of the net cash receipts from a principal asset that is subject to depreciation, but may not transfer any amount for depreciation:

(1) of that portion of real property used or available for use by a beneficiary as a residence or of tangible personal property held or made available for the personal use or enjoyment of a beneficiary;

(2) during the administration of a decedent's estate; or

(3) under this section if the trustee is accounting under Section 116.153 for the business or activity in which the asset is used.

(c) An amount transferred to principal need not be held as a separate fund.

History of Prop. Code §116.203: Acts 2003, 78th Leg., ch. 659, §1, eff. Jan. 1, 2004.

PROP §116.204. TRANSFERS FROM INCOME TO REIMBURSE PRINCIPAL

(a) If a trustee makes or expects to make a principal disbursement described in this section, the trustee may transfer an appropriate amount from income to principal in one or more accounting periods to reimburse principal or to provide a reserve for future principal disbursements.

(b) Principal disbursements to which Subsection (a) applies include the following, but only to the extent that the trustee has not been and does not expect to be reimbursed by a third party:

(1) an amount chargeable to income but paid from principal because it is unusually large, including extraordinary repairs;

(2) a capital improvement to a principal asset, whether in the form of changes to an existing asset or the construction of a new asset, including special assessments;

(3) disbursements made to prepare property for rental, including tenant allowances, leasehold improvements, and broker's commissions;

(4) periodic payments on an obligation secured by a principal asset to the extent that the amount transferred from income to principal for depreciation is less than the periodic payments; and

(5) disbursements described in Section 116.202(a)(7).

(c) If the asset whose ownership gives rise to the disbursements becomes subject to a successive income interest after an income interest ends, a trustee may continue to transfer amounts from income to principal as provided in Subsection (a).

History of Prop. Code §116.204: Acts 2003, 78th Leg., ch. 659, §1, eff. Jan. 1, 2004.

PROP §116.205. INCOME TAXES

(a) A tax required to be paid by a trustee based on receipts allocated to income must be paid from income.

(b) A tax required to be paid by a trustee based on receipts allocated to principal must be paid from principal, even if the tax is called an income tax by the taxing authority.

(c) A tax required to be paid by a trustee on the trust's share of an entity's taxable income must be paid:

(1) from income to the extent that receipts from the entity are allocated only to income;

(2) from principal to the extent that receipts from the entity are allocated only to principal;

(3) proportionately from principal and income to the extent that receipts from the entity are allocated to both principal and income; and

(4) from principal to the extent that the tax exceeds the total receipts from the entity.

(d) After applying the other provisions of this section, the trustee shall adjust income or principal re-

ceipts to the extent that the trust's taxes are reduced because the trust receives a deduction for payments made to a beneficiary.

History of Prop. Code §116.205: Acts 2003, 78th Leg., ch. 659, §1, eff. Jan. 1, 2004. Amended by Acts 2011, 82nd Leg., ch. 657, §8, eff. Sept. 1, 2011.

PROP §116.206. ADJUSTMENTS BETWEEN PRINCIPAL & INCOME BECAUSE OF TAXES

(a) A fiduciary may make adjustments between principal and income to offset the shifting of economic interests or tax benefits between income beneficiaries and remainder beneficiaries which arise from:

(1) elections and decisions, other than those described in Subsection (b), that the fiduciary makes from time to time regarding tax matters;

(2) an income tax or any other tax that is imposed upon the fiduciary or a beneficiary as a result of a transaction involving or a distribution from the estate or trust; or

(3) the ownership by an estate or trust of an interest in an entity whose taxable income, whether or not distributed, is includable in the taxable income of the estate, trust, or a beneficiary.

(b) If the amount of an estate tax marital deduction or charitable contribution deduction is reduced because a fiduciary deducts an amount paid from principal for income tax purposes instead of deducting it for estate tax purposes, and as a result estate taxes paid from principal are increased and income taxes paid by an estate, trust, or beneficiary are decreased, each estate, trust, or beneficiary that benefits from the decrease in income tax shall reimburse the principal from which the increase in estate tax is paid. The total reimbursement must equal the increase in the estate tax to the extent that the principal used to pay the increase would have qualified for a marital deduction or charitable contribution deduction but for the payment. The proportionate share of the reimbursement for each estate, trust, or beneficiary whose income taxes are reduced must be the same as its proportionate share of the total decrease in income tax. An estate or trust shall reimburse principal from income.

History of Prop. Code §116.206: Acts 2003, 78th Leg., ch. 659, §1, eff. Jan. 1, 2004.

CHAPTER 117. UNIFORM PRUDENT INVESTOR ACT

PROP §117.001. SHORT TITLE

This chapter may be cited as the "Uniform Prudent Investor Act."

History of Prop. Code §117.001: Acts 2003, 78th Leg., ch. 1103, §1, eff. Jan. 1, 2004.

PROP §117.002. UNIFORMITY OF APPLICATION & CONSTRUCTION

This chapter shall be applied and construed to effectuate its general purpose to make uniform the law with respect to the subject of this chapter among the states enacting it.

History of Prop. Code §117.002: Acts 2003, 78th Leg., ch. 1103, §1, eff. Jan. 1, 2004.

PROP §117.003. PRUDENT INVESTOR RULE

(a) Except as otherwise provided in Subsection (b), a trustee who invests and manages trust assets owes a duty to the beneficiaries of the trust to comply with the prudent investor rule set forth in this chapter.

(b) The prudent investor rule, a default rule, may be expanded, restricted, eliminated, or otherwise altered by the provisions of a trust. A trustee is not liable to a beneficiary to the extent that the trustee acted in reasonable reliance on the provisions of the trust.

History of Prop. Code §117.003: Acts 2003, 78th Leg., ch. 1103, §1, eff. Jan. 1, 2004.

PROP §117.004. STANDARD OF CARE; PORTFOLIO STRATEGY; RISK & RETURN OBJECTIVES

(a) A trustee shall invest and manage trust assets as a prudent investor would, by considering the purposes, terms, distribution requirements, and other circumstances of the trust. In satisfying this standard, the trustee shall exercise reasonable care, skill, and caution.

(b) A trustee's investment and management decisions respecting individual assets must be evaluated

not in isolation but in the context of the trust portfolio as a whole and as a part of an overall investment strategy having risk and return objectives reasonably suited to the trust.

(c) Among circumstances that a trustee shall consider in investing and managing trust assets are such of the following as are relevant to the trust or its beneficiaries:

(1) general economic conditions;

(2) the possible effect of inflation or deflation;

(3) the expected tax consequences of investment decisions or strategies;

(4) the role that each investment or course of action plays within the overall trust portfolio, which may include financial assets, interests in closely held enterprises, tangible and intangible personal property, and real property;

(5) the expected total return from income and the appreciation of capital;

(6) other resources of the beneficiaries;

(7) needs for liquidity, regularity of income, and preservation or appreciation of capital; and

(8) an asset's special relationship or special value, if any, to the purposes of the trust or to one or more of the beneficiaries.

(d) A trustee shall make a reasonable effort to verify facts relevant to the investment and management of trust assets.

(e) Except as otherwise provided by and subject to this subtitle, a trustee may invest in any kind of property or type of investment consistent with the standards of this chapter.

(f) A trustee who has special skills or expertise, or is named trustee in reliance upon the trustee's representation that the trustee has special skills or expertise, has a duty to use those special skills or expertise.

History of Prop. Code §117.004: Acts 2003, 78th Leg., ch. 1103, §1, eff. Jan. 1, 2004.

PROP §117.005. DIVERSIFICATION

A trustee shall diversify the investments of the trust unless the trustee reasonably determines that, because of special circumstances, the purposes of the trust are better served without diversifying.

History of Prop. Code §117.005: Acts 2003, 78th Leg., ch. 1103, §1, eff. Jan. 1, 2004.

PROP §117.006. DUTIES AT INCEPTION OF TRUSTEESHIP

Within a reasonable time after accepting a trusteeship or receiving trust assets, a trustee shall review the trust assets and make and implement decisions concerning the retention and disposition of assets, in order to bring the trust portfolio into compliance with the purposes, terms, distribution requirements, and other circumstances of the trust, and with the requirements of this chapter.

History of Prop. Code §117.006: Acts 2003, 78th Leg., ch. 1103, §1, eff. Jan. 1, 2004.

PROP §117.007. LOYALTY

A trustee shall invest and manage the trust assets solely in the interest of the beneficiaries.

History of Prop. Code §117.007: Acts 2003, 78th Leg., ch. 1103, §1, eff. Jan. 1, 2004.

PROP §117.008. IMPARTIALITY

If a trust has two or more beneficiaries, the trustee shall act impartially in investing and managing the trust assets, taking into account any differing interests of the beneficiaries.

History of Prop. Code §117.008: Acts 2003, 78th Leg., ch. 1103, §1, eff. Jan. 1, 2004.

PROP §117.009. INVESTMENT COSTS

In investing and managing trust assets, a trustee may only incur costs that are appropriate and reasonable in relation to the assets, the purposes of the trust, and the skills of the trustee.

History of Prop. Code §117.009: Acts 2003, 78th Leg., ch. 1103, §1, eff. Jan. 1, 2004.

PROP §117.010. REVIEWING COMPLIANCE

Compliance with the prudent investor rule is determined in light of the facts and circumstances existing at the time of a trustee's decision or action and not by hindsight.

History of Prop. Code §117.010: Acts 2003, 78th Leg., ch. 1103, §1, eff. Jan. 1, 2004.

PROP §117.011. DELEGATION OF INVESTMENT & MANAGEMENT FUNCTIONS

(a) A trustee may delegate investment and management functions that a prudent trustee of comparable skills could properly delegate under the circumstances. The trustee shall exercise reasonable care, skill, and caution in:

(1) selecting an agent;

(2) establishing the scope and terms of the delegation, consistent with the purposes and terms of the trust; and

(3) periodically reviewing the agent's actions in order to monitor the agent's performance and compliance with the terms of the delegation.

(b) In performing a delegated function, an agent owes a duty to the trust to exercise reasonable care to comply with the terms of the delegation.

(c) A trustee who complies with the requirements of Subsection (a) is not liable to the beneficiaries or to the trust for the decisions or actions of the agent to whom the function was delegated, unless:

(1) the agent is an affiliate of the trustee; or

(2) under the terms of the delegation:

(A) the trustee or a beneficiary of the trust is required to arbitrate disputes with the agent; or

(B) the period for bringing an action by the trustee or a beneficiary of the trust with respect to an agent's actions is shortened from that which is applicable to trustees under the law of this state.

(d) By accepting the delegation of a trust function from the trustee of a trust that is subject to the law of this state, an agent submits to the jurisdiction of the courts of this state.

History of Prop. Code §117.011: Acts 2003, 78th Leg., ch. 1103, §1, eff. Jan. 1, 2004.

PROP §117.012. LANGUAGE INVOKING STANDARD OF CHAPTER

The following terms or comparable language in the provisions of a trust, unless otherwise limited or modified, authorizes any investment or strategy permitted under this chapter: "investments permissible by law for investment of trust funds," "legal investments," "authorized investments," "using the judgment and care under the circumstances then prevailing that persons of prudence, discretion, and intelligence exercise in the management of their own affairs, not in regard to speculation but in regard to the permanent disposition of their funds, considering the probable income as well as the probable safety of their capital," "prudent man rule," "prudent trustee rule," "prudent person rule," and "prudent investor rule."

History of Prop. Code §117.012: Acts 2003, 78th Leg., ch. 1103, §1, eff. Jan. 1, 2004.

Chapters 118-120 reserved for expansion

SUBTITLE C. MISCELLANEOUS TRUSTS

CHAPTER 121. EMPLOYEES' TRUSTS

SUBCHAPTER A. PENSION TRUSTS

PROP §121.001. PENSION TRUSTS

(a) For the purposes of this subchapter, a pension trust is an express trust:

(1) containing or relating to property;

(2) created by an employer as part of a stock-bonus plan, pension plan, disability or death benefit plan, or profit-sharing plan for the benefit of some or all of the employer's employees;

(3) to which contributions are made by the employer, by some or all of the employees, or by both; and

(4) created for the principal purpose of distributing to the employees, or the successor to their beneficial interest in the trust, the principal or income, or both, of the property held in trust.

(b) This subchapter applies to a pension trust regardless of when the trust was created.

History of Prop. Code §121.001: Acts 1983, 68th Leg., ch. 576, §1, eff. Jan. 1, 1984. Source: TRCS art. 7425d, §1.

PROP §121.002. EMPLOYEES OF CONTROLLED CORPORATIONS

For the purposes of this subchapter, the relationship of employer and employee exists between a corporation and its own employees, and between a corporation and the employees of each other corporation that it controls, by which it is controlled, or with which it is under common control through the exercise by one or more persons of a majority of voting rights in one or more corporations.

History of Prop. Code §121.002: Acts 1983, 68th Leg., ch. 576, §1, eff. Jan. 1, 1984. Source: TRCS art. 7425d, §1.

PROP §121.003. APPLICATION OF TEXAS TRUST CODE

The Texas Trust Code (Chapters 111 through 117) applies to a pension trust.

History of Prop. Code §121.003: Acts 1983, 68th Leg., ch. 576, §1, eff. Jan. 1, 1984. Amended by Acts 2005, 79th Leg., ch. 148, §27, eff. Jan. 1, 2006. Source: TRCS art. 7425d, §2.

PROP §121.004. RULE AGAINST PERPETUITIES

A pension trust may continue for as long as is necessary to accomplish the purposes of the trust and is not invalid under the rule against perpetuities or any other law restricting or limiting the duration of a trust.

History of Prop. Code §121.004: Acts 1983, 68th Leg., ch. 576, §1, eff. Jan. 1, 1984. Source: TRCS art. 7425d, §3.

PROP §121.005. ACCUMULATION OF INCOME

Notwithstanding any law limiting the time during which trust income may be accumulated, the income of a pension trust may be accumulated under the terms of the trust for as long as is necessary to accomplish the purposes of the trust.

History of Prop. Code §121.005: Acts 1983, 68th Leg., ch. 576, §1, eff. Jan. 1, 1984. Source: TRCS art. 7425d, §5.

Sections 121.006-121.050 reserved for expansion

SUBCHAPTER B. DEATH BENEFITS UNDER EMPLOYEES' TRUSTS

PROP §121.051. DEFINITIONS

(a) In this subchapter:

(1) "Death benefit" means a benefit of any kind, including the proceeds of a life insurance policy or any other payment, in cash or property, under an employees' trust or a retirement account, a contract purchased by an employees' trust or a retirement account, or a retirement-annuity contract that is payable because of an employee's, participant's, or beneficiary's death to or for the benefit of the employee's, participant's, or beneficiary's beneficiary.

(2) "Employee" means a person covered by an employees' trust or a retirement account that provides a death benefit or a person whose interest in an employees' trust or a retirement account has not been fully distributed.

(3) "Employees' trust" means:

(A) a trust forming a part of a stock-bonus, pension, or profit-sharing plan under Section 401, Internal Revenue Code of 1954 (26 U.S.C.A. Sec. 401 (1986));

(B) a pension trust under Chapter 111; and

(C) an employer-sponsored benefit plan or program, or any other retirement savings arrangement, including a pension plan created under Section 3, Employee Retirement Income Security Act of 1974 (29 U.S.C.A. Sec. 1002 (1986)), regardless of whether the plan, program, or arrangement is funded through a trust.

(4) "Individual retirement account" means a trust, custodial arrangement, or annuity under Section 408(a) or (b), Internal Revenue Code of 1954 (26 U.S.C.A. Sec. 408 (1986)).

(5) "Participant" means a person covered by an employees' trust or a retirement account that provides a death benefit or a person whose interest in an employees' trust or a retirement account has not been fully distributed.

(6) "Retirement account" means a retirement-annuity contract, an individual retirement account, a simplified employee pension, or any other retirement savings arrangement.

(7) "Retirement-annuity contract" means an annuity contract under Section 403, Internal Revenue Code of 1954 (26 U.S.C.A. Sec. 403 (1986)).

(8) "Simplified employee pension" means a trust, custodial arrangement, or annuity under Section 408, Internal Revenue Code of 1954 (26 U.S.C.A. Sec. 408 (1986)).

(9) "Trust" and "trustee" have the meanings assigned by the Texas Trust Code (Chapters 111 through 115), except that "trust" includes any trust, regardless of when it is created.

(b) References to specific provisions of the Internal Revenue Code of 1954 (26 U.S.C.A.) include corresponding provisions of any subsequent federal tax laws.

History of Prop. Code §121.051: Acts 1983, 68th Leg., ch. 576, §1, eff. Jan. 1, 1984. Amended by Acts 1987, 70th Leg., ch. 741, §3, eff. Aug. 31, 1987. Source: TRCS art. 7425d-1, §1.

PROP §121.052. PAYMENT OF DEATH BENEFIT TO TRUSTEE

(a) A death benefit is payable to a trustee of a trust evidenced by a written instrument or declaration existing on the date of an employee's or participant's death, or to a trustee named or to be named as trustee of a trust created under an employee's or participant's will, if the trustee is designated as beneficiary under the plan containing the employees' trust or under the retirement account.

(b) A trustee of a testamentary trust may be designated under Subsection (a) prior to the execution of the will.

(c) A death benefit under a will is not payable until the will is probated.

(d) The trustee shall hold, administer, and dispose of a death benefit payable under this section in accordance with the terms of the trust on the date of the employee's death.

(e) A death benefit is payable to a trustee of a trust created by the will of a person other than the employee if:

(1) the will has been probated at the time of the employee's death; and

(2) the death benefit is payable to the trustee to be held, administered, and disposed of in accordance with the terms of the testamentary trust.

History of Prop. Code §121.052: Acts 1983, 68th Leg., ch. 576, §1, eff. Jan. 1, 1984. Amended by Acts 1987, 70th Leg., ch. 741, §4, eff. Aug. 31, 1987. Source: TRCS art. 7425d-1, §§2, 3.

PROP §121.053. VALIDITY OF TRUST DECLARATION

The validity of a trust agreement or declaration is not affected by:

(1) the absence of a corpus other than the right of the trustee to receive a death benefit as beneficiary;

(2) the employee's reservation of the right to designate another beneficiary of the death benefit; or

(3) the existence of authority to amend, modify, revoke, or terminate the agreement or declaration.

History of Prop. Code §121.053: Acts 1983, 68th Leg., ch. 576, §1, eff. Jan. 1, 1984. Source: TRCS art. 7425d-1, §2.

PROP §121.054. UNCLAIMED BENEFITS

If a trustee does not claim a death benefit on or before the first anniversary of the employee's or participant's death or if satisfactory evidence is provided to a trustee, custodian, other fiduciary, or other obligor of the employees' trust, contract purchased by the employees' trust, or the retirement account before the first anniversary of the employee's or participant's death that there is or will be no trustee to receive the death benefit, the death benefit shall be paid:

(1) according to the beneficiary designation under the plan, trust, contract, or arrangement providing the death benefit under the employees' trust or retirement account; or

(2) if there is no designation in the employees' trust or retirement account, to the personal representative of the deceased employee's or participant's estate.

History of Prop. Code §121.054: Acts 1983, 68th Leg., ch. 576, §1, eff. Jan. 1, 1984. Amended by Acts 1987, 70th Leg., ch. 741, §5, eff. Aug. 31, 1987. Source: TRCS art. 7425d-1, §4.

PROP §121.055. EXEMPTION FROM TAXES & DEBTS

Unless the trust agreement, declaration of trust, or will provides otherwise, a death benefit payable to a trustee under this subchapter is not:

(1) part of the deceased employee's estate;

(2) subject to the debts of the deceased employee or the employee's estate, or to other charges enforceable against the estate; or

(3) subject to the payment of taxes enforceable against the deceased employee's estate to a greater extent than if the death benefit is payable, free of trust, to a beneficiary other than the executor or administrator of the estate of the employee.

History of Prop. Code §121.055: Acts 1983, 68th Leg., ch. 576, §1, eff. Jan. 1, 1984. Source: TRCS art. 7425d-1, §5.

PROP §121.056. COMMINGLING OF ASSETS

A trustee who receives a death benefit under this subchapter may commingle the property with other assets accepted by the trustee and held in trust, either before or after the death benefit is received.

History of Prop. Code §121.056: Acts 1983, 68th Leg., ch. 576, §1, eff. Jan. 1, 1984. Source: TRCS art. 7425d-1, §6.

PROP §121.057. PRIOR DESIGNATIONS NOT AFFECTED

This subchapter does not affect the validity of a beneficiary designation made by an employee before April 3, 1975, that names a trustee as beneficiary of a death benefit.

History of Prop. Code §121.057: Acts 1983, 68th Leg., ch. 576, §1, eff. Jan. 1, 1984. Source: TRCS art. 7425d-1, §7.

PROP §121.058. CONSTRUCTION

(a) This subchapter is intended to be declaratory of the common law of this state.

(b) A court shall liberally construe this subchapter to effect the intent that a death benefit received by a trustee under this subchapter is not subject to the obligations of the employee or the employee's estate unless the trust receiving the benefit expressly provides otherwise.

(c) A death benefit shall not be included in property administered as part of a testator's estate or in an

inventory filed with the county court because of a reference in a will to the death benefit or because of the naming of the trustee of a testamentary trust.

History of Prop. Code §121.058: Acts 1983, 68th Leg., ch. 576, §1, eff. Jan. 1, 1984. Source: TRCS art. 7425d-1, §8.

CHAPTER 122. REPEALED

Repealed by Acts 1983, 68th Leg., ch. 567, art. 2, §9, eff. Jan. 1, 1984.

CHAPTER 123. ATTORNEY GENERAL PARTICIPATION IN PROCEEDINGS INVOLVING CHARITABLE TRUSTS

PROP §123.001. DEFINITIONS

In this chapter:

(1) "Charitable entity" means a corporation, trust, community chest, fund, foundation, or other entity organized for scientific, educational, philanthropic, or environmental purposes, social welfare, the arts and humanities, or another civic or public purpose described by Section 501(c)(3) of the Internal Revenue Code of 1986 (26 U.S.C. 501(c)(3)).

(2) "Charitable trust" means a charitable entity, a trust the stated purpose of which is to benefit a charitable entity, or an inter vivos or testamentary gift to a charitable entity.

(3) "Proceeding involving a charitable trust" means a suit or other judicial proceeding the object of which is to:

(A) terminate a charitable trust or distribute its assets to other than charitable donees;

(B) depart from the objects of the charitable trust stated in the instrument creating the trust, including a proceeding in which the doctrine of cy-pres is invoked;

(C) construe, nullify, or impair the provisions of a testamentary or other instrument creating or affecting a charitable trust;

(D) contest or set aside the probate of an alleged will under which money, property, or another thing of value is given for charitable purposes;

(E) allow a charitable trust to contest or set aside the probate of an alleged will;

(F) determine matters relating to the probate and administration of an estate involving a charitable trust; or

(G) obtain a declaratory judgment involving a charitable trust.

(4) "Fiduciary or managerial agent" means an individual, corporation, or other entity acting either as a trustee, a member of the board of directors, an officer, an executor, or an administrator for a charitable trust.

History of Prop. Code §123.001: Acts 1987, 70th Leg., ch. 147, §4, eff. Sept. 1, 1987. Amended by Acts 1995, 74th Leg., ch. 172, §2, eff. Sept. 1, 1995. Source: TRCS art. 4412a, §1.

PROP §123.002. ATTORNEY GENERAL'S PARTICIPATION

For and on behalf of the interest of the general public of this state in charitable trusts, the attorney general is a proper party and may intervene in a proceeding involving a charitable trust. The attorney general may join and enter into a compromise, settlement agreement, contract, or judgment relating to a proceeding involving a charitable trust.

History of Prop. Code §123.002: Acts 1987, 70th Leg., ch. 147, §4, eff. Sept. 1, 1987. Source: TRCS art. 4412a, §§1, 5.

A PROP §123.003. NOTICE

(a) Any party initiating a proceeding involving a charitable trust shall give notice of the proceeding to the attorney general by sending to the attorney general, by registered or certified mail, a true copy of the petition or other instrument initiating the proceeding involving a charitable trust within 30 days of the filing of such petition or other instrument, but no less than 25 days prior to a hearing in such a proceeding. This subsection does not apply to a proceeding that is initiated by an application that exclusively seeks the admission of a will to probate, regardless of whether the application seeks the appointment of a personal representative, if the application:

(1) is uncontested; and

(2) is not subject to Subchapter C, Chapter 256, Estates [~~Section 83, Texas Probate~~] Code.

(b) Notice shall be given to the attorney general of any pleading which adds new causes of action or additional parties to a proceeding involving a charitable trust in which the attorney general has previously waived participation or in which the attorney general has otherwise failed to intervene. Notice shall be given by sending to the attorney general by registered or certified mail a true copy of the pleading within 30 days of

the filing of the pleading, but no less than 25 days prior to a hearing in the proceeding.

(c) The party or the party's attorney shall execute and file in the proceeding an affidavit stating the facts of the notice and shall attach to the affidavit the customary postal receipts signed by the attorney general or an assistant attorney general.

History of Prop. Code §123.003: Acts 1987, 70th Leg., ch. 147, §4, eff. Sept. 1, 1987. Amended by Acts 1995, 74th Leg., ch. 172, §3, eff. Sept. 1, 1995; Acts 2005, 79th Leg., ch. 1017, §1, eff. Sept. 1, 2005; Acts 2007, 80th Leg., ch. 451, §15, eff. Sept. 1, 2007; S.B. 1488, §22.061, 85th Leg., eff. Sept. 1, 2017. Source: TRCS art. 4412a, §3.

PROP §123.004. VOIDABLE JUDGMENT OR AGREEMENT

(a) A judgment in a proceeding involving a charitable trust is voidable if the attorney general is not given notice of the proceeding as required by this chapter. On motion of the attorney general after the judgment is rendered, the judgment shall be set aside.

(b) A compromise, settlement agreement, contract, or judgment relating to a proceeding involving a charitable trust is voidable on motion of the attorney general if the attorney general is not given notice as required by this chapter unless the attorney general has:

(1) declined in writing to be a party to the proceeding; or

(2) approved and joined in the compromise, settlement agreement, contract, or judgment.

History of Prop. Code §123.004: Acts 1987, 70th Leg., ch. 147, §4, eff. Sept. 1, 1987. Source: TRCS art. 4412a, §4.

A PROP §123.005. BREACH OF FIDUCIARY DUTY: VENUE; JURISDICTION

(a) Venue in a proceeding brought by the attorney general alleging breach of a fiduciary duty by a charitable entity or a fiduciary or managerial agent of a charitable trust shall be a court of competent jurisdiction in Travis County or in the county where the defendant resides or has its principal office. To the extent of a conflict between this subsection and any provision of the Estates [~~Texas Probate~~] Code providing for venue of a proceeding brought with respect to a charitable trust created by a will that has been admitted to probate, this subsection controls.

(b) A statutory probate court of Travis County has concurrent jurisdiction with any other court on which jurisdiction is conferred by Section 32.001, Estates [~~4A, Texas Probate~~] Code, in a proceeding brought by the attorney general alleging breach of a fiduciary duty with respect to a charitable trust created by a will that has been admitted to probate.

History of Prop. Code §123.005: Acts 1987, 70th Leg., ch. 147, §4, eff. Sept. 1, 1987. Amended by Acts 1995, 74th Leg., ch. 172, §4, eff. Sept. 1, 1995; Acts 2009, 81st Leg., ch. 133, §1 (eff. Sept. 1, 2009), ch. 1351, §12(g) (eff. Sept. 1, 2009); Acts 2011, 82nd Leg., ch. 91, §21.003 (eff. Sept. 1, 2011), ch. 401, §1 (eff. June 17, 2011); S.B. 1488, §22.062, 85th Leg., eff. Sept. 1, 2017. Source: TRCS art. 4412a, §7.

PROP §123.006. ATTORNEY'S FEES

(a) In a proceeding subject to Section 123.005, the attorney general, if successful in the proceeding, is entitled to recover from the charitable entity or fiduciary or managerial agent of the charitable trust actual costs incurred in bringing the suit and may recover reasonable attorney's fees.

(b) In a proceeding in which the attorney general intervenes under this chapter, other than a proceeding subject to Section 123.005, a court may award the attorney general court costs and reasonable and necessary attorney's fees as may seem equitable and just.

History of Prop. Code §123.006: Acts 2009, 81st Leg., ch. 133, §2, eff. Sept. 1, 2009.

CHAPTER 124. PARTITION OF MINERAL INTERESTS OF CHARITABLE TRUST

PROP §124.001. DEFINITIONS

In this chapter:

(1) "Charitable entity" means a corporation, trust, community chest, fund, foundation, or other entity organized for scientific, educational, philanthropic, or environmental purposes, social welfare, the arts and humanities, or another civic or public purpose described by Section 501(c)(3), Internal Revenue Code of 1986.

(2) "Charitable trust" means a charitable entity, a trust the stated purpose of which is to benefit a charitable entity, or an inter vivos or testamentary gift to a charitable entity.

(3) "Mineral interest" means an interest in oil, gas, or other mineral substance in place or that otherwise constitutes real property without regard to the depth at which such mineral substance is found.

History of Prop. Code §124.001: Acts 2013, 83rd Leg., ch. 480, §1, eff. June 14, 2013.

PROP §124.002. COMPULSORY DIVESTMENT PROHIBITED

In a suit or other judicial proceeding the object or effect of which is to compel the partition of a mineral interest owned or claimed by a charitable trust, a sale or other action that would divest the charitable trust of the trust's ownership of a mineral interest may not be ordered unless the trust has refused to execute a mineral lease, the terms of which are fair and reasonable, to the plaintiff or petitioner in the proceeding.

History of Prop. Code §124.002: Acts 2013, 83rd Leg., ch. 480, §1, eff. June 14, 2013.

Chapters 125-140 reserved for expansion

TITLE 10. MISCELLANEOUS BENEFICIAL PROPERTY INTERESTS

SUBTITLE A. PERSONS UNDER DISABILITY

CHAPTER 141. TRANSFERS TO MINORS

PROP §141.001. SHORT TITLE

This chapter may be cited as the Texas Uniform Transfers to Minors Act.

History of Prop. Code §141.001: Acts 1983, 68th Leg., ch. 576, §1, eff. Jan. 1, 1984. Amended by Acts 1995, 74th Leg., ch. 1043, §1, eff. Sept. 1, 1995. Renumbered from Prop. Code ch. 141, §1 by Acts 1997, 75th Leg., ch. 165, §31.01(72), eff. Sept. 1, 1997. Source: TRCS art. 5923-101, §10.

PROP §141.002. DEFINITIONS

In this chapter:

(1) "Adult" means an individual who is at least 21 years of age.

(2) "Benefit plan" means a retirement plan, including an interest described by Sections 111.004(19)-(23).

(3) "Broker" means a person lawfully engaged in the business of effecting transactions in securities or commodities for the person's own account or for the account of another.

(4) "Court" means a court with original probate jurisdiction.

(5) "Custodial property" means:

(A) any interest in property transferred to a custodian under this chapter; and

(B) the income from and proceeds of that interest in property.

(6) "Custodian" means a person designated as a custodian under Section 141.010 or a successor or substitute custodian designated under Section 141.019.

(7) "Financial institution" means a bank, trust company, savings institution, or credit union chartered and supervised under state or federal law.

(8) "Guardian" means a person appointed or qualified by a court to act as general, limited, or temporary guardian of a minor's property or a person legally authorized to perform substantially the same functions.

(9) "Legal representative" means an executor, independent executor, administrator or independent administrator of a decedent's estate, an obligor under a benefit plan or other governing instrument, a successor legal representative, or a person legally authorized to perform substantially the same functions.

(10) "Member of the minor's family" means the minor's parent, stepparent, spouse, grandparent, brother, sister, uncle, or aunt, whether of whole or half blood or by adoption.

(11) "Minor" means an individual who is younger than 21 years of age.

(12) "Transfer" means a transaction that creates custodial property under Section 141.010.

(12-a) "Qualified minor's trust" means a trust to which a gift is considered a present interest under Section 2503(c), Internal Revenue Code of 1986.

(13) "Transferor" means a person who makes a transfer under this chapter.

(14) "Trust company" means a financial institution, corporation, or other legal entity authorized to exercise general trust powers.

History of Prop. Code §141.002: Acts 1983, 68th Leg., ch. 576, §1, eff. Jan. 1, 1984. Amended by Acts 1995, 74th Leg., ch. 1043, §1, eff. Sept. 1, 1995. Renumbered from Prop. Code ch. 141, §2 by Acts 1997, 75th Leg., ch. 165, §31.01(72), eff. Sept. 1, 1997. Amended by Acts 2007, 80th Leg., ch. 451, §16, eff. Sept. 1, 2007. Source: TRCS art. 5923-101, §1.

PROP §141.003. SCOPE & JURISDICTION

(a) This chapter applies to a transfer that refers to the Texas Uniform Transfers to Minors Act in the designation under Section 141.010(a) by which the transfer is made if at the time of the transfer, the transferor, the minor, or the custodian is a resident of this state or the custodial property is located in this state. The custodianship created under Section 141.010 remains subject to this chapter despite a subsequent change in residence of a transferor, the minor, or the custodian or the removal of custodial property from this state.

(b) A person designated as custodian under this chapter is subject to personal jurisdiction in this state with respect to any matter relating to the custodianship.

(c) A transfer that purports to be made and that is valid under the Uniform Transfers to Minors Act, the Uniform Gifts to Minors Act, or a substantially similar act of another state is governed by the law of the designated state and may be executed and is enforceable in this state if at the time of the transfer, the transferor, the minor, or the custodian is a resident of the designated state or the custodial property is located in the designated state.

History of Prop. Code §141.003: Acts 1995, 74th Leg., ch. 1043, §1, eff. Sept. 1, 1995. Renumbered from Prop. Code ch. 141, §3 by Acts 1997, 75th Leg., ch. 165, §31.01(72), eff. Sept. 1, 1997.

PROP §141.004. NOMINATION OF CUSTODIAN

(a) A person having the right to designate the recipient of property transferable on the occurrence of a future event may revocably nominate a custodian to receive the property for a minor beneficiary on the occurrence of that event by naming the custodian followed in substance by the words: "as custodian for (name of minor) under the Texas Uniform Transfers to Minors Act." The nomination may name one or more persons as substitute custodians to whom the property must be transferred, in the order named, if the first nominated custodian dies before the transfer or is unable, declines, or is ineligible to serve. The nomination may be made in a will, a trust, a deed, an instrument exercising a power of appointment, or in a writing designating a beneficiary of contractual rights, including the right to receive payments from a benefit plan, that is registered with or delivered to the payor, issuer, or other obligor of the contractual rights.

(b) A custodian nominated under this section must be a person to whom a transfer of property of that kind may be made under Section 141.010(a).

(c) The nomination of a custodian under this section does not create custodial property until the nominating instrument becomes irrevocable or a transfer to the nominated custodian is completed under Section 141.010. Unless the nomination of a custodian has been revoked, the custodianship becomes effective on the occurrence of the future event, and the custodian shall enforce a transfer of the custodial property under Section 141.010.

History of Prop. Code §141.004: Acts 1995, 74th Leg., ch. 1043, §1, eff. Sept. 1, 1995. Renumbered from Prop. Code ch. 141, §4 by Acts 1997, 75th Leg., ch. 165, §31.01(72), eff. Sept. 1, 1997. Amended by Acts 2007, 80th Leg., ch. 451, §17, eff. Sept. 1, 2007.

PROP §141.005. TRANSFER BY GIFT OR EXERCISE OF POWER OF APPOINTMENT

A person may make a transfer by irrevocable gift to, or the irrevocable exercise of a power of appointment in favor of, a custodian for the benefit of a minor under Section 141.010.

History of Prop. Code §141.005: Acts 1995, 74th Leg., ch. 1043, §1, eff. Sept. 1, 1995. Renumbered from Prop. Code ch. 141, §5 by Acts 1997, 75th Leg., ch. 165, §31.01(72), eff. Sept. 1, 1997.

PROP §141.006. TRANSFER AUTHORIZED BY WILL OR TRUST

(a) A legal representative or trustee may make an irrevocable transfer under Section 141.010 to a custodian for a minor's benefit as authorized in the governing will or trust.

(b) If the testator or settlor has nominated a custodian under Section 141.004 to receive the custodial property, the transfer must be made to that person.

(c) If the testator or settlor has not nominated a custodian under Section 141.004, or all persons nominated as custodian die before the transfer or are unable, decline, or are ineligible to serve, the legal representative or the trustee shall designate the custodian from among those persons eligible to serve as custodian for property of that kind under Section 141.010(a).

History of Prop. Code §141.006: Acts 1995, 74th Leg., ch. 1043, §1, eff. Sept. 1, 1995. Renumbered from Prop. Code ch. 141, §6 by Acts 1997, 75th Leg., ch. 165, §31.01(72), eff. Sept. 1, 1997.

PROP §141.007. OTHER TRANSFER BY FIDUCIARY

(a) Subject to Subsections (b) and (c), a guardian, legal representative, or trustee may make an irrevocable transfer to another adult or trust company as custodian for a minor's benefit under Section 141.010 in the absence of a will or under a will or trust that does not contain an authorization to do so.

(b) With the approval of the court supervising the guardianship, a guardian may make an irrevocable transfer to another adult or trust company as custodian for the minor's benefit under Section 141.010.

(c) A transfer under Subsection (a) or (b) may be made only if:

(1) the legal representative or trustee considers the transfer to be in the best interest of the minor;

(2) the transfer is not prohibited by or inconsistent with provisions of the applicable will, trust agreement, or other governing instrument; and

(3) the transfer is authorized by the court if it exceeds $25,000 in value.

History of Prop. Code §141.007: Acts 1983, 68th Leg., ch. 576, §1, eff. Jan. 1, 1984. Renumbered from §141.003 by Acts 1995, 74th Leg., ch. 1043, §1, eff. Sept. 1, 1995. Renumbered from Prop. Code ch. 141, §7 by Acts 1997, 75th Leg., ch. 165, §31.01(72), eff. Sept. 1, 1997. Amended by Acts 2015, 84th Leg., ch. 622, §1, eff. Sept. 1, 2015. Source: TRCS art. 5923-101, §2.

PROP §141.008. TRANSFER BY OBLIGOR

(a) Subject to Subsections (b) and (c), a person who is not subject to Section 141.006 or 141.007 and who holds property, including a benefit plan of a minor who does not have a guardian, or who owes a liquidated debt to a minor who does not have a guardian may make an irrevocable transfer to a custodian for the benefit of the minor under Section 141.010.

(b) If a person who has the right to nominate a custodian under Section 141.004 has nominated a custodian under that section to receive the custodial property, the transfer must be made to that person.

(c) If a custodian has not been nominated under Section 141.004, or all persons nominated as custodian die before the transfer or are unable, decline, or are ineligible to serve, a transfer under this section may be made to an adult member of the minor's family or to a trust company unless the property exceeds $25,000 in value.

History of Prop. Code §141.008: Acts 1983, 68th Leg., ch. 576, §1, eff. Jan. 1, 1984. Renumbered from §141.003 by Acts 1995, 74th Leg., ch. 1043, §1, eff. Sept. 1, 1995. Renumbered from Prop. Code ch. 141, §8 by Acts 1997, 75th Leg., ch. 165, §31.01(72), eff. Sept. 1, 1997. Amended by Acts 2007, 80th Leg., ch. 451, §18, eff. Sept. 1, 2007; Acts 2015, 84th Leg., ch. 622, §2, eff. Sept. 1, 2015. Source: TRCS art. 5923-101, §2.

PROP §141.009. RECEIPT FOR CUSTODIAL PROPERTY

A written acknowledgment of delivery by a custodian constitutes a sufficient receipt and discharge for custodial property transferred to the custodian under this chapter.

History of Prop. Code §141.009: Acts 1983, 68th Leg., ch. 576, §1, eff. Jan. 1, 1984. Renumbered from §141.003 by Acts 1995, 74th Leg., ch. 1043, §1, eff. Sept. 1, 1995. Renumbered from Prop. Code ch. 141, §9 by Acts 1997, 75th Leg., ch. 165, §31.01(72), eff. Sept. 1, 1997. Source: TRCS art. 5923-101, §2.

PROP §141.010. MANNER OF CREATING CUSTODIAL PROPERTY & EFFECTING TRANSFER; DESIGNATION OF INITIAL CUSTODIAN; CONTROL

(a) Custodial property is created and a transfer is made when:

(1) an uncertificated security or a certificated security in registered form is:

(A) registered in the name of the transferor, an adult other than the transferor, or a trust company, followed in substance by the words: "as custodian for (name of minor) under the Texas Uniform Transfers to Minors Act"; or

(B) delivered if in certificated form, or any document necessary for the transfer of an uncertificated security is delivered, with any necessary endorsement to an adult other than the transferor or to a trust company as custodian, accompanied by an instrument in substantially the form set forth in Subsection (b);

(2) money is paid or delivered, or a security held in the name of a broker, financial institution, or its nominee is transferred, to a broker or financial institution for credit to an account in the name of the transferor, an adult other than the transferor, or a trust company, followed in substance by the words: "as custodian for (name of minor) under the Texas Uniform Transfers to Minors Act";

(3) the ownership of a life or endowment insurance policy or annuity contract is:

(A) registered with the issuer in the name of the transferor, an adult other than the transferor, or a trust company, followed in substance by the words: "as custodian for (name of minor) under the Texas Uniform Transfers to Minors Act"; or

(B) assigned in a writing delivered to an adult other than the transferor or to a trust company whose name in the assignment is followed in substance by the words: "as custodian for (name of minor) under the Texas Uniform Transfers to Minors Act";

(4) an irrevocable exercise of a power of appointment or an irrevocable present right to future payment under a contract is the subject of a written notification delivered to the payor, issuer, or other obligor that the right is transferred to the transferor, an adult other than the transferor, or a trust company, whose name in the notification is followed in substance by the words: "as custodian for (name of minor) under the Texas Uniform Transfers to Minors Act";

(5) an interest in real property is conveyed by instrument recorded in the real property records in the county in which the real property is located to the transferor, an adult other than the transferor, or a trust company, followed in substance by the words: "as custodian for (name of minor) under the Texas Uniform Transfers to Minors Act";

(6) a certificate of title issued by a department or agency of a state or of the United States that evidences title to tangible personal property is:

(A) issued in the name of the transferor, an adult other than the transferor, or a trust company, followed in substance by the words: "as custodian for (name of minor) under the Texas Uniform Transfers to Minors Act"; or

(B) delivered to an adult other than the transferor or to a trust company, endorsed to that person followed in substance by the words: "as a custodian for (name of minor) under the Texas Uniform Transfers to Minors Act"; or

(7) an interest in any property not described in Subdivisions (1)-(6) is transferred to an adult other than the transferor or to a trust company by a written instrument in substantially the form set forth in Subsection (b).

(b) An instrument in the following form satisfies the requirements of Subsections (a)(1)(B) and (7):

TRANSFER UNDER THE TEXAS UNIFORM TRANSFERS TO MINORS ACT

I, ____________ (name of transferor or name and representative capacity if a fiduciary) hereby transfer to ____________ (name of custodian), as custodian for ____________ (name of minor) under the Texas Uniform Transfers to Minors Act, the following: (insert a description of the custodial property sufficient to identify it).

Dated: ____________

____________ (Signature)

____________ (name of custodian) acknowledges receipt of the property described above as custodian for the minor named above under the Texas Uniform Transfers to Minors Act.

Dated: ____________

____________ (Signature of Custodian)

(c) A transferor shall place the custodian in control of the custodial property as soon as practicable.

History of Prop. Code §141.010: Acts 1983, 68th Leg., ch. 576, §1, eff. Jan. 1, 1984. Renumbered from §141.004 by Acts 1995, 74th Leg., ch. 1043, §1, eff. Sept. 1, 1995. Renumbered from Prop. Code ch. 141, §10 by Acts 1997, 75th Leg., ch. 165, §31.01(72), eff. Sept. 1, 1997. Source: TRCS art. 5923-101, §2(a).

PROP §141.011. SINGLE CUSTODIANSHIP

A transfer may be made only for one minor, and only one person may be the custodian. All custodial property held under this chapter by the same custodian for the benefit of the same minor constitutes a single custodianship.

History of Prop. Code §141.011: Acts 1983, 68th Leg., ch. 576, §1, eff. Jan. 1, 1984. Renumbered from §141.003 by Acts 1995, 74th Leg., ch. 1043, §1, eff. Sept. 1, 1995. Renumbered from Prop. Code ch. 141, §11 by Acts 1997, 75th Leg., ch. 165, §31.01(72), eff. Sept. 1, 1997. Source: TRCS art. 5923-101, §2.

PROP §141.012. VALIDITY & EFFECT OF TRANSFER

(a) The validity of a transfer made in a manner prescribed by this chapter is not affected by the:

(1) transferor's failure to comply with Section 141.010(c) concerning possession and control;

(2) designation of an ineligible custodian, except designation of the transferor in the case of property for which the transferor is ineligible to serve as custodian under Section 141.010(a); or

(3) death or incapacity of a person nominated under Section 141.004 or designated under Section 141.010 as custodian or the disclaimer of the office by that person.

(b) A transfer made under Section 141.010 is irrevocable, and the custodial property is indefeasibly vested in the minor. The custodian has all the rights, powers, duties, and authority provided in this chapter, and the minor or the minor's legal representative does not have any right, power, duty, or authority with respect to the custodial property except as provided by this chapter.

(c) By making a transfer, the transferor incorporates all the provisions of this chapter in the disposition and grants to the custodian, or to any third person dealing with a person designated as custodian, the respective powers, rights and immunities provided by this chapter.

History of Prop. Code §141.012: Acts 1983, 68th Leg., ch. 576, §1, eff. Jan. 1, 1984. Renumbered from §§141.003, 141.005 by Acts 1995, 74th Leg., ch. 1043, §1, eff. Sept. 1, 1995. Renumbered from Prop. Code ch. 141, §12 by Acts 1997, 75th Leg., ch. 165, §31.01(72), eff. Sept. 1, 1997. Source: TRCS art. 5923-101, §§2, 3.

PROP §141.013. CARE OF CUSTODIAL PROPERTY

(a) A custodian shall:

(1) take control of custodial property;

(2) register or record title to custodial property if appropriate; and

(3) collect, hold, manage, sell, convey, invest, and reinvest custodial property.

(b) In dealing with custodial property, a custodian shall observe the standard of care that would be observed by a prudent person dealing with property of another and is not limited by any other statute restricting investments by fiduciaries. If a custodian has a special skill or expertise, the custodian shall use that skill or expertise. However, a custodian, in the custodian's discretion and without liability to the minor or the minor's estate, may retain any custodial property received from a transferor.

(c) A custodian may invest in or pay premiums on life insurance or endowment policies on the life of:

(1) the minor only if the minor or the minor's estate is the sole beneficiary; or

(2) another person in whom the minor has an insurable interest only to the extent that the minor, the minor's estate, or the custodian in the capacity of the custodian is the irrevocable beneficiary.

(d) A custodian at all times shall keep custodial property separate and distinct from all other property in a manner sufficient to identify it clearly as custodial property of the minor. Custodial property consisting of an undivided interest is so identified if the minor's interest is held as a tenant in common and is fixed. Custodial property subject to recordation is so identified if it is recorded, and custodial property subject to registration is so identified if it is registered, or held in an account designated, in the name of the custodian followed in substance by the words: "as custodian for (name of minor) under the Texas Uniform Transfers to Minors Act."

(e) A custodian shall keep records of all transactions with respect to custodial property, including information necessary for the preparation of the minor's tax returns, and shall make the records available for inspection at reasonable intervals by a parent or legal representative of the minor or by the minor if the minor is at least 14 years of age.

History of Prop. Code §141.013: Acts 1983, 68th Leg., ch. 576, §1, eff. Jan. 1, 1984. Renumbered from §141.006 by Acts 1995, 74th Leg., ch. 1043, §1, eff. Sept. 1, 1995. Renumbered from Prop. Code ch. 141, §13 by Acts 1997, 75th Leg., ch. 165, §31.01(72), eff. Sept. 1, 1997. Source: TRCS art. 5923-101, §3.

PROP §141.014. POWERS OF CUSTODIAN

(a) A custodian, acting in a custodial capacity, has all the rights, powers, and authority over custodial property that unmarried adult owners have over their own property, but a custodian may exercise those rights, powers, and authority in that capacity only.

(b) This section does not relieve a custodian from liability for breach of Section 141.013.

History of Prop. Code §141.014: Acts 1983, 68th Leg., ch. 576, §1, eff. Jan. 1, 1984. Renumbered from §141.006 by Acts 1995, 74th Leg., ch. 1043, §1, eff. Sept. 1, 1995. Renumbered from Prop. Code ch. 141, §14 by Acts 1997, 75th Leg., ch. 165, §31.01(72), eff. Sept. 1, 1997. Source: TRCS art. 5923-101, §3.

PROP §141.015. USE OF CUSTODIAL PROPERTY

(a) A custodian may deliver or pay to the minor or expend for the minor's benefit as much of the custodial property as the custodian considers advisable for the use and benefit of the minor, without court order and without regard to:

(1) the duty or ability of the custodian personally or of any other person to support the minor; or

(2) any other income or property of the minor that may be applicable or available for that purpose.

(b) On petition of an interested person or the minor if the minor is at least 14 years of age, the court may order the custodian to deliver or pay to the minor or expend for the minor's benefit as much of the custodial property as the court considers advisable for the use and benefit of the minor.

(b-1) A custodian may, without a court order, transfer all or part of the custodial property to a qualified minor's trust. A transfer of property under this subsection terminates the custodianship to the extent of the property transferred.

(c) A delivery, payment, or expenditure under this section is in addition to, not in substitution for, and does not affect any obligation of a person to support the minor.

History of Prop. Code §141.015: Acts 1983, 68th Leg., ch. 576, §1, eff. Jan. 1, 1984. Renumbered from §§141.006, 141.011 by Acts 1995, 74th Leg., ch. 1043, §1, eff. Sept. 1, 1995. Renumbered from Prop. Code ch. 141, §15 by Acts 1997, 75th Leg., ch. 165, §31.01(72), eff. Sept. 1, 1997. Amended by Acts 2007, 80th Leg., ch. 451, §19, eff. Sept. 1, 2007. Source: TRCS art. 5923-101, §4(a)-(i).

PROP §141.016. CUSTODIAN'S EXPENSES, COMPENSATION, & BOND

(a) A custodian is entitled to reimbursement from custodial property for reasonable expenses incurred in the performance of the custodian's duties.

(b) Except for one who is a transferor under Section 141.005, a custodian has a noncumulative election during each calendar year to charge reasonable compensation for services performed by the custodian during that year.

(c) Except as provided by Section 141.019(f), a custodian is not required to give a bond.

History of Prop. Code §141.016: Acts 1983, 68th Leg., ch. 576, §1, eff. Jan. 1, 1984. Renumbered from §141.007 by Acts 1995, 74th Leg., ch. 1043, §1, eff. Sept. 1, 1995. Renumbered from Prop. Code ch. 141, §16 by Acts 1997, 75th Leg., ch. 165, §31.01(72), eff. Sept. 1, 1997. Source: TRCS art. 5923-101, §5.

PROP §141.017. EXEMPTION OF THIRD PERSON FROM LIABILITY

A third person, in good faith and without court order, may act on the instructions of or otherwise deal with any person purporting to make a transfer or act in the capacity of a custodian and, in the absence of knowledge, is not responsible for determining the:

(1) validity of the purported custodian's designation;

(2) propriety of, or the authority under this chapter for, any act of the purported custodian;

(3) validity or propriety under this chapter of any instrument or instructions executed or given by the person purporting to make a transfer or by the purported custodian; or

(4) propriety of the application of the minor's property delivered to the purported custodian.

History of Prop. Code §141.017: Acts 1983, 68th Leg., ch. 576, §1, eff. Jan. 1, 1984. Renumbered from §141.008 by Acts 1995, 74th Leg., ch. 1043, §1, eff. Sept. 1, 1995. Renumbered from Prop. Code ch. 141, §17 by Acts 1997, 75th Leg., ch. 165, §31.01(72), eff. Sept. 1, 1997. Source: TRCS art. 5923-101, §6.

PROP §141.018. LIABILITY TO THIRD PERSON

(a) A claim based on a contract entered into by a custodian acting in a custodial capacity, an obligation arising from the ownership or control of custodial property, or a tort committed during the custodianship may be asserted against the custodial property by proceeding against the custodian in the custodian's custodial capacity, whether or not the custodian or the minor is personally liable for the claim.

(b) A custodian is not personally liable:

(1) on a contract properly entered into in the custodian's custodial capacity unless the custodian fails to reveal that capacity and to identify the custodianship in the contract; or

(2) for an obligation arising from control of custodial property or for a tort committed during the custodianship unless the custodian is personally at fault.

(c) A minor is not personally liable for an obligation arising from ownership of custodial property or for a tort committed during the custodianship unless the minor is personally at fault.

History of Prop. Code §141.018: Acts 1995, 74th Leg., ch. 1043, §1, eff. Sept. 1, 1995. Renumbered from Prop. Code ch. 141, §18 by Acts 1997, 75th Leg., ch. 165, §31.01(72), eff. Sept. 1, 1997.

PROP §141.019. RENUNCIATION, RESIGNATION, DEATH, OR REMOVAL OF CUSTODIAN; DESIGNATION OF SUCCESSOR CUSTODIAN

(a) A person nominated to serve as a custodian under Section 141.004 or designated to serve as a custodian under Section 141.010 may decline to serve as custodian by delivering written notice to the person who made the nomination or to the transferor's legal representative. If the event giving rise to a transfer has not occurred and no substitute custodian who is able, willing, and eligible to serve was nominated under Section 141.004, the person who made the nomination may nominate a substitute custodian under Section 141.004; otherwise the transferor or the transferor's legal representative shall designate a substitute custodian at the time of the transfer, in either case from among the persons eligible to serve as custodian for that kind of property under Section 141.010(a). A substitute custodian designated under this section has the rights of a successor custodian.

(b) A custodian at any time may designate as successor custodian a trust company or an adult other than a transferor under Section 141.005 by executing and dating an instrument of designation before a subscribing witness other than the successor. If the instrument of designation does not contain or is not accompanied by the custodian's resignation, the designation of the successor does not take effect until the custodian resigns, dies, becomes incapacitated, or is removed.

(c) A custodian may resign at any time by delivering:

(1) written notice to the successor custodian and to the minor if the minor is at least 14 years of age; and

(2) the custodial property to the successor custodian.

(d) If a custodian is ineligible, dies, or becomes incapacitated without having effectively designated a successor and the minor is at least 14 years of age, the minor may designate as successor custodian an adult member of the minor's family, a guardian of the minor, or a trust company in the manner prescribed by Subsection (b). If the minor is younger than 14 years of age or fails to act within 60 days after the ineligibility, death, or incapacity of the custodian, the minor's guardian becomes successor custodian. If the minor has no guardian or the minor's guardian declines to act, the transferor, the legal representative of the transferor or of the custodian, an adult member of the minor's family, or any other interested person may petition the court to designate a successor custodian.

(e) As soon as practicable, a custodian who declines to serve under Subsection (a) or resigns under Subsection (c), or the legal representative of a deceased or incapacitated custodian, shall put the custodial property and records in the possession and control of the successor custodian. The successor custodian by action may enforce the obligation to deliver custodial property and records and becomes responsible for each item as received.

(f) A transferor, the legal representative of a transferor, an adult member of the minor's family, a guardian of the person of the minor, the guardian of the minor, or the minor if the minor is at least 14 years of age may petition the court to:

(1) remove the custodian for cause and designate a successor custodian other than a transferor under Section 141.005; or

(2) require the custodian to give appropriate bond.

History of Prop. Code §141.019: Acts 1983, 68th Leg., ch. 576, §1, eff. Jan. 1, 1984. Renumbered from §§141.009, 141.010 by Acts 1995, 74th Leg., ch. 1043, §1, eff. Sept. 1, 1995. Renumbered from Prop. Code ch. 141, §19 by Acts 1997, 75th Leg., ch. 165, §31.01(72), eff. Sept. 1, 1997. Source: TRCS art. 5923-101, §7(a)-(f).

PROP §141.020. ACCOUNTING BY & DETERMINATION OF LIABILITY

(a) A minor who is at least 14 years of age, the minor's guardian of the person or legal representative, an adult member of the minor's family, a transferor, or a transferor's legal representative may petition the court for:

(1) an accounting by the custodian or the custodian's legal representative; or

(2) a determination of responsibility, as between the custodial property and the custodian personally, for claims against the custodial property unless the responsibility has been adjudicated in an action under Section 141.018 to which the minor or the minor's legal representative was a party.

(b) A successor custodian may petition the court for an accounting by the predecessor custodian.

(c) The court, in a proceeding under this chapter or in any other proceeding, may require or permit the custodian or the custodian's legal representative to account.

(d) If a custodian is removed under Section 141.019(f), the court shall require an accounting and order delivery of the custodial property and records to the successor custodian and the execution of all instruments required for transfer of the custodial property.

History of Prop. Code §141.020: Acts 1983, 68th Leg., ch. 576, §1, eff. Jan. 1, 1984. Renumbered from §141.012 by Acts 1995, 74th Leg., ch. 1043, §1, eff. Sept. 1, 1995. Renumbered from Prop. Code ch. 141, §20 by Acts 1997, 75th Leg., ch. 165, §31.01(72), eff. Sept. 1, 1997. Source: TRCS art. 5923-101, §8.

PROP §141.021. TERMINATION OF CUSTODIANSHIP

The custodian shall transfer in an appropriate manner the custodial property to the minor or to the minor's estate on the earlier of the date:

(1) the minor attains 21 years of age, with respect to custodial property transferred under Section 141.005 or 141.006;

(2) the minor attains the age of majority under the laws of this state other than this chapter, with respect to custodial property transferred under Section 141.007 or 141.008; or

(3) the minor's death.

History of Prop. Code §141.021: Acts 1995, 74th Leg., ch. 1043, §1, eff. Sept. 1, 1995. Renumbered from Prop. Code ch. 141, §21 by Acts 1997, 75th Leg., ch. 165, §31.01(72), eff. Sept. 1, 1997.

PROP §141.022. APPLICABILITY

Except as provided by Section 141.025, this chapter applies to a transfer within the scope of Section 141.003 made after September 1, 1995, if:

(1) the transfer purports to have been made under the Texas Uniform Gifts to Minors Act; or

(2) the instrument by which the transfer purports to have been made uses in substance the designation "as custodian under the Uniform Gifts to Minors Act" or "as custodian under the Uniform Transfers to Minors Act" of any other state, and the application of this chapter is necessary to validate the transfer.

History of Prop. Code §141.022: Acts 1995, 74th Leg., ch. 1043, §1, eff. Sept. 1, 1995. Amended by Acts 1997, 75th Leg., ch. 221, §1, eff. Sept. 1, 1997. Renumbered from Prop. Code ch. 141, §22 by Acts 1997, 75th Leg., ch. 165, §31.01(72), eff. Sept. 1, 1997.

PROP §141.023. EFFECT ON EXISTING CUSTODIANSHIPS

(a) Any transfer of custodial property under this chapter made before September 1, 1995, is validated notwithstanding that there was no specific authority in this chapter for the coverage of custodial property of that kind or for a transfer from that source at the time the transfer was made.

(b) Sections 141.002 and 141.021, with respect to the age of a minor for whom custodial property is held under this chapter, do not apply to custodial property held in a custodianship that terminated because the minor attained the age of 18 after August 26, 1973, and before September 1, 1995.

History of Prop. Code §141.023: Acts 1983, 68th Leg., ch. 576, §1, eff. Jan. 1, 1984. Renumbered from §141.014 by Acts 1995, 74th Leg., ch. 1043, §1, eff. Sept. 1, 1995. Renumbered from Prop. Code ch. 141, §23 by Acts 1997, 75th Leg., ch. 165, §31.01(72), eff. Sept. 1, 1997. Source: TRCS art. 5923b, §2.

PROP §141.024. UNIFORMITY OF APPLICATION & CONSTRUCTION

This chapter shall be applied and construed to effect its general purpose, to make uniform the law with respect to the subject of this chapter among states enacting that law.

History of Prop. Code §141.024: Acts 1983, 68th Leg., ch. 576, §1, eff. Jan. 1, 1984. Renumbered from §141.013 by Acts 1995, 74th Leg., ch. 1043, §1, eff. Sept. 1, 1995. Renumbered from Prop. Code ch. 141, §24 by Acts 1997, 75th Leg., ch. 165, §31.01(72), eff. Sept. 1, 1997. Source: TRCS art. 5923-101, §9.

PROP §141.025. ADDITIONAL TRANSFERS TO CUSTODIANSHIPS IN EXISTENCE BEFORE EFFECTIVE DATE OF ACT

(a) This section applies only to a transfer within the scope of Section 141.003 made after September 1, 1995, to a custodian of a custodianship established before September 1, 1995, under the Texas Uniform Gifts to Minors Act.

(b) This chapter does not prevent a person from making additional transfers to a custodianship described by Subsection (a). On the direction of the transferor or custodian, custodial property that is transferred to the custodianship shall be commingled with the custodial property of the custodianship established under the Texas Uniform Gifts to Minors Act. The additional transfers to the custodianship shall be administered and distributed on termination of the custodianship, as prescribed by this chapter, except that for purposes of Section 141.021, the custodian shall transfer the custodial property to:

(1) the beneficiary on the date the beneficiary attains 18 years of age or an earlier date as prescribed by Section 141.021; or

(2) the beneficiary's estate if the individual dies before the date prescribed by Subdivision (1).

History of Prop. Code §141.025: Acts 1997, 75th Leg., ch. 221, §2, eff. Sept. 1, 1997. Amended by Acts 1997, 75th Leg., ch. 165, §31.01(72), eff. Sept. 1, 1997. Renumbered from Prop. Code ch. 141, §25 by Acts 1999, 76th Leg., ch. 62, §19.01(91), eff. Sept. 1, 1999.

CHAPTER 142. MANAGEMENT OF PROPERTY RECOVERED IN SUIT BY A NEXT FRIEND OR GUARDIAN AD LITEM

PROP §142.001. MANAGEMENT BY DECREE

(a) In a suit in which a minor or incapacitated person who has no legal guardian is represented by a next friend or an appointed guardian ad litem, the court, on application and hearing, may provide by decree for the investment of funds accruing to the minor or other person under the judgment in the suit.

(b) If the decree is made during vacation, it must be recorded in the minutes of the succeeding term of the court.

History of Prop. Code §142.001: Acts 1983, 68th Leg., ch. 576, §1, eff. Jan. 1, 1984. Amended by Acts 1984, 68th Leg., 2nd C.S., ch. 18, §14(b), eff. Oct. 2, 1984; Acts 1999, 76th Leg., ch. 195, §§1, 2, eff. Sept. 1, 1999.

PROP §142.002. MANAGEMENT BY BONDED MANAGER

(a) In a suit in which a minor or incapacitated person who has no legal guardian is represented by a next friend or an appointed guardian ad litem, the court in which a judgment is rendered may by an order entered of record authorize the next friend, the guardian ad litem, or another person to take possession of money or other personal property recovered under the judgment for the minor or other person represented.

(b) The next friend, guardian ad litem, or other person may not take possession of the property until the person has executed a bond as principal that:

(1) is in an amount at least double the value of the property or, if a surety on the bond is a solvent surety company authorized under the law of this state to execute the bond, is in an amount at least equal to the value of the property;

(2) is payable to the county judge; and

(3) is conditioned on the obligation of the next friend, guardian ad litem, or other person to use the property under the direction of the court for the benefit of its owner and to return the property, with interest or other increase, to the person entitled to receive the property when ordered by the court to do so.

History of Prop. Code §142.002: Acts 1983, 68th Leg., ch. 576, §1, eff. Jan. 1, 1984. Amended by Acts 1984, 68th Leg., 2nd C.S., ch. 18, §14(c), eff. Oct. 2, 1984; Acts 1999, 76th Leg., ch. 195, §3, eff. Sept. 1, 1999.

PROP §142.003. COMPENSATION & DUTIES OF MANAGERS

(a) A person who manages property under Section 142.001 or 142.002 is entitled to receive compensation as allowed by the court.

(b) The person shall make dispositions of the property as ordered by the court and shall return the property into court on the order of the court.

History of Prop. Code §142.003: Acts 1983, 68th Leg., ch. 576, §1, eff. Jan. 1, 1984.

A PROP §142.004. INVESTMENT OF FUNDS

(a) In a suit in which a minor or incapacitated person who has no legal guardian is represented by a next friend or an appointed guardian ad litem, any money recovered by the plaintiff, if not otherwise managed under this chapter, may be invested:

(1) by the next friend or guardian ad litem in:

(A) a higher education savings plan established under Subchapter G, Chapter 54, Education Code, [~~or~~] a prepaid tuition program established under Subchapter H, Chapter 54, Education Code, or an ABLE account established in accordance with the Texas Achieving a Better Life Experience (ABLE) Program under Subchapter J, Chapter 54, Education Code; or

(B) interest-bearing time deposits in a financial institution doing business in this state and insured by the Federal Deposit Insurance Corporation; or

(2) by the clerk of the court, on written order of the court of proper jurisdiction, in:

(A) a higher education savings plan established under Subchapter G, Chapter 54, Education Code, [~~or~~] a prepaid tuition program established under Subchapter H, Chapter 54, Education Code, or an ABLE account established in accordance with the Texas Achieving a Better Life Experience (ABLE) Program under Subchapter J, Chapter 54, Education Code;

(B) interest-bearing deposits in a financial institution doing business in this state and insured by the Federal Deposit Insurance Corporation;

(C) United States treasury bills;

(D) an eligible interlocal investment pool that meets the requirements of Sections 2256.016, 2256.017, and 2256.019, Government Code; or

(E) a no-load money market mutual fund, if the fund:

(i) is regulated by the Securities and Exchange Commission;

(ii) has a dollar weighted average stated maturity of 90 days or fewer; and

(iii) includes in its investment objectives the maintenance of a stable net asset value of $1 for each share.

(b) If the money invested under this section may not be withdrawn from the financial institution without an order of the court, a next friend or guardian ad litem who makes the investment is not required to execute a bond with respect to the money.

(c) When money invested under this section is withdrawn, the court may:

(1) on a finding that the person entitled to receive the money is no longer under the disability, order the funds turned over to the person; or

(2) order management of the funds under another provision of this chapter.

(d) Interest earned on an account invested by the clerk of the court shall be paid in the same manner as interest earned on an account under Chapter 117, Local Government Code.

(e) If money is invested under Subsection (a)(2)(E), the court may waive any bonding requirement.

History of Prop. Code §142.004: Acts 1983, 68th Leg., ch. 576, §1, eff. Jan. 1, 1984. Amended by Acts 1984, 68th Leg., 2nd C.S., ch. 18, §14(d), eff. Oct. 2, 1984; Acts 1997, 75th Leg., ch. 505, §22, eff. Sept. 1, 1997; Acts 1999, 76th Leg., ch. 94, §1 (eff. May 17, 1999), ch. 195, §4 (eff. Sept. 1, 1999); Acts 2001, 77th Leg., ch. 1420, §17.002, eff. Sept. 1, 2001; Acts 2015, 84th Leg., ch. 289, §1, eff. Sept. 1, 2015; S.B. 1764, §3, 85th Leg., eff. Sept. 1, 2017.

PROP §142.005. TRUST FOR PROPERTY

(a) Any court of record with jurisdiction to hear a suit involving a beneficiary may, on application and on a finding that the creation of a trust would be in the best interests of the beneficiary, enter a decree in the record directing the clerk to deliver any funds accruing to the beneficiary under the judgment to a financial institution, except as provided by Subsections (m) and (n).

(b) The decree shall provide for the creation of a trust for the management of the funds for the benefit of the beneficiary and for terms, conditions, and limitations of the trust, as determined by the court, that are not in conflict with the following mandatory provisions:

(1) The beneficiary shall be the sole beneficiary of the trust.

(2) The trustee may disburse amounts of the trust's principal, income, or both as the trustee in the trustee's sole discretion determines to be reasonably necessary for the health, education, support, or maintenance of the beneficiary. The trustee may conclusively presume that medicine or treatments approved by a licensed physician are appropriate for the health of the beneficiary.

(3) The income of the trust not disbursed under Subdivision (2) shall be added to the principal of the trust.

(4) If the beneficiary is a minor, the trust shall terminate on the death of the beneficiary, on the beneficiary's attaining an age stated in the trust, or on the 25th birthday of the beneficiary, whichever occurs first, or if the beneficiary is an incapacitated person, the trust shall terminate on the death of the beneficiary or when the beneficiary regains capacity.

(5) A trustee that is a financial institution shall serve without bond.

(6) The trustee shall receive reasonable compensation paid from trust's income, principal, or both on application to and approval of the court.

(7) The first page of the trust instrument shall contain the following notice:

NOTICE: THE BENEFICIARY AND CERTAIN PERSONS INTERESTED IN THE WELFARE OF THE BENEFICIARY MAY HAVE REMEDIES UNDER SECTION 114.008 OR 142.005, PROPERTY CODE.

(c) A trust established under this section may provide that:

(1) distributions of the trust principal before the termination of the trust may be made from time to time as the beneficiary attains designated ages and at designated percentages of the principal; and

(2) distributions, payments, uses, and applications of all trust funds may be made to the legal or natural guardian of the beneficiary or to the person having custody of the beneficiary or may be made directly to or expended for the benefit, support, or maintenance of the beneficiary without the intervention of any legal guardian or other legal representative of the beneficiary.

(d) A court that creates a trust under this section has continuing jurisdiction and supervisory power over the trust, including the power to construe, amend, revoke, modify, or terminate the trust. A trust created under this section is not subject to revocation by the beneficiary or a guardian of the beneficiary's estate. If the trust is revoked by the court before the beneficiary is 18 years old, the court may provide for the management of the trust principal and any undistributed income as authorized by this chapter. If the trust is revoked by the court after the beneficiary is 18 years old, the trust principal and any undistributed income shall be delivered to the beneficiary after the payment of all proper and necessary expenses.

(e) On the termination of the trust under its terms or on the death of the beneficiary, the trust principal and any undistributed income shall be paid to the beneficiary or to the representative of the estate of the deceased beneficiary.

(f) A trust established under this section prevails over any other law concerning minors, incapacitated persons, or their property, and the trust continues in force and effect until terminated or revoked, notwithstanding the appointment of a guardian of the estate of the minor or incapacitated person, or the attainment of the age of majority by the minor.

(g) Notwithstanding any other provision of this chapter, if the court finds that it would be in the best interests of the beneficiary for whom a trust is established under this section, the court may omit or modify any terms required by Subsection (b) if the court determines that the omission or modification is necessary or appropriate to allow the beneficiary to be eligible to receive public benefits or assistance under a state or federal program. This section does not require a distribution from a trust if the distribution is discretionary under the terms of the trust.

(h) A trust created under this section is subject to Subtitle B, Title 9.

(i) Notwithstanding Subsection (h), this section prevails over a provision in Subtitle B, Title 9, that is in conflict or inconsistent with this section.

(j) A provision in a trust created under this section that relieves a trustee from a duty, responsibility, or liability imposed by this section or Subtitle B, Title 9, is enforceable only if:

(1) the provision is limited to specific facts and circumstances unique to the property of that trust and is not applicable generally to the trust; and

(2) the court creating or modifying the trust makes a specific finding that there is clear and convincing evidence that the inclusion of the provision is in the best interests of the beneficiary of the trust.

(k) In addition to ordering other appropriate remedies and grounds, the court may appoint a guardian ad litem to investigate and report to the court whether the trustee should be removed for failing or refusing to make distributions for the health, education, support, or maintenance of the beneficiary required under the terms of the trust if the court is petitioned by:

(1) a parent of the beneficiary;

(2) a next friend of the beneficiary;

(3) a guardian of the beneficiary;

(4) a conservator of the beneficiary;

(5) a guardian ad litem for the beneficiary; or

(6) an attorney ad litem for the beneficiary.

(*l*) A person listed in Subsection (k) shall be reimbursed from the trust for reasonable attorney's fees, not to exceed $1,000, incurred in bringing the petition.

(m) If the value of the trust's principal is $50,000 or less, the court may appoint a person other than a financial institution to serve as trustee of the trust only if the court finds the appointment is in the beneficiary's best interests.

(n) If the value of the trust's principal is more than $50,000, the court may appoint a person other than a financial institution to serve as trustee of the trust only if the court finds that:

(1) no financial institution is willing to serve as trustee; and

(2) the appointment is in the beneficiary's best interests.

(o) In this section:

(1) "Beneficiary" means:

(A) a minor or incapacitated person who:

(i) has no legal guardian; and

(ii) is represented by a next friend or an appointed guardian ad litem; or

(B) a person with a physical disability.

(2) "Financial institution" means a financial institution, as defined by Section 201.101, Finance Code, that has trust powers, exists, and does business under the laws of this or another state or the United States.

History of Prop. Code §142.005: Acts 1983, 68th Leg., ch. 576, §1, eff. Jan. 1, 1984. Amended by Acts 1984, 68th Leg., 2nd C.S., ch. 18, §14(e), (f), eff. Oct. 2, 1984; Acts 1997, 75th Leg., ch. 128, §1, eff. Sept. 1, 1997; Acts 2003, 78th Leg., ch. 1154, §3, eff. Sept. 1, 2003; Acts 2005, 79th Leg., ch. 148, §28, eff. Jan. 1, 2006; Acts 2007, 80th Leg., ch. 451, §20, eff. Sept. 1, 2007.

PROP §142.006. CLAIMS AGAINST PROPERTY

If any person claims an interest in property subject to management under this chapter, the court having authority over the property may hear evidence on the interest and may order the claim or the portion of the claim found to be just to be paid to the person entitled to receive it.

History of Prop. Code §142.006: Acts 1983, 68th Leg., ch. 576, §1, eff. Jan. 1, 1984.

PROP §142.007. INCAPACITATED PERSON

For the purposes of this chapter, "incapacitated person" means a person who is impaired because of mental illness, mental deficiency, physical illness or disability, advanced age, chronic use of drugs, chronic intoxication, or any other cause except status as a minor to the extent that the person lacks sufficient understanding or capacity to make or communicate responsible decisions concerning his person.

History of Prop. Code §142.007: Acts 1984, 68th Leg., 2nd C.S., ch. 18, §14(g), eff. Oct. 2, 1984.

PROP §142.008. STRUCTURED SETTLEMENT

(a) In a suit in which a minor or incapacitated person who has no legal guardian is represented by a next friend or an appointed guardian ad litem, the court, on a motion from the parties, may provide for a structured settlement that:

(1) provides for periodic payments; and

(2) is funded by:

(A) an obligation guaranteed by the United States government; or

(B) an annuity contract that meets the requirements of Section 142.009.

(b) The person obligated to fund a structured settlement shall provide to the court:

(1) a copy of the instrument that provides funding for the structured settlement; or

(2) an affidavit from an independent financial consultant that specifies the present value of the structured settlement and the method by which the value is calculated.

(c) A structured settlement provided for under this section is solely for the benefit of the beneficiary of the structured settlement and is not subject to the interest payment calculations contained in Section 117.054, Local Government Code.

History of Prop. Code §142.008: Acts 1999, 76th Leg., ch. 195, §5, eff. Sept. 1, 1999.

PROP §142.009. ANNUITY CONTRACT REQUIREMENTS FOR STRUCTURED SETTLEMENT

(a) An insurance company providing an annuity contract for a structured settlement as provided by Section 142.008 must:

(1) be licensed to write annuity contracts in this state;

(2) have a minimum of $1 million of capital and surplus; and

(3) be approved by the court and comply with any requirements imposed by the court to ensure funding to satisfy periodic settlement payments.

(b) In approving an insurance company under Subsection (a)(3), the court may consider whether the company:

(1) holds an industry rating equivalent to at least two of the following rating organizations:

(A) A. M. Best Company: A++ or A+;

(B) Duff & Phelps Credit Rating Company Insurance Company Claims Paying Ability Rating: AA-, AA, AA+, or AAA;

(C) Moody's Investors Service Claims Paying Ability Rating: Aa3, Aa2, Aa1, or aaa; or

(D) Standard & Poor's Corporation Insurer Claims-Paying Ability Rating: AA-, AA, AA+, or AAA;

(2) is an affiliate, as that term is described by Section 823.003, Insurance Code, of a liability insurance carrier involved in the suit for which the structured settlement is created; or

(3) is connected in any way to a person obligated to fund the structured settlement.

History of Prop. Code §142.009: Acts 1999, 76th Leg., ch. 195, §5, eff. Sept. 1, 1999. Amended by Acts 2001, 77th Leg., ch. 96, §2, eff. Sept. 1, 2001; Acts 2003, 78th Leg., ch. 1276, §10A.551, eff. Sept. 1, 2003.

Chapters 143-160 reserved for expansion

SUBTITLE B. FIDUCIARIES

CHAPTER 161. MANAGEMENT & CONTROL OF SECURITIES

SUBCHAPTER A. GENERAL PROVISIONS

PROP §161.001. DEFINITIONS

In this chapter:

(1) "Fiduciary" means an executor, administrator, or trustee of an express trust, including a corporation or a natural person acting as fiduciary, and a successor or substitute, whether or not designated in a trust instrument.

(2) "Clearing corporation" has the meaning assigned by Section 8.102, Business & Commerce Code, as amended.

History of Prop. Code §161.001: Acts 1983, 68th Leg., ch. 576, §1, eff. Jan. 1, 1984. Source: TRCS arts. 7425a-2, §1; 7425a-3, §1.

PROP §161.002. DECREE OR GOVERNING INSTRUMENT CONTROLS

The authority granted in this chapter is subject to contrary or limiting provisions in the instrument or court order appointing the fiduciary of the securities or in a subsequent court order.

History of Prop. Code §161.002: Acts 1983, 68th Leg., ch. 576, §1, eff. Jan. 1, 1984. Source: TRCS arts. 7425a-2, §2(A); 7425a-3, §§2, 3(a).

Sections 161.003-161.020 reserved for expansion

SUBCHAPTER B. CUSTODIAN OF SECURITIES

PROP §161.021. AUTHORITY OF FIDUCIARY

A fiduciary who holds a security in a fiduciary capacity may:

(1) employ a bank incorporated in this state or a national bank located in this state as custodian of the security; and

(2) whether the fiduciary is an individual or a bank and if any individual who is a cofiduciary with the bank consents, authorize the security to be registered and held in the name of a nominee of the bank without disclosing the fiduciary relationship.

History of Prop. Code §161.021: Acts 1983, 68th Leg., ch. 576, §1, eff. Jan. 1, 1984. Source: TRCS art. 7425a-2, §2.

PROP §161.022. SEPARATE ASSETS

(a) A bank holding a security under this subchapter, whether in registered or bearer form, at all times shall keep the security separate from the bank's assets. The bank may:

(1) hold separately the certificates representing securities that periodically comprise the assets of a particular fiduciary account from those of all other accounts; or

(2) without certification as to ownership attached, hold in bulk certificates representing the same class of securities of the same issuer that periodically comprise the assets of different fiduciary accounts and, to the extent feasible, merge certificates of small denomination into one or more certificates of large denomination.

(b) A bank that holds security certificates in bulk is subject to the regulations issued by the Finance Commission of Texas if the bank is chartered by this state or by the comptroller of the currency if the bank is a national banking association.

History of Prop. Code §161.022: Acts 1983, 68th Leg., ch. 576, §1, eff. Jan. 1, 1984. Source: TRCS art. 7425a-2, §2.

PROP §161.023. EXPENSE OF CUSTODIANSHIP

Unless the fiduciary is a corporation, the cost of employing a bank as a custodian of securities under this subchapter is a charge against the estate or trust.

History of Prop. Code §161.023: Acts 1983, 68th Leg., ch. 576, §1, eff. Jan. 1, 1984. Source: TRCS art. 7425a-2, §2(A).

PROP §161.024. RECORDS

A bank holding a security under Section 161.021, whether in registered or bearer form, at all times shall keep records showing the ownership of the security.

History of Prop. Code §161.024: Acts 1983, 68th Leg., ch. 576, §1, eff. Jan. 1, 1984. Source: TRCS art. 7425a-2, §2.

PROP §161.025. REDELIVERY OF SECURITY HELD BY NOMINEE

(a) A bank holding a security in the name of a nominee of the bank under this subchapter may not redeliver the security to the individual fiduciary who authorized its registration in the name of the nominee without registering the security in the name of the individual fiduciary, as fiduciary.

(b) A sale of the security by the bank at the direction of the individual fiduciary is not a redelivery.

History of Prop. Code §161.025: Acts 1983, 68th Leg., ch. 576, §1, eff. Jan. 1, 1984. Source: TRCS art. 7425a-2, §2(B).

PROP §161.026. DISPOSITION OF SECURITY HELD BY NOMINEE

A bank holding a security in the name of a nominee under this subchapter may make any disposition of the security that is authorized or ordered by a court having jurisdiction of the estate or trust.

History of Prop. Code §161.026: Acts 1983, 68th Leg., ch. 576, §1, eff. Jan. 1, 1984. Source: TRCS art. 7425a-2, §2(B).

PROP §161.027. LIABILITY

A bank holding a security in the name of a nominee under this subchapter is liable for a loss resulting from the acts of the bank's nominee with respect to the security.

History of Prop. Code §161.027: Acts 1983, 68th Leg., ch. 576, §1, eff. Jan. 1, 1984. Source: TRCS art. 7425a-2, §2(B).

PROP §161.028. CERTIFICATION

(a) On the demand of a fiduciary employing a bank to hold a security as custodian under this subchapter, the bank shall identify in a written certification the securities it holds for the fiduciary.

(b) On the demand of a party, or the attorney of a party, to an accounting by a bank holding a security in the name of a nominee under this subchapter, the bank shall identify in a written certification the securities it holds as fiduciary.

History of Prop. Code §161.028: Acts 1983, 68th Leg., ch. 576, §1, eff. Jan. 1, 1984. Source: TRCS art. 7425a-2, §2.

Sections 161.029-161.050 reserved for expansion

SUBCHAPTER C. DEPOSIT OF SECURITY WITH FEDERAL RESERVE BANK OR CLEARING CORPORATION

PROP §161.051. APPLICATION

(a) Except as provided by Subsection (b), this subchapter applies to a fiduciary holding a security in its fiduciary capacity and to a bank, trust company, or private banker holding a security as a fiduciary, custodian, custodian for a fiduciary, or managing agent, regardless of:

(1) the date of the agreement, instrument, or court order by which the fiduciary, custodian, or managing agent is appointed; and

(2) ownership by the fiduciary, custodian, or managing agent of capital stock of the clearing corporation.

(b) This subchapter does not apply to a security held by a fiduciary, bank, trust company, or private banker on behalf of a domestic insurance company, unless the prior express approval of the State Board of Insurance is obtained. The board may grant approval to all domestic insurance companies generally, or to specific insurance companies on a case-by-case basis.

(c) For the purposes of this subchapter, "fiduciary" includes a state or national bank acting in a fiduciary capacity.

History of Prop. Code §161.051: Acts 1983, 68th Leg., ch. 576, §1, eff. Jan. 1, 1984. Source: TRCS art. 7425a-3, §§1, 4.

PROP §161.052. AUTHORITY OF FIDUCIARY

A fiduciary holding a security in its fiduciary capacity and a bank, trust company, or private banker holding a security as a custodian for a fiduciary, a managing agent, or a custodian may deposit or arrange for the deposit of the security with:

(1) the Federal Reserve Bank of Dallas if the United States has agreed to pay or has guaranteed payment of the security's principal and interest; or

(2) a clearing corporation, either in this state or elsewhere, regardless of whether the clearing corporation conducts or is authorized to conduct business in this state.

History of Prop. Code §161.052: Acts 1983, 68th Leg., ch. 576, §1, eff. Jan. 1, 1984. Source: TRCS art. 7425a-3, §§2, 3(a).

PROP §161.053. BULK HOLDINGS

A clearing corporation may merge and hold in bulk certificates representing the same class of securities of the same issuer that are deposited with it under this subchapter, together with any other securities deposited with the clearing corporation by any person in the name of the nominee of the clearing corporation, regardless of the ownership of the securities. Certificates of small denomination may be merged into one or more certificates of larger denomination.

History of Prop. Code §161.053: Acts 1983, 68th Leg., ch. 576, §1, eff. Jan. 1, 1984. Source: TRCS art. 7425a-3, §3(a).

PROP §161.054. RECORDS

A fiduciary, bank, trust company, or private banker depositing a security under this subchapter shall show in its records at all times the ownership of the securities deposited in the account.

History of Prop. Code §161.054: Acts 1983, 68th Leg., ch. 576, §1, eff. Jan. 1, 1984. Source: TRCS art. 7425a-3, §§2, 3(a).

PROP §161.055. REGULATION

A bank, trust company, or private banker depositing securities under this subchapter is subject to the regulations issued by the Finance Commission of Texas if the institution is chartered by this state or is private or by the comptroller of the currency if the institution is a national banking association.

History of Prop. Code §161.055: Acts 1983, 68th Leg., ch. 576, §1, eff. Jan. 1, 1984. Source: TRCS art. 7425a-3, §§2, 3(a).

PROP §161.056. BOOK TRANSFERS

The Federal Reserve Bank of Dallas or a clearing corporation holding securities deposited under this subchapter may transfer ownership of or other interests in the securities by making entries in the books of the bank or corporation and without physical delivery of certificates representing the securities.

History of Prop. Code §161.056: Acts 1983, 68th Leg., ch. 576, §1, eff. Jan. 1, 1984. Source: TRCS art. 7425a-3, §§2, 3(a).

PROP §161.057. LIABILITY

A fiduciary who deposits securities in a clearing corporation is liable to the beneficial owner of the securities for a loss resulting from the acts or omissions of the clearing corporation. This subchapter does not affect a liability between the fiduciary and the clearing corporation.

History of Prop. Code §161.057: Acts 1983, 68th Leg., ch. 576, §1, eff. Jan. 1, 1984. Source: TRCS art. 7425a-3, §3(b).

PROP §161.058. CERTIFICATION

(a) On the demand of a fiduciary for whom a bank, trust company, or private banker is acting as custodian, the bank, trust company, or private banker shall identify in a written certification the securities deposited by the bank, trust company, or private banker with the federal reserve bank or in the clearing corporation for the account of the fiduciary.

(b) On the demand of a party, or the attorney of a party, to an accounting by a fiduciary or by a bank, trust company, or private banker that is acting as a fiduciary, a custodian, a custodian for a fiduciary, or a managing agent, the fiduciary, bank, trust company, or private banker shall identify in a written certification to the party the securities deposited by the fiduciary, bank, trust company, or private banker with the federal reserve bank or the clearing corporation.

History of Prop. Code §161.058: Acts 1983, 68th Leg., ch. 576, §1, eff. Jan. 1, 1984. Source: TRCS art. 7425a-3, §§2, 3(a).

CHAPTER 162. CONSTRUCTION PAYMENTS, LOAN RECEIPTS, & MISAPPLICATION OF TRUST FUNDS

SUBCHAPTER A. CONSTRUCTION PAYMENTS & LOAN RECEIPTS

PROP §162.001. CONSTRUCTION PAYMENTS & LOAN RECEIPTS AS TRUST FUNDS

(a) Construction payments are trust funds under this chapter if the payments are made to a contractor or subcontractor or to an officer, director, or agent of a contractor or subcontractor, under a construction contract for the improvement of specific real property in this state.

(b) Loan receipts are trust funds under this chapter if the funds are borrowed by a contractor, subcontractor, or owner or by an officer, director, or agent of a contractor, subcontractor, or owner for the purpose of improving specific real property in this state, and the loan is secured in whole or in part by a lien on the property.

(c) A fee payable to a contractor is not considered trust funds if:

(1) the contractor and property owner have entered into a written construction contract for the improvement of specific real property in this state before the commencement of construction of the improvement and the contract provides for the payment by the owner of the costs of construction and a reasonable fee specified in the contract payable to the contractor; and

(2) the fee is earned as provided by the contract and paid to the contractor or disbursed from a construction account described by Section 162.006, if applicable.

(d) Trust funds paid to a creditor under this chapter are not property or an interest in property of a debtor who is a trustee described by Section 162.002.

History of Prop. Code §162.001: Acts 1983, 68th Leg., ch. 576, §1, eff. Jan. 1, 1984. Amended by Acts 1997, 75th Leg., ch. 1018, §1, eff. Sept. 1, 1997; Acts 2009, 81st Leg., ch. 1277, §§1, 2, eff. Sept. 1, 2009. Source: TRCS art. 5472e, §1.

ANNOTATIONS

Kelly v. General Interior Constr., Inc., 301 S.W.3d 653, 660-61 (Tex.2010). For in personam jurisdiction, "merely pleading that [Ds] violated the Texas [Construction] Trust Fund Act is not enough; [P] must also plead and, when challenged by [Ds], present evidence that [Ds'] relevant acts (i.e., those connected to [P's] claims) occurred, at least in part, in Texas."

Dealers Elec. Sup. v. Scoggins Constr. Co., 292 S.W.3d 650, 658 (Tex.2009). "[T]he [Texas Construction] Trust Fund Act was enacted for the protection of laborers and materialmen, and is a remedial statute that should be given a broad construction. Interpreting the McGregor Act [Gov't Code ch. 2253] to provide an exclusive remedy for unpaid claims would contravene, rather than further, the purpose of both the McGregor Act and the [Texas Construction] Trust Fund Act. To hold that one impliedly abrogates the other absent the Legislature's expression would undermine both Acts' clear purpose. *At 660:* While Texas cases and the statute itself support a conclusion that the McGregor Act provides a laborer or materialman's mandatory and exclusive remedy against a surety and obligor on a public-work payment bond, that exclusivity does not extend beyond suit against the bond itself."

Ulusal v. Lentz Eng'g, L.C., 491 S.W.3d 910, 919 (Tex.App.—Houston [1st Dist.] 2016, no pet.). "[D] argues that attorneys' fees are not authorized under the Texas Construction Trust Fund Act. [¶] [P] pleaded it was entitled to attorneys' fees under [CPRC] §38.001.... Pursuant to that section, a party can recover reasonable attorneys' fees from claims for, among other things, rendered services, performed labor, furnished materials, and a contract. [T]he Texas Construction Trust Fund[ ] Act creates a cause of action for failure to make payments under a construction contract. Accordingly, §38.001 permits attorneys' fees to be awarded for claims under the ... Act."

C&G, Inc. v. Jones, 165 S.W.3d 450, 453 (Tex. App.—Dallas 2005, pet. denied). "[A] party who misapplies ... trust funds is subject to civil liability if (1) the party breaches the duty imposed by ch. 162, (2) with the requisite scienter, and (3) the claimants are within the class of people ch. 162 was designed to protect and have asserted the type of injury ch. 162 was intended to prohibit. *At 455:* Even though the stipulated facts state that [Ds] did not 'independently' determine to whom the funds should be paid, the word 'independently' does not exclude the participation of [Ds] in the decision to divert funds. Further, the stipulation that [Ds] made the payments 'in accordance with the instructions' of the parent company officers does not exclude [Ds] from the 'decision' to divert the funds." *See also* ***Lively v. Carpet Servs.***, 904 S.W.2d 868, 873 (Tex.App.—Houston [1st Dist.] 1995, writ denied).

Park Envtl. Equip., Ltd. v. Texas Capital Funding, Inc., 102 S.W.3d 243, 245 (Tex.App.—Houston [14th Dist.] 2003, pet. denied). "If a construction company uses project payments to buy cars for its officers instead of paying subcontractors, there is no question that company has misappropriated trust funds under the [Texas Construction Trust Fund] Act. But it does not follow that the car dealership who received the funds is a party to the fiduciary breach. ... While the legislature certainly meant to protect materialmen ..., there is no indication it meant to do so at the expense (not to mention the risk of felony) of a third party who provides necessary services for fair value."

McCoy v. Nelson Utils. Servs., 736 S.W.2d 160, 164 (Tex.App.—Tyler 1987, writ ref'd n.r.e.). Property Code §162.001 "was enacted to give protection to materialmen in addition to that provided by the materialman's lien statutes. This act declares that all funds paid to a contractor or subcontractor under a construction contract for the improvement of specified real property, and all funds borrowed by a contractor, subcontractor, or owner for the purpose of improving such real property, which are secured in whole or in part by a lien on the specific property to be improved, are 'Trust Funds for the benefit of the artisans, laborers, mechanics, contractors, subcontractors, or materialmen who may labor or furnish labor or materials for' the improvements, and appoints the contractor, subcontractor, or owner receiving such funds as Trustee. There is no requirement that the materialman must comply with procedural requisites of [TRCS art. 5469, now Prop. Code §53.105,] to qualify as a beneficiary of these trust funds." *See also* ***Panhandle Bank & Trust Co. v. Graybar Elec. Co.***, 492 S.W.2d 76, 81 (Tex.App.—Amarillo 1973, writ ref'd n.r.e.).

Holley v. NL Indus., 718 S.W.2d 813, 815 (Tex. App.—Austin 1986, writ ref'd n.r.e.). As a matter of law, "drilling an oil and gas well is not the construction of an improvement on real property within the meaning of Ch. 162...."

Trenholm v. B.J. Tidwell Indus., 631 S.W.2d 545, 546-47 (Tex.App.—Eastland 1982, no writ). Section 162.001 "affords protection to materialmen without any requirement for filing or notice. We think, however, it is clear that moneys received from the 'sale' of properties do not constitute a trust fund under the statute. [¶] The statute does not cover proceeds received from the sale of specific real property."

PROP §162.002. CONTRACTORS AS TRUSTEES

A contractor, subcontractor, or owner or an officer, director, or agent of a contractor, subcontractor, or owner, who receives trust funds or who has control or direction of trust funds, is a trustee of the trust funds.

History of Prop. Code §162.002: Acts 1983, 68th Leg., ch. 576, §1, eff. Jan. 1, 1984. Source: TRCS art. 5472e, §1.

ANNOTATIONS

Lively v. Carpet Servs., 904 S.W.2d 868, 873 (Tex. App.—Houston [1st Dist.] 1995, writ denied). "[A]ny officer or director who has control or direction over the funds is also a trustee of the funds, and is therefore personally liable."

Don Hill Constr. Co. v. Dealers Elec. Sup., 790 S.W.2d 805, 811-12 (Tex.App.—Beaumont 1990, no writ), *overruled on other grounds*, ***Morrell Masonry***

Sup. v. Lupe's Shenandoah Reserve, LLC, 363 S.W.3d 901 (Tex.App.—Beaumont 2012, no pet.). "The mere transfer of those funds from the owner to the general contractor does not defeat the funds classification as trust funds."

PROP §162.003. BENEFICIARIES OF TRUST FUNDS

(a) An artisan, laborer, mechanic, contractor, subcontractor, or materialman who labors or who furnishes labor or material for the construction or repair of an improvement on specific real property in this state is a beneficiary of any trust funds paid or received in connection with the improvement.

(b) A property owner is a beneficiary of trust funds described by Section 162.001 in connection with a residential construction contract, including funds deposited into a construction account described by Section 162.006.

History of Prop. Code §162.003: Acts 1983, 68th Leg., ch. 576, §1, eff. Jan. 1, 1984. Amended by Acts 1997, 75th Leg., ch. 1018, §2, eff. Sept. 1, 1997; Acts 2009, 81st Leg., ch. 1277, §3, eff. Sept. 1, 2009. Source: TRCS art. 5472e, §1.

PROP §162.004. APPLICATION

(a) This chapter does not apply to:

(1) a bank, savings and loan, or other lender;

(2) a title company or other closing agent; or

(3) a corporate surety who issues a payment bond covering the contract for the construction or repair of the improvement.

(b) The Texas Trust Act (Chapters 111 through 115) does not apply to any trust created under this chapter, nor does this chapter affect any provision of the Texas Trust Act.

(c) Regardless of whether a construction contract is covered by a statutory or common law payment bond, this chapter applies to a public or private construction contract for the improvement of specific real property in this state.

History of Prop. Code §162.004: Acts 1983, 68th Leg., ch. 576, §1, eff. Jan. 1, 1984. Amended by Acts 1987, 70th Leg., ch. 578, §2, eff. Aug. 31, 1987; Acts 2009, 81st Leg., ch. 1277, §4, eff. Sept. 1, 2009. Source: TRCS art. 5472e, §§4, 7.

ANNOTATIONS

RepublicBank v. Interkal, Inc., 691 S.W.2d 605, 607 (Tex.1985). "[D] argues that [§162.004] means only that a bank cannot be subject to liability for using trust funds over which the bank already has control. Language supporting such a qualification or limitation upon [§162.004] cannot be found in the statute. The legislature clearly stated that the act protecting materialmen's liens is not applicable to any transaction involving a bank." *See also* ***J.P. Morgan Chase Bank v. Texas Contract Carpet, Inc.***, 302 S.W.3d 515, 528 (Tex.App.—Austin 2009, no pet.).

PROP §162.005. DEFINITIONS

In this chapter:

(1) A trustee acts with "intent to defraud" when the trustee:

(A) retains, uses, disburses, or diverts trust funds with the intent to deprive the beneficiaries of the trust funds;

(B) retains, uses, disburses, or diverts trust funds and fails to establish or maintain a construction account as required by Section 162.006 or fails to establish or maintain an account record for the construction account as required by Section 162.007; or

(C) uses, disburses, or diverts trust funds that were paid to the trustee in reliance on an affidavit furnished by the trustee under Section 53.085 if the affidavit contains false information relating to the trustee's payment of current or past due obligations.

(2) "Current or past due obligations" are those obligations incurred or owed by the trustee for labor or materials furnished in the direct prosecution of the work under the construction contract prior to the receipt of the trust funds and which are due and payable by the trustee no later than 30 days following receipt of the trust funds.

(3) "Direct cost" means a cost included under a construction contract that is specific to the construction of the improvement that is the subject of the contract.

(4) "Indirect cost" means a cost included under a construction contract that is not specific to the construction of the improvement that is the subject of the contract.

(5) "Financial institution" means a bank, savings association, savings bank, credit union, or savings and loan association authorized to do business in the state.

(6) "Construction account" means an account in a financial institution into which only trust funds and funds deposited by the contractor that are necessary to pay charges imposed on the account by the financial institution may be maintained.

History of Prop. Code §162.005: Acts 1987, 70th Leg., ch. 578, §3, eff. Aug. 31, 1987. Amended by Acts 1997, 75th Leg., ch. 1018, §3, eff. Sept. 1, 1997.

ANNOTATIONS

Choy v. Graziano Roofing, 322 S.W.3d 276, 291 (Tex.App.—Houston [1st Dist.] 2009, no pet.). "We hold that, by the plain language of the [Texas Construction Trust Fund] Act, the words 'due and payable … no later than 30 days' after a trustee's receipt of construction trust funds include invoices already due and payable at the time trust funds are requested by a trustee."

PROP §162.006. CONSTRUCTION ACCOUNT REQUIRED IN CERTAIN CIRCUMSTANCES

(a) A contractor who enters into a written contract with a property owner to construct improvements to a residential homestead for an amount exceeding $5,000 shall deposit the trust funds in a construction account in a financial institution.

(b) The periodic statement received from the financial institution must refer to the account as a "construction account" to satisfy the requirements of this section.

History of Prop. Code §162.006: Acts 1997, 75th Leg., ch. 1018, §4, eff. Sept. 1, 1997.

PROP §162.007. MANAGEMENT OF CONSTRUCTION ACCOUNTS

(a) A contractor required to maintain a construction account under this subchapter shall maintain an account record for the construction account that provides information relating to:

(1) the source and amount of the funds in the account and the date the funds were deposited;

(2) the date and amount of each disbursement from the account and the person to whom the funds were disbursed; and

(3) the current balance of the account.

(b) The contractor shall maintain an account record for each construction project that specifies the direct costs and indirect costs charged to the owner.

(c) The contractor shall retain all invoices and other supporting documentation received relating to funds that were disbursed from the construction account.

(d) The contractor shall ensure that all deposit and disbursement documentation includes the construction account number or information that provides a direct connection between the documentation and the account.

(e) The contractor may not destroy information required to be maintained under this section before the first anniversary of the date the improvement that is the subject of the contract is completed.

History of Prop. Code §162.007: Acts 1997, 75th Leg., ch. 1018, §4, eff. Sept. 1, 1997.

Sections 162.008-162.030 reserved for expansion

SUBCHAPTER B. MISAPPLICATION OF TRUST FUNDS

PROP §162.031. MISAPPLICATION OF TRUST FUNDS

(a) A trustee who, intentionally or knowingly or with intent to defraud, directly or indirectly retains, uses, disburses, or otherwise diverts trust funds without first fully paying all current or past due obligations incurred by the trustee to the beneficiaries of the trust funds, has misapplied the trust funds.

(b) It is an affirmative defense to prosecution or other action brought under Subsection (a) that the trust funds not paid to the beneficiaries of the trust were used by the trustee to pay the trustee's actual expenses directly related to the construction or repair of the improvement or have been retained by the trustee, after notice to the beneficiary who has made a request for payment, as a result of the trustee's reasonable belief that the beneficiary is not entitled to such funds or have been retained as authorized or required by Chapter 53.

(c) It is also an affirmative defense to prosecution or other action brought under Subsection (a) that the trustee paid the beneficiaries all trust funds which they are entitled to receive no later than 30 days following written notice to the trustee of the filing of a criminal complaint or other notice of a pending criminal investigation.

(d) A trustee who commingles trust funds with other funds in the trustee's possession does not defeat a trust created by this chapter.

History of Prop. Code §162.031: Acts 1983, 68th Leg., ch. 576, §1, eff. Jan. 1, 1984. Amended by Acts 1987, 70th Leg., ch. 578, §4, eff. Aug. 31, 1987; Acts 2009, 81st Leg., ch. 1277, §5, eff. Sept. 1, 2009. Source: TRCS art. 5472e, §§1, 2.

ANNOTATIONS

Direct Value, L.L.C. v. Stock Bldg. Sup., 388 S.W.3d 386, 392-93 (Tex.App.—Amarillo 2012, no pet.). "[D] contends that, in order to establish personal liability as a trustee, the beneficiary must prove the officer, director, or agent has the ability to sign the company's checks. Although this type of evidence has been used to establish an officer's ability to control or direct payment …, the [Texas Construction Trust Fund] Act does not require direct evidence of such an ability.

Rather, the Act requires that a beneficiary establish that an officer, director, or agent '*directly or indirectly retains, uses, disburses, or otherwise diverts trust funds* without first fully paying all current and past due obligations.' Further, if [D's] bright-line test were allowed, any officer, director, or agent could circumvent liability under the Act by simply directing an employee without disbursement authority to sign all company checks even though an officer, director, or agent has the ultimate authority to decide whether to pay a beneficiary. Such an interpretation would emasculate those provisions of the Act related to a trustee's liability leading to absurd and unintended consequences."

Holladay v. CW&A, Inc., 60 S.W.3d 243, 246 (Tex. App.—Corpus Christi 2001, pet. denied). "A party who misapplies [construction-payment] trust funds is subject to civil liability if (1) it breaches the duty imposed by the Texas Construction [Trust] Fund Act, and (2) the requisite plaintiffs are within the class of people that the act was designed to protect and have asserted the type of injury the act was intended to prohibit. *At 247-48:* The affirmative defense provided in the Texas Construction [Trust] Fund Act can be based on two different situations: (1) the trustee retains funds to construct or repair the improvement; or (2) the trustee retains funds to determine entitlement thereto after notice to the beneficiary." *See also* ***Lively v. Carpet Servs.***, 904 S.W.2d 868, 876 (Tex.App.—Houston [1st Dist.] 1995, writ denied).

Kirschner v. State, 997 S.W.2d 335, 340 (Tex. App.—Austin 1999, pet. ref'd). "The affirmative defense provided for by §162.031(b) is a justification for what would otherwise be culpable conduct. *At 342:* The trustee of a construction trust cannot simultaneously be a beneficiary of the trust. Under the statute, the trustee must justify any payments to himself as being for actual expenses directly relating to the construction. *At 343:* The misapplication of construction trust funds is a felony only if it is committed with the intent to defraud the trust beneficiaries. A trustee acts with intent to defraud when he retains, uses, disburses, or diverts trust funds with the intent to deprive the beneficiaries of the trust funds." *See also* ***Morrell Masonry Sup. v. Lupe's Shenandoah Reserve, LLC***, 363 S.W.3d 901, 908 (Tex.App.—Beaumont 2012, no pet.). *But see* ***Morelli v. State***, 9 S.W.3d 909, 915 (Tex.App.—Austin 2000, pet. ref'd) (no requirement that all expenditures be for "sticks and bricks").

In re Nicholas, 956 F.2d 110, 113 (5th Cir.1992). "[P] argues that [§162.031] was amended post-***Boyle*** [***v. Abilene Lumber, Inc.***, 819 F.2d 583 (5th Cir.1987),] to prohibit all intentional diversions of funds—and not just fraudulent diversions.... The essential element of our inquiry continues to be determining what *fiduciary* duties are imposed on the fund holder and the manner in which the state's statutory construction funds trust interacts with the Bankruptcy Code debt discharge exception for these debts arising from fiduciary activities. ***Boyle*** interpreted the former Texas statute to create a fiduciary duty only to the extent that a trustee should not divert trust funds with intent to defraud. ... Relevant to this discussion, no criminal penalty attaches to the retention, use or disbursement of funds to pay the trustee's *actual* expenses *directly related* to the construction or repair of the improvement—whether or not such expenses were owed to beneficiaries of the trust fund. If, however, trust funds were knowingly or intentionally paid for *more* than the actual expenses, or for expenses *not* directly related to the construction or repair project, criminal sanctions could be imposed, and ***Boyle*** renders such actions subject to nondischargeability. [¶] Under the affirmative defense to the Texas Construction Trust Fund Statute, there is no such express prohibition; general contractors may use the payments they receive from construction projects to keep those projects going even if, in some instances, the beneficiaries are not paid first." (Internal quotes omitted.)

PROP §162.032. PENALTIES

(a) A trustee who misapplies trust funds amounting to $500 or more in violation of this chapter commits a Class A misdemeanor.

(b) A trustee who misapplies trust funds amounting to $500 or more in violation of this chapter, with intent to defraud, commits a felony of the third degree.

(c) A trustee who fails to establish or maintain a construction account in violation of Section 162.006 or fails to establish or maintain an account record for the construction account in violation of Section 162.007 commits a Class A misdemeanor.

History of Prop. Code §162.032: Acts 1983, 68th Leg., ch. 576, §1, eff. Jan. 1, 1984. Amended by Acts 1987, 70th Leg., ch. 578, §5, eff. Aug. 31, 1987; Acts 1997, 75th Leg., ch. 1018, §5, eff. Sept. 1, 1997. Source: TRCS art. 5472e, §2.

ANNOTATIONS

Fisk-Allied v. Manhattan Constr., 835 F.Supp. 334, 335 (E.D.Tex.1993). "[I]njunctive relief is not available for the kind of trust created by the Texas Con-

struction Trust Fund Statute. [Section 162.032] provides only for criminal penalties. Furthermore, the Fifth Circuit's analysis of the statute finds that it 'falls far short of statutes ... creating classic, expressed trust arrangement[s]' for which injunctive relief is normally available."

PROP §162.033. ELECTION OF OFFENSES

If the misapplication of trust funds by a trustee constitutes another offense punishable under the laws of this state, the state may elect the offense for which it will prosecute the trustee.

History of Prop. Code §162.033: Acts 1983, 68th Leg., ch. 576, §1, eff. Jan. 1, 1984. Source: TRCS art. 5472e, §3.

CHAPTER 163. MANAGEMENT, INVESTMENT, & EXPENDITURE OF INSTITUTIONAL FUNDS

NCCUSL Prefatory Comment*

Reasons for Revision

The Uniform Prudent Management of Institutional Funds Act (UPMIFA) replaces the Uniform Management of Institutional Funds Act (UMIFA). The National Conference of Commissioners on Uniform State Laws approved UMIFA in 1972, and 47 jurisdictions have enacted the act. UMIFA provided guidance and authority to charitable organizations within its scope concerning the management and investment of funds held by those organizations, UMIFA provided endowment spending rules that did not depend on trust accounting principles of income and principal, and UMIFA permitted the release of restrictions on the use or management of funds under certain circumstances. The changes UMIFA made to the law permitted charitable organizations to use modern investment techniques such as total-return investing and to determine endowment fund spending based on spending rates rather than on determinations of "income" and "principal."

UMIFA was drafted almost 35 years ago, and portions of it are now out of date. The prudence standards in UMIFA have provided useful guidance, but prudence norms evolve over time. The new Act provides modern articulations of the prudence standards for the management and investment of charitable funds and for endowment spending. The Uniform Prudent Investor Act (UPIA), an Act promulgated in 1994 and already enacted in 43 jurisdictions, served as a model for many of the revisions. UPIA updates rules on investment decision making for trusts, including charitable trusts, and imposes additional duties on trustees for the protection of beneficiaries. UPMIFA applies these rules and duties to charities organized as nonprofit corporations. UPMIFA does not apply to trusts managed by corporate and other fiduciaries that are not charities, because UPIA provides management and investment standards for those trusts.

In applying principles based on UPIA to charities organized as nonprofit corporations, UPMIFA combines the approaches taken by UPIA and by the Revised Model Nonprofit Corporation Act (RMNCA). UPMIFA reflects the fact that standards for managing and investing institutional funds are and should be the same regardless of whether a charitable organization is organized as a trust, a nonprofit corporation, or some other entity. *See* Bevis Longstreth, Modern Investment Management and the Prudent Man Rule 7 (1986) (stating "[t]he modern paradigm of prudence applies to all fiduciaries who are subject to some version of the prudent man rule, whether under ERISA, the private foundation provisions of the Code, UMIFA, other state statutes, or the common law."); Harvey P. Dale, *Nonprofit Directors and Officers—Duties and Liabilities for Investment Decisions*, 1994 N.Y.U. Conf. Tax Plan. 501(c)(3) Org's. Ch. 4.

UPMIFA provides guidance and authority to charitable organizations concerning the management and investment of funds held by those organizations, and UPMIFA imposes additional duties on those who manage and invest charitable funds. These duties provide additional protections for charities and also protect the interests of donors who want to see their contributions used wisely.

UPMIFA modernizes the rules governing expenditures from endowment funds, both to provide stricter guidelines on spending from endowment funds and to give institutions the ability to cope more easily with fluctuations in the value of the endowment.

Finally, UPMIFA updates the provisions governing the release and modification of restrictions on charitable funds to permit more efficient management of these funds. These provisions derive from the approach taken in the Uniform Trust Code (UTC) for modifying charitable trusts. Like the UTC provisions, UPMIFA's modification rules preserve the historic position of the attorneys general in most states as the overseers of charities.

As under UMIFA, the new Act applies to charities organized as charitable trusts, as nonprofit corporations, or in some other manner, but the rules do not apply to funds managed by trustees that are not charities. Thus, the Act does not apply to trusts managed by corporate or individual trustees, but the Act does apply to trusts managed by charities.

Prudent Management and Investment

UMIFA applied the 1972 prudence standard to investment decision making. In contrast, UPMIFA will give charities updated and more useful guidance by incorporating language from UPIA, modified to fit the special needs of charities. The revised Act spells out more of the factors a charity should consider in making investment decisions, thereby imposing a modern, well accepted, prudence standard based on UPIA.

Among the expressly enumerated prudence factors in UPMIFA is "the preservation of the endowment fund," a standard not articulated in UMIFA.

In addition to identifying factors that a charity must consider in making management and investment decisions, UPMIFA requires a charity and those who manage and invest its funds to:

(1) Give primary consideration to donor intent as expressed in a gift instrument,

(2) Act in good faith, with the care an ordinarily prudent person would exercise,

(3) Incur only reasonable costs in investing and managing charitable funds,

(4) Make a reasonable effort to verify relevant facts,

(5) Make decisions about each asset in the context of the portfolio of investments, as part of an overall investment strategy,

(6) Diversify investments unless due to special circumstances, the purposes of the fund are better served without diversification,

(7) Dispose of unsuitable assets, and

---

* **Editor's note:**

The NCCUSL comments have been edited to reflect the Texas Legislature's omission of sections and changing of section numbers from the original uniform act. The Texas Legislature did not adopt the NCCUSL comments when it adopted the Uniform Prudent Management of Institutional Funds Act. The full uniform act and comments can be found at www.uniformlaws.org.

(8) In general, develop an investment strategy appropriate for the fund and the charity.

UMIFA did not articulate these requirements.

Thus, UPMIFA strengthens the rules governing management and investment decision making by charities and provides more guidance for those who manage and invest the funds.

Donor Intent with Respect to Endowments

UPMIFA improves the protection of donor intent with respect to expenditures from endowments. When a donor expresses intent clearly in a written gift instrument, the Act requires that the charity follow the donor's instructions. When a donor's intent is not so expressed, UPMIFA directs the charity to spend an amount that is prudent, consistent with the purposes of the fund, relevant economic factors, and the donor's intent that the fund continue in perpetuity. This approach allows the charity to give effect to donor intent, protect its endowment, assure generational equity, and use the endowment to support the purposes for which the endowment was created.

Retroactivity

Like UMIFA, UPIA, the Uniform Principal and Income Act of 1961, and the Uniform Principal and Income Act of 1997, UPMIFA applies retroactively to institutional funds created before and prospectively to institutional funds created after enactment of the statute. Regarding the considerations motivating this treatment of the issues, see the comment to Section 163.005.

Endowment Spending

UPMIFA improves the endowment spending rule by eliminating the concept of historic dollar value and providing better guidance regarding the operation of the prudence standard. Under UMIFA a charity can spend amounts above historic dollar value that the charity determines to be prudent. The Act directs the charity to focus on the purposes and needs of the charity rather than on the purposes and perpetual nature of the fund. Amounts below historic dollar value cannot be spent. The Drafting Committee concluded that this endowment spending rule created numerous problems and that restructuring the rule would benefit charities, their donors, and the public. The problems include:

(1) Historic dollar value fixes valuation at a moment in time, and that moment is arbitrary. If a donor provides for a gift in the donor's will, the date of valuation for the gift will likely be the donor's date of death. (UMIFA left uncertain what the appropriate date for valuing a testamentary gift was.) The determination of historic dollar value can vary significantly depending upon when in the market cycle the donor dies. In addition, the fund may be below historic dollar value at the time the charity receives the gift if the value of the asset declines between the date of the donor's death and the date the asset is actually distributed to the charity from the estate.

(2) After a fund has been in existence for a number of years, historic dollar value may become meaningless. Assuming reasonable long term investment success, the value of the typical fund will be well above historic dollar value, and historic dollar value will no longer represent the purchasing power of the original gift. Without better guidance on spending the increase in value of the fund, historic dollar value does not provide adequate protection for the fund. If a charity views the restriction on spending simply as a direction to preserve historic dollar value, the charity may spend more than it should.

(3) The Act does not provide clear answers to questions a charity faces when the value of an endowment fund drops below historic dollar value. A fund that is so encumbered is commonly called an "underwater" fund. Conflicting advice regarding whether an organization could spend from an underwater fund has led to difficulties for those managing charities. If a charity concluded that it could continue to spend trust accounting income until a fund regained its historic dollar value, the charity might invest for income rather than on a total-return basis. Thus, the historic dollar value rule can cause inappropriate distortions in investment policy and can ultimately lead to a decline in a fund's real value. If, instead, a charity with an underwater fund continues to invest for growth, the charity may be unable to spend anything from an underwater endowment fund for several years. The inability of a charity to spend anything from an endowment is likely to be contrary to donor intent, which is to provide current benefits to the charity.

The Drafting Committee concluded that providing clearly articulated guidance on the prudence rule for spending from an endowment fund, with emphasis on the permanent nature of the fund, would provide the best protection of the purchasing power of endowment funds.

Presumption of Imprudence

UPMIFA includes as an optional provision a presumption of imprudence if a charity spends more than seven percent of an endowment fund in any one year. The presumption is meant to protect against spending an endowment too quickly. Although the Drafting Committee believes that the prudence standard of UPMIFA provides appropriate and adequate protection for endowments, the Committee provided the option for states that want to include a mechanical guideline in the statute. A major drawback to any statutory percentage is that it is unresponsive to changes in the rate of inflation or deflation.

Modification of Restrictions on Charitable Funds

UPMIFA clarifies that the doctrines of cy pres and deviation apply to funds held by nonprofit corporations as well as to funds held by charitable trusts. Courts have applied trust law rules to nonprofit corporations in the past, but the Drafting Committee believed that statutory authority for applying these principles to nonprofit corporations would be helpful. UMIFA permitted release of restrictions but left the application of cy pres uncertain. Under UPMIFA, as under trust law, the court will determine whether and how to apply cy pres or deviation and the attorney general will receive notice and have the opportunity to participate in the proceeding. The one addition to existing law is that UPMIFA gives a charity the authority to modify a restriction on a fund that is both old and small. For these funds, the expense of a trip to court will often be prohibitive. By permitting a charity to make an appropriate modification, money is saved for the charitable purposes of the charity. Even with respect to small, old funds, however, the charity must notify the attorney general of the charity's intended action. Of course, if the attorney general has concerns, he or she can seek the agreement of the charity to change or abandon the modification, and if that fails, can commence a court action to enjoin it. Thus, in all types of modification the attorney general continues to be the protector both of the donor's intent and of the public's interest in charitable funds.

Other Organizational Law

For matters not governed by UPMIFA, a charitable organization will continue to be governed by rules applicable to charitable trusts, if it is organized as a trust, or rules applicable to nonprofit corporations, if it is organized as a nonprofit corporation.

Relation to Trust Law

Although UPMIFA applies a number of rules from trust law to institutions organized as nonprofit corporations, in two respects UPMIFA creates rules that do not exist under the common law applicable to trusts. The endowment spending rule of Section 4 and the provision for modifying a small, old fund in subsection (d) of Section 6 have no counterparts in the common law or the UTC. The Drafting Committee believes that these rules could be useful to charities organized as trusts, and the Committee recommends conforming amendments to the UTC and the Principal and Income Act to incorporate these changes into trust law.

PROP §163.001. SHORT TITLE

This chapter may be cited as the Uniform Prudent Management of Institutional Funds Act.

History of Prop. Code §163.001: Acts 2007, 80th Leg., ch. 834, §1, eff. Sept. 1, 2007.

PROP §163.002. LEGISLATIVE FINDINGS & PURPOSE

(a) The legislature finds that:

(1) institutions organized and operated exclusively for a charitable purpose perform essential and needed services in the state;

(2) uncertainty exists regarding the prudence standards for the management and investment of charitable funds and for endowment spending by institutions described by Subdivision (1); and

(3) the institutions, their officers, directors, and trustees, and the citizens of this state will benefit from

removal of the uncertainty regarding applicable prudence standards and by permitting endowment funds to be invested for the long-term goals of achieving growth and maintaining purchasing power without adversely affecting the availability of funds for current expenditure.

(b) The purpose of this chapter is to provide guidance and authority through modern articulations of prudence standards for the management and investment of charitable funds and for endowment spending by institutions organized and operated exclusively for a charitable purpose in order to provide uniformity and remove uncertainty regarding those standards.

History of Prop. Code §163.002: Acts 2007, 80th Leg., ch. 834, §1, eff. Sept. 1, 2007.

PROP §163.003. DEFINITIONS

In this chapter:

(1) "Charitable purpose" means the promotion of a scientific, educational, philanthropic, or environmental purpose, social welfare, the arts and humanities, or another civic or public purpose described by Section 501(c)(3) of the Internal Revenue Code of 1986.

(2) "Endowment fund" means an institutional fund or part thereof that, under the terms of a gift instrument, is not wholly expendable by the institution on a current basis. The term does not include assets that an institution designates as an endowment fund for its own use.

(3) "Gift instrument" means a record or records, including an institutional solicitation, under which property is granted to, transferred to, or held by an institution as an institutional fund.

(4) "Institution" means:

(A) a person, other than an individual, organized and operated exclusively for charitable purposes;

(B) a government or governmental subdivision, agency, or instrumentality, to the extent that it holds funds exclusively for a charitable purpose; and

(C) a trust that had both charitable and noncharitable interests, after all noncharitable interests have terminated.

(5) "Institutional fund" means a fund held by an institution exclusively for charitable purposes. The term does not include:

(A) program-related assets;

(B) a fund held for an institution by a trustee that is not an institution; or

(C) a fund in which a beneficiary that is not an institution has an interest, other than an interest that could arise upon violation or failure of the purposes of the fund.

(6) "Person" means an individual, corporation, business trust, estate, trust, partnership, limited liability company, association, joint venture, public corporation, government or governmental subdivision, agency, or instrumentality, or any other legal or commercial entity.

(7) "Program-related asset" means an asset held by an institution primarily to accomplish a charitable purpose of the institution and not primarily for investment.

(8) "Record" means information that is inscribed on a tangible medium or that is stored in an electronic or other medium and is retrievable in perceivable form.

History of Prop. Code §163.003: Acts 2007, 80th Leg., ch. 834, §1, eff. Sept. 1, 2007.

NCCUSL Comment*

Subsection (1). Charitable Purpose

The definition of charitable purpose as adopted by the Drafting Committee follows that of UTC §405 and Restatement (Third) of Trusts §28 (2003). This long-familiar standard derives from the English Statute of Charitable Uses, enacted in 1601.

Some 17 states, including Texas in §163.003(1) above, have created statutory definitions of charitable purpose for various purposes. *See, e.g.*, 10 PA. CONS. STAT. §162.3 (2005) (defining charitable purpose within the Solicitation of Funds for Charitable Purposes Act to include "humane," "patriotic," social welfare and advocacy," and "civic" purposes). The definition in subsection (1) as adopted by the Drafting Committee applies for purposes of this Act and does not affect other definitions of charitable purpose.

Subsection (2). Endowment Fund

An endowment fund is an institutional fund or a part of an institutional fund that is not wholly expendable by the institution on a current basis. A restriction that makes a fund an endowment fund arises from the terms of a gift instrument. If an institution has more than one endowment fund, under Section 163.004 the institution can manage and invest some or all endowment funds together. Section 163.005 and Section 163.007 must be applied to individual funds and cannot be applied to a group of funds that may be managed collectively for investment purposes.

Board-designated funds are institutional funds but not endowment funds. The rules on expenditures and modification of restrictions in this Act do not apply to restrictions that an institution places on an otherwise unrestricted fund that the institution holds for its own benefit. The institution may be able to change these restrictions itself, subject to internal rules and to the fiduciary duties that apply to those that manage the institution.

If an institution transfers assets to another institution, subject to the restriction that the other institution hold the assets as an endowment, then the second institution will hold the assets as an endowment fund.

Subsection (3). Gift Instrument

The term gift instrument refers to the records that establish the terms of a gift and may consist of more than one document. The definition clarifies that the only legally binding restrictions on a gift are the terms set forth in writing.

As used in this definition, "record" is an expansive concept and means a writing in any form, including electronic. The term includes a will, deed, grant, conveyance, agreement, or memorandum, and also includes writings that do

* See footnote on p. 583.

not have a donative purpose. For example, under some circumstances the bylaws of the institution, minutes of the board of directors, or canceled checks could be a gift instrument or be one of several records constituting a gift instrument. Although the term can include any of these records, a record will only become a gift instrument if both the donor and the institution were or should have been aware of its terms when the donor made the gift. For example, if a donor sends a contribution to an institution for its general purposes, then the articles of incorporation may be used to clarify those purposes. If, in contrast, the donor sends a letter explaining that the institution should use the contribution for its "educational projects concerning teenage depression," then any funds received in response must be used for that purpose and not for broader purposes otherwise permissible under the articles of incorporation.

Solicitation materials may constitute a gift instrument. For example, a solicitation that suggests in writing that any gifts received pursuant to the solicitation will be held as an endowment may be integrated with other writings and may be considered part of the gift instrument. Whether the terms of the solicitation become part of the gift instrument will depend upon the circumstances, including whether a subsequent writing superseded the terms of the solicitation. Each gift received in response to a solicitation will be subject to any restrictions indicated in the gift instrument pertaining to that gift. For example, if an initial gift establishes an endowment fund, and the charity then solicits additional gifts "to be held as part of the Charity X Endowment Fund," those additional gifts will each be subject to the restriction that the gifts be held as part of that endowment fund.

The term gift instrument includes matching funds provided by an employer or some other person. Whether matching funds are treated as part of the endowment fund or otherwise will depend on the terms of the matching gift.

The term gift instrument also includes an appropriation by a legislature or other public or governmental body for the benefit of an institution.

Subsection (4). Institution

The Act applies generally to institutions organized and operated exclusively for charitable purposes. The term includes charitable organizations created as nonprofit corporations, unincorporated associations, governmental subdivisions or agencies, or any form of entity, however organized, that is organized and operated exclusively for charitable purposes. The term includes a trust organized and operated exclusively for charitable purposes, but only if a charity acts as trustee. This approach leaves unchanged the coverage of UMIFA. The exclusion of "individual" from the definition of institution is not intended to exclude a corporation sole.

Although UPMIFA does not apply to all charitable trusts, many of UPMIFA's provisions derive from trust law. Prudent investor standards apply to trustees of charitable trusts in states that have adopted UPIA. Trustees of charitable trusts can use the doctrines of cy pres and deviation to modify trust provisions, and the UTC includes a number of modification provisions. The Uniform Principal and Income Act permits allocation between principal and income to facilitate total-return investing. Charitable trusts not included in UPMIFA, primarily those managed by corporate trustees and individuals, will lose the benefits of UPMIFA's endowment spending rule and the provision permitting a charity to apply cy pres, without court supervision, for modifications to a small, old fund. Enacting jurisdictions may choose to incorporate these rules into existing trust statutes to provide the benefits to charitable funds managed by corporate trustees.

The definition of institution includes governmental organizations that hold funds exclusively for the purposes listed in the definition. A governmental entity created by state law may fall outside the definition on account of the form of organization under which the state created it. Because state arrangements are so varied, creating a definition that encompasses all charitable entities created by states is not feasible. States should consider applying the core principles of UPMIFA to such governmental institutions. For example, the control over a state university may be held by a State Board of Regents. In that situation, the state may have created a governing structure by statute or in the state constitution so that the university is, in effect, privately chartered. The Drafting Committee does not intend to exclude these universities from the definition of institution, but additional state legislation may be necessary to address particular situations.

Subsection (5). Institutional Fund

The term institutional fund includes any fund held by an institution for charitable purposes, whether the fund is expendable currently or subject to restrictions. The term does not include a fund held by a trustee that is not an institution.

Some institutions combine assets from multiple funds for investment purposes, and some institutions invest funds from different institutions in a common fund. Typically each fund is assigned units representing the share value of the individual fund. The assets are invested collectively, permitting more efficient investment and improved diversification of the overall portfolio. The collective fund makes annual distributions to the individual funds based on the units held by each fund. For purposes of Section 163.004 and Section 163.006, the collective fund is considered one institutional fund. Section 163.005 and Section 163.007 apply to each fund individually and not to the collective fund.

Assets held by an institution primarily for program-related purposes rather than exclusively for investment are not subject to UPMIFA. For example, a university may purchase land adjacent to its campus for future development. The purchase might not meet prudent investor standards for commercial real estate, but the purchase may be appropriate because the university needs to build a new dormitory. The classroom buildings, administration buildings, and dormitories held by the university all have value as property, but the university does not hold those buildings as financial assets for investment purposes. The Act excludes from the prudent investor norms those assets that a charity uses to conduct its charitable activities, but does not exclude assets that have a tangential tie to the charitable purpose of the institution but are held primarily for investment purposes.

A fund held by an institution is not an institutional fund if any beneficiary of the fund is not an institution. For example, a charitable remainder trust held by a charity as trustee for the benefit of the donor during the donor's lifetime, with the remainder interest held by the charity, is not an institutional fund. However, this subsection treats as an institution a charitable remainder trust that continues to operate for charitable purposes after the termination of the noncharitable interests. The Act will have only a limited effect on a charitable remainder trust that terminates after the noncharitable interest ends. During the period required to complete the distribution of the trust's property, the prudence norm will apply to the actions of the trustee, but the short timeframe will affect investment decision making.

Subsection (6). Person

The Act uses as the definition of person the definition approved by the National Conference of Commissioners on Uniform State Laws. The definition of institution uses the term person, but to be an institution a person must be organized and operated exclusively for charitable purposes. A person with a commercial purpose cannot be an institution. Thus, although the definition of person includes "business trust" and "any other ... commercial entity," the Act does not apply to an entity organized for business purposes and not exclusively for charitable purposes. Further, the definition of person includes trusts, but only trusts managed by charities can be institutional funds. UPMIFA does not apply to trusts managed by corporate trustees or by individual trustees.

If a governing instrument provides that a fund will revert to the donor if, and only if, the institution ceases to exist or the purposes of the fund fail, then the fund will be considered an institutional fund until such contingency occurs.

Subsection (7). Program-Related Asset

Although UPMIFA does not apply to program-related assets, if program-related assets serve, in part, as investments for an institution, then the institution should identify categories for reporting those investments and should establish investment criteria for the investments that are reasonably related to achieving the institution's charitable purposes. For example, a program providing below-market loans to inner-city businesses may be "primarily to accomplish a charitable purpose of the institution" but also can be considered, in part, an investment. The institution should create reasonable credit standards and other guidelines for the program to increase the likelihood that the loans will be repaid.

Subsection (8). Record

This definition was added to clarify that the definition of instrument includes electronic records as defined in Section 2(8) of the Uniform Electronic Transactions Act (1999).

PROP §163.004. STANDARD OF CONDUCT IN MANAGING & INVESTING INSTITUTIONAL FUND

(a) Subject to the intent of a donor expressed in a gift instrument, an institution, in managing and invest-

ing an institutional fund, shall consider the charitable purposes of the institution and the purposes of the institutional fund.

(b) In addition to complying with the duty of loyalty imposed by law other than this chapter, each person responsible for managing and investing an institutional fund shall manage and invest the fund in good faith and with the care an ordinarily prudent person in a like position would exercise under similar circumstances.

(c) In managing and investing an institutional fund, an institution:

(1) may incur only costs that are appropriate and reasonable in relation to the assets, the purposes of the institution, and the skills available to the institution; and

(2) shall make a reasonable effort to verify facts relevant to the management and investment of the fund.

(d) An institution may pool two or more institutional funds for purposes of management and investment.

(e) Except as otherwise provided by a gift instrument, the following rules apply:

(1) In managing and investing an institutional fund, the following factors, if relevant, must be considered:

(A) general economic conditions;

(B) the possible effect of inflation or deflation;

(C) the expected tax consequences, if any, of investment decisions or strategies;

(D) the role that each investment or course of action plays within the overall investment portfolio of the fund;

(E) the expected total return from income and the appreciation of investments;

(F) other resources of the institution;

(G) the needs of the institution and the fund to make distributions and to preserve capital; and

(H) an asset's special relationship or special value, if any, to the charitable purposes of the institution.

(2) Management and investment decisions about an individual asset must be made not in isolation but rather in the context of the institutional fund's portfolio of investments as a whole and as a part of an overall investment strategy having risk and return objectives reasonably suited to the fund and to the institution.

(3) Except as otherwise provided by law other than this chapter, an institution may invest in any kind of property or type of investment consistent with this section.

(4) An institution shall diversify the investments of an institutional fund unless the institution reasonably determines that, because of special circumstances, the purposes of the fund are better served without diversification.

(5) Within a reasonable time after receiving property, an institution shall make and carry out decisions concerning the retention or disposition of the property or to rebalance a portfolio, in order to bring the institutional fund into compliance with the purposes, terms, and distribution requirements of the institution as necessary to meet other circumstances of the institution and the requirements of this chapter.

(6) A person that has special skills or expertise, or is selected in reliance upon the person's representation that the person has special skills or expertise, has a duty to use those skills or that expertise in managing and investing institutional funds.

History of Prop. Code §163.004: Acts 2007, 80th Leg., ch. 834, §1, eff. Sept. 1, 2007.

NCCUSL Comment*

Purpose and Scope of Revisions

This section adopts the prudence standard for investment decision making. The section directs directors or others responsible for managing and investing the funds of an institution to act as a prudent investor would, using a portfolio approach in making investments and considering the risk and return objectives of the fund. The section lists the factors that commonly bear on decisions in fiduciary investing and incorporates the duty to diversify investments absent a conclusion that special circumstances make a decision not to diversify reasonable. Thus, the section follows modern portfolio theory for investment decision making. Section 163.004 applies to all funds held by an institution, regardless of whether the institution obtained the funds by gift or otherwise and regardless of whether the funds are restricted.

The Drafting Committee discussed extensively the standard that should govern nonprofit managers. UMIFA (former §163.007) states the standard as "ordinary business care and prudence under the facts and circumstances prevailing at the time of the action or decision." Since the decision in *Stern v. Lucy Webb Hayes National Training School for Deaconesses*, 381 F.Supp. 1003 (1974), the trend has been to hold directors of nonprofit corporations to a standard nominally similar to the corporate standard but with the recognition that the facts and circumstances considered include the fact that the entity is a charity and not a business corporation.

The language of the prudence standard adopted in UPMIFA is derived from the RMNCA and from the prudent investor rule of UPIA. The standard is consistent with the business judgment standard under corporate law, *as applied to charitable institutions*. That is, a manager operating a charitable organization under the business judgment rule would look to the same factors as those identified by the prudent investor rule. The standard for prudent investment set forth in Section 163.004 first states the duty of care as articulated in the RMNCA, but provides more specific guidance for those managing and investing institutional funds by incorporating language from UPIA. The criteria derived from UPIA are consistent with good practice under current law applicable to nonprofit corporations.

* See footnote on p. 583.

Trust law norms already inform managers of nonprofit corporations. The Preamble to UPIA explains: "Although the Uniform Prudent Investor Act by its terms applies to trusts and not to charitable corporations, the standards of the Act can be expected to inform the investment responsibilities of directors and officers of charitable corporations." *See also*, Restatement (Third) of Trusts: Prudent Investor Rule §379, Comment b, at 190 (1992) (stating that "absent a contrary statute or other provision, the prudent investor rule applies to investment of funds held for charitable corporations."). Trust precedents have routinely been found to be helpful but not binding authority in corporate cases.

The Drafting Committee decided that by adopting language from both the RMNCA and UPIA, UPMIFA could clarify that common standards of prudent investing apply to all charitable institutions. Although the principal trust authorities, UPIA §(2)(a), Restatement (Third) of Trusts §337, UTC §804, and Restatement (Second) of Trusts §174 (prudent administration) use the phrase "care, skill and caution," the Drafting Committee decided to use the more familiar corporate formulation as found in RMNCA. The standard also appears in Sections 163.004, 163.005 and 163.006 of UPMIFA. The Drafting Committee does not intend any substantive change to the UPIA standard and believes that "reasonable care, skill, and caution" are implicit in the term "care" as used in the RMNCA. The Drafting Committee included the detailed provisions from UPIA, because the Committee believed that the greater precision of the prudence norms of the Restatement and UPIA, as compared with UMIFA, could helpfully inform managers of charitable institutions. For an explanation of the Prudent Investor Act, see John H. Langbein, *The Uniform Prudent Investor Act and the Future of Trust Investing*, 81 Iowa L. Rev. 641 (1996), and for a discussion of the effect UPIA has had on investment decision making, see Max M. Schanzenbach & Robert H. Sitkoff, *Did Reform of Prudent Trust Investment Laws Change Trust Portfolio Allocation?*, 50 J. L. & Econ. (forthcoming 2007).

Section 163.004 has incorporated the provisions of UPIA with only a few exceptions. UPIA applies to private trusts and is entirely default law. The settlor of a private trust has complete control over virtually all trust provisions. See UTC §105. Because UPMIFA applies to charitable organizations, UPMIFA makes the duty of care, the duty to minimize costs, and the duty to investigate mandatory. The duty of loyalty is mandatory under applicable organization law, corporate or trust. Other than these duties, the provisions of Section 163.004 are default rules. A gift instrument or the governing instruments of an institution can modify these duties, but the charitable purpose doctrine limits the extent to which an institution or a donor can restrict these duties. In addition, subsection (a) of Section 163.004 reminds the decision maker that the intent of a donor expressed in a gift instrument will control decision making. Further, the decision maker must consider the charitable purposes of the institution and the purposes of the institutional fund for which decisions are being made. These factors are specific to charitable organizations; UPIA §2(a) states the duty to consider similar factors in the private trust context.

UPMIFA does not include the duty of impartiality, stated in UPIA §6, because nonprofit corporations do not confront the multiple beneficiaries problem to which the duty is addressed. Under UPIA, a trustee must treat the current beneficiaries and the remainder beneficiaries with due regard to their respective interests, subject to alternative direction from the trust document. A nonprofit corporation typically creates one charity. The institution may serve multiple beneficiaries, but those beneficiaries do not have enforceable rights in the institution in the same way that beneficiaries of a private trust do. Of course, if a charitable trust is created to benefit more than one charity, rather than being created to carry out a charitable purpose, then UPIA will apply the duty of impartiality to that trust.

In other respects, the Drafting Committee made changes to language from UPIA only where necessary to adapt the language for charitable institutions. No material differences are intended. Subsection (e)(1)(D) of Section 163.004 of UPMIFA does not include a clause that appears at the end of UPIA §2(c)(4) ("which may include financial assets, interest in closely held enterprises, tangible and intangible personal property, and real property."). The Drafting Committee deemed this clause unnecessary for charitable institutions. The language of subsection (e)(1)(G) reflects a modification of the language of UPIA §(2)(c)(7). Other minor modifications to the UPIA provisions make the language more appropriate for charitable institutions.

The duties imposed by this section apply to those who govern an institution, including directors and trustees, and to those to whom the directors or managers delegate responsibility for investment and management of institutional funds. The standard applies to officers and employees of an institution and to agents who invest and manage institutional funds. Volunteers who work with an institution will be subject to the duties imposed here, but state and federal statutes may provide reduced liability for persons who act without compensation. UPMIFA does not affect the application of those shield statutes.

Subsection (a). Donor Intent and Charitable Purposes

Subsection (a) states the overarching duty to comply with donor intent as expressed in the terms of the gift instrument. The emphasis in the Act on giving effect to donor intent does not mean that the donor can or should control the management of the institution. The other fundamental duty is the duty to consider the charitable purposes of the institution and of the institutional fund in making management and investment decisions. UPIA §2(a) states a similar duty to consider the purposes of a trust in investing and managing assets of a trust.

Subsection (b). Duty of Loyalty

Subsection (b) reminds those managing and investing institutional funds that the duty of loyalty will apply to their actions, but Section 163.004 does not state the loyalty standard that applies. The Drafting Committee was concerned, at least nominally, that different standards of loyalty may apply to directors of nonprofit corporations and to trustees of charitable trusts. The RMNCA provides that under the duty of loyalty a director of a nonprofit corporation should act "in a manner the director reasonably believes to be in the best interests of the corporation." RMNCA §8.30. The trust law articulation of the loyalty standard uses "sole interests" rather than "best interests." As the Restatement of Trusts explains, "[t]he trustee is under a duty to the beneficiary to administer the trust solely in the interest of the beneficiary." Restatement (Second) of Trusts §170 (1). Although the standards for loyalty, like the standard of care, are merging, *see* Evelyn Brody, *Charitable Governance: What's Trust Law Got to do With It?* Chi.-Kent L. Rev. (2005); John H. Langbein, *Questioning the Trust Law Duty of Loyalty: Sole Interest or Best Interest*, 114 Yale L.J. 929 (2005), the Drafting Committee concluded that formulating a duty of loyalty provision for UPMIFA was unnecessary. Thus the duty of loyalty under nonprofit corporation law will apply to charities organized as nonprofit corporations, and the duty of loyalty under trust law will apply to charitable trusts.

Subsection (b). Duty of Care

Subsection (b) also applies the duty of care to performance of investment duties. The language derives from §8.30 of the RMNCA. This subsection states the duty to act in good faith, "with the care an ordinarily prudent person in a like position would exercise under similar circumstances." Although the language in the RMNCA and in UPMIFA is similar to that of §8.30 of the Model Business Corporation Act (3d ed. 2002), the standard as applied to persons making decisions for charities is informed by the fact that the institution is a charity and not a business corporation. Thus, in UPMIFA the references to "like position" and "similar circumstances" mean that the charitable nature of the institution affects the decision making of a prudent person acting under the standard set forth in subsection (b). The duty of care involves considering the factors set forth in subsection (e)(1).

Subsection (c)(1). Duty to Minimize Costs

Subsection (c)(1) tracks the language of UPIA §7 and requires an institution to minimize costs. An institution may prudently incur costs by hiring an investment advisor, but the costs incurred should be appropriate under the circumstances. *See* UPIA §7 cmt; Restatement (Third) of Trusts: Prudent Investor Rule §227, cmt. M, at 58 (1992); Restatement (Second) of Trusts §188 (1959). The duty is consistent with the duty to act prudently under §8.30 of the RMNCA.

Subsection (c)(2). Duty to Investigate

This subsection incorporates the traditional fiduciary duty to investigate, using language from UPIA §2(d). The subsection requires persons who make investment and management decisions to investigate the accuracy of the information used in making decisions.

Subsection (d). Pooling Funds

An institution holding more than one institutional fund may find that pooling its funds for investment and management purposes will be economically beneficial. The Act permits pooling for these purposes. The prohibition against commingling no longer prevents pooling funds for investment and management purposes. *See* UPIA §3, cmt. (duty to diversify aided by pooling); UPIA §7, cmt. (pooling to minimize costs); Restatement (Third) of Trusts: Duty to Segregate and Identify Trust Property §84 (T.D. No. 4 2005). Funds will be considered individually for other purposes of the Act, including for the spending rule for endowment funds of Section 163.005 and the modification rules of Section 163.007.

Subsection (e)(1). Prudent Decision Making

Subsection (e)(1) takes much of its language from UPIA §2(c). In making decisions about whether to acquire or retain an asset, the institution should consider the institution's mission, its current programs, and the desire to cultivate additional donations from a donor, in addition to factors related more directly to the asset's potential as an investment.

Subsection (e)(1)(C) reflects the fact that some organizations will invest in taxable investments that may generate unrelated business taxable income for income tax purposes.

Assets held primarily for program-related purposes are not subject to UPMIFA. The management of those assets will continue to be governed by other laws applicable to the institution. Other assets may not be held primarily for program-related purposes but may have both investment purposes and program-related purposes. Subsections (a) and (e)(1)(H) indicate that a prudent decision maker can take into consideration the relationship between an investment and the purposes of the institution and of the institutional fund in making an investment that may have a program-related purpose but not be primarily program-related. The degree to which an institution uses an asset to accomplish a charitable purpose will affect the weight given that factor in a decision to acquire or retain the asset.

Subsection (e)(2). Portfolio Approach

This subsection reflects the use of portfolio theory in modern investment practice. The language comes from UPIA §2(b), which follows the articulation of the prudent investor standard in Restatement (Third) of Trusts: Prudent Investor Rule §227(a) (1992).

Subsection (e)(3). Broad Investment Authority

Consistent with the portfolio theory of investment, this subsection permits a broad range of investments. The language derives from UPIA §2(e).

Section 4 of UMIFA (former §163.005) indicated that an institution could invest "without restriction to investments a fiduciary may make." The committee removed this language from subsection (e)(3) as unnecessary, because states no longer have legal lists restricting fiduciary investing to the specific types of investments identified in statutory lists.

Subsection (e)(3) also provides that other law may limit the authority under this subsection. In addition, all of subsection (e) is subject to contrary provisions in a gift instrument, and a gift instrument may restrict the ability to invest in particular assets. For example, the gift instrument for a particular institutional fund might preclude the institution from investing the assets of the fund in companies that produce tobacco products.

In her book, Governing Nonprofit Organizations: Federal and State Law and Regulation 434 (Harv. Univ. Press 2004), Marion R. Fremont-Smith reports that some large charities pledge their endowment funds as security for loans. Subsection (e)(3) permits this sort of debt financing, subject to the guidelines of subsection (e)(1).

Subsection (e)(4). Duty to Diversify

This subsection assumes that prudence requires diversification but permits an institution to determine that nondiversification is appropriate under exceptional circumstances. A decision not to diversify must be based on the needs of the charity and not solely for the benefit of a donor. A decision to retain property in the hope of obtaining additional contributions from the same donor may be considered made for the benefit of the charity, but the appropriateness of that decision will depend on the circumstances. This subsection derives its language from UPIA §3. *See* UPIA §3 cmt. (discussing the rationale for diversification); Restatement (Third) of Trusts: Prudent Investor Rule §227 (1992).

Subsection (e)(5). Disposing of Unsuitable Assets

This subsection imposes a duty on an institution to review the suitability of retaining property contributed to the institution within a reasonable period of time after the institution receives the property. Subsection (e)(5) requires the institution to make a decision but does not require a particular outcome. The institution may consider a variety of factors in making its decision, and a decision to retain the property either for a period of time or indefinitely may be a prudent decision.

Section 4(2) (former §163.005(2) of the Texas Property Code) of UMIFA specifically authorized an institution to retain property contributed by a donor. The comment explained that an institution might retain property in the hope of obtaining additional contributions from the donor. Under UPMIFA the potential for developing additional contributions by retaining property contributed to the institution would be among the "other circumstances" that the institution might consider in deciding whether to retain or dispose of the property. The institution must weigh the potential for obtaining additional contributions with all other factors that affect the suitability of retaining the property in the investment portfolio.

The language of subsection (e)(5) comes from UPIA §4, which restates Restatement (Third) of Trusts: Prudent Investor Rule §229 (1992), which adopted language from Restatement (Second) of Trusts §231 (1959). *See* UPIA §4 cmt.

Subsection (e)(6). Special Skills or Expertise

Subsection (e)(6) states the rule provided in UPIA §2(f) requiring a trustee to use the trustee's own skills and expertise in carrying out the trustee's fiduciary duties. The comment to RMNCA §8.30 describes the existence of a similar rule under the law of nonprofit corporations. Section 8.30(a)(2) provides that in discharging duties a director must act "with the care an ordinarily prudent person in a like position would exercise under similar circumstances...." The comment explains that "[t]he concept of 'under similar circumstances' relates not only to the circumstances of the corporation but to the special background, qualifications, and management experience of the individual director and the role the director plays in the corporation." After describing directors chosen for their ability to raise money, the comment notes that "[n]o special skill or expertise should be expected from such directors unless their background or knowledge evidences some special ability."

The intent of subsection (e)(6) is that a person managing or investing institutional funds must use the person's own judgment and experience, including any particular skills or expertise, in carrying out the management or investment duties. For example, if a charity names a person as a director in part because the person is a lawyer, the lawyer's background may allow the lawyer to recognize legal issues in connection with funds held by the charity. The lawyer should identify the issues for the board, but the lawyer is not expected to provide legal advice. A lawyer is not expected to be able to recognize every legal issue, particularly issues outside the lawyer's area of expertise, simply because the board member is lawyer. *See* ALI Principles of the Law of Nonprofit Organizations, Preliminary Draft No. 3 (May 12, 2005) §315 (Duty of Care), cmt. c.

UMIFA contained two provisions that authorized investments in pooled or common investment funds. UMIFA §§4(3), 4(4) (former §§163.005(3), 163.005(4)). The Drafting Committee concluded that Section 163.004(e)(3) of UPMIFA authorizes these investments. The decision not to include the two provisions in UPMIFA implies no disapproval of such investments.

PROP §163.005. APPROPRIATION FOR EXPENDITURE OR ACCUMULATION OF ENDOWMENT FUND; RULES OF CONSTRUCTION

(a) Subject to the intent of a donor expressed in the gift instrument and to Subsections (d) and (e), an institution may appropriate for expenditure or accumulate so much of an endowment fund as the institution determines is prudent for the uses, benefits, purposes, and duration for which the endowment fund is established. Unless stated otherwise in the gift instrument, the assets in an endowment fund are donor-restricted assets until appropriated for expenditure by the institution. In making a determination to appropriate or accumulate, the institution shall act in good faith, with the care that an ordinarily prudent person in a like position would exercise under similar circumstances, and shall consider, if relevant, the following factors:

(1) the duration and preservation of the endowment fund;

(2) the purposes of the institution and the endowment fund;

(3) general economic conditions;

(4) the possible effect of inflation or deflation;

(5) the expected total return from income and the appreciation of investments;

(6) other resources of the institution; and

(7) the investment policy of the institution.

(b) To limit the authority to appropriate for expenditure or accumulate under Subsection (a), a gift instrument must specifically state the limitation.

(c) Terms in a gift instrument designating a gift as an endowment, or a direction or authorization in the gift instrument to use only "income," "interest," "dividends," or "rents, issues, or profits," or "to preserve the principal intact," or words of similar import:

(1) create an endowment fund of permanent duration unless other language in the gift instrument limits the duration or purpose of the fund; and

(2) do not otherwise limit the authority to appropriate for expenditure or accumulate under Subsection (a).

(d) Except as provided in Subsection (f), appropriation for expenditure in any year of an amount greater than seven percent of the fair market value of an endowment fund with an aggregate value of $1 million or more, calculated on the basis of market values determined at least quarterly and averaged over a period of not less than three years immediately preceding the year in which the appropriation for expenditure was made, creates a rebuttable presumption of imprudence. For an endowment fund in existence for fewer than three years, the fair market value of the endowment fund must be calculated for the period the endowment fund has been in existence. This subsection does not:

(1) apply to an appropriation for expenditure permitted under law other than this chapter or by the gift instrument; or

(2) create a presumption of prudence for an appropriation for expenditure of an amount less than or equal to seven percent of the fair market value of the endowment fund.

(e) For an institution with an endowment fund with an aggregate value of less than $1 million, a rebuttable presumption of imprudence is created if more than five percent of the fair market value of the endowment fund is appropriated for expenditure in any year, calculated on the basis of market values determined at least quarterly and averaged over a period of not less than three years immediately preceding the year in which the appropriation for expenditure was made. For an endowment fund in existence for fewer than three years, the fair market value of the endowment fund must be calculated for the period the endowment fund has been in existence. This subsection does not:

(1) apply to an appropriation for expenditure permitted under law other than this chapter or by the gift instrument; or

(2) create a presumption of prudence for an appropriation for expenditure of an amount less than or equal to five percent of the fair market value of the endowment fund.

(f) This subsection applies only to a university system, as defined by Section 61.003(10), Education Code. The appropriation for expenditure in any year of any amount greater than nine percent of the fair market value of an endowment fund with an aggregate value of $450 million or more, calculated on the basis of market values determined at least quarterly and averaged over a period of not less than three years immediately preceding the year in which the appropriation for expenditure was made, creates a rebuttable presumption of imprudence. For an endowment fund in existence for fewer than three years, the fair market value of the endowment fund must be calculated for the period the endowment fund has been in existence. This subsection does not:

(1) apply to an appropriation for expenditure permitted under law other than this chapter or by the gift instrument; or

(2) create a presumption of prudence for an appropriation for expenditure of an amount less than or equal to nine percent of the fair market value of the endowment fund.

(g) If an institution pools the assets of individual endowment funds for collective investment, this section applies to the pooled fund and does not apply to individual endowment funds, including individual endowment funds for which the nature of the underlying asset or donor restrictions preclude inclusion in a pool but which are managed by the institution in accordance with a collective investment policy.

History of Prop. Code §163.005: Acts 2007, 80th Leg., ch. 834, §1, eff. Sept. 1, 2007.

NCCUSL Comment*

Purpose and Scope of Revisions

This section revises the provision in UMIFA that permitted the expenditure of appreciation of an endowment fund to the extent the fund had appreciated in value above the fund's historic dollar value. UMIFA defined historic dollar value to mean all contributions to the fund, valued at the time of contribution. Instead of using historic dollar value as a limitation, UPMIFA applies a more carefully articulated prudence standard to the process of making decisions about expenditures from an endowment fund. The expenditure rule of Section 163.005 applies only to the extent that a donor and an institution have not reached some other agreement about spending from an endowment. If a gift instrument sets forth specific requirements for spending, then the charity must comply with those requirements. However, if the gift instrument uses more general language, for example directing the charity to "hold the fund as an endowment" or "retain principal and spend income," then Section 163.005 provides a rule of construction to guide the charity.

Prior to the promulgation of UMIFA, "income" for trust accounting purposes meant interest and dividends but not capital gains, whether or not realized. Many institutions assumed that trust accounting principles applied to charities organized as nonprofit corporations, and the rules limited the institutions' ability to invest their endowment funds effectively. UMIFA addressed this problem by construing "income" in gift instruments to include a prudent amount of capital gains, both realized and unrealized. Under UMIFA an institution could spend appreciation in addition to spending income determined under trust accounting rules. This rule of construction likely carried out the intent of the donor better than a rule limiting spending to trust accounting income, while permitting the charity to invest in a manner that could generate better returns for the fund.

UPMIFA also applies a rule of construction to terms like "income" or "endowment." The assumption in the Act is that a donor who uses one of these terms intends to create a fund that will generate sufficient gains to be able to make ongoing distributions from the fund while at the same time preserving the purchasing power of the fund. Because historic dollar value under UMIFA was a number fixed in time, the use of that approach may not have adequately captured the intent of a donor who wanted the endowment fund to continue to maintain its value in current dollars. UPMIFA takes a different approach, directing the institution to determine spending based on the total assets of the endowment fund rather than determining spending by adding a prudent amount of appreciation to trust accounting income.

UPMIFA requires the persons making spending decisions for an endowment fund to focus on the purposes of the endowment fund as opposed to the purposes of the institution more generally, as was the case under UMIFA. When the institution considers the purposes and duration of the fund, the institution will give priority to the donor's general intent that the fund be maintained permanently. Although the Act does not require that a specific amount be set aside as "principal," the Act assumes that the charity will act to preserve "principal" (i.e., to maintain the purchasing power of the amounts contributed to the fund) while spending "income" (i.e. making a distribution each year that represents a reasonable spending rate, given investment performance and general economic conditions). Thus, an institution should monitor principal in an accounting sense, identifying the original value of the fund (the historic dollar value) and the increases in value necessary to maintain the purchasing power of the fund.

Subsection (a). Expenditure of Endowment Funds

Subsection (a) uses the RMNCA articulation of the standard of care for decision making under Section 163.005. The change in language does not reflect a substantive change. The comment to Section 163.004 more fully describes that standard of care.

Section 163.005 permits expenditures from an endowment fund to the extent the institution determines that the expenditures are prudent after considering the factors listed in subsection (a). These factors emphasize the importance of the intent of the donor, as expressed in a gift instrument. Section 163.005 looks to written documents as evidence of donor's intent and does not require an institution to rely on oral expressions of intent. By requiring written evidence of intent, the Act protects reliance by the donor and the institution on the written terms of a donative agreement. Informal conversations may be misremembered and may be subject to multiple interpretations. Of course, oral expressions of intent may guide an institution in further carrying out a donor's wishes and in understanding a donor's intent.

The factors in subsection (a) require attention to the purposes of the institution and the endowment fund, economic conditions, and present and reasonably anticipated resources of the institution. As under UMIFA, determinations under Section 163.005 do not depend on the characterization of assets as income or principal and are not limited to the amount of income and unrealized appreciation. The authority in Section 163.005 is permissive, however, and an institution organized as a trust may continue to make spending decisions under trust accounting principles so long as doing so is prudent.

Institutions have operated effectively under UMIFA and have operated more conservatively than the historic dollar value rule would have permitted. Institutions have little incentive to maximize allowable spending. Good practice has been to provide for modest expenditures while maintaining the purchasing power of a fund. Institutions have followed this practice even though UMIFA (1) does not require an institution to maintain a fund's purchasing power and (2) does allow an institution to spend any amounts in a fund above historic dollar value, subject to the prudence standard. The Drafting Committee concluded that eliminating historic dollar value and providing institutions with more discretion would not lead to depletion of endowment funds. Instead, UPMIFA should encourage institutions to establish a spending policy that will be responsive to short-term fluctuations in the value of the fund. Section 163.005 allows an institution to maintain appropriate levels of expenditures in times of economic downturn or economic strength. In some years, accumulation rather than spending will be prudent, and in other years an institution may appropriately make expenditures even if a fund has not generated investment return that year.

Several levels of safeguard exist to prevent an institution from depleting an endowment fund or diverting assets from the purposes for which the fund was created. In comparison with UMIFA, UPMIFA provides greater direction to the institution with respect to making a prudent determination about spending from an endowment. UMIFA (former §163.007) told the decision maker to consider "long and short term needs of the institution in carrying out its educational, religious, charitable, or other eleemosynary purposes, its present and anticipated financial requirements, expected total return on its investments, price level trends, and general economic conditions." UPMIFA clarifies that in making spending decisions the institution should attempt to ensure that the value of the fund endures while still providing that some amounts be spent for the purposes of the endowment fund. In UPMIFA prudent decision making emphasizes the endowment aspect of the fund, rather than the overall purposes or needs of the institution.

In addition to the guidance provided by Section 163.005, other safeguards exist. Donors can restrict gifts and can provide specific instructions to donee institutions regarding appropriate uses for assets contributed. Within institutions, fiduciary duties govern the persons making decisions on expenditures. Those persons must operate both with the best interests of the institution in mind and in keeping with the intent of donors. If an institution diverts an institutional fund from the charitable purposes of the institution, the state attorney general can enforce the charitable interests of the public. By relying on these safeguards while providing institutions with adequate discretion to make appropriate expenditures, the Act creates a standard that takes into consideration the diversity of the charitable sector. The committee expects that accumulated experience with such spending formulas will continue to inform institutional practice under the Act.

Distinguishing Legal and Accounting Standards

Deleting historic dollar value does not transform any portion of an endowment fund into unrestricted assets from a legal standpoint. An endowment fund is restricted because of the donor's intent that the fund be restricted by the prudent spending rule, that the fund not be spent in the current year, and that the fund continue to maintain its value for a long time. Regardless of the treatment of endowment fund from an accounting standpoint, legally an endowment fund should not be considered unrestricted. Subsection (a) states that endowment funds will be legally restricted until the institution appropriates funds for expenditure. The UMIFA statutes in Utah and Maine contain similar language. 13 Me. Rev. Stat. Ann. tit. 13 §4106 (West 2005); Utah Code Ann. 1953 §13-29-3 (2005). *See, also*, advisory published by Mass. Attorney General, "The Attorney General's Position on FASB Statement of Financial Accounting Standards No. 117, ¶ 22 and Related G.L.C. 180A Issues" (January 2004) http://www.ago.state.ma.us/filelibrary/fasb.pdf[1] (last visited May 22, 2006) (concerning the treatment of endowments as legally restricted assets).

* See footnote on p. 583.

The term "endowment fund" includes funds that may last in perpetuity but also funds that are created to last for a fixed term of years or until the institution achieves a specified objective. Section 163.005 requires the institution to consider the intended duration of the fund in making determinations about spending. For example, if a donor directs that a fund be spent over 20 years, Section 163.005 will guide the institution in making distribution decisions. The institution would amortize the fund over 20 years rather than try to maintain the fund in perpetuity. For an endowment fund of limited duration, spending at a rate higher than rates typically used for endowment spending will be both necessary and prudent.

Subsection (c). Rule of Construction

Donor's intent must be respected in the process of making decisions to expend endowment funds. Section 163.005 does not allow an institution to convert an endowment fund into a non-endowment fund nor does the section allow the institution to ignore a donor's intent that a fund be maintained as an endowment. Rather, subsection (c) provides rules of construction to assist institutions in interpreting donor's intent. Subsection (c) assumes that if a donor wants an institution to spend "only the income" from a fund, the donor intends that the fund both support current expenditures and be preserved permanently. The donor is unlikely to be concerned about designation of particular returns as "income" or "principal" under accounting principles. Rather the donor is more likely to assume that the institution will use modern total-return investing techniques to generate enough funds to distribute while maintaining the long-term viability of the fund. Subsection (c) is an intent effectuating provision that provides default rules to construe donor's intent.

As subsection (b) explains, a donor who wants to specify particular spending guidelines can do so. For example, a donor might require that a charity spend between three and five percent of an endowed gift each year, regardless of investment performance or other factors. Because the charity agrees to the restriction in accepting the gift, the restriction will govern spending decisions by the charity. Another donor might want to limit expenditures to trust accounting income and not want the institution to be able to expend appreciation. An instruction to "pay only the income" will not be specific enough, but an instruction to "pay only interest and dividend income earned by the fund and not to make other distributions of the kind authorized by Section 163.005 of UPMIFA" should be sufficient. If a donor indicates that the rules on investing or expenditures under Section 163.005 do not apply to a particular fund, then as a practical matter the institution will probably invest the fund separately. Thus, a decision by a donor to require fund specific expenditure rules will likely also have consequences in the way the institution invests the fund.

Retroactive Application of the Rule of Construction

A constructional rule resolves an ambiguity, in this case, because donors use words like endowment or income without specific directions regarding the intended meaning. Changing a statutory constructional rule does not change the underlying intent, and instead changes the way an ambiguity is resolved, in an attempt to increase the likelihood of giving effect to the intent of most donors.

If a donor has stated in a gift instrument specific directions as to spending, then the institution must respect those wishes, but many donors do not give precise instructions about how to spend endowment funds. In Section 163.005 UPMIFA provides guidance for giving effect to a donor's intent when the donor has not been specific. Like Section 3 of UMIFA (roughly corresponding with former §163.004(d)), Section 163.005 of UPMIFA is a rule of construction, so it does not violate either donor intent or the Constitution.

The issue of whether to apply a rule of construction retroactively was considered in connection with UMIFA. When the New Hampshire legislature considered UMIFA, the Senate asked the New Hampshire Supreme Court for an opinion regarding whether UMIFA, if adopted, would violate a provision of the state constitution prohibiting retrospective laws, and also whether the statute would encroach on the functions of the judicial branch. The opinion answered no to both questions. Opinion of the Justices, Request of the Senate No. 6667, 113 N.H. 287, 306 A.2d 55 (1973).

More recently the Colorado Supreme Court considered the retroactive application of another constructional statute, one that deems the designation of a spouse as the beneficiary of a life insurance policy to be revoked in a case in which the marriage was dissolved after the naming of the spouse as beneficiary. In re Estate of DeWitt, 54 P. 3d 849 (Colo. 2002). In holding that retroactive application of the statute did not violate the Contracts Clause, the court cited approvingly from a statement prepared by the Joint Editorial Board for Uniform Trusts and Estates Acts (JEB). JEB Statement Regarding the Constitutionality of Changes in Default Rules as Applied to Pre-Existing Documents, 17 Am. Coll. Tr. & Est. Couns. Notes 184 app. II (1991).

The JEB Statement explains that the purpose of the anti-retroactivity norm is to protect a transferor who relies on existing rules of law. By definition, however, rules of construction apply only in situations in which a transferor did not spell out his or her intent and hence did not rely on the then-current rule of construction. *See also In re Gardner's Trust*, 266 Minn. 127, 132, 123 N.W. 2d 69, 73 (1963) ("[I]t is doubtful whether the testatrix had any clear intention in mind at the time the will was executed. It is equally plausible that if she had thought about it at all she would have desired to have the dividends go where the law required them to go at the time they were received by the trustee.") (Uniform Principal and Income Act).

Non-retroactivity would produce serious practical problems: If the Act were not retroactive, a charity would need to keep two sets of books for each endowment fund created before the enactment of UPMIFA, if new funds were added after the enactment. The burden that such a rule would impose is out of proportion to the benefit sought.

Subsection (d). Rebuttable Presumption of Imprudence

The Drafting Committee debated at length whether to include a presumption of imprudence for spending above a fixed percentage of the value of the fund. The Drafting Committee decided to include a ... discussion of the advantages and disadvantages of including a presumption in the Act.

Some who commented on the Act viewed the presumption as linked to the retroactive application of the rule of construction of subsection (c). A donor who contributed to an endowment fund under UMIFA may have assumed that the historic dollar value of the gift would be subject to a no-spending rule under the statute. Because UPMIFA removes the concept of historic dollar value, the bracketed presumption of imprudence would assure the donor that spending from an endowment fund will be so limited.

Those in favor of the presumption of imprudence argued that the presumption would curb the temptation that a charity might have to spend endowment assets too rapidly. Although the presumption would be rebuttable, and spending above the identified percentage might, in some years and for some charities, be prudent, institutions would likely be reluctant to authorize spending above seven percent. In addition, the presumption would give the attorney general a benchmark of sorts.

A variety of considerations cut against including a presumption of imprudence in the statute. A fixed percentage in the statute might be perceived as a safe harbor that could lead institutions to spend more than is prudent. Although the provision should not be read to imply that spending below seven percent will be considered prudent, some charities might interpret the statute in that way. Decision makers might be pressured to spend up to the percentage, and in doing so spend more than is prudent, without adequate review of the prudence factors as required under the Act.

Perhaps the biggest problem with including a presumption in the statute is the difficulty of picking a number that will be appropriate in view of the range of institutions and charitable purposes and the fact that economic conditions will change over time. Under recent economic conditions, a spending rate of seven percent is too high for most funds, but in a period of high inflation, seven percent might be too low. In making a prudent decision regarding how much to spend from an endowment fund, each institution must consider a variety of factors, including the particular purposes of the fund, the wishes of the donors, changing economic factors, and whether the fund will receive future donations.

Whether or not a statute includes the presumption, institutions must remember that prudence controls decision making. Each institution must make decisions on expenditures based on the circumstances of the particular charity.

Application of Presumption

For a state wishing to adopt a presumption of imprudence, subsection (d) provides language. Under subsection (d), a rebuttable presumption of imprudence will arise if expenditures in one year exceed seven percent of the assets of an endowment fund. The subsection applies a rolling average of three or more years in determining the value of the fund for purposes of calculating the seven-percent amount. An institution can rebut the presumption of imprudence if circumstances in a particular year make expenditures above that amount prudent. The concept and the language for the presumption of imprudence comes from Mass. Gen. L. ch. 180A, §2 (2004). Massachusetts enacted this rule in 1975 as part of its UMIFA statute. New Mexico adopted the same presumption in 1978. N.M.S.A. §46-9-2 (C) (2004). New Hampshire has a similar provision. N.H. Rev. Stat. §292-B:6.

The period that a charity uses to calculate the presumption (three or more years) and the frequency of valuation (at least quarterly) will be binding in any determination of whether the presumption applies. For example, if a charity values an endowment fund on a quarterly basis and averages the quarterly values over three years to determine the fair market value of the fund for purposes calculating seven percent of the fund, the charity's choices of three years as a smoothing period and quarterly as a valuation period cannot be challenged. If the charity makes an appropriation that is less than seven percent of this value, then the presumption of imprudence does not arise even if the appropriation would exceed seven percent of the value of the fund calculated based on monthly valuations averaged over five years.

If sufficient evidence establishes, by the preponderance of the evidence, the facts necessary to raise the presumption of imprudence, then the institution will have to carry the burden of production of (i.e., the burden of going forward with) other evidence that would tend to demonstrate that its decision was prudent. The existence of the presumption does not shift the burden of persuasion to the charity.

Expenditures from an endowment fund may include distributions for charitable purposes and amounts used for the management and administration of the fund, including annual charges for fundraising. The value of a fund, as calculated for purposes of determining the seven percent amount, will reflect increases due to contributions and investment gains and decreases due to distributions and investment losses. The seven percent figure includes charges for fundraising and administrative expenses other than investment management expenses. All costs or fees associated with an endowment fund are factors that prudent decision makers consider. High costs or fees of investment management could be considered imprudent regardless of whether spending exceeds seven percent of the fund's value.

The presumption of imprudence does not create an automatic safe harbor. Expenditures at six percent might well be imprudently high. *See* James P. Garland, *The Fecundity of Endowments and Long-Duration Trusts*, The Journal of Portfolio Management (2005). Evidence reviewed by the Drafting Committee suggests that at present few funds can sustain spending at a rate above five percent. *See* Roger G. Ibbotson & Rex A. Sinquefield, Stocks, Bonds, Bills, and Inflation: Historical Returns (1926-1987) (Research Foundation of the Institute of Chartered Financial Analysts, 1989). Indeed, under current conditions five percent can be too high. *See* Joel C. Dobris, *Why Five? The Strange, Magnetic, and Mesmerizing Affect of the Five Percent Unitrust and Spending Rate on Settlors, Their Advisers, and Retirees*, 40 Real Prop. Prob. & Tr. J. 39 (2005). Further, spending at a lower rate, particularly in the early years of an endowment, may result in greater distributions over time. *See* DeMarche Associates, Inc, Spending Policies and Investment Planning for Foundations: A Structure for Determining a Foundation's Asset Mix (Council on Foundations: 3d ed. 1999). A presumption of imprudence can serve as a reminder that spending at too high a rate will jeopardize the long-term nature of an endowment fund. If an endowment fund is intended to continue permanently, the institution should take special care to limit annual spending to a level that protects the purchasing power of the fund.

Subsection (d) provides that the terms of the gift instrument can provide additional spending authority. For example, if a gift instrument directs that an institution expend a fund over a ten-year period, exhausting the fund after ten years, spending at a rate higher than seven percent will be necessary.

Subsection (d) does not require an institution to spend a minimum amount each year. The prudence standard and the needs of the institution will supply sufficient guidance regarding whether to accumulate rather than to spend in a particular year.

Spending above seven percent in any one year will not necessarily be imprudent. For some endowment funds fluctuating spending rates may be appropriate. Although the Act does not apply the percentage for the presumption on a rolling basis (e.g., 21 percent over three years), some endowment funds may prudently spend little or nothing in some years and more than seven percent in other years. For example, a charity planning a construction project might decide to spend nothing from an endowment for three years and then in the fourth year might spend 20 percent of the value of the fund for construction costs. The decision to accumulate in years one through three and then to spend 20 percent in the fourth year might be prudent for the charity, depending on the other factors. The charity should maintain adequate records during the accumulation period and should document the decision-making process in the fourth year to be able to meet the burden of production associated with the presumption. Another charity might prudently spend 20 percent in year one and nothing for the following three years. That charity would also need to document the decision-making process through which the decision to spend occurred and maintain records explaining why the decision was prudent under the circumstances.

A charity might establish a "capital replacement fund" designed to provide funds to the institution for repair or replacement of major items of equipment. Disbursements from such a fund will likely fluctuate, with limited expenditures in some years and big expenditures in others. The fund would not exhibit a uniform spending rate. Indeed, an advantage of a capital replacement fund is the ability to absorb a significant capital expenditure in a single year without a negative impact on the operating budget of the institution. Disbursements might average five percent per year but would vary, with spending in some years more and in some years less. Even if this fund is an endowment fund subject to Section 163.005, spending above seven percent in a particular year could well be prudent. Subsection (d) does not preclude spending above seven percent.

A charity creating a capital replacement fund or a building fund might chose to adopt spending rules for the fund that would not be subject to UPMIFA. Specific donor intent can supersede the rules of UPMIFA. If the charity creates a gift instrument that establishes appropriate rules on spending for the fund, and if donors agree to those restrictions, then the UPMIFA rules on spending, including the bracketed presumption, will not apply.

Institutions with Limited Investment and Spending Experience

Several attorneys general and other charity officials raised concerns about whether small institutions would be able to adjust to a spending rule based solely on prudence, without the bright-line guidance of historic dollar value. Some charity regulators who spoke with the Drafting Committee noted that large institutions have sophisticated investment strategies, access to good investment advisors, and experience with spending rules that maintain purchasing power for endowment funds. For these institutions, the rules of UPMIFA should work well. For smaller institutions, however, the state regulators thought that additional guidance could be helpful. After discussing strategies to address this concern, the Drafting Committee decided to include in these comments an additional optional provision that a state could choose to include in its UPMIFA statute.

The optional provision focuses on institutions with endowment funds valued, in the aggregate, at less than $2,000,000. The number is in brackets to indicate that it could be set higher or lower. The number was chosen to address the concern of the state regulators that some small charities might be more likely to spend imprudently than large charities. The Drafting Committee selected $2,000,000 as the value that might include most unsophisticated institutions but would not be overinclusive.

The optional provision creates a notification requirement for an institution with a small endowment that plans to spend below historic dollar value. If an institution subject to the provision decides to appropriate an amount that would cause the value of its endowment funds to drop below the aggregate historic dollar value for all of its endowment funds, then the institution will have to notify the attorney general before proceeding with the expenditure. The provision does not require that the institution obtain the approval of the attorney general before making the distribution. Rather, the notification requirement gives the attorney general the opportunity to take a closer look at the institution and its spending decision, to educate the institution on prudent decision making for endowment funds, and to intervene if the attorney general determines that the spending would be imprudent for the institution. Although the Drafting Committee thinks that the prudence standard in UPMIFA provides adequate guidance to all institutions within the scope of the Act, if a state chooses to adopt a notification provision for institutions with small endowments, the Drafting Committee recommends the following language:

(-) If an institution has endowment funds with an aggregate value of less than [$2,000,000], the institution shall notify the [Attorney General] at least [60 days] prior to an appropriation for expenditure of an amount that would cause the value of the institution's endowment funds to fall below the aggregate historic dollar value of the institution's endowment funds, unless the expenditure is permitted or required under law other than this [act] or in the gift instrument. For purposes of this subsection, "historic dollar value" means the aggregate value in dollars of (i) each endowment fund at the time it became an endowment fund, (ii) each subsequent donation to the fund at the time the donation is made, and (iii) each accumulation made pursuant to a direction in the applicable gift instrument at the time the accumulation is added to the fund. The institution's determination of historic dollar value made in good faith is conclusive.

1. **Editor's note:** This URL no longer exists.

PROP §163.006. DELEGATION OF MANAGEMENT & INVESTMENT FUNCTIONS

(a) Subject to any specific limitation set forth in a gift instrument or in law other than this chapter, an institution may delegate to an external agent the management and investment of an institutional fund to the extent that an institution could prudently delegate under the circumstances. An institution shall act in good faith, with the care that an ordinarily prudent person in a like position would exercise under similar circumstances, in:

(1) selecting an agent;

(2) establishing the scope and terms of the delegation, consistent with the purposes of the institution and the institutional fund; and

(3) periodically reviewing the agent's actions in order to monitor the agent's performance and compliance with the scope and terms of the delegation.

(b) In performing a delegated function, an agent owes a duty to the institution to exercise reasonable care to comply with the scope and terms of the delegation.

(c) An institution that complies with Subsection (a) is not liable for the decisions or actions of an agent to which the function was delegated.

(d) By accepting delegation of a management or investment function from an institution that is subject to the laws of this state, an agent submits to the jurisdiction of the courts of this state in all proceedings arising from or related to the delegation or the performance of the delegated function.

(e) An institution may delegate management and investment functions to its committees, officers, or employees as authorized by law of this state other than this chapter.

History of Prop. Code §163.006: Acts 2007, 80th Leg., ch. 834, §1, eff. Sept. 1, 2007.

NCCUSL Comment*

The prudent investor standard in Section 163.005 presupposes the power to delegate. For some types of investment, prudence requires diversification, and diversification may best be accomplished through the use of pooled investment vehicles that entail delegation. Enacting delegation rules that duplicate existing rules could be confusing and might create conflicts. For charitable trusts, UPIA provides the same delegation rules as those in Section 163.006. For nonprofit corporations, nonprofit corporation statutes often provide comparable rules. A state enacting UPMIFA must be certain that its laws authorize delegation, either through other statutes or by enacting Section 163.006.

Section 163.006 incorporates the delegation rule found in UPIA §9, updating the delegation rules in UMIFA §5 (former §163.006). Section 163.006 permits the decision makers in an institution to delegate management and investment functions to external agents if the decision makers exercise reasonable skill, care, and caution in selecting the agent, defining the scope of the delegation and reviewing the performance of the agent. In some circumstances, the scope of the delegation may include redelegation. For example, an institution may select an investment manager to assist with investment decisions. The delegation may include the authority to redelegate to investment managers with expertise in particular investment areas. All decisions to delegate require the exercise of reasonable care, skill, and caution in selecting, instructing, and monitoring agents. Further, decision makers cannot delegate the authority to make decisions concerning expenditures and can only delegate management and investment functions. Subsection (c) protects decision makers who comply with the requirement for proper delegation from liability for actions or decisions of the agents. In making decisions concerning delegation, the institution must be mindful of Section 163.004(c)(1) of UPMIFA, the provision that directs the institution to incur only reasonable costs in managing and investing an institutional fund.

Section 163.006 does not address issues of internal delegation and potential liability for internal delegation, and subsection (c) does not affect laws that govern personal liability of directors or trustees for matters outside the scope of Section 163.006. Directors will look to nonprofit corporation laws for these rules, while trustees will look to trust law. *See, e.g.*, RMNCA, §8.30(b) (permitting directors to rely on information prepared by an officer or employee of the institution if the director reasonably believes the officer or employee to be reliable and competent in the matters presented).

The language of subsection (c) is similar to that of UPIA §9(c) and RMNCA §8.30(d). The decision not to include the terms "beneficiaries" or "members" in subsection (c) does not indicate a decision that this section does not create immunity from claims brought by beneficiaries or members. Instead, a decision maker who complies with Section 163.006 will be protected from any liability resulting from actions or decisions made by an external agent.

Subsection (d) creates personal jurisdiction over the agent. This subsection is not a choice of law rule.

Subsection (e) notes that law other than this Act governs internal delegation. Section 163.006 of UMIFA included internal delegation as well as external delegation, due to a concern at that time that trust law concepts might govern internal delegation in nonprofit corporations. With the widespread adoption of nonprofit corporation statutes, that concern no longer exists. The decision not to address internal delegation in UPMIFA does not suggest that a governing board of a nonprofit corporation cannot delegate to committees, officers, or employees. Rather, a nonprofit corporation must look to other law, typically a nonprofit corporation statute, for the rules governing internal delegation.

PROP §163.007. RELEASE OR MODIFICATION OF RESTRICTIONS ON MANAGEMENT, INVESTMENT, OR PURPOSE

(a) If the donor consents in a record, an institution may release or modify, in whole or in part, a restriction contained in a gift instrument on the management, investment, or purpose of an institutional fund. A release or modification may not allow a fund to be used for a purpose other than a charitable purpose of the institution.

(b) The court, upon application of an institution, may modify a restriction contained in a gift instrument regarding the management or investment of an institutional fund if the restriction has become impracticable or wasteful, if it impairs the management or investment of the fund, or if, because of circumstances not anticipated by the donor, a modification of a restriction will further the purposes of the fund. Chapter 123 ap-

* See footnote on p. 583.

plies to a proceeding under this subsection. To the extent practicable, any modification must be made in accordance with the donor's probable intention.

(c) If a particular charitable purpose or a restriction contained in a gift instrument on the use of an institutional fund becomes unlawful, impracticable, impossible to achieve, or wasteful, the court, upon application of an institution, may modify the purpose of the fund or the restriction on the use of the fund in a manner consistent with the charitable purposes expressed in the gift instrument. Chapter 123 applies to a proceeding under this subsection.

(d) If an institution determines that a restriction contained in a gift instrument on the management, investment, or purpose of an institutional fund is unlawful, impracticable, impossible to achieve, or wasteful, the institution, 60 days after receipt of notice by the attorney general, may release or modify the restriction, in whole or part, if:

(1) the institutional fund subject to the restriction has a total value of less than $25,000;

(2) more than 20 years have elapsed since the fund was established; and

(3) the institution uses the property in a manner consistent with the charitable purposes expressed in the gift instrument.

(e) The notification to the attorney general under Subsection (d) must be accompanied by a copy of the gift instrument and a statement of facts sufficient to evidence compliance with Subsections (d)(1), (2), and (3).

History of Prop. Code §163.007: Acts 2007, 80th Leg., ch. 834, §1, eff. Sept. 1, 2007.

NCCUSL Comment*

Section 163.007 expands the rules on releasing or modifying restrictions that are found in Section 163.008 of UMIFA. Subsection (a) restates the rule from UMIFA allowing the release of a restriction with donor consent. Subsections (b) and (c) make clear that an institution can always ask a court to apply equitable deviation or cy pres to modify or release a restriction, under appropriate circumstances. Subsection (d), a new provision, permits an institution to apply cy pres on its own for small funds that have existed for a substantial period of time, after giving notice to the state attorney general.

Although UMIFA stated that it did not "limit the application of the doctrine of *cy pres*," UMIFA §7(d) (former §163.008(d)), what that statement meant under the Act was unclear. UMIFA itself appeared to permit only a release of a restriction and not a modification. That all-or-nothing approach did not adequately protect donor intent. *See Yale Univ. v. Blumenthal*, 621 A.2d 1304 (Conn. 1993). By expressly including deviation and cy pres, UPMIFA requires an institution to seek modifications that are "in accordance with the donor's probable intention" for deviation and "in a manner consistent with the charitable purposes expressed in the gift instrument" for cy pres.

Individual Funds

The rules on modification require that the institution, or a court applying a court-ordered doctrine, review each institutional fund separately. Although an institution may manage institutional funds collectively, for purposes of this Section each fund must be considered individually.

Subsection (a). Donor Release

Subsection (a) permits the release of a restriction if the donor consents. A release with donor consent cannot change the charitable beneficiary of the fund. Although the donor has the power to consent to a release of a restriction, this section does not create a power in the donor that will cause a federal tax problem for the donor. The gift to the institution is a completed gift for tax purposes, the property cannot be diverted from the charitable beneficiary, and the donor cannot redirect the property to another use by the charity. The donor has no retained interest in the fund.

Subsection (b). Equitable Deviation

Subsection (b) applies the rule of equitable deviation, adapting the language of UTC §412 to this section. *See also* Restatement (Third) of Trusts §66 (2003). Under the deviation doctrine, a court may modify restrictions on the way an institution manages or administers a fund in a manner that furthers the purposes of the fund. Deviation implements the donor's intent. A donor commonly has a predominating purpose for a gift and, secondarily, an intent that the purpose be carried out in a particular manner. Deviation does not alter the purpose but rather modifies the means in order to carry out the purpose.

Sometimes deviation is needed on account of circumstances unanticipated when the donor created the restriction. In other situations the restriction may impair the management or investment of the fund. Modification of the restriction may permit the institution to carry out the donor's purposes in a more effective manner. A court applying deviation should attempt to follow the donor's probable intention in deciding how to modify the restriction. Consistent with the doctrine of equitable deviation in trust law, subsection (b) does not require an institution to notify donors of the proposed modification. Good practice dictates notifying any donors who are alive and can be located with a reasonable expenditure of time and money. Consistent with the doctrine of deviation under trust law, the institution must notify the attorney general who may choose to participate in the court proceeding. The attorney general protects donor intent as well as the public's interest in charitable assets. Attorney general is in brackets in the Act because in some states another official enforces the law of charities.

Subsection (c). Cy Pres

Subsection (c) applies the rule of cy pres from trust law, authorizing the court to modify the purpose of an institutional fund. The term "modify" encompasses the release of a restriction as well as an alteration of a restriction and also permits a court to order that the fund be paid to another institution. A court can apply the doctrine of cy pres only if the restriction in question has become unlawful, impracticable, impossible to achieve, or wasteful. This standard, which comes from UTC §413, updates the circumstances under which cy pres may be applied by adding "wasteful" to the usual common law articulation of the doctrine. Any change must be made in a manner consistent with the charitable purposes expressed in the gift instrument. *See also* Restatement (Third) of Trusts §67 (2003). Consistent with the doctrine of cy pres, subsection (c) does not require an institution seeking cy pres to notify donors. Good practice will be to notify donors whenever possible. As with deviation, the institution must notify the attorney general who must have the opportunity to be heard in the proceeding.

Subsection (d). Modification of Small, Old Funds

Subsection (d) permits an institution to release or modify a restriction according to cy pres principles but without court approval if the amount of the institutional fund involved is small and if the institutional fund has been in existence for more than 20 years. The rationale is that under some circumstances a restriction may no longer make sense but the cost of a judicial cy pres proceeding will be too great to warrant a change in the restriction. The Drafting Committee discussed at length the parameters for allowing an institution to apply cy pres without court supervision. The Committee drafted subsection (d) to balance the needs of an institution to serve its charitable purposes efficiently with the policy of enforcing donor intent. The Committee concluded that an institutional fund with a value of $25,000 or less is sufficiently small that the cost of a judicial proceeding will be out of proportion to its protective purpose. The Committee included a requirement that the institutional fund be in existence at least 20 years, as a further safeguard for fidelity to donor intent. The 20-year

* See footnote on p. 583.

period begins to run from the date of inception of the fund and not from the date of each gift to the fund. The amount and the number of years have been placed in brackets to signal to an enacting jurisdiction that it may wish to designate a higher or lower figure. Because the amount should reflect the cost of a judicial proceeding to obtain a modification, the number may be higher in some states and lower in others.

As under judicial cy pres, an institution acting under subsection (d) must change the restriction in a manner that is in keeping with the intent of the donor and the purpose of the fund. For example, if the value of a fund is too small to justify the cost of administration of the fund as a separate fund, the term "wasteful" would allow the institution to combine the fund with another fund with similar purposes. If a fund has been created for nursing scholarships and the institution closes its nursing school, the institution might appropriately decide to use the fund for other scholarships at the institution. In using the authority granted under subsection (d), the institution must determine which alternative use for the fund reasonably approximates the original intent of the donor. The institution cannot divert the fund to an entirely different use. For example, the fund for nursing scholarships could not be used to build a football stadium.

An institution seeking to modify a provision under subsection (d) must notify the attorney general of the planned modification. The institution must wait 60 days before proceeding; the attorney general may take action if the proposed modification appears inappropriate.

Notice to Donors

The Drafting Committee decided not to require notification of donors under subsections (b), (c), and (d). The trust law rules of equitable deviation and cy pres do not require donor notification and instead depend on the court and the attorney general to protect donor intent and the public's interest in charitable assets.

With regard to subsection (d), the Drafting Committee concluded that an institution should not be required to give notice to donors. Subsection (d) can only be used for an old and small fund. Locating a donor who contributed to the fund more than 20 years earlier may be difficult and expensive. If multiple donors each gave a small amount to create a fund 20 years earlier, the task of locating all of those donors would be harder still. The Drafting Committee concluded that an institution's concern for donor relations would serve as a sufficient incentive for notifying donors when donors can be located.

PROP §163.008. REVIEWING COMPLIANCE

Compliance with this chapter is determined in light of the facts and circumstances existing at the time a decision is made or action is taken, and not by hindsight.

History of Prop. Code §163.008: Acts 2007, 80th Leg., ch. 834, §1, eff. Sept. 1, 2007.

PROP §163.009. RELATION TO ELECTRONIC SIGNATURES IN GLOBAL & NATIONAL COMMERCE ACT

This chapter modifies, limits, and supersedes the provisions of the Electronic Signatures in Global and National Commerce Act (15 U.S.C. Section 7001 et seq.) but does not modify, limit, or supersede Section 101 of that Act (15 U.S.C. Section 7001(a)) or authorize electronic delivery of any of the notices described in Section 103 of that Act (15 U.S.C. Section 7003(b)).

History of Prop. Code §163.009: Acts 2007, 80th Leg., ch. 834, §1, eff. Sept. 1, 2007.

PROP §163.010. UNIFORMITY OF APPLICATION & CONSTRUCTION

In applying and construing this chapter, consideration must be given to the need to promote uniformity of the law with respect to the subject matter of this chapter among states that enact a law substantially similar to this chapter.

History of Prop. Code §163.010: Acts 2007, 80th Leg., ch. 834, §1, eff. Sept. 1, 2007.

Ⓐ PROP §163.011. APPLICABILITY OF OTHER PARTS OF CODE

Chapters 116 and 117 do ~~[Subtitle B, Title 9 (the Texas Trust Code), does]~~ not apply to any institutional fund subject to this chapter.

History of Prop. Code §163.011: Acts 2007, 80th Leg., ch. 834, §1, eff. Sept. 1, 2007. Amended by S.B. 617, §14, 85th Leg., eff. Sept. 1, 2017.

Chapters 164-180 reserved for expansion

SUBTITLE C. POWERS OF APPOINTMENT

CHAPTER 181. POWERS OF APPOINTMENT

SUBCHAPTER A. GENERAL PROVISIONS

PROP §181.001. DEFINITIONS

In this chapter:

(1) "Donee" means a person, whether or not a resident of this state, who, either alone or in conjunction with others, may exercise a power.

(1-a) "Object of the power of appointment" means a person to whom the donee is given the power to appoint.

(2) "Power" means the authority to appoint or designate the recipient of property, to invade or consume

property, to alter, amend, or revoke an instrument under which an estate or trust is created or held, and to terminate a right or interest under an estate or trust, and any authority remaining after a partial release of a power.

(3) "Property" means all property and interests in property, real or personal, including parts of property, partial interests, and all or any part of the income from property.

(4) "Release" means a renunciation, relinquishment, surrender, refusal to accept, extinguishment, and any other form of release, including a covenant not to exercise all or part of a power.

History of Prop. Code §181.001: Acts 1983, 68th Leg., ch. 576, §1, eff. Jan. 1, 1984. Amended by Acts 2003, 78th Leg., ch. 551, §1, eff. Sept. 1, 2003. Source: TRCS art. 7425c, §1.

PROP §181.002. APPLICATION

(a) Except as provided by Subsection (b), this chapter applies:

(1) to a power or a release of a power, regardless of the date the power is created;

(2) to a vested, contingent, or conditional power; and

(3) to a power classified as a power in gross, a power appurtenant, a power appendant, a collateral power, a general, limited, or special power, an exclusive or nonexclusive power, or any other power.

(b) This chapter applies regardless of the time or manner a power is created or reserved or the release is made and regardless of the time, manner, or in whose favor a power may be exercised.

(c) This chapter does not apply to a power in trust that is imperative.

History of Prop. Code §181.002: Acts 1983, 68th Leg., ch. 576, §1, eff. Jan. 1, 1984. Source: TRCS art. 7425c, §1(a).

PROP §181.003. CHAPTER NOT EXCLUSIVE

The provisions of this chapter concerning the release of a power are not exclusive.

History of Prop. Code §181.003: Acts 1983, 68th Leg., ch. 576, §1, eff. Jan. 1, 1984. Source: TRCS art. 7425c, §11.

PROP §181.004. CONSTRUCTION

This chapter is intended to be declarative of the common law of this state, and it shall be liberally construed to make all powers, except imperative powers in trust, releasable unless the instrument creating the trust expressly provides otherwise.

History of Prop. Code §181.004: Acts 1983, 68th Leg., ch. 576, §1, eff. Jan. 1, 1984.

Sections 181.005-181.050 reserved for expansion

SUBCHAPTER B. RELEASE OF POWERS OF APPOINTMENT

PROP §181.051. AUTHORITY OF DONEE TO RELEASE POWER

Unless the instrument creating the power specifically provides to the contrary, a donee may at any time:

(1) completely release the power;

(2) release the power as to any property subject to the power;

(3) release the power as to a person in whose favor a power may be exercised; or

(4) limit in any respect the extent to which the power may be exercised.

History of Prop. Code §181.051: Acts 1983, 68th Leg., ch. 576, §1, eff. Jan. 1, 1984. Source: TRCS art. 7425c, §2.

PROP §181.052. REQUISITES OF RELEASE

(a) A partial or complete release of a power, with or without consideration, is valid if the donee executes and acknowledges, in the manner required by law for the execution and recordation of deeds, an instrument evidencing an intent to make the release, and the instrument is delivered:

(1) to the person or in the manner specified in the instrument creating the power;

(2) to an adult, other than the donee releasing the power, who may take any of the property subject to the power if the power is not exercised or in whose favor it may be exercised after the partial release;

(3) to a trustee or cotrustee of the property subject to the power; or

(4) to an appropriate county clerk for recording.

(b) An instrument releasing a power may be recorded in a county in this state in which:

(1) property subject to the power is located;

(2) a donee in control of the property resides;

(3) a trustee in control of the property resides;

(4) a corporate trustee in control of the property has its principal office; or

(5) the instrument creating the power is probated or recorded.

History of Prop. Code §181.052: Acts 1983, 68th Leg., ch. 576, §1, eff. Jan. 1, 1984. Source: TRCS art. 7425c, §3.

PROP §181.053. RELEASE BY GUARDIAN

If a person under a disability holds a power, the guardian of the person's estate may release the power in the manner provided in this chapter on the order of the court in this state in which the guardian was appointed or in which the guardianship proceeding is pending.

History of Prop. Code §181.053: Acts 1983, 68th Leg., ch. 576, §1, eff. Jan. 1, 1984. Source: TRCS art. 7425c, §8.

PROP §181.054. EFFECT OF RELEASE ON MULTIPLE DONEES

Unless the instrument creating a power provides otherwise, the complete or partial release by one or more donees of a power that may be exercised by two or more donees, either as an individual or a fiduciary, together or successively, does not prevent or limit the exercise or participation in the exercise of the power by the other donee or donees.

History of Prop. Code §181.054: Acts 1983, 68th Leg., ch. 576, §1, eff. Jan. 1, 1984. Source: TRCS art. 7425c, §4.

PROP §181.055. NOTICE OF RELEASE

(a) A fiduciary or other person in possession or control of property subject to a power, other than the donee, does not have notice of a release of the power until the original release or a copy is delivered to the fiduciary or other person.

(b) A purchaser, lessee, or mortgagee of real property subject to a power who has paid a valuable consideration and who is without actual notice does not have notice of a release of the power until the instrument releasing the power is filed for record with the county clerk of the county in which the real property is located.

History of Prop. Code §181.055: Acts 1983, 68th Leg., ch. 576, §1, eff. Jan. 1, 1984. Source: TRCS art. 7425c, §5.

PROP §181.056. RECORDING

(a) A county clerk shall record a release of a power in the county deed records, and the clerk shall index the release, with the name of the donee entered in the grantor index.

(b) The county clerk shall charge the same fee for recording the release of a power as the clerk is authorized to charge for recording a deed.

History of Prop. Code §181.056: Acts 1983, 68th Leg., ch. 576, §1, eff. Jan. 1, 1984. Source: TRCS art. 7425c, §6.

PROP §181.057. EFFECT OF FAILURE TO DELIVER OR FILE

Failure to deliver or file an instrument releasing a power under Sections 181.052 and 181.055 does not affect the validity of the release as to the donee, the person in whose favor the power may be exercised, or any other person except those expressly protected by Sections 181.052 and 181.055.

History of Prop. Code §181.057: Acts 1983, 68th Leg., ch. 576, §1, eff. Jan. 1, 1984. Source: TRCS art. 7425c, §7.

PROP §181.058. RESTRAINTS ON ALIENATION OR ANTICIPATION

The release of a power that otherwise may be released is not prevented merely by provisions of the instrument creating the power that restrain alienation or anticipation.

History of Prop. Code §181.058: Acts 1983, 68th Leg., ch. 576, §1, eff. Jan. 1, 1984. Source: TRCS art. 7425c, §8.

Sections 181.059-181.080 blank

SUBCHAPTER C. EXERCISE OF POWERS OF APPOINTMENT

PROP §181.081. EXTENT OF POWER

Unless an instrument creating a power expressly provides to the contrary, a donee may exercise a power in any manner consistent with this subchapter.

History of Prop. Code §181.081: Acts 2003, 78th Leg., ch. 551, §2, eff. Sept. 1, 2003.

PROP §181.082. GENERAL EXERCISE

In exercising a power, a donee may make an appointment:

(1) of present, future, or present and future interests;

(2) with conditions and limitations;

(3) with restraints on alienation;

(4) of interests to a trustee for the benefit of one or more objects of the power; and

(5) that creates any right existing under common law.

History of Prop. Code §181.082: Acts 2003, 78th Leg., ch. 551, §2, eff. Sept. 1, 2003.

PROP §181.083. CREATING ADDITIONAL POWERS

(a) In exercising a power, a donee may make appointments that create in the objects of the power additional powers of appointment. The additional powers of appointment must be exercisable in favor of objects of the power who would have been permissible objects under the original donee's power.

(b) In exercising a power, a donee who may appoint outright to an object of the power may make appointments that create in the object of the power pow-

ers exercisable in favor of persons that the original donee may direct, even though the objects of the secondary power of appointment may not have been permissible objects of the original donee's power.

History of Prop. Code §181.083: Acts 2003, 78th Leg., ch. 551, §2, eff. Sept. 1, 2003.

Chapters 182-200 blank

TITLE 11. RESTRICTIVE COVENANTS

CHAPTER 201. RESTRICTIVE COVENANTS APPLICABLE TO CERTAIN SUBDIVISIONS

PROP §201.001. APPLICATION

(a) This chapter applies to a residential real estate subdivision that is located in whole or in part:

(1) within a city that has a population of more than 100,000, or within the extraterritorial jurisdiction of such a city;

(2) in the unincorporated area of:

(A) a county having a population of 3.3 million or more; or

(B) a county having a population of 40,000 or more that is adjacent to a county having a population of 3.3 million or more; or

(3) in the incorporated area of a county having a population of 40,000 or more that is adjacent to a county having a population of 3.3 million or more.

(b) The provisions of this chapter relating to extension of the term of, renewal of, or creation of restrictions do not apply to a subdivision if, by the express terms of the instrument creating existing restrictions, some or all of the restrictions affecting the real property within the subdivision provide:

(1) for automatic extensions of the term of the restrictions for an indefinite number of successive specified periods of at least 10 years subject to a right of waiver or termination, in whole or in part, by a specified percentage of less than 50 percent plus one of the owners of real property interests in the subdivision, as set forth in the instrument creating the restrictions; or

(2) for an indefinite number of successive extensions of at least 10 years of the term of the restrictions by written and filed agreement of a specified percentage of less than 50 percent plus one of the owners of real property interests in the subdivision, as authorized by the instrument creating the restrictions.

(c) The provisions of this chapter relating to addition to or modification of existing restrictions do not apply to a subdivision if, by the express terms of the instrument creating the restrictions, the restrictions affecting the real property within the subdivision provide for addition to or modification of the restrictions by written and filed agreement of a specified percentage of less than 75 percent of the owners of real property interests in the subdivision, as set forth in the instrument creating the restrictions. A subdivision is excluded under this subsection regardless of whether a provision in the restrictions requires the consent of the developer of the subdivision or an architectural control committee for an addition to or modification of the restrictions.

(d) A residential real estate subdivision that is or was subject to this chapter at any time remains subject to this chapter regardless of a change in circumstances that removes the subdivision from the applicability requirements of Subsection (a).

History of Prop. Code §201.001: Acts 1985, 69th Leg., ch. 309, §1, eff. Sept. 1, 1985. Amended by Acts 1987, 70th Leg., ch. 712, §2, eff. June 18, 1987; Acts 1989, 71st Leg., ch. 556, §1, eff. June 14, 1989; Acts 1991, 72nd Leg., ch. 821, §1, eff. Sept. 1, 1991; Acts 1997, 75th Leg., ch. 451, §§1, 2, eff. Sept. 1, 1997; Acts 1999, 76th Leg., ch. 1127, §1, eff. Sept. 1, 1999; Acts 2005, 79th Leg., ch. 1004, §1, eff. Sept. 1, 2005; Acts 2007, 80th Leg., ch. 1367, §3, eff. Sept. 1, 2007; Acts 2011, 82nd Leg., ch. 1163, §109, eff. Sept. 1, 2011.

PROP §201.002. FINDINGS & PURPOSE

(a) The legislature finds that:

(1) the pending expiration of property restrictions applicable to real estate subdivisions in municipalities and in the extraterritorial jurisdiction area of municipalities where there is no zoning creates uncertainty in living conditions and discourages investments in affected subdivisions;

(2) owners of land in affected subdivisions are reluctant or unable to provide proper maintenance, up-

keep, and repairs of structures because of the pending expiration of the restrictions;

(3) financial institutions cannot or will not lend money for investments, maintenance, upkeep, or repairs in affected subdivisions;

(4) these conditions cause dilapidation of housing and other structures and cause unhealthful and unsanitary conditions in affected subdivisions, contrary to the health, safety, and welfare of the citizens; and

(5) the existence of racial covenants in subdivisions, regardless of their unenforceability, is offensive, repugnant, and harmful to members of racial or ethnic minority groups, and public policy requires that these covenants be deleted.

(b) The purpose of this chapter is to provide a procedure for extending the term of, creation of, additions to, or modification of restrictions and to provide for the removal of any restriction or other provision relating to race, religion, or national origin that is void and unenforceable under either the United States Constitution or Section 5.026.

History of Prop. Code §201.002: Acts 1985, 69th Leg., ch. 309, §1, eff. Sept. 1, 1985.

PROP §201.003. DEFINITIONS

In this chapter:

(1) "Restrictions" means one or more restrictive covenants contained or incorporated by reference in a properly recorded map, plat, replat, declaration, or other instrument filed in the county real property records, map records, or deed records.

(2) "Residential real estate subdivision" or "subdivision" means:

(A) all land encompassed within one or more maps or plats of land that is divided into two or more parts if the maps or plats cover land within a city, town, or village, or within the extraterritorial jurisdiction of a city, town, or village and are recorded in the deed, map, or real property records of a county, and the land encompassed within the maps or plats is or was burdened by restrictions limiting all or at least a majority of the land area covered by the map or plat, excluding streets and public areas, to residential use only; or

(B) all land located within a city, town, or village, or within the extraterritorial jurisdiction of a city, town, or village that has been divided into two or more parts and that is or was burdened by restrictions limiting at least a majority of the land area burdened by restrictions, excluding streets and public areas, to residential use only, if the instrument or instruments creating the restrictions are recorded in the deed or real property records of a county.

(3) "Owner" means an individual, fiduciary, partnership, joint venture, corporation, association, or other entity that owns record title to real property in a subdivision, or the personal representative of an individual who owns record title to subdivision property.

(4) "Petition" means one or more instruments, however designated or entitled, by which one or more of the purposes authorized by this chapter are sought to be accomplished.

(5) "Real property records" means the applicable records of a county clerk in which conveyances of real property are recorded.

(6) "Lienholder" means an individual, corporation, financial institution, or other entity that holds a vendor's or deed of trust lien secured by land within the subdivision.

(7) "Petition committee" or "committee" means a group of three or more owners who file with the county clerk a notice as required by Section 201.005(a) and who prepare and circulate a petition as allowed under this chapter.

History of Prop. Code §201.003: Acts 1985, 69th Leg., ch. 309, §1, eff. Sept. 1, 1985. Amended by Acts 1991, 72nd Leg., ch. 822, §2, eff. Sept. 1, 1991.

PROP §201.004. EXTENSION, RENEWAL, CREATION, MODIFICATION OF, OR ADDITION TO, RESTRICTIONS

(a) A petition may be filed under this chapter to:

(1) extend or renew an unexpired restriction;

(2) create a restriction;

(3) add to or modify an existing restriction; or

(4) modify an existing provision in an instrument creating a restriction that provides for extension of those restrictions.

(b) A petition is not effective to extend, renew, create, add to, or modify a restriction unless the petition is filed with the county clerk's office in the county where the subdivision is located before the second anniversary of the date the committee files with the county clerk the notice required by Section 201.005(a).

(c) If a petition meeting the requirements of this chapter is filed with the county clerk within the required period, the provisions of the petition extending, renewing, creating, adding to, or modifying a restriction apply to and burden all of the property in the subdi-

vision except property excluded under Section 201.009. If a petition contains provisions extending or renewing the term of a restriction, the petition may provide for an initial extension or renewal period of not more than 10 years and additional automatic extensions of the term for not more than 10 years each. The extension, renewal, creation, or modification of, or addition to, a restriction takes effect on the later of the dates the petition is filed with the county clerk or a date specified in the petition.

(d) If existing originally applicable restrictions provide a procedure for extension, that procedure may be used for successive extensions of the originally applicable restrictions unless the original restriction instrument expressly prohibits the procedure from being used for successive extensions.

History of Prop. Code §201.004: Acts 1985, 69th Leg., ch. 309, §1, eff. Sept. 1, 1985. Amended by Acts 1991, 72nd Leg., ch. 822, §3, eff. Sept. 1, 1991; Acts 2007, 80th Leg., ch. 1367, §4, eff. Sept. 1, 2007; Acts 2009, 81st Leg., ch. 821, §1, eff. June 19, 2009.

See also ***Real Estate Forms***, FORM 6:1.

PROP §201.005. PETITION COMMITTEE

(a) At least three owners may form a petition committee. The committee shall file written notice of its formation with the county clerk of each county in which the subdivision is located.

(b) A notice filed under this chapter must contain:

(1) a statement that a petition committee has been formed for the extension of the term of, creation of, addition to, or modification of one or more restrictions;

(2) the name and residential address of each member of the committee;

(3) the name of the subdivision to which the restrictions apply and a reference to the real property records or map or plat records where the instrument or instruments that contain the restrictions sought to be extended, added to, or modified are recorded or, if the creation of a restriction is proposed, a reference to the place where the map or other document, if any, is recorded;

(4) a general statement of the matters to be included in the petition;

(5) if the creation of a restriction for a subdivision is proposed, a copy of the proposed petition creating the restriction; and

(6) if the amendment or modification of a restriction is proposed, a copy of the proposed instrument creating the amendment or modification, containing the original restriction that is affected and indicating by appropriate deletion and insertion the change to the restriction that is proposed to be amended or modified.

(c) Each member of the committee must sign and acknowledge the notice before a notary or other official authorized to take acknowledgments.

(d) The county clerk shall enter on the notice the date it is filed and record it in the real property records of the county.

(e) An individual's membership on the committee terminates if the individual ceases to own land in the subdivision. If a vacancy on the committee occurs, either because a member ceases to own land in the subdivision or because a member resigns or dies, a majority of the remaining members may appoint as a successor an individual who owns land in the subdivision and who consents to serve as a committee member. If one or more successor committee members are appointed, the surviving committee members shall file written notice of the name and address of each successor committee member with the county clerk not later than the 10th day after the date of the appointment.

(f) After August 31, 1989, only one committee in a subdivision may file to operate under this chapter at one time. Before September 1, 1989, there is no limit on the number of committees in a subdivision with power to act under this chapter at one time. If more than one committee in a subdivision files a notice after August 31, 1989, the committee that files its notice first is the committee with the power to act. A committee that does not effect a successful petition within the time provided by this chapter is dissolved by operation of law. Except as provided by Section 201.006(c), a new committee for that subdivision may not be validly created under this chapter before the fifth anniversary of the date of dissolution of the previous committee. A petition circulated by a dissolved committee is ineffective for any of the purposes of this chapter.

History of Prop. Code §201.005: Acts 1985, 69th Leg., ch. 309, §1, eff. Sept. 1, 1985. Amended by Acts 1987, 70th Leg., ch. 712, §3, eff. June 18, 1987.

See also ***Real Estate Forms***, FORMS 11:1, 11:2.

PROP §201.0051. SPECIAL PETITION APPROVAL REQUIRED FOR CERTAIN RESTRICTIONS

A right created or an obligation imposed by an existing restriction that relates to the developer of the subdivision or an architectural control committee estab-

lished by the instrument creating the restriction cannot be altered unless the person who has the right or obligation signs and acknowledges the petition.

History of Prop. Code §201.0051: Acts 1997, 75th Leg., ch. 451, §3, eff. Sept. 1, 1997.

See also *Real Estate Forms*, FORMS 11:1, 11:2.

PROP §201.006. PETITION PROCEDURE

(a) A petition may be circulated, signed, acknowledged, and filed by or on behalf of owners at any time during the circulating committee's existence. The petition must conform to the requirements of Section 201.007.

(b) The petition may be filed not later than one year after the date on which the notice required by Section 201.005(a) is filed. The petition must be signed and acknowledged by owners who own, in the aggregate:

(1) a majority of the total number of lots in the subdivision, in order to extend, renew, or create restrictions;

(2) a majority of the total number of separately owned parcels, tracts, or building sites in the subdivision, whether or not the parcels, tracts, or building sites contain part or all of one or more platted lots or combinations of lots, in order to extend, renew, or create restrictions;

(3) a majority of the square footage within all of the lots in the subdivision, excluding any area dedicated or used exclusively for roadways or public purposes or by utilities, in order to extend, renew, or create restrictions;

(4) at least 75 percent of the total number of lots in the subdivision, in order to modify or add to existing restrictions;

(5) at least 75 percent of the total number of separately owned parcels, tracts, or building sites in the subdivision, whether or not the parcels, tracts, or building sites contain part or all of one or more platted lots or combination of lots, in order to modify or add to existing restrictions; or

(6) at least 75 percent of the square footage within all of the lots in the subdivision, excluding any area dedicated or used exclusively for roadways or public purposes or by utilities, in order to modify or add to existing restrictions.

(c) If, after August 31, 1988, a court of competent jurisdiction holds any provision of a restrictive covenant affecting a subdivision to which this chapter applies invalid, a petition committee authorized by this chapter may file a petition not later than one year after the date on which the judgment is rendered. For this purpose, the five-year limitation period in Section 201.005(f) does not apply.

(d) The petition is effective if signed and acknowledged by the required number of owners of any one of the classifications of property specified in Subsection (b) and is filed as provided by Subsection (f).

(e) After an owner signs a petition, the fact that the owner subsequently conveys the land in the subdivision does not affect the previous signing of the petition.

(f) The petition must be filed with the county clerk of each county in which the subdivision is located.

History of Prop. Code §201.006: Acts 1985, 69th Leg., ch. 309, §1, eff. Sept. 1, 1985. Amended by Acts 1987, 70th Leg., ch. 712, §4, eff. June 18, 1987; Acts 1991, 72nd Leg., ch. 822, §4, eff. Sept. 1, 1991.

See also *Real Estate Forms*, FORMS 11:1, 11:2.

PROP §201.007. CONTENTS OF PETITION

(a) A petition filed under this chapter must contain or be supplemented by one or more instruments containing:

(1) the name of the subdivision;

(2) a reference to the real property records or map or plat records where the instrument or instruments that contain any restriction sought to be extended, added to, or modified are recorded or, in the case of the creation of a restriction, a reference to the place where the map or other document identifying the subdivision is recorded;

(3) a verbatim statement of any provisions for extension of the term of, or addition to, the restriction;

(4) if a restriction is being amended or modified, the text of the proposed instrument creating the amendment or modification, together with a comparison of the original restriction that is affected indicating by appropriate deletion and insertion the change to the restriction that is proposed to be amended or modified;

(5) if a restriction is being created, the text of the proposed instrument creating the restriction;

(6) original acknowledged signatures of the required number of owners as provided by Section 201.006;

(7) alternate boxes, clearly identified in a conspicuous manner next to the place for signing the peti-

tion, that enable each record owner to mark the appropriate box to show the exercise of the owner's option of either including or excluding the owner's property from being burdened by the restrictions being extended, created, added to, or modified;

(8) a statement that owners who do not sign the petition must file suit under Section 201.010 before the 181st day after the date on which the certificate called for by Section 201.008(e) is filed in order to challenge the procedures followed in extending, creating, adding to, or modifying a restriction; and

(9) a statement that owners who do not sign the petition may delete their property from the operation of the extended, created, added to, or modified restriction by filing a statement described in the fourth listed category in Section 201.009(b) before one year after the date on which the owner receives actual notice of the filing of the petition authorized by this chapter.

(b) If a restriction being added to, modified, or extended contains any provision relating to race, religion, or national origin that is void and unenforceable under either the United States Constitution or Section 5.026, the void and unenforceable restriction shall, by the provisions of the petition, be declared to be deleted from the restriction as if the provision had never been contained in the restriction.

(c) Each petition filed under this chapter must contain an assertion from the signing owners that they own record title to property within the subdivision, and the legal description and street address of the property of each signing owner must be shown beside or above the signature. If there is more than one record owner of a tract, each record owner must sign the petition before the property can be counted as a part of the number required by Section 201.006.

History of Prop. Code §201.007: Acts 1985, 69th Leg., ch. 309, §1, eff. Sept. 1, 1985.

See also *Real Estate Forms*, FORMS 6:1, 11:1, 11:2.

PROP §201.008. NOTICE & CERTIFICATE OF COMPLIANCE

(a) Not later than the 60th day after the date on which a petition that meets the requirements of this chapter is filed, the committee shall give notice directed to all persons who then are record owners of property in the subdivision. The notice must contain:

(1) the name of the subdivision covered by the petition;

(2) a copy of the petition;

(3) a statement that the proper number of property owners in the subdivision have signed and acknowledged the petition; and

(4) the date the petition was filed with the county clerk.

(b) Except as provided by Subsection (d), the notice required by Subsection (a) must be:

(1) published once a week for two consecutive weeks in a newspaper of general circulation in the county or counties where the subdivision is located; and

(2) sent by certified mail, return receipt requested, to each person who owned land in the subdivision as of the date the notice is given, excluding the owners of land dedicated for public use or for use by utilities.

(c) If the committee acts in good faith in determining ownership and giving notice as required by this section, the failure to give personal notice to an owner does not affect the application of an extension, modification, or creation of, or addition to, a restriction under this chapter to the property of a person who signed the petition.

(d) Instead of the information required by Subsection (a)(2), a notice published as required by Subsection (b)(1) may contain a general description of the purpose and effect of the petition.

(e) On compliance with the notice requirements of this section, a majority of the members of the committee shall execute a certificate of compliance and file the certificate with the county clerk of each county where the subdivision is located.

(f) The county clerk of each county shall record the certificate in the real property records of the county.

History of Prop. Code §201.008: Acts 1985, 69th Leg., ch. 309, §1, eff. Sept. 1, 1985.

PROP §201.009. PROPERTY WITHIN SUBDIVISION NOT AFFECTED BY PETITION

(a) The procedures called for under this chapter are considered complete and regular in all respects unless challenged by a declaratory judgment suit under Section 201.010.

(b) A restriction added, modified, created, or extended under this chapter does not affect or encumber property within the subdivision that is included within one of the following categories:

(1) property exclusively dedicated for use by the public or for use by utilities;

(2) property of an owner who elected in the petition to exclude the property from the restriction;

(3) property of an owner who did not sign the petition and has not received actual notice of the filing of the petition;

(4) property of an owner who did not sign the petition and who files, before one year after the date on which the owner received actual notice of the filing of the petition, an acknowledged statement describing the owner's property by reference to the recorded map or plat of the subdivision and stating that the owner elects to have the property deleted and excluded from the operation of the extended, modified, changed, or created restriction; and

(5) property owned by a minor or a person judicially declared to be incompetent at the time the certificate is filed, unless:

(A) actual notice of the filing of the petition is given to a guardian of the minor or incompetent person, and the guardian has not filed the statement described in the fourth listed category in this subsection;

(B) a predecessor in title to the minor or incompetent person signed a petition that was filed while the property was owned by the predecessor; or

(C) the incompetent person signed a petition that was filed before the judicial declaration of the person's incompetency.

(c) The county clerk shall file a statement described in the fourth listed category in Subsection (b) in the same manner as the petition and certificate. Substantial compliance by an owner with the requirements for the statement prevents the owner's property from being burdened by an extended, created, added to, or modified restriction if the statement is filed within the time required.

(d) A lienholder whose lien was established before the effective date of a petition is not bound by the petition unless the lienholder signs it and it is later filed. If such a lienholder who does not sign the filed petition later acquires title to the property in the subdivision through foreclosure, the acquisition is free of the restrictions added, modified, created, or extended by the petition. However, if any other person acquires the title to the property at a foreclosure sale, that person takes the property subject to the restriction added, modified, created, or extended by the petition, if any prior owner of the foreclosed property signed and acknowledged the petition.

(e) Notwithstanding any other provision of this chapter, property that is excluded in any manner from the operation of restrictions that are modified, added to, or created by a petition under this chapter is, unless the petition expressly provides otherwise, subject to those restrictions, if any, affecting the excluded property as the restrictions existed immediately before the effective date of the petition, and those restrictions are continued in effect to the extent originally applicable to the excluded property. After the filing of such a petition, those restrictions may be added to, modified, or extended by a specified percentage of the owners of real property interests in accordance with this chapter or the instruments evidencing the restrictions as they existed immediately before the effective date of the petition, if otherwise still applicable. Any petition filed under this chapter that creates, adds to, or modifies restrictions may provide for the subsequent addition to or extension, creation, or modification of, the resulting restrictions by a specified percentage of the owners of real property interests in the subdivision as set forth in the instruments evidencing the continued restrictions. This subsection does not abrogate, alter, affect, or impair the rights of a lienholder under Subsection (d) to not be bound by a petition adopted under this chapter when the lienholder subsequently acquires title to the excluded property through foreclosure.

History of Prop. Code §201.009: Acts 1985, 69th Leg., ch. 309, §1, eff. Sept. 1, 1985. Amended by Acts 1987, 70th Leg., ch. 712, §5, eff. June 18, 1987.

See also *Real Estate Forms*, FORMS 11:1, 11:2.

PROP §201.010. ACTION & LIMITATIONS OF REMEDIES

(a) If an owner and the owner's predecessors in interest neither signed the petition nor filed the statement described in the fourth listed category in Section 201.009(b), the owner may file a suit for declaratory judgment in a court of competent jurisdiction:

(1) to challenge the completeness or regularity of the procedures leading to the recordation of a certificate, if the suit is filed before the 181st day after the date on which the certificate is filed with the county clerk; or

(2) to exclude the owner's property from the operation of the extended, modified, added to, or created restriction.

(b) A suit for a declaratory judgment must name as defendants the final members of the petition committee who are owners of property in the subdivision at the time of the filing of the suit. In addition, a suit for a declaratory judgment must name all other owners of property in the subdivision as defendants, either as individuals or as members of a class.

(c) An owner who files a suit for the second listed purpose in Subsection (a) is entitled to relief only if the owner pleads and establishes that the conditions of land use within the subdivision at the time the certificate was filed were incompatible with the restriction. As an alternative to excluding a specific parcel of land from the operation of the restriction, a court may alter the restriction as it applies to the parcel to better conform to the incompatible conditions.

(d) The remedies in this section are exclusive of all others in actions brought to challenge a restriction extended, modified, added to, or created under this chapter. The filing of an action for the first listed purpose in Subsection (a) does not prevent the restriction from taking effect in accordance with its terms pending a final judgment.

History of Prop. Code §201.010: Acts 1985, 69th Leg., ch. 309, §1, eff. Sept. 1, 1985.

ANNOTATIONS

Wilchester W. Concerned Homeowners LDEF, Inc. v. Wilchester W. Fund, Inc., 177 S.W.3d 552, 560-61 (Tex.App.—Houston [1st Dist.] 2005, pet. denied). "In light of ***Brooks*** [***v. Northglen Ass'n***, 141 S.W.3d 158 (Tex.2004),] and ***Simpson*** [***v. Afton Oaks Civic Club, Inc.***, 145 S.W.3d 169 (Tex.2004)], we must reject the argument that a court does not have jurisdiction to hear a case ... unless all property owners are joined. Instead, ... the Club and the homeowners' associations should have sought abatement or joinder to protect their interests, and if the trial court denied such relief, then they should have sought review of the trial court's denial of their efforts to seek such relief."

PROP §201.011. PROHIBITION OF CLAIM OF LACK OF MUTUALITY

If a petition procedure is completed under this chapter, the owners of property within the subdivision whose property is covered by the petition may not raise in any judicial proceeding the issue that the restrictions added, modified, created, or extended under this chapter are not enforceable on the grounds that the restrictions are not applicable to all of the property in the subdivision.

History of Prop. Code §201.011: Acts 1985, 69th Leg., ch. 309, §1, eff. Sept. 1, 1985.

PROP §201.012. MULTIPLE FILING; COMPUTATION OF FILING DATE

For purposes of this chapter, an instrument required to be filed with the clerk of more than one county is considered filed on the date on which the last required filing is made.

History of Prop. Code §201.012: Acts 1985, 69th Leg., ch. 309, §1, eff. Sept. 1, 1985.

PROP §201.013. CUMULATIVE EFFECT

The procedure prescribed by this chapter for adding to, modifying, creating, or extending the term of a restriction is cumulative and not in lieu of other methods of adding to, modifying, creating, or extending a restriction.

History of Prop. Code §201.013: Acts 1985, 69th Leg., ch. 309, §1, eff. Sept. 1, 1985.

CHAPTER 202. CONSTRUCTION & ENFORCEMENT OF RESTRICTIVE COVENANTS

PROP §202.001. DEFINITIONS

In this chapter:

(1) "Dedicatory instrument" means each document governing the establishment, maintenance, or operation of a residential subdivision, planned unit development, condominium or townhouse regime, or any similar planned development. The term includes a declaration or similar instrument subjecting real property to:

(A) restrictive covenants, bylaws, or similar instruments governing the administration or operation of a property owners' association;

(B) properly adopted rules and regulations of the property owners' association; or

(C) all lawful amendments to the covenants, bylaws, instruments, rules, or regulations.

(2) "Property owners' association" means an incorporated or unincorporated association owned by or whose members consist primarily of the owners of the property covered by the dedicatory instrument and through which the owners, or the board of directors or similar governing body, manage or regulate the residential subdivision, planned unit development, condominium or townhouse regime, or similar planned development.

(3) "Petition" means one or more instruments, however designated or entitled, by which one or more actions relating to restrictive covenants are sought to be accomplished.

(4) "Restrictive covenant" means any covenant, condition, or restriction contained in a dedicatory instrument, whether mandatory, prohibitive, permissive, or administrative.

(5) "Front yard" means a yard within a lot having a front building setback line with a setback of not less than 15 feet extending the full width of the lot between the front lot line and the front building setback line.

History of Prop. Code §202.001: Acts 1987, 70th Leg., ch. 712, §1, eff. June 18, 1987. Amended by Acts 2011, 82nd Leg., ch. 1142, §2, eff. Jan. 1, 2012; Acts 2013, 83rd Leg., ch. 1389, §1, eff. June 14, 2013.

ANNOTATIONS

Anderson v. New Prop. Owners' Ass'n, 122 S.W.3d 378, 384 (Tex.App.—Texarkana 2003, pet. denied). "An association has standing to sue when it satisfies a three-pronged test. First, the members must otherwise have standing to sue in their own right. Second, the interests it seeks to protect must be germane to the organization's purpose. Finally, neither the claim asserted nor the relief requested may require the participation of individual members in the lawsuit. [¶] Ordinarily, any person entitled to benefit under a restrictive covenant may enforce it. This means that, generally, an interested property owner may enforce a restrictive covenant." *See also* ***Musgrave v. Brookhaven Lake Prop. Owners Ass'n***, 990 S.W.2d 386, 393-94 (Tex.App.—Texarkana 1999, pet. denied).

PROP §202.002. APPLICABILITY OF CHAPTER

(a) This chapter applies to all restrictive covenants regardless of the date on which they were created.

(b) This chapter does not affect the requirements of the Community Homes for Disabled Persons Location Act (Article 1011n, Vernon's Texas Civil Statutes).

History of Prop. Code §202.002: Acts 1987, 70th Leg., ch. 712, §1, eff. June 18, 1987.

PROP §202.003. CONSTRUCTION OF RESTRICTIVE COVENANTS

(a) A restrictive covenant shall be liberally construed to give effect to its purposes and intent.

(b) In this subsection, "family home" is a residential home that meets the definition of and requirements applicable to a family home under the Community Homes for Disabled Persons Location Act (Article 1011n, Vernon's Texas Civil Statutes). A dedicatory instrument or restrictive covenant may not be construed to prevent the use of property as a family home. However, any restrictive covenant that applies to property used as a family home shall be liberally construed to give effect to its purposes and intent except to the extent that the construction would restrict the use as a family home.

History of Prop. Code §202.003: Acts 1987, 70th Leg., ch. 712, §1, eff. June 18, 1987.

See also ***Real Estate Forms***, FORM 6:1.

ANNOTATIONS

Pilarcik v. Emmons, 966 S.W.2d 474, 478 (Tex. 1998). "[R]estrictive covenants are subject to the general rules of contract construction. Whether restrictive covenants are ambiguous is a question of law. Courts must examine the covenants as a whole in light of the circumstances present when the parties entered the agreement. Like a contract, covenants are 'unambiguous as a matter of law if [they] can be given a definite or certain legal meaning.' On the other hand, if the covenants are susceptible to more than one reasonable interpretation, they are ambiguous." *See also* ***Sanchez v. Southampton Civic Club, Inc.***, 367 S.W.3d 429, 434 (Tex.App.—Houston [14th Dist.] 2012, no pet.); ***Leake v. Campbell***, 352 S.W.3d 180, 184 (Tex.App.—Fort Worth 2011, no pet.); ***Uptegraph v. Sandalwood Civic Club***, 312 S.W.3d 918, 925-26 (Tex.App.—Houston [1st Dist.] 2010, no pet.).

Tarr v. Timberwood Park Owners Ass'n, 510 S.W.3d 725, 730-31 (Tex.App.—San Antonio 2016, pet.

filed 12-29-16). "[T]he term 'used solely for residential purposes' [from the restrictive covenant] has a definite legal meaning and is unambiguous. Therefore, ... we apply §202.003 ... and liberally construe the restrictive covenant to give effect to its purpose and intent. [¶] One leasing his home to be used for transient purposes is not complying with the restrictive covenant that it be used *solely* for residential purposes. [¶] Here, [t]he leasing agreement is not consistent with a renter who has the intent to remain at the home; the agreement thus shows that the home is being used for transient purposes rather than residential purposes." *But see* ***Zgabay v. NBRC Prop. Owners Ass'n***, No. 03-14-00660-CV (Tex.App.—Austin 2015, pet. denied) (memo op.; 8-28-15) (term "used for single family residential purposes" was ambiguous; court did not apply §202.003 requirement).

Baywood Estates Prop. Owners Ass'n v. Caolo, 392 S.W.3d 776, 782 (Tex.App.—Tyler 2012, no pet.). "A restrictive covenant is a contractual agreement between the seller and the purchaser of real property. A property owner may subdivide property into lots and create a subdivision in which all property owners agree to the same or similar restrictive covenants designed to further the owner's general plan or scheme of development. A covenant runs with the land when it touches and concerns the land; relates to a thing in existence or specifically binds the parties and their assigns; is intended by the original parties to run with the land; and when the successor to the burden has notice. Neighborhood and subdivision developers in Texas have been using covenants that run with the land as described in the seminal 1914 case of ***Hooper v. Lottman***, 171 S.W. 270 (Tex.App.—El Paso 1914, no writ).... *At 783:* Where an owner of a tract subdivides and sells the subdivided parcels to separate grantees, imposing restrictions on the use of each parcel pursuant to a general plan or scheme of development, each grantee may enforce the restrictions against each other grantee. A neighborhood scheme of restrictions, to be effective and enforceable, must apply to all lots of like character within the subdivision. The theory which sustains a scheme or plan of this character is that the restrictions are a benefit to all. If the restrictions upon all lots similarly located are not alike, or some lots are not subject to the restrictions while others are, then a burden would be carried by some owners without a corresponding benefit."

Uptegraph v. Sandalwood Civic Club, 312 S.W.3d 918, 926 (Tex.App.—Houston [1st Dist.] 2010, no pet.). "Some courts of appeals have recognized that the common-law requirement of construing restrictions strictly and §202.003(a)'s requirement of construing residential covenants liberally to effectuate their purposes and intent might appear contradictory. As a result, some courts of appeals have held or implied that §202.003(a)'s liberal-construction rule concerning residential covenants supersedes the common-law rule of strict construction. In contrast, other courts of appeals, including ours, have concluded that there is no discernable conflict between the common law and §202.003(a). *At 927:* The Texas Supreme Court has noted, but not yet resolved, the potential conflict between the common law and §202.003(a). *At 928:* In this case, neither party asserts that the covenant is ambiguous. The trial court found that the covenant is unambiguous, and we agree. Because the covenant is unambiguous, our interpretation of the ... covenant is the same under both the common law and §202.003(a). Because the Supreme Court has not yet spoken on the issue, and because the outcome of this case does not rely on our resolving any ambiguity between the common law and §202.003(a), it is unnecessary for us to address that question." *Compare* ***City of Pasadena v. Gennedy***, 125 S.W.3d 687, 693-95 (Tex.App.—Houston [1st Dist.] 2003, pet. denied) (§202.003(a) does not trump common-law rules of construction), *and* ***Reagan Nat'l Adver. v. Capital Outdoors, Inc.***, 96 S.W.3d 490, 493 n.2 (Tex.App.—Austin 2002, pet. granted, judgm't vacated w.r.m.) (same), *with* ***Village of Pheasant Run Homeowners Ass'n v. Kastor***, 47 S.W.3d 747, 751 (Tex.App.—Houston [14th Dist.] 2001, pet. denied) (noting that §202.003(a) constitutes statutory exception to common-law rules), *and* ***Benard v. Humble***, 990 S.W.2d 929, 930-31 (Tex. App.—Beaumont 1999, pet. denied) (giving priority to Property Code's rule of construction over common-law rules).

Hourani v. Katzen, 305 S.W.3d 239, 251 (Tex. App.—Houston [1st Dist.] 2009, pet. denied). "In construing a restrictive covenant, the court's primary task is to determine the intent of its framers. Covenants restricting the free use of land are not favored by the courts, but when they are confined to a lawful purpose and are clearly worded, they are generally enforceable. 'All doubts must be resolved in favor of the free and unrestricted use of the premises, and the restrictive

clause must be strictly construed against the party seeking to enforce it.'" *See also* ***Raman Chandler Props., L.C. v. Caldwell's Creek Homeowners Ass'n***, 178 S.W.3d 384, 390-91 (Tex.App.—Fort Worth 2005, pet. denied); ***Ostrowski v. Ivanhoe Prop. Owners Imprv. Ass'n***, 38 S.W.3d 248, 252-53 (Tex.App.—Texarkana 2001, pet. denied).

Meehl v. Wise, 285 S.W.3d 561, 567 (Tex.App.—Houston [14th Dist.] 2009, no pet.). "The tension between [Prop. Code] §202.003(b) ... and [Hum. Res. Code] §123.003(b) ... is readily apparent with respect to enforceability of a restrictive covenant depending on the date in which the covenant was created. The Human Resources Code bars enforcement of a covenant restricting the use of property as a community home created after September 1, 1985, while the Property Code bars enforcement of the same covenant regardless of the date in which the instrument was created. Because §202.003(b) is the later statute, enacted in 1987, its general prohibition controls the less restrictive section of 123.003(b) passed in 1985. We conclude that the universal applicability of ... §202.003(b) controls if the use of property comports with definition of a community home articulated in the Human Resources Code."

Voice of Cornerstone Ch. Corp. v. Pizza Prop. Partners, 160 S.W.3d 657, 669 (Tex.App.—Austin 2005, no pet.). "In restrictive covenants, the word 'structure' may be used in a broad sense or in a restricted one. The broad definition of a structure is 'any production or piece of work artificially built up, or composed of parts joined together in some definite manner; any construction.' In a restricted sense, 'structure' means 'a building of any kind, chiefly a building of some size or of magnificence; an edifice.' Inclusion of a particular object within the term, or its exclusion therefrom, usually depends upon the context and the purpose sought to be accomplished by the provision of which the term is a part."

PROP §202.004. ENFORCEMENT OF RESTRICTIVE COVENANTS

(a) An exercise of discretionary authority by a property owners' association or other representative designated by an owner of real property concerning a restrictive covenant is presumed reasonable unless the court determines by a preponderance of the evidence that the exercise of discretionary authority was arbitrary, capricious, or discriminatory.

(b) A property owners' association or other representative designated by an owner of real property may initiate, defend, or intervene in litigation or an administrative proceeding affecting the enforcement of a restrictive covenant or the protection, preservation, or operation of the property covered by the dedicatory instrument.

(c) A court may assess civil damages for the violation of a restrictive covenant in an amount not to exceed $200 for each day of the violation.

History of Prop. Code §202.004: Acts 1987, 70th Leg., ch. 712, §1, eff. June 18, 1987.

See also *Real Estate Forms*, FORMS 6:1-6:3.

ANNOTATIONS

KBG Invs. v. Greenspoint Prop. Owners' Ass'n, 478 S.W.3d 111, 116 (Tex.App.—Houston [14th Dist.] 2015, no pet.). "[D] argues that because [damages under Prop. Code §202.004(c)] are punitive rather than compensatory, ... they constitute exemplary damages under [CPRC] Ch. 41.... [D] then argues that because [P] recovered no actual damages, the award of statutory civil damages is precluded. *At 122-23:* Chapter 41 defines exemplary damages as any damages awarded as a penalty or by way of punishment but not for compensatory purposes. Exemplary damages includes punitive damages. Our court already has determined that the civil damages under §202.004(c) ... are punitive rather than compensatory. Under this precedent, civil damages under §202.004(c) ... fall squarely within Ch. 41's definition of exemplary damages. [¶] Chapter 41 is broad in scope, and with certain limited exceptions that are inapplicable here, its provisions prevail over all other law to the extent of any conflict. While the ... Property Code would allow the recovery of these civil damages without any proof of actual damages, Ch. 41 does not, and Ch. 41 prevails." (Internal quotes omitted.)

Moran v. Memorial Point Prop. Owners Ass'n, 410 S.W.3d 397, 403 (Tex.App.—Houston [14th Dist.] 2013, no pet.). "To determine whether a restrictive covenant has been abandoned or its enforcement waived, we consider such factors as the number, nature, and severity of the existing violations, any prior enforcements of the restriction, and whether it is still possible to realize to a substantial degree ... the benefits of the restriction despite the violations. To defeat enforcement of the restrictive covenant ..., the property user must

prove that violations then existing are so great as to lead the mind of the average man to reasonably conclude that the restriction in question has been abandoned and its enforcement waived." (Internal quotes omitted.) *See also* ***Finkelstein v. Southampton Civic Club***, 675 S.W.2d 271, 278 (Tex.App.—Houston [1st Dist.] 1984, writ ref'd n.r.e.).

Wiese v. Heathlake Cmty. Ass'n, 384 S.W.3d 395, 404-05 (Tex.App.—Houston [14th Dist.] 2012, no pet.). Section 202.004 "does not define the scope of an association's discretionary authority. Other courts have considered this provision when reviewing issues bearing on an association's decision to grant or deny a homeowner's request for a variance permit. If we assume for argument's sake that this provision also applies to an association's interpretation of its covenants, then [homeowner] must show that the interpretation is arbitrary, capricious, or discriminatory. We conclude that [association's] interpretation is arbitrary on its face when evaluated in light of the Declaration's language as a whole. Therefore, even if a presumption of reasonableness applies in this case, it was overcome." *See also* ***Marmic Props., L.L.C. v. Silverglen Townhomes Homeowners Ass'n***, No. 14-12-00312-CV (Tex. App.—Houston [14th Dist.] 2013, no pet.) (memo op.; 8-29-13).

Summers v. Highland Composite Prop. Owners Ass'n, 363 S.W.3d 210, 214 (Tex.App.—Corpus Christi 2011, no pet.). "[I]n order to hold the fees collected, [P] was required to show that it is a valid property owners association. *At 215:* We hold that even if [P] were designated by certain homeowners within the subdivisions at issue to enforce deed restrictions, and, if we further assume, but not hold, that this designation is the designation referred to in [Prop. Code] §§204.004 and 209.002 ..., it is insufficient to establish that [P] is a duly constituted property owners association absent a showing that [P] manages or regulates these residential subdivisions for the benefit of the owners of property in these subdivisions. [¶] In the absence of a showing that it is a valid property owners association, [P] is not entitled to hold the fees that it has collected. The judgment should have required that any maintenance fees collected be held in the registry of the court for the benefit of the entity entitled to hold such funds under the applicable restrictions." *See also* ***Musgrave v. Brookhaven Lake Prop. Owners Ass'n***, 990 S.W.2d 386, 394 (Tex.App.—Texarkana 1999, pet. denied).

Uptegraph v. Sandalwood Civic Club, 312 S.W.3d 918, 937 (Tex.App.—Houston [1st Dist.] 2010, no pet.). "The damages awarded under [§202.004(c)] are clearly discretionary with the court, and the language of §202.004(c) suggests that the damages that may be assessed thereunder are punitive, rather than compensatory, in nature. [¶] Notably, the amount of damages that may be assessed ... is not related to the showing of any type of injury or harm or the extent of such injury or harm; rather, it is related to the number of days that the violation takes place.... *At 938:* We ... hold that the damages that may be assessed under §202.004(c) are not limited to compensation for actual harm or injury from the violation of a restrictive covenant. [A] trial court does not abuse its discretion in assessing damages under §202.004(c) in the absence of evidence of actual damages." *See also* ***Sanchez v. Southampton Civic Club, Inc.***, 367 S.W.3d 429, 436 (Tex.App.—Houston [14th Dist.] 2012, no pet.).

Jennings v. Bindseil, 258 S.W.3d 190, 198 (Tex. App.—Austin 2008, no pet.). "A purchaser is bound by restrictive covenants of which he has notice, regardless of whether he believed that his actions violated the restriction." *See also* ***Village of Pheasant Run Homeowners Ass'n v. Kastor***, 47 S.W.3d 747, 753-54 (Tex. App.—Houston [14th Dist.] 2001, pet. denied) (owners aware of deed restrictions and accompanying guidelines are considered on notice of restrictions despite believing guidelines unclear and inapplicable); ***Tien Tao Ass'n v. Kingsbridge Park Cmty. Ass'n***, 953 S.W.2d 525, 529 (Tex.App.—Houston [1st Dist.] 1997, no pet.) (owner could not argue no notice of restrictions because guidelines were unclear when owner acknowledged having copy of such restrictions).

Indian Beach Prop. Owners' Ass'n v. Linden, 222 S.W.3d 682, 690 (Tex.App.—Houston [1st Dist.] 2007, no pet.). "A party must substantially violate a deed restriction before the trial court may issue a permanent injunction. *At 691:* A party seeking an injunction has the burden of showing that a clear equity demands the injunction. A party seeking enforcement of a deed restriction always has the burden at trial to demonstrate the enforceability of the restriction." *See also* ***Marcus v. Whispering Springs Homeowners Ass'n***, 153 S.W.3d 702, 707 (Tex.App.—Dallas 2005, no pet.).

Voice of Cornerstone Ch. Corp. v. Pizza Prop. Partners, 160 S.W.3d 657, 666 (Tex.App.—Austin 2005, no pet.). Successor grantor and original grantor "were

in privity of estate when the restrictive covenant was created. The special warranty deed conveying the property from [original grantor] to [successor grantor] contained the terms of the covenant, which attempts to make the property unusable for purposes other than commercial or light industrial uses. The covenant burdens the property itself, and its terms make clear that [successor grantor] and [original grantor] intended for it to bind future owners of the property. The explicit terms of the covenant also evidence the parties' intention that it run with the land. ... Thus, [current owner] is charged with notice of the deed's terms and those of the other agreements made between [successor grantor] and [original grantor]. Accordingly, we find that this restrictive covenant runs with the land and that [successor-in-interest] properly had standing to seek its enforcement."

Youssefzadeh v. Brown, 131 S.W.3d 641, 644-45 (Tex.App.—Fort Worth 2004, no pet.). "A subdivision developer is generally free to amend restrictions in covenants for the subdivision prior to the sale of lots in the subdivision, assuming the amendments do not violate public policy. However, the sale of subdivision lots triggers any amendment mechanism set forth in the dedication. When the power to amend the land use restriction is reserved in the developer, the amendment of a restrictive covenant must be in the precise manner authorized by the dedicating agreement. The same 'precise manner' requirement should logically be required when the amendment mechanism lies other than with the developer."

PROP §202.005. WITHDRAWAL OF SIGNATURE

(a) A signature may be withdrawn from a petition authorized to be filed in connection with terminating restrictive covenants, as provided by this section.

(b) To withdraw a signature, the signer must request that the signature be withdrawn.

(c) To be effective, a withdrawal request must:

(1) be in writing and be signed and acknowledged by the signer of the petition;

(2) be filed with the authority with whom the petition is required to be filed not later than the day before the petition filing deadline, if any; and

(3) be delivered in the form of a copy of the request to the circulator of the petition not later than the date the request is filed or by the effective date of this chapter, whichever is later.

(d) A withdrawal request or copy filed or delivered by mail is considered to be filed or delivered at the time of its receipt by the appropriate person.

(e) The filing of an effective withdrawal request nullifies the signature on the petition and places the signer in the same position as if the signer had not signed the petition.

History of Prop. Code §202.005: Acts 1987, 70th Leg., ch. 712, §1, eff. June 18, 1987.

See also ***Real Estate Forms***, FORMS 11:1, 11:2.

PROP §202.006. PUBLIC RECORDS

(a) A property owners' association shall file all dedicatory instruments in the real property records of each county in which the property to which the dedicatory instruments relate is located.

(b) A dedicatory instrument has no effect until the instrument is filed in accordance with this section.

History of Prop. Code §202.006: Acts 1999, 76th Leg., ch. 1420, §2, eff. Sept. 1, 1999. Amended by Acts 2011, 82nd Leg., ch. 1142, §3, eff. Jan. 1, 2012.

See also ***Real Estate Forms***, FORMS 6:1-6:3, 6:16-6:18.

PROP §202.007. CERTAIN RESTRICTIVE COVENANTS PROHIBITED

(a) A property owners' association may not include or enforce a provision in a dedicatory instrument that prohibits or restricts a property owner from:

(1) implementing measures promoting solid-waste composting of vegetation, including grass clippings, leaves, or brush, or leaving grass clippings uncollected on grass;

(2) installing rain barrels or a rainwater harvesting system;

(3) implementing efficient irrigation systems, including underground drip or other drip systems; or

(4) using drought-resistant landscaping or water-conserving natural turf.

(b) A provision that violates Subsection (a) is void.

(c) A property owners' association may restrict the type of turf used by a property owner in the planting of new turf to encourage or require water-conserving turf.

(d) This section does not:

(1) restrict a property owners' association from regulating the requirements, including size, type, shielding, and materials, for or the location of a composting device if the restriction does not prohibit the economic installation of the device on the property owner's property where there is reasonably sufficient area to install the device;

(2) require a property owners' association to permit a device described by Subdivision (1) to be installed in or on property:

(A) owned by the property owners' association;

(B) owned in common by the members of the property owners' association; or

(C) in an area other than the fenced yard or patio of a property owner;

(3) prohibit a property owners' association from regulating the installation of efficient irrigation systems, including establishing visibility limitations for aesthetic purposes;

(4) prohibit a property owners' association from regulating the installation or use of gravel, rocks, or cacti;

(5) restrict a property owners' association from regulating yard and landscape maintenance if the restrictions or requirements do not restrict or prohibit turf or landscaping design that promotes water conservation;

(6) require a property owners' association to permit a rain barrel or rainwater harvesting system to be installed in or on property if:

(A) the property is:

(i) owned by the property owners' association;

(ii) owned in common by the members of the property owners' association; or

(iii) located between the front of the property owner's home and an adjoining or adjacent street; or

(B) the barrel or system:

(i) is of a color other than a color consistent with the color scheme of the property owner's home; or

(ii) displays any language or other content that is not typically displayed by such a barrel or system as it is manufactured;

(7) restrict a property owners' association from regulating the size, type, and shielding of, and the materials used in the construction of, a rain barrel, rainwater harvesting device, or other appurtenance that is located on the side of a house or at any other location that is visible from a street, another lot, or a common area if:

(A) the restriction does not prohibit the economic installation of the device or appurtenance on the property owner's property; and

(B) there is a reasonably sufficient area on the property owner's property in which to install the device or appurtenance; or

(8) prohibit a property owners' association from requiring an owner to submit a detailed description or a plan for the installation of drought-resistant landscaping or water-conserving natural turf for review and approval by the property owners' association to ensure, to the extent practicable, maximum aesthetic compatibility with other landscaping in the subdivision.

(d-1) A property owners' association may not unreasonably deny or withhold approval of a proposed installation of drought-resistant landscaping or water-conserving natural turf under Subsection (d)(8) or unreasonably determine that the proposed installation is aesthetically incompatible with other landscaping in the subdivision.

(e) This section does not apply to a property owners' association that:

(1) is located in a municipality with a population of more than 175,000 that is located in a county in which another municipality with a population of more than one million is predominantly located; and

(2) manages or regulates a development in which at least 4,000 acres of the property is subject to a covenant, condition, or restriction designating the property for commercial use, multifamily dwellings, or open space.

History of Prop. Code §202.007: Acts 2003, 78th Leg., ch. 1024, §1, eff. Sept. 1, 2003. Amended by Acts 2011, 82nd Leg., ch. 1311, §6, eff. Sept. 1, 2011; Acts 2013, 83rd Leg., ch. 736, §1, eff. Sept. 1, 2013.

Section 202.008 blank

PROP §202.009. REGULATION OF DISPLAY OF POLITICAL SIGNS

(a) Except as otherwise provided by this section, a property owners' association may not enforce or adopt a restrictive covenant that prohibits a property owner from displaying on the owner's property one or more signs advertising a political candidate or ballot item for an election:

(1) on or after the 90th day before the date of the election to which the sign relates; or

(2) before the 10th day after that election date.

(b) This section does not prohibit the enforcement or adoption of a covenant that:

(1) requires a sign to be ground-mounted; or

(2) limits a property owner to displaying only one sign for each candidate or ballot item.

(c) This section does not prohibit the enforcement or adoption of a covenant that prohibits a sign that:

(1) contains roofing material, siding, paving materials, flora, one or more balloons or lights, or any other similar building, landscaping, or nonstandard decorative component;

(2) is attached in any way to plant material, a traffic control device, a light, a trailer, a vehicle, or any other existing structure or object;

(3) includes the painting of architectural surfaces;

(4) threatens the public health or safety;

(5) is larger than four feet by six feet;

(6) violates a law;

(7) contains language, graphics, or any display that would be offensive to the ordinary person; or

(8) is accompanied by music or other sounds or by streamers or is otherwise distracting to motorists.

(d) A property owners' association may remove a sign displayed in violation of a restrictive covenant permitted by this section.

History of Prop. Code §202.009: Acts 2005, 79th Leg., ch. 1010, §1, eff. June 18, 2005.

PROP §202.010. REGULATION OF SOLAR ENERGY DEVICES

(a) In this section:

(1) "Development period" means a period stated in a declaration during which a declarant reserves:

(A) a right to facilitate the development, construction, and marketing of the subdivision; and

(B) a right to direct the size, shape, and composition of the subdivision.

(1-a) "Residential unit" means a structure or part of a structure intended for use as a single residence and that is:

(A) a single-family house; or

(B) a separate living unit in a duplex, a triplex, or a quadplex.

(2) "Solar energy device" has the meaning assigned by Section 171.107, Tax Code.

(b) Except as otherwise provided by Subsection (d), a property owners' association may not include or enforce a provision in a dedicatory instrument that prohibits or restricts a property owner from installing a solar energy device.

(c) A provision that violates Subsection (b) is void.

(d) A property owners' association may include or enforce a provision in a dedicatory instrument that prohibits a solar energy device that:

(1) as adjudicated by a court:

(A) threatens the public health or safety; or

(B) violates a law;

(2) is located on property owned or maintained by the property owners' association;

(3) is located on property owned in common by the members of the property owners' association;

(4) is located in an area on the property owner's property other than:

(A) on the roof of the home or of another structure allowed under a dedicatory instrument; or

(B) in a fenced yard or patio owned and maintained by the property owner;

(5) if mounted on the roof of the home:

(A) extends higher than or beyond the roofline;

(B) is located in an area other than an area designated by the property owners' association, unless the alternate location increases the estimated annual energy production of the device, as determined by using a publicly available modeling tool provided by the National Renewable Energy Laboratory, by more than 10 percent above the energy production of the device if located in an area designated by the property owners' association;

(C) does not conform to the slope of the roof and has a top edge that is not parallel to the roofline; or

(D) has a frame, a support bracket, or visible piping or wiring that is not in a silver, bronze, or black tone commonly available in the marketplace;

(6) if located in a fenced yard or patio, is taller than the fence line;

(7) as installed, voids material warranties; or

(8) was installed without prior approval by the property owners' association or by a committee created in a dedicatory instrument for such purposes that provides decisions within a reasonable period or within a period specified in the dedicatory instrument.

(e) A property owners' association or the association's architectural review committee may not withhold approval for installation of a solar energy device if the provisions of the dedicatory instruments to the extent authorized by Subsection (d) are met or exceeded, unless the association or committee, as applicable, determines in writing that placement of the device as pro-

posed by the property owner constitutes a condition that substantially interferes with the use and enjoyment of land by causing unreasonable discomfort or annoyance to persons of ordinary sensibilities. For purposes of making a determination under this subsection, the written approval of the proposed placement of the device by all property owners of adjoining property constitutes prima facie evidence that such a condition does not exist.

(f) During the development period for a development with fewer than 51 planned residential units, the declarant may prohibit or restrict a property owner from installing a solar energy device.

History of Prop. Code §202.010: Acts 2011, 82nd Leg., ch. 939, §1, eff. June 17, 2011. Amended by Acts 2015, 84th Leg., ch. 126, §§1, 2, eff. Sept. 1, 2015.

PROP §202.011. REGULATION OF CERTAIN ROOFING MATERIALS

A property owners' association may not include or enforce a provision in a dedicatory instrument that prohibits or restricts a property owner who is otherwise authorized to install shingles on the roof of the owner's property from installing shingles that:

(1) are designed primarily to:

(A) be wind and hail resistant;

(B) provide heating and cooling efficiencies greater than those provided by customary composite shingles; or

(C) provide solar generation capabilities; and

(2) when installed:

(A) resemble the shingles used or otherwise authorized for use on property in the subdivision;

(B) are more durable than and are of equal or superior quality to the shingles described by Paragraph (A); and

(C) match the aesthetics of the property surrounding the owner's property.

History of Prop. Code §202.011: Acts 2011, 82nd Leg., ch. 939, §1, eff. June 17, 2011.

PROP §202.012. FLAG DISPLAY

(a) A property owners' association may not, except as provided in this section, adopt or enforce a dedicatory instrument provision that prohibits, restricts, or has the effect of prohibiting or restricting an owner from the display of:

(1) the flag of the United States of America;

(2) the flag of the State of Texas; or

(3) an official or replica flag of any branch of the United States armed forces.

(b) A property owners' association may adopt or enforce reasonable dedicatory instrument provisions:

(1) that require:

(A) the flag of the United States be displayed in accordance with 4 U.S.C. Sections 5-10;

(B) the flag of the State of Texas be displayed in accordance with Chapter 3100, Government Code;

(C) a flagpole attached to a dwelling or a freestanding flagpole be constructed of permanent, long-lasting materials, with a finish appropriate to the materials used in the construction of the flagpole and harmonious with the dwelling;

(D) the display of a flag, or the location and construction of the supporting flagpole, to comply with applicable zoning ordinances, easements, and setbacks of record; and

(E) a displayed flag and the flagpole on which it is flown be maintained in good condition and that any deteriorated flag or deteriorated or structurally unsafe flagpole be repaired, replaced, or removed;

(2) that regulate the size, number, and location of flagpoles on which flags are displayed, except that the regulation may not prevent the installation or erection of at least one flagpole per property that:

(A) is not more than 20 feet in height and, subject to applicable zoning ordinances, easements, and setbacks of record, is located in the front yard of the property; or

(B) is attached to any portion of a residential structure owned by the property owner and not maintained by the property owners' association;

(3) that govern the size of a displayed flag;

(4) that regulate the size, location, and intensity of any lights used to illuminate a displayed flag;

(5) that impose reasonable restrictions to abate noise caused by an external halyard of a flagpole; or

(6) that prohibit a property owner from locating a displayed flag or flagpole on property that is:

(A) owned or maintained by the property owners' association; or

(B) owned in common by the members of the association.

(c) A property owner who has a front yard and who otherwise complies with any permitted property owners' association regulations may elect to install a flagpole in accordance with either Subsection (b)(2)(A) or Subsection (b)(2)(B).

History of Prop. Code §202.012: Acts 2011, 82nd Leg., ch. 1028, §1, eff. June 17, 2011. Amended by Acts 2013, 83rd Leg., ch. 1389, §2, eff. June 14, 2013. Renumbered from §202.011 by Acts 2013, 83rd Leg., ch. 161, §22.001(40), eff. Sept. 1, 2013.

Sections 202.013-202.017 blank

PROP §202.018. REGULATION OF DISPLAY OF CERTAIN RELIGIOUS ITEMS

(a) Except as otherwise provided by this section, a property owners' association may not enforce or adopt a restrictive covenant that prohibits a property owner or resident from displaying or affixing on the entry to the owner's or resident's dwelling one or more religious items the display of which is motivated by the owner's or resident's sincere religious belief.

(b) This section does not prohibit the enforcement or adoption of a covenant that, to the extent allowed by the constitution of this state and the United States, prohibits the display or affixing of a religious item on the entry to the owner's or resident's dwelling that:

(1) threatens the public health or safety;

(2) violates a law;

(3) contains language, graphics, or any display that is patently offensive to a passerby;

(4) is in a location other than the entry door or door frame or extends past the outer edge of the door frame of the owner's or resident's dwelling; or

(5) individually or in combination with each other religious item displayed or affixed on the entry door or door frame has a total size of greater than 25 square inches.

(c) Except as otherwise provided by this section, this section does not authorize an owner or resident to use a material or color for an entry door or door frame of the owner's or resident's dwelling or make an alteration to the entry door or door frame that is not authorized by the restrictive covenants governing the dwelling.

(d) A property owners' association may remove an item displayed in violation of a restrictive covenant permitted by this section.

History of Prop. Code §202.018: Acts 2011, 82nd Leg., ch. 263, §1, eff. June 17, 2011.

PROP §202.019. STANDBY ELECTRIC GENERATORS

(a) In this section, "standby electric generator" means a device that converts mechanical energy to electrical energy and is:

(1) powered by natural gas, liquefied petroleum gas, diesel fuel, biodiesel fuel, or hydrogen;

(2) fully enclosed in an integral manufacturer-supplied sound attenuating enclosure;

(3) connected to the main electrical panel of a residence by a manual or automatic transfer switch; and

(4) rated for a generating capacity of not less than seven kilowatts.

(b) Except as provided by this section, a property owners' association may not adopt or enforce a dedicatory instrument provision that prohibits, restricts, or has the effect of prohibiting or restricting an owner from owning, operating, installing, or maintaining a permanently installed standby electric generator.

(c) A property owners' association may adopt or enforce any of the following dedicatory instrument provisions to regulate the operation and installation of standby electric generators:

(1) a dedicatory instrument provision that requires a standby electric generator to be installed and maintained in compliance with:

(A) the manufacturer's specifications; and

(B) applicable governmental health, safety, electrical, and building codes;

(2) a dedicatory instrument provision that requires all electrical, plumbing, and fuel line connections to be installed only by licensed contractors;

(3) a dedicatory instrument provision that requires all electrical connections to be installed in accordance with applicable governmental health, safety, electrical, and building codes;

(4) a dedicatory instrument provision that requires all natural gas, diesel fuel, biodiesel fuel, or hydrogen fuel line connections to be installed in accordance with applicable governmental health, safety, electrical, and building codes;

(5) a dedicatory instrument provision that requires all liquefied petroleum gas fuel line connections to be installed in accordance with rules and standards promulgated and adopted by the Railroad Commission of Texas and other applicable governmental health, safety, electrical, and building codes;

(6) a dedicatory instrument provision that requires nonintegral standby electric generator fuel tanks to be installed and maintained to comply with applicable municipal zoning ordinances and governmental health, safety, electrical, and building codes;

(7) a dedicatory instrument provision that requires the standby electric generator and its electrical lines and fuel lines to be maintained in good condition;

(8) a dedicatory instrument provision that requires the repair, replacement, or removal of any deteriorated or unsafe component of a standby electric generator, including electrical or fuel lines;

(9) a dedicatory instrument provision that requires an owner to screen a standby electric generator if the standby electric generator is:

(A) visible from the street faced by the dwelling;

(B) located in an unfenced side or rear yard of a residence and is visible either from an adjoining residence or from adjoining property owned by the property owners' association; or

(C) located in a side or rear yard fenced by a wrought iron or residential aluminum fence and is visible through the fence either from an adjoining residence or from adjoining property owned by the property owners' association;

(10) a dedicatory instrument provision that sets reasonable times, consistent with the manufacturer's recommendations, for the periodic testing of a standby electric generator;

(11) a dedicatory instrument provision that prohibits the use of a standby electric generator to generate all or substantially all of the electrical power to a residence, except when utility-generated electrical power to the residence is not available or is intermittent due to causes other than nonpayment for utility service to the residence;

(12) a dedicatory instrument provision that regulates the location of the standby electric generator; or

(13) a dedicatory instrument provision that prohibits an owner from locating a standby electric generator on property:

(A) owned or maintained by the property owners' association; or

(B) owned in common by the property owners' association members.

(d) A dedicatory instrument provision permitted by Subsection (c), if adopted, must be reasonably applied and enforced.

(e) A dedicatory instrument provision that regulates the location of a standby electric generator is unenforceable if:

(1) it increases the cost of installing the standby electric generator by more than 10 percent; or

(2) it increases the cost of installing and connecting the electrical and fuel lines for the standby electric generator by more than 20 percent.

(f) If a dedicatory instrument requires that the installation of a standby electric generator be approved before installation, approval may not be withheld if the proposed installation meets or exceeds the dedicatory instrument provisions permitted by Subsection (c).

(g) If a dedicatory instrument provision requires an owner to submit an application for approval of improvements located exterior to a residence, this section does not negate the requirement, but the information required to be submitted as part of the application for the installation of a standby electric generator may not be greater or more detailed than the application for any other improvement.

(h) In a hearing, action, or proceeding to determine whether a proposed or installed standby electric generator complies with the requirements of a dedicatory instrument provision permitted by Subsection (c), the party asserting noncompliance bears the burden of proof.

History of Prop. Code §202.019: Acts 2015, 84th Leg., ch. 1014, §1, eff. June 19, 2015.

See also *Real Estate Forms*, FORM 6:15.

CHAPTER 203. ENFORCEMENT OF LAND USE RESTRICTIONS IN CERTAIN COUNTIES

PROP §203.001. APPLICABILITY OF CHAPTER

This chapter applies only to a county with a population of more than 200,000.

History of Prop. Code §203.001: Acts 1987, 70th Leg., ch. 712, §1, eff. June 18, 1987. Amended by Acts 1997, 75th Leg., ch. 274, §2, eff. May 26, 1997.

PROP §203.002. DEFINITION

In this chapter, "restriction" means a limitation that affects the use to which real property may be put, fixes the distance at which buildings or other struc-

tures must be set back from property, street, or lot lines, affects the size of lots, or affects the size, type, or number of buildings or other structures that may be built on the property.

History of Prop. Code §203.002: Acts 1987, 70th Leg., ch. 712, §1, eff. June 18, 1987.

PROP §203.003. COUNTY ATTORNEY AUTHORIZED TO ENFORCE RESTRICTIONS

(a) The county attorney may sue in a court of competent jurisdiction to enjoin or abate violations of a restriction contained or incorporated by reference in a properly recorded plan, plat, replat, or other instrument affecting a real property subdivision located in the county, regardless of the date on which the instrument was recorded.

(b) The county attorney may not enforce a restriction relating to race or any other restriction that violates the state or federal constitution.

History of Prop. Code §203.003: Acts 1987, 70th Leg., ch. 712, §1, eff. June 18, 1987.

PROP §203.004. ADMINISTRATIVE FEE

(a) A complaint filed in connection with Section 203.003 must be accompanied by an administrative fee prescribed by the county commissioners court. The amount of the fee may not exceed the administrative costs to be incurred by the county in pursuing the matter.

(b) The administrative fee shall be deposited in a special county fund. The fund may be used only to administer this chapter.

(c) The commissioners court may waive the administrative fee if the complainant files with the complaint a hardship affidavit in a form approved by the commissioners court.

History of Prop. Code §203.004: Acts 1987, 70th Leg., ch. 712, §1, eff. June 18, 1987.

PROP §203.005. COURT COSTS & ATTORNEY'S FEES

(a) The county may be awarded court costs and attorney's fees in a successful action under this chapter.

(b) If the court costs and attorney's fees awarded to the county, together with the administrative fee collected under Section 203.004, exceed the county's expenses in a successful action under this chapter, any portion of the excess that does not exceed the amount of the administrative fee collected by the county shall be refunded to the complainant.

History of Prop. Code §203.005: Acts 1987, 70th Leg., ch. 712, §1, eff. June 18, 1987.

CHAPTER 204. POWERS OF PROPERTY OWNERS' ASSOCIATION RELATING TO RESTRICTIVE COVENANTS IN CERTAIN SUBDIVISIONS

PROP §204.001. DEFINITIONS

In this chapter:

(1) "Restrictions," "residential real estate subdivision," "subdivision," "owner," "real property records," and "lienholder" have the meanings assigned by Section 201.003.

(2) "Dedicatory instrument," "petition," and "restrictive covenant" have the meanings assigned by Section 202.001.

(3) "Regular assessment" means an assessment, charge, fee, or dues that each owner of property within a subdivision is required to pay to the property owners' association on a regular basis and that are to be used by the association for the benefit of the subdivision in accordance with the original, extended, added, or modified restrictions.

(4) "Special assessment" means an assessment, charge, fee, or dues that each owner of property within a subdivision is required to pay to the property owners' association, after a vote of the membership, for the purpose of paying for the costs of capital improvements to the common areas that are incurred or will be incurred by the association during the fiscal year. A special assessment may be assessed before or after the association incurs the capital improvement costs.

History of Prop. Code §204.001: Acts 1995, 74th Leg., ch. 1040, §2, eff. Aug. 28, 1995.

ANNOTATIONS

Hodas v. Scenic Oaks Prop. Ass'n., 21 S.W.3d 524, 528 (Tex.App.—San Antonio 2000, pet. denied). "We refuse to hold that the security assessment is a 'special

assessment' based solely on the fact that [D] termed it a 'special assessment' in the meeting notification and minutes. Instead, we turn to the wording of the property restriction itself. It is the restriction which embodies the intent of a covenant, not the notification to the property owners. *At 529:* [T]he fact that the general term 'special' was used to describe the … assessment in the property owners' notice does not foreclose our inquiry [into the nature of the assessment]."

PROP §204.002. APPLICATION

(a) This chapter applies only to a residential real estate subdivision, excluding a condominium development governed by Title 7, Property Code, that is located in whole or in part:

(1) in a county with a population of 3.3 million or more;

(2) in a county with a population of not less than 285,000 and not more than 300,000 that is adjacent to the Gulf of Mexico and that is adjacent to a county having a population of 3.3 million or more; or

(3) in a county with a population of 275,000 or more that:

(A) is adjacent to a county with a population of 3.3 million or more; and

(B) contains part of a national forest.

(b) This chapter applies to a restriction regardless of its effective date.

(c) This chapter does not apply to portions of a subdivision that are zoned for or that contain a commercial structure, an industrial structure, an apartment complex, or a condominium development governed by Title 7, Property Code. For purposes of this subsection, "apartment complex" means two or more dwellings in one or more buildings that are owned by the same owner, located on the same lot or tract, and managed by the same owner, agent, or management company.

History of Prop. Code §204.002: Acts 1995, 74th Leg., ch. 1040, §2, eff. Aug. 28, 1995. Amended by Acts 2003, 78th Leg., ch. 547, §1, eff. Sept. 1, 2003; Acts 2005, 79th Leg., ch. 1078, §1, eff. Sept. 1, 2005; Acts 2011, 82nd Leg., ch. 1163, §110, eff. Sept. 1, 2011.

PROP §204.003. APPLICATION OF PROVISIONS OF RESTRICTIVE COVENANTS IN CERTAIN CIRCUMSTANCES

(a) An express designation in a document creating restrictions applicable to a residential real estate subdivision that provides for the extension of, addition to, or modification of existing restrictions by a designated number of owners of real property in the subdivision prevails over the provisions of this chapter.

(b) Notwithstanding Subsection (a), for a residential subdivision described by Subsection (c), the provisions of this chapter prevail over an express designation in a document described by Subsection (a) if:

(1) the designated number of owners of real property in the subdivision required for approval of an extension of, addition to, or modification of the document is more than 75 percent; or

(2) the designation prohibits the extension of, addition to, or modification of an existing restriction for a certain time period and that time period has not expired.

(c) Subsection (b) applies to a residential subdivision that is located in a county described by Section 204.002(a)(3) other than a gated community with private streets.

(d) A document creating restrictions that provides for the extension or renewal of restrictions and does not provide for modification or amendment of restrictions may be modified under this chapter, including modifying the provision that provides for extension or renewal of the restrictions.

History of Prop. Code §204.003: Acts 1995, 74th Leg., ch. 1040, §2, eff. Aug. 28, 1995. Amended by Acts 2007, 80th Leg., ch. 767, §1 (eff. Sept. 1, 2007), ch. 1367, §5 (eff. Sept. 1, 2007); Acts 2009, 81st Leg., ch. 87, §20.004, eff. Sept. 1, 2009.

PROP §204.004. PROPERTY OWNERS' ASSOCIATION

(a) A property owners' association is a designated representative of the owners of property in a subdivision and may be referred to as a "homeowners association," "community association," "civic association," "civic club," "association," "committee," or similar term contained in the restrictions. The membership of the association consists of the owners of property within the subdivision.

(b) The association must be nonprofit and may be incorporated as a Texas nonprofit corporation. An unincorporated association may incorporate under the Texas Non-Profit Corporation Act (Article 1396-1.01 et seq., Vernon's Texas Civil Statutes).

(c) The association's board of directors or trustees must be elected or appointed in accordance with the applicable provisions of the restrictions and the association's articles of incorporation or bylaws.

History of Prop. Code §204.004: Acts 1995, 74th Leg., ch. 1040, §2, eff. Aug. 28, 1995.

See also *Real Estate Forms*, FORMS 6:2, 6:3, 6:18.

ANNOTATIONS

Anderson v. New Prop. Owners' Ass'n, 122 S.W.3d 378, 384 (Tex.App.—Texarkana 2003, pet. denied). "An association has standing to sue when it satisfies a three-pronged test. First, the members must otherwise have standing to sue in their own right. Second, the interests it seeks to protect must be germane to the organization's purpose. Finally, neither the claim asserted nor the relief requested may require the participation of individual members in the lawsuit."

PROP §204.005. EXTENSION OF, ADDITION TO, OR MODIFICATION OF EXISTING RESTRICTIONS

(a) A property owners' association has authority to approve and circulate a petition relating to the extension of, addition to, or modification of existing restrictions. A property owners' association is not required to comply with Sections 201.009-201.012.

(b) A petition to extend, add to, or modify existing restrictions approved and circulated by a property owners' association is effective if:

(1) the petition is approved by the owners, excluding lienholders, contract purchasers, and the owners of mineral interests, of at least 75 percent of the real property in the subdivision or a smaller percentage required by the original dedicatory instrument; and

(2) the petition is filed as a dedicatory instrument with the county clerk of the county in which the subdivision is located.

(c) If a subdivision consisting of multiple sections, each with its own restrictions, is represented by a single property owners' association, the approval requirement may be satisfied by obtaining approval of at least 75 percent of the owners on a section-by-section basis or of the total number of properties in the property owners' association's jurisdiction.

(d) If approved, the petition is binding on all properties in the subdivision or section, as applicable.

(e) A property owners' association that circulates a petition must notify all record owners of property in the subdivision in writing of the proposed extension, addition to, or modification of the existing restrictions. Notice may be hand-delivered to residences within the subdivision or sent by regular mail to the owner's last known mailing address as reflected in the ownership records maintained by the property owners' association. The approval of multiple owners of a property may be reflected by the signature of a single co-owner.

History of Prop. Code §204.005: Acts 1995, 74th Leg., ch. 1040, §2, eff. Aug. 28, 1995.

ANNOTATIONS

Brooks v. Northglen Ass'n, 76 S.W.3d 162, 173-74 (Tex.App.—Texarkana 2002), *rev'd in part on other grounds*, 141 S.W.3d 158 (Tex.2004). Section 204.005 "intends to address the problem of the extension, addition, or modification to existing subdivision restrictions by providing an alternative means, i.e., the circulation of a petition, by which such restrictions may be amended. ... The language of §204.005 will not support an interpretation that would permit increasing maintenance fees in direct contravention of limitations specifically set out in the restrictions. If the Legislature in this statute intended to grant homeowners' associations the authority simply to increase assessments above limitations stated within the restrictions, without some kind of amending procedure, there would be no need to place in the statute the mechanism for circulating a petition."

Dahl v. Hartman, 14 S.W.3d 434, 436-37 (Tex. App.—Houston [14th Dist.] 2000, pet. denied). "[T]he only mandatory power given to a [property owners' association] under Ch. 204 is the power to approve and circulate petitions relating to changing existing deed restrictions."

PROP §204.006. CREATION OF PROPERTY OWNERS' ASSOCIATION

(a) If existing restrictions applicable to a subdivision do not provide for a property owners' association and require approval of more than 60 percent of the owners to add to or modify the original dedicating instrument, a petition to add to or modify the existing restrictions for the sole purpose of creating and operating a property owners' association with mandatory membership, mandatory regular or special assessments, and equivalent voting rights for each of the owners in the subdivision is effective if:

(1) a petition committee has been formed as prescribed by Section 201.005;

(2) the petition is approved by the owners, excluding lienholders, contract purchasers, and the owners of mineral interests, of at least 60 percent of the real property in the subdivision; and

(3) the procedure employed in the circulation and approval of the petition to add to or amend the existing restrictions for the specified purpose complies with the requirements of this chapter.

(b) If the circulated petition is not approved by the required percentage of owners within one year of the creation of the petition committee, the petition is void and another petition committee may be formed.

(c) If the petition is approved, the petition is binding on all properties in the subdivision or section, as applicable.

History of Prop. Code §204.006: Acts 1995, 74th Leg., ch. 1040, §2, eff. Aug. 28, 1995.

ANNOTATIONS

Gillebaard v. Bayview Acres Ass'n, 263 S.W.3d 342, 350 (Tex.App.—Houston [1st Dist.] 2007, pet. denied). "The plain meaning of the term 'sole,' as used in [Prop. Code] §204.006(a), is 'the only one; only.' The petition that §204.006(a) sanctions is one that seeks to amend or to modify existing deed restrictions for 'the *sole* purpose' of creating and operating a property owners' association. That means that the only purpose of that petition can be, ultimately, to create and to operate a property owners' association. [¶] A property owners' association cannot conduct the preliminary steps of proposing, approving, and circulating a petition, as required to invoke [Prop. Code] §204.005, if the deed restrictions have not yet been amended to create an association with the power to do these things on the homeowners' behalf. *At 351:* Considering the overall scheme of ch. 204 and the plain language of §204.006(a) discussed above, we hold that the phrase 'for the sole purpose of creating and operating a property owners' association' in §204.006(a) means for the sole purpose of creating the association and establishing the terms under which it will operate, e.g., the association's powers and duties."

Simpson v. Afton Oaks Civic Club, Inc., 155 S.W.3d 674, 675 (Tex.App.—Texarkana 2005, pet. denied). "The initial and dispositive question is whether the subdivision could use the procedures set out by [§204.006] to amend the restrictions—when the deeds provided a different, and specific, procedure to be followed in making such an amendment. [¶] Even assuming the dedicating instrument does not provide for a property owners' association, its terms provide that to amend the restrictions requires only a simple majority—not more than 60%. Thus, the second part of the statute is not satisfied, and it will not support the petition filed in this case. [¶] [Property owners' association] suggests that, because a specific window for amendments is set out by the dedicating document—six months every ten years—the procedures in the [Property] Code should take the place of the procedures set out by the restrictions and allow amendment at any time as permitted by the Code. There is no support for this position either in caselaw or the Code. In fact, the Code specifically states otherwise."

PROP §204.007. EFFECT ON LIENHOLDERS

(a) Extensions of, additions to, or modifications of restrictions under this chapter are binding on a lienholder, excluding restrictions relating to regular or special assessment increases if the assessment is not subordinated to purchase money or home improvement liens.

(b) If the assessment lien of the property owners' association is subordinate to purchase money or home improvement liens, the lienholder is not entitled to notice of the proposed dedicatory instrument and the lienholder is bound by the instrument if the instrument is approved. If the assessment lien is not subordinated, a lienholder who is not a signatory to the dedicatory instrument and whose lien was established before the effective date of the dedicatory instrument is not bound by the portion of the dedicatory instrument that increases the amount of the regular or special assessment during any period of ownership by the lienholder.

(c) A person who acquires title to the property at a foreclosure sale or by deed from a foreclosing lienholder is bound by the assessment increase.

History of Prop. Code §204.007: Acts 1995, 74th Leg., ch. 1040, §2, eff. Aug. 28, 1995.

PROP §204.008. METHOD OF ADOPTION

An extension, addition to, or modification of restrictions proposed by a property owners' association may be adopted:

(1) by a written ballot that states the substance of the amendment and specifies the date by which a ballot must be received to be counted;

(2) at a meeting of the members represented by the property owners' association if written notice of the meeting stating the purpose of the meeting is delivered to each owner of property in the subdivision;

(3) by door-to-door circulation of a petition by the property owners' association or a person authorized by the property owners' association;

(4) by a method permitted by the existing restrictions; or

(5) by a combination of the methods described by this section.

History of Prop. Code §204.008: Acts 1995, 74th Leg., ch. 1040, §2, eff. Aug. 28, 1995.

PROP §204.009. TEXAS NONPROFIT CORPORATIONS

(a) If the property owners' association is referenced in the existing, extended, added to, or modified restrictions as a Texas nonprofit corporation, the instrument contemplates the interaction of a nonprofit corporation, its articles of incorporation, and its bylaws.

(b) The property owners' association has the powers and shall promote the purposes enumerated in the articles of incorporation and bylaws. These powers and purposes necessarily modify the express provisions of the restrictions to include the referenced powers and purposes.

History of Prop. Code §204.009: Acts 1995, 74th Leg., ch. 1040, §2, eff. Aug. 28, 1995.

See also *Real Estate Forms*, FORMS 6:2, 6:3.

PROP §204.010. POWERS OF PROPERTY OWNERS' ASSOCIATION

(a) Unless otherwise provided by the restrictions or the association's articles of incorporation or bylaws, the property owners' association, acting through its board of directors or trustees, may:

(1) adopt and amend bylaws;

(2) adopt and amend budgets for revenues, expenditures, and reserves and collect regular assessments or special assessments for common expenses from property owners;

(3) hire and terminate managing agents and other employees, agents, and independent contractors;

(4) institute, defend, intervene in, settle, or compromise litigation or administrative proceedings on matters affecting the subdivision;

(5) make contracts and incur liabilities relating to the operation of the subdivision and the property owners' association;

(6) regulate the use, maintenance, repair, replacement, modification, and appearance of the subdivision;

(7) make additional improvements to be included as a part of the common area;

(8) grant easements, leases, licenses, and concessions through or over the common area;

(9) impose and receive payments, fees, or charges for the use, rental, or operation of the common area and for services provided to property owners;

(10) impose interest, late charges, and, if applicable, returned check charges for late payments of regular assessments or special assessments;

(11) if notice and an opportunity to be heard are given, collect reimbursement of actual attorney's fees and other reasonable costs incurred by the property owners' association relating to violations of the subdivision's restrictions or the property owners' association's bylaws and rules;

(12) charge costs to an owner's assessment account and collect the costs in any manner provided in the restrictions for the collection of assessments;

(13) adopt and amend rules regulating the collection of delinquent assessments and the application of payments;

(14) impose reasonable charges for preparing, recording, or copying amendments to the restrictions, resale certificates, or statements of unpaid assessments;

(15) purchase insurance and fidelity bonds, including directors' and officers' liability insurance, that the board considers appropriate or necessary;

(16) if the restrictions allow for an annual increase in the maximum regular assessment without a vote of the membership, assess the increase annually or accumulate and assess the increase after a number of years;

(17) subject to the requirements of the Texas Non-Profit Corporation Act (Article 1396-1.01 et seq., Vernon's Texas Civil Statutes) and by majority vote of its board of directors, indemnify a director or officer of the property owners' association who was, is, or may be made a named defendant or respondent in a proceeding because the person is or was a director;

(18) if the restrictions vest the architectural control authority in the property owners' association or if the authority is vested in the property owners' association under Section 204.011:

(A) implement written architectural control guidelines for its own use or record the guidelines in the real property records of the applicable county; and

(B) modify the guidelines as the needs of the subdivision change;

(19) exercise other powers conferred by the restrictions, its articles of incorporation, or its bylaws;

(20) exercise other powers that may be exercised in this state by a corporation of the same type as the property owners' association; and

(21) exercise other powers necessary and proper for the governance and operation of the property owners' association.

(b) Powers enumerated by this section are in addition to any other powers granted to a property owners' association by this chapter or other law.

History of Prop. Code §204.010: Acts 1995, 74th Leg., ch. 1040, §2, eff. Aug. 28, 1995.

See also *Real Estate Forms*, FORMS 6:2, 6:3.

ANNOTATIONS

Brooks v. Northglen Ass'n, 141 S.W.3d 158, 167-68 (Tex.2004). Section 204.010 "does not apply if the deed restrictions 'otherwise provide.' [¶] [Association's] deed restrictions for [subdivisions] 'otherwise provide' that accumulation is not permitted. … By specifically tying any increase to the previous year's annual assessment, the deed restrictions do not permit accumulation over multiple years. [¶] The voting mechanism, combined with the increase being tied to the previous year's assessment, establishes that the deed restrictions 'otherwise provide.' [¶] [W]e conclude that [§204.010] does not permit accumulation or fee increases above the deed restrictions…."

Evans v. Davis, No. 14-12-01053-CV (Tex.App.—Houston [14th Dist.] 2013, no pet.) (memo op.; 11-19-13). "[D] argues that demolishing the structures on [Ps'] property was within [its] regulatory power. We disagree. [¶] Because the statute specifically grants … limited enforcement powers, we do not construe its authorization to 'regulate' as conferring the power to enforce regulations by any means an association deems appropriate. Indeed, if the authority to regulate in [§204.010](a)(6) included an unrestricted power to enforce, the specific enforcement mechanisms [in §204.010] would be superfluous. We therefore reject [D's] argument that §204.010(a)(6) authorized its demolition of the structures on [Ps'] property."

Truong v. City of Houston, 99 S.W.3d 204, 214 (Tex.App.—Houston [1st Dist.] 2002, no pet.). "Our reading of [Prop. Code] §204.004, in harmony with [Prop. Code] §204.010, suggests that the owners' associations may compromise litigation on behalf of the subdivision owners, but not on behalf of parties who are not subdivision owners."

Cottonwood Valley Home Owners Ass'n v. Hudson, 75 S.W.3d 601, 603 (Tex.App.—Eastland 2002, no pet.). "As an inherent part of the property interest, the purchase of a lot in a subdivision with deed restrictions carries the obligation to pay association fees for maintenance and ownership of common facilities and services. The remedy of foreclosure is an inherent characteristic of that property right. [¶] [W]hile the remedy of foreclosure may seem harsh especially when a small sum is due, the court is bound to enforce the agreements the homeowners enter into concerning the payment of assessments. [A] homeowners' association is entitled to foreclose on homesteads of owners who have not paid their homeowners' assessments [and] property [that] does not have the homestead protections."

Dahl v. Hartman, 14 S.W.3d 434, 436 (Tex.App.—Houston [14th Dist.] 2000, pet. denied). "The permissive language of [§204.010] allows the [property owners' association] to defend litigation on behalf of the entire subdivision, but does not require the [property owners' association] to represent the interests of all property owners in the community once litigation has begun."

PROP §204.011. ARCHITECTURAL CONTROL COMMITTEE

(a) This section applies to restrictions providing for the creation and operation of an architectural control committee with the power to approve or deny applications for proposed original construction or modification of a building, structure, or improvement.

(b) Unless the restrictions applicable to a residential real estate subdivision vest the architectural control committee authority in the property owners' association before either of the following events, the architectural control committee authority automatically vests in the property owners' association when:

(1) the term of the architectural control committee authority expires as prescribed by the restrictions;

(2) a residence on the last available building site is completed and sold;

(3) the person or entity designated as the architectural control committee in the restrictions assigns, in writing, authority to the property owners' association; or

(4) an assignee of the original holder abandons its authority for more than one year.

(c) If the architectural control committee authority is transferred to the property owners' association, the authority is vested in the property owners' association until:

(1) the restrictions are modified to reflect otherwise;

(2) the restrictions are terminated; or

(3) the property owners' association ceases to exist.

(d) If existing restrictions applicable to a subdivision do not provide for a property owners' association and a property owners' association has not been formed, the architectural control committee authority over the entire subdivision vests in a civic association other than a property owners' association if:

(1) an architectural control committee created by the restrictions exercised the architectural control committee authority as provided by the restrictions over all the lots in the subdivision for at least 10 years and over a majority of the lots in the subdivision for at least 20 years;

(2) an architectural control committee created by the restrictions assigned the civic association the architectural control committee authority over a majority of the lots in the subdivision;

(3) the civic association was assigned the architectural control committee authority over a majority of the lots in the subdivision and has exercised that authority over all the lots in the subdivision for at least 10 years; and

(4) the architectural control committee authority has lapsed in the lots in which the civic association lacks authority, and the lapse is solely the result of:

(A) the automatic termination of the architectural control committee authority; or

(B) the death of a member of the architectural control committee or another cause resulting from the inability to locate a member of the architectural control committee or the member's assigns.

History of Prop. Code §204.011: Acts 1995, 74th Leg., ch. 1040, §2, eff. Aug. 28, 1995. Amended by Acts 2007, 80th Leg., ch. 711, §1, eff. Sept. 1, 2007.

CHAPTER 205. RESTRICTIVE COVENANTS APPLICABLE TO REVISED SUBDIVISIONS IN CERTAIN COUNTIES

PROP §205.001. DEFINITIONS

In this chapter:

(1) "Restrictions" and "subdivision" have the meanings assigned by Section 201.003.

(2) "Property owners' association" has the meaning assigned by Section 202.001.

History of Prop. Code §205.001: Acts 1995, 74th Leg., ch. 1040, §3, eff. Aug. 28, 1995. Amended by Acts 1997, 75th Leg., ch. 451, §4, eff. Sept. 1, 1997.

PROP §205.002. APPLICABILITY

This chapter applies only to a county with a population of 65,000 or more.

History of Prop. Code §205.002: Acts 1995, 74th Leg., ch. 1040, §3, eff. Aug. 28, 1995.

PROP §205.003. RESTRICTIONS APPLICABLE TO REVISED SUBDIVISIONS

(a) If all or part of a subdivision plat is revised to provide for another subdivision of land within all or part of the earlier subdivision, the restrictions that apply to the subdivision before the revision apply to the newly created subdivision.

(b) The property owners of the newly created subdivision must comply with the petition procedures prescribed by Chapter 204 to modify the restrictions.

History of Prop. Code §205.003: Acts 1995, 74th Leg., ch. 1040, §3, eff. Aug. 28, 1995.

PROP §205.004. AMENDMENT OF RESTRICTIONS BY GOVERNING BODY OF PROPERTY OWNERS' ASSOCIATION

(a) The governing body of a property owners' association may amend the restrictions for the limited purpose of complying with United States Department of Housing and Urban Development or United States Department of Veterans Affairs requirements for subdivision property to qualify for insured or guaranteed mortgage loans.

(b) An amendment adopted under this section must:

(1) indicate that the amendment is adopted under authority of this section by specifically referencing this section;

(2) be signed by a majority of the governing body; and

(3) be filed in the real property records of the county in which the subdivision is located.

History of Prop. Code §205.004: Acts 1997, 75th Leg., ch. 451, §5, eff. Sept. 1, 1997.

CHAPTER 206. EXTENSION OF RESTRICTIONS IMPOSING REGULAR ASSESSMENTS IN CERTAIN SUBDIVISIONS

PROP §206.001. DEFINITIONS

In this chapter:

(1) "Community association" means an incorporated association created to enforce restrictions.

(2) "Dedicatory instrument" and "restrictive covenant" have the meanings assigned by Section 202.001.

(3) "Lienholder," "owner," "real property records," "residential real estate subdivision," and "restrictions" have the meanings assigned by Section 201.003.

(4) "Regular assessment" means an assessment, charge, fee, or dues that each owner is required to pay to the community association on a regular basis and that is to be used by the association for the benefit of the subdivision in accordance with the original, extended, added, or modified restrictions.

History of Prop. Code §206.001: Acts 1997, 75th Leg., ch. 1249, §1, eff. Sept. 1, 1997.

PROP §206.002. APPLICABILITY OF CHAPTER

This chapter applies only to:

(1) a residential real estate subdivision that:

(A) consists of at least 4,600 homes;

(B) is located in whole or in part in a municipality with a population of more than 1.6 million located in a county with a population of 2.8 million or more; and

(C) has restrictions the terms of which are automatically extended but has a regular assessment that is established by a separate document that permits the assessment to expire and does not provide for extension of the term of the assessment; or

(2) a residential real estate subdivision that:

(A) consists of at least 750 homes;

(B) is located in two adjacent municipalities in a county with a population of 2.8 million or more; and

(C) has use restrictions the terms of which are automatically extended but has a regular assessment that is established by two separate documents that permit the assessment to expire and do not provide for extension of the term of the assessment.

History of Prop. Code §206.002: Acts 1997, 75th Leg., ch. 1249, §1, eff. Sept. 1, 1997. Amended by Acts 2001, 77th Leg., ch. 597, §1, eff. Sept. 1, 2001.

PROP §206.003. EXTENSION OF RESTRICTION IMPOSING REGULAR ASSESSMENT

(a) A community association may approve and submit to a vote of the owners an extension of a restriction imposing a regular assessment.

(b) The extension of a restriction imposing a regular assessment is approved if a majority of the owners in the subdivision who vote on the issue in accordance with Section 206.004 vote in favor of the extension.

(c) An extension approved in accordance with this section and Section 206.004 applies to all real property in the subdivision, including residential and commercial property.

(d) A document certifying that a majority of the owners voting on the issue approved the extension of the restriction must be recorded in the real property records of the county in which the subdivision is located.

History of Prop. Code §206.003: Acts 1997, 75th Leg., ch. 1249, §1, eff. Sept. 1, 1997.

PROP §206.004. METHOD OF VOTING

(a) An extension of a restriction that imposes a regular assessment must be voted on:

(1) by a written ballot that states the substance of the amendment extending the restriction and specifies the date by which the community association must receive a ballot for the ballot to be counted; or

(2) at a meeting of the property owners in the subdivision.

(b) The community association shall provide for mailing to each owner, as applicable:

(1) the ballot under Subsection (a)(1); or

(2) notice of the meeting under Subsection (a)(2) that states the purpose of the meeting.

(c) In conjunction with a vote by ballot or at a meeting under Subsection (a), the community association may provide for circulation of a petition in the subdivision.

(d) The vote of multiple owners of a property may be reflected by the signature or vote of one of the owners.

(e) The community association shall record a copy of the ballot or petition in the real property records in the county in which the subdivision is located prior to submission of the extension to a vote of the owners.

History of Prop. Code §206.004: Acts 1997, 75th Leg., ch. 1249, §1, eff. Sept. 1, 1997.

CHAPTER 207. DISCLOSURE OF INFORMATION BY PROPERTY OWNERS' ASSOCIATIONS

PROP §207.001. DEFINITIONS

In this chapter:

(1) "Restrictions" has the meaning assigned by Section 201.003.

(2) "Dedicatory instrument," "property owners' association," and "restrictive covenant" have the meanings assigned by Section 209.002.

(3) "Owner" means a person who owns record title to property in a subdivision or the personal representative of an individual who owns record title to property in a subdivision.

(4) "Regular assessment" and "special assessment" have the meanings assigned by Section 204.001.

(5) "Resale certificate" means a written statement issued, signed, and dated by an officer or authorized agent of a property owners' association that contains the information specified by Section 207.003(b).

(6) "Subdivision" means all land that has been divided into two or more parts and that is or was burdened by restrictions limiting at least the majority of the land area burdened by restrictions, excluding streets and public areas, to residential use only, if the instrument or instruments creating the restrictions are recorded in the deed or real property records of a county.

History of Prop. Code §207.001: Acts 1999, 76th Leg., ch. 1198, §1, eff. Sept. 1, 1999. Amended by Acts 2015, 84th Leg., ch. 1183, §2, eff. Sept. 1, 2015.

PROP §207.002. APPLICABILITY

(a) This chapter applies to a subdivision with a property owners' association that is entitled to levy regular or special assessments.

(b) This chapter does not apply to a condominium council of owners governed by Chapter 81 or a condominium unit owners' association governed by Chapter 82.

History of Prop. Code §207.002: Acts 1999, 76th Leg., ch. 1198, §1, eff. Sept. 1, 1999. Amended by Acts 2015, 84th Leg., ch. 1183, §3, eff. Sept. 1, 2015.

PROP §207.003. DELIVERY OF SUBDIVISION INFORMATION TO OWNER

(a) Not later than the 10th business day after the date a written request for subdivision information is received from an owner or the owner's agent, a purchaser of property in a subdivision or the purchaser's agent, or a title insurance company or its agent acting on behalf of the owner or purchaser and the evidence of the requestor's authority to order a resale certificate under Subsection (a-1) is received and verified, the property owners' association shall deliver to the owner or the owner's agent, the purchaser or the purchaser's agent, or the title insurance company or its agent:

(1) a current copy of the restrictions applying to the subdivision;

(2) a current copy of the bylaws and rules of the property owners' association; and

(3) a resale certificate prepared not earlier than the 60th day before the date the certificate is delivered that complies with Subsection (b).

(a-1) For a request from a purchaser of property in a subdivision or the purchaser's agent, the property owners' association may require the purchaser or purchaser's agent to provide to the association, before the association begins the process of preparing or delivers the items listed in Subsection (a), reasonable evidence that the purchaser has a contractual or other right to acquire property in the subdivision.

(b) A resale certificate under Subsection (a) must contain:

(1) a statement of any right of first refusal, other than a right of first refusal that is prohibited by statute, and any other restraint contained in the restrictions or restrictive covenants that restricts the owner's right to transfer the owner's property;

(2) the frequency and amount of any regular assessments;

(3) the amount and purpose of any special assessment that has been approved before and is due after the resale certificate is delivered;

(4) the total of all amounts due and unpaid to the property owners' association that are attributable to the owner's property;

(5) capital expenditures, if any, approved by the property owners' association for the property owners' association's current fiscal year;

(6) the amount of reserves, if any, for capital expenditures;

(7) the property owners' association's current operating budget and balance sheet;

(8) the total of any unsatisfied judgments against the property owners' association;

(9) the style and cause number of any pending lawsuit in which the property owners' association is a party, other than a lawsuit relating to unpaid ad valorem taxes of an individual member of the association;

(10) a copy of a certificate of insurance showing the property owners' association's property and liability insurance relating to the common areas and common facilities;

(11) a description of any conditions on the owner's property that the property owners' association board has actual knowledge are in violation of the restrictions applying to the subdivision or the bylaws or rules of the property owners' association;

(12) a summary or copy of notices received by the property owners' association from any governmental authority regarding health or housing code violations existing on the preparation date of the certificate relating to the owner's property or any common areas or common facilities owned or leased by the property owners' association;

(13) the amount of any administrative transfer fee charged by the property owners' association for a change of ownership of property in the subdivision;

(14) the name, mailing address, and telephone number of the property owners' association's managing agent, if any;

(15) a statement indicating whether the restrictions allow foreclosure of a property owners' association's lien on the owner's property for failure to pay assessments; and

(16) a statement of all fees associated with the transfer of ownership, including a description of each fee, to whom each fee is paid, and the amount of each fee.

(c) A property owners' association may charge a reasonable fee to assemble, copy, and deliver the information required by this section and may charge a reasonable fee to prepare and deliver an update of a resale certificate under Subsection (f).

(c-1) The property owners' association may require payment before beginning the process of providing a resale certificate but may not process a payment for a resale certificate until the certificate is available for delivery. The association may not charge a fee if the certificate is not provided in the time prescribed by Subsection (a).

(d) The property owners' association shall deliver the information required by Subsection (a) or (f) to the person specified in the written request. A written request that does not specify the name and location to which the information is to be sent is not effective. The property owners' association may deliver the information required by Subsection (a) and any update to the resale certificate required by Subsection (f) by mail, hand delivery, or alternative delivery means specified in the written request.

(e) Unless required by a dedicatory instrument, neither a property owners' association or its agent is required to inspect a property before issuing a resale certificate or an update to a resale certificate.

(f) Not later than the seventh business day after the date a written request for an update of a resale certificate delivered under Subsection (a) is received from an owner, owner's agent, or title insurance company or its agent acting on behalf of the owner, the property owners' association shall deliver to the owner, owner's agent, or title insurance company or its agent an updated resale certificate that contains the following information:

(1) if a right of first refusal or other restraint on sale is contained in the restrictions, a statement of whether the property owners' association waives the restraint on sale;

(2) the status of any unpaid special assessments, dues, or other payments attributable to the owner's property; and

(3) any changes to the information provided in the resale certificate issued under Subsection (a).

(g) Requests for an updated resale certificate pursuant to Subsection (f) must be made within 180 days of the date a resale certificate is issued under Subsection (a). The update request may be made only by the party requesting the original resale certificate.

History of Prop. Code §207.003: Acts 1999, 76th Leg., ch. 1198, §1, eff. Sept. 1, 1999. Amended by Acts 2009, 81st Leg., ch. 147, §1, eff. Sept. 1, 2009; Acts 2011, 82nd Leg., ch. 1142, §4, eff. Jan. 1, 2012.

See also *Real Estate Forms*, FORM 6:18.

ANNOTATIONS

Webb v. Voga, 316 S.W.3d 809, 814 (Tex.App.—Dallas 2010, no pet.). "In [P's] affidavit in support of her motion for summary judgment, [P] attested she 'own[s] land which has a mandatory homeowners association.' *At 815:* [P's] contention that she had standing in a representative capacity for the record title owner is unfounded. [P's] suits as consolidated were brought in her individual capacity and not as a representative or fiduciary of the record title owner, and there is no pleading or evidence in the record to support a contention that [P] brought claims other than on her own behalf. Further, [P] acknowledges [her husband] as the record owner of the property [at issue] at all relevant times. [¶] The evidence shows [P] was not a property owner. We conclude that [P] lacked standing for her causes of action against [Ds] and, therefore, the trial court lacked subject matter jurisdiction over those causes of action."

PROP §207.004. OWNER'S REMEDIES FOR FAILURE BY PROPERTY OWNERS' ASSOCIATION TO TIMELY DELIVER INFORMATION

(a) If a property owners' association does not timely deliver information in accordance with Section 207.003, the owner, owner's agent, or title insurance company or its agent acting on behalf of the owner may submit a second request for the information.

(b) If a property owners' association fails to deliver the information required under Section 207.003 before the seventh day after the second request for the information was mailed by certified mail, return receipt requested, or hand delivered, evidenced by receipt, the owner:

(1) may seek one or any combination of the following:

(A) a court order directing the property owners' association to furnish the required information;

(B) a judgment against the property owners' association for not more than $500;

(C) a judgment against the property owners' association for court costs and attorney's fees; or

(D) a judgment authorizing the owner or the owner's assignee to deduct the amounts awarded under Paragraphs (B) and (C) from any future regular or special assessments payable to the property owners' association; and

(2) may provide a buyer under contract to purchase the owner's property an affidavit that states that the owner, owner's agent, or title insurance company or its agent acting on behalf of the owner made, in accordance with this chapter, two written requests to the property owners' association for the information described in Section 207.003 and that the association did not timely provide the information.

(c) If the owner provides a buyer under contract to purchase the owner's property an affidavit in accordance with Subsection (b)(2):

(1) the buyer, lender, or title insurance company or its agent is not liable to the property owners' association for:

(A) any money that is due and unpaid to the property owners' association on the date the affidavit was prepared; and

(B) any debt to the property owners' association or claim by the property owners' association that accrued before the date the affidavit was prepared; and

(2) the property owners' association's lien to secure the amounts due the property owners' association on the owner's property on the date the affidavit was prepared shall automatically terminate.

History of Prop. Code §207.004: Acts 1999, 76th Leg., ch. 1198, §1, eff. Sept. 1, 1999.

PROP §207.005. EFFECT OF RESALE CERTIFICATE; LIABILITY

(a) A property owners' association may not deny the validity of any statement in the resale certificate. The property owners' association's lien to secure undisclosed amounts due the property owners' association on the date the resale certificate is prepared shall automatically terminate as a lien securing the undisclosed amount. A buyer, buyer's agent, owner, owner's agent, lender, and title insurance company and its agent are not liable for any debt or claim exist-

ing on the preparation date of the resale certificate that is not disclosed in the resale certificate.

(b) A resale certificate does not affect:

(1) the right of a property owners' association to recover debts or claims that arise or become due after the date the resale certificate is prepared; or

(2) a lien on a property securing payment of future assessments held by the property owners' association.

(c) The owner's agent and the title insurance company and its agent are not liable to a buyer for any delay or failure by the property owners' association in delivering the information required by Section 207.003.

(d) Except as provided by Section 207.004, the property owners' association is not liable to an owner selling property in the subdivision for delay or failure to deliver the information required by Section 207.003. An officer or agent of the property owners' association is not liable for a delay or failure to furnish a resale certificate.

History of Prop. Code §207.005: Acts 1999, 76th Leg., ch. 1198, §1, eff. Sept. 1, 1999.

See also *Real Estate Forms*, FORM 6:19.

PROP §207.006. ONLINE SUBDIVISION INFORMATION REQUIRED

A property owners' association shall make dedicatory instruments relating to the association or subdivision and filed in the county deed records available on a website if the association has, or a management company on behalf of the association maintains, a publicly accessible website.

History of Prop. Code §207.006: Acts 2011, 82nd Leg., ch. 1142, §5, eff. Jan. 1, 2012.

CHAPTER 208. AMENDMENT & TERMINATION OF RESTRICTIVE COVENANTS IN HISTORIC NEIGHBORHOODS

PROP §208.001. DEFINITIONS

In this chapter:

(1) "Owner" and "real property records" have the meanings assigned by Section 201.003.

(2) "Dedicatory instrument," "property owners' association," "petition," and "restrictive covenant" have the meanings assigned by Section 202.001.

(3) "Regular assessment" and "special assessment" have the meanings assigned by Section 204.001.

(4) "Apartment complex" has the meaning assigned by Section 204.002(c).

(5) "Historic neighborhood" means:

(A) an area incorporated as a separate municipality before 1900 and subsequently annexed into another municipality;

(B) an area described by a municipal map or subdivision plat filed in real property records of the county in which the area is located before 1900; or

(C) an area designated as a historic district or similar designation by the municipality in which the area is located, the Texas Historical Commission, or the National Register of Historic Places.

History of Prop. Code §208.001: Acts 1999, 76th Leg., ch. 871, §2, eff. June 18, 1999. Renumbered from §207.001 by Acts 2001, 77th Leg., ch. 1420, §21.001(98), eff. Sept. 1, 2001.

PROP §208.002. APPLICABILITY

(a) This chapter applies only to a historic neighborhood that is located in whole or in part in a municipality with a population of 1.6 million or more located in a county with a population of 2.8 million or more.

(b) This chapter applies to a restrictive covenant regardless of the date on which it was created.

(c) This chapter applies to property in the area of a historic neighborhood that is zoned for or that contains a commercial structure, an industrial structure, an apartment complex, or a condominium development covered by Title 7 only if the owner of the property signed a restrictive covenant that includes the property in a common scheme for preservation of historic property as described by Section 208.004.

History of Prop. Code §208.002: Acts 1999, 76th Leg., ch. 871, §2, eff. June 18, 1999. Renumbered from §207.002 by Acts 2001, 77th Leg., ch. 1420, §21.001(98), eff. Sept. 1, 2001. Amended by Acts 2001, 77th Leg., ch. 1420, §21.002(17), eff. Sept. 1, 2001.

PROP §208.003. HISTORIC NEIGHBORHOOD PRESERVATION ASSOCIATION

(a) A historic neighborhood preservation association must:

(1) be a Texas nonprofit corporation or limited liability company organized, in part, to encourage the preservation of property in a historic neighborhood; and

(2) open its membership to all owners of property in the historic neighborhood.

(b) A historic neighborhood preservation association may be composed of only a portion of the owners of property in the historic neighborhood.

(c) A historic neighborhood preservation association may be a property owners' association or an organization that is qualified as a charitable organization under Section 501(c)(3) of the Internal Revenue Code of 1986.

(d) A statement in the articles of incorporation or association, bylaws, regulations, or operating agreement of the historic neighborhood preservation association is prima facie evidence of compliance with Subsection (a).

History of Prop. Code §208.003: Acts 1999, 76th Leg., ch. 871, §2, eff. June 18, 1999. Renumbered from §207.003 by Acts 2001, 77th Leg., ch. 1420, §21.001(98), eff. Sept. 1, 2001.

PROP §208.004. COMMON SCHEME FOR PRESERVATION OF PROPERTY IN HISTORIC NEIGHBORHOOD

(a) A common scheme for preservation of historic property exists in a historic neighborhood if:

(1) the restrictive covenants were created by individual dedicatory instruments signed by an owner of one or more separately owned parcels or tracts in the historic neighborhood; and

(2) the restrictive covenants authorize a historic neighborhood preservation association to enforce the restrictive covenants.

(b) A common scheme for preservation of historic property does not include property that is not subject to restrictive covenants that authorize a historic neighborhood preservation association to enforce the restrictive covenants.

(c) Restrictive covenants included in a common scheme for preservation of historic property exist for the benefit of all owners of property subject to the common scheme for preservation as if each owner were referenced in each dedicatory instrument.

(d) Each owner of property subject to a common scheme for preservation of historic property may enforce restrictive covenants on other property included in the common scheme for preservation.

History of Prop. Code §208.004: Acts 1999, 76th Leg., ch. 871, §2, eff. June 18, 1999. Renumbered from §207.004 by Acts 2001, 77th Leg., ch. 1420, §21.001(98), eff. Sept. 1, 2001.

PROP §208.005. AMENDMENT OR TERMINATION OF RESTRICTIVE COVENANTS UNDER COMMON SCHEME FOR PRESERVATION

(a) A restrictive covenant applicable to property that is included in a common scheme for preservation of historic property may not be amended or terminated except as provided by this section.

(b) A historic neighborhood preservation association may approve and submit to a vote of the owners of property that is included in a common scheme for preservation of historic property an amendment of the restrictive covenants or the termination of all or part of the restrictive covenants included in the common scheme for preservation of historic property.

(c) The amendment or termination of a restrictive covenant is effective and applies to each separately owned parcel or tract subject to the common scheme for preservation of historic property if the owners of at least 75 percent of the parcels or tracts who vote on the issue in accordance with Section 208.006 vote in favor of the amendment or termination of the restrictive covenant.

(d) A document certifying that 75 percent of the owners voting on the issue approved the amendment or termination of the restrictive covenant must be recorded by the historic neighborhood preservation association in the real property records of the county in which the historic neighborhood is located. The document is prima facie evidence that the requisite percentage of votes was attained and the required formalities for the action were taken.

History of Prop. Code §208.005: Acts 1999, 76th Leg., ch. 871, §2, eff. June 18, 1999. Renumbered from §207.005 by Acts 2001, 77th Leg., ch. 1420, §21.001(98), eff. Sept. 1, 2001. Amended by Acts 2001, 77th Leg., ch. 1420, §21.002(18), eff. Sept. 1, 2001.

PROP §208.006. METHOD OF VOTING

(a) An amendment or termination of a restrictive covenant must be voted on:

(1) by a written ballot that states the substance of the amendment or termination of the restrictive covenant and specifies the date by which the historic neighborhood preservation association must receive a ballot for the ballot to be counted;

(2) at a meeting of the historic neighborhood preservation association;

(3) by circulation of a petition by the historic neighborhood preservation association or a person authorized by the historic neighborhood preservation association; or

(4) by any combination of methods described by this subsection.

(b) If the vote occurs at a meeting of the historic neighborhood preservation association under Subsection (a)(2), the historic neighborhood preservation association shall:

(1) before the meeting, deliver written notice of the meeting stating the purpose of the meeting to each owner of property subject to the common scheme for preservation of historic property; and

(2) provide each owner of property subject to the common scheme for preservation with the opportunity to appear and vote at the meeting.

(c) The historic neighborhood preservation association shall provide for the mailing to each owner, as applicable:

(1) the ballot under Subsection (a)(1);

(2) notice of the meeting under Subsection (a)(2); or

(3) the petition under Subsection (a)(3).

(d) The vote of multiple owners of a property may be reflected by signature or vote of one of the owners.

(e) The historic neighborhood preservation association shall record a copy of the ballot or petition, as applicable, in the real property records of the county in which the historic neighborhood is located before the vote of the owners.

History of Prop. Code §208.006: Acts 1999, 76th Leg., ch. 871, §2, eff. June 18, 1999. Renumbered from §207.006 by Acts 2001, 77th Leg., ch. 1420, §21.001(98), eff. Sept. 1, 2001.

PROP §208.007. REGULAR & SPECIAL ASSESSMENTS

The procedure established by this chapter for the amendment of restrictive covenants may not be used to establish a regular or special assessment.

History of Prop. Code §208.007: Acts 1999, 76th Leg., ch. 871, §2, eff. June 18, 1999. Renumbered from §207.007 by Acts 2001, 77th Leg., ch. 1420, §21.001(98), eff. Sept. 1, 2001.

PROP §208.008. BUILDING LINES

The procedure established by this chapter for the amendment of restrictive covenants may not be used to modify a building line established by a restrictive covenant, municipal map, or subdivision plat.

History of Prop. Code §208.008: Acts 1999, 76th Leg., ch. 871, §2, eff. June 18, 1999. Renumbered from §207.008 by Acts 2001, 77th Leg., ch. 1420, §21.001(98), eff. Sept. 1, 2001.

PROP §208.009. DEFENSE TO ENFORCEMENT OF RESTRICTIVE COVENANT

An owner may not assert as a defense to the enforcement of a restrictive covenant that is part of a common scheme for preservation of historic property that the owner or a predecessor in title signed a blank signature page or similar procedural defect if the signature page was attached to a dedicatory instrument adopted by a historic neighborhood preservation association and:

(1) the dedicatory instrument has been recorded for more than two years; or

(2) the restrictive covenant is referenced in the owner's title insurance policy obtained by the owner when the property was purchased.

History of Prop. Code §208.009: Acts 1999, 76th Leg., ch. 871, §2, eff. June 18, 1999. Renumbered from §207.009 by Acts 2001, 77th Leg., ch. 1420, §21.001(98), eff. Sept. 1, 2001.

CHAPTER 209. TEXAS RESIDENTIAL PROPERTY OWNERS PROTECTION ACT

PROP §209.001. SHORT TITLE

This chapter may be cited as the Texas Residential Property Owners Protection Act.

History of Prop. Code §209.001: Acts 2001, 77th Leg., ch. 926, §1, eff. Jan. 1, 2002.

PROP §209.002. DEFINITIONS

In this chapter:

(1) "Assessment" means a regular assessment, special assessment, or other amount a property owner is required to pay a property owners' association under the dedicatory instrument or by law.

(2) "Board" means the governing body of a property owners' association.

(3) "Declaration" means an instrument filed in the real property records of a county that includes restrictive covenants governing a residential subdivision.

(4) "Dedicatory instrument" means each governing instrument covering the establishment, maintenance, and operation of a residential subdivision. The term includes restrictions or similar instruments subjecting property to restrictive covenants, bylaws, or similar instruments governing the administration or operation of a property owners' association, to properly adopted rules and regulations of the property owners' association, and to all lawful amendments to the covenants, bylaws, rules, or regulations.

(4-a) "Development period" means a period stated in a declaration during which a declarant reserves:

(A) a right to facilitate the development, construction, and marketing of the subdivision; or

(B) a right to direct the size, shape, and composition of the subdivision.

(5) "Lot" means any designated parcel of land located in a residential subdivision, including any improvements on the designated parcel.

(6) "Owner" means a person who holds record title to property in a residential subdivision and includes the personal representative of a person who holds record title to property in a residential subdivision.

(7) "Property owners' association" or "association" means an incorporated or unincorporated association that:

(A) is designated as the representative of the owners of property in a residential subdivision;

(B) has a membership primarily consisting of the owners of the property covered by the dedicatory instrument for the residential subdivision; and

(C) manages or regulates the residential subdivision for the benefit of the owners of property in the residential subdivision.

(8) "Regular assessment" means an assessment, a charge, a fee, or dues that each owner of property within a residential subdivision is required to pay to the property owners' association on a regular basis and that is designated for use by the property owners' association for the benefit of the residential subdivision as provided by the restrictions.

(9) "Residential subdivision" or "subdivision" means a subdivision, planned unit development, townhouse regime, or similar planned development in which all land has been divided into two or more parts and is subject to restrictions that:

(A) limit a majority of the land subject to the dedicatory instruments, excluding streets, common areas, and public areas, to residential use for single-family homes, townhomes, or duplexes only;

(B) are recorded in the real property records of the county in which the residential subdivision is located; and

(C) require membership in a property owners' association that has authority to impose regular or special assessments on the property in the subdivision.

(10) "Restrictions" means one or more restrictive covenants contained or incorporated by reference in a properly recorded map, plat, replat, declaration, or other instrument filed in the real property records or map or plat records. The term includes any amendment or extension of the restrictions.

(11) "Restrictive covenant" means any covenant, condition, or restriction contained in a dedicatory instrument, whether mandatory, prohibitive, permissive, or administrative.

(12) "Special assessment" means an assessment, a charge, a fee, or dues, other than a regular assessment, that each owner of property located in a residential subdivision is required to pay to the property owners' association, according to procedures required by the dedicatory instruments, for:

(A) defraying, in whole or in part, the cost, whether incurred before or after the assessment, of any construction or reconstruction, unexpected repair, or replacement of a capital improvement in common areas owned by the property owners' association, including the necessary fixtures and personal property related to the common areas;

(B) maintenance and improvement of common areas owned by the property owners' association; or

(C) other purposes of the property owners' association as stated in its articles of incorporation or the dedicatory instrument for the residential subdivision.

(13) "Verified mail" means any method of mailing for which evidence of mailing is provided by the United States Postal Service or a common carrier.

History of Prop. Code §209.002: Acts 2001, 77th Leg., ch. 926, §1, eff. Jan. 1, 2002. Amended by Acts 2013, 83rd Leg., ch. 863, §1, eff. Sept. 1, 2013; Acts 2015, 84th Leg., ch. 1183, §4, eff. Sept. 1, 2015.

ANNOTATIONS

Storck v. Tres Lagos Prop. Owners Ass'n, 442 S.W.3d 730, 738 (Tex.App.—Texarkana 2014, pet. denied). "We do not believe the definition of dedicatory instrument in the Property Code was intended to establish a definitive list of documents to be considered dedicatory instruments. Instead, we interpret the phrase 'subjecting property to' as modifying 'restrictions or similar instruments.' The list of various instruments in the statute is included in the definition to indicate the types of documents that make restrictions or other similar instruments into dedicatory instruments. So, for example, an instrument which subjects property to bylaws is a dedicatory instrument, although the bylaws may not fall within this category."

Summers v. Highland Composite Prop. Owners Ass'n, 363 S.W.3d 210, 215 (Tex.App.—Corpus Christi 2011, no pet.). "The fact that [P] was formed [for purposes listed in its articles of incorporation] does not necessarily mean that it in fact manages or regulates any of these residential subdivisions for the benefit of the owners of property in these subdivisions. [¶] We hold that even if [P] were designated by certain homeowners within the subdivisions at issue to enforce deed restrictions, and, if we further assume, but not hold, that this designation is the designation referred to in [Prop. Code] §§204.004 and 209.002 ..., it is insufficient to establish that [P] is a duly constituted property owners association absent a showing that [P] manages or regulates these residential subdivisions for the benefit of the owners of property in these subdivisions."

Khyber Holdings, LLC v. BAC Home Loans Servicing, LP, 349 S.W.3d 178, 180 (Tex.App.—Dallas 2011, no pet.). Purchaser "asserts the trial court erred in granting [loan-servicing company] summary judgment because [loan-servicing company] is not a 'person' entitled to redeem property within the meaning of the [Texas Residential Property Owners Protection] Act. [¶] The ... Act defines 'Owner' as a person who holds record title to property in a residential subdivision and includes the personal representative of a person who holds record title to property in a residential subdivision. The word 'person' is not defined in the Act. Under the Code Construction Act, however, the following definition of 'person' applies unless the statute or context in which the word or phrase is used requires a different definition: 'Person' includes corporation, organization, government or governmental subdivision or agency, business trust, partnership association and any other legal entity. Thus, we conclude that [loan-servicing company] is a 'person' entitled to redeem property under the Act." (Internal quotes omitted.)

PROP §209.003. APPLICABILITY OF CHAPTER

(a) This chapter applies only to a residential subdivision that is subject to restrictions or provisions in a declaration that authorize the property owners' association to collect regular or special assessments on all or a majority of the property in the subdivision.

(b) Except as otherwise provided by this chapter, this chapter applies only to a property owners' association that requires mandatory membership in the association for all or a majority of the owners of residential property within the subdivision subject to the association's dedicatory instruments.

(c) This chapter applies to a residential property owners' association regardless of whether the entity is designated as a "homeowners' association," "commu-

nity association," or similar designation in the restrictions or dedicatory instrument.

(d) This chapter does not apply to a condominium as defined by Section 81.002 or 82.003.

(e) The following provisions of this chapter do not apply to a property owners' association that is a mixed-use master association that existed before January 1, 1974, and that does not have the authority under a dedicatory instrument or other governing document to impose fines:

(1) Section 209.005(c);

(2) Section 209.0056;

(3) Section 209.0057;

(4) Section 209.0058;

(5) Section 209.00592; and

(6) Section 209.0062.

History of Prop. Code §209.003: Acts 2001, 77th Leg., ch. 926, §1, eff. Jan. 1, 2002. Amended by Acts 2007, 80th Leg., ch. 1367, §7, eff. Sept. 1, 2007; Acts 2011, 82nd Leg., ch. 1026, §1 (eff. Jan. 1, 2012), ch. 1142, §6 (eff. Jan. 1, 2012), ch. 1217, §1 (eff. Sept. 1, 2011), ch. 1282, §1 (eff. Jan. 1, 2012); Acts 2013, 83rd Leg., ch. 161, §17.002, eff. Sept. 1, 2013; Acts 2015, 84th Leg., ch. 1183, §5, eff. Sept. 1, 2015.

ANNOTATIONS

Western Hills Harbor Owners Ass'n v. Baker, 516 S.W.3d 215, 224 (Tex.App.—El Paso 2017, n.p.h.). "Although [Ps] correctly point out that the Declaration does not expressly state that membership in the Association is mandatory, the Declaration nevertheless imposes *mandatory* assessments on all lot owners, giving the owners no choice but to pay those assessments. Further, the Declaration provides that those assessments are for the construction of 'swimming pools, parks, roads and other improvements' in the subdivision, which were to be utilized solely by 'members' of the Association and their families. From this language, we conclude that the subdivision developer made clear its intent to create a mandatory-membership association for the benefit of its members, as opposed to one that was simply voluntary. *At 225:* [Ps] contend [that] the Association [has] the discretion to refuse membership to a particular lot owner and to expel the lot owner from membership, and that therefore membership cannot be considered mandatory. This position is incorrect. The fact that a subdivision's declaration gives a homeowner's association the discretion to refuse membership to a property owner or to expel an owner from membership in accordance with its internal rules and regulations, does not render membership in the Association any less mandatory, where an individual purchasing property within the subdivision otherwise agrees to pay those assessments in accordance with the subdivision's restrictive covenants. [¶] We therefore conclude that … the subdivision was intended to be developed as a mandatory-membership Association, and therefore, Ch. 209 … is applicable…."

PROP §209.004. MANAGEMENT CERTIFICATES

(a) A property owners' association shall record in each county in which any portion of the residential subdivision is located a management certificate, signed and acknowledged by an officer or the managing agent of the association, stating:

(1) the name of the subdivision;

(2) the name of the association;

(3) the recording data for the subdivision;

(4) the recording data for the declaration;

(5) the name and mailing address of the association;

(6) the name and mailing address of the person managing the association or the association's designated representative; and

(7) other information the association considers appropriate.

(a-1) The county clerk of each county in which a management certificate is filed as required by this section shall record the management certificate in the real property records of the county and index the document as a "Property Owners' Association Management Certificate."

(b) The property owners' association shall record an amended management certificate not later than the 30th day after the date the association has notice of a change in any information in the recorded certificate required by Subsection (a).

(c) Except as provided under Subsections (d) and (e), the property owners' association and its officers, directors, employees, and agents are not subject to liability to any person for a delay in recording or failure to record a management certificate, unless the delay or failure is wilful or caused by gross negligence.

(d) If a property owners' association fails to record a management certificate or an amended management certificate under this section, the purchaser, lender, or title insurance company or its agent in a transaction involving property in the property owners' association is not liable to the property owners' association for:

(1) any amount due to the association on the date of a transfer to a bona fide purchaser; and

(2) any debt to or claim of the association that accrued before the date of a transfer to a bona fide purchaser.

(e) A lien of a property owners' association that fails to file a management certificate or an amended management certificate under this section to secure an amount due on the effective date of a transfer to a bona fide purchaser is enforceable only for an amount incurred after the effective date of sale.

(f) For purposes of this section, "bona fide purchaser" means:

(1) a person who pays valuable consideration without notice of outstanding rights of others and acts in good faith; or

(2) a third-party lender who acquires a security interest in the property under a deed of trust.

History of Prop. Code §209.004: Acts 2001, 77th Leg., ch. 926, §1, eff. Jan. 1, 2002. Amended by Acts 2009, 81st Leg., ch. 148, §1, eff. Sept. 1, 2009; Acts 2013, 83rd Leg., ch. 1108, §1, eff. Sept. 1, 2013.

See also *Real Estate Forms*, FORMS 6:5, 6:16-6:18, 11:1, 11:2.

PROP §209.0041. ADOPTION OR AMENDMENT OF CERTAIN DEDICATORY INSTRUMENTS

(a) Repealed by Acts 2015, 84th Leg., ch. 1183, §24, eff. Sept. 1, 2015.

(b) This section applies to a residential subdivision in which property owners are subject to mandatory membership in a property owners' association.

(c) This section does not apply to a property owners' association that is subject to Chapter 552, Government Code, by application of Section 552.0036, Government Code.

(d) This section does not apply to the amendment of a declaration during a development period.

(e) This section applies to a dedicatory instrument regardless of the date on which the dedicatory instrument was created.

(f) This section supersedes any contrary requirement in a dedicatory instrument.

(g) To the extent of any conflict with another provision of this title, this section prevails.

(h) Except as provided by Subsection (h-1) or (h-2), a declaration may be amended only by a vote of 67 percent of the total votes allocated to property owners entitled to vote on the amendment of the declaration, in addition to any governmental approval required by law.

(h-1) If the declaration contains a lower percentage than prescribed by Subsection (h), the percentage in the declaration controls.

(h-2) If the declaration is silent as to voting rights for an amendment, the declaration may be amended by a vote of owners owning 67 percent of the lots subject to the declaration.

(i) A bylaw may not be amended to conflict with the declaration.

History of Prop. Code §209.0041: Acts 2011, 82nd Leg., ch. 1217, §2, eff. Sept. 1, 2011. Amended by Acts 2015, 84th Leg., ch. 1183, §§6, 24, eff. Sept. 1, 2015.

PROP §209.0042. METHODS OF PROVIDING NOTICES TO OWNERS

(a) Subject to this section, a property owners' association may adopt a method that may be used by the association to provide a notice from the association to a property owner.

(b) A property owners' association may use an alternative method of providing notice adopted under this section to provide a notice for which another method is prescribed by law only if the property owner to whom the notice is provided has affirmatively opted to allow the association to use the alternative method of providing notice to provide to the owner notices for which another method is prescribed by law.

(c) A property owners' association may not require an owner to allow the association to use an alternative method of providing notice adopted under this section to provide to the owner any notice for which another method of providing notice is prescribed by law.

History of Prop. Code §209.0042: Acts 2015, 84th Leg., ch. 1183, §7, eff. Sept. 1, 2015.

PROP §209.005. ASSOCIATION RECORDS

(a) Except as provided by Subsection (b), this section applies to all property owners' associations and controls over other law not specifically applicable to a property owners' association.

(b) This section does not apply to a property owners' association that is subject to Chapter 552, Government Code, by application of Section 552.0036, Government Code.

(c) Notwithstanding a provision in a dedicatory instrument, a property owners' association shall make the books and records of the association, including financial records, open to and reasonably available for examination by an owner, or a person designated in a

writing signed by the owner as the owner's agent, attorney, or certified public accountant, in accordance with this section. An owner is entitled to obtain from the association copies of information contained in the books and records.

(d) Except as provided by this subsection, an attorney's files and records relating to the property owners' association, excluding invoices requested by an owner under Section 209.008(d), are not records of the association and are not subject to inspection by the owner or production in a legal proceeding. If a document in an attorney's files and records relating to the association would be responsive to a legally authorized request to inspect or copy association documents, the document shall be produced by using the copy from the attorney's files and records if the association has not maintained a separate copy of the document. This subsection does not require production of a document that constitutes attorney work product or that is privileged as an attorney-client communication.

(e) An owner or the owner's authorized representative described by Subsection (c) must submit a written request for access or information under Subsection (c) by certified mail, with sufficient detail describing the property owners' association's books and records requested, to the mailing address of the association or authorized representative as reflected on the most current management certificate filed under Section 209.004. The request must contain an election either to inspect the books and records before obtaining copies or to have the property owners' association forward copies of the requested books and records and:

(1) if an inspection is requested, the association, on or before the 10th business day after the date the association receives the request, shall send written notice of dates during normal business hours that the owner may inspect the requested books and records to the extent those books and records are in the possession, custody, or control of the association; or

(2) if copies of identified books and records are requested, the association shall, to the extent those books and records are in the possession, custody, or control of the association, produce the requested books and records for the requesting party on or before the 10th business day after the date the association receives the request, except as otherwise provided by this section.

(f) If the property owners' association is unable to produce the books or records requested under Subsection (e) on or before the 10th business day after the date the association receives the request, the association must provide to the requestor written notice that:

(1) informs the requestor that the association is unable to produce the information on or before the 10th business day after the date the association received the request; and

(2) states a date by which the information will be sent or made available for inspection to the requesting party that is not later than the 15th business day after the date notice under this subsection is given.

(g) If an inspection is requested or required, the inspection shall take place at a mutually agreed on time during normal business hours, and the requesting party shall identify the books and records for the property owners' association to copy and forward to the requesting party.

(h) A property owners' association may produce books and records requested under this section in hard copy, electronic, or other format reasonably available to the association.

(i) A property owners' association board must adopt a records production and copying policy that prescribes the costs the association will charge for the compilation, production, and reproduction of information requested under this section. The prescribed charges may include all reasonable costs of materials, labor, and overhead but may not exceed costs that would be applicable for an item under 1 T.A.C. Section 70.3. The policy required by this subsection must be recorded as a dedicatory instrument in accordance with Section 202.006. An association may not charge an owner for the compilation, production, or reproduction of information requested under this section unless the policy prescribing those costs has been recorded as required by this subsection. An owner is responsible for costs related to the compilation, production, and reproduction of the requested information in the amounts prescribed by the policy adopted under this subsection. The association may require advance payment of the estimated costs of compilation, production, and reproduction of the requested information. If the estimated costs are lesser or greater than the actual costs, the association shall submit a final invoice to the owner on or before the 30th business day after the date the information is delivered. If the final invoice includes additional amounts due from the owner, the additional amounts, if not reimbursed to the association before the 30th busi-

ness day after the date the invoice is sent to the owner, may be added to the owner's account as an assessment. If the estimated costs exceeded the final invoice amount, the owner is entitled to a refund, and the refund shall be issued to the owner not later than the 30th business day after the date the invoice is sent to the owner.

(j) A property owners' association must estimate costs under this section using amounts prescribed by the policy adopted under Subsection (i).

(k) Except as provided by Subsection (*l*) and to the extent the information is provided in the meeting minutes, the property owners' association is not required to release or allow inspection of any books or records that identify the dedicatory instrument violation history of an individual owner of an association, an owner's personal financial information, including records of payment or nonpayment of amounts due the association, an owner's contact information, other than the owner's address, or information related to an employee of the association, including personnel files. Information may be released in an aggregate or summary manner that would not identify an individual property owner.

(*l*) The books and records described by Subsection (k) shall be released or made available for inspection if:

(1) the express written approval of the owner whose records are the subject of the request for inspection is provided to the property owners' association; or

(2) a court orders the release of the books and records or orders that the books and records be made available for inspection.

(m) A property owners' association composed of more than 14 lots shall adopt and comply with a document retention policy that includes, at a minimum, the following requirements:

(1) certificates of formation, bylaws, restrictive covenants, and all amendments to the certificates of formation, bylaws, and covenants shall be retained permanently;

(2) financial books and records shall be retained for seven years;

(3) account records of current owners shall be retained for five years;

(4) contracts with a term of one year or more shall be retained for four years after the expiration of the contract term;

(5) minutes of meetings of the owners and the board shall be retained for seven years; and

(6) tax returns and audit records shall be retained for seven years.

(n) A member of a property owners' association who is denied access to or copies of association books or records to which the member is entitled under this section may file a petition with the justice of the peace of a justice precinct in which all or part of the property that is governed by the association is located requesting relief in accordance with this subsection. If the justice of the peace finds that the member is entitled to access to or copies of the records, the justice of the peace may grant one or more of the following remedies:

(1) a judgment ordering the property owners' association to release or allow access to the books or records;

(2) a judgment against the property owners' association for court costs and attorney's fees incurred in connection with seeking a remedy under this section; or

(3) a judgment authorizing the owner or the owner's assignee to deduct the amounts awarded under Subdivision (2) from any future regular or special assessments payable to the property owners' association.

(o) If the property owners' association prevails in an action under Subsection (n), the association is entitled to a judgment for court costs and attorney's fees incurred by the association in connection with the action.

(p) On or before the 10th business day before the date a person brings an action against a property owners' association under this section, the person must send written notice to the association of the person's intent to bring the action. The notice must:

(1) be sent certified mail, return receipt requested, or delivered by the United States Postal Service with signature confirmation service to the mailing address of the association or authorized representative as reflected on the most current management certificate filed under Section 209.004; and

(2) describe with sufficient detail the books and records being requested.

(q) For the purposes of this section, "business day" means a day other than Saturday, Sunday, or a state or federal holiday.

History of Prop. Code §209.005: Acts 2001, 77th Leg., ch. 926, §1, eff. Jan. 1, 2002. Amended by Acts 2007, 80th Leg., ch. 1367, §6, eff. Sept. 1, 2007; Acts 2011, 82nd Leg., ch. 1026, §2, eff. Jan. 1, 2012.

PROP §209.0051. OPEN BOARD MEETINGS

(a) This section does not apply to a property owners' association that is subject to Chapter 551, Government Code, by application of Section 551.0015, Government Code.

(b) In this section, "board meeting":

(1) means a deliberation between a quorum of the voting board of the property owners' association, or between a quorum of the voting board and another person, during which property owners' association business is considered and the board takes formal action; and

(2) does not include the gathering of a quorum of the board at a social function unrelated to the business of the association or the attendance by a quorum of the board at a regional, state, or national convention, ceremonial event, or press conference, if formal action is not taken and any discussion of association business is incidental to the social function, convention, ceremonial event, or press conference.

(c) Regular and special board meetings must be open to owners, subject to the right of the board to adjourn a board meeting and reconvene in closed executive session to consider actions involving personnel, pending or threatened litigation, contract negotiations, enforcement actions, confidential communications with the property owners' association's attorney, matters involving the invasion of privacy of individual owners, or matters that are to remain confidential by request of the affected parties and agreement of the board. Following an executive session, any decision made in the executive session must be summarized orally and placed in the minutes, in general terms, without breaching the privacy of individual owners, violating any privilege, or disclosing information that was to remain confidential at the request of the affected parties. The oral summary must include a general explanation of expenditures approved in executive session.

(c-1) Except for a meeting held by electronic or telephonic means under Subsection (c-2), a board meeting must be held in a county in which all or part of the property in the subdivision is located or in a county adjacent to that county.

(c-2) A board meeting may be held by electronic or telephonic means provided that:

(1) each board member may hear and be heard by every other board member;

(2) except for any portion of the meeting conducted in executive session:

(A) all owners in attendance at the meeting may hear all board members; and

(B) owners are allowed to listen using any electronic or telephonic communication method used or expected to be used by a board member to participate; and

(3) the notice of the meeting includes instructions for owners to access any communication method required to be accessible under Subdivision (2)(B).

(d) The board shall keep a record of each regular or special board meeting in the form of written minutes of the meeting. The board shall make meeting records, including approved minutes, available to a member for inspection and copying on the member's written request to the property owners' association's managing agent at the address appearing on the most recently filed management certificate or, if there is not a managing agent, to the board.

(e) Members shall be given notice of the date, hour, place, and general subject of a regular or special board meeting, including a general description of any matter to be brought up for deliberation in executive session. The notice shall be:

(1) mailed to each property owner not later than the 10th day or earlier than the 60th day before the date of the meeting; or

(2) provided at least 72 hours before the start of the meeting by:

(A) posting the notice in a conspicuous manner reasonably designed to provide notice to property owners' association members:

(i) in a place located on the association's common property or, with the property owner's consent, on other conspicuously located privately owned property within the subdivision; or

(ii) on any Internet website maintained by the association or other Internet media; and

(B) sending the notice by e-mail to each owner who has registered an e-mail address with the association.

(f) It is an owner's duty to keep an updated e-mail address registered with the property owners' association under Subsection (e)(2)(B).

(g) If the board recesses a regular or special board meeting to continue the following regular business day, the board is not required to post notice of the continued

meeting if the recess is taken in good faith and not to circumvent this section. If a regular or special board meeting is continued to the following regular business day, and on that following day the board continues the meeting to another day, the board shall give notice of the continuation in at least one manner prescribed by Subsection (e)(2)(A) within two hours after adjourning the meeting being continued.

(h) Except as provided by this subsection, a board may take action outside of a meeting, including voting by electronic or telephonic means, without prior notice to owners under Subsection (e), if each board member is given a reasonable opportunity to express the board member's opinion to all other board members and to vote. Any action taken without notice to owners under Subsection (e) must be summarized orally, including an explanation of any known actual or estimated expenditures approved at the meeting, and documented in the minutes of the next regular or special board meeting. The board may not, unless done in an open meeting for which prior notice was given to owners under Subsection (e), consider or vote on:

(1) fines;

(2) damage assessments;

(3) initiation of foreclosure actions;

(4) initiation of enforcement actions, excluding temporary restraining orders or violations involving a threat to health or safety;

(5) increases in assessments;

(6) levying of special assessments;

(7) appeals from a denial of architectural control approval;

(8) a suspension of a right of a particular owner before the owner has an opportunity to attend a board meeting to present the owner's position, including any defense, on the issue;

(9) lending or borrowing money;

(10) the adoption or amendment of a dedicatory instrument;

(11) the approval of an annual budget or the approval of an amendment of an annual budget that increases the budget by more than 10 percent;

(12) the sale or purchase of real property;

(13) the filling of a vacancy on the board;

(14) the construction of capital improvements other than the repair, replacement, or enhancement of existing capital improvements; or

(15) the election of an officer.

(i) This section applies to a meeting of a property owners' association board during the development period only if the meeting is conducted for the purpose of:

(1) adopting or amending the governing documents, including declarations, bylaws, rules, and regulations of the association;

(2) increasing the amount of regular assessments of the association or adopting or increasing a special assessment;

(3) electing non-developer board members of the association or establishing a process by which those members are elected; or

(4) changing the voting rights of members of the association.

History of Prop. Code §209.0051: Acts 2011, 82nd Leg., ch. 1026, §3, eff. Jan. 1, 2012. Amended by Acts 2015, 84th Leg., ch. 1183, §8, eff. Sept. 1, 2015.

PROP §209.0052. ASSOCIATION CONTRACTS

(a) This section does not apply to a contract entered into by an association during the development period.

(b) An association may enter into an enforceable contract with a current association board member, a person related to a current association board member within the third degree by consanguinity or affinity, as determined under Chapter 573, Government Code, a company in which a current association board member has a financial interest in at least 51 percent of profits, or a company in which a person related to a current association board member within the third degree by consanguinity or affinity, as determined under Chapter 573, Government Code, has a financial interest in at least 51 percent of profits only if the following conditions are satisfied:

(1) the board member, relative, or company bids on the proposed contract and the association has received at least two other bids for the contract from persons not associated with the board member, relative, or company, if reasonably available in the community;

(2) the board member:

(A) is not given access to the other bids;

(B) does not participate in any board discussion regarding the contract; and

(C) does not vote on the award of the contract;

(3) the material facts regarding the relationship or interest with respect to the proposed contract are dis-

closed to or known by the association board and the board, in good faith and with ordinary care, authorizes the contract by an affirmative vote of the majority of the board members who do not have an interest governed by this subsection; and

(4) the association board certifies that the other requirements of this subsection have been satisfied by a resolution approved by an affirmative vote of the majority of the board members who do not have an interest governed by this subsection.

History of Prop. Code §209.0052: Acts 2013, 83rd Leg., ch. 863, §2, eff. Sept. 1, 2013.

PROP §209.0055. VOTING

(a) This section applies only to a property owners' association that:

(1) provides maintenance, preservation, and architectural control of residential and commercial property within a defined geographic area in a county with a population of 2.8 million or more or in a county adjacent to a county with a population of 2.8 million or more; and

(2) is a corporation that:

(A) is governed by a board of trustees who may employ a general manager to execute the association's bylaws and administer the business of the corporation;

(B) does not require membership in the corporation by the owners of the property within the defined area; and

(C) was incorporated before January 1, 2006.

(b) A property owners' association described by Subsection (a) may not bar a property owner from voting in an association election solely based on the fact that:

(1) there is a pending enforcement action against the property owner; or

(2) the property owner owes the association any delinquent assessments, fees, or fines.

History of Prop. Code §209.0055: Acts 2007, 80th Leg., ch. 1367, §8, eff. Sept. 1, 2007.

PROP §209.0056. NOTICE OF ELECTION OR ASSOCIATION VOTE

(a) For an election or vote taken at a meeting of the owners, not later than the 10th day or earlier than the 60th day before the date of the election or vote, a property owners' association shall give written notice of the election or vote to:

(1) each owner of property in the property owners' association, for purposes of an association-wide election or vote; or

(2) each owner of property in the property owners' association entitled under the dedicatory instruments to vote in a particular representative election, for purposes of a vote that involves election of representatives of the association who are vested under the dedicatory instruments of the property owners' association with the authority to elect or appoint board members of the property owners' association.

(a-1) For an election or vote of owners not taken at a meeting, the property owners' association shall give notice of the election or vote to all owners entitled to vote on any matter under consideration. The notice shall be given not later than the 20th day before the latest date on which a ballot may be submitted to be counted.

(b) This section supersedes any contrary requirement in a dedicatory instrument.

(c) This section does not apply to a property owners' association that is subject to Chapter 552, Government Code, by application of Section 552.0036, Government Code.

History of Prop. Code §209.0056: Acts 2011, 82nd Leg., ch. 1026, §3, eff. Jan. 1, 2012. Amended by Acts 2015, 84th Leg., ch. 1183, §9, eff. Sept. 1, 2015.

PROP §209.0057. RECOUNT OF VOTES

(a) This section does not apply to a property owners' association that is subject to Chapter 552, Government Code, by application of Section 552.0036, Government Code.

(b) Any owner may, not later than the 15th day after the later of the date of any meeting of owners at which the election or vote was held or the date of the announcement of the results of the election or vote, require a recount of the votes. A demand for a recount must be submitted in writing either:

(1) by verified mail or by delivery by the United States Postal Service with signature confirmation service to the property owners' association's mailing address as reflected on the latest management certificate filed under Section 209.004; or

(2) in person to the property owners' association's managing agent as reflected on the latest management certificate filed under Section 209.004 or to the address to which absentee and proxy ballots are mailed.

(b-1) The property owners' association must estimate the costs for performance of the recount by a person qualified to tabulate votes under Subsection (c) and must send an invoice for the estimated costs to the

requesting owner at the owner's last known address according to association records not later than the 20th day after the date the association receives the owner's demand for the recount.

(b-2) The owner demanding a recount under this section must pay the invoice described by Subsection (b-1) in full to the property owners' association on or before the 30th day after the date the invoice is sent to the owner.

(b-3) If the invoice described by Subsection (b-1) is not paid by the deadline prescribed by Subsection (b-2), the owner's demand for a recount is considered withdrawn and a recount is not required.

(b-4) If the estimated costs under Subsection (b-1) are lesser or greater than the actual costs, the property owners' association must send a final invoice to the owner on or before the 30th business day after the date the results of the recount are provided. If the final invoice includes additional amounts owed by the owner, any additional amounts not paid to the association before the 30th business day after the date the invoice is sent to the owner may be added to the owner's account as an assessment. If the estimated costs exceed the final invoice amount, the owner is entitled to a refund. The refund shall be paid to the owner at the time the final invoice is sent under this subsection.

(c) Following receipt of payment under Subsection (b-2), the property owners' association shall, at the expense of the owner requesting the recount, retain for the purpose of performing the recount the services of a person qualified to tabulate votes under this subsection. The association shall enter into a contract for the services of a person who:

(1) is not a member of the association or related to a member of the association board within the third degree by consanguinity or affinity, as determined under Chapter 573, Government Code; and

(2) is:

(A) a current or former:

(i) county judge;

(ii) county elections administrator;

(iii) justice of the peace; or

(iv) county voter registrar; or

(B) a person agreed on by the association and each person requesting the recount.

(d) On or before the 30th day after the date of receipt of payment for a recount in accordance with Subsection (b-2), the recount must be completed and the property owners' association must provide each owner who requested the recount with notice of the results of the recount. If the recount changes the results of the election, the association shall reimburse the requesting owner for the cost of the recount not later than the 30th day after the date the results of the recount are provided. Any action taken by the board in the period between the initial election vote tally and the completion of the recount is not affected by any recount.

History of Prop. Code §209.0057: Acts 2011, 82nd Leg., ch. 1026, §3, eff. Jan. 1, 2012. Amended by Acts 2015, 84th Leg., ch. 1183, §10, eff. Sept. 1, 2015.

PROP §209.0058. BALLOTS

☠ *Subsection (a) was amended by Acts 2015, 84th Leg., ch. 249, §1, enacted May 19, 2015, effective May 29, 2015, without reference to the conflicting amendment made by Acts 2015, 84th Leg., ch. 1183, §11, enacted May 28, 2015, effective Sept. 1, 2015. For harmonizing conflicts, see p. V.*

(a) Except as provided by Subsection (d), any vote cast in an election or vote by a member of a property owners' association must be in writing and signed by the member.

☠ *Subsection (a) was amended by Acts 2015, 84th Leg., ch. 1183, §11, enacted May 28, 2015, effective Sept. 1, 2015, without reference to the conflicting amendment made by Acts 2015, 84th Leg., ch. 249, §1, enacted May 19, 2015, effective May 29, 2015. For harmonizing conflicts, see p. V.*

(a) Except as provided by Subsection (d), a vote cast by a member of a property owners' association must be in writing and signed by the member if the vote is cast:

(1) outside of a meeting;

(2) in an election to fill a position on the board;

(3) on a proposed adoption or amendment of a dedicatory instrument;

(4) on a proposed increase in the amount of a regular assessment or the proposed adoption of a special assessment; or

(5) on the proposed removal of a board member.

(a-1) If a property owners' association elects to use a ballot for a vote on a matter other than a matter described by Subsection (a), the ballot must be:

(1) in writing and signed by the member; or

(2) cast by secret ballot in accordance with Subsection (d).

(b) Electronic votes cast under Section 209.00592 constitute written and signed ballots.

(c) In a property owners' association election, written and signed ballots are not required for uncontested races.

Subsection (d) was enacted by Acts 2015, 84th Leg., ch. 249, §1, enacted May 19, 2015, effective May 29, 2015, without reference to the conflicting enactment made by Acts 2015, 84th Leg., ch. 1183, §11, enacted May 28, 2015, effective Sept. 1, 2015. For harmonizing conflicts, see p. V.

(d) A property owners' association may adopt rules to allow voting by secret ballot by members of the association. The association must take measures to reasonably ensure that:

(1) a member cannot cast more votes than the member is eligible to cast in an election or vote; and

(2) the association counts every vote cast by a member that is eligible to cast a vote.

Subsection (d) was enacted by Acts 2015, 84th Leg., ch. 1183, §11, enacted May 28, 2015, effective Sept. 1, 2015, without reference to the conflicting enactment made by Acts 2015, 84th Leg., ch. 249, §1, enacted May 19, 2015, effective May 29, 2015. For harmonizing conflicts, see p. V.

(d) A property owners' association may adopt rules to allow voting by secret ballot by association members. The association must take measures to reasonably ensure that:

(1) a member cannot cast more votes than the member is eligible to cast in an election or vote;

(2) the association counts each vote cast by a member that the member is eligible to cast; and

(3) in any election for the board, each candidate may name one person to observe the counting of the ballots, provided that this does not entitle any observer to see the name of the person who cast any ballot, and that any disruptive observer may be removed.

History of Prop. Code §209.0058: Acts 2011, 82nd Leg., ch. 1026, §3 (eff. Jan. 1, 2012), ch. 1217, §3 (eff. Sept. 1, 2011). Amended by Acts 2013, 83rd Leg., ch. 161, §17.003, eff. Sept. 1, 2013; Acts 2015, 84th Leg., ch. 249, §1 (eff. May 29, 2015), ch. 1183, §11 (eff. Sept. 1, 2015).

PROP §209.0059. RIGHT TO VOTE

(a) A provision in a dedicatory instrument that would disqualify a property owner from voting in a property owners' association election of board members or on any matter concerning the rights or responsibilities of the owner is void.

(b) This section does not apply to a property owners' association that is subject to Chapter 552, Government Code, by application of Section 552.0036, Government Code.

(c) In a residential development with 10 or fewer lots for which the declaration was recorded before January 1, 2015, a person may not vote in a property owners' association election unless the person is subject to a dedicatory instrument governing the association through which the association exercises its authority.

History of Prop. Code §209.0059: Acts 2011, 82nd Leg., ch. 1026, §3 (eff. Jan. 1, 2012), ch. 1217, §3 (eff. Sept. 1, 2011). Amended by Acts 2013, 83rd Leg., ch. 161, §17.003, eff. Sept. 1, 2013; Acts 2015, 84th Leg., ch. 1183, §12, eff. Sept. 1, 2015.

ANNOTATIONS

Storck v. Tres Lagos Prop. Owners Ass'n, 442 S.W.3d 730, 737 (Tex.App.—Texarkana 2014, pet. denied). "The issue before this Court is whether the restricted vote …, limited to members in good standing, violates §209.0059(a)…. *At 739-40:* To conclude that [a restrictive voting provision] in the bylaws is valid, when the Legislature has declared all such provisions in dedicatory instruments void, would essentially eviscerate the purpose of the statute. Here, the dedicatory instrument specifically subjects Association property to the Association bylaws…. The bylaws … effectively suspend a property owner's voting rights when that owner's assessments are unpaid. Because the bylaws have effectively been incorporated into the dedicatory instrument and because the bylaws include a voting restriction which would be invalid if set out directly in the dedicatory instrument, we conclude that the voting restriction in the bylaws is void."

PROP §209.00591. BOARD MEMBERSHIP

(a) Except as provided by this section, a provision in a dedicatory instrument that restricts a property owner's right to run for a position on the board of the property owners' association is void.

(a-1) Notwithstanding any other provision of this chapter, a property owners' association's bylaws may require one or more board members to reside in the subdivision subject to the dedicatory instruments but may not require all board members to reside in that subdivision. A requirement described by this subsection is not applicable during the development period.

(b) If a board is presented with written, documented evidence from a database or other record main-

tained by a governmental law enforcement authority that a board member was convicted of a felony or crime involving moral turpitude not more than 20 years before the date the board is presented with the evidence, the board member is immediately ineligible to serve on the board of the property owners' association, automatically considered removed from the board, and prohibited from future service on the board.

(c) The declaration may provide for a period of declarant control of the association during which a declarant, or persons designated by the declarant, may appoint and remove board members and the officers of the association, other than board members or officers elected by members of the property owners' association. Regardless of the period of declarant control provided by the declaration, on or before the 120th day after the date 75 percent of the lots that may be created and made subject to the declaration are conveyed to owners other than a declarant or a builder in the business of constructing homes who purchased the lots from the declarant for the purpose of selling completed homes built on the lots, at least one-third of the board members must be elected by owners other than the declarant. If the declaration does not include the number of lots that may be created and made subject to the declaration, at least one-third of the board members must be elected by owners other than the declarant not later than the 10th anniversary of the date the declaration was recorded.

History of Prop. Code §209.00591: Acts 2011, 82nd Leg., ch. 1026, §3, eff. Jan. 1, 2012. Amended by Acts 2015, 84th Leg., ch. 649, §1 (eff. Sept. 1, 2015), ch. 1183, §13 (eff. Sept. 1, 2015).

A PROP §209.00592. VOTING; QUORUM

(a) Subject to Subsection (a-1), the voting rights of an owner may be cast or given:

(1) in person or by proxy at a meeting of the property owners' association;

(2) by absentee ballot in accordance with this section;

(3) by electronic ballot in accordance with this section; or

(4) by any method of representative or delegated voting provided by a dedicatory instrument.

Subsection (a-1) as added by Acts 2015, 84th Leg., ch. 248, §1, eff. Sept. 1, 2015, was repealed as duplicative by S.B. 1488, §16.001, 85th Leg., eff. Sept. 1, 2017.

(a-1) Except as provided by this subsection, unless a dedicatory instrument provides otherwise, a property owners' association is not required to provide an owner with more than one voting method. An owner must be allowed to vote by absentee ballot or proxy.

(b) An absentee or electronic ballot:

(1) may be counted as an owner present and voting for the purpose of establishing a quorum only for items appearing on the ballot;

(2) may not be counted, even if properly delivered, if the owner attends any meeting to vote in person, so that any vote cast at a meeting by a property owner supersedes any vote submitted by absentee or electronic ballot previously submitted for that proposal; and

(3) may not be counted on the final vote of a proposal if the motion was amended at the meeting to be different from the exact language on the absentee or electronic ballot.

(b-1) For purposes of Subsection (b), a nomination taken from the floor in a board member election is not considered an amendment to the proposal for the election.

(c) A solicitation for votes by absentee ballot must include:

(1) an absentee ballot that contains each proposed action and provides an opportunity to vote for or against each proposed action;

(2) instructions for delivery of the completed absentee ballot, including the delivery location; and

(3) the following language: "By casting your vote via absentee ballot you will forgo the opportunity to consider and vote on any action from the floor on these proposals, if a meeting is held. This means that if there are amendments to these proposals your votes will not be counted on the final vote on these measures. If you desire to retain this ability, please attend any meeting in person. You may submit an absentee ballot and later choose to attend any meeting in person, in which case any in-person vote will prevail."

(d) For the purposes of this section, "electronic ballot" means a ballot:

(1) given by:

(A) e-mail;

(B) facsimile; or

(C) posting on an Internet website;

(2) for which the identity of the property owner submitting the ballot can be confirmed; and

(3) for which the property owner may receive a receipt of the electronic transmission and receipt of the owner's ballot.

(e) If an electronic ballot is posted on an Internet website, a notice of the posting shall be sent to each owner that contains instructions on obtaining access to the posting on the website.

(f) This section supersedes any contrary provision in a dedicatory instrument.

(g) This section does not apply to a property owners' association that is subject to Chapter 552, Government Code, by application of Section 552.0036, Government Code.

History of Prop. Code §209.00592: Acts 2011, 82nd Leg., ch. 1026, §3 (eff. Jan. 1, 2012), ch. 1217, §3 (eff. Sept. 1, 2011). Amended by Acts 2013, 83rd Leg., ch. 161, §17.003, eff. Sept. 1, 2013; Acts 2015, 84th Leg., ch. 248, §1 (eff. Sept. 1, 2015), ch. 1183, §14 (eff. Sept. 1, 2015); S.B. 1488, §16.001, 85th Leg., eff. Sept. 1, 2017.

PROP §209.00593. ELECTION OF BOARD MEMBERS

(a) Notwithstanding any provision in a dedicatory instrument, any board member whose term has expired must be elected by owners who are members of the property owners' association. A board member may be appointed by the board to fill a vacancy on the board. A board member appointed to fill a vacant position shall serve for the remainder of the unexpired term of the position.

(a-1) At least 10 days before the date a property owners' association composed of more than 100 lots disseminates absentee ballots or other ballots to association members for purposes of voting in a board member election, the association must provide notice to the association members soliciting candidates interested in running for a position on the board. The notice must contain instructions for an eligible candidate to notify the association of the candidate's request to be placed on the ballot and the deadline to submit the candidate's request. The deadline may not be earlier than the 10th day after the date the association provides the notice required by this subsection.

(a-2) The notice required by Subsection (a-1) must be:

(1) mailed to each owner; or

(2) provided by:

(A) posting the notice in a conspicuous manner reasonably designed to provide notice to association members:

(i) in a place located on the association's common property or, with the property owner's consent, on other conspicuously located privately owned property within the subdivision; or

(ii) on any Internet website maintained by the association or other Internet media; and

(B) sending the notice by e-mail to each owner who has registered an e-mail address with the association.

(a-3) An association described by Subsection (a-1) shall include on each absentee ballot or other ballot for a board member election the name of each eligible candidate from whom the association received a request to be placed on the ballot in accordance with this section.

(b) The board of a property owners' association may amend the bylaws of the property owners' association to provide for elections to be held as required by Subsection (a).

(c) The appointment of a board member in violation of this section is void.

(d) This section does not apply to the appointment of a board member during a development period.

(e) This section does not apply to a representative board whose members or delegates are elected or appointed by representatives of a property owners' association who are elected by owner members of a property owners' association.

History of Prop. Code §209.00593: Acts 2011, 82nd Leg., ch. 1026, §3 (eff. Jan. 1, 2012), ch. 1217, §3 (eff. Sept. 1, 2011). Amended by Acts 2013, 83rd Leg., ch. 161, §17.003 (eff. Sept. 1, 2013), ch. 1062, §1 (eff. June 14, 2013); Acts 2015, 84th Leg., ch. 1183, §15, eff. Sept. 1, 2015.

PROP §209.00594. TABULATION OF & ACCESS TO BALLOTS

(a) Notwithstanding any other provision of this chapter or any other law, a person who is a candidate in a property owners' association election or who is otherwise the subject of an association vote, or a person related to that person within the third degree by consanguinity or affinity, as determined under Chapter 573, Government Code, may not tabulate or otherwise be given access to the ballots cast in that election or vote except as provided by this section.

(b) A person other than a person described by Subsection (a) may tabulate votes in an association election or vote.

(b-1) A person who tabulates votes under Subsection (b) or who performs a recount under Section 209.0057(c) may not disclose to any other person how an individual voted.

(c) Notwithstanding any other provision of this chapter or any other law, only a person who tabulates votes under Subsection (b) or who performs a recount under Section 209.0057(c) may be given access to the ballots cast in the election or vote.

(d) This section may not be construed to affect a person's obligation to comply with a court order for the release of ballots or other voting records.

History of Prop. Code §209.00594: Acts 2011, 82nd Leg., ch. 1217, §3, eff. Sept. 1, 2011. Amended by Acts 2015, 84th Leg., ch. 1183, §16, eff. Sept. 1, 2015.

PROP §209.006. NOTICE REQUIRED BEFORE ENFORCEMENT ACTION

(a) Before a property owners' association may suspend an owner's right to use a common area, file a suit against an owner other than a suit to collect a regular or special assessment or foreclose under an association's lien, charge an owner for property damage, or levy a fine for a violation of the restrictions or bylaws or rules of the association, the association or its agent must give written notice to the owner by certified mail.

(b) The notice must:

(1) describe the violation or property damage that is the basis for the suspension action, charge, or fine and state any amount due the association from the owner;

(2) except as provided by Subsection (d), inform the owner that the owner:

(A) is entitled to a reasonable period to cure the violation and avoid the fine or suspension if the violation is of a curable nature and does not pose a threat to public health or safety;

(B) may request a hearing under Section 209.007 on or before the 30th day after the date the notice was mailed to the owner; and

(C) may have special rights or relief related to the enforcement action under federal law, including the Servicemembers Civil Relief Act (50 U.S.C. App. Section 501 et seq.), if the owner is serving on active military duty;

(3) specify the date by which the owner must cure the violation if the violation is of a curable nature and does not pose a threat to public health or safety; and

(4) be sent by verified mail to the owner at the owner's last known address as shown on the association records.

(c) The date specified in the notice under Subsection (b)(3) must provide a reasonable period to cure the violation if the violation is of a curable nature and does not pose a threat to public health or safety.

(d) Subsections (a) and (b) do not apply to a violation for which the owner has been previously given notice under this section and the opportunity to exercise any rights available under this section in the preceding six months.

(e) If the owner cures the violation before the expiration of the period for cure described by Subsection (c), a fine may not be assessed for the violation.

(f) For purposes of this section, a violation is considered a threat to public health or safety if the violation could materially affect the physical health or safety of an ordinary resident.

(g) For purposes of this section, a violation is considered uncurable if the violation has occurred but is not a continuous action or a condition capable of being remedied by affirmative action. For purposes of this subsection, the nonrepetition of a one-time violation or other violation that is not ongoing is not considered an adequate remedy.

(h) The following are examples of acts considered uncurable for purposes of this section:

(1) shooting fireworks;

(2) an act constituting a threat to health or safety;

(3) a noise violation that is not ongoing;

(4) property damage, including the removal or alteration of landscape; and

(5) holding a garage sale or other event prohibited by a dedicatory instrument.

(i) The following are examples of acts considered curable for purposes of this section:

(1) a parking violation;

(2) a maintenance violation;

(3) the failure to construct improvements or modifications in accordance with approved plans and specifications; and

(4) an ongoing noise violation such as a barking dog.

History of Prop. Code §209.006: Acts 2001, 77th Leg., ch. 926, §1, eff. Jan. 1, 2002. Amended by Acts 2011, 82nd Leg., ch. 252, §3, eff. Jan. 1, 2012; Acts 2015, 84th Leg., ch. 1183, §17, eff. Sept. 1, 2015.

ANNOTATIONS

Park v. Escalera Ranch Owners' Ass'n, 457 S.W.3d 571, 587 (Tex.App.—Austin 2015, no pet.). "[D] and [P] dispute whether §209.006's notice requirement is jurisdictional ... or is mandatory but not juris-

dictional. This is a question of first impression. [D] asserts that the notice requirement is jurisdictional, and therefore, [P's] failure to provide notice requires the trial court to dismiss its case. [P] responds that the requirement is mandatory, but not jurisdictional, and that [D] waived the requirement by failing to timely object and request an abatement. *At 590:* [W]e conclude that the Legislature did not intend to make notice under §209.006 jurisdictional. … Therefore, a complete lack of notice may be cured by a defendant's timely request for abatement to allow for provision of the notice."

Haas v. Ashford Hollow Cmty. Imprv. Ass'n, 209 S.W.3d 875, 885 (Tex.App.—Houston [14th Dist.] 2006, no pet.). See annotation under Property Code §209.008, p. 646.

PROP §209.0062. ALTERNATIVE PAYMENT SCHEDULE FOR CERTAIN ASSESSMENTS

(a) A property owners' association composed of more than 14 lots shall adopt reasonable guidelines to establish an alternative payment schedule by which an owner may make partial payments to the property owners' association for delinquent regular or special assessments or any other amount owed to the association without accruing additional monetary penalties. For purposes of this section, monetary penalties do not include reasonable costs associated with administering the payment plan or interest.

(b) The minimum term for a payment plan offered by a property owners' association is three months.

(c) A property owners' association is not required to allow a payment plan for any amount that extends more than 18 months from the date of the owner's request for a payment plan. The association is not required to enter into a payment plan with an owner who failed to honor the terms of a previous payment plan during the two years following the owner's default under the previous payment plan. The association is not required to make a payment plan available to an owner after the period for cure described by Section 209.0064(b)(3) expires. The association is not required to allow an owner to enter into a payment plan more than once in any 12-month period.

(d) A property owners' association shall file the association's guidelines under this section in the real property records of each county in which the subdivision is located.

(e) A property owners' association's failure to file as required by this section the association's guidelines in the real property records of each county in which the subdivision is located does not prohibit a property owner from receiving an alternative payment schedule by which the owner may make partial payments to the property owners' association for delinquent regular or special assessments or any other amount owed to the association without accruing additional monetary penalties, as defined by Subsection (a).

History of Prop. Code §209.0062: Acts 2011, 82nd Leg., ch. 1282, §2, eff. Jan. 1, 2012. Amended by Acts 2013, 83rd Leg., ch. 161, §17.004, eff. Sept. 1, 2013; Acts 2015, 84th Leg., ch. 1183, §18, eff. Sept. 1, 2015.

See also *Real Estate Forms*, FORM 6:8.

PROP §209.0063. PRIORITY OF PAYMENTS

(a) Except as provided by Subsection (b), a payment received by a property owners' association from the owner shall be applied to the owner's debt in the following order of priority:

(1) any delinquent assessment;

(2) any current assessment;

(3) any attorney's fees or third party collection costs incurred by the association associated solely with assessments or any other charge that could provide the basis for foreclosure;

(4) any attorney's fees incurred by the association that are not subject to Subdivision (3);

(5) any fines assessed by the association; and

(6) any other amount owed to the association.

(b) If, at the time the property owners' association receives a payment from a property owner, the owner is in default under a payment plan entered into with the association:

(1) the association is not required to apply the payment in the order of priority specified by Subsection (a); and

(2) in applying the payment, a fine assessed by the association may not be given priority over any other amount owed to the association.

History of Prop. Code §209.0063: Acts 2011, 82nd Leg., ch. 1282, §2, eff. Jan. 1, 2012.

PROP §209.0064. THIRD PARTY COLLECTIONS

(a) In this section, "collection agent" means a debt collector, as defined by Section 803 of the federal Fair Debt Collection Practices Act (15 U.S.C. Section 1692a).

(b) A property owners' association may not hold an owner liable for fees of a collection agent retained by the association unless the association first provides written notice to the owner by certified mail that:

(1) specifies each delinquent amount and the total amount of the payment required to make the account current;

(2) if the association is subject to Section 209.0062 or the association's dedicatory instruments contain a requirement to offer a payment plan, describes the options the owner has to avoid having the account turned over to a collection agent, including information regarding availability of a payment plan through the association; and

(3) provides a period of at least 30 days for the owner to cure the delinquency before further collection action is taken.

(c) An owner is not liable for fees of a collection agent retained by the property owners' association if:

(1) the obligation for payment by the association to the association's collection agent for fees or costs associated with a collection action is in any way dependent or contingent on amounts recovered; or

(2) the payment agreement between the association and the association's collection agent does not require payment by the association of all fees to a collection agent for the action undertaken by the collection agent.

(d) The agreement between the property owners' association and the association's collection agent may not prohibit the owner from contacting the association board or the association's managing agent regarding the owner's delinquency.

(e) A property owners' association may not sell or otherwise transfer any interest in the association's accounts receivables for a purpose other than as collateral for a loan.

History of Prop. Code §209.0064: Acts 2011, 82nd Leg., ch. 1282, §2, eff. Jan. 1, 2012. Amended by Acts 2015, 84th Leg., ch. 1183, §19, eff. Sept. 1, 2015.

PROP §209.007. HEARING BEFORE BOARD; ALTERNATIVE DISPUTE RESOLUTION

(a) If the owner is entitled to an opportunity to cure the violation, the owner has the right to submit a written request for a hearing to discuss and verify facts and resolve the matter in issue before a committee appointed by the board of the property owners' association or before the board if the board does not appoint a committee.

(b) If a hearing is to be held before a committee, the notice prescribed by Section 209.006 must state that the owner has the right to appeal the committee's decision to the board by written notice to the board.

(c) The association shall hold a hearing under this section not later than the 30th day after the date the board receives the owner's request for a hearing and shall notify the owner of the date, time, and place of the hearing not later than the 10th day before the date of the hearing. The board or the owner may request a postponement, and, if requested, a postponement shall be granted for a period of not more than 10 days. Additional postponements may be granted by agreement of the parties. The owner or the association may make an audio recording of the meeting.

(d) The notice and hearing provisions of Section 209.006 and this section do not apply if the association files a suit seeking a temporary restraining order or temporary injunctive relief or files a suit that includes foreclosure as a cause of action. If a suit is filed relating to a matter to which those sections apply, a party to the suit may file a motion to compel mediation. The notice and hearing provisions of Section 209.006 and this section do not apply to a temporary suspension of a person's right to use common areas if the temporary suspension is the result of a violation that occurred in a common area and involved a significant and immediate risk of harm to others in the subdivision. The temporary suspension is effective until the board makes a final determination on the suspension action after following the procedures prescribed by this section.

(e) An owner or property owners' association may use alternative dispute resolution services.

History of Prop. Code §209.007: Acts 2001, 77th Leg., ch. 926, §1, eff. Jan. 1, 2002.

ANNOTATIONS

Tees v. East Lake Woods Homeowners Ass'n, No. 12-04-00020-CV (Tex.App.—Tyler 2006, no pet.) (memo op.; 1-18-06). "Association's petition clearly stated that it sought a temporary injunction restraining [owners] from using the garage on [subdivision lot] as a residence without proper approval. However, [owners] assert that the Association should not be allowed to avoid the notice requirements of the Property Code by merely including a request for a temporary injunction in the petition. [¶] We do not agree that the Asso-

ciation did not seek a temporary injunction. [¶] [W]e conclude that [owners] waived their right to a hearing on temporary relief and agreed to proceed to a hearing on the merits. They cannot now use the lack of such a hearing to argue that the Association was not truly seeking an injunction. Because the Association sought a temporary injunction, the notice provision of [Prop. Code] §209.006 is not applicable."

PROP §209.008. ATTORNEY'S FEES

(a) A property owners' association may collect reimbursement of reasonable attorney's fees and other reasonable costs incurred by the association relating to collecting amounts, including damages, due the association for enforcing restrictions or the bylaws or rules of the association only if the owner is provided a written notice that attorney's fees and costs will be charged to the owner if the delinquency or violation continues after a date certain.

(b) An owner is not liable for attorney's fees incurred by the association relating to a matter described by the notice under Section 209.006 if the attorney's fees are incurred before the conclusion of the hearing under Section 209.007 or, if the owner does not request a hearing under that section, before the date by which the owner must request a hearing. The owner's presence is not required to hold a hearing under Section 209.007.

(c) All attorney's fees, costs, and other amounts collected from an owner shall be deposited into an account maintained at a financial institution in the name of the association or its managing agent. Only members of the association's board or its managing agent or employees of its managing agent may be signatories on the account.

(d) On written request from the owner, the association shall provide copies of invoices for attorney's fees and other costs relating only to the matter for which the association seeks reimbursement of fees and costs.

(e) The notice provisions of Subsection (a) do not apply to a counterclaim of an association in a lawsuit brought against the association by a property owner.

(f) If the dedicatory instrument or restrictions of an association allow for nonjudicial foreclosure, the amount of attorney's fees that a property owners' association may include in a nonjudicial foreclosure sale for an indebtedness covered by a property owners' association's assessment lien is limited to the greater of:

(1) one-third of the amount of all actual costs and assessments, excluding attorney's fees, plus interest and court costs, if those amounts are permitted to be included by law or by the restrictive covenants governing the property; or

(2) $2,500.

(g) Subsection (f) does not prevent a property owners' association from recovering or collecting attorney's fees in excess of the amounts prescribed by Subsection (f) by other means provided by law.

History of Prop. Code §209.008: Acts 2001, 77th Leg., ch. 926, §1, eff. Jan. 1, 2002.

ANNOTATIONS

Haas v. Ashford Hollow Cmty. Imprv. Ass'n, 209 S.W.3d 875, 885 (Tex.App.—Houston [14th Dist.] 2006, no pet.). "Based on the language of [Prop. Code] §209.008(a), we conclude that it does not apply to attorney's fees incurred merely to collect delinquent assessments or enforce a lien due to nonpayment of the assessments [under Prop. Code §5.006(a)]. [Section 209.008(a)] specifically applies to attorney's fees 'relating to collecting amounts, including damages, due the association *for enforcing* restrictions.' The assessments [for which attorney fees were awarded under §5.006(a)] are not 'amounts, including damages, due the association *for enforcing* restrictions.' *At 886:* Therefore, an association is not even required to give a homeowner notice and an opportunity to cure pursuant to [Prop. Code] §209.006 before filing suit to collect assessments or foreclose a lien due to unpaid assessments."

PROP §209.009. FORECLOSURE SALE PROHIBITED IN CERTAIN CIRCUMSTANCES

A property owners' association may not foreclose a property owners' association's assessment lien if the debt securing the lien consists solely of:

(1) fines assessed by the association;

(2) attorney's fees incurred by the association solely associated with fines assessed by the association; or

(3) amounts added to the owner's account as an assessment under Section 209.005(i) or 209.0057(b-4).

History of Prop. Code §209.009: Acts 2001, 77th Leg., ch. 926, §1, eff. Jan. 1, 2002. Amended by Acts 2011, 82nd Leg., ch. 1026, §4, eff. Jan. 1, 2012; Acts 2015, 84th Leg., ch. 1183, §20, eff. Sept. 1, 2015.

PROP §209.0091. PREREQUISITES TO FORECLOSURE: NOTICE & OPPORTUNITY TO CURE FOR CERTAIN OTHER LIENHOLDERS

(a) A property owners' association may not file an application for an expedited court order authorizing foreclosure of the association's assessment lien as described by Section 209.0092(a) or a petition for judicial foreclosure of the association's assessment lien as described by Section 209.0092(d) unless the association has:

(1) provided written notice of the total amount of the delinquency giving rise to the foreclosure to any other holder of a lien of record on the property whose lien is inferior or subordinate to the association's lien and is evidenced by a deed of trust; and

(2) provided the recipient of the notice an opportunity to cure the delinquency before the 61st day after the date the association mails the notice described in Subdivision (1).

(b) Notice under this section must be sent by certified mail to the address for the lienholder shown in the deed records relating to the property that is subject to the property owners' association assessment lien.

(c) Notwithstanding any other law, notice under this section may be provided to any holder of a lien of record on the property.

History of Prop. Code §209.0091: Acts 2011, 82nd Leg., ch. 1282, §2, eff. Jan. 1, 2012. Amended by Acts 2015, 84th Leg., ch. 1183, §21, eff. Sept. 1, 2015.

PROP §209.0092. JUDICIAL FORECLOSURE REQUIRED

(a) Except as provided by Subsection (c) or (d) and subject to Section 209.009, a property owners' association may not foreclose a property owners' association assessment lien unless the association first obtains a court order in an application for expedited foreclosure under the rules adopted by the supreme court under Subsection (b). A property owners' association may use the procedure described by this subsection to foreclose any lien described by the association's dedicatory instruments. A property owners' association whose dedicatory instruments grant a right of foreclosure is considered to have any power of sale required by law as a condition of using the procedure described by this subsection.

(b) The supreme court, as an exercise of the court's authority under Section 74.024, Government Code, shall adopt rules establishing expedited foreclosure proceedings for use by a property owners' association in foreclosing an assessment lien of the association. The rules adopted under this subsection must be substantially similar to the rules adopted by the supreme court under Section 50(r), Article XVI, Texas Constitution.

(c) Expedited foreclosure is not required under this section if the owner of the property that is subject to foreclosure agrees in writing at the time the foreclosure is sought to waive expedited foreclosure under this section. A waiver under this subsection may not be required as a condition of the transfer of title to real property.

(d) A property owners' association authorized to use the procedure described by Subsection (a) may in its discretion elect not to use that procedure and instead foreclose the association's assessment lien under court judgment foreclosing the lien and ordering the sale, pursuant to Rules 309 and 646a, Texas Rules of Civil Procedure.

(e) This section does not affect any right an association that is not authorized to use the procedure described by Subsection (a) may have to judicially foreclose the association's assessment lien as described by Subsection (d).

History of Prop. Code §209.0092: Acts 2011, 82nd Leg., ch. 1282, §2, eff. Jan. 1, 2012. Amended by Acts 2015, 84th Leg., ch. 1183, §22, eff. Sept. 1, 2015.

PROP §209.0093. REMOVAL OR ADOPTION OF FORECLOSURE AUTHORITY

A provision granting a right to foreclose a lien on real property for unpaid amounts due to a property owners' association may be removed from a dedicatory instrument or adopted in a dedicatory instrument by a vote of at least 67 percent of the total votes allocated to property owners in the property owners' association. Owners holding at least 10 percent of all voting interests in the property owners' association may petition the association and require a special meeting to be called for the purposes of taking a vote for the purposes of this section.

History of Prop. Code §209.0093: Acts 2011, 82nd Leg., ch. 1282, §2, eff. Jan. 1, 2012.

PROP §209.0094. ASSESSMENT LIEN FILING

A lien, lien affidavit, or other instrument evidencing the nonpayment of assessments or other charges owed to a property owners' association and filed in the official public records of a county is a legal instrument affecting title to real property.

History of Prop. Code §209.0094: Acts 2011, 82nd Leg., ch. 1282, §2, eff. Jan. 1, 2012.

PROP §209.010. NOTICE AFTER FORECLOSURE SALE

(a) A property owners' association that conducts a foreclosure sale of an owner's lot must send to the lot owner and to each lienholder of record, not later than the 30th day after the date of the foreclosure sale, a written notice stating the date and time the sale occurred and informing the lot owner and each lienholder of record of the right of the lot owner and lienholder to redeem the property under Section 209.011.

(b) The notice must be sent by certified mail, return receipt requested, to:

(1) the lot owner's last known mailing address, as reflected in the records of the property owners' association;

(2) the address of each holder of a lien on the property subject to foreclosure evidenced by the most recent deed of trust filed of record in the real property records of the county in which the property is located; and

(3) the address of each transferee or assignee of a deed of trust described by Subdivision (2) who has provided notice to a property owners' association of such assignment or transfer. Notice provided by a transferee or assignee to a property owners' association shall be in writing, shall contain the mailing address of the transferee or assignee, and shall be mailed by certified mail, return receipt requested, or United States mail with signature confirmation to the property owners' association according to the mailing address of the property owners' association pursuant to the most recent management certificate filed of record pursuant to Section 209.004.

(b-1) If a recorded instrument does not include an address for the lienholder, the association does not have a duty to notify the lienholder as provided by this section.

(b-2) For purposes of this section, the lot owner is deemed to have given approval for the association to notify the lienholder.

(c) Not later than the 30th day after the date the association sends the notice required by Subsection (a), the association must record an affidavit in the real property records of the county in which the lot is located, stating the date on which the notice was sent and containing a legal description of the lot. Any person is entitled to rely conclusively on the information contained in the recorded affidavit.

(d) The notice requirements of this section also apply to the sale of an owner's lot by a sheriff or constable conducted as provided by a judgment obtained by the property owners' association.

History of Prop. Code §209.010: Acts 2001, 77th Leg., ch. 926, §1, eff. Jan. 1, 2002. Amended by Acts 2009, 81st Leg., ch. 1176, §2, eff. Sept. 1, 2009.

PROP §209.011. RIGHT OF REDEMPTION AFTER FORECLOSURE

(a) A property owners' association or other person who purchases occupied property at a sale foreclosing a property owners' association's assessment lien must commence and prosecute a forcible entry and detainer action under Chapter 24 to recover possession of the property.

(b) The owner of property in a residential subdivision or a lienholder of record may redeem the property from any purchaser at a sale foreclosing a property owners' association's assessment lien not later than the 180th day after the date the association mails written notice of the sale to the owner and the lienholder under Section 209.010. A lienholder of record may not redeem the property as provided herein before 90 days after the date the association mails written notice of the sale to the lot owner and the lienholder under Section 209.010, and only if the lot owner has not previously redeemed.

(c) A person who purchases property at a sale foreclosing a property owners' association's assessment lien may not transfer ownership of the property to a person other than a redeeming lot owner during the redemption period.

(d) To redeem property purchased by the property owners' association at the foreclosure sale, the lot owner or lienholder must pay to the association:

(1) all amounts due the association at the time of the foreclosure sale;

(2) interest from the date of the foreclosure sale to the date of redemption on all amounts owed the association at the rate stated in the dedicatory instruments for delinquent assessments or, if no rate is stated, at an annual interest rate of 10 percent;

(3) costs incurred by the association in foreclosing the lien and conveying the property to the lot owner, including reasonable attorney's fees;

(4) any assessment levied against the property by the association after the date of the foreclosure sale;

(5) any reasonable cost incurred by the association, including mortgage payments and costs of repair, maintenance, and leasing of the property; and

(6) the purchase price paid by the association at the foreclosure sale less any amounts due the association under Subdivision (1) that were satisfied out of foreclosure sale proceeds.

(e) To redeem property purchased at the foreclosure sale by a person other than the property owners' association, the lot owner or lienholder:

(1) must pay to the association:

(A) all amounts due the association at the time of the foreclosure sale less the foreclosure sales price received by the association from the purchaser;

(B) interest from the date of the foreclosure sale through the date of redemption on all amounts owed the association at the rate stated in the dedicatory instruments for delinquent assessments or, if no rate is stated, at an annual interest rate of 10 percent;

(C) costs incurred by the association in foreclosing the lien and conveying the property to the redeeming lot owner, including reasonable attorney's fees;

(D) any unpaid assessments levied against the property by the association after the date of the foreclosure sale; and

(E) taxable costs incurred in a proceeding brought under Subsection (a); and

(2) must pay to the person who purchased the property at the foreclosure sale:

(A) any assessments levied against the property by the association after the date of the foreclosure sale and paid by the purchaser;

(B) the purchase price paid by the purchaser at the foreclosure sale;

(C) the amount of the deed recording fee;

(D) the amount paid by the purchaser as ad valorem taxes, penalties, and interest on the property after the date of the foreclosure sale; and

(E) taxable costs incurred in a proceeding brought under Subsection (a).

(f) If a lot owner or lienholder redeems the property under this section, the purchaser of the property at foreclosure shall immediately execute and deliver to the redeeming party a deed transferring the property to the lot owner. If a purchaser fails to comply with this section, the lot owner or lienholder may file an action against the purchaser and may recover reasonable attorney's fees from the purchaser if the lot owner or the lienholder is the prevailing party in the action.

(g) If, before the expiration of the redemption period, the redeeming lot owner or lienholder fails to record the deed from the foreclosing purchaser or fails to record an affidavit stating that the lot owner or lienholder has redeemed the property, the lot owner's or lienholder's right of redemption as against a bona fide purchaser or lender for value expires after the redemption period.

(h) The purchaser of the property at the foreclosure sale or a person to whom the person who purchased the property at the foreclosure sale transferred the property may presume conclusively that the lot owner or a lienholder did not redeem the property unless the lot owner or a lienholder files in the real property records of the county in which the property is located:

(1) a deed from the purchaser of the property at the foreclosure sale; or

(2) an affidavit that:

(A) states that the property has been redeemed;

(B) contains a legal description of the property; and

(C) includes the name and mailing address of the person who redeemed the property.

(i) If the property owners' association purchases the property at foreclosure, all rent and other income collected by the association from the date of the foreclosure sale to the date of redemption shall be credited toward the amount owed the association under Subsection (d), and if there are excess proceeds, they shall be refunded to the lot owner. If a person other than the association purchases the property at foreclosure, all rent and other income collected by the purchaser from the date of the foreclosure sale to the date of redemption shall be credited toward the amount owed the purchaser under Subsection (e), and if there are excess proceeds, those proceeds shall be refunded to the lot owner.

(j) If a person other than the property owners' association is the purchaser at the foreclosure sale, before executing a deed transferring the property to the lot owner, the purchaser shall obtain an affidavit from the association or its authorized agent stating that all amounts owed the association under Subsection (e) have been paid. The association shall provide the purchaser with the affidavit not later than the 10th day af-

ter the date the association receives all amounts owed to the association under Subsection (e). Failure of a purchaser to comply with this subsection does not affect the validity of a redemption.

(k) Property that is redeemed remains subject to all liens and encumbrances on the property before foreclosure. Any lease entered into by the purchaser of property at a sale foreclosing an assessment lien of a property owners' association is subject to the right of redemption provided by this section and the lot owner's right to reoccupy the property immediately after redemption.

(*l*) If a lot owner makes partial payment of amounts due the association at any time before the redemption period expires but fails to pay all amounts necessary to redeem the property before the redemption period expires, the association shall refund any partial payments to the lot owner by mailing payment to the owner's last known address as shown in the association's records not later than the 30th day after the expiration date of the redemption period.

(m) If a lot owner or lienholder sends by certified mail, return receipt requested, a written request to redeem the property on or before the last day of the redemption period, the lot owner's or lienholder's right of redemption is extended until the 10th day after the date the association and any third party foreclosure purchaser provides written notice to the redeeming party of the amounts that must be paid to redeem the property.

(n) After the redemption period and any extended redemption period provided by Subsection (m) expires without a redemption of the property, the association or third party foreclosure purchaser shall record an affidavit in the real property records of the county in which the property is located stating that the lot owner or a lienholder did not redeem the property during the redemption period or any extended redemption period.

(o) The association or the person who purchased the property at the foreclosure sale may file an affidavit in the real property records of the county in which the property is located that states the date the citation was served in a suit under Subsection (a) and contains a legal description of the property. Any person may rely conclusively on the information contained in the affidavit.

(p) The rights of a lot owner and a lienholder under this section also apply if the sale of the lot owner's property is conducted by a constable or sheriff as provided by a judgment obtained by the property owners' association.

History of Prop. Code §209.011: Acts 2001, 77th Leg., ch. 926, §1, eff. Jan. 1, 2002. Amended by Acts 2009, 81st Leg., ch. 1176, §3, eff. Sept. 1, 2009.

ANNOTATIONS

Laguan v. Lloyd, 493 S.W.3d 720, 723-24 (Tex. App.—Houston [1st Dist.] 2016, no pet.). "It has long been the practice in Texas to liberally construe redemption statutes in favor of redemption. For redemption under §209.011, the owners ... bear the burden at trial of proving a right to redemption. [¶] For many redemption statutes, the owner carries her burden of establishing her right of redemption by showing 'substantial compliance' with the statutory requirements. We must determine if that standard applies here. [¶] The longstanding practice of liberally construing redemption statutes in favor of redemption weighs in favor of not strictly construing the requirements of the statute and, instead, of weighing multiple factors to determine whether the payment was sufficient to avoid seriously hindering the legislature's purpose in imposing the requirement. Another factor in determining whether a substantial-compliance burden is proper is whether proof of compliance is based on subjective or disputable requirements. [¶] Here, the amount for some of the items for which §209.011 requires reimbursement for redemption might be known only by the purchaser. The statute implicitly acknowledges this by allowing the owner to request an itemization of costs from the purchaser and extending the redemption period until 10 days after the purchaser responds. Accordingly, we hold the owner carries her burden by showing substantial compliance with the statute." (Internal quotes omitted.)

WaiWai, LLC v. Alvarado, No. 03-13-00540-CV (Tex.App.—Austin 2014, no pet.) (memo op.; 11-26-14). The issue "is whether a foreclosure purchaser's alleged failure to follow §209.011(a)'s requirements when evicting the property's occupant can serve as the basis for an extension of the 180-day redemption period given to property owners under §209.011(b).... [¶] There are only two provisions within §209.011 that directly address the time period in which a property owner must invoke its right to redeem property sold at a foreclosure—subsections (b) and (m). ... The existence of subsection (m) ... demonstrates that the legislature knew how to extend the redemption period if it

so desired, yet did not do so elsewhere in the statute. [¶] Section 209.011(a) contains no requirement that the property owner receive notice of an eviction during the 180-day redemption period. Given this legislative omission, it is difficult to envision how the legislature could have intended for the purpose of this provision to be that owners receive notice and one last opportunity for redemption of the property.... If anything, §209.011(a) appears to be the legislature's effort to make clear to foreclosure purchasers that possession of the property is not self-executing and must be accomplished through normal eviction procedures."

Khyber Holdings, LLC v. BAC Home Loans Servicing, LP, 349 S.W.3d 178, 180 (Tex.App.—Dallas 2011, no pet.). See annotation under Property Code §209.002, p. 631.

PROP §209.012. RESTRICTIVE COVENANTS GRANTING EASEMENTS TO CERTAIN PROPERTY OWNERS' ASSOCIATIONS

(a) A property owners' association may not amend a dedicatory instrument to grant the property owners' association an easement through or over an owner's lot without the consent of the owner.

(b) This section does not prohibit a property owners' association from adopting or enforcing a restriction in a dedicatory instrument that allows the property owners' association to access an owner's lot to remedy a violation of the dedicatory instrument.

History of Prop. Code §209.012: Acts 2007, 80th Leg., ch. 887, §1, eff. Sept. 1, 2007. Amended by Acts 2013, 83rd Leg., ch. 161, §17.004, eff. Sept. 1, 2013.

PROP §209.013. AUTHORITY OF ASSOCIATION TO AMEND DEDICATORY INSTRUMENT

(a) A dedicatory instrument created by a developer of a residential subdivision or by a property owners' association in which the developer has a majority of the voting rights or that the developer otherwise controls under the terms of the dedicatory instrument may not be amended during the period between the time the developer loses the majority of the voting rights or other form of control of the property owners' association and the time a new board of directors of the association assumes office following the loss of the majority of the voting rights or other form of control.

(b) A provision in a dedicatory instrument that violates this section is void and unenforceable.

History of Prop. Code §209.013: Acts 2007, 80th Leg., ch. 887, §2, eff. Sept. 1, 2007.

PROP §209.014. MANDATORY ELECTION REQUIRED AFTER FAILURE TO CALL REGULAR MEETING

(a) Notwithstanding any provision in a dedicatory instrument, a board of a property owners' association shall call an annual meeting of the members of the association.

(b) If a board of a property owners' association does not call an annual meeting of the association members, an owner may demand that a meeting of the association members be called not later than the 30th day after the date of the owner's demand. The owner's demand must be made in writing and sent by certified mail, return receipt requested, to the registered agent of the property owners' association and to the association at the address for the association according to the most recently filed management certificate. A copy of the notice must be sent to each property owner who is a member of the association.

(c) If the board does not call a meeting of the members of the property owners' association on or before the 30th day after the date of a demand under Subsection (b), three or more owners may form an election committee. The election committee shall file written notice of the committee's formation with the county clerk of each county in which the subdivision is located.

(d) A notice filed by an election committee must contain:

(1) a statement that an election committee has been formed to call a meeting of owners who are members of the property owners' association for the sole purpose of electing board members;

(2) the name and residential address of each committee member; and

(3) the name of the subdivision over which the property owners' association has jurisdiction under a dedicatory instrument.

(e) Each committee member must sign and acknowledge the notice before a notary or other official authorized to take acknowledgments.

(f) The county clerk shall enter on the notice the date the notice is filed and record the notice in the county's real property records.

(g) Only one committee in a subdivision may operate under this section at one time. If more than one committee in a subdivision files a notice, the first committee that files a notice, after having complied with all

other requirements of this section, is the committee with the power to act under this section. A committee that does not hold or conduct a successful election within four months after the date the notice is filed with the county clerk is dissolved by operation of law. An election held or conducted by a dissolved committee is ineffective for any purpose under this section.

(h) The election committee may call meetings of the owners who are members of the property owners' association for the sole purpose of electing board members. Notice, quorum, and voting provisions contained in the bylaws of the property owners' association apply to any meeting called by the election committee.

History of Prop. Code §209.014: Acts 2011, 82nd Leg., ch. 1026, §5, eff. Jan. 1, 2012.

PROP §209.015. REGULATION OF LAND USE: RESIDENTIAL PURPOSE

(a) In this section:

(1) "Adjacent lot" means:

(A) a lot that is contiguous to another lot that fronts on the same street;

(B) with respect to a corner lot, a lot that is contiguous to the corner lot by either a side property line or a back property line; or

(C) if permitted by the dedicatory instrument, any lot that is contiguous to another lot at the back property line.

(2) "Residential purpose" with respect to the use of a lot:

(A) means the location on the lot of any building, structure, or other improvement customarily appurtenant to a residence, as opposed to use for a business or commercial purpose; and

(B) includes the location on the lot of a garage, sidewalk, driveway, parking area, children's swing or playscape, fence, septic system, swimming pool, utility line, or water well and, if otherwise specifically permitted by the dedicatory instrument, the parking or storage of a recreational vehicle.

(b) Except as provided by this section, a property owners' association may not adopt or enforce a provision in a dedicatory instrument that prohibits or restricts the owner of a lot on which a residence is located from using for residential purposes an adjacent lot owned by the property owner.

(c) An owner must obtain the approval of the property owners' association or, if applicable, an architectural committee established by the association or the association's dedicatory instruments, based on criteria prescribed by the dedicatory instruments specific to the use of a lot for residential purposes, including reasonable restrictions regarding size, location, shielding, and aesthetics of the residential purpose, before the owner begins the construction, placement, or erection of a building, structure, or other improvement for the residential purpose on an adjacent lot.

(d) An owner who elects to use an adjacent lot for residential purposes under this section shall, on the sale or transfer of the lot containing the residence:

(1) include the adjacent lot in the sales agreement and transfer the lot to the new owner under the same dedicatory conditions; or

(2) restore the adjacent lot to the original condition before the addition of the improvements allowed under this section to the extent that the lot would again be suitable for the construction of a separate residence as originally platted and provided for in the conveyance to the owner.

(e) An owner may sell the adjacent lot separately only for the purpose of the construction of a new residence that complies with existing requirements in the dedicatory instrument unless the lot has been restored as described by Subsection (d)(2).

(f) A provision in a dedicatory instrument that violates this section is void.

History of Prop. Code §209.015: Acts 2013, 83rd Leg., ch. 219, §1, eff. June 14, 2013.

PROP §209.016. REGULATION OF RESIDENTIAL LEASES OR RENTAL AGREEMENTS

(a) In this section, "sensitive personal information" means an individual's:

(1) social security number;

(2) driver's license number;

(3) government-issued identification number; or

(4) account, credit card, or debit card number.

(b) A property owners' association may not adopt or enforce a provision in a dedicatory instrument that:

(1) requires a lease or rental applicant or a tenant to be submitted to and approved for tenancy by the property owners' association; or

(2) requires the following information to be submitted to a property owners' association regarding a lease or rental applicant or current tenant:

(A) a consumer or credit report; or

(B) a lease or rental application submitted by the applicant, tenant, or that person's agent to the property owner or property owner's agent when applying for tenancy.

(c) If a copy of the lease or rental agreement is required by the property owners' association, any sensitive personal information may be redacted or otherwise made unreadable or indecipherable.

(d) Except as provided by Subsection (b), nothing in this section shall be construed to prohibit the adoption or enforcement of a provision in a dedicatory instrument establishing a restriction relating to occupancy or leasing.

History of Prop. Code §209.016: Acts 2015, 84th Leg., ch. 1077, §1, eff. June 19, 2015.

CHAPTER 210. EXTENSION OR MODIFICATION OF RESIDENTIAL RESTRICTIVE COVENANTS BY PETITION IN CERTAIN SUBDIVISIONS

PROP §210.001. DEFINITIONS

In this chapter:

(1) "Dedicatory instrument" has the meaning assigned by Section 202.001.

(2) "Owner" has the meaning assigned by Section 201.003.

(3) "Property owners' association" has the meaning assigned by Section 202.001.

(4) "Residential real estate subdivision" or "subdivision" has the meaning assigned by Section 201.003, except that in a county described by Section 210.002(1) a subdivision that is a gated community with private streets need not be located in a city, town, or village or within the extraterritorial jurisdiction of a city, town, or village.

(5) "Restrictions" has the meaning assigned by Section 201.003.

History of Prop. Code §210.001: Acts 2005, 79th Leg., ch. 1180, §1, eff. Sept. 1, 2005. Amended by Acts 2009, 81st Leg., ch. 821, §2, eff. June 19, 2009; Acts 2011, 82nd Leg., ch. 954, §1, eff. June 17, 2011.

PROP §210.002. APPLICABILITY OF CHAPTER

This chapter applies to a residential real estate subdivision that is located in a county with a population of:

(1) more than 200,000 and less than 220,000; or

(2) more than 45,000 and less than 80,000 that is adjacent to a county with a population of more than 200,000 and less than 220,000.

History of Prop. Code §210.002: Acts 2005, 79th Leg., ch. 1180, §1, eff. Sept. 1, 2005. Amended by Acts 2011, 82nd Leg., ch. 1163, §111, eff. Sept. 1, 2011.

PROP §210.003. FINDINGS & PURPOSE

(a) The legislature finds that:

(1) the pending expiration of and the inability of owners to extend or modify property restrictions applicable to certain real estate subdivisions in this state creates uncertainty in living conditions and discourages investments in those subdivisions;

(2) owners of land in affected subdivisions are reluctant or unable to provide proper maintenance, upkeep, and repairs of structures because of the pending expiration of restrictions;

(3) financial institutions cannot or will not lend money for investments, maintenance, upkeep, or repairs in affected subdivisions;

(4) these conditions cause dilapidation of housing and other structures and cause unhealthful and unsanitary conditions in affected subdivisions, contrary to the health, safety, and welfare of the public; and

(5) the existence of race-related covenants in restrictions, regardless of their unenforceability, is offensive, repugnant, and harmful to members of racial or ethnic minority groups and public policy requires that those covenants be removed.

(b) The purpose of this chapter is to provide a procedure for extending or modifying residential restrictions and to provide for the removal of any restriction or other provision relating to race, religion, or national origin that is void and unenforceable under either the United States Constitution or Section 5.026.

History of Prop. Code §210.003: Acts 2005, 79th Leg., ch. 1180, §1, eff. Sept. 1, 2005.

PROP §210.004. EXTENSION OR MODIFICATION OF RESTRICTIONS

(a) In addition to any procedures provided in a subdivision's restrictions, a property owners' association, or a petition committee comprised of at least three owners, may circulate a petition proposing to extend or modify existing restrictions.

(b) An extension or modification of existing restrictions that is approved by the owners becomes effective when the resolution required by Section 210.008 is filed as a dedicatory instrument with the county clerk of each county in which the subdivision is located.

(c) An extension or modification of existing restrictions that is approved by the owners under this chapter is binding on all properties in the subdivision.

History of Prop. Code §210.004: Acts 2005, 79th Leg., ch. 1180, §1, eff. Sept. 1, 2005.

PROP §210.005. PETITION PROCEDURE

(a) The property owners' association or petition committee shall deliver to each record owner of property in the subdivision a petition describing the exact terms of the proposed extension or modification of the existing restrictions.

(b) The petition must state the date by which a response must be received in order to be counted.

(c) The petition may allow each owner to indicate approval or disapproval of:

(1) the entire proposal; or

(2) specific provisions of the proposal.

(d) Separate signature pages may be delivered if the proposed extension or modification is stated fully or referenced on each signature page. A reference may be made by the following or substantially similar wording: "We the undersigned owners of property in the __________ Subdivision indicate by our signatures on this document our approval or disapproval of the proposal(s) circulated by __________ on or about [date] to [extend or modify] our restrictive covenants. We acknowledge that we have fully reviewed the proposal(s)."

(e) The petition must be sent by certified mail, return receipt requested, to each owner's mailing address as reflected in the appraisal records maintained by the appraisal district in which the owner's property is located.

(f) The signature of an owner on the petition conclusively establishes that the owner received the petition.

History of Prop. Code §210.005: Acts 2005, 79th Leg., ch. 1180, §1, eff. Sept. 1, 2005.

PROP §210.006. VOTE ON PROPOSAL

(a) If the petition allows owners to indicate only approval or disapproval of the entire proposal, the proposal is adopted if owners of at least 66 percent of the real property in the subdivision vote in favor of the proposal. If the petition allows owners to indicate approval or disapproval of specific provisions of the proposal, a provision is adopted if owners of at least 66 percent of the real property in the subdivision vote in favor of the provision.

(b) The property owners' association or petition committee shall exclude votes by lienholders, contract purchasers, and owners of mineral interests.

(c) Except as provided by this subsection, the approval or disapproval of multiple owners of a property may be reflected by the signatures of a majority of the co-owners. The approval or disapproval of owners who are married may be reflected by the signature of one of those owners.

(d) An owner is considered to have cast a vote if the owner signs the petition indicating approval or disapproval of the proposal or one or more specific provisions of the proposal.

(e) The property owners' association or petition committee may only count a vote if the association or committee receives the vote before the deadline stated in the petition.

History of Prop. Code §210.006: Acts 2005, 79th Leg., ch. 1180, §1, eff. Sept. 1, 2005.

PROP §210.007. SUBDIVISION CONSISTING OF MULTIPLE SECTIONS

If a subdivision consisting of multiple sections, each with its own restrictions, is represented by a single property owners' association, a proposal or specific provision of a proposal is adopted if owners of at least 66 percent of the total number of properties in the subdivision vote in favor of the proposal or provision.

History of Prop. Code §210.007: Acts 2005, 79th Leg., ch. 1180, §1, eff. Sept. 1, 2005.

PROP §210.008. RESOLUTION CERTIFYING RESULTS OF VOTE

(a) The property owners' association or petition committee shall certify the results of a vote under this chapter by a written resolution specifying the number of votes for and against the proposal, or for and against each provision of the proposal, and shall also certify that the petition was delivered to each record owner of property in the subdivision as required by Section 210.005.

(b) The association or committee shall attach to the resolution a statement of the exact terms of the proposed extension or modification of the existing restrictions.

(c) The association or committee shall make the resolution, petition, and signature pages available to any owner on request.

History of Prop. Code §210.008: Acts 2005, 79th Leg., ch. 1180, §1, eff. Sept. 1, 2005.

PROP §210.009. ADDITIONAL PROCEDURES

The procedures provided by this chapter are in addition to any procedures provided in a subdivision's restrictions for the extension or modification of existing restrictions. The property owners' association or petition committee may propose the extension or modification of restrictions either in accordance with the procedures provided by the subdivision's restrictions or the procedures provided by this chapter.

History of Prop. Code §210.009: Acts 2005, 79th Leg., ch. 1180, §1, eff. Sept. 1, 2005.

CHAPTER 211. AMENDMENT & ENFORCEMENT OF RESTRICTIONS IN CERTAIN SUBDIVISIONS

PROP §211.001. DEFINITIONS

In this chapter:

(1) "Dedicatory instrument" means each governing instrument covering the establishment, maintenance, and operation of a residential subdivision or any similar planned development. The term includes a declaration or similar instrument subjecting real property to restrictive covenants, bylaws, or similar instruments governing the administration or operation of a property owners' association, to properly adopted rules and regulations of the property owners' association, or to all lawful amendments to the covenants, bylaws, instruments, rules, or regulations.

(2) "Lienholder," "owner," "real property records," and "restrictions" have the meanings assigned by Section 201.003.

(3) "Property owners' association" means an incorporated or unincorporated association owned by or whose members consist primarily of the owners of the property covered by the dedicatory instrument and through which the owners, or the board of directors or similar governing body, manage or regulate the residential subdivision or similar planned development.

(4) "Residential real estate subdivision" or "subdivision" means all land encompassed within one or more maps or plats of land that is divided into two or more parts if:

(A) the maps or plats cover land all or part of which is not located within a municipality and:

(i) for a county with a population of less than 65,000, is not located within the extraterritorial jurisdiction of a municipality;

(ii) for a county with a population of at least 65,000 and less than 135,000, is located wholly within the extraterritorial jurisdiction of a municipality; or

(iii) for a county that borders Lake Buchanan and has a population of at least 18,500 and less than 19,500, is located wholly within the extraterritorial jurisdiction of a municipality;

(B) the land encompassed within the maps or plats is or was burdened by restrictions limiting all or at least a majority of the land area covered by the map or plat, excluding streets and public areas, to residential use only; and

(C) all instruments creating the restrictions are recorded in the deed or real property records of a county.

History of Prop. Code §211.001: Acts 2005, 79th Leg., ch. 1077, §1, eff. Sept. 1, 2005. Amended by Acts 2011, 82nd Leg., ch. 1125, §1, eff. June 17, 2011; Acts 2013, 83rd Leg., ch. 1242, §1, eff. Sept. 1, 2013.

PROP §211.002. APPLICABILITY OF CHAPTER

(a) This chapter applies only to a residential real estate subdivision or any unit or parcel of a subdivision:

(1) all or part of which is located within an unincorporated area of a county if the county has a population of less than 65,000;

(2) all of which is located within the extraterritorial jurisdiction of a municipality located in a county that has a population of at least 65,000 and less than 135,000;

(3) all of which is located within the extraterritorial jurisdiction of a municipality located in a county that borders Lake Buchanan and has a population of at least 18,500 and less than 19,500; or

(4) all or part of which is located within a county that borders Lake Livingston and has a population of less than 50,000.

(b) This chapter applies only to restrictions that affect real property within a residential real estate subdivision or any units or parcels of the subdivision and that, by the express terms of the instrument creating the restrictions:

(1) are not subject to a procedure by which the restrictions may be amended;

(2) may not be amended without the unanimous consent of:

(A) all property owners in the subdivision; or

(B) all property owners in any unit or parcel of the subdivision; or

(3) may not be amended without a written instrument that is:

(A) signed by a majority or more than a majority of the owners of the lots in the subdivision; and

(B) filed in the real property records of each county in which all or part of the subdivision is located.

(b-1) In addition to restrictions and units or parcels of a subdivision that are subject to this chapter under Subsection (b), this chapter applies to restrictions that affect real property within a residential real estate subdivision or any units or parcels of the subdivision and that, by the express terms of the instrument creating the restrictions, provide that amendments to the restrictions are not operative or effective until a specified date or the expiration of a specified period. An amendment under this chapter of a restriction described by this subsection is effective as provided by this chapter, regardless of whether the date specified in the restrictions has occurred or the period prescribed by the restrictions has expired. This subsection expires September 1, 2019.

(c) This chapter applies to a restriction regardless of the date on which it was created.

(d) An amendment of a restriction under this chapter is effective on the filing of an instrument reflecting the amendment in the real property records of each county in which all or part of the subdivision is located after the approval of the owners in accordance with the amendment procedure adopted under Section 211.004.

History of Prop. Code §211.002: Acts 2005, 79th Leg., ch. 1077, §1, eff. Sept. 1, 2005. Amended by Acts 2011, 82nd Leg., ch. 1125, §2, eff. June 17, 2011; Acts 2013, 83rd Leg., ch. 1242, §2, eff. Sept. 1, 2013; Acts 2015, 84th Leg., ch. 901, §1, eff. June 18, 2015.

PROP §211.003. FINDINGS & PURPOSE

(a) The legislature finds that:

(1) owners of land in certain real estate subdivisions are unable to govern the subdivisions by democratic principles of self-government;

(2) requiring unanimous consent to amend or modify restrictions in affected subdivisions or units or parcels of the subdivisions is impractical and unworkable to bring needed change and improvement;

(3) the inability of owners to amend or modify property restrictions in certain real estate subdivisions in which no zoning regulations apply creates uncertainty in living conditions and discourages investments in those subdivisions;

(4) owners of land in affected subdivisions are reluctant or unable to provide proper maintenance, upkeep, and repairs of structures because of the inability to amend or modify the restrictions in response to changing circumstances;

(5) financial institutions are reluctant to or will not lend money for investments, maintenance, upkeep, or repairs in affected subdivisions;

(6) these conditions will cause dilapidation of housing and other structures and cause unhealthful and unsanitary conditions in affected subdivisions, contrary to the health, safety, and welfare of the public; and

(7) the existence of race-related covenants in restrictions, regardless of their unenforceability, is offensive, repugnant, and harmful to members of racial or ethnic minority groups and public policy requires that those covenants be removed.

(b) The purpose of this chapter is to provide a procedure for creating, modifying, or adding to residential restrictions and to provide for the removal of any restriction or other provision relating to race, religion, or national origin that is void and unenforceable under either the United States Constitution or Section 5.026.

History of Prop. Code §211.003: Acts 2005, 79th Leg., ch. 1077, §1, eff. Sept. 1, 2005.

PROP §211.004. CREATION OR MODIFICATION OF PROCEDURE TO AMEND RESTRICTIONS

(a) A property owners' association by a two-thirds vote of the association's governing body may submit a procedure for amending restrictions to a vote of the property owners in the subdivision or in the unit or parcel of the subdivision governed by restrictions.

(b) An amendment procedure submitted to a vote under Subsection (a) binds all property owners in the subdivision or the unit or parcel of the subdivision to which the procedure applies if more than two-thirds of the voting property owners vote in favor of the procedure.

(c) Not later than the 30th day before the date a ballot for a vote under this section must be received to be counted, the property owners' association shall mail to each affected property owner a notice that includes:

(1) the exact wording of the amendment procedure; and

(2) the date by which a property owner's ballot must be received to be counted.

(d) The property owners' association shall pay all costs of:

(1) printing and mailing the required notices and ballots; and

(2) canvassing, tabulating, and certifying the vote.

(e) A property owner may not cast more than one vote, regardless of the number of lots the person owns. If more than one person owns an interest in a lot, the owners may cast only one vote for that lot. A person may not vote if the person has an interest in a lot only by virtue of being a lienholder.

(f) A ballot cast under this section is secret and may not be counted unless it is placed inside an unmarked envelope that is placed inside another envelope that bears the signature and printed name of the property owner casting the enclosed ballot.

(g) The presiding officer of the property owners' association shall appoint an election canvassing committee and a committee chairperson to canvass and count the votes and determine the outcome.

(h) If the amendment procedure receives the number of votes required under Subsection (b), the election canvassing committee chairperson shall certify the result to the presiding officer of the property owners' association. The presiding officer shall file in the real property records of each county in which all or part of the subdivision is located an instrument that indicates that the procedure was adopted.

(i) If the amendment procedure is not adopted, the property owners' association may not submit the same amendment procedure to a vote under this section on or before the first anniversary of the date the previous votes on the procedure were certified.

History of Prop. Code §211.004: Acts 2005, 79th Leg., ch. 1077, §1, eff. Sept. 1, 2005.

PROP §211.005. EFFECT OF ADOPTING AMENDMENT PROCEDURE

After the effective date of the adoption of the amendment procedure under this chapter, any proposed amendment to the restrictions described by Section 211.002(b) applicable to the subdivision or unit or parcel of the subdivision, as applicable, must be submitted for approval to the owners under the amendment procedure.

History of Prop. Code §211.005: Acts 2005, 79th Leg., ch. 1077, §1, eff. Sept. 1, 2005.

CHAPTER 212. EXTENSION OF RESTRICTIONS BY MAJORITY VOTE IN CERTAIN SUBDIVISIONS

PROP §212.001. DEFINITIONS

In this chapter, "lienholder," "owner," "restrictions," and "residential real estate subdivision" or "subdivision" have the meanings assigned by Section 201.003.

History of Prop. Code §212.001: Acts 2011, 82nd Leg., ch. 954, §2, eff. June 17, 2011.

PROP §212.002. APPLICABILITY OF CHAPTER

This chapter applies only to a residential real estate subdivision that:

(1) is located wholly or partly in a municipality with a population of more than two million located in a county with a population of 3.3 million or more; and

(2) is subject to restrictions the terms of which:

(A) provide that the restrictions expire;

(B) permit the restrictions to be extended after the initial restriction period expires if a majority of the owners of lots in the subdivision, by a written instrument

that is acknowledged and filed for record, signify consent to the extension of the restrictions for a further period the maximum length of which is specified by the restrictions; and

(C) do not expressly provide for or expressly prohibit successive extensions of the restrictions after the expiration of the initial extension period.

History of Prop. Code §212.002: Acts 2011, 82nd Leg., ch. 954, §2, eff. June 17, 2011.

PROP §212.003. PROCEDURE FOR SUCCESSIVE EXTENSIONS

(a) Restrictions may be extended under this chapter by the written consent of the owners of a majority of the lots in the subdivision, without respect to the number of lots owned by a particular owner.

(b) Consent for the purposes of this section may be reflected by an owner's signature on a petition or written ballot.

(c) Petitions, written ballots, or both may be distributed to the owners of lots in the subdivision by any method, including one or both of the following methods:

(1) by door-to-door circulation; or

(2) at a meeting of the owners of lots in the subdivision called for the purpose of voting on the proposed extension.

(d) The required signatures must be obtained during the same extension period. The petitions, written ballots, or both, as applicable, must be filed for record in the county in which the subdivision is located before the earlier of:

(1) the first anniversary of the date on which the first signature is obtained; or

(2) the expiration of the extension period during which the signatures are collected.

(e) Restrictions may be extended under this chapter only once during each unexpired extension period.

History of Prop. Code §212.003: Acts 2011, 82nd Leg., ch. 954, §2, eff. June 17, 2011.

PROP §212.004. EFFECT OF OWNER SIGNATURE

(a) The vote of multiple owners of a lot may be reflected by the signature of one of the owners.

(b) After an owner signs a petition or ballot under Section 212.003 or 212.007, the owner's subsequent conveyance of the owner's interest in a lot or unplatted real property in the subdivision does not affect the validity of the signature for the purposes of that section.

History of Prop. Code §212.004: Acts 2011, 82nd Leg., ch. 954, §2, eff. June 17, 2011.

PROP §212.005. PROPERTY OWNERS' ASSOCIATION NOT REQUIRED

Restrictions may be extended under this chapter without the creation of or action by a property owners' association, homeowners association, community association, civic club, or similar organization.

History of Prop. Code §212.005: Acts 2011, 82nd Leg., ch. 954, §2, eff. June 17, 2011.

PROP §212.006. EFFECTIVE DATE OF EXTENSION; LENGTH OF EXTENSION PERIOD

(a) An extension of restrictions under this chapter takes effect on the date the petitions, written ballots, or both, as applicable, sufficient to reflect the consent required by Section 212.003 are filed and recorded in the real property records of the county in which the subdivision is located.

(b) Subject to Section 212.007, an extension of restrictions under this chapter is for a period equal to the original term of the restrictions or a shorter period agreed to by the owners of a majority of the lots in the subdivision in the petitions, written ballots, or both, as applicable, signed under Section 212.003.

History of Prop. Code §212.006: Acts 2011, 82nd Leg., ch. 954, §2, eff. June 17, 2011.

PROP §212.007. TERMINATION OF RESTRICTIONS

(a) Restrictions extended under this chapter may be terminated before their expiration date if:

(1) the consent of the owners of a majority of the lots in the subdivision to the termination of the restrictions on a specified date is obtained in the same manner as consent to the extension of restrictions is obtained under this chapter; and

(2) the petitions, written ballots, or both, as applicable, sufficient to reflect the required consent to termination are filed for record in the real property records of the county in which the subdivision is located before the earlier of:

(A) the first anniversary of the date on which the first signature consenting to termination is obtained; or

(B) a date specified under Subsection (b)(2).

(b) Petitions, written ballots, or both, as applicable, used to extend restrictions under this section may provide that:

(1) the restrictions may be terminated only on one or more termination dates specified in the petitions, written ballots, or both, as applicable, used to extend the restrictions; or

(2) the petitions, written ballots, or both, as applicable, sufficient to reflect the required consent to termination must be filed for record before a time specified in the petitions, written ballots, or both, as applicable.

History of Prop. Code §212.007: Acts 2011, 82nd Leg., ch. 954, §2, eff. June 17, 2011.

PROP §212.008. APPLICABILITY OF EXTENDED RESTRICTIONS

(a) An extension of restrictions under this chapter is binding on all lots and all unplatted real property in the subdivision, without regard to whether the owner or owners of any individual lot or unplatted real property signify consent to extend the restrictions. Any statute authorizing a property owner to opt out of the applicability of restrictions to the owner's property does not apply to restrictions extended under this chapter.

(b) An extension of restrictions under this chapter is binding on a lienholder or a person who acquires title to property at a foreclosure sale or by deed from a foreclosing lienholder.

History of Prop. Code §212.008: Acts 2011, 82nd Leg., ch. 954, §2, eff. June 17, 2011.

PROP §212.009. UNCONSTITUTIONAL RESTRICTIONS NOT EXTENDED

If a provision in restrictions extended under this chapter is void and unenforceable under the United States Constitution, the restrictions are considered as if the void and unenforceable provision was never contained in the restrictions.

History of Prop. Code §212.009: Acts 2011, 82nd Leg., ch. 954, §2, eff. June 17, 2011.

PROP §212.010. USE OF ORIGINAL EXTENSION PROCEDURE; PROCEDURES CUMULATIVE

(a) In addition to the procedure provided by this chapter for the extension of restrictions, the procedure provided by the original restrictions for the initial extension of the restrictions, including the requirement that a specified percentage of a specified class approve the extension, may be used for successive extensions of the original restrictions, provided that the approval obtained includes the approval of the owners of not less than a majority of the lots in the subdivision.

(b) An extension of the restrictions as described by Subsection (a) is for a period equal to the original term of the restrictions or a shorter period agreed to by the owners of a majority of the lots in the subdivision.

(c) The procedure provided by this chapter for the extension or termination of restrictions is cumulative of and not in lieu of any other method by which restrictions of a subdivision to which this chapter applies may be added to, modified, created, extended, or terminated.

History of Prop. Code §212.010: Acts 2011, 82nd Leg., ch. 954, §2, eff. June 17, 2011.

PROP §212.011. CONSTRUCTION OF CHAPTER & EXTENDED RESTRICTIONS

(a) This chapter and any petition or ballot made or action taken in connection with an attempt to comply with this chapter shall be liberally construed to effectuate the intent of this chapter and the petition, ballot, or action.

(b) A deed restriction that is extended under this chapter shall be liberally construed to give effect to the restriction's purposes and intent.

History of Prop. Code §212.011: Acts 2011, 82nd Leg., ch. 954, §2, eff. June 17, 2011.

CHAPTER 213. MODIFICATION OR TERMINATION OF RESTRICTIONS IN CERTAIN REAL ESTATE DEVELOPMENTS BY PROPERTY OWNERS' ASSOCIATION OR PROPERTY OWNER PETITION

PROP §213.001. DEFINITIONS

In this chapter:

(1) "Amenity property" means real property the use of which is restricted by a dedicatory instrument to use as a golf course or country club.

(2) "Council of owners" has the meaning assigned by Section 81.002 as it relates to an existing condominium in a development.

(3) "Dedicatory instrument" means a governing instrument that:

(A) restricts amenity property to use as amenity property;

(B) designates real property in the development, other than amenity property, as a beneficiary of a restriction described by Paragraph (A); and

(C) addresses the establishment, maintenance, and operation of amenity property.

(4) "Development" means:

(A) amenity property; and

(B) all real property designated as beneficiary property in the dedicatory instrument.

(5) "Owner" means a person, or the person's personal representative, who holds record title to:

(A) a lot or parcel of real property in a development; or

(B) a unit or apartment of a condominium in the development.

(6) "Petition circulator" means a person authorized to circulate a petition under Section 213.005.

(7) "Property owners' association" means an incorporated or unincorporated association that:

(A) is designated as the representative of the owners of lots or parcels of real property in a development;

(B) has a membership primarily consisting of those owners; and

(C) manages or regulates all or part of the development for the benefit of those owners.

(8) "Restrictions" means one or more restrictive covenants contained or incorporated by reference in a properly recorded map, plat, replat, declaration, or other instrument filed in the real property records or map or plat records. The term includes any amendment or extension of the restrictions.

(9) "Restrictive covenant" means any covenant, condition, or restriction contained in a dedicatory instrument, whether mandatory, prohibitive, permissive, or administrative.

(10) "Unit owners' association" means an association of unit owners organized under Section 82.101 for a condominium in a development.

History of Prop. Code §213.001: Acts 2015, 84th Leg., ch. 1183, §23, eff. Sept. 1, 2015.

PROP §213.002. FINDINGS & PURPOSE

(a) The legislature finds that:

(1) a restriction on the use of an amenity property may create uncertainty if the owners of an amenity property are reluctant or unable to properly maintain or operate the amenity property;

(2) such uncertainty may discourage investment and negatively impact property values in the development;

(3) investors may be reluctant to or will not invest funds to revitalize an amenity property burdened with a restriction on its use;

(4) financial institutions may be reluctant to or will not provide financing to revitalize an amenity property burdened with a restriction on its use; and

(5) establishing a procedural option to allow for the modification or termination of the restriction would alleviate the uncertainty and encourage revitalization of the amenity property.

(b) The purpose of this chapter is to provide a procedural option for the modification or termination of a restriction on the use of an amenity property.

History of Prop. Code §213.002: Acts 2015, 84th Leg., ch. 1183, §23, eff. Sept. 1, 2015.

PROP §213.003. MODIFICATION OR TERMINATION BY PETITION

(a) Except as provided by Subsection (b), a restriction on the use of an amenity property may be modified or terminated by petition in accordance with this chapter.

(b) This chapter does not apply if:

(1) a dedicatory instrument includes a procedure to modify or terminate a restriction on the use of an amenity property on approval of the owners of less than 75 percent of, as applicable, the lots or parcels of land and units or apartments of condominiums in the development; or

(2) a restriction on the use of an amenity property may be modified or terminated under the procedures of Chapter 81, 82, 201, or 209.

History of Prop. Code §213.003: Acts 2015, 84th Leg., ch. 1183, §23, eff. Sept. 1, 2015.

PROP §213.004. PREREQUISITES FOR CIRCULATION

A petition may not be circulated under this chapter unless:

(1) for a continuous period of at least 36 months, the amenity property has not been in operation; and

(2) if zoning regulations apply to the amenity property, the owner of the amenity property has received all required zoning approvals for any proposed redevelopment of the amenity property.

History of Prop. Code §213.004: Acts 2015, 84th Leg., ch. 1183, §23, eff. Sept. 1, 2015.

PROP §213.005. PETITION CIRCULATOR

A petition authorized by Section 213.003 may be circulated by:

(1) an owner;

(2) a property owners' association that owns and manages the amenity property; or

(3) a unit owners' association or council of owners that owns and manages the amenity property.

History of Prop. Code §213.005: Acts 2015, 84th Leg., ch. 1183, §23, eff. Sept. 1, 2015.

PROP §213.006. CONTENTS OF PETITION

(a) The petition must include all relevant information about the proposed modification or termination, including:

(1) the name of the development, if any;

(2) the name of the amenity property, if any;

(3) the recording information of the restriction to be modified or terminated;

(4) the text of the restriction subject to modification or termination;

(5) the text of the restriction as modified or terminated; and

(6) a comparison of the original language of the restriction and the restriction as modified or terminated, showing any insertion and deletion of language or punctuation.

(b) The petition must state:

(1) reasonable times and dates the petition circulator will be available at a location in the development to receive a signed statement required by Section 213.008;

(2) a mailing address, e-mail address, and facsimile number to which a signed statement may be delivered; and

(3) the date by which a signed statement must be received to be counted.

History of Prop. Code §213.006: Acts 2015, 84th Leg., ch. 1183, §23, eff. Sept. 1, 2015.

PROP §213.007. CIRCULATION PROCEDURE

(a) A petition circulator shall deliver a copy of the petition to:

(1) all owners of:

(A) each lot or parcel of real property in the development; and

(B) each unit or apartment of each condominium, if any, in the development; and

(2) each property owners' association, unit owners' association, and council of owners in the development.

(b) The petition circulator may deliver a copy of the petition in any reasonable manner, including:

(1) by regular mail or certified mail, return receipt requested, to the last known address of the owners or entities described by Subsections (a)(1) and (2);

(2) personal delivery to the owners or entities described by Subsections (a)(1) and (2); or

(3) at a regular meeting of a property owners' association, unit owners' association, or council of owners.

(c) If the petition circulator acts in good faith in determining ownership and delivering copies of the petition as required by this section, an owner's lack of receipt of a copy of the petition does not affect the application of a modification or termination of a restriction under this chapter to the amenity property.

History of Prop. Code §213.007: Acts 2015, 84th Leg., ch. 1183, §23, eff. Sept. 1, 2015.

PROP §213.008. VOTE ON PROPOSAL

(a) The modification or termination of the restriction is adopted if the owners of at least 75 percent of the total number, as applicable, of the lots or parcels of land and the units or apartments of condominiums in the development, including the owner of the amenity property, vote in favor of the modification or termination of the restriction.

(b) An owner may cast a vote only by delivering to the petition circulator in accordance with Section 213.009 a signed statement that includes:

(1) the owner's name, the legal description or street address of the owner's property, and the owner's mailing address;

(2) a statement that the owner holds record title to the property;

(3) if more than one person owns an interest in the property, the name and mailing address of each co-owner; and

(4) a statement indicating whether the owner is in favor of or against the modification or termination proposed by the petition.

(c) An owner may vote only in favor of or against the modification or termination as proposed in the petition.

(d) If more than one person owns an interest in a lot or parcel of land or a unit or apartment of a condominium, the owners may cast only one vote for that lot, parcel, unit, or apartment. Except as otherwise provided by this subsection, the vote of multiple owners in favor of or against the modification or termination may be reflected by the signatures of a majority of the co-owners who return a signed statement. The vote of owners who are married may be reflected by the signature of only one of those owners.

(e) A person whose only property interest in a lot or parcel of land or unit or apartment of a condominium is that of a contract purchaser, lienholder, or mineral interest holder may not cast a vote for that property under this chapter.

(f) A vote may be counted only if the vote is received before the deadline stated in the petition as required by Section 213.006(b).

(g) The signed statement of an owner conclusively establishes that:

(1) the petition was received by the owner in accordance with Section 213.007; and

(2) the statement accurately reflects the vote of the owner.

History of Prop. Code §213.008: Acts 2015, 84th Leg., ch. 1183, §23, eff. Sept. 1, 2015.

PROP §213.009. DELIVERY OF SIGNED STATEMENT

(a) The petition circulator must accept a signed statement described by Section 213.008 that is delivered:

(1) in person under Section 213.006(b) or otherwise;

(2) by first class mail to an address stated in the petition;

(3) by e-mail to an address stated in the petition; or

(4) by facsimile to a facsimile number stated in the petition.

(b) This section supersedes any contrary provision in a dedicatory instrument.

History of Prop. Code §213.009: Acts 2015, 84th Leg., ch. 1183, §23, eff. Sept. 1, 2015.

PROP §213.010. CERTIFICATION OF RESULTS BY RECORDED AFFIDAVIT

(a) The petition circulator shall certify the result of the votes by filing an affidavit with the county clerk of the county in which the restriction modified or terminated is recorded.

(b) The affidavit required by Subsection (a) must state:

(1) the name of the development, if any;

(2) the name of the amenity property, if any;

(3) the recording information of the restriction that was modified or terminated;

(4) the text of the restriction before modification or termination;

(5) the text of the restriction as modified or terminated;

(6) the number of votes in favor of and against the proposed modification or termination;

(7) the name and address of the petition circulator; and

(8) the name, address, and telephone number of the person maintaining the documents in accordance with Section 213.013.

(c) The petition circulator must affirm in the affidavit that the petition was delivered in accordance with Section 213.007.

History of Prop. Code §213.010: Acts 2015, 84th Leg., ch. 1183, §23, eff. Sept. 1, 2015.

PROP §213.011. NOTICE

(a) The recording of the affidavit required by Section 213.010 constitutes notice that the restriction is modified or terminated.

(b) Notwithstanding Subsection (a), the petition circulator must deliver to each person who resides within 200 feet of the boundary of the amenity property a copy of the affidavit. The affidavit may be delivered by regular mail, by certified mail, return receipt requested, or by personal delivery.

History of Prop. Code §213.011: Acts 2015, 84th Leg., ch. 1183, §23, eff. Sept. 1, 2015.

PROP §213.012. EFFECTIVE DATE OF MODIFICATION OR TERMINATION

The modification or termination of the restriction takes effect on the later of:

(1) the date the affidavit required by Section 213.010 is filed with the county clerk; or

(2) the date, if any, specified as the effective date in the petition.

History of Prop. Code §213.012: Acts 2015, 84th Leg., ch. 1183, §23, eff. Sept. 1, 2015.

PROP §213.013. DOCUMENTATION AVAILABLE

At least one year after the date the affidavit is filed with the county clerk, the petition circulator shall make available for inspection and copying the original petition, the signed statements described by Section 213.008, and the affidavit required by Section 213.010.

History of Prop. Code §213.013: Acts 2015, 84th Leg., ch. 1183, §23, eff. Sept. 1, 2015.

PROP §213.014. EXPIRATION

This chapter expires September 1, 2021.

History of Prop. Code §213.014: Acts 2015, 84th Leg., ch. 1183, §23, eff. Sept. 1, 2015.

Chapter 214 blank

CHAPTER 215. MASTER MIXED-USE PROPERTY OWNERS' ASSOCIATIONS

PROP §215.001. DEFINITIONS

In this chapter:

(1) "Appraised value" means the property value determined by the appraisal district that establishes property values for taxing entities levying taxes on property in a mixed-use development.

(2) "Property owners' association" or "association" means, unless otherwise indicated, a master mixed-use property owners' association.

(3) "Dedicatory instrument" has the meaning assigned by Section 209.002.

(4) "Self-help" means the process by which a property owners' association takes remedial action with regard to property governed by the association.

History of Prop. Code §215.001: Acts 2011, 82nd Leg., ch. 1167, §1, eff. Sept. 1, 2011.

PROP §215.002. APPLICABILITY OF CHAPTER

(a) This chapter applies to a property owners' association that:

(1) includes:

(A) commercial properties, including hotel and retail properties, that constitute at least 35 percent of the total appraised property value of the mixed-use development governed by the association;

(B) single-family attached and detached properties that constitute at least 25 percent of the total appraised property value of the mixed-use development governed by the association; and

(C) multifamily properties that constitute at least 10 percent of the total appraised property value of the mixed-use development governed by the association;

(2) governs at least 6,000 acres of deed-restricted property;

(3) has at least 10 incorporated residential or commercial property owners' associations that are members of and subject to the dedicatory instruments of the master mixed-use property owners' association;

(4) has at least 3,400 platted and developed single-family residential properties and at least 400 separately platted commercial properties, including office, industrial, hotel, and retail properties, which together constitute at least 30 million square feet of building area available for rental; and

(5) participates in the maintenance of public space, including parks, medians, and lakefronts, owned by local, including county, or state governmental entities.

(b) This chapter applies to property that is:

(1) governed by a property owners' association described by Subsection (a);

(2) located in a master mixed-use development; and

(3) subject to a provision, including a restriction, in a declaration that:

(A) requires mandatory membership in the association; and

(B) authorizes the association to collect a regular or special assessment on all or a majority of the property in the development.

(c) Except as otherwise provided by this chapter, this chapter applies only to a master mixed-use property owners' association and not to the independent property owners' associations that are members of the master mixed-use property owners' association.

History of Prop. Code §215.002: Acts 2011, 82nd Leg., ch. 1167, §1, eff. Sept. 1, 2011.

PROP §215.003. APPLICABILITY OF CHAPTER 209

Chapter 209 does not apply to a property owners' association subject to this chapter.

History of Prop. Code §215.003: Acts 2011, 82nd Leg., ch. 1167, §1, eff. Sept. 1, 2011. Amended by Acts 2013, 83rd Leg., ch. 673, §1, eff. Sept. 1, 2013.

PROP §215.004. CONFLICTS OF LAW

Notwithstanding any other provision of law, the provisions of this chapter prevail over a conflicting or inconsistent provision of law relating to independent property owners' associations.

History of Prop. Code §215.004: Acts 2011, 82nd Leg., ch. 1167, §1, eff. Sept. 1, 2011.

PROP §215.005. BOARD POWERS

In addition to any other powers provided by applicable law and this chapter, and unless otherwise provided by the dedicatory instruments of the property owners' association, the association, acting through its board of directors, may:

(1) adopt and amend bylaws;

(2) adopt and amend budgets for revenues, expenditures, and reserves and collect assessments for common expenses from property owners;

(3) adopt reasonable rules;

(4) hire and terminate managing agents and other agents, employees, and independent contractors;

(5) institute, defend, intervene in, settle, or compromise litigation or administrative proceedings on matters affecting a property governed by the association;

(6) make contracts and incur liabilities relating to the operation of the association;

(7) regulate the use, maintenance, repair, replacement, modification, and appearance of the property governed by the association;

(8) make improvements to be included as a part of the common area;

(9) acquire, hold, encumber, and convey in its own name any right, title, or interest to real or personal property;

(10) purchase an investment property that is not part of the common area;

(11) grant easements, leases, licenses, and concessions through or over the common elements;

(12) impose and receive payments, fees, or charges for the use, rental, or operation of the common area and for services provided to property owners;

(13) impose interest, late charges, and, if applicable, returned check charges for late payments of regular assessments or special assessments;

(14) charge costs to an owner's assessment account and collect the costs in any manner provided in the restrictions for the collection of assessments;

(15) adopt and amend rules regulating the collection of delinquent assessments;

(16) impose reasonable charges for preparing, recording, or copying amendments to resale certificates or statements of unpaid assessments;

(17) purchase insurance and fidelity bonds, including directors' and officers' liability insurance, that the board considers appropriate or necessary;

(18) subject to the requirements of the provisions described by Section 1.008(d), Business Organizations Code, and by majority vote of the board, indemnify a director or officer of the association who was, is, or may be made a named defendant or respondent in a proceeding because the person is or was a director or officer;

(19) if the restrictions vest the architectural control authority in the association:

(A) implement written architectural control guidelines for its own use, or record the guidelines in the real property records of the applicable county; and

(B) modify the guidelines as the needs of the development change;

(20) exercise self-help with regard to property governed by the association;

(21) exercise other powers conferred by the dedicatory instruments;

(22) exercise other powers necessary and proper for the governance and operation of the association; and

(23) exercise any other powers that may be exercised in this state by a corporation of the same type as the association.

History of Prop. Code §215.005: Acts 2011, 82nd Leg., ch. 1167, §1, eff. Sept. 1, 2011.

PROP §215.006. ANNUAL MEETING OF ASSOCIATION MEMBERS; NOTICE OF ANNUAL OR SPECIAL MEETING

(a) An annual meeting of members of a property owners' association must be conducted in accordance with the association's dedicatory instruments.

(b) Unless otherwise provided by a dedicatory instrument, an annual meeting of the property owners' association members is open to association members and must be held in a county in which all or part of the property governed by the association is located or in a county adjacent to that county.

(c) Unless otherwise provided by a dedicatory instrument, the board shall give members notice of the date, time, place, and subject of an annual or special meeting of the members. The notice must be delivered to each member not later than the 10th day and not earlier than the 60th day before the date of the meeting.

(d) A notice under Subsection (c) must be posted in a conspicuous manner reasonably designed to provide notice to association members:

(1) in a place located outside the corporate offices of the association that is accessible by the general membership during normal business hours; or

(2) on any Internet website maintained by the association.

(e) Unless otherwise provided by a dedicatory instrument, any number of the members may attend the meeting by use of videoconferencing or a similar telecommunication method for purposes of establishing full participation in the meeting.

History of Prop. Code §215.006: Acts 2011, 82nd Leg., ch. 1167, §1, eff. Sept. 1, 2011.

PROP §215.007. BOARD MEETINGS

(a) A meeting of the board of directors of a property owners' association must be conducted in accordance with the association's dedicatory instruments.

(b) Unless otherwise provided by a dedicatory instrument, elected directors who represent the commercial and residential membership attend and conduct the business of the property owners' association at a meeting under this section.

(c) In this section, a board meeting has the meaning assigned by a dedicatory instrument. Notwithstanding this subsection, the term does not include the gathering of a quorum of the board at any other venue, including at a social function unrelated to the business of the association, or the attendance by a quorum of the board at a regional, state, or national convention, workshop, ceremonial event, or press conference, if formal action is not taken and any discussion of association business is incidental to the social function, convention, workshop, ceremonial event, or press conference.

(d) Unless otherwise provided by a dedicatory instrument, the board shall keep a record of each regular, emergency, or special board meeting in the form of written minutes or an audio recording of the meeting. A record of a meeting must state the subject of each motion or inquiry, regardless of whether the board takes action on the motion or inquiry, and indicate each vote, order, decision, or other action taken by the board. The board shall make meeting records, including approved minutes, available to a member for inspection and copying, at the member's expense, during the normal business hours of the association on the member's written request to the board or the board's representative. The board shall approve the minutes of a board meeting not later than the next regular board meeting.

(e) Unless otherwise provided by a dedicatory instrument, before the board calls an executive session, the board shall convene in a regular or special board meeting for which notice has been given as provided by this section. During that board meeting, the presiding board member may call an executive session by announcing that an executive session will be held to deliberate a matter described by Subsection (f) and identifying the specific subdivision of Subsection (f) under which the executive session will be held. A vote or other action item may not be taken in executive session. An executive session is not subject to the requirements of Subsection (d).

(f) Unless otherwise provided by a dedicatory instrument, a property owners' association board may meet in executive session to deliberate:

(1) anticipated or pending litigation, settlement offers, or interpretations of the law with the association's legal counsel;

(2) complaints or charges against or issues regarding a board member or an agent, employee, contractor, or other representative of the association;

(3) all financial matters concerning a specific property owner;

(4) a payment plan for an association member who has a financial obligation to the association;

(5) a foreclosure of a lien;

(6) an enforcement action against an association member, including for nonpayment of amounts due;

(7) the purchase, exchange, lease, or value of real property, if the board determines in good faith that deliberation in an open board meeting may have a detrimental effect on the association;

(8) business and financial issues relating to the negotiation of a contract, if the board determines in good faith that deliberation in an open board meeting may have a detrimental effect on the position of the association;

(9) matters involving the invasion of privacy of an individual owner;

(10) an employee matter; and

(11) any other matter the board considers necessary or reasonable to further assist the association's operation.

History of Prop. Code §215.007: Acts 2011, 82nd Leg., ch. 1167, §1, eff. Sept. 1, 2011.

PROP §215.008. VOTING

(a) The number of votes to which an individual or corporation who is a member of a property owners' association is entitled is determined by the dedicatory instruments of the association.

(b) Each corporation or individual who is a member of the property owners' association may vote by proxy as provided for nonprofit corporations under Sections 22.160(b) and (c), Business Organizations Code.

(c) Notwithstanding any provision of the certificate of formation or bylaws to the contrary, a member vote on any matter may be conducted by mail, by facsimile transmission, by e-mail, or by any combination of those methods.

(d) Notwithstanding any provision of the certificate of formation, declaration, or bylaws to the contrary, the declaration and any supplementary declaration, including amendments, modifications, or corrections, may be amended by a simple majority of the eligible votes being cast in favor of the amendment.

History of Prop. Code §215.008: Acts 2011, 82nd Leg., ch. 1167, §1, eff. Sept. 1, 2011. Amended by Acts 2013, 83rd Leg., ch. 673, §2, eff. Sept. 1, 2013.

PROP §215.009. RESTRICTIVE COVENANTS

(a) A property owners' association may enforce its restrictive covenants as follows:

(1) by exercising discretionary authority relating to a restrictive covenant unless a court has determined by a preponderance of the evidence that the exercise of discretionary authority was arbitrary, capricious, or discriminatory; and

(2) by initiating, defending, or intervening in litigation or an administrative proceeding affecting the enforcement of a restrictive covenant or the protection, preservation, or operation of property subject to the association's dedicatory instruments.

(b) If the association prevails in an action to enforce restrictive covenants, the association may recover reasonable attorney's fees and costs incurred.

(c) An association may use self-help to enforce its restrictive covenants against a residential or commercial property owner as necessary to prevent immediate harm to a person or property, or as otherwise reasonable. If a property owner commits a subsequent repeat violation of the restrictive covenants within 12 months of the initial violation, the association is not required to provide the property owner with advance notice before the association implements self-help.

(d) For purposes of Subsection (c), an advance, annual notice of maintenance requirements is considered notice to the extent notice is required.

History of Prop. Code §215.009: Acts 2011, 82nd Leg., ch. 1167, §1, eff. Sept. 1, 2011.

PROP §215.010. ATTORNEY'S FEES IN BREACH OF RESTRICTIVE COVENANT ACTION

In an action based on breach of a restrictive covenant, the prevailing party is entitled to reasonable attorney's fees, costs, and actual damages.

History of Prop. Code §215.010: Acts 2011, 82nd Leg., ch. 1167, §1, eff. Sept. 1, 2011.

PROP §215.011. COMMON AREAS

A property owners' association may adopt reasonable rules regulating common areas.

History of Prop. Code §215.011: Acts 2011, 82nd Leg., ch. 1167, §1, eff. Sept. 1, 2011.

PROP §215.012. RESALE CERTIFICATES

A property owners' association shall provide resale certificates only for residential properties and in the manner provided by Section 207.003.

History of Prop. Code §215.012: Acts 2011, 82nd Leg., ch. 1167, §1, eff. Sept. 1, 2011.

PROP §215.013. MANAGEMENT CERTIFICATE

(a) A property owners' association shall record in each county in which any portion of the development governed by the association is located a management certificate, signed and acknowledged by an officer of the association, stating:

(1) the name of the development;

(2) the name of the association;

(3) the recording data for the declaration and all supplementary declarations;

(4) the applicability of any supplementary declarations to residential communities;

(5) the name and mailing address of the association; and

(6) other information the association considers appropriate.

(b) A property owners' association shall record an amended management certificate not later than the 30th day after the date the association has notice of a change in information in the recorded certificate required by Subsection (a).

(c) The association and its officers, directors, employees, and agents are not liable to any person or corporation for delay in recording or failure to record a management certificate unless the delay or failure is willful or caused by gross negligence.

History of Prop. Code §215.013: Acts 2011, 82nd Leg., ch. 1167, §1, eff. Sept. 1, 2011.

PROP §215.0135. ASSOCIATION RECORDS

(a) To the extent of any conflict or inconsistency, this section prevails over other provisions of law and the dedicatory instruments of a property owners' association subject to this chapter. This section is the exclusive procedure for a property owner to inspect the books and records of the association.

(b) Except as provided by Subsection (c) or (j), a property owners' association shall, on written request as provided by this section, make the books and records of the association open to and reasonably available for examination by an owner or a person designated in a written instrument signed by the owner as the owner's agent, attorney, or certified public accountant. Except as provided by Subsection (c) or (j), an owner is entitled to obtain copies of the books and records from the association.

(c) An attorney's files and records relating to the property owners' association, excluding invoices, are not records of the association and are not subject to inspection by the owner or the owner's authorized representative or to production in a legal proceeding. This subsection does not require production of a document that is covered by the attorney-client privilege.

(d) An owner or the owner's authorized representative described by Subsection (b) must submit a written request by certified mail to the mailing address of the property owners' association or the association's authorized representative, as reflected on the most current management certificate filed under Section 215.013, for access to the books and records of the association. The request must describe, in sufficient detail, the association's books and records requested by the owner or the owner's representative and:

(1) if an inspection is requested, the association shall, on or before the 10th business day after the date the association receives the request, send written notice of dates that the owner may inspect, during normal business hours, the requested books and records to the extent those books and records are in the actual physical possession, custody, and control of the association; or

(2) if copies of identified books and records are requested, the association shall, to the extent those books and records are in the actual physical possession, custody, and control of the association, produce copies of the requested books and records on or before the 10th business day after the date the association receives the request, except as otherwise provided by this section.

(e) If the property owners' association fails to produce the books or records requested under Subsection (d) on or before the 10th business day after the date the association receives the request, the association must provide to the requestor written notice that:

(1) informs the requestor that the association is unable to produce the information and the specific reasons for that inability on or before the 10th business day after the date the association received the request; and

(2) if the association can produce the information, notifies the requestor of the date by which the information will be sent or made available for inspection to the requesting party, which may not be later than the 15th day after the date notice under this subsection is given.

(f) If an inspection is requested or required, the inspection shall take place at a mutually agreed on time during normal business hours of the property owners' association, and the requesting party shall identify the books and records for the association to copy and forward to the requesting party.

(g) A property owners' association may produce books and records requested under this section in hard copy, electronic, or other format reasonably available to the association.

(h) A property owners' association board must adopt a records production and copying policy that prescribes the costs the association will charge for the compilation, production, and reproduction of information requested under this section. The prescribed charges may include all reasonable costs of materials, labor, and overhead. The policy required by this subsection must be recorded as a dedicatory instrument. If the policy is not recorded, the association may not charge an owner for the compilation, production, or reproduction of information requested under this section. If the policy is recorded, the requesting owner or the owner's representative is responsible for all costs related to the compilation, production, and reproduction of the requested information based on the amounts prescribed by the policy. The association may require advance payment of the estimated costs of compilation, production, and reproduction of the requested information. If the total of the estimated costs differs from the total of the actual costs, the association shall submit a final invoice to the owner on or before the 30th business day after the date the requested copies are delivered. If the actual total cost is higher than the estimated total cost, and the owner fails to reimburse the association before the 30th business day after the date the invoice is sent to the owner, the association may add the amount due to the owner's account as an assessment. If the actual total cost is less than the estimated total cost, the association shall issue a refund to the owner not later than the 30th business day after the date the requested copies are delivered.

(i) A property owners' association must estimate costs under this section using amounts prescribed by the policy adopted under Subsection (h).

(j) Information may be released in an aggregate or summary manner that would not identify an individual property owner. Except as provided by Subsection (k) and to the extent the information is provided in the meeting minutes, the property owners' association is not required to release or allow inspection of any books or records that identify:

(1) the dedicatory instrument violation history of an individual owner;

(2) an owner's personal financial information, including records of payment or nonpayment of amounts due the association;

(3) an owner's contact information, other than the owner's address;

(4) an owner's property files or building plans;

(5) books or records described by Subsection (c);

(6) any information to which an owner objects to releasing or has not granted approval for releasing; or

(7) information related to an employee of the association, including personnel files.

(k) The books and records described by Subsection (j) shall be released or made available for inspection if:

(1) the express written approval of the owner whose records are the subject of the request for inspection is provided to the property owners' association; or

(2) a court orders the release of the books and records or orders that the books and records be made available for inspection.

(*l*) A property owners' association shall adopt and comply with a document retention policy that includes, at a minimum, the following requirements:

(1) certificates of formation, bylaws, restrictive covenants, and all amendments to the certificates of formation, bylaws, and covenants shall be retained permanently;

(2) financial books and records shall be retained for seven years;

(3) account records of current owners shall be retained for five years;

(4) contracts with a term of one year or more shall be retained for four years after the expiration of the contract term;

(5) minutes of meetings of the owners and the board shall be retained for seven years; and

(6) tax returns and audit records shall be retained for seven years.

(m) A member of a property owners' association who is denied access to or copies of the association books or records to which the member is entitled under this section may file a petition with the county court at law in which all or part of the property that is governed by the association is located requesting relief in accordance with this subsection. If the county court at law finds that the member is entitled to access to or copies of the records, the county court at law may grant one or more of the following remedies:

(1) a judgment ordering the association to release or allow access to the books or records;

(2) a judgment against the association for court costs and attorney's fees incurred in connection with seeking a remedy under this section; or

(3) a judgment authorizing the owner or the owner's assignee to deduct the amounts awarded under Subdivision (2) from any future regular or special assessments payable to the association.

(n) If the property owners' association prevails in an action under Subsection (m), the association is entitled to a judgment for court costs and attorney's fees incurred by the association in connection with the action.

(o) On or before the 10th business day before the date a person brings an action against a property owners' association under this section, the person must send written notice to the association of the person's intent to bring the action. The notice must:

(1) be sent certified mail, return receipt requested, or delivered by the United States Postal Service with signature confirmation service, to the mailing address of the association or the association's authorized representative as reflected on the most current management certificate filed under Section 215.013; and

(2) describe with sufficient detail the books and records being requested.

(p) For the purposes of this section, "business day" means a day other than Saturday, Sunday, or a state or federal holiday.

History of Prop. Code §215.0135: Acts 2013, 83rd Leg., ch. 673, §3, eff. Sept. 1, 2013.

PROP §215.014. PRIORITY OF PAYMENTS

Unless otherwise provided in writing by the property owner at the time payment is made, a payment received by a property owners' association from the owner shall be applied to the owner's debt in the following order of priority:

(1) any delinquent assessment;

(2) any current assessment;

(3) any attorney's fees incurred by the association associated solely with assessments or any other charge that could provide the basis for foreclosure;

(4) any fines assessed by the association;

(5) any attorney's fees incurred by the association that are not subject to Subdivision (3); and

(6) any other amount owed to the association.

History of Prop. Code §215.014: Acts 2011, 82nd Leg., ch. 1167, §1, eff. Sept. 1, 2011.

PROP §215.015. FORECLOSURE

A property owners' association may not foreclose an association assessment lien unless the association first obtains a court order of sale.

History of Prop. Code §215.015: Acts 2011, 82nd Leg., ch. 1167, §1, eff. Sept. 1, 2011.

PROP §215.016. NOTICE REQUIRED BEFORE CERTAIN ENFORCEMENT ACTIONS

(a) Before a property owners' association may file a suit against an owner, other than a suit to collect a regular or special assessment or judicial foreclosure under the association's lien, or charge an owner for property damage, the association or its agent must give written notice sent to the owner by certified mail, return receipt requested, to the property address of the owner.

(b) The notice must:

(1) describe the violation of the declaration or property damage that is the basis for the suit or charge and state any amount due to the association from the owner; and

(2) inform the owner that the owner:

(A) is entitled, as applicable, to a reasonable period to cure the violation and avoid the suit unless the owner was previously given notice and a reasonable opportunity to cure by the association for the same or a similar violation within the preceding six months;

(B) may request a hearing under Section 215.017 on or before the 30th day after the date the owner receives the notice; and

(C) may have special rights or relief related to the suit or charge under federal law, including, without limitation, the Servicemembers Civil Relief Act (50 U.S.C. app. Section 501 et seq.), if the owner is serving on active military duty.

History of Prop. Code §215.016: Acts 2013, 83rd Leg., ch. 673, §4, eff. Sept. 1, 2013.

PROP §215.017. HEARING BEFORE BOARD

(a) Except as provided by Section 215.009(c), if the owner is entitled to an opportunity to cure a violation, the owner has the right to submit a written request for a hearing to discuss and verify facts and resolve the matter at issue before a committee appointed by the board of the property owners' association or before the board if the board does not appoint a committee.

(b) The association shall hold a hearing under this section not later than the 30th day after the date the board receives the owner's request for a hearing and shall notify the owner of the date, time, and place of the hearing not later than the 10th day before the date of the hearing. The board or committee or the owner may request a postponement, and if requested, a postponement shall be granted for a period of not more than 10 days. Additional postponements may be granted by agreement of the parties.

(c) The notice and hearing provisions of this section and Section 215.016 do not apply if the association files a suit seeking a temporary restraining order or temporary injunctive relief or a suit that includes foreclosure as a cause of action.

History of Prop. Code §215.017: Acts 2013, 83rd Leg., ch. 673, §4, eff. Sept. 1, 2013.

PROP §215.018. ALTERNATIVE PAYMENT SCHEDULE FOR CERTAIN ASSESSMENTS

(a) A property owners' association shall adopt reasonable guidelines to establish an alternative payment schedule by which an owner may make partial payments to the association for delinquent regular or special assessments or any other amount owed to the association without accruing additional monetary penalties. For purposes of this section, monetary penalties do not include reasonable costs associated with administering the payment plan or interest.

(b) A property owners' association is not required to enter into a payment plan with an owner who failed to honor the terms of a previous payment plan.

(c) A property owners' association shall file the association's guidelines under this section in the real property records of each county in which any portion of the subdivision is located.

History of Prop. Code §215.018: Acts 2013, 83rd Leg., ch. 673, §4, eff. Sept. 1, 2013.

Chapters 216-220 blank

TITLE 12. MISCELLANEOUS SHARED REAL PROPERTY INTERESTS

CHAPTER 221. TEXAS TIMESHARE ACT

SUBCHAPTER A. GENERAL PROVISIONS

PROP §221.001. SHORT TITLE

This chapter shall be known and may be cited as the Texas Timeshare Act.

History of Prop. Code §221.001: Acts 1987, 70th Leg., ch. 167, §6.03, eff. Sept. 1, 1987. Renumbered from §201.001 by Acts 1989, 71st Leg., ch. 2, §13.03(b), eff. Aug. 28, 1989. Source: TRCS art. 6573c, §1.

PROP §221.002. DEFINITIONS

As used in this chapter:

(1) "Accommodation" means any apartment, condominium or cooperative unit, hotel or motel room, cabin, lodge, or other private or commercial structure that:

(A) is affixed to real property;

(B) is designed for occupancy or use by one or more individuals; and

(C) is part of a timeshare plan.

(2) "Advertisement" means any written, oral, or electronic communication that is directed to or targeted at individuals in this state and contains a promotion, inducement, or offer to sell a timeshare interest, including a promotion, inducement, or offer to sell:

(A) contained in a brochure, pamphlet, or radio or television transcript;

(B) communicated by electronic media or telephone; or

(C) solicited through direct mail.

(3) "Amenities" means all common areas and includes recreational and maintenance facilities of the timeshare plan.

(4) "Assessment" means an amount assessed against or collected from a purchaser by an association or its managing entity in a fiscal year, regardless of the frequency with which the amount is assessed or collected, to cover expenditures, charges, reserves, or liabilities related to the operation of a timeshare plan or timeshare properties managed by the same managing entity.

(5) "Association" means a council or association composed of all persons who have purchased a timeshare interest.

(5-a) "Board" means the governing body of a timeshare association designated in a project instrument to act on behalf of the association.

(6) "Commission" means the Texas Real Estate Commission.

(7) "Component site" means a specific geographic location where accommodations that are part of a multisite timeshare plan are located. Separate phases of a single timeshare property in a specific geographic location and under common management are a single component site.

(8) "Developer" means:

(A) any person, excluding a sales agent, who creates a timeshare plan or is in the business of selling timeshare interests or employs a sales agent to sell timeshare interests; or

(B) any person who succeeds in the developer's interest by sale, lease, assignment, mortgage, or other transfer if the person:

(i) offers at least 12 timeshare interests in a particular timeshare plan; and

(ii) is in the business of selling timeshare interests or employs a sales agent to sell timeshare interests.

(9) "Dispose" or "disposition" means a voluntary transfer of any legal or equitable timeshare interest but does not include the transfer or release of a real estate lien or of a security interest.

(10) "Escrow agent" means a bonded escrow company, a financial institution whose accounts are insured by a governmental agency or instrumentality, or an attorney or title insurance agent licensed in this state who is responsible for the receipt and disbursement of funds in accordance with this chapter.

(11) "Exchange company" means any person who owns or operates an exchange program.

(12) "Exchange disclosure statement" means a written statement that includes the information required by Section 221.033.

(13) "Exchange program" means any method, arrangement, or procedure for the voluntary exchange of timeshare interests among purchasers or owners.

(14) "Incidental use right" means the right to use accommodations and amenities at one or more timeshare properties that is not guaranteed and is administered by the managing entity of the timeshare properties that makes vacant accommodations at the timeshare properties available to owners of timeshare interests in the timeshare properties.

(15) "Managing entity" means the person responsible for operating and maintaining a timeshare property.

(16) "Multisite timeshare plan" means a plan in which a timeshare purchaser has:

(A) a specific timeshare interest, which is the right to use and occupy accommodations at a specific timeshare property and the right to use and occupy accommodations at one or more other component sites created by or acquired solely through the reservation system of the timeshare plan; or

(B) a nonspecific timeshare interest, which is the right to use and occupy accommodations at more than one component site created by or acquired solely through the reservation system of the timeshare plan but which does not include a right to use and occupy a particular accommodation.

(17) "Offering" or "offer" means any advertisement, inducement, or solicitation and includes any attempt to encourage a person to purchase a timeshare interest other than as a security for an obligation.

(18) "Project instrument" means a timeshare instrument or one or more recordable documents, by whatever name denominated, applying to the whole of a timeshare project and containing restrictions or covenants regulating the use, occupancy, or disposition of units in a project, including a declaration for a condominium, association articles of incorporation, association bylaws, and rules for a condominium in which a timeshare plan is created.

(19) "Promotion" means any program, activity, contest, or gift, prize, or other item of value used to induce any person to attend a timeshare sales presentation.

(20) "Purchaser" means any person, other than a developer, who by means of a voluntary transfer acquires a legal or equitable interest in a timeshare interest other than as a security for an obligation.

(21) "Reservation system" means the method, arrangement, or procedure by which a purchaser, in order to reserve the use and occupancy of an accommodation of a multisite timeshare plan for one or more timeshare periods, is required to compete with other purchasers in the same multisite timeshare plan, regardless of whether the reservation system is operated and maintained by the multisite timeshare plan, a managing entity, an exchange company, or any other person. If a purchaser is required to use an exchange program as the purchaser's principal means of obtaining the right to use and occupy the accommodations and facilities of the plan, the arrangement is considered a reservation system. If the exchange company uses a mechanism to exchange timeshare periods among members of the exchange program, the use of the mechanism is not considered a reservation system of the multisite timeshare plan.

(22) "Single-site timeshare plan" means a timeshare plan in which a timeshare purchaser's right to use and occupy accommodations is limited to a single timeshare property. A single-site timeshare plan that includes an incidental use right or a program under which the owner of a timeshare interest at a specific timeshare property may exchange a timeshare period for another timeshare period at the same or another timeshare property under common management does not transform the single-site timeshare plan into a multisite timeshare plan.

(23) "Timeshare disclosure statement" means a written statement that includes the information required by Section 221.032.

(24) "Timeshare estate" means an arrangement under which the purchaser receives a right to occupy a timeshare property and an estate interest in the real property.

(25) "Timeshare interest" means a timeshare estate or timeshare use.

(26) "Timeshare instrument" means a master deed, master lease, declaration, or any other instrument used in the creation of a timeshare plan.

(27) "Timeshare period" means the period within which the purchaser of a timeshare interest is entitled to the exclusive possession, occupancy, and use of an accommodation.

(28) "Timeshare plan" means any arrangement, plan, scheme, or similar method, excluding an exchange program but including a membership agreement, sale, lease, deed, license, or right-to-use agreement, by which a purchaser, in exchange for consideration, receives an ownership right in or the right to use accommodations for a period of time less than a year during a given year, but not necessarily consecutive years.

(29) "Timeshare property" means:

(A) one or more accommodations and any related amenities subject to the same timeshare instrument; and

(B) any other property or property rights appurtenant to the accommodations and amenities.

(30) "Timeshare use" means any arrangement under which the purchaser receives a right to occupy a timeshare property, but under which the purchaser does not receive an estate interest in the timeshare property.

(31) to **(34)** Deleted by Acts 2005, 79th Leg., ch. 539, §1, eff. Jan. 15, 2006.

History of Prop. Code §221.002: Acts 1987, 70th Leg., ch. 167, §6.03, eff. Sept. 1, 1987. Renumbered from §201.002 by Acts 1989, 71st Leg., ch. 2, §13.03(b), eff. Aug. 28, 1989. Amended by Acts 1993, 73rd Leg., ch. 443, §1, eff. Sept. 1, 1993; Acts 2005, 79th Leg., ch. 539, §1, eff. Jan. 15, 2006; Acts 2013, 83rd Leg., ch. 1352, §3, eff. Sept. 1, 2013. Source: TRCS art. 6573c, §2.

PROP §221.003. APPLICABILITY

(a) This chapter applies to all timeshare properties that are located in this state or offered for sale in this state.

(b) Timeshare properties located outside this state are subject only to Subchapters C through H and J.

(c) This chapter applies to any timeshare property in existence on or after August 26, 1985, but does not affect a timeshare contract in existence before that date.

(d) A timeshare property subject to this chapter is not subject to:

(1) Section 5.008 or 5.012;

(2) Chapter 202;

(3) Chapter 207; or

(4) Chapter 209, unless an individual timeshare owner continuously occupies a single timeshare property as the owner's primary residence 12 months of the year.

(e) If a person with a specific program that might otherwise be subject to this chapter received from the commission, before January 31, 2005, a written determination that the program is exempt from this chapter as the chapter existed when the determination was made, the program remains exempt from this chapter if:

(1) the program does not vary materially from the terms on which the exemption was granted; or

(2) the program varies materially from the terms on which the exemption was granted, but the person receives from the commission a new written determination that the program is exempt from this chapter.

History of Prop. Code §221.003: Acts 1987, 70th Leg., ch. 167, §6.03, eff. Sept. 1, 1987. Renumbered from §201.003 by Acts 1989, 71st Leg., ch. 2, §13.03(b), eff. Aug. 28, 1989. Amended by Acts 2005, 79th Leg., ch. 539, §1, eff. Jan. 15, 2006; Acts 2013, 83rd Leg., ch. 1352, §4, eff. Sept. 1, 2013; Acts 2015, 84th Leg., ch. 554, §1, eff. Sept. 1, 2015. Source: TRCS art. 6573c, §§17, 18.

PROP §221.004. CONFLICTS OF LAW

(a) The provisions of this chapter prevail over a conflicting or inconsistent provision of law applicable to timeshare owners' associations.

(b) Provisions of this code relating to property owners' associations do not apply to an association subject to this chapter.

History of Prop. Code §221.004: Acts 2013, 83rd Leg., ch. 1352, §5, eff. Sept. 1, 2013.

Sections 221.005-221.010 reserved for expansion

SUBCHAPTER B. CREATION OF TIMESHARE REGIME

PROP §221.011. DECLARATION

(a) The developer of a timeshare plan any part of which is located in this state must record the timeshare instrument in this state. When a person expressly declares an intent to subject the property to a timeshare

plan through the recordation of a timeshare instrument that sets forth the information provided in Subsection (b), that property shall be established thenceforth as a timeshare plan.

(b) The declaration made in a timeshare instrument recorded under this section must include:

(1) a legal description of the timeshare property, including a ground plan indicating the location of each existing or proposed building included in the timeshare plan;

(2) a description of each existing or proposed accommodation, including the location and square footage of each unit and an interior floor plan of each existing or proposed building;

(3) a description of any amenities furnished or to be furnished to the purchaser;

(4) a statement of the fractional or percentage part that each timeshare interest bears to the entire timeshare plan;

(5) if applicable, a statement that the timeshare property is part of a multisite timeshare plan;

(6) any additional provisions that are consistent with this section; and

(7) the provisions required by Subchapter I to be included in a project instrument unless the provisions are included in one or more other project instruments.

(c) Any timeshare interest created under this section is subject to Section 1101.002(5), Occupations Code, but Sections 1101.351(a)(1) and (c), Occupations Code, do not apply to the acts of an exchange company in exchanging timeshare periods.

(d) Deleted by Acts 2005, 79th Leg., ch. 539, §3, eff. Jan. 15, 2006.

History of Prop. Code §221.011: Acts 1987, 70th Leg., ch. 167, §6.03, eff. Sept. 1, 1987. Renumbered from §201.011 by Acts 1989, 71st Leg., ch. 2, §13.03(b), eff. Aug. 28, 1989. Amended by Acts 1993, 73rd Leg., ch. 443, §2, eff. Sept. 1, 1993; Acts 2003, 78th Leg., ch. 1276, §14A.809, eff. Sept. 1, 2003; Acts 2005, 79th Leg., ch. 539, §2, eff. Jan. 15, 2006; Acts 2013, 83rd Leg., ch. 1352, §6, eff. Sept. 1, 2013. Source: TRCS art. 6573c, §3.

PROP §221.012. CONVEYANCE & ENCUMBRANCE

Once the property is established as a timeshare plan, each timeshare interest may be individually conveyed or encumbered and shall be entirely independent of all other timeshare interests in the same timeshare property. Any title or interest in a timeshare interest may be recorded.

History of Prop. Code §221.012: Acts 1987, 70th Leg., ch. 167, §6.03, eff. Sept. 1, 1987. Renumbered from §201.012 by Acts 1989, 71st Leg., ch. 2, §13.03(b), eff. Aug. 28, 1989. Amended by Acts 2005, 79th Leg., ch. 539, §3, eff. Jan. 15, 2006. Source: TRCS art. 6573c, §4.

PROP §221.013. COMMON OWNERSHIP

(a) Any timeshare interest may be jointly or commonly owned by more than one person.

(b) A timeshare estate may be jointly or commonly owned in the same manner as any other real property interest in this state.

History of Prop. Code §221.013: Acts 1987, 70th Leg., ch. 167, §6.03, eff. Sept. 1, 1987. Renumbered from §201.013 by Acts 1989, 71st Leg., ch. 2, §13.03(b) eff. Aug. 28, 1989. Amended by Acts 2005, 79th Leg., ch. 539, §3, eff. Jan. 15, 2006. Source: TRCS art. 6573c, §5.

PROP §221.014. PARTITION

An action for partition of a timeshare interest may not be maintained during the term of a timeshare plan.

History of Prop. Code §221.014: Acts 1987, 70th Leg., ch. 167, §6.03, eff. Sept. 1, 1987. Renumbered from §201.014 by Acts 1989, 71st Leg., ch. 2, §13.03(b), eff. Aug. 28, 1989. Amended by Acts 2005, 79th Leg., ch. 539, §3, eff. Jan. 15, 2006. Source: TRCS art. 6573c, §14.

Sections 221.015-221.020 reserved for expansion

SUBCHAPTER C. REGISTRATION

PROP §221.021. REGISTRATION REQUIRED

(a) Except as provided by Subsection (b) or (d) of this section or another provision of this chapter, a person may not offer or dispose of a timeshare interest unless the timeshare plan is registered with the commission.

(b) Before a registration application for a timeshare plan is submitted or completed, a developer or any person acting on the developer's behalf may accept a reservation and a deposit from a prospective purchaser if the deposit is placed in a segregated escrow account with an independent escrow agent and if the deposit is fully refundable at any time at the request of the purchaser. The deposit may not be forfeited unless the purchaser affirmatively creates a binding obligation by a subsequent written instrument.

(c) A developer or any person acting on the developer's behalf may not offer or dispose of a timeshare interest during any period within which there is in effect an order by the commission or by any court of competent jurisdiction revoking or suspending the registration of the timeshare plan of which such timeshare interest is a part.

(d) At the developer's request, the commission may authorize the developer to conduct presales before a timeshare plan is registered if the registration application is administratively complete, as determined by the commission or as established by commission rule.

The authorization for presales permits the developer to offer and dispose of timeshare interests during the period the application is in process. To obtain a presales authorization, the developer must:

(1) submit a written request to the commission for an authorization to conduct presales;

(2) submit an administratively complete application for registration, including appropriate fees and exhibits required by the commission; and

(3) provide evidence acceptable to the commission that all funds received by the developer will be placed with an escrow agent with instructions requiring the funds to be retained until a registration application is complete as determined by the commission.

(e) During the presales authorization period, the developer must:

(1) provide to each purchaser and prospective purchaser a copy of the proposed timeshare disclosure statement that the developer submitted to the commission with the initial registration application; and

(2) offer each purchaser the opportunity to cancel the purchase contract as provided by Section 221.041.

(f) After the final timeshare disclosure statement is approved by the commission, the developer must:

(1) give each purchaser and prospective purchaser a copy of the final timeshare disclosure statement; and

(2) if the commission determines that a materially adverse change exists between the disclosures contained in the proposed timeshare disclosure statement and the final timeshare disclosure statement, provide the purchaser a second opportunity to cancel the purchase contract as provided by Section 221.041.

(g) The requirements of this subchapter remain in effect during the period the developer offers or disposes of timeshare interests of the timeshare plan registered with the commission. The developer must notify the commission in writing when all of the timeshare interests of a timeshare plan have been disposed of.

History of Prop. Code §221.021: Acts 1987, 70th Leg., ch. 167, §6.03, eff. Sept. 1, 1987. Renumbered from §201.021 by Acts 1989, 71st Leg., ch. 2, §13.03(b), eff. Aug. 28, 1989. Amended by Acts 2005, 79th Leg., ch. 539, §4, eff. Jan. 15, 2006. Source: TRCS art. 6573c, §6(a).

PROP §221.022. APPLICATION FOR REGISTRATION

(a) An application for registration filed under this section must include a timeshare disclosure statement and any required exchange disclosure statement required by Section 221.033, recorded copies of all timeshare instruments, and other information as may be required by the commission. If the timeshare property is a newly developed property, recorded copies of the timeshare instruments must be provided promptly after recorded copies are available from the entity with which the instruments are recorded. If existing or proposed accommodations are in a condominium, an applicant who complies with this section is not required to prepare or deliver a condominium information statement or a resale certificate as described by Chapter 82.

(b) If existing or proposed accommodations are in a condominium or similar development, the application for registration must contain the project instruments of that development and affirmatively indicate that the creation and disposition of timeshare interests are not prohibited by those instruments. If the project instruments do not expressly authorize the creation and disposition of timeshare interests, the application must contain evidence that existing owners of the condominium development were provided written notice, at least 60 days before the application for registration, that timeshare interests would be created and sold. If the project instruments prohibit the creation or disposition of timeshare interests, the application must contain a certification by the authorized representative of all existing owners that the project instruments have been properly amended to permit that creation and disposition.

(c) The commission may accept an abbreviated registration application from a developer of a timeshare plan for any accommodations in the plan located outside this state. The developer must file written notice of the intent to register under this section not later than the 15th day before the date the abbreviated application is submitted.

(d) A developer of a timeshare plan with any accommodation located in this state may not file an abbreviated application unless:

(1) the developer is a:

(A) successor in interest after a merger or acquisition; or

(B) joint venture in which the previous developer or its affiliate is a partner or a member; and

(2) the previous developer registered the timeshare plan in this state preceding the merger, acquisition, or joint venture.

(e) A developer filing an abbreviated application must provide:

(1) the legal name and any assumed names and the principal office location, mailing address, telephone number, and primary contact person of the developer;

(2) the name, location, mailing address, telephone number, and primary contact person of the timeshare plan;

(3) the name and address of the developer's authorized or registered agent for service of process in this state;

(4) the name, primary office location, mailing address, and telephone number of the managing entity of the timeshare plan;

(5) the certificate or other evidence of registration from any jurisdiction in which the timeshare plan is approved or accepted;

(6) the certificate or other evidence of registration from the appropriate regulatory agency of any other jurisdiction in the United States in which some or all of the accommodations are located;

(7) a declaration stating whether the timeshare plan is a single-site timeshare plan or a multisite timeshare plan;

(8) if the plan is a multisite timeshare plan, a declaration stating whether the plan consists of specific timeshare interests or nonspecific timeshare interests;

(9) a disclosure of each jurisdiction in which the developer has applied for registration of the timeshare plan and whether the timeshare plan, the developer, or the managing entity used were denied registration or, during the five-year period before the registration application date, were the subject of a final adverse disposition in a disciplinary proceeding;

(10) if requested by the commission, copies of any disclosure documents required to be provided to purchasers or filed with any jurisdiction that approved or accepted the timeshare plan;

(11) the appropriate filing fee; and

(12) any other information reasonably requested by the commission or required by commission rule.

(f) A foreign jurisdiction providing evidence of registration as provided by Subsection (e)(6) must have registration and disclosure requirements that are substantially similar to or stricter than the requirements of this chapter.

(g) The commission shall investigate all matters relating to the application and may in its discretion require a personal inspection of the proposed timeshare property by any persons designated by it. All direct expenses incurred by the commission in inspecting the property shall be borne by the applicant. The commission may require the applicant to pay an advance deposit sufficient to cover those expenses.

History of Prop. Code §221.022: Acts 1987, 70th Leg., ch. 167, §6.03, eff. Sept. 1, 1987. Renumbered from §201.022 by Acts 1989, 71st Leg., ch. 2, §13.03(b), eff. Aug. 28, 1989. Amended by Acts 2005, 79th Leg., ch. 539, §4, eff. Jan. 15, 2006; Acts 2009, 81st Leg., ch. 279, §1, eff. Sept. 1, 2009. Source: TRCS art. 6573c, §6(b), (d), (e).

PROP §221.023. AMENDMENT OF REGISTRATION

The developer shall file amendments to the registration reporting to the commission any materially adverse change in any document contained in the registration not later than the 30th day after the date the developer knows or reasonably should know of the change. The developer may continue to offer and dispose of timeshare interests under the existing registration pending review of the amendments by the commission if the materially adverse change is disclosed to prospective purchasers.

History of Prop. Code §221.023: Acts 1987, 70th Leg., ch. 167, §6.03, eff. Sept. 1, 1987. Renumbered from §201.023 by Acts 1989, 71st Leg., ch. 2, §13.03(b), eff. Aug. 28, 1989. Amended by Acts 2005, 79th Leg., ch. 539, §4, eff. Jan. 15, 2006. Source: TRCS art. 6573c, §6(c).

PROP §221.024. POWERS OF COMMISSION

(a) The commission may prescribe and publish forms and adopt rules necessary to carry out the provisions of this chapter and may suspend or revoke the registration of any developer, place on probation the registration of a developer that has been suspended or revoked, reprimand a developer, impose an administrative penalty of not more than $10,000, or take any other disciplinary action authorized by this chapter if, after notice and hearing, the commission determines that a developer has materially violated this chapter, the Deceptive Trade Practices-Consumer Protection Act (Subchapter E, Chapter 17, Business & Commerce Code), or the Contest and Gift Giveaway Act (Chapter 621, Business & Commerce Code).

(b) The commission:

(1) shall authorize the State Office of Administrative Hearings to conduct hearings in contested cases; and

(2) may establish reasonable fees for forms and documents it provides to the public and for the filing or registration of documents required by this chapter.

(c) If the commission initiates a disciplinary proceeding under this chapter, the person is entitled to a hearing before the State Office of Administrative Hearings. The commission by rule shall adopt procedures to permit an appeal to the commission from a determination made by the State Office of Administrative Hearings in a disciplinary action.

(d) The commission shall set the time and place of the hearing.

(e) A disciplinary procedure under this chapter is governed by the contested case procedures of Chapter 2001, Government Code.

(f) The commission may file a suit in a district court of Travis County to prevent a violation of this chapter or for any other appropriate relief.

(g) Judicial review of a commission order imposing an administrative penalty is:

(1) instituted by filing a petition as provided by Subchapter G, Chapter 2001, Government Code; and

(2) by trial de novo.

History of Prop. Code §221.024: Acts 1987, 70th Leg., ch. 167, §6.03, eff. Sept. 1, 1987. Renumbered from §201.024 by Acts 1989, 71st Leg., ch. 2, §13.03(b), eff. Aug. 28, 1989. Amended by Acts 1989, 71st Leg., ch. 381, §1, eff. June 14, 1989; Acts 1999, 76th Leg., ch. 62, §7.87, eff. Sept. 1, 1999; Acts 2005, 79th Leg., ch. 539, §4, eff. Jan. 15, 2006; Acts 2007, 80th Leg., ch. 885, §2.34, eff. Apr. 1, 2009; Acts 2009, 81st Leg., ch. 23, §8, eff. May 12, 2009. Source: TRCS art. 6573c, §6(f), (g).

PROP §221.025. EFFECT OF REGISTRATION ON OTHER LAWS: EXEMPTION FROM CERTAIN LAWS

(a) A developer's compliance with this chapter exempts the developer's offer and disposition of timeshare interests subject to this chapter from securities and dealer registration under The Securities Act (Article 581-1 et seq., Vernon's Texas Civil Statutes).

(b) A timeshare plan created as a condominium regime before January 1, 1994, that complies with this chapter is exempt from the requirements of Section 81.112 relating to club membership.

(c) A timeshare plan subject to Chapter 82 that complies with this chapter is exempt from the requirements of:

(1) Section 82.0675 relating to club membership; and

(2) Sections 82.103(c)-(e) relating to declarant control.

(c-1) The exemption provided by Subsection (c)(2) applies to a timeshare plan created before September 1, 2013, and to the project instrument governing the timeshare property subject to the timeshare plan only if the developer and the association agree to the application of the exemption in writing and the project instrument is amended to provide for the application of the exemption. If the conditions provided by this subsection are not satisfied, a timeshare plan created before September 1, 2013, and the timeshare property subject to the timeshare plan are governed by any developer control provisions provided in the project instrument, notwithstanding any other law.

(d) A developer's compliance with this chapter as to any timeshare plan exempts any company, as defined by Chapter 181, Finance Code (Texas Trust Company Act), that holds title to the timeshare interests in the timeshare plan from compliance with the Texas Trust Company Act as to the company's activities relating to the holding of that title.

History of Prop. Code §221.025: Acts 1987, 70th Leg., ch. 167, §6.03, eff. Sept. 1, 1987. Renumbered from §201.025 by Acts 1989, 71st Leg., ch. 2, §13.03(b), eff. Aug. 28, 1989. Amended by Acts 2005, 79th Leg., ch. 539, §4, eff. Jan. 15, 2006; Acts 2013, 83rd Leg., ch. 1352, §7, eff. Sept. 1, 2013. Source: TRCS art. 6573c, §13.

PROP §221.026. ISSUANCE & RENEWAL OF REGISTRATION

(a) The commission by rule shall adopt requirements for the issuance and renewal of a developer's registration under this chapter, including:

(1) the form required for application for registration or a renewal of registration; and

(2) any supporting documentation required for registration or renewal of registration.

(b) The commission shall issue or renew a registration under this chapter for a period not to exceed 24 months.

(c) The commission may assess and collect a fee for the issuance or renewal of a registration under this chapter.

(d) The commission may assess and collect a late fee if the commission has not received the fee or any supporting documentation required before the 61st day after the date a registration is issued or renewed under this section.

(e) Failure to pay a renewal fee or late fee is a violation of this chapter.

History of Prop. Code §221.026: Acts 2005, 79th Leg., ch. 539, §4, eff. Jan. 15, 2006.

PROP §221.027. TEMPORARY SUSPENSION

(a) The presiding officer of the commission shall appoint a disciplinary panel consisting of three com-

mission members to determine whether the registration for a timeshare plan under this chapter should be temporarily suspended.

(b) If the disciplinary panel determines from the information presented to the panel that a timeshare plan registered under this chapter would, by the continued disposition of the timeshare property, constitute a continuing threat to the public welfare, the panel shall temporarily suspend the registration of the timeshare plan.

(c) A registration may be suspended under this section without notice or hearing on the complaint if:

(1) institution of proceedings for a hearing before the State Office of Administrative Hearings is initiated simultaneously with the temporary suspension; and

(2) a hearing is held under Chapter 2001, Government Code, and this chapter as soon as possible.

(d) Notwithstanding Chapter 551, Government Code, the disciplinary panel may hold a meeting by telephone conference call if immediate action is required and convening the panel at one location is inconvenient for any member of the panel.

History of Prop. Code §221.027: Acts 2007, 80th Leg., ch. 1411, §58, eff. Sept. 1, 2007. Amended by Acts 2009, 81st Leg., ch. 23, §9, eff. May 12, 2009.

Sections 221.028-221.030 reserved for expansion

SUBCHAPTER D. DISCLOSURE

PROP §221.031. ADVERTISEMENTS & PROMOTIONS

(a) At any time, the commission may request a developer to file for review by the commission any advertisement used in this state by the developer in connection with offering a timeshare interest. The developer shall provide the advertisement not later than the 15th day after the date the commission makes the request. If the commission determines that the advertisement violates this chapter or Chapter 621, Business & Commerce Code, the commission shall notify the developer in writing, stating the specific grounds for the commission's determination not later than the 15th day after the date the commission makes its determination. The commission may grant the developer provisional approval for the advertisement if the developer agrees to correct the deficiencies identified by the commission. A developer, on its own initiative, may submit any proposed advertisement to the commission for review and approval by the commission.

(b) Any advertisement that contains a promotion in connection with the offering of a timeshare interest must comply with Chapter 621, Business & Commerce Code.

(c) As provided by Subsections (d) and (e), an advertisement that contains a promotion in connection with the offering of a timeshare interest must include, in addition to any disclosures required under Chapter 621, Business & Commerce Code, the following:

(1) a statement to the effect that the promotion is intended to solicit purchasers of timeshare interests;

(2) if applicable, a statement to the effect that any person whose name is obtained during the promotion may be solicited to purchase a timeshare interest;

(3) the full name of the developer of the timeshare property; and

(4) if applicable, the full name and address of any marketing company involved in the promotion of the timeshare property, excluding the developer or an affiliate or subsidiary of the developer.

(d) An advertisement containing the disclosures required by Chapter 621, Business & Commerce Code, and Subsection (c) must be provided in writing or electronically:

(1) at least once before a scheduled sales presentation; and

(2) in a reasonable period before the scheduled sales presentation to ensure that the recipient receives the disclosures before leaving to attend the sales presentation.

(e) The developer is not required to provide the disclosures required by this section in every advertisement or other written, oral, or electronic communication provided or made to a recipient before a scheduled sales presentation.

History of Prop. Code §221.031: Acts 1987, 70th Leg., ch. 167, §6.03, eff. Sept. 1, 1987. Renumbered from §201.031 by Acts 1989, 71st Leg., ch. 2, §13.03(b), eff. Aug. 28, 1989. Amended by Acts 1989, 71st Leg., ch. 381, §2, eff. June 14, 1989; Acts 2005, 79th Leg., ch. 539, §5, eff. Jan. 15, 2006; Acts 2007, 80th Leg., ch. 885, §2.35, eff. Apr. 1, 2009. Source: TRCS art. 6573c, §7(a).

PROP §221.032. TIMESHARE DISCLOSURE STATEMENT

(a) Before the signing of any agreement to acquire a timeshare interest, the developer shall provide a timeshare disclosure statement to the prospective purchaser and shall obtain from the purchaser a written acknowledgement of receipt of the timeshare disclosure statement.

(b) The timeshare disclosure statement for a single-site timeshare plan or a multisite timeshare plan that includes a specific timeshare interest must include:

(1) the type of timeshare plan offered and the name and address of:

(A) the developer; and

(B) the single site or specific site offered for the multisite timeshare plan;

(2) a description of the duration and operation of the timeshare plan;

(3) a description of the existing or proposed accommodations, including the type and number of timeshare interests in the accommodations expressed in periods of seven-day use availability or other time increment applicable to the timeshare plan. The description of each type of accommodation included in the timeshare plan shall be categorized by the number of bedrooms, the number of bathrooms, and sleeping capacity, and shall include a statement indicating whether the accommodation contains a full kitchen, which means a kitchen that has a minimum of a dishwasher, range, sink, oven, and refrigerator. If the accommodations are proposed or incomplete, a schedule for commencement, completion, and availability of the accommodations shall be provided;

(4) a description of any existing or proposed amenities of the timeshare plan and, if the amenities are proposed or incomplete, a schedule for commencement, completion, and availability of the amenities;

(5) the extent to which financial arrangements have been provided for the completion of all promised accommodations and amenities that are committed to be built;

(6) a description of the method and timing for performing maintenance of the accommodations;

(7) a statement indicating that, on an annual basis, the sum of the nights that purchasers are entitled to use the accommodations does not exceed the number of nights the accommodations are available for use by the purchasers;

(8) a description of the method by which purchasers' use of the accommodations is scheduled;

(9) a statement that an association exists or is expected to be created or that such an association does not exist and is not expected to be created and, if such an association exists or is reasonably contemplated, a description of its powers and responsibilities;

(10) relating to the single-site timeshare plan or the specific timeshare interest of a multisite timeshare plan, copies of the following documents, if applicable, including any amendments to the documents, unless separately provided to the purchaser simultaneously with the timeshare disclosure statement:

(A) the declaration;

(B) the association articles of incorporation;

(C) the association bylaws;

(D) the association rules; and

(E) any lease or contract, excluding the purchase contract and other loan documents required to be signed by the purchaser at closing;

(11) the name and principal address of the managing entity and a description of the procedures, if any, for altering the powers and responsibilities of the managing entity and for removing or replacing it;

(12) the current annual budget, if available, or the projected annual budget for the timeshare plan or timeshare properties managed by the same managing entity if assessments are deposited in a common account. The budget must include:

(A) a statement of the amount reserved or budgeted for repairs, replacements, and refurbishment;

(B) the projected common expense liability, if any, by category of expenditure for the timeshare plan or timeshare properties managed by the same managing entity; and

(C) the assumptions on which the operating budget is based;

(13) the projected assessments and a description of the method for calculating and apportioning those assessments among purchasers;

(14) any initial fee or special fee due from the purchaser at closing, together with a description of the purpose and method of calculating the fee;

(15) a description of any lien, defect, or encumbrance on or affecting title to the timeshare interest and, if applicable, a copy of each written warranty provided by the developer;

(16) a description of any bankruptcy that is pending or that has occurred within the past five years, pending civil or criminal suit, adjudication, or disciplinary actions material to the timeshare plan of which the developer has knowledge;

(17) a description of any financing offered by or available through the developer;

(18) any current or anticipated fees or charges to be paid by timeshare purchasers for the use of any accommodations or amenities related to the timeshare plan, and a statement that the fees or charges are subject to change;

(19) a description and amount of insurance coverage provided for the protection of the purchaser;

(20) the extent to which a timeshare interest may become subject to a tax lien or other lien arising out of claims against purchasers of different timeshare interests;

(21) a description of those matters required by Section 221.041;

(22) a statement disclosing any right of first refusal or other restraint on the transfer of all or any portion of a timeshare interest;

(23) a statement disclosing that any deposit made in connection with the purchase of a timeshare interest must be held by an escrow agent until expiration of any right to cancel the contract and that any deposit must be returned to the purchaser if the purchaser elects to exercise the right of cancellation; or, if the commission accepts from the developer a surety bond, irrevocable letter of credit, or other form of financial assurance instead of an escrow deposit, a statement disclosing that the developer has provided a surety bond, irrevocable letter of credit, or other form of financial assurance in an amount equal to or in excess of the funds that would otherwise be held by an escrow agent and that the deposit must be returned if the purchaser elects to exercise the right of cancellation;

(24) if applicable, a statement that the assessments collected from the purchasers may be placed in a common account with the assessments collected from the purchasers of other timeshare properties managed by the same managing entity;

(25) if the timeshare plan provides purchasers with the opportunity to participate in an exchange program, a description of the name and address of the exchange company and the method by which a purchaser accesses the exchange program; and

(26) any other information the commission determines is necessary to protect prospective purchasers or to implement the purpose of this chapter.

(c) A developer who offers a specific timeshare interest in a multisite timeshare plan also must fully disclose the following information in written, graphic, or tabular form:

(1) a description of each component site, including the name and address of each component site;

(2) a description of each type of accommodation in each component site, categorized by the number of bedrooms, the number of bathrooms, and sleeping capacity, and a statement indicating whether the accommodation contains a full kitchen, which means a kitchen that has a minimum of a dishwasher, range, sink, oven, and refrigerator;

(3) a description of the amenities at each component site available for use by the purchasers;

(4) a description of the reservation system, which must include:

(A) the entity responsible for operating the reservation system, its relationship to the developer, and the duration of any agreement for operation of the reservation system;

(B) a summary or the rules governing access to and use of the reservation system; and

(C) the existence of and explanation regarding any priority reservation features that affect a purchaser's ability to make reservations for the use of a given accommodation on a first-come, first-served basis;

(5) the name and principal address of the managing entity for the multisite timeshare plan and a description of the procedures, if any, for altering the powers and responsibilities of the managing entity and for removing or replacing it;

(6) a description of any right to make additions to, substitutions in, or deletions from accommodations, amenities, or component sites, and a description of the basis on which accommodations, amenities, or component sites may be added to, substituted in, or deleted from the multisite timeshare plan;

(7) a description of the purchaser's liability for any fees associated with the multisite timeshare plan;

(8) the location of each component site of the multisite timeshare plan, the historical occupancy of each component site for the prior 12-month period, if the component site was part of the multisite timeshare plan during such 12-month time period, as well as any periodic adjustment or amendment to the reservation system that may be needed in order to respond to actual purchaser use patterns and changes in purchaser use demand for the accommodations existing at the time within the multisite timeshare plan; and

(9) any other information the commission determines is necessary to protect prospective purchasers or to implement the purpose of this chapter.

(d) A developer who offers a nonspecific timeshare interest in a multisite timeshare plan must disclose the following information in written, graphic, or tabular form:

(1) the name and address of the developer;

(2) a description of the type of interest and the usage rights the purchaser will receive;

(3) a description of the duration and operation of the timeshare plan;

(4) a description of the type of insurance coverage provided for each component site;

(5) an explanation of who holds title to the accommodations of each component site;

(6) a description of each component site, including the name and address of each component site;

(7) a description of the existing or proposed accommodations, expressed in periods of seven-day use availability or any other time increment applicable to the timeshare plan. The description of each type of accommodation included in the timeshare plan shall be categorized by the number of bedrooms, the number of bathrooms, and sleeping capacity, and shall include a statement indicating whether the accommodation contains a full kitchen, which means a kitchen that has a minimum of a dishwasher, range, sink, oven, and refrigerator. If the accommodations are proposed or incomplete, a schedule for commencement, completion, and availability of the accommodations shall be provided;

(8) a statement that an association exists or is expected to be created or that such an association does not exist and is not expected to be created and, if such an association exists or is reasonably contemplated, a description of its powers and responsibilities;

(9) if applicable, copies of the following documents applicable to the multisite timeshare plan, including any amendments to the documents, unless separately provided to the purchaser simultaneously with the timeshare disclosure statement:

(A) the declaration;

(B) the association articles of incorporation;

(C) the association bylaws;

(D) the association rules; and

(E) any lease or contract, excluding the purchase contract and other loan documents required to be signed by the purchaser at closing;

(10) a description of the method and timing for performing maintenance of the accommodations;

(11) a statement indicating that, on an annual basis, the sum of the nights that purchasers are entitled to use the accommodations does not exceed the number of nights the accommodations are available for use by the purchasers;

(12) a description of each type of accommodation included in the timeshare plan, categorized by the number of bedrooms, the number of bathrooms, and sleeping capacity, and a statement indicating whether the accommodation contains a full kitchen, which means a kitchen that has a minimum of a dishwasher, range, sink, oven, and refrigerator;

(13) a description of amenities available for use by the purchaser at each component site;

(14) the location of each component site of the multisite timeshare plan, the historical occupancy of each component site for the prior 12-month period, if the component site was part of the multisite timeshare plan during such 12-month time period, as well as any periodic adjustment or amendment to the reservation system that may be needed in order to respond to actual purchaser use patterns and changes in purchaser use demand for the accommodations existing at the time within the multisite timeshare plan;

(15) a description of the right to make any additions, substitutions, or deletions of accommodations, amenities, or component sites, and a description of the basis upon which accommodations, amenities, or component sites may be added to, substituted in, or deleted from the multisite timeshare plan;

(16) a description of the reservation system that shall include all of the following:

(A) the entity responsible for operating the reservation system, its relationship to the developer, and the duration of any agreement for operation of the reservation system;

(B) a summary of the rules governing access to and use of the reservation system; and

(C) the existence of and an explanation regarding any priority reservation features that affect a purchaser's ability to make reservations for the use of a given accommodation on a first-come, first-served basis;

(17) the name and principal address of the managing entity for the multisite timeshare plan and a description of the procedures, if any, for altering the powers and responsibilities of the managing entity and for removing or replacing it, and a description of the relationship between the multisite timeshare plan managing entity and the managing entity of the component sites of the multisite timeshare plan, if different from the multisite timeshare plan managing entity;

(18) the current annual budget of the multisite timeshare plan, if available, or the projected annual budget for the multisite timeshare plan, which must include:

(A) a statement of the amount reserved or budgeted for repairs, replacements, and refurbishment;

(B) the projected common expense liability, if any, by category of expenditure for the multisite timeshare plan; and

(C) the assumptions on which the operating budget is based;

(19) the projected assessments and a description of the method for calculating and apportioning those assessments among purchasers of the multisite timeshare plan;

(20) if applicable, a statement that the assessments collected from the purchasers may be placed in a common account with the assessments collected from the purchasers of other timeshare properties managed by the same managing entity;

(21) any current fees or charges to be paid by timeshare purchasers for the use of any amenities related to the timeshare plan and a statement that the fees or charges are subject to change;

(22) any initial or special fee due from the purchaser at closing, together with a description of the purpose of and method of calculating the fee;

(23) a description of the purchaser's liability for any fees associated with the multisite timeshare plan;

(24) a description of any lien, defect, or encumbrance on or affecting title to the timeshare interest and, if applicable, a copy of each written warranty provided by the developer;

(25) the extent to which a timeshare interest may become subject to a tax lien or other lien arising out of claims against purchasers of different timeshare interests;

(26) a description of those matters required by Section 221.041;

(27) a description of any financing offered by or available through the developer;

(28) a description of any bankruptcy that is pending or that has occurred within the past five years, pending civil or criminal suits, adjudications, or disciplinary actions material to the timeshare plan of which the developer has knowledge;

(29) a statement disclosing any right of first refusal or other restraint on the transfer of all or a portion of a timeshare interest;

(30) a statement disclosing that any deposit made in connection with the purchase of a timeshare interest must be held by an escrow agent until expiration of any right to cancel the contract and that any deposit must be returned to the purchaser if the purchaser elects to exercise the right of cancellation; or, if the commission accepts from the developer a surety bond, irrevocable letter of credit, or other form of financial assurance instead of an escrow deposit, a statement disclosing that the developer has provided a surety bond, irrevocable letter of credit, or other form of financial assurance in an amount equal to or in excess of the funds that would otherwise be held by an escrow agent and that the deposit must be returned if the purchaser elects to exercise the right of cancellation;

(31) if the timeshare plan provides purchasers with the opportunity to participate in an exchange program, a description of the name and address of the exchange company and the method by which a purchaser accesses the exchange program; and

(32) any other information the commission determines is necessary to protect prospective purchasers or to implement the purpose of this chapter.

(e) A developer may include any other information in a timeshare disclosure statement required by this section on approval by the commission.

(f) If a timeshare plan is located wholly outside this state, the commission may permit the developer to submit a timeshare disclosure statement the developer is currently providing purchasers or an equivalent timeshare disclosure statement filed for the timeshare plan in another state if the current statement or the equivalent statement substantially complies with the requirements of this subchapter. This subsection does not exempt the developer from other requirements of this chapter.

History of Prop. Code §221.032: Acts 1987, 70th Leg., ch. 167, §6.03, eff. Sept. 1, 1987. Renumbered from §201.032 by Acts 1989, 71st Leg., ch. 2, §13.03(b), eff. Aug. 28, 1989. Amended by Acts 1993, 73rd Leg., ch. 443, §3, eff. Sept. 1, 1993; Acts 2005, 79th Leg., ch. 539, §5, eff. Jan. 15, 2006; Acts 2009, 81st Leg., ch. 279, §2, eff. Sept. 1, 2009. Source: TRCS art. 6573c, §7(b).

PROP §221.033. EXCHANGE DISCLOSURE STATEMENT

(a) Before the signing of any agreement to purchase a timeshare interest in which a prospective purchaser is also offered participation in any exchange program, the developer shall also deliver to the prospective purchaser the exchange disclosure statement of any exchange company whose service is advertised or offered by the developer or other person in connection with the disposition.

(b) If participation in an exchange program is offered for the first time after a disposition has occurred, any person offering that participation shall also deliver an exchange disclosure statement to the purchaser before the execution by the purchaser of any instrument relating to participation in the exchange program.

(c) In all cases, the person offering participation in the exchange program shall obtain from the purchaser a written acknowledgement of receipt of the exchange disclosure statement.

(d) The exchange disclosure statement must include the following information:

(1) the name and address of the exchange company;

(2) if the exchange company is not the developer, a statement describing the legal relationship, if any, between the exchange company and the developer;

(3) a statement indicating the conditions under which the exchange program might terminate or become unavailable;

(4) whether membership or participation or both in the exchange program is voluntary or mandatory;

(5) a complete description of the required procedure for executing an exchange of timeshare periods;

(6) the fee required for membership or participation or both in the program and whether the fee is subject to change;

(7) a statement to the effect that participation in the exchange program is conditioned on compliance with the terms of a contract between the exchange company and the purchaser;

(8) a statement in conspicuous and bold-faced print to the effect that all exchanges are arranged on a space-available basis and that neither the developer nor the exchange company guarantees that a particular timeshare period can be exchanged; and

(9) a description of seasonal demand and unit occupancy restrictions employed in the exchange program.

History of Prop. Code §221.033: Acts 1987, 70th Leg., ch. 167, §6.03, eff. Sept. 1, 1987. Renumbered from §201.033 by Acts 1989, 71st Leg., ch. 2, §13.03(b), eff. Aug. 28, 1989. Amended by Acts 2005, 79th Leg., ch. 539, §6, eff. Jan. 15, 2006. Source: TRCS art. 6573c, §7(c).

PROP §221.034. EXEMPT OFFERINGS & DISPOSITIONS; COMMUNICATIONS

(a) An offering or disposition is exempt from this chapter if it is:

(1) a gratuitous offering or disposition of a timeshare interest;

(2) a disposition pursuant to a court order;

(3) a disposition by a governmental agency;

(4) a disposition by foreclosure or deed in lieu of foreclosure;

(5) an offering or disposition by an association of its own timeshare interest acquired through foreclosure, deed in lieu of foreclosure, or gratuitous transfer;

(6) an offering or disposition of all timeshare interests in a timeshare plan to not more than five persons;

(7) an offering or disposition of a timeshare interest in a timeshare property situated wholly outside this state under a contract executed wholly outside this state, if there has been no offering to the purchaser within this state;

(8) an offering or disposition of a timeshare interest to a purchaser who is not a resident of this state under a contract executed wholly outside this state, if there has been no offering to the purchaser within this state;

(9) the offering or redisposition of a timeshare interest by a purchaser who acquired the interest for the purchaser's personal use; or

(10) the offering or disposition of a rental of an accommodation for a period of three years or less.

(b) If a developer has a timeshare plan registered under this chapter and is subject to Section 221.024, the developer may offer or dispose of an interest in a timeshare plan that is not registered under this chapter to a person who is the owner of a timeshare interest in a timeshare plan created by the developer. A developer under this subsection is exempt from Sections 221.021,

221.022, 221.023, 221.032, 221.041, 221.042, 221.043, 221.061, 221.071(a)(1) and (8), 221.074, and 221.075 if the developer:

(1) permits the purchaser to cancel the purchase contract before the sixth day after the date the contract is signed; and

(2) provides the purchaser all timeshare disclosure documents required by law to be provided in the jurisdiction in which the timeshare property is located.

(c) The following communications are not advertisements under this chapter:

(1) any stockholder communication, including an annual report or interim financial report, proxy material, registration statement, securities prospectus, timeshare disclosure statement, or other material required to be delivered to a prospective purchaser by a state or federal governmental entity;

(2) any oral or written statement disseminated by a developer to broadcast or print media, excluding:

(A) paid advertising or promotional material relating to plans for acquiring or developing timeshare property; and

(B) the rebroadcast or other dissemination of any oral statements by a developer to a prospective purchaser or the distribution or other dissemination of written statements, including newspaper or magazine articles or press releases, by a developer to prospective purchasers;

(3) the offering of a timeshare interest in a national publication or by electronic media that is not directed to or targeted at any individual located in this state;

(4) any audio, written, or visual publication or material relating to the availability of any accommodations for transient rental if:

(A) a sales presentation is not a term or condition of the availability of the accommodations; and

(B) the failure of the transient renter to take a tour of the timeshare property or attend a sales presentation does not result in a reduction in the level of services or an increase in the rental price that would otherwise be available to the renter; or

(5) any follow-up communication with a person relating to a promotion if the person previously received an advertisement relating to the promotion that complied with Section 221.031.

(d) The following communications are exempt from this chapter if they are delivered to a person who has previously executed a contract for the purchase of or is an owner of a timeshare interest in a timeshare plan:

(1) any communication addressed to and relating to the account of the person; or

(2) any audio, written, or visual publication or material relating to an exchange company or program if the person is a member of that exchange company or program.

History of Prop. Code §221.034: Acts 1987, 70th Leg., ch. 167, §6.03, eff. Sept. 1, 1987. Renumbered from §201.034 by Acts 1989, 71st Leg., ch. 2, §13.03(b), eff. Aug. 28, 1989. Amended by Acts 2005, 79th Leg., ch. 539, §7, eff. Jan. 15, 2006. Source: TRCS art. 6573c, §7(d).

PROP §221.035. SUPERVISORY DUTIES OF DEVELOPER

Notwithstanding obligations placed upon any other persons by this chapter, the developer shall supervise, manage, and control all aspects of the offering of a timeshare interest, including but not limited to promotion, advertising, contracting, and closing. Any violation of this chapter which occurs during such offering activities is considered to be a violation by the developer as well as by the person actually committing the violation.

History of Prop. Code §221.035: Acts 1989, 71st Leg., ch. 381, §3, eff. June 14, 1989.

PROP §221.036. DEVELOPER PREPARATION & COMPLETION OF DOCUMENTS

(a) A developer may charge a reasonable fee for completion of a contract form, closing document, or disclosure document required for the sale, exchange, option, lease, or rental of a timeshare interest.

(b) The action of a developer under Subsection (a) does not constitute the unauthorized or illegal practice of law in this state if the contract or document has been:

(1) accepted by the commission for use in the particular type of transaction involved; or

(2) prepared by an attorney licensed to practice law in this state for use in the particular type of transaction involved.

History of Prop. Code §221.036: Acts 2003, 78th Leg., ch. 1244, §1, eff. June 20, 2003.

PROP §221.037. ALTERNATIVE TERMINOLOGY OR NAME

(a) In providing the disclosures required by this chapter, the use of the terms "vacation ownership interest" or "vacation ownership plan" to refer to the

timeshare interest or plan offered by the developer, or the use of other terms that are substantially similar and that are regularly used by the developer to denote a timeshare interest or plan, is sufficient and complies with the requirements of this chapter.

(b) In providing the full name of a developer or a marketing company as required by this chapter, the disclosure of an assumed name of the developer or the marketing company, if the entity has complied with the requirements of the applicable assumed business names statutes or other laws regarding the use of the assumed name, is sufficient and complies with this chapter.

History of Prop. Code §221.037: Acts 2009, 81st Leg., ch. 279, §3, eff. Sept. 1, 2009.

Sections 221.038-221.040 reserved for expansion

SUBCHAPTER E. CANCELLATION OF PURCHASE CONTRACT

PROP §221.041. PURCHASER'S RIGHT TO CANCEL

(a) A purchaser may cancel a purchase contract before the sixth day after the date the purchaser signs and receives a copy of the purchase contract or receives the required timeshare disclosure statement, whichever is later.

(b) A purchaser may not waive the right of cancellation under this section. A contract containing a waiver is voidable by the purchaser.

(c) Deleted by Acts 2005, 79th Leg., ch. 539, §8, eff. Jan. 15, 2006.

History of Prop. Code §221.041: Acts 1987, 70th Leg., ch. 167, §6.03, eff. Sept. 1, 1987. Renumbered from §201.041 by Acts 1989, 71st Leg., ch. 2, §13.03(b), eff. Aug. 28, 1989. Amended by Acts 1989, 71st Leg., ch. 381, §4, eff. June 14, 1989; Acts 1993, 73rd Leg., ch. 443, §4, eff. Sept. 1, 1993; Acts 2005, 79th Leg., ch. 539, §8, eff. Jan. 15, 2006. Source: TRCS art. 6573c, §8(a).

PROP §221.042. NOTICE; REFUND

(a) If a purchaser elects to cancel a purchase contract under Section 221.041, the purchaser may do so by hand-delivering notice of cancellation to the developer, by mailing notice by prepaid United States mail to the developer or to the developer's agent for service of process, or by providing notice by overnight common carrier delivery service to the developer or the developer's agent for service of process.

(b) Cancellation is without penalty, and all payments made by the purchaser before cancellation must be refunded on or before the 30th day after the date on which the developer receives a timely notice of cancellation or on or before the fifth day after the date the developer receives good funds from the purchaser, whichever is later.

History of Prop. Code §221.042: Acts 1987, 70th Leg., ch. 167, §6.03, eff. Sept. 1, 1987. Renumbered from §201.042 by Acts 1989, 71st Leg., ch. 2, §13.03(b), eff. Aug. 28, 1989. Amended by Acts 2005, 79th Leg., ch. 539, §8, eff. Jan. 15, 2006. Source: TRCS art. 6573c, §8(b).

PROP §221.043. CONTRACT REQUIREMENTS

(a) Each purchase contract shall contain the following information. The statements required by this subsection and Subsection (c)(8) shall be provided in a conspicuous manner and in the exact language set forth in this section with the developer's name and address, the date of the last day of the fiscal year, and the address of the managing entity inserted where indicated:

"PURCHASER'S RIGHT TO CANCEL.

"(1) BY SIGNING THIS CONTRACT YOU ARE INCURRING AN OBLIGATION TO PURCHASE A TIMESHARE INTEREST. YOU MAY, HOWEVER, CANCEL THIS CONTRACT WITHOUT PENALTY OR OBLIGATION BEFORE THE SIXTH DAY AFTER THE DATE YOU SIGN AND RECEIVE A COPY OF THE PURCHASE CONTRACT, OR RECEIVE THE REQUIRED TIMESHARE DISCLOSURE STATEMENT, WHICHEVER IS LATER.

"(2) IF YOU DECIDE TO CANCEL THIS CONTRACT, YOU MAY DO SO BY EITHER HAND-DELIVERING NOTICE OF CANCELLATION TO THE DEVELOPER, BY MAILING NOTICE BY PREPAID UNITED STATES MAIL TO THE DEVELOPER OR THE DEVELOPER'S AGENT FOR SERVICE OF PROCESS, OR BY PROVIDING NOTICE BY OVERNIGHT COMMON CARRIER DELIVERY SERVICE TO THE DEVELOPER OR THE DEVELOPER'S AGENT FOR SERVICE OF PROCESS. YOUR NOTICE OF CANCELLATION IS EFFECTIVE ON THE DATE SENT OR DELIVERED TO (INSERT NAME OF DEVELOPER) AT (INSERT ADDRESS OF DEVELOPER). FOR YOUR PROTECTION, SHOULD YOU DECIDE TO CANCEL YOU SHOULD EITHER SEND YOUR NOTICE OF CANCELLATION BY CERTIFIED MAIL WITH A RETURN RECEIPT REQUESTED OR OBTAIN A SIGNED AND DATED RECEIPT IF DELIVERING IT IN PERSON OR BY OVERNIGHT COMMON CARRIER.

"(3) A PURCHASER SHOULD NOT RELY ON STATEMENTS OTHER THAN THOSE INCLUDED IN THIS CONTRACT AND THE DISCLOSURE STATEMENT."

(b) Immediately following the required statements in Subsection (a) shall be a space reserved for the signature of the purchaser.

(c) The purchase contract must also include the following:

(1) the name and address of the developer and the address of the timeshare property or the address of any available timeshare interest being offered;

(2) an agreement describing the cancellation policy prescribed by Section 221.041;

(3) the name of the person or persons primarily involved in the sales presentation on behalf of the developer;

(4) a statement disclosing the amount of the periodic assessments currently assessed against or collected from the purchasers of the timeshare interest, immediately followed by a statement providing that collected assessments will be used by the managing entity to pay for expenditures, charges, reserves, or liabilities relating to the operation of the timeshare plan or timeshare properties managed by the managing entity;

(5) the date the purchaser signs the contract; and

(6) the following statement:

"AS A TIMESHARE OWNER, YOU HAVE A RIGHT TO REQUEST A WRITTEN ANNUAL TIMESHARE FEE AND EXPENSE STATEMENT. THIS STATEMENT IS PREPARED ANNUALLY BY THE MANAGING ENTITY AND WILL BE AVAILABLE NOT LATER THAN FIVE MONTHS AFTER (INSERT THE DATE OF THE LAST DAY OF THE FISCAL YEAR). YOU MAY REQUEST THE STATEMENT BY WRITING TO (INSERT NAME AND ADDRESS OF THE MANAGING ENTITY)."

(d) The information required to be provided by this section may be provided in the purchase contract or in an exhibit to the purchase contract, or it may be provided in part in both if all of the information is provided.

History of Prop. Code §221.043: Acts 1987, 70th Leg., ch. 167, §6.03, eff. Sept. 1, 1987. Renumbered from §201.043 by Acts 1989, 71st Leg., ch. 2, §13.03(b), eff. Aug. 28, 1989. Amended by Acts 1989, 71st Leg., ch. 381, §5, eff. June 14, 1989; Acts 1993, 73rd Leg., ch. 443, §5, eff. Sept. 1, 1993; Acts 2005, 79th Leg., ch. 539, §8, eff. Jan. 15, 2006; Acts 2009, 81st Leg., ch. 279, §4, eff. Sept. 1, 2009. Source: TRCS art. 6573c, §8(c), (d).

Sections 221.044-221.050 reserved for expansion

SUBCHAPTER F. EXCHANGE PROGRAM

PROP §221.051. OPERATION REQUIREMENT

An exchange company shall employ seasonal demand and unit occupancy restrictions in the operation of its exchange program.

History of Prop. Code §221.051: Acts 1987, 70th Leg., ch. 167, §6.03, eff. Sept. 1, 1987. Renumbered from §201.051 by Acts 1989, 71st Leg., ch. 2, §13.03(b), eff. Aug. 28, 1989. Source: TRCS art. 6573c, §9(a).

PROP §221.052. LIABILITY OF DEVELOPER & EXCHANGE COMPANY

(a) A developer does not incur any liability arising out of the use, delivery, or publication to a purchaser of written information or audio-visual materials provided to it by the exchange company in accordance with Subchapter D, unless the developer knows or has reason to know that the materials are inaccurate or false.

(b) No exchange company shall have any liability with respect to any violation under this chapter arising out of the use by a developer of information relating to an exchange program other than that provided to the developer by the exchange company.

(c) An exchange company that denies exchange privileges to an owner whose use of accommodations in the owner's timeshare plan is denied is not liable to any member of the exchange company or exchange program or any third party because of the denial of the owner's exchange privileges.

History of Prop. Code §221.052: Acts 1987, 70th Leg., ch. 167, §6.03, eff. Sept. 1, 1987. Renumbered from §201.052 by Acts 1989, 71st Leg., ch. 2, §13.03(b), eff. Aug. 28, 1989. Amended by Acts 2005, 79th Leg., ch. 539, §9, eff. Jan. 15, 2006. Source: TRCS art. 6573c, §9(b).

PROP §221.053. EXCHANGE COMPANY LIABILITY

Except for written information or audio-visual materials provided to a developer by an exchange company, an exchange company does not incur liability as a result of:

(1) a representation made by a developer that relates to any exchange program or exchange company; or

(2) the use, delivery, or publication by a developer of information that relates to an exchange program or exchange company.

History of Prop. Code §221.053: Acts 1987, 70th Leg., ch. 167, §6.03, eff. Sept. 1, 1987. Renumbered from §201.053 by Acts 1989, 71st Leg., ch. 2, §13.03(b), eff. Aug. 28, 1989. Source: TRCS art. 6573c, §9(c).

Sections 221.054-221.060 reserved for expansion

SUBCHAPTER G. ESCROW DEPOSITS

PROP §221.061. ESCROW OR TRUST ACCOUNT REQUIRED

(a) A developer or escrow agent of a timeshare plan shall deposit in an escrow or trust account in a federally insured depository 100 percent of all funds received during the purchaser's cancellation period.

(b) An escrow agent owes the purchaser a fiduciary duty.

(c) The escrow agent and the developer shall execute an agreement that includes a statement providing that:

(1) funds may be disbursed to the developer from the escrow or trust account by the agent only:

(A) after the purchaser's cancellation period has expired; and

(B) as provided by the purchase contract, subject to this subchapter; and

(2) if the purchaser cancels the purchase contract as provided by the contract, the funds must be paid to:

(A) the purchaser; or

(B) the developer if the purchaser's funds have been refunded previously by the developer.

(d) If a developer contracts to sell a timeshare interest and the construction of the building in which the timeshare interest is located has not been completed when the cancellation period expires, the developer shall continue to maintain all funds received from the purchaser under the purchase agreement in the escrow or trust account until construction of the building is completed. The documentation required for evidence of completion of construction includes:

(1) a certificate of occupancy;

(2) a certificate of substantial completion;

(3) evidence of a public safety inspection equivalent to Subdivision (1) or (2) from a government agency in the applicable jurisdiction; or

(4) any other evidence acceptable to the commission.

History of Prop. Code §221.061: Acts 1987, 70th Leg., ch. 167, §6.03, eff. Sept. 1, 1987. Renumbered from §201.061 by Acts 1989, 71st Leg., ch. 2, §13.03(b), eff. Aug. 28, 1989. Amended by Acts 2005, 79th Leg., ch. 539, §10, eff. Jan. 15, 2006. Source: TRCS art. 6573c, §10(a).

PROP §221.062. RELEASE OF ESCROW

(a) The funds or property constituting the escrow or trust deposit may be released from escrow only in accordance with this section.

(b) If the purchaser cancels the purchase contract as provided by the contract, the funds shall be paid to:

(1) the purchaser; or

(2) the developer if the purchaser's funds have been refunded previously by the developer.

(c) If the purchaser defaults in the performance of obligations under the terms of the purchase contract, the funds shall be paid to the developer.

(d) If the developer defaults in the performance of obligations under the purchase contract, the funds shall be paid to the purchaser.

(e) If the funds of the purchaser have not been disbursed previously as provided by Subsections (a)-(d), the funds may be disbursed to the developer by the escrow or trust agent if acceptable evidence of completion of construction is provided.

(f) If there is a dispute relating to the funds in the escrow or trust account, the agent shall maintain the funds in the account until:

(1) the agent receives written directions agreed to and signed by all parties; or

(2) a civil action relating to the disputed funds is filed.

(g) If a civil action is filed under Subsection (f)(2), the escrow or trust account agent shall deposit the funds with the court in which the action is filed.

(h) Excluding any encumbrance placed against the purchaser's timeshare interest that secures the purchaser's payment of purchase money financing for the purchase, the developer is not entitled to the release of any funds escrowed with respect to each timeshare interest until the developer has provided the commission with satisfactory evidence that:

(1) the timeshare interest and any other property or rights to property appurtenant to the timeshare interest, including any amenities represented to the purchaser as being part of the timeshare plan, are free and clear of any of the claims of the developer, any owner of the underlying fee, a mortgagee, judgment creditor, or other lienor, or any other person having an interest in or lien or encumbrance against the timeshare interest or appurtenant property or property rights;

(2) the developer, any owner of the underlying fee, a mortgagee, judgment creditor, or other lienor, or any other person having an interest in or lien or encumbrance against the timeshare interest or appurtenant property or property rights, including any amenities represented to the purchaser as being part of the timeshare plan, has recorded a subordination and notice to creditors document in the jurisdiction in which the timeshare interest is located that expressly and effectively provides that the interest holder's right, lien, or encumbrance does not adversely affect and is subordinate to the rights of the owners of the timeshare interests in the timeshare plan, regardless of the date of purchase, on and after the effective date of the subordination document;

(3) the developer, any owner of the underlying fee, a mortgagee, judgment creditor, or other lienor, or any

other person having an interest in or lien or encumbrance against the timeshare interest or appurtenant property or property rights, including any amenities represented to the purchaser as being part of the timeshare plan, has transferred the subject accommodations or amenities or all use rights therein to a nonprofit organization or an owners' association to be held for the use and benefit of the purchasers of the timeshare plan, which entity shall act as a fiduciary to the purchasers, provided that the developer has transferred control of that entity to the purchasers or does not exercise its voting rights in that entity with respect to the subject accommodations or amenities and, prior to the transfer, any lien or other encumbrance against the accommodation or facility is subject to a subordination and notice to creditors instrument pursuant to this subsection; or

(4) alternative arrangements have been made that are adequate to protect the rights of the purchasers of the timeshare interests and are approved by the commission.

History of Prop. Code §221.062: Acts 1987, 70th Leg., ch. 167, §6.03, eff. Sept. 1, 1987. Renumbered from §201.063 by Acts 1989, 71st Leg., ch. 2, §13.03(b), eff. Aug. 28, 1989. Renumbered from §221.063 and amended by Acts 2005, 79th Leg., ch. 539, §10, eff. Jan. 15, 2006. Amended by Acts 2009, 81st Leg., ch. 279, §5, eff. Sept. 1, 2009. Source: TRCS art. 6573c, §10(b).

PROP §221.063. ALTERNATIVE TO ESCROW OR TRUST ACCOUNT: FINANCIAL ASSURANCE

(a) Instead of the deposit of funds in an escrow or trust account as provided by Section 221.061, the commission may accept from the developer a surety bond, irrevocable letter of credit, or other form of financial assurance, including financial assurance posted in another state or jurisdiction.

(b) The amount of the financial assurance provided under this section must be an amount equal to or more than the amount of funds that would otherwise be placed in an escrow or trust account under Section 221.061(a).

(c) The amount of the financial assurance provided under this section for timeshare property under construction as provided by Section 221.061(d) must be the lesser of:

(1) an amount equal to or more than the amount of funds that would otherwise be placed in an escrow or trust account under that subsection; or

(2) the amount necessary to assure completion of the building in which the timeshare interest is located.

History of Prop. Code §221.063: Acts 2005, 79th Leg., ch. 539, §10, eff. Jan. 15, 2006.

History of Former Prop. Code §221.063: Acts 1987, 70th Leg., ch. 167, §6.03, eff. Sept. 1, 1987. Renumbered from §201.063 by Acts 1989, 71st Leg., ch. 2, §13.03(b), eff. Aug. 28, 1989. Renumbered as §221.062 by Acts 2005, 79th Leg., ch. 539, §10, eff. Jan. 15, 2006. Source: TRCS art. 6573c, §10(b).

PROP §221.064. DOCUMENTATION REQUIRED

The escrow or trust account agent or developer shall make documents related to the escrow or trust account or the financial assurance provided available to the commission at the commission's request.

History of Prop. Code §221.064: Acts 2005, 79th Leg., ch. 539, §10, eff. Jan. 15, 2006.

Sections 221.065-221.070 reserved for expansion

SUBCHAPTER H. MISCELLANEOUS PROVISIONS

PROP §221.071. DECEPTIVE TRADE PRACTICES

(a) A developer or other person commits a false, misleading, or deceptive act or practice within the meaning of Subsections (a) and (b) of Section 17.46 of the Texas Deceptive Trade Practices-Consumer Protection Act (Article 17.46 et seq., Business & Commerce Code), by engaging in any of the following acts:

(1) failing to disclose information concerning a timeshare interest required by Subchapter D;

(2) making false or misleading statements of fact concerning the characteristics of accommodations or amenities available to a consumer;

(3) predicting specific or immediate increases in the value of a timeshare interest without a reasonable basis for such predictions;

(4) making false or misleading statements of fact concerning the duration that accommodations or amenities will be available to a consumer;

(5) making false or misleading statements of fact concerning the conditions under which a purchaser of a timeshare interest may exchange the right to occupy a unit for the right to occupy a unit in the same or another timeshare property;

(6) representing that a prize, gift, or other benefit will be awarded in connection with a promotion with the intent not to award that prize, gift, or benefit in the manner represented;

(7) failing to provide a copy of the purchase contract to the purchaser at the time the contract is signed by the purchaser;

(8) failing to provide the annual statement as required by Section 221.074(a); or

(9) exceeding a one-to-one purchaser-to-accommodation ratio for a timeshare plan during a consecutive 12-month period, as determined under Subsection (c).

(b) The provisions of this section are not exclusive and are in addition to provisions provided for in any other law.

(c) A developer complies with the one-to-one purchaser-to-accommodation ratio referred to in Subsection (a)(9) if the total number of purchasers eligible to use the accommodations of the timeshare plan during a consecutive 12-month period never exceeds the total number of accommodations available for use in the timeshare plan during that same period. A purchaser-to-accommodation ratio is computed by dividing the number of purchasers eligible to use an accommodation in a timeshare plan on any given day by the number of accommodations within the plan available for use on that day. For purposes of computing the purchaser-to-accommodation ratio:

(1) each purchaser is counted at least once each consecutive 12-month period;

(2) each accommodation is counted not more than 365 times each consecutive 12-month period, excluding a leap year, in which each accommodation may be counted 366 times; and

(3) a purchaser who is delinquent in paying timeshare assessments is considered eligible to use timeshare plan accommodations.

(d) If a developer has substantially complied with this chapter in good faith, a nonmaterial error or omission is not actionable. Any nonmaterial error or omission is not sufficient to permit a purchaser to cancel a purchase contract after the period provided for cancellation expires under this chapter.

(e) A person, other than an owner of a timeshare interest who purchased the interest from a developer for the person's own personal use and occupancy, commits a false, misleading, or deceptive act or practice within the meaning of Sections 17.46(a) and (b), Business & Commerce Code, and an unconscionable action or course of action as defined by Section 17.45, Business & Commerce Code, by knowingly participating, for consideration or with the expectation of consideration, in any plan or scheme a purpose of which is to transfer a timeshare interest to a transferee who does not have the ability, means, or intent to pay all assessments and taxes for the timeshare interest. An association or other managing entity does not commit an act or action as described by this subsection by performing administrative acts and collecting fees or expenses as customary or required by law or under the project instruments in connection with a transfer by an owner of a timeshare interest in the timeshare property.

History of Prop. Code §221.071: Acts 1987, 70th Leg., ch. 167, §6.03, eff. Sept. 1, 1987. Renumbered from §201.071 by Acts 1989, 71st Leg., ch. 2, §13.03(b), eff. Aug. 28, 1989. Amended by Acts 1993, 73rd Leg., ch. 443, §6, eff. Sept. 1, 1993; Acts 2005, 79th Leg., ch. 539, §11, eff. Jan. 15, 2006; Acts 2013, 83rd Leg., ch. 1352, §8, eff. Sept. 1, 2013. Source: TRCS art. 6573c, §11.

PROP §221.072. INSURANCE

Before the disposition of any timeshare interest, the developer or managing entity shall maintain the following insurance with respect to the timeshare property:

(1) property insurance on the timeshare property and any personal property for use by purchasers, other than personal property separately owned by a purchaser, insuring against all risks of direct physical loss commonly insured against, in a total amount, after application of deductibles, of the full replacement cost of the accommodations and amenities of the timeshare property; and

(2) liability insurance covering all occurrences commonly insured against for death, bodily injury, and property damage arising out of or in connection with the use, ownership, and maintenance of the timeshare property.

History of Prop. Code §221.072: Acts 1987, 70th Leg., ch. 167, §6.03, eff. Sept. 1, 1987. Renumbered from §201.072 by Acts 1989, 71st Leg., ch. 2, §13.03(b), eff. Aug. 28, 1989. Amended by Acts 2005, 79th Leg., ch. 539, §12, eff. Jan. 15, 2006. Source: TRCS art. 6573c, §12.

PROP §221.073. PENALTY

(a) A developer subject to this chapter commits an offense if the developer offers or disposes of a timeshare interest in a timeshare property which has not been registered with the commission.

(b) It is not a violation of this section for a developer subject to this chapter to accept reservations and deposits from prospective purchasers in accordance with Section 221.021(b) or (d).

(c) An offense under this section is a Class A misdemeanor. A person may not be prosecuted for more than one offense involving the same promotion, even if mailed or distributed to more than one person.

History of Prop. Code §221.073: Acts 1989, 71st Leg., ch. 381, §6, eff. June 14, 1989. Amended by Acts 1999, 76th Leg., ch. 1382, §9, eff. June 19, 1999; Acts 2005, 79th Leg., ch. 539, §13, eff. Jan. 15, 2006.

PROP §221.074. ANNUAL TIMESHARE FEE & EXPENSE STATEMENT

(a) Notwithstanding any contrary provision of the required timeshare disclosure statement, project instrument, timeshare instrument, or bylaws adopted pursuant to a timeshare instrument, the managing entity shall make a written annual accounting of the operation of the timeshare properties managed by the managing entity to each purchaser who requests an accounting not later than five months after the last day of each fiscal year. The statement shall fairly and accurately represent the collection and expenditure of assessments and include:

(1) a balance sheet;

(2) an income and expense statement;

(3) the current budget for the timeshare property, timeshare properties managed by the same managing entity, or multisite timeshare plan required by Section 221.032(b)(12); and

(4) the name, address, and telephone number of a designated representative of the managing entity.

(5) Deleted by Acts 2005, 79th Leg., ch. 539, §14, eff. Jan. 15, 2006.

(b) On the request of an owner, the managing entity of the timeshare plan shall provide the owner with the name and address of each member of the board of directors of the owners' association, if one exists.

(c) A developer or managing entity shall have an annual independent audit of the financial statements of the timeshare plan or timeshare properties managed by the managing entity performed by a certified public accountant or an accounting firm. The audit must be:

(1) conducted in accordance with generally accepted auditing standards as prescribed by the American Institute of Certified Public Accountants, the Governmental Accounting Standards Board, the United States General Accounting Office, or other professionally recognized entities that prescribe auditing standards; and

(2) completed not later than five months after the last day of the fiscal year of the timeshare plan or timeshare property.

(d) Knowingly furnishing false information in the annual timeshare fee and expense statement is a violation of the Deceptive Trade Practices-Consumer Protection Act (Section 17.41 et seq., Business & Commerce Code).

(e) The managing entity of any accommodation located in this state shall post prominently in the registration area of the accommodations the following notice, with the date of the last day of the current fiscal year and the address of the managing entity inserted where indicated:

"AS A TIMESHARE OWNER YOU HAVE A RIGHT TO REQUEST A WRITTEN ANNUAL TIMESHARE FEE AND EXPENSE STATEMENT. THIS STATEMENT IS PREPARED ANNUALLY BY THE MANAGING ENTITY AND WILL BE AVAILABLE NO LATER THAN FIVE MONTHS FOLLOWING (INSERT THE DATE OF THE LAST DAY OF THE CURRENT FISCAL YEAR). YOU MAY REQUEST THE STATEMENT, BY WRITING TO (INSERT ADDRESS OF THE MANAGING ENTITY)."

(f) Deleted by Acts 2005, 79th Leg., ch. 539, §14, eff. Jan. 15, 2006.

History of Prop. Code §221.074: Acts 1993, 73rd Leg., ch. 443, §7, eff. Jan. 1, 1995. Amended by Acts 2005, 79th Leg., ch. 539, §14, eff. Jan. 15, 2006.

PROP §221.075. CIVIL PENALTY FOR LATE STATEMENT; INJUNCTION

(a) On receipt of a written request filed with the commission by a managing entity before the date on which the statement required by Section 221.074 must be made available, the commission for good cause shown may grant the managing entity an extension of no more than 30 days in which to provide the statement.

(b) If the statement required by Section 221.074 is late and an extension has not been granted under Subsection (a), the managing entity required to provide the statement is liable to the state for a civil penalty not to exceed:

(1) $500 per day for each of the first 10 days that the statement is late; and

(2) $1,500 per day for each day after the 10th day, until the managing entity has complied with Section 221.074.

(c) In no event shall the civil penalties exceed $30,000 for any one statement period.

(d) A managing entity may not assess against or collect from the purchasers of a timeshare property the amount of a penalty incurred under this section.

(e) If it appears that a managing entity has violated Section 221.074, the attorney general may institute an action for injunctive relief, a civil penalty, or both.

History of Prop. Code §221.075: Acts 1993, 73rd Leg., ch. 443, §7, eff. Jan. 1, 1995. Amended by Acts 1999, 76th Leg., ch. 1382, §10, eff. June 19, 1999; Acts 2005, 79th Leg., ch. 539, §15, eff. Jan. 15, 2006.

PROP §221.076. MANAGING ENTITIES THAT MANAGE MORE THAN ONE TIMESHARE PROPERTY

(a) A managing entity that manages two or more single-site timeshare plans may commingle the assessments collected from purchasers of one timeshare plan with the assessments collected from purchasers of any other single-site plan for which it is the managing entity only if the practice is disclosed in the timeshare disclosure statement for each timeshare property and the appropriate statement is included in the declaration for each timeshare property as required by Subchapter B.

(b) A managing entity which manages a multisite timeshare plan may deposit assessments collected from purchasers of one timeshare property into a common account with assessments collected from purchasers of other timeshare properties participating in the same multisite timeshare plan only if the practice is disclosed in the timeshare disclosure statement for each timeshare property in the multisite timeshare plan and the appropriate statement is included in the declaration for each timeshare plan as required by Subchapter B.

(c) Nothing in this section shall be construed to allow a managing entity to commingle assessments of a multisite timeshare plan with the assessments of a separate multisite timeshare plan or a timeshare plan that is not a part of the multisite timeshare plan.

History of Prop. Code §221.076: Acts 1993, 73rd Leg., ch. 443, §8, eff. Sept. 1, 1993. Amended by Acts 2005, 79th Leg., ch. 539, §16, eff. Jan. 15, 2006.

PROP §221.077. AVAILABILITY OF BOOKS & RECORDS; RECORDS RETENTION

(a) A developer or managing entity, on written request of an owner, shall make available for examination at its registered office or principal place of business and at any reasonable time or times the relevant books and records relating to the collection and expenditure of assessments.

(b) A developer or managing entity shall maintain in its records a copy of each purchase contract for an accommodation sold by the developer for a timeshare period unless the contract has been canceled. If a sale of the timeshare estate is pending, the developer shall retain a copy of the contract until a deed of conveyance, agreement for deed, or lease is recorded in the real property records of the county in which the timeshare property is located.

History of Prop. Code §221.077: Acts 1993, 73rd Leg., ch. 443, §8, eff. Sept. 1, 1993. Amended by Acts 2005, 79th Leg., ch. 539, §16, eff. Jan. 15, 2006.

Sections 221.078-221.080 blank

SUBCHAPTER I. TIMESHARE OWNERS' ASSOCIATIONS

PROP §221.081. APPLICABILITY

(a) Except as provided by this section, this subchapter applies to a timeshare plan, the project instrument governing the timeshare property subject to the timeshare plan, and the association related to the timeshare plan, regardless of the date on which the timeshare plan was created.

(b) Except as provided by Section 221.083(f), this subchapter applies to a timeshare plan, the project instrument governing the timeshare property subject to the timeshare plan, and the association related to the timeshare plan, created before September 1, 2013, unless the project instrument is amended before September 1, 2013, to provide that this subchapter does not apply.

History of Prop. Code §221.081: Acts 2013, 83rd Leg., ch. 1352, §2, eff. Sept. 1, 2013.

PROP §221.082. POWERS & LIMITATIONS OF BOARD

(a) An association may be governed by a board of directors. Except as provided in the project instrument, or this chapter, the board may act in all instances on behalf of the association.

(b) Except as expressly authorized in the project instrument or otherwise permitted by the association, the board may not act on behalf of the association to:

(1) amend the project instrument;

(2) terminate the timeshare plan;

(3) elect or remove board members; or

(4) determine the qualifications, powers, duties, or terms of office of board members.

(c) Subject to the project instrument, the board may appoint a member to fill a vacancy on the board and the member appointed serves for the unexpired portion of the term of the predecessor board member.

History of Prop. Code §221.082: Acts 2013, 83rd Leg., ch. 1352, §2, eff. Sept. 1, 2013.

PROP §221.083. PERIOD OF DEVELOPER CONTROL

(a) Except as otherwise provided in this section, the project instrument may provide for a period of developer control of an association during which the de-

veloper, or a person designated by the developer, may appoint and remove board members and officers of the association.

(b) Regardless of the period of developer control provided in the project instrument, that period expires not later than the earlier of:

(1) the 120th day after the date that at least 95 percent of the timeshare interests that were created by the timeshare instrument are conveyed to owners other than the developer; or

(2) the fifth anniversary of the date the developer ceased to offer timeshare interests for sale in the ordinary course of business under the timeshare plan or under another timeshare plan in which the timeshare interests are included, whichever date is later.

(c) A developer may voluntarily surrender the developer's right to appoint and remove board members and officers of the association during the period of developer control by executing a written instrument stating that the developer's rights are surrendered and providing a copy of the instrument to the owners. The developer may provide in the surrender instrument that, during the remaining period otherwise designated for developer control, specified actions of the association or board as described in the project instrument are effective only on approval of the developer. The surrender instrument must be recorded in the real property records of the county in which the timeshare property is located.

(d) If the project instrument provides for a developer control period of shorter duration than any period prescribed by this section, the project instrument controls.

(e) During the period of developer control and subject to the project instrument, the developer may determine all matters governing the association, including the occurrence of special or regular meetings of the members and the notice requirements and rules for those meetings.

(f) This section applies to a timeshare plan created before September 1, 2013, and to the project instrument governing the timeshare property subject to the timeshare plan only if the developer and the association agree to the application in writing and the project instrument is amended to provide for that application. If the conditions provided by this subsection are not satisfied, a timeshare plan created before September 1, 2013, and the timeshare property subject to the timeshare plan are governed by any developer control provisions provided in the project instrument, notwithstanding any other law.

History of Prop. Code §221.083: Acts 2013, 83rd Leg., ch. 1352, §2, eff. Sept. 1, 2013.

PROP §221.084. ELECTION OF INITIAL BOARD MEMBERS & OFFICERS

(a) Not later than the termination, by expiration or surrender, of any period of developer control, the owners, including the developer to the extent of any developer-owned timeshare interests, must elect a board of at least three members. The board may include one or more representatives of the developer.

(b) The board shall elect the officers of the association.

(c) The board members and officers of the association take office on election.

History of Prop. Code §221.084: Acts 2013, 83rd Leg., ch. 1352, §2, eff. Sept. 1, 2013.

PROP §221.085. REMOVAL OF BOARD MEMBERS

Notwithstanding any provision of a project instrument to the contrary, the owners, by a vote of at least two-thirds of the voting rights of persons entitled to vote and voting in person or by proxy at any meeting of the owners, may remove a member of the board, with or without cause, other than a member appointed by the developer during the period of developer control under Section 221.083, provided that the developer remains in control of the association.

History of Prop. Code §221.085: Acts 2013, 83rd Leg., ch. 1352, §2, eff. Sept. 1, 2013.

PROP §221.086. QUORUM

(a) Unless the project instrument provides for a larger quorum requirement, the percentage of voting interests constituting a quorum at a meeting of the members of an association is 10 percent of the voting interests of owners who are not delinquent in assessments, voting in person or by proxy.

(b) If a quorum is not present at any meeting of the association at which board members will be elected, the meeting may be adjourned and reconvened not later than the 90th day after the date of adjournment for the sole purpose of electing board members. Unless the project instrument provides for a larger quorum requirement, the quorum for the reconvened meeting is 10 percent of the voting interests of owners who are not delinquent in assessments, voting in person or by proxy.

(c) Unless the project instrument provides otherwise, a quorum of the board is considered present throughout a board meeting if the members entitled to cast a majority of the votes are present at the beginning of the meeting.

History of Prop. Code §221.086: Acts 2013, 83rd Leg., ch. 1352, §2, eff. Sept. 1, 2013.

PROP §221.087. VOTES

(a) If only one of the multiple owners of a timeshare interest is present at a meeting of the association, that owner may cast all votes allocated to that timeshare interest. If more than one of the multiple owners are present, the votes allocated to that timeshare interest may be cast only in accordance with the agreement of a majority of the timeshare interest held by the multiple owners unless the timeshare instrument expressly provides otherwise. For purposes of this subsection, there is a majority agreement if any one of the multiple owners casts the votes allocated to that timeshare interest and no protest is made promptly to the person presiding over the meeting by any of the other owners of the timeshare interest.

(b) Votes allocated to a timeshare interest may be cast under a proxy duly executed by an owner. A proxy must expressly state the dates of execution and termination. An owner may only revoke a proxy given under this section by actual notice of revocation to the person presiding over a meeting of the association. A proxy is revoked on presentation of a later dated proxy or other written revocation executed by the same owner. A proxy terminates the 25th month after the date the proxy is executed, unless the proxy specifies a shorter period or states that the proxy is coupled with an interest and is irrevocable.

(c) The project instrument for a timeshare plan may authorize votes of members of an association to be cast by mail only if:

(1) mail ballots are mailed or sent to each member in the manner prescribed for a notice of a special meeting under Section 221.089;

(2) the period for return of mail ballots is not later than the 30th day after the date the ballots are mailed or sent to members; and

(3) the required minimum number of ballots that must be returned by members for the vote to be effective represents at least the percentage of voting interests required for a quorum as prescribed by Section 221.086(a).

(d) Only timeshare interests included in the timeshare plan have voting rights.

(e) Unless the project instrument provides otherwise, owners who are delinquent in assessments do not have the right to cast a vote. The right to cast a vote is also subject to any additional limitations provided in the project instrument.

History of Prop. Code §221.087: Acts 2013, 83rd Leg., ch. 1352, §2, eff. Sept. 1, 2013.

PROP §221.088. OPEN MEETINGS; EXCEPTIONS

(a) Notwithstanding any provision in the project instrument to the contrary and except as provided in this section, after the period of developer control under Section 221.083, all meetings of the association and board are open to all members of the association and all members must be permitted to attend and listen to the deliberations and proceedings. Meetings must be conducted as provided in the project instrument. The board may adjourn a board meeting and reconvene in a closed executive session to consider:

(1) legal advice from an attorney for the board or the association;

(2) pending or contemplated litigation;

(3) financial information about an individual member of the association, an individual employee of the association, an individual employee of the managing entity, or an individual employee of a contractor for the association or managing entity; or

(4) matters relating to the job performance of, compensation of, health records of, or specific complaints against an individual employee of the association, an individual employee of the managing entity, or an individual employee of a contractor of the association or managing entity who works under the direction of the association or the managing entity.

(b) If a board meeting is closed as provided by Subsection (a)(1) or (2), the board, on final resolution of any matter for which the board received legal advice or that concerned pending or contemplated litigation, may disclose information about that matter in an open meeting, except to the extent that those matters are required to remain confidential by the terms of a settlement agreement or judgment.

History of Prop. Code §221.088: Acts 2013, 83rd Leg., ch. 1352, §2, eff. Sept. 1, 2013.

PROP §221.089. NOTICE

(a) A meeting of the members of the association must be held annually after the termination of the pe-

riod of developer control under Section 221.083. Special meetings of the members of the association may be called by the president, by a majority of the board, or by owners having at least 25 percent of the votes allocated to timeshare interests in the association or any lower percentage specified in the project instrument.

(b) Unless the project instrument provides otherwise, the association or managing entity must send notice of the meeting to the mailing address of each owner on record with the association:

(1) not later than the 30th day or earlier than the 90th day before the date of an annual meeting; and

(2) not later than the 10th day or earlier than the 60th day before the date of a special meeting.

(c) The notice of a meeting of the owners must state the date, time, and place of the meeting. The notice of a special meeting of the owners must also state the purpose of the meeting. A notice of a meeting may be included in a list of upcoming meetings sent to owners, and the list is not required to be specific to one meeting. The failure of an owner to receive actual notice of a meeting of the owners does not affect the validity of any action taken at that meeting.

(d) Unless the project instrument provides otherwise, the association or managing entity must send notice of a board meeting held after the date the developer control period terminates to the mailing address of each owner on record with the association not later than the 10th day before the date of the meeting. Notice to owners of a board meeting is not required if emergency circumstances require action by the board before notice can be given. A notice of a board meeting must state the date, time, and place of the meeting. A notice of a meeting may be included in a list of upcoming meetings sent to owners, and the list is not required to be specific to one meeting. The failure of an owner to receive actual notice of a board meeting does not affect the validity of any action taken at that meeting.

(e) A notice may be provided in a newsletter or a similar mailing. Notice may be provided by prepaid United States mail, e-mail for those owners who have provided an e-mail address, or any other reasonable method selected by the board.

(f) Notwithstanding Subsections (a)-(d) or any other law related to notice by an association, a notice to an owner may be provided by conspicuous disclosure on the association's website if the owner has consented to that alternative notice. Consent to that alternative notice must be in writing and may be revoked by the owner at any time.

(g) An affidavit of notice by an officer of the association or the managing entity is prima facie evidence that notice was provided under this section.

History of Prop. Code §221.089: Acts 2013, 83rd Leg., ch. 1352, §2, eff. Sept. 1, 2013.

PROP §221.090. DUTIES; LIST OF OWNERS

(a) The association or managing entity of the association must maintain among its records a complete and current list of the names and addresses of all owners of timeshare interests in the timeshare plan. The association or managing entity must update this list not less than quarterly.

(b) The association or managing entity may not publish the owners list or provide a copy of the list to any owner or to any third party, except:

(1) as reasonably required to conduct legitimate association business; or

(2) as authorized or required by law.

(c) On the termination of the period of developer control under Section 221.083 and on the written request of an owner, the association or managing entity shall send by first class mail to owners on the list described by Subsection (a) any materials provided by any owner if the purpose of the mailing is for legitimate association business, including a proxy solicitation for the recall of a board member elected by the owners or the discharge of the managing entity. The use of the solicited proxies must comply with the project instrument and this chapter. Materials required to be provided under this subsection must be mailed not later than the 30th day after the date the request is received from an owner.

(d) The board or the managing entity is responsible for determining the appropriateness of a mailing requested under Subsection (c) and establishing reasonable procedures for exercising rights under this section. The association or managing entity does not have an obligation to mail an item that the board or managing entity reasonably believes based on advice of legal counsel may be libelous or otherwise actionable. An owner who requests the mailing of materials under Subsection (c) must reimburse the association or managing entity in advance for the actual costs of perform-

ing the mailing or a proportionate share of actual costs if the mailing is included in a mailing with other items.

(e) After the termination of the period of developer control under Section 221.083, it is a violation of this subchapter to refuse to mail material provided by a requesting owner who has complied with the reasonable procedures established by the board or managing entity, if:

(1) the sole purpose of the materials is to advance legitimate association business; and

(2) the requesting owner has:

(A) tendered to the association or managing entity payment of the cost under Subsection (d); or

(B) requested an invoice for that cost and has not received the invoice before the 10th day after the date the request was delivered to the association or managing entity.

(f) Except as otherwise authorized or required by law, the association or other managing entity may not furnish the name, address, telephone number, or e-mail address of any owner to any other owner or authorized agent of an owner unless the owner whose name, address, phone number, or e-mail address is requested first approves the disclosure in writing.

History of Prop. Code §221.090: Acts 2013, 83rd Leg., ch. 1352, §2, eff. Sept. 1, 2013.

Sections 221.091-221.100 blank

SUBCHAPTER J. SERVICE AGREEMENTS TO TRANSFER OR TERMINATE A TIMESHARE INTEREST

PROP §221.101. TRANSFER OR TERMINATION OF TIMESHARE INTEREST

In this subchapter:

(1) "Termination" with respect to a timeshare interest:

(A) means:

(i) the release of contractual obligations relating to a timeshare interest by the developer, association, or managing entity; or

(ii) the invalidation, cancellation, nullification, or cessation of contractual obligations related to a timeshare interest by a judgment or court order; and

(B) does not include the cancellation of a purchase contract governed by Subchapter E.

(2) "Transfer" with respect to a timeshare interest means the conveyance of all or substantially all of a timeshare interest.

History of Prop. Code §221.101: Acts 2015, 84th Leg., ch. 554, §2, eff. Sept. 1, 2015.

PROP §221.102. APPLICABILITY

(a) This subchapter applies to a timeshare interest if the timeshare interest has been acquired only for the purchaser's personal, family, or household use and:

(1) the timeshare interest is owned by a resident of this state;

(2) the timeshare property is located in this state; or

(3) the timeshare interest acquired is in a multisite timeshare plan required to be registered under Subchapter C.

(b) Except as provided by Subsection (c), this subchapter applies to a person who:

(1) is acting in the ordinary course of business; and

(2) directly or indirectly, regardless of whether acting in person, by mail, by telephone, or by any mode of Internet or electronic communication, offers or advertises an offer to engage in, for consideration, the following activities:

(A) obtaining or attempting to obtain on behalf of a timeshare interest owner a termination of contractual obligations relating to a timeshare interest;

(B) selling, renting, listing, or advertising a timeshare interest on behalf of a timeshare interest owner;

(C) purchasing a timeshare interest from a timeshare interest owner; or

(D) assisting in the transfer of an owner's timeshare interest.

(c) This subchapter does not apply to:

(1) a license holder under Chapter 1101, Occupations Code, acting as a broker, agent, or salesperson under that person's license in connection with the transfer or termination of a timeshare interest;

(2) a developer, association, or managing entity for a timeshare interest to be transferred or terminated or a third party acting at the specific request of the developer, association, or managing entity; or

(3) an attorney, title agent, title company, or escrow company that:

(A) provides only closing, settlement, or other comparable transaction services in connection with the transfer or termination of a timeshare interest; and

(B) does not otherwise engage in activities described by Subsection (b).

History of Prop. Code §221.102: Acts 2015, 84th Leg., ch. 554, §2, eff. Sept. 1, 2015.

PROP §221.103. GENERAL DISCLOSURES REQUIRED

A person subject to this subchapter who enters into an agreement with a timeshare interest owner to facilitate the transfer or termination of a timeshare interest shall provide to the timeshare interest owner, before the third day before the date the timeshare interest owner enters into the agreement the following written disclosures, as applicable:

(1) the name, telephone number, and physical address of the person providing services under the agreement and any affiliate, agent, or third-party representative of that person;

(2) if the person identified in Subdivision (1), or an affiliate, agent, or third-party representative of that person providing services under the agreement, is an attorney licensed to practice law in this state, a disclosure of whether the attorney will be providing services under the agreement and representing the timeshare interest owner in connection with the transfer or termination of the timeshare interest;

(3) a description, legally sufficient for identification, of the timeshare interest to be transferred or terminated;

(4) a description of the method of transfer or termination or a copy of the instrument that will be used for transferring or terminating the timeshare interest;

(5) a description of any interest the timeshare interest owner retains after the transfer;

(6) a description of the scope of a power of attorney or other delegation of authority, if any, that the timeshare interest owner is required to give to complete the transfer of the timeshare interest;

(7) an itemized statement of any amounts the timeshare owner is required to pay as consideration or reimbursement for services provided in connection with the agreement;

(8) the name of each recipient of amounts described by Subdivision (7);

(9) the estimated date for completing all services sufficient to transfer or terminate the timeshare interest; and

(10) a statement that, on completion of the transfer or termination of the timeshare interest, the person will give written notice of the transfer or termination to:

(A) the developer, association, or managing entity, as applicable; and

(B) if applicable, the exchange company for the timeshare interest.

History of Prop. Code §221.103: Acts 2015, 84th Leg., ch. 554, §2, eff. Sept. 1, 2015.

PROP §221.104. DISCLOSURE OF AUTHORIZED USE OF TIMESHARE INTEREST

(a) A person subject to this subchapter who enters into an agreement with a timeshare interest owner to facilitate the transfer or termination of a timeshare interest shall disclose in writing to the timeshare interest owner the name of any person, other than the timeshare interest owner, who may occupy, rent, exchange, or otherwise use the timeshare interest during the term of the agreement.

(b) If a person is authorized to occupy, rent, exchange, or otherwise use the timeshare interest during the term of the agreement, the agreement must state the name of each person receiving consideration for the occupation, rent, exchange, or use of the timeshare interest.

History of Prop. Code §221.104: Acts 2015, 84th Leg., ch. 554, §2, eff. Sept. 1, 2015.

PROP §221.105. DISCLOSURES RELATING TO PAYMENT OF FEES FOR TRANSFER SERVICES

A person subject to this subchapter who enters into an agreement with a timeshare interest owner to facilitate the transfer of the timeshare interest must conspicuously disclose in writing to the timeshare interest owner that the timeshare interest owner is not required to pay any consideration or reimbursement under the agreement until the timeshare interest owner receives:

(1) a written acknowledgement from the developer, the association, or the managing entity that the person facilitating the transfer under the agreement complied with all applicable policies of the developer, association, or managing entity, if any, governing the transfer of the timeshare interest; and

(2) a copy of the instrument transferring the timeshare interest, recorded, if required by applicable law,

in the real property records of the county in which the timeshare property is located.

History of Prop. Code §221.105: Acts 2015, 84th Leg., ch. 554, §2, eff. Sept. 1, 2015.

PROP §221.106. REQUIRED NOTICE FOR TRANSFER SERVICES

A person subject to this subchapter who enters into an agreement with a timeshare interest owner to facilitate the transfer of the timeshare interest must provide to the timeshare interest owner a statement printed in 14-point boldface type or 14-point uppercase typewritten letters that reads substantially similar to the following:

I (name of the person facilitating the transfer) WILL ACT IN GOOD FAITH AND IN A COMMERCIALLY REASONABLE MANNER TO COMPLETE THE TRANSFER OF OWNERSHIP OF YOUR TIMESHARE INTEREST NOT LATER THAN THE 180TH DAY AFTER THE DATE OF THIS AGREEMENT.

YOUR OBLIGATION TO PAY ALL COSTS AND FEES ASSOCIATED WITH YOUR TIMESHARE INTEREST, INCLUDING ANY REGULAR OR SPECIAL ASSESSMENTS OR REAL OR PERSONAL PROPERTY TAXES, DOES NOT CEASE BY VIRTUE OF THE EXECUTION OF THIS AGREEMENT.

IF THE TRANSFER OF YOUR TIMESHARE INTEREST IS NOT COMPLETED BEFORE THE 180TH DAY AFTER THE DATE OF THIS AGREEMENT, YOU WILL CONTINUE TO BE RESPONSIBLE FOR THE PAYMENT OF ALL COSTS AND FEES ASSOCIATED WITH YOUR TIMESHARE INTEREST, INCLUDING ANY REGULAR OR SPECIAL ASSESSMENTS OR REAL OR PERSONAL PROPERTY TAXES.

History of Prop. Code §221.106: Acts 2015, 84th Leg., ch. 554, §2, eff. Sept. 1, 2015.

PROP §221.107. REQUIRED NOTICE FOR TERMINATION SERVICES

A person subject to this subchapter who enters into an agreement with a timeshare interest owner to facilitate the termination of the timeshare interest must provide to the timeshare interest owner a statement printed in 14-point boldface type or 14-point uppercase typewritten letters that reads substantially similar to the following:

I (name of the person facilitating the termination of the timeshare interest) WILL ACT IN GOOD FAITH AND IN A COMMERCIALLY REASONABLE MANNER TO COMPLETE THE TERMINATION OF YOUR TIMESHARE INTEREST NOT LATER THAN THE 180TH DAY AFTER THE DATE OF THIS AGREEMENT BY OBTAINING:

(1) A VALID AND ENFORCEABLE RELEASE FROM THE DEVELOPER, ASSOCIATION, OR MANAGING ENTITY; OR

(2) A JUDGMENT OR COURT ORDER INVALIDATING THE PURCHASE OR OWNERSHIP OF YOUR TIMESHARE INTEREST.

YOUR OBLIGATION TO PAY ALL COSTS AND FEES ASSOCIATED WITH YOUR TIMESHARE INTEREST, INCLUDING ANY REGULAR OR SPECIAL ASSESSMENTS OR REAL OR PERSONAL PROPERTY TAXES, DOES NOT CEASE BY VIRTUE OF THE EXECUTION OF THIS AGREEMENT.

I CANNOT GUARANTEE THAT I WILL SUCCESSFULLY COMPLETE THE TERMINATION OF YOUR TIMESHARE INTEREST. IF I FAIL TO COMPLETE THE TERMINATION OF YOUR TIMESHARE INTEREST, YOU WILL CONTINUE TO BE RESPONSIBLE FOR THE PAYMENT OF ALL COSTS AND FEES ASSOCIATED WITH YOUR TIMESHARE INTEREST, INCLUDING ANY REGULAR OR SPECIAL ASSESSMENTS OR REAL OR PERSONAL PROPERTY TAXES.

History of Prop. Code §221.107: Acts 2015, 84th Leg., ch. 554, §2, eff. Sept. 1, 2015.

PROP §221.108. RELIANCE

In making disclosures required by this subchapter, a person facilitating the transfer or termination of a timeshare interest may rely on written information provided by the timeshare interest owner, the developer, the association, or the managing entity.

History of Prop. Code §221.108: Acts 2015, 84th Leg., ch. 554, §2, eff. Sept. 1, 2015.

PROP §221.109. DUTY OF GOOD FAITH REGARDING TRANSFER OR TERMINATION SERVICES

A person facilitating the transfer or termination of a timeshare interest must act in good faith to accomplish the transfer or termination not later than the 180th day after the date the person enters into an agreement with the timeshare interest owner.

History of Prop. Code §221.109: Acts 2015, 84th Leg., ch. 554, §2, eff. Sept. 1, 2015.

PROP §221.110. DECEPTIVE TRADE PRACTICES

A person subject to this subchapter commits a false, misleading, or deceptive act or practice within the meaning of Sections 17.46(a) and (b), Business & Commerce Code, by engaging in any of the following acts:

(1) failing to disclose information as required by this subchapter;

(2) making false or misleading statements concerning:

(A) the existence of an offer related to the purchase or rent of a timeshare interest;

(B) the likelihood of the completion or the time necessary to complete any sale, rental, transfer, or termination of a timeshare interest;

(C) the value of a timeshare interest;

(D) the current or future costs, including assessments, maintenance fees, or taxes, of owning a timeshare interest;

(E) the method by which or source from which a timeshare interest owner's name, address, telephone number, or other contact information was obtained;

(F) the identity of the person providing services to facilitate the transfer or termination of a timeshare interest or any affiliate, agent, or third-party representative of that person;

(G) the terms and conditions under which services to facilitate a transfer or termination of a timeshare interest are offered;

(H) the willingness of a developer, association, or managing entity to:

(i) agree to the transfer or termination of a timeshare interest; or

(ii) execute instruments necessary to transfer or terminate the timeshare interest; or

(I) the manner in which consideration or reimbursements paid by a timeshare interest owner will be used or applied;

(3) encouraging or inducing a timeshare interest owner to stop paying the developer, the association, or the managing entity in violation of a contract with or any other legally enforceable obligation to the developer, the association, or the managing entity before the completion of a transfer or termination; or

(4) receiving or collecting consideration for or reimbursement related to the facilitation of the transfer of a timeshare interest before the timeshare interest owner receives the documents described by Sections 221.105(1) and (2).

History of Prop. Code §221.110: Acts 2015, 84th Leg., ch. 554, §2, eff. Sept. 1, 2015.

PROP §221.111. SUPERVISORY DUTIES

(a) The person who enters into an agreement to facilitate the transfer or termination of a timeshare interest shall supervise, manage, and control all aspects of the services provided under the agreement.

(b) Any violation of this subchapter that occurs during the provision of services is considered a violation by the person who enters into the agreement and any affiliate, agent, or third-party representative of that person.

(c) Section 221.035 does not apply to a person providing services under this subchapter.

History of Prop. Code §221.111: Acts 2015, 84th Leg., ch. 554, §2, eff. Sept. 1, 2015.

CHAPTER 222. TEXAS MEMBERSHIP CAMPING RESORT ACT

PROP §222.001. SHORT TITLE

This chapter may be cited as the Texas Membership Camping Resort Act.

History of Prop. Code §222.001: Acts 1989, 71st Leg., ch. 2, §13.03(d), eff. Aug. 28, 1989. Source: TRCS art. 8880, §1.

PROP §222.002. APPLICATION OF CHAPTER

(a) This chapter applies to all membership camping resorts located in this state.

(b) Sections 222.003-222.013 also apply to membership camping resorts located outside this state but offered for sale in this state.

(c) This chapter does not affect a membership camping contract made before August 31, 1987.

History of Prop. Code §222.002: Acts 1989, 71st Leg., ch. 2, §13.03(d), eff. Aug. 28, 1989. Source: TRCS art. 8880, §§15, 16.

PROP §222.003. DEFINITIONS

In this chapter:

(1) "Advertising" means a direct or indirect solicitation or inducement to purchase and includes but is not necessarily limited to a solicitation or inducement made by print or electronic media, through the mail, or by personal contact.

(2) "Amenities" means all common areas of real property occupied by a membership camping resort and includes but is not necessarily limited to camping sites, swimming pools, stables, tennis courts, recreation buildings, restrooms and showers, laundry rooms, trading posts, grocery stores, and maintenance facilities.

(3) "Blanket encumbrance" means a mortgage, deed of trust, option to purchase, or vendor's lien, an interest obtained under a contract or agreement of sale, or other financing lien or encumbrance granted by an operator that secures or evidences the obligation to pay money or to sell or convey any campgrounds located in this state that are made available to purchasers by the operator, and that authorizes, permits, or requires the foreclosure or other disposition of the affected campground.

(4) "Business day" means any day other than a Saturday, Sunday, or federal holiday.

(5) "Camping site" means a space designed and promoted for the purpose of locating a trailer, tent, tent trailer, pickup camper, recreational vehicle, or similar device designed for camping.

(6) "Dispose" or "disposition" means a voluntary transfer of any membership interest or membership right but does not include the transfer or release of a real estate lien or of a security interest.

(7) "Home resort" means the camping resort to which the purchaser has purchased a right of membership. The term does not include a resort that a purchaser may use as a result of a reciprocal program among operators.

(8) "Membership camping contract" means an agreement under which a purchaser pays for or becomes obligated to pay for a membership interest or membership right in a membership camping resort.

(9) "Membership camping contract broker" means a person who resells a membership camping contract to a new purchaser on behalf of the former purchaser. The term does not include a membership camping operator or that person's agent.

(10) "Membership camping resort disclosure statement" means a written statement that includes the information that is required by Section 222.006(b).

(11) "Membership camping resort" means real property owned or operated by a membership camping operator that is available for camping by purchasers of a membership right.

(12) "Membership interest" means a membership camping resort estate.

(13) "Membership right" means a license, contract right, or other right entitling a purchaser to use camping sites or amenities at a membership camping resort.

(14) "Offering" or "offer" means any advertisement, inducement, or solicitation and includes but is not necessarily limited to any attempt to encourage a person to purchase a membership interest or membership right.

(15) "Operator" means a person who owns or provides a camping site or an amenity to a purchaser. The term does not include:

(A) a person who owns or otherwise provides a mobile home park or a camping or recreational trailer park open to the general public with camping sites that are rented on a fee for use basis and who does not solicit purchases of membership camping contracts; or

(B) an outdoor service, facility, enterprise, or park that is owned or operated by or under the control of the United States, this state, or a political subdivision of this state.

(16) "Promotion" means any program or activity that is used to induce any person to attend a membership camping resort sales presentation.

(17) "Promotional disclosure statement" means a written statement that includes the information required by Section 222.006(a).

(18) "Purchaser" means a person, other than an operator, seller, or broker, who by means of voluntary transfer acquires a membership interest or membership right in a membership camping resort other than as security for an obligation.

(19) "Reciprocal company" means any person, including an operator, who operates a reciprocal program.

(20) "Reciprocal program disclosure statement" means a written statement that includes the information required by Section 222.006(c).

(21) "Reciprocal program" means any program under which the purchaser of a membership interest or membership right in a membership camping resort may use the facilities of a membership camping resort other than those of the purchaser's home resort.

(22) "Seller" means a person, including an operator, who in the ordinary course of business offers a membership interest or membership right for sale to the public but does not include a person who acquires a membership interest or membership right for his use and subsequently offers it for resale.

History of Prop. Code §222.003: Acts 1989, 71st Leg., ch. 2, §13.03(d), eff. Aug. 28, 1989. Amended by Acts 1989, 71st Leg., ch. 1039, §3.20, eff. Sept. 1, 1989. Source: TRCS art. 8880, §2.

PROP §222.004. REGISTRATION; ADMINISTRATION

(a) A person may not offer or dispose of a membership interest or membership right under a membership camping contract in this state unless the operator is registered with the secretary of state. If an operator also sells membership camping contracts, that operator must also comply with the registration requirements for membership camping contract brokers imposed by Section 222.005.

(b) A registration filed under this section must be on a form prescribed by the secretary of state and must include, to the extent applicable, the following information:

(1) the operator's name, address, and the organizational form of the operator's business, including the date and jurisdiction under which the business was organized, the name and address of each of its officers in this state, and the name and address of each membership camping resort located in this state that is owned or operated in whole or in part by the operator;

(2) a list of all owners of 10 percent or more of the capital stock of the operator's business if the operator is not required to report under the Securities Exchange Act of 1934 (15 U.S.C. Sec. 78a et seq.);

(3) a brief description and certified copy of the instrument creating the operator's ownership of or other right to use the membership camping resort and the amenities that are to be available for use by purchasers, together with a copy of any lease, license, franchise, reciprocal agreement, or other agreement entitling the operator to use the membership camping resort and the amenities, and any material provision of the agreement that restricts a purchaser's use of the membership camping resort or the amenities;

(4) a sample copy of each instrument to be delivered to a purchaser to evidence the purchaser's membership in the membership camping resort and a sample copy of each agreement that a purchaser is required to execute;

(5) financial statements of the operator for the most recent fiscal quarter;

(6) a narrative description of the promotional plan for the offering of membership interests or membership rights;

(7) a copy of any agreement between the operator and any person owning, controlling, or managing the membership camping resort;

(8) a complete list of the locations and addresses of any sales offices located in this state;

(9) the names of any other states or foreign countries in which a registration of the operator or the membership camping contract has been filed;

(10) complete information concerning any adverse order, judgment, or decree entered by any court or administrative agency in connection with a membership camping resort operated by the operator or in which the operator had an interest at the time of the order, judgment, or decree;

(11) a description of any blanket encumbrance on the membership camping resort; and

(12) a membership camping resort disclosure statement and any required reciprocal program disclosure statement required by Section 222.006.

(c) The registration must be signed by the operator, by an officer or general partner of the operator, or by another person who holds a power of attorney for this purpose from the operator. If the registration is signed under a power of attorney, a copy of the power of attorney must be included with the registration. The registration must be submitted with the registration fee set by the secretary of state pursuant to Section 222.010.

(d) The operator shall promptly file amendments to the registration reporting to the secretary of state any material and adverse change in any document contained in such registration. For the purposes of this subsection, a material and adverse change includes any

change that significantly reduces or terminates either the applicant's or a purchaser's right to use the membership camping resort or any of the amenities described by the membership camping contract but does not include minor changes covering the use of the membership camping resort, its amenities, or any reciprocal program.

(e) The secretary of state shall investigate all matters relating to the registration and may in his discretion require a personal inspection of the proposed membership camping resort by any persons designated by him.

(f) The secretary of state may prescribe and publish forms necessary to carry out the provisions of this chapter. The secretary of state may not approve or disapprove any registration, and an operator may not represent to any person that the secretary of state endorses or approves the membership camping resort or membership camping contract.

History of Prop. Code §222.004: Acts 1989, 71st Leg., ch. 2, §13.03(d), eff. Aug. 28, 1989. Amended by Acts 1989, 71st Leg., ch. 1039, §3.21, eff. Sept. 1, 1989. Source: TRCS art. 8880, §3.

PROP §222.005. REGISTRATION OF SELLERS & MEMBERSHIP CAMPING CONTRACT BROKERS

(a) A person may not offer a membership interest or membership right in a membership camping resort or resell membership camping contracts in this state unless the person is registered with the secretary of state. Each application for registration as a seller or membership camping contract broker must be in writing and must be signed by the applicant.

(b) The application must state:

(1) the name and address of the applicant;

(2) the name and place of business of the applicant's employer, if any;

(3) whether the applicant has been convicted of a felony or a misdemeanor involving moral turpitude and if so, the nature of the felony, where and when it was committed, and the disposition of the conviction; and

(4) whether the applicant has been refused a real estate broker's or salesman's license or any other occupational license in this or any other state or whether the applicant's license as a real estate broker or salesman in this or any other state has been revoked or suspended.

(c) The secretary of state may require any additional information that is reasonably necessary to determine the good moral character of an applicant for registration.

(d) Each application for registration as a seller or membership camping contract broker must be accompanied by the required registration fee set by the secretary of state pursuant to Section 222.010.

(e) The secretary of state may prescribe and publish forms to carry out the provisions of this section.

History of Prop. Code §222.005: Acts 1989, 71st Leg., ch. 2, §13.03(d), eff. Aug. 28, 1989. Amended by Acts 1989, 71st Leg., ch. 1039, §3.22, eff. Sept. 1, 1989. Source: TRCS art. 8880, §4.

PROP §222.006. DISCLOSURE STATEMENTS

(a) Before or at the time of the use of any promotion in connection with the offering of a membership interest or membership right in a membership camping resort, the person who intends to use the promotion shall include the following information in its advertisements to the prospective purchaser:

(1) a statement to the effect that the promotion is intended to solicit purchasers of membership interests or membership rights in a membership camping resort;

(2) the full name of the operator and seller of the membership interest or membership right in the membership camping resort;

(3) if applicable, the full name and address of any marketing company involved in the promotion of the membership camping resort;

(4) the complete rules of the promotion;

(5) the method of awarding, the odds of winning, and the approximate retail value of prizes, gifts, or other benefits under the promotion and the date by which each prize, gift, or other benefit will be awarded or conferred;

(6) any restrictions, qualifications, or other conditions that the recipient must satisfy before the recipient is entitled to receive a prize, gift, or other benefit, including:

(A) any deadline by which the recipient must visit the membership camping resort, attend the sales presentation, or contact a seller in order to receive the prize, gift, or other benefit;

(B) the date on which the offer expires; and

(C) any other conditions, including minimum age qualifications, financial qualifications, or a requirement that if the recipient is married both husband and wife must be present in order to receive the prize, gift, or other benefit;

(7) if applicable, a statement that the operator or seller reserves the right to provide a certificate with

which to redeem or claim the prize, gift, or other benefit awarded and that the prize, gift, or other benefit shall be shipped or delivered to the recipient within 30 days following the mailing of the certificate; and

(8) if applicable, a statement that the operator or seller reserves the right to substitute a prize, gift, or other benefit of equal value for the prize, gift, or other benefit awarded if the item is not available to the operator or seller after the purchaser or prospect has complied with the provisions of the promotion.

(b) Before or at the time of the signing of any agreement or membership camping contract to acquire a membership interest or membership right in a membership camping resort, the operator shall provide a membership camping resort disclosure statement to the prospective purchaser and shall obtain from the purchaser a written acknowledgement of receipt of the membership camping resort disclosure statement. The membership camping resort disclosure statement must include:

(1) the name and address of the operator and the name and specific location of the membership camping resort;

(2) a description of the amenities, membership camping resort, and any project or development within which the membership camping resort is located or of which it is a part. The disclosure statement must also state the total number of camping sites in the membership camping resort and whether and under what circumstances that number may be increased or decreased; if a membership interest or membership right includes amenities not yet in existence, the disclosure statement must provide the approximate commencement and completion schedule of those proposed amenities;

(3) a description of the membership interests and membership rights currently available for disposition;

(4) a statement that a council of purchasers exists or is expected to be created or that such a council does not exist and is not expected to be created; if such a council exists or is reasonably contemplated, the disclosure statement must contain a description of its powers and responsibilities;

(5) the name and principal address of the managing entity;

(6) a description and amount of any current or expected dues, assessments, fees, taxes, or charges to be paid by purchasers for the use of amenities or for any other purpose;

(7) a description and amount of insurance coverage provided for the protection of the purchaser; and

(8) a statement that any deposit made in connection with the purchase of a membership interest or membership right will be held until expiration of any right to cancel the contract or any later time specified in the contract and will be returned to the purchaser if he elects to exercise his right of cancellation.

(c) Before or at the time of the signing of any agreement or membership camping contract in which a prospective purchaser is also offered participation in a reciprocal program, the operator shall also deliver to the prospective purchaser the reciprocal program disclosure statement of the reciprocal company whose reciprocal program is advertised or offered by the operator or seller in connection with the disposition. If participation in a reciprocal program is offered for the first time after a disposition has occurred, any person offering the participation shall also deliver a reciprocal program disclosure statement to the purchaser before the execution by the purchaser of any instrument relating to participation in the reciprocal program. In all cases, the person offering the participation shall obtain from the purchaser a written acknowledgement of receipt of the reciprocal program disclosure statement. The reciprocal program disclosure statement must include the following information:

(1) the name and address of the reciprocal company;

(2) if the reciprocal company is not the operator, a statement describing the legal relationship, if any, between the reciprocal company and the operator;

(3) a statement that the reciprocal program might terminate or become unavailable;

(4) whether membership or participation, or both, in the reciprocal program is voluntary or mandatory;

(5) a complete description of the required procedure for using the reciprocal program;

(6) the fee required for membership or participation, or both, in the reciprocal program and whether the fee is subject to change;

(7) a statement to the effect that participation in the reciprocal program is conditioned on compliance with the terms of a contract between the reciprocal company and the purchaser; and

(8) a statement in conspicuous and bold-faced print to the effect that all reciprocal campgrounds are arranged on a space-available basis and that neither the operator nor the reciprocal company guarantees that a particular reciprocal campground can be used.

(d) A disclosure statement need not be delivered in the case of:

(1) a gratuitous disposition of a membership interest or membership right;

(2) a disposition pursuant to a court order;

(3) a disposition by a governmental agency;

(4) a disposition by foreclosure or deed in lieu of foreclosure;

(5) a disposition that may be canceled by the purchaser without penalty at any time and for any reason;

(6) a disposition of a membership interest or membership right in a membership camping resort situated wholly outside this state under a contract executed wholly outside this state, if there has been no offering to the purchaser within this state;

(7) a disposition of a membership interest or membership right to a purchaser who is not a resident of this state under a contract executed wholly outside this state, if there has been no offering to the purchaser within this state; or

(8) the redisposition of a membership interest or membership right by a purchaser who acquired the interest or right for his personal use.

History of Prop. Code §222.006: Acts 1989, 71st Leg., ch. 2, §13.03(d), eff. Aug. 28, 1989. Source: TRCS art. 8880, §5.

PROP §222.007. CONTRACT

(a) Each sale of a membership interest or membership right in a membership camping resort must be evidenced by a membership camping contract written in the language principally used in any promotional presentation made to the purchaser. The seller must give the purchaser a copy of the contract at the time it is signed.

(b) Each contract must contain the following:

(1) the name and address of the operator and the seller and the location of the membership camping resort;

(2) the signature of the operator or seller;

(3) the signature of the purchaser;

(4) the date on which the purchaser signs the contract;

(5) the name of the person who closed the transaction described in the membership camping contract;

(6) a brief description of the nature of the purchaser's interest in and right or license to use the membership camping resort;

(7) a summary or copy of the rules, restrictions, or covenants regulating the purchaser's use of the operator's properties, including a statement of whether and how the rules, restrictions, or covenants may be changed;

(8) any restraints on the transfer of the membership camping contract;

(9) any grounds for forfeiture of a purchaser's membership camping contract;

(10) if applicable, a statement of the purchaser's right to cancel the membership camping contract as provided by Section 222.008(c);

(11) a statement of whether the purchaser visited the location of the membership camping resort before signing the contract; and

(12) if applicable, a statement by the seller that if the purchaser timely exercises any right of cancellation under the contract, all payments made by the purchaser to the seller in connection with the contract shall be returned to the purchaser before the 21st day after the seller receives notice of cancellation as required under Section 222.008.

(c) The contract must also contain a brief description of the existing amenities available for use by purchasers at the home resort and of any proposed amenities or amenities not yet complete or fully functional.

(d) The contract must also contain a brief statement of the operator's ownership of or other right to use the camping properties represented to be available for use by purchasers, together with the duration of any lease, license, franchise, or reciprocal program entitling the operator to use the property, and material provisions of any agreements that restrict a purchaser's use of the property.

(e) The contract must be revised annually to include any changes to the information required by this section, if applicable.

History of Prop. Code §222.007: Acts 1989, 71st Leg., ch. 2, §13.03(d), eff. Aug. 28, 1989. Source: TRCS art. 8880, §6.

PROP §222.008. PURCHASER'S RIGHT TO CANCEL

(a) A purchaser may cancel a membership camping contract to purchase a membership interest or

membership right before the fourth business day after the contract is executed if the purchaser did not visit the location of the membership camping resort being offered for sale before the contract was signed. A purchaser may not waive his right of cancellation under this section. A contract containing a waiver is voidable by the purchaser.

(b) If a purchaser elects to cancel a membership camping contract under Subsection (a), he may do so by hand delivering notice of cancellation to the seller or by mailing notice by prepaid United States mail to the seller or to the seller's agent for service of process. Cancellation is without penalty, and all payments made by the purchaser before cancellation must be refunded before the 21st day after the date on which the seller receives notice of cancellation.

(c) If applicable, immediately before the space reserved in the contract for the signature of the purchaser, in bold-faced and conspicuous type or print that is larger than the type of print in the remaining text of the contract, substantially the following statement must appear:

"If you have not visited the location of the membership camping resort in which you are acquiring an interest or membership right, you may cancel this contract without penalty or obligation before the fourth business day after the date on which you signed this contract. If you decide to cancel this contract, you may do so by hand delivering notice of cancellation to the seller or by mailing notice by prepaid United States mail to the seller or the seller's agent for service of process. Your notice of cancellation is effective on the date sent or delivered to (name of seller) at (address of seller). A purchaser should not rely on statements other than those included in this contract and the disclosure statement."

History of Prop. Code §222.008: Acts 1989, 71st Leg., ch. 2, §13.03(d), eff. Aug. 28, 1989. Source: TRCS art. 8880, §7.

PROP §222.009. RECIPROCAL PROGRAM

An operator does not incur any liability arising out of use, delivery, or publication by the operator to the purchaser of written information or audio-visual materials provided to it by the reciprocal company pursuant to Section 222.006; provided, however, that an operator is subject to liability arising out of the use, delivery, or publication to the purchaser of materials provided by the reciprocal company if the operator knows that the materials are inaccurate or false.

History of Prop. Code §222.009: Acts 1989, 71st Leg., ch. 2, §13.03(d), eff. Aug. 28, 1989. Source: TRCS art. 8880, §8.

PROP §222.010. FEES

(a) The secretary of state shall set all fees imposed by this chapter in amounts reasonable and necessary to cover the costs of administering this chapter.

(b) The secretary of state shall deposit all fees received under this chapter in the state treasury to the credit of a special fund to be used in the administration of this chapter.

History of Prop. Code §222.010: Acts 1989, 71st Leg., ch. 2, §13.03(d), eff. Aug. 28, 1989. Amended by Acts 1989, 71st Leg., ch. 1039, §3.23, eff. Sept. 1, 1989. Source: TRCS art. 8880, §9.

PROP §222.011. VIOLATIONS

(a) A person commits a false, misleading, or deceptive act or practice within the meaning of Subsections (a) and (b), Section 17.46, Deceptive Trade Practices-Consumer Protection Act (Section 17.46, Business & Commerce Code), by engaging in any of the following acts:

(1) failing to disclose information concerning a membership interest or membership right required by Section 222.006;

(2) failing to provide a purchaser with a copy of the membership camping contract and any other document signed by the purchaser or the operator in connection with the purchase of a membership interest or membership right;

(3) making false or misleading statements of a material nature concerning camping sites or amenities available to the purchaser;

(4) predicting specific or immediate increases in the value of a membership interest or membership right without a reasonable basis for such predictions;

(5) making false or misleading statements of a material nature concerning the conditions under which a purchaser of a membership interest or membership right may use or occupy other membership camping resort camping sites or amenities;

(6) representing that a prize, gift, or other benefit will be awarded in connection with a promotion with intent not to award that prize, gift, or other benefit;

(7) representing that registration with the secretary of state under Section 222.004 constitutes approval or endorsement by the secretary of state of the operator, the membership camping contract, or the membership camping resort;

(8) offering or disposing of a membership interest or membership right under a membership camping contract without having complied with the registration requirements under Section 222.004; and

(9) offering for sale a membership interest or membership right in a membership camping resort without having complied with the registration requirements under Section 222.005.

(b) The provisions of this section are not exclusive and are in addition to provisions provided for in any other law.

History of Prop. Code §222.011: Acts 1989, 71st Leg., ch. 2, §13.03(d), eff. Aug. 28, 1989. Amended by Acts 1989, 71st Leg., ch. 1039, §3.24, eff. Sept. 1, 1989. Source: TRCS art. 8880, §10.

PROP §222.012. INSURANCE

Before the disposition of any membership interest or membership right in a membership camping resort, the operator shall maintain the following insurance with respect to the membership camping resort:

(1) property insurance on any personal property for use by purchasers, other than personal property separately owned by a purchaser, insuring against all risks of direct physical loss commonly insured against in a total amount, after application of deductibles, of the insurable value of the personal property of the membership camping resort; and

(2) liability insurance covering all occurrences commonly insured against for death, bodily injury, and property damage arising out of or in connection with the use, ownership, and maintenance of the membership camping resort.

History of Prop. Code §222.012: Acts 1989, 71st Leg., ch. 2, §13.03(d), eff. Aug. 28, 1989. Source: TRCS art. 8880, §11.

PROP §222.013. EXEMPT FROM SECURITIES ACT

The filing of a registration under this chapter exempts the sale of a membership interest or membership right in a membership camping resort subject to this chapter from registration under The Securities Act (Article 581-1 et seq., Vernon's Texas Civil Statutes).

History of Prop. Code §222.013: Acts 1989, 71st Leg., ch. 2, §13.03(d), eff. Aug. 28, 1989. Source: TRCS art. 8880, §12.

Chapters 223-239 blank

TITLE 13. DISCLAIMER OF PROPERTY INTERESTS

NCCUSL Prefatory Comment*

The Uniform Disclaimer of Property Interests Acts (UDPIA) replaces three Uniform Acts promulgated in 1978 (Uniform Disclaimer of Property Interests Act, Uniform Disclaimer of Transfers by Will, Intestacy or Appointment Act, and Uniform Disclaimer of Transfers under Nontestatmentary Instruments Act) and is incorporated into the Uniform Probate Code to replace former UPC §2-801. The new Act is the most comprehensive disclaimer statute ever written. It is designed to allow every sort of disclaimer, including those that are useful for tax planning purposes. It does not, however, include a specific time limit on the making of any disclaimer. Because a disclaimer is a refusal to accept, the only bar to a disclaimer should be acceptance of the offer. In addition, in almost all jurisdictions disclaimers can be used for more than tax planning. A proper disclaimer will often keep the disclaimed property from the disclaimant's creditors. In short, the new Act is an enabling statute which prescribes all the rules for refusing a proffered interest in or power over property and the effect of that refusal on the power or interest while leaving the effect of the refusal itself to other law. ...

The decision not to include a specific time limit—to "decouple" the disclaimer statute from the time requirement applicable to a "qualified disclaimer" under IRC §2518 is also designed to reduce confusion. The older Uniform Acts and almost all the current state statutes (many of which are based on those Acts) were drafted in the wake of the passage of IRC §2518 in 1976. That provision replaced the "reasonable time" requirement of prior law with a requirement that a disclaimer must be made within nine months of the creation of the interest disclaimed if the disclaimer is to be a "qualified disclaimer" which is not regarded as transfer by the disclaimant. The statutes that were written in response to this new provision of tax law reflected the nine month time limit. Under most of these statutes (including the older Uniform Acts and former §2-801) a disclaimer must be made within nine months of the creation of a present interest (for example, as disclaimer of an outright gift under a will must be made within nine months of the decedent's death), which corresponds to the requirement of IRC §2518. A future interest, however, may be disclaimed within nine months of the time the interest vests in possession or enjoyment (for example, a remainder whether or not contingent on surviving the holder of the life income interest must be disclaimed within nine months of the death of the life income beneficiary). The time limit for future interests does not correspond to IRC §2518 which generally requires that a qualified disclaimer of a future interest be made within nine months of the interest's creation, no matter how contingent it may then be. The nine-month time limit of the existing statutes really is a trap. While it superficially conforms to IRC §2518, its application to the disclaimer of future interests does not. The removal of all mention of time limits will clearly signal the practitioner that the requirements for a tax qualified disclaimer are set by different law.

... UDPIA creates rules for several types of disclaimers that have not been explicitly addressed in previous statutes. The Act provides detailed rules for the disclaimer of interests in jointly held property (§240.052). Such disclaimers have important uses especially in tax planning, but their status under current law is not clear. Furthermore, although current statutes mention the disclaimer of jointly held property, they provide no details. Recent developments in the law of qualified disclaimers of jointly held property make fuller treatment of such disclaimers necessary. Section 240.053 addresses the disclaimer by trustees of property that would otherwise become part of the trust. The disclaimer of powers of appointment and other powers not held in a fiduciary capacity is treated in §240.054 and disclaimers by appointees, objects, and takers in default of exercise of a power of appointment is the subject of §240.055. Finally, §240.056 provides rules for the disclaimer of powers held in a fiduciary capacity.

CHAPTER 240. TEXAS UNIFORM DISCLAIMER OF PROPERTY INTERESTS ACT

Subchapter A. General Provisions

The NCCUSL comments have been edited to reflect the Texas Legislature's omission of sections and changing of section numbers from the original uniform act. The Texas Legislature did not adopt the NCCUSL comments when it adopted the Uniform Disclaimer of Property Interests Act. The full uniform act and comments can be found at www.uniformlaws.org.

SUBCHAPTER A. GENERAL PROVISIONS

PROP §240.001. SHORT TITLE

This chapter may be cited as the Texas Uniform Disclaimer of Property Interests Act.

History of Prop. Code §240.001: Acts 2015, 84th Leg., ch. 562, §15, eff. Sept. 1, 2015.

PROP §240.002. DEFINITIONS

In this chapter:

(1) "Charity" means a charitable entity or a charitable trust, as those terms are defined by Section 123.001.

(1-a) "Current beneficiary" and "presumptive remainder beneficiary" have the meanings assigned by Section 112.071.

(2) "Disclaim" means to refuse to accept an interest in or power over property, including an interest or power the person is entitled to:

(A) by inheritance;

(B) under a will;

(C) by an agreement between spouses for community property with a right of survivorship;

(D) by a joint tenancy with a right of survivorship;

(E) by a survivorship agreement, account, or interest in which the interest of the decedent passes to a surviving beneficiary;

(F) by an insurance, annuity, endowment, employment, deferred compensation, or other contract or arrangement;

(G) under a pension, profit sharing, thrift, stock bonus, life insurance, survivor income, incentive, or other plan or program providing retirement, welfare, or fringe benefits with respect to an employee or a self-employed individual; or

(H) by an instrument creating a trust.

(3) "Disclaimant" means:

(A) the person to whom a disclaimed interest or power would have passed had the disclaimer not been made;

(B) the estate to which a disclaimed interest or power would have passed had the disclaimer not been made by the personal representative of the estate; or

(C) the trust into which a disclaimed interest or power would have passed had the disclaimer not been made by the trustee of the trust.

(4) "Disclaimed interest" means the interest that would have passed to the disclaimant had the disclaimer not been made.

(5) "Disclaimed power" means the power that would have been possessed by the disclaimant had the disclaimer not been made.

(6) "Disclaimer" means the refusal to accept an interest in or power over property.

(7) "Estate" has the meaning assigned by Section 22.012, Estates Code.

(8) "Fiduciary" means a personal representative, a trustee, an attorney in fact or agent acting under a power of attorney, or any other person authorized to act as a fiduciary with respect to the property of another person.

(9) "Guardian" has the meaning assigned by Section 1002.012, Estates Code.

(10) Notwithstanding Section 311.005, Government Code, "person" means an individual, corporation, including a public corporation, business trust, partnership, limited liability company, association, joint venture, governmental entity, including a political subdivision, agency, or instrumentality, or any other legal entity.

(11) "Personal representative" has the meanings assigned by Sections 22.031 and 1002.028, Estates Code.

(12) "State" means a state of the United States, the District of Columbia, Puerto Rico, the United States Virgin Islands, or any territory or insular possession subject to the jurisdiction of the United States. The term includes an Indian tribe or band, or Alaskan native village, recognized by federal law or formally acknowledged by a state.

(13) "Survivorship property" means property held in the name of two or more persons under an arrangement in which, on the death of one of the persons, the property passes to and is vested in the other person or persons. The term includes:

(A) property held by an agreement described in Section 111.001, Estates Code;

(B) property held by a community property survivorship agreement defined in Section 112.001, Estates Code; and

(C) property in a joint account held by an agreement described in Section 113.151, Estates Code.

(14) "Trust" has the meaning assigned by Section 111.003.

(15) "Ward" has the meaning assigned by Section 22.033, Estates Code.

History of Prop. Code §240.002: Acts 2015, 84th Leg., ch. 562, §15, eff. Sept. 1, 2015. Amended by S.B. 617, §15, 85th Leg., eff. Sept. 1, 2017.

NCCUSL Comment*

...

The term "disclaimed interest" (subsection (4)) refers to the subject matter of a disclaimer of an interest in property and provides a compact term the use of which simplifies the drafting of §§240.051-240.0512.

The definition of "disclaimer" (subsection (6)) expands previous definitions. Prior Uniform Acts provided for a disclaimer of "the right of succession to any property or interest therein" and former UPC §2-801 referred to "an interest in or with respect to property or an interest therein." These previously authorized types of disclaimers are continued by the present language referring to "an interest in ... property." The language referring to "power over property" broadens the permissible scope of disclaimers to include any power over property that gives the power-holder a right to control property, whether it be cast in the form of a power of appointment or a fiduciary's management power over property or discretionary power of distribution over income or corpus.

Under the Act, a "fiduciary" (defined in subsection (8)) is given the power to disclaim except where specifically prohibited by state law or by the document creating the fiduciary relationship. *See* §240.007.

...

PROP §240.003. APPLICABILITY OF CHAPTER

This chapter applies to disclaimers of any interest in or power over property, whenever created.

History of Prop. Code §240.003: Acts 2015, 84th Leg., ch. 562, §15, eff. Sept. 1, 2015.

PROP §240.004. CHAPTER SUPPLEMENTED BY OTHER LAW

(a) Unless displaced by a provision of this chapter, the principles of law and equity supplement this chapter.

(b) This chapter does not limit any right of a person to waive, release, disclaim, or renounce an interest in or power over property under a statute other than this chapter.

History of Prop. Code §240.004: Acts 2015, 84th Leg., ch. 562, §15, eff. Sept. 1, 2015.

NCCUSL Comment*

The supplementation of the provisions of the Act by the principles of law and equity in §2-1104(a) is important because the Act is not a complete statement of the law relating to disclaimers. For example, §2-1105(b) permits a trustee to disclaim, yet the disclaiming trustee must still adhere to all applicable fiduciary duties. *See* Restatement (Third) of Trusts §86 Reporter's Notes to cmt. f. Similarly, the provisions of §2-1113 on bars to disclaiming are subject to supplementation by equitable principles. *See Badouh v. Hale*, 22 S.W.3d 392 (Tex. 2000) (invalidating a disclaimer of an expectancy as contrary to equity, on the ground that the putative disclaimant had earlier pledged it to a third party).

Not only are the provisions of the Act supplemented by the principles of law and equity, but under §2-1104(b) the provisions of the Act do not preempt other law that creates the right to reject an interest in or power over property. The growth of the law would be unduly restricted were the provisions of the Act completely to displace other law.

PROP §240.005. UNIFORMITY OF APPLICATION & CONSTRUCTION

In applying and construing this chapter, consideration must be given to the need to promote uniformity

* See footnote on p. 705.

of the law, with respect to the subject matter of this chapter, among states that enact a law based on the uniform act on which this chapter is based.

History of Prop. Code §240.005: Acts 2015, 84th Leg., ch. 562, §15, eff. Sept. 1, 2015.

PROP §240.006. POWER TO DISCLAIM BY PERSON OTHER THAN FIDUCIARY

(a) A person other than a fiduciary may disclaim, in whole or in part, any interest in or power over property, including a power of appointment.

(b) A person other than a fiduciary may disclaim an interest or power under this section even if the creator of the interest or power imposed a spendthrift provision or similar restriction on transfer or a restriction or limitation on the right to disclaim.

History of Prop. Code §240.006: Acts 2015, 84th Leg., ch. 562, §15, eff. Sept. 1, 2015.

NCCUSL Comment*

Sections 240.006-240.008 give both persons (as defined in §240.002(10)) and fiduciaries (as defined in §240.002(8)) a broad power to disclaim both interests in and powers over property. In both instances, the ability to disclaim interests is comprehensive; it does not matter whether the disclaimed interest is vested, either in interest or in possession. For example, Father's will creates a testamentary trust which is to pay income to his descendants and after the running of the traditional perpetuities period is to terminate and be distributed to his descendants then living by representation. If at any time there are no descendants, the trust is to terminate and be distributed to collateral relatives. At the time of Father's death he has many descendants and the possibility of his line dying out and the collateral relatives taking under the trust is remote in the extreme. Nevertheless, under the Act the collateral relatives may disclaim their contingent remainders. (In order to make a qualified disclaimer for tax purposes, however, they must disclaim them within nine months of Father's death.) Every sort of power may also be disclaimed.

Section 240.006 continues the provisions of current law by making ineffective any attempt to limit the right to disclaim which the creator of an interest or non-fiduciary power seeks to impose on a person. This provision follows from the principle behind all disclaimers—no one can be forced to accept property—and extends that principle to powers over property.

PROP §240.007. POWER TO DISCLAIM POWER HELD IN FIDUCIARY CAPACITY BY PERSON DESIGNATED TO SERVE AS OR SERVING AS FIDUCIARY

(a) Subject to Subsection (b) and except to the extent the person's right to disclaim is expressly restricted or limited by a law of this state or by the instrument creating the fiduciary relationship, a person designated to serve or serving as a fiduciary may disclaim, in whole or in part, any power over property, including a power of appointment and the power to disclaim, held in a fiduciary capacity.

(b) If a power being disclaimed under Subsection (a) by a person designated to serve or serving as a trustee affects the distributive rights of any beneficiary of the trust:

(1) the person may disclaim only on or after accepting the trust;

(2) the disclaimer must be compatible with the trustee's fiduciary obligations; and

(3) if the disclaimer is made on accepting the trust, the trustee is considered to have never possessed the power disclaimed.

(c) A person designated to serve or serving as a fiduciary may disclaim a power under this section even if the creator of the power imposed a spendthrift provision or similar restriction on transfer.

History of Prop. Code §240.007: Acts 2015, 84th Leg., ch. 562, §15, eff. Sept. 1, 2015.

PROP §240.008. POWER TO DISCLAIM BY FIDUCIARY ACTING IN FIDUCIARY CAPACITY

(a) Subject to this section and except to the extent the fiduciary's right to disclaim is expressly restricted or limited by a law of this state or by the instrument creating the fiduciary relationship, a fiduciary acting in a fiduciary capacity may disclaim, in whole or in part, any interest in or power over property, including a power of appointment and the power to disclaim, that would have passed to the ward, estate, trust, or principal with respect to which the fiduciary was acting had the disclaimer not been made even if:

(1) the creator of the interest or power imposed a spendthrift provision or similar restriction on transfer or a restriction or limitation on the right to disclaim; or

(2) an instrument other than the instrument that created the fiduciary relationship imposed a restriction or limitation on the right to disclaim.

(b) Except as provided by Subsection (c), (d), or (f), a disclaimer by a fiduciary acting in a fiduciary capacity does not require court approval to be effective unless the instrument that created the fiduciary relationship requires court approval.

(c) The following disclaimers by a fiduciary acting in a fiduciary capacity are not effective unless approved by a court of competent jurisdiction:

(1) a disclaimer by a personal representative who is not an independent administrator or independent executor;

* See footnote on p. 705.

(2) a disclaimer by the trustee of a management trust created under Chapter 1301, Estates Code;

(3) a disclaimer by the trustee of a trust created under Section 142.005; or

(4) a disclaimer that would result in an interest in or power over property passing to the person making the disclaimer.

(d) A trustee acting in a fiduciary capacity may not disclaim an interest in property that would cause the interest in property not to become trust property unless:

(1) a court of competent jurisdiction approves the disclaimer; or

(2) the trustee provides written notice of the disclaimer in accordance with Section 240.0081.

(e) In the absence of a court-appointed guardian, without court approval, a natural guardian as described by Section 1104.051, Estates Code, may disclaim on behalf of a minor child of the natural guardian, in whole or in part, any interest in or power over property, including a power of appointment, that the minor child is to receive solely as a result of another disclaimer, but only if the disclaimed interest or power does not pass to or for the benefit of the natural guardian as a result of the disclaimer.

(f) Unless a court of competent jurisdiction approves the disclaimer, a disclaimer by a fiduciary acting in a fiduciary capacity must be compatible with the fiduciary's fiduciary obligations. A disclaimer by a fiduciary acting in a fiduciary capacity is not a per se breach of the fiduciary's fiduciary obligations.

(g) Possible remedies for a breach of fiduciary obligations do not include declaring an otherwise effective disclaimer void or granting other legal or equitable relief that would make the disclaimer ineffective.

History of Prop. Code §240.008: Acts 2015, 84th Leg., ch. 562, §15, eff. Sept. 1, 2015.

NCCUSL Comment*

This Act ... gives fiduciaries broad powers to disclaim both interests and powers. A fiduciary who may also be a beneficiary of the fiduciary arrangement may disclaim in either capacity. For example, a trustee who is also one of several beneficiaries of a trust may have the power to invade trust principal for the beneficiaries. The trustee may disclaim the power as trustee under §240.056 or may disclaim as a holder of a power of appointment under §240.054. Section 240.008 also gives fiduciaries the right to disclaim in spite of spendthrift or similar restrictions given, but subjects that right to a restriction applicable only to fiduciaries. As a policy matter, the creator of a trust or other arrangement creating a fiduciary relationship should be able to prevent a fiduciary accepting office under the arrangement from altering the parameters of the relationship. This reasoning also applies to fiduciary relationships created by statute such as those governing conservatorships and guardianships. Section 240.008 therefore does not override express restrictions on disclaimers contained in the instrument creating the fiduciary relationship or in other statutes of the state.

Ⓐ PROP §240.0081. NOTICE REQUIRED BY TRUSTEE DISCLAIMING CERTAIN INTERESTS IN PROPERTY; EFFECT OF NOTICE

(a) A trustee acting in a fiduciary capacity may disclaim an interest in property that would cause the interest in property not to become trust property without court approval if the trustee provides written notice of the disclaimer to all of the current beneficiaries and presumptive remainder beneficiaries of the trust.

(b) For the purpose of determining who is a current beneficiary or presumptive remainder beneficiary entitled to the notice under Subsection (a), a beneficiary is determined as of the date the notice is sent.

(c) Except as provided by Subsection (e-1), in [~~In~~] addition to the notice required under Subsection (a), the trustee shall give written notice of the trustee's disclaimer to the attorney general if:

(1) a charity is entitled to notice;

(2) a charity entitled to notice is no longer in existence;

(3) the trustee has the authority to distribute trust assets to one or more charities that are not named in the trust instrument; or

(4) the trustee has the authority to make distributions for a charitable purpose described in the trust instrument, but no charity is named as a beneficiary for that purpose.

(d) If the beneficiary has a court-appointed guardian or conservator, the notice required to be given by this section must be given to that guardian or conservator. If the beneficiary is a minor for whom no guardian or conservator has been appointed, the notice required to be given by this section must be given to a parent of the minor.

(e) The trustee is not required to provide the notice to a beneficiary who:

(1) is known to the trustee and cannot be located by the trustee after reasonable diligence;

(2) is not known to the trustee;

(3) waives the requirement of the notice under this section; or

(4) is a descendant of a beneficiary to whom the trustee has given notice if the beneficiary and the ben-

* See footnote on p. 705.

eficiary's ancestor have similar interests in the trust and no apparent conflict of interest exists between them.

(e-1) The trustee is not required to give notice to the attorney general under Subsection (c) if the attorney general waives that requirement in writing.

(e-2) For purposes of Subsection (e)(3), a beneficiary is considered to have waived the requirement that notice be given under this section if a person to whom notice is required to be given with respect to that beneficiary under Subsection (d) waives the requirement that notice be given under this section.

(f) The notice required under Subsection (a) must:

(1) include a statement that:

(A) the trustee intends to disclaim an interest in property;

(B) if the trustee makes the disclaimer, the property will not become trust property and will not be available to distribute to the beneficiary from the trust;

(C) the beneficiary has the right to object to the disclaimer; and

(D) the beneficiary may petition a court to approve, modify, or deny the disclaimer;

(2) describe the interest in property the trustee intends to disclaim;

(3) specify the earliest date the trustee intends to make the disclaimer;

(4) include the name and mailing address of the trustee;

(5) be given not later than the 30th day before the date the disclaimer is made; and

(6) be sent by personal delivery, first-class mail, facsimile, e-mail, or any other method likely to result in the notice's receipt.

(g) A beneficiary is not considered to have accepted the disclaimed interest solely because the beneficiary acts or does not act on receipt of a notice provided under this section.

(h) If the trustee makes the disclaimer for which notice is provided under this section, the beneficiary does not lose the beneficiary's right, if any, to sue the trustee for breach of the trustee's fiduciary obligations in connection with making the disclaimer. Section 240.008(g) applies to remedies sought in connection with the alleged breach.

History of Prop. Code §240.0081: Acts 2015, 84th Leg., ch. 562, §15, eff. Sept. 1, 2015. Amended by S.B. 617, §16, 85th Leg., eff. Sept. 1, 2017.

PROP §240.009. POWER TO DISCLAIM; GENERAL REQUIREMENTS; WHEN IRREVOCABLE

(a) To be effective, a disclaimer must:

(1) be in writing;

(2) declare the disclaimer;

(3) describe the interest or power disclaimed;

(4) be signed by the person making the disclaimer; and

(5) be delivered or filed in the manner provided by Subchapter C.

(b) A partial disclaimer may be expressed as a fraction, percentage, monetary amount, term of years, limitation of a power, or any other interest or estate in the property.

(c) A disclaimer is irrevocable on the later of the date the disclaimer:

(1) is delivered or filed under Subchapter C; or

(2) takes effect as provided in Sections 240.051-240.056.

(d) A disclaimer made under this chapter is not a transfer, assignment, or release.

History of Prop. Code §240.009: Acts 2015, 84th Leg., ch. 562, §15, eff. Sept. 1, 2015.

NCCUSL Comment*

...

Section 240.009(b) specifically allows a partial disclaimer of an interest in property or of a power over property, and gives the disclaimant wide latitude in describing the portion disclaimed. For example, a residuary beneficiary of an estate may disclaim a fraction or percentage of the residue or may disclaim specific property included in the residue (all the shares of X corporation or a specific number of shares). A devisee or donee may disclaim specific acreage or an undivided fraction or carve out a life estate or remainder from a larger interest in real or personal property. (It must be noted, however, that a disclaimer by a devisee or donee which seeks to "carve out" a remainder or life estate is not a "qualified disclaimer" for tax purposes, Treas. Reg. §25.2518-3(b).)

Section 240.009(c) makes the disclaimer irrevocable on the later to occur of (i) delivery or filing or (ii) its becoming effective under the section governing the disclaimer of the particular power or interest. A disclaimer must be "irrevocable" in order to be a qualified disclaimer for tax purposes. Since a disclaimer under this Act becomes effective at the time significant for tax purposes, a disclaimer under this Act will always meet the irrevocability requirement for tax qualification. The interaction of the Act and the requirements for a tax qualified disclaimer can be illustrated by analyzing a disclaimer of an interest in a revocable lifetime trust.

> **Example 1.** G creates a revocable lifetime trust which will terminate on G's death and distribute the trust property to G's surviving descendants by representation. G's son, S, determines that he would prefer his share of G's estate to pass to his descendants and executes a disclaimer of his interest in the revocable trust. The disclaimer is then delivered to G (*see* §240.104(2)). The disclaimer is not irrevocable at that time, however, because it will not become effective until G's

* See footnote on p. 705.

death when the trust becomes irrevocable (*see* §240.051). Because the disclaimer will not become irrevocable until it becomes effective at G's death, S may recall the disclaimer before G's death and, if he does so, the disclaimer will have no effect.

Section 240.009(d) restates the long standing rule that a disclaimer is a true refusal to accept and not an act by which the disclaimant transfers, assigns, or releases the disclaimed interest. This subsection states the effect and meaning of the traditional "relation back" doctrine of prior Acts. It also makes it clear that the disclaimed interest passes without direction by the disclaimant, a requirement of tax qualification.

Sections 240.010-240.0500 blank

SUBCHAPTER B. TYPE & EFFECT OF DISCLAIMER

PROP §240.0501. DEFINITION

In this subchapter, "future interest" means an interest that:

(1) takes effect in possession or enjoyment, if at all, later than the time at which the instrument creating the interest becomes irrevocable; and

(2) passes to the holder of the interest at the time of the event that causes the taker of the interest to be finally ascertained and the interest to be indefeasibly vested.

History of Prop. Code §240.0501: Acts 2015, 84th Leg., ch. 562, §15, eff. Sept. 1, 2015.

PROP §240.051. DISCLAIMER OF INTEREST IN PROPERTY

(a) This section and Sections 240.0511 and 240.0512 apply to a disclaimer of an interest in property other than a disclaimer subject to Section 240.052 or 240.053.

(b) If an interest in property passes because of the death of a decedent:

(1) a disclaimer of the interest:

(A) takes effect as of the time of the decedent's death; and

(B) relates back for all purposes to the time of the decedent's death; and

(2) the disclaimed interest is not subject to the claims of any creditor of the disclaimant.

(c) If an interest in property passes because of an event not related to the death of a decedent:

(1) a disclaimer of the interest:

(A) takes effect:

(i) as of the time the instrument creating the interest became irrevocable; or

(ii) in the case of an irrevocable transfer made without an instrument, at the time of the irrevocable transfer; and

(B) relates back for all purposes to the time the instrument became irrevocable or the time of the irrevocable transfer, as applicable; and

(2) the disclaimed interest is not subject to the claims of any creditor of the disclaimant.

(d) A disclaimed interest passes according to any provision in the instrument creating the interest that provides for:

(1) the disposition of the interest if the interest were to be disclaimed; or

(2) the disposition of disclaimed interests in general.

(e) If the instrument creating the disclaimed interest does not contain a provision described by Subsection (d) and:

(1) if the disclaimant is not an individual, the disclaimed interest passes as if the disclaimant did not exist; or

(2) if the disclaimant is an individual:

(A) except as provided by Section 240.0511, if the interest is passing because of the death of a decedent, the disclaimed interest passes as if the disclaimant had died immediately before the time as of which the disclaimer takes effect under Subsection (b); or

(B) except as provided by Section 240.0512, if the interest is passing because of an event not related to the death of a decedent, the disclaimed interest passes as if the disclaimant had died immediately before the time as of which the disclaimer takes effect under Subsection (c).

(f) A disclaimed interest that passes by intestacy passes as if the disclaimant died immediately before the decedent.

History of Prop. Code §240.051: Acts 2015, 84th Leg., ch. 562, §15, eff. Sept. 1, 2015.

See also Karisch, et al., *To Disclaim or Not to Disclaim: "How?" Is the Real Question*, Advanced Estate Planning & Probate Course, State Bar of Texas CLE, ch. 4 (2015).

NCCUSL Comment*

...

Subsections (b) and (c) make a disclaimer of an interest in property effective as of the time the instrument creating the interest becomes irrevocable or at the decedent's death if the interest is created by intestate succession. A will and a revocable trust are irrevocable at the testator's or settlor's death. Inter vivos trusts may also be irrevocable at their creation or may become irrevocable before the settlor's death. A beneficiary designation is also irrevocable at death, unless it is made irrevocable at an earlier time. This provision continues the provision of Uniform Acts on this subject, but with different wording. ...

Section 240.051(d) allows the creator of the instrument to control the disposition of the disclaimed interest by express provision in the instrument. The

* See footnote on p. 705.

provision may apply to a particular interest. "I give to my cousin A the sum of ten thousand dollars ($10,000) and should he disclaim any part of this gift, I give the part disclaimed to my cousin B." The provision may also apply to all disclaimed interests. A residuary clause beginning "I give my residuary estate, including all disclaimed interests to…." is such a provision.

Sections 240.051(e)(2) and 240.0511(a), (b) apply if §240.051(d) does not and if the disclaimant is an individual. Because "disclaimant" is defined as the person to whom the disclaimed interest would have passed had the disclaimer not been made (§240.002(3)(A)), these paragraphs would apply to disclaimers by fiduciaries on behalf of individuals. The general rule is that the disclaimed interest passes as if the disclaimant had died immediately before the time of distribution…. The application of this general rule to present interests given to named individuals is illustrated by the following examples:

Example 1(a). T's will devised "ten thousand dollars ($10,000) to my brother, B." B disclaims the entire devise. B is deemed to have predeceased T, and, therefore B's gift has lapsed. If the state's antilapse statute applies, it will direct the passing of the disclaimed interest. Under UPC §2-603(b)(1), for example, B's descendants who survive T by 120 hours will take the devise by representation.

Example 1(b). T's will devised "ten thousand dollars ($10,000) to my friend, F." F disclaims the entire devise. F is deemed to predecease T and the gift has lapsed. Few antilapse statutes apply to devises to non-family members. Under UPC §2-603(b), which saves from lapse only gifts made to certain relatives, the devise would lapse and pass through the residuary clause of the will.

Example 1(c). T's will devised "ten thousand dollars ($10,000) to my brother, B, but if B does not survive me, to my children." If B disclaims the devise, he will be deemed to have predeceased T and the alternative gift to T's children will dispose of the devise.

Present interests are also given to the surviving members of a class or group of persons. Perhaps the most common example of this gift is a devise of the testator's residuary estate "to my descendants who survive me by representation." Under the system of distribution among multigenerational classes used in the Uniform Probate Code §2-709 and similar statutes, division of the property to be distributed begins in the eldest generation in which there are living people. The following example illustrates a problem that can arise.

Example 2(a). T's will devised "the residue of my estate to my descendants who survive me by representation." T is survived by son S and daughter D. Son has two living children and D has one. S disclaims his interest. The disclaimed interest is one-half of the residuary estate, the interest S would have received had he not disclaimed. Section 240.051(e)(2) provides that the disclaimed interest passes as if S had predeceased T. If §240.051(e) stopped there, S's children would take one-half of the disclaimed interest and D would take the other half under every system of "representation" that commonly exists. S's disclaimer should not have that effect, however, but should pass what he would have taken to his children. Section 240.0511(a)(1) solves the problem. It provides that the entire disclaimed interest passes only to S's descendants because they would share in the interest had S truly predeceased T.

The provision also solves a problem that exists when the disclaimant is the only representative of an older generation.

Example 2(b). Assume the same facts as **Example 2(a)**, but D has predeceased T. T is survived, therefore, by S, S's two children, and D's child. S disclaims. Again, the disclaimed interest is one-half of the residuary estate and it passes as if S had predeceased T. Had S actually predeceased T, the three grandchildren of S would have shared equally in T's residuary estate because they are all in the same generation. Were the three grandchildren to share equally in the disclaimed interest, S's two children would each receive one-third of the one-half while D's child would receive one-third of the one-half in addition to the one-half of the residuary estate received as the representative of his or her late parent. Section 240.0511(a)(1) again applies to insure that S's children receive one-half of the residue, exactly the interest S would have received but for the disclaimer.

The disclaimer of future interests created by will leads to a different problem. The effective date of the disclaimer of the future interest, the testator's death, is earlier in time than the distribution date. This in turn leads to a possible anomaly illustrated by the following example.

Example 3. Father's will creates a testamentary trust for Mother who is to receive all the income for life. At her death, the trust is to be distributed to Father and Mother's surviving descendants by representation. Mother is survived by son S and daughter D. Son has two living children and D has one. Son decides that he would prefer his share of the trust to pass to his children and disclaims. The disclaimer must be made within nine months of Father's death if it is to be a qualified disclaimer for tax purposes. Under prior Acts and former UPC §2-801, the interest would have passed as if Son had predeceased Father. A problem could arise if, at Mother's death, one or more of S's children living at that time were born after Father's death. It would be possible to argue that had S predeceased Father the afterborn children would not exist and that D and S's two children living at the time of Father's death are entitled to all of the trust property.

The problem illustrated in **Example 3** is solved by §240.051(e)(2). The disclaimed interest would have taken effect in possession or enjoyment, that is, Son would be entitled to receive one-half of the trust property, at Mother's death. Under paragraph (e)(2) Son is deemed to have died immediately before Mother's death even though under §240.051(b) the disclaimer is effective as of Father's death. There is no doubt, therefore, that S's children living at the distribution date, whenever born, are entitled to the share of the trust property S would have received and, as **Examples 2(a)** and **2(b)** show, they will take exactly what S would have received but for the disclaimer. Had S actually died before Mother, he would have received nothing at Mother's death whether or not the disclaimer had been made. There is nothing to pass to S's children and they take as representatives of S under the representational scheme in effect.

Future interests may or may not be conditioned on survivorship. The following examples illustrate disclaimers of future interests not expressly conditioned on survival.

Example 4(a). G's revocable trust directs the trustee to pay "ten thousand dollars ($10,000) to the grantor's brother, B" at the termination of the trust on G's death. B disclaims the entire gift immediately after G's death. B is deemed to have predeceased G because it is at G's death that the interest given B will come into possession and enjoyment. Had B not disclaimed he would have received $10,000 at that time. The recipient of the disclaimed interest will be determined by the law that applies to gifts of future interests to persons who die before the interest comes into possession and enjoyment. Traditional analysis would regard the gift to B as a vested interest subject to divestment by G's power to revoke the trust. So long as G has not revoked the gift, the interest would pass through B's estate to B's successors in interest. Yet If B's successors in interest are selected by B's will, the disclaimer cannot be a qualified disclaimer for tax purposes. This problem does not arise in a jurisdiction with UPC §2-707(b), because the interest passes not through B's estate but rather to B's descendants who survive G by 120 hours by representation. Because the antilapse mechanism of UPC §2-707 is not limited to gifts to relatives, a disclaimer by a friend rather than a brother would have the same result. For jurisdictions without UPC §2-707, however, §240.0511(a)(2) provides an equivalent solution: a disclaimed interest that would otherwise pass through B's estate instead passes to B's descendants who survive G by representation.

Example 4(b). G's revocable trust directed that on his death the trust property is to be distributed to his three children, A, B, and C. A disclaims immediately after G's death and is deemed to predecease the distribution date, which is G's death. The traditional analysis applies exactly as it does in **Example 4(a)**. The only condition on A's gift would be G's not revoking the trust. A is not explicitly required to survive G. (*See First National Bank of Bar Harbor v. Anthony*, 557 A.2d 957 (Me. 1989).) The interest would pass to A's successors in interest. If those successors are selected by A's will, the disclaimer cannot be a qualified disclaimer for tax purposes. UPC §2-707(b) provides

that A's interest passes by representation to A's descendants who survive G by 120 hours. For jurisdictions without UPC §2-707, §240.0511(a)(2) reaches the same result.

Example 4(c). G conveys land "to A for life, remainder to B." B disclaims immediately after the conveyance. Traditional analysis regards B's remainder as vested; it is not contingent on surviving A. This classification is unaffected by whether or not the jurisdiction has adopted UPC §2-707, because that section only applies to future interests in trust; it does not apply to future interests not in trust, such as the one in this example created directly in land. To the extent that B's remainder is transmissible through B's estate, B's disclaimer cannot be a qualified disclaimer for tax purposes. Section 240.0511(a)(2) resolves the problem: a disclaimed interest that would otherwise pass through B's estate instead passes as if it were controlled by UPC §§2-707 and 2-711. ...

Section 240.051(e)(1) provides a rule for the passing of property interests disclaimed by persons other than individuals. Because §240.053 applies to disclaimers by trustees of property that would otherwise pass to the trust, §240.051(e)(1) principally applies to disclaimers by corporations, partnerships, and the other entities listed in the definition of "person" in §240.002(10). A charity, for example, might wish to disclaim property the acceptance of which would be incompatible with its purposes.

PROP §240.0511. DISPOSITION OF INTEREST PASSING BECAUSE OF DECEDENT'S DEATH & DISCLAIMED BY INDIVIDUAL

(a) Subject to Subsection (b):

(1) if by law or under the instrument creating the disclaimed interest the descendants of a disclaimant of an interest passing because of the death of a decedent would share in the disclaimed interest by any method of representation under Section 240.051(e)(2)(A), the disclaimed interest passes only to the descendants of the disclaimant who survive the decedent; or

(2) if the disclaimed interest would have passed to the disclaimant's estate under Section 240.051(e)(2)(A), the disclaimed interest instead passes by representation to the descendants of the disclaimant who survive the decedent.

(b) If no descendant of the disclaimant survives the decedent, the disclaimed interest passes to those persons, including the state but excluding the disclaimant, and in such shares as would succeed to the transferor's intestate estate under the intestate succession law of the transferor's domicile had the transferor died immediately before the decedent, except that if the transferor's surviving spouse is living but remarried before the decedent's death, the transferor is considered to have died unmarried immediately before the decedent's death.

(c) On the disclaimer of a preceding interest, a future interest held by a person other than the disclaimant takes effect as if the disclaimant had died immediately before the decedent, but a future interest held by the disclaimant is not accelerated in possession or enjoyment.

History of Prop. Code §240.0511: Acts 2015, 84th Leg., ch. 562, §15, eff. Sept. 1, 2015.

NCCUSL Comment*

Section 240.0511(c) continues the provision of prior Uniform Acts and UPC §2-801 on this subject providing for the acceleration of future interests on the making of the disclaimer, except that future interests in the disclaimant do not accelerate. The workings of §240.0511(c) are illustrated by the following examples.

Example 5(a). Father's will creates a testamentary trust to pay income to his son S for his life, and on his death to pay the remainder to S's descendants then living, by representation. If S disclaims his life income interest in the trust, he will be deemed to have died immediately before Father's death. The disclaimed interest, S's income interest, came into possession and enjoyment at Father's death as would any present interest created by will (*see* **Examples 1(a), (b), and (c)**), and, therefore, the time of distribution is Father's death. If at the income beneficiary of a testamentary trust does not survive the testator, the income interest is not created and the next interest in the trust takes effect. Since the next interest in Father's trust is the remainder in S's descendants, the trust property will pass to S's descendants who survive Father by representation. It is immaterial under the statute that the actual situation at the S's death might be different with different descendants entitled to the remainder.

Example 5(b). Mother's will creates a testamentary trust to pay the income to her daughter D until she reaches age 35 at which time the trust is to terminate and the trust property distributed in equal shares to D and her three siblings. D disclaims her income interest. The remainder interests in her three siblings accelerate and they each receive one-fourth of the trust property. D's remainder interest does not accelerate, however, and she must wait until she is 35 to receive her fourth of the trust property.

PROP §240.0512. DISPOSITION OF INTEREST PASSING BECAUSE OF EVENT OTHER THAN DECEDENT'S DEATH & DISCLAIMED BY INDIVIDUAL

(a) Subject to Subsection (b):

(1) if by law or under the instrument creating the disclaimed interest the descendants of a disclaimant of an interest passing because of an event not related to the death of a decedent would share in the disclaimed interest by any method of representation under Section 240.051(e)(2)(B), the disclaimed interest passes only to the descendants of the disclaimant living at the time of the event that causes the interest to pass; or

(2) if the disclaimed interest would have passed to the disclaimant's estate under Section 240.051(e)(2)(B), the disclaimed interest instead passes by representation to the descendants of the disclaimant living at the time of the event that causes the interest to pass.

---

* See footnote on p. 705.

(b) If no descendant of the disclaimant is living at the time of the event described by Subsection (a)(1), the disclaimed interest passes to those persons, including the state but excluding the disclaimant, and in such shares as would succeed to the transferor's intestate estate under the intestate succession law of the transferor's domicile had the transferor died immediately before the event described by Subsection (a)(1), except that if the transferor's surviving spouse is living but remarried before the event, the transferor is considered to have died unmarried immediately before the event.

(c) On the disclaimer of a preceding interest, a future interest held by a person other than the disclaimant takes effect as if the disclaimant had died immediately before the time the disclaimer takes effect under Section 240.051(c)(1)(A), but a future interest held by the disclaimant is not accelerated in possession or enjoyment.

History of Prop. Code §240.0512: Acts 2015, 84th Leg., ch. 562, §15, eff. Sept. 1, 2015.

PROP §240.052. DISCLAIMER OF RIGHTS IN SURVIVORSHIP PROPERTY

(a) On the death of a holder of survivorship property, a surviving holder may disclaim, in whole or in part, an interest in the property of the deceased holder that would have otherwise passed to the surviving holder by reason of the deceased holder's death.

(b) If an interest in survivorship property is disclaimed by a surviving holder of the property:

(1) the disclaimer:

(A) takes effect as of the time of the deceased holder's death; and

(B) relates back for all purposes to the time of the deceased holder's death; and

(2) the disclaimed interest is not subject to the claims of any creditor of the disclaimant.

(c) An interest in survivorship property disclaimed by a surviving holder of the property passes as if the disclaimant predeceased the holder to whose death the disclaimer relates.

History of Prop. Code §240.052: Acts 2015, 84th Leg., ch. 562, §15, eff. Sept. 1, 2015.

NCCUSL Comment*

... The common law was unsettled whether a surviving joint tenant had any right to renounce his interest in jointly-owned property and if so to what extent. *See* Casner, Estate Planning, 5th ed. §10.7. Specifically, if A and B owned real estate or securities as joint tenants with right of survivorship and A died, the problem was whether B might disclaim what was given to him originally upon creation of the estate, or, if not, whether he could nevertheless reject the incremental portion derived through the right of survivorship. There was also a question of whether a joint bank account should be treated differently from jointly-owned securities or real estate for the purpose of disclaimer.

This common law of disclaimers of jointly held property must be set against the rapid developments in the law of tax qualified disclaimers of jointly held property. Since the previous Uniform Acts were drafted, the law regarding tax qualified disclaimers of joint property interests has been clarified. Courts have repeatedly held that a surviving joint tenant may disclaim that portion of the jointly held property to which the survivor succeeds by operation of law on the death of the other joint tenant so long as the joint tenancy was severable during the life of the joint tenants (*Kennedy v. Commissioner*, 804 F.2d 1332 (7th Cir 1986), *McDonald v. Commissioner*, 853 F.2d 1494 (9th Cir 1988), *Dancy v. Commissioner*, 872 F.2d 84 (4th Cir 1989).) On December 30, 1997 the Service published T.D. 8744 making final proposed amendments of the Regulations under IRC §2518 to reflect the decisions regarding disclaimers of joint property interests.

The amended final Regulations, §25.2518-2(c)(4)(i) allow a surviving joint tenant or tenant by the entireties to disclaim that portion of the tenancy to which he or she succeeds upon the death of the first joint tenant (½ where there are two joint tenants) whether or not the tenancy could have been unilaterally severed under local law and regardless of the proportion of consideration furnished by the disclaimant. The Regulations also create a special rule for joint tenancies between spouses created after July 14, 1988 where the spouse of the donor is not a United States citizen. In that case, the donee spouse may disclaim any portion of the joint tenancy includible in the donor spouse's gross estate under IRC §2040, which creates a contribution rule. Thus the surviving non-citizen spouse may disclaim all of the joint tenancy property if the deceased spouse provided all the consideration for the tenancy's creation.

The amended final Regulations, §25.2518-2(c)(4)(iii) also recognize the unique features of joint bank accounts, and allow the disclaimer by a survivor of that part of the account contributed by the decedent, so long as the decedent could have regained that portion during life by unilateral action, bar the disclaimer of that part of the account attributable to the survivor's contributions, and explicitly extend the rule governing joint bank accounts to brokerage and other investment accounts, such as mutual fund accounts, held in joint name.

... In the usual joint tenancy or tenancy by the entireties between husband and wife, the survivor will always be able to disclaim one-half of the property. If the disclaimer conforms to the requirements of IRC §2518, it will be a qualified disclaimer. In addition the surviving spouse can disclaim all of the property attributable to the decedent's contribution, a provision which will allow the non-citizen spouse to take advantage of the contribution rule of the final Regulations. ...

Subsection (b) provides that the disclaimer is effective as of the death of the joint holder which triggers the survivorship feature of the joint property arrangement. The disclaimant, therefore, has no interest in and has not transferred the disclaimed interest.

Subsection (c) provides that the disclaimed interest passes as if the disclaimant had predeceased the holder to whose death the disclaimer relates. Where there are two joint holders, a disclaimer by the survivor results in the disclaimed property passing as part of the deceased joint holder's estate because under this subsection, the deceased joint holder is the survivor as to the portion disclaimed. ...

In a multiple holder joint property arrangement, the disclaimed interest will belong to the other joint holder or holders.

> **Example 1.** A, B, and C make equal contributions to the purchase of Blackacre, to which they take title as joint tenants with right of survivorship. On partition each would receive 1/3 of Blackacre and any of them could convert his or her interest to a 1/3 tenancy in common interest by unilateral severance (which, of course, would have to be accomplished in accordance with state law). On A's death, B and C may each, if they wish, disclaim up to 1/3 of the property under 2-1107(a)(1). Should one of them disclaim the full 1/3, the disclaimant will be deemed to predecease A.
>
> Assume that B so disclaims. With respect to the 1/3 undivided interest that now no longer belongs to A the only surviving joint holder is C. C therefore owns that 1/3 interest as tenant in common with the joint tenancy. Should C predecease B, the 1/3 tenancy in common interest

* See footnote on p. 705.

will pass through C's estate and B will be the sole owner of an undivided 2/3 interest in Blackacre as the survivor of the joint tenancy. Should B predecease C, C will be the sole owner of Blackacre in fee simple absolute.

Alternatively, assume that both B and C make valid disclaimers after A's death. They are both deemed to have predeceased A, A is the sole survivor of the joint tenancy and Blackacre passes through A's estate.

Finally, assume that A provided all the consideration for the purchase of Blackacre. On A's death, B and C can each disclaim the entire property under 2-1107(a)(2). If they both do so, Blackacre will pass through A's estate. If only one of B or C disclaims the entire property, the one who does not will be the sole owner of Blackacre as the only surviving joint tenant. Such a disclaimer would not be completely tax qualified, however. The Regulations limit a tax qualified disclaimer to no more than 1/3 of the property. If, however, B or C were the first to die, A could still disclaim the 1/3 interest that no longer belongs to the decedent under §240.052(a) [UPC §2-1107(a)(1)], the disclaimer would be a qualified disclaimer for tax purposes under the Regulations, and the result is that the other surviving joint tenant owns 1/3 of Blackacre as tenant in common with the joint tenancy.

PROP §240.053. DISCLAIMER OF INTEREST BY TRUSTEE

(a) If a trustee disclaims an interest in property that otherwise would have become trust property:

(1) the interest does not become trust property;

(2) the disclaimer:

(A) takes effect as of the time the trust became irrevocable; and

(B) relates back for all purposes to the time the trust became irrevocable; and

(3) the disclaimed interest is not subject to the claims of any creditor of the trustee, the trust, or any trust beneficiary.

(b) If the instrument creating the disclaimed interest contains a provision that provides for the disposition of the interest if the interest were to be disclaimed, the disclaimed interest passes according to that provision.

(c) If the instrument creating the disclaimed interest does not contain a provision described by Subsection (b), the disclaimed interest passes as if:

(1) all of the current beneficiaries, presumptive remainder beneficiaries, and contingent beneficiaries of the trust affected by the disclaimer who are individuals died before the trust became irrevocable; and

(2) all beneficiaries of the trust affected by the disclaimer who are not individuals ceased to exist without successor organizations and without substitution of beneficiaries under the cy pres doctrine before the trust became irrevocable.

(d) Subsection (c) applies only for purposes of determining the disposition of an interest in property disclaimed by a trustee that otherwise would have become trust property and applies only with respect to the trust affected by the disclaimer. Subsection (c) does not apply with respect to other trusts governed by the instrument and does not apply for other purposes under the instrument or under the laws of intestacy.

History of Prop. Code §240.053: Acts 2015, 84th Leg., ch. 562, §15, eff. Sept. 1, 2015.

NCCUSL Comment*

Section 240.053 deals with disclaimer of a right to receive property into a trust, and thus applies only to trustees. (A disclaimer of a right to receive property by a fiduciary acting on behalf of an individual, such as a personal representative, conservator, guardian, or agent is governed by the section of the statute applicable to the type of interest being disclaimed.) The instrument under which the right to receive the property was created may govern the disposition of the property in the event of a disclaimer by providing for a disposition when the trust does not exist. When the instrument does not make such a provision, the doctrine of resulting trust will carry the property back to the donor. The effect of the actions of co-trustees will depend on the state law governing the action of multiple trustees. Every disclaimer by a trustee must be compatible with the trustee's fiduciary obligations.

PROP §240.054. DISCLAIMER OF POWER OF APPOINTMENT OR OTHER POWER NOT HELD IN FIDUCIARY CAPACITY

(a) If a holder disclaims a power of appointment or other power not held in a fiduciary capacity, this section applies.

(b) If the holder:

(1) has not exercised the power, the disclaimer takes effect as of the time the instrument creating the power becomes irrevocable; or

(2) has exercised the power and the disclaimer is of a power other than a presently exercisable general power of appointment, the disclaimer takes effect immediately after the last exercise of the power.

(c) The instrument creating the power is construed as if the power had expired when the disclaimer became effective.

History of Prop. Code §240.054: Acts 2015, 84th Leg., ch. 562, §15, eff. Sept. 1, 2015.

NCCUSL Comment*

Section 240.006 authorizes a person to disclaim an interest in or power over property. Section 240.054 provides rules for disclaimers of powers which are not held in a fiduciary capacity. The most common non-fiduciary power is a power of appointment. Section 240.006 also authorizes the partial disclaimer of a power as well as of an interest. For example, the disclaimer could be of a portion of the power to appoint one's self, while retaining the right to appoint to others. The effect of a disclaimer of a power under §240.054 depends on whether or not the holder has exercised the power and on what sort of power is held. If a holder disclaims a power before exercising it, the power expires and can never be exercised. If the power has been exercised, the power is construed as having expired immediately after its last exercise by the holder. The disclaimer affects only the holder of the power and will not affect other aspects of the power.

* See footnote on p. 705.

Example 1. T creates a testamentary trust to pay the income to A for life, remainder as A shall appoint by will among her descendants living at A's death and four named charities. If A does not exercise her power, the remainder passes to her descendants living at her death by representation. A disclaims the power. The power can no longer be exercised and on A's death the remainder will pass to the takers in default.

PROP §240.055. DISCLAIMER BY APPOINTEE OF, OR OBJECT OR TAKER IN DEFAULT OF EXERCISE OF, POWER OF APPOINTMENT

(a) A disclaimer of an interest in property by an appointee of a power of appointment takes effect as of the time the instrument by which the holder exercises the power becomes irrevocable.

(b) A disclaimer of an interest in property by an object or taker in default of an exercise of a power of appointment takes effect as of the time the instrument creating the power becomes irrevocable.

History of Prop. Code §240.055: Acts 2015, 84th Leg., ch. 562, §15, eff. Sept. 1, 2015.

NCCUSL Comment*

Section 240.055 governs disclaimers by those who may or do receive an interest in property through the exercise of a power of appointment. At the time of the creation of a power of appointment, the creator of the power, besides giving the power to the holder of the power, can also limit the objects of the power (the permissible appointees of the property subject to the power) and also name those who are to take if the power is not exercised, persons referred to as takers in default.

Section 240.055 provides rules for disclaimers by all of these persons: subsection (a) is concerned with a disclaimer by a person who actually receives an interest in property through the exercise of a power of appointment, and subsection (b) recognizes a disclaimer by a taker in default or permissible appointee before the power is exercised. These two situations are quite different. An appointee is in the same position as any devisee or beneficiary of a trust. He or she may receive a present or future interest depending on how the holder of the power exercises it. Subsection (a), therefore, makes the disclaimer effective as of the time the instrument exercising the power—giving the interest to the disclaimant—becomes irrevocable. If the holder of the power created an interest in the appointee, the effect of the disclaimer is governed by §240.051. If the holder created another power in the appointee, the effect of the disclaimer is governed by §240.054.

Example 1. Mother's will creates a testamentary trust for daughter D. The trustees are to pay all income to D for her life and have discretion to invade principal for D's maintenance. On D's death she may appoint the trust property by will among her then living descendants. In default of appointment the property is to be distributed by representation to D's descendants who survive her. D is the donee, her descendants are the permissible appointees and the takers in default. D exercises her power by appointing the trust property in three equal shares to her children A, B, and C. The three children are the appointees. A disclaims. Under subsection (a) A's disclaimer is effective as of D's death (the time at which the will exercising the power became irrevocable). Because A disclaimed an interest in property, the effect of the disclaimer is governed by §240.051(b). If D's will makes no provisions for the disposition of the interest should it be disclaimed or of disclaimed interests in general (§240.051(d)), the interest passes as if A predeceased the time of distribution which is D's death. An appointment to a person who is dead at the time of the appointment is ineffective except as provided by an antilapse statute. *See* Restatement, Second, Property (Donative Transfers) §18.5. The Restatement, Second, Property (Donative Transfers), §18.6 suggests that any requirement of the antilapse statute that the deceased devisee be related in some way to the testator be applied as if the appointive property were owned either by the donor or the holder of the power. (*See also* Restatement, Third, Property (Wills and Other Donative Transfers) §5.5, Comment *l*.) That is the position taken by UPC §2-603. Since antilapse statutes usually apply to devises to children and grandchildren, the disclaimed interest would pass to A's descendants by representation.

A taker in default or a permissible object of appointment is traditionally regarded as having a type of future interest. *See* Restatement, Second, Property (Donative Transfers) §11.2, *Comments c and d*. The future interest will come into possession and enjoyment when the question of whether or not the power is to be exercised is resolved. For testamentary powers that time is the death of the holder.

Subsection (b) provides that a disclaimer by an object or taker in default takes effect as of the time the instrument creating the power becomes effective. Because the disclaimant is disclaiming an interest in property, albeit a future interest, the effect of the disclaimer is governed by §240.051. The effect of these rules is illustrated by the following examples.

Example 2(a). The facts are the same as **Example 1**, except A disclaims before D's death and D's will does not exercise the power. Under subsection (b) A's disclaimer is effective as of Mother's death which is the time when the instrument creating the power, Mother's will, became irrevocable. Because A disclaimed an interest in property, the effect of the disclaimer is governed by §240.051(b). If Mother's will makes no provision for the disposition of the interest should it be disclaimed or of disclaimed interests in general (§240.051(d)), the interest passes under §240.051(e) as if the disclaimant had died immediately before the time of distribution. Thus, A is deemed to have died immediately before D's death, which is the time of distribution. If A actually survives D, the disclaimed interest is one-third of the trust property; it will pass as if A predeceased D, and the result is the same as in **Example 1**. If A does predecease D he would have received nothing and there is no disclaimed interest. The disclaimer has no effect on the passing of the trust property.

Example 2(b). The facts are the same as in **Example 2(a)** except D does exercise her power of appointment to give one-third of the trust property to each of her three children, A, B, and C. A's disclaimer means the disclaimed interest will pass as if he predeceased D and the result is the same as in **Example 1**.

In addition, if all the objects and takers in default disclaim before the power is exercised the power of appointment is destroyed. *See* Restatement, Second, Property (Donative Transfers) §12.1, *Comment g*.

PROP §240.056. DISCLAIMER OF POWER HELD IN FIDUCIARY CAPACITY

(a) If a person designated to serve or serving as a fiduciary disclaims a power held or to be held in a fiduciary capacity that has not been exercised, the disclaimer takes effect as of the time the instrument creating the power becomes irrevocable.

(b) If a person designated to serve or serving as a fiduciary disclaims a power held or to be held in a fiduciary capacity that has been exercised, the disclaimer takes effect immediately after the last exercise of the power.

* See footnote on p. 705.

(c) A disclaimer subject to this section is effective as to another person designated to serve or serving as a fiduciary if:

(1) the disclaimer provides that it is effective as to another person designated to serve or serving as a fiduciary; and

(2) the person disclaiming has the authority to bind the estate, trust, or other person for whom the person is acting.

History of Prop. Code §240.056: Acts 2015, 84th Leg., ch. 562, §15, eff. Sept. 1, 2015.

NCCUSL Comment*

Section 240.056 governs disclaimers by fiduciaries of powers held in their fiduciary capacity. Examples include a right to remove and replace a trustee or a trustee's power to make distributions of income or principal. Such disclaimers have not been specifically dealt with in prior Uniform Acts although they could prove useful in several situations. A trustee who is also a beneficiary may want to disclaim a power to invade principal for himself for tax purposes. A trustee of a trust for the benefit for a surviving spouse who also has the power to invade principal for the decedent's descendants may wish to disclaim the power in order to qualify the trust for the marital deduction. (The use of a disclaimer in just that situation was approved in *Cleaveland v. U.S.*, 62 A.F.T.R.2d 88-5992, 88-1 USTC ¶13,766 (C.D.Ill. 1988).)

The section refers to fiduciary in the singular. It is possible, of course, for a trust to have two or more co-trustees and an estate to have two or more co-personal representatives. This Act leaves the effect of actions of multiple fiduciaries to the general rules in effect in each state relating to multiple fiduciaries. For example, if the general rule is that a majority of trustees can make binding decisions, a disclaimer by two of three co-trustees of a power is effective. A dissenting co-trustee could follow whatever procedure state law prescribes for disassociating him or herself from the action of the majority. A sole trustee burdened with a power to invade principal for a group of beneficiaries including him or herself who wishes to disclaim the power but yet preserve the possibility of another trustee exercising the power would seek the appointment of a disinterested co-trustee to exercise the power and then disclaim the power for him or herself. The subsection thus makes the disclaimer effective only as to the disclaiming fiduciary unless the disclaimer states otherwise. If the disclaimer does attempt to bind other fiduciaries, be they co-fiduciaries or successor fiduciaries, the effect of the disclaimer will depend on local law.

As with any action by a fiduciary, a disclaimer of fiduciary powers must be compatible with the fiduciary's duties.

PROP §240.057. TAX QUALIFIED DISCLAIMER

(a) In this section, "Internal Revenue Code" has the meaning assigned by Section 111.004.

(b) Notwithstanding any other provision of this chapter, if, as a result of a disclaimer or transfer, the disclaimed or transferred interest is treated under the Internal Revenue Code as never having been transferred to the disclaimant, the disclaimer or transfer is effective as a disclaimer under this chapter.

History of Prop. Code §240.057: Acts 2015, 84th Leg., ch. 562, §15, eff. Sept. 1, 2015.

NCCUSL Comment*

This section coordinates the Act with the requirements of a qualified disclaimer for transfer tax purposes under IRC §2518. Any disclaimer which is qualified for estate and gift tax purposes is a valid disclaimer under this Act even if it does not otherwise meet the Act's more specific requirements.

PROP §240.058. PARTIAL DISCLAIMER BY SPOUSE

A disclaimer by a decedent's surviving spouse of an interest in property transferred as the result of the death of the decedent is not a disclaimer by the surviving spouse of any other transfer from the decedent to or for the benefit of the surviving spouse, regardless of whether the interest that would have passed under the disclaimed transfer passes because of the disclaimer to or for the benefit of the surviving spouse by the other transfer.

History of Prop. Code §240.058: Acts 2015, 84th Leg., ch. 562, §15, eff. Sept. 1, 2015.

Sections 240.059-240.100 blank

SUBCHAPTER C. DELIVERY OR FILING

PROP §240.101. DELIVERY OR FILING GENERALLY

(a) Subject to applicable requirements of this subchapter, a disclaimant may deliver a disclaimer by personal delivery, first-class mail, facsimile, e-mail, or any other method likely to result in the disclaimer's receipt.

(b) If a disclaimer is mailed to the intended recipient by certified mail, return receipt requested, at an address the disclaimant in good faith believes is likely to result in the disclaimer's receipt, delivery is considered to have occurred on the date of mailing regardless of receipt.

History of Prop. Code §240.101: Acts 2015, 84th Leg., ch. 562, §15, eff. Sept. 1, 2015.

PROP §240.102. DISCLAIMER OF INTEREST CREATED UNDER INTESTATE SUCCESSION OR WILL

In the case of an interest created under the law of intestate succession or an interest created by will, other than an interest in a testamentary trust:

(1) a disclaimer must be delivered to the personal representative of the decedent's estate; or

(2) if no personal representative is then serving, a disclaimer must be filed in the official public records of any county in which the decedent:

(A) was domiciled on the date of the decedent's death; or

(B) owned real property.

History of Prop. Code §240.102: Acts 2015, 84th Leg., ch. 562, §15, eff. Sept. 1, 2015.

NCCUSL Comment*

The rules set forth in §240.102 are designed to provide notice of the disclaimer. For example, a disclaimer of an interest in a decedent's estate must be

* See footnote on p. 705.

delivered to the personal representative of the estate. A disclaimer is required to be filed in court only in very limited circumstances.

PROP §240.103. DISCLAIMER OF INTEREST IN TESTAMENTARY TRUST

In the case of an interest in a testamentary trust:

(1) a disclaimer must be delivered to the trustee then serving;

(2) if no trustee is then serving, a disclaimer must be delivered to the personal representative of the decedent's estate; or

(3) if no trustee or personal representative is then serving, a disclaimer must be filed in the official public records of any county in which the decedent:

(A) was domiciled on the date of the decedent's death; or

(B) owned real property.

History of Prop. Code §240.103: Acts 2015, 84th Leg., ch. 562, §15, eff. Sept. 1, 2015.

PROP §240.104. DISCLAIMER OF INTEREST IN INTER VIVOS TRUST

In the case of an interest in an inter vivos trust:

(1) a disclaimer must be delivered to the trustee then serving, or, if no trustee is then serving, a disclaimer must be filed:

(A) with a court having jurisdiction to enforce the trust; or

(B) in the official public records of the county in which:

(i) the situs of administration of the trust is maintained; or

(ii) the settlor is domiciled or was domiciled on the date of the settlor's death; and

(2) if a disclaimer is made before the time the instrument creating the trust becomes irrevocable, a disclaimer must be delivered to the settlor of a revocable trust or the transferor of the interest.

History of Prop. Code §240.104: Acts 2015, 84th Leg., ch. 562, §15, eff. Sept. 1, 2015.

PROP §240.105. DISCLAIMER OF INTEREST CREATED BY BENEFICIARY DESIGNATION

(a) In this section, "beneficiary designation" means an instrument, other than an instrument creating a trust, naming the beneficiary of:

(1) an annuity or insurance policy;

(2) an account with a designation for payment on death;

(3) a security registered in beneficiary form;

(4) a pension, profit-sharing, retirement, or other employment-related benefit plan; or

(5) any other nonprobate transfer at death.

(b) In the case of an interest created by a beneficiary designation that is disclaimed before the designation becomes irrevocable, the disclaimer must be delivered to the person making the beneficiary designation.

(c) In the case of an interest created by a beneficiary designation that is disclaimed after the designation becomes irrevocable:

(1) a disclaimer of an interest in personal property must be delivered to the person obligated to distribute the interest; and

(2) a disclaimer of an interest in real property must be recorded in the official public records of the county where the real property that is the subject of the disclaimer is located.

History of Prop. Code §240.105: Acts 2015, 84th Leg., ch. 562, §15, eff. Sept. 1, 2015.

PROP §240.106. DISCLAIMER BY SURVIVING HOLDER OF SURVIVORSHIP PROPERTY

In the case of a disclaimer by a surviving holder of survivorship property, the disclaimer must be delivered to the person to whom the disclaimed interest passes.

History of Prop. Code §240.106: Acts 2015, 84th Leg., ch. 562, §15, eff. Sept. 1, 2015.

PROP §240.107. DISCLAIMER BY OBJECT OR TAKER IN DEFAULT OF EXERCISE OF POWER OF APPOINTMENT

In the case of a disclaimer by an object or taker in default of an exercise of a power of appointment at any time after the power was created:

(1) the disclaimer must be delivered to the holder of the power or to the fiduciary acting under the instrument that created the power; or

(2) if no fiduciary is then serving, the disclaimer must be filed:

(A) with a court having authority to appoint the fiduciary; or

(B) in the official public records of the county in which the creator of the power is domiciled or was domiciled on the date of the creator's death.

History of Prop. Code §240.107: Acts 2015, 84th Leg., ch. 562, §15, eff. Sept. 1, 2015.

PROP §240.108. DISCLAIMER BY CERTAIN APPOINTEES

In the case of a disclaimer by an appointee of a nonfiduciary power of appointment:

(1) the disclaimer must be delivered to the holder, the personal representative of the holder's estate, or the fiduciary under the instrument that created the power; or

(2) if no fiduciary is then serving, the disclaimer must be filed:

(A) with a court having authority to appoint the fiduciary; or

(B) in the official public records of the county in which the creator of the power is domiciled or was domiciled on the date of the creator's death.

History of Prop. Code §240.108: Acts 2015, 84th Leg., ch. 562, §15, eff. Sept. 1, 2015.

PROP §240.109. DISCLAIMER BY CERTAIN FIDUCIARIES

In the case of a disclaimer by a fiduciary of a power over a trust or estate, the disclaimer must be delivered as provided by Section 240.102, 240.103, or 240.104 as if the power disclaimed were an interest in property.

History of Prop. Code §240.109: Acts 2015, 84th Leg., ch. 562, §15, eff. Sept. 1, 2015.

PROP §240.110. DISCLAIMER OF POWER BY AGENT

In the case of a disclaimer of a power by an agent, the disclaimer must be delivered to the principal or the principal's representative.

History of Prop. Code §240.110: Acts 2015, 84th Leg., ch. 562, §15, eff. Sept. 1, 2015.

PROP §240.111. RECORDING OF DISCLAIMER

If an instrument transferring an interest in or power over property subject to a disclaimer is required or authorized by law to be filed, recorded, or registered, the disclaimer may be filed, recorded, or registered as that instrument. Except as otherwise provided by Section 240.105(c)(2), failure to file, record, or register the disclaimer does not affect the disclaimer's validity between the disclaimant and persons to whom the property interest or power passes by reason of the disclaimer.

History of Prop. Code §240.111: Acts 2015, 84th Leg., ch. 562, §15, eff. Sept. 1, 2015.

NCCUSL Comment*

This section permits the recordation of a disclaimer of an interest in property ownership of or title to which is the subject of a recording system. This section expands on the corresponding provision of previous Uniform Acts which referred to permissive recording of a disclaimer of an interest in real property. While local practice may vary, disclaimants should realize that in order to establish the chain of title to real property, and to ward off creditors and bona fide purchasers, the disclaimer may have to be recorded. This section does not change the law of the state governing notice. The reference to §240.105(c)(2) concerns the disclaimer of an interest in real property created by a "beneficiary designation" as that term is defined in §240.105(a). Such a disclaimer must be recorded.

Sections 240.112-240.150 blank

SUBCHAPTER D. DISCLAIMER BARRED OR LIMITED

PROP §240.151. WHEN DISCLAIMER BARRED OR LIMITED

(a) A disclaimer is barred by a written waiver of the right to disclaim.

(b) A disclaimer of an interest in property is barred if any of the following events occur before the disclaimer becomes effective:

(1) the disclaimant accepts the interest sought to be disclaimed by:

(A) taking possession of the interest; or

(B) exercising dominion and control over the interest;

(2) the disclaimant voluntarily assigns, conveys, encumbers, pledges, or transfers the interest sought to be disclaimed or contracts to do so; or

(3) the interest sought to be disclaimed is sold under a judicial sale.

(c) The acceptance of an interest in property by a person in the person's fiduciary capacity is not an acceptance of the interest in the person's individual capacity and does not bar the person from disclaiming the interest in the person's individual capacity.

(d) A disclaimer, in whole or in part, of the future exercise of a power held in a fiduciary capacity is not barred by the previous exercise of the power.

(e) A disclaimer, in whole or in part, of the future exercise of a power not held in a fiduciary capacity is not barred by the previous exercise of the power unless the power is exercisable in favor of the disclaimant.

(f) A disclaimer of:

(1) a power over property that is barred by this section is ineffective; and

(2) an interest in property that is barred by this section takes effect as a transfer of the interest disclaimed to the persons who would have taken the interest under Subchapter B had the disclaimer not been barred.

* See footnote on p. 705.

(g) A disclaimer by a child support obligor is barred as to disclaimed property that could be applied to satisfy the disclaimant's child support obligations if those obligations have been:

(1) administratively determined by the Title IV-D agency as defined by Section 101.033, Family Code, in a Title IV-D case as defined by Section 101.034, Family Code; or

(2) confirmed and reduced to judgment as provided by Section 157.263, Family Code.

(h) If Subsection (g) applies, the child support obligee to whom child support arrearages are owed may enforce the child support obligation against the disclaimant as to disclaimed property by a lien or by any other remedy provided by law.

History of Prop. Code §240.151: Acts 2015, 84th Leg., ch. 562, §15, eff. Sept. 1, 2015.

NCCUSL Comment*

The 1978 Act required that an effective disclaimer be made within nine months of the event giving rise to the right to disclaim (e.g., nine months from the death of the decedent or donee of a power or the vesting of a future interest). The nine month period corresponded in some situations with the Internal Revenue Code provisions governing qualified tax disclaimers. Under the common law an effective disclaimer had to be made only within a "reasonable" time.

This Act specifically rejects a time requirement for making a disclaimer. Recognizing that disclaimers are used for purposes other than tax planning, a disclaimer can be made effectively under the Act so long as the disclaimant is not barred from disclaiming the property or interest or has not waived the right to disclaim. Persons seeking to make tax qualified disclaimers will continue to have to conform to the requirements of the Internal Revenue Code.

The events resulting in a bar to the right to disclaim set forth in this section are similar to those found in the 1978 Acts and former UPC §2-801. Subsection (a) provides that a written waiver of the right to disclaim is effective to bar a disclaimer. Such a waiver might be sought, for example, by a creditor who wishes to make sure that property acquired in the future will be available to satisfy the debt.

Whether particular actions by the disclaimant amount to accepting the interest sought to be disclaimed within the meaning of subsection (b)(1) will necessarily be determined by the courts based upon the particular facts. (*See Leipham v. Adams*, 77 Wash. App. 827, 894 P.2d 576 (1995); *Matter of Will of Hall*, 318 S.C. 188, 456 S.E.2d 439 (Ct. App. 1995); *Jordan v. Trower*, 208 Ga. App. 552, 431 S.E.2d 160 (1993); *Matter of Gates*, 189 A.D.2d 427, 595 N.Y.S.2d 194 (3d Dept. 1993); "What Constitutes or Establishes Beneficiary's Acceptance or Renunciation of Devise or Bequest," 93 ALR2d 8.)

The addition in this Act of the word "voluntary" to the list of actions barring a disclaimer which also appears in the earlier Acts reflects the numerous cases holding that only actions by the disclaimant taken after the right to disclaim has arisen will act as a bar. (*See Troy v. Hart*, 116 Md. App. 468, 697 A.2d 113 (1997), *Estate of Opatz*, 554 N.W.2d 813 (N.D. 1996), *Frances Slocum Bank v. Martin*, 666 N.E.2d 411 (Ind. App. 1996), *Brown v. Momar, Inc.*, 201 Ga. App. 542, 411 S.E.2d 718 (1991), *Tompkins State Bank v. Niles*, 127 Ill.2d 209, 130 Ill. Dec. 207, 537 N.E.2d 274 (1989).) An existing lien, therefore, will not prevent a disclaimer, although the disclaimant's actions before the right to disclaim arises may work an estoppel. *See Hale v. Bardouh*, 975 S.W.2d 419 (Tex. Ct. App. 1998). With regard to joint property, the event giving rise to the right to disclaim is the death of a joint holder, not the creation of the joint interest and any benefit received during the deceased joint tenant's life is ignored.

The reference to judicial sale in subsection (b)(3) continues a provision from the earlier Acts and ensures that title gained from a judicial sale by a personal representative will not be clouded by a possible disclaimer.

Subsection (d) rephrases the rules of §240.056 governing the effect of disclaimers of powers.

Subsection (e) is applicable to powers which can be disclaimed under §240.054. It bars the disclaimer of a general power of appointment once it has been exercised. A general power of appointment allows the holder to take the property subject to the power for him or herself, whether outright or by using it to pay his or her creditors (for estate and gift tax purposes, a general power is one that allows the holder to appoint to himself, his estate, his creditors, or the creditors of his estate). The power is presently exercisable if the holder need not wait to some time or for some event to occur before exercising the power. If the holder has exercised such a power, it can no longer be disclaimed.

Subsection (f) provides a rule stating what happens if an attempt is made to disclaim a power or property interest whose disclaimer is barred by this section. A disclaimer of a power is ineffective, but the attempted disclaimer of the property interest, although invalid as a disclaimer, will operate as a transfer of the disclaimed property interest to the person or persons who would have taken the interest had the disclaimer not been barred. This provision removes the ambiguity that would otherwise be caused by an ineffective refusal to accept property. Whoever has control of the property will know to whom to deliver it and the person attempting the disclaimer will bear any transfer tax consequences.

* See footnote on p. 705.

Title 14 blank

TITLE 15. FAIR HOUSING PRACTICES

CHAPTER 301. TEXAS FAIR HOUSING ACT

SUBCHAPTER A. TITLE, PURPOSE, & DEFINITIONS

PROP §301.001. SHORT TITLE

This chapter may be cited as the Texas Fair Housing Act.

History of Prop. Code §301.001: Acts 1993, 73rd Leg., ch. 268, §40, eff. Sept. 1, 1993. Source: TRCS art. 1f, §1.01.

PROP §301.0015. TEXAS WORKFORCE COMMISSION

The powers and duties exercised by the Commission on Human Rights under this chapter are transferred to the Texas Workforce Commission. A reference in this chapter to the "commission" means the Texas Workforce Commission.

History of Prop. Code §301.0015: Acts 2003, 78th Leg., ch. 302, §3, eff. Apr. 1, 2004. Amended by Acts 2015, 84th Leg., ch. 1138, §29, eff. Sept. 1, 2015.

PROP §301.002. PURPOSES

The purposes of this chapter are to:

(1) provide for fair housing practices in this state;

(2) create a procedure for investigating and settling complaints of discriminatory housing practices; and

(3) provide rights and remedies substantially equivalent to those granted under federal law.

History of Prop. Code §301.002: Acts 1993, 73rd Leg., ch. 268, §40, eff. Sept. 1, 1993. Source: TRCS art. 1f, §1.02.

See also 42 U.S.C. §3601.

PROP §301.003. DEFINITIONS

In this chapter:

(1) "Aggrieved person" includes any person who:

(A) claims to have been injured by a discriminatory housing practice; or

(B) believes that the person will be injured by a discriminatory housing practice that is about to occur.

(2) "Complainant" means a person, including the commission, that files a complaint under Section 301.081.

(3) Repealed by Acts 2003, 78th Leg., ch. 302, §4(3), eff. Apr. 1, 2004.

(4) "Conciliation" means the informal negotiations among an aggrieved person, the respondent, and the commission to resolve issues raised by a complaint or by the investigation of the complaint.

(5) "Conciliation agreement" means a written agreement resolving the issues in conciliation.

(6) "Disability" means a mental or physical impairment that substantially limits at least one major life activity, a record of the impairment, or being regarded as having the impairment. The term does not include current illegal use or addiction to any drug or illegal or federally controlled substance and does not apply to an individual because of an individual's sexual orientation or because that individual is a transvestite.

(7) "Discriminatory housing practice" means an act prohibited by Subchapter B or conduct that is an offense under Subchapter I.

(8) "Dwelling" means any:

(A) structure or part of a structure that is occupied as, or designed or intended for occupancy as, a residence by one or more families; or

(B) vacant land that is offered for sale or lease for the construction or location of a structure or part of a structure described by Paragraph (A).

(9) "Family" includes a single individual.

(10) "Respondent" means:

(A) a person accused of a violation of this chapter in a complaint of discriminatory housing practice; or

(B) a person identified as an additional or substitute respondent under Section 301.084 or an agent of an additional or substitute respondent.

(11) "To rent" includes to lease, sublease, or let, or to grant in any other manner, for a consideration, the right to occupy premises not owned by the occupant.

(12) "Person" means:

(A) an individual;

(B) a corporation, partnership, association, unincorporated organization, labor organization, mutual company, joint-stock company, and trust; and

(C) a legal representative, a trustee, a trustee in a case under Title 11, U.S.C., a receiver, and a fiduciary.

History of Prop. Code §301.003: Acts 1993, 73rd Leg., ch. 268, §40, eff. Sept. 1, 1993. Amended by Acts 2001, 77th Leg., ch. 1420, §17.003, eff. Sept. 1, 2001; Acts 2003, 78th Leg., ch. 302, §4(3), eff. Apr. 1, 2004. Source: TRCS art. 1f, §1.03.

See also 42 U.S.C. §3602.

PROP §301.004. FAMILIAL STATUS

A discriminatory act is committed because of familial status if the act is committed because the person who is the subject of discrimination is:

(1) pregnant;

(2) domiciled with an individual younger than 18 years of age in regard to whom the person:

(A) is the parent or legal custodian; or

(B) has the written permission of the parent or legal custodian for domicile with that person; or

(3) in the process of obtaining legal custody of an individual younger than 18 years of age.

History of Prop. Code §301.004: Acts 1993, 73rd Leg., ch. 268, §40, eff. Sept. 1, 1993. Source: TRCS art. 1f, §1.04.

See also 42 U.S.C. §3602(k).

PROP §301.005. CONSTRUCTION OF CHAPTER

The statutory civil remedies or theories of recovery created by this chapter may not be expanded beyond their express statutory terms.

History of Prop. Code §301.005: Acts 1993, 73rd Leg., ch. 268, §40, eff. Sept. 1, 1993. Source: TRCS art. 1f, §10.01.

Sections 301.006-301.020 reserved for expansion

SUBCHAPTER B. DISCRIMINATION PROHIBITED

PROP §301.021. SALE OR RENTAL

(a) A person may not refuse to sell or rent, after the making of a bona fide offer, refuse to negotiate for the sale or rental of, or in any other manner make unavailable or deny a dwelling to another because of race, color, religion, sex, familial status, or national origin.

(b) A person may not discriminate against another in the terms, conditions, or privileges of sale or rental of a dwelling or in providing services or facilities in connection with a sale or rental of a dwelling because of race, color, religion, sex, familial status, or national origin.

(c) This section does not prohibit discrimination against a person because the person has been convicted under federal law or the law of any state of the illegal manufacture or distribution of a controlled substance.

History of Prop. Code §301.021: Acts 1993, 73rd Leg., ch. 268, §40, eff. Sept. 1, 1993. Source: TRCS art. 1f, §3.01.

See also 42 U.S.C. §3604(a), (b).

PROP §301.022. PUBLICATION

A person may not make, print, or publish or effect the making, printing, or publishing of a notice, statement, or advertisement that is about the sale or rental of a dwelling and that indicates any preference, limitation, or discrimination or the intention to make a preference, limitation, or discrimination because of race, color, religion, sex, disability, familial status, or national origin.

History of Prop. Code §301.022: Acts 1993, 73rd Leg., ch. 268, §40, eff. Sept. 1, 1993. Source: TRCS art. 1f, §3.02.

See also 42 U.S.C. §3604(c).

PROP §301.023. INSPECTION

A person may not represent to another because of race, color, religion, sex, disability, familial status, or national origin that a dwelling is not available for inspection for sale or rental when the dwelling is available for inspection.

History of Prop. Code §301.023: Acts 1993, 73rd Leg., ch. 268, §40, eff. Sept. 1, 1993. Source: TRCS art. 1f, §3.03.

See also 42 U.S.C. §3604(d).

PROP §301.024. ENTRY INTO NEIGHBORHOOD

A person may not, for profit, induce or attempt to induce another to sell or rent a dwelling by representations regarding the entry or prospective entry into a

neighborhood of a person of a particular race, color, religion, sex, disability, familial status, or national origin.

History of Prop. Code §301.024: Acts 1993, 73rd Leg., ch. 268, §40, eff. Sept. 1, 1993. Source: TRCS art. 1f, §3.04.

See also 42 U.S.C. §3604(e).

PROP §301.025. DISABILITY

(a) A person may not discriminate in the sale or rental of, or make unavailable or deny, a dwelling to any buyer or renter because of a disability of:

(1) the buyer or renter;

(2) a person residing in or intending to reside in that dwelling after it is sold, rented, or made available; or

(3) any person associated with the buyer or renter.

(b) A person may not discriminate against another in the terms, conditions, or privileges of sale or rental of a dwelling or in the provision of services or facilities in connection with the dwelling because of a disability of:

(1) the other person;

(2) a person residing in or intending to reside in that dwelling after it is sold, rented, or made available; or

(3) any person associated with the other person.

(c) In this section, discrimination includes:

(1) a refusal to permit, at the expense of the person having a disability, a reasonable modification of existing premises occupied or to be occupied by the person if the modification may be necessary to afford the person full enjoyment of the premises;

(2) a refusal to make a reasonable accommodation in rules, policies, practices, or services if the accommodation may be necessary to afford the person equal opportunity to use and enjoy a dwelling; or

(3) the failure to design and construct a covered multifamily dwelling in a manner:

(A) that allows the public use and common use portions of the dwellings to be readily accessible to and usable by persons having a disability;

(B) that allows all doors designed to allow passage into and within all premises within the dwellings to be sufficiently wide to allow passage by a person who has a disability and who is in a wheelchair; and

(C) that provides all premises within the dwellings contain the following features of adaptive design:

(i) an accessible route into and through the dwelling;

(ii) light switches, electrical outlets, thermostats, and other environmental controls in accessible locations;

(iii) reinforcements in bathroom walls to allow later installation of grab bars; and

(iv) kitchens and bathrooms that are usable and have sufficient space in which an individual in a wheelchair can maneuver.

(d) Compliance with the appropriate requirements of the American National Standard for buildings and facilities providing accessibility and usability for persons having physical disabilities, commonly cited as "ANSI A 117.1," satisfies the requirements of Subsection (c)(3)(C).

(e) Subsection (c)(3) does not apply to a building the first occupancy of which occurred on or before March 13, 1991.

(f) This section does not require a dwelling to be made available to an individual whose tenancy would constitute a direct threat to the health or safety of other individuals or whose tenancy would result in substantial physical damage to the property of others.

(g) In this subsection, the term "covered multifamily dwellings" means:

(1) buildings consisting of four or more units if the buildings have one or more elevators; and

(2) ground floor units in other buildings consisting of four or more units.

History of Prop. Code §301.025: Acts 1993, 73rd Leg., ch. 268, §40, eff. Sept. 1, 1993. Source: TRCS art. 1f, §3.05.

See also 42 U.S.C. §3604(f).

PROP §301.026. RESIDENTIAL REAL ESTATE RELATED TRANSACTION

(a) A person whose business includes engaging in residential real estate related transactions may not discriminate against another in making a real estate related transaction available or in the terms or conditions of a real estate related transaction because of race, color, religion, sex, disability, familial status, or national origin.

(b) In this section, "residential real estate related transaction" means:

(1) the making or purchasing of loans or the provision of other financial assistance:

(A) to purchase, construct, improve, repair, or maintain a dwelling; or

(B) to secure residential real estate; or

(2) the selling, brokering, or appraising of residential real property.

History of Prop. Code §301.026: Acts 1993, 73rd Leg., ch. 268, §40, eff. Sept. 1, 1993. Source: TRCS art. 1f, §3.06.

See also 42 U.S.C. §3605(a), (b).

PROP §301.027. BROKERAGE SERVICES

A person may not deny another access to, or membership or participation in, a multiple-listing service, real estate brokers' organization, or other service, organization, or facility relating to the business of selling or renting dwellings, or discriminate against a person in the terms or conditions of access, membership, or participation in such an organization, service, or facility because of race, color, religion, sex, disability, familial status, or national origin.

History of Prop. Code §301.027: Acts 1993, 73rd Leg., ch. 268, §40, eff. Sept. 1, 1993. Source: TRCS art. 1f, §3.07.

See also 42 U.S.C. §3606.

Sections 301.028-301.040 reserved for expansion

SUBCHAPTER C. EXEMPTIONS

PROP §301.041. SALES & RENTALS EXEMPTED

(a) Subchapter B does not apply to:

(1) the sale or rental of a single-family house sold or rented by the owner if:

(A) the owner does not:

(i) own more than three single-family houses at any one time; or

(ii) own any interest in, nor is there owned or reserved on the person's behalf, under any express or voluntary agreement, title to or any right to any part of the proceeds from the sale or rental of more than three single-family houses at any one time; and

(B) the house is sold or rented without:

(i) the use of the sales or rental facilities or services of a broker, agent, or salesperson licensed under Chapter 1101, Occupations Code, or of an employee or agent of a licensed broker, agent, or salesperson, or the facilities or services of the owner of a dwelling designed or intended for occupancy by five or more families; or

(ii) the publication, posting, or mailing of a notice, statement, or advertisement prohibited by Section 301.022; or

(2) the sale or rental of the rooms or units in a dwelling containing living quarters occupied by or intended to be occupied by not more than four families living independently of each other, if the owner maintains and occupies one of the living quarters as the owner's residence.

(b) The exemption in Subsection (a)(1) applies only to one sale or rental in a 24-month period if the owner was not the most recent resident of the house at the time of the sale or rental.

History of Prop. Code §301.041: Acts 1993, 73rd Leg., ch. 268, §40, eff. Sept. 1, 1993. Amended by Acts 2003, 78th Leg., ch. 1276, §14A.810, eff. Sept. 1, 2003. Source: TRCS art. 1f, §1.05.

See also 42 U.S.C. §3603.

PROP §301.042. RELIGIOUS ORGANIZATION, PRIVATE CLUB, & APPRAISAL EXEMPTION

(a) This chapter does not prohibit a religious organization, association, or society or a nonprofit institution or organization operated, supervised, or controlled by or in conjunction with a religious organization, association, or society from:

(1) limiting the sale, rental, or occupancy of dwellings that it owns or operates for other than a commercial purpose to persons of the same religion; or

(2) giving preference to persons of the same religion, unless membership in the religion is restricted because of race, color, or national origin.

(b) This chapter does not prohibit a private club that is not open to the public and that, as an incident to its primary purpose, provides lodging that it owns or operates for other than a commercial purpose from limiting the rental or occupancy of the lodging to its members or from giving preference to its members.

(c) This chapter does not prohibit a person engaged in the business of furnishing appraisals of real property from considering in those appraisals factors other than race, color, religion, sex, disability, familial status, or national origin.

History of Prop. Code §301.042: Acts 1993, 73rd Leg., ch. 268, §40, eff. Sept. 1, 1993. Source: TRCS art. 1f, §§1.06, 1.08.

See also 42 U.S.C. §§3605(c), 3607(a).

PROP §301.043. HOUSING FOR ELDERLY EXEMPTED

The provisions of this chapter relating to familial status do not apply to housing:

(1) that the commission determines is specifically designed and operated to assist elderly individuals under a federal or state program;

(2) intended for, and solely occupied by, individuals 62 years of age or older; or

(3) intended and operated for occupancy by at least one individual 55 years of age or older for each unit as determined by commission rules.

History of Prop. Code §301.043: Acts 1993, 73rd Leg., ch. 268, §40, eff. Sept. 1, 1993. Source: TRCS art. 1f, §1.07.

See also 42 U.S.C. §3607(b).

PROP §301.044. EFFECT ON OTHER LAW

(a) This chapter does not affect a reasonable local or state restriction on the maximum number of occupants permitted to occupy a dwelling or a restriction relating to health or safety standards.

(b) This chapter does not affect a requirement of nondiscrimination in any other state or federal law.

History of Prop. Code §301.044: Acts 1993, 73rd Leg., ch. 268, §40, eff. Sept. 1, 1993. Source: TRCS art. 1f, §1.09.

See also 42 U.S.C. §3607(b).

Sections 301.045-301.060 reserved for expansion

SUBCHAPTER D. ADMINISTRATIVE PROVISIONS

PROP §301.061. REPEALED

Repealed by Acts 2003, 78th Leg., ch. 302, §4(3), eff. Apr. 1, 2004.

PROP §301.062. RULES

The commission may adopt rules necessary to implement this chapter, but substantive rules adopted by the commission shall impose obligations, rights, and remedies that are the same as are provided in federal fair housing regulations.

History of Prop. Code §301.062: Acts 1993, 73rd Leg., ch. 268, §40, eff. Sept. 1, 1993. Source: TRCS art. 1f, §2.02.

See also 40 T.A.C. ch. 819, subchs. G-L; 42 U.S.C. §3614a.

PROP §301.063. COMPLAINTS

As provided by Subchapters E and F, the commission shall receive, investigate, seek to conciliate, and act on complaints alleging violations of this chapter.

History of Prop. Code §301.063: Acts 1993, 73rd Leg., ch. 268, §40, eff. Sept. 1, 1993. Source: TRCS art. 1f, §2.03.

See also Prop. Code §§301.081-301.093, 301.111-301.115, 301.131.

PROP §301.064. REPEALED

Repealed by Acts 2003, 78th Leg., ch. 302, §4(3), eff. Apr. 1, 2004.

PROP §301.065. REPORTS & STUDIES

(a) The commission shall, at least annually, publish a written report recommending legislative or other action to carry out the purposes of this chapter.

(b) The commission shall make studies relating to the nature and extent of discriminatory housing practices in this state.

History of Prop. Code §301.065: Acts 1993, 73rd Leg., ch. 268, §40, eff. Sept. 1, 1993. Source: TRCS art. 1f, §2.05.

See also 42 U.S.C. §§3608(e), 3608a, 3609.

PROP §301.066. COOPERATION WITH OTHER ENTITIES

The commission shall cooperate with and may provide technical and other assistance to federal, state, local, and other public or private entities that are designing or operating programs to prevent or eliminate discriminatory housing practices.

History of Prop. Code §301.066: Acts 1993, 73rd Leg., ch. 268, §40, eff. Sept. 1, 1993. Source: TRCS art. 1f, §2.06.

See also 42 U.S.C. §§3608(d), 3609, 3616.

PROP §301.067. SUBPOENAS & DISCOVERY

(a) The commission may issue subpoenas and order discovery in investigations and hearings under this chapter.

(b) The subpoenas and discovery may be ordered to the same extent and are subject to the same limitations as subpoenas and discovery in a civil action in district court.

History of Prop. Code §301.067: Acts 1993, 73rd Leg., ch. 268, §40, eff. Sept. 1, 1993. Source: TRCS art. 1f, §2.07.

See also 42 U.S.C. §3611.

PROP §301.068. REFERRAL TO MUNICIPALITY

The commission may defer proceedings under this chapter and refer a complaint to a municipality that has been certified by the federal Department of Housing and Urban Development as a substantially equivalent fair housing agency.

History of Prop. Code §301.068: Acts 1993, 73rd Leg., ch. 268, §40, eff. Sept. 1, 1993. Source: TRCS art. 1f, §2.08(b).

PROP §301.069. GIFTS & GRANTS

(a) The commission may accept gifts and grants from any public or private source for administering this chapter.

(b) Gifts and grants received shall be deposited to the credit of the fair housing fund in the state treasury.

(c) Money deposited to the credit of the fund may be used only for administering this chapter.

History of Prop. Code §301.069: Acts 1993, 73rd Leg., ch. 268, §40, eff. Sept. 1, 1993. Source: TRCS art. 1f, §§2.09, 7.01.

PROP §301.070. ACCESSIBILITY ASSISTANCE & INFORMATION FOR LANDLORDS

The commission shall provide to landlords technical and other assistance relating to the accessibility requirements under this chapter.

History of Prop. Code §301.070: Acts 1999, 76th Leg., ch. 872, §16, eff. Sept. 1, 1999. Source: TRCS art. 1f, §4.01.

Sections 301.071-301.080 reserved for expansion

SUBCHAPTER E. ADMINISTRATIVE ENFORCEMENT

PROP §301.081. COMPLAINT

(a) The commission shall investigate complaints of alleged discriminatory housing practices.

(b) A complaint must be:

(1) in writing;

(2) under oath; and

(3) in the form prescribed by the commission.

(c) An aggrieved person may file a complaint with the commission alleging the discriminatory housing practice. The commission may file a complaint.

(d) A complaint must be filed on or before the first anniversary of the date the alleged discriminatory housing practice occurs or terminates, whichever is later.

(e) A complaint may be amended at any time.

(f) On the filing of a complaint, the commission shall:

(1) give the aggrieved person notice that the complaint has been received;

(2) advise the aggrieved person of the time limits and choice of forums under this chapter; and

(3) not later than the 20th day after the date of the filing of the complaint or the identification of an additional or substitute respondent under Section 301.084, serve on each respondent:

(A) a notice identifying the alleged discriminatory housing practice and advising the respondent of the procedural rights and obligations of a respondent under this chapter; and

(B) a copy of the original complaint.

History of Prop. Code §301.081: Acts 1993, 73rd Leg., ch. 268, §40, eff. Sept. 1, 1993. Source: TRCS art. 1f, §4.01.

See also 42 U.S.C. §3610(a).

PROP §301.082. ANSWER

(a) Not later than the 10th day after the date of receipt of the notice and copy of the complaint under Section 301.081(f)(3), a respondent may file an answer to the complaint.

(b) An answer must be:

(1) in writing;

(2) under oath; and

(3) in the form prescribed by the commission.

(c) An answer may be amended at any time.

(d) An answer does not inhibit the investigation of a complaint.

History of Prop. Code §301.082: Acts 1993, 73rd Leg., ch. 268, §40, eff. Sept. 1, 1993. Source: TRCS art. 1f, §4.02.

See also 42 U.S.C. §3610(a).

PROP §301.083. INVESTIGATION

(a) If the federal government has referred a complaint to the commission or has deferred jurisdiction over the subject matter of the complaint to the commission, the commission shall promptly investigate the allegations set forth in the complaint.

(b) The commission shall investigate all complaints and, except as provided by Subsection (c), shall complete an investigation not later than the 100th day after the date the complaint is filed or, if it is unable to complete the investigation within the 100-day period, shall dispose of all administrative proceedings related to the investigation not later than the first anniversary after the date the complaint is filed.

(c) If the commission is unable to complete an investigation within the time periods prescribed by Subsection (b), the commission shall notify the complainant and the respondent in writing of the reasons for the delay.

History of Prop. Code §301.083: Acts 1993, 73rd Leg., ch. 268, §40, eff. Sept. 1, 1993. Source: TRCS art. 1f, §4.03.

See also 42 U.S.C. §3610(a).

PROP §301.084. ADDITIONAL OR SUBSTITUTE RESPONDENT

(a) The commission may join a person not named in the complaint as an additional or substitute respondent if during the investigation the commission determines that the person should be accused of a discriminatory housing practice.

(b) In addition to the information required in the notice under Section 301.081(f), the commission shall include in a notice to a respondent joined under this section the reasons for the determination that the person is properly joined as a respondent.

History of Prop. Code §301.084: Acts 1993, 73rd Leg., ch. 268, §40, eff. Sept. 1, 1993. Source: TRCS art. 1f, §4.04.

See also 42 U.S.C. §3610(a).

PROP §301.085. CONCILIATION

(a) The commission shall, during the period beginning with the filing of a complaint and ending with the

filing of a charge or a dismissal by the commission, to the extent feasible, engage in conciliation with respect to the complaint.

(b) A conciliation agreement between a respondent and the complainant is subject to commission approval.

(c) A conciliation agreement may provide for binding arbitration or another method of dispute resolution. Dispute resolution that results from a conciliation agreement may authorize appropriate relief, including monetary relief.

(d) A conciliation agreement is public information unless:

(1) the complainant and respondent agree that it is not; and

(2) the commission determines that disclosure is not necessary to further the purposes of this chapter.

(e) Statements made or actions taken in the conciliation may not be made public or used as evidence in a subsequent proceeding under this chapter without the written consent of the persons concerned.

(f) After completion of the commission's investigation, the commission shall make available to the aggrieved person and the respondent, at any time, information derived from the investigation and the final investigative report relating to that investigation.

History of Prop. Code §301.085: Acts 1993, 73rd Leg., ch. 268, §40, eff. Sept. 1, 1993. Source: TRCS art. 1f, §4.05.

See also 42 U.S.C. §3610(b).

ANNOTATIONS

Tex. Atty. Gen. Op. No. OR-04147 (2007). Requestor claims that "submitted documents were created during [civil-rights-division] conciliation attempts and are therefore confidential under [Prop. Code] §301.085…. [Government Code] §552.101 … excepts from disclosure 'information considered to be confidential by law, either constitutional, statutory, or by judicial decision.' Section 552.101 encompasses information protected by §301.085…. [¶] [Submitted] documents were created during the conciliation attempts and no written consent for their release exists. [W]e find that the submitted information is confidential under §301.085(e) … and must be withheld under §552.101."

PROP §301.086. TEMPORARY OR PRELIMINARY RELIEF

(a) The commission may authorize a civil action for temporary or preliminary relief pending the final disposition of a complaint if the commission concludes after the filing of the complaint that prompt judicial action is necessary to carry out the purposes of this chapter.

(b) On receipt of the commission's authorization, the attorney general shall promptly file the action.

(c) A temporary restraining order or other order granting preliminary or temporary relief under this section is governed by the applicable Texas Rules of Civil Procedure.

(d) The filing of a civil action under this section does not affect the initiation or continuation of administrative proceedings under Section 301.111.

History of Prop. Code §301.086: Acts 1993, 73rd Leg., ch. 268, §40, eff. Sept. 1, 1993. Source: TRCS art. 1f, §4.06.

See also 42 U.S.C. §3610(e).

PROP §301.087. INVESTIGATIVE REPORT

(a) The commission shall prepare a final investigative report including:

(1) the names of and dates of contacts with witnesses;

(2) a summary of correspondence and other contacts with the aggrieved person and the respondent showing the dates of the correspondence and contacts;

(3) a summary description of other pertinent records;

(4) a summary of witness statements; and

(5) answers to interrogatories.

(b) A final report under this section may be amended if additional evidence is discovered.

History of Prop. Code §301.087: Acts 1993, 73rd Leg., ch. 268, §40, eff. Sept. 1, 1993. Source: TRCS art. 1f, §4.07.

See also 42 U.S.C. §3610(b).

PROP §301.088. REASONABLE CAUSE DETERMINATION

(a) The commission shall determine from the facts whether reasonable cause exists to believe that a discriminatory housing practice has occurred or is about to occur.

(b) The commission shall make the determination under Subsection (a) not later than the 100th day after the date a complaint is filed unless:

(1) making the determination is impracticable; or

(2) the commission approves a conciliation agreement relating to the complaint.

(c) If within the period provided by Subsection (b) making the determination is impracticable, the com-

mission shall give in writing to the complainant and the respondent the reasons for the delay.

(d) If the commission determines that reasonable cause exists to believe that a discriminatory housing practice has occurred or is about to occur, the commission shall, except as provided by Section 301.090, immediately issue a charge on behalf of the aggrieved person.

History of Prop. Code §301.088: Acts 1993, 73rd Leg., ch. 268, §40, eff. Sept. 1, 1993. Source: TRCS art. 1f, §4.08.

See also 42 U.S.C. §3610(g).

PROP §301.089. CHARGE

(a) A charge issued under Section 301.088:

(1) must consist of a short and plain statement of the facts on which the commission finds reasonable cause to believe that a discriminatory housing practice has occurred or is about to occur;

(2) must be based on the final investigative report; and

(3) is not limited to the facts or grounds alleged in the complaint.

(b) Not later than the 20th day after the date the commission issues a charge, the commission shall send a copy of the charge with information about the election under Section 301.093 to:

(1) each respondent; and

(2) each aggrieved person on whose behalf the complaint was filed.

(c) The commission shall include with a charge sent to a respondent a notice of the opportunity for a hearing under Section 301.111.

History of Prop. Code §301.089: Acts 1993, 73rd Leg., ch. 268, §40, eff. Sept. 1, 1993. Source: TRCS art. 1f, §4.09.

See also 42 U.S.C. §3610(g).

PROP §301.090. LAND USE LAW

If the commission determines that the matter involves the legality of a state or local zoning or other land use law or ordinance, the commission may not issue a charge and shall immediately refer the matter to the attorney general for appropriate action.

History of Prop. Code §301.090: Acts 1993, 73rd Leg., ch. 268, §40, eff. Sept. 1, 1993. Source: TRCS art. 1f, §4.10.

See also 42 U.S.C. §3610(g).

PROP §301.091. DISMISSAL

(a) If the commission determines that no reasonable cause exists to believe that a discriminatory housing practice that is the subject of a complaint has occurred or is about to occur, the commission shall promptly dismiss the complaint.

(b) The commission shall make public disclosure of each dismissal.

History of Prop. Code §301.091: Acts 1993, 73rd Leg., ch. 268, §40, eff. Sept. 1, 1993. Source: TRCS art. 1f, §4.11.

See also 42 U.S.C. §3610(g).

PROP §301.092. PENDING CIVIL TRIAL

The commission may not issue a charge alleging a discriminatory housing practice after the beginning of the trial of a civil action commenced by the aggrieved party under federal or state law seeking relief with respect to that discriminatory housing practice.

History of Prop. Code §301.092: Acts 1993, 73rd Leg., ch. 268, §40, eff. Sept. 1, 1993. Source: TRCS art. 1f, §4.12.

See also 42 U.S.C. §3610(g).

PROP §301.093. ELECTION OF JUDICIAL DETERMINATION

(a) A complainant, a respondent, or an aggrieved person on whose behalf a complaint was filed may elect to have the claims asserted in the charge decided in a civil action as provided by Section 301.131.

(b) The election must be made not later than the 20th day after the date the person having the election receives service under Section 301.089(b) or, in the case of the commission, not later than the 20th day after the date the charge is issued.

(c) The person making the election shall give notice to the commission and to all other complainants and respondents to whom the charge relates.

History of Prop. Code §301.093: Acts 1993, 73rd Leg., ch. 268, §40, eff. Sept. 1, 1993. Source: TRCS art. 1f, §4.13.

See also 42 U.S.C. §3612(a).

Sections 301.094-301.110 reserved for expansion

SUBCHAPTER F. ADMINISTRATIVE HEARINGS

PROP §301.111. ADMINISTRATIVE HEARING

(a) If a timely election is not made under Section 301.093, the commission shall provide for a hearing on the charge.

(b) Except as provided by Subsection (c), Chapter 2001, Government Code, governs a hearing and an appeal of a hearing.

(c) A hearing under this section on an alleged discriminatory housing practice may not continue after the beginning of the trial of a civil action commenced by the aggrieved person under federal or state law seeking relief with respect to the discriminatory housing practice.

History of Prop. Code §301.111: Acts 1993, 73rd Leg., ch. 268, §40, eff. Sept. 1, 1993. Source: TRCS art. 1f, §4.15.

See also 42 U.S.C. §3612(b); Gov't Code ch. 2001.

PROP §301.112. ADMINISTRATIVE PENALTIES

(a) If the commission determines at a hearing under Section 301.111 that a respondent has engaged in or is about to engage in a discriminatory housing practice, the commission may order the appropriate relief, including actual damages, reasonable attorney fees, court costs, and other injunctive or equitable relief.

(b) To vindicate the public's interest, the commission may assess a civil penalty against the respondent in an amount that does not exceed:

(1) $10,000 if the respondent has been found by order of the commission or a court to have committed a prior discriminatory housing practice; or

(2) except as provided by Subsection (c):

(A) $25,000 if the respondent has been found by order of the commission or a court to have committed one other discriminatory housing practice during the five-year period ending on the date of the filing of the charges; or

(B) $50,000 if the respondent has been found by the commission or a court to have committed two or more discriminatory housing practices during the seven-year period ending on the date of filing of the charge.

(c) If the acts constituting the discriminatory housing practice that is the object of the charge are committed by the same individual who has previously been found to have committed acts constituting a discriminatory housing practice, the civil penalties in Subsection (b)(2) may be imposed without regard to the period of time within which any other discriminatory housing practice occurred.

(d) At the request of the commission, the attorney general shall sue to recover a civil penalty due under this section. Funds collected under this section shall be paid to the comptroller for deposit in the state treasury to the credit of the fair housing fund.

History of Prop. Code §301.112: Acts 1993, 73rd Leg., ch. 268, §40, eff. Sept. 1, 1993. Amended by Acts 1997, 75th Leg., ch. 1423, §16.39, eff. Sept. 1, 1997. Source: TRCS art. 1f, §4.16.

See also 42 U.S.C. §3612(g).

PROP §301.113. EFFECT OF COMMISSION ORDER

A commission order under Section 301.112 does not affect a contract, sale, encumbrance, or lease that:

(1) is consummated before the commission issues the order; and

(2) involves a bona fide purchaser, encumbrancer, or tenant who did not have actual notice of the charge filed under this chapter.

History of Prop. Code §301.113: Acts 1993, 73rd Leg., ch. 268, §40, eff. Sept. 1, 1993. Source: TRCS art. 1f, §4.17.

See also 42 U.S.C. §3612(g).

PROP §301.114. LICENSED OR REGULATED BUSINESS

If the commission issues an order with respect to a discriminatory housing practice that occurs in the course of a business subject to a licensing or regulation by a governmental agency, the commission shall, not later than the 30th day after the date the order is issued:

(1) send copies of the findings and the order to the governmental agency; and

(2) recommend to the governmental agency appropriate disciplinary action.

History of Prop. Code §301.114: Acts 1993, 73rd Leg., ch. 268, §40, eff. Sept. 1, 1993. Source: TRCS art. 1f, §4.18.

See also 42 U.S.C. §3612(g).

PROP §301.115. ORDER IN PRECEDING FIVE YEARS

If the commission issues an order against a respondent against whom another order was issued within the preceding five years under Section 301.112, the commission shall send a copy of each order to the attorney general.

History of Prop. Code §301.115: Acts 1993, 73rd Leg., ch. 268, §40, eff. Sept. 1, 1993. Source: TRCS art. 1f, §4.19.

See also 42 U.S.C. §3612(g).

Sections 301.116-301.130 reserved for expansion

SUBCHAPTER G. ENFORCEMENT BY ATTORNEY GENERAL

PROP §301.131. ATTORNEY GENERAL ACTION FOR ENFORCEMENT

(a) If a timely election is made under Section 301.093, the commission shall authorize and not later than the 30th day after the date the election is made the attorney general shall file in a district court a civil action seeking relief on behalf of the aggrieved person.

(b) Venue for an action is in the county in which the alleged discriminatory housing practice occurred or is about to occur.

(c) An aggrieved person may intervene in the action.

(d) If the court finds that a discriminatory housing practice has occurred or is about to occur, the court may grant as relief any relief that a court may grant in a civil action under Subchapter H.

(e) If monetary relief is sought for the benefit of an aggrieved person who does not intervene in the civil action, the court may not award the monetary relief if that aggrieved person has not complied with discovery orders entered by the court.

History of Prop. Code §301.131: Acts 1993, 73rd Leg., ch. 268, §40, eff. Sept. 1, 1993. Source: TRCS art. 1f, §4.14.

See also 42 U.S.C. §3612(o).

PROP §301.132. PATTERN OR PRACTICE CASE

(a) On the request of the commission, the attorney general may file a civil action in district court for appropriate relief if the commission has reasonable cause to believe that:

(1) a person is engaged in a pattern or practice of resistance to the full enjoyment of a right granted under this chapter; or

(2) a person has been denied a right granted by this chapter and that denial raises an issue of general public importance.

(b) In an action under this section the court may:

(1) award preventive relief, including a permanent or temporary injunction, restraining order, or other order against the person responsible for a violation of this chapter as necessary to assure the full enjoyment of the rights granted by this chapter;

(2) award other appropriate relief, including monetary damages, reasonable attorney fees, and court costs; and

(3) to vindicate the public interest, assess a civil penalty against the respondent in an amount that does not exceed:

(A) $50,000 for a first violation; and

(B) $100,000 for a second or subsequent violation.

(c) A person may intervene in an action under this section if the person is:

(1) a person aggrieved by the discriminatory housing practice; or

(2) a party to a conciliation agreement concerning the discriminatory housing practice.

History of Prop. Code §301.132: Acts 1993, 73rd Leg., ch. 268, §40, eff. Sept. 1, 1993. Source: TRCS art. 1f, §6.01.

See also 42 U.S.C. §3614(a), (d).

PROP §301.133. SUBPOENA ENFORCEMENT

The attorney general, on behalf of the commission or another party at whose request a subpoena is issued under this chapter, may enforce the subpoena in appropriate proceedings in district court.

History of Prop. Code §301.133: Acts 1993, 73rd Leg., ch. 268, §40, eff. Sept. 1, 1993. Source: TRCS art. 1f, §6.02.

See also 42 U.S.C. §§3611, 3614(c).

Sections 301.134-301.150 reserved for expansion

SUBCHAPTER H. ENFORCEMENT BY PRIVATE PERSONS

PROP §301.151. CIVIL ACTION

(a) An aggrieved person may file a civil action in district court not later than the second year after the date of the occurrence or the termination of an alleged discriminatory housing practice or the breach of a conciliation agreement entered under this chapter, whichever occurs last, to obtain appropriate relief with respect to the discriminatory housing practice or breach.

(b) The two-year period does not include any time during which an administrative hearing under this chapter is pending with respect to a complaint or charge under this chapter based on the discriminatory housing practice. This subsection does not apply to actions arising from the breach of a conciliation agreement.

(c) An aggrieved person may file an action whether a complaint has been filed under Section 301.081 and without regard to the status of any complaint filed under that section.

(d) If the commission has obtained a conciliation agreement with the consent of an aggrieved person, the aggrieved person may not file an action with respect to the alleged discriminatory housing practice that forms the basis of the complaint except to enforce the terms of the agreement.

(e) An aggrieved person may not file an action with respect to an alleged discriminatory housing practice that forms the basis of a charge issued by the commission if the commission has begun a hearing on the record under this chapter with respect to the charge.

History of Prop. Code §301.151: Acts 1993, 73rd Leg., ch. 268, §40, eff. Sept. 1, 1993. Source: TRCS art. 1f, §5.01.

See also 42 U.S.C. §3613(a).

PROP §301.152. COURT-APPOINTED ATTORNEY

On application by a person alleging a discriminatory housing practice or by a person against whom a dis-

criminatory housing practice is alleged, the court may appoint an attorney for the person.

History of Prop. Code §301.152: Acts 1993, 73rd Leg., ch. 268, §40, eff. Sept. 1, 1993. Source: TRCS art. 1f, §5.02.

See also 42 U.S.C. §3613(b).

PROP §301.153. RELIEF GRANTED

If the court finds that a discriminatory housing practice has occurred or is about to occur, the court may award to the plaintiff:

(1) actual and punitive damages;

(2) reasonable attorney fees;

(3) court costs; and

(4) subject to Section 301.154, a permanent or temporary injunction, temporary restraining order, or other order, including an order enjoining the defendant from engaging in the practice or ordering appropriate affirmative action.

History of Prop. Code §301.153: Acts 1993, 73rd Leg., ch. 268, §40, eff. Sept. 1, 1993. Source: TRCS art. 1f, §5.03.

See also 42 U.S.C. §3613(c).

PROP §301.154. EFFECT OF RELIEF GRANTED

Relief granted under this subchapter does not affect a contract, sale, encumbrance, or lease that:

(1) is consummated before the granting of the relief; and

(2) involves a bona fide purchaser, encumbrancer, or tenant who did not have actual notice of the filing of a complaint or civil action under this chapter.

History of Prop. Code §301.154: Acts 1993, 73rd Leg., ch. 268, §40, eff. Sept. 1, 1993. Source: TRCS art. 1f, §5.04.

See also 42 U.S.C. §3613(d).

PROP §301.155. INTERVENTION BY ATTORNEY GENERAL

(a) On request of the commission, the attorney general may intervene in an action under this subchapter if the commission certifies that the case is of general public importance.

(b) The attorney general may obtain the same relief as is available to the attorney general under Section 301.132(b).

History of Prop. Code §301.155: Acts 1993, 73rd Leg., ch. 268, §40, eff. Sept. 1, 1993. Source: TRCS art. 1f, §5.05.

See also 42 U.S.C. §3613(e).

PROP §301.156. PREVAILING PARTY

A court in a civil action brought under this chapter or the commission in an administrative hearing under Section 301.111 may award reasonable attorney fees to the prevailing party and asscss court costs against the nonprevailing party.

History of Prop. Code §301.156: Acts 1993, 73rd Leg., ch. 268, §40, eff. Sept. 1, 1993. Source: TRCS art. 1f, §8.01.

See also 42 U.S.C. §3613(c).

ANNOTATIONS

Texas Comm'n on Human Rights v. Kinnear, 986 S.W.2d 828, 832 (Tex.App.—Beaumont 1999), *rev'd in part on other grounds*, 14 S.W.3d 299 (Tex.2000). "The [Texas] Fair Housing Act provides the court in a civil action brought under the Act may award reasonable attorney fees to the prevailing party. An award against the State of Texas may be granted only if the State has waived sovereign immunity. [Section 301.156] does not provide that the State shall be liable for attorney fees in the same manner as private litigants. In the context of attorney fees, sovereign immunity is waived if a state agency files an action that is frivolous, unreasonable, or without foundation, and the action is dismissed or judgment is awarded to the other party."

Sections 301.157-301.170 reserved for expansion

SUBCHAPTER I. CRIMINAL PENALTY

PROP §301.171. INTIMIDATION OR INTERFERENCE

(a) A person commits an offense if the person, without regard to whether the person is acting under color of law, by force or threat of force intentionally intimidates or interferes with a person:

(1) because of the person's race, color, religion, sex, disability, familial status, or national origin and because the person is or has been selling, purchasing, renting, financing, occupying, or contracting or negotiating for the sale, purchase, rental, financing, or occupation of any dwelling or applying for or participating in a service, organization, or facility relating to the business of selling or renting dwellings; or

(2) because the person is or has been or to intimidate the person from:

(A) participating, without discrimination because of race, color, religion, sex, disability, familial status, or national origin, in an activity, service, organization, or facility described by Subdivision (1); or

(B) affording another person opportunity or protection to so participate; or

(C) lawfully aiding or encouraging other persons to participate, without discrimination because of race, color, religion, sex, disability, familial status, or national origin, in an activity, service, organization, or facility described by Subdivision (1).

(b) An offense under this section is a Class A misdemeanor.

History of Prop. Code §301.171: Acts 1993, 73rd Leg., ch. 268, §40, eff. Sept. 1, 1993. Source: TRCS art. 1f, §9.01.

See also 42 U.S.C. §§3617, 3631.

CHAPTERS 401-446. EXPIRED

***Editor's note:** The Texas Residential Construction Commission was not renewed by the Texas Legislature in 2009, following the Texas Sunset Advisory Commission's recommendation. For more information, visit www.sunset.texas.gov. See also **O'Connor's Texas COA**, "Common Law: Implied Warranty of Good & Workmanlike Services—Home Construction," ch. 32-I, p. 1129; "Common Law: Implied Warranty of Habitability," ch. 32-J, p. 1137.*

TEXAS TITLE EXAMINATION STANDARDS

TABLE OF CONTENTS

TEXAS TITLE EXAMINATION STANDARDS

TABLE OF CONTENTS

TEXAS TITLE EXAMINATION STANDARDS

By

The Title Standards Joint Editorial Board of the Section of Real Estate, Probate & Trust Law & the Oil, Gas & Energy Resources Law Section of the State Bar of Texas

Executive Editor:

William B. Burford

Editor:

Owen L. Anderson

Assistant Editors:

Douglas W. Becker
Terry I. Cross
Celia C. Flowers
H. Martin Gibson
James L. Gosdin
Mari C. Haley
Peter E. Hosey
G. Roland Love
George A. Snell, III
Robert "Doc" Watson
Roderick E. Wetsel

Past Editors:

William A. Abney (served 1990-2006)
A. W. Clem (served 1990-2011)
David R. Duckworth (served 1990-2006)
Charles B. Harris (served 1990-2016)
Edward H. Hill (served as Executive Editor 1990-2015)
Nancy A. Lynch (served 2000-2008)
Jan E. Rehler (served 1990-2016)

Adopted June 27, 1997
Last revised June 2017

PREFACE

In 1989, the Council of the Section of Real Estate, Probate and Trust Law of the State Bar of Texas approved the formation of a committee to study the formulation and development of title examination standards. Through the newsletter of that Section, Section members were notified of the project. Lawyers from all parts of Texas responded evidencing their interest in working as active participants on this project. Subsequently, the Oil, Gas and Mineral Law Section (now the Oil, Gas and Energy Resources Law Section) of the State Bar of Texas asked to co-sponsor this project.

After substantial study of the use of title examination standards and many hours of drafting and meeting time, proposed standards were published for comment in 1996 in the newsletters of both of the sponsoring sections. Following the receipt of comments from lawyers across Texas, additional revisions were made by the committee (now the "Title Standards Joint Editorial Board") and the proposed standards were once again published for comment in the Spring of 1997.

At the State Bar of Texas Convention on June 27, 1997, 33 standards were approved by both the Section of Real Estate, Probate and Trust Law and the Oil, Gas and Mineral Law Section. The initial standards constituted the beginning of title examination standards in Texas. Under current procedure, the Title Standards Joint Editorial Board, appointed by these two sections, meets at least semiannually to consider amendments to existing standards and additional standards. As with the initial standards, amendments or new standards are presented to the membership of these two sections prior to formal adoption; however, the Board makes changes to the comments and cautions as needed. In keeping with this process, the Comments, Cautions, Sources, and Histories have been updated from the initial Standards.

DISCLAIMER & INTRODUCTION

Disclaimer: These title examination standards represent the collective consensus of The Title Standards Joint Editorial Board established by the Section of Real Estate, Probate and Trust Law and the Oil, Gas and Energy Resources Law Section of the State Bar of Texas. These standards should not be construed as reflecting the opinion of the State Bar of Texas, its officers, members or staff. These standards are presented with the understanding that neither the publisher nor the Joint Editorial Board is engaged in rendering legal services. In no event shall the Joint Editorial Board, the reviewers, or the publisher be liable for any direct, indirect, or consequential damages resulting from the use of this publication, including damages resulting from the sole or concurrent negligence of the Joint Editorial Board, its members, the reviewers, or the publisher.

Because statutory law prohibits title insurance companies from insuring against loss by reason of unmarketable title, these standards do not apply to title examination for purposes of title insurance. *See* Tex. Ins. Code Ann. Section 2502.002. Moreover, these standards do not apply to the exercise of discretion by a title insurance company in determining the insurability of title. Title insurance is a contract of indemnity. *Southern Title Guaranty Co., Inc. v. Prendergast*, 494 S.W.2d 154 (Tex. 1973).

Standards for real estate title examinations are statements that declare an answer to a question or a so-

lution for a problem that is commonly encountered in the process of a title examination. Their purpose is to alleviate disagreements among members of the bar regarding real estate transactions and to set forth propositions (standards) with which title lawyers can generally agree concerning title documents to promote uniformity in the preparation, use, and meaning of such documents. In other words, title standards can be viewed as a reference that can be consulted in the preparation and examination of title documents. Although standards do not, by themselves, impose compulsory legal requirements, they do establish guidelines upon which a reasonable and practical examination can be based. And although standards should state fundamental and enduring principles, they are subject to amendment as required by changes in governing law and in title and conveyancing practice.

Title standards may address a variety of concerns, including the attitudes and relationships among examiners and between examiners and the public, the appropriate duration of a title search, the effect of the lapse of time on a defective or improperly recorded title document, the appropriate presumptions of fact that can be relied upon in the course of an examination, and the law applicable to commonly encountered situations. Standards should represent the near unanimous opinion of the experienced and competent title bar.

Even with title standards, however, title examiners should advise their clients honestly as to their beliefs and opinions regarding the ownership of a particular interest in land. The judgment of an examiner should necessarily reflect rules of law (both legislative and case law) as well as justifiable presumptions that are applicable to title documents and to fact situations arising from the chain of title appearing of record. For example, when the name of a grantee in one deed corresponds with the name of the grantor in a later deed, the universal practice is to presume that they are the same person. And although there is nothing of record to show that the grantor was competent, that the signature is genuine, or that the deed was actually delivered, the universal practice is to presume that these are facts. Indeed, any attempt to require proof of these matters regarding each document in the chain of title would create chaos.

Of course, when minor title questions do arise, the reaction of different examiners may not always be the same. For example, title examiners may respond differently regarding the effect of a recorded, unacknowledged deed; of a deed that fails to state the marital status of the grantor; or of a deed from a married grantor that does not contain the signature of the grantor's spouse. Thus, a chief objective of title standards is to set forth uniform principles to resolve certain common title problems.

Users of these Standards are cautioned that individual Standards, Comments, and Cautions may not reflect current case law and statutes. There is a lapse of time between the time that changes in law occur and the updating of the Standards, Comments, and Cautions. Users are invited to notify the Joint Editorial Board if they believe that any of the Standards, Comments, or Cautions fail to reflect current law.

CHAPTER I. TITLE EXAMINER

STANDARD 1.10. PURPOSE OF TITLE EXAMINER

The purpose of an examination of title and comments, objections, and requirements is to advise an examiner's client of the status of title and of the methods by which the client may secure marketable title to real property. Based upon the materials examined, the title opinion should advise an examiner's client of all irregularities, defects, and encumbrances that may reasonably be expected to affect materially the value or use of the property or that may expose the owner to litigation or adverse claims even if the litigation or adverse claims can reasonably be expected to be successfully defended. The examiner does not ordinarily determine the validity or priority of irregularities, defects and encumbrances.

COMMENT

A major goal of title standards is to eliminate technical objections that do not impair marketability and common objections that are based upon a misapplication of law. An examiner should determine what irregularities, defects, and encumbrances have been discovered by the examination. Then an examiner should determine, to the extent reasonably possible, who, if anyone, can take advantage of each irregularity, defect, or encumbrance against the owner and/or client, and if there are consequent risks.

Source:
Lewis M. Simes & Clarence B. Taylor, *Model Title Standards*, Std. 2.1 (1960).

History:

Adopted June 27, 1997; amended June 16, 2006. The original standard provided:

"The purpose of an examination of title and comments, objections, and requirements is to advise an examiner's client of the status of title and of the methods by which the client may secure marketable title to real property. Based upon the materials examined, the title opinion should advise an examiner's client of all irregularities, defects, and encumbrances that may reasonably be expected to affect materially the value or use of the property; or that may expose the owner to litigation or adverse claims even if the litigation or adverse claims can reasonably be expected to be successfully defended."

STANDARD 1.20. REVIEW BY EXAMINER

Based upon the intended scope of the examination, an examiner should review any documents, records, deeds, abstracts, affidavits, or other reliable materials that are necessary to form a legal opinion as to the status of title to the property. The materials that are examined should be set forth in the title opinion or as an exhibit to the opinion.

COMMENT

An examiner's opinion will usually be based upon the entire chain of title. The chain of title is the successive conveyances, commencing with the severance of title from the sovereign down to and including the conveyance to the present holder. *Munawar v. Cadle Company*, 2 S.W.3d 12, 18 (Tex. App.—Corpus Christi 1999, pet. denied). Note that severance from the sovereign occurs on the date of the survey of the property for severance purposes, not on the date of the patent, which always post-dates severance—sometimes by many years. Occasionally, an examiner may base an opinion upon a chain of title covering a shorter time period. For example, an examiner may limit the examination to instruments in the chain of title that were recorded after the period covered by a prior title opinion that was submitted by the client and prepared by another attorney; however, in this instance, the examiner is well advised to make certain that the client understands that the client assumes the risk of any deficiencies in the prior opinion.

The documents that are available for examination may vary, but they should be sufficient for an examiner to be legally satisfied as to the status of title to the property. Disclosure of the documents examined is necessary to advise the client of the basis for the opinion and to protect an examiner from documents and matters not considered. The examining attorney is usually not responsible for identifying or gathering the documents to be examined, but should assess the acceptability of the methods employed in doing so and should disclose any instance in which the methods employed are not generally considered to be the most reliable.

The scope of an examiner's opinion may be limited at the request of the client or to suit the client's particular purpose or property interest. The nature and scope of the documents examined may be limited accordingly. Under such circumstances, an examiner should carefully set forth the limited scope of the opinion, and an examiner should be reasonably certain that the opinion is adequate for the client's purpose.

Source:

Title Standards Joint Editorial Board.

History:

Adopted June 27, 1997.

STANDARD 1.30. CONSULTATION WITH PRIOR EXAMINER

When an examiner discovers a situation that creates a question regarding the status of title and an examiner has knowledge that another examiner has examined the title, or is familiar with the situation in the context of other property, an examiner may, before preparing the opinion, communicate with the other examiner if such communication is in the best interests of an examiner's client and does not violate the Texas Disciplinary Rules of Professional Conduct.

COMMENT

Communication with the prior attorney is a discretionary matter. A prior examiner may not be readily available for consultation, or communication with the prior examiner may not be economically justified.

CAUTION

A prior examiner may represent an adverse or potentially adverse party, making such communication inappropriate.

Source:

Oklahoma Title Examination Standards, Std. 1.2; Lewis M. Simes & Clarence B. Taylor, *Model Title Standards*, Std. 2.2 (1960).

History:

Adopted June 27, 1997.

CHAPTER II. MARKETABLE TITLE

STANDARD 2.10. MARKETABLE TITLE DEFINED

All title examinations should be based on marketability of title. A marketable title is a record title that is free from reasonable doubt such that a prudent person, with knowledge of all salient facts and circumstances and their legal significance, would be willing to accept

it. To be marketable, a title need not be absolutely free from every possible suspicion. The mere possibility of a defect that has no probable basis does not show an unmarketable title.

COMMENT

Except as otherwise provided in these standards, if a title examination reveals the need to rely on facts outside of the record, the title is unmarketable. An example would be facts that must be proven by parol evidence or by presumptions of fact that would probably, in the event of suit, become genuine issues of fact. Whether the potential lawsuit would likely be won by the party with apparent record title is immaterial, because threat or probable likelihood of litigation renders the title unmarketable. On the other hand, a title need not be perfect to be marketable. A doubt about title must be a reasonable doubt and be serious enough to affect its value.

Usually, the buyer's attorney examines the title and identifies any title defects. If the examiner prepares a written opinion, any title defects will be listed together with a statement of the necessary requirement(s) to cure each defect. The opinion may also contain comments about the title that are intended to inform the buyer of any concerns about the title that do not affect marketability. Usually in response, the seller's attorney or other agent obtains the curative instruments or takes other necessary action to cure any title defects. Such curative efforts are usually submitted to the buyer's attorney for approval prior to closing. If a title defect cannot be cured prior to closing, the buyer must decide whether to accept the defective title or rescind the transaction.

CAUTION

In Texas, an owner cannot be a bona fide purchaser if the owner derives its title under a quitclaim deed. *Woodward v. Ortiz*, 237 S.W.2d 286, 291-92 (Tex. 1951) (purchaser under a quitclaim deed takes with notice of all prior unrecorded conveyances and equitable claims of third persons). Nevertheless, because quitclaim deeds are often found in chains of title, an examiner does not typically question marketability merely because a quitclaim deed is found within a chain of title. Moreover, case law is not clear as to what constitutes a quitclaim. *See, e.g.*, *Bryan v. Thomas*, 365 S.W.2d 628 (Tex. 1963) (conveyance of all of grantor's interest in a tract is not a quitclaim deed).

Matters that may make a title unmarketable include:

(1) Land acquired by limitation title, *Greer v. International Stock Yards Co.*, 43 Tex. Civ. App. 370, 96 S.W. 79 (Tex. Civ. App. 1906, writ ref'd).

(2) Land acquired by accretion, *Gaines v. Dillard*, 545 S.W.2d 845 (Tex. Civ. App.—Fort Worth 1976, writ ref'd n.r.e.).

(3) Title that is subject to an outstanding oil and gas lease, *Roberts & Corley v. McFaddin, Weiss & Kyle*, 74 S.W. 105 (Tex. Civ. App. 1903, writ denied).

(4) Title that is subject to an outstanding royalty interest, *Sweet v. Berry*, 236 S.W. 531 (Tex. Civ. App.—Amarillo 1921, writ dism'd).

(5) Title that is subject to an outstanding covenant, *Dupree v. Savage*, 154 S.W. 701 (Tex. Civ. App.—Amarillo 1913, writ ref'd).

(6) Title that is subject to an outstanding easement, *Shaw v. Morrison*, 14 S.W.2d 953 (Tex. Civ. App.—Eastland 1929, no writ).

(7) Title that is subject to a mortgage, judgment lien, or tax lien, *Crutcher v. Aiken*, 252 S.W. 844 (Tex. Civ. App.—El Paso 1923, no writ).

Effective September 1, 2011, the Texas Property Code was revised to authorize the correction of instruments containing incorrect or ambiguous property descriptions, as well as mistakes relating to the names of parties, acknowledgments, marital status, dates, and recording data. Tex. Prop. Code Ann. §§5.027-5.031, as amended. These statutes were enacted in response[1] *Myrad Properties, Inc. v. LaSalle Bank Nat'l Ass'n*, 300 S.W.3d 746 (Tex. 2009) (holding that a particular correction deed was void as a matter of law). Until these statutes are either amended or construed by the Texas courts, an examiner should be wary of relying upon any correction deed issued under these new statutes.

1. **Editor's note:** So in original. Probably should add "to."

Source:

Lund v. Emerson, 204 S.W.2d 639 (Tex. Civ. App.—Amarillo 1947, no writ); *Owens v. Jackson*, 35 S.W.2d 186 (Tex. Civ. App.—Austin 1931, writ dism'd w.o.j.); *Texas Auto Co. v. Arbetter*, 1 S.W.2d 334 (Tex. Civ. App.—San Antonio 1927, writ dism'd w.o.j.); *Austin v. Carter*, 296 S.W. 649 (Tex. Civ. App.—Eastland 1927, writ dism'd); *Alling v. Vander Stucken*, 194 S.W. 443 (Tex. Civ. App.—San Antonio 1917, writ ref'd); *Adkins v. Gillespie*, 189 S.W. 275 (Tex. Civ. App.—Dallas 1916, no writ); 3A Aloysius A. Leopold, *Land Titles and Title Examination* §10.6 n.1 (Texas Practice 3d ed. 2005).

History:

Adopted June 27, 1997.

STANDARD 2.20. CORRECTION INSTRUMENTS

An examiner may rely on a correction instrument to establish, or as an aid to establishing, marketable title. However, a correction instrument materially altering the effect of a prior conveyance or other instrument that it purports to correct should be considered effective only if joined by all parties whose interests are affected.

COMMENT

Tex. Prop. Code. Ann. §§5.027-.031, enacted in 2011 and subsequently revised, expressly sanction use of correction instruments to correct errors and omissions in conveyances. The legislation is a reaction to *Myrad Properties, Inc. v. LaSalle Bank*, 300 S.W.3d 746 (Tex. 2009), which held that a correction deed was void because it added a tract of land that was not included in the earlier deed that it purported to correct, but might be read to suggest that a correction deed is inherently unreliable. As Tex. Prop. Code Ann. §5.028 directly contemplates, an examiner should liberally rely on information provided in a correction instrument purporting to correct a clerical error to give effect to a previous instrument's clarified intent where there is no apparent reason to question the correction instrument's factual accuracy.

CAUTION

An examiner should not rely on a purported correction instrument that makes a material correction to an earlier instrument unless all who could be adversely affected by the correction, including subsequent purchasers, have joined in its execution. *See* Tex. Prop. Code Ann. §5.029. Because of the difficulty in determining the materiality of a correction, absent a judicial resolution, the examiner should exercise caution in relying on a correction instrument in which not all affected persons have joined.

Source:
Citations in the Comment.
History:
Adopted July 17, 2014.

CHAPTER III. NAME VARIANCES

STANDARD 3.10. IDEM SONANS

An examiner may presume that differently spelled names refer to the same person when the names sound alike or when their sounds cannot be distinguished easily or when common usage by corruption or abbreviation has made their pronunciation identical.

COMMENT

This standard expresses the common law rule of "idem sonans." If a name in a legal document is incorrectly spelled but, when commonly pronounced, conveys to the ear a sound practically identical to the correct name as commonly pronounced, then the name thus given can be accepted as sufficient identification. *Means v. Protestant Episcopal Church Council*, 503 S.W.2d 591, 592 (Tex. Civ. App.—Houston [1st Dist.] 1973, writ ref'd n.r.e.); *Dingler v. State*, 705 S.W.2d 144, 145 (Tex. Crim. App. 1984). Thus, if the grantee in one deed is "John Macomber" and the grantor in the next deed is "John McOmber," these names are presumed to refer to the same person. Or, if the grantee in one deed is "William Conolly" and the grantor in the next deed is "William Conley," the same presumption may be made.

In *Cockrell v. Estevez*, 737 S.W.2d 138, 139 n.1 (Tex. App.—San Antonio 1987, no writ), the court noted that under the rule of idem sonans, absolute accuracy in the spelling of a name is not required in a legal document. As long as the incorrect spelling sounds practically identical to the correct name (in this instance "Cockrall" and "Cockrell"), there is sufficient identification of the named person. *See also Chumney v. Craig*, 805 S.W.2d 864 (Tex. App.—Waco 1991, writ denied) ("Damon" and "Damond"); *O'Brien v. Cole*, 532 S.W.2d 151 (Tex. Civ. App.—Dallas 1976, no writ) ("O'Brian" and "O'Brien"). In *Hill v. Foster*, 181 S.W.2d 299, 304 (Tex. Civ. App.—Amarillo 1944), aff'd, 186 S.W.2d 343 (Tex. 1945), the court applied the rule of idem sonans and held that it is immaterial if a slight discrepancy exists between the name used in the body of the deed and the name signed thereto. The court determined that, through typographical error, the name "Barclay" used in the body of the deed was intended to be "Baxley," but the two names, although spelled differently, sounded enough alike to be idem sonans.

CAUTION

Similarity of names is never more than a mere rebuttable presumption of identity. *Turner v. Roberts*, 513 S.W.2d 957, 959 (Tex. Civ. App.—Fort Worth 1974, no writ). Texas law is unclear where the difference in spelling regards the first letter of the surname (e.g., "Pfister" and "Fister," "Pharnsworth" and "Farnsworth"). Because the official title indices in Texas are grantor-grantee and grantee-grantor (in contrast with a

tract index), names like "Fister" and "Pfister" would not be indexed in the same portion of the indices.

Source:
Citations in the Comment; Lewis M. Simes & Clarence B. Taylor, *Model Title Standards*, Std. 5.1 (1960); 5 Aloysius A. Leopold, *Land Titles and Title Examination* §32.4 (Texas Practice 3d ed. 2005).

History:
Adopted June 27, 1997.

STANDARD 3.20. MIDDLE NAMES OR INITIALS

Unless otherwise put on inquiry, an examiner may presume that the use of a middle name or initial in one instrument and its nonuse in another instrument does not raise an issue of identity that affects title.

COMMENT

Similarity of names is ordinarily sufficient identity in the chain of title. In the absence of evidence casting doubt upon the identity of a party to a conveyance, such similarity is controlling in nearly every instance. *Knox v. Gruhlkey*, 192 S.W. 334 (Tex. Civ. App.—Amarillo 1917, writ ref'd). The similarity of "H. Percy Forster" to "H. P. Forster" was found to be sufficient evidence of identity in a trespass-to-try title action in *Corder v. Foster*, 505 S.W.2d 645, 649 (Tex. Civ. App.—Houston [1st Dist.] 1973, writ ref'd n.r.e.).

CAUTION

Similarity of names is never more than a mere rebuttable presumption of identity. *Turner v. Roberts*, 513 S.W.2d 957, 959 (Tex. Civ. App.—Fort Worth 1974, no writ).

Source:
Citations in the Comment; Lewis M. Simes & Clarence B. Taylor, *Model Title Standards*, Std. 5.2 (1960).

History:
Adopted June 27, 1997.

STANDARD 3.30. ABBREVIATIONS

An examiner may presume that any customary and generally accepted abbreviation of a first or middle name is the equivalent of the full name.

COMMENT

A commonly known diminutive or abbreviation is sufficient to identify a person in the absence of evidence indicating that a different person was intended. *Salazar v. Tower*, 683 S.W.2d 797, 799 (Tex. App.—Corpus Christi 1984, no writ). "Terry" is a sufficient identification of "Terrance." *O'Brien v. Cole*, 532 S.W.2d 151 (Tex. Civ. App.—Dallas 1976, no writ).

CAUTION

Similarity of names is never more than a mere rebuttable presumption of identity. *Turner v. Roberts*, 513 S.W.2d 957, 959 (Tex. Civ. App.—Fort Worth 1974, no writ).

Source:
Citations in the Comment; Lewis M. Simes & Clarence B. Taylor, *Model Title Standards*, Std. 5.3 (1960).

History:
Adopted June 27, 1997.

STANDARD 3.40. RECITALS OF IDENTITY

An examiner may rely upon a recital of identity contained in a conveyance executed by the party whose identity is recited, unless the examiner has a reasonable basis for questioning the recital. If title is held in a name that appears to be a business name, an examiner may rely on a recital of identity that incorporates the words "doing business as" ("dba") or similar words (e.g., "John Smith, dba Wholesome Grocery Store"), unless the form of name or other facts appearing from the materials examined raise a contrary inference.

COMMENT

An examiner often encounters conveyances in which the grantor's name is not the same as that of the record owner, but which recite the identity between the two. Frequent examples include instruments using words such as "also known as" ("aka") ("Robert T. Jones, Jr., aka Bobby Jones"); "formerly" or "formerly known as" ("fka") ("Mary Smith, formerly Mary Jones"); and "nee," which means "born as" ("Mary Lincoln, nee Todd"). Even though these instruments are usually executed only by the person whose identity is recited and might technically be regarded as self-serving, such recitals are, practically universally, accepted as fact to complete the chain of title.

The rule here expressed is grounded in the notion that similarity of names is sufficient to establish identity of persons when there is no evidence to the contrary. *See Chamblee v. Tarbox*, 27 Tex. 139, 144-45 (1863). *Cf., Dittman v. Cornelius*, 234 S.W. 880 (Tex. Comm'n App. 1921, judgm't adopted) (holding that proof of identity need not be conclusive). In *Haney v. Gartin*, 113 S.W. 166 (Tex. Civ. App. 1908, writ denied), the objection was made that "Mary E. Kurtz," one of the grantors, was not shown to have a connection with the title, although the deed contained a recital that "Mary E. Kurtz" was "formerly Mary E. Newlin." This recital

was sufficient, said the court, to show that "Mary E. Kurtz," who signed the deed, was the same person as "Mary E. Newlin," to whom the land had been devised. Recitals of identity were likewise deemed sufficient to explain discrepancies between the names of grantors and the record owners in *Auerbach v. Wylie*, 19 S.W. 856 (Tex. 1892) and *Russell v. Oliver*, 14 S.W. 264 (Tex. 1890).

With some exceptions, the Assumed Business or Professional Name Act, Tex. Bus. & Com. Code Ann. Ch. 71, requires persons and entities doing business under an assumed name to file a certificate thereof in specified offices. Failure to file the required certificate does not void or impair transactions by the offending party. *Paragon Oil Syndicate v. Rhoades Drilling Co.*, 277 S.W. 1036 (Tex. 1925); Tex. Bus. & Com. Code Ann. §71.201. Reference to a county's assumed name certificate records may be helpful in resolving identity questions and may be relied upon in the absence of inconsistent information.

As to the use of recitals generally, see Standard 13.40. For guidance generally concerning conveyances involving business entities, see Chapters VI and VII, infra.

CAUTION

On occasion an examiner may be presented with names which, although recited to be alternative names of the same person, are entirely dissimilar. Under such circumstances the examiner should bear in mind the presumption that names that are not the same refer to different persons. *See Fox v. Grand Union Tea Co.*, 236 S.W.2d 561, 563 (Tex. Civ. App.—Austin 1951, no writ). Unless the instrument recites some further explanation or qualifies as an ancient document (see Comment to Standard 13.40), or supporting facts otherwise appear in the record, an examiner should require further inquiry.

Although recitals of identity may be relied upon for business entities in the chain of title as well as for individuals, authority for reliance may be weaker in the case of business entities. *See Texas Co. v. Lee*, 157 S.W.2d 628, 630-31 (Tex. 1941). Prudence dictates the exercise of greater care in considering recitals of the identity of business entities, particularly when it is practical to obtain documentation. *See* Standard 6.70.

The name of a business entity may raise an inference contrary to a recital of identity. For example, appellations such as "Inc." or "Corporation," ordinarily denoting a particular form of organization, would contradict a recital that the entity is an individual, or a different kind of entity, doing business under the corporate name. If a business entity's name tends to contradict a recital of identity, a requirement of further investigation and proof of identity is warranted. Other examples of words and abbreviations that connote a particular kind of entity are "L.L.C.," "L.C.," or "Ltd. Co." for a limited liability company, "Ltd." or "L.P." for a limited partnership; and "L.L.P." for a limited liability partnership. On the other hand, the word "Company" or "Co." in the name of a business entity is widely used in many different forms of business and should not be regarded as signifying any particular one. (The examiner should bear in mind that words and abbreviations occurring in the names of entities incorporated or registered in other jurisdictions might have connotations different from those that would apply to Texas entities.)

Source:

Citations in the Comment; Lewis M. Simes & Clarence B. Taylor, *Model Title Standards*, Std. 5.4 (1960); 5 Aloysius A. Leopold, *Land Titles and Title Examination* §§32.6, 32.9 (Texas Practice 3d ed. 2005).

History:

Adopted June 27, 1997; amended June 15, 2001. This amendment was primarily adopted for the purpose of accommodating a new chapter on affidavits and recitals. (Chapter XIII). The original standard provided: "Absent actual or constructive notice that a recital of identity may be untrue, an examiner may rely upon a recital of identity contained in a conveyance executed by the person whose identity is recited. A recital of a statement of fact, marital status or identity of heirship is prima facie evidence of the truth of the recital if the document containing such statement has been of record in the deed records of the applicable county for at least five years. A recital in an 'ancient document' is admissible as evidence of the recited facts."

STANDARD 3.50. SUFFIXES

Although identity of a name raises a presumption of identity of a person, an examiner should take note of the addition of a suffix, such as "Jr." or "II," to the name of a subsequent grantor because such a suffix may rebut the presumption of identity with the prior grantee.

COMMENT

Ordinarily a suffix is not considered a part of the name. Thus, where the grantee in one instrument is "John Doe, M.D." and the grantor in the next instrument is merely "John Doe," it would be presumed that they are the same person. However, if the grantee in one instrument is "John Doe, Sr." and the grantor in the next instrument is "John Doe, Jr.," the presumption that they are the same person would be rebutted. Or, if the grantee in one instrument is "John Doe," and in another instrument the grantor is "John Doe, Jr.," the presumption of identity may be rebutted.

The Texas Supreme Court, in a case concerning service of process, reversed a court of appeals' decision that had held that the addition or omission of the suffix "Sr." or "Jr." was immaterial. *Uvalde Country Club v. Martin Linen Supply Co.*, 690 S.W.2d 884 (Tex. 1985). The issue in the case was whether a citation that had been issued in the name of "Henry Bunting" satisfied the rules of civil procedure where the registered agent was listed as "Henry Bunting, Jr." Without elaborating, the Texas Supreme Court held that the discrepancy in names invalidated the service of process under the rules of civil procedure.

Source:

Citations in the Comment; Lewis M. Simes & Clarence B. Taylor, *Model Title Standards*, Std. 5.5 (1960).

History:

Adopted June 27, 1997.

STANDARD 3.60. VARIANCE IN NAME WITHIN AN INSTRUMENT

Where a grantor's signature differs from the grantor's name as it appears in the body of the deed, but the name given in the acknowledgment agrees with either the signature or the name as it appears in the body of the deed, an examiner should accept the certificate of acknowledgment as providing adequate identification.

COMMENT

An officer may not take an acknowledgment unless the officer knows or has satisfactory evidence that the acknowledging person is in fact the person who executed the instrument. Tex. Civ. Prac. & Rem. Code Ann. §121.005. This requirement is sufficient to create a presumption of identity when the signature differs from the body of the deed but the acknowledgment agrees with one or the other. Numerous cases have held that a certificate of acknowledgment is considered prima facie evidence of all facts therein recited and that the recitals are conclusive unless fraud or duress is shown.

CAUTION

This general rule should not be extended beyond relatively minor variances, such as the use of a full given name in one place and initials in another, or a variance between a middle initial used in the body of the deed and a different one in the signature. A deed purporting to be from Robert Jones but signed by John Smith certainly should not be passed.

Source:

Bell v. Sharif-Munir-Davidson Dev. Corp., 738 S.W.2d 326 (Tex. App.—Dallas 1987, writ denied); *Stout v. Oliveira*, 153 S.W.2d 590 (Tex. Civ. App.—El Paso 1941, writ ref'd w.o.m.); *Oklahoma Title Examination Standards*, Std. 5.2; Lewis A. Simes & Clarence B. Taylor, *Model Title Standards*, Std. 5.6 (1960); 5 Aloysius A. Leopold, *Land Titles and Title Examination* §§32.6, 32.9 (Texas Practice 3d ed. 2005).

History:

Adopted June 27, 1997.

STANDARD 3.70. VARIANCES IN NAME OF SPOUSE

If a grantee spouse in one instrument of conveyance is identified only by a title and last name (e.g., "John Smith and Mrs. John Smith, grantees") and such spouse is apparently identified in a succeeding instrument in the chain of title by both a given and last name (e.g., "John Smith and Mary Smith, grantors"), an examiner should require further evidence showing that such spouse (e.g., Mrs. John Smith) in the first instrument is the same person as the spouse (e.g., Mary Smith) in the second instrument. The same requirement should be made if these succeeding forms of identification are reversed (e.g., the grantees in the first instrument are "John Smith and Mary Smith" and the grantors in a succeeding instrument in the chain of title are "John Smith and Mrs. John Smith").

COMMENT

This standard conforms to the practice of Texas title examiners.

CAUTION

Although this standard conforms to title examination practice, no Texas cases are directly on point.

Source:

Lewis M. Simes & Clarence B. Taylor, *Model Title Standards*, Std. 5.8 (1960).

History:

Adopted June 27, 1997.

CHAPTER IV. EXECUTION, ACKNOWLEDGMENT & RECORDATION

STANDARD 4.10. OMISSIONS & INCONSISTENCIES

Omission of the date of execution from an instrument affecting title does not, in itself, impair marketability. An examiner may presume that an undated instrument has been timely executed if the dates of acknowledgment and recordation, and other circumstances of record, support the presumption.

Inconsistencies in recitals or dates (such as among dates of execution, attestation, acknowledgment, or recordation) do not, in themselves, impair marketability,

and an examiner may presume that a proper sequence of formalities occurred.

COMMENT

The date of execution is not essential to an instrument's validity or delivery. *Dunn v. Taylor*, 113 S.W. 265, 268 (Tex. 1908); *Webb v. Huff*, 61 Tex. 677, 679 (1884); *Owen v. State*, 26 S.W.2d 251, 253 (Tex. Crim. App. 1930). *See generally* 5 Aloysius A. Leopold, *Land Titles and Title Examination* §36.2 (Texas Practice 3d ed. 2005). The date on an instrument, like other recitals, is important, if the date is in issue, and the given date is presumptively correct, but subject to rebuttal or explanation. *Farrell v. Comer*, 84 S.W.2d 300, 303 (Tex. Civ. App.—Fort Worth 1935, no writ); *Owens v. Jackson*, 35 S.W.2d 186, 188 (Tex. Civ. App.—Austin 1931, writ dism'd w.o.j.); *Brown v. Rodgers*, 248 S.W. 750 (Tex. Civ. App.—Amarillo 1923, no writ). The same is true of the date of attestation and, generally, of acknowledgment. *Wilson v. Curry*, 151 S.W.2d 356, 358 (Tex. Civ. App.—Fort Worth 1941, writ dism'd).

The critical date—that of delivery—is not normally found in the instrument. *See* Standard 4.30. Hence, omission of the date from one conveyance in an ordinary series of conveyances may be disregarded. Even though special importance may attach to the date of execution, as in the case of a power of attorney, there is a presumption of timely execution (i.e., in proper sequence in relation to other instruments) if such is supported by other dates and circumstances of record.

Because recitals of dates may be omitted or explained, are notoriously inaccurate, and are more generally in error than are the actual sequences of formalities, inconsistencies in the indicated dates of formalities (e.g., acknowledgment dated prior to execution or execution dated subsequent to indicated date of recordation) should be disregarded. Further, the inconsistency or impossibility of a recited date should not be regarded as vitiating the particular formality involved. *Brown v. Rodgers*, supra; *Wilson v. Curry*, supra; *Owen v. State*, supra; *Panhandle Construction Co. v. Flesher*, 87 S.W.2d 273, 275 (Tex. Civ. App.—Amarillo 1935, writ dism'd).

Regarding instruments that have been filed for record, an examiner should consider Tex. Civ. Prac. & Rem. Code Ann. §16.033, which contains a two-year statute of limitations that bars certain actions to recover real property based upon acts and omissions specified in the statute. For further discussion, see Comment and Caution to Standard 4.20. In addition, Tex. Loc. Gov't Code Ann. §191.007(k) provides that a recorded instrument that fails to meet certain specifications relating to page size, paper weight, font size, legibility, and other technical matters, is deemed to have been properly recorded.

Tex. Prop. Code Ann. §12.0011 addresses the requirements for recordation. Effective September 1, 2007, this was amended to provide that a paper document attached as an exhibit to a paper affidavit or other document having an original signature or signatures and acknowledged, sworn to with a proper jurat, or proved according to law, may be recorded and, if recorded, imparts notice.

CAUTION

If, under the circumstances indicated by the record, a date has a particular significance (e.g., for a priority or for an important presumption), an inconsistency or impossibility should not be disregarded.

Source:

Citations in the Comment; Lewis M. Simes & Clarence B. Taylor, *Model Title Standards*, Std. 6.2 (1960); 5 Aloysius A. Leopold, *Land Titles and Title Examination* §36.2 (Texas Practice 3d ed. 2005).

History:

Adopted June 27, 1997.

STANDARD 4.20. DEFECTIVE ACKNOWLEDGMENTS

If a certificate of acknowledgment does not conform to the exact wording of the applicable statute, but shows substantial compliance with the statutory requirements for acknowledgments, an examiner should not require corrective action. If a deed or other instrument contains an acknowledgment in substantial noncompliance with the applicable statute or does not contain any acknowledgment whatever, an examiner should not require that such defects be cured if the instrument has been of record for at least twenty years and no adverse claim appears. Otherwise, the examiner should require a corrected acknowledgment and rerecord the instrument, or require and record a new, corrected instrument. A proper jurat may substitute for an acknowledgment for instruments recorded on or after September 1, 1989.

COMMENT

In general, an instrument is entitled to be recorded only if acknowledged or proven by witnesses according to law. Tex. Prop. Code Ann. §12.001. The proper forms for acknowledgments are expressed by statute. Tex. Civ.

Prac. & Rem. Code Ann. §§121.001-121.015. A jurat may substitute for an acknowledgment in instruments recorded on or after September 1, 1989. Tex. Prop. Code Ann. §12.001(a).

A jurat is a certificate signed by the officer before whom an instrument was executed, stating that the instrument was subscribed and sworn to before the officer by the person executing the instrument. *Carpenter v. State*, 218 S.W.2d 207, 208 (Tex. Crim. App. 1949); *Robertson v. State*, 8 S.W. 659 (Tex. Crim. App. 1888). Subject to an exception (discussed in the following paragraph), an acknowledgment certificate must include the officer's seal of office, Tex. Civ. Prac. & Rem. Code Ann. §121.004, and this is also presumably true for a proper jurat, if the officer has a seal. *Missouri Pacific Railway Co. v. Brown*, 53 S.W. 1019 (Tex. 1899). For a listing of the officers who may take acknowledgments or proofs, see Tex. Civ. Prac. & Rem. Code Ann. §121.001. For a listing of officers who may administer oaths and supply a jurat, see Tex. Gov't Code Ann. §§602.002-602.005.

An acknowledgment or jurat that does not include an official seal and that is taken in the United States or its territories is invalid only if the jurisdiction in which the acknowledgment or jurat is taken requires the attachment of an official seal. Tex. Civ. Prac. & Rem. Code Ann. §121.004. The secretary of state must annually furnish the county clerks with a list of states that require an official seal. Tex. Gov't Code Ann. §405.019.

An acknowledgment or jurat that does not include an embossed or printed seal is not invalid on an electronically transmitted authenticated document that legibly reproduces the required elements of the seal. Tex. Gov't Code Ann. §406.013.

An acknowledgment or jurat may be satisfied by the electronic signature of the notary public so long as all required information is attached to or logically associated with the signature or record. Tex. Bus. & Com. Code Ann. §322.011.

Subject to the Caution noted below, the absence or presence of a proper acknowledgment does not affect the validity of a deed or other instrument. Tex. Prop. Code Ann. §13.001(b); *Haile v. Holtzclaw*, 414 S.W.2d 916, 928 (Tex. 1967). Substantial compliance with the statutory acknowledgment requirements is sufficient. "If the strict compliance with the letter of the law was exacted, we have no doubt that it would destroy and invalidate thousands of records, long since made and believed to have been in accordance with the law." *Dorn v. Best*, 15 Tex. 62, 66 (1855). Omission of mere formal parts of the acknowledgment certificate, such as the recitation that the instrument was executed "for the consideration and purposes therein stated," will not invalidate it, so long as the material parts are present, though all such parts should be included for the sake of regularity. *Monroe v. Arledge*, 23 Tex. 478 (1859). No particular form of words is required, so long as the certificate shows on its face that all prerequisites to a valid acknowledgment were in fact complied with. *Williams v. Cruse*, 130 S.W.2d 908 (Tex. Civ. App.—Beaumont 1939, writ ref'd).

The necessary prerequisites for an acknowledgment are that the signer personally appeared before the officer, that the signer was known to the officer to be the person whose name is subscribed to the instrument, and that the signer acknowledged that the signer executed the same for the purposes and considerations therein stated. *Sheldon v. Farinacci*, 535 S.W.2d 938, 942 (Tex. Civ. App.—San Antonio 1976, no writ). Since August 31, 1981, these essential elements may be fulfilled by a simple certificate stating that the instrument "was acknowledged" by the signer (and, if other than as an individual, the signer's particular capacity). Tex. Civ. Prac. & Rem. Code Ann. §§121.006, 121.008. An acknowledgment may be considered in connection with the deed to which it is attached to supply some missing ingredient. Thus, where the acknowledgment is made by a corporate officer but fails to state the officer's capacity or that the acknowledgment is that of the corporation, it is nonetheless sufficient if it states that the deed was executed for the purposes therein expressed and the deed purports to be the act of the corporation. *Ballard v. Carmichael*, 18 S.W. 734 (Tex. 1892); *Muller v. Boone*, 63 Tex. 91 (1885).

If an acknowledgment is defective because it was made "in an individual, rather than a representative or official, capacity" or fails "to show an acknowledgment or jurat that complies with applicable law," a person with a right of action to recover real property or an interest therein must bring suit within two years after an instrument is filed for record; however, this limitations period does not apply to a forged instrument. Tex. Civ. Prac. & Rem. Code Ann. §16.033. In addition, an instrument "filed for record containing a ministerial defect, omission, or informality in the certificate of acknowledgment that has been filed for record for longer than

two years … is considered to have been lawfully recorded and to be notice of the existence of the instrument on and after the date the instrument is filed." Tex. Civ. Prac. & Rem. Code Ann. §16.033(c). *But see* Caution, below.

To prove title, an instrument in the chain of title to land may be admitted into evidence as an "ancient document," without further proof of its execution, if it has been in existence for at least twenty years. (See discussion of the "ancient document" rule in the comment to Standard 13.40.) This rule of evidence does not require the instrument to have been acknowledged. A former statute, deemed repealed upon promulgation of the rules of evidence effective September 1, 1983, provided that an instrument without a proper acknowledgment is admissible if it has been of record for at least ten years. There is no similar specific provision in the current rules of evidence. Arguably, the record of an unacknowledged, or improperly acknowledged, instrument which has been of record for at least twenty years is admissible into evidence under the ancient document rule, but this is not certain. *See generally* 3 Aloysius A. Leopold, *Land Titles and Title Examination* §§8.6, 8.48 (Texas Practice 3d ed. 2005) and 5 *Id.* §35.18. Even if admissible into evidence to prove title, an instrument improperly acknowledged, although of record for at least twenty years, still cannot be regarded as having been validly recorded so as to impart constructive notice. Of course, one who has examined the instrument or the record of the instrument would have actual notice of it. Where no adverse claim appears from the record after twenty years, marketability would not ordinarily be questioned because the possibility of a successful adverse claim based on a defective acknowledgment is remote.

CAUTION

An examiner should exercise caution in relying on the two-year statute of limitations discussed in the Comment. Tex. Civ. Prac. & Rem. Code Ann. §16.033. Except for a "ministerial defect, omission, or informality" in the certificate of acknowledgment that has been filed for record for longer than two years, Tex. Civ. Prac. & Rem. Code §16.033(c), this statute does not expressly validate the recording of an improperly acknowledged instrument. The statute does not explain what constitutes "a ministerial defect, omission, or informality." Moreover, the period of limitation will not run against persons under disability. A defectively acknowledged instrument probably cannot be proven through a certified copy from the public records, at least until it qualifies as an "ancient document." Tex. R. Evid. 902(4).

An instrument executed by a married woman prior to August 22, 1963, but not "privily and apart" acknowledged in the manner then prescribed by statute, was void as to her. Tex. Rev. Civ. Stat. art. 1299 (repealed by Acts 1963, 58th Leg., p. 1189, ch. 473, §1); *Humble Oil & Refining Co. v. Downey*, 183 S.W.2d 426 (Tex. 1944); *Sun Oil Co. v. Rhodes*, 71 S.W.2d 413 (Tex. Civ. App.—Beaumont 1943, writ ref'd). The supreme court declared former Article 1299 to be unconstitutional in *Wessely Energy Co. v. Jennings*, 736 S.W.2d 624 (Tex. 1987) (affirming a married woman's pre-repeal conveyance despite its noncompliance with Article 1299). However, the ruling was made prospective only. 736 S.W.2d at 629. Thus, an examiner should still be alert to a deed which: pre-dates August 22, 1963, is executed by a married woman, but is not "privily and apart" acknowledged.

An unacknowledged and unrecorded instrument is void as to creditors and subsequent purchasers for value without notice. Tex. Prop. Code Ann. §13.001(a). Further, the recordation of an instrument does not impart constructive notice unless the instrument has been properly acknowledged or proved. *Hill v. Taylor*, 14 S.W. 366 (Tex. 1890). Moreover, the acknowledgment of the grantee only, without that of the grantor, is insufficient. *Sweeney v. Vasquez*, 229 S.W.2d 96, 97 (Tex. Civ. App.—San Antonio 1950, writ ref'd). Of course, an examiner who encounters such an instrument in the course of examining title would gain actual notice of its contents and such notice would likely be imputed to the examiner's client.

Caution should be exercised in determining that an acknowledgment is in substantial, though not literal, compliance. The general rule is that omitted words can be supplied by inference if it is clear what they should be. *Sheldon v. Farinacci*, 535 S.W.2d 938 (Tex. Civ. App.—San Antonio 1976, no writ). However, an acknowledgment was held insufficient where the certificate recited that the subscribing party, by name, had appeared and "acknowledged that ______ had signed, sealed and delivered" the instrument, omitting only the personal pronoun. *Huff v. Webb*, 64 Tex. 284 (1885).

A jurat (as distinguished from an acknowledgment) is required for the perfection of certain claims (e.g., a mechanic's lien). Tex. Prop. Code Ann. §58.004.

Source:

Citations in the Comment; *Oklahoma Title Examination Standards*, Stds. 6.1, 6.2; 3 Aloysius A. Leopold, *Land Titles and Title Examination* §§8.6, 8.48 (Texas Practice 3d ed. 2005) and 5 *Id.* §35.18.

History:

Adopted June 27, 1997.

STANDARD 4.30. DELIVERY; EFFECTIVE DATE; DELAY IN RECORDATION

An examiner may presume the delivery of instruments acknowledged and recorded. Delay in recordation, with or without record evidence of the intervening death of the grantor, does not rebut the presumption or create an unmarketable title; however, as an added exceptional protection to the client, an examiner may choose to make an inquiry outside of the record.

COMMENT

Delivery is a formality essential to the effectiveness of conveyances, recorded or otherwise. *Dikes v. Miller*, 24 Tex. 417 (1859). Delivery may be actual or constructive. An example of constructive (or conditional) delivery is the typical situation where a deed is delivered to a closing agent to be subsequently delivered to a buyer upon the satisfaction of all contractual conditions to closing. Delivery is a question of fact focusing on two elements: (1) was the instrument placed within the control of the grantee by the grantor, and (2) did the grantor intend that the instrument operate as a conveyance? *Ragland v. Kelner*, 221 S.W.2d 357 (Tex. 1949); *Bell v. Rudd*, 191 S.W.2d 841 (Tex. 1946); *Steffian v. Milmo National Bank*, 6 S.W. 823 (Tex. 1888).

Unless it provides its own effective date, a deed takes effect from the date of its delivery to the grantee. *Rosenberg v. Levin*, 181 S.W.2d 832 (Tex. Civ. App.—Dallas 1944, writ ref'd w.o.m.). Possession of a deed raises the presumption of its due delivery. *Tuttle v. Turner*, Wilson & Co., 28 Tex. 759 (1866). The date affixed to an instrument is prima facie evidence of the date of delivery. *Lichtenstein v. F&M Nat'l Bank*, 372 S.W.2d 716 (Tex. Civ. App.—Dallas 1963, no writ). In the absence of contrary evidence, a deed must be presumed to have been delivered on the date it was executed and acknowledged. *Hooks v. Vanderburg*, 328 S.W.2d 467 (Tex. Civ. App.—Fort Worth 1959, no writ). Where a deed is dated one date and the acknowledgment is on a different date, however, it is presumed that it was delivered on the date of the deed and not on the date of the acknowledgment in the absence of evidence showing the date it was actually delivered. *Rogers v. Gunn*, 545 S.W.2d 861 (Tex. Civ. App.—Amarillo 1976, no writ); *Popplewell v. City of Mission*, 342 S.W.2d 52 (Tex. Civ. App.—San Antonio 1960, writ ref'd n.r.e.).

A conveyance to a person who is deceased on the effective day of the conveyance is void for lack of an existing grantee, and no title passes in that conveyance to the heirs or devisees of such deceased person. *Vineyard v. Heard*, 167 S.W. 22 (Tex. Civ. App.—San Antonio 1914), aff'd, 212 S.W. 489 (Tex. 1919); *Sparks v. Humble Oil & Refining Co.*, 129 S.W.2d 468 (Tex. Civ. App.—Texarkana 1939, writ ref'd). However, a conveyance to a living grantee and the grantee's "heirs and assigns" or to "the estate of" a dead grantee is valid. *Haile v. Holtzclaw*, 414 S.W.2d 916, 927 (Tex. 1967) (holding that a conveyance to the "estate" of a grantee was sufficient because the "estate" or heirs were capable of being ascertained).

CAUTION

Neither a delay in recordation nor a post-mortem recordation presumptively impairs marketability; however, if the record reflects either the death of the grantee prior to the recording of the instrument, or a long delay in recording, the examiner should inquire outside the record if the examiner reasonably believes, based upon the facts, that a claim of non-delivery is probable. *Burris v. McDougald*, 832 S.W.2d 707 (Tex. App.—Corpus Christi 1992, no writ); *Perkins v. Damme*, 774 S.W.2d 765 (Tex. App.—Corpus Christi 1989, writ denied).

Because recorded instruments raise a prima facie presumption of delivery, an examiner is usually not concerned with evidentiary questions; however, because this presumption may be overcome, an examiner may have a duty to inquire further when an examiner knows, or reasonably should know, of facts or circumstances indicating: (1) that the deed was delivered or recorded for a different purpose; (2) that fraud, accident or mistake accompanied the delivery or recording; or, (3) that the grantor had no intention of divesting title. *Stephens County Museum, Inc. v. Swenson*, 517 S.W.2d 257, 261-262 (Tex. 1974); *Thornton v. Rains*, 299 S.W.2d 287 (Tex. 1957); *Vannerberg v. Anderson*, 206 S.W.2d 217, 219 (Tex. 1947). Moreover, a deed must be accepted by the grantee. Recordation of a deed is also prima facie evidence of acceptance; however, this pre-

sumption can also be overcome. *Martin v. Uvalde Savings & Loan Ass'n*, 773 S.W.2d 808 (Tex. App.—San Antonio 1989, no writ).

Source:

Citations in the Comment; *Oklahoma Title Examination Standards*, Std. 6.4; Lewis M. Simes & Clarence B. Taylor, *Model Title Standards*, Std. 6.3 (1960); 5 Aloysius A. Leopold, *Land Titles and Title Examination* §§36.2, 36.6 (Texas Practice 3d ed. 2005).

History:

Adopted June 27, 1997.

STANDARD 4.40. NOTICE RECORDING SYSTEM

Because Texas has a "notice" recordation statute, an examiner should not presume that the order of filing or recording of competing instruments establishes priority of right or that unrecorded instruments are subordinate to recorded instruments.

COMMENT

Common Law Background: "Our system of registration was unknown to the common law." *Ball v. Norton*, 238 S.W. 889, 890 (Tex. Comm'n App. 1922, judgm't adopted). "At common law in England, there was no system of registration or recording, and the rule between claimants of the same title was found in the maxim 'prior in tempore potior est in jure,' which means, he who is first in time has the better right." 2 Maurice Merrill, *Merrill on Notice* §921 (Vernon 1952). This is still the law except as abrogated by statute. Thus, as between claimants who are not entitled to the special protections conferred by recording statutes, the first in time is first in right.

Types of Recording Statutes: In general, recording statutes limit the first-in-time, first-in-right rule and were enacted to protect a bona fide purchaser, as defined in the comments to Standard 4.90, including a lienholder, who is without notice of prior unrecorded claims to real property. Three basic types of recording systems are recognized in the United States: race, race-notice, and notice.

A race statute provides that a purchaser or lienholder who is second in time of conveyance prevails if she records first, regardless of whether that person has notice of other unrecorded interests.

Under a race-notice statute, the subsequent purchaser or lienholder must acquire an interest without notice of the prior unrecorded interest and also must file for record before recordation of the prior unrecorded interest.

A notice statute protects a subsequent purchaser or lienholder who acquires an interest without notice of a prior unrecorded conveyance or lien, regardless of when the subsequent purchaser's deed is recorded, if ever. Nevertheless, because a party who takes without notice may lose out to another subsequent purchaser or lienholder who takes without notice, every grantee should promptly record. Texas has a notice recordation statute. Tex. Prop. Code Ann. §13.001.

How A Notice Recordation Statute Operates: Under a notice statute, if the subsequent instrument is executed and delivered before the prior instrument is filed for record and if the subsequent purchaser or lienholder pays value and has no notice of the prior instrument, then the subsequent instrument prevails regardless of whether the prior instrument is filed for record before the subsequent instrument is filed. *Houston Oil Co. v. Kimball*, 122 S.W. 533 (Tex. 1909); *Watkins v. Edwards*, 23 Tex. 443 (1859); *White v. McGregor*, 50 S.W. 564 (Tex. 1899); *Penny v. Adams*, 420 S.W.2d 820 (Tex. Civ. App.—Tyler 1967, writ ref'd); *Matthews v. Houston Oil Co.*, 299 S.W. 450 (Tex. Civ. App.—Beaumont 1927, no writ); *Raposa v. Johnson*, 693 S.W.2d 43 (Tex. App.—Ft. Worth 1985, writ ref'd n.r.e.). For example, assume that Homeowner grants an oil and gas lease on February 1 to A, who does not file for record. Thereafter, Homeowner gives another oil and gas lease to B, a bona fide purchaser, as defined in the comments to Standard 4.90, on February 5. As between A and B, B prevails regardless of whether either A or B records. And, under Texas case law, if A assigned his lease to C on February 10, B would also prevail over C even if B has not recorded. *Houston Oil Co. v. Kimball*, 122 S.W. 533 (Tex. 1909). However, if Homeowner, on February 15, granted a third oil and gas lease to D for value, who took without notice of B's lease (and assuming that B has still not recorded), D would prevail over B.

Filing and Recording: A paper document filed for record may not be validly recorded or serve as notice of the paper document unless: (1) the paper document contains an original signature or signatures that are acknowledged, sworn to with a proper jurat, or proved according to law; or (2) on or after September 1, 2007, the paper document is attached as an exhibit to a paper affidavit or other document that has an original signature or signatures that are acknowledged, sworn to with a proper jurat, or proved according to law. Tex. Prop. Code Ann. §12.0011. An original signature is not re-

quired for an electronic document that complies with the requirements of Chapter 15, Tex. Prop. Code Ann. (Uniform Real Property Electronic Recording Act); Chapter 195, Tex. Local Gov't Code Ann. (electronic filing of records); Chapter 322, Tex. Bus. & Comm. Code Ann. (Uniform Electronic Transactions Act); "or other applicable law." Tex. Prop. Code Ann. §12.0011. *See* Standard 4.120. If made as provided by law, a certified copy, when recorded, has the same effect as the original. Tex. Local Gov't Code Ann. §191.005 and Tex. Evid. Rules 902(4).

An instrument meeting the requirements of the preceding paragraph imparts constructive notice upon filing. An instrument is filed "when deposited for that purpose in the county clerk's office, together with the proper recording fees." *Jones v. MacCorquodale*, 218 S.W. 59, 61 (Tex. Civ. App.—Galveston 1919, writ ref'd). Tex. Local Gov't Code Ann. §191.003. "The county clerk [is] not authorized to 'impose additional requirements' for filing or recording a legal paper such as the removal of irrelevant notations." *Ready Cable, Inc. v. RJP Southern Comfort Homes*, Inc., 295 S.W.3d 763 (Tex. App.—Austin 2009, no pet.) (the words "unofficial document" on the top of an exhibit was an irrelevant notation). Tex. Local Gov't Code Ann. §191.007(k).

"[A]n electronic document or other instrument is filed with the county clerk when it is received by the county clerk, unless the county clerk rejects the filing within the time and manner provided by this chapter and rules adopted under this chapter." Tex. Local Gov't Code Ann. §195.009. "An electronic document or other instrument that is recorded electronically ... is considered to be recorded in compliance with a law relating to the recording of electronic documents or other instruments as of the county clerk's business day on which the electronic document or other instrument is filed electronically." *Id.* §195.005. In general, the county clerk must confirm or reject an electronic filing "not later than the first business day after the date the electronic document or other instrument is filed." *Id.* §195.004. *See* Standard 4.110.

County Clerk's Records: The county clerk is required to:

(1) Record instruments in a well-bound book, microfilm records, or other medium (such as optical imaging). Tex. Local Gov't Code Ann. §191.002;

(2) Record, within a reasonable time after delivery, any instrument that is authorized or required to be recorded in that clerk's office and that is proved, acknowledged, or sworn to according to law. Tex. Prop. Code Ann. §11.004(a)(1);

(3) Record instruments relating to the same property in the order the instruments are filed. Tex. Prop. Code Ann. §11.004(a)(3); and

(4) Make a record of the names of the parties to the instrument in alphabetical order, the date of the instrument, the nature of the instrument, and the time the instrument was filed. Tex. Local Gov't Code Ann. §193.001.

Although local practice varies, county clerks may maintain separate books with corresponding indices for:

(1) Deed Records (since 1836)
(2) Probate Records (since 1836)
(3) Release Records (since 1836)
(4) Marriage Records (since 1837)
(5) Deed of Trust Records (since 1879)
(6) Abstract of Judgment Records (since 1879)
(7) Vendor's Lien Records (since 1879)
(8) Lis Pendens Records (since 1905)
(9) Oil and Gas Lease Records (since 1917)
(10) Federal Tax Lien Records (since 1923)
(11) Mechanic's and Materialmen's Lien Records (since 1939)
(12) State Tax Lien Records (since 1961)
(13) Financing Statements (since 1966)
(14) Utility Security Records (since 1966)

As of September 1, 1987, a clerk may consolidate the real property records into a single class known as "Official Public Records of Real Property" or "Official Public Records." Tex. Local Gov't Code Ann. §§193.002, 193.008.

The clerk must maintain alphabetical indices, Direct (Grantor) Index and Reverse (Grantee) Index, for all recorded deeds, powers of attorney, mortgages, and other instruments relating to real property. The Grantor Index must refer to the names of the corresponding grantees, and the Grantee Index must refer to the names of the corresponding grantors. If the instrument is executed by a representative (e.g., executor, administrator, guardian, agent, attorney in fact, or trustee), then both that person and the principal's

name must be indexed. Tex. Local Gov't Code Ann. §§193.003, 193.004. The index entries for a correction instrument must contain the names of the grantors and grantees as stated in the correction instrument. Tex. Local Gov't Code Ann. §193.003. Records maintained on microfilm and microfiche must also contain a brief description of the property, if any, and the location of the microfilm or microfiche image. Tex. Local Gov't Code Ann. §§193.009 and 193.010.

CAUTION

An instrument properly filed for record but not yet indexed or not properly indexed nevertheless imparts constructive notice upon filing. *See* Standard 4.50.

A properly filed instrument imparts constructive notice even if the records have been destroyed. For a list of Texas counties whose records are not complete because of fires or other record deficiencies, see 3 Aloysius A. Leopold, *Land Titles and Title Examination* §38.7 (Texas Practice 3d ed. 2005). In some cases, copies of or information pertaining to destroyed records may have been maintained by an independent abstract or title company, and examiners customarily rely on such records.

Source:

Citations in the Comment.

History:

Adopted Aug. 2, 2013; amended July 17, 2014.

The prior standard provided: "Because Texas has a 'notice' recordation statute, an examiner must not assume that the order of filing or recording of competing instruments establishes priority of right or that unrecorded instruments are subordinate to recorded instruments."

STANDARD 4.50. CONSTRUCTIVE NOTICE

An examiner should examine all instruments within the record chain of title as of the date and time of the examination, including instruments that have been recently filed for record but not yet indexed.

COMMENT

Definition: Instruments filed for record within the chain of title impart constructive notice. Constructive notice is notice imputed as a matter of law as a result of an instrument having been filed for record. "An instrument that is properly recorded in the proper county is ... notice to all persons of the existence of the instrument." Tex. Prop. Code Ann. §13.002. An instrument that appears of record but does not meet the statutory requirements for recordation does not impart constructive notice, *Hill v. Taylor*, 14 S.W. 366 (Tex. 1890); however, such an instrument may impart actual or inquiry notice to one who learns of its existence. *See Farmers Mut. Royalty Synd. v. Isaacks*, 138 S.W.2d 228 (Tex. Civ. App.—Amarillo 1940, no writ).

Effect of filing: Except for abstracts of judgment and lis pendens, instruments that meet the statutory requirements for recordation, once filed, impart constructive notice even though never actually or accurately recorded or indexed. A party claiming under a properly filed instrument has no duty to verify that the clerk actually or accurately recorded it. *William Carlisle & Co. v. King*, 133 S.W. 241 (Tex. 1910); *Throckmorton v. Price*, 28 Tex. 605 (1866); *David v. Roe*, 271 S.W. 196 (Tex. Civ. App.—Fort Worth 1925, writ dism'd w.o.j.). Recordation in the wrong records (such as a mortgage in the deed records) does not defeat constructive notice. *Kennard v. Mabry*, 14 S.W. 272 (Tex. 1890); *Knowles v. Ott*, 34 S.W. 295 (Tex. Civ. App. 1895, writ ref'd).

An electronic instrument is deemed filed and generally imparts constructive notice when it is received by the county clerk, unless rejected by the next business day. Tex. Local Gov't Code Ann. §195.009 and 13 Tex. Admin. Code Ann. §7.144.

Abstracts of judgment are not effective to create judgment liens until recorded and indexed. *Belbaze v. Ratto*, 7 S.W. 501 (Tex. 1888). *See* Standard 15.30. However, a federal tax lien is effective as constructive notice from the time filed, even though it was never recorded or indexed. *Hanafy v. United States*, 991 F.Supp. 794 (N.D. Tex. 1998).

"To be effectively recorded [to impart constructive notice], an instrument relating to real property must be eligible for recording and must be recorded in the county in which a part of the property is located." Tex. Prop. Code Ann. §11.001(a). Thus, if a tract of land is partly located in more than one county, recordation of an instrument affecting the tract in any of the counties imparts constructive notice in each of the counties of its existence and contents. *Hancock v. Tram Lumber Co.*, 65 Tex. 225, 232 (1885); *Aston Meadows, Ltd. v. Devon Energy Production Co.*, 359 S.W.3d 856 (Tex. App.—Fort Worth 2012, pet. denied).

If an instrument was recorded in the proper county at the time but a new county containing the land conveyed was subsequently created, that event does not affect the validity of the prior recording. Tex. Prop. Code Ann. §11.001(b); *Lumpkin v. Muncey*, 17 S.W. 732 (Tex. 1886).

STANDARD 4.50

Like most instruments, a lis pendens filed for record before September 1, 2011, imparts constructive notice from date of filing; thus proper indexing of a lis pendens was not required. A lis pendens filed for record on or after September 1, 2011 must be filed for record and indexed in order to be constructive notice. Tex. Prop. Code Ann. §13.004. However, a lis pendens does not impart constructive notice of matters not appearing on the face of the pleadings as of the time of the title examination, although it is effective as to papers that were lost by the clerk. *Kropp v. Prather*, 526 S.W.2d 283 (Tex. Civ. App.—Tyler 1975, writ ref'd n.r.e.); *Latta v. Wiley*, 92 S.W. 433 (Tex. Civ. App. 1905, writ ref'd). A lis pendens imparts constructive notice only while the underlying cause of action is pending; however, it may nevertheless impart actual or inquiry notice, unless "expunged." Tex. Prop. Code Ann. §12.0071(f). For more information on lis pendens, including termination of constructive notice, see Standard 15.110.

Interests Not Subject To The Recording Statutes: Various rights and interests are not subject to the recording statutes and thus are not rendered void by the recording statutes as to a subsequent purchaser or lienholder without notice even though the rights or interests are not of record in the county clerk's office. Those rights and interests include:

(1) Patents. *Arrowood v. Blount*, 41 S.W.2d 412 (Tex. 1931) (holding that the record of a patent in the General Land Office is notice to the world).

(2) Heirship. *New York & T. Land Co. v. Hyland*, 28 S.W. 206 (Tex. Civ. App. 1894, writ ref'd); *Ross v. Morrow*, 19 S.W. 1090 (Tex. 1892). *See* Standard 11.70.

(3) The appointment of a receiver. *First Southern Properties, Inc. v. Vallone*, 533 S.W.2d 339 (Tex. 1976) (the property is in custodia legis).

(4) An equitable interest or title. However, equity may protect a bona fide purchaser, as defined in the comments to Standard 4.90, against outstanding equitable interests. *Cetti v. Wilson*, 168 S.W. 996, 998 (Tex. Civ. App. 1914, writ ref'd).

(5) A forfeiture order in favor of the United States. *United States v. Colonial National Bank, N.A.*, 74 F.3d 486 (4th Cir. 1996) (if the United States recovers land by forfeiture order, it does not have to file the order in the real property records or to file a lis pendens to protect its interest from the effect of a subsequent lien or conveyance by the former owner of the land).

(6) Title acquired by prescription or adverse possession. *Houston Oil Co. v. Olive Sternenberg & Co.*, 222 S.W. 534 (Tex. Comm'n App. 1920, judgm't adopted); *Heard v. Bowen*, 184 S.W. 234 (Tex. Civ. App.—San Antonio 1916, writ ref'd); *MacGregor v. Thompson*, 26 S.W. 649 (Tex. Civ. App. 1894, no writ).

(7) An easement by necessity. *Fletcher v. Watson*, No. 14-02-00508, 2003 WL 22901026 at *8, 2003 Tex. App. LEXIS 10493 at *25 (Tex. App.—Houston [14th Dist.] Dec. 4, 2003, pet. denied) ("[I]t makes sense that an easement by estoppel could be defeated by a purchaser in good faith without notice, but that an estoppel by necessity would not be defeated.").

(8) Uniform Commercial Code (UCC) filings covering growing crops and promissory notes, whether or not secured by an interest in land. These security interests are perfected by filing in the central filing office of the state of location of the debtor, whether they specifically or generally describe the collateral and with or without a legal description of the affected lands. Tex. Bus. & Com. Code Ann. §§9.301, 9.501. However, security interests in fixtures, in as-extracted collateral (oil, gas, and other minerals), and in timber to be cut are perfected by filing in the real property records of the county where the property is located. Tex. Bus. & Com. Code Ann. §9.501.

(9) A bankruptcy court order (confirming a reorganization plan) that extends the maturity date of a mortgage debt. *Wind Mountain Ranch, LLC v. City of Temple*, 333 S.W.3d 580 (Tex. 2010).

Title under a will probated in Texas may not be subject to the recording statutes, so that notwithstanding that the will is not of record in the county where the land is located, a purchaser from the decedent's intestate heirs without knowledge of the will cannot acquire title free of the devisees' title. *See Howth v. Farrar*, 94 F.2d 654 (5th Cir. 1938) (holding that the probate of a will is an in rem proceeding and notice to the world). Although that case has never been overruled, some commentators have expressed serious doubt that it accurately represents Texas law. *See* 17 M. K. Woodward & Ernest E. Smith, III, *Tex. Prac., Prob. & Decedents' Estates* §87 (1971), in which the authors, pointing out that a purchaser should not be expected to search all of the counties in the state, offer the opinion that to impart notice to persons other than the parties to a probate proceeding and their privies as to land outside the county of probate, the decree must be recorded in the

records of the county in which the land lies. The authors further note that title examiners customarily require the recording of proceedings for the probate of a will in the county where the land under examination is located. In view of the uncertainty whether a will and its Texas probate must be recorded in the county where the land is located, in addition to the county where the will was probated, to impart constructive notice of the devisees' title, the only prudent course for the examiner is to require that any known will and its probate be recorded in the county where the land under examination is located.

Chain Of Title: A bona fide purchaser, as defined in the comments to Standard 4.90, of property is not charged with constructive notice of instruments that, although recorded, are outside of the chain of title. "Chain of title" refers to the documents that show the successive ownership history of a tract of land, commencing with the severance of title from the sovereign down to and including the conveyance to the present holder. *Munawar v. Cadle Co.*, 2 S.W.3d 12, 18 (Tex. App.—Corpus Christi 1999, pet. denied). Note that severance from the sovereign occurs on the date of the survey of the property for severance purposes, not on the date of the patent, which always post-dates severance—sometimes by many years.

Examples of instruments that are not in the chain of title and that do not impart constructive notice include:

(1) Instruments executed by a grantor and recorded before the grantor acquired title. *Breen v. Morehead*, 136 S.W. 1047 (Tex. 1911).

(2) Mortgages covering land by an after-acquired property clause. *First Nat'l Bank v. Southwestern Lumber Co.*, 75 F.2d 814 (5th Cir. 1935).

(3) Disclosure of an unrecorded deed by a grantee's affidavit recorded in the real property records. *Reserve Petroleum Co. v. Hutcheson*, 254 S.W.2d 802 (Tex. Civ. App.—Amarillo 1952, writ ref'd n.r.e.).

(4) Instruments executed by a stranger to title. *Lone Star Gas Co. v. Sheaner*, 297 S.W.2d 855, 857 (Tex. Civ. App.—Waco 1956), rev'd in part on other grounds, 305 S.W.2d 150 (Tex. 1957) ("It is the law of this state that the record of a deed or mortgage by a stranger to the title to real estate, although duly recorded, is not constructive notice to a subsequent purchaser from the record owner of the property, because such instrument is not in the chain of title to such property.").

(5) Instruments executed by the grantee of a prior unrecorded instrument from a common grantor. *Southwest Title Ins. Co. v. Woods*, 449 S.W.2d 773 (Tex. 1970).

(6) Instruments executed by a grantor after the grantor has previously conveyed the property.

> If a grantor conveys the same property twice, and the second grantee puts his deed upon record, is it notice to one who subsequently purchases from the first grantee? We think not. The record is not notice to the first grantee, for he is a prior purchaser. Nor do we think it was intended to be notice to any one who should purchase from him. In other words, we think the subsequent purchasers who are meant are only those the origin of whose title is subsequent to the title of the grantee in the recorded deed. And it is such subsequent purchasers alone to whom the registry acts extend. The language of these statutes, so far as they affect deeds, is that, unless recorded, such deeds shall be void as against subsequent purchasers. When recorded, therefore, they have been held to operate as notice to such persons. The object of all the registry acts, however expressed, is the same. They were intended to affect with notice such persons only as have reason to apprehend some transfer or encumbrance prior to their own, because none arising afterwards can, in its own nature, affect them; and after they have once, on a search instituted upon this principle, secured themselves against the imputation of notice, it follows that every one coming into their place by title derived from them may insist on the same principle in respect to himself.

White v. McGregor, 50 S.W. 564, 565 (Tex. 1899).

Texas cases that discuss chain of title issues are based upon a grantor-grantee title examination, not a tract index examination; however, an abstract company may provide a means of locating instruments on a geographic or tract basis.

Process Of Examination: While county clerks do not maintain tract indices, most abstract and title companies maintain records by tract, usually by section, survey, or subdivision. Unless the examiner is provided an abstract of title compiled by an abstract company, the examiner will usually use or prepare a run sheet (list of instruments in chain of title) from an abstract company's tract records and general name indices or from the

indices and register of the county clerk. The information provided or used should identify all instruments affecting title that have been recorded or filed for record. The examiner should identify the source and the time interval of the records examined.

Index Search: Because Texas maintains only official grantor and grantee indices, an examiner should search under the name of each grantor from the date the grantor acquired the property forward to the date of filing for record the instrument that transfers the property to a grantee. *White v. McGregor*, 50 S.W. 564, 565-566 (Tex. 1899). The date of the conveyance itself, not the date of filing for record, controls whether an instrument is within the chain. *Fitzgerald v. Le Grande*, 187 S.W.2d 155 (Tex. Civ. App.—El Paso 1945, no writ).

However, Texas case law provides that: "A purchaser is required to look only for conveyances made prior to his purchase by his immediate vendor, or by any remote vendor through whom he derives his title." *Houston Oil Co. v. Kimball*, 122 S.W. 533, 540 (Tex. 1909). The decision in *Delay v. Truitt*, 182 S.W. 732 (Tex. Civ. App.—Amarillo 1916, writ ref'd), illustrates that late-recording grantees who recorded their instrument outside the chain of title may prevail over a later grantee who recorded first. Consider the following example: O conveys Blackacre to A, who does not immediately record. Thereafter, O conveys to B, who records but with actual notice of O's prior conveyance to A. Thus, B cannot be a bona fide purchaser, as defined in the comments to Standard 4.90. Thereafter, A records. If B subsequently conveys to C, C must look beyond the date of recordation of B's deed for the late recorded O to A deed because the O to A deed imparts constructive notice under Texas law (in most states, the late-recorded O to A deed would be "outside the chain of title" and thus not impart constructive notice). In this example in Texas, A would defeat C. In the absence of a judicial determination of such facts, the record will not reveal whether B had actual notice of O's prior conveyance to A. Thus, the record alone will not determine title between A and C. Because this scenario is unlikely to occur, an examiner often considers it reasonably safe to forgo this extended forward search, instead opting to do the more limited search described above immediately under this subheading, especially where the risk is mitigated by factors such as the passage of time since a remote grantor's deed or the examiner's reliance on an abstract company's indices.

Source:
Citations in the Comment.
History:
Adopted Aug. 2, 2013.

STANDARD 4.60. RECITALS IN INSTRUMENTS IN CHAIN OF TITLE

The examiner should advise the client of outstanding encumbrances and other matters apparently affecting the title and disclosed by recitals in instruments appearing in the chain of title.

COMMENT

A purchaser will be charged with constructive notice of the contents of instruments in that person's chain of title, including instruments incorporated by reference or otherwise identified in a series of unrecorded instruments where a reference in the chain of title would lead an examiner to become aware of them. *Westland Oil Dev. Corp. v. Gulf Oil Corp.*, 637 S.W.2d 903 (Tex. 1982); *Houston Title Co. v. Ojeda De Toca*, 733 S.W.2d 325 (Tex. App.—Houston [14th Dist.] 1987), rev'd on other grounds, *Ojeda de Toca v. Wise*, 748 S.W.2d 449 (Tex. 1988); *Abercrombie v. Bright*, 271 S.W.2d 734 (Tex. Civ. App.—Eastland 1954, writ ref'd n.r.e.); *MBank Abilene, N.A. v. Westwood Energy, Inc.*, 723 S.W.2d 246 (Tex. App.—Eastland 1986, no writ). A purchaser is charged with constructive notice of the referenced instrument unless the purchaser can prove that the purchaser made a diligent search to obtain the instrument and was unable to obtain it. *Loomis v. Cobb*, 159 S.W. 305 (Tex. Civ. App.—El Paso 1913, writ ref'd); *Westland Oil Dev. Corp. v. Gulf Oil Corp.*, 637 S.W.2d 903 (Tex. 1982); *Waggoner v. Morrow*, 932 S.W.2d 627 (Tex. App.—Houston [14th Dist.] 1996, no writ).

> The rationale of the rule is that any description, recital of fact, or reference to other documents puts the purchaser upon inquiry, and he is bound to follow up this inquiry, step by step, from one discovery to another and from one instrument to another, until the whole series of title deeds is exhausted and a complete knowledge of all the matters referred to and affecting the estate is obtained.

Loomis v. Cobb, 159 S.W. 305, 307 (Tex. Civ. App.—El Paso 1913, writ ref'd). Other examples of the binding effect of such references include:

(1) A reference to a vendor's lien even though the deed that created the lien was unrecorded, *Gilbough v. Runge*, 91 S.W. 566 (Tex. 1906).

(2) A reference in a deed to an unrecorded deed of trust, *Garrett v. Parker*, 39 S.W. 147 (Tex. Civ. App. 1896, writ ref'd).

(3) A recitation in a deed to a prior contract covering the land, *Houston Ice & Brewing Co. v. Henson*, 93 S.W. 713 (Tex. Civ. App. 1906, no writ); *Cumming v. Johnson*, 616 F.2d 1069, 1075 (9th Cir. 1979).

(4) A recitation in a deed to other deeds that granted easements over the land. *Jones v. Fuller*, 856 S.W.2d 597 (Tex. App.—Waco 1993, writ denied).

(5) A reference to a deed of trust in an assignment of oil and gas leases. *MBank Abilene, N.A. v. Westwood Energy, Inc.*, 723 S.W.2d 246 (Tex. App.—Eastland 1986, no writ).

Source:
Citations in the Comment.
History:
Adopted Aug. 2, 2013.

STANDARD 4.70. DUTY OF INQUIRY BASED ON ACTUAL NOTICE

The examiner should advise the client of matters affecting the title that are known by the examiner even though not revealed by the record, including unfiled instruments and facts known to the examiner that would impart either actual or inquiry notice of matters affecting title.

COMMENT

A purchaser is charged with notice (a) of information appearing of record (constructive notice), (b) of information within the purchaser's knowledge (actual notice), and (c) of information that the purchaser would have learned arising from circumstances that would prompt a good-faith purchaser to make a diligent inquiry (inquiry notice).

While constructive notice serves as notice as a matter of law, actual notice is notice as a matter of fact. Inquiry notice results as a matter of law from facts that would prompt a reasonable person to inquire about the possible existence of an interest in property. *Noble Mortgage & Investments, LLC v. D&M Vision Investments, LLC*, 340 S.W.3d 65 (Tex. App.—Houston [1st Dist.] 2011, no pet.); *Mann v. Old Republic National Title Insurance Co.*, 975 S.W.2d 347 (Tex. Civ. App.—Houston [14th Dist.] 1998, no writ); *City of Richland Hills v. Bertelsen*, 724 S.W.2d 428, 430 (Tex. App.—Ft. Worth 1987, writ denied). *Also see* Standard 4.80.

Actual notice includes, not only known information, but also facts that a reasonably diligent inquiry would have disclosed. *Hexter v. Pratt*, 10 S.W.2d 692 (Tex. Comm'n App. 1928, judgm't adopted); *Mann v. Old Republic National Title Insurance Co.*, 975 S.W.2d 347 (Tex. Civ. App.—Houston [14th Dist.] 1998, no writ).

> In common parlance "actual notice" generally consists in express information of a fact, but in law the term is more comprehensive.... So that, in legal parlance, actual knowledge embraces those things of which the one sought to be charged has express information, and likewise those things which a reasonably diligent inquiry and exercise of the means of information at hand would have disclosed.

Hexter v. Pratt, 10 S.W.2d 692, 693 (Tex. Comm'n App. 1928, judgm't adopted). *See also Flack v. First Nat'l Bank*, 226 S.W.2d 628, 632 (Tex. 1950).

Circumstances that give rise to a duty to inquire include obvious ones, such as a person's assertion of a claim to an interest in property, *Zamora v. Vela*, 202 S.W. 215 (Tex. Civ. App.—San Antonio 1918, no writ); *Price v. Cole*, 35 Tex. 461 (1871), rev'd on other grounds, 45 Tex. 522 (1876), as well as others that merely arouse suspicion. For example, the refusal of a spouse to sign an instrument may give notice of the inability of the other spouse to execute it. *Williams v. Portland State Bank*, 514 S.W.2d 124 (Tex. Civ. App.—Beaumont 1974, writ dism'd).

A purchaser with constructive notice of a deed of trust is put on inquiry to determine the status of the deed of trust, such as whether it had been released or foreclosed. *Realty Portfolio, Inc. v. Hamilton*, 125 F.3d 292 (5th Cir. 1997); *Clarkson v. Ruiz*, 140 S.W.2d 206 (Tex. Civ. App.—San Antonio 1940, writ dism'd).

Notice to an agent will constitute notice to the principal if the agent is one who had the power to act with reference to the subject matter to which the notice relates. *J.M. Radford Grocery Co. v. Citizens Nat'l Bank*, 37 S.W.2d 1080 (Tex. Civ. App.—El Paso 1931, writ dism'd). Accordingly, a purchaser is generally legally charged with such facts that come to his or her attorney's knowledge in the course of employment as an attorney to examine title, *Hexter v. Pratt*, 10 S.W.2d 692 (Tex. Comm'n App. 1928, judgm't adopted) and *Ramirez v. Bell*, 298 S.W. 924 (Tex. Civ. App.—Austin 1927, writ ref'd), or with such facts that would have become known to the purchaser's attorney upon further inquiry into irregularities arising in connection with the closing of a transaction. *Carter v. Converse*, 550 S.W.2d 322

(Tex. Civ. App.—Tyler 1977, writ ref'd n.r.e.). Therefore, even though a case may have been dismissed for want of prosecution, the attorney and principal have a further obligation to investigate the suit to determine if there is any claim which may remain outstanding although the lis pendens does not continue as constructive notice to the world. *Hexter v. Pratt*, 10 S.W.2d 692 (Tex. Comm'n App. 1928, judgm't adopted). In contrast, a title company does not become an insured's agent in examining title or in acting as escrow agent, and notice that the title company acquires is not imputed to the insured. *Tamburine v. Center Savings Assoc.*, 583 S.W.2d 942 (Tex. Civ. App.—Tyler 1979, writ ref'd n.r.e.) (in examining title in order to issue a title insurance policy, the title company does not act on behalf of the parties to the real estate transaction but acts exclusively for itself; in supervising the transfer of title in accordance with the commitment, the title company acts for its own benefit and protection; and in acting as escrow agent, the authority of the title company does not extend to examination of title).

If notice is given to a party, that party only has a reasonable obligation of investigation at that time and does not have a continued obligation of monitoring to see if an event transpires at a later day. For example, if tax agents of the Internal Revenue Service are notified that a divorce is pending, this fact does not obligate the IRS to continue to monitor to see if the divorce later occurs, and if the land is awarded to the non-taxpayer. *Prewitt v. United States*, 792 F.2d 1353 (5th Cir. 1986).

Source:
Citations in the Comment.
History:
Adopted Aug. 2, 2013.

STANDARD 4.80. DUTY OF INQUIRY BASED ON POSSESSION

The examiner should advise the client to inspect the land to determine possible rights in third parties that may not be reflected in the record, such as an apparent easement or third parties in possession.

COMMENT

Notice of title given by possession or apparent use of property is equivalent to the notice that is afforded by recording a deed. *Strong v. Strong*, 98 S.W.2d 346 (Tex. 1936). The duty to inquire arises only if the possession or apparent use is inconsistent with record title and is (1) visible, (2) open, (3) exclusive, and (4) unequivocal, implying exclusive dominion over the property. *Strong*, 98 S.W.2d at 350 (holding that possession by a member of the record title-owner's family was not open or exclusive).

Possession by a tenant creates a duty to inquire. *Mainwarring v. Templeman*, 51 Tex. 205, 209 (1879). Possession of a single rental-unit dwelling was sufficient to create constructive notice. *See, e.g.*, *Moore v. Chamberlain*, 195 S.W. 1135 (Tex. 1917); *Collum v. Sanger Bros.*, 82 S.W. 459 (Tex. 1904). A purchaser is charged with constructive notice of each tenant's rights in occupied units of a multi-unit property. Inquiry of a tenant's rights may result in actual notice of the tenant's claim to additional units; however, possession of a unit in a multi-unit structure may not satisfy the criteria for claiming rights in more than just the occupied unit. *Madison v. Gordon*, 39 S.W.3d 604 (Tex. 2001).

Ordinarily, a subsequent purchaser need not inquire whether a grantor who remains in possession has any claim to the property. For example, there is no obligation to inquire whether the grantor's deed was, instead, a mortgage, whether the deed was fraudulently secured, or whether the deed was executed by mutual mistake. *Eylar v. Eylar*, 60 Tex. 315 (1883). However, special circumstances may impart constructive notice of a possible claim by a grantor. *See, e.g.*, *Anderson v. Barnwell*, 52 S.W.2d 96 (Tex. Civ. App.—Texarkana 1932), aff'd sub nom. *Anderson v. Brawley*, 86 S.W.2d 41 (Tex. 1935) (grantor was in possession over six years after conveying the property and conveyed additional interests in the property).

If possession by a third party has terminated before the buyer acquires an interest in the land, then the buyer need not inquire as to the rights of the third party in the property, even if the buyer knew of the former possession. *Maxfield v. Pure Oil Co.*, 91 S.W.2d 892 (Tex. Civ. App.—Dallas 1936, writ dism'd w.o.j.).

Not all possession or apparent use gives rise to a duty to inquire, e.g.:

(1) A nonvisible buried pipeline. *Shaver v. National Title & Abstract Co.*, 361 S.W.2d 867, 869 (Tex. 1962).

(2) Minor children's occupancy of mother's homestead. *Boyd v. Orr*, 170 S.W.2d 829, 834 (Tex. Civ. App.—Texarkana 1943, writ ref'd).

(3) A crop. *De Guerin v. Jackson*, 50 S.W.2d 443, 448 (Tex. Civ. App.—Texarkana 1932), aff'd 77 S.W.2d 1041 (Tex. 1935).

CAUTION

The above comments do not address adverse possession and prescription. *See* comments to Standard 4.50, supra, under subheading "Interests Not Subject To The Recording Statutes," and comments to Standard 4.90, infra, under subheading "Bona Fide Purchaser Not Protected."

Source:
Citations in the Comment.
History:
Adopted Aug. 2, 2013.

STANDARD 4.90. QUALIFICATION AS BONA FIDE PURCHASER

An examiner cannot determine whether any party in the chain of title is a bona fide purchaser. Accordingly, an examiner should not disregard any interest in the chain of title based solely on an assumption that it was extinguished by a bona fide purchaser under the recording laws. However, if title passed by a quitclaim deed, then the grantee and the grantee's successors are not bona fide purchasers as to claims existing at the time of the quitclaim deed.

COMMENT

Definition: A bona fide purchaser is one who, in good faith, pays valuable consideration without actual, constructive, or inquiry notice of an adverse claim. *Sparks v. Taylor*, 99 Tex. 411, 90 S.W. 485 (1906). The terms "good faith purchaser" and "bona fide purchaser" have the same meaning. *Bank of America v. Babu*, 340 S.W.3d 917 (Tex. App.—Dallas 2011, no pet.).

A lender acquiring a mortgage, deed of trust, or other lien based on sufficient consideration and without notice of a prior claim is a bona fide purchaser. *Graves v. Guaranty Bond State Bank*, 161 S.W.2d 118 (Tex. Civ. App.—Texarkana 1942, no writ). For discussion of the Texas recording law, see Standard 4.40.

This discussion will make numerous references to the following terms that were previously defined:

Constructive notice—*See* Standard 4.50;

Actual notice—*See* Standard 4.70; and

Inquiry notice—*See* Standards 4.70 and 4.80.

Consideration: To be a bona fide purchaser, the party must show that, before the party had actual, constructive, or inquiry notice of an interest, the purchaser's deed was delivered and value was paid. *La Fon v. Grimes*, 86 F.2d 809 (5th Cir. 1936). A recital in the deed that consideration was paid is not sufficient. That consideration was paid must be independently proven, *Watkins v. Edwards*, 23 Tex. 443, 448 (1859), although a recital of consideration may be an element of that proof, *Davidson v. Ryle*, 124 S.W. 616, 619 (Tex. 1910).

The purchaser may be a bona fide purchaser even if the purchaser has paid less than the "real value" of the land, unless the price paid is grossly inadequate. *Nichols-Stewart v. Crosby*, 29 S.W. 380, 382 (Tex. 1895) ($5 paid for land then worth $8,000 is grossly inadequate); *McAnally v. Panther*, 26 S.W.2d 478, 480 (Tex. Civ. App.—Eastland 1930, no writ) (providing numerous examples of inadequate consideration). To show that the purchaser has paid valuable consideration, the purchaser must pay more value than merely cancelling an antecedent debt. Similarly, where a grantor executes a deed of trust or mortgage for an antecedent debt, the grantee has not paid sufficient value. *Turner v. Cochran*, 61 S.W. 923 (Tex. 1901); *Jackson v. Waldstein*, 30 S.W. 47 (Tex. Civ. App.—Austin 1895, writ ref'd).

Good Faith: To be a bona fide purchaser, a purchaser must take the property in good faith. "A transferee who takes property with knowledge of such facts as would excite the suspicions of a person of ordinary prudence and put him on inquiry of the fraudulent nature of an alleged transfer does not take the property in good faith and is not a bona fide purchaser." *Hahn v. Love*, 321 S.W.3d 517, 527 (Tex. App.—Houston [1st Dist.] 2009, pet. denied). Whether a person takes in good faith depends on whether the purchaser is aware of circumstances within or outside the chain of title that would place the purchaser on notice of an unrecorded claim or that would excite the suspicion of a person of ordinary prudence. *Noble Mortgage & Investments, LLC v. D&M Vision Investments, LLC*, 340 S.W.3d 65 (Tex. App.—Houston [1st Dist.] 2011, no pet.).

Quitclaim Deed: In Texas the grantee of a quitclaim deed cannot qualify as a bona fide purchaser for value against unrecorded instruments and equities that existed at the time of the quitclaim, *Threadgill v. Bickerstaff*, 29 S.W. 757 (Tex. 1895); *Rodgers v. Burchard*, 34 Tex. 441 (1870-71). The rationale is that the fact that a quitclaim deed was used, in and of itself, attests to the dubiousness of the title. *See Richardson v. Levi*, 3 S.W. 444, 447-48 (Tex. 1887). Although a quitclaim is fully effective to convey whatever interest the grantor owns in the property described in the deed, *Harrison Oil Co. v. Sherman*, 66 S.W.2d 701, 705 (Tex. Civ. App.—Beau-

mont 1933, writ ref'd), the grantee takes title subject to any outstanding interest or defect, whether or not recorded and whether or not the grantee is aware of it or has any means of discovering it. *See, e.g.*, *Woodward v. Ortiz*, 237 S.W.2d 286, 291-92 (Tex. 1951). Moreover, in Texas not only is the grantee under a quitclaim deed subject to any outstanding claims or equities, all subsequent purchasers in his chain of title, however remote, are likewise subject to any unknown and unrecorded interests that were outstanding at the time of the quitclaim. *Houston Oil Co. v. Niles*, 255 S.W. 604, 609-11 (Tex. Comm'n App. 1923, judgm't adopted).

Any title dependent on a quitclaim as a link in the chain of title cannot be marketable title, since it might at any time be defeated by some unknown claimant. Accordingly, absent passage of time or other factors that may remove the practical risk, if the chain of title includes a quitclaim, then the examiner should advise the client of its existence in the chain of title and of its effect.

Unfortunately, it is often difficult for a title examiner to reach a definite conclusion whether a deed is a quitclaim. A quitclaim deed, as traditionally defined, is one that purports to convey not the land or a specific interest but only the grantor's right, title and interest in it. *See Rogers v. Ricane Enters.*, Inc., 884 S.W.2d 763, 769 (Tex. 1994); *Richardson v. Levi*, 3 S.W. 444 (Tex. 1887). Nevertheless, building on a line of reasoning that seems to have originated with *F. J. Harrison & Co. v. Boring & Kennard*, 44 Tex. 255 (1875), in which the court's discussion of the issue does not bear on its ultimate decision, Texas courts have developed and liberally applied the notion that if the language of a deed as a whole reasonably implies a purpose to effect a transfer of particular rights in the land, it will be treated as a conveyance of those rights, not a mere quitclaim, despite the presence of traditional quitclaim language and even the word "quitclaim" itself. *See, e.g.*, *Cook v. Smith*, 174 S.W. 1094 (Tex. 1915); *Benton Land Co. v. Jopling*, 300 S.W. 28 (Tex. Comm'n App. 1927, judgm't adopted). (This manner of construction of apparent quitclaims has been treated by at least one authority as being peculiar to Texas. *See* Annotation, *Grantee or Mortgagee by Quitclaim Deed or Mortgage in Quitclaim Form as Within Protection of Recording Laws*, 59 A.L.R. 632, 648-49 (1929).) Construing a deed in which the grantors conveyed "all of our undivided interest" in the minerals in a tract of land, the court in *Bryan v. Thomas*, 365 S.W.2d 628, 630 (Tex. 1963), stated unequivocally, "To remove the question from speculation and doubt we now hold that the grantee in a deed which purports to convey all of the grantor's undivided interest in a particular tract of land, if otherwise entitled, will be accorded the protection of a bona fide purchaser." *See also Miller v. Hodges*, 260 S.W. 168, 171 (Tex. Comm'n App. 1924, judgm't adopted).

Notwithstanding that many deeds in traditional quitclaim form have been held otherwise by Texas courts, the principle that a deed is a mere quitclaim if it conveys only a grantor's "right, title, and interest," as opposed to a specific interest in described land, has never been overruled. *See Geodyne Energy Income Prod. P'ship I-E v. Newton Corp.*, 161 S.W.3d 482 (Tex. 2005); *Rogers v. Ricane Enters, Inc.*, 884 S.W.2d 763 (Tex. 1994). Although neither of the latter supreme court decisions addressed whether the grantee was deprived of the status of bona fide purchaser for value under the recording laws because of the nature of the conveyance, and cases such as *Bryan v. Thomas* might be distinguished on that basis, they are unequivocal in denominating a conveyance of a grantor's right, title and interest as a quitclaim. Unless a conveyance of only a grantor's right, title, and interest contains words that otherwise amply demonstrate the parties' intention that some particular interest be conveyed, a determination that may be very difficult for a title examiner to make objectively, the deed's quitclaim form must be considered to pose the risk that the grantee's title might be defeated by some unrecorded and unknown claim. *See Enerlex, Inc. v. Amerada Hess, Inc.*, 302 S.W.3d 351 (Tex. App.—Eastland 2009, no writ); *Riley v. Brown*, 452 S.W.2d 548 (Tex. Civ. App.—Tyler 1970, no writ). Further, it is frequently overlooked that blanket conveyances, for example of all the grantor's interests in land in a particular county or in the entire state, have generally been held to be quitclaims. *See, e.g.*, *Miller v. Pullman*, 72 S.W.2d 379 (Tex. Civ. App.—Galveston 1934, writ ref'd). In case of doubt the examiner should err on the side of construing deeds as quitclaims.

There are two statutory exceptions to the general rule that a grantee under a quitclaim deed cannot be a bona fide purchaser. Tex. Civ. Prac. & Rem. Code Ann. §34.045 provides that the officer who has sold a judgment creditor's property at an execution sale is to deliver to the purchaser a conveyance of "all the right, title, interest, and claim" that the defendant in execu-

tion had in the property sold. Tex. Civ. Prac. & Rem. Code Ann. §34.046 then provides, "The purchaser of property sold under execution is considered to be an innocent purchaser without notice if the purchaser would have been considered an innocent purchaser without notice had the sale been made voluntarily and in person by the defendant." Although the statute appears dispositive, and the status of a purchaser at an execution sale as a bona fide purchaser has been upheld, *Triangle Supply Co. v. Fletcher*, 408 S.W.2d 765 (Tex. Civ. App.—Eastland 1966, writ ref'd n.r.e.), officers' deeds resulting from execution sales have nevertheless been construed as quitclaims, affording the grantee no protection as a bona fide purchaser. *Diversified, Inc. v. Hall*, 23 S.W.3d 403 (Tex. App.—Houston [1st Dist.] 2000, pet. denied); *Smith v. Morris & Co.*, 694 S.W.2d 37 (Tex. App.—Corpus Christi 1985, writ ref'd n.r.e.) (neither case addressing the effect of Tex. Civ. Prac. & Rem. Code Ann. §34.046 or its predecessor statute). Under Tex. Tax Code Ann. §34.21(j), "A quitclaim deed to an owner redeeming property under this section is not notice of an unrecorded instrument. The grantee of a quitclaim and a successor or assign of the grantee may be a bona fide purchaser in good faith for value under the recording laws."

Statutes Permitting Or Requiring Recordation: Although not a complete list, the following statutes permit or require recording of particular instruments:

- Tex. Bus. Org. Code Ann. §252.005 (reliance on recorded statement of authority of unincorporated nonprofit association).
- Tex. Civ. Prac. & Rem. Code Ann. §§16.035-16.037 (extension of liens).
- Tex. Civ. Prac. & Rem. Code Ann. §34.046 (purchaser of property sold under execution considered to be an innocent purchaser without notice, if the purchaser would have been so considered had the sale been made voluntarily and in person by the defendant).
- Tex. Family Code Ann. §3.004 (schedule of spouse's separate property).
- Tex. Family Code Ann. §3.104 (presumed authority of spouse who is record owner).
- Tex. Family Code Ann. §§3.306, 3.308 (order affecting the management of community).
- Tex. Family Code Ann. §4.106 (a partition or exchange agreement of spouses).
- Tex. Family Code Ann. §4.206 (an agreement converting separate property to community property).
- Tex. Occ. Code Ann. §1201.2055 (a real property election for a manufactured home is not considered perfected until a certified copy of the statement of ownership and location has been filed in the real property records).
- Tex. Estates Code Ann. §33.055 ("a bona fide purchaser of real property who relied on a probate proceeding that was not the first commenced proceeding, without knowledge that the proceeding was not the first commenced proceeding, shall be protected with respect to the purchase unless before the purchase an order rendered in the first commenced proceeding admitting the decedent's will to probate, determining the decedent's heirs, or granting administration of the decedent's estate was recorded in the office of the county clerk of the county in which the purchased property is located.").
- Tex. Estates Code Ann. §114.055 (to be *valid*, a statutory transfer on death deed must be recorded before the transferor's death in the county where the property is located). *See* Standard 11.10.
- Tex. Estates Code Ann. §201.053 (good faith purchaser relying on affidavit of heirship takes free of interest of child not disclosed in affidavit if child not found under court decree to be entitled to treatment as child and not otherwise recognized).
- Tex. Estates Code Ann. §256.003 (if will is not probated within four years of date of death, purchaser can rely upon deed from heir).
- Tex. Estates Code Ann. §256.201 (certified copies of the will and order probating the will may be recorded in other counties).
- Tex. Estates Code Ann. §§503.051, 503.052 (ancillary probate).
- Tex. Estates Code Ann. §205.006 (reliance on small estates affidavit).
- Tex. Estates Code Ann. §§751.054, 751.055 (conclusive reliance on affidavit of lack of knowledge of termination of Power of Attorney).
- Tex. Prop. Code Ann. §5.030 (correction instrument). *See* Standard 5.10.
- Tex. Prop. Code Ann. §5.063(c) (affidavit stating that executory contract is properly forfeited).
- Tex. Prop. Code Ann. §12.0012 (regarding foreclosure sales, appointment of a trustee or successor trustee, notice of sale, notice of default, documentation that a debtor was not on military duty, proof of notice,

STANDARD 4.90

and statements of an attorney representing a trustee or mortgage servicer, even if not in recordable form, may be recorded if attached as exhibits to recordable trustee's deed or affidavit).

• Tex. Prop. Code Ann. §12.005 (a court order partitioning or allowing recovery of title to land must be recorded).

• Tex. Prop. Code Ann. §12.007 (a party seeking affirmative relief may file a notice of pending action in an eminent domain proceeding or a pending suit affecting title).

• Tex. Prop. Code Ann. §12.0071 (procedure to expunge lis pendens).

• Tex. Prop. Code Ann. §12.008 (procedure for cancellation of lis pendens).

• Tex. Prop. Code Ann. §12.017 (affidavit as release of lien).

• Tex. Prop. Code Ann. §12.018 (affidavit or memorandum of sale, transfer, purchase or acquisition agreement between receiver and conservator of failed depository institution and another depository institution).

• Tex. Prop. Code Ann. §13.004 (a recorded lis pendens is notice to the world of its contents).

• Tex. Prop. Code Ann. §64.052 (recordation and perfection of security interest in rents).

• Tex. Prop. Code Ann. §101.001 (conveyance by trustee if trust not identified and names of beneficiaries not disclosed).

• Tex. Prop. Code Ann. §141.017 (third party, "in the absence of knowledge," may deal with any person acting as custodian under Texas Uniform Transfers to Minors Act).

• Tex. Prop. Code Ann. §202.006 (effective January 1, 2012, a dedicatory instrument has no effect until the instrument is filed in the real property records).

• Tex. Prop. Code Ann. §209.004(e) (a lien of a property owners' association that fails to file a management certificate to secure an amount due on the effective date of a transfer to a bona fide purchaser is enforceable only for an amount incurred after the effective date of sale).

• Tex. Transp. Code Ann. §251.058(b) (a copy of the order closing, abandoning, and vacating a public road shall be filed in the deed records).

• 11 U.S.C. §§362(b)(20), 362(d)(4) (lift of stay order finding that filing of bankruptcy petition part of scheme to delay, hinder, or defraud creditors shall be binding in any other bankruptcy case filed within two years of order, if recorded in real property records).

• 11 U.S.C. §544 (trustee and debtor in possession are treated as bona fide purchasers and lien creditors for avoidance of unperfected interests).

• 11 U.S.C. §547 (deed, mortgage, or other instrument may be avoidable preference in bankruptcy unless perfected within 30 days after it takes effect).

• 11 U.S.C. §549(c) (protection of transfer from debtor to good faith purchaser without knowledge of commencement of bankruptcy case unless a copy or notice of the bankruptcy petition is filed).

• Bankruptcy Rule 4001(c)(1)(B)(vii) (a motion for authority to obtain a mortgage during a bankruptcy case may include a waiver or modification of the applicability of non-bankruptcy law relating to the perfection of a lien on property of the estate).

• 28 U.S.C. §1964 (recordation of notice of action concerning real property pending in a United States district court, if required by state law).

<u>Equitable Interests:</u> A bona fide purchaser will be protected as a matter of equity and take title free of unrecorded equitable interests. *Hill v. Moore*, 62 Tex. 610, 613 (1884). For example, a bona fide purchaser may take free and clear of the following equitable interests:

• A right to reform due to a mutual mistake. *Farley v. Deslande*, 69 Tex. 458, 6 S.W. 786 (1888).

• A claim that the deed was induced by fraud. *Pure Oil Co. v. Swindall*, 58 S.W.2d 7 (Tex. Comm'n App. 1933, holding approved); *Ramirez v. Bell*, 298 S.W. 924 (Tex. Civ. App.—Austin 1927, writ ref'd); *Hickman v. Hoffman*, 11 Tex. Civ. App. 605, 33 S.W. 257 (1895, writ ref'd).

• Any rights of parties based on adoption by estoppel. *Moran v. Adler*, 570 S.W.2d 883 (Tex. 1978).

• A claim of equitable subrogation, *AMC Mortgage Services Inc. v. Watts*, 260 S.W.3d 582 (Tex. App.—Dallas 2008, no pet.).

• An easement by estoppel. *Cleaver v. Cundiff*, 203 S.W.3d 373 (Tex. App.—Eastland 2006, pet. denied). (However, if possession and use are sufficient to place the purchaser on inquiry, then the purchaser will not be bona fide).

• A claim that the deed was, in actuality, given as a mortgage. *Brown v. Wilson*, 29 S.W. 530 (Tex. Civ. App. 1895, no writ).

A party also can be a bona fide purchaser even though the party acquires only an equitable title (such as a contract purchaser who has paid the contract price). *Batts & Dean v. Scott*, 37 Tex. 59, 64 (1872).

Bona Fide Purchaser Not Protected: Even a bona fide purchaser's title is subject to certain claims, whether or not these claims are disclosed in the real property records:

- A claim of title by adverse possession or prescription, *Houston Oil Co. v. Olive Sternenberg & Co.*, 222 S.W. 534 (Tex. Comm'n App. 1920, judgm't adopted); *Heard v. Bowen*, 184 S.W. 234 (Tex. Civ. App.—San Antonio 1916, writ ref'd); *MacGregor v. Thompson*, 26 S.W. 649 (Tex. Civ. App. 1894, no writ).
- A claim that a deed was given while the person was a minor or insane, *Gaston v. Bruton*, 358 S.W.2d 207 (Tex. Civ. App.—El Paso 1962, writ dism'd w.o.j.); *Pure Oil Co. v. Swindall*, 58 S.W.2d 7 (Tex. Comm'n App. 1933, holding approved); *McLean v. Stith*, 112 S.W. 355 (Tex. Civ. App. 1908, writ ref'd).
- A claim that the deed was forged, *Pure Oil Co. v. Swindall*, 58 S.W.2d 7 (Tex. Comm'n App. 1933, holding approved).
- A claim of heirs, regardless of whether known by the bona fide purchaser, *New York & Tex. Land Co. v. Hyland*, 28 S.W. 206 (Tex. Civ. App. 1894, writ ref'd).
- A conveyance by a person who had the identical name of the record owner but who was not the same person, *Blocker v. Davis*, 241 S.W.2d 698 (Tex. Civ. App.—Fort Worth 1951, writ ref'd n.r.e.); *Pure Oil Co. v. Swindall*, 58 S.W.2d 7 (Tex. Comm'n App. 1933, holding approved).

Burden Of Proof: Although status as a bona fide purchaser is an affirmative defense in a title dispute, *Madison v. Gordon*, 39 S.W.3d 604, 607 (Tex. 2001), a person claiming title through principles of equity has the burden to establish that the subsequent purchaser is not a bona fide purchaser. *Noble Mortgage & Investments, LLC v. D&M Vision Investments, LLC*, 340 S.W.3d 65 (Tex. App.—Houston [1st Dist.] 2011, no pet.); *NRG Expl., Inc. v. Rauch*, 671 S.W.2d 649 (Tex. App.—Austin 1984, writ ref'd n.r.e.); *see Westland Oil Dev. Corp. v. Gulf Oil Corp.*, 637 S.W.2d 903 (Tex. 1982). On the other hand, a claimant under a junior deed has the burden to prove bona fide purchaser status against a prior unrecorded conveyance of legal title, *Watkins v. Edwards*, 23 Tex. 443 (1859); *Ryle v. Davidson*, 115 S.W. 28 (Tex. 1909); *Raposa v. Johnson*, 693 S.W.2d 43 (Tex. App.—Fort Worth 1985, writ ref'd n.r.e.), unless the junior deed was delivered before the passage of the registration act of 1840. *Kimball v. Houston Oil Co.*, 99 S.W. 852 (Tex. 1907).

Source:
Citations in the Comment.
History:
Adopted Aug. 2, 2013; amended July 17, 2014.

The prior standard provided: "An examiner cannot determine whether any party in the chain of title is a bona fide purchaser. Accordingly, an examiner must not disregard any interest in the chain of title based solely on an assumption that it was extinguished by a bona fide purchaser under the recording laws. However, if title passed by a quitclaim deed, then the grantee and the grantee's successors are not bona fide purchasers as to claims existing at the time of the quitclaim deed."

STANDARD 4.100. QUALIFICATION AS LIEN CREDITOR

A lien creditor without notice has a status similar to a bona fide purchaser.

COMMENT

The recording statutes provide that a lien creditor without notice takes free of a prior deed, mortgage, or other instrument that has not been acknowledged, sworn to, or proved and filed for record. Tex. Prop. Code Ann. §13.001. A "creditor" is a claimant whose claim is fixed by some legal process as a lien on the land, such as by attachment, execution, judgment, landlord or mechanic's lien, or a tax lien (such as IRS or state tax lien). *Johnson v. Darr*, 272 S.W. 1098, 1100 (Tex. 1925) ("The Texas courts have construed the words 'all creditors' of the statute to mean creditors who acquired a lien by legal proceedings without notice of the unrecorded instrument."); *Prewitt v. United States*, 792 F.2d 1353 (5th Cir. 1986); *United States v. Creamer Industries, Inc.*, 349 F.2d 625 (5th Cir. 1965); *Underwood v. United States*, 118 F.2d 760 (5th Cir. 1941); *Bowen v. Lansing Wagon Works*, 43 S.W. 872 (Tex. 1898). A junior lender whose mortgage secures an antecedent debt is not a lien creditor and cannot take priority over a prior unrecorded deed. *Turner v. Cochran*, 61 S.W. 923 (Tex. 1901). A trustee or debtor-in-possession in a bankruptcy will be treated as a judgment creditor in order to set aside unrecorded interests. 11 U.S.C. §544; *Faires v. Billman*, 849 S.W.2d 455 (Tex. App.—Austin 1993, no pet.); *Segrest v. Hale*, 164 S.W.2d 793 (Tex. Civ. App.—Galveston, 1941, writ ref'd w.o.m.).

A lien creditor will take free and clear of prior unrecorded (but recordable) interests, unless the creditor has notice of them. Examples of such recordable interests are:

(1) An equitable right to have a deed corrected to convey a lot originally intended to be included in the conveyance (but not included due to mutual mistake), *United States v. Creamer Industries, Inc.*, 349 F.2d 625 (5th Cir. 1965); *Henderson v. Odessa Building & Finance Co.*, 24 S.W.2d 393 (Tex. Comm'n App. 1930); *North East Independent School District v. Aldridge*, 528 S.W.2d 341 (Tex. Civ. App.—Amarillo 1975, writ ref'd n.r.e.).

(2) An unrecorded contract for sale, *Linn v. Le Compte*, 47 Tex. 440 (1877).

(3) A prior unrecorded deed, *Whitaker v. Farris*, 101 S.W. 456 (Tex. Civ. App. 1907, writ ref'd).

(4) A divorce decree not filed of record in the real property records; *Prewitt v. United States*, 792 F.2d 1353 (5th Cir. 1986).

(5) An unrecorded sheriff's deed; *Wiggins v. Sprague*, 40 S.W. 1019 (Tex. Civ. App. 1897, no writ).

(6) An unrecorded extension of deed of trust. *Cadle Co. v. Butler*, 951 S.W.2d 901 (Tex. App.—Corpus Christi 1997, no writ).

(7) An entry of a constable's sale in the litigation records (execution docket) of the county clerk's office. *Noble Mortgage & Investments, LLC v. D&M Vision Investments, LLC*, 340 S.W.3d 65 (Tex. App.—Houston [1st Dist.] 2011, no pet.).

Bona fide purchasers for value are protected against the assertion of equitable titles because of the doctrine of estoppel, and not because of the registration statutes. *Johnson v. Darr*, 272 S.W. 1098 (Tex. 1925). Unlike a bona fide purchaser, a lien creditor cannot invoke estoppel, and must rely solely upon the recording statute to assert that its rights are superior to an unrecorded interest. The lien creditor will not extinguish "unrecorded equities" such as:

(1) An executory contract to convey real property where the purchaser goes into possession of the property. *Cadle Co. v. Harvey*, 46 S.W.3d 282, 287 (Tex. App.—Fort Worth 2001, pet. denied).

(2) A completed contract for sale where no deed had been executed to the purchaser, *Texas American Bank v. Resendez*, 706 S.W.2d 343 (Tex. App.—Amarillo 1986, no writ).

(3) A deed intended as a mortgage, *Michael v. Knapp*, 23 S.W. 280 (Tex. Civ. App. 1893, no writ).

(4) A deed of trust released by mutual mistake, *First State Bank v. Jones*, 183 S.W. 874 (Tex. 1916).

(5) A right to reform a deed where by mutual mistake the grantor conveyed a greater interest than intended, *Cetti v. Wilson*, 168 S.W. 996 (Tex. Civ. App.—Fort Worth 1914, writ ref'd).

Source:
Citations in the Comment.
History:
Adopted Aug. 2, 2013.

STANDARD 4.110. ELECTRONIC FILING & RECORDATION

An examiner may presume that any additional requirements for electronic filing of instruments (beyond those required for recordation of paper instruments) have been met.

COMMENT

Electronic filing of instruments in the real property records is governed by (1) the Uniform Electronic Transactions Act (Tex. Bus. & Com. Code Ann. §§322.001-322.021) (UETA), (2) the Uniform Real Property Electronic Recording Act (Tex. Prop. Code Ann. §§15.001-15.008) (URPERA), (3) Tex. Local Gov't Code Ann. §§195.001-195.009, and (4) 13 Tex. Admin. Code Ann. §§7.141-7.145. The federal Electronic Signatures in Global and National Commerce Act (15 U.S.C. §7001 et seq.) (E-SIGN) has been largely modified, limited, and superseded by Texas law. Tex. Prop. Code Ann. §15.007; Tex. Bus. & Com. Code Ann. §322.019. The Texas State Library and Archives Commission has adopted rules by which a county clerk may accept electronic documents by electronic filing and record electronic documents and other instruments. Tex. Local Gov't Code Ann. §195.002(a).

The persons (authorized filers) who may file electronic documents or other documents electronically with a county clerk that accepts electronic filing and recording are specified in Tex. Local Gov't Code Ann. §195.003.

An electronic instrument or instrument filed electronically must be available for public inspection in the same manner and at the same time as an instrument filed by other means. Tex. Local Gov't Code Ann. §195.007(a). An electronic document or instrument filed electronically is filed with the county clerk when it is received, unless the county clerk rejects the filing within the time and manner provided by Chapter 195 or by applicable rules. Tex. Local Gov't Code Ann. §195.009. A county clerk that accepts an electronic filing shall confirm or reject the filing no later than the first business

day after the date of filing. If the county clerk fails to provide notice of rejection within the time provided, the filing is considered accepted and may not subsequently be rejected. Tex. Local Gov't Code Ann. §195.004. An electronic document or other instrument that is filed electronically is considered recorded in compliance with a law relating to electronic filing as of the county clerk's business day of filing. Tex. Local Gov't Code Ann. §195.005.

If a law requires as a condition for recording that a document be an original or be in writing, the requirement is satisfied by an electronic document (a document received by a county clerk in an electronic form) that complies with Chapter 15, Texas Prop. Code Ann. If a law requires as a condition for recording that a document be signed, the requirement is satisfied by an electronic signature. A requirement that a document be notarized, acknowledged, verified, witnessed, or made under oath is satisfied if the electronic signature of the person authorized to perform that act, and all other information required to be included, is attached or logically associated with the document or signature. A physical or electronic image of a stamp, impression, or seal need not accompany an electronic signature. Tex. Prop. Code Ann. §15.004; Tex. Bus. & Com. Code Ann. §322.011. An original signature may not be required for an electronic instrument or other document that complies with Chapter 15, Tex. Prop. Code Ann.; Chapter 195, Tex. Loc. Gov't. Code Ann.; Chapter 322, Tex. Bus. & Com. Code Ann., or other applicable law. Tex. Prop. Code Ann. §12.0011.

Source:

Citations in the Comment.

History:

Adopted Aug. 2, 2013; amended July 17, 2014.

The prior standard provided: "An examiner may assume that any additional requirements for electronic filing of instruments (beyond those required for recordation of paper instruments) have been met."

STANDARD 4.120. ESTOPPEL BY DEED

The examiner may rely upon the doctrine of estoppel by deed for vesting of an interest in title, where applicable.

COMMENT

If a grantor does not own the interest he purports to convey, estoppel by deed (also called the doctrine of after-acquired title) will automatically vest title in the grantee or the grantee's successors if the grantor later acquires title to the interest. Estoppel by deed also applies more broadly to bind the parties to a deed by the recitals in the deed. *Box v. Lawrence*, 14 Tex. 545 (1855); *Surtees v. Hobson*, 4 S.W.2d 245 (Tex. Civ. App.—El Paso 1928), aff'd, 13 S.W.2d 345 (Tex. Comm'n App. 1929); *XTO Energy Inc. v. Nikolai*, 357 S.W.3d 47 (Tex. App.—Fort Worth 2011, pet. denied).

A deed will operate to vest the after-acquired title of the grantor in the grantee if the deed is not a quitclaim deed, *Wilson v. Wilson*, 118 S.W.2d 403 (Tex. Civ. App.—Beaumont 1938, no writ), and it is not essential that a deed contain a warranty in order for the doctrine to apply. *Wilson v. Beck*, 286 S.W. 315, 320 (Tex. Civ. App.—Dallas 1926, writ ref'd); *Lindsay v. Freeman*, 18 S.W. 727 (Tex. 1892); *Blanton v. Bruce*, 688 S.W.2d 908 (Tex. App.—Eastland 1985, writ ref'd n.r.e.); *Texas Pacific Coal & Oil Co. v. Fox*, 228 S.W. 1021 (Tex. Civ. App.—Fort Worth 1921, no writ). Estoppel will apply even in the case of a gift deed. *Robinson v. Douthit*, 64 Tex. 101 (1885). See discussion of quitclaim deeds in the comment to Standard 4.90.

If the grantor conveys without excepting to a lien and thereafter acquires title (at a foreclosure sale or later), then the title it acquires will inure to its prior grantee. *Burns v. Goodrich*, 392 S.W.2d 689 (Tex. 1965); *Robinson v. Douthit*, 64 Tex. 101 (1885). Presumably the benefits to a grantee of the doctrine of estoppel by deed are assigned to a later grantee who receives a quitclaim from the first grantee. *Burns v. Goodrich*, 392 S.W.2d 689 (Tex. 1965); *Robinson v. Douthit*, 64 Tex. 101 (1885).

The rule of after-acquired title also applies to mortgages. *Shield v. Donald*, 253 S.W.2d 710 (Tex. Civ. App.—Fort Worth 1952, writ ref'd n.r.e.). A party who executes notes and mortgages on land (or assumes existing liens) cannot take title under a foreclosure of a prior lien without discharging the notes secured by inferior mortgages; the mortgagees' liens will be reinstated. *Milford v. Culpepper*, 40 S.W.2d 163 (Tex. Civ. App.—Dallas 1931, writ ref'd).

Where a deed conveys land and reserves a mineral interest, but fails to except prior reserved minerals, thus creating an overconveyance, the grantor loses his title as necessary to make his grantee whole. *Duhig v. Peavy-Moore Lumber Co*, 144 S.W.2d 878 (Tex. 1940). The Duhig rule of estoppel will not apply, however, if the deed refers to a prior deed reserving a mineral interest by language such as "reference to which is made

for all purposes" or "for all legal purposes." *Harris v. Windsor*, 294 S.W.2d 798 (Tex. 1956).

A grantee in a deed will be bound by the deed's contents, including a reference to a disputed prior reservation of minerals, and may not thereafter acquire superior title free of the reservation. *Adams v. Duncan*, 215 S.W.2d 599 (Tex. 1948); *Greene v. White*, 153 S.W.2d 575 (Tex. 1941). However, before the grantor can secure a mineral interest by estoppel, the grantee must have all of the interest that the grantor purported to convey. *Dean v. Hidalgo County Water Imp. Dist. No. Two*, 320 S.W.2d 29 (Tex. Civ. App.—San Antonio 1959, writ ref'd n.r.e.).

A conveyance signed by a party only in a representative capacity will, nevertheless, convey whatever interest that person owns individually where that party's deed purports to convey the property (as opposed to a quitclaim deed). Conveyances where such estoppel has been recognized include those by an estate representative, *Tomlinson v. H.P. Drought & Co.*, 127 S.W. 262 (Tex. Civ. App. 1910, writ ref'd); agents on behalf of principals, *Ford v. Warner*, 176 S.W. 885 (Tex. Civ. App.—Amarillo 1915, no writ); trustee, *Grange v. Kayser*, 80 S.W.2d 1007 (Tex. Civ. App.—El Paso 1935, no writ); and corporations by officers, *Carothers v. Alexander*, 12 S.W. 4 (Tex. 1889) (where the issue was discussed although estoppel was inapplicable); *see also American Savings & Loan Assoc. v. Musick*, 517 S.W.2d 627 (Tex. Civ. App.—Houston [14th Dist.] 1974), rev'd on other grounds, 531 S.W.2d 581 (Tex. 1975).

Source:
Citations in the Comment.
History:
Adopted Aug. 2, 2013.

CHAPTER V. LAND DESCRIPTIONS

STANDARD 5.10. LAND DESCRIPTIONS GENERALLY

Although an examiner does not determine actual boundaries on the ground, an examiner should determine whether each land description in the chain of title is sufficient to identify the land under examination.

COMMENT

A legal description affords the means of identifying the land. *Morrow v. Shotwell*, 477 S.W.2d 538, 539 (Tex. 1972); *Wilson v. Fisher*, 188 S.W.2d 150, 152 (Tex. 1945); *Chandler v. Kountze*, 130 S.W.2d 327, 331 (Tex. Civ. App.—Galveston 1939, writ ref'd); 4 Aloysius A. Leopold, *Land Titles and Title Examination* §15.2 (Texas Practice 3d ed. 2005). A conveyance in the chain of title that does not identify the land under examination is ineffective to pass title. *Greer v. Greer*, 191 S.W.2d 848 (Tex. 1946).

The intention of the parties concerning the identification of the land conveyed and its boundaries is determined from the face of the instrument in light of surrounding circumstances. *Stafford v. King*, 30 Tex. 257 (1867). The intention of the parties to a deed containing a metes and bounds description is presumed to be the same as that of the surveyor who surveyed the tract. *Strong v. Sunray DX Oil Co.*, 448 S.W.2d 728 (Tex. Civ. App.—Corpus Christi 1969, writ ref'd n.r.e.). The instrument need not contain such a full description as will enable the property to be ascertained without the aid of extrinsic evidence. *Chandler v. Kountze*, 130 S.W.2d 327 (Tex. Civ. App.—Galveston 1939, writ ref'd). However, the description contained in an instrument must furnish, within itself or by reference to other existing writing, the means by which the property can be identified with reasonable certainty. *Broaddus v. Grout*, 258 S.W.2d 308 (Tex. 1953). A legally sufficient description depicts the tract's boundaries as located on the ground by the surveyor.

The boundaries of a tract as originally surveyed are described by the field notes of the surveyor and are commonly found in the patent or other grant from the sovereign. The footsteps of the original surveyor, if they can be ascertained, should be followed. *Silver Oil & Gas, Inc. v. EOG Resources, Inc.*, 246 S.W.3d 197 (Tex. App.—San Antonio 2007, no pet.). In the case of a conflict between two or more patented surveys, the senior (oldest) survey controls over any junior (younger) survey. *Silver Oil & Gas, Inc. v. EOG Resources, Inc.*, 246 S.W.3d 197, 204 (Tex. App.—San Antonio 2007, no pet.) ("The description in a senior survey controls when locating a line of that survey over any junior survey of that line, unless the evidence proves that the senior survey is in error."). When the senior survey can be easily identified, a junior survey cannot be made to control the senior survey. *Hill v. Whiteside*, 749 S.W.2d 144, 151 (Tex. App.—Fort Worth 1988, writ denied). If the actual boundary lines and corners run by the original surveyor can be found they are controlling, even if they are inconsistent with the calls and references found in the field notes. If the footsteps of the original surveyor cannot be ascertained with the reasonable

certainty, the surrounding facts and circumstances should be considered in order to arrive at the intent and purpose of the surveyor. *Silver Oil & Gas, Inc. v. EOG Resources, Inc.*, 246 S.W.3d 197 (Tex. App.—San Antonio 2007, no pet.).

An examiner is not responsible for identifying a boundary defect, such as an encroachment or a survey conflict or error, that is not apparent from the instruments examined unless the examiner has other notice of the defect. Moreover, not all boundary defects are apparent from the record.

In determining the legal sufficiency of a description, an examiner may presume that errors, irregularities, deficiencies, and inconsistencies in a land description in the chain of title are not material unless, under the circumstances, a substantial uncertainty exists as to the identity of the land or the description fails to satisfy the minimal requirements essential to an effective conveyance. When examining a marginally sufficient or questionable land description, the examiner should consider all relevant factors, including the lapse of time, subsequent conveyances, the manifest or typographical nature of an error or omission, and accepted rules of construction.

While any title is only as good as the weakest link in the chain of descriptions, practical considerations justify reliance upon corrections or improved land descriptions appearing in later conveyances and upon the passage of time if no apparent difficulties have arisen from a less than perfect land description. Further, all matters of record (e.g., adjoining descriptions, other land owned by the grantor, and the like) may become sources of explanation for what might be a dubious description by itself. *Pickett v. Bishop*, 223 S.W.2d 222, 223 (Tex. 1949); *Abercrombie v. Bright*, 271 S.W.2d 734 (Tex. Civ. App.—Eastland 1954, writ ref'd n.r.e.). Likewise, typographical mistakes and similar apparent errors and omissions in land descriptions do not detract from the obvious intent of instruments. *Reserve Petroleum Co. v. Harp*, 226 S.W.2d 839, 841 (Tex. 1950); *Barnard v. Good*, 44 Tex. 638 (1876); *Rhoden v. Bergman*, 75 S.W.2d 993 (Tex. Civ. App.—Beaumont 1934, writ ref'd); *Holman v. Houston Oil Co.*, 152 S.W. 885 (Tex. Civ. App.—Galveston 1912, writ dism'd).

Where elements of the description conflict or where the calls do not close, the examiner may utilize rules of construction to construe descriptive calls that are conflicting or ambiguous. The order of dignity of calls is summarized in the following provision from the Texas Administrative Code, which is consistent with Texas case law:

The order of dignity of calls in a survey is as follows:

1. Natural objects (rivers, etc.).
2. Artificial objects (marked trees, stone mounds, adjoinder calls, etc.).
3. Courses (bearings).
4. Distances.
5. Acreage.

31 Tex. Admin. Code §7.5 (General Land Office surveying rules for licensed state surveyors). *See also, Frost v. Socony Mobil Oil Co., Inc.*, 433 S.W.2d 387 (Tex. 1968) (holding that calls to course and distance control over mistaken calls for an unmarked line which was not located on the ground); *Stafford v. King*, 30 Tex. 257 (1867) (recognizing that the general rules as to controlling calls are: "natural objects; artificial objects; course and distance."); *Mohnke v. Greenwood*, 915 S.W.2d 585 (Tex. App.—Houston [14th Dist.] 1996, no writ) (holding that the law of legal preferences gives dignity to calls in the following order: natural objects; artificial objects; course; and distance and that where there is a conflict, calls to natural objects will prevail over calls to artificial objects); *Cox v. Piwonka*, 257 S.W.2d 955 (Tex. Civ. App.—Galveston 1953, writ dism'd) (holding that a line of a located survey is an artificial object that controls over distance); *Duff v. Moore*, 68 Tex. 270 (1887) (calls to an adjoining tract shall control over distance). Calls for adjoinder prevail even if the adjoinder is with an unmarked but ascertainable line. *Frost v. Socony Mobil Oil Co.*, 433 S.W.2d 387 (Tex. 1968). An exception exists if the call for adjoinder was made upon mistake, apprehension, or conjecture. *Turner v. Smith*, 61 S.W.2d 792 (Tex. 1933). A call for course is considered more reliable and will prevail over a call for distance. *Lilley v. Blum*, 6 S.W. 279 (Tex. 1887). Calls for quantity of acreage will be given the least priority. *Collins v. Warfield*, 140 S.W. 107 (Tex. Civ. App.—Galveston 1911, no writ). Nevertheless, if the instrument shows that the parties intended that other objects or calls should prevail, then their intention should be given effect over the usual order of priority or dignity. *Port Aransas Properties, Inc. v. Ellis*, 129 S.W.2d 699 (Tex. Civ. App.—San Antonio 1939, writ dism'd judgm't cor.); *Stuart v. Coldwell Banker & Co.*, 552 S.W.2d 904 (Tex. Civ. App.—Houston [1st Dist.] 1977, writ ref'd n.r.e.).

Global or blanket descriptions of all of the grantor's real property wherever located in a specified city, county, or state are sufficient to satisfy the Statute of Frauds, even if other tracts are also specifically described. *Witt v. Harlan*, 2 S.W. 41 (Tex. 1886); *Holloway's Unknown Heirs v. Whatley*, 131 S.W.2d 89 (Tex. 1939). However, in *J. Hiram Moore, Ltd. v. Greer*, 172 S.W.3d 609 (Tex. 2005), the deed at issue contained both a specific description and a global description. Because the specific description failed, the court refused to enforce the global description on the ground that the deed was ambiguous. Moreover, a global or blanket description is distinguishable from a "Mother Hubbard" or "cover-all" clause, which is ordinarily construed as including in the description only small strips of land adjacent to the land described. *Cf.*, *J. Hiram Moore, Ltd. v. Greer*, 172 S.W.3d 609 (Tex. 2005); *Sun Oil Co. v. Burns*, 84 S.W.2d 442 (Tex. 1935). An examiner should be aware that it is not always easy to distinguish global or blanket descriptions, which are broadly construed, from Mother Hubbard or cover-all clauses that apply only to small strips of land. *See* Caution to Standard 15.10.

Boundaries may be established by means other than through the calls recited in the instrument, including by express agreement, by the passage of time, or by the action or acquiescence of the parties.

Written Agreements: Boundary lines may be established by written agreement, but all parties with an interest in the property must join in the written agreement for it to be effective as to all interests in the property. The agreement must be filed for record with the county clerk of the county where the land is located to be binding upon subsequent purchasers without notice. Where the boundary separates two platted lots, a boundary agreement that includes a conveyance of land may be valid between the parties, but, absent replatting, the agreement may violate subdivision regulations, leading to civil and criminal penalties and possible denial of city and utility services. Tex. Loc. Gov't Code Ann. §212.004.

Oral Agreements: Where the location of the boundary described in the conveyance is doubtful, uncertain, or disputed, the parties may agree upon a division line through an oral boundary agreement without violating the Statute of Frauds. *Duval County Ranch Co. v. Foster*, 318 S.W.2d 25 (Tex. Civ. App.—San Antonio 1958, writ ref'd n.r.e.). The oral agreement must be definite, unconditional, and "executed" by the parties through (1) erection of monuments on the agreed line or by otherwise marking it and by the actual and physical possession or use to the line or (2) improving or developing the property with reference to the line. *Farmer v. Kornfuehrer*, 271 S.W.2d 501 (Tex. Civ. App.—San Antonio 1954, no writ). Otherwise, an oral agreement does not bind subsequent purchasers.

Acquiescence: Where there is uncertainty, doubt, or dispute as to the true boundary, the location may be resolved, without an express agreement, by acquiescence. *Taylor v. Benton*, 390 S.W.2d 509 (Tex. Civ. App.—Eastland 1965, no writ). The acquiesced line becomes the new boundary line by subsequent transfers that describe it. *Sullivan v. Michael*, 87 S.W. 1061 (Tex. Civ. App. 1905, no writ).

CAUTION

A defective description is one of the most frequent causes of title failure. In general, courts construe land descriptions objectively, i.e., how the land was described in the instrument, and not subjectively, i.e., what the parties intended to describe in the instrument but did not. Thus, ordinarily, if the land description is unambiguous, the parties' subjective intent not expressed in the instrument is of no consequence. Accordingly, the examiner should ascertain that the description in the instruments involved in a chain of title sufficiently describes the land so that it can be identified and located on the ground with reasonable certainty. If extrinsic evidence is necessary to determine the boundaries, then the descriptive words in the deed, or deeds, must furnish a basis or guide for its admission.

Source:

Citations in the Comment; 4 Aloysius A. Leopold, *Land Titles and Title Examination*, ch. 15 (Texas Practice 3d ed. 2005).

History:

Adopted June 27, 1997; replaced June 11, 2010; amended July 17, 2014.

The prior standard provided: "Although examiners do not determine actual boundaries on the ground, an examiner must determine whether each land description in the chain of title is sufficient to identify the land under examination."

The original standard provided: "An examiner may presume that errors, irregularities, deficiencies, and inconsistencies in land descriptions in the chain of title do not impair marketability unless, after considering all circumstances of record, (a) a substantial uncertainty exists as to the land involved or (b) the description falls beneath the minimal requirements of sufficiency and definiteness essential to an effective conveyance. When examining marginally sufficient or questionable descriptions, the examiner should consider all relevant factors, including the lapse of time, subsequent conveyances, the manifest or typographical nature of errors or omissions, and accepted rules of construction."

STANDARD 5.20. LAND DESCRIPTIONS IN PATENTS

An examiner may ordinarily rely on the land description contained in a patent recorded in the county records.

COMMENT

Titles to Texas land are derived from land grants by Spain and Mexico and from patents issued by the Republic of Texas and the State of Texas. In each case, in the absence of evidence indicating an error, an examiner may rely upon the land description in the land grant or patent in considering whether the sovereign's title has been divested.

Regarding patents issued by the Republic or State of Texas, the laws have always required that before a patent may be issued for an unsevered tract, the tract must be surveyed and the field notes returned to the General Land Office. Those field notes are then incorporated in the patent. *See Atlantic Refining Co. v. Noel*, 443 S.W.2d 35 (Tex. 1968). Patents are not required to be recorded in the county where the land is situated, *Mathews v. Caldwell*, 258 S.W. 810, 813-14 (Tex. Comm'n App. 1924), although the patent—or a certified copy obtained from the General Land Office—usually is recorded. It is possible, although uncommon, for the field notes in the patent to differ from those of the original survey. In such a case the original field notes control. *State v. Sun Oil Co.*, 114 S.W.2d 936, 944 (Tex. Civ. App.—Austin 1938, writ ref'd). However, unless the conflict is disclosed in the course of the examination, an examiner may reasonably and customarily rely on the patent as it appears in the county records. If there is evidence of a conflict, it may be necessary for the examiner to consult the records of the General Land Office to resolve the issue.

CAUTION

As to patents to lands sold by the State of Texas between September 1, 1895 (the effective date of the General Mineral Release Act of 1895) and August 21, 1931 (the effective date of the Sales Act of 1931), the examiner should not rely on the patent to ascertain whether the State reserved minerals in the patented lands but should obtain from the General Land Office a letter or certificate of classification or Certificate of Facts, which will indicate any reservation of minerals.

Source:
Citations in the Comment.

History:
Adopted June 11, 2010.

STANDARD 5.30. WATER BOUNDARIES

Although an examiner does not determine actual water boundaries on the ground or the character of waters, an examiner should be aware of the following general principles governing riparian and littoral boundaries along tidelands, lakes, and streams.

Riparian and littoral boundaries are governed by the applicable law in effect on the date of severance of title from the sovereign.

The boundary of a tract bounded by a non-navigable stream is generally located at the thread of the stream.

Title to the bed of tidelands and to natural navigable lakes is in the State.

Title to the bed of navigable streams is determined by the common law and by the "thirty-foot" statute. Title to other streams is determined by the law in effect on the date of severance of title from the sovereign. State title to the bed of parts of some streams may be relinquished under the "Small Bill."

COMMENT

Tidelands: The owner of land adjacent to a shore is a "littoral owner." Tex. Nat. Res. Code Ann. §61.001(6). The location of the littoral boundaries is determined by the date of severance from the sovereign. After the Republic of Texas adopted the common law on January 20, 1840, the boundary of the sea was established as the mean high tide of the sea waters. Prior to that time, the boundary of the sea was controlled by civil law, which established the boundary as the mean higher high tide. The civil law line is calculated over regular tidal cycles of 18.6 years. *Luttes v. State*, 324 S.W.2d 167 (Tex. 1958). *See also Kenedy Memorial Foundation v. Dewhurst*, 90 S.W.3d 268, 272 (Tex. 2002) ("A mean daily higher high tide—which the parties agree in this case is synonymous with mean daily higher high water—is calculated by averaging the highest elevations reached by water each day over a tidal epoch of 18.6 years. Of course, as we recognized in Luttes, water level data is not available at all locations on the coast, and where it is available it may cover only part of the lengthy epochal cycle. But averages may nevertheless be obtained by extrapolation from data that is available, adjusting for known, cyclical variations. At times on the Texas coast there are two daily high tides and two daily low tides.

Mean higher high tide is an average of only the higher of the daily levels. Mean high tide is an average of both high levels. This distinction is immaterial in areas of the Laguna Madre where tidal influences and daily fluctuations in water levels are ordinarily quite small. Thus, for purposes of this case, daily higher high water is indistinguishable from daily high water.").

In the case of a Spanish land grant, a Mexican land grant, or a Republic of Texas patent issued prior to January 20, 1840, littoral ownership may not be encumbered by a migratory easement in favor of the public in the beach area between mean higher high tide and the line of natural vegetation. In the case of a patent issued on or after January 20, 1840, littoral ownership may not be encumbered by a migratory easement in favor of the public in the beach area between mean high tide and the line of natural vegetation. In any case, absent proof of establishment of such easement by grant, reservation, prescription, dedication, or by virtue of the continuous right in the public since time immemorial, littoral ownership may not be encumbered by an easement in favor of the public in the above mentioned beach areas.

When an avulsive event dramatically changes the coastline (e.g., the location of the natural vegetation line), no easement in favor of the public to access the beach area is created encumbering an entirely new portion of a landowner's property or a different parcel that had not been previously subject to an easement. *Severance v. Patterson*, 370 S.W.3d 705 (Tex. 2012) ("…when a beachfront vegetation line is suddenly and dramatically pushed landward by acts of nature, an existing public easement on the public beach does not 'roll' inland to other parts of the parcel or onto a new parcel of land").

The Texas Open Beach Act (OBA) does not create substantive rights and thus does not recognize a public easement where none previously existed. The OBA does provide the State with a means of enforcing the public's right to use state-owned beaches. *See* Tex. Nat. Res. Code Ann. §§61.011(a), 61.013(a). *See also* Tex. Nat. Res. Code Ann. §61.001(7-a) (defining a "meteorological event" which alters the location of the line of vegetation); Tex. Nat. Res. Code Ann. §61.001(8) (defining the public beach area); Tex. Nat. Res. Code Ann. §61.0011(d) (allowing the Commissioner of the General Land Office to temporarily suspend the determination of the line of vegetation or natural line of vegetation under Section 61.071 during which time the public beach shall extend to a line 200 feet inland from the line of mean low tide as established by a licensed state surveyor); Tex. Nat. Res. Code Ann. §61.013 (prohibiting littoral owners from constructing improvements on the public beach or from interfering with public use of a public beach); Tex. Nat. Res. Code Ann. §61.016 (establishing the boundary in the absence of a line of natural vegetation).

Streams: Title to the bed of streams may depend upon whether a stream was perennial or torrential, or is navigable or non-navigable, and on whether the stream has been affected by erosion, accretion, or avulsion.

In land grants made prior to January 20, 1840, in accordance with Spanish or Mexican civil law, the sovereign retained title to the bed of a perennial stream (including all minerals) flowing through or along the granted land, whether navigable or not. *Manry v. Robison*, 56 S.W.2d 438, 446 (Tex. 1932) (addressing mineral title to a portion of the Brazos River, a perennial stream). A perennial stream flows most of the year, as opposed to a torrential stream, which flows only after substantial rainfall. Title to the bed of a torrential stream was deemed granted to the riparian owners. *McCurdy v. Morgan*, 265 S.W.2d 269 (Tex. Civ. App.—San Antonio 1954, writ ref'd) (addressing mineral title to a portion of the Chiltipin Creek in San Patricio County, a torrential stream).

The Republic of Texas modified Mexican civil law, effective December 14, 1837, by adding the so called "thirty foot" statute and by no longer referring to torrential and perennial streams, but distinguishing navigable and non-navigable streams. Under this statute, a stream that has an "average width of 30 feet from the mouth up" is defined as a navigable stream. Tex. Nat. Res. Code Ann. §21.001(3). Thus, regarding land grants made on or after December 14, 1837, the sovereign retains title to the bed of such streams (including all minerals) as to their entire length. *Motl v. Boyd*, 286 S.W. 458 (Tex. 1926) (addressing Spring Creek, a tributary of the South Concho River, located in Tom Green County). *See Hix v. Robertson*, 211 S.W.3d 423, 425 (Tex. App.—Waco 2006, pet. denied) (finding that there is no single methodology that must be followed to measure this width to determine whether a particular stream falls within the statute). Therefore, regarding severances from the Republic of Texas between Decem-

ber 14, 1837, and January 20, 1840, Texas retained sovereign title to the beds of perennial streams and to any streams that meet the requirements of the "thirty-foot" statute.

Texas adopted the common law in 1840. Act approved Jan. 20, 1840, 4th Cong., R.S., §1, 1840 Republic of Texas Laws 3, 3-4, reprinted in 2 H.P.N. Gammel, *Laws of Texas* 177, 177-178 (1898) (current version at Tex. Civ. Prac. & Rem. Code Ann. §5.001). Since then, the thirty-foot statute remains in effect and the sovereign also retains, as a matter of common law, title to the beds of streams that are navigable in fact regardless of the width of the stream.

To determine the boundary line between the bed of a navigable stream and riparian land (between public and private ownership), the law requires compliance with the gradient boundary methodology. The gradient boundary methodology utilizes two factors: (i) the location of the "key bank," and (ii) the gradient or rate of fall of the water. The gradient boundary of a navigable stream is "the water-washed and relatively permanent elevation or acclivity at the outer line of the riverbed that separates the bed from the adjacent upland, whether valley or hill, and serves to confine the water within the bed and to preserve the course of the river." *Oklahoma v. Texas*, 260 U.S. 606, 631 32 (1923). The boundary is the bank at the average or mean level attained by the water when it washes the bank without overflowing. *Brainard v. State*, 12 S.W.3d 6, 16 (Tex. 1999). The boundary between the private riparian landowner and the State of Texas is the inner bank at the mean level midway between the line made by the flowing water as it reaches the cut bank and the top of the cut bank. *Diversion Lake Club v. Heath*, 86 S.W.2d 441 (Tex. 1935). The stream width includes the entire bed whether the full bed has water over the entire width or not. *Motl v. Boyd*, 286 S.W. 458 (Tex. 1926).

The boundary rules related to erosion and accretion are applicable to navigable and non-navigable streams. *Maufrais v. State*, 180 S.W.2d 144 (Tex. 1944); *Tyler v. Gonzales*, 189 S.W.2d 519 (Tex. Civ. App.—San Antonio 1945, writ ref'd w.o.m.). Where a stream gradually or imperceptibly changes or shifts by accretion or erosion, the body of water that makes up the boundary also shifts or changes for both surface and mineral rights. *Brainard v. State*, 12 S.W.3d 6 (Tex. 1999).

Accretion is the gradual and imperceptible process of adding land by the action of water thereby creating dry land that was previously covered by the water. Land may be added or accreted by alluvian or reliction. Accretion by alluvian is the gradual addition made to the land by the action of the water depositing solid material or mud. Accretion by reliction is the gradual and imperceptible addition of land by the recession of the water, whereby water recedes below its previously normal watermark, thereby uncovering previously submerged land. *Brainard v. State*, supra. A change in the boundary is gradual or imperceptible when a person witnessing the boundary from time to time can see that progress is being made but cannot perceive it while the process is occurring. *Denny v. Cotton*, 22 S.W. 122 (Tex. Civ. App. 1893, writ ref'd).

Avulsion is the sudden and perceptible loss or addition of land by the action of the water resulting in a sudden change in the bed or course of the stream. Where a navigable stream suddenly and perceptibly creates a new bed, the owner through whose property the stream now passes loses title to the bed, except for a possibility of reverter, which may again ripen into fee title should the stream bed return to its previous location. The State obtains a determinable fee interest in the newly washed land. The former riparian owners of land abutting on the abandoned bed are entitled to claim the abandoned bed. *Manry v. Robison*, 56 S.W.2d 438 (Tex. 1932). However, the owner of the land lying between the old and the new bed does not lose title to it, even if the land is an island washed by the stream on both sides. *Maufrais v. State*, 180 S.W.2d 144 (Tex. 1944).

Patent survey lines are not supposed to cross navigable streams, Tex. Nat. Res. Code Ann. §21.012(b). Nevertheless, the Small Bill (Tex. Rev. Civ. Stat. Ann. art. 5414a, effective March 3, 1929) validated patents to lands crossing navigable streams where the patent had been issued at least ten years prior to the enactment of the statute (March 3, 1919) and passed title to the bed to the patentee to the extent necessary to convey the number of acres contained in the patent. *Strayhorn v. Jones*, 300 S.W.2d 623 (Tex. 1957) (addressing the Salt Fork of the Brazos Kent County). With regard to stream beds, if a resurvey of the patented acreage reveals more acreage than stated in the patent, then any excess land outside the stream bed must first be utilized to satisfy the patented acreage before any portion of the stream bed acreage will be relinquished to the land owner. If a resurvey reveals excess acreage outside the stream bed, the landowner may make an application for a Deed

of Acquittance to pay for such excess acreage. 31 Tex. Admin. Code Ann. §7.3 (addressing General Land Office, Deeds of Acquittance).

Beginning in 1837, grants by the Republic of Texas and the State of Texas have included title to the beds of non-navigable streams. Thus, if a tract granted on December 14, 1837 or thereafter is bounded by a non-navigable stream, the non-navigable stream bed is owned by the riparian owners to the center or thread of the stream. *City of Victoria v. Schott*, 29 S.W. 681 (Tex. Civ. App. 1895, no writ); *Muller v. Landa*, 31 Tex. 265 (Tex. 1868). The "thread" is typically defined as the center line of the stream as measured from opposite banks. *Border Island Co. v. Cowles Shipyard Co.*, 94 Misc. 340, 348 (N.Y. Sup. Ct. Eq. 1914).

If a non-navigable water course that serves as a boundary changes its location by the gradual and imperceptible processes of accretion and erosion, the boundary will move with movement of the stream and continue to be the center of the stream. *Maufrais v. State*, 180 S.W.2d 144 (Tex. 1944); *Tyler v. Gonzales*, 189 S.W.2d 519 (Tex. Civ. App.—San Antonio 1945, writ ref'd w.o.m.). If a non-navigable stream changes location suddenly through avulsion, leaving its old banks to form new ones, the boundary will remain in the middle of the pre avulsion channel even if the boundary is no longer washed by the waters. *Maufrais v. State*, 180 S.W.2d 144 (Tex. 1944).

Calls in a deed contiguous to a non-navigable stream are presumed to pass title to the center of the stream. *Strayhorn v. Jones*, 300 S.W.2d 623 (Tex. 1957) (applying the "strip-and-gore" doctrine to a stream). This presumption applies even if the land is described by metes and bounds without mention of the stream, or where the description refers to marked corners on the bank that do not correspond to the center of the stream. *Muller v. Landa*, 31 Tex. 265 (1868). If boundary descriptions along non-navigable streams incorporate meander lines, the meander lines do not determine the boundary of the property conveyed, but generally describe the curvature of the banks of the stream, thereby assisting in locating the general course of the stream. Absent avulsion, the actual course of the stream, not surveyed meander lines, determines the boundary. *Strayhorn v. Jones*, 300 S.W.2d 623 (Tex. 1957); *Stover v. Gilbert*, 247 S.W. 841 (Tex. 1923).

For general discussion of streams, see *Brainard v. State*, 12 S.W.3d 6 (Tex. 1999).

Lakes: A natural lake that is navigable belongs to the state. *State v. Bradford*, 50 S.W.2d 1065 (Tex. 1932). A grant from the sovereign of a natural lake that is non-navigable includes the bed of the lake if the patent shows an unmistakable intention to convey the bed. *Taylor Fishing Club v. Hammett*, 88 S.W.2d 127 (Tex. Civ. App.—Waco 1935, writ dism'd). A lake is navigable if "its natural and ordinary condition affords a channel for useful commerce." The "thirty foot statute" discussed above has no application in determining navigability. *Id.*

Calls in an instrument to the edge of the water, high or low watermark, the shore, or the bank of a lake establish the boundary at the edge of the water and exclude the bed of the lake. *Welder v. State*, 196 S.W. 868 (Tex. Civ. App.—Austin 1917, writ ref'd). A boundary may be established by a call for a contour elevation line. *See Ulbricht v. Friedsam*, 325 S.W.2d 669 (Tex. 1959).

CAUTION

This Standard and related comments refer to severances from the sovereign. For purposes of this Standard, the time of "severance" is measured from the effective date of the segregation of the tract from the public domain. An examiner may consult the General Land Office for further information on severance.

Source:

Citations in the Comment; 3 Aloysius A. Leopold, *Land Titles and Title Examination*, ch. 6 (Texas Practice 3d ed. 2005).

History:

Adopted June 11, 2010; amended July 17, 2014.

The prior standard provided: "Although examiners do not determine actual water boundaries on the ground or the character of waters, the following general principles govern riparian and littoral boundaries along tidelands, lakes, and streams. Riparian and littoral boundaries are governed by the applicable law in effect on the date of severance of title from the sovereign. The boundary of a tract bounded by a non-navigable stream is generally located at the thread of the stream. Title to the bed of tidelands and to natural navigable lakes is in the State. Title to the bed of navigable streams is determined by the common law and by the 'thirty-foot' statute. Title to other streams is determined by the law in effect on the date of severance of title from the sovereign. State title to the bed of parts of some streams may be relinquished under the 'Small Bill.'"

STANDARD 5.40. ROADS

Although an examiner does not determine actual land boundaries on the ground, an examiner should consider the possible application of the "strip-and-gore" doctrine. Where applicable, the doctrine generally provides as follows: Unless the instrument expresses a contrary intent, in a conveyance where a road is a boundary of a tract, the conveyance of the tract presumptively conveys the grantor's title to the center of the road and in some cases to the entire road.

Comment

This standard applies the "strip-and-gore" doctrine in the context of roads. For purposes of this standard, "road" includes highways, streets, alleys, railroad rights-of-way, and other types of roads.

The strip-and-gore doctrine is a rule of construction that creates a rebuttable presumption that the grantor of a tract bordering a road intended to convey the grantor's interest in the road—usually to the center of the road—even though apparently excluded or excepted by the terms of the conveyance unless the grantor expressed a clear and unequivocal intent to the contrary. *Rio Bravo Oil Co. v. Weed*, 50 S.W.2d 1080 (Tex. 1932). The doctrine is justified both as a matter of public policy, *Cantley v. Gulf Production Co.*, 143 S.W.2d 912 (Tex. 1940), and on the theory that a grantor is presumed to convey all appurtenant rights incident to the enjoyment of the tract conveyed. *Reagan v. Marathon Oil Co.*, 50 S.W.3d 70 (Tex. App.—Waco 2001, no pet.) The court in *Reagan* discusses the history of the application of the doctrine and applies it to severed minerals.

The doctrine applies even though the calls contained in the metes and bounds description extend only to the edge of the road. *Cox v. Campbell*, 143 S.W.2d 361 (Tex. 1940) (applies the general rule, which the Supreme Court had previously affirmed as to highways and streams, to a railroad right of way). Conveyances with phrases such as "save and except" or "not including the road" are not sufficient to overcome the presumption. *Reagan v. Marathon Oil Co.*, 50 S.W.3d 70 (Tex. App.—Waco 2001, no pet.).

Under the strip-and-gore doctrine, a conveyance of a tract adjoining multiple, adjacent road easements will convey to the center of the easements in the same manner as if they constituted a single easement. *Haines v. McLean*, 276 S.W.2d 777 (Tex. 1955). The doctrine extends to a small tract, even though not a "strip," where the tract is of no further benefit to the grantor. *Alkas v. United Savings Ass'n*, 672 S.W.2d 852 (Tex. App.—Corpus Christi 1984, writ ref'd n.r.e.). A reservation of minerals in the streets of a platted subdivision noted in a developer's dedication plat will not overcome the presumption that the developer's subsequent deed of a lot joining the street conveyed the minerals to the center of the street. *Lackner v. Bybee*, 159 S.W.2d 215 (Tex. Civ. App.—Galveston 1942, writ ref'd w.o.m.).

The doctrine may also apply to governmental entities. *Joslin v. State*, 146 S.W.2d 208 (Tex. Civ. App.—Austin 1940, writ ref'd) (general rule, that adjacent owners own minerals to the center of road easements, applies to patents). *But see Town of Refugio v. Strauch*, 29 S.W.2d 1041 (Tex. Comm'n App. 1930, judgm't adopted) (title to minerals under streets described in a land grant in what were Mexican town lots, such as located in Gonzales, Refugio, Bastrop, Liberty, and Victoria, were vested in the town and not in the lot owners fronting the streets; the term "streets" does not apply in its usual sense where the "street" is not in existence at the time of the conveyance of the property in question) and *Mitchell v. Bass*, 33 Tex. 259 (1870) (applying civil law and rejecting strip-and-gore doctrine where the land at issue had been granted by the Mexican government).

For application of the doctrine to streams see Comments to Standard 5.30.

Caution

The presumption created by the strip-and-gore doctrine may not apply where the land within the easement is relatively "larger and perhaps more valuable" when compared to the adjoining tract specifically conveyed in the instrument. *Angelo v. Biscamp*, 441 S.W.2d 524, 527 (Tex. 1969).

The presumption will not apply where no road, alley, or easement exists at the time of the grant, and the property description excludes the narrow strip from the acreage being conveyed. *Goldsmith v. Humble Oil & Ref'g Co.*, 199 S.W.2d 773 (Tex. 1947).

Nevertheless, the doctrine similarly applies where the roadway is located entirely within the grantor's land, although along a boundary, and the grantor does not own land on the other side of the road. Thus, where the conveyance contained a property description that referred to the edge of the road as the boundary, the instrument was construed to convey the grantor's interest underlying the entire road. *Cantley v. Gulf Production Co.*, 143 S.W.2d 912 (Tex. 1940). Likewise, when a road is adjacent to navigable waters, a deed describing the land bounded by a road conveys the fee of the entire tract including the land underlying the marginal roadway. *State v. Arnim*, 173 S.W.2d 503 (Tex. Civ. App.—San Antonio, 1943, writ ref'd w.o.m.) (road was adjacent to Nueces Bay and lots were adjacent to the road).

Finally, although this standard is limited to roads, the doctrine has been applied to small strips or parcels

of land that do not comprise a road or easement. *See, e.g., Alkas v. United Savings Ass'n*, 672 S.W.2d 852, 857 (Tex. App.—Corpus Christi 1984, writ ref'd n.r.e.) (applying the doctrine to a 2.1467-acre non-road tract out of a 146.584-acre tract). In *Alkas*, the court stated that, for the doctrine to apply: (1) the tract must be small in comparison to the land conveyed; (2) the tract must be adjacent to or surrounded by the land conveyed; (3) title to the tract and the adjacent or surrounding tract must be in the same grantor at the time of the conveyance; and (4) the tract, by itself, must be of no apparent benefit or importance to the grantor at the time of the conveyance. *Id.* at 857. At least one court has cited the four principles of Alkas in a road context. *See Escondido Services, LLC v. VKM Holdings, LP*, 321 S.W.3d 102 (Tex. App.—Eastland 2010, no pet.).

Whether application of the strip-and-gore doctrine grants marketable title to a strip or a gore is uncertain. *See* Standard 2.10 (discussing marketable title).

Source:

Citations in the Comment.

History:

Adopted June 24, 2011; amended July 17, 2014.

The prior standard provided: "Although examiners do not determine actual land boundaries on the ground, an examiner should consider the possible application of the 'strip-and-gore' doctrine. Where applicable, the doctrine generally provides as follows: Unless the instrument expresses a contrary intent, in a conveyance where a road is a boundary of a tract, the conveyance of the tract presumptively conveys the grantor's title to the center of the road and in some cases to the entire road."

STANDARD 5.50. EASEMENTS

An examiner should identify and note as an encumbrance all easements of record affecting the title under examination. Certain title examinations may require the examiner to determine additional information about easements.

COMMENT

Customarily, when conducting an examination of surface title, mineral title, or both an examiner does not trace and determine ownership resulting from transfers of an easement or provide detailed information concerning the easement unless such information is material to the transaction prompting the title examination.

Unrecorded easements may encumber the property under examination. The existence of such easements can only be determined by a physical inspection of the property. An examiner typically does not conduct an on-the-ground inspection of the property. If a physical inspection of the property is conducted to determine the existence or location of easements, the client typically arranges it.

An examiner may be retained to examine easement title. In this circumstance, the examiner should ascertain what information the client needs and conduct the examination accordingly.

An easement is a non-possessory right to use the property of another. The owner of the burdened property is bound to permit certain acts by another, such as to pass over it (affirmative easement) or to not do certain acts that would otherwise be lawful, such as constructing a building if it would interrupt another's view (negative easement). *Miller v. Babb*, 263 S.W. 253, 254 (Tex. Comm'n App.1924, judgm't adopted). An easement is an interest in land, distinguishable from a license or permit that merely confers a personal and generally revocable privilege to do some act on the land and is generally not assignable. A license in land does not grant any interest in or title to the real property, and a license need not be in writing. *Arant v. Jaffe*, 436 S.W.2d 169 (Tex. Civ. App.—Dallas 1968, no writ).

An easement may be private or public. There are two types of easements: an easement in gross and an easement appurtenant. An easement appurtenant attaches to and runs with the benefitted land. The benefitted land is the dominant estate, and the land burdened by the easement is the servient estate. *Pokorny v. Yudin*, 188 S.W.2d 185 (Tex. Civ. App.—El Paso 1945, no writ). An easement is not presumed to be in gross when it can fairly be construed to be appurtenant. *Ginther v. Bammel*, 336 S.W.2d 759, 763 (Tex. Civ. App.—Waco 1960, no writ). "Whether an easement is in gross or appurtenant must be determined by the fair interpretation of the grant or reservation creating the easement, aided, if necessary, by the situation of the property and the surrounding circumstances." *Stuart v. Larrabee*, 14 S.W.2d 316, 318 (Tex. Civ. App.—Beaumont 1929, writ ref'd) quoting 19 C.J. 868.

Generally, easements of passage or of ingress and egress are easements appurtenant. *Coleman v. Forister*, 514 S.W.2d 899 (Tex. 1974). When a dominant estate is conveyed, the conveyance transfers the benefit of all appurtenant easements even though not expressed in the deed. *West v. Giesen*, 242 S.W. 312, 319 (Tex. Civ. App.—Austin 1922, writ ref'd).

Easements in gross benefit a party rather than a dominant estate. Generally, public road, railroad, utility,

and pipeline easements are in gross; however, oil and gas gathering lines are typically appurtenant. At common law an easement in gross is not transferable since allowing the transfer of the personal privilege would be an added servitude on the land unless the instrument creating the easement expressly states that the easement is being transferred to the grantee and its successors and assigns or other language expressing an intent that the easement is assignable. *Southtex 66 Pipeline Co. v. Spoor*, 238 S.W.3d 538 (Tex. App.—Houston [14th Dist.] 2007, pet. denied); *Cantu v. Central Power & Light Co.*, 38 S.W.2d 876 (Tex. Civ. App. 1931, writ refused) and *Williams v. Humble Pipe Line Co.*, 417 S.W.2d 453 (Tex. Civ. App.—Houston 1967, no writ). Absent language to the contrary in the instrument or consent of the owner of the burdened land, the owner of an easement in gross cannot transfer part of its easement to another party. *Fort Worth & R.G. Ry. Co. v. Jennings*, 13 S.W. 270 (Tex. 1890) (addressing the conveyance of part of an easement not in use to another party to build a road); *Marcus Cable Associates, L.P. v. Krohn*, 90 S.W.3d 697 (Tex. 2002) (holding that an electric company owning an easement for constructing and maintaining transmission or distribution lines could not authorize a cable company to use the easement for installing cable television lines). However, pipeline easements are ordinarily assignable in whole or in part where the resulting use does not burden the underlying land beyond what was contemplated in the original grant. *Orange County, Inc. v. Citgo Pipeline Co.*, 934 S.W.2d 472 (Tex. App.—Beaumont 1996, writ denied).

The Texas Utility Code provides for use of public rights-of-way (roads, streets, alleys, water and other municipal property with the consent of the governing body) by gas companies (§181.005 and §181.022), by electric utilities (§181.042), by telephone and telegraph companies (§181.082), and by television cable services (§181.102). Once created, the uses to which public right-of-way easements can be used have been broadly construed. An easement for city streets includes the right for the municipality to lay sewer, gas, and water lines. *West Texas Utilities Co. v. City of Baird*, 286 S.W.2d 185 (Tex. Civ. App.—Eastland 1956, writ ref'd n.r.e.). An easement for a state highway includes the right for a public utility company to lay a gas pipeline within the easement. *Grimes v. Corpus Christi Transmission Co.*, 829 S.W.2d 335, 337 (Tex. App.—Corpus Christi 1992, writ denied).

Private easements may be created by deed, implication, estoppel and prescription. Public easements may be created by deed, dedication, prescription, and condemnation.

An easement is an incorporeal interest in land and may be created by grant, covenant, or agreement, express or implied. *Settegast v. Foley Bros. Dry Goods Co.*, 270 S.W. 1014 (Tex. 1925). Where an easement is conveyed or transferred by deed it may be recorded. Tex. Prop. Code Ann. §12.001. The Statute of Frauds applies to conveyances of easements. *Callan v. Walters*, 190 S.W. 829 (Tex. Civ. App.—Austin 1916, no writ). Land descriptions must be described with the same certainty in instruments that create easements as in other instruments. *Compton v. Texas Southeastern Gas Co.*, 315 S.W.2d 345 (Tex. Civ. App.—Houston 1958, writ ref'd n.r.e.). *See* Standard 5.10 for additional discussion of land descriptions.

The exact location of the easement need not be established in the instrument, but the burdened tract must be sufficiently identified. *Elias v. Horak*, 292 S.W. 288 (Tex. Civ. App.—Austin 1927, writ ref'd). A grant in general terms of a right to lay a pipeline across the land of the grantor without specifying the place for laying it or the size of the pipe is made certain by the act of the grantee in laying the pipe. Once the pipe is laid with the acquiescence of the grantor, the grant, which was general and indefinite, becomes fixed and certain, and the grantee cannot change the easement either by relocating the pipe or by increasing its size. *Dwyer v. Houston Pipe Line Co.*, 374 S.W.2d 662 (Tex.1964) (holding that the rights created by the easement had become fixed when the 18-inch line had been constructed and that the pipeline company had no right to remove the line and replace it with a 30-inch high pressure line). In *Pioneer Natural Gas Co. v. Russell*, 453 S.W.2d 882, 886 (Tex. Civ. App.—Amarillo 1970, writ ref'd n.r.e.) the deed at issue granted a right-of-way of sufficient width to permit grantee to lay parallel pipelines. When the grantee laid an eight-inch pipe the grant became fixed and certain, and the grantee could not, 40 years later, lay a ten-inch pipe parallel to the first.

Implied easements for road access may arise by necessity. *Bains v. Parker*, 182 S.W.2d 397 (Tex. 1944). Implied easements by way of necessity for road access may be created by implication where a grantor conveys part of a tract in a manner that results in landlocking either the part conveyed or the part retained. Strict ne-

cessity only exists when there is no other way of access. *Duff v. Matthews*, 311 S.W.2d 637 (Tex. 1958). In addition the necessity must have existed at the time of the severance of the tract. *Waggoner v. Cleburne*, 378 S.W.2d 47 (Tex. 1964). Implied easements by way of necessity terminate when the necessity terminates. *Bains v. Parker*, 182 S.W.2d 397 (Tex. 1944).

An implied easement by prior use, sometimes called a quasi-easement, can be established in appropriate circumstances for purposes other than roads. An implied easement for a road cannot be established by prior use in the absence of necessity, *Hamrick v. Ward*, 446 S.W.3d 377 (Tex. 2014); however, other existing uses may give rise to an implied easement by prior use. *See, e.g.*, *Westbrook v. Wright*, 477 S.W.2d 663 (Tex. Civ. App.—Houston [14th Dist.] 1972, no writ) (sewer line) and *Seber v. Union Pac. R.R. Co.*, 350 S.W.3d 640 (Tex. App.—Houston [14th Dist.] 2011, no pet.) (private railroad crossing). A quasi-easement rests upon the principle that where an owner who grants part of a tract also grants by implication all those apparent and visible easements that are necessary for the reasonable use of the property granted. Reasonable necessity is sufficient for an implied easement by prior use to arise in favor of the granted land across the retained land even though alternate but inconvenient access may exist. Strict necessity is generally required for an implied easement by prior use to arise in favor of the retained land across the granted land. *Scarborough v. Anderson Bros. Constr. Co.*, 90 S.W.2d 305 (Tex. Civ. App.—El Paso 1936, writ dism'd); *Heard v. Roos*, 885 S.W.2d 592 (Tex. App.—Corpus Christi 1994, no writ). Unlike easements by necessity, easements established by prior use do not terminate when alternative access becomes available. *Harrington v. Dawson Conway Ranch, Ltd.*, 372 S.W.3d 711 (Tex. App.—Eastland 2012, pet. denied).

An easement by estoppel may arise when a representation recognizing an easement was (1) communicated, (2) believed and (3) relied upon. *Doss v. Blackstock*, 466 S.W.2d 59 (Tex. Civ. App.—Austin 1971, writ ref'd n.r.e.) For example, the principle of estoppel applies where the grantor has exhibited a map or plat showing the existence of an easement, such as a street or alley, and the grantee has been induced to accept the grant, where the natural inference of those who consulted the map or plat with a view to purchase would be that the street or alley would be available for the benefit of their use. *Birnberg v. Sparks*, 410 S.W.2d 789 (Tex. Civ. App.—Corpus Christi 1966, writ ref n.r.e.) An easement by estoppel cannot arise solely from passive acquiescence; where there has been no promise or representation there can be no estoppel. *Stallman v. Newman*, 9 S.W.3d 243 (Tex. App.—Houston [14th Dist.] 1999, pet. denied).

Prescriptive easements arise in much the same manner as title accrues by adverse possession; however adverse possession ripens into title to the land and a prescriptive right matures into an easement. To burden a party's land with an easement by prescription, the plaintiff must show that his use of the land was: (1) open and notorious; (2) adverse to the owner's claim of right; (3) exclusive; (4) uninterrupted; and (5) continuous for a period of ten years. *Brooks v. Jones*, 578 S.W.2d 669 (Tex.1979). Burdening another's property with a prescriptive easement is not well regarded in the law. *Wiegand v. Riojas*, 547 S.W.2d 287 (Tex. Civ. App.—Austin 1977, no writ). A mere use by permission or license never ripens into an easement by prescription, no matter how long it continues. *Dailey v. Alarid*, 486 S.W.2d 620 (Tex. Civ. App.—Tyler 1972, writ ref n.r.e.); *Othen v. Rosier*, 226 S.W.2d 622 (Tex.1950).

Both public and private easements may arise by prescription, but the public easement requires continuous use by the public for ten years, rather than by one or a few individuals. On the other hand, a person may not acquire through adverse possession any right or title to real property dedicated to public use. Tex. Civ. Prac. & Rem. Code Ann. §16.030. In effect the public can acquire a public prescriptive easement over private land, but a private individual cannot acquire a private prescriptive easement across public land.

A public easement may be acquired through condemnation, exercisable through the power of eminent domain by a governmental entity as conferred by statute. *Crawford v. Frio County*, 153 S.W. 388 (Tex. Civ. App.—San Antonio 1913, no writ). For condemnation procedure, see Tex. Prop. Code Ann. §§21.011 through 21.016. Unless otherwise provided in the judgment, a pipeline easement created through the power of eminent domain is presumed to create an easement that extends only to a width of 50 feet as to each pipeline laid under the judgment. Tex. Nat. Res. Code Ann. §111.0194.

Dedication is the most common means by which a public easement arises. *Scott v. Cannon*, 959 S.W.2d 712(Tex. App.—Austin 1998, pet. denied). There are

two types of dedication: statutory and common law, but both types require intent on the part of the landowner to dedicate (or set apart) the easement for use by the public and a reciprocal acceptance of the easement by the public. Statutory dedication must be carried out in compliance with all relevant statutes. If land is located in a municipality or its extraterritorial jurisdiction Chapter 212 of the Texas Local Government Code governs. If the land is located in a rural area (outside of the extra-territorial jurisdiction of a municipality), Chapter 232 of the Texas Local Government Code controls. As for dedications occurring after 1980 in counties having a population of 50,000 or less Chapter 281 of the Texas Transportation Code addresses the procedure. Chapter 183 of the Texas Natural Resources Code and Chapter 184 of the Texas Parks and Wildlife Code authorize and govern conservation easements that impose restrictions or obligations concerning land use designed to protect natural, environmental, historical, and other specified values.

Common law dedications may be either express or implied. *Jezek v. City of Midland*, 605 S.W.2d 544 (Tex. 1980); however in 1981 the Legislature abolished the common law doctrine of implied dedication as a means of establishing that a particular road running through private property was a public road. *See* Act of May 31, 1981, 67th Leg., R.S., ch. 613, §§1, 2 & 4, 1981 Tex. Gen. Laws 2412 (current version at Tex. Transp. Code Ann. §§281.002, 281.003). An express dedication may be declared orally or in writing; however in a county with a population of less than 50,000 the dedication must be in writing. Tex. Transp. Code Ann. §281.003. For a dedication to the public to occur certain elements must be present: (1) an intention of the landowner to devote his land to public use, (2) a manifestation of the landowner's intention through his words or acts, and a communication to the public or some portion thereof and (3) an acceptance of the use of the property by the public. *King v. Walton*, 576 S.W.2d 460, (Tex. Civ. App.—San Antonio 1979, writ ref'd n.r.e.). Acceptance may be implied by the conduct of the public, which binds the dedicator. *Gilder v. City of Brenham*, 3 S.W. 309 (Tex. 1887).

The recording of a map or plat, which shows streets or roadways thereon, without more, does not as a matter of law constitute a dedication of such streets as public roadways. *Aransas County v. Reif*, 532 S.W.2d 131 (Tex. Civ. App.—Corpus Christi 1975, writ ref'd n.r.e.), citing *County of Calhoun v. Wilson*, 425 S.W.2d 846 (Tex. Civ. App.—Corpus Christi 1968, writ ref'd n.r.e.). However, the filing and approval of a plat, which undertakes to dedicate streets and roads does not make them public roads since dedication is a mere offer and filing does not constitute an acceptance. *Langford v. Kraft*, 498 S.W.2d 42 (Tex. Civ. App.—Beaumont 1973, writ ref'd n.r.e.).

Easements may terminate through abandonment, operation of law, adverse possession, merger, or cessation of purpose. An easement may be lost by abandonment through a long period of non-use, coupled with intent to abandon. Intent to abandon an easement "must be established by clear and satisfactory evidence." *Milligan v. Niebuhr*, 990 S.W.2d 823, 826 (Tex. App.—Austin 1999, no pet.). Abandonment of an easement will not result from non-use alone; instead, the "circumstances must disclose some definite act showing an intention to abandon and terminate the right possessed by the easement owner." *Id. Dallas County v. Miller*, 166 S.W.2d 922 (Tex. 1942). "Abandonment occurs where the use for which the property is dedicated becomes impossible of execution or the object of the use wholly fails. In general, misuser does not constitute abandonment unless the dedicated use becomes impossible; but an abandonment may be effected by the substitution of new property for the old for a particular use." *Adams v. Rowles*, 228 S.W.2d 849, 852 (Tex. 1950) citing 26 C.J.S., Dedication, §63a, p. 151. An easement may be abandoned by cessation of the defined purpose of the easement or terminated by the completion of the purpose for which it is granted. *Woodmen of the World v. Goodman*, 193 S.W.2d 739 (Tex. Civ. App.—Dallas 1945, no writ.) A county road is abandoned when its use has become so infrequent that one or more adjoining property owners have enclosed the road with a fence continuously for at least 20 years. Tex. Trans. Code Ann. §251.057(a); the section does not apply to a road to a cemetery or an access road that is reasonably necessary to reach adjoining real property.

An easement may be extinguished by operation of law, such as a sale under a deed of trust created prior to the easement. *Cousins v. Sperry*, 139 S.W.2d 665 (Tex. Civ. App.—Beaumont 1940, no writ.); *Lavigne v. Holder*, 186 S.W.3d 625 (Tex. App.—Fort Worth 2006, no pet.)

Easements may also be lost by adverse possession; however, continued use of the property subject to the

easement by the party granting the easement would not be deemed adverse unless the continued use was inconsistent with and hostile to the grantees and their assigns over the limitation period. *Henry v. Roundtree*, 354 S.W.2d 604 (Tex. Civ. App.—Dallas 1962, writ ref'd n.r.e.).

An easement may also be extinguished by merger. Since the dominant and the servient tenements must be held by different parties for an appurtenant easement to exist a merger of the two tenements, as in the case of the dominant owner's purchase of the servient tenement, extinguishes the existing easement. *Howell v. Estes*, 12 S.W. 62 (Tex. 1888).

An easement is extinguished when the purpose and reason for which it was acquired or granted ceases or has been fulfilled. *Scott v. Walden*, 165 S.W.2d 449 (Tex. 1942).

Where a road easement forms a boundary of the land, the underlying title ordinarily extends to the center of the road, but may extend, in some cases, to the entire road. *See* Standard 5.40, Roads (discussing the "strip-and-gore" doctrine).

Where land is adjacent to a shore title, it may be encumbered by an easement in favor of the public in a beach area. *See* Comment to Standard 5.30, Water Boundaries (discussing Tidelands).

Effective October 1, 1991, Procedural Rule P-37 was adopted by the Texas State Board of Insurance regarding guaranteeing the right of access in a title insurance policy. All title policies issued after that date ensure the right of access unless a specific exception is added. Neither the width of the access nor access to a public thoroughfare is insured.

CAUTION

The examiner must carefully examine instruments labeled "easements" to determine if the fee to the land is conveyed instead of a mere right of use. Where the instrument conveys the land, and not a "right-of-way, privilege or easement over the land," it is a conveyance in fee simple, as distinguished from an easement, even though such instrument may contain recitals attempting to limit the use of the land for a recited purpose. *Texas Elec. Ry. Co. v. Neale*, 252 S.W.2d 451 (Tex. 1952). The term "right-of-way" in an instrument is generally construed as describing or denoting only an easement. *Right of Way Oil Co. v. Gladys City Oil, Gas & Mfg. Co.*, 157 S.W. 737 (Tex. 1913). However, in *S.H. Oil & Royalty Co. v. Texas & New Orleans R. Co.* 295 S.W.2d 227 (Tex. Civ. App.—Beaumont 1956, writ ref'd n.r.e.), the court held that the reservation of "the 100 foot right-of-way" retained in the railroad title in fee to the land covered by the "right-of-way" and that the term "right-of-way" did not imply reservation of an easement.

Source:

Citations in the Comment; 3 Aloysius A. Leopold, *Land Titles and Title Examination* §§331-332, 356, 371-385, 436 (Texas Practice 3d ed. 2005).

History:

Adopted July 17, 2014.

CHAPTER VI. CORPORATE CONVEYANCES

STANDARD 6.10. CORPORATE EXISTENCE

Where a corporation is a named party to an instrument in the chain of title, an examiner may presume that the corporation was legally in existence at the time the instrument took effect, if the instrument is executed and acknowledged in the proper form.

COMMENT

A corporation may exist in fact without being legally constituted. It is therefore unnecessary, in examining title, to investigate in detail whether all measures have been taken for valid incorporation, so long as the record shows the existence of a corporation de facto. Rufford G. Patton & Carroll G. Patton, *Patton on Land Titles* §405 (2d ed. 1957 and Supp. 1997) and Paul E. Basye, *Clearing Land Titles* §§296-301 (2d ed. 1970).

CAUTION

This standard conforms to the standard practice of Texas title examiners. No Texas cases are directly on point. However, in *Allday v. Drummond*, 280 S.W.2d 381 (Tex. Civ. App.—Fort Worth 1955, writ ref'd n.r.e.), the court sustained a conveyance by a foreign corporation at a time when the corporate grantor's charter had been forfeited by the State of Delaware for nonpayment of taxes. A primary basis for the court's holding was that the conveyance in question had been of record more than 10 years.

Source:

Lewis M. Simes & Clarence B. Taylor, *Model Title Standards*, Std. 12.4 (1960); 4 Aloysius A. Leopold, *Land Titles and Title Examination* §22.16 (Texas Practice 3d ed. 2005).

History:

Adopted June 27, 1997.

STANDARD 6.20. CORPORATE AUTHORITY PRESUMED

In the absence of actual or constructive notice to the contrary, an examiner may presume that the action of the corporation in acquiring or selling the real property affected by an instrument is within its power.

COMMENT

Any action taken by a corporation that is beyond the power conferred upon it by its articles of incorporation or by the laws of the state of its incorporation is ultra vires. This may include action contrary to public policy or to some statute expressly prohibiting such action. This excess or abuse of power is ordinarily not within the scope of an examiner to determine or question, without some type of actual or constructive notice.

Source:

Lewis M. Simes & Clarence B. Taylor, *Model Title Standards*, Std. 12.5 (1960); 4 Aloysius A. Leopold, *Land Titles and Title Examination* §22.16 (Texas Practice 3d ed. 2005).

History:

Adopted June 27, 1997.

STANDARD 6.30. FOREIGN CORPORATIONS

Where a corporation organized and doing business under the laws of another state is a named party to an instrument in the chain of title, an examiner may presume that the corporation was authorized to do business in this state or authorized to acquire and dispose of the real property affected by the instrument, if the instrument is executed and acknowledged in the proper form.

COMMENT

At one time, both foreign and domestic corporations were prohibited from owning land in Texas except under certain narrow circumstances. However, those statutory prohibitions were repealed in 1981. *See* Historical and Statutory Notes at Misc. Corp. Laws Act, Tex. Rev. Civ. Stat. Ann. arts. 1302-4.01 to 1302-4.07. Even then a foreign corporation without qualifying to do business in Texas could own and convey title unless its right to do so was challenged by the state. *Byerly v. Camey*, 161 S.W.2d 1105, 1110 (Tex. Civ. App.—Fort Worth 1942, writ ref'd w.o.m.). Under present law, the holding of title in Texas land by a foreign corporation may constitute the doing of business in Texas, but its failure to register will not "affect the validity of any contract or act" of the corporation. Tex. Bus. Org. Code Ann. §§9.051, 9.202.

Source:

Citations in the Comment; Lewis M. Simes & Clarence B. Taylor, *Model Title Standards*, Std. 12.6 (1960).

History:

Adopted June 27, 1997.

STANDARD 6.40. CORPORATE SEAL

An examiner may presume that a corporate seal does not have to appear on an instrument, unless the examiner has actual or constructive notice that the bylaws of the corporation require the seal to have been placed on the instrument.

COMMENT

Subject to any approval required by the Texas Business Organizations Code or by the governing body of the corporation, a corporation may convey land by a deed, with or without the seal of the corporation, that is signed by an officer, authorized attorney-in-fact, or other authorized person.

Source:

Tex. Bus. Org. Code Ann. §§9.202, 10.251, 10.253.

History:

Adopted June 27, 1997.

STANDARD 6.50. AUTHORITY OF PARTICULAR OFFICERS

Where a corporation is a named party to an instrument in the chain of title, an examiner may presume that the persons executing the instrument were the officers they purported to be and that such officers were authorized to execute the instrument on behalf of the corporation, if the instrument is executed and acknowledged in the proper form.

COMMENT

A conveyance that is signed and acknowledged by an officer, an authorized attorney-in-fact, or other authorized person of a corporation and recorded is prima facie evidence that the conveyance was duly authorized under the Texas Business Organizations Code and the governing documents of the corporation. Tex. Bus. Org. Code Ann. §§9.202, 10.253.

Prior to August 28, 1989, the presumption of corporate authority only extended to conveyances executed by the president or a vice president. Acts 1955, 54th Leg., p. 239, ch. 64. Accordingly, instruments that are executed by another officer prior to the amendments should be accompanied by a showing of the officer's authority. However, if the instrument has been recorded for more than four years (two years, effective September 1, 2007, prospective only), such authority may be

presumed. Tex. Civ. Prac. & Rem. Code Ann. §16.033. Act of June 15, 2007, 80th Leg., R.S., ch. 819, §2, 2007 Tex. Gen. Laws 1695 (nonretroactivity provision).

CAUTION

The presumption of corporate authority applies to corporate officers and not to an attorney in fact. The examiner should look to the power of attorney to determine the authority of the attorney in fact. For further information on attorneys in fact, see Standards 8.10 and 8.20.

Source:

Paul E. Basye, *Clearing Land Titles* §293 (2d ed. 1970); Lewis M. Simes & Clarence B. Taylor, *Model Title Standards*, Std. 12.3 (1960).

History:

Adopted June 27, 1997.

STANDARD 6.60. CORPORATE NAME OR SIGNER'S REPRESENTATIVE CAPACITY OMITTED FROM SIGNATURE

Where a corporation appears as a party in the body of the instrument, an examiner may presume that the signature on the instrument by a corporate representative is sufficient notwithstanding the omission of the corporate name or the signer's representative capacity, or both, within the signature block.

COMMENT

There are no reported Texas cases validating corporate deeds where no corporate capacity of the signer is disclosed. However, analogous Texas case law generally holds that a deed executed by an individual acting in an apparent representative capacity passes whatever title the individual has the authority to convey. Regarding the failure of an instrument to reflect the authority of the signer, see generally *Hough v. Hill*, 47 Tex. 148, 153 (1877); *Odell v. Kennedy*, 64 S.W. 802 (Tex. Civ. App.1901, writ ref'd); *Bennett v. Virginia Ranch, Land & Cattle Co.*, 21 S.W. 126 (Tex. Civ. App.1892, no writ); *Pride Exploration, Inc. v. Marshall Exploration, Inc.*, 798 F.2d 864, 866-67 (5th Cir.1986); *Sheldon v. Farinacci*, 535 S.W.2d 938 (Tex. Civ. App.—San Antonio 1976, no writ).

Although some courts have broadly stated that an instrument conveys whatever right the person making it had to convey, in whatever capacity, a conveyance by an individual who is an officer of a corporation does not convey the interest of the corporation unless the name of the corporation appears in the instrument as grantor. *Rogers v. Ricane Enterprises, Inc.*, 884 S.W.2d 763 (Tex. 1994).

Note that Tex. Civ. Prac. & Rem. Code Ann. §16.033 may cure the problems addressed by this standard. For further discussion, see comments to Standards 4.10 and 4.20.

Source:

Lewis M. Simes & Clarence B. Taylor, *Model Title Standards*, Std. 12.2 (1960).

History:

Adopted June 27, 1997; amended July 17, 2014.

The prior standard provided: "Where a corporation appears as a party in the body of the instrument and the instrument is otherwise properly executed and acknowledged, an examiner may presume that the signature on the instrument by a corporate representative is sufficient notwithstanding the omission of the corporate name over such signature."

STANDARD 6.70. NAME VARIANCES

Although their exact names are not used and variations exist from instrument to instrument, an examiner may presume that a corporation is satisfactorily identified if, from the name(s) used and other circumstances of record, the identity of the corporation can be inferred with reasonable certainty. Variances that an examiner may ordinarily ignore include the addition or omission of the word "the" preceding the name; the use or non-use of the symbol "&" for the word "and"; the use or non-use of abbreviations for "company," "limited," "corporation" or "incorporated"; and the inclusion or omission of all or part of a place or a location. An examiner may exercise a greater degree of liberality with a greater lapse of time and in the absence of circumstances appearing of record that raise reasonable doubt as to the identity of the corporation. An examiner may rely on affidavits and recitals of identity to obviate variances too substantial or too significant to be ignored.

COMMENT

Although corporations frequently have closely corresponding names, a purported conveyance by an interloper seems extremely unlikely. The significance of a variance should be evaluated on the basis of ascertaining the actual identity of the corporation, and not on the basis of mechanical perfection. Although Texas courts, in the context of a conveyance, have not addressed the effect of a variance in a corporate name, several cases in which slight name variances were held immaterial amply support this standard. *Wandelohr v. Rainey*, 100 S.W. 1155, 1157 (Tex. 1907) (holding that an appeal bond was effective despite the omission of the words "of Sherman" from the name of a bank); *Texas Electric Service Co. v. Commercial Standard Insurance Co.*, 592 S.W.2d 677, 683-84 (Tex. Civ. App.—

Fort Worth 1979, writ ref'd n.r.e.) (holding a suit on a performance bond could be maintained despite the principal's misnomer in the bond as Everman Park Development "Corporation" instead of its true name, Everman Park Development "Co., Inc."); *Houston Land & Loan Co. v. Danley*, 131 S.W. 1143 (Tex. Civ. App. 1910, no writ) (holding that a note executed in the name of "Houston Land & Loan Company" could be enforced against the maker under its true name of "Houston Loan & Land Company"). An entity doing business in Texas is prohibited from using a name that is the same as, deceptively similar to, or similar to, a name of another existing filing entity or that is reserved or registered under the Tex. Bus. Org. Code Ann. §§5.053, 5.102, 5.153, 9.105.

Source:

Lewis M. Simes & Clarence B. Taylor, *Model Title Standards*, Std. 12.1 (1960); *Oklahoma Title Examination Standards*, Std 12.1; Paul E. Basye, *Clearing Land Titles* §19 (2d ed. 1970).

History:

Adopted June 27, 1997.

PROPOSED STANDARD 6.70. NAME VARIANCES

Although their exact names are not used and variations exist from instrument to instrument, an examiner may presume that a corporation is satisfactorily identified if, from the name(s) used and other circumstances of record, the identity of the corporation can be inferred with reasonable certainty. Variances that an examiner may ordinarily ignore include the addition or omission of the word "the" preceding the name; the use or non-use of the symbol "&" for the word "and"; the use or non-use of abbreviations for "company," "limited," "corporation," "incorporated," "limited liability company," "partnership," and the like; and the inclusion or omission of all or part of a place or a location. An examiner may exercise a greater degree of liberality with a greater lapse of time and in the absence of circumstances appearing of record that raise reasonable doubt as to the identity of the corporation. An examiner may rely on affidavits and recitals of identity to obviate variances too substantial or too significant to be ignored.

COMMENT

Although corporations frequently have closely corresponding names, a purported conveyance by an interloper seems extremely unlikely. The significance of a variance should be evaluated on the basis of ascertaining the actual identity of the corporation, and not on the basis of mechanical perfection. Although Texas courts, in the context of a conveyance, have not addressed the effect of a variance in a corporate name, several cases in which slight name variances were held immaterial amply support this standard. *Wandelohr v. Rainey*, 100 S.W. 1155, 1157 (Tex. 1907) (holding that an appeal bond was effective despite the omission of the words "of Sherman" from the name of a bank); *Texas Electric Service Co. v. Commercial Standard Insurance Co.*, 592 S.W.2d 677, 683-84 (Tex. Civ. App.—Fort Worth 1979, writ ref'd n.r.e.) (holding a suit on a performance bond could be maintained despite the principal's misnomer in the bond as Everman Park Development "Corporation" instead of its true name, Everman Park Development "Co., Inc."); *Houston Land & Loan Co. v. Danley*, 131 S.W. 1143 (Tex. Civ. App. 1910, no writ) (holding that a note executed in the name of "Houston Land & Loan Company" could be enforced against the maker under its true name of "Houston Loan & Land Company"). An entity doing business in Texas is prohibited from using a name that is the same as, deceptively similar to, or similar to, a name of another existing filing entity or that is reserved or registered under the Tex. Bus. Org. Code Ann. §§5.053, 5.102, 5.153, 9.105.

Some examiners choose to rely on information from the Secretary of State that, although not imparting constructive notice, indicates a change in entity name or status, merger, or conversion.

Source:

Lewis M. Simes & Clarence B. Taylor, *Model Title Standards*, Std. 12.1 (1960); *Oklahoma Title Examination Standards*, Std 12.1; Paul E. Basye, *Clearing Land Titles* §19 (2d ed. 1970).

History:

As of the date of publication, the proposed amendments to Standard 6.70 have not been adopted.

CHAPTER VII. CONVEYANCES INVOLVING PARTNERSHIPS, JOINT VENTURES, LIMITED LIABILITY COMPANIES, & UNINCORPORATED ASSOCIATIONS

STANDARD 7.10. CONVEYANCE OF REAL PROPERTY HELD IN PARTNERSHIP OR JOINT VENTURE NAME

When title to real property is held in the name of a partnership or joint venture, an examiner may rely upon a conveyance by a general partner on behalf of the partnership or by a joint venturer on behalf of the joint venture if the conveyance appears to be a transfer in the ordinary course of business of the partnership or joint venture.

COMMENT

Each partner is an agent of the partnership for the purpose of its business. The act of a partner performed for the apparent purpose of carrying on in the ordinary course the partnership business or business of the kind carried on by the partnership binds the partnership unless: (1) the partner in fact had no such authority, and (2) the person with whom the partner is dealing had knowledge of the lack of authority. Tex. Bus. Org. Code Ann. §§152.301, 152.302.

The Texas Uniform Partnership Act, effective January 1, 1962, which expired January 1, 1999, applied to all general partnerships formed under its provisions prior to January 1, 1994, except those that timely elected to adopt the Texas Revised Partnership Act. Tex. Rev. Partnership Act, Tex. Rev. Civ. Stat. Ann. art. 6132b-11.04. The Texas Revised Partnership Act applies to all partnerships formed on or after January 1, 1994, to all partnerships formed before that date and that, before January 1, 1999, elected to adopt the Act, and to all partnerships formed after December 31, 1998, but before January 1, 2006. The Texas Bus. Org. Code, effective January 1, 2006, applies to all partnerships formed on or after January 1, 2006, to all partnerships formed before that date and that elect to adopt the Code, and to all partnerships after December 31, 2009. Tex. Bus. Org. Code Ann. §401.001.

A general partner of a limited partnership has the rights and powers of a partner in a partnership without limited partners. Tex. Rev. Ltd. Partnership Act, Tex. Bus. Org. Code Ann. §153.152 provides that such rights and powers may be negated by the Code, other limited partnership provisions, or the limited partnership agreement.

Source:

Citations in the Comment; 4 Aloysius A. Leopold, *Land Titles and Title Examination* §22.17 (Texas Practice 3d ed. 2005).

History:

Adopted June 27, 1997.

STANDARD 7.20. AUTHORITY OF LESS THAN ALL PARTNERS REGARDING TRANSACTIONS THAT ARE NOT IN THE ORDINARY COURSE OF BUSINESS

If a conveyance of a joint venture or a partnership that is executed by less than all of the joint venturers or partners appears not to be in the ordinary course of business (such as a sale of the sole asset of the partnership), an examiner should review a copy of the partnership or joint venture agreement or other satisfactory evidence to verify the authority of the signing partner(s) or joint venturer(s) to act on behalf of the partnership or joint venture.

COMMENT

A partnership is not bound by an act of a partner that is not apparently for the carrying on of the business of the partnership in the usual way, unless that act has been authorized by the partners. Tex. Rev. Partnership Act, Tex. Bus. Org. Code Ann. §152.302. Unless authorized by the other partners or unless the other partners have abandoned the business, one or more but less than all the partners have no authority to do any act that is not apparently for carrying on business in the ordinary course. Tex. Bus. Org. Code Ann. §152.302. *See* Comment to Standard 7.10.

A general partner of a limited partnership is subject to the restrictions of a partner in a partnership without limited partners. Tex. Rev. Ltd. Partnership Act, Tex. Bus. Org. Code Ann. §153.152.

Source:

Citations in the Comment.

History:

Adopted June 27, 1997.

STANDARD 7.30. PRIOR CONVEYANCE IN CHAIN BY PARTNERSHIP OR JOINT VENTURE

An examiner may presume the authority of an apparent partner or a joint venturer who has executed a prior conveyance in the chain of title on behalf of the partnership or joint venture.

COMMENT

See Comment and Caution to Standard 7.40, below.

Source:

Citations in the Comment.

History:

Adopted June 27, 1997; amended July 17, 2014.

The prior standard provided: "An examiner may assume the authority of an apparent partner or a joint venturer who has executed a prior conveyance in the chain of title on behalf of the partnership or joint venture."

STANDARD 7.40. CONVEYANCE OF PARTNERSHIP PROPERTY HELD IN NAME OF PARTNERS

If title to the property is in the name of the partners, the named partners must execute the conveyance.

COMMENT

Where title to real property is in the name of one or more of the partners, and without an indication in the

instrument transferring title of the person's capacity as a partner or of the existence of the partnership, and without use of partnership property, the property is presumed to be the partner's property under the provisions of Tex. Bus. Org. Code Ann. §152.102.

See Comment to Standard 7.10.

CAUTION

Every partner is an agent of the partnership for the purpose of its business, and the act of every partner, including the execution in the partnership name of any instrument, for apparently carrying on in the usual way the business of the partnership of which the partner is a member binds the partnership, unless the partner so acting has in fact no authority to act for the partnership in the particular matter, and the person with whom the partner is dealing has knowledge of the fact that the partner has no such authority.

An act of a partner that is not apparently for the carrying on of the partnership business or business of the kind carried on by the partnership does not bind the partnership unless authorized by the other partners. Tex. Rev. Partnership Act, Tex. Bus. Org. Code Ann. §§152.301, 152.302, 153.152. *See* Comment to Standard 7.10.

Source:
Citations in the Comment.
History:
Adopted June 27, 1997.

STANDARD 7.50. CONVEYANCE OF REAL PROPERTY HELD IN NAME OF LIMITED LIABILITY COMPANY

If title is held by a limited liability company, an examiner may rely upon a conveyance that is executed by an officer, agent, manager, or member thereof if the conveyance appears *to be consistent* with the limited liability company's usual way of doing business.

COMMENT

The act of an officer, agent, manager, or member of a limited liability company binds the company when that person is apparently conducting in the usual way the business of the company, unless the person lacks authority to act and the purchaser has knowledge of the lack of authority. Tex. Ltd. Liability Co. Act, Tex. Bus. Org. Code Ann. §§101.253, 101.254.

Effective September 1, 2009, a limited liability company agreement may provide for one or more designated series of members, managers, membership interests, or assets to have separate rights, powers, or duties concerning specified property or obligations. Tex. Bus. Org. Code Ann. §101.601. The debts, liabilities, obligations, and expenses of a particular series shall be enforceable against the assets of the series only, and none of the debts, liabilities, obligations, and expenses of the limited liability company generally or of any other series shall be enforceable against the assets of a particular series, provided the records, company agreement, and company's certificate of formation conform to applicable requirements. Tex. Bus. Org. Code Ann. §101.602. Assets associated with a series may be held directly or indirectly, including being held in the name of the series, in the name of the limited liability company, through a nominee, or otherwise. Tex. Bus. Org. Code Ann. §101.603. A series has the power and capacity, in the series' own name, to hold title to assets of the series, including real property and to grant liens and security interests in assets of the series. Tex. Bus. Org. Code Ann. §101.605.

Source:
Citations in the Comment.
History:
Adopted June 27, 1997; amended Oct. 9, 1999. The original standard provided: "If title is held by a limited liability company, an examiner may rely upon the conveyance that is executed by a manager or officer if the conveyance appears to be consistent with the limited liability company's usual way of doing business."

CHAPTER VIII. POWERS OF ATTORNEY

STANDARD 8.10. VALIDITY OF INSTRUMENT EXECUTED BY AN AGENT

An examiner should determine that the power of attorney granted sufficient authority to the agent and that the power of attorney was in effect on the date of the agent's act.

COMMENT

There are two types of powers of attorney: a "special" power of attorney, and "general" or "universal" power of attorney. In a special power, the principal grants authority to the agent (also called an attorney-in-fact) to perform a specific act or acts, such as selling the principal's residence. In a general or universal power, the principal grants the agent (attorney-in-fact) broad or universal powers, sometimes expressed as authority "to exercise all legal powers possessed by the principal." A power of attorney signed on or after September 1, 1993 that complies with Section 490 of the Durable Power of Attorney Act, Tex. Estates Code Ann. §§751.001-752.115) (a "statutory power"), provides an

STANDARD 8.10

abbreviated form for delegating general and special powers. The authority granted to an agent to convey land must be in writing, Tex. Prop. Code Ann. §5.021, and if properly acknowledged, the power of attorney may be recorded.

In examining a document signed by an agent for a principal, an examiner should determine that the power of attorney granted sufficient authority to validate the act of the agent and that it was not revoked prior to the act. Causes of revocation include a specific act of revocation by the principal, the terms of the power-of-attorney document, the death of the principal, or the incapacity of the principal unless the power-of-attorney provides that it survives incapacity. In the absence of information to the contrary, an examiner frequently relies upon an affidavit from a person knowledgeable of the facts that on the date of the agent's act the principal was alive, that the power of attorney had not been revoked, and that the principal was not incapacitated.

The problems of revocation by incapacity were largely eliminated effective January 1, 1972, after which time a power of attorney, whether a special or general power, could be expressly made "durable." The Durable Power of Attorney Act provides that a durable power is one that is in writing, signed by the principal, and acknowledged and that contains the words: "This power of attorney is not affected by subsequent disability," or "This power of attorney becomes effective on the disability or incapacity of the principal," or similar words showing the intent of the principal. Although not affected by disability, a durable power is revoked: (1) by the appointment of a permanent guardian (and in some instances the appointment of a temporary guardian) of the estate of the principal, Tex. Estates Code Ann. §751.052; (2) by the divorce or annulment of the marriage of the principal and the agent unless otherwise provided by the durable power (Tex. Estates Code Ann. §751.053); or (3) by the death of the principal, *Cleveland v. Williams*, 29 Tex. 204 (1867).

The Durable Power of Attorney Act provides that an affidavit executed by an agent under a durable power is conclusive proof as between the agent and a person, other than the principal or the principal's personal representative, that the power had not been revoked or terminated at that time if the affidavit provides that the agent did not, at the time of the exercise of the power, have actual notice of the termination of the power by:

(1) revocation;

(2) the principal's death;

(3) the principal's divorce or annulment of the marriage of the principal in the circumstance where the agent was the spouse of the principal; or

(4) the qualification of the guardian of the estate of the principal.

Id. Tex. Estates Code Ann. §751.055(a). Similarly, regarding a durable power that becomes effective upon the disability or incapacity of the principal, an affidavit executed by the agent stating that the principal is disabled or incapacitated, as defined in the power, is conclusive proof as between the agent and a person other than the principal or the principal's personal representative of the disability or incapacity of the principal at that time. *Id.* Tex. Estates Code Ann. §751.055(b). Unless otherwise noted in the power-of-attorney document, a revocation of a durable power is not effective as to a third party until the third party receives actual notice of the revocation. Tex. Estates Code Ann. §751.058. Tex. Prop. Code Ann. §12.016. Tex. Estates Code Ann. §751.151 requires the recordation of a durable power for a real property transaction in the county where the property is located.

Special powers of attorney are strictly construed. The following examples illustrate how Texas courts have applied this rule of strict construction:

(1) A "naked" power to sell does not include the right to execute an oil and gas lease. *Bean v. Bean*, 79 S.W.2d 652, 654 (Tex. Civ. App.—Texarkana 1935, writ ref'd);

(2) The power to sell land does not authorize a conveyance in exchange or a partition of lands. *Frost v. Erath Cattle Co.*, 17 S.W. 52, 54 (Tex. 1891); and

(3) The power to sell does not include the power to encumber. *First Nat'l Bank v. Blades*, 93 F.2d 154, 155 (5th Cir. 1937).

Nevertheless, the Durable Power of Attorney Act provides that a power that grants authority concerning "real estate transactions" would permit the actions involved in the three examples above. Tex. Estates Code Ann. §§752.051, 752.102.

Courts construe a general power of attorney more liberally than a special power. For example, *Dockstader v. Brown*, 204 S.W.2d 352, 353 (Tex. Civ. App.—Fort Worth 1947, writ ref'd n.r.e.) involved a power of attorney authorizing a party "to do any and every act, and ex-

ercise any and every power that [the principal] might, or could do or exercise through any other person." Since there was no reference to any specific acts and since it was not qualified in any manner, the court held that the language quoted authorized any lawful act.

Where the authority of an agent is not documented by any instrument of record, but the deed purportedly executed pursuant to the authority has been of record for at least twenty years, the examiner may presume that the recited authority is valid under the "ancient document" rule. See discussion in Comment to Standard 13.40.

An agent cannot delegate its authority without express power to that effect. *C. H. McCormick & Bro. v. Bush*, 38 Tex. 314 (1873).

Military powers of attorney are exempt from certain formalities that would otherwise be required by state law. 10 U.S.C. §§1044a and 1044b.

CAUTION

As originally enacted in 1993, Tex. Estates Code Ann. §752.102 did not include the authority to execute conveyances of oil, gas, and other minerals under a statutory power. Thus, the holding in *Bean v. Bean* (discussed above) may apply to statutory powers created through August 31, 1997. Effective September 1, 1997, the Act was amended to authorize the holder of a statutory power concerning "real estate transactions" to execute oil, gas, and mineral leases.

A power of attorney coupled with an interest, whether durable or not, cannot be revoked, even by death of the principal. A power coupled with an interest arises when the agent receives an interest in the property that is the subject of the agency contemporaneous with the power of attorney. *Superior Oil Co. v. Stanolind Oil & Gas Co.*, 230 S.W.2d 346 (Tex. Civ. App.—Eastland 1950), aff'd, 240 S.W.2d 281 (Tex. 1951). Because powers of attorney coupled with an interest are rare, there is little relevant case law.

Effective September 1, 2015, Tex. Estates Code Ann. §751.151 was amended to provide that the power of attorney must be filed not later than 30 days after an instrument executed pursuant to the power was filed. The legal effect of this amendment is uncertain.

Source:

Citations in the Comment; 4 Aloysius A. Leopold, *Land Titles and Title Examination* §§22.19-22.23 (Texas Practice 3d ed. 2005).

History:

The current Standard 8.10 effective June 5, 2012 replaces the prior Standard 8.10 and Standard 8.20, each of which became effective June 27, 1997.

Prior Standard 8.10 provided: An examiner should determine that a power of attorney grants sufficient authority to validate the actions of the agent. Any instrument affecting real estate may be executed by an attorney in fact, duly appointed and empowered, unless: (1) The power of attorney was not executed in writing; (2) The principal has died or an order of a court has appointed a guardian of the principal's person or estate, or both, unless the court order otherwise provides; or (3) The power of attorney has expired or terminated by its own terms or by operation of law. A power of attorney and instruments executed by one having apparent agency power may qualify as "ancient documents."

STANDARD 8.20. [REPEALED]

History:

Standard 8.20 was replaced by new Standard 8.10, which combines previous Standard 8.10 and Standard 8.20, effective June 5, 2012.

Prior Standard 8.20 provided: An examiner should determine that a power of attorney grants sufficient authority to validate the actions of the agent. Any instrument affecting real estate may be executed by an attorney in fact, duly appointed and empowered, unless the attorney in fact or the third party dealing with the attorney in fact had actual notice that:

(1) The power of attorney was not executed, acknowledged, and recorded as required by law;

(2) A revocation of the power of attorney has been recorded in the same office in which the instrument containing the power of attorney was recorded;

(3) The principal has died or an order of a court has appointed a guardian of the principal's estate, unless the court order otherwise provides;

(4) The principal was not disabled or incapacitated, as defined by the power; or

(5) The power of attorney has expired or terminated by its own terms or by operation of law.

CHAPTER IX. CONVEYANCES INVOLVING TRUSTEES

STANDARD 9.10. POWERS OF TRUSTEE

An examiner should confirm the identity and powers of the trustee and whether the trust was in effect at the time of a trust transaction.

COMMENT

Prior to April 19, 1943, the effective date of the Texas Trust Act, a trustee had only those powers granted by or reasonably implied from the trust instrument. Under the current Texas Trust Code, a trustee of an express trust has the powers enumerated in Texas Prop. Code Ann. §§113.003-.030—including the power to convey, lease, and encumber trust property and any additional powers that are necessary or appropriate to carry out the purposes of the trust—unless limited by the trust instrument, a subsequent court order, or another provision of the Code that conflicts with or limits the power. Tex. Prop. Code Ann. §§113.001-.002. Although subject to certain limitations, the terms of an express trust prevail over any provision of the Code. Tex. Prop. Code Ann. §111.0035(b). Thus, an examiner should examine both the trust instrument and the Code to confirm that the trustee had the authority to perform

the act under consideration. As an alternative to being furnished a copy of the trust agreement, an examiner may rely upon a certification of trust that complies with Tex. Prop. Code §114.086.

Where the authority of a trustee is not documented by any instrument of record, but the deed by the trustee has been of record for at least twenty years, the examiner is aided by a presumption of the grantor's recited authority under the "ancient document" rule. See discussion in Comment to Standard 13.40. An examiner may also be aided by the statutory requirement that an action to recover property conveyed by an instrument signed by a trustee without record of the authority of the trustee or proof of the facts recited in the instrument must be brought within four years of the date that the instrument was "recorded," if it was recorded before September 1, 2007, or within two years of the date that the instrument was "filed for record," if it was filed on or after September 1, 2007. Tex. Civ. Prac. & Rem. Code Ann. §16.033(a)(7). Act of June 15, 2007, 80th Leg., R.S., ch. 819, §2, 2007 Tex. Gen. Laws 1695 (nonretroactivity provision).

If the purpose of an examination concerns dealing with a trustee over an extended period of time (e.g., paying the trust proceeds from oil or gas production), then the examiner may need to review the trust instrument to: (1) identify successor trustees; (2) determine what facts may cause the trust to terminate; and (3) identify the beneficiaries of the trust property at the time of trust termination.

CAUTION

Unless the trust agreement expressly grants the power of delegation to the trustee, *Transamerican Leasing Co. v. Three Bears, Inc.*, 586 S.W.2d 472 (Tex. 1979), the general rule is that a trustee may not delegate the trustee's authority to another. *West v. Hapgood*, 174 S.W.2d 963 (Tex. 1943). At least for purposes of conveying or encumbering real property, an examiner should not presume that this general rule has been altered by the Texas Trust Code. *See, e.g.*, Tex. Prop. Code Ann. §§114.081, 114.086, 117.004, 117.011. Accordingly, a title examiner encountering a conveyance by a person purporting to act as agent or attorney in fact for a trustee must, in addition to examining the power of attorney or other document granting the power, carefully review the trust agreement to verify that it expressly enables the trustee to delegate the trustee's discretionary authority.

If property is conveyed to a person identified as "trustee" but the conveyance does not identify the trust or disclose a beneficiary, then the examiner should follow the guidance of Standard 9.20, its Comment, and Caution.

Source:

Citations in the Comment; *Oklahoma Title Examination Standards*, Std. 15.1; 3A Aloysius A. Leopold, *Land Titles and Title Examination* §12.36 (Texas Practice 3d ed. 2005).

History:

Adopted June 27, 1997; amended June 27, 2008; amended June 11, 2010; amended July 17, 2014.

The prior standard: "An examiner must confirm the identity and powers of the trustee and whether the trust was in effect at the time of a trust transaction."

The amended standard of June 27, 2008, provided: "Unless a trustee's power is restricted by the trust instrument or by law, the trustee of an express trust has the power to convey, lease, and encumber the real property interest that is subject to the trust."

The original standard provided: "Unless a trustee's power is restricted by the trust instrument or by law, the trustee of an express trust has the power to convey, lease, and encumber the real property interest that is subject to the trust. A trustee's act binds the trust and all beneficiaries as against successors who are without actual or constructive notice of restrictions or limitations upon the trustee's powers."

STANDARD 9.20. TITLE AS "TRUSTEE" WITHOUT FURTHER IDENTIFICATION OF TRUST

If property is conveyed to a person identified as "trustee," but the conveyance does not identify the trust or disclose the names of the beneficiaries, an examiner may presume the authority of the trustee to convey, transfer or encumber the title to the property.

COMMENT

The mere designation of a party as "Trustee," "as Trustee," or "Agent" following the name of a grantee, without additional language actually identifying a trust, does not in itself create a trust and it does not give notice or put an examiner upon inquiry that a trust does exist or that any person other than the present grantee has a beneficial interest. *Barker v. Temple Lumber Co.*, 12 S.W.2d 175 (Tex. Comm'n App. 1929, judgm't aff'd), rev'd on rehearing on other grounds, 120 Tex. 244, 37 S.W.2d 721 (1931), 137 A.L.R. 460, 462-65 (1942); *Nolana Dev. Ass'n. v. Corsi*, 682 S.W.2d 246, 249 (Tex. 1984). This "blind trustee" concept was first enacted into statutory form as a conveyancing statute. Acts 1925, 39th Leg., ch. 120, p. 305, §1. This statute was used for many years to avoid filing trust instruments of record and to escape the formality of creating a trust where title was held by a "nominee." For example, when a conveyance is made to "Jack Smith, Trustee" and the creating instrument does not identify a trust or the name of any beneficiary, the trustee may "convey,

transfer, or encumber the title of the property without subsequent question by a person who claims to be a beneficiary under a trust or who claims by, through, or under any undisclosed beneficiary or by, through, or under the person designated as trustee in that person's individual capacity." Tex. Prop. Code Ann. §101.001. Moreover, in this situation, "the trust property is not liable to satisfy the personal obligations of the trustee." Tex. Prop. Code Ann. §101.002. *See also* Tex. Prop. Code Ann. §114.082 and *Gulf Production Co. v. Continental Oil Co.*, 164 S.W.2d 488 (Tex. 1942).

If there is no subsequent conveyance out of the "blind trust" and no other evidence that a trust exists, record title to the property interest in question is deemed to be in the named trustee or the trustee's successors. *Jordan v. Exxon Corp.*, 802 S.W.2d 880 (Tex. App.—Texarkana 1991, no writ).

CAUTION

If a conveyance to a person designated as a trustee identifies the trust or discloses the name of the beneficiary, then an examiner should follow the guidance of Standard 9.10 and its Comment and Caution.

A governmental entity (defined as a state agency or political subdivision) may not purchase property held in trust until the governmental entity receives from the trustee a copy of the trust agreement identifying the true owner of the property. Likewise, a governmental entity may not sell property to a trustee until the governmental entity receives from the trustee a copy of the trust agreement identifying the person who will be the true owner of the property. In either case, the trustee must identify the true owner of the property to the governmental entity. Texas Gov't Code Ann. §2252.092. If a governmental entity fails to comply with this provision, the conveyance is void. *Id.* §2252.093.

Source:

Citations in the Comment; Tex. Prop. Code Ann. §§101.001, 101.002, 114.082, 114.0821; 5 Aloysius A. Leopold, *Land Titles and Title Examination* §32.10 (Texas Practice 3d ed. 2005).

History:

Adopted June 27, 1997.

CHAPTER X. CAPACITY TO CONVEY

STANDARD 10.10. MINORITY

In the absence of actual or constructive notice to the contrary, a grantor is presumed to be an adult. If it appears that a person acquired title as a minor, an examiner should first determine that a conveyance from that person occurred after:

(1) the person obtained the age of majority as defined at the time of the conveyance;

(2) the person had the disability of minority removed by a court of competent jurisdiction; or

(3) the person was legally married.

A conveyance that has not been disaffirmed within a reasonable time after the minor attains the age of majority is valid.

COMMENT

Texas law presumes that any party to a legal contract has sufficient capacity. Thus, deeds executed by minors are voidable, not void, and convey title until set aside. *Neill v. Pure Oil Co.*, 101 S.W.2d 402 (Tex. Civ. App.—Dallas 1937, writ ref'd). In order to avoid a conveyance that a minor executed while the minor was under the disability of minority, the minor must disaffirm the conveyance within a reasonable time after attaining the age of majority or after removal of disability or after marriage. *Searcy v. Hunter*, 17 S.W. 372, 373 (Tex. 1891).

A minor who has been legally married or whose disabilities have been removed by a court has the capacity and power of an adult. Texas Fam. Code Ann. §§1.104, 31.006.

CAUTION

The question of reasonable time is one of fact, not of law. There is no certain period for the minor to disaffirm, but what is a "reasonable time" is determined by all facts and circumstances. *Miller v. McAden*, 253 S.W. 901 (Tex. Civ. App.—Austin 1923, no writ). Examples of attempts to disaffirm that were found not to have occurred within a reasonable time are as follows:

(1) Disaffirmance about one year after reaching majority. *Askey v. Williams*, 11 S.W. 1101, 1102 (Tex. 1889).

(2) Waiting two years after reaching majority. *Ferguson v. Houston, E. & W. T. Ry. Co.*, 11 S.W. 347, 348 (Tex. 1889).

(3) Minor accepted proceeds of sale and waited nearly three years to disaffirm. *Daimwood v. Driscoll*, 151 S.W. 621, 623 (Tex. Civ. App.—San Antonio 1912, writ ref'd).

Any positive act of the minor after the minor reaches majority should satisfy an examiner. As long as the minor continues to take a position that the minor intends to stand by the conveyance, it will be considered as a ratification of the executed deed.

If a legally married minor is divorced or if the marriage is annulled, the minor most likely retains capacity pursuant to Texas Fam. Code Ann. §1.104. *See generally* [***O'Connor's Fam. Law Handbook***, "Losing minority status," ch. 1-B, §5.2, p. 33]. The capacity of the minor is uncertain in the hypothetical circumstance where the marriage of a minor is declared void in a suit to declare the marriage void by reason of a prior existing marriage or incest. *See* Texas Fam. Code Ann. §§6.201-6.203. In these instances, because the marriage is void, the minor may have never obtained capacity by such marriage in the first place; however, the issue of such minor's capacity may turn on whether the minor knew that the marriage was incestuous or bigamous.

Source:

Citations in the Comment; 5 Aloysius A. Leopold, *Land Titles and Title Examination* §32.22 (Texas Practice 3d ed. 2005); *Oklahoma Title Examination Standards*, Std. 4.1.

History:

Adopted June 27, 1997; amended July 17, 2014.

The prior standard provided: "In the absence of actual or constructive notice to the contrary, a grantor is presumed to be an adult. If it appears that a person acquired title as a minor, an examiner must first determine that a conveyance from that person occurred after: (1) the person obtained the age of majority as defined at the time of the conveyance; (2) the person had the disability of minority removed by a court of competent jurisdiction; or (3) the person was legally married. A conveyance that has not been disaffirmed within a reasonable time after the minor attains the age of majority is valid."

STANDARD 10.20. MENTAL CAPACITY

In the absence of actual or constructive notice to the contrary, an examiner may presume that a grantor has the mental capacity to convey. If the lack of capacity has been established, restoration of capacity may be accomplished pursuant to statute.

COMMENT

Texas law presumes that the grantor of the deed has sufficient mental capacity at the time of execution to understand the grantor's legal rights. The party alleging incapacity has the burden of proof. *Bradshaw v. Naumann*, 528 S.W.2d 869, 873 (Tex. Civ. App.—Austin 1975, writ dism'd). The Texas Supreme Court has held that an insane person's deed is voidable and not void, evidently reaching this conclusion based upon the similarity between the deed of an insane person and that of a minor. *Williams v. Sapieha*, 61 S.W. 115, 116 (Tex. 1901).

Upon the adjudication of incompetency of a spouse, the other spouse acquires full power to dispose of the community property. Tex. Estates Code Ann. §1353.002. However, if a lack of mental capacity of a spouse has been previously established, a court, upon determining that the mental capacity of such spouse has been restored, may enter an order terminating the other spouse's full power to dispose of the community property. Tex. Estates Code Ann. §1353.103.

CAUTION

If capacity is challenged, the legal standards in Texas for determining the existence of mental capacity for purposes of executing a will or a deed are substantially the same as mental capacity for executing a contract. To have the requisite mental capacity, the testator or grantor must appreciate the effect of what is happening and understand the nature and consequences of the act and of the business being transacted. *Bach v. Hudson*, 596 S.W.2d 673, 675-76 (Tex. Civ. App.—Corpus Christi 1980, no writ).

Source:

Citations in the Comment; *Oklahoma Title Examination Standards*, Std. 4.2; 5 Aloysius A. Leopold, *Land Titles and Title Examination* §32.15 (Texas Practice 3d ed. 2005).

History:

Adopted June 27, 1997.

STANDARD 10.30. GUARDIANS

In reviewing a sale or encumbrance of property by a guardian, an examiner should determine that all statutory requirements have been met.

COMMENT

In considering a guardian's sale of property, including leases and mineral leases, or mortgage or other encumbrance of property, the examiner should first review the documents involved in the appointment of the guardian. Among these are:

(1) the application for appointment,

(2) the citation and return,

(3) the order appointing the guardian, and

(4) the guardian's oath and bond.

The examiner must also determine that the guardian's appointment was in effect at the time of the sale or lease. Unless otherwise discharged, a guardian remains in office until the estate is closed. Tex. Estates Code Ann. §§1202.001, 1204.001. A guardianship terminates in any of the following circumstances:

(1) when the ward dies;

(2) when a minor ward marries, reaches majority (age 18), or has disabilities removed;

(3) when a court issues an order of restoration in the case of an incapacitated ward; or

(4) when a court determines the guardianship is no longer necessary.

Specific requirements relating to sales are found in Tex. Estates Code Ann. §1158.001 et seq. In general, a guardian's sale requires:

(1) an application by a duly appointed and acting guardian for authority to sell,

(2) a citation and return,

(3) an order of sale,

(4) notice as required by the court in the order of sale,

(5) a sale by the guardian, as evidenced by a report of sale,

(6) an additional guardian's bond if the general bond is inadequate,

(7) a decree confirming the sale, and

(8) a conveyance by the guardian.

The examiner should review each of the above documents. If two years have elapsed from the date of the decree confirming the sale, an examiner may rely on the decree as evidence that the requirements of the order of sale were met unless, on its face, the decree indicates that the sale was not conducted in the manner required. *See* Tex. Estates Code Ann. §§55.251, 55.252. If the two-year period has not elapsed, evidence of compliance with the requirements of the order of sale is necessary.

For provisions relating to mineral leases, see Tex. Estates Code Ann. §§1160.001-1160.254. For provisions relating to mortgages, see Tex. Estates Code Ann. §§1151.201-1151.203. For provisions relating to gifts, see Tex. Estates Code Ann. §§1162.001-1162.053.

A guardian may be appointed as the guardian of the person of the ward or as guardian of the estate of the ward or both. In general, only the guardian of the estate of the ward may sell or lease the property of the ward. Subject to statutory limitations on net value of the minor's interest, a minor's property may be sold by a parent or the managing conservator without the appointment of a guardian. Tex. Estates Code Ann. §1351.001. Similarly, subject to statutory limitations on the net value of the ward's interest, the property of a ward, not just that of a minor, may be sold by the guardian of the person of the ward without appointment as guardian of the estate of the ward. Tex. Estates Code Ann. §1351.052. Both statutes require that these sales be approved by a court.

For related standards, see Standard 10.10, Minority, and Standard 10.20, Mental Capacity. The holder of a durable power of attorney may have authority to convey the property of an incapacitated person. *See* Chapter VIII, Powers of Attorney. However, if a guardian of the estate of the ward has been appointed, the durable power of attorney is no longer effective. Tex. Estates Code Ann. §751.052.

CAUTION

A decree confirming a sale may not be issued until five days after the date the report of sale is filed. Tex. Estates Code Ann. §§1158.552, 1158.556. The appointment of a guardian in another jurisdiction does not give the guardian any authority over a ward's estate in Texas. *American Surety Co. v. Fitzgerald*, 36 S.W.2d 1104 (Tex. Civ. App.—Dallas 1931, writ ref'd). A foreign guardian may be appointed by a Texas court, without notice or citation, in the manner prescribed by Tex. Estates Code Ann. §1252.051.

The statutes governing guardianships were extensively modified effective September 1, 1993. Thus, when reviewing more recent sales by guardians, an examiner should be cautious in relying upon court decisions based upon the law that existed prior to that date. Like the current statutes, prior law required that the guardian be duly appointed and acting and required court orders authorizing and approving the sale. An examiner encountering a guardian's sale made under earlier statutes should verify compliance with those statutes.

Source:
Citations in the Comment.
History:
Adopted June 22, 2007; amended July 17, 2014.
The prior standard provided: "In reviewing a sale or encumbrance of property by a guardian, an examiner must determine that all statutory requirements have been met."

CHAPTER XI. DECEDENTS' ESTATES

STANDARD 11.10. PASSAGE OF TITLE UPON DEATH

A decedent's property passes to his or her heirs at law or devisees immediately upon death, subject in each instance, except for exempt property, to payment of debts, including estate and inheritance taxes.

COMMENT

Notwithstanding the passage of title at death, if letters testamentary or letters of administration are issued, the personal representative of the estate has the

right to possession and control of the estate assets for purposes of estate administration.

With respect to the property of an intestate person, Tex. Estates Code Ann. §201.003 states the manner in which community property passes, and Tex. Estates Code Ann. §201.002 governs the passage of separate property. A will is not valid to pass title until it has been probated. Tex. Estates Code Ann. §256.001.

Source:

Citations in the Comment; Stanley M. Johanson, *Johanson's Texas Estates Code Annotated* §§101.001, 101.003, 101.051 (2014).

History:

Adopted Oct. 9, 1999.

PROPOSED STANDARD 11.10. PASSAGE OF TITLE UPON DEATH

A decedent's property passes to his or her heirs at law or devisees or to the grantee of a transfer on death deed immediately upon death, subject to payment of debts, including federal estate taxes.

COMMENT

Notwithstanding the passage of title at death, if letters testamentary or letters of administration are issued, the personal representative of the estate has the right to possession and control of the estate assets for purposes of estate administration.

Regarding the property of an intestate person, Tex. Estates Code Ann. §201.003 states the manner in which community property passes, and Tex. Estates Code Ann. §201.002 governs the passage of separate property. A will is not valid to pass title until it has been probated. Tex. Estates Code Ann. §256.001.

For decedents dying after September 1, 2015, a statutory "transfer on death deed" under Tex. Estates Code Ann. ch. 14 provides a means of passage of title at death other than by intestate succession or by will. Such a deed must be filed for record before the grantor's death and is revocable and subject to any conveyance or encumbrances on the part of the grantor until the grantor has died.

A decedent's heir or, unless the will provides to the contrary, any devisee who fails to survive the decedent by at least 120 hours is considered as though predeceased. Tex. Estates Code Ann. §§121.052, 121.102. No right of inheritance accrues to any person unless the person is born before, or is in gestation at, the time of intestate decedent's death. Tex. Estates Code Ann. §201.256. No person may take as a member of a class under a class gift unless born or in gestation before the decedent's death. Tex. Estates Code Ann. §255.401. If a testator's marriage is dissolved by divorced or annulment or declared void before the testator's death, all provisions of the will are read as though the former spouse and all relatives of the former spouse who are not also relatives of the testator had failed to survive the testator unless the will expressly provides otherwise. Tex. Estates Code Ann. §123.001.

Tex. Prop. Code Ann. ch. 240 allows the beneficiary of property passing by various means, including inheritance or devise, to disclaim it. The examiner should be alert to this possibility, which results in the property's passing as though the disclaiming beneficiary had predeceased the decedent.

Source:

Citations in the Comment; Stanley M. Johanson, *Johanson's Texas Estates Code Annotated* §§101.001, 101.003, 101.051 (2014).

History:

As of the date of publication, the proposed amendments to Standard 11.10 have not been adopted.

STANDARD 11.20. ESTATE PROCEEDINGS

If an owner of property dies, the examiner should determine whether the owner left a will, whether there is a probate proceeding or administration pending, and whether a personal representative is acting.

COMMENT

If the records of the county where the land is located do not indicate that a will has been filed for probate, and in the absence of information to the contrary, the affidavit of a person who has knowledge of the facts is usually accepted as satisfactory evidence that the owner died intestate.

See also, Standard 11.70, addressing affidavits of heirship, and Standard 13.20, addressing reliance on affidavits.

Source:

Title Standards Joint Editorial Board.

History:

Adopted Oct. 9, 1999; amended June 5, 2012; amended July 17, 2014.

The prior standard provided: "If an owner of property dies, the examiner must determine whether the owner left a will, whether there is a probate proceeding or administration pending, and whether a personal representative is acting."

The original standard provided: "If an owner of property dies, the examiner must determine whether the owner left a will, whether there is a probate proceeding or administration pending, and whether a personal representative is acting. If the records of the county where the land is located do not indicate that a will has been filed for probate, and in the absence of information to the contrary, the affidavit of a person who has knowledge of the facts is usually accepted as satisfactory evidence that the owner died intestate."

STANDARD 11.30. CONVEYANCES BY AN EXECUTOR OR AN INDEPENDENT ADMINISTRATOR

Before accepting a deed from an executor or an independent administrator, an examiner should be satisfied that all statutory requirements were met in the appointment of the representative, that the representative is qualified to execute the deed, and that the representative's act is authorized by the will or by law.

COMMENT

If a representative (an executor or an independent administrator) executes a deed to the decedent's property, then the examiner should determine the representative's qualifications. When determining the qualification of a representative to execute a deed, the examiner should examine the will, the order probating the will and appointing the executor, the representative's bond (if required), and recent letters testamentary or of administration. In addition to the above, the examiner should examine other relevant documents that may be of record, including the application for the representative's appointment. If the probate proceedings took place in another county, the examiner should require the filing of certified copies of the order appointing the representative and any will and any codicils in the county where the land is located. Tex. Estates Code Ann. §256.201.

A qualified executor, even one under court order, may convey real property belonging to the estate if authorized to do so by the will. Tex. Estates Code Ann. §356.002. If the owner of real property died intestate, or if a will does not give the authority to convey real property, a qualified independent executor or a qualified independent administrator may convey real property with the consent of the decedent's distributees in the application for independent administration or in their consent to the independent administration and if authorized by the order of appointment. Tex. Estates Code Ann. §401.006.

Unless limited by the terms of a will, an independent executor or an independent administrator has the power of sale, without court approval, to:

(1) Pay expenses of administration, funeral expenses and expenses of last sickness, and allowances and claims against the estate of a decedent. Tex. Estates Code Ann. §§402.002 and 403.051.

(2) Dispose of any interest in real property "when it is deemed to [be in] the best interest of the estate to sell such interest." Tex. Estates Code Ann. §356.251(2).

A person who is not a devisee or an heir is not required to look into the power of sale or the propriety of a sale by an independent executor or independent administrator or to obtain the joinder of the decedent's distributees if the person deals in good faith and:

(1) the sale is by an independent executor and a power of sale is granted to the independent executor in the will;

(2) effective September 1, 2011, a power of sale is granted under Tex. Estates Code Ann. §401.006 in the order appointing the independent executor or independent administrator; or

(3) effective September 1, 2011, the independent executor or independent administrator provides an affidavit, that is recorded in the deed records of the county where the land is located, stating that the sale is necessary or advisable for any of the purposes described in Tex. Estates Code Ann. §356.251(1).

A sale of estate property by an executor to an innocent purchaser, for a valuable consideration, in good faith, and without notice of any illegality in the sale continues to be valid notwithstanding that the acts or the authority under which the acts were performed is later set aside. Tex. Estates Code Ann. §307.001.

The powers of an independent executor continue until there is no longer any necessity for the executor to act, typically when all debts of the estate have been paid and the assets of the estate have been distributed. Although Tex. Estates Code Ann. §§405.004-405.009 provide methods of closing an independent administration, the procedures are rarely followed. This practice presents problems for the examiner, because there frequently is no convenient way to determine conclusively that an executor no longer has authority to act. In case of doubt as to whether the executor continues to act, the examiner should require the joinder of the devisees in any conveyance of estate property.

An examiner may rely upon a will that has been duly admitted to probate and that has not been challenged. However, during the two-year period after the date of the order admitting the will to probate, the order is subject to contest by bill of review filed in the proper court by any interested person. Tex. Estates Code Ann. §55.251. Moreover, any interested person may institute

suit to cancel a will for forgery or other fraud within two years after the discovery of the forgery or fraud, and persons non compos mentis and minors have two years after the removal of their disabilities within which to commence such a suit. Tex. Estates Code Ann. §256.204.

During the two-year period after a decision, order, or judgment, the decision, order, or judgment is subject to attack by any interested person by bill of review filed in the same court, and if error is shown, the decision, order, or judgment can be revised or corrected. Tex. Estates Code Ann. §55.251.

CAUTION

If the order of appointment of an independent administrator did not give authority to sell real property, the examiner should require the joinder of the parties who would have otherwise received the property.

A good-faith, third-party purchaser who relies upon an affidavit described in Tex. Estates Code Ann. §402.053 is protected only if the sale was made for the reasons set out in Tex. Estates Code Ann. §356.251(1), that is, for administrative expenses, allowances, and claims. There is no similar protection regarding a sale made because it was deemed by the representative to be in the best interest of the estate.

An examiner should question an apparent delegation of authority by the executor because, while an executor may delegate ministerial duties, an executor may not delegate discretionary authority. *Terrell v. McCown*, 43 S.W. 2 (Tex. 1897).

If a will does not give an executor the power of sale or if the executor is not given the power of sale in the order of appointment, then the executor must follow the same procedure for a sale as is prescribed for an administrator.

Source:

Citations in the Comment; Tex. Estates Code Ann. §§356.002, 356.251, 401.002, 401.003; *Roy v. Whitaker*, 48 S.W. 892 (Tex. 1898); Stanley M. Johanson, *Johanson's Texas Estates Code Annotated* §§301.001, 356.002, 401.001 through .008, 402.001, 402.002, 402.051, 402.053, 405.004 through .009 (2014); 17 M. K. Woodward & Ernest E. Smith, III, *Tex. Prac., Prob. & Decedents' Estates* §§497, 499 (1971).

History:

Adopted Oct. 9, 1999; amended June 5, 2012; amended July 17, 2014.

The prior standard provided: "Before accepting a deed from an executor or an independent administrator, an examiner must be satisfied that all statutory requirements were met in the appointment of the representative, that the representative is qualified to execute the deed, and that the representative's act is authorized by the will or by law."

The original standard provided: "Before accepting an executor's deed, an examiner should be satisfied that all statutory requirements were met in the appointment of the executor and that the executor is qualified to act. A qualified executor, even one under court order, may convey property belonging to the estate if authorized to do so by the will. In addition, a qualified independent executor, even though not authorized by will, may convey if not prohibited by the will and if there are one or more unpaid debts of the estate that are not barred by limitations. In the absence of information to the contrary, the examiner may rely upon an affidavit of an executor or other person who has knowledge of the facts that there are existing debts of the estate."

STANDARD 11.40. CONVEYANCES BY AN ADMINISTRATOR

Before accepting an administrator's conveyance, an examiner should determine that all statutory requirements have been met in the appointment of the administrator and that the administrator is qualified to act and is authorized to make the sale.

COMMENT

An administrator may convey property of a decedent only with authority of the court. Determining the qualification of an administrator requires an examination of the application for appointment, the order appointing the administrator, recent letters of administration, and the administrator's bond. A sale of estate property requires, in addition, an application for sale, order of sale, additional bond (if required by the court), report of sale, and order approving sale.

Unless the examiner determines that an administrator has the authority to convey, all parties who would otherwise take the property must join the administrator in any conveyance.

During the two-year period after a decision, order, or judgment, the decision, order, or judgment is subject to attack by any interested person by bill of review filed in the same court, and if error is shown, the decision, order, or judgment can be revised or corrected. Tex. Estates Code Ann. §55.251.

A sale of estate property by an administrator to an innocent purchaser, for a valuable consideration, in good faith, and without notice of any illegality in the sale continues to be valid notwithstanding that the acts or the authority under which the acts were performed is later set aside. Tex. Estates Code Ann. §307.001. The recitals in a deed by a personal representative made pursuant to a court order are prima facie evidence that the sale met all applicable requirements of the law. Tex. Estates Code Ann. §356.557.

If a will does not give an executor the power of sale or if the executor is not given the power of sale in the order of appointment, then the executor must follow the same procedure for a sale as is prescribed for an administrator.

Source:

Citations in the Comment; Tex. Estates Code Ann. §356.001.

History:

Adopted Oct. 9, 1999; amended June 5, 2012; amended July 17, 2014.

The prior standard provided: "Before accepting an administrator's conveyance, an examiner must determine that all statutory requirements have been met in the appointment of the administrator and that the administrator is qualified to act and is authorized to make the sale."

The original standard provided: "An administrator may convey property only with authority of the court. Therefore, before accepting an administrator's conveyance, an examiner should determine that all statutory requirements have been met in the appointment of the administrator and that the administrator is qualified to act and is authorized to make the sale."

STANDARD 11.50. CONVEYANCES BY HEIRS OF AN ESTATE

If the property owner died intestate, or if the owner died testate but the will is not probated, the examiner should, in the absence of administration, identify the heirs of the decedent, along with the devisees in any unprobated will, and require that all of them join in a conveyance of the property of the decedent.

COMMENT

Beneficiaries of a will frequently agree not to probate the will, in some instances because the estate is small and does not justify the cost. A commonly accepted procedure is to attach a copy of the will, if available, to an affidavit of heirship and to file the documents in the county records. In those cases, the examiner should require the joinder in the conveyance of each party who would take by intestacy and each party who would take under the will. If the will was not attached to the affidavit, but is available, the examiner should obtain a copy of the will in order to confirm the identity of the devisees under the will.

Regarding the property of an intestate person, Tex. Estates Code Ann. §201.003 states the manner in which community property passes, and Tex. Estates Code Ann. §201.002 governs the passage of separate property. For estates of decedents dying intestate after September 1, 1993, Tex. Estates Code Ann. §201.003 provides that title to community property passes to the surviving spouse if all the decedent's descendants are also the surviving spouse's descendants. If a husband or wife dies intestate and the community property passes to the surviving spouse, no administration on the community property is necessary. Tex. Estates Code Ann. §453.002.

A purchaser who buys real property from an heir, for value, in good faith, and without knowledge of a will, more than four years after the death of the decedent is protected from the claims of any devisees if a will is later offered for probate. Tex. Estates Code Ann. §256.003.

Source:

Citations in the Comment; Stanley M. Johanson, *Johanson's Texas Estates Code Annotated* §§201.003, 453.001, 453.002 (2014).

History:

Adopted Oct. 9, 1999; amended July 17, 2014.

The prior standard provided: "If the property owner died intestate, or if the owner died testate but the will is not probated, the examiner must, in the absence of administration, identify the heirs of the decedent, along with the devisees in any unprobated will, and require that all of them join in a conveyance of the property of the decedent."

STANDARD 11.60. LIENS FOR DEBTS & TAXES

An examiner should determine whether an estate of an owner owes taxes or debts that are not barred by limitations.

COMMENT

Property of a decedent passes subject to unpaid debts and taxes of the estate, and the examiner should determine whether any exist.

Absent information to the contrary, an examiner may rely upon the affidavit of an executor, administrator, or other person who has knowledge of the facts that all debts of the estate have been paid. As evidence that an estate is not large enough to incur federal estate taxes, an examiner may rely upon a court approved inventory, or in the absence of an inventory, the affidavit of a person who has knowledge of the facts. An order of the court probating a will as a muniment of title may be accepted as evidence that all obligations of the estate have been paid other than debts secured by liens on real property. In the latter case, the examiner should determine that the liens do not affect the property under examination.

An examiner may accept, as proof that debts and taxes have been paid, an order closing a court supervised administration or an affidavit closing an independent administration. If federal estate taxes are due, satisfaction of the taxes may be proven by a Federal Estate and Generation-Skipping Transfer Tax Closing Letter together with proof of payment of the taxes shown by the letter to be due to the United States.

Tex. Estates Code Ann. §101.051 creates a statutory lien on the decedent's estate in favor of the decedent's creditors. *Blinn v. McDonald*, 46 S.W. 787 (Tex. 1898). The statutory lien is not a lien in the usual sense and is not upon specific property but is a general lien upon all property that is subject to payment of debts. *Moore v.*

Moore, 33 S.W. 217 (Tex. 1895). Because a personal representative can sell property to pay debts, it follows that property sold by a personal representative in an authorized sale passes free of the statutory lien. Debts for which an estate is obligated, and which are secured by the statutory lien, include court ordered child support payments that were delinquent at the date of death. Delinquent payments may also be secured by a Child Support Lien as provided in Tex. Fam. Code Ann. §§157.311-157.326. As liens of the latter type must be recorded in the county judgment records, they will be apparent from a customary search for abstracts of judgment.

While an inventory, appraisement, and list of claims may contain information that is useful concerning the size and composition of the estate, the examiner should be aware that the information may be erroneous or incomplete. For example, the personal representative must list only property that is considered part of the probate estate with the result that there may be additional property that is part of the estate for estate tax purposes but which is not listed. Moreover, debts of the estate are not required to be listed on the inventory. A United States Estate (and Generation-Skipping Transfer) Tax Return (Form 706), if available, is a more reliable source of information of the character and extent of a decedent's property. Effective September 1, 2011, an independent executor or independent administrator may, in lieu of filing an inventory, file an affidavit stating that there are no unpaid debts, other than secured debts, taxes, and administration expenses. Tex. Estates Code Ann. §309.056. In the latter situation, the examiner should determine that any secured debts do not affect the land under examination.

A lien for federal estate taxes attaches to the gross estate of a decedent as of the date of death and, in general, exists for a period of ten years. 26 U.S.C. §6324. There is no requirement for filing notice in the county records. The State of Texas does not impose an estate or inheritance tax.

Federal estate taxes may be payable for taxable estates exceeding certain thresholds ($5,000,000 for decedents dying in or after 2010, adjusted upward annually for inflation for decedents dying after 2011, except that no estate tax was levied against the estates of decedents who died in 2010 if the estate opted out of a stepped-up basis). Any unused estate tax exemption of a married person who died in 2011 or later can be transferred to the surviving spouse under a concept commonly called "portability." 26 U.S.C. §2010(c).

If estate taxes are due and have not been paid, the District Director of the Internal Revenue Service has the authority to release the lien upon being furnished a bond conditioned on the payment of the tax. U.S. Treas. Reg. 301.6325-1(a)(2). Similarly, the District Director may release the lien if the fair market value of the remaining property is at least double the amount of the outstanding tax plus all prior liens against the property. U.S. Treas. Reg. 301.6325-1(b)(1). Other release authority is set out in U.S. Treas. Reg. 301.6325-1. An estate tax lien is divested regarding property sold under court order to pay debts and administration expenses. 26 U.S.C. §6324(a)(1).

In some instances, upon satisfaction that adequate liquid assets are available, an examiner frequently relies upon an affidavit of the personal representative that the taxes will be paid.

CAUTION

An examiner should check for updated information regarding possible estate-tax liability.

Source:

Citations in the Comment; Tex. Estates Code Ann. §101.051; Stanley M. Johanson, *Johanson's Texas Estates Code Annotated* §§101.001, 101.051 (2014).

History:

Adopted Oct. 9, 1999; amended June 5, 2012; amended July 17, 2014.

The prior standard provided: "An examiner must determine whether an estate of an owner owes taxes or debts that are not barred by limitations."

The original standard provided: "Property of a decedent passes subject to unpaid debts and taxes of the estate. Therefore, the examiner must determine whether these are unpaid. In the absence of information to the contrary, an examiner may rely upon the affidavit of an executor, administrator, or other person who has knowledge of the facts that all debts of the estate have been paid. As evidence that an estate is not large enough to incur federal estate and Texas inheritance taxes, an examiner may rely upon a court approved inventory, or in the absence of an inventory, the affidavit of a person who has knowledge of the facts. An order of the court probating a will as a muniment of title may be accepted as evidence that all obligations of the estate have been paid other than debts secured by liens on real property. In the latter case, the examiner must determine that the liens do not affect the property under examination.

An examiner may accept, as proof that debts and taxes have been paid, an order closing a court supervised administration or an affidavit closing an independent administration. If federal estate and Texas inheritance taxes are due, satisfaction of the taxes may be proven by a Federal Estate and Generation-Skipping Transfer Tax Closing Letter together with proof of payment of the taxes shown by the letter to be due to the United States and to the State of Texas."

STANDARD 11.70. HEIRSHIP AFFIDAVITS

In the absence of information to the contrary, an examiner may rely upon an affidavit of heirship with respect to the family history and the identity of heirs of a decedent.

COMMENT

An examiner commonly relies upon affidavits of heirship when the family history and the identity of the heirs of a decedent are not otherwise known. Heirs can also be determined in an action to declare heirship as provided in Tex. Estates Code Ann. §§202.001-202.206.

In addition, Tex. Estates Code Ann. §203.001 provides that, subject to rebuttal, a statement of facts concerning family history shall be received as prima facie evidence in any proceeding to declare heirship or suit involving title if contained in a document legally executed and acknowledged or sworn to and if the document has been of record five years in the county where the land is located or the county where the decedent had his domicile or residence at the time of his death.

Recent affidavits are also commonly accepted. In obtaining an affidavit of heirship, it is desirable for the affiant to be a person related to the decedent but who does not inherit from the decedent. If none is available, a person possessing personal knowledge of the decedent is the next choice. If neither is available, an interested heir can be used. In the latter case, it is also desirable to obtain a supporting affidavit from a person who has no interest in the estate.

Tex. Estates Code Ann. §203.002 sets out a suggested form for an affidavit of heirship.

The Texas Rules of Evidence provide exceptions to the hearsay rule that permit hearsay evidence of family history. Tex. R. Evid. 803, 804. *See also* Standard 3.40 and Chapter XIII.

See also, comments to Standard 11.20, addressing affidavits of intestacy, and Standard 13.20, addressing reliance on affidavits.

Source:

Citations in the Comment; 5A Aloysius A. Leopold, *Land Titles and Title Examination* §41.23 (Texas Practice 3d ed. 2005); Stanley M. Johanson, *Johanson's Texas Estates Code Annotated* §§203.001, 203.002 (2014); 17 M. K. Woodward & Ernest E. Smith, III, *Tex. Prac., Prob. & Decedents' Estates* §208 (1971); J. Howard Hayden, *Affidavits of Heirship*, 31 Tex. B. J. 741 (1968).

History:

Adopted Oct. 9, 1999; title changed and comment modified by Board, May 22, 2000.

STANDARD 11.80. COMMUNITY SURVIVORS

If no one has qualified as executor or administrator of the estate of a decedent who was married, the examiner may rely upon a conveyance of community property from the surviving spouse, acting as community survivor pursuant to Tex. Estates Code Ann. §453.003, made for the purpose of paying community debts.

COMMENT

A surviving spouse who acts as community survivor under the authority of Tex. Estates Code Ann. §453.003 is commonly called an "unqualified survivor" as opposed to a surviving spouse who "qualified" pursuant to Tex. Prob. Code Ann. §161 [repealed in 2007].

The doctrine embodied by Tex. Estates Code Ann. §453.003, that the surviving spouse may sell community property to pay community debts, is based on analogy to a surviving partner's authority in discharging the debts of a partnership and long predates the legislation. *See Jones's Adm'r v. Jones*, 15 Tex. 143, 148 (1855). Although the burden is on the purchaser under an unqualified community survivor's deed to prove the property was sold to pay community debts, *Moody v. Butler*, 63 Tex. 210 (1885), it is discharged upon proof of the existence of some community debt. *Jones v. Harris*, 139 S.W. 69, 78 (Tex. Civ. App.—San Antonio 1911, writ ref'd), and it is presumed that a debt existing at the date of death continued to exist at the time of the conveyance. *Wilson v. Meredith, Clegg & Hunt*, 268 S.W.2d 511 (Tex. Civ. App.—Beaumont 1954, writ ref'd n.r.e.). The purchaser need not inquire into the community survivor's application of the sale proceeds to the community debt. *Griffin v. Stanolind Oil & Gas Co.*, 125 S.W.2d 545 (Tex. 1939); *Kinard v. Sims*, 53 S.W.2d 803 (Tex. Civ. App.—Amarillo 1932, writ ref'd). In any event, the burden of proof is on a party asserting that an unqualified community survivor had no authority to sell the community property to show that the purchaser was not an innocent purchaser for value. *Johnson v. Masterson Irr. Co.*, 217 S.W. 407 (Tex. Civ. App.—Beaumont 1919, writ ref'd). It follows that in the absence of anything in the record indicating that an unqualified community survivor lacked authority to sell and convey community property, the examiner may presume that he or she did have the requisite authority. *See Kinard v. Sims*, 53 S.W.2d 803, 806 (Tex. Civ. App.—Amarillo 1932, writ ref'd).

A conveyance by a community survivor that purports to convey the entire interest owned by the community passes the deceased spouse's interest notwithstanding that the grantor purports to convey only on behalf of the grantor, without any indication of his or her capacity as community survivor. *Davis v. Magnolia Petroleum Co.*, 134 S.W.2d 1042 (Tex. 1940); *Griffin v. Stanolind Oil & Gas*, 125 S.W.2d 545 (Tex. 1939).

For estates of decedents dying intestate after September 1, 1993, title to community property passes to the surviving spouse if all the decedent's descendants are also the surviving spouse's descendants, in which case no administration on the community property is necessary. Tex. Estates Code Ann. §§201.003, 453.002.

Source:

Citations in the Comment; Tex. Estates Code Ann. §453.003; 4 Aloysius A. Leopold, *Land Titles and Title Examination* §20.12 (Texas Practice 3d ed. 2005); Stanley M. Johanson, *Johanson's Texas Estates Code Annotated* §453.003 (2014); 17 M. K. Woodward & Ernest E. Smith, III, *Tex. Prac., Prob. & Decedents' Estates* §544 (1971).

History:

Adopted Oct. 9, 1999.

STANDARD 11.90. COMMUNITY ADMINISTRATION

If a surviving spouse of a decedent who died before September 1, 2007, has qualified as a statutory community administrator, an examiner may rely upon a deed of community property from the administrator without further court order.

COMMENT

Tex. Prob. Code Ann. §§161 through 167, prior to September 1, 2007, governed the appointment and activities of a community administrator. Those sections were repealed as of that date, but the law in effect at the date of death of a decedent who died before that date governs a community administration of the estate of the decedent.

A community administrator who qualified concerning a decedent who died before September 1, 2007, had broader powers than those of an unqualified community survivor. For example, a community administrator could sell community property without regard to the existence of community debts.

For estates of decedents dying intestate after September 1, 1993, title to community property passes to the surviving spouse if all the decedent's descendants are also the surviving spouse's descendants, in which case no administration on the community property is necessary. Tex. Estates Code Ann. §§201.003, 453.002.

Source:

Citations in the Comment; 4 Aloysius A. Leopold, *Land Titles and Title Examination* §20.12 (Texas Practice 3d ed. 2005); Stanley M. Johanson, *Johanson's Texas Probate Code Annotated* §§161-177 (2011) (prior codification); 17 M. K. Woodward & Ernest E. Smith, III, *Tex. Prac., Prob. & Decedents' Estates* §574 (1971).

History:

Adopted Oct. 9, 1999; amended June 27, 2008. The original standard provided: "If a surviving spouse has qualified as community administrator in the manner prescribed in Tex. Prob. Code Ann. §§161-167, an examiner may rely upon a deed of community property from the administrator without further court order."

STANDARD 11.100. FOREIGN WILLS

An examiner may rely upon an exemplified copy of a will probated outside of Texas, as being effective to pass title to property in Texas owned by a decedent, if the will and the order admitting the will to probate are probated in Texas pursuant to Tex. Estates Code Ann. §§501.001-501.008 or are filed in the deed records pursuant to Tex. Estates Code Ann. §503.001.

COMMENT

A foreign will is one probated outside of Texas in any of the United States, its territories, the District of Columbia, or any foreign nation. In cases where the appointment of a personal representative in Texas is unnecessary, Tex. Estates Code Ann. §503.001 permits an authenticated copy of the foreign will and of the order admitting the will to probate to be filed in the records of the county where the land is located. If a personal representative is needed, Tex. Estates Code Ann. §§501.001-501.008 provide a simplified procedure for the probate in Texas of the foreign will.

This procedure is rarely used, however, as the recording of the will in the deed records is usually sufficient for most purposes.

If a foreign will that is recorded in the deed records gives an executor a power of sale, that power may be exercised in Texas without court order. Tex. Estates Code Ann. §505.052.

Although only the will and the order probating the will are necessary, a complete copy of the foreign probate, including the application to probate and the order closing the estate, is desirable as it may contain important information, such as the date of the decedent's death and the names and addresses of surviving heirs.

CAUTION

An exemplified copy is not a mere certified copy. To be exemplified, the foreign will and the order admitting it to probate must be authenticated in the manner prescribed in Tex. Estates Code Ann. §§501.002, 503.002. The required documentation is commonly called a "three-way certificate."

Although there is scant authority, it appears that a foreign executor's power to convey Texas real property, if granted by the foreign will, may not be relied upon unless the foreign will has been probated or authenticated copies of the foreign will and its probate filed for record in at least one Texas county before the time of

the executor's deed. Unfortunately, the court in *Mills v. Herndon*, 60 Tex. 353, 355-56 (1883), stated unequivocally, albeit as dictum, that a foreign executor has no authority to convey Texas property until the statutory filing has been accomplished and that subsequent compliance would not relate back and give validity to prior acts done without authority. *See also Coy v. Gaye*, 84 S.W. 441 (Tex. Civ. App.—San Antonio 1904, no writ); 17 M. K. Woodward and Ernest E. Smith, III, *Tex. Prac., Prob. & Decedents' Estates* §434 (1971).

Source:

Citations in the Comment; Tex. Estates Code Ann. §§501.001-501.008, 503.001, 505.052; 17 M. K. Woodward & Ernest E. Smith, III, *Tex. Prac., Prob & Decedents' Estates* §421 (1971).

History:

Adopted Oct. 9, 1999.

CHAPTER XII. BANKRUPTCIES

STANDARD 12.10. RELEVANCE OF BANKRUPTCY CASES TO REAL ESTATE TRANSACTIONS

The examiner should consider whether a person in the chain of title or in a proposed transaction is or was a debtor in a bankruptcy proceeding. If the person in the chain of title has been or is a debtor in a bankruptcy proceeding, the land may have been or may be property of the estate, subject to the jurisdiction and control of the bankruptcy proceeding.

COMMENT

A "debtor" is a person or municipality concerning which a bankruptcy case has been commenced since October 1, 1979, the effective date of the Bankruptcy Code. 11 U.S.C. §101(13). Formerly, the person subject to a bankruptcy case was commonly known as a "bankrupt." There are generally four types of bankruptcy cases: a Chapter 7 "liquidation"; a Chapter 11 "reorganization"; a Chapter 12 "adjustment of debts of a family farmer or fisherman with regular annual income"; and a Chapter 13 "adjustment of debts of an individual with regular income." A Chapter 9 case applies only to a political subdivision or public agency or instrumentality of a state. A Chapter 15 case concerns ancillary and other cross-border cases. The commencement of a voluntary case (filed by the debtor alone or jointly with a spouse) or an involuntary case (filed by another person, such as a creditor) creates an estate. The estate includes all legal and equitable interests of the debtor in property as of the commencement of the case. The estate also includes property that the debtor acquires or becomes entitled to acquire within 180 days after the commencement of the case by bequest, devise or inheritance, by property settlement agreement with the debtor's spouse or in an interlocutory or final divorce decree, or as a beneficiary of a life insurance policy or death benefit plan. 11 U.S.C. §541. The trustee may avoid postpetition transactions (transactions occurring after the commencement of the bankruptcy case of the debtor), unless protected under §§549(b) and (c) of Title 11 or unless the transaction is authorized by the bankruptcy court or the Bankruptcy Code. 11 U.S.C. §549(a). The trustee may not avoid a transfer made by the debtor in an involuntary bankruptcy case before the order for relief, to the extent any value is given in exchange for the transfer, notwithstanding any notice or knowledge of the bankruptcy case that the transferee has. 11 U.S.C. §549(b). The trustee may not avoid a transfer of an interest in real property to a good faith purchaser without knowledge of the commencement of the case and for present fair equivalent value unless a copy or notice of the petition was filed in the real property records before the transfer was perfected. 11 U.S.C. §549(c). A "purchaser" is a transferee of a voluntary transfer and includes the immediate or mediate transferee of such transferee. 11 U.S.C. §101(43). A "transfer" includes the creation of a lien, a foreclosure, and each mode, direct or indirect, absolute or conditional, voluntary or involuntary, of disposing or parting with property or an interest in property. 11 U.S.C. §101(54). The automatic stay does not apply to a transfer that is not avoidable under 11 U.S.C. §544 and that is not avoidable under Section 549. 11 U.S.C. §362(b)(24). An action or proceeding under 11 U.S.C. §549 to set aside a postpetition transaction must be commenced no later than the earlier of (1) two years after the date of the transfer or (2) the time the case is closed or dismissed. 11 U.S.C. §549(d).

Source:

Citations in the Comment; 5 *Collier on Bankruptcy*, Chapters 541, 549 (Alan N. Resnick & Henry J. Sommer eds. Matthew Bender & Company, Inc., a member of LexisNexis, 16th Revised 2014).

History:

Adopted Oct. 9, 1999.

STANDARD 12.20. AUTHORITY FOR PRIOR TRANSFER

If the examiner has knowledge that the owner or transferor in a prior real estate transaction recorded within two years prior to the current examination was then a debtor in a bankruptcy case, the examiner should determine that the prior transfer was authorized in that case. If the chain of title discloses that the

owner or transferor in a prior real estate transaction in the chain of title was then a debtor in a bankruptcy case, the examiner should determine that the prior transfer was authorized in that case.

COMMENT

If a prior real estate transaction in the chain of title was recorded more than two years prior to the current examination and if a bankruptcy case filed by or against the transferor or owner in that prior transaction is not disclosed in the chain of title, the examiner is not required to determine whether the prior real estate transaction was authorized in a bankruptcy proceeding, regardless of whether the examiner has knowledge that the owner or transferor in the prior transaction was then a debtor in a bankruptcy case. Notice is commonly given by a copy or notice of the bankruptcy petition filed by or against the owner or transferor. 11 U.S.C. §549(c).

The trustee in a bankruptcy case may not avoid a transfer of an interest in real property to a good faith purchaser without knowledge of the commencement of the case and for present fair equivalent value unless a copy or notice of the petition was filed in the real property records before the transfer was perfected. 11 U.S.C. §549(c). An action or proceeding under 11 U.S.C. §549 to set aside a post-petition transaction must be commenced no later than the earlier of (1) two years after the date of the transfer or (2) the time the case is closed or dismissed. 11 U.S.C. §549(d).

CAUTION

A mortgagee purchasing at a foreclosure of its mortgage encumbering an interest owned by the debtor may not be protected under 11 U.S.C. §549(c) (absent lift or annulment of the automatic stay) because it has not paid present consideration. *In re Penfil*, 40 B.R. 474 (Bankr. E.D. Mich. 1984); *In re Major*, 218 B.R. 501 (Bankr. W.D. Mo. 1998). A third-party bona fide purchaser without knowledge buying at a foreclosure may not be protected—at least unless the third party establishes that it paid fair present equivalent value, which may not be established solely by the amount bid at the foreclosure sale. *In re Miller*, 454 F.3d 899 (8th Cir. 2006). Although Section 362(b)(24) provides that the automatic stay does not apply to a transfer that is not avoidable under §549, the purchaser may not be treated as a protected purchaser because the definition of "purchaser" means "transferee of a voluntary transfer." 11 U.S.C. §101 (43).

Prior to the 2005 amendments to the Bankruptcy Code, a beneficiary of a deed of trust from the debtor was not protected under 11 U.S.C. §549(c). *In re McConville*, 110 F.3d 47 (9th Cir. 1997). The postpetition bona fide mortgagee will now be protected if a copy or notice of the bankruptcy petition is not filed before the mortgage is filed, provided that the mortgagee acquired the mortgage in good faith without knowledge of the bankruptcy and the lender provided present fair equivalent value (or fair market value). *Hopkins v. Suntrust Mortg., Inc.*, 441 B.R. 656 (Bankr. D. Idaho 2010). An amendment to §549(c) protects a post-petition transfer of "an interest in" real property, the addition of §362(b)(24) provides that the stay does not apply to a transfer that is not avoidable under §549, and the expansion of the definition of "transfer" in §101(54) includes the creation of a lien. 11 U.S.C. §§101(54), 362(b)(24), 549(c). However, this protection is contingent upon the lender being a "bona fide" lender without knowledge of the bankruptcy.

An assignee of a deed of trust from a debtor apparently will not be protected by 11 U.S.C. §549(c) because the assignment involves a sale of a promissory note secured by a deed of trust, and the note "retains its identity as personal property" which is not protected by §549(c). *In re Rice*, 83 B.R. 8, 11 (Bankr. 9th Cir. 1987).

Source:
Standard 1.20; Citations in the Comment; 5 *Collier on Bankruptcy*, Chapter 549 (Alan N. Resnick & Henry J. Sommer eds. Matthew Bender & Company, Inc., a member of LexisNexis, 16th Ed. Revised 2014).

History:
Adopted Oct. 9, 1999.

STANDARD 12.30. RELIANCE UPON RECITALS OF AUTHORITY FOR PRIOR TRANSFER

If a copy of an order in the bankruptcy case authorizing a prior real estate transaction in the chain of title has been recorded, the examiner may rely upon the order to determine that the transaction was authorized in the bankruptcy case. If the instrument evidencing the transaction was recorded more than two years prior to the examination, the examiner may rely upon any recitals in the chain of title that the transaction was authorized in bankruptcy case. Recitals may include a statement in the instrument in the chain of title that the grantor was acting as trustee or debtor in possession, that the property had been exempted or abandoned,

that the automatic stay had been lifted or annulled to authorize a foreclosure, or that the transaction evidenced by the instrument had been otherwise authorized in the bankruptcy case.

COMMENT

Although the Bankruptcy Code does not explicitly authorize reliance upon recitals in an instrument executed by the debtor or trustee, there are numerous legal principles that will generally justify reliance upon the apparent authority set forth in an instrument in the chain of title. An action or proceeding by the trustee to set aside a transfer of property of the estate made after the commencement of the bankruptcy case and that is not properly authorized may not be commenced after the earlier of (1) two years after the date of the transfer sought to be avoided or (2) the time the case is closed or dismissed. 11 U.S.C. §549(d). A motion to set aside a judgment or order must be made within one year if for (1) mistake, inadvertence, surprise, or excusable neglect; (2) newly discovered evidence which by due diligence could not have been discovered in time to move for a new trial; or (3) fraud, misrepresentation, or other misconduct of an adverse party. This time limit to file a motion to set aside a judgment or order does not apply if the judgment is void. Fed. R. Civ. P. 60(b). The Bankruptcy Code also favors reliance upon court orders, notwithstanding appeals from those orders. The reversal or modification of an authorization of sale or lease under 11 U.S.C. §363(b) or (c) does not affect the validity of the sale or lease to an entity that purchased or leased in good faith, whether or not the entity knew of the pendency of an appeal, unless the sale or lease was stayed pending appeal. 11 U.S.C. §363(m). The reversal or modification on appeal of an authorization to obtain credit and grant a lien does not affect the validity or priority of the lien to an entity that extended such credit in good faith, whether or not the entity knew of the pendency of the appeal, unless the granting of the lien was stayed pending appeal. 11 U.S.C. §364(e). A motion to revoke a confirmation of a plan must be filed before 180 days after entry of the order of confirmation. 11 U.S.C. §§1144, 1230, 1330.

CAUTION

If the examiner has knowledge that the transaction was not properly authorized or is in dispute, the examiner may make additional requirements. For example, if the taxing authority has refused to remove delinquent taxes from the tax rolls based upon a sale free and clear of liens, the examiner may require an additional court order or except to the taxes. Note that [11 U.S.C. §]106, which waives sovereign immunity of certain governmental units, may be unconstitutional, at least in part as to Section 106(a), because of the limitations of U. S. Const. amend XI. *See In re Mitchell*, 209 F.3d 1111 (9th Cir. 2000) (filing of adversary proceeding against non-consenting state violates sovereign immunity). However, Section 106(b), which provides that the filing of a claim may be a valid partial waiver of sovereign immunity regarding the same transaction or occurrence, may be constitutional. *Arecibo Community Health Care, Inc. v. Commonwealth of Puerto Rico*, 270 F.3d 17 (1st Cir. 2001) (citing cases considering whether Section 106(b), which waives immunity based on filing of claim, is constitutional). In addition, states are not immune from preference avoidance or other in rem proceedings. *Central Virginia Comm. College v. Katz*, 546 U.S. 356, 126 S.Ct. 990, 163 L.Ed. 2d 945 (2006). A sale free and clear of a state lien will not violate sovereign immunity.

> [I]n *Van Huffel v. Harkelrode*, 284 U.S. 225, 228-229, 76 L. Ed. 256, 52 S.Ct. 115 (1931), we held that the Bankruptcy Court had the authority to sell a debtor's property "free and clear" of a State's tax lien. At least when the bankruptcy court's jurisdiction over the res is unquestioned our cases indicate that the exercise of its in rem jurisdiction to discharge a debt does not infringe state sovereignty... In *Van Huffel*, we affirmed the bankruptcy courts' power to sell property free from encumbrances, including States' liens, and approvingly noted that some courts had chosen specifically to discharge States' liens for taxes....

Tennessee Student Assistance Corp. v. Hood, 541 U.S. 440, 450-451, 124 S.Ct. 1905, 158 L. Ed. 2d 764 (2004).

Source:

Citations in the Comment; Standard 3.40; 3 *Collier on Bankruptcy*, ¶s 363.11, 364.06; 5 *Collier on Bankruptcy*, ¶549.07; 8 *Collier on Bankruptcy*, Chapters 1144, 1230, 1330 (Alan N. Resnick & Henry J. Sommer eds. Matthew Bender & Company, Inc., a member of LexisNexis, 16th Ed. Revised 2014).

History:

Adopted Oct. 9, 1999.

STANDARD 12.40. AUTHORITY FOR PROPOSED TRANSFER BY DEBTOR OR TRUSTEE

If the examiner has knowledge that the owner is the debtor in a bankruptcy case or if the bankruptcy is disclosed in the chain of title in the real property records,

the examiner should determine whether the proposed transaction is authorized in that case and should require that a certified copy of the order or other evidence of authority be recorded in the real property records.

COMMENT

The commencement of a bankruptcy case creates an estate, which includes legal or equitable interests of the debtor in property as of the commencement of the case, and in property the debtor acquires within 180 days after the commencement of the case by bequest, devise or inheritance, or as a result of a property settlement agreement with the debtor's spouse. 11 U.S.C. §541(a). The estate does not include certain interests in liquid or gaseous hydrocarbons to the extent the debtor has transferred or agreed to transfer the interests pursuant to a farmout agreement or any written agreement directly related to a farmout agreement, or to the extent the debtor has transferred such interest pursuant to a written conveyance of a production payment to an entity that does not participate in the operation of the property. 11 U.S.C. §§541(b)(4), 101(21A), 101(42A), 101(56A). A bankruptcy petition creates an automatic stay, which includes a stay against enforcement against the debtor or property of the debtor of a claim that arose before the commencement of the case. 11 U.S.C. §362. The debtor or trustee may not sell or mortgage property of the estate, except as authorized by 11 U.S.C. §§363, 364. The trustee in a bankruptcy proceeding may not avoid a transfer of an interest in real property to a good faith purchaser without knowledge of the commencement of the case and for present fair equivalent value unless a copy or notice of the petition was filed in the real property records before the transfer was perfected. 11 U.S.C. §549(c). An action or proceeding under 11 U.S.C. §549 to set aside a post-petition transaction must be commenced no later than the earlier of (1) two years after the date of the transfer or (2) the time the case is closed or dismissed. 11 U.S.C. §549(d). If the examiner has knowledge that the current owner is a debtor in a bankruptcy case, the examiner should require satisfactory evidence that the current transaction is authorized.

CAUTION

See Standard 12.20.

Source:

Citations in the Comment; 3 *Collier on Bankruptcy*, Chapters 362, 363, 364; 5 *Collier on Bankruptcy*, Chapters 541, 549 (Alan N. Resnick & Henry J. Sommer eds. Matthew Bender & Company, Inc., a member of LexisNexis, 16th Ed. Revised 2014).

History:

Adopted Oct. 9, 1999.

STANDARD 12.50. AUTHORITY TO CONVEY EXEMPTED LAND IN PROPOSED TRANSACTION

If the examiner has knowledge that the current owner is the debtor in a bankruptcy case and the property is to be sold by the debtor based on the debtor's claim of exemptions in the bankruptcy case, the examiner should require evidence that (1) the land was claimed in the Schedule of Exempt Property as exempt under state law and (2) no objections were made within 30 days after the conclusion of the "first" meeting of creditors or the filing of any amendment to the list or supplemental schedules or such longer time for objection as was granted by the court. The examiner should require that evidence that the property has been exempted be recorded in the real property records.

COMMENT

An individual debtor may exempt from property of the estate that property claimed as exempt under state law or under the applicable federal exemptions. In a joint case, both spouses must choose the same exemptions. 11 U.S.C. §522(b)(1). Fed. R. Bankr. P. 4003(b) provides that the trustee or any creditor may file objection to the claimed exemptions within 30 days after the conclusion of the meeting of creditors or the filing of any amendment to the list or supplemental schedules, unless the court grants additional time for objection within that period. If objection has been filed, the examiner should also be furnished for review any order by the bankruptcy court overruling or otherwise resolving such objection.

The exemptions are scheduled in the Schedule of Real Property (Schedule "B-1" for cases filed prior to August 1, 1991, or Schedule "A" for cases filed on or after August 1, 1991) and the Schedule of Exempt Property (Schedule "B-4" for cases filed prior to August 1, 1991, or Schedule "C" for cases filed on or after August 1, 1991). The Schedules should be reviewed to verify whether the exemptions under state law (pursuant to 11 U.S.C. §522(b)(3)) are chosen or whether the federal exemptions (pursuant to 11 U.S.C. §§522(b)(2), 522(d)) are chosen. If the federal exemptions are chosen, only an equity interest is exempted (subject to indexing of the allowed amount pursuant to 11 U.S.C. §104) and the remaining value of the land remains part of the estate until abandoned. If the state exemptions

are chosen, the exemptions are subject to the limitations set forth in 11 U.S.C. §522. The title examiner also should be aware that even though property is exempt, a mortgagee or other lien creditor may not commence or continue a foreclosure action against the debtor or obtain a conveyance from the debtor, so long as the automatic stay continues in effect. Unless relief from the automatic stay has been obtained (by final order of the bankruptcy court to permit the action) or an exception to the stay applies under §362(b), the stay continues until the earliest of (a) the closing of the bankruptcy case, (b) the dismissal of the bankruptcy case or (c), in a Chapter 7 case concerning an individual or in a case under Chapters 9, 11, 12 or 13, the grant or denial of discharge. 11 U.S.C. §362; Fed. R. Bankr. P. 4001.

CAUTION

An examiner should not rely upon evidence that the land has been exempted in a Chapter 12 or Chapter 13 bankruptcy case prior to the court's discharge after completion of the plan, unless the court authorizes the conveyance or encumbrance by the debtor in the plan or a separate order. *In re Turek*, 346 B.R. 350 (Bankr. M.D. Pa. 2006). The sale or encumbrance by the debtor may require a modification of the plan or may require court approval because of local rules or provisions of the plan.

Source:

Citations in the Comment; Fed R. Bankr. P. 1007(c); 4 *Collier on Bankruptcy*, Chapter 522, ¶522.05 (Alan N. Resnick & Henry J. Sommer eds. Matthew Bender & Company, Inc., a member of LexisNexis, 16th Ed. Revised 2014).

History:

Adopted Oct. 9, 1999.

STANDARD 12.60. AUTHORITY TO CONVEY ABANDONED LAND IN PROPOSED TRANSACTION

If the examiner has knowledge that the current owner is the debtor in a bankruptcy case and the property is to be sold by the debtor based on abandonment of the property in the bankruptcy case, the examiner should require evidence that (1) the trustee in the bankruptcy case or the debtor in possession gave notice of intent to abandon the property and that no objections were filed within 14 days after the mailing of the notice or such other time fixed by the court, (2) the bankruptcy court ordered the property abandoned, by a final nonappealable court order, or (3) the property is scheduled in the bankruptcy case and is not dealt with prior to the closing of the case. The examiner should require that a certified copy of the order of abandonment or other evidence of authority to abandon be recorded in the real property records.

COMMENT

After notice and a hearing, the trustee (or debtor in possession) may abandon property of the bankruptcy estate. On request of a party in interest and after notice and a hearing, the court may order the trustee to abandon property of the estate. A party in interest must file and serve an objection to the notice of proposed abandonment by the trustee or debtor in possession within 14 days of the mailing of the notice, or within the time fixed by the court. 11 U.S.C. §§554, 1107; Fed. R. Bankr. P. 6007. Upon abandonment, control of the property abandoned reverts to and revests in the debtor. In such event, unless the automatic stay has terminated, a mortgagee or other lien creditor must obtain relief from the automatic stay as to the debtor by final order of the bankruptcy court before foreclosing the debtor's interest. 11 U.S.C. §362; Fed. R. Bankr. P. 4001. An order of abandonment is not final and nonappealable until 14 days after the entry of the order. Fed. R. Bankr. P. 8002. Unless the court orders otherwise, property scheduled and not otherwise administered at the time of the closing of the estate is abandoned to the debtor. Property that is not abandoned and that is not administered (such as property never scheduled or dealt with) remains property of the estate. 11 U.S.C. §554.

CAUTION

The examiner should not rely upon the final report of the trustee as constituting a closing of the estate. The final report and final account constitute a presumption of full administration if no objections are filed within 30 days, but are not equivalent to an order closing the estate. Fed. R. Bankr. P. 5009; *In re Reed*, 89 B.R. 100 (Bankr. C.D.Cal.1988), aff'd 940 F.2d 1317 (9th Cir. 1991) (discussing "no asset" report); *In re Ginsberg*, 164 B.R. 870 (Bankr. S.D. N.Y. 1994); *In re Schoenewerk*, 304 B.R. 59 (Bankr. E.D. N.Y. 2003).

Source:

Citations in the Comment; 5 *Collier on Bankruptcy*, Chapter 554 (Alan N. Resnick & Henry J. Sommer eds. Matthew Bender & Company, Inc., a member of LexisNexis, 16th Ed. Revised 2014).

History:

Adopted Oct. 9, 1999.

STANDARD 12.70. AUTHORITY TO FORECLOSE LAND IN PROPOSED TRANSACTION

If a deed of trust encumbering property of the estate or property of the debtor is to be foreclosed and the automatic stay has not otherwise terminated, the examiner should require satisfactory evidence that the mort-

gagee filed a motion to lift stay, that notice of the motion for relief from the automatic stay was served in accordance with the Bankruptcy Rules and applicable local rules, and that the bankruptcy court granted the motion prior to commencement of the foreclosure. The examiner should require that a certified copy of the order lifting stay or other evidence of lift of stay be recorded in the real property records.

COMMENT

The filing of a bankruptcy petition operates as an automatic stay that prevents enforcement of any lien against property of the estate and that prevents enforcement of a lien that secured a claim that arose before the commencement of the case. 11 U.S.C. §362. A motion for relief from the automatic stay must be served in accordance with Fed. R. Bankr. P. 4001 and 9014. The motion must be served on the official committees, or on scheduled creditors, if there are no committees appointed. The motion also must be served on such other entities as the court may order and as provided by local rules. Fed. R. Bankr. P. 4001(a)(1). For example, Rule 4001 of the Bankruptcy Rules for the Southern District of Texas requires that, in addition to service required by Fed. R. Bankr. P. 4001, the motion must be served on the debtor, debtor's attorney, parties requesting notice, parties with an interest in collateral that is the subject of the requested relief (e.g., other lienholders), co-debtors under 11 U.S.C. §1301, parties who are identified as a party against whom relief is sought in the motion, and the trustee. An agreement for relief from the stay may be granted after notice, unless objections are filed within 15 days after mailing of notice (or such other time fixed by the court). Fed. R. Bankr. P. 4001(d).

A bankruptcy court may terminate, lift, or annul a stay. The automatic stay may be lifted or, for a variety of reasons, may not exist, such as (1) without court order after passage of 30 days after motion for relief, unless the court continues the stay (or after 60 days, if the debtor is an individual in a Chapter 7, 11, or 13 proceeding), 11 U.S.C. §362(e), Advisory Committee Note to R4001; (2) by court order recorded in the real property records and effective for two years that finds the petition was part of a scheme to delay, hinder, and defraud creditors involving multiple filings or transfers without lender consent, 11 U.S.C. §§362(b), 362(d)(4); (3) where a case is filed in violation of a bankruptcy court order in a prior case, 11 U.S.C. §362(b)(21)(B); or (4) by court order confirming that the stay has been terminated because of certain frequent filings, 11 U.S.C. §362(j). The court may annul a stay after a foreclosure has been commenced or conducted. 11 U.S.C. §362(d). The stay does not otherwise terminate until the case is closed, until the case is dismissed, or, if the case is under Chapter 7 concerning an individual or under Chapter 9, 11, 12, or 13, until the time the discharge is granted or denied. The discharge is granted or denied in a case under Chapter 11 upon confirmation of the plan, unless the debtor is an individual. 11 U.S.C.A. §1141(d). The discharge is granted or denied in a case under Chapter 12 or 13, or in a case of an individual under Chapter 11, after completion of the plan. 11 U.S.C.A. §§1141(d), 1228, 1328. An order granting a lift or annulment of stay is not final and nonappealable until 14 days after the entry of the order. Fed. R. Bankr. P. 8002. An order granting a motion for relief from the automatic stay is stayed until the expiration of 14 days after the entry of the order, unless the court orders otherwise. Fed. R. Bankr. P. 4001(a)(3).

Source:

Citations in the Comment; 3 *Collier on Bankruptcy*, Chapter 362 (Alan N. Resnick & Henry J. Sommer eds. Matthew Bender & Company, Inc., a member of LexisNexis, 16th Ed. Revised 2014).

History:

Adopted Oct. 9, 1999; amended June 16, 2006; amended June 27, 2008. The amended standard of June 16, 2006 provided: "If a deed of trust encumbering property of the estate or property of the debtor is to be foreclosed and the automatic stay has not otherwise terminated, the examiner should require satisfactory evidence that (1) the mortgagee filed a motion to lift stay; (2) notice of the motion for relief from the automatic stay was served in accordance with the Bankruptcy Rules and applicable local rules; and (3) the bankruptcy court granted the motion prior to commencement of the foreclosure; or, if no order grants or denies relief or continues the stay more than 60 days from the date of the request for relief from the stay prior to commencement of the foreclosure if the debtor is an individual in a Chapter 7, 11 or 13 case or otherwise more than 30 days from the date of the request for relief from the stay prior to commencement of the foreclosure. The examiner should require that a certified copy of the order lifting stay or other evidence of lift of stay be recorded in the real property records."

The original standard provided: "If a deed of trust encumbering property of the estate or property of the debtor is to be foreclosed and the automatic stay has not otherwise terminated, the examiner should require satisfactory evidence that (1) the mortgagee filed a motion to lift stay; (2) notice of the motion for relief from the automatic stay was served in accordance with the Bankruptcy Rules and applicable local rules; and (3) the bankruptcy court granted the motion prior to commencement of the foreclosure; or, if no order grants or denies relief or continues the stay, more than 30 days passed from the date of the request for relief from the stay prior to commencement of the foreclosure. The examiner should require that a certified copy of the order lifting stay or other evidence of lift of stay be recorded in the real property records."

STANDARD 12.80. AUTHORITY TO CONVEY OR LEASE PROPERTY OF THE BANKRUPTCY ESTATE NOT IN THE ORDINARY COURSE OF BUSINESS IN PROPOSED TRANSACTION

If property will be sold or leased by the bankruptcy trustee or debtor in possession, other than in the ordi-

nary course of business, the examiner should require evidence of the following: (1) 21 days' notice of sale to the debtor, the trustee, all creditors and indenture trustees by mail, unless the court orders the time shortened; (2) no objections to the sale were made or the court by order overruled the objections and authorized the sale; and (3) the order of sale, if any, is nonappealable or is not stayed pending appeal. The examiner should require that a certified copy of the order or other evidence of authority to sell or lease be recorded in the real property records.

COMMENT

The trustee or debtor in possession, after notice and a hearing, may sell property of the estate other than in the ordinary course of business. 11 U.S.C. §§363, 1107. The clerk or some other person as the court may direct must give the debtor, the trustee, all creditors and indenture trustees at least 21 days' notice by mail of a proposed sale of property of the estate other than in the ordinary course of business, unless the court for cause shortens the time or directs another method of notice. Fed. R. Bankr. P. 2002(a), 6004. The reversal or modification on appeal of an order of sale does not affect the finality or validity of a sale to an entity that bought the property in good faith, whether or not the entity knew of the appeal, unless the sale was stayed pending appeal. 11 U.S.C. §363(m). An order authorizing a sale is not final and nonappealable until 14 days after the entry of the order. Fed. R. Bankr. P. 8002. An order authorizing the use, sale, or lease of property other than cash collateral is stayed until the expiration of 14 days after entry of the order, unless the court orders otherwise. Fed. R. Bankr. P. 6004(h). An objection to a proposed sale must be filed and served no less than seven days before the date set for the proposed action or in the time set by the court. Fed. R. Bankr. P. 6004(b). If timely objection is not made, court approval of the sale is not required. Fed. R. Bankr. P. 6004(e); 11 U.S.C. §§102(1), 363(b). A grant or transfer of rights under an oil and gas lease would be governed by the requirements for a sale of property of the estate and would not be controlled by the provisions relating to rejection, assumption, and assignment of executory contracts and unexpired leases. *In re Topco, Inc.*, 894 F.2d 727, 739 (5th Cir. 1990) reh'g denied, en banc; *River Production Co. v. Webb*, 902 F.2d 955 (5th Cir. 1990) (dictum at footnote 17 asserts that state law determines whether oil and gas leases are subject to §365 as unexpired leases, and that such oil and gas "leases" in Texas are conveyances of determinable fee interests subject to the provisions of §363 regarding sales, rather than subject to §365 as unexpired "leases"); *K&D Energy v. KY USA Energy, Inc. (In re KY USA Energy, Inc.)*, 444 B.R. 734 (Bankr. W.D. Ky. 2011) (holding that, because a farmout assignment assigns interests in oil and gas leases, it is not an executory contract because the rights assigned were interests in real estate and not a true lease); *In re WRT Energy Corporation*, 202 B.R. 579 (Bankr. W.D.La.1996) (Louisiana mineral lease was not an unexpired lease or executory contract subject to assumption or rejection under 11 U.S.C. §365).

CAUTION

In certain circumstances, an examiner should not rely upon a court order authorizing a sale from the time that the order is signed or entered on the docket. For example, the issue of the good faith of the purchaser may be considered on appeal, even though no stay was granted. *In re Paolo Gucci*, 105 F.3d 837 (2d Cir. 1997); *In re Abbotts Dairies of Pennsylvania, Inc.*, 788 F.2d 143 (3d Cir. 1986). Also, an order authorizing a sale is automatically "stayed" for 14 days after entry of the order, unless the court orders otherwise. Fed. R. Bank. P. 6004(h).

Source:

Citations in the Comment; 3 *Collier on Bankruptcy*, Chapter 363 (Alan N. Resnick & Henry J. Sommer eds. Matthew Bender & Company, Inc., a member of LexisNexis, 16th Ed. Revised 2014).

History:

Adopted Oct. 9, 1999.

STANDARD 12.90. AUTHORITY TO CONVEY PROPERTY OF THE BANKRUPTCY ESTATE IN THE ORDINARY COURSE OF BUSINESS IN PROPOSED TRANSACTION

If property will be sold or leased by the bankruptcy trustee or debtor in possession, in the ordinary course of business, the examiner should require evidence of the following: (1) if the trustee is acting in a Chapter 7 case, the court must authorize the trustee to operate the business and should authorize real estate sales in the ordinary course of business; or (2) if the debtor in possession or trustee is acting in a Chapter 11 case, the authority of the debtor or trustee has not been limited by court order (and no plan has been confirmed). The examiner also should require evidence that the sale will be made in the ordinary course of business be recorded in the real property records.

COMMENT

The trustee or debtor in possession may sell or lease property of the estate in the ordinary course of business if authorized to operate the business under 11 U.S.C. §§721, 1108, 1203, 1204 or 1304. 11 U.S.C. §363(c)(1). The court may authorize the trustee to operate the business of the debtor for a limited period in a Chapter 7 case. 11 U.S.C. §721. Unless the court orders otherwise, the trustee may operate the debtor's business in a Chapter 11 case. 11 U.S.C. §1108. A debtor in possession in a Chapter 12 case has the rights of a trustee serving in a Chapter 11 case, unless the court orders otherwise. 11 U.S.C. §1203. Unless the court orders otherwise, a debtor engaged in business may operate the business of the debtor and has the powers of a trustee under §363(c). 11 U.S.C. §1303.

CAUTION

In order to accomplish an ordinary course of business sale or lease, some examiners will require (1) an order authorizing the trustee or debtor in possession to sell or lease in the ordinary course of business, (2) a specific order authorizing the sale or lease, or (3) notice of a proposed sale or lease and evidence that no objection to the sale or lease was filed. However, many examiners do not believe that a sale or lease of real property in the ordinary course of business may be made in a Chapter 12 or Chapter 13 proceeding. If the sale or lease is not made in the ordinary course of business and is not otherwise authorized, it may be avoidable as a post-petition transaction. 11 U.S.C. §549.

Source:

Citations in the Comment; 3 *Collier on Bankruptcy*, Chapter 363 (Alan N. Resnick & Henry J. Sommer eds. Matthew Bender & Company, Inc., a member of LexisNexis, 16th Ed. Revised 2014).

History:

Adopted Oct. 9, 1999.

STANDARD 12.100. AUTHORITY TO CONVEY PROPERTY OF THE BANKRUPTCY ESTATE FREE & CLEAR OF LIENS IN PROPOSED TRANSACTION

If property will be sold by the bankruptcy trustee or debtor in possession free and clear of liens, the examiner should require evidence that: (1) 21 days' notice of sale disclosing that the sale would be made free and clear of liens was given to the debtor, the trustee, all creditors, including the creditors secured by liens on the land, and indenture trustees by mail, unless the court orders the time shortened; (2) the court by order authorized the sale free and clear of liens; and (3) the order of sale is nonappealable or is not stayed pending appeal. The examiner should require that a certified copy of the order be recorded in the real property records.

COMMENT

The trustee or debtor in possession, after notice and a hearing, may sell property of the estate free and clear of liens. 11 U.S.C. §§363(f), 1107. The clerk or some other person as the court may direct must give the debtor, the trustee, all creditors and indenture trustees at least 21 days' notice by mail of a proposed sale of property of the estate, unless the court for cause shortens the time or directs another method of notice. Fed. R. Bankr. P. 2002(a), 6004. A motion for authority to sell free and clear of liens must be served on the parties who have liens or other interests in the property. The notice shall include the date of the hearing on the motion and the time within which objections may be filed and served. Fed. R. Bankr. P. 6004(c). The reversal or modification on appeal of an order of sale does not affect the finality or validity of a sale to an entity that bought the property in good faith, whether or not the entity knew of the appeal, unless the sale was stayed pending appeal. 11 U.S.C. §363(m). An order authorizing a sale is not final and nonappealable until 14 days after the entry of the order. Fed. R. Bankr. P. 8002. The date of "entry" of an order is the date that the order is noted on the docket; the date of signature of an order is not determinative of the date of entry. Fed. R. Bankr. P. 5003(a). An order authorizing the use, sale, or lease of property other than cash collateral is stayed until the expiration of 14 days after entry of the order, unless the court orders otherwise. Fed. R. Bankr. P. 6004(h).

CAUTION

In certain circumstances, an examiner should not rely upon a court order authorizing a sale from the time that the order is signed or entered on the docket. For example, the issue of the good faith of the purchaser may be considered on appeal, even though no stay was granted. *In re Paolo Gucci*, 105 F.3d 837 (2d Cir.1997); *In re Abbotts Dairies of Pennsylvania, Inc.*, 788 F.2d 143 (3d Cir.1986). The Bankruptcy Code §363(f) provides several bases to sell free and clear of liens, including a sale if the price is greater than the aggregate "value" of all liens, or a sale if the lien is in bona fide dispute. Many orders free and clear of liens provide that the

liens attach to the proceeds, and an examiner may wish to include such requirement. Given the reluctance of taxing authorities to recognize such sales, the examiner may require payment of taxes, absent approval of the order by the taxing authority. For the sale to be made free and clear of an IRS lien, notice must have been given to (1) the IRS, (2) the United States attorney for the district in which the action is brought, and (3) the Attorney General. Fed. R. Bankr. P. 6004(c), 7004 (b)(4), 9014. Notice to an insured depository institution must include notice by certified mail to an officer, unless the institution has appeared by its attorney in the bankruptcy case or unless the court orders otherwise after certified mail notice of an application to authorize service by first class mail, or the institution has waived right to service by certified mail. Fed. R. Bankr. P. 7004(h) [amended by 2014 US Order 0011 (C.O. 0011)]. The 2005 amendments to the Bankruptcy Code changed the requirements for various notices, 11 USC §342 (notice to the current account number and address at which the creditor requests notice pursuant to Section 342(c)(2)(A)); however, an examiner reasonably and customarily relies on certificates confirming notice as evidence of compliance with the notice requirements. A sale may be made free and clear of the interest of a co-owner pursuant to §363(h). However, the sale must be made pursuant to an adversary proceeding. Fed. R. Bankr. P. 7001(3).

The bankruptcy estate does not include PACA (Perishable Agricultural Commodities Act, 7 U.S.C. §499a, et seq.) and P&SA (Packers and Stockyards Act, 7 U.S.C. §181, et seq.) trust assets. Thus, a sale cannot be made free and clear of such rights. *See In re Kornblum & Co.*, 81 F.3d 280 (2d Cir. 1996) (holding that a single PACA trust exists for the benefit of all sellers to a produce dealer); *In re Panache Cuisine*, 2013 WL 5350613, 58 Bankr. Ct. Dec. (LRP) 129 (Bankr. D. Md. Sept. 23, 2013) (holding that disputed claims under PACA should be resolved by adversary proceedings and not by claims objections).

Various decisions conclude that a sale cannot be made free and clear of certain third party interests in real property that are not in dispute, including easements (*In re Pintlar Corp.*, 187 B.R. 680 (Bankr. D. Idaho 1995), restrictions of record that run with the land (*In re Oyster Bay Cove*, 196 B.R. 251 (E.D. N.Y. 1996), and certain leases (*In re MMH Auto Group, LLC*, 385 B.R. 47 (Bankr. S.D. 2008). *But see Precision Industries, Inc. v. Qualitech Steel SBQ, LLC*, 327 F.3d 537 (7th Cir. 2003), which allowed such a sale involving a lease).

The *Clear Channel* case concerned a particular type of sale free and clear of liens: "This appeal presents a simple issue: outside a plan of reorganization, does Section 363(f) of the Bankruptcy Code permit a secured creditor to credit bid its debt and purchase estate property, taking title free and clear of valid, nonconsenting junior liens? We hold that it does not." *In re PW, LLC (Clear Channel Outdoor, Inc. v. Knupfer)*, 391 B.R. 25, 29 (9th Cir. BAP 2008). This case has been "widely criticized." Kevin J. Walsh & Ella Shenhav, "Are Bankruptcy Sales Finally Final," http://www.mintz.com/newsletter/2011/Advisories/1229-0611-NAT-BRC/web.htm (July 8, 2011).

The Supreme Court has cast doubt on reliance on numerous bankruptcy court decisions, absent a district court order, because the issues were not within core bankruptcy jurisdiction under 28 U.S.C. Section 157 and thus could only be finally adjudicated by a U.S. Const. Article III (district) judge. In *Stern v. Marshall.*, 131 S.Ct. 2594, 2620, 180 L.Ed.2d 475, 79 U.S.L.W. 4564 (2011), the Supreme Court held that "Article III of the Constitution provides that the judicial power of the United States may be vested only in courts whose judges enjoy the protections set forth in that Article. We conclude today that Congress, in one isolated respect, exceeded that limitation in the Bankruptcy Act of 1984. The Bankruptcy Court [whose judge is now appointed by federal courts of appeals pursuant to 28 U.S.C. Section 152] below lacked the constitutional authority to enter a final judgment on a state law counterclaim that is not resolved in the process of ruling on a creditor's proof of claim." Subsequently, the Supreme Court held in *Executive Benefits Ins. Agency v. Arkison*, 189 L.Ed. 2d 83, 2014 U.S. LEXIS 3993, 82 U.S.L.W. 4450 (June 9, 2014) that the bankruptcy court should have entered findings of fact and conclusions of law in a fraudulent conveyance action (which is not core), and should not have granted summary judgment; however, the district court's de novo review of the bankruptcy court order cured possible error in the bankruptcy court order. The Supreme Court has not addressed whether consent by a party may be given to a bankruptcy court order on a non-core proceeding that is related to the bankruptcy proceeding. As suggested by *In re Teleservices Group, Inc. (Meoli v. Huntington Nat'l Bank)*, 456 B.R. 318, 332-334 (Bankr. W.D. Mich. 2011), numerous actions

approved by a bankruptcy court, without district court review, may be called into question. Those may include an avoidance action under Section 544 (incorporating state law for avoidance), Section 547 (preference), Section 548 (fraudulent transfer), or Section 363(h) (sale free and clear of the rights of a co-owner).

The examiner also should be aware that there is an automatic stay for 14 days after entry of the order of sale, unless the court orders otherwise. Fed. R. Bankr. P. 6004(h). *See* Standard 12.30.

Source:
Citations in the Comment; 3 *Collier on Bankruptcy*, Chapters 342, 363 (Alan N. Resnick & Henry J. Sommer eds. Matthew Bender & Company, Inc., a member of LexisNexis, 16th Ed. Revised 2014).

History:
Adopted Oct. 9, 1999.

STANDARD 12.110. AUTHORITY TO CONVEY PROPERTY AFTER CONFIRMATION OF PLAN

If the debtor is selling land and the debtor's bankruptcy plan has been confirmed, the examiner should (1) review the confirmed plan and order confirming plan to determine that the land is revested in the debtor and to determine that the plan and order do not limit the authority of the debtor to convey and (2) determine that the order is final and nonappealable. The examiner should require that a certified copy of the order confirming the plan be recorded in the real property records.

COMMENT

Except as provided in the plan or order confirming the plan, the confirmation of the plan vests all property of the estate in the debtor. 11 U.S.C. §§1141(b), 1227(b), 1327(b). A notice of appeal must be filed with the clerk within 14 days of the date of the entry (on the docket) of the order of confirmation. A timely motion to amend or make additional findings of fact, to alter or amend the judgment, for a new trial, or for relief from a judgment because of mistakes, inadvertence, excusable neglect, newly discovered evidence, or fraud, must be filed within 14 days of the entry of the order of confirmation; in the event of such motion, the time for appeal runs from the entry of the order disposing of the motion. Fed. R. Bankr. P. 8002. An order confirming a Chapter 9 (Municipality) or a Chapter 11 (Reorganization) plan is stayed until the expiration of 14 days after the entry of the order, unless the court orders otherwise. Fed. R. Bankr. P. 3020(e).

CAUTION

If the sale involves substantially all of the assets of the debtor or nonexempt assets in a Chapter 12 or 13 case, then the sale may be viewed as a modification of the plan. The sale or encumbrance by the debtor after confirmation of a Chapter 12 or 13 plan also may require court approval because of local rules or provisions of the plan. A cautious examiner may require an order authorizing the sale. Although an appeal from a confirmation order may be moot if no stay is secured, based upon established case law, this doctrine may not be as clearly reliable as the statutorily based mootness provisions of §§363 and 364. *In re Seidler*, 44 F.3d 945 (11th Cir. 1995). The examiner also should be aware that there is an automatic stay for 14 days after entry of the order confirming the plan, unless the court orders otherwise. Fed. R. Bankr. P. 3020(e).

Source:
Citations in the Comment; 8 *Collier on Bankruptcy*, Chapters 1141, 1227, 1327 (Alan N. Resnick & Henry J. Sommer eds. Matthew Bender & Company, Inc., a member of LexisNexis, 16th Ed. Revised 2014).

History:
Adopted Oct. 9, 1999.

STANDARD 12.120. AUTHORITY TO MORTGAGE IN PROPOSED TRANSACTION

If property will be mortgaged by the bankruptcy trustee or debtor in possession, the examiner should require evidence of the following: (1) notice of the proposed mortgage to interested parties, including the debtor, all creditors and indenture trustees, by mail; (2) no objections to the mortgage were made or the court by order overruled the objections and authorized the mortgage; and (3) the mortgage is nonappealable or is not stayed pending appeal. The examiner should require that a certified copy of the order be recorded in the real property records.

COMMENT

The debtor in possession, or the trustee if the trustee is authorized to operate the business, may, after notice and a hearing, be authorized by the bankruptcy court to incur debt secured by a lien on the land. 11 U.S.C. §364(c). The reversal or modification on appeal of the authorization does not affect the priority or lien granted to an entity that extended the credit in good faith, unless the authority was stayed pending appeal. 11 U.S.C. §364(e).

CAUTION

If the loan has not been fully disbursed, the appeal may not be moot due to failure to obtain a stay because meaningful relief could be granted. *In re Swedeland Develop. Group, Inc.*, 16 F.3d 552 (3d Cir. 1994). The cautious examiner may require proof that the order is final and nonappealable. Unless the order provides otherwise, the grant of a mortgage may remain subject to the automatic stay until later lifted. *Gibraltar Savings v. Commonwealth Land Title Insurance Co.*, 905 F.2d 1203 (8th Cir. 1990).

Source:

Citations in the Comment; 3 *Collier on Bankruptcy*, ¶364.01, et seq. (Alan N. Resnick & Henry J. Sommer eds. Matthew Bender & Company, Inc., a member of LexisNexis, 16th Ed. Revised 2014).

History:

Adopted Oct. 9, 1999.

STANDARD 12.130. FILINGS IN VIOLATION OF THE AUTOMATIC STAY

The examiner should not disregard a judgment lien, tax lien notice, or other instrument filed after the commencement of a bankruptcy case and in apparent violation of the automatic stay, because the filing of the instrument may be treated as voidable and may not be considered void, absent action in the bankruptcy case to avoid the instrument.

COMMENT

The automatic stay prevents any act to create or perfect any lien against property of the estate or any act to create or perfect against property of the debtor any lien to the extent the claim arose prior to the commencement of the case. 11 U.S.C. §362(a)(4), (a)(5). However, there are different opinions as to whether the violation of a stay is automatically void or is simply voidable. *Bronson v. U.S.*, 46 F.3d 1573 (Fed. Cir. 1995); *In re Soares,* 107 F.3d 969 (1st Cir. 1997).

Source:

Citations in the Comment; 3 *Collier on Bankruptcy*, ¶362.11 (Alan N. Resnick & Henry J. Sommer eds. Matthew Bender & Company, Inc., a member of LexisNexis, 16th Ed. Revised 2014).

History:

Adopted Oct. 9, 1999.

STANDARD 12.140. THE DISCHARGE & JUDGMENT LIENS

An examiner may presume that an abstract of judgment filed against a person who was a debtor in a bankruptcy case is extinguished as a lien against property of the debtor if: (1) the debtor files a motion in the bankruptcy case pursuant to 11 U.S.C. §522(f) to extinguish the lien as to homestead, notifies the creditor in accordance with the applicable Bankruptcy Rules and local rules, and secures a final order of the bankruptcy court removing the lien; (2) the debtor acquires the property after receiving a discharge from the debt evidenced by the abstract of judgment; or, (3) the property is exempt or is not abandoned in the bankruptcy proceeding, and the debtor receives a discharge from the debt.

COMMENT

A proceeding under 11 U.S.C.A. §522(f) by the debtor to avoid a judicial lien must be treated as a contested matter, and notice must be served in accordance with Fed. R. Bankr. P. 7004. Fed. R. Bankr. P. 4003(d), 9014. An order will not be final until 14 days after the entry of the order (or after a timely motion to amend, or alter a judgment, or for mistake or fraud). Fed. R. Bankr. P. 8002(c)(2). A dismissal of the bankruptcy case will reinstate a judgment lien, unless the court orders otherwise. 11 U.S.C. §349. The judgment lien may not be extinguished pursuant to 11 U.S.C. §522(f) if the lien secures a domestic support obligation. 11 U.S.C.A. §§101(14A), 522(f)(1)(A). If the judgment debtor receives a discharge from the debt of the judgment, property acquired by the debtor after the bankruptcy discharge will not be encumbered by the abstract of judgment. *In re Fuller*, 134 B.R. 945 (Bankr. 9th Cir. 1992) (relating to tax lien); Tex. Prop. Code Ann. §52.025 (prior to September 1, 1993). A judgment lien (evidencing a discharged debt) will not attach to property acquired after the petition for debtor relief is filed. Tex. Prop. Code Ann. §52.042 (effective September 1, 1993). A judgment lien is automatically released if the debt is discharged and the land is exempt or is otherwise not abandoned. The examiner should review the bankruptcy docket and abstract of judgment to verify that the debt was discharged, and should review the docket and Schedule "A" to verify that the property was scheduled, and was exempt or otherwise was not abandoned.

Source:

Citations in the Comment.

History:

Adopted Oct. 9, 1999; amended June 16, 2006; amended June 27, 2008; amended July 17, 2014.

The prior standard, amended June 27, 2008, provided: "An examiner may assume that an abstract of judgment filed against a person who was a debtor in a bankruptcy case is extinguished as a lien against property of the debtor if: (1) the debtor files a motion in the bankruptcy case pursuant to 11 U.S.C. §522(f) to extinguish the lien as to homestead, notifies the creditor in accordance with the applicable Bankruptcy Rules and local rules, and secures a final order of the bankruptcy court removing the lien; (2) the debtor acquires the

property after receiving a discharge from the debt evidenced by the abstract of judgment; or, (3) the property is exempt or is not abandoned in the bankruptcy proceeding, and the debtor receives a discharge from the debt."

The amended June 16, 2006 standard provided: "An examiner may assume that an abstract of judgment filed against a person who was a debtor in a bankruptcy case is extinguished as a lien against property of the debtor if: (1) the debtor files a motion in the bankruptcy case pursuant to 11 U.S.C. 522(f) to extinguish the lien as to homestead, notifies the creditor in accordance with the applicable Bankruptcy Rules and local rules, and secures a final order of the bankruptcy court removing the lien; (2) the debtor acquires the property after receiving a discharge from the debt evidenced by the abstract of judgment; or, (3) the property is exempt or is not abandoned in the bankruptcy proceeding, and the debtor receives a discharge from the debt."

The original standard provided: "An examiner may assume that an abstract of judgment filed against a person who was a debtor in a bankruptcy case is extinguished as a lien against property of the debtor if: (1) the debtor files a motion in the bankruptcy case pursuant to 11 U.S.C. 522(f) to extinguish the lien as to homestead, notifies the creditor in accordance with the applicable Bankruptcy Rules and local rules, and secures a final order of the bankruptcy court removing the lien; (2) the debtor acquires the property after receiving a discharge from the debt evidenced by the abstract of judgment; (3) the abstract of judgment is recorded before September 1, 1993, and the property is exempt or is not abandoned in the bankruptcy case, and the debt is discharged, and the court which granted the judgment reflected by the abstract of judgment removes the judgment lien by court order more than one year after the bankruptcy discharge is granted, and a copy of the order is recorded; or, (4) the abstract of judgment is recorded on or after September 1, 1993, and the property is exempt or is not abandoned in the bankruptcy proceeding, and the debtor receives a discharge from the debt."

STANDARD 12.150. EXTENSION OF TIME

An examiner should be aware that the filing of the bankruptcy case tolls the limitation period in which the trustee may commence an action, if the limitation period had not expired at the time of the filing of the case, until the later of (1) the end of the period under other law or (2) two years after the order for relief (filing of voluntary bankruptcy). The filing of the bankruptcy case tolls the period in which the trustee may file a pleading or cure a default until the later of (a) the end of the period under other law or (2) 60 days after the order for relief. If applicable nonbankruptcy law or an agreement fixes a period for commencing an action on a claim against the debtor, then the limitation period does not expire until the later of (1) the end of the period under other law or (2) 30 days after the notice of termination or expiration of the stay as to the claim.

COMMENT

The Bankruptcy Code tolls the time for enforcement of contracts, options, deeds of trust, mechanic's liens and other claims by or against the debtor and debtor's property if they have not expired at the time of the filing of the bankruptcy case. 11 U.S.C. §108.

CAUTION

Some cases indicate that the provisions requiring delay rentals or production will not be tolled by the automatic stay (or otherwise), because of the filing of a bankruptcy by a lessee. *Champlin Petroleum Co. v. Mingo Oil Producers*, 628 F.Supp. 557 (D.Wyo.1986) (force majeure clause did not extend the lease because of bankruptcy proceedings), aff'd without op., *Champlin Petroleum Co. v. Mingo Oil Producers*, 841 F.2d 1131 (10th Cir. 1987); *Good Hope Refineries, Inc. v. Benavides*, 602 F.2d 998 (1st Cir. 1979) (rejecting the argument that §108 extended time for performance); *In re Anne Cara Oil Co*, 32 B.R. 643 (Bankr. D. Mass. 1983) (Section 108 is not applicable and does not extend the time for performance).

Source:

Citations in the Comment; 2 *Collier on Bankruptcy*, Chapter 108 (Alan N. Resnick & Henry J. Sommer eds. Matthew Bender & Company, Inc., a member of LexisNexis, 16th Ed. Revised 2014).

History:

Adopted Oct. 9, 1999.

STANDARD 12.160. EFFECT OF DISMISSAL OF CASE

The examiner should be aware that the dismissal of a bankruptcy case reinstates any transfer or lien avoided in the bankruptcy, vacates orders, and revests the property of the estate in the debtor.

COMMENT

The dismissal of the bankruptcy case will revest title in the debtor and vacates orders entered in the bankruptcy case. The goal is to undo the bankruptcy case and restore property rights as they were vested before the case. 11 U.S.C. §349. However, the bankruptcy court has discretion to protect rights acquired in reliance on the case (such as the rights of a purchaser from the estate).

Source:

Citations in the Comment; 3 *Collier on Bankruptcy*, Chapter 349 (Alan N. Resnick & Henry J. Sommer eds. Matthew Bender & Company, Inc., a member of LexisNexis, 16th Ed. Revised 2014).

History:

Adopted Oct. 9, 1999.

CHAPTER XIII. AFFIDAVITS & RECITALS

STANDARD 13.10. AFFIDAVIT DEFINED

An affidavit is a written statement, under oath, signed by the affiant and evidenced by a jurat.

COMMENT

A jurat is a certificate signed by an officer authorized to administer oaths before whom an instrument was executed, stating that the instrument was subscribed and sworn to before the officer by the person

executing the instrument. An affidavit must contain a jurat to be effective. A form of a jurat is as follows:

Subscribed and sworn to this _______ day of __________, _____, by _______________.

____

Notary Public, State of Texas

My commission expires:

For a listing of officers who may administer oaths and supply a jurat, see Tex. Gov't Code Ann. §§602.002-602.005.

In the past, it was typical for an affidavit to contain both a jurat and an acknowledgment. An acknowledgment merely requires that the signing party acknowledge that he or she executed the instrument. Prior to September 1, 1989, an acknowledgment was required in order for an affidavit to be recorded. As of that date, an affidavit need only contain a jurat to be recorded.

The admissibility of affidavits in a court proceeding is governed by Tex. R. Evid. 803, 804 and Tex. Estates Code Ann. §203.001. *See also Albright v. Bouldin*, 394 S.W.2d 681 (Tex. Civ. App.—Eastland 1965, writ ref'd) and *Compton v. WWV Enterprises*, 679 S.W.2d 668 (Tex. App.—Eastland 1984, no writ).

See Standard 4.20 for a further discussion of the use of the jurat and acknowledgment and Standard 11.70 concerning affidavits of heirship.

CAUTION

An instrument containing an acknowledgment, but not a jurat, is not an affidavit since the facts stated therein are not sworn to by the affiant.

Source:

Citations in the Comment; 3A Aloysius A. Leopold, *Land Titles and Title Examination* §§10.18, 10.19 (Texas Practice 3d ed. 2005); Tex. Gov't Code Ann. §§312.011(1); 602.002-602.005; Tex. Prop. Code Ann. §12.001(a); Tex. Estates Code Ann. §§205.001-205.003; 2 Tex. Jur. 3d *Affidavits* §§1-30 (1995).

History:

Adopted June 15, 2001.

STANDARD 13.20. RELIANCE UPON AFFIDAVITS

An examiner may rely upon an affidavit unless the examiner has a reasonable basis to question its reliability.

COMMENT

Unlike the other standards, there is little authority for the use of affidavits. Nevertheless, the employment of affidavits in determining title to real property is based upon long established custom and practice.

During the course of title examination, an examiner may encounter many types of affidavits, such as affidavits relating to heirship, family history, identity, marital status, use and possession of property, adverse possession, payment of debts, non-production of oil and gas, lack of drilling operations, and boundaries.

The examiner may find it necessary to rely upon affidavits in the interpretation of title documents, clarification of title ownership, or establishment of title. In deciding whether to rely upon an affidavit, the title examiner may consider relevant factors, such as:

(1) The date on which the affidavit was made and, if recorded, the length of time it has been recorded;

(2) Whether the party or parties making the affidavit were interested or disinterested;

(3) The completeness of the affidavit, whether it recites facts or merely draws conclusions, and whether it discloses the basis of the maker's knowledge;

(4) The value of the interest in the property under examination;

(5) Whether more reliable and readily obtainable proof is available; and

(6) The cost and feasibility of alternative procedures to establish title.

On many occasions, the examiner has no practical alternative but to rely upon an affidavit. However, in relying upon an affidavit, an examiner does not become a guarantor of the truth of the affidavit. An affidavit may qualify as an ancient document. *See* Comment to Standard 13.40.

See also, Standard 11.20, addressing affidavits of intestacy, and Standard 11.70, addressing affidavits of heirship.

CAUTION

Title based upon an affidavit may not be marketable. *See* Standard 2.10.

An examiner should be very hesitant to rely upon an affidavit in lieu of more reliable and readily obtainable proof, such as a conveyance or the existing proceedings of a court of record.

Source:

Title Standards Joint Editorial Board.

History:

Adopted June 15, 2001.

STANDARD 13.20

STANDARD 13.30. AFFIDAVITS OF NON-PRODUCTION

Concerning an instrument creating an interest that depends upon production (e.g., an oil and gas lease, a mineral or royalty deed, or an assignment), an examiner may rely upon an affidavit which includes facts sufficient to show that the interest has expired by its own terms, although it is preferable to obtain a release from the owner of the interest.

COMMENT

The affidavit of non-production is a curative device of necessity. The form and content of these affidavits vary widely. Because it is often not feasible to obtain a release, the examiner may rely upon an affidavit of non-production to show that a term interest has expired. The affidavit should be carefully examined, however, to ascertain that the stated facts are sufficient to show that the interest has expired by its own terms. *See* Comment to Standard 13.20.

CAUTION

There is no statutory authority for this procedure; however, the use of the affidavit of non-production is a long established custom and practice. The affidavit itself does not terminate the interest. The affidavit only contains facts that the examiner may consider in forming an opinion as to the status of the term interest.

The examiner should carefully review the instrument creating the interest to determine whether the term continues for reasons other than actual production (e.g., operations, payment of shut-in royalties, pooling, force majeure, etc.).

Additionally, the examiner may suggest that the client consult the records of the Texas Railroad Commission as another source of information regarding expiration of the interest; however, such records are subject to amendment and may be self-serving since they are prepared by, or at the direction of, the leasehold operator.

Source:
Title Standards Joint Editorial Board.
History:
Adopted June 15, 2001.

STANDARD 13.40. RELIANCE UPON RECITALS

Recitals are statements of fact made in deeds, leases, mortgages and other documents. Because documents containing recitals are not typically sworn statements, recitals should generally be regarded as having less probative force than affidavits; however, an examiner having no reasonable basis for doubt or suspicion may rely upon recitals as establishing the recited facts.

COMMENT

Recitals, as distinguished from affidavits, occur within deeds, mortgages, leases and other instruments affecting real property. *Compton v. WWV Enterprises*, 679 S.W.2d 668 (Tex. App.—Eastland 1984, no writ). Like affidavits, recitals encountered during the course of title examination often remove doubt or explain apparent gaps in the chain of title. Recitals are not sworn statements, however, and are often much less thorough than affidavits intended to establish similar facts. They should therefore be appraised somewhat more critically than affidavits, although the indicia of reliability the examiner should consider are much the same as those mentioned for affidavits in the Comment to Standard 13.20. Reliance on a recital is particularly warranted if it occurs in an ancient document (one in existence at least twenty years, in a condition that arouses no suspicion, and in a place where it would likely be if authentic). *See* Tex. R. Evid. 803(16) & 901(b)(8). Recitals in an ancient document are prima facie evidence of the facts recited. *Zobel v. Slim*, 576 S.W.2d 362, 365 (Tex. 1978); *Moses v. Chapman*, 280 S.W. 911, 913-14 (Tex. Civ. App.—Texarkana 1926, no writ). A particularly useful application of the "ancient document" rule is that it permits an examiner to presume the authority of a fiduciary, such as an attorney-in-fact or a trustee, whose capacity is recited in the deed but does not otherwise appear in the record. For example, in *West v. Hapgood*, 174 S.W.2d 963, 967-71 (Tex. 1943), the court pointed out that, while not conclusive and subject to rebuttal, the power and authority of a grantor in an ancient deed may be presumed from a bare recital. If an instrument has been recorded for the requisite period, the record itself ordinarily will qualify as an ancient document. *See, e.g.*, *Holmes v. Coryell*, 58 Tex. 680, 688-89 (1883). *See also* Wickes, *Ancient Documents and Hearsay*, 8 Tex. L. Rev. 451 (1930) (discussing the necessity for such a rule and its rationale).

If an instrument legally executed and acknowledged or sworn to has been of record for five years or more in the county where the land is located or where the decedent resided at the time of his death, the facts contained therein concerning the family history, genealogy, marital status, or the identity of the heirs of a de-

cedent are admissible in suits to declare heirship or involving title to property as prima facie evidence of the stated facts. Tex. Estates Code Ann. §203.001. Such recitals, if not controverted by other facts, will support a determination of heirship against any claimant, whether or not in privity with a party to the deed. *Gramm v. Coffield*, 116 S.W.2d 1089 (Tex. Civ. App.—Austin 1938, writ dism'd). *See* Standard 3.40 concerning recitals of identity.

CAUTION

This standard is intended to recognize the examiner's latitude in accepting the truth of a recital whose source appears to be reliable; nevertheless, some degree of subjective judgment is required to appraise the likelihood that a person in the declarant's position would misstate the pertinent facts, either from lack of knowledge or from self-interest. The value of recitals is certainly tempered by the traditional rule that they are only binding on parties to the instrument and their privies and are inadmissible as evidence against the claims of others. *See, e.g.*, *Watkins v. Smith*, 45 S.W. 560 (Tex. 1898). Although Tex R. Evid. 803(15) may have relaxed this rule by allowing the admission into evidence of any statement contained in a deed if the matter stated is relevant to the purpose of the document, apparently without regard to privity, a prudent examiner will not treat recitals, although admissible into evidence, as established facts against all the world without sufficient indicia of their reliability. The examiner should also bear in mind that the special legislative endorsement of reliance on recitals represented by Tex. Estates Code Ann. §203.001 is limited to matters of family history, genealogy, marital status and heirship.

Further, the existence and contents of necessary written documents may not rest on a mere recital. For example, see Standards 8.10 and 8.20, regarding the necessity for examination of powers of attorney, and the Caution to Standard 9.10, indicating that an examiner's assessment of a trustee's authority must be based on the provisions of the trust instrument. It should go without saying that a recital of the existence of an essential deed should not take the place of the deed itself. For example, a recital identifying a grantor as "John Smith, successor by conveyance to the interest of William Jones" may not be accepted in lieu of the recorded deed from Jones to Smith. Reliance on recitals is misplaced where any circumstances appear to cast suspicion on their accuracy.

For example, recitals even in ancient documents should not be relied upon if they consist of mere conclusions that are uncorroborated and self-serving, such as a grantor's bare recital of heirship in a deed. *See, e.g.*, *Slattery v. Adams*, 279 S.W.2d 445, 451-52 (Tex. Civ. App.—Beaumont 1954), aff'd on other grounds, 295 S.W.2d 859 (Tex. 1956). And a grantor's power will not be presumed where it emanates from a court whose proceedings are required by law to be entered of record unless it is shown that the court records have been lost or destroyed. *Baumgarten v. Frost*, 186 S.W.2d 982, 985 (Tex. 1945).

Where the primary source of the grantor's recited authority is presumably readily available, as from court records, the primary source must be examined. *Jobe v. Osborne*, 97 S.W.2d 939, 940 (Tex. 1936); *Tucker v. Murphy*, 1 S.W. 76 (Tex. 1886). While recitals in ancient documents are admissible as evidence of the facts recited, they are not conclusive proof. *Bruni v. Vidaurri*, 166 S.W.2d 81, 90-91 (Tex. 1942).

A purchaser is bound by every recital or reference to other documents contained in or fairly disclosed by any instrument that forms an essential link in his chain of title. *Westland Oil Dev. Corp. v. Gulf Oil Corp.*, 637 S.W.2d 903, 908 (Tex. 1982). Therefore, no material recital can be safely ignored.

Source:

Citations in the Comment; 4 Aloysius A. Leopold, *Land Titles and Title Examination* §§21.10, 21.10A (Texas Practice 3d ed. 2005); 5 *Id.* §35.18.

History:

Adopted June 15, 2001.

CHAPTER XIV. MARITAL INTERESTS

STANDARD 14.10. COMMUNITY PROPERTY PRESUMPTION

Except as otherwise provided in this Chapter, an examiner should presume that real property acquired during marriage is community property, whether acquired in the name of one or both spouses.

COMMENT

On June 26, 2015, the United States Supreme Court held that a lawful marriage of a same-sex couple must be recognized by all states and held that marriages between parties of the same sex are valid, notwithstanding state law to the contrary. *Obergefell v. Hodges*, ___ U.S. ___, 135 S.Ct. 2584, 192 L. Ed. 2d 609 (2015).

Tex. Fam. Code Ann. §3.002 defines community property as all property, other than separate property, acquired by either spouse during marriage. This defini-

tion applies regardless of whether the marriage is ceremonial or at common law. *See In re Glasco*, 619 S.W.2d 567, 571 (Tex. Civ. App.—San Antonio 1981, no writ). (Since the constitutional amendment of 1999, effective January 1, 2000, community property may also include property converted from separate property by the spouses' agreement. Tex. Fam. Code Ann. §§4.202-4.206.) Under Tex. Fam. Code Ann. §3.001, separate property consists only of that acquired before marriage and that acquired during marriage by gift, devise, or descent or as recovery for personal injuries. The character of property as separate or community is determined and becomes fixed at the time of acquisition. *Smith v. Buss*, 144 S.W.2d 529, 532 (Tex. 1940); *Welder v. Lambert*, 44 S.W. 281 (Tex. 1898). It is not changed from one to the other by subsequent events; for example, use of community funds to pay installments on the purchase price for property acquired by one spouse before marriage does not vest a community property interest in the other spouse. *Colden v. Alexander*, 171 S.W.2d 328 (Tex. 1943).

The community property presumption has long been a settled rule of property in Texas, *see, e.g., Stiles v. Japhet*, 19 S.W. 450 (Tex. 1892), and is codified as Tex. Fam. Code Ann. §3.003. The presumption is rebuttable by clear and convincing evidence that the property is separate property. Tex. Fam. Code Ann. §3.003; *e.g., Janes v. Gulf Production Co.*, 15 S.W.2d 1102 (Tex. Civ. App.—Beaumont 1929, writ ref'd). It is conclusive, however, in favor of purchasers for value without notice. *Houston Oil Co. v. Choate*, 232 S.W. 285, 287 (Tex. Comm'n App. 1921, judgm't adopted). For further reference and guidance concerning the community property presumption, see [***O'Connor's Fam. Law Handbook***, "Community-property presumption," ch. 2-A, §3.2, p. 97; "Rebutting community-property presumption," ch. 2-A, §3.3, p. 97].

See Standards 14.20, 14.30, 14.40 and 14.50, which describe circumstances in which an examiner may instead presume property acquired by conveyance to be separate property.

Source:

Citations in the Comment.

History:

Adopted June 15, 2001; amended July 17, 2014.

The prior standard provided: "Except as otherwise provided in this Chapter, an examiner must presume that real property acquired during marriage is community property, whether acquired in the name of one or both spouses."

STANDARD 14.20. GIFTS, DEVISE & DESCENT

An examiner should consider property acquired during marriage by gift, devise or descent to be the acquiring spouse's separate property. Where the grantor's donative intent is clearly demonstrated on the face of the deed, an examiner may presume the property conveyed to be the grantee's separate property.

COMMENT

Property acquired during marriage by gift, devise or descent is separate property. Tex. Fam. Code Ann. §3.001(2). If the deed to a married person states that the conveyance is being made as a gift or otherwise clearly expresses donative intent, such as by stating the consideration to be love and affection, such a statement may be relied upon as establishing the separate character of the property conveyed. *Janes v. Gulf Production Co.*, 15 S.W.2d 1102 (Tex. Civ. App.—Beaumont 1929, writ ref'd). Even where the gift is made to both spouses, it vests one half in each of them, as separate property and not community. *Bradley v. Love*, 60 Tex. 472, 477-78 (1883); *McLemore v. McLemore*, 641 S.W.2d 395, 397 (Tex. App.—Tyler 1982, no writ).

One occasionally encounters deeds recited to be for love and affection and a nominal sum paid or "other good and valuable consideration." Where a deed recites love and affection as consideration or otherwise clearly demonstrates on its face donative intent, an examiner should accept these expressions as ample evidence that the property conveyed was a gift and therefore the grantee's separate property, notwithstanding further recitals of nominal or unspecified other consideration. *Hall v. Barrett*, 126 S.W.2d 1045 (Tex. Civ. App.—Fort Worth 1939, no writ); *see also Banks v. Banks*, 229 S.W.2d 99 (Tex. Civ. App.—Austin 1950, writ ref'd n.r.e.); *Williams v. Nettles*, 56 S.W.2d 321 (Tex. Civ. App.—Waco 1932, writ dism'd).

CAUTION

The community property presumption can be overcome by a showing that no consideration actually was paid. *See, e.g., Lowe v. Ragland*, 297 S.W.2d 668 (Tex. 1957). In such cases an examiner may rely on an affidavit or other extrinsic evidence to show that no valuable consideration changed hands in the transaction. See Chapter XIII of these standards concerning the use of and reliance upon affidavits generally.

Conversely, the presumption of a gift that may arise from recitals in a deed may be overcome by contrary evidence as well. *See Hall v. Barrett*, 126 S.W.2d 1045 (Tex. Civ. App.—Fort Worth 1939, no writ); *see also Somer v. Bogart*, 749 S.W.2d 202 (Tex. App.—Dallas 1988, writ denied) (presumption of gift resulting from parents' placing title in son-in-law's name was rebuttable).

Source:

Citations in the Comment.

History:

Adopted June 15, 2001; amended July 17, 2014.

The prior standard provided: "An examiner must consider property acquired during marriage by gift, devise or descent to be the acquiring spouse's separate property. Where the grantor's donative intent is clearly demonstrated on the face of the deed, an examiner may presume the property conveyed to be the grantee's separate property."

STANDARD 14.30. CONVEYANCES BETWEEN SPOUSES

An examiner should consider property conveyed by one spouse to another to have become the grantee's separate property regardless of whether consideration is recited. However, effective January 1, 2000, a conveyance or agreement signed by both spouses may convert separate property to community property if such intention is specified.

COMMENT

Texas courts have always held that a deed from husband to wife, absent evidence of any contrary intention, vests the estate in the wife as her separate property. *See, e.g., Taylor v. Hollingsworth*, 176 S.W.2d 733, 736 (Tex. 1943); *Story v. Marshall*, 24 Tex. 305 (1859). This is true whether the property is the husband's separate property or community property, and whether or not consideration is given. *Dalton v. Pruett*, 483 S.W.2d 926, 928-29 (Tex. Civ. App.—Texarkana 1972, no writ). Although the principal cases deal with conveyances from husband to wife, there seems no reason that the same law would not be applied to deeds from either spouse to the other after the statutory equalization of the rights of spouses regarding marital property. *See In re Marriage of Morrison*, 913 S.W.2d 689 (Tex. App.—Texarkana 1995, writ denied).

Tex. Const. Ann. art. XVI, §15, effective January 1, 2000, now permits the conversion of separate property to community property by the spouses' agreement. However, the mere transfer of separate property by one spouse to the other spouse or to both spouses is not sufficient to accomplish the conversion. Tex. Fam. Code Ann. §4.203(b). A conveyance signed by both spouses clearly stating their intention may be relied upon.

CAUTION

Prior to its repeal, effective August 23, 1963, Tex. Rev. Civ. Stat. Ann. art. 1299 (1925) (repealed by Acts 1963, 58th Leg., p. 1189, ch. 473, §1) required the joinder of the husband in any conveyance of his wife's separate property, as well as her privy acknowledgment. *See* Caution to Standard 4.20. Further, before January 1, 1968, the husband was statutorily the sole manager of the community estate. Tex. Rev. Civ. Stat. Ann. art. 4619 (1925) (amended 1967, repealed 1969). Before either of these changes in the law, therefore, a wife could not convey her separate property or her community property interest directly to her husband. *See, e.g., Graham v. Struwe*, 13 S.W. 381 (Tex. 1890). However, a conveyance by wife to husband could be accomplished, if desired, by conveyance from husband and wife to a nominee, who would then convey to the husband. *Kellett v. Trice*, 66 S.W. 51 (Tex. 1902). Although Article 1299 was held unconstitutional in *Wessely Energy Co. v. Jennings*, 736 S.W.2d 624 (Tex. 1987), on the basis of its disparate treatment of husbands and wives, the ruling was prospective only. 736 S.W.2d at 629. Thus, an examiner may not presume that a pre-repeal deed from wife to husband can be given effect.

Source:

Citations in the Comment.

History:

Adopted June 15, 2001; amended July 17, 2014.

The prior standard provided: "An examiner must consider property conveyed by one spouse to another to have become the grantee's separate property regardless of whether consideration is recited. However, effective January 1, 2000, a conveyance or agreement signed by both spouses may convert separate property to community property if such intention is specified."

STANDARD 14.40. SEPARATE PROPERTY CONSIDERATION

If an examiner determines that the consideration for a conveyance came from a married grantee's separate estate, the community property presumption is rebutted, and the examiner should consider the property to be the grantee's separate property. For example, an examiner without knowledge of contrary evidence may rely on a recital in the deed (1) that the consideration was paid out of the grantee's separate property, or (2) that the property is conveyed to the grantee as separate property.

COMMENT

All property acquired during marriage for consideration is presumed to be community property, and this presumption is conclusive in the absence of contrary

evidence. *Lockhart v. Garner*, 298 S.W.2d 108, 110 (Tex. 1957). The presumption obtains even where the parties are closely related so that a gift otherwise might be inferred. *See, e.g.*, *Kitchens v. Kitchens*, 372 S.W.2d 249, 255 (Tex. Civ. App.—Waco 1963, writ dism'd). The presumption is overcome, however, by proof that the property was acquired with one spouse's separate funds or separate credit. *See, e.g.*, *Huston v. Curl*, 8 Tex. 239, 242 (1852); *Whorrall v. Whorrall*, 691 S.W.2d 32, 35 (Tex. App.—Austin 1985, writ dism'd); *Coggin v. Coggin*, 204 S.W.2d 47, 51-52 (Tex. Civ. App.—Amarillo 1947, no writ). Property purchased with one spouse's separate property is itself separate property (a concept commonly called "mutation"). *Lewis v. Lewis*, 944 S.W.2d 630 (Tex. 1997); *Love v. Robertson*, 7 Tex. 6 (1851).

Property may be partly separate and partly community in character, in a kind of tenancy in common between the two estates, if acquired partly with one spouse's separate funds and partly with community funds or credit. *Gleich v. Bongio*, 99 S.W.2d 881 (Tex. 1937). Under such circumstances the interest of each estate is established proportionately to the fractional share of the purchase consideration furnished out of each. 99 S.W.2d at 884.

Many cases have held that recitals in a deed that the consideration was paid out of the grantee's separate property or that the conveyance is to the grantee as his or her separate property displace the usual community property presumption and establish in its place a contrary presumption that the property is the grantee's separate property. *See, e.g.*, *Henry S. Miller Co. v. Evans*, 452 S.W.2d 426 (Tex. 1970); *Smith v. Buss*, 144 S.W.2d 529 (Tex. 1940); *McCutchen v. Purinton*, 19 S.W. 710 (Tex. 1892). Even if only community funds were in fact used in the purchase, a spouse who participated in the transaction is deemed to have intended a gift to the grantee. *Hodge v. Ellis*, 277 S.W.2d 900, 905 (Tex. 1955). Accordingly, an innocent purchaser for value relying on such a separate property recital would take free of the claim of one asserting a community property interest in the other spouse. *See generally* 4 Aloysius A. Leopold, *Land Titles and Title Examination* §20.6 (Texas Practice 3d ed. 2005) and 5 *Id.* §§28.4, 28.8, 33.22.

CAUTION

The presumption that arises from separate property recitals is rebuttable. If a spouse can show no participation in or knowledge of the transaction, that spouse will be allowed to show that the consideration was not the grantee's separate property and that no gift to the grantee was intended, so that the property is community property. *Hodge v. Ellis*, 277 S.W.2d 900, 905-07 (Tex. 1955); *Kearse v. Kearse*, 276 S.W. 690 (Tex. Comm'n App. 1925, judgm't adopted); *Morris v. Neie*, 212 S.W.2d 981 (Tex. Civ. App.—Eastland 1948, writ ref'd n.r.e.). The examiner should be watchful for any evidence that might be construed to place a purchaser on notice of the unreliability of separate property recitals. The separate property presumption arising from deed recitals seems particularly vulnerable given that it has been applied almost exclusively for the benefit of wives and was developed during an era in which courts felt justified in providing special protection to wives (as indicated, for example, by the court's remarks in *McCutchen v. Purinton*, 19 S.W. 710, 711 (Tex. 1892), noting the husband's authority over the wife's property, both separate and community). The Constitution and statutes, of course (not to mention political and cultural reality), no longer allow courts to indulge in the protection of wives while not affording similar protection to husbands.

Source:
Citations in the Comment.
History:
Adopted June 15, 2001.

STANDARD 14.50. COMMUNITY PROPERTY PRESUMPTION MAY BE REBUTTED BY SHOWING OF DOMICILE IN COMMON LAW JURISDICTION

An examiner may consider the community property presumption to be rebutted if it is shown the acquiring spouse was domiciled in a common law jurisdiction at the time of acquisition and if there is no indication that community funds or credit were used in the purchase.

COMMENT

Under the common law as generally applied in noncommunity property states, a spouse's funds are his or her separate estate. *See Oliver v. Robertson*, 41 Tex. 422, 425 (1874). It follows that if money earned in a common law state, being separate property, is paid for Texas real property, the real property takes on the same separate character. *Huston v. Colonial Trust Co.*, 266 S.W.2d 231, 233 (Tex. Civ. App.—El Paso 1954, writ ref'd n.r.e.). Citing that case and others, the court in *Orr v. Pope*, 400 S.W.2d 614, 616-17 (Tex. Civ. App.—Amarillo 1966, no writ), declared it to be the law of this state that

where a spouse acquires Texas real property while residing in a common law state, the real property is separate property.

Community property laws now prevail in Texas, Louisiana, New Mexico, Arizona, California, Washington, Idaho and Nevada, as well as in many foreign countries. 7 Richard R. Powell & Patrick J. Rohan, *Powell on Real Property* §53.01(3), at 53-6 (1997). Wisconsin's Uniform Marital Property Act, enacted in 1983, establishes a system analogous to community property. *Id.* at 53-7. The Alaska Community Property Act, Alaska Stat. §§34.77.010-34.77.995, in 1998 established a community property system applicable only to spouses who have chosen it by written agreement. The examiner may not apply a separate property presumption on the basis of residency outside Texas if it appears the owner was domiciled in another community property jurisdiction.

CAUTION

This standard should be applied narrowly and cautiously. The fact of domicile in a common law jurisdiction should be clear, and the separate character of property should not be presumed if there are any indications that community property consideration could have been paid, such as past residence in Texas or another community property state. The examiner may apply the standard more liberally as time passes without any apparent spousal claim.

Establishment of the fact of the grantee's domicile to a sufficient certainty will often require inquiry outside the record. The laws of any jurisdiction are, of course, subject to change and interpretation. Prudence may require verification that the common law has not been altered in the foreign jurisdiction in question in a manner that might render the acquiring spouse's consideration community property in the analysis of a Texas court. *See Huston v. Colonial Trust Co.*, 266 S.W.2d 231, 233-34 (Tex. Civ. App.—El Paso 1954, writ ref'd n.r.e.), in which the court complains of being almost worn down with citation of Pennsylvania authorities in an unsuccessful effort to convince it that the wife had some interest akin to community property. During the 1940s several states, including Hawaii, Michigan, Nebraska, Oklahoma and Oregon, enacted community property systems to take advantage of federal tax laws then effective. Those states repealed their community property laws after legislation removed the tax advantages of community property in 1948. 7 Richard R. Powell & Patrick J. Rohan, *Powell on Real Property* §53.08(1), at 53-108 (1997).

Tex. Fam. Code Ann. §7.002 authorizes the court, in a decree of divorce or annulment, to order a division of property acquired by either spouse while domiciled in another state that would have been community property if the acquiring spouse had been domiciled in Texas. Although Tex. Const. Ann. art. I, §19 prohibits the divestiture of separate property acquired as such by a Texas resident, *Eggemeyer v. Eggemeyer*, 554 S.W.2d 137 (Tex. 1977), the constitutionality of the divorce court's authority over "quasicommunity" property under Family Code §7.002 has been upheld. *Cameron v. Cameron*, 641 S.W.2d 210 (Tex. 1982); *Ismail v. Ismail*, 702 S.W.2d 216 (Tex. App.—Houston [1st Dist.] 1985, writ ref'd n.r.e.). An examiner who is aware of a divorce involving a person who acquired Texas real property for consideration while residing in a common law jurisdiction should investigate the court's division of the property, if any, in the same manner as for the spouses' community property. (Note, however, that §7.002 only empowers the court to order division of this kind of property in a decree of divorce or annulment. If the spouses' divorce was granted outside Texas, it appears the statute has no application.)

Source:
Citations in the Comment.
History:
Adopted June 15, 2001.

STANDARD 14.60. NECESSITY FOR JOINDER WHEN COMMUNITY PROPERTY IS IN NAME OF BOTH SPOUSES

If property is acquired during marriage by a deed naming both spouses as grantees, an examiner should not give effect to a subsequent conveyance of the property unless (1) it is joined by both spouses or (2) it was made by the husband before January 1, 1968, and did not convey homestead property.

COMMENT

Community property not subject to the sole management of one of the spouses is subject to their joint management, control and disposition. Tex. Fam. Code Ann. §3.102(c). Tex. Fam. Code Ann. §3.104(a) establishes the presumption that property held in one spouse's name is subject to his or her sole management, leaving property acquired in both spouses' names subject to joint management. It seems to follow that if property is held in the names of both spouses, a deed from one

spouse alone is ineffective as to either the entire community interest or the granting spouse's share, *Dalton v. Don J. Jackson, Inc.*, 691 S.W.2d 765 (Tex. App.—Austin 1985, no writ), except where it is from one spouse to the other. *In re Marriage of Morrison*, 913 S.W.2d 689 (Tex. App.—Texarkana 1995, writ denied). Although there is authority that a conveyance by one of the spouses may be given effect as to that spouse's half of the property, *Williams v. Portland State Bank*, 514 S.W.2d 124 (Tex. Civ. App.—Beaumont 1974, writ dism'd); *see Vallone v. Miller*, 663 S.W.2d 97, 98 (Tex. App.—Houston [14th Dist.] 1983, writ ref'd n.r.e.), the Dalton court points out that this would, in effect, permit one spouse unilaterally to partition joint management community property. Since community property may only be partitioned upon strict compliance with Tex. Const. Ann. art. XVI, §15, one spouse's purported conveyance of only his or her interest is ineffective. 691 S.W.2d at 768.

Before January 1, 1968, the Texas statutes vested the management of the entire community estate in the husband. Tex. Rev. Civ. Stat. Ann. art. 4619 (1925) (amended 1967, repealed 1969). During the period of the husband's management, a deed from him alone was considered sufficient to convey the community's interest in all property except homestead, regardless of how legal title was held.

There are unusual circumstances under which property subject to joint management may be conveyed by one spouse alone. Tex. Fam. Code Ann. §§3.301 and 3.302 expressly authorize the remaining spouse to petition the court for sole management if the other spouse has disappeared, has permanently abandoned the petitioning spouse, or the spouses are permanently separated, and case law supports the remaining spouse's authority to convey when the other has disappeared or has become incapacitated or incarcerated. *See, e.g., Reed v. Beheler*, 198 S.W.2d 625, 628 (Tex. Civ. App.—Fort Worth 1946, no writ). When one spouse has been judicially declared incapacitated, Tex. Estates Code Ann. §1353.002 gives sole management of the community estate to the other spouse.

CAUTION

If the examiner encounters a deed of joint management community property executed by only one spouse, it may not be ignored as being invalid. The grantee may be able to argue, for example, that the non-signing spouse consented to the conveyance. At the very least, such a deed casts a cloud on title that should be investigated.

Source:
Citations in the Comment.
History:
Adopted June 15, 2001; amended July 17, 2014.

The prior standard provided: "If property is acquired during marriage by a deed naming both spouses as grantees, an examiner may not give effect to a subsequent conveyance of the property unless (1) it is joined by both spouses or (2) it was made by the husband before January 1, 1968, and did not convey homestead property."

STANDARD 14.70. NECESSITY FOR JOINDER WHEN COMMUNITY PROPERTY IS IN NAME OF ONLY ONE SPOUSE

Subject to Standard 14.90, where community property has been acquired in the name of only one spouse, an examiner may rely on the grantee's authority to execute a subsequent conveyance as grantor, without joinder of the other spouse; however, the examiner should not pass a conveyance of community property held in the name of the wife made before January 1, 1968, without the husband's joinder or consent.

COMMENT

During marriage each spouse has the sole management, control and disposition of the community property that the spouse would have owned if single. Tex. Fam. Code Ann. §3.102(a). (Exceptions involving unusual circumstances such as the permanent abandonment of the petitioning spouse, permanent separation or disappearance of the managing spouse are allowed, with court approval, by Tex. Fam. Code. Ann. §§3.301 and 3.302; and these kinds of circumstances may validate a conveyance by the nonmanaging spouse regardless of judicial action. *See, e.g., Reed v. Beheler*, 198 S.W.2d 625, 628 (Tex. Civ. App.—Fort Worth 1946, no writ). To the same effect are Tex. Estates Code Ann. §§1353.002, 1353.003 regarding a spouse judicially declared to be incapacitated.) Property is presumed subject to a spouse's sole management, control, and disposition if it is held in that spouse's name, and a third party may rely on the presumption. Tex. Fam. Code Ann. §3.104. The sale of homestead, however, whether it consists of separate or community property, generally requires the joinder of both spouses. Tex. Fam. Code Ann. §5.001; *see* Standard 14.90.

CAUTION

On termination of the marriage by death or divorce, the community having been dissolved, the spouse in

whose name community property was acquired no longer has any authority to convey the other's community share, *Burnham v. Hardy Oil Co.*, 195 S.W. 1139 (Tex. 1917), except as may be authorized by the laws concerning community survivorship. *See* Standards 11.80 and 11.90. Therefore, if the record discloses the marriage's dissolution or facts that would, on inquiry, lead a prudent person to discover it, the examiner may not rely on the power of the holder of legal title over the entire interest of the community. *See, e.g., Myers v. Crenshaw*, 116 S.W.2d 1125, 1130 (Tex. Civ. App.—Texarkana 1938), aff'd, 137 S.W.2d 7 (Tex. 1940).

The Texas statutes formerly vested the entire management of community property in the husband. Tex. Rev. Civ. Stat. Ann. art. 4619 (1925) (amended 1967, repealed 1969). Before the effective date of the amendment, January 1, 1968, therefore, the general rule expressed in this standard would not apply to a conveyance of community property acquired in a married woman's name. Such property could instead be conveyed only by the husband, or at least with his consent. *Lockhart v. Garner*, 298 S.W.2d 108 (Tex. 1957). The constitutionality of the former statute may be subject to challenge on the basis of its disparate treatment of husbands and wives. *See Wessely Energy Co. v. Jennings*, 736 S.W.2d 624 (Tex. 1987), which held unconstitutional the long repealed statute requiring the husband's joinder in his wife's conveyance of her separate property. The ruling in *Wessely Energy* was prospective only, however, 736 S.W.2d at 629, and the examiner should presume that the exception noted in this Caution still governs pre-1968 conveyances.

Source:
Citations in the Comment.
History:
Adopted June 15, 2001.

STANDARD 14.80. NO PRESUMPTION OF MARRIAGE

Where the examiner is not aware that the grantor was married at the time of acquisition, the examiner need not inquire into the possible existence of a spouse's community property interest. The examiner should not infer that the grantor was married at the time of acquisition merely from a recital that the grantor is a widow or a widower.

COMMENT

A purchaser without actual knowledge or constructive notice that the grantor was married at the time of acquisition will take free of any claim by the former spouse or the spouse's heirs or devisees. *Hill v. Moore*, 62 Tex. 610 (1884); *McClenny v. Humble Oil & Refining Co.*, 179 S.W.2d 798 (Tex. Civ. App.—Texarkana 1944, writ ref'd w.o.m.). For example, a purchaser without notice of a former spouse's interest pursuant to a prior marriage will take free of it unless a certified copy of the divorce decree or other evidence of the dissolution has been recorded in the real property records of the county where the land is located. *Benn v. Security Realty & Development Co.*, 54 S.W.2d 146, 150 (Tex. Civ. App.—Beaumont 1932, writ ref'd). Even if the purchaser is put on notice that the grantor was formerly married and that the marriage has terminated, for example by a recital that the grantor is a widow or widower, the purchaser will still take free of claims under the spouse, as a bona fide purchaser for value, where the purchaser has no knowledge that the grantor had a spouse living at the time the property was acquired. *Gilmer's Estate v. Veatch*, 117 S.W. 430 (Tex. 1909); *Griggs v. Houston Oil Co.*, 213 S.W. 261 (Tex. Comm'n App. 1919, judgm't adopted); *Strong v. Strong*, 66 S.W.2d 751 (Tex. Civ. App.—Texarkana 1933), aff'd on other grounds, 98 S.W.2d 346 (Tex. 1936).

CAUTION

If the record discloses that the grantor was married at the time of acquisition, or discloses facts that would lead a prudent person to inquire and thereupon discover the marriage, a purchaser will be subject to claims by or under the former spouse. For example, the court in *Hill v. Moore*, 19 S.W. 162 (Tex. 1892), held that where a Republic of Texas land grant, although in the name of the husband only, was of a type available only to the head of a family, a purchaser was on notice to inquire into the identity of the man's family members and would have discovered that he had been married at the time of the grant. In *Myers v. Crenshaw*, 116 S.W.2d 1125, 1130 (Tex. Civ. App.—Texarkana 1938), aff'd, 137 S.W.2d 7 (Tex. 1940), the joinder of several of a deceased wife's children with their father in the execution of a deed, where there was no question of the reason for their joinder, was held to put a purchaser on notice of the wife's interest.

If the spouses (whether in a formal or common law marriage) actually occupy the property and use it as a home, a purchaser is on notice of its probable homestead character. *First State Bank v. Zeanon*, 169 S.W.2d 735, 739 (Tex. Civ. App.—Waco 1943, writ ref'd w.o.m.).

Accordingly, an examiner should, when appropriate, require inquiry into the possibility that the property is homestead, which would require joinder of both spouses in any conveyance. In case of any doubt, both spouses should be required to join in the conveyance. See Standard 14.90 regarding conveyances of homestead generally.

This standard is meant to apply to the examiner's consideration of a conveyance made by a grantor who acquired title by deed, not necessarily by passage of title through a decedent's estate. Because a purchaser of an interest that has passed through a decedent's estate is charged with notice of the beneficiaries' identity, *Sanburn v. Schuler*, 23 S.W. 641 (Tex. 1893), an examiner should consider the possibility that a community property or homestead interest may exist or have existed in a surviving or predeceased spouse. An examiner considering a decedent's estate will rarely, if ever, encounter circumstances in which available information reveals the identity of the decedent's heirs or devisees with sufficient certainty but does not somehow disclose, or at least lead to inquiry concerning, the decedent's marital status and history. *See Ross v. Morrow*, 19 S.W. 1090 (Tex. 1892).

Source:
Citations in the Comment.
History:
Adopted June 15, 2001.

STANDARD 14.90. HOMESTEAD

If the property conveyed is or may be the homestead of married persons, whether community property or separate property, an examiner should require the joinder of both spouses, unless it is conclusively shown that the property is not, or is no longer, homestead.

COMMENT

Homestead is defined by Tex. Const. Ann. art. XVI, §51 as not more than 200 acres not in a town or city, which may be one or more parcels, or not more than ten contiguous acres in a city, town or village, including improvements. For a single person, a rural homestead is limited by Tex. Prop. Code Ann. §41.002(b)(2) to 100 acres. An urban homestead must be used for purposes of a home, or as both a home and place of business, on one contiguous tract. Tex. Const. Ann. art. XVI, §51; Tex. Prop. Code Ann. §41.002(a). The constitution makes no provision for business use of a rural homestead, but the rural acreage need not all be contiguous to the tract used as a home. Tex. Const. Ann. art. XVI, §51; Tex. Prop. Code Ann. §41.002(b); *Riley v. Riley*, 972 S.W.2d 149 (Tex. App.—Texarkana 1998, no pet.). The establishment of a tract's character as homestead requires physical occupancy, or at least overt acts of preparation, with the intent to reside on the land as a home. *Gilmore v. Dennison*, 115 S.W.2d 902 (Tex. 1938); 39 Aloysius A. Leopold, *Marital Property and Homesteads* §25.3 (Texas Practice 1993). A homestead claimant need not actually reside on the land for it to become impressed with homestead character. *See, e.g.*, *Bartels v. Huff*, 67 S.W.2d 411 (Tex. Civ. App.—San Antonio 1933, writ ref'd). Mere intent to reside on the land, however, without some overt act in preparation for physical occupancy, is insufficient. *Cheswick v. Freeman*, 287 S.W.2d 171 (Tex. 1956). The homestead character extends to the unsevered minerals underlying the homestead, so that, for example, both spouses must join in oil and gas leases. *Gulf Production Co. v. Continental Oil Co.*, 164 S.W.2d 488 (Tex. 1939). Because the requirement for occupancy as a home necessarily implies surface ownership, however, no homestead character attaches to a severed mineral interest in a tract where the owner holds no right to occupy the surface other than for mineral development.

Whether the homestead is separate property of one spouse or community property, Tex. Fam. Code Ann. §5.001 provides that neither spouse may convey it, except under certain unusual circumstances, without the other's joinder. The unusual circumstances, which now require judicial authorization, are generally set out in Tex. Fam. Code Ann. §§5.002 (spouse's incapacity) and 5.101-102 (spouse's disappearance or abandonment). The current statute carries forward a policy long a feature of Texas law, embodied in Tex. Const. Ann. art. XVI, §50, and formerly in Tex. Rev. Civ. Stat. Ann. art. 1300 (1925) (repealed 1967), requiring the joinder of both spouses and formerly requiring adherence to strict requirements concerning the wife's acknowledgment.

A tract's homestead character, however, does not make a conveyance of the land (other than a mortgage or a deed of trust) by one spouse alone void. If the record title is in the name of the executing spouse, such a deed is merely inoperative while the property remains the non-signing spouse's homestead. *Grissom v. Anderson*, 79 S.W.2d 619, 621 (Tex. 1935); *Zable v. Henry*, 649 S.W.2d 136, 137 (Tex. App.—Dallas 1983, no writ). Obviously, factors such as the passage of time should be taken into consideration in assessing

whether it is necessary that inquiry be made into whether a tract of land conveyed by one spouse alone was homestead.

Unlike a deed, a mortgage or deed of trust granting a lien on homestead property is absolutely void unless joined by both spouses. *Inge v. Cain*, 65 Tex. 75 (1885). This is because the Texas Constitution provides that no mortgage, trust deed, or other lien "shall ever be valid" except as authorized thereby. Tex. Const. Ann. art. XVI, §50(c). (Joinder by both spouses is only one of many strict requirements and limitations the constitution places on the mortgaging of homestead.) Thus, the failure of one of the spouses to join in a deed of trust or other mortgage is not cured even though the property ceases to be homestead. *Toler v. Fertitta*, 67 S.W.2d 229 (Tex. Comm'n App. 1934, judgm't adopted). However, effective June 17, 2011, the occupying co-owner of residential homestead property may, upon proof of certain conditions, act as agent and attorney-in-fact for the other co-owner in encumbering the property for purposes of preserving or improving the property. Tex. Prop. Code Ann. §§65.001 to .004. Nonetheless, a deed of trust or other mortgage to secure the purchase money for property that is to be acquired by one spouse and is to become homestead need only be executed by the acquiring spouse. *Skelton v. Washington Mut. Bank, F.A.*, 61 S.W.3d 56 (Tex. App.—Amarillo 2001, no pet.) (at least if the deed retains an express vendor's lien); *Minnehoma Financial Co. v. Ditto*, 566 S.W.2d 354 (Tex. Civ. App.—Fort Worth 1978, writ ref'd n.r.e.); *Farmer v. Simpson*, 6 Tex. 303, 310 (1851).

For a discussion of judgment liens clouding homesteads, see Standard 15.30. For discussion of trusts that include homestead property, see Caution to Standard 9.10.

CAUTION

The examiner should always begin with the assumption that a tract of land that includes surface ownership is homestead and, before relying on a conveyance by one spouse alone, require a definite showing that it is not. An examiner should exercise a great deal of care in relying on extrinsic evidence to confirm that the property is not homestead. A purchaser or lender may be charged with the fact that a tract is homestead if it is occupied by the owner as a home, *Texas Land & Loan Co. v. Blalock*, 13 S.W.12 (Tex. 1890); *Gibraltar Savings & Building Ass'n v. Harper*, 41 S.W.2d 130 (Tex. Civ. App.—Austin 1931, writ ref'd); and the public records seldom reveal sufficiently definite and complete evidence of a tract's homestead character. In case of any reasonable doubt, an affidavit of the owners designating other property as homestead and stating that the property to be conveyed or encumbered is not homestead is now conclusive in favor of a purchaser or lender without contrary knowledge and should be required. Tex. Const. Ann. art. XVI, §50. If any question remains after investigation, an examiner should require that both spouses join in the conveyance. Where the property is separate property of one of the spouses or is community property held in the name of only one of them, the other spouse may be recited to be joining "pro forma." Because a spouse may have homestead rights arising from a common law marriage the same as from a formal one, a cautious examiner might consider requiring joinder of any two persons who occupy the same residence absent conclusive evidence that they are not married. Of course, both spouses should be required to join in a deed for any property that is not clearly non-homestead in character. *See* Standard 14.60.

Source:
Citations in the Comment.
History:
Adopted June 15, 2001; amended July 17, 2014.
The prior standard provided: "If the property conveyed is or may be the homestead of married persons, whether community property or separate property, an examiner must require the joinder of both spouses, unless it is conclusively shown that the property is not, or is no longer, homestead."

STANDARD 14.100. DIVORCE OR ANNULMENT

Absent a conveyance or agreement between the parties providing otherwise or a judicial decree imposing an equitable lien, the examiner should treat the separate property of each spouse as unaffected by a divorce or annulment. The examiner should examine the judgment of dissolution and any accompanying property settlement agreement for their effect on community property. Community property not divided by the court or by the spouses is owned equally by the former spouses as tenants in common.

COMMENT

In a decree of divorce or annulment, the court divides the marital estate in a manner it deems just and right, having due regard for the rights of each party and any children of the marriage. Tex. Fam. Code Ann. §7.001. The division need not be equal, *Williams v. Williams*, 325 S.W.2d 682 (Tex. 1959), and the court may even award all of the community property to just one of

the spouses. *Reardon v. Reardon*, 359 S.W.2d 329 (Tex. 1962). The court may incorporate the parties' agreement for division of their property in its decree. Tex. Fam. Code Ann. §7.006. The court is not empowered, however, to divest one spouse of his or her separate real property and award it to the other, *Eggemeyer v. Eggemeyer*, 554 S.W.2d 137 (Tex. 1977); however, a court may impose an equitable lien to secure reimbursement for improvements made with community funds. *Heggen v. Pemelton*, 836 S.W.2d 145, 146 (Tex. 1992). Subject to homestead restrictions, an equitable lien may be imposed by a court on property of a marital estate to secure a claim for economic contribution by another marital estate. Tex. Fam. Code Ann. §3.406. If the court and the parties fail to make a division of their community property, the former spouses become equal tenants in common, the same as if they had never been married. *Kirkwood v. Domnau*, 16 S.W. 428 (Tex. 1891).

Following a divorce or annulment affecting community property, it is important that a certified copy of the divorce decree, as well as any property settlement agreement that it incorporates, or a conveyance between the spouses be recorded in the real property records of the county where the property is located; otherwise there is no constructive notice of the new status of the spouses and their property. *Myers v. Crenshaw*, 116 S.W.2d 1125, 1131 (Tex. Civ. App.—Texarkana 1938), aff'd, 137 S.W.2d 7 (Tex. 1940); *Benn v. Security Realty & Development Co.*, 54 S.W.2d 146, 150 (Tex. Civ. App.—Beaumont 1932, writ ref'd); *Prewitt v. United States*, 792 F.2d 1353 (5th Cir. 1986).

The court's division of community property amounts to a partition, and its judgment vests title to the real property in the spouse to whom it is awarded. *Hailey v. Hailey*, 331 S.W.2d 299 (Tex. 1960). A certified copy of the divorce decree may be recorded in the real property records of the county where the land is located, Tex. Prop. Code Ann. §12.013. So long as the decree adequately describes the property in question, either in specific terms or generally (e.g., "all real property held in the name of Wife"), and is clear in its intent to vest the title in the spouse to whom it is awarded, such recordation, without a conveyance from the other spouse or other formality, is sufficient to evidence record title in the spouse to whom the tract has been allotted. *See Brinkley v. Brinkley*, 381 S.W.2d 725 (Tex. Civ. App.—Houston 1964, no writ).

CAUTION

The courts of one state have no jurisdiction to divide marital real property in another state. *See Fall v. Eastin*, 215 U.S. 1 (1909); *McElreath v. McElreath*, 345 S.W.2d 722 (Tex. 1961); *Morris v. Hand*, 8 S.W. 210 (Tex. 1888); *Keith v. Keith*, 763 S.W.2d 950, 954 (Tex. App.—Fort Worth 1989, no writ). Thus, although presumptively effective to have dissolved the marriage, a judgment of divorce or annulment from a jurisdiction other than Texas cannot be given effect to the extent it purports to divide the spouses' real property in Texas. Unless a conveyance or other self-executing agreement between the spouses provides for a different division, community property of spouses divorcing outside Texas must be considered to be owned by each of them equally after the divorce.

Source:

Citations in the Comment.

History:

Adopted June 15, 2001; amended July 17, 2014.

The prior standard provided: "Absent a conveyance or agreement between the parties providing otherwise or a judicial decree imposing an equitable lien, the examiner must treat the separate property of each spouse as unaffected by a divorce or annulment. The examiner must examine the judgment of dissolution and any accompanying property settlement agreement for their effect on community property. Community property not divided by the court or by the spouses is owned equally by the former spouses as tenants in common."

CHAPTER XV. LIENS & LIS PENDENS

STANDARD 15.10. LIENS GENERALLY

An examiner should identify all liens, both contractual and statutory, relevant to the interests under examination and advise the client regarding any actions that are appropriate to the purpose of the examination. An examiner need not identify a lien that is barred by limitations or is otherwise unenforceable.

COMMENT

Determining the significance of a lien or encumbrance and drafting appropriate requirements for a particular situation requires careful and skillful analysis by the examiner. The examiner ordinarily disclaims coverage of liens that might not appear of record or ripen until after the closing date of the opinion (such as involuntary mechanics' and materialmen's liens); however, if the purpose of the examination is to determine the validity and priority of liens, an examiner should caution the client about the possible existence of unrecorded liens.

Mortgage or Deed of Trust: A mortgage or deed of trust is an interest in real property providing security for the performance of an obligation, usually evidenced by a note. On default, the mortgage or deed of trust may be foreclosed, the property may be sold, and the proceeds applied for the mortgagee's benefit. While a mortgage is a two party instrument between a mortgagor and mortgagee, a deed of trust is a conveyance to a trustee for the benefit of the mortgagee and, in Texas, gives the trustee the power of nonjudicial foreclosure and sale. *Johnson v. Snell*, 504 S.W.2d 397, 399 (Tex. 1973). The general practice in Texas is to use a deed of trust; however, lenders and attorneys commonly use the terms "mortgage" and "deed of trust" interchangeably. The secured creditor under a deed of trust is often identified as the "beneficiary" or "mortgagee," the debtor is often identified as the "borrower," "grantor," or "mortgagor," and the party having the power of nonjudicial foreclosure and sale in the event of default is identified as the "trustee."

Mortgaged Property: Absent some statutory or other legal inhibition, any alienable interest in real property may be mortgaged. *Cadle Co. v. Caamano*, 930 S.W.2d 917, 920 (Tex. App.—Houston [14th Dist.] 1996, no writ). Appurtenances are rights and interests in related real property that are essential to the full enjoyment of the subject property. A security interest in real property automatically extends to appurtenances. *Pine v. Gibraltar Savings Assoc.*, 519 S.W.2d 238, 242 (Tex. Civ. App.—Houston [1st Dist.] 1974, writ ref'd n.r.e.). Rights and interests in other property that are useful but not essential for the full enjoyment of the described property are not considered appurtenances. Thus, a security interest in the described property does not automatically extend to those rights and interests. *Balcar v. Lee County Cotton Oil Co.*, 193 S.W. 1094, 1095 (Tex. Civ. App.—Austin 1917, no writ).

Lien Theory: Texas follows the "lien theory" of mortgages and deeds of trust, under which the creditor or the trustee, despite granting language in the instrument, is not regarded as the owner of the property securing the debt. *Taylor v. Brennan*, 621 S.W.2d 592, 593 (Tex. 1981); *NCNB Tex. Nat'l Bank v. Sterling Projects, Inc.*, 789 S.W.2d 358, 359 (Tex. App.—Dallas 1990, writ dism'd w.o.j.). Legal title does not pass from the mortgagor, and the mortgagee receives only a lien or equitable title. *Flag-Redfern Oil Co. v. Humble Exploration Co.*, 744 S.W.2d 6, 8 (Tex. 1987); *First Baptist Church v. Baptist Bible Seminary*, 347 S.W.2d 587, 590-591 (Tex. 1961). A mortgagee ordinarily has no right of possession. The mortgagor remains entitled to possession of the land and is entitled to use the land without being accountable to the mortgagee, except for waste. *State v. First Interstate Bank*, 880 S.W.2d 427, 429-430 (Tex. App.—Austin 1994, writ denied); *NCNB Tex. Nat'l Bank v. Sterling Projects, Inc.*, 789 S.W.2d 358, 359 (Tex. App.—Dallas 1990, writ dism'd w.o.j.).

Vendor's Lien: A vendor's lien is a lien in favor of the seller of real property to secure payment of the unpaid purchase price. The usual practice in Texas is to expressly reserve a vendor's lien in the deed so that, when the deed is recorded, third parties will have notice of the lien. Even if the lien is not reserved in the deed, an express vendor's lien may be created by acknowledging the lien in the purchase money note. *Simms v. Espindola*, 310 S.W.2d 364, 366 (Tex. Civ. App.—San Antonio 1958, writ ref'd n.r.e.). An express vendor's lien makes the deed an executory sales contract and gives the seller superior title to the real property until the purchase price is paid. Under an express vendor's lien, the seller has an election of remedies on the buyer's default: (1) sue for the balance of the purchase money and foreclose the lien; (2) rescind the contract and take possession; or (3) sue to recover title and possession. *Hampton v. Minton*, 785 S.W.2d 854 (Tex. App.—Austin 1990, writ den.); *Lusk v. Mintz*, 625 S.W.2d 774 (Tex. Civ. App.—Houston [14th Dist.] 1981, no writ). A vendor's lien is an assignable interest. *Cadle Co. v. Caamano*, 930 S.W.2d 917, 919-920 (Tex. App.—Houston [14th Dist.] 1996, no writ). For a discussion of implied vendor's liens, see Standard 15.40.

Even if an express lien is not reserved in the deed, the seller still has, by operation of law, an implied or equitable vendor's lien to secure payment of any unpaid portion of the purchase money. However, when there is no express vendor's lien in the deed, the buyer receives full title to the property, and the seller's only remedy under an equitable vendor's lien is a judicial foreclosure. *Zapata v. Torres*, 464 S.W.2d 926, 928 (Tex. Civ. App.—Dallas 1971, no writ).

Other Contractual Liens: A lien may be created by contract to secure practically any obligation. Commonly encountered voluntary liens include:

(a) Mechanics' and Materialmen's Contract Lien.

A contract granting a lien for improvements on real property is commonly made separately from a mortgage

or deed of trust in order to address special requirements relating to the placement of liens on homesteads. For a lien contract validly to impose a lien on homestead property, it must be executed before any labor is performed or material furnished, must be filed for record in the county clerk's office, and must meet certain other requirements. Tex. Prop. Code Ann. §53.254.

(b) Oil and Gas Operating Agreement Lien.

Commonly, oil and gas joint operating agreements impose a lien upon the interest of a party to the agreement who defaults in the performance of its obligations under the agreement. Record notice of the lien may be shown by a memorandum of the operating agreement filed in the records of the county clerk. However, even without recording, a third party may be on notice of the lien for other reasons, including a reference to the operating agreement in the chain of title. *Mbank Abilene, N.A. v. Westwood Energy, Inc.*, 723 S.W.2d 246 (Tex. App.—Eastland 1986, no writ). *See also Enduro Oil Co. v. Parish & Ellison*, 834 S.W.2d 547 (Tex. App.—Houston [14th Dist.] 1992, writ denied). *See generally* 3 Ernest E. Smith and Jacqueline Lang Weaver, *Texas Law of Oil and Gas* §17.3(C)(2) (2d ed. 2006).

(c) Homeowners' Association Lien for Assessments.

Unless there is a subordination, a homeowners' association assessment lien provided for in the declaration of restrictions has priority over subsequent rights (such as homestead rights) and transfers that occurred before the assessment was due. *Inwood North Homeowners' Association v. Harris*, 736 S.W.2d 632 (Tex. 1987). Regarding condominiums, however, the unit owners' association lien for unpaid assessments is given statutory priority over any other lien except those listed in Tex. Prop. Code. Ann. §82.113(b). A deed restriction or other covenant running with the land and applicable to residential real estate that requires payment of a fee for a future transfer of the property (including any lien in support thereof) by a transferee is void and unenforceable; however, this invalidity does not apply to a restriction or covenant in favor of a residential "property owners' association" (as defined in Tex. Prop. Code Ann. §209.002), a tax exempt entity (26 U.S.C. §501(c)(3)), or a governmental entity. Tex. Prop. Code Ann. §5.017, repealed by Acts 2011, 82nd Leg., ch. 211 (H.B. 8), §2, eff. June 17, 2011.

Formalities: Generally applicable conveyancing rules govern mortgages and deeds of trust. A mortgage, deed of trust, or other contractual lien on real estate falls within the statute of frauds. Tex. Bus. & Com. Code Ann. §26.01(a), (b)(4); *West v. First Baptist Church*, 71 S.W.2d 1090, 1100 (Tex. 1934); *Edward Scharf Assocs., Inc. v. Skiba*, 538 S.W.2d 501, 502-503 (Tex. Civ. App.—Waco 1976, no writ). Recordation of a mortgage or a deed of trust is not essential to make it a valid and binding obligation between the immediate parties. *Denson v. First Bank & Trust*, 728 S.W.2d 876, 877 (Tex. App.—Beaumont 1987, no writ). An unrecorded deed of trust is effective between the parties and against any other person who has notice of it. Tex. Prop. Code Ann. §13.001(b); *Biggs & Co. v. Caldwell*, 115 S.W.2d 461, 463 (Tex. Civ. App.—Fort Worth 1938, writ dism'd). If after the execution of a mortgage or a deed of trust, the mortgagor subsequently acquires title to property described in the mortgage or deed of trust, the title is automatically encumbered by the lien by virtue of the doctrine of after-acquired title (estoppel by deed). *Clark v. Gauntt*, 161 S.W.2d 270, 271 (Tex. 1942); *Shield v. Donald*, 253 S.W.2d 710, 712 (Tex. Civ. App.—Fort Worth 1952, writ ref'd n.r.e.). The doctrine of estoppel by deed does not apply to quitclaim instruments.

Judgments or documents purporting to create a lien from a purported court not expressly created or established under the Texas or U.S. constitution or not consented to by the debtor, are presumed fraudulent. For example, a document purporting to establish or assert a lien against real property and filed by a prison inmate is presumed fraudulent. Tex. Civ. Prac. & Rem. Code Ann. §§12.001, 12.002; Tex. Gov't Code Ann. §§51.901(e) and (f).

Rents, Issues and Profits: Unless the mortgage or deed of trust provides otherwise, the property owner generally retains the right to rents, issues, and profits while the property is subject to the lien. However, the deed of trust or a separate instrument commonly includes a provision assigning to the mortgagee the mortgagor's interest in rents or other income accruing after the date of the mortgage as additional security. *NCNB Tex. Nat'l Bank v. Sterling Projects, Inc.*, 789 S.W.2d 358, 360 (Tex. App.—Dallas 1990, writ dism'd w.o.j.); *McGeorge v. Henrie*, 94 S.W.2d 761, 762 (Tex. Civ. App.—Texarkana 1936, no writ).

If an assignment of rents is given as additional security for the debt, the assignment does not become operative until the creditor takes affirmative action, such as obtaining possession of the property, impounding the rents, or securing the appointment of a receiver. *Summers v. Consol. Capital Special Trust*, 783 S.W.2d 580, 583 (Tex. 1989). On the other hand, if the assignment of rentals is an "absolute assignment," it does not create a security interest, but instead automatically gives the creditor title to the rent on the occurrence of a specified condition, such as default. *NCNB Tex. Nat'l Bank v. Sterling Projects, Inc.*, 789 S.W.2d 358, 360 (Tex. App.—Dallas 1990, writ dism'd w.o.j.). Whether the assignment is an absolute assignment or is given as additional security depends on the intent of the parties, as determined by examining both the assignment of rents clause and the security agreement executed contemporaneously with it. *Oryx Energy Co. v. Union Nat'l Bank of Tex.*, 895 S.W.2d 409, 415 (Tex. App.—San Antonio 1995, writ denied). Absolute assignments are not favored by the courts. If the assignment agreement or deed of trust states that the assignment of rents is given as "further" security for the debt and permits the creditor on default to enter the premises and collect the rents, the assignment will be construed to be a security, which must be foreclosed, not an absolute assignment. *Taylor v. Brennan*, 621 S.W.2d 592 (Tex. 1981).

Unless the security instrument provides otherwise, every deed of trust, mortgage, or other lien instrument signed and delivered on or after June 17, 2011, creates an assignment of rents arising from real property securing an obligation under the security instrument. Tex. Prop. Code Ann. §64.051. A security instrument signed and delivered before June 17, 2011, is governed by the law that applied to the instrument immediately before that date, as discussed above; however, Tex. Prop. Code Ann. §§64.100 et seq. govern the enforcement of an assignment of rents, the perfection and priority of a security interest in rents, and the attachment and perfection of a security interest in proceeds even if signed and delivered prior to June 17, 2011. "Rents" are defined in Tex. Prop. Code Ann. §64.001.

Landlord-Tenant: By statute, a tenant's leasehold interest is not a transferable interest and will not be subject to a security interest unless the landlord consents to subletting by the tenant. Tex. Prop. Code Ann. §91.005; *Am. Nat'l Bank & Trust v. First Wis. Mtg. Trust*, 577 S.W.2d 312, 316 (Tex. Civ. App.—Beaumont 1979, writ ref'd n.r.e.). A lease provision allowing the tenant to sublet without further consent by the landlord empowers the tenant to create a security interest in the leasehold. *Menger v. Ward*, 30 S.W. 853, 854 (Tex. 1895). Unless the parties provide otherwise in the lease, a landlord may create a security interest in the reversion, because the landlord's reversionary interest is alienable. *Wilson v. Beck*, 286 S.W. 315, 321-322 (Tex. Civ. App.—Dallas 1926, writ ref'd). A security interest in the reversion is subject to any then existing lease unless the lease provides for a subordination of interests. *F. Groos & Co. v. Chittim*, 100 S.W. 1006, 1010-1011 (Tex. Civ. App. 1907, no writ).

Future Advance Clause: A future advance clause in a mortgage or deed of trust creates an inchoate security interest in the subject property. If and when a debt arises that is covered by the instrument, the inchoate security interest immediately and automatically ripens into a lien. *Robinson v. Nat'l Bank of Commerce*, 515 S.W.2d 166, 168 (Tex. Civ. App.—Dallas 1974, no writ). The future advance clause in a recorded deed of trust has the same priority over subsequent conveyances and encumbrances as the deed of trust because the clause is sufficient to put third parties on notice of the possibility of future indebtedness, and the duty to inquire is on the third party. *Regold Mfg. Co. v. Maccabees*, 348 S.W.2d 864, 865 (Tex. Civ. App.—Fort Worth 1961, writ ref'd n.r.e.); *Coke Lumber & Mfg. Co. v. First Nat'l Bank*, 529 S.W.2d 612, 615 (Tex. Civ. App.—Dallas 1975, writ ref'd).

Dragnet Clause: A dragnet clause provides that the deed of trust secures payment of not only a specific debt, but all obligations of any kind that the debtor owes or may owe to the creditor, past, present or future. A dragnet clause may read "all other indebtedness, obligations, and liabilities of any kind or character of grantor to lender, now or hereafter existing, absolute or contingent, arising by operation of law or otherwise, or direct or indirect, primary or secondary, joint, several, fixed or contingent, and whether incurred by grantor as principal, surety, endorser, guarantor, or otherwise." The dragnet clause applies only to indebtedness which was reasonably within the contemplation of the parties to the mortgage or deed of trust at the time of execution. *Moss v. Hipp*, 387 S.W.2d 656, 658 (Tex. 1965); *FDIC v. Bodin Concrete Co.*, 869 S.W.2d 372, 377 (Tex. App.—Dallas 1993, writ denied). If as a result of the dragnet clause, other debt is owed at the time the specific debt is paid, the borrower will not be entitled to a release.

For discussion of involuntary or constitutional or statutory liens, including constitutional and statutory mechanics' and materialmen's liens, see Standards 15.20, 15.50, and 15.60. For judgment liens, see Standard 15.30. For implied vendor's liens, see Standard 15.40. For ad valorem tax liens, see Standards 15.70 and 15.80. For lien priority and subordination, see Standard 15.90. For removal of liens, see Standard 15.100. For lis pendens, see Standard 15.110. For nonjudicial foreclosures, see Standard 16.10. For judicial foreclosures and execution sales, see Standard 16.20. For foreclosure of home equity loans and reverse mortgages, see Standard 16.30. For deeds in lieu of foreclosure, see Standard 16.40. Bankruptcy issues are addressed in Chapter XII. Financing statements, fixtures, and crops are not within the scope of this chapter. For mortgages or deeds of trust on homestead property, see Standard 14.90.

CAUTION

Once perfected, many involuntary liens, including judgment liens and federal and state tax liens but excluding liens securing ad valorem taxes, encumber all of the debtor's nonexempt property located in the county where notice of the lien is recorded. The lien attaches to nonexempt property owned at the time of perfection as well as to nonexempt property acquired thereafter until the debt is discharged or enforcement is barred by limitations. Thus, an examiner should not rely on a search of the relevant indices only from the time of the party's acquisition forward. Rather, the search for liens concerning each party in the chain of title should also extend back from the time that a party acquires an interest for the longest possible period of limitation. In this regard, for child support liens filed on or after September 1, 1997 and prior to May 26, 2009, the duration of the Texas lien for unpaid child support is indefinite, Tex. Fam. Code Ann. §157.318, and federal judgment liens and federal tax liens may be renewed multiple times, see Standards 15.30 and 15.60. Child support liens filed on or after May 26, 2009 are effective regarding real property until the tenth anniversary of the date on which the lien notice was filed and may be renewed for subsequent 10-year periods if a renewed lien notice is filed before the applicable tenth anniversary. Tex. Fam. Code Ann. §157.318. Nevertheless, a title examiner reasonably relies exclusively on materials furnished to the examiner, such as an abstract of title or a landman's run sheets. When doing a stand-up examination, the practice of examiners regarding the scope of search for involuntary liens varies. To avoid an unreasonably expansive scope of search, many examiners reasonably limit their stand-up examination for involuntary liens back twenty years from the date of examination under the names of current interest owners and parties who disposed of their interest within twenty years of the date of examination. *See* Standard 1.20 and accompanying Comment.

Cover-all and Mother Hubbard Clauses: A mortgage or deed of trust typically includes general language that purports to cover lands or interests that are not specifically described. This language is often called, but seldom labeled in the instrument, a "cover-all" clause or "Mother Hubbard" clause. An examiner should examine any mortgage or deed of trust within the chain of title in a grantor index that does not specifically cover the lands under examination to determine whether that instrument, by reason of the scope of any "cover-all" clause or "Mother Hubbard" clause, may encumber the lands under examination. The typical cover-all or Mother Hubbard clause includes real property interests appurtenant to the land described, such as easements, strips and gores, etc.; however, the clause may be much broader by also referring to all of the mortgagor's land in the county or all of the grantor's land, as described in another document. *Compare Jones v. Colle*, 727 S.W.2d 262 (Tex. 1987); *Smith v. Allison*, 301 S.W.2d 608 (Tex. 1957); *Broaddus v. Grout*, 258 S.W.2d 308 (Tex. 1953); *Sun Oil Co. v. Bennett*, 84 S.W.2d 447 (Tex. 1935); *Sun Oil Co. v. Burns*, 84 S.W.2d 442 (Tex. 1935); *Smith v. Westall*, 13 S.W. 540 (Tex. 1890); *Witt v. Harlan*, 2 S.W. 41 (Tex. 1886); *Holloway's Unknown Heirs v. Whatley*, 131 S.W.2d 89 (Tex. 1939); *Sanderson v. Sanderson*, 109 S.W.2d 744 (Tex. 1937); *J. Hiram Moore, Ltd. v. Greer*, 172 S.W.3d 609 (Tex. 2005); and *Lauchheimer v. Saunders*, 65 S.W. 500 (Tex. Civ. App. 1901, no writ).

Claim for conveyance of residential property encumbered by a lien: Effective January 1, 2008, a person may not contract to sell or convey an interest in residential real property that will remain encumbered by a recorded lien unless, before the conveyance, the seller provides a detailed disclosure of the lien and of any insurance relating to the property to the buyer and each lienholder. There are numerous requirements regarding, as well as numerous exceptions to, the duty of disclosure. A violation of the duty to disclose allows the buyer to terminate a contract for sale but does not in-

validate a conveyance; however, the transferee, in certain circumstances, may have a cause of action for damages. Tex. Prop. Code. Ann. §5.016. Although the law appears to have been passed to address sales of residences, the law is broadly worded to apply to a contract of sale or conveyance of any interest in "residential real property" (undefined), including easements and oil and gas leases, but is also subject to numerous exceptions—e.g., the law does not apply to a transfer where the purchaser obtains a title insurance policy or to a person "who has purchased, conveyed, or entered into contracts to purchase or convey an interest in real property four or more times in the preceding 12 months." *Id.* At 5.016(c).

Source:
Citations in the Comment.
History:
Adopted June 13, 2003.

STANDARD 15.20. INVOLUNTARY MECHANICS' & MATERIALMEN'S LIENS

The examiner should identify recorded mechanics' and materialmen's lien affidavits affecting the title under examination.

COMMENT

The Texas constitution provides that "[m]echanics, artisans and materialmen, of every class, shall have a lien upon the buildings and articles made or repaired by them for the value of their labor done thereon, or material furnished therefor; and the Legislature shall provide by law for the speedy and efficient enforcement of said liens." Tex. Const. art. XVI, §37. The constitutional lien attaches not only to the 'building' for which the work was done or material furnished but to so much of the land on which it stands as is necessary for its enjoyment, which is a question of fact. *Ferrell v. Ertel*, 100 S.W.2d 1084 (Tex. Civ. App.—Fort Worth 1936, writ dism'd). What constitutes a "building" has been construed broadly. *See Ambrose & Co. v. Hutchison*, 356 S.W.2d 215 (Tex. Civ. App.—Fort Worth 1962, no writ) (holding that a pier is a building); *Moore v. Carey Bros. Oil Co.*, 269 S.W. 75 (Tex. Comm'n App. 1925, judgm't adopted) (holding that oil well casing is a building). The constitutional lien is self-executing as between the property owner and original contractors, and one providing labor or materials directly to the owner is not subject to statutory conditions to enforcement such as the timely filing of an affidavit claiming the lien. *Hayek v. Western Steel Co.*, 478 S.W.2d 786, 790 (Tex. 1972); *Strang v. Pray*, 35 S.W. 1054 (Tex. 1896). While, generally, the constitutional lien may be either oral or written, for it to be a valid construction or improvement lien on homestead, the contract must be in writing. *Cavazos v. Munoz*, 305 B.R. 661, 680 (S.D. Tex. 2004). The constitutional lien is not binding on third parties without notice or unless the contractor has followed the statutory lien provisions. *Strang v. Pray*, 35 S.W. at 1056. Only original contractors may claim the constitutional lien; subcontractors face the more onerous burden of perfecting a statutory lien. *Da-Col Paint Manufacturing Co. v. American Indemnity Co.*, 517 S.W.2d 270, 273 (Tex. 1974); *First National Bank v. Lyon-Gray Lumber Co.*, 217 S.W. 133 (Tex. 1919). Special rules apply to renovation and repair on existing improvements on a homestead. Tex Const. art XVI, §50(a)(5)(A)-(D). For mechanics' and materialmen's liens affecting homestead property, see Standard 14.90.

In addition to the constitutional lien, a statutory lien is available to one who provides labor or materials, either as an original contractor or as a subcontractor: (1) for a house, building or improvement, a levee or embankment, a railroad, or landscaping, Tex. Prop. Code Ann. §53.021; or (2) for an oil, gas or water well, an oil or gas pipeline, or a mine or quarry, Tex. Prop. Code Ann. §§56.001-56.002. The existence and enforceability of the statutory lien is entirely dependent on the contractor's or subcontractor's compliance with specified prerequisites, though substantial compliance is sufficient. *First National Bank v. Sledge*, 653 S.W.2d 283 (Tex. 1983). Of primary importance to the title examiner are the statutes' requirements for the recording of an affidavit claiming the lien. The pertinent requirements are generally as follows:

General Mechanic's Lien: The affidavit claiming a lien for labor or materials furnished to a house, building, or improvements, a levee or embankment, or a railroad must be filed in the office of the county clerk of the county in which the property is located not later than the 15th day of the fourth calendar month after the day on which the indebtedness accrues, except that for a lien arising from a residential construction project, it must be filed not later than the 15th day of the third calendar month after such accrual. Tex. Prop. Code Ann. §53.052(a) & (b). The indebtedness generally accrues on the last day of the month the contract was completed or terminated for an original contractor and on the last day of the last month labor was performed or material

furnished by a subcontractor or material supplier. Tex. Prop. Code Ann. §53.053. The affidavit must be signed and sworn to by the person claiming the lien or another person on the claimant's behalf and contain the items specified in Tex. Prop. Code Ann. §53.054, including the amount of the claim; the name and last known address of the owner, the person who employed the claimant, and the original contractor; the kind of work done and material furnished (and, for a subcontractor, each month in which the work was done or material furnished); a legal description of the property; and, for subcontractors, the date and method of notice to the owner.

The inception of a mechanic's lien is the commencement of visible construction, Tex. Prop. Code Ann. §53.124(a) and (b). However, the inception of a architect's, engineer's, surveyor's, landscaper's, or demolition contractor's lien is the date of recording of the lien, provided that the underlying contract for work is in writing. *Id.* §53.124(e).

<u>Mineral Contractor's or Subcontractor's Lien:</u> One who furnishes labor or material for an oil, gas or water well, an oil or gas pipeline, or a mine or quarry must file an affidavit in the office of the county clerk of the county where the property is located not later than six months after the day the indebtedness accrues. Tex. Prop. Code Ann. §56.021(a). A mineral subcontractor must have served notice of the claim on the property owner at least ten days before filing the affidavit. Tex. Prop. Code Ann. §56.021(b). The indebtedness for labor performed by the day or week accrues at the end of each week during which the labor is performed. Tex. Prop. Code Ann. §56.005(a). The indebtedness for material or services otherwise accrues on the date they were last furnished; all material or services furnished by the same person to the same property are considered furnished under a single contract unless more than six months elapse between the dates the material or services are furnished. Tex. Prop. Code Ann. §56.005(b). The affidavit must contain the items specified in Tex. Prop. Code Ann. §56.022, including the name and mailing address of the claimant; the name of the mineral property owner, if known; an itemized list of the amounts claimed and the dates of performance or furnishing; a description of the land, leasehold interest, pipeline or pipeline right-of-way involved; and, if the claimant is a subcontractor, the name of the person for whom the labor was performed or material furnished and a statement that the claimant served timely notice on the owner or the owner's representative. The lien attaches to leasehold interests and is not limited to the wells or to the proration units around the wells. Thus, the lien claimant for a well will acquire a lien in other wells on the same lease and in nonproductive acreage covered by the lease. *Mercantile Nat'l Bank v. McCullough Tool Co.*, 259 S.W.2d 724 (Tex. 1953). The lien attaches only to the leasehold interest of the owner who contracts with the lien claimant. The lien does not attach to the undivided interest of co-owners who did not contract with the lien claimant unless the lien claimant can establish that the co-owners are mining partners or joint venturers or that an agency relationship exists. *Youngstown Sheet and Tube Co. v. Penn*, 357 S.W.2d 239 (Tex. Civ. App.—Austin 1962), modified on other grounds, 363 S.W.2d 230 (Tex. 1962). Typically, the co-owners of the leasehold will designate an operator as an independent contractor under a joint operating agreement, and so long as the parties' conduct is not inconsistent with that characterization, they will not be mining partners or joint venturers and the operator will not be regarded as an agent of the nonoperators. *Ayco Devel. Corp. v. G.E.T. Service Co.*, 616 S.W.2d 184 (Tex. 1981); Tex. Prop. Code Ann. §§56.001-56.006.

Tex. Prop. Code ch. 62 also enables a broker to perfect a statutory lien on a seller's or lessor's commercial non-residential real estate for the broker's commission. A broker claiming the lien must have earned the commission under a written commission agreement and comply with the filing and notice requirements of Tex. Prop. Code Ann. §§62.024-62.026, 62.041.

Enforcement of an original contractor's constitutional lien, unlike a statutory lien, is not barred if the contractor fails to meet the statutory requirements for, among other things, filing an affidavit. *Farmers' & Mechanics' National Bank v. Taylor*, 40 S.W. 876 (Tex. Civ. App.—Fort Worth 1897), aff'd, 40 S.W. 966 (Tex. 1897); *Texas Builders' Supply Co. v. Beaumont Construction Co.*, 150 S.W. 770 (Tex. Civ. App.—Galveston 1912, writ dism'd). The statutory requirements must be satisfied, however, for a constitutional lien to be enforceable against a bona fide purchaser. *Black, Sivalls & Bryson, Inc. v. Operators' Oil & Gas Co.*, 37 S.W.2d 313, 315 (Tex. Civ. App.—Eastland 1931, writ dism'd). Thus, where a bona fide purchaser is involved, any inquiry for the existence of unfiled liens ordinarily need extend no further for constitutional liens than for statutory liens.

However, a purchaser who knows or should have known of facts and circumstances giving rise to a constitutional lien or a donee acquires the property subject to it. *See Apex Financial Corp. v. Brown*, 7 S.W.3d 820, 831 (Tex. App.—Texarkana 1999, no pet.).

A suit to foreclose a statutory lien must generally be filed within two years (or one year for a claim arising from a residential construction contract) after the last day the claimant may file the lien affidavit, or within one year after completion, termination, or abandonment of the work under the original contract, whichever is later. Tex. Prop. Code Ann. §§53.158, 56.041(a). After the passage of that period, the title examiner may presume that the lien is no longer effective unless a foreclosure suit has been filed, or unless the lien being claimed is or may be a constitutional one. In the latter event the general four-year statute of limitation for debt actions, Tex. Civ. Prac. & Rem. Code Ann. §16.004(a), would apply.

The right to enforce a lien for performance of labor or furnishing material may be waived by express agreement or by acts inconsistent with the lien's continued existence, but waiver will not be inferred unless the lienholder's intention to do so is clear. *See Jones v. White*, 12 S.W. 179 (Tex. 1888); *McBride v. Beakley*, 203 S.W. 1137 (Tex. Civ. App.—Amarillo 1918, no writ). A statutory mechanics' and materialmen's lien may be avoided by the filing of a bond for payment in compliance with Tex. Prop. Code Ann. §§53.171-53.175 or §§53.201-53.211.

For contracts executed on or after January 1, 2012, any waiver and release of a lien or payment bond claim is unenforceable unless it complies with Tex. Prop. Code Ann. §53.281 et seq., including being signed and delivered using a waiver and release form substantially in compliance with prescribed statutory forms.

For a discussion of voluntary mechanics' and materialmen's liens, see Standard 15.10.

CAUTION

A mechanics' and materialmen's lien relates back to the beginning of the work or the furnishing of materials. Tex. Prop. Code Ann. §53.124; *Denny v. White House Lumber Co.*, 54 S.W.2d 86 (Tex. Comm'n App. 1932, holding approved). The lien of a contractor or subcontractor who complies with the statutory filing and other requirements will be superior to the title of a subsequent purchaser, regardless of notice of the lien. Accordingly, prospective purchasers and lenders must make some inquiry outside the public records into activity on the property at least as far back as the length of the filing periods and seek to assure themselves that any potential claimants have been paid.

Source:
Citations in the Comment.
History:
Adopted June 16, 2006.

STANDARD 15.30. JUDGMENT LIENS

An examiner should identify recorded abstracts of judgment affecting the title under examination.

COMMENT

If a court-certified "abstract of judgment" is properly prepared, recorded, and indexed, a judgment lien attaches to the judgment debtor's non-homestead real property, then owned or thereafter acquired, located in the county or counties where the abstract of judgment is of record. Tex. Prop. Code Ann. §§52.001, 52.002. The term "real property" includes any interest in land including any undivided interest. *Robertson v. Scott*, 172 S.W.2d 478 (Tex. 1943); *Stroble v. Tearl*, 221 S.W.2d 556 (Tex. 1949).

An examiner should identify potentially enforceable liens evidenced by recorded abstracts of judgment and advise the client as appropriate to the circumstances of the examination. Typically, an examiner will require that any lien evidenced by a recorded abstract of judgment be released.

In general, neither the entry of a money judgment nor the recordation of a judgment creates a lien. *White v. FDIC*, 19 F.3d 249, 251 n.5 (5th Cir. 1994). Although a judgment may create a separate judicial lien by its express language, a certified copy of a judgment does not qualify as an abstract of judgment and does not create a lien by recordation. *Citicorp Real Estate, Inc. v. Banque Arabe Internationale D'Investissement*, 747 S.W.2d 926, 929 (Tex. App.—Dallas 1988, writ denied). An examiner may usually presume that a recorded document appearing to be an abstract of judgment creates an enforceable lien. However, occasionally an examiner may have to consider the validity of a recorded abstract of judgment, as for example where a title examination is being conducted for a judgment creditor. To create an enforceable judgment lien, the abstract of judgment must contain all of the mandatory items required by Tex. Prop. Code Ann. §52.003:

1. The names of the plaintiff and defendant;
2. The birth date of the defendant, if available;
3. The last three numbers of the driver's license number of the defendant, if available;
4. The last three numbers of the social security number of the defendant, if available;
5. The number of the suit in which the judgment was rendered;
6. The defendant's address, or if the address is not shown in the suit, the nature of citation (i.e., service of process) and the date and place of service of citation;
7. The date on which the judgment was rendered;
8. The amount for which the judgment was rendered and the balance due;
9. The amount of the balance due, if any, for child support arrearage; and
10. The rate of interest specified in the judgment.

The above requirements summarize current law and do not reflect prior statutory requirements.

Womack v. Paris Grocer Co., 166 S.W.2d 366 (Tex. Civ. App.—Galveston 1942), writ ref'd, 168 S.W.2d 645 (Tex. 1943). While each and every statutory element must be met to establish a lien, the standard for establishing a lien is substantial compliance with the statute. *Apostolic Church v. American Honda Motor Co.*, 833 S.W.2d 553, 554 (Tex. App.—Tyler 1992, writ denied). While older cases suggest strict compliance with the statutory elements, more recent cases suggest that the abstract of judgment must contain sufficient facts to put a subsequent purchaser on notice of a lien. *See Thompson v. Clay*, 367 S.W.2d 917, 920 (Tex. Civ. App.—Amarillo 1963, writ ref'd n.r.e.).

The lien comes into existence only when the abstract of judgment has been recorded and indexed as to each plaintiff and each defendant. *J. M. Radford Grocery Co. v. Speck*, 152 S.W.2d 787, 789 (Tex. Civ. App.—Amarillo 1941, writ ref'd). An abstract of judgment may not be enforced if it is indexed under an incorrect name. For example, in *Wicker v. Jenkins*, 108 S.W. 188 (Tex. Civ. App. 1908, no writ), the court held that the abstract of judgment was invalid where record title was in W. F. B. Wicker, but the abstract of judgment was indexed against the Plaintiff as "W. B. F. Wicker." Likewise, in *Anthony v. Taylor*, 4 S.W. 531 (Tex. 1887), the court held that the abstract of judgment was invalid where a judgment recovered by "Joan and William Bankhead" was abstracted as a judgment recovered by "Joan and William Burkhead". The cases dealing with the validity of abstracts of judgment do not seem to apply idem sonans. *See* Standard 3.10.

All names must be indexed to create a valid lien. *Shirey v. Trust Co. of Texas*, 69 S.W.2d 835 (Tex. Civ. App.—Texarkana 1934, writ ref'd) (holding that abstract of judgment was fatally defective where it was indexed in the names of all defendants against whom a personal judgment was rendered but not in the name of one additional defendant against whom costs only had been awarded); *McGlothlin v. Coody*, 59 S.W.2d 819 (Tex. Comm'n App. 1922, judgm't adopted) (holding that abstract of judgment failed to create a judgment lien where it was indexed under the name of the defendant against whom a money judgment was rendered but not in the name of an additional defendant against whom a foreclosure was ordered); *Reynolds v. Kessler*, 669 S.W.2d 801, 805 (Tex. App.—El Paso 1984, no writ) ("The names of all the parties to the judgment must appear alphabetically in the index, direct and reverse"). The names of defendants must correctly appear in the direct index, and names of the plaintiffs must appear in the indirect index. *Guaranty State Bank v. Marion County Nat'l Bank*, 293 S.W. 248 (Tex. Civ. App.—San Antonio 1927, no writ.) (holding that no lien was created where the abstract was correctly indexed as to all defendants but not indexed for any of the plaintiffs).

The judgment creditor has the burden to prove that the abstract of judgment complied with the statute and that it was properly recorded and indexed. *Alkas v. United Sav. Ass'n of Texas, Inc.*, 672 S.W.2d 852, 859 (Tex. App.—Corpus Christi 1984, writ ref'd n.r.e.). The judgment creditor cannot use as a defense the fact that the error was caused by the clerk. *Caruso v. Shropshire*, 954 S.W.2d 115, 116 (Tex. App.—San Antonio 1997, no pet.).

An examiner may presume that a judgment lien has ceased to exist ten years after recording and indexing. A judgment lien continues for a period of ten years following the date of recording and indexing the abstract of judgment; however, if the underlying judgment becomes dormant during this time period, then the judgment lien ceases to exist unless it has been timely revived. Tex. Prop. Code Ann. §52.006. To determine whether a judgment has become dormant, see Tex. Civ. Prac. & Rem. Code Ann. §34.001. A dormant judgment may be revived within two years after the date of dormancy by filing a scire facias proceeding. Tex. Civ. Prac.

& Rem. Code Ann. §31.006. In addition, dormancy may be prevented by filing suit to foreclose the judgment lien, which is regarded as an action for debt sufficient to preserve the judgment. *Churchill v. Russey*, 692 S.W.2d 596, 597-98 (Tex. App.—Ft. Worth 1985, no writ).

If a judgment is not dormant, an abstract of judgment can be re-recorded and re-indexed. Each recording and indexing of an abstract of judgment seems to create a new lien with a new priority date. *Burton Lingo Co. v. Warren*, 45 S.W.2d 750 (Tex. Civ. App.—Eastland 1931, writ ref'd).

There are three exceptions to the general rule that a judgment lien lasts for ten years:

(1) Judgment liens in favor of the United States are effective for twenty years and may be extended with the same priority another twenty years. 28 U.S.C.A. §3201.

(2) Child support liens filed on or after September 1, 1997, and prior to May 26, 2009, are effective indefinitely. Child support liens filed on or after May 26, 2009, are effective for real property until the tenth anniversary of the date on which the lien notice was filed and may be extended for subsequent 10-year periods by filing a renewal lien notice before the tenth anniversary. Tex. Fam. Code Ann. §157.318. *In the Interest of S.C.S. and M.D.S.*, 48 S.W.3d 831 (Tex. App.—Houston [14th Dist.] 2001, pet. denied); and

(3) Judgment liens in favor of the state or a state agency are effective for twenty years and may be renewed for an additional twenty years. Tex. Prop. Code Ann. §52.006(b).

An abstract of judgment creates a judgment lien only if issued by a Texas state court under Tex. Prop. Code Ann. §§52.001, 52.002, or by a United States district court located in Texas, as authorized by Tex. Prop. Code Ann. §52.007. *See Reynolds v. Kessler*, 669 S.W.2d 801, 806 (Tex. App.—El Paso 1984, no writ); 28 U.S.C. §1962. A foreign judgment must first be domesticated as provided in Tex. Civ. Prac. & Rem. Code Ann. ch. 35 and ch. 36, whereupon an abstract of judgment may be issued and recorded in the same manner as any other Texas judgment. *Hennessy v. Marshall*, 682 S.W.2d 340, 343 (Tex. App.—Dallas 1984, no writ).

An abstract of judgment lien cannot attach to a homestead; however, whether particular property constitutes a homestead is not always clear in the record. Thus, an abstract of judgment lien clouds a homestead title. For abstract of judgment liens recorded and indexed on or after September 1, 2007, Tex. Prop. Code Ann. §52.0012 creates a nonjudicial procedure for clearing such cloud by filing an affidavit that operates to release the abstract of judgment regarding the homestead unless the creditor files a contradicting affidavit within the time provided by the statute. For abstracts of judgment liens recorded and indexed prior to September 1, 2007, the cloud on the homestead could be released by a declaratory judgment action.

An obligor who believes that a child support lien has attached to the homestead of the obligor may file an affidavit to release the lien against the homestead in the same manner as a judgment debtor may file an affidavit to release a judgment lien against the homestead, provided the obligor complies with the requirements of the statute. Tex. Prop. Code Ann. §52.0012. The obligor is required to send the letter and affidavit to the claimant under the child support lien at the claimant's last known address. The affidavit filed by the obligor has the same effect regarding a child support lien as an affidavit filed regarding a judgment lien. The claimant may file a contradicting affidavit in the same manner as provided by *Id.* §52.0012(e). *See* Tex. Fam. Code Ann. §157.3171.

For the effect of bankruptcy upon judgment liens, see Standard 12.140.

CAUTION

The above comments only briefly identify the issues inherent in proving up an abstract of judgment. There are many cases, particularly older cases, which conclude that an abstract of judgment lien was not created based upon what today might appear to be very technical and rigid mistakes. An examiner asked to opine on the enforceability of a particular judgment should carefully research this issue.

Source:

Citations in the Comment; Steven C. Haley, *Texas Abstracts of Judgment and Judgment Liens*, State Bar of Tex. Prof. Dev. Prog., Advanced Real Estate Law Course (2000); C. M. (Hank) Hudspeth, *Judgment Liens and Abstracts of Judgment in Texas*, 32 Tex. B. J. 520 (1969); S. Bradley Todes and Rosa S. Silbert, *Judgment Liens in Texas*, Houston Lawyer, May/June, 1994, at 28.

History:

Adopted June 16, 2006.

STANDARD 15.40. IMPLIED VENDOR'S LIENS

Absent an express vendor's lien, if the record indicates, or the examiner otherwise knows that purchase money remains unpaid, the examiner should consider the possible existence of an implied vendor's lien.

Comment

Although liens are most commonly created by express contract or by statute, certain liens may arise by implication. *Williams v. Greer*, 122 S.W.2d 247 (Tex. Civ. App.—Dallas 1938, no writ). For example, where no express lien is reserved in the deed and the purchase money is not paid, an implied lien arises in favor of the vendor to secure payment of the purchase money. *McGoodwin v. McGoodwin*, 671 S.W.2d 880 (Tex. 1984). If the purchase price is not paid, a vendor may sue for the debt and enforce an implied lien, although the vendor is not entitled to rescind the sale and recover the property. *Rhiddlehoover v. Boren*, 260 S.W.2d 431 (Tex. Civ. App.—Texarkana 1953, no writ). Thus, for example, if the examiner encounters a deed reciting that part of the consideration is an obligation not yet paid, such as a promissory note, the examiner should consider an implied vendor's lien to exist notwithstanding that no express vendor's lien is received and no deed of trust or mortgage appears.

An equitable or implied vendor's lien is not recordable, but rests upon the principle that it would be inequitable to allow one to retain the property of another without paying for it. It is good against all except subsequent bona fide purchasers and encumbrancers. *United States v. Morrison*, 247 F.2d 285 (5th Cir. 1957); *Scull v. Davis*, 434 S.W.2d 391 (Tex. Civ. App.—El Paso 1968, writ ref'd n.r.e.).

If an express lien is retained affirmatively showing the party's intention to rely solely upon the security provided within the written agreement, any implied or equitable lien is presumptively waived. Equity does not infer that the vendor is entitled to a different and additional security from that specified in the contract. *GXG, Inc. v. Texacal Oil & Gas*, 977 S.W.2d 403 (Tex. App.—Corpus Christi 1998, pet. denied). Similarly, where a note was secured by a deed of trust and the parties struck out of the deed the printed language concerning the reservation of a vendor's lien, the deletion affirmatively showed the seller's intention to rely solely on the deed of trust. *Zapata v. Torres*, 464 S.W.2d 926 (Tex. Civ. App.—Dallas 1971, no writ). Under these circumstances, no equitable lien will arise, because the purpose of an implied equitable lien is to enforce a purchase money obligation not otherwise secured.

Where part of the consideration for a conveyance is the purchaser's assumption of the seller's indebtedness to a third party, the third-party creditor thereby becomes entitled to an implied vendor's lien against the property. *Delley v. Unknown Stockholders of Brotherly and Sisterly Club of Christ, Inc.*, 509 S.W.2d 709 (Tex. Civ. App.—Tyler 1974, writ ref'd n.r.e.). An implied vendor's lien will also be created under the terms of a divorce judgment, where a promissory note is executed by one party in consideration of a conveyance of the other party's interest in real property, where no express lien was created in the divorce decree to secure the note. *Colquette v. Forbes*, 680 S.W.2d 536 (Tex. App.—Austin 1984, no writ).

An implied lien may arise in cotenancy situations. For example, where a cotenant pays expenses and advances taxes on behalf of another cotenant, the advancing cotenant may enforce an implied lien for recovery of the advancements. *Cox v. Davison*, 397 S.W.2d 200 (Tex. 1965). In partition, a court may divide the property into shares of unequal value and impose a payment obligation, commonly called owelty. The owelty is secured by an implied vendor's lien. *Sayers v. Pyland*, 161 S.W.2d 769 (Tex. 1942).

Any implied vendor's lien is lost when the debt is barred by the statute of limitations. *See* comments to Standard 15.100, "Removal of Lien." Where the wording of the stated consideration in an instrument "may or might create an implied lien in favor of the grantor," an action for the recovery of the property conveyed by that instrument must be brought within four years of the date that the instrument was "recorded," if it was recorded before September 1, 2007, or within two years of the date that the instrument was "filed for record," if it was filed on or after September 1, 2007. Tex. Civ. Prac. & Rem. Code Ann. §16.033(a)(9). Act of June 15, 2007, 80th Leg., R.S. ch. 819, §2, 2007 Gen. Laws 1695 (nonretroactivity provision).

Upon encountering an outstanding implied vendor's lien, the examiner would ordinarily require a release of the vendor's lien, a quitclaim deed from the holder of the obligation, or a subordination of the vendor's lien to the interest being examined.

An implied vendee's lien may arise where the vendee advances consideration for property without receiving valid title from the seller; however, a bona fide purchaser without notice of the vendee's lien would take the property free of the lien. *See Morris v. Holland*, 31 S.W. 690 (Tex. Civ. App. 1895, no writ); *Stockwell v. Melbern*, 185 S.W. 399 (Tex. Civ. App.—Galveston 1916,

writ ref'd); *Martin v. Bell-Woods Co.*, 57 S.W.2d 271 (Tex. Civ. App.—San Antonio 1932, no writ).

For a further discussion of vendor's liens, see comments to Standard 15.10.

Source:
Citations in the Comment.
History:
Adopted June 16, 2006.

STANDARD 15.50. OTHER INVOLUNTARY STATUTORY LIENS

The examiner should identify other recorded statutory liens affecting the title under examination.

COMMENT

A host of specialized involuntary statutory liens may affect Texas real property. Among them are the following:

Child Support Lien, Tex. Fam. Code Ann. §§157.311-.331.

Cotton Pests (Texas Department of Agriculture), Tex. Agric. Code Ann. §74.004(e)-(g).

County Assessments For Road Improvements,* Tex. Transp. Code Ann. §253.009.

County Litter Lien, Tex. Health & Safety Code Ann. §365.034(c).

County Weed and Sanitary Lien, Tex. Health & Safety Code Ann. §343.023.

Federal Lien Securing a Judgment Imposing a Criminal Fine, 18 U.S.C. §3613.

Miscellaneous State Tax Liens, Tex. Tax Code Ann. ch. 113.

Municipal Assessments for Street Improvements,* Tex. Transp. Code Ann. §§312.002, 312.064, 313.042, 313.051, 313.054.

Municipal Assessments for Water/Sewer Systems,* Tex. Loc. Gov't Code Ann. §§214.013(b), 214.014, 522.065, 522.067.

Municipal Demolition Lien,* Tex. Loc. Gov't Code Ann. §214.0015-.004.

Municipal Floodplain Management Lien,* Tex. Loc. Gov't Code Ann. §54.020.

Municipal Utility Services Lien,* Tex. Loc. Gov't Code Ann. §402.0025(d)-(h).

Municipal Weed and Sanitary Lien,* Tex. Health & Safety Code Ann. §342.007.

Solid Waste Facility Remedial Lien, Tex. Health & Safety Code Ann. §361.194.

State Hospital Lien (for support, maintenance, and treatment of a patient with mental illness or intellectual disability), Tex. Health & Safety Code Ann. §§533.004, 533A.004.

Surface Coal Mining Reclamation,* Tex. Nat. Res. Code Ann. §134.150.

Texas Workforce Lien,* Tex. Lab. Code Ann. §§61.081-.085.

Unemployment Taxes, Tex. Lab. Code Ann. §§213.057-.058.

Water District Standby Fees,* Tex. Water Code Ann. §49.231.

Water District Taxes,* Tex. Water Code Ann. §55.604, Texas Tax Code Ann. §32.01.

For a discussion of mechanics' and materialmen's liens generally, see Standard 15.20. For a discussion of state ad valorem taxes and the lien securing them, see Standards 15.70 and 15.80.

CAUTION

In most instances, a statutory lien is not perfected until a notice has been filed for record in the pertinent county clerk's office, and the lien's priority is determined according to the time of filing. However, the liens marked with an asterisk (*) in the above listing may have special priority independent of the time or fact of filing over other titles and encumbrances.

Source:
Citations in the Comment.
History:
Adopted June 22, 2007.

STANDARD 15.60. FEDERAL TAX LIENS

The examiner should determine whether the land under examination is subject to a federal tax lien.

COMMENT

Various federal tax liens may constitute a claim against a taxpayer's property. These include a general tax lien (26 U.S.C. §6321), a gift tax lien (26 U.S.C. §6324(b)), an estate tax lien (26 U.S.C. §6324(a)), a generation-skipping transfer tax lien (26 U.S.C. §2661), and special liens relating to recapture of deferred or reduced taxes such as special use valuation of a farm or closely held business (26 U.S.C. §§6324A and 6324B).

Most federal tax liens attach to the taxpayer's property following certain statutory notice from the Internal

Revenue Service and other procedures involving the taxpayer (26 U.S.C. §6320). No filing is required for perfection of the estate tax lien or gift tax lien. Except for the federal estate tax lien, a lien is not perfected against a purchaser, a holder of a security interest, a holder of a mechanic's lien, or a judgment creditor until a notice is filed in the records of the county where the land is located (26 U.S.C. §6323).

Procedures relating to release of liens and discharge of property from liens are set out in 26 U.S.C. §6325.

Subject to renewal (26 U.S.C. §6323(g)), a notice of federal tax lien is valid for ten years and thirty days from date of assessment (26 U.S.C. §§6322, 6502, and 6503). Although rarely done, a notice of federal tax lien may be filed for estate and gift taxes; if a notice is not filed, a federal estate tax lien is valid for ten years from the taxpayer's date of death (26 U.S.C. §6324(a)(1)), and a gift tax lien is valid for ten years from the date of the gift (26 U.S.C. §6324(b)). For more information concerning liens against a decedent's estate, see Standard 11.60.

A federal tax lien may be extended by agreement of the taxpayer and the government, as well as for other reasons. Unless an examiner has record notice or actual notice of an extension, an examiner may presume that a federal tax lien has lapsed if the limitation periods in the prior paragraph have expired.

An examiner should require a release of any lien held by the United States, any agency of the United States, or any assignee of such a lien unless the lien is no longer enforceable under federal law.

CAUTION

See first paragraph of Caution to Standard 15.10.

Source:
Citations in the Comment.
History:
Adopted June 22, 2007.

STANDARD 15.70. PAYMENT OF AD VALOREM TAXES

The examiner should ordinarily determine the status of payment of ad valorem taxes.

COMMENT

Ad valorem taxes are assessed as of January 1 of each year. They are due and payable on the following October 1 but are not delinquent if paid before February 1 of the following year (or, in the case of a residence homestead and certain classes of individuals, including disabled veterans and persons over 65, if paid in four bimonthly installments beginning on February 1). A tax lien attaches on January 1 of each year to secure payment of taxes, penalties, and interest ultimately imposed for that year. Tex. Tax Code Ann. §§32.01, 32.02, 32.031, 32.032.

In determining the status of payment of ad valorem taxes, an examiner customarily relies upon a tax certificate issued by a collector for a taxing unit. The methods of assessment and collection are not uniform. The collection of taxes may be consolidated in one collector of taxes or may be separately maintained by separate tax units. Tex. Tax Code Ann. §§6.23, 6.26. Any person may request a tax certificate, which must be issued by the collector for the taxing unit. The certificate shows the amount of delinquent taxes, penalties, and interest due according to the unit's current records. The effect of a tax certificate is as follows: "[I]f a person transfers property accompanied by a tax certificate erroneously showing that no delinquent taxes, penalties, or interest are due a taxing unit on the property, the unit's tax lien on the property is extinguished and the purchaser of the property is absolved of liability to the unit for delinquent taxes, penalties, or interest on the property. The person who was liable for the tax for the year it was imposed remains personally liable for the delinquent tax, penalties, and interest." Tex. Tax Code Ann. §31.08. However, a tax certificate issued through fraud or collusion is void.

Although examiners frequently rely on a tax receipt to indicate the payment of taxes for the specified year, a tax receipt is only prima facie evidence that the tax has been paid. Tex. Tax Code Ann. §31.075.

The assessor is required to mail the tax bill by October 1 of each year, or as soon thereafter as practicable. The tax bill, or a separate statement accompanying the tax bill, shall include: (1) the appraised value, assessed value and taxable value of the land (including improvements); (2) the market value and taxable value of the land, as provided in §23.46 (agricultural assessment), §23.55 (qualified open-space land), §23.76 (qualified timber land), and §23.9807 (restricted-use timber land); and (3) the amount and type of any partial exemption. Tex. Tax Code Ann. §31.01.

If there is a sale or change in use of land qualified for special valuation as agricultural land or if there is a change in the use of land qualified for special valuation

as open space or timber land, an additional rollback tax may be imposed. Tex. Tax Code Ann. §§23.46, 23.55, 23.76, and 23.9807. As to when a rollback tax lien attaches, see *Compass Bank v. Bent Creek Investments, Inc.*, 52 S.W.3d 419 (Tex. App.—Fort Worth 2001, no pet.) (addressing agricultural rollback tax liens).

Land is subject to foreclosure for nonpayment of delinquent taxes; however, if there has been no foreclosure or if there is no pending foreclosure for delinquent taxes, the collector for a taxing unit must cancel and remove from the delinquent tax rolls a tax that has been delinquent for more than twenty years. Tex. Tax Code Ann. §33.05. For further information on foreclosure, see Standard 16.20.

If the examiner does not determine the status of payment of ad valorem taxes, the examiner should advise the client to make this determination.

CAUTION

As previously indicated, the most reliable protection for a purchaser is a current tax certificate; however, the examiner should verify that the certificate covers all of the relevant land and improvements and encompasses all taxing units. Tex. Tax Code Ann. §31.08. Moreover, a tax certificate procured by fraud or collusion is void. *Id.* In addition, an erroneous tax certificate does not protect a non-purchaser. *Id.*

Ad valorem taxes are subject to reassessment. For example, the property may no longer qualify for the over-65 homestead tax exemption (e.g., the over-65 owner has died or is no longer domiciled on the subject property), or there may have been a failure to include the land in a taxing unit or a failure to assess improvements. In general, ad valorem property taxes may be reassessed for up to five years. *See, e.g.*, Tex. Tax Code Ann. §§25.21, 1.04(2). *Harris County Appraisal District v. Reynolds/Texas, J.V.*, 884 S.W.2d 526 (Tex. App.—El Paso 1994, no writ) (improvements had not been assessed).

Source:
Citations in the Comment.
History:
Adopted June 24, 2005; amended July 17, 2014.
The prior standard provided: "The examiner ordinarily determines the status of payment of ad valorem taxes."

STANDARD 15.80. PRIORITY OF AD VALOREM TAX LIEN

The examiner should ordinarily assume that an ad valorem tax lien is superior to any mortgage, judgment, other lien, or homestead right.

COMMENT

All ad valorem tax liens have equal priority. The ad valorem tax lien is superior to a federal tax lien. Tex. Tax Code Ann. §32.04; 26 U.S.C. §6323(b)(6). Except as hereafter provided, a tax lien takes priority over the claim of any holder of a lien on the land encumbered by the tax lien, regardless of whether the debt or lien existed before the tax lien. Tex. Tax Code Ann. §32.05.

The above standard is subject to the following qualifications:

The ad valorem tax lien is subordinate to survivor's allowance, funeral expenses, or expenses of last illness of a decedent made against the estate.

The ad valorem tax lien is subordinate to a restrictive covenant running with the land, other than a restrictive covenant in favor of a property owner's association recorded before January 1 of the year the tax lien arose, and is subordinate to an easement recorded before January 1 of the year the tax lien arose. Tex. Tax Code Ann. §32.05.

Tex. Tax Code Ann. §32.06 provides a procedure whereby a taxpayer may authorize a third party to pay ad valorem taxes and to obtain a transfer of the taxing unit's lien. Effective September 1, 2007, changes were made in this procedure that are prospective only.

Amendments in 2013 tightened the statute by, for example, preventing nonjudicial foreclosure and prohibiting waivers and certain transfers, and made related changes to Tex. Fin. Code, Annot., Subchapter A, Chapter 351. The examiner should be aware of this statute if the title chain contains a foreclosure of an ad valorem tax lien by other than a taxing authority.

Source:
Citations in the Comments.
History:
Adopted June 24, 2005.

STANDARD 15.90. LIEN PRIORITY & SUBORDINATION

Subject to exceptions, an examiner may presume that a lien created and filed for record has priority over a subsequently created competing lien or interest in the same property unless the priority has been altered by a subordination agreement.

COMMENT

After a senior lien is validly foreclosed, junior liens and junior interests in the same property are extinguished. *Arnold v. Eaton*, 910 S.W.2d 181 (Tex. App.—

STANDARD 15.90

Eastland 1995, no writ). Under common law, the lienholder whose lien first attaches to the property has the right to satisfy the lien against the property before the holders of subsequently attached liens. *Windham v. Citizens Nat'l Bank*, 105 S.W.2d 348 (Tex. Civ. App.—Austin 1937, writ dism'd). However, recording statutes have modified the common law rules of lien priority. Generally, the first lien filed for recordation is superior to a lien or other interest created subsequent to the first lien filed because subsequent creditors and owners of junior interests are charged with constructive notice of the earlier recorded lien. *Regold Mfg. Co. v. Maccabees*, 348 S.W.2d 864 (Tex. Civ. App.—Fort Worth 1961, writ ref'd n.r.e.); Tex. Prop. Code Ann. §13.002. A deed of trust or mortgage that has not been recorded is void as to a creditor or subsequent purchaser for valuable consideration without notice of the unrecorded encumbrance. Tex. Prop. Code Ann. §13.001(a).

A subordination agreement is a contractual modification of lien priorities which establishes different lien priorities than those provided under the statutory or common law rules. In agreeing to subordinate a superior lien secured by real property to a subsequent lien or other interest in the same property, the superior lienholder voluntarily contracts to be paid after a junior lienholder if the liens are foreclosed or agrees that foreclosure will not extinguish a previously junior interest. *Vahlsing Christina Corp. v. First Nat. Bank of Hobbs*, 491 S.W.2d 954 (Tex. Civ. App.—El Paso 1973, writ ref'd n.r.e.).

If there are more than two liens against a real property interest at the time of subordination, the subordinated lien is placed directly after the lien to which it is subordinated. Any liens not participating in the subordination agreement that have a priority ranking between the liens participating in the subordination move up in priority, becoming superior to the liens involved in the subordination. Liens that have a lower priority ranking than the liens involved in the subordination do not move up in priority. For example, if four liens against a parcel of real property are ranked A, B, C, and D, and lien A is contractually subordinated to lien C, the ranking after subordination would be B, C, A, and D. *McConnell v. Mortgage Inv. Co. of El Paso*, 292 S.W.2d 636 (Tex. Civ. App.—El Paso 1955), aff'd, 305 S.W.2d 280 (Tex. 1957). Note, however, different rules apply to a subordination agreement in a non-real estate situation. *See ITT Diversified Credit Corp. v. First City Capital Corporation*, 737 S.W.2d 803 (Tex. 1987).

If a landlord-tenant lease is executed before a lien is created, the lease is superior to the lien and continues in effect after the foreclosure unless the mortgagee is a bona fide mortgagee without notice of the lease (i.e., the mortgagee does not have actual or constructive notice of the lease and the tenant is not in possession at the time the lien is created). *Groos v. Chittim*, 100 S.W. 1006 (Tex. Civ. App. 1907, no writ); *Gill v. First Nat. Bank of Harlingen*, 114 S.W.2d 428 (Tex. Civ. App.—San Antonio 1938, no writ); *Boyd v. United Bank, N.A.*, 794 S.W.2d 839 (Tex. App.—El Paso 1990, writ denied); *United General Ins. v. American Nat. Ins.*, 740 S.W.2d 885 (Tex. App.—El Paso 1987, no writ), disapproved in part, *ICM Mortgage Corp. v. Jacob*, 902 S.W.2d 527 (Tex. App.—El Paso 1994, writ denied).

There has been some confusion in the cases over the effect of a foreclosure of an existing lien on a subsequent landlord-tenant lease. The basic rule appears to be that the junior lease terminates on foreclosure. However, the parties are free to enter a new lease (as opposed to "continuing" the old one). The post-foreclosure conduct of the parties determines whether a new lease, with terms supplied by the previous lease, is created by implication. *Twelve Oaks Tower I v. Premier Allergy*, 938 S.W.2d 102 (Tex. App.—Houston [14th Dist.] 1996, no writ); *Peterson v. NCNB Texas Nat. Bank*, 838 S.W.2d 263 (Tex. App.—Dallas 1992, no writ).

Under Tex. Prop. Code Ann. §66.001, the foreclosure of a mortgage on a surface tract that includes minerals underlying the land does not extinguish an oil and gas lease that is subsequent to the mortgage if the lease was recorded before the foreclosure sale. The foreclosure sale does extinguish the oil and gas lessee's right to use the surface, and any royalty and other lease benefits accruing to the mortgagor pass to the purchaser at the foreclosure sale. Cautious examiners should consider whether this legislation applies to mortgages in effect before the enactment of the legislation, which was effective January 1, 2016.

CAUTION

A recorded lien may be inferior to a subsequent lien created under an instrument actually recorded before the first lien, such as a deed of trust with a future advance clause, because the first lienholder is charged with constructive notice of the lien that may arise in

the future. *Coke Lbr. & Mfg. Co. v. First Nat. Bank*, 529 S.W.2d 612 (Tex. Civ. App.—Dallas 1975, writ ref'd).

There are several exceptions to the general rule under recording statutes that the first lien recorded is the first in priority. If a creditor has actual or constructive notice of a prior unrecorded lien, the general priority rules under the recording statute may not apply. For instance, a lender's deed of trust is inferior to a contractor's lien if construction or construction materials are visible from an inspection of the land before the deed of trust is executed, because the lender is charged with notice of the possible existence of an unrecorded prior lien. *Hagler v. Continental Nat. Bank of Fort Worth*, 549 S.W.2d 250 (Tex. Civ. App.—Texarkana, 1977, writ ref'd n.r.e.). Texas has a notice system of recording, in contrast with race notice or race recording systems. Under a notice system of recording, a prior mortgage not filed for record at the time of delivery of a subsequent mortgage to a good faith lender for valuable consideration may not have priority over that subsequent mortgage, even if the prior mortgage is filed for record first. Tex. Prop. Code Ann. §13.001. However, a vendor's lien retained in a deed will be prior to a previously recorded judgment lien against a purchaser. *Donie State Bank v. Parker*, 554 S.W.2d 858 (Tex. Civ. App.—Waco 1977, writ ref'd n.r.e.).

Mechanic's Liens: An involuntary mechanic's lien may attach to the building or improvement and take priority over a previously recorded lien or interest on the land on which the building or improvement is located if the previously recorded lien encumbers the property after the inception of the involuntary mechanic's lien. Tex. Prop. Code Ann. §53.124. The involuntary mechanic's lien does not affect any lien on the land or improvement at the inception of the mechanic's lien, and the lienholder does not need to be made a party to a suit to foreclose the mechanic's lien. Tex. Prop. Code Ann. §53.123. An involuntary mechanic's lien against improvements to real property may be superior to an earlier recorded deed of trust secured by the real property if the improvements are removable without injury to the land, preexisting improvements, or improvements removed. *First National Bank in Dallas v. Whirlpool Corp.*, 517 S.W.2d 262 (Tex. 1974). *See also* Standard 15.20.

Fixture Filing: A purchase-money security interest in a fixture may have priority over a prior, recorded real property lien provided the purchase-money security interest is filed as a fixture filing in the real property records before the goods become fixtures or within twenty days thereafter. Tex. Bus. & Com. Code Ann. §9.334(d).

Federal Tax Liens: Special seniority rules govern federal tax liens. 26 U.S.C. §§6321-6323. In general, if the notice of a federal lien is filed prior to the time that the debtor acquires the property, the federal tax lien has priority over any subsequently created lien or other interest. *United States v. McDermott*, 507 U.S. 447, 455 (1993). However, a federal tax lien does not have priority over a purchase money mortgage—at least if secured by an express vendor's lien. *Slodov v. U.S.*, 436 U.S. 238 (1978) (recognizing priority of purchase money lien); *Minix v. Maggard*, 652 S.W.2d 93 (Ky. Ct. App. 1983); *Belland v. OK Lumber Company, Inc.*, 797 P.2d 638 (Alas. 1990); Rev. Rul. 68-57 (1977). *See also* Standard 15.60.

Possession: Similarly, a creditor may be put on notice of the equitable interest or adverse claim of a person in prior possession of property. The creditor's lien will be inferior to the possessor's interest or estate if the possession is such that the creditor has a duty to ask the possessor about the nature of the possessor's claim. *Boyd v. United Bank, N.A.*, 794 S.W.2d 839 (Tex. App.—El Paso 1990, writ denied).

Source:
Citations in the Comment.
History:
Adopted June 13, 2003.

STANDARD 15.100. REMOVAL OF LIEN

Subject to exceptions, an examiner may presume that a lien on real property is extinguished upon establishing that the secured debt (1) has been paid or (2) has become unenforceable upon expiration of the applicable limitations period.

COMMENT

Regardless of whether a written release is delivered, the lien ceases to exist when the underlying debt is paid; however, the lienholder has a duty to issue a written release. *Knox v. Farmers' State Bank*, 7 S.W.2d 918 (Tex. Civ. App.—Eastland 1928, writ ref'd); *Spencer-Sauer Lumber Co. v. Ballard*, 98 S.W.2d 1054 (Tex. Civ. App.—San Antonio 1936, no writ) (full release); *Cook v. Leslie*, 59 S.W.2d 302 (Tex. Civ. App.—San Antonio 1933, no writ) (partial release). Preferably a written release should be obtained whenever reasonably possible. To give notice to third parties dealing with the property, a written release must be recorded in the county in which the lien was recorded. Tex. Prop. Code Ann. §§11.001, 13.002.

A title insurance company or its expressly authorized title insurance agent may file an affidavit releasing a mortgage that exclusively encumbers (1) a one-to-four family residence or (2) other property if the face amount of the secured indebtedness is less than $1.5 million. Tex. Prop. Code Ann. §12.017.

Commonly, a release of a mortgage or deed of trust may fail to expressly release a related assignment of rents or leases or a separate financing statement which may have been given to the same lender as additional security. If a deed of trust or other mortgage was filed for record at or about the same time as the filing of a financing statement or the recordation of an assignment of rents, leases, production, or other collateral to the same lender and appears to be part of the same transaction evidenced by the deed of trust or other mortgage, it is common practice for an examiner to presume that a full release of the deed of trust or other mortgage without specific reference to the financing statement or assignment is sufficient as a release of the financing statement or assignment.

A sale of real property under a power of sale in a mortgage or deed of trust must be made not later than four years after the date the cause of action accrues. Generally, the cause of action accrues on the maturity date of the debt. Upon expiration of the four-year limitations period, the real property lien and any power of sale to enforce the lien are void. The running of the statute of limitations is not suspended against a bona fide purchaser. An examiner who does not have notice or knowledge of the suspension of the limitations period (e.g., unrecorded extension agreement) may presume that the lien is unenforceable when a cause of action on an outstanding real property lien has accrued for more than four years, except as provided by the provisions governing suspension in the event of death. Tex. Civ. Prac. & Rem. Code Ann. §§16.035, 16.036, 16.062.

If a series of notes or obligations or a note or obligation payable in installments is secured by a real property lien, the four-year limitations period does not begin to run until the maturity date of the last note, obligation, or installment. The limitations period in the preceding paragraph is not affected by the Uniform Commercial Code provision containing limitations periods applying to negotiable instruments. *Cf.*, Tex. Civ. Prac. & Rem. Code Ann. §16.035 and Tex. Bus. & Com. Code Ann. §3.118.

If a promissory note is payable on demand, there are two limitations periods. A promissory note is "payable on demand" if it states that it is payable on demand, payable at sight, or otherwise indicates that it is payable at the will of the holder, or does not state any time for payment. Tex. Bus. & Com. Code Ann. §3.108. If demand for payment is made to the maker, an action to enforce payment must be commenced within six years after the demand. However, if no demand for payment is made, an action to enforce the note is barred if neither principal nor interest on the note has been paid for a continuous period of ten years. *See* Tex. Bus. & Com. Code Ann. §3.118(b). Note, however, that prior to the amendment of §3.118, effective May 22, 2001, Texas case law held that the limitations period for a demand note began to run on the date the note was made. *See, e.g.*, *G & R Inv. v. Nance*, 683 S.W.2d 727 (Tex. App.—Houston [14th Dist.] 1984, writ ref'd n.r.e.). Although enforcement of a lien may be barred by the four-year limitations period (under §16.035 Tex. Civ. Prac. & Rem. Code Ann.), payment of the debt may continue to be enforceable as an unsecured debt provided an action to enforce payment is commenced within the limitations periods set forth in Tex. Bus. & Com. Code Ann. §3.118; *Aguero v. Ramirez*, 70 S.W.3d 372 (Tex. App.—Corpus Christi 2002, pet. denied).

A party primarily liable for an obligation secured by a real property lien may suspend the running of the four-year limitations period through a written extension agreement. Regarding that party's interest, the limitations period is suspended, and the lien remains in effect for four years after the extended maturity date of the obligation if the extension agreement is signed, acknowledged, and filed for record in the county clerk's office of the county where the real property is located. A lien may be further extended by additional extension agreements. The maturity date stated in the original instrument or in the recorded renewal and extension is conclusive evidence of the maturity date of the debt or obligation. This limitation period is not affected by the Uniform Commercial Code limitations provision governing notes and other negotiable instruments. Tex. Civ. Prac. & Rem. Code Ann. §16.035; Tex. Bus. & Com. Code Ann. §3.118.

Although valid between the parties, an oral extension of a note is not effective against a third party. An extension agreement is invalid as to a bona fide purchaser for value, a lienholder, or a lessee who deals with real property affected by an extended real property lien without actual notice of the extension agreement and before the agreement is filed for recordation. Tex. Civ. Prac. & Rem. Code Ann. §16.037.

If the maturity date of the debt is omitted from a deed of trust, the deed of trust is read together with the underlying note as if the two constituted one instrument. *Cadle Co. v. Butler*, 951 S.W.2d 901 (Tex. App.—Corpus Christi 1997, no writ). An omission of the date of maturity does not toll the statute of limitations for the payment of the debt. The limitations period begins to run on the date the last installment payment is due, even if not stated in the deed of trust. *Swedlund v. Banner*, 970 S.W.2d 107 (Tex. App.—Corpus Christi 1998, pet. denied).

For the removal of abstract of judgment liens clouding homesteads, see Standard 15.30.

For a waiver and release of a mechanics', contractors', or materialmen's lien or payment bond claim arising under a contract executed on or after January 1, 2012, see Standard 15.20 and Tex. Prop. Code Ann. §53.281.

CAUTION

If payment of the existing indebtedness is not made by the debtor, but by another creditor as a part of a legitimate business transaction, the lien is not extinguished. Instead, the lien is transferred to the new creditor. *Baccus v. Westgate Management Corp.*, 981 S.W.2d 383 (Tex. App.—San Antonio 1998, pet. denied); *Chicago Title Ins. v. Lawrence Invest.*, 782 S.W.2d 332 (Tex. App.—Fort Worth 1989, writ ref'd).

Federal Agencies: If a lien is held by the United States or any agency of the United States, Texas statutes prescribing limitations periods generally do not apply to foreclosure of the lien. *Farmers Home Administration v. Muirhead*, 42 F.3d 964 (5th Cir. 1995). *See* 12 U.S.C.A. §1821(d)(14), enacted as part of the Financial Institutions Reform, Recovery, and Enforcement Act of 1989 (FIRREA), and 28 U.S.C.A. §2415(a); *Jackson v. Thweatt*, 883 S.W.2d 171 (Tex. 1994); *Cadle Co. v. Estate of Weaver*, 883 S.W.2d 179 (Tex. 1994); *Jon Luce Builder, Inc. v. First Gibraltar Bank*, 849 S.W.2d 451 (Tex. App.—Austin 1993, writ denied). Unless the lien is no longer enforceable under federal law, an examiner should require a release of any lien held by the United States, any agency of the United States, or any assignee of such a lien.

Property Acquired By Farm Credit System: After January 6, 1988, agricultural real estate acquired by an institution of the Farm Credit System (a Federal Land Bank, a Farm Credit Bank or a Production Credit Association) as a result of a loan foreclosure or a voluntary conveyance from a borrower is subject to a right of first refusal vested in the "previous owner" to repurchase or lease the property. A "previous owner" is the person or entity from which or from whom the Farm Credit System lender acquired title. If the previous owner waived his right of first refusal, the original or an authentic copy of the executed waiver should be furnished and recorded. *See* 12 U.S.C.A. §2219a (Farm Credit Act of 1971, §4.36, as amended by Agricultural Credit Act of 1987, Pub. L. No. 100-233 (January 6, 1988), tit. I. §108, 101 Stat. 1582 and Agricultural Credit Technical Corrections Act of 1988, Pub. L. No. 100-399 (August 17, 1988), tit. I, §104, 102 Stat. 990).

Property Acquired By Farmers Home Administration: After January 6, 1988, agricultural real estate acquired by the Farmers Home Administration as a result of a loan foreclosure or a voluntary conveyance from a borrower is subject to a number of rights and preferences in favor of the borrower, and certain other entities (e.g., the party from which or from whom the Farmers Home Administration acquired title), to repurchase or lease the property. The examiner should be furnished satisfactory evidence that, in compliance with the applicable statutes, regulations and cases, the Farmers Home Administration has either obtained waivers from the borrower and other protected entities, or has complied with the appropriate notice procedures, and that all administrative appeal rights, if any, have been exhausted. *See* 7 U.S.C.A. §1985 (Consolidated Farm and Rural Development Act, Pub. L. No. 87-128 (August 8, 1961), tit. VII, §335(c), 75 Stat. §315, as amended by Agricultural Credit Act of 1987, Pub. L. No. 100-233 (January 6, 1988), tit. VII, §610, 101 Stat. 1568); 7 C.F.R. §1951.911; Food, Agricultural, Conservation and Trade Act of 1990, Pub. L. No. 101-624 (November 28, 1990), 103 Stat. §3359.

Source:
Citations in the Comment.
History:
Adopted June 13, 2003.

Standard 15.110. Lis Pendens

The examiner should inquire as to the nature of the cause of action giving rise to a notice of lis pendens, should evaluate whether the pending litigation may be relevant to the interests under examination, and should advise the client regarding any actions that are appropriate to the purpose of the examination.

Comment

The filing of a lis pendens notice gives notice of a pending cause of action involving eminent domain, title to real property, establishment of an interest in real property, or enforcement of an encumbrance against real property. The party filing a lis pendens, or the party's agent or attorney, must sign the lis pendens, stating:

(1) the style and number, if any, of the proceeding;

(2) the court in which the proceeding is pending;

(3) the names of the parties;

(4) the kind of proceeding; and

(5) a description of the property affected.

Tex. Prop. Code Ann. §12.007; *Prappas v. Meyerland Community Improvement Assoc.*, 795 S.W.2d 794 (Tex. App.—Houston [14th Dist.] 1990, writ denied); *King v. Tubb*, 551 S.W.2d 436 (Tex. Civ. App.—Corpus Christi 1977, no writ).

Tex. Prop. Code Ann. §12.007(c) provides that the county clerk shall record the notice in a lis pendens record and shall index the record in a direct and reverse index under the name of each party to the proceeding.

Effective September 1, 2009, a person who files a notice of lis pendens must serve a copy of the notice on each party to the action who has an interest in the real property affected by the notice. The notice must be served not later than the third day after the person files the notice. Tex. Prop. Code Ann. §12.007(d).

Effective September 1, 2009, a court may expunge a notice of lis pendens if the lis pendens claimant cannot establish a real property claim or has not given the required notice. Tex. Prop. Code Ann. §12.0071. After a certified copy of an order expunging the notice of lis pendens is recorded, the notice of lis pendens and any information derived from the notice:

(1) does not: (A) constitute constructive or actual notice of any matter contained in the notice or of any matter relating to the proceeding; (B) create any duty of inquiry in a person concerning the property described in the notice; or (C) affect the validity of a conveyance to a purchaser for value or of a mortgage to a lender for value; and (2) is not enforceable against a purchaser or lender described in Subdivision (1)(C), regardless of whether the purchaser or lender knew of the lis pendens action.

Id.

Tex. Prop. Code Ann. §12.008 contains provisions regarding cancellation of a lis pendens.

Tex. Prop. Code Ann. §13.004 provides:

(a) A recorded lis pendens is notice to the world of its contents. The notice is effective from the time it is filed for record and indexed, as provided by Tex. Prop. Code §12.007(c), regardless of whether service has been made on the parties to the proceeding.

(b) A transfer or encumbrance of real property involved in a proceeding by a party to the proceeding to a third party who has paid a valuable consideration and who does not have actual or constructive notice of the proceeding is effective, even though the judgment is against the party transferring or encumbering the property, unless a notice of the pendency of the proceeding has been recorded and indexed under that party's name, as provided by Tex. Prop. Code §12.007(c), in each county in which the property is located.

A properly filed lis pendens notice effectively prevents a grantee from being an innocent purchaser. The doctrine does not void a conveyance during the pendency of a suit, but the interest of the grantor merely passes subject to the results of the cause. *Cherokee Water Co. v. Advance Oil & Gas Co.*, 843 S.W.2d 132 (Tex. App.—Texarkana 1992, writ den.). The lis pendens notice is considered part of the judicial process, and the resulting absolute privilege bars a suit for damages arising from the filing of the lis pendens. *Bayou Terrace Inv. Corp. v. Lyles*, 881 S.W.2d 810 (Tex. App.—Houston [1st Dist.] 1994, no writ).

Caution

A lis pendens only gives constructive notice while the underlying cause of action is pending and has no existence separate and apart from the litigation of which it gives notice. *Taliaferro v. Smith*, 804 S.W.2d 548 (Tex. App.—Houston [14th Dist.] 1991, no writ); *Wagner v. Oliver*, 256 S.W. 302 (Tex. Civ. App.—Amarillo 1923, writ dism'd). However, a lis pendens notice is rarely released and may remain on record many years after the litigation is terminated. Thus, unless the underlying litiga-

tion has been dismissed or resolved, an unreleased lis pendens continues to cloud title, regardless of its age.

Source:
Citations in the Comment.
History:
Adopted June 13, 2003; amended July 17, 2014.
The prior standard provided: "The existence of a lis pendens notice requires the examiner to inquire as to the nature of the cause of action, evaluate whether the pending litigation may be relevant to the interests under examination, and advise the client regarding any actions that are appropriate to the purpose of the examination."

Chapter XVI. Foreclosures

Standard 16.10. Nonjudicial Foreclosure

An examiner should determine that all statutory and contractual requirements for a nonjudicial foreclosure sale have been satisfied. Specifically, an examiner should determine: (1) that the security instrument confers the power of sale; (2) that there has been a default under the terms of the instrument; (3) that the trustee or substitute trustee was properly appointed; (4) that all statutory requirements in effect at the time of sale have been met; (5) that all additional requirements, if any, contained in the security instrument have been met; and (6) that a trustee's deed has been delivered.

Comment

The first determination should be made from an examination of the security instrument. The other determinations may be made by examining the trustee's deed and other related instruments that may be available or of record. These may include an affidavit by the trustee, a copy of the notice of the trustee's sale, and an appointment of substitute trustee.

Ordinarily, the examiner may determine default from the recitals in affidavits accompanying or incorporated in the trustee's deed. If not, the examiner should search for other evidence or take into consideration other factors, such as the passage of time since the foreclosure.

The trustee or trustees are customarily appointed in the security instrument. The provisions for the appointment of a substitute trustee are usually set out in the security instrument, and the beneficiary must strictly comply with these provisions. *Slaughter v. Qualls*, 162 S.W.2d 671 (Tex. 1942); *Michael v. Crawford*, 193 S.W. 1070 (Tex. 1917). If the instrument makes no provision for appointment of a substitute trustee, the district court is authorized to appoint one, in which case the examiner should review the proceedings for the appointment.

In addition to the statutory requirements, there must be strict compliance with any other requirements the security instrument may contain pertaining to foreclosure. *See, e.g.*, *Ogden v. Gibraltar Sav. Ass'n*, 640 S.W.2d 232 (Tex. 1982); *Houston First American Sav. v. Musick*, 650 S.W.2d 764 (Tex. 1983).

The trustee's deed must contain all of the formalities of a deed, disclose the status of the grantor as a trustee, and be delivered. Delivery may be presumed from recordation. Once the foreclosure sale is complete, the trustee may not rescind the foreclosure nor cancel the trustee's deed. *Bonilla v. Roberson*, 918 S.W.2d 17 (Tex. App.—Corpus Christi 1996, no writ).

An examiner may rely on recitals in appropriate circumstances. *See* Standards 13.20 and 13.40, pertaining to recitals. Where the security instrument expressly provides that the recitals in the trustee's deed are evidence of the facts therein stated, a presumption arises that the recitals are true. *Adams v. Zellner*, 183 S.W. 1143 (Tex. 1916); *Birdwell v. Kidd*, 240 S.W.2d 488 (Tex. Civ. App.—Texarkana 1951, no writ). An examiner may also be aided by the statutory requirement that an action to recover property conveyed by an instrument signed by a trustee without record of the authority of the trustee or proof of the facts recited in the instrument must be brought within four years of the date that the instrument was "recorded," if it was recorded before September 1, 2007, or within two years of the date that the instrument was "filed for record," if it was filed on or after September 1, 2007. Tex. Civ. Prac. & Rem. Code Ann. 16.033(a)(7). Act of June 15, 2007, 80th Leg., R.S., ch. 819, 2, 2007 Tex. Gen. Laws 1695 (nonretroactivity provision).

Statutory History: Tex. Prop. Code Ann. 51.002 (formerly codified as Tex. Rev. Civ. Stat. Ann. art. 3810) sets out the current procedures that must be followed for sale of real estate under a power of sale conferred by a deed of trust or other contract lien. Texas law pertaining to nonjudicial foreclosure as initially enacted did not change substantially until 1976.

The basic statutory requirements for sales prior to January 1, 1976, are as follows: A Notice of Sale must be posted for three consecutive weeks prior to the day of sale in three public places in the county or counties where the sale is to be made, but one notice must be posted at the courthouse door of each county where any part of the land is located. If the property is located in more than one county, then the Notice of Sale must be

given in all counties and must designate the county where the sale will be made. The sale must be public and held between the hours of 10:00 A.M. and 4:00 P.M. on the first Tuesday in any month. Upon written application, the owner may require that the land be sold as provided in the security instrument.

For sales held on or after January 1, 1976, and prior to January 1, 1984:

The basic requirements remain the same except as follows. The Notice of Sale requirement was changed to require posting for at least 21 days preceding the date of sale at the courthouse door of the county where the property is located. If the property is located in more than one county, the Notice of Sale must be posted in each county in which the property is located. The provisions allowing the owner to demand sale in accordance with the security instrument were not carried forward; however, as previously established, to the extent that the provisions of the security instrument do not conflict with the statutory requirements, the provisions of the security instrument must also be met.

For sales held on or after January 1, 1984, and prior to January 1, 1988:

The basic requirements remain the same except as follows. In addition to the requirements prior to January 1, 1984, the Notice of Sale must also be filed in the office of the county clerk of each county where the subject property is located 21 days preceding the sale. (On or after January 1, 1984, and prior to October 2, 1984, the Notice of Sale had to be filed only with the county clerk of the county where the sale was to be held.) In addition, the holder of the debt must give Notice of Sale to the debtor 21 days preceding the sale by certified mail, which is accomplished when sent to the debtor's most recent address as shown by the records of the holder and deposited in the mail, postage paid. An affidavit of mailing stating the date of mailing, debtors, and addresses is prima facie evidence that this notice requirement was met.

For sales held on or after January 1, 1988, and prior to September 1, 1993:

The basic requirements remain the same except as follows. In addition to the requirements prior to January 1, 1988, the county commissioners shall designate the area at the courthouse where foreclosure sales are to take place and shall record this designation in the real property records. All sales must occur in this area. The sale must not begin prior to the time stated in the Notice of Sale nor later than three hours thereafter. If the subject property is the residence of the debtor, notice of default must be given to the debtor by certified mail to the debtor's last known address giving the debtor at least 20 days to cure the default before Notice of Sale can be given. Prima facie evidence of notice of default may be established by affidavit of mailing showing the date of mailing, debtors, and addresses.

For sales held on or after September 1, 1993, and prior to January 1, 2004:

The basic requirements remain the same except as follows. The following statutory clarifications were made, effective September 1, 1993. Regarding the Notice of Sale, the entire calendar day on which the Notice of Sale is given is included in computing the 21-day notice period and the entire calendar day of the foreclosure sale is excluded. In the case of a debtor's residence, the entire calendar day on which notice of default is given is included in computing the 20-day notice period and the entire calendar day on which notice of sale is given is excluded in computing the 20-day notice period and the entire calendar day on which notice of sale is given is excluded in computing the 20 day notice period.

For sales held on or after January 1, 2004, and prior to June 17, 2005:

The basic requirements remain the same except that a "mortgage servicer" is given authority to perform certain prerequisites to foreclose on behalf of a holder of the debt.

For sales held on or after June 17, 2005, and prior to September 1, 2005:

The basic requirements remain the same, except that by a recorded designation of the commissioners court the location of the place of sale may be a public place other than an area at the courthouse.

For sales held on or after September 1, 2005, and prior to June 15, 2007:

The basic requirements remain the same except as to the appointment of substitute trustees and the notices required under Tex. Prop. Code Ann. §§51.002, 51.0025.

For sales held on or after June 15, 2007, and prior to September 1, 2009:

The basic requirements remain the same except: (1) if the courthouse or county clerk's office is closed because of inclement weather, natural disaster, or

other act of God, a notice required to be posted or filed may be posted or filed up to 48 hours after the courthouse or county clerk's office reopens, Tex. Prop. Code §51.002(b-1); (2) a sale may not be held at an area designated by the county commissioners other than an area at the courthouse before the 90th day after the date the designation is recorded, Tex. Prop. Code Ann. §51.002(h); (3) one or more persons may be authorized to execute the power of sale under a security agreement, Tex. Prop. Code Ann. §51.0074; and (4) the purchase price is payable immediately upon acceptance of the bid, Tex. Prop. Code Ann. §51.0075(f).

For sales held on or after September 1, 2009:

The basic requirements remain the same except: (1) the purchase price in a sale by a trustee or substitute trustee is due and payable "without delay" on acceptance of the bid, or (2) "within such reasonable time as may be agreed upon by the purchaser and the trustee or substitute trustee if the purchaser makes such request for additional time to deliver the purchase price." Payment is no longer required to be paid "immediately" upon acceptance of the bid. Tex. Prop. Code Ann. §51.0075(f).

The foreclosure sale of a dwelling owned by a military servicemember, foreclosing a lien that originated before the servicemember's active duty began, is prohibited without a court order or the servicemember's written waiver during the servicemember's active duty and for nine months thereafter, if the creditor's notice of default was sent on or after June 19, 2009. Tex. Prop. Code Ann. §51.015. For notices of default or sale on or after September 1, 2011, the notice to the debtor must include a boldface or underlined notice that if the debtor or the debtor's spouse is serving on active military duty, including active military duty as a member of the Texas National Guard or another state's National Guard or as a member of a reserve component of the United States armed forces, the debtor should send notice of the active duty to the sender of the notice immediately. Tex. Prop. Code Ann. §51.002(i).

For sales held on or after September 1, 2013, the basic requirements remain the same except:

(1) Effective September 1, 2013, a new Section 51.002(f-1) is added to the Property Code, providing that if a county maintains an internet website, the county must post a notice of sale filed with the county clerk under Section 51.000 (b)(2) on the website on a page that is publicly available for viewing without charge or registration;

(2) Effective October 1, 2013, Section 51.002(h) of the Property Code is amended to provide that a commissioners court of a county may designate an area other than an area of the county courthouse where public sales of land will take place that is in a public place within a reasonable proximity of the county courthouse as determined by the commissioners court and in a location as accessible to the public as the courthouse door. The designation shall be recorded in the real property records. Any sale held on or after the 90th day after the recording of the designation shall be held at the location so designated.

For sales held on or after September 1, 2015, the basic requirements remain the same except that (1) the appointment of a trustee or substitute trustee, a notice of sale, a notice of default, documentation that the debtor was not on active military duty at the time of the sale, and an attorney's statement of proof of notice of the sale are expressly authorized to be recorded as exhibits to a trustee's recordable foreclosure deed or affidavit, Tex. Prop. Code Ann. §12.0012; and (2) the appointment or authorization of a trustee or substitute trustee made in a notice of sale otherwise in compliance with the statutes is expressly made effective on the date of the notice if signed by an attorney as agent for the mortgagee or mortgage servicer and if it contains specific statutory wording in all capital, boldface letters. Tex. Prop. Code Ann. §51.0076.

Home Equity and Reverse Mortgage Foreclosures: Not all of the above provisions apply to home equity and reverse mortgage foreclosures, and there are additional requirements. *See* Standard 16.30.

Condominiums: A power of sale conferred by statute or contained in a condominium declaration is sufficient to foreclose by sale an assessment lien, unless the assessment consists solely of fines. There is a right of redemption within 90 days for residential property. Tex. Prop. Code Ann. §82.113.

Property Owners' Association: A dedicatory instrument or restrictions of a residential property owners' association may provide for nonjudicial foreclosure of a lien for assessments, but unless the property owner executes a written waiver at the time foreclosure is sought, a court order authorizing the foreclosure is required for foreclosure on or after September 1, 2011. Tex. Prop. Code Ann. §209.0092. Moreover, without ex-

ception, a master mixed-use property owner's association, governing a large subdivision that includes both single-family residential properties and commercial properties within the criteria described in Tex. Prop. Code Ann. §215.002, is prohibited from foreclosing an assessment lien without a judicial order of sale. Tex. Prop. Code Ann. §215.015. Notice to junior lienholders and an opportunity to cure is a prerequisite to foreclosure, Tex. Prop. Code Ann. §209.0091, and the association may not foreclose a lien solely for fines or attorney's fees relating to fines. Tex. Prop. Code Ann. §209.009. The association must send the owner written notice not later than 30 days after the foreclosure sale informing the owner of the right of redemption. A residential debtor has a right of redemption within 180 days after the association has mailed a written notice to the owner informing the owner of the sale and right of redemption. Tex. Prop. Code Ann. §209.011. Effective September 1, 2009, a property owners' association that conducts a foreclosure sale must also send written notice by certified mail, return receipt requested, to each lot owner and each lienholder of record not less than the 30th day after the date of the foreclosure sale informing them of their right to redeem. Tex. Prop. Code Ann. §209.010. The owner or a lienholder of record may redeem the property from any purchaser at the foreclosure sale not later than the 180th day after the date the association mails written notice of the sale to the owner and lienholder. A lienholder of record may not redeem the property before 90 days after the association mails written notice of the sale to the lot owner and the lienholder and then only if the lot owner has not previously redeemed. Tex. Prop. Code Ann. §209.011.

Limitations: The statute of limitations for foreclosure of a lien runs four years from date of maturity of the obligation, unless otherwise tolled. Tex. Civ. Prac. & Rem. Code Ann. §16.035. The trustee's authority expires when the debt is barred; therefore, a sale subsequent to the running of the statute of limitations is void. *Stubbs v. Lowrey's Heirs*, 253 S.W.2d 312 (Tex. Civ. App.—Eastland 1952, writ ref'd n.r.e.). Moreover, the statute of limitations begins to run when a note is accelerated, *Curtis v. Speck*, 130 S.W.2d 348 (Tex. Civ. App.—Galveston 1939, writ ref'd) or, for lien foreclosure purposes, when the note is executed if it is a demand note, *Seaman v. Seaman*, 425 S.W.2d 339 (Tex. 1968), unless demand is specifically required in the instrument. *Loomis v. Republic Nat'l Bank*, 653 S.W.2d 75 (Tex. App.—Dallas 1983, writ ref'd n.r.e.). If the deed of trust itself does not state the maturity date of the note, then the note itself must be examined. An extension of the maturity date of the note extends the period of time for foreclosure. *Southland Life Ins. Co. v. Egan*, 86 S.W.2d 722 (Tex. 1935). Tex. Civ. Prac. & Rem. Code Ann. §16.036 prescribes the requirements for a valid extension. To be effective as to a bona fide purchaser, a lienholder, or lessee without actual notice, the extension must be recorded. *Id.* §16.037.

Rescission: A mortgagee or trustee may rescind a foreclosure sale within 15 days after its occurrence if the statutory requirements for the sale were not met, the debtor's default was cured before the sale, or other specified circumstances existed. For the rescission to be effective against anyone other than parties to the foreclosure sale and purchasers with notice or without valuable consideration, evidence of notice to the purchaser, if not the mortgagee, and return of the purchase price must be recorded. Bona fide purchasers for value without actual or constructive notice of the rescission are not affected by it. Tex. Prop. Code Ann. §51.016. The examiner should consult the statutory requirements and verify that their fulfillment appears of record.

CAUTION

Even though a federal tax lien may be subordinate to the lien of the security instrument being foreclosed, a federal tax lien is not cut off by the foreclosure unless there has been compliance with I.R.C. §7425. Thus, where an unreleased subordinate federal tax lien has been filed or recorded more than 30 days prior to the date of the foreclosure sale, the examiner should determine either that the notice of lien has expired (I.R.C. §6323) or that the Internal Revenue Service was notified in compliance with I.R.C. §7425. If the examiner determines that this notice was given by mail, the examiner should confirm that the mailing complied with I.R.C. §7502 and the applicable regulations, 26 C.F.R. §301.7502-1. If notified, the Internal Revenue Service has the right to redeem foreclosed property for a period of 120 days after the date of sale. I.R.C. §7425(d). If the required notice is not given, any transfer remains subject to the federal tax lien. *Id.* §7425(b)(1). In making the [determination, the examiner may] consider (a) a copy of the notice, (b) an affidavit of mailing, (c) recitals in the trustee's deed, and (d) a receipt from the United States Postal Service indicating that the notice

was timely sent to the Internal Revenue Service or other evidence that the Service received timely notice. However, the Service is not bound by affidavits of mailing and recitals.

The filing of a petition in bankruptcy generally results in an automatic stay against the enforcement of a lien and any action to obtain possession of property of the bankrupt estate. 11 U.S.C. §§362, 922. An examiner who becomes aware of a bankruptcy filing should require evidence that the stay was lifted.

The Servicemembers Civil Relief Act of 2003, formerly the Soldiers' and Sailors' Civil Relief Act of 1940, as amended by the Housing and Economic Recovery Act of 2008, prohibits foreclosure of property against an owner who acquired the property before military service and who is currently in the military service of the United States or has been in the military service within a specified number of days (e.g., 90 days effective January 1, 2015) prior to the attempted foreclosure. These limitations do not apply to obligations that were incurred during military service. 50 U.S.C. App. §§511, 517, 527, 533.

Source:

Citations in the Comment; Tex. Prop. Code Ann. §51.002; John M. Nolan & Michael F. Alessio, *Texas Annotated Deed of Trust* in Univ. Tex. 38th Annual Mortgage Lending Inst. (2004).

History:

Adopted June 25, 2004; amended July 17, 2014.

The prior standard provided: "An examiner must determine that all statutory and contractual requirements for a nonjudicial foreclosure sale have been satisfied. Specifically, an examiner must determine (1) that the security instrument confers the power of sale; (2) that there has been a default under the terms of the instrument; (3) that the trustee or substitute trustee was properly appointed; (4) that all statutory requirements in effect at the time of sale have been met; (5) that all additional requirements, if any, contained in the security instrument have been met; and (6) that a trustee's deed has been delivered."

Law Review & Journal Commentaries:

Limiting the foreclosure power of Texas HOAs with a percentage threshold, Laci Ehlers, 43 St. Mary's L.J. 187 (2011).

STANDARD 16.20. JUDICIAL FORECLOSURE & EXECUTION SALES

When title is based on a court's foreclosure of a lien or an execution sale, an examiner may rely on the deed of the officer who conducted the sale only after verifying the existence and apparent validity of the judgment conferring authority to make the sale and of the order of sale or writ of execution and levy.

COMMENT

A deed by an officer, typically a sheriff or constable, purporting to convey a judgment defendant's interest in real property may form an essential link in the chain of title under examination. Sheriffs' deeds are commonly encountered in two situations: those involving the judicial foreclosure of liens and those resulting from execution on money judgments. A foreclosure judgment describes the specific property upon which the plaintiff's lien is being foreclosed and orders it sold, whereupon the court clerk issues an order to any sheriff or constable within the State of Texas, directing the officer to seize and sell the property described in the judgment, first giving public notice of the time and place of sale. Tex. R. Civ. P. 309 and 631. An execution sale requires the clerk's issuance of a writ of execution, likewise directed to any sheriff or constable, specifying the sum recovered and due and the interest rate, and requiring the officer to satisfy the judgment and costs out of the defendant's property. Tex. R. Civ. P. 622 and 630. The officer indorses the levy on the writ, using a sufficient legal description. Tex. R. Civ. P. 639; *see Riordan v. Britton*, 7 S.W. 50 (Tex. 1887). The manner in which the officer effects the sale of the defendant's property is essentially the same in either case. The defendant's property is sold at public auction, after advertisement by newspaper publication, at the courthouse door of the county where situated, on the first Tuesday of any month between the hours of 10:00 A.M. and 4:00 P.M. Tex. R. Civ. P. 646a and 647. Once the sale has been made and its terms complied with, the officer must execute and deliver to the purchaser a conveyance of all the right, title, and interest the defendant had in the property sold. Tex. Civ. Prac. & Rem. Code Ann. §34.045.

Three documents should be represented in the record under examination: (1) the court's judgment, (2) the clerk's order of sale or writ of execution and levy, and (3) the sheriff's or constable's deed resulting from the sale. Unless the sale is conducted pursuant to the court's authority, a sheriff's or constable's deed conveys no title. *Mills v. Pitts*, 48 S.W.2d 941 (Tex. 1932). For this reason it is essential to the establishment of title that the court's judgment and the order of sale or writ of execution and levy be examined. *See Tudor v. Hodges*, 9 S.W. 443 (Tex. 1888); *Atkinson v. Dailey*, 238 S.W.2d 584, 587 (Tex. Civ. App.—Amarillo 1951, no writ). The only exception is where the requisite court records are unavailable and the sheriff's deed qualifies as an ancient document, in which case the examiner may rely on recitals in the deed. *W. T. Carter & Bro. v. Bendy*, 251 S.W. 265 (Tex. Civ. App.—Beaumont 1923), aff'd, 269 S.W. 1037 (Tex. Comm'n App. 1925, judgm't

adopted); *Sledge v. Craven*, 254 S.W.2d 888 (Tex. Civ. App.—Galveston 1953, no writ). If necessary, the authority for the deed may be established by secondary evidence. *Richards v. Rule*, 207 S.W. 912 (Tex. Comm'n App. 1919, judgm't adopted). See the Comment to Standard 13.40 regarding recitals and ancient documents generally.

Moreover, the judgment upon which the sale is based must be a valid one. A sale based on a void judgment is likewise a nullity. For example, where a judgment of foreclosure describes the land too indefinitely to identify it, the sheriff's deed made pursuant to it conveys no title even if the deed contains an adequate description. *Adams v. Duncan*, 215 S.W.2d 599, 603-604 (Tex. 1948). A title examiner should therefore be satisfied that the court had jurisdiction to enter the judgment and that the sale complied with the court's order. Because recitals in a judgment are conclusive against anything else in the record on collateral attack, they ordinarily may be regarded as sufficient without further inquiry into the record. *Levy v. Roper*, 256 S.W. 251 (Tex. 1923); *see Pure Oil Co. v. Reece*, 78 S.W.2d 932 (Tex. 1935); *Crawford v. McDonald*, 33 S.W. 325, 327-328 (Tex. 1895). If the judgment does not include such recitals, so that reference to the rest of the record in the underlying proceeding becomes necessary, the judgment is still presumed valid unless lack of jurisdiction or some other fatal defect affirmatively appears. *Fitch v. Boyer*, 51 Tex. 336, 344 (1879); *Cox v. Campbell*, 257 S.W.2d 462 (Tex. Civ. App.—Dallas 1953, writ ref'd). The presumption that a judgment is valid is rebutted only if the record itself, uncontradicted by recitals in the judgment, discloses facts showing the judgment void. *Fowler v. Simpson*, 15 S.W. 682 (Tex. 1891).

Although the officer's sale must comply with a valid judgment and order of sale or execution, mere irregularities in the conduct of the sale will not invalidate it. *Coffee v. Silvan*, 15 Tex. 354 (1855); *Hendron v. Yount-Lee Oil Co.*, 119 S.W.2d 171 (Tex. Civ. App.—Texarkana 1938, writ ref'd); *see Howard v. North*, 5 Tex. 290 (1849). For example, a return by the sheriff or constable following the sale is not essential. It will be presumed from the judgment and the sheriff's deed that the officer did his duty unless this is rebutted by proof to the contrary. *Harris v. Mayfield*, 260 S.W. 835 (Tex. Comm'n App. 1924, holding approved). For this reason a sheriff's deed may be regarded as reliable if regular on its face. But if the record discloses that the officer acted beyond his authority, the sale cannot be given effect. *Mills v. Pitts*, 48 S.W.2d 941 (Tex. 1932); *Howard v. North*, 5 Tex. 290 (1849).

Unlike some other varieties of judicial sales, foreclosure and execution sales do not require an order of confirmation after the sale. In the case of judicial foreclosures, the order of sale itself authorizes the executing officer to place the purchaser in possession. *See* Tex. R. Civ. P. 309 and 310; *Efficient Energy Systems, Inc. v. J. Hoyt Kniveton, Inc.*, 631 S.W.2d 538, 542 (Tex. App.—El Paso 1982, no writ); *Darlington v. Allison*, 12 S.W.2d 839 (Tex. Civ. App.—Amarillo 1928, writ dism'd). Following an execution sale the officer is required to file a return of the sale with the clerk of the court, Tex. R. Civ. P. 654, but it is well established that irregularities in the return, or even the complete absence of a return, do not void the sale. *See Willis v. Smith*, 17 S.W. 247 (Tex. 1886); *Donald v. Davis*, 208 S.W.2d 571, 573 (Tex. Civ. App.—Fort Worth 1948, writ ref'd); *Tyler v. Henderson*, 162 S.W.2d 170, 174-175 (Tex. Civ. App.—Fort Worth 1942, writ ref'd w.o.m.).

CAUTION

On collateral attack, the rule that recitals in judgments control the rest of the record does not apply to judgments against nonresidents of Texas. *Pellow v. Cade*, 990 S.W.2d 307 (Tex. App.—Texarkana 1999, no pet.); *Hicks v. Sias*, 102 S.W.2d 460 (Tex. Civ. App.—Beaumont 1937, writ ref'd). Accordingly, if the defendant sought to be bound by a proceeding was not a Texas resident, an examiner should review the entire record in the underlying proceeding.

After foreclosure of a real estate tax lien, the prior owner has the right to redeem the property within 180 days; however, if the land is the residence homestead, is designated for agricultural use, or is a mineral interest, the redemption period is two years. The redemption period runs from the date the purchaser's deed is filed for record. Tex. Tax Code Ann. §34.21. Note, however, that the Texas Constitution provides that the former owner has a right to redeem within six months, which may not be synonymous with 180 days, upon payment of the amount of money paid for the property at foreclosure, including the tax deed recording fee and all taxes, penalties, interest, and costs paid plus an amount not exceeding 25% of aggregate total. Tex. Const. art. VIII, §13.

The owner of property sold on foreclosure of a federal tax lien may redeem it within 180 days after the sale. 26 U.S.C. §6337(b)(1).

The owner of property and each lienholder of record in a residential subdivision may redeem property sold on foreclosure of a property owners' association's assessment lien within 180 days for the owner (but not before ninety days for a lienholder of record if the owner has not redeemed) after the association's mailing of notice of the sale to the owner and to each such lienholder. Tex. Prop. Code Ann. §209.011(b). The purchaser at foreclosure shall immediately execute and deliver to a redeeming lot owner or lienholder a deed transferring the property to the "lot owner." *Id.* §209.011(f). If, before the expiration of such redemption period, the redeeming owner or lienholder fails to record the deed from the foreclosing purchaser or fails to record an affidavit stating that the owner or lienholder has redeemed the property, the owner's or lienholder's right of redemption as against a bona fide purchaser or lender for value expires after the redemption period. *Id.* §209.011(g).

If a residential condominium unit is purchased by the unit owners' association on foreclosure of the association's lien for assessments, the owner may redeem the unit within 90 days after the foreclosure sale. Tex. Prop. Code Ann. §82.113(g).

Other types of lien foreclosures are not subject to redemption after the sale has taken place.

An action to set aside a tax sale is subject to the limitations periods in Tex. Tax Code Ann. §§33.54, 34.08.

Source:

Citations in the Comment; 4 Aloysius A. Leopold, *Land Titles and Title Examination* §§22.25-22.29 (Texas Practice 3d ed. 2005); and 5 *Id.* §28.14; Gus M. Hodges, *Collateral Attacks on Judgments*, 41 Tex. L. Rev. 499 (1963).

History:

Adopted June 13, 2003.

Law Review & Journal Commentaries:

Limiting the foreclosure power of Texas HOAs with a percentage threshold, Laci Ehlers, 43 St. Mary's L.J. 187 (2011).

STANDARD 16.30. FORECLOSURE OF HOME EQUITY LOANS & REVERSE MORTGAGES

An examiner should verify the judicial authority for foreclosures of home equity loans. An examiner should verify the judicial authority for foreclosure of a reverse mortgage unless, before the foreclosure, (1) all borrowers have died or have ceased to occupy the property for more than twelve consecutive months, or (2) the property has been sold or otherwise transferred.

COMMENT

Upon strictly limited terms, the Texas Constitution authorizes the mortgage of homestead property to secure loans for purposes other than payment of purchase money, taxes, or the cost of improvements. These are denominated as home equity loans, subject to Tex. Const. art. XVI, §50(a)(6), and reverse mortgages, subject to Tex. Const. art. XVI, §§50(a)(7) and 50(k). Home equity loans and reverse mortgages are similar in that the purpose of both is to allow homestead mortgages without restriction on the use of the loan proceeds. The principal distinction between the two types of loans, as defined in the constitution, is that in the case of reverse mortgage, the borrower or the borrower's spouse must be at least 62 years old, and no payment of principal or interest is generally required until the borrowers have died, the property is sold or otherwise transferred, or the borrowers have ceased to occupy it for twelve months. Except in the case of reverse mortgages that are foreclosed after all borrowers have died or have ceased to occupy the property for twelve consecutive months, or after the homestead property has been sold or otherwise transferred, both types of liens may be foreclosed only after a court order. Tex. Const. art. XVI, §§50(a)(6)(D), 50(k)(11).

Under Tex. R. Civ. P. 735 a party seeking an order to foreclose such a lien may either (1) seek judicial foreclosure, (2) pursue a suit for an order allowing foreclosure under the security instrument, or (3) apply for an order allowing foreclosure under the security instrument using the expedited procedure prescribed by Tex. R. Civ. P. 736. *See* Standard 16.20 concerning judicial foreclosure. If the property has been sold by a trustee appointed in the deed of trust securing the loan, the examiner should examine the court proceeding and verify the validity of the order authorizing the lender to proceed with foreclosure, unless one of the above mentioned exceptions relevant to reverse mortgages applies.

Tex. R. Civ. P. 735 and 736 both contemplate that any sale will be conducted in compliance with Tex. Prop. Code Ann. §51.002. For guidance, see Standard 16.10 concerning nonjudicial foreclosure. Both home equity loans and reverse mortgages are subject to a host of restrictions and conditions. In particular, the validity of a lien securing a home equity loan depends on circumstances that may not be easily verifiable from recorded documents. However, if the mortgage document dis-

closes that the loan is the type defined by Section 50(a)(6) of Article XVI of the Texas Constitution, a purchaser for value without actual knowledge, other than the lender or its assignee, may conclusively presume the validity of a home equity mortgage lien. Tex. Const. art. XVI, §50(I).

A reverse mortgage that permits nonjudicial foreclosure may be foreclosed without a court order only if the borrowers have all died or if the property has been sold or otherwise transferred-facts that may not appear affirmatively from examination of the record. The examiner may verify the requisite circumstances through death certificates, affidavits or other means. *See* Standard 13.20 regarding reliance on affidavits generally.

CAUTION

For guidance regarding the customs and practices of home equity mortgage loans, see the Joint Financial Regulatory Agencies Home Equity Lending Rules. Tex. Admin. Code, Title 7, Part 8, Chapters 151, 153. *See also* Tex. Const. art. XVI, §50(u); Tex. Fin. Code §§11.308, 15.413.

There is scant reported authority construing the constitutional provisions allowing home equity loans and reverse mortgages and the rules for their foreclosure. The examiner should be extremely cautious in passing on any deviation from the rules. *See LaSalle Bank v. White*, 246 S.W.3d 616 (Tex. 2007) (applying the doctrine of equitable subrogation even though the loan violated the constitutional provision prohibiting a home equity loan from being secured by homestead property designated for agricultural use).

An order obtained in an "expedited" foreclosure proceeding under Tex. R. Civ. P. 736, authorizing a mortgagee to proceed with sale on foreclosure of a home equity loan or reverse mortgage, is not res judicata and does not constitute collateral estoppel or estoppel by judgment in any other proceeding. Tex. R. Civ. P. 736(9). Such an order, it would seem, is therefore not entitled to the presumptions usually accorded judgments rendered in judicial foreclosures. *See* the Comment to Standard 16.20.

Source:

Citations in the Comment; 15 Mike Baggett, *Texas Foreclosure: Law and Practice* §§2.176, 2.191 (Texas Practice 2014).

History:

Adopted June 13, 2003; amended July 17, 2014.

The prior standard provided: "An examiner must verify the judicial authority for foreclosures of home equity loans. An examiner must verify the judicial authority for foreclosure of a reverse mortgage unless, before the foreclosure, (1) all borrowers have died or have ceased to occupy the property for more than twelve consecutive months, or (2) the property has been sold or otherwise transferred."

STANDARD 16.40. DEEDS IN LIEU OF FORECLOSURE

When examining a deed taken by a lienholder in satisfaction of its secured debt, the examiner should consider the possible right of redemption of a junior lienholder and the validity of a subordinate interest created during the existence of the extinguished debt.

COMMENT

Frequently a mortgagor will convey mortgaged land to a mortgagee in satisfaction of the debt. These conveyances, commonly called deeds in lieu of foreclosure, are sometimes taken, not only to avoid the problems inherent in foreclosures, but in the belief that they extinguish all subordinate liens and interests. The intended result does not always follow.

If there are senior and junior liens, and if the holder of the senior lien accepts a deed in satisfaction of the debt secured by that lien, there is a question of whether the lien merges into the fee simple title. If there is a merger of title, the grantee would own the land subject to a new first lien held by the original junior lienholder. However, if the mortgagee did not intend that a merger occur, but rather that the lien remain in existence, there will be no merger. As a merger would most commonly be disadvantageous to the mortgagee, unless there is evidence that the parties intended a merger, Texas courts assume that no intent to merge existed and none will result. The junior lienholder will thereafter have a right to redeem within a reasonable period of time. *See North Texas Building & Loan Ass'n v. Overton*, 86 S.W.2d 738 (Tex. 1935).

Because of the judicial presumption that no merger has occurred, a provision in a deed that none is intended is not necessary; however, practitioners commonly insert language to that effect.

Subordinate interests other than junior liens present additional concerns. If a mortgagor conveys the land or an interest in land subject to an existing lien to a third party prior to a deed in lieu of foreclosure, the effect upon the third-party's interest depends upon whether the lien is a vendor's lien. In a sale that retains a vendor's lien, title remains in the vendor until the purchase price is paid. Among other remedies, the vendor may rescind the sale upon default in the payment of the purchase price. Accordingly, before satisfaction of the vendor's lien, if the vendee transfers an interest in the land to a third party and subsequently

reconveys to the vendor, the third party is left only with the vendee's right to redeem. The result is different where the security instrument secures an obligation other than a vendor's lien. In that case, the debtor can convey the land or an interest in the land to a third party, and the interest conveyed to the third party will not be affected by a deed in lieu of foreclosure; however, the land or interest will remain subject to the original lien. *See Yett v. Houston Farms Development Co.*, 41 S.W.2d 305 (Tex. Civ. App.—Galveston 1931, writ ref'd) (mineral deed); *Flag-Redfern Oil Co. v. Humble Exploration Co.*, 744 S.W.2d 6 (Tex. 1987) (mineral deed).

The problems that might arise from accepting a deed in lieu of foreclosure were remedied somewhat by Tex. Prop. Code Ann. §51.006, which became effective on August 28, 1995. This provision permits the holder of a debt under a deed of trust to void the deed within four years of its date if the debtor did not disclose a lien or other encumbrance before executing the deed to the holder of the debt and the holder had no personal knowledge of the undisclosed lien or encumbrance. A third party may rely conclusively upon an affidavit of the holder stating that the holder has voided the deed as provided in the section. Voiding a deed in lieu of foreclosure does not affect the priority of the deed of trust. The holder may also foreclose the deed of trust without voiding the deed in lieu of foreclosure.

A potentially abusive practice, no longer frequently encountered, is for a lender or credit seller to require a purchaser or borrower to execute a deed conveying fee title to real property, to be delivered to the lender or seller and held as security for the debt. If the debt is not paid, the seller or lender files the deed for record to recover title to the property and avoid ordinary foreclosure procedures. Such deeds are prohibited when they involve residential real estate under Tex. Bus. & Com. Code Ann. §21.002 and are voidable within four years after being recorded unless a subsequent purchaser without notice of the violation has acquired an interest in the property.

Source:

Citations in the Comment; 5A Aloysius A. Leopold, *Land Titles and Title Examination* §38.7 (Texas Practice 3d ed. 2005); Sara E. Dysart, *The Continued Existence of Deeds in Lieu of Foreclosure* in State Bar of Tex. Prof. Dev. Prog., Advanced Real Estate Law Course (1989).

History:

Adopted June 25, 2004.

TEXAS CONSTITUTION

TEXAS CONSTITUTION

ARTICLE 1. BILL OF RIGHTS

ART. 1, §17. TAKING, DAMAGING, OR DESTROYING PROPERTY FOR PUBLIC USE; SPECIAL PRIVILEGES & IMMUNITIES; CONTROL OF PRIVILEGES & FRANCHISES

(a) No person's property shall be taken, damaged, or destroyed for or applied to public use without adequate compensation being made, unless by the consent of such person, and only if the taking, damage, or destruction is for:

(1) the ownership, use, and enjoyment of the property, notwithstanding an incidental use, by:

(A) the State, a political subdivision of the State, or the public at large; or

(B) an entity granted the power of eminent domain under law; or

(2) the elimination of urban blight on a particular parcel of property.

(b) In this section, "public use" does not include the taking of property under Subsection (a) of this section for transfer to a private entity for the primary purpose of economic development or enhancement of tax revenues.

(c) On or after January 1, 2010, the legislature may enact a general, local, or special law granting the power of eminent domain to an entity only on a two-thirds vote of all the members elected to each house.

(d) When a person's property is taken under Subsection (a) of this section, except for the use of the State, compensation as described by Subsection (a) shall be first made, or secured by a deposit of money; and no irrevocable or uncontrollable grant of special privileges or immunities shall be made; but all privileges and franchises granted by the Legislature, or created under its authority, shall be subject to the control thereof.

ART. 1, §33. ACCESS & USE OF PUBLIC BEACHES

(a) In this section, "public beach" means a state-owned beach bordering on the seaward shore of the Gulf of Mexico, extending from mean low tide to the landward boundary of state-owned submerged land, and any larger area extending from the line of mean low tide to the line of vegetation bordering on the Gulf of Mexico to which the public has acquired a right of use or easement to or over the area by prescription or dedication or has established and retained a right by virtue of continuous right in the public under Texas common law.

(b) The public, individually and collectively, has an unrestricted right to use and a right of ingress to and egress from a public beach. The right granted by this subsection is dedicated as a permanent easement in favor of the public.

(c) The legislature may enact laws to protect the right of the public to access and use a public beach and to protect the public beach easement from interference and encroachments.

(d) This section does not create a private right of enforcement.

ARTICLE 8. TAXATION & REVENUE

ART. 8, §1. EQUALITY & UNIFORMITY; TAX IN PROPORTION TO VALUE; INCOME TAX; EXEMPTION OF CERTAIN TANGIBLE PERSONAL PROPERTY FROM AD VALOREM TAXATION

(a) Taxation shall be equal and uniform.

(b) All real property and tangible personal property in this State, unless exempt as required or permitted by this Constitution, whether owned by natural persons or corporations, other than municipal, shall be taxed in

proportion to its value, which shall be ascertained as may be provided by law.

(c) The Legislature may provide for the taxation of intangible property and may also impose occupation taxes, both upon natural persons and upon corporations, other than municipal, doing any business in this State. Subject to the restrictions of Section 24 of this article, it may also tax incomes of both natural persons and corporations other than municipal. Persons engaged in mechanical and agricultural pursuits shall never be required to pay an occupation tax.

(d) The Legislature by general law shall exempt from ad valorem taxation household goods not held or used for the production of income and personal effects not held or used for the production of income. The Legislature by general law may exempt from ad valorem taxation:

(1) all or part of the personal property homestead of a family or single adult, "personal property homestead" meaning that personal property exempt by law from forced sale for debt;

(2) subject to Subsections (e) and (g) of this section, all other tangible personal property, except structures which are substantially affixed to real estate and are used or occupied as residential dwellings and except property held or used for the production of income;

(3) subject to Subsection (e) of this section, a leased motor vehicle that is not held primarily for the production of income by the lessee and that otherwise qualifies under general law for exemption; and

(4) one motor vehicle, as defined by general law, owned by an individual that is used in the course of the individual's occupation or profession and is also used for personal activities of the owner that do not involve the production of income.

(e) The governing body of a political subdivision may provide for the taxation of all property exempt under a law adopted under Subdivision (2) or (3) of Subsection (d) of this section and not exempt from ad valorem taxation by any other law. The Legislature by general law may provide limitations to the application of this subsection to the taxation of vehicles exempted under the authority of Subdivision (3) of Subsection (d) of this section.

(f) The occupation tax levied by any county, city or town for any year on persons or corporations pursuing any profession or business, shall not exceed one half of the tax levied by the State for the same period on such profession or business.

(g) The Legislature may exempt from ad valorem taxation tangible personal property that is held or used for the production of income and has a taxable value of less than the minimum amount sufficient to recover the costs of the administration of the taxes on the property, as determined by or under the general law granting the exemption.

(h) The Legislature may exempt from ad valorem taxation a mineral interest that has a taxable value of less than the minimum amount sufficient to recover the costs of the administration of the taxes on the interest, as determined by or under the general law granting the exemption.

(i) Notwithstanding Subsections (a) and (b) of this section, the Legislature by general law may limit the maximum appraised value of a residence homestead for ad valorem tax purposes in a tax year to the lesser of the most recent market value of the residence homestead as determined by the appraisal entity or 110 percent, or a greater percentage, of the appraised value of the residence homestead for the preceding tax year. A limitation on appraised values authorized by this subsection:

(1) takes effect as to a residence homestead on the later of the effective date of the law imposing the limitation or January 1 of the tax year following the first tax year the owner qualifies the property for an exemption under Section 1-b of this article; and

(2) expires on January 1 of the first tax year that neither the owner of the property when the limitation took effect nor the owner's spouse or surviving spouse qualifies for an exemption under Section 1-b of this article.

(j) The Legislature by general law may provide for the taxation of real property that is the residence homestead of the property owner solely on the basis of the property's value as a residence homestead, regardless of whether the residential use of the property by the owner is considered to be the highest and best use of the property.

ART. 8, §1-L. PROPERTY USED FOR CONTROL OF AIR, WATER, OR LAND POLLUTION; EXEMPTION FROM AD VALOREM TAXATION

(a) The legislature by general law may exempt from ad valorem taxation all or part of real and personal

property used, constructed, acquired, or installed wholly or partly to meet or exceed rules or regulations adopted by any environmental protection agency of the United States, this state, or a political subdivision of this state for the prevention, monitoring, control, or reduction of air, water, or land pollution.

(b) This section applies to real and personal property used as a facility, device, or method for the control of air, water, or land pollution that would otherwise be taxable for the first time on or after January 1, 1994.

(c) This section does not authorize the exemption from ad valorem taxation of real or personal property that was subject to a tax abatement agreement executed before January 1, 1994.

ART. 8, §13. SALES OF LANDS & OTHER PROPERTY FOR TAXES; REDEMPTION

(a) Provision shall be made by the Legislature for the sale of a sufficient portion of all lands and other property for the taxes due thereon that have not been paid.

(b) The deed of conveyance to the purchaser for all lands and other property thus sold shall be held to vest a good and perfect title in the purchaser thereof, subject only to redemption as provided by this section or impeachment for actual fraud.

(c) The former owner of a residence homestead, land designated for agricultural use, or a mineral interest sold for unpaid taxes shall within two years from date of the filing for record of the Purchaser's Deed have the right to redeem the property on the following basis:

(1) Within the first year of the redemption period, upon the payment of the amount of money paid for the property, including the Tax Deed Recording Fee and all taxes, penalties, interest, and costs paid plus an amount not exceeding 25 percent of the aggregate total; and

(2) Within the last year of the redemption period, upon the payment of the amount of money paid for the property, including the Tax Deed Recording Fee and all taxes, penalties, interest, and costs paid plus an amount not exceeding 50 percent of the aggregate total.

(d) If the residence homestead or land designated for agricultural use is sold pursuant to a suit to enforce the collection of the unpaid taxes, the Legislature may limit the application of Subsection (c) of this section to property used as a residence homestead when the suit was filed and to land designated for agricultural use when the suit was filed.

(e) The former owner of real property not covered by Subsection (c) of this section sold for unpaid taxes shall within six months from the date of filing for record of the Purchaser's Deed have the right to redeem the property upon the payment of the amount of money paid for the property, including the Tax Deed Recording Fee and all taxes, penalties, interest, and costs paid plus an amount not exceeding 25 percent of the aggregate total.

ART. 8, §15. LIEN OF ASSESSMENT; SEIZURE & SALE OF PROPERTY

The annual assessment made upon landed property shall be a special lien thereon; and all property, both real and personal, belonging to any delinquent taxpayer shall be liable to seizure and sale for the payment of all the taxes and penalties due by such delinquent; and such property may be sold for the payment of the taxes and penalties due by such delinquent, under such regulations as the Legislature may provide.

ART. 8, §21. INCREASE IN TOTAL PROPERTY TAXES; NOTICE & HEARING; CALCULATION

(a) Subject to any exceptions prescribed by general law, the total amount of property taxes imposed by a political subdivision in any year may not exceed the total amount of property taxes imposed by that subdivision in the preceding year unless the governing body of the subdivision gives notice of its intent to consider an increase in taxes and holds a public hearing on the proposed increase before it increases those total taxes. The legislature shall prescribe by law the form, content, timing, and methods of giving the notice and the rules for the conduct of the hearing.

(b) In calculating the total amount of taxes imposed in the current year for the purposes of Subsection (a) of this section, the taxes on property in territory added to the political subdivision since the preceding year and on new improvements that were not taxable in the preceding year are excluded. In calculating the total amount of taxes imposed in the preceding year for the purposes of Subsection (a) of this section, the taxes imposed on real property that is not taxable by the subdivision in the current year are excluded.

(c) The legislature by general law shall require that, subject to reasonable exceptions, a property owner be given notice of a revaluation of his property and a

reasonable estimate of the amount of taxes that would be imposed on his property if the total amount of property taxes for the subdivision were not increased according to any law enacted pursuant to Subsection (a) of this section. The notice must be given before the procedures required in Subsection (a) are instituted.

ART. 8, §23. APPRAISAL OF PROPERTY; ENFORCEMENT OF STANDARDS

(a) There shall be no statewide appraisal of real property for ad valorem tax purposes; however, this shall not preclude formula distribution of tax revenues to political subdivisions of the state.

(b) Administrative and judicial enforcement of uniform standards and procedures for appraisal of property for ad valorem tax purposes shall be prescribed by general law.

ARTICLE 16. GENERAL PROVISIONS

ART. 16, §15. SEPARATE & COMMUNITY PROPERTY

All property, both real and personal, of a spouse owned or claimed before marriage, and that acquired afterward by gift, devise or descent, shall be the separate property of that spouse; and laws shall be passed more clearly defining the rights of the spouses, in relation to separate and community property; provided that persons about to marry and spouses, without the intention to defraud pre-existing creditors, may by written instrument from time to time partition between themselves all or part of their property, then existing or to be acquired, or exchange between themselves the community interest of one spouse or future spouse in any property for the community interest of the other spouse or future spouse in other community property then existing or to be acquired, whereupon the portion or interest set aside to each spouse shall be and constitute a part of the separate property and estate of such spouse or future spouse; spouses also may from time to time, by written instrument, agree between themselves that the income or property from all or part of the separate property then owned or which thereafter might be acquired by only one of them, shall be the separate property of that spouse; if one spouse makes a gift of property to the other that gift is presumed to include all the income or property which might arise from that gift of property; spouses may agree in writing that all or part of their community property becomes the property of the surviving spouse on the death of a spouse; and spouses may agree in writing that all or part of the separate property owned by either or both of them shall be the spouses' community property.

ART. 16, §37. LIENS OF MECHANICS, ARTISANS, & MATERIAL MEN

Mechanics, artisans and material men, of every class, shall have a lien upon the buildings and articles made or repaired by them for the value of their labor done thereon, or material furnished therefor; and the Legislature shall provide by law for the speedy and efficient enforcement of said liens.

18 ART. 16, §50. HOMESTEAD; PROTECTION FROM FORCED SALE; MORTGAGES, TRUST DEEDS, & LIENS

The amended text in subsection (a), proposed as a constitutional amendment by S.J.R. 60, §1, will be voted on during the Nov. 7, 2017 general election. If approved by the voters, the amendment will become effective Jan. 1, 2018.

(a) The homestead of a family, or of a single adult person, shall be, and is hereby protected from forced sale, for the payment of all debts except for:

(1) the purchase money thereof, or a part of such purchase money;

(2) the taxes due thereon;

(3) an owelty of partition imposed against the entirety of the property by a court order or by a written agreement of the parties to the partition, including a debt of one spouse in favor of the other spouse resulting from a division or an award of a family homestead in a divorce proceeding;

(4) the refinance of a lien against a homestead, including a federal tax lien resulting from the tax debt of both spouses, if the homestead is a family homestead, or from the tax debt of the owner;

(5) work and material used in constructing new improvements thereon, if contracted for in writing, or work and material used to repair or renovate existing improvements thereon if:

(A) the work and material are contracted for in writing, with the consent of both spouses, in the case of a family homestead, given in the same manner as is required in making a sale and conveyance of the homestead;

(B) the contract for the work and material is not executed by the owner or the owner's spouse before the

fifth day after the owner makes written application for any extension of credit for the work and material, unless the work and material are necessary to complete immediate repairs to conditions on the homestead property that materially affect the health or safety of the owner or person residing in the homestead and the owner of the homestead acknowledges such in writing;

(C) the contract for the work and material expressly provides that the owner may rescind the contract without penalty or charge within three days after the execution of the contract by all parties, unless the work and material are necessary to complete immediate repairs to conditions on the homestead property that materially affect the health or safety of the owner or person residing in the homestead and the owner of the homestead acknowledges such in writing; and

(D) the contract for the work and material is executed by the owner and the owner's spouse only at the office of a third-party lender making an extension of credit for the work and material, an attorney at law, or a title company;

(6) an extension of credit that:

(A) is secured by a voluntary lien on the homestead created under a written agreement with the consent of each owner and each owner's spouse;

(B) is of a principal amount that when added to the aggregate total of the outstanding principal balances of all other indebtedness secured by valid encumbrances of record against the homestead does not exceed 80 percent of the fair market value of the homestead on the date the extension of credit is made;

(C) is without recourse for personal liability against each owner and the spouse of each owner, unless the owner or spouse obtained the extension of credit by actual fraud;

(D) is secured by a lien that may be foreclosed upon only by a court order;

(E) does not require the owner or the owner's spouse to pay, in addition to any interest or any bona fide discount points used to buy down the interest rate, any fees to any person that are necessary to originate, evaluate, maintain, record, insure, or service the extension of credit that exceed, in the aggregate, two [~~three~~] percent of the original principal amount of the extension of credit, excluding fees for:

(i) an appraisal performed by a third party appraiser;

(ii) a property survey performed by a state registered or licensed surveyor;

(iii) a state base premium for a mortgagee policy of title insurance with endorsements established in accordance with state law; or

(iv) a title examination report if its cost is less than the state base premium for a mortgagee policy of title insurance without endorsements established in accordance with state law;

(F) is not a form of open-end account that may be debited from time to time or under which credit may be extended from time to time unless the open-end account is a home equity line of credit;

(G) is payable in advance without penalty or other charge;

(H) is not secured by any additional real or personal property other than the homestead;

(I) (repealed) [~~is not secured by homestead property that on the date of closing is designated for agricultural use as provided by statutes governing property tax, unless such homestead property is used primarily for the production of milk~~];

(J) may not be accelerated because of a decrease in the market value of the homestead or because of the owner's default under other indebtedness not secured by a prior valid encumbrance against the homestead;

(K) is the only debt secured by the homestead at the time the extension of credit is made unless the other debt was made for a purpose described by Subsections (a)(1)-(a)(5) or Subsection (a)(8) of this section;

(L) is scheduled to be repaid:

(i) in substantially equal successive periodic installments, not more often than every 14 days and not less often than monthly, beginning no later than two months from the date the extension of credit is made, each of which equals or exceeds the amount of accrued interest as of the date of the scheduled installment; or

(ii) if the extension of credit is a home equity line of credit, in periodic payments described under Subsection (t)(8) of this section;

(M) is closed not before:

(i) the 12th day after the later of the date that the owner of the homestead submits a loan application to the lender for the extension of credit or the date that the lender provides the owner a copy of the notice prescribed by Subsection (g) of this section;

TEXAS CONSTITUTION

(ii) one business day after the date that the owner of the homestead receives a copy of the loan application if not previously provided and a final itemized disclosure of the actual fees, points, interest, costs, and charges that will be charged at closing. If a bona fide emergency or another good cause exists and the lender obtains the written consent of the owner, the lender may provide the documentation to the owner or the lender may modify previously provided documentation on the date of closing; and

(iii) the first anniversary of the closing date of any other extension of credit described by Subsection (a)(6) of this section secured by the same homestead property, except a refinance described by Paragraph (Q)(x)(f) of this subdivision, unless the owner on oath requests an earlier closing due to a state of emergency that:

(a) has been declared by the president of the United States or the governor as provided by law; and

(b) applies to the area where the homestead is located;

(N) is closed only at the office of the lender, an attorney at law, or a title company;

(O) permits a lender to contract for and receive any fixed or variable rate of interest authorized under statute;

(P) is made by one of the following that has not been found by a federal regulatory agency to have engaged in the practice of refusing to make loans because the applicants for the loans reside or the property proposed to secure the loans is located in a certain area:

(i) a bank, savings and loan association, savings bank, or credit union doing business under the laws of this state or the United States, including a subsidiary of a bank, savings and loan association, savings bank, or credit union described by this subparagraph;

(ii) a federally chartered lending instrumentality or a person approved as a mortgagee by the United States government to make federally insured loans;

(iii) a person licensed to make regulated loans, as provided by statute of this state;

(iv) a person who sold the homestead property to the current owner and who provided all or part of the financing for the purchase;

(v) a person who is related to the homestead property owner within the second degree of affinity or consanguinity; or

(vi) a person regulated by this state as a mortgage banker or mortgage company [~~broker~~]; and

(Q) is made on the condition that:

(i) the owner of the homestead is not required to apply the proceeds of the extension of credit to repay another debt except debt secured by the homestead or debt to another lender;

(ii) the owner of the homestead not assign wages as security for the extension of credit;

(iii) the owner of the homestead not sign any instrument in which blanks relating to substantive terms of agreement are left to be filled in;

(iv) the owner of the homestead not sign a confession of judgment or power of attorney to the lender or to a third person to confess judgment or to appear for the owner in a judicial proceeding;

(v) at the time the extension of credit is made, the owner of the homestead shall receive a copy of the final loan application and all executed documents signed by the owner at closing related to the extension of credit;

(vi) the security instruments securing the extension of credit contain a disclosure that the extension of credit is the type of credit defined by Subsection (a)(6) of this section [~~Section 50(a)(6), Article XVI, Texas Constitution~~];

(vii) within a reasonable time after termination and full payment of the extension of credit, the lender cancel and return the promissory note to the owner of the homestead and give the owner, in recordable form, a release of the lien securing the extension of credit or a copy of an endorsement and assignment of the lien to a lender that is refinancing the extension of credit;

(viii) the owner of the homestead and any spouse of the owner may, within three days after the extension of credit is made, rescind the extension of credit without penalty or charge;

(ix) the owner of the homestead and the lender sign a written acknowledgment as to the fair market value of the homestead property on the date the extension of credit is made;

(x) except as provided by Subparagraph (xi) of this paragraph, the lender or any holder of the note for the extension of credit shall forfeit all principal and interest of the extension of credit if the lender or holder fails to comply with the lender's or holder's obligations under the extension of credit and fails to correct the failure to comply not later than the 60th day after the date

the lender or holder is notified by the borrower of the lender's failure to comply by:

(a) paying to the owner an amount equal to any overcharge paid by the owner under or related to the extension of credit if the owner has paid an amount that exceeds an amount stated in the applicable Paragraph (E), (G), or (O) of this subdivision;

(b) sending the owner a written acknowledgement that the lien is valid only in the amount that the extension of credit does not exceed the percentage described by Paragraph (B) of this subdivision, if applicable, or is not secured by property described under Paragraph (H) [~~or (I)~~] of this subdivision, if applicable;

(c) sending the owner a written notice modifying any other amount, percentage, term, or other provision prohibited by this section to a permitted amount, percentage, term, or other provision and adjusting the account of the borrower to ensure that the borrower is not required to pay more than an amount permitted by this section and is not subject to any other term or provision prohibited by this section;

(d) delivering the required documents to the borrower if the lender fails to comply with Subparagraph (v) of this paragraph or obtaining the appropriate signatures if the lender fails to comply with Subparagraph (ix) of this paragraph;

(e) sending the owner a written acknowledgement, if the failure to comply is prohibited by Paragraph (K) of this subdivision, that the accrual of interest and all of the owner's obligations under the extension of credit are abated while any prior lien prohibited under Paragraph (K) remains secured by the homestead; or

(f) if the failure to comply cannot be cured under Subparagraphs (x)(a)-(e) of this paragraph, curing the failure to comply by a refund or credit to the owner of $1,000 and offering the owner the right to refinance the extension of credit with the lender or holder for the remaining term of the loan at no cost to the owner on the same terms, including interest, as the original extension of credit with any modifications necessary to comply with this section or on terms on which the owner and the lender or holder otherwise agree that comply with this section; and

(xi) the lender or any holder of the note for the extension of credit shall forfeit all principal and interest of the extension of credit if the extension of credit is made by a person other than a person described under Paragraph (P) of this subdivision or if the lien was not created under a written agreement with the consent of each owner and each owner's spouse, unless each owner and each owner's spouse who did not initially consent subsequently consents;

(7) a reverse mortgage; or

(8) the conversion and refinance of a personal property lien secured by a manufactured home to a lien on real property, including the refinance of the purchase price of the manufactured home, the cost of installing the manufactured home on the real property, and the refinance of the purchase price of the real property.

(b) An owner or claimant of the property claimed as homestead may not sell or abandon the homestead without the consent of each owner and the spouse of each owner, given in such manner as may be prescribed by law.

(c) No mortgage, trust deed, or other lien on the homestead shall ever be valid unless it secures a debt described by this section, whether such mortgage, trust deed, or other lien, shall have been created by the owner alone, or together with his or her spouse, in case the owner is married. All pretended sales of the homestead involving any condition of defeasance shall be void.

(d) A purchaser or lender for value without actual knowledge may conclusively rely on an affidavit that designates other property as the homestead of the affiant and that states that the property to be conveyed or encumbered is not the homestead of the affiant.

(e) A refinance of debt secured by a homestead and described by any subsection under Subsections (a)(1)-(a)(5) that includes the advance of additional funds may not be secured by a valid lien against the homestead unless:

(1) the refinance of the debt is an extension of credit described by Subsection (a)(6) of this section; or

(2) the advance of all the additional funds is for reasonable costs necessary to refinance such debt or for a purpose described by Subsection (a)(2), (a)(3), or (a)(5) of this section.

The amended text in subsection (f), proposed as a constitutional amendment by S.J.R. 60, §1, will be voted on during the Nov. 7, 2017 general election. If approved by the voters, the amendment will become effective Jan. 1, 2018.

(f) A refinance of debt secured by the homestead, any portion of which is an extension of credit described

by Subsection (a)(6) of this section, may not be secured by a valid lien against the homestead unless either:

(1) the refinance of the debt is an extension of credit described by Subsection (a)(6) or (a)(7) of this section; or

(2) all of the following conditions are met:

(A) the refinance is not closed before the first anniversary of the date the extension of credit was closed;

(B) the refinanced extension of credit does not include the advance of any additional funds other than:

(i) funds advanced to refinance a debt described by Subsections (a)(1) through (a)(7) of this section; or

(ii) actual costs and reserves required by the lender to refinance the debt;

(C) the refinance of the extension of credit is of a principal amount that when added to the aggregate total of the outstanding principal balances of all other indebtedness secured by valid encumbrances of record against the homestead does not exceed 80 percent of the fair market value of the homestead on the date the refinance of the extension of credit is made; and

(D) the lender provides the owner the following written notice on a separate document not later than the third business day after the date the owner submits the loan application to the lender and at least 12 days before the date the refinance of the extension of credit is closed:

"YOUR EXISTING LOAN THAT YOU DESIRE TO REFINANCE IS A HOME EQUITY LOAN. YOU MAY HAVE THE OPTION TO REFINANCE YOUR HOME EQUITY LOAN AS EITHER A HOME EQUITY LOAN OR AS A NON-HOME EQUITY LOAN, IF OFFERED BY YOUR LENDER.

"HOME EQUITY LOANS HAVE IMPORTANT CONSUMER PROTECTIONS. A LENDER MAY ONLY FORECLOSE A HOME EQUITY LOAN BASED ON A COURT ORDER. A HOME EQUITY LOAN MUST BE WITHOUT RECOURSE FOR PERSONAL LIABILITY AGAINST YOU AND YOUR SPOUSE.

"IF YOU HAVE APPLIED TO REFINANCE YOUR EXISTING HOME EQUITY LOAN AS A NON-HOME EQUITY LOAN, YOU WILL LOSE CERTAIN CONSUMER PROTECTIONS. A NON-HOME EQUITY REFINANCED LOAN:

"(1) WILL PERMIT THE LENDER TO FORECLOSE WITHOUT A COURT ORDER;

"(2) WILL BE WITH RECOURSE FOR PERSONAL LIABILITY AGAINST YOU AND YOUR SPOUSE; AND

"(3) MAY ALSO CONTAIN OTHER TERMS OR CONDITIONS THAT MAY NOT BE PERMITTED IN A TRADITIONAL HOME EQUITY LOAN.

"BEFORE YOU REFINANCE YOUR EXISTING HOME EQUITY LOAN TO MAKE IT A NON-HOME EQUITY LOAN, YOU SHOULD MAKE SURE YOU UNDERSTAND THAT YOU ARE WAIVING IMPORTANT PROTECTIONS THAT HOME EQUITY LOANS PROVIDE UNDER THE LAW AND SHOULD CONSIDER CONSULTING WITH AN ATTORNEY OF YOUR CHOOSING REGARDING THESE PROTECTIONS.

"YOU MAY WISH TO ASK YOUR LENDER TO REFINANCE YOUR LOAN AS A HOME EQUITY LOAN. HOWEVER, A HOME EQUITY LOAN MAY HAVE A HIGHER INTEREST RATE AND CLOSING COSTS THAN A NON-HOME EQUITY LOAN."

The enacted text in subsection (f-1), proposed as a constitutional amendment by S.J.R. 60, §1, will be voted on during the Nov. 7, 2017 general election. If approved by the voters, the enactment will become effective Jan. 1, 2018.

(f-1) A lien securing a refinance of debt under Subsection (f)(2) of this section is deemed to be a lien described by Subsection (a)(4) of this section. An affidavit executed by the owner or the owner's spouse acknowledging that the requirements of Subsection (f)(2) of this section have been met conclusively establishes that the requirements of Subsection (a)(4) of this section have been met.

The amended text in subsection (g), proposed as a constitutional amendment by S.J.R. 60, §1, will be voted on during the Nov. 7, 2017 general election. If approved by the voters, the amendment will become effective Jan. 1, 2018.

(g) An extension of credit described by Subsection (a)(6) of this section may be secured by a valid lien against homestead property if the extension of credit is not closed before the 12th day after the lender provides the owner with the following written notice on a separate instrument:

"NOTICE CONCERNING EXTENSIONS OF CREDIT DEFINED BY SECTION 50(a)(6), ARTICLE XVI, TEXAS CONSTITUTION:

"SECTION 50(a)(6), ARTICLE XVI, OF THE TEXAS CONSTITUTION ALLOWS CERTAIN LOANS TO BE SE-

CURED AGAINST THE EQUITY IN YOUR HOME. SUCH LOANS ARE COMMONLY KNOWN AS EQUITY LOANS. IF YOU DO NOT REPAY THE LOAN OR IF YOU FAIL TO MEET THE TERMS OF THE LOAN, THE LENDER MAY FORECLOSE AND SELL YOUR HOME. THE CONSTITUTION PROVIDES THAT:

"(A) THE LOAN MUST BE VOLUNTARILY CREATED WITH THE CONSENT OF EACH OWNER OF YOUR HOME AND EACH OWNER'S SPOUSE;

"(B) THE PRINCIPAL LOAN AMOUNT AT THE TIME THE LOAN IS MADE MUST NOT EXCEED AN AMOUNT THAT, WHEN ADDED TO THE PRINCIPAL BALANCES OF ALL OTHER LIENS AGAINST YOUR HOME, IS MORE THAN 80 PERCENT OF THE FAIR MARKET VALUE OF YOUR HOME;

"(C) THE LOAN MUST BE WITHOUT RECOURSE FOR PERSONAL LIABILITY AGAINST YOU AND YOUR SPOUSE UNLESS YOU OR YOUR SPOUSE OBTAINED THIS EXTENSION OF CREDIT BY ACTUAL FRAUD;

"(D) THE LIEN SECURING THE LOAN MAY BE FORECLOSED UPON ONLY WITH A COURT ORDER;

"(E) FEES AND CHARGES TO MAKE THE LOAN MAY NOT EXCEED 2 ~~[3]~~ PERCENT OF THE LOAN AMOUNT, EXCEPT FOR A FEE OR CHARGE FOR AN APPRAISAL PERFORMED BY A THIRD PARTY APPRAISER, A PROPERTY SURVEY PERFORMED BY A STATE REGISTERED OR LICENSED SURVEYOR, A STATE BASE PREMIUM FOR A MORTGAGEE POLICY OF TITLE INSURANCE WITH ENDORSEMENTS, OR A TITLE EXAMINATION REPORT;

"(F) THE LOAN MAY NOT BE AN OPEN-END ACCOUNT THAT MAY BE DEBITED FROM TIME TO TIME OR UNDER WHICH CREDIT MAY BE EXTENDED FROM TIME TO TIME UNLESS IT IS A HOME EQUITY LINE OF CREDIT;

"(G) YOU MAY PREPAY THE LOAN WITHOUT PENALTY OR CHARGE;

"(H) NO ADDITIONAL COLLATERAL MAY BE SECURITY FOR THE LOAN;

"(I) (repealed) ~~[THE LOAN MAY NOT BE SECURED BY HOMESTEAD PROPERTY THAT IS DESIGNATED FOR AGRICULTURAL USE AS OF THE DATE OF CLOSING, UNLESS THE AGRICULTURAL HOMESTEAD PROPERTY IS USED PRIMARILY FOR THE PRODUCTION OF MILK]~~;

"(J) YOU ARE NOT REQUIRED TO REPAY THE LOAN EARLIER THAN AGREED SOLELY BECAUSE THE FAIR MARKET VALUE OF YOUR HOME DECREASES OR BECAUSE YOU DEFAULT ON ANOTHER LOAN THAT IS NOT SECURED BY YOUR HOME;

"(K) ONLY ONE LOAN DESCRIBED BY SECTION 50(a)(6), ARTICLE XVI, OF THE TEXAS CONSTITUTION MAY BE SECURED WITH YOUR HOME AT ANY GIVEN TIME;

"(L) THE LOAN MUST BE SCHEDULED TO BE REPAID IN PAYMENTS THAT EQUAL OR EXCEED THE AMOUNT OF ACCRUED INTEREST FOR EACH PAYMENT PERIOD;

"(M) THE LOAN MAY NOT CLOSE BEFORE 12 DAYS AFTER YOU SUBMIT A LOAN APPLICATION TO THE LENDER OR BEFORE 12 DAYS AFTER YOU RECEIVE THIS NOTICE, WHICHEVER DATE IS LATER; AND MAY NOT WITHOUT YOUR CONSENT CLOSE BEFORE ONE BUSINESS DAY AFTER THE DATE ON WHICH YOU RECEIVE A COPY OF YOUR LOAN APPLICATION IF NOT PREVIOUSLY PROVIDED AND A FINAL ITEMIZED DISCLOSURE OF THE ACTUAL FEES, POINTS, INTEREST, COSTS, AND CHARGES THAT WILL BE CHARGED AT CLOSING; AND IF YOUR HOME WAS SECURITY FOR THE SAME TYPE OF LOAN WITHIN THE PAST YEAR, A NEW LOAN SECURED BY THE SAME PROPERTY MAY NOT CLOSE BEFORE ONE YEAR HAS PASSED FROM THE CLOSING DATE OF THE OTHER LOAN, UNLESS ON OATH YOU REQUEST AN EARLIER CLOSING DUE TO A DECLARED STATE OF EMERGENCY;

"(N) THE LOAN MAY CLOSE ONLY AT THE OFFICE OF THE LENDER, TITLE COMPANY, OR AN ATTORNEY AT LAW;

"(O) THE LENDER MAY CHARGE ANY FIXED OR VARIABLE RATE OF INTEREST AUTHORIZED BY STATUTE;

"(P) ONLY A LAWFULLY AUTHORIZED LENDER MAY MAKE LOANS DESCRIBED BY SECTION 50(a)(6), ARTICLE XVI, OF THE TEXAS CONSTITUTION;

"(Q) LOANS DESCRIBED BY SECTION 50(a)(6), ARTICLE XVI, OF THE TEXAS CONSTITUTION MUST:

"(1) NOT REQUIRE YOU TO APPLY THE PROCEEDS TO ANOTHER DEBT EXCEPT A DEBT THAT IS SECURED BY YOUR HOME OR OWED TO ANOTHER LENDER;

"(2) NOT REQUIRE THAT YOU ASSIGN WAGES AS SECURITY;

"(3) NOT REQUIRE THAT YOU EXECUTE INSTRUMENTS WHICH HAVE BLANKS FOR SUBSTANTIVE TERMS OF AGREEMENT LEFT TO BE FILLED IN;

"(4) NOT REQUIRE THAT YOU SIGN A CONFESSION OF JUDGMENT OR POWER OF ATTORNEY TO ANOTHER PERSON TO CONFESS JUDGMENT OR APPEAR IN A LEGAL PROCEEDING ON YOUR BEHALF;

"(5) PROVIDE THAT YOU RECEIVE A COPY OF YOUR FINAL LOAN APPLICATION AND ALL EXECUTED DOCUMENTS YOU SIGN AT CLOSING;

"(6) PROVIDE THAT THE SECURITY INSTRUMENTS CONTAIN A DISCLOSURE THAT THIS LOAN IS A LOAN DEFINED BY SECTION 50(a)(6), ARTICLE XVI, OF THE TEXAS CONSTITUTION;

"(7) PROVIDE THAT WHEN THE LOAN IS PAID IN FULL, THE LENDER WILL SIGN AND GIVE YOU A RELEASE OF LIEN OR AN ASSIGNMENT OF THE LIEN, WHICHEVER IS APPROPRIATE;

"(8) PROVIDE THAT YOU MAY, WITHIN 3 DAYS AFTER CLOSING, RESCIND THE LOAN WITHOUT PENALTY OR CHARGE;

"(9) PROVIDE THAT YOU AND THE LENDER ACKNOWLEDGE THE FAIR MARKET VALUE OF YOUR HOME ON THE DATE THE LOAN CLOSES; AND

"(10) PROVIDE THAT THE LENDER WILL FORFEIT ALL PRINCIPAL AND INTEREST IF THE LENDER FAILS TO COMPLY WITH THE LENDER'S OBLIGATIONS UNLESS THE LENDER CURES THE FAILURE TO COMPLY AS PROVIDED BY SECTION 50(a)(6)(Q)(x), ARTICLE XVI, OF THE TEXAS CONSTITUTION; AND

"(R) IF THE LOAN IS A HOME EQUITY LINE OF CREDIT:

"(1) YOU MAY REQUEST ADVANCES, REPAY MONEY, AND REBORROW MONEY UNDER THE LINE OF CREDIT;

"(2) EACH ADVANCE UNDER THE LINE OF CREDIT MUST BE IN AN AMOUNT OF AT LEAST $4,000;

"(3) YOU MAY NOT USE A CREDIT CARD, DEBIT CARD, OR SIMILAR DEVICE, OR PREPRINTED CHECK THAT YOU DID NOT SOLICIT, TO OBTAIN ADVANCES UNDER THE LINE OF CREDIT;

"(4) ANY FEES THE LENDER CHARGES MAY BE CHARGED AND COLLECTED ONLY AT THE TIME THE LINE OF CREDIT IS ESTABLISHED AND THE LENDER MAY NOT CHARGE A FEE IN CONNECTION WITH ANY ADVANCE;

"(5) THE MAXIMUM PRINCIPAL AMOUNT THAT MAY BE EXTENDED, WHEN ADDED TO ALL OTHER DEBTS SECURED BY YOUR HOME, MAY NOT EXCEED 80 PERCENT OF THE FAIR MARKET VALUE OF YOUR HOME ON THE DATE THE LINE OF CREDIT IS ESTABLISHED;

"(6) IF THE PRINCIPAL BALANCE UNDER THE LINE OF CREDIT AT ANY TIME EXCEEDS 80 [50] PERCENT OF THE FAIR MARKET VALUE OF YOUR HOME, AS DETERMINED ON THE DATE THE LINE OF CREDIT IS ESTABLISHED, YOU MAY NOT CONTINUE TO REQUEST ADVANCES UNDER THE LINE OF CREDIT UNTIL THE BALANCE IS LESS THAN 80 [50] PERCENT OF THE FAIR MARKET VALUE; AND

"(7) THE LENDER MAY NOT UNILATERALLY AMEND THE TERMS OF THE LINE OF CREDIT.

"THIS NOTICE IS ONLY A SUMMARY OF YOUR RIGHTS UNDER THE TEXAS CONSTITUTION. YOUR RIGHTS ARE GOVERNED BY SECTION 50, ARTICLE XVI, OF THE TEXAS CONSTITUTION, AND NOT BY THIS NOTICE."

If the discussions with the borrower are conducted primarily in a language other than English, the lender shall, before closing, provide an additional copy of the notice translated into the written language in which the discussions were conducted.

(h) A lender or assignee for value may conclusively rely on the written acknowledgment as to the fair market value of the homestead property made in accordance with Subsection (a)(6)(Q)(ix) of this section if:

(1) the value acknowledged to is the value estimate in an appraisal or evaluation prepared in accordance with a state or federal requirement applicable to an extension of credit under Subsection (a)(6); and

(2) the lender or assignee does not have actual knowledge at the time of the payment of value or advance of funds by the lender or assignee that the fair market value stated in the written acknowledgment was incorrect.

(i) This subsection shall not affect or impair any right of the borrower to recover damages from the lender or assignee under applicable law for wrongful foreclosure. A purchaser for value without actual knowledge may conclusively presume that a lien securing an extension of credit described by Subsection (a)(6) of this section was a valid lien securing the extension of credit with homestead property if:

(1) the security instruments securing the extension of credit contain a disclosure that the extension of

credit secured by the lien was the type of credit defined by Section 50(a)(6), Article XVI, Texas Constitution;

(2) the purchaser acquires the title to the property pursuant to or after the foreclosure of the voluntary lien; and

(3) the purchaser is not the lender or assignee under the extension of credit.

(j) Subsection (a)(6) and Subsections (e)-(i) of this section are not severable, and none of those provisions would have been enacted without the others. If any of those provisions are held to be preempted by the laws of the United States, all of those provisions are invalid. This subsection shall not apply to any lien or extension of credit made after January 1, 1998, and before the date any provision under Subsection (a)(6) or Subsections (e)-(i) is held to be preempted.

(k) "Reverse mortgage" means an extension of credit:

(1) that is secured by a voluntary lien on homestead property created by a written agreement with the consent of each owner and each owner's spouse;

(2) that is made to a person who is or whose spouse is 62 years or older;

(3) that is made without recourse for personal liability against each owner and the spouse of each owner;

(4) under which advances are provided to a borrower:

(A) based on the equity in a borrower's homestead; or

(B) for the purchase of homestead property that the borrower will occupy as a principal residence;

(5) that does not permit the lender to reduce the amount or number of advances because of an adjustment in the interest rate if periodic advances are to be made;

(6) that requires no payment of principal or interest until:

(A) all borrowers have died;

(B) the homestead property securing the loan is sold or otherwise transferred;

(C) all borrowers cease occupying the homestead property for a period of longer than 12 consecutive months without prior written approval from the lender;

(C-1) if the extension of credit is used for the purchase of homestead property, the borrower fails to timely occupy the homestead property as the borrower's principal residence within a specified period after the date the extension of credit is made that is stipulated in the written agreement creating the lien on the property; or

(D) the borrower:

(i) defaults on an obligation specified in the loan documents to repair and maintain, pay taxes and assessments on, or insure the homestead property;

(ii) commits actual fraud in connection with the loan; or

(iii) fails to maintain the priority of the lender's lien on the homestead property, after the lender gives notice to the borrower, by promptly discharging any lien that has priority or may obtain priority over the lender's lien within 10 days after the date the borrower receives the notice, unless the borrower:

(a) agrees in writing to the payment of the obligation secured by the lien in a manner acceptable to the lender;

(b) contests in good faith the lien by, or defends against enforcement of the lien in, legal proceedings so as to prevent the enforcement of the lien or forfeiture of any part of the homestead property; or

(c) secures from the holder of the lien an agreement satisfactory to the lender subordinating the lien to all amounts secured by the lender's lien on the homestead property;

(7) that provides that if the lender fails to make loan advances as required in the loan documents and if the lender fails to cure the default as required in the loan documents after notice from the borrower, the lender forfeits all principal and interest of the reverse mortgage, provided, however, that this subdivision does not apply when a governmental agency or instrumentality takes an assignment of the loan in order to cure the default;

(8) that is not made unless the prospective borrower and the spouse of the prospective borrower attest in writing that the prospective borrower and the prospective borrower's spouse received counseling regarding the advisability and availability of reverse mortgages and other financial alternatives that was completed not earlier than the 180th day nor later than the 5th day before the date the extension of credit is closed;

(9) that is not closed before the 12th day after the date the lender provides to the prospective borrower the following written notice on a separate instrument,

which the lender or originator and the borrower must sign for the notice to take effect:

"IMPORTANT NOTICE TO BORROWERS

RELATED TO YOUR REVERSE MORTGAGE

"UNDER THE TEXAS TAX CODE, CERTAIN ELDERLY PERSONS MAY DEFER THE COLLECTION OF PROPERTY TAXES ON THEIR RESIDENCE HOMESTEAD. BY RECEIVING THIS REVERSE MORTGAGE YOU MAY BE REQUIRED TO FORGO ANY PREVIOUSLY APPROVED DEFERRAL OF PROPERTY TAX COLLECTION AND YOU MAY BE REQUIRED TO PAY PROPERTY TAXES ON AN ANNUAL BASIS ON THIS PROPERTY.

"THE LENDER MAY FORECLOSE THE REVERSE MORTGAGE AND YOU MAY LOSE YOUR HOME IF:

"(A) YOU DO NOT PAY THE TAXES OR OTHER ASSESSMENTS ON THE HOME EVEN IF YOU ARE ELIGIBLE TO DEFER PAYMENT OF PROPERTY TAXES;

"(B) YOU DO NOT MAINTAIN AND PAY FOR PROPERTY INSURANCE ON THE HOME AS REQUIRED BY THE LOAN DOCUMENTS;

"(C) YOU FAIL TO MAINTAIN THE HOME IN A STATE OF GOOD CONDITION AND REPAIR;

"(D) YOU CEASE OCCUPYING THE HOME FOR A PERIOD LONGER THAN 12 CONSECUTIVE MONTHS WITHOUT THE PRIOR WRITTEN APPROVAL FROM THE LENDER OR, IF THE EXTENSION OF CREDIT IS USED FOR THE PURCHASE OF THE HOME, YOU FAIL TO TIMELY OCCUPY THE HOME AS YOUR PRINCIPAL RESIDENCE WITHIN A PERIOD OF TIME AFTER THE EXTENSION OF CREDIT IS MADE THAT IS STIPULATED IN THE WRITTEN AGREEMENT CREATING THE LIEN ON THE HOME;

"(E) YOU SELL THE HOME OR OTHERWISE TRANSFER THE HOME WITHOUT PAYING OFF THE LOAN;

"(F) ALL BORROWERS HAVE DIED AND THE LOAN IS NOT REPAID;

"(G) YOU COMMIT ACTUAL FRAUD IN CONNECTION WITH THE LOAN; OR

"(H) YOU FAIL TO MAINTAIN THE PRIORITY OF THE LENDER'S LIEN ON THE HOME, AFTER THE LENDER GIVES NOTICE TO YOU, BY PROMPTLY DISCHARGING ANY LIEN THAT HAS PRIORITY OR MAY OBTAIN PRIORITY OVER THE LENDER'S LIEN WITHIN 10 DAYS AFTER THE DATE YOU RECEIVE THE NOTICE, UNLESS YOU:

"(1) AGREE IN WRITING TO THE PAYMENT OF THE OBLIGATION SECURED BY THE LIEN IN A MANNER ACCEPTABLE TO THE LENDER;

"(2) CONTEST IN GOOD FAITH THE LIEN BY, OR DEFEND AGAINST ENFORCEMENT OF THE LIEN IN, LEGAL PROCEEDINGS SO AS TO PREVENT THE ENFORCEMENT OF THE LIEN OR FORFEITURE OF ANY PART OF THE HOME; OR

"(3) SECURE FROM THE HOLDER OF THE LIEN AN AGREEMENT SATISFACTORY TO THE LENDER SUBORDINATING THE LIEN TO ALL AMOUNTS SECURED BY THE LENDER'S LIEN ON THE HOME.

"IF A GROUND FOR FORECLOSURE EXISTS, THE LENDER MAY NOT COMMENCE FORECLOSURE UNTIL THE LENDER GIVES YOU WRITTEN NOTICE BY MAIL THAT A GROUND FOR FORECLOSURE EXISTS AND GIVES YOU AN OPPORTUNITY TO REMEDY THE CONDITION CREATING THE GROUND FOR FORECLOSURE OR TO PAY THE REVERSE MORTGAGE DEBT WITHIN THE TIME PERMITTED BY SECTION 50(k)(10), ARTICLE XVI, OF THE TEXAS CONSTITUTION. THE LENDER MUST OBTAIN A COURT ORDER FOR FORECLOSURE EXCEPT THAT A COURT ORDER IS NOT REQUIRED IF THE FORECLOSURE OCCURS BECAUSE:

"(1) ALL BORROWERS HAVE DIED; OR

"(2) THE HOMESTEAD PROPERTY SECURING THE LOAN IS SOLD OR OTHERWISE TRANSFERRED."

"YOU SHOULD CONSULT WITH YOUR HOME COUNSELOR OR AN ATTORNEY IF YOU HAVE ANY CONCERNS ABOUT THESE OBLIGATIONS BEFORE YOU CLOSE YOUR REVERSE MORTGAGE LOAN. TO LOCATE AN ATTORNEY IN YOUR AREA, YOU MAY WISH TO CONTACT THE STATE BAR OF TEXAS."

"THIS NOTICE IS ONLY A SUMMARY OF YOUR RIGHTS UNDER THE TEXAS CONSTITUTION. YOUR RIGHTS ARE GOVERNED IN PART BY SECTION 50, ARTICLE XVI, OF THE TEXAS CONSTITUTION, AND NOT BY THIS NOTICE.";

(10) that does not permit the lender to commence foreclosure until the lender gives notice to the borrower, in the manner provided for a notice by mail related to the foreclosure of liens under Subsection (a)(6) of this section, that a ground for foreclosure exists and gives the borrower at least 30 days, or at least 20 days in the event of a default under Subdivision (6)(D)(iii) of this subsection, to:

(A) remedy the condition creating the ground for foreclosure;

(B) pay the debt secured by the homestead property from proceeds of the sale of the homestead property by the borrower or from any other sources; or

(C) convey the homestead property to the lender by a deed in lieu of foreclosure; and

(11) that is secured by a lien that may be foreclosed upon only by a court order, if the foreclosure is for a ground other than a ground stated by Subdivision (6)(A) or (B) of this subsection.

(*l*) Advances made under a reverse mortgage and interest on those advances have priority over a lien filed for record in the real property records in the county where the homestead property is located after the reverse mortgage is filed for record in the real property records of that county.

(m) A reverse mortgage may provide for an interest rate that is fixed or adjustable and may also provide for interest that is contingent on appreciation in the fair market value of the homestead property. Although payment of principal or interest shall not be required under a reverse mortgage until the entire loan becomes due and payable, interest may accrue and be compounded during the term of the loan as provided by the reverse mortgage loan agreement.

(n) A reverse mortgage that is secured by a valid lien against homestead property may be made or acquired without regard to the following provisions of any other law of this state:

(1) a limitation on the purpose and use of future advances or other mortgage proceeds;

(2) a limitation on future advances to a term of years or a limitation on the term of open-end account advances;

(3) a limitation on the term during which future advances take priority over intervening advances;

(4) a requirement that a maximum loan amount be stated in the reverse mortgage loan documents;

(5) a prohibition on balloon payments;

(6) a prohibition on compound interest and interest on interest;

(7) a prohibition on contracting for, charging, or receiving any rate of interest authorized by any law of this state authorizing a lender to contract for a rate of interest; and

(8) a requirement that a percentage of the reverse mortgage proceeds be advanced before the assignment of the reverse mortgage.

(o) For the purposes of determining eligibility under any statute relating to payments, allowances, benefits, or services provided on a means-tested basis by this state, including supplemental security income, low-income energy assistance, property tax relief, medical assistance, and general assistance:

(1) reverse mortgage loan advances made to a borrower are considered proceeds from a loan and not income; and

(2) undisbursed funds under a reverse mortgage loan are considered equity in a borrower's home and not proceeds from a loan.

(p) The advances made on a reverse mortgage loan under which more than one advance is made must be made according to the terms established by the loan documents by one or more of the following methods:

(1) an initial advance at any time and future advances at regular intervals;

(2) an initial advance at any time and future advances at regular intervals in which the amounts advanced may be reduced, for one or more advances, at the request of the borrower;

(3) an initial advance at any time and future advances at times and in amounts requested by the borrower until the credit limit established by the loan documents is reached;

(4) an initial advance at any time, future advances at times and in amounts requested by the borrower until the credit limit established by the loan documents is reached, and subsequent advances at times and in amounts requested by the borrower according to the terms established by the loan documents to the extent that the outstanding balance is repaid; or

(5) at any time by the lender, on behalf of the borrower, if the borrower fails to timely pay any of the following that the borrower is obligated to pay under the loan documents to the extent necessary to protect the lender's interest in or the value of the homestead property:

(A) taxes;

(B) insurance;

(C) costs of repairs or maintenance performed by a person or company that is not an employee of the lender or a person or company that directly or indirectly controls, is controlled by, or is under common control with the lender;

(D) assessments levied against the homestead property; and

(E) any lien that has, or may obtain, priority over the lender's lien as it is established in the loan documents.

(q) To the extent that any statutes of this state, including without limitation, Section 41.001 of the Texas Property Code, purport to limit encumbrances that may properly be fixed on homestead property in a manner that does not permit encumbrances for extensions of credit described in Subsection (a)(6) or (a)(7) of this section, the same shall be superseded to the extent that such encumbrances shall be permitted to be fixed upon homestead property in the manner provided for by this amendment.

(r) The supreme court shall promulgate rules of civil procedure for expedited foreclosure proceedings related to the foreclosure of liens under Subsection (a)(6) of this section and to foreclosure of a reverse mortgage lien that requires a court order.

(s) The Finance Commission of Texas shall appoint a director to conduct research on the availability, quality, and prices of financial services and research the practices of business entities in the state that provide financial services under this section. The director shall collect information and produce reports on lending activity of those making loans under this section. The director shall report his or her findings to the legislature not later than December 1 of each year.

The amended text in subsection (t), proposed as a constitutional amendment by S.J.R. 60, §1, will be voted on during the Nov. 7, 2017 general election. If approved by the voters, the amendment will become effective Jan. 1, 2018.

(t) A home equity line of credit is a form of an open-end account that may be debited from time to time, under which credit may be extended from time to time and under which:

(1) the owner requests advances, repays money, and reborrows money;

(2) any single debit or advance is not less than $4,000;

(3) the owner does not use a credit card, debit card, or similar device, or preprinted check unsolicited by the borrower, to obtain an advance;

(4) any fees described by Subsection (a)(6)(E) of this section are charged and collected only at the time the extension of credit is established and no fee is charged or collected in connection with any debit or advance;

(5) the maximum principal amount that may be extended under the account, when added to the aggregate total of the outstanding principal balances of all indebtedness secured by the homestead on the date the extension of credit is established, does not exceed an amount described under Subsection (a)(6)(B) of this section;

(6) (repealed) [~~no additional debits or advances are made if the total principal amount outstanding exceeds an amount equal to 50 percent of the fair market value of the homestead as determined on the date the account is established~~];

(7) the lender or holder may not unilaterally amend the extension of credit; and

(8) repayment is to be made in regular periodic installments, not more often than every 14 days and not less often than monthly, beginning not later than two months from the date the extension of credit is established, and:

(A) during the period during which the owner may request advances, each installment equals or exceeds the amount of accrued interest; and

(B) after the period during which the owner may request advances, installments are substantially equal.

(u) The legislature may by statute delegate one or more state agencies the power to interpret Subsections (a)(5)-(a)(7), (e)-(p), and (t), of this section. An act or omission does not violate a provision included in those subsections if the act or omission conforms to an interpretation of the provision that is:

(1) in effect at the time of the act or omission; and

(2) made by a state agency to which the power of interpretation is delegated as provided by this subsection or by an appellate court of this state or the United States.

(v) A reverse mortgage must provide that:

(1) the owner does not use a credit card, debit card, preprinted solicitation check, or similar device to obtain an advance;

(2) after the time the extension of credit is established, no transaction fee is charged or collected solely in connection with any debit or advance; and

(3) the lender or holder may not unilaterally amend the extension of credit.

ART. 16, §52. DESCENT & DISTRIBUTION OF HOMESTEAD; RESTRICTIONS ON PARTITION

On the death of the husband or wife, or both, the homestead shall descend and vest in like manner as other real property of the deceased, and shall be governed by the same laws of descent and distribution, but it shall not be partitioned among the heirs of the deceased during the lifetime of the surviving husband or wife, or so long as the survivor may elect to use or occupy the same as a homestead, or so long as the guardian of the minor children of the deceased may be permitted, under the order of the proper court having the jurisdiction, to use and occupy the same.

ART. 16, §73. VETERANS HOSPITALS

The state may contribute money, property, and other resources for the establishment, maintenance, and operation of veterans hospitals in this state.

Business & Commerce Code

Selected Provisions

Table of Contents

For the complete Business & Commerce Code with annotations, see the current edition of ***O'Connor's Texas Business & Commerce Code Plus***. To order, call 1-800-OCONNOR (1-800-626-6667) or visit www.oconnors.com.

Title 1. Uniform Commercial Code

B&CC

Business & Commerce Code

Selected Provisions

Table of Contents

B&CC

Business & Commerce Code

Selected Provisions
Table of Contents

B&CC

Title 1. Uniform Commercial Code

Chapter 7. Documents of Title

Subchapter A. General Provisions

B&CC §7.101. Short Title

This chapter may be cited as Uniform Commercial Code—Documents of Title.

B&CC §7.102. Definitions & Index of Definitions

(a) In this chapter, unless the context otherwise requires:

(1) "Bailee" means a person that by a warehouse receipt, bill of lading, or other document of title acknowledges possession of goods and contracts to deliver them.

(2) "Carrier" means a person that issues a bill of lading.

(3) "Consignee" means a person named in a bill of lading to which or to whose order the bill promises delivery.

(4) "Consignor" means a person named in a bill of lading as the person from which the goods have been received for shipment.

(5) "Delivery order" means a record that contains an order to deliver goods directed to a warehouse, carrier, or other person that in the ordinary course of business issues warehouse receipts or bills of lading.

(6) [Reserved.]

(7) "Goods" means all things that are treated as movable for the purposes of a contract for storage or transportation.

(8) "Issuer" means a bailee that issues a document of title or, in the case of an unaccepted delivery order, the person that orders the possessor of goods to deliver. The term includes a person for which an agent or employee purports to act in issuing a document if the agent or employee has real or apparent authority to issue documents, even if the issuer did not receive any goods, the goods were misdescribed, or in any other respect the agent or employee violated the issuer's instructions.

(9) "Person entitled under the document" means the holder, in the case of a negotiable document of title, or the person to which delivery of the goods is to be made by the terms of, or pursuant to instructions in a record under, a nonnegotiable document of title.

(10) [Reserved.]

(11) "Shipper" means a person that enters into a contract of transportation with a carrier.

(12) "Sign" means, with present intent to authenticate or adopt a record:

(A) to execute or adopt a tangible symbol; or

(B) to attach to or logically associate with the record an electronic sound, symbol, or process.

(13) "Warehouse" means a person engaged in the business of storing goods for hire.

(b) Definitions in other chapters applying to this chapter and the sections in which they appear are:

(1) "Contract for sale," Section 2.106.

(2) "Lessee in ordinary course of business," Section 2A.103.

(3) "'Receipt' of goods," Section 2.103.

(c) In addition, Chapter 1 contains general definitions and principles of construction and interpretation applicable throughout this chapter.

B&CC §7.103. Relation of Article to Treaty or Statute

(a) This chapter is subject to any treaty or statute of the United States or a regulatory statute of this state to the extent the treaty, statute, or regulatory statute is applicable.

(b) This chapter does not repeal or modify any law prescribing the form or contents of a document of title or the services or facilities to be afforded by a bailee, or otherwise regulating a bailee's businesses in respects not specifically treated in this chapter. However, violation of these laws does not affect the status of a document of title that otherwise complies with the definition of a document of title.

(c) This chapter modifies, limits, and supersedes the federal Electronic Signatures in Global and National Commerce Act (15 U.S.C. Section 7001 et seq.) but does not modify, limit, or supersede Section 101(c) of that Act (15 U.S.C. Section 7001(c)) or authorize electronic delivery of any of the notices described in Section 103(b) of that Act (15 U.S.C. Section 7003(b)).

(d) To the extent there is a conflict between Chapter 322 and this chapter, this chapter governs.

B&CC §7.104. Negotiable & Nonnegotiable Document of Title

(a) A document of title is negotiable if by its terms the goods are to be delivered to bearer or to the order of a named person.

(b) A document of title other than one described in Subsection (a) is nonnegotiable. A bill of lading that states that the goods are consigned to a named person is not made negotiable by a provision that the goods are to be delivered only against an order in a record signed by the same or another named person.

(c) A document of title is nonnegotiable if, at the time it is issued, the document has a conspicuous legend, however expressed, that it is nonnegotiable.

B&CC §7.105. REISSUANCE IN ALTERNATIVE MEDIUM

(a) Upon request of a person entitled under an electronic document of title, the issuer of the electronic document may issue a tangible document of title as a substitute for the electronic document if:

(1) the person entitled under the electronic document surrenders control of the document to the issuer; and

(2) the tangible document when issued contains a statement that it is issued in substitution for the electronic document.

(b) Upon issuance of a tangible document of title in substitution for an electronic document of title in accordance with Subsection (a):

(1) the electronic document ceases to have any effect or validity; and

(2) the person that procured issuance of the tangible document warrants to all subsequent persons entitled under the tangible document that the warrantor was a person entitled under the electronic document when the warrantor surrendered control of the electronic document to the issuer.

(c) Upon request of a person entitled under a tangible document of title, the issuer of the tangible document may issue an electronic document of title as a substitute for the tangible document if:

(1) the person entitled under the tangible document surrenders possession of the document to the issuer; and

(2) the electronic document when issued contains a statement that it is issued in substitution for the tangible document.

(d) Upon issuance of the electronic document of title in substitution for a tangible document of title in accordance with Subsection (c):

(1) the tangible document ceases to have any effect or validity; and

(2) the person that procured issuance of the electronic document warrants to all subsequent persons entitled under the electronic document that the warrantor was a person entitled under the tangible document when the warrantor surrendered possession of the tangible document to the issuer.

B&CC §7.106. CONTROL OF ELECTRONIC DOCUMENT OF TITLE

(a) A person has control of an electronic document of title if a system employed for evidencing the transfer of interests in the electronic document reliably establishes that person as the person to which the electronic document was issued or transferred.

(b) A system satisfies Subsection (a), and a person is deemed to have control of an electronic document of title, if the document is created, stored, and assigned in such a manner that:

(1) a single authoritative copy of the document exists which is unique, identifiable, and, except as otherwise provided in Subdivisions (4), (5), and (6), unalterable;

(2) the authoritative copy identifies the person asserting control as:

(A) the person to which the document was issued; or

(B) if the authoritative copy indicates that the document has been transferred, the person to which the document was most recently transferred;

(3) the authoritative copy is communicated to and maintained by the person asserting control or its designated custodian;

(4) copies or amendments that add or change an identified assignee of the authoritative copy can be made only with the consent of the person asserting control;

(5) each copy of the authoritative copy and any copy of a copy is readily identifiable as a copy that is not the authoritative copy; and

(6) any amendment of the authoritative copy is readily identifiable as authorized or unauthorized.

Sections 7.107-7.200 blank

SUBCHAPTER B. WAREHOUSE RECEIPTS: SPECIAL PROVISIONS

B&CC §7.201. PERSON THAT MAY ISSUE A WAREHOUSE RECEIPT; STORAGE UNDER BOND

(a) A warehouse receipt may be issued by any warehouse.

(b) If goods, including distilled spirits and agricultural commodities, are stored under a statute requiring a bond against withdrawal or a license for the issuance of receipts in the nature of warehouse receipts, a receipt issued for the goods is deemed to be a warehouse receipt even if issued by a person that is the owner of the goods and is not a warehouse.

B&CC §7.202. FORM OF WAREHOUSE RECEIPT

(a) A warehouse receipt need not be in any particular form.

(b) Unless a warehouse receipt provides for each of the following, the warehouse is liable for damages caused to a person injured by its omission:

(1) the location of the warehouse facility where the goods are stored;

(2) the date of issue of the receipt;

(3) the unique identification code of the receipt;

(4) a statement whether the goods received will be delivered to the bearer, to a named person, or to a named person or its order;

(5) the rate of storage and handling charges, but if goods are stored under a field warehousing arrangement, a statement of that fact is sufficient on a nonnegotiable receipt;

(6) a description of the goods or the packages containing them;

(7) the signature of the warehouse or its agent;

(8) if the receipt is issued for goods that the warehouse owns, either solely, jointly, or in common with others, the fact of that ownership; and

(9) a statement of the amount of advances made and of liabilities incurred for which the warehouse claims a lien or security interest, but if the precise amount of advances made or of liabilities incurred is, at the time of the issue of the receipt, unknown to the warehouse or to its agent that issued the receipt, a statement of the fact that advances have been made or liabilities incurred and the purpose of the advances or liabilities is sufficient.

(c) A warehouse may insert in its receipt any terms that are not contrary to this title and do not impair its obligation of delivery under Section 7.403 or its duty of care under Section 7.204. Any contrary provisions are ineffective.

B&CC §7.203. LIABILITY FOR NONRECEIPT OR MISDESCRIPTION

A party to or purchaser for value in good faith of a document of title, other than a bill of lading, that relies upon the description of the goods in the document may recover from the issuer damages caused by the nonreceipt or misdescription of the goods, except to the extent that:

(1) the document conspicuously indicates that the issuer does not know whether all or part of the goods in fact were received or conform to the description, such as a case in which the description is in terms of marks or labels or kind, quantity, or condition, or the receipt or description is qualified by "contents, condition, and quality unknown," "said to contain," or words of similar import, if the indication is true; or

(2) the party or purchaser otherwise has notice of the nonreceipt or misdescription.

B&CC §7.204. DUTY OF CARE; CONTRACTUAL LIMITATION OF WAREHOUSE'S LIABILITY

(a) A warehouse is liable for damages for loss of or injury to the goods caused by its failure to exercise care with regard to the goods that a reasonably careful person would exercise under similar circumstances. However, unless otherwise agreed, the warehouse is not liable for damages that could not have been avoided by the exercise of that care.

(b) Damages may be limited by a term in the warehouse receipt or storage agreement limiting the amount of liability in case of loss or damage beyond which the warehouse is not liable. Such a limitation is not effective with respect to the warehouse's liability for conversion to its own use. The warehouse's liability, on request of the bailor in a record at the time of signing such storage agreement or within a reasonable time after receipt of the warehouse receipt, may be increased on part or all of the goods covered by the storage agreement or the warehouse receipt. In this event, increased rates may be charged based on an increased valuation of the goods.

(c) Reasonable provisions as to the time and manner of presenting claims and commencing actions based on the bailment may be included in the warehouse receipt or storage agreement.

B&CC §7.205. TITLE UNDER WAREHOUSE RECEIPT DEFEATED IN CERTAIN CASES

A buyer in ordinary course of business of fungible goods sold and delivered by a warehouse that is also in the business of buying and selling such goods takes the goods free of any claim under a warehouse receipt even if the receipt is negotiable and has been duly negotiated.

B&CC §7.206. TERMINATION OF STORAGE AT WAREHOUSE'S OPTION

(a) A warehouse, by giving notice to the person on whose account the goods are held and any other person known to claim an interest in the goods, may require payment of any charges and removal of the goods from the warehouse at the termination of the period of storage fixed by the document of title or, if a period is not fixed, within a stated period not less than 30 days after the warehouse gives notice. If the goods are not removed before the date specified in the notice, the warehouse may sell them pursuant to Section 7.210.

(b) If a warehouse in good faith believes that goods are about to deteriorate or decline in value to less than the amount of its lien within the time provided in Subsection (a) and Section 7.210, the warehouse may specify in the notice given under Subsection (a) any reasonable shorter time for removal of the goods and, if the goods are not removed, may sell them at public sale held not less than one week after a single advertisement or posting.

(c) If, as a result of a quality or condition of the goods of which the warehouse did not have notice at the time of deposit, the goods are a hazard to other property, the warehouse facilities, or other persons, the warehouse may sell the goods at public or private sale without advertisement or posting on reasonable notification to all persons known to claim an interest in the goods. If the warehouse, after a reasonable effort, is unable to sell the goods, it may dispose of them in any lawful manner and does not incur liability by reason of that disposition.

(d) A warehouse shall deliver the goods to any person entitled to them under this chapter upon due demand made at any time before sale or other disposition under this section.

(e) A warehouse may satisfy its lien from the proceeds of any sale or disposition under this section but shall hold the balance for delivery on the demand of any person to which the warehouse would have been bound to deliver the goods.

B&CC §7.207. GOODS MUST BE KEPT SEPARATE; FUNGIBLE GOODS

(a) Unless the warehouse receipt provides otherwise, a warehouse shall keep separate the goods covered by each receipt so as to permit at all times identification and delivery of those goods. However, different lots of fungible goods may be commingled.

(b) If different lots of fungible goods are commingled, the goods are owned in common by the persons entitled thereto and the warehouse is severally liable to each owner for that owner's share. If, because of overissue, a mass of fungible goods is insufficient to meet all the receipts the warehouse has issued against it, the persons entitled include all holders to which overissued receipts have been duly negotiated.

B&CC §7.208. ALTERED WAREHOUSE RECEIPTS

If a blank in a negotiable tangible warehouse receipt has been filled in without authority, a good faith purchaser for value and without notice of the lack of authority may treat the insertion as authorized. Any other unauthorized alteration leaves any tangible or electronic warehouse receipt enforceable against the issuer according to its original tenor.

B&CC §7.209. LIEN OF WAREHOUSE

(a) A warehouse has a lien against the bailor on the goods covered by a warehouse receipt or storage agreement or on the proceeds thereof in its possession for charges for storage or transportation, including demurrage and terminal charges, insurance, labor, or other charges, present or future, in relation to the goods, and for expenses necessary for preservation of the goods or reasonably incurred in their sale pursuant to law. If the person on whose account the goods are held is liable for similar charges or expenses in relation to other goods whenever deposited and it is stated in the warehouse receipt or storage agreement that a lien is claimed for charges and expenses in relation to other goods, the warehouse also has a lien against the goods covered by the warehouse receipt or storage agreement or on the proceeds thereof in its possession for those charges and expenses, whether or not the other goods have been delivered by the warehouse. However, as against a person to which a negotiable warehouse receipt is duly negotiated, a warehouse's lien is limited to

charges in an amount or at a rate specified in the warehouse receipt or, if no charges are so specified, to a reasonable charge for storage of the specific goods covered by the receipt subsequent to the date of the receipt.

(b) The warehouse may also reserve a security interest under Chapter 9 against the bailor for the maximum amount specified on the receipt for charges other than those specified in Subsection (a), such as for money advanced and interest. A security interest is governed by Chapter 9.

(c) A warehouse's lien for charges and expenses under Subsection (a) or a security interest under Subsection (b) is also effective against any person that so entrusted the bailor with possession of the goods that a pledge of them by the bailor to a good faith purchaser for value would have been valid. However, the lien or security interest is not effective against a person that before issuance of a document of title had a legal interest or a perfected security interest in the goods and that did not:

(1) deliver or entrust the goods or any document covering the goods to the bailor or the bailor's nominee with actual or apparent authority to ship, store, or sell; or with power to obtain delivery under Section 7.403; or with power of disposition under Section 2.403, 2A.304(a)(2), 2A.305(a)(2), or 9.320 or other statute or rule of law; or

(2) acquiesce in the procurement by the bailor or its nominee of any document.

(d) A warehouse's lien on household goods for charges and expenses in relation to the goods under Subsection (a) is also effective against all persons if the depositor was the legal possessor of the goods at the time of deposit. In this subsection, "household goods" means furniture, furnishings, or personal effects used by the depositor in a dwelling.

(e) A warehouse loses its lien on any goods that it voluntarily delivers or unjustifiably refuses to deliver.

B&CC §7.210. ENFORCEMENT OF WAREHOUSE'S LIEN

(a) Except as otherwise provided in Subsection (b), a warehouse's lien may be enforced by public or private sale of the goods, in bulk or in packages, at any time or place and on any terms that are commercially reasonable, after notifying all persons known to claim an interest in the goods. The notification must include a statement of the amount due, the nature of the proposed sale, and the time and place of any public sale. The fact that a better price could have been obtained by a sale at a different time or in a different method from that selected by the warehouse is not of itself sufficient to establish that the sale was not made in a commercially reasonable manner. The warehouse has sold in a commercially reasonable manner if the warehouse sells the goods in the usual manner in any recognized market therefor, sells at the price current in that market at the time of the sale, or has otherwise sold in conformity with commercially reasonable practices among dealers in the type of goods sold. A sale of more goods than apparently necessary to be offered to ensure satisfaction of the obligation is not commercially reasonable, except in cases covered by the preceding sentence.

(b) A warehouse's lien on goods, other than goods stored by a merchant in the course of its business, may be enforced only if the following requirements are satisfied:

(1) All persons known to claim an interest in the goods must be notified.

(2) The notification must include an itemized statement of the claim, a description of the goods subject to the lien, a demand for payment within a specified time not less than 10 days after receipt of the notification, and a conspicuous statement that unless the claim is paid within that time the goods will be advertised for sale and sold by auction at a specified time and place.

(3) The sale must conform to the terms of the notification.

(4) The sale must be held at the nearest suitable place to where the goods are held or stored.

(5) After the expiration of the time given in the notification, an advertisement of the sale must be published once a week for two weeks consecutively in a newspaper of general circulation where the sale is to be held. The advertisement must include a description of the goods, the name of the person on whose account the goods are being held, and the time and place of the sale. The sale must take place at least 15 days after the first publication. If there is no newspaper of general circulation where the sale is to be held, the advertisement must be posted at least 10 days before the sale in not less than six conspicuous places in the neighborhood of the proposed sale.

(c) Before any sale pursuant to this section, any person claiming a right in the goods may pay the amount necessary to satisfy the lien and the reasonable expenses incurred in complying with this section. In that event, the goods may not be sold but must be retained by the warehouse subject to the terms of the receipt and this chapter.

(d) A warehouse may buy at any public sale held pursuant to this section.

(e) A purchaser in good faith of goods sold to enforce a warehouse's lien takes the goods free of any rights of persons against which the lien was valid, despite the warehouse's noncompliance with this section.

(f) A warehouse may satisfy its lien from the proceeds of any sale pursuant to this section but shall hold the balance, if any, for delivery on demand to any person to which the warehouse would have been bound to deliver the goods.

(g) The rights provided by this section are in addition to all other rights allowed by law to a creditor against a debtor.

(h) If a lien is on goods stored by a merchant in the course of its business, the lien may be enforced in accordance with Subsection (a) or (b).

(i) A warehouse is liable for damages caused by failure to comply with the requirements for sale under this section and, in case of wilful violation, is liable for conversion.

Sections 7.211-7.300 blank

SUBCHAPTER C. BILLS OF LADING: SPECIAL PROVISIONS

B&CC §7.301. LIABILITY FOR NONRECEIPT OR MISDESCRIPTION; "SAID TO CONTAIN"; "SHIPPER'S LOAD & COUNT"; IMPROPER HANDLING

(a) A consignee of a nonnegotiable bill of lading which has given value in good faith, or a holder to which a negotiable bill has been duly negotiated, relying upon the description of the goods in the bill or upon the date shown in the bill, may recover from the issuer damages caused by the misdating of the bill or the nonreceipt or misdescription of the goods, except to the extent that the document of title indicates that the issuer does not know whether any part or all of the goods in fact were received or conform to the description, such as in a case in which the description is in terms of marks or labels or kind, quantity, or condition, or the receipt or description is qualified by "contents or condition of contents of packages unknown," "said to contain," "shipper's weight, load and count," or words of similar import, if that indication is true.

(b) If goods are loaded by the issuer of the bill of lading, the issuer shall count the packages of goods if shipped in packages and ascertain the kind and quantity if shipped in bulk and words such as "shipper's weight, load and count," or words of similar import indicating that the description was made by the shipper are ineffective except as to goods concealed by packages.

(c) If bulk goods are loaded by a shipper that makes available to the issuer of the bill of lading adequate facilities for weighing those goods, the issuer shall ascertain the kind and quantity within a reasonable time after receiving the shipper's request in a record to do so. In that case, "shipper's weight" or words of similar import are ineffective.

(d) The issuer, by including in the bill of lading the words "shipper's weight, load and count," or words of similar import, may indicate that the goods were loaded by the shipper, and, if that statement is true, the issuer is not liable for damages caused by the improper loading. However, omission of such words does not imply liability for damages caused by improper loading.

(e) A shipper guarantees to the issuer the accuracy at the time of shipment of the description, marks, labels, number, kind, quantity, condition, and weight, as furnished by the shipper, and the shipper shall indemnify the issuer against damage caused by inaccuracies in those particulars. This right of the issuer to that indemnity does not limit its responsibility or liability under the contract of carriage to any person other than the shipper.

B&CC §7.302. THROUGH BILLS OF LADING & SIMILAR DOCUMENTS OF TITLE

(a) The issuer of a through bill of lading or other document of title embodying an undertaking to be performed in part by a person acting as its agent or by a performing carrier is liable to any person entitled to recover on the document for any breach by the other person or the performing carrier of its obligation under the document. However, to the extent that the bill covers an undertaking to be performed overseas or in territory not contiguous to the continental United States or an

undertaking including matters other than transportation, this liability for breach by the other person or the performing carrier may be varied by agreement of the parties.

(b) If goods covered by a through bill of lading or other document of title embodying an undertaking to be performed in part by a person other than the issuer are received by that person, the person is subject, with respect to its own performance while the goods are in its possession, to the obligation of the issuer. The person's obligation is discharged by delivery of the goods to another person pursuant to the document and does not include liability for breach by any other person or by the issuer.

(c) The issuer of a through bill of lading or other document of title described in Subsection (a) is entitled to recover from the performing carrier, or other person in possession of the goods when the breach of the obligation under the document occurred:

(1) the amount it may be required to pay to any person entitled to recover on the document for the breach, as may be evidenced by any receipt, judgment, or transcript of judgment; and

(2) the amount of any expense reasonably incurred by the issuer in defending any action commenced by any person entitled to recover on the document for the breach.

B&CC §7.303. DIVERSION; RECONSIGNMENT; CHANGE OF INSTRUCTIONS

(a) Unless the bill of lading otherwise provides, a carrier may deliver the goods to a person or destination other than that stated in the bill or may otherwise dispose of the goods, without liability for misdelivery, on instructions from:

(1) the holder of a negotiable bill;

(2) the consignor on a nonnegotiable bill even if the consignee has given contrary instructions;

(3) the consignee on a nonnegotiable bill in the absence of contrary instructions from the consignor, if the goods have arrived at the billed destination or if the consignee is in possession of the tangible bill or in control of the electronic bill; or

(4) the consignee on a nonnegotiable bill, if the consignee is entitled as against the consignor to dispose of the goods.

(b) Unless instructions described in Subsection (a) are included in a negotiable bill of lading, a person to which the bill is duly negotiated may hold the bailee according to the original terms.

B&CC §7.304. TANGIBLE BILLS OF LADING IN SET

(a) Except as customary in international transportation, a tangible bill of lading may not be issued in a set of parts. The issuer is liable for damages caused by violation of this subsection.

(b) If a tangible bill of lading is lawfully issued in a set of parts, each of which contains an identification code and is expressed to be valid only if the goods have not been delivered against any other part, the whole of the parts constitutes one bill.

(c) If a tangible negotiable bill of lading is lawfully issued in a set of parts and different parts are negotiated to different persons, the title of the holder to which the first due negotiation is made prevails as to both the document of title and the goods even if any later holder may have received the goods from the carrier in good faith and discharged the carrier's obligation by surrendering its part.

(d) A person that negotiates or transfers a single part of a tangible bill of lading issued in a set is liable to holders of that part as if it were the whole set.

(e) The bailee is obliged to deliver in accordance with Subchapter D against the first presented part of a tangible bill of lading lawfully issued in a set. Delivery in this manner discharges the bailee's obligation on the whole bill.

B&CC §7.305. DESTINATION BILLS

(a) Instead of issuing a bill of lading to the consignor at the place of shipment, a carrier, at the request of the consignor, may procure the bill to be issued at destination or at any other place designated in the request.

(b) Upon request of any person entitled as against a carrier to control the goods while in transit and on surrender of possession or control of any outstanding bill of lading or other receipt covering the goods, the issuer, subject to Section 7.105, may procure a substitute bill to be issued at any place designated in the request.

B&CC §7.306. ALTERED BILLS OF LADING

An unauthorized alteration or filling in of a blank in a bill of lading leaves the bill enforceable according to its original tenor.

B&CC §7.307. LIEN OF CARRIER

(a) A carrier has a lien on the goods covered by a bill of lading or on the proceeds thereof in its possession for charges after the date of the carrier's receipt of the goods for storage or transportation, including demurrage and terminal charges, and for expenses necessary for preservation of the goods incident to their transportation or reasonably incurred in their sale pursuant to law. However, against a purchaser for value of a negotiable bill of lading, a carrier's lien is limited to charges stated in the bill or the applicable tariffs or, if no charges are stated, a reasonable charge.

(b) A lien for charges and expenses under Subsection (a) on goods that the carrier was required by law to receive for transportation is effective against the consignor or any person entitled to the goods unless the carrier had notice that the consignor lacked authority to subject the goods to those charges and expenses. Any other lien under Subsection (a) is effective against the consignor and any person that permitted the bailor to have control or possession of the goods unless the carrier had notice that the bailor lacked authority.

(c) A carrier loses its lien on any goods that it voluntarily delivers or unjustifiably refuses to deliver.

B&CC §7.308. ENFORCEMENT OF CARRIER'S LIEN

(a) A carrier's lien on goods may be enforced by public or private sale of the goods, in bulk or in packages, at any time or place and on any terms that are commercially reasonable, after notifying all persons known to claim an interest in the goods. The notification must include a statement of the amount due, the nature of the proposed sale, and the time and place of any public sale. The fact that a better price could have been obtained by a sale at a different time or in a different method from that selected by the carrier is not of itself sufficient to establish that the sale was not made in a commercially reasonable manner. The carrier has sold goods in a commercially reasonable manner if the carrier sells the goods in the usual manner in any recognized market therefor, sells at the price current in that market at the time of the sale, or has otherwise sold in conformity with commercially reasonable practices among dealers in the type of goods sold. A sale of more goods than apparently necessary to be offered to ensure satisfaction of the obligation is not commercially reasonable, except in cases covered by the preceding sentence.

(b) Before any sale pursuant to this section, any person claiming a right in the goods may pay the amount necessary to satisfy the lien and the reasonable expenses incurred in complying with this section. In that event, the goods may not be sold but must be retained by the carrier, subject to the terms of the bill of lading and this chapter.

(c) A carrier may buy at any public sale pursuant to this section.

(d) A purchaser in good faith of goods sold to enforce a carrier's lien takes the goods free of any rights of persons against which the lien was valid, despite the carrier's noncompliance with this section.

(e) A carrier may satisfy its lien from the proceeds of any sale pursuant to this section but shall hold the balance, if any, for delivery on demand to any person to which the carrier would have been bound to deliver the goods.

(f) The rights provided by this section are in addition to all other rights allowed by law to a creditor against a debtor.

(g) A carrier's lien may be enforced pursuant to either Subsection (a) or the procedure set forth in Section 7.210(b).

(h) A carrier is liable for damages caused by failure to comply with the requirements for sale under this section and, in case of wilful violation, is liable for conversion.

B&CC §7.309. DUTY OF CARE; CONTRACTUAL LIMITATION OF CARRIER'S LIABILITY

(a) A carrier that issues a bill of lading, whether negotiable or nonnegotiable, shall exercise the degree of care in relation to the goods which a reasonably careful person would exercise under similar circumstances. This subsection does not affect any statute, regulation, or rule of law that imposes liability upon a common carrier for damages not caused by its negligence.

(b) Damages may be limited by a term in the bill of lading or in a transportation agreement that the carrier's liability may not exceed a value stated in the bill or transportation agreement if the carrier's rates are dependent upon value and the consignor is afforded an opportunity to declare a higher value and is advised of the opportunity. However, such a limitation is not effective with respect to the carrier's liability for conversion to its own use.

(c) Reasonable provisions as to the time and manner of presenting claims and commencing actions based on the shipment may be included in a bill of lading or a transportation agreement.

Sections 7.310-7.400 blank

SUBCHAPTER D. WAREHOUSE RECEIPTS & BILLS OF LADING: GENERAL OBLIGATIONS

B&CC §7.401. IRREGULARITIES IN ISSUE OF RECEIPT OR BILL OR CONDUCT OF ISSUER

The obligations imposed by this chapter on an issuer apply to a document of title even if:

(1) the document does not comply with the requirements of this chapter or of any other statute, rule, or regulation regarding its issue, form, or content;

(2) the issuer violated laws regulating the conduct of its business;

(3) the goods covered by the document were owned by the bailee when the document was issued; or

(4) the person issuing the document is not a warehouse but the document purports to be a warehouse receipt.

B&CC §7.402. DUPLICATE DOCUMENT OF TITLE; OVERISSUE

A duplicate or any other document of title purporting to cover goods already represented by an outstanding document of the same issuer does not confer any right in the goods, except as provided in the case of tangible bills of lading in a set of parts, overissue of documents for fungible goods, substitutes for lost, stolen, or destroyed documents, or substitute documents issued pursuant to Section 7.105. The issuer is liable for damages caused by its overissue or failure to identify a duplicate document by a conspicuous notation.

B&CC §7.403. OBLIGATION OF WAREHOUSE OR CARRIER TO DELIVER; EXCUSE

(a) A bailee shall deliver the goods to a person entitled under a document of title if the person complies with Subsections (b) and (c), unless and to the extent that the bailee establishes any of the following:

(1) delivery of the goods to a person whose receipt was rightful as against the claimant;

(2) damage to or delay, loss, or destruction of the goods for which the bailee is not liable;

(3) previous sale or other disposition of the goods in lawful enforcement of a lien or on a warehouse's lawful termination of storage;

(4) the exercise by a seller of its right to stop delivery pursuant to Section 2.705 or by a lessor of its right to stop delivery pursuant to Section 2A.526;

(5) a diversion, reconsignment, or other disposition pursuant to Section 7.303;

(6) release, satisfaction, or any other fact affording a personal defense against the claimant; or

(7) any other lawful excuse.

(b) A person claiming goods covered by a document of title shall satisfy the bailee's lien if the bailee so requests or the bailee is prohibited by law from delivering the goods until the charges are paid.

(c) Unless a person claiming the goods is one against which the document of title does not confer a right under Section 7.503(a):

(1) the person claiming under a document shall surrender possession or control of any outstanding negotiable document covering the goods for cancellation or indication of partial deliveries; and

(2) the bailee shall cancel the document or conspicuously indicate in the document the partial delivery or be liable to any person to which the document is duly negotiated.

B&CC §7.404. NO LIABILITY FOR GOOD FAITH DELIVERY PURSUANT TO DOCUMENT OF TITLE

A bailee that in good faith has received goods and delivered or otherwise disposed of the goods according to the terms of a document of title or pursuant to this chapter is not liable for the goods even if:

(1) the person from which the bailee received the goods did not have authority to procure the document or to dispose of the goods; or

(2) the person to which the bailee delivered the goods did not have authority to receive the goods.

Sections 7.405-7.500 blank

SUBCHAPTER E. WAREHOUSE RECEIPTS & BILLS OF LADING: NEGOTIATION & TRANSFER

B&CC §7.501. FORM OF NEGOTIATION & REQUIREMENTS OF DUE NEGOTIATION

(a) The following rules apply to a negotiable tangible document of title:

(1) If the document's original terms run to the order of a named person, the document is negotiated by the named person's indorsement and delivery. After the named person's indorsement in blank or to bearer, any person may negotiate the document by delivery alone.

(2) If the document's original terms run to bearer, it is negotiated by delivery alone.

(3) If the document's original terms run to the order of a named person and it is delivered to the named person, the effect is the same as if the document had been negotiated.

(4) Negotiation of the document after it has been indorsed to a named person requires indorsement by the named person as well as delivery.

(5) A document is duly negotiated if it is negotiated in the manner stated in this subsection to a holder that purchases it in good faith, without notice of any defense against or claim to it on the part of any person, and for value, unless it is established that the negotiation is not in the regular course of business or financing or involves receiving the document in settlement or payment of a monetary obligation.

(b) The following rules apply to a negotiable electronic document of title:

(1) If the document's original terms run to the order of a named person or to bearer, the document is negotiated by delivery of the document to another person. Indorsement by the named person is not required to negotiate the document.

(2) If the document's original terms run to the order of a named person and the named person has control of the document, the effect is the same as if the document had been negotiated.

(3) A document is duly negotiated if it is negotiated in the manner stated in this subsection to a holder that purchases it in good faith, without notice of any defense against or claim to it on the part of any person, and for value, unless it is established that the negotiation is not in the regular course of business or financing or involves taking delivery of the document in settlement or payment of a monetary obligation.

(c) Indorsement of a nonnegotiable document of title neither makes it negotiable nor adds to the transferee's rights.

(d) The naming in a negotiable bill of lading of a person to be notified of the arrival of the goods does not limit the negotiability of the bill or constitute notice to a purchaser of the bill of any interest of that person in the goods.

B&CC §7.502. RIGHTS ACQUIRED BY DUE NEGOTIATION

(a) Subject to Sections 7.205 and 7.503, a holder to which a negotiable document of title has been duly negotiated acquires thereby:

(1) title to the document;

(2) title to the goods;

(3) all rights accruing under the law of agency or estoppel, including rights to goods delivered to the bailee after the document was issued; and

(4) the direct obligation of the issuer to hold or deliver the goods according to the terms of the document free of any defense or claim by the issuer except those arising under the terms of the document or under this chapter. In the case of a delivery order, the bailee's obligation accrues only upon the bailee's acceptance of the delivery order and the obligation acquired by the holder is that the issuer and any indorser will procure the acceptance of the bailee.

(b) Subject to Section 7.503, title and rights acquired by due negotiation are not defeated by any stoppage of the goods represented by the document of title or by surrender of the goods by the bailee and are not impaired even if:

(1) the due negotiation or any prior due negotiation constituted a breach of duty;

(2) any person has been deprived of possession of a negotiable tangible document or control of a negotiable electronic document by misrepresentation, fraud, accident, mistake, duress, loss, theft, or conversion; or

(3) a previous sale or other transfer of the goods or document has been made to a third person.

B&CC §7.503. DOCUMENT OF TITLE TO GOODS DEFEATED IN CERTAIN CASES

(a) A document of title confers no right in goods against a person that before issuance of the document had a legal interest or a perfected security interest in the goods and that did not:

(1) deliver or entrust the goods or any document covering the goods to the bailor or the bailor's nominee with actual or apparent authority to ship, store, or sell; with power to obtain delivery under Section 7.403;

or with power of disposition under Section 2.403, 2A.304(a)(2), 2A.305(a)(2), or 9.320 or other statute or rule of law; or

(2) acquiesce in the procurement by the bailor or its nominee of any document.

(b) Title to goods based upon an unaccepted delivery order is subject to the rights of any person to which a negotiable warehouse receipt or bill of lading covering the goods has been duly negotiated. That title may be defeated under Section 7.504 to the same extent as the rights of the issuer or a transferee from the issuer.

(c) Title to goods based upon a bill of lading issued to a freight forwarder is subject to the rights of any person to which a bill issued by the freight forwarder is duly negotiated. However, delivery by the carrier in accordance with Subchapter D pursuant to its own bill of lading discharges the carrier's obligation to deliver.

B&CC §7.504. RIGHTS ACQUIRED IN ABSENCE OF DUE NEGOTIATION; EFFECT OF DIVERSION; STOPPAGE OF DELIVERY

(a) A transferee of a document of title, whether negotiable or nonnegotiable, to which the document has been delivered but not duly negotiated, acquires the title and rights that its transferor had or had actual authority to convey.

(b) In the case of a nonnegotiable document of title, until but not after the bailee receives notice of the transfer, the rights of the transferee may be defeated:

(1) by those creditors of the transferor that could treat the transfer as void under Section 2.402 or 2A.308;

(2) by a buyer from the transferor in ordinary course of business if the bailee has delivered the goods to the buyer or received notification of the buyer's rights;

(3) by a lessee from the transferor in ordinary course of business if the bailee has delivered the goods to the lessee or received notification of the lessee's rights; or

(4) as against the bailee, by good faith dealings of the bailee with the transferor.

(c) A diversion or other change of shipping instructions by the consignor in a nonnegotiable bill of lading which causes the bailee not to deliver the goods to the consignee defeats the consignee's title to the goods if the goods have been delivered to a buyer in ordinary course of business or a lessee in ordinary course of business and in any event defeats the consignee's rights against the bailee.

(d) Delivery of the goods pursuant to a nonnegotiable document of title may be stopped by a seller under Section 2.705 or a lessor under Section 2A.526, subject to the requirements of due notification in those sections. A bailee honoring the seller's or lessor's instructions is entitled to be indemnified by the seller or lessor against any resulting loss or expense.

B&CC §7.505. INDORSER NOT GUARANTOR FOR OTHER PARTIES

The indorsement of a tangible document of title issued by a bailee does not make the indorser liable for any default by the bailee or previous indorsers.

B&CC §7.506. DELIVERY WITHOUT INDORSEMENT; RIGHT TO COMPEL INDORSEMENT

The transferee of a negotiable tangible document of title has a specifically enforceable right to have its transferor supply any necessary indorsement, but the transfer becomes a negotiation only as of the time the indorsement is supplied.

B&CC §7.507. WARRANTIES ON NEGOTIATION OR DELIVERY OF DOCUMENT OF TITLE

If a person negotiates or delivers a document of title for value, otherwise than as a mere intermediary under Section 7.508, unless otherwise agreed, the transferor warrants to its immediate purchaser only in addition to any warranty made in selling or leasing the goods that:

(1) the document is genuine;

(2) the transferor does not have knowledge of any fact that would impair the document's validity or worth; and

(3) the negotiation or delivery is rightful and fully effective with respect to the title to the document and the goods it represents.

B&CC §7.508. WARRANTIES OF COLLECTING BANK AS TO DOCUMENTS OF TITLE

A collecting bank or other intermediary known to be entrusted with documents of title on behalf of another or with collection of a draft or other claim against delivery of documents warrants by the delivery of the documents only its own good faith and authority even if the collecting bank or other intermediary has purchased or made advances against the claim or draft to be collected.

B&CC §7.509. ADEQUATE COMPLIANCE WITH COMMERCIAL CONTRACT

Whether a document of title is adequate to fulfill the obligations of a contract for sale, a contract for lease, or the conditions of a letter of credit is determined by Chapter 2, 2A, or 5.

Sections 7.510-7.600 blank

Subchapter F. Warehouse Receipts & Bills of Lading: Miscellaneous Provisions

B&CC §7.601. LOST, STOLEN, OR DESTROYED DOCUMENTS OF TITLE

(a) If a document of title is lost, stolen, or destroyed, a court may order delivery of the goods or issuance of a substitute document and the bailee may without liability to any person comply with the order. If the document was negotiable, a court may not order delivery of the goods or issuance of a substitute document without the claimant's posting security unless it finds that any person that may suffer loss as a result of nonsurrender of possession or control of the document is adequately protected against the loss. If the document was nonnegotiable, the court may require security. The court may also order payment of the bailee's reasonable costs and attorney's fees in any action under this subsection.

(b) A bailee that without court order delivers goods to a person claiming under a missing negotiable document of title is liable to any person injured thereby. If the delivery is not in good faith, the bailee is liable for conversion. Delivery in good faith is not conversion if the claimant posts security with the bailee in an amount at least double the value of the goods at the time of posting to indemnify any person injured by the delivery that files a notice of claim within one year after the delivery.

B&CC §7.602. ATTACHMENT OF GOODS COVERED BY NEGOTIABLE DOCUMENT OF TITLE

Unless a document of title was originally issued upon delivery of the goods by a person that did not have power to dispose of them, a lien does not attach by virtue of any judicial process to goods in the possession of a bailee for which a negotiable document of title is outstanding unless possession or control of the document is first surrendered to the bailee or the document's negotiation is enjoined. The bailee may not be compelled to deliver the goods pursuant to process until possession or control of the document is surrendered to the bailee or to the court. A purchaser of the document for value without notice of the process or injunction takes free of the lien imposed by judicial process.

B&CC §7.603. CONFLICTING CLAIMS; INTERPLEADER

If more than one person claims title to or possession of the goods, the bailee is excused from delivery until the bailee has a reasonable time to ascertain the validity of the adverse claims or to commence an action for interpleader. The bailee may assert an interpleader either in defending an action for nondelivery of the goods or by original action.

Chapter 9. Secured Transactions

Subchapter C. Perfection & Priority

B&CC §9.301. LAW GOVERNING PERFECTION & PRIORITY OF SECURITY INTERESTS

Except as otherwise provided in Sections 9.303 through 9.306, the following rules determine the law governing perfection, the effect of perfection or nonperfection, and the priority of a security interest in collateral:

(1) Except as otherwise provided in this section, while a debtor is located in a jurisdiction, the local law of that jurisdiction governs perfection, the effect of perfection or nonperfection, and the priority of a security interest in collateral.

(2) While collateral is located in a jurisdiction, the local law of that jurisdiction governs perfection, the effect of perfection or nonperfection, and the priority of a possessory security interest in that collateral.

(3) Except as otherwise provided in Subdivision (4), while tangible negotiable documents, goods, instruments, money, or tangible chattel paper is located in a jurisdiction, the local law of that jurisdiction governs:

(A) perfection of a security interest in the goods by filing a fixture filing;

(B) perfection of a security interest in timber to be cut; and

(C) the effect of perfection or nonperfection and the priority of a nonpossessory security interest in the collateral.

(4) The local law of the jurisdiction in which the wellhead or minehead is located governs perfection,

the effect of perfection or nonperfection, and the priority of a security interest in as-extracted collateral.

B&CC §9.302. LAW GOVERNING PERFECTION & PRIORITY OF AGRICULTURAL LIENS

While farm products are located in a jurisdiction, the local law of that jurisdiction governs perfection, the effect of perfection or nonperfection, and the priority of an agricultural lien on the farm products.

B&CC §9.303. LAW GOVERNING PERFECTION & PRIORITY OF SECURITY INTERESTS IN GOODS COVERED BY A CERTIFICATE OF TITLE

(a) This section applies to goods covered by a certificate of title, even if there is no other relationship between the jurisdiction under whose certificate of title the goods are covered and the goods or the debtor.

(b) Goods become covered by a certificate of title when a valid application for the certificate of title and the applicable fee are delivered to the appropriate authority. Goods cease to be covered by a certificate of title at the earlier of the time the certificate of title ceases to be effective under the law of the issuing jurisdiction or the time the goods become covered subsequently by a certificate of title issued by another jurisdiction.

(c) The local law of the jurisdiction under whose certificate of title the goods are covered governs perfection, the effect of perfection or nonperfection, and the priority of a security interest in goods covered by a certificate of title from the time the goods become covered by the certificate of title until the goods cease to be covered by the certificate of title.

B&CC §9.304. LAW GOVERNING PERFECTION & PRIORITY OF SECURITY INTERESTS IN DEPOSIT ACCOUNTS

(a) The local law of a bank's jurisdiction governs perfection, the effect of perfection or nonperfection, and the priority of a security interest in a deposit account maintained with that bank.

(b) The following rules determine a bank's jurisdiction for purposes of this subchapter:

(1) If an agreement between the bank and its customer governing the deposit account expressly provides that a particular jurisdiction is the bank's jurisdiction for purposes of this subchapter, this chapter, or this title, that jurisdiction is the bank's jurisdiction.

(2) If Subdivision (1) does not apply and an agreement between the bank and its customer governing the deposit account expressly provides that the agreement is governed by the law of a particular jurisdiction, that jurisdiction is the bank's jurisdiction.

(3) If neither Subdivision (1) nor Subdivision (2) applies and an agreement between the bank and its customer governing the deposit account expressly provides that the deposit account is maintained at an office in a particular jurisdiction, that jurisdiction is the bank's jurisdiction.

(4) If none of the preceding subdivisions applies, the bank's jurisdiction is the jurisdiction in which the office identified in an account statement as the office serving the customer's account is located.

(5) If none of the preceding subdivisions applies, the bank's jurisdiction is the jurisdiction in which the chief executive office of the bank is located.

B&CC §9.305. LAW GOVERNING PERFECTION & PRIORITY OF SECURITY INTERESTS IN INVESTMENT PROPERTY

(a) Except as otherwise provided in Subsection (c), the following rules apply:

(1) While a security certificate is located in a jurisdiction, the local law of that jurisdiction governs perfection, the effect of perfection or nonperfection, and the priority of a security interest in the certificated security represented thereby.

(2) The local law of the issuer's jurisdiction as specified in Section 8.110(d) governs perfection, the effect of perfection or nonperfection, and the priority of a security interest in an uncertificated security.

(3) The local law of the securities intermediary's jurisdiction as specified in Section 8.110(e) governs perfection, the effect of perfection or nonperfection, and the priority of a security interest in a security entitlement or securities account.

(4) The local law of the commodity intermediary's jurisdiction governs perfection, the effect of perfection or nonperfection, and the priority of a security interest in a commodity contract or commodity account.

(b) The following rules determine a commodity intermediary's jurisdiction for purposes of this subchapter:

(1) If an agreement between the commodity intermediary and commodity customer governing the com-

modity account expressly provides that a particular jurisdiction is the commodity intermediary's jurisdiction for purposes of this subchapter, this chapter, or this title, that jurisdiction is the commodity intermediary's jurisdiction.

(2) If Subdivision (1) does not apply and an agreement between the commodity intermediary and commodity customer governing the commodity account expressly provides that the agreement is governed by the law of a particular jurisdiction, that jurisdiction is the commodity intermediary's jurisdiction.

(3) If neither Subdivision (1) nor Subdivision (2) applies and an agreement between the commodity intermediary and commodity customer governing the commodity account expressly provides that the commodity account is maintained at an office in a particular jurisdiction, that jurisdiction is the commodity intermediary's jurisdiction.

(4) If none of the preceding subdivisions applies, the commodity intermediary's jurisdiction is the jurisdiction in which the office identified in an account statement as the office serving the commodity customer's account is located.

(5) If none of the preceding subdivisions applies, the commodity intermediary's jurisdiction is the jurisdiction in which the chief executive office of the commodity intermediary is located.

(c) The local law of the jurisdiction in which the debtor is located governs:

(1) perfection of a security interest in investment property by filing;

(2) automatic perfection of a security interest in investment property created by a broker or securities intermediary; and

(3) automatic perfection of a security interest in a commodity contract or commodity account created by a commodity intermediary.

B&CC §9.306. LAW GOVERNING PERFECTION & PRIORITY OF SECURITY INTERESTS IN LETTER-OF-CREDIT RIGHTS

(a) Subject to Subsection (c), the local law of the issuer's jurisdiction or a nominated person's jurisdiction governs perfection, the effect of perfection or nonperfection, and the priority of a security interest in a letter-of-credit right if the issuer's jurisdiction or nominated person's jurisdiction is a state.

(b) For purposes of this subchapter, an issuer's jurisdiction or nominated person's jurisdiction is the jurisdiction whose law governs the liability of the issuer or nominated person with respect to the letter-of-credit right as provided in Section 5.116.

(c) This section does not apply to a security interest that is perfected only under Section 9.308(d).

B&CC §9.307. LOCATION OF DEBTOR

(a) In this section, "place of business" means a place where a debtor conducts its affairs.

(b) Except as otherwise provided in this section, the following rules determine a debtor's location:

(1) A debtor who is an individual is located at the individual's principal residence.

(2) A debtor that is an organization and has only one place of business is located at its place of business.

(3) A debtor that is an organization and has more than one place of business is located at its chief executive office.

(c) Subsection (b) applies only if a debtor's residence, place of business, or chief executive office, as applicable, is located in a jurisdiction whose law generally requires information concerning the existence of a nonpossessory security interest to be made generally available in a filing, recording, or registration system as a condition or result of the security interest's obtaining priority over the rights of a lien creditor with respect to the collateral. If Subsection (b) does not apply, the debtor is located in the District of Columbia.

(d) A person that ceases to exist, have a residence, or have a place of business continues to be located in the jurisdiction specified by Subsections (b) and (c).

(e) A registered organization that is organized under the law of a state is located in that state.

(f) Except as otherwise provided in Subsection (i), a registered organization that is organized under the law of the United States and a branch or agency of a bank that is not organized under the law of the United States or a state are located:

(1) in the state that the law of the United States designates, if the law designates a state of location;

(2) in the state that the registered organization, branch, or agency designates, if the law of the United States authorizes the registered organization, branch, or agency to designate its state of location, including by designating its main office, home office, or other comparable office; or

(3) in the District of Columbia, if neither Subdivision (1) nor Subdivision (2) applies.

(g) A registered organization continues to be located in the jurisdiction specified by Subsection (e) or (f) notwithstanding:

(1) the suspension, revocation, forfeiture, or lapse of the registered organization's status as such in its jurisdiction of organization; or

(2) the dissolution, winding up, or cancellation of the existence of the registered organization.

(h) The United States is located in the District of Columbia.

(i) A branch or agency of a bank that is not organized under the law of the United States or a state is located in the state in which the branch or agency is licensed, if all branches and agencies of the bank are licensed in only one state.

(j) A foreign air carrier under the Federal Aviation Act of 1958, as amended, is located at the designated office of the agent upon which service of process may be made on behalf of the carrier.

(k) This section applies only for purposes of this subchapter.

B&CC §9.308. WHEN SECURITY INTEREST OR AGRICULTURAL LIEN IS PERFECTED; CONTINUITY OF PERFECTION

(a) Except as otherwise provided in this section and Section 9.309, a security interest is perfected if it has attached and all of the applicable requirements for perfection in Sections 9.310 through 9.316 have been satisfied. A security interest is perfected when it attaches if the applicable requirements are satisfied before the security interest attaches.

(b) An agricultural lien is perfected if it has become effective and all of the applicable requirements for perfection in Section 9.310 have been satisfied. An agricultural lien is perfected when it becomes effective if the applicable requirements are satisfied before the agricultural lien becomes effective.

(c) A security interest or agricultural lien is perfected continuously if it is originally perfected by one method under this chapter and is later perfected by another method under this chapter, without an intermediate period when it was unperfected.

(d) Perfection of a security interest in collateral also perfects a security interest in a supporting obligation for the collateral.

(e) Perfection of a security interest in a right to payment or performance also perfects a security interest in a security interest, mortgage, or other lien on personal or real property securing the right.

(f) Perfection of a security interest in a securities account also perfects a security interest in the security entitlements carried in the securities account.

(g) Perfection of a security interest in a commodity account also perfects a security interest in the commodity contracts carried in the commodity account.

B&CC §9.309. SECURITY INTEREST PERFECTED UPON ATTACHMENT

The following security interests are perfected when they attach:

(1) a purchase money security interest in consumer goods, except as otherwise provided in Section 9.311(b) with respect to consumer goods that are subject to a statute or treaty described in Section 9.311(a);

(2) an assignment of accounts or payment intangibles that does not by itself or in conjunction with other assignments to the same assignee transfer a significant part of the assignor's outstanding accounts or payment intangibles;

(3) a sale of a payment intangible;

(4) a sale of a promissory note;

(5) a security interest created by the assignment of a health-care-insurance receivable to the provider of the health care goods or services;

(6) a security interest arising under Section 2.401, 2.505, 2.711(c), or 2A.508(e), until the debtor obtains possession of the collateral;

(7) a security interest of a collecting bank arising under Section 4.210;

(8) a security interest of an issuer or nominated person arising under Section 5.118;

(9) a security interest arising in the delivery of a financial asset under Section 9.206(c);

(10) a security interest in investment property created by a broker or securities intermediary;

(11) a security interest in a commodity contract or a commodity account created by a commodity intermediary;

(12) an assignment for the benefit of all the creditors of the transferor and subsequent transfers by the assignee thereunder;

(13) a security interest created by an assignment of a beneficial interest in a decedent's estate; and

(14) a sale by an individual of an account that is a right to payment of winnings in a lottery or other game of chance.

B&CC §9.310. WHEN FILING REQUIRED TO PERFECT SECURITY INTEREST OR AGRICULTURAL LIEN; SECURITY INTERESTS & AGRICULTURAL LIENS TO WHICH FILING PROVISIONS DO NOT APPLY

(a) Except as otherwise provided in Subsection (b) and Section 9.312(b), a financing statement must be filed to perfect all security interests and agricultural liens.

(b) The filing of a financing statement is not necessary to perfect a security interest:

(1) that is perfected under Section 9.308(d), (e), (f), or (g);

(2) that is perfected under Section 9.309 when it attaches;

(3) in property subject to a statute, regulation, or treaty described in Section 9.311(a);

(4) in goods in possession of a bailee that is perfected under Section 9.312(d)(1) or (2);

(5) in certificated securities, documents, goods, or instruments which is perfected without filing, control or possession under Section 9.312(e), (f), or (g);

(6) in collateral in the secured party's possession under Section 9.313;

(7) in a certificated security that is perfected by delivery of the security certificate to the secured party under Section 9.313;

(8) in deposit accounts, electronic chattel paper, electronic documents, investment property, or letter-of-credit rights that is perfected by control under Section 9.314;

(9) in proceeds that is perfected under Section 9.315;

(10) that is perfected under Section 9.316; or

(11) in oil or gas production or their proceeds under Section 9.343.

(c) If a secured party assigns a perfected security interest or agricultural lien, a filing under this Chapter is not required to continue the perfected status of the security interest against creditors of and transferees from the original debtor.

B&CC §9.311. PERFECTION OF SECURITY INTERESTS IN PROPERTY SUBJECT TO CERTAIN STATUTES, REGULATIONS, & TREATIES

(a) Except as otherwise provided in Subsection (d), the filing of a financing statement is not necessary or effective to perfect a security interest in property subject to:

(1) a statute, regulation, or treaty of the United States whose requirements for a security interest's obtaining priority over the rights of a lien creditor with respect to the property preempt Section 9.310(a);

(2) the following statutes of this state: a certificate of title statute of this state or rules adopted under the statute to the extent the statute or rules provide for a security interest to be indicated on the certificate of title as a condition or result of perfection or such alternative to notation as may be prescribed by those statutes or rules of this state; or Chapter 261, relating to utility security instruments; or

(3) a statute of another jurisdiction that provides for a security interest to be indicated on a certificate of title as a condition or result of the security interest's obtaining priority over the rights of a lien creditor with respect to the property.

(b) Compliance with the requirements of a statute, regulation, or treaty described in Subsection (a) for obtaining priority over the rights of a lien creditor is equivalent to the filing of a financing statement under this Chapter. Except as otherwise provided in Subsection (d) and Sections 9.313 and 9.316(d) and (e) for goods covered by a certificate of title, a security interest in property subject to a statute, regulation, or treaty described in Subsection (a) may be perfected only by compliance with those requirements, and a security interest so perfected remains perfected notwithstanding a change in the use or transfer of possession of the collateral.

(c) Except as otherwise provided in Subsection (d) and Sections 9.316(d) and (e), duration and renewal of perfection of a security interest perfected by compliance with the requirements prescribed by a statute, regulation, or treaty described in Subsection (a) are governed by the statute, regulation, or treaty. In other respects, the security interest is subject to this Chapter.

(d) During any period in which collateral subject to a statute specified in Subsection (a)(2) is inventory held for sale or lease by a person or leased by that person as lessor and that person is in the business of sell-

ing goods of that kind, this section does not apply to a security interest in that collateral created by that person.

B&CC §9.312. PERFECTION OF SECURITY INTERESTS IN CHATTEL PAPER, DEPOSIT ACCOUNTS, DOCUMENTS, & GOODS COVERED BY DOCUMENTS, INSTRUMENTS, INVESTMENT PROPERTY, LETTER-OF-CREDIT RIGHTS, & MONEY; PERFECTION BY PERMISSIVE FILING; TEMPORARY PERFECTION WITHOUT FILING OR TRANSFER OF POSSESSION

(a) A security interest in chattel paper, negotiable documents, instruments, or investment property may be perfected by filing.

(b) Except as otherwise provided in Sections 9.315(c) and (d) for proceeds:

(1) a security interest in a deposit account may be perfected only by control under Section 9.314;

(2) and except as otherwise provided in Section 9.308(d), a security interest in a letter-of-credit right may be perfected only by control under Section 9.314; and

(3) a security interest in money may be perfected only by the secured party's taking possession under Section 9.313.

(c) While goods are in the possession of a bailee that has issued a negotiable document covering the goods:

(1) a security interest in the goods may be perfected by perfecting a security interest in the document; and

(2) a security interest perfected in the document has priority over any security interest that becomes perfected in the goods by another method during that time.

(d) While goods are in the possession of a bailee that has issued a nonnegotiable document covering the goods, a security interest in the goods may be perfected by:

(1) issuance of a document in the name of the secured party;

(2) the bailee's receipt of notification of the secured party's interest; or

(3) filing as to the goods.

(e) A security interest in certificated securities, negotiable documents, or instruments is perfected without filing or the taking of possession or control for a period of 20 days from the time it attaches to the extent that it arises for new value given under an authenticated security agreement.

(f) A perfected security interest in a negotiable document or goods in possession of a bailee, other than one that has issued a negotiable document for the goods, remains perfected for 20 days without filing if the secured party makes available to the debtor the goods or documents representing the goods for the purpose of:

(1) ultimate sale or exchange; or

(2) loading, unloading, storing, shipping, transshipping, manufacturing, processing, or otherwise dealing with them in a manner preliminary to their sale or exchange.

(g) A perfected security interest in a certificated security or instrument remains perfected for 20 days without filing if the secured party delivers the security certificate or instrument to the debtor for the purpose of:

(1) ultimate sale or exchange; or

(2) presentation, collection, enforcement, renewal, or registration of transfer.

(h) After the 20-day period specified in Subsection (e), (f), or (g) expires, perfection depends upon compliance with this chapter.

B&CC §9.313. WHEN POSSESSION BY OR DELIVERY TO SECURED PARTY PERFECTS SECURITY INTEREST WITHOUT FILING

(a) Except as otherwise provided in Subsection (b), a secured party may perfect a security interest in tangible negotiable documents, goods, instruments, money, or tangible chattel paper by taking possession of the collateral. A secured party may perfect a security interest in certificated securities by taking delivery of the certificated securities under Section 8.301.

(b) With respect to goods covered by a certificate of title issued by this state, a secured party may perfect a security interest in the goods by taking possession of the goods only in the circumstances described in Section 9.316(d).

(c) With respect to collateral other than certificated securities and goods covered by a document, a secured party takes possession of collateral in the possession of a person other than the debtor, the secured

party, or a lessee of the collateral from the debtor in the ordinary course of the debtor's business when:

(1) the person in possession authenticates a record acknowledging that it holds possession of the collateral for the secured party's benefit; or

(2) the person takes possession of the collateral after having authenticated a record acknowledging that it will hold possession of collateral for the secured party's benefit.

(d) If perfection of a security interest depends upon possession of the collateral by a secured party, perfection occurs no earlier than the time the secured party takes possession and continues only while the secured party retains possession.

(e) A security interest in a certificated security in registered form is perfected by delivery when delivery of the certificated security occurs under Section 8.301 and remains perfected by delivery until the debtor obtains possession of the security certificate.

(f) A person in possession of collateral is not required to acknowledge that it holds possession for a secured party's benefit.

(g) If a person acknowledges that it holds possession for the secured party's benefit:

(1) the acknowledgment is effective under Subsection (c) or Section 8.301(a), even if the acknowledgment violates the rights of a debtor; and

(2) unless the person otherwise agrees or law other than this chapter otherwise provides, the person does not owe any duty to the secured party and is not required to confirm the acknowledgment to another person.

(h) A secured party having possession of collateral does not relinquish possession by delivering the collateral to a person other than the debtor or a lessee of the collateral from the debtor in the ordinary course of the debtor's business if the person was instructed before the delivery or is instructed contemporaneously with the delivery:

(1) to hold possession of the collateral for the secured party's benefit; or

(2) to redeliver the collateral to the secured party.

(i) A secured party does not relinquish possession, even if a delivery under Subsection (h) violates the rights of a debtor. A person to which collateral is delivered under Subsection (h) does not owe any duty to the secured party and is not required to confirm the delivery to another person unless the person otherwise agrees or law other than this chapter otherwise provides.

B&CC §9.314. PERFECTION BY CONTROL

(a) A security interest in investment property, deposit accounts, letter-of-credit rights, electronic chattel paper, or electronic documents may be perfected by control of the collateral under Section 7.106, 9.104, 9.105, 9.106, or 9.107.

(b) A security interest in deposit accounts, electronic chattel paper, letter-of-credit rights, or electronic documents is perfected by control under Section 7.106, 9.104, 9.105, or 9.107 when the secured party obtains control and remains perfected by control only while the secured party retains control.

(c) A security interest in investment property is perfected by control under Section 9.106 from the time the secured party obtains control and remains perfected by control until:

(1) the secured party does not have control; and

(2) one of the following occurs:

(A) if the collateral is a certificated security, the debtor has or acquires possession of the security certificate;

(B) if the collateral is an uncertificated security, the issuer has registered or registers the debtor as the registered owner; or

(C) if the collateral is a security entitlement, the debtor is or becomes the entitlement holder.

B&CC §9.315. SECURED PARTY'S RIGHTS ON DISPOSITION OF COLLATERAL & IN PROCEEDS

(a) Except as otherwise provided in this chapter and Section 2.403(b):

(1) a security interest or agricultural lien continues in collateral notwithstanding sale, lease, license, exchange, or other disposition thereof unless the secured party authorized the disposition free of the security interest or agricultural lien; and

(2) a security interest attaches to any identifiable proceeds of collateral.

(b) Proceeds that are commingled with other property are identifiable proceeds:

(1) if the proceeds are goods, to the extent provided by Section 9.336; and

(2) if the proceeds are not goods, to the extent that the secured party identifies the proceeds by a method of tracing, including application of equitable principles, that is permitted under law other than this chapter with respect to commingled property of the type involved.

(c) A security interest in proceeds is a perfected security interest if the interest in the original collateral was perfected.

(d) A perfected security interest in proceeds becomes unperfected on the 21st day after the security interest attaches to receipt of the proceeds unless:

(1) the following conditions are satisfied:

(A) a filed financing statement covers the original collateral;

(B) the proceeds are collateral in which a security interest may be perfected by filing in the office in which the financing statement has been filed; and

(C) the proceeds are not acquired with cash proceeds;

(2) the proceeds are identifiable cash proceeds; or

(3) the security interest in the proceeds is perfected other than under Subsection (c) when the security interest attaches to the proceeds or within 20 days thereafter.

(e) If a filed financing statement covers the original collateral, a security interest in proceeds that remains perfected under Subsection (d)(1) becomes unperfected at the later of:

(1) when the effectiveness of the filed financing statement lapses under Section 9.515 or is terminated under Section 9.513; or

(2) the 21st day after the security interest attaches to the proceeds.

B&CC §9.316. EFFECT OF CHANGE IN GOVERNING LAW

(a) A security interest perfected pursuant to the law of the jurisdiction designated in Section 9.301(1) or 9.305(c) remains perfected until the earliest of:

(1) the time perfection would have ceased under the law of that jurisdiction;

(2) the expiration of four months after a change of the debtor's location to another jurisdiction; or

(3) the expiration of one year after a transfer of collateral to a person that thereby becomes a debtor and is located in another jurisdiction.

(b) If a security interest described in Subsection (a) becomes perfected under the law of the other jurisdiction before the earliest time or event described in that subsection, it remains perfected thereafter. If the security interest does not become perfected under the law of the other jurisdiction before the earliest time or event, it becomes unperfected and is deemed never to have been perfected as against a purchaser of the collateral for value.

(c) A possessory security interest in collateral, other than goods covered by a certificate of title and as-extracted collateral consisting of goods, remains continuously perfected if:

(1) the collateral is located in one jurisdiction and subject to a security interest perfected under the law of that jurisdiction;

(2) thereafter the collateral is brought into another jurisdiction; and

(3) upon entry into the other jurisdiction, the security interest is perfected under the law of the other jurisdiction.

(d) Except as otherwise provided in Subsection (e), a security interest in goods covered by a certificate of title that is perfected by any method under the law of another jurisdiction when the goods become covered by a certificate of title from this state remains perfected until the security interest would have become unperfected under the law of the other jurisdiction had the goods not become so covered.

(e) A security interest described in Subsection (d) becomes unperfected as against a purchaser of the goods for value and is deemed never to have been perfected as against a purchaser of the goods for value if the applicable requirements for perfection under Section 9.311(b) or 9.313 are not satisfied before the earlier of:

(1) the time the security interest would have become unperfected under the law of the other jurisdiction had the goods not become covered by a certificate of title from this State; or

(2) the expiration of four months after the goods had become so covered.

(f) A security interest in deposit accounts, letter-of-credit rights, or investment property that is perfected under the law of the bank's jurisdiction, the issuer's jurisdiction, a nominated person's jurisdiction, the securities intermediary's jurisdiction, or the commodity intermediary's jurisdiction, as applicable, remains perfected until the earlier of:

(1) the time the security interest would have become unperfected under the law of that jurisdiction; or

(2) the expiration of four months after a change of the applicable jurisdiction to another jurisdiction.

(g) If a security interest described in Subsection (f) becomes perfected under the law of the other jurisdiction before the earlier of the time or the end of the period described in that subsection, it remains perfected thereafter. If the security interest does not become perfected under the law of the other jurisdiction before the earlier of that time or the end of that period, it becomes unperfected and is deemed never to have been perfected as against a purchaser of the collateral for value.

(h) The following rules apply to collateral to which a security interest attaches within four months after the debtor changes its location to another jurisdiction:

(1) A financing statement filed before the change of the debtor's location pursuant to the law of the jurisdiction designated in Section 9.301(1) or 9.305(c) is effective to perfect a security interest in the collateral if the financing statement would have been effective to perfect a security interest in the collateral if the debtor had not changed its location.

(2) If a security interest that is perfected by a financing statement that is effective under Subdivision (1) becomes perfected under the law of the other jurisdiction before the earlier of the time the financing statement would have become ineffective under the law of the jurisdiction designated in Section 9.301(1) or 9.305(c) or the expiration of the four-month period, it remains perfected thereafter. If the security interest does not become perfected under the law of the other jurisdiction before the earlier time or event, it becomes unperfected and is deemed never to have been perfected as against a purchaser of the collateral for value.

(i) If a financing statement naming an original debtor is filed pursuant to the law of the jurisdiction designated in Section 9.301(1) or 9.305(c) and the new debtor is located in another jurisdiction, the following rules apply:

(1) The financing statement is effective to perfect a security interest in collateral in which the new debtor has or acquires rights before or within four months after the new debtor becomes bound under Section 9.203(d), if the financing statement would have been effective to perfect a security interest in the collateral if the collateral had been acquired by the original debtor.

(2) A security interest that is perfected by the financing statement and that becomes perfected under the law of the other jurisdiction before the earlier of the expiration of the four-month period or the time the financing statement would have become ineffective under the law of the jurisdiction designated in Section 9.301(1) or 9.305(c) remains perfected thereafter. A security interest that is perfected by the financing statement but that does not become perfected under the law of the other jurisdiction before the earlier time or event becomes unperfected and is deemed never to have been perfected as against a purchaser of the collateral for value.

B&CC §9.317. INTERESTS THAT TAKE PRIORITY OVER OR TAKE FREE OF SECURITY INTEREST OR AGRICULTURAL LIEN

(a) A security interest or agricultural lien is subordinate to the rights of:

(1) a person entitled to priority under Section 9.322; and

(2) except as otherwise provided in Subsection (e), a person that becomes a lien creditor before the earlier of the time:

(A) the security interest or agricultural lien is perfected; or

(B) one of the conditions specified in Section 9.203(b)(3) is met and a financing statement covering the collateral is filed.

(b) Except as otherwise provided in Subsection (e), a buyer, other than a secured party, of tangible chattel paper, tangible documents, goods, instruments, or a certificated security takes free of a security interest or agricultural lien if the buyer gives value and receives delivery of the collateral without knowledge of the security interest or agricultural lien and before it is perfected.

(c) Except as otherwise provided in Subsection (e), a lessee of goods takes free of a security interest or agricultural lien if the lessee gives value and receives delivery of the collateral without knowledge of the security interest or agricultural lien and before it is perfected.

(d) A licensee of a general intangible or a buyer, other than a secured party, of collateral other than tangible chattel paper, tangible documents, goods, instruments, or a certificated security takes free of a security

interest if the licensee or buyer gives value without knowledge of the security interest and before it is perfected.

(e) Except as otherwise provided in Sections 9.320 and 9.321, if a person files a financing statement with respect to a purchase-money security interest before or within 20 days after the debtor receives delivery of the collateral, the security interest takes priority over the rights of a buyer, lessee, or lien creditor that arise between the time the security interest attaches and the time of filing.

B&CC §9.318. No Interest Retained in Right to Payment That Is Sold; Rights & Title of Seller of Account or Chattel Paper with Respect to Creditors & Purchasers

(a) A debtor that has sold an account, chattel paper, payment intangible, or promissory note does not retain a legal or equitable interest in the collateral sold.

(b) For purposes of determining the rights of creditors of, and purchasers for value of an account or chattel paper from, a debtor that has sold an account or chattel paper, while the buyer's security interest is unperfected, the debtor is deemed to have rights and title to the account or chattel paper identical to those the debtor sold.

B&CC §9.319. Rights & Title of Consignee with Respect to Creditors & Purchasers

(a) Except as otherwise provided in Subsection (b), for purposes of determining the rights of creditors of, and purchasers for value of goods from, a consignee, while the goods are in the possession of the consignee, the consignee is deemed to have rights and title to the goods identical to those the consignor had or had power to transfer.

(b) For purposes of determining the rights of a creditor of a consignee, law other than this chapter determines the rights and title of a consignee while goods are in the consignee's possession if, under this subchapter, a perfected security interest held by the consignor would have priority over the rights of the creditor.

B&CC §9.320. Buyers of Goods

(a) Except as otherwise provided by Subsection (e), a buyer in ordinary course of business, other than a person buying farm products from a person engaged in farming operations, takes free of a security interest created by the buyer's seller, even if the security interest is perfected and the buyer knows of its existence.

(b) Except as otherwise provided in Subsection (e), a buyer of goods from a person who used or bought the goods for use primarily for personal, family, or household purposes takes free of a security interest, even if perfected, if the buyer buys:

(1) without knowledge of the security interest;

(2) for value;

(3) primarily for the buyer's personal, family, or household purposes; and

(4) before the filing of a financing statement covering the goods.

(c) To the extent that it affects the priority of a security interest over a buyer of goods under Subsection (b), the period of effectiveness of a filing made in the jurisdiction in which the seller is located is governed by Sections 9.316(a) and (b).

(d) A buyer in ordinary course of business buying oil, gas, or other minerals at the wellhead or minehead or after extraction takes free of an interest arising out of an encumbrance.

(e) Subsections (a) and (b) do not affect a security interest in goods in the possession of the secured party under Section 9.313.

B&CC §9.321. Licensee of General Intangible & Lessee of Goods in Ordinary Course of Business

(a) In this section, "licensee in ordinary course of business" means a person that becomes a licensee of a general intangible in good faith, without knowledge that the license violates the rights of another person in the general intangible, and in the ordinary course from a person in the business of licensing general intangibles of that kind. A person becomes a licensee in the ordinary course if the license to the person comports with the usual or customary practices in the kind of business in which the licensor is engaged or with the licensor's own usual or customary practices.

(b) A licensee in ordinary course of business takes its rights under a nonexclusive license free of a security interest in the general intangible created by the licensor, even if the security interest is perfected and the licensee knows of its existence.

(c) A lessee in ordinary course of business takes its leasehold interest free of a security interest in the

goods created by the lessor, even if the security interest is perfected and the lessee knows of its existence.

B&CC §9.322. PRIORITIES AMONG CONFLICTING SECURITY INTERESTS IN & AGRICULTURAL LIENS ON SAME COLLATERAL

(a) Except as otherwise provided in this section, priority among conflicting security interests and agricultural liens in the same collateral is determined according to the following rules:

(1) Conflicting perfected security interests and agricultural liens rank according to priority in time of filing or perfection. Priority dates from the earlier of the time a filing covering the collateral is first made or the security interest or agricultural lien is first perfected, if there is no period thereafter when there is neither filing nor perfection.

(2) A perfected security interest or agricultural lien has priority over a conflicting unperfected security interest or agricultural lien.

(3) The first security interest or agricultural lien to attach or become effective has priority if conflicting security interests and agricultural liens are unperfected.

(b) For the purposes of Subsection (a)(1):

(1) the time of filing or perfection as to a security interest in collateral is also the time of filing or perfection as to a security interest in proceeds; and

(2) the time of filing or perfection as to a security interest in collateral supported by a supporting obligation is also the time of filing or perfection as to a security interest in the supporting obligation.

(c) Except as otherwise provided in Subsection (f), a security interest in collateral that qualifies for priority over a conflicting security interest under Section 9.327, 9.328, 9.329, 9.330, or 9.331 also has priority over a conflicting security interest in:

(1) any supporting obligation for the collateral; and

(2) proceeds of the collateral if:

(A) the security interest in proceeds is perfected;

(B) the proceeds are cash proceeds or of the same type as the collateral; and

(C) in the case of proceeds that are proceeds of proceeds, all intervening proceeds are cash proceeds, proceeds of the same type as the collateral, or an account relating to the collateral.

(d) Subject to Subsection (e) and except as otherwise provided in Subsection (f), if a security interest in chattel paper, deposit accounts, negotiable documents, instruments, investment property, or letter-of-credit rights is perfected by a method other than filing, conflicting perfected security interests in proceeds of the collateral rank according to priority in time of filing.

(e) Subsection (d) applies only if the proceeds of the collateral are not cash proceeds, chattel paper, negotiable documents, instruments, investment property, or letter-of-credit rights.

(f) Subsections (a)-(e) are subject to:

(1) Subsection (g) and the other provisions of this subchapter;

(2) Section 4.210 with respect to a security interest of a collecting bank;

(3) Section 5.118 with respect to a security interest of an issuer or nominated person; and

(4) Section 9.110 with respect to a security interest arising under Chapter 2 or 2A.

(g) A perfected agricultural lien on collateral has priority over a conflicting security interest in or agricultural lien on the same collateral if the statute creating the agricultural lien so provides.

B&CC §9.323. FUTURE ADVANCES

(a) Except as otherwise provided in Subsection (c), for purposes of determining the priority of a perfected security interest under Section 9.322(a)(1), perfection of the security interest dates from the time an advance is made to the extent that the security interest secures an advance that:

(1) is made while the security interest is perfected only:

(A) under Section 9.309 when it attaches; or

(B) temporarily under Section 9.312(e), (f), or (g); and

(2) is not made pursuant to a commitment entered into before or while the security interest is perfected by a method other than under Section 9.309 or 9.312(e), (f), or (g).

(b) Except as otherwise provided in Subsection (c), a security interest is subordinate to the rights of a person that becomes a lien creditor to the extent that the security interest secures an advance made more than 45 days after the person becomes a lien creditor unless the advance is made:

(1) without knowledge of the lien; or

(2) pursuant to a commitment entered into without knowledge of the lien.

(c) Subsections (a) and (b) do not apply to a security interest held by a secured party that is a buyer of accounts, chattel paper, payment intangibles, or promissory notes or a consignor.

(d) Except as otherwise provided in Subsection (e), a buyer of goods other than a buyer in ordinary course of business takes free of a security interest to the extent that it secures advances made after the earlier of:

(1) the time the secured party acquires knowledge of the buyer's purchase; or

(2) 45 days after the purchase.

(e) Subsection (d) does not apply if the advance is made pursuant to a commitment entered into without knowledge of the buyer's purchase and before the expiration of the 45-day period.

(f) Except as otherwise provided in Subsection (g), a lessee of goods, other than a lessee in ordinary course of business, takes the leasehold interest free of a security interest to the extent that it secures advances made after the earlier of:

(1) the time the secured party acquires knowledge of the lease; or

(2) 45 days after the lease contract becomes enforceable.

(g) Subsection (f) does not apply if the advance is made pursuant to a commitment entered into without knowledge of the lease and before the expiration of the 45-day period.

B&CC §9.324. PRIORITY OF PURCHASE-MONEY SECURITY INTERESTS

(a) Except as otherwise provided in Subsection (g), a perfected purchase-money security interest in goods other than inventory or livestock has priority over a conflicting security interest in the same goods, and, except as otherwise provided in Section 9.327, a perfected security interest in its identifiable proceeds also has priority, if the purchase-money security interest is perfected when the debtor receives possession of the collateral or within 20 days thereafter.

(b) Subject to Subsection (c) and except as otherwise provided in Subsection (g), a perfected purchase-money security interest in inventory has priority over a conflicting security interest in the same inventory, has priority over a conflicting security interest in chattel paper or an instrument constituting proceeds of the inventory and in proceeds of the chattel paper, if so provided in Section 9.330, and, except as otherwise provided in Section 9.327, also has priority in identifiable cash proceeds of the inventory to the extent the identifiable cash proceeds are received on or before the delivery of the inventory to a buyer, if:

(1) the purchase-money security interest is perfected when the debtor receives possession of the inventory;

(2) except where excused by Section 9.343 (oil and gas production), the purchase-money secured party sends an authenticated notification to the holder of the conflicting security interest;

(3) the holder of the conflicting security interest receives any required notification within five years before the debtor receives possession of the inventory; and

(4) the notification states that the person sending the notification has or expects to acquire a purchase-money security interest in inventory of the debtor and describes the inventory.

(c) Subsections (b)(2)-(4) apply only if the holder of the conflicting security interest had filed a financing statement covering the same types of inventory:

(1) if the purchase-money security interest is perfected by filing, before the date of the filing; or

(2) if the purchase-money security interest is temporarily perfected without filing or possession under Section 9.312(f), before the beginning of the 20-day period under that subsection.

(d) Subject to Subsection (e) and except as otherwise provided in Subsection (g), a perfected purchase-money security interest in livestock that are farm products has priority over a conflicting security interest in the same livestock, and, except as otherwise provided in Section 9.327, a perfected security interest in their identifiable proceeds and identifiable products in their unmanufactured states also has priority, if:

(1) the purchase-money security interest is perfected when the debtor receives possession of the livestock;

(2) the purchase-money secured party sends an authenticated notification to the holder of the conflicting security interest;

(3) the holder of the conflicting security interest receives the notification within six months before the debtor receives possession of the livestock; and

(4) the notification states that the person sending the notification has or expects to acquire a purchase-

money security interest in livestock of the debtor and describes the livestock.

(e) Subsections (d)(2)-(4) apply only if the holder of the conflicting security interest had filed a financing statement covering the same types of livestock:

(1) if the purchase-money security interest is perfected by filing, before the date of the filing; or

(2) if the purchase-money security interest is temporarily perfected without filing or possession under Section 9.312(f), before the beginning of the 20-day period under that subsection.

(f) Except as otherwise provided in Subsection (g), a perfected purchase-money security interest in software has priority over a conflicting security interest in the same collateral, and, except as otherwise provided in Section 9.327, a perfected security interest in its identifiable proceeds also has priority, to the extent that the purchase-money security interest in the goods in which the software was acquired for use has priority in the goods and proceeds of the goods under this section.

(g) If more than one security interest qualifies for priority in the same collateral under Subsection (a), (b), (d), or (f):

(1) a security interest securing an obligation incurred as all or part of the price of the collateral has priority over a security interest securing an obligation incurred for value given to enable the debtor to acquire rights in or the use of collateral; and

(2) in all other cases, Section 9.322(a) applies to the qualifying security interests.

B&CC §9.325. PRIORITY OF SECURITY INTERESTS IN TRANSFERRED COLLATERAL

(a) Except as otherwise provided in Subsection (b), a security interest created by a debtor is subordinate to a security interest in the same collateral created by another person if:

(1) the debtor acquired the collateral subject to the security interest created by the other person;

(2) the security interest created by the other person was perfected when the debtor acquired the collateral; and

(3) there is no period thereafter when the security interest is unperfected.

(b) Subsection (a) subordinates a security interest only if the security interest:

(1) otherwise would have priority solely under Section 9.322(a) or 9.324; or

(2) arose solely under Section 2.711(c) or 2A.508(e).

B&CC §9.326. PRIORITY OF SECURITY INTERESTS CREATED BY NEW DEBTOR

(a) Subject to Subsection (b), a security interest that is created by a new debtor in collateral in which the new debtor has or acquires rights and perfected by a filed financing statement that would be ineffective to perfect the security interest but for the application of Section 9.508 or of Sections 9.508 and 9.316(i)(1) is subordinate to a security interest in the same collateral that is perfected other than by such a filed financing statement.

(b) The other provisions of this subchapter determine the priority among conflicting security interests in the same collateral perfected by filed financing statements described in Subsection (a). However, if the security agreements to which a new debtor became bound as debtor were not entered into by the same original debtor, the conflicting security interests rank according to priority in time of the new debtor's having become bound.

B&CC §9.327. PRIORITY OF SECURITY INTERESTS IN DEPOSIT ACCOUNT

The following rules govern priority among conflicting security interests in the same deposit account:

(1) A security interest held by a secured party having control of the deposit account under Section 9.104 has priority over a conflicting security interest held by a secured party that does not have control.

(2) Except as otherwise provided in Subdivisions (3) and (4), security interests perfected by control under Section 9.314 rank according to priority in time of obtaining control.

(3) Except as otherwise provided in Subdivision (4), a security interest held by the bank with which the deposit account is maintained has priority over a conflicting security interest held by another secured party.

(4) A security interest perfected by control under Section 9.104(a)(3) has priority over a security interest held by the bank with which the deposit account is maintained.

B&CC §9.328. PRIORITY OF SECURITY INTERESTS IN INVESTMENT PROPERTY

The following rules govern priority among conflicting security interests in the same investment property:

(1) A security interest held by a secured party having control of investment property under Section 9.106 has priority over a security interest held by a secured party that does not have control of the investment property.

(2) Except as otherwise provided in Subdivisions (3) and (4), conflicting security interests held by secured parties each of which has control under Section 9.106 rank according to priority in time of:

(A) if the collateral is a security, obtaining control;

(B) if the collateral is a security entitlement carried in a securities account and:

(i) if the secured party obtained control under Section 8.106(d)(1), the secured party's becoming the person for which the securities account is maintained;

(ii) if the secured party obtained control under Section 8.106(d)(2), the securities intermediary's agreement to comply with the secured party's entitlement orders with respect to security entitlements carried or to be carried in the securities account; or

(iii) if the secured party obtained control through another person under Section 8.106(d)(3), the time on which priority would be based under this subdivision if the other person were the secured party; or

(C) if the collateral is a commodity contract carried with a commodity intermediary, the satisfaction of the requirement for control specified in Section 9.106(b)(2) with respect to commodity contracts carried or to be carried with the commodity intermediary.

(3) A security interest held by a securities intermediary in a security entitlement or a securities account maintained with the securities intermediary has priority over a conflicting security interest held by another secured party.

(4) A security interest held by a commodity intermediary in a commodity contract or a commodity account maintained with the commodity intermediary has priority over a conflicting security interest held by another secured party.

(5) A security interest in a certificated security in registered form that is perfected by taking delivery under Section 9.313(a) and not by control under Section 9.314 has priority over a conflicting security interest perfected by a method other than control.

(6) Conflicting security interests created by a broker, securities intermediary, or commodity intermediary that are perfected without control under Section 9.106 rank equally.

(7) In all other cases, priority among conflicting security interests in investment property is governed by Sections 9.322 and 9.323.

B&CC §9.329. PRIORITY OF SECURITY INTERESTS IN LETTER-OF-CREDIT RIGHT

The following rules govern priority among conflicting security interests in the same letter-of-credit right:

(1) A security interest held by a secured party having control of the letter-of-credit right under Section 9.107 has priority to the extent of its control over a conflicting security interest held by a secured party that does not have control.

(2) Security interests perfected by control under Section 9.314 rank according to priority in time of obtaining control.

B&CC §9.330. PRIORITY OF PURCHASER OF CHATTEL PAPER OR INSTRUMENT

(a) A purchaser of chattel paper has priority over a security interest in the chattel paper that is claimed merely as proceeds of inventory subject to a security interest if:

(1) in good faith and in the ordinary course of the purchaser's business, the purchaser gives new value and takes possession of the chattel paper or obtains control of the chattel paper under Section 9.105; and

(2) the chattel paper does not indicate that it has been assigned to an identified assignee other than the purchaser.

(b) A purchaser of chattel paper has priority over a security interest in the chattel paper that is claimed other than merely as proceeds of inventory subject to a security interest if the purchaser gives new value and takes possession of the chattel paper or obtains control of the chattel paper under Section 9.105 in good faith, in the ordinary course of the purchaser's business, and without knowledge that the purchase violates the rights of the secured party.

(c) Except as otherwise provided in Section 9.327, a purchaser having priority in chattel paper under Sub-

section (a) or (b) also has priority in proceeds of the chattel paper to the extent that:

(1) Section 9.322 provides for priority in the proceeds; or

(2) the proceeds consist of the specific goods covered by the chattel paper or cash proceeds of the specific goods, even if the purchaser's security interest in the proceeds is unperfected.

(d) Except as otherwise provided in Section 9.331(a), a purchaser of an instrument has priority over a security interest in the instrument perfected by a method other than possession if the purchaser gives value and takes possession of the instrument in good faith and without knowledge that the purchase violates the rights of the secured party.

(e) For purposes of Subsections (a) and (b), the holder of a purchase-money security interest in inventory gives new value for chattel paper constituting proceeds of the inventory.

(f) For purposes of Subsections (b) and (d), if chattel paper or an instrument indicates that it has been assigned to an identified secured party other than the purchaser, a purchaser of the chattel paper or instrument has knowledge that the purchase violates the rights of the secured party.

B&CC §9.331. PRIORITY OF RIGHTS OF PURCHASERS OF INSTRUMENTS, DOCUMENTS, & SECURITIES UNDER OTHER CHAPTERS; PRIORITY OF INTERESTS IN FINANCIAL ASSETS & SECURITY ENTITLEMENTS UNDER CHAPTER 8

(a) This chapter does not limit the rights of a holder in due course of a negotiable instrument, a holder to which a negotiable document of title has been duly negotiated, or a protected purchaser of a security. These holders or purchasers take priority over an earlier security interest, even if perfected, to the extent provided in Chapters 3, 7, and 8.

(b) This chapter does not limit the rights of or impose liability on a person to the extent that the person is protected against the assertion of a claim under Chapter 8.

(c) Filing under this chapter does not constitute notice of a claim or defense to the holders, or purchasers, or persons described in Subsections (a) and (b).

B&CC §9.332. TRANSFER OF MONEY; TRANSFER OF FUNDS FROM DEPOSIT ACCOUNT

(a) A transferee of money takes the money free of a security interest unless the transferee acts in collusion with the debtor in violating the rights of the secured party.

(b) A transferee of funds from a deposit account takes the funds free of a security interest in the deposit account unless the transferee acts in collusion with the debtor in violating the rights of the secured party.

B&CC §9.333. PRIORITY OF CERTAIN LIENS ARISING BY OPERATION OF LAW

(a) In this section, "possessory lien" means an interest, other than a security interest or an agricultural lien:

(1) that secures payment or performance of an obligation for services or materials furnished with respect to goods by a person in the ordinary course of the person's business;

(2) that is created by statute or rule of law in favor of the person; and

(3) whose effectiveness depends on the person's possession of the goods.

(b) A possessory lien on goods has priority over a security interest in the goods unless the lien is created by a statute that expressly provides otherwise.

B&CC §9.334. PRIORITY OF SECURITY INTERESTS IN FIXTURES & CROPS

(a) A security interest under this chapter may be created in goods that are fixtures or may continue in goods that become fixtures. A security interest does not exist under this chapter in ordinary building materials incorporated into an improvement on land.

(b) This chapter does not prevent creation of an encumbrance upon fixtures under real property law.

(c) In cases not governed by Subsections (d)-(h), a security interest in fixtures is subordinate to a conflicting interest of an encumbrancer or owner of the related real property other than the debtor.

(d) Except as otherwise provided in Subsection (h), a perfected security interest in fixtures has priority over the conflicting interest of an encumbrancer or owner of the real property if the debtor has an interest of record in or is in possession of the real property and:

(1) the security interest is a purchase-money security interest;

(2) the interest of the encumbrancer or owner arises before the goods become fixtures; and

(3) the security interest is perfected by a fixture filing before the goods become fixtures or within 20 days thereafter.

(e) A perfected security interest in fixtures has priority over a conflicting interest of an encumbrancer or owner of the real property if:

(1) the debtor has an interest of record in the real property or is in possession of the real property and the security interest:

(A) is perfected by a fixture filing before the interest of the encumbrancer or owner is of record; and

(B) has priority over any conflicting interest of a predecessor in title of the encumbrancer or owner;

(2) before the goods become fixtures, the security interest is perfected by any method permitted by this chapter and the fixtures are readily removable:

(A) factory or office machines;

(B) equipment that is not primarily used or leased for use in the operation of the real property; or

(C) replacements of domestic appliances that are consumer goods;

(3) the conflicting interest is a lien on the real property obtained by legal or equitable proceedings after the security interest was perfected by any method permitted by this chapter; or

(4) the security interest is:

(A) created in a manufactured home in a manufactured-home transaction; and

(B) perfected pursuant to a statute described in Section 9.311(a)(2).

(f) A security interest in fixtures, whether or not perfected, has priority over the conflicting interest of an encumbrancer or owner of the real property if:

(1) the encumbrancer or owner has, in an authenticated record, consented to the security interest or disclaimed an interest in the goods as fixtures; or

(2) the debtor has a right to remove the goods as against the encumbrancer or owner.

(g) The priority of the security interest under Subsection (f)(2) continues for a reasonable time if the debtor's right to remove the goods as against the encumbrancer or owner terminates.

(h) A mortgage is a construction mortgage to the extent that it secures an obligation incurred for the construction of an improvement on land, including the acquisition cost of the land, if a recorded record of the mortgage so indicates. Except as otherwise provided in Subsections (e) and (f), a security interest in fixtures is subordinate to a construction mortgage if a record of the mortgage is recorded before the goods become fixtures before the completion of the construction. A mortgage has this priority to the same extent as a construction mortgage to the extent that it is given to refinance a construction mortgage.

(i) A perfected security interest in crops growing on real property has priority over a conflicting interest of an encumbrancer or owner of the real property if the debtor has an interest of record in or is in possession of the real property.

B&CC §9.335. ACCESSIONS

(a) A security interest may be created in an accession and continues in collateral that becomes an accession.

(b) If a security interest is perfected when the collateral becomes an accession, the security interest remains perfected in the collateral.

(c) Except as otherwise provided in Subsection (d), the other provisions of this subchapter determine the priority of a security interest in an accession.

(d) A security interest in an accession is subordinate to a security interest in the whole that is perfected by compliance with the requirements of a certificate-of-title statute under Section 9.311(b).

(e) After default, subject to Subchapter F, a secured party may remove an accession from other goods if the security interest in the accession has priority over the claims of every person having an interest in the whole.

(f) A secured party that removes an accession from other goods under Subsection (e) shall promptly reimburse any holder of a security interest or other lien on, or owner of, the whole or the other goods, other than the debtor, for the cost of repair of any physical injury to the whole or the other goods. The secured party need not reimburse the holder or owner for any diminution in value of the whole or the other goods caused by the absence of the accession removed or by any necessity for replacing it. A person entitled to reimbursement may refuse permission to remove until the secured party gives adequate assurance for the performance of the obligation to reimburse.

B&CC §9.336. COMMINGLED GOODS

(a) In this section, "commingled goods" means goods that are physically united with other goods in such a manner that their identity is lost in a product or mass.

(b) A security interest does not exist in commingled goods as such. However, a security interest may attach to a product or mass that results when goods become commingled goods.

(c) If collateral becomes commingled goods, a security interest attaches to the product or mass.

(d) If a security interest in collateral is perfected before the collateral becomes commingled goods, the security interest that attaches to the product or mass under Subsection (c) is perfected.

(e) Except as otherwise provided in Subsection (f), the other provisions of this subchapter determine the priority of a security interest that attaches to the product or mass under Subsection (c).

(f) If more than one security interest attaches to the product or mass under Subsection (c), the following rules determine priority:

(1) A security interest that is perfected under Subsection (d) has priority over a security interest that is unperfected at the time the collateral becomes commingled goods.

(2) If more than one security interest is perfected under Subsection (d), the security interests rank equally in proportion to the value of the collateral at the time it became commingled goods.

B&CC §9.337. PRIORITY OF SECURITY INTERESTS IN GOODS COVERED BY CERTIFICATE OF TITLE

If, while a security interest in goods is perfected by any method under the law of another jurisdiction, this state issues a certificate of title that does not show that the goods are subject to the security interest or contain a statement that they may be subject to security interests not shown on the certificate:

(1) a buyer of the goods, other than a person in the business of selling goods of that kind, takes free of the security interest if the buyer gives value and receives delivery of the goods after issuance of the certificate and without knowledge of the security interest; and

(2) the security interest is subordinate to a conflicting security interest in the goods that attaches, and is perfected under Section 9.311(b), after issuance of the certificate and without the conflicting secured party's knowledge of the security interest.

B&CC §9.338. PRIORITY OF SECURITY INTEREST OR AGRICULTURAL LIEN PERFECTED BY FILED FINANCING STATEMENT PROVIDING CERTAIN INCORRECT INFORMATION

If a security interest or agricultural lien is perfected by a filed financing statement providing information described in Section 9.516(b)(5) that is incorrect at the time the financing statement is filed:

(1) the security interest or agricultural lien is subordinate to a conflicting perfected security interest in the collateral to the extent that the holder of the conflicting security interest gives value in reasonable reliance upon the incorrect information; and

(2) a purchaser, other than a secured party, of the collateral takes free of the security interest or agricultural lien to the extent that, in reasonable reliance upon the incorrect information, the purchaser gives value and, in the case of tangible chattel paper, tangible documents, goods, instruments, or a security certificate, receives delivery of the collateral.

B&CC §9.339. PRIORITY SUBJECT TO SUBORDINATION

This chapter does not preclude subordination by agreement by a person entitled to priority.

B&CC §9.340. EFFECTIVENESS OF RIGHT OF RECOUPMENT OR SET-OFF AGAINST DEPOSIT ACCOUNT

(a) Except as otherwise provided in Subsection (c), a bank with which a deposit account is maintained may exercise any right of recoupment or set-off against a secured party that holds a security interest in the deposit account.

(b) Except as otherwise provided in Subsection (c), the application of this chapter to a security interest in a deposit account does not affect a right of recoupment or set-off of the secured party as to a deposit account maintained with the secured party.

(c) The exercise by a bank of a set-off against a deposit account is ineffective against a secured party that holds a security interest in the deposit account that is perfected by control under Section 9.104(a)(3), if the set-off is based on a claim against the debtor.

B&CC §9.341. BANK'S RIGHTS & DUTIES WITH RESPECT TO DEPOSIT ACCOUNT

Except as otherwise provided in Section 9.340(c), and unless the bank otherwise agrees in an authenticated record, a bank's rights and duties with respect to a deposit account maintained with the bank are not terminated, suspended, or modified by:

(1) the creation, attachment, or perfection of a security interest in the deposit account;

(2) the bank's knowledge of the security interest; or

(3) the bank's receipt of instructions from the secured party.

B&CC §9.342. BANK'S RIGHT TO REFUSE TO ENTER INTO OR DISCLOSE EXISTENCE OF CONTROL AGREEMENT

This chapter does not require a bank to enter into an agreement of the kind described in Section 9.104(a)(2), even if its customer so requests or directs. A bank that has entered into such an agreement is not required to confirm the existence of the agreement to another person unless requested to do so by its customer.

B&CC §9.343. OIL & GAS INTERESTS: SECURITY INTEREST PERFECTED WITHOUT FILING; STATUTORY LIEN

(a) This section provides a security interest in favor of interest owners, as secured parties, to secure the obligations of the first purchaser of oil and gas production, as debtor, to pay the purchase price. An authenticated record giving the interest owner a right under real property law operates as a security agreement created under this chapter. The act of the first purchaser in signing an agreement to purchase oil or gas production, in issuing a division order, or in making any other voluntary communication to the interest owner or any governmental agency recognizing the interest owner's right operates as an authentication of a security agreement in accordance with Section 9.203(b) for purposes of this chapter.

(b) The security interest provided by this section is perfected automatically without the filing of a financing statement. If the interest of the secured party is evidenced by a deed, mineral deed, reservation in either, oil or gas lease, assignment, or any other such record recorded in the real property records of a county clerk, that record is effective as a filed financing statement for purposes of this chapter, but no fee is required except a fee that is otherwise required by the county clerk, and there is no requirement of refiling every five years to maintain effectiveness of the filing.

(c) The security interest exists in oil and gas production, and also in the identifiable proceeds of that production owned by, received by, or due to the first purchaser:

(1) for an unlimited time if:

(A) the proceeds are oil or gas production, inventory of raw, refined, or manufactured oil or gas production, or rights to or products of any of those, although the sale of those proceeds by a first purchaser to a buyer in the ordinary course of business as provided in Subsection (e) cuts off the security interest in those proceeds;

(B) the proceeds are accounts, chattel paper, instruments, documents, or payment intangibles; or

(C) the proceeds are cash proceeds, as defined in Section 9.102; and

(2) for the length of time provided in Section 9.315 for all other proceeds.

(d) This section creates a lien that secures the payment of all taxes that are or should be withheld or paid by the first purchaser and a lien that secures the rights of any person who would be entitled to a security interest under Subsection (a) except for lack of any adoption of a security agreement by the first purchaser or a lack of possession or record required by Section 9.203 for the security interest to be enforceable.

(e) The security interests and liens created by this section have priority over any purchaser who is not a buyer in the ordinary course of the first purchaser's business, but are cut off by the sale to a buyer from the first purchaser who is in the ordinary course of the first purchaser's business under Section 9.320(a). But in either case, whether or not the buyer from the first purchaser is in ordinary course, a security interest will continue in the proceeds of the sale by the first purchaser as provided in Subsection (c).

(f) The security interests and all liens created by this section have the following priorities over other Chapter 9 security interests:

(1) A security interest created by this section is treated as a purchase-money security interest for purposes of determining its relative priority under Section 9.324 over other security interests not provided for by

this section. A holder of a security interest created under this section is not required to give the written notice every five years as provided in Section 9.324(b)(3) to have purchase-money priority over a security interest with a prior financing statement covering inventory.

(2) A statutory lien is subordinate to all other perfected Chapter 9 security interests and has priority over unperfected Chapter 9 security interests and the lien creditors, buyers, and transferees mentioned in Section 9.317.

(g) The security interests and liens created by this section have the following priorities among themselves:

(1) If a record effective as a filed financing statement under Subsection (b) exists, the security interests perfected by that record have priority over a security interest automatically perfected without filing under Subsection (b). If several security interests perfected by records exist, they have the same priority among themselves as established by real property law for interests in oil and gas in place. If real property law establishes no priority among them, they share priority pro rata.

(2) A security interest perfected automatically without filing under Subsection (b) has priority over a lien created under Subsection (d).

(3) A nontax lien under Subsection (d) has priority over a lien created under that subsection that secures the payment of taxes.

(h) The priorities for statutory liens mentioned in Section 9.333 do not apply to any security interest or statutory lien created by this section. But if a pipeline common carrier has a statutory or tariff lien that is effective and enforceable against a trustee in bankruptcy and not invalidated by the Federal Tax Lien Act, that lien has priority over the security interests and statutory liens created by this section.

(i) If oil or gas production in which there are security interests or statutory liens created by this section is commingled with inventory or other production, the rules of Section 9.336 apply.

(j) A security interest or statutory lien created by this section remains effective against the debtor and perfected against the debtor's creditors even if assigned, regardless of whether the assignment is perfected against the assignor's creditors. If a deed, mineral deed, assignment of oil and gas lease, or other such record evidencing the assignment is filed in the real property records of the county, it will have the same effect as filing an amended financing statement under Section 9.514.

(k) This section does not impair an operator's right to set-off or withhold funds from other interest owners as security for or in satisfaction of any debt or security interest. In case of a dispute between an operator and another interest owner, a good faith tender of funds by anyone to the person who the operator and other interest owner agree on, to a person who otherwise shows himself or herself to be the one entitled to the funds, or to a court of competent jurisdiction in the event of litigation or bankruptcy operates as a tender of the funds to both.

(*l*) A first purchaser who acts in good faith may terminate an interest owner's security interest or statutory lien under this section by paying, or by making and keeping open a tender of, the amount the first purchaser believes to be due to the interest owner:

(1) if the interest owner's rights are to oil or gas production or its proceeds, either to the operator alone, in which event the operator is considered the first purchaser, or to some combination of the interest owner and the operator, as the first purchaser chooses;

(2) whatever the nature of the production to which the interest owner has rights, to the person that the interest owner agreed to or acquiesced in; or

(3) to a court of competent jurisdiction in the event of litigation or bankruptcy.

(m) A person who buys from a first purchaser can ensure that the person buys free and clear of an interest owner's security interest or statutory lien under this section:

(1) by buying in the ordinary course of the first purchaser's business from the first purchaser under Section 9.320(a);

(2) by obtaining the interest owner's consent to the sale under Section 9.315(a)(1);

(3) by ensuring that the first purchaser has paid the interest owner or, provided that gas production is involved, or the interest owner has so agreed or acquiesced, by ensuring that the first purchaser has paid the interest owner's operator; or

(4) by ensuring that the person or the first purchaser or some other person has withheld funds sufficient to pay amounts in dispute and has maintained a tender of those funds to whoever shows himself or herself to be the person entitled.

(n) If a tender under Subsection (m)(4) that is valid thereafter fails, the security interest and liens governed by this section remain effective.

(o) In addition to the usual remedy of sequestration available to secured parties, and the remedies given in Subchapter F, the holders of security interests and liens created by this section have available to them, to the extent constitutionally permitted, the remedies of replevin, attachment, and garnishment to assist them in realizing upon their rights.

(p) The rights of any person claiming under a security interest or lien created by this section are governed by the other provisions of this chapter except to the extent that this section necessarily displaces those provisions. This section does not invalidate or otherwise affect the interests of any person in any real property before severance of any oil or gas production.

(q) The security interest created under Subsections (a) and (b) do not apply to proceeds of gas production that have been withheld, in cash or account form, by a purchaser under Section 201.204(c), Tax Code.

(r) In this section:

(1) "Oil and gas production" means any oil, natural gas, condensate of either, natural gas liquids, other gaseous, liquid, or dissolved hydrocarbons, sulfur, or helium, or other substance produced as a by-product or adjunct to their production, or any combination of these, which is severed, extracted, or produced from the ground, the seabed, or other submerged lands within the jurisdiction of this state. Any such substance, including recoverable or recovered natural gas liquids, that is transported to or in a natural gas pipeline or natural gas gathering system, or otherwise transported or sold for use as natural gas, or is transported or sold for the extraction of helium or natural gas liquids is "gas production." Any such substance that is transported or sold to persons and for purposes not included in the foregoing natural gas definition is "oil production."

(2) "Interest owner" means a person owning an entire or fractional interest of any kind or nature in oil or gas production at the time of severance, or a person who has an express, implied, or constructive right to receive a monetary payment determined by the value of oil or gas production or by the amount of production.

(3) "First purchaser" means the first person that purchases oil or gas production from an operator or interest owner after the production is severed, or an operator that receives production proceeds from a third-party purchaser who acts in good faith under a division order or other agreement authenticated by the operator under which the operator collects proceeds of production on behalf of other interest owners. To the extent the operator receives proceeds attributable to the interest of other interest owners from a third-party purchaser who acts in good faith under a division order or other agreement authenticated by such operator, the operator is considered to be the first purchaser of the production for all purposes under this section, notwithstanding the characterization of other persons as first purchasers under other laws or regulations. To the extent the operator has not received from the third-party purchaser proceeds attributable to the operator's interest and the interest of other interest owners, the operator is not considered the first purchaser for the purposes of this section and is entitled to all rights and benefits under this section. Nothing in this section impairs or affects any rights otherwise held by a royalty owner to take its share of oil in kind or receive payment directly from a third-party purchaser for the royalty owner's share of oil production with or without a previously made agreement.

(4) "Operator" means a person engaged in the business of severing oil or gas production from the ground, whether for the person alone, only for other persons, or for the person and others.

TITLE 2. COMPETITION & TRADE PRACTICES

CHAPTER 21. REGULATION OF CERTAIN RESIDENTIAL FORECLOSURE CONSULTING SERVICES

SUBCHAPTER A. GENERAL PROVISIONS

B&CC §21.001. DEFINITIONS

(a) In this chapter:

(1) "Foreclosure consultant" means a person who makes a solicitation, representation, or offer to a homeowner to perform for compensation, or who for compensation performs, a service that the person represents will do any of the following:

(A) prevent or postpone a foreclosure sale;

(B) obtain a forbearance from:

(i) a mortgagee;

(ii) a beneficiary of a deed of trust; or

(iii) another person who holds a lien secured by the residence in foreclosure;

(C) assist the homeowner:

(i) to cure the default giving rise to the foreclosure action; or

(ii) to exercise the right of reinstatement of the homeowner's obligation secured by the residence in foreclosure;

(D) obtain an extension of the period within which the homeowner may reinstate the homeowner's obligation secured by the residence in foreclosure;

(E) obtain a waiver of an acceleration clause contained in a promissory note or contract secured by a deed of trust or mortgage on a residence in foreclosure or contained in the deed of trust or mortgage;

(F) assist the homeowner to obtain a loan or advance of funds to prevent foreclosure;

(G) avoid or ameliorate the impairment of the homeowner's credit resulting from the recording of a notice of default or the conduct of a foreclosure sale;

(H) save the homeowner's residence from foreclosure; or

(I) assist the homeowner in obtaining excess proceeds from a foreclosure sale of the homeowner's residence.

(2) "Homeowner" means a person that holds record title to a residence in foreclosure at the time the foreclosure action has been commenced.

(3) "Mortgage servicer" has the meaning assigned by Section 51.0001, Property Code.

(4) "Residence in foreclosure" means residential real property consisting of not more than four single-family dwelling units, at least one of which is occupied as the property owner's principal place of residence, and against which a foreclosure action has been commenced.

(b) For purposes of Subsections (a)(2) and (4), a foreclosure action has been commenced if:

(1) notice of sale has been filed under Section 51.002(b), Property Code; or

(2) a judicial foreclosure action has been commenced.

B&CC §21.002. EXCEPTION FROM APPLICABILITY OF CHAPTER

(a) Except as provided by Subsection (b), this chapter does not apply to the following persons that perform foreclosure consulting services:

(1) an attorney admitted to practice in this state who performs those services in relation to the attorney's attorney-client relationship with a homeowner or the beneficiary of the lien being foreclosed;

(2) a person that holds or is owed an obligation secured by a lien on a residence in foreclosure if the person performs those services in connection with the obligation or lien;

(3) a mortgage servicer of an obligation secured by a lien on a residence in foreclosure if the servicer performs those services in connection with the obligation or lien;

(4) a person that regulates banks, trust companies, savings and loan associations, credit unions, or insurance companies under the laws of this state or the United States if the person performs those services as part of the person's normal business activities;

(5) an affiliate of a person described by Subdivision (4) if the affiliate performs those services as part of the affiliate's normal business activities;

(6) a judgment creditor of the homeowner of the residence in foreclosure, if:

(A) the legal action giving rise to the judgment was commenced before the notice of default required under Section 5.064, 5.066, or 51.002(d), Property Code; and

(B) the judgment is recorded in the real property records of the clerk of the county where the residence in foreclosure is located;

(7) a licensed title insurer, title insurance agent, or escrow officer authorized to transact business in this state if the person is performing those services in conjunction with title insurance or settlement services;

(8) a licensed real estate broker or real estate salesperson if the person is engaging in an activity for which the person is licensed;

(9) a person licensed or registered under Chapter 156, Finance Code, if the person is engaging in an activity for which the person is licensed or registered under that chapter;

(10) a person licensed or registered under Chapter 157, Finance Code, if the person is engaging in an activity for which the person is licensed or registered under that chapter;

(11) a nonprofit organization that provides solely counseling or advice to homeowners who have a residence in foreclosure or have defaulted on their home loans, unless the organization is an associate of the foreclosure consultant;

(12) a depository institution, as defined by Section 31.002, Finance Code, subject to regulation or supervision by a state or federal regulatory agency; or

(13) an affiliate or subsidiary of a depository institution described by Subdivision (12).

(b) This chapter applies to a person described by Subsection (a) if the person is providing foreclosure consulting services to a homeowner designed or intended to transfer title, directly or indirectly, to a residence in foreclosure to that person or the person's associate, unless the person is a mortgagee or mortgage servicer that negotiates with or accepts from the mortgagor a deed in lieu of foreclosure for the benefit of the mortgagee.

B&CC §21.003. CONFLICT WITH OTHER LAW

To the extent of a conflict between this chapter and Chapter 393, Finance Code, this chapter controls.

Sections 21.004-21.050 reserved for expansion

SUBCHAPTER B. CONTRACT FOR SERVICES

B&CC §21.051. FORM & TERMS OF CONTRACT

Each contract for the purchase of the services of a foreclosure consultant by a homeowner of a residence in foreclosure must be in writing, dated, and signed by each homeowner and the foreclosure consultant.

B&CC §21.052. REQUIRED DISCLOSURE

Before entering into a contract with a homeowner of a residence in foreclosure for the purchase of the services of a foreclosure consultant, the foreclosure consultant shall provide the homeowner written notice stating the following, in at least 14-point boldfaced type:

NOTICE REQUIRED BY TEXAS LAW

________ (Name) or an associate of ________ (Name) cannot ask you to sign or have you sign any document that transfers any interest in your home or property to ________ (Name) or ________ (Name's) associate.

________(Name) or ________ (Name's) associate cannot guarantee you that they will be able to refinance your home or arrange for you to keep your home.

You may, at any time, cancel or rescind this contract, without penalty of any kind.

If you want to cancel this contract, mail or deliver a signed and dated copy of this notice of cancellation or rescission, or any other written notice, indicating your intent to cancel or rescind to ________ (Name and address of foreclosure consultant) at ________ (Address of foreclosure consultant, including facsimile and electronic mail address).

As part of any cancellation or rescission, you (the homeowner) must repay any money spent on your behalf by ________ (Name of foreclosure consultant) prior to receipt of this notice and as a result of this agreement, within 60 days, along with interest calculated at the rate of eight percent per year.

Sections 21.053-21.100 reserved for expansion

SUBCHAPTER C. LIMITATIONS, PROHIBITIONS, & DUTIES REGARDING SERVICES

B&CC §21.101. RESTRICTIONS ON CHARGE OR RECEIPT OF CONSIDERATION

A foreclosure consultant may not:

(1) charge or receive compensation until the foreclosure consultant has fully performed each service the foreclosure consultant has contracted to perform or has represented the foreclosure consultant can or will perform unless the foreclosure consultant has obtained a surety bond or established and maintained a surety account for each location at which the foreclosure consultant conducts business in the manner that Subchapter E, Chapter 393, Finance Code, provides for credit services organizations; or

(2) receive any consideration from a third party in connection with foreclosure consulting services provided to the homeowner of a residence in foreclosure unless the consideration is fully disclosed in writing to the homeowner.

B&CC §21.102. PROHIBITED CONDUCT

A foreclosure consultant may not:

(1) take any power of attorney from a homeowner for any purpose other than to inspect documents;

(2) for purposes of securing payment of compensation, acquire an interest, directly or indirectly, in the real or personal property of the homeowner of a residence in foreclosure with whom the foreclosure consultant has contracted to perform services; or

(3) take an assignment of wages to secure payment of compensation.

B&CC §21.103. RETENTION OF RECORDS

(a) A foreclosure consultant shall keep each record and document, including the foreclosure consultant contract, related to foreclosure consulting services performed on behalf of a homeowner.

(b) A foreclosure consultant shall retain the records described by Subsection (a) until at least the third anniversary of the day the foreclosure consultant contract entered into by the consultant and the homeowner was terminated or concluded.

Sections 21.104-21.150 reserved for expansion

SUBCHAPTER D. ENFORCEMENT

B&CC §21.151. CRIMINAL PENALTY

(a) A person commits an offense if the person violates this chapter.

(b) An offense under this chapter is a Class C misdemeanor.

CHAPTER 21A. EXECUTION OF DEEDS IN CERTAIN TRANSACTIONS INVOLVING RESIDENTIAL REAL ESTATE

B&CC §21A.001. DEFINITION

In this chapter, "residential real estate" means real property on which a dwelling designed for occupancy for one to four families is constructed or intended to be constructed.

B&CC §21A.002. PROHIBITION OF EXECUTION OF DEEDS CONVEYING RESIDENTIAL REAL ESTATE IN CERTAIN TRANSACTIONS

(a) A seller of residential real estate or a person who makes an extension of credit and takes a security interest or mortgage against residential real estate may not, before or at the time of the conveyance of the residential real estate to the purchaser or the extension of credit to the borrower, request or require the purchaser or borrower to execute and deliver to the seller or person making the extension of credit a deed conveying the residential real estate to the seller or person making the extension of credit.

(b) A deed executed in violation of this section is voidable unless a subsequent purchaser of the residential real estate, for valuable consideration, obtains an interest in the property after the deed was recorded without notice of the violation, including notice provided by actual possession of the property by the grantor of the deed. The residential real estate continues to be subject to the security interest of a creditor who, without notice of the violation, granted an extension of credit to a borrower based on the deed executed in violation of this section.

(c) A purchaser or borrower must bring an action to void a deed executed in violation of this section not later than the fourth anniversary of the date the deed was recorded.

(d) A purchaser or borrower who is a prevailing party in an action to void a deed under this section may recover reasonable and necessary attorney's fees.

B&CC §21A.003. ACTION BY ATTORNEY GENERAL

(a) The attorney general may bring an action on behalf of the state:

(1) for injunctive relief to require compliance with this chapter;

(2) to recover a civil penalty of $500 for each violation of this chapter; or

(3) for both injunctive relief and to recover the civil penalty.

(b) The attorney general is entitled to recover reasonable expenses incurred in obtaining injunctive relief or a civil penalty, or both, under this section, including court costs and reasonable attorney's fees.

(c) The court may make such additional orders or judgments as are necessary to return to the purchaser a deed conveying residential real estate that the court finds was acquired by means of any violation of this chapter.

(d) In bringing or participating in an action under this chapter, the attorney general acts in the name of the state and does not establish an attorney-client relationship with another person, including a person to whom the attorney general requests that the court award relief.

(e) An action by the attorney general must be brought not later than the fourth anniversary of the date the deed was recorded.

E

CHAPTER 22. PUBLIC SALE OF RESIDENTIAL REAL PROPERTY UNDER POWER OF SALE

B&CC §22.001. DEFINITIONS

In this chapter:

(1) "Auction company" has the meaning assigned by Section 1802.001, Occupations Code.

B&CC §22.001

(2) "Residential real property" means:

(A) a single-family house;

(B) a duplex, triplex, or quadraplex; or

(C) a unit in a multiunit residential structure in which title to an individual unit is transferred to the owner of the unit under a condominium or cooperative system.

(3) "Security instrument," "substitute trustee," and "trustee" have the meanings assigned by Section 51.0001, Property Code.

2017 Legislation: Enacted by H.B. 1470, §1, 85th Leg., eff. Sept. 1, 2017.

B&CC §22.002. APPLICABILITY

This chapter applies only to a public sale of residential real property conducted under a power of sale in a security instrument.

2017 Legislation: Enacted by H.B. 1470, §1, 85th Leg., eff. Sept. 1, 2017.

B&CC §22.003. CONTRACTS CONCERNING SALE

A trustee or substitute trustee conducting a sale to which this chapter applies may contract with:

(1) an attorney to advise the trustee or substitute trustee or to administer or perform any of the trustee's or substitute trustee's functions or responsibilities under a security instrument or this chapter; or

(2) an auction company to arrange, manage, sponsor, or advertise a public sale.

2017 Legislation: Enacted by H.B. 1470, §1, 85th Leg., eff. Sept. 1, 2017.

B&CC §22.004. INFORMATION FROM WINNING BIDDER

(a) A winning bidder at a sale, other than the foreclosing mortgagee or mortgage servicer, shall provide the following information to the trustee or substitute trustee at the time the trustee or substitute trustee completes the sale:

(1) the name, address, telephone number, and e-mail address of the bidder and of each individual tendering or who will tender the sale price for the winning bid;

(2) if the bidder is acting on behalf of another individual or organization, the name, address, telephone number, and e-mail address of the individual or organization and the name of a contact person for the organization;

(3) the name and address of any person to be identified as the grantee in a trustee's or substitute trustee's deed;

(4) the purchaser's tax identification number;

(5) a government-issued photo identification to confirm the identity of each individual tendering funds for the winning bid; and

(6) any other information reasonably needed to complete the trustee's or substitute trustee's duties and functions concerning the sale.

(b) If a winning bidder required to provide information under Subsection (a) fails or refuses to provide the information, the trustee or substitute trustee may decline to complete the transaction or deliver a deed.

2017 Legislation: Enacted by H.B. 1470, §1, 85th Leg., eff. Sept. 1, 2017.

B&CC §22.005. RECEIPT & DEED

The trustee or substitute trustee shall:

(1) provide the winning bidder with a receipt for the sale proceeds tendered; and

(2) except when prohibited by law, within a reasonable time:

(A) deliver the deed to the winning bidder; or

(B) file the deed for recording.

2017 Legislation: Enacted by H.B. 1470, §1, 85th Leg., eff. Sept. 1, 2017.

B&CC §22.006. SALE PROCEEDS

(a) The trustee or substitute trustee shall ensure that funds received at the sale are maintained in a separate account until distributed. The trustee or substitute trustee shall cause to be maintained a written record of deposits to and disbursements from the account.

(b) The trustee or substitute trustee shall make reasonable attempts to identify and locate the persons entitled to all or any part of the sale proceeds.

(c) In connection with the sale and related post-sale actions to identify persons with legal claims to sale proceeds, determine the priority of any claims, and distribute proceeds to pay claims, a trustee or substitute trustee may receive:

(1) reasonable actual costs incurred, including costs for evidence of title;

(2) a reasonable trustee's or substitute trustee's fee; and

(3) reasonable trustee's or substitute trustee's attorney's fees.

(d) A fee described by Subsection (c):

(1) is considered earned at the time of the sale;

(2) may be paid from sale proceeds in excess of the payoff of the lien being foreclosed; and

(3) is conclusively presumed to be reasonable if the fee:

(A) is not more than the lesser of 2.5 percent of the sale proceeds or $5,000, for a trustee's or substitute trustee's fee; or

(B) is not more than 1.5 percent of the sale proceeds, for trustee's or substitute trustee's attorney's fees incurred to identify persons with legal claims to sale proceeds and determine the priority of the claims.

(e) A trustee or substitute trustee who prevails in a suit based on a claim that relates to the sale and that is found by a court to be groundless in fact or in law is entitled to recover reasonable attorney's fees necessary to defend against the claim, which may be paid from the excess sale proceeds, if any.

(f) Nothing in this section precludes the filing of an interpleader action or the depositing of funds in a court registry.

2017 Legislation: Enacted by H.B. 1470, §1, 85th Leg., eff. Sept. 1, 2017.

TITLE 3. INSOLVENCY, FRAUDULENT TRANSFERS, & FRAUD

CHAPTER 24. UNIFORM FRAUDULENT TRANSFER ACT

B&CC §24.001. SHORT TITLE

This chapter may be cited as the Uniform Fraudulent Transfer Act.

See also *O'Connor's Texas COA*, "Uniform Fraudulent Transfer Act (UFTA)," ch. 12-A, §7.9, p. 298.

B&CC §24.002. DEFINITIONS

In this chapter:

(1) "Affiliate" means:

(A) a person who directly or indirectly owns, controls, or holds with power to vote, 20 percent or more of the outstanding voting securities of the debtor, other than a person who holds the securities:

(i) as a fiduciary or agent without sole discretionary power to vote the securities; or

(ii) solely to secure a debt, if the person has not exercised the power to vote;

(B) a corporation 20 percent or more of whose outstanding voting securities are directly or indirectly owned, controlled, or held with power to vote, by the debtor or a person who directly or indirectly owns, controls, or holds, with power to vote, 20 percent or more of the outstanding voting securities of the debtor, other than a person who holds the securities:

(i) as a fiduciary or agent without sole power to vote the securities; or

(ii) solely to secure a debt, if the person has not in fact exercised the power to vote;

(C) a person whose business is operated by the debtor under a lease or other agreement, or a person substantially all of whose assets are controlled by the debtor; or

(D) a person who operates the debtor's business under a lease or other agreement or controls substantially all of the debtor's assets.

(2) "Asset" means property of a debtor, but the term does not include:

(A) property to the extent it is encumbered by a valid lien;

(B) property to the extent it is generally exempt under nonbankruptcy law; or

(C) an interest in property held in tenancy by the entireties to the extent it is not subject to process by a creditor holding a claim against only one tenant, under the law of another jurisdiction.

(3) "Claim" means a right to payment or property, whether or not the right is reduced to judgment, liquidated, unliquidated, fixed, contingent, matured, unmatured, disputed, undisputed, legal, equitable, secured, or unsecured.

(4) "Creditor" means a person, including a spouse, minor, person entitled to receive court or administratively ordered child support for the benefit of a child, or ward, who has a claim.

(5) "Debt" means a liability on a claim.

(6) "Debtor" means a person who is liable on a claim.

(7) "Insider" includes:

(A) if the debtor is an individual:

(i) a relative of the debtor or of a general partner of the debtor;

(ii) a partnership in which the debtor is a general partner;

(iii) a general partner in a partnership described in Subparagraph (ii) of this paragraph; or

(iv) a corporation of which the debtor is a director, officer, or person in control;

(B) if the debtor is a corporation:

(i) a director of the debtor;

(ii) an officer of the debtor;

(iii) a person in control of the debtor;

(iv) a partnership in which the debtor is a general partner;

(v) a general partner in a partnership described in Subparagraph (iv) of this paragraph; or

(vi) a relative of a general partner, director, officer, or person in control of the debtor;

(C) if the debtor is a partnership:

(i) a general partner in the debtor;

(ii) a relative of a general partner in, a general partner of, or a person in control of the debtor;

(iii) another partnership in which the debtor is a general partner;

(iv) a general partner in a partnership described in Subparagraph (iii) of this paragraph; or

(v) a person in control of the debtor;

(D) an affiliate, or an insider of an affiliate as if the affiliate were the debtor; and

(E) a managing agent of the debtor.

(8) "Lien" means a charge against or an interest in property to secure payment of a debt or performance of an obligation, and includes a security interest created by agreement, a judicial lien obtained by legal or equitable process or proceedings, a common-law lien, or a statutory lien.

(9) "Person" means an individual, partnership, corporation, association, organization, government or governmental subdivision or agency, business trust, estate, trust, or any other legal or commercial entity.

(10) "Property" means anything that may be the subject of ownership.

(11) "Relative" means an individual related by consanguinity within the third degree as determined by the common law, a spouse, or an individual related to a spouse within the third degree as so determined, and includes an individual in an adoptive relationship within the third degree.

(12) "Transfer" means every mode, direct or indirect, absolute or conditional, voluntary or involuntary, of disposing of or parting with an asset or an interest in an asset, and includes payment of money, release, lease, and creation of a lien or other encumbrance. The term does not include a transfer under a disclaimer filed under Chapter 240, Property Code.

(13) "Valid lien" means a lien that is effective against the holder of a judicial lien subsequently obtained by legal or equitable process or proceedings.

B&CC §24.003. INSOLVENCY

(a) A debtor is insolvent if the sum of the debtor's debts is greater than all of the debtor's assets at a fair valuation.

(b) A debtor who is generally not paying the debtor's debts as they become due is presumed to be insolvent.

(c) Repealed by Acts 2013, 83rd Leg., ch. 9, §11, eff. Sept. 1, 2013.

(d) Assets under this section do not include property that has been transferred, concealed, or removed with intent to hinder, delay, or defraud creditors or that has been transferred in a manner making the transfer voidable under this chapter.

(e) Debts under this section do not include an obligation to the extent it is secured by a valid lien on property of the debtor not included as an asset.

B&CC §24.004. VALUE

(a) Value is given for a transfer or an obligation if, in exchange for the transfer or obligation, property is transferred or an antecedent debt is secured or satisfied, but value does not include an unperformed promise made otherwise than in the ordinary course of the promisor's business to furnish support to the debtor or another person.

(b) For the purposes of Sections 24.005(a)(2) and 24.006 of this code, a person gives a reasonably equivalent value if the person acquires an interest of the debtor in an asset pursuant to a regularly conducted, noncollusive foreclosure sale or execution of a power of sale for the acquisition or disposition of the interest of the debtor upon default under a mortgage, deed of trust, or security agreement.

(c) A transfer is made for present value if the exchange between the debtor and the transferee is intended by them to be contemporaneous and is in fact substantially contemporaneous.

(d) "Reasonably equivalent value" includes without limitation, a transfer or obligation that is within the range of values for which the transferor would have sold the assets in an arm's length transaction.

B&CC §24.005. TRANSFERS FRAUDULENT AS TO PRESENT & FUTURE CREDITORS

(a) A transfer made or obligation incurred by a debtor is fraudulent as to a creditor, whether the creditor's claim arose before or within a reasonable time af-

ter the transfer was made or the obligation was incurred, if the debtor made the transfer or incurred the obligation:

(1) with actual intent to hinder, delay, or defraud any creditor of the debtor; or

(2) without receiving a reasonably equivalent value in exchange for the transfer or obligation, and the debtor:

(A) was engaged or was about to engage in a business or a transaction for which the remaining assets of the debtor were unreasonably small in relation to the business or transaction; or

(B) intended to incur, or believed or reasonably should have believed that the debtor would incur, debts beyond the debtor's ability to pay as they became due.

(b) In determining actual intent under Subsection (a)(1) of this section, consideration may be given, among other factors, to whether:

(1) the transfer or obligation was to an insider;

(2) the debtor retained possession or control of the property transferred after the transfer;

(3) the transfer or obligation was concealed;

(4) before the transfer was made or obligation was incurred, the debtor had been sued or threatened with suit;

(5) the transfer was of substantially all the debtor's assets;

(6) the debtor absconded;

(7) the debtor removed or concealed assets;

(8) the value of the consideration received by the debtor was reasonably equivalent to the value of the asset transferred or the amount of the obligation incurred;

(9) the debtor was insolvent or became insolvent shortly after the transfer was made or the obligation was incurred;

(10) the transfer occurred shortly before or shortly after a substantial debt was incurred; and

(11) the debtor transferred the essential assets of the business to a lienor who transferred the assets to an insider of the debtor.

See also *O'Connor's Texas COA*, "Proving actual fraud," ch. 38-F, §2.2.2, p. 1262; "Actions involving a fraudulent conveyance," ch. 52, §2.7.5, p. 1553.

B&CC §24.006. TRANSFERS FRAUDULENT AS TO PRESENT CREDITORS

(a) A transfer made or obligation incurred by a debtor is fraudulent as to a creditor whose claim arose before the transfer was made or the obligation was incurred if the debtor made the transfer or incurred the obligation without receiving a reasonably equivalent value in exchange for the transfer or obligation and the debtor was insolvent at that time or the debtor became insolvent as a result of the transfer or obligation.

(b) A transfer made by a debtor is fraudulent as to a creditor whose claim arose before the transfer was made if the transfer was made to an insider for an antecedent debt, the debtor was insolvent at that time, and the insider had reasonable cause to believe that the debtor was insolvent.

See also *O'Connor's Texas COA*, "Proving actual fraud," ch. 38-F, §2.2.2, p. 1262; "Actions involving a fraudulent conveyance," ch. 52, §2.7.5, p. 1553.

B&CC §24.007. WHEN TRANSFER IS MADE OR OBLIGATION IS INCURRED

For the purposes of this chapter:

(1) a transfer is made:

(A) with respect to an asset that is real property other than a fixture, but including the interest of a seller or purchaser under a contract for the sale of the asset, when the transfer is so far perfected that a good faith purchaser of the asset from the debtor against whom applicable law permits the transfer to be perfected cannot acquire an interest in the asset that is superior to the interest of the transferee; and

(B) with respect to an asset that is not real property or that is a fixture, when the transfer is so far perfected that a creditor on a simple contract cannot acquire a judicial lien otherwise than under this chapter that is superior to the interest of the transferee;

(2) if applicable law permits the transfer to be perfected as provided in Subdivision (1) of this section and the transfer is not so perfected before the commencement of an action for relief under this chapter, the transfer is deemed made immediately before the commencement of the action;

(3) if applicable law does not permit the transfer to be perfected as provided in Subdivision (1) of this section, the transfer is made when it becomes effective between the debtor and the transferee;

(4) a transfer is not made until the debtor has acquired rights in the asset transferred; and

(5) an obligation is incurred:

(A) if oral, when it becomes effective between the parties; or

(B) if evidenced by a writing, when the writing executed by the obligor is delivered to or for the benefit of the obligee.

B&CC §24.008. REMEDIES OF CREDITORS

(a) In an action for relief against a transfer or obligation under this chapter, a creditor, subject to the limitations in Section 24.009 of this code, may obtain:

(1) avoidance of the transfer or obligation to the extent necessary to satisfy the creditor's claim;

(2) an attachment or other provisional remedy against the asset transferred or other property of the transferee in accordance with the applicable Texas Rules of Civil Procedure and the Civil Practice and Remedies Code relating to ancillary proceedings; or

(3) subject to applicable principles of equity and in accordance with applicable rules of civil procedure:

(A) an injunction against further disposition by the debtor or a transferee, or both, of the asset transferred or of other property;

(B) appointment of a receiver to take charge of the asset transferred or of other property of the transferee; or

(C) any other relief the circumstances may require.

(b) If a creditor has obtained a judgment on a claim against the debtor, the creditor, if the court so orders, may levy execution on the asset transferred or its proceeds.

B&CC §24.009. DEFENSES, LIABILITY, & PROTECTION OF TRANSFEREE

(a) A transfer or obligation is not voidable under Section 24.005(a)(1) of this code against a person who took in good faith and for a reasonably equivalent value or against any subsequent transferee or obligee.

(b) Except as otherwise provided in this section, to the extent a transfer is voidable in an action by a creditor under Section 24.008(a)(1) of this code, the creditor may recover judgment for the value of the asset transferred, as adjusted under Subsection (c) of this section, or the amount necessary to satisfy the creditor's claim, whichever is less. The judgment may be entered against:

(1) the first transferee of the asset or the person for whose benefit the transfer was made; or

(2) any subsequent transferee other than a good faith transferee who took for value or from any subsequent transferee.

(c)(1) Except as provided by Subdivision (2) of this subsection, if the judgment under Subsection (b) of this section is based upon the value of the asset transferred, the judgment must be for an amount equal to the value of the asset at the time of the transfer, subject to adjustment as the equities may require.

(2) The value of the asset transferred is not to be adjusted to include the value of improvements made by a good faith transferee, including:

(A) physical additions or changes to the asset transferred;

(B) repairs to the asset;

(C) payment of any tax on the asset;

(D) payment of any debt secured by a lien on the asset that is superior or equal to the rights of a voiding creditor under this chapter; and

(E) preservation of the asset.

(d)(1) Notwithstanding voidability of a transfer or an obligation under this chapter, a good faith transferee or obligee is entitled, at the transferee's or obligee's election, to the extent of the value given the debtor for the transfer or obligation, to:

(A) a lien, prior to the rights of a voiding creditor under this chapter, or a right to retain any interest in the asset transferred;

(B) enforcement of any obligation incurred; or

(C) a reduction in the amount of the liability on the judgment.

(2) Notwithstanding voidability of a transfer under this chapter, to the extent of the value of any improvements made by a good faith transferee, the good faith transferee is entitled to a lien on the asset transferred prior to the rights of a voiding creditor under this chapter.

(e) A transfer is not voidable under Section 24.005(a)(2) or Section 24.006 of this code if the transfer results from:

(1) termination of a lease upon default by the debtor when the termination is pursuant to the lease and applicable law; or

(2) enforcement of a security interest in compliance with Chapter 9 of this code.

(f) A transfer is not voidable under Section 24.006(b) of this code:

(1) to the extent the insider gave new value to or for the benefit of the debtor after the transfer was made unless the new value was secured by a valid lien;

(2) if made in the ordinary course of business or financial affairs of the debtor and the insider; or

(3) if made pursuant to a good-faith effort to rehabilitate the debtor and the transfer secured present value given for that purpose as well as an antecedent debt of the debtor.

B&CC §24.01. DELETED

B&CC §24.010. EXTINGUISHMENT OF CAUSE OF ACTION

(a) Except as provided by Subsection (b) of this section, a cause of action with respect to a fraudulent transfer or obligation under this chapter is extinguished unless action is brought:

(1) under Section 24.005(a)(1) of this code, within four years after the transfer was made or the obligation was incurred or, if later, within one year after the transfer or obligation was or could reasonably have been discovered by the claimant;

(2) under Section 24.005(a)(2) or 24.006(a) of this code, within four years after the transfer was made or the obligation was incurred; or

(3) under Section 24.006(b) of this code, within one year after the transfer was made.

(b) A cause of action on behalf of a spouse, minor, or ward with respect to a fraudulent transfer or obligation under this chapter is extinguished unless the action is brought:

(1) under Section 24.005(a) or 24.006(a) of this code, within two years after the cause of action accrues, or if later, within one year after the transfer or obligation was or could reasonably have been discovered by the claimant; or

(2) under Section 24.006(b) of this code within one year after the date the transfer was made.

(c) If a creditor entitled to bring an action under this chapter is under a legal disability when a time period prescribed by this section starts, the time of the disability is not included in the period. A disability that arises after the period starts does not suspend the running of the period. A creditor may not tack one legal disability to another to extend the period. For the purposes of this subsection, a creditor is under a legal disability if the creditor is:

(1) younger than 18 years of age, regardless of whether the person is married; or

(2) of unsound mind.

See also *O'Connor's Texas COA*, "Actions involving a fraudulent conveyance," ch. 52, §2.7.5, p. 1553.

B&CC §24.011. SUPPLEMENTARY PROVISIONS

Unless displaced by the provisions of this chapter, the principles of law and equity, including the law merchant and the law relating to principal and agent, estoppel, laches, fraud, misrepresentation, duress, coercion, mistake, insolvency, or other validating or invalidating cause, supplement its provisions.

B&CC §24.012. UNIFORMITY OF APPLICATION & CONSTRUCTION

This chapter shall be applied and construed to effectuate its general purpose to make uniform the law with respect to the subject of this chapter among states enacting it.

B&CC §24.013. COSTS

In any proceeding under this chapter, the court may award costs and reasonable attorney's fees as are equitable and just.

B&CC §§24.02 TO 24.05. DELETED

CHAPTER 26. STATUTE OF FRAUDS

B&CC §26.01. PROMISE OR AGREEMENT MUST BE IN WRITING

(a) A promise or agreement described in Subsection (b) of this section is not enforceable unless the promise or agreement, or a memorandum of it, is

(1) in writing; and

(2) signed by the person to be charged with the promise or agreement or by someone lawfully authorized to sign for him.

(b) Subsection (a) of this section applies to:

(1) a promise by an executor or administrator to answer out of his own estate for any debt or damage due from his testator or intestate;

(2) a promise by one person to answer for the debt, default, or miscarriage of another person;

(3) an agreement made on consideration of marriage or on consideration of nonmarital conjugal cohabitation;

(4) a contract for the sale of real estate;

(5) a lease of real estate for a term longer than one year;

(6) an agreement which is not to be performed within one year from the date of making the agreement;

(7) a promise or agreement to pay a commission for the sale or purchase of:

(A) an oil or gas mining lease;

(B) an oil or gas royalty;

(C) minerals; or

(D) a mineral interest; and

(8) an agreement, promise, contract, or warranty of cure relating to medical care or results thereof made by a physician or health care provider as defined in Section 74.001, Civil Practice and Remedies Code. This section shall not apply to pharmacists.

See also Prop. Code §5.021; ***O'Connor's Texas COA***, "Statute of Frauds," ch. 50, p. 1505; ***Real Estate Forms***, FORMS 1.3, 2.1.

B&CC §26.02. LOAN AGREEMENT MUST BE IN WRITING

(a) In this section:

(1) "Financial institution" means a state or federally chartered bank, savings bank, savings and loan association, or credit union, a holding company, subsidiary, or affiliate of such an institution, or a lender approved by the United States Secretary of Housing and Urban Development for participation in a mortgage insurance program under the National Housing Act (12 U.S.C. Section 1701 et seq.).

(2) "Loan agreement" means one or more promises, promissory notes, agreements, undertakings, security agreements, deeds of trust or other documents, or commitments, or any combination of those actions or documents, pursuant to which a financial institution loans or delays repayment of or agrees to loan or delay repayment of money, goods, or another thing of value or to otherwise extend credit or make a financial accommodation. The term does not include a promise, promissory note, agreement, undertaking, document, or commitment relating to:

(A) a credit card or charge card; or

(B) an open-end account, as that term is defined by Section 301.002, Finance Code, intended or used primarily for personal, family, or household use.

(b) A loan agreement in which the amount involved in the loan agreement exceeds $50,000 in value is not enforceable unless the agreement is in writing and signed by the party to be bound or by that party's authorized representative.

(c) The rights and obligations of the parties to an agreement subject to Subsection (b) of this section shall be determined solely from the written loan agreement, and any prior oral agreements between the parties are superseded by and merged into the loan agreement.

(d) An agreement subject to Subsection (b) of this section may not be varied by any oral agreements or discussions that occur before or contemporaneously with the execution of the agreement.

(e) In a loan agreement subject to Subsection (b) of this section, the financial institution shall give notice to the debtor or obligor of the provisions of Subsections (b) and (c) of this section. The notice must be in a separate document signed by the debtor or obligor or incorporated into one or more of the documents constituting the loan agreement. The notice must be in type that is boldface, capitalized, underlined, or otherwise set out from surrounding written material so as to be conspicuous. The notice must state substantially the following:

"This written loan agreement represents the final agreement between the parties and may not be contradicted by evidence of prior, contemporaneous, or subsequent oral agreements of the parties.

"There are no unwritten oral agreements between the parties.

______________	______________
"Debtor or Obligor	Financial Institution"

(f) If the notice required by Subsection (e) of this section is not given on or before execution of the loan agreement or is not conspicuous, this section does not apply to the loan agreement, but the validity and enforceability of the loan agreement and the rights and obligations of the parties are not impaired or affected.

(g) All financial institutions shall conspicuously post notices that inform borrowers of the provisions of this section. The notices shall be located in such a manner and in places in the institutions so as to fully inform borrowers of the provisions of this section. The Finance Commission of Texas shall prescribe the language of the notice.

See also ***Real Estate Forms***, FORMS 3.1, 3.2, 3.7.

Title 4. Business Opportunities & Agreements

Chapter 56. Agreement for Payment of Construction Subcontractor

Subchapter A. General Provisions

B&CC §56.001. Definitions

In this chapter:

(1) "Contingent payee" means a party to a contract with a contingent payment clause, other than an architect or engineer, whose receipt of payment is conditioned on the contingent payor's receipt of payment from another person.

(2) "Contingent payment clause" means a provision in a contract for construction management, or for the construction of improvements to real property or the furnishing of materials for the construction, that provides that the contingent payor's receipt of payment from another is a condition precedent to the obligation of the contingent payor to make payment to the contingent payee for work performed or materials furnished.

(3) "Contingent payor" means a party to a contract with a contingent payment clause that conditions payment by the party on the receipt of payment from another person.

(4) "Improvement" includes new construction, remodeling, or repair.

(5) "Obligor" means the person obligated to make payment to the contingent payor for an improvement.

(6) "Primary obligor" means the owner of the real property to be improved or repaired under the contract, or the contracting authority if the contract is for a public project. A primary obligor may be an obligor.

B&CC §56.002. Inapplicability of Chapter to Certain Contracts

This chapter does not apply to a contract that is solely for:

(1) design services;

(2) the construction or maintenance of a road, highway, street, bridge, utility, water supply project, water plant, wastewater plant, water and wastewater distribution or conveyance facility, wharf, dock, airport runway or taxiway, drainage project, or related type of project associated with civil engineering construction; or

(3) improvements to or the construction of a structure that is a:

(A) detached single-family residence;

(B) duplex;

(C) triplex; or

(D) quadruplex.

B&CC §56.003. Effect of Chapter on Timing of Payment Provisions

This chapter does not affect a provision that affects the timing of a payment in a contract for construction management or for the construction of improvements to real property if the payment is to be made within a reasonable period.

B&CC §56.004. Waiver of Chapter Prohibited

A person may not waive this chapter by contract or other means. A purported waiver of this chapter is void.

Sections 56.005-56.050 reserved for expansion

Subchapter B. Contingent Payment Clause

B&CC §56.051. Enforcement of Clause Prohibited to Extent Certain Contractual Obligations Not Met

A contingent payor or its surety may not enforce a contingent payment clause to the extent that the obligor's nonpayment to the contingent payor is the result of the contractual obligations of the contingent payor not being met, unless the nonpayment is the result of the contingent payee's failure to meet the contingent payee's contractual requirements.

B&CC §56.052. Enforcement of Clause Prohibited Following Notice from Contingent Payee

(a) Except as provided by Subsection (d), a contingent payor or its surety may not enforce a contingent payment clause as to work performed or materials delivered after the contingent payor receives written notice from the contingent payee objecting to the further enforceability of the contingent payment clause as provided by this chapter and the notice becomes effective as provided by Subsection (b). The contingent payee may send written notice only after the 45th day after the date the contingent payee submits a written request for payment to the contingent payor that is in a form substantially in accordance with the contingent payee's contract requirements for the contents of a regular progress payment request or an invoice.

(b) For purposes of Subsection (a), the written notice becomes effective on the latest of:

(1) the 10th day after the date the contingent payor receives the notice;

(2) the eighth day after the date interest begins to accrue against the obligor under:

(A) Section 28.004, Property Code, under a contract for a private project governed by Chapter 28, Property Code; or

(B) 31 U.S.C. Section 3903(a)(6), under a contract for a public project governed by 40 U.S.C. Section 3131; or

(3) the 11th day after the date interest begins to accrue against the obligor under Section 2251.025, Government Code, under a contract for a public project governed by Chapter 2251, Government Code.

(c) A notice given by a contingent payee under Subsection (a) does not prevent enforcement of a contingent payment clause if:

(1) the obligor has a dispute under Chapter 28, Property Code, Chapter 2251, Government Code, or 31 U.S.C. Chapter 39 as a result of the contingent payee's failure to meet the contingent payee's contractual requirements; and

(2) the contingent payor gives notice in writing to the contingent payee that the written notice given under Subsection (a) does not prevent enforcement of the contingent payment clause under this subsection and the contingent payee receives the notice under this subdivision not later than the later of:

(A) the fifth day before the date the written notice from the contingent payee under Subsection (a) becomes effective under Subsection (b); or

(B) the fifth day after the date the contingent payor receives the written notice from the contingent payee under Subsection (a).

(d) A written notice given by a contingent payee under Subsection (a) does not prevent the enforcement of a contingent payment clause to the extent that the funds are not collectible as a result of a primary obligor's successful assertion of a defense of sovereign immunity, if the contingent payor has exhausted all of its rights and remedies under its contract with the primary obligor and under Chapter 2251, Government Code. This subsection does not:

(1) create or validate a defense of sovereign immunity; or

(2) extend to a primary obligor a defense or right that did not exist before September 1, 2007.

(e) On receipt of payment by the contingent payee of the unpaid indebtedness giving rise to the written notice provided by the contingent payee under Subsection (a), the contingent payment clause is reinstated as to work performed or materials furnished after the receipt of the payment, subject to the provisions of this chapter.

B&CC §56.053. ENFORCEMENT OF CLAUSE PROHIBITED IF EXISTENCE OF SHAM RELATIONSHIP

A contingent payor or its surety may not enforce a contingent payment clause if the contingent payor is in a sham relationship with the obligor, as described by the sham relationships in Section 53.026, Property Code.

B&CC §56.054. ENFORCEMENT OF CLAUSE PROHIBITED IF UNCONSCIONABLE

(a) A contingent payor or its surety may not enforce a contingent payment clause if the enforcement would be unconscionable. The party asserting that a contingent payment clause is unconscionable has the burden of proving that the clause is unconscionable.

(b) The enforcement of a contingent payment clause is not unconscionable if the contingent payor:

(1) proves that the contingent payor has exercised diligence in ascertaining and communicating in writing to the contingent payee, before the contract in which the contingent payment clause has been asserted becomes enforceable against the contingent payee, the financial viability of the primary obligor and the existence of adequate financial arrangements to pay for the improvements; and

(2) has done the following:

(A) made reasonable efforts to collect the amount owed to the contingent payor; or

(B) made or offered to make, at a reasonable time, an assignment by the contingent payor to the contingent payee of a cause of action against the obligor for the amounts owed to the contingent payee by the contingent payor and offered reasonable cooperation to the contingent payee's collection efforts, if the assigned

cause of action is not subject to defenses caused by the contingent payor's action or failure to act.

(c) A cause of action brought on an assignment made under Subsection (b)(2)(B) is enforceable by a contingent payee against an obligor or a primary obligor.

(d) A contingent payor is considered to have exercised diligence for purposes of Subsection (b)(1) under a contract for a private project governed by Chapter 53, Property Code, if the contingent payee receives in writing from the contingent payor:

(1) the name, address, and business telephone number of the primary obligor;

(2) a description, legally sufficient for identification, of the property on which the improvements are being constructed;

(3) the name and address of the surety on any payment bond provided under Subchapter I, Chapter 53, Property Code, to which any notice of claim should be sent;

(4) if a loan has been obtained for the construction of improvements:

(A) a statement, furnished by the primary obligor and supported by reasonable and credible evidence from all applicable lenders, of the amount of the loan;

(B) a summary of the terms of the loan;

(C) a statement of whether there is foreseeable default of the primary obligor; and

(D) the name, address, and business telephone number of the borrowers and lenders; and

(5) a statement, furnished by the primary obligor and supported by reasonable and credible evidence from all applicable banks or other depository institutions, of the amount, source, and location of funds available to pay the balance of the contract amount if there is no loan or the loan is not sufficient to pay for all of the construction of the improvements.

(e) A contingent payor is considered to have exercised diligence for purposes of Subsection (b)(1) under a contract for a public project governed by Chapter 2253, Government Code, if the contingent payee receives in writing from the contingent payor:

(1) the name, address, and primary business telephone number of the primary obligor;

(2) the name and address of the surety on the payment bond provided to the primary obligor to which any notice of claim should be sent; and

(3) a statement from the primary obligor that funds are available and have been authorized for the full contract amount for the construction of the improvements.

(f) A contingent payor is considered to have exercised diligence for purposes of Subsection (b)(1) under a contract for a public project governed by 40 U.S.C. Section 3131 if the contingent payee receives in writing from the contingent payor:

(1) the name, address, and primary business telephone number of the primary obligor;

(2) the name and address of the surety on the payment bond provided to the primary obligor; and

(3) the name of the contracting officer, if known at the time of the execution of the contract.

(g) A primary obligor shall furnish the information described by Subsection (d) or (e), as applicable, to the contingent payor not later than the 30th day after the date the primary obligor receives a written request for the information. If the primary obligor fails to provide the information under the written request, the contingent payor, the contingent payee, and their sureties are relieved of the obligation to initiate or continue performance of the construction contracts of the contingent payor and contingent payee.

B&CC §56.055. USE OF CLAUSE TO INVALIDATE ENFORCEABILITY OR PERFECTION OF MECHANIC'S LIEN PROHIBITED

A contingent payment clause may not be used as a basis for invalidation of the enforceability or perfection of a mechanic's lien under Chapter 53, Property Code.

B&CC §56.056. ASSERTION OF CLAUSE AS AFFIRMATIVE DEFENSE

The assertion of a contingent payment clause is an affirmative defense to a civil action for payment under a contract.

B&CC §56.057. ALLOCATION OF RISK PERMITTED

An obligor or a primary obligor may not prohibit a contingent payor from allocating risk by means of a contingent payment clause.

TITLE 9. APPLICABILITY OF LAW TO COMMERCIAL TRANSACTIONS

A CHAPTER 272. LAW APPLICABLE TO CERTAIN CONSTRUCTION CONTRACTS [~~FOR CONSTRUCTION OR REPAIR OF REAL PROPERTY IMPROVEMENTS~~]

E B&CC §272.0001. DEFINITION

In this chapter, "construction contract" means a contract, subcontract, or agreement entered into or made by an owner, architect, engineer, contractor, construction manager, subcontractor, supplier, or material or equipment lessor for the design, construction, alteration, renovation, remodeling, or repair of, or for the furnishing of material or equipment for, a building, structure, appurtenance, or other improvement to or on public or private real property, including moving, demolition, and excavation connected with the real property. The term includes an agreement to which an architect, engineer, or contractor and an owner's lender are parties regarding an assignment of the construction contract or other modifications thereto.

2017 Legislation: Enacted by S.B. 807, §2, 85th Leg., eff. Sept. 1, 2017.

A B&CC §272.001. VOIDABLE CONTRACT PROVISION

The amended text in §272.001 is effective for contracts or agreements collateral to or affecting contracts entered into on or after Sept. 1, 2017. Contracts or agreements entered into before Sept. 1, 2017, are governed by the former law in effect at that time.

(a) This section applies only to a construction contract concerning [~~that is principally for the construction or repair of an improvement to~~] real property located in this state.

(b) If a construction contract or an agreement collateral to or affecting the construction contract contains a provision making the contract or agreement or any conflict arising under the contract or agreement subject to another state's law, litigation in the courts of another state, or arbitration in another state, that provision is voidable by a [~~the~~] party obligated by the contract or agreement to perform the work that is the subject of the construction contract [~~or repair~~].

2017 Legislation: Amended by S.B. 807, §§1, 2, 85th Leg., eff. Sept. 1, 2017.

A B&CC §272.002. INAPPLICABILITY OF CHAPTER [~~CONTRACT PRINCIPALLY FOR CONSTRUCTION OR REPAIR OF REAL PROPERTY IMPROVEMENTS~~]

The amended text in §272.002 is effective for contracts or agreements collateral to or affecting contracts entered into on or after Sept. 1, 2017. Contracts or agreements entered into before Sept. 1, 2017, are governed by the former law in effect at that time.

This chapter does not apply to a construction [~~(a)~~] [~~For purposes of this chapter, a contract is principally for the construction or repair of an improvement to real property located in this state if the contract obligates a party, as the party's principal obligation under the contract, to provide labor or labor and materials as a general contractor or subcontractor for the construction or repair of an improvement to real property located in this state.~~]

[~~(b)~~] [~~For purposes of this chapter, a contract is not principally for the construction or repair of an improvement to real property located in this state if the~~] contract that:

(1) is a partnership agreement or other agreement governing an entity or trust;

(2) provides for a loan or other extension of credit and the party promising to perform the work that is the subject of the construction contract [~~construct or repair the improvement~~] is doing so as part of the party's agreements with the lender or other person who extends credit; or

(3) is for the management of real property or improvements and the obligation to perform the work that is the subject of the construction contract [~~construct or repair the improvement~~] is part of that management.

[~~(c)~~] [~~Subsections (a) and (b) do not provide an exclusive list of the situations in which a contract is or is not principally for the construction or repair of an improvement to real property located in this state.~~]

2017 Legislation: Amended by S.B. 807, §2, 85th Leg., eff. Sept. 1, 2017.

TITLE 12. RIGHTS & DUTIES OF CONSUMERS & MERCHANTS

CHAPTER 601. CANCELLATION OF CERTAIN CONSUMER TRANSACTIONS

SUBCHAPTER A. GENERAL PROVISIONS

B&CC §601.001. DEFINITIONS

In this chapter:

(1) "Consumer" means an individual who seeks or acquires real property, money or other personal property, services, or credit for personal, family, or household purposes.

(2) "Consumer transaction" means a transaction between a merchant and one or more consumers.

(3) "Merchant" means a party to a consumer transaction other than a consumer.

(4) "Merchant's place of business" means a merchant's main or permanent branch office or local address. For a state or national bank or savings and loan association, the term includes an approved branch office and a registered loan production office.

B&CC §601.002. APPLICABILITY OF CHAPTER; EXCEPTION

(a) This chapter applies only to a consumer transaction in which:

(1) the merchant or the merchant's agent engages in a personal solicitation of a sale to the consumer at a place other than the merchant's place of business;

(2) the consumer's agreement or offer to purchase is given to the merchant or the merchant's agent at a place other than the merchant's place of business; and

(3) the agreement or offer is for:

(A) the purchase of goods or services for consideration that exceeds $25, payable in installments or in cash; or

(B) the purchase of real property for consideration that exceeds $100, payable in installments or in cash.

(b) Notwithstanding Subsection (a), this chapter does not apply to:

(1) a purchase of farm equipment;

(2) an insurance sale regulated by the Texas Department of Insurance;

(3) a sale of goods or services made:

(A) under a preexisting revolving charge account or retail charge agreement; or

(B) after negotiations between the parties at a business establishment in a fixed location where goods or services are offered or exhibited for sale; or

(4) a sale of real property if:

(A) the purchaser is represented by a licensed attorney;

(B) the transaction is negotiated by a licensed real estate broker; or

(C) the transaction is negotiated at a place other than the consumer's residence by the person who owns the property.

Sections 601.003-601.050 reserved for expansion

SUBCHAPTER B. CONSUMER'S RIGHT TO CANCEL TRANSACTION

B&CC §601.051. CONSUMER'S RIGHT TO CANCEL

In addition to any other rights or remedies available, a consumer may cancel a consumer transaction not later than midnight of the third business day after the date the consumer signs an agreement or offer to purchase.

B&CC §601.052. NOTICE OF CONSUMER'S RIGHT TO CANCEL REQUIRED

(a) A merchant must provide a consumer with a complete receipt or copy of a contract pertaining to the consumer transaction at the time of its execution.

(b) The document provided under Subsection (a) must:

(1) be in the same language as that principally used in the oral sales presentation;

(2) contain the date of the transaction;

(3) contain the name and address of the merchant; and

(4) contain a statement:

(A) in immediate proximity to the space reserved in the contract for the signature of the consumer or on the front page of the receipt if a contract is not used; and

(B) in boldfaced type of a minimum size of 10 points in substantially the following form:

"YOU, THE BUYER, MAY CANCEL THIS TRANSACTION AT ANY TIME PRIOR TO MIDNIGHT OF THE THIRD BUSINESS DAY AFTER THE DATE OF THIS TRANSACTION. SEE THE ATTACHED NOTICE OF CANCELLATION FORM FOR AN EXPLANATION OF THIS RIGHT."

B&CC §601.053. COMPLETED CANCELLATION FORM REQUIRED

(a) A merchant that provides a document under Section 601.052 must attach to the document a completed notice of cancellation form in duplicate. The form must:

(1) be easily detachable;

(2) be in the same language as the document provided under Section 601.052; and

(3) contain the following information and statements in 10-point boldfaced type:

"NOTICE OF CANCELLATION

(enter date of transaction)

"YOU MAY CANCEL THIS TRANSACTION, WITHOUT ANY PENALTY OR OBLIGATION, WITHIN THREE BUSINESS DAYS FROM THE ABOVE DATE.

"IF YOU CANCEL, ANY PROPERTY TRADED IN, ANY PAYMENTS MADE BY YOU UNDER THE CONTRACT OR SALE, AND ANY NEGOTIABLE INSTRUMENT EXECUTED BY YOU WILL BE RETURNED WITHIN 10 BUSINESS DAYS FOLLOWING RECEIPT BY THE MERCHANT OF YOUR CANCELLATION NOTICE, AND ANY SECURITY INTEREST ARISING OUT OF THE TRANSACTION WILL BE CANCELLED.

"IF YOU CANCEL, YOU MUST MAKE AVAILABLE TO THE MERCHANT AT YOUR RESIDENCE, IN SUBSTANTIALLY AS GOOD CONDITION AS WHEN RECEIVED, ANY GOODS DELIVERED TO YOU UNDER THIS CONTRACT OR SALE; OR YOU MAY IF YOU WISH, COMPLY WITH THE INSTRUCTIONS OF THE MERCHANT REGARDING THE RETURN SHIPMENT OF THE GOODS AT THE MERCHANT'S EXPENSE AND RISK.

"IF YOU DO NOT AGREE TO RETURN THE GOODS TO THE MERCHANT OR IF THE MERCHANT DOES NOT PICK THEM UP WITHIN 20 DAYS OF THE DATE OF YOUR NOTICE OF CANCELLATION, YOU MAY RETAIN OR DISPOSE OF THE GOODS WITHOUT ANY FURTHER OBLIGATION.

"TO CANCEL THIS TRANSACTION, MAIL OR DELIVER A SIGNED AND DATED COPY OF THIS CANCELLATION NOTICE OR ANY OTHER WRITTEN NOTICE, OR SEND A TELEGRAM, TO (name of merchant), AT (address of merchant's place of business) NOT LATER THAN MIDNIGHT OF (date).

I HEREBY CANCEL THIS TRANSACTION.

(date)

(buyer's signature)"

(b) A merchant may not fail to include on both copies of the form described by Subsection (a):

(1) the name of the merchant;

(2) the address of the merchant's place of business;

(3) the date of the transaction; and

(4) a date not earlier than the third business day after the date of the transaction by which the consumer must give notice of cancellation.

B&CC §601.054. USE OF FORMS & NOTICES PRESCRIBED BY THE FEDERAL TRADE COMMISSION AUTHORIZED

The use of the forms and notices of the right to cancel prescribed by the Federal Trade Commission's trade-regulation rule providing a cooling-off period for door-to-door sales constitutes compliance with Sections 601.052 and 601.053.

B&CC §601.055. ALTERNATIVE NOTICE AUTHORIZED FOR CERTAIN CONSUMER TRANSACTIONS

A consumer transaction in which the contract price does not exceed $200 complies with the notice requirements of Sections 601.052 and 601.053 if:

(1) the consumer may at any time cancel the order, refuse to accept delivery of the goods without incurring any obligation to pay for the goods, or return the goods to the merchant and receive a full refund of the amount the consumer has paid; and

(2) the consumer's right to cancel the order, refuse delivery, or return the goods without obligation or charge at any time is clearly and conspicuously stated on the face or reverse side of the sales ticket.

Sections 601.056-601.100 reserved for expansion

SUBCHAPTER C. RIGHTS & DUTIES OF CONSUMER & MERCHANT

B&CC §601.101. MERCHANT'S COMPENSATION

A merchant is not entitled to compensation for services performed under a consumer transaction canceled under this chapter.

B&CC §601.102. CONSUMER'S RETENTION OF GOODS OR TITLE TO REAL PROPERTY AUTHORIZED

Until a merchant has complied with this chapter, a consumer with possession of goods or the right or title to real property delivered by the merchant:

(1) may retain possession of the goods or the right or title to the real property; and

(2) has a lien on the goods or real property to the extent of any recovery to which the consumer is entitled.

B&CC §601.103. CONSUMER'S DUTIES WITH RESPECT TO DELIVERED GOODS OR REAL PROPERTY

(a) Within a reasonable time after a cancellation under this chapter, the consumer must, on demand,

tender to the merchant any goods or any right or title to real property delivered by the merchant under the consumer transaction.

(b) The consumer is not obligated to tender goods at a place other than the consumer's residence.

(c) If the merchant fails to demand possession of the goods or the right or title to real property within a reasonable time after cancellation, the goods or real property become the property of the consumer without obligation to pay.

(d) Goods or real property in possession of the consumer are at the risk of the merchant, except that the consumer shall take reasonable care of the goods or the real property both before and for a reasonable time after cancellation.

(e) For purposes of this section, 20 days is presumed to be a reasonable time.

Sections 601.104-601.150 reserved for expansion

Subchapter D. Prohibited Acts & Conduct by Merchant

B&CC §601.151. Confession of Judgment or Waiver of Rights

A merchant may not include in a contract or receipt pertaining to a consumer transaction a confession of judgment or a waiver of any of the rights to which the consumer is entitled under this chapter.

B&CC §601.152. Failure to Inform or Misrepresentation of Right to Cancel

A merchant may not:

(1) at the time the consumer signs the contract pertaining to a consumer transaction or purchases the goods, services, or real property, fail to inform the consumer orally of the right to cancel the transaction; or

(2) misrepresent in any manner the consumer's right to cancel.

B&CC §601.153. Transfer of Indebtedness During Certain Period

A merchant may not negotiate, transfer, sell, or assign a note or other evidence of indebtedness to a finance company or other third party before midnight of the fifth business day after the date the contract pertaining to a consumer transaction was signed or the goods or services were purchased.

B&CC §601.154. Failure to Take Certain Actions Following Receipt of Notice of Cancellation

A merchant may not:

(1) fail to notify the consumer before the end of the 10th business day after the date the merchant receives the notice of cancellation whether the merchant intends to repossess or abandon any shipped or delivered goods;

(2) fail or refuse to honor a valid cancellation under this chapter by a consumer; or

(3) fail before the end of the 10th business day after the date the merchant receives a valid notice of cancellation to:

(A) refund all payments made under the contract or sale;

(B) return any goods or property traded in to the merchant in substantially the same condition as when received by the merchant;

(C) cancel and return a negotiable instrument executed by the consumer in connection with the contract of sale;

(D) take any action appropriate to terminate promptly any security interest created in the transaction; or

(E) restore improvements on real property to the same condition as when the merchant took title to or possession of the real property unless the consumer requests otherwise.

Sections 601.155-601.200 reserved for expansion

Subchapter E. Enforcement

B&CC §601.201. Certain Sales or Contracts Void

A sale or contract entered into under a consumer transaction in violation of Section 601.053(b) or Subchapter D is void.

B&CC §601.202. Liability for Damages

A merchant who violates this chapter is liable to the consumer for:

(1) actual damages suffered by the consumer as a result of the violation;

(2) reasonable attorney's fees; and

(3) court costs.

B&CC §601.203. ALTERNATIVE RECOVERY UNDER CERTAIN CIRCUMSTANCES

If the merchant fails to tender goods or property traded to the merchant in substantially the same condition as when received by the merchant, the consumer may elect to recover an amount equal to the trade-in allowance stated in the agreement.

B&CC §601.204. DECEPTIVE TRADE PRACTICE

A violation of this chapter is a false, misleading, or deceptive act or practice as defined by Section 17.46(b). In addition to any remedy under this chapter, a remedy under Subchapter E, Chapter 17, is also available for a violation of this chapter.

B&CC §601.205. INJUNCTION

If the attorney general believes that a person is violating or about to violate this chapter, the attorney general may bring an action in the name of the state to restrain or enjoin the person from violating this chapter.

Civil Practice & Remedies Code

Selected Provisions

Table of Contents

For the complete Civil Practice & Remedies Code with annotations, see the current edition of ***O'Connor's Texas Civil Practice & Remedies Code Plus***. To order, call 1-800-OCONNOR (1-800-626-6667) or visit www.oconnors.com.

CPRC

Civil Practice & Remedies Code
Selected Provisions
Table of Contents

TITLE 2. TRIAL, JUDGMENT, & APPEAL

SUBTITLE A. GENERAL PROVISIONS

CHAPTER 12. LIABILITY RELATED TO A FRAUDULENT COURT RECORD OR A FRAUDULENT LIEN OR CLAIM FILED AGAINST REAL OR PERSONAL PROPERTY

CPRC §12.001. DEFINITIONS

In this chapter:

(1) "Court record" has the meaning assigned by Section 37.01, Penal Code.

(2) "Exemplary damages" has the meaning assigned by Section 41.001.

(2-a) "Filing office" has the meaning assigned by Section 9.102, Business & Commerce Code.

(2-b) "Financing statement" has the meaning assigned by Section 9.102, Business & Commerce Code.

(2-c) "Inmate" means a person housed in a secure correctional facility.

(3) "Lien" means a claim in property for the payment of a debt and includes a security interest.

(4) "Public servant" has the meaning assigned by Section 1.07, Penal Code, and includes officers and employees of the United States.

(5) "Secure correctional facility" has the meaning assigned by Section 1.07, Penal Code.

CPRC §12.002. LIABILITY

(a) A person may not make, present, or use a document or other record with:

(1) knowledge that the document or other record is a fraudulent court record or a fraudulent lien or claim against real or personal property or an interest in real or personal property;

(2) intent that the document or other record be given the same legal effect as a court record or document of a court created by or established under the constitution or laws of this state or the United States or another entity listed in Section 37.01, Penal Code, evidencing a valid lien or claim against real or personal property or an interest in real or personal property; and

(3) intent to cause another person to suffer:

(A) physical injury;

(B) financial injury; or

(C) mental anguish or emotional distress.

(a-1) Except as provided by Subsection (a-2), a person may not file an abstract of a judgment or an instrument concerning real or personal property with a court or county clerk, or a financing statement with a filing office, if the person:

(1) is an inmate; or

(2) is not licensed or regulated under Title 11, Insurance Code, and is filing on behalf of another person who the person knows is an inmate.

(a-2) A person described by Subsection (a-1) may file an abstract, instrument, or financing statement described by that subsection if the document being filed includes a statement indicating that:

(1) the person filing the document is an inmate; or

(2) the person is filing the document on behalf of a person who is an inmate.

(b) A person who violates Subsection (a) or (a-1) is liable to each injured person for:

(1) the greater of:

(A) $10,000; or

(B) the actual damages caused by the violation;

(2) court costs;

(3) reasonable attorney's fees; and

(4) exemplary damages in an amount determined by the court.

(c) A person claiming a lien under Chapter 53, Property Code, is not liable under this section for the making, presentation, or use of a document or other record in connection with the assertion of the claim unless the person acts with intent to defraud.

CPRC §12.003. CAUSE OF ACTION

(a) The following persons may bring an action to enjoin violation of this chapter or to recover damages under this chapter:

(1) the attorney general;

(2) a district attorney;

(3) a criminal district attorney;

(4) a county attorney with felony responsibilities;

(5) a county attorney;

(6) a municipal attorney;

(7) in the case of a fraudulent judgment lien, the person against whom the judgment is rendered; and

(8) in the case of a fraudulent lien or claim against real or personal property or an interest in real or personal property, the obligor or debtor, or a person who owns an interest in the real or personal property.

(b) Notwithstanding any other law, a person or a person licensed or regulated by Title 11, Insurance

CPRC §12.003

Code (the Texas Title Insurance Act), does not have a duty to disclose a fraudulent, as described by Section 51.901(c), Government Code, court record, document, or instrument purporting to create a lien or purporting to assert a claim on real property or an interest in real property in connection with a sale, conveyance, mortgage, or other transfer of the real property or interest in real property.

(c) Notwithstanding any other law, a purported judgment lien or document establishing or purporting to establish a judgment lien against property in this state, that is issued or purportedly issued by a court or a purported court other than a court established under the laws of this state or the United States, is void and has no effect in the determination of any title or right to the property.

CPRC §12.007. EFFECT ON OTHER LAW

This law is cumulative of other law under which a person may obtain judicial relief with respect to a recorded document or other record.

SUBTITLE B. TRIAL MATTERS

CHAPTER 15. VENUE

SUBCHAPTER A. DEFINITIONS; GENERAL RULES

CPRC §15.001. DEFINITIONS

In this chapter:

(a) "Principal office" means a principal office of the corporation, unincorporated association, or partnership in this state in which the decision makers for the organization within this state conduct the daily affairs of the organization. The mere presence of an agency or representative does not establish a principal office.

(b) "Proper venue" means:

(1) the venue required by the mandatory provisions of Subchapter B or another statute prescribing mandatory venue; or

(2) if Subdivision (1) does not apply, the venue provided by this subchapter or Subchapter C.

See also TRCP 86, 87; *O'Connor's Texas Rules*, "Choosing the Court—Venue," ch. 2-G, p. 175; "Motion to Transfer—Challenging Venue," ch. 3-C, p. 235.

SUBCHAPTER B. MANDATORY VENUE

CPRC §15.011. LAND

Actions for recovery of real property or an estate or interest in real property, for partition of real property, to remove encumbrances from the title to real property, for recovery of damages to real property, or to quiet title to real property shall be brought in the county in which all or a part of the property is located.

See also TRCP 86, 87; *O'Connor's Texas Appeals*, "Transfer of venue," ch. 10-B, §5.1.8, p. 383; *O'Connor's Texas COA*, "Venue," ch. 22-A, §6.1, p. 765; "Venue for suit," ch. 24-A, §3.2, p. 868; *O'Connor's Texas Rules*, "Choosing the Court—Venue," ch. 2-G, p. 175; "Motion to Transfer—Challenging Venue," ch. 3-C, p. 235.

CPRC §15.0115. LANDLORD-TENANT

(a) Except as provided by another statute prescribing mandatory venue, a suit between a landlord and a tenant arising under a lease shall be brought in the county in which all or a part of the real property is located.

(b) In this section, "lease" means any written or oral agreement between a landlord and a tenant that establishes or modifies the terms, conditions, or other provisions relating to the use and occupancy of the real property that is the subject of the agreement.

See also TRCP 86, 87; *O'Connor's Texas Appeals*, "Transfer of venue," ch. 10-B, §5.1.8, p. 383; *O'Connor's Texas COA*, "Venue for suit," ch. 24-A, §3.2, p. 868; *O'Connor's Texas Rules*, "Choosing the Court—Venue," ch. 2-G, p. 175; "Motion to Transfer—Challenging Venue," ch. 3-C, p. 235.

CPRC §15.020. MAJOR TRANSACTIONS: SPECIFICATION OF VENUE BY AGREEMENT

(a) In this section, "major transaction" means a transaction evidenced by a written agreement under which a person pays or receives, or is obligated to pay or entitled to receive, consideration with an aggregate stated value equal to or greater than $1 million. The term does not include a transaction entered into primarily for personal, family, or household purposes, or to settle a personal injury or wrongful death claim, without regard to the aggregate value.

(b) An action arising from a major transaction shall be brought in a county if the party against whom the action is brought has agreed in writing that a suit arising from the transaction may be brought in that county.

(c) Notwithstanding any other provision of this title, an action arising from a major transaction may not be brought in a county if:

(1) the party bringing the action has agreed in writing that an action arising from the transaction may not be brought in that county, and the action may be brought in another county of this state or in another jurisdiction; or

(2) the party bringing the action has agreed in writing that an action arising from the transaction

must be brought in another county of this state or in another jurisdiction, and the action may be brought in that other county, under this section or otherwise, or in that other jurisdiction.

(d) This section does not apply to an action if:

(1) the agreement described by this section was unconscionable at the time that it was made;

(2) the agreement regarding venue is voidable under Chapter 272, Business & Commerce Code; or

(3) venue is established under a statute of this state other than this title.

(e) This section does not affect venue and jurisdiction in an action arising from a transaction that is not a major transaction.

See also TRCP 86, 87; ***O'Connor's Texas Appeals***, "Transfer of venue," ch. 10-B, §5.1.8, p. 383; ***O'Connor's Texas COA***, "Written contractual venue," ch. 5-B, §6.2.4, p. 104; "Venue for suit," ch. 24-A, §3.2, p. 868; ***O'Connor's Texas Rules***, "Choosing the Court—Venue," ch. 2-G, p. 175; "Motion to Transfer—Challenging Venue," ch. 3-C, p. 235; "Forum-Selection Clause," ch. 3-D, §6, p. 259.

SUBCHAPTER D. GENERAL PROVISIONS

CPRC §15.065. WATERCOURSE OR ROADWAY FORMING COUNTY BOUNDARY

If a river, watercourse, highway, road, or street forms the boundary line between two counties, the courts of each county have concurrent jurisdiction over the parts of the watercourse or roadway that form the boundary of the county in the same manner as if the watercourse or roadway were in that county.

SUBCHAPTER E. SUITS BROUGHT IN JUSTICE COURT

CPRC §15.084. FORCIBLE ENTRY & DETAINER

A suit for forcible entry and detainer shall be brought in the precinct in which all or part of the premises is located.

See also TRCP 500.3, 502.4, 510.

CPRC §15.090. PERSONAL PROPERTY

A suit to recover personal property may be brought in the county and precinct in which the property is located.

See also TRCP 502.4.

CPRC §15.091. RENTS

A suit to recover rents may be brought in the county and precinct in which all or part of the rented premises is located.

See also TRCP 502.4.

CHAPTER 16. LIMITATIONS

SUBCHAPTER A. LIMITATIONS OF PERSONAL ACTIONS

Editor's note: *For an extensive list of limitations in property-related actions, see chart, "Statutes of Limitations in Property-Law Proceedings," p. 1520.*

CPRC §16.003. TWO-YEAR LIMITATIONS PERIOD

(a) Except as provided by Sections 16.010, 16.0031, and 16.0045, a person must bring suit for trespass for injury to the estate or to the property of another, conversion of personal property, taking or detaining the personal property of another, personal injury, forcible entry and detainer, and forcible detainer not later than two years after the day the cause of action accrues.

(b) A person must bring suit not later than two years after the day the cause of action accrues in an action for injury resulting in death. The cause of action accrues on the death of the injured person.

See also ***O'Connor's Texas COA***, "Limitations," ch. 52, p. 1537.

CPRC §16.004. FOUR-YEAR LIMITATIONS PERIOD

(a) A person must bring suit on the following actions not later than four years after the day the cause of action accrues:

(1) specific performance of a contract for the conveyance of real property;

(2) penalty or damages on the penal clause of a bond to convey real property;

(3) debt;

(4) fraud; or

(5) breach of fiduciary duty.

(b) A person must bring suit on the bond of an executor, administrator, or guardian not later than four years after the day of the death, resignation, removal, or discharge of the executor, administrator, or guardian.

(c) A person must bring suit against his partner for a settlement of partnership accounts, and must bring an action on an open or stated account, or on a mutual and current account concerning the trade of merchandise between merchants or their agents or factors, not later than four years after the day that the cause of action accrues. For purposes of this subsection, the cause of action accrues on the day that the dealings in which the parties were interested together cease.

See also ***O'Connor's Texas COA***, "Limitations," ch. 52, p. 1537.

CPRC §16.0045. LIMITATIONS PERIOD FOR CLAIMS ARISING FROM CERTAIN OFFENSES

(a) A person must bring suit for personal injury not later than 15 years after the day the cause of action accrues if the injury arises as a result of conduct that violates:

(1) Section 22.011(a)(2), Penal Code (sexual assault of a child);

(2) Section 22.021(a)(1)(B), Penal Code (aggravated sexual assault of a child);

(3) Section 21.02, Penal Code (continuous sexual abuse of young child or children);

(4) Section 20A.02(a)(7)(A), (B), (C), (D), or (H) or Section 20A.02(a)(8), Penal Code, involving an activity described by Section 20A.02(a)(7)(A), (B), (C), (D), or (H) or sexual conduct with a child trafficked in the manner described by Section 20A.02(a)(7), Penal Code (certain sexual trafficking of a child);

(5) Section 43.05(a)(2), Penal Code (compelling prostitution by a child); or

(6) Section 21.11, Penal Code (indecency with a child).

(b) A person must bring suit for personal injury not later than five years after the day the cause of action accrues if the injury arises as a result of conduct that violates:

(1) Section 22.011(a)(1), Penal Code (sexual assault);

(2) Section 22.021(a)(1)(A), Penal Code (aggravated sexual assault);

(3) Section 20A.02, Penal Code (trafficking of persons), other than conduct described by Subsection (a)(4); or

(4) Section 43.05(a)(1), Penal Code (compelling prostitution).

(c) In an action for injury resulting in death arising as a result of conduct described by Subsection (a) or (b), the cause of action accrues on the death of the injured person.

(d) A limitations period under this section is tolled for a suit on the filing of a petition by any person in an appropriate court alleging that the identity of the defendant in the suit is unknown and designating the unknown defendant as "John or Jane Doe." The person filing the petition shall proceed with due diligence to discover the identity of the defendant and amend the petition by substituting the real name of the defendant for "John or Jane Doe" not later than the 30th day after the date that the defendant is identified to the plaintiff. The limitations period begins running again on the date that the petition is amended.

CPRC §16.005. ACTION FOR CLOSING STREET OR ROAD

(a) A person must bring suit for any relief from the following acts not later than two years after the day the cause of action accrues:

(1) the passage by a governing body of an incorporated city or town of an ordinance closing and abandoning, or attempting to close and abandon, all or any part of a public street or alley in the city or town, other than a state highway; or

(2) the adoption by a commissioners court of an order closing and abandoning, or attempting to close and abandon, all or any part of a public road or thoroughfare in the county, other than a state highway.

(b) The cause of action accrues when the order or ordinance is passed or adopted.

(c) If suit is not brought within the period provided by this section, the person in possession of the real property receives complete title to the property by limitations and the right of the city or county to revoke or rescind the order or ordinance is barred.

See also *O'Connor's Texas COA*, "Limitations," ch. 52, p. 1537.

CPRC §16.008. ARCHITECTS, ENGINEERS, INTERIOR DESIGNERS, & LANDSCAPE ARCHITECTS FURNISHING DESIGN, PLANNING, OR INSPECTION OF CONSTRUCTION OF IMPROVEMENTS

(a) A person must bring suit for damages for a claim listed in Subsection (b) against a registered or licensed architect, engineer, interior designer, or landscape architect in this state, who designs, plans, or inspects the construction of an improvement to real property or equipment attached to real property, not later than 10 years after the substantial completion of the improvement or the beginning of operation of the equipment in an action arising out of a defective or unsafe condition of the real property, the improvement, or the equipment.

(b) This section applies to suit for:

(1) injury, damage, or loss to real or personal property;

CPRC §16.0045

(2) personal injury;

(3) wrongful death;

(4) contribution; or

(5) indemnity.

(c) If the claimant presents a written claim for damages, contribution, or indemnity to the architect, engineer, interior designer, or landscape architect within the 10-year limitations period, the period is extended for two years from the day the claim is presented.

See also *O'Connor's Texas COA*, "Actions against architects, engineers & design professionals," ch. 52, §2.7.1, p. 1552.

CPRC §16.009. PERSONS FURNISHING CONSTRUCTION OR REPAIR OF IMPROVEMENTS

(a) A claimant must bring suit for damages for a claim listed in Subsection (b) against a person who constructs or repairs an improvement to real property not later than 10 years after the substantial completion of the improvement in an action arising out of a defective or unsafe condition of the real property or a deficiency in the construction or repair of the improvement.

(b) This section applies to suit for:

(1) injury, damage, or loss to real or personal property;

(2) personal injury;

(3) wrongful death;

(4) contribution; or

(5) indemnity.

(c) If the claimant presents a written claim for damages, contribution, or indemnity to the person performing or furnishing the construction or repair work during the 10-year limitations period, the period is extended for two years from the date the claim is presented.

(d) If the damage, injury, or death occurs during the 10th year of the limitations period, the claimant may bring suit not later than two years after the day the cause of action accrues.

(e) This section does not bar an action:

(1) on a written warranty, guaranty, or other contract that expressly provides for a longer effective period;

(2) against a person in actual possession or control of the real property at the time that the damage, injury, or death occurs; or

(3) based on wilful misconduct or fraudulent concealment in connection with the performance of the construction or repair.

(f) This section does not extend or affect a period prescribed for bringing an action under any other law of this state.

See also *O'Connor's Texas COA*, "Actions against persons furnishing construction," ch. 52, §2.7.2, p. 1552.

SUBCHAPTER B. LIMITATIONS OF REAL PROPERTY ACTIONS

CPRC §16.021. DEFINITIONS

In this subchapter:

(1) "Adverse possession" means an actual and visible appropriation of real property, commenced and continued under a claim of right that is inconsistent with and is hostile to the claim of another person.

(2) "Color of title" means a consecutive chain of transfers to the person in possession that:

(A) is not regular because of a muniment that is not properly recorded or is only in writing or because of a similar defect that does not want of intrinsic fairness or honesty; or

(B) is based on a certificate of headright, land warrant, or land scrip.

(3) "Peaceable possession" means possession of real property that is continuous and is not interrupted by an adverse suit to recover the property.

(4) "Title" means a regular chain of transfers of real property from or under the sovereignty of the soil.

CPRC §16.022. EFFECT OF DISABILITY

(a) For the purposes of this subchapter, a person is under a legal disability if the person is:

(1) younger than 18 years of age, regardless of whether the person is married;

(2) of unsound mind; or

(3) serving in the United States Armed Forces during time of war.

(b) If a person entitled to sue for the recovery of real property or entitled to make a defense based on the title to real property is under a legal disability at the time title to the property vests or adverse possession commences, the time of the disability is not included in a limitations period.

(c) Except as provided by Sections 16.027 and 16.028, after the termination of the legal disability, a

person has the same time to present a claim that is allowed to others under this chapter.

See also *O'Connor's Texas COA*, "Tolling limitations," ch. 52, §2.5, p. 1546.

CPRC §16.023. TACKING OF SUCCESSIVE INTERESTS

To satisfy a limitations period, peaceable and adverse possession does not need to continue in the same person, but there must be privity of estate between each holder and his successor.

CPRC §16.024. ADVERSE POSSESSION: THREE-YEAR LIMITATIONS PERIOD

A person must bring suit to recover real property held by another in peaceable and adverse possession under title or color of title not later than three years after the day the cause of action accrues.

CPRC §16.025. ADVERSE POSSESSION: FIVE-YEAR LIMITATIONS PERIOD

(a) A person must bring suit not later than five years after the day the cause of action accrues to recover real property held in peaceable and adverse possession by another who:

(1) cultivates, uses, or enjoys the property;

(2) pays applicable taxes on the property; and

(3) claims the property under a duly registered deed.

(b) This section does not apply to a claim based on a forged deed or a deed executed under a forged power of attorney.

CPRC §16.026. ADVERSE POSSESSION: 10-YEAR LIMITATIONS PERIOD

(a) A person must bring suit not later than 10 years after the day the cause of action accrues to recover real property held in peaceable and adverse possession by another who cultivates, uses, or enjoys the property.

(b) Without a title instrument, peaceable and adverse possession is limited in this section to 160 acres, including improvements, unless the number of acres actually enclosed exceeds 160. If the number of enclosed acres exceeds 160 acres, peaceable and adverse possession extends to the real property actually enclosed.

(c) Peaceable possession of real property held under a duly registered deed or other memorandum of title that fixes the boundaries of the possessor's claim extends to the boundaries specified in the instrument.

E CPRC §16.0265. ADVERSE POSSESSION BY COTENANT HEIR: 15-YEAR COMBINED LIMITATIONS PERIOD

(a) In this section, "cotenant heir" means one of two or more persons who simultaneously acquire identical, undivided ownership interests in, and rights to possession of, the same real property by operation of the applicable intestate succession laws of this state or a successor in interest of one of those persons.

(b) One or more cotenant heirs of real property may acquire the interests of other cotenant heirs in the property by adverse possession under this section if, for a continuous, uninterrupted 10-year period immediately preceding the filing of the affidavits required by Subsection (c):

(1) the possessing cotenant heir or heirs:

(A) hold the property in peaceable and exclusive possession;

(B) cultivate, use, or enjoy the property; and

(C) pay all property taxes on the property not later than two years after the date the taxes become due; and

(2) no other cotenant heir has:

(A) contributed to the property's taxes or maintenance;

(B) challenged a possessing cotenant heir's exclusive possession of the property;

(C) asserted any other claim against a possessing cotenant heir in connection with the property, such as the right to rental payments from a possessing cotenant heir;

(D) acted to preserve the cotenant heir's interest in the property by filing notice of the cotenant heir's claimed interest in the deed records of the county in which the property is located; or

(E) entered into a written agreement with the possessing cotenant heir under which the possessing cotenant heir is allowed to possess the property but the other cotenant heir does not forfeit that heir's ownership interest.

(c) To make a claim of adverse possession against a cotenant heir under this section, the cotenant heir or heirs claiming adverse possession must:

(1) file in the deed records of the county in which the real property is located an affidavit of heirship in the

form prescribed by Section 203.002, Estates Code, and an affidavit of adverse possession that complies with the requirements of Subsection (d);

(2) publish notice of the claim in a newspaper of general circulation in the county in which the property is located for the four consecutive weeks immediately following the date the affidavits required by Subdivision (1) are filed; and

(3) provide written notice of the claim to the last known addresses of all other cotenant heirs by certified mail, return receipt requested.

(d) The affidavits required by Subsection (c) may be filed separately or combined into a single instrument. The affidavit of adverse possession must include:

(1) a legal description of the property that is the subject of the adverse possession;

(2) an attestation that each affiant is a cotenant heir of the property who has been in peaceable and exclusive possession of the property for a continuous, uninterrupted period during the 10 years preceding the filing of the affidavit;

(3) an attestation of cultivation, use, or enjoyment of the property by each affiant during the 10 years preceding the filing of the affidavit;

(4) evidence of payment by the affiant or affiants of all property taxes on the property as provided by Subsection (b) during the 10 years preceding the filing of the affidavit; and

(5) an attestation that there has been no action described by Subsection (b)(2) by another cotenant heir during the 10 years preceding the filing of the affidavit.

(e) A cotenant heir must file a controverting affidavit or bring suit to recover the cotenant heir's interest in real property adversely possessed by another cotenant heir under this section not later than the fifth anniversary of the date a right of adverse possession is asserted by the filing of the affidavits required by Subsection (c).

(f) If a controverting affidavit or judgment is not filed before the fifth anniversary of the date the affidavits required by Subsection (c) are filed and no notice described by Subsection (b)(2)(D) was filed in the 10-year period preceding the filing of the affidavits under Subsection (c), title vests in the adversely possessing cotenant heir or heirs in the manner provided by Section 16.030, precluding all claims by other cotenant heirs.

(g) A bona fide lender for value without notice accepting a voluntary lien against the real property to secure the adversely possessing cotenant heir's indebtedness or a bona fide purchaser for value without notice may conclusively rely on the affidavits required by Subsection (c) if:

(1) the affidavits have been filed of record for the period prescribed by Subsection (e); and

(2) a controverting affidavit or judgment has not been filed during that period.

(h) Without a title instrument, peaceable and adverse possession is limited in this section to 160 acres, including improvements, unless the number of acres actually enclosed exceeds 160 acres. If the number of enclosed acres exceeds 160 acres, peaceable and adverse possession extends to the real property actually enclosed.

(i) Peaceable possession of real property held under a duly registered deed or other memorandum of title that fixes the boundaries of the possessor's claim extends to the boundaries specified in the instrument.

2017 Legislation: Enacted by S.B. 1249, §1, 85th Leg., eff. Sept. 1, 2017.

CPRC §16.027. ADVERSE POSSESSION: 25-YEAR LIMITATIONS PERIOD NOTWITHSTANDING DISABILITY

A person, regardless of whether the person is or has been under a legal disability, must bring suit not later than 25 years after the day the cause of action accrues to recover real property held in peaceable and adverse possession by another who cultivates, uses, or enjoys the property.

CPRC §16.028. ADVERSE POSSESSION WITH RECORDED INSTRUMENT: 25-YEAR LIMITATIONS PERIOD

(a) A person, regardless of whether the person is or has been under a legal disability, may not maintain an action for the recovery of real property held for 25 years before the commencement of the action in peaceable and adverse possession by another who holds the property in good faith and under a deed or other instrument purporting to convey the property that is recorded in the deed records of the county where any part of the real property is located.

(b) Adverse possession of any part of the real property held under a recorded deed or other recorded instrument that purports to convey the property extends to and includes all of the property described in the instrument, even though the instrument is void on its face or in fact.

(c) A person who holds real property and claims title under this section has a good and marketable title to the property regardless of a disability arising at any time in the adverse claimant or a person claiming under the adverse claimant.

CPRC §16.029. EVIDENCE OF TITLE TO LAND BY LIMITATIONS

(a) In a suit involving title to real property that is not claimed by this state, it is prima facie evidence that the title to the property has passed from the person holding apparent record title to an opposing party if it is shown that:

(1) for one or more years during the 25 years preceding the filing of the suit the person holding apparent record title to the property did not exercise dominion over or pay taxes on the property; and

(2) during that period the opposing parties and those whose estate they own have openly exercised dominion over and have asserted a claim to the land and have paid taxes on it annually before becoming delinquent for as long as 25 years.

(b) This section does not affect a statute of limitations, a right to prove title by circumstantial evidence under the case law of this state, or a suit between a trustee and a beneficiary of the trust.

CPRC §16.030. TITLE THROUGH ADVERSE POSSESSION

(a) If an action for the recovery of real property is barred under this chapter, the person who holds the property in peaceable and adverse possession has full title, precluding all claims.

(b) A person may not acquire through adverse possession any right or title to real property dedicated to public use.

CPRC §16.031. ENCLOSED LAND

(a) A tract of land that is owned by one person and that is entirely surrounded by land owned, claimed, or fenced by another is not considered enclosed by a fence that encloses any part of the surrounding land.

(b) Possession of the interior tract by the owner or claimant of the surrounding land is not peaceable and adverse possession as described by Section 16.026 unless:

(1) the interior tract is separated from the surrounding land by a fence; or

(2) at least one-tenth of the interior tract is cultivated and used for agricultural purposes or is used for manufacturing purposes.

CPRC §16.032. ADJACENT LAND

Possession of land that belongs to another by a person owning or claiming 5,000 or more fenced acres that adjoin the land is not peaceable and adverse as described by Section 16.026 unless:

(1) the land is separated from the adjacent enclosed tract by a substantial fence;

(2) at least one-tenth of the land is cultivated and used for agricultural purposes or used for manufacturing purposes; or

(3) there is actual possession of the land.

CPRC §16.033. TECHNICAL DEFECTS IN INSTRUMENT

(a) A person with a right of action for the recovery of real property or an interest in real property conveyed by an instrument with one of the following defects must bring suit not later than two years after the day the instrument was filed for record with the county clerk of the county where the real property is located:

(1) lack of the signature of a proper corporate officer, partner, or company officer, manager, or member;

(2) lack of a corporate seal;

(3) failure of the record to show the corporate seal used;

(4) failure of the record to show authority of the board of directors or stockholders of a corporation, partners of a partnership, or officers, managers, or members of a company;

(5) execution and delivery of the instrument by a corporation, partnership, or other company that had been dissolved, whose charter had expired, or whose franchise had been canceled, withdrawn, or forfeited;

(6) acknowledgment of the instrument in an individual, rather than a representative or official, capacity;

(7) execution of the instrument by a trustee without record of the authority of the trustee or proof of the facts recited in the instrument;

(8) failure of the record or instrument to show an acknowledgment or jurat that complies with applicable law; or

(9) wording of the stated consideration that may or might create an implied lien in favor of the grantor.

(b) This section does not apply to a forged instrument.

CPRC §16.028

(c) For the purposes of this section, an instrument affecting real property containing a ministerial defect, omission, or informality in the certificate of acknowledgment that has been filed for record for longer than two years in the office of the county recorder of the county in which the property is located is considered to have been lawfully recorded and to be notice of the existence of the instrument on and after the date the instrument is filed.

CPRC §16.034. ATTORNEY'S FEES

(a) In a suit for the possession of real property between a person claiming under record title to the property and one claiming by adverse possession, if the prevailing party recovers possession of the property from a person unlawfully in actual possession, the court:

(1) shall award costs and reasonable attorney's fees to the prevailing party if the court finds that the person unlawfully in actual possession made a claim of adverse possession that was groundless and made in bad faith; and

(2) may award costs and reasonable attorney's fees to the prevailing party in the absence of a finding described by Subdivision (1).

(b) To recover attorney's fees, the person seeking possession must give the person unlawfully in possession a written demand for that person to vacate the premises. The demand must be given by registered or certified mail at least 10 days before filing the claim for recovery of possession.

(c) The demand must state that if the person unlawfully in possession does not vacate the premises within 10 days and a claim is filed by the person seeking possession, the court may enter a judgment against the person unlawfully in possession for costs and attorney's fees in an amount determined by the court to be reasonable.

See also *O'Connor's Texas COA*, "Award of Attorney Fees," ch. 45-A, §5, p. 1417.

CPRC §16.035. LIEN ON REAL PROPERTY

(a) A person must bring suit for the recovery of real property under a real property lien or the foreclosure of a real property lien not later than four years after the day the cause of action accrues.

(b) A sale of real property under a power of sale in a mortgage or deed of trust that creates a real property lien must be made not later than four years after the day the cause of action accrues.

(c) The running of the statute of limitations is not suspended against a bona fide purchaser for value, a lienholder, or a lessee who has no notice or knowledge of the suspension of the limitations period and who acquires an interest in the property when a cause of action on an outstanding real property lien has accrued for more than four years, except as provided by:

(1) Section 16.062, providing for suspension in the event of death; or

(2) Section 16.036, providing for recorded extensions of real property liens.

(d) On the expiration of the four-year limitations period, the real property lien and a power of sale to enforce the real property lien become void.

(e) If a series of notes or obligations or a note or obligation payable in installments is secured by a real property lien, the four-year limitations period does not begin to run until the maturity date of the last note, obligation, or installment.

(f) The limitations period under this section is not affected by Section 3.118, Business & Commerce Code.

(g) In this section, "real property lien" means:

(1) a superior title retained by a vendor in a deed of conveyance or a purchase money note; or

(2) a vendor's lien, a mortgage, a deed of trust, a voluntary mechanic's lien, or a voluntary materialman's lien on real estate, securing a note or other written obligation.

CPRC §16.036. EXTENSION OF REAL PROPERTY LIEN

(a) The party or parties primarily liable for a debt or obligation secured by a real property lien, as that term is defined in Section 16.035, may suspend the running of the four-year limitations period for real property liens through a written extension agreement as provided by this section.

(b) The limitations period is suspended and the lien remains in effect for four years after the extended maturity date of the debt or obligation if the extension agreement is:

(1) signed and acknowledged as provided by law for a deed conveying real property; and

(2) filed for record in the county clerk's office of the county where the real property is located.

(c) The parties may continue to extend the lien by entering, acknowledging, and recording additional extension agreements.

(d) The maturity date stated in the original instrument or in the date of the recorded renewal and extension is conclusive evidence of the maturity date of the debt or obligation.

(e) The limitations period under this section is not affected by Section 3.118, Business & Commerce Code.

See also *Real Estate Forms*, FORMS 11:1, 11:2.

CPRC §16.037. EFFECT OF EXTENSION OF REAL PROPERTY LIEN ON THIRD PARTIES

An extension agreement is void as to a bona fide purchaser for value, a lienholder, or a lessee who deals with real property affected by a real property lien without actual notice of the agreement and before the agreement is acknowledged, filed, and recorded.

See also *Real Estate Forms*, FORMS 11:1, 11:2.

CPRC §16.038. RESCISSION OR WAIVER OF ACCELERATED MATURITY DATE

(a) If the maturity date of a series of notes or obligations or a note or obligation payable in installments is accelerated, and the accelerated maturity date is rescinded or waived in accordance with this section before the limitations period expires, the acceleration is deemed rescinded and waived and the note, obligation, or series of notes or obligations shall be governed by Section 16.035 as if no acceleration had occurred.

(b) Rescission or waiver of acceleration is effective if made by a written notice of a rescission or waiver served as provided in Subsection (c) by the lienholder, the servicer of the debt, or an attorney representing the lienholder on each debtor who, according to the records of the lienholder or the servicer of the debt, is obligated to pay the debt.

(c) Service of a notice under Subsection (b) must be by first class or certified mail and is complete when the notice is deposited in the United States mail, postage prepaid and addressed to the debtor at the debtor's last known address. The affidavit of a person knowledgeable of the facts to the effect that service was completed is prima facie evidence of service.

(d) A notice served under this section does not affect a lienholder's right to accelerate the maturity date of the debt in the future nor does it waive past defaults.

(e) This section does not create an exclusive method for waiver and rescission of acceleration or affect the accrual of a cause of action and the running of the related limitations period under Section 16.035(e) on any subsequent maturity date, accelerated or otherwise, of the note or obligation or series of notes or obligations.

See also *Real Estate Forms*, FORM 4A:11.

SUBCHAPTER C. RESIDUAL LIMITATIONS PERIOD

CPRC §16.051. RESIDUAL LIMITATIONS PERIOD

Every action for which there is no express limitations period, except an action for the recovery of real property, must be brought not later than four years after the day the cause of action accrues.

See also *O'Connor's Texas COA*, "Limitations," ch. 52, p. 1537.

SUBCHAPTER D. MISCELLANEOUS PROVISIONS

CPRC §16.061. RIGHTS NOT BARRED

(a) A right of action of this state or a political subdivision of the state, including a county, an incorporated city or town, a navigation district, a municipal utility district, a port authority, an entity acting under Chapter 54, Transportation Code, a school district, or an entity created under Section 52, Article III, or Section 59, Article XVI, Texas Constitution, is not barred by any of the following sections: 16.001-16.004, 16.006, 16.007, 16.021-16.028, 16.030-16.032, 16.035-16.037, 16.051, 16.062, 16.063, 16.065-16.067, 16.070, 16.071, 31.006, or 71.021.

(b) In this section:

(1) "Navigation district" means a navigation district organized under Section 52, Article III, or Section 59, Article XVI, Texas Constitution.

(2) "Port authority" has the meaning assigned by Section 60.402, Water Code.

(3) "Municipal utility district" means a municipal utility district created under Section 52, Article III, or Section 59, Article XVI, Texas Constitution.

See also *O'Connor's Texas COA*, "Governmental exemptions from limitations," ch. 52, §2.2, p. 1538.

CPRC §16.070. CONTRACTUAL LIMITATIONS PERIOD

(a) Except as provided by Subsection (b), a person may not enter a stipulation, contract, or agreement that purports to limit the time in which to bring suit on the stipulation, contract, or agreement to a period shorter than two years. A stipulation, contract, or agreement that establishes a limitations period that is shorter than two years is void in this state.

(b) This section does not apply to a stipulation, contract, or agreement relating to the sale or purchase of a business entity if a party to the stipulation, contract, or agreement pays or receives or is obligated to pay or entitled to receive consideration under the stipulation, contract, or agreement having an aggregate value of not less than $500,000.

CHAPTER 17. PARTIES; CITATION; LONG-ARM JURISDICTION

SUBCHAPTER A. PARTIES TO SUIT

CPRC §17.002. SUIT AGAINST ESTATE FOR LAND TITLE

In a suit against the estate of a decedent involving the title to real property, the executor or administrator, if any, and the heirs must be made parties defendant.

CPRC §17.003. SUIT AGAINST NONRESIDENT OR TRANSIENT PROPERTY OWNER

For the purpose of establishing title to property, settling a lien or encumbrance on property, or determining an estate, interest, lien, or encumbrance, a person who claims an interest in the property may sue another person who claims an adverse interest or a lien or encumbrance but resides outside this state, resides in an unknown place, or is a transient. The plaintiff is not required to have actual possession of the property.

See also *O'Connor's Texas Rules*, "Special Appearance—Challenging Personal Jurisdiction," ch. 3-B, p. 218.

CPRC §17.005. SUIT AGAINST UNKNOWN LANDOWNER

(a) A person may sue the unknown owner or claimant of an interest in land if:

(1) the person bringing suit claims ownership of an interest in the land or has a claim or cause of action related to the land against the unknown owner or claimant; and

(2) the unknown owner or claimant:

(A) takes or holds the beneficial interest under a conveyance, lease, or written contract that conveyed an interest in the land to a trustee without disclosing the name of the owner of the beneficial interest; or

(B) takes or holds the interest of a dissolved association, joint-stock company, partnership, or other organization under an instrument that did not disclose his name, and the organization had acquired the interest under a conveyance, lease, or written contract that conveyed the interest to the organization in its name without disclosing the names of the members, shareholders, partners, or other persons owning an interest in the organization.

(b) A person may not sue the unknown stockholders of a corporation under this section, but if the plaintiff did not know that the organization was incorporated and the corporate character of the organization was not disclosed in the instrument under which title was acquired, the court retains jurisdiction over the unknown owners even if the organization was in fact incorporated.

See also TRCP 112, 113; *O'Connor's Texas Rules*, "Special Appearance—Challenging Personal Jurisdiction," ch. 3-B, p. 218.

CHAPTER 19. LOST RECORDS

CPRC §19.001. APPLICATION OF CHAPTER

This chapter applies to:

(1) a deed, bond, bill of sale, mortgage, deed of trust, power of attorney, or conveyance that is required or permitted by law to be acknowledged or recorded and that has been acknowledged or recorded; or

(2) a judgment, order, or decree of a court of record of this state.

See also *Real Estate Forms*, FORMS 11:1, 11:2.

CPRC §19.002. PAROL PROOF

A person may supply a lost, destroyed, or removed record by parol proof of the record's contents as provided by this chapter.

CPRC §19.003. APPLICATION FOR RELIEF

(a) To supply a record that has been lost, destroyed, or removed:

(1) a person interested in an instrument or in a judgment, order, or decree of the district court may file an application with the district clerk of the county in which the record was lost or destroyed or from which the record was removed; or

(2) a person interested in a judgment, order, or decree of a county court may file an application with the clerk of the court to which the record belonged.

(b) The application must be in writing and must set forth the facts that entitle the applicant to relief.

CPRC §19.004. CITATION

(a) If an application is filed to supply a record, the clerk shall issue a citation to the following, as applicable, or to the person's heirs or legal representatives:

(1) each grantor of property, in the case of a record of a deed;

(2) an interested party, in the case of an instrument other than a deed; or

(3) a party adversely interested to the applicant at the time of the rendition, in the case of a judgment, order, or decree.

(b) The citation must direct the person to whom it is issued to appear at a designated term of the court to contest the applicant's right to record a substitute.

(c) Process must be served in the manner provided by law for civil cases.

CPRC §19.005. ORDER

(a) On hearing an application to supply a record, if the court is satisfied from the evidence of the previous existence and content of the record and of its loss, destruction, or removal, the court shall enter on its minutes an order containing its findings and a description of the record and its contents.

(b) A certified copy of the order may be recorded in the proper county.

CPRC §19.006. EFFECT OF ORDER

The order supplying the record:

(1) stands in the place of the original record;

(2) has the same effect as the original record;

(3) if recorded, may be used as evidence in a court of the state as though it were the original record; and

(4) carries the same rights as the original record, including:

(A) preserving liens from the date of the original record; and

(B) giving parties the right to issue execution under the order as under the original record.

CPRC §19.007. METHOD NOT EXCLUSIVE

The method provided by this chapter for supplying a record is in addition to other methods provided by law.

CPRC §19.008. RERECORDATION OF ORIGINAL DOCUMENT

Rerecordation of the original document within four years after the date a record of an instrument, judgment, order, or decree was lost, destroyed, or removed is effective from the time of the original recordation.

CPRC §19.009. CERTIFIED COPY

If the loss, destruction, or removal of an original county record is established, a certified copy of the record from the records of that county or from the records of the county from which that county was created may be recorded in the county.

SUBTITLE C. JUDGMENTS

CHAPTER 31. JUDGMENTS

CPRC §31.001. PASSAGE OF TITLE

A judgment for the conveyance of real property or the delivery of personal property may pass title to the property without additional action by the party against whom the judgment is rendered.

A CPRC §31.002. COLLECTION OF JUDGMENT THROUGH COURT PROCEEDING

(a) A judgment creditor is entitled to aid from a court of appropriate jurisdiction through injunction or other means in order to reach property to obtain satisfaction on the judgment if the judgment debtor owns property, including present or future rights to property, that[~~:~~]

[~~(1)~~] [~~cannot readily be attached or levied on by ordinary legal process; and~~]

[~~(2)~~] is not exempt from attachment, execution, or seizure for the satisfaction of liabilities.

(b) The court may:

(1) order the judgment debtor to turn over nonexempt property that is in the debtor's possession or is subject to the debtor's control, together with all documents or records related to the property, to a designated sheriff or constable for execution;

(2) otherwise apply the property to the satisfaction of the judgment; or

(3) appoint a receiver with the authority to take possession of the nonexempt property, sell it, and pay the proceeds to the judgment creditor to the extent required to satisfy the judgment.

(c) The court may enforce the order by contempt proceedings or by other appropriate means in the event of refusal or disobedience.

(d) The judgment creditor may move for the court's assistance under this section in the same proceeding in which the judgment is rendered or in an independent proceeding.

(e) The judgment creditor is entitled to recover reasonable costs, including attorney's fees.

(f) A court may not enter or enforce an order under this section that requires the turnover of the proceeds of, or the disbursement of, property exempt under any statute, including Section 42.0021, Property Code. This subsection does not apply to the enforcement of a child support obligation or a judgment for past due child support.

(g) With respect to turnover of property held by a financial institution in the name of or on behalf of the judgment debtor as customer of the financial institution, the rights of a receiver appointed under Subsection (b)(3) do not attach until the financial institution receives service of a certified copy of the order of receivership in the manner specified by Section 59.008, Finance Code.

(h) A court may enter or enforce an order under this section that requires the turnover of nonexempt property without identifying in the order the specific property subject to turnover.

2017 Legislation: Amended by H.B. 1066, §1, 85th Leg., eff. June 15, 2017.
See also Tex. Const. art. 16, §28; B&CC §17.59; CPRC §31.0025; Fam. Code §§157.261-157.269; Prop. Code §41.001.

CPRC §31.0025. Authority of Court to Order Turnover of Wages

(a) Notwithstanding any other law, a court may not, at any time before a judgment debtor is paid wages for personal services performed by the debtor, enter or enforce an order that requires the debtor or any other person to turn over the wages for the satisfaction of the judgment.

(b) This section applies to wages in any form, including paycheck, cash, or property.

(c) This section does not apply to the enforcement of a child support obligation or a judgment for past due child support.

See also Tex. Const. art. 16, §28; CPRC §31.002(f); Prop. Code §42.001(b)(1).

CPRC §31.003. Judgment Against Partnership

If a suit is against several partners who are jointly indebted under a contract and citation has been served on at least one but not all of the partners, the court may render judgment against the partnership and against the partners who were actually served, but may not award a personal judgment or execution against any partner who was not served.

See also CPRC §17.022.

Chapter 34. Execution on Judgments

Subchapter A. Issuance & Levy of Writ

CPRC §34.001. No Execution on Dormant Judgment

(a) If a writ of execution is not issued within 10 years after the rendition of a judgment of a court of record or a justice court, the judgment is dormant and execution may not be issued on the judgment unless it is revived.

(b) If a writ of execution is issued within 10 years after rendition of a judgment but a second writ is not issued within 10 years after issuance of the first writ, the judgment becomes dormant. A second writ may be issued at any time within 10 years after issuance of the first writ.

(c) This section does not apply to a judgment for child support under the Family Code.

See also CPRC §31.006.

CPRC §34.002. Effect of Plaintiff's Death

(a) If a plaintiff dies after judgment, any writ of execution must be issued in the name of the plaintiff's legal representative, if any, and in the name of any other plaintiff. An affidavit of death and a certificate of appointment of the legal representative, given under the hand and seal of the clerk of the appointing court, must be filed with the clerk of the court issuing the writ of execution.

(b) If a plaintiff dies after judgment and his estate is not administered, the writ of execution must be issued in the name of all plaintiffs shown in the judgment. An affidavit showing that administration of the estate is unnecessary must be filed with the clerk of the court that rendered judgment. Money collected under the execution shall be paid into the registry of the court, and the court shall order the money partitioned and paid to the parties entitled to it.

(c) Death of a plaintiff after a writ of execution has been issued does not abate the execution, and the writ shall be levied and returned as if the plaintiff were living.

See also TRAP 7.1(a); TRCP 150, 151, 156.

CPRC §34.003. Effect of Defendant's Death

The death of the defendant after a writ of execution is issued stays the execution proceedings, but any lien acquired by levy of the writ must be recognized and enforced by the county court in the payment of the debts of the deceased.

See also TRAP 7.1(a); TRCP 150, 152, 156.

CPRC §34.004. LEVY ON PROPERTY CONVEYED TO THIRD PARTY

Property that the judgment debtor has sold, mortgaged, or conveyed in trust may not be seized in execution if the purchaser, mortgagee, or trustee points out other property of the debtor in the county that is sufficient to satisfy the execution.

CPRC §34.005. LEVY ON PROPERTY OF SURETY

(a) If the face of a writ of execution or the endorsement of the clerk shows that one of the persons against whom it is issued is surety for another, the officer must first levy on the principal's property that is subject to execution and is located in the county in which the judgment is rendered.

(b) If property of the principal cannot be found that, in the opinion of the officer, is sufficient to satisfy the execution, the officer shall levy first on the principal's property that can be found and then on as much of the property of the surety as is necessary to satisfy the execution.

CPRC §34.003

SUBCHAPTER B. RECOVERY OF SEIZED PROPERTY

CPRC §34.021. RECOVERY OF PROPERTY BEFORE SALE

A person is entitled to recover his property that has been seized through execution of a writ issued by a court if the judgment on which execution is issued is reversed or set aside and the property has not been sold at execution.

CPRC §34.022. RECOVERY OF PROPERTY VALUE AFTER SALE

(a) A person is entitled to recover from the judgment creditor the market value of the person's property that has been seized through execution of a writ issued by a court if the judgment on which execution is issued is reversed or set aside but the property has been sold at execution.

(b) The amount of recovery is determined by the market value at the time of sale of the property sold.

SUBCHAPTER C. SALE

Ⓐ CPRC §34.041. SALE AT PLACE OTHER THAN COURTHOUSE DOOR; DATE & TIME OF SALE

(a) If the public sale of real property is required by court order or other law to be made at a place other than the courthouse door, sales under this chapter shall be made at the place designated by that court order or other law.

(b) The commissioners court of a county may designate an area other than an area at the county courthouse where public sales of real property under this chapter will take place that is in a public place within a reasonable proximity of the county courthouse as determined by the commissioners court and in a location as accessible to the public as the courthouse door. The commissioners court shall record that designation in the real property records of the county. A designation by a commissioners court under this section is not a ground for challenging or invalidating any sale. Except for a sale under Subsection (a), a sale must be held at an area designated under this subsection if the sale is held on or after the 90th day after the date the designation is recorded. The commissioners court may by order authorize a county official or employee to identify separate locations within the designated area for the conduct of sales under this section and for the conduct of sales by peace officers under other laws.

(c) A sale of real property under this subchapter must take place between 10 a.m. and 4 p.m. on the first Tuesday of a month or, if the first Tuesday of a month occurs on January 1 or July 4, between 10 a.m. and 4 p.m. on the first Wednesday of the month. Notwithstanding Section 22.004, Government Code, the supreme court may not amend or adopt rules in conflict with this subsection.

2017 Legislation: Amended by H.B. 1128, §§1, 2, 85th Leg., eff. Sept. 1, 2017.

CPRC §34.042. SALE OF CITY LOTS

If real property taken in execution consists of several lots, tracts, or parcels in a city or town, each lot, tract, or parcel must be offered for sale separately unless not susceptible to separate sale because of the character of improvements.

CPRC §34.043. SALE OF RURAL PROPERTY

(a) If real property taken in execution is not located in a city or town, the defendant in the writ who

holds legal or equitable title to the property may divide the property into lots of not less than 50 acres and designate the order in which those lots shall be sold.

(b) The defendant must present to the executing officer:

(1) a plat of the property as divided and as surveyed by the county surveyor of the county in which the property is located; and

(2) field notes of each numbered lot with a certificate of the county surveyor certifying that the notes are correct.

(c) The defendant must present the plat and field notes to the executing officer before the sale at a time that will not delay the sale as advertised.

(d) When a sufficient number of the lots are sold to satisfy the amount of the execution, the officer shall stop the sale.

(e) The defendant shall pay the expenses of the survey and the sale, and those expenses do not constitute an additional cost in the case.

CPRC §34.044. STOCK SHARES SUBJECT TO SALE

Shares of stock in a corporation or joint-stock company that are owned by a defendant in execution may be sold on execution.

CPRC §34.0445. PERSONS ELIGIBLE TO PURCHASE REAL PROPERTY

(a) An officer conducting a sale of real property under this subchapter may not execute or deliver a deed to the purchaser of the property unless the purchaser exhibits to the officer:

(1) an unexpired written statement issued to the person in the manner prescribed by Section 34.015, Tax Code, showing that the county assessor-collector of the county in which the sale is conducted has determined that:

(A) there are no delinquent ad valorem taxes owed by the person to that county; and

(B) for each school district or municipality having territory in the county there are no known or reported delinquent ad valorem taxes owed by the person to that school district or municipality; or

(2) the written registration statement issued to the person in the manner prescribed by Section 34.011, Tax Code, showing that the person is a registered bidder at the sale at which the property is sold.

(b) An individual may not bid on or purchase the property in the name of any other individual. An officer conducting a sale under this subchapter may not execute a deed in the name of or deliver a deed to any person other than the person who was the successful bidder.

(c) The deed executed by the officer conducting the sale must name the successful bidder as the grantee and recite that the successful bidder exhibited to that officer:

(1) an unexpired written statement issued to the person in the manner prescribed by Section 34.015, Tax Code, showing that the county assessor-collector of the county in which the sale was conducted determined that:

(A) there are no delinquent ad valorem taxes owed by the person to that county; and

(B) for each school district or municipality having territory in the county there are no known or reported delinquent ad valorem taxes owed by the person to that school district or municipality; or

(2) the written registration statement issued to the person in the manner prescribed by Section 34.011, Tax Code, showing that the person is a registered bidder at the sale at which the property is sold.

(d) If a deed contains the recital required by Subsection (c), it is conclusively presumed that this section was complied with.

(e) A person who knowingly violates this section commits an offense. An offense under this subsection is a Class B misdemeanor.

(f) To the extent of a conflict between this section and any other law, this section controls.

(g) This section applies only to a sale of real property under this subchapter that is conducted in:

(1) a county with a population of 250,000 or more; or

(2) a county with a population of less than 250,000 in which the commissioners court by order has adopted the provisions of this section.

CPRC §34.045. CONVEYANCE OF TITLE AFTER SALE

(a) When the sale has been made and its terms complied with, the officer shall execute and deliver to the purchaser a conveyance of all the right, title, interest, and claim that the defendant in execution had in the property sold.

(b) If the purchaser complies with the terms of the sale but dies before the conveyance is executed, the officer shall execute the conveyance to the purchaser, and the conveyance has the same effect as if it had been executed in the purchaser's lifetime.

CPRC §34.046. PURCHASER CONSIDERED INNOCENT PURCHASER WITHOUT NOTICE

The purchaser of property sold under execution is considered to be an innocent purchaser without notice if the purchaser would have been considered an innocent purchaser without notice had the sale been made voluntarily and in person by the defendant.

CPRC §34.047. DISTRIBUTION OF SALE PROCEEDS

(a) An officer shall deliver money collected on execution to the entitled party at the earliest opportunity.

(b) The officer is entitled to retain from the proceeds of a sale of personal property an amount equal to the reasonable expenses incurred by him in making the levy and keeping the property.

(c) If more money is received from the sale of property than is sufficient to satisfy the executions held by the officer, the officer shall immediately pay the surplus to the defendant or the defendant's agent or attorney.

CHAPTER 35. ENFORCEMENT OF JUDGMENTS OF OTHER STATES

CPRC §35.001. DEFINITION

In this chapter, "foreign judgment" means a judgment, decree, or order of a court of the United States or of any other court that is entitled to full faith and credit in this state.

CPRC §35.002. SHORT TITLE

This chapter may be cited as the Uniform Enforcement of Foreign Judgments Act.

CPRC §35.003. FILING & STATUS OF FOREIGN JUDGMENTS

(a) A copy of a foreign judgment authenticated in accordance with an act of congress or a statute of this state may be filed in the office of the clerk of any court of competent jurisdiction of this state.

(b) The clerk shall treat the foreign judgment in the same manner as a judgment of the court in which the foreign judgment is filed.

(c) A filed foreign judgment has the same effect and is subject to the same procedures, defenses, and proceedings for reopening, vacating, staying, enforcing, or satisfying a judgment as a judgment of the court in which it is filed.

CPRC §35.004. AFFIDAVIT; NOTICE OF FILING

(a) At the time a foreign judgment is filed, the judgment creditor or the judgment creditor's attorney shall file with the clerk of the court an affidavit showing the name and last known post office address of the judgment debtor and the judgment creditor.

(b) The judgment creditor or the judgment creditor's attorney shall:

(1) promptly mail notice of the filing of the foreign judgment to the judgment debtor at the address provided for the judgment debtor under Subsection (a); and

(2) file proof of mailing of the notice with the clerk of the court.

(c) The notice must include the name and post office address of the judgment creditor and if the judgment creditor has an attorney in this state, the attorney's name and address.

(d) On receipt of proof of mailing under Subsection (b), the clerk of the court shall note the mailing in the docket.

CPRC §35.005. REPEALED

CPRC §35.006. STAY

(a) If the judgment debtor shows the court that an appeal from the foreign judgment is pending or will be taken, that the time for taking an appeal has not expired, or that a stay of execution has been granted, has been requested, or will be requested, and proves that the judgment debtor has furnished or will furnish the security for the satisfaction of the judgment required by the state in which it was rendered, the court shall stay enforcement of the foreign judgment until the appeal is concluded, the time for appeal expires, or the stay of execution expires or is vacated.

(b) If the judgment debtor shows the court a ground on which enforcement of a judgment of the court of this state would be stayed, the court shall stay enforcement of the foreign judgment for an appropriate period and require the same security for suspending enforcement of the judgment that is required in this state in accordance with Section 52.006.

CPRC §35.007. FEES

(a) A person filing a foreign judgment shall pay to the clerk of the court the amount as otherwise provided by law for filing suit in the courts of this state.

(b) Filing fees are due and payable at the time of filing.

(c) Fees for other enforcement proceedings are as provided by law for judgments of the courts of this state.

CPRC §35.008. OPTIONAL PROCEDURE

A judgment creditor retains the right to bring an action to enforce a judgment instead of proceeding under this chapter.

Chapter 36. Repealed [~~Enforcement of Judgments of Other Countries~~]

CPRC §36.001. REPEALED [~~DEFINITIONS~~]

[~~In this chapter:~~]

[~~(1)~~] [~~"Foreign country" means a governmental unit other than:~~]

[~~(A)~~] [~~the United States;~~]

[~~(B)~~] [~~a state, district, commonwealth, territory, or insular possession of the United States;~~]

[~~(C)~~] [~~the Panama Canal Zone; or~~]

[~~(D)~~] [~~the Trust Territory of the Pacific Islands.~~]

[~~(2)~~] [~~"Foreign country judgment" means a judgment of a foreign country granting or denying a sum of money other than a judgment for:~~]

[~~(A)~~] [~~taxes, a fine, or other penalty; or~~]

[~~(B)~~] [~~support in a matrimonial or family matter.~~]

Repealed by S.B. 944, §2, 85th Leg., eff. June 1, 2017.

CPRC §36.002. REPEALED [~~APPLICABILITY~~]

[~~(a)~~] [~~This chapter applies to a foreign country judgment:~~]

[~~(1)~~] [~~that is final and conclusive and enforceable where rendered, even though an appeal is pending or the judgment is subject to appeal; or~~]

[~~(2)~~] [~~that is in favor of the defendant on the merits of the cause of action and is final and conclusive where rendered, even though an appeal is pending or the judgment is subject to appeal.~~]

[~~(b)~~] [~~This chapter does not apply to a judgment rendered before June 17, 1981.~~]

Repealed by S.B. 944, §2, 85th Leg., eff. June 1, 2017.

CPRC §36.003. REPEALED [~~SHORT TITLE~~]

[~~This chapter may be cited as the Uniform Foreign Country Money-Judgment Recognition Act.~~]

Repealed by S.B. 944, §2, 85th Leg., eff. June 1, 2017.

CPRC §36.004. REPEALED [~~RECOGNITION & ENFORCEMENT~~]

[~~Except as provided by Section 36.005, a foreign country judgment that is filed with notice given as provided by this chapter, that meets the requirements of Section 36.002, and that is not refused recognition under Section 36.0044 is conclusive between the parties to the extent that it grants or denies recovery of a sum of money. The judgment is enforceable in the same manner as a judgment of a sister state that is entitled to full faith and credit.~~]

Repealed by S.B. 944, §2, 85th Leg., eff. June 1, 2017.

CPRC §36.0041. REPEALED [~~FILING~~]

[~~A copy of a foreign country judgment authenticated in accordance with an act of congress, a statute of this state, or a treaty or other international convention to which the United States is a party may be filed in the office of the clerk of a court in the county of residence of the party against whom recognition is sought or in any other court of competent jurisdiction as allowed under the Texas venue laws.~~]

Repealed by S.B. 944, §2, 85th Leg., eff. June 1, 2017.

CPRC §36.0042. REPEALED [~~AFFIDAVIT; NOTICE OF FILING~~]

[~~(a)~~] [~~At the time a foreign country judgment is filed, the party seeking recognition of the judgment or the party's attorney shall file with the clerk of the court an affidavit showing the name and last known post office address of the judgment debtor and the judgment creditor.~~]

[~~(b)~~] [~~The clerk shall promptly mail notice of the filing of the foreign country judgment to the party against whom recognition is sought at the address given and shall note the mailing in the docket.~~]

[~~(c)~~] [~~The notice must include the name and post office address of the party seeking recognition and that party's attorney, if any, in this state.~~]

Repealed by S.B. 944, §2, 85th Leg., eff. June 1, 2017.

CPRC §36.0043. REPEALED [~~ALTERNATE NOTICE OF FILING~~]

[~~(a)~~] [~~The party seeking recognition may mail a notice of the filing of the foreign country judgment to the other party and may file proof of mailing with the clerk.~~]

[~~(b)~~] [~~A clerk's lack of mailing the notice of filing does not affect the conclusive recognition of the foreign country judgment under this chapter if proof of mailing by the party seeking recognition has been filed.~~]

Repealed by S.B. 944, §2, 85th Leg., eff. June 1, 2017.

CPRC §36.0044. REPEALED [~~CONTESTING RECOGNITION~~]

[~~(a)~~] [~~A party against whom recognition of a foreign country judgment is sought may contest recognition of the judgment if, not later than the 30th day after the date of service of the notice of filing, the party files with the court, and serves the opposing party with a copy of, a motion for nonrecognition of the judgment on the basis of one or more grounds under Section 36.005. If the party is domiciled in a foreign country, the party must file the motion for nonrecognition not later than the 60th day after the date of service of the notice of filing.~~]

[~~(b)~~] [~~The party filing the motion for nonrecognition shall include with the motion all supporting affidavits, briefs, and other documentation.~~]

[~~(c)~~] [~~A party opposing the motion must file any response, including supporting affidavits, briefs, and other documentation, not later than the 20th day after the date of service on that party of a copy of the motion for nonrecognition.~~]

[~~(d)~~] [~~The court may, on motion and notice, grant an extension of time, not to exceed 20 days unless good cause is shown, for the filing of a response or any document that is required to establish a ground for nonrecognition but that is not available within the time for filing the document.~~]

[~~(e)~~] [~~A party filing a motion for nonrecognition or responding to the motion may request an evidentiary hearing that the court may allow in its discretion.~~]

[~~(f)~~] [~~The court may at any time permit or require the submission of argument, authorities, or supporting material in addition to that provided for by this section.~~]

[~~(g)~~] [~~The court may refuse recognition of the foreign country judgment if the motions, affidavits, briefs, and other evidence before it establish grounds for nonrecognition as specified in Section 36.005, but the court may not, under any circumstances, review the foreign country judgment in relation to any matter not specified in Section 36.005.~~]

Repealed by S.B. 944, §2, 85th Leg., eff. June 1, 2017.

CPRC §36.005. REPEALED [~~GROUNDS FOR NONRECOGNITION~~]

[~~(a)~~] [~~A foreign country judgment is not conclusive if:~~]

[~~(1)~~] [~~the judgment was rendered under a system that does not provide impartial tribunals or procedures compatible with the requirements of due process of law;~~]

[~~(2)~~] [~~the foreign country court did not have personal jurisdiction over the defendant; or~~]

[~~(3)~~] [~~the foreign country court did not have jurisdiction over the subject matter.~~]

[~~(b)~~] [~~A foreign country judgment need not be recognized if:~~]

[~~(1)~~] [~~the defendant in the proceedings in the foreign country court did not receive notice of the proceedings in sufficient time to defend;~~]

[~~(2)~~] [~~the judgment was obtained by fraud;~~]

[~~(3)~~] [~~the cause of action on which the judgment is based is repugnant to the public policy of this state;~~]

[~~(4)~~] [~~the judgment conflicts with another final and conclusive judgment;~~]

[~~(5)~~] [~~the proceeding in the foreign country court was contrary to an agreement between the parties under which the dispute in question was to be settled otherwise than by proceedings in that court;~~]

[~~(6)~~] [~~in the case of jurisdiction based only on personal service, the foreign country court was a seriously inconvenient forum for the trial of the action; or~~]

[~~(7)~~] [~~it is established that the foreign country in which the judgment was rendered does not recognize judgments rendered in this state that, but for the fact that they are rendered in this state, conform to the definition of "foreign country judgment."~~]

Repealed by S.B. 944, §2, 85th Leg., eff. June 1, 2017.

CPRC §36.006. REPEALED [~~PERSONAL JURISDICTION~~]

[~~(a)~~] [~~A court may not refuse to recognize a foreign country judgment for lack of personal jurisdiction if:~~]

[~~(1)~~] [~~the defendant was served personally in the foreign country;~~]

[~~(2)~~] [~~the defendant voluntarily appeared in the proceedings, other than for the purpose of protecting property seized or threatened with seizure in the proceedings or of contesting the jurisdiction of the court over him;~~]

[~~(3)~~] [~~the defendant prior to the commencement of the proceedings had agreed to submit to the jurisdiction of the foreign country court with respect to the subject matter involved;~~]

[~~(4)~~] [~~the defendant was domiciled in the foreign country when the proceedings were instituted or, if the defendant is a body corporate, had its principal place of business, was incorporated, or had otherwise acquired corporate status in the foreign country;~~]

[~~(5)~~] [~~the defendant had a business office in the foreign country and the proceedings in the foreign country court involved a cause of action arising out of business done by the defendant through that office in the foreign country; or~~]

[~~(6)~~] [~~the defendant operated a motor vehicle or airplane in the foreign country and the proceedings involved a cause of action arising out of operation of the motor vehicle or airplane.~~]

[~~(b)~~] [~~A court of this state may recognize other bases of jurisdiction.~~]

Repealed by S.B. 944, §2, 85th Leg., eff. June 1, 2017.

CPRC §36.007. REPEALED [~~STAY IN CASE OF APPEAL~~]

[~~If the defendant satisfies the court either that an appeal is pending or that the defendant is entitled and intends to appeal from the foreign country judgment, the court may stay the proceedings until the appeal has been determined or until a period of time sufficient to enable the defendant to prosecute the appeal has expired.~~]

Repealed by S.B. 944, §2, 85th Leg., eff. June 1, 2017.

CPRC §36.008. REPEALED [~~OTHER FOREIGN COUNTRY JUDGMENTS~~]

[~~This chapter does not prevent the recognition of a foreign country judgment in a situation not covered by this chapter.~~]

Repealed by S.B. 944, §2, 85th Leg., eff. June 1, 2017.

E

Chapter 36A. Enforcement of Judgments of Other Countries

NCCUSL Prefatory Comment*

This Act is a revision of the Uniform Foreign Money-Judgments Recognition Act of 1962. That Act codified the most prevalent common law rules with regard to the recognition of money judgments rendered in other countries. The hope was that codification by a state of its rules on the recognition of foreign-country money judgments, by satisfying reciprocity concerns of foreign courts, would make it more likely that money judgments rendered in that state would be recognized in other countries. Towards this end, the Act sets out the circumstances in which the courts in states that have adopted the Act must recognize foreign-country money judgments. It delineates a minimum of foreign-country judgments that must be recognized by the courts of adopting states, leaving those courts free to recognize other foreign-country judgments not covered by the Act under principles of comity or otherwise. Since its promulgation over forty years ago, the 1962 Act has been adopted in a majority of the states and has been in large part successful in carrying out its purpose of establishing uniform and clear standards under which state courts will enforce the foreign-country money judgments that come within its scope.

This Act continues the basic policies and approach of the 1962 Act. Its purpose is not to depart from the basic rules or approach of the 1962 Act, which have withstood well the test of time, but rather to update the 1962 Act, to clarify its provisions, and to correct problems created by the interpretation of the provisions of that Act by the courts over the years since its promulgation. Among the more significant issues that have arisen under the 1962 Act which are addressed in this Revised Act are (1) the need to update and clarify the definitions section; (2) the need to reorganize and clarify the scope provisions, and to allocate the burden of proof with regard to establishing application of the Act; (3) the need to set out the procedure by which recognition of a foreign-country money judgment under the Act must be sought; (4) the need to clarify and, to a limited extent, expand upon the grounds for denying recognition in light of differing interpretations of those provisions in the current case law; (5) the need to expressly allocate the burden of proof with regard to the grounds for denying recognition; and (6) the need to establish a statute of limitations for recognition actions.

In the course of drafting this Act, the drafters revisited the decision made in the 1962 Act not to require reciprocity as a condition to recognition of the foreign-country money judgments covered by the Act. After much discussion, the drafters decided that the approach of the 1962 Act continues to be the wisest course with regard to this issue. While recognition of U.S. judgments continues to be problematic in a number of foreign countries, there was insufficient evidence to establish that a reciprocity requirement would have a greater effect on encouraging foreign recognition of U.S. judgments than does the approach taken by the Act. At the same time, the certainty and uniformity provided by the approach of the 1962 Act, and continued in this Act, creates a stability in this area that facilitates international commercial transactions.

CPRC §36A.001. SHORT TITLE

This chapter may be cited as the Uniform Foreign-Country Money Judgments Recognition Act.

2017 Legislation: Enacted by S.B. 944, §1, 85th Leg., eff. June 1, 2017.

CPRC §36A.002. DEFINITIONS

In this chapter:

(1) "Foreign country" means a government other than:

(A) the United States;

(B) a state, district, commonwealth, territory, or insular possession of the United States; or

(C) any other government with respect to which the decision in this state as to whether to recognize a judgment of that government's court is initially subject to determination under Section 1, Article IV, United States Constitution (the full faith and credit clause).

(2) "Foreign-country judgment" means a judgment of a court of a foreign country.

2017 Legislation: Enacted by S.B. 944, §1, 85th Leg., eff. June 1, 2017.

* **Editor's note:**

The NCCUSL comments have been edited to reflect the Texas Legislature's omission of sections and changing of section numbers from the original uniform act. The Texas Legislature did not adopt the NCCUSL comments when it adopted the Revised Uniform Fiduciary Access to Digital Assets Act. The full uniform act and comments can be found at www.uniformlaws.org.

NCCUSL Comment*

1. The defined terms "foreign state" and "foreign judgment" in the 1962 Act have been changed to "foreign country" and "foreign-country judgment" in order to make it clear that the Act does not apply to recognition of sister-state judgments. Some courts have noted that the "foreign state" and "foreign judgment" definitions of the 1962 Act have caused confusion as to whether the Act should apply to sister-state judgments because "foreign state" and "foreign judgment" are terms of art generally used in connection with recognition and enforcement of sister-state judgments. *See, e.g.*, Eagle Leasing v. Amandus, 476 N.W.2d 35 (S.Ct. Iowa 1991) (reversing lower court's application of UFMJRA to a sister-state judgment, but noting lower court's confusion was understandable as "foreign judgment" is term of art normally applied to sister-state judgments). *See also*, Uniform Enforcement of Foreign Judgments Act §1 (defining "foreign judgment" as the judgment of a sister state or federal court).

The 1962 Act defines a "foreign state" as "any governmental unit other than the United States, or any state, district, commonwealth, territory, insular possession thereof, or the Panama Canal Zone, the Trust Territory of the Pacific Islands, or the Ryuku Islands." Rather than simply updating the list in the 1962 Act's definition of "foreign state," the new definition of "foreign country" in this Act combines the "listing" approach of the 1962 Act's "foreign state" definition with a provision that defines "foreign country" in terms of whether the judgments of the particular government's courts are initially subject to the Full Faith and Credit Clause standards for determining whether those judgments will be recognized. Under this new definition, a governmental unit is a "foreign country" if it is (1) not the United States or a state, district, commonwealth, territory or insular possession of the United States; and (2) its judgments are not initially subject to Full Faith and Credit Clause standards.

The Full Faith and Credit Clause, Art. IV, §1, provides that "Full Faith and Credit shall be given in each State to the public Acts, Records, and judicial Proceedings of every other State. And the Congress may by general Laws prescribe the Manner in which such Acts, Records, and Proceedings shall be proved, and the Effect thereof." Whether the judgments of a governmental unit are subject to the Full Faith and Credit Clause may be determined by judicial interpretation of the Full Faith and Credit Clause or by statute, or by a combination of these two sources. For example, pursuant to the authority granted by the second sentence of the Full Faith and Credit Clause, Congress has passed 28 U.S.C.A. §1738, which provides *inter alia* that court records from "any State, Territory, or Possession of the United States" are entitled to full faith and credit under the Full Faith and Credit Clause. In *Stoll v. Gottlieb*, 305 U.S. 165, 170 (1938), the United States Supreme Court held that this statute also requires that full faith and credit be given to judgments of federal courts. States also have made determinations as to whether certain types of judgments are subject to the Full Faith and Credit Clause. *E.g.* Day v. Montana Dept. Of Social & Rehab. Servs., 900 P.2d 296 (Mont. 1995) (tribal court judgment not subject to Full Faith and Credit, and should be treated with same deference shown foreign-country judgments). Under the definition of "foreign country" in this Act, the determination as to whether a governmental unit's judgments are subject to full faith and credit standards should be made by reference to any relevant law, whether statutory or decisional, that is applicable "in this state."

The definition of "foreign country" in terms of those judgments not subject to Full Faith and Credit standards also has the advantage of more effectively coordinating the Act with the Uniform Enforcement of Foreign Judgments Act. That Act, which establishes a registration procedure for the enforcement of sister state and equivalent judgments, defines a "foreign judgment" as "any judgment, decree, or order of a court of the United States or of any other court which is entitled to full faith and credit in this state." Uniform Enforcement of Foreign Judgments Act, §1 (1964). By defining "foreign country" in the Recognition Act in terms of those judgments not subject to full faith and credit standards, this Act makes it clear that the Enforcement Act and the Recognition Act are mutually exclusive—if a foreign money judgment is subject to full faith and credit standards, then the Enforcement Act's registration procedure is available with regard to its enforcement; if the foreign money judgment is not subject to full faith and credit standards, then the foreign money judgment may not be enforced until recognition of it has been obtained in accordance with the provisions of the Recognition Act.

2. The definition of "foreign-country judgment" in this Act differs significantly from the 1962 Act's definition of "foreign judgment." The 1962 Act's definition served in large part as a scope provision for the Act. The part of the definition defining the scope of the Act has been moved to §36A.003, which is the scope section.

3. The definition of "foreign-country judgment" in this Act refers to "a judgment" of "a court" of the foreign country. The foreign-country judgment need not take a particular form—any order or decree that meets the requirements of this section and comes within the scope of the Act under §36A.003 is subject to the Act. Similarly, any competent government tribunal that issues such a "judgment" comes within the term "court" for purposes of this Act. The judgment, however, must be a judgment of an adjudicative body of the foreign country, and not the result of an alternative dispute mechanism chosen by the parties. Thus, foreign arbitral awards and agreements to arbitrate are not covered by this Act. They are governed instead by federal law, Chapter 2 of the U.S. Arbitration Act, 9 U.S.C. §§201-208, implementing the United Nations Convention on the Recognition and Enforcement of Foreign Arbitral Awards and Chapter 3 of the U.S. Arbitration Act, 9 U.S.C. §§301-307, implementing the Inter-American Convention on International Commercial Arbitration. A judgment of a foreign court confirming or setting aside an arbitral award, however, would be covered by this Act.

4. The definition of "foreign-country judgment" does not limit foreign-country judgments to those rendered in litigation between private parties. Judgments in which a governmental entity is a party also are included, and are subject to this Act if they meet the requirements of this section and are within the scope of the Act under §36A.003.

CPRC §36A.003. APPLICABILITY

(a) Except as otherwise provided in Subsection (b), this chapter applies to a foreign-country judgment to the extent that the judgment:

(1) grants or denies recovery of a sum of money; and

(2) under the law of the foreign country in which the judgment is rendered, is final, conclusive, and enforceable.

(b) This chapter does not apply to a foreign-country judgment that grants or denies recovery of a sum of money to the extent that the judgment is:

(1) a judgment for taxes;

(2) a fine or other penalty; or

(3) a judgment for divorce, support, or maintenance, or other judgment rendered in connection with domestic relations.

(c) A party seeking recognition of a foreign-country judgment has the burden of establishing that this chapter applies to the foreign-country judgment.

2017 Legislation: Enacted by S.B. 944, §1, 85th Leg., eff. June 1, 2017.

NCCUSL Comment*

1. Like the 1962 Act, this Act sets out in §36A.003(a) two basic requirements that a foreign-country judgment must meet before it comes within the scope of this Act—the foreign-country judgment must (1) grant or deny recovery of a sum of money and (2) be final, conclusive and enforceable under the law of the foreign country where it was rendered. Subsection (b) then sets out three types of foreign-country judgments that are excluded from the coverage of this Act, even though they meet the criteria of subsection (a)—judgments for taxes, judgments constituting fines and other penalties, and judgments in domestic relations matters. These exclusions are comparable to those contained in Section 1(2) of the 1962 Act.

2. This Act applies to a foreign-country judgment only to the extent the foreign-country judgment grants or denies recovery of a sum of money. If a for-

* See footnote on p. 933.

eign-country judgment both grants or denies recovery of a sum money and provides for some other form of relief, this Act would apply to the portion of the judgment that grants or denies monetary relief, but not to the portion that provides for some other form of relief. The U.S. court, however, would be left free to decide to recognize and enforce the non-monetary portion of the judgment under principles of comity or other applicable law. See §36A.011.

3. In order to come within the scope of this Act, a foreign-country judgment must be final, conclusive, and enforceable under the law of the foreign country in which it was rendered. This requirement contains three distinct, although inter-related concepts. A judgment is final when it is not subject to additional proceedings in the rendering court other than execution. A judgment is conclusive when it is given effect between the parties as a determination of their legal rights and obligations. A judgment is enforceable when the legal procedures of the state to ensure that the judgment debtor complies with the judgment are available to the judgment creditor to assist in collection of the judgment.

While the first two of these requirements—finality and conclusiveness—will apply with regard to every foreign-country money judgment, the requirement of enforceability is only relevant when the judgment is one granting recovery of a sum of money. A judgment denying a sum of money obviously is not subject to enforcement procedures, as there is no monetary award to enforce. This Act, however, covers both judgments granting and those denying recovery of a sum of money. Thus, the fact that a foreign-country judgment denying recovery of a sum of money is not enforceable does not mean that such judgments are not within the scope of the Act. Instead, the requirement that the judgment be enforceable should be read to mean that, if the foreign-country judgment grants recovery of a sum of money, it must be enforceable in the foreign country in order to be within the scope of the Act.

Like the 1962 Act, §36A.003(b) requires that the determinations as to finality, conclusiveness and enforceability be made using the law of the foreign country in which the judgment was rendered. Unless the foreign-country judgment is final, conclusive, and (to the extent it grants recovery of a sum of money) enforceable in the foreign country where it was rendered, it will not be within the scope of this Act.

4. Section 36A.003(b) follows the 1962 Act by excluding three categories of foreign-country money judgments from the scope of the Act—judgments for taxes, judgments that constitute fines and penalties, and judgments in domestic relations matters. The domestic relations exclusion has been redrafted to make it clear that all judgments in domestic relations matters are excluded from the Act, not just judgments "for support" as provided in the 1962 Act. This is consistent with interpretation of the 1962 Act by the courts, which extended the "support" exclusion in the 1962 Act beyond its literal wording to exclude other money judgments in connection with domestic matters. *E.g.*, Wolff v. Wolff, 389 A.2d 413 (My. App. 1978) ("support" includes alimony).

Recognition and enforcement of domestic relations judgments traditionally has been treated differently from recognition and enforcement of other judgments. The considerations with regard to those judgments, particularly with regard to jurisdiction and finality, differ from those with regard to other money judgments. Further, national laws with regard to domestic relations vary widely, and recognition and enforcement of such judgments thus is more appropriately handled through comity than through use of this uniform Act. Finally, other statutes, such as the Uniform Interstate Family Support Act and the federal International Child Support Enforcement Act, 42 U.S.C. §659a (1996), address various aspects of the recognition and enforcement of domestic relations awards. Under §36A.011 of this Act, courts are free to recognize money judgments in domestic relations matters under principles of comity or otherwise, and U.S. courts routinely enforce money judgments in domestic relations matters under comity principles.

Foreign-country judgments for taxes and judgments that constitute fines or penalties traditionally have not been recognized and enforced in U.S. courts. *See, e.g.*, Restatement (Third) of the Foreign Relations Law of the United States §483 (1986). Both the "revenue rule," under which the courts of one country will not enforce the revenue laws of another country, and the prohibition on enforcement of penal judgments seem to be grounded in the idea that one country does not enforce the public laws of another. *See id.* Reporters' Note 2. The exclusion of tax judgments and judgments constituting fines or penalties from the scope of the Act reflects this tradition. Under §36A.011, however, courts remain free to consider whether such judgments should be recognized and enforced under comity or other principles.

A judgment for taxes is a judgment in favor of a foreign country or one of its subdivisions based on a claim for an assessment of a tax. Thus, a judgment awarding a plaintiff restitution of the purchase price paid for an item would not be considered in any part a judgment for taxes, even though one element of the recovery was the sales tax paid by the plaintiff at the time of purchase. Such a judgment would not be one designed to enforce the revenue laws of the foreign country, but rather one designed to compensate the plaintiff. Courts generally hold that the test for whether a judgment is a fine or penalty is determined by whether its purpose is remedial in nature, with its benefits accruing to private individuals, or it is penal in nature, punishing an offense against public justice. *E.g.*, Chase Manhattan Bank, N.A. v. Hoffman, 665 F.Supp. 73 (D. Mass. 1987) (finding that Belgium judgment was not penal even though the proceeding forming the basis of the suit was primarily criminal where Belgium court considered damage petition a civil remedy, the judgment did not constitute punishment for an offense against public justice of Belgium, and benefit of the judgment accrued to private judgment creditor, not Belgium). Thus, a judgment that awards compensation or restitution for the benefit of private individuals should not automatically be considered penal in nature and therefore outside the scope of the Act simply because the action is brought on behalf of the private individuals by a government entity. *Cf.* U.S.-Australia Free Trade Agreement, art. 14.7.2, U.S.-Austl., May 18, 2004 (providing that when government agency obtains a civil monetary judgment for purpose of providing restitution to consumers, investors, or customers who suffered economic harm due to fraud, judgment generally should not be denied recognition and enforcement on ground that it is penal or revenue in nature, or based on other foreign public law).

5. Under §36A.003(b), a foreign-country money judgment is not within the scope of this Act "to the extent" that it comes within one of the excluded categories. Therefore, if a foreign-country money judgment is only partially within one of the excluded categories, the nonexcluded portion will be subject to this Act.

6. Section 36A.003(c) is new. The 1962 Act does not expressly allocate the burden of proof with regard to establishing whether a foreign-country judgment is within the scope of the Act. Courts applying the 1962 Act generally have held that the burden of proof is on the person seeking recognition to establish that the judgment is final, conclusive and enforceable where rendered. *E.g.*, Mayekawa Mfg. Co. Ltd. v. Sasaki, 888 P.2d 183, 189 (Wash. App. 1995) (burden of proof on creditor to establish judgment is final, conclusive, and enforceable where rendered); Bridgeway Corp. v. Citibank, 45 F.Supp.2d 276, 285 (S.D.N.Y. 1999) (party seeking recognition must establish that there is a final judgment, conclusive and enforceable where rendered); S.C.Chimexim S.A. v. Velco Enterprises, Ltd., 36 F.Supp.2d 206, 212 (S.D.N.Y. 1999) (plaintiff has the burden of establishing conclusive effect). Subsection (c) places the burden of proof to establish whether a foreign-country judgment is within the scope of the Act on the party seeking recognition of the foreign-country judgment with regard to both subsection (a) and subsection (b).

CPRC §36A.004. STANDARDS FOR RECOGNITION OF FOREIGN-COUNTRY JUDGMENT

(a) Except as otherwise provided in Subsections (b) and (c), a court of this state shall recognize a foreign-country judgment to which this chapter applies.

(b) A court of this state may not recognize a foreign-country judgment if:

(1) the judgment was rendered under a judicial system that does not provide impartial tribunals or procedures compatible with the requirements of due process of law;

(2) the foreign court did not have personal jurisdiction over the defendant; or

(3) the foreign court did not have jurisdiction over the subject matter.

(c) A court of this state is not required to recognize a foreign-country judgment if:

(1) the defendant in the proceeding in the foreign court did not receive notice of the proceeding in sufficient time to enable the defendant to defend;

(2) the judgment was obtained by fraud that deprived the losing party of an adequate opportunity to present the party's case;

(3) the judgment or the cause of action on which the judgment is based is repugnant to the public policy of this state or the United States;

(4) the judgment conflicts with another final and conclusive judgment;

(5) the proceeding in the foreign court was contrary to an agreement between the parties under which the dispute in question was to be determined otherwise than by proceedings in the foreign court;

(6) jurisdiction was based only on personal service and the foreign court was a seriously inconvenient forum for the trial of the action;

(7) the judgment was rendered in circumstances that raise substantial doubt about the integrity of the rendering court with respect to the judgment;

(8) the specific proceeding in the foreign court leading to the judgment was not compatible with the requirements of due process of law; or

(9) it is established that the foreign country in which the judgment was rendered does not recognize judgments rendered in this state that, but for the fact that they are rendered in this state, would constitute foreign-country judgments to which this chapter would apply under Section 36A.003.

(d) A party resisting recognition of a foreign-country judgment has the burden of establishing that a ground for nonrecognition stated in Subsection (b) or (c) exists.

2017 Legislation: Enacted by S.B. 944, §1, 85th Leg., eff. June 1, 2017.

NCCUSL Comment*

1. This Section provides the standards for recognition of a foreign-country money judgment. Section 36A.007 sets out the effect of recognition of a foreign-country money judgment under this Act.

2. Recognition of a judgment means that the forum court accepts the determination of legal rights and obligations made by the rendering court in the foreign country. *See, e.g.* Restatement (Second) of Conflicts of Laws, Ch. 5, Topic 3, Introductory Note (recognition of foreign judgment occurs to the extent the forum court gives the judgment "the same effect with respect to the parties, the subject matter of the action and the issues involved that it has in the state where it was rendered."). Recognition of a foreign-country judgment must be distinguished from enforcement of that judgment. Enforcement of the foreign-country judgment involves the application of the legal procedures of the state to ensure that the judgment debtor obeys the foreign-country judgment. Recognition of a foreign-country money judgment often is associated with enforcement of the judgment, as the judgment creditor usually seeks recognition of the foreign-country judgment primarily for the purpose of invoking the enforcement procedures of the forum state to assist the judgment creditor's collection of the judgment from the judgment debtor. Because the forum court cannot enforce the foreign-country judgment until it has determined that the judgment will be given effect, recognition is a prerequisite to enforcement of the foreign-country judgment. Recognition, however, also has significance outside the enforcement context because a foreign-country judgment also must be recognized before it can be given preclusive effect under res judicata and collateral estoppel principles. The issue of whether a foreign-country judgment will be recognized is distinct from both the issue of whether the judgment will be enforced, and the issue of the extent to which it will be given preclusive effect.

3. Section 36A.004(a) places an affirmative duty on the forum court to recognize a foreign-country money judgment unless one of the grounds for nonrecognition stated in subsection (b) or (c) applies. Subsection (b) states three mandatory grounds for denying recognition to a foreign-country money judgment. If the forum court finds that one of the grounds listed in subsection (b) exists, then it must deny recognition to the foreign-country money judgment. Subsection (c) states eight nonmandatory grounds for denying recognition. The forum court has discretion to decide whether or not to refuse recognition based on one of these grounds. Subsection (d) places the burden of proof on the party resisting recognition of the foreign-country judgment to establish that one of the grounds for nonrecognition exists.

4. The mandatory grounds for nonrecognition stated in §36A.004(b) are identical to the mandatory grounds stated in Section 4 of the 1962 Act. The discretionary grounds stated in subsections (c)(1) through (6) are based on subsections 4(b)(1) through (6) of the 1962 Act. The discretionary grounds stated in subsections (c)(7) and (8) are new.

5. Under §36A.004(b)(1), the forum court must deny recognition to the foreign-country money judgment if that judgment was "rendered under a judicial system that does not provide impartial tribunals or procedures compatible with the requirements of due process of law." The standard for this ground for nonrecognition "has been stated authoritatively by the Supreme Court of the United States in *Hilton v. Guyot*, 159 U.S. 113, 205 (1895). As indicated in that decision, a mere difference in the procedural system is not a sufficient basis for nonrecognition. A case of serious injustice must be involved." Cmt §4, Uniform Foreign Money-Judgment Recognition Act (1962). The focus of inquiry is not whether the procedure in the rendering country is similar to U.S. procedure, but rather on the basic fairness of the foreign-country procedure. Kam-Tech Systems, Ltd. V. Yardeni, 74 A.2d 644, 649 (N.J. App. 2001) (interpreting the comparable provision in the 1962 Act); *accord*, Society of Lloyd's v. Ashenden, 233 F.3d 473 (7th Cir. 2000) (procedures need not meet all the intricacies of the complex concept of due process that has emerged from U.S. case law, but rather must be fair in the broader international sense) (interpreting comparable provision in the 1962 Act). Procedural differences, such as absence of jury trial or different evidentiary rules are not sufficient to justify denying recognition under subsection (b)(1), so long as the essential elements of impartial administration and basic procedural fairness have been provided in the foreign proceeding. As the U.S. Supreme Court stated in *Hilton*:

> Where there has been opportunity for a full and fair trial abroad before a court of competent jurisdiction conducting the trial upon regular proceedings, after due citation or voluntary appearance of the defendant, and under a system of jurisprudence likely to secure an impartial administration of justice between the citizens of its own country and those of other countries, and there is nothing to show either prejudice in the court, or in the system of laws under which it was sitting, or fraud in procuring the judgment, or any other special reason why the comity of this nation should not allow it full effect then a foreign-country judgment should be recognized.

Hilton, 159 U.S. at 202.

6. Under §36A.004(b)(2), the forum court must deny recognition to the foreign-country judgment if the foreign court did not have personal jurisdiction over the defendant. Section 36A.005(a) lists six bases for personal jurisdiction that are adequate as a matter of law to establish that the foreign court had personal jurisdiction. Section 36A.005(b) makes clear that other grounds for personal jurisdiction may be found sufficient.

7. Section 36A.004(c)(2) limits the type of fraud that will serve as a ground for denying recognition to extrinsic fraud. This provision is consistent with the

* See footnote on p. 933.

interpretation of the comparable provision in subsection 4(b)(2) of the 1962 Act by the courts, which have found that only extrinsic fraud—conduct of the prevailing party that deprived the losing party of an adequate opportunity to present its case—is sufficient under the 1962 Act. Examples of extrinsic fraud would be when the plaintiff deliberately had the initiating process served on the defendant at the wrong address, deliberately gave the defendant wrong information as to the time and place of the hearing, or obtained a default judgment against the defendant based on a forged confession of judgment. When this type of fraudulent action by the plaintiff deprives the defendant of an adequate opportunity to present its case, then it provides grounds for denying recognition of the foreign-country judgment. Extrinsic fraud should be distinguished from intrinsic fraud, such as false testimony of a witness or admission of a forged document into evidence during the foreign proceeding. Intrinsic fraud does not provide a basis for denying recognition under subsection (c)(2), as the assertion that intrinsic fraud has occurred should be raised and dealt with in the rendering court.

8. The public policy exception in §36A.004(c)(3) is based on the public policy exception in subsection 4(b)(3) of the 1962 Act, with one difference. The public policy exception in the 1962 Act states that the relevant inquiry is whether "the [cause of action] [claim for relief] on which the judgment is based" is repugnant to public policy. Based on this "cause of action" language, some courts interpreting the 1962 Act have refused to find that a public policy challenge based on something other than repugnancy of the foreign cause of action comes within this exception. *E.g.*, Southwest Livestock & Trucking Co., Inc. v. Ramon, 169 F.3d 317 (5th Cir. 1999) (refusing to deny recognition to Mexican judgment on promissory note with interest rate of 48% because cause of action to collect on promissory note does not violate public policy); Guinness PLC v. Ward, 955 F.2d 875 (4th Cir. 1992) (challenge to recognition based on post-judgment settlement could not be asserted under public policy exception); The Society of Lloyd's v. Turner, 303 F.3d 325 (5th Cir. 2002) (rejecting argument legal standards applied to establish elements of breach of contract violated public policy because cause of action for breach of contract itself is not contrary to state public policy); *cf.* Bachchan v. India Abroad Publications, Inc., 585 N.Y.S.2d 661 (N.Y. Sup. Ct. 1992) (judgment creditor argued British libel judgment should be recognized despite argument it violated First Amendment because New York recognizes a cause of action for libel). Subsection (c)(3) rejects this narrow focus by providing that the forum court may deny recognition if either the cause of action or the judgment itself violates public policy. *Cf.* Restatement (Third) of the Foreign Relations Law of the United States, §482(2)(d) (1986) (containing a similarly-worded public policy exception to recognition).

Although §36A.004(c)(3) of this Act rejects the narrow focus on the cause of action under the 1962 Act, it retains the stringent test for finding a public policy violation applied by courts interpreting the 1962 Act. Under that test, a difference in law, even a marked one, is not sufficient to raise a public policy issue. Nor is it relevant that the foreign law allows a recovery that the forum state would not allow. Public policy is violated only if recognition or enforcement of the foreign-country judgment would tend clearly to injure the public health, the public morals, or the public confidence in the administration of law, or would undermine "that sense of security for individual rights, whether of personal liberty or of private property, which any citizen ought to feel." Hunt v. BP Exploration Co. (Libya) Ltd., 492 F.Supp. 885, 901 (N.D. Tex. 1980).

The language "or of the United States" in subsection (c)(3), which does not appear in the 1962 Act provision, makes it clear that the relevant public policy is that of both the State in which recognition is sought and that of the United States. This is the position taken by the vast majority of cases interpreting the 1962 public policy provision. *E.g.*, Bachchan v. India Abroad Publications, Inc., 585 N.Y.S.2d 661 (Sup.Ct. N.Y. 1992) (British libel judgment denied recognition because it violates First Amendment).

9. Section 36A.004(c)(5) allows the forum court to refuse recognition of a foreign-country judgment when the parties had a valid agreement, such as a valid forum selection clause or agreement to arbitrate, providing that the relevant dispute would be resolved in a forum other than the forum issuing the foreign-country judgment. Under this provision, the forum court must find both the existence of a valid agreement and that the agreement covered the subject matter involved in the foreign litigation resulting in the foreign-country judgment.

10. Section 36A.004(c)(6) authorizes the forum court to refuse recognition of a foreign-country judgment that was rendered in the foreign country solely on the basis of personal service when the forum court believes the original action should have been dismissed by the court in the foreign country on grounds of *forum non conveniens*.

11. Section 36A.004(c)(7) is new. Under this subsection, the forum court may deny recognition to a foreign-country judgment if there are circumstances that raise substantial doubt about the integrity of the rendering court with respect to that judgment. It requires a showing of corruption in the particular case that had an impact on the judgment that was rendered. This provision may be contrasted with §36A.004(b)(1), which requires that the forum court refuse recognition to the foreign-country judgment if it was rendered under a judicial system that does not provide impartial tribunals. Like the comparable provision in subsection 4(a)(1) of the 1962 Act, §36A.004(b)(1) focuses on the judicial system of the foreign country as a whole, rather than on whether the particular judicial proceeding leading to the foreign-country judgment was impartial and fair. *See, e.g.*, The Society of Lloyd's v. Turner, 303 F.3d 325, 330 (5th Cir. 2002) (interpreting the 1962 Act); CIBC Mellon Trust Co. v. Mora Hotel Corp., N.V., 743 N.Y.S.2d 408, 415 (N.Y. App. 2002) (interpreting the 1962 Act); Society of Lloyd's v. Ashenden, 233 F.3d 473, 477 (7th Cir. 2000) (interpreting the 1962 Act). On the other hand, §36A.004(c)(7) allows the court to deny recognition to the foreign-country judgment if it finds a lack of impartiality and fairness of the tribunal in the individual proceeding leading to the foreign-country judgment. Thus, the difference is that between showing, for example, that corruption and bribery is so prevalent throughout the judicial system of the foreign country as to make that entire judicial system one that does not provide impartial tribunals versus showing that bribery of the judge in the proceeding that resulted in the particular foreign-country judgment under consideration had a sufficient impact on the ultimate judgment as to call it into question.

12. Section 36A.004(c)(8) also is new. It allows the forum court to deny recognition to the foreign-country judgment if the court finds that the specific proceeding in the foreign court was not compatible with the requirements of fundamental fairness. Like subsection (c)(7), it can be contrasted with subsection (b)(1), which requires the forum court to deny recognition to the foreign-country judgment if the forum court finds that the entire judicial system in the foreign country where the foreign-country judgment was rendered does not provide procedures compatible with the requirements of fundamental fairness. While the focus of subsection (b)(1) is on the foreign country's judicial system as a whole, the focus of subsection (c)(8) is on the particular proceeding that resulted in the specific foreign-country judgment under consideration. Thus, the difference is that between showing, for example, that there has been such a breakdown of law and order in the particular foreign country that judgments are rendered on the basis of political decisions rather than the rule of law throughout the judicial system versus a showing that for political reasons the particular party against whom the foreign-country judgment was entered was denied fundamental fairness in the particular proceedings leading to the foreign-country judgment.

Subsections (c)(7) and (8) both are discretionary grounds for denying recognition, while subsection (b)(1) is mandatory. Obviously, if the entire judicial system in the foreign country fails to satisfy the requirements of impartiality and fundamental fairness, a judgment rendered in that foreign country would be so compromised that the forum court should refuse to recognize it as a matter of course. On the other hand, if the problem is evidence of a lack of integrity or fundamental fairness with regard to the particular proceeding leading to the foreign-country judgment, then there may or may not be other factors in the particular case that would cause the forum court to decide to recognize the foreign-country judgment. For example, a forum court might decide not to exercise its discretion to deny recognition despite evidence of corruption or procedural unfairness in a particular case because the party resisting recognition failed to raise the issue on appeal from the foreign-country judgment in the foreign country, and the evidence establishes that, if the party had done so, appeal would have been an adequate mechanism for correcting the transgressions of the lower court.

13. Under §36A.004(d), the party opposing recognition of the foreign-country judgment has the burden of establishing that one of the grounds for nonrecognition set out in subsection (b) or (c) applies. The 1962 Act was silent as to who had the burden of proof to establish a ground for nonrecognition and courts applying the 1962 Act took different positions on the issue. *Compare* Bridgeway Corp. v. Citibank, 45 F.Supp. 2d 276, 285 (S.D.N.Y. 1999) (plaintiff has burden to show no mandatory basis for nonrecognition exists; defendant has burden regarding discretionary bases) *with* The Courage Co. LLC v. The ChemShare Corp., 93 S.W.3d 323, 331 (Tex. App. 2002) (party seeking to avoid recognition has burden to prove ground for nonrecognition). Because the grounds for nonrecognition in §36A.004 are in the nature of defenses to recog-

nition, the burden of proof is most appropriately allocated to the party opposing recognition of the foreign-country judgment.

CPRC §36A.005. PERSONAL JURISDICTION

(a) A foreign-country judgment may not be refused recognition for lack of personal jurisdiction if:

(1) the defendant was served with process personally in the foreign country;

(2) the defendant voluntarily appeared in the proceeding, other than for the purpose of protecting property seized or threatened with seizure in the proceeding or of contesting the jurisdiction of the court over the defendant;

(3) the defendant, before commencement of the proceeding, agreed to submit to the jurisdiction of the foreign court with respect to the subject matter involved;

(4) the defendant was domiciled in the foreign country when the proceeding was instituted or was a corporation or other form of business organization whose principal place of business was in, or that was organized under the laws of, the foreign country;

(5) the defendant had a business office in the foreign country and the proceeding in the foreign court involved a cause of action arising out of business done by the defendant through that office in the foreign country; or

(6) the defendant operated a motor vehicle or airplane in the foreign country and the proceeding involved a cause of action arising out of that operation.

(b) The list of bases for personal jurisdiction in Subsection (a) is not exclusive. A court of this state may recognize bases of personal jurisdiction other than those listed in Subsection (a) as sufficient to support a foreign-country judgment.

2017 Legislation: Enacted by S.B. 944, §1, 85th Leg., eff. June 1, 2017.

NCCUSL Comment*

1. Under §36A.004(b)(2), the forum court must deny recognition to the foreign-country judgment if the foreign court did not have personal jurisdiction over the defendant. Section 36A.005(a) lists six bases for personal jurisdiction that are adequate as a matter of law to establish that the foreign court had personal jurisdiction. Section 36A.005(b) makes it clear that these bases of personal jurisdiction are not exclusive. The forum court may find that the foreign court had personal jurisdiction over the defendant on some other basis.

2. Subsection 5(a)(4) of the 1962 Act provides that the foreign court had personal jurisdiction over the defendant if the defendant was "a body corporate" that "had its principal place of business, was incorporated, or had otherwise acquired corporate status, in the foreign state." Section 36A.005(a)(4) of this Act extends that concept to forms of business organization other than corporations.

3. Section 36A.005(a)(3) provides that the foreign court has personal jurisdiction over the defendant if the defendant agreed before commencement of the proceeding leading to the foreign-country judgment to submit to the jurisdiction of the foreign court with regard to the subject matter involved. Under this provision, the forum court must find both the existence of a valid agreement to submit to the foreign court's jurisdiction and that the agreement covered the subject matter involved in the foreign litigation resulting in the foreign-country judgment.

CPRC §36A.006. PROCEDURE FOR RECOGNITION OF FOREIGN-COUNTRY JUDGMENT

(a) If recognition of a foreign-country judgment is sought as an original matter, the issue of recognition may be raised by filing an action seeking recognition of the foreign-country judgment.

(b) If recognition of a foreign-country judgment is sought in a pending action, the issue of recognition may be raised by counterclaim, cross-claim, or affirmative defense.

2017 Legislation: Enacted by S.B. 944, §1, 85th Leg., eff. June 1, 2017.

NCCUSL Comment*

1. Unlike the 1962 Act, which was silent as to the proper procedure for seeking recognition of a foreign-country judgment, §36A.006 of this Act expressly sets out the ways in which the issue of recognition may be raised. Under §36A.006, the issue of recognition always must be raised in a court proceeding. Thus, §36A.006 rejects decisions under the 1962 Act holding that the registration procedure found in the Uniform Enforcement of Foreign Judgments Act could be utilized with regard to recognition of a foreign-country judgment. *E.g.* Society of Lloyd's v. Ashenden, 233 F.3d 473 (7th Cir. 2000). The Enforcement Act deals solely with the *enforcement* of sister-state judgments and other judgments entitled to full faith and credit, not with the *recognition* of foreign-country judgments.

More broadly, §36A.006 rejects the use of any registration procedure in the context of the foreign-country judgments covered by this Act. A registration procedure represents a balance between the interest of the judgment creditor in obtaining quick and efficient recognition and enforcement of a judgment when the judgment debtor has already been provided with an opportunity to litigate the underlying issues, and the interest of the judgment debtor in being provided an adequate opportunity to raise and litigate issues regarding whether the foreign-country judgment should be recognized. In the context of sister-state judgments, this balance favors use of a truncated procedure such as that found in the Enforcement Act. Recognition of sister-state judgments normally is mandated by the Full Faith and Credit Clause. Courts recognize only a very limited number of grounds for denying full faith and credit to a sister-state judgment—that the rendering court lacked jurisdiction, that the judgment was procured by fraud, that the judgment has been satisfied, or that the limitations period has expired. Thus, the judgment debtor with regard to a sister-state judgment normally does not have any grounds for opposing recognition and enforcement of the judgment. The extremely limited grounds for denying full faith and credit to a sister-state judgment reflect the fact such judgments will have been rendered by a court that is subject to the same due process limitations and the same overlap of federal statutory and constitutional law as the forum state's courts, and, to a large extent, the same body of court precedent and socio-economic ideas as those shaping the law of the forum state. Therefore, there is a strong presumption of fairness and competence attached to a sister-state judgment that justifies use of a registration procedure.

The balance between the benefits and costs of a registration procedure is significantly different, however, in the context of recognition and enforcement of foreign-country judgments. Unlike the limited grounds for denying full faith and credit to a sister-state judgment, this Act provides a number of grounds upon which recognition of a foreign-country judgment may be denied. Determination of whether these grounds apply requires the forum court to look behind the foreign-country judgment to evaluate the law and the judicial system under which the foreign-country judgment was rendered. The existence of these grounds for nonrecognition reflects the fact there is less expectation that for-

* See footnote on p. 933.

eign-country courts will follow procedures comporting with U.S. notions of fundamental fairness and jurisdiction or that those courts will apply laws viewed as substantively tolerable by U.S. standards than there is with regard to sister-state courts. In some situations, there also may be suspicions of corruption or fraud in the foreign-country proceedings. These differences between sister-state judgments and foreign-country judgments provide a justification for requiring judicial involvement in the decision whether to recognize a foreign-country judgment in all cases in which that issue is raised. Although the threshold for establishing that a foreign-country judgment is not entitled to recognition under §36A.004 is high, there is a sufficiently greater likelihood that significant recognition issues will be raised so as to require a judicial proceeding.

2. This Section contemplates that the issue of recognition may be raised either as an original matter or in the context of a pending proceeding. Subsection (a) provides that in order to raise the issue of recognition of a foreign-country judgment as an initial matter, the party seeking recognition must file an action for recognition of the foreign-country judgment. Subsection (b) provides that when the recognition issue is raised in a pending proceeding, it may be raised by counterclaim, cross-claim or affirmative defense, depending on the context in which it is raised. These rules are consistent with the way the issue of recognition most often was raised in most states under the 1962 Act.

3. An action seeking recognition of a foreign-country judgment under this Section is an action on the foreign-country judgment itself, not an action on the underlying cause of action that gave rise to that judgment. The parties to an action under §36A.006 may not relitigate the merits of the underlying dispute that gave rise to the foreign-country judgment.

4. While this Section sets out the ways in which the issue of recognition of a foreign-country judgment may be raised, it is not intended to create any new procedure not currently existing in the state or to otherwise effect existing state procedural requirements. The parties to an action in which recognition of a foreign-country judgment is sought under §36A.006 must comply with all state procedural rules with regard to that type of action. Nor does this Act address the question of what constitutes a sufficient basis for jurisdiction to adjudicate with regard to an action under §36A.006. Courts have split over the issue of whether the presence of assets of the debtor in a state is a sufficient basis for jurisdiction in light of footnote 36 of the U.S. Supreme Court decision in Shaffer v. Heitner, 433 U.S. 186, 210 n.36 (1977). This Act takes no position on that issue.

5. In states that have adopted the Uniform Foreign-Money Claims Act, that Act will apply to the determination of the amount of a money judgment recognized under this Act.

CPRC §36A.007. EFFECT OF RECOGNITION OF FOREIGN-COUNTRY JUDGMENT

If the court in a proceeding under Section 36A.006 finds that the foreign-country judgment is entitled to recognition under this chapter, then, to the extent that the foreign-country judgment grants or denies recovery of a sum of money, the foreign-country judgment is:

(1) conclusive between the parties to the same extent as the judgment of a sister state entitled to full faith and credit in this state would be conclusive; and

(2) enforceable in the same manner and to the same extent as a judgment rendered in this state.

2017 Legislation: Enacted by S.B. 944, §1, 85th Leg., eff. June 1, 2017.

NCCUSL Comment*

1. Section 36A.005 of this Act sets out the standards for the recognition of foreign-country judgments within the scope of this Act, and places an affirmative duty on the forum court to recognize any foreign-country judgment that meets those standards. Section 36A.006 of this Act sets out the procedures by which the issue of recognition may be raised. This Section sets out the consequences of the decision by the forum court that the foreign-country judgment is entitled to recognition.

2. Under §36A.007(1), the first consequence of recognition of a foreign-country judgment is that it is treated as conclusive between the parties in the forum state. Subsection (1) does not attempt to establish directly the extent of that conclusiveness. Instead, it provides that the foreign-country judgment is treated as conclusive to the same extent that a judgment of a sister state that had been determined to be entitled to full faith and credit would be conclusive. This means that the foreign-country judgment generally will be given the same effect in the forum state that it has in the foreign country where it was rendered. Subsection (1), however, sets out the minimum effect that must be given to the foreign-country judgment once recognized. The forum court remains free to give the foreign-country judgment a greater preclusive effect in the forum state than the judgment would have in the foreign country where it was rendered. *Cf.* Restatement (Third) of the Foreign Relations Law of the United States, §481 cmt c (1986).

3. Under §36A.007(2), the second consequence of recognition of a foreign-country judgment is that, to the extent it grants a sum of money, it is enforceable in the forum state in accordance with the procedures for enforcement in the forum state and to the same extent that a judgment of the forum state would be enforceable. *Cf.* Restatement (Third) of the Foreign Relations Law of the United States §481 (1986) (judgment entitled to recognition is enforceable in accordance with the procedure for enforcement of judgments applicable where enforcement is sought). Thus, under subsection (2), once recognized, the foreign-country judgment has the same effect and is subject to the same procedures, defenses and proceedings for reopening, vacating, or staying a judgment of a comparable court in the forum state, and can be enforced or satisfied in the same manner as such a judgment of the forum state.

CPRC §36A.008. STAY OF PROCEEDINGS PENDING APPEAL OF FOREIGN-COUNTRY JUDGMENT

If a party establishes that an appeal from a foreign-country judgment is pending or will be taken, the court may stay any proceedings with regard to the foreign-country judgment until:

(1) the appeal is concluded;

(2) the time for appeal expires; or

(3) the appellant has had sufficient time to prosecute the appeal and has failed to do so.

2017 Legislation: Enacted by S.B. 944, §1, 85th Leg., eff. June 1, 2017.

NCCUSL Comment*

1. Under §36A.003 of this Act, a foreign-country judgment is not within the scope of this Act unless it is conclusive and enforceable where rendered. Thus, if the effect of appeal under the law of the foreign country in which the judgment was rendered is to prevent it from being conclusive or enforceable between the parties, the existence of a pending appeal in the foreign country would prevent the application of this Act. Section 36A.008 addresses a different situation. It deals with the situation in which either (1) the party seeking a stay has demonstrated that it intends to file an appeal in the foreign country, although the appeal has not yet been filed or (2) an appeal has been filed in the foreign country, but under the law of the foreign country filing of an appeal does not affect the conclusiveness or enforceability of the judgment. Section 36A.008 allows the forum court in those situations to determine in its discretion that a stay of proceedings is appropriate.

CPRC §36A.009. STATUTE OF LIMITATIONS

An action to recognize a foreign-country judgment must be brought within the earlier of:

(1) the time during which the foreign-country judgment is effective in the foreign country; or

* See footnote on p. 933.

(2) 15 years from the date that the foreign-country judgment became effective in the foreign country.

2017 Legislation: Enacted by S.B. 944, §1, 85th Leg., eff. June 1, 2017.

NCCUSL Comment*

1. Under §36A.003 of this Act, this Act only applies to foreign-country judgments that are conclusive, and if the judgment grants recovery of a sum of money, enforceable where rendered. Thus, if the period of effectiveness of the foreign-country judgment has expired in the foreign country where the judgment was rendered, the foreign-country judgment would not be subject to this Act. This means that the period of time during which a foreign-country judgment may be recognized under this Act normally is measured by the period of time during which that judgment is effective (that is, conclusive and, if applicable, enforceable) in the foreign country that rendered the judgment. If, however, the foreign-country judgment remains effective for more than fifteen years after the date on which it became effective in the foreign country, §36A.009 places an additional time limit on recognition of a foreign-country judgment. It provides that, if the foreign-country judgment remains effective between the parties for more than fifteen years, then an action to recognize the foreign-country judgment under this Act must be commenced within that fifteen year period.

2. Section 36A.009 does not address the issue of whether a foreign-country judgment that can no longer be the basis of a recognition action under this Act because of the application of the fifteen-year limitations period in §36A.009 may be used for other purposes. For example, a common rule with regard to judgments barred by a statute of limitations is that they still may be used defensively for purposes of offset and for their preclusive effect. The extent to which a foreign-country judgment with regard to which a recognition action is barred by §36A.009 may be used for these or other purposes is left to the other law of the forum state.

CPRC §36A.010. UNIFORMITY OF INTERPRETATION

In applying and construing this chapter, consideration must be given to the need to promote uniformity of the law with respect to the subject matter of this chapter among states that enact a law based on the uniform act on which this chapter is based.

2017 Legislation: Enacted by S.B. 944, §1, 85th Leg., eff. June 1, 2017.

CPRC §36A.011. SAVING CLAUSE

This chapter does not prevent the recognition under principles of comity or otherwise of a foreign-country judgment not within the scope of this chapter.

2017 Legislation: Enacted by S.B. 944, §1, 85th Leg., eff. June 1, 2017.

NCCUSL Comment*

1. Section 36A.003 of this Act provides that this Act applies only to certain foreign-country judgments that grant or deny recovery of a sum of money. The purpose of this Act is to establish the minimum standards for recognition of those judgments. Section 36A.011 makes clear that no negative implication should be read from the fact that this Act does not provide for recognition of other foreign-country judgments. Rather, this Act simply does not address the issue of whether foreign-country judgments not within its scope under §36A.003 should be recognized. Courts are free to recognize those foreign-country judgments not within the scope of this Act under common law principles of comity or other applicable law.

CHAPTER 37. DECLARATORY JUDGMENTS

CPRC §37.004. SUBJECT MATTER OF RELIEF

(a) A person interested under a deed, will, written contract, or other writings constituting a contract or whose rights, status, or other legal relations are affected by a statute, municipal ordinance, contract, or franchise may have determined any question of construction or validity arising under the instrument, statute, ordinance, contract, or franchise and obtain a declaration of rights, status, or other legal relations thereunder.

(b) A contract may be construed either before or after there has been a breach.

(c) Notwithstanding Section 22.001, Property Code, a person described by Subsection (a) may obtain a determination under this chapter when the sole issue concerning title to real property is the determination of the proper boundary line between adjoining properties.

See also *O'Connor's Texas Rules*, "Declaratory Judgment," ch. 2-D, p. 149.

CPRC §37.005. DECLARATIONS RELATING TO TRUST OR ESTATE

A person interested as or through an executor or administrator, including an independent executor or administrator, a trustee, guardian, other fiduciary, creditor, devisee, legatee, heir, next of kin, or cestui que trust in the administration of a trust or of the estate of a decedent, an infant, mentally incapacitated person, or insolvent may have a declaration of rights or legal relations in respect to the trust or estate:

(1) to ascertain any class of creditors, devisees, legatees, heirs, next of kin, or others;

(2) to direct the executors, administrators, or trustees to do or abstain from doing any particular act in their fiduciary capacity;

(3) to determine any question arising in the administration of the trust or estate, including questions of construction of wills and other writings; or

(4) to determine rights or legal relations of an independent executor or independent administrator regarding fiduciary fees and the settling of accounts.

See also *O'Connor's Texas Rules*, "Declaratory Judgment," ch. 2-D, p. 149.

CPRC §37.0055. DECLARATIONS RELATING TO LIABILITY FOR SALES & USE TAXES OF ANOTHER STATE

(a) In this section, "state" includes any political subdivision of that state.

(b) A district court has original jurisdiction of a proceeding seeking a declaratory judgment that involves:

(1) a party seeking declaratory relief that is a business that is:

* See footnote on p. 933.

(A) organized under the laws of this state or is otherwise owned by a resident of this state; or

(B) a retailer registered with the comptroller under Section 151.106, Tax Code; and

(2) a responding party that:

(A) is an official of another state; and

(B) asserts a claim that the party seeking declaratory relief is required to collect sales or use taxes for that state based on conduct of the business that occurs in whole or in part within this state.

(c) A business described by Subsection (b)(1) is entitled to declaratory relief on the issue of whether the requirement of another state that the business collect and remit sales or use taxes to that state constitutes an undue burden on interstate commerce under Section 8, Article I, United States Constitution.

(d) In determining whether to grant declaratory relief to a business under this section, a court shall consider:

(1) the factual circumstances of the business's operations that give rise to the demand by the other state; and

(2) the decisions of other courts interpreting Section 8, Article I, United States Constitution.

TITLE 4. LIABILITY IN TORT

CHAPTER 75. LIMITATION OF LANDOWNERS' LIABILITY

CPRC §75.001. DEFINITIONS

In this chapter:

(1) "Agricultural land" means land that is located in this state and that is suitable for:

(A) use in production of plants and fruits grown for human or animal consumption, or plants grown for the production of fibers, floriculture, viticulture, horticulture, or planting seed;

(B) forestry and the growing of trees for the purpose of rendering those trees into lumber, fiber, or other items used for industrial, commercial, or personal consumption; or

(C) domestic or native farm or ranch animals kept for use or profit.

(2) "Premises" includes land, roads, water, watercourse, private ways, and buildings, structures, machinery, and equipment attached to or located on the land, road, water, watercourse, or private way.

(3) "Recreation" means an activity such as:

(A) hunting;

(B) fishing;

(C) swimming;

(D) boating;

(E) camping;

(F) picnicking;

(G) hiking;

(H) pleasure driving, including off-road motorcycling and off-road automobile driving and the use of all-terrain vehicles and recreational off-highway vehicles;

(I) nature study, including bird-watching;

(J) cave exploration;

(K) waterskiing and other water sports;

(L) any other activity associated with enjoying nature or the outdoors;

(M) bicycling and mountain biking;

(N) disc golf;

(O) on-leash and off-leash walking of dogs; or

(P) radio control flying and related activities.

(4) "Governmental unit" has the meaning assigned by Section 101.001.

See also *O'Connor's Texas COA*, "Recreational use," ch. 23-A, §1.2.2(2), p. 780; "Liability Under the Recreational Use Statute," ch. 23-F, p. 830; "Injury While Engaged in Recreation," ch. 26-F, p. 979.

CPRC §75.002. LIABILITY LIMITED

(a) An owner, lessee, or occupant of agricultural land:

(1) does not owe a duty of care to a trespasser on the land; and

(2) is not liable for any injury to a trespasser on the land, except for wilful or wanton acts or gross negligence by the owner, lessee, or other occupant of agricultural land.

(b) If an owner, lessee, or occupant of agricultural land gives permission to another or invites another to enter the premises for recreation, the owner, lessee, or occupant, by giving the permission, does not:

(1) assure that the premises are safe for that purpose;

(2) owe to the person to whom permission is granted or to whom the invitation is extended a greater degree of care than is owed to a trespasser on the premises; or

(3) assume responsibility or incur liability for any injury to any individual or property caused by any act of

the person to whom permission is granted or to whom the invitation is extended.

(c) If an owner, lessee, or occupant of real property other than agricultural land gives permission to another to enter the premises for recreation, the owner, lessee, or occupant, by giving the permission, does not:

(1) assure that the premises are safe for that purpose;

(2) owe to the person to whom permission is granted a greater degree of care than is owed to a trespasser on the premises; or

(3) assume responsibility or incur liability for any injury to any individual or property caused by any act of the person to whom permission is granted.

(d) Subsections (a), (b), and (c) shall not limit the liability of an owner, lessee, or occupant of real property who has been grossly negligent or has acted with malicious intent or in bad faith.

(e) In this section, "recreation" means, in addition to its meaning under Section 75.001, the following activities only if the activities take place on premises owned, operated, or maintained by a governmental unit for the purposes of those activities:

(1) hockey and in-line hockey;

(2) skating, in-line skating, roller-skating, skateboarding, and roller-blading;

(3) soap box derby use; and

(4) paintball use.

(f) Notwithstanding Subsections (b) and (c), if a person enters premises owned, operated, or maintained by a governmental unit and engages in recreation on those premises, the governmental unit does not owe to the person a greater degree of care than is owed to a trespasser on the premises.

(g) Any premises a governmental unit owns, operates, or maintains and on which the recreational activities described in Subsections (e)(1)-(4) are conducted shall post and maintain a clearly readable sign in a clearly visible location on or near the premises. The sign shall contain the following warning language:

WARNING

TEXAS LAW (CHAPTER 75, CIVIL PRACTICE AND REMEDIES CODE) LIMITS THE LIABILITY OF A GOVERNMENTAL UNIT FOR DAMAGES ARISING DIRECTLY FROM HOCKEY, IN-LINE HOCKEY, SKATING, IN-LINE SKATING, ROLLER-SKATING, SKATEBOARDING, ROLLER-BLADING, PAINTBALL USE, OR SOAP BOX DERBY USE ON PREMISES THAT THE GOVERNMENTAL UNIT OWNS, OPERATES, OR MAINTAINS FOR THAT PURPOSE.

(h) An owner, lessee, or occupant of real property in this state is liable for trespass as a result of migration or transport of any air contaminant, as defined in Section 382.003(2), Health and Safety Code, other than odor, only upon a showing of actual and substantial damages by a plaintiff in a civil action.

(i) Subsections (b) and (c) do not affect any liability of an owner, lessee, or occupant of real property for an injury occurring outside the boundaries of the real property caused by an activity described by Section 75.001(3)(P) that originates within the boundaries of the real property.

See also *O'Connor's Texas COA*, "Recreational use," ch. 23-A, §1.2.2(2), p. 780; "Liability Under the Recreational Use Statute," ch. 23-F, p. 830; "Injury While Engaged in Recreation," ch. 26-F, p. 979.

CPRC §75.0021. REPEALED [~~LIMITED LIABILITY OF CERTAIN PUBLIC UTILITIES~~]

The repealed text of former §75.0021 is effective for causes of action that accrue before Sept. 1, 2017.

[~~(a)~~] [~~In this section:~~]

[~~(1)~~] [~~"Person" includes an individual as defined by Section 71.001.~~]

[~~(2)~~] [~~"Public utility" means an electric utility as defined by Section 31.002, Utilities Code.~~]

[~~(b)~~] [~~A public utility that, as the owner, easement holder, occupant, or lessee of land, signs an agreement with a municipality, county, or political subdivision to allow public access to or use of the premises for recreation by allowing the public access or use does not assume responsibility or incur liability beyond that provided by Chapter 75 of the Civil Practice and Remedies Code to a third party who enters the premises for recreation to the extent the municipality, county, or political subdivision purchases a general liability insurance policy in amounts required by Chapter 75 of the Civil Practice and Remedies Code insuring the public utility for liability arising from the condition of the premises for such recreational use.~~]

[~~(c)~~] [~~This section applies only to a public utility located in a county with a population of 800,000 or more and located on the international border.~~]

Repealed by H.B. 931, §2, 85th Leg., eff. Sept. 1, 2017.

A CPRC §75.0022. LIMITED LIABILITY OF CERTAIN ELECTRIC UTILITIES

(a) In this section:

(1) "Electric utility" has the meaning assigned by Section 31.002, Utilities Code.

(2) "Person" includes an individual, as defined by Section 71.001.

(3) "Premises" includes the land owned, occupied, or leased by an electric utility, or covered by an easement owned by an electric utility, with respect to which public access and use is allowed in a written agreement with a political subdivision under Subsection (c).

(4) "Serious bodily injury" means an injury that creates a substantial risk of death or that causes serious permanent disfigurement or protracted loss or impairment of the function of a body part or organ.

The repealed text of former subsection (b) is effective for causes of action that accrue before Sept. 1, 2017.

(b) Repealed by H.B. 931, §2, 85th Leg., eff. Sept. 1, 2017.

~~[(b)]~~ [~~This section applies only to an electric utility located in a county with a population of four million or more.~~]

(c) An electric utility, as the owner, easement holder, occupant, or lessee of land, may enter into a written agreement with a political subdivision to allow public access to and use of the premises of the electric utility for recreation, exercise, relaxation, travel, or pleasure.

(d) The electric utility, by entering into an agreement under this section or at any time during the term of the agreement, does not:

(1) assure that the premises are safe for recreation, exercise, relaxation, travel, or pleasure;

(2) owe to a person entering the premises for recreation, exercise, relaxation, travel, or pleasure, or accompanying another person entering the premises for recreation, exercise, relaxation, travel, or pleasure, a greater degree of care than is owed to a trespasser on the premises; or

(3) except as provided by Subsection (e), assume responsibility or incur any liability for:

(A) damages arising from or related to bodily or other personal injury to or death of any person who enters the premises for recreation, exercise, relaxation, travel, or pleasure or accompanies another person entering the premises for recreation, exercise, relaxation, travel, or pleasure;

(B) property damage sustained by any person who enters the premises for recreation, exercise, relaxation, travel, or pleasure or accompanies another person entering the premises for recreation, exercise, relaxation, travel, or pleasure; or

(C) an act of a third party that occurs on the premises, regardless of whether the act is intentional.

(e) Subsection (d) does not limit the liability of an electric utility for serious bodily injury or death of a person proximately caused by the electric utility's wilful or wanton acts or gross negligence with respect to a dangerous condition existing on the premises.

(f) The limitation on liability provided by this section applies only to a cause of action brought by a person who enters the premises for recreation, exercise, relaxation, travel, or pleasure or accompanies another person entering the premises for recreation, exercise, relaxation, travel, or pleasure.

(g) The doctrine of attractive nuisance does not apply to a claim that is subject to this section.

(h) A written agreement entered into under this section may require the political subdivision to provide or pay for insurance coverage for any defense costs or other litigation costs incurred by the electric utility for damage claims under this section.

2017 Legislation: Amended by H.B. 931, §2, 85th Leg., eff. Sept. 1, 2017.

CPRC §75.0025. LIMITED LIABILITY OF PERSONS ALLOWING CERTAIN USES OF LAND

(a) In this section, "community garden" means the premises used for recreational gardening by a group of people residing in a neighborhood or community for the purpose of providing fresh produce for the benefit of the residents of the neighborhood or community.

(b) An owner, lessee, or occupant of land that gives permission to another person to enter and use the land as a community garden does not by giving that permission:

(1) ensure that the premises are safe; or

(2) assume responsibility or incur any liability for:

(A) damages arising from or related to any bodily or other personal injury to or death of any person who enters the premises for a purpose related to a community garden;

(B) property damage sustained by any person who enters the premises for a purpose related to a community garden; or

(C) an act of a third party that occurs on the premises.

(c) The doctrine of attractive nuisance does not apply to a claim that is subject to this section.

(d) This section does not limit the liability of an owner, lessee, or occupant of land for an injury caused by wilful or wanton acts or gross negligence by the owner, lessee, or occupant.

(e) An owner, lessee, or occupant of land that allows the use of the premises as a community garden shall post and maintain a clearly readable sign in a clearly visible location on or near the premises. The sign must contain the following warning language:

WARNING

TEXAS LAW (CHAPTER 75, CIVIL PRACTICE AND REMEDIES CODE) LIMITS THE LIABILITY OF THE LANDOWNER, LESSEE, OR OCCUPANT FOR DAMAGES ARISING FROM THE USE OF THIS PROPERTY AS A COMMUNITY GARDEN.

CPRC §75.003. APPLICATION & EFFECT OF CHAPTER

(a) This chapter does not relieve any owner, lessee, or occupant of real property of any liability that would otherwise exist for deliberate, wilful, or malicious injury to a person or to property.

(b) This chapter does not affect the doctrine of attractive nuisance, except:

(1) as provided by Section 75.0022(g) or 75.0025(c); and

(2) the doctrine of attractive nuisance may not be the basis for liability of an owner, lessee, or occupant of agricultural land for any injury to a trespasser over the age of 16 years.

(c) Except for a governmental unit, this chapter applies only to an owner, lessee, or occupant of real property who:

(1) does not charge for entry to the premises;

(2) charges for entry to the premises, but whose total charges collected in the previous calendar year for all recreational use of the entire premises of the owner, lessee, or occupant are not more than 20 times the total amount of ad valorem taxes imposed on the premises for the previous calendar year; or

(3) has liability insurance coverage in effect on an act or omission described by Section 75.004(a) and in the amounts equal to or greater than those provided by that section.

(d) This chapter does not create any liability.

(e) Except as otherwise provided, this chapter applies to a governmental unit.

(f) This chapter does not waive sovereign immunity.

(g) To the extent that this chapter limits the liability of a governmental unit under circumstances in which the governmental unit would be liable under Chapter 101, this chapter controls.

(h) In the case of agricultural land, an owner, lessee, or occupant of real property who does not charge for entry to the premises because the individuals entering the premises for recreation are invited social guests satisfies the requirement of Subsection (c)(1).

See also *O'Connor's Texas COA*, "Recreational use," ch. 23-A, §1.2.2(2), p. 780; "Liability Under the Recreational Use Statute," ch. 23-F, p. 830; "Injury While Engaged in Recreation," ch. 26-F, p. 979.

CPRC §75.004. LIMITATION ON MONETARY DAMAGES FOR PRIVATE LANDOWNERS

(a) Subject to Subsection (b), the liability of an owner, lessee, or occupant of agricultural land used for recreational purposes for an act or omission by the owner, lessee, or occupant relating to the premises that results in damages to a person who has entered the premises is limited to a maximum amount of $500,000 for each person and $1 million for each single occurrence of bodily injury or death and $100,000 for each single occurrence for injury to or destruction of property. In the case of agricultural land, the total liability of an owner, lessee, or occupant for a single occurrence is limited to $1 million, and the liability also is subject to the limits for each single occurrence of bodily injury or death and each single occurrence for injury to or destruction of property stated in this subsection.

(b) This section applies only to an owner, lessee, or occupant of agricultural land used for recreational purposes who has liability insurance coverage in effect on an act or omission described by Subsection (a) and in the amounts equal to or greater than those provided by Subsection (a). The coverage may be provided under a contract of insurance or other plan of insurance authorized by statute. The limit of liability insurance coverage applicable with respect to agricultural land may be

a combined single limit in the amount of $1 million for each single occurrence.

(c) This section does not affect the liability of an insurer or insurance plan in an action under Chapter 541, Insurance Code, or an action for bad faith conduct, breach of fiduciary duty, or negligent failure to settle a claim.

(d) This section does not apply to a governmental unit.

See also *O'Connor's Texas COA*, "Liability Under the Recreational Use Statute," ch. 23-F, p. 830; "Injury While Engaged in Recreation," ch. 26-F, p. 979.

CPRC §75.006. LIABILITY LIMITED FOR ACTIONS OF FIREFIGHTER, FEDERAL LAW ENFORCEMENT OFFICER, OR PEACE OFFICER

(a) In this section:

(1) "Federal law enforcement officer" means a law enforcement officer as defined by 5 U.S.C. Section 8331(20).

(2) "Firefighter" means a member of a fire department who performs a function listed in Section 419.021(3)(C), Government Code.

(3) "Livestock" has the meaning assigned by Section 1.003, Agriculture Code.

(4) "Peace officer" has the meaning assigned by Section 1.07, Penal Code, or other state or federal law.

(b) A landowner is not liable for damages arising from an incident or accident caused by livestock of the landowner due to an act or omission of a firefighter or a peace officer who has entered the landowner's property with or without the permission of the landowner, regardless of whether the damage occurs on the landowner's property.

(c) An owner, lessee, or occupant of agricultural land is not liable for any damage or injury to any person or property that arises from the actions of a peace officer or federal law enforcement officer when the officer enters or causes another person to enter the agricultural land with or without the permission of the owner, lessee, or occupant, regardless of whether the damage or injury occurs on the agricultural land.

(d) The owner, lessee, or occupant of agricultural land is not liable for any damage or injury to any person or property that arises from the actions of an individual who, because of the actions of a peace officer or federal law enforcement officer, enters or causes another person to enter the agricultural land without the permission of the owner, lessee, or occupant.

(e) This section does not limit the liability of an owner, lessee, or occupant of agricultural land for any damage or injury that arises from a wilful or wanton act or gross negligence by the owner, lessee, or occupant.

CHAPTER 80. TRESPASS: OUTDOOR SIGN

CPRC §80.001. DEFINITION

In this chapter, "sign" means an outdoor structure, sign, display, light device, figure, painting, drawing, message, plaque, poster, billboard, or any other thing that is designed, intended, or used to advertise or inform.

CPRC §80.002. TRESPASS

A trespass occurs when an individual:

(1) erects or places a sign on premises without the permission of the owner of the premises; or

(2) after the expiration or termination of an agreement with the owner of the premises for the erection, placement, or maintenance of a sign on the premises and before the expiration of the period described by Section 80.003(b)(2), fails to remove or abandons a sign or fails to obtain from the owner of the premises permission for the continued use or maintenance of the sign on the premises.

CPRC §80.003. DAMAGES

(a) The owner of the premises is entitled to recover damages equal to the amount of payments received by or accruing to the owner of the sign from the rental, sale, lease, or other use of the sign during the period after the expiration of the 30th day after the date on which the written notice required by Subsection (b)(1) is received and before the date on which the sign is removed or permission for the continued use or maintenance of the sign is obtained.

(b) The owner of the premises may not recover damages for trespass under this section unless:

(1) the owner of the premises sends, by certified mail, return receipt requested, to the owner of the sign written demand for removal of the sign, stating in detail the act constituting the trespass and the location where the sign has been erected, placed, or maintained; and

(2) the owner of the sign fails to remove the sign or obtain permission from the owner of the premises for the continued use or maintenance of the sign before the 30th day after the date on which the notice described by Subdivision (1) was received.

CHAPTER 95. PROPERTY OWNER'S LIABILITY FOR ACTS OF INDEPENDENT CONTRACTORS & AMOUNT OF RECOVERY

CPRC §95.001. DEFINITIONS

In this chapter:

(1) "Claim" means a claim for damages caused by negligence, including a counterclaim, cross-claim, or third party claim.

(2) "Claimant" means a party making a claim subject to this chapter.

(3) "Property owner" means a person or entity that owns real property primarily used for commercial or business purposes.

See also *O'Connor's Texas COA*, "Real-property-improvement cases," ch. 23-B, §5.1.4, p. 807.

CPRC §95.002. APPLICABILITY

This chapter applies only to a claim:

(1) against a property owner, contractor, or subcontractor for personal injury, death, or property damage to an owner, a contractor, or a subcontractor or an employee of a contractor or subcontractor; and

(2) that arises from the condition or use of an improvement to real property where the contractor or subcontractor constructs, repairs, renovates, or modifies the improvement.

See also *O'Connor's Texas COA*, "Real-property-improvement cases," ch. 23-B, §5.1.4, p. 807.

CPRC §95.003. LIABILITY FOR ACTS OF INDEPENDENT CONTRACTORS

A property owner is not liable for personal injury, death, or property damage to a contractor, subcontractor, or an employee of a contractor or subcontractor who constructs, repairs, renovates, or modifies an improvement to real property, including personal injury, death, or property damage arising from the failure to provide a safe workplace unless:

(1) the property owner exercises or retains some control over the manner in which the work is performed, other than the right to order the work to start or stop or to inspect progress or receive reports; and

(2) the property owner had actual knowledge of the danger or condition resulting in the personal injury, death, or property damage and failed to adequately warn.

See also *O'Connor's Texas COA*, "Real-property-improvement cases," ch. 23-B, §5.1.4, p. 807.

CPRC §95.004. EVIDENCE ADMISSIBLE

In the trial of a case against a contractor, subcontractor, or property owner for personal injury, property damage, or death to a contractor, a subcontractor, or an employee of a contractor or subcontractor that arises from the condition or use of an improvement to real property where the contractor or subcontractor constructs, repairs, renovates, or modifies the improvement, the trial judge, outside the presence of the jury, shall receive evidence of workers' compensation benefits paid and shall deduct the amount of the benefits from the damages awarded by the trier of fact. The deduction for workers' compensation benefits does not apply unless the workers' compensation carrier's subrogation rights have been waived.

See also *O'Connor's Texas COA*, "Real-property-improvement cases," ch. 23-B, §5.1.4, p. 807.

TITLE 6. MISCELLANEOUS PROVISIONS

CHAPTER 125. COMMON & PUBLIC NUISANCES

SUBCHAPTER A. SUIT TO ABATE CERTAIN COMMON NUISANCES

A CPRC §125.001. DEFINITIONS

In this chapter:

(1) "Common nuisance" is a nuisance described by Section 125.0015.

(1-a) "Computer network" means the interconnection of two or more computers or computer systems by satellite, microwave, line, or other communication medium with the capability to transmit information between the computers.

(2) "Public nuisance" is a nuisance described by Section 125.062 or 125.063.

(3) "Multiunit residential property" means improved real property with at least three dwelling units, including an apartment building, condominium, hotel, or motel. The term does not include a single-family home or duplex.

(4) "Web address" means a website operating on the Internet.

2017 Legislation: Amended by H.B. 2552, §2, 85th Leg., eff. Sept. 1, 2017; S.B. 1196, §1, 85th Leg., eff. Sept. 1, 2017.

A CPRC §125.0015. COMMON NUISANCE

(a) A person who maintains a place to which persons habitually go for the following purposes and who

knowingly tolerates the activity and furthermore fails to make reasonable attempts to abate the activity maintains a common nuisance:

(1) discharge of a firearm in a public place as prohibited by the Penal Code;

(2) reckless discharge of a firearm as prohibited by the Penal Code;

(3) engaging in organized criminal activity as a member of a combination as prohibited by the Penal Code;

(4) delivery, possession, manufacture, or use of a [~~controlled~~] substance or other item in violation of Chapter 481, Health and Safety Code;

(5) gambling, gambling promotion, or communicating gambling information as prohibited by the Penal Code;

(6) prostitution, promotion of prostitution, or aggravated promotion of prostitution as prohibited by the Penal Code;

(7) compelling prostitution as prohibited by the Penal Code;

(8) commercial manufacture, commercial distribution, or commercial exhibition of obscene material as prohibited by the Penal Code;

(9) aggravated assault as described by Section 22.02, Penal Code;

(10) sexual assault as described by Section 22.011, Penal Code;

(11) aggravated sexual assault as described by Section 22.021, Penal Code;

(12) robbery as described by Section 29.02, Penal Code;

(13) aggravated robbery as described by Section 29.03, Penal Code;

(14) unlawfully carrying a weapon as described by Section 46.02, Penal Code;

(15) murder as described by Section 19.02, Penal Code;

(16) capital murder as described by Section 19.03, Penal Code;

(17) continuous sexual abuse of young child or children as described by Section 21.02, Penal Code;

(18) massage therapy or other massage services in violation of Chapter 455, Occupations Code;

(19) employing a minor at a sexually oriented business as defined by Section 243.002, Local Government Code;

(20) trafficking of persons as described by Section 20A.02, Penal Code;

(21) sexual conduct or performance by a child as described by Section 43.25, Penal Code; [~~or~~]

(22) employment harmful to a child as described by Section 43.251, Penal Code;

(23) criminal trespass as described by Section 30.05, Penal Code;

(24) disorderly conduct as described by Section 42.01, Penal Code;

(25) arson as described by Section 28.02, Penal Code;

(26) criminal mischief as described by Section 28.03, Penal Code, that causes a pecuniary loss of $500 or more; or

(27) a graffiti offense in violation of Section 28.08, Penal Code.

(b) A person maintains a common nuisance if the person maintains a multiunit residential property to which persons habitually go to commit acts listed in Subsection (a) and knowingly tolerates the acts and furthermore fails to make reasonable attempts to abate the acts.

(c) A person operating a web address or computer network in connection with an activity described by Subsection (a)(3), (6), (7), (10), (11), (17), (18), (19), (20), (21), or (22) maintains a common nuisance.

(d) Subsection (c) does not apply to:

(1) a provider of remote computing services or electronic communication services to the public;

(2) a provider of an interactive computer service as defined by 47 U.S.C. Section 230;

(3) an Internet service provider;

(4) a search engine operator;

(5) a browsing or hosting company;

(6) an operating system provider; or

(7) a device manufacturer.

(e) This section does not apply to an activity exempted, authorized, or otherwise lawful activity regulated by federal law.

2017 Legislation: Amended by H.B. 2359, §1, 85th Leg., eff. Sept. 1, 2017; H.B. 2552, §3, 85th Leg., eff. Sept. 1, 2017; S.B. 1196, §2, 85th Leg., eff. Sept. 1, 2017.

See also *O'Connor's Texas COA*, "Public Nuisance," ch. 22-B, p. 767; *O'Connor's Texas Rules*, "Injunctive Relief," ch. 2-C, p. 135.

A CPRC §125.002. SUIT TO ABATE CERTAIN COMMON NUISANCES [~~NUISANCE~~]; BOND

(a) A suit to enjoin and abate a common nuisance described by Section 125.0015(a) or (b) may be brought by an individual, by the attorney general, or by a district, county, or city attorney. The suit must be brought in the county in which it is alleged to exist against the person who is maintaining or about to maintain the nuisance. The suit must be brought in the name of the state if brought by the attorney general or a district or county attorney, in the name of the city if brought by a city attorney, or in the name of the individual if brought by a private citizen. Verification of the petition or proof of personal injury by the acts complained of need not be shown. For purposes of this subsection, personal injury may include economic or monetary loss.

(b) A person may bring a suit under Subsection (a) against any person who maintains, owns, uses, or is a party to the use of a place for purposes constituting a nuisance under this subchapter and may bring an action in rem against the place itself. A council of owners, as defined by Section 81.002, Property Code, or a unit owners' association organized under Section 82.101, Property Code, may be sued under this subsection if the council or association maintains, owns, uses, or is a party to the use of the common areas of the council's or association's condominium for purposes constituting a nuisance.

(c) Service of any order, notice, process, motion, or ruling of the court on the attorney of record of a cause pending under this subchapter is sufficient service of the party represented by an attorney.

(d) A person who violates a temporary or permanent injunctive order under this subchapter is subject to the following sentences for civil contempt:

(1) a fine of not less than $1,000 or more than $10,000;

(2) confinement in jail for a term of not less than 10 or more than 30 days; or

(3) both fine and confinement.

(e) If judgment is in favor of the petitioner, the court shall grant an injunction ordering the defendant to abate the nuisance and enjoining the defendant from maintaining or participating in the nuisance and may include in its order reasonable requirements to prevent the use or maintenance of the place as a nuisance. If the petitioner brings an action in rem, the judgment is a judgment in rem against the property as well as a judgment against the defendant. The judgment must order that the place where the nuisance exists be closed for one year after the date of judgment.

(f) Repealed by Acts 2007, 80th Leg., ch. 1023, §3, eff. June 15, 2007.

(f-1) If the defendant required to execute the bond is a hotel, motel, or similar establishment that rents overnight lodging to the public and the alleged common nuisance is under Section 125.0015(a)(6) or (7), the bond must also be conditioned that the defendant will, in each of the defendant's lodging units on the premises that are the subject of the suit, post in a conspicuous place near the room rate information required to be posted under Section 2155.001, Occupations Code, an operating toll-free telephone number of a nationally recognized information and referral hotline for victims of human trafficking.

(g) In an action brought under this chapter, other than an action brought under Section 125.0025, the petitioner may file a notice of lis pendens and a certified copy of an order of the court in the office of the county clerk in each county in which the land is located. The notice of lis pendens must conform to the requirements of Section 12.007, Property Code, and constitutes notice as provided by Section 13.004, Property Code. A certified copy of an order of the court filed in the office of the county clerk constitutes notice of the terms of the order and is binding on subsequent purchasers and lienholders.

(h) A person who may bring a suit under Subsection (a) [~~Section 125.0015~~] shall consider, among other factors, whether the property owner, the owner's authorized representative, or the operator or occupant of the business, dwelling, or other place where the criminal acts occurred:

(1) promptly notifies the appropriate governmental entity or the entity's law enforcement agency of the occurrence of criminal acts on the property; and

(2) cooperates with the governmental entity's law enforcement investigation of criminal acts occurring at the property.

2017 Legislation: Amended by H.B. 2552, §§5, 6, 85th Leg., eff. Sept. 1, 2017; S.B. 1196, §§4, 5, 85th Leg., eff. Sept. 1, 2017.

See also *O'Connor's Texas COA*, "Equitable relief," ch. 22-B, §3.4, p. 772; *O'Connor's Texas Rules*, "Injunctive Relief," ch. 2-C, p. 135.

CHAPTER 130. INDEMNIFICATION IN CERTAIN CONSTRUCTION CONTRACTS

CPRC §130.001. DEFINITION

In this chapter "construction contract" means a contract or agreement made and entered into by an owner, contractor, subcontractor, registered architect, licensed engineer, or supplier concerning the design, construction, alteration, repair, or maintenance of a building, structure, appurtenance, road, highway, bridge, dam, levee, or other improvement to or on real property, including moving, demolition, and excavation connected with the real property.

CPRC §130.002. COVENANT OR PROMISE VOID & UNENFORCEABLE

(a) A covenant or promise in, in connection with, or collateral to a construction contract is void and unenforceable if the covenant or promise provides for a contractor who is to perform the work that is the subject of the construction contract to indemnify or hold harmless a registered architect, licensed engineer or an agent, servant, or employee of a registered architect or licensed engineer from liability for damage that:

(1) is caused by or results from:

(A) defects in plans, designs, or specifications prepared, approved, or used by the architect or engineer; or

(B) negligence of the architect or engineer in the rendition or conduct of professional duties called for or arising out of the construction contract and the plans, designs, or specifications that are a part of the construction contract; and

(2) arises from:

(A) personal injury or death;

(B) property injury; or

(C) any other expense that arises from personal injury, death, or property injury.

(b) A covenant or promise in, in connection with, or collateral to a construction contract other than a contract for a single family or multifamily residence is void and unenforceable if the covenant or promise provides for a registered architect or licensed engineer whose engineering or architectural design services are the subject of the construction contract to indemnify or hold harmless an owner or owner's agent or employee from liability for damage that is caused by or results from the negligence of an owner or an owner's agent or employee.

CPRC §130.003. INSURANCE CONTRACT; WORKERS' COMPENSATION

This chapter does not apply to:

(1) an insurance contract; or

(2) a workers' compensation agreement.

CPRC §130.004. OWNER OF INTEREST IN REAL PROPERTY

(a) Except as provided by Section 130.002(b), this chapter does not apply to an owner of an interest in real property or persons employed solely by that owner.

(b) Except as provided by Section 130.002(b), this chapter does not prohibit or make void or unenforceable a covenant or promise to:

(1) indemnify or hold harmless an owner of an interest in real property and persons employed solely by that owner; or

(2) allocate, release, liquidate, limit, or exclude liability in connection with a construction contract between an owner or other person for whom a construction contract is being performed and a registered architect or licensed engineer.

CPRC §130.005. APPLICATION OF CHAPTER

This chapter does not apply to a contract or agreement in which an architect or engineer or an agent, servant, or employee of an architect or engineer is indemnified from liability for:

(1) negligent acts other than those described by this chapter; or

(2) negligent acts of the contractor, any subcontractor, any person directly or indirectly employed by the contractor or a subcontractor, or any person for whose acts the contractor or a subcontractor may be liable.

ESTATES CODE

SELECTED PROVISIONS
TABLE OF CONTENTS

For the complete Estates Code with annotations, see the current edition of ***O'Connor's Texas Estates Code Plus***. To order, call 1-800-OCONNOR (1-800-626-6667) or visit www.oconnors.com.

ESTATES CODE

SELECTED PROVISIONS
TABLE OF CONTENTS

ESTATES CODE

TITLE 2. ESTATES OF DECEDENTS; DURABLE POWERS OF ATTORNEY

SUBTITLE C. PASSAGE OF TITLE & DISTRIBUTION OF DECEDENTS' PROPERTY IN GENERAL

CHAPTER 101. ESTATE ASSETS IN GENERAL

SUBCHAPTER A. PASSAGE & POSSESSION OF DECEDENT'S ESTATE ON DEATH

EST §101.001. PASSAGE OF ESTATE ON DECEDENT'S DEATH

(a) Subject to Section 101.051, if a person dies leaving a lawful will:

(1) all of the person's estate that is devised by the will vests immediately in the devisees;

(2) all powers of appointment granted in the will vest immediately in the donees of those powers; and

(3) all of the person's estate that is not devised by the will vests immediately in the person's heirs at law.

(b) Subject to Section 101.051, the estate of a person who dies intestate vests immediately in the person's heirs at law.

EST §101.001

EST §101.002. EFFECT OF JOINT OWNERSHIP OF PROPERTY

If two or more persons hold an interest in property jointly and one joint owner dies before severance, the interest of the decedent in the joint estate:

(1) does not survive to the remaining joint owner or owners; and

(2) passes by will or intestacy from the decedent as if the decedent's interest had been severed.

EST §101.003. POSSESSION OF ESTATE BY PERSONAL REPRESENTATIVE

On the issuance of letters testamentary or of administration on an estate described by Section 101.001, the executor or administrator has the right to possession of the estate as the estate existed at the death of the testator or intestate, subject to the exceptions provided by Section 101.051. The executor or administrator shall recover possession of the estate and hold the estate in trust to be disposed of in accordance with the law.

Sections 101.004-101.050 reserved for expansion

SUBCHAPTER B. LIABILITY OF ESTATE FOR DEBTS

EST §101.051. LIABILITY OF ESTATE FOR DEBTS IN GENERAL

(a) A decedent's estate vests in accordance with Section 101.001(a) subject to the payment of:

(1) the debts of the decedent, except as exempted by law; and

(2) any court-ordered child support payments that are delinquent on the date of the decedent's death.

(b) A decedent's estate vests in accordance with Section 101.001(b) subject to the payment of, and is still liable for:

(1) the debts of the decedent, except as exempted by law; and

(2) any court-ordered child support payments that are delinquent on the date of the decedent's death.

EST §101.052. LIABILITY OF COMMUNITY PROPERTY FOR DEBTS OF DECEASED SPOUSE

(a) The community property subject to the sole or joint management, control, and disposition of a spouse during marriage continues to be subject to the liabilities of that spouse on death.

(b) The interest that the deceased spouse owned in any other nonexempt community property passes to the deceased spouse's heirs or devisees charged with the debts that were enforceable against the deceased spouse before death.

(c) This section does not prohibit the administration of community property under other provisions of this title relating to the administration of an estate.

See also Fam. Code §§3.002, 3.003, 3.102, 3.202; Featherston, *Creditors' Rights in & to the Marital Estate: What Property is Liable for Which Debts?*, Advanced Estate Planning & Probate Course, State Bar of Texas CLE, ch. 9 (2013).

CHAPTER 111. NONPROBATE ASSETS IN GENERAL

SUBCHAPTER A. RIGHT OF SURVIVORSHIP AGREEMENTS BETWEEN JOINT TENANTS

EST §111.001. RIGHT OF SURVIVORSHIP AGREEMENTS AUTHORIZED

(a) Notwithstanding Section 101.002, two or more persons who hold an interest in property jointly may agree in writing that the interest of a joint owner who dies survives to the surviving joint owner or owners.

(b) An agreement described by Subsection (a) may not be inferred from the mere fact that property is held in joint ownership.

EST §111.002. AGREEMENTS CONCERNING COMMUNITY PROPERTY

(a) Section 111.001 does not apply to an agreement between spouses regarding the spouses' community property.

(b) An agreement between spouses regarding a right of survivorship in community property is governed by Chapter 112.

Chapter 114. Transfer on Death Deed

NCCUSL Prefatory Comment*

One of the main innovations in the property law of the twentieth century has been the development of asset-specific will substitutes for the transfer of property at death. By these mechanisms, an owner may designate beneficiaries to receive the property at the owner's death without waiting for probate and without the beneficiary designation needing to comply with the witnessing requirements of wills. Examples of specific assets that today routinely pass outside of probate include the proceeds of life insurance policies and pension plans, securities registered in transfer on death (TOD) form, and funds held in pay on death (POD) bank accounts.

Today, nonprobate transfers are widely accepted. The trend has largely focused on assets that are personal property, such as the assets described in the preceding paragraph. However, long-standing uniform law speaks more broadly. Section 6-101 of the Uniform Probate Code (UPC) provides: "*A provision for a nonprobate transfer on death in* an insurance policy, contract of employment, bond, mortgage, promissory note, certificated or uncertificated security, account agreement, custodial agreement, deposit agreement, compensation plan, pension plan, individual retirement plan, employee benefit plan, trust, *conveyance*, *deed of gift*, marital property agreement, *or other written instrument of a similar nature is nontestamentary*" (emphasis supplied).

A small but growing number of jurisdictions have implemented the principle of UPC §6-101 by enacting statutes providing an asset-specific mechanism for the nonprobate transfer of land. This is done by permitting owners of interests in real property to execute and record a transfer on death (TOD) deed. By this deed, the owner identifies the beneficiary or beneficiaries who will succeed to the property at the owner's death. During the owner's lifetime, the beneficiaries have no interest in the property, and the owner retains full power to transfer or encumber the property or to revoke the TOD deed.

Thirteen states have enacted statutes authorizing TOD deeds. In the chronological order of the statutes' enactment, the states are: Missouri (1989), Kansas (1997), Ohio (2000), New Mexico (2001), Arizona (2002), Nevada (2003), Colorado (2004), Arkansas (2005), Wisconsin (2006), Montana (2007), Oklahoma (2008), Minnesota (2008), and Indiana (2009).

The time is ripe for a Uniform Act to facilitate this emerging form of nonprobate transfer and to bring uniformity and clarity to its use and operation.

Subchapter A. General Provisions

EST §114.001. SHORT TITLE

This chapter may be cited as the Texas Real Property Transfer on Death Act.

---

* **Editor's note:**

The NCCUSL comments have been edited to reflect the Texas Legislature's omission of sections and changing of section numbers from the original uniform act. The Texas Legislature did not adopt the NCCUSL comments when it adopted the Uniform Real Property Transfer on Death Act. The full uniform act and comments can be found at www.uniformlaws.org.

EST §114.002. DEFINITIONS

(a) In this chapter:

(1) "Beneficiary" means a person who receives real property under a transfer on death deed.

(2) "Designated beneficiary" means a person designated to receive real property in a transfer on death deed.

(3) "Joint owner with right of survivorship" or "joint owner" means an individual who owns real property concurrently with one or more other individuals with a right of survivorship. The term does not include a tenant in common or an owner of community property with or without a right of survivorship.

(4) "Person" has the meaning assigned by Section 311.005, Government Code.

(5) "Real property" means an interest in real property located in this state.

(6) "Transfer on death deed" means a deed authorized under this chapter and does not refer to any other deed that transfers an interest in real property on the death of an individual.

(7) "Transferor" means an individual who makes a transfer on death deed.

(b) In this chapter, the terms "cancel" and "revoke" are synonymous.

NCCUSL Comment*

Subsection (1) defines a beneficiary as a person that receives property under a transfer on death deed. This links the definition of a "beneficiary" to the definition of a "person." A beneficiary can be any person, including the trustee of a revocable trust.

Subsection (2) defines a designated beneficiary as a person designated to receive property in a transfer on death deed. This links the definition of a "designated beneficiary" to the definition of a "person." A designated beneficiary can be any person, including a revocable trust.

The distinction between a "beneficiary" and a "designated beneficiary" is easily illustrated. Section 114.103 provides that, on the transferor's death, the property that is the subject of a transfer on death deed is transferred to the designated beneficiaries who survive the transferor. If *X* and *Y* are the designated beneficiaries but only *Y* survives the transferor, then *Y* is a beneficiary and *X* is not. A further illustration comes into play if §114.103 is made subject to the state's antilapse statute. If *X* fails to survive the transferor but has a descendant, *Z*, who survives the transferor, the antilapse statute may create a substitute gift in favor of *Z*. In such a case, the designated beneficiaries are *X* and *Y*, but the beneficiaries are *Y* and *Z*.

Subsection (3) provides a definition of a "joint owner" as an individual who owns property with one or more other individuals with a right of survivorship. The term is used in §§114.057 and 114.103.

...

Subsection (6) provides that a "transfer on death deed" is a deed authorized under this act. In some states with existing transfer on death deed legislation, the legislation has instead used the term "beneficiary deed." The term "transfer on death deed" is preferred, to be consistent with the transfer on death registration of securities. *See* Article 6, Part 3, of the Uniform Probate Code, containing the Uniform TOD Security Registration Act.

Subsection (7) limits the definition of a "transferor" to an individual. The term "transferor" does not include a corporation, business trust, estate,

trust, partnership, limited liability company, association, joint venture, public corporation, government or governmental subdivision, agency, or instrumentality, or any legal or commercial entity other than an individual. The term also does not include an agent or other representative. If a transfer on death deed is made by an agent on behalf of a principal or by a conservator, guardian, or judge on behalf of a ward, the principal or ward is the transferor. By way of analogy, *see* Uniform Trust Code (2000/2005) §103(15) (defining "settlor") and the accompanying Comment (excluding an individual "acting as the agent for the person who will be funding the trust"). The power of an agent to make or revoke a transfer on death deed on behalf of a principal is determined by other law, such as the Uniform Power of Attorney Act (2006) (UPC Article 5B), as indicated in the Comments to §§114.055 and 114.057 (UPC §§6-409 and 6-411).

EST §114.003. APPLICABILITY

This chapter applies to a transfer on death deed executed and acknowledged on or after September 1, 2015, by a transferor who dies on or after September 1, 2015.

NCCUSL Comment*

This section provides that the act applies to a transfer on death deed made … on or after the effective date of the act by a transferor dying on or after the effective date of the act. This section is consistent with the Uniform Probate Code's provisions governing transfer on death registration of securities. Those provisions "appl[y] to registrations of securities in beneficiary form made before or after [effective date], by decedents dying on or after [effective date]." UPC §6-311.

EST §114.004. NONEXCLUSIVITY

This chapter does not affect any method of transferring real property otherwise permitted under the laws of this state.

NCCUSL Comment*

This section provides that the act is nonexclusive. The act does not affect any method of transferring property otherwise permitted under state law.

One such method is a present transfer with a retained legal life estate. Consider the following examples:

Example 1. A conveys Blackacre to *B* while reserving *A*'s right to remain in possession until *A*'s death. By this conveyance, *A* has made a present transfer of a future interest to *B*. The transfer is irrevocable. The future interest will ripen into possession at *A*'s death, even if *B* fails to survive *A*.

Example 2. A executes, acknowledges, and records a transfer on death deed for Blackacre, naming *B* as the designated beneficiary. During *A*'s lifetime, no interest passes to *B*, and *A* may revoke the deed. If unrevoked, the deed will transfer possession to *B* at *A*'s death only if *B* survives *A*.

As illustrated in these examples, the two methods of transfer have different effects and are governed by different rules.

EST §114.005. UNIFORMITY OF APPLICATION & CONSTRUCTION

In applying and construing this chapter, consideration must be given to the need to promote uniformity of the law with respect to the subject matter of this chapter among states that enact a law similar to this chapter.

* See footnote on p. 955.

EST §114.006. RELATION TO ELECTRONIC SIGNATURES IN GLOBAL & NATIONAL COMMERCE ACT

This chapter modifies, limits, and supersedes the federal Electronic Signatures in Global and National Commerce Act (15 U.S.C. Section 7001 et seq.), except that this chapter does not modify, limit, or supersede Section 101(c) of that Act (15 U.S.C. Section 7001(c)) or authorize electronic delivery of any of the notices described in Section 103(b) of that Act (15 U.S.C. Section 7003(b)).

Sections 114.007-114.050 blank

SUBCHAPTER B. AUTHORIZATION, EXECUTION, & REVOCATION OF TRANSFER ON DEATH DEED

EST §114.051. TRANSFER ON DEATH DEED AUTHORIZED

An individual may transfer the individual's interest in real property to one or more beneficiaries effective at the transferor's death by a transfer on death deed.

NCCUSL Comment*

This section authorizes a transfer on death deed and makes it clear that the transfer is not an inter vivos transfer. The transfer occurs at the transferor's death.

The transferor is an individual, but the singular includes the plural. Multiple individuals can readily act together to transfer property by a transfer on death deed, as in the common case of a husband and wife who own the property as joint tenants or as tenants by the entirety. On the effect of a transfer on death deed made by joint owners, see §114.103(b) and the accompanying Comment.

The transferor may select any form of ownership, concurrent or successive, absolute or conditional, contingent or vested, valid under state law. Among many other things, this permits the transferor to reserve interests for his estate (e.g., mineral interests); to specify the nature and extent of the beneficiary's interest; and to designate one or more primary beneficiaries and one or more alternate beneficiaries to take in the event the primary beneficiaries fail to survive the transferor. This freedom to specify the form and terms of the transferee's interest comports with the fundamental principle of American law recognized by the Restatement (Third) of Property (Wills and Other Donative Transfers) §10.1 that the donor's intention should be "given effect to the maximum extent allowed by law." As the Restatement explains in Comment c to §10.1, "American law curtails freedom of disposition only to the extent that the donor attempts to make a disposition or achieve a purpose that is prohibited or restricted by an overriding rule of law."

Notwithstanding this freedom of disposition, transferors are encouraged as a practical matter to avoid formulating dispositions that would complicate title. Dispositions containing conditions or class gifts, for example, may require a court proceeding to sort out the beneficiaries' interests. Other estate planning mechanisms, such as trusts, may be more appropriate in such cases.

EST §114.052. TRANSFER ON DEATH DEED REVOCABLE

A transfer on death deed is revocable regardless of whether the deed or another instrument contains a contrary provision.

NCCUSL Comment*

A fundamental feature of a transfer on death deed under this Act is that the transferor retains the power to revoke the deed. Section 114.052 is framed as a mandatory rule, for two reasons. First, the rule prevents an off-record instrument from affecting the revocability of a transfer on death deed. Second, the rule protects the transferor who may wish later to revoke the deed.

If the transferor promises to make the deed irrevocable or not to revoke the deed, the promisee may have a remedy under other law if the promise is broken. The deed remains revocable despite the promise.

EST §114.053. TRANSFER ON DEATH DEED NONTESTAMENTARY

A transfer on death deed is a nontestamentary instrument.

NCCUSL Comment*

This section is consistent with Uniform Probate Code §6-101(a), which provides: "A provision for a nonprobate transfer on death in an insurance policy, contract of employment, bond, mortgage, promissory note, certificated or uncertificated security, account agreement, custodial agreement, deposit agreement, compensation plan, pension plan, individual retirement plan, employee benefit plan, trust, conveyance, deed of gift, marital property agreement, or other written instrument of a similar nature is nontestamentary."

As the Comment to Uniform Probate Code §6-101 explains, because the mode of transfer is declared to be nontestamentary, the instrument of transfer is not a will and does not have to be executed in compliance with the formalities for wills, nor does the instrument need to be probated.

Whether a document that is ineffective as a transfer on death deed (e.g., because it has not been recorded before the transferor's death) should be given effect as a testamentary instrument will depend on the applicable facts and on the wills law of the jurisdiction. Section 2-503 of the Uniform Probate Code provides in pertinent part: "Although a document ... was not executed in compliance with §2-502, the document ... is treated as if it had been executed in compliance with that section if the proponent of the document ... establishes by clear and convincing evidence that the decedent intended the document ... to constitute ... (iii) an addition to or alteration of the [decedent's] will...."

EST §114.054. CAPACITY OF TRANSFEROR; USE OF POWER OF ATTORNEY

(a) The capacity required to make or revoke a transfer on death deed is the same as the capacity required to make a contract.

(b) A transfer on death deed may not be created through use of a power of attorney.

NCCUSL Comment*

...

A transfer on death deed is not affected if the transferor subsequently loses capacity. On the ability of an agent under a power of attorney to make or revoke a transfer on death deed, see the Comments to §114.055 and 114.057.

EST §114.055. REQUIREMENTS

To be effective, a transfer on death deed must:

(1) except as otherwise provided in Subdivision (2), contain the essential elements and formalities of a recordable deed;

(2) state that the transfer of an interest in real property to the designated beneficiary is to occur at the transferor's death; and

(3) be recorded before the transferor's death in the deed records in the county clerk's office of the county where the real property is located.

NCCUSL Comment*

Subsection (1) requires a transfer on death deed to contain the same essential elements and formalities, other than a present intention to convey, as are required for a properly recordable inter vivos deed under state law. "Essential elements" is a term with a long usage in the law of deeds of real property. The essential elements of a deed vary from one state to another but commonly include the names of the grantor and grantee, a clause transferring title, a description of the property transferred, and the grantor's signature. In all states, the essential elements of a properly recordable deed include the requirement that the deed be acknowledged by the grantor before a notary public or other individual authorized by law to take acknowledgments. *See* Thompson on Real Property §92.04(c) (observing that a "certificate of acknowledgment or attestation is universally required to qualify an instrument for recordation"). In the context of transfer on death deeds, the requirement of acknowledgment fulfills at least four functions. First, it cautions a transferor that he or she is performing an act with legal consequences. Such caution is important where, as here, the transferor does not experience the wrench of delivery because the transfer occurs at death. Second, acknowledgment helps to prevent fraud. Third, acknowledgment facilitates the recording of the deed. Fourth, acknowledgment enables the rule in §114.057 that a later acknowledged deed prevails over an earlier acknowledged deed.

Subsection (2) emphasizes an important distinction between an inter vivos transfer and a transfer on death. An inter vivos transfer reflects an intention to transfer, at the time of the conveyance, an interest in property, either a present interest or a future interest. In contrast, a transfer on death reflects an intention that the transfer occur at the transferor's death. Under no circumstances should a transfer on death be given effect inter vivos; to do so would violate the transferor's intention that the transfer occur at the transferor's death.

Subsection (3) requires a transfer on death deed to be recorded before the transferor's death in the county (or other appropriate administrative division of a state, such as a parish) where the land is located. If the property described in the deed is in more than one county, the deed is effective only with respect to the property in the county or counties where the deed is recorded. The requirement of recordation before death helps to prevent fraud by ensuring that all steps necessary to the effective transfer on death deed are completed during the transferor's lifetime. The requirement of recordation before death also enables all parties to rely on the recording system.

An individual's agent may execute a transfer on death deed on the individual's behalf to the extent permitted by other law, such as the Uniform Power of Attorney Act (2006). This act does not define, but instead relies on other law to determine, the authority of an agent.

EST §114.056. NOTICE, DELIVERY, ACCEPTANCE, OR CONSIDERATION NOT REQUIRED

A transfer on death deed is effective without:

(1) notice or delivery to or acceptance by the designated beneficiary during the transferor's life; or

(2) consideration.

NCCUSL Comment*

This section makes it clear that a transfer on death deed is effective without notice or delivery to or acceptance by the beneficiary during the transferor's lifetime (subsection (1)) and without consideration (subsection (2)).

Subsection (1) is consistent with the fundamental distinction under this Act between a transfer on death deed and an inter vivos deed. Under the former, but not under the latter, the transfer occurs at the transferor's death. Therefore, there is no requirement of notice, delivery, or acceptance during the transferor's life. This does not mean that the beneficiary is required to accept the property. The beneficiary may disclaim the property, as explained in §114.105 and the accompanying Comment.

Subsection (2) is consistent with the law of donative transfers. A deed need not be supported by consideration.

* See footnote on p. 955.

EST §114.057. REVOCATION BY CERTAIN INSTRUMENTS; EFFECT OF WILL OR MARRIAGE DISSOLUTION

(a) Subject to Subsections (d) and (e), an instrument is effective to revoke a recorded transfer on death deed, or any part of it, if the instrument:

(1) is one of the following:

(A) a subsequent transfer on death deed that revokes the preceding transfer on death deed or part of the deed expressly or by inconsistency; or

(B) except as provided by Subsection (b), an instrument of revocation that expressly revokes the transfer on death deed or part of the deed;

(2) is acknowledged by the transferor after the acknowledgment of the deed being revoked; and

(3) is recorded before the transferor's death in the deed records in the county clerk's office of the county where the deed being revoked is recorded.

(b) A will may not revoke or supersede a transfer on death deed.

(c) If a marriage between the transferor and a designated beneficiary is dissolved after a transfer on death deed is recorded, a final judgment of the court dissolving the marriage operates to revoke the transfer on death deed as to that designated beneficiary if notice of the judgment is recorded before the transferor's death in the deed records in the county clerk's office of the county where the deed is recorded, notwithstanding Section 111.052.

(d) If a transfer on death deed is made by more than one transferor, revocation by a transferor does not affect the deed as to the interest of another transferor who does not make that revocation.

(e) A transfer on death deed made by joint owners with right of survivorship is revoked only if it is revoked by all of the living joint owners.

(f) This section does not limit the effect of an inter vivos transfer of the real property.

NCCUSL Comment*

This section concerns revocation by instrument and revocation by act. On revocation by change of circumstances, such as by divorce or homicide, see §114.103 and the accompanying Comment.

Subsection (a) provides the exclusive methods of revoking, in whole or in part, a recorded transfer on death deed by a subsequent instrument. Revocation by an instrument not specified, such as the transferor's will, is not permitted.

The rule that a transfer on death deed may not be revoked by the transferor's subsequent will is a departure from the Restatement (Third) of Property (Wills and Other Donative Transfers) §7.2 comment e (see also the corresponding Reporter's Note), which encourages the revocability of will substitutes by will. However, there is a sound reason for the departure in the specific case of a transfer on death deed. A transfer on death deed operates on real property, for which certainty of title is essential. This certainty would be difficult, and in many cases impossible, to achieve if an off-record instrument, such as the grantor's will, could revoke a recorded transfer on death deed. The rule in this Act against revocation by will is also consistent with the uniform acts governing multiple-party bank accounts. *See* Uniform Probate Code §6-213(b) ("A right of survivorship arising from the express terms of the account, §6-212, or a POD designation, may not be altered by will.").

A recorded transfer on death deed may be revoked by instrument only by (1) a subsequently acknowledged transfer on death deed, (2) a subsequently acknowledged instrument of revocation, such as the form in §114.152.... Consider the following examples:

Example 1. T executes, acknowledges, and records a transfer on death deed for Blackacre. Later, *T* executes, acknowledges, and records a second transfer on death deed for Blackacre, containing an express revocation clause revoking "all my prior transfer on death deeds concerning this property." The second deed revokes the first deed. The revocation occurs when the second deed is recorded. (For the result if the second deed had not contained the express revocation clause, see Example 5.)

Example 2. T executes, acknowledges, and records two transfer on death deeds for Blackacre. Both deeds expressly revoke "all my prior transfer on death deeds concerning this property." The dates of acknowledgment determine which deed revoked the other. The first deed is acknowledged November 1; the second deed is acknowledged December 15. The second deed is the later acknowledged, so it revokes the first deed. The revocation occurs when the second deed is recorded.

Example 3. T executes and acknowledges a transfer on death deed for Blackacre. *T* later executes and acknowledges a revocation form. Both instruments are recorded. Because the revocation form is acknowledged later than the deed, the form revokes the deed. The revocation occurs when the form is recorded.

...

The same rules apply whether the revocation is total or partial. In the previous examples, suppose instead that the initial transfer on death deed provides for the transfer of two parcels, Blackacre and Whiteacre, and that the subsequent instrument revokes the transfer on death deed as to Blackacre. The subsequent instrument revokes the transfer on death deed in part.

If the property described in the original deed is in more than one county, the revocation is effective only with respect to the property in the county or counties where the revoking deed or instrument is recorded.

Subsection (a)(1)(A) speaks of revocation "expressly or by inconsistency." This provision references the well-established law of revocation by inconsistency of wills. Consider the following examples:

Example 5. T executes, acknowledges, and records a transfer on death deed for Blackacre naming *X* as the designated beneficiary. Later, *T* executes, acknowledges, and records a transfer on death deed for the same property, Blackacre, containing no express revocation of the earlier deed but naming *Y* as the designated beneficiary. Later, *T* dies. The recording of the deed in favor of *Y* revokes the deed in favor of *X* by inconsistency. At *T*'s death, *Y* is the owner of Blackacre.

Example 6. T, the owner of Blackacre in fee simple absolute, executes, acknowledges, and records a transfer on death deed for Blackacre naming *X* as the designated beneficiary. Later, *T* executes, acknowledges, and records a transfer on death deed containing no express revocation of the earlier deed but naming *Y* as the designated beneficiary of a life estate (or a mineral interest) in Blackacre. Later, *T* dies. The recording of the deed in favor of *Y* partially revokes the deed in favor of *X* by inconsistency. At *T*'s death, *Y* is the owner of a life estate (or a mineral interest) in Blackacre, and *X* is the owner of the remainder.

... Revocation means that the instrument is rendered void. Ademption by extinction means that the transfer of the property cannot occur because the property is not owned by the transferor at death. The doctrines are different.

In some instances, revocation and ademption have the same practical effect: the designated beneficiary of the property receives nothing. Nothing in this section changes that fact, as indicated in subsection (f). However, there

* See footnote on p. 955.

EST §114.057

are other instances where the doctrines have differing effects. Consider the following illustration, drawn from the law of wills.

Example 7. T executes a will devising Blackacre to *A*. Later, *T* becomes legally incompetent, and *G* is appointed as *T*'s conservator. *G*, acting within the scope of his authority, sells Blackacre to *B* for $100,000. Later, *T* dies.

The law of wills provides that the devise to *A* is adeemed rather than revoked. This means that *A* is not entitled to Blackacre but is entitled to a pecuniary devise in the amount of $100,000. *See* UPC §2-606(b); Atkinson on Wills §134; *Wasserman v. Cohen*, 606 N.E.2d 901, 903 (Mass. 1993). The result is designed to effectuate *T*'s presumed intention.

The Joint Editorial Board for Uniform Trust and Estate Acts has begun a conversation on whether the Uniform Probate Code's provisions on ademption should be extended to nonprobate transfers, thus harmonizing the treatment of wills and will substitutes on this aspect of the law. This act accepts the well recognized distinction between revocation and ademption in order to leave the door open for such future harmonization, which would effectuate the presumed intention of nonprobate grantors.

Subsections (d) and (e) supply rules governing revocation by instrument in the event of a transfer on death deed made by multiple owners. Subsection (d) provides that revocation by a transferor does not affect a transfer on death deed as to the interest of another transferor. Subsection (e) provides that a transfer on death deed of joint owners is revoked only if it is revoked by all of the living joint owners. This rule is consistent with Uniform Probate Code §6-306, which provides in pertinent part: "A registration of a security in beneficiary form may be canceled or changed at any time by the sole owner or all then surviving owners without the consent of the beneficiary." Subsection (e) applies only to a deed of joint owners. A joint tenant who severs the joint tenancy, thereby destroying the right of survivorship, is no longer a joint owner.

...

This act does not define, but instead looks to other law to determine, the authority of an agent. An individual's agent may revoke a transfer on death deed on the individual's behalf to the extent permitted by other law, such as the Uniform Power of Attorney Act (2006).

Sections 114.058-114.100 blank

SUBCHAPTER C. EFFECT OF TRANSFER ON DEATH DEED; LIABILITY OF TRANSFERRED PROPERTY FOR CREDITORS' CLAIMS

EST §114.101. EFFECT OF TRANSFER ON DEATH DEED DURING TRANSFEROR'S LIFE

During a transferor's life, a transfer on death deed does not:

(1) affect an interest or right of the transferor or any other owner, including:

(A) the right to transfer or encumber the real property that is the subject of the deed;

(B) homestead rights in the real property, if applicable; and

(C) ad valorem tax exemptions, including exemptions for residence homestead, persons 65 years of age or older, persons with disabilities, and veterans;

(2) affect an interest or right of a transferee of the real property that is the subject of the deed, even if the transferee has actual or constructive notice of the deed;

(3) affect an interest or right of a secured or unsecured creditor or future creditor of the transferor, even if the creditor has actual or constructive notice of the deed;

(4) affect the transferor's or designated beneficiary's eligibility for any form of public assistance, subject to applicable federal law;

(5) constitute a transfer triggering a "due on sale" or similar clause;

(6) invoke statutory real estate notice or disclosure requirements;

(7) create a legal or equitable interest in favor of the designated beneficiary; or

(8) subject the real property to claims or process of a creditor of the designated beneficiary.

NCCUSL Comment*

A fundamental feature of a transfer on death deed under this Act is that it does not operate until the transferor's death. The transfer occurs at the transferor's death, not before.

Subsection (1): A transfer on death deed, during the transferor's lifetime, does not affect the interests or property rights of the transferor or any other owners. Therefore, the deed does not, among many other things: affect the transferor's right to transfer or encumber the property inter vivos; sever a joint tenancy or a joint tenant's right of survivorship; trigger a due-on-sale clause in the transferor's mortgage; trigger the imposition of real estate transfer tax; or affect the transferor's homestead or real estate tax exemptions, if any.

Subsection (2): A transfer on death deed does not affect transferees, whether or not they have notice of the deed. Like a will, the transfer on death deed is ambulatory. It has no effect on inter vivos transfers.

Subsection (3): A transfer on death deed, during the transferor's lifetime, does not affect pre-existing or future creditors, secured or unsecured, whether or not they have an interest in the property or notice of the deed.

Subsection (4): A transfer on death deed, during the transferor's lifetime, does not affect the transferor's or designated beneficiary's eligibility for any form of public assistance, including Medicaid. ...

Subsection (7): During the transferor's lifetime, a transfer on death deed does not create a legal or equitable interest in the designated beneficiary. The beneficiary does not have an interest that can be assigned or encumbered. Note, however, that this rule would not preclude the doctrine of after-acquired title. A warranty deed from a designated beneficiary to a third party would operate to pass the beneficiary's title to the third party after the transferor's death.

Subsection (8): A transfer on death deed, during the transferor's lifetime, does not make the property subject to claims or process of the designated beneficiary's creditors. The deed has no more effect than a will.

If a transferor combines an inter vivos transfer of an interest in property (such as a mineral interest) with a transfer on death of the remainder interest, the inter vivos transfer may have present effect even though the transfer on death does not occur until the transferor's death.

EST §114.102. EFFECT OF SUBSEQUENT CONVEYANCE ON TRANSFER ON DEATH DEED

An otherwise valid transfer on death deed is void as to any interest in real property that is conveyed by the transferor during the transferor's lifetime after the transfer on death deed is executed and recorded if:

* See footnote on p. 955.

(1) a valid instrument conveying the interest is recorded in the deed records in the county clerk's office of the same county in which the transfer on death deed is recorded; and

(2) the recording of the instrument occurs before the transferor's death.

EST §114.103. EFFECT OF TRANSFER ON DEATH DEED AT TRANSFEROR'S DEATH

The amended text in §114.103 is effective for transfer-on-death deeds executed and acknowledged on or after Sept. 1, 2017. Deeds executed and acknowledged before Sept. 1, 2017, are governed by the former law in effect at that time.

(a) Except as otherwise provided in the transfer on death deed, this section, or any other statute or the common law of this state governing a decedent's estate, on the death of the transferor, the following rules apply to an interest in real property that is the subject of a transfer on death deed and owned by the transferor at death:

(1) if the designated beneficiary survives the transferor by 120 hours, the interest in the real property is transferred to the designated beneficiary in accordance with the deed;

(2) the share [~~interest~~] of any [~~a~~] designated beneficiary that fails to survive the transferor by 120 hours lapses, notwithstanding Section 111.052, and is subject to and passes in accordance with Subchapter D, Chapter 255, as if the transfer on death deed were a devise made in a will; and

(3) subject to Subdivision (2) [~~(4)~~], concurrent interests are transferred to the beneficiaries in equal and undivided shares with no right of survivorship [~~; and~~]

[~~(4)~~] [~~notwithstanding Subdivision (2), if the transferor has identified two or more designated beneficiaries to receive concurrent interests in the real property, the share of a designated beneficiary who predeceases the transferor lapses and is subject to and passes in accordance with Subchapter D, Chapter 255, as if the transfer on death deed were a devise made in a will~~].

(b) If a transferor is a joint owner with right of survivorship who is survived by one or more other joint owners, the real property that is the subject of the transfer on death deed belongs to the surviving joint owner or owners. If a transferor is a joint owner with right of survivorship who is the last surviving joint owner, the transfer on death deed is effective.

(c) If a transfer on death deed is made by two or more transferors who are joint owners with right of survivorship, the last surviving joint owner may revoke the transfer on death deed subject to Section 114.057.

(d) A transfer on death deed transfers real property without covenant of warranty of title even if the deed contains a contrary provision.

2017 Legislation: Amended by S.B. 2150, §1, 85th Leg., eff. Sept. 1, 2017.

NCCUSL Comment*

Subsection (a) states three default rules, except as otherwise provided by the transfer on death deed, by this section, or by other provisions of state law governing nonprobate transfers. ...

The three default rules established by subsection (a) are these. First, the property that is the subject of an effective transfer on death deed and owned by the transferor at death is transferred at the transferor's death to the designated beneficiaries as provided in the deed. The rule implements the transferor's intention as described in the deed. Consider the following example:

Example 1. A executes, acknowledges, and records a transfer on death deed for Blackacre naming *X* as the primary beneficiary and *Y* as the alternate beneficiary if *X* fails to survive *A*. Both *X* and *Y* survive *A*. Blackacre is transferred to *X* at *A*'s death in accordance with the provisions of the deed.

This default rule implements the fundamental principle that the provisions of the deed control the disposition of the property, unless otherwise provided by state law.

The drafting committee approves of the result in *In re Estate of Roloff*, 143 P.3d 406 (Kan. Ct. App. 2006) (holding that crops should be transferred with the land under a transfer on death deed because this result would be reached on the same facts with any other deed).

...

Example 2. A executes, acknowledges, and records a transfer on death deed for Blackacre naming *X* as the primary beneficiary and *Y* as the alternate beneficiary if *X* fails to survive *A*. In fact, *X* and *Y* fail to survive *A*, who is survived only by *X*'s child, *Z*. Assume that the state's antilapse statute applies to transfer on death deeds and creates a substitute gift in *Z*. (For such a statute, see Uniform Probate Code §2-706.) Blackacre is transferred to *Z* at *A*'s death in accordance with the provisions of the deed as modified by the antilapse statute.

Example 3. A executes, acknowledges, and records a transfer on death deed for Blackacre naming her spouse, *X*, as the primary beneficiary and *Y* as the alternate beneficiary if *X* fails to survive *A*. Later, *A* and *X* divorce. Assume that the state's statute on revocation by divorce applies to transfer on death deeds and revokes the designation in favor of *X*, with the effect that the provisions of the transfer on death deed are given effect as if *X* had disclaimed. (For such a statute, see Uniform Probate Code §2-804.) Assume further that the effect of the putative disclaimer is that *X* is treated as having failed to survive *A*. (See the Uniform Disclaimer of Property Interests Act (1999/2006) §6(a)(3)(B) (UPC §2-1106(a)(3)(B).) Blackacre is transferred to *Y* at *A*'s death in accordance with the provisions of the deed as modified by the revocation on divorce and disclaimer statutes.

Note that the property must be owned by the transferor at death. Property no longer owned by the transferor at death cannot be transferred by a transfer on death deed, just as it cannot be transferred by a will. This is the principle of ademption by extinction, discussed in the Comment to §114.057.

* See footnote on p. 955.

In almost every instance, the transferor will own the property not only at death but also when the transfer on death deed is executed, but the latter is not imperative. Consider the following example. *H* and *W*, a married couple, hold Blackacre as tenants by the entirety. *H* executes, acknowledges, and records a transfer on death deed for Blackacre in favor of *X*. *W* later dies, at which point *H* owns Blackacre in fee simple absolute. Later, *H* dies. Under the law of some states, there may be a question whether the transfer on death deed is effective, given that *H* executed it when Blackacre was owned, not by *H* and *W*, but by the marital entity. The correct answer is that the transfer on death deed is effective at *H*'s death because Blackacre is owned by *H* at *H*'s death. *See, e.g., Mitchell v. Wilmington Trust Co.*, 449 A.2d 1055 (Del. Ch. 1982) (mortgage granted by one tenant by the entirety is not void upon execution but remains inchoate during the lives of both spouses, and becomes a valid lien if the spouse who executed the mortgage survives the other spouse or if the spouses get divorced).

The second default rule established by subsection (a) is that the share of any designated beneficiary is contingent on surviving the transferor. This default rule treats wills and will substitutes alike. The share of any designated beneficiary who fails to survive the transferor lapses. ...

The third default rule established by subsection (a) is that concurrent beneficiaries receive equal and undivided interests with no right of survivorship among them. This default rule is consistent with the general presumption in favor of tenancy in common. *See* Powell on Real Property §51.02. The rule is also consistent with Uniform Probate Code §6-212 governing multiple-party accounts and §6-307 governing the transfer on death registration of securities.

Subsection (b) provides that the survivorship right of a joint owner takes precedence over the transfer on death deed. This rule is consistent with the law of joint tenancy and wills: the right of survivorship takes precedence over a provision in a joint tenant's will.

Subsection (d) states the mandatory rule that a transfer on death deed transfers the property without covenant or warranty of title. The rule is mandatory for two reasons: first, to prevent mishaps by uninformed grantors; and second, to recognize that a transfer on death deed is a will substitute. The rule of this section is consistent with the longstanding law of wills. As stated by Sir Edward Coke, "an express warranty cannot be created by will." Coke on Littleton 386a.

EST §114.104. TRANSFER ON DEATH DEED PROPERTY SUBJECT TO LIENS & ENCUMBRANCES AT TRANSFEROR'S DEATH; CREDITORS' CLAIMS

(a) Subject to Section 13.001, Property Code, a beneficiary takes the real property subject to all conveyances, encumbrances, assignments, contracts, mortgages, liens, and other interests to which the real property is subject at the transferor's death. For purposes of this subsection and Section 13.001, Property Code, the recording of the transfer on death deed is considered to have occurred at the transferor's death.

(b) If a personal representative has been appointed for the transferor's estate, an administration of the estate has been opened, and the real property transferring under a transfer on death deed is subject to a lien or security interest, including a deed of trust or mortgage, the personal representative shall give notice to the creditor of the transferor as the personal representative would any other secured creditor under Section 308.053. The creditor shall then make an election under Section 355.151 in the period prescribed by Section 355.152 to have the claim treated as a matured secured claim or a preferred debt and lien claim, and the claim is subject to the claims procedures prescribed by this section.

(c) If the secured creditor elects to have the claim treated as a preferred debt and lien claim, Sections 355.154 and 355.155 apply as if the transfer on death deed were a devise made in a will, and the creditor may not pursue any other claims or remedies for any deficiency against the transferor's estate.

(d) If the secured creditor elects to have the claim treated as a matured secured claim, Section 355.153 applies as if the transfer on death deed were a devise made in a will, and the claim is subject to the procedural provisions of this title governing creditor claims.

NCCUSL Comment*

Subsection (a) concerns the effect of transactions during the transferor's life. The subsection states an intermediate rule between two extremes. One extreme would provide that transactions during the transferor's life affect the beneficiary only if the transactions are recorded before the transferor's death. This would unfairly disadvantage the transferor's creditors and inter vivos transferees. The other extreme would provide that transactions during the transferor's life always supersede the beneficiary's interest, even if the recording act would provide otherwise. Between these two positions is the rule of subsection (a).

Subsection (a) provides that the beneficiary's interest is subject to *all* conveyances, encumbrances, assignments, contracts, mortgages, liens, and other interests to which the property is subject at the transferor's death. "Liens" includes liens arising by operation of law, such as state Medicaid liens.

The only exception to this rule arises when the state recording act so provides. The state recording act will so provide only when two conditions are met: (1) the inter vivos conveyance or encumbrance is unrecorded throughout the transferor's life (the legal fiction in this subsection protects persons who transact with the transferor and record any time before the transferor's death); and (2) the beneficiary is protected by the recording act. These two conditions will be met only in rare instances. Most beneficiaries of transfer on death deeds are gratuitous, whereas state recording acts typically protect only purchasers for value. *See* Powell on Real Property §82.02.

EST §114.105. DISCLAIMER

A designated beneficiary may disclaim all or part of the designated beneficiary's interest as provided by Chapter 122.

NCCUSL Comment*

A beneficiary of a transfer on death deed may disclaim the property interest the deed attempts to transfer. While this section relies on other law, such as the Uniform Disclaimer of Property Interests Act (1999/2006), to govern the disclaimer, two general principles should be noted.

First, there is no need under the law of disclaimers to execute a disclaimer in advance. During the transferor's life, a designated beneficiary has no interest in the property. *See* §114.101. Nothing passes to the designated beneficiary while the transferor is alive, hence there is no need to execute a disclaimer during that time.

Second, an effective disclaimer executed after the testator's death "relates back" to the moment of the attempted transfer, here the death of the transferor. Because the disclaimer "relates back," the beneficiary is regarded as never having had an interest in the disclaimed property. ...

---

* See footnote on p. 955.

EST §114.106. LIABILITY FOR CREDITOR CLAIMS; ALLOWANCES IN LIEU OF EXEMPT PROPERTY & FAMILY ALLOWANCES

(a) To the extent the transferor's estate is insufficient to satisfy a claim against the estate, expenses of administration, any estate tax owed by the estate, or an allowance in lieu of exempt property or family allowance to a surviving spouse, minor children, or incapacitated adult children, the personal representative may enforce that liability against real property transferred at the transferor's death by a transfer on death deed to the same extent the personal representative could enforce that liability if the real property were part of the probate estate.

(b) Notwithstanding Subsection (a), real property transferred at the transferor's death by a transfer on death deed is not considered property of the probate estate for any purpose, including for purposes of Section 531.077, Government Code.

(c) If a personal representative does not commence a proceeding to enforce a liability under Subsection (a) on or before the 90th day after the date the representative receives a demand for payment, a proceeding to enforce the liability may be brought by a creditor, a distributee of the estate, a surviving spouse of the decedent, a guardian or other appropriate person on behalf of a minor child or adult incapacitated child of the decedent, or any taxing authority.

(d) If more than one real property interest is transferred by one or more transfer on death deeds or if there are other nonprobate assets of the transferor that may be liable for the claims, expenses, and other payments specified in Subsection (a), the liability for those claims, expenses, and other payments may be apportioned among those real property interests and other assets in proportion to their net values at the transferor's death.

(e) A proceeding to enforce liability under this section must be commenced not later than the second anniversary of the transferor's death, except for any rights arising under Section 114.104(d).

(f) In connection with any proceeding brought under this section, a court may award costs and reasonable and necessary attorney's fees in amounts the court considers equitable and just.

NCCUSL Comment*

...

§114.106 provides an *in rem* liability rule applying to transfer on death deeds. The property transferred under a transfer on death deed is liable to the transferor's probate estate for properly allowed claims and statutory allowances to the extent the estate is insufficient.

One of the functions of probate is creditor protection. ... §114.106 provides more creditor protection than is typically available under current law. For many transferors, the transfer on death deed will be used in lieu of joint tenancy with right of survivorship. Under the usual law of joint tenancy, the unsecured creditors of a deceased joint tenant have no recourse against the property or against the other joint tenant. Instead, the property passes automatically to the survivor, free of the decedent's debts. *See* Comment 5 to UPC §6-102. If the debts cannot be paid from the probate estate, the creditor is out of luck. Under §114.106, in contrast, the property transferred under a transfer on death deed is liable to the probate estate for properly allowed claims and statutory allowances to the extent the estate is insufficient.

Sections 114.107-114.150 blank

SUBCHAPTER D. FORMS FOR TRANSFER ON DEATH DEED

(A) EST §114.151. OPTIONAL FORM FOR TRANSFER ON DEATH DEED

The amended text in §114.151 is effective for transfer-on-death deeds executed and acknowledged on or after Sept. 1, 2017. Deeds executed and acknowledged before Sept. 1, 2017, are governed by the former law in effect at that time.

The following form may be used to create a transfer on death deed.

REVOCABLE TRANSFER ON DEATH DEED

NOTICE OF CONFIDENTIALITY RIGHTS: IF YOU ARE A NATURAL PERSON, YOU MAY REMOVE OR STRIKE ANY OF THE FOLLOWING INFORMATION FROM THIS INSTRUMENT BEFORE IT IS FILED FOR RECORD IN THE PUBLIC RECORDS: YOUR SOCIAL SECURITY NUMBER OR YOUR DRIVER'S LICENSE NUMBER.

IMPORTANT NOTICE TO OWNER: You should carefully read all the information included in the instructions to this form. You may want to consult a lawyer before using this form.

MUST RECORD DEED: Before your death, this deed must be recorded with the county clerk where the property is located, or it will not be effective.

MARRIED PERSONS: If you are married and want your spouse to own the property on your death, you must name your spouse as the primary beneficiary. If your spouse does not survive you, the property will transfer to any listed alternate beneficiary or beneficiaries on your death.

* See footnote on p. 955.

EST §114.106

1. Owner (Transferor) Making this Deed:

_______________ _______________

Printed name Mailing address

2. Legal Description of the Property:

____

3. Address of the Property (if any) (include county):

____

4. Primary Beneficiary (Transferee) or Beneficiaries (Transferees)

I designate the following beneficiary or beneficiaries, if the beneficiary survives me:

_______________ _______________

Printed name Mailing address

5. Alternate Beneficiary or Beneficiaries (Optional)

[~~If no primary beneficiary survives me,~~] I designate the following alternate beneficiary or beneficiaries, if the alternate beneficiary survives me:

_______________ _______________

Printed name Mailing address

6. Transfer on Death: (Choose an option under both A and B below, and if you have designated any alternate beneficiaries, choose an option under C.)

At my death, I grant and convey to the primary beneficiary or beneficiaries my interest in the property, to have and hold forever. [~~If at my death I am not survived by any primary beneficiary, I grant and convey to the alternate beneficiary or beneficiaries, if designated, my interest in the property, to have and hold forever. If the primary and alternate beneficiaries do not survive me, this transfer on death deed shall be deemed canceled by me.~~]

A. IF AT LEAST ONE PRIMARY BENEFICIARY SURVIVES ME

(Select either option (1) or (2) by placing your initials next to the option chosen. If you do not choose an option, then option (1), which is the anti-lapse election, will apply.)

If at least one primary beneficiary survives me, I grant and convey the primary beneficiaries' share or shares of the property, to have and hold forever, as follows:

___ (1) Anti-Lapse Election. To the surviving primary beneficiary or beneficiaries, but if a deceased primary beneficiary, if any, was a child or other descendant of mine or of one or both of my parents, that deceased primary beneficiary's share will pass to the surviving children or other descendants of that deceased primary beneficiary.

___ (2) Surviving Primary Beneficiaries Election. To the surviving primary beneficiary or beneficiaries only. If a deceased primary beneficiary, if any, was a child or other descendant of mine or of one or both of my parents, I do not want that deceased primary beneficiary's share to pass to the children or other descendants of that deceased primary beneficiary.

B. IF NO PRIMARY BENEFICIARY SURVIVES ME

(Select either option (1) or (2) by placing your initials next to the option chosen. If you do not choose an option, then option (1), which is the anti-lapse election, will apply.)

If no primary beneficiary survives me, I grant and convey the share of the property that would have transferred to a deceased primary beneficiary, to have and hold forever, as follows:

___ (1) Anti-Lapse Election. To the surviving children or other descendants of the deceased primary beneficiary, if the deceased primary beneficiary was a child or other descendant of mine or of one or both of my parents.

___ (2) Surviving Alternate Beneficiaries Election. To the alternate beneficiary or beneficiaries designated above. If the deceased primary beneficiary was a child or other descendant of mine or of one or both of my parents, I do not want that deceased primary beneficiary's share to pass to the children or other descendants of that deceased primary beneficiary.

If no primary beneficiary survives me and the anti-lapse election is not chosen or that election is chosen, but a deceased primary beneficiary is not a child or other descendant of mine or of one or both of my parents, I grant and convey to the alternate beneficiary or beneficiaries my share in the property that otherwise would have transferred to the deceased primary beneficiary, to have and hold forever. If I have not designated alternate beneficiaries, this transfer on death deed shall be considered cancelled by me.

C. IF AN ALTERNATE BENEFICIARY DOES NOT SURVIVE ME

(Select either option (1) or (2) by placing your initials next to the option chosen. If you do not choose an option, then option (1), which is the anti-lapse election, will apply.)

EST §114.151

If an alternate beneficiary does not survive me, I grant and convey that alternate beneficiary's share of the property as follows:

___ (1) Anti-Lapse Election. To the surviving alternate beneficiary or beneficiaries, but if the deceased alternate beneficiary was a child or other descendant of mine or of one or both of my parents, that deceased alternate beneficiary's share will pass to the surviving children or other descendants of that deceased alternate beneficiary.

___ (2) Surviving Alternate Beneficiaries Election. To the surviving alternate beneficiary or beneficiaries only. If the deceased alternate beneficiary was a child or other descendant of mine or of one or both of my parents, I do not want that deceased alternate beneficiary's share to pass to the children or other descendants of that deceased alternate beneficiary.

If no alternate beneficiary survives me and the anti-lapse election is not chosen or that election is chosen, but no deceased alternate beneficiary was a child or other descendant of mine or of one or both of my parents, this transfer on death deed shall be considered cancelled by me.

7. Printed Name and Signature of Owner Making this Deed:

________________ ________________

Printed Name Date

____

Signature

BELOW LINE FOR NOTARY ONLY

____

Acknowledgment

STATE OF ________

COUNTY OF ________

This instrument was acknowledged before me on the _____ day of ________, 20____,

by ________________.

____

Notary Public, State of ________

After recording, return to:

(insert name and mailing address)

____

____

INSTRUCTIONS FOR TRANSFER ON DEATH DEED

DO NOT RECORD THESE INSTRUCTIONS

Instructions for Completing the Form

1. Owner (Transferor) Making this Deed: Enter your first, middle (if any), and last name here, along with your mailing address.

2. Legal Description of the Property: Enter the formal legal description of the property. This information is different from the mailing and physical address for the property and is necessary to complete the form. To find this information, look on the deed you received when you became an owner of the property. This information may also be available in the office of the county clerk for the county where the property is located. Do NOT use your tax bill to find this information. If you are not absolutely sure, consult a lawyer.

3. Address of the Property: Enter the physical address of the property.

4. Primary Beneficiary or Beneficiaries: Enter the first and last name of each person you want to get the property when you die. If you are married and want your spouse to get the property when you die, enter your spouse's first and last name (even if you and your spouse own the property together).

5. Alternate Beneficiary or Beneficiaries: Enter the first and last name of each person you want to get the property if no primary beneficiary survives you.

6. Transfer on Death: You should carefully read the language describing the options and choose an option under both A and B of Paragraph 6, and if you have listed any alternate beneficiaries, choose an option under C of Paragraph 6 [~~No action needed~~].

7. Printed Name and Signature of Owner: Do not sign your name or enter the date until you are before a notary. Include your printed name.

8. Acknowledgment: This deed must be signed before a notary. The notary will fill out this section of the deed.

2017 Legislation: Amended by S.B. 2150, §2, 85th Leg., eff. Sept. 1, 2017.

NCCUSL Comment*

The form in this section is optional. The section is based on §4 of the Uniform Health-Care Decisions Act (1993).

The transfer on death deed is likely to be used by consumers for whom the preparation of a tailored inter vivos revocable trust is too costly. The form in this section is designed to be understandable and consumer friendly.

...

* See footnote on p. 955.

EST §114.151

EST §114.152. OPTIONAL FORM OF REVOCATION

The following form may be used to create an instrument of revocation under this chapter.

CANCELLATION OF TRANSFER ON DEATH DEED

IMPORTANT NOTICE TO OWNER: You should carefully read all the information included in the instructions to this form. You may want to consult a lawyer before using this form.

MUST RECORD FORM: Before your death, this cancellation form must be recorded with the county clerk where the property is located, or it will not be effective. This cancellation is effective only as to the interests in the property of owners who sign this cancellation form.

1. Owner (Transferor) Making this Cancellation:

________________ ________________

Printed name Mailing address

2. Legal Description of the Property:

____

3. Address of the Property (if any) (include county):

____

4. Cancellation

I cancel all my previous transfers of this property by transfer on death deed.

5. Printed Name and Signature of Owner (Transferor) Making this Cancellation:

________________ ________________

Printed Name Date

____

Signature

BELOW LINE FOR NOTARY ONLY

____

Acknowledgment

STATE OF __________

COUNTY OF __________

This instrument was acknowledged before me on the _____ day of __________, 20_____,

by ____________________.

____

Notary Public, State of __________

After recording, return to:

(insert name and mailing address)

____

____

INSTRUCTIONS FOR CANCELING A TRANSFER ON DEATH (TOD) DEED

DO NOT RECORD THESE INSTRUCTIONS

Instructions for Completing the Form

1. Owner (Transferor) Making this Cancellation: Enter your first, middle (if any), and last name here, along with your mailing address.

2. Legal Description of the Property: Enter the formal legal description of the property. This information is different from the mailing and physical address for the property and is necessary to complete the form. To find this information, look on the deed you received when you became an owner of the property. This information may also be available in the office of the county clerk for the county where the property is located. Do NOT use your tax bill to find this information. If you are not absolutely sure, consult a lawyer.

3. Address of the Property: Enter the physical address of the property.

4. Cancellation: No action needed.

5. Printed Name and Signature of Owner: Do not sign your name or enter the date until you are before a notary. Include your printed name.

6. Acknowledgment: This cancellation form must be signed before a notary. The notary will fill out this section of the form.

NCCUSL Comment*

The form in this section is optional. The section is based on §4 of the Uniform Health-Care Decisions Act (1993).

The aim of the form in this section is to be understandable and consumer friendly.

CHAPTER 121. SURVIVAL REQUIREMENTS

SUBCHAPTER A. GENERAL PROVISIONS

EST §121.001. APPLICABILITY OF CHAPTER

This chapter does not apply if provision has been made by will, living trust, deed, or insurance contract, or in any other manner, for a disposition of property that is different from the disposition of the property that would be made if the provisions of this chapter applied.

Sections 121.002-121.050 reserved for expansion

* See footnote on p. 955.

EST §121.001

Subchapter B. Survival Requirement for Intestate Succession & Certain Other Purposes

EST §121.051. Applicability of Subchapter

This subchapter does not apply if the application of this subchapter would result in the escheat of an intestate estate.

EST §121.052. Required Period of Survival for Intestate Succession & Certain Other Purposes

A person who does not survive a decedent by 120 hours is considered to have predeceased the decedent for purposes of the homestead allowance, exempt property, and intestate succession, and the decedent's heirs are determined accordingly, except as otherwise provided by this chapter.

EST §121.053. Intestate Succession: Failure to Survive Presumed Under Certain Circumstances

A person who, if the person survived a decedent by 120 hours, would be the decedent's heir is considered not to have survived the decedent for the required period if:

(1) the time of death of the decedent or of the person, or the times of death of both, cannot be determined; and

(2) the person's survival for the required period after the decedent's death cannot be established.

Sections 121.054-121.100 reserved for expansion

Subchapter C. Survival Requirements for Certain Beneficiaries

EST §121.101. Required Period of Survival for Devisee

A devisee who does not survive the testator by 120 hours is treated as if the devisee predeceased the testator unless the testator's will contains some language that:

(1) deals explicitly with simultaneous death or deaths in a common disaster; or

(2) requires the devisee to survive the testator, or to survive the testator for a stated period, to take under the will.

EST §121.102. Required Period of Survival for Contingent Beneficiary

(a) If property is disposed of in a manner that conditions the right of a beneficiary to succeed to an interest in the property on the beneficiary surviving another person, the beneficiary is considered not to have survived the other person unless the beneficiary survives the person by 120 hours, except as provided by Subsection (b).

(b) If an interest in property is given alternatively to one of two or more beneficiaries, with the right of each beneficiary to take being dependent on that beneficiary surviving the other beneficiary or beneficiaries, and all of the beneficiaries die within a period of less than 120 hours, the property shall be divided into as many equal portions as there are beneficiaries. The portions shall be distributed respectively to those who would have taken if each beneficiary had survived.

Sections 121.103-121.150 reserved for expansion

Subchapter D. Distribution of Certain Property on Person's Failure to Survive for Required Period

EST §121.151. Distribution of Community Property

(a) This section applies to community property, including the proceeds of life or accident insurance that are community property and become payable to the estate of either the husband or wife.

(b) If a husband and wife die leaving community property but neither survives the other by 120 hours, one-half of all community property shall be distributed as if the husband had survived, and the other one-half shall be distributed as if the wife had survived.

EST §121.152. Distribution of Property Owned by Joint Owners

If property, including community property with a right of survivorship, is owned so that one of two joint owners is entitled to the whole of the property on the death of the other, but neither survives the other by 120 hours, one-half of the property shall be distributed as if one joint owner had survived, and the other one-half shall be distributed as if the other joint owner had survived. If there are more than two joint owners and all of the joint owners die within a period of less than 120 hours, the property shall be divided into as many equal portions as there are joint owners and the portions

shall be distributed respectively to those who would have taken if each joint owner survived.

EST §121.153. DISTRIBUTION OF CERTAIN INSURANCE PROCEEDS

(a) If the insured under a life or accident insurance policy and a beneficiary of the proceeds of that policy die within a period of less than 120 hours, the insured is considered to have survived the beneficiary for the purpose of determining the rights under the policy of the beneficiary or beneficiaries as such.

(b) This section does not prevent the applicability of Section 121.151 to proceeds of life or accident insurance that are community property.

CHAPTER 122. DISCLAIMERS & ASSIGNMENTS

SUBCHAPTER A. DISCLAIMER OF INTEREST OR POWER

A EST §122.001. DEFINITIONS

In this subchapter:

(1) "Beneficiary" includes a person who would have been entitled, if the person had not made a disclaimer, to receive property as a result of the death of another person:

(A) by inheritance;

(B) under a will;

(C) by an agreement between spouses for community property with a right of survivorship;

(D) by a joint tenancy with a right of survivorship;

(E) by a survivorship agreement, account, or interest in which the interest of the decedent passes to a surviving beneficiary;

(F) by an insurance, annuity, endowment, employment, deferred compensation, or other contract or arrangement;

(G) under a pension, profit sharing, thrift, stock bonus, life insurance, survivor income, incentive, or other plan or program providing retirement, welfare, or fringe benefits with respect to an employee or a self-employed individual; [~~or~~]

(H) by a transfer on death deed; or

(I) by a beneficiary designation as defined by Section 115.001.

(2) "Disclaim" and "disclaimer" have the meanings assigned by Section 240.002, Property Code.

2017 Legislation: Amended by S.B. 869, §2, 85th Leg., eff. Sept. 1, 2017.

EST §122.002. DISCLAIMER

A person who may be entitled to receive property as a beneficiary may disclaim the person's interest in or power over the property in accordance with Chapter 240, Property Code.

See also Karisch et al., *To Disclaim or Not to Disclaim: "How?" Is the Real Question*, Advanced Estate Planning & Probate Course, State Bar of Texas CLE, ch. 4 (2015).

EST §§122.003 TO 122.005. REPEALED

SUBCHAPTERS B TO D. REPEALED

SUBCHAPTER E. ASSIGNMENT OF INTEREST

EST §122.201. ASSIGNMENT

A person who is entitled to receive property or an interest in property from a decedent under a will, by inheritance, or as a beneficiary under a life insurance contract, and does not disclaim the property under Chapter 240, Property Code, may assign the property or interest in property to any person.

EST §122.202. FILING OF ASSIGNMENT

An assignment may, at the request of the assignor, be delivered or filed as provided for the delivery or filing of a disclaimer under Subchapter C, Chapter 240, Property Code.

EST §122.203. REPEALED

EST §122.204. FAILURE TO COMPLY

Failure to comply with Chapter 240, Property Code, does not affect an assignment.

EST §122.205. GIFT

An assignment under this subchapter is a gift to the assignee and is not a disclaimer under Chapter 240, Property Code.

EST §122.206. SPENDTHRIFT PROVISION

An assignment of property or interest that would defeat a spendthrift provision imposed in a trust may not be made under this subchapter.

CHAPTER 123. DISSOLUTION OF MARRIAGE

SUBCHAPTER A. EFFECT OF DISSOLUTION OF MARRIAGE ON WILL

EST §123.001. WILL PROVISIONS MADE BEFORE DISSOLUTION OF MARRIAGE

(a) In this section:

(1) "Irrevocable trust" means a trust:

(A) for which the trust instrument was executed before the dissolution of a testator's marriage; and

(B) that the testator was not solely empowered by law or by the trust instrument to revoke.

(2) "Relative" means an individual related to another individual by:

(A) consanguinity, as determined under Section 573.022, Government Code; or

(B) affinity, as determined under Section 573.024, Government Code.

(b) If, after the testator makes a will, the testator's marriage is dissolved by divorce, annulment, or a declaration that the marriage is void, unless the will expressly provides otherwise:

(1) all provisions in the will, including all fiduciary appointments, shall be read as if the former spouse and each relative of the former spouse who is not a relative of the testator had failed to survive the testator; and

(2) all provisions in the will disposing of property to an irrevocable trust in which a former spouse or a relative of a former spouse who is not a relative of the testator is a beneficiary or is nominated to serve as trustee or in another fiduciary capacity or that confers a general or special power of appointment on a former spouse or a relative of a former spouse who is not a relative of the testator shall be read to instead dispose of the property to a trust the provisions of which are identical to the irrevocable trust, except any provision in the irrevocable trust:

(A) conferring a beneficial interest or a general or special power of appointment to the former spouse or a relative of the former spouse who is not a relative of the testator shall be treated as if the former spouse and each relative of the former spouse who is not a relative of the testator had disclaimed the interest granted in the provision; and

(B) nominating the former spouse or a relative of the former spouse who is not a relative of the testator to serve as trustee or in another fiduciary capacity shall be treated as if the former spouse and each relative of the former spouse who is not a relative of the testator had died immediately before the dissolution of the marriage.

(c) Subsection (b)(2) does not apply if one of the following provides otherwise:

(1) a court order; or

(2) an express provision of a contract relating to the division of the marital estate entered into between the testator and the testator's former spouse before, during, or after the marriage.

See also Est. Code §123.052; Fam. Code §§9.301, 9.302.

EST §123.002. TREATMENT OF DECEDENT'S FORMER SPOUSE

A person is not a surviving spouse of a decedent if the person's marriage to the decedent has been dissolved by divorce, annulment, or a declaration that the marriage is void, unless:

(1) as the result of a subsequent marriage, the person is married to the decedent at the time of death; and

(2) the subsequent marriage is not declared void under Subchapter C.

Sections 123.003-123.050 reserved for expansion

SUBCHAPTER B. EFFECT OF DISSOLUTION OF MARRIAGE ON CERTAIN NONTESTAMENTARY TRANSFERS

EST §123.051. DEFINITIONS

In this subchapter:

(1) "Disposition or appointment of property" includes a transfer of property to or a provision of another benefit to a beneficiary under a trust instrument.

(2) "Divorced individual" means an individual whose marriage has been dissolved by divorce, annulment, or a declaration that the marriage is void.

(2-a) "Relative" means an individual who is related to another individual by consanguinity or affinity, as determined under Sections 573.022 and 573.024, Government Code, respectively.

(3) "Revocable," with respect to a disposition, appointment, provision, or nomination, means a disposition to, appointment of, provision in favor of, or nomination of an individual's spouse that is contained in a trust instrument executed by the individual before the dissolution of the individual's marriage to the spouse and that the individual was solely empowered by law or by the trust instrument to revoke regardless of whether the individual had the capacity to exercise the power at that time.

A EST §123.052. REVOCATION OF CERTAIN NONTESTAMENTARY TRANSFERS; TREATMENT OF FORMER SPOUSE AS BENEFICIARY UNDER CERTAIN POLICIES OR PLANS

(a) The dissolution of the marriage revokes a provision in a trust instrument that was executed by a di-

vorced individual as settlor before the divorced individual's marriage was dissolved and that:

(1) is a revocable disposition or appointment of property made to the divorced individual's former spouse or any relative of the former spouse who is not a relative of the divorced individual;

(2) revocably confers a general or special power of appointment on the divorced individual's former spouse or any relative of the former spouse who is not a relative of the divorced individual; or

(3) revocably nominates the divorced individual's former spouse or any relative of the former spouse who is not a relative of the divorced individual to serve:

(A) as a personal representative, trustee, conservator, agent, or guardian; or

(B) in another fiduciary or representative capacity.

(b) Subsection (a) does not apply if one of the following provides otherwise:

(1) a court order;

(2) the express terms of a trust instrument executed by the divorced individual before the individual's marriage was dissolved; or

(3) an express provision of a contract relating to the division of the marital estate entered into between the divorced individual and the individual's former spouse before, during, or after the marriage.

(c) Sections 9.301 and 9.302, Family Code, govern the designation of a former spouse as a beneficiary of certain life insurance policies or as a beneficiary under certain retirement benefit plans or other financial plans.

2017 Legislation: Amended by H.B. 2271, §5, 85th Leg., eff. Sept. 1, 2017.

EST §123.053. EFFECT OF REVOCATION

(a) An interest granted in a provision of a trust instrument that is revoked under Section 123.052(a)(1) or (2) passes as if the former spouse of the divorced individual who executed the trust instrument and each relative of the former spouse who is not a relative of the divorced individual disclaimed the interest granted in the provision.

(b) An interest granted in a provision of a trust instrument that is revoked under Section 123.052(a)(3) passes as if the former spouse and each relative of the former spouse who is not a relative of the divorced individual died immediately before the dissolution of the marriage.

EST §123.054. LIABILITY OF CERTAIN PURCHASERS OR RECIPIENTS OF CERTAIN PAYMENTS, BENEFITS, OR PROPERTY

A bona fide purchaser of property from a divorced individual's former spouse or any relative of the former spouse who is not a relative of the divorced individual or a person who receives from the former spouse or any relative of the former spouse who is not a relative of the divorced individual a payment, benefit, or property in partial or full satisfaction of an enforceable obligation:

(1) is not required by this subchapter to return the payment, benefit, or property; and

(2) is not liable under this subchapter for the amount of the payment or the value of the property or benefit.

EST §123.055. LIABILITY OF FORMER SPOUSE FOR CERTAIN PAYMENTS, BENEFITS, OR PROPERTY

A divorced individual's former spouse or any relative of the former spouse who is not a relative of the divorced individual who, not for value, receives a payment, benefit, or property to which the former spouse or the relative of the former spouse who is not a relative of the divorced individual is not entitled as a result of Sections 123.052(a) and (b):

(1) shall return the payment, benefit, or property to the person who is entitled to the payment, benefit, or property under this subchapter; or

(2) is personally liable to the person described by Subdivision (1) for the amount of the payment or the value of the benefit or property received, as applicable.

E EST §123.056. CERTAIN TRUSTS WITH DIVORCED INDIVIDUALS AS JOINT SETTLORS

(a) This section applies only to a trust created under a trust instrument that:

(1) was executed by two married individuals as settlors whose marriage to each other is subsequently dissolved; and

(2) includes a provision described by Section 123.052(a).

(b) On the death of one of the divorced individuals who is a settlor of a trust to which this section applies, the trustee shall divide the trust into two trusts, each of

which shall be composed of the property attributable to the contributions of only one of the divorced individuals.

(c) An action authorized in a trust instrument described by Subsection (a) that requires the actions of both divorced individuals may be taken with respect to a trust established in accordance with Subsection (b) from the surviving divorced individual's contributions solely by that divorced individual.

(d) The provisions of this subchapter apply independently to each trust established in accordance with Subsection (b) as if the divorced individual from whose contributions the trust was established had been the only settlor to execute the trust instrument described by Subsection (a).

(e) This section does not apply if one of the following provides otherwise:

(1) a court order;

(2) the express terms of a trust instrument executed by the two divorced individuals before their marriage was dissolved; or

(3) an express provision of a contract relating to the division of the marital estate entered into between the two divorced individuals before, during, or after their marriage.

2017 Legislation: Enacted by H.B. 2271, §6, 85th Leg., eff. Sept. 1, 2017.

Sections 123.057-123.100 reserved for expansion

SUBCHAPTER C. CERTAIN MARRIAGES VOIDABLE AFTER DEATH

EST §123.101. PROCEEDING TO VOID MARRIAGE BASED ON MENTAL CAPACITY PENDING AT TIME OF DEATH

(a) If a proceeding under Chapter 6, Family Code, to declare a marriage void based on the lack of mental capacity of one of the parties to the marriage is pending on the date of death of one of those parties, or if a guardianship proceeding in which a court is requested under Chapter 6, Family Code, to declare a ward's or proposed ward's marriage void based on the lack of mental capacity of the ward or proposed ward is pending on the date of the ward's or proposed ward's death, the court may make the determination and declare the marriage void after the decedent's death.

(b) In making a determination described by Subsection (a), the court shall apply the standards for an annulment prescribed by Section 6.108(a), Family Code.

EST §123.102. APPLICATION TO VOID MARRIAGE AFTER DEATH

(a) Subject to Subsection (c), if a proceeding described by Section 123.101(a) is not pending on the date of a decedent's death, an interested person may file an application with the court requesting that the court void the marriage of the decedent if:

(1) on the date of the decedent's death, the decedent was married; and

(2) that marriage commenced not earlier than three years before the date of the decedent's death.

(b) The notice applicable to a proceeding for a declaratory judgment under Chapter 37, Civil Practice and Remedies Code, applies to a proceeding under Subsection (a).

(c) An application authorized by Subsection (a) may not be filed after the first anniversary of the date of the decedent's death.

EST §123.103. ACTION ON APPLICATION TO VOID MARRIAGE AFTER DEATH

(a) Except as provided by Subsection (b), in a proceeding brought under Section 123.102, the court shall declare the decedent's marriage void if the court finds that, on the date the marriage occurred, the decedent did not have the mental capacity to:

(1) consent to the marriage; and

(2) understand the nature of the marriage ceremony, if a ceremony occurred.

(b) A court that makes a finding described by Subsection (a) may not declare the decedent's marriage void if the court finds that, after the date the marriage occurred, the decedent:

(1) gained the mental capacity to recognize the marriage relationship; and

(2) did recognize the marriage relationship.

EST §123.104. EFFECT OF VOIDED MARRIAGE

If the court declares a decedent's marriage void in a proceeding described by Section 123.101(a) or brought under Section 123.102, the other party to the marriage is not considered the decedent's surviving spouse for purposes of any law of this state.

Sections 123.105-123.150 blank

EST §123.056

SUBCHAPTER D. EFFECT OF DISSOLUTION OF MARRIAGE ON CERTAIN MULTIPLE-PARTY ACCOUNTS

A EST §123.151. DESIGNATION OF FORMER SPOUSE OR RELATIVE OF FORMER SPOUSE ON CERTAIN MULTIPLE-PARTY ACCOUNTS

(a) In this section:

(1) "Beneficiary," "multiple-party account," "party," "P.O.D. account," and "P.O.D. payee" have the meanings assigned by Chapter 113.

(2) "Public retirement system" has the meaning assigned by Section 802.001, Government Code.

(3) "Relative" has the meaning assigned by Section 123.051.

(4) "Survivorship agreement" means an agreement described by Section 113.151.

(b) If [~~, after~~] a decedent established [~~designates a spouse or a relative of a spouse who is not a relative of the decedent as a P.O.D. payee or beneficiary, including alternative P.O.D. payee or beneficiary, on~~] a P.O.D. account or other multiple-party account and [~~,~~] the decedent's marriage was later [~~is~~] dissolved by divorce, annulment, or a declaration that the marriage is void, any payable on request after death [~~the~~] designation provision or provision of a survivorship agreement with respect to that account in favor of the decedent's former spouse or a relative of the former spouse who is not a relative of the decedent [~~on the account~~] is not effective as to that [~~the former~~] spouse or [~~the former spouse's~~] relative unless:

(1) the court decree dissolving the marriage:

(A) designates the former spouse or the former spouse's relative as the P.O.D. payee or beneficiary; or

(B) reaffirms the survivorship agreement or the relevant provision of the survivorship agreement in favor of the former spouse or the former spouse's relative;

(2) after the marriage was dissolved, the decedent:

(A) redesignated the former spouse or the former spouse's relative as the P.O.D[1] payee or beneficiary; or

(B) reaffirmed the survivorship agreement in writing [~~after the marriage was dissolved~~]; or

(3) the former spouse or the former spouse's relative is designated to receive, or under the survivorship agreement would receive, the proceeds or benefits in trust for, on behalf of, or for the benefit of a child or dependent of either the decedent or the former spouse.

(c) If a designation is not effective under Subsection (b), a multiple-party account is payable to the named alternative P.O.D. payee or beneficiary or, if an alternative P.O.D. payee or beneficiary is not named, to the estate of the decedent.

(c-1) If the provision of a survivorship agreement is not effective under Subsection (b), for purposes of determining the disposition of the decedent's interest in the account, the former spouse or former spouse's relative who would have received the decedent's interest if the provision were effective is treated as if that spouse or relative predeceased the decedent.

(d) A financial institution or other person obligated to pay an account described by Subsection (b) that pays the account to the former spouse or the former spouse's relative as P.O.D. payee or beneficiary under a designation that is not effective under Subsection (b) is liable for payment of the account to the person provided by Subsection (c) only if:

(1) before payment of the account to the designated P.O.D. payee or beneficiary, the payor receives written notice at the home office or principal office of the payor from an interested person that the designation of the P.O.D. payee or beneficiary is not effective under Subsection (b); and

(2) the payor has not interpleaded the account funds into the registry of a court of competent jurisdiction in accordance with the Texas Rules of Civil Procedure.

Subsection (d-1) is effective for causes of action that accrue on or after Sept. 1, 2017.

(d-1) A financial institution is not liable for payment of an account to a former spouse or the former spouse's relative as a party to the account, notwithstanding the fact that a designation or provision of a survivorship agreement in favor of that person is not effective under Subsection (b).

(e) This section does not affect the right of a former spouse to assert an ownership interest in an undivided multiple-party account described by Subsection (b).

(f) This section does not apply to the disposition of a beneficial interest in a retirement benefit or other financial plan of a public retirement system.

1. **Editor's note:** Probably should be "P.O.D."

2017 Legislation: Amended by H.B. 2271, §7, 85th Leg., eff. Sept. 1, 2017.

SUBTITLE E. INTESTATE SUCCESSION

CHAPTER 201. DESCENT & DISTRIBUTION

SUBCHAPTER A. INTESTATE SUCCESSION

EST §201.001. ESTATE OF AN INTESTATE NOT LEAVING SPOUSE

(a) If a person who dies intestate does not leave a spouse, the estate to which the person had title descends and passes in parcenary to the person's kindred in the order provided by this section.

(b) The person's estate descends and passes to the person's children and the children's descendants.

(c) If no child or child's descendant survives the person, the person's estate descends and passes in equal portions to the person's father and mother.

(d) If only the person's father or mother survives the person, the person's estate shall:

(1) be divided into two equal portions, with:

(A) one portion passing to the surviving parent; and

(B) one portion passing to the person's siblings and the siblings' descendants; or

(2) be inherited entirely by the surviving parent if there is no sibling of the person or siblings' descendants.

(e) If neither the person's father nor mother survives the person, the person's entire estate passes to the person's siblings and the siblings' descendants.

(f) If none of the kindred described by Subsections (b)-(e) survive the person, the person's estate shall be divided into two moieties, with:

(1) one moiety passing to the person's paternal kindred as provided by Subsection (g); and

(2) one moiety passing to the person's maternal kindred as provided by Subsection (h).

(g) The moiety passing to the person's paternal kindred passes in the following order:

(1) if both paternal grandparents survive the person, equal portions pass to the person's paternal grandfather and grandmother;

(2) if only the person's paternal grandfather or grandmother survives the person, the person's estate shall:

(A) be divided into two equal portions, with:

(i) one portion passing to the surviving grandparent; and

(ii) one portion passing to the descendants of the deceased grandparent; or

(B) pass entirely to the surviving grandparent if no descendant of the deceased grandparent survives the person; and

(3) if neither the person's paternal grandfather nor grandmother survives the person, the moiety passing to the decedent's paternal kindred passes to the descendants of the person's paternal grandfather and grandmother, and so on without end, passing in like manner to the nearest lineal ancestors and their descendants.

(h) The moiety passing to the person's maternal kindred passes in the same order and manner as the other moiety passes to the decedent's paternal kindred under Subsection (g).

EST §201.002. SEPARATE ESTATE OF AN INTESTATE

(a) If a person who dies intestate leaves a surviving spouse, the estate, other than a community estate, to which the person had title descends and passes as provided by this section.

(b) If the person has one or more children or a descendant of a child:

(1) the surviving spouse takes one-third of the personal estate;

(2) two-thirds of the personal estate descends to the person's child or children, and the descendants of a child or children; and

(3) the surviving spouse is entitled to a life estate in one-third of the person's land, with the remainder descending to the person's child or children and the descendants of a child or children.

(c) Except as provided by Subsection (d), if the person has no child and no descendant of a child:

(1) the surviving spouse is entitled to all of the personal estate;

(2) the surviving spouse is entitled to one-half of the person's land without a remainder to any person; and

(3) one-half of the person's land passes and is inherited according to the rules of descent and distribution.

(d) If the person described by Subsection (c) does not leave a surviving parent or one or more surviving

EST §201.001

siblings, or their descendants, the surviving spouse is entitled to the entire estate.

See also Fam. Code §§3.001-3.006.

EST §201.003. COMMUNITY ESTATE OF AN INTESTATE

(a) If a person who dies intestate leaves a surviving spouse, the community estate of the deceased spouse passes as provided by this section.

(b) The community estate of the deceased spouse passes to the surviving spouse if:

(1) no child or other descendant of the deceased spouse survives the deceased spouse; or

(2) all of the surviving children and descendants of the deceased spouse are also children or descendants of the surviving spouse.

(c) If the deceased spouse is survived by a child or other descendant who is not also a child or descendant of the surviving spouse, one-half of the community estate is retained by the surviving spouse and the other one-half passes to the deceased spouse's children or descendants. The descendants inherit only the portion of that estate to which they would be entitled under Section 201.101. In every case, the community estate passes charged with the debts against the community estate.

See also Fam. Code §§3.001-3.006.

Sections 201.004-201.050 reserved for expansion

SUBCHAPTER B. MATTERS AFFECTING INHERITANCE

EST §201.051. MATERNAL INHERITANCE

(a) For purposes of inheritance, a child is the child of the child's biological or adopted mother, and the child and the child's issue shall inherit from the child's mother and the child's maternal kindred, both descendants, ascendants, and collateral kindred in all degrees, and they may inherit from the child and the child's issue. However, if a child has intended parents, as defined by Section 160.102, Family Code, under a gestational agreement validated under Subchapter I, Chapter 160, Family Code, the child is the child of the intended mother and not the biological mother or gestational mother unless the biological mother is also the intended mother.

(b) This section does not permit inheritance by a child for whom no right of inheritance accrues under Section 201.056 or by the child's issue.

EST §201.052. PATERNAL INHERITANCE

(a) For purposes of inheritance, a child is the child of the child's biological father if:

(1) the child is born under circumstances described by Section 160.201, Family Code;

(2) the child is adjudicated to be the child of the father by court decree under Chapter 160, Family Code;

(3) the child was adopted by the child's father; or

(4) the father executed an acknowledgment of paternity under Subchapter D, Chapter 160, Family Code, or a similar statement properly executed in another jurisdiction.

(a-1) Notwithstanding Subsection (a), if a child has intended parents, as defined by Section 160.102, Family Code, under a gestational agreement validated under Subchapter I, Chapter 160, Family Code, the child is the child of the intended father and not the biological father unless the biological father is also the intended father.

(b) A child described by Subsection (a) or (a-1) and the child's issue shall inherit from the child's father and the child's paternal kindred, both descendants, ascendants, and collateral kindred in all degrees, and they may inherit from the child and the child's issue.

(c) A person may petition the probate court for a determination of right of inheritance from a decedent if the person:

(1) claims to be a biological child of the decedent and is not otherwise presumed to be a child of the decedent; or

(2) claims inheritance through a biological child of the decedent who is not otherwise presumed to be a child of the decedent.

(d) If under Subsection (c) the court finds by clear and convincing evidence that the purported father was the biological father of the child:

(1) the child is treated as any other child of the decedent for purposes of inheritance; and

(2) the child and the child's issue may inherit from the child's paternal kindred, both descendants, ascendants, and collateral kindred in all degrees, and they may inherit from the child and the child's issue.

(e) This section does not permit inheritance by a purported father of a child, recognized or not, if the purported father's parental rights have been terminated.

(f) This section does not permit inheritance by a child for whom no right of inheritance accrues under Section 201.056 or by the child's issue.

See also Fam. Code ch. 160; Elsom & Powers, *Defining Descendants: Building the Family You Want*, Estate Planning & Probate Drafting Course, State Bar of Texas CLE, ch. 2 (2012).

EST §201.053. EFFECT OF RELIANCE ON AFFIDAVIT OF HEIRSHIP

(a) A person who purchases for valuable consideration any interest in property of the heirs of a decedent acquires good title to the interest that the person would have received, as purchaser, in the absence of a claim of the child described by Subdivision (1), if the person:

(1) in good faith relies on the declarations in an affidavit of heirship that does not include a child who at the time of the sale or contract of sale of the property:

(A) is not a presumed child of the decedent; and

(B) has not under a final court decree or judgment been found to be entitled to treatment under Section 201.052 as a child of the decedent; and

(2) is without knowledge of the claim of the child described by Subdivision (1).

(b) Subsection (a) does not affect any liability of the heirs for the proceeds of a sale described by Subsection (a) to the child who was not included in the affidavit of heirship.

EST §201.054. ADOPTED CHILD

(a) For purposes of inheritance under the laws of descent and distribution, an adopted child is regarded as the child of the adoptive parent or parents, and the adopted child and the adopted child's descendants inherit from and through the adoptive parent or parents and their kindred as if the adopted child were the natural child of the adoptive parent or parents. The adoptive parent or parents and their kindred inherit from and through the adopted child as if the adopted child were the natural child of the adoptive parent or parents.

(b) The natural parent or parents of an adopted child and the kindred of the natural parent or parents may not inherit from or through the adopted child, but the adopted child inherits from and through the child's natural parent or parents, except as provided by Section 162.507(c), Family Code.

(c) This section does not prevent an adoptive parent from disposing of the parent's property by will according to law.

(d) This section does not diminish the rights of an adopted child under the laws of descent and distribution or otherwise that the adopted child acquired by virtue of inclusion in the definition of "child" under Section 22.004.

(e) For purposes of this section, "adopted child" means a child:

(1) adopted through an existing or former statutory procedure; or

(2) considered by a court to be equitably adopted or adopted by acts of estoppel.

2017 Legislation: Amended by H.B. 2271, §9, 85th Leg., eff. Sept. 1, 2017.
See also Fam. Code ch. 162.

EST §201.055. ISSUE OF VOID OR VOIDABLE MARRIAGE

The issue of a marriage declared void or voided by annulment shall be treated in the same manner as the issue of a valid marriage.

EST §201.056. PERSONS NOT IN BEING

No right of inheritance accrues to any person unless the person is born before, or is in gestation at, the time of the intestate's death and survives for at least 120 hours. A person is:

(1) considered to be in gestation at the time of the intestate's death if insemination or implantation occurs at or before the time of the intestate's death; and

(2) presumed to be in gestation at the time of the intestate's death if the person is born before the 301st day after the date of the intestate's death.

EST §201.057. COLLATERAL KINDRED OF WHOLE & HALF BLOOD

If the inheritance from an intestate passes to the collateral kindred of the intestate and part of the collateral kindred are of whole blood and the other part are of half blood of the intestate, each of the collateral kindred who is of half blood inherits only half as much as that inherited by each of the collateral kindred who is of whole blood. If all of the collateral kindred are of half blood of the intestate, each of the collateral kindred inherits a whole portion.

EST §201.058. CONVICTED PERSONS

(a) No conviction shall work corruption of blood or forfeiture of estate except as provided by Subsection (b).

(b) If a beneficiary of a life insurance policy or contract is convicted and sentenced as a principal or accomplice in wilfully bringing about the death of the in-

sured, the proceeds of the insurance policy or contract shall be paid in the manner provided by the Insurance Code.

EST §201.059. PERSON WHO DIES BY CASUALTY

Death by casualty does not result in forfeiture of estate.

EST §201.060. ALIENAGE

A person is not disqualified to take as an heir because the person, or another person through whom the person claims, is or has been an alien.

EST §201.061. ESTATE OF PERSON WHO DIES BY SUICIDE

The estate of a person who commits suicide descends or vests as if the person died a natural death.

EST §201.062. TREATMENT OF CERTAIN PARENT-CHILD RELATIONSHIPS

(a) A probate court may enter an order declaring that the parent of a child under 18 years of age may not inherit from or through the child under the laws of descent and distribution if the court finds by clear and convincing evidence that the parent has:

(1) voluntarily abandoned and failed to support the child in accordance with the parent's obligation or ability for at least three years before the date of the child's death, and did not resume support for the child before that date;

(2) voluntarily and with knowledge of the pregnancy:

(A) abandoned the child's mother beginning at a time during her pregnancy with the child and continuing through the birth;

(B) failed to provide adequate support or medical care for the mother during the period of abandonment before the child's birth; and

(C) remained apart from and failed to support the child since birth; or

(3) been convicted or has been placed on community supervision, including deferred adjudication community supervision, for being criminally responsible for the death or serious injury of a child under the following sections of the Penal Code or adjudicated under Title 3, Family Code, for conduct that caused the death or serious injury of a child and that would constitute a violation of one of the following sections of the Penal Code:

(A) Section 19.02 (murder);

(B) Section 19.03 (capital murder);

(C) Section 19.04 (manslaughter);

(D) Section 21.11 (indecency with a child);

(E) Section 22.01 (assault);

(F) Section 22.011 (sexual assault);

(G) Section 22.02 (aggravated assault);

(H) Section 22.021 (aggravated sexual assault);

(I) Section 22.04 (injury to a child, elderly individual, or disabled individual);

(J) Section 22.041 (abandoning or endangering child);

(K) Section 25.02 (prohibited sexual conduct);

(L) Section 43.25 (sexual performance by a child); or

(M) Section 43.26 (possession or promotion of child pornography).

(b) On a determination under Subsection (a) that the parent of a child may not inherit from or through the child, the parent shall be treated as if the parent predeceased the child for purposes of:

(1) inheritance under the laws of descent and distribution; and

(2) any other cause of action based on parentage.

Sections 201.063-201.100 reserved for expansion

SUBCHAPTER C. DISTRIBUTION TO HEIRS

EST §201.101. DETERMINATION OF PER CAPITA WITH REPRESENTATION DISTRIBUTION

(a) The children, descendants, brothers, sisters, uncles, aunts, or other relatives of an intestate who stand in the first or same degree of relationship alone and come into the distribution of the intestate's estate take per capita, which means by persons.

(b) If some of the persons described by Subsection (a) are dead and some are living, each descendant of those persons who have died is entitled to a distribution of the intestate's estate. Each descendant inherits only that portion of the property to which the parent through whom the descendant inherits would be entitled if that parent were alive.

EST §201.102. NO DISTINCTION BASED ON PROPERTY'S SOURCE

A distinction may not be made, in regulating the descent and distribution of an estate of a person dying intestate, between property derived by gift, devise, or descent from the intestate's father, and property derived by gift, devise, or descent from the intestate's mother.

EST §201.103. TREATMENT OF INTESTATE'S ESTATE

All of the estate to which an intestate had title at the time of death descends and vests in the intestate's heirs in the same manner as if the intestate had been the original purchaser.

Sections 201.104-201.150 reserved for expansion

SUBCHAPTER D. ADVANCEMENTS

EST §201.151. DETERMINATION OF ADVANCEMENT; DATE OF VALUATION

(a) If a decedent dies intestate as to all or part of the decedent's estate, property that the decedent gave during the decedent's lifetime to a person who, on the date of the decedent's death, is the decedent's heir, or property received by the decedent's heir under a nontestamentary transfer under Subchapter B, Chapter 111, or Chapter 112 or 113, is an advancement against the heir's intestate share of the estate only if:

(1) the decedent declared in a contemporaneous writing, or the heir acknowledged in writing, that the gift or nontestamentary transfer is an advancement; or

(2) the decedent's contemporaneous writing or the heir's written acknowledgment otherwise indicates that the gift or nontestamentary transfer is to be considered in computing the division and distribution of the decedent's intestate estate.

(b) For purposes of Subsection (a), property that is advanced is valued as of the earlier of:

(1) the time that the heir came into possession or enjoyment of the property; or

(2) the time of the decedent's death.

EST §201.152. SURVIVAL OF RECIPIENT REQUIRED

If the recipient of property described by Section 201.151 does not survive the decedent, the property is not considered in computing the division and distribution of the decedent's intestate estate unless the decedent's contemporaneous writing provides otherwise.

CHAPTER 202. DETERMINATION OF HEIRSHIP

SUBCHAPTER A. AUTHORIZATION & PROCEDURES FOR COMMENCEMENT OF PROCEEDING TO DECLARE HEIRSHIP

EST §202.001. GENERAL AUTHORIZATION FOR & NATURE OF PROCEEDING TO DECLARE HEIRSHIP

In the manner provided by this chapter, a court may determine through a proceeding to declare heirship:

(1) the persons who are a decedent's heirs and only heirs; and

(2) the heirs' respective shares and interests under the laws of this state in the decedent's estate or, if applicable, in the trust.

EST §202.002. CIRCUMSTANCES UNDER WHICH PROCEEDING TO DECLARE HEIRSHIP IS AUTHORIZED

A court may conduct a proceeding to declare heirship when:

(1) a person dies intestate owning or entitled to property in this state and there has been no administration in this state of the person's estate;

(2) there has been a will probated in this state or elsewhere or an administration in this state of a decedent's estate, but:

(A) property in this state was omitted from the will or administration; or

(B) no final disposition of property in this state has been made in the administration; or

(3) it is necessary for the trustee of a trust holding assets for the benefit of a decedent to determine the heirs of the decedent.

EST §202.0025. ACTION BROUGHT AFTER DECEDENT'S DEATH

Notwithstanding Section 16.051, Civil Practice and Remedies Code, a proceeding to declare heirship of a decedent may be brought at any time after the decedent's death.

EST §202.003. REPEALED

EST §202.004. PERSONS WHO MAY COMMENCE PROCEEDING TO DECLARE HEIRSHIP

A proceeding to declare heirship of a decedent may be commenced and maintained under a circumstance specified by Section 202.002 by:

EST §201.102

(1) the personal representative of the decedent's estate;

(2) a person claiming to be a creditor or the owner of all or part of the decedent's estate;

(3) if the decedent was a ward with respect to whom a guardian of the estate had been appointed, the guardian of the estate, provided that the proceeding is commenced and maintained in the probate court in which the proceedings for the guardianship of the estate were pending at the time of the decedent's death;

(4) a party seeking the appointment of an independent administrator under Section 401.003; or

(5) the trustee of a trust holding assets for the benefit of a decedent.

EST §202.005. APPLICATION FOR PROCEEDING TO DECLARE HEIRSHIP

A person authorized by Section 202.004 to commence a proceeding to declare heirship must file an application in a court specified by Section 33.004 to commence the proceeding. The application must state:

(1) the decedent's name and date and place of death;

(2) the names and physical addresses where service can be had of the decedent's heirs, the relationship of each heir to the decedent, whether each heir is an adult or minor, and the true interest of the applicant and each of the heirs in the decedent's estate or in the trust, as applicable;

(3) if the date or place of the decedent's death or the name or physical address where service can be had of an heir is not definitely known to the applicant, all the material facts and circumstances with respect to which the applicant has knowledge and information that might reasonably tend to show the date or place of the decedent's death or the name or physical address where service can be had of the heir;

(4) that all children born to or adopted by the decedent have been listed;

(5) that each of the decedent's marriages has been listed with:

(A) the date of the marriage;

(B) the name of the spouse;

(C) the date and place of termination if the marriage was terminated; and

(D) other facts to show whether a spouse has had an interest in the decedent's property;

(6) whether the decedent died testate and, if so, what disposition has been made of the will;

(7) a general description of all property belonging to the decedent's estate or held in trust for the benefit of the decedent, as applicable; and

(8) an explanation for the omission from the application of any of the information required by this section.

EST §202.006. REQUEST FOR DETERMINATION OF NECESSITY FOR ADMINISTRATION

A person who files an application under Section 202.005 not later than the fourth anniversary of the date of the death of the decedent who is the subject of the application may request that the court determine whether there is a need for administration of the decedent's estate. The court shall hear evidence on the issue and, in the court's judgment, make a determination of the issue.

EST §202.007. AFFIDAVIT SUPPORTING APPLICATION REQUIRED

(a) An application filed under Section 202.005 must be supported by the affidavit of each applicant.

(b) An affidavit of an applicant under Subsection (a) must state that, to the applicant's knowledge:

(1) all the allegations in the application are true; and

(2) no material fact or circumstance has been omitted from the application.

EST §202.008. REQUIRED PARTIES TO PROCEEDING TO DECLARE HEIRSHIP

Each of the following persons must be made a party to a proceeding to declare heirship:

(1) each unknown heir of the decedent who is the subject of the proceeding;

(2) each person who is named as an heir of the decedent in the application filed under Section 202.005; and

(3) each person who is, on the filing date of the application, shown as owning a share or interest in any real property described in the application by the deed records of the county in which the property is located.

EST §202.009. ATTORNEY AD LITEM

(a) The court shall appoint an attorney ad litem in a proceeding to declare heirship to represent the interests of heirs whose names or locations are unknown.

(b) The court may expand the appointment of the attorney ad litem appointed under Subsection (a) to include representation of an heir who is an incapacitated person on a finding that the appointment is necessary to protect the interests of the heir.

Sections 202.010-202.050 reserved for expansion

SUBCHAPTER B. NOTICE OF PROCEEDING TO DECLARE HEIRSHIP

EST §202.051. SERVICE OF CITATION BY MAIL WHEN RECIPIENT'S NAME & ADDRESS ARE KNOWN OR ASCERTAINABLE

Except as provided by Section 202.054, citation in a proceeding to declare heirship must be served by registered or certified mail on:

(1) each distributee who is 12 years of age or older and whose name and address are known or can be ascertained through the exercise of reasonable diligence; and

(2) the parent, managing conservator, or guardian of each distributee who is younger than 12 years of age if the name and address of the parent, managing conservator, or guardian are known or can be reasonably ascertained.

EST §202.052. SERVICE OF CITATION BY PUBLICATION ~~[WHEN RECIPIENT'S NAME OR ADDRESS IS NOT ASCERTAINABLE]~~

If the address of a person or entity on whom citation is required to be served cannot be ascertained, citation must be served on the person or entity by publication in the county in which the proceeding to declare heirship is commenced and in the county of the last residence of the decedent who is the subject of the proceeding, if that residence was in a county other than the county in which the proceeding is commenced. To determine whether a decedent has any other heirs, citation must be served on unknown heirs by publication in the manner provided by this section.

2017 Legislation: Amended by H.B. 2271, §10, 85th Leg., eff. Sept. 1, 2017.

EST §202.053. REQUIRED POSTING OF CITATION

Except in a proceeding in which citation is served by publication as provided by Section 202.052, citation in a proceeding to declare heirship must be posted in:

(1) the county in which the proceeding is commenced; and

(2) the county of the last residence of the decedent who is the subject of the proceeding.

EST §202.054. PERSONAL SERVICE OF CITATION MAY BE REQUIRED

The court may require that service of citation in a proceeding to declare heirship be made by personal service on some or all of those named as distributees in the application filed under Section 202.005.

EST §202.055. SERVICE OF CITATION ON CERTAIN PERSONS NOT REQUIRED

A party to a proceeding to declare heirship who executed the application filed under Section 202.005, entered an appearance in the proceeding, or waived citation under this subchapter is not required to be served by any method.

EST §202.056. WAIVER OF SERVICE OF CITATION

(a) Except as provided by Subsection (b)(2), a distributee may waive citation required by this subchapter to be served on the distributee.

(b) A parent, managing conservator, guardian, attorney ad litem, or guardian ad litem of a minor distributee who:

(1) is younger than 12 years of age may waive citation required by this subchapter to be served on the distributee; and

(2) is 12 years of age or older may not waive citation required by this subchapter to be served on the distributee.

EST §202.057. AFFIDAVIT OF SERVICE OF CITATION

The amended text in §202.057 is effective for applications for a proceeding to declare heirship filed on or after Sept. 1, 2017. Applications filed before Sept. 1, 2017, are governed by the former law in effect at that time.

(a) A person who files an application under Section 202.005 shall file with the court:

(1) a copy of any citation required by this subchapter and the proof of delivery of service of the citation; and

(2) an affidavit sworn to by the applicant or a certificate signed by the applicant's attorney stating:

(A) that the citation was served as required by this subchapter;

(B) the name of each person to whom the citation was served, if the person's name is not shown on the proof of delivery; and

(C) if service of citation is waived under Section 202.056:

(i) the name of each person who waived citation under that section; and

(ii) if citation is waived under Section 202.056(b)(1), the name of the distributee and the representative capacity of the person who waived citation required to be served on the distributee ~~[Section 202.056]~~.

(b) The court may not enter an order in the proceeding to declare heirship under Subchapter E until the affidavit or certificate required by Subsection (a) is filed.

2017 Legislation: Amended by H.B. 2271, §11, 85th Leg., eff. Sept. 1, 2017.

Sections 202.058-202.100 reserved for expansion

SUBCHAPTER C. TRANSFER OF PENDING PROCEEDING TO DECLARE HEIRSHIP

EST §202.101. REQUIRED TRANSFER OF PENDING PROCEEDING TO DECLARE HEIRSHIP UNDER CERTAIN CIRCUMSTANCES

If, after a proceeding to declare heirship is commenced, an administration of the estate of the decedent who is the subject of the proceeding is granted in this state or the decedent's will is admitted to probate in this state, the court in which the proceeding to declare heirship is pending shall, by an order entered of record in the proceeding, transfer the proceeding to the court in which the administration was granted or the will was probated.

EST §202.102. TRANSFER OF RECORDS

The clerk of the court from which a proceeding to declare heirship is transferred under Section 202.101 shall, on entry of the order under that section, send to the clerk of the court named in the order a certified transcript of all pleadings, entries in the judge's probate docket, and orders of the court in the proceeding. The clerk of the court to which the proceeding is transferred shall:

(1) file the transcript;

(2) record the transcript in the judge's probate docket of that court; and

(3) docket the proceeding.

EST §202.103. PROCEDURES APPLICABLE TO TRANSFERRED PROCEEDING TO DECLARE HEIRSHIP; CONSOLIDATION WITH OTHER PROCEEDING

A proceeding to declare heirship that is transferred under Section 202.101 shall proceed as though the proceeding was originally filed in the court to which the proceeding is transferred. The court may consolidate the proceeding with the other proceeding pending in that court.

Sections 202.104-202.150 reserved for expansion

SUBCHAPTER D. EVIDENCE RELATING TO DETERMINATION OF HEIRSHIP

EST §202.151. EVIDENCE IN PROCEEDING TO DECLARE HEIRSHIP

(a) The court may require that any testimony admitted as evidence in a proceeding to declare heirship be reduced to writing and subscribed and sworn to by the witnesses, respectively.

(b) Testimony in a proceeding to declare heirship must be taken in open court, by deposition in accordance with Section 51.203, or in accordance with the Texas Rules of Civil Procedure.

Sections 202.152-202.200 reserved for expansion

SUBCHAPTER E. JUDGMENT IN PROCEEDING TO DECLARE HEIRSHIP

EST §202.201. REQUIRED STATEMENTS IN JUDGMENT

(a) The judgment in a proceeding to declare heirship must state:

(1) the names of the heirs of the decedent who is the subject of the proceeding; and

(2) the heirs' respective shares and interests in the decedent's property.

(b) If the proof in a proceeding to declare heirship is in any respect deficient, the judgment in the proceeding must state that.

EST §202.202. FINALITY & APPEAL OF JUDGMENT

(a) The judgment in a proceeding to declare heirship is a final judgment.

(b) At the request of an interested person, the judgment in a proceeding to declare heirship may be appealed or reviewed within the same time limits and in the same manner as other judgments in probate matters.

See also King, *"Final Enough": Finality of Probate Orders For Appeal*, Advanced Estate Planning & Probate Course, State Bar of Texas CLE, ch. 23 (2009).

EST §202.203. CORRECTION OF JUDGMENT AT REQUEST OF HEIR NOT PROPERLY SERVED

If an heir of a decedent who is the subject of a proceeding to declare heirship is not served with citation by registered or certified mail or personal service in the proceeding, the heir may:

(1) have the judgment in the proceeding corrected by bill of review:

(A) at any time, but not later than the fourth anniversary of the date of the judgment; or

(B) after the passage of any length of time, on proof of actual fraud; and

(2) recover the heir's just share of the property or the value of that share from:

(A) the heirs named in the judgment; and

(B) those who claim under the heirs named in the judgment and who are not bona fide purchasers for value.

EST §202.204. LIMITATION OF LIABILITY OF CERTAIN PERSONS ACTING IN ACCORDANCE WITH JUDGMENT

(a) The judgment in a proceeding to declare heirship is conclusive in a suit between an heir omitted from the judgment and a bona fide purchaser for value who purchased property after entry of the judgment without actual notice of the claim of the omitted heir, regardless of whether the judgment is subsequently modified, set aside, or nullified.

(b) A person is not liable to another person for the following actions performed in good faith after a judgment is entered in a proceeding to declare heirship:

(1) delivering the property of the decedent who was the subject of the proceeding to the persons named as heirs in the judgment; or

(2) engaging in any other transaction with the persons named as heirs in the judgment.

EST §202.205. EFFECT OF CERTAIN JUDGMENTS ON LIABILITY TO CREDITORS

(a) A judgment in a proceeding to declare heirship stating that there is no necessity for administration of the estate of the decedent who is the subject of the proceeding constitutes authorization for a person who owes money to the estate, has custody of estate property, acts as registrar or transfer agent of an evidence of interest, indebtedness, property, or right belonging to the estate, or purchases from or otherwise deals with an heir named in the judgment to take the following actions without liability to a creditor of the estate or other person:

(1) to pay, deliver, or transfer the property or the evidence of property rights to an heir named in the judgment; or

(2) to purchase property from an heir named in the judgment.

(b) An heir named in a judgment in a proceeding to declare heirship is entitled to enforce the heir's right to payment, delivery, or transfer described by Subsection (a) by suit.

(c) Except as provided by this section, this chapter does not affect the rights or remedies of the creditors of a decedent who is the subject of a proceeding to declare heirship.

EST §202.206. FILING & RECORDING OF JUDGMENT

(a) A certified copy of the judgment in a proceeding to declare heirship may be:

(1) filed for record in the office of the county clerk of the county in which any real property described in the judgment is located;

(2) recorded in the deed records of that county; and

(3) indexed in the name of the decedent who was the subject of the proceeding as grantor and in the names of the heirs named in the judgment as grantees.

(b) On the filing of a judgment in accordance with Subsection (a), the judgment constitutes constructive notice of the facts stated in the judgment.

CHAPTER 203. NONJUDICIAL EVIDENCE OF HEIRSHIP

EST §203.001. RECORDED STATEMENT OF FACTS AS PRIMA FACIE EVIDENCE OF HEIRSHIP

(a) A court shall receive in a proceeding to declare heirship or a suit involving title to property a statement of facts concerning the family history, genealogy, marital status, or the identity of the heirs of a decedent as prima facie evidence of the facts contained in the statement if:

(1) the statement is contained in:

(A) an affidavit or other instrument legally executed and acknowledged or sworn to before, and certi-

EST §202.202

fied by, an officer authorized to take acknowledgments or oaths, as applicable; or

(B) a judgment of a court of record; and

(2) the affidavit or instrument containing the statement has been of record for five years or more in the deed records of a county in this state in which the property is located at the time the suit involving title to property is commenced, or in the deed records of a county in this state in which the decedent was domiciled or had a fixed place of residence at the time of the decedent's death.

(b) If there is an error in a statement of facts in a recorded affidavit or instrument described by Subsection (a), anyone interested in a proceeding in which the affidavit or instrument is offered in evidence may prove the true facts.

(c) An affidavit of facts concerning the identity of a decedent's heirs as to an interest in real property that is filed in a proceeding or suit described by Subsection (a) may be in the form prescribed by Section 203.002.

(d) An affidavit of facts concerning the identity of a decedent's heirs does not affect the rights of an omitted heir or creditor of the decedent as otherwise provided by law. This section is cumulative of all other statutes on the same subject and may not be construed as abrogating any right to present evidence or rely on an affidavit of facts conferred by any other statute or rule.

EST §203.002. FORM OF AFFIDAVIT CONCERNING IDENTITY OF HEIRS

An affidavit of facts concerning the identity of a decedent's heirs may be in substantially the following form:

AFFIDAVIT OF FACTS CONCERNING
THE IDENTITY OF HEIRS

Before me, the undersigned authority, on this day personally appeared __________ ("Affiant") (insert name of affiant) who, being first duly sworn, upon his/her oath states:

1. My name is __________ (insert name of affiant), and I live at __________ (insert address of affiant's residence). I am personally familiar with the family and marital history of __________ ("Decedent") (insert name of decedent), and I have personal knowledge of the facts stated in this affidavit.

2. I knew decedent from __________ (insert date) until __________ (insert date). Decedent died on __________ (insert date of death). Decedent's place of death was __________ (insert place of death). At the time of decedent's death, decedent's residence was __________ (insert address of decedent's residence).

3. Decedent's marital history was as follows: __________ (insert marital history and, if decedent's spouse is deceased, insert date and place of spouse's death).

4. Decedent had the following children: __________ (insert name, birth date, name of other parent, and current address of child or date of death of child and descendants of deceased child, as applicable, for each child).

5. Decedent did not have or adopt any other children and did not take any other children into decedent's home or raise any other children, except: __________ (insert name of child or names of children, or state "none").

6. (Include if decedent was not survived by descendants.) Decedent's mother was: __________ (insert name, birth date, and current address or date of death of mother, as applicable).

7. (Include if decedent was not survived by descendants.) Decedent's father was: __________ (insert name, birth date, and current address or date of death of father, as applicable).

8. (Include if decedent was not survived by descendants or by both mother and father.) Decedent had the following siblings: __________ (insert name, birth date, and current address or date of death of each sibling and parents of each sibling and descendants of each deceased sibling, as applicable, or state "none").

9. (Optional.) The following persons have knowledge regarding the decedent, the identity of decedent's children, if any, parents, or siblings, if any: __________ (insert names of persons with knowledge, or state "none").

10. Decedent died without leaving a written will. (Modify statement if decedent left a written will.)

11. There has been no administration of decedent's estate. (Modify statement if there has been administration of decedent's estate.)

12. Decedent left no debts that are unpaid, except: __________ (insert list of debts, or state "none").

13. There are no unpaid estate or inheritance taxes, except: __________ (insert list of unpaid taxes, or state "none").

14. To the best of my knowledge, decedent owned an interest in the following real property: ______ (insert list of real property in which decedent owned an interest, or state "none").

15. (Optional.) The following were the heirs of decedent: ______ (insert names of heirs).

16. (Insert additional information as appropriate, such as size of the decedent's estate.)

Signed this ____ day of ________, ____.

____
(signature of affiant)

State of ________

County of ________

Sworn to and subscribed to before me on (date) by ________ (insert name of affiant).

____
(signature of notarial officer)

(Seal, if any, of notary) ________________
(printed name)

My commission expires: ________

CHAPTER 204. GENETIC TESTING IN PROCEEDINGS TO DECLARE HEIRSHIP

SUBCHAPTER A. GENERAL PROVISIONS

EST §204.001. PROCEEDINGS & RECORDS PUBLIC

A proceeding under this chapter or Chapter 202 involving genetic testing is open to the public as in other civil cases. Papers and records in the proceeding are available for public inspection.

Sections 204.002-204.050 reserved for expansion

SUBCHAPTER B. COURT ORDERS FOR GENETIC TESTING IN PROCEEDINGS TO DECLARE HEIRSHIP

EST §204.051. ORDER FOR GENETIC TESTING

(a) In a proceeding to declare heirship under Chapter 202, the court may, on the court's own motion, and shall, on the request of a party to the proceeding, order one or more specified individuals to submit to genetic testing as provided by Subchapter F, Chapter 160, Family Code. If two or more individuals are ordered to be tested, the court may order that the testing of those individuals be done concurrently or sequentially.

(b) The court may enforce an order under this section by contempt.

EST §204.052. ADVANCEMENT OF COSTS

Subject to any assessment of costs following a proceeding to declare heirship in accordance with Rule 131, Texas Rules of Civil Procedure, the cost of genetic testing ordered under Section 204.051 must be advanced:

(1) by a party to the proceeding who requests the testing;

(2) as agreed by the parties and approved by the court; or

(3) as ordered by the court.

EST §204.053. ORDER & ADVANCEMENT OF COSTS FOR SUBSEQUENT GENETIC TESTING

(a) Subject to Subsection (b), the court shall order genetic testing subsequent to the testing conducted under Section 204.051 if:

(1) a party to the proceeding to declare heirship contests the results of the genetic testing ordered under Section 204.051; and

(2) the party contesting the results requests that additional testing be conducted.

(b) If the results of the genetic testing ordered under Section 204.051 identify a tested individual as an heir of the decedent, the court may order additional genetic testing in accordance with Subsection (a) only if the party contesting those results pays for the additional testing in advance.

EST §204.054. SUBMISSION OF GENETIC MATERIAL BY OTHER RELATIVE UNDER CERTAIN CIRCUMSTANCES

If a sample of an individual's genetic material that could identify another individual as the decedent's heir is not available for purposes of conducting genetic testing under this subchapter, the court, on a finding of good cause and that the need for genetic testing outweighs the legitimate interests of the individual to be tested, may order any of the following individuals to submit a sample of genetic material for the testing under circumstances the court considers just:

(1) a parent, sibling, or child of the individual whose genetic material is not available; or

(2) any other relative of that individual, as necessary to conduct the testing.

EST §204.055. GENETIC TESTING OF DECEASED INDIVIDUAL

On good cause shown, the court may order:

(1) genetic testing of a deceased individual under this subchapter; and

(2) if necessary, removal of the remains of the deceased individual as provided by Section 711.004, Health and Safety Code, for that testing.

EST §204.056. CRIMINAL PENALTY

(a) An individual commits an offense if:

(1) the individual intentionally releases an identifiable sample of the genetic material of another individual that was provided for purposes of genetic testing ordered under this subchapter; and

(2) the release:

(A) is for a purpose not related to the proceeding to declare heirship; and

(B) was not ordered by the court or done in accordance with written permission obtained from the individual who provided the sample.

(b) An offense under this section is a Class A misdemeanor.

Sections 204.057-204.100 reserved for expansion

SUBCHAPTER C. RESULTS OF GENETIC TESTING

EST §204.101. RESULTS OF GENETIC TESTING; ADMISSIBILITY

A report of the results of genetic testing ordered under Subchapter B:

(1) must comply with the requirements for a report prescribed by Section 160.504, Family Code; and

(2) is admissible in a proceeding to declare heirship under Chapter 202 as evidence of the truth of the facts asserted in the report.

EST §204.102. PRESUMPTION REGARDING RESULTS OF GENETIC TESTING; REBUTTAL

The presumption under Section 160.505, Family Code:

(1) applies to the results of genetic testing ordered under Subchapter B; and

(2) may be rebutted as provided by Section 160.505, Family Code.

EST §204.103. CONTESTING RESULTS OF GENETIC TESTING

(a) A party to a proceeding to declare heirship who contests the results of genetic testing may call one or more genetic testing experts to testify in person or by telephone, videoconference, deposition, or another method approved by the court.

(b) Unless otherwise ordered by the court, the party offering the testimony under Subsection (a) bears the expense for the expert testifying.

Sections 204.104-204.150 reserved for expansion

SUBCHAPTER D. USE OF RESULTS OF GENETIC TESTING IN CERTAIN PROCEEDINGS TO DECLARE HEIRSHIP

EST §204.151. APPLICABILITY OF SUBCHAPTER

This subchapter applies in a proceeding to declare heirship of a decedent only with respect to an individual who claims to be a biological child of the decedent or claims to inherit through a biological child of the decedent.

EST §204.152. PRESUMPTION; REBUTTAL

The presumption under Section 160.505, Family Code, that applies in establishing a parent-child relationship also applies in determining heirship in the probate court using the results of genetic testing ordered with respect to an individual described by Section 204.151, and the presumption may be rebutted in the same manner provided by Section 160.505, Family Code.

EST §204.153. EFFECT OF INCONCLUSIVE RESULTS OF GENETIC TESTING

If the results of genetic testing ordered under Subchapter B do not identify or exclude a tested individual as the ancestor of the individual described by Section 204.151:

(1) the court may not dismiss the proceeding to declare heirship; and

(2) the results of the genetic testing and other relevant evidence are admissible in the proceeding.

Sections 204.154-204.200 reserved for expansion

SUBCHAPTER E. ADDITIONAL ORDERS FOLLOWING RESULTS OF GENETIC TESTING

EST §204.201. ORDER FOR CHANGE OF NAME

On the request of an individual determined by the results of genetic testing to be the heir of a decedent and for good cause shown, the court may:

(1) order the name of the individual to be changed; and

(2) if the court orders a name change under Subdivision (1), order the bureau of vital statistics to issue an amended birth record for the individual.

SUBTITLE F. WILLS

CHAPTER 255. CONSTRUCTION & INTERPRETATION OF WILLS

SUBCHAPTER C. LIFETIME GIFTS AS SATISFACTION OF DEVISE

EST §255.101. CERTAIN LIFETIME GIFTS CONSIDERED SATISFACTION OF DEVISE

Property that a testator gives to a person during the testator's lifetime is considered a satisfaction, either wholly or partly, of a devise to the person if:

(1) the testator's will provides for deduction of the lifetime gift from the devise;

(2) the testator declares in a contemporaneous writing that the lifetime gift is to be deducted from, or is in satisfaction of, the devise; or

(3) the devisee acknowledges in writing that the lifetime gift is in satisfaction of the devise.

EST §255.102. VALUATION OF PROPERTY

Property given in partial satisfaction of a devise shall be valued as of the earlier of:

(1) the date the devisee acquires possession of or enjoys the property; or

(2) the date of the testator's death.

FINANCE CODE

SELECTED PROVISIONS
TABLE OF CONTENTS

TITLE 3. FINANCIAL INSTITUTIONS & BUSINESSES

SUBTITLE A. BANKS

CHAPTER 59. MISCELLANEOUS PROVISIONS

SUBCHAPTER A. GENERAL PROVISIONS

FIN §59.006. DISCOVERY OF CUSTOMER RECORDS

(a) This section provides the exclusive method for compelled discovery of a record of a financial institution relating to one or more customers but does not create a right of privacy in a record. This section does not apply to and does not require or authorize a financial institution to give a customer notice of:

(1) a demand or inquiry from a state or federal government agency authorized by law to conduct an examination of the financial institution;

(2) a record request from a state or federal government agency or instrumentality under statutory or administrative authority that provides for, or is accompanied by, a specific mechanism for discovery and protection of a customer record of a financial institution, including a record request from a federal agency subject to the Right to Financial Privacy Act of 1978 (12 U.S.C. Section 3401 et seq.), as amended, or from the Internal Revenue Service under Section 1205, Internal Revenue Code of 1986;

(3) a record request from or report to a government agency arising out of:

(A) the investigation or prosecution of a criminal offense;

(B) the investigation of alleged abuse, neglect, or exploitation of an elderly or disabled person in accordance with Chapter 48, Human Resources Code; or

(C) the assessment for or provision of guardianship services under Subchapter E, Chapter 161, Human Resources Code;

(4) a record request in connection with a garnishment proceeding in which the financial institution is garnishee and the customer is debtor;

(5) a record request by a duly appointed receiver for the customer;

(6) an investigative demand or inquiry from a state legislative investigating committee;

(7) an investigative demand or inquiry from the attorney general of this state as authorized by law other than the procedural law governing discovery in civil cases;

(8) the voluntary use or disclosure of a record by a financial institution subject to other applicable state or federal law; or

(9) a record request in connection with an investigation conducted under Section 1054.151, 1054.152, or 1102.001, Estates Code.

(b) A financial institution shall produce a record in response to a record request only if:

(1) it is served with the record request not later than the 24th day before the date that compliance with the record request is required;

(2) before the financial institution complies with the record request the requesting party pays the financial institution's reasonable costs of complying with the record request, including costs of reproduction, postage, research, delivery, and attorney's fees, or posts a cost bond in an amount estimated by the financial institution to cover those costs; and

(3) if the customer is not a party to the proceeding in which the request was issued, the requesting party complies with Subsections (c) and (d) and:

(A) the financial institution receives the customer's written consent to release the record after a request under Subsection (c)(3); or

(B) the tribunal takes further action based on action initiated by the requesting party under Subsection (d).

(b-1) If the requesting party has not paid a financial institution's costs or posted a cost bond as required by Subsection (b)(2), a court may not:

(1) order the financial institution to produce a record in response to the record request; or

(2) find the financial institution to be in contempt of court for failing to produce the record.

(c) If the affected customer is not a party to the proceeding in which the record request was issued, in addition to serving the financial institution with a record request, the requesting party shall:

(1) give notice stating the rights of the customer under Subsection (e) and a copy of the request to each affected customer in the manner and within the time provided by Rule 21a, Texas Rules of Civil Procedure;

(2) file a certificate of service indicating that the customer has been mailed or served with the notice and a copy of the record request as required by this subsection with the tribunal and the financial institution; and

(3) request the customer's written consent authorizing the financial institution to comply with the request.

(d) If the customer that is not a party to the proceeding does not execute the written consent requested under Subsection (c)(3) on or before the date that compliance with the request is required, the requesting party may by written motion seek an in camera inspection of the requested record as its sole means of obtaining access to the requested record. In response to a motion for in camera inspection, the tribunal may inspect the requested record to determine its relevance to the matter before the tribunal. The tribunal may order redaction of portions of the records that the tribunal determines should not be produced and shall enter a protective order preventing the record that it orders produced from being:

(1) disclosed to a person who is not a party to the proceeding before the tribunal; and

(2) used by a person for any purpose other than resolving the dispute before the tribunal.

(e) A customer that is a party to the proceeding bears the burden of preventing or limiting the financial institution's compliance with a record request subject to this section by seeking an appropriate remedy, including filing a motion to quash the record request or a motion for a protective order. Any motion filed shall be served on the financial institution and the requesting party before the date that compliance with the request is required. A financial institution is not liable to its customer or another person for disclosure of a record in compliance with this section.

(f) A financial institution may not be required to produce a record under this section before the later of:

(1) the 24th day after the date of receipt of the record request as provided by Subsection (b)(1);

(2) the 15th day after the date of receipt of a customer consent to disclose a record as provided by Subsection (b)(3); or

(3) the 15th day after the date a court orders production of a record after an in camera inspection of a requested record as provided by Subsection (d).

(g) An order to quash or for protection or other remedy entered or denied by the tribunal under Subsection (d) or (e) is not a final order and an interlocutory appeal may not be taken.

See also *O'Connor's Texas Rules*, "Securing Documents from a Financial Institution," ch. 6-I, §7, p. 655.

SUBTITLE E. OTHER FINANCIAL BUSINESSES

CHAPTER 180. RESIDENTIAL MORTGAGE LOAN ORIGINATORS

SUBCHAPTER A. GENERAL PROVISIONS

FIN §180.001. SHORT TITLE

This chapter may be cited as the Texas Secure and Fair Enforcement for Mortgage Licensing Act of 2009.

FIN §180.002. DEFINITIONS

In this chapter:

(1) "Clerical or support duties," following the receipt of an application from a consumer, includes:

(A) the receipt, collection, distribution, and analysis of information related to the processing or underwriting of a residential mortgage loan; and

(B) communication with a consumer to obtain information necessary to process or underwrite a loan, to the extent that the communication does not include offering or negotiating loan rates or terms or counseling the consumer about residential mortgage loan rates or terms.

(2) "Credit union" means a state or federal credit union operating in this state.

(3) "Credit union subsidiary organization" means an agency, association, or company wholly or partly owned by a credit union that is designed primarily to serve or otherwise assist credit union operations. The term includes a credit union service organization authorized by:

(A) Section 124.351(a)(1);

(B) Credit Union Commission rule; or

(C) Part 712 of the National Credit Union Administration's Rules and Regulations.

(4) "Depository institution" has the meaning assigned by Section 3, Federal Deposit Insurance Act (12 U.S.C. Section 1813). The term includes a credit union but does not include a credit union subsidiary organization.

(5) "Dwelling" has the meaning assigned by Section 103(v) of the Truth in Lending Act (15 U.S.C. Section 1602(v)).

(6) "Federal banking agency" means:

(A) the Board of Governors of the Federal Reserve System;

(B) the Office of the Comptroller of the Currency;

(C) the Office of Thrift Supervision;

(D) the National Credit Union Administration;

(E) the Federal Deposit Insurance Corporation; or

(F) the successor of any of those agencies.

(7) "Finance commission" means the Finance Commission of Texas.

(8) "Immediate family member" means the spouse, child, sibling, parent, grandparent, or grandchild of an individual. The term includes a stepparent, stepchild, and stepsibling and a relationship established by adoption.

(9) "Individual" means a natural person.

(10) "License" means a license issued under the laws of this state to an individual acting as or engaged in the business of a residential mortgage loan originator.

(11) "Loan processor or underwriter" means an individual who performs clerical or support duties as an employee at the direction of and subject to the supervision and instruction of an individual licensed as a residential mortgage loan originator or exempt from licensure under Section 180.003.

(12) "Nationwide Mortgage Licensing System and Registry" means a mortgage licensing system developed and maintained by the Conference of State Bank Supervisors and the American Association of Residential Mortgage Regulators for the licensing and registration of state residential mortgage loan originators.

(13) "Nontraditional mortgage product" means a mortgage product other than a 30-year fixed rate mortgage.

(14) "Person" means an individual, corporation, company, limited liability company, partnership, or association.

(15) "Real estate brokerage activity" means an activity that involves offering or providing real estate brokerage services to the public, including:

(A) acting as a real estate broker or salesperson for a buyer, seller, lessor, or lessee of real property;

(B) bringing together parties interested in the sale, purchase, lease, rental, or exchange of real property;

(C) negotiating, on a party's behalf, any provision of a contract relating to the sale, purchase, lease, rental, or exchange of real property, other than a negotiation conducted in connection with providing financing with respect to such a transaction;

(D) engaging in an activity for which a person is required to be registered or licensed by the state as a real estate broker or salesperson; and

(E) offering to engage in an activity described by Paragraphs (A) through (D) or to act in the same capacity as a person described by Paragraphs (A) through (D).

(16) "Registered mortgage loan originator" means an individual who:

(A) is a residential mortgage loan originator and is an employee of:

(i) a depository institution;

(ii) a subsidiary that is:

(a) owned and controlled by a depository institution; and

(b) regulated by a federal banking agency; or

(iii) an institution regulated by the Farm Credit Administration; and

(B) is registered with, and maintains a unique identifier through, the Nationwide Mortgage Licensing System and Registry.

(17) "Regulatory official" means:

(A) with respect to Subtitles A, F, and G of this title, the banking commissioner of Texas;

(B) with respect to Chapters 156 and 157, the savings and mortgage lending commissioner; and

(C) with respect to Chapters 342, 347, 348, and 351, the consumer credit commissioner.

(18) "Residential mortgage loan" means a loan primarily for personal, family, or household use that is secured by a mortgage, deed of trust, or other equivalent consensual security interest on a dwelling or on residential real estate.

(19) "Residential mortgage loan originator":

(A) means an individual who for compensation or gain or in the expectation of compensation or gain:

(i) takes a residential mortgage loan application; or

(ii) offers or negotiates the terms of a residential mortgage loan; and

(B) does not include:

(i) an individual who performs solely administrative or clerical tasks on behalf of an individual licensed as a residential mortgage loan originator or exempt from licensure under Section 180.003, except as otherwise provided by Section 180.051;

(ii) an individual who performs only real estate brokerage activities and is licensed or registered by the state as a real estate broker or salesperson, unless the individual is compensated by:

(a) a lender or other residential mortgage loan originator; or

(b) an agent of a lender or other residential mortgage loan originator;

(iii) an individual licensed under Chapter 1201, Occupations Code, unless the individual is directly compensated for arranging financing for activities regulated under that chapter by:

(a) a lender or other residential mortgage loan originator; or

(b) an agent of a lender or other residential mortgage loan originator;

(iv) an individual who receives the same benefits from a financed transaction as the individual would receive if the transaction were a cash transaction; or

(v) an individual who is involved solely in providing extensions of credit relating to timeshare plans, as defined by 11 U.S.C. Section 101(53D).

(20) "Residential real estate" means real property located in this state on which a dwelling is constructed or intended to be constructed.

(21) "Rulemaking authority" means the finance commission.

(22) "S.A.F.E. Mortgage Licensing Act" means the federal Secure and Fair Enforcement for Mortgage Licensing Act of 2008 (Pub. L. No. 110-289).

(23) "Unique identifier" means a number or other identifier assigned by protocols established by the Nationwide Mortgage Licensing System and Registry.

FIN §180.003. EXEMPTION

(a) The following persons are exempt from this chapter:

(1) a registered mortgage loan originator when acting for an entity described by Section 180.002(16)(A)(i), (ii), or (iii);

(2) an individual who offers or negotiates terms of a residential mortgage loan with or on behalf of an immediate family member of the individual;

(3) a licensed attorney who negotiates the terms of a residential mortgage loan on behalf of a client as an ancillary matter to the attorney's representation of the client, unless the attorney:

(A) takes a residential mortgage loan application; and

(B) offers or negotiates the terms of a residential mortgage loan;

(4) an individual who offers or negotiates terms of a residential mortgage loan secured by a dwelling that serves as the individual's residence;

(5) an owner of residential real estate who in any 12-consecutive-month period makes no more than five residential mortgage loans to purchasers of the property for all or part of the purchase price of the residential real estate against which the mortgage is secured; and

(6) an owner of a dwelling who in any 12-consecutive-month period makes no more than five residential mortgage loans to purchasers of the property for all or part of the purchase price of the dwelling against which the mortgage or security interest is secured.

(b) An individual is exempt from this chapter, other than Section 180.171, if the individual:

(1) in any 12-consecutive-month period originates five or fewer closed residential mortgage loans exclusively for a single federally chartered depository institution and the loans are closed within that period;

(2) is contractually prohibited from soliciting, processing, negotiating, or placing a residential mortgage loan with a person other than the depository institution described by Subdivision (1); and

(3) is sponsored by a life insurance company, or an affiliate of the company, authorized to engage in business in this state.

(c) The finance commission may grant an exemption from the licensing requirements of this chapter to a municipality, county, community development corporation, or public or private grant administrator to the extent the entity is administering the Texas HOME Investment Partnerships program if the commission determines that granting the exemption is not inconsistent with the intentions of the federal Secure and Fair Enforcement for Mortgage Licensing Act of 2008 (Pub. L. No. 110-289).

FIN §180.004. ADMINISTRATIVE AUTHORITY; RULEMAKING

(a) A regulatory official has broad authority to administer, interpret, and enforce this chapter.

(b) The finance commission may implement rules necessary to comply with this chapter and as required

to carry out the intentions of the federal Secure and Fair Enforcement for Mortgage Licensing Act of 2008 (Pub. L. No. 110-289).

(c) This chapter does not limit the authority of a regulatory official to take disciplinary action against a license holder for a violation of this chapter or the rules adopted by the regulatory official under this chapter. A regulatory official has broad authority to investigate, revoke a license, and inform the proper authority when fraudulent conduct or a violation of this chapter occurs.

See also 7 T.A.C. ch. 80, subch. D, ch. 81, subch. D.

FIN §180.005. SEVERABILITY

The provisions of this chapter or applications of those provisions are severable as provided by Section 311.032(c), Government Code.

Sections 180.006-180.050 reserved for expansion

SUBCHAPTER B. LICENSING & REGISTRATION REQUIREMENTS

FIN §180.051. STATE LICENSE REQUIRED; RENEWAL

(a) Unless exempted by Section 180.003, an individual may not engage in business as a residential mortgage loan originator with respect to a dwelling located in this state unless the individual:

(1) is licensed to engage in that business under Chapter 156, 157, 342, 347, 348, or 351; and

(2) complies with the requirements of this chapter.

(b) Unless exempted by Section 180.003, a loan processor or underwriter who is an independent contractor may not engage in the activities of a loan processor or underwriter unless the independent contractor loan processor or underwriter obtains and maintains the appropriate residential mortgage loan originator license and complies with the requirements of this chapter.

(c) The individual must renew the license annually to be considered licensed for purposes of this section.

(d) Notwithstanding any provision of law listed in Subsection (a)(1), the regulatory official shall provide for annual renewal of licenses for individuals seeking to engage in residential mortgage loan origination activities.

See also 7 T.A.C. ch. 80, subch. B, ch. 81, subch. B.

FIN §180.052. ENROLLMENT OR REGISTRATION WITH NATIONWIDE MORTGAGE LICENSING SYSTEM & REGISTRY

(a) A licensed residential mortgage loan originator must enroll with and maintain a valid unique identifier issued by the Nationwide Mortgage Licensing System and Registry.

(b) A non-federally insured credit union that employs loan originators, as defined by the S.A.F.E. Mortgage Licensing Act, shall register those employees with the Nationwide Mortgage Licensing System and Registry by furnishing the information relating to the employees' identity set forth in Section 1507(a)(2) of the S.A.F.E. Mortgage Licensing Act.

(c) Each independent contractor loan processor or underwriter licensed as a residential mortgage loan originator must have and maintain a valid unique identifier issued by the Nationwide Mortgage Licensing System and Registry.

(d) The regulatory official who administers the law under which a residential mortgage loan originator is licensed shall require the residential mortgage loan originator to be enrolled with the Nationwide Mortgage Licensing System and Registry.

(e) For purposes of implementing Subsection (d), the regulatory official may participate in the Nationwide Mortgage Licensing System and Registry.

See also 7 T.A.C. §§80.100, 80.102, 80.103, 80.106, 81.100, 81.101, 81.104, 81.107.

FIN §180.053. APPLICATION FORM

(a) A regulatory official shall prescribe application forms for a license as a residential mortgage loan originator.

(b) A regulatory official may change or update an application form as necessary to carry out the purposes of this chapter.

FIN §180.054. CRIMINAL & OTHER BACKGROUND CHECKS

(a) In connection with an application for a license as a residential mortgage loan originator, the applicant shall, at a minimum, furnish in the form and manner prescribed by the regulatory official and acceptable to the Nationwide Mortgage Licensing System and Registry information concerning the applicant's identity, including:

(1) fingerprints for submission to the Federal Bureau of Investigation and any governmental agency or

entity authorized to receive the information to conduct a state, national, and international criminal background check; and

(2) personal history and experience information in a form prescribed by the Nationwide Mortgage Licensing System and Registry, including the submission of authorization for the Nationwide Mortgage Licensing System and Registry and the appropriate regulatory official to obtain:

(A) an independent credit report obtained from a consumer reporting agency described by Section 603(p), Fair Credit Reporting Act (15 U.S.C. Section 1681a(p)); and

(B) information related to any administrative, civil, or criminal findings by a governmental jurisdiction.

(b) For purposes of this section and to reduce the points of contact that the Federal Bureau of Investigation may have to maintain for purposes of Subsection (a)(1), a regulatory official may use the Nationwide Mortgage Licensing System and Registry as a channeling agent for requesting information from and distributing information to the United States Department of Justice, any governmental agency, or any source at the regulatory official's direction.

(c) For purposes of this section and to reduce the points of contact that a regulatory official may have to maintain for purposes of Subsection (a) or (b), the regulatory official may use the Nationwide Mortgage Licensing System and Registry as a channeling agent for requesting information from and distributing information to and from any source as directed by the regulatory official.

See also 7 T.A.C. §§80.104, 81.108.

FIN §180.055. ISSUANCE OF LICENSE

(a) The regulatory official may not issue a residential mortgage loan originator license to an individual unless the regulatory official determines, at a minimum, that the applicant:

(1) has not had a residential mortgage loan originator license revoked in any governmental jurisdiction;

(2) has not been convicted of, or pled guilty or nolo contendere to, a felony in a domestic, foreign, or military court:

(A) during the seven-year period preceding the date of application; or

(B) at any time preceding the date of application, if the felony involved an act of fraud, dishonesty, breach of trust, or money laundering;

(3) demonstrates financial responsibility, character, and general fitness so as to command the confidence of the community and to warrant a determination that the individual will operate honestly, fairly, and efficiently as a residential mortgage loan originator within the purposes of this chapter and any other appropriate regulatory law of this state;

(4) provides satisfactory evidence that the applicant has completed prelicensing education courses described by Section 180.056;

(5) provides satisfactory evidence of having passed a written test that meets the requirements of Section 180.057; and

(6) has paid a recovery fund fee or obtained a surety bond as required under the appropriate state regulatory law.

(b) A revocation that has been formally vacated may not be considered a license revocation for purposes of Subsection (a)(1).

(c) A conviction for which a full pardon has been granted may not be considered a conviction for purposes of Subsection (a)(2).

(d) For purposes of Subsection (a)(3), an individual is considered not to be financially responsible if the individual has shown a lack of regard in managing the individual's own financial affairs or condition. A determination that an individual has not shown financial responsibility may include:

(1) an outstanding judgment against the individual, other than a judgment imposed solely as a result of medical expenses;

(2) an outstanding tax lien or other governmental liens and filings;

(3) a foreclosure during the three-year period preceding the date of the license application; and

(4) a pattern of seriously delinquent accounts during the three-year period preceding the date of the application.

A FIN §180.056. PRELICENSING EDUCATIONAL COURSES

(a) An applicant for a residential mortgage loan originator license must complete education courses that include at least the minimum number of hours and type of courses required by the S.A.F.E. Mortgage Li-

censing Act and the minimum number of hours of training related to lending standards for the nontraditional mortgage product marketplace required by that Act and any additional requirements established by the regulatory official and adopted by rule of the rulemaking authority.

(b) Education courses required under this section must be reviewed and approved by the Nationwide Mortgage Licensing System and Registry in accordance with the S.A.F.E. Mortgage Licensing Act.

(c) Nothing in this section precludes any education course approved in accordance with the S.A.F.E. Mortgage Licensing Act from being provided by:

(1) an applicant's employer;

(2) an entity affiliated with the applicant by an agency contract; or

(3) a subsidiary or affiliate of the employer or entity.

(d) Education courses required under this section may be offered in a classroom, online, or by any other means approved by the Nationwide Mortgage Licensing System and Registry.

(e) An individual who has successfully completed prelicensing education requirements approved by the Nationwide Mortgage Licensing System and Registry for another state shall be given credit toward completion of the prelicensing education requirements of this section.

(f) An applicant who has previously held a residential mortgage loan originator license that meets the requirements of this chapter and other appropriate regulatory law, before being issued a new original license, must demonstrate to the appropriate regulatory official that the applicant has completed all continuing education requirements for the calendar year in which the license was last held by the applicant.

(g) If the appropriate federal regulators and the Nationwide Mortgage Licensing System and Registry establish additional educational requirements for licensed residential mortgage loan originators, the rulemaking authority shall adopt necessary rules to implement the changes to the educational requirements of this section.

(h) An individual who fails to maintain a residential mortgage loan originator license for <u>the period of time established by rule of the rulemaking authority</u> [~~at least five consecutive years~~] must retake the prelicensing education requirements prescribed by the S.A.F.E. Mortgage Licensing Act.

2017 Legislation: Amended by H.B. 3342, §1, 85th Leg., eff. Jan. 1, 2018. See also 7 T.A.C. §81.106.

FIN §180.057. TESTING REQUIREMENTS

(a) An applicant for a residential mortgage loan originator license must pass a qualified, written test that:

(1) meets the standards and requirements established by the S.A.F.E. Mortgage Licensing Act;

(2) is developed by the Nationwide Mortgage Licensing System and Registry; and

(3) is administered by a test provider in accordance with the S.A.F.E. Mortgage Licensing Act.

(b) An individual may retake the test the number of times and within the period prescribed by the S.A.F.E. Mortgage Licensing Act.

(c) An individual who fails to maintain a residential mortgage loan originator license for at least five consecutive years must retake the test.

(d) This section does not prohibit a test provider approved in accordance with the S.A.F.E. Mortgage Licensing Act from providing a test at the location of:

(1) the license applicant's employer;

(2) a subsidiary or affiliate of the applicant's employer; or

(3) an entity with which the applicant holds an exclusive arrangement to conduct the business of a residential mortgage loan originator.

FIN §180.058. RECOVERY FUND FEE OR SURETY BOND REQUIREMENT

(a) A regulatory official may not issue a residential mortgage loan originator license unless the official determines that the applicant meets the surety bond requirement or has paid a recovery fund fee, as applicable, in accordance with the requirements of the S.A.F.E. Mortgage Licensing Act.

(b) Each regulatory official shall adopt rules requiring an individual licensed as a residential mortgage loan originator to obtain a surety bond or pay a recovery fund fee as the official determines appropriate to comply with the S.A.F.E. Mortgage Licensing Act.

FIN §180.059. STANDARDS FOR LICENSE RENEWAL

A license to act as a residential mortgage loan originator may be renewed on or before its expiration date if the license holder:

(1) continues to meet the minimum requirements for license issuance;

(2) pays all required fees for the renewal of the license; and

(3) provides satisfactory evidence that the license holder has completed the continuing education requirements of Section 180.060.

FIN §180.060. CONTINUING EDUCATION COURSES

(a) To renew a residential mortgage loan originator license, a license holder must annually complete the minimum number of hours and type of continuing education courses required by the S.A.F.E. Mortgage Licensing Act, the minimum requirements established by the Nationwide Mortgage Licensing System and Registry, and any additional requirements established by the regulatory official.

(b) Continuing education courses, including the course provider, must be reviewed and approved by the Nationwide Mortgage Licensing System and Registry as required by the S.A.F.E. Mortgage Licensing Act. Course credit must be granted in accordance with that Act.

(c) Nothing in this section precludes any continuing education course approved in accordance with the S.A.F.E. Mortgage Licensing Act from being provided by:

(1) the employer of the license holder;

(2) an entity affiliated with the license holder by an agency contract; or

(3) a subsidiary or affiliate of the employer or entity.

(d) A person who successfully completes continuing education requirements approved by the Nationwide Mortgage Licensing System and Registry for another state shall be given credit toward completion of the continuing education requirements of this section.

FIN §180.061. RULEMAKING AUTHORITY

A rulemaking authority may adopt rules establishing requirements as necessary for:

(1) conducting background checks by obtaining:

(A) criminal history information through fingerprint or other databases;

(B) civil administrative records;

(C) credit history information; or

(D) any other information considered necessary by the Nationwide Mortgage Licensing System and Registry;

(2) payment of fees to apply for or renew licenses through the Nationwide Mortgage Licensing System and Registry;

(3) setting or resetting, as necessary, license renewal dates or reporting periods;

(4) amending or surrendering a license or any other activity a regulatory official considers necessary for participation in the Nationwide Mortgage Licensing System and Registry; and

(5) investigation and examination authority for purposes of investigating a violation or complaint arising under this chapter or for purposes of examining, reviewing, or investigating any license holder or individual subject to this chapter.

FIN §180.062. CONFIDENTIALITY OF INFORMATION

(a) Except as otherwise provided by this section, a requirement under federal or state law regarding the privacy or confidentiality of information or material provided to the Nationwide Mortgage Licensing System and Registry, and a privilege arising under federal or state law, or under the rules of a federal or state court, continue to apply to the information or material after the disclosure of the information or material to the Nationwide Mortgage Licensing System and Registry. The information and material may be shared with federal and state regulatory officials with mortgage industry oversight authority without the loss of any privilege or confidentiality protections afforded by federal or state laws.

(b) Information or material subject to a privilege or confidential under Subsection (a) may not be subject to:

(1) disclosure under any federal or state law governing the disclosure to the public of information held by an officer or an agency of the federal government or this state; or

(2) subpoena, discovery, or admission into evidence in a private civil action or administrative proceeding.

(c) A person who is the subject of information or material in the Nationwide Mortgage Licensing System and Registry may waive, wholly or partly, any privilege held by the Nationwide Mortgage Licensing System and Registry with respect to the information or material.

(d) A regulatory official may enter into an agreement or sharing arrangement with another govern-

mental agency, the Conference of State Bank Supervisors, the American Association of Residential Mortgage Regulators, or other associations representing appropriate governmental agencies as established by rule of the rulemaking authority or order issued by the regulatory official. A protection provided by Subsection (a) also applies to information and material shared under an agreement or sharing arrangement entered into under this subsection.

(e) To the extent of a conflict between Subsection (a) and Chapter 552, Government Code, or another state law relating to the disclosure of confidential information or information or material described by Subsection (a), Subsection (a) controls to the extent Chapter 552, Government Code, or the other law provides less confidentiality or a weaker privilege than is provided by Subsection (a).

(f) This section does not apply to information or material relating to the employment history of, and publicly adjudicated disciplinary and enforcement actions against, a residential mortgage loan originator that is included in the Nationwide Mortgage Licensing System and Registry for access by the public.

Sections 180.063-180.100 reserved for expansion

SUBCHAPTER C. REPORTING & OTHER REQUIREMENTS REGARDING NATIONWIDE MORTGAGE LICENSING SYSTEM & REGISTRY

FIN §180.101. MORTGAGE CALL REPORTS

Each licensed residential mortgage loan originator shall submit to the Nationwide Mortgage Licensing System and Registry a report of condition that is in the form and contains the information required by the Nationwide Mortgage Licensing System and Registry.

See also 7 T.A.C. §§80.205, 81.205.

FIN §180.102. REPORT OF VIOLATIONS & ENFORCEMENT ACTIONS

Subject to the confidentiality provisions of this chapter, a regulatory official shall report to the Nationwide Mortgage Licensing System and Registry on a regular basis regarding violations of, enforcement actions under, or information relevant to this chapter or the S.A.F.E. Mortgage Licensing Act under the regulatory official's licensure, regulation, or examination of a licensed residential mortgage loan originator or person registered under the S.A.F.E. Mortgage Licensing Act.

FIN §180.103. INFORMATION CHALLENGE PROCESS

The applicable rulemaking authority by rule shall establish a process by which licensed residential mortgage loan originators may dispute information submitted by the regulatory official to the Nationwide Mortgage Licensing System and Registry.

Sections 180.104-180.150 reserved for expansion

SUBCHAPTER D. BUSINESS PRACTICES; PROHIBITED ACTS

FIN §180.151. DISPLAY OF UNIQUE IDENTIFIER

The unique identifier of a person originating a residential mortgage loan must be clearly shown on each residential mortgage loan application form, solicitation, or advertisement, including business cards and websites, and any other document required by rule of the rulemaking authority.

FIN §180.152. REPRESENTATIONS

An individual who is engaged exclusively in loan processor or underwriter activities may not represent to the public, through the use of advertising, business cards, stationery, brochures, signs, rate lists, or other means, that the individual can or will perform any of the activities of a residential mortgage loan originator unless the individual is licensed as a residential mortgage loan originator.

FIN §180.153. PROHIBITED ACTS & PRACTICES

An individual or other person subject to regulation under this chapter may not:

(1) employ, directly or indirectly, a scheme, device, or artifice to defraud or mislead borrowers or lenders or to defraud a person;

(2) engage in an unfair or deceptive practice toward a person;

(3) obtain property by fraud or misrepresentation;

(4) solicit or enter into a contract with a borrower that provides in substance that the individual or other person subject to this chapter may earn a fee or commission through "best efforts" to obtain a loan even though no loan was actually obtained for the borrower;

(5) solicit, advertise, or enter into a contract for specific interest rates, points, or other financing terms

unless the terms are actually available at the time of soliciting, advertising, or contracting;

(6) conduct any business regulated by this chapter without holding a license as required by this chapter;

(7) assist, aid, or abet an individual in the conduct of business without a license required by this chapter;

(8) fail to make disclosures as required by this chapter and any other applicable state or federal law, including rules or regulations under applicable state or federal law;

(9) fail to comply with this chapter or rules adopted under this chapter;

(10) fail to comply with any other state or federal law, including rules or regulations adopted under that law, applicable to a business or activity regulated by this chapter;

(11) make, in any manner, a false or deceptive statement or representation;

(12) negligently make a false statement or knowingly or wilfully make an omission of material fact in connection with:

(A) information or a report filed with a governmental agency or the Nationwide Mortgage Licensing System and Registry; or

(B) an investigation conducted by the regulatory official or another governmental agency;

(13) make a payment, threat, or promise, directly or indirectly, to a person for purposes of influencing the person's independent judgment in connection with a residential mortgage loan, or make a payment, threat, or promise, directly or indirectly, to an appraiser of property, for purposes of influencing the appraiser's independent judgment with respect to the property's value;

(14) collect, charge, attempt to collect or charge, or use or propose an agreement purporting to collect or charge a fee prohibited by this chapter;

(15) cause or require a borrower to obtain property insurance coverage in an amount that exceeds the replacement cost of the improvements as established by the property insurer; or

(16) fail to truthfully account for money belonging to a party to a residential mortgage loan transaction.

Sections 180.154-180.170 reserved for expansion

SUBCHAPTER D-1. REQUIREMENT FOR INDIVIDUALS ORIGINATING RESIDENTIAL MORTGAGE LOANS EXCLUSIVELY FOR CERTAIN DEPOSITORY INSTITUTION

FIN §180.171. ENROLLMENT WITH DEPARTMENT OF SAVINGS & MORTGAGE LENDING

(a) This section applies only to an individual who:

(1) in any 12-consecutive-month period originates five or fewer residential mortgage loans exclusively for a single federally chartered depository institution and the loans are closed within that period;

(2) is contractually prohibited from soliciting, processing, negotiating, or placing a residential mortgage loan with a person other than the depository institution described by Subdivision (1); and

(3) is sponsored by a life insurance company, or an affiliate of the company, authorized to engage in business in this state.

(b) Before conducting business in this state with respect to a residential mortgage loan, an individual to whom this section applies must enroll as a financial exclusive agent with the Department of Savings and Mortgage Lending until the time any registration with the Nationwide Mortgage Licensing System and Registry is required for the individual by federal law or regulation and a suitable category is created for that registration with that nationwide registry.

(c) An enrollment under this section must be renewed annually.

(d) An individual required under this section to enroll as a financial exclusive agent shall pay to the savings and mortgage lending commissioner an annual fee in an amount not to exceed $40 as prescribed by the commissioner.

Sections 180.172-180.200 reserved for expansion

SUBCHAPTER E. ENFORCEMENT PROVISIONS

FIN §180.201. ENFORCEMENT AUTHORITY

To ensure the effective supervision and enforcement of this chapter, a regulatory official may:

(1) deny, suspend, revoke, condition, or decline to renew a license for a violation of this chapter, a rule adopted under this chapter, or an order or directive issued under this chapter;

(2) deny, suspend, revoke, condition, or decline to renew a license if an applicant or license holder:

(A) fails to meet the requirements of Subchapter B; or

(B) withholds information or makes a material misstatement in an application for a license or renewal of a license;

(3) order restitution against a person subject to regulation under this chapter for a violation of this chapter;

(4) impose an administrative penalty on a person subject to regulation under this chapter, subject to Section 180.202; or

(5) issue orders or directives as provided by Section 180.203.

See also 7 T.A.C. §§80.202, 81.202.

FIN §180.202. ADMINISTRATIVE PENALTY

(a) A regulatory official may impose an administrative penalty on a residential mortgage loan originator or other person subject to regulation under this chapter, if the official, after notice and opportunity for hearing, determines that the residential mortgage loan originator or other person subject to regulation under this chapter has violated or failed to comply with:

(1) this chapter;

(2) a rule adopted under this chapter; or

(3) an order issued under this chapter.

(b) The penalty may not exceed $25,000 for each violation.

(c) The amount of the penalty shall be based on:

(1) the seriousness of the violation, including the nature, circumstances, extent, and gravity of the violation;

(2) the economic harm to property caused by the violation;

(3) the history of previous violations;

(4) the amount necessary to deter a future violation;

(5) efforts to correct the violation; and

(6) any other matter that justice may require.

See also 7 T.A.C. §80.301.

FIN §180.203. CEASE & DESIST ORDERS

A regulatory official may:

(1) order or direct a person subject to regulation under this chapter to cease and desist from conducting business, including issuing an immediate temporary order to cease and desist from conducting business;

(2) order or direct a person subject to regulation under this chapter to cease a violation of this chapter or a harmful activity in violation of this chapter, including issuing an immediate temporary order to cease and desist;

(3) enter immediate temporary orders against a person subject to regulation under this chapter to cease engaging in business under a license if the regulatory official determines that the license was erroneously granted or the license holder is in violation of this chapter; and

(4) order or direct other affirmative action as the regulatory official considers necessary.

See also 7 T.A.C. §80.301.

Sections 180.204-180.250 reserved for expansion

SUBCHAPTER F. DUTIES OF REGULATORY OFFICIALS

FIN §180.251. GENERAL DUTIES OF REGULATORY OFFICIALS

(a) The savings and mortgage lending commissioner shall administer and enforce this chapter with respect to individuals licensed under Chapter 157.

(b) Repealed by Acts 2013, 83rd Leg., ch. 160, §87(9), eff. Sept. 1, 2013.

(c) The consumer credit commissioner shall administer and enforce this chapter with respect to individuals licensed under Chapter 342, 347, 348, or 351.

(d) To the extent permitted or required by this chapter and as reasonably necessary for the implementation and enforcement of the S.A.F.E. Mortgage Licensing Act, the banking commissioner of Texas may administer and enforce this chapter with respect to a person otherwise under the commissioner's jurisdiction under Subtitle A, F, or G of this title.

See also 7 T.A.C. ch. 80, subch. D, ch. 81, subch. D.

FIN §180.252. AUTHORITY OF REGULATORY OFFICIALS TO ESTABLISH RELATIONSHIP WITH NATIONWIDE MORTGAGE LICENSING SYSTEM & REGISTRY; CONTRACTING AUTHORITY

To fulfill the purposes of this chapter, a regulatory official may establish a relationship with or contract with the Nationwide Mortgage Licensing System and Registry or an entity designated by the Nationwide Mortgage Licensing System and Registry to collect and

FIN §180.201

maintain records and process transaction fees or other fees related to licensed residential mortgage loan originators or other persons subject to regulation under this chapter.

TITLE 4. REGULATION OF INTEREST, LOANS, & FINANCED TRANSACTIONS

SUBTITLE A. INTEREST

CHAPTER 301. GENERAL PROVISIONS

FIN §301.002. DEFINITIONS

(a) In this subtitle:

(1) "Contract interest" means interest that an obligor has paid or agreed to pay to a creditor under a written contract of the parties. The term does not include judgment interest.

(2) "Credit card transaction" means a transaction for personal, family, or household use in which a credit card, plate, coupon book, or credit card cash advance check may be used or is used to debit an open-end account in connection with:

(A) a purchase or lease of goods or services; or

(B) a loan of money.

(3) "Creditor" means a person who loans money or otherwise extends credit. The term does not include a judgment creditor.

(4) "Interest" means compensation for the use, forbearance, or detention of money. The term does not include time price differential, regardless of how it is denominated. The term does not include compensation or other amounts that are determined or stated by this code or other applicable law not to constitute interest or that are permitted to be contracted for, charged, or received in addition to interest in connection with an extension of credit.

(5) "Judgment creditor" means a person to whom a money judgment is payable.

(6) "Judgment debtor" means a person obligated to pay a money judgment.

(7) "Judgment interest" means interest on a money judgment, whether the interest accrues before, on, or after the date the judgment is rendered.

(8) "Legal interest" means interest charged or received in the absence of any agreement by an obligor to pay contract interest. The term does not include judgment interest.

(9) "Lender credit card agreement":

(A) means an agreement between a creditor and an obligor that provides that:

(i) the obligor, by means of a credit card transaction for personal, family, or household use, may:

(a) obtain loans from the creditor directly or through other participating persons; and

(b) lease or purchase goods or services from more than one participating lessor or seller who honors the creditor's credit card;

(ii) the creditor or another person acting in cooperation with the creditor is to reimburse the participating persons, lessors, or sellers for the loans or the goods or services purchased or leased;

(iii) the obligor is to pay the creditor the amount of the loan or cost of the lease or purchase;

(iv) the unpaid balance of the loan, lease, or purchase and interest on that unpaid balance are debited to the obligor's account under the agreement;

(v) interest may be computed on the balances of the obligor's account but is not precomputed; and

(vi) the obligor and the creditor may agree that payment of part of the balance may be deferred;

(B) includes an agreement under Section 342.455 or Section 346.003(b) or (c) for an open-end account under which credit card transactions may be made or a merchant discount may be taken; and

(C) does not include:

(i) an agreement, including an open-end account credit agreement, between a seller and a buyer or between a lessor and a lessee; or

(ii) an agreement under which:

(a) the entire balance is due in full each month; and

(b) no interest is charged if the obligor pays the entire balance each month.

(10) "Loan" means an advance of money that is made to or on behalf of an obligor, the principal amount of which the obligor has an obligation to pay the creditor. The term does not include a judgment.

(11) "Merchant discount" means the consideration, including a fee, charge, discount, or compensating balance, that a creditor requires, or that a creditor, subsidiary, or parent company of the creditor, or subsidiary of the creditor's parent company, receives directly or indirectly from a person other than the obligor in connection with a credit card transaction under a lender credit card agreement between the obligor and the creditor. The term does not include consideration received by a creditor from the obligor in connection with the credit card transaction.

(12) "Money judgment" means a judgment for money. For purposes of this subtitle, the term includes legal interest or contract interest, if any, that is payable to a judgment creditor under a judgment.

(13) "Obligor" means a person to whom money is loaned or credit is otherwise extended. The term does not include:

(A) a judgment debtor; or

(B) a surety, guarantor, or similar person.

(14) "Open-end account":

(A) means an account under a written contract between a creditor and an obligor in connection with which:

(i) the creditor reasonably contemplates repeated transactions and the obligor is authorized to make purchases or borrow money;

(ii) interest or time price differential may be charged from time to time on an outstanding unpaid balance; and

(iii) the amount of credit that may be extended during the term of the account is generally made available to the extent that any outstanding balance is repaid; and

(B) includes an account under an agreement described by Section 342.455 or Chapter 345 or 346.

(15) "Prepayment penalty" means consideration agreed on and contracted for a discharge of a loan, other than a loan governed by Chapter 306, before its maturity or a regularly scheduled date of payment, as a result of an obligor's election to pay all of the principal amount before its stated maturity or a regularly scheduled date of payment.

(16) "Time price differential" means an amount, however denominated or expressed, that is:

(A) added to the price at which a seller offers to sell services or property to a purchaser for cash payable at the time of sale; and

(B) paid or payable to the seller by the purchaser for the privilege of paying the offered sales price after the time of sale.

(17) "Usurious interest" means interest that exceeds the applicable maximum amount allowed by law.

(b) The Finance Commission of Texas by rule may adopt other definitions to accomplish the purposes of this title.

See also *O'Connor's Texas COA*, "Usury," ch. 31, p. 1057.

CHAPTER 302. INTEREST RATES

SUBCHAPTER A. USURIOUS INTEREST

FIN §302.002. ACCRUAL OF INTEREST WHEN NO RATE SPECIFIED

If a creditor has not agreed with an obligor to charge the obligor any interest, the creditor may charge and receive from the obligor legal interest at the rate of six percent a year on the principal amount of the credit extended beginning on the 30th day after the date on which the amount is due. If an obligor has agreed to pay to a creditor any compensation that constitutes interest, the obligor is considered to have agreed on the rate produced by the amount of that interest, regardless of whether that rate is stated in the agreement.

CHAPTER 304. JUDGMENT INTEREST

SUBCHAPTER A. GENERAL PROVISIONS

FIN §304.001. INTEREST RATE REQUIRED IN JUDGMENT

A money judgment of a court in this state must specify the postjudgment interest rate applicable to that judgment.

See also *O'Connor's Texas COA*, "Postjudgment Interest," ch. 43, §3, p. 1387; *O'Connor's Texas Rules*, "Postjudgment interest," ch. 9-C, §4.6, p. 868.

FIN §304.002. JUDGMENT INTEREST RATE: INTEREST RATE OR TIME PRICE DIFFERENTIAL IN CONTRACT

A money judgment of a court of this state on a contract that provides for interest or time price differential earns postjudgment interest at a rate equal to the lesser of:

(1) the rate specified in the contract, which may be a variable rate; or

(2) 18 percent a year.

See also *O'Connor's Texas COA*, "Computing postjudgment interest," ch. 43, §3.3, p. 1387; *O'Connor's Texas Rules*, "Calculating postjudgment interest," ch. 9-C, §4.6.2, p. 868.

FIN §304.003. JUDGMENT INTEREST RATE: INTEREST RATE OR TIME PRICE DIFFERENTIAL NOT IN CONTRACT

(a) A money judgment of a court of this state to which Section 304.002 does not apply, including court costs awarded in the judgment and prejudgment interest, if any, earns postjudgment interest at the rate determined under this section.

(b) On the 15th day of each month, the consumer credit commissioner shall determine the postjudgment

FIN §301.002

interest rate to be applied to a money judgment rendered during the succeeding calendar month.

(c) The postjudgment interest rate is:

(1) the prime rate as published by the Board of Governors of the Federal Reserve System on the date of computation;

(2) five percent a year if the prime rate as published by the Board of Governors of the Federal Reserve System described by Subdivision (1) is less than five percent; or

(3) 15 percent a year if the prime rate as published by the Board of Governors of the Federal Reserve System described by Subdivision (1) is more than 15 percent.

See also *O'Connor's Texas Appeals*, "Calculation of interest," ch. 4-B, §3.1.1(2), p. 178; *O'Connor's Texas COA*, "Computing postjudgment interest," ch. 43, §3.3, p. 1387; *O'Connor's Texas Rules*, "Calculating postjudgment interest," ch. 9-C, §4.6.2, p. 868.

FIN §304.004. PUBLICATION OF JUDGMENT INTEREST RATE

The consumer credit commissioner shall send to the secretary of state the postjudgment interest rate for publication, and the secretary shall publish the rate in the Texas Register.

FIN §304.005. ACCRUAL OF JUDGMENT INTEREST

(a) Except as provided by Subsection (b), postjudgment interest on a money judgment of a court in this state accrues during the period beginning on the date the judgment is rendered and ending on the date the judgment is satisfied.

(b) If a case is appealed and a motion for extension of time to file a brief is granted for a party who was a claimant at trial, interest does not accrue for the period of extension.

See also *O'Connor's Texas COA*, "Computing postjudgment interest," ch. 43, §3.3, p. 1387; *O'Connor's Texas Rules*, "Calculating postjudgment interest," ch. 9-C, §4.6.2, p. 868.

FIN §304.006. COMPOUNDING OF JUDGMENT INTEREST

Postjudgment interest on a judgment of a court in this state compounds annually.

See also *O'Connor's Texas COA*, "Computing postjudgment interest," ch. 43, §3.3, p. 1387; *O'Connor's Texas Rules*, "Calculating postjudgment interest," ch. 9-C, §4.6.2, p. 868.

FIN §304.007. JUDICIAL NOTICE OF JUDGMENT INTEREST RATE

A court of this state shall take judicial notice of a published postjudgment interest rate.

Sections 304.008-304.100 reserved for expansion

SUBCHAPTER B. PREJUDGMENT INTEREST IN WRONGFUL DEATH, PERSONAL INJURY, OR PROPERTY DAMAGE CASE

FIN §304.101. APPLICABILITY OF SUBCHAPTER

This subchapter applies only to a wrongful death, personal injury, or property damage case of a court of this state.

FIN §304.102. PREJUDGMENT INTEREST REQUIRED IN CERTAIN CASES

A judgment in a wrongful death, personal injury, or property damage case earns prejudgment interest.

See also *O'Connor's Texas COA*, "Prejudgment Interest," ch. 43, §2, p. 1383; *O'Connor's Texas Rules*, "Prejudgment interest," ch. 9-C, §4.5, p. 866.

FIN §304.103. PREJUDGMENT INTEREST RATE FOR WRONGFUL DEATH, PERSONAL INJURY, OR PROPERTY DAMAGE CASE

The prejudgment interest rate is equal to the postjudgment interest rate applicable at the time of judgment.

See also *O'Connor's Texas COA*, "Prejudgment Interest," ch. 43, §2, p. 1383; *O'Connor's Texas Rules*, "Prejudgment interest," ch. 9-C, §4.5, p. 866.

FIN §304.104. ACCRUAL OF PREJUDGMENT INTEREST

Except as provided by Section 304.105 or 304.108, prejudgment interest accrues on the amount of a judgment during the period beginning on the earlier of the 180th day after the date the defendant receives written notice of a claim or the date the suit is filed and ending on the day preceding the date judgment is rendered. Prejudgment interest is computed as simple interest and does not compound.

See also *O'Connor's Texas COA*, "Computing prejudgment interest," ch. 43, §2.3, p. 1385; *O'Connor's Texas Rules*, "Calculating prejudgment interest," ch. 9-C, §4.5.2, p. 866.

FIN §304.1045. FUTURE DAMAGES

Prejudgment interest may not be assessed or recovered on an award of future damages.

See also *O'Connor's Texas COA*, "Future damages," ch. 43, §2.1.2(1)(b), p. 1384; *O'Connor's Texas Rules*, "Prejudgment interest not permitted," ch. 9-C, §4.5.3, p. 867.

FIN §304.105. EFFECT OF SETTLEMENT OFFER ON ACCRUAL OF PREJUDGMENT INTEREST

(a) If judgment for a claimant is equal to or less than the amount of a settlement offer of the defendant, prejudgment interest does not accrue on the amount of the judgment during the period that the offer may be accepted.

(b) If judgment for a claimant is more than the amount of a settlement offer of the defendant, prejudgment interest does not accrue on the amount of the settlement offer during the period that the offer may be accepted.

See also *O'Connor's Texas COA*, "Settlement offer," ch. 43, §2.3.3(4)(b), p. 1387.

FIN §304.106. SETTLEMENT OFFER REQUIREMENTS TO PREVENT PREJUDGMENT INTEREST ACCRUAL

To prevent the accrual of prejudgment interest under this subchapter, a settlement offer must be in writing and delivered to the claimant or the claimant's attorney or representative.

FIN §304.107. VALUE OF SETTLEMENT OFFER FOR COMPUTING PREJUDGMENT INTEREST

If a settlement offer does not provide for cash payment at the time of settlement, the amount of the settlement offer for the purpose of computing prejudgment interest is the cost or fair market value of the settlement offer at the time it is made.

FIN §304.108. REPEALED

Sections 304.109-304.200 reserved for expansion

SUBCHAPTER C. OTHER PREJUDGMENT INTEREST PROVISIONS

FIN §304.201. PREJUDGMENT INTEREST RATE FOR CONDEMNATION CASE

The prejudgment interest rate in a condemnation case is equal to the postjudgment interest rate at the time of judgment and is computed as simple interest.

See also *O'Connor's Texas COA*, "Statutory interest," ch. 43, §2.2.1(1), p. 1385.

Sections 304.202-304.300 reserved for expansion

SUBCHAPTER D. EXCEPTIONS TO APPLICATION OF CHAPTER

FIN §304.301. EXCEPTION FOR DELINQUENT TAXES

This chapter does not apply to a judgment:

(1) in favor of a taxing unit in a delinquent tax suit under Subchapter C, Chapter 33, Tax Code; or

(2) that earns interest at a rate set by Title 2, Tax Code.

FIN §304.302. EXCEPTION FOR DELINQUENT CHILD SUPPORT

This chapter does not apply to interest that accrues on an amount of unpaid child support under Section 157.265, Family Code.

Government Code

Selected Provisions
Table of Contents

Title 4. Executive Branch

Title 10. General Government

Subtitle F. State & Local Contracts & Fund Management

Chapter 2253. Public Work Performance & Payment Bonds

Subchapter A. General Provisions

Subchapter B. General Requirements; Liability

Subchapter C. Notice Requirements

Subchapter D. Claims on Bonds; Enforcement

TITLE 4. EXECUTIVE BRANCH

SUBTITLE D. HISTORY, CULTURE, & EDUCATION

CHAPTER 442. TEXAS HISTORICAL COMMISSION

SUBCHAPTER A. GENERAL PROVISIONS

A GOVT §442.002. COMMISSION; MEMBERS; SUNSET ACT

(a) The Texas Historical Commission is an agency of the state.

(b) The commission is composed of 15 [~~nine~~] members appointed by the governor with the advice and consent of the senate. One member must have expertise in archeology, preferably as a professional archeologist, one must have expertise in history, preferably as a professional historian, and one must have expertise in architecture, preferably as a professional architect who is licensed in this state and has expertise in historic preservation and architectural history. The remaining members must represent the general public. A person is [~~may~~] not eligible for appointment as [~~be~~] a member of the commission if the person or the person's spouse:

(1) owns or controls, directly or indirectly, more than a 10 percent interest in a business entity or other organization regulated by the commission or receiving money other than grant money from the commission;

(2) uses or receives a substantial amount of tangible goods, services, or money from the commission, other than compensation or reimbursement authorized by law for commission membership, attendance, or expenses; or

(3) is employed by or participates in the management of a business entity or other organization regulated by or receiving money other than grant money from the commission.

(c) Members serve for staggered six-year terms, with the terms of one-third of the members expiring February 1 of each odd-numbered year.

(d) Any vacancy occurring on the commission shall be filled for the unexpired term.

(e) A member of the commission must be a citizen of this state who has demonstrated an interest in the preservation of the state's historical or archeological heritage. In making appointments to the commission, the governor shall seek to have each geographical section of the state represented as nearly as possible.

(f) A person may not serve as a member of the commission or act as the general counsel to the commission if the person is required to register as a lobbyist under Chapter 305 because of the person's activities for compensation on behalf of a profession related to the operation of the commission.

(g) The commission shall hold at least one regular meeting in each calendar quarter of each year. The commission may hold other meetings at times and places scheduled by it in formal session or called by the chairman of the commission.

(h) The governor shall designate a member of the commission as the presiding officer of the commission to serve in that capacity at the pleasure of the governor. At its first meeting in each odd-numbered year, the commission shall select from its membership an assistant presiding officer and a secretary.

(i) A member of the commission serves without pay but shall be reimbursed for actual expenses incurred in attending a meeting of the commission.

(j) The commission is subject to the open meetings law, Chapter 551, and the administrative procedure law, Chapter 2001. The commission shall develop and implement policies that provide the public with a reasonable opportunity to appear before the commission and to speak on any issue under the jurisdiction of the commission.

(k) The Texas Historical Commission is subject to Chapter 325 (Texas Sunset Act). Unless continued in existence as provided by that chapter, the commission is abolished and this chapter expires September 1, 2019.

(*l*) Appointments to the commission shall be made without regard to the race, color, disability, sex, religion, age, or national origin of the appointees.

2017 Legislation: Amended by S.B. 763, §1, 85th Leg., eff. Sept. 1, 2017.

GOVT §442.005. GENERAL POWERS & DUTIES OF COMMISSION

(a) The commission shall furnish leadership, coordination, and services to county historical commissions, historical societies, and the organizations, agencies, institutions, museums, and individuals of this state interested in the preservation of archeological or historical heritage and shall act as a clearinghouse and information center for that work in this state.

(b) The commission is responsible for the administration of the Antiquities Code of Texas, Chapter 191, Natural Resources Code, and shall strive to establish ef-

fective working relationships among individuals primarily interested in history, architecture, and archeology.

(c) The commission shall furnish professional consultant services to museums and to agencies, individuals, and organizations interested in the preservation and restoration of archeological or historic structures, sites, or landmarks.

(d) Repealed by Acts 2011, 82nd Leg., ch. 1083, §25(41), eff. June 17, 2011.

(e) The commission shall administer the federal National Historic Preservation Act of 1966 and may prepare, maintain, and keep up to date a statewide comprehensive historic preservation plan.

(f) The commission by rule may establish a reasonable fee to recover its costs arising from review of a rehabilitation project on an income-producing property included in the National Register of Historic Places. Any fee established is payable by the applicant for the rehabilitation project.

(g) The commission may apply to any appropriate agency or officer of the United States for participation in any federal program pertaining to historic preservation.

(h) The commission may certify to another state agency the worthiness of preservation of any historic district, site, structure, or object significant in Texas or American history, architecture, archeology, or culture.

(i) The commission may provide matching grants to assist the preservation of a historic structure significant in Texas or American history, architecture, archeology, or culture.

(j) The commission shall use its facilities and leadership to stimulate the development and protection of archeological or historical resources in every locality of this state, emphasizing responsibility and privilege of local effort except in a case in which the project or problem clearly demands a broader approach.

(k) The commission may provide matching grants to preserve collections of small history museums in this state if the collections are significant in Texas or American history, architecture, archeology, or culture.

(*l*) The commission may conduct educational programs, seminars, and workshops throughout this state covering any phase of historic preservation.

(m) The commission shall continue cooperative studies and surveys of the various aspects of historical heritage.

(n) Not later than December 1 before each regular session of the legislature, the commission shall make a report of its activities to the governor and to the legislature.

(o) The commission may enter into contracts with other state agencies or institutions, qualified private institutions, and other persons, including for-profit corporations, to carry out the purposes of this chapter. A contract with a for-profit corporation under this chapter may not permit any property preserved, maintained, or administered by the commission under this chapter to display any corporate name, logo, or product other than a discreet plaque or similar acknowledgment that does not detract from the property's historic purpose.

(p) The commission may accept a gift, grant, devise, or bequest of money, securities, services, or property to carry out any purpose of this chapter, including funds raised or services provided by a volunteer or volunteer group to promote the work of the commission. The commission may participate in the establishment and operation of an affiliated nonprofit organization whose purpose is to raise funds for or provide services or other benefits to the commission.

(q) The commission may adopt rules as it considers proper for the effective administration of this chapter.

(r) The commission may establish advisory committees to advise the commission on archeological and historical matters, including an advisory committee to consider matters relating to Chapter 191, Natural Resources Code.

(s) The commission may promote the appreciation of historic sites, structures, or objects in the state through a program designed to develop tourism in the state.

(t) The commission shall promote heritage tourism by assisting persons, including local governments, organizations, and individuals, in the preservation, enhancement, and promotion of heritage and cultural attractions in this state. The program must include efforts to:

(1) raise the standards of heritage and cultural attractions around this state;

(2) foster heritage preservation and education;

(3) encourage regional cooperation and promotion of heritage and cultural attractions; and

(4) foster effective local tourism leadership and organizational skills.

(u) The commission may:

(1) maintain the historic character of the sites and structures entrusted to its care;

(2) use its resources to develop the historic sites through promotional and educational activities, including the purchase of items for resale or donation and the purchase of plants and landscaping services; and

(3) accept advertisements in selected agency publications, including print and electronic publications, at a rate that offsets development and production costs.

(v) The commission may accept a gift of real property, whether of historical value or not. When the gift is received, the commission may:

(1) arrange for the preservation, maintenance, and public exhibition of the property; or

(2) at the commission's discretion, sell the property at fair market value and use the proceeds to carry out any purpose of this chapter.

GOVT §442.0055. AFFILIATED NONPROFIT ORGANIZATION; RULES; GUIDELINES

(a) The commission shall adopt rules governing the relationship between the commission and an affiliated nonprofit organization formed under Section 442.005(p), including rules that, at a minimum:

(1) define the extent to which commission employees with regulatory responsibilities, including the executive director, may participate in activities that raise funds for an affiliated nonprofit organization, which may not include the direct solicitation of funds; and

(2) define the relationship between commission employees and an affiliated nonprofit organization.

(b) The commission shall establish guidelines for identifying and defining the administrative and financial support the commission may provide for an affiliated nonprofit organization formed under Section 442.005(p).

GOVT §442.007. STATE ARCHEOLOGICAL PROGRAM

(a) The commission, through the state archeologist, shall direct the state archeological program.

(b) The program must include:

(1) a continuing inventory of nonrenewable archeological resources;

(2) evaluation of known sites through testing and excavation;

(3) maintenance of extensive field and laboratory data, including data on collections of antiquities;

(4) consultation with state agencies and organizations and local groups concerning archeological and historical problems; and

(5) publication of the results of the program through various sources, including a regular series of reports.

(c) The commission may enter into contracts or cooperative agreements with the federal government, other state agencies, state or private museums or educational institutions, or qualified persons, including for-profit corporations, for prehistoric or historic archeological investigations, surveys, excavations, or restorations in this state.

(d) The state archeologist has general jurisdiction and supervision over archeological work, reports, surveys, excavations, and archeological programs of the commission and of cooperating state agencies.

(e) The duties of the state archeologist include:

(1) maintaining an inventory of significant historic or prehistoric sites of archeological or historic interest;

(2) providing public information and education in the fields of archeology and history;

(3) conducting surveys and excavations with respect to significant archeological or historic sites in this state;

(4) preparing reports and publications concerning the work of the office of the state archeologist;

(5) doing cooperative and contract work in prehistoric and historic archeology with other state agencies, the federal government, state or private institutions, or individuals;

(6) maintaining and determining the repository of catalogued collections of artifacts and other materials of archeological or historic interest; and

(7) preserving the archeological and historical heritage of this state.

(f) The state archeologist shall withhold from disclosure to the public information relating to the location or character of archeological or historic resources if the state archeologist determines that the disclosure of the information may create a substantial risk of harm, theft, or destruction to the resources or to the area or place where the resources are located.

GOVT §442.016. LIABILITY FOR ADVERSELY AFFECTING HISTORIC STRUCTURE OR PROPERTY

(a) In this section, "historic structure or property" means a historic structure or a structure or property that is designated as historic by a political subdivision of the state, the state, or the federal government.

(b) A person is liable to the commission for damages if the person:

(1) demolishes, causes to be demolished, or otherwise adversely affects the structural, physical, or visual integrity of a historic structure or property that is not located in a municipality that has a demolition permit and a building permit procedure; and

(2) does not obtain written permission from the commission before beginning to demolish, cause the demolition of, or otherwise adversely affect the structural, physical, or visual integrity of the structure or property.

(c) If the structural, physical, or visual integrity of the structure or property is adversely affected to the extent that it is not feasible to restore the structural, physical, or visual integrity substantially to its former level, the damages are equal to the cost of constructing, using as many of the original materials as possible, a new structure or property that is a reasonable facsimile of the historic structure or property and the cost of attorney's, architect's, and appraiser's fees and other costs related to the enforcement of this section. If it is feasible to restore the structural, physical, or visual integrity of the structure or property substantially to its former level, the damages are equal to the cost of the restoration, using as many of the original materials as possible, and the cost of attorney's, architect's, and appraiser's fees and other costs related to the enforcement of this section.

(d) Instead of accepting monetary damages, the commission may permit the liable person to construct, using as many of the original materials as possible, a structure or property that is a reasonable facsimile of the demolished historic structure or property or to restore, using as many of the original materials as possible, the historic structure or property and to pay the cost of attorney's, architect's, and appraiser's fees and other costs related to the enforcement of this section.

(e) Damages recovered under this section shall be deposited in the Texas preservation trust fund account.

(f) The construction of a facsimile structure or property under Subsection (d) must be undertaken at the location designated by the commission, which may be the same location as that of the demolished historic structure or property.

(g) The commission may make contracts and adopt rules as necessary to carry out this section.

(h) The commission shall file in the real property records of the county clerk's office in each county in which a historic structure or property that is included on the National Register of Historic Places or that is designated as a Recorded Texas Historic Landmark is located a verified written instrument listing each structure or property located in that county by:

(1) the street address, if available in the commission files;

(2) the legal description of the real property on which the structure or property is located; and

(3) the name of the owner of the real property, if available in the commission files.

(i) Subsections (a) through (g) of this section apply only to a historic structure or property on or after the date the instrument has been filed under Subsection (h) and indexed.

GOVT §442.017. IDENTIFICATION & PRESERVATION OF ABANDONED CEMETERIES

(a) The commission should establish a program to identify and preserve abandoned cemeteries across the state.

(b) The commission is encouraged to use volunteers to the maximum extent possible to implement the program and to model the program to the extent appropriate on the "Adopt-A-Beach" program conducted by the General Land Office.

(c) The commission may accept gifts, grants, and in-kind donations from public and private entities for the implementation of the program. The legislature may appropriate money to the commission to implement the program.

(d) The commission may adopt rules reasonably necessary to implement the program.

GOVT §442.018. IDENTIFICATION & PRESERVATION OF TEXAS UNDERGROUND RAILROAD HISTORICAL SITES

(a) The commission should establish a program to identify and preserve Texas Underground Railroad Historical Sites.

(b) The commission is encouraged to use volunteers to the maximum extent possible to implement the program and to model the program to the extent appropriate on the "Adopt-A-Beach" program conducted by the General Land Office.

(c) The commission may accept gifts, grants, and in-kind donations from public and private entities for the implementation of the program. The legislature may appropriate money to the commission to implement the program.

(d) The commission may adopt rules reasonably necessary to implement the program.

TITLE 10. GENERAL GOVERNMENT

SUBTITLE A. ADMINISTRATIVE PROCEDURE & PRACTICE

CHAPTER 2007. GOVERNMENTAL ACTION AFFECTING PRIVATE PROPERTY RIGHTS

SUBCHAPTER A. GENERAL PROVISIONS

GOVT §2007.001. SHORT TITLE

This chapter may be cited as the Private Real Property Rights Preservation Act.

GOVT §2007.002. DEFINITIONS

In this chapter:

(1) "Governmental entity" means:

(A) a board, commission, council, department, or other agency in the executive branch of state government that is created by constitution or statute, including an institution of higher education as defined by Section 61.003, Education Code; or

(B) a political subdivision of this state.

(2) "Owner" means a person with legal or equitable title to affected private real property at the time a taking occurs.

(3) "Market value" means the price a willing buyer would pay a willing seller after considering all factors in the marketplace that influence the price of private real property.

(4) "Private real property" means an interest in real property recognized by common law, including a groundwater or surface water right of any kind, that is not owned by the federal government, this state, or a political subdivision of this state.

(5) "Taking" means:

(A) a governmental action that affects private real property, in whole or in part or temporarily or permanently, in a manner that requires the governmental entity to compensate the private real property owner as provided by the Fifth and Fourteenth Amendments to the United States Constitution or Section 17 or 19, Article I, Texas Constitution; or

(B) a governmental action that:

(i) affects an owner's private real property that is the subject of the governmental action, in whole or in part or temporarily or permanently, in a manner that restricts or limits the owner's right to the property that would otherwise exist in the absence of the governmental action; and

(ii) is the producing cause of a reduction of at least 25 percent in the market value of the affected private real property, determined by comparing the market value of the property as if the governmental action is not in effect and the market value of the property determined as if the governmental action is in effect.

GOVT §2007.003. APPLICABILITY

(a) This chapter applies only to the following governmental actions:

(1) the adoption or issuance of an ordinance, rule, regulatory requirement, resolution, policy, guideline, or similar measure;

(2) an action that imposes a physical invasion or requires a dedication or exaction of private real property;

(3) an action by a municipality that has effect in the extraterritorial jurisdiction of the municipality, excluding annexation, and that enacts or enforces an ordinance, rule, regulation, or plan that does not impose identical requirements or restrictions in the entire extraterritorial jurisdiction of the municipality; and

(4) enforcement of a governmental action listed in Subdivisions (1) through (3), whether the enforcement of the governmental action is accomplished through the use of permitting, citations, orders, judicial or quasi-judicial proceedings, or other similar means.

(b) This chapter does not apply to the following governmental actions:

(1) an action by a municipality except as provided by Subsection (a)(3);

(2) a lawful forfeiture or seizure of contraband as defined by Article 59.01, Code of Criminal Procedure;

(3) a lawful seizure of property as evidence of a crime or violation of law;

(4) an action, including an action of a political subdivision, that is reasonably taken to fulfill an obligation mandated by federal law or an action of a political subdivision that is reasonably taken to fulfill an obligation mandated by state law;

(5) the discontinuance or modification of a program or regulation that provides a unilateral expectation that does not rise to the level of a recognized interest in private real property;

(6) an action taken to prohibit or restrict a condition or use of private real property if the governmental entity proves that the condition or use constitutes a public or private nuisance as defined by background principles of nuisance and property law of this state;

(7) an action taken out of a reasonable good faith belief that the action is necessary to prevent a grave and immediate threat to life or property;

(8) a formal exercise of the power of eminent domain;

(9) an action taken under a state mandate to prevent waste of oil and gas, protect correlative rights of owners of interests in oil or gas, or prevent pollution related to oil and gas activities;

(10) a rule or proclamation adopted for the purpose of regulating water safety, hunting, fishing, or control of nonindigenous or exotic aquatic resources;

(11) an action taken by a political subdivision:

(A) to regulate construction in an area designated under law as a floodplain;

(B) to regulate on-site sewage facilities;

(C) under the political subdivisions's statutory authority to prevent waste or protect rights of owners of interest in groundwater; or

(D) to prevent subsidence;

(12) the appraisal of property for purposes of ad valorem taxation;

(13) an action that:

(A) is taken in response to a real and substantial threat to public health and safety;

(B) is designed to significantly advance the health and safety purpose; and

(C) does not impose a greater burden than is necessary to achieve the health and safety purpose; or

(14) an action or rulemaking undertaken by the Public Utility Commission of Texas to order or require the location or placement of telecommunications equipment owned by another party on the premises of a certificated local exchange company.

(c) Sections 2007.021 and 2007.022 do not apply to the enforcement or implementation of a statute, ordinance, order, rule, regulation, requirement, resolution, policy, guideline, or similar measure that was in effect September 1, 1995, and that prevents the pollution of a reservoir or an aquifer designated as a sole source aquifer under the federal Safe Drinking Water Act (42 U.S.C. Section 300h-3(e)).

(d) This chapter applies to a governmental action taken by a county only if the action is taken on or after September 1, 1997.

(e) This chapter does not apply to the enforcement or implementation of Subchapter B, Chapter 61, Natural Resources Code, as it existed on September 1, 1995, or to the enforcement or implementation of any rule or similar measure that was adopted under that subchapter and was in existence on September 1, 1995.

GOVT §2007.004. WAIVER OF GOVERNMENTAL IMMUNITY; PERMISSION TO SUE

(a) Sovereign immunity to suit and liability is waived and abolished to the extent of liability created by this chapter.

(b) This section does not authorize a person to execute a judgment against property of the state or a governmental entity.

GOVT §2007.005. ALTERNATIVE DISPUTE RESOLUTION

Chapter 154, Civil Practice and Remedies Code, applies to a suit filed under this chapter.

GOVT §2007.006. CUMULATIVE REMEDIES

(a) The provisions of this chapter are not exclusive. The remedies provided by this chapter are in addition to other procedures or remedies provided by law.

(b) A person may not recover under this chapter and also recover under another law or in an action at common law for the same economic loss.

Sections 2007.007-2007.020 reserved for expansion

SUBCHAPTER B. ACTION TO DETERMINE TAKING

GOVT §2007.021. SUIT AGAINST POLITICAL SUBDIVISION

(a) A private real property owner may bring suit under this subchapter to determine whether the gov-

ernmental action of a political subdivision results in a taking under this chapter. A suit under this subchapter must be filed in a district court in the county in which the private real property owner's affected property is located. If the affected private real property is located in more than one county, the private real property owner may file suit in any county in which the affected property is located.

(b) A suit under this subchapter must be filed not later than the 180th day after the date the private real property owner knew or should have known that the governmental action restricted or limited the owner's right in the private real property.

GOVT §2007.022. ADMINISTRATIVE PROCEEDING AGAINST STATE AGENCY

(a) A private real property owner may file a contested case with a state agency to determine whether a governmental action of the state agency results in a taking under this chapter.

(b) A contested case must be filed with the agency not later than the 180th day after the date the private real property owner knew or should have known that the governmental action restricted or limited the owner's right in the private real property.

(c) A contested case filed under this section is subject to Chapter 2001 except to the extent of a conflict with this subchapter.

GOVT §2007.023. ENTITLEMENT TO INVALIDATION OF GOVERNMENTAL ACTION

(a) Whether a governmental action results in a taking is a question of fact.

(b) If the trier of fact in a suit or contested case filed under this subchapter finds that the governmental action is a taking under this chapter, the private real property owner is only entitled to, and the governmental entity is only liable for, invalidation of the governmental action or the part of the governmental action resulting in the taking.

See also *O'Connor's Texas COA*, "Invalidation of government takings," ch. 22-A, §7.2, p. 765.

GOVT §2007.024. JUDGMENT OR FINAL DECISION OR ORDER

(a) The court's judgment in favor of a private real property owner under Section 2007.021 or a final decision or order issued under Section 2007.022 that determines that a taking has occurred shall order the governmental entity to rescind the governmental action, or the part of the governmental action resulting in the taking, as applied to the private real property owner not later than the 30th day after the date the judgment is rendered or the decision or order is issued.

(b) The judgment or final decision or order shall include a fact finding that determines the monetary damages suffered by the private real property owner as a result of the taking. The amount of damages is determined from the date of the taking.

(c) A governmental entity may elect to pay the damages as compensation to the private real property owner who prevails in a suit or contested case filed under this subchapter. Sovereign immunity to liability is waived to the extent the governmental entity elects to pay compensation under this subsection.

(d) If a governmental entity elects to pay compensation to the private real property owner:

(1) the court that rendered the judgment in the suit or the state agency that issued the final order or decision in the case shall withdraw the part of the judgment or final decision or order rescinding the governmental action; and

(2) the governmental entity shall pay to the owner the damages as determined in the judgment or final order not later than the 30th day after the date the judgment is rendered or the final decision or order is issued.

(e) If the governmental entity does not pay compensation to the private real property owner as provided by Subsection (d), the court or the state agency shall reinstate the part of the judgment or final decision or order previously withdrawn.

(f) A state agency that elects to pay compensation to the private real property owner shall pay the compensation from funds appropriated to the agency.

GOVT §2007.025. APPEAL

(a) A person aggrieved by a judgment rendered in a suit filed under Section 2007.021 may appeal as provided by law.

(b) A person who has exhausted all administrative remedies available within the state agency and is aggrieved by a final decision or order in a contested case filed under Section 2007.022 is entitled to judicial review under Chapter 2001. Review by a court under this subsection is by trial de novo.

(c) If a private real property owner prevails in a suit or contested case filed under this subchapter and the governmental entity appeals, the court or the state agency shall enjoin the governmental entity from invoking the governmental action or the part of the governmental action resulting in the taking, pending the appeal of the suit or contested case.

GOVT §2007.026. FEES & COSTS

(a) The court or the state agency shall award a private real property owner who prevails in a suit or contested case filed under this subchapter reasonable and necessary attorney's fees and court costs.

(b) The court or the state agency shall award a governmental entity that prevails in a suit or contested case filed under this subchapter reasonable and necessary attorney's fees and court costs.

Sections 2007.027-2007.040 reserved for expansion

SUBCHAPTER C. REQUIREMENTS FOR PROPOSED GOVERNMENTAL ACTION

GOVT §2007.041. GUIDELINES

(a) The attorney general shall prepare guidelines to assist governmental entities in identifying and evaluating those governmental actions described in Section 2007.003(a)(1) through (3) that may result in a taking.

(b) The attorney general shall file the guidelines with the secretary of state for publication in the Texas Register in the manner prescribed by Chapter 2002.

(c) The attorney general shall review the guidelines at least annually and revise the guidelines as necessary to ensure consistency with the actions of the legislature and the decisions of the United States Supreme Court and the supreme court of this state.

(d) A person may make comments or suggestions or provide information to the attorney general concerning the guidelines. The attorney general shall consider the comments, suggestions, and information in the annual review process required by this section.

(e) Material provided to the attorney general under Subsection (d) is public information.

GOVT §2007.042. PUBLIC NOTICE

(a) A political subdivision that proposes to engage in a governmental action described in Section 2007.003(a)(1) through (3) that may result in a taking shall provide at least 30 days' notice of its intent to engage in the proposed action by providing a reasonably specific description of the proposed action in a notice published in a newspaper of general circulation published in the county in which affected private real property is located. If a newspaper of general circulation is not published in that county, the political subdivision shall publish a notice in a newspaper of general circulation located in a county adjacent to the county in which affected private real property is located. The political subdivision shall, at a minimum, include in the notice a reasonably specific summary of the takings impact assessment that was prepared as required by this subchapter and the name of the official of the political subdivision from whom a copy of the full assessment may be obtained.

(b) A state agency that proposes to engage in a governmental action described in Section 2007.003(a)(1) or (2) that may result in a taking shall:

(1) provide notice in the manner prescribed by Section 2001.023; and

(2) file with the secretary of state for publication in the Texas Register in the manner prescribed by Chapter 2002 a reasonably specific summary of the takings impact assessment that was prepared by the agency as required by this subchapter.

GOVT §2007.043. TAKINGS IMPACT ASSESSMENT

(a) A governmental entity shall prepare a written takings impact assessment of a proposed governmental action described in Section 2007.003(a)(1) through (3) that complies with the evaluation guidelines developed by the attorney general under Section 2007.041 before the governmental entity provides the public notice required under Section 2007.042.

(b) The takings impact assessment must:

(1) describe the specific purpose of the proposed action and identify:

(A) whether and how the proposed action substantially advances its stated purpose; and

(B) the burdens imposed on private real property and the benefits to society resulting from the proposed use of private real property;

(2) determine whether engaging in the proposed governmental action will constitute a taking; and

(3) describe reasonable alternative actions that could accomplish the specified purpose and compare, evaluate, and explain:

GOVT §2007.025

(A) how an alternative action would further the specified purpose; and

(B) whether an alternative action would constitute a taking.

(c) A takings impact assessment prepared under this section is public information.

GOVT §2007.044. SUIT TO INVALIDATE GOVERNMENTAL ACTION

(a) A governmental action requiring a takings impact assessment is void if an assessment is not prepared. A private real property owner affected by a governmental action taken without the preparation of a takings impact assessment as required by this subchapter may bring suit for a declaration of the invalidity of the governmental action.

(b) A suit under this section must be filed in a district court in the county in which the private real property owner's affected property is located. If the affected property is located in more than one county, the private real property owner may file suit in any county in which the affected property is located.

(c) The court shall award a private real property owner who prevails in a suit under this section reasonable and necessary attorney's fees and court costs.

GOVT §2007.045. UPDATING OF CERTAIN ASSESSMENTS REQUIRED

A state agency that proposes to adopt a governmental action described in Section 2007.003(a)(1) or (2) that may result in a taking as indicated by the takings impact assessment shall update the assessment if the action is not adopted before the 180th day after the date the notice is given as required by Section 2001.023.

SUBTITLE D. STATE PURCHASING & GENERAL SERVICES

CHAPTER 2165. STATE BUILDINGS, GROUNDS, & PROPERTY

SUBCHAPTER D. LEASE OF PUBLIC GROUNDS

GOVT §2165.151. AUTHORITY TO LEASE PUBLIC GROUNDS

All public grounds belonging to the state under the commission's charge and control may be leased for agricultural or commercial purposes.

GOVT §2165.152. LEASE OF BUILDING SPACE NOT AFFECTED

This subchapter does not apply to space in a building that the commission may lease to a private tenant under Subchapter E.

GOVT §2165.153. ADVERTISEMENT OF LEASE PROPOSALS

The commission shall advertise a lease proposal under this subchapter once a week for four consecutive weeks in at least two newspapers, one of which is published in the municipality in which the property is located or in the daily paper nearest to the property, and the other of which has statewide circulation.

GOVT §2165.155. APPROVAL BY ATTORNEY GENERAL

Each lease under this subchapter is subject to the approval of the attorney general regarding both substance and form.

GOVT §2165.156. DEPOSIT OF LEASE PROCEEDS

Money received from a lease under this subchapter, minus the amount spent for advertising and leasing expenses, shall be deposited:

(1) in the state treasury to the credit of the general revenue fund; or

(2) if the land leased belongs to an eleemosynary institution for which there is an appropriate special fund, to the credit of the institution in the appropriate special fund.

GOVT §2165.157. FORMS, RULES, & CONTRACTS

The commission shall adopt proper forms, rules, and contracts that will in its best judgment protect the interest of the state.

GOVT §2165.158. REJECTION OF BIDS

The commission may reject any and all bids under this subchapter.

SUBCHAPTER E. LEASE OF SPACE IN STATE-OWNED BUILDINGS TO PRIVATE TENANTS

GOVT §2165.201. PURPOSE OF SUBCHAPTER

The purpose of this subchapter is to:

(1) encourage the most efficient use of valuable space in state office buildings and parking garages;

GOVT §2165.201

(2) serve the needs of employees and visitors in the buildings;

(3) provide child care services for state employees; and

(4) enhance the social, cultural, and economic environment in and near the buildings.

GOVT §2165.202. APPLICABILITY

This subchapter applies only to the lease of space in a state-owned building to a private tenant.

GOVT §2165.203. LEASE; FAIR MARKET VALUE

In a state-owned building that is under the commission's control and that is used primarily for office space or vehicle parking for state government, the commission may lease at fair market value space to private tenants for commercial, cultural, educational, or recreational activities.

GOVT §2165.2035. LEASE OF SPACE IN STATE-OWNED PARKING LOTS & GARAGES; PRIVATE COMMERCIAL USE

(a) In this section, "lease" includes a management agreement.

(b) The commission shall develop private, commercial uses for state-owned parking lots and garages located in the city of Austin at locations the commission determines are appropriate for commercial uses outside of regular business hours.

(c) The commission may contract with a private vendor to manage the commercial use of state-owned parking lots and garages.

(d) Money received from a lease under this program shall be deposited to the credit of the general revenue fund.

(d-1) From the money received under Subsection (d), an amount equal to the costs associated with the lease of state parking lots and garages, including costs of trash collection and disposal, grounds and other property maintenance, and the remedying of any damage to state property, may be appropriated only to the commission to pay those costs.

Subsection (e) was repealed by Acts 2013, 83rd Leg., ch. 1312, §99(23), enacted May 23, 2013, effective Sept. 1, 2013, without reference to the conflicting amendment made by Acts 2013, 83rd Leg., ch. 1153, §10, enacted May 26, 2013, effective June 14, 2013. For harmonizing conflicts, see p. V.

(e) Repealed by Acts 2013, 83rd Leg., ch. 1312, §99(23), eff. Sept. 1, 2013.

Subsection (e) was amended by Acts 2013, 83rd Leg., ch. 1153, §10, enacted May 26, 2013, effective June 14, 2013, without reference to the conflicting repeal made by Acts 2013, 83rd Leg., ch. 1312, §99(23), enacted May 23, 2013, effective Sept. 1, 2013. For harmonizing conflicts, see p. V.

(e) On or before December 1 of each even-numbered year, the commission shall electronically submit a report to the legislature and the Legislative Budget Board describing the effectiveness of the program under this section.

(f) The limitation on the amount of space allocated to private tenants prescribed by Section 2165.205(b) does not apply to the lease of a state-owned parking lot or garage under this section.

(g) Any lease of a state-owned parking lot or garage under this section must contain a provision that allows state employees who work hours other than regular working hours under Section 658.005 to retain their parking privileges in a state-owned parking lot or garage. Such a lease must also provide that any state employee showing a State of Texas employee identification card is permitted to park in any state-owned parking lot or garage free of charge after normal business hours and on weekends. The foregoing provision does not apply to a lease to an institution of higher education under which all spaces in a parking lot or garage are leased for a time certain if parking in an alternate state-owned parking lot or garage is available to state employees.

(h) Nonprofit, charitable, and other community organizations may apply to use state parking lots and garages located in the city of Austin in the area bordered by West Fourth Street, Lavaca Street, West Third Street, and Nueces Street free of charge or at a reduced rate. The executive director of the commission shall develop a form to be used to make such applications. The form shall require information related to:

(1) the dates and times of the free use requested;

(2) the nature of the applicant's activities associated with the proposed use of state parking lots and garages; and

(3) any other information determined by the executive director of the commission to be necessary to evaluate an application.

(i) To be considered timely, an application must be submitted at least one month before the proposed use, unless this provision is waived by the executive director of the commission.

(j) The executive director of the commission may approve or reject an application made under Subsection (h).

GOVT §2165.204. LEASE OF SPACE IN STATE-OWNED PARKING LOTS & GARAGES; PRIVATE INDIVIDUAL USE OF EXCESS INDIVIDUAL PARKING SPACES

(a) The commission may lease to a private individual an individual parking space in a state-owned parking lot or garage located in the city of Austin if the commission determines the parking space to be in excess of the number of parking spaces sufficient to accommodate the regular parking requirements of state employees employed near the lot or garage and visitors to nearby state government offices.

(b) Money received from a lease under this section shall be deposited to the credit of the general revenue fund.

(c) In leasing a parking space under Subsection (a), the commission must ensure that the lease does not restrict uses for parking lots and garages developed under Section 2165.2035, including special event parking related to institutions of higher education.

(d) In leasing or renewing a lease for a parking space under Subsection (a), the commission shall give preference to an individual who is currently leasing or previously leased the parking space.

GOVT §2165.2045. LEASE OF SPACE IN STATE-OWNED PARKING LOTS & GARAGES; CERTAIN GOVERNMENTAL ENTITIES' USE OF EXCESS BLOCKS OF PARKING SPACE

(a) The commission may lease to an institution of higher education or a local government all or a significant block of a state-owned parking lot or garage located in the city of Austin if the commission determines the parking spaces located in the lot or garage to be in excess of the number of parking spaces sufficient to accommodate the regular parking requirements of state employees employed near the lot or garage and visitors to nearby state government offices.

(b) Money received from a lease under this section shall be deposited to the credit of the general revenue fund.

(c) In leasing all or a block of a state-owned parking lot or garage under Subsection (a), the commission must ensure that the lease does not restrict uses for parking lots and garages developed under Section 2165.2035, including special event parking related to institutions of higher education.

(d) In leasing or renewing a lease for all or a block of a state-owned parking lot or garage under Subsection (a), the commission shall give preference to an entity that is currently leasing or previously leased the lot or garage or a block of the lot or garage.

GOVT §2165.2046. REPORTS ON PARKING PROGRAMS

On or before December 1 of each even-numbered year, the commission shall electronically submit a report to the legislature and Legislative Budget Board describing the effectiveness of parking programs developed by the commission under this subchapter. The report must, at a minimum, include:

(1) the yearly revenue generated by the programs;

(2) the yearly administrative and enforcement costs of each program;

(3) yearly usage statistics for each program; and

(4) initiatives and suggestions by the commission to:

(A) modify administration of the programs; and

(B) increase revenue generated by the programs.

GOVT §2165.205. LIMITATIONS ON AMOUNT, LOCATION, & USE OF LEASED SPACE

(a) The commission may not lease space to a private tenant for use as private office space unless the private office space is related and incidental to another commercial, cultural, educational, recreational, or child care activity of the tenant in the building.

(b) Except as provided by this subchapter and Chapter 663, the commission shall determine the amount of space in a building to be allocated to private tenants and the types of activities in which the tenants may engage according to the market for certain activities among employees and visitors in the building and in the vicinity of the building.

(c) Except as provided by Section 2165.215, the amount of space allocated to private tenants may not exceed 15 percent of the total space in the building. Space leased to provide child care services for state employees does not count toward the 15 percent maximum.

(d) If the commission allocates space in a building to a private tenant, it shall encourage the tenant to lease space with street frontage or space in another area of heavy pedestrian activity.

GOVT §2165.206. LEASE OF SPACE FOR CHILD CARE FACILITY

(a) Providing a site for a child care facility in a state-owned building has first priority over all other uses of a building, except for the purposes essential to the official functions of the agencies housed in the building.

(b) If the commission allocates space for the purpose of providing child care services for state employees, the commission shall designate the use of the space most appropriate for child care.

(c) Notwithstanding any other provision of this subtitle, the commission shall lease at a rate set by the commission suitable space in state-owned buildings to child care providers selected as provided by Chapter 663.

GOVT §2165.207. METHOD OF SELECTING TENANT

(a) The commission may lease space in a building by negotiating a lease with a tenant or by selecting the tenant through competitive bidding. In either event, the commission shall follow procedures that promote competition and protect the state's interests.

(b) If the space is leased for the purpose of providing child care services for state employees, the commission may select the child care provider through procedures other than competitive bidding.

GOVT §2165.208. UTILITIES & CUSTODIAL SERVICES

(a) The commission may furnish utilities and custodial services to a private tenant at cost.

(b) The commission shall furnish utilities and custodial services to a child care provider selected by the commission under Chapter 663 at cost.

GOVT §2165.209. SUBLEASES & ASSIGNMENTS

The commission may permit a private tenant to sublease or assign space that the tenant leases. The commission must approve in writing all subleases and assignments of leases.

GOVT §2165.210. REFUSAL TO LEASE SPACE OR PERMIT AN ACTIVITY

The commission may refuse to lease space to a person or to permit an activity in a space if the commission considers the refusal to be in the state's best interests.

GOVT §2165.211. USE OF LEASE PROCEEDS

Money received from a lease under this subchapter may be used only for building and property services performed by the commission.

GOVT §2165.212. VENDING FACILITIES; TEXAS COMMISSION FOR THE BLIND

(a) The commission shall request the Texas Commission for the Blind to determine under Section 94.003, Human Resources Code, whether it is feasible to install a vending facility in a building in which the commission intends to lease space to a private tenant, other than a child care provider. If the installation of the facility is feasible, the commission shall permit the installation in accordance with Chapter 94, Human Resources Code.

(b) If a vending facility is installed, the commission may not lease space in the building to a tenant that the commission, after consultation with the Texas Commission for the Blind, determines would be in direct competition with the vending facility.

(c) If the Texas Commission for the Blind determines that the installation of a vending facility is not feasible, the commission shall lease space to at least one private tenant whose activity in the building will be managed by a blind person or by a person with a disability who is not blind.

GOVT §2165.213. AD VALOREM TAXATION

(a) Space leased to a private tenant is subject to ad valorem taxation in accordance with Section 11.11(d), Tax Code.

(b) The space is not subject to taxation if:

(1) the private tenant would be entitled to an exemption from taxation of the space if the tenant owned the space instead of leasing it; or

(2) the tenant uses the space for a child care facility.

GOVT §2165.214. PREFERENCE IN LEASING TO CERTAIN EXISTING VENDING FACILITIES

Notwithstanding the other provisions of this subchapter or Chapters 2155, 2156, 2157, and 2158, the commission shall give a preference, when leasing

space in a state-owned building for the operation of a vending facility as defined by Chapter 94, Human Resources Code, to an existing lessee, licensee, or contractor who operates a vending facility on the property if:

(1) the existing lessee, licensee, or contractor has operated a vending facility on the property for not less than 10 years;

(2) Chapter 94, Human Resources Code, does not apply to the property;

(3) the commission finds there is a history of quality and reliable service; and

(4) the proposal of the existing lessee, licensee, or contractor for the right to continue operation of the facility is consistent with the historical quality of service and the historical retail pricing structure at the facility.

GOVT §2165.215. PURCHASE OF BUILDING SUBJECT TO EXISTING LEASES

(a) If the commission determines under Section 2166.452 or 2166.453 that the purchase of an existing building is more advantageous to the state than constructing a new building or continuing to lease space for a state agency, but a purchase of the building would be subject to existing leases to private tenants that exceed 15 percent of the building's total space, the commission may purchase the building subject to existing leases notwithstanding Section 2165.205.

(b) On expiration of a private tenant's existing lease, the commission may renew the lease subject to this subchapter, including Section 2165.205.

SUBTITLE E. GOVERNMENT PROPERTY

CHAPTER 2206. EMINENT DOMAIN

SUBCHAPTER A. LIMITATIONS ON PURPOSE & USE OF PROPERTY ACQUIRED THROUGH EMINENT DOMAIN

GOVT §2206.001. LIMITATION ON EMINENT DOMAIN FOR PRIVATE PARTIES OR ECONOMIC DEVELOPMENT PURPOSES

(a) This section applies to the use of eminent domain under the laws of this state, including a local or special law, by any governmental or private entity, including:

(1) a state agency, including an institution of higher education as defined by Section 61.003, Education Code;

(2) a political subdivision of this state; or

(3) a corporation created by a governmental entity to act on behalf of the entity.

(b) A governmental or private entity may not take private property through the use of eminent domain if the taking:

(1) confers a private benefit on a particular private party through the use of the property;

(2) is for a public use that is merely a pretext to confer a private benefit on a particular private party;

(3) is for economic development purposes, unless the economic development is a secondary purpose resulting from municipal community development or municipal urban renewal activities to eliminate an existing affirmative harm on society from slum or blighted areas under:

(A) Chapter 373 or 374, Local Government Code, other than an activity described by Section 373.002(b)(5), Local Government Code; or

(B) Section 311.005(a)(1)(I), Tax Code; or

(4) is not for a public use.

(b-1) Expired.

(c) This section does not affect the authority of an entity authorized by law to take private property through the use of eminent domain for:

(1) transportation projects, including, but not limited to, railroads, airports, or public roads or highways;

(2) entities authorized under Section 59, Article XVI, Texas Constitution, including:

(A) port authorities;

(B) navigation districts; and

(C) any other conservation or reclamation districts that act as ports;

(3) water supply, wastewater, flood control, and drainage projects;

(4) public buildings, hospitals, and parks;

(5) the provision of utility services;

(6) a sports and community venue project approved by voters at an election held on or before December 1, 2005, under Chapter 334 or 335, Local Government Code;

(7) the operations of:

(A) a common carrier pipeline; or

(B) an energy transporter, as that term is defined by Section 186.051, Utilities Code;

(8) a purpose authorized by Chapter 181, Utilities Code;

(9) underground storage operations subject to Chapter 91, Natural Resources Code;

(10) a waste disposal project; or

(11) a library, museum, or related facility and any infrastructure related to the facility.

(d) This section does not affect the authority of a governmental entity to condemn a leasehold estate on property owned by the governmental entity.

(e) The determination by the governmental or private entity proposing to take the property that the taking does not involve an act or circumstance prohibited by Subsection (b) does not create a presumption with respect to whether the taking involves that act or circumstance.

GOVT §2206.002. LIMITATIONS ON EASEMENTS

(a) This section applies only to an easement acquired by an entity for the purpose of a pipeline to be used for oil or gas exploration or production activities.

(b) A property owner whose property is acquired through the use of eminent domain under Chapter 21, Property Code, for the purpose of creating an easement through that owner's property may construct streets or roads, including gravel, asphalt, or concrete streets or roads, at any locations above the easement that the property owner chooses.

(c) The portion of a street or road constructed under this section that is within the area covered by the easement:

(1) must cross the easement at or near 90 degrees; and

(2) may not:

(A) exceed 40 feet in width;

(B) cause a violation of any applicable pipeline regulation; or

(C) interfere with the operation and maintenance of any pipeline.

(d) At least 30 days before the date on which construction of an asphalt or concrete street or road that will be located wholly or partly in an area covered by an easement used for a pipeline is scheduled to begin, the property owner must submit plans for the proposed construction to the owner of the easement.

(e) Notwithstanding the provisions of this section, a property owner and the owner of the easement may agree to terms other than those stated in Subsection (c).

Sections 2206.003-2206.050 blank

SUBCHAPTER B. PROCEDURES REQUIRED TO INITIATE EMINENT DOMAIN PROCEEDINGS

GOVT §2206.051. SHORT TITLE

This subchapter may be cited as the Truth in Condemnation Procedures Act.

GOVT §2206.052. APPLICABILITY

The procedures in this subchapter apply only to the use of eminent domain under the laws of this state by a governmental entity.

GOVT §2206.053. VOTE ON USE OF EMINENT DOMAIN

(a) Before a governmental entity initiates a condemnation proceeding by filing a petition under Section 21.012, Property Code, the governmental entity must:

(1) authorize the initiation of the condemnation proceeding at a public meeting by a record vote; and

(2) include in the notice for the public meeting as required by Subchapter C, Chapter 551, in addition to other information as required by that subchapter, the consideration of the use of eminent domain to condemn property as an agenda item.

(b) A single ordinance, resolution, or order may be adopted for all units of property to be condemned if:

(1) the motion required by Subsection (e) indicates that the first record vote applies to all units of property to be condemned; and

(2) the minutes of the governmental entity reflect that the first vote applies to all of those units.

(c) If more than one member of the governing body objects to adopting a single ordinance, resolution, or order by a record vote for all units of property for which condemnation proceedings are to be initiated, a separate record vote must be taken for each unit of property.

(d) For the purposes of Subsections (a) and (c), if two or more units of real property are owned by the same person, the governmental entity may treat those units of property as one unit of property.

(e) The motion to adopt an ordinance, resolution, or order authorizing the initiation of condemnation proceedings under Chapter 21, Property Code, must be made in a form substantially similar to the following: "I move that the (name of governmental entity) authorize the use of the power of eminent domain to acquire (describe the property) for (describe the public use)." The description of the property required by this subsection is sufficient if the description of the location of and interest in the property that the governmental entity seeks to acquire is substantially similar to the description that is or could properly be used in a petition to condemn the property under Section 21.012, Property Code.

(f) If a project for a public use described by Section 2206.001(c)(3) will require a governmental entity to acquire multiple tracts or units of property to construct facilities connecting one location to another location, the governing body of the governmental entity may adopt a single ordinance, resolution, or order by a record vote that delegates the authority to initiate condemnation proceedings to the chief administrative official of the governmental entity.

(g) An ordinance, resolution, or order adopted under Subsection (f) is not required to identify specific properties that the governmental entity will acquire. The ordinance, resolution, or order must identify the general area to be covered by the project or the general route that will be used by the governmental entity for the project in a way that provides property owners in and around the area or along the route reasonable notice that the owners' properties may be subject to condemnation proceedings during the planning or construction of the project.

Sections 2206.054-2206.100 blank

SUBCHAPTER C. EXPIRATION OF CERTAIN EMINENT DOMAIN AUTHORITY

GOVT §2206.101. REPORT OF EMINENT DOMAIN AUTHORITY; EXPIRATION OF AUTHORITY

(a) This section does not apply to an entity that was created or that acquired the power of eminent domain on or after December 31, 2012.

(b) Not later than December 31, 2012, an entity, including a private entity, authorized by the state by a general or special law to exercise the power of eminent domain shall submit to the comptroller a letter stating that the entity is authorized by the state to exercise the power of eminent domain and identifying each provision of law that grants the entity that authority. The entity must send the letter by certified mail, return receipt requested.

(c) The authority of an entity to exercise the power of eminent domain expires on September 1, 2013, unless the entity submits a letter in accordance with Subsection (b).

(d) Not later than March 1, 2013, the comptroller shall submit to the governor, the lieutenant governor, the speaker of the house of representatives, the presiding officers of the appropriate standing committees of the senate and the house of representatives, and the Texas Legislative Council a report that contains:

(1) the name of each entity that submitted a letter in accordance with this section; and

(2) a corresponding list of the provisions granting eminent domain authority as identified by each entity that submitted a letter.

(e) The Texas Legislative Council shall prepare for consideration by the 84th Legislature, Regular Session, a nonsubstantive revision of the statutes of this state as necessary to reflect the state of the law after the expiration of an entity's eminent domain authority effective under Subsection (c).

Sections 2206.102-2206.150 blank

SUBCHAPTER D. EMINENT DOMAIN AUTHORITY REPORTING; PUBLIC AVAILABILITY

GOVT §2206.151. APPLICABILITY

This subchapter applies to public and private entities, including common carriers, authorized by the state by a general or special law to exercise the power of eminent domain.

GOVT §2206.152. CREATION DATE

For the purposes of this subchapter, an entity described by Section 2206.151 is considered to have been created on:

(1) the earliest date on which the entity existed if the entity was authorized to exercise the power of eminent domain on that date; or

(2) the earliest date on which the entity was authorized to exercise the power of eminent domain if the entity did not have that authority on the earliest date on which the entity existed.

GOVT §2206.153. EMINENT DOMAIN DATABASE

(a) The comptroller shall create and make accessible on an Internet website maintained by the comptroller an eminent domain database as provided by this section.

(b) The eminent domain database must include with respect to each entity described by Section 2206.151:

(1) the name of the entity;

(2) the entity's address and public contact information;

(3) the name of the appropriate officer or other person representing the entity and that person's contact information;

(4) the type of entity;

(5) each provision of law that grants the entity eminent domain authority;

(6) the focus or scope of the eminent domain authority granted to the entity;

(7) the earliest date on which the entity had the authority to exercise the power of eminent domain;

(8) the entity's taxpayer identification number, if any;

(9) whether the entity exercised the entity's eminent domain authority in the preceding calendar year by the filing of a condemnation petition under Section 21.012, Property Code; and

(10) the entity's Internet website address or, if the entity does not operate an Internet website, contact information to enable a member of the public to obtain information from the entity.

(c) The comptroller may consult with the appropriate officer of, or other person representing, each entity to obtain the information necessary to maintain the eminent domain database.

(d) To the extent information required in the eminent domain database is otherwise collected or maintained by a state agency or political subdivision, the comptroller may request and the state agency or political subdivision shall provide that information and any update to the information as necessary for inclusion in the eminent domain database.

(e) At least annually, the comptroller shall update information in the eminent domain database for each entity, as appropriate.

(f) To the extent possible, the comptroller shall present information in the eminent domain database in a manner that is searchable and intuitive to users. The comptroller may enhance and organize the presentation of the information through the use of graphical representations as the comptroller considers appropriate.

(g) The comptroller may not charge a fee to the public to access the eminent domain database.

GOVT §2206.154. REPORTING OF INFORMATION TO COMPTROLLER

(a) Except as provided by Subsection (b), not later than February 1 of each year, an entity described by Section 2206.151 shall submit to the comptroller a report containing records and other information specified by this subchapter for the purpose of providing the comptroller with information to maintain the eminent domain database under Section 2206.153. The entity shall submit the report in a form and in the manner prescribed by the comptroller.

(a-1) Expired.

(b) An entity described by Section 2206.151 created on or after September 1, 2015, is not required to submit the entity's initial report under Subsection (a) before the 180th day after the date of the entity's creation.

(c) In addition to the annual report required under Subsection (a), an entity described by Section 2206.151 shall report to the comptroller any changes to the entity's eminent domain authority information reported under this section not later than the 90th day after the date on which the change occurred.

GOVT §2206.155. PENALTIES FOR NONCOMPLIANCE

(a) If an entity does not timely submit a report that complies with Section 2206.154, the comptroller shall provide written notice to the entity:

(1) informing the entity of the entity's violation of that section; and

(2) notifying the entity that the entity will be subject to a penalty of $1,000 if the entity does not report the required information on or before the 30th day after the date the notice is provided.

(b) Not later than the 30th day after the date the comptroller provides notice to an entity under Subsection (a), the entity must report the required information.

(c) If an entity does not report the required information as prescribed by Subsection (b):

(1) the entity is liable to the state for a civil penalty of $1,000; and

(2) the comptroller shall provide written notice to the entity:

(A) informing the entity of the entity's liability for the penalty; and

(B) notifying the entity that if the entity does not report the required information on or before the 30th day after the date the notice is provided:

(i) the entity will be subject to an additional penalty of $1,000; and

(ii) the entity's noncompliance will be reflected in the eminent domain database maintained by the comptroller.

(d) Not later than the 30th day after the date the comptroller provides notice to an entity under Subsection (c), the entity must report the required information.

(e) If an entity does not report the required information as prescribed by Subsection (d):

(1) the entity is liable to the state for a civil penalty of $1,000; and

(2) the comptroller shall:

(A) reflect the entity's noncompliance in the database required by this subchapter by including the entity on a separately maintained list of noncomplying entities and in any other manner determined appropriate by the comptroller until the entity reports all information required under Section 2206.154; and

(B) provide written notice to the entity that the entity's noncompliance will be reflected in the database until the entity reports the required information.

(f) The attorney general may sue to collect a civil penalty imposed by this section.

GOVT §2206.156. EMINENT DOMAIN AUTHORITY NOT AFFECTED

The reporting, failure to report, or late submission of a report by a public or private entity, including a common carrier, under this subchapter does not affect the entity's authority to exercise the power of eminent domain.

GOVT §2206.157. RULES

The comptroller may adopt rules and establish policies and procedures to implement this subchapter.

SUBTITLE F. STATE & LOCAL CONTRACTS & FUND MANAGEMENT

CHAPTER 2253. PUBLIC WORK PERFORMANCE & PAYMENT BONDS

SUBCHAPTER A. GENERAL PROVISIONS

GOVT §2253.001. DEFINITIONS

In this chapter:

(1) "Governmental entity" means a governmental or quasi-governmental authority authorized by state law to make a public work contract, including:

(A) the state, a county, or a municipality;

(B) a department, board, or agency of the state, a county, or a municipality; and

(C) a school district or a subdivision of a school district.

(2) "Payment bond beneficiary" means a person for whose protection and use this chapter requires a payment bond.

(3) "Prime contractor" means a person, firm, or corporation that makes a public work contract with a governmental entity.

(4) "Public work contract" means a contract for constructing, altering, or repairing a public building or carrying out or completing any public work.

(5) "Public work labor" means labor used directly to carry out a public work.

(6) "Public work material" means:

(A) material used, or ordered and delivered for use, directly to carry out a public work;

(B) specially fabricated material;

(C) reasonable rental and actual running repair costs for construction equipment used, or reasonably required and delivered for use, directly to carry out work at the project site; or

(D) power, water, fuel, and lubricants used, or ordered and delivered for use, directly to carry out a public work.

(7) "Retainage" means the part of the payments under a public work contract that are not required to be paid within the month after the month in which the public work labor is performed or public work material is delivered under the contract.

(8) "Specially fabricated material" means material ordered by a prime contractor or subcontractor that is:

(A) specially fabricated for use in a public work; and

(B) reasonably unsuitable for another use.

(9) "Subcontractor" means a person, firm, or corporation that provides public work labor or material to fulfill an obligation to a prime contractor or to a subcontractor for the performance and installation of any of the work required by a public work contract.

GOVT §2253.002. EXEMPTION

This chapter does not apply to a public work contract entered into by a state agency relating to an action taken under Subchapter F or I, Chapter 361, Health and Safety Code, or Subchapter I, Chapter 26, Water Code.

Sections 2253.003-2253.020 reserved for expansion

SUBCHAPTER B. GENERAL REQUIREMENTS; LIABILITY

GOVT §2253.021. PERFORMANCE & PAYMENT BONDS REQUIRED

(a) A governmental entity that makes a public work contract with a prime contractor shall require the contractor, before beginning the work, to execute to the governmental entity:

(1) a performance bond if the contract is in excess of $100,000; and

(2) a payment bond if:

(A) the contract is in excess of $25,000, and the governmental entity is not a municipality or a joint board created under Subchapter D, Chapter 22, Transportation Code; or

(B) the contract is in excess of $50,000, and the governmental entity is a municipality or a joint board created under Subchapter D, Chapter 22, Transportation Code.

(b) The performance bond is:

(1) solely for the protection of the state or governmental entity awarding the public work contract;

(2) in the amount of the contract; and

(3) conditioned on the faithful performance of the work in accordance with the plans, specifications, and contract documents.

(c) The payment bond is:

(1) solely for the protection and use of payment bond beneficiaries who have a direct contractual relationship with the prime contractor or a subcontractor to supply public work labor or material; and

(2) in the amount of the contract.

(d) A bond required by this section must be executed by a corporate surety in accordance with Section 1, Chapter 87, Acts of the 56th Legislature, Regular Session, 1959 (Article 7.19-1, Vernon's Texas Insurance Code).

(e) A bond executed for a public work contract with the state or a department, board, or agency of the state must be payable to the state and its form must be approved by the attorney general. A bond executed for a public work contract with another governmental entity must be payable to and its form must be approved by the awarding governmental entity.

(f) A bond required under this section must clearly and prominently display on the bond or on an attachment to the bond:

(1) the name, mailing address, physical address, and telephone number, including the area code, of the surety company to which any notice of claim should be sent; or

(2) the toll-free telephone number maintained by the Texas Department of Insurance under Subchapter B, Chapter 521, Insurance Code, and a statement that the address of the surety company to which any notice of claim should be sent may be obtained from the Texas Department of Insurance by calling the toll-free telephone number.

(g) A governmental entity may not require a contractor for any public building or other construction contract to obtain a surety bond from any specific insurance or surety company, agent, or broker.

(h) A reverse auction procedure may not be used to obtain services related to a public work contract for which a bond is required under this section. In this subsection, "reverse auction procedure" has the meaning assigned by Section 2155.062 or a procedure similar to that described by Section 2155.062.

GOVT §2253.022. PERFORMANCE & PAYMENT BONDS; INSURED LOSS

(a) A governmental entity shall ensure that an insurance company that is fulfilling its obligation under a contract of insurance by arranging for the replacement of a loss, rather than by making a cash payment directly to the governmental entity, furnishes or has furnished by a contractor, in accordance with this chapter:

(1) a performance bond as described by Section 2253.021(b) for the benefit of the governmental entity; and

(2) a payment bond as described in Section 2253.021(c) for the benefit of the beneficiaries described by that subsection.

(b) The bonds required to be furnished under Subsection (a) must be furnished before the contractor begins work.

(c) It is an implied obligation under a contract of insurance for the insurance company to furnish the bonds required by this section.

(d) To recover in a suit with respect to which the insurance company has furnished or caused to be furnished a payment bond, the only notice required of a payment bond beneficiary is the notice given to the surety in accordance with Subchapter C.

(e) This section does not apply to a governmental entity when a surety company is complying with an obligation under a bond that had been issued for the benefit of the governmental entity.

(f) If the payment bond required by Subsection (a) is not furnished, the governmental entity is subject to the same liability that a surety would have if the surety had issued the payment bond and the governmental entity had required the bond to be provided. To recover in a suit under this subsection, the only notice required of a payment bond beneficiary is a notice given to the governmental entity, as if the governmental entity were the surety, in accordance with Subchapter C.

GOVT §2253.023. ATTEMPTED COMPLIANCE

(a) A bond furnished by a prime contractor in an attempt to comply with this chapter shall be construed to comply with this chapter regarding the rights created, limitations on those rights, and remedies provided.

(b) A provision in a bond furnished by a prime contractor in an attempt to comply with this chapter that expands or restricts a right or liability under this chapter shall be disregarded, and this chapter shall apply to that bond.

GOVT §2253.024. INFORMATION FROM CONTRACTOR OR SUBCONTRACTOR

(a) A prime contractor, on the written request of a person who provides public work labor or material and when required by Subsection (c), shall provide to the person:

(1) the name and last known address of the governmental entity with whom the prime contractor contracted for the public work;

(2) a copy of the payment and performance bonds for the public work, including bonds furnished by or to the prime contractor; and

(3) the name of the surety issuing the payment bond and the performance bond and the toll-free telephone number maintained by the Texas Department of Insurance under Subchapter B, Chapter 521, Insurance Code, for obtaining information concerning licensed insurance companies.

(b) A subcontractor, on the written request of a governmental entity, the prime contractor, a surety on a bond that covers the public work contract, or a person providing work under the subcontract and when required by Subsection (c), shall provide to the person requesting the information:

(1) the name and last known address of each person from whom the subcontractor purchased public work labor or material, other than public work material from the subcontractor's inventory;

(2) the name and last known address of each person to whom the subcontractor provided public work labor or material;

(3) a statement of whether the subcontractor furnished a bond for the benefit of its subcontractors and materialmen;

(4) the name and last known address of the surety on the bond the subcontractor furnished; and

(5) a copy of that bond.

(c) Information requested shall be provided within a reasonable time but not later than the 10th day after the receipt of the written request for the information.

(d) A person from whom information is requested may require payment of the actual cost, not to exceed $25, for providing the requested information if the person does not have a direct contractual relationship with the person requesting information that relates to the public work.

(e) A person who fails to provide information required by this section is liable to the requesting person for that person's reasonable and necessary costs incurred in getting the requested information.

GOVT §2253.025. INFORMATION FROM PAYMENT BOND BENEFICIARY

(a) A payment bond beneficiary, not later than the 30th day after the date the beneficiary receives a writ-

ten request from the prime contractor or a surety on a bond on which a claim is made, shall provide to the contractor or surety:

(1) a copy of any applicable written agreement or purchase order; and

(2) any statement or payment request of the beneficiary that shows the amount claimed and the work performed by the beneficiary for which the claim is made.

(b) If requested, the payment bond beneficiary shall provide the estimated amount due for each calendar month in which the beneficiary performed public work labor or provided public work material.

GOVT §2253.026. COPY OF PAYMENT BOND & CONTRACT

(a) A governmental entity shall furnish the information required by Subsection (d) to any person who applies for the information and who submits an affidavit that the person:

(1) has supplied public work labor or material for which the person has not been paid;

(2) has contracted for specially fabricated material for which the person has not been paid; or

(3) is being sued on a payment bond.

(b) The copy of the payment bond or public work contract is prima facie evidence of the content, execution, and delivery of the original.

(c) An applicant under this section shall pay any reasonable fee set by the governmental entity for the actual cost of preparation of the copies.

(d) A governmental entity shall furnish the following information to a person who makes a request under Subsection (a):

(1) a certified copy of a payment bond and any attachment to the bond;

(2) the public work contract for which the bond was given; and

(3) the toll-free telephone number maintained by the Texas Department of Insurance under Subchapter B, Chapter 521, Insurance Code, for obtaining information concerning licensed insurance companies.

GOVT §2253.027. LIABILITY OF GOVERNMENTAL ENTITY

(a) If a governmental entity fails to obtain from a prime contractor a payment bond as required by Section 2253.021:

(1) the entity is subject to the same liability that a surety would have if the surety had issued a payment bond and if the entity had obtained the bond; and

(2) a payment bond beneficiary is entitled to a lien on money due to the prime contractor in the same manner and to the same extent as if the public work contract were subject to Subchapter J, Chapter 53, Property Code.

(b) To recover in a suit under Subsection (a), the only notice a payment bond beneficiary is required to provide to the governmental entity is a notice provided in the same manner as described by Subchapter C. The notice must be provided as if the governmental entity were a surety.

Sections 2253.028-2253.040 reserved for expansion

SUBCHAPTER C. NOTICE REQUIREMENTS

GOVT §2253.041. NOTICE REQUIRED FOR CLAIM FOR PAYMENT FOR LABOR OR MATERIAL

(a) To recover in a suit under Section 2253.073 on a payment bond for a claim for payment for public work labor performed or public work material delivered, a payment bond beneficiary must mail to the prime contractor and the surety written notice of the claim.

(b) The notice must be mailed on or before the 15th day of the third month after each month in which any of the claimed labor was performed or any of the claimed material was delivered.

(c) The notice must be accompanied by a sworn statement of account that states in substance:

(1) the amount claimed is just and correct; and

(2) all just and lawful offsets, payments, and credits known to the affiant have been allowed.

(d) The statement of account shall include the amount of any retainage applicable to the account that has not become due under the terms of the public work contract between the payment bond beneficiary and the prime contractor or between the payment bond beneficiary and a subcontractor.

GOVT §2253.042. COPY OF AGREEMENT AS NOTICE OF CLAIM FOR UNPAID LABOR OR MATERIAL

A payment bond beneficiary has the option to enclose with the sworn statement of account, as the notice for a claim under a written agreement for payment for public work labor performed or public work material

delivered, a copy of the written agreement and a statement of the completion or the value of partial completion of the agreement.

GOVT §2253.043. NOTICE OF CLAIM FOR UNPAID LABOR OR MATERIAL WHEN WRITTEN AGREEMENT DOES NOT EXIST

(a) Except as provided by Section 2253.044, if a written agreement does not exist between the payment bond beneficiary and the prime contractor or between the payment bond beneficiary and the subcontractor, the notice for a claim for unpaid bills must contain:

(1) the name of the party for whom the public work labor was performed or to whom the public work material was delivered;

(2) the approximate date of performance or delivery;

(3) a description of the public work labor or material for reasonable identification; and

(4) the amount due.

(b) The payment bond beneficiary must generally itemize the claim and include with it copies of documents, invoices, or orders that reasonably identify:

(1) the public work labor performed or public work material delivered for which the claim is made;

(2) the job; and

(3) the destination of delivery.

GOVT §2253.044. NOTICE OF CLAIM FOR MULTIPLE ITEMS OF LABOR OR MATERIAL

The notice for a claim for lump-sum payment for multiple items of public work labor or material must:

(1) describe the labor or material in a manner that reasonably identifies the labor or material;

(2) state the name of the party for whom the labor was performed or to whom the material was delivered;

(3) state the approximate date of performance or delivery;

(4) state whether the contract is written or oral;

(5) state the amount of the contract; and

(6) state the amount claimed.

GOVT §2253.045. NOTICE OF CLAIM FOR UNPAID LABOR OR MATERIAL UNDER WRITTEN UNIT PRICE AGREEMENT

The notice for a claim for public work labor performed or public work material delivered by a payment bond beneficiary who is a subcontractor or materialman to the prime contractor or to a subcontractor and who has a written unit price agreement that is wholly or partially completed is sufficient if the beneficiary attaches to the sworn statement of account:

(1) a list of units and unit prices set by the contract; and

(2) a statement of those completed and partially completed units.

GOVT §2253.046. NOTICE REQUIRED FOR CLAIM FOR PAYMENT OF RETAINAGE

(a) To recover in a suit under Section 2253.073 on a payment bond for a claim for payment of retainage, a payment bond beneficiary whose contract with a prime contractor or subcontractor provides for retainage must mail written notice of the claim to the prime contractor and the surety on or before the 90th day after the date of final completion of the public work contract.

(b) The notice shall consist of a statement of:

(1) the amount of the contract;

(2) any amount paid; and

(3) the outstanding balance.

(c) Notice of a claim for payment of retainage is not required if the amount claimed is part of a prior claim made under this subchapter.

GOVT §2253.047. ADDITIONAL NOTICE REQUIRED FOR PAYMENT BOND BENEFICIARY WITHOUT DIRECT CONTRACTUAL RELATIONSHIP WITH PRIME CONTRACTOR

(a) To recover in a suit under Section 2253.073 on a payment bond, a payment bond beneficiary who does not have a direct contractual relationship with the prime contractor for public work labor or material must mail notice as required by this section.

(b) A payment bond beneficiary who contracts with a subcontractor for retainage must mail, on or before the 15th day of the second month after the date of the beginning of the delivery of public work material or the performance of public work labor, written notice to the prime contractor that:

(1) the contract provides for retainage; and

(2) generally indicates the nature of the retainage.

(c) The payment bond beneficiary must mail to the prime contractor written notice of a claim for any unpaid public work labor performed or public work material delivered. The notice must be mailed on or before

the 15th day of the second month after each month in which the labor was performed or the material was delivered. A copy of the statement sent to a subcontractor is sufficient as notice under this subsection.

(d) The payment bond beneficiary must mail to the prime contractor, on or before the 15th day of the second month after the receipt and acceptance of an order for specially fabricated material, written notice that the order has been received and accepted.

(e) This section applies only to a payment bond beneficiary who is not an individual mechanic or laborer and who makes a claim for wages.

GOVT §2253.048. MAILING NOTICE

(a) A notice required by this subchapter to be mailed must be sent by certified or registered mail.

(b) A notice required by this subchapter to be mailed to a prime contractor must be addressed to the prime contractor at the contractor's residence or last known business address.

(c) A person satisfies the requirements of this subchapter relating to providing notice to the surety if the person mails the notice by certified or registered mail to the surety:

(1) at the address stated on the bond or on an attachment to the bond;

(2) at the address on file with the Texas Department of Insurance; or

(3) at any other address allowed by law.

Sections 2253.049-2253.070 reserved for expansion

Subchapter D. Claims on Bonds; Enforcement

GOVT §2253.071. TERMINATION OR ABANDONMENT OF CONTRACT; PROCEEDS OF CONTRACT

(a) The proceeds of a public work contract are not payable, until all costs of completion of the contract work are paid by the contractor or the contractor's surety, to a contractor who furnishes a bond required by this chapter if:

(1) the contractor abandons performance of the contract; or

(2) the contractor's right to proceed with performance of the contract is lawfully terminated by the awarding governmental entity because of the contractor's default.

(b) The balance of the public work contract proceeds remaining after the costs of completion are paid shall be paid according to the contractor's and the surety's interests as may be established by agreement or by judgment of a court.

(c) A surety that completes a public work contract or incurs a loss under a performance bond required under this chapter has a claim to the proceeds of the contract prior to all other creditors of the prime contractor to the full extent of the surety's loss. That priority does not excuse the surety from paying an obligation under a payment bond.

GOVT §2253.072. STATE NOT LIABLE FOR COSTS

The state is not liable for payment of a cost or expense of a suit brought by any party on a payment bond furnished under this chapter.

GOVT §2253.073. SUIT ON PAYMENT BOND

(a) A payment bond beneficiary who has provided public work labor or material under a public work contract for which a payment bond is furnished under this chapter may sue the principal or surety, jointly or severally, on the payment bond if the claim is not paid before the 61st day after the date the notice for the claim is mailed.

(b) Suit may be brought under Subsection (a) for:

(1) the unpaid balance of the beneficiary's claim at the time the claim was mailed or the suit is brought; and

(2) reasonable attorney fees.

GOVT §2253.074. COSTS & ATTORNEY FEES

A court may award costs and reasonable attorney fees that are equitable in a proceeding to enforce a claim on a payment bond or to declare that any part of a claim is invalid.

GOVT §2253.075. ASSIGNMENT OF CLAIM

A third party to whom a claim is assigned is in the same position as a payment bond beneficiary if notice is given as required by this chapter.

GOVT §2253.076. LIMITATIONS ON CERTAIN CLAIMS; MAXIMUM RETAINAGE

(a) The amount of a subcontractor's claim, including previous payments, may not exceed the proportion of the subcontract price that the work done bears to the total of the work covered by the subcontract.

(b) A claim for specially fabricated material that has not been delivered or incorporated into the public work is limited to material that conforms to and complies with the plans, specifications, and contract documents for the material. The amount of the claim may not exceed the reasonable cost, less the fair salvage value, of the specially fabricated material.

(c) A claim for retainage in a notice under this subchapter is not valid for an amount greater than the amount of retainage specified in the public work contract between the payment bond beneficiary and the prime contractor or between the payment bond beneficiary and the subcontractor. A claim for retainage is never valid for an amount greater than 10 percent of the amount of that contract.

GOVT §2253.077. VENUE

A suit under this chapter shall be brought in a court in a county in which any part of the public work is located.

GOVT §2253.078. STATUTE OF LIMITATIONS

(a) A suit on a performance bond may not be brought after the first anniversary of the date of final completion, abandonment, or termination of the public work contract.

(b) A suit on a payment bond may not be brought by a payment bond beneficiary after the first anniversary of the date notice for a claim is mailed under this chapter.

GOVT §2253.079. CRIMINAL OFFENSE FOR FALSE & FRAUDULENT CLAIM

(a) A person commits an offense if the person wilfully files a false and fraudulent claim under this chapter.

(b) An offense under this section is subject to the penalty for false swearing.

Selected Provisions
Table of Contents

Title 9. Safety

Subtitle A. Public Safety

Subtitle C. Fire

TITLE 9. SAFETY

SUBTITLE A. PUBLIC SAFETY

CHAPTER 756. MISCELLANEOUS HAZARDOUS CONDITIONS

SUBCHAPTER A. COVERING WELLS, CISTERNS, & HOLES

H&SC §756.001. COVERING LARGE WELL OR CISTERN; CRIMINAL PENALTY

(a) The owner or operator of a well or cistern that is at least 10 feet deep and not less than 10 inches nor more than six feet in diameter shall keep it entirely covered at all times except when the owner or operator is actually using the well or cistern.

(b) The cover required by this section must be capable of sustaining at least 200 pounds of weight.

(c) A person commits an offense if the person fails to cover a well or cistern as required by this section. An offense under this subsection is a misdemeanor punishable by a fine of not less than $100 or more than $500.

H&SC §756.002. COVERING OR PLUGGING SMALL WELL OR HOLE; CRIMINAL PENALTY

(a) A person who drills, digs, or otherwise creates or causes to be drilled, dug, or otherwise created a well or hole that is at least 10 feet deep and less than 10 inches in diameter may not abandon the hole unless the person first:

(1) completely fills the well or hole from its total depth to the surface; or

(2) plugs the well or hole with a permanent plug not less than 10 feet from the surface and completely fills the well or hole from the plug to the surface.

(b) A person commits an offense if the person abandons a well or hole in violation of this section. An offense under this subsection is a misdemeanor punishable by a fine of not less than $100 or more than $500.

Sections 756.003-756.010 reserved for expansion

SUBCHAPTER B. REFRIGERATORS & OTHER CONTAINERS

H&SC §756.011. TYPES OF REFRIGERATORS & CONTAINERS COVERED

This subchapter applies only to a refrigerator, ice box, or other airtight or semi-airtight container that has:

(1) a capacity of at least 1-½ cubic feet;

(2) an opening of at least 50 square inches; and

(3) a door or lid equipped with a latch or other fastening device capable of securing the door or lid shut.

H&SC §756.012. LEAVING REFRIGERATOR OR CONTAINER ACCESSIBLE TO CHILDREN

(a) A person may not place a container described by Section 756.011 outside of a structure or in a warehouse, storage room, or unoccupied or abandoned structure so that the container is accessible to children.

(b) A person may not permit a container described by Section 756.011 to remain in an area specified by Subsection (a) so that the container is accessible to children.

H&SC §756.013. CRIMINAL PENALTY

(a) A person commits an offense if the person violates Section 756.012.

(b) An offense under this section is a misdemeanor punishable by a fine of not less than $5 or more than $200.

(c) Each day of a continuing violation constitutes a separate offense.

Sections 756.014-756.020 reserved for expansion

SUBCHAPTER C. TRENCH SAFETY

H&SC §756.021. DEFINITION

In this subchapter, "trench" has the meaning assigned by the standards adopted by the Occupational Safety and Health Administration.

H&SC §756.022. TRENCH EXCAVATION IN STATE

(a) The bid documents, if bids are used, and the contract for a construction project in this state on which a contractor is employed and that includes a trench excavation exceeding a depth of five feet must include:

(1) a reference to the Occupational Safety and Health Administration standards for trench safety that will be in effect during the period of construction of the project;

(2) a copy of special shoring requirements, if any, of the state or of a political subdivision in which the construction project is located, with a separate pay item for the special shoring requirements;

(3) a copy of any geotechnical information that was obtained by the owner for use in the design of the trench safety system; and

(4) a separate pay item for trench excavation safety protection.

(b) The separate pay item for trench excavation safety protection must be based on the linear feet of trench excavated. The separate pay item for special shoring requirements, if any, of the state or of any political subdivision in which the construction project is located must be based on the square feet of shoring used.

(c) A municipality may adopt an ordinance that requires the refusal of a building permit to a person who fails to certify in writing that the requirement of Subsection (a) has been satisfied. A municipality, in lieu of or in addition to the written certification, may require an applicant for a building permit to produce for inspection or file with the municipality a copy of a contract that complies with Subsection (a) as a condition of issuance of a building permit.

(d) This section does not apply to a contract:

(1) governed by Section 756.023;

(2) governed by Subtitle D, Title 10, Government Code; or

(3) entered into by a person subject to the safety standards adopted under and the administrative penalty provisions of Subchapter E, Chapter 121, Utilities Code.

H&SC §756.023. TRENCH EXCAVATION FOR POLITICAL SUBDIVISION

(a) On a project for a political subdivision of the state in which trench excavation will exceed a depth of five feet, the bid documents provided to all bidders and the contract must include:

(1) a reference to the Occupational Safety and Health Administration standards for trench safety in effect during the period of construction of the project;

(2) a copy of special shoring requirements, if any, of the political subdivision, with a separate pay item for the special shoring requirements;

(3) a copy of any geotechnical information that was obtained by the owner for use by the contractor in the design of the trench safety system; and

(4) a separate pay item for trench excavation safety protection.

(b) The separate pay item for trench excavation safety protection must be based on the linear feet of trench excavated. The separate pay item for special shoring requirements, if any, of the political subdivision must be based on the square feet of shoring used.

(c) A political subdivision may require a bidder to attend a prebid conference to coordinate a geotechnical investigation of the project site by bidders. In awarding a contract, a political subdivision may not consider a bid from a bidder who failed to attend a required prebid conference.

(d) This section does not apply to a person subject to the safety standards adopted under and the administrative penalty provisions of Subchapter E, Chapter 121, Utilities Code.

Sections 756.024-756.040 blank

SUBCHAPTER D. OUTDOOR SHOOTING RANGES

H&SC §756.041. DEFINITION

In this subchapter, "outdoor shooting range" means an outdoor shooting range, outdoor firing range, or other open property on which persons may fire a weapon for a fee or other remuneration but does not include a deer lease or other similar leases of property for the purpose of hunting or an archery range.

H&SC §756.0411. APPLICABILITY

This subchapter applies only to an outdoor shooting range located in a county with a population of more than 150,000.

H&SC §756.042. CONSTRUCTION STANDARDS

The owner of an outdoor shooting range shall construct and maintain the range according to standards that are at least as stringent as the standards printed in the National Rifle Association range manual.

H&SC §756.043. CIVIL PENALTY

(a) The owner of an outdoor shooting range who fails to comply with Section 756.042 is liable within 60 days after a finding of noncompliance for a civil penalty of $50 for each day of noncompliance; the aggregate amount not to exceed $500.

(b) The attorney general or the appropriate district attorney, criminal district attorney, or county attorney shall recover the civil penalty in a suit on behalf of the state. If the attorney general brings the suit, the penalty

shall be deposited in the state treasury to the credit of the general revenue fund. If another attorney brings the suit, the penalty shall be deposited in the general fund of the county in which the violation occurred.

H&SC §756.044. CRIMINAL PENALTIES

(a) The owner of an outdoor shooting range commits an offense if the owner intentionally or recklessly fails to comply with Section 756.042 and that failure results in injury to another person.

(b) An offense under this section is a Class C misdemeanor, except that if it is shown on the trial of the defendant that the defendant has previously been convicted of an offense under this section, the offense is a Class A misdemeanor.

H&SC §756.045. INSURANCE REQUIRED

(a) The owner of an outdoor shooting range shall purchase and maintain an insurance policy that provides coverage of at least $500,000 for bodily injuries or death and another policy that provides that level of coverage for property damage resulting from firing any weapon while on the shooting range.

(b) The owner of an outdoor shooting range shall prominently display a sign at the shooting range stating that the owner has purchased insurance to cover bodily injury, death, or property damage occurring from activities at the shooting range.

Sections 756.046-756.060 blank

SUBCHAPTER E. PUBLICLY FUNDED PLAYGROUNDS

H&SC §756.061. COMPLIANCE WITH SAFETY STANDARDS

(a) Notwithstanding any other rule or statute, and except as provided by Subsection (b), on or after September 1, 2009, public funds may not be used:

(1) to purchase playground equipment that:

(A) does not comply with each applicable provision of ASTM Standard F1487-07ae1, "Consumer Safety Performance Specification for Playground Equipment for Public Use" published by ASTM International; or

(B) has a horizontal bare metal platform or a bare metal step or slide, unless the bare metal is shielded from direct sun by a covering provided with the equipment or by a shaded area in the location where the equipment is installed;

(2) to purchase surfacing for the area under and around playground equipment if the surfacing will not comply, on completion of installation of the surfacing, with each applicable provision of ASTM Standard F2223-04e1, "Standard Guide for ASTM Standards on Playground Surfacing" published by ASTM International; or

(3) to pay for installation of playground equipment or surfacing if the installation will not comply, on completion of the installation, with each applicable provision of the specifications described by Subdivision (1) or (2), as applicable.

(b) Public funds may be used for maintenance of playground equipment or surfacing for the area under and around playground equipment that was purchased before September 1, 2009, even if the equipment or surfacing does not comply, on completion of the maintenance, with each applicable provision of the specifications described by Subsections (a)(1) and (a)(2).

(c) This section:

(1) does not create, increase, decrease, or otherwise affect a person's liability for damages for injury, death, or other harm caused by playground equipment, surfacing, or the installation of the equipment or surfacing; and

(2) is not a waiver of sovereign immunity of any governmental entity.

Sections 756.062-756.080 blank

SUBCHAPTER F. SECURITY BARS

H&SC §756.081. DEFINITIONS

In this chapter:

(1) "Bedroom" means an area of a dwelling intended as sleeping quarters.

(2), (3) Repealed by Acts 2015, 84th Leg., ch. 1, §3.1639(113), eff. Apr. 2, 2015.

(4) "Residential dwelling" includes a single-family home, a duplex, a triplex, an apartment, a motel or hotel, and a mobile home.

(5) "Security bars" means burglar bars or other bars located on the inside or outside of a door or window of a residential dwelling.

H&SC §756.082. SECURITY BARS ON RESIDENTIAL DWELLING

A person may not install security bars on a door or window of a bedroom in a residential dwelling unless:

(1) the security bars on at least one door or window in the bedroom have an interior release mechanism; or

(2) at least one window or door from the bedroom to the exterior may be opened for emergency escape or rescue.

H&SC §756.083. LABELING REQUIREMENT

(a) Except as provided by Subsection (b), a person may not sell security bars or offer security bars for sale in this state unless the security bars or their packaging are labeled in accordance with rules adopted by the state fire marshal. The required label must state the requirements of Section 756.082.

(b) A person who is not regularly and actively engaged in business as a wholesale or retail dealer may sell or offer to sell security bars in this state provided that proper written notice of the requirements of Section 756.082 is provided to the buyer in a form approved by the state fire marshal.

H&SC §756.084. RECOMMENDED RELEASE MECHANISM

(a) The state fire marshal or a testing laboratory under conditions and procedures approved by the state fire marshal may recommend an interior release mechanism that has been shown to be effective.

(b) The state fire marshal shall adopt rules to implement this section.

Sections 756.085-756.100 blank

SUBCHAPTER G. MUNICIPAL LANDSCAPING SERVICES

H&SC §756.101. AUTHORIZATION

To protect the public health, safety, or welfare, a municipality may provide landscaping services, including tree-trimming, tree disposal, remediation, cleanup, and recycling services, to any person who resides or business that operates inside or outside the corporate limits of the municipality only if the governing body of the municipality makes written findings as required by Section 756.102.

H&SC §756.102. FINDINGS REQUIRED

The written findings must:

(1) identify the problem requiring the need for providing municipal landscaping services;

(2) identify the public health, safety, or welfare concern;

(3) describe any reasonable actions previously taken to alleviate the problem; and

(4) specify a period of definite duration necessary to address the problem.

H&SC §756.103. EXCEPTION

The limitations and requirements of this subchapter do not apply to a municipality in times of emergency, catastrophe, or other calamity.

Sections 756.104-756.120 blank

SUBCHAPTER H. CONSTRUCTION AFFECTING PIPELINE EASEMENTS & RIGHTS-OF-WAY

H&SC §756.121. DEFINITIONS

In this subchapter:

(1) "Construction" means a building, structure, driveway, roadway, or other construction any part of which is physically located on, across, over, or under the easement or right-of-way of a pipeline facility or that physically impacts or creates a risk to a pipeline facility.

(2) "Constructor" means a person that builds, operates, repairs, replaces, or maintains a construction or causes a construction to be built, operated, repaired, maintained, or replaced.

(3) "Pipeline facility" means a pipeline used to transmit or distribute natural gas or to gather or transmit oil, gas, or the products of oil or gas.

H&SC §756.122. APPLICABILITY

(a) This subchapter applies to a construction or the repair, replacement, or maintenance of a construction unless there is a written agreement, including a Texas Department of Transportation right-of-way agreement, to the contrary between the owner or operator of the affected pipeline facility and the person that places or causes a construction to be placed on the easement or right-of-way of a pipeline facility.

(b) This subchapter does not apply to:

(1) construction done by a municipality on property owned by the municipality, unless the construction is for private commercial use; or

(2) construction or repair, replacement, or maintenance of construction on property owned by a navigation district or port authority created or operating under Section 52, Article III, or Section 59, Article XVI, Texas Constitution.

H&SC §756.123. PROHIBITION OF CONSTRUCTION WITHOUT NOTICE

A person may not build, repair, replace, or maintain a construction on, across, over, or under the easement or right-of-way for a pipeline facility unless notice of the construction is given the operator of the pipeline facility and:

(1) the operator of the pipeline facility determines that the construction will not increase a risk to the public or increase a risk of a break, leak, rupture, or other damage to the pipeline facility;

(2) if the operator of the pipeline facility determines that the construction will increase risk to the public or the pipeline facility, the constructor pays the reasonable, necessary, and documented cost of the additional fortifications, barriers, conduits, or other changes or improvements necessary to protect the public or pipeline facility from that risk before proceeding with the construction;

(3) the building, repair, replacement, or maintenance is conducted under an existing written agreement; or

(4) the building, repair, replacement, or maintenance is required to be done promptly by a regulated utility company because of the effects of a natural disaster.

H&SC §756.124. CIVIL LIABILITY

A constuctor[1] who violates this subchapter is liable to the owner or operator of a pipeline facility for damages to the facility proximately caused by the violation, including any liability the owner or operator of the pipeline facility incurs as a result of the violation. This section does not affect the right of a surface owner to recover for any damages to the owner's property.

1. **Editor's note:** Probably should be "constructor."

H&SC §756.125. INJUNCTIVE RELIEF

(a) A suit for injunctive relief to prevent or abate the violation of this subchapter may be brought by the county attorney for the county in which the pipeline facility is located, by the attorney general, or by the owner or operator of the pipeline facility.

(b) The court in which the suit is brought may grant any prohibitory or mandatory injunction the facts warrant, including a temporary restraining order, temporary injunction, or permanent injunction. The court may grant the relief without requiring a bond or other undertaking.

(A) H&SC §756.126. SAFETY STANDARDS & BEST PRACTICES

The Railroad Commission of Texas shall adopt and enforce rules prescribing safety standards and best practices, including those described by 49 U.S.C. Section 6105 et seq., relating to the prevention of damage by a person to a facility, including an interstate or intrastate pipeline facility, under the jurisdiction of the commission.

2017 Legislation: Amended by H.B. 1818, §8, 85th Leg., eff. Sept. 1, 2017.

CHAPTER 757. POOL YARD ENCLOSURES

H&SC §757.001. DEFINITIONS

In this chapter:

(1) "Self-closing and self-latching device" means a device that causes a gate to automatically close without human or electrical power after it has been opened and to automatically latch without human or electrical power when the gate closes.

(2) "Doorknob lock" means a lock that is in a doorknob and that is operated from the exterior by a key, card, or combination and from the interior without a key, card, or combination.

(3) "Dwelling" or "rental dwelling" means one or more rooms rented to one or more tenants for use as a permanent residence under a lease. The term does not include a room rented to overnight guests.

(4) "French doors" means double doors, sometimes called double-hinged patio doors, that provide access from a dwelling interior to the exterior and in which each of the two doors are hinged and closable so that the edge of one door closes immediately adjacent to the edge of the other door with no partition between the doors. "French door" means either one of the two doors.

(5) "Keyed dead bolt" means a door lock that is not in the doorknob, that locks by a bolt in the doorjamb, that has a bolt with at least a one-inch throw if installed after September 1, 1993, and that is operated from the exterior by a key, card, or combination and operated from the interior by a knob or lever without a key, card, or combination. The term includes a doorknob lock that contains a bolt with at least a one-inch throw.

(6)(A) "Keyless bolting device" means a door lock not in the doorknob that locks:

(i) with a bolt with a one-inch throw into a strike plate screwed into the portion of the doorjamb surface

that faces the edge of the door when the door is closed or into a metal doorjamb that serves as the strike plate, operable only by knob or lever from the door's interior and not in any manner from the door's exterior, and that is commonly known as a keyless dead bolt;

(ii) by a drop bolt system operated by placing a central metal plate over a metal doorjamb restraint which protrudes from the doorjamb and which is affixed to the doorjamb frame by means of three case-hardened screws at least three inches in length. One half of the central plate must overlap the interior surface of the door and the other half of the central plate must overlap the doorjamb when the plate is placed over the doorjamb restraint. The drop bolt system must prevent the door from being opened unless the central plate is lifted off of the doorjamb restraint by a person who is on the interior side of the door; or

(iii) by a metal bar or metal tube that is placed across the entire interior side of the door and secured in place at each end of the bar or tube by heavy-duty metal screw hooks. The screw hooks must be at least three inches in length and must be screwed into the door frame stud or wall stud on each side of the door. The bar or tube must be capable of being secured to both of the screw hooks and must be permanently attached in some way to the door frame stud or wall stud. When secured to the screw hooks, the bar or tube must prevent the door from being opened unless the bar or tube is removed by a person who is on the interior side of the door.

(B) The term does not include a chain latch, flip latch, surface-mounted slide bolt, mortise door bolt, surface-mounted barrel bolt, surface-mounted swing bar door guard, spring-loaded nightlatch, foot bolt, or other lock or latch.

(7) "Multiunit rental complex" means two or more dwelling units in one or more buildings that are under common ownership, managed by the same owner, managing agent, or management company, and located on the same lot or tract of land or adjacent lots or tracts of land. The term includes a condominium project. The term does not include:

(A) a facility primarily renting rooms to overnight guests; or

(B) a single-family home or adjacent single-family homes that are not part of a condominium project.

(8) "Pool" means a permanent swimming pool, permanent wading or reflection pool, or permanent hot tub or spa over 18 inches deep, located at ground level, above ground, below ground, or indoors.

(9) "Pool yard" means an area that contains a pool.

(10) "Pool yard enclosure" or "enclosure" means a fence, wall, or combination of fences, walls, gates, windows, or doors that completely surround a pool.

(11) "Property owners association" means an association of property owners for a residential subdivision, condominium, cooperative, town home project, or other project involving residential dwellings.

(12) "Sliding door handle latch" means a latch or lock that is near the handle on a sliding glass door, that is operated with or without a key, and that is designed to prevent the door from being opened.

(13) "Sliding door pin lock" means a pin or rod that is inserted from the interior side of a sliding glass door at the side opposite the door's handle and that is designed to prevent the door from being opened or lifted.

(14) "Sliding door security bar" means a bar or rod that can be placed at the bottom of or across the interior side of the fixed panel of a sliding glass door and that is designed to prevent the sliding panel of the door from being opened.

(15) "Tenant" means a person who is obligated to pay rent or other consideration and who is authorized to occupy a dwelling, to the exclusion of others, under a verbal or written lease or rental agreement.

(16) "Window latch" means a device on a window or window screen that prevents the window or window screen from being opened and that is operated without a key and only from the interior.

H&SC §757.002. APPLICATION

This chapter applies only to:

(1) a pool owned, controlled, or maintained by the owner of a multiunit rental complex or by a property owners association; and

(2) doors and windows of rental dwellings opening into the pool yard of a multiunit rental complex or condominium, cooperative, or town home project.

H&SC §757.003. ENCLOSURE FOR POOL YARD

(a) Except as otherwise provided by Section 757.005, the owner of a multiunit rental complex with a pool or a property owners association that owns, controls, or maintains a pool shall completely enclose the pool yard with a pool yard enclosure.

(b) The height of the pool yard enclosure must be at least 48 inches as measured from the ground on the side away from the pool.

(c) Openings under the pool yard enclosure may not allow a sphere four inches in diameter to pass under the pool yard enclosure.

(d) If the pool yard enclosure is constructed with horizontal and vertical members and the distance between the tops of the horizontal members is at least 45 inches, the openings may not allow a sphere four inches in diameter to pass through the enclosure.

(e) If the pool yard enclosure is constructed with horizontal and vertical members and the distance between the tops of the horizontal members is less than 45 inches, the openings may not allow a sphere 1-¾ inches in diameter to pass through the enclosure.

(f) The use of chain link fencing materials is prohibited entirely for a new pool yard enclosure that is constructed after January 1, 1994. The use of diagonal fencing members that are lower than 49 inches above the ground is prohibited for a new pool yard enclosure that is constructed after January 1, 1994.

(g) Decorative designs or cutouts on or in the pool yard enclosure may not contain any openings greater than 1-¾ inches in any direction.

(h) Indentations or protrusions in a solid pool yard enclosure without any openings may not be greater than normal construction tolerances and tooled masonry joints on the side away from the pool.

(i) Permanent equipment or structures may not be constructed or placed in a manner that makes them readily available for climbing over the pool yard enclosure.

(j) The wall of a building may be part of the pool yard enclosure only if the doors and windows in the wall comply with Sections 757.006 and 757.007.

(k) The owner of a multiunit rental complex with a pool or a property owners association that owns, controls, or maintains a pool is not required to:

(1) build a pool yard enclosure at specified locations or distances from the pool other than distances for minimum walkways around the pool; or

(2) conform secondary pool yard enclosures, located inside or outside the primary pool yard enclosure, to the requirements of this chapter.

H&SC §757.004. GATES

(a) Except as otherwise provided by Section 757.005, a gate in a fence or wall enclosing a pool yard as required by Section 757.003 must:

(1) have a self-closing and self-latching device;

(2) have hardware enabling it to be locked, at the option of whoever controls the gate, by a padlock or a built-in lock operated by key, card, or combination; and

(3) open outward away from the pool yard.

(b) Except as otherwise provided by Subsection (c) and Section 757.005, a gate latch must be installed so that it is at least 60 inches above the ground, except that it may be installed lower if:

(1) the latch is installed on the pool yard side of the gate only and is at least three inches below the top of the gate; and

(2) the gate or enclosure has no opening greater than one-half inch in any direction within 18 inches from the latch, including the space between the gate and the gate post to which the gate latches.

(c) A gate latch may be located 42 inches or higher above the ground if the gate cannot be opened except by key, card, or combination on both sides of the gate.

H&SC §757.005. EXISTING POOL YARD ENCLOSURES

(a) If a pool yard enclosure is constructed or modified before January 1, 1994, and no municipal ordinance containing standards for pool yard enclosures were applicable at the time of construction or modification, the enclosure must comply with the requirements of Sections 757.003 and 757.004, except that:

(1) if the enclosure is constructed with chain link metal fencing material, the openings in the enclosure may not allow a sphere 2-¼ inches in diameter to pass through the enclosure; or

(2) if the enclosure is constructed with horizontal and vertical members and the distance between the tops of the horizontal members is at least 36 inches, the openings in the enclosure may not allow a sphere four inches in diameter to pass through the enclosure.

(b) If a pool yard enclosure is constructed or modified before January 1, 1994, and if the enclosure is in compliance with applicable municipal ordinances existing on January 1, 1994, and containing standards for pool yard enclosures, Sections 757.003, 757.004(a)(3), and 757.004(b) do not apply to the enclosure.

H&SC §757.006. DOOR

(a) A door, sliding glass door, or French door may not open directly into a pool yard if the date of electrical service for initial construction of the building or pool is on or after January 1, 1994.

(b) A door, sliding glass door, or French door may open directly into a pool yard if the date of electrical service for initial construction of the building or pool is before January 1, 1994, and the pool yard enclosure complies with Subsection (c), (d), or (e), as applicable.

(c) If a door of a building, other than a sliding glass door or screen door, opens into the pool yard, the door must have a:

(1) latch that automatically engages when the door is closed;

(2) spring-loaded door-hinge pin, automatic door closer, or similar device to cause the door to close automatically; and

(3) keyless bolting device that is installed not less than 36 inches or more than 48 inches above the interior floor.

(d) If French doors of a building open to the pool yard, one of the French doors must comply with Subsection (c)(1) and the other door must have:

(1) a keyed dead bolt or keyless bolting device capable of insertion into the doorjamb above the door, and a keyless bolting device capable of insertion into the floor or threshold; or

(2) a bolt with at least a ¾-inch throw installed inside the door and operated from the edge of the door that is capable of insertion into the doorjamb above the door and another bolt with at least a ¾-inch throw installed inside the door and operated from the edge of the door that is capable of insertion into the floor or threshold.

(e) If a sliding glass door of a building opens into the pool yard, the sliding glass door must have:

(1) a sliding door handle latch or sliding door security bar that is installed not more than 48 inches above the interior floor; and

(2) a sliding door pin lock that is installed not more than 48 inches above the interior floor.

(f) A door, sliding glass door, or French door that opens into a pool yard from an area of a building that is not used by residents and that has no access to an area outside the pool yard is not required to have a lock, latch, dead bolt, or keyless bolting device.

(g) A keyed dead bolt, keyless bolting device, sliding door pin lock, or sliding door security bar installed before September 1, 1993, may be installed not more than 54 inches from the floor.

(h) A keyed dead bolt or keyless dead bolt, as described by Section 757.001(6)(A)(i), installed in a dwelling on or after September 1, 1993, must have a bolt with a throw of not less than one inch.

H&SC §757.007. WINDOW & WINDOW SCREENS

A wall of a building constructed before January 1, 1994, may not be used as part of a pool yard enclosure unless each window in the wall has a latch and unless each window screen on a window in the wall is affixed by a window screen latch, screws, or similar means. This section does not require the installation of window screens. A wall of a building constructed on or after January 1, 1994, may not be used as part of a pool yard enclosure unless each ground floor window in the wall is permanently closed and unable to be opened.

H&SC §757.008. BUILDING IN POOL YARD

Each door, sliding glass door, window, and window screen of each dwelling unit in a residential building located in the enclosed pool yard must comply with Sections 757.006 and 757.007.

H&SC §757.009. INSPECTION, REPAIR, & MAINTENANCE

(a) An owner of a multiunit rental complex or a rental dwelling in a condominium, cooperative, or town home project with a pool or a property owners association that owns, controls, or maintains a pool shall exercise ordinary and reasonable care to inspect, maintain, repair, and keep in good working order the pool yard enclosures, gates, and self-closing and self-latching devices required by this chapter and within the control of the owner or property owners association.

(b) An owner of a multiunit rental complex or a rental dwelling in a condominium, cooperative, or town home project with a pool or a property owners association that owns, controls, or maintains a pool shall exercise ordinary and reasonable care to maintain, repair, and keep in good working order the window latches, sliding door handle latches, sliding door pin locks, and sliding door security bars required by this chapter and within the control of the owner or property owners association after request or notice from the tenant that

those devices are malfunctioning or in need of repair or replacement. A request or notice under this subsection may be given orally unless a written lease applicable to the tenant or written rules governing the property owners association require the request or notice to be in writing. The requirement in the lease or rules must be in capital letters and underlined or in 10-point boldfaced print.

(c) An owner of a multiunit rental complex or a rental dwelling in a condominium, cooperative, or town home project with a pool or a property owners association that owns, controls, or maintains a pool shall inspect the pool yard enclosures, gates, and self-closing and self-latching devices on gates no less than once every 31 days.

(d) An owner's or property owners association's duty of inspection, repair, and maintenance under this section may not be waived under any circumstances and may not be enlarged except by written agreement with a tenant or occupant of a multiunit rental complex or a member of a property owners association or as may be otherwise allowed by this chapter.

H&SC §757.010. COMPLIANCE WITH CHAPTER

(a) Except as provided by Subsection (b) and Section 757.011, a person who constructs or modifies a pool yard enclosure to conform with this chapter may not be required to construct the enclosure differently by a local governmental entity, common law, or any other law.

(b) An owner of a multiunit rental complex or a rental dwelling in a condominium, cooperative, or town home project with a pool or a property owners association that owns, controls, or maintains a pool may, at the person's option, exceed the standards of this chapter or those adopted under Section 757.011. A tenant or occupant in a multiunit rental complex and a member of a property owners association may, by express written agreement, require the owner of the complex or the association to exceed those standards.

(c) A municipality may continue to require greater overall height requirements for pool yard enclosures if the requirements exist under the municipality's ordinances on January 1, 1994.

H&SC §757.011. RULEMAKING AUTHORITY

The executive commissioner of the Health and Human Services Commission may adopt rules requiring standards for design and construction of pool yard enclosures that exceed the requirements of this chapter and that apply to all pools and pool yards subject to this chapter. An owner of a multiunit rental complex or a rental dwelling in a condominium, cooperative, or town home project with a pool or a property owners association that owns, controls, or maintains a pool shall comply with and shall be liable for failure to comply with those rules to the same extent as if they were part of this chapter.

H&SC §757.012. ENFORCEMENT

(a) A tenant of an owner of a multiunit rental complex, a member of a property owners association, a governmental entity, or any other person or the person's representative may maintain an action against the owner or property owners association for failure to comply with the requirements of this chapter. In that action, the person may obtain:

(1) a court order directing the owner or property owners association to comply with this chapter;

(2) a judgment against the owner or property owners association for actual damages resulting from the failure to comply with the requirements of this chapter;

(3) a judgment against the owner or property owners association for punitive damages resulting from the failure to comply with the requirements of this chapter if the actual damages to the person were caused by the owner's or property owners association's intentional, malicious, or grossly negligent actions;

(4) a judgment against the owner or property owners association for actual damages, and if appropriate, punitive damages, where the owner or association was in compliance with this chapter at the time of the pool-related damaging event but was consciously indifferent to access being repeatedly gained to the pool yard by unauthorized persons; or

(5) a judgment against the owner or property owners association for a civil penalty of not more than $5,000 if the owner or property owners association fails to comply with this chapter within a reasonable time after written notice by a tenant of the multiunit rental complex or a member of the property owners association.

(b) A court may award reasonable attorney fees and costs to the prevailing party in an action brought under Subsection (a)(5).

(c) The attorney general, a local health department, a municipality, or a county having jurisdiction

may enforce this chapter by any lawful means, including inspections, permits, fees, civil fines, criminal prosecutions, injunctions, and, after required notice, governmental construction or repair of pool yard enclosures that do not exist or that do not comply with this chapter.

H&SC §757.013. Tenant's Request for Repairs

A tenant in a multiunit rental complex with a pool may verbally request repair of a keyed dead bolt, keyless bolting device, sliding door latch, sliding door pin lock, sliding door security bar, window latch, or window screen latch unless a provision of a written lease executed by the tenant requires that the request be made in writing and the provision is in capital letters and underlined or in 10-point boldfaced print. A request for repair may be given to the owner or the owner's managing agent.

H&SC §757.014. Application to Other Bodies of Water & Related Facilities

The owner of a multiunit rental complex or a property owners association is not required to enclose a body of water or construct barriers between the owner's or property owners association's property and a body of water such as an ocean, bay, lake, pond, bayou, river, creek, stream, spring, reservoir, stock tank, culvert, drainage ditch, detention pond, or other flood or drainage facility.

H&SC §757.015. Effect on Other Laws

(a) The duties established by this chapter for an owner of a multiunit dwelling project, an owner of a dwelling in a condominium, cooperative, or town home project, and a property owners association supersede those established by common law, the Property Code, the Health and Safety Code, the Local Government Code other than Section 214.101, and local ordinances relating to duties to inspect, install, repair, or maintain:

(1) pool yard enclosures;

(2) pool yard enclosure gates and gate latches, including self-closing and self-latching devices;

(3) keyed dead bolts, keyless bolting devices, sliding door handle latches, sliding door security bars, self-latching and self-closing devices, and sliding door pin locks on doors that open into a pool yard area and that are owned and controlled by the owner or property owners association; and

(4) latches on windows that open into a pool yard area and that are owned and controlled by the owner or property owners association.

(b) This chapter does not affect any duties of a rental dwelling owner, lessor, sublessor, management company, or managing agent under Subchapter D, Chapter 92, Property Code.

H&SC §757.016. Nonexclusive Remedies

The remedies contained in this chapter are not exclusive and are not intended to affect existing remedies allowed by law or other procedure.

H&SC §757.017. Interpretation & Application

The provisions of this chapter shall be liberally construed to promote its underlying purpose which is to prevent swimming pool deaths and injuries in this state.

Subtitle C. Fire

Chapter 791. Fire Escapes

Subchapter A. General Provisions

H&SC §791.001. Definitions

In this chapter:

(1) "Owner" includes an individual, firm, association, or private corporation.

(2) "Story" has its usual architectural meaning and includes:

(A) a basement that extends five feet or more above the grade line on one or more sides of a building;

(B) a balcony or mezzanine floor of a building;

(C) a roof garden; or

(D) an attic used for any purpose.

H&SC §791.002. Fire Escape Required

(a) The owner of a building shall equip the building with at least one fire escape and with additional fire escapes as required by Subchapters C and D if the building has at least:

(1) three stories and is used as a facility subject to Subchapter C; or

(2) two stories and is used as a school.

(b) A fire escape required by this chapter must meet the specifications provided by this chapter for an exterior stairway fire escape, an exterior chute fire es-

cape, a combination of those exterior fire escapes, or an interior fire escape.

H&SC §791.003. COMPLIANCE

A building constructed after September 1, 1925, and subject to this chapter shall be equipped with fire escapes and must meet all other requirements of this chapter before the building is wholly or partially occupied or used.

H&SC §791.004. EXEMPTIONS

(a) This chapter does not apply to the construction of a structure in a municipality that has in effect a nationally recognized model building code governing the construction if the building code requires at least one one-hour fire-resistive means of escape with a total width equal to or greater than the total exit width required under this chapter for a structure of three or more stories.

(b) This chapter does not apply to a grain elevator constructed of:

(1) steel;

(2) steel and concrete; or

(3) wood if fewer than five persons are employed at the grain elevator.

H&SC §791.005. LOCATION OF FIRE ESCAPES

Consistent with accessibility, each fire escape subject to this chapter must be located as far as possible from stairways, elevator hatchways, and other openings in the floors of the building served by the fire escape. If possible, each fire escape must be located at the end of a hallway or unobstructed passageway and as far apart as is consistent with the construction and location of the building.

H&SC §791.006. INSPECTION; APPROVAL

(a) A fire escape subject to this chapter and each extension or addition to that fire escape shall be inspected before being approved for use.

(b) The inspection may be conducted by:

(1) the state fire marshal;

(2) an inspector of the State Board of Insurance;

(3) the chief of a municipal fire department; or

(4) a municipal fire marshal.

(c) A fire escape or an addition or extension to a fire escape may not be approved unless it meets the requirements of this chapter.

H&SC §791.007. TESTS; AFFIDAVIT

(a) The person who erects a fire escape shall test the fire escape, on its completion and before final approval of the fire escape, by the application of a live load of 160 pounds per square foot of area of balcony floor and stair treads, or a dead load of 240 pounds per square foot of area of balcony floor and stair treads. The weight must be simultaneously imposed on each balcony and the stairways connecting the balconies that lead both up and down.

(b) Sand, gravel, concrete blocks, or any other suitable commodity may be used in performing the tests. The load must be accurately weighed and applied as specified in this section.

(c) A dead load must be placed in position in whole or in part by mechanical means without a person present on the fire escape when the test is made. A live load must be placed in position by mechanical means or by persons, and persons must be present on the fire escape as part of the load when the test is made.

(d) The person who erects the fire escape shall conduct the tests in the presence of:

(1) the state fire marshal;

(2) an appointed representative of the state fire marshal;

(3) the chief of a fire department; or

(4) a municipal fire marshal.

(e) If an official listed in Subsection (d) cannot be present to witness the test, any of the officials instead may accept an affidavit from the person who erects the fire escape that states that the minimum required test has been made and that the fire escape has passed the test.

Sections 791.008-791.010 reserved for expansion

SUBCHAPTER B. MINIMUM SPECIFICATIONS FOR FIRE ESCAPES

H&SC §791.011. GENERAL REQUIREMENTS

(a) A fire escape shall be constructed and arranged in a manner that:

(1) permits exit on the fire escape from each floor of the building above the first floor; and

(2) provides an uninterrupted exit from the building to the grade.

(b) The materials, construction, erection, and test of a fire escape must comply with the minimum specifications established under this subchapter for that type of fire escape.

H&SC §791.012. MINIMUM SPECIFICATIONS FOR EXTERIOR STAIRWAY FIRE ESCAPES

(a) An exterior stairway fire escape is a structure that:

(1) is located on the exterior of a building;

(2) is constructed of iron, steel, or reinforced concrete; and

(3) consists of balconies and stairways.

(b) An exterior stairway fire escape may be constructed in:

(1) superimposed form;

(2) straight run form;

(3) superimposed form with intermediate balconies; or

(4) a combination of those forms.

(c) The balconies for a superimposed form stairway fire escape attached to the building at two or more floors must equal in length the horizontal length of the stair runs plus an amount at each end equal to the width of the stairs. Each balcony must be as long as the width of the exit opening in the building wall and must be at least 50 inches wide inside the balcony railings.

(d) The balconies for a superimposed form stairway fire escape with intermediate balconies attached to the building at two or more floors must be at least equal in width to the combined width of the stairways connected by the balconies leading both up and down. The landings at the head and foot of the stairs must be as deep as the width of the stairs and as long as the width of the exit opening in the building wall.

(e) The balconies for a straight run form stairway fire escape must be at least equal in width to the width of the stairs and as long as the width of the exit opening in the building wall.

(f) The floor of an iron or steel balcony must be either solid or slatted. If solid, the floor must have a scored surface to prevent slipping and, to provide drainage, must be pitched at a slope of not less than one-half inch in 10 feet. If slatted, the slats may not be placed more than three-quarters inch apart and must be secured with rivets or bolts. Material used in the floor must be at least three-sixteenths inch thick.

(g) The railing enclosures of a balcony must be at least two feet nine inches high. If of vertical and horizontal slat or grill construction, a space between slats or within the grill may not have a horizontal width of more than eight inches. If of truss construction, the span of a panel may not exceed three feet. An opening in the railing enclosures on any type of construction may not exceed two square feet. A railing enclosure must be free throughout its length from obstructions that tend to break handholds, and the passage space must be smooth and free from obstructions or projections. A railing enclosure must be designed to withstand a horizontal pressure of 200 pounds per running foot of railing without serious deflection.

(h) A balcony must be anchored to the building with bolts at least one inch in diameter, extending through the wall of the building and provided with a wall bearing plate on the interior that is at least five inches square and three-eighths inch thick, or must be anchored by such bolts set in concrete or masonry or made integral in new buildings. A balcony may not be placed above or more than one foot below the top of the sill of the exit opening in the building wall and preferably should be level with the sill.

(i) A concrete balcony must meet the requirements of this section and must be made of reinforced concrete composed of one part cement, two parts sand, and four parts stone or gravel. The railing enclosure of a concrete balcony must meet the specifications of this section or be made of reinforced concrete, with balusters spaced not more than one foot apart.

(j) The pitch of a fire escape stairway may not exceed 45 degrees.

(k) The stairway treads must be at least eight inches wide, excluding nosings, and at least 24 inches long. Treads must be placed so that the rise, either open or closed, does not exceed eight inches. If solid, treads must have a scored surface. If slatted, the slats must be placed not more than three-quarters inch apart and be well secured by bolts or rivets. Material used in the treads must be at least three-sixteenths inch thick.

(*l*) Railings must be provided on both sides of stairs. The railings must be at least two feet nine inches high, measured vertically from the center of the stair treads, and must be supported by balusters spaced not more than one foot apart. If an intermediate rail is provided, it shall be provided halfway between the top rail and the stair stringers and the balusters must be

placed not more than five feet apart. Stair railings must permit at least 24 inches of unobstructed passageway and must be designed to withstand a horizontal pressure of 200 pounds per running foot of railing without serious deflection.

(m) Concrete stairs must comply with the requirements of this section and must be made of reinforced concrete composed in the same mix as provided by Subsection (i). Railing enclosures for concrete stairs must be either as provided by Subsection (g) or of reinforced concrete balustrade with balusters spaced not more than one foot apart.

(n) Stairways must be built stationary to grade where possible and must be built stationary to grade for buildings such as schools or hospitals.

(o) If a fire escape terminates over a street, alley, private driveway, or other similar situation and terminates in a hinged and counterbalanced section of stairway, the construction of that section of stairs must conform to the stationary parts of the stairway and must be balanced so that the weight of one person on the third or fourth tread will lower the stairway to the landing. Bearings for counterbalanced stairs must be either bronze bushings or have sufficient clearance to prevent sticking caused by corrosion. A latch or lock may not be attached to the counterbalanced stairs in the up position, but a latch must be provided to hold the stairs in the down position when they have been swung to the ground. The connection between stair railings on the stationary part of the stairway and the counterbalanced part of the stairway must be designed to prevent the probability of injury to persons who use the fire escape. If necessary, a suitable opening must be provided in any awning, roof, or other intervening obstruction to admit the counterbalanced stairs and permit the passage of persons on the stairs.

(p) The fire escape must be connected to the roof of the building to which it is attached. If the roof of the building is designed in such a way that escape by way of the roof may be necessary, the fire escape must extend to the roof. If the connection is only for use by the fire department, it must be made with a gooseneck-type ladder with stringers made of material at least three-eighths inch thick, and rungs at least three-quarters inch in diameter, 16 inches long, and not more than 14 inches apart. The ladder must be anchored to the wall.

(q) The minimum unobstructed width of an exterior passageway in the fire escape, whether parallel to the building or at right angles to it, is 24 inches.

(r) The clearance at all points on balconies and stairs, as measured vertically, must be at least six feet six inches.

H&SC §791.013. MINIMUM SPECIFICATIONS FOR EXTERIOR CHUTE FIRE ESCAPES

(a) An exterior chute fire escape is a structure that is located on the exterior of a building and constructed of iron or steel and that consists of balconies and a straight or spiral gravity chute.

(b) An exterior straight chute fire escape may be in:

(1) superimposed form parallel to or at right angles to the building;

(2) straight run form parallel to or at right angles to the building; or

(3) a combination of those two forms.

(c) An exterior spiral chute fire escape must be constructed in a spiral form around a central column and must rest on and be anchored to a concrete base at least 18 inches thick.

(d) The chute and any intervening balconies must be constructed in a manner that provides a continuous gravity slide from the top floor to the grade and must be accessible from all floors of the building. An exterior straight chute must be placed at an angle that does not exceed 45 degrees.

(e) The balconies must meet the specifications imposed under Section 791.012 for the balconies of exterior stairway fire escapes.

(f) A straight chute must be composed of material equal to at least 14-gauge iron or steel. A spiral chute must be composed of material equal to at least 16-gauge iron or steel. The material used must be blue annealed or of equal type and must be capable of taking a smooth or polished surface.

(g) The interior of a straight chute must be 20 inches wide and 18 inches deep, and in cross section must have a concave bottom and straight sides. The interior of a spiral chute must be at least 30 inches wide. The interior of either form of chute must be free from obstructions or sharp edges.

(h) The top edges of a straight chute must be stiffened and protected throughout the length of the chute

with iron or steel angles free from sharp edges. The angles must be of the size necessary to carry the maximum possible load. The chute must be reinforced crosswise underneath with iron or steel angles.

(i) The slideway of a spiral chute must be banked at the outer edge to prevent a passenger from being thrown against a guardrail or enclosure and must be enclosed by either a continuous wall or guardrail at least 30 inches high constructed of at least 18-gauge iron or steel. A spiral chute may not terminate more than two feet above the grade and must be constructed and arranged so that a normal landing is in a standing position.

(j) A landing composed of the same material as the chute must be provided at the lower end of a straight chute and must be of sufficient length in proportion to the length of the chute and the concavity of its surface to check the momentum attained through gravity and to provide a safe stop. The landing must be six inches wider than the chute on each side if wall construction does not interfere and must be without sharp edges or ragged projections. The landing must rest on and be anchored to a concrete base at least six inches thick.

(k) All rivets exposed inside a chute and on the top side of a landing of a straight chute must be countersunk and ground smooth.

H&SC §791.014. MINIMUM SPECIFICATIONS FOR INTERIOR FIRE ESCAPES

(a) An interior fire escape may be:

(1) a stairway composed of iron, steel, or concrete; or

(2) a straight or spiral chute composed of iron or steel.

(b) The fire escape must be enclosed with a noncombustible material. All door and window openings in the enclosure must be protected with self-closing fireproof shutters.

(c) Balconies or landings used with an interior fire escape must meet the construction requirements imposed under Section 791.012, except that a balcony used with an interior fire escape must permit at least 40 inches of unobstructed passageway, and the balconies or landings must be located on a level with the floors of the building.

(d) The stairs of an interior stairway fire escape must meet the requirements imposed under Section 791.012, except that the stairs must permit at least 40 inches of unobstructed passageway in all parts. An interior stairway fire escape may not use stairs of the types known as "spirals" or "winders."

(e) An interior stairway fire escape must be continuous, starting at the ground floor, and may not descend to any basement. It must extend through the roof of the building and must terminate in a penthouse constructed of noncombustible material equipped with a self-closing fire door as specified in this section.

(f) An interior chute fire escape must meet the requirements of Section 791.013.

(g) An interior fire escape must be accessible from all parts of the building it is designed to serve. Each lobby, hall, or passageway that leads to a fire escape and is used in connection with it must be at least 36 inches wide and at least six feet six inches high and must be level with the floor on which the fire escape opens and which it serves. The fire escape must be constructed at the lower end in a manner that permits direct exit to the outside of the building at the grade.

(h) The enclosing walls of an interior fire escape may be constructed of:

(1) brick;

(2) plain solid concrete;

(3) reinforced stone or gravel concrete;

(4) reinforced cinder concrete;

(5) hollow terra-cotta blocks;

(6) hollow concrete blocks composed of stone or cinder concrete mortar;

(7) gypsum blocks; or

(8) metal lath on steel studding.

(i) If the enclosing walls are of brick or plain solid concrete, they must be at least eight inches thick for the top 30 feet, increasing four inches in thickness for each lower section of 30 feet or fraction of 30 feet, or at least eight inches thick for the entire height if the walls are wholly supported at intervals not to exceed 30 feet. If the enclosing walls are of reinforced stone or gravel concrete, they must be at least five inches thick for the top 30 feet, increasing two inches in thickness for each lower section of 30 feet or fraction of 30 feet, or at least three inches thick for the entire height if supported at vertical intervals not to exceed 20 feet and if braced as necessary with lateral supports or suitable steel uprights. If the enclosing walls are of reinforced cinder concrete, the concrete must be at least five inches thick

for the entire height of the enclosing walls, and the walls must be supported at vertical intervals not to exceed 15 feet and must be braced as necessary with lateral supports or suitable steel uprights.

(j) If the enclosing walls are composed of hollow terra-cotta blocks, the blocks must be laid in cement mortar, and the walls must be at least five inches thick overall. If the enclosing walls are composed of hollow concrete blocks of either stone or cinder concrete mortar, the enclosing walls must be at least five inches thick overall. If the walls are constructed of gypsum blocks, the blocks may be either solid or hollow but must contain not more than 25 percent by weight of cinders, asbestos fiber, wood chips, or vegetable fiber. The gypsum blocks must be laid in gypsum plaster or cement mortar tempered with lime, and the enclosing walls must be at least five inches thick overall. If the walls are constructed of metal lath on steel studding, they must be covered with portland cement mortar or gypsum plaster of a finished thickness of at least two inches in the case of solid partitions or of at least three inches in the case of hollow partitions. Each opening in a wall or partition must have substantial steel framing, the vertical members of which must be securely attached to the floor construction above and below.

(k) Each door opening in an interior fire escape must be protected by the use of an automatic or self-closing fire door of standard manufacture, bearing the Underwriters Laboratory label. If an automatic fire door is used, it must be enclosed in a recessed partition. All doors must be arranged and equipped to remain in closed positions at all times and under all conditions except during actual use.

(l) Each window opening must be equipped with a metal sash bearing the Underwriters Laboratory label and with wire glass.

(m) Each interior fire escape must be provided at each landing with at least one light equal in power to a 10-watt electric globe. The lighting must be on a separate circuit from that of the rest of the building and must be designed to operate if the regular lighting system of the building is disabled.

H&SC §791.015. EXIT LIGHTS; GUIDE SIGNS

(a) At least one red light must be installed and maintained in good condition at each exit to a fire escape in a building subject to Section 791.002. An exit light must be painted with the words "fire escape exit."

(b) One guide sign must be installed and maintained in good condition at each hallway intersection. An additional guide sign must be provided for every 25 lineal feet of hallway leading to a fire escape. A guide sign must be painted with the words "fire escape" and with an arrow or hand pointing to the nearest fire escape exit.

H&SC §791.016. PAINTING & MAINTENANCE REQUIREMENTS

(a) A fire escape constructed of iron or steel must be painted with at least two coats of good metallic paint when erected. The fire escape must be repainted at least every two years or more frequently if necessary to preserve the fire escape from rust or climatic influences.

(b) The slideway of a straight or spiral chute fire escape must be thoroughly cleaned and painted at least once each year.

Sections 791.017-791.020 reserved for expansion

SUBCHAPTER C. ADDITIONAL FIRE ESCAPE REQUIREMENTS FOR CERTAIN FACILITIES

H&SC §791.021. ADDITIONAL FIRE ESCAPES FOR CERTAIN FACILITIES

(a) This section applies to:

(1) a hospital;

(2) a seminary;

(3) a college;

(4) an academy;

(5) a school;

(6) a dormitory;

(7) a hotel or other facility for the accommodation of transient guests;

(8) a lodging house, apartment house, rooming house, or boardinghouse;

(9) a lodge hall;

(10) a theater or other public place of amusement; or

(11) any other facility used for public gatherings.

(b) Each facility subject to this section and Section 791.002 that has a lot area greater than 5,000 square feet shall provide, in addition to the fire escape required by Section 791.002, one additional fire escape for:

(1) each 5,000 square feet of area in excess of the initial 5,000 square feet; and

(2) the area in excess of the largest multiple of 5,000 square feet contained in the facility's lot area if that excess is more than 2,000 square feet.

H&SC §791.022. ADDITIONAL FIRE ESCAPES FOR CERTAIN OFFICE BUILDINGS, STORES, OR INDUSTRIAL PLANTS

(a) This section applies to:

(1) an office building;

(2) a wholesale or retail mercantile establishment or store;

(3) a workshop or manufacturing establishment; or

(4) an industrial plant.

(b) Each facility subject to this section and Section 791.002 that has a lot area greater than 6,000 square feet shall provide, in addition to the fire escape required by Section 791.002, one additional fire escape for:

(1) each 6,000 square feet of area in excess of the initial 6,000 square feet; and

(2) the area in excess of the largest multiple of 6,000 square feet contained in the facility's lot area if that excess is more than 2,500 square feet.

H&SC §791.023. ADDITIONAL FIRE ESCAPES FOR CERTAIN WAREHOUSES & MILLS

(a) This section applies to a warehouse, storehouse, or mill building.

(b) Each facility subject to this section and Section 791.002 that has a lot area greater than 8,000 square feet shall provide, in addition to the fire escape required by Section 791.002, one additional fire escape for:

(1) each 8,000 square feet of area in excess of the initial 8,000 square feet; and

(2) the area in excess of the largest multiple of 8,000 square feet contained in the facility's lot area if that excess is more than 3,500 square feet.

H&SC §791.024. ADDITIONAL FIRE ESCAPES FOR NONSCHOOL PUBLIC BUILDINGS

(a) This section applies to a building, other than a school building, that is owned by this state or by a municipality or county of this state and in which public assemblies or sleeping apartments are permitted on any floor above the first floor.

(b) Each building subject to this section and Section 791.002 that has a lot area greater than 5,000 square feet shall provide, in addition to the fire escape required by Section 791.002, one additional fire escape for:

(1) each 5,000 square feet of area in excess of the initial 5,000 square feet; and

(2) the area in excess of the largest multiple of 5,000 square feet contained in the building's lot area if that excess is more than 2,000 square feet.

(c) Each person who has charge or supervision of a facility subject to this section, or who has charge or supervision of the letting of contracts for the construction of the facility, shall comply with this chapter.

Sections 791.025-791.030 reserved for expansion

SUBCHAPTER D. ADDITIONAL FIRE ESCAPE REQUIREMENTS FOR CERTAIN SCHOOL BUILDINGS

H&SC §791.031. DEFINITIONS

(a) In this subchapter, "story" means the space between two successive floor levels of a building, and a basement is a story if the floor level immediately above the basement is at least 10 feet above the grade line on at least one side of the building.

(b) In this subchapter, types of construction are classified as "fireproof," "semifireproof," or "ordinary," as those terms are defined in the most recent edition of the building code published by the successor organization to the National Board of Fire Underwriters.

H&SC §791.032. APPLICATION

This subchapter applies to a building in which a school of any kind is conducted and that is:

(1) at least two stories high; and

(2) owned by a school district.

H&SC §791.033. COMPLIANCE REQUIREMENTS

Each person who has charge or supervision of a school building subject to this subchapter, or who has charge or supervision of the letting of contracts for the construction of the building, shall comply with this chapter.

H&SC §791.034. ADMINISTRATION; ENFORCEMENT

(a) The state fire marshal shall administer and supervise the enforcement of this subchapter and Section 791.024.

(b) The state fire marshal, an inspector of the State Board of Insurance, the chief of any fire depart-

ment, and any municipal fire marshal shall enforce this subchapter and Section 791.024 by all lawful means.

H&SC §791.035. FIRE ESCAPE REQUIREMENT

(a) A school building of at least three stories and of fireproof construction, semifireproof construction, or ordinary construction shall have one fire escape for each group of 250 pupils, or each major fraction of that number, who are housed in the building at a level above the first floor.

(b) A school building of two stories and of ordinary construction shall have one fire escape for each group of 250 pupils, or each major fraction of that number, who are housed in the building at a level above the first floor.

(c) A school building of two stories that is of fireproof or semifireproof construction or that has stairways and hallways of that type of construction is not required to have a fire escape.

H&SC §791.036. REQUIRED TYPES OF FIRE ESCAPES; SPECIFICATIONS

(a) A fire escape for a school building constructed before March 17, 1950, may be either an interior fire escape or an exterior fire escape.

(b) A school building constructed on or after March 17, 1950, that consists of at least three stories of fireproof construction or at least two stories of ordinary construction shall have interior fire escapes.

(c) An exterior fire escape for a school building constructed before March 17, 1950, may be:

(1) an iron, steel, or concrete stairway;

(2) an iron or steel straight chute;

(3) an iron or steel spiral chute; or

(4) a fire escape that is a combination of those types.

(d) Exterior fire escapes used in school buildings must meet the construction requirements of this section or similar construction requirements approved by the successor organization to the National Board of Fire Underwriters. Except as otherwise provided by this section, exterior fire escapes must be:

(1) constructed throughout of noncombustible materials;

(2) designed for a live load of 100 pounds per square foot; and

(3) supported by vertical steel columns.

(e) If it is impossible to use vertical steel columns in the construction of an exterior fire escape, the use of steel brackets with bolts extending through the entire thickness of the wall may be approved.

(f) The landings and treads of exterior fire escapes must be of solid hatched steel plate or of steel gratings with interstices that do not exceed three-fourths inch and must be designed so that any accumulation of ice and snow is reduced to a minimum.

(g) The guardrails of exterior fire escapes must be at least three feet six inches high and must be substantially constructed. The guardrails must be faced either with heavy wire mesh or by steel balusters or rails not more than 9-½ inches o.c.

(h) The fire escape must have handrails on each side of the stairs that must be securely attached to the guardrails or to the building walls. Handrails must be two feet four inches to two feet six inches above the nosings.

(i) The calculated live load of an exterior fire escape must be clearly stated on the plans submitted for approval.

(j) Exterior fire escapes must be:

(1) free from obstruction;

(2) constructed in a manner that provides a safe exit for children;

(3) conveniently accessible from each floor above the first floor; and

(4) of sufficient width and strength so that each step and landing may accommodate two adults at the same time.

(k) If the Texas Education Agency approves that construction as providing a convenient and safe passage, doorways may be used as exits from each floor. The base of a doorway must be at the same level as the corresponding floor of the building and the landing of the fire escape to which the doorway leads. A doorway must be at least three feet wide and six feet six inches high and must be fitted with panic hardware approved by the successor organization to the National Board of Fire Underwriters. If there are two or more rooms or hallways adjacent and convenient to the landing of a fire escape, each room or hallway must have a doorway leading to that landing.

(*l*) The design of an interior fire escape used in a school building must meet the specifications required under Section 791.014, and must have:

(1) stairs and landings at least three feet six inches long and at least three feet wide;

(2) treads at least nine inches wide with a one inch nosing; and

(3) risers of not more than 7-¼ inches.

(m) A rise in a single run may not exceed nine feet six inches. A longer run must be interrupted by landings at least as deep as the width of the stairs.

(n) Stairs must extend continuously to the ground. Counterbalanced or swinging sections may not be approved.

H&SC §791.037. EXTERIOR FIRE ESCAPE EXITS

(a) An exit door leading to an exterior fire escape must open on a landing that is at least the width of the doors. The door must swing outward and be:

(1) at least three feet by six feet six inches;

(2) glazed with wire glass; and

(3) level at the bottom with the floors of the rooms or hallways and landings that it serves.

(b) An exit door may be secured only by panic hardware approved by the successor organization to the National Board of Fire Underwriters. Hooks, latches, bolts, locks, and similar devices are prohibited.

(c) A window may not be used as a means of access to an exterior fire escape.

H&SC §791.038. WINDOWS

A window located beneath or within 10 feet of a fire escape must be glazed with wire glass.

Sections 791.039-791.050 reserved for expansion

SUBCHAPTER E. ENFORCEMENT & PENALTY PROVISIONS

H&SC §791.051. ENFORCEMENT

(a) The attorney general, the county attorney of a county in which a building is maintained in violation of this chapter, or the district attorney of a district in which such a building is located may bring an action in the name of the state for an injunction or other process to enforce this chapter against the owner or person in charge of the building.

(b) The action shall be brought in the district court of the county in which the building is located.

(c) The action may be prosecuted by the attorney general, the county attorney, or the district attorney on that person's own motion, or on the relation of any individual, including the state fire marshal, an inspector of the State Board of Insurance, the chief of a municipal fire department, or a municipal fire marshal.

(d) A district judge may issue a mandatory injunction or other writ against a person to enforce this chapter. Disobedience of the injunction constitutes contempt of court and is punishable in the manner provided for contempt.

(e) The court may hear the case and may grant an injunction after the defendant has received 10 days' notice of the time and place set for the hearing on the injunction.

H&SC §791.052. CRIMINAL PENALTY

(a) A person commits an offense if the person obstructs a fire escape or a hallway or entrance leading to a fire escape in a manner that prevents free access to or use of the fire escape. A door equipped with a lock requiring a key to operate is an obstruction.

(b) A person commits an offense if the person is the owner of a building required to be equipped with fire escapes and the person fails or refuses to comply with this chapter.

(c) A person commits an offense if the person serves as an agent in the care, management, supervision, control, or renting of a building for an owner who is not a resident of this state and the owner fails or refuses to comply with this chapter as it applies to that building.

(d) An offense under this section is punishable by a fine of not less than $20 or more than $50. If the defendant is a corporation, each officer or member of the board of directors of the corporation is subject to the fine.

(e) Each day's failure or refusal to comply constitutes a separate offense. Each day that an agent represents a nonresident owner who is not in compliance constitutes a separate offense.

(b) The action shall be brought in the district court of the county in which the building is located.

(c) The [illegible] may be [illegible] by the attorney general, the county attorney, or the district attorney on [illegible] of a violation of [illegible], including the state fire marshal, an inspector of the State Board of Insurance, [illegible] of a municipality [illegible].

(d) [illegible] injunction [illegible] of this chapter [illegible] constitutes [illegible] court [illegible] when [illegible].

(e) The court may [illegible] of [illegible] for [illegible] and [illegible].

§ [illegible] CRIMINAL PENALTY

(a) A person commits an offense if the person [illegible] a [illegible] in a manner that prevents [illegible] access [illegible] with a [illegible].

(b) A person commits an offense if the person is the owner of a building required to be equipped with fire escapes and the person fails or refuses to comply with this chapter.

(c) A person commits an offense if the person serves as an agent in the care, management, supervision, control, or renting of a building for an owner who is not a resident of this state and the owner fails or refuses to comply with this chapter as it applies to that building.

(d) An offense under this section is punishable by a fine of not less than [illegible] nor more than [illegible]. If the defendant is a corporation, each officer or member of the board of directors of the corporation is subject to the fine.

(e) Each day of a failure or refusal to comply constitutes a separate offense. Each day that an agent serves a nonresident owner who is not in compliance constitutes a separate offense.

(1) [illegible] and [illegible] [illegible]

(2) [illegible]

(3) [illegible]

(4) a metal [illegible] sixty inches [illegible] long [illegible] at least [illegible] the stairs.

(b) [illegible] Commercial [illegible] may not be approved.

§ [illegible] EXTERIOR [illegible]

(a) An exterior [illegible] shall [illegible] at least [illegible]. The door [illegible] outward and:

(1) [illegible] sixty inches;

(2) [illegible] with [illegible]; and

(3) [illegible] at the [illegible] with the [illegible] of the [illegible] or [illegible].

(b) [illegible] may be [illegible] from the [illegible] are prohibited.

(c) A window may not be [illegible] than [illegible].

§ [illegible].036. WINDOWS

A window [illegible] each [illegible] must be [illegible].

[illegible]

§ [illegible] PENALTY PROVISIONS

§ [illegible] ENFORCEMENT

(a) The attorney general, the county attorney of the county in which a building is situated in violation of this chapter, or the district attorney [illegible] in which such a building is located may bring an action in the name of the state [illegible] injunction or another order [illegible] to enforce this chapter against the owner or person in charge of the building.

SELECTED PROVISIONS
TABLE OF CONTENTS

TITLE 2. ORGANIZATION OF MUNICIPAL GOVERNMENT

Subtitle C. Municipal Boundaries & Annexation

Chapter 42. Extraterritorial Jurisdiction of Municipalities

Chapter 43. Municipal Annexation

Local Government Code

Selected Provisions

Table of Contents

Title 7. Regulation of Land Use, Structures, Businesses, & Related Activities

Subtitle A. Municipal Regulatory Authority

Chapter 211. Municipal Zoning Authority

SELECTED PROVISIONS
TABLE OF CONTENTS

Local Government Code

Selected Provisions
Table of Contents

Local Government Code

Selected Provisions

Table of Contents

SELECTED PROVISIONS
TABLE OF CONTENTS

TITLE 2. ORGANIZATION OF MUNICIPAL GOVERNMENT

SUBTITLE C. MUNICIPAL BOUNDARIES & ANNEXATION

CHAPTER 42. EXTRATERRITORIAL JURISDICTION OF MUNICIPALITIES

SUBCHAPTER A. GENERAL PROVISIONS

LGOVT §42.001. PURPOSE OF EXTRATERRITORIAL JURISDICTION

The legislature declares it the policy of the state to designate certain areas as the extraterritorial jurisdiction of municipalities to promote and protect the general health, safety, and welfare of persons residing in and adjacent to the municipalities.

Sections 42.002-42.020 reserved for expansion

SUBCHAPTER B. DETERMINATION OF EXTRATERRITORIAL JURISDICTION

LGOVT §42.021. EXTENT OF EXTRATERRITORIAL JURISDICTION

(a) The extraterritorial jurisdiction of a municipality is the unincorporated area that is contiguous to the corporate boundaries of the municipality and that is located:

(1) within one-half mile of those boundaries, in the case of a municipality with fewer than 5,000 inhabitants;

(2) within one mile of those boundaries, in the case of a municipality with 5,000 to 24,999 inhabitants;

(3) within two miles of those boundaries, in the case of a municipality with 25,000 to 49,999 inhabitants;

(4) within 3½ miles of those boundaries, in the case of a municipality with 50,000 to 99,999 inhabitants; or

(5) within five miles of those boundaries, in the case of a municipality with 100,000 or more inhabitants.

(b) Regardless of Subsection (a), the extraterritorial jurisdiction of a municipality is the unincorporated area that is contiguous to the corporate boundaries of the municipality and that is located:

(1) within five miles of those boundaries on a barrier island; or

(2) within one-half mile of those boundaries off a barrier island.

(c) Subsection (b) applies to a municipality that has:

(1) a population of 2,000 or more; and

(2) territory located:

(A) entirely on a barrier island in the Gulf of Mexico; and

(B) within 30 miles of an international border.

(d) Regardless of Subsection (a), the extraterritorial jurisdiction of a municipality is the unincorporated area that is contiguous to the corporate boundaries of the municipality and that is located within three miles of those boundaries if the municipality:

(1) has a population of not less than 20,000 or more than 29,000; and

(2) is located in a county that has a population of 45,000 or more and borders the Trinity River.

LGOVT §42.022. EXPANSION OF EXTRATERRITORIAL JURISDICTION

(a) When a municipality annexes an area, the extraterritorial jurisdiction of the municipality expands with the annexation to comprise, consistent with Section 42.021, the area around the new municipal boundaries.

(b) The extraterritorial jurisdiction of a municipality may expand beyond the distance limitations imposed by Section 42.021 to include an area contiguous to the otherwise existing extraterritorial jurisdiction of the municipality if the owners of the area request the expansion.

(c) The expansion of the extraterritorial jurisdiction of a municipality through annexation, request, or increase in the number of inhabitants may not include any area in the existing extraterritorial jurisdiction of another municipality, except as provided by Subsection (d).

(d) The extraterritorial jurisdiction of a municipality may be expanded through annexation to include area that on the date of annexation is located in the extraterritorial jurisdiction of another municipality if a written agreement between the municipalities in effect on the date of annexation allocates the area to the extraterritorial jurisdiction of the annexing municipality.

LGOVT §42.0225. EXTRATERRITORIAL JURISDICTION AROUND CERTAIN MUNICIPALLY OWNED PROPERTY

(a) This section applies only to an area owned by a municipality that is:

(1) annexed by the municipality; and

(2) not contiguous to other territory of the municipality.

(b) Notwithstanding Section 42.021, the annexation of an area described by Subsection (a) does not expand the extraterritorial jurisdiction of the municipality.

LGOVT §42.023. REDUCTION OF EXTRATERRITORIAL JURISDICTION

The extraterritorial jurisdiction of a municipality may not be reduced unless the governing body of the municipality gives its written consent by ordinance or resolution, except:

(1) in cases of judicial apportionment of overlapping extraterritorial jurisdictions under Section 42.901;

(2) in accordance with an agreement under Section 42.022(d); or

(3) as necessary to comply with Section 42.0235.

Ⓐ LGOVT §42.0235. LIMITATION ON EXTRATERRITORIAL JURISDICTION OF CERTAIN MUNICIPALITIES

(a) Notwithstanding Section 42.021, and except as provided by Subsection (d), the extraterritorial jurisdiction of a municipality with a population of more than 175,000 located in a county that contains an international border and borders the Gulf of Mexico terminates two miles from the extraterritorial jurisdiction of a neighboring municipality if extension of the extraterritorial jurisdiction beyond that limit would:

(1) completely surround the corporate boundaries or extraterritorial jurisdiction of the neighboring municipality; and

(2) limit the growth of the neighboring municipality by precluding the expansion of the neighboring municipality's extraterritorial jurisdiction.

(b) A municipality shall release extraterritorial jurisdiction as necessary to comply with Subsection (a).

(c) Notwithstanding any other law, a municipality that owns an electric system and that releases extraterritorial jurisdiction under Subsection (b) may provide electric service in the released area to the same extent that the service would have been provided if the municipality had annexed the area.

(d) Extraterritorial jurisdiction for a municipality subject to this section is determined under Section 42.021 if the governing body of the municipality and the governing body of the neighboring municipality each adopt, on or after June 1, 2017, resolutions stating that the determination of extraterritorial jurisdiction under Section 42.0235(a) is not in the best interest of the municipality.

2017 Legislation: Amended by S.B. 468, §1, 85th Leg., eff. Sept. 1, 2017.

LGOVT §42.024. TRANSFER OF EXTRATERRITORIAL JURISDICTION BETWEEN CERTAIN MUNICIPALITIES

(a) In this section:

(1) "Adopting municipality" means a home-rule municipality with a population of less than 25,000 that purchases and appropriates raw water for its water utility through a transbasin diversion permit from one or two river authorities in which the municipality has territory.

(2) "Releasing municipality" means a home-rule municipality with a population of more than 450,000 that owns an electric utility, that has a charter provision allowing for limited-purpose annexation, and that has annexed territory for a limited purpose.

(b) The governing body of an adopting municipality may by resolution include in its extraterritorial jurisdiction an area that is in the extraterritorial jurisdiction of a releasing municipality if:

(1) the releasing municipality does not provide water, sewer services, and electricity to the released area;

(2) the owners of a majority of the land within the released area request that the adopting municipality include in its extraterritorial jurisdiction the released area;

(3) the released area is:

(A) adjacent to the territory of the adopting municipality;

(B) wholly within a county in which both municipalities have territory; and

(C) located in one or more school districts, each of which has the majority of its territory outside the territory of the releasing municipality;

(4) the adopting municipality adopts ordinances or regulations within the released area for water quality standards relating to the control or abatement of water pollution that are in conformity with those of the Texas Natural Resource Conservation Commission applicable to the released area on January 1, 1995;

(5) the adopting municipality has adopted a service plan to provide water and sewer service to the area acceptable to the owners of a majority of the land within the released area; and

(6) the size of the released area does not exceed the difference between the total area within the extraterritorial jurisdiction of the adopting municipality, exclusive of the extraterritorial jurisdiction of the releasing municipality, on the date the resolution was adopted under this subsection, as determined by Section 42.021, and the total area within the adopting municipality's extraterritorial jurisdiction on the date of the resolution.

(c)(1) The service plan under Subsection (b)(5) shall include an assessment of the availability and feasibility of participation in any regional facility permitted by the Texas Natural Resource Conservation Commission in which the releasing municipality is a participant and had plans to provide service to the released area. The plan for regional service shall include:

(A) proposed dates for providing sewer service through the regional facility;

(B) terms of financial participation to provide sewer service to the released area, including rates proposed for service sufficient to reimburse the regional participants over a reasonable time for any expenditures associated with that portion of the regional facility designed or constructed to serve the released area as of January 1, 1993; and

(C) participation by the adopting municipality in governance of the regional facility based on the percentage of land to be served by the regional facility in the released area compared to the total land area to be served by the regional facility.

(2) The adopting municipality shall deliver a copy of the service plan to the releasing municipality and any other participant in any regional facility described in this subsection at least 30 days before the resolution to assume extraterritorial jurisdiction. The releasing municipality and any other participant in any regional facility described in this subsection by resolution shall, within 30 days of delivery of the service plan, either accept that portion of the service plan related to participation by the adopting municipality in the regional facility or propose alternative terms of participation.

(3) If the adopting municipality, the releasing municipality, and any other participant in any regional facility described in this subsection fail to reach agreement on the service plan within 60 days after the service plan is delivered, any municipality that is a participant in the regional facility or any owner of land within the area to be released may appeal the matter to the Texas Natural Resource Conservation Commission. The Texas Natural Resource Conservation Commission shall, in its resolution of any differences between proposals submitted for review in this subsection, use a cost-of-service allocation methodology which treats each service unit in the regional facility equally, with any variance in rates to be based only on differences in costs based on the time service is provided to an area served by the regional facility. The Texas Natural Resource Conservation Commission may allow the adopting municipality, the releasing municipality, or any other participant in any regional facility described in this subsection to withdraw from participation in the regional facility on a showing of undue financial hardship.

(4) A decision by the Texas Natural Resource Conservation Commission under this subsection is not subject to judicial review, and any costs associated with the commission's review shall be assessed to the parties to the decision in proportion to the percentage of land served by the regional facility subject to review in the jurisdiction of each party.

(5) The releasing municipality shall not, prior to January 1, 1997, discontinue or terminate any interlocal agreement, contract, or commitment relating to water or sewer service that it has as of January 1, 1995, with the adopting municipality without the consent of the adopting municipality.

(d) On the date the adopting municipality delivers a copy of the resolution under Subsection (b) to the municipal clerk of the releasing municipality, the released area shall be included in the extraterritorial jurisdiction of the adopting municipality and excluded from the extraterritorial jurisdiction of the releasing municipality.

(e) If any part of a tract of land, owned either in fee simple or under common control or undivided ownership, was or becomes split, before or after the dedication or deed of a portion of the land for a public purpose, between the extraterritorial jurisdiction of a releasing municipality and the jurisdiction of another municipality, or is land described in Subsection (b)(3)(C), the authority to act under Chapter 212 and the authority to regulate development and building with respect to the tract of land is, on the request of the owner to the municipality, with the municipality selected by the owner

of the tract of land. The municipality selected under this subsection may also provide or authorize another person or entity to provide municipal services to land subject to this subsection.

(f) Nothing in this section requires the releasing municipality to continue to participate in a regional wastewater treatment plant providing service, or to provide new services, to any territory within the released area.

(g) This section controls over any conflicting provision of this subchapter.

LGOVT §42.025. RELEASE OF EXTRATERRITORIAL JURISDICTION BY CERTAIN MUNICIPALITIES

(a) In this section, "eligible property" means any portion of a contiguous tract of land:

(1) that is located in the extraterritorial jurisdiction of a municipality within one-half mile of the territory of a proposed municipal airport;

(2) for which a contract for land acquisition services was awarded by the municipality; and

(3) that has not been acquired through the contract described by Subdivision (2) for the proposed municipal airport.

(b) The owner of eligible property may petition the municipality to release the property from the municipality's extraterritorial jurisdiction not later than June 1, 1996. The petition must be filed with the secretary or clerk of the municipality.

(c) Not later than the 10th day after the date the secretary or clerk receives a petition under Subsection (b), the municipality by resolution shall release the eligible property from the extraterritorial jurisdiction of the municipality.

(d) Eligible property that is released from the extraterritorial jurisdiction of a municipality under Subsection (c) may be included in the extraterritorial jurisdiction of another municipality if:

(1) any part of the other municipality is located in the same county as the property; and

(2) the other municipality and the owner agree to the inclusion of the property in the extraterritorial jurisdiction.

LGOVT §42.0251. RELEASE OF EXTRATERRITORIAL JURISDICTION BY CERTAIN GENERAL-LAW MUNICIPALITIES

(a) This section applies only to a general-law municipality:

(1) that has a population of less than 3,000;

(2) that is located in a county with a population of more than 500,000 that is adjacent to a county with a population of more than four million; and

(3) in which at least two-thirds of the residents reside within a gated community.

(b) A municipality shall release an area from its extraterritorial jurisdiction not later than the 10th day after the date the municipality receives a petition requesting that the area be released that is signed by at least 80 percent of the owners of real property located in the area requesting release.

LGOVT §42.026. LIMITATION ON EXTRATERRITORIAL JURISDICTION OF CERTAIN MUNICIPALITIES

(a) In this section, "navigable stream" has the meaning assigned by Section 21.001, Natural Resources Code.

(b) This section applies only to an area that is:

(1) located in the extraterritorial jurisdiction of a home-rule municipality that has a population of 60,000 or less and is located in whole or in part in a county with a population of 240,000 or less;

(2) located outside the county in which a majority of the land area of the municipality is located; and

(3) separated from the municipality's corporate boundaries by a navigable stream.

(c) A municipality that, on August 31, 1999, includes that area in its extraterritorial jurisdiction shall, before January 1, 2000:

(1) adopt an ordinance removing that area from the municipality's extraterritorial jurisdiction; or

(2) enter into an agreement with a municipality located in the county in which that area is located to transfer that area to the extraterritorial jurisdiction of that municipality.

(d) If the municipality that is required to act under Subsection (c) does not do so as provided by that subsection, the area is automatically removed from the extraterritorial jurisdiction of that municipality on January 1, 2000.

(e) Section 42.021 does not apply to a transfer of extraterritorial jurisdiction under Subsection (c)(2).

Sections 42.027-42.040 reserved for expansion

SUBCHAPTER C. CREATION OR EXPANSION OF GOVERNMENTAL ENTITIES IN EXTRATERRITORIAL JURISDICTION

LGOVT §42.041. MUNICIPAL INCORPORATION IN EXTRATERRITORIAL JURISDICTION GENERALLY

(a) A municipality may not be incorporated in the extraterritorial jurisdiction of an existing municipality unless the governing body of the existing municipality gives its written consent by ordinance or resolution.

(b) If the governing body of the existing municipality refuses to give its consent, a majority of the qualified voters of the area of the proposed municipality and the owners of at least 50 percent of the land in the proposed municipality may petition the governing body to annex the area. If the governing body fails or refuses to annex the area within six months after the date it receives the petition, that failure or refusal constitutes the governing body's consent to the incorporation of the proposed municipality.

(c) The consent to the incorporation of the proposed municipality is only an authorization to initiate incorporation proceedings as provided by law.

(d) If the consent to initiate incorporation proceedings is obtained, the incorporation must be initiated within six months after the date of the consent and must be finally completed within 18 months after the date of the consent. Failure to comply with either time requirement terminates the consent.

(e) This section applies only to the proposed municipality's area located in the extraterritorial jurisdiction of the existing municipality.

LGOVT §42.0411. MUNICIPAL INCORPORATION IN EXTRATERRITORIAL JURISDICTION OF CERTAIN MUNICIPALITIES

(a) This section applies only to:

(1) an area located north and east of Interstate Highway 10 that is included in the extraterritorial jurisdiction, or the limited-purpose annexation area, of a municipality with a population of one million or more that has operated under a three-year annexation plan similar to the municipal annexation plan described by Section 43.052 for at least 10 years; or

(2) an area located north and east of Interstate Highway 10:

(A) that is included in the extraterritorial jurisdiction, or the limited-purpose annexation area, of a municipality with a population of one million or more that has operated under a three-year annexation plan similar to the municipal annexation plan described by Section 43.052 for at least 10 years;

(B) that has not been included in the municipality's annexation plan described by Section 43.052 before the 180th day before the date consent for incorporation is requested under Section 42.041(a); and

(C) for which the municipality refused to give its consent to incorporation under Section 42.041(a).

(b) The residents of the area described by Subsection (a)(2) may initiate an attempt to incorporate as a municipality by filing a written petition signed by at least 10 percent of the registered voters of the area of the proposed municipality with the county judge of the county in which the proposed municipality is located. The petition must request the county judge to order an election to determine whether the area of the proposed municipality will incorporate. An incorporation election under this section shall be conducted in the same manner as an incorporation election under Subchapter A, Chapter 8. The consent of the municipality that previously refused to give consent is not required for the incorporation.

(c) In this subsection, "deferred annexation area" means an area that has entered into an agreement with a municipality under which the municipality defers annexation of the area for at least 10 years. An area described by Subsection (a)(1) that is located within 1½ miles of a municipality's deferred annexation area or adjacent to the corporate boundaries of the municipality may not be annexed for limited or full purposes during the period provided under the agreement. During the period provided under the agreement, the residents of the area may incorporate in accordance with the incorporation proceedings provided by law, except that the consent of the municipality is not required for the incorporation. This subsection expires on the later of:

(1) September 1, 2009; or

(2) the date that all areas entitled to incorporate under this subsection have incorporated.

(d) This subsection applies only to an area that is described by Subsection (a)(1) and removed from a municipality's annexation plan under Section 43.052(e) two times or more. The residents of the area and any adjacent territory that is located within the extraterritorial

jurisdiction of the municipality or located within an area annexed for limited purposes by the municipality and that is adjacent to the corporate boundaries of the municipality may incorporate in accordance with the incorporation proceedings provided by law, except that the consent of the municipality is not required for the incorporation. This subsection expires on the later of:

(1) September 1, 2009; or

(2) the date that all areas entitled to incorporate under this subsection have incorporated.

LGOVT §42.042. CREATION OF POLITICAL SUBDIVISION TO SUPPLY WATER OR SEWER SERVICES, ROADWAYS, OR DRAINAGE FACILITIES IN EXTRATERRITORIAL JURISDICTION

(a) A political subdivision, one purpose of which is to supply fresh water for domestic or commercial use or to furnish sanitary sewer services, roadways, or drainage, may not be created in the extraterritorial jurisdiction of a municipality unless the governing body of the municipality gives its written consent by ordinance or resolution in accordance with this subsection and the Water Code. In giving its consent, the municipality may not place any conditions or other restrictions on the creation of the political subdivision other than those expressly permitted by Sections 54.016(e) and (i), Water Code.

(b) If the governing body fails or refuses to give its consent for the creation of the political subdivision on mutually agreeable terms within 90 days after the date it receives a written request for the consent, a majority of the qualified voters of the area of the proposed political subdivision and the owners of at least 50 percent of the land in the proposed political subdivision may petition the governing body to make available to the area the water, sanitary sewer services, or both that would be provided by the political subdivision.

(c) If, within 120 days after the date the governing body receives the petition, the governing body fails to make a contract with a majority of the qualified voters of the area of the proposed political subdivision and the owners of at least 50 percent of the land in the proposed political subdivision to provide the services, that failure constitutes the governing body's consent to the creation of the proposed political subdivision.

(d) The consent to the creation of the political subdivision is only an authorization to initiate proceedings to create the political subdivision as provided by law.

(e) Repealed by Acts 1997, 75th Leg., ch. 1070, §55, eff. Sept. 1, 1997.

(f) If the municipality fails or refuses to give its consent to the creation of the political subdivision or fails or refuses to execute a contract providing for the water or sanitary sewer services requested within the time limits prescribed by this section, the applicant may petition the Texas Natural Resource Conservation Commission for the creation of the political subdivision or the inclusion of the land in a political subdivision. The commission shall allow creation of the political subdivision or inclusion of the land in a proposed political subdivision on finding that the municipality either does not have the reasonable ability to serve or has failed to make a legally binding commitment with sufficient funds available to provide water and wastewater service adequate to serve the proposed development at a reasonable cost to the landowner. The commitment must provide that construction of the facilities necessary to serve the land will begin within two years and will be substantially completed within 4½ years after the date the petition was filed with the municipality.

(g) On an appeal taken to the district court from the Texas Natural Resource Conservation Commission's ruling, all parties to the commission hearing must be made parties to the appeal. The court shall hear the appeal within 120 days after the date the appeal is filed. If the case is continued or appealed to a higher court beyond the 120-day period, the court shall require the appealing party or party requesting the continuance to post a bond or other adequate security in the amount of damages that may be incurred by any party as a result of the appeal or delay from the commission action. The amount of the bond or other security shall be determined by the court after notice and hearing. On final disposition, a court may award damages, including any damages for delays, attorney's fees, and costs of court to the prevailing party.

(h) A municipality may not unilaterally extend the time limits prescribed by this section through the adoption of preapplication periods or by passage of any rules, resolutions, ordinances, or charter provisions. However, the municipality and the petitioner may jointly petition the Texas Natural Resource Conservation Commission to request an extension of the time limits.

(i) Repealed by Acts 1989, 71st Leg., ch. 1058, §1, eff. Sept. 1, 1989.

(j) The consent requirements of this section do not apply to the creation of a special utility district under Chapter 65, Water Code. If a special utility district is to be converted to a district with taxing authority that provides utility services, this section applies to the conversion.

(k) This section, except Subsection (i), applies only to the proposed political subdivision's area located in the extraterritorial jurisdiction of the municipality.

LGOVT §42.0425. ADDITION OF LAND IN EXTRATERRITORIAL JURISDICTION OF MUNICIPALITY TO CERTAIN POLITICAL SUBDIVISIONS

(a) A political subdivision, one purpose of which is to supply fresh water for domestic or commercial use or to furnish sanitary sewer services, roadways, or drainage, may not add land that is located in the extraterritorial jurisdiction of a municipality unless the governing body of the municipality gives its written consent by ordinance or resolution in accordance with this section and the Water Code. In giving its consent, the municipality may not place any conditions or other restrictions on the expansion of the political subdivision other than those expressly permitted by Section 54.016(e), Water Code.

(b) The procedures under Section 42.042 governing a municipality's refusal to consent to the creation of a political subdivision apply to a municipality that refuses to consent to the addition of land to a political subdivision under this section.

(c) An owner of land in the area proposed to be added to the political subdivision may not unreasonably refuse to enter into a contract for water or sanitary sewer services with the municipality under Section 42.042(c).

(d) This section does not apply to a political subdivision created by Chapter 289, Acts of the 73rd Legislature, Regular Session, 1993.

LGOVT §42.043. REQUIREMENTS APPLYING TO PETITION

(a) A petition under Section 42.041 or 42.042 must:

(1) be written;

(2) request that the area be annexed or that the services be made available, as appropriate;

(3) be signed in ink or indelible pencil by the appropriate voters and landowners;

(4) be signed, in the case of a person signing as a voter, as the person's name appears on the most recent official list of registered voters;

(5) contain, in the case of a person signing as a voter, a note made by the person stating the person's residence address and the precinct number and voter registration number that appear on the person's voter registration certificate;

(6) contain, in the case of a person signing as a landowner, a note made by the person opposite the person's name stating the approximate total acreage that the person owns in the area to be annexed or serviced;

(7) describe the area to be annexed or serviced and have a plat of the area attached; and

(8) be presented to the secretary or clerk of the municipality.

(b) The signatures to the petition need not be appended to one paper.

(c) Before the petition is circulated among the voters and landowners, notice of the petition must be given by posting a copy of the petition for 10 days in three public places in the area to be annexed or serviced and by publishing the notice once, in a newspaper of general circulation serving the area, before the 15th day before the date the petition is first circulated. Proof of posting and publication must be made by attaching to the petition presented to the secretary or clerk:

(1) the affidavit of any voter who signed the petition, stating the places and dates of the posting;

(2) the affidavit of the publisher of the newspaper in which the notice was published, stating the name of the newspaper and the issue and date of publication; and

(3) the affidavit of at least three voters who signed the petition, if there are that many, stating the total number of voters residing in the area and the approximate total acreage in the area.

LGOVT §42.044. CREATION OF INDUSTRIAL DISTRICT IN EXTRATERRITORIAL JURISDICTION

(a) In this section, "industrial district" has the meaning customarily given to the term but also includes any area in which tourist-related businesses and facilities are located.

(b) The governing body of a municipality may designate any part of its extraterritorial jurisdiction as an industrial district and may treat the designated area in

a manner considered by the governing body to be in the best interests of the municipality.

(c) The governing body may make written contracts with owners of land in the industrial district:

(1) to guarantee the continuation of the extraterritorial status of the district and its immunity from annexation by the municipality for a period not to exceed 15 years; and

(2) with other lawful terms and considerations that the parties agree to be reasonable, appropriate, and not unduly restrictive of business activities.

(d) The parties to a contract may renew or extend it for successive periods not to exceed 15 years each. In the event any owner of land in an industrial district is offered an opportunity to renew or extend a contract, then all owners of land in that industrial district must be offered an opportunity to renew or extend a contract subject to the provisions of Subsection (c).

(e) A municipality may provide for adequate fire-fighting services in the industrial district by:

(1) directly furnishing fire-fighting services that are to be paid for by the property owners of the district;

(2) contracting for fire-fighting services, whether or not all or a part of the services are to be paid for by the property owners of the district; or

(3) contracting with the property owners of the district to have them provide for their own fire-fighting services.

(f) A property owner who provides for his own fire-fighting services under this section may not be required to pay any part of the cost of the fire-fighting services provided by the municipality to other property owners in the district.

LGOVT §42.045. CREATION OF POLITICAL SUBDIVISION IN INDUSTRIAL DISTRICT

(a) A political subdivision, one purpose of which is to provide services of a governmental or proprietary nature, may not be created in an industrial district designated under Section 42.044 by a municipality unless the municipality gives its written consent by ordinance or resolution. The municipality shall give or deny consent within 60 days after the date the municipality receives a written request for consent. Failure to give or deny consent in the allotted period constitutes the municipality's consent to the initiation of the creation proceedings.

(b) If the consent is obtained, the creation proceedings must be initiated within six months after the date of the consent and must be finally completed within 18 months after the date of the consent. Failure to comply with either time requirement terminates the consent for the proceedings.

LGOVT §42.046. DESIGNATION OF A PLANNED UNIT DEVELOPMENT DISTRICT IN EXTRATERRITORIAL JURISDICTION

(a) The governing body of a municipality that has disannexed territory previously annexed for limited purposes may designate an area within its extraterritorial jurisdiction as a planned unit development district by written agreement with the owner of the land under Subsection (b). The agreement shall be recorded in the deed records of the county or counties in which the land is located. A planned unit development district designated under this section shall contain no less than 250 acres. If there are more than four owners of land to be designated as a single planned unit development, each owner shall appoint a single person to negotiate with the municipality and authorize that person to bind each owner for purposes of this section.

(b) An agreement governing the creation, development, and existence of a planned unit development district established under this section shall be between the governing body of the municipality and the owner of the land subject to the agreement. The agreement shall not be effective until signed by both parties and by any other person with an interest in the land, as that interest is evidenced by an instrument recorded in the deed records of the county or counties in which the land is located. The parties may agree:

(1) to guarantee continuation of the extraterritorial status of the planned unit development district and its immunity from annexation by the municipality for a period not to exceed 15 years after the effective date of the agreement;

(2) to authorize certain land uses and development within the planned unit development;

(3) to authorize enforcement by the municipality of certain municipal land use and development regulations within the planned unit development district, in the same manner such regulations are enforced within the municipality's boundaries, as may be agreed by the landowner and the municipality;

(4) to vary any watershed protection regulations;

(5) to authorize or restrict the creation of political subdivisions within the planned unit development district; and

(6) to such other terms and considerations the parties consider appropriate.

(c) The agreement between the governing body of the municipality and the owner of the land within the planned unit development district shall be binding upon all subsequent governing bodies of the municipality and subsequent owners of the land within the planned unit development district for the term of the agreement.

(d) An agreement or a decision made under this section and an action taken under the agreement by the parties to the agreement are not subject to an approval or an appeal brought under Section 26.177, Water Code.

LGOVT §42.047. CREATION OF A POLITICAL SUBDIVISION IN AN AREA PROPOSED FOR A PLANNED UNIT DEVELOPMENT DISTRICT

If the governing body of a municipality that has disannexed territory previously annexed for limited purposes refuses to designate a planned unit development district under Section 42.046 no later than 180 days after the date a request for the designation is filed with the municipality by the owner of the land to be included in the planned unit development district, the municipality shall be considered to have given the consent required by Section 42.041 to the incorporation of a proposed municipality including within its boundaries all or some of such land. If consent to incorporation is granted by this subsection, the consenting municipality waives all rights to challenge the proposed incorporation in any court.

LGOVT §42.048. EXPIRED

LGOVT §42.049. AUTHORITY OF WELLS BRANCH MUNICIPAL UTILITY DISTRICT

(a) Wells Branch Municipal Utility district is authorized to contract with a municipality:

(1) to provide for payments to be made to the municipality for purposes that the governing body of the district determines will further regional cooperation between the district and the municipality; and

(2) to provide other lawful terms and considerations that the district and the municipality agree are reasonable and appropriate.

(b) A contract entered into under this section may be for a term that is mutually agreeable to the parties. The parties to such a contract may renew or extend the contract.

(c) A municipality may contract with the district to accomplish the purposes set forth in Subsection (a) of this section. In a contract entered into under this section, a municipality may agree that the district will remain in existence and be exempt from annexation by the municipality for the term of the contract.

(d) A contract entered into under this section will be binding on all subsequent governing bodies of the district and of the municipality for the term of the contract.

(e) The district may make annual appropriations from its operations and maintenance tax or other revenues lawfully available to the district to make payments to a municipality under a contract entered into under this section.

Sections 42.050-42.900 reserved for expansion

SUBCHAPTER Z. MISCELLANEOUS PROVISIONS

LGOVT §42.901. APPORTIONMENT OF EXTRATERRITORIAL JURISDICTIONS THAT OVERLAPPED ON AUGUST 23, 1963

(a) If, on August 23, 1963, the extraterritorial jurisdiction of a municipality overlapped the extraterritorial jurisdiction of one or more other municipalities, the governing bodies of the affected municipalities may apportion the overlapped area by a written agreement approved by an ordinance or a resolution adopted by the governing bodies.

(b) A municipality having a claim of extraterritorial jurisdiction to the overlapping area may bring an action as plaintiff in the district court of the judicial district in which the largest municipality having a claim to the area is located. The plaintiff municipality must name as a defendant each municipality having a claim of extraterritorial jurisdiction to the area and must request the court to apportion the area among the affected municipalities. In apportioning the area, the court shall consider population densities, patterns of growth, transportation, topography, and land use in the municipalities and the overlapping area. The area must be apportioned among the municipalities:

(1) so that each municipality's part is contiguous to the extraterritorial jurisdiction of the municipality

or, if the extraterritorial jurisdiction of the municipality is totally overlapped, is contiguous to the boundaries of the municipality;

(2) so that each municipality's part is in a substantially compact shape; and

(3) in the same ratio, to one decimal, that the respective populations of the municipalities bear to each other, but with each municipality receiving at least one-tenth of the area.

(c) An apportionment under this section must consider existing property lines. A tract of land or adjoining tracts of land that were under one ownership on August 23, 1963, and that do not exceed 160 acres may not be apportioned so as to be in the extraterritorial jurisdiction of more than one municipality unless the landowner gives written consent to that apportionment.

Sections 42.902-42.904 omitted by editor

Chapter 43. Municipal Annexation
Subchapter A. General Provisions

LGOVT §43.001. DEFINITION

In this chapter, "extraterritorial jurisdiction" means extraterritorial jurisdiction as determined under Chapter 42.

Subchapter C. Annexation Procedure for Areas Annexed Under Municipal Annexation Plan

LGOVT §43.052. MUNICIPAL ANNEXATION PLAN REQUIRED

(a) In this section, "special district" means a municipal utility district, water control and improvement district, or other district created under Section 52, Article III, or Section 59, Article XVI, Texas Constitution.

(b) A municipality may annex an area identified in the annexation plan only as provided by this section.

(c) A municipality shall prepare an annexation plan that specifically identifies annexations that may occur beginning on the third anniversary of the date the annexation plan is adopted. The municipality may amend the plan to specifically identify annexations that may occur beginning on the third anniversary of the date the plan is amended.

(d) At any time during which an area is included in a municipality's annexation plan, a municipal utility district or other special district that will be abolished as a result of the annexation, excluding an emergency services district, in which the area is located may not without consent of the municipality:

(1) reduce the tax rate applicable to the area if the amount that would remain in the debt service fund after the reduction and after subtracting the amount due for debt service in the following year is less than 25 percent of the debt service requirements for the following year;

(2) voluntarily transfer an asset without consideration; or

(3) enter into a contract for services that extends beyond the three-year annexation plan period other than a contract with another political subdivision for the operation of water, wastewater, and drainage facilities.

(e) A municipality may amend its annexation plan at any time to remove an area proposed for annexation. If, before the end of the 18th month after the month an area is included in the three-year annexation cycle, a municipality amends its annexation plan to remove the area, the municipality may not amend the plan to again include the area in its annexation plan until the first anniversary of the date the municipality amended the plan to remove the area. If, during or after the 18 months after the month an area is included in the three-year annexation cycle, a municipality amends its annexation plan to remove the area, the municipality may not amend the plan to again include the area in its annexation plan until the second anniversary of the date the municipality amended the plan to remove the area.

(f) Before the 90th day after the date a municipality adopts or amends an annexation plan under this section, the municipality shall give written notice to:

(1) each property owner in the affected area, as indicated by the appraisal records furnished by the appraisal district for each county in which the affected area is located, that the area has been included in or removed from the municipality's annexation plan;

(2) each public entity, as defined by Section 43.053, or private entity that provides services in the area proposed for annexation; and

(3) each railroad company that serves the municipality and is on the municipality's tax roll if the company's right-of-way is in the area proposed for annexation.

(g) If an area is not removed from the municipality's annexation plan, the annexation of the area under the plan must be completed before the 31st day after

the third anniversary of the date the area was included in the annexation plan. If the annexation is not completed within the period prescribed by this subsection, the municipality may not annex the area proposed for annexation before the fifth anniversary of the last day for completing an annexation under this subsection.

(h) This section does not apply to an area proposed for annexation if:

(1) the area contains fewer than 100 separate tracts of land on which one or more residential dwellings are located on each tract;

(2) the area will be annexed by petition of more than 50 percent of the real property owners in the area proposed for annexation or by vote or petition of the qualified voters or real property owners as provided by Subchapter B;

(3) the area is or was the subject of:

(A) an industrial district contract under Section 42.044; or

(B) a strategic partnership agreement under Section 43.0751;

(4) the area is located in a colonia, as that term is defined by Section 2306.581, Government Code;

(5) the area is annexed under Section 43.026, 43.027, 43.029, or 43.031;

(6) the area is located completely within the boundaries of a closed military installation; or

(7) the municipality determines that the annexation of the area is necessary to protect the area proposed for annexation or the municipality from:

(A) imminent destruction of property or injury to persons; or

(B) a condition or use that constitutes a public or private nuisance as defined by background principles of nuisance and property law of this state.

(i) A municipality may not circumvent the requirements of this section by proposing to separately annex two or more areas described by Subsection (h)(1) if no reason exists under generally accepted municipal planning principles and practices for separately annexing the areas. If a municipality proposes to separately annex areas in violation of this section, a person residing or owning land in the area may petition the municipality to include the area in the municipality's annexation plan. If the municipality fails to take action on the petition, the petitioner may request arbitration of the dispute. The petitioner must request the appointment of an arbitrator in writing to the municipality. Sections 43.0564(b), (c), and (e) apply to the appointment of an arbitrator and the conduct of an arbitration proceeding under this subsection. Except as provided by this subsection, the municipality shall pay the cost of arbitration. If the arbitrator finds that the petitioner's request for arbitration was groundless or requested in bad faith or for the purposes of harassment, the arbitrator shall require the petitioner to pay the costs of arbitration.

(j) If a municipality has an Internet website, the municipality shall:

(1) post and maintain the posting of its annexation plan on its Internet website;

(2) post and maintain the posting on its Internet website of any amendments to include an area in its annexation plan until the date the area is annexed; and

(3) post and maintain the posting on its Internet website of any amendments to remove an area from its annexation plan until the date the municipality may again include the area in its annexation plan.

(k) Notwithstanding the restrictions imposed by Subsections (e) and (g), under an agreement described by Section 43.0563 a municipality may annex an area for full or limited purposes at any time on petition of the owner of the area for the annexation if the area:

(1) is in the municipality's annexation plan; or

(2) was previously in the municipality's annexation plan but removed under Subsection (e).

LGOVT §43.053. INVENTORY OF SERVICES & FACILITIES REQUIRED

(a) In this section, "public entity" includes a municipality, county, fire protection service provider, including a volunteer fire department, emergency medical services provider, including a volunteer emergency medical services provider, or a special district, as that term is defined by Section 43.052.

(b) After adopting an annexation plan or amending an annexation plan to include additional areas under Section 43.052, a municipality shall compile a comprehensive inventory of services and facilities provided by public and private entities, directly or by contract, in each area proposed for annexation. The inventory of services and facilities must include all services and facilities the municipality is required to provide or maintain following the annexation.

(c) The municipality shall request, in the notice provided under Section 43.052(f), the information necessary to compile the inventory from each public or private entity that provides services or facilities in each area proposed for annexation. The public or private entity shall provide to the municipality the information held by the entity that is necessary to compile the inventory not later than the 90th day after the date the municipality requests the information unless the entity and the municipality agree to extend the period for providing the information. The information provided under this subsection must include the type of service provided, the method of service delivery, and all information prescribed by Subsections (e) and (f). If a service provider fails to provide the required information within the 90-day period, the municipality is not required to include the information in an inventory prepared under this section.

(d) The information required in the inventory shall be based on the services and facilities provided during the year preceding the date the municipality adopted the annexation plan or amended the annexation plan to include additional areas.

(e) For utility facilities, roads, drainage structures, and other infrastructure provided or maintained by public or private entities, the inventory must include:

(1) an engineer's report that describes the physical condition of all infrastructure elements in the area; and

(2) a summary of capital, operational, and maintenance expenditures for that infrastructure.

(f) For police, fire, and emergency medical services provided by public or private entities, the inventory must include for each service:

(1) the average dispatch and delivery time;

(2) a schedule of equipment, including vehicles;

(3) a staffing schedule that discloses the certification and training levels of personnel; and

(4) a summary of operating and capital expenditures.

(g) The municipality shall complete the inventory and make the inventory available for public inspection on or before the 60th day after the date the municipality receives the required information from the service providers under Subsection (c).

(h) The municipality may monitor the services provided in an area proposed for annexation and verify the inventory information provided by the service provider.

LGOVT §43.054. WIDTH REQUIREMENTS

(a) A municipality with a population of less than 1.6 million may not annex a publicly or privately owned area, including a strip of area following the course of a road, highway, river, stream, or creek, unless the width of the area at its narrowest point is at least 1,000 feet.

(b) The prohibition established by Subsection (a) does not apply if:

(1) the boundaries of the municipality are contiguous to the area on at least two sides;

(2) the annexation is initiated on the written petition of the owners or of a majority of the qualified voters of the area; or

(3) the area abuts or is contiguous to another jurisdictional boundary.

(c) Notwithstanding Subsection (a), a municipality with a population of 21,000 or more located in a county with a population of 100,000 or more may annex a publicly owned strip or similar area following the course of a road or highway for the purpose of annexing territory contiguous to the strip or area if the territory contiguous to the strip or area was formerly used or was to be used in connection with or by a superconducting super collider high-energy research facility.

LGOVT §43.0545. ANNEXATION OF CERTAIN ADJACENT AREAS

(a) A municipality may not annex an area that is located in the extraterritorial jurisdiction of the municipality only because the area is contiguous to municipal territory that is less than 1,000 feet in width at its narrowest point.

(b) A municipality may not annex an area that is located in the extraterritorial jurisdiction of the municipality only because the area is contiguous to municipal territory that:

(1) was annexed before September 1, 1999; and

(2) was in the extraterritorial jurisdiction of the municipality at the time of annexation only because the territory was contiguous to municipal territory that was less than 1,000 feet in width at its narrowest point.

(c) Subsections (a) and (b) do not apply to an area:

(1) completely surrounded by incorporated territory of one or more municipalities;

(2) for which the owners of the area have requested annexation by the municipality;

(3) that is owned by the municipality; or

(4) that is the subject of an industrial district contract under Section 42.044.

(d) Subsection (b) does not apply if the minimum width of the narrow territory described by Subsection (b)(2), following subsequent annexation, is no longer less than 1,000 feet in width at its narrowest point.

(e) For purposes of this section, roads, highways, rivers, lakes, or other bodies of water are not included in computing the 1,000-foot distance unless the area being annexed includes land in addition to a road, highway, river, lake, or other body of water.

LGOVT §43.0546. ANNEXATION OF CERTAIN ADJACENT AREAS BY POPULOUS MUNICIPALITIES

(a) In this section, "municipal area" means the area within the corporate boundaries of a municipality other than:

(1) an area annexed before September 1, 1999, that is less than 1,000 feet wide at any point;

(2) an area within the corporate boundaries of the municipality that was annexed by the municipality before September 1, 1999, and at the time of the annexation the area was contiguous to municipal territory that was less than 1,000 feet wide at any point;

(3) an area annexed after December 1, 1995, and before September 1, 1999;

(4) municipally owned property; or

(5) an area contiguous to municipally owned property if the municipally owned property was annexed in an annexation that included an area that was less than 1,000 feet wide at its narrowest point.

(b) This section applies only to a municipality with a population of 1.6 million or more.

(c) A municipality to which this section applies may not annex an area that is less than 1,500 feet wide at any point. At least 1,500 feet of the perimeter of the area annexed by a municipality must be coterminous with the boundary of the municipal area of the municipality.

(d) This section does not apply to territory:

(1) that is completely surrounded by municipal area;

(2) for which the owners of the area have requested annexation by the municipality;

(3) within a district whose elected board of directors has by a majority vote requested annexation;

(4) owned by the municipality; or

(5) that contains fewer than 50 inhabitants.

LGOVT §43.055. MAXIMUM AMOUNT OF ANNEXATION EACH YEAR

(a) In a calendar year, a municipality may not annex a total area greater than 10 percent of the incorporated area of the municipality as of January 1 of that year, plus any amount of area carried over to that year under Subsection (b). In determining the total area annexed in a calendar year, an area annexed for limited purposes is included, but an annexed area is not included if it is:

(1) annexed at the request of a majority of the qualified voters of the area and the owners of at least 50 percent of the land in the area;

(2) owned by the municipality, a county, the state, or the federal government and used for a public purpose;

(3) annexed at the request of at least a majority of the qualified voters of the area; or

(4) annexed at the request of the owners of the area.

(b) If a municipality fails to annex in a calendar year the entire 10 percent amount permitted under Subsection (a), the municipality may carry over the unused allocation for use in subsequent calendar years.

(c) A municipality carrying over an allocation may not annex in a calendar year a total area greater than 30 percent of the incorporated area of the municipality as of January 1 of that year.

Ⓐ LGOVT §43.056. PROVISION OF SERVICES TO ANNEXED AREA

The amended text in §43.056 is effective for annexations of an area for which all parts of the statutory annexation process are begun on or after Sept. 1, 2017. Annexations for which any part of the process was begun before Sept. 1, 2017, are governed by the former law in effect at that time.

(a) Before the first day of the 10th month after the month in which the inventory is prepared as provided by Section 43.053, the municipality proposing the annexation shall complete a service plan that provides for the extension of full municipal services to the area to be annexed. The municipality shall provide the services by any of the methods by which it extends the services to any other area of the municipality.

(b) The service plan, which must be completed in the period provided by Subsection (a) before the annexation, must include a program under which the municipality will provide full municipal services in the annexed area no later than 2½ years after the effective date of the annexation, in accordance with Subsection (e), unless certain services cannot reasonably be provided within that period and the municipality proposes a schedule for providing those services, and must include a list of all services required by this section to be provided under the plan. If the municipality proposes a schedule to extend the period for providing certain services, the schedule must provide for the provision of full municipal services no later than 4½ years after the effective date of the annexation. However, under the program if the municipality provides any of the following services within the corporate boundaries of the municipality before annexation, the municipality must provide those services in the area proposed for annexation on the effective date of the annexation of the area:

(1) police protection;

(2) fire protection;

(3) emergency medical services;

(4) solid waste collection, except as provided by Subsection (o);

(5) operation and maintenance of water and wastewater facilities in the annexed area that are not within the service area of another water or wastewater utility;

(6) operation and maintenance of roads and streets, including road and street lighting;

(7) operation and maintenance of parks, playgrounds, and swimming pools; and

(8) operation and maintenance of any other publicly owned facility, building, or service.

(c) For purposes of this section, "full municipal services" means services provided by the annexing municipality within its full-purpose boundaries, including water and wastewater services and excluding gas or electrical service.

(d) A municipality with a population of 1.5 million or more may provide all or part of the municipal services required under the service plan by contracting with service providers. If the municipality owns a water and wastewater utility, the municipality shall, subject to this section, extend water and wastewater service to any annexed area not within the service area of another water or wastewater utility. If the municipality annexes territory included within the boundaries of a municipal utility district or a water control and improvement district, the municipality shall comply with applicable state law relating to annexation of territory within a municipal utility district or a water control and improvement district. The service plan shall summarize the service extension policies of the municipal water and wastewater utility.

(e) The service plan must also include a program under which the municipality will initiate after the effective date of the annexation the acquisition or construction of capital improvements necessary for providing municipal services adequate to serve the area. The construction shall be substantially completed within the period provided in the service plan. The service plan may be amended to extend the period for construction if the construction is proceeding with all deliberate speed. The acquisition or construction of the facilities shall be accomplished by purchase, lease, or other contract or by the municipality succeeding to the powers, duties, assets, and obligations of a conservation and reclamation district as authorized or required by law. The construction of the facilities shall be accomplished in a continuous process and shall be completed as soon as reasonably possible, consistent with generally accepted local engineering and architectural standards and practices. However, the municipality does not violate this subsection if the construction process is interrupted for any reason by circumstances beyond the direct control of the municipality. The requirement that construction of capital improvements must be substantially completed within the period provided in the service plan does not apply to a development project or proposed development project within an annexed area if the annexation of the area was initiated by petition or request of the owners of land in the annexed area and the municipality and the landowners have subsequently agreed in writing that the development project within that area, because of its size or projected manner of development by the developer, is not reasonably expected to be completed within that period.

(f) A service plan may not:

(1) require the creation of another political subdivision;

(2) require a landowner in the area to fund the capital improvements necessary to provide municipal

services in a manner inconsistent with Chapter 395 unless otherwise agreed to by the landowner;

(3) provide services in the area in a manner that would have the effect of reducing by more than a negligible amount the level of fire and police protection and emergency medical services provided within the corporate boundaries of the municipality before annexation;

(4) provide services in the area in a manner that would have the effect of reducing by more than a negligible amount the level of fire and police protection and emergency medical services provided within the area before annexation; or

(5) cause a reduction in fire and police protection and emergency medical services within the area to be annexed below that of areas within the corporate boundaries of the municipality with similar topography, land use, and population density.

(g) If the annexed area had a lower level of services, infrastructure, and infrastructure maintenance than the level of services, infrastructure, and infrastructure maintenance provided within the corporate boundaries of the municipality before annexation, a service plan must provide the annexed area with a level of services, infrastructure, and infrastructure maintenance that is comparable to the level of services, infrastructure, and infrastructure maintenance available in other parts of the municipality with topography, land use, and population density similar to those reasonably contemplated or projected in the area. If the annexed area had a level of services, infrastructure, and infrastructure maintenance equal to the level of services, infrastructure, and infrastructure maintenance provided within the corporate boundaries of the municipality before annexation, a service plan must maintain that same level of services, infrastructure, and infrastructure maintenance. Except as provided by this subsection, if the annexed area had a level of services superior to the level of services provided within the corporate boundaries of the municipality before annexation, a service plan must provide the annexed area with a level of services that is comparable to the level of services available in other parts of the municipality with topography, land use, and population density similar to those reasonably contemplated or projected in the area. If the annexed area had a level of services for operating and maintaining the infrastructure of the area, including the facilities described by Subsections (b)(5)-(8), superior to the level of services provided within the corporate boundaries of the municipality before annexation, a service plan must provide for the operation and maintenance of the infrastructure of the annexed area at a level of services that is equal or superior to that level of services.

(h) A municipality with a population of 1.6 million or more may not impose a fee in the annexed area, over and above ad valorem taxes and fees imposed within the corporate boundaries of the municipality before annexation, to maintain the level of services that existed in the area before annexation. This subsection does not prohibit the municipality from imposing a fee for a service in the area annexed if the same fee is imposed within the corporate boundaries of the municipality before annexation.

(i) If only a part of the area to be annexed is actually annexed, the governing body shall direct the department to prepare a revised service plan for that part.

(j) The proposed service plan must be made available for public inspection and explained to the inhabitants of the area at the public hearings held under Section 43.0561. The plan may be amended through negotiation at the hearings, but the provision of any service may not be deleted. On completion of the public hearings, the service plan shall be attached to the ordinance annexing the area and approved as part of the ordinance.

(k) On approval by the governing body, the service plan is a contractual obligation that is not subject to amendment or repeal except that if the governing body determines at the public hearings required by this subsection that changed conditions or subsequent occurrences make the service plan unworkable or obsolete, the governing body may amend the service plan to conform to the changed conditions or subsequent occurrences. An amended service plan must provide for services that are comparable to or better than those established in the service plan before amendment. Before any amendment is adopted, the governing body must provide an opportunity for interested persons to be heard at public hearings called and held in the manner provided by Section 43.0561.

(*l*) A service plan is valid for 10 years. Renewal of the service plan is at the discretion of the municipality. A person residing or owning land in an annexed area in a municipality with a population of 1.6 million or more may enforce a service plan by petitioning the municipality for a change in policy or procedures to ensure

compliance with the service plan. If the municipality fails to take action with regard to the petition, the petitioner may request arbitration of the dispute under Section 43.0565. A person residing or owning land in an annexed area in a municipality with a population of less than 1.6 million may enforce a service plan by applying for a writ of mandamus not later than the second anniversary of the date the person knew or should have known that the municipality was not complying with the service plan. If a writ of mandamus is applied for, the municipality has the burden of proving that the services have been provided in accordance with the service plan in question. If a court issues a writ under this subsection, the court:

(1) must provide the municipality the option of disannexing the area within a reasonable period specified by the court;

(2) may require the municipality to comply with the service plan in question before a reasonable date specified by the court if the municipality does not disannex the area within the period prescribed by the court under Subdivision (1);

(3) may require the municipality to refund to the landowners of the annexed area money collected by the municipality from those landowners for services to the area that were not provided;

(4) may assess a civil penalty against the municipality, to be paid to the state in an amount as justice may require, for the period in which the municipality is not in compliance with the service plan;

(5) may require the parties to participate in mediation; and

(6) may require the municipality to pay the person's costs and reasonable attorney's fees in bringing the action for the writ.

(m) This section does not require that a uniform level of full municipal services be provided to each area of the municipality if different characteristics of topography, land use, and population density constitute a sufficient basis for providing different levels of service. Any disputes regarding the level of services provided under this subsection are resolved in the same manner provided by Subsection (*l*). Nothing in this subsection modifies the requirement under Subsection (g) for a service plan to provide a level of services in an annexed area that is equal or superior to the level of services provided within the corporate boundaries of the municipality before annexation. To the extent of any conflict between this subsection and Subsection (g), Subsection (g) prevails.

(n) Before the second anniversary of the date an area is included within the corporate boundaries of a municipality by annexation, the municipality may not:

(1) prohibit the collection of solid waste in the area by a privately owned solid waste management service provider; or

(2) impose a fee for solid waste management services on a person who continues to use the services of a privately owned solid waste management service provider.

(o) A municipality is not required to provide solid waste collection services under Subsection (b) to a person who continues to use the services of a privately owned solid waste management service provider as provided by Subsection (n).

(p) This subsection applies only to a municipality in a county with a population of more than one million and less than 1.75 [~~1.5~~] million. For a municipality that has adopted Chapter 143 and directly employs firefighters, a service plan that includes the provision of services to an area that, at the time the service plan is adopted, is located in the territory of an emergency services district:

(1) must require the municipality's fire department to provide initial response to the annexed territory that is equivalent to that provided to other areas within the corporate boundaries of the municipality with similar topography, land use, and population density;

(2) may not provide for municipal fire services to the annexed area solely or primarily by means of an automatic aid or mutual aid agreement with the affected emergency services district or other third-party provider of services; and

(3) may authorize the emergency services district to provide supplemental fire and emergency medical services to the annexed area by means of an automatic aid or mutual aid agreement.

(q) This chapter does not affect the obligation of a municipality that has adopted Chapter 143 to provide police, fire, or emergency medical services within the municipality's corporate boundaries by means of personnel classified in accordance with that chapter.

2017 Legislation: Amended by S.B. 1878, §1, 85th Leg., eff. Sept. 1, 2017.

LGOVT §43.0561. ANNEXATION HEARING REQUIREMENTS

(a) Before a municipality may institute annexation proceedings, the governing body of the municipality must conduct two public hearings at which persons interested in the annexation are given the opportunity to be heard. The hearings must be conducted not later than the 90th day after the date the inventory is available for inspection.

(b) At least one of the hearings must be held in the area proposed for annexation if a suitable site is reasonably available and more than 20 adults who are permanent residents of the area file a written protest of the annexation with the secretary of the municipality within 10 days after the date of the publication of the notice required by this section. The protest must state the name, address, and age of each protester who signs. If a suitable site is not reasonably available in the area proposed for annexation, the hearing may be held outside the area proposed for annexation if the hearing is held in the nearest suitable public facility.

(c) The municipality must post notice of the hearings on the municipality's Internet website if the municipality has an Internet website and publish notice of the hearings in a newspaper of general circulation in the municipality and in the area proposed for annexation. The notice for each hearing must be published at least once on or after the 20th day but before the 10th day before the date of the hearing. The notice for each hearing must be posted on the municipality's Internet website on or after the 20th day but before the 10th day before the date of the hearing and must remain posted until the date of the hearing. The municipality must give additional notice by certified mail to:

(1) each public entity, as defined by Section 43.053, and utility service provider that provides services in the area proposed for annexation; and

(2) each railroad company that serves the municipality and is on the municipality's tax roll if the company's right-of-way is in the area proposed for annexation.

LGOVT §43.0562. NEGOTIATIONS REQUIRED

(a) After holding the hearings as provided by Section 43.0561:

(1) if a municipality has a population of less than 1.6 million, the municipality and the property owners of the area proposed for annexation shall negotiate for the provision of services to the area after annexation or for the provision of services to the area in lieu of annexation under Section 43.0563; or

(2) if a municipality proposes to annex a special district, as that term is defined by Section 43.052, the municipality and the governing body of the district shall negotiate for the provision of services to the area after annexation or for the provision of services to the area in lieu of annexation under Section 43.0751.

(b) For purposes of negotiations under Subsection (a)(1), the commissioners court of the county in which the area proposed for annexation is located shall select five representatives to negotiate with the municipality for the provision of services to the area after annexation. If the area proposed for annexation is located in more than one county, the commissioners court of the county in which the greatest number of residents reside shall select three representatives to negotiate with the municipality, and the commissioners courts of the remaining counties jointly shall select two representatives to negotiate with the municipality.

(c) For purposes of negotiations under Subsection (a)(2), if more than one special district is located in the area proposed for annexation, the governing boards of the districts may jointly select five representatives to negotiate with the municipality on behalf of all the affected districts.

LGOVT §43.0563. CONTRACTS FOR PROVISION OF SERVICES IN LIEU OF ANNEXATION

(a) The governing body of a municipality with a population of less than 1.6 million may negotiate and enter into a written agreement for the provision of services and the funding of the services in an area with:

(1) representatives designated under Section 43.0562(b), if the area is included in the municipality's annexation plan; or

(2) an owner of an area within the extraterritorial jurisdiction of the municipality if the area is not included in the municipality's annexation plan.

(a-1) An agreement under this section may also include an agreement related to permissible land uses and compliance with municipal ordinances.

(b) An agreement under this section is in lieu of annexation by the municipality of the area.

(c) In negotiating an agreement under this section, the parties may agree to:

(1) any term allowed under Section 42.044 or 43.0751, regardless of whether the municipality or the area proposed for annexation would have been able to agree to the term under Section 42.044 or 43.0751; and

(2) any other term to which both parties agree to satisfactorily resolve any dispute between the parties, including the creation of any type of special district otherwise allowed by state law.

LGOVT §43.0564. ARBITRATION REGARDING NEGOTIATIONS FOR SERVICES

(a) If the municipality and the representatives of the area proposed for annexation cannot reach an agreement for the provision of services under Section 43.0562 or if the municipality and the property owner representatives described by Section 43.0563(a)(1) cannot reach an agreement for the provision of services in lieu of annexation under Section 43.0563, either party by majority decision of the party's representatives may request the appointment of an arbitrator to resolve the service plan issues in dispute. The request must be made in writing to the other party before the 60th day after the date the service plan is completed under Section 43.056. The municipality may not annex the area under another section of this chapter during the pendency of the arbitration proceeding or an appeal from the arbitrator's decision.

(b) The parties to the dispute may agree on the appointment of an arbitrator. If the parties cannot agree on the appointment of an arbitrator before the 11th business day after the date arbitration is requested, the mayor of the municipality shall immediately request a list of seven neutral arbitrators from the American Arbitration Association or the Federal Mediation and Conciliation Service or their successors in function. An arbitrator included in the list must be a resident of this state and may not be a resident of a county in which any part of the municipality or any part of the district proposed for annexation is located. The parties to the dispute may agree on the appointment of an arbitrator included in the list. If the parties cannot agree on the appointment of an arbitrator before the 11th business day after the date the list is provided to the parties, each party or the party's designee may alternately strike a name from the list. The remaining person on the list shall be appointed as the arbitrator. In this subsection, "business day" means a day other than a Saturday, Sunday, or state or national holiday.

(c) The arbitrator shall:

(1) set a hearing to be held not later than the 10th day after the date the arbitrator is appointed; and

(2) notify the parties to the arbitration in writing of the time and place of the hearing not later than the eighth day before the date of the hearing.

(d) The authority of the arbitrator is limited to issuing a decision relating only to the service plan issues in dispute.

(e) The arbitrator may:

(1) receive in evidence any documentary evidence or other information the arbitrator considers relevant;

(2) administer oaths; and

(3) issue subpoenas to require:

(A) the attendance and testimony of witnesses; and

(B) the production of books, records, and other evidence relevant to an issue presented to the arbitrator for determination.

(f) Unless the parties to the dispute agree otherwise, the arbitrator shall complete the hearing within two consecutive days. The arbitrator shall permit each party one day to present evidence and other information. The arbitrator, for good cause shown, may schedule an additional hearing to be held not later than the seventh day after the date of the first hearing. Unless otherwise agreed to by the parties, the arbitrator must issue a decision in writing and deliver a copy of the decision to the parties not later than the 14th day after the date of the final hearing.

(g) Either party may appeal any provision of an arbitrator's decision that exceeds the authority granted under Subsection (d) to a district court in a county in which the area proposed for annexation is located.

(h) If the municipality does not agree with the terms of the arbitrator's decision, the municipality may not annex the area proposed for annexation before the fifth anniversary of the date of the arbitrator's decision.

(i) Except as provided by this subsection, the municipality shall pay the cost of arbitration. If the arbitrator finds that the request for arbitration submitted by the representatives of the area proposed for annexation was groundless or requested in bad faith or for the purposes of harassment, the arbitrator may require the area proposed for annexation to pay all or part of the cost of arbitration.

LGOVT §43.0565. ARBITRATION REGARDING ENFORCEMENT OF SERVICE PLAN

(a) A person who requests arbitration as provided by Section 43.056(*l*) must request the appointment of an arbitrator in writing to the municipality.

(b) Sections 43.0564(b), (c), and (e) apply to appointment of an arbitrator and the conduct of an arbitration proceeding under this section.

(c) In an arbitration proceeding under this section, the municipality has the burden of proving that the municipality is in compliance with the service plan requirements.

(d) If the arbitrator finds that the municipality has not complied with the service plan requirements:

(1) the municipality may disannex the area before the 31st day after the date the municipality receives a copy of the arbitrator's decision; and

(2) the arbitrator may:

(A) require the municipality to comply with the service plan in question before a reasonable date specified by the arbitrator if the municipality does not disannex the area;

(B) require the municipality to refund to the landowners of the annexed area money collected by the municipality from those landowners for services to the area that were not provided; and

(C) require the municipality to pay the costs of arbitration, including the reasonable attorney's fees and arbitration costs of the person requesting arbitration.

(e) If the arbitrator finds that the municipality has complied with the service plan requirements, the arbitrator may require the person requesting arbitration to pay all or part of the cost of arbitration, including the reasonable attorney's fees of the municipality.

LGOVT §43.0567. PROVISION OF WATER OR SEWER SERVICE IN POPULOUS MUNICIPALITY

(a) The requirements of this section are in addition to those prescribed by Section 43.056.

(b) A municipality with a population of more than 1.6 million that includes within its boundaries annexed areas without water service, sewer service, or both:

(1) shall develop a service plan that:

(A) must identify developed tracts in annexed areas of the municipality that do not have water service, sewer service, or both and must provide a procedure for providing water service, sewer service, or both to those developed tracts;

(B) must establish a timetable for providing service based on a priority system that considers potential health hazards, population density, the number of existing buildings, the reasonable cost of providing service, and the desires of the residents;

(C) must include a capital improvements plan committing the necessary financing;

(D) may relieve the municipality from an obligation to provide water service, sewer service, or both in an area described in the service plan if a majority of the households in the area sign a petition stating they do not want to receive the services; and

(E) may require property owners to connect to service lines constructed to serve their area;

(2) shall provide water service, sewer service, or both to at least 75 percent of the residential buildings in annexed areas of the municipality that did not have water service, sewer service, or both on September 1, 1991;

(3) shall provide water service to each area annexed before January 1, 1993, if the area or subdivision as described in the service plan contains at least 25 residences without water service, unless a majority of the households in the area state in a petition that they do not want municipal water service; and

(4) is subject to the penalty prescribed by Section 5.235(n)(6), Water Code, for the failure to provide services.

LGOVT §43.057. ANNEXATION THAT SURROUNDS AREA: FINDINGS REQUIRED

If a proposed annexation would cause an area to be entirely surrounded by the annexing municipality but would not include the area within the municipality, the governing body of the municipality must find, before completing the annexation, that surrounding the area is in the public interest.

SUBCHAPTER C-1. ANNEXATION PROCEDURE FOR AREAS EXEMPTED FROM MUNICIPAL ANNEXATION PLAN

LGOVT §43.061. APPLICABILITY

This subchapter applies to an area proposed for annexation that is not required to be included in a municipal annexation plan under Section 43.052.

LGOVT §43.062. PROCEDURES APPLICABLE

(a) Sections 43.051, 43.054, 43.0545, 43.055, 43.0565, 43.0567, and 43.057 apply to the annexation of an area to which this subchapter applies.

(b) This subsection applies only to an area described by Section 43.052(h)(1). Before the 30th day before the date of the first hearing required under Section 43.063, a municipality shall give written notice of its intent to annex the area to:

(1) each property owner in an area proposed for annexation, as indicated by the appraisal records furnished by the appraisal district for each county in which the area is located;

(2) each public entity, as defined by Section 43.053, or private entity that provides services in the area proposed for annexation; and

(3) each railroad company that serves the municipality and is on the municipality's tax roll if the company's right-of-way is in the area proposed for annexation.

LGOVT §43.063. ANNEXATION HEARING REQUIREMENTS

(a) Before a municipality may institute annexation proceedings, the governing body of the municipality must conduct two public hearings at which persons interested in the annexation are given the opportunity to be heard. The hearings must be conducted on or after the 40th day but before the 20th day before the date of the institution of the proceedings.

(b) At least one of the hearings must be held in the area proposed for annexation if a suitable site is reasonably available and more than 10 percent of the adults who are permanent residents of the area file a written protest of the annexation with the secretary of the municipality within 10 days after the date of the publication of the notice required by this section. The protest must state the name, address, and age of each protester who signs.

(c) The municipality must post notice of the hearings on the municipality's Internet website if the municipality has an Internet website and publish notice of the hearings in a newspaper of general circulation in the municipality and in the area proposed for annexation. The notice for each hearing must be published at least once on or after the 20th day but before the 10th day before the date of the hearing. The notice for each hearing must be posted on the municipality's Internet website on or after the 20th day but before the 10th day before the date of the hearing and must remain posted until the date of the hearing. The municipality must give additional notice by certified mail to each railroad company that serves the municipality and is on the municipality's tax roll if the company's right-of-way is in the area proposed for annexation.

LGOVT §43.064. PERIOD FOR COMPLETION OF ANNEXATION; EFFECTIVE DATE

(a) The annexation of an area must be completed within 90 days after the date the governing body institutes the annexation proceedings or those proceedings are void. Any period during which the municipality is restrained or enjoined by a court from annexing the area is not included in computing the 90-day period.

(b) Notwithstanding any provision of a municipal charter to the contrary, the governing body of a municipality with a population of 1.6 million or more may provide that an annexation take effect on any date within 90 days after the date of the adoption of the ordinance providing for the annexation.

LGOVT §43.065. PROVISION OF SERVICES TO ANNEXED AREA

(a) Before the publication of the notice of the first hearing required under Section 43.063, the governing body of the municipality proposing the annexation shall direct its planning department or other appropriate municipal department to prepare a service plan that provides for the extension of full municipal services to the area to be annexed. The municipality shall provide the services by any of the methods by which it extends the services to any other area of the municipality.

(b) Sections 43.056(b)-(o) apply to the annexation of an area to which this subchapter applies.

SUBCHAPTER D. ANNEXATION PROVISIONS RELATING TO SPECIAL DISTRICTS

LGOVT §43.071. AUTHORITY TO ANNEX WATER OR SEWER DISTRICT

(a) In this section, "water or sewer district" means a district or authority created under Article III, Section 52, Subsections (b)(1) and (2), or under Article XVI, Section 59, of the Texas Constitution that provides or proposes to provide, as its principal function, water services or sewer services or both to household users. The

term does not include a district or authority the primary function of which is the wholesale distribution of water.

(b) A municipality may not annex area in a water or sewer district unless it annexes the entire part of the district that is outside the municipality's boundaries. This restriction does not apply to the annexation of area in a water or sewer district if the district is wholly or partly in the extraterritorial jurisdiction of more than one municipality.

(c) An annexation subject to Subsection (b) is exempt from the provisions of this chapter that limit annexation authority to a municipality's extraterritorial jurisdiction if:

(1) immediately before the annexation, at least one-half of the area of the water or sewer district is in the municipality or its extraterritorial jurisdiction; and

(2) the municipality does not annex in the annexation proceeding any area outside its extraterritorial jurisdiction except the part of the district that is outside its extraterritorial jurisdiction.

(d) Area annexed under Subsection (b) is included in computing the amount of area that a municipality may annex under Section 43.055 in a calendar year. If the area to be annexed exceeds the amount of area the municipality would otherwise be able to annex, the municipality may annex the area but may not annex additional area during the remainder of that calendar year, except area subject to Subsection (b) and area that is excluded from the computation under Section 43.055.

(e) Subsections (b)-(d) do not apply to the annexation of:

(1) an area within a water or sewer district if:

(A) the governing body of the district consents to the annexation;

(B) the owners in fee simple of the area to be annexed consent to the annexation; and

(C) the annexed area does not exceed 525 feet in width at its widest point;

(2) a water or sewer district that has a noncontiguous part that is not within the extraterritorial jurisdiction of the municipality; or

(3) a part of a special utility district created or operating under Chapter 65, Water Code.

(f) To annex the entire part of a water or sewer district that is outside the municipality's boundaries, a general-law municipality incorporated after 1983 that is, after incorporation of the district, incorporated over all or any part of the district may annex territory by ordinance without the consent of the inhabitants or property owners of the territory.

(g) For an annexation of an area in a water or sewer district that is wholly or partly in the overlapping extraterritorial jurisdiction of two or more municipalities, any one of those municipalities is not required to obtain under Section 42.023 the written consent of any of the other municipalities in order to annex the area if:

(1) the area contains less than 100 acres;

(2) the annexing municipality, before June 1, 2005, annexed more than 50 percent of the territory of the water or sewer district, as the district existed on the date of its creation; and

(3) the entire water or sewer district would be contained in the annexing municipality after completion of the annexation.

LGOVT §43.0712. INVALIDATION OF ANNEXATION OF SPECIAL DISTRICT; REIMBURSEMENT OF DEVELOPER

(a) If a municipality enacts an ordinance to annex a special district and assumes control and operation of utilities within the district, and the annexation is invalidated by a final judgment of a court after all appeals have been exhausted, the municipality is deemed, by enactment of its annexation ordinance, to have acquired title to utilities owned by a developer within the special district and is obligated to pay the developer all amounts related to the utilities as provided in Section 43.0715.

(b) Upon resumption of the functions of the special district:

(1) the municipality shall succeed to the contractual rights of the developer to be reimbursed by the special district for the utilities the municipality acquires from the developer; and

(2) the special district shall resume the use of the utilities acquired and paid for by the municipality and shall thereafter acquire the utilities from the municipality and reimburse the municipality for amounts the municipality paid the developer. The payment to the municipality shall be governed by the requirements of the Texas Natural Resource Conservation Commission.

LGOVT §43.0715. ANNEXATION OF WATER-RELATED SPECIAL DISTRICT: REIMBURSEMENT OF LANDOWNER OR DEVELOPER; CONTINUATION OF DISTRICT & TAXING AUTHORITY

(a) In this section:

(1) "Special district" means a political subdivision one purpose of which is to supply fresh water for domestic or commercial use or to furnish sanitary sewer services or drainage.

(2) "Delinquent sum" means the sum a municipality has failed to timely pay to a landowner or developer under Subsection (b).

(b) If a municipality with a population of less than 1.5 million annexes a special district for full or limited purposes and the annexation precludes or impairs the ability of the district to issue bonds, the municipality shall, prior to the effective date of the annexation, pay in cash to the landowner or developer of the district a sum equal to all actual costs and expenses incurred by the landowner or developer in connection with the district that the district has, in writing, agreed to pay and that would otherwise have been eligible for reimbursement from bond proceeds under the rules and requirements of the Texas Natural Resource Conservation Commission as such rules and requirements exist on the date of annexation. For an annexation that is subject to preclearance by a federal authority, a payment will be considered timely if the municipality:

(i) escrows the reimbursable amounts determined in accordance with Subsection (c) prior to the effective date of the annexation; and

(ii) subsequently causes the escrowed funds and accrued interest to be disbursed to the developer within five business days after the municipality receives notice of the preclearance.

(c) At the time notice of the municipality's intent to annex the land within the district is first published in accordance with Section 43.052, the municipality shall proceed to initiate and complete a report for each developer conducted in accordance with the format approved by the Texas Natural Resource Conservation Commission for audits. In the event the municipality is unable to complete the report prior to the effective date of the annexation as a result of the developer's failure to provide information to the municipality which cannot be obtained from other sources, the municipality shall obtain from the district the estimated costs of each project previously undertaken by a developer which are eligible for reimbursement. The amount of such costs, as estimated by the district, shall be escrowed by the municipality for the benefit of the persons entitled to receive payment in an insured interest-bearing account with a financial institution authorized to do business in the state. To compensate the developer for the municipality's use of the infrastructure facilities pending the determination of the reimbursement amount or federal preclearance, all interest accrued on the escrowed funds shall be paid to the developer whether or not the annexation is valid. Upon placement of the funds in the escrow account, the annexation may become effective. In the event a municipality timely escrows all estimated reimbursable amounts as required by this subsection and all such amounts, determined to be owed, including interest, are subsequently disbursed to the developer within five days of final determination in immediately available funds as required by this section, no penalties or interest shall accrue during the pendency of the escrow. Either the municipality or developer may, by written notice to the other party, require disputes regarding the amount owed under this section to be subject to nonbinding arbitration in accordance with the rules of the American Arbitration Association.

(d) A delinquent sum incurs a penalty of six percent of the amount of the sum for the first calendar month it is delinquent plus one percent for each additional month or portion of a month the sum remains unpaid. For an annexation occurring prior to the effective date of the changes in law made by this Act in amending Subsection (b), a delinquent sum begins incurring a penalty on the first day of the eighth month following the month in which the municipality enacted its annexation ordinance. For an annexation occurring after the effective date of this Act, a delinquent sum begins incurring a penalty on the first day after the date the municipality enacts its annexation ordinance.

LGOVT §43.072. AUTHORITY TO ANNEX MUNICIPAL UTILITY DISTRICT BY HOME-RULE MUNICIPALITY

(a) This section applies to a municipal utility district that is located entirely in the extraterritorial jurisdiction of a single general-law municipality and that has a common boundary with at least one home-rule municipality.

(b) A home-rule municipality having a common boundary with a district subject to this section may annex the area of the district if:

(1) the annexation is approved by a majority of the qualified voters who vote on the question at an election held under this section;

(2) the annexation is completed before the date that is one year after the date of the election; and

(3) all the area of the district is annexed.

(c) Area annexed under Subsection (b) is included in computing the amount of area that a municipality may annex under Section 43.055 in a calendar year. If the area to be annexed exceeds the amount of area the municipality would otherwise be able to annex, the municipality may annex the area but may not annex additional area during the remainder of that calendar year, except area subject to Subsection (b) and area that is excluded from the computation under Section 43.055.

(d) Annexation of area under this section is exempt from the provisions of this chapter that prohibit:

(1) a municipality from annexing area outside its extraterritorial jurisdiction;

(2) annexation of area narrower than the minimum width prescribed by Section 43.054; or

(3) reduction of the extraterritorial jurisdiction of a municipality without the written consent of the municipality's governing body.

(e) If the district is composed of two or more tracts, at least one of which is not contiguous to the home-rule municipality, the fact that the annexation will result in one or more parts of the home-rule municipality being not contiguous to the rest of the municipality does not affect the municipality's authority to annex the district.

(f) The extraterritorial jurisdiction of a home-rule municipality is not expanded by the annexation of area under this section.

(g) The board of directors of the district may order an election under this section. The board shall conduct the election in the area composed of the district and the general-law municipality. A person who is qualified to vote in the general-law municipality or the district is eligible to vote in the election.

(h) The board of directors shall set the date of the election for the first uniform election date that falls on or after the 30th day after the date of the order. If a state law prescribing uniform election dates is not in effect on the date of the order, the board shall set the election for a date that falls on or after the 30th day but before the 60th day after the date of the order.

(i) The board of directors shall give notice of the election in the manner provided for an election of the members of the board. The ballot for the election shall be printed to provide for voting for or against the proposition: "Authorizing the municipality of (name of the home-rule municipality) to annex the unincorporated area of the (name of the district)."

(j) Promptly after the board of directors declares the result of the election:

(1) the board shall mail or deliver a certified copy of the resolution declaring the result of the election to the mayor and the secretary of each of the two affected municipalities; and

(2) if the election authorizes annexation of the district by the home-rule municipality, the board shall file a certified copy of the resolution in the deed records of each county in which the district is located.

(k) During the time that an election under this section is pending, the general-law municipality may not annex area in the district. For the purposes of this requirement, an election is pending during the period that begins on the date the board of directors adopts the election order and ends on the date the board declares the result of the election. If, on the date the election order is adopted, the general-law municipality has instituted but not completed proceedings to annex area in the district, the general-law municipality may complete the annexation while the election is pending. If proceedings are completed while the election is pending, the annexation, to the extent that it includes area in the district, takes effect only if the election results in the defeat of the question and, in that case, it takes effect on the date the result of the election is officially declared.

(l) If the question is approved, the period during which the general-law municipality is prohibited from annexing area in the district is extended to the date that is one year after the date of the election.

(m) If a district holds an election under this section, the district may not hold another election under this section before the date that is one year after the date of the earlier election, except that if an election is held on a uniform election date prescribed by law, the subsequent election may be held on the corresponding uniform election date of the following year.

LGOVT §43.073. ABOLITION OF, OR DIVISION OF FUNCTIONS OF, LEVEE IMPROVEMENT DISTRICT ANNEXED BY MUNICIPALITY WITH POPULATION OF MORE THAN 500,000

(a) This section applies to a municipality with a population of more than 500,000 that annexes all or part of the area in a levee improvement district organized under the laws of this state.

(b) If the municipality annexes all the area in the district, the municipality:

(1) shall take over the property and other assets of the district;

(2) assumes all the debts, liabilities, and obligations of the district; and

(3) shall perform all the functions of the district, including the provision of services.

(c) The district is abolished on the annexation of all of its area by the municipality. The abolition of the district does not impair or otherwise affect a contract between the district and a flood control district or other governmental agency for the operation or maintenance of levees or other flood control works, but the municipality assumes the rights and obligations of the district under the contract. On the annexation of all of the area of the district, the municipality may refund, in whole or in part, any outstanding bonded indebtedness and may provide for a sufficient sinking fund to meet any refunding bonds issued.

(d) If the municipality annexes only part of the area in the district, the governing bodies of the municipality and the district may make contracts relating to the division and allocation between themselves of their duplicate and overlapping powers, duties, and other functions and relating to the use, management, control, purchase, conveyance, assumption, and disposition of the property and other assets, debts, liabilities, and obligations of the district. The amount of taxes levied by the district against a parcel of real estate subsequently annexed by the municipality shall be credited against any property taxes levied against the parcel by the municipality.

(e) If the municipality annexes only part of the area in the district, the district may contract with the municipality for the municipal operation of the district's utility systems and other property and for the transfer, conveyance, or sale of those systems and that property, regardless of kind or location inside or outside municipal boundaries, to the municipality on terms to which the governing bodies of the district and municipality agree. That operating contract may extend for a period, not to exceed 30 years, stipulated in the contract and is subject to amendment, renewal, or termination by the mutual consent of the governing bodies. The contract may not impair the obligation of another contract of the municipality or district. In the absence of such a contract, the district may continue to exercise, unaffected by the annexation, the powers, duties, and other functions granted or imposed on the district by law. The municipality may not be required to perform any drainage functions in the district. The municipality may, with the consent of the district, construct and maintain drainage facilities in the district that are consistent with the reclamation plan of the district. The municipality may perform all other municipal functions that the municipality is authorized to perform and that the district is not engaged in performing nor authorized to perform.

LGOVT §43.074. ABOLITION OF WATER-RELATED SPECIAL DISTRICT CREATED WHOLLY IN MUNICIPALITY

(a) A water control and improvement district, fresh water supply district, or municipal utility district created from area that, at the time of the district's creation, is located wholly in a municipality may be abolished as provided by this section.

(b) On a vote of at least two-thirds of the entire membership of the governing body of the municipality, the governing body may adopt an ordinance abolishing the district if the governing body finds:

(1) that:

(A) the district is no longer needed; or

(B) the services furnished and functions performed by the district can be furnished and performed by the municipality; and

(2) that the abolition of the district is in the best interests of the residents and property in the municipality and the district.

(c) If before the effective date of the ordinance or if within 30 days after the effective date or the date of the publication of the ordinance, a petition that is signed and verified by a number of qualified voters of the municipality equal to at least 10 percent of the total votes cast at the most recent election for municipal officers is filed with the secretary of the municipality pro-

testing the enactment or enforcement of the ordinance, the ordinance is suspended and any action taken under the ordinance is void. Immediately after the filing of the petition, the secretary shall present it to the governing body. Immediately after the presentation of the petition, the governing body shall reconsider the ordinance. If the governing body does not repeal the ordinance, the governing body shall submit it to a popular vote at the next municipal election or at a special election the governing body may order for that purpose. The ordinance does not take effect unless a majority of the votes received in the election favor the ordinance.

(d) On the adoption of the ordinance, the district is abolished, the property and other assets of the district vest in the municipality, and the municipality assumes and becomes liable for the bonds and other obligations of the district. The municipality shall perform the services and other functions that were performed by the district.

(e) If a district bond, warrant, or other obligation payable in whole or in part from property taxes is assumed by the municipality, the governing body shall levy and collect taxes on all taxable property in the municipality in an amount sufficient to pay the principal of and interest on the bond, warrant, or other obligation as it becomes due and payable.

(f) The municipality may issue refunding bonds in its own name to refund bonds, warrants, or other obligations, including unpaid accrued interest on an obligation, that is assumed by the municipality. The refunding bonds must be issued in the manner provided by Chapter 1207, Government Code.

LGOVT §43.075. ABOLITION OF, OR DIVISION OF FUNCTIONS OF, WATER-RELATED SPECIAL DISTRICT THAT BECOMES PART OF NOT MORE THAN ONE MUNICIPALITY

(a) This section applies to:

(1) a municipality that annexes all or part of the area in a water control and improvement district, fresh water supply district, or municipal utility district organized for the primary purpose of providing municipal functions such as the supplying of fresh water for domestic or commercial uses or the furnishing of sanitary sewer service or drainage service; or

(2) a municipality:

(A) that, by incorporation of the municipality, includes in the municipality all or part of the area in a district described by Subdivision (1); and

(B) the governing body of which adopts, by a vote of at least two-thirds of its entire membership, an ordinance making this section applicable to the municipality.

(b) This section does not apply if the district includes area located in more than one municipality.

(c) The municipality succeeds to the powers, duties, assets, and obligations of the district as provided by this section. This section does not prohibit the municipality from continuing to operate utility facilities in the district that are owned and operated by the municipality on the date the area becomes a part of the municipality.

(d) If all the area in the district becomes a part of the municipality, the municipality:

(1) shall take over all the property and other assets of the district;

(2) assumes all the debts, liabilities, and obligations of the district; and

(3) shall perform all the functions of the district, including the provision of services.

(e) The governing body of the municipality by ordinance shall designate the date on which the duties and the assumption under Subsection (d) take effect. The date must be set for a day within 90 days after the date the area becomes a part of the municipality. If the governing body fails to adopt the ordinance, the duties and the assumption automatically take effect on the 91st day after the date the area becomes a part of the municipality. The district is abolished on the date the duties and assumption take effect.

(f) If only part of the area in the district becomes a part of the municipality, the governing bodies of the municipality and the district may make contracts relating to the division and allocation between themselves of their duplicate and overlapping powers, duties, and other functions and relating to the use, management, control, purchase, conveyance, assumption, and disposition of the property and other assets, debts, liabilities, and obligations of the district.

(g) If only part of the area in the district becomes a part of the municipality, the district may contract with the municipality for the municipal operation of the district's utility systems and other property and for the transfer, conveyance, or sale of those systems and that property, regardless of kind or location inside or outside municipal boundaries, to the municipality on terms to

which the governing bodies of the district and municipality agree. That operating contract may extend for a period, not to exceed 30 years, stipulated in the contract and is subject to amendment, renewal, or termination by the mutual consent of the governing bodies. The contract may not impair the obligation of another contract of the municipality or district. In the absence of such a contract, the district may continue to exercise the powers and other functions that it was authorized to exercise before the area became a part of the municipality, and the municipality may not, without the district's consent, duplicate the services rendered by the district in the district. However, the municipality may perform in the district all other municipal functions in which the district is not engaged.

(h) If a district bond, warrant, or other obligation payable in whole or in part from property taxes is assumed under this section by the municipality, the governing body shall levy and collect taxes on all taxable property in the municipality in an amount sufficient to pay the principal of and interest on the bond, warrant, or other obligation as it becomes due and payable. The municipality may issue refunding bonds or warrants to refund bonds, warrants, or other obligations, including unpaid earned interest on them, that is assumed by the municipality. The refunding bonds or warrants must be issued in the manner provided by Chapter 1207, Government Code. A refunding bond must bear interest at the same rate or at a lower rate than that borne by the refunded obligation unless it is shown mathematically that a different rate results in a savings in the total amount of interest to be paid.

(i) If all the area in the district becomes a part of the municipality and if the district has outstanding bonds, warrants, or other obligations payable solely from the net revenues from the operation of any utility system or property, the municipality shall take over and operate the system or property and shall apply the net revenues from the operation to the payment of the outstanding revenue bonds, warrants, or other obligations as if the district had not been abolished. The municipality may combine the district system or property with the municipality's similar system or property if:

(1) the municipality has no outstanding revenue bonds, warrants, or other obligations payable from and secured by a pledge of the net revenue of its own utility system or property; or

(2) the municipality:

(A) has outstanding obligations payable from and secured by a pledge of net revenues sufficient to meet the outstanding obligations; and

(B) those revenues have produced, during the five-year period before May 30, 1959, an annual surplus in an amount sufficient to meet the annual obligations for which the district revenues are pledged.

(j) If the municipality combines the systems or property as provided by Subsection (i), it shall levy on all property subject to taxation by the municipality an annual property tax at a rate that, when combined with other available municipal funds and revenues, is sufficient to pay the principal of and interest on the outstanding obligations.

(k) If all the area in the district becomes a part of the municipality, the municipality, unless the refunding authorized by Subsection (*l*) has been accomplished, shall separately operate the district and municipal systems and property and may not commingle revenue if the municipality has outstanding bonds, warrants, or other bonded obligations payable from and secured by a pledge of the net revenue of its own utility system or property and does not have an amount annually accruing to its surplus revenue fund that exceeds the amount of the fund pledged to the payment of outstanding municipal obligations and that is sufficient to meet the annual obligations for which the district revenues are pledged. The municipality shall perform the duties and other functions imposed by law or contract on the governing body of the district relating to the district's outstanding bonds, warrants, or other obligations and shall separately perform the duties and other functions relating to the bonds, warrants, and other obligations of the municipal system. The municipality may allocate overhead expenses between any two or more systems in direct proportion to the gross income of each system.

(*l*) The municipality may issue revenue refunding bonds in its own name for the purpose of refunding outstanding district revenue bonds, warrants, or other obligations, including unpaid accrued interest on them, that are assumed by the municipality under this section. The municipality may combine different issues of district and municipal revenue bonds, warrants, or other obligations into one series of revenue refunding bonds and may pledge the net revenues of the utility systems or property to the payment of the refunding

bonds as the governing body considers proper. Except as otherwise provided by this section, Chapter 1502, Government Code, applies to the revenue refunding bonds, but an election for the issuance of the bonds is not required. Refunding bonds must bear interest at the same rate or at a lower rate than that borne by the refunded obligations unless it is shown mathematically that a different rate results in a savings in the total amount of interest to be paid.

LGOVT §43.0751. STRATEGIC PARTNERSHIPS FOR CONTINUATION OF CERTAIN DISTRICTS

(a) In this section:

(1) "District" means a conservation and reclamation district operating under Chapter 49, Water Code. The term does not include a groundwater conservation district operating under Chapter 36, Water Code, or a special utility district operating under Chapter 65, Water Code.

(2) "Limited district" means a district that, pursuant to a strategic partnership agreement, continues to exist after full-purpose annexation by a municipality in accordance with the terms of a strategic partnership agreement.

(3) "Strategic partnership agreement" means a written agreement described by this section between a municipality and a district.

(b) The governing bodies of a municipality and a district may negotiate and enter into a written strategic partnership agreement for the district by mutual consent. The governing body of a municipality, on written request from a district included in the municipality's annexation plan under Section 43.052, shall negotiate and enter into a written strategic partnership agreement with the district. A district included in a municipality's annexation plan under Section 43.052:

(1) may not submit its written request before the date of the second hearing required under Section 43.0561; and

(2) must submit its written request before the 61st day after the date of the second hearing required under Section 43.0561.

(c) A strategic partnership agreement shall not be effective until adopted by the governing bodies of the municipality and the district. The agreement shall be recorded in the deed records of the county or counties in which the land included within the district is located and shall bind each owner and each future owner of land included within the district's boundaries on the date the agreement becomes effective.

(d) Before the governing body of a municipality or a district adopts a strategic partnership agreement, it shall conduct two public hearings at which members of the public who wish to present testimony or evidence regarding the proposed agreement shall be given the opportunity to do so. Notice of public hearings conducted by the governing body of a municipality under this subsection shall be published in a newspaper of general circulation in the municipality and in the district. The notice must be in the format prescribed by Section 43.123(b) and must be published at least once on or after the 20th day before each date. Notice of public hearings conducted by the governing body of a district under this subsection shall be given in accordance with the district's notification procedures for other matters of public importance. Any notice of a public hearing conducted under this subsection shall contain a statement of the purpose of the hearing, the date, time, and place of the hearing, and the location where copies of the proposed agreement may be obtained prior to the hearing. The governing bodies of a municipality and a district may conduct joint public hearings under this subsection, provided that at least one public hearing is conducted within the district.

(e) The governing body of a municipality may not annex a district for limited purposes under this section or under the provisions of Subchapter F until it has adopted a strategic partnership agreement with the district. The governing body of a municipality may not adopt a strategic partnership agreement before the agreement has been adopted by the governing body of the affected district.

(f) A strategic partnership agreement may provide for the following:

(1) limited-purpose annexation of the district on terms acceptable to the municipality and the district provided that the district shall continue in existence during the period of limited-purpose annexation;

(2) limited-purpose annexation of a district located in a county with a population of more than 3.3 million:

(A) only if the municipality does not require services, permits, or inspections or impose fees for services, permits, or inspections within the district; and

LGOVT §43.075

(B) provided that this subsection does not prevent the municipality from providing services within the district if:

(i) the provision of services is specified and agreed to in the agreement;

(ii) the provision of services is not solely the result of a regulatory plan adopted by the municipality in connection with the limited-purpose annexation of the district; and

(iii) the district has obtained the authorization of the governmental entity currently providing the service;

(3) payments by the municipality to the district for services provided by the district;

(4) annexation of any commercial property in a district for full purposes by the municipality, notwithstanding any other provision of this code or the Water Code, except for the obligation of the municipality to provide, directly or through agreement with other units of government, full provision of municipal services to annexed territory, in lieu of any annexation of residential property or payment of any fee on residential property in lieu of annexation of residential property in the district authorized by this subsection;

(5) a full-purpose annexation provision on terms acceptable to the municipality and the district;

(6) conversion of the district to a limited district including some or all of the land included within the boundaries of the district, which conversion shall be effective on the full-purpose annexation conversion date established under Subdivision (5);

(7) agreements existing between districts and governmental bodies and private providers of municipal services in existence on the date a municipality evidences its intention by adopting a resolution to negotiate for a strategic partnership agreement with the district shall be continued and provision made for modifications to such existing agreements; and

(8) such other lawful terms that the parties consider appropriate.

(g) A strategic partnership agreement that provides for the creation of a limited district under Subsection (f)(6) shall include provisions setting forth the following:

(1) the boundaries of the limited district;

(2) the functions of the limited district and the term during which the limited district shall exist after full-purpose annexation, which term may be renewed successively by the governing body of the municipality, provided that no such original or renewed term shall exceed 10 years;

(3) the name by which the limited district shall be known; and

(4) the procedure by which the limited district may be dissolved prior to the expiration of any term established under Subdivision (2).

(h) On the full-purpose annexation conversion date set forth in the strategic partnership agreement pursuant to Subsection (f)(5)(A), the land included within the boundaries of the district shall be deemed to be within the full-purpose boundary limits of the municipality without the need for further action by the governing body of the municipality. The full-purpose annexation conversion date established by a strategic partnership agreement may be altered only by mutual agreement of the district and the municipality. However, nothing herein shall prevent the municipality from terminating the agreement and instituting proceedings to annex the district, on request by the governing body of the district, on any date prior to the full-purpose annexation conversion date established by the strategic partnership agreement. Land annexed for limited or full purposes under this section shall not be included in calculations prescribed by Section 43.055(a).

(i) A strategic partnership agreement may provide that the district shall not incur additional debt, liabilities, or obligations, to construct additional utility facilities, or sell or otherwise transfer property without prior approval of the municipality.

(j) Except as limited by this section or the terms of a strategic partnership agreement, a district that has been annexed for limited purposes by a municipality and a limited district shall have and may exercise all functions, powers, and authority otherwise vested in a district.

(k) A municipality that has annexed all or part of a district for limited purposes under this section may impose a sales and use tax within the boundaries of the part of the district that is annexed for limited purposes. Except to the extent it is inconsistent with this section, Chapter 321, Tax Code, governs the imposition, computation, administration, governance, and abolition of the sales and use tax.

(*l*) An agreement or a decision made under this section and an action taken under the agreement by

the parties to the agreement are not subject to approval or an appeal brought under the Water Code unless it is an appeal of a utility rate charged by a municipality to customers outside the corporate boundaries of the municipality.

(m) A municipality that may annex a district for limited purposes to implement a strategic partnership agreement under this section shall not annex for full purposes any territory within a district created pursuant to a consent agreement with that municipality executed before August 27, 1979. The prohibition on annexation established by this subsection shall expire on September 1, 1997, or on the date on or before which the municipality and any district may have separately agreed that annexation would not take place whichever is later.

(n) This subsection applies only to a municipality any portion of which is located in a county that has a population of not less than 285,000 and not more than 300,000 and that borders the Gulf of Mexico and is adjacent to a county with a population of more than 3.3 million. A municipality may impose within the boundaries of a district a municipal sales and use tax authorized by Chapter 321, Tax Code, or a municipal hotel occupancy tax authorized by Chapter 351, Tax Code, that is imposed in the municipality if:

(1) the municipality has annexed the district for limited purposes under this section; or

(2) following two public hearings on the matter, the municipality and the district enter a written agreement providing for the imposition of the tax or taxes.

(n-1) At the conclusion of the term of an agreement between a municipality and a district under Subsection (n), the district and the municipality may extend the agreement for a period not to exceed 10 years. An agreement may be extended only once under this subsection.

(o) If a municipality required to negotiate with a district under this section and the requesting district fail to agree on the terms of a strategic partnership agreement, either party may seek binding arbitration of the issues relating to the agreement in dispute under Section 43.0752.

(p) An agreement under this section:

(1) may not require the district to provide revenue to the municipality solely for the purpose of obtaining an agreement with the municipality to forgo annexation of the district; and

(2) must provide benefits to each party, including revenue, services, and regulatory benefits, that must be reasonable and equitable with regard to the benefits provided by the other party.

(q) Except for Sections 43.130(a) and (b), Subchapter F does not apply to a limited-purpose annexation under a strategic partnership agreement.

(r) A district or the area of a district annexed for limited purposes under this section must be:

(1) in the municipality's extraterritorial jurisdiction; and

(2) contiguous to the corporate boundaries of the municipality or an area annexed by the municipality for limited purposes, unless the district consents to noncontiguous annexation under a strategic partnership agreement with the municipality.

LGOVT §43.07515. REGULATION OF FIREWORKS UNDER STRATEGIC PARTNERSHIP AGREEMENT LAW

(a) A municipality may not regulate under Section 43.0751 or 43.0752 the sale, use, storage, or transportation of fireworks outside of the municipality's boundaries.

(b) To the extent of a conflict with any other law, this section controls.

LGOVT §43.0752. ARBITRATION OF STRATEGIC PARTNERSHIP AGREEMENT

(a) If the municipality and the district cannot reach an agreement on the terms of a strategic partnership agreement under Section 43.0751, either party may request the appointment of an arbitrator to resolve the issues in dispute. The request must be made in writing to the other party before the 60th day after the date the district submits its written request for negotiations under Section 43.0751(b). The municipality may not annex the district under another section of this chapter during the pendency of the arbitration proceeding or an appeal from the arbitrator's decision.

(b) Sections 43.0564(b), (c), (e), (f), (g), and (h) apply to appointment of an arbitrator and the conduct of an arbitration proceeding under this section.

(c) The authority of the arbitrator is limited to determining whether the offer of a party complies with Section 43.0751(p).

(d) If the arbitrator finds that an offer complies with Section 43.0751(p), the arbitrator may issue a de-

cision that incorporates the offer as part of the strategic partnership agreement.

(e) The municipality and the district shall equally pay the costs of arbitration.

LGOVT §43.0753. REGIONAL DEVELOPMENT AGREEMENTS

(a) In this section:

(1) "District" means a conservation and reclamation district that is created or operating under Chapters 49 and 54, Water Code, and that is located entirely within the boundaries of a planned community and entirely within the extraterritorial jurisdiction of a municipality.

(2) "Municipality" means a municipality with a population of 1.6 million or more.

(3) "Planned community" means a planned community of 10,000 acres or more that is subject in whole or in part to a restrictive covenant that contains an ad valorem-based assessment on real property used or to be used, in any part, to fund governmental or quasi-governmental services and facilities within and for the planned community.

(4) "Regional development agreement" means a contract or agreement entered into under this section or in anticipation of the enactment of this section and any amendment, modification, supplement, addition, renewal, or extension to or of the contract or agreement or any proceeding relating to the contract or agreement.

(b) Notwithstanding any contrary law or municipal charter provision, the governing body of a municipality and the governing body of one or more districts may enter into a regional development agreement to further regional cooperation between the municipality and the district.

(c) A regional development agreement may allow:

(1) any type of annexation of any part of the land in the district to be deferred for a mutually agreeable period of time;

(2) facilities or services to be provided to the land within the district by any party to the agreement or by any other person, including optional, backup, emergency, mutual aid, or supplementary facilities or services;

(3) payments to be made by the municipality to the district or another person or by the district or another person to the municipality for services provided to the district or municipality;

(4) standards for requesting and receiving any form of required consent or approval from the municipality;

(5) a district to issue bonds, notes, refunding bonds, or other forms of indebtedness;

(6) the coordination of local, regional, and area-wide planning;

(7) remedies for breach of the agreement;

(8) the modification, amendment, renewal, extension, or termination of the agreement;

(9) any other district to join the agreement at any time;

(10) third-party beneficiaries to be specifically designated and conferred rights or remedies under the agreement; and

(11) any other term to which the parties agree.

(d) A regional development agreement must be:

(1) in writing;

(2) approved by the governing body of the municipality and the district; and

(3) recorded:

(A) in the real property records of any county in which any part of a district that is party to the agreement is located; and

(B) in any manner that complies with Subchapter J, Chapter 49, Water Code.

(e) Subject to compliance with Subsection (d)(1) and (3), another district may join or become a party to a regional development agreement in the manner authorized in the agreement.

(f) A regional development agreement does not need to describe the land contained within the boundaries of a district that is a party to the agreement. The agreement must be recorded in the deed records of any county in which any land in the district is located.

(g) A regional development agreement binds each party to the agreement and each owner and future owner of land that is subject to the agreement. If a party or landowner is excluded or removed from an agreement, the removal or exclusion is effective on the recordation requirement of Subsection (d)(3).

(h) A regional development agreement may not require a district to provide public services and facilities to a person to whom the district is not otherwise authorized to provide services or facilities or to make payments from any source from which the district is not otherwise authorized to make payments.

(i) A district may contract with any person for services or facilities to be provided at no cost to the district or for the payment of funds by the person in support of a regional development agreement.

(j) A regional development agreement and any action taken under the agreement is not subject to any method of approval under the Water Code or any method of appeal under the Water Code.

(k) Notwithstanding any defect, ambiguity, discrepancy, invalidity, or unenforceability of a regional development agreement that has been voluntarily entered into and fully executed by the parties thereto, or any contrary law, common law doctrine, or municipal charter provision, and for the duration of any annexation deferral period established in the regional development agreement during which a district continues to perform its obligations under the regional development agreement:

(1) Sections 42.023 and 42.041(b)-(e) do not apply to any land or owner of land within a district that is a party to the regional development agreement; and

(2) the governing body of the municipality may not include the area covered by the regional development agreement in a municipal annexation plan and may not initiate or continue an annexation proceeding relating to that area after the effective date of this section.

(*l*) This section shall be liberally construed so as to give effect to its legislative purposes and to sustain the validity of a regional development agreement if the agreement was entered into under or in anticipation of this section.

LGOVT §43.0754. REGIONAL PARTICIPATION AGREEMENTS

(a) In this section:

(1) "District" means a political subdivision created by general or special law that has the powers of a municipal management district under Chapter 375 and a conservation and reclamation district under Chapters 49 and 54, Water Code, a majority by area of the territory of which is located within a planned community and within the extraterritorial jurisdiction of one or more municipalities.

(2) "Eligible municipality" means a municipality:

(A) that has a population of 1.5 million or more and that includes in its extraterritorial jurisdiction at least 90 percent by area of the territory of a district;

(B) that includes in its extraterritorial jurisdiction not more than 10 percent of the territory of a district that has entered into a regional participation agreement under this section with another eligible municipality described by Paragraph (A); or

(C) with corporate boundaries contiguous to the boundaries of a district that has entered into a regional participation agreement under this section with another eligible municipality described by Paragraph (A).

(3) "Party" means a district, eligible municipality, or person that is a party to a regional participation agreement approved and entered into under this section.

(4) "Planned community" means a planned community of 20 square miles or more with a population of 50,000 or more that is subject in whole or in part to a restrictive covenant that contains an ad valorem-based assessment on real property used or to be used, in any part, to fund governmental or quasi-governmental services and facilities within and for the planned community.

(5) "Regional participation agreement" means a contract or agreement entered into under this section or in anticipation of the enactment of this section and any amendment, modification, supplement, addition, renewal, or extension to or of the contract or agreement or any proceeding relating to the contract or agreement.

(b) Notwithstanding any contrary law or municipal charter provision, the governing body of an eligible municipality, the governing body of a district, and, if applicable, a person may approve and authorize execution and performance of a regional participation agreement to further regional participation in the funding of eligible programs or projects. A regional participation agreement must include as parties at least one eligible municipality and one district and may include as parties other eligible municipalities, districts, or persons.

(c) A regional participation agreement may provide or allow for:

(1) the establishment, administration, use, investment, and application of a regional participation fund, which shall be a special fund or escrow account to be used solely for funding the costs and expenses of eligible programs or projects;

(2) payments to be made by a party into the regional participation fund for application, currently or in the future, toward eligible programs or projects;

(3) the methods and procedures by which eligible programs or projects are prioritized, identified, and se-

lected for implementation and are planned, designed, bid, constructed, administered, inspected, and completed;

(4) the methods and procedures for accounting for amounts on deposit in, to the credit of, or expended from the regional participation fund, as well as any related investment income or amounts due and owing to or from any party to the fund;

(5) credits against payments otherwise due by any party under the agreement resulting from taxes, charges, fees, assessments, tolls, or other payments in support of or related to the usage or costs of eligible programs or projects that are levied or imposed upon, assessed against, or made applicable to a party or its citizens, ratepayers, taxpayers, or constituents after the effective date of the agreement;

(6) any type of annexation of any part of the territory of a district to be deferred by an eligible municipality that is a party for a mutually agreeable period;

(7) the release of territory from the extraterritorial jurisdiction of an eligible municipality that is a party at a specified time or upon the occurrence of specified events;

(8) the consent of an eligible municipality that is a party to the incorporation of, or the adoption of an alternate form of government by, all or part of the territory of a district at a specified time or upon the occurrence of specified events;

(9) remedies for breach of the agreement;

(10) the modification, amendment, renewal, extension, or termination of the agreement;

(11) other districts, eligible municipalities, or persons to join the agreement as a party at any time;

(12) third-party beneficiaries to be specifically designated and conferred rights or remedies under the agreement;

(13) the duration of the agreement, including an unlimited term;

(14) the creation and administration of a nonprofit corporation, joint powers agency, local government corporation, or other agency for the purpose of administration and management of a regional participation fund, program, or project under the agreement; and

(15) any other provision or term to which the parties agree.

(d) A regional participation agreement may provide for the funding of any program or project, whether individual, intermittent, or continuing and whether located or conducted within or outside the boundaries of a party, for the planning, design, construction, acquisition, lease, rental, installment purchase, improvement, provision of furnishings or equipment, rehabilitation, repair, reconstruction, relocation, preservation, beautification, use, execution, administration, management, operation, or maintenance of any works, improvements, or facilities, or for providing any functions or services, whether provided to, for, by, or on behalf of a party, that provide a material benefit to each party in the accomplishment of the purposes of each party, related to:

(1) mobility or transportation, including mass transportation, traffic circulation, or ground, air, rail, water, or other means of transportation or movement of people, freight, goods, or materials;

(2) health care treatment, research, teaching, or education facilities or infrastructure;

(3) parks or recreation, open space, and scenic, wildlife, wetlands, or wilderness areas;

(4) public assembly or shelter, including halls, arenas, stadiums or similar facilities for sporting events, exhibitions, conventions, or other mass assembly purposes;

(5) environmental preservation or enhancement, including air or water quality protection, improvement, preservation, or enhancement, and noise abatement;

(6) the supply, conservation, transportation, treatment, disposal, or reuse of water or wastewater;

(7) drainage, stormwater management or detention, and flood control or prevention;

(8) solid waste collection, transfer, processing, reuse, resale, disposal, and management; or

(9) public safety and security, including law enforcement, firefighting and fire prevention, emergency services and facilities, and homeland security.

(e) A regional participation agreement must be:

(1) in writing;

(2) approved by the governing body of each eligible municipality or district that is or that becomes a party to the agreement; and

(3) must be recorded in the deed records of any county in which is located any territory of a district that is or that becomes a party to the agreement.

(f) A district, eligible municipality, or person may join or become a party to a regional participation agreement in the manner authorized in the agreement.

(g) A regional participation agreement is not required to describe the land contained within the boundaries of a party to the agreement, but any territory to be released from the extraterritorial jurisdiction of an eligible municipality that is a party under an agreement must be described in sufficient detail to convey title to land and the description must be made a part of the agreement.

(h) A regional participation agreement binds each party and its legal successor, including a municipality or other form of local government, to the agreement for the term specified in the agreement and each owner and future owner of land that is subject to the agreement during any annexation deferral period established in the agreement. If a party, land, or landowner is excluded or removed from an agreement, the removal or exclusion is effective on the recordation of the amendment, supplement, modification, or restatement of the agreement implementing the removal or exclusion.

(i) A regional participation agreement may not require a party to make payments from any funds that are restricted, encumbered, or pledged for the payment of contractual obligations or indebtedness of the party. Otherwise, any party may commit or pledge or may issue bonds payable from or secured by a pledge of any available source of funds, including unencumbered sales and use taxes, to make payments due or to become due under an agreement.

(j) Notwithstanding any other law, a program or project to be funded and any bonds to be issued by a district to make payments under a regional participation agreement are not subject to review or approval by the Texas Commission on Environmental Quality.

(k) A regional participation agreement and any action taken under the agreement are not subject to any method of approval or appeal under the Water Code.

(*l*) After due authorization, execution, delivery, and recordation as provided by this section, a regional participation agreement, including any related amendment, supplement, modification, or restatement, and a pledge of funds to make payments under an agreement shall be final and incontestable in any court of this state.

(m) Notwithstanding any defect, ambiguity, discrepancy, invalidity, or unenforceability of a regional participation agreement that has been voluntarily entered into and fully executed by the parties, or any contrary law, common law doctrine, or municipal charter provision, and for the duration of any annexation deferral period established in the agreement during which a district continues to perform its obligations under the agreement:

(1) Section 42.023 and any other law or municipal charter provision relating to the reduction of the extraterritorial jurisdiction of an eligible municipality that is a party do not apply, and Sections 42.041(b)-(e) do not apply to any land or owner of land within a district that is a party;

(2) the governing body of an eligible municipality that is a party may not initiate or continue an annexation proceeding relating to that area but may include the area covered by the agreement in a municipal annexation plan; and

(3) any area that is to be released from the extraterritorial jurisdiction of an eligible municipality that is a party under an agreement, or that is to be incorporated or included within an alternate form of government with the consent of a municipality that is a party under an agreement, shall, by operation of law and without further action by a party or its governing body, be released from the extraterritorial jurisdiction, or consent of the municipality to the incorporation or adoption of an alternate form of government by the district shall be deemed to have been given, as appropriate under the agreement, at the time or upon the occurrence of the events specified in the agreement.

(n) Notwithstanding the provisions of any municipal charter or other law, a district or an eligible municipality is not required to hold an election to authorize a regional participation agreement. As long as such funds remain restricted for use under an agreement, payments to or income from a regional participation fund shall not be deemed revenues to an eligible municipality for purposes of any law or municipal charter provision relating to revenue or property tax caps or limits.

(o) This section is cumulative of all other authority to make, enter into, and perform a regional participation agreement. In case of any conflict or ambiguity between this section and any other law or municipal charter provision, this section shall prevail and control.

(p) This section shall be liberally construed so as to give effect to its legislative purposes and to sustain the validity of a regional participation agreement if the agreement was entered into under or in anticipation of enactment of this section.

(q) For purposes of Subchapter I, Chapter 271:

(1) a district or eligible municipality is a "local governmental entity" within the meaning of Section 271.151(3); and

(2) a regional participation agreement is a "contract subject to this subchapter" within the meaning of Section 271.151(2), without regard to whether the agreement is for providing goods or services.

E LGOVT §43.0755. PROCEDURES FOR INCORPORATION OR ESTABLISHMENT OF ANOTHER FORM OF LOCAL GOVERNMENT FOR CERTAIN AREAS SUBJECT TO REGIONAL PARTICIPATION AGREEMENT

(a) In this section, "district," "eligible municipality," and "regional participation agreement" have the meanings assigned by Section 43.0754.

(b) This section applies only to a district and an eligible municipality that have entered into a regional participation agreement under Section 43.0754 that authorizes any of the actions described by Section 43.0754(c)(6), (7), or (8).

(c) Notwithstanding any other law, including laws prescribing population or territorial requirements for incorporation under Section 5.901, 6.001, 7.001, or 8.001, the governing body of a district may order an election as provided by this subsection to be held on a uniform election date prescribed by Section 41.001, Election Code. An election under this subsection may, consistent with the regional participation agreement, be ordered for the purpose of:

(1) submitting to the qualified voters of the district the question of whether the territory of the district should be incorporated as a municipality;

(2) submitting to the qualified voters of a designated area of the district the question of whether that designated area should be incorporated as a municipality;

(3) submitting to the qualified voters of the district the question of whether the territory of the district should adopt a specific alternate form of local government other than a municipality; or

(4) submitting to the qualified voters of a designated area of the district the question of whether that designated area should adopt a specific alternate form of local government other than a municipality.

(d) Notwithstanding any other law:

(1) the authority of the governing body of a district to order an election under Subsection (c) is separate and independent and is the exclusive means of ordering any such election;

(2) all or any part of the territory of a district may be incorporated as a Type A, Type B, or Type C municipality, as determined by the governing body of the district ordering the incorporation election under Subsection (c)(1) or (2); and

(3) the requirements of Sections 7.002 and 8.002 do not apply to an election ordered under Subsection (c)(1) or (2).

(e) In an election ordered under Subsection (c)(2) or (4), the governing body of the district may order elections in multiple designated areas on the same date or order elections in designated areas periodically on a uniform election date.

(f) In any election ordered under Subsection (c), the governing body of the district shall also submit for confirmation to the voters voting in the election the proposed initial property tax rate determined for the municipality or alternate form of government, as applicable, which may not exceed the maximum rate authorized by law. The ballot in an election held under Subsection (c) shall be printed to permit voting for or against the proposition: "Authorizing the (specify the incorporation of or the adoption of an alternate form of local government for) (insert name of local government) and the adoption of an initial property tax rate of not more than (specify the maximum rate determined)."

(g) In any election ordered under Subsection (c), the governing body of the district may also submit to the voters voting in the election any other measure the governing body considers necessary and convenient to effectuate the transition to a municipal or alternate form of local government, including a measure on the question of whether, on incorporation as a municipality or establishment of an alternate form of local government, any rights, powers, privileges, duties, purposes, functions, or responsibilities of the district or the dis-

LGOVT §43.0755

trict's authority to issue bonds and impose a tax is transferred to the municipality or alternate form of local government.

(h) If a majority of the voters voting in an election under Subsection (c)(2) or (4) approve the proposition submitted on the form of local government, the county judge of the county in which the municipality or alternate form of local government is located shall order an election for the governing body of the municipality or alternate form of local government to be held on a date that complies with the provisions of the Election Code, except that Section 41.001(a), Election Code, does not apply. A municipality or alternate form of local government resulting from an election described by this subsection is incorporated or established on the date a majority of the members of the governing body qualify and take office.

(i) If a majority of the voters voting in an election under Subsection (c)(1) or (3) approve the proposition submitted on the form of local government, the district is dissolved and the governing body of the district will serve as the temporary governing body of the municipality or alternate form of local government until a permanent governing body is elected as provided by Subsection (j).

(j) The temporary governing body under Subsection (i) shall order an election to elect the permanent governing body of the municipality or alternate form of local government to occur on a date that complies with the provisions of the Election Code, except that Section 41.001(a), Election Code, does not apply.

(k) An election ordered under Subsection (h) or (j) to elect members of the governing body of a municipality must be held under the applicable provisions of Chapter 22, 23, or 24, to the extent consistent with this section. An election for members of the governing body of an alternate form of government must be held under the law applicable to that form of government, to the extent consistent with this section.

(l) If a majority of the voters voting in an election under Subsection (c)(1) or (3) approve the proposition submitted on the form of local government for the territory of the district, the assets, liabilities, and obligations of the district are transferred to the form of government approved at the election.

(m) If a majority of the voters voting in an election under Subsection (c)(2) or (4) approve the proposition submitted on the form of local government in a designated area of the district and if, on the date of the election approving the form of local government, the district owes any debts, by bond or otherwise, the designated area is not released from its pro rata share of the indebtedness.

(n) For purposes of determining the initial tax rate of a municipality or an alternate form of local government, the tax rate of the district when the territory incorporated or established as an alternate form of government was part of the district is not considered for purposes of the calculations required by Section 26.04(c), Tax Code.

2017 Legislation: Enacted by S.B. 1015, §1, 85th Leg., eff. June 9, 2017.

LGOVT §43.076. ABOLITION OF WATER-RELATED SPECIAL DISTRICT THAT BECOMES PART OF MORE THAN ONE MUNICIPALITY

(a) This section applies to a municipality that contains, as a result of the annexation by or the incorporation of the municipality, any part of the area in a water control and improvement district, fresh water supply district, or municipal utility district organized for the primary purpose of providing municipal functions such as the supplying of fresh water for domestic or commercial uses or the furnishing of sanitary sewer service, if:

(1) the balance of the area in the district is located in one or more other municipalities;

(2) the district is not created by a special act of the legislature and the balance of the area is located in one or more other municipalities and in an unincorporated area; or

(3) the district is a conservation and reclamation district of more than 10,000 acres which provides water and sanitary sewer service to households and parts of which are located in two or more municipalities, one of which has a population of more than 1.6 million.

(b) The municipality succeeds to the powers, duties, assets, and obligations of the district as provided by this section. This section does not prohibit the municipality from continuing to operate utility facilities in the district that are owned and operated by the municipality on the date the part of the district area becomes a part of the municipality.

(c) If the district is located wholly in two or more municipalities, the district may be abolished by agreement among the district and the municipalities in which the district is located. Subject to Subsection (f), the agreement must provide for the distribution among

the municipalities of the property and other assets of the district and for the pro rata assumption by the municipalities of all the debts, liabilities, and obligations of the district. The assumption by each municipality must be based on the ratio that the value of the property and other assets distributed to that municipality bears to the total value of all the property and other assets of the district. The determination of value may be made on an original cost basis, a reproduction cost basis, a fair market value basis, or by any other valuation method agreed on by the parties that reasonably reflects the value of the property and other assets, debts, liabilities, and obligations of the district. The agreement must specify the date on which the district is abolished.

(d) If the district is located wholly in two or more municipalities and in unincorporated area, the district may be abolished by agreement among the district and all of the municipalities in which parts of the district are located. The abolition agreement must provide for the distribution of assets and liabilities as provided by Subsection (c). The agreement must also provide for the distribution among one or more of the municipalities of the pro rata assets and liabilities located in the unincorporated area and must provide for service to customers in unincorporated areas in the service area of the abolished district. The municipality that provides the service in the unincorporated area may charge its usual and customary fees and assessments to the customers in that area.

(e) An agreement made under Subsection (c) or (d) must be approved by an ordinance adopted by the governing body of each municipality and by an order or resolution adopted by the governing board of the district before the date specified in the agreement for the abolition, distribution, and assumption.

(f) If the abolished district has outstanding bonds, warrants, or other obligations payable in whole or in part from the net revenue from the operation of the district utility system or property, the affected municipalities shall take over and operate the system or property through a board of trustees as provided by this section. The municipalities shall apply the net revenue from the operation of the system or property to the payment of outstanding revenue bonds, warrants, or other obligations as if the district had not been abolished. The system or property shall be operated in that manner until all the revenue bonds, warrants, or obligations are retired in full by payment or by the refunding of the bonds, warrants, or other obligations into municipal obligations. The board of trustees must be composed of not more than five members appointed by the governing bodies of the municipalities. The trustees are appointed for the terms and shall perform the duties as provided by the agreement made under Subsection (c) or (d). The board also shall perform the duties and other functions that are imposed by law or by contract on the abolished district and its governing board and that relate to the outstanding revenue bonds. The board shall charge and collect sufficient rates for the services of the system or property and shall apply the revenue to comply with each covenant or agreement contained in the proceedings relating to the revenue bonds, warrants, or other obligations with respect to the payment of principal and interest and the maintenance of reserves and other funds. When all the revenue bonds, warrants, and other obligations are retired in full, the property and other assets of the district shall be distributed among the municipalities as provided by Subsection (c) or (d). On the distribution, the board is abolished.

(g) When the pro rata share of any district bonds, warrants, or other obligations payable in whole or in part from property taxes has been assumed by the municipality, the governing body of the municipality shall levy and collect taxes on all taxable property in the municipality to pay the principal of and interest on its share as the principal and interest become due and payable.

(h) The municipality may issue general obligation refunding bonds in its own name to refund in whole or in part its pro rata share of any outstanding district bonds, warrants, or other obligations, including unpaid earned interest on them, that are assumed by the municipality and that are payable in whole or in part from property taxes. The refunding bonds must be issued in the manner provided by Chapter 1207, Government Code. Refunding bonds must bear interest at the same rate or at a lower rate than that borne by the refunded obligations unless it is shown mathematically that a different rate results in a savings in the total amount of interest to be paid.

(i) The municipality may issue revenue refunding bonds or general obligation refunding bonds in its own name to refund in whole or in part its pro rata share of any outstanding district bonds, warrants, or other obli-

gations, including unpaid earned interest on them, that are assumed by the municipality and that are payable solely from net revenues. The municipality may combine the different issues or the bonds of different issues of both district and municipal revenue bonds, warrants, or other obligations into one or more series of revenue refunding bonds. The municipality may pledge the net revenues of the district utility system or property to the payment of those bonds, warrants, or other obligations. The municipality may also combine the different issues or the bonds of the different issues into one or more series of general obligation refunding bonds. An originally issued municipal revenue bond may not be refunded into municipal general obligation refunding bonds. Except as otherwise provided by this section, Subchapter B, Chapter 1502, Government Code, applies to the revenue refunding bonds, but an election for the issuance of the bonds is not required. Revenue refunding bonds or general obligation refunding bonds must be issued in the manner provided by Chapter 1207, Government Code. The revenue refunding bonds and the general obligation refunding bonds must bear interest at the same rate or at a lower rate than that borne by the refunded obligations unless it is shown mathematically that a different rate results in a savings in the total amount of interest to be paid.

LGOVT §43.0761. PROVISION OF WATER & SANITARY SEWER UTILITY SERVICE

(a) A district existing on September 1, 1997, that, within 10 years after the date of its creation, has not provided water and sanitary sewer utility service from its facilities to all household users in its territory shall:

(1) provide water and sanitary sewer utility service from its facilities to all household users in its territory not later than September 1, 1998; or

(2) for that part of the district for which the district does not provide water and sanitary sewer utility service, and for which a municipality does provide those services, provide for periodic payments, as described by Subsection (b), by the district to the municipality that provides the services.

(b) Payments made under Subsection (a)(2) are operation and maintenance expenses of the district and shall be made at least every three months. The total annual amount of the payments may not exceed the lesser of:

(1) the total annual cost to the municipality of providing the water and sanitary sewer utility service, including both capital and operation and maintenance costs and expenses; or

(2) the total annual amount of maintenance and operation taxes and debt service or bond taxes paid to the district by the owners of taxable property within the district that receives water and sanitary sewer utility service from the municipality.

(c) For purposes of Subsection (b)(2), the value of taxable property that receives the utility service shall be determined by the most recent certified tax roll provided by the central appraisal district in which the property is located. The amount of the taxes shall be determined using rates from the district's most recent tax levies.

(d) A district that on January 1, 1997, was providing water and sanitary sewer utility service to households outside the territory of the district may not discontinue that service and shall continue to provide that service on the basis of rates established by the district in accordance with Chapter 13, Water Code.

(e) In this section, "district" means a conservation and reclamation district of more than 10,000 acres that provides water and sanitary sewer utility service to households and parts of which are located in two or more municipalities, one of which has a population of more than 1.6 million.

LGOVT §43.079. CONSENT REQUIREMENT FOR ANNEXATION OF AREA IN CERTAIN CONSERVATION & RECLAMATION DISTRICTS

(a) This section applies only to a conservation and reclamation district, including a municipal utility district, that:

(1) is located wholly in more than one municipality, but on April 1, 1971, was not wholly in more than one municipality;

(2) was created or exists under Section 59, Article XVI, Texas Constitution;

(3) provides or has provided a fresh water supply, sanitary sewer services, and drainage services; and

(4) was not, on April 1, 1971, a party to a contract providing for a federal grant for research and development under 33 U.S.C. Sections 1155(a)(2) and (d).

(b) A municipality that has annexed area in the district is not required to obtain the consent of any mu-

nicipality to annex additional area located wholly in the district other than the consent of the other municipalities that have annexed area in the district and have extraterritorial jurisdiction over the area proposed to be annexed.

LGOVT §43.080. MUNICIPAL BONDS USED TO CARRY OUT PURPOSES OF ABOLISHED CONSERVATION & RECLAMATION DISTRICT

(a) This section applies only to each municipality that under any other law, including Section 43.075, abolishes a conservation and reclamation district created under Article XVI, Section 59, of the Texas Constitution, including a water control and improvement district, fresh water supply district, or municipal utility district.

(b) If, before its abolition, the district voted to issue bonds to provide waterworks, sanitary sewer facilities, or drainage facilities and if some or all of the bonds were not issued, sold, and delivered before the abolition, the governing body of the municipality may issue and sell municipal bonds in an amount not to exceed the amount of the unissued district bonds to carry out the purposes for which the district bonds were voted.

(c) The bonds must be authorized by ordinance of the governing body of the municipality. The ordinance must provide for the levy of taxes on all taxable property in the municipality to pay the principal of and interest on the bonds when due. The bonds must be sold at not less than par value and accrued interest, and must mature, bear interest, and be subject to approval by the attorney general and to registration by the comptroller of public accounts as provided by law for other general obligation bonds of the municipality.

(d) A bond that is approved, registered, and sold as provided by this section is incontestable.

(e) This section repeals a municipal charter provision to the extent of a conflict with this section. This section does not affect the authority of a municipality to issue bonds for other purposes.

LGOVT §43.081. CONTINUATION OF CERTAIN MUNICIPAL WATER BOARDS ON ANNEXATION OF WATER CONTROL & IMPROVEMENT DISTRICT

(a) A municipal water board that was created by Section 6, Chapter 134, Acts of the 52nd Legislature, Regular Session, 1951, and that continues to exist to preserve a vested right created under that law, remains in existence with full power after the municipality annexes all the area of the water control and improvement district whose functions the municipality assumed and delegated to the water board, so long as the land located in the board's jurisdiction is used for farming, ranching, or orchard purposes.

(b) The municipal water board shall select and designate one or more depositories for the proceeds of the maintenance and water charges and other charges levied by the water control and improvement district and for any other income or other funds of the district. The water board may select a depository regardless of the fact that one or more members of the board are members of the board of directors or are stockholders of the depository.

(c) The funds of the water control and improvement district may be kept in one or more separate accounts in the depository if the funds deposited in each separate account are to be used for a different designated purpose from the funds deposited in any other separate account. The funds deposited in the depository must be insured by an official agency of the United States and must be at least as well insured and protected as funds deposited in the official municipal depository of the municipality.

LGOVT §43.082. ANNEXATION BY CERTAIN MUNICIPALITIES OF LAND OWNED BY NAVIGATION DISTRICT

A municipality with a population of less than 30,000, that is in a county that borders the Gulf of Mexico and that is adjacent to a county with a population of one million or more, and that seeks to annex land owned by a navigation district operating under Section 59, Article XVI, Texas Constitution, must have the consent of the district to annex the land.

SUBCHAPTER E. ANNEXATION PROVISIONS RELATING TO RESERVOIRS, AIRPORTS, STREETS, & CERTAIN OTHER AREAS

LGOVT §43.101. ANNEXATION OF MUNICIPALLY OWNED RESERVOIR BY GENERAL-LAW MUNICIPALITY

(a) A general-law municipality may annex:

(1) a reservoir owned by the municipality and used to supply water to the municipality;

(2) any land contiguous to the reservoir and subject to an easement for flood control purposes in favor of the municipality; and

(3) the right-of-way of any public road or highway connecting the reservoir to the municipality by the most direct route.

(b) The municipality may annex the area if:

(1) none of the area is more than five miles from the municipality's boundaries;

(2) none of the area is in another municipality's extraterritorial jurisdiction; and

(3) the area, excluding road or highway right-of-way, is less than 600 acres.

(c) The area may be annexed without the consent of the owners or residents of the area.

(d) The municipality may annex the area even if part of the area is outside the municipality's extraterritorial jurisdiction or is narrower than the minimum width prescribed by Section 43.054. Section 43.055, which relates to the amount of area a municipality may annex in a calendar year, does not apply to the annexation.

LGOVT §43.102. ANNEXATION OF MUNICIPALLY OWNED AIRPORT

(a) A municipality may annex:

(1) an airport owned by the municipality; and

(2) the right-of-way of any public road or highway connecting the airport to the municipality by the most direct route.

(b) The municipality may annex the area if:

(1) none of the area is more than eight miles from the municipality's boundaries; and

(2) each municipality in whose extraterritorial jurisdiction the airport is located agrees to the annexation.

(c) The area may be annexed without the consent of the owners or residents of the area.

(d) The municipality may annex the area even if the area is outside the municipality's extraterritorial jurisdiction, is in another municipality's extraterritorial jurisdiction, or is narrower than the minimum width prescribed by Section 43.054. Section 43.055, which relates to the amount of area a municipality may annex in a calendar year, does not apply to the annexation.

(e) The annexation under this section of area outside the extraterritorial jurisdiction of the annexing municipality does not expand the extraterritorial jurisdiction of the municipality.

LGOVT §43.1025. ANNEXATION OF NONCONTIGUOUS MUNICIPALLY OWNED AIRPORT BY CERTAIN MUNICIPALITIES

(a) This section applies only to a home-rule municipality that has a population of less than 11,000 and is located primarily in a county with a population of more than 3.3 million.

(b) The municipality may annex the unincorporated area of an airport owned by the municipality that is noncontiguous to the boundaries of the municipality regardless of whether the airport is located in the municipality's extraterritorial jurisdiction. The annexation may include any unincorporated area located in the proximity of the airport.

(c) The area described by Subsection (b) may be annexed without the consent of the owners or residents of the area, but the annexation may not occur unless each municipality in whose extraterritorial jurisdiction the area may be located:

(1) consents to the annexation; and

(2) reduces its extraterritorial jurisdiction over the area as provided by Section 42.023.

(d) If the area proposed for annexation is completely surrounded by territory under the jurisdiction of another municipality, regardless of whether that jurisdiction is full-purpose, limited-purpose, or extraterritorial, that municipality must find that the annexation is in the public interest.

(e) Following annexation, territory annexed under this section is not required to be contiguous to the boundaries of the annexing municipality.

(f) The annexation of area under this section outside the extraterritorial jurisdiction of the annexing municipality does not expand the extraterritorial jurisdiction of the municipality.

(g) The municipality may annex the area if the area is narrower than the minimum width prescribed by Section 43.054. Section 43.055 does not apply to the annexation.

LGOVT §43.103. ANNEXATION OF STREETS, HIGHWAYS, & OTHER WAYS BY GENERAL-LAW MUNICIPALITY

(a) A general-law municipality with a population of 500 or more may annex, by ordinance and without the

consent of any person, the part of a street, highway, alley, or other public or private way, including a railway line, spur, or roadbed, that is adjacent and runs parallel to the boundaries of the municipality.

(b) The requirements imposed by Section 43.054 regarding the width of the area to be annexed do not apply to an area annexed under this section.

LGOVT §43.105. ANNEXATION OF STREETS BY CERTAIN SMALL GENERAL-LAW MUNICIPALITIES

(a) A general-law municipality that has a population of 1,066-1,067 and is located in a county with a population of 85,000 or more that is not adjacent to a county with a population of 2 million or more, or that has a population of 6,000-6,025 may annex, by ordinance and without the consent of any person, a public street, highway, road, or alley adjacent to the municipality.

(b) The requirements imposed by Section 43.054 regarding the width of the area to be annexed do not apply to an area annexed under this section.

(c) The requirements imposed by Section 43.056 regarding service plans shall apply to an area annexed under this section. The service plan required by this section shall address drainage issues.

LGOVT §43.106. ANNEXATION OF COUNTY ROADS REQUIRED IN CERTAIN CIRCUMSTANCES

(a) A municipality that proposes to annex any portion of a county road or territory that abuts a county road must also annex the entire width of the county road and the adjacent right-of-way on both sides of the county road.

(b) If a road annexed under Subsection (a) is a gravel road, the county retains control of granting access to the road and its right-of-way from property that:

(1) is not located in the boundaries of the annexing municipality; and

(2) is adjacent to the road and right-of-way.

SUBCHAPTER F. LIMITED PURPOSE ANNEXATION

LGOVT §43.121. AUTHORITY OF POPULOUS HOME-RULE MUNICIPALITIES TO ANNEX FOR LIMITED PURPOSES; OTHER AUTHORITY NOT AFFECTED

(a) The governing body of a home-rule municipality with more than 225,000 inhabitants by ordinance may annex an area for the limited purposes of applying its planning, zoning, health, and safety ordinances in the area.

(b) To be annexed for limited purposes, an area must be:

(1) within the municipality's extraterritorial jurisdiction; and

(2) contiguous to the corporate boundaries of the municipality, unless the owner of the area consents to noncontiguous annexation.

(c) The provisions of this subchapter, other than Section 43.136, do not affect the authority of a municipality to annex an area for limited purposes under Section 43.136 or any other statute granting the authority to annex for limited purposes.

LGOVT §43.122. CERTAIN STRIP ANNEXATIONS PROHIBITED

A municipality may not annex for limited purposes any strip of territory, including a strip following the course of a road, highway, river, stream, or creek, that is, at its narrowest point, less than 1,000 feet in width and is located farther than three miles from the preexisting boundaries of the municipality, unless the area is annexed under Section 43.129.

LGOVT §43.123. REPORT REGARDING PLANNING STUDY & REGULATORY PLAN

(a) Before the 10th day before the date the first hearing required by Section 43.124 is held, the municipality must prepare a report regarding the proposed annexation of an area for limited purposes and make the report available to the public. The report must contain the results of the planning study conducted for the area in accordance with Subsection (c) and must contain the regulatory plan prepared for the area in accordance with Subsection (d).

(b) Notice of the availability of the report shall be published at least twice in a newspaper of general circulation in the area proposed to be annexed. The notice may not be smaller than one-quarter page of a standard-size or tabloid-size newspaper, and the headline on the notice must be in 18-point or larger type.

(c) The planning study must:

(1) project the kinds and levels of development that will occur in the area in the next 10 years if the area is not annexed for limited purposes and also if the area is annexed for limited purposes;

(2) describe the issues the municipality considers to give rise to the need for the annexation of the area for limited purposes and the public benefits to result from the limited-purpose annexation;

(3) analyze the economic, environmental, and other impacts the annexation of the area for limited purposes will have on the residents, landowners, and businesses in the area; and

(4) identify the proposed zoning of the area on annexation and inform the public that any comments regarding the proposed zoning will be considered at the public hearings for the proposed limited-purpose annexation.

(d) The regulatory plan must:

(1) identify the kinds of land use and other regulations that will be imposed in the area if it is annexed for limited purposes; and

(2) state the date on or before which the municipality shall annex the area for full purposes, which date must be within three years after the date the area is annexed for limited purposes.

(e) The deadline imposed by Subsection (d)(2) does not apply to an area that:

(1) is owned by the United States, this state, or a political subdivision of this state;

(2) is located outside the boundaries of a water control and improvement district or a municipal utility district; and

(3) is annexed for limited purposes in connection with a strategic partnership agreement under Section 43.0751.

LGOVT §43.124. PUBLIC HEARINGS

(a) Before instituting proceedings for annexing an area for limited purposes, the governing body of the municipality must hold two public hearings on the proposed annexation. Each member of the public who wishes to present testimony or evidence regarding the proposed limited-purpose annexation must be given the opportunity to do so. At the hearing, the municipality shall hear and consider the appropriateness of the application of rural and urban ordinances in the area to be annexed for limited purposes.

(b) The hearings must be held on or after the 40th day but before the 20th day before the date the annexation proceedings are instituted. A notice of the hearings must be published in a newspaper of general circulation in the municipality and in the area proposed for annexation. The notice must be in the format prescribed by Section 43.123(b). Before the date of each hearing, the notice must be published at least once on or after the 20th day before the hearing date and must contain:

(1) a statement of the purpose of the hearing;

(2) a statement of the date, time, and place of the hearing; and

(3) a general description of the location of the area proposed to be annexed for limited purposes.

LGOVT §43.125. ADOPTION OF REGULATORY PLAN

(a) At the time the governing body of the municipality adopts an ordinance annexing an area for limited purposes, the governing body must also adopt by ordinance a regulatory plan for the area.

(b) The adopted regulatory plan must be the same as the regulatory plan prepared under Section 43.123 unless the governing body finds and states in the ordinance the reasons for the adoption of a different regulatory plan.

(c) The governing body by ordinance may change a regulatory plan adopted under Subsection (b) if, in the ordinance making the change, the governing body finds and states the reasons for the adoption of the change.

LGOVT §43.126. PERIOD FOR COMPLETION OF ANNEXATION

The annexation of an area for limited purposes must be completed within 90 days after the date the governing body institutes the annexation proceedings.

LGOVT §43.127. ANNEXATION FOR FULL PURPOSES

(a) Except as provided by Section 43.123(e), on or before the date prescribed by the regulatory plan under Section 43.123(d)(2), the municipality must annex the area for full purposes. This requirement may be waived and the date for full-purpose annexation postponed by written agreement between the municipality and a majority of the affected landowners. A written agreement to waive the municipality's obligation to annex the area for full purposes binds all future owners of land annexed for limited purposes pursuant to that waiver.

(b) In each of the three years for which an area may be annexed for limited purposes, the municipality must take the steps prescribed by this subsection toward the full-purpose annexation of the area. By the

end of the first year after the date an area is annexed for limited purposes, the municipality must develop a land use and intensity plan as a basis for services and capital improvements projects planning. By the end of the second year after that date, the municipality must include the area in the municipality's long-range financial forecast and in the municipality's program to identify future capital improvements projects. By the end of the third year after that date, the municipality must include in its adopted capital improvements program the projects intended to serve the area and must identify potential sources of funding for capital improvements.

LGOVT §43.128. JUDICIAL REMEDIES: FORCED ANNEXATION OR DISANNEXATION

(a) If the municipality fails to annex the area for full purposes as required by Section 43.127(a), any affected person may petition the district court to compel the annexation of the area for full purposes or the disannexation of the area. On finding that the municipality has failed to annex the area as required by Section 43.127(a), the court shall enter an order requiring the municipality to annex the area for full purposes or to disannex the area. If an area is disannexed, the area may not be annexed again by the municipality for five years.

(b) If the municipality fails to take the steps required by Section 43.127(b), any affected person may petition the district court to compel the annexation of a particular area for full purposes or the disannexation of the area. On finding that the municipality has failed to take the steps required by Section 43.127(b), the court shall enter an order requiring the municipality to annex the area for full purposes or to disannex the area.

LGOVT §43.129. CONSENSUAL ANNEXATION

The municipality may annex for limited purposes any land for which the landowner requests annexation and provides to the municipality before the effective date of the annexation the landowner's written consent to annexation for limited purposes. With respect to any larger parcels of property, consent of the owners of at least 51 percent of the total affected territory must be evidenced by appropriate signatures on the limited-purpose annexation request. A landowner's written consent to limited-purpose annexation is binding on all future owners of land in the area annexed for limited purposes pursuant to the consent.

LGOVT §43.130. EFFECT OF ANNEXATION ON VOTING RIGHTS, ELIGIBILITY FOR OFFICE, & TAXING AUTHORITY

(a) The qualified voters of an area annexed for limited purposes are entitled to vote in municipal elections regarding the election or recall of members of the governing body of the municipality, the election or recall of the controller, if the office of controller is an elective position of the municipality, and the amendment of the municipal charter. The voters may not vote in any bond election. On or after the 15th day but before the fifth day before the date of the first election held in which the residents of an area annexed for limited purposes are entitled to vote, the municipality shall publish notice in the form of a quarter-page advertisement in a newspaper of general circulation in the municipality notifying the residents that they are eligible to vote in the election and stating the location of all polling places for the residents.

(b) A resident of an area annexed for limited purposes is not eligible to be a candidate for or to be elected to a municipal office.

(c) The municipality may not impose a tax on any property in an area annexed for limited purposes or on any resident of the area for an activity occurring in the area. The municipality may impose reasonable charges, such as building inspection and permit fees, on residents or landowners for actions or procedures performed by the municipality in connection with the limited purposes for which the area is annexed.

LGOVT §43.131. EFFECT OF ANNEXATION ON EXTRATERRITORIAL JURISDICTION

The annexation of an area for limited purposes does not extend the municipality's extraterritorial jurisdiction.

LGOVT §43.132. MUNICIPAL INCORPORATION IN ANNEXED AREA

A municipality may not be incorporated in an area annexed for limited purposes unless the annexing municipality gives its consent.

LGOVT §43.136. AUTHORITY OF SPECIAL-LAW MUNICIPALITY TO ANNEX FOR LIMITED PURPOSES ALONG NAVIGABLE STREAM

(a) The governing body of a special-law municipality located along or on a navigable stream may extend the boundaries of the municipality to include the area designated by Subsection (b) only to:

(1) improve navigation on the stream by the United States, the municipality, or a navigation or other improvement district; and

(2) establish and maintain wharves, docks, railway terminals, side tracks, warehouses, or other facilities or aids relating to navigation or wharves.

(b) The municipality by ordinance may extend the boundaries to include an area composed of the navigable stream and the land on each side of the stream. The area may not exceed 2,500 feet in width on either side of the stream as measured from the thread of the stream and may not exceed 20 miles in length as measured in a direct line from the ordinary municipal boundaries, either above or below the boundaries, or both. Consequently, the area subject to the boundary extension is a strip 5,000 feet wide and 20 miles in length, or as much of that strip as the governing body considers advisable to add to the municipality. The boundaries are extended on the adoption of the ordinance.

(c) The governing body may acquire land in the added area by purchase, condemnation, or gift. If condemnation is used, the municipality shall follow the condemnation procedure applying to the condemnation of land by the municipality for the purchase of streets.

(d) This section does not authorize the municipality to extend its boundaries to include area that is part of or belongs to another municipality.

(e) A municipality may not tax the property over which the boundaries are extended under this section unless the property is within the general municipal boundaries.

(f) After the adoption of the ordinance extending the municipal boundaries, the municipality may fully regulate navigation, wharfage, including wharfage rates, and all facilities, conveniences, and aids to navigation or wharfage. The municipality may adopt ordinances, including those imposing criminal penalties, and may otherwise police navigation on the stream and the use of the wharves or other facilities and aids to navigation or wharfage.

(g) The municipality may designate all or part of the added area as an industrial district, as the term is customarily used, and may treat the designated area in a manner considered by the governing body to be in the best interest of the municipality. The governing body may make written contracts or agreements with the owners of land in the industrial district, to guarantee the continuation of the limited purpose annexation status of the district and its immunity from general purpose annexation for a period not to exceed 10 years. The contract or agreement may contain other terms considered appropriate by the parties. The governing body and landowners may renew or extend the contract for successive periods not to exceed 10 years each.

(h) Notwithstanding any other law, including a municipal ordinance or charter provision, the governing body by ordinance may change the status of an area previously annexed for general purposes to limited purpose annexation status governed by this section if:

(1) the area previously annexed at any time was eligible to be included within the municipal boundaries under Subsection (b);

(2) the owners of the area petition the governing body for the change in status; and

(3) the governing body includes the area in an industrial district designated as provided by Subsection (g) or any other law.

SUBCHAPTER G. DISANNEXATION

LGOVT §43.141. DISANNEXATION FOR FAILURE TO PROVIDE SERVICES

(a) A majority of the qualified voters of an annexed area may petition the governing body of the municipality to disannex the area if the municipality fails or refuses to provide services or to cause services to be provided to the area within the period specified by Section 43.056 or by the service plan prepared for the area under that section.

(b) If the governing body fails or refuses to disannex the area within 60 days after the date of the receipt of the petition, any one or more of the signers of the petition may bring a cause of action in a district court of the county in which the area is principally located to request that the area be disannexed. On the filing of an answer by the governing body, and on application of either party, the case shall be advanced and heard without further delay in accordance with the Texas Rules of Civil Procedure. The district court shall enter an order disannexing the area if the court finds that a valid petition was filed with the municipality and that the municipality failed to perform its obligations in accor-

dance with the service plan or failed to perform in good faith.

(c) If the area is disannexed under this section, it may not be annexed again within 10 years after the date of the disannexation.

(d) The petition for disannexation must:

(1) be written;

(2) request the disannexation;

(3) be signed in ink or indelible pencil by the appropriate voters;

(4) be signed by each voter as that person's name appears on the most recent official list of registered voters;

(5) contain a note made by each voter stating the person's residence address and the precinct number and voter registration number that appear on the person's voter registration certificate;

(6) describe the area to be disannexed and have a plat or other likeness of the area attached; and

(7) be presented to the secretary of the municipality.

(e) The signatures to the petition need not be appended to one paper.

(f) Before the petition is circulated among the voters, notice of the petition must be given by posting a copy of the petition for 10 days in three public places in the annexed area and by publishing a copy of the petition once in a newspaper of general circulation serving the area before the 15th day before the date the petition is first circulated. Proof of the posting and publication must be made by attaching to the petition presented to the secretary:

(1) the sworn affidavit of any voter who signed the petition, stating the places and dates of the posting; and

(2) the sworn affidavit of the publisher of the newspaper in which the notice was published, stating the name of the newspaper and the issue and date of publication.

LGOVT §43.142. DISANNEXATION ACCORDING TO MUNICIPAL CHARTER IN HOME-RULE MUNICIPALITY

A home-rule municipality may disannex an area in the municipality according to rules as may be provided by the charter of the municipality and not inconsistent with the procedural rules prescribed by this chapter.

LGOVT §43.143. DISANNEXATION BY PETITION & ELECTION IN GENERAL-LAW MUNICIPALITY

(a) When at least 50 qualified voters of an area located in a general-law municipality sign and present a petition to the mayor of the municipality that describes the area by metes and bounds and requests that the area be declared no longer part of the municipality, the mayor shall order an election on the question in the municipality. The election shall be held on the first uniform election date prescribed by Chapter 41, Election Code, that occurs after the date on which the petition is filed and that affords enough time to hold the election in the manner required by law.

(b) When a majority of the votes received in the election favor discontinuing the area as part of the municipality, the mayor shall declare that the area is no longer a part of the municipality and shall enter an order to that effect in the minutes or records of the governing body of the municipality. The area ceases to be a part of the municipality on the date of the order. However, the area may not be discontinued as part of the municipality if the discontinuation would result in the municipality having less area than one square mile or one mile in diameter around the center of the original municipal boundaries.

(c) If the area withdraws from a municipality as provided by this section and if, at the time of the withdrawal, the municipality owes any debts, by bond or otherwise, the area is not released from its pro rata share of that indebtedness. The governing body shall continue to levy a property tax each year on the property in the area at the same rate that is levied on other property in the municipality until the taxes collected from the area equal its pro rata share of the indebtedness. Those taxes may be charged only with the cost of levying and collecting the taxes, and the taxes shall be applied exclusively to the payment of the pro rata share of the indebtedness. This subsection does not prevent the inhabitants of the area from paying in full at any time their pro rata share of the indebtedness.

LGOVT §43.144. DISANNEXATION OF SPARSELY POPULATED AREA IN GENERAL-LAW MUNICIPALITY

(a) The mayor and governing body of a general-law municipality by ordinance may discontinue an area as a part of the municipality if:

(1) the area consists of at least 10 acres contiguous to the municipality; and

(2) the area:

(A) is uninhabited; or

(B) contains fewer than one occupied residence or business structure for every two acres and fewer than three occupied residences or business structures on any one acre.

(b) On adoption of the ordinance, the mayor shall enter in the minutes or records of the governing body an order discontinuing the area. The area ceases to be a part of the municipality on the date of the entry of the order.

LGOVT §43.145. DISANNEXATION OF UNIMPROVED AREA OR NONTAXABLE AREA IN CERTAIN MUNICIPALITIES

(a) The governing body of a municipality by ordinance may discontinue an area as a part of the municipality if:

(1) the municipality has a population of 4,000 or more and is located in a county with a population of more than 205,000, and the area is composed of at least three contiguous acres that are unimproved and adjoining the municipal boundaries; or

(2) the municipality has a population of 596,000 or more, and the area is an improved area that is not taxable by the municipality and is contiguous to the municipal boundary.

(b) On adoption of the ordinance, the governing body shall enter in the minutes or records of the municipality an order discontinuing the area. The area ceases to be a part of the municipality on the date of the entry of the order.

LGOVT §43.146. DISANNEXATION OF LAND IN A MUNICIPAL UTILITY DISTRICT

Notwithstanding any provision of any other law related to the annexation or disannexation of territory, including but not limited to the requirement that the minimum width of any territory annexed be at least 1,000 feet in width, a municipality that has exercised limited purpose annexation may disannex any land located within a municipal utility district. Such disannexation shall not affect the validity of the annexation of other territory. Such municipality may refund any taxes paid or waive any taxes due to the municipality by the owners of the property disannexed pursuant to the provisions of this section.

LGOVT §43.147. WIDTH REQUIREMENT FOR DISANNEXATION

(a) A municipality disannexing a road or highway shall also disannex a strip of area that is equal in size to the minimum area that the municipality is required to annex in order to comply with the width requirements of Section 43.054 unless such disannexation is undertaken with the mutual agreement of the county government and the municipality.

(b) The strip of area to be disannexed must:

(1) be adjacent to either side of the road or highway; and

(2) follow the course of the road or highway.

LGOVT §43.148. REFUND OF TAXES & FEES

(a) If an area is disannexed, the municipality disannexing the area shall refund to the landowners of the area the amount of money collected by the municipality in property taxes and fees from those landowners during the period that the area was a part of the municipality less the amount of money that the municipality spent for the direct benefit of the area during that period.

(b) A municipality shall proportionately refund the amount under Subsection (a) to the landowners according to a method to be developed by the municipality that identifies each landowner's approximate pro rata payment of the taxes and fees being refunded.

(c) A municipality required to refund money under this section shall refund the money to current landowners in the area not later than the 180th day after the date the area is disannexed. Money that is not refunded within the period prescribed by this subsection accrues interest at the rate of:

(1) six percent each year after the 180th day and until the 210th day after the date the area is disannexed; and

(2) one percent each month after the 210th day after the date the area is disannexed.

SUBCHAPTER H. ALTERATION OF ANNEXATION STATUS

LGOVT §43.201. DEFINITIONS

In this subchapter:

(1) "Consent agreement" means an agreement between a district and a municipality under Section 42.042.

(2) "Limited-purpose annexation" means annexation authorized under Section 43.121.

LGOVT §43.202. APPLICABILITY

This subchapter applies to:

(1) a municipal utility district operating under Chapter 54, Water Code, that:

(A) was annexed for full purposes by a municipality as a condition of the municipality granting consent to the creation of the district;

(B) was annexed by the municipality on the same date as at least five other districts; and

(C) has not had on the eighth anniversary of the district's annexation by the municipality more than 10 percent of the housing units or commercial square footage authorized in its consent agreement constructed; and

(2) a municipality that has:

(A) annexed territory for limited purposes;

(B) disannexed territory that previously was annexed for limited purposes; and

(C) previously disannexed territory in a municipal utility district originally annexed for full purposes on the same date as a district to which this section applies.

LGOVT §43.203. ALTERATION OF ANNEXATION STATUS

(a) The governing body of a district by resolution may petition a municipality to alter the annexation status of land in the district from full-purpose annexation to limited-purpose annexation.

(b) On receipt of the district's petition, the governing body of the municipality shall enter into negotiations with the district for an agreement to alter the status of annexation that must:

(1) specify the period, which may not be less than 10 years beginning on January 1 of the year following the date of the agreement, in which limited-purpose annexation is in effect;

(2) provide that, at the expiration of the period, the district's annexation status will automatically revert to full-purpose annexation without following procedures provided by Sections 43.051 through 43.055 or any other procedural requirement for annexation not in effect on January 1, 1995; and

(3) specify the financial obligations of the district during and after the period of limited-purpose annexation for:

(A) facilities constructed by the municipality that are in or that serve the district;

(B) debt incurred by the district for water and sewer infrastructure that will be assumed by the municipality at the end of the period of limited-purpose annexation; and

(C) use of the municipal sales taxes collected by the municipality for facilities or services in the district.

(c) If an agreement is not reached within 90 days after the date the municipality receives a petition submitted by a district:

(1) the district's status is automatically altered from full-purpose annexation to limited-purpose annexation for a period of not less than 10 years, beginning January 1 of the year following the date of the submission of a petition, unless the voters of the district have approved the dissolution of the district through an election authorized by this section; and

(2) on the expiration of the 10-year period of Subdivision (1), notwithstanding any other provision of law, the district may be restored to full-purpose annexation at the option of the municipality, provided that the municipality assumes all obligations otherwise assigned by law to a municipality that annexes a district; and

(3) the municipality may collect a waste and wastewater surcharge for customers in the district after restoration of full-purpose annexation provided that:

(A) notice of such proposed surcharge is provided to the board of a district six months prior to restoration of full-purpose annexation;

(B) the surcharge does not exceed the cost of a post-annexation surcharge to any other district annexed by the municipality; and

(C) the surcharge is in effect only during the period in which bonds issued by the district or refunded by the municipality are not fully retired.

(d) Upon the request of any residents of a district subject to this section the municipality may conduct an election on a uniform election date at which election voters who are residents of the district may vote for or against a ballot proposal to dissolve the district. If more than one district was created on the same date and the districts are contiguous, the election shall be a combined election of all such districts, with a majority of votes cast by all residents of the districts combined required for dissolution of the districts. If a majority of votes are in favor of dissolution, the date of dissolution

shall be December 31 of the same year in which the election is held. Upon dissolution of the district, all property and obligations of a dissolved district become the responsibility of the municipality.

(e) The municipality shall have no responsibility to reimburse the developer of the district or its successors for more than reasonable and actual engineering and construction costs to design and build internal water treatment and distribution facilities, wastewater treatment and collection facilities, or drainage facilities, whether temporary or permanent, installed after September 1, 1995. Any obligation to reimburse the developer may be paid in installments over a three-year period.

(f) During the period of limited-purpose annexation:

(1) the district may not use bond proceeds to pay for impact fees but must comply with other items in its consent agreement with the municipality;

(2) the municipality:

(A) must continue to provide wholesale water and sewer service as provided by the consent agreement; and

(B) is relieved of service obligations in the district that are not provided to other territory annexed for limited purposes or required by the annexation alteration agreement between the municipality and the district; and

(3) retail sales in the boundaries of the district will be treated for municipal sales tax purposes as if the district were annexed by the municipality for full purposes.

(g) This section does not allow a change in annexation status for land or facilities in a district to which the municipality granted a property tax abatement before September 1, 1995.

TITLE 7. REGULATION OF LAND USE, STRUCTURES, BUSINESSES, & RELATED ACTIVITIES

SUBTITLE A. MUNICIPAL REGULATORY AUTHORITY

CHAPTER 211. MUNICIPAL ZONING AUTHORITY

SUBCHAPTER A. GENERAL ZONING REGULATIONS

LGOVT §211.001. PURPOSE

The powers granted under this subchapter are for the purpose of promoting the public health, safety, morals, or general welfare and protecting and preserving places and areas of historical, cultural, or architectural importance and significance.

LGOVT §211.002. ADOPTION OF REGULATION OR BOUNDARY INCLUDES AMENDMENT OR OTHER CHANGE

A reference in this subchapter to the adoption of a zoning regulation or a zoning district boundary includes the amendment, repeal, or other change of a regulation or boundary.

LGOVT §211.003. ZONING REGULATIONS GENERALLY

(a) The governing body of a municipality may regulate:

(1) the height, number of stories, and size of buildings and other structures;

(2) the percentage of a lot that may be occupied;

(3) the size of yards, courts, and other open spaces;

(4) population density;

(5) the location and use of buildings, other structures, and land for business, industrial, residential, or other purposes; and

(6) the pumping, extraction, and use of groundwater by persons other than retail public utilities, as defined by Section 13.002, Water Code, for the purpose of preventing the use or contact with groundwater that presents an actual or potential threat to human health.

(b) In the case of designated places and areas of historical, cultural, or architectural importance and significance, the governing body of a municipality may regulate the construction, reconstruction, alteration, or razing of buildings and other structures.

(c) The governing body of a home-rule municipality may also regulate the bulk of buildings.

LGOVT §211.0035. ZONING REGULATIONS & DISTRICT BOUNDARIES APPLICABLE TO PAWNSHOPS

(a) In this section, "pawnshop" has the meaning assigned by Section 371.003, Finance Code.

(b) For the purposes of zoning regulation and determination of zoning district boundaries, the governing body of a municipality shall designate pawnshops that have been licensed to transact business by the

Consumer Credit Commissioner under Chapter 371, Finance Code, as a permitted use in one or more zoning classifications.

(c) The governing body of a municipality may not impose a specific use permit requirement or any requirement similar in effect to a specific use permit requirement on a pawnshop that has been licensed to transact business by the Consumer Credit Commissioner under Chapter 371, Finance Code.

LGOVT §211.004. COMPLIANCE WITH COMPREHENSIVE PLAN

(a) Zoning regulations must be adopted in accordance with a comprehensive plan and must be designed to:

(1) lessen congestion in the streets;

(2) secure safety from fire, panic, and other dangers;

(3) promote health and the general welfare;

(4) provide adequate light and air;

(5) prevent the overcrowding of land;

(6) avoid undue concentration of population; or

(7) facilitate the adequate provision of transportation, water, sewers, schools, parks, and other public requirements.

(b) Repealed by Acts 1997, 75th Leg., ch. 459, §2, eff. Sept. 1, 1997.

LGOVT §211.005. DISTRICTS

(a) The governing body of a municipality may divide the municipality into districts of a number, shape, and size the governing body considers best for carrying out this subchapter. Within each district, the governing body may regulate the erection, construction, reconstruction, alteration, repair, or use of buildings, other structures, or land.

(b) Zoning regulations must be uniform for each class or kind of building in a district, but the regulations may vary from district to district. The regulations shall be adopted with reasonable consideration, among other things, for the character of each district and its peculiar suitability for particular uses, with a view of conserving the value of buildings and encouraging the most appropriate use of land in the municipality.

LGOVT §211.006. PROCEDURES GOVERNING ADOPTION OF ZONING REGULATIONS & DISTRICT BOUNDARIES

(a) The governing body of a municipality wishing to exercise the authority relating to zoning regulations and zoning district boundaries shall establish procedures for adopting and enforcing the regulations and boundaries. A regulation or boundary is not effective until after a public hearing on the matter at which parties in interest and citizens have an opportunity to be heard. Before the 15th day before the date of the hearing, notice of the time and place of the hearing must be published in an official newspaper or a newspaper of general circulation in the municipality.

(b) In addition to the notice required by Subsection (a), a general-law municipality that does not have a zoning commission shall give notice of a proposed change in a zoning classification to each property owner who would be entitled to notice under Section 211.007(c) if the municipality had a zoning commission. That notice must be given in the same manner as required for notice to property owners under Section 211.007(c). The governing body may not adopt the proposed change until after the 30th day after the date the notice required by this subsection is given.

(c) If the governing body of a home-rule municipality conducts a hearing under Subsection (a), the governing body may, by a two-thirds vote, prescribe the type of notice to be given of the time and place of the public hearing. Notice requirements prescribed under this subsection are in addition to the publication of notice required by Subsection (a).

(d) If a proposed change to a regulation or boundary is protested in accordance with this subsection, the proposed change must receive, in order to take effect, the affirmative vote of at least three-fourths of all members of the governing body. The protest must be written and signed by the owners of at least 20 percent of either:

(1) the area of the lots or land covered by the proposed change; or

(2) the area of the lots or land immediately adjoining the area covered by the proposed change and extending 200 feet from that area.

(e) In computing the percentage of land area under Subsection (d), the area of streets and alleys shall be included.

(f) The governing body by ordinance may provide that the affirmative vote of at least three-fourths of all its members is required to overrule a recommendation of the municipality's zoning commission that a proposed change to a regulation or boundary be denied.

LGOVT §211.007. ZONING COMMISSION

(a) To exercise the powers authorized by this subchapter, the governing body of a home-rule municipality shall, and the governing body of a general-law municipality may, appoint a zoning commission. The commission shall recommend boundaries for the original zoning districts and appropriate zoning regulations for each district. If the municipality has a municipal planning commission at the time of implementation of this subchapter, the governing body may appoint that commission to serve as the zoning commission.

(b) The zoning commission shall make a preliminary report and hold public hearings on that report before submitting a final report to the governing body. The governing body may not hold a public hearing until it receives the final report of the zoning commission unless the governing body by ordinance provides that a public hearing is to be held, after the notice required by Section 211.006(a), jointly with a public hearing required to be held by the zoning commission. In either case, the governing body may not take action on the matter until it receives the final report of the zoning commission.

(c) Before the 10th day before the hearing date, written notice of each public hearing before the zoning commission on a proposed change in a zoning classification shall be sent to each owner, as indicated by the most recently approved municipal tax roll, of real property within 200 feet of the property on which the change in classification is proposed. The notice may be served by its deposit in the municipality, properly addressed with postage paid, in the United States mail. If the property within 200 feet of the property on which the change is proposed is located in territory annexed to the municipality and is not included on the most recently approved municipal tax roll, the notice shall be given in the manner provided by Section 211.006(a).

(c-1) Before the 10th day before the hearing date, written notice of each public hearing before the zoning commission on a proposed change in a zoning classification affecting residential or multifamily zoning shall be sent to each school district in which the property for which the change in classification is proposed is located. The notice may be served by its deposit in the municipality, properly addressed with postage paid, in the United States mail.

(c-2) Subsection (c-1) does not apply to a municipality the majority of which is located in a county with a population of 100,000 or less, except that such a municipality must give notice under Subsection (c-1) to a school district that has territory in the municipality and requests the notice. For purposes of this subsection, if a school district makes a request for notice under Subsection (c-1), the municipality must give notice of each public hearing held following the request unless the school district requests that no further notices under Subsection (c-1) be given to the school district.

(d) The governing body of a home-rule municipality may, by a two-thirds vote, prescribe the type of notice to be given of the time and place of a public hearing held jointly by the governing body and the zoning commission. If notice requirements are prescribed under this subsection, the notice requirements prescribed by Subsections (b) and (c) and by Section 211.006(a) do not apply.

(e) If a general-law municipality exercises zoning authority without the appointment of a zoning commission, any reference in a law to a municipal zoning commission or planning commission means the governing body of the municipality.

LGOVT §211.0075. COMPLIANCE WITH OPEN MEETINGS LAW

A board or commission established by an ordinance or resolution adopted by the governing body of a municipality to assist the governing body in developing an initial comprehensive zoning plan or initial zoning regulations for the municipality, or a committee of the board or commission that includes one or more members of the board or commission, is subject to Chapter 551, Government Code, regardless of whether the board, commission, or committee has rulemaking or quasi-judicial powers or functions only in an advisory capacity.

LGOVT §211.008. BOARD OF ADJUSTMENT

(a) The governing body of a municipality may provide for the appointment of a board of adjustment. In the regulations adopted under this subchapter, the governing body may authorize the board of adjustment, in appropriate cases and subject to appropriate conditions and safeguards, to make special exceptions to the terms of the zoning ordinance that are consistent with the general purpose and intent of the ordinance and in accordance with any applicable rules contained in the ordinance.

(b) A board of adjustment must consist of at least five members to be appointed for terms of two years. The governing body must provide the procedure for appointment. The governing body may authorize each member of the governing body, including the mayor, to appoint one member to the board. The appointing authority may remove a board member for cause, as found by the appointing authority, on a written charge after a public hearing. A vacancy on the board shall be filled for the unexpired term.

(c) The governing body, by charter or ordinance, may provide for the appointment of alternate board members to serve in the absence of one or more regular members when requested to do so by the mayor or city manager. An alternate member serves for the same period as a regular member and is subject to removal in the same manner as a regular member. A vacancy among the alternate members is filled in the same manner as a vacancy among the regular members.

(d) Each case before the board of adjustment must be heard by at least 75 percent of the members.

(e) The board by majority vote shall adopt rules in accordance with any ordinance adopted under this subchapter. Meetings of the board are held at the call of the presiding officer and at other times as determined by the board. The presiding officer or acting presiding officer may administer oaths and compel the attendance of witnesses. All meetings of the board shall be open to the public.

(f) The board shall keep minutes of its proceedings that indicate the vote of each member on each question or the fact that a member is absent or fails to vote. The board shall keep records of its examinations and other official actions. The minutes and records shall be filed immediately in the board's office and are public records.

(g) The governing body of a Type A general-law municipality by ordinance may grant the members of the governing body the authority to act as a board of adjustment under this chapter.

LGOVT §211.009. AUTHORITY OF BOARD

(a) The board of adjustment may:

(1) hear and decide an appeal that alleges error in an order, requirement, decision, or determination made by an administrative official in the enforcement of this subchapter or an ordinance adopted under this subchapter;

(2) hear and decide special exceptions to the terms of a zoning ordinance when the ordinance requires the board to do so;

(3) authorize in specific cases a variance from the terms of a zoning ordinance if the variance is not contrary to the public interest and, due to special conditions, a literal enforcement of the ordinance would result in unnecessary hardship, and so that the spirit of the ordinance is observed and substantial justice is done; and

(4) hear and decide other matters authorized by an ordinance adopted under this subchapter.

(b) In exercising its authority under Subsection (a)(1), the board may reverse or affirm, in whole or in part, or modify the administrative official's order, requirement, decision, or determination from which an appeal is taken and make the correct order, requirement, decision, or determination, and for that purpose the board has the same authority as the administrative official.

(c) The concurring vote of 75 percent of the members of the board is necessary to:

(1) reverse an order, requirement, decision, or determination of an administrative official;

(2) decide in favor of an applicant on a matter on which the board is required to pass under a zoning ordinance; or

(3) authorize a variation from the terms of a zoning ordinance.

LGOVT §211.010. APPEAL TO BOARD

(a) Except as provided by Subsection (e), any of the following persons may appeal to the board of adjustment a decision made by an administrative official:

(1) a person aggrieved by the decision; or

(2) any officer, department, board, or bureau of the municipality affected by the decision.

(b) The appellant must file with the board and the official from whom the appeal is taken a notice of appeal specifying the grounds for the appeal. The appeal must be filed within a reasonable time as determined by the rules of the board. On receiving the notice, the official from whom the appeal is taken shall immediately transmit to the board all the papers constituting the record of the action that is appealed.

(c) An appeal stays all proceedings in furtherance of the action that is appealed unless the official from

whom the appeal is taken certifies in writing to the board facts supporting the official's opinion that a stay would cause imminent peril to life or property. In that case, the proceedings may be stayed only by a restraining order granted by the board or a court of record on application, after notice to the official, if due cause is shown.

(d) The board shall set a reasonable time for the appeal hearing and shall give public notice of the hearing and due notice to the parties in interest. A party may appear at the appeal hearing in person or by agent or attorney. The board shall decide the appeal within a reasonable time.

(e) A member of the governing body of the municipality who serves on the board of adjustment under Section 211.008(g) may not bring an appeal under this section.

LGOVT §211.011. JUDICIAL REVIEW OF BOARD DECISION

(a) Any of the following persons may present to a district court, county court, or county court at law a verified petition stating that the decision of the board of adjustment is illegal in whole or in part and specifying the grounds of the illegality:

(1) a person aggrieved by a decision of the board;

(2) a taxpayer; or

(3) an officer, department, board, or bureau of the municipality.

(b) The petition must be presented within 10 days after the date the decision is filed in the board's office.

(c) On the presentation of the petition, the court may grant a writ of certiorari directed to the board to review the board's decision. The writ must indicate the time by which the board's return must be made and served on the petitioner's attorney, which must be after 10 days and may be extended by the court. Granting of the writ does not stay the proceedings on the decision under appeal, but on application and after notice to the board the court may grant a restraining order if due cause is shown.

(d) The board's return must be verified and must concisely state any pertinent and material facts that show the grounds of the decision under appeal. The board is not required to return the original documents on which the board acted but may return certified or sworn copies of the documents or parts of the documents as required by the writ.

(e) If at the hearing the court determines that testimony is necessary for the proper disposition of the matter, it may take evidence or appoint a referee to take evidence as directed. The referee shall report the evidence to the court with the referee's findings of fact and conclusions of law. The referee's report constitutes a part of the proceedings on which the court shall make its decision.

(f) The court may reverse or affirm, in whole or in part, or modify the decision that is appealed. Costs may not be assessed against the board unless the court determines that the board acted with gross negligence, in bad faith, or with malice in making its decision.

(g) The court may not apply a different standard of review to a decision of a board of adjustment that is composed of members of the governing body of the municipality under Section 211.008(g) than is applied to a decision of a board of adjustment that does not contain members of the governing body of a municipality.

LGOVT §211.012. ENFORCEMENT; PENALTY; REMEDIES

(a) The governing body of a municipality may adopt ordinances to enforce this subchapter or any ordinance or regulation adopted under this subchapter.

(b) A person commits an offense if the person violates this subchapter or an ordinance or regulation adopted under this subchapter. An offense under this subsection is a misdemeanor, punishable by fine, imprisonment, or both, as provided by the governing body. The governing body may also provide civil penalties for a violation.

(c) If a building or other structure is erected, constructed, reconstructed, altered, repaired, converted, or maintained or if a building, other structure, or land is used in violation of this subchapter or an ordinance or regulation adopted under this subchapter, the appropriate municipal authority, in addition to other remedies, may institute appropriate action to:

(1) prevent the unlawful erection, construction, reconstruction, alteration, repair, conversion, maintenance, or use;

(2) restrain, correct, or abate the violation;

(3) prevent the occupancy of the building, structure, or land; or

(4) prevent any illegal act, conduct, business, or use on or about the premises.

LGOVT §211.013. CONFLICT WITH OTHER LAWS; EXCEPTIONS

(a) If a zoning regulation adopted under this subchapter requires a greater width or size of a yard, court, or other open space, requires a lower building height or fewer number of stories for a building, requires a greater percentage of lot to be left unoccupied, or otherwise imposes higher standards than those required under another statute or local ordinance or regulation, the regulation adopted under this subchapter controls. If the other statute or local ordinance or regulation imposes higher standards, that statute, ordinance, or regulation controls.

(b) This subchapter does not authorize the governing body of a municipality to require the removal or destruction of property that exists at the time the governing body implements this subchapter and that is actually and necessarily used in a public service business.

(c) This subchapter does not apply to a building, other structure, or land under the control, administration, or jurisdiction of a state or federal agency.

(d) This subchapter applies to a privately owned building or other structure and privately owned land when leased to a state agency.

LGOVT §211.014. PANEL OF BOARD OF ADJUSTMENT

(a) This section applies only to a municipality with a population of 500,000 or more.

(b) A board of adjustment shall consist of one or more panels of at least five members each to be appointed for terms of two years. If more than one panel of the board is appointed, the board consists of the regular members of all of the panels. The board may adopt rules for the assignment of appeals to a panel.

(c) If the board consists of more than one panel, only one panel may hear, handle, or render a decision in a particular case. A decision of a panel of the board on a case constitutes the decision of the board.

(d) Meetings of a panel of the board are held at the call of the presiding officer of the panel and at other times as determined by the panel or the board.

(e) A panel of a board of adjustment:

(1) has the powers and duties that a board of adjustment has under Sections 211.008, 211.009, 211.010, and 211.011; and

(2) is to be treated as a board of adjustment for purposes of the requirement imposed by Section 211.008(d).

LGOVT §211.015. ZONING REFERENDUM IN HOME-RULE MUNICIPALITY

(a) Notwithstanding other requirements of this subchapter, the voters of a home-rule municipality may repeal the municipality's zoning regulations adopted under this subchapter by either:

(1) a charter election conducted under law; or

(2) on the initial adoption of zoning regulations by a municipality, the use of any referendum process that is authorized under the charter of the municipality for public protest of the adoption of an ordinance.

(b) Notwithstanding any procedural or other requirements of this chapter to the contrary, the governing body of a home-rule municipality may on its own motion submit the repeal of the municipality's zoning regulations, as adopted under this chapter, in their entirety to the electors by use of any process that is authorized under the charter of the municipality for a popular vote on the rejection or repeal of ordinances in general.

(c) The provisions of this chapter shall not be construed to prohibit the adoption or application of any charter provision of a home-rule municipality that requires a waiting period prior to the adoption of zoning regulations or the submission of the initial adoption of zoning regulations to a binding referendum election, or both, provided that all procedural requirements of this chapter for the adoption of the zoning regulation are otherwise complied with. This subsection does not apply to the adoption of airport zoning regulations under Chapter 241.

(d) Notwithstanding any charter provision to the contrary, a governing body of a municipality may adopt a zoning ordinance and condition its taking effect upon the ordinance receiving the approval of the electors at an election held for that purpose.

(e) The provisions of this section may only be utilized for the repeal of a municipality's zoning regulations in their entirety or for determinations of whether a municipality should initially adopt zoning regulations, except the governing body of a municipality may amend, modify, or repeal a zoning ordinance adopted, approved, or ratified at an election conducted pursuant to this section.

(f) The provisions of this section shall not authorize the repeal of:

(1) an ordinance approving land-use regulations adopted under the provisions of this chapter by a board of directors of a reinvestment zone under the authority of Section 311.010(c), Tax Code; or

(2) an ordinance approving airport zoning regulations adopted under Chapter 241.

LGOVT §211.016. ZONING REGULATION AFFECTING APPEARANCE OF BUILDINGS OR OPEN SPACE

(a) This section applies only to a zoning regulation that affects:

(1) the exterior appearance of a single-family house, including the type and amount of building materials; or

(2) the landscaping of a single-family residential lot, including the type and amount of plants or landscaping materials.

(b) A zoning regulation adopted after the approval of a residential subdivision plat does not apply to that subdivision until the second anniversary of the later of:

(1) the date the plat was approved; or

(2) the date the municipality accepts the subdivision improvements offered for public dedication.

(c) This section does not prevent a municipality from adopting or enforcing applicable building codes or prohibiting the use of building materials that have been proven to be inherently dangerous.

LGOVT §211.017. CONTINUATION OF LAND USE IN NEWLY INCORPORATED AREAS

(a) A municipality incorporated after September 1, 2003, may not prohibit a person from:

(1) continuing to use land in the area in the manner in which the land was being used on the date of incorporation if the land use was legal at that time; or

(2) beginning to use land in the area in the manner that was planned for the land before the 90th day before the effective date of the incorporation if:

(A) one or more licenses, certificates, permits, approvals, or other forms of authorization by a governmental entity were required by law for the planned land use; and

(B) a completed application for the initial authorization was filed with the governmental entity before the date of incorporation.

(b) For purposes of this section, a completed application is filed if the application includes all documents and other information designated as required by the governmental entity in a written notice to the applicant.

(c) This section does not prohibit a municipality from imposing:

(1) a regulation relating to the location of sexually oriented businesses, as that term is defined by Section 243.002;

(2) a municipal ordinance, regulation, or other requirement affecting colonias, as that term is defined by Section 2306.581, Government Code;

(3) a regulation relating to preventing imminent destruction of property or injury to persons;

(4) a regulation relating to public nuisances;

(5) a regulation relating to flood control;

(6) a regulation relating to the storage and use of hazardous substances;

(7) a regulation relating to the sale and use of fireworks; or

(8) a regulation relating to the discharge of firearms.

(d) A municipal ordinance or rule in conflict with this section is void.

E LGOVT §211.018. CONTINUATION OF LAND USE REGARDING MANUFACTURED HOME COMMUNITIES

(a) In this section, "manufactured home," "manufactured home community," and "manufactured home lot" have the meanings assigned by Section 94.001, Property Code.

(b) The governing body of a municipality may not require a change in the nonconforming use of any manufactured home lot within the boundaries of a manufactured home community if:

(1) the nonconforming use of the land constituting the manufactured home community is authorized by law; and

(2) at least 50 percent of the manufactured home lots in the manufactured home community are physically occupied by a manufactured home used as a residence.

(c) For purposes of Subsection (b), requiring a change in the nonconforming use includes:

(1) requiring the number of manufactured home lots designated as a nonconforming use to be decreased; and

(2) declaring that the nonconforming use of the manufactured home lots has been abandoned based on a period of continuous abandonment of use as a manufactured home lot of any lot for less than 12 months.

(d) A manufactured home owner may install a new or used manufactured home, regardless of the size, or any appurtenance on a manufactured home lot located in a manufactured home community for which a nonconforming use is authorized by law, provided that the manufactured home or appurtenance and the installation of the manufactured home or appurtenance comply with:

(1) nonconforming land use standards, including standards relating to separation and setback distances and lot size, applicable on the date the nonconforming use of the land constituting the manufactured home community was authorized by law; and

(2) all applicable state and federal law and standards in effect on the date of the installation of the manufactured home or appurtenance.

(e) A municipality that prohibits the construction of new single-family residences or the construction of additions to existing single-family residences on a site located in a designated floodplain may, notwithstanding Subsection (b), (c), or (d), prohibit the installation of a manufactured home in a manufactured home community on a manufactured home lot that is located in an equivalently designated floodplain.

2017 Legislation: Enacted by S.B. 1248, §1, 85th Leg., eff. Sept. 1, 2017.

Sections 211.019 & 211.020 reserved for expansion

SUBCHAPTER B. ADDITIONAL ZONING REGULATIONS IN MUNICIPALITY WITH POPULATION OF MORE THAN 290,000

LGOVT §211.021. ADDITIONAL ZONING REGULATIONS

(a) The governing body of a municipality with a population of more than 290,000 that has adopted a comprehensive zoning ordinance under Subchapter A may, by ordinance, divide the municipality into neighborhood zoning areas after a public hearing on the matter at which parties in interest and citizens have an opportunity to be heard. Before the 15th day before the date of the hearing, notice of the time and place of the hearing must be published in an official newspaper or a newspaper of general circulation in the municipality.

(b) The mayor of the municipality, with the approval of the governing body, may appoint a neighborhood advisory zoning council for each of the neighborhood zoning areas. Each zoning council must be composed of five citizens who reside in the neighborhood zoning area. A zoning council member is appointed for a term of two years.

(c) Each neighborhood advisory zoning council shall provide the zoning commission with information, advice, and recommendations relating to each application filed with the zoning commission for zoning regulation changes that affect property within that neighborhood zoning area.

(d) On the filing of a zoning change application with the zoning commission, the zoning commission shall provide the appropriate neighborhood advisory zoning council with a copy of the application. The zoning council shall conduct a public hearing on the application and must publish notice of the time and place of the hearing in an official newspaper or a newspaper of general circulation in the municipality before the 10th day before the date of the hearing.

(e) At or before the zoning commission's hearing on the zoning change application, the neighborhood advisory zoning council shall submit to the zoning commission any information, advice, and recommendations relating to that application that the zoning council considers proper. The zoning commission may not overrule a recommendation of the zoning council with respect to the disposition of the application unless at least three-fourths of the members of the zoning commission who are present at the meeting vote to overrule the recommendation.

Sections 211.022-211.030 blank

SUBCHAPTER C. REGULATION OF COTTAGE FOOD PRODUCTION OPERATIONS

LGOVT §211.031. DEFINITIONS

In this subchapter, "cottage food production operation" and "home" have the meanings assigned by Section 437.001, Health and Safety Code.

LGOVT §211.032. CERTAIN ZONING REGULATIONS PROHIBITED

A municipal zoning ordinance may not prohibit the use of a home for cottage food production operations.

LGOVT §211.033. ACTION FOR NUISANCE OR OTHER TORT

This subchapter does not affect the right of a person to bring a cause of action under other law against an individual for nuisance or another tort arising out of the

individual's use of the individual's home for cottage food production operations.

CHAPTER 212. MUNICIPAL REGULATION OF SUBDIVISIONS & PROPERTY DEVELOPMENT

SUBCHAPTER A. REGULATION OF SUBDIVISIONS

LGOVT §212.001. DEFINITIONS

In this subchapter:

(1) "Extraterritorial jurisdiction" means a municipality's extraterritorial jurisdiction as determined under Chapter 42, except that for a municipality that has a population of 5,000 or more and is located in a county bordering the Rio Grande River, "extraterritorial jurisdiction" means the area outside the municipal limits but within five miles of those limits.

(2) "Plat" includes a replat.

LGOVT §212.002. RULES

After a public hearing on the matter, the governing body of a municipality may adopt rules governing plats and subdivisions of land within the municipality's jurisdiction to promote the health, safety, morals, or general welfare of the municipality and the safe, orderly, and healthful development of the municipality.

LGOVT §212.0025. CHAPTER-WIDE PROVISION RELATING TO REGULATION OF PLATS & SUBDIVISIONS IN EXTRATERRITORIAL JURISDICTION

The authority of a municipality under this chapter relating to the regulation of plats or subdivisions in the municipality's extraterritorial jurisdiction is subject to any applicable limitation prescribed by an agreement under Section 242.001.

LGOVT §212.003. EXTENSION OF RULES TO EXTRATERRITORIAL JURISDICTION

(a) The governing body of a municipality by ordinance may extend to the extraterritorial jurisdiction of the municipality the application of municipal ordinances adopted under Section 212.002 and other municipal ordinances relating to access to public roads or the pumping, extraction, and use of groundwater by persons other than retail public utilities, as defined by Section 13.002, Water Code, for the purpose of preventing the use or contact with groundwater that presents an actual or potential threat to human health. However, unless otherwise authorized by state law, in its extraterritorial jurisdiction a municipality shall not regulate:

(1) the use of any building or property for business, industrial, residential, or other purposes;

(2) the bulk, height, or number of buildings constructed on a particular tract of land;

(3) the size of a building that can be constructed on a particular tract of land, including without limitation any restriction on the ratio of building floor space to the land square footage;

(4) the number of residential units that can be built per acre of land; or

(5) the size, type, or method of construction of a water or wastewater facility that can be constructed to serve a developed tract of land if:

(A) the facility meets the minimum standards established for water or wastewater facilities by state and federal regulatory entities; and

(B) the developed tract of land is:

(i) located in a county with a population of 2.8 million or more; and

(ii) served by:

(a) on-site septic systems constructed before September 1, 2001, that fail to provide adequate services; or

(b) on-site water wells constructed before September 1, 2001, that fail to provide an adequate supply of safe drinking water.

(b) A fine or criminal penalty prescribed by the ordinance does not apply to a violation in the extraterritorial jurisdiction.

(c) The municipality is entitled to appropriate injunctive relief in district court to enjoin a violation of municipal ordinances or codes applicable in the extraterritorial jurisdiction.

LGOVT §212.004. PLAT REQUIRED

(a) The owner of a tract of land located within the limits or in the extraterritorial jurisdiction of a municipality who divides the tract in two or more parts to lay out a subdivision of the tract, including an addition to a municipality, to lay out suburban, building, or other lots, or to lay out streets, alleys, squares, parks, or other parts of the tract intended to be dedicated to public use or for the use of purchasers or owners of lots fronting on or adjacent to the streets, alleys, squares, parks, or other parts must have a plat of the subdivision prepared. A division of a tract under this subsection in-

cludes a division regardless of whether it is made by using a metes and bounds description in a deed of conveyance or in a contract for a deed, by using a contract of sale or other executory contract to convey, or by using any other method. A division of land under this subsection does not include a division of land into parts greater than five acres, where each part has access and no public improvement is being dedicated.

(b) To be recorded, the plat must:

(1) describe the subdivision by metes and bounds;

(2) locate the subdivision with respect to a corner of the survey or tract or an original corner of the original survey of which it is a part; and

(3) state the dimensions of the subdivision and of each street, alley, square, park, or other part of the tract intended to be dedicated to public use or for the use of purchasers or owners of lots fronting on or adjacent to the street, alley, square, park, or other part.

(c) The owner or proprietor of the tract or the owner's or proprietor's agent must acknowledge the plat in the manner required for the acknowledgment of deeds.

(d) The plat must be filed and recorded with the county clerk of the county in which the tract is located.

(e) The plat is subject to the filing and recording provisions of Section 12.002, Property Code.

See also *Real Estate Forms*, FORMS 11:1, 11:2.

LGOVT §212.0045. EXCEPTION TO PLAT REQUIREMENT: MUNICIPAL DETERMINATION

(a) To determine whether specific divisions of land are required to be platted, a municipality may define and classify the divisions. A municipality need not require platting for every division of land otherwise within the scope of this subchapter.

(b) In lieu of a plat contemplated by this subchapter, a municipality may require the filing of a development plat under Subchapter B if that subchapter applies to the municipality.

LGOVT §212.0046. EXCEPTION TO PLAT REQUIREMENT: CERTAIN PROPERTY ABUTTING AIRCRAFT RUNWAY

An owner of a tract of land is not required to prepare a plat if the land:

(1) is located wholly within a municipality with a population of 5,000 or less;

(2) is divided into parts larger than 2½ acres; and

(3) abuts any part of an aircraft runway.

LGOVT §212.005. APPROVAL BY MUNICIPALITY REQUIRED

The municipal authority responsible for approving plats must approve a plat or replat that is required to be prepared under this subchapter and that satisfies all applicable regulations.

LGOVT §212.006. AUTHORITY RESPONSIBLE FOR APPROVAL GENERALLY

(a) The municipal authority responsible for approving plats under this subchapter is the municipal planning commission or, if the municipality has no planning commission, the governing body of the municipality. The governing body by ordinance may require the approval of the governing body in addition to that of the municipal planning commission.

(b) In a municipality with a population of more than 1.5 million, at least two members of the municipal planning commission, but not more than 25 percent of the membership of the commission, must be residents of the area outside the limits of the municipality and in which the municipality exercises its authority to approve subdivision plats.

LGOVT §212.0065. DELEGATION OF APPROVAL RESPONSIBILITY

(a) The governing body of a municipality may delegate to one or more officers or employees of the municipality or of a utility owned or operated by the municipality the ability to approve:

(1) amending plats described by Section 212.016;

(2) minor plats or replats involving four or fewer lots fronting on an existing street and not requiring the creation of any new street or the extension of municipal facilities; or

(3) a replat under Section 212.0145 that does not require the creation of any new street or the extension of municipal facilities.

(b) The designated person or persons may, for any reason, elect to present the plat for approval to the municipal authority responsible for approving plats.

(c) The person or persons shall not disapprove the plat and shall be required to refer any plat which the person or persons refuse to approve to the municipal authority responsible for approving plats within the time period specified in Section 212.009.

LGOVT §212.007. AUTHORITY RESPONSIBLE FOR APPROVAL: TRACT IN EXTRATERRITORIAL JURISDICTION OF MORE THAN ONE MUNICIPALITY

(a) For a tract located in the extraterritorial jurisdiction of more than one municipality, the authority responsible for approving a plat under this subchapter is the authority in the municipality with the largest population that under Section 212.006 has approval responsibility. The governing body of that municipality may enter into an agreement with any other affected municipality or with any other municipality having area that, if unincorporated, would be in the extraterritorial jurisdiction of the governing body's municipality delegating to the other municipality the responsibility for plat approval within specified parts of the affected area.

(b) Either party to an agreement under Subsection (a) may revoke the agreement after 20 years have elapsed after the date of the agreement unless the parties agree to a shorter period.

(c) A copy of the agreement shall be filed with the county clerk.

LGOVT §212.008. APPLICATION FOR APPROVAL

A person desiring approval of a plat must apply to and file a copy of the plat with the municipal planning commission or, if the municipality has no planning commission, the governing body of the municipality.

LGOVT §212.009. APPROVAL PROCEDURE

(a) The municipal authority responsible for approving plats shall act on a plat within 30 days after the date the plat is filed. A plat is considered approved by the municipal authority unless it is disapproved within that period.

(b) If an ordinance requires that a plat be approved by the governing body of the municipality in addition to the planning commission, the governing body shall act on the plat within 30 days after the date the plat is approved by the planning commission or is considered approved by the inaction of the commission. A plat is considered approved by the governing body unless it is disapproved within that period.

(c) If a plat is approved, the municipal authority giving the approval shall endorse the plat with a certificate indicating the approval. The certificate must be signed by:

(1) the authority's presiding officer and attested by the authority's secretary; or

(2) a majority of the members of the authority.

(d) If the municipal authority responsible for approving plats fails to act on a plat within the prescribed period, the authority on request shall issue a certificate stating the date the plat was filed and that the authority failed to act on the plat within the period. The certificate is effective in place of the endorsement required by Subsection (c).

(e) The municipal authority responsible for approving plats shall maintain a record of each application made to the authority and the authority's action taken on it. On request of an owner of an affected tract, the authority shall certify the reasons for the action taken on an application.

LGOVT §212.010. STANDARDS FOR APPROVAL

(a) The municipal authority responsible for approving plats shall approve a plat if:

(1) it conforms to the general plan of the municipality and its current and future streets, alleys, parks, playgrounds, and public utility facilities;

(2) it conforms to the general plan for the extension of the municipality and its roads, streets, and public highways within the municipality and in its extraterritorial jurisdiction, taking into account access to and extension of sewer and water mains and the instrumentalities of public utilities;

(3) a bond required under Section 212.0106, if applicable, is filed with the municipality; and

(4) it conforms to any rules adopted under Section 212.002.

(b) However, the municipal authority responsible for approving plats may not approve a plat unless the plat and other documents have been prepared as required by Section 212.0105, if applicable.

LGOVT §212.0101. ADDITIONAL REQUIREMENTS: USE OF GROUNDWATER

(a) If a person submits a plat for the subdivision of a tract of land for which the source of the water supply intended for the subdivision is groundwater under that land, the municipal authority responsible for approving plats by ordinance may require the plat application to have attached to it a statement that:

(1) is prepared by an engineer licensed to practice in this state or a geoscientist licensed to practice in this state; and

(2) certifies that adequate groundwater is available for the subdivision.

(b) The Texas Commission on Environmental Quality by rule shall establish the appropriate form and content of a certification to be attached to a plat application under this section.

(c) The Texas Commission on Environmental Quality, in consultation with the Texas Water Development Board, by rule shall require a person who submits a plat under Subsection (a) to transmit to the Texas Water Development Board and any groundwater conservation district that includes in the district's boundaries any part of the subdivision information that would be useful in:

(1) performing groundwater conservation district activities;

(2) conducting regional water planning;

(3) maintaining the state's groundwater database; or

(4) conducting studies for the state related to groundwater.

LGOVT §212.0105. WATER & SEWER REQUIREMENTS IN CERTAIN COUNTIES

(a) This section applies only to a person who:

(1) is the owner of a tract of land in a county in which a political subdivision that is eligible for and has applied for financial assistance through Subchapter K, Chapter 17, Water Code;

(2) divides the tract in a manner that creates any lots that are intended for residential purposes and are five acres or less; and

(3) is required under this subchapter to have a plat prepared for the subdivision.

(b) The owner of the tract:

(1) must:

(A) include on the plat or have attached to the plat a document containing a description of the water and sewer service facilities that will be constructed or installed to service the subdivision and a statement of the date by which the facilities will be fully operable; and

(B) have attached to the plat a document prepared by an engineer registered to practice in this state certifying that the water and sewer service facilities described by the plat or on the document attached to the plat are in compliance with the model rules adopted under Section 16.343, Water Code; or

(2) must:

(A) include on the plat a statement that water and sewer service facilities are unnecessary for the subdivision; and

(B) have attached to the plat a document prepared by an engineer registered to practice in this state certifying that water and sewer service facilities are unnecessary for the subdivision under the model rules adopted under Section 16.343, Water Code.

(c) The governing body of the municipality may extend, beyond the date specified on the plat or on the document attached to the plat, the date by which the water and sewer service facilities must be fully operable if the governing body finds the extension is reasonable and not contrary to the public interest. If the facilities are fully operable before the expiration of the extension period, the facilities are considered to have been made fully operable in a timely manner. An extension is not reasonable if it would allow a residence in the subdivision to be inhabited without water or sewer services.

LGOVT §212.0106. BOND REQUIREMENTS & OTHER FINANCIAL GUARANTEES IN CERTAIN COUNTIES

(a) This section applies only to a person described by Section 212.0105(a).

(b) If the governing body of a municipality in a county described by Section 212.0105(a)(1)(A) or (B) requires the owner of the tract to execute a bond, the owner must do so before subdividing the tract unless an alternative financial guarantee is provided under Subsection (c). The bond must:

(1) be payable to the presiding officer of the governing body or to the presiding officer's successors in office;

(2) be in an amount determined by the governing body to be adequate to ensure the proper construction or installation of the water and sewer service facilities to service the subdivision but not to exceed the estimated cost of the construction or installation of the facilities;

(3) be executed with sureties as may be approved by the governing body;

(4) be executed by a company authorized to do business as a surety in this state if the governing body requires a surety bond executed by a corporate surety; and

(5) be conditioned that the water and sewer service facilities will be constructed or installed:

(A) in compliance with the model rules adopted under Section 16.343, Water Code; and

(B) within the time stated on the plat or on the document attached to the plat for the subdivision or within any extension of that time.

(c) In lieu of the bond an owner may deposit cash, a letter of credit issued by a federally insured financial institution, or other acceptable financial guarantee.

(d) If a letter of credit is used, it must:

(1) list as the sole beneficiary the presiding officer of the governing body; and

(2) be conditioned that the water and sewer service facilities will be constructed or installed:

(A) in compliance with the model rules adopted under Section 16.343, Water Code; and

(B) within the time stated on the plat or on the document attached to the plat for the subdivision or within any extension of that time.

LGOVT §212.011. EFFECT OF APPROVAL ON DEDICATION

(a) The approval of a plat is not considered an acceptance of any proposed dedication and does not impose on the municipality any duty regarding the maintenance or improvement of any dedicated parts until the appropriate municipal authorities make an actual appropriation of the dedicated parts by entry, use, or improvement.

(b) The disapproval of a plat is considered a refusal by the municipality of the offered dedication indicated on the plat.

LGOVT §212.0115. CERTIFICATION REGARDING COMPLIANCE WITH PLAT REQUIREMENTS

(a) For the purposes of this section, land is considered to be within the jurisdiction of a municipality if the land is located within the limits or in the extraterritorial jurisdiction of the municipality.

(b) On the approval of a plat by the municipal authority responsible for approving plats, the authority shall issue to the person applying for the approval a certificate stating that the plat has been reviewed and approved by the authority.

(c) On the written request of an owner of land, a purchaser of real property under a contract for deed, executory contract, or other executory conveyance, an entity that provides utility service, or the governing body of the municipality, the municipal authority responsible for approving plats shall make the following determinations regarding the owner's land or the land in which the entity or governing body is interested that is located within the jurisdiction of the municipality:

(1) whether a plat is required under this subchapter for the land; and

(2) if a plat is required, whether it has been prepared and whether it has been reviewed and approved by the authority.

(d) The request made under Subsection (c) must identify the land that is the subject of the request.

(e) If the municipal authority responsible for approving plats determines under Subsection (c) that a plat is not required, the authority shall issue to the requesting party a written certification of that determination. If the authority determines that a plat is required and that the plat has been prepared and has been reviewed and approved by the authority, the authority shall issue to the requesting party a written certification of that determination.

(f) The municipal authority responsible for approving plats shall make its determination within 20 days after the date it receives the request under Subsection (c) and shall issue the certificate, if appropriate, within 10 days after the date the determination is made.

(g) If both the municipal planning commission and the governing body of the municipality have authority to approve plats, only one of those entities need make the determinations and issue the certificates required by this section.

(h) The municipal authority responsible for approving plats may adopt rules it considers necessary to administer its functions under this section.

(i) The governing body of a municipality may delegate, in writing, the ability to perform any of the responsibilities under this section to one or more persons. A binding decision of the person or persons under this subsection is appealable to the municipal authority responsible for approving plats.

LGOVT §212.012. CONNECTION OF UTILITIES

(a) Except as provided by Subsection (c), (d), or (j), an entity described by Subsection (b) may not serve or connect any land with water, sewer, electricity, gas, or other utility service unless the entity has been presented with or otherwise holds a certificate applicable to the land issued under Section 212.0115.

(b) The prohibition established by Subsection (a) applies only to:

(1) a municipality and officials of a municipality that provides water, sewer, electricity, gas, or other utility service;

(2) a municipally owned or municipally operated utility that provides any of those services;

(3) a public utility that provides any of those services;

(4) a water supply or sewer service corporation organized and operating under Chapter 67, Water Code, that provides any of those services;

(5) a county that provides any of those services; and

(6) a special district or authority created by or under state law that provides any of those services.

(c) An entity described by Subsection (b) may serve or connect land with water, sewer, electricity, gas, or other utility service regardless of whether the entity is presented with or otherwise holds a certificate applicable to the land issued under Section 212.0115 if:

(1) the land is covered by a development plat approved under Subchapter B or under an ordinance or rule relating to the development plat;

(2) the land was first served or connected with service by an entity described by Subsection (b)(1), (b)(2), or (b)(3) before September 1, 1987; or

(3) the land was first served or connected with service by an entity described by Subsection (b)(4), (b)(5), or (b)(6) before September 1, 1989.

(d) In a county to which Subchapter B, Chapter 232, applies, an entity described by Subsection (b) may serve or connect land with water, sewer, electricity, gas, or other utility service that is located in the extraterritorial jurisdiction of a municipality regardless of whether the entity is presented with or otherwise holds a certificate applicable to the land issued under Section 212.0115, if the municipal authority responsible for approving plats issues a certificate stating that:

(1) the subdivided land:

(A) was sold or conveyed by a subdivider by any means of conveyance, including a contract for deed or executory contract, before:

(i) September 1, 1995, in a county defined under Section 232.022(a)(1);

(ii) September 1, 1999, in a county defined under Section 232.022(a)(1) if, on August 31, 1999, the subdivided land was located in the extraterritorial jurisdiction of a municipality as determined by Chapter 42; or

(iii) September 1, 2005, in a county defined under Section 232.022(a)(2);

(B) has not been subdivided after September 1, 1995, September 1, 1999, or September 1, 2005, as applicable under Paragraph (A);

(C) is the site of construction of a residence, evidenced by at least the existence of a completed foundation, that was begun on or before:

(i) May 1, 2003, in a county defined under Section 232.022(a)(1); or

(ii) September 1, 2005, in a county defined under Section 232.022(a)(2); and

(D) has had adequate sewer services installed to service the lot or dwelling, as determined by an authorized agent responsible for the licensing or permitting of on-site sewage facilities under Chapter 366, Health and Safety Code;

(2) the subdivided land is a lot of record as defined by Section 232.021(6-a) that is located in a county defined by Section 232.022(a)(1) and has adequate sewer services installed that are fully operable to service the lot or dwelling, as determined by an authorized agent responsible for the licensing or permitting of on-site sewage facilities under Chapter 366, Health and Safety Code; or

(3) the land was not subdivided after September 1, 1995, in a county defined under Section 232.022(a)(1), or September 1, 2005, in a county defined under Section 232.022(a)(2), and:

(A) water service is available within 750 feet of the subdivided land; or

(B) water service is available more than 750 feet from the subdivided land and the extension of water service to the land may be feasible, subject to a final determination by the water service provider.

(e) An entity described by Subsection (b) may provide utility service to land described by Subsection (d)(1), (2), or (3) only if the person requesting service:

(1) is not the land's subdivider or the subdivider's agent; and

(2) provides to the entity a certificate described by Subsection (d).

(f) A person requesting service may obtain a certificate under Subsection (d)(1), (2), or (3) only if the person is the owner or purchaser of the subdivided land and provides to the municipal authority responsible for approving plats documentation containing:

(1) a copy of the means of conveyance or other documents that show that the land was sold or conveyed by a subdivider before September 1, 1995, before September 1, 1999, or before September 1, 2005, as applicable under Subsection (d);

(2) for a certificate issued under Subsection (d)(1), a notarized affidavit by the person requesting service that states that construction of a residence on the land, evidenced by at least the existence of a completed foundation, was begun on or before May 1, 2003, in a county defined by Section 232.022(a)(1) or September 1, 2005, in a county defined by Section 232.022(a)(2), and the request for utility connection or service is to connect or serve a residence described by Subsection (d)(1)(C);

(3) a notarized affidavit by the person requesting service that states that the subdivided land has not been further subdivided after September 1, 1995, September 1, 1999, or September 1, 2005, as applicable under Subsection (d); and

(4) evidence that adequate sewer service or facilities have been installed and are fully operable to service the lot or dwelling from an entity described by Subsection (b) or the authorized agent responsible for the licensing or permitting of on-site sewage facilities under Chapter 366, Health and Safety Code.

(g) On request, the municipal authority responsible for approving plats shall provide to the attorney general and any appropriate local, county, or state law enforcement official a copy of any document on which the municipal authority relied in determining the legality of providing service.

(h) This section may not be construed to abrogate any civil or criminal proceeding or prosecution or to waive any penalty against a subdivider for a violation of a state or local law, regardless of the date on which the violation occurred.

(i) In this section:

(1) "Foundation" means the lowest division of a residence, usually consisting of a masonry slab or a pier and beam structure, that is partly or wholly below the surface of the ground and on which the residential structure rests.

(2) "Subdivider" has the meaning assigned by Section 232.021.

(j) Except as provided by Subsection (k), this section does not prohibit a water or sewer utility from providing in a county defined by Section 232.022(a)(1) water or sewer utility connection or service to a residential dwelling that:

(1) is provided water or wastewater facilities under or in conjunction with a federal or state funding program designed to address inadequate water or wastewater facilities in colonias or to residential lots located in a county described by Section 232.022(a)(1);

(2) is an existing dwelling identified as an eligible recipient for funding by the funding agency providing adequate water and wastewater facilities or improvements;

(3) when connected, will comply with the minimum state standards for both water and sewer facilities and as prescribed by the model subdivision rules adopted under Section 16.343, Water Code; and

(4) is located in a project for which the municipality with jurisdiction over the project or the approval of plats within the project area has approved the improvement project by order, resolution, or interlocal agreement under Chapter 791, Government Code.

(k) A utility may not serve any subdivided land with water utility connection or service under Subsection (j) unless the entity receives a determination that adequate sewer services have been installed to service the lot or dwelling from the municipal authority responsible for approving plats, an entity described by Subsection (b), or the authorized agent responsible for the licensing or permitting of on-site sewage facilities under Chapter 366, Health and Safety Code.

LGOVT §212.013. VACATING PLAT

(a) The proprietors of the tract covered by a plat may vacate the plat at any time before any lot in the plat is sold. The plat is vacated when a signed, acknowl-

edged instrument declaring the plat vacated is approved and recorded in the manner prescribed for the original plat.

(b) If lots in the plat have been sold, the plat, or any part of the plat, may be vacated on the application of all the owners of lots in the plat with approval obtained in the manner prescribed for the original plat.

(c) The county clerk shall write legibly on the vacated plat the word "Vacated" and shall enter on the plat a reference to the volume and page at which the vacating instrument is recorded.

(d) On the execution and recording of the vacating instrument, the vacated plat has no effect.

See also *Real Estate Forms*, FORMS 11:1, 11:2.

LGOVT §212.014. REPLATTING WITHOUT VACATING PRECEDING PLAT

A replat of a subdivision or part of a subdivision may be recorded and is controlling over the preceding plat without vacation of that plat if the replat:

(1) is signed and acknowledged by only the owners of the property being replatted;

(2) is approved, after a public hearing on the matter at which parties in interest and citizens have an opportunity to be heard, by the municipal authority responsible for approving plats; and

(3) does not attempt to amend or remove any covenants or restrictions.

See also *Real Estate Forms*, FORMS 11:1, 11:2.

LGOVT §212.0145. REPLATTING WITHOUT VACATING PRECEDING PLAT: CERTAIN SUBDIVISIONS

(a) A replat of a part of a subdivision may be recorded and is controlling over the preceding plat without vacation of that plat if the replat:

(1) is signed and acknowledged by only the owners of the property being replatted; and

(2) involves only property:

(A) of less than one acre that fronts an existing street; and

(B) that is owned and used by a nonprofit corporation established to assist children in at-risk situations through volunteer and individualized attention.

(b) An existing covenant or restriction for property that is replatted under this section does not have to be amended or removed if:

(1) the covenant or restriction was recorded more than 50 years before the date of the replat; and

(2) the replatted property has been continuously used by the nonprofit corporation for at least 10 years before the date of the replat.

(c) Sections 212.014 and 212.015 do not apply to a replat under this section.

See also *Real Estate Forms*, FORMS 11:1, 11:2.

LGOVT §212.0146. REPLATTING WITHOUT VACATING PRECEDING PLAT: CERTAIN MUNICIPALITIES

(a) This section applies only to a replat of a subdivision or a part of a subdivision located in a municipality or the extraterritorial jurisdiction of a municipality with a population of 1.3 million or more.

(b) A replat of a subdivision or part of a subdivision may be recorded and is controlling over the preceding plat without vacation of that plat if:

(1) the replat is signed and acknowledged by each owner and only the owners of the property being replatted;

(2) the municipal authority responsible for approving plats holds a public hearing on the matter at which parties in interest and citizens have an opportunity to be heard;

(3) the replat does not amend, remove, or violate, or have the effect of amending, removing, or violating, any covenants or restrictions that are contained or referenced in a dedicatory instrument recorded in the real property records separately from the preceding plat or replat;

(4) the replat does not attempt to amend, remove, or violate, or have the effect of amending, removing, or violating, any existing public utility easements without the consent of the affected utility companies; and

(5) the municipal authority responsible for approving plats approves the replat after determining that the replat complies with this subchapter and rules adopted under Section 212.002 and this section in effect at the time the application for the replat is filed.

(c) The governing body of a municipality may adopt rules governing replats, including rules that establish criteria under which covenants, restrictions, or plat notations that are contained only in the preceding plat or replat without reference in any dedicatory instrument recorded in the real property records separately from the preceding plat or replat may be amended or removed.

See also *Real Estate Forms*, FORMS 11:1, 11:2.

LGOVT §212.015. ADDITIONAL REQUIREMENTS FOR CERTAIN REPLATS

(a) In addition to compliance with Section 212.014, a replat without vacation of the preceding plat must conform to the requirements of this section if:

(1) during the preceding five years, any of the area to be replatted was limited by an interim or permanent zoning classification to residential use for not more than two residential units per lot; or

(2) any lot in the preceding plat was limited by deed restrictions to residential use for not more than two residential units per lot.

(b) Notice of the hearing required under Section 212.014 shall be given before the 15th day before the date of the hearing by:

(1) publication in an official newspaper or a newspaper of general circulation in the county in which the municipality is located; and

(2) by written notice, with a copy of Subsection (c) attached, forwarded by the municipal authority responsible for approving plats to the owners of lots that are in the original subdivision and that are within 200 feet of the lots to be replatted, as indicated on the most recently approved municipal tax roll or in the case of a subdivision within the extraterritorial jurisdiction, the most recently approved county tax roll of the property upon which the replat is requested. The written notice may be delivered by depositing the notice, properly addressed with postage prepaid, in a post office or postal depository within the boundaries of the municipality.

(c) If the proposed replat requires a variance and is protested in accordance with this subsection, the proposed replat must receive, in order to be approved, the affirmative vote of at least three-fourths of the members present of the municipal planning commission or governing body, or both. For a legal protest, written instruments signed by the owners of at least 20 percent of the area of the lots or land immediately adjoining the area covered by the proposed replat and extending 200 feet from that area, but within the original subdivision, must be filed with the municipal planning commission or governing body, or both, prior to the close of the public hearing.

(d) In computing the percentage of land area under Subsection (c), the area of streets and alleys shall be included.

(e) Compliance with Subsections (c) and (d) is not required for approval of a replat of part of a preceding plat if the area to be replatted was designated or reserved for other than single or duplex family residential use by notation on the last legally recorded plat or in the legally recorded restrictions applicable to the plat.

LGOVT §212.0155. ADDITIONAL REQUIREMENTS FOR CERTAIN REPLATS AFFECTING A SUBDIVISION GOLF COURSE

(a) This section applies to land located wholly or partly:

(1) in the corporate boundaries of a municipality if the municipality:

(A) has a population of more than 50,000; and

(B) is located wholly or partly in:

(i) a county with a population of more than three million;

(ii) a county with a population of more than 400,000 that is adjacent to a county with a population of more than three million; or

(iii) a county with a population of more than 1.4 million:

(a) in which two or more municipalities with a population of 300,000 or more are primarily located; and

(b) that is adjacent to a county with a population of more than two million; or

(2) in the corporate boundaries or extraterritorial jurisdiction of a municipality with a population of 1.9 million or more.

(b) In this section:

(1) "Management certificate" means a certificate described by Section 209.004, Property Code.

(2) "New plat" means a development plat, replat, amending plat, or vacating plat that would change the existing plat or the current use of the land that is the subject of the new plat.

(3) "Property owners' association" and "restrictive covenant" have the meanings assigned by Section 202.001, Property Code.

(4) "Restrictions," "subdivision," and "owner" have the meanings assigned by Section 201.003, Property Code.

(5) "Subdivision golf course" means an area of land:

(A) that was originally developed as a golf course or a country club within a common scheme of development for a predominantly residential single-family development project;

(B) that was at any time in the seven years preceding the date on which a new plat for the land is filed:

(i) used as a golf course or a country club;

(ii) zoned as a community facility;

(iii) benefited from restrictive covenants on adjoining homeowners; or

(iv) designated on a recorded plat as a golf course or a country club; and

(C) that is not separated entirely from the predominantly residential single-family development project by a public street.

(c) In addition to any other requirement of this chapter, a new plat must conform to the requirements of this section if any of the area subject to the new plat is a subdivision golf course. The exception in Section 212.004(a) excluding divisions of land into parts greater than five acres for platting requirements does not apply to a subdivision golf course.

(d) A new plat that is subject to this section may not be approved until each municipal authority reviewing the new plat conducts a public hearing on the matter at which the parties in interest and citizens have an adequate opportunity to be heard, present evidence, and submit statements or petitions for consideration by the municipal authority. The number, location, and procedure for the public hearings may be designated by the municipal authority for a particular hearing. The municipal authority may abate, continue, or reschedule, as the municipal authority considers appropriate, any public hearing in order to receive a full and complete record on which to make a decision. If the new plat would otherwise be administratively approved, the municipal planning commission is the approving body for the purposes of this section.

(e) The municipal authority may not approve the new plat without adequate consideration of testimony and the record from the public hearings and making the findings required by Subsection (k). Not later than the 30th day after the date on which all proceedings necessary for the public hearings have concluded, the municipal authority shall take action on the application for the new plat. Sections 212.009(a) and (b) do not apply to the approval of plats under this section.

(f) The municipality may provide notice of the initial hearing required by Subsection (d) only after the requirements of Subsections (m) and (n) are met. The notice shall be given before the 15th day before the date of the hearing by:

(1) publishing notice in an official newspaper or a newspaper of general circulation in the county in which the municipality is located;

(2) providing written notice, with a copy of this section attached, by the municipal authority responsible for approving plats to:

(A) each property owners' association for each neighborhood benefited by the subdivision golf course, as indicated in the most recently filed management certificates; and

(B) the owners of lots that are within 200 feet of the area subject to the new plat, as indicated:

(i) on the most recently approved municipal tax roll; and

(ii) in the most recent online records of the central appraisal district of the county in which the lots are located; and

(3) any other manner determined by the municipal authority to be necessary to ensure that full and fair notice is provided to all owners of residential single-family lots in the general vicinity of the subdivision golf course.

(g) The written notice required by Subsection (f)(2) may be delivered by depositing the notice, properly addressed with postage prepaid, in the United States mail.

(h) The cost of providing the notices under Subsection (f) shall be paid by the plat applicant.

(i) If written instruments protesting the proposed new plat are signed by the owners of at least 20 percent of the area of the lots or land immediately adjacent to the area covered by a proposed new plat and extending 200 feet from that area and are filed with the municipal planning commission or the municipality's governing body before the conclusion of the public hearings, the proposed new plat must receive, to be approved, the affirmative vote of at least three-fifths of the members of the municipal planning commission or governing body.

(j) In computing the percentage of land area under Subsection (i), the area of streets and alleys is included.

(k) The municipal planning commission or the municipality's governing body may not approve a new plat under this section unless it determines that:

(1) there is adequate existing or planned infrastructure to support the future development of the subdivision golf course;

(2) based on existing or planned facilities, the development of the subdivision golf course will not have a materially adverse effect on:

(A) traffic, parking, drainage, water, sewer, or other utilities;

(B) the health, safety, or general welfare of persons in the municipality; or

(C) safe, orderly, and healthful development of the municipality;

(3) the development of the subdivision golf course will not have a materially adverse effect on existing single-family property values;

(4) the new plat is consistent with all applicable land use regulations and restrictive covenants and the municipality's land use policies as described by the municipality's comprehensive plan or other appropriate public policy documents; and

(5) if any portion of a previous plat reflected a restriction on the subdivision golf course whether:

(A) that restriction is an implied covenant or easement benefiting adjacent residential properties; or

(B) the restriction, covenant, or easement has been legally released or has expired.

(*l*) The municipal authority may adopt rules to govern the platting of a subdivision golf course that do not conflict with this section, including rules that require more detailed information than is required by Subsection (n) for plans for development and new plat applications.

(m) The application for a new plat under this section is not complete and may not be submitted for review for administrative completeness unless the tax certificates required by Section 12.002(e), Property Code, are attached, notwithstanding that the application is for a type of plat other than a plat specified in that section.

(n) A plan for development or a new plat application for a subdivision golf course is not considered to provide fair notice of the project and nature of the permit sought unless it contains the following information, complete in all material respects:

(1) street layout;

(2) lot and block layout;

(3) number of residential units;

(4) location of nonresidential development, by type of development;

(5) drainage, detention, and retention plans;

(6) screening plan for adjacent residential properties, including landscaping or fencing; and

(7) an analysis of the effect of the project on values in the adjacent residential neighborhoods.

(o) A municipal authority with authority over platting may require as a condition for approval of a plat for a golf course that:

(1) the area be platted as a restricted reserve for the proposed use; and

(2) the plat be incorporated into the plat for any adjacent residential lots.

(p) An owner of a lot that is within 200 feet of a subdivision golf course may seek declaratory or injunctive relief from a district court to enforce the provisions in this section.

LGOVT §212.016. AMENDING PLAT

(a) The municipal authority responsible for approving plats may approve and issue an amending plat, which may be recorded and is controlling over the preceding plat without vacation of that plat, if the amending plat is signed by the applicants only and is solely for one or more of the following purposes:

(1) to correct an error in a course or distance shown on the preceding plat;

(2) to add a course or distance that was omitted on the preceding plat;

(3) to correct an error in a real property description shown on the preceding plat;

(4) to indicate monuments set after the death, disability, or retirement from practice of the engineer or surveyor responsible for setting monuments;

(5) to show the location or character of a monument that has been changed in location or character or that is shown incorrectly as to location or character on the preceding plat;

(6) to correct any other type of scrivener or clerical error or omission previously approved by the municipal authority responsible for approving plats, including lot numbers, acreage, street names, and identification of adjacent recorded plats;

(7) to correct an error in courses and distances of lot lines between two adjacent lots if:

(A) both lot owners join in the application for amending the plat;

(B) neither lot is abolished;

(C) the amendment does not attempt to remove recorded covenants or restrictions; and

(D) the amendment does not have a material adverse effect on the property rights of the other owners in the plat;

(8) to relocate a lot line to eliminate an inadvertent encroachment of a building or other improvement on a lot line or easement;

(9) to relocate one or more lot lines between one or more adjacent lots if:

(A) the owners of all those lots join in the application for amending the plat;

(B) the amendment does not attempt to remove recorded covenants or restrictions; and

(C) the amendment does not increase the number of lots;

(10) to make necessary changes to the preceding plat to create six or fewer lots in the subdivision or a part of the subdivision covered by the preceding plat if:

(A) the changes do not affect applicable zoning and other regulations of the municipality;

(B) the changes do not attempt to amend or remove any covenants or restrictions; and

(C) the area covered by the changes is located in an area that the municipal planning commission or other appropriate governing body of the municipality has approved, after a public hearing, as a residential improvement area; or

(11) to replat one or more lots fronting on an existing street if:

(A) the owners of all those lots join in the application for amending the plat;

(B) the amendment does not attempt to remove recorded covenants or restrictions;

(C) the amendment does not increase the number of lots; and

(D) the amendment does not create or require the creation of a new street or make necessary the extension of municipal facilities.

(b) Notice, a hearing, and the approval of other lot owners are not required for the approval and issuance of an amending plat.

LGOVT §212.017. CONFLICT OF INTEREST; PENALTY

(a) In this section, "subdivided tract" means a tract of land, as a whole, that is subdivided. The term does not mean an individual lot in a subdivided tract of land.

(b) A person has a substantial interest in a subdivided tract if the person:

(1) has an equitable or legal ownership interest in the tract with a fair market value of $2,500 or more;

(2) acts as a developer of the tract;

(3) owns 10 percent or more of the voting stock or shares of or owns either 10 percent or more or $5,000 or more of the fair market value of a business entity that:

(A) has an equitable or legal ownership interest in the tract with a fair market value of $2,500 or more; or

(B) acts as a developer of the tract; or

(4) receives in a calendar year funds from a business entity described by Subdivision (3) that exceed 10 percent of the person's gross income for the previous year.

(c) A person also is considered to have a substantial interest in a subdivided tract if the person is related in the first degree by consanguinity or affinity, as determined under Chapter 573, Government Code, to another person who, under Subsection (b), has a substantial interest in the tract.

(d) If a member of the municipal authority responsible for approving plats has a substantial interest in a subdivided tract, the member shall file, before a vote or decision regarding the approval of a plat for the tract, an affidavit stating the nature and extent of the interest and shall abstain from further participation in the matter. The affidavit must be filed with the municipal secretary or clerk.

(e) A member of the municipal authority responsible for approving plats commits an offense if the member violates Subsection (d). An offense under this subsection is a Class A misdemeanor.

(f) The finding by a court of a violation of this section does not render voidable an action of the municipal authority responsible for approving plats unless the measure would not have passed the municipal authority without the vote of the member who violated this section.

LGOVT §212.0175. ENFORCEMENT IN CERTAIN COUNTIES; PENALTY

(a) The attorney general may take any action necessary to enforce a requirement imposed by or under Section 212.0105 or 212.0106 or to ensure that water and sewer service facilities are constructed or installed to service a subdivision in compliance with the model rules adopted under Section 16.343, Water Code.

(b) A person who violates Section 212.0105 or 212.0106 or fails to timely provide for the construction or installation of water or sewer service facilities that the person described on the plat or on the document attached to the plat, as required by Section 212.0105, is subject to a civil penalty of not less than $500 nor more than $1,000 plus court costs and attorney's fees.

(c) An owner of a tract of land commits an offense if the owner knowingly or intentionally violates a requirement imposed by or under Section 212.0105 or 212.0106 or fails to timely provide for the construction or installation of water or sewer service facilities that the person described on a plat or on a document attached to a plat, as required by Section 212.0105. An offense under this subsection is a Class B misdemeanor.

(d) A reference in this section to an "owner of a tract of land" does not include the owner of an individual lot in a subdivided tract of land.

LGOVT §212.018. ENFORCEMENT IN GENERAL

(a) At the request of the governing body of the municipality, the municipal attorney or any other attorney representing the municipality may file an action in a court of competent jurisdiction to:

(1) enjoin the violation or threatened violation by the owner of a tract of land of a requirement regarding the tract and established by, or adopted by the governing body under, this subchapter; or

(2) recover damages from the owner of a tract of land in an amount adequate for the municipality to undertake any construction or other activity necessary to bring about compliance with a requirement regarding the tract and established by, or adopted by the governing body under, this subchapter.

(b) A reference in this section to an "owner of a tract of land" does not include the owner of an individual lot in a subdivided tract of land.

Sections 212.019-212.040 reserved for expansion

Subchapter B. Regulation of Property Development

LGOVT §212.041. MUNICIPALITY COVERED BY SUBCHAPTER

This subchapter applies only to a municipality whose governing body chooses by ordinance to be covered by this subchapter or chose by ordinance to be covered by the law codified by this subchapter.

LGOVT §212.042. APPLICATION OF SUBCHAPTER A

The provisions of Subchapter A that do not conflict with this subchapter apply to development plats.

LGOVT §212.043. DEFINITIONS

In this subchapter:

(1) "Development" means the new construction or the enlargement of any exterior dimension of any building, structure, or improvement.

(2) "Extraterritorial jurisdiction" means a municipality's extraterritorial jurisdiction as determined under Chapter 42.

LGOVT §212.044. PLANS, RULES, & ORDINANCES

After a public hearing on the matter, the municipality may adopt general plans, rules, or ordinances governing development plats of land within the limits and in the extraterritorial jurisdiction of the municipality to promote the health, safety, morals, or general welfare of the municipality and the safe, orderly, and healthful development of the municipality.

LGOVT §212.045. DEVELOPMENT PLAT REQUIRED

(a) Any person who proposes the development of a tract of land located within the limits or in the extraterritorial jurisdiction of the municipality must have a development plat of the tract prepared in accordance with this subchapter and the applicable plans, rules, or ordinances of the municipality.

(b) A development plat must be prepared by a registered professional land surveyor as a boundary survey showing:

(1) each existing or proposed building, structure, or improvement or proposed modification of the external configuration of the building, structure, or improvement involving a change of the building, structure, or improvement;

(2) each easement and right-of-way within or abutting the boundary of the surveyed property; and

(3) the dimensions of each street, sidewalk, alley, square, park, or other part of the property intended to be dedicated to public use or for the use of purchasers or owners of lots fronting on or adjacent to the street, sidewalk, alley, square, park, or other part.

(c) New development may not begin on the property until the development plat is filed with and approved by the municipality in accordance with Section 212.047.

(d) If a person is required under Subchapter A or an ordinance of the municipality to file a subdivision plat, a development plat is not required in addition to the subdivision plat.

LGOVT §212.046. RESTRICTION ON ISSUANCE OF BUILDING & OTHER PERMITS BY MUNICIPALITY, COUNTY, OR OFFICIAL OF OTHER GOVERNMENTAL ENTITY

The municipality, a county, or an official of another governmental entity may not issue a building permit or any other type of permit for development on lots or tracts subject to this subchapter until a development plat is filed with and approved by the municipality in accordance with Section 212.047.

LGOVT §212.047. APPROVAL OF DEVELOPMENT PLAT

The municipality shall endorse approval on a development plat filed with it if the plat conforms to:

(1) the general plans, rules, and ordinances of the municipality concerning its current and future streets, sidewalks, alleys, parks, playgrounds, and public utility facilities;

(2) the general plans, rules, and ordinances for the extension of the municipality or the extension, improvement, or widening of its roads, streets, and public highways within the municipality and in its extraterritorial jurisdiction, taking into account access to and extension of sewer and water mains and the instrumentalities of public utilities; and

(3) any general plans, rules, or ordinances adopted under Section 212.044.

LGOVT §212.048. EFFECT OF APPROVAL ON DEDICATION

The approval of a development plat is not considered an acceptance of any proposed dedication for public use or use by persons other than the owner of the property covered by the plat and does not impose on the municipality any duty regarding the maintenance or improvement of any purportedly dedicated parts until the municipality's governing body makes an actual appropriation of the dedicated parts by formal acceptance, entry, use, or improvement.

LGOVT §212.049. BUILDING PERMITS IN EXTRATERRITORIAL JURISDICTION

This subchapter does not authorize the municipality to require municipal building permits or otherwise enforce the municipality's building code in its extraterritorial jurisdiction.

LGOVT §212.050. ENFORCEMENT; PENALTY

(a) If it appears that a violation or threat of a violation of this subchapter or a plan, rule, or ordinance adopted under this subchapter or consistent with this subchapter exists, the municipality is entitled to appropriate injunctive relief against the person who committed, is committing, or is threatening to commit the violation.

(b) A suit for injunctive relief may be brought in the county in which the defendant resides, the county in which the violation or threat of violation occurs, or any county in which the municipality is wholly or partly located.

(c) In a suit to enjoin a violation or threat of a violation of this subchapter or a plan, rule, ordinance, or other order adopted under this subchapter, the court may grant the municipality any prohibitory or mandatory injunction warranted by the facts including a temporary restraining order, temporary injunction, or permanent injunction.

(d) A person commits an offense if the person violates this subchapter or a plan, rule, or ordinance adopted under this subchapter or consistent with this subchapter within the limits of the municipality. An offense under this subsection is a Class C misdemeanor. Each day the violation continues constitutes a separate offense.

(e) A suit under this section shall be given precedence over all other cases of a different nature on the docket of the trial or appellate court.

(f) It is no defense to a criminal or civil suit under this section that an agency of government other than the municipality issued a license or permit authorizing the construction, repair, or alteration of any building, structure, or improvement. It also is no defense that the

defendant had no knowledge of this subchapter or of an applicable plan, rule, or ordinance.

Sections 212.051-212.070 blank

SUBCHAPTER C. DEVELOPER PARTICIPATION IN CONTRACT FOR PUBLIC IMPROVEMENTS

LGOVT §212.071. DEVELOPER PARTICIPATION CONTRACT

Without complying with the competitive sealed bidding procedure of Chapter 252, a municipality with 5,000 or more inhabitants may make a contract with a developer of a subdivision or land in the municipality to construct public improvements, not including a building, related to the development. If the contract does not meet the requirements of this subchapter, Chapter 252 applies to the contract if the contract would otherwise be governed by that chapter.

LGOVT §212.072. DUTIES OF PARTIES UNDER CONTRACT

(a) Under the contract, the developer shall construct the improvements and the municipality shall participate in their cost.

(b) The contract:

(1) must establish the limit of participation by the municipality at a level not to exceed 30 percent of the total contract price, if the municipality has a population of less than 1.8 million; or

(2) may allow participation by a municipality at a level not to exceed 70 percent of the total contract price, if the municipality has a population of 1.8 million or more.

(b-1) In addition, if the municipality has a population of 1.8 million or more, the municipality may participate at a level not to exceed 100 percent of the total contract price for all required drainage improvements related to the development and construction of affordable housing. Under this subsection, affordable housing is defined as housing which is equal to or less than the median sales price, as determined by the Real Estate Center at Texas A&M University, of a home in the Metropolitan Statistical Area (MSA) in which the municipality is located.

(c) In addition, the contract may also allow participation by the municipality at a level not to exceed 100 percent of the total cost for any oversizing of improvements required by the municipality, including but not limited to increased capacity of improvements to anticipate other future development in the area.

(d) The municipality is liable only for the agreed payment of its share of the contract, which shall be determined in advance either as a lump sum or as a factor or percentage of the total actual cost as determined by municipal ordinance.

LGOVT §212.073. PERFORMANCE BOND

The developer must execute a performance bond for the construction of the improvements to ensure completion of the project. The bond must be executed by a corporate surety in accordance with Chapter 2253, Government Code.

LGOVT §212.074. ADDITIONAL SAFEGUARDS; INSPECTION OF RECORDS

(a) In the ordinance adopted by the municipality under Section 212.072(b), the municipality may include additional safeguards against undue loading of cost, collusion, or fraud.

(b) All of the developer's books and other records related to the project shall be available for inspection by the municipality.

Sections 212.075-212.100 blank

SUBCHAPTER D. REGULATION OF PROPERTY DEVELOPMENT PROHIBITED IN CERTAIN CIRCUMSTANCES

LGOVT §212.101. APPLICATION OF SUBCHAPTER TO CERTAIN HOME-RULE MUNICIPALITY

This subchapter applies only to a home-rule municipality that:

(1) has a charter provision allowing for limited-purpose annexation; and

(2) has annexed territory for a limited purpose.

LGOVT §212.102. DEFINITIONS

In this subchapter:

(1) "Affected area" means an area that is:

(A) in a municipality or a municipality's extraterritorial jurisdiction;

(B) in a county other than the county in which a majority of the territory of the municipality is located;

(C) within the boundaries of one or more school districts other than the school district in which a majority of the territory of the municipality is located; and

(D) within the area of or within 1,500 feet of the boundary of an assessment road district in which there are two state highways.

(2) "Assessment road district" means a road district that has issued refunding bonds and that has imposed assessments on each parcel of land under Subchapter C, Chapter 1471, Government Code.

(3) "State highway" means a highway that is part of the state highway system under Section 221.001, Transportation Code.

LGOVT §212.103. TRAFFIC OR TRAFFIC OPERATIONS

(a) A municipality may not deny, limit, delay, or condition the use or development of land, any part of which is within an affected area, because of:

(1) traffic or traffic operations that would result from the proposed use or development of the land; or

(2) the effect that the proposed use or development of the land would have on traffic or traffic operations.

(b) In this section, an action to deny, limit, delay, or condition the use or development of land includes a decision or other action by the governing body of the municipality or by a commission, board, department, agency, office, or employee of the municipality related to zoning, subdivision, site planning, the construction or building permit process, or any other municipal process, approval, or permit.

(c) This subchapter does not prevent a municipality from exercising its authority to require the dedication of right-of-way.

LGOVT §212.104. PROVISION NOT ENFORCEABLE

A provision in a covenant or agreement relating to land in an affected area that would have the effect of denying, limiting, delaying, or conditioning the use or development of the land because of its effect on traffic or traffic operations may not be enforced by a municipality.

LGOVT §212.105. SUBCHAPTER CONTROLS

This subchapter controls over any other law relating to municipal regulation of land use or development based on traffic.

Sections 212.106-212.130 blank

SUBCHAPTER E. MORATORIUM ON PROPERTY DEVELOPMENT IN CERTAIN CIRCUMSTANCES

LGOVT §212.131. DEFINITIONS

In this subchapter:

(1) "Essential public facilities" means water, sewer, or storm drainage facilities or street improvements provided by a municipality or private utility.

(2) "Residential property" means property zoned for or otherwise authorized for single-family or multifamily use.

(3) "Property development" means the construction, reconstruction, or other alteration or improvement of residential or commercial buildings or the subdivision or replatting of a subdivision of residential or commercial property.

(4) "Commercial property" means property zoned for or otherwise authorized for use other than single-family use, multifamily use, heavy industrial use, or use as a quarry.

LGOVT §212.132. APPLICABILITY

This subchapter applies only to a moratorium imposed on property development affecting only residential property, commercial property, or both residential and commercial property.

LGOVT §212.133. PROCEDURE FOR ADOPTING MORATORIUM

A municipality may not adopt a moratorium on property development unless the municipality:

(1) complies with the notice and hearing procedures prescribed by Section 212.134; and

(2) makes written findings as provided by Section 212.135, 212.1351, or 212.1352, as applicable.

LGOVT §212.134. NOTICE & PUBLIC HEARING REQUIREMENTS

(a) Before a moratorium on property development may be imposed, a municipality must conduct public hearings as provided by this section.

(b) A public hearing must provide municipal residents and affected parties an opportunity to be heard. The municipality must publish notice of the time and place of a hearing in a newspaper of general circulation in the municipality on the fourth day before the date of the hearing.

(c) Beginning on the fifth business day after the date a notice is published under Subsection (b), a temporary moratorium takes effect. During the period of the temporary moratorium, a municipality may stop accepting permits, authorizations, and approvals necessary for the subdivision of, site planning of, or construction on real property.

(d) One public hearing must be held before the governing body of the municipality. Another public

hearing must be held before the municipal zoning commission, if the municipality has a zoning commission.

(e) If a general-law municipality does not have a zoning commission, two public hearings separated by at least four days must be held before the governing body of the municipality.

(f) Within 12 days after the date of the first public hearing, the municipality shall make a final determination on the imposition of a moratorium. Before an ordinance adopting a moratorium may be imposed, the ordinance must be given at least two readings by the governing body of the municipality. The readings must be separated by at least four days. If the municipality fails to adopt an ordinance imposing a moratorium within the period prescribed by this subsection, an ordinance imposing a moratorium may not be adopted, and the temporary moratorium imposed under Subsection (c) expires.

LGOVT §212.135. JUSTIFICATION FOR MORATORIUM: SHORTAGE OF ESSENTIAL PUBLIC FACILITIES; WRITTEN FINDINGS REQUIRED

(a) If a municipality adopts a moratorium on property development, the moratorium is justified by demonstrating a need to prevent a shortage of essential public facilities. The municipality must issue written findings based on reasonably available information.

(b) The written findings must include a summary of:

(1) evidence demonstrating the extent of need beyond the estimated capacity of existing essential public facilities that is expected to result from new property development, including identifying:

(A) any essential public facilities currently operating near, at, or beyond capacity;

(B) the portion of that capacity committed to the development subject to the moratorium; and

(C) the impact fee revenue allocated to address the facility need; and

(2) evidence demonstrating that the moratorium is reasonably limited to:

(A) areas of the municipality where a shortage of essential public facilities would otherwise occur; and

(B) property that has not been approved for development because of the insufficiency of existing essential public facilities.

LGOVT §212.1351. JUSTIFICATION FOR MORATORIUM: SIGNIFICANT NEED FOR PUBLIC FACILITIES; WRITTEN FINDINGS REQUIRED

(a) Except as provided by Section 212.1352, a moratorium that is not based on a shortage of essential public facilities is justified only by demonstrating a significant need for other public facilities, including police and fire facilities. For purposes of this subsection, a significant need for public facilities is established if the failure to provide those public facilities would result in an overcapacity of public facilities or would be detrimental to the health, safety, and welfare of the residents of the municipality. The municipality must issue written findings based on reasonably available information.

(b) The written findings must include a summary of:

(1) evidence demonstrating that applying existing development ordinances or regulations and other applicable laws is inadequate to prevent the new development from causing the overcapacity of municipal infrastructure or being detrimental to the public health, safety, and welfare in an affected geographical area;

(2) evidence demonstrating that alternative methods of achieving the objectives of the moratorium are unsatisfactory; and

(3) evidence demonstrating that the municipality has approved a working plan and time schedule for achieving the objectives of the moratorium.

LGOVT §212.1352. JUSTIFICATION FOR COMMERCIAL MORATORIUM IN CERTAIN CIRCUMSTANCES; WRITTEN FINDINGS REQUIRED

(a) If a municipality adopts a moratorium on commercial property development that is not based on a demonstrated shortage of essential public facilities, the municipality must issue written findings based on reasonably available information that the moratorium is justified by demonstrating that applying existing commercial development ordinances or regulations and other applicable laws is inadequate to prevent the new development from being detrimental to the public health, safety, or welfare of the residents of the municipality.

(b) The written findings must include a summary of:

(1) evidence demonstrating the need to adopt new ordinances or regulations or to amend existing ordi-

nances, including identification of the harm to the public health, safety, or welfare that will occur if a moratorium is not adopted;

(2) the geographical boundaries in which the moratorium will apply;

(3) the specific types of commercial property to which the moratorium will apply; and

(4) the objectives or goals to be achieved by adopting new ordinances or regulations or amending existing ordinances or regulations during the period the moratorium is in effect.

LGOVT §212.136. EXPIRATION OF MORATORIUM; EXTENSION

A moratorium adopted under Section 212.135 or 212.1351 expires on the 120th day after the date the moratorium is adopted unless the municipality extends the moratorium by:

(1) holding a public hearing on the proposed extension of the moratorium; and

(2) adopting written findings that:

(A) identify the problem requiring the need for extending the moratorium;

(B) describe the reasonable progress made to alleviate the problem; and

(C) specify a definite duration for the renewal period of the moratorium.

LGOVT §212.1361. NOTICE FOR EXTENSION REQUIRED

A municipality proposing an extension of a moratorium under this subchapter must publish notice in a newspaper of general circulation in the municipality not later than the 15th day before the date of the hearing required by this subchapter.

LGOVT §212.1362. EXPIRATION OF MORATORIUM ON COMMERCIAL PROPERTY IN CERTAIN CIRCUMSTANCES; EXTENSION

(a) A moratorium on commercial property adopted under Section 212.1352 expires on the 90th day after the date the moratorium is adopted unless the municipality extends the moratorium by:

(1) holding a public hearing on the proposed extension of the moratorium; and

(2) adopting written findings that:

(A) identify the problem requiring the need for extending the moratorium;

(B) describe the reasonable progress made to alleviate the problem;

(C) specify a definite duration for the renewal period of the moratorium; and

(D) include a summary of evidence demonstrating that the problem will be resolved within the extended duration of the moratorium.

(b) A municipality may not adopt a moratorium on commercial property under Section 212.1352 that exceeds an aggregate of 180 days. A municipality may not adopt a moratorium on commercial property under Section 212.1352 before the second anniversary of the expiration date of a previous moratorium if the subsequent moratorium addresses the same harm, affects the same type of commercial property, or affects the same geographical area identified by the previous moratorium.

LGOVT §212.137. WAIVER PROCEDURES REQUIRED

(a) A moratorium adopted under this subchapter must allow a permit applicant to apply for a waiver from the moratorium relating to the property subject to the permit by:

(1) claiming a right obtained under a development agreement; or

(2) providing the public facilities that are the subject of the moratorium at the landowner's cost.

(b) The permit applicant must submit the reasons for the request to the governing body of the municipality in writing. The governing body of the municipality must vote on whether to grant the waiver request within 10 days after the date of receiving the written request.

LGOVT §212.138. EFFECT ON OTHER LAW

A moratorium adopted under this subchapter does not affect the rights acquired under Chapter 245 or common law.

LGOVT §212.139. LIMITATION ON MORATORIUM

(a) A moratorium adopted under this subchapter does not affect an application for a project in progress under Chapter 245.

(b) A municipality may not adopt a moratorium under this subchapter that:

(1) prohibits a person from filing or processing an application for a project in progress under Chapter 245; or

(2) prohibits or delays the processing of an application for zoning filed before the effective date of the moratorium.

Sections 212.140-212.150 blank

SUBCHAPTER F. ENFORCEMENT OF LAND USE RESTRICTIONS CONTAINED IN PLATS & OTHER INSTRUMENTS

LGOVT §212.151. MUNICIPALITY COVERED BY SUBCHAPTER

This subchapter applies only to a municipality with a population of 1.5 million or more that passes an ordinance that requires uniform application and enforcement of this subchapter with regard to all property and residents or to a municipality that does not have zoning ordinances and passes an ordinance that requires uniform application and enforcement of this subchapter with regard to all property and residents.

LGOVT §212.152. DEFINITION

In this subchapter, "restriction" means a land-use regulation that:

(1) affects the character of the use to which real property, including residential and rental property, may be put;

(2) fixes the distance that a structure must be set back from property lines, street lines, or lot lines;

(3) affects the size of a lot or the size, type, and number of structures that may be built on the lot;

(4) regulates or restricts the type of activities that may take place on the property, including commercial activities, sweepstakes activities, keeping of animals, use of fire, nuisance activities, vehicle storage, and parking;

(5) regulates architectural features of a structure, construction of fences, landscaping, garbage disposal, or noise levels; or

(6) specifies the type of maintenance that must be performed on a lot or structure, including maintenance of a yard or fence.

LGOVT §212.153. SUIT TO ENFORCE RESTRICTIONS

(a) Except as provided by Subsection (b), the municipality may sue in any court of competent jurisdiction to enjoin or abate a violation of a restriction contained or incorporated by reference in a properly recorded plan, plat, or other instrument that affects a subdivision located inside the boundaries of the municipality.

(b) The municipality may not initiate or maintain a suit to enjoin or abate a violation of a restriction if a property owners' association with the authority to enforce the restriction files suit to enforce the restriction.

(c) In a suit by a property owners' association to enforce a restriction, the association may not submit into evidence or otherwise use the work product of the municipality's legal counsel.

(d) In a suit filed under this section alleging that any of the following activities violates a restriction limiting property to residential use, it is not a defense that the activity is incidental to the residential use of the property:

(1) storing a tow truck, crane, moving van or truck, dump truck, cement mixer, earth-moving device, or trailer longer than 20 feet; or

(2) repairing or offering for sale more than two motor vehicles in a 12-month period.

(e) A municipality may not enforce a deed restriction which purports to regulate or restrict the rights granted to public utilities to install, operate, maintain, replace, and remove facilities within easements and private or public rights-of-way.

LGOVT §212.1535. FORECLOSURE BY PROPERTY OWNERS' ASSOCIATION

(a) A municipality may not participate in a suit or other proceeding to foreclose a property owners' association's lien on real property.

(b) In a suit or other proceeding to foreclose a property owners' association's lien on real property in the subdivision, the association may not submit into evidence or otherwise use the work product of the municipality's legal counsel.

LGOVT §212.154. LIMITATION ON ENFORCEMENT

A restriction contained in a plan, plat, or other instrument that was properly recorded before August 30, 1965, may be enforced as provided by Section 212.153, but a violation of a restriction that occurred before that date may not be enjoined or abated by the municipality as long as the nature of the violation remains unchanged.

LGOVT §212.155. NOTICE TO PURCHASERS

(a) The governing body of the municipality may require, in the manner prescribed by law for official ac-

tion of the municipality, any person who sells or conveys restricted property located inside the boundaries of the municipality to first give to the purchaser written notice of the restrictions and notice of the municipality's right to enforce compliance.

(b) If the municipality elects under this section to require that notice be given, the notice to the purchaser shall contain the following information:

(1) the name of each purchaser;

(2) the name of each seller;

(3) a legal description of the property;

(4) the street address of the property;

(5) a statement that the property is subject to deed restrictions and the municipality is authorized to enforce the restrictions;

(6) a reference to the volume and page, clerk's file number, or film code number where the restrictions are recorded; and

(7) a statement that provisions that restrict the sale, rental, or use of the real property on the basis of race, color, religion, sex, or national origin are unenforceable.

(c) If the municipality elects under this section to require that notice be given, the following procedure shall be followed to ensure the delivery and recordation of the notice:

(1) the notice shall be given to the purchaser at or before the final closing of the sale and purchase;

(2) the seller and purchaser shall sign and acknowledge the notice; and

(3) following the execution, acknowledgment, and closing of the sale and purchase, the notice shall be recorded in the real property records of the county in which the property is located.

(d) If the municipality elects under this section to require that notice be given:

(1) the municipality shall file in the real property records of the county clerk's office in each county in which the municipality is located a copy of the form of notice, with its effective date, that is prescribed for use by any person who sells or conveys restricted property located inside the boundaries of the municipality;

(2) all sellers and all persons completing the prescribed notice on the seller's behalf are entitled to rely on the currently effective form filed by the municipality;

(3) the municipality may prescribe a penalty against a seller, not to exceed $500, for the failure of the seller to obtain the execution and recordation of the notice; and

(4) an action may not be maintained by the municipality against a seller to collect a penalty for the failure to obtain the execution and recordation of the notice if the municipality has not filed for record the form of notice with the county clerk of the appropriate county.

(e) This section does not limit the seller's right to recover a penalty, or any part of a penalty, imposed pursuant to Subsection (d)(3) from a third party for the negligent failure to obtain the execution or proper recordation of the notice.

(f) The failure of the seller to comply with the requirements of this section and the implementing municipal regulation does not affect the validity or enforceability of the sale or conveyance of restricted property or the validity or enforceability of restrictions covering the property.

(g) For the purposes of this section, an executory contract of purchase and sale having a performance period of more than six months is considered a sale under Subsection (a).

(h) For the purposes of the disclosure required by this section, restrictions may not include provisions that restrict the sale, rental, or use of property on the basis of race, color, religion, sex, or national origin and may not include any restrictions that by their express provisions have terminated.

See also *Real Estate Forms*, FORMS 11:1, 11:2.

LGOVT §212.156. ENFORCEMENT BY ORDINANCE; CIVIL PENALTY

(a) The governing body of the municipality by ordinance may require compliance with a restriction contained or incorporated by reference in a properly recorded plan, plat, or other instrument that affects a subdivision located inside the boundaries of the municipality.

(b) The municipality may bring a civil action to recover a civil penalty for a violation of the restriction. The municipality may bring an action and recover the penalty in the same manner as a municipality may bring an action and recover a penalty under Subchapter B, Chapter 54.

(c) For the purposes of an ordinance adopted under this section, restrictions do not include provisions

that restrict the sale, rental, or use of property on the basis of race, color, religion, sex, or national origin and do not include any restrictions that by their express provisions have terminated.

LGOVT §212.157. GOVERNMENTAL FUNCTION

An action filed by a municipality under this subchapter to enforce a land use restriction is a governmental function of the municipality.

LGOVT §212.158. EFFECT ON OTHER LAW

This subchapter does not prohibit the exhibition, play, or necessary incidental action thereto of a sweepstakes not prohibited by Chapter 622, Business & Commerce Code.

Sections 212.159-212.170 blank

SUBCHAPTER G. AGREEMENT GOVERNING CERTAIN LAND IN A MUNICIPALITYS[1] EXTRATERRITORIAL JURISDICTION

LGOVT §212.171. APPLICABILITY

This subchapter does not apply to land located in the extraterritorial jurisdiction of a municipality with a population of 1.9 million or more.

1. **Editor's note:** Probably should be "Municipality's."

LGOVT §212.172. DEVELOPMENT AGREEMENT

(a) In this subchapter, "extraterritorial jurisdiction" means a municipality's extraterritorial jurisdiction as determined under Chapter 42.

(b) The governing body of a municipality may make a written contract with an owner of land that is located in the extraterritorial jurisdiction of the municipality to:

(1) guarantee the continuation of the extraterritorial status of the land and its immunity from annexation by the municipality;

(2) extend the municipality's planning authority over the land by providing for a development plan to be prepared by the landowner and approved by the municipality under which certain general uses and development of the land are authorized;

(3) authorize enforcement by the municipality of certain municipal land use and development regulations in the same manner the regulations are enforced within the municipality's boundaries;

(4) authorize enforcement by the municipality of land use and development regulations other than those that apply within the municipality's boundaries, as may be agreed to by the landowner and the municipality;

(5) provide for infrastructure for the land, including:

(A) streets and roads;

(B) street and road drainage;

(C) land drainage; and

(D) water, wastewater, and other utility systems;

(6) authorize enforcement of environmental regulations;

(7) provide for the annexation of the land as a whole or in parts and to provide for the terms of annexation, if annexation is agreed to by the parties;

(8) specify the uses and development of the land before and after annexation, if annexation is agreed to by the parties; or

(9) include other lawful terms and considerations the parties consider appropriate.

(c) An agreement under this subchapter must:

(1) be in writing;

(2) contain an adequate legal description of the land;

(3) be approved by the governing body of the municipality and the landowner; and

(4) be recorded in the real property records of each county in which any part of the land that is subject to the agreement is located.

(d) The total duration of the contract and any successive renewals or extensions may not exceed 45 years.

(e) A municipality in an affected county, as defined by Section 16.341, Water Code, may not enter into an agreement under this subchapter that is inconsistent with the model rules adopted under Section 16.343, Water Code.

(f) The agreement between the governing body of the municipality and the landowner is binding on the municipality and the landowner and on their respective successors and assigns for the term of the agreement. The agreement is not binding on, and does not create any encumbrance to title as to, any end-buyer of a fully developed and improved lot within the development, except for land use and development regulations that may apply to a specific lot.

(g) An agreement under this subchapter constitutes a permit under Chapter 245.

(h) An agreement between a municipality and a landowner entered into prior to the effective date of this section and that complies with this section is validated.

LGOVT §212.173. CERTAIN COASTAL AREAS

This subchapter does not apply to, limit, or otherwise affect any ordinance, order, rule, plan, or standard adopted by this state or a state agency, county, municipality, or other political subdivision of this state under the federal Coastal Zone Management Act of 1972 (16 U.S.C. Section 1451 et seq.), and its subsequent amendments, or Subtitle E, Title 2, Natural Resources Code.

LGOVT §212.174. MUNICIPAL UTILITIES

A municipality may not require an agreement under this subchapter as a condition for providing water, sewer, electricity, gas, or other utility service from a municipally owned or municipally operated utility that provides any of those services.

Sections 212.175-212.900 blank

SUBCHAPTER Z. MISCELLANEOUS PROVISIONS

LGOVT §212.901. DEVELOPER REQUIRED TO PROVIDE SURETY

(a) To ensure that it will not incur liabilities, a municipality may require, before it gives approval of the plans for a development, that the owner of the development provide sufficient surety to guarantee that claims against the development will be satisfied if a default occurs.

(b) This section does not preclude a claimant from seeking recovery by other means.

LGOVT §212.902. SCHOOL DISTRICT LAND DEVELOPMENT STANDARDS

(a) This section applies to agreements between school districts and any municipality which has annexed territory for limited purposes.

(b) On request by a school district, a municipality shall enter an agreement with the board of trustees of the school district to establish review fees, review periods, and land development standards ordinances and to provide alternative water pollution control methodologies for school buildings constructed by the school district. The agreement shall include a provision exempting the district from all land development ordinances in cases where the district is adding temporary classroom buildings on an existing school campus.

(c) If the municipality and the school district do not reach an agreement on or before the 120th day after the date on which the municipality receives the district's request for an agreement, proposed agreements by the school district and the municipality shall be submitted to an independent arbitrator appointed by the presiding district judge whose jurisdiction includes the school district. The arbitrator shall, after a hearing at which both the school district and municipality make presentations on their proposed agreements, prepare an agreement resolving any differences between the proposals. The agreement prepared by the arbitrator will be final and binding upon both the school district and the municipality. The cost of the arbitration proceeding shall be borne equally by the school district and the municipality.

(d) A school district that requests an agreement under this section, at the time it makes the request, shall send a copy of the request to the commissioner of education. At the end of the 120-day period, the requesting district shall report to the commissioner the status or result of negotiations with the municipality. A municipality may send a separate status report to the commissioner. The district shall send to the commissioner a copy of each agreement between the district and a municipality under this section.

(e) In this section, "land development standards" includes impervious cover limitations, building setbacks, floor to area ratios, building coverage, water quality controls, landscaping, development setbacks, compatibility standards, traffic analyses, and driveway cuts, if applicable.

(f) Nothing in this section shall be construed to limit the applicability of or waive fees for fire, safety, health, or building code ordinances of the municipality prior to or during construction of school buildings, nor shall any agreement waive any fee or modify any ordinance of a municipality for an administration, service, or athletic facility proposed for construction by a school district.

LGOVT §212.903. CONSTRUCTION & RENOVATION WORK ON COUNTY-OWNED BUILDINGS OR FACILITIES IN CERTAIN COUNTIES

(a) This section applies only to a county with a population of 250,000 or more.

(b) A municipality is not authorized to require a county to notify the municipality or obtain a building permit for any new construction or renovation work performed within the limits of the municipality by the county's personnel or by county personnel acting as general contractor on county-owned buildings or facilities. Such construction or renovation work shall be inspected by a registered professional engineer or architect licensed in this state in accordance with any other applicable law. A municipality may require a building permit for construction or renovation work performed on county-owned buildings or facilities by private general contractors.

(c) This section does not exempt a county from complying with a municipality's building code standards when performing construction or renovation work.

LGOVT §212.904. APPORTIONMENT OF MUNICIPAL INFRASTRUCTURE COSTS

(a) If a municipality requires as a condition of approval for a property development project that the developer bear a portion of the costs of municipal infrastructure improvements by the making of dedications, the payment of fees, or the payment of construction costs, the developer's portion of the costs may not exceed the amount required for infrastructure improvements that are roughly proportionate to the proposed development as approved by a professional engineer who holds a license issued under Chapter 1001, Occupations Code, and is retained by the municipality.

(b) A developer who disputes the determination made under Subsection (a) may appeal to the governing body of the municipality. At the appeal, the developer may present evidence and testimony under procedures adopted by the governing body. After hearing any testimony and reviewing the evidence, the governing body shall make the applicable determination within 30 days following the final submission of any testimony or evidence by the developer.

(c) A developer may appeal the determination of the governing body to a county or district court of the county in which the development project is located within 30 days of the final determination by the governing body.

(d) A municipality may not require a developer to waive the right of appeal authorized by this section as a condition of approval for a development project.

(e) A developer who prevails in an appeal under this section is entitled to applicable costs and to reasonable attorney's fees, including expert witness fees.

(f) This section does not diminish the authority or modify the procedures specified by Chapter 395.

CHAPTER 213. MUNICIPAL COMPREHENSIVE PLANS

LGOVT §213.001. PURPOSE

The powers granted under this chapter are for the purpose of promoting sound development of municipalities and promoting public health, safety, and welfare.

LGOVT §213.002. COMPREHENSIVE PLAN

(a) The governing body of a municipality may adopt a comprehensive plan for the long-range development of the municipality. A municipality may define the content and design of a comprehensive plan.

(b) A comprehensive plan may:

(1) include but is not limited to provisions on land use, transportation, and public facilities;

(2) consist of a single plan or a coordinated set of plans organized by subject and geographic area; and

(3) be used to coordinate and guide the establishment of development regulations.

(c) A municipality may define, in its charter or by ordinance, the relationship between a comprehensive plan and development regulations and may provide standards for determining the consistency required between a plan and development regulations.

(d) Land use assumptions adopted in a manner that complies with Subchapter C, Chapter 395, may be incorporated in a comprehensive plan.

LGOVT §213.003. ADOPTION OR AMENDMENT OF COMPREHENSIVE PLAN

(a) A comprehensive plan may be adopted or amended by ordinance following:

(1) a hearing at which the public is given the opportunity to give testimony and present written evidence; and

(2) review by the municipality's planning commission or department, if one exists.

(b) A municipality may establish, in its charter or by ordinance, procedures for adopting and amending a comprehensive plan.

LGOVT §213.004. EFFECT ON OTHER MUNICIPAL PLANS

This chapter does not limit the ability of a municipality to prepare other plans, policies, or strategies as required.

LGOVT §213.005. NOTATION ON MAP OF COMPREHENSIVE PLAN

A map of a comprehensive plan illustrating future land use shall contain the following clearly visible statement: "A comprehensive plan shall not constitute zoning regulations or establish zoning district boundaries."

CHAPTER 214. MUNICIPAL REGULATION OF HOUSING & OTHER STRUCTURES

SUBCHAPTER A. DANGEROUS STRUCTURES

LGOVT §214.001. AUTHORITY REGARDING SUBSTANDARD BUILDING

(a) A municipality may, by ordinance, require the vacation, relocation of occupants, securing, repair, removal, or demolition of a building that is:

(1) dilapidated, substandard, or unfit for human habitation and a hazard to the public health, safety, and welfare;

(2) regardless of its structural condition, unoccupied by its owners, lessees, or other invitees and is unsecured from unauthorized entry to the extent that it could be entered or used by vagrants or other uninvited persons as a place of harborage or could be entered or used by children; or

(3) boarded up, fenced, or otherwise secured in any manner if:

(A) the building constitutes a danger to the public even though secured from entry; or

(B) the means used to secure the building are inadequate to prevent unauthorized entry or use of the building in the manner described by Subdivision (2).

(b) The ordinance must:

(1) establish minimum standards for the continued use and occupancy of all buildings regardless of the date of their construction;

(2) provide for giving proper notice, subject to Subsection (b-1), to the owner of a building; and

(3) provide for a public hearing to determine whether a building complies with the standards set out in the ordinance.

(b-1) For a condominium, as defined by Section 81.002 or 82.003, Property Code, located wholly or partly in a municipality with a population of more than 1.9 million, notice to a unit owner in accordance with Section 82.118, Property Code, and notice to the registered agent for the unit owners' association in the manner provided for service of process to a condominium association under Section 54.035(a-1) satisfy the notice requirements under this section.

(c) A notice of a hearing sent to an owner, lienholder, or mortgagee under this section must include a statement that the owner, lienholder, or mortgagee will be required to submit at the hearing proof of the scope of any work that may be required to comply with the ordinance and the time it will take to reasonably perform the work.

(d) After the public hearing, if a building is found in violation of standards set out in the ordinance, the municipality may order that the building be vacated, secured, repaired, removed, or demolished by the owner within a reasonable time as provided by this section. The municipality also may order that the occupants be relocated within a reasonable time. If the owner does not take the ordered action within the allotted time, the municipality shall make a diligent effort to discover each mortgagee and lienholder having an interest in the building or in the property on which the building is located. The municipality shall personally deliver, send by certified mail with return receipt requested, or deliver by the United States Postal Service using signature confirmation service, to each identified mortgagee and lienholder a notice containing:

(1) an identification, which is not required to be a legal description, of the building and the property on which it is located;

(2) a description of the violation of municipal standards that is present at the building; and

(3) a statement that the municipality will vacate, secure, remove, or demolish the building or relocate the occupants of the building if the ordered action is not taken within a reasonable time.

(e) As an alternative to the procedure prescribed by Subsection (d), the municipality may make a dili-

gent effort to discover each mortgagee and lienholder before conducting the public hearing and may give them a notice of and an opportunity to comment at the hearing. In addition, the municipality may file notice of the hearing in the Official Public Records of Real Property in the county in which the property is located. The notice must contain the name and address of the owner of the affected property if that information can be determined, a legal description of the affected property, and a description of the hearing. The filing of the notice is binding on subsequent grantees, lienholders, or other transferees of an interest in the property who acquire such interest after the filing of the notice, and constitutes notice of the hearing on any subsequent recipient of any interest in the property who acquires such interest after the filing of the notice. If the municipality operates under this subsection, the order issued by the municipality may specify a reasonable time as provided by this section for the building to be vacated, secured, repaired, removed, or demolished by the owner or for the occupants to be relocated by the owner and an additional reasonable time as provided by this section for the ordered action to be taken by any of the mortgagees or lienholders in the event the owner fails to comply with the order within the time provided for action by the owner. Under this subsection, the municipality is not required to furnish any notice to a mortgagee or lienholder other than a copy of the order in the event the owner fails to timely take the ordered action.

(f) Within 10 days after the date that the order is issued, the municipality shall:

(1) file a copy of the order in the office of the municipal secretary or clerk, if the municipality has a population of 1.9 million or less; and

(2) publish in a newspaper of general circulation in the municipality in which the building is located a notice containing:

(A) the street address or legal description of the property;

(B) the date of the hearing;

(C) a brief statement indicating the results of the order; and

(D) instructions stating where a complete copy of the order may be obtained.

(g) After the hearing, the municipality shall promptly mail by certified mail with return receipt requested, deliver by the United States Postal Service using signature confirmation service, or personally deliver a copy of the order to the owner of the building and to any lienholder or mortgagee of the building. The municipality shall use its best efforts to determine the identity and address of any owner, lienholder, or mortgagee of the building.

(h) In conducting a hearing authorized under this section, the municipality shall require the owner, lienholder, or mortgagee of the building to within 30 days:

(1) secure the building from unauthorized entry; or

(2) repair, remove, or demolish the building, unless the owner or lienholder establishes at the hearing that the work cannot reasonably be performed within 30 days.

(i) If the municipality allows the owner, lienholder, or mortgagee more than 30 days to repair, remove, or demolish the building, the municipality shall establish specific time schedules for the commencement and performance of the work and shall require the owner, lienholder, or mortgagee to secure the property in a reasonable manner from unauthorized entry while the work is being performed, as determined by the hearing official.

(j) A municipality may not allow the owner, lienholder, or mortgagee more than 90 days to repair, remove, or demolish the building or fully perform all work required to comply with the order unless the owner, lienholder, or mortgagee:

(1) submits a detailed plan and time schedule for the work at the hearing; and

(2) establishes at the hearing that the work cannot reasonably be completed within 90 days because of the scope and complexity of the work.

(k) If the municipality allows the owner, lienholder, or mortgagee more than 90 days to complete any part of the work required to repair, remove, or demolish the building, the municipality shall require the owner, lienholder, or mortgagee to regularly submit progress reports to the municipality to demonstrate compliance with the time schedules established for commencement and performance of the work. The order may require that the owner, lienholder, or mortgagee appear before the hearing official or the hearing official's designee to demonstrate compliance with the time schedules. If the owner, lienholder, or mortgagee owns property, including structures or improvements on property, within the municipal boundaries that exceeds $100,000 in total value, the municipality may require the owner,

lienholder, or mortgagee to post a cash or surety bond in an amount adequate to cover the cost of repairing, removing, or demolishing a building under this subsection. In lieu of a bond, the municipality may require the owner, lienholder, or mortgagee to provide a letter of credit from a financial institution or a guaranty from a third party approved by the municipality. The bond must be posted, or the letter of credit or third party guaranty provided, not later than the 30th day after the date the municipality issues the order.

(*l*) In a public hearing to determine whether a building complies with the standards set out in an ordinance adopted under this section, the owner, lienholder, or mortgagee has the burden of proof to demonstrate the scope of any work that may be required to comply with the ordinance and the time it will take to reasonably perform the work.

(m) If the building is not vacated, secured, repaired, removed, or demolished, or the occupants are not relocated within the allotted time, the municipality may vacate, secure, remove, or demolish the building or relocate the occupants at its own expense. This subsection does not limit the ability of a municipality to collect on a bond or other financial guaranty that may be required by Subsection (k).

(n) If a municipality incurs expenses under Subsection (m), the municipality may assess the expenses on, and the municipality has a lien against, unless it is a homestead as protected by the Texas Constitution, the property on which the building was located. The lien is extinguished if the property owner or another person having an interest in the legal title to the property reimburses the municipality for the expenses. The lien arises and attaches to the property at the time the notice of the lien is recorded and indexed in the office of the county clerk in the county in which the property is located. The notice must contain the name and address of the owner if that information can be determined with a reasonable effort, a legal description of the real property on which the building was located, the amount of expenses incurred by the municipality, and the balance due.

(o) If the notice is given and the opportunity to relocate the tenants of the building or to repair, remove, or demolish the building is afforded to each mortgagee and lienholder as authorized by Subsection (d), (e), or (g), the lien is a privileged lien subordinate only to tax liens.

(p) A hearing under this section may be held by a civil municipal court.

(q) A municipality satisfies the requirements of this section to make a diligent effort, to use its best efforts, or to make a reasonable effort to determine the identity and address of an owner, a lienholder, or a mortgagee if the municipality searches the following records:

(1) county real property records of the county in which the building is located;

(2) appraisal district records of the appraisal district in which the building is located;

(3) records of the secretary of state;

(4) assumed name records of the county in which the building is located;

(5) tax records of the municipality; and

(6) utility records of the municipality.

(r) When a municipality mails a notice in accordance with this section to a property owner, lienholder, mortgagee, or registered agent and the United States Postal Service returns the notice as "refused" or "unclaimed," the validity of the notice is not affected, and the notice is considered delivered.

LGOVT §214.0011. ADDITIONAL AUTHORITY TO SECURE SUBSTANDARD BUILDING

(a) A municipality by ordinance may establish minimum standards for the use and occupancy of buildings in the municipality regardless of the date of their construction and may adopt other ordinances as necessary to carry out this section.

(b) The municipality may secure a building the municipality determines:

(1) violates the minimum standards; and

(2) is unoccupied or is occupied only by persons who do not have a right of possession to the building.

(c) Before the 11th day after the date the building is secured, the municipality shall give notice to the owner by:

(1) personally serving the owner with written notice;

(2) depositing the notice in the United States mail addressed to the owner at the owner's post office address;

(3) publishing the notice at least twice within a 10-day period in a newspaper of general circulation in the county in which the building is located if personal ser-

vice cannot be obtained and the owner's post office address is unknown; or

(4) posting the notice on or near the front door of the building if personal service cannot be obtained and the owner's post office address is unknown.

(d) The notice must contain:

(1) an identification, which is not required to be a legal description, of the building and the property on which it is located;

(2) a description of the violation of the municipal standards that is present at the building;

(3) a statement that the municipality will secure or has secured, as the case may be, the building; and

(4) an explanation of the owner's entitlement to request a hearing about any matter relating to the municipality's securing of the building.

(e) The municipality shall conduct a hearing at which the owner may testify or present witnesses or written information about any matter relating to the municipality's securing of the building if, within 30 days after the date the municipality secures the building, the owner files with the municipality a written request for the hearing. The municipality shall conduct the hearing within 20 days after the date the request is filed.

(f) A municipality has the same authority to assess expenses under this section as it has to assess expenses under Section 214.001(n). A lien is created under this section in the same manner that a lien is created under Section 214.001(n) and is subject to the same conditions as a lien created under that section.

(g) The authority granted by this section is in addition to that granted by Section 214.001.

LGOVT §214.00111. ADDITIONAL AUTHORITY TO PRESERVE SUBSTANDARD BUILDING AS HISTORIC PROPERTY

(a) This section applies only to a municipality that is designated as a certified local government by the state historic preservation officer as provided by 16 U.S.C.A. Section 470 et seq.

(b) This section does not apply to an owner-occupied, single-family dwelling.

(c) Before a notice is sent or a hearing is conducted under Section 214.001, the historic preservation board of a municipality may review a building described by Section 214.001(a) to determine whether the building can be rehabilitated and designated:

(1) on the National Register of Historic Places;

(2) as a Recorded Texas Historic Landmark; or

(3) as historic property through a municipal historic designation.

(d) If a municipal historic preservation board reviews a building, the board shall submit a written report to the municipality indicating the results of the review conducted under this section before a public hearing is conducted under Section 214.001.

(e) If the municipal historic preservation board report determines that the building may not be rehabilitated and designated as historic property, the municipality may proceed as provided by Section 214.001.

(f) If the municipal historic preservation board report determines that the building may be rehabilitated and designated as historic property, the municipality may not permit the building to be demolished for at least 90 days after the date the report is submitted. During this 90-day period, the municipality shall notify the owner and attempt to identify a feasible alternative use for the building or locate an alternative purchaser to rehabilitate and maintain the building. If the municipality is not able to locate the owner or if the owner does not respond within the 90-day period, the municipality may appoint a receiver as provided by Section 214.003.

(g) The municipality may require the building to be demolished as provided by Section 214.001 after the expiration of the 90-day period if the municipality is not able to:

(1) identify a feasible alternative use for the building;

(2) locate an alternative purchaser to rehabilitate and maintain the building; or

(3) appoint a receiver for the building as provided by Section 214.003.

(h) An owner of a building described by Section 214.001(a) is not liable for penalties related to the building that accrue during the 90-day period provided for disposition of historic property under this section.

LGOVT §214.0012. JUDICIAL REVIEW

(a) Any owner, lienholder, or mortgagee of record of property jointly or severally aggrieved by an order of a municipality issued under Section 214.001 may file in district court a verified petition setting forth that the decision is illegal, in whole or in part, and specifying the grounds of the illegality. The petition must be filed by an owner, lienholder, or mortgagee within 30 calen-

dar days after the respective dates a copy of the final decision of the municipality is personally delivered to them, mailed to them by first class mail with certified return receipt requested, or delivered to them by the United States Postal Service using signature confirmation service, or such decision shall become final as to each of them upon the expiration of each such 30 calendar day period.

(b) On the filing of the petition, the court may issue a writ of certiorari directed to the municipality to review the order of the municipality and shall prescribe in the writ the time within which a return on the writ must be made, which must be longer than 10 days, and served on the relator or the relator's attorney.

(c) The municipality may not be required to return the original papers acted on by it, but it is sufficient for the municipality to return certified or sworn copies of the papers or of parts of the papers as may be called for by the writ.

(d) The return must concisely set forth other facts as may be pertinent and material to show the grounds of the decision appealed from and shall be verified.

(e) The issuance of the writ does not stay proceedings on the decision appealed from.

(f) Appeal in the district court shall be limited to a hearing under the substantial evidence rule. The court may reverse or affirm, in whole or in part, or may modify the decision brought up for review.

(g) Costs may not be allowed against the municipality.

(h) If the decision of the municipality is affirmed or not substantially reversed but only modified, the district court shall allow to the municipality all attorney's fees and other costs and expenses incurred by it and shall enter a judgment for those items, which may be entered against the property owners, lienholders, or mortgagees as well as all persons subject to the proceedings before the municipality.

LGOVT §214.0015. ADDITIONAL AUTHORITY REGARDING SUBSTANDARD BUILDING

(a) This section applies only to a municipality that has adopted an ordinance under Section 214.001.

(b) In addition to the authority granted to the municipality by Section 214.001, after the expiration of the time allotted under Section 214.001(d) or (e) for the repair, removal, or demolition of a building, the municipality may:

(1) repair the building at the expense of the municipality and assess the expenses on the land on which the building stands or to which it is attached and may provide for that assessment, the mode and manner of giving notice, and the means of recovering the repair expenses; or

(2) assess a civil penalty against the property owner for failure to repair, remove, or demolish the building and provide for that assessment, the mode and manner of giving notice, and the means of recovering the assessment.

(c) The municipality may repair a building under Subsection (b) only to the extent necessary to bring the building into compliance with the minimum standards and only if the building is a residential building with 10 or fewer dwelling units. The repairs may not improve the building to the extent that the building exceeds minimum housing standards.

(d) The municipality shall impose a lien against the land on which the building stands or stood, unless it is a homestead as protected by the Texas Constitution, to secure the payment of the repair, removal, or demolition expenses or the civil penalty. Promptly after the imposition of the lien, the municipality must file for record, in recordable form in the office of the county clerk of the county in which the land is located, a written notice of the imposition of the lien. The notice must contain a legal description of the land.

(e) Except as provided by Section 214.001, the municipality's lien to secure the payment of a civil penalty or the costs of repairs, removal, or demolition is inferior to any previously recorded bona fide mortgage lien attached to the real property to which the municipality's lien attaches if the mortgage lien was filed for record in the office of the county clerk of the county in which the real property is located before the date the civil penalty is assessed or the repair, removal, or demolition is begun by the municipality. The municipality's lien is superior to all other previously recorded judgment liens.

(f) Any civil penalty or other assessment imposed under this section accrues interest at the rate of 10 percent a year from the date of the assessment until paid in full.

(g) The municipality's right to the assessment lien may not be transferred to third parties.

(h) In any judicial proceeding regarding enforcement of municipal rights under this section, the pre-

vailing party is entitled to recover reasonable attorney's fees from the nonprevailing party.

(i) A lien acquired under this section by a municipality for repair expenses may not be foreclosed if the property on which the repairs were made is occupied as a residential homestead by a person 65 years of age or older.

(j) The municipality by order may assess and recover a civil penalty against a property owner at the time of an administrative hearing on violations of an ordinance, in an amount not to exceed $1,000 a day for each violation or, if the owner shows that the property is the owner's lawful homestead, in an amount not to exceed $10 a day for each violation, if the municipality proves:

(1) the property owner was notified of the requirements of the ordinance and the owner's need to comply with the requirements; and

(2) after notification, the property owner committed an act in violation of the ordinance or failed to take an action necessary for compliance with the ordinance.

(k) An assessment of a civil penalty under Subsection (j) is final and binding and constitutes prima facie evidence of the penalty in any suit brought by a municipality in a court of competent jurisdiction for a final judgment in accordance with the assessed penalty.

(*l*) To enforce a civil penalty under this subchapter, the clerk or secretary of the municipality must file with the district clerk of the county in which the municipality is located a certified copy of an order issued under Subsection (j) stating the amount and duration of the penalty. No other proof is required for a district court to enter a final judgment on the penalty.

LGOVT §214.002. REQUIRING REPAIR, REMOVAL, OR DEMOLITION OF BUILDING OR OTHER STRUCTURE

(a) If the governing body of a municipality finds that a building, bulkhead or other method of shoreline protection, fence, shed, awning, or other structure, or part of a structure, is likely to endanger persons or property, the governing body may:

(1) order the owner of the structure, the owner's agent, or the owner or occupant of the property on which the structure is located to repair, remove, or demolish the structure, or the part of the structure, within a specified time; or

(2) repair, remove, or demolish the structure, or the part of the structure, at the expense of the municipality, on behalf of the owner of the structure or the owner of the property on which the structure is located, and assess the repair, removal, or demolition expenses on the property on which the structure was located.

(b) The governing body shall provide by ordinance for:

(1) the assessment of repair, removal, or demolition expenses incurred under Subsection (a)(2);

(2) a method of giving notice of the assessment; and

(3) a method of recovering the expenses.

(c) The governing body may punish by a fine, confinement in jail, or both a person who does not comply with an order issued under Subsection (a)(1).

LGOVT §214.003. RECEIVER

(a) A home-rule municipality may bring an action in district court against an owner of property that is not in substantial compliance with:

(1) the municipal ordinances regarding:

(A) fire protection;

(B) structural integrity;

(C) zoning; or

(D) disposal of refuse; or

(2) a municipal ordinance described by Section 54.012(1), (2), (5), (6), (7), or (9).

(b) Except as provided by Subsection (c), the court may appoint as a receiver for the property a nonprofit organization or an individual with a demonstrated record of rehabilitating properties if the court finds that:

(1) the structures on the property are in violation of the standards set forth in Section 214.001(b) and an ordinance described by Subsection (a);

(2) notice of violation was given to the record owner of the property; and

(3) a public hearing as required by Section 214.001(b) has been conducted.

(c) A receiver appointed under Subsection (b) may act as a receiver for any property, including historic property subject to Section 214.00111.

(d) For the purposes of this section, if the record owner does not appear at the hearing required by Section 214.001(b), the hearing shall be conducted as if the owner had personally appeared.

(e) In the action, the record owners and any lienholders of record of the property shall be served with personal notice of the proceedings or, if not available after due diligence, may be served by publication. Actual service or service by publication on the record owners or lienholders constitutes notice to all unrecorded owners or lienholders.

(f) The court may issue, on a showing of imminent risk of injury to any person occupying the property or a person in the community, any mandatory or prohibitory temporary restraining orders and temporary injunctions necessary to protect the public health and safety.

(g) A receiver appointed by the court may:

(1) take control of the property;

(2) collect rents due on the property;

(3) make or have made any repairs necessary to bring the property into compliance with:

(A) minimum standards in local ordinances; or

(B) guidelines for rehabilitating historic properties established by the secretary of the interior under 16 U.S.C.A. Section 470 et seq. or the municipal historic preservation board, if the property is considered historic property under Section 214.00111;

(4) make payments necessary for the maintenance or restoration of utilities to the properties;

(5) purchase materials necessary to accomplish repairs;

(6) renew existing rental contracts and leases;

(7) enter into new rental contracts and leases;

(8) affirm, renew, or enter into a new contract providing for insurance coverage on the property; and

(9) exercise all other authority that an owner of the property would have except for the authority to sell the property.

(h) On the completion of the restoration of the property to the minimum code standards of the municipality or guidelines for rehabilitating historic property, or before petitioning a court for termination of the receivership under Subsection (*l*):

(1) the receiver shall file with the court a full accounting of all costs and expenses incurred in the repairs, including reasonable costs for labor and supervision, all income received from the property, and, at the receiver's discretion, a receivership fee of 10 percent of those costs and expenses;

(2) if the income exceeds the total of the cost and expense of rehabilitation and any receivership fee, the rehabilitated property shall be restored to the owners and any net income shall be returned to the owners; and

(3) if the total of the costs and expenses and any receivership fee exceeds the income received during the receivership, the receiver may maintain control of the property until the time all rehabilitation and maintenance costs and any receivership fee are recovered, or until the receivership is terminated.

(h-1) A receiver shall have a lien on the property under receivership for all of the receiver's unreimbursed costs and expenses and any receivership fee.

(i) Any record lienholder may, after initiation of an action by a municipality:

(1) intervene in the action; and

(2) request appointment as a receiver:

(A) under the same conditions as the nonprofit organization or individual; and

(B) on a demonstration to the court of an ability and willingness to rehabilitate the property.

(j) For the purposes of this section, the interests and rights of an unrecorded lienholder or unrecorded property owner are, in all respects, inferior to the rights of a duly appointed receiver.

(k) The court may not appoint a receiver for any property that is an owner-occupied, single-family residence.

(*l*) A receiver appointed by a district court under this section, or the home-rule municipality that filed the action under which the receiver was appointed, may petition the court to terminate the receivership and order the sale of the property after the receiver has been in control of the property for more than one year, if an owner has been served with notice but has failed to assume control or repay all rehabilitation and maintenance costs and any receivership fee of the receiver.

(m) In the action, the record owners and any lienholders of record of the property shall be served with personal notice of the proceedings or, if not found after due diligence, may be served by publication. Actual service or service by publication on all record owners and lienholders of record constitutes notice to all unrecorded owners and lienholders.

(n) The court may order the sale of the property if the court finds that:

(1) notice was given to each record owner of the property and each lienholder of record;

(2) the receiver has been in control of the property for more than one year and an owner has failed to repay all rehabilitation and maintenance costs and any receivership fee of the receiver; and

(3) no lienholder of record has intervened in the action and offered to repay the costs and any receivership fee of the receiver and assume control of the property.

(o) The court shall order the sale to be conducted by the petitioner in the same manner that a sale is conducted under Chapter 51, Property Code. If the record owners and lienholders are identified, notice of the date and time of the sale must be sent in the same manner as provided by Chapter 51, Property Code. If the owner cannot be located after due diligence, the owner may be served notice by publication. The receiver may bid on the property at the sale and may use a lien granted under Subsection (h-1) as credit toward the purchase. The petitioner shall make a report of the sale to the court.

(p) The court shall confirm the sale and order a distribution of the proceeds of the sale in the following order:

(1) court costs;

(2) costs and expenses of the receiver, and any lien held by the receiver; and

(3) other valid liens.

(q) Any remaining sums must be paid to the owner. If the owner is not identified or cannot be located, the court shall order the remaining sums to be deposited in an interest-bearing account with the district clerk's office in the district in which the action is pending, and the clerk shall hold the funds as provided by other law.

(r) After the proceeds are distributed, the court shall award fee title to the purchaser subject to any recorded bona fide liens that were not paid by the proceeds of the sale.

LGOVT §214.0031. ADDITIONAL AUTHORITY TO APPOINT RECEIVER FOR HAZARDOUS PROPERTIES

(a) In this section:

(1) "Eligible nonprofit housing organization" means a nonprofit housing organization that is certified by a home-rule municipality to bring an action under this section.

(2) "Multifamily residential property" means any residential dwelling complex consisting of four or more units.

(b) A home-rule municipality may annually certify one or more nonprofit housing organizations to bring an action under this section after making the following findings:

(1) the nonprofit housing organization has a record of community involvement; and

(2) the certification will further the home-rule municipality's goal to rehabilitate hazardous properties.

(c) A home-rule municipality or an eligible nonprofit housing organization may bring an action under this section in district court against an owner of property that is not in substantial compliance with one or more municipal ordinances regarding:

(1) the prevention of substantial risk of injury to any person; or

(2) the prevention of an adverse health impact to any person.

(d) A municipality that grants authority to an eligible nonprofit housing organization to initiate an action under this section has standing to intervene in the proceedings at any time as a matter of right.

(e) The court may appoint a receiver if the court finds that:

(1) the property is in violation of one or more ordinances of the municipality described by Subsection (c);

(2) the condition of the property constitutes a serious and imminent public health or safety hazard; and

(3) the property is not an owner-occupied, single-family residence.

(f) The following are eligible to serve as court-appointed receivers:

(1) an entity with, as determined by the court, sufficient capacity and experience rehabilitating properties; and

(2) an individual with, as determined by the court, sufficient resources and experience rehabilitating properties.

(g) Notwithstanding Subsection (f), an entity is ineligible to serve as a receiver for a multifamily residential property if the nonprofit housing organization that brought the action under this section has an ownership interest or a right to income in the entity.

(h) The home-rule municipality or eligible nonprofit housing organization must send by certified mail notice of any ordinance violation alleged to exist on the property on or before the 30th day before the date an action is filed under this section to:

(1) the physical address of the property; and

(2) the address as indicated on the most recently approved municipal tax roll for the property owner or the property owner's agent.

(i) In an action under this section, each record owner and each lienholder of record of the property shall be served with notice of the proceedings or, if not available after due diligence, may be served by alternative means, including publication, as prescribed by the Texas Rules of Civil Procedure. Actual service or service by publication on a record owner or lienholder constitutes notice to each unrecorded owner or lienholder.

(j) On a showing of imminent risk of injury to a person occupying the property or present in the community, the court may issue a mandatory or prohibitory temporary restraining order or temporary injunction as necessary to protect the public health or safety.

(k) Unless inconsistent with this section or other law, the rules of equity govern all matters relating to a court action under this section.

(*l*) Subject to control of the court, a court-appointed receiver has all powers necessary and customary to the powers of a receiver under the laws of equity and may:

(1) take possession and control of the property;

(2) operate and manage the property;

(3) establish and collect rents and income on the property;

(4) lease the property;

(5) make any repairs and improvements necessary to bring the property into compliance with local codes and ordinances and state laws, including:

(A) performing and entering into contracts for the performance of work and the furnishing of materials for repairs and improvements; and

(B) entering into loan and grant agreements for repairs and improvements to the property;

(6) pay expenses, including paying for utilities and paying taxes and assessments, insurance premiums, and reasonable compensation to a property management agent;

(7) enter into contracts for operating and maintaining the property;

(8) exercise all other authority of an owner of the property other than the authority to sell the property unless authorized by the court under Subsection (n); and

(9) perform other acts regarding the property as authorized by the court.

(m) A court-appointed receiver may demolish a single-family structure on the property under this section on authorization by the court and only if the court finds:

(1) it is not economically feasible to bring the structure into compliance with local codes and ordinances and state laws; and

(2) the structure is:

(A) unfit for human habitation or is a hazard to the public health or safety;

(B) regardless of its structural condition:

(i) unoccupied by its owners or lessees or other invitees; and

(ii) unsecured from unauthorized entry to the extent that it could be entered or used by vagrants or other uninvited persons as a place of harborage or could be entered or used by children; or

(C) boarded, fenced, or otherwise secured, but:

(i) the structure constitutes a danger to the public even though secured from entry; or

(ii) the means used to secure the structure are inadequate to prevent unauthorized entry or use of the structure in the manner described by Paragraph (B)(ii).

(n) On demolition of the structure, the court may authorize the receiver to sell the property to an individual or organization that will bring the property into productive use.

(o) On completing the repairs or demolishing the structure or before petitioning a court for termination of the receivership, the receiver shall file with the court a full accounting of all costs and expenses incurred in the repairs or demolition, including reasonable costs for labor and supervision, all income received from the property, and, at the receiver's discretion, a receivership fee of 10 percent of those costs and expenses. If the property was sold under Subsection (n) and the revenue exceeds the total of the costs and expenses incurred by the receiver plus any receivership fee, any net income shall be returned to the owner. If the property is not sold and the income produced exceeds the total of the costs and expenses incurred by the receiver plus any receivership fee, the rehabilitated property shall be restored to the owner and any net income shall be returned to the owner. If the total of the costs and ex-

penses incurred by the receiver plus any receivership fee exceeds the income produced during the receivership, the receiver may maintain control of the property until all rehabilitation and maintenance costs plus any receivership fee are recovered or until the receivership is terminated.

(p) A receiver shall have a lien on the property for all of the receiver's unreimbursed costs and expenses, plus any receivership fee.

(q) Any lienholder of record may, after initiation of an action under this section:

(1) intervene in the action; and

(2) request appointment as a receiver under this section if the lienholder demonstrates to the court an ability and willingness to rehabilitate the property.

(r) A receiver appointed under this section or the home-rule municipality or eligible nonprofit housing organization that filed the action under which the receiver was appointed may petition the court to terminate the receivership and order the sale of the property if an owner has been served with notice but has failed to repay all of the receiver's outstanding costs and expenses plus any receivership fee on or before the 180th day after the date the notice was served.

(s) The court may order the sale of the property if the court finds that:

(1) notice was given to each record owner of the property and each lienholder of record;

(2) the receiver has been in control of the property and the owner has failed to repay all the receiver's outstanding costs and expenses of rehabilitation plus any receivership fee within the period prescribed by Subsection (r); and

(3) no lienholder of record has intervened in the action and tendered the receiver's costs and expenses, plus any receivership fee, and assumed control of the property.

(t) The court may order the property sold:

(1) to a land bank or other party as the court may direct, excluding, for multifamily residential properties, an eligible nonprofit housing organization that initiated the action under this section; or

(2) at public auction.

(u) The receiver, if an entity not excluded under Subsection (t), may bid on the property at the sale described by Subsection (t)(2) and may use a lien granted under Subsection (p) as credit toward the purchase.

(v) The court shall confirm a sale under this section and order a distribution of the proceeds of the sale in the following order:

(1) court costs;

(2) costs and expenses, plus a receivership fee, and any lien held by the receiver; and

(3) other valid liens.

(w) Any remaining amount shall be paid to the owner. If the owner cannot be identified or located, the court shall order the remaining amount to be deposited in an interest-bearing account with the district clerk's office in the district court in which the action is pending. The district clerk shall hold the funds as provided by other law.

(x) After the proceeds are distributed, the court shall award fee title to the purchaser. If the proceeds of the sale are insufficient to pay all liens, claims, and encumbrances on the property, the court shall extinguish all unpaid liens, claims, and encumbrances on the property and award title to the purchaser free and clear.

(y) This section does not foreclose any right or remedy that may be available under Section 214.003, other state law, or the laws of equity.

LGOVT §214.004. SEIZURE & SALE OF PROPERTY TO RECOVER EXPENSES

A Type A general-law municipality or home-rule municipality may foreclose a lien on property under this subchapter:

(1) in a proceeding relating to the property brought under Subchapter E, Chapter 33, Tax Code; or

(2) in a judicial proceeding, if:

(A) a building or other structure on the property has been demolished;

(B) a lien for the cost of the demolition of the building or other structure on the property has been created and that cost has not been paid more than 180 days after the date the lien was filed; and

(C) ad valorem taxes are delinquent on all or part of the property.

LGOVT §214.005. PROPERTY BID OFF TO MUNICIPALITY

A municipality may adopt an ordinance under Section 214.001(a) that applies to property that has been bid off to the municipality under Section 34.01(j), Tax Code.

Sections 214.006-214.010 reserved for expansion

Subchapter B. Plumbing & Sewers

LGOVT §214.011. Plumbing Inspector

(a) If a municipality does not have a special charter that provides for an inspector of plumbing, the governing body of the municipality may appoint an inspector of plumbing for a term fixed by the governing body.

(b) The same individual may serve as plumbing inspector and municipal engineer.

LGOVT §214.012. Sewers & Plumbing

A municipality that has underground sewers or cesspools shall regulate by ordinance:

(1) the tapping of the sewers and cesspools; and

(2) house draining and plumbing.

LGOVT §214.013. Sewer Connections

(a) A municipality may:

(1) provide for a sanitary sewer system; and

(2) require property owners to connect to the sewer system.

(b) If an owner does not connect to the sewer system, the municipality may:

(1) fix a lien against the owner's property;

(2) charge the cost of the connection to the owner as a personal liability; and

(3) impose a penalty on the owner.

LGOVT §214.014. Drains, Sinks, & Privies

(a) The governing body of a Type A general-law municipality may, by resolution or ordinance, order the owner of a private drain, sink, or privy to fill up, clean, drain, alter, relay, repair, or improve the drain, sink, or privy.

(b) If the order cannot be served on a person in the municipality, the municipality may have the work done on behalf of the owner. The municipality may fix a lien on the owner's property for expenses incurred in having the work done. The lien is created when the mayor of the municipality files and records a memorandum, under the seal of the municipality, with the clerk of the district court.

(c) The municipality may enforce the lien and may obtain in any court having jurisdiction a judgment against the owner for the amount of the expenses.

(d) The governing body may punish by a fine a person who does not comply with an order adopted under this section.

LGOVT §214.015. Seizure & Sale of Property to Recover Expenses

A home-rule municipality or Type A general-law municipality may foreclose a lien on property under this subchapter in a proceeding relating to the property brought under Subchapter E, Chapter 33, Tax Code.

Sections 214.016-214.100 reserved for expansion

Subchapter C. Swimming Pool Enclosures

LGOVT §214.101. Authority Regarding Swimming Pool Enclosures

(a) A municipality may by ordinance establish minimum standards for swimming pool fences and enclosures and may adopt other ordinances as necessary to carry out this subchapter. A municipal ordinance containing standards for a pool yard enclosure as defined by Chapter 757, Health and Safety Code, as added by Section 2, Chapter 517, Acts of the 73rd Legislature, 1993, must contain the same standards for that enclosure as are required or permitted by that chapter of the Health and Safety Code.

(b) A municipality that adopts an ordinance under this subchapter may repair, replace, secure, or otherwise remedy an enclosure or fence that is damaged, deteriorated, substandard, dilapidated, or otherwise in a state that poses a hazard to the public health, safety, and welfare.

(c) A municipality may require the owner of the property on which the swimming pool or enclosure or fence is situated, after notice and hearing as provided in Sections 214.001(d) and (e), to repair, replace, secure, or otherwise remedy an enclosure or fence of a swimming pool that the municipality or an appropriate municipal official, agent, or employee determines violates the minimum standards adopted under this subchapter.

(d) If the enclosure or fence is on unoccupied property or is on property occupied only by persons who do not have a right of possession to the property, the municipality shall give notice to the owner, in accordance with the procedures set out in Sections 214.0011(c) and (d), of the municipality's action to re-

pair, replace, secure, or otherwise remedy an enclosure or fence of a swimming pool.

(e) If a municipality incurs expenses under this subchapter, the municipality may assess the expenses on, and the municipality has a lien against, unless it is a homestead as protected by the Texas Constitution, the property on which the swimming pool or the enclosure or fence is situated. The lien is extinguished if the property owner or another person having an interest in the legal title to the property reimburses the municipality for the expenses. The lien arises and attaches to the property at the time the notice of the lien is recorded in the office of the county clerk in the county in which the property is situated. The notice must contain the name and address of the owner if that information can be determined with a reasonable effort, a legal description of the real property on which the swimming pool or the enclosure or fence is situated, the amount of expenses incurred by the municipality, and the balance due. The lien is a privileged lien subordinate only to tax liens and all previously recorded bona fide mortgage liens attached to the real property to which the municipality's lien attaches.

(f) An ordinance adopted under this subchapter may provide for a penalty, not to exceed $1,000, for a violation of the ordinance. The ordinance may provide that each day a violation occurs constitutes a separate offense.

(g) A municipal official, agent, or employee, acting under the authority granted by this subchapter or any ordinance adopted under this subchapter, may enter any unoccupied premises at a reasonable time to inspect, investigate, or enforce the powers granted under this subchapter or any ordinance adopted pursuant to this subchapter. After providing a minimum of 24 hours notice to the occupant, a municipal official, agent, or employee, acting under the authority granted by this subchapter or any ordinance adopted under this subchapter, may enter any occupied premises to inspect, investigate, or enforce the powers granted under this subchapter or any ordinance adopted pursuant to this subchapter. A municipality and its officials, agents, or employees shall be immune from liability for any acts or omissions not knowingly done that are associated with actions taken in an effort to eliminate the dangerous conditions posed by an enclosure or fence that is damaged, deteriorated, substandard, dilapidated, or otherwise in a state that poses a hazard to the public health, safety, and welfare and for any previous or subsequent conditions on the property.

(h) The authority granted by this subchapter is in addition to that granted by any other law.

LGOVT §214.102. SEIZURE & SALE OF PROPERTY TO RECOVER EXPENSES

A municipality may foreclose a lien on property under this subchapter in a proceeding relating to the property brought under Subchapter E, Chapter 33, Tax Code.

Sections 214.103-214.130 reserved for expansion

SUBCHAPTER D. BUILDING LINES

LGOVT §214.131. DEFINITIONS

In this subchapter:

(1) "Street" means a public highway, boulevard, parkway, square, or street, or a part or side of any of these.

(2) "Structure" means a building or other structure, or a part of a building or other structure.

LGOVT §214.132. BUILDING LINES AUTHORIZED

The governing body of a municipality may, by resolution or ordinance, establish a building line on a street in the municipality.

LGOVT §214.133. ACTIVITY PROHIBITED WITHIN BUILDING LINE

In the area between a street and a building line established under this subchapter for the street, the erection, re-erection, reconstruction, or substantial repair of a structure is prohibited.

LGOVT §214.134. RESOLUTION OR ORDINANCE

(a) In adopting a resolution or ordinance that establishes a building line, a municipality must follow the same procedure that it is authorized by law to use to acquire land for the opening of streets.

(b) The resolution or ordinance must:

(1) describe the street affected and the location of the building line; and

(2) provide a period, not to exceed 25 years after the date on which the line is established, during which structures extending into the area between the street and the building line must be brought into conformance with the line.

LGOVT §214.135. CONDEMNATION OF EASEMENTS & INTERESTS; ASSESSMENTS

(a) A municipality must follow the same procedure that it is authorized by law to use to open streets when the municipality:

(1) institutes and conducts a condemnation proceeding to condemn an easement or interest necessary to establish a building line; or

(2) imposes and collects an assessment based on the benefits arising out of the establishment of a building line against the property owner and property abutting or in the vicinity of the building line.

(b) If, in the condemnation of a tract, the ownership of the tract or the interests in the tract are in controversy or unknown, an award for the tract may be made in bulk and paid into court for the use of the parties owning or interested in the tract as their ownership or interest appears.

(c) When the award and findings of the special commissioners, who are appointed under Chapter 21, Property Code, are filed with the court having jurisdiction over the condemnation proceedings, the award and findings are final and shall be made the judgment of the court. Compensation is due and payable on rendition of the judgment by the court adopting the award.

LGOVT §214.136. CONDEMNATION OF PROPERTY

(a) Before or after expiration of the period for conformance set under Section 213.134(b)(2),[1] a municipality, following the same procedure that it is authorized by law to use to institute condemnation proceedings, may:

(1) remove a structure and condemn property in the area between a street and a building line; and

(2) impose an assessment against property owners and property that is benefitted by the establishment of the building line to the extent of the benefit.

(b) The municipality must provide notice and a hearing to the owner of affected property for the determination of:

(1) additional damages sustained by the removal of a structure or the taking of land in the area between a street and a building line; or

(2) the assessment to be imposed against a property owner and the property.

1. **Editor's note:** Probably should be "Section 214.134(b)(2)."

Sections 214.137-214.160 reserved for expansion

Subchapter E. Commercial Building Permits in Certain Populous Municipalities

LGOVT §214.161. MUNICIPALITY COVERED BY SUBCHAPTER

This subchapter applies only to a municipality with a population of more than 1.18 million located primarily in a county with a population of 2 million or more.

LGOVT §214.162. DEFINITIONS

In this subchapter:

(1) "Commercial building" means a building that is not a single family residence.

(2) "Permit department" means the municipal agency that is authorized to issue commercial building permits.

(3) "Subdivider" means a person who divides a tract of real property under circumstances to which Subchapter A, Chapter 212 applies.

LGOVT §214.163. PERMIT APPLICATION REQUIREMENTS; ISSUANCE OF PERMIT

(a) A person who desires to obtain a commercial building permit must file with the permit application a certified copy of any instrument that contains a restriction on the use of or on construction on the affected property and must also include a certified copy of any amendment, judgment, or other document that affects the use of the property.

(b) The permit department shall issue a permit for construction or repair that conforms to all restrictions relating to the use of the property described in the application if the applicant for the permit has complied with this subchapter and with local ordinances relating to commercial building permits.

LGOVT §214.164. FILING OF PLAT & RESTRICTIONS; EFFECT ON PERMIT

(a) At the time that a subdivider files a plat of a proposed subdivision for recording, the subdivider shall file with the permit department two copies of the subdivision plat and of any restrictions relating to the property included in the plat.

(b) The permit department shall securely keep one copy of the plat and restrictions as a permanent record.

(c) A person who desires to obtain a commercial building permit for property that is included in a plat or restrictions on file with the permit department is not

LGOVT §214.164

required to file a copy of the plat and the restrictions with the permit application.

LGOVT §214.165. REPAIRS; CONVERSIONS

(a) A person who proposes to substantially repair or remodel a commercial building located within a subdivision or to convert a single family residence into a commercial building must obtain a commercial building permit from the permit department.

(b) This section does not apply to a violation of a restrictive covenant that occurred before May 18, 1965, if the violation retains the status existing on that date.

LGOVT §214.166. INJUNCTION

(a) A person who, without obtaining a permit, attempts to construct or repair any structure for which a commercial building permit is required may be enjoined from any further construction activity until the person complies with this subchapter.

(b) The municipality may join with an interested property owner in a suit to enjoin further construction activity by a person who does not have a permit issued in compliance with this subchapter if the structure or proposed structure violates a restriction contained in the deed or other instrument.

(c) A municipality may join with an interested property owner in a suit to enjoin the maintenance of a commercial building by a person who does not have a permit in compliance with this subchapter.

LGOVT §214.167. REVIEW OF REFUSAL TO ISSUE PERMIT

(a) An administrative refusal to issue a commercial building permit based on a violation of restrictions contained in a deed or other instrument is reviewable by a court of competent jurisdiction if, during the 90-day period after the day on which the permit is refused, the person contesting the refusal gives notice to the permit department that the suit has been filed.

(b) If conditions in a subdivision change or if other legally sufficient reasons to modify the restrictions occur, a person who has been refused a commercial building permit may petition a court of competent jurisdiction to alter the restrictions to better conform to present conditions.

LGOVT §214.168. VOID PERMITS

A commercial permit obtained without full compliance with this subchapter is void.

Sections 214.169-214.190 reserved for expansion

SUBCHAPTER F. BURGLAR ALARM SYSTEMS IN CERTAIN MUNICIPALITIES WHOLLY LOCATED IN CERTAIN COUNTIES

LGOVT §214.191. DEFINITIONS

In this subchapter:

(1) "Alarm system" means a device or system that transmits a signal intended to summon police of a municipality in response to a burglary. The term includes an alarm that emits an audible signal on the exterior of a structure. The term does not include an alarm installed on a vehicle, unless the vehicle is used for a habitation at a permanent site, or an alarm designed to alert only the inhabitants within the premises.

(2) "Permit" means a certificate, license, permit, or other form of permission that authorizes a person to engage in an action.

LGOVT §214.1915. APPLICABILITY

This subchapter applies only to a municipality with a population of less than 100,000 that is located wholly in a county with a population of less than 500,000.

LGOVT §214.192. CATEGORIES OF ALARM SYSTEMS

The category of alarm system to be regulated is burglary.

LGOVT §214.193. DURATION OF MUNICIPAL PERMIT

(a) If a municipality adopts an ordinance that requires a person to obtain a permit from the municipality before a person may use an alarm system in the municipality, the ordinance must provide that the permit is valid for at least one year.

(b) This requirement does not affect the authority of the municipality to:

(1) revoke, suspend, or otherwise affect the duration of a permit for disciplinary reasons at any time during the period for which the permit is issued; or

(2) make a permit valid for a period of less than one year if necessary to conform the permit to the termination schedule established by the municipality for permits.

LGOVT §214.194. MUNICIPAL PERMIT FEE GENERALLY

(a) If a municipality adopts an ordinance that requires a person to pay an annual fee to obtain a permit from the municipality before the person may use an

alarm system in the municipality, the fee shall be used for the general administration of this subchapter, including the provision of responses generally required to implement this subchapter other than specific responses to false alarms.

(b) A municipal permit fee imposed under this section may not exceed the rate of $50 a year for a residential location.

LGOVT §214.195. NONRENEWAL OR REVOCATION OF PERMIT & TERMINATION OF MUNICIPAL RESPONSE; DISCRIMINATION PROHIBITED

(a) Except as provided in Subsection (d), a municipality may not terminate its law enforcement response to a residential permit holder because of excess false alarms if the false alarm fees are paid in full.

(b) In permitting free false alarm responses and in setting false alarm fees, a municipality must administer any ordinance on a fair and equitable basis as determined by the governing body.

(c) A municipality may not terminate an alarm permit for nonrenewal without providing at least 30 days' notice.

(d) A municipality may revoke or refuse to renew the permit of an alarm system that has had eight or more false alarms during the preceding 12-month period.

LGOVT §214.1955. MULTIUNIT HOUSING FACILITIES

(a) A municipality may not refuse to issue an alarm system permit for a residential location solely because the residential location is an individual residential unit located in a multiunit housing facility.

(b) In issuing an alarm system permit for an alarm installed in an individual residential unit of a multiunit housing facility, the municipality shall issue the permit to the person occupying the individual residential unit.

(c) A municipality may impose a penalty under Section 214.197 for the signaling of a false alarm on the premises of a multiunit housing facility for a facility other than an individual residential unit only if the permit holder is notified of:

(1) the date of the signaling of the false alarm;

(2) the address of the multiunit housing facility where the signaling of the false alarm occurred; and

(3) the identification of the individual facility, if applicable, located on the multiunit housing facility premises where the signaling of the false alarm occurred.

LGOVT §214.196. ON-SITE INSPECTION REQUIRED

A municipality may not consider a false alarm to have occurred unless a response is made by an agency of the municipality within 30 minutes of the alarm notification and the agency determines from an inspection of the interior or exterior of the premises that the alarm was false.

LGOVT §214.197. PENALTIES FOR FALSE ALARMS

A municipality may impose a penalty for the signaling of a false alarm by a burglar alarm system if at least three other false alarms have occurred during the preceding 12-month period. The amount of the penalty for the signaling of a false alarm as described by Section 214.196 may not exceed:

(1) $50, if the location has had more than three but fewer than six other false alarms in the preceding 12-month period;

(2) $75, if the location has had more than five but fewer than eight other false alarms in the preceding 12-month period; or

(3) $100, if the location has had eight or more other false alarms in the preceding 12-month period.

LGOVT §214.198. VERIFICATION

A municipality may require an alarm systems monitor to attempt to contact the occupant of the alarm system location twice before the municipality responds to the alarm signal.

LGOVT §214.199. EXCEPTION OF MUNICIPALITY FROM ALARM SYSTEM RESPONSE

(a) The governing body of a municipality may not adopt an ordinance providing that law enforcement personnel of the municipality will not respond to any alarm signal indicated by an alarm system in the municipality unless, before adopting the ordinance, the governing body of the municipality:

(1) makes reasonable efforts to notify permit holders of its intention to adopt the ordinance; and

(2) conducts a public hearing at which persons interested in the response of the municipality to alarm systems are given the opportunity to be heard.

(b) A municipality that adopts an ordinance under this section may not impose or collect any fine, fee, or penalty otherwise authorized by this subchapter.

(c) A municipality that adopts or proposes to adopt an ordinance under this section may notify permit holders that a permit holder may contract with a security services provider licensed by the Texas Private Security Board under Chapter 1702, Occupations Code, to respond to an alarm. The notice, if given, must include the board's telephone number and Internet website address.

LGOVT §214.200. PRIORITY OR LEVEL OF RESPONSE NOT AFFECTED; LIABILITY OF MUNICIPALITY FOR NONRESPONSE

(a) Nothing in this subchapter:

(1) affects the priority or level of response provided by a municipality to a permitted location; or

(2) waives the governmental immunity provided by law for a municipality.

(b) A municipality that does not respond to an alarm signal is not liable for damages that may occur relating to the cause of the alarm signal.

SUBCHAPTER F-1. BURGLAR ALARM SYSTEMS IN LARGE MUNICIPALITIES & MUNICIPALITIES WHOLLY OR PARTLY LOCATED IN LARGE COUNTIES

LGOVT §214.201. DEFINITIONS

In this subchapter:

(1) "Alarm system" and "permit" have the meanings assigned by Section 214.191.

(2) "Alarm systems monitor" means a person who acts as an alarm systems company under Section 1702.105, Occupations Code.

(3) "False alarm" means a notification of possible criminal activity reported to law enforcement:

(A) that is based solely on electronic information remotely received by an alarm systems monitor;

(B) that is uncorroborated by eyewitness, video, or photographic evidence that an emergency exists; and

(C) concerning which an agency of the municipality has verified that no emergency exists after an on-site inspection of the location from which the notification originated.

LGOVT §214.2015. APPLICABILITY

This subchapter does not apply to a municipality to which Subchapter F applies.

LGOVT §214.202. CATEGORIES OF ALARM SYSTEMS

The category of alarm system to be regulated is burglary.

LGOVT §214.203. DURATION OF MUNICIPAL PERMIT

(a) If a municipality adopts an ordinance that requires a person to obtain a permit from the municipality before a person may use an alarm system in the municipality, the ordinance must provide that the permit is valid for at least one year.

(b) This requirement does not affect the authority of the municipality to:

(1) revoke, suspend, or otherwise affect the duration of a permit for disciplinary reasons at any time during the period for which the permit is issued; or

(2) make a permit valid for a period of less than one year if necessary to conform the permit to the termination schedule established by the municipality for permits.

LGOVT §214.204. MUNICIPAL PERMIT FEE GENERALLY

(a) If a municipality adopts an ordinance that requires a person to pay an annual fee to obtain a permit from the municipality before the person may use an alarm system in the municipality, the fee shall be used for the general administration of this subchapter, including the provision of responses generally required to implement this subchapter other than specific responses to false alarms.

(b) A municipal permit fee imposed under this section for an alarm system may not exceed the rate of:

(1) $50 a year for a residential location; and

(2) $250 a year for other alarm system locations.

LGOVT §214.205. NONRENEWAL OR REVOCATION OF PERMIT; TERMINATION OF MUNICIPAL RESPONSE; DISCRIMINATION PROHIBITED

(a) Except as provided by Subsection (d), a municipality may not terminate its law enforcement response to a residential permit holder because of excess false alarms if the false alarm fees are paid in full.

(b) In permitting free false alarm responses and in setting false alarm fees, a municipality must administer any ordinance on a fair and equitable basis as determined by the governing body.

(c) A municipality may not terminate an alarm permit for nonrenewal without providing at least 30 days' notice.

(d) A municipality may revoke or refuse to renew the permit of an alarm system that has had eight or more false alarms during the preceding 12-month period.

LGOVT §214.2055. MULTIUNIT HOUSING FACILITIES

(a) A municipality may not refuse to issue an alarm system permit for a residential location solely because the residential location is an individual residential unit located in a multiunit housing facility.

(b) In issuing an alarm system permit for an alarm installed in an individual residential unit of a multiunit housing facility, the municipality shall issue the permit to the person occupying the individual residential unit.

(c) A municipality may impose a penalty under Section 214.207 for the signaling of a false alarm on the premises of a multiunit housing facility for a facility other than an individual residential unit only if the permit holder is notified of:

(1) the date of the signaling of the false alarm;

(2) the address of the multiunit housing facility where the signaling of the false alarm occurred; and

(3) the identification of the individual facility, if applicable, located on the multiunit housing facility premises where the signaling of the false alarm occurred.

LGOVT §214.206. ON-SITE INSPECTION REQUIRED

A municipality may not consider a false alarm to have occurred unless a response is made by an agency of the municipality within a reasonable time and the agency determines from an inspection of the interior or exterior of the premises that the alarm report by an alarm systems monitor was false.

LGOVT §214.207. PENALTIES FOR FALSE ALARMS

(a) A municipality may impose a penalty on a person who uses an alarm system in the municipality for the report of a false alarm by an alarm systems monitor if at least three other false alarms have occurred at that location during the preceding 12-month period. The amount of the penalty for the report of a false alarm as described by Section 214.206 may not exceed:

(1) $50, if the location has had more than three but fewer than six other false alarms in the preceding 12-month period;

(2) $75, if the location has had more than five but fewer than eight other false alarms in the preceding 12-month period; or

(3) $100, if the location has had eight or more other false alarms in the preceding 12-month period.

(b) A municipality may not impose a penalty authorized under Subsection (a) if reasonable visual proof of possible criminal activity recorded by an alarm systems monitor is provided to the municipality before the inspection of the premises by an agency of the municipality.

(c) A municipality that adopts an ordinance requiring a person to obtain a permit from the municipality before the person may use an alarm system in the municipality may impose a penalty, not to exceed $250, for the report of a false alarm by an alarm systems monitor on a person who has not obtained a permit for the alarm system as required by the municipal ordinance.

(d) A municipality:

(1) may impose a penalty, not to exceed $250, for the report of a false alarm on a person not licensed under Chapter 1702, Occupations Code, that to any extent is reported or facilitated by the unlicensed person; and

(2) may not impose a penalty for the report of a false alarm on a person licensed under Chapter 1702, Occupations Code.

(e) A municipality may not impose or collect any fine, fee, or penalty, other than collection fees, related to a false alarm or alarm system unless the fine, fee, or penalty is defined in the ordinance in accordance with this subchapter.

LGOVT §214.208. PROCEDURES FOR REDUCING FALSE ALARMS

A municipality may require an alarm systems monitor to attempt to contact the occupant of the alarm system location twice before the municipality responds to the alarm signal.

LGOVT §214.209. EXCEPTION OF MUNICIPALITY FROM ALARM SYSTEM RESPONSE

(a) The governing body of a municipality may not adopt an ordinance providing that law enforcement personnel of the municipality will not respond to any alarm

signal indicated by an alarm system in the municipality unless, before adopting the ordinance, the governing body of the municipality:

(1) makes reasonable efforts to notify permit holders of its intention to adopt the ordinance; and

(2) conducts a public hearing at which persons interested in the response of the municipality to alarm systems are given the opportunity to be heard.

(b) A municipality that adopts an ordinance under this section may not impose or collect any fine, fee, or penalty otherwise authorized by this subchapter.

(c) A municipality that adopts or proposes to adopt an ordinance under this section may notify permit holders that a permit holder may contract with a security services provider licensed by the Texas Private Security Board under Chapter 1702, Occupations Code, to respond to an alarm. The notice, if given, must include the board's telephone number and Internet website address.

LGOVT §214.210. PRIORITY OR LEVEL OF RESPONSE NOT AFFECTED; LIABILITY OF MUNICIPALITY FOR NONRESPONSE

(a) Nothing in this subchapter:

(1) affects the priority or level of response provided by a municipality to a permitted location; or

(2) waives the governmental immunity provided by law for a municipality.

(b) A municipality that does not respond to an alarm system signal is not liable for damages that may occur relating to the cause of the alarm system signal.

LGOVT §214.2105. EXCLUSION OF CERTAIN ALARM SYSTEMS BY OWNER

(a) A property owner or an agent of the property owner authorized to make decisions regarding the use of the property may elect to exclude the municipality from receiving an alarm signal by an alarm system located on the owner's property. A municipality may adopt an ordinance that specifies the requirements a property owner must satisfy for an election to be made under this section.

(b) If an election is made under Subsection (a), the municipality:

(1) may not impose a fee to obtain a permit to use the alarm system;

(2) may impose a fee on the property owner, not to exceed $250, for each law enforcement response to a signal from the alarm system requested by an alarm systems monitor; and

(3) may not impose or collect any other fine, penalty, or fee, other than a collection fee, related to the alarm system.

SUBCHAPTER G. BUILDING & REHABILITATION CODES

LGOVT §214.211. DEFINITIONS

In this subchapter:

(1) "International Residential Code" means the International Residential Code for One- and Two-Family Dwellings promulgated by the International Code Council.

(2) "National Electrical Code" means the electrical code published by the National Fire Protection Association.

(3) "Residential" means having the character of a detached one-family or two-family dwelling or a multiple single-family dwelling that is not more than three stories high with separate means of egress, including the accessory structures of the dwelling, and that does not have the character of a facility used for the accommodation of transient guests or a structure in which medical, rehabilitative, or assisted living services are provided in connection with the occupancy of the structure.

(4) "International Building Code" means the International Building Code promulgated by the International Code Council.

(5) "Commercial" means a building for the use or occupation of people for:

(A) a public purpose or economic gain; or

(B) a residence if the building is a multifamily residence that is not defined as residential by this section.

LGOVT §214.212. INTERNATIONAL RESIDENTIAL CODE

(a) To protect the public health, safety, and welfare, the International Residential Code, as it existed on May 1, 2001, is adopted as a municipal residential building code in this state.

(b) The International Residential Code applies to all construction, alteration, remodeling, enlargement, and repair of residential structures in a municipality.

(c) A municipality may establish procedures:

(1) to adopt local amendments to the International Residential Code; and

(2) for the administration and enforcement of the International Residential Code.

(d) A municipality may review and consider amendments made by the International Code Council to the International Residential Code after May 1, 2001.

LGOVT §214.213. EXCEPTIONS

(a) The International Residential Code and the International Building Code do not apply to the installation and maintenance of electrical wiring and related components.

(b) A municipality is not required to review and consider adoption of amendments to the International Residential Code or the International Building Code regarding electrical provisions.

LGOVT §214.214. NATIONAL ELECTRICAL CODE

(a) Except as provided by Subsection (c), the National Electrical Code, as it existed on May 1, 2001, is adopted as the municipal electrical construction code in this state and applies to all residential and commercial electrical construction applications.

(b) A municipality may establish procedures:

(1) to adopt local amendments to the National Electrical Code; and

(2) for the administration and enforcement of the National Electrical Code.

(c) The National Electrical Code applies to all commercial buildings in a municipality for which construction begins on or after January 1, 2006, and to any alteration, remodeling, enlargement, or repair of those commercial buildings.

LGOVT §214.215. ADOPTION OF REHABILITATION CODES OR PROVISIONS

(a) In this section, "rehabilitation" means the alteration, remodeling, enlargement, or repair of an existing structure.

(b) A municipality that adopts a building code, other than the International Residential Code adopted under Section 214.212, shall adopt one of the following:

(1) prescriptive provisions for rehabilitation as part of the municipality's building code; or

(2) the rehabilitation code that accompanies the building code adopted by the municipality.

(c) The rehabilitation code or prescriptive provisions do not apply to the rehabilitation of a structure to which the International Residential Code applies or to the construction of a new structure.

(d) A municipality may:

(1) adopt the rehabilitation code or prescriptive provisions for rehabilitation recommended by the Texas Board of Architectural Examiners; or

(2) amend its rehabilitation code or prescriptive provisions for rehabilitation.

(e) A municipality shall enforce the prescriptive provisions for rehabilitation or the rehabilitation code in a manner consistent with the enforcement of the municipality's building code.

LGOVT §214.216. INTERNATIONAL BUILDING CODE

(a) To protect the public health, safety, and welfare, the International Building Code, as it existed on May 1, 2003, is adopted as a municipal commercial building code in this state.

(b) The International Building Code applies to all commercial buildings in a municipality for which construction begins on or after January 1, 2006, and to any alteration, remodeling, enlargement, or repair of those commercial buildings.

(c) A municipality may establish procedures:

(1) to adopt local amendments to the International Building Code; and

(2) for the administration and enforcement of the International Building Code.

(d) A municipality may review and consider amendments made by the International Code Council to the International Building Code after May 1, 2003.

(e) A municipality that has adopted a more stringent commercial building code before January 1, 2006, is not required to repeal that code and may adopt future editions of that code.

LGOVT §214.217. NOTICE REGARDING MODEL CODE ADOPTION OR AMENDMENT IN CERTAIN MUNICIPALITIES

(a) In this section, "national model code" means a publication that is developed, promulgated, and periodically updated at a national level by organizations consisting of industry and government fire and building safety officials through a legislative or consensus process and that is intended for consideration by units

of government as local law. National model codes include the International Residential Code, the National Electrical Code, and the International Building Code.

(b) This section applies only to a municipality with a population of more than 100,000.

(c) On or before the 21st day before the date the governing body of a municipality takes action to consider, review, and recommend the adoption of or amendment to a national model code governing the construction, renovation, use, or maintenance of buildings and building systems in the municipality, the governing body shall publish notice of the proposed action conspicuously on the municipality's Internet website.

(d) The governing body of the municipality shall make a reasonable effort to encourage public comment from persons affected by the proposed adoption of or amendment to a national model code under this section.

(e) On the written request from five or more persons, the governing body of the municipality shall hold a public hearing open to public comment on the proposed adoption of or amendment to a national model code under this section. The hearing must be held on or before the 14th day before the date the governing body adopts the ordinance that adopts or amends a national model code under this section.

(f) If the governing body of a municipality has established an advisory board or substantially similar entity for the purpose of obtaining public comment on the proposed adoption of or amendment to a national model code, this section does not apply.

LGOVT §214.218. IMMEDIATE EFFECT OF CERTAIN CODES OR PROVISIONS DELAYED

(a) In this section, "national model code" has the meaning assigned by Section 214.217.

(b) Except as provided by Subsection (c), the governing body of a municipality with a population of more than 100,000 that adopts an ordinance or national model code provision that is intended to govern the construction, renovation, use, or maintenance of buildings and building systems in the municipality shall delay implementing and enforcing the ordinance or code provision for at least 30 days after final adoption to permit persons affected to comply with the ordinance or code provision.

(c) If a delay in implementing or enforcing the ordinance or code provision would cause imminent harm to the health or safety of the public, the municipality may enforce the ordinance or code provision immediately on the effective date of the ordinance or code provision.

LGOVT §214.219. MINIMUM HABITABILITY STANDARDS FOR MULTI-FAMILY RENTAL BUILDINGS IN CERTAIN MUNICIPALITIES

(a) This section applies only to a municipality with a population of 1.7 million or more. This section does not affect the authority of a municipality to which this section does not apply to enact or enforce laws relating to multi-family rental buildings.

(b) In this section:

(1) "Multi-family rental building" means a building that has three or more single-family residential units.

(2) "Unit" means one or more rooms rented for use as a permanent residence under a single lease to one or more tenants.

(c) A municipality shall adopt an ordinance to establish minimum habitability standards for multi-family rental buildings, including requiring maintenance of proper operating conditions.

(d) A municipality may establish other standards as necessary to reduce material risks to the physical health or safety of tenants of multi-family rental buildings.

(e) A municipality shall establish a program for the inspection of multi-family rental buildings to determine if the buildings meet the minimum required habitability standards. The program shall include inspections under the direction of:

(1) the municipality's building official, as defined by the International Building Code or by a local amendment to the code under Section 214.216;

(2) the chief executive of the municipality's fire department; and

(3) the municipality's health authority, as defined by Section 121.021, Health and Safety Code.

(f) A municipality may not order the closure of a multi-family rental building due to a violation of an ordinance adopted by the municipality relating to habitability unless the municipality makes a good faith effort to locate housing with comparable rental rates in the same school district for the residents displaced by the closure.

(g) The owner of a multi-family rental building commits an offense if the owner violates an ordinance adopted under this section. An offense under this subsection is a Class C misdemeanor. Each day the violation continues constitutes a separate offense.

(h) A municipality may impose a civil penalty under Section 54.017 for a violation of this section.

Sections 214.220-214.230 reserved for expansion

SUBCHAPTER H. REGISTRATION OF VACANT BUILDINGS

LGOVT §214.231. DEFINITIONS

In this subchapter:

(1) "Building" means any enclosed structure designed for use as a habitation or for a commercial use, including engaging in trade or manufacture.

(2) "Owner" means the person that owns the real property on which a building is situated, according to:

(A) the real property records of the county in which the property is located; or

(B) the records of the appraisal district in which the property is located.

(3) "Unit" means an enclosed area designed:

(A) for habitation by a single family; or

(B) for a commercial use, including engaging in trade or manufacture, by a tenant.

LGOVT §214.232. PRESUMPTION OF VACANCY

A building is presumed to be vacant under this subchapter if:

(1) all lawful residential, commercial, recreational, charitable, or construction activity at the building has ceased, or reasonably appears to have ceased, for more than 150 days; or

(2) the building contains more than three units, 75 percent or more of which have not been used lawfully, or reasonably appear not to have been used lawfully, for more than 150 days.

LGOVT §214.233. REGISTRATION

(a) A municipality located in a county with a population of two million or more may adopt an ordinance requiring owners of vacant buildings to register their buildings by filing a registration form with a designated municipal official.

(b) A municipality, in an ordinance adopted under this subchapter, may exempt certain classifications of buildings as determined reasonable and appropriate by the governing body of the municipality.

LGOVT §214.234. FORM

An ordinance adopted under this subchapter may require a designated municipal official to adopt a form for registration. The form adopted may require the disclosure of information reasonably necessary for the municipality to minimize the threat to health, safety, and welfare that a vacant building may present to the public.

Sections 214.235-214.300 reserved for expansion

SUBCHAPTER I. EXPIRED

Sections 214.305-214.900 reserved for expansion

SUBCHAPTER Z. MISCELLANEOUS POWERS & DUTIES

LGOVT §214.901. ENERGY CONSERVATION

A home-rule municipality may require that the construction of buildings comply with the energy conservation standards in the municipal building code.

LGOVT §214.902. RENT CONTROL

(a) The governing body of a municipality may, by ordinance, establish rent control if:

(1) the governing body finds that a housing emergency exists due to a disaster as defined by Section 418.004, Government Code; and

(2) the governor approves the ordinance.

(b) The governing body shall continue or discontinue rent control in the same manner that the governor continues or discontinues a state of disaster under Section 418.014, Government Code.

LGOVT §214.903. FAIR HOUSING ORDINANCES

(a) The governing body of a municipality may adopt fair housing ordinances that provide fair housing rights, compliance duties, and remedies that are substantially equivalent to those granted under federal law. Enforcement procedures and remedies in fair housing ordinances may vary from state or federal fair housing law.

(b) Fair housing ordinances that were in existence on January 1, 1991, and are more restrictive than federal fair housing law shall remain in effect.

LGOVT §214.904. TIME FOR ISSUANCE OF MUNICIPAL BUILDING PERMIT

(a) This section applies only to a permit required by a municipality to erect or improve a building or other structure in the municipality or its extraterritorial jurisdiction.

(b) Not later than the 45th day after the date an application for a permit is submitted, the municipality must:

(1) grant or deny the permit;

(2) provide written notice to the applicant stating the reasons why the municipality has been unable to grant or deny the permit application; or

(3) reach a written agreement with the applicant providing for a deadline for granting or denying the permit.

(c) For a permit application for which notice is provided under Subsection (b)(2), the municipality must grant or deny the permit not later than the 30th day after the date the notice is received.

(d) If a municipality fails to grant or deny a permit application in the time required by Subsection (c) or by an agreement under Subsection (b)(3), the municipality:

(1) may not collect any permit fees associated with the application; and

(2) shall refund to the applicant any permit fees associated with the application that have been collected.

LGOVT §214.905. PROHIBITION OF CERTAIN MUNICIPAL REQUIREMENTS REGARDING SALES OF HOUSING UNITS OR RESIDENTIAL LOTS

(a) A municipality may not adopt a requirement in any form, including through an ordinance or regulation or as a condition for granting a building permit, that establishes a maximum sales price for a privately produced housing unit or residential building lot.

(b) This section does not affect any authority of a municipality to:

(1) create or implement an incentive, contract commitment, density bonus, or other voluntary program designed to increase the supply of moderate or lower-cost housing units; or

(2) adopt a requirement applicable to an area served under the provisions of Chapter 373A, Local Government Code, which authorizes homestead preservation districts, if such chapter is created by an act of the legislature.

(c) This section does not apply to a requirement adopted by a municipality for an area as a part of a development agreement entered into before September 1, 2005.

(d) This section does not apply to property that is part of an urban land bank program.

E LGOVT §214.906. REGULATION OF MANUFACTURED HOME COMMUNITIES

(a) "Manufactured home" has the meaning assigned by Section 1201.003, Occupations Code.

(b) Notwithstanding any other law, the governing body of a municipality may not regulate a tract or parcel of land as a manufactured home community, park, or subdivision unless the tract or parcel contains at least four spaces offered for lease for installing and occupying manufactured homes.

2017 Legislation: Enacted by S.B. 1248, §2, 85th Leg., eff. Sept. 1, 2017.

CHAPTER 215. MUNICIPAL REGULATION OF BUSINESSES & OCCUPATIONS

SUBCHAPTER B. REGULATION BY TYPE A GENERAL-LAW MUNICIPALITY

LGOVT §215.024. TANNERIES; STABLES; SLAUGHTERHOUSES; OTHER BUSINESSES

(a) As necessary for the health, comfort, and convenience of the residents of the municipality, the governing body of the municipality may compel the owner or occupant to clean, abate, or remove:

(1) a grocery;

(2) a soap, tallow, or chandler establishment;

(3) a blacksmith shop;

(4) a tannery;

(5) a stable;

(6) a slaughterhouse;

(7) a sewer;

(8) a privy;

(9) a hide house; or

(10) any other unwholesome or nauseous house or place.

(b) The governing body may direct the location of:

(1) businesses;

(2) tanneries;

(3) blacksmith shops;

(4) foundries;

(5) livery stables; and

(6) manufacturing establishments.

(c) Within the limits of a municipality, the governing body may restrain, abate, prohibit, direct the location of, or regulate the management or construction of:

(1) slaughtering establishments;

(2) hide houses;

(3) establishments for making soap;

(4) establishments for steaming or rendering lard, tallow, offal, or any other substances that may be rendered; and

(5) any other establishments or places at which any nauseous, offensive, or unwholesome business may be conducted.

LGOVT §215.025. ANIMAL DRIVES

The governing body of the municipality may prohibit or otherwise regulate the driving of cattle, horses, or other animals in the municipality.

LGOVT §215.026. ANIMALS AT LARGE

(a) The governing body of the municipality may establish and regulate public pounds.

(b) The governing body may prohibit or otherwise regulate the running at large of horses, mules, cattle, sheep, swine, or goats.

(c) If an animal is at large in violation of an ordinance adopted under this section, the governing body may authorize:

(1) the capture and impounding of the animal;

(2) the sale of the animal for the costs of the sale proceedings and any penalties imposed;

(3) the destruction of the animal if the animal cannot be sold; and

(4) the imposition of a penalty on the owner.

LGOVT §215.027. BREEDING ANIMALS

The governing body of the municipality by ordinance may prohibit a person from keeping a jack, bull, or stallion in the municipality for breeding purposes.

LGOVT §215.028. MARKETS

(a) The governing body of the municipality may establish or erect markets or market houses.

(b) The governing body may designate and regulate market places and privileges and may inspect and determine the manner of inspecting meat, fish, vegetables and other produce, and any other article brought for sale at a market.

LGOVT §215.032. EXHIBITIONS; SHOWS; AMUSEMENTS

(a) The governing body of the municipality may license, tax, suppress, prevent, or otherwise regulate keepers of theatrical or other exhibitions, shows, or amusements.

(b) The governing body may license, tax, or otherwise regulate:

(1) theaters;

(2) circuses;

(3) exhibitions of common showmen;

(4) shows of any kind;

(5) exhibitions of natural or artificial curiosities;

(6) caravans;

(7) menageries; and

(8) musical exhibitions or performances.

SUBCHAPTER C. REGULATION BY TYPE B GENERAL-LAW MUNICIPALITY

LGOVT §215.052. MARKETS

The governing body of the municipality may establish markets.

SUBCHAPTER D. REGULATION BY HOME-RULE MUNICIPALITY

LGOVT §215.072. DAIRIES; SLAUGHTERHOUSES

The municipality may inspect dairies, slaughterhouses, or slaughter pens, in or outside the municipal limits, from which milk or meat is furnished to the residents of the municipality.

LGOVT §215.074. THEATERS; SHOWS; AMUSEMENTS

The municipality may regulate the location and conduct of:

(1) theaters;

(2) movie theaters;

(3) bowling alleys; and

(4) other places of public amusements.

LGOVT §215.075. POLICE POWER

The municipality may license any lawful business or occupation that is subject to the police power of the municipality.

CHAPTER 216. REGULATION OF SIGNS BY MUNICIPALITIES

SUBCHAPTER A. RELOCATION, RECONSTRUCTION, OR REMOVAL OF SIGN

LGOVT §216.001. LEGISLATIVE INTENT

(a) This subchapter is not intended to require a municipality to provide for the relocation, reconstruction, or removal of any sign in the municipality, nor is it intended to prohibit a municipality from requiring the relocation, reconstruction, or removal of any sign. This subchapter is intended only to authorize a municipality to take that action and to establish the procedure by which the municipality may do so.

(b) This subchapter is not intended to require a municipality to make a cash payment to compensate the owner of a sign that the municipality requires to be relocated, reconstructed, or removed. Cash payment is established as only one of several methods from which a municipality may choose in compensating the owner of a sign.

(c) This subchapter is not intended to affect any eminent domain proceeding in which the taking of a sign is only an incidental part of the exercise of the eminent domain power.

LGOVT §216.002. DEFINITIONS

In this subchapter:

(1) "Sign" means an outdoor structure, sign, display, light device, figure, painting, drawing, message, plaque, poster, billboard, or other thing that is designed, intended, or used to advertise or inform.

(2) "On-premise sign" means a freestanding sign identifying or advertising a business, person, or activity, and installed and maintained on the same premises as the business, person, or activity.

(3) "Off-premise sign" means a sign displaying advertising copy that pertains to a business, person, organization, activity, event, place, service, or product not principally located or primarily manufactured or sold on the premises on which the sign is located.

LGOVT §216.003. MUNICIPAL REGULATION

(a) Subject to the requirements of this subchapter, a municipality may require the relocation, reconstruction, or removal of any sign within its corporate limits or extraterritorial jurisdiction.

(b) Except as provided by Subsection (e), the owner of a sign that is required to be relocated, reconstructed, or removed is entitled to be compensated by the municipality for costs associated with the relocation, reconstruction, or removal.

(c) If application of a municipal regulation would require reconstruction of a sign in a manner that would make the sign ineffective for its intended purpose, such as by substantially impairing the sign's visibility, application of the regulation is treated as the required removal of the sign for purposes of this subchapter.

(d) In lieu of paying compensation, a municipality may exempt from required relocation, reconstruction, or removal those signs lawfully in place on the effective date of the requirement.

(e) A municipality that exercises authority under this subchapter may, without paying compensation as provided by this subchapter, require the removal of an on-premise sign or sign structure not sooner than the first anniversary of the date the business, person, or activity that the sign or sign structure identifies or advertises ceases to operate on the premises on which the sign or sign structure is located. If the premises containing the sign or sign structure is leased, a municipality may not require removal under this subsection sooner than the second anniversary after the date the most recent tenant ceases to operate on the premises. The removal of a sign or sign structure as described by this subsection does not require the appointment of a board under Section 216.004.

(f) A municipality acting under Subsection (e) may agree with the owner of the sign or sign structure to remove only a portion of the sign or sign structure.

LGOVT §216.0035. REGULATORY AUTHORITY NOT APPLICABLE TO ON-PREMISES SIGNS UNDER CERTAIN CIRCUMSTANCES

The authority granted to a municipality by this subchapter to require the relocation, reconstruction, or removal of signs does not apply to:

(1) on-premises signs in the extraterritorial jurisdiction of municipalities in a county described by Section 394.063, Transportation Code, if the circumstances described by that section occur; and

(2) on-premises signs in a municipality's extraterritorial jurisdiction in a county that borders a county described by that law.

LGOVT §216.004. MUNICIPAL BOARD

(a) If a municipality requires the relocation, reconstruction, or removal of a sign within its corporate limits or extraterritorial jurisdiction, the presiding officer of the governing body of the municipality shall appoint a municipal board on sign control. The board must be composed of:

(1) two real estate appraisers, each of whom must be a member in good standing of a nationally recognized professional appraiser society or trade organization that has an established code of ethics, educational program, and professional certification program;

(2) one person engaged in the sign business in the municipality;

(3) one employee of the Texas Department of Transportation who is familiar with real estate valuations in eminent domain proceedings; and

(4) one architect or landscape architect licensed by this state.

(b) A member of the board is appointed for a term of two years.

LGOVT §216.005. DETERMINATION OF AMOUNT OF COMPENSATION

(a) The municipal board on sign control shall determine the amount of the compensation to which the owner of a sign that is required to be relocated, reconstructed, or removed is entitled. The determination shall be made after the owner of the sign is given the opportunity for a hearing before the board about the issues involved in the matter.

(b) In any court proceeding in which the reasonableness of compensation is at issue and the compensation is to be provided over a period longer than one year, the court shall consider whether the duration of the period is reasonable under the circumstances.

LGOVT §216.006. COMPENSATION FOR RELOCATED SIGN

The compensable costs for a sign that is required to be relocated include the expenses of dismantling the sign, transporting it to another site, and reerecting it. The board shall determine the compensable costs according to the standards applicable in a proceeding under Chapter 21, Property Code. In addition, the municipality shall issue to the owner of the sign an appropriate permit or other authority to operate a substitute sign of the same type at an alternative site of substantially equivalent value. Whether an alternative site is of substantially equivalent value is determined by standards generally accepted in the outdoor advertising industry, including visibility, traffic count, and demographic factors. The municipality shall compensate the owner for any increased operating costs, including increased rent, at the new location. The owner is responsible for designating an alternative site where the erection of the sign would be in compliance with the sign ordinance.

LGOVT §216.007. COMPENSATION FOR RECONSTRUCTED SIGN

The compensable costs for a sign that is required to be reconstructed include expenses of labor and materials and any loss in the value of the sign due to the reconstruction in excess of 15 percent of that value. The board shall determine the compensable costs according to standards applicable in a proceeding under Chapter 21, Property Code.

LGOVT §216.008. COMPENSATION FOR REMOVAL OF OFF-PREMISE SIGN

(a) For an off-premise sign that is required to be removed, the compensable cost is an amount computed by determining the average annual gross revenue received by the owner from the sign during the two years preceding September 1, 1985, or the two years preceding the month in which the removal date of the sign occurs, whichever is less, and by multiplying that amount by three. If the sign has not been in existence for all of either two-year period, the average annual gross revenue for that period, for the purpose of this computation, is an amount computed by dividing 12 by the number of months that the sign has been in existence, and multiplying that result by the total amount of the gross revenue received for the period that the sign has been in existence. However, if the sign did not generate revenue for at least one month preceding September 1, 1985, this computation of compensable costs is to be made using only the average annual gross revenue received during the two years preceding the month in which the removal date of the sign occurs, and by multiplying that amount by three. In determining the amounts under this paragraph, a sign is treated as if it were in existence for the entire month if it was in existence for more than 15 days of the month and is treated as if it were not in existence for any part of the month if it was in existence for 15 or fewer days of the month.

(b) The owner of the real property on which the sign was located is entitled to be compensated for any decrease in the value of the real property. The compensable cost is to be determined by the board according to standards applicable in a proceeding under Chapter 21, Property Code.

LGOVT §216.009. COMPENSATION FOR REMOVAL OF ON-PREMISE SIGN

For an on-premise sign that is required to be removed, the compensable cost is an amount computed by determining a reasonable balance between the original cost of the sign, less depreciation, and the current replacement cost of the sign, less an adjustment for the present age and condition of the sign.

LGOVT §216.010. METHOD OF COMPENSATION

(a) To pay the compensable costs required under this subchapter, the governing body of a municipality may use only a method, or a combination of the methods, prescribed by this section.

(b) If any sign is required to be relocated or reconstructed, or an on-premise sign is required to be removed, the municipality, acting pursuant to the Property Redevelopment and Tax Abatement Act (Chapter 312, Tax Code), may abate municipal property taxes that otherwise would be owed by the owner of the sign. The abated taxes may be on any real or personal property owned by the owner of the sign except residential property. The right to the abatement of taxes is assignable by the holder, and the assignee may use the right to abatement with respect to taxes on any nonresidential property in the same taxing jurisdiction. In a municipality where tax abatement is used to pay compensable costs, the costs include reasonable interest and the abatement period may not exceed five years.

(c) The municipality may allocate to a special fund in the municipal treasury, to be known as the sign abatement and community beautification fund, all or any part of the municipal property taxes paid on signs, on the real property on which the signs are located, or on other real or personal property owned by the owner of the sign. The municipality may make payments from that fund to reimburse compensable costs to owners of signs required to be relocated, reconstructed, or removed.

(d) The municipality may provide for the issuance of sign abatement revenue bonds and use the proceeds to make payments to reimburse costs to the owners of signs within the corporate limits of such municipality that are required to be relocated, reconstructed, or removed.

(e) The municipality may pay compensable costs in cash.

(f) Except as prohibited by federal law, a municipality with a population of more than 1.9 million may pay the compensable costs to the owner of an on-premise sign by allowing the sign to remain in place for a period sufficient to recover the compensable cost of the sign as determined under Section 216.009, based on a determination by the municipal board of the average annual gross revenue as determined under Section 216.008 that would be generated by the sign in its specific location if the sign were used as an off-premise sign rather than an on-premise sign. During the period in which a sign remains in place under this subsection, the owner of the sign shall maintain the sign in compliance with all other regulations applicable to the sign, including structural regulations.

LGOVT §216.011. TAX APPRAISAL OF PROPERTY WITH NONCONFORMING SIGN

For each nonconforming sign, the board shall file with the appropriate property tax appraisal office the board's compensable costs value appraisal of the sign. The appraisal office shall consider the board's appraisal when the office, for property tax purposes, determines the appraised value of the real property to which the sign is attached.

LGOVT §216.012. SPECIAL PROVISIONS FOR SIGNS UNDER SIGN ORDINANCE IN EFFECT ON JUNE 1, 1985

(a) This section applies to compensation for the required relocation, reconstruction, or removal of a sign under a municipal ordinance in effect on June 1, 1985, that provided for compensation to the sign owner under an amortization plan.

(b) For a nonconforming sign erected after September 1, 1985, or for a sign in place on that date that later is made nonconforming by an extension of or strengthening of an ordinance that was in effect on June 1, 1985, and that provided an amortization plan, the amortization period is the entire useful life of the sign. If it has not already done so, the board shall determine the entire useful life of signs by type or category,

such as mono-pole signs, metal signs, and wood signs. The useful life may not be solely determined by the natural life expectancy of a sign.

(c) Compensation for the relocation, reconstruction, or removal of a sign that, on September 1, 1985, was not in compliance with the sign ordinance shall be made in accordance with the applicable procedures of Section 6, Chapter 221, Acts of the 69th Legislature, Regular Session, 1985 (Article 1015o, Vernon's Texas Civil Statutes), and that law is continued in effect for this purpose.

LGOVT §216.013. EXCEPTIONS

(a) The requirements of this subchapter do not apply to a sign that was erected in violation of local ordinances, laws, or regulations applicable at the time of its erection.

(b) The requirements of this subchapter do not apply to a sign that, having been permitted to remain in place as a nonconforming use, is required to be removed by a municipality because the sign, or a substantial part of it, is blown down or otherwise destroyed or dismantled for any purpose other than maintenance operations or for changing the letters, symbols, or other matter on the sign.

(c) For purposes of Subsection (b), a sign or substantial part of it is considered to have been destroyed only if the cost of repairing the sign is more than 60 percent of the cost of erecting a new sign of the same type at the same location.

(d) This subchapter does not limit or restrict the compensation provisions of the highway beautification provisions contained in Chapter 391, Transportation Code.

LGOVT §216.014. APPEAL

(a) Any person aggrieved by a decision of the board may file in district court a verified petition setting forth that the decision is illegal, in whole or in part, and specifying the grounds of the illegality. The petition must be filed within 20 days after the date the decision is rendered by the board.

(b) On the filing of the petition, the court may issue a writ of certiorari directed to the board to review the decision of the board and shall prescribe in the writ the time within which a return must be made, which must be longer than 10 days and may be extended by the court.

(c) The board is not required to return the original papers acted on by it, but it shall be sufficient to return certified or sworn copies of the papers. The return must concisely set forth all other facts as may be pertinent and material to show the grounds of the decision appealed from and must be verified.

(d) The court may reverse or affirm, wholly or partly, or modify the decision brought up for review.

(e) Costs may not be allowed against the board unless it appears to the court that the board acted with gross negligence, in bad faith, or with malice in making the decision appealed from.

LGOVT §216.015. EFFECT OF PARTIAL INVALIDITY

(a) The legislature declares that it would not have enacted the following without the inclusion of Section 216.010(a), to the extent that provision excludes methods of compensation not specifically authorized by that provision:

(1) this subchapter;

(2) Section 216.902;

(3) Article 2, Chapter 221, Acts of the 69th Legislature, Regular Session, 1985 (codified as Chapter 394, Transportation Code); and

(4) the amendments made to Section 3, Property Redevelopment and Tax Abatement Act (codified as Chapter 312, Tax Code) by Article 4, Chapter 221, Acts of the 69th Legislature, Regular Session, 1985.

(b) If that exclusion of alternative methods of compensation is held invalid for any reason by a final judgment of a court of competent jurisdiction, the enactments described by Subsection (a) are void.

Sections 216.016-216.900 reserved for expansion

SUBCHAPTER Z. MISCELLANEOUS PROVISIONS

LGOVT §216.901. REGULATION OF SIGNS BY HOME-RULE MUNICIPALITY

(a) A home-rule municipality may license, regulate, control, or prohibit the erection of signs or billboards by charter or ordinance.

(b) Subsection (a) does not authorize a municipality to regulate the relocation, reconstruction, or removal of a sign in violation of Subchapter A.

LGOVT §216.902. REGULATION OF OUTDOOR SIGNS IN MUNICIPALITY'S EXTRATERRITORIAL JURISDICTION

(a) A municipality may extend the provisions of its outdoor sign regulatory ordinance and enforce the ordinance within its area of extraterritorial jurisdiction as defined by Chapter 42. However, any municipality, in lieu of the regulatory ordinances, may allow the Texas Transportation Commission to regulate outdoor signs in the municipality's extraterritorial jurisdiction by filing a written notice with the commission.

(b) If a municipality extends its outdoor sign ordinance within its area of extraterritorial jurisdiction, the municipal ordinance supersedes the regulations imposed by or adopted under Chapter 394, Transportation Code.

(c) The authority granted to a municipality by this section to extend its outdoor sign ordinance does not apply to:

(1) on-premises signs in the extraterritorial jurisdiction of municipalities in a county described by Section 394.063, Transportation Code, if the circumstances described by that section occur;

(2) on-premises signs in a municipality's extraterritorial jurisdiction in a county that borders a county described by that law; and

(3) on-premises signs in the extraterritorial jurisdiction of a municipality with a population of 1.5 million or more that are located in a county that is adjacent to the county in which the majority of the land of the municipality is located.

LGOVT §216.903. REGULATION OF POLITICAL SIGNS BY MUNICIPALITY

(a) In this section, "private real property" does not include real property subject to an easement or other encumbrance that allows a municipality to use the property for a public purpose.

(b) A municipal charter provision or ordinance that regulates signs may not, for a sign that contains primarily a political message and that is located on private real property with the consent of the property owner:

(1) prohibit the sign from being placed;

(2) require a permit or approval of the municipality or impose a fee for the sign to be placed;

(3) restrict the size of the sign; or

(4) provide for a charge for the removal of a political sign that is greater than the charge for removal of other signs regulated by ordinance.

(c) Subsection (b) does not apply to a sign, including a billboard, that contains primarily a political message on a temporary basis and that is generally available for rent or purchase to carry commercial advertising or other messages that are not primarily political.

(d) Subsection (b) does not apply to a sign that:

(1) has an effective area greater than 36 feet;

(2) is more than eight feet high;

(3) is illuminated; or

(4) has any moving elements.

SUBTITLE B. COUNTY REGULATORY AUTHORITY

CHAPTER 232. COUNTY REGULATION OF SUBDIVISIONS

SUBCHAPTER A. SUBDIVISION PLATTING REQUIREMENTS IN GENERAL

LGOVT §232.001. PLAT REQUIRED

(a) The owner of a tract of land located outside the limits of a municipality must have a plat of the subdivision prepared if the owner divides the tract into two or more parts to lay out:

(1) a subdivision of the tract, including an addition;

(2) lots; or

(3) streets, alleys, squares, parks, or other parts of the tract intended to be dedicated to public use or for the use of purchasers or owners of lots fronting on or adjacent to the streets, alleys, squares, parks, or other parts.

(a-1) A division of a tract under Subsection (a) includes a division regardless of whether it is made by using a metes and bounds description in a deed of conveyance or in a contract for a deed, by using a contract of sale or other executory contract to convey, or by using any other method.

(b) To be recorded, the plat must:

(1) describe the subdivision by metes and bounds;

(2) locate the subdivision with respect to an original corner of the original survey of which it is a part; and

(3) state the dimensions of the subdivision and of each lot, street, alley, square, park, or other part of the tract intended to be dedicated to public use or for the

use of purchasers or owners of lots fronting on or adjacent to the street, alley, square, park, or other part.

(c) The owner or proprietor of the tract or the owner's or proprietor's agent must acknowledge the plat in the manner required for the acknowledgment of deeds.

(d) The plat must be filed and recorded with the county clerk of the county in which the tract is located.

(e) The plat is subject to the filing and recording provisions of Section 12.002, Property Code.

(f) The commissioners court may require a plat application submitted for approval to include a digital map that is compatible with other mapping systems used by the county and that georeferences the subdivision plat and related public infrastructure using the Texas Coordinate Systems adopted under Section 21.071, Natural Resources Code. A digital map required under this subsection may be required only in a format widely used by common geographic information system software. A requirement adopted under this subsection must provide for an exemption from the requirement if the owner of the tract submits with the plat application an acknowledged statement indicating that the digital mapping technology necessary to submit a map that complies with this subsection was not reasonably accessible.

See also *Real Estate Forms*, FORMS 11:1, 11:2.

LGOVT §232.0013. CHAPTER-WIDE PROVISION RELATING TO REGULATION OF PLATS & SUBDIVISIONS IN EXTRATERRITORIAL JURISDICTION

The authority of a county under this chapter relating to the regulation of plats or subdivisions in the extraterritorial jurisdiction of a municipality is subject to any applicable limitation prescribed by an agreement under Section 242.001 or by Section 242.002.

LGOVT §232.0015. EXCEPTIONS TO PLAT REQUIREMENT

(a) To determine whether specific divisions of land are required to be platted, a county may define and classify the divisions. A county need not require platting for every division of land otherwise within the scope of this subchapter.

(b) Except as provided by Section 232.0013, this subchapter does not apply to a subdivision of land to which Subchapter B applies.

(c) A county may not require the owner of a tract of land located outside the limits of a municipality who divides the tract into two or more parts to have a plat of the subdivision prepared if:

(1) the owner does not lay out a part of the tract described by Section 232.001(a)(3); and

(2) the land is to be used primarily for agricultural use, as defined by Section 1-d, Article VIII, Texas Constitution, or for farm, ranch, wildlife management, or timber production use within the meaning of Section 1-d-1, Article VIII, Texas Constitution.

(d) If a tract described by Subsection (c) ceases to be used primarily for agricultural use or for farm, ranch, wildlife management, or timber production use, the platting requirements of this subchapter apply.

(e) A county may not require the owner of a tract of land located outside the limits of a municipality who divides the tract into four or fewer parts and does not lay out a part of the tract described by Section 232.001(a)(3) to have a plat of the subdivision prepared if each of the lots is to be sold, given, or otherwise transferred to an individual who is related to the owner within the third degree by consanguinity or affinity, as determined under Chapter 573, Government Code. If any lot is sold, given, or otherwise transferred to an individual who is not related to the owner within the third degree by consanguinity or affinity, the platting requirements of this subchapter apply.

(f) A county may not require the owner of a tract of land located outside the limits of a municipality who divides the tract into two or more parts to have a plat of the subdivision prepared if:

(1) all of the lots of the subdivision are more than 10 acres in area; and

(2) the owner does not lay out a part of the tract described by Section 232.001(a)(3).

(g) A county may not require the owner of a tract of land located outside the limits of a municipality who divides the tract into two or more parts and does not lay out a part of the tract described by Section 232.001(a)(3) to have a plat of the subdivision prepared if all the lots are sold to veterans through the Veterans' Land Board program.

(h) The provisions of this subchapter shall not apply to a subdivision of any tract of land belonging to the state or any state agency, board, or commission or owned by the permanent school fund or any other dedicated funds of the state unless the subdivision lays out a part of the tract described by Section 232.001(a)(3).

(i) A county may not require the owner of a tract of land located outside the limits of a municipality who divides the tract into two or more parts to have a plat of the subdivision prepared if:

(1) the owner of the land is a political subdivision of the state;

(2) the land is situated in a floodplain; and

(3) the lots are sold to adjoining landowners.

(j) A county may not require the owner of a tract of land located outside the limits of a municipality who divides the tract into two parts to have a plat of the subdivision prepared if:

(1) the owner does not lay out a part of the tract described by Section 232.001(a)(3); and

(2) one new part is to be retained by the owner, and the other new part is to be transferred to another person who will further subdivide the tract subject to the plat approval requirements of this chapter.

(k) A county may not require the owner of a tract of land located outside the limits of a municipality who divides the tract into two or more parts to have a plat of the subdivision prepared if:

(1) the owner does not lay out a part of the tract described by Section 232.001(a)(3); and

(2) all parts are transferred to persons who owned an undivided interest in the original tract and a plat is filed before any further development of any part of the tract.

LGOVT §232.002. APPROVAL BY COUNTY REQUIRED

(a) The commissioners court of the county in which the land is located must approve, by an order entered in the minutes of the court, a plat required by Section 232.001. The commissioners court may refuse to approve a plat if it does not meet the requirements prescribed by or under this chapter or if any bond required under this chapter is not filed with the county.

(b) The commissioners court may not approve a plat unless the plat and other documents have been prepared as required by Section 232.0035, if applicable.

(c) If no portion of the land subdivided under a plat approved under this section is sold or transferred before January 1 of the 51st year after the year in which the plat was approved, the approval of the plat expires, and the owner must resubmit a plat of the subdivision for approval. A plat resubmitted for approval under this subsection is subject to the requirements prescribed by this chapter at the time the plat is resubmitted.

LGOVT §232.0021. PLAT APPLICATION FEE

(a) The commissioners court may impose an application fee to cover the cost of the county's review of a subdivision plat and inspection of street, road, and drainage improvements described by the plat.

(b) The fee may vary based on the number of proposed lots in the subdivision, the acreage described by the plat, the type or extent of proposed street and drainage improvements, or any other reasonable criteria as determined by the commissioners court.

(c) The owner of the tract to be subdivided must pay the fee at the time directed by the county before the county conducts a review of the plat.

(d) The fee is subject to refund under Section 232.0025(i).

LGOVT §232.0025. TIMELY APPROVAL OF PLATS

(a) The commissioners court of a county or a person designated by the commissioners court shall issue a written list of the documentation and other information that must be submitted with a plat application. The documentation or other information must relate to a requirement authorized under this section or other applicable law. An application submitted to the commissioners court or the person designated by the commissioners court that contains the documents and other information on the list is considered complete.

(b) If a person submits a plat application to the commissioners court that does not include all of the documentation or other information required by Subsection (a), the commissioners court or the court's designee shall, not later than the 10th business day after the date the commissioners court receives the application, notify the applicant of the missing documents or other information. The commissioners court shall allow an applicant to timely submit the missing documents or other information.

(c) An application is considered complete when all documentation or other information required by Subsection (a) is received. Acceptance by the commissioners court or the court's designee of a completed plat application with the documentation or other information required by Subsection (a) shall not be construed as approval of the documentation or other information.

(d) Except as provided by Subsection (f), the commissioners court or the court's designee shall take final action on a plat application, including the resolution of all appeals, not later than the 60th day after the date a completed plat application is received by the commissioners court or the court's designee.

(e) If the commissioners court or the court's designee disapproves a plat application, the applicant shall be given a complete list of the reasons for the disapproval.

(f) The 60-day period under Subsection (d):

(1) may be extended for a reasonable period, if agreed to in writing by the applicant and approved by the commissioners court or the court's designee;

(2) may be extended 60 additional days if Chapter 2007, Government Code, requires the county to perform a takings impact assessment in connection with a plat application; and

(3) applies only to a decision wholly within the control of the commissioners court or the court's designee.

(g) The commissioners court or the court's designee shall make the determination under Subsection (f)(2) of whether the 60-day period will be extended not later than the 20th day after the date a completed plat application is received by the commissioners court or the court's designee.

(h) The commissioners court or the court's designee may not compel an applicant to waive the time limits contained in this section.

(i) If the commissioners court or the court's designee fails to take final action on the plat as required by Subsection (d):

(1) the commissioners court shall refund the greater of the unexpended portion of any plat application fee or deposit or 50 percent of a plat application fee or deposit that has been paid;

(2) the plat application is granted by operation of law; and

(3) the applicant may apply to a district court in the county where the tract of land is located for a writ of mandamus to compel the commissioners court to issue documents recognizing the plat's approval.

LGOVT §232.003. SUBDIVISION REQUIREMENTS

By an order adopted and entered in the minutes of the commissioners court, and after a notice is published in a newspaper of general circulation in the county, the commissioners court may:

(1) require a right-of-way on a street or road that functions as a main artery in a subdivision, of a width of not less than 50 feet or more than 100 feet;

(2) require a right-of-way on any other street or road in a subdivision of not less than 40 feet or more than 70 feet;

(3) require that the shoulder-to-shoulder width on collectors or main arteries within the right-of-way be not less than 32 feet or more than 56 feet, and that the shoulder-to-shoulder width on any other street or road be not less than 25 feet or more than 35 feet;

(4) adopt, based on the amount and kind of travel over each street or road in a subdivision, reasonable specifications relating to the construction of each street or road;

(5) adopt reasonable specifications to provide adequate drainage for each street or road in a subdivision in accordance with standard engineering practices;

(6) require that each purchase contract made between a subdivider and a purchaser of land in the subdivision contain a statement describing the extent to which water will be made available to the subdivision and, if it will be made available, how and when;

(7) require that the owner of the tract to be subdivided execute a good and sufficient bond in the manner provided by Section 232.004;

(8) adopt reasonable specifications that provide for drainage in the subdivision to:

(A) efficiently manage the flow of stormwater runoff in the subdivision; and

(B) coordinate subdivision drainage with the general storm drainage pattern for the area; and

(9) require lot and block monumentation to be set by a registered professional surveyor before recordation of the plat.

LGOVT §232.0031. STANDARD FOR ROADS IN SUBDIVISION

A county may not impose under Section 232.003 a higher standard for streets or roads in a subdivision than the county imposes on itself for the construction of streets or roads with a similar type and amount of traffic.

LGOVT §232.0032. ADDITIONAL REQUIREMENTS: USE OF GROUNDWATER

(a) If a person submits a plat for the subdivision of a tract of land for which the source of the water supply

intended for the subdivision is groundwater under that land, the commissioners court of a county by order may require the plat application to have attached to it a statement that:

(1) is prepared by an engineer licensed to practice in this state or a geoscientist licensed to practice in this state; and

(2) certifies that adequate groundwater is available for the subdivision.

(b) The Texas Commission on Environmental Quality by rule shall establish the appropriate form and content of a certification to be attached to a plat application under this section.

(c) The Texas Commission on Environmental Quality, in consultation with the Texas Water Development Board, by rule shall require a person who submits a plat under Subsection (a) to transmit to the Texas Water Development Board and any groundwater conservation district that includes in the district's boundaries any part of the subdivision information that would be useful in:

(1) performing groundwater conservation district activities;

(2) conducting regional water planning;

(3) maintaining the state's groundwater database; or

(4) conducting studies for the state related to groundwater.

LGOVT §232.0033. ADDITIONAL REQUIREMENTS: FUTURE TRANSPORTATION CORRIDORS

(a) This section applies to each county in the state. The requirements provided by this section are in addition to the other requirements of this chapter.

(b) If all or part of a subdivision for which a plat is required under this chapter is located within a future transportation corridor identified in an agreement under Section 201.619, Transportation Code:

(1) the commissioners court of a county in which the land is located:

(A) may refuse to approve the plat for recordation unless the plat states that the subdivision is located within the area of the alignment of a transportation project as shown in the final environmental decision document that is applicable to the future transportation corridor; and

(B) may refuse to approve the plat for recordation if all or part of the subdivision is located within the area of the alignment of a transportation project as shown in the final environmental decision document that is applicable to the future transportation corridor; and

(2) each purchase contract or lease between the subdivider and a purchaser or lessee of land in the subdivision must contain a conspicuous statement that the land is located within the area of the alignment of a transportation project as shown in the final environmental decision document that is applicable to the future transportation corridor.

LGOVT §232.0034. ADDITIONAL REQUIREMENTS: ACCESS BY EMERGENCY VEHICLES

(a) This section applies only to a residential subdivision that is subdivided into 1,000 or more lots in the unincorporated area of a county.

(b) The commissioners court shall adopt infrastructure standards requiring at least two means of ingress and egress in the subdivision to provide for sufficient routes of travel for use by emergency vehicles and for use during evacuations resulting from fire or other natural disasters.

(c) This section does not limit the authority of a commissioners court under other existing laws, as applicable, to adopt infrastructure standards that are more stringent than standards required by this section.

LGOVT §§232.0035, 232.0036. REPEALED

LGOVT §232.004. BOND REQUIREMENTS

If the commissioners court requires the owner of the tract to execute a bond, the owner must do so before subdividing the tract unless an alternative financial guarantee is provided under Section 232.0045. The bond must:

(1) be payable to the county judge of the county in which the subdivision will be located or to the judge's successors in office;

(2) be in an amount determined by the commissioners court to be adequate to ensure proper construction of the roads and streets in and drainage requirements for the subdivision, but not to exceed the estimated cost of construction of the roads, streets, and drainage requirements;

(3) be executed with sureties as may be approved by the court;

(4) be executed by a company authorized to do business as a surety in this state if the court requires a surety bond executed by a corporate surety; and

(5) be conditioned that the roads and streets and the drainage requirements for the subdivision will be constructed:

(A) in accordance with the specifications adopted by the court; and

(B) within a reasonable time set by the court.

LGOVT §232.0045. FINANCIAL GUARANTEE IN LIEU OF BOND

(a) In lieu of the bond an owner may deposit cash, a letter of credit issued by a federally insured financial institution, or other acceptable financial guarantee.

(b) If a letter of credit is used, it must:

(1) list as the sole beneficiary the county judge of the county in which the subdivision is located; and

(2) be conditioned that the owner of the tract of land to be subdivided will construct any roads or streets in the subdivision:

(A) in accordance with the specifications adopted by the commissioners court; and

(B) within a reasonable time set by the court.

LGOVT §§232.0046, 232.0047. REPEALED

LGOVT §232.0048. CONFLICT OF INTEREST; PENALTY

(a) In this section, "subdivided tract" means a tract of land, as a whole, that is subdivided. The term does not mean an individual lot in a subdivided tract of land.

(b) A person has a substantial interest in a subdivided tract if the person:

(1) has an equitable or legal ownership interest in the tract with a fair market value of $2,500 or more;

(2) acts as a developer of the tract;

(3) owns 10 percent or more of the voting stock or shares of or owns either 10 percent or more or $5,000 or more of the fair market value of a business entity that:

(A) has an equitable or legal ownership interest in the tract with a fair market value of $2,500 or more; or

(B) acts as a developer of the tract; or

(4) receives in a calendar year funds from a business entity described by Subdivision (3) that exceed 10 percent of the person's gross income for the previous year.

(c) A person also is considered to have a substantial interest in a subdivided tract if the person is related in the first degree by consanguinity or affinity, as determined under Chapter 573, Government Code, to another person who, under Subsection (b), has a substantial interest in the tract.

(d) If a member of the commissioners court of a county has a substantial interest in a subdivided tract, the member shall file, before a vote or decision regarding the approval of a plat for the tract, an affidavit stating the nature and extent of the interest and shall abstain from further participation in the matter. The affidavit must be filed with the county clerk.

(e) A member of the commissioners court of a county commits an offense if the member violates Subsection (d). An offense under this subsection is a Class A misdemeanor.

(f) The finding by a court of a violation of this section does not render voidable an action of the commissioners court unless the measure would not have passed the commissioners court without the vote of the member who violated this section.

LGOVT §232.0049. REPEALED

LGOVT §232.005. ENFORCEMENT IN GENERAL; PENALTY

(a) At the request of the commissioners court, the county attorney or other prosecuting attorney for the county may file an action in a court of competent jurisdiction to:

(1) enjoin the violation or threatened violation of a requirement established by, or adopted by the commissioners court under a preceding section of this chapter; or

(2) recover damages in an amount adequate for the county to undertake any construction or other activity necessary to bring about compliance with a requirement established by, or adopted by the commissioners court under a preceding section of this chapter.

(b) A person commits an offense if the person knowingly or intentionally violates a requirement established by, or adopted by the commissioners court under a preceding section of this chapter. An offense under this subsection is a Class B misdemeanor. This subsection does not apply to a violation for which a criminal penalty is prescribed by Section 232.0048.

(c) A requirement that was established by or adopted under Chapter 436, Acts of the 55th Legislature,

Regular Session, 1957 (Article 6626a, Vernon's Texas Civil Statutes), or Chapter 151, Acts of the 52nd Legislature, Regular Session, 1951 (Article 2372k, Vernon's Texas Civil Statutes), before September 1, 1983, and that, after that date, continues to apply to a subdivision of land is enforceable under Subsection (a). A knowing or intentional violation of the requirement is an offense under Subsection (b).

LGOVT §232.006. EXCEPTIONS FOR POPULOUS COUNTIES OR CONTIGUOUS COUNTIES

(a) This section applies to a county:

(1) that has a population of more than 3.3 million or is contiguous with a county that has a population of more than 3.3 million; and

(2) in which the commissioners court by order elects to operate under this section.

(b) If a county elects to operate under this section, Section 232.005 does not apply to the county. The sections of this chapter preceding Section 232.005 do apply to the county in the same manner that they apply to other counties except that:

(1) they apply only to tracts of land located outside municipalities and the extraterritorial jurisdiction of municipalities, as determined under Chapter 42;

(2) the commissioners court of the county, instead of having the powers granted by Sections 232.003(2) and (3), may:

(A) require a right-of-way on a street or road that does not function as a main artery in the subdivision of not less than 40 feet or more than 50 feet; and

(B) require that the street cut on a main artery within the right-of-way be not less than 30 feet or more than 45 feet, and that the street cut on any other street or road within the right-of-way be not less than 25 feet or more than 35 feet; and

(3) Section 232.004(5)(B) does not apply to the county.

LGOVT §232.007. MANUFACTURED HOME RENTAL COMMUNITIES

(a) In this section:

(1) "Manufactured home rental community" means a plot or tract of land that is separated into two or more spaces or lots that are rented, leased, or offered for rent or lease, for a term of less than 60 months without a purchase option, for the installation of manufactured homes for use and occupancy as residences.

(2) "Business day" means a day other than a Saturday, Sunday, or holiday recognized by this state.

(b) A manufactured home rental community is not a subdivision, and Sections 232.001-232.006 do not apply to the community.

(c) After a public hearing and after notice is published in a newspaper of general circulation in the county, the commissioners court of a county, by order adopted and entered in the minutes of the commissioners court, may establish minimum infrastructure standards for manufactured home rental communities located in the county outside the limits of a municipality. The minimum standards may include only:

(1) reasonable specifications to provide adequate drainage in accordance with standard engineering practices, including specifying necessary drainage culverts and identifying areas included in the 100-year flood plain;

(2) reasonable specifications for providing an adequate public or community water supply, including specifying the location of supply lines, in accordance with Subchapter C, Chapter 341, Health and Safety Code;

(3) reasonable requirements for providing access to sanitary sewer lines, including specifying the location of sanitary sewer lines, or providing adequate on-site sewage facilities in accordance with Chapter 366, Health and Safety Code;

(4) a requirement for the preparation of a survey identifying the proposed manufactured home rental community boundaries and any significant features of the community, including the proposed location of manufactured home rental community spaces, utility easements, and dedications of rights-of-way; and

(5) reasonable specifications for streets or roads in the manufactured rental home community to provide ingress and egress access for fire and emergency vehicles.

(d) The commissioners court may not adopt minimum infrastructure standards that are more stringent than requirements adopted by the commissioners court for subdivisions. The commissioners court may only adopt minimum infrastructure standards for ingress and egress access by fire and emergency vehicles that are reasonably necessary.

(e) If the commissioners court adopts minimum infrastructure standards for manufactured home rental

communities, the owner of land located outside the limits of a municipality who intends to use the land for a manufactured home rental community must have an infrastructure development plan prepared that complies with the minimum infrastructure standards adopted by the commissioners court under Subsection (c).

(f) Not later than the 60th day after the date the owner of a proposed manufactured home rental community submits an infrastructure development plan for approval, the county engineer or another person designated by the commissioners court shall approve or reject the plan in writing. If the plan is rejected, the written rejection must specify the reasons for the rejection and the actions required for approval of the plan. The failure to reject a plan within the period prescribed by this subsection constitutes approval of the plan.

(g) Construction of a proposed manufactured home rental community may not begin before the date the county engineer or another person designated by the commissioners court approves the infrastructure development plan. The commissioners court may require inspection of the infrastructure during or on completion of its construction. If a final inspection is required, the final inspection must be completed not later than the second business day after the date the commissioners court or the person designated by the commissioners court receives a written confirmation from the owner that the construction of the infrastructure is complete. If the inspector determines that the infrastructure complies with the infrastructure development plan, the commissioners court shall issue a certificate of compliance not later than the fifth business day after the date the final inspection is completed. If a final inspection is not required, the commissioners court shall issue a certificate of compliance not later than the fifth business day after the date the commissioners court or the person designated by the commissioners court receives written certification from the owner that construction of the infrastructure has been completed in compliance with the infrastructure development plan.

(h) A utility may not provide utility services, including water, sewer, gas, and electric services, to a manufactured home rental community subject to an infrastructure development plan or to a manufactured home in the community unless the owner provides the utility with a copy of the certificate of compliance issued under Subsection (g). This subsection applies only to:

(1) a municipality that provides utility services;

(2) a municipally owned or municipally operated utility that provides utility services;

(3) a public utility that provides utility services;

(4) a nonprofit water supply or sewer service corporation organized and operating under Chapter 67, Water Code, that provides utility services;

(5) a county that provides utility services; and

(6) a special district or authority created by state law that provides utility services.

LGOVT §232.008. CANCELLATION OF SUBDIVISION

(a) This section applies only to real property located outside municipalities and the extraterritorial jurisdiction of municipalities, as determined under Chapter 42.

(b) A person owning real property in this state that has been subdivided into lots and blocks or into small subdivisions may apply to the commissioners court of the county in which the property is located for permission to cancel all or part of the subdivision, including a dedicated easement or roadway, to reestablish the property as acreage tracts as it existed before the subdivision. If, on the application, it is shown that the cancellation of all or part of the subdivision does not interfere with the established rights of any purchaser who owns any part of the subdivision, or it is shown that the purchaser agrees to the cancellation, the commissioners court by order shall authorize the owner of the subdivision to file an instrument canceling the subdivision in whole or in part. The instrument must describe the subdivision or the part of it that is canceled. The court shall enter the order in its minutes. After the cancellation instrument is filed and recorded in the deed records of the county, the county tax assessor-collector shall assess the property as if it had never been subdivided.

(c) The commissioners court shall publish notice of an application for cancellation. The notice must be published in a newspaper, published in the English language, in the county for at least three weeks before the date on which action is taken on the application. The court shall take action on an application at a regular term. The published notice must direct any person who is interested in the property and who wishes to protest the proposed cancellation to appear at the time specified in the notice.

(d) If delinquent taxes are owed on the subdivided tract for any preceding year, and if the application to cancel the subdivision is granted as provided by this section, the owner of the tract may pay the delinquent taxes on an acreage basis as if the tract had not been subdivided. For the purpose of assessing the tract for a preceding year, the county tax assessor-collector shall back assess the tract on an acreage basis.

(e) On application for cancellation of a subdivision or any phase or identifiable part of a subdivision, including a dedicated easement or roadway, by the owners of 75 percent of the property included in the subdivision, phase, or identifiable part, the commissioners court by order shall authorize the cancellation in the manner and after notice and a hearing as provided by Subsections (b) and (c). However, if the owners of at least 10 percent of the property affected by the proposed cancellation file written objections to the cancellation with the court, the grant of an order of cancellation is at the discretion of the court.

(f) To maintain an action to enjoin the cancellation or closing of a roadway or easement in a subdivision, a person must own a lot or part of the subdivision that:

(1) abuts directly on the part of the roadway or easement to be canceled or closed; or

(2) is connected by the part of the roadway or easement to be canceled or closed, by the most direct feasible route, to:

(A) the nearest remaining public highway, county road, or access road to the public highway or county road; or

(B) any uncanceled common amenity of the subdivision.

(g) A person who appears before the commissioners court to protest the cancellation of all or part of a subdivision may maintain an action for damages against the person applying for the cancellation and may recover as damages an amount not to exceed the amount of the person's original purchase price for property in the canceled subdivision or part of the subdivision. The person must bring the action within one year after the date of the entry of the commissioners court's order granting the cancellation.

(h) Regardless of the date land is subdivided or a plat is filed for a subdivision, the commissioners court may deny a cancellation under this section if the commissioners court determines the cancellation will prevent the proposed interconnection of infrastructure to pending or existing development as defined by Section 232.0085.

LGOVT §232.0083. CANCELLATION OF CERTAIN SUBDIVISION PLATS IF EXISTING PLAT OBSOLETE

(a) This section applies only to a subdivision for which:

(1) a plat has been filed for 75 years or more;

(2) the most recent plat describes at least a portion of the property as acreage tracts;

(3) a previous plat described at least a portion of the property as lots and blocks; and

(4) the county tax assessor-collector lists the property in the subdivision on the tax rolls based on the description in the previous plat and assesses taxes on the basis of that description.

(b) A person owning real property in the subdivision may apply to the commissioners court of the county in which the property is located for permission to cancel an existing subdivision plat in whole or part and to reestablish the property using lots and blocks descriptions that, to the extent practicable, are consistent with the previous subdivision plat.

(c) After notice and hearing, the commissioners court may order the cancellation of the existing subdivision plat and the reestablishment of the property in accordance with the application submitted under Subsection (b) if the court finds that:

(1) the cancellation and reestablishment does not interfere with the established rights of:

(A) any owner of a part of the subdivision; or

(B) a utility company with a right to use a public easement in the subdivision; or

(2) each owner or utility whose rights may be interfered with has agreed to the cancellation and reestablishment.

(d) The commissioners court shall publish notice of an application for the cancellation and reestablishment. The notice must be published at least three weeks before the date on which action is taken on the application and must direct any person who is interested in the property and who wishes to protest the proposed cancellation and reestablishment to appear at the time specified in the notice. The notice must be published in a newspaper that has general circulation in the county.

(e) If the commissioners court authorizes the cancellation and reestablishment, the court by order shall authorize the person making the application under this section to record an instrument showing the cancellation and reestablishment. The court shall enter the order in its minutes.

LGOVT §232.0085. CANCELLATION OF CERTAIN SUBDIVISIONS IF LAND REMAINS UNDEVELOPED

(a) This section applies only to real property located:

(1) outside municipalities and the extraterritorial jurisdiction of municipalities, as determined under Chapter 42; and

(2) in an affected county, as defined by Section 16.341, Water Code, that has adopted the model rules developed under Section 16.343, Water Code, and is located along an international border.

(b) The commissioners court of a county may cancel, after notice and a hearing as required by this section, a subdivision for which the plat was filed and approved before September 1, 1989, if:

(1) the development of or the making of improvements in the subdivision was not begun before the effective date of this section; and

(2) the commissioners court by resolution has made a finding that the land in question is likely to be developed as a colonia.

(c) The commissioners court must publish notice of a proposal to cancel a subdivision under this section and the time and place of the required hearing in a newspaper of general circulation in the county for at least 21 days immediately before the date a cancellation order is adopted under this section. The county tax assessor-collector shall, not later than the 14th day before the date of the hearing, deposit with the United States Postal Service a similar notice addressed to each owner of land in the subdivision, as determined by the most recent county tax roll.

(d) At the hearing, the commissioners court shall permit any interested person to be heard. At the conclusion of the hearing, the court shall adopt an order on whether to cancel the subdivision. The commissioners court may adopt an order canceling a subdivision if the court determines the cancellation is in the best interest of the public. The court may not adopt an order canceling a subdivision if:

(1) the cancellation interferes with the established rights of a person who is a nondeveloper owner and owns any part of the subdivision, unless the person agrees to the cancellation; or

(2) the owner of the entire subdivision is able to show that:

(A) the owner of the subdivision is able to comply with the minimum state standards and model political subdivision rules developed under Section 16.343, Water Code, including any bonding requirements; or

(B) the land was developed or improved within the period described by Subsection (b).

(e) The commissioners court shall file the cancellation order for recording in the deed records of the county. After the cancellation order is filed and recorded, the property shall be treated as if it had never been subdivided, and the county chief appraiser shall assess the property accordingly. Any liens against the property shall remain against the property as it was previously subdivided.

(f) In this section:

(1) "Development" means the making, installing, or constructing of buildings and improvements.

(2) "Improvements" means water supply, treatment, and distribution facilities; wastewater collection and treatment facilities; and other utility facilities. The term does not include roadway facilities.

LGOVT §232.009. REVISION OF PLAT

(a) This section applies only to real property located outside municipalities and the extraterritorial jurisdiction of municipalities with a population of 1.5 million or more, as determined under Chapter 42.

(b) A person who owns real property in a tract that has been subdivided and that is subject to the subdivision controls of the county in which the property is located may apply in writing to the commissioners court of the county for permission to revise the subdivision plat that applies to the property and that is filed for record with the county clerk.

(c) Except as provided by Subsection (c-1), after the application is filed with the commissioners court, the court shall publish a notice of the application in a newspaper of general circulation in the county. The notice must include a statement of the time and place at which the court will meet to consider the application and to hear protests to the revision of the plat. The no-

tice must be published at least three times during the period that begins on the 30th day and ends on the seventh day before the date of the meeting. Except as provided by Subsection (f), if all or part of the subdivided tract has been sold to nondeveloper owners, the court shall also give notice to each of those owners by certified or registered mail, return receipt requested, at the owner's address in the subdivided tract.

(c-1) If the commissioners court determines that the revision to the subdivision plat does not affect a public interest or public property of any type, including, but not limited to, a park, school, or road, the notice requirements under Subsection (c) do not apply to the application and the commissioners court shall:

(1) provide written notice of the application to the owners of the lots that are within 200 feet of the subdivision plat to be revised, as indicated in the most recent records of the central appraisal district of the county in which the lots are located; and

(2) if the county maintains an Internet website, post notice of the application continuously on the website for at least 30 days preceding the date of the meeting to consider the application until the day after the meeting.

(d) During a regular term of the commissioners court, the court shall adopt an order to permit the revision of the subdivision plat if it is shown to the court that:

(1) the revision will not interfere with the established rights of any owner of a part of the subdivided land; or

(2) each owner whose rights may be interfered with has agreed to the revision.

(e) If the commissioners court permits a person to revise a subdivision plat, the person may make the revision by filing for record with the county clerk a revised plat or part of a plat that indicates the changes made to the original plat.

(f) The commissioners court is not required to give notice by mail under Subsection (c) if the plat revision only combines existing tracts.

(g) The commissioners court may impose a fee for filing an application under this section. The amount of the fee must be based on the cost of processing the application, including publishing the notices required under Subsection (c) or (c-1).

LGOVT §232.0095. ALTERNATIVE PROCEDURES FOR PLAT REVISION

(a) This section applies only to real property located outside municipalities and outside the extraterritorial jurisdiction, as determined under Chapter 42, of municipalities with a population of 1.5 million or more.

(b) As an alternative to the provisions in Section 232.009 governing the revision of plats, a county by order may adopt the provisions in Sections 212.013, 212.014, 212.015, and 212.016 governing plat vacations, replatting, and plat amendment. A county that adopts the provisions in those sections may approve a plat vacation, a replat, and an amending plat in the same manner and under the same conditions, including the notice and hearing requirements, as a municipal authority responsible for approving plats under those sections.

(c) Instead of the purpose described by Section 212.016(a)(10), an amended plat may be approved and issued by the county to make necessary changes to the preceding plat to create six or fewer lots in the subdivision or a part of the subdivision covered by the preceding plat if:

(1) the changes do not affect applicable county regulations, including zoning regulations if the county has authority to adopt zoning regulations; and

(2) the changes do not attempt to amend or remove any covenants or restrictions.

LGOVT §232.010. EXCEPTION TO PLAT REQUIREMENT: COUNTY DETERMINATION

A commissioners court of the county may allow conveyance of portions of one or more previously platted lots by metes and bounds description without revising the plat.

LGOVT §232.011. AMENDING PLAT

(a) The commissioners court may approve and issue an amending plat, if the amending plat is signed by the applicants and filed for one or more of the following purposes:

(1) to correct an error in a course or distance shown on the preceding plat;

(2) to add a course or distance that was omitted on the preceding plat;

(3) to correct an error in a real property description shown on the preceding plat;

(4) to show the location or character of a monument that has been changed in location or character or that is shown incorrectly as to location or character on the preceding plat;

(5) to correct any other type of scrivener or clerical error or omission of the previously approved plat, including lot numbers, acreage, street names, and identification of adjacent recorded plats; or

(6) to correct an error in courses and distances of lot lines between two adjacent lots if:

(A) both lot owners join in the application for amending the plat;

(B) neither lot is abolished;

(C) the amendment does not attempt to remove recorded covenants or restrictions; and

(D) the amendment does not have a material adverse effect on the property rights of the other owners of the property that is the subject of the plat.

(b) The amending plat controls over the preceding plat without the vacation, revision, or cancellation of the preceding plat.

(c) Notice, a hearing, and the approval of other lot owners are not required for the filing, recording, or approval of an amending plat.

Sections 232.012-232.020 blank

SUBCHAPTER B. SUBDIVISION PLATTING REQUIREMENTS IN COUNTY NEAR INTERNATIONAL BORDER

LGOVT §232.021. DEFINITIONS

In this subchapter:

(1) "Board" means the Texas Water Development Board.

(2) "Common promotional plan" means any plan or scheme of operation undertaken by a single subdivider or a group of subdividers acting in concert, either personally or through an agent, to offer for sale or lease lots when the land is:

(A) contiguous or part of the same area of land; or

(B) known, designated, or advertised as a common unit or by a common name.

(3) "Executive administrator" means the executive administrator of the Texas Water Development Board.

(4) "Floodplain" means any area in the 100-year floodplain that is susceptible to being inundated by water from any source or that is identified by the Federal Emergency Management Agency under the National Flood Insurance Act of 1968 (42 U.S.C. Sections 4001 through 4127).

(5) "Lease" includes an offer to lease.

(6) "Lot" means a parcel into which land that is intended for residential use is divided.

(6-a) "Lot of record" means:

(A) a lot, the boundaries of which were established by a plat recorded in the office of the county clerk before September 1, 1989, that has not been subdivided after September 1, 1989; or

(B) a lot, the boundaries of which were established by a metes and bounds description in a deed of conveyance, a contract of sale, or other executory contract to convey real property that has been legally executed and recorded in the office of the county clerk before September 1, 1989, that has not been subdivided after September 1, 1989.

(7) "Minimum state standards" means the minimum standards set out for:

(A) adequate drinking water by or under Section 16.343(b)(1), Water Code;

(B) adequate sewer facilities by or under Section 16.343(c)(1), Water Code; or

(C) the treatment, disposal, and management of solid waste by or under Chapters 361 and 364, Health and Safety Code.

(8) "Plat" means a map, chart, survey, plan, or replat containing a description of the subdivided land with ties to permanent landmarks or monuments.

(9) "Sell" includes an offer to sell.

(10) "Sewer," "sewer services," or "sewer facilities" means treatment works as defined by Section 17.001, Water Code, or individual, on-site, or cluster treatment systems such as septic tanks and includes drainage facilities and other improvements for proper functioning of septic tank systems.

(11) "Subdivide" means to divide the surface area of land into lots intended primarily for residential use.

(12) "Subdivider" means an individual, firm, corporation, or other legal entity that directly or indirectly subdivides land into lots for sale or lease as part of a common promotional plan in the ordinary course of business.

(13) "Subdivision" means an area of land that has been subdivided into lots for sale or lease.

(14) "Utility" means a person, including a legal entity or political subdivision, that provides the services of:

(A) an electric utility, as defined by Section 31.002, Utilities Code;

(B) a gas utility, as defined by Section 101.003, Utilities Code; and

(C) a water and sewer utility, as defined by Section 13.002, Water Code.

LGOVT §232.022. APPLICABILITY

(a) This subchapter applies only to:

(1) a county any part of which is located within 50 miles of an international border; or

(2) a county:

(A) any part of which is located within 100 miles of an international border;

(B) that contains the majority of the area of a municipality with a population of more than 250,000; and

(C) to which Subdivision (1) does not apply.

(b) This subchapter applies only to land that is subdivided into two or more lots that are intended primarily for residential use in the jurisdiction of the county. A lot is presumed to be intended for residential use if the lot is five acres or less. This subchapter does not apply if the subdivision is incident to the conveyance of the land as a gift between persons related to each other within the third degree by affinity or consanguinity, as determined under Chapter 573, Government Code.

(c) Except as provided by Subsection (c-1), for purposes of this section, land is considered to be in the jurisdiction of a county if the land is located in the county and outside the corporate limits of municipalities.

(c-1) Land in a municipality's extraterritorial jurisdiction is not considered to be in the jurisdiction of a county for purposes of this section if the municipality and the county have entered into a written agreement under Section 242.001 that authorizes the municipality to regulate subdivision plats and approve related permits in the municipality's extraterritorial jurisdiction.

(d) This subchapter does not apply if all of the lots of the subdivision are more than 10 acres.

LGOVT §232.023. PLAT REQUIRED

(a) A subdivider of land must have a plat of the subdivision prepared if at least one of the lots of the subdivision is five acres or less. A commissioners court by order may require each subdivider of land to prepare a plat if none of the lots is five acres or less but at least one of the lots of a subdivision is more than five acres but not more than 10 acres.

(a-1) A subdivision of a tract under this section includes a subdivision of real property by any method of conveyance, including a contract for deed, oral contract, contract of sale, or other type of executory contract, regardless of whether the subdivision is made by using a metes and bounds description.

(b) A plat required under this section must:

(1) be certified by a surveyor or engineer registered to practice in this state;

(2) define the subdivision by metes and bounds;

(3) locate the subdivision with respect to an original corner of the original survey of which it is a part;

(4) describe each lot, number each lot in progression, and give the dimensions of each lot;

(5) state the dimensions of and accurately describe each lot, street, alley, square, park, or other part of the tract intended to be dedicated to public use or for the use of purchasers or owners of lots fronting on or adjacent to the street, alley, square, park, or other part;

(6) include or have attached a document containing a description in English and Spanish of the water and sewer facilities and roadways and easements dedicated for the provision of water and sewer facilities that will be constructed or installed to service the subdivision and a statement specifying the date by which the facilities will be fully operable;

(7) have attached a document prepared by an engineer registered to practice in this state certifying that the water and sewer service facilities proposed under Subdivision (6) are in compliance with the model rules adopted under Section 16.343, Water Code, and a certified estimate of the cost to install water and sewer service facilities;

(8) provide for drainage in the subdivision to:

(A) avoid concentration of storm drainage water from each lot to adjacent lots;

(B) provide positive drainage away from all buildings; and

(C) coordinate individual lot drainage with the general storm drainage pattern for the area;

(9) include a description of the drainage requirements as provided in Subdivision (8);

(10) identify the topography of the area;

(11) include a certification by a surveyor or engineer registered to practice in this state describing any area of the subdivision that is in a floodplain or stating that no area is in a floodplain; and

(12) include certification that the subdivider has complied with the requirements of Section 232.032 and that:

(A) the water quality and connections to the lots meet, or will meet, the minimum state standards;

(B) sewer connections to the lots or septic tanks meet, or will meet, the minimum requirements of state standards;

(C) electrical connections provided to the lot meet, or will meet, the minimum state standards; and

(D) gas connections, if available, provided to the lot meet, or will meet, the minimum state standards.

(c) A subdivider may meet the requirements of Subsection (b)(12)(B) through the use of a certificate issued by the appropriate county or state official having jurisdiction over the approval of septic systems stating that lots in the subdivision can be adequately and legally served by septic systems.

(d) The subdivider of the tract must acknowledge the plat by signing the plat and attached documents and attest to the veracity and completeness of the matters asserted in the attached documents and in the plat.

(e) The plat must be filed and recorded with the county clerk of the county in which the tract is located. The plat is subject to the filing and recording provisions of Section 12.002, Property Code.

(f) The commissioners court may require a plat application submitted for approval to include a digital map that is compatible with other mapping systems used by the county and that georeferences the subdivision plat and related public infrastructure using the Texas Coordinate Systems adopted under Section 21.071, Natural Resources Code. A digital map required under this subsection may be required only in a format widely used by common geographic information system software. A requirement adopted under this subsection must provide for an exemption from the requirement if the subdivider of the tract submits with the plat application an acknowledged statement indicating that the digital mapping technology necessary to submit a map that complies with this subsection was not reasonably accessible.

LGOVT §232.024. APPROVAL BY COUNTY REQUIRED

(a) A plat filed under Section 232.023 is not valid unless the commissioners court of the county in which the land is located approves the plat by an order entered in the minutes of the court. The commissioners court shall refuse to approve a plat if it does not meet the requirements prescribed by or under this subchapter or if any bond required under this subchapter is not filed with the county clerk.

(b) If any part of a plat applies to land intended for residential housing and any part of that land lies in a floodplain, the commissioners court shall not approve the plat unless:

(1) the subdivision is developed in compliance with the minimum requirements of the National Flood Insurance Program and local regulations or orders adopted under Section 16.315, Water Code; and

(2) the plat evidences a restrictive covenant prohibiting the construction of residential housing in any area of the subdivision that is in a floodplain unless the housing is developed in compliance with the minimum requirements of the National Flood Insurance Program and local regulations or orders adopted under Section 16.315, Water Code.

(c) On request, the county clerk shall provide the attorney general or the Texas Water Development Board:

(1) a copy of each plat that is approved under this subchapter; or

(2) the reasons in writing and any documentation that support a variance granted under Section 232.042.

(d) The commissioners court of the county in which the land is located may establish a planning commission as provided by Subchapter D. The planning commission, including its findings and decisions, is subject to the same provisions applicable to the commissioners court under this subchapter, including Section 232.034 relating to conflicts of interest.

LGOVT §232.025. SUBDIVISION REQUIREMENTS

By an order adopted and entered in the minutes of the commissioners court, and after a notice is published in English and Spanish in a newspaper of general circulation in the county, the commissioners court shall for each subdivision:

(1) require a right-of-way on a street or road that functions as a main artery in a subdivision, of a width of not less than 50 feet or more than 100 feet;

(2) require a right-of-way on any other street or road in a subdivision of not less than 40 feet or more than 70 feet;

(3) require that the shoulder-to-shoulder width on collectors or main arteries within the right-of-way be not less than 32 feet or more than 56 feet, and that the shoulder-to-shoulder width on any other street or road be not less than 25 feet or more than 35 feet;

(4) adopt, based on the amount and kind of travel over each street or road in a subdivision, reasonable specifications relating to the construction of each street or road;

(5) adopt reasonable specifications to provide adequate drainage for each street or road in a subdivision in accordance with standard engineering practices;

(6) require that each purchase contract made between a subdivider and a purchaser of land in the subdivision contain a statement describing how and when water, sewer, electricity, and gas services will be made available to the subdivision; and

(7) require that the subdivider of the tract execute a bond in the manner provided by Section 232.027.

LGOVT §232.026. WATER & SEWER SERVICE EXTENSION

(a) The commissioners court may extend, beyond the date specified on the plat or on the document attached to the plat, the date by which the water and sewer service facilities must be fully operable if the commissioners court finds the extension is reasonable and not contrary to the public interest.

(b) The commissioners court may not grant an extension under Subsection (a) if it would allow an occupied residence to be without water or sewer services.

(c) If the commissioners court provides an extension, the commissioners court shall notify the attorney general of the extension and the reason for the extension. The attorney general shall notify all other state agencies having enforcement power over subdivisions of the extension.

LGOVT §232.027. BOND REQUIREMENTS

(a) Unless a person has completed the installation of all water and sewer service facilities required by this subchapter on the date that person applies for final approval of a plat under Section 232.024, the commissioners court shall require the subdivider of the tract to execute and maintain in effect a bond or, in the alternative, a person may make a cash deposit in an amount the commissioners court determines will ensure compliance with this subchapter. A person may not meet the requirements of this subsection through the use of a letter of credit unless that letter of credit is irrevocable and issued by an institution guaranteed by the FDIC. The subdivider must comply with the requirement before subdividing the tract.

(b) The bond must be conditioned on the construction or installation of water and sewer service facilities that will be in compliance with the model rules adopted under Section 16.343, Water Code.

LGOVT §232.028. CERTIFICATION REGARDING COMPLIANCE WITH PLAT REQUIREMENTS

(a) On the approval of a plat by the commissioners court, the commissioners court shall issue to the person applying for the approval a certificate stating that the plat has been reviewed and approved by the commissioners court.

(b) On the commissioners court's own motion or on the written request of a subdivider, an owner or resident of a lot in a subdivision, or an entity that provides a utility service, the commissioners court shall make the following determinations regarding the land in which the entity or commissioners court is interested that is located within the jurisdiction of the county:

(1) whether a plat has been prepared and whether it has been reviewed and approved by the commissioners court;

(2) whether water service facilities have been constructed or installed to service the lot or subdivision under Section 232.023 and are fully operable;

(3) whether sewer service facilities have been constructed or installed to service the lot or subdivision under Section 232.023 and are fully operable, or if septic systems are used, whether the lot is served by a permitted on-site sewage facility or lots in the subdivision can be adequately and legally served by septic systems under Section 232.023; and

(4) whether electrical and gas facilities, if available, have been constructed or installed to service the lot or subdivision under Section 232.023.

(c) The request made under Subsection (b) must identify the land that is the subject of the request.

(d) Whenever a request is made under Subsection (b), the commissioners court shall issue the requesting party a written certification of its determinations under that subsection.

(e) The commissioners court shall make its determinations within 20 days after the date it receives the request under Subsection (b) and shall issue the certificate, if appropriate, within 10 days after the date the determinations are made.

(f) The commissioners court may adopt rules it considers necessary to administer its duties under this section.

(g) The commissioners court may impose a fee for a certificate issued under this section for a subdivision which is located in the county and not within the limits of a municipality. The amount of the fee may be the greater of $30 or the amount of the fee imposed by the municipality for a subdivision that is located entirely in the extraterritorial jurisdiction of the municipality for a certificate issued under Section 212.0115. A person who obtains a certificate under this section is not required to obtain a certificate under Section 212.0115.

LGOVT §232.029. CONNECTION OF UTILITIES IN COUNTIES WITHIN 50 MILES OF INTERNATIONAL BORDER

(a) This section applies only to a county defined under Section 232.022(a)(1).

(a-1) Except as provided by Subsection (c) or Section 232.037(c), a utility may not serve or connect any subdivided land with water or sewer services unless the utility receives a certificate issued by the commissioners court under Section 232.028(a) or receives a determination from the commissioners court under Section 232.028(b)(1) that the plat has been reviewed and approved by the commissioners court.

(b) Except as provided by Subsections (c) and (k) or Section 232.037(c), a utility may not serve or connect any subdivided land with electricity or gas unless the entity receives a determination from the county commissioners court under Sections 232.028(b)(2) and (3) that adequate water and sewer services have been installed to service the lot or subdivision.

(c) An electric, gas, water, or sewer service utility may serve or connect subdivided land with water, sewer, electricity, gas, or other utility service regardless of whether the utility receives a certificate issued by the commissioners court under Section 232.028(a) or receives a determination from the commissioners court under Section 232.028(b) if the utility is provided with a certificate issued by the commissioners court that states that:

(1) the subdivided land:

(A) was sold or conveyed by a subdivider by any means of conveyance, including a contract for deed or executory contract:

(i) before September 1, 1995; or

(ii) before September 1, 1999, if the subdivided land on August 31, 1999, was located in the extraterritorial jurisdiction of a municipality as determined by Chapter 42;

(B) has not been subdivided after September 1, 1995, or September 1, 1999, as applicable under Paragraph (A);

(C) is the site of construction of a residence, evidenced by at least the existence of a completed foundation, that was begun on or before May 1, 2003; and

(D) has had adequate sewer services installed to service the lot or dwelling, as determined by an authorized agent responsible for the licensing or permitting of on-site sewage facilities under Chapter 366, Health and Safety Code;

(2) the subdivided land is a lot of record and has adequate sewer services installed that are fully operable to service the lot or dwelling, as determined by an authorized agent responsible for the licensing or permitting of on-site sewage facilities under Chapter 366, Health and Safety Code; or

(3) the land was not subdivided after September 1, 1995, and:

(A) water service is available within 750 feet of the subdivided land; or

(B) water service is available more than 750 feet from the subdivided land and the extension of water service to the land may be feasible, subject to a final determination by the water service provider.

(d) A utility may provide utility service to subdivided land described by Subsection (c)(1), (2), or (3) only if the person requesting service:

(1) is not the land's subdivider or the subdivider's agent; and

(2) provides to the utility a certificate described by Subsection (c).

(e) A person requesting service may obtain a certificate under Subsection (c)(1), (2), or (3) only if the

person is the owner or purchaser of the subdivided land and provides to the commissioners court documentation containing:

(1) a copy of the means of conveyance or other documents that show that the land was sold or conveyed by a subdivider before September 1, 1995, or before September 1, 1999, as applicable under Subsection (c);

(2) a notarized affidavit by that person requesting service under Subsection (c)(1) that states that construction of a residence on the land, evidenced by at least the existence of a completed foundation, was begun on or before May 1, 2003, and the request for utility connection or service is to connect or serve a residence described by Subsection (c)(1)(C);

(3) a notarized affidavit by the person requesting service that states that the subdivided land has not been further subdivided after September 1, 1995, or September 1, 1999, as applicable under Subsection (c); and

(4) evidence that adequate sewer service or facilities have been installed and are fully operable to service the lot or dwelling from an entity described by Section 232.021(14) or the authorized agent responsible for the licensing or permitting of on-site sewage facilities under Chapter 366, Health and Safety Code.

(f) Repealed by Acts 2009, 81st Leg., ch. 1239, §6, eff. June 19, 2009.

(g) On request, the commissioners court shall provide to the attorney general and any appropriate local, county, or state law enforcement official a copy of any document on which the commissioners court relied in determining the legality of providing service.

(h) This section may not be construed to abrogate any civil or criminal proceeding or prosecution or to waive any penalty against a subdivider for a violation of a state or local law, regardless of the date on which the violation occurred.

(i) The prohibition established by this section shall not prohibit a water, sewer, electric, or gas utility from providing water, sewer, electric, or gas utility connection or service to a lot sold, conveyed, or purchased through a contract for deed or executory contract or other device by a subdivider prior to July 1, 1995, or September 1, 1999, if on August 31, 1999, the subdivided land was located in the extraterritorial jurisdiction of a municipality that has adequate sewer services installed that are fully operable to service the lot, as determined by an authorized agent responsible for the licensing or permitting of on-site sewage facilities under Chapter 366, Health and Safety Code, and was subdivided by a plat approved prior to September 1, 1989.

(j) In this section, "foundation" means the lowest division of a residence, usually consisting of a masonry slab or a pier and beam structure, that is partly or wholly below the surface of the ground and on which the residential structure rests.

(k) Subject to Subsections (*l*) and (m), a utility that does not hold a certificate issued by, or has not received a determination from, the commissioners court under Section 232.028 to serve or connect subdivided property with electricity or gas may provide that service to a single-family residential dwelling on that property if:

(1) the person requesting utility service:

(A) is the owner and occupant of the residential dwelling; and

(B) on or before January 1, 2001, owned and occupied the residential dwelling;

(2) the utility previously provided the utility service on or before January 1, 2001, to the property for the person requesting the service;

(3) the utility service provided as described by Subdivision (2) was terminated not earlier than five years before the date on which the person requesting utility service submits an application for that service; and

(4) providing the utility service will not result in:

(A) an increase in the volume of utility service provided to the property; or

(B) more than one utility connection for each single-family residential dwelling located on the property.

(*l*) A utility may provide service under Subsection (k) only if the person requesting the service provides to the commissioners court documentation that evidences compliance with the requirements of Subsection (k) and that is satisfactory to the commissioners court.

(m) A utility may not serve or connect subdivided property as described by Subsection (k) if, on or after September 1, 2007, any existing improvements on that property are modified.

(n) Except as provided by Subsection (o), this section does not prohibit a water or sewer utility from providing water or sewer utility connection or service to a residential dwelling that:

LGOVT §232.029

(1) is provided water or wastewater facilities under or in conjunction with a federal or state funding program designed to address inadequate water or wastewater facilities in colonias or to residential lots located in a county described by Section 232.022(a)(1);

(2) is an existing dwelling identified as an eligible recipient for funding by the funding agency providing adequate water and wastewater facilities or improvements;

(3) when connected, will comply with the minimum state standards for both water and sewer facilities and as prescribed by the model subdivision rules adopted under Section 16.343, Water Code; and

(4) is located in a project for which the municipality with jurisdiction over the project or the approval of plats within the project area has approved the improvement project by order, resolution, or interlocal agreement under Chapter 791, Government Code, if applicable.

(o) A utility may not serve any subdivided land with water utility connection or service under Subsection (n) unless the entity receives a determination from the county commissioners court under Section 232.028(b)(3) that adequate sewer services have been installed to service the lot or dwelling.

(p) The commissioners court may impose a fee for a certificate issued under this section for a subdivision which is located in the county and not within the limits of a municipality. The amount of the fee may be the greater of $30 or the amount of the fee imposed by the municipality for a subdivision that is located entirely in the extraterritorial jurisdiction of the municipality for a certificate issued under Section 212.0115. A person who obtains a certificate under this section is not required to obtain a certificate under Section 212.0115.

LGOVT §232.0291. CONNECTION OF UTILITIES IN CERTAIN COUNTIES WITHIN 100 MILES OF INTERNATIONAL BORDER

(a) This section applies only to a county defined under Section 232.022(a)(2).

(b) Except as provided by Subsection (d) or Section 232.037(c), a utility may not serve or connect any subdivided land with water or sewer services unless the utility receives a certificate issued by the commissioners court under Section 232.028(a) or receives a determination from the commissioners court under Section 232.028(b)(1) that the plat has been reviewed and approved by the commissioners court.

(c) Except as provided by Subsection (d) or Section 232.037(c), a utility may not serve or connect any subdivided land with electricity or gas unless the entity receives a determination from the county commissioners court under Section 232.028(b)(2) that adequate water and sewer services have been installed to service the subdivision.

(d) An electric, gas, water, or sewer service utility may serve or connect subdivided land with water, sewer, electricity, gas, or other utility service regardless of whether the utility receives a certificate issued by the commissioners court under Section 232.028(a) or receives a determination from the commissioners court under Section 232.028(b) if the utility is provided with a certificate issued by the commissioners court that states that:

(1) the subdivided land:

(A) was sold or conveyed to the person requesting service by any means of conveyance, including a contract for deed or executory contract before September 1, 2005;

(B) is located in a subdivision in which the utility has previously provided service; and

(C) is the site of construction of a residence, evidenced by at least the existence of a completed foundation, that was begun on or before September 1, 2005; or

(2) the subdivided land was not subdivided after September 1, 2005, and:

(A) water service is available within 750 feet of the subdivided land; or

(B) water service is available more than 750 feet from the subdivided land and the extension of water service to the land may be feasible, subject to a final determination by the water service provider.

(e) A utility may provide utility service to subdivided land described by Subsection (d)(1) only if the person requesting service:

(1) is not the land's subdivider or the subdivider's agent; and

(2) provides to the utility a certificate described by Subsection (d)(1).

(f) A person requesting service may obtain a certificate under Subsection (d)(1) only if the person provides to the commissioners court either:

(1) documentation containing:

(A) a copy of the means of conveyance or other documents that show that the land was sold or conveyed to the person requesting service before September 1, 2005; and

(B) a notarized affidavit by that person that states that construction of a residence on the land, evidenced by at least the existence of a completed foundation, was begun on or before September 1, 2005; or

(2) a notarized affidavit by the person requesting service that states that:

(A) the property was sold or conveyed to that person before September 1, 2005; and

(B) construction of a residence on the land, evidenced by at least the existence of a completed foundation, was begun on or before September 1, 2005.

(g) A person requesting service may obtain a certificate under Subsection (d)(2) only if the person provides to the commissioners court an affidavit that states that the property was not sold or conveyed to that person from a subdivider or the subdivider's agent after September 1, 2005.

(h) On request, the commissioners court shall provide to the attorney general and any appropriate local, county, or state law enforcement official a copy of any document on which the commissioners court relied in determining the legality of providing service.

(i) This section may not be construed to abrogate any civil or criminal proceeding or prosecution or to waive any penalty against a subdivider for a violation of a state or local law, regardless of the date on which the violation occurred.

(j) The prohibition established by this section does not prohibit an electric or gas utility from providing electric or gas utility connection or service to a lot:

(1) sold, conveyed, or purchased through a contract for deed or executory contract or other device by a subdivider before September 1, 2005;

(2) located within a subdivision where the utility has previously established service; and

(3) subdivided by a plat approved before September 1, 1989.

(k) In this section, "foundation" means the lowest division of a residence, usually consisting of a masonry slab or a pier and beam structure, that is partly or wholly below the surface of the ground and on which the residential structure rests.

LGOVT §232.030. SUBDIVISION REGULATION; COUNTY AUTHORITY

(a) The commissioners court for each county shall adopt and enforce the model rules developed under Section 16.343, Water Code.

(b) Except as provided by Section 16.350(d), Water Code, or Section 232.042 or 232.043, the commissioners court may not grant a variance or adopt regulations that waive any requirements of this subchapter.

(c) The commissioners court shall adopt regulations setting forth requirements for:

(1) potable water sufficient in quality and quantity to meet minimum state standards;

(2) solid waste disposal meeting minimum state standards and rules adopted by the county under Chapter 364, Health and Safety Code;

(3) sufficient and adequate roads that satisfy the standards adopted by the county;

(4) sewer facilities meeting minimum state standards;

(5) electric service and gas service; and

(6) standards for flood management meeting the minimum standards set forth by the Federal Emergency Management Agency under the National Flood Insurance Act of 1968 (42 U.S.C. Sections 4001 through 4127).

(d) In adopting regulations under Subsection (c)(2), the commissioners court may allow one or more commercial providers to provide solid waste disposal services as an alternative to having the service provided by the county.

LGOVT §232.0305. COUNTY INSPECTOR

(a) The commissioners court may impose a fee on a subdivider of property under this subchapter for an inspection of the property to ensure compliance with the subdivision regulations adopted under this subchapter, Section 16.343, Water Code, or other law.

(b) Fees collected under this section may be used only to fund inspections conducted under this section.

LGOVT §232.031. REQUIREMENTS PRIOR TO SALE OR LEASE

(a) Except as provided by Subsection (d), a subdivider may not sell or lease land in a subdivision first platted or replatted after July 1, 1995, unless the subdivision plat is approved by the commissioners court in accordance with Section 232.024.

(b) Not later than the 30th day after the date a lot is sold, a subdivider shall record with the county clerk all sales contracts, including the attached disclosure statement required by Section 232.033, leases, and any other documents that convey an interest in the subdivided land.

(c) A document filed under Subsection (b) is a public record.

(d) In a county defined under Section 232.022(a)(2), a subdivider may not sell or lease land in a subdivision first platted or replatted after September 1, 2005, unless the subdivision plat is approved by the commissioners court in accordance with Section 232.024.

LGOVT §232.0315. NOTICE OF WATER & WASTEWATER REQUIREMENTS BY COUNTIES

(a) This section applies only to a county that sells:

(1) under Section 34.01, Tax Code, real property presumed to be for residential use under Section 232.022; or

(2) under Section 3, Part VI, Texas Rules of Civil Procedure, and Chapter 34, Civil Practice and Remedies Code, real property presumed to be for residential use under Section 232.022, taken by virtue of a writ of execution.

(b) A county shall include in the public notice of sale of the property and the deed conveying the property a statement substantially similar to the following:

"THIS SALE IS BEING CONDUCTED PURSUANT TO STATUTORY OR JUDICIAL REQUIREMENTS. BIDDERS WILL BID ON THE RIGHTS, TITLE, AND INTERESTS, IF ANY, IN THE REAL PROPERTY OFFERED.

"THE PROPERTY IS SOLD AS IS, WHERE IS, AND WITHOUT ANY WARRANTY, EITHER EXPRESS OR IMPLIED. NEITHER THE COUNTY NOR THE SHERIFF'S DEPARTMENT WARRANTS OR MAKES ANY REPRESENTATIONS ABOUT THE PROPERTY'S TITLE, CONDITION, HABITABILITY, MERCHANTABILITY, OR FITNESS FOR A PARTICULAR PURPOSE. BUYERS ASSUME ALL RISKS.

"IN SOME SITUATIONS, A LOT OF FIVE ACRES OR LESS IS PRESUMED TO BE INTENDED FOR RESIDENTIAL USE. HOWEVER, IF THE PROPERTY LACKS WATER OR WASTEWATER SERVICE, THE PROPERTY MAY NOT QUALIFY FOR RESIDENTIAL USE. A POTENTIAL BUYER WHO WOULD LIKE MORE INFORMATION SHOULD MAKE ADDITIONAL INQUIRIES OR CONSULT WITH PRIVATE COUNSEL."

(c) The statement required by Subsection (b) must be:

(1) printed:

(A) in English and Spanish; and

(B) in 14-point boldface type or 14-point uppercase typewritten letters; and

(2) read aloud at the sale, in English and Spanish, by an agent of the county.

(d) A sale conducted in violation of this section is void.

LGOVT §232.032. SERVICES PROVIDED BY SUBDIVIDER

A subdivider having an approved plat for a subdivision shall:

(1) furnish a certified letter from the utility provider stating that water is available to the subdivision sufficient in quality and quantity to meet minimum state standards required by Section 16.343, Water Code, and consistent with the certification in the letter, and that water of that quality and quantity will be made available to the point of delivery to all lots in the subdivision;

(2) furnish sewage treatment facilities that meet minimum state standards to fulfill the wastewater requirements of the subdivision or furnish certification by the appropriate county or state official having jurisdiction over the approval of the septic systems indicating that lots in the subdivision can be adequately and legally served by septic systems as provided under Chapter 366, Health and Safety Code;

(3) furnish roads satisfying minimum standards as adopted by the county;

(4) furnish adequate drainage meeting standard engineering practices; and

(5) make a reasonable effort to have electric utility service and gas utility service installed by a utility.

LGOVT §232.033. ADVERTISING STANDARDS & OTHER REQUIREMENTS BEFORE SALE; OFFENSE

(a) Brochures, publications, and advertising of any form relating to subdivided land:

(1) may not contain any misrepresentation; and

(2) except for a for-sale sign posted on the property that is no larger than three feet by three feet, must accurately describe the availability of water and sewer service facilities and electric and gas utilities.

(b) The subdivider shall provide a copy in Spanish of all written documents relating to the sale of subdivided land under an executory contract, including the contract, disclosure notice, and annual statement required by this section and a notice of default required by Subchapter D, Chapter 5, Property Code, if:

(1) negotiations that precede the execution of the executory contract are conducted primarily in Spanish; or

(2) the purchaser requests the written documents to be provided in Spanish.

(c) Before an executory contract is signed by the purchaser, the subdivider shall provide the purchaser with a written notice, which must be attached to the executory contract, informing the purchaser of the condition of the property that must, at a minimum, be executed by the subdivider and purchaser, be acknowledged, and read substantially similar to the following:

IF ANY OF THE ITEMS BELOW HAVE NOT BEEN CHECKED, YOU MAY NOT BE ABLE TO LIVE ON THE PROPERTY.

WARNING

CONCERNING THE PROPERTY AT (street address or legal description and municipality)

THIS DOCUMENT STATES THE TRUE FACTS ABOUT THE LAND YOU ARE CONSIDERING PURCHASING.

CHECK OFF THE ITEMS THAT ARE TRUE:

___ The property is in a recorded subdivision.

___ The property has water service that provides potable water.

___ The property has sewer service or a septic system.

___ The property has electric service.

___ The property is not in a flood-prone area.

___ The roads are paved.

___ No person other than the subdivider:

(1) owns the property;

(2) has a claim of ownership to the property; or

(3) has an interest in the property.

___ No person has a lien filed against the property.

___ There are no back taxes owed on the property.

NOTICE

SELLER ADVISES PURCHASER TO:

(1) OBTAIN A TITLE ABSTRACT OR TITLE COMMITMENT REVIEWED BY AN ATTORNEY BEFORE SIGNING A CONTRACT OF THIS TYPE; AND

(2) PURCHASE AN OWNER'S POLICY OF TITLE INSURANCE COVERING THE PROPERTY.

__________ __________

(Date) (Signature of Subdivider)

__________ __________

(Date) (Signature of Purchaser)

(d) The subdivider shall provide any purchaser who is sold a lot under an executory contract with an annual statement in January of each year for the term of the executory contract. If the subdivider mails the statement to the purchaser, the statement must be postmarked not later than January 31.

(e) The statement under Subsection (d) must include the following information:

(1) the amount paid under the contract;

(2) the remaining amount owed under the contract;

(3) the annual interest rate charged under the contract during the preceding 12-month period; and

(4) the number of payments remaining under the contract.

(f) If the subdivider fails to comply with Subsections (d) and (e), the purchaser may:

(1) notify the subdivider that the purchaser has not received the statement and will deduct 15 percent of each monthly payment due until the statement is received; and

(2) not earlier than the 25th day after the date the purchaser provides the subdivider notice under this subsection, deduct 15 percent of each monthly payment due until the statement is received by the purchaser.

(g) A purchaser who makes a deduction under Subsection (f) is not required to reimburse the subdivider for the amount deducted.

(h) A person who is a seller of lots in a subdivision, or a subdivider or an agent of a seller or subdivider, commits an offense if the person knowingly authorizes or assists in the publication, advertising, distribution,

or circulation of any statement or representation that the person knows is false concerning any subdivided land offered for sale or lease. An offense under this section is a Class A misdemeanor.

LGOVT §232.034. CONFLICT OF INTEREST; PENALTY

(a) In this section, "subdivided tract" means a tract of land, as a whole, that is subdivided into tracts or lots. The term does not mean an individual lot in a subdivided tract of land.

(b) A person has an interest in a subdivided tract if the person:

(1) has an equitable or legal ownership interest in the tract;

(2) acts as a developer of the tract;

(3) owns voting stock or shares of a business entity that:

(A) has an equitable or legal ownership interest in the tract; or

(B) acts as a developer of the tract; or

(4) receives in a calendar year money or any thing of value from a business entity described by Subdivision (3).

(c) A person also is considered to have an interest in a subdivided tract if the person is related in the second degree by consanguinity or affinity, as determined under Chapter 573, Government Code, to a person who, under Subsection (b), has an interest in the tract.

(d) If a member of the commissioners court has an interest in a subdivided tract, the member shall file, before a vote or decision regarding the approval of a plat for the tract, an affidavit with the county clerk stating the nature and extent of the interest and shall abstain from further participation in the matter. The affidavit must be filed with the county clerk.

(e) A member of the commissioners court of a county commits an offense if the member violates Subsection (d). An offense under this subsection is a Class A misdemeanor.

(f) The finding by a court of a violation of this section does not render voidable an action of the commissioners court unless the measure would not have passed the commissioners court but for the vote of the member who violated this section.

(g) A conviction under Subsection (e) constitutes official misconduct by the member and is grounds for removal from office.

LGOVT §232.035. CIVIL PENALTIES

(a) A subdivider or an agent of a subdivider may not cause, suffer, allow, or permit a lot to be sold in a subdivision if the subdivision has not been platted as required by this subchapter.

(b) Notwithstanding any other remedy at law or equity, a subdivider or an agent of a subdivider may not cause, suffer, allow, or permit any part of a subdivision over which the subdivider or an agent of the subdivider has control, or a right of ingress and egress, to become a public health nuisance as defined by Section 341.011, Health and Safety Code.

(c) A subdivider who fails to provide, in the time and manner described in the plat, for the construction or installation of water or sewer service facilities described on the plat or on the document attached to the plat or who otherwise violates this subchapter or a rule or requirement adopted by the commissioners court under this subchapter is subject to a civil penalty of not less than $500 or more than $1,000 for each violation and for each day of a continuing violation but not to exceed $5,000 each day and shall also pay court costs, investigative costs, and attorney's fees for the governmental entity bringing the suit.

(d) Except as provided by Subsection (e), a person who violates Subsection (a) or (b) is subject to a civil penalty of not less than $10,000 or more than $15,000 for each lot conveyed or each subdivision that becomes a nuisance. The person must also pay court costs, investigative costs, and attorney's fees for the governmental entity bringing the suit.

(e) A person who violates Subsection (b) is not subject to a fine under Subsection (d) if the person corrects the nuisance not later than the 30th day after the date the person receives notice from the attorney general or a local health authority of the nuisance.

(f) Venue for an action under this section is in a district court of Travis County, a district court in the county in which the defendant resides, or a district court in the county in which the violation or threat of violation occurs.

LGOVT §232.036. CRIMINAL PENALTIES

(a) A subdivider commits an offense if the subdivider knowingly fails to file a plat required by this subchapter. An offense under this subsection is a Class A misdemeanor.

(b) A subdivider who owns a subdivision commits an offense if the subdivider knowingly fails to timely provide for the construction or installation of water or sewer service as required by Section 232.032 or fails to make a reasonable effort to have electric utility service and gas utility service installed by a utility as required by Section 232.032. An offense under this subsection is a Class A misdemeanor.

(c) If it is shown at the trial of an offense under Subsection (a) that the defendant caused five or more residences in the subdivision to be inhabited, the offense is a state jail felony.

(d) A subdivider commits an offense if the subdivider allows the conveyance of a lot in the subdivision without the appropriate water and sewer utilities as required by Section 232.032 or without having made a reasonable effort to have electric utility service and gas utility service installed by a utility as required by Section 232.032. An offense under this section is a Class A misdemeanor. Each lot conveyed constitutes a separate offense.

(e) Venue for prosecution for a violation under this section is in the county in which any element of the violation is alleged to have occurred or in Travis County.

LGOVT §232.037. ENFORCEMENT

(a) The attorney general, or the district attorney, criminal district attorney, county attorney with felony responsibilities, or county attorney of the county may take any action necessary in a court of competent jurisdiction on behalf of the state or on behalf of residents to:

(1) enjoin the violation or threatened violation of the model rules adopted under Section 16.343, Water Code;

(2) enjoin the violation or threatened violation of a requirement of this subchapter or a rule adopted by the commissioners court under this subchapter;

(3) recover civil or criminal penalties, attorney's fees, litigation costs, and investigation costs; and

(4) require platting or replatting under Section 232.040.

(b) The attorney general, at the request of the district or county attorney with jurisdiction, may conduct a criminal prosecution under Section 232.033(h) or 232.036.

(c) During the pendency of any enforcement action brought, any resident of the affected subdivision, or the attorney general, district attorney, or county attorney on behalf of a resident, may file a motion against the provider of utilities to halt termination of pre-existing utility services. The services may not be terminated if the court makes an affirmative finding after hearing the motion that termination poses a threat to public health, safety, or welfare of the residents.

(d) This subchapter is subject to the applicable enforcement provisions prescribed by Sections 16.352, 16.353, 16.354, and 16.3545, Water Code.

LGOVT §232.038. SUIT BY PRIVATE PERSON IN ECONOMICALLY DISTRESSED AREA

(a) Except as provided by Subsection (b), a person who has purchased or is purchasing a lot after July 1, 1995, in a subdivision for residential purposes that does not have water and sewer services as required by this subchapter and is located in an economically distressed area, as defined by Section 17.921, Water Code, from a subdivider, may bring suit in the district court in which the property is located or in a district court in Travis County to:

(1) declare the sale of the property void, require the subdivider to return the purchase price of the property, and recover from the subdivider:

(A) the market value of any permanent improvements the person placed on the property;

(B) actual expenses incurred as a direct result of the failure to provide adequate water and sewer facilities;

(C) court costs; and

(D) reasonable attorney's fees; or

(2) enjoin a violation or threatened violation of Section 232.032, require the subdivider to plat or replat under Section 232.040, and recover from the subdivider:

(A) actual expenses incurred as a direct result of the failure to provide adequate water and sewer facilities;

(B) court costs; and

(C) reasonable attorney's fees.

(b) If the lot is located in a county defined under Section 232.022(a)(2), a person may only bring suit under Subsection (a) if the person purchased or is purchasing the lot after September 1, 2005.

LGOVT §232.039. CANCELLATION OF SUBDIVISION

(a) A subdivider of land may apply to the commissioners court to cancel all or part of the subdivision in the manner provided by Section 232.008 after notice and hearing as provided by this section.

(b) A resident of a subdivision for which the subdivider has applied for cancellation under Subsection (a) has the same rights as a purchaser of land under Section 232.008.

(c) The notice required by Section 232.008(c) must also be published in Spanish in the newspaper of highest circulation and in a Spanish-language newspaper in the county if available.

(d) Not later than the 14th day before the date of the hearing, the county chief appraiser shall by regular and certified mail provide notice containing the information described by Section 232.008(c) to:

(1) each person who pays property taxes in the subdivision, as determined by the most recent tax roll; and

(2) each person with an interest in the property.

(e) The commissioners court may require a subdivider to provide the court with the name and last known address of each person with an interest in the property. For purposes of this subsection, a person residing on a lot purchased through an executory contract has an interest in the property.

(f) A person who fails to provide information requested under Subsection (e) before the 31st day after the date the request is made is liable to the state for a penalty of $500 for each week the person fails to provide the information.

(g) The commissioners court may cancel a subdivision only after a public hearing. At the hearing, the commissioners court shall permit any interested person to be heard. At the conclusion of the hearing, the commissioners court shall adopt an order on whether to cancel the subdivision.

LGOVT §232.040. REPLATTING

(a) A subdivision plat must accurately reflect the subdivision as it develops. If there is any change, either by the intentional act of the subdivider or by the forces of nature, including changes in the size or dimension of lots or the direction or condition of the roads, a plat must be revised in accordance with Section 232.041.

(b) Except as provided by Subsection (c), a lot in a subdivision may not be sold if the lot lacks water and sewer services as required by this subchapter unless the lot is platted or replatted as required by this subchapter. A subdivider or agent of a subdivider may not transfer a lot through an executory contract or other similar conveyance to evade the requirements of this subchapter. The prohibition in this subsection includes the sale of a lot:

(1) by a subdivider who regains possession of a lot previously exempt under Subsection (c) through the exercise of a remedy described in Section 5.064, Property Code; or

(2) for which it is shown at a proceeding brought in the district court in which the property is located that the sale of a lot otherwise exempt under Subsection (c) was made for the purpose of evading the requirements of this subchapter.

(c) Subsection (b) does not apply if a seller other than a subdivider or agent of a subdivider resides on the lot.

(d) The attorney general or a district or county attorney with jurisdiction may bring a proceeding under Subsection (b).

(e) Existing utility services to a subdivision that must be platted or replatted under this section may not be terminated under Section 232.029 or 232.0291.

LGOVT §232.041. REVISION OF PLAT

(a) A person who has subdivided land that is subject to the subdivision controls of the county in which the land is located may apply in writing to the commissioners court of the county for permission to revise the subdivision plat filed for record with the county clerk.

(b) Except as provided by Subsection (b-1), after the application is filed with the commissioners court, the court shall publish a notice of the application in a newspaper of general circulation in the county. The notice must include a statement of the time and place at which the court will meet to consider the application and to hear protests to the revision of the plat. The notice must be published at least three times during the period that begins on the 30th day and ends on the seventh day before the date of the meeting. If all or part of the subdivided tract has been sold to nondeveloper owners, the court shall also give notice to each of those owners by certified or registered mail, return receipt requested, at the owner's address in the subdivided tract.

(b-1) If the commissioners court determines that the revision to the subdivision plat does not affect a public interest or public property of any type, including, but not limited to, a park, school, or road, the notice requirements under Subsection (b) do not apply to the application and the commissioners court shall:

(1) provide written notice of the application to the owners of the lots that are within 200 feet of the subdivision plat to be revised, as indicated in the most recent records of the central appraisal district of the county in which the lots are located; and

(2) if the county maintains an Internet website, post notice of the application continuously on the website for at least 30 days preceding the date of the meeting to consider the application until the day after the meeting.

(c) During a regular term of the commissioners court, the court shall adopt an order to permit the revision of the subdivision plat if it is shown to the court that:

(1) the revision will not interfere with the established rights of any owner of a part of the subdivided land; or

(2) each owner whose rights may be interfered with has agreed to the revision.

(d) If the commissioners court permits a person to revise a subdivision plat, the person may make the revision by filing for record with the county clerk a revised plat or part of a plat that indicates the changes made to the original plat.

(e) The commissioners court may impose a fee for filing an application under this section. The amount of the fee must be based on the cost of processing the application, including publishing the notices required under Subsection (b) or (b-1).

LGOVT §232.042. VARIANCES FROM REPLATTING REQUIREMENTS

(a) On request of a subdivider or resident purchaser, the commissioners court may grant a delay or a variance from compliance with Section 232.040 as provided by this section.

(b) The commissioners court may grant a delay of two years if the reason for the delay is to install utilities. A person may apply for one renewal of a delay under this subsection. To obtain an initial delay under this subsection, a subdivider must:

(1) identify the affected utility providers;

(2) provide the terms and conditions on which service may be provided; and

(3) provide a certified letter from each utility provider stating that it has the right to serve the area and it will serve the area.

(c) The commissioners court may grant a delay or a variance for a reason other than a reason described by Subsection (b) if it is shown that compliance would be impractical or would be contrary to the health and safety of residents of the subdivision. The commissioners court must issue written findings stating the reasons why compliance is impractical.

(d) A delay or a variance granted by the commissioners court is valid only if the commissioners court notifies the attorney general of the delay or variance and the reasons for the delay or variance not later than the 30th day after the date the commissioners court grants the delay or variance.

(e) Until approved water and sewer services are made available to the subdivision, the subdivider of land for which a delay is granted under this section must provide at no cost to residents:

(1) 25 gallons of potable water a day for each resident and a suitable container for storing the water; and

(2) suitable temporary sanitary wastewater disposal facilities.

LGOVT §232.043. VARIANCES FROM PLATTING REQUIREMENTS

(a) On the request of a subdivider who created an unplatted subdivision or a resident purchaser of a lot in the subdivision, the commissioners court of a county may grant:

(1) a delay or variance from compliance with the subdivision requirements prescribed by Section 232.023(b)(8) or (9), 232.025(1), (2), (3), (4), or (5), or 232.030(c)(2), (3), (5), or (6); or

(2) a delay or variance for an individual lot from compliance with the requirements prescribed by the model subdivision rules adopted under Section 16.343, Water Code, for:

(A) the distance that a structure must be set back from roads or property lines; or

(B) the number of single-family, detached dwellings that may be located on a lot.

(b) If the commissioners court makes a written finding that the subdivider who created the unplatted subdivision no longer owns property in the subdivision,

the commissioners court may grant a delay or variance under this section only if:

(1) a majority of the lots in the subdivision were sold before:

(A) September 1, 1995, in a county defined under Section 232.022(a)(1); or

(B) September 1, 2005, in a county defined under Section 232.022(a)(2);

(2) a majority of the resident purchasers in the subdivision sign a petition supporting the delay or variance;

(3) the person requesting the delay or variance submits to the commissioners court:

(A) a description of the water and sewer service facilities that will be constructed or installed to service the subdivision;

(B) a statement specifying the date by which the water and sewer service facilities will be fully operational; and

(C) a statement signed by an engineer licensed in this state certifying that the plans for the water and sewer facilities meet the minimum state standards;

(4) the commissioners court finds that the unplatted subdivision at the time the delay or variance is requested is developed in a manner and to an extent that compliance with specific platting requirements is impractical or contrary to the health or safety of the residents of the subdivision; and

(5) the subdivider who created the unplatted subdivision has not violated local law, federal law, or state law, excluding this chapter, in subdividing the land for which the delay or variance is requested, if the subdivider is the person requesting the delay or variance.

(c) If the commissioners court makes a written finding that the subdivider who created the unplatted subdivision owns property in the subdivision, the commissioners court may grant a provisional delay or variance only if the requirements of Subsection (b) are satisfied. The commissioners court may issue a final grant of the delay or variance only if the commissioners court has not received objections from the attorney general before the 91st day after the date the commissioners court submits the record of its proceedings to the attorney general as prescribed by Subsection (d).

(d) If the commissioners court grants a delay or variance under this section, the commissioners court shall:

(1) make findings specifying the reason compliance with each requirement is impractical or contrary to the health or safety of residents of the subdivision;

(2) keep a record of its proceedings and include in the record documentation of the findings and the information submitted under Subsection (b); and

(3) submit a copy of the record to the attorney general.

(e) The failure of the attorney general to comment or object to a delay or variance granted under this section does not constitute a waiver of or consent to the validity of the delay or variance granted.

(f) This section does not affect a civil suit filed against, a criminal prosecution of, or the validity of a penalty imposed on a subdivider for a violation of law, regardless of the date on which the violation occurred.

LGOVT §232.044. AMENDING PLAT

The commissioners court may approve and issue an amending plat under this subchapter in the same manner, for the same purposes, and subject to the same related provisions as provided by Section 232.011.

Sections 232.045-232.070 blank

SUBCHAPTER C. SUBDIVISION PLATTING REQUIREMENTS IN CERTAIN ECONOMICALLY DISTRESSED COUNTIES

LGOVT §232.071. APPLICABILITY

This subchapter applies only to the subdivision of land located:

(1) outside the corporate limits of a municipality; and

(2) in a county:

(A) in which is located a political subdivision that is eligible for and has applied for financial assistance under Section 15.407, Water Code, or Subchapter K, Chapter 17, Water Code; and

(B) to which Subchapter B does not apply.

LGOVT §232.072. PLAT REQUIRED

(a) The owner of a tract of land that divides the tract in any manner that creates at least one lot of five acres or less intended for residential purposes must have a plat of the subdivision prepared. A commissioners court by order may require each subdivider of land to prepare a plat if none of the lots is five acres or less but at least one of the lots of the subdivision is more than five acres but not more than 10 acres.

(a-1) A subdivision of a tract under this section includes a subdivision of real property by any method of conveyance, including a contract for deed, oral contract, contract of sale, or other type of executory contract, regardless of whether the subdivision is made by using a metes and bounds description.

(b) A plat required under this section must:

(1) include on the plat or have attached to the plat a document containing a description of the water and sewer service facilities that will be constructed or installed to service the subdivision and a statement of the date by which the facilities will be fully operable; and

(2) have attached to the plat a document prepared by an engineer registered to practice in this state certifying that the water and sewer service facilities described by the plat or the document attached to the plat are in compliance with the model rules adopted under Section 16.343, Water Code.

(c) A plat required under this section must be filed and recorded with the county clerk of the county in which the tract is located. The plat is subject to the filing and recording provisions of Section 12.002, Property Code.

(d) The commissioners court may require a plat application submitted for approval to include a digital map that is compatible with other mapping systems used by the county and that georeferences the subdivision plat and related public infrastructure using the Texas Coordinate Systems adopted under Section 21.071, Natural Resources Code. A digital map required under this subsection may be required only in a format widely used by common geographic information system software. A requirement adopted under this subsection must provide for an exemption from the requirement if the owner of the tract submits with the plat application an acknowledged statement indicating that the digital mapping technology necessary to submit a map that complies with this subsection was not reasonably accessible.

LGOVT §232.073. APPROVAL BY COUNTY REQUIRED

(a) A plat filed under Section 232.072 is not valid unless the commissioners court of the county in which the land is located approves the plat by an order entered in the minutes of the court. The commissioners court shall refuse to approve a plat if it does not meet the requirements prescribed by or under this subchapter or if any bond required under this subchapter is not filed with the county clerk.

(b) The commissioners court of the county in which the land is located may establish a planning commission as provided by Subchapter D. The planning commission, including its findings and decisions, is subject to the same provisions applicable to the commissioners court under this subchapter, including Section 232.078 relating to conflicts of interest.

LGOVT §232.074. BOND REQUIREMENTS

(a) Unless a person has completed the installation of all water and sewer service facilities required by this subchapter on the date that person applies for final approval of a plat under Section 232.073, the commissioners court shall require the subdivider of the tract to execute and maintain in effect a bond or, in the alternative, a person may make a cash deposit in an amount the commissioners court determines will ensure compliance with this subchapter. A person may not meet the requirements of this subsection through the use of a letter of credit unless that letter of credit is irrevocable and issued by an institution guaranteed by the Federal Deposit Insurance Corporation. The subdivider must comply with the requirement before subdividing the tract.

(b) The bond must be conditioned on the construction or installation of water and sewer service facilities that will be in compliance with the model rules adopted under Section 16.343, Water Code.

LGOVT §232.075. WATER & SEWER SERVICE EXTENSION

(a) The commissioners court may extend, beyond the date specified on the plat or on the document attached to the plat, the date by which the water and sewer service facilities must be fully operable if the commissioners court finds the extension is reasonable and not contrary to the public interest.

(b) The commissioners court may not grant an extension under Subsection (a) if it would allow an occupied residence to be without water or sewer services.

LGOVT §232.076. CERTIFICATION REGARDING COMPLIANCE WITH PLAT REQUIREMENTS

(a) On the approval of a plat by the commissioners court, the commissioners court shall issue to the person applying for the approval a certificate stating that

the plat has been reviewed and approved by the commissioners court.

(b) On its own motion or on the written request of a subdivider, an owner or resident of a lot in a subdivision, or an entity that provides a utility service, the commissioners court shall:

(1) determine whether a plat is required under this subchapter for an identified tract of land that is located within the jurisdiction of the county; and

(2) if a plat is required for the identified tract, determine whether a plat has been reviewed and approved by the commissioners court.

(c) The request made under Subsection (b) must adequately identify the land that is the subject of the request.

(d) Whenever a request is made under Subsection (b), the commissioners court shall issue the requesting party a written certification of its determinations.

(e) The commissioners court shall make its determinations within 20 days after the date it receives the request under Subsection (b) and shall issue the certificate, if appropriate, within 10 days after the date the determinations are made.

(f) The commissioners court may adopt rules it considers necessary to administer its duties under this section.

LGOVT §232.077. CONNECTION OF UTILITIES IN CERTAIN COUNTIES

(a) This section applies only to a tract of land for which a plat is required under this subchapter.

(b) An entity described by Subsection (c) may not serve or connect any land with water, sewer, electricity, gas, or other utility service unless the entity has been presented with or otherwise holds a certificate applicable to the land issued under Section 232.076 stating that a plat has been reviewed and approved for the land.

(c) The prohibition established by Subsection (b) applies only to:

(1) a municipality, and officials of the municipality, that provides water, sewer, electricity, gas, or other utility service;

(2) a municipally owned or municipally operated utility that provides any of those services;

(3) a public utility that provides any of those services;

(4) a water supply or sewer service corporation organized and operating under Chapter 67, Water Code, that provides any of those services;

(5) a county that provides any of those services; and

(6) a special district or authority created by or under state law that provides any of those services.

(d) The prohibition established by Subsection (b) applies only to land that an entity described by Subsection (c) first serves or first connects with services:

(1) between September 1, 1989, and June 16, 1995; or

(2) after the effective date of this subchapter.

LGOVT §232.0775. COUNTY INSPECTOR

(a) The commissioners court may impose a fee on a subdivider of property under this subchapter for an inspection of the property to ensure compliance with the subdivision regulations adopted under this subchapter, Section 16.343, Water Code, or other law.

(b) Fees collected under this section may be used only to fund inspections conducted under this section.

LGOVT §232.078. CONFLICT OF INTEREST; PENALTY

(a) In this section, "subdivided tract" means a tract of land, as a whole, that is subdivided into tracts or lots. The term does not mean an individual lot in a subdivided tract of land.

(b) A person has an interest in a subdivided tract if the person:

(1) has an equitable or legal ownership interest in the tract;

(2) acts as a developer of the tract;

(3) owns voting stock or shares of a business entity that:

(A) has an equitable or legal ownership interest in the tract; or

(B) acts as a developer of the tract; or

(4) receives in a calendar year money or any thing of value from a business entity described by Subdivision (3).

(c) A person also is considered to have an interest in a subdivided tract if the person is related in the second degree by consanguinity or affinity, as determined under Chapter 573, Government Code, to a person who, under Subsection (b), has an interest in the tract.

(d) If a member of the commissioners court has an interest in a subdivided tract, the member shall file, before a vote or decision regarding the approval of a plat for the tract, an affidavit with the county clerk stating the nature and extent of the interest and shall abstain from further participation in the matter. The affidavit must be filed with the county clerk.

(e) A member of the commissioners court of a county commits an offense if the member violates Subsection (d). An offense under this subsection is a Class A misdemeanor.

(f) The finding by a court of a violation of this section does not render voidable an action of the commissioners court unless the measure would not have passed the commissioners court but for the vote of the member who violated this section.

(g) A conviction under Subsection (e) constitutes official misconduct by the member and is grounds for removal from office.

LGOVT §232.079. CIVIL PENALTIES

(a) A subdivider or an agent of a subdivider may not cause, suffer, allow, or permit a lot to be sold in a subdivision if the subdivision has not been platted as required by this subchapter.

(b) A subdivider who fails to provide, in the time and manner described in the plat, for the construction or installation of water or sewer service facilities described on the plat or on the document attached to the plat or who otherwise violates this subchapter or a rule or requirement adopted by the commissioners court under this subchapter is subject to a civil penalty of not less than $500 or more than $1,000 for each violation and for each day of a continuing violation but not to exceed $5,000 each day and shall also pay court costs, investigative costs, and attorney's fees for the governmental entity bringing the suit.

(c) Venue for an action under this section is in a district court of Travis County, a district court in the county in which the defendant resides, or a district court in the county in which the violation or threat of violation occurs.

LGOVT §232.080. ENFORCEMENT

(a) The attorney general, or the district attorney, criminal district attorney, or county attorney, may take any action necessary in a court of competent jurisdiction on behalf of the state or on behalf of residents to:

(1) enjoin the violation or threatened violation of applicable model rules adopted under Section 16.343, Water Code;

(2) enjoin the violation or threatened violation of a requirement of this subchapter or a rule adopted by the commissioners court under this subchapter;

(3) recover civil or criminal penalties, attorney's fees, litigation costs, and investigation costs; and

(4) require platting as required by this subchapter.

(b) During the pendency of any enforcement action brought, any resident of the affected subdivision, or the attorney general, district attorney, or county attorney on behalf of a resident, may file a motion against the provider of utilities to halt termination of preexisting utility services. The services may not be terminated if the court makes an affirmative finding after hearing the motion that termination poses a threat to public health or to the health, safety, or welfare of the residents. This subsection does not prohibit a provider of utilities from terminating services under other law to a resident who has failed to timely pay for services.

(c) This subchapter is subject to the applicable enforcement provisions prescribed by Sections 16.352, 16.353, 16.354, and 16.3545, Water Code.

LGOVT §232.081. AMENDING PLAT

The commissioners court may approve and issue an amending plat under this subchapter in the same manner, for the same purposes, and subject to the same related provisions as provided by Section 232.011.

Sections 232.082-232.090 blank

SUBCHAPTER D. COUNTY PLANNING COMMISSION

LGOVT §232.091. APPLICABILITY

This subchapter applies only to a county:

(1) authorized to establish a planning commission under Subchapter B or C; and

(2) in which the commissioners court by order elects to operate under this subchapter.

LGOVT §232.092. ESTABLISHMENT & ABOLITION OF PLANNING COMMISSION

(a) To promote the general public welfare, the commissioners court of a county by order may:

(1) establish a planning commission under this section; and

(2) abolish a planning commission established under this section.

(b) The commissioners court may authorize the planning commission to act on behalf of the commissioners court in matters relating to:

(1) the duties and authority of the commissioners court under Subchapter A, B, or C; and

(2) land use, health and safety, planning and development, or other enforcement provisions specifically authorized by law.

(c) If the commissioners court establishes a planning commission, the commissioners court by order shall adopt reasonable rules and procedures necessary to administer this subchapter.

(d) This subchapter does not grant a commissioners court or a planning commission the power to regulate the use of property for which a permit has been issued to engage in a federally licensed activity.

LGOVT §232.093. APPOINTMENT OF MEMBERS OF PLANNING COMMISSION

(a) The commissioners court may appoint a planning commission consisting of five members. Members are appointed for staggered terms of two years.

(b) A person appointed as a member of the planning commission must be a citizen of the United States and reside in the county.

(c) The commissioners court shall file with the county clerk a certificate of appointment for each commission member.

(d) The commissioners court shall fill any vacancy on the commission.

(e) Before a planning commission member undertakes the duties of the office, the member must:

(1) take the official oath; and

(2) swear in writing that the member will promote the interest of the county as a whole and not only a private interest or the interest of a special group or location in the county.

(f) A member of the planning commission serves at the pleasure of the commissioners court and is subject to removal as provided by Chapter 87.

LGOVT §232.094. FINANCIAL DISCLOSURE

(a) The commissioners court of a county may require each member of the planning commission to file a financial disclosure report in the same manner as required for county officers under Subchapter B, Chapter 159.

(b) If the commissioners court requires a financial disclosure report but has not adopted a financial disclosure reporting system under Subchapter B, Chapter 159, the planning commission member shall file a financial disclosure report in the same manner as required for county officers under Subchapter A, Chapter 159.

LGOVT §232.095. OFFICERS, QUORUM, & MEETINGS

(a) At the first meeting of each calendar year, the planning commission shall elect a presiding officer and assistant presiding officer. The presiding officer presides over the meetings and executes all documentation required on behalf of the planning commission. The assistant presiding officer represents the presiding officer during the presiding officer's absence.

(b) There is no limitation on the number of terms a member may serve on the commission.

(c) Minutes of the planning commission's proceedings must be filed with the county clerk or other county officer or employee designated by the commissioners court. The minutes of the planning commission's proceedings are a public record.

(d) The planning commission is subject to Chapters 551 and 552, Government Code.

(e) The planning commission may adopt rules necessary to administer this subchapter. Rules adopted under this subsection are subject to approval by the commissioners court.

LGOVT §232.096. TIMELY APPROVAL OF PLATS

(a) The planning commission shall issue a written list of the documentation and other information that must be submitted with a plat application. The documentation or other information must relate to a requirement authorized by law. An application submitted to the planning commission that contains the documents and other information on the list is considered complete.

(b) If a person submits an incomplete plat application to the planning commission, the planning commission or its designee shall, not later than the 15th business day after the date the planning commission or its designee receives the application, notify the applicant of the missing documents or other information. The

planning commission or its designee shall allow an applicant to timely submit the missing documents or other information.

(c) An application is considered complete on the date all documentation and other information required by Subsection (a) is received by the planning commission.

(d) If the approval of the plat is within the exclusive jurisdiction of the planning commission, the planning commission shall take final action on a plat application, including the resolution of all appeals, not later than the 60th day after the date a completed plat application is received by the planning commission.

(e) The time period prescribed by Subsection (d) may be extended for:

(1) a reasonable period if requested by the applicant; and

(2) an additional 60 days if the county is required under Chapter 2007, Government Code, to perform a takings impact assessment in connection with a plat submitted for approval.

(f) The planning commission may not compel an applicant to waive the time limits prescribed by this section.

(g) If the planning commission fails to take final action on the completed plat application as required by this section, the applicant may apply to a district court in the county in which the land is located for a mandamus order to compel the planning commission to approve or disapprove the plat. A planning commission subject to a mandamus order under this subsection shall make a decision approving or disapproving the plat not later than the 20th business day after the date a copy of the mandamus order is served on the presiding officer of the planning commission. If the planning commission approves the plat, the planning commission, within the 20-day period prescribed by this subsection, shall:

(1) refund the greater of the unexpended portion of any plat application fee or deposit or 50 percent of a plat application fee or deposit that has been paid;

(2) determine the appropriate amount of any bond or other financial guarantee required in connection with the plat approval; and

(3) issue documents recognizing the plat's approval.

(h) Except as provided by this subsection, an approval of a plat by the planning commission is final on the 31st day after the date the planning commission votes to approve the plat. On the request of a county commissioner, the commissioners court shall review a plat approved by the planning commission not later than the 30th day after the date the planning commission votes to approve the plat. The commissioners court may disapprove the plat if the plat fails to comply with state law or rules adopted by the county or the planning commission. If the commissioners court fails to take action within the 30-day period prescribed by this subsection, the decision of the planning commission is final.

(i) In this section, "business day" means a day other than a Saturday, Sunday, or holiday recognized by this state.

LGOVT §232.097. REASONS FOR DISAPPROVAL OF PLAT REQUIRED

If the planning commission refuses to approve a plat, the planning commission shall provide to the person requesting approval a notice specifying the reason for the disapproval.

Sections 232.098 & 232.099 blank

SUBCHAPTER E. INFRASTRUCTURE PLANNING PROVISIONS IN CERTAIN URBAN COUNTIES

LGOVT §232.100. REPEALED

LGOVT §232.101. RULES

(a) By an order adopted and entered in the minutes of the commissioners court and after a notice is published in a newspaper of general circulation in the county, the commissioners court may adopt rules governing plats and subdivisions of land within the unincorporated area of the county to promote the health, safety, morals, or general welfare of the county and the safe, orderly, and healthful development of the unincorporated area of the county.

(b) Unless otherwise authorized by state law, a commissioners court shall not regulate under this section:

(1) the use of any building or property for business, industrial, residential, or other purposes;

(2) the bulk, height, or number of buildings constructed on a particular tract of land;

(3) the size of a building that can be constructed on a particular tract of land, including without limitation and restriction on the ratio of building floor space to the land square footage;

(4) the number of residential units that can be built per acre of land;

(5) a plat or subdivision in an adjoining county; or

(6) road access to a plat or subdivision in an adjoining county.

(c) The authority granted under Subsection (a) is subject to the exemptions to plat requirements provided for in Section 232.0015.

LGOVT §232.102. MAJOR THOROUGHFARE PLAN

By an order adopted and entered in the minutes of the commissioners court and after a notice is published in a newspaper of general circulation in the county, the commissioners court may:

(1) require a right-of-way on a street or road that functions as a major thoroughfare of a width of not more than 120 feet; or

(2) require a right-of-way on a street or road that functions as a major thoroughfare of a width of more than 120 feet, if such requirement is consistent with a transportation plan adopted by the metropolitan planning organization of the region.

LGOVT §232.103. LOT FRONTAGES

By an order adopted and entered in the minutes of the commissioners court and after a notice is published in a newspaper of general circulation in the county, the commissioners court may adopt reasonable standards for minimum lot frontages on existing county roads and establish reasonable standards for the lot frontages in relation to curves in the road.

LGOVT §232.104. SET-BACKS

By an order adopted and entered in the minutes of the commissioners court and after a notice is published in a newspaper of general circulation in the county, the commissioners court may establish reasonable building and set-back lines as provided by Chapter 233 without the limitation period provided by Section 233.004(c).

LGOVT §232.105. DEVELOPER PARTICIPATION CONTRACTS

(a) Without complying with the competitive sealed bidding procedure of Chapter 262, a commissioners court may make a contract with a developer of a subdivision or land in the unincorporated area of the county to construct public improvements, not including a building, related to the development. If the contract does not meet the requirements of this subchapter, Chapter 262 applies to the contract if the contract would otherwise be governed by that chapter.

(b) Under the contract, the developer shall construct the improvements, and the county shall participate in the cost of the improvements.

(c) The contract must establish the limit of participation by the county at a level not to exceed 30 percent of the total contract price. In addition, the contract may also allow participation by the county at a level not to exceed 100 percent of the total cost for any oversizing of improvements required by the county, including but not limited to increased capacity of improvements to anticipate other future development in the area. The county is liable only for the agreed payment of its share, which shall be determined in advance either as a lump sum or as a factor or percentage of the total actual cost as determined by an order of the commissioners court.

(d) The developer must execute a performance bond for the construction of the improvements to ensure completion of the project. The bond must be executed by a corporate surety in accordance with Chapter 2253, Government Code.

(e) In the order adopted by the commissioners court under Subsection (c), the county may include additional safeguards against undue loading of cost, collusion, or fraud.

LGOVT §232.106. CONNECTION OF UTILITIES

By an order adopted and entered in the minutes of the commissioners court, and after a notice is published in a newspaper of general circulation in the county, the commissioners court may impose the requirements of Section 232.029 or 232.0291.

LGOVT §232.107. PROVISIONS CUMULATIVE

The authorities under this subchapter are cumulative of and in addition to the authorities granted under this chapter and all other laws to counties to regulate the subdivision of land.

LGOVT §232.108. PLAT REQUIREMENTS

(a) The commissioners court, in addition to having the authority to adopt rules under Section 232.101 and other authority granted by this chapter, may impose the plat requirements prescribed by Section 232.023. If the commissioners court imposes the plat requirements

prescribed by Section 232.023, any rules adopted under Section 232.101 must be consistent with those requirements.

(b) If a county imposing the plat requirements prescribed by Section 232.023 is not described by Section 232.022(a):

(1) the document required by Section 232.023(b)(6) is not required to be in Spanish; and

(2) the plat requirements related to drainage shall be those authorized by Section 232.003(8) rather than those authorized by Section 232.023(b)(8).

LGOVT §232.109. FIRE SUPPRESSION SYSTEM

In a subdivision that is not served by fire hydrants as part of a centralized water system certified by the Texas Commission on Environmental Quality as meeting minimum standards for water utility service, the commissioners court may require a limited fire suppression system that requires a developer to construct:

(1) for a subdivision of fewer than 50 houses, 2,500 gallons of storage; or

(2) for a subdivision of 50 or more houses, 2,500 gallons of storage with a centralized water system or 5,000 gallons of storage.

CHAPTER 233. COUNTY REGULATION OF HOUSING & OTHER STRUCTURES

SUBCHAPTER A. DANGEROUS SUBSTANCES[1]

LGOVT §233.001. REQUIRING REPAIR, REMOVAL, OR DEMOLITION OF BUILDING OR OTHER STRUCTURE

(a) If the commissioners court of a county that borders the Gulf of Mexico and is adjacent to a county with a population of more than 3.3 million finds that a bulkhead or other method of shoreline protection, hereafter called "structure," in an unincorporated area of the county is likely to endanger persons or property, the commissioners may:

(1) order the owner of the structure, the owner's agent, or the owner or occupant of the property on which the structure is located to repair, remove, or demolish the structure or the part of the structure within a specified time; or

(2) repair, remove, or demolish the structure or the part of the structure at the expense of the county on behalf of the owner of the structure or the owner of the property on which the structure is located and assess the repair, removal, or demolition expenses on the property on which the structure was located.

(b) The commissioners court shall provide by order for:

(1) the assessment of repair, removal, or demolition expenses incurred under Subsection (a)(2);

(2) a method of giving notice of the assessment; and

(3) a method of recovering the expenses.

(c) Promptly after the assessment, the county must file for record, in recordable form in the office of the county clerk in which the property is located, a written notice of the imposition of a lien, if any, that is imposed on the property. The notice must contain a legal description of the property, the amount of the assessment, and the owner if known. The lien arises and attaches to the property at the time the notice of the assessment is recorded and indexed in the office of the county clerk in the county in which the property is located. The notice to secure the assessment is inferior to any previously recorded bona fide mortgage lien attached to the property to which the county's lien attaches if the mortgage lien was filed for record in the office of the county clerk of the county in which the property is located before the date the notice is recorded and indexed in the office of the county clerk. The assessment lien is superior to all other previously recorded judgment liens.

(d) A person commits an offense if the person does not comply with an order issued under Subsection (a)(1). An offense under this section is a Class C misdemeanor.

(e) This section does not apply to a:

(1) residential building; or

(2) building or other structure that is owned or held in trust by the state or a political subdivision of this state; or

(3) building or structure used on or in connection with an agricultural operation.

1. Editor's note: Probably should be "Structures."

SUBCHAPTER B. BUILDING & SETBACK LINES

LGOVT §233.031. AUTHORITY LIMITED TO UNINCORPORATED AREAS; CONFLICT WITH MUNICIPAL AUTHORITY

(a) The authority under this subchapter to establish building and set-back lines applies only to areas outside the corporate limits of municipalities.

(b) If the lines conflict with lines adopted by a municipality, the municipal lines prevail if they are in the extraterritorial jurisdiction of the municipality.

LGOVT §233.032. POWERS & DUTIES OF COMMISSIONERS COURT

(a) If the commissioners court of a county determines that the general welfare will be promoted, the court may:

(1) establish by order building or set-back lines on the public roads, including major highways and roads, in the county; and

(2) prohibit the location of a new building within those building or set-back lines.

(b) A building or set-back line established under this subchapter may not extend:

(1) more than 25 feet from the edge of the right-of-way on all public roads other than major highways and roads; or

(2) more than 50 feet from the edge of the right-of-way of major highways and roads.

(c) The commissioners court may designate the public roads that are major highways and roads.

LGOVT §233.033. HEARING; ADOPTION OF LINES

(a) Before the establishment or change of building or set-back lines, the commissioners court must hold at least one public hearing on the establishment or change. The court shall publish notice of the time and place of the hearing in a newspaper of general circulation in the county before the 15th day before the date of the hearing. The court may adjourn the hearing from time to time.

(b) The commissioners court may establish or change a building or set-back line only by an order passed by at least a majority vote of the full membership of the court.

LGOVT §233.034. NOTICE; LIMITATIONS PERIOD

(a) An owner of real property that fronts along a road that has a building or set-back line established under this subchapter is charged with notice of the building or set-back line order.

(b) The commissioners court shall show in a general manner each building or set-back line established under this subchapter on a map. The map shall be filed with the county clerk.

(c) If the county does not begin the construction of the improvement or widening of a road along which a building or set-back line has been established within four years after the date the building or set-back line is established, the building or set-back line becomes void, unless the county and the affected property owners agree to extend the time period for the improvements or widening.

LGOVT §233.035. BOARD OF BUILDING LINE ADJUSTMENT

(a) The commissioners court may appoint a board of building line adjustment consisting of five freeholders of the county. Members must be appointed for staggered terms of two years, with two members' terms expiring in one year and three members' terms expiring the next year. However, in making the initial appointments, the commissioners court shall designate two members for one-year terms and three members for two-year terms. The court may remove a member for cause on a written charge after a public hearing. The court shall fill a vacancy on the board for the unexpired term of the member whose term becomes vacant.

(b) The board shall elect its own chairman and shall adopt rules of procedure. The meetings of the board are open to the public. The board shall keep minutes of its proceedings that shall be filed in the board's office. The minutes of board meetings constitute a public record.

(c) Subject to appropriate conditions and safeguards, the board may modify or vary the regulations affecting building or set-back lines in a case in which unnecessary hardship may result from a literal enforcement of those regulations, in order to do substantial justice and to observe the purpose of the regulations in protecting the public welfare and safety.

(d) The board shall hear and decide an appeal in a case in which, because of exceptional narrowness, shallowness, shape, topography, existing building development, or another exceptional and extraordinary situation or condition of a specific piece of property, the strict application of a building line established under this subchapter would result in peculiar and exceptional difficulties or hardships to the owner of the property. On appeal, the board may authorize a variance from the strict application of the regulation, under conditions imposed by the board, to relieve the hardship or difficulty if that relief can be granted without substantially impairing the intent and purpose of the building line or set-back line.

(e) With appropriate safeguards, the board shall authorize the construction of an improvement or a structure that may encroach on a building or set-back line. However, if the county proceeds with projected improvements of the affected road within the time provided by Section 233.034(c), the owner of the improvement or structure must remove it at no expense to the county.

LGOVT §233.036. ENFORCEMENT

If a structure is erected, constructed, or reconstructed in violation of a building or set-back line established under this subchapter, the commissioners court, the district or county attorney, or an owner of real property in the county may institute an injunction, mandamus, abatement, or other appropriate action to prevent, abate, remove, or enjoin the unlawful erection, construction, or reconstruction.

LGOVT §233.037. APPEAL

(a) An owner of property who is aggrieved by an action or order adopted by the board of building line adjustment may appeal to the commissioners court. The person must bring the appeal within 30 days after the date the action or order was adopted.

(b) A property owner in the county who is aggrieved by a final order of the board or of the commissioners court may appeal to the district court or to another court with proper jurisdiction. The appellant must bring the appeal within 30 days after the date on which the final order in question was adopted. The appellant must execute an appeal bond in an amount fixed by the court.

SUBCHAPTER C. FIRE CODE IN UNINCORPORATED AREA

LGOVT §233.061. AUTHORITY TO ADOPT & ENFORCE FIRE CODE

(a) The commissioners court of a county with a population of over 250,000 or a county adjacent to a county with a population of over 250,000 may adopt a fire code and rules necessary to administer and enforce the fire code.

(b) The commissioners court, or any municipality in the county, may contract with one another for the administration and enforcement of the fire code.

LGOVT §233.0615. DEFINITIONS; SUBSTANTIAL IMPROVEMENT; CONSTRUCTION

(a) In this subchapter:

(1) "Building" includes an establishment or multifamily dwelling.

(2) "Substantial improvement" means:

(A) the repair, restoration, reconstruction, improvement, or remodeling of a building for which the cost exceeds 50 percent of the building's value according to the certified tax appraisal roll for the county for the year preceding the year in which the work was begun; or

(B) a change in occupancy classification involving a change in the purpose or level of activity in a building, including the renovation of a warehouse into a loft apartment.

(b) For purposes of this subchapter, substantial improvement begins on the date that the repair, restoration, reconstruction, improvement, or remodeling or the change in occupancy classification begins or on the date materials are first delivered for that purpose.

(c) For purposes of this subchapter, construction begins on the date that ground is broken for a building, or if no ground is broken, on the date that:

(1) the first materials are added to the original property;

(2) foundation pilings are installed on the original property; or

(3) a manufactured building or relocated structure is placed on a foundation on the original property.

LGOVT §233.062. APPLICATION & CONTENT OF FIRE CODE

(a) The fire code applies only to the following buildings constructed in an unincorporated area of the county:

(1) a commercial establishment;

(2) a public building; and

(3) a multifamily residential dwelling consisting of four or more units.

(b) The fire code does not apply to an industrial facility having a fire brigade that conforms to requirements of the Occupational Health and Safety Administration.

(c) The fire code must:

(1) conform to:

(A) the International Fire Code, as published by the International Code Council, as the code existed on May 1, 2005; or

(B) the Uniform Fire Code, as published by the National Fire Protection Association, as the code existed on May 1, 2005; or

(2) establish protective measures that exceed the standards of the codes described by Subdivision (1).

(d) The commissioners court may adopt later editions of a fire code listed in Subsection (c).

LGOVT §233.063. BUILDING PERMIT; APPLICATION

(a) A person may not construct or substantially improve a building described by Section 233.062(a) in an unincorporated area of the county unless the person obtains a building permit issued in accordance with this subchapter.

(b) A person may apply for a building permit by providing to the commissioners court:

(1) a plan of the proposed building containing information required by the commissioners court; and

(2) an application fee in an amount set by the commissioners court.

(c) Within 30 days after the date the commissioners court receives an application and fee in accordance with Subsection (b), the commissioners court shall:

(1) issue the permit if the plan complies with the fire code; or

(2) deny the permit if the plan does not comply with the fire code.

(d) If the commissioners court receives an application and fee in accordance with Subsection (b) and the commissioners court does not issue the permit or deny the application within 30 days after receiving the application and fee, the construction or substantial improvement of the building that is the subject of the application is approved for the purposes of this subchapter.

LGOVT §233.064. INSPECTIONS

(a) The county shall inspect a building subject to this subchapter to determine whether the building complies with the fire code.

(b) The commissioners court may provide that a county employee or an employee of another governmental entity under intergovernmental contract may perform the inspection.

(c) A building inspector may enter and perform the inspection at a reasonable time at any stage of the building's construction or substantial improvement and after completion of the building.

(d) On or before the date that construction or substantial improvement of a building subject to this subchapter is completed, the owner of the building shall request in writing that the county inspect the building for compliance with the fire code.

(e) The county shall begin the inspection of the building within five business days after the date of the receipt of the written inspection request. If an inspection is properly requested and the county does not begin the inspection within the time permitted by this subsection, the building that is the subject of the request is considered approved for the purposes of this subchapter.

(f) The county shall issue a final certificate of compliance to the owner of a building inspected under this section if the inspector determines, after an inspection of the completed building, that the building complies with the fire code. For a building or complex of buildings involving phased completion or build-out, the county may issue a partial certificate of compliance for any portion of the building or complex the inspector determines is in substantial compliance with the fire code.

(g) If the inspector determines, after an inspection of the completed building, that the building does not comply with the fire code, the county may:

(1) deny the certificate of compliance; or

(2) issue a conditional or partial certificate of compliance and allow the building to be occupied.

(h) A county that issues a conditional certificate of compliance under Subsection (g) shall notify the owner of the building of the violations of the fire code and establish a reasonable time to remedy the violations. A county may revoke a conditional certificate of compliance if the owner does not remedy the violations within the time specified on the conditional certificate of compliance.

(i) A building may not be occupied until a county issues a final, conditional, or partial certificate of compliance for the building.

LGOVT §233.065. FEES

(a) The commissioners court may develop a fee schedule based on building type and may set and charge fees for an inspection and the issuance of a building permit and final certificate of compliance under this subchapter.

(b) The fees must be set in amounts necessary to cover the cost of administering and enforcing this subchapter.

(c) The county shall deposit fees received under this subchapter in a special fund in the county treasury, and money in that fund may be used only for the administration and enforcement of the fire code.

(d) The fee for a fire code inspection under this subchapter must be reasonable and reflect the approximate cost of the inspection personnel, materials, and administrative overhead.

LGOVT §233.066. INJUNCTION

The appropriate attorney representing the county in the district court may seek injunctive relief to prevent the violation or threatened violation of the fire code.

LGOVT §233.067. CIVIL PENALTY

(a) The appropriate attorney representing the county in civil cases may file a civil action in a court of competent jurisdiction to recover from a person who violates the fire code a civil penalty in an amount not to exceed $200 for each day on which the violation exists. In determining the amount of the penalty, the court shall consider the seriousness of the violation.

(b) The county shall deposit amounts collected under this section in the fund and for the purposes described by Section 233.065(c).

SUBCHAPTER D. ALARM SYSTEMS

LGOVT §233.091. DEFINITIONS

In this subchapter:

(1) "Alarm site" means the specific property or area of the premises on or within which an alarm system is installed or placed.

(2) "Alarm system" means an alarm signal device, burglar alarm, heat or motion sensor, or other electrical, mechanical, or electronic device used:

(A) to prevent or detect burglary, theft, pilferage, fire, or other loss of property;

(B) to prevent or detect intrusion; or

(C) primarily to detect and summon aid for other emergencies.

(3) "False alarm" means an alarm signal received by a law enforcement official that is later determined not to involve a criminal offense, attempted criminal offense, fire, or other emergency.

LGOVT §233.092. AUTHORITY TO REGULATE; ADOPTION OF RULES

(a) The commissioners court of a county by order may authorize the sheriff of a county to:

(1) propose rules to implement this subchapter;

(2) regulate the incidence of and response to false alarms in accordance with the rules proposed by the sheriff and adopted or modified by the commissioners court under this subchapter;

(3) establish procedures for application for and renewal and revocation of an alarm system permit;

(4) establish procedures that include notice to the permit holder and an opportunity for a hearing for permit revocation or suspension if the permit holder violates this subchapter or an order of the commissioners court or a rule adopted under this subchapter;

(5) establish fees in accordance with this subchapter for the issuance of the permits;

(6) require that any permit issued under this subchapter be kept at the alarm site and produced for inspection on request of the sheriff or the sheriff's representative;

(7) require that a permit must be issued and unrevoked before a sheriff or other law enforcement official may respond; and

(8) establish a number of free false alarms for each category of alarm system and impose a service response fee for any alarm in excess of the number of free responses within the preceding 12-month period.

(b) Repealed by Acts 2005, 79th Leg., ch. 1296, §5, eff. June 18, 2005.

(c) A penalty or fee imposed for a false alarm must be established by rule based on the type and level of emergency response provided. The fee for more than five false alarms shall not exceed $75 per false alarm above the number of free responses. If there are more than nine false alarms in a one-year period, the alarm system permit may be revoked.

(d) Notwithstanding the other provisions of this section, the owner or lessee of premises on which an alarm system is installed may be charged the full costs incurred by the county when the owner or lessee or the agent or employee of the owner or lessee intentionally or knowingly activates the alarm system for any reason other than an emergency or threat of an emergency of the kind for which the alarm system was designed to give notice.

(e) The sheriff or the sheriff's representative shall provide a copy of the rules to a person and assess a fee for the copy in accordance with Chapter 552, Government Code.

LGOVT §233.093. PERMIT REQUIRED; EXCEPTIONS

(a) In a county in which the sheriff regulates alarm systems under this subchapter, a person may not use an alarm system without a permit issued in accordance with this subchapter.

(b) This subchapter does not apply to:

(1) emergency response systems managed by health care facilities licensed by the Texas Department of Health; or

(2) alarm systems installed on:

(A) a motor vehicle;

(B) premises occupied by the United States, this state, or the county; or

(C) premises located in an incorporated area within the county.

LGOVT §233.094. PERMIT FEES

(a) The sheriff of a county who regulates alarm systems under this subchapter may authorize the county auditor to assess and collect fees for the issuance or renewal of a permit under this subchapter in reasonable amounts set by the commissioners court.

(b) All fees received under this subchapter shall be remitted to the county treasurer to be deposited to the credit of the general fund of the county.

LGOVT §233.095. MUNICIPAL AUTHORITY UNAFFECTED

This subchapter does not affect the authority of a municipality in the county to enact ordinances regulating alarm systems.

LGOVT §233.096. CRIMINAL PENALTY

(a) A person who violates this subchapter, an order of the commissioners court, or a rule adopted under this subchapter commits an offense.

(b) An offense under this section is a Class C misdemeanor.

LGOVT §233.097. COUNTY LIABILITY

The county, the commissioners court, the sheriff, and the sheriff's employees or agents are not liable for an action arising out of the regulation of or failure to regulate alarm systems.

LGOVT §233.098. ENFORCED COLLECTION

The appropriate attorney representing the county may file a civil action in a court of competent jurisdiction to recover a penalty or fee imposed by a county under this subchapter.

Chapter 240. Miscellaneous Regulatory Authority of Counties

Subchapter A. Regulation of Keeping of Wild Animals

LGOVT §240.001. DEFINITION

In this subchapter, "wild animal" means a nondomestic animal that the commissioners court of a county determines is dangerous and is in need of control in that county.

LGOVT §240.002. REGULATION

(a) The commissioners court of a county by order may prohibit or regulate the keeping of a wild animal in the county.

(b) The order does not apply inside the limits of a municipality.

LGOVT §240.003. OFFENSE

(a) A person commits an offense if the person violates an order adopted under this subchapter and the order defines the violation as an offense.

(b) An offense under this section is prosecuted in the same manner as an offense defined under state law.

(c) An offense under this section is a Class C misdemeanor.

LGOVT §240.004. INJUNCTION

The county attorney or an attorney representing the county may file an action in a district court to enjoin a violation or threatened violation of an order adopted under this subchapter. The court may grant appropriate relief.

Subchapter Z. Miscellaneous Provisions

LGOVT §240.901. LAND USE REGULATION FOR FLOOD CONTROL IN COASTAL COUNTIES

(a) This state recognizes the personal hardships and economic distress caused by flood disasters since it has become uneconomical for the private insurance industry alone to make flood insurance available to those in need of protection on reasonable terms and conditions. Recognizing the burden on the nation's resources, congress enacted the National Flood Insurance Act of 1968, under which flood insurance can be made available through the coordinated efforts of the

federal government and the private insurance industry by pooling risks and by the positive cooperation of state and local governments. The purpose of this subchapter is to evidence a positive interest in securing flood insurance coverage under the federal program, thus procuring coverage for the citizens of this state who desire to participate, to promote the public interest by providing appropriate protection against the perils of flood losses, and to encourage sound land use by minimizing exposure of property to flood losses.

(b) A county bordering on the Gulf of Mexico or on the tidewater limits of the gulf may determine the boundaries of any flood-prone area of the county. The suitability of that determination is conclusively established when the commissioners court of the county adopts a resolution finding that the area is a flood-prone area.

(c) The commissioners court may adopt and enforce rules that regulate the management and use of land, structures, and other development in a flood-prone area of the county in order to reduce the extent of damage caused by flooding. The matters to which the rules may apply include:

(1) the floodproofing of structures located or to be constructed in the area;

(2) the minimum elevation of a structure permitted to be constructed or improved in the area;

(3) specifications for drainage;

(4) the prohibition of the connection of land with water, sewer, electricity, and gas utility service, if a structure or other development on the land is not in compliance with a rule adopted by the commissioners court; and

(5) any other action feasible to minimize flooding and rising water damage.

(d) In this section, "flood-prone area" means an area that is subject to damage from rising water or flooding from the Gulf of Mexico or its tidal waters, including lakes, bays, inlets, and lagoons.

(e) Rules and regulations adopted by counties under this section shall comply with rules and regulations promulgated by the Commissioner of the General Land Office under Sections 16.320 and 16.321, Water Code.

(f) If the commissioners court prohibits the connection of land with water, sewer, electricity, and gas utility service under Subsection (c)(4), a person may not provide utility services that connect the land with utility services without written certification from the county that the property complies with rules adopted under this section.

(g) A commissioners court may authorize procedures for filing a notice in the real property records of the county in which a property is located that identifies any condition on the property that the county determines violates the rules adopted under this section or a permit issued under this section. The notice is not a final legal determination and is meant only to provide notice of the county's determination that a violation of the rules or a permit exists on the property. The notice must include a description legally sufficient for identification of the property and the name of the owner of the property.

LGOVT §240.902. CLOSING OF GULF BEACHES

(a) The commissioners court of a county in which a public beach is located may by order close a part of the beach for a maximum of three days each year to allow a nonprofit organization to hold an event on the beach to which the public is invited and to which the organization charges no more than a nominal admission fee.

(b) In this section, "public beach" means a beach located on a bay or inlet of the Gulf of Mexico to which the general public or a substantial part of the general public has free access.

Subtitle C. Regulatory Authority Applying to More Than One Type of Local Government

Chapter 241. Municipal & County Zoning Authority Around Airports

Subchapter A. General Provisions

LGOVT §241.003. DEFINITIONS

In this chapter:

(1) "Airport" means an area of land or water, publicly or privately owned, designed and set aside for the landing and taking off of aircraft and used or to be used in the interest of the public for that purpose. The term includes an area with installations relating to flights, including installations, facilities, and bases of operations for tracking flights or acquiring data concerning flights.

(2) "Airport hazard" means a structure or object of natural growth that obstructs the air space required for the taking off, landing, and flight of aircraft or that in-

terferes with visual, radar, radio, or other systems for tracking, acquiring data relating to, monitoring, or controlling aircraft.

(3) "Airport hazard area" means an area of land or water on which an airport hazard could exist.

(4) "Airport zoning regulation" means an airport hazard area zoning regulation and an airport compatible land use zoning regulation adopted under this chapter.

(5) "Centerline" means a line extending through the midpoint of each end of a runway.

(6) "Compatible land use" means a use of land adjacent to an airport that does not endanger the health, safety, or welfare of the owners, occupants, or users of the land because of levels of noise or vibrations or the risk of personal injury or property damage created by the operations of the airport, including the taking off and landing of aircraft.

(7) "Controlled compatible land use area" means an area of land located outside airport boundaries and within a rectangle bounded by lines located no farther than 1½ statute miles from the centerline of an instrument or primary runway and lines located no farther than five statute miles from each end of the paved surface of an instrument or primary runway.

(8) "Instrument runway" means an existing or planned runway of at least 3,200 feet for which an instrument landing procedure published by a defense agency of the federal government or the Federal Aviation Administration exists or is planned.

(9) "Obstruction" means a structure, growth, or other object, including a mobile object, that exceeds a limiting height established by federal regulations or by an airport hazard area zoning regulation.

(10) "Political subdivision" means a municipality or county.

(11) "Primary runway" means an existing or planned paved runway, as shown in the official airport layout plan (ALP) of the airport, of at least 3,200 feet on which a majority of the approaches to and departures from the airport occur.

(12) "Runway" means a defined area of an airport prepared for the landing and taking off of aircraft along its length.

(13) "Structure" means an object constructed or installed by one or more persons and includes a building, tower, smokestack, and overhead transmission line.

SUBCHAPTER B. ADOPTION OF AIRPORT ZONING REGULATIONS

LGOVT §241.011. AIRPORT HAZARD AREA ZONING REGULATIONS

(a) To prevent the creation of an airport hazard, a political subdivision in which an airport hazard area is located may adopt, administer, and enforce, under its police power, airport hazard area zoning regulations for the airport hazard area.

(b) The airport hazard area zoning regulations may divide an airport hazard area into zones and for each zone:

(1) specify the land uses permitted;

(2) regulate the type of structures; and

(3) restrict the height of structures and objects of natural growth to prevent the creation of an obstruction to flight operations or air navigation.

LGOVT §241.012. AIRPORT COMPATIBLE LAND USE ZONING REGULATIONS

(a) A political subdivision may adopt, administer, and enforce, under its police power, airport compatible land use zoning regulations for the part of a controlled compatible land use area located within the political subdivision if the airport is:

(1) used in the interest of the public to the benefit of the political subdivision; or

(2) located within the political subdivision and owned or operated by a federal defense agency or by the state.

(b) The political subdivision by ordinance or resolution may implement, in connection with airport compatible land use zoning regulations, any federal law or rules controlling the use of land located adjacent to or in the immediate vicinity of the airport.

(c) The airport compatible land use zoning regulations must include a statement that the airport fulfills an essential community purpose.

LGOVT §241.013. EXTRATERRITORIAL ZONING IN POLITICAL SUBDIVISIONS WITH POPULATION OF MORE THAN 45,000

(a) A political subdivision with a population of more than 45,000 in which an airport used in the interest of the public to the benefit of the political subdivision is located may adopt, administer, and enforce:

(1) airport hazard area zoning regulations applicable to an airport hazard area relating to the airport and located outside the political subdivision; and

(2) airport compatible land use zoning regulations applicable to a controlled compatible land use area relating to the airport and located outside the political subdivision.

(b) The political subdivision has the same power to adopt, administer, and enforce airport hazard area zoning regulations or airport compatible land use zoning regulations under this section as that given a political subdivision by Sections 241.011 and 241.012.

(c) The airport hazard area zoning regulations or airport compatible land use zoning regulations must include a statement that the airport fulfills an essential community purpose.

LGOVT §241.014. JOINT AIRPORT ZONING BOARD

(a) A political subdivision to whose benefit an airport is used in the interest of the public or in which an airport owned or operated by a defense agency of the federal government or the state is located may create a joint airport zoning board with another political subdivision in which an airport hazard area or a controlled compatible land use area relating to the airport is located. The political subdivisions must act by resolution or ordinance in creating the joint board.

(b) The joint airport zoning board has the same power to adopt, administer, and enforce airport hazard area zoning regulations or airport compatible land use zoning regulations under this section as that given a political subdivision by Sections 241.011 and 241.012.

(c) The joint airport zoning board must consist of two members appointed by each of the political subdivisions creating the board and, in addition, a chairman elected by a majority of the appointed members.

(d) If an agency of the state owns and operates an airport located within an airport hazard area or controlled compatible land use area governed by a joint airport zoning board, the agency is entitled to have two members on the board.

(e) The joint airport zoning board for an airport that is owned or operated by a defense agency of the federal government and that is closed by the federal government may provide that zoning regulations adopted by the board continue in effect until the fourth anniversary of the date the airport is closed.

LGOVT §241.015. INCORPORATION OF AIRPORT ZONING REGULATION INTO COMPREHENSIVE ZONING ORDINANCE

A political subdivision may incorporate an airport zoning regulation in a comprehensive zoning ordinance and administer and enforce it in connection with the administration and enforcement of the comprehensive zoning ordinance if:

(1) the two zoning regulations apply, in whole or in part, to the same area; and

(2) the comprehensive zoning ordinance includes, among other matters, a regulation on the height of buildings.

LGOVT §241.016. AIRPORT ZONING COMMISSION

(a) Before an airport zoning regulation may be adopted, a political subdivision acting unilaterally under Section 241.013 must appoint an airport zoning commission. If the political subdivision has a planning commission or comprehensive zoning commission, that commission may be designated as the airport zoning commission.

(b) The commission shall recommend the boundaries of the zones to be established and the regulations for these zones.

(c) The commission shall make a preliminary report and hold public hearings on the report before submitting a final report.

(d) Before the 15th day before the date of a hearing under Subsection (c), notice of the hearing shall be published in an official newspaper or a newspaper of general circulation in each political subdivision in which the airport hazard area or controlled compatible land use area to be zoned is located.

(e) A joint airport zoning board created under Section 241.014 is not required to appoint a commission under this section.

LGOVT §241.017. PROCEDURAL LIMITATIONS APPLYING TO ADOPTION OF ZONING REGULATIONS

(a) The governing body of a political subdivision may not hold a public hearing or take other action concerning an airport zoning regulation until it receives the final report of the airport zoning commission.

(b) An airport zoning regulation may not be adopted except by action of the governing body of the

political subdivision or a joint airport zoning board after the political subdivision or joint airport zoning board holds a public hearing on the matter at which parties in interest and citizens have an opportunity to be heard.

(c) Before the 15th day before the date of a hearing under Subsection (b), notice of the hearing must be published in an official newspaper or a newspaper of general circulation in each political subdivision in which the area to be zoned is located.

(d) A procedural requirement adopted or applied by a political subdivision, including any requirement in the charter of a home-rule municipality, that imposes a waiting period before the adoption of a zoning regulation or requires the submission of a zoning regulation to a binding referendum election does not apply to this chapter.

LGOVT §241.018. REASONABLENESS OF AIRPORT ZONING REGULATIONS

(a) An airport zoning regulation must be reasonable and may impose a requirement or restriction only if the requirement or restriction is reasonably necessary to achieve the purposes of this chapter.

(b) In determining which airport zoning regulations to adopt, the governing body of a political subdivision or a joint airport zoning board shall consider, among other things:

(1) the character of the flying operations expected to be conducted at the airport;

(2) the nature of the terrain within the airport hazard area;

(3) the character of the neighborhood; and

(4) the current and possible uses of the property to be zoned.

LGOVT §241.019. NONCONFORMING USES & STRUCTURES

Except as provided by Section 241.035, airport zoning regulations may not require:

(1) changes in nonconforming land use existing on the date of the adoption of the regulations;

(2) the removal, lowering, or other change of a structure that does not conform to the regulations on the date of their adoption, including all phases or elements of a multiphase structure, regardless of whether actual construction has commenced, that received a determination of no hazard by the Federal Aviation Administration under 14 C.F.R., Part 77, before the regulations were adopted;

(3) the removal, lowering, or other change of an object of natural growth that does not conform to the regulations on the date of their adoption; or

(4) any other interference in the continuation of a use that does not conform to the regulations on the date of their adoption.

LGOVT §241.020. PERMITS

(a) Airport zoning regulations may require that a permit be obtained before:

(1) a new structure is constructed;

(2) an existing structure is substantially changed or repaired;

(3) a new use is established; or

(4) an existing use is substantially changed.

(b) Airport zoning regulations must provide that a permit be obtained from the administrative agency authorized to administer and enforce the regulations before:

(1) a nonconforming structure may be replaced, rebuilt, or substantially changed or repaired; or

(2) a nonconforming object of natural growth may be replaced, substantially changed, allowed to grow higher, or replanted.

(c) A permit may not allow:

(1) the establishment of an airport hazard;

(2) a nonconforming use to be made;

(3) a nonconforming structure or object of natural growth to become higher than it was at the time of the adoption of the airport zoning regulations relating to the structure or object of natural growth or at the time of the application for the permit; or

(4) a nonconforming structure, object of natural growth, or use to become a greater hazard to air navigation than it was at the time of the adoption of the airport zoning regulations relating to the structure, object of natural growth, or use or at the time of the application for the permit.

(d) Except as provided by Subsection (c), an application for a permit shall be granted.

Subchapter Z. Miscellaneous Provisions

LGOVT §241.901. Conflict of an Airport Hazard Area Zoning Regulation with Another Regulation

(a) If an airport hazard area zoning regulation conflicts with any other regulation applicable to the same area, the more stringent limitation or requirement controls.

(b) Subsection (a) applies to any conflict with respect to the height of a structure or object of natural growth or any other matter.

(c) Subsection (a) applies to any regulation that conflicts with an airport hazard area zoning regulation whether the regulation was adopted by the political subdivision that adopted the airport zoning regulation or by another political subdivision.

LGOVT §241.902. Conflict of an Airport Compatible Land Use Zoning Regulation with Another Regulation

(a) If an airport compatible land use zoning regulation conflicts with any other regulation applicable to the same area, the airport compatible land use zoning regulation controls.

(b) Subsection (a) applies to any conflict with respect to the use of land or any other matter.

(c) Subsection (a) applies to any regulation that conflicts with an airport compatible land use zoning regulation, whether the regulation was adopted by the political subdivision that adopted the airport compatible land use zoning regulation or by another political subdivision.

LGOVT §241.903. Acquisition of Air Rights or Other Property

(a) A political subdivision may acquire from a person or other political subdivision an air right, aviation easement, or other estate or interest in property or in a nonconforming structure or use if:

(1) the acquisition is necessary to accomplish the purposes of this chapter;

(2) the property or nonconforming structure or use is located within the political subdivision, the political subdivision owns the airport, or the political subdivision is served by the airport; and

(3)(A) the political subdivision desires to remove, lower, or terminate the nonconforming structure or use;

(B) airport zoning regulations are not sufficient to provide necessary approach protection because of constitutional limitations; or

(C) the acquisition of a property right is more advisable than an airport zoning regulation in providing necessary approach protection.

(b) An acquisition under this section may be by purchase, grant, or condemnation in the manner provided by Subchapter B, Chapter 21, Property Code.

Chapter 242. Authority of Municipality & County to Regulate Subdivisions in & Outside Municipality's Extraterritorial Jurisdiction

LGOVT §242.001. Regulation of Subdivisions in Extraterritorial Jurisdiction Generally

(a) This section applies only to a county operating under Sections 232.001-232.005 or Subchapter B, C, or E, Chapter 232, and a municipality that has extraterritorial jurisdiction in that county. Subsections (b)-(g) do not apply:

(1) within a county that contains extraterritorial jurisdiction of a municipality with a population of 1.9 million or more;

(2) within a county within 50 miles of an international border, or to which Subchapter C, Chapter 232, applies; or

(3) to a tract of land subject to a development agreement under Subchapter G, Chapter 212, or other provisions of this code.

(b) For an area in a municipality's extraterritorial jurisdiction, as defined by Section 212.001, a plat may not be filed with the county clerk without the approval of the governmental entity authorized under Subsection (c) or (d) to regulate subdivisions in the area.

(c) Except as provided by Subsections (d)(3) and (4), a municipality and a county may not both regulate subdivisions and approve related permits in the extraterritorial jurisdiction of a municipality after an agreement under Subsection (d) is executed. The municipality and the county shall enter into a written agreement that identifies the governmental entity authorized to regulate subdivision plats and approve related permits in the extraterritorial jurisdiction. For a municipality in existence on September 1, 2001, the municipality and county shall enter into a written agreement under this

subsection on or before April 1, 2002. For a municipality incorporated after September 1, 2001, the municipality and county shall enter into a written agreement under this subsection not later than the 120th day after the date the municipality incorporates. On reaching an agreement, the municipality and county shall certify that the agreement complies with the requirements of this chapter. The municipality and the county shall adopt the agreement by order, ordinance, or resolution. The agreement must be amended by the municipality and the county if necessary to take into account an expansion or reduction in the extraterritorial jurisdiction of the municipality. The municipality shall notify the county of any expansion or reduction in the municipality's extraterritorial jurisdiction. Any expansion or reduction in the municipality's extraterritorial jurisdiction that affects property that is subject to a preliminary or final plat, a plat application, or an application for a related permit filed with the municipality or the county or that was previously approved under Section 212.009 or Chapter 232 does not affect any rights accrued under Chapter 245. The approval of the plat, any permit, a plat application, or an application for a related permit remains effective as provided by Chapter 245 regardless of the change in designation as extraterritorial jurisdiction of the municipality.

(d) An agreement under Subsection (c) may grant the authority to regulate subdivision plats and approve related permits in the extraterritorial jurisdiction of a municipality as follows:

(1) the municipality may be granted exclusive jurisdiction to regulate subdivision plats and approve related permits in the extraterritorial jurisdiction and may regulate subdivisions under Subchapter A of Chapter 212 and other statutes applicable to municipalities;

(2) the county may be granted exclusive jurisdiction to regulate subdivision plats and approve related permits in the extraterritorial jurisdiction and may regulate subdivisions under Sections 232.001-232.005, Subchapter B or C, Chapter 232, and other statutes applicable to counties;

(3) the municipality and the county may apportion the area within the extraterritorial jurisdiction of the municipality with the municipality regulating subdivision plats and approving related permits in the area assigned to the municipality and the county regulating subdivision plats and approving related permits in the area assigned to the county; or

(4) the municipality and the county may enter into an interlocal agreement that:

(A) establishes one office that is authorized to:

(i) accept plat applications for tracts of land located in the extraterritorial jurisdiction;

(ii) collect municipal and county plat application fees in a lump-sum amount; and

(iii) provide applicants one response indicating approval or denial of the plat application; and

(B) establishes a single set of consolidated and consistent regulations related to plats, subdivision construction plans, and subdivisions of land as authorized by Chapter 212, Sections 232.001-232.005, Subchapters B and C, Chapter 232, and other statutes applicable to municipalities and counties that will be enforced in the extraterritorial jurisdiction.

(e) In an unincorporated area outside the extraterritorial jurisdiction of a municipality, the municipality may not regulate subdivisions or approve the filing of plats, except as provided by The Interlocal Cooperation Act, Chapter 791, Government Code.

(f) If a certified agreement between a county and municipality as required by Subsection (c) is not in effect on or before the applicable date prescribed by Section 242.0015(a), the municipality and the county must enter into arbitration as provided by Section 242.0015. If the arbitrator or arbitration panel, as applicable, has not reached a decision in the 60-day period as provided by Section 242.0015, the arbitrator or arbitration panel, as applicable, shall issue an interim decision regarding the regulation of plats and subdivisions and approval of related permits in the extraterritorial jurisdiction of the municipality. The interim decision shall provide for a single set of regulations and authorize a single entity to regulate plats and subdivisions. The interim decision remains in effect only until the arbitrator or arbitration panel reaches a final decision.

(g) If a regulation or agreement adopted under this section relating to plats and subdivisions of land or subdivision development establishes a plan for future roads that conflicts with a proposal or plan for future roads adopted by a metropolitan planning organization, the proposal or plan of the metropolitan planning organization prevails.

(h) This subsection applies only to a county to which Subsections (b)-(g) do not apply, except that this

subsection does not apply to a county subject to Section 242.002 or a county that has entered into an agreement under Section 242.003. For an area in a municipality's extraterritorial jurisdiction, as defined by Section 212.001, a plat may not be filed with the county clerk without the approval of both the municipality and the county. If a municipal regulation and a county regulation relating to plats and subdivisions of land conflict, the more stringent regulation prevails. However, if one governmental entity requires a plat to be filed for the subdivision of a particular tract of land in the extraterritorial jurisdiction of the municipality and the other governmental entity does not require the filing of a plat for that subdivision, the authority responsible for approving plats for the governmental entity that does not require the filing shall issue on request of the subdivider a written certification stating that a plat is not required to be filed for that subdivision of the land. The certification must be attached to a plat required to be filed under this subsection.

(i) Property subject to pending approval of a preliminary or final plat application filed after September 1, 2002, that is released from the extraterritorial jurisdiction of a municipality shall be subject only to county approval of the plat application and related permits and county regulation of that plat. This subsection does not apply to the simultaneous exchange of extraterritorial jurisdiction between two or more municipalities or an exchange of extraterritorial jurisdiction that is contingent on the subsequent approval by the releasing municipality.

LGOVT §242.0015. ARBITRATION REGARDING SUBDIVISION REGULATION AGREEMENT

(a) This section applies only to a county and a municipality that are required to make an agreement as described under Section 242.001(f). If a certified agreement between a county and a municipality with an extraterritorial jurisdiction that extends 3.5 miles or more from the corporate boundaries of the municipality is not in effect on or before January 1, 2004, the parties must arbitrate the disputed issues. If a certified agreement between a county and a municipality with an extraterritorial jurisdiction that extends less than 3.5 miles from the corporate boundaries of the municipality is not in effect on or before January 1, 2006, the parties must arbitrate the disputed issues. A party may not refuse to participate in arbitration requested under this section. An arbitration decision under this section is binding on the parties.

(b) The county and the municipality must agree on an individual to serve as arbitrator. If the county and the municipality cannot agree on an individual to serve as arbitrator, the county and the municipality shall each select an arbitrator and the arbitrators selected shall select a third arbitrator.

(c) The third arbitrator selected under Subsection (b) presides over the arbitration panel.

(d) Not later than the 30th day after the date the county and the municipality are required to have an agreement in effect under Section 242.001(f), the arbitrator or arbitration panel, as applicable, must be selected.

(e) The authority of the arbitrator or arbitration panel is limited to issuing a decision relating only to the disputed issues between the county and the municipality regarding the authority of the county or municipality to regulate plats, subdivisions, or development plans.

(f) Each party is equally liable for the costs of an arbitration conducted under this section.

(g) The arbitrator or arbitration panel, as applicable, shall render a decision under this section not later than the 60th day after the date the arbitrator or arbitration panel is selected. If after a good faith effort the arbitrator or panel has not reached a decision as provided under this subsection, the arbitrator or panel shall continue to arbitrate the matter until the arbitrator or panel reaches a decision.

(h) A municipality and a county may not arbitrate the subdivision of an individual plat under this section.

LGOVT §242.002. REGULATION OF SUBDIVISIONS IN POPULOUS COUNTIES OR CONTIGUOUS COUNTIES

(a) This section applies only to a county operating under Section 232.006.

(b) For an area in a municipality's extraterritorial jurisdiction, as defined by Section 212.001, a subdivision plat may not be filed with the county clerk without the approval of the municipality.

(c) In the extraterritorial jurisdiction of a municipality, the municipality has exclusive authority to regulate subdivisions under Subchapter A of Chapter 212 and other statutes applicable to municipalities.

(d) In an unincorporated area outside the extraterritorial jurisdiction of a municipality, the municipality may not regulate subdivisions or approve the filing of plats, except as provided by The Interlocal Cooperation Act (Article 4413(32c), Vernon's Texas Civil Statutes).

LGOVT §242.003. AUTHORITY OF CERTAIN BORDER COUNTIES & MUNICIPALITIES TO REGULATE SUBDIVISIONS IN EXTRATERRITORIAL JURISDICTION BY AGREEMENT

(a) This section applies only to a county having a population of more than 800,000 and located on the international border and a municipality that has extraterritorial jurisdiction, as defined by Section 212.001, in that county.

(b) A county and a municipality may enter into an agreement that identifies the governmental entity authorized to regulate subdivision plats and approve related permits in the extraterritorial jurisdiction of the municipality in a manner consistent with Section 242.001(d). The county and the municipality shall adopt the agreement by order, ordinance, or resolution.

(c) The agreement must be amended by the county and the municipality if necessary to take into account an expansion or reduction in the extraterritorial jurisdiction of the municipality. The municipality shall notify the county of any expansion or reduction in the municipality's extraterritorial jurisdiction. Any expansion or reduction in the municipality's extraterritorial jurisdiction that affects property that is subject to a preliminary or final plat, a plat application, or an application for a related permit filed with the municipality or the county or that was previously approved under Section 212.009 or Chapter 232 does not affect any rights accrued under Chapter 245. The approval of the plat, any permit, a plat application, or an application for a related permit remains effective as provided by Chapter 245 regardless of the change in designation as extraterritorial jurisdiction of the municipality.

(d) In an unincorporated area outside the extraterritorial jurisdiction of a municipality, the municipality may not regulate subdivisions or approve the filing of plats, except as provided by Chapter 791, Government Code.

(e) Property subject to pending approval of a preliminary or final plat is governed by Section 242.001(i).

CHAPTER 243. MUNICIPAL & COUNTY AUTHORITY TO REGULATE SEXUALLY ORIENTED BUSINESS

LGOVT §243.001. PURPOSE; EFFECT ON OTHER REGULATORY AUTHORITY

(a) The legislature finds that the unrestricted operation of certain sexually oriented businesses may be detrimental to the public health, safety, and welfare by contributing to the decline of residential and business neighborhoods and the growth of criminal activity. The purpose of this chapter is to provide local governments a means of remedying this problem.

(b) This chapter does not diminish the authority of a local government to regulate sexually oriented businesses with regard to any matters.

LGOVT §243.002. DEFINITION

In this chapter, "sexually oriented business" means a sex parlor, nude studio, modeling studio, love parlor, adult bookstore, adult movie theater, adult video arcade, adult movie arcade, adult video store, adult motel, or other commercial enterprise the primary business of which is the offering of a service or the selling, renting, or exhibiting of devices or any other items intended to provide sexual stimulation or sexual gratification to the customer.

LGOVT §243.003. AUTHORITY TO REGULATE

(a) A municipality by ordinance or a county by order of the commissioners court may adopt regulations regarding sexually oriented businesses as the municipality or county considers necessary to promote the public health, safety, or welfare.

(b) A regulation adopted by a municipality applies only inside the municipality's corporate limits.

(c) A regulation adopted by a county applies only to the parts of the county outside the corporate limits of a municipality.

(d) In adopting a regulation, a municipality that has in effect a comprehensive zoning ordinance adopted under Chapter 211 must comply with all applicable procedural requirements of that chapter if the regulation is within the scope of that chapter.

LGOVT §243.004. EXEMPT BUSINESS

The following are exempt from regulation under this chapter:

(1) a bookstore, movie theater, or video store, unless that business is an adult bookstore, adult movie theater, or adult video store under Section 243.002;

(2) a business operated by or employing a licensed psychologist, licensed physical therapist, licensed athletic trainer, licensed cosmetologist, or licensed barber engaged in performing functions authorized under the license held; or

(3) a business operated by or employing a licensed physician or licensed chiropractor engaged in practicing the healing arts.

LGOVT §243.005. BUSINESS LICENSED UNDER ALCOHOLIC BEVERAGE CODE: BUSINESS HAVING COIN-OPERATED MACHINES

(a) A business is not exempt from regulation under this chapter because it holds a license or permit under the Alcoholic Beverage Code authorizing the sale or service of alcoholic beverages or because it contains one or more coin-operated machines that are subject to regulation or taxation, or both, under Chapter 8, Title 132, Revised Statutes.

(b) A regulation adopted under this chapter may not discriminate against a business on the basis of whether the business holds a license or permit under the Alcoholic Beverage Code or on the basis of whether it contains one or more coin-operated machines that are subject to regulation or taxation, or both, under Chapter 8, Title 132, Revised Statutes.

(c) This chapter does not affect the existing preemption by the state of the regulation of alcoholic beverages and the alcoholic beverage industry as provided by Section 1.06, Alcoholic Beverage Code.

LGOVT §243.006. SCOPE OF REGULATION

(a) The location of sexually oriented businesses may be:

(1) restricted to particular areas; or

(2) prohibited within a certain distance of a school, regular place of religious worship, residential neighborhood, or other specified land use the governing body of the municipality or county finds to be inconsistent with the operation of a sexually oriented business.

(b) A municipality or county may restrict the density of sexually oriented businesses.

LGOVT §243.007. LICENSES OR PERMITS

(a) A municipality or county may require that an owner or operator of a sexually oriented business obtain a license or other permit or renew a license or other permit on a periodic basis for the operation of a sexually oriented business. An application for a license or other permit must be made in accordance with the regulations adopted by the municipality or county.

(b) The municipal or county regulations adopted under this chapter may provide for the denial, suspension, or revocation of a license or other permit by the municipality or county.

(c) A district court has jurisdiction of a suit that arises from the denial, suspension, or revocation of a license or other permit by a municipality or county.

LGOVT §243.0075. NOTICE BY SIGN

(a) An applicant for a license or permit issued under Section 243.007 for a location not currently licensed or permitted shall, not later than the 60th day before the date the application is filed, prominently post an outdoor sign at the location stating that a sexually oriented business is intended to be located on the premises and providing the name and business address of the applicant.

(b) A person who intends to operate a sexually oriented business in the jurisdiction of a municipality or county that does not require the owner or operator of a sexually oriented business to obtain a license or permit shall, not later than the 60th day before the date the person intends to begin operation of the business, prominently post an outdoor sign at the location stating that a sexually oriented business is intended to be located on the premises and providing the name and business address of the owner and operator.

(c) The sign must be at least 24 by 36 inches in size and must be written in lettering at least two inches in size. The municipality or county in which the sexually oriented business is to be located may require the sign to be both in English and a language other than English if it is likely that a substantial number of the residents in the area speak a language other than English as their familiar language.

LGOVT §243.008. INSPECTION

A municipality or county may inspect a sexually oriented business to determine compliance with this chapter and regulations adopted under this chapter by the municipality or county.

LGOVT §243.009. FEES

A municipality or county may impose fees on applicants for a license or other permit issued under this chapter or for the renewal of the license or other permit. The fees must be based on the cost of processing the applications and investigating the applicants.

LGOVT §243.010. ENFORCEMENT

(a) A municipality or county may sue in the district court for an injunction to prohibit the violation of a regulation adopted under this chapter.

(b) A person commits an offense if the person violates a municipal or county regulation adopted under this chapter. An offense under this subsection is a Class A misdemeanor.

LGOVT §243.011. EFFECT ON OTHER LAWS

This chapter does not legalize anything prohibited under the Penal Code or other state law.

CHAPTER 244. LOCATION OF CERTAIN FACILITIES & SHELTERS

SUBCHAPTER A. CORRECTIONAL OR REHABILITATION FACILITY

LGOVT §244.001. DEFINITIONS

In this subchapter:

(1) "Correctional or rehabilitation facility" means a probation or parole office or a residential facility that:

(A) is operated by an agency of the state, a political subdivision of the state, or a private vendor operating under a contract with an agency of the state or a political subdivision of the state; and

(B) houses persons convicted of misdemeanors or felonies or children found to have engaged in delinquent conduct, regardless of whether the persons are housed in the residential facility:

(i) while serving a sentence of confinement following conviction of an offense;

(ii) as a condition of probation, parole, or mandatory supervision; or

(iii) under a court order for out-of-home placement under Title 3, Family Code, other than in a foster home operated under a contract with the juvenile board of the county in which the foster home is located or under a contract with the Texas Juvenile Justice Department.

(2) "Residential area" means:

(A) an area designated as a residential zoning district by a governing ordinance or code or an area in which the principal permitted land use is for private residences;

(B) a subdivision for which a plat is recorded in the real property records of the county and that contains or is bounded by public streets or parts of public streets that are abutted by residential property occupying at least 75 percent of the front footage along the block face; or

(C) a subdivision for which a plat is recorded in the real property records of the county and a majority of the lots of which are subject to deed restrictions limiting the lots to residential use.

LGOVT §244.002. NOTICE OF PROPOSED LOCATION

(a) An agency of the state, a political subdivision of the state, or a private vendor operating under a contract with an agency or political subdivision of the state that proposes to construct or operate a correctional or rehabilitation facility within 1,000 feet of a residential area, a primary or secondary school, property designated as a public park or public recreation area by the state or a political subdivision of the state, or a church, synagogue, or other place of worship shall:

(1) provide written notice to:

(A) the commissioners court of any county with an unincorporated area that includes all or part of the land within 1,000 feet of the proposed correctional or rehabilitation facility; and

(B) the governing body of any municipality that includes within its boundaries all or part of the land within 1,000 feet of the proposed correctional or rehabilitation facility; and

(2) post the notice required by Subsection (d).

(b) An entity required to give notice under Subsection (a) shall give notice not later than the 60th day before the date the entity begins construction or operation of the correctional or rehabilitation facility, whichever date is earlier. The entity shall include in the notice:

(1) a statement of the entity's intent to construct or operate a correctional or rehabilitation facility in an area described by Subsection (a);

(2) a description of the proposed location of the facility; and

(3) a statement that this subchapter governs the procedure for notice of and consent to the facility.

(c) For purposes of this subchapter, distance is measured along the shortest straight line between the nearest property line of the correctional or rehabilitation facility and the nearest property line of the residential area, school, park, recreation area, or place of worship, as appropriate.

(d) An entity described by Subsection (a) shall prominently post an outdoor sign at the proposed location of the correctional or rehabilitation facility stating that a correctional or rehabilitation facility is intended to be located on the premises and providing the name and business address of the entity. The sign must be at least 24 by 36 inches in size and must be written in lettering at least two inches in size. The municipality or county in which the correctional or rehabilitation facility is to be located may require the sign to be both in English and a language other than English if it is likely that a substantial number of the residents in the area speak a language other than English as their familiar language.

LGOVT §244.003. PROXIMITY OF CORRECTIONAL OR REHABILITATION FACILITY

(a) Unless local consent is denied under Section 244.004, an agency of the state, a political subdivision of the state, or a private vendor operating under a contract with an agency or political subdivision of the state may operate a correctional or rehabilitation facility within 1,000 feet of a residential area, a primary or secondary school, property designated as a public park or public recreation area by the state or a political subdivision of the state, or a church, synagogue, or other place of worship.

(b) The governing body of a church, synagogue, or other place of worship may waive the distance requirements of Section 244.002 between a correctional or rehabilitation facility and the place of worship by filing an acknowledged written statement of the waiver in the deed records of the county in which the facility is located.

LGOVT §244.004. LOCAL CONSENT

(a) Local consent to the operation of a correctional or rehabilitation facility at a location within 1,000 feet of a residential area, a primary or secondary school, property designated as a park or public recreation area by the state or a political subdivision of the state, or a church, synagogue, or other place of worship is granted unless, not later than the 60th day after the date on which notice is received by a commissioners court or governing body of a municipality under Section 244.002(a), the commissioners court or governing body, as appropriate, determines by resolution after a public hearing that the operation of a correctional or rehabilitation facility at the proposed location is not in the best interest of the county or municipality, as appropriate.

(b) The public hearing requirement established under Subsection (a) may be met by a public meeting held under Section 508.119 or 509.010, Government Code, if:

(1) the Texas Department of Criminal Justice receives written approval from the commissioners court of a county or governing body of a municipality allowing the public meeting to satisfy the public hearing requirement of this section; and

(2) during the public meeting, a determination is made as to whether operating the facility in the proposed location would be in the best interest of the county or municipality.

(c) If the public hearing requirement established under Subsection (a) is met in the manner described by Subsection (b), the commissioners court of a county or governing body of a municipality may adopt a resolution under Subsection (a) without holding a public hearing under that subsection. The commissioners court or governing body, as appropriate, retains the discretion to hold a separate public hearing under Subsection (a) as the commissioners court or governing body considers necessary or appropriate.

(d) A commissioners court or governing body of a municipality may rescind a resolution adopted under Subsection (a).

LGOVT §244.005. REPEALED

LGOVT §244.006. EXEMPTIONS

This subchapter does not apply to the operation of a correctional or rehabilitation facility at a location subject to this subchapter if:

(1) on September 1, 1997, the correctional or rehabilitation facility was in operation, under construction, under contract for operation or construction, or planned for construction at the location on land owned or leased by an agency or political subdivision of the state and designated for use as a correctional or rehabilitation facility;

(2) the correctional or rehabilitation facility was in operation or under construction before the establishment of a residential area the location of which makes the facility subject to this subchapter;

(3) the correctional or rehabilitation facility is a temporary correctional or rehabilitation facility that will be operated at the location for less than one year;

(4) the correctional or rehabilitation facility is required to obtain a special use permit or a conditional use permit from the municipality in which the facility is located before beginning operation;

(5) the correctional or rehabilitation facility is an expansion of a facility operated by the correctional institutions division of the Texas Department of Criminal Justice for the imprisonment of individuals convicted of felonies other than state jail felonies or by the Texas Juvenile Justice Department;

(6) the correctional or rehabilitation facility is a county jail or a pre-adjudication or post-adjudication juvenile detention facility operated by a county or county juvenile board;

(7) the facility is:

(A) a juvenile probation office located at, and operated in conjunction with, a juvenile justice alternative education center; and

(B) used exclusively by students attending the juvenile justice alternative education center;

(8) the facility is a public or private institution of higher education or vocational training to which admission is open to the general public;

(9) the facility is operated primarily as a treatment facility for juveniles under contract with the Department of Aging and Disability Services or the Department of State Health Services or a local mental health or mental retardation authority;

(10) the facility is operated as a juvenile justice alternative education program;

(11) the facility:

(A) is not operated primarily as a correctional or rehabilitation facility; and

(B) only houses persons or children described by Section 244.001(1)(B) for a purpose related to treatment or education; or

(12) the facility is a probation or parole office located in a commercial use area.

LGOVT §244.007. CONFLICT WITH OTHER LAW

To the extent of any conflict between this subchapter and Sections 508.119 and 509.010, Government Code, this subchapter prevails.

LGOVT §244.008. REPEALED

Sections 244.009-244.020 blank

SUBCHAPTER B. SHELTER FOR HOMELESS INDIVIDUALS

LGOVT §244.021. DEFINITION

In this subchapter, "shelter for homeless individuals" means a supervised private facility that provides temporary living accommodations for homeless individuals.

LGOVT §244.022. APPLICATION OF SUBCHAPTER

This subchapter applies only to construction or operation of a shelter for homeless individuals that is located or proposed to be located within the boundaries of a municipality with a population of 1.6 million or more.

LGOVT §244.023. RESTRICTION

Unless municipal consent is granted under Section 244.025, a person may not construct or operate a shelter for homeless individuals within 1,000 feet of another shelter for homeless individuals or a primary or secondary school.

LGOVT §244.024. NOTICE

(a) A person who intends to construct or operate a shelter for homeless individuals subject to Section 244.023 shall:

(1) post notice of the proposed location of the shelter at that location; and

(2) provide notice of the proposed location of the shelter to the governing body of the municipality within the boundaries of which the shelter is proposed to be located.

(b) The person shall post and provide the notice required by Subsection (a) before the 61st day before the date the person begins construction or operation of the shelter for homeless individuals, whichever date is earlier.

LGOVT §244.025. MUNICIPAL CONSENT

(a) Municipal consent to the construction or operation of a shelter for homeless individuals subject

to Section 244.023 is considered granted unless, before the 61st day after the date notice is received by the governing body of the municipality under Section 244.024(a)(2), the governing body determines by resolution after a public hearing that the construction or operation of a shelter at the proposed location is not in the best interest of the municipality.

(b) The governing body of the municipality may rescind a resolution adopted under Subsection (a).

LGOVT §244.026. DISTANCE MEASUREMENT

For purposes of this subchapter, distance is measured along the shortest straight line between the nearest property line of the shelter for homeless individuals and the nearest property line of another shelter for homeless individuals or a primary or secondary school, as appropriate.

CHAPTER 245. ISSUANCE OF LOCAL PERMITS

LGOVT §245.001. DEFINITIONS

In this chapter:

(1) "Permit" means a license, certificate, approval, registration, consent, permit, contract or other agreement for construction related to, or provision of, service from a water or wastewater utility owned, operated, or controlled by a regulatory agency, or other form of authorization required by law, rule, regulation, order, or ordinance that a person must obtain to perform an action or initiate, continue, or complete a project for which the permit is sought.

(2) "Political subdivision" means a political subdivision of the state, including a county, a school district, or a municipality.

(3) "Project" means an endeavor over which a regulatory agency exerts its jurisdiction and for which one or more permits are required to initiate, continue, or complete the endeavor.

(4) "Regulatory agency" means the governing body of, or a bureau, department, division, board, commission, or other agency of, a political subdivision acting in its capacity of processing, approving, or issuing a permit.

LGOVT §245.002. UNIFORMITY OF REQUIREMENTS

(a) Each regulatory agency shall consider the approval, disapproval, or conditional approval of an application for a permit solely on the basis of any orders, regulations, ordinances, rules, expiration dates, or other properly adopted requirements in effect at the time:

(1) the original application for the permit is filed for review for any purpose, including review for administrative completeness; or

(2) a plan for development of real property or plat application is filed with a regulatory agency.

(a-1) Rights to which a permit applicant is entitled under this chapter accrue on the filing of an original application or plan for development or plat application that gives the regulatory agency fair notice of the project and the nature of the permit sought. An application or plan is considered filed on the date the applicant delivers the application or plan to the regulatory agency or deposits the application or plan with the United States Postal Service by certified mail addressed to the regulatory agency. A certified mail receipt obtained by the applicant at the time of deposit is prima facie evidence of the date the application or plan was deposited with the United States Postal Service.

(b) If a series of permits is required for a project, the orders, regulations, ordinances, rules, expiration dates, or other properly adopted requirements in effect at the time the original application for the first permit in that series is filed shall be the sole basis for consideration of all subsequent permits required for the completion of the project. All permits required for the project are considered to be a single series of permits. Preliminary plans and related subdivision plats, site plans, and all other development permits for land covered by the preliminary plans or subdivision plats are considered collectively to be one series of permits for a project.

(c) After an application for a project is filed, a regulatory agency may not shorten the duration of any permit required for the project.

(d) Notwithstanding any provision of this chapter to the contrary, a permit holder may take advantage of recorded subdivision plat notes, recorded restrictive covenants required by a regulatory agency, or a change to the laws, rules, regulations, or ordinances of a regulatory agency that enhance or protect the project, including changes that lengthen the effective life of the permit after the date the application for the permit was made, without forfeiting any rights under this chapter.

(e) A regulatory agency may provide that a permit application expires on or after the 45th day after the date the application is filed if:

(1) the applicant fails to provide documents or other information necessary to comply with the agency's technical requirements relating to the form and content of the permit application;

(2) the agency provides to the applicant not later than the 10th business day after the date the application is filed written notice of the failure that specifies the necessary documents or other information and the date the application will expire if the documents or other information is not provided; and

(3) the applicant fails to provide the specified documents or other information within the time provided in the notice.

(f) This chapter does not prohibit a regulatory agency from requiring compliance with technical requirements relating to the form and content of an application in effect at the time the application was filed even though the application is filed after the date an applicant accrues rights under Subsection (a-1).

(g) Notwithstanding Section 245.003, the change in law made to Subsection (a) and the addition of Subsections (a-1), (e), and (f) by S.B. No. 848, Acts of the 79th Legislature, Regular Session, 2005, apply only to a project commenced on or after the effective date of that Act.

LGOVT §245.003. APPLICABILITY OF CHAPTER

This chapter applies only to a project in progress on or commenced after September 1, 1997. For purposes of this chapter a project was in progress on September 1, 1997, if:

(1) before September 1, 1997:

(A) a regulatory agency approved or issued one or more permits for the project; or

(B) an application for a permit for the project was filed with a regulatory agency; and

(2) on or after September 1, 1997, a regulatory agency enacts, enforces, or otherwise imposes:

(A) an order, regulation, ordinance, or rule that in effect retroactively changes the duration of a permit for the project;

(B) a deadline for obtaining a permit required to continue or complete the project that was not enforced or did not apply to the project before September 1, 1997; or

(C) any requirement for the project that was not applicable to or enforced on the project before September 1, 1997.

LGOVT §245.004. EXEMPTIONS

This chapter does not apply to:

(1) a permit that is at least two years old, is issued for the construction of a building or structure intended for human occupancy or habitation, and is issued under laws, ordinances, procedures, rules, or regulations adopting only:

(A) uniform building, fire, electrical, plumbing, or mechanical codes adopted by a recognized national code organization; or

(B) local amendments to those codes enacted solely to address imminent threats of destruction of property or injury to persons;

(2) municipal zoning regulations that do not affect landscaping or tree preservation, open space or park dedication, property classification, lot size, lot dimensions, lot coverage, or building size or that do not change development permitted by a restrictive covenant required by a municipality;

(3) regulations that specifically control only the use of land in a municipality that does not have zoning and that do not affect landscaping or tree preservation, open space or park dedication, lot size, lot dimensions, lot coverage, or building size;

(4) regulations for sexually oriented businesses;

(5) municipal or county ordinances, rules, regulations, or other requirements affecting colonias;

(6) fees imposed in conjunction with development permits;

(7) regulations for annexation that do not affect landscaping or tree preservation or open space or park dedication;

(8) regulations for utility connections;

(9) regulations to prevent imminent destruction of property or injury to persons from flooding that are effective only within a flood plain established by a federal flood control program and enacted to prevent the flooding of buildings intended for public occupancy;

(10) construction standards for public works located on public lands or easements; or

(11) regulations to prevent the imminent destruction of property or injury to persons if the regulations do not:

(A) affect landscaping or tree preservation, open space or park dedication, lot size, lot dimensions, lot coverage, building size, residential or commercial density, or the timing of a project; or

(B) change development permitted by a restrictive covenant required by a municipality.

LGOVT §245.005. DORMANT PROJECTS

(a) After the first anniversary of the effective date of this chapter, a regulatory agency may enact an ordinance, rule, or regulation that places an expiration date on a permit if as of the first anniversary of the effective date of this chapter: (i) the permit does not have an expiration date; and (ii) no progress has been made towards completion of the project. Any ordinance, rule, or regulation enacted pursuant to this subsection shall place an expiration date of no earlier than the fifth anniversary of the effective date of this chapter.

(b) A regulatory agency may enact an ordinance, rule, or regulation that places an expiration date of not less than two years on an individual permit if no progress has been made towards completion of the project. Notwithstanding any other provision of this chapter, any ordinance, rule, or regulation enacted pursuant to this section shall place an expiration date on a project of no earlier than the fifth anniversary of the date the first permit application was filed for the project if no progress has been made towards completion of the project. Nothing in this subsection shall be deemed to affect the timing of a permit issued solely under the authority of Chapter 366, Health and Safety Code, by the Texas Commission on Environmental Quality or its authorized agent.

(c) Progress towards completion of the project shall include any one of the following:

(1) an application for a final plat or plan is submitted to a regulatory agency;

(2) a good-faith attempt is made to file with a regulatory agency an application for a permit necessary to begin or continue towards completion of the project;

(3) costs have been incurred for developing the project including, without limitation, costs associated with roadway, utility, and other infrastructure facilities designed to serve, in whole or in part, the project (but exclusive of land acquisition) in the aggregate amount of five percent of the most recent appraised market value of the real property on which the project is located;

(4) fiscal security is posted with a regulatory agency to ensure performance of an obligation required by the regulatory agency; or

(5) utility connection fees or impact fees for the project have been paid to a regulatory agency.

Ⓐ LGOVT §245.006. ENFORCEMENT OF CHAPTER

(a) This chapter may be enforced only through mandamus or declaratory or injunctive relief.

(b) A political subdivision's immunity from suit is waived in regard to an action under this chapter.

(c) A court may award court costs and reasonable and necessary attorney's fees to the prevailing party in an action under this chapter.

2017 Legislation: Amended by H.B. 1704, §1, 85th Leg., eff. May 29, 2017.

LGOVT §245.007. CONSTRUCTION & RENOVATION WORK ON COUNTY-OWNED BUILDINGS & FACILITIES IN CERTAIN COUNTIES

(a) This section applies only to a building or facility that is owned by a county with a population of 3.3 million or more and is located within the boundaries of another political subdivision.

(b) A political subdivision may not require a county to notify the political subdivision or obtain a building permit for any new construction or any renovation of a building or facility owned by the county if the construction or renovation work is supervised and inspected by an engineer or architect licensed in this state.

(c) This section does not exempt a county from complying with the building standards of the political subdivision during the construction or renovation of the building or facility.

CHAPTER 246. CONSTRUCTION OF CERTAIN TELECOMMUNICATIONS FACILITIES

LGOVT §246.001. DEFINITIONS

In this chapter:

(1) "Commission" means the Public Utility Commission of Texas.

(2) "Critical facility" means a central office that contains:

(A) a switching unit for a telecommunications system that provides service to the general public; and

(B) equipment and operating arrangements necessary for terminating and interconnecting:

(i) customer lines and trunks; or

(ii) trunks.

(3) "Impervious lot coverage regulation" means an ordinance, regulation, rule, or other enactment by a county, municipality, or other authority that limits the development of real property based on the amount of impervious lot coverage to be constructed. The term does not include a flood control regulation.

(4) "Regulating authority" means a county, municipality, or other political subdivision of this state that has adopted an impervious lot coverage regulation or a sedimentation, retention, or erosion regulation by ordinance, order, resolution, rule, or other enactment.

(5) "Sedimentation, retention, or erosion regulation" means an ordinance, regulation, rule, or other enactment by a county, municipality, or other authority that limits or regulates the development of real property based on the development's effect on water quality resulting from sedimentation, retention, or erosion. The term does not include a:

(A) flood control regulation; or

(B) requirement for silt fences, vegetative cover, or other similar requirement.

(6) "Telecommunications utility" has the meaning assigned by Section 51.002, Utilities Code.

LGOVT §246.002. APPLICABILITY

This chapter applies only to a critical facility that:

(1) existed on April 1, 2001; and

(2) is being expanded to provide space and facilities for competing telecommunications utilities because of requirements in:

(A) the Communications Act of 1934 (47 U.S.C. Section 151 et seq.), as amended; or

(B) Subchapters G and H, Chapter 60, Utilities Code.

LGOVT §246.003. REQUEST PROCESS

(a) A regulating authority that receives a written request by a telecommunications utility to expand a critical facility on real property owned, leased, or occupied by the telecommunications utility in an area governed by impervious lot coverage regulation or sedimentation, retention, or erosion regulation shall approve or deny the request not later than the 60th day after the date the request is received.

(b) The regulating authority shall approve the request unless the regulating authority finds, after a hearing, that:

(1) additional, suitable vacant land contiguous with the proposed building site that is sufficient to satisfy the impervious lot coverage regulation or sedimentation, retention, or erosion regulation is not available, except:

(A) through the use of condemnation; or

(B) at a price that exceeds the average fair market value of vacant land within a one-mile radius of the property that is the subject of the request under Subsection (a); or

(2) the telecommunications utility did not provide an affidavit containing the statement described in Subdivision (1).

(c) The regulating authority shall provide written notice of a denial. The notice must specify the findings on which the authority relied in denying the request.

(d) If a regulating authority does not make a decision before the deadline prescribed by Subsection (a):

(1) the request is approved; and

(2) the regulating authority may not apply the authority's impervious lot coverage regulations or sedimentation, retention, or erosion regulations to the expansion that is the subject of the request under Subsection (a).

LGOVT §246.004. COMMISSION JURISDICTION

The commission has jurisdiction to enforce this chapter and to ensure that legal requirements are enforced in a competitively neutral, nondiscriminatory, and reasonable manner.

TITLE 8. ACQUISITION, SALE, OR LEASE OF PROPERTY

SUBTITLE A. MUNICIPAL ACQUISITION, SALE, OR LEASE OF PROPERTY

CHAPTER 251. MUNICIPAL RIGHT OF EMINENT DOMAIN

LGOVT §251.001. RIGHT OF EMINENT DOMAIN

(a) When the governing body of a municipality considers it necessary, the municipality may exercise the right of eminent domain for a public use to acquire public or private property, whether located inside or outside the municipality, for any of the following uses:

(1) the providing, enlarging, or improving of a municipally owned city hall; police station; jail or other law enforcement detention facility; fire station; library; school or other educational facility; academy; audito-

rium; hospital; sanatorium; market house; slaughterhouse; warehouse; elevator; railroad terminal; airport; ferry; ferry landing; pier; wharf; dock or other shipping facility; loading or unloading facility; alley, street, or other roadway; park, playground, or other recreational facility; square; water works system, including reservoirs, other water supply sources, watersheds, and water storage, drainage, treatment, distribution, transmission, and emptying facilities; sewage system including sewage collection, drainage, treatment, disposal, and emptying facilities; electric or gas power system; cemetery; and crematory;

(2) the determining of riparian rights relative to the municipal water works;

(3) the straightening or improving of the channel of any stream, branch, or drain;

(4) the straightening, widening, or extending of any alley, street, or other roadway; and

(5) any other municipal public use the governing body considers advisable.

(b) A municipality condemning land under this section may take a fee simple title to the property if the governing body expresses the intention to do so.

LGOVT §251.002. PROCEDURE

An exercise of the power of eminent domain granted by this chapter is governed by Chapter 21 of the Property Code.

SUBTITLE B. COUNTY ACQUISITION, SALE, OR LEASE OF PROPERTY

CHAPTER 261. COUNTY RIGHT OF EMINENT DOMAIN

LGOVT §261.001. RIGHT OF EMINENT DOMAIN

(a) A county may exercise the right of eminent domain to condemn and acquire land, an easement in land, or a right-of-way if the acquisition is necessary for the construction of a jail, courthouse, hospital, or library, or for another public use authorized by law.

(b) The right of eminent domain conferred by this section extends to public or private land, but not to land used for cemetery purposes.

LGOVT §261.002. PROCEDURE

The condemnation proceedings must be instituted in the name of the county and under the direction of the commissioners court.

LGOVT §261.003. APPEAL

(a) An appeal from a finding and assessment of damages made as prescribed by Chapter 21, Property Code, does not suspend work by the county that relates to the land the county seeks to acquire.

(b) A county is not required to give a bond in an appealed case.

NATURAL RESOURCES CODE
SELECTED PROVISIONS
TABLE OF CONTENTS

NATURAL RESOURCES CODE
SELECTED PROVISIONS
TABLE OF CONTENTS

TITLE 12. WETLANDS

Chapter 221. Wetland Mitigation

Subchapter A. General Provisions

Subchapter B. Wetland Mitigation Banking & Contracts

Subchapter C. Provisions for Political Subdivisions

Title 3. Oil & Gas

Subtitle B. Conservation & Regulation of Oil & Gas

Chapter 92. Mineral Use of Subdivided Land

NatRes §92.001. Purpose

It is the finding of the legislature that the rapidly expanding population and development of the cities and towns of this state and the concomitant need for adequate and affordable housing and suitable job opportunities call for full and efficient utilization and development of all the land resources of this state, as well as the full development of all the minerals of this state. In view of that finding, it is the intent of the legislature that the mineral resources of this state be fully and effectively exploited and that all land in this state be maintained and utilized to its fullest and most efficient use. It is the further finding of this legislature that it is necessary to exercise the authority of the legislature pursuant to Article XVI, Section 59, of the Constitution of the State of Texas to assure proper and orderly development of both the mineral and land resources of this state and that the enactment of this chapter will protect the rights and welfare of the citizens of this state.

NatRes §92.002. Definitions

In this chapter:

(1) "Operations site" means a surface area of two or more acres located in whole or in part within a qualified subdivision, designated on the subdivision plat, that an owner of a possessory mineral interest may use to explore for and produce minerals.

(2) "Possessory mineral interest" means a mineral interest that includes the right to use the land surface for exploration and production of minerals.

(3) "Qualified subdivision" means a tract of land of not more than 640 acres:

(A) that is located in a county having a population in excess of 400,000, or in a county having a population in excess of 140,000 that borders a county having a population in excess of 400,000 or located on a barrier island;

(B) that has been subdivided in a manner authorized by law by the surface owners for residential, commercial, or industrial use; and

(C) that contains an operations site for each separate 80 acres within the 640-acre tract and provisions for road and pipeline easements to allow use of the operations site.

(4) "Barrier island" means an island bordering on the Gulf of Mexico and entirely surrounded by water.

NatRes §92.003. Creation of Subdivision

The surface owners of a parcel of land may create a qualified subdivision on the land if a plat of the subdivision has been approved by the railroad commission and filed with the clerk of the county in which the subdivision is to be located.

NatRes §92.004. Hearing & Order by Railroad Commission

(a) The railroad commission shall adopt rules governing the contents of an application for a qualified subdivision. An application must be accompanied by a plat of the subdivision showing the applicant's proposed location of operations sites and road and pipeline easements.

(b) The railroad commission shall, on notice to the applicant and owners of possessory mineral interests, hold a hearing on the application at which the commission shall consider the adequacy of the number and location of operations sites and road and pipeline easements. At the hearing on the application, evidence may be presented by the applicant and the owners of possessory mineral interests. After considering the evidence, the commission shall approve, reject, or amend the application to ensure that the mineral resources of the subdivision are fully and effectively exploited. The applicant or the owner of the possessory mineral interest may appeal the order of the railroad commission as provided by law.

NatRes §92.005. Use of Operations Site

(a) An owner of a possessory mineral interest within a qualified subdivision may use only the surface contained in designated operations sites for exploration, development, and production of minerals and the designated easements only as necessary to adequately use the operations sites.

(b) The owner of the possessory mineral interest may drill wells or extend well bores from an operations site or from a site outside of the qualified subdivision under the surface of other parts of the qualified subdivision if the operations do not unreasonably interfere with the use of the surface of the qualified subdivision outside the operations site.

(c) This section ceases to apply to a subdivision if, by the third anniversary of the date on which the order of the commission becomes final:

(1) the surface owner has not commenced actual construction of roads or utilities within the qualified subdivision; and

(2) a lot within the qualified subdivision has not been sold to a third party.

NatRes §92.006. Amendment, Replat, or Abandonment

All or any portion of a qualified subdivision may be amended, replatted, or abandoned by the surface owner. An amendment or replat, however, may not alter, diminish, or impair the usefulness of an operations site or appurtenant road or pipeline easement unless the amendment or replat is approved by the commission in accordance with Section 92.003 of this code.

NatRes §92.007. Municipal Authority

This chapter does not affect the authority of a municipality to require approval of subdivision plats or the authority of a home-rule city to regulate exploration and development of mineral interests within its boundaries.

Subtitle D. Regulation of Specific Businesses & Occupations

Chapter 111. Common Carriers, Public Utilities, & Common Purchasers

Subchapter A. General Provisions

NatRes §111.001. Definitions

In this chapter:

(1) "Commission" means the Railroad Commission of Texas.

(2) "Public utility" means a person, association of persons, or corporation that owns, operates, or manages crude petroleum storage tanks or storage facilities for the public for hire, either in connection with a pipeline, pipelines, or otherwise. The term does not include an electric cooperative, as that term is defined by Section 11.003, Utilities Code, or its subsidiary, that sells electricity at wholesale and that owns or operates an underground storage facility and provides gas storage services to the public for hire if the gas storage facility is predominantly operated to support the integration of renewable resources. Such a gas storage facility may not have a working gas capacity of greater than five billion cubic feet.

Subchapter B. Common Carriers

NatRes §111.019. Right of Eminent Domain

(a) Common carriers have the right and power of eminent domain.

(b) In the exercise of the power of eminent domain granted under the provisions of Subsection (a) of this section, a common carrier may enter on and condemn the land, rights-of-way, easements, and property of any person or corporation necessary for the construction, maintenance, or operation of the common carrier pipeline.

(c) Upon written request by a resident or owner of land crossed by a common carrier pipeline, the common carrier must disclose material data safety sheets concerning the commodities transported by the common carrier required by the commission and the Emergency Planning and Community Right-to-Know Act of 1986 (42 U.S.C. Section 11001 et seq.). Such disclosure must be in writing and must be mailed or delivered to the resident or landowner within 30 days of receipt of the request.

NatRes §111.0191. Costs of Relocation of Property

In the event a common carrier pipeline in the exercise of the power of eminent domain or police power or any other power granted under this chapter makes necessary the relocation, raising, lowering, rerouting, or changing the grade of, or altering the construction of any railroad, electric transmission, telegraph or telephone lines, properties and facilities, or pipeline, all such relocation, raising, lowering, rerouting, changing of grade, or alteration of construction shall be accomplished at the sole expense of such common carrier pipeline. The term "sole expense" means the actual cost of the relocation, raising, lowering, rerouting, or change in grade or alteration of construction in providing comparable replacement without enhancement of the facilities, after deducting therefrom the net salvage value derived from the old facility.

NatRes §111.0192. Limitations on the Powers of Eminent Domain in Certain Situations

(a) The right of eminent domain granted under this chapter to any pipelines transporting coal in what-

ever form shall not include and cannot be used to condemn water or water rights for use in the transportation of coal by pipeline, and no Texas water from any source shall be used in connection with the transportation, maintenance, or operation of a coal slurry pipeline (except water used for drinking, toilet, bath, or other personal uses at pumping stations or offices) within the State of Texas unless the Texas Natural Resource Conservation Commission shall determine, after public hearing, that the use will not be detrimental to the water supply of the area from which the water is sought to be extracted.

(b) The right of eminent domain granted under this chapter to any pipeline transporting coal in whatever form shall not include the power to take land or any interest in land, by exercise of the power of eminent domain, for the purpose of drilling for, mining, or producing any oil, gas, geothermal, geothermal/geopressured, lignite, coal, sulphur, uranium, plutonium, or other mineral, but this provision does not impair the right of any such entity to acquire title to real property for pipelines, including cooling ponds and related surface installations and equipment.

NATRES §111.0193. RESTORATION OF PROPERTY

Every condemnation award granted under this chapter shall require that the condemnor restore the property which is the subject of the award to its former condition as near as reasonably practicable.

NATRES §111.0194. PIPELINE EASEMENTS

(a) Unless the terms of the grant or the condemnation judgment expressly provide otherwise, or the easement rights otherwise prescriptively owned through actual use are greater, an easement created through grant or through the power of eminent domain for the benefit of a single common carrier pipeline for which the power of eminent domain is available under Section 111.019 of this code as of January 1, 1994, is presumed to create an easement in favor of the common carrier pipeline, or a successor in interest to the common carrier pipeline, that extends only a width of 50 feet as to each pipeline laid under the grant or judgment in eminent domain prior to January 1, 1994.

(b) The presumption in Subsection (a) of this section is not applicable to pipeline easements of a common carrier pipeline granted under the terms of an oil and gas lease or oil, gas, and mineral lease, or to any easement which authorizes the construction of gathering lines.

(c) The presumption set out in Subsection (a) of this section on the limitation of width may be rebutted by evidence on behalf of the common carrier pipeline that a greater width is reasonably needed for purposes of operation, construction of additional lines under the grant or judgment in an eminent domain proceeding, maintenance, repair, replacement, safety, surveillance, or as a buffer zone for protection of the safe operation of the common carrier pipeline, together with such other evidence as a court may deem relevant to establish the extent of an easement in excess of 50 feet in width.

(d) The presumption in Subsection (a) of this section shall apply separately as to each pipeline under a grant or judgment which allows more than one pipeline on the subservient estate.

(e) This section shall not be deemed to limit any rights of ingress to or egress from easements that may exist under the original grant, prescriptive rights, or common law.

(f) This section does not limit or otherwise affect the rights of parties engaged in litigation before January 1, 1994.

NATRES §111.020. PIPELINE ON PUBLIC STREAM OR HIGHWAY

(a) Subject to the provisions of Subsection (b) of this section, all common carriers are entitled to lay, maintain, and operate along, across, or under a public stream or highway in this state pipelines, together with telegraph and telephone lines incidental to and designed for use only in connection with the operation of the pipelines.

(b) The right to run a pipeline or telegraph or telephone line along, across, or over a public road or highway may be exercised only on condition that:

(1) it does not interfere with traffic on the road or highway;

(2) the road or highway is promptly restored to its former condition of usefulness;

(3) the restoration of the road or highway is subject also to the supervision of the commissioners court or other proper local authority; and

(4) no pipes or pipelines are laid parallel with and on a public highway closer than 15 feet from the improved section of the highway except with the approval and under the direction of the commissioners court of the county in which the public highway is located.

(c) The common carrier shall compensate the county or road district, respectively, for any damage done to the public road in the exercise of the privileges conferred.

(d) A person may acquire the right conferred in this section by filing with the commission a written acceptance of the provisions of this chapter expressly agreeing that, in consideration of the rights acquired, it becomes a common carrier subject to the duties and obligations conferred or imposed by this chapter.

NatRes §111.021. Pipeline Under Railroad, Street Railroad, or Canal

A common carrier is entitled to lay its pipe or pipeline under any railroad, railroad right-of-way, street railroad, or canal in this state.

NatRes §111.022. Right to Use Street or Alley in City or Town

The provisions of this chapter do not grant a pipeline company the right to use a public street or alley in an incorporated or unincorporated city or town except with express permission of the governing body of the city or town or the right to lay its pipes or pipelines along and under a street or alley in an incorporated city or town except with the consent and under the direction of the governing body of the city or town.

NatRes §111.023. Exchange of Facilities

(a) A common carrier shall exchange crude petroleum tonnage with each like common carrier.

(b) When a necessity exists, the commission may require connections and facilities for the interchange of crude petroleum tonnage to be made at every locality reached by both pipelines, subject to the rules and rates made by the commission.

(c) A common carrier pipeline under like rules shall be required to install and maintain facilities for the receipt and delivery of crude petroleum of patrons at all points on the pipeline.

Title 6. Timber

Chapter 153. Prescribed Burning

Subchapter A. General Provisions

NatRes §153.001. Definitions

In this chapter:

(1) "Board" means the Prescribed Burning Board.

(2) "Department" means the Department of Agriculture.

(3) "Prescribed burning organization" means an organization described by Section 153.049.

NatRes §153.002. Landowner's Right to Conduct Burns Not Limited

This chapter does not limit a landowner's right to conduct burns on the landowner's property.

NatRes §153.003. Liability

This chapter does not modify a landowner's liability for property damage, personal injury, or death resulting from a burn that is not conducted as provided by this chapter.

NatRes §153.004. Prescribed Burning in State of Emergency or Disaster

A certified and insured prescribed burn manager or the members of a prescribed burning organization may conduct a burn in a county in which a state of emergency or state of disaster has been declared by the governor or the president of the United States, unless the declaration expressly prohibits all outdoor burning.

Sections 153.005-153.040 reserved for expansion

Subchapter B. Prescribed Burning Board

NatRes §153.041. Establishment

(a) The Prescribed Burning Board is established within the department and is composed of:

(1) an employee of the Texas Forest Service designated by the director of the Texas Forest Service;

(2) an employee of the Parks and Wildlife Department appointed by the executive director of the Parks and Wildlife Department;

(3) an employee of the Texas Commission on Environmental Quality appointed by the executive director of the Texas Commission on Environmental Quality;

(4) an employee of the Texas AgriLife Extension Service appointed by the executive director of the Texas AgriLife Extension Service;

(5) an employee of Texas AgriLife Research appointed by the director of Texas AgriLife Research;

(6) an employee of the Texas Tech University Range and Wildlife Department appointed by the dean

of the Texas Tech University College of Agricultural Sciences and Natural Resources;

(7) an employee of the department appointed by the commissioner of agriculture;

(8) an employee of the State Soil and Water Conservation Board appointed by the executive director of the State Soil and Water Conservation Board; and

(9) five persons who are:

(A) owners of agricultural land, as that term is defined by Section 153.081;

(B) self-employed or employed by a person other than a governmental entity; and

(C) appointed by the commissioner of agriculture.

(b) A member serves for a two-year term.

(c) The board shall, by majority vote, elect a presiding officer from the members of the board.

(d) Appointments to the board shall be made without regard to the race, creed, sex, disability, age, religion, or national origin of the appointees.

(e) It is a ground for removal from the board that a member:

(1) does not have at the time of appointment the qualifications required by Subsection (a) for appointment to the board;

(2) does not maintain during the service on the board the qualifications required by Subsection (a) for appointment to the board;

(3) cannot because of illness or disability discharge the member's duties for a substantial part of the term for which the member is appointed; or

(4) is absent from more than half of the regularly scheduled board meetings that the member is eligible to attend during a calendar year unless the absence is excused by majority vote of the board.

(f) The validity of an action of the board is not affected by the fact that it was taken when a ground for removal of a member of the board existed.

NATRES §153.042. INFORMATION RELATING TO STANDARDS OF CONDUCT

The presiding officer of the board or the presiding officer's designee shall provide to members of the board, as often as necessary, information regarding their qualification for office under this chapter and their responsibilities under applicable laws relating to standards of conduct for state officers.

NATRES §153.043. MEMBER TRAINING

(a) A person appointed to the board is not eligible for membership on the board unless the person completes at least one training program that complies with this section.

(b) The training program must provide information to the member regarding:

(1) this chapter;

(2) the programs operated by the board;

(3) the role and functions of the board;

(4) the requirements of Chapters 551, 552, and 2001, Government Code;

(5) the requirements of the conflict of interest laws and other laws relating to public officials; and

(6) any applicable ethics policies adopted by the board or the Texas Ethics Commission.

(c) A person appointed to the board is entitled to reimbursement for travel expenses incurred in attending the training program as provided by the General Appropriations Act as if the person were a member of the board.

NATRES §153.044. SUNSET PROVISION

The Prescribed Burning Board is subject to Chapter 325, Government Code (Texas Sunset Act). The board shall be reviewed during the period in which the Department of Agriculture is reviewed.

NATRES §153.045. ADVISORY BOARD

(a) The board shall establish an advisory board of members of the public, including individuals representing:

(1) property owners;

(2) agriculture, forestry, and livestock producers;

(3) conservation interests;

(4) environmental interests; and

(5) insurance interests.

(b) The board shall determine the number of persons and manner of selection of the advisory board.

NATRES §153.046. DUTIES

The board shall:

(1) establish standards for prescribed burning;

(2) develop a comprehensive training curriculum for certified and insured prescribed burn managers;

(3) establish standards for certification, recertification, and training for certified and insured prescribed burn managers;

(4) establish minimum education and professional requirements for instructors for the approved curriculum;

(5) establish insurance requirements for certified and insured prescribed burn managers in amounts not less than those required by Section 153.082; and

(6) establish minimum insurance requirements for prescribed burning organizations.

NATRES §153.047. PRESCRIBED BURNING STANDARDS

Minimum standards established by the board for prescribed burning must:

(1) ensure that prescribed burning is the controlled application of fire to naturally occurring or naturalized vegetative fuels under specified environmental conditions in accordance with a written prescription plan:

(A) designed to confine the fire to a predetermined area and to accomplish planned land management objectives; and

(B) that conforms to the standards established under this section;

(2) require that:

(A) at least one certified and insured prescribed burn manager is present on site during the conduct of the prescribed burn; or

(B) the burn be conducted by the members of a prescribed burning organization;

(3) establish appropriate guidelines for size of burning crews sufficient to:

(A) conduct the burn in accordance with the prescription plan; and

(B) provide adequate protection for the safety of persons and of adjacent property;

(4) include standards for notification to adjacent land owners, the Texas Commission on Environmental Quality, and local fire authorities; and

(5) include minimum insurance requirements for certified and insured prescribed burn managers and prescribed burning organizations.

NATRES §153.048. CERTIFIED & INSURED PRESCRIBED BURN MANAGERS

(a) Minimum standards established by the board for certification as a certified and insured prescribed burn manager must require the completion of the approved training curriculum to be developed and promulgated by the board and taught by an approved instructor.

(b) The board shall certify a person as a certified and insured prescribed burn manager if the person:

(1) applies to the board for certification;

(2) demonstrates completion of an approved training program by an approved instructor;

(3) pays a fee to the board in an amount determined by the board; and

(4) meets the insurance requirements established by the board under Section 153.046.

(c) The certification is for two years.

(d) A person may renew certification only by completing a continuing education program established by the board.

(e) The board shall maintain a register of certified and insured prescribed burn managers and dates of completion of initial and continuing training.

NATRES §153.049. PRESCRIBED BURNING ORGANIZATIONS

The members of a charitable organization, as defined by Section 84.003, Civil Practice and Remedies Code, that is organized and operated for prescribed burning purposes may conduct a burn under this chapter if:

(1) the member in charge of the burn has completed the approved training curriculum described by Section 153.048(a); and

(2) the organization has insurance coverage in an amount not less than the amount established by the board under Section 153.046.

Sections 153.050-153.080 reserved for expansion

SUBCHAPTER C. LIMITATIONS ON LIABILITY

NATRES §153.081. LIMITATION OF OWNER LIABILITY

(a) Subject to Section 153.082, an owner, lessee, or occupant of agricultural or conservation land is not liable for property damage or for injury or death to persons caused by or resulting from prescribed burning conducted on the land owned by, leased by, or occupied by the person if the prescribed burning is conducted:

(1) under the supervision of a certified and insured prescribed burn manager; or

(2) by the members of a prescribed burning organization.

(b) This section does not apply to an owner, lessee, or occupant of agricultural or conservation land who is a certified and insured prescribed burn manager and conducts a burn on that land.

(c) In this section, "agricultural or conservation land" means land that is located in this state and that is suitable for:

(1) use and production of plants and fruits for human or animal consumption or plants grown for the production of fibers, floriculture, viticulture, horticulture, or planting seed;

(2) forestry and the growing of trees for the purpose of rendering those trees into lumber, fiber, or other items used for industrial, commercial, or personal consumption;

(3) domestic or native farm or ranch animals kept for use or profit;

(4) management of native or exotic wildlife; or

(5) conservation or management of an ecosystem, a forest, a habitat, a species, water, or wildlife.

NATRES §153.082. INSURANCE

The limitation on liability under Section 153.081 does not apply to an owner, lessee, or occupant of agricultural or conservation land unless:

(1) the burn is conducted under the supervision of a certified and insured prescribed burn manager who has liability insurance coverage:

(A) of at least $1 million for each single occurrence of bodily injury or death, or injury to or destruction of property; and

(B) with a policy period minimum aggregate limit of at least $2 million;

(2) the owner, lessee, or occupant is a governmental unit, as that term is defined by Section 2259.001, Government Code, that has a self-insurance program that provides the amount of coverage required by Subdivision (1); or

(3) the burn is conducted by the members of a prescribed burning organization that has insurance coverage in an amount not less than the amount established by the board under Section 153.046.

Sections 153.083-153.100 blank

SUBCHAPTER D. COMPLAINTS, ENFORCEMENT, & PENALTIES

NATRES §153.101. COMPLAINTS

The department shall receive and process complaints concerning certified and insured prescribed burn managers in the manner described by Section 12.026, Agriculture Code, and rules adopted under that section.

NATRES §153.102. DISCIPLINARY ACTION; SCHEDULE OF SANCTIONS

(a) The department may impose an administrative sanction, including an administrative penalty, as provided by Sections 12.020, 12.0201, 12.0202, and 12.0261, Agriculture Code, for a violation of this chapter.

(b) The department by rule shall adopt a schedule of the disciplinary sanctions that the department may impose under this chapter. In adopting the schedule of sanctions, the department shall ensure that the severity of the sanction imposed is appropriate to the type of violation or conduct that is the basis for disciplinary action.

(c) In determining the appropriate disciplinary action, including the amount of any administrative penalty to assess, the department shall consider:

(1) whether the person:

(A) is being disciplined for multiple violations of either this chapter or a rule or order adopted under this chapter; or

(B) has previously been the subject of disciplinary action by the department under this chapter and has previously complied with department rules and this chapter;

(2) the seriousness of the violation;

(3) the threat to public safety; and

(4) any mitigating factors.

NATRES §153.103. INJUNCTION

(a) The department may apply to a district court in any county for an injunction to restrain a person who is not a certified and insured prescribed burn manager from representing that the person is a certified and insured prescribed burn manager.

(b) At the request of the department, the attorney general shall initiate and conduct an action in a district court in the state's name to obtain an injunction under this section.

NATRES §153.104. EMERGENCY SUSPENSION

(a) On determining that a certification holder is engaged in or about to engage in a violation of this chapter and that the certification holder's continued practice constitutes an immediate threat to the public welfare, the department may issue an order suspending the certification holder's certification without notice or a hearing. The department shall immediately serve notice of the suspension on the certification holder.

(b) The notice required by Subsection (a) must:

(1) be personally served on the certification holder or be sent by registered or certified mail, return receipt requested, to the certification holder's last known address according to the department's records;

(2) state the grounds for the suspension; and

(3) inform the certification holder of the right to a hearing on the suspension order.

(c) A certification holder whose certification is suspended under this section is entitled to request a hearing on the suspension not later than the 30th day after the date of receipt of notice of the suspension. Not later than the fifth day after the date a hearing is requested, the department shall issue a notice of hearing.

(d) A hearing on a suspension order under this section is subject to Chapter 2001, Government Code. If the hearing is before an administrative law judge, after the hearing, the administrative law judge shall recommend to the department whether to uphold, vacate, or modify the suspension order.

(e) A suspension order issued under this section remains in effect until further action is taken by the department. If the administrative law judge's recommendation under Subsection (d) is to vacate the order, the department shall determine whether to vacate the order not later than the second day after the date of the recommendation.

TITLE 8. ACQUISITION OF RESOURCES

CHAPTER 183. CONSERVATION EASEMENTS

SUBCHAPTER A. CONSERVATION EASEMENTS GENERALLY

NATRES §183.001. DEFINITIONS

In this chapter:

(1) "Conservation easement" means a nonpossessory interest of a holder in real property that imposes limitations or affirmative obligations designed to:

(A) retain or protect natural, scenic, or open-space values of real property or assure its availability for agricultural, forest, recreational, or open-space use;

(B) protect natural resources;

(C) maintain or enhance air or water quality; or

(D) preserve the historical, architectural, archeological, or cultural aspects of real property.

(2) "Holder" means:

(A) a governmental body empowered to hold an interest in real property under the laws of this state or the United States; or

(B) a charitable corporation, charitable association, or charitable trust created or empowered to:

(i) retain or protect the natural, scenic, or open-space values of real property;

(ii) assure the availability of real property for agricultural, forest, recreational, or open-space use;

(iii) protect natural resources;

(iv) maintain or enhance air or water quality; or

(v) preserve the historical, architectural, archeological, or cultural aspects of real property.

(3) "Third-party right of enforcement" means a right provided in a conservation easement to enforce any of its terms granted to a governmental body, charitable corporation, charitable association, or charitable trust that is eligible to be a holder but is not a holder.

(4) "Servient estate" means the real property burdened by the conservation easement.

NATRES §183.002. CREATION, CONVEYANCES, ACCEPTANCES, & DURATION

(a) Except as otherwise provided in this chapter, a conservation easement may be created, conveyed, recorded, assigned, released, modified, terminated, or otherwise altered or affected in the same manner as other easements.

(b) A right or duty in favor of or against a holder and a right in favor of a person having a third-party right of enforcement does not arise under a conservation easement before its acceptance by the holder and the recordation of the acceptance.

(c) Except as provided by Section 183.003(b) of this code, a conservation easement is unlimited in duration unless the instrument creating it makes some other provision.

(d) An interest that exists in real property at the time a conservation easement is created is not impaired

unless the owner of the interest is a party to the conservation easement or consents to it.

(e) A conservation easement must be created in writing, acknowledged and recorded in the deed records of the county in which the servient estate is located, and must include a legal description of the real property which constitutes the servient estate.

(f) If land that has been subject to a conservation easement is no longer subject to such easement, an additional tax is imposed on the land equal to the difference, if any, between the taxes imposed on the land for each of the five years preceding the year in which the easement terminates and the taxes that would have been imposed had the land not been subject to a conservation easement in each of those years, plus interest at an annual rate of seven percent calculated from the dates on which the differences would have become due.

See also *Real Estate Forms*, FORMS 11:1, 11:2.

NATRES §183.003. JUDICIAL ACTIONS

(a) An action affecting a conservation easement may be brought by:

(1) an owner of an interest in the real property burdened by the easement;

(2) a holder of the easement;

(3) a person having a third-party right of enforcement; or

(4) a person authorized by some other law.

(b) This chapter does not affect the power of a court to modify or terminate a conservation easement in accordance with the principles of law and equity.

NATRES §183.004. VALIDITY

A conservation easement is valid even though:

(1) it is not appurtenant to an interest in real property;

(2) it can be or has been assigned to another holder;

(3) it is not of a character that has been recognized traditionally at common law;

(4) it imposes a negative burden;

(5) it imposes affirmative obligations on the owner of an interest in the burdened property or on the holder;

(6) the benefit does not touch or concern real property; or

(7) there is no privity of estate or of contract.

NATRES §183.005. APPLICABILITY

(a) This chapter applies to any interest created on or after September 1, 1983, that complies with this chapter, whether designated as a conservation easement or as a covenant, equitable servitude, restriction, easement, or otherwise.

(b) This chapter applies to any interest created before September 1, 1983, if it would have been enforceable had it been created on or after September 1, 1983, unless retroactive application contravenes the constitution or laws of this state or the United States.

(c) This chapter does not invalidate any interest, whether designated as a conservation or preservation easement or as a covenant, equitable servitude, restriction, easement, or otherwise, that is enforceable under other law of this state.

Section 183.006 omitted by editor

TITLE 9. HERITAGE

CHAPTER 191. ANTIQUITIES CODE

SUBCHAPTER A. GENERAL PROVISIONS

NATRES §191.001. TITLE

This chapter may be cited as the Antiquities Code of Texas.

NATRES §191.002. DECLARATION OF PUBLIC POLICY

It is the public policy and in the public interest of the State of Texas to locate, protect, and preserve all sites, objects, buildings, pre-twentieth century shipwrecks, and locations of historical, archeological, educational, or scientific interest, including but not limited to prehistoric and historical American Indian or aboriginal campsites, dwellings, and habitation sites, archeological sites of every character, treasure imbedded in the earth, sunken or abandoned ships and wrecks of the sea or any part of their contents, maps, records, documents, books, artifacts, and implements of culture in any way related to the inhabitants, pre-history, history, natural history, government, or culture in, on, or under any of the land in the State of Texas, including the tidelands, submerged land, and the bed of the sea within the jurisdiction of the State of Texas.

NATRES §191.003. DEFINITIONS

In this chapter:

(1) "Committee" means the Texas Historical Commission.

(2) "Landmark" means a state archeological landmark.

(3) "State agency" means a department, commission, board, office, or other agency that is a part of state government and that is created by the constitution or a statute of this state. The term includes an institution of higher education as defined by Section 61.003, Texas Education Code.

(4) "Political subdivision" means a local governmental entity created and operating under the laws of this state, including a city, county, school district, or special district created under Article III, Section 52(b)(1) or (2), or Article XVI, Section 59, of the Texas Constitution.

NatRes §191.004. Certain Records Not Public Information

(a) Information specifying the location of any site or item declared to be a state archeological landmark under Subchapter D of this chapter is not public information.

(b) Information specifying the location or nature of an activity covered by a permit or an application for a permit under this chapter is not public information.

(c) Information specifying details of a survey to locate state archeological landmarks under this chapter is not public information.

Subchapter B. Administrative Provisions

NatRes §191.021. Compliance with Open Meetings Act & Administrative Procedure & Texas Register Act

(a) Repealed by Acts 1995, 74th Leg., ch. 109, §29, eff. Aug. 30, 1995.

(b) If an institution of higher education notifies the committee in a timely manner (as established by the committee's rules) that it protests the proposed designation of a building or land under its control as a landmark, the matter becomes a contested case under the provisions of Sections 12 through 20 of the Administrative Procedure and Texas Register Act. In the conduct of proceedings under the Administrative Procedure and Texas Register Act, both the hearing officer in his or her recommendations to the committee and the committee in its determinations of findings of fact and conclusions of law shall consider, in addition to such other objective criteria as the committee may establish pursuant to Section 191.091 of this chapter:

(1) that the primary mission of institutions of higher education is the provision of educational services to the state's citizens;

(2) that the authority for expenditure of the portion of the state's resources allocated to institutions of higher education for construction and repair purposes is entrusted to the governing boards of institutions of higher education for the purpose of the furtherance of the primary mission of the respective institutions of higher education;

(3) whether the benefit to the state from landmark designation outweighs the potential inflexibility of use that may be a consequence of the designation; and

(4) whether the cost of remodeling and/or restoration that might be required under the permit procedures of the committee if the building were designated as a landmark may be so substantially greater than remodeling under procedures established by law for the review of remodeling projects for higher education buildings not so designated as to impair the proper use of funds designated by the state for educational purposes at the institution.

(c) If an institution of higher education notifies the committee in a timely manner (as established by the committee's rules) that it protests the terms of a permit proposed to be granted to an institution of higher education under this chapter, the matter becomes a contested case under the provisions of Sections 12 through 20 of the Administrative Procedure and the Texas Register Act. The hearing officer in his or her recommendations to the committee and the committee in its determination of findings of fact and conclusions of law shall consider:

(1) that the primary mission of institutions of higher education is the provision of educational services to the state's citizens;

(2) that the authority for expenditure of the portion of the state's resources allocated to institutions of higher education for construction and repair purposes is entrusted to the governing boards of institutions of higher education for the purpose of the furtherance of the primary mission of the respective institutions of higher education;

(3) whether the legislature has provided extra funds that may be required to implement any proposed requirements;

(4) the effect of any proposed requirements on maintenance costs;

(5) the effect of any proposed requirements on energy costs; and

(6) the appropriateness of any proposed permit requirements to the uses to which a public building has been or will be dedicated by the governing board of the institution of higher education.

(d) Weighing the criteria set forth in Subsections (b) and (c) of this section against the criteria it adopts pursuant to Section 191.092 of this chapter and such criteria as it may adopt with regard to permit requirements, the committee shall designate a building or land under the control of an institution of higher education as a landmark or include a requirement in a permit only if the record before the committee establishes by clear and convincing evidence that such designation or inclusion would be in the public interest.

SUBCHAPTER C. POWERS & DUTIES

NATRES §191.051. IN GENERAL

(a) The committee is the legal custodian of all items described in this chapter that have been recovered and retained by the State of Texas.

(b) The committee shall:

(1) maintain an inventory of the items recovered and retained by the State of Texas, showing the description and depository of them;

(2) determine the site of and designate landmarks and remove from the designation certain sites, as provided in Subchapter D of this chapter;

(3) contract or otherwise provide for discovery operations and scientific investigations under the provisions of Section 191.053 of this code;

(4) consider the requests for and issue the permits provided for in Section 191.054 of this code;

(5) prepare and make available to the general public and appropriate state agencies and political subdivisions information of consumer interest describing the functions of the committee and the procedures by which complaints are filed with and resolved by the committee; and

(6) protect and preserve the archeological and historical resources of Texas.

NATRES §191.052. RULES

The committee may promulgate rules and require contract or permit conditions to reasonably effect the purposes of this chapter.

NATRES §191.0525. NOTICE REQUIRED

(a) Before breaking ground at a project location on state or local public land, the person primarily responsible for the project or the person's agent shall notify the committee. The committee shall promptly determine whether:

(1) a historically significant archeological site is likely to be present at the project location;

(2) additional action, if any, is needed to protect the site; and

(3) an archeological survey is necessary.

(b) Except as provided by Subsection (c), the committee shall make a determination not later than the 30th day after the date the committee receives notice under Subsection (a). If the committee fails to respond in the 30-day period, the person may proceed with the project without further notice to the committee. If the committee determines that an archeological survey is necessary at the project location, the project may not commence until the archeological survey is completed.

(c) The committee shall make a determination not later than the 15th day after the date the committee receives notice under Subsection (a) for project locations regarding oil, gas, or other mineral exploration, production, processing, marketing, refining, or transportation facility or pipeline projects. If the committee fails to respond in the 15-day period, the person may proceed with the project without further notice to the committee. If the committee determines that an archeological survey is necessary at the project location, the project may not commence until the archeological survey is completed.

(d) A project for a county, municipality, or an entity created under Section 52, Article III, or Section 59, Article XVI, Texas Constitution, requires advance project review only if the project affects a cumulative area larger than five acres or disturbs a cumulative area of more than 5,000 cubic yards, whichever measure is triggered first, or if the project is inside a designated historic district or recorded archeological site.

(e) There exist categorical exclusions since many activities conducted on nonfederal public land have little, if any, chance to damage archeological sites, and therefore should not require notification under this section. The following are categorical exclusions at a minimum:

(1) water injection into existing oil and gas wells;

(2) upgrading of electrical transmission lines when there will be no new disturbance of the existing easement;

(3) seismic exploration activity when there is no ground penetration or disturbance;

(4) building and repairing fences that do not require construction or modification of associated roads, fire breaks, or previously disturbed ground;

(5) road maintenance that does not involve widening or lengthening the road;

(6) installation or replacement of meter taps;

(7) controlled burning of fields;

(8) animal grazing;

(9) plowing, if the techniques are similar to those used previously;

(10) installation of monuments and sign posts unless within the boundaries of designated historic districts;

(11) maintenance of existing trails;

(12) land sales and trades of land held by the permanent school fund and permanent university fund;

(13) permanent school fund and permanent university fund leases, easements, and permits, including mineral leases and pooling agreements, in which the lessee, grantee, or permittee is specifically required to comply with the provisions of this chapter;

(14) oil, gas, or other mineral exploration, production, processing, marketing, refining, or transportation facility or pipeline project in an area where the project will cross state or local public roads, rivers, and streams, unless they contain a recorded archeological site or a designated state land tract in Texas' submerged lands;

(15) maintenance, operation, replacement, or minor modification of an existing oil, gas, or other mineral exploration, production, processing, marketing, refining, or transportation facility or pipeline; and

(16) any project for which a state permit application has been made prior to promulgation of rules under this section.

(f) This section does not apply to any state agency or political subdivision that has entered into a memorandum of understanding for coordination with the committee.

(g)(1) If, during the course of a project or class of projects that have complied with the notification requirements of this section, a person encounters an archeological site, the person shall abate activity on the project at the project location and shall promptly notify the committee. Within two business days of notification under this subsection, the committee shall determine whether:

(A) a historically significant archeological site is likely to be present in the project area;

(B) additional action, if any, is needed to protect the site; and

(C) an archeological investigation is necessary.

(2) If the committee fails to respond within two business days, the person may proceed without further notice to the committee.

(h) The notification required by this section does not apply to a response to a fire, spill, or other emergency associated with an existing facility located on state or local public lands if the emergency requires an immediate response.

(i) The committee by rule shall establish procedures to implement this section.

NATRES §191.053. CONTRACT FOR DISCOVERY & SCIENTIFIC INVESTIGATION

(a) The committee may contract with other state agencies or political subdivisions and with qualified private institutions, corporations, or individuals for the discovery and scientific investigation of sunken or abandoned ships or wrecks of the sea, or any part of the contents of them, or archeological deposits or treasure imbedded in the earth.

(b) The contract shall:

(1) be on a form approved by the attorney general;

(2) specify the location, nature of the activity, and the time period covered by the contract; and

(3) provide for the termination of any right in the investigator or permittee under the contract on the violation of any of the terms of the contract.

(c) The executed contract shall be recorded by the person, firm, or corporation obtaining the contract in the office of the county clerk in the county or counties in which the operations are to be conducted prior to the commencement of the operation.

(d) Title to all objects recovered is retained by the State of Texas unless and until it is released by the committee.

NATRES §191.054. PERMIT FOR SURVEY & DISCOVERY, EXCAVATION, RESTORATION, DEMOLITION, OR STUDY

(a) The committee may issue a permit to other state agencies or political subdivisions or to qualified private institutions, companies, or individuals for the survey and discovery, excavation, demolition, or restoration of, or the conduct of scientific or educational studies at, in, or on landmarks, or for the discovery of eligible landmarks on public land if it is the opinion of the committee that the permit is in the best interest of the State of Texas.

(b) Restoration shall be defined as any rehabilitation of a landmark excepting normal maintenance or alterations to nonpublic interior spaces.

(c) The permit shall:

(1) be on a form approved by the attorney general;

(2) specify the location, nature of the activity, and the time period covered by the permit; and

(3) provide for the termination of any right in the investigator or permittee under the permit on the violation of any of the terms of the permit.

NATRES §191.055. SUPERVISION

All scientific investigations or recovery operations conducted under the contract provisions in Section 191.053 of this code and all operations conducted under permits or contracts set out in Section 191.054 of this code must be carried out:

(1) under the general supervision of the committee;

(2) in accordance with reasonable rules adopted by the committee; and

(3) in such manner that the maximum amount of historic, scientific, archeological, and educational information may be recovered and preserved in addition to the physical recovery of items.

NATRES §191.056. ACCEPTANCE OF GIFTS

The committee may accept gifts, grants, devises, or bequests of money, securities, or property to be used in the pursuance of its activities and the performance of its duties.

NATRES §191.057. SURVEY, EXCAVATION, OR RESTORATION FOR PRIVATE PARTIES

The committee may survey, excavate, or restore antiquities for private parties under rules promulgated by the committee. All real and administrative costs incurred in the survey, excavation, or restoration shall be paid by the private party.

NATRES §191.058. CURATION OF ARTIFACTS

(a) As far as is consistent with the public policy of this chapter, the committee, on a majority vote, may arrange or contract with other state agencies or political subdivisions, and qualified private institutions, corporations, or individuals, for public display of artifacts and other items in its custody through permanent exhibits established in the locality or region in which the artifacts were discovered or recovered. The committee, on a majority vote, may also arrange or contract with these same persons and groups for portable or mobile displays.

(b) The committee is the legal custodian of the items described in this chapter and shall adopt appropriate rules, terms, and conditions to assure appropriate security, qualification of personnel, insurance, facilities for preservation, restoration, and display of the items loaned under the contracts.

(c) Arrangements for curation of artifacts, data, and other materials recovered under Texas Antiquities Committee permits are specified in the body of the permit. Should a state agency or political subdivision lack the facilities or for any reason be unable to curate or provide responsible storage for such artifacts, data, or other materials, the Texas Antiquities Committee will arrange for curation at a suitable institution. The Texas Antiquities Committee may by rule assess costs for the curation.

(d) The committee may contract with a qualified institution for the institution to serve as a repository for artifacts and other items in the custody of the committee. The Corpus Christi Museum of Science and History is the repository for marine artifacts. The committee may contract with other qualified institutions to serve as additional repositories for marine artifacts. The committee may authorize an archeological repository to loan artifacts and other items curated by the repository to a qualified institution for public display. The Corpus Christi Museum of Science and History:

(1) does not own the artifacts for which it serves as a repository; and

(2) shall make available for loan to a qualified institution for display the marine artifacts for which it serves as a repository.

NatRes §191.059. Complaints

(a) The committee shall keep an information file about each complaint filed with the committee.

(b) If a written complaint is filed with the committee, the committee, at least as frequently as quarterly and until final disposition of the complaint, shall notify the parties to the complaint of the status of the complaint.

Subchapter D. State Archeological Landmarks

NatRes §191.091. Ships, Wrecks of the Sea, & Treasure Imbedded in Earth

Sunken or abandoned pre-twentieth century ships and wrecks of the sea, and any part or the contents of them, and all treasure imbedded in the earth, located in, on, or under the surface of land belonging to the State of Texas, including its tidelands, submerged land, and the beds of its rivers and the sea within jurisdiction of the State of Texas, are declared to be state archeological landmarks and are eligible for designation.

NatRes §191.092. Other Sites, Artifacts, or Articles

(a) Sites, objects, buildings, artifacts, implements, and locations of historical, archeological, scientific, or educational interest, including those pertaining to prehistoric and historical American Indians or aboriginal campsites, dwellings, and habitation sites, their artifacts and implements of culture, as well as archeological sites of every character that are located in, on, or under the surface of any land belonging to the State of Texas or to any county, city, or political subdivision of the state are state archeological landmarks and are eligible for designation.

(b) For the purposes of this section, a structure or a building has historical interest if the structure or building:

(1) was the site of an event that has significance in the history of the United States or the State of Texas;

(2) was significantly associated with the life of a famous person;

(3) was significantly associated with an event that symbolizes an important principle or ideal;

(4) represents a distinctive architectural type and has value as an example of a period, style, or construction technique; or

(5) is important as part of the heritage of a religious organization, ethnic group, or local society.

(c) An individual or a private group that desires to nominate a building or site owned by a political subdivision as a state archeological landmark must give notice of the nomination at the individual's or group's own expense in a newspaper of general circulation published in the city, town, or county in which the building or site is located. If no newspaper of general circulation is published in the city, town, or county, the notice must be published in a newspaper of general circulation published in an adjoining or neighboring county that is circulated in the county of the applicant's residence. The notice must:

(1) be printed in 12-point boldface type;

(2) include the exact location of the building or site; and

(3) include the name of the group or individual nominating the building or site.

(d) An original copy of the notice and an affidavit of publication signed by the newspaper's publisher must be submitted to the commission with the application for nomination.

(e) The commission may not consider for designation as a state archeological landmark a building or site owned by a political subdivision unless the notice and affidavit required by Subsection (d) are attached to the application.

(f) Before the committee may designate a structure or building as a state archeological landmark, the structure or building must be listed on the National Register of Historic Places.

(g) The committee shall adopt rules establishing criteria for the designation of a structure or building as a state archeological landmark.

(h) The committee shall consider any and all fiscal impact on local political subdivisions before any structure or building owned by a local political subdivision may be designated as a state archeological landmark.

NatRes §191.093. Prerequisites to Removal, Altering, Damaging, Destroying, Salvaging, or Excavating Certain Landmarks

Landmarks under Section 191.091 or 191.092 of this code are the sole property of the State of Texas and may not be removed, altered, damaged, destroyed, salvaged, or excavated without a contract with or permit from the committee.

NatRes §191.098. Notification of Alteration or Demolition of Possible Landmark

(a) A state agency may not alter, renovate, or demolish a building possessed by the state that was constructed at least 50 years before the alteration, renovation, or demolition and that has not been designated a landmark by the committee, without notifying the committee of the proposed alteration, renovation, or demolition not later than the 60th day before the day on which the agency begins the alteration, renovation, or demolition.

(b) After receipt of the notice the committee may waive the waiting period; however, if the committee institutes proceedings to determine whether the building is a state archeological landmark under Section 191.092 of this code not later than the 60th day after the day on which the notice is received by the committee, the agency must obtain a permit from the committee before beginning an alteration, renovation, or demolition of the building during the time that the committee's proceedings are pending.

(c) Should the committee fail to provide a substantive response within 60 days to a request for a review of project plans, application for permit, draft report review, or other business required under the Antiquities Code, the applicant may proceed without further reference to the committee.

Subchapter E. Prohibitions

NatRes §191.131. Contract or Permit Requirement

(a) No person, firm, or corporation may conduct a salvage or recovery operation without first obtaining a contract.

(b) No person, firm, or corporation may conduct an operation on any landmark without first obtaining a permit and having the permit in his or its possession at the site of the operation, or conduct the operation in violation of the provisions of the permit.

NatRes §191.132. Damage or Destruction

(a) No person may intentionally and knowingly deface American Indian or aboriginal paintings, hieroglyphics, or other marks or carvings on rock or elsewhere that pertain to early American Indian or aboriginal habitation of the country.

(b) A person who is not the owner shall not wilfully injure, disfigure, remove, or destroy a historical structure, monument, marker, medallion, or artifact without lawful authority.

NatRes §191.133. Entry Without Consent

No person who is not the owner, and does not have the consent of the owner, proprietor, lessee, or person in charge, may enter or attempt to enter on the enclosed land of another and intentionally injure, disfigure, remove, excavate, damage, take, dig into, or destroy any historical structure, monument, marker, medallion, or artifact, or any prehistoric or historic archeological site, American Indian or aboriginal campsite, artifact, burial, ruin, or other archeological remains located in, on, or under any private land within the State of Texas.

Subchapter F. Enforcement

NatRes §191.171. Criminal Penalty

(a) A person violating any of the provisions of this chapter is guilty of a misdemeanor, and on conviction shall be punished by a fine of not less than $50 and not more than $1,000, by confinement in jail for not more than 30 days, or by both.

(b) Each day of continued violation of any provision of this chapter constitutes a separate offense for which the offender may be punished.

NatRes §191.172. Civil Action by Attorney General

(a) In addition to, and without limiting the other powers of the attorney general, and without altering or waiving any criminal penalty provided in this chapter, the attorney general may bring an action in the name of the State of Texas in any court of competent jurisdiction for restraining orders and injunctive relief to restrain and enjoin violations or threatened violations of this chapter, and for the return of items taken in violation of the provisions of this chapter.

(b) Venue for an action instituted by the attorney general lies either in Travis County or in the county

in which the activity sought to be restrained is alleged to be taking place or from which the items were taken.

NATRES §191.173. CIVIL ACTION BY CITIZEN

(a) A citizen of the State of Texas may bring an action in any court of competent jurisdiction for restraining orders and injunctive relief to restrain and enjoin violations or threatened violations of this chapter, and for the return of items taken in violation of the provisions of this chapter.

(b) Venue of an action by a citizen lies in the county in which the activity sought to be restrained is alleged to be taking place or from which the items were taken.

NATRES §191.174. ASSISTANCE FROM STATE AGENCIES, POLITICAL SUBDIVISIONS, & LAW ENFORCEMENT OFFICERS

(a) The chief administrative officers of all state agencies and political subdivisions are directed to cooperate and assist the committee and the attorney general in carrying out the intent of this chapter.

(b) All state and local law enforcement agencies and officers are directed to assist in enforcing the provisions and carrying out the intent of this chapter.

TITLE 12. WETLANDS

CHAPTER 221. WETLAND MITIGATION

SUBCHAPTER A. GENERAL PROVISIONS

NATRES §221.001. DEFINITIONS

In this chapter:

(1) "Buffer zone" means a strip of land adjoining a wetland mitigation bank to protect the wetland habitat and wildlife within the bank from the impact of an activity outside the zone. The term includes a strip of land composed primarily of water or a strip of land that includes a fence, wall, or screen of vegetation.

(2) "Eligible political subdivision" means:

(A) a county with a population of 3.3 million or more or a county adjacent to such a county; or

(B) a conservation and reclamation district:

(i) that is established under Section 59, Article XVI, Texas Constitution;

(ii) the boundaries of which are within a county that has a population of 3.3 million or more; and

(iii) that is authorized under other law to participate in a program under this chapter.

(3) "Federal requirement" means a requirement of the federal government contained in a statute, regulation, or guideline for an eligible mitigation bank program or a wetland regulation program.

(4) "Mitigation bank" means a parcel of land that has undergone or is proposed to undergo a physical change necessary to create or optimize the acreage or quality of wetland habitat on the parcel expressly to provide a mitigation credit to offset an adverse impact to wetland caused by an approved project located elsewhere.

(5) "Mitigation credit" means a unit of measured area that supports wetland habitat or wetland habitat value that did not exist at the mitigation bank site before the mitigation bank was developed.

(6) "Wetland" means land that:

(A) has a predominance of hydric soil;

(B) is inundated or saturated by surface or groundwater at a frequency and duration sufficient to support a prevalence of hydrophytic vegetation typically adapted for life in saturated soil conditions; and

(C) under normal circumstances does support a prevalence of that vegetation.

(7) "Wetland regulation program" means a program of the state, a state agency, or an eligible political subdivision under which the state, agency, or subdivision administers its own individual or general permit program regulating the use of wetland.

NATRES §221.002. USE OF MONEY

A state agency or an eligible political subdivision may use any money to accomplish a purpose of this chapter.

NATRES §221.003. COST OF MOVING OR CHANGING FACILITY

If a state agency, eligible political subdivision, or nonprofit corporation, in exercising a power under this chapter, makes it necessary to move, raise, lower, reroute, or change the grade of or alter the construction of a pipeline, highway, railroad, electric transmission or distribution line, or telephone or telegraph property or facility, the agency, subdivision, or corporation must bear the sole expense of the action.

Sections 221.004-221.020 reserved for expansion

SUBCHAPTER B. WETLAND MITIGATION BANKING & CONTRACTS

NATRES §221.021. ACTIONS TO ESTABLISH OR MAINTAIN MITIGATION BANK

(a) With the approval of the General Land Office, a state agency or eligible political subdivision may take any necessary and reasonable action to comply with a federal requirement to establish or maintain a mitigation bank. An action under this section may include:

(1) authorizing or making a continuing study of wetland areas and wetland mitigation programs;

(2) consistent with federal requirements, engaging in a wetland mitigation program and adopting and enforcing permanent land use and control measures on land the agency or subdivision owns in a mitigation bank;

(3) consulting with, providing information to, and entering into an agreement with a federal agency to identify and publish information about wetland areas;

(4) cooperating with a federal or state agency in connection with a study or investigation regarding the adequacy of a local measure with respect to a federal or state wetland program;

(5) improving the long-range management or use of wetland or a wetland mitigation bank;

(6) purchasing, leasing, condemning, or otherwise acquiring property inside or outside the eligible political subdivision that is necessary for a wetland mitigation bank or buffer zone and, as necessary, improving the land or other property as a wetland mitigation bank, including any adjacent buffer zone, to comply with a federal requirement;

(7) requesting or receiving aid from a federal or state agency or an eligible political subdivision;

(8) purchasing, selling, or contracting to purchase or sell a mitigation credit in a mitigation bank;

(9) incurring a liability or borrowing money on terms approved by the governing body of the subdivision;

(10) acquiring, holding, using, selling, leasing, or disposing of real or personal property, including a license, patent, right, or interest, that is necessary, convenient, or useful for the full exercise of a power under this chapter;

(11) contracting with any operator to use or operate any part of a mitigation bank; and

(12) procuring any type of insurance and paying an insurance premium in an amount the governing body of the eligible political subdivision considers necessary or advisable.

(b) The power of eminent domain granted by this section does not enable a state agency or eligible political subdivision to acquire by condemnation an interest in land that is owned or used by a public utility. In this subsection, "public utility" has the meaning assigned by the Public Utility Regulatory Act of 1995 (Article 1446c-0, Vernon's Texas Civil Statutes).

NATRES §221.022. OPTIONAL MITIGATION BANK PROVISIONS

A mitigation bank project may include a provision for:

(1) a park;

(2) recreation;

(3) a scenic area; or

(4) flood control.

NATRES §221.023. MITIGATION BANK CONTRACTS; CONTRACT PAYMENTS

(a) A state agency or eligible political subdivision may contract with another state agency or eligible political subdivision to pay jointly any part of the cost to acquire, design, construct, improve, or maintain a wetland mitigation bank or a buffer zone.

(b) Payment of the cost of a project or a payment required to be made under a contract may be made out of bond proceeds, taxes, or any other money available for the payment.

(c) If a contract provides for payment over a term of years, an eligible political subdivision may impose a tax in an amount necessary to:

(1) create a sinking fund for the contract payments; and

(2) make the payments when due.

Sections 221.024-221.040 reserved for expansion

SUBCHAPTER C. PROVISIONS FOR POLITICAL SUBDIVISIONS

NATRES §221.041. APPLICATION TO FEDERAL AGENCY

On behalf of an eligible political subdivision that proposes to administer its own individual or general wetland regulation program, the governor may apply to the appropriate federal agency for program approval.

NATRES §221.042. COMPLIANCE WITH FEDERAL PROGRAM

An eligible political subdivision authorized to implement a wetland mitigation program may comply with a program established by the federal government with respect to the implementation of a wetland regulation program or for the acquisition, ownership, or operation of a wetland mitigation bank.

NATRES §221.043. COUNTY APPROVAL OF POLITICAL SUBDIVISION PROGRAM

An eligible political subdivision may not institute a wetland regulation program unless the commissioners court of each county in which the eligible political subdivision lies approves the program after conducting a public hearing.

NATRES §221.044. RULES FOR WETLAND DELINEATION

(a) An eligible political subdivision authorized to implement a wetland mitigation program may adopt and compile reasonably necessary rules.

(b) An eligible political subdivision by rule may set standards for delineating land as wetland for purposes of:

(1) this chapter; or

(2) a federal requirement.

(c) A rule under Subsection (b) may be adopted after consultation with federal agencies, including the United States Fish and Wildlife Service, the United States Environmental Protection Agency, the United States Army Corps of Engineers, and the Soil Conservation Service of the United States Department of Agriculture.

(d) A standard for delineating wetland must comply with federal requirements for delineating wetland.

NATRES §221.045. PERMIT

(a) An eligible political subdivision authorized to implement a wetland mitigation program may issue a permit that incorporates, and assures compliance with, an applicable:

(1) requirement of this chapter; or

(2) federal requirement.

(b) A permit may be terminated or modified for cause, including:

(1) violation of a permit condition;

(2) obtaining a permit by misrepresentation or not fully disclosing all relevant facts; or

(3) a change in a condition that requires temporarily or permanently reducing or eliminating the permitted activity.

NATRES §221.046. MITIGATION BANK FINANCING

(a) A mitigation project participant may issue a bond, note, or other obligation to acquire land for, to pay any part of the cost of, or to acquire, construct, improve, operate, or maintain a wetland mitigation bank.

(b) The subdivision may issue a bond, note, or obligation:

(1) in one or more series; and

(2) payable from and secured by:

(A) a tax;

(B) an assessment;

(C) an impact fee;

(D) revenue;

(E) a grant or gift;

(F) a lease or contract; or

(G) a combination of resources listed in Paragraphs (A)-(F).

(c) In this section, "mitigation project participant" means an eligible political subdivision that seeks to:

(1) implement a project the unavoidable result of which would adversely affect wetland; and

(2) compensate for the loss of wetland acreage or wetland habitat value through participation in a mitigation bank.

NATRES §221.047. BOND REQUIREMENTS

(a) A bond issued under Section 221.046 is a negotiable instrument within the meaning and for purposes of the Business & Commerce Code.

(b) The bond may be:

(1) issued registrable as to principal or as to both principal and interest; or

(2) made redeemable before maturity.

(c) The bond may be:

(1) issued in the form, denominations, and manner and under the terms provided by the order or resolution authorizing the issuance of the bond; and

(2) sold in the manner, at the price, and under the terms provided by the order or resolution authorizing the issuance of the bond.

(d) The bond shall:

(1) be executed in accordance with the order or resolution authorizing the issuance of the bond; and

(2) bear interest at the rate provided by the order or resolution authorizing the issuance of the bond.

(e) The bond may bear interest and may be issued in accordance with:

(1) Chapters 1201, 1204, and 1371, Government Code; or

(2) Subchapters A-C, Chapter 1207, Government Code.

(f) The bond may be additionally secured by a:

(1) mortgage or deed of trust on real property that is related to the mitigation bank; or

(2) chattel mortgage, lien, or security interest on personal property appurtenant to that real property.

(g) The eligible political subdivision may authorize the execution of a trust indenture, mortgage, deed of trust, or other encumbrance to evidence the indebtedness.

(h) The eligible political subdivision may pledge to the payment of the bond any part of a grant, a donation, revenue, or income received or to be received from the United States or any other source.

NATRES §221.048. BOND PROCEEDS

If the use authorized by the order or resolution authorizing the issuance of a bond under Section 221.046, the bond proceeds may be used to:

(1) pay interest on the bond during or after the acquisition or construction of an improvement project financed by the bond issue;

(2) pay administrative and operation expenses;

(3) create a reserve fund for payment of the principal of and interest on the bonds; or

(4) create any other fund.

Occupations Code
Selected Provisions

OCCUPATIONS CODE

SELECTED PROVISIONS
TABLE OF CONTENTS

TITLE 7. PRACTICES & PROFESSIONS RELATED TO REAL PROPERTY & HOUSING

OCCUPATIONS CODE

SELECTED PROVISIONS
TABLE OF CONTENTS

Occupations Code

Selected Provisions
Table of Contents

TITLE 7. PRACTICES & PROFESSIONS RELATED TO REAL PROPERTY & HOUSING

SUBTITLE A. PROFESSIONS RELATED TO REAL ESTATE

CHAPTER 1101. REAL ESTATE BROKERS & SALES AGENTS

SUBCHAPTER A. GENERAL PROVISIONS

OCC §1101.0045. EQUITABLE INTERESTS IN REAL PROPERTY

(a) A person may acquire an option or an interest in a contract to purchase real property and then sell or offer to sell the option or assign or offer to assign the contract without holding a license issued under this chapter if the person:

(1) does not use the option or contract to purchase to engage in real estate brokerage; and

(2) discloses the nature of the equitable interest to any potential buyer.

(b) A person selling or offering to sell an option or assigning or offering to assign an interest in a contract to purchase real property without disclosing the nature of that interest to a potential buyer is engaging in real estate brokerage.

2017 Legislation: Enacted by S.B. 2212, §1, 85th Leg., eff. Sept. 1, 2017.

SUBCHAPTER D. COMMISSION POWERS & DUTIES

OCC §1101.155. RULES RELATING TO CONTRACT FORMS

(a) The commission may adopt rules in the public's best interest that require license holders to use contract forms prepared by the Texas Real Estate Broker-Lawyer Committee and adopted by the commission.

(b) The commission may not prohibit a license holder from using for the sale, exchange, option, or lease of an interest in real property a contract form that is:

(1) prepared by the property owner; or

(2) prepared by an attorney and required by the property owner.

(c) A listing contract form adopted by the commission that relates to the contractual obligations between a seller of real estate and a license holder acting as an agent for the seller must include:

(1) a provision informing the parties to the contract that real estate commissions are negotiable; and

(2) a provision explaining the availability of Texas coastal natural hazards information important to coastal residents, if that information is appropriate.

OCC §1101.156. RULES RESTRICTING ADVERTISING OR COMPETITIVE BIDDING

(a) The commission may not adopt a rule restricting advertising or competitive bidding by a person regulated by the commission except to prohibit a false, misleading, or deceptive practice by the person.

(b) The commission may not include in rules to prohibit false, misleading, or deceptive practices by a person regulated by the commission a rule that:

(1) restricts the use of any advertising medium;

(2) restricts the person's personal appearance or use of the person's voice in an advertisement;

(3) relates to the size or duration of an advertisement used by the person; [or]

(4) restricts the person's advertisement under an assumed or [a] trade name that is authorized by a law of this state and registered with the commission; or

(5) requires the term "broker," "agent," or a similar designation or term, a reference to the commission, or the person's license number to be included in the person's advertisement.

2017 Legislation: Amended by S.B. 2212, §2, 85th Leg., eff. Sept. 1, 2017.

CHAPTER 1103. REAL ESTATE APPRAISERS

SUBCHAPTER A. GENERAL PROVISIONS

OCC §1103.001. SHORT TITLE

This chapter may be cited as the Texas Appraiser Licensing and Certification Act.

OCC §1103.002. PURPOSE

The purpose of this chapter is to:

(1) conform state law relating to the regulation of real estate appraisers to the requirements adopted under Title XI, Financial Institutions Reform, Recovery, and Enforcement Act of 1989; and

(2) enforce standards for the appraisal of real property.

OCC §1103.003. DEFINITIONS

In this chapter:

(1) "Appraisal" means, regardless of whether prepared for a federally related transaction:

(A) an opinion of value; or

(B) the act or process of developing an opinion of value.

(2) "Appraisal Foundation" means The Appraisal Foundation, as defined by 12 U.S.C. Section 3350, or its successor.

(2-a) "Appraisal review" has the meaning assigned by Section 1104.003.

(2-b) "Appraisal Standards Board" means the Appraisal Standards Board of the Appraisal Foundation, or its successor.

(3) "Appraisal Subcommittee" means the Appraisal Subcommittee of the Federal Financial Institutions Examination Council, or its successor.

(4) "Appraiser Qualifications Board" means the Appraiser Qualifications Board of the Appraisal Foundation, or its successor.

(4-a) "Appraiser trainee" means an appraiser trainee licensed under this chapter.

(5) "Board" means the Texas Appraiser Licensing and Certification Board.

(5-a) "Certified appraiser" means a person who is certified under this chapter to practice as a certified general or certified residential appraiser.

(6) "Commissioner" means the commissioner of the Texas Appraiser Licensing and Certification Board.

(6-a) "Federally related transaction" means a real estate-related transaction that:

(A) requires the services of an appraiser; and

(B) is engaged in, contracted for, or regulated by a federal financial institution regulatory agency.

(6-b) "Federal financial institution regulatory agency" means:

(A) the Board of Governors of the Federal Reserve System;

(B) the Federal Deposit Insurance Corporation;

(C) the Office of the Comptroller of the Currency;

(D) the Consumer Financial Protection Bureau;

(E) the National Credit Union Administration; or

(F) the successors of any of those agencies.

(7) "Licensed appraiser" means a person who is licensed under this chapter to practice as a residential real estate appraiser.

(8) "Supervisory appraiser" means a supervisory appraiser as defined by the Appraiser Qualifications Board.

OCC §1103.004. EFFECT OF CHAPTER

This chapter does not prohibit:

(1) a person authorized by law from performing an evaluation of real property for or providing an evaluation of real property to another person;

(2) a real estate broker licensed under Chapter 1101 or a sales agent acting under the authority of a sponsoring broker from providing to another person a written analysis, opinion, or conclusion relating to the estimated price of real property if the analysis, opinion, or conclusion:

(A) is not referred to as an appraisal;

(B) is given in the ordinary course of the broker's business; and

(C) is related to the actual or potential acquisition, disposition, encumbrance, or management of an interest in real property; or

(3) an appraiser who is certified by a jurisdiction other than this state from performing an appraisal review of an appraisal performed on real property in this state, if the appraiser does not offer an opinion of value as part of the appraisal review.

OCC §1103.005. REPEALED

OCC §1103.006. APPLICATION OF SUNSET ACT

The Texas Appraiser Licensing and Certification Board is subject to Chapter 325, Government Code (Texas Sunset Act). Unless continued in existence as provided by that chapter, the board is abolished and this chapter and Chapter 1104 expire September 1, 2019.

SUBTITLE C. REGULATION OF CERTAIN TYPES OF HOUSING & BUILDINGS

CHAPTER 1201. MANUFACTURED HOUSING

SUBCHAPTER A. GENERAL PROVISIONS

OCC §1201.001. SHORT TITLE

This chapter may be cited as the Texas Manufactured Housing Standards Act.

OCC §1201.002. LEGISLATIVE FINDINGS & PURPOSES; LIBERAL CONSTRUCTION

(a) The legislature finds that:

(1) there is a growing need to provide state residents with safe, affordable, and well-constructed housing;

(2) manufactured housing has become a primary housing source for many state residents;

(3) statutes and rules in effect before September 1, 1969, were inadequate to:

(A) fully protect the consumer; and

(B) prevent certain discrimination in this state regarding manufactured housing;

(4) the state is responsible for:

(A) protecting state residents who want to purchase manufactured housing by regulating the construction and installation of manufactured housing;

(B) providing economic stability to manufactured housing manufacturers, retailers, installers, and brokers; and

(C) providing fair and effective consumer remedies; and

(5) the expansion of certain regulatory powers is:

(A) necessary to address the problems described by Subdivisions (1)-(4); and

(B) the most economical and efficient means to address those problems and serve the public interest.

(b) The purposes of this chapter are to:

(1) encourage the construction of housing for state residents; and

(2) improve the general welfare and safety of purchasers of manufactured housing in this state.

(c) This chapter shall be liberally construed to promote its policies and accomplish its purposes.

A OCC §1201.003. DEFINITIONS

In this chapter:

(1) "Advertisement" means a commercial message that promotes the sale or[,] exchange[~~, or lease-purchase~~] of a manufactured home and that is presented on radio, television, a public-address system, or electronic media or appears in a newspaper, a magazine, a flyer, a catalog, direct mail literature, an inside or outside sign or window display, point-of-sale literature, a price tag, or other printed material. The term does not include educational material or material required by law.

(2) "Affiliate" means a person who is under common control.

(3) "Alteration" means the replacement, addition, modification, or removal of equipment in a new manufactured home after sale by a manufacturer to a retailer but before sale and installation by a retailer to a purchaser in a manner that may affect the home's construction, fire safety, occupancy, or plumbing, heating, or electrical system. The term includes the modification of a manufactured home in a manner that may affect the home's compliance with the appropriate standards but does not include:

(A) the repair or replacement of a component or appliance that requires plug-in to an electrical receptacle, if the replaced item is of the same configuration and rating as the replacement; or

(B) the addition of an appliance that requires plug-in to an electrical receptacle and that was not provided with the manufactured home by the manufacturer, if the rating of the appliance does not exceed the rating of the receptacle to which the appliance is connected.

(4) "Attached" in reference to a manufactured home means that the home has been:

(A) installed in compliance with the rules of the department; and

(B) connected to a utility, including a utility providing water, electric, natural gas, propane or butane gas, or wastewater service.

(5) "Board" means the Manufactured Housing Board within the Texas Department of Housing and Community Affairs.

(6) "Broker" means a person engaged by one or more other persons to negotiate or offer to negotiate a bargain or contract for the sale or[,] exchange[~~, or lease-purchase~~] of a manufactured home for which a certificate or other document of title has been issued and is outstanding. The term does not include a person who maintains a location for the display of manufactured homes.

(7) "Business use" means the use of a manufactured home in conjunction with operating a business, for a purpose other than as a permanent or temporary residential dwelling.

(8) "Consumer" means a person, other than a person licensed under this chapter, who seeks to acquire or acquires by purchase or[,] exchange[~~, or lease-purchase~~] a manufactured home.

(9) "Control" means, with respect to another person, the possession of the power, directly or indirectly, to vote an interest of 25 percent or more.

(9-a) "Credit transaction" has the meaning assigned by Section 347.002(a)(3), Finance Code.

(10) "Department" means the Texas Department of Housing and Community Affairs operating through its manufactured housing division.

(11) "Director" means the executive director of the manufactured housing division of the Texas Department of Housing and Community Affairs.

(12) "HUD-code manufactured home":

(A) means a structure:

(i) constructed on or after June 15, 1976, according to the rules of the United States Department of Housing and Urban Development;

(ii) built on a permanent chassis;

(iii) designed for use as a dwelling with or without a permanent foundation when the structure is connected to the required utilities;

(iv) transportable in one or more sections; and

(v) in the traveling mode, at least eight body feet in width or at least 40 body feet in length or, when erected on site, at least 320 square feet;

(B) includes the plumbing, heating, air conditioning, and electrical systems of the home; and

(C) does not include a recreational vehicle as defined by 24 C.F.R. Section 3282.8(g).

(13) "Installation" means the temporary or permanent construction of the foundation system and the placement of a manufactured home or manufactured home component on the foundation. The term includes supporting, blocking, leveling, securing, anchoring, and properly connecting multiple or expandable sections or components and making minor adjustments.

(14) "Installer" means a person, including a retailer or manufacturer, who contracts to perform or performs an installation function on manufactured housing.

(15) "Label" means a device or insignia that is:

(A) issued by the director to indicate compliance with the standards, rules, and regulations established by the United States Department of Housing and Urban Development; and

(B) permanently attached to each transportable section of each HUD-code manufactured home constructed after June 15, 1976, for sale to a consumer.

(16) Repealed by H.B. 2019, §85(1), 85th Leg., eff. Sept. 1, 2017.

[~~(16)~~] [~~"Lease purchase" means entering into a lease contract for a manufactured home, in which the lessor retains title, containing a provision or, in another agreement, conferring on the lessee an option to purchase a manufactured home.~~]

(17) "License holder" or "licensee" means a person who holds a department-issued license as a manufacturer, retailer, broker, salesperson, or installer.

(18) "Manufactured home" or "manufactured housing" means a HUD-code manufactured home or a mobile home.

(19) "Manufacturer" means a person who constructs or assembles manufactured housing for sale or[~~,~~] exchange[~~, or lease-purchase~~] in this state.

(20) "Mobile home":

(A) means a structure:

(i) constructed before June 15, 1976;

(ii) built on a permanent chassis;

(iii) designed for use as a dwelling with or without a permanent foundation when the structure is connected to the required utilities;

(iv) transportable in one or more sections; and

(v) in the traveling mode, at least eight body feet in width or at least 40 body feet in length or, when erected on site, at least 320 square feet; and

(B) includes the plumbing, heating, air conditioning, and electrical systems of the home.

(21) "New manufactured home" means a manufactured home that is not a used manufactured home, regardless of its age.

(21-a) "Nonresidential use" means use of a manufactured home for a purpose other than as a permanent or temporary residential dwelling.

(22) "Person" means an individual or a partnership, company, corporation, association, or other group, however organized.

(23) "Related person" means a person who:

(A) directly [~~or indirectly~~] participates in management or policy decisions; and

(B) is designated by an entity and satisfies the requirements of Sections 1201.104 and 1201.113 on behalf of the entity, if the entity is licensed or seeking licensure under this chapter.

(24) "Retailer" means a person who:

(A) is engaged in the business of buying for resale, selling, or exchanging manufactured homes or offering manufactured homes for sale or[~~,~~] exchange[~~, or lease-purchase~~] to consumers, including a person who maintains a location for the display of manufactured homes; and

(B) sells or[~~,~~] exchanges[~~, or lease-purchases~~] at least two manufactured homes to consumers in a 12-month period.

(25) "Rules" means the rules of the department.

(26) "Salesperson" means a person who, as an employee or agent of a retailer or broker, sells [~~or lease-purchases~~] or offers to sell [~~or lease-purchase~~] manufactured housing to a consumer.

(26-a) "Sales purchase contract" means the contract between a retailer and a consumer for the purchase of a manufactured home from the retailer.

(27) "Salvaged manufactured home" means a manufactured home determined to be salvaged under Section 1201.461.

(28) "Seal" means a device or insignia issued by the director that, for title purposes, is to be attached to a used manufactured home as required by the director.

(29) "Standards code" means the Texas Manufactured Housing Standards Code.

(30) "Statement of ownership [~~and location~~]" means a statement issued by the department and setting forth:

(A) the ownership [~~and location~~] of a manufactured home in this state as provided by Section 1201.205; and

(B) other information required by this chapter.

(31) Repealed by H.B. 2019, §85(1), 85th Leg., eff. Sept. 1, 2017.

[~~(31)~~] [~~"Trust fund" means the manufactured homeowners' recovery trust fund.~~]

(32) "Used manufactured home" means a manufactured home which has been occupied for any use or for which a statement of ownership [~~and location~~] has been issued. The term does not include:

(A) a manufactured home that was used as a sales model at a licensed retail location; or

(B) a manufactured home that:

(i) was sold as a new manufactured home and installed but never occupied;

(ii) had a statement of ownership [~~and location~~]; and

(iii) was taken back from the consumer or transferee because of a first payment default or agreement to rescind or unwind the transaction.

2017 Legislation: Amended by H.B. 2019, §§1, 85(1), 85th Leg., eff. Sept. 1, 2017.

OCC §1201.004. DEFINITIONS BINDING

The definitions of "mobile home," "HUD-code manufactured home," and "manufactured housing" provided by Section 1201.003 are binding as a matter of law on each person and agency in this state, including a home-rule municipality or other political subdivision. A mobile home is not a HUD-code manufactured home and a HUD-code manufactured home is not a mobile home for any purpose under state law. Those terms may not be defined in a manner that is not identical to the definitions provided by Section 1201.003.

OCC §1201.005. CONSUMER WAIVER VOID

A waiver by a consumer of this chapter is contrary to public policy and void.

OCC §1201.006. APPLICABILITY OF BUSINESS & COMMERCE CODE

The Business & Commerce Code applies to transactions relating to manufactured housing except to the extent that it conflicts with this chapter.

OCC §1201.007. EXCEPTION FOR REAL ESTATE BROKERS & SALESPERSONS

This chapter does not:

(1) modify or amend Chapter 1101 or 1102; or

(2) apply to a person who is licensed as a real estate broker or salesperson under Chapter 1101 and who, as agent of a buyer or seller, negotiates the sale or lease of a manufactured home and the real property to which the home is attached if:

(A) the same person is the record owner of both the manufactured home and the real property; and

(B) the sale or lease occurs in a single real estate transaction.

OCC §1201.008. REGULATION BY MUNICIPALITY

(a) A municipality may prohibit the installation of a mobile home for use as a dwelling in the municipality. The prohibition must be prospective and may not apply to a mobile home previously legally permitted by and used as a dwelling in the municipality. If a mobile home is replaced by a HUD-code manufactured home in the municipality, the municipality shall grant a permit for use of the manufactured home as a dwelling in the municipality.

(b) On application, the municipality shall permit the installation of a HUD-code manufactured home for use as a dwelling in any area determined appropriate by the municipality, including a subdivision, planned unit development, single lot, and rental community or park. An application to install a new HUD-code manufactured home for use as a dwelling is considered to be granted unless the municipality in writing denies the application and states the reason for the denial not later than the 45th day after the date the application is received.

(c) Subsections (a) and (b) do not affect the validity of an otherwise valid deed restriction.

(d) Except as approved by the department, a local governmental unit may not require a permit, a fee, a bond, or insurance for the transportation and installation of manufactured housing by a licensed retailer or installer. This subsection does not prohibit the collection of actual costs incurred by a local governmental unit that result from the transportation of a manufactured home.

(e) Notwithstanding any zoning or other law, in the event that a manufactured home occupies a lot in a municipality, the owner of the manufactured home may remove the manufactured home from its location and place another manufactured home on the same property, provided that the replacement is a newer manufactured home and is at least as large in living space as the prior manufactured home.

(f) An owner's ability to replace the home as a result of a fire or natural disaster cannot be restricted. Other than in the case of a fire or natural disaster, a general-rule or home-rule municipality by an ordinance or charter may limit the ability of the owner to replace his home to a single replacement.

OCC §1201.009. ELECTRONIC MEANS AUTHORIZED

If feasible, any action required under this chapter may be accomplished by electronic means.

E OCC §1201.010. ELECTRONIC PUBLIC RECORDS REQUIRED

The department shall provide to the public through the department's Internet website searchable and downloadable information regarding manufactured home ownership records, lien records, installation records, license holder records, and enforcement actions.

2017 Legislation: Enacted by H.B. 2019, §2, 85th Leg., eff. Sept. 1, 2017.

Sections 1201.011-1201.050 reserved for expansion

SUBCHAPTER B. DEPARTMENT POWERS & DUTIES

OCC §1201.051. ADMINISTRATION & ENFORCEMENT OF CHAPTER

The director shall administer and enforce this chapter.

OCC §1201.052. GENERAL RULEMAKING AUTHORITY

(a) The director shall adopt rules, issue orders, and otherwise act as necessary to ensure compliance with the purposes of this chapter to implement and provide for uniform enforcement of this chapter and the standards code.

(b) To protect the public health, safety, and welfare and to ensure the availability of low cost manufactured housing for all consumers, the director shall adopt rules to:

(1) protect the interests of consumers who occupy or want to purchase or install manufactured housing; and

(2) govern the business conduct of license holders.

OCC §1201.053. RULES RELATING TO COMPLIANCE WITH NATIONAL STANDARDS FOR MANUFACTURED HOUSING CONSTRUCTION & SAFETY; STATE PLAN

(a) The board shall adopt rules and otherwise act as necessary to:

(1) comply with the National Manufactured Housing Construction and Safety Standards Act of 1974 (42 U.S.C. Section 5401 et seq.), including adopting and enforcing rules reasonably required to implement the notification and correction procedures provided by 42 U.S.C. Section 5414; and

(2) provide for the effective enforcement of all HUD-code manufactured housing construction and safety standards in order to have the state plan authorized by the National Manufactured Housing Construction and Safety Standards Act of 1974 (42 U.S.C. Section 5401 et seq.) approved by the secretary of housing and urban development.

(b) The state plan described by Subsection (a)(2) must provide for a third-party inspection agency approved by the United States Department of Housing and Urban Development to act as an in-plant inspection agency.

Ⓐ OCC §1201.054. PROCEDURE FOR ADOPTING RULES

(a) Rules must be adopted in accordance with Chapter 2001, Government Code, and with this section.

(b) If requested, the board shall, after at least 10 days' notice, hold a hearing on any rule that it proposes to adopt, other than a rule that is to be adopted under emergency rulemaking, in which case only the requirements of Chapter 2001, Government Code, shall apply.

(c) A rule takes effect on the 30th day after the date of publication of notice that the rule has been adopted, except that a rule relating to installation standards may not take effect earlier than the 60th day after the date of publication of notice unless the board has determined that an earlier effective date is required to meet an emergency and the standard was adopted under the emergency rulemaking provisions of Chapter 2001, Government Code.

(d) To maintain affordability of manufactured homes in this state, the board shall:

(1) conduct a cost benefit analysis for any rule, process, or policy change that will increase a fee or another incurred cost by more than $50 for license holders or consumers; and

(2) present at the next board meeting an analysis detailing whether the need for the rule, process, or policy change justifies the increase.

2017 Legislation: Amended by H.B. 2019, §3, 85th Leg., eff. Sept. 1, 2017.

Ⓐ OCC §1201.055. INSPECTION, REVIEW, & RELATED FEES

(a) With guidance from the federal Housing and Community Development Act of 1974 (42 U.S.C. Section 5301 et seq.) and from the rules and regulations adopted under the National Manufactured Housing Construction and Safety Standards Act of 1974 (42 U.S.C. Section 5401 et seq.), the board shall establish fees as follows:

(1) if the department acts as a design approval primary inspection agency, a schedule of fees for the review of HUD-code manufactured home blueprints and supporting information, to be paid by the manufacturer seeking approval of the blueprints and supporting information;

(2) except as provided by Subsection (e), a fee for the inspection of each HUD-code manufactured home manufactured or assembled in this state, to be paid by the manufacturer of the home;

(3) a fee for the inspection of an alteration made to the structure or plumbing, heating, or electrical system of a HUD-code manufactured home, to be charged on an hourly basis and to be paid by the person making the alteration;

(4) a fee for the inspection of the rebuilding of a salvaged manufactured home, to be paid by the retailer;

(5) a fee for the inspection of a used manufactured home to determine whether the home is habitable for the issuance of a new statement of ownership [~~and location~~]; and

(6) a fee for the issuance of a seal for a used mobile or HUD-code manufactured home.

(b) In addition to the fees imposed under Subsections (a)(2), (3), and (4), a manufacturer or a person making an alteration, as appropriate, shall be charged for the actual cost of travel of a department representative to and from:

(1) the manufacturing facility, for an inspection described by Subsection (a)(2); or

(2) the place of inspection, for an inspection described by Subsection (a)(3) or (4).

(c) The board shall establish a fee for the inspection of the installation of a mobile or HUD-code manufactured home, to be paid by the installer of the home.

(c-1) The department may permit the use of any device or procedure that has been reviewed and approved by a licensed engineer provided that such use or procedure complies with any instructions, conditions, or other requirements specified by that engineer.

(d) The board shall charge a fee for a consumer complaint home inspection requested by a manufacturer or retailer under Section 1201.355(b), to be paid by the manufacturer or retailer.

(e) The fee described by Subsection (a)(2) does not apply if an inspection agency authorized by the United States Department of Housing and Urban Development, other than the department, acts as the in-plant inspection agency.

(f) The fee described by Subsection (c) must accompany notice to the department of the exact location of the mobile or HUD-code manufactured home. The department shall make an appropriate fee distribution to a local governmental unit that performs an inspection under a contract or other official designation if that unit does not collect a local inspection fee.

2017 Legislation: Amended by H.B. 2019, §4, 85th Leg., eff. Sept. 1, 2017.

OCC §1201.056. LICENSE FEES

(a) The board shall establish fees for the issuance and renewal of licenses for:

(1) manufacturers;

(2) retailers;

(3) brokers;

(4) salespersons; and

(5) installers.

(b) The board by rule may establish a fee for reprinting a license issued under this chapter.

OCC §1201.057. INSTRUCTION FEE

The board shall charge a fee to each person attending a course of instruction described by Section 1201.104.

OCC §1201.058. AMOUNT OF FEES

(a) The board shall establish reasonable fees for all matters under this chapter providing for fees. If the department's rules provide an option to file a document electronically, the department may charge a discounted fee for the electronic filing.

(b) Repealed by H.B. 2019, §85(2), 85th Leg., eff. Sept. 1, 2017.

[~~(b)~~] [~~Ten dollars of the fee for each purchase, exchange, or lease-purchase of a manufactured home shall be deposited to the credit of the trust fund and used for the protection programs described by Subchapter I.~~]

(c) All fees established by this chapter or the rules are deemed to be earned and not subject to refund after receipt by the department.

(d) Notwithstanding Subsection (c), the director may, in limited and appropriate circumstances and in accordance with rules adopted by the board, approve the refund of fees.

(e) If the governor by executive order or proclamation declares a state of disaster under Chapter 418, Government Code, the director, in accordance with rules adopted by the board, may waive the imposition of any fee under this chapter in the affected area.

2017 Legislation: Amended by H.B. 2019, §85(2), 85th Leg., eff. Sept. 1, 2017.

OCC §1201.059. REPEALED

OCC §1201.060. VENUE FOR HEARING

A hearing under this chapter shall be held in Travis County unless all parties agree to another location.

OCC §1201.061. COOPERATION WITH LOCAL GOVERNMENTAL UNITS

The department shall cooperate with all local governmental units in this state.

OCC §1201.062. SEAL PROPERTY OF DEPARTMENT

A seal is the property of the department.

Sections 1201.063-1201.100 reserved for expansion

SUBCHAPTER C. LICENSING

OCC §1201.101. LICENSE REQUIRED

(a) A person may not construct or assemble in this state or ship into this state a new HUD-code manufactured home unless the person holds, at the time the home is constructed or assembled, a manufacturer's license.

(b) Except as otherwise provided by this chapter, a person may not sell or [~~,~~] exchange, or [~~lease-purchase or~~] offer to sell or [~~,~~] exchange, [~~or lease-purchase~~] two or more manufactured homes to consumers in this state in a 12-month period unless the person holds a retailer's license.

(c) A person may not offer to negotiate or negotiate for others a bargain or contract for the sale or [~~,~~] exchange [~~, or lease-purchase~~] of two or more manufactured homes to consumers in this state in a 12-month period unless the person holds a broker's license.

(d) A person may not act as an installer in this state unless the person holds an installer's license.

(e) A person may not repair, rebuild, or otherwise alter a salvaged manufactured home unless the person holds a retailer's license.

(f) A person may not act as a salesperson of manufactured housing unless the person holds a salesperson's license. A retailer or broker may not employ or otherwise use the services of a salesperson who is not licensed. A licensed salesperson may not participate in a sale of a manufactured home unless the sale is through the retailer or broker who sponsored the salesperson's application as required by Section 1201.103(d).

(f-1) A retailer may not be licensed to operate more than one location under a single license.

(g) A person may not make an announcement concerning the sale or [~~,~~] exchange [~~, or lease-purchase~~] of, or offer to sell or [~~,~~] exchange [~~, or lease-purchase~~],

a manufactured home to a consumer in this state through an advertisement unless the person holds a manufacturer's, retailer's, or broker's license. This subsection does not apply to:

(1) a person exempt from licensing; or

(2) an advertisement concerning real property on which there is a manufactured home that has been converted to real property in accordance with Section 1201.2055.

2017 Legislation: Amended by H.B. 2019, §5, 85th Leg., eff. Sept. 1, 2017.

A OCC §1201.102. EXCEPTIONS TO LICENSE REQUIREMENT

(a) A licensed installer may employ unlicensed persons to assist in performing installation functions provided that the licensed installer maintains a list of the persons so employed. The director may issue an order to prohibit a person who is not licensed as an installer from performing installation functions under the oversight of a licensed installer.

(b) A licensee may engage another person who is not licensed under this chapter but possesses another license issued by the State of Texas to provide goods and services subject to that other license. Without limiting the generality of the foregoing, this includes engaging others to install, connect, or otherwise work on air conditioning, plumbing, and electrical systems.

(c) An individual who holds a retailer's license or broker's license or who is a related person of such a licensee is not required to apply for a salesperson's license.

(c-1) An individual who is listed as an owner, principal, partner, corporate officer, registered agent, or related person of an entity that is licensed as a retailer or broker may act on behalf of that license holder in the capacity of a retailer, broker, or salesperson without holding the appropriate license if at least one individual who is listed as an owner, principal, partner, corporate officer, registered agent, or related person of the entity has satisfied the requirements of Sections 1201.104 and 1201.113.

(d) A person who holds a real estate broker's or salesperson's license under Chapter 1101 may act as a broker or salesperson under this chapter without holding a license or filing a bond or other security as required by this chapter if negotiations for the sale or [~~,~~] exchange [~~, or lease purchase~~] of a manufactured home are conducted for a consumer for whom the person is also acting as a real estate broker or salesperson under Chapter 1101 consistent with Section 1201.007.

2017 Legislation: Amended by H.B. 2019, §6, 85th Leg., eff. Sept. 1, 2017.

OCC §1201.1025. EXEMPTION FROM RETAILER'S LICENSE REQUIREMENT

(a) Notwithstanding any other law, in any 12-month period a person is exempt from holding a retailer's license as required by Section 1201.101(b) if during that period the person sells or offers to sell not more than three manufactured homes.

(b) The department by rule shall develop a form necessary for a person to establish eligibility for the exemption provided by this section.

(c) A person who is eligible for an exemption under this section remains subject to the other applicable provisions of this subchapter regarding the sale of manufactured homes.

OCC §1201.103. LICENSE APPLICATION

(a) An applicant for a license as a manufacturer, retailer, broker, or installer must file with the director a license application containing:

(1) the legal name, address, and telephone number of the applicant and each person who will be a related person at the time the requested license is issued;

(2) all trade names, and the names of all other business organizations, under which the applicant does business subject to this chapter, the name of each such business organization registered with the secretary of state, and the address of such business organization;

(3) the dates on which the applicant became the owner and operator of the business; and

(4) the location to which the license will apply.

(a-1) All required records of a licensee under Subsection (a) are to be maintained at the licensee's principal office or such other location within this state as the licensee may designate.

(b) A license application must be accompanied by:

(1) proof of the security required by this subchapter;

(2) payment of the fee required for issuance of the license; and

(3) the information and the cost required under Section 1201.1031.

(c) If a change occurs in the information filed with the director under Subsection (a), the applicant shall amend the application to state the correct information.

(d) An applicant for a salesperson's license must:

(1) file with the director an application that provides any information the director considers necessary and that is sponsored by a currently licensed retailer or broker; and

(2) pay the required fee.

OCC §1201.1031. CRIMINAL HISTORY RECORD INFORMATION REQUIREMENT FOR LICENSE

(a) The department shall require that an applicant for a license or renewal of an unexpired license submit a complete and legible set of fingerprints, on a form prescribed by the board, to the department or to the Department of Public Safety for the purpose of obtaining criminal history record information from the Department of Public Safety and the Federal Bureau of Investigation. The applicant is required to submit a set of fingerprints only once under this section unless a replacement set is otherwise needed to complete the criminal history check required by this section.

(b) The department shall refuse to issue a license to or renew the license of a person who does not comply with the requirement of Subsection (a).

(c) The department shall conduct a criminal history check of each applicant for a license or renewal of a license using information:

(1) provided by the individual under this section; and

(2) made available to the department by the Department of Public Safety, the Federal Bureau of Investigation, and any other criminal justice agency under Chapter 411, Government Code.

(d) The department may enter into an agreement with the Department of Public Safety to administer a criminal history check required under this section.

(e) The applicant shall pay the cost of a criminal history check under this section.

Ⓐ OCC §1201.104. QUALIFICATIONS FOR LICENSE

(a) Except as provided by Subsection (g), as a requirement for a manufacturer's, retailer's, broker's, installer's, or salesperson's license, a person who was not licensed or registered with the department or a predecessor agency on September 1, 1987, must, not more than 12 months before applying for the person's first license under this chapter, attend and successfully complete eight hours of instruction in the law, including instruction in consumer protection regulations.

(a-1) If the applicant is not an individual, the applicant must have at least one related person who satisfies the requirements of Subsection (a). If that applicant is applying for a retailer's license, the related person must be a management official who satisfies the requirements of Subsections (a) and (a-2) for [~~at~~] each retail location operated by the applicant.

(a-2) An applicant for a retailer's license must complete four hours of specialized instruction relevant to the sale and[~~,~~] exchange[~~, and lease purchase~~] of manufactured homes. The instruction under this subsection is in addition to the instruction required under Subsection (a).

(a-3) An applicant for an installer's license must complete four hours of specialized instruction relevant to the installation of manufactured homes. The instruction under this subsection is in addition to the instruction required under Subsection (a).

(a-4) An applicant for a joint installer-retailer license must comply with Subsections (a-2) and (a-3), for a total of eight hours of specialized instruction. The instruction under this subsection is in addition to the instruction required under Subsection (a).

(b) Except in the case of an applicant for a salesperson's license, successful completion of the course of instruction is a prerequisite to obtaining the license.

(c) An applicant for a salesperson's license may apply for a license without having completed the course of instruction if the person successfully completes the course not later than the 90th day after the date of the person's licensure. If the person fails to complete such course successfully and in a timely manner, the person's license is automatically suspended until the person successfully completes the course.

(d) The course of instruction must be offered at least quarterly.

(e) The board shall adopt rules relating to course content and approval.

(f) An applicant for an initial installer's license shall receive a license on a provisional basis. The person's provisional status remains in effect until a sufficient number of installations completed by the person have been inspected by the department and found not

to have any identified material violations of the department's rules. The board, with the advice of the advisory committee to be established under Section 1201.251, shall adopt rules to establish what constitutes a sufficient number of installations under this subsection.

(g) Subsections (a), (a-2), (a-3), and (a-4) do not apply to a license holder who applies:

(1) for a license for an additional business location; or

(2) to renew or reinstate a license.

(h) An examination must be a requirement of successful completion of any initial required course of instruction under this section. The period needed to complete an examination under this subsection may not be used to satisfy the minimum education requirements under Subsection (a), (a-2), (a-3), or (a-4). If the examination failure rate exceeds 25 percent, the board shall:

(1) review the examination and the examination procedures; and

(2) adopt rules intended to maintain the historical passage rate for the examination.

2017 Legislation: Amended by H.B. 2019, §7, 85th Leg., eff. Sept. 1, 2017.

OCC §1201.105. SECURITY REQUIRED

(a) The department may not issue or renew a license unless a bond or other security in a form prescribed by the director is filed with the department as provided by this subchapter. The bond or other security is payable to the manufactured homeowner consumer claims program [~~trust fund~~].

(b) If a bond is filed, the bond must be issued by a company authorized to do business in this state and must conform to applicable provisions of the Insurance Code. If other security is filed, that security must be maintained in or by a federally insured depository institution located in this state.

(c) If the department experiences significant problems in obtaining timely reimbursements from a surety or the surety has experienced a deterioration in its financial condition, the board may direct the director to stop accepting bonds issued by the surety.

2017 Legislation: Amended by H.B. 2019, §8, 85th Leg., eff. Sept. 1, 2017.

OCC §1201.106. SECURITY: AMOUNT

(a) An applicant for a license or a license holder shall file a bond or other security under Section 1201.105 for the issuance or renewal of a license in the following amount:

(1) $100,000 for a manufacturer;

(2) $50,000 for a retailer;

(3) $50,000 for a broker; or

(4) $25,000 for an installer.

(a-1) Notwithstanding the provisions of Subsection (a), the director may require additional security for the licensing, renewal, or relicensing of a person, or the sponsoring of a salesperson, who, either directly, as a related person, or through a related person, has been the subject of a license revocation, has caused the manufactured homeowner consumer claims program [~~trust fund~~] to incur unreimbursed costs or liabilities in excess of available surety bond coverage, or has failed to pay an administrative penalty that has been assessed by final order.

(b) To ensure the availability of prompt and satisfactory warranty service, a manufacturer that does not have a licensed manufacturing plant or other facility in this state from which warranty service and repairs can be provided shall file a bond or other security in the additional amount of $100,000.

(c) The bond or other security is open to successive claims up to the face value of the bond or other security. The surety is not liable for successive claims in excess of the face value of the bond, regardless of the number of years the bond remains in force.

2017 Legislation: Amended by H.B. 2019, §9, 85th Leg., eff. Sept. 1, 2017.

OCC §1201.107. SECURITY: LOCATION

(a) A manufacturer, retailer, broker, or installer who maintains a place of business at one or more locations shall file with the department a separate bond or other security for each location.

(b) Property used for the business that is not contiguous to, or located within 300 feet of, a bonded location requires a separate bond. A location at which a manufactured home is shown to the public or at which the home is offered for sale or [~~,~~] exchange [~~, or lease-purchase~~] by a retailer to consumers requires a bond.

(c) A manufactured home installed on a permanent foundation system and offered for sale as real property does not require a bond. A temporary location for a bona fide trade show sponsored by a nonprofit corporation that qualifies for an exemption from federal income taxation under Section 501(a), Internal Rev-

enue Code of 1986, by being listed as an exempt organization under Section 501(c) of that code does not require a bond.

(d) If a retailer or broker offers for sale or participates in any way in the sale of a manufactured home at a location other than an undivided parcel of real property where more than one manufactured home is located and offered for sale or[~~,~~] exchange[~~, or lease-purchase~~] by a retailer or broker to the public, the retailer or broker must:

(1) identify the bond on file with the department in conjunction with that person's license; and

(2) provide contractually in the sales transaction that the identified bond applies to the sale.

2017 Legislation: Amended by H.B. 2019, §10, 85th Leg., eff. Sept. 1, 2017.

OCC §1201.108. SECURITY: CHANGE IN OWNERSHIP OR LOCATION

(a) A new bond is not required for a change in:

(1) ownership of a licensee or a business entity under which a license holder conducts business; or

(2) location.

(b) A licensee shall notify the department of a change described by Subsection (a) not later than the 10th day before the date the change occurs.

(c) After a change described by Subsection (a), the licensee shall provide to the department a proper endorsement to the original bond showing that the bond continues to apply to the license without interruption.

OCC §1201.109. SECURITY: CANCELLATION OR OTHER IMPAIRMENT

(a) If a bond required by this subchapter is canceled, the license for which the security is filed is suspended on the effective date of cancellation. The surety shall provide written notice to the director before the 60th day preceding the effective date of cancellation.

(b) If a surety files for liquidation or reorganization in bankruptcy or is placed in receivership, the license holder shall obtain other security not later than the 60th day after the date that notice of the filing or receivership is received.

(c) If the required face amount of a security is impaired by the payment of a claim, the license holder shall restore the security to the required face amount not later than the 60th day after the date of impairment.

OCC §1201.110. SECURITY: DURATION

The department shall maintain on file a security other than a bond canceled as provided by Section 1201.109(a) until the later of:

(1) the second anniversary of the date the manufacturer, retailer, broker, or installer ceases doing business; or

(2) the date the director determines that a claim does not exist against the security.

OCC §1201.111. EXCEPTIONS TO SECURITY & INSTRUCTION REQUIREMENTS

(a) Notwithstanding any other provision of this chapter, a state or national bank, state or federal savings and loan association, federal savings bank, or state or federal credit union engaged in the business of selling or[~~,~~] exchanging, [~~or lease-purchasing~~] or offering for sale or[~~,~~] exchange, [~~or lease-purchase~~] manufactured homes that the institution has acquired through repossession of collateral is not required to attend a course of instruction or file a bond or other security to be licensed as a retailer.

(b) A licensed retailer is not required to file a bond or other security to be licensed as a broker or installer.

2017 Legislation: Amended by H.B. 2019, §11, 85th Leg., eff. Sept. 1, 2017.

OCC §1201.112. REPEALED

OCC §1201.113. [~~CERTIFICATION &~~] CONTINUING EDUCATION PROGRAMS

(a) The board shall approve [~~or administer~~] continuing education programs for licensees under this chapter. A continuing education program must be at least eight hours long and must include the current rules of the department and such other matters as the board may deem relevant.

(b) Completion of an approved [~~or administered~~] continuing education program [~~course~~] described by Subsection (a) is a prerequisite to renewal of a license.

Subsection (c) was amended by Acts 2007, 80th Leg., ch. 863, §13, enacted May 26, 2007, effective Jan. 1, 2008, without reference to the conflicting repeal made by Acts 2007, 80th Leg., ch. 863, §73(a)(3), enacted May 26, 2007, effective Jan. 1, 2008. For harmonizing conflicts, see p. V.

(c) No test shall be given in relation to any continuing education program.

Subsection (c) was repealed by Acts 2007, 80th Leg., ch. 863, §73(a)(3), enacted May 26, 2007, effective Jan. 1, 2008, without reference to the conflicting amendment made by Acts 2007, 80th Leg., ch. 863, §13, enacted May 26, 2007, effective Jan. 1, 2008. For harmonizing conflicts, see p. V.

(c) Repealed by Acts 2007, 80th Leg., ch. 863, §73(a)(3), eff. Jan. 1, 2008.

(d) If the approval of a continuing education program expires between regularly scheduled board meetings, the director may, on receipt of the required renewal application, fee, and necessary documentation of education material, approve the continued administration of the program until the next board meeting.

(e) to **(g)** Repealed by Acts 2007, 80th Leg., ch. 863, §73(a)(3), eff. Jan. 1, 2008.

2017 Legislation: Amended by H.B. 2019, §§12, 13, 85th Leg., eff. Sept. 1, 2017.

OCC §1201.114. LICENSE EXPIRATION

Any license under this chapter is valid for two years. A license may be renewed as provided by the director. A person whose license has been suspended or revoked or whose license has expired may not engage in activities that require a license until the license has been reinstated or renewed.

OCC §1201.115. NOTICE OF LICENSE EXPIRATION

Not later than the 30th day before the date a person's license is scheduled to expire, the department shall send written notice of the impending expiration to the person at the person's last known address according to the records of the department.

OCC §1201.116. PROCEDURE FOR LICENSE RENEWAL

(a) The department shall renew a license if, before the expiration date of the license, the department receives the renewal application and payment of the required fee as well as the cost required under Section 1201.1031.

(b) If the department needs additional information for the renewal application or verification of continuing insurance or bond coverage, the license holder must provide the requested information or verification not later than the 20th day after the date of receipt of notice from the department.

(c) The renewal license expires on the second anniversary of the date the license was renewed.

(d) A person whose license has been expired for 90 days or less may renew the license by paying to the department a renewal fee that is equal to 1-½ times the normally required renewal fee.

(e) A person whose license has been expired for more than 90 days but less than one year may renew the license by paying to the department a renewal fee that is equal to two times the normally required renewal fee.

(f) A person whose license has been expired for one year or more may not renew the license. The person may obtain a new license by complying with the requirements and procedures for obtaining an original license.

OCC §1201.117. RENEWAL OF EXPIRED LICENSE BY OUT-OF-STATE PRACTITIONER

(a) A person who was licensed in this state, moved to another state, and is currently licensed and has been in practice in the other state for the two years preceding the date of application may obtain a new license without fulfilling the instruction requirements of Section 1201.104(a).

(b) The person must pay to the department a fee that is equal to two times the normally required renewal fee for the license.

A OCC §1201.118. RULES RELATING TO CERTAIN PERSONS

The board shall adopt rules providing for additional review and scrutiny of any application for an initial or renewal license that involves a person who has previously:

(1) been found in a final order to have participated in one or more violations of this chapter that served as grounds for the suspension or revocation of a license;

(2) been found to have engaged in activity subject to this chapter without possessing the required license;

(3) caused the manufactured homeowner consumer claims program [~~trust fund~~] to incur unreimbursed payments or claims; or

(4) failed to abide by the terms of a final order, including the payment of any assessed administrative penalties.

2017 Legislation: Amended by H.B. 2019, §14, 85th Leg., eff. Sept. 1, 2017.

Sections 1201.119-1201.150 reserved for expansion

Subchapter D. Practice

OCC §1201.1505. DEPOSIT ON SPECIALLY ORDERED MANUFACTURED HOMES

A retailer may require a deposit on a specially ordered manufactured home.

A OCC §1201.151. REFUNDS

(a) Except as otherwise provided by this section, a retailer must refund a consumer's deposit not later than the 15th day after the date that a written request for the refund is received from the consumer.

(b) The deposit may be retained only if:

(1) the consumer specially orders from the manufacturer a manufactured home that is not in the retailer's inventory;

(2) the home conforms to the specifications of the special order and any representations made to the consumer;

(3) the consumer fails or refuses to accept delivery and installation of the home by the retailer; and

(4) the consumer was given conspicuous written notice of the requirements for retaining the deposit.

(c) The retailer may not retain more than five percent of the estimated cash price of the specially ordered home and must refund any amount that exceeds five percent.

(d) This section does not apply to:

(1) a deposit held in escrow in a real estate transaction; or

(2) money stated to be a down payment in an executed retail sales contract.

(e) A deposit becomes a down payment upon execution of a sales purchase contract [~~binding written agreement~~]. Thereafter, if the consumer exercises the consumer's three-day [~~a~~] right of rescission in accordance with Section 1201.1521, the retailer shall, not later than the 15th day after the date of the rescission, refund to the consumer all money and other consideration received from the consumer, with only the allowable [~~without offset or~~] deduction for real property appraisal and title work expenses in accordance with Section 1201.1511.

(f) Retention of real property appraisal and title work expenses authorized by Subsection (e) is not allowed if the consumer exercises the right of rescission in accordance with 12 C.F.R. Section 1026.23.

2017 Legislation: Amended by H.B. 2019, §15, 85th Leg., eff. Sept. 1, 2017.

E OCC §1201.1511. REAL PROPERTY APPRAISAL & TITLE WORK EXPENSES

(a) Notwithstanding Section 1201.151 or 1201.1521, a retailer may collect from a consumer in advance or deduct from the consumer's deposit or down payment any expenses incurred by the retailer if, after receiving a conditional notification of approval from a lender chosen by the consumer, the consumer:

(1) contracts with the retailer to arrange for services that are performed by an appraiser of real property or a title company in connection with real property that will be included in the purchase or exchange or is intended to be pledged by the consumer as collateral for the consumer's purchase or exchange of a manufactured home;

(2) is provided notice of laws relating to rescission and real property appraisal and title work expenses before signing the contract for real property appraisal and title work services; and

(3) is provided an itemized list of the specific real property appraisal and title work expenses incurred by the retailer.

(b) A retailer may not charge to the consumer any fees or expenses other than the real property appraisal and title work expenses disclosed to the consumer under Subsection (a)(3).

(c) The department may demand copies of contracts, invoices, receipts, or other proof of any real property appraisal and title work expenses retained by a retailer.

2017 Legislation: Enacted by H.B. 2019, §16, 85th Leg., eff. Sept. 1, 2017.

A OCC §1201.152. VOIDABLE CONTRACT

(a) If a retailer purchases a new manufactured home from an unlicensed manufacturer in violation of Section 1201.505, a consumer's contract with the retailer for the purchase or [~~,~~] exchange [~~, or lease-purchase~~] of the home is voidable until the second anniversary of the date of purchase or [~~,~~] exchange [~~, or lease-purchase~~] of the home.

(b) If an unlicensed retailer, broker, or installer enters into a contract with a consumer concerning a manufactured home, the consumer may void the contract until the second anniversary of the date of purchase of the home.

2017 Legislation: Amended by H.B. 2019, §17, 85th Leg., eff. Sept. 1, 2017.

A OCC §1201.1521. RESCISSION OF CONTRACT FOR SALE OR[~~,~~] EXCHANGE[~~, OR LEASE-PURCHASE~~] OF HOME

(a) A person who acquires a manufactured home from or through a licensee by purchase or[~~,~~] exchange[~~, or lease-purchase~~] may, in a cash transaction occurring not later than the third day after the date the sales purchase [~~applicable~~] contract is signed, rescind the contract without penalty or charge other than the real property appraisal and title work expenses incurred in accordance with Section 1201.1511.

(b) A person who acquires a manufactured home from or through a licensee by purchase or exchange may, in a transfer that is based wholly or partly on a credit transaction occurring not later than the third day after the date of the signing of the binding note, security agreement, or other financing credit contract with respect to which the consumer's purchased manufactured home will serve as collateral for the credit transaction, rescind the contract without penalty or charge other than the real property appraisal and title work expenses incurred in accordance with Section 1201.1511.

(c) [~~(b)~~] Subject to rules adopted by the board, a consumer may waive a right of rescission in the event of a bona fide emergency. Such rules shall, to the extent practical, be modeled on the federal rules for the waiver of a right of rescission under 12 C.F.R. Part 1026 [~~226~~].

2017 Legislation: Amended by H.B. 2019, §18, 85th Leg., eff. Sept. 1, 2017.

OCC §1201.153. FORMALDEHYDE HEALTH NOTICE

(a) A retailer or manufacturer may not transfer ownership of a HUD-code manufactured home or otherwise sell, assign, or convey a HUD-code manufactured home to a consumer unless the retailer or manufacturer delivers to the consumer a formaldehyde health notice, subject to the director's rules concerning the notice.

(b) The notice must be delivered before the execution of a mutually binding sales agreement or retail installment sales contract.

(c) The notice must:

(1) contain the information required by the United States Department of Housing and Urban Development; and

(2) be of the type, size, and format required by the director.

(d) A retailer or manufacturer may not vary the content or form of the notice.

OCC §1201.154. SUFFICIENCY OF FORMALDEHYDE HEALTH NOTICE; RETAILER & MANUFACTURER COMPLIANCE

(a) The formaldehyde health notice required by Section 1201.153 is sufficient, as a matter of law, to advise a consumer of the risks of occupying a HUD-code manufactured home.

(b) The consumer's written acknowledgement of the receipt of the notice is conclusive proof of the delivery of the notice and the posting of the notice in compliance with federal regulations.

(c) A retailer's or manufacturer's compliance with United States Department of Housing and Urban Development regulations and the director's rules concerning the notice is conclusive proof that:

(1) the consumer received sufficient notice of the risks of occupying the home; and

(2) the home is habitable with respect to formaldehyde emissions.

(d) A retailer's or manufacturer's compliance, from September 1, 1981, to September 1, 1985, with Section 1201.153 and the revised formaldehyde warning as adopted by the department is conclusive proof that:

(1) the consumer received sufficient notice of the risks of occupying the home; and

(2) the home is habitable with respect to formaldehyde emissions.

(e) A retailer's or manufacturer's knowing and wilful failure to comply with the regulations and rules described by Subsection (c) is conclusive proof that:

(1) the retailer or manufacturer breached the duty to notify the consumer about formaldehyde; and

(2) the home is not habitable.

(f) A retailer's or manufacturer's knowing and wilful failure, from September 1, 1981, to September 1, 1985, to comply with Section 1201.153 and the revised formaldehyde warning as adopted by the department is conclusive proof that:

(1) the retailer or manufacturer breached the duty to notify the consumer about formaldehyde; and

(2) the home is not habitable.

OCC §1201.155. DISCLAIMER OF IMPLIED WARRANTY

The seller's proper provision of the warranties and notices as required by Subchapter H or J is a valid disclaimer of an implied warranty of fitness for a particu-

lar purpose or of merchantability as described by Chapter 2, Business & Commerce Code.

A OCC §1201.156. ADVERTISEMENT AS OFFER

An advertisement relating to manufactured housing is an offer to sell or [,] exchange [, or lease-purchase] manufactured housing to consumers.

2017 Legislation: Amended by H.B. 2019, §19, 85th Leg., eff. Sept. 1, 2017.

A OCC §1201.157. RETAILER AS WAREHOUSE [WAREHOUSEMAN]

(a) With respect to the storage of manufactured homes for hire, a [A] licensed retailer is:

(1) a "warehouse" ["warehouseman"] as defined by Section 7.102, Business & Commerce Code; and

(2) a "warehouseman" under Chapter 24, Property Code [, for the storage of manufactured homes for hire].

(b) The provisions of the Business & Commerce Code relating to the storage of goods for hire apply to a licensed retailer acting as a warehouse [warehouseman].

(c) A licensed retailer acting as a warehouse and warehouseman satisfies all storage, bonding, insurance, public sale, and security requirements if the storage of a manufactured home occurs on the retailer's lot and the home is secured in the same manner the retailer secures a manufactured home held on the lot as inventory.

(d) In accordance with the provisions of Section 7.210, Business & Commerce Code, a licensed retailer acting as a warehouse to enforce a warehouse's lien is considered to have sold a manufactured home in a commercially reasonable manner if the retailer sells the manufactured home in the same manner the retailer would sell a manufactured home at retail.

2017 Legislation: Amended by H.B. 2019, §20, 85th Leg., eff. Sept. 1, 2017.

OCC §1201.158. SALESPERSON

A licensed salesperson may work only for the salesperson's sponsoring retailer or broker.

OCC §1201.159. BROKER

(a) Except as provided by Section 1201.456, a broker shall ensure that the seller gives the buyer the applicable disclosures and warranties that the buyer would have received if the buyer had purchased the manufactured home through a licensed retailer.

(b) A person is not required to be a broker licensed under this chapter but may be required to be a real estate broker or salesperson licensed under Chapter 1101 if:

(1) the manufactured home is attached; and

(2) the home is offered as real property.

(c) A broker shall provide any person who engages the broker's services with a written disclosure of which interests in the transaction, if any, the broker represents.

(d) If the seller is required to possess a license by this chapter, a broker may assist in the sale of a manufactured home only if that seller has a current license.

OCC §1201.160. REPEALED

OCC §1201.161. TRANSPORTATION OF MANUFACTURED HOUSING

(a) Notwithstanding any other statute or rule or ordinance, a licensed retailer or licensed installer is not required to obtain a permit, certificate, or license or pay a fee to transport manufactured housing to the place of installation except as required by the Texas Department of Motor Vehicles under Subchapter E, Chapter 623, Transportation Code.

(b) The department shall cooperate with the Texas Department of Motor Vehicles by providing current lists of licensed manufacturers, retailers, and installers.

(c) The Texas Department of Motor Vehicles shall send the department monthly:

(1) a copy of each permit issued in the preceding month for the movement of manufactured housing on the highways; or

(2) a list of the permits issued in the preceding month and the information on the permits.

(d) Unless the information provided for in Subsection (c) is provided electronically, the department shall pay the reasonable cost of providing the copies or the list and information under Subsection (c).

(e) The copies and lists to be provided under this section may be provided electronically.

A OCC §1201.162. DISCLOSURE BY RETAILER & LENDER

(a) Before the completion of a credit application or more than one day before entering into any agreement for a sale or [,] exchange [, or the exercise of the lease purchase option] that will not be financed, the retailer must provide to the consumer a written disclosure in

the form promulgated by the board. The disclosure shall be in at least 12-point type and must address matters of concern relating to costs and obligations that may be associated with home ownership, matters to be considered in making financing decisions, related costs that may arise when purchasing a manufactured home, and such other matters as the board may deem appropriate to promote informed purchase, financing, and related decisions regarding the acquisition and ownership of a manufactured home. The form shall also conspicuously disclose the consumer's right of rescission.

(b) A federally insured financial institution or lender approved or authorized by the United States Department of Housing and Urban Development as a mortgagee with direct endorsement underwriting authority that fully complies with federal Truth in Lending disclosures concerning the terms of a manufactured housing transaction is exempt from the disclosure provisions of this section.

(c) The right of rescission described in Subsection (a) shall apply only to the sale transaction between the retailer and the consumer. Failure by the retailer to comply with the disclosure provisions of this section does not affect the validity of a subsequent conveyance or transfer of title of a manufactured home or otherwise impair a title or lien position of a person other than the retailer. The consumer shall continue to have the right of rescission with regard to the retailer until the end of the third day after the retailer delivers a copy of the disclosure required by Subsection (a). The consumer's execution of a signed receipt of a copy of the disclosure required by Subsection (a) shall constitute conclusive proof of the delivery of the disclosure. If the consumer grants a person other than the retailer a lien on the manufactured home, the right of rescission shall immediately cease on the filing of the lien with the department.

2017 Legislation: Amended by H.B. 2019, §21, 85th Leg., eff. Sept. 1, 2017.

OCC §1201.163. REPEALED

OCC §1201.164. ADVANCE COPY OF SALES PURCHASE CONTRACT & DISCLOSURE STATEMENTS; OFFER BY RETAILER

(a) In a transaction that is to be financed and that will not be subject to the federal Real Estate Settlement Procedures Act of 1974 (Pub. L. No. 93-533) and its implementing regulations, a retailer shall deliver to a consumer at least 24 hours before the sales purchase contract is fully executed the contract, with all required information included, signed by the retailer. The delivery of the contract, with all required information included, signed by the retailer constitutes a firm offer by the retailer. Except as provided for by [~~in~~] Subsection (b), the consumer may accept the offer not earlier than 24 hours after the delivery of the contract. If the consumer has not accepted the offer within 72 hours after the delivery of the contract, the retailer may withdraw the offer.

(b) Before the execution of the sales purchase contract, the [~~The~~] consumer may modify or waive the right to rescind and the deadlines for disclosures [~~before the execution of the contract~~] that are provided by Subsection (a) if the consumer determines that the purchase of the manufactured home is needed to meet a bona fide personal emergency. If the consumer has a bona fide personal emergency that necessitates the immediate purchase of the manufactured home, the consumer shall give the retailer a dated written statement that describes the emergency, specifically modifies or waives the notice periods and any right of rescission, and bears the signature of all of the consumers entitled to the disclosures and right of rescission. In such event the retailer shall immediately give the consumer all of the disclosures required by this code and sell the manufactured home without the required waiting periods or the right of rescission. The department shall verify with the consumer the consumer's bona fide personal emergency before issuing the statement of ownership [~~Printed forms for this purpose are prohibited except in a county that has been declared by the governor to be a major disaster area. If the governor declares a county to be a major disaster area, the retailer may use printed forms promulgated by the department. This exception shall expire one year after the county has been declared a major disaster area~~].

2017 Legislation: Amended by H.B. 2019, §22, 85th Leg., eff. Sept. 1, 2017.

OCC §1201.165. REPEALED

Sections 1201.166-1201.200 reserved for expansion

SUBCHAPTER E. MANUFACTURED HOME STATEMENTS OF OWNERSHIP [~~& LOCATION~~]

OCC §1201.201. DEFINITIONS

In this subchapter:

(1) "Certificate of attachment" means a written instrument issued solely by and under the authority of the director before September 1, 2001, that provides the

information required by former Section 19(*l*), Texas Manufactured Housing Standards Act (Article 5221f, Vernon's Texas Civil Statutes), as that subsection existed before that date. Beginning September 1, 2003, a certificate of attachment is considered to be a statement of ownership and may be exchanged for a statement of ownership as provided by Section 1201.214.

(1-a) "Debtor" has the meaning assigned by Section 9.102, Business & Commerce Code.

(2) "Document of title" means a written instrument issued solely by and under the authority of the director before September 1, 2003, that provides the information required by Section 1201.205, as that section existed before that date. Beginning September 1, 2003, a document of title is considered to be a statement of ownership [~~and location~~] and may be exchanged for a statement of ownership [~~and location~~] as provided by Section 1201.214.

(3) "First retail sale" means a consumer's initial acquisition of a new manufactured home from a retailer by purchase or [~~,~~] exchange [~~, or lease-purchase~~]. The term includes a bargain, sale, transfer, or delivery of a manufactured home for which the director has not previously issued a statement of ownership [~~and location~~], with intent to pass an interest in the home, other than a lien.

(4) "Identification number" means the number permanently attached to or imprinted on a manufactured home or section of the home as prescribed by department rule.

(5) "Inventory" means new and used manufactured homes that:

(A) a retailer has designated as the retailer's inventory for sale pursuant to the process implemented by the department; and

(B) are not used as residential dwellings when so designated [~~has the meaning assigned by Section 9.102, Business & Commerce Code~~].

(6) "Lien" means:

(A) a security interest created by a lease, conditional sales contract, deed of trust, chattel mortgage, trust receipt, reservation of title, or other security agreement if an interest other than an absolute title is sought to be held or given in a manufactured home; or

(B) a lien on a manufactured home created by the constitution or a statute.

(7) "Manufacturer's certificate" means a document that meets the requirements prescribed by Section 1201.204.

(8) "Secured party" has the meaning assigned by Section 9.102, Business & Commerce Code.

(9) "Security agreement" has the meaning assigned by Section 9.102, Business & Commerce Code.

(10) "Security interest" has the meaning assigned by Section 1.201, Business & Commerce Code.

(11) "Subsequent sale" means a bargain, sale, transfer, or delivery of a manufactured home, with intent to pass an interest in the home, other than a lien, from one person to another after the first retail sale and initial issuance of a statement of ownership [~~and location~~].

2017 Legislation: Amended by H.B. 2019, §§23, 24, 85th Leg., eff. Sept. 1, 2017.

OCC §1201.202. APPLICATION OF CHAPTER TO CERTAIN CERTIFICATES OF TITLE OR LIENS

(a) This chapter applies to a certificate of title to a manufactured home issued before March 1, 1982, under Chapter 501, Transportation Code.

(b) A lien recorded before March 1, 1982, with the Texas Department of Transportation or a predecessor agency of that department is recorded with the department for the purposes of this chapter.

OCC §1201.203. FORMS; RULES

(a) The board shall adopt rules and forms relating to:

(1) the manufacturer's certificate;

(2) the statement of ownership [~~and location~~];

(3) the application for a statement of ownership [~~and location~~]; and

(4) the issuance of an initial or revised statement of ownership.

(b) The board shall adopt rules for the documenting of the ownership [~~and location~~] of a manufactured home that has been previously owned in this state or another state. The rules must protect a lienholder recorded with the department.

2017 Legislation: Amended by H.B. 2019, §25, 85th Leg., eff. Sept. 1, 2017.

OCC §1201.204. MANUFACTURER'S CERTIFICATE

(a) A manufacturer's certificate must show:

(1) on a form prescribed by the director, the original transfer of a manufactured home from the manufacturer to the retailer; and

(2) on a form prescribed by the director, each subsequent transfer of a manufactured home between retailers and from retailer to owner, if the transfer from retailer to owner involves a completed application for the issuance of a statement of ownership [~~and location~~].

(b) At the first retail sale of a manufactured home, a manufacturer's certificate automatically converts to a document that does not evidence any ownership interest in the manufactured home described in the document. A security interest in inventory evidenced by a properly recorded inventory finance lien automatically converts to a security interest in proceeds and cash proceeds.

(c) After the first retail sale of a manufactured home, the retailer must submit the original manufacturer's certificate for that home to the department. If an application for an initial statement of ownership is made without the required manufacturer's certificate and the retailer does not provide it as required, the department shall, on or before the issuance of the requested statement of ownership [~~and location~~], send written notice to each party currently reflected on the department's records as having a recorded lien on the inventory of that retailer with respect to that home. Failure to include the original manufacturer's certificate with such an application does not impair a consumer's ability to obtain, on submittal of an otherwise complete application, a statement of ownership [~~and location~~] free and clear of any liens other than liens created by or consented to by the consumer.

2017 Legislation: Amended by H.B. 2019, §26, 85th Leg., eff. Sept. 1, 2017.

Ⓐ OCC §1201.205. STATEMENT OF OWNERSHIP [~~& LOCATION~~] FORM

A statement of ownership [~~and location~~] must be evidenced by a board-approved form issued by the department setting forth:

(1) the name and address of the seller and the name and, if it is different from the location of the home, the mailing address of the new owner;

(2) the manufacturer's name and address and any model designation, if available;

(3) in accordance with the board's rules:

(A) the outside dimensions of the manufactured home when installed for occupancy, as measured to the nearest one-half foot at the base of the home, exclusive of the tongue or other towing device; and

(B) the approximate square footage of the home when installed for occupancy;

(4) the identification number for each section or module of the home;

(5) the physical address where the home is installed for occupancy, including the name of the county, and, if it is different from the physical address, the mailing address of the owner of the home;

(6) in chronological order of recordation, the date of each lien, other than a tax lien, on the home and the name and address of each lienholder, or, if a lien is not recorded, a statement of that fact;

(7) a statement regarding tax liens as follows:

"On January 1st of each year, a new tax lien comes into existence on a manufactured home in favor of each taxing unit having jurisdiction where the home is actually located on January 1st. In order to be enforced, any such lien must be recorded with the Texas Department of Housing and Community Affairs—Manufactured Housing Division as provided by law. You may check that division's records through its website or contact that division to learn any recorded tax liens. To find out about the amount of any unpaid tax liabilities, contact the tax office for the county where the home was actually located on January 1st of that year.";

(8) a statement that if two or more eligible persons, as determined by Section 1201.213, file with the application for the issuance of a statement of ownership [~~and location~~] an agreement signed by all the persons providing that the home is to be held jointly with a right of survivorship, the director shall issue the statement of ownership [~~and location~~] in all the names;

(9) the location of the home;

(10) a statement of whether the owner has elected to treat the home as real property [~~or personal property~~];

(11) statements of whether the home is a salvaged manufactured home and whether the home is reserved for business use only or for another nonresidential use; and

(12) any other information the board requires.

2017 Legislation: Amended by H.B. 2019, §27, 85th Leg., eff. Sept. 1, 2017.

Ⓐ OCC §1201.2055. ELECTION BY OWNER

(a) In completing an application for the issuance of a statement of ownership [~~and location~~], an owner of a manufactured home shall indicate whether the

owner elects to treat the home as [~~personal property or~~] real property. An owner may elect to treat a manufactured home as real property only if the home is attached to:

(1) real property that is owned by the owner of the home; or

(2) land leased to the owner of the home under a long-term lease, as defined by department rule.

(b) Repealed by Acts 2009, 81st Leg., ch. 77, §15(2), eff. Sept. 1, 2009.

(c) If the department issues a statement of ownership [~~and location~~] to an owner of a manufactured home treated as personal property [~~who has elected to treat a manufactured home as personal property~~], the statement of ownership [~~and location~~] on file with the department is evidence of ownership of the home. A lien, charge, or other encumbrance on a home treated as personal property may be made only by filing the appropriate document with the department.

(d) If an owner elects to treat a manufactured home as real property, the department shall issue to the owner a [~~certified~~] copy of the statement of ownership [~~and location~~] that on its face reflects that the owner has elected to treat the manufactured home as real property at the location listed on the statement. Not later than the 60th day after the date the department issues a [~~certified~~] copy of the statement of ownership [~~and location~~] to the owner, the owner must:

(1) file the [~~certified~~] copy in the real property records of the county in which the home is located; and

(2) notify the department and the chief appraiser of the applicable appraisal district that the [~~certified~~] copy has been filed.

(e) A real property election for a manufactured home is not considered to be perfected until a [~~certified~~] copy of the statement of ownership [~~and location~~] has been filed and the department and the chief appraiser of the applicable appraisal district have been notified of the filing as provided by Subsection (d).

(f) Repealed by Acts 2011, 82nd Leg., ch. 46, §8(1), eff. Sept. 1, 2011.

(g) After a real property election is perfected under Subsection (e):

(1) the home is considered to be real property for all purposes; and

(2) no additional issuance of a statement of ownership [~~and location~~] is required with respect to the manufactured home, unless:

(A) the home is moved from the location specified on the statement of ownership [~~and location~~];

(B) the real property election is changed; or

(C) the use of the property is changed as described by Section 1201.216.

(h) The provisions of this chapter relating to the construction or installation of a manufactured home or to warranties for a manufactured home apply to a home regardless of whether the home is considered to be real or personal property.

(i) Notwithstanding the 60-day deadline specified in Subsection (d), if the closing of a mortgage loan to be secured by real property including the manufactured home is held, the loan is funded, and a deed of trust covering the real property and all improvements on the property is recorded and the licensed title company or attorney who closed the loan failed to complete the conversion to real property in accordance with this chapter, the holder or servicer of the loan may apply for a statement of ownership [~~and location~~] electing real property status, obtain a [~~certified~~] copy of the statement of ownership [~~and location~~], and make the necessary filings and notifications to complete such conversion at any time provided that:

(1) the record owner of the home, as reflected on the department's records, has been given at least 60 days' prior written notice at:

(A) the location of the home and, if it is different, the mailing address of the owner as specified in the department records; and

(B) any other location the holder or servicer knows or believes, after a reasonable inquiry, to be an address where the owner may have been or is receiving mail or is an address of record;

(2) such notification shall be given by certified mail; and

(3) the department by rule shall require evidence that the holder or servicer requesting such after-the-fact completion of a real property election has complied with the requirements of this subsection.

2017 Legislation: Amended by H.B. 2019, §28, 85th Leg., eff. Sept. 1, 2017.

Ⓐ OCC §1201.206. APPLICATION FOR ISSUANCE OF STATEMENT OF OWNERSHIP [~~& LOCATION~~]

(a) At the first retail sale of a manufactured home, the retailer shall provide for the installation of the home and ensure that the application for the issuance

of a statement of ownership [~~and location~~] is properly completed. The consumer shall return the completed application to the retailer. In accordance with Section 1201.204, the retailer shall surrender to the department the original manufacturer's statement of origin at the same time that the retailer applies for the first statement of ownership [~~and location~~].

(b) Not later than the 60th day after the date of the retail sale, the retailer shall provide to the department the completed application for the issuance of a statement of ownership [~~and location~~]. If for any reason the retailer does not timely comply with the requirements of this subsection, the consumer may apply for the issuance of the statement.

(c) Not later than the 60th day after the date of each subsequent sale or transfer of a home that is considered to be personal property, the seller or transferor shall provide to the department a completed application for the issuance of a new statement of ownership [~~and location~~]. If for any reason the seller or transferor does not timely comply with the requirements of this subsection, the consumer may apply for the issuance of the statement.

(d) Repealed by Acts 2011, 82nd Leg., ch. 46, §8(2), eff. Sept. 1, 2011.

(e) Ownership of a manufactured home does not pass or vest at a sale or transfer of the home until a completed application for the issuance of a statement of ownership [~~and location~~] is filed with the department.

(f) If the owner of a manufactured home relocates the home, the owner shall apply for the issuance of a new statement of ownership [~~and location~~] not later than the 60th day after the date the home is relocated. The department shall require that the owner submit evidence that the home was relocated in accordance with the requirements of the Texas Department of Motor Vehicles.

(g) When an application is filed for the issuance of a statement of ownership [~~and location~~] for a used manufactured home that is not in a retailer's inventory or is being converted from personal property to real property in accordance with Section 1201.2075 [~~is filed~~], a statement from the tax assessor-collector for the taxing unit having power to tax the manufactured home shall also be filed with the department. The statement from the tax assessor-collector must indicate that, with respect to each January 1 occurring in the 18-month period preceding the date of the sale, there are no perfected and enforceable tax liens on the manufactured home that have not been extinguished and canceled in accordance with Section 32.015, Tax Code, or personal property taxes due on the manufactured home [~~that may have accrued on each January 1 that falls within the 18 months before the date of the sale~~].

(h) If a person selling a manufactured home to a consumer for residential use fails to file with the department the application for the issuance of a statement of ownership [~~and location~~] and the appropriate filing fee before the 61st day after the date of the sale, the department may assess a fee of at least $100 against the seller. The department shall have the authority to enforce the collection of any fee from the seller through judicial means. The department shall place on the application for the issuance of a statement of ownership [~~and location~~] the following legend in a clear and conspicuous manner:

"THE FILING OF AN APPLICATION FOR THE ISSUANCE OF A STATEMENT OF OWNERSHIP [~~AND LOCATION~~] LATER THAN SIXTY (60) DAYS AFTER THE DATE OF A SALE TO A CONSUMER FOR RESIDENTIAL USE MAY RESULT IN A FEE OF UP TO ONE HUNDRED DOLLARS ($100.00). ANY SUCH APPLICATION THAT IS SUBMITTED LATE MAY BE DELAYED UNTIL THE FEE IS PAID IN FULL."

(i) to **(j)** Repealed by H.B. 2019, §85(3), 85th Leg., eff. Sept. 1, 2017.

[~~(i)~~] [~~When a properly completed notice of installation on the department's promulgated form is filed that relates to a secondary move, the notice must be accompanied by either:~~]

[~~(1)~~] [~~one true and correct copy of the original notice of installation; or~~]

[~~(2)~~] [~~a certification that a true and correct copy of the notice of installation has been provided to the chief appraiser for the county in which the home was installed; the delivery of the copy of the notice to the chief appraiser may be accomplished either by certified mail or by electronic mailing of the electronically reproduced document in a commonly readable format.~~]

[~~(i-1)~~] [~~If the method specified in Subsection (i)(2) is used to report the installation, the department may adopt a discounted fee for the filing of the notice of installation.~~]

[~~(j)~~] [~~In addition to providing each chief appraiser the monthly report required by Section 1201.220, the~~]

~~department shall, on request, provide the tax collector one copy of any requested reported notice of installation.~~]

(k) Notwithstanding any provision in this chapter to the contrary, if a person has acquired a manufactured home and the owner of record or any intervening owners of liens or equitable interests cannot be located to assist in documenting the chain of title, the department may issue a statement of ownership [~~and location~~] to the person claiming ownership if the person can provide a supporting affidavit describing the chain of title and such reasonable supporting proof as the director may require.

2017 Legislation: Amended by H.B. 2019, §§29, 30, 85(3), 85th Leg., eff. Sept. 1, 2017.

A OCC §1201.207. ISSUANCE OF STATEMENT OF OWNERSHIP [~~& LOCATION~~]

(a) Except as provided for in Subsection (a-1), the department shall process any completed application for the issuance of a statement of ownership [~~and location~~] not later than the 15th working day after the date the application is received by the department. If the department rejects an application, the department shall provide a clear and complete explanation of the reason for the rejection and instructions on how to cure any defects, if possible.

(a-1) For the period immediately following June 30 of each year, the department shall, except for applications relating to new manufactured homes and applications accompanied by a tax certificate, cease issuing statements of ownership [~~and location~~] until all tax liens filed with the department before June 30 have been processed and either recorded or rejected. During this period the department will post on its Internet website a notice as to when it is anticipated that processing statements of ownership [~~and location~~] will resume and when it is anticipated that such processing will be within the 15-working-day time frame provided by Subsection (a).

(b) If the department issues a statement of ownership [~~and location~~] for a manufactured home, the department shall maintain a record of the issuance in its electronic records and shall mail a copy to the owner and each lienholder. The department shall make available to the public on the department's Internet website in a searchable and downloadable format all ownership and lienholder information contained on the statement of ownership.

(c) Except with respect to any change in use, servicing of a loan on a manufactured home, release of a lien on a manufactured home by an authorized lienholder, or change in ownership of a lien on a manufactured home, but subject to Section 1201.2075, if the department has issued a statement of ownership [~~and location~~] for a manufactured home, the department may issue a subsequent statement of ownership [~~and location~~] for the home only if all parties reflected in the department's records as having an interest in the manufactured home give their written consent or release their interest, either in writing or by operation of law, or the department has followed the procedures provided by Section 1201.206(k) to document ownership and lien status. Once the department issues a statement of ownership [~~and location~~], the department shall not alter the record of the ownership or lien status, other than to change the record to accurately reflect the proper owner's or lienholder's identity or to release a lien if an authorized lienholder files with the department a request for that release, of a manufactured home for any activity occurring before the issuance of the statement of ownership [~~and location~~] without either the written permission of the owner of record for the manufactured home, their legal representative, or a court order.

(d) Notwithstanding any other provision of this chapter, if the consumer purchases a new manufactured home from a licensed retailer in the ordinary course of business, whether or not a statement of ownership [~~and location~~] has been issued for the manufactured home, the consumer is a bona fide purchaser for value without notice and is entitled to ownership of the manufactured home free and clear of all liens and to a statement of ownership [~~and location~~] reflecting the same on payment by the consumer of the purchase price to the retailer. If there is an existing lien on the new manufactured home perfected with the department, the owner of the lien is entitled to recover the value of the lien from the retailer.

(e) Notwithstanding any other provision of this chapter, if the consumer purchases a used manufactured home from a retailer in the ordinary course of business, the consumer takes the manufactured home free and clear of any liens created by the selling retailer even if they are recorded.

2017 Legislation: Amended by H.B. 2019, §§31, 32, 85th Leg., eff. Sept. 1, 2017.

OCC §1201.2075. CONVERSION FROM PERSONAL PROPERTY TO REAL PROPERTY

(a) Except as provided by Subsection (b) or Section 1201.206(k), the department may not issue a statement of ownership [~~and location~~] for a manufactured home that is being converted from personal property to real property until:

(1) each lien on the home is released by the lienholder; or

(2) each lienholder gives written consent, to be placed on file with the department.

(b) The department may issue a statement of ownership [~~and location~~] before the release of any liens or before receiving the consent of any lienholders as required by this section, or without receiving the statement required by Section 1201.206(g), if the department releases a [~~certified~~] copy of the statement to:

(1) a licensed title insurance company that has issued a commitment to issue a title insurance policy covering all prior liens on the home in connection with a loan that the title company has closed; or

(2) a federally insured financial institution or licensed attorney who has obtained from a licensed title insurance company a title insurance policy covering all prior liens on the home.

2017 Legislation: Amended by H.B. 2019, §33, 85th Leg., eff. Sept. 1, 2017.

OCC §1201.2076. CONVERSION FROM REAL PROPERTY TO PERSONAL PROPERTY

(a) The department may not issue a statement of ownership [~~and location~~] for a manufactured home that is being converted from real property to personal property until the department has inspected the home and determined that it is habitable and:

(1) each lien, including a tax lien, on the home is released by the lienholder; or

(2) each lienholder, including a taxing unit, gives written consent, to be placed on file with the department.

(a-1) Notwithstanding Subsection (a), the department may not require an inspection for habitability before issuing a statement of ownership with respect to a manufactured home if the home is being sold to or ownership is otherwise being transferred to a retailer. The department remains subject to the other requirements of Subsection (a).

(b) For the purposes of Subsection (a)(1), the department may rely on a commitment for title insurance, a title insurance policy, or a lawyer's title opinion to determine that any liens on real property have been released.

2017 Legislation: Amended by H.B. 2019, §34, 85th Leg., eff. Sept. 1, 2017.

OCC §1201.208. PAYMENT OF TAXES REQUIRED FOR ISSUANCE OF STATEMENT OF OWNERSHIP [~~& LOCATION~~]

(a) Any licensee who sells or[~~,~~] exchanges[~~, or lease purchases~~] a new manufactured home to any consumer is responsible for the payment of all required sales and use tax on such home.

(b) If it is determined that a new manufactured home was sold or[~~,~~] exchanged[~~, or lease-purchased~~] without the required sales and use tax being paid, the payment shall be made from the fund, up to the available penal amount of the licensee's bond or the remaining balance of the security for the license, and a claim for reimbursement shall be filed with the licensee's surety or the amount deducted from the security for the license.

2017 Legislation: Amended by H.B. 2019, §35, 85th Leg., eff. Sept. 1, 2017.

OCC §1201.209. GROUNDS FOR REFUSAL TO ISSUE OR FOR SUSPENSION OR REVOCATION OF STATEMENT OF OWNERSHIP [~~& LOCATION~~]

The department may not refuse to issue a statement of ownership [~~and location~~] and may not suspend or revoke a statement of ownership [~~and location~~] unless:

(1) the application for issuance of the statement of ownership [~~and location~~] contains a false or fraudulent statement, the applicant failed to provide information required by the director, or the applicant is not entitled to issuance of the statement of ownership [~~and location~~];

(2) the director has reason to believe that the manufactured home is stolen or unlawfully converted, or the issuance of a statement of ownership [~~and location~~] would defraud the owner or a lienholder of the manufactured home;

(3) the director has reason to believe that the manufactured home is salvaged, and an application for the issuance of a new statement of ownership [~~and location~~] that indicates that the home is salvaged has not been filed;

(4) the required fee has not been paid;

(5) the state sales and use tax has not been paid in accordance with Chapter 158, Tax Code, and Section 1201.208; or

(6) a tax lien was filed and recorded under Section 1201.219 and the lien has not been extinguished.

2017 Legislation: Amended by H.B. 2019, §36, 85th Leg., eff. Sept. 1, 2017.

A OCC §1201.210. PROCEDURE FOR REFUSAL TO ISSUE OR SUSPENSION OR REVOCATION OF STATEMENT OF OWNERSHIP [~~& LOCATION~~]

(a) If the director refuses to issue or suspends or revokes a statement of ownership [~~and location~~], the director shall give, by certified mail, written notice of that action to:

(1) the seller and purchaser or transferor and transferee, as applicable; and

(2) the holder of a lien or security interest of record.

(b) An action by the director under Subsection (a) is a contested case under Chapter 2001, Government Code.

(c) A notice of appeal and request for hearing must be filed with the director not later than the 30th day after the date of notice of the director's action. If appeal is not timely made, the revocation or suspension described in the notice of the director's action becomes final.

(d) Repealed by H.B. 2019, §85(4), 85th Leg., eff. Sept. 1, 2017.

[~~(d)~~] [~~Until a revocation or suspension has become final, the department shall place a hold on any activity relating to the statement of ownership and location other than the recordation of liens, including tax liens.~~]

2017 Legislation: Amended by H.B. 2019, §§37, 38, 85(4), 85th Leg., eff. Sept. 1, 2017.

OCC §1201.211. REPEALED

A OCC §1201.212. TRANSFER OF OWNERSHIP BY OPERATION OF LAW

(a) If the ownership of a manufactured home in this state is transferred by inheritance, devise, or bequest, by bankruptcy, receivership, judicial sale, or other involuntary divestiture of ownership, or by any other operation of law, the department shall issue a new statement of ownership [~~and location~~] after receiving a [~~certified~~] copy of:

(1) the order or bill of sale from an officer making a judicial sale;

(2) the order appointing a temporary administrator;

(3) the probate proceedings;

(4) the letters testamentary or the letters of administration; or

(5) if administration of an estate is not necessary, an affidavit by all of the heirs at law showing:

(A) that administration is not necessary; and

(B) the name in which the statement of ownership [~~and location~~] should be issued.

(b) The department may issue a new statement of ownership [~~and location~~] in the name of the purchaser at a foreclosure sale:

(1) for a lien or security interest foreclosed according to law by nonjudicial means, if the lienholder or secured party files an affidavit showing the nonjudicial foreclosure according to law; or

(2) for a foreclosed constitutional or statutory lien, if the person entitled to the lien files an affidavit showing the creation of the lien and the resulting divestiture of title according to law.

(c) The department shall issue a new statement of ownership [~~and location~~] to a survivor if:

(1) an agreement providing for a right of survivorship is signed by two or more eligible persons, as determined under Section 1201.213; and

(2) on the death of one of the persons, the department is provided with a copy of the death certificate of that person.

2017 Legislation: Amended by H.B. 2019, §39, 85th Leg., eff. Sept. 1, 2017.

A OCC §1201.213. ELIGIBILITY TO SIGN RIGHT OF SURVIVORSHIP AGREEMENT

(a) A person is eligible to sign a right of survivorship agreement under this subchapter if the person:

(1) is married and the spouse of the signing person is the only other party to the agreement;

(2) is unmarried and attests to that unmarried status by affidavit; or

(3) is married and provides the department with an affidavit from the signing person's spouse that attests that the signing person's interest in the manufactured home is the signing person's separate property.

(b) If the statement of ownership [~~and location~~] is being issued in connection with the sale of the home, the seller is not eligible to sign a right of survivorship agreement under this subchapter unless the seller is

the child, grandchild, parent, grandparent, or sibling of each other person signing the agreement. A family relationship required by this subsection may be a relationship established by adoption.

2017 Legislation: Amended by H.B. 2019, §40, 85th Leg., eff. Sept. 1, 2017.

Ⓐ OCC §1201.214. DOCUMENT OF TITLE; CERTIFICATE OF ATTACHMENT

(a) Effective September 1, 2003, all outstanding documents of title or certificates of attachment are considered to be statements of ownership [~~and location~~].

(b) An owner or lienholder may provide to the department a document of title or certificate of attachment and any additional information required by the department and request that the department issue a statement of ownership [~~and location~~] to replace the document of title or certificate of attachment. The department shall mail to the owner or lienholder a copy of the statement of ownership [~~and location~~] issued under this subsection.

(c), (d) Repealed by Acts 2007, 80th Leg., ch. 863, §73(a)(5), eff. Jan. 1, 2008.

2017 Legislation: Amended by H.B. 2019, §41, 85th Leg., eff. Sept. 1, 2017.

OCC §1201.215. REPEALED

Ⓐ OCC §1201.216. CHANGE IN USE

(a) If the owner of a manufactured home notifies the department that the owner intends to treat the home as real property or intends to treat the home as a salvaged manufactured home or reserve the home [~~its use~~] for a business use [~~purpose~~] or another nonresidential use [~~salvage~~], the department shall indicate on the statement of ownership [~~and location~~] for the home that:

(1) the owner of the home has elected to treat the home as described by this subsection [~~as real property or to reserve its use for a business purpose or salvage~~]; and

(2) except as provided by Section 1201.2055(h), the home is no longer a manufactured home for purposes of regulation under this chapter or of recordation of liens, including tax liens.

(b) On application and subject to Sections 1201.2076 and 1201.209, the department shall issue for the structure described in the application a new statement of ownership [~~and location~~] restoring the structure's designation as a manufactured home only after an inspection and determination that the structure is habitable as provided by Section 1201.453.

(c), (d) Repealed by Acts 2005, 79th Leg., ch. 1284, §34(1), eff. June 18, 2005.

2017 Legislation: Amended by H.B. 2019, §42, 85th Leg., eff. Sept. 1, 2017.

Ⓐ OCC §1201.217. MANUFACTURED HOME ABANDONED

(a) The owner of real property on which a manufactured home owned by another is located may declare the home abandoned as provided by this section if:

(1) the home has been continuously unoccupied for at least four months; and

(2) any indebtedness secured by the home or related to a lease agreement between the owner of the real property and the owner of the home is considered delinquent.

(b) Before declaring a manufactured home abandoned, the owner of real property on which the home is located must send a notice of intent to declare the home abandoned to the record owner of the home, all lienholders at the addresses listed on the home's statement of ownership [~~and location~~] on file with the department, the tax collector for each taxing unit that imposes ad valorem taxes on the real property where the home is located, and any intervening owners of liens or equitable interests. The notice must include the address where the home is currently located. If the person giving such notice knows that a person to whom the notice is being given no longer resides and is no longer receiving mail at a known address, a reasonable effort shall be made to locate the person and give the person notice at an address where the person is receiving mail. Mailing of the notice by certified mail, return receipt requested, postage prepaid, to the persons required to be notified by this subsection constitutes conclusive proof of compliance with this subsection.

(c) On receipt of a notice of intent to declare a manufactured home abandoned, the record owner of the home, a lienholder, a tax assessor-collector for a taxing unit that imposes ad valorem taxes on the real property on which the home is located, or an intervening owner of a lien or equitable interest may enter the real property on which the home is located to remove the home. The real property owner must disclose to the record owner, lienholder, tax assessor-collector, or intervening owner seeking to remove the home the location of the home and grant the person reasonable access to the home. A person removing a home is responsible to the real property owner for any damage to the real property resulting from the removal of the home.

(d) If the manufactured home remains on the real property for at least 45 days after the date the notice is postmarked:

(1) all liens on the home are extinguished; and

(2) the real property owner may declare the home abandoned and may apply to the department for a statement of ownership [~~and location~~] listing the real property owner as the owner of the manufactured home.

(d-1) When applying for a statement of ownership under this section, the real property owner shall include with the application an affidavit stating that:

(1) the person owns the real property where the manufactured home is located; and

(2) the name of the person to whom title to the home will be transferred under this section is the same name that is listed in the real property or tax records indicating the current ownership of the real property.

(e) A new statement of ownership [~~and location~~] issued by the department under this section transfers, free of any liens, if there is evidence of United States Postal Service return receipt from all lienholders, title to the manufactured home to the real property owner.

(f) This section does not apply if the person who owns the real property on which the manufactured home is located and who is declaring that the home is abandoned, or any person who is related to or affiliated with that person, has now, or has ever owned, an interest in the manufactured home.

(g) Notwithstanding Subsection (f), an owner of real property on which a manufactured home has been abandoned may apply for a new statement of ownership with respect to a home that was previously declared abandoned and then resold and abandoned again.

2017 Legislation: Amended by H.B. 2019, §43, 85th Leg., eff. Sept. 1, 2017.

OCC §1201.218. REPEALED

OCC §1201.219. PERFECTION, EFFECT, & RELEASE OF LIENS

(a) A lien on manufactured homes in inventory is perfected only by filing the lien with the department on the required form. Once perfected, the lien applies to the manufactured homes in the inventory as well as to any proceeds from the sale of those homes. The department may suspend or revoke the license of a retailer who fails to satisfy a perfected inventory lien.

(b) Except as provided by Subsection (a) and subject to Subsection (d), a lien on a manufactured home is perfected only by filing with the department the notice of lien on a form provided by the department. The department shall disclose on its website the date of each lien filing. A lien recorded with the department has priority, according to the chronological order of recordation, over another lien or claim against the manufactured home.

(b-1) Notwithstanding any other law, a lien perfected with the department may be released only by filing a request for the release with the department on the form provided by the department or by following the department's procedures for electronic lien release on the department's Internet website. This subsection does not apply to the release of a tax lien perfected with the department.

(c) Notwithstanding any other provision of this section or any other law, the filing of a lien security agreement on the inventory of a retailer does not prevent a buyer in the ordinary course of business, as defined by Section 1.201, Business & Commerce Code, from acquiring good and marketable title free of that lien, and the department may not consider that lien for the purpose of title issuance.

(d) A tax lien on a manufactured home not held in a retailer's inventory is perfected only by filing with the department the notice of the tax lien on a form provided by the department in accordance with the requirements of Chapter 32, Tax Code. The form must require the disclosure of the original dollar amount of the tax lien and the name and address of the person in whose name the manufactured home is listed on the tax roll. The department shall disclose on its Internet website the date of each tax lien filing, the original amount of the tax lien claimed by each filing, and the fact that the amount shown does not include additional sums, including interest, penalties, and attorney's fees. The statement required by Section 1201.205(7) is notice to all persons that the tax lien exists. A tax lien recorded with the department has priority over another lien or claim against the manufactured home. Tax liens shall be filed by the tax collector for any taxing unit having the power to tax the manufactured home. A single filing by a tax collector is a filing for all the taxing units for which the tax collector is empowered to collect.

(e) A tax lien perfected with the department may be released only by:

(1) filing with the department a tax certificate or tax paid receipt in accordance with Section 32.015, Tax Code;

(2) filing a request for the release with the department on the form provided by the department;

(3) following the department's procedures for electronic tax lien release on the department's Internet website;

(4) a tax collector filing a tax lien release with the department as provided by Subsection (f); or

(5) the department in the manner provided by Subsection (h).

(f) On request by any person, a tax collector shall file a tax lien release with the department if the four-year statute of limitations to file a suit for collection of personal property taxes in Section 33.05(a)(1), Tax Code, has expired.

(g) The department may request that a tax collector confirm that no tax suit has been timely filed on any manufactured home tax lien more than four years in delinquency. The department may make a request under this subsection electronically, and a taxing authority may provide notice of the existence or absence of a timely filed tax suit electronically.

(h) The department shall remove from a manufactured home's statement of ownership [~~and location~~] a reference to any tax lien delinquent more than four years for which no suit has been timely filed in accordance with Section 33.05(a)(1), Tax Code, if:

(1) a tax collector confirms no suit has been filed; or

(2) the department:

(A) has submitted to a tax collector two requests under Subsection (g) sent not fewer than 15 days apart; and

(B) has not received any response from the tax collector before the 60th day after the tax collector's receipt of the second request.

2017 Legislation: Amended by H.B. 2019, §44, 85th Leg., eff. Sept. 1, 2017.

A OCC §1201.220. REPORT TO CHIEF APPRAISER

(a) The department shall make available in electronic format, or in hard-copy format on request, to each chief appraiser of an appraisal district in this state a monthly report that, for each manufactured home reported as having been installed during the preceding month in the county for which the district was established and for each manufactured home previously installed in the county for which a transfer of ownership was recorded by the issuance of a statement of ownership [~~and location~~] during the preceding month, lists:

(1) the name of the owner of the home;

(2) the name of the manufacturer of the home, if available;

(3) the model designation of the home, if available;

(4) the identification number of each section or module of the home;

(5) the address or location where the home was reported as installed; and

(6) the reported date of the installation of the home.

(b) The department shall make the report required by this section available to the public on the department's Internet website in a searchable and downloadable format.

2017 Legislation: Amended by H.B. 2019, §45, 85th Leg., eff. Sept. 1, 2017.

A OCC §1201.221. INFORMATION ON OWNERSHIP & TAX LIEN

(a) On written request, the department shall provide information held by the department on:

(1) the current ownership and location of a manufactured home; and

(2) the existence of all tax liens on that home for which notice has been filed with the department.

(b) A request under Subsection (a) must contain:

(1) the name of the owner of the home as reflected on the statement of ownership [~~and location~~]; or

(2) the identification number of the home.

2017 Legislation: Amended by H.B. 2019, §46, 85th Leg., eff. Sept. 1, 2017.

A OCC §1201.222. CERTAIN MANUFACTURED HOMES CONSIDERED REAL PROPERTY

(a) A manufactured home is treated as real property only if:

(1) the owner of the home has elected to treat the home as real property as provided by Section 1201.2055; and

(2) a [~~certified~~] copy of the statement of ownership [~~and location~~] for the home has been filed in the real property records of the county in which the home is located.

(b) Repealed by Acts 2005, 79th Leg., ch. 1284, §34(1), eff. June 18, 2005.

(c) Installation of a manufactured home considered to be real property under this chapter must occur

in a manner that satisfies the lending requirements of the Federal Housing Administration (FHA), Fannie Mae, or Freddie Mac for long-term mortgage loans or for FHA insurance. The installation of a new manufactured home must meet, in addition to applicable state standards, the manufacturer's specifications required to validate the manufacturer's warranty.

(d) A civil action to enjoin a violation of this section may be brought by:

(1) a purchaser in the county in which the violation occurs; or

(2) the county in which the violation occurs.

(e) Repealed by Acts 2003, 78th Leg., ch. 338, §51, eff. June 1, 2003.

(f) This section does not require a retailer or retailer's agent to obtain a license under Chapter 1101.

2017 Legislation: Amended by H.B. 2019, §47, 85th Leg., eff. Sept. 1, 2017.

Sections 1201.223-1201.250 reserved for expansion

SUBCHAPTER F. STANDARDS

OCC §1201.251. STANDARDS & REQUIREMENTS ADOPTED BY BOARD

(a) The board shall adopt standards and requirements for:

(1) the installation and construction of manufactured housing that are reasonably necessary to protect the health, safety, and welfare of the occupants and the public; and

(2) the construction of HUD-code manufactured homes in compliance with the federal standards and requirements established under the National Manufactured Housing Construction and Safety Standards Act of 1974 (42 U.S.C. Section 5401 et seq.).

(b) The standards and requirements adopted under Subsection (a)(1) are the standards code.

(c) The standards adopted under Subsection (a)(1) must ensure that manufactured housing installed on both permanent and nonpermanent foundation systems resists overturning and lateral movement, according to the design loads for the particular wind zone for which the housing was constructed.

(d) In order to ensure that the determinations required by this section are properly made by qualified persons:

(1) the board's rules may provide for the approval of foundation systems and devices that have been approved by licensed engineers; and

(2) any generic installation standards promulgated by rule shall first be reviewed by an advisory committee established by the board comprised of representatives of manufacturers, installers, and manufacturers of stabilization systems or devices, including one or more licensed engineers.

(e) The advisory committee established by Subsection (d) shall make a report to the board setting forth each comment and concern over any proposed rules. The members of the committee shall have no personal liability for providing this advice.

OCC §1201.252. POWER OF LOCAL GOVERNMENTAL UNIT TO ADOPT DIFFERENT STANDARD

(a) A local governmental unit of this state may not adopt a standard for the construction or installation of manufactured housing in the local governmental unit that is different from a standard adopted by the board unless, after a hearing, the board expressly approves the proposed standard.

(b) To adopt a different standard under this section, the local governmental unit must demonstrate that public health and safety require the different standard.

OCC §1201.253. HEARING ON STANDARD OR REQUIREMENT

The director shall publish notice and conduct a public hearing before:

(1) adopting a standard or requirement authorized by this subchapter;

(2) amending a standard authorized by this subchapter; or

(3) approving a standard proposed by a local governmental unit under Section 1201.252.

OCC §1201.254. EFFECTIVE DATE OF REQUIREMENT OR STANDARD

Each requirement or standard that is adopted, modified, amended, or repealed by the board must state its effective date.

A OCC §1201.255. INSTALLATION OF MANUFACTURED HOUSING

(a) Except as authorized under Section 1201.252, manufactured housing that is installed must be installed in compliance with the standards and rules adopted and orders issued by the department. An uninstalled manufactured home may not be occupied for any purpose other than to view the home on a retailer's sales lot.

(b) An installer may not install a used manufactured home at a location on a site that has evidence of ponding, runoff under heavy rains, or bare uncompacted soil unless the installer first obtains the owner's signature on a form promulgated by the board disclosing that such conditions may contribute to problems with the stabilization system for that manufactured home, including possible damage to that home, and the owner accepts that risk.

2017 Legislation: Amended by H.B. 2019, §48, 85th Leg., eff. Sept. 1, 2017.

OCC §1201.256. WIND ZONE REGULATIONS

(a) Aransas, Brazoria, Calhoun, Cameron, Chambers, Galveston, Jefferson, Kenedy, Kleberg, Matagorda, Nueces, Orange, Refugio, San Patricio, and Willacy counties are in Wind Zone II. All other counties are in Wind Zone I.

(b) To be installed in a Wind Zone II county, a manufactured home constructed on or after September 1, 1997, must meet the Wind Zone II standards adopted by the United States Department of Housing and Urban Development.

(c) A manufactured home constructed before September 1, 1997, may be installed in a Wind Zone I or II county without restriction.

(d) A retailer who sells a manufactured home constructed on or after September 1, 1997, to Wind Zone I standards must, before the execution of a mutually binding sales agreement or retail installment sales contract, give the consumer notice that:

(1) the home was not designed or constructed to withstand a hurricane force wind occurring in a Wind Zone II or III area;

(2) installation of the home is not permitted in a Wind Zone II county in this state; and

(3) another state may prohibit installation of the home in a Wind Zone II or III area.

Sections 1201.257-1201.300 reserved for expansion

SUBCHAPTER G. INSPECTIONS & MONITORING

OCC §1201.301. STATE INSPECTORS

(a) The director may employ state inspectors to:

(1) carry out the functions the department is required to perform under this chapter;

(2) implement this chapter; and

(3) enforce the rules adopted and orders issued under this chapter.

(b) In enforcing this chapter, the director may authorize a state inspector to travel inside or outside of the state to inspect a licensee.

OCC §1201.302. INSPECTION BY LOCAL GOVERNMENTAL UNITS

(a) To ensure that a manufactured home sold or installed in this state complies with the standards code, the director may by contract provide for a federal agency or an agency or political subdivision of this state or another state to perform an inspection or inspection program under this chapter or under rules adopted by the board.

(b) On request, the department shall authorize a local governmental unit in this state to perform an inspection or enforcement activity related to the construction of a foundation system or the erection or installation of manufactured housing at a homesite under a contract or other official designation and rules adopted by the board. The department may withdraw the authorization if the local governmental unit fails to follow the rules, interpretations, and written instructions of the department.

(c) The department:

(1) shall advise each local governmental unit biennially in writing of the program for contracting installation inspections;

(2) shall encourage local building inspection officials to perform enforcement and inspection activities for manufactured housing installed in the local governmental unit; and

(3) may establish cooperative inspection training programs.

Ⓐ OCC §1201.303. INSPECTIONS

(a) The director may inspect manufactured homes at the state border and adopt rules necessary for the inspection of manufactured homes entering this state to ensure:

(1) compliance with:

(A) the National Manufactured Housing Construction and Safety Standards Act of 1974 (42 U.S.C. Section 5401 et seq.);

(B) the standards code; and

(C) the rules adopted by the director; and

(2) payment of any use tax owed to the state.

(b) The department shall establish an installation inspection program in which at least 75 percent of in-

stalled manufactured homes are inspected on a sample basis for compliance with the standards and rules adopted and orders issued by the director. The program must place priority on inspecting multisection homes and homes installed in Wind Zone II counties.

(c) to **(g)** Repealed by H.B. 2019, §85(5), 85th Leg., eff. Sept. 1, 2017.

[~~(c)~~] [~~On or after January 1, 2015, the director by rule shall establish a third-party installation inspection program to supplement the inspections of the department if the department is not able to inspect at least 75 percent of manufactured homes installed in each of the calendar years 2012, 2013, and 2014.~~]

[~~(d)~~] [~~The third-party installation inspection program established under Subsection (c) must:~~]

[~~(1)~~] [~~establish qualifications for third party inspectors to participate in the program;~~]

[~~(2)~~] [~~require third-party inspectors to register with the department before participating in the program;~~]

[~~(3)~~] [~~establish a biennial registration and renewal process for third-party inspectors;~~]

[~~(4)~~] [~~require the list of registered third-party inspectors to be posted on the department's Internet website;~~]

[~~(5)~~] [~~establish clear processes governing inspection fees and payment to third-party inspectors;~~]

[~~(6)~~] [~~establish the maximum inspection fee that may be charged to a consumer;~~]

[~~(7)~~] [~~require a third-party inspection to occur not later than the 14th day after the date of installation of the manufactured home;~~]

[~~(8)~~] [~~establish a process for a retailer or broker to contract, as part of the sale of a new or used manufactured home, with an independent third-party inspector to inspect the installation of the home;~~]

[~~(9)~~] [~~establish a process for an installer to schedule an inspection for each consumer-to-consumer sale where a home is reinstalled;~~]

[~~(10)~~] [~~if a violation is noted in an inspection, require the installer to:~~]

[~~(A)~~] [~~remedy the violations noted;~~]

[~~(B)~~] [~~have the home reinspected at the installer's expense; and~~]

[~~(C)~~] [~~certify to the department that all violations have been corrected;~~]

[~~(11)~~] [~~require an inspector to report inspection results to the retailer, installer, and the department;~~]

[~~(12)~~] [~~require all persons receiving inspection results under Subdivision (11) to maintain a record of the results at least until the end of the installation warranty period;~~]

[~~(13)~~] [~~authorize the department to charge a filing fee and an inspection fee for third-party inspections;~~]

[~~(14)~~] [~~authorize the department to continue to conduct no-charge complaint inspections under Section 1201.355 on request, but only after an initial installation inspection is completed;~~]

[~~(15)~~] [~~establish procedures to revoke the registration of inspectors who fail to comply with rules adopted under this section; and~~]

[~~(16)~~] [~~require the department to notify the relevant state agency if the department revokes an inspector registration based on a violation that is relevant to a license issued to the applicable person by another state agency.~~]

[~~(e)~~] [~~Not later than January 1, 2015, the department shall submit to the Legislative Budget Board, the Governor's Office of Budget, Planning, and Policy, and the standing committee of each house of the legislature having primary jurisdiction over housing a report concerning whether the department inspected at least 75 percent of manufactured homes installed in each of the calendar years 2012, 2013, and 2014.~~]

[~~(f)~~] [~~Not later than December 1, 2015, the director shall adopt rules as necessary to implement Subsections (c) and (d) if the department did not inspect at least 75 percent of manufactured homes installed in each of the calendar years 2012, 2013, and 2014. Not later than January 1, 2016, the department shall begin registering third-party inspectors under Subsections (c) and (d) if the department inspections did not occur as described by this subsection.~~]

[~~(g)~~] [~~If the department is not required to establish a third-party installation inspection program as provided by Subsection (c), Subsections (c), (d), (e), and (f) and this subsection expire September 1, 2016.~~]

2017 Legislation: Amended by H.B. 2019, §85(5), 85th Leg., eff. Sept. 1, 2017.

OCC §1201.304. INSPECTION SEARCH WARRANTS

If required by law or otherwise necessary, the director may obtain an inspection search warrant.

OCC §1201.305. PROGRAM MONITORING

The director may enter into a contract with the United States Department of Housing and Urban Development or its designee to monitor the programs of that department.

Sections 1201.306-1201.350 reserved for expansion

SUBCHAPTER H. WARRANTIES

OCC §1201.351. MANUFACTURER'S WARRANTY

(a) The manufacturer of a new HUD-code manufactured home shall warrant, in a separate written document, that:

(1) the home is constructed or assembled in accordance with all building codes, standards, requirements, and regulations prescribed by the United States Department of Housing and Urban Development under the National Manufactured Housing Construction and Safety Standards Act of 1974 (42 U.S.C. Section 5401 et seq.); and

(2) the home and all appliances and equipment included in the home are free from defects in materials or workmanship except for cosmetic defects.

(b) The manufacturer's warranty is in effect until at least the first anniversary of the date of initial installation of the home at the consumer's homesite or the closing of the consumer's purchase or acquisition of an already installed new home, whichever is later.

(c) At the time the manufacturer delivers the home to the retailer, the manufacturer shall also deliver to the retailer:

(1) the manufacturer's warranty; and

(2) the warranties given by the manufacturers of appliances or equipment installed in the home.

OCC §1201.352. RETAILER'S WARRANTY ON A NEW HUD-CODE MANUFACTURED HOME

(a) The retailer of a new HUD-code manufactured home shall warrant to the consumer in writing that:

(1) installation of the home at the initial homesite was or will be, as applicable, completed in accordance with all department standards, rules, orders, and requirements; and

(2) appliances and equipment included with the sale of the home and installed by the retailer are or will be:

(A) installed in accordance with the instructions or specifications of the manufacturers of the appliances or equipment; and

(B) free from defects in materials or workmanship.

The warranty may expressly disclaim or limit any warranty regarding cosmetic defects.

(b) The retailer's warranty on a new HUD-code manufactured home is in effect until the first anniversary of the later of the date of initial installation of the home at the consumer's homesite or the closing of the consumer's purchase or acquisition of the home.

(c) Before the signing of a binding retail installment sales contract or other binding purchase agreement on a new HUD-code manufactured home, the retailer must give the consumer a copy of:

(1) the manufacturer's warranty;

(2) the retailer's warranty;

(3) the warranties given by the manufacturers of appliances or equipment included with the home; and

(4) the name and address of the manufacturer or retailer to whom the consumer is to give notice of a warranty service request.

(d) Not later than the 30th day after the installation of a new HUD-code manufactured home, the retailer shall deliver to the consumer a copy of the warranty given by the licensed installer.

OCC §1201.353. NOTICE OF NEED FOR WARRANTY SERVICE

(a) The consumer shall give written notice to the manufacturer, retailer, or installer, as applicable, of a need for warranty service or repairs.

(b) Written notice to the department is deemed to be notice to the manufacturer, retailer, or installer commencing three business days after receipt and forwarding of the notice by the department to the licensee by regular mail or electronic mail of a scanned copy of the notice.

OCC §1201.354. CORRECTIVE ACTION REQUIRED

The manufacturer, retailer, or installer, as applicable, shall take appropriate corrective action within a reasonable period as required by department rules to fulfill the written warranty obligation.

OCC §1201.355. CONSUMER COMPLAINT HOME INSPECTION

(a) If the manufacturer, retailer, or installer does not provide the consumer with proper warranty service,

the consumer may, at any time, request the department to perform a consumer complaint home inspection. The department may not charge a fee for the inspection.

(b) On payment of the required inspection fee, the manufacturer, retailer, or installer may request the department to perform a consumer complaint home inspection if the manufacturer, retailer, or installer:

(1) believes the consumer's complaints are not covered by the warranty of the manufacturer, retailer, or installer, as applicable;

(2) believes that the warranty service was properly provided; or

(3) disputes responsibility concerning the warranty obligation.

(c) The department shall perform a consumer complaint home inspection not later than the 30th day after the date of receipt of a request for the inspection.

(d) Notwithstanding any other provision of this section, the department may make an inspection at any time if it believes that there is a reasonable possibility that a condition exists that would present an imminent threat to health or safety.

OCC §1201.356. REPORT & ORDER; AMENDMENT; COMPLIANCE

(a) Not later than the 10th day after the date of a consumer complaint home inspection, the department shall send a written report and any order to the consumer, manufacturer, retailer, and installer by certified mail, return receipt requested.

(b) The report shall specify:

(1) each of the consumer's complaints; and

(2) whether the complaint is covered by the manufacturer's, retailer's, or installer's warranty and, if so, which of those warranties.

(c) The director shall issue to the manufacturer, retailer, or installer an appropriate order for corrective action by the manufacturer, retailer, or installer specifying a reasonable period for completion of the corrective action. With regard to new manufactured homes, both the installer and the retailer are responsible for the warranty of installation. If the department determines that a complaint is covered by the installation warranty, the director shall issue the order to the installer for the corrective action. If the installer fails to perform the corrective action, the installer shall be subject to the provisions of Section 1201.357. In that instance, the director shall issue the same order for corrective action to the retailer with a new time frame not to exceed 10 days unless additional time is needed for compliance upon a showing of good cause. If the retailer is compelled to perform corrective action because of the failure of the installer to comply with the director's order, the retailer may seek reimbursement from the installer. The period for the performance of any required warranty work may be shortened by the director as much as is feasible if the warranty work is believed necessary to address a possible imminent threat to health or safety.

(d) The department may issue an amended report and order if all parties receive notice of and are given an opportunity to respond to that report and order. The amended report and order supersede the initial report and order.

(e) The manufacturer, retailer, or installer shall comply with the report and order of the director.

OCC §1201.357. FAILURE TO PROVIDE WARRANTY SERVICE

(a) If the manufacturer, retailer, or installer, as applicable, fails to provide warranty service within a period specified by the director, the manufacturer, retailer, or installer must show good cause in writing as to why the manufacturer, retailer, or installer failed to provide the service.

(b) If the manufacturer, retailer, or installer, as applicable, fails or refuses to provide warranty service in accordance with the department order under Section 1201.356, the director shall hold an informal meeting at which the manufacturer, retailer, or installer must show cause as to why the manufacturer's, retailer's, or installer's license should not be suspended or revoked and at which the consumer may express the person's views. Following the meeting, the director shall either resolve the matter by agreed order, dismiss the matter if no violation is found to have occurred, or institute an administrative action, which may include license suspension or revocation, the assessment of administrative penalties, or a combination of such actions.

(b-1) As authorized by Section 1201.6041, the director may order a manufacturer, retailer, or installer, as applicable, to pay a refund directly to a consumer as part of an agreed order described by Subsection (b) instead of or in addition to instituting an administrative action under this chapter.

(c) If the manufacturer, retailer, or installer is unable to provide warranty service in accordance with the

department order under Section 1201.356 as a result of an action of the consumer, the manufacturer, retailer, or installer must make that allegation in the written statement required by Subsection (a). The department shall investigate the allegation, and if the department determines that the allegation is credible, the department shall issue a new order specifying the date and time of the proposed corrective action. The department shall send the order to the consumer and the manufacturer, retailer, or installer, as applicable, by certified mail, return receipt requested. If the consumer refuses to comply with the department's new order, the manufacturer, retailer, or installer, as applicable:

(1) is discharged from the obligations imposed by the relevant department orders;

(2) has no liability to the consumer with regard to that warranty; and

(3) is not subject to an action by the department for failure to provide warranty service.

Ⓐ OCC §1201.358. FAILURE TO SHOW GOOD CAUSE; HEARING RESULTS

(a) Failure by the manufacturer, retailer, or installer to show good cause under Section 1201.357(a) is a sufficient basis for suspension or revocation of the manufacturer's, retailer's, or installer's license.

(b) If the director determines that an order was incorrect regarding a warranty obligation, the director shall issue a final order stating the correct warranty obligation and the right of the manufacturer, retailer, or installer to indemnification from one of the other parties.

(c) The director may issue an order:

(1) directing a manufacturer, retailer, or installer whose license is not revoked, suspended, or subject to an administrative sanction under Section 1201.357(b) and who is not out of business to perform the warranty obligation of a manufacturer, retailer, or installer whose license is revoked, suspended, or subject to an administrative sanction under Section 1201.357(b) or who is out of business; and

(2) giving the manufacturer, retailer, or installer performing the obligation the right of indemnification against another party.

(d) A manufacturer, retailer, or installer entitled to indemnification under this section is a consumer for purposes of Subchapter I and may recover actual damages from the manufactured homeowner consumer claims program [~~trust fund~~].

2017 Legislation: Amended by H.B. 2019, §49, 85th Leg., eff. Sept. 1, 2017.

OCC §1201.359. APPLICATION OF WARRANTIES IF HUD-CODE MANUFACTURED HOME MOVED

(a) The manufacturer's and retailer's warranties do not apply to any defect or damage caused by moving a new HUD-code manufactured home from the initial installation site.

(b) Conspicuous notice of the warranty exception under Subsection (a) must be given to the consumer at the time of sale.

(c) The warrantor has the burden of proof to show that the defect or damage is caused by the move.

Ⓐ OCC §1201.360. WARRANTY FOR HUD-CODE MANUFACTURED HOME PERMANENTLY ATTACHED TO REAL PROPERTY

(a) The seller of real property to which a new HUD-code manufactured home is permanently attached may give the initial purchaser a written warranty that combines the manufacturer's warranty and the retailer's warranty required by this subchapter if:

(1) the statement of ownership [~~and location~~] reflects that the owner has elected to treat the home as real property;

(2) the home is actually located where the statement of ownership [~~and location~~] reflects that it is located; and

(3) a [~~certified~~] copy of the statement of ownership [~~and location~~] has been filed in the real property records for the county in which the home is located.

(b) If a combination warranty is given under this section, the manufacturer and retailer are not required to give separate written warranties, but the manufacturer and retailer are jointly liable with the seller of the real property to the purchaser for the performance of their respective warranty obligations.

2017 Legislation: Amended by H.B. 2019, §50, 85th Leg., eff. Sept. 1, 2017.

OCC §1201.361. INSTALLER'S WARRANTY

(a) For all installations, the installer shall give the manufactured home owner a written warranty that the installation of the home was performed in accordance with all department standards, rules, orders, and requirements. The warranty for the installation of a new HUD-code manufactured home is to be given by the re-

tailer, who is responsible for installation. If the retailer subcontracts this function to a licensed installer, the retailer and installer are jointly and severally responsible for performance of the warranty.

(b) The warranty must conspicuously disclose the requirement that the consumer notify the installer of any claim in writing in accordance with the terms of the warranty. Unless the warranty provides for a longer period, the installer or retailer has no obligation or liability under the person's warranty for any defect described in a written notice received from the consumer more than two years after the later of the date of purchase or the date of installation.

OCC §1201.362. INSPECTIONS NOT LIMITED; CORRECTIONS

(a) Nothing in this chapter shall limit the ability of the department to inspect a manufactured home at any time.

(b) Notwithstanding the limitations and terms of any warranty, the director may, whenever the department identifies any aspect of an installation that does not conform to applicable requirements, order the licensee who performed the installation to correct it, or, if that licensee is no longer licensed, reassign correction to a licensed installer and reimburse the person from the fund for the costs of correction.

Sections 1201.363-1201.400 reserved for expansion

SUBCHAPTER I. MANUFACTURED HOMEOWNER CONSUMER CLAIMS PROGRAM [~~HOMEOWNERS' RECOVERY TRUST FUND~~]

OCC §1201.401. MANUFACTURED HOMEOWNER CONSUMER CLAIMS PROGRAM [~~HOMEOWNERS' RECOVERY TRUST FUND~~]

(a) The department shall administer the manufactured homeowner consumer claims program to provide a remedy for damages resulting from prohibited conduct by a person licensed under this chapter [~~homeowners' recovery trust fund is an account in the general revenue fund~~].

(b) The department may make a payment under the manufactured homeowner consumer claims program only after all other departmental operating expenses are sufficiently funded.

2017 Legislation: Amended by H.B. 2019, §§51, 52, 85th Leg., eff. Sept. 1, 2017.

OCC §1201.402. REPEALED [~~ADMINISTRATION OF TRUST FUND~~]

[~~(a)~~] [~~The director shall administer the trust fund.~~]

[~~(b)~~] [~~The director is not required to file a bond or other security to serve as administrator of the trust fund.~~]

[~~(c)~~] [~~The trust fund, fees collected for the trust fund, and income earned from investment of the trust fund may be used only for the protection programs prescribed by this subchapter.~~]

[~~(d)~~] [~~Money in the trust fund may be invested and reinvested in the same manner as the funds of the Employees Retirement System of Texas. An investment may not be made that would impair the liquidity necessary to fund the protection programs prescribed by this subchapter. Income from the trust fund shall be deposited to the credit of the fund.~~]

Repealed by H.B. 2019, §85(6), 85th Leg., eff. Sept. 1, 2017.

OCC §1201.403. REPEALED [~~AMOUNT RESERVED IN TRUST FUND; PAYMENT OF COSTS~~]

[~~(a)~~] [~~One million dollars shall be reserved in the trust fund for payment of valid consumer claims.~~]

[~~(b)~~] [~~Unless the balance of the trust fund is less than $1 million, the costs of the director and the department in administering the trust fund, keeping books and records, investigating consumer complaints, and conducting the informal dispute resolution process shall be paid from the trust fund.~~]

Repealed by H.B. 2019, §85(7), 85th Leg., eff. Sept. 1, 2017.

OCC §1201.404. CONSUMER COMPENSATION

(a) Except as otherwise provided by Subchapter C, a payment made under the manufactured homeowner consumer claims program [~~the trust fund~~] shall be paid directly to a consumer or, at the director's option, to a third party on behalf of a consumer to compensate a consumer who sustains actual damages resulting from an unsatisfied claim against a licensed manufacturer, retailer, broker, or installer if the unsatisfied claim results from a violation of:

(1) this chapter;

(2) a rule adopted by the director;

(3) the National Manufactured Housing Construction and Safety Standards Act of 1974 (42 U.S.C. Section 5401 et seq.);

(4) a rule or regulation of the United States Department of Housing and Urban Development; or

(5) Subchapter E, Chapter 17, Business & Commerce Code.

(b) The department is [~~trust fund and the director are~~] not liable to the consumer if the manufactured homeowner consumer claims program [~~trust fund~~] does not have the money necessary to pay the actual damages determined to be payable. The director shall record the date and time of receipt of each verified complaint and, as money becomes available, pay the consumer whose claim is the earliest by date and time to have been found to be verified and properly payable.

2017 Legislation: Amended by H.B. 2019, §53, 85th Leg., eff. Sept. 1, 2017.

A OCC §1201.405. LIMITATIONS ON CLAIMS

(a) The payment of actual damages is limited to the lesser of:

(1) the amount of actual, reasonable costs, not including attorney's fees, that the consumer has incurred or will incur to resolve the act or omission found to be a violation under Section 1201.404; or

(2) $35,000.

(b) Repealed by Acts 2009, 81st Leg., ch. 77, §15(3), eff. Sept. 1, 2009.

(c) Under the manufactured homeowner consumer claims program, the department [~~The trust fund~~] is not liable for and the director may not pay:

(1) punitive, exemplary, double, or treble damages; or

(2) damages for pain and suffering, mental anguish, emotional distress, or other analogous tort claims.

(d) Notwithstanding other provisions of this subchapter, this subchapter does not apply to, and a consumer may not recover through the manufactured homeowner consumer claims program [~~against the trust fund~~] as a result of, a claim against a license holder that results from a cause of action directly related to the sale, [~~lease-purchase,~~] exchange, brokerage, or installation of a manufactured home before September 1, 1987.

(e) In determining the amount of actual damages under this section, the director shall make an independent inquiry as to the damages actually incurred, unless the damages have been previously established through a contested trial.

(f) Under the manufactured homeowner consumer claims program, the department [~~The trust fund~~] is not liable for and the director may not pay:

(1) actual damages to reimburse an affiliate or related person of a licensee, except when the director issues an order under Sections 1201.358(b) and (c);

(2) actual damages to correct matters that are solely cosmetic in nature;

(3) for attorney's fees; or

(4) actual damages to address other matters, unless the matters involve:

(A) a breach of warranty;

(B) a failure to return or apply as agreed money received from a consumer or money for which the consumer was obligated; [~~or~~]

(C) the breach of an agreement to provide goods or services necessary to the safe and habitable use of a manufactured home such as steps, air conditioning, access to utilities, or access to sewage and wastewater treatment; or

(D) perfected and enforceable tax liens not extinguished and canceled in accordance with Section 32.015, Tax Code.

(g) The board by rule may place reasonable limits on the costs that may be approved for payment under the manufactured homeowner consumer claims program [~~from the trust fund~~], including the costs of reassigned warranty work, and require consumers making claims that may be subject to reimbursement under the manufactured homeowner consumer claims program [~~from the trust fund~~] to provide estimates establishing that the cost will be reasonable. Such rules may also specify such procedures and requirements as the board may deem necessary and advisable for the administration of the manufactured homeowner consumer claims program [~~trust fund~~].

2017 Legislation: Amended by H.B. 2019, §54, 85th Leg., eff. Sept. 1, 2017.

A OCC §1201.406. PROCEDURE FOR RECOVERY UNDER MANUFACTURED HOMEOWNER CONSUMER CLAIMS PROGRAM [~~FROM TRUST FUND~~]

(a) To recover under the manufactured homeowner consumer claims program [~~from the trust fund~~], a consumer must file a written, sworn complaint in the form required by the director not later than the second anniversary of:

(1) the date of the alleged act or omission causing the actual damages; or

(2) the date the act or omission is discovered or should reasonably have been discovered.

(b) On receipt of a verified complaint, the department shall:

(1) notify each appropriate license holder and the issuer of any surety bond issued in connection with their licenses; and

(2) investigate the claim and issue a preliminary determination, giving the consumer, the licensee, and any surety an opportunity to resolve the matter by agreement or to dispute the preliminary determination.

(c) If the matter being investigated is not resolved by agreement or is disputed by written notice to the director before the 31st day after the date of the preliminary determination, the preliminary determination shall automatically become final and the director shall make demand on the surety or deduct any payable amount of the claim from the licensee's security.

2017 Legislation: Amended by H.B. 2019, §§55, 56, 85th Leg., eff. Sept. 1, 2017.

OCC §1201.407. DISAGREEMENT OF PARTIES; INFORMAL DISPUTE RESOLUTION PROCESS

(a) If a preliminary determination is disputed, the department shall conduct an informal dispute resolution process, including a home inspection if appropriate, to resolve the dispute.

(b) For a preliminary determination that has been disputed to become final and valid, the department shall make any changes the director determines to be appropriate and issue another written preliminary determination as to the responsibility and liability of the manufacturer, retailer, broker, and installer.

(c) Before making a final determination, the department shall allow a license holder 10 days to comment on this preliminary determination.

(d) After consideration of the comments, if any, the director shall issue a final determination.

(e) The final determination may be appealed to the board on or before the 10th day after the date of its issuance by giving written notice to the director, who shall place the matter before the board at the next meeting held on a date for which the matter could be publicly posted as required by Chapter 551, Government Code.

(f) Any license holder or surety, as applicable, is bound by the department's final determination of responsibility and liability.

OCC §1201.408. REPEALED

OCC §1201.409. PAYMENT BY SURETY OR FROM OTHER SECURITY

(a) Except as otherwise provided by Subchapter C, the manufactured homeowner consumer claims program [~~trust fund~~] shall be reimbursed by the surety on a bond or from other security filed under Subchapter C for the amount of a claim that is paid out under the manufactured homeowner consumer claims program [~~of the trust fund~~] by the director to a consumer in accordance with this subchapter.

(b) Payment by the surety or from the other security must be made not later than the 30th day after the date of notice from the director that a consumer claim has been paid.

(c) If payment to the manufactured homeowner consumer claims program [~~trust fund~~] of a claim is not made by the surety or from the other security in a timely manner, the attorney general shall file suit for recovery of the amount due the manufactured homeowner consumer claims program [~~trust fund~~]. Venue for the suit is in Travis County.

2017 Legislation: Amended by H.B. 2019, §57, 85th Leg., eff. Sept. 1, 2017.

OCC §1201.410. INFORMATION ON RECOVERY UNDER MANUFACTURED HOMEOWNER CONSUMER CLAIMS PROGRAM [~~FROM TRUST FUND~~]

The director shall prepare information for notifying consumers of their rights to recover under the manufactured homeowner consumer claims program [~~from the trust fund~~], shall post the information on the department's website, and shall make printed copies available on request.

2017 Legislation: Amended by H.B. 2019, §58, 85th Leg., eff. Sept. 1, 2017.

Sections 1201.411-1201.450 reserved for expansion

SUBCHAPTER J. USED OR SALVAGED MANUFACTURED HOMES

OCC §1201.451. TRANSFER OF GOOD & MARKETABLE TITLE REQUIRED

(a) Except as otherwise provided by this subchapter, a person may not sell or [~~,~~] exchange [~~, or lease-purchase~~] a used manufactured home without the appropriate transfer of good and marketable title to the home.

(b) Not later than the 60th day after the effective date of the transfer of ownership or the date the seller or transferor obtains possession of the necessary and

properly executed documents, the seller or transferor shall forward to the purchaser or transferee the necessary, executed documents. If the seller or transferor fails to forward the documents on a timely basis, the purchaser or transferee may apply directly for the documents. On receipt of the documents, the purchaser or transferee shall apply for the issuance of a statement of ownership [~~and location~~].

2017 Legislation: Amended by H.B. 2019, §59, 85th Leg., eff. Sept. 1, 2017.

A OCC §1201.452. SEAL OR LABEL REQUIRED

(a) Except as otherwise provided by this subchapter, a person may not sell or [~~,~~] exchange [~~, or lease-purchase~~] or negotiate for the sale or [~~,~~] exchange [~~, or lease-purchase~~] of a used manufactured home to a consumer unless the appropriate seal or label is attached to the home.

(b) If the home does not have the appropriate seal or label, the person must:

(1) apply to the department for a seal; and

(2) pay the fee.

2017 Legislation: Amended by H.B. 2019, §60, 85th Leg., eff. Sept. 1, 2017.

OCC §1201.453. HABITABILITY

Manufactured housing is habitable only if:

(1) there is no defect or deterioration in or damage to the home that creates a dangerous situation;

(2) the plumbing, heating, and electrical systems are in safe working order;

(3) the walls, floor, and roof are:

(A) free from a substantial opening that was not designed; and

(B) structurally sound; and

(4) all exterior doors and windows are in place and operate properly.

OCC §1201.454. HABITABILITY: PROHIBITED ALTERATION OR REPLACEMENT

A manufacturer, retailer, broker, installer, or lienholder may not repair or otherwise alter a used manufactured home or replace a component or system of a used manufactured home in a way that makes the home not habitable.

A OCC §1201.455. WRITTEN DISCLOSURE & WARRANTY OF HABITABILITY REQUIRED

(a) Except as otherwise provided by this subchapter, a person may not sell or [~~,~~] exchange [~~, or lease-purchase~~] a used manufactured home to a consumer for use as a dwelling without providing:

(1) a written disclosure, on a form not to exceed two pages prescribed by the department, describing the condition of the home and of any appliances that are included in the home; and

(2) a written warranty that the home is and will remain habitable until the 60th day after the later of the installation date or the date of the purchase agreement.

(b) Unless, not later than the 65th day after the later of the installation date or the date of the sale or [~~,~~] exchange [~~, or lease-purchase agreement~~], the consumer notifies the seller in writing of a defect that makes the home not habitable, any obligation or liability of the seller under this subchapter is terminated. The warranty must conspicuously disclose that notice requirement to the consumer.

2017 Legislation: Amended by H.B. 2019, §61, 85th Leg., eff. Sept. 1, 2017.

A OCC §1201.456. HABITABILITY: EXCEPTION TO WARRANTY REQUIREMENT

The warranty requirement imposed by Section 1201.455 does not apply to a sale or [~~,~~] exchange [~~, or lease-purchase~~] of a used manufactured home from one consumer to another.

2017 Legislation: Amended by H.B. 2019, §62, 85th Leg., eff. Sept. 1, 2017.

A OCC §1201.457. HABITABILITY: CHANGE TO OR FROM NONRESIDENTIAL [~~BUSINESS~~] USE OR SALVAGE

(a) If the sale or [~~,~~] exchange [~~, or lease-purchase~~] of a used manufactured home is to a purchaser for the purchaser's business use, the home is not required to be habitable unless the purchaser discloses to the retailer in writing at the time of purchase that the purchaser intends for a person to be present in the home for regularly scheduled work shifts of not less than eight hours each day. The purchaser of the home shall file with the department an application for the issuance of a statement of ownership [~~and location~~] indicating that the home is reserved for a business use.

(a-1) If the sale or exchange of a used manufactured home is for the purchaser's nonresidential use other than a business use, the home is not required to be habitable. The purchaser of the home shall file with the department an application for the issuance of a statement of ownership indicating that the home is for a nonresidential use other than a business use.

(b) If a used manufactured home is reserved for a business use or another nonresidential use or is salvaged, a person may not knowingly allow any person to occupy or use the home as a dwelling unless the director issues a new statement of ownership [~~and location~~] indicating that the home is no longer reserved for that [~~business~~] use or is no longer salvaged [~~salvage~~]. On the purchaser's application to the department for issuance of a new statement of ownership [~~and location~~], the department shall inspect the home and, if the department determines that the home is habitable, issue a new statement of ownership [~~and location~~].

2017 Legislation: Amended by H.B. 2019, §63, 85th Leg., eff. Sept. 1, 2017.

OCC §1201.458. HABITABILITY: EXCEPTION FOR CERTAIN GOVERNMENTAL OR NONPROFIT ENTITIES

(a) Notwithstanding any other provision of this subchapter and on a written application by the purchaser or transferee, the director may give express written authorization to a licensed retailer to sell or exchange a used manufactured home that is not or may not be habitable to or with a governmental housing agency or authority or to a nonprofit organization that provides housing for the homeless.

(b) As a part of the application, the purchaser or transferee must certify to the receipt of a written notice that the home is not or may not be habitable. The consumer protection division of the attorney general's office shall prepare the form of the notice, which must be approved by the director.

(c) The purchaser or transferee may not occupy or allow occupation of the home as a dwelling until the completion of any repair necessary to make the home habitable.

OCC §1201.459. COMPLIANCE NOT REQUIRED FOR SALE FOR COLLECTION OF DELINQUENT TAXES

(a) In selling a manufactured home to collect delinquent taxes, a tax assessor-collector is not required to comply with this subchapter or another provision of this chapter relating to the sale of a used manufactured home.

(b) If a home does not have a serial number, seal, or label, the tax appraiser or tax assessor-collector may apply to the department for a seal if the tax appraiser or assessor-collector assumes full responsibility for the affixation of a seal to the home and the seal is actually affixed on the home.

(c) A seal issued to a tax appraiser or tax assessor-collector is for identification purposes only and does not imply that:

(1) the home is habitable; or

(2) a purchaser of the home at a tax sale may obtain a new statement of ownership [~~and location~~] from the department without an inspection for habitability.

2017 Legislation: Amended by H.B. 2019, §64, 85th Leg., eff. Sept. 1, 2017.

OCC §1201.460. COMPLIANCE NOT REQUIRED FOR LIENHOLDER

(a) A holder of a lien recorded on the statement of ownership [~~and location~~] of a manufactured home that has not been converted to real property who sells or [~~,~~] exchanges [~~, or lease-purchases~~] a repossessed manufactured home covered by that statement of ownership [~~and location~~] is not required to comply with this chapter if the sale or [~~,~~] exchange [~~, or lease-purchase~~] is:

(1) to or through a licensed retailer; or

(2) to a purchaser for the purchaser's business use or another nonresidential use.

(b) If the sale or [~~,~~] exchange [~~, or lease-purchase~~] of the repossessed manufactured home is to or through a licensed retailer, the retailer is responsible and liable for compliance with this chapter and department rules. The lienholder may not be joined as a party in any litigation relating to the sale or [~~,~~] exchange [~~, or lease-purchase~~] of the home.

(c) If the sale or [~~,~~] exchange [~~, or lease-purchase~~] of the repossessed manufactured home is to a purchaser for the purchaser's business use or another nonresidential use, the lienholder shall apply to the department for the issuance of a new statement of ownership [~~and location~~] indicating that the home is reserved for a business use or another nonresidential use.

2017 Legislation: Amended by H.B. 2019, §65, 85th Leg., eff. Sept. 1, 2017.

OCC §1201.461. SALVAGED MANUFACTURED HOME; CRIMINAL PENALTY

(a) For the purposes of this chapter, a manufactured home is salvaged if the home is scrapped, dismantled, or destroyed or if an insurance company pays the full insured value of the home. The reasonableness of the insurer's judgment that the cost of repairing the

home would exceed the full insured value of the home does not affect whether the home is salvaged.

(b) A person who owns a used manufactured home that is salvaged shall apply to the director for the issuance of a new statement of ownership [~~and location~~] that indicates that the home is salvaged.

(c) If a new manufactured home is salvaged, the retailer shall remove the label and surrender the label and the manufacturer's certificate under Section 1201.204 to the director for issuance of a statement of ownership [~~and location~~] that indicates that the home is salvaged.

(d) A person may not sell, convey, or otherwise transfer to a consumer in this state a manufactured home that is salvaged. A salvaged manufactured home may be sold only to a licensed retailer.

(e) A person may not repair, rebuild, or otherwise refurbish [~~alter~~] a salvaged manufactured home unless the person complies with the rules of the director relating to rebuilding a salvaged manufactured home. For purposes of this subsection, "refurbish" means any general repairs, improvements, or aesthetic changes to a manufactured home that do not constitute the rebuilding of a salvaged manufactured home.

(f) If a salvaged manufactured home is rebuilt in accordance with this chapter and the rules of the director, the director shall, on application, issue a new statement of ownership [~~and location~~] that indicates that the home is no longer salvaged.

(g) A county or other unit of local government that identifies a manufactured home within its jurisdiction that has been declared salvage may impose on that home such inspection, correction, and other requirements as it could apply if the home were not a manufactured home.

(h) A licensee may not participate in the sale, exchange, [~~lease-purchase,~~] or installation for use as a dwelling of a manufactured home that is salvage and that has not been repaired in accordance with this chapter and the department's rules. An act that is prohibited by this subsection is deemed to be a practice that constitutes an imminent threat to health or safety and is subject to the imposition of penalties and other sanctions provided for by this chapter. A violation of this subsection is a Class B misdemeanor.

2017 Legislation: Amended by H.B. 2019, §66, 85th Leg., eff. Sept. 1, 2017.

Sections 1201.462-1201.500 reserved for expansion

SUBCHAPTER K. PROHIBITED PRACTICES

OCC §1201.501. PROHIBITED CONSTRUCTION BY MANUFACTURER

A manufacturer may not construct a HUD-code manufactured home in this state for sale or resale unless the manufacturer:

(1) supplies the department with proof of acceptance by a design approval primary inspection agency authorized by the United States Department of Housing and Urban Development;

(2) purchases the required labels; and

(3) has the home inspected by an in-plant inspection agency authorized by the United States Department of Housing and Urban Development.

OCC §1201.502. PROHIBITED SHIPPING BY MANUFACTURER

A manufacturer may not ship a HUD-code manufactured home into this state for sale or resale unless the manufacturer complies with:

(1) all requirements of the National Manufactured Housing Construction and Safety Standards Act of 1974 (42 U.S.C. Section 5401 et seq.); and

(2) all standards, rules, and regulations of the United States Department of Housing and Urban Development.

OCC §1201.503. PROHIBITED ALTERATION

Before the sale to a consumer of a new manufactured home to which a label has been attached and before installation of the home, a manufacturer, retailer, broker, or installer may not alter the home or cause the home to be altered without obtaining prior written approval from a licensed engineer and providing evidence of such approval to the department.

A OCC §1201.504. PROHIBITED SALE OR[~~,~~] EXCHANGE[~~, OR LEASE-PURCHASE~~]

(a) A manufacturer may not sell or[~~,~~] exchange, [~~or lease-purchase~~] or offer to sell or[~~,~~] exchange, [~~or lease-purchase~~] a manufactured home to a person in this state who is not a licensed retailer.

(b) A retailer may not sell or[~~,~~] exchange, [~~or lease-purchase~~] or offer to sell or[~~,~~] exchange, [~~or lease-purchase~~] a new HUD-code manufactured home that was constructed by a manufacturer who was not licensed by the department at the time of construction.

(c) A retailer, broker, or salesperson may not sell or[~~,~~] exchange, [~~or lease-purchase~~] or offer to sell or[~~,~~] exchange, [~~or lease-purchase~~] a manufactured home to a consumer in this state for use as a dwelling unless the appropriate seal or label is attached to the home.

2017 Legislation: Amended by H.B. 2019, §67, 85th Leg., eff. Sept. 1, 2017.

OCC §1201.505. PROHIBITED PURCHASE

A retailer may not purchase for resale to a consumer a new HUD-code manufactured home that was constructed by a manufacturer who was not licensed by the department at the time of construction.

OCC §1201.506. CREDIT

(a) A retailer or broker:

(1) shall comply with Subtitles A and B, Title 4, Finance Code, and the Truth in Lending Act (15 U.S.C. Section 1601 et seq.);

(2) may not advertise an interest rate or finance charge that is not expressed as an annual percentage rate; and

(3) shall comply with all applicable provisions of the Finance Code.

(b) A violation of this section does not create a cause of action or claim for damages for a consumer. The consumer may not recover more than the penalties provided by Subtitles A and B, Title 4, Finance Code, and the Truth in Lending Act (15 U.S.C. Section 1601 et seq.).

OCC §1201.507. FALSE OR MISLEADING INFORMATION

(a) A retailer or salesperson may not:

(1) assist a consumer in preparing or providing false or misleading information on a document related to the purchase or financing of a manufactured home; or

(2) submit to a credit underwriter or lending institution information known to be false or misleading.

(b) A salesperson may not submit to a retailer information known to be false or misleading.

OCC §1201.508. DOWN PAYMENT

(a) A retailer may not state payment of a down payment in a retail installment sales contract or other credit document unless the retailer has actually received the entire down payment at the time of execution of the document.

(b) If part of the down payment is consideration other than cash, including a loan or trade-in, the retailer must expressly state that fact in the retail installment sales contract or other credit document.

(c) A cash down payment may not be derived in any part from a rebate or other consideration received by, or to be given to, the consumer from the retailer or manufacturer.

(d) The retailer may not require a consumer to make a down payment on the acquisition of a manufactured home from the retailer's inventory until the time the installment contract is executed.

OCC §1201.509. PROHIBITED RETENTION OF DEPOSIT

A retailer, salesperson, or agent of the retailer may not refuse to refund a consumer's deposit except as provided by Section 1201.151.

OCC §1201.510. PROHIBITED INSTALLATION OF AIR CONDITIONING EQUIPMENT

A retailer or an installer may not contract with a person for the installation of air conditioning equipment in connection with the installation of a manufactured home unless the person is licensed by the state as an air conditioning and refrigeration contractor.

OCC §1201.511. PROHIBITED REAL ESTATE TRANSACTION

(a) This section applies to a transaction in which a manufactured home is sold as personal property.

(b) A retailer may not sell, represent for sale, or offer for sale real property in conjunction with the sale of a manufactured home except as authorized by the department consistent with Chapter 1101.

(c) A retailer, broker, or salesperson or a person acting on behalf of a retailer or broker may not receive or accept compensation or consideration of any kind from the seller of the real property or a person acting on the seller's behalf. No part of the down payment on the purchase of the manufactured home or any fees, points, or other charges or "buy-downs" may be paid from money from the seller of the real property or a person acting on the seller's behalf.

OCC §1201.512. PROHIBITED DELIVERY OR INSTALLATION OF MANUFACTURED HOME

(a) In this section, "homesite" means the land on which the foundation system for a manufactured home is or will be located.

(b) Unless the retailer, broker, or salesperson complies with the requirements of the National Flood Insurance Act of 1968 (42 U.S.C. Section 4001 et seq.), Subchapter I, Chapter 16, Water Code, and any other applicable local, state, or federal law, and ensures the consumer's compliance with applicable law by requiring the evidence described by Subsection (c), a retailer, broker, or salesperson who sells or[~~,~~] exchanges[~~, or lease-purchases~~] a new or used manufactured home to a consumer for use as a permanent dwelling in this state may not:

(1) deliver or arrange for the delivery of the home to a homesite in a special flood hazard area designated by the director of the Federal Emergency Management Agency;

(2) install or arrange for the installation of the home at a homesite in that area; or

(3) assist the consumer in the delivery or installation of, or in making arrangements for the delivery or installation of, the home to or at a homesite in that area.

(c) Before closing on the acquisition of a new or used manufactured home for use as a permanent dwelling in this state, a consumer seeking to acquire the home must provide to the retailer, broker, or salesperson selling or[~~,~~] exchanging[~~, or lease-purchasing~~] the home satisfactory evidence that the home will not be located, in a manner that violates local, state, or federal law, on a homesite in a special flood hazard area designated by the director of the Federal Emergency Management Agency. A consumer may satisfy the evidentiary requirement of this subsection by providing the retailer, broker, or salesperson, as applicable, with a copy of any required permit to install a septic tank on the homesite.

(d) The following are exempt from the application of this section:

(1) a manufactured home that on August 31, 2003, was inhabited and located on real property zoned before September 1, 2003, by a local political subdivision for the purpose of developing homesites in a special flood hazard area designated by the director of the Federal Emergency Management Agency, if the home will remain on or be relocated to real property zoned as described by this subsection; and

(2) real property zoned before September 1, 2003, by a local political subdivision for the purpose of developing homesites in a special flood hazard area designated by the director of the Federal Emergency Management Agency.

2017 Legislation: Amended by H.B. 2019, §68, 85th Leg., eff. Sept. 1, 2017.

OCC §1201.513. DISPOSITION OF TRADE-INS & OCCUPANCY OF HOMES BEFORE CLOSING

(a) A retailer may not sell a trade-in manufactured home before the closing of the sale in connection with which the retailer receives the trade-in.

(b) A retailer may not knowingly permit a consumer to occupy a manufactured home that is the subject of a sale or[~~,~~] exchange[~~, or lease-purchase~~] to that consumer before the closing of any required financing unless the consumer is first given a form adopted by the board disclosing that if for any reason the financing does not close, the consumer may be required to vacate the home.

2017 Legislation: Amended by H.B. 2019, §69, 85th Leg., eff. Sept. 1, 2017.

Sections 1201.514-1201.550 reserved for expansion

SUBCHAPTER L. DISCIPLINARY PROCEDURES

OCC §1201.551. DENIAL OF LICENSE; DISCIPLINARY ACTION

(a) The director may deny, permanently revoke, or suspend for a definite period and specified sales location or geographic area a license if the director determines that the applicant or license holder:

(1) knowingly and wilfully violated this chapter or a rule adopted or order issued under this chapter;

(2) unlawfully retained or converted money, property, or any other thing of value from a consumer in the form of a down payment, sales or use tax, deposit, or insurance premium;

(3) failed repeatedly to file with the department a completed application for a statement of ownership [~~and location~~] before the 61st day after the date of the sale of a manufactured home as required by Section 1201.206 or the date of the installation, whichever occurred later;

(4) failed to give or breached a manufactured home warranty required by this chapter or by the Federal Trade Commission;

(5) engaged in a false, misleading, or deceptive act or practice as described by Subchapter E, Chapter 17, Business & Commerce Code;

(6) failed to provide or file a report required by the department for the administration or enforcement of this chapter;

(7) provided false information on an application, report, or other document filed with the department;

(8) acquired a criminal record during the five-year period preceding the application date that, in the opinion of the director, makes the applicant unfit for licensing;

(9) failed to file a bond or other security for each location as required by Subchapter C; [~~or~~]

(10) has had another license issued by this state revoked or suspended; or

(11) failed to pay the required fee to obtain or renew a license.

(b) The director may suspend or revoke a license if, after receiving notice of a claim, the license holder or the license holder's surety fails or refuses to pay a final claim paid under the manufactured homeowner consumer claims program [~~from the trust fund~~] for which demand for reimbursement was made.

2017 Legislation: Amended by H.B. 2019, §70, 85th Leg., eff. Sept. 1, 2017.

OCC §1201.552. LICENSE REVOCATION, SUSPENSION, OR DENIAL; HEARING

The director may issue an order to revoke, suspend, or deny a new or renewal license. If, before the 31st day after an order revoking, suspending, or denying a license is issued, the person against whom the order is issued requests a hearing by giving written notice to the director, the director shall set a hearing before the State Office of Administrative Hearings. If the person does not request a hearing before the 31st day after the date the order is issued, the order becomes final. Any administrative proceedings relating to the revocation, suspension, or denial of a license under this subsection shall be a contested case under Chapter 2001, Government Code. The board shall issue an order after receiving a proposal for decision.

OCC §1201.553. JUDICIAL REVIEW

Judicial review of any order, decision, or determination of the board is instituted by filing a petition with a district court in Travis County as provided by Chapter 2001, Government Code.

OCC §1201.554. PROBATION

The department may place on probation a person whose license is suspended. If a license suspension is probated, the department may require the person to:

(1) report regularly to the department on matters that are the basis of the probation;

(2) limit practice to the areas prescribed by the department; or

(3) continue or review professional education until the person attains a degree of skill satisfactory to the department in those areas that are the basis of the probation.

Sections 1201.555-1201.600 reserved for expansion

SUBCHAPTER M. ENFORCEMENT PROVISIONS & PENALTIES

OCC §1201.601. ACTION AGAINST RETAILER OR MANUFACTURER: HOLDER OF DEBT INSTRUMENT

(a) If a consumer files a cause of action against a retailer or manufacturer, a claim based on an act of the retailer or manufacturer that the consumer could assert against the holder of the manufactured home debt instrument must be asserted against the holder in the primary suit against the retailer or manufacturer.

(b) A judgment obtained in the primary suit against the retailer or manufacturer is conclusive proof as to the holder of the debt instrument and admissible in an action by the consumer against the holder only if the consumer joins the holder in the primary suit.

(c) The holder of the debt instrument is entitled to full indemnity from the retailer or manufacturer for a claim based on an act or omission of the retailer or manufacturer.

(d) If the consumer asserts against the holder of the debt instrument a claim or defense that arises from a claim or defense of the consumer against the retailer, the consumer's relief against the holder arising from claims and defenses of the consumer against the retailer is limited to recovery of an amount not to exceed the total amount paid by the consumer to the holder and to cancellation of the balance remaining on the instrument. If the balance remaining on the instrument is canceled, the manufactured home shall be returned to the holder.

OCC §1201.602. ACTION AGAINST MANUFACTURER, INSTALLER, OR RETAILER: ABATEMENT OR BAR

(a) Notwithstanding any other law, a suit alleging that a manufacturer, installer, or retailer failed to perform warranty service or failed to comply with a written or implied warranty is abated if:

(1) a plea in abatement is filed with the court not later than the 45th day after the movant's answer date; and

(2) the manufacturer, installer, or retailer requests a consumer complaint home inspection under Section 1201.355.

(b) The abatement continues until the earlier of:

(1) the date on which the department performs a consumer complaint home inspection and the manufacturer, installer, or retailer is given an opportunity to comply with the inspection report, determinations, and orders of the director; or

(2) the expiration of a period not to exceed 150 days.

(c) A consumer's refusal to allow the manufacturer, installer, or retailer to perform warranty service in accordance with the inspection report, determinations, and orders of the director bars a cause of action relating to an alleged failure to:

(1) comply with a written or implied warranty; or

(2) perform warranty service.

OCC §1201.603. DECEPTIVE TRADE PRACTICES

(a) A person's violation of this chapter or the failure by a manufacturer, installer, or retailer to comply with an implied warranty is a deceptive trade practice actionable under Subchapter E, Chapter 17, Business & Commerce Code.

(b) The venue provisions of Subchapter E, Chapter 17, Business & Commerce Code, apply to a claim under Subsection (a). The remedies available under Subchapter E, Chapter 17, Business & Commerce Code, are cumulative of the remedies under this chapter.

OCC §1201.604. CONSUMER RECOVERY FOR PROHIBITED RETENTION OF DEPOSIT

In addition to any other remedy, a consumer may recover from a retailer, salesperson, or agent of the retailer who violates Section 1201.151:

(1) three times the amount of the deposit; and

(2) reasonable attorney's fees.

OCC §1201.6041. DIRECT CONSUMER COMPENSATION

(a) Instead of requiring a consumer to apply for compensation under the manufactured homeowner consumer claims program ~~[from the trust fund]~~ under Subchapter I, the director may order a manufacturer, retailer, broker, or installer, as applicable, to pay a refund directly to a consumer who sustains actual damages resulting from an unsatisfied claim against a licensed manufacturer, retailer, broker, or installer if the unsatisfied claim results from a violation of:

(1) this chapter;

(2) a rule adopted by the director;

(3) the National Manufactured Housing Construction and Safety Standards Act of 1974 (42 U.S.C. Section 5401 et seq.);

(4) a rule or regulation of the United States Department of Housing and Urban Development; or

(5) Subchapter E, Chapter 17, Business & Commerce Code.

(b) For purposes of this section, the refund of a consumer's actual damages is determined according to Section 1201.405.

(c) The director shall prepare information for notifying consumers of the director's option to order a direct refund under this section, shall post the information on the department's Internet website, and shall make printed copies available on request.

2017 Legislation: Amended by H.B. 2019, §71, 85th Leg., eff. Sept. 1, 2017.

OCC §1201.605. ADMINISTRATIVE PENALTY

(a) The director may assess against a person who fails to comply with this chapter, the rules adopted under this chapter, or any final order of the department an administrative penalty in an amount not to exceed $10,000 for each violation of this chapter and:

(1) reasonable attorney's fees;

(2) administrative costs;

(3) witness fees;

(4) investigative costs; and

(5) deposition expenses.

(b) The director may assess against a licensee who fails to provide information to a consumer as required by this chapter an administrative penalty in an amount not to exceed:

(1) $1,000 for the first violation;

(2) $2,000 for the second violation; and

(3) $4,000 for each subsequent violation.

(c) In determining the amount of an administrative penalty assessed under this section, the director shall consider:

(1) the seriousness of the violation;

(2) the history of previous violations;

(3) the amount necessary to deter future violations;

(4) efforts made to correct the violation; and

(5) any other matters that justice may require.

(d) The director may impose an administrative penalty in accordance with this section. If, before the 31st day after the date a person receives notice of the imposition of an administrative penalty, the person requests a hearing by giving written notice to the director, the director shall set a hearing before the State Office of Administrative Hearings. If the person does not request a hearing before the 31st day after the date the person receives notice of the imposition of the administrative penalty, the penalty becomes final. Any administrative proceedings relating to the imposition of an administrative penalty under this subsection shall be a contested case under Chapter 2001, Government Code. The board shall issue an order after receiving a proposal for decision.

OCC §1201.606. CRIMINAL PENALTY

(a) A person or a director, officer, or agent of a corporation commits an offense if the person, director, officer, or agent knowingly and wilfully violates this chapter or a rule adopted or order issued by the department in a manner that threatens consumer health or safety.

(b) An offense under this section is a Class A misdemeanor punishable by:

(1) a fine of not more than $4,000;

(2) confinement in county jail for a term of not more than one year; or

(3) both the fine and confinement.

OCC §1201.607. ISSUANCE OF ORDERS & REQUESTS FOR HEARINGS

Any order issued by the director under this chapter, if not appealed before the 31st day after the date the order was issued, shall automatically become a final order. If the person made the subject of the order files a written request for a hearing with the director, the order shall be deemed to have been appealed and shall be a contested case under Chapter 2001, Government Code. The director shall set any appealed order for a hearing before the State Office of Administrative Hearings, and the board shall issue a final order after receiving and reviewing the proposal for decision issued pursuant to such hearing.

OCC §1201.608. INSPECTION OF LICENSEE RECORDS

(a) The department may inspect a licensee's records during normal business hours without advance notice if the director believes that such inspection is necessary to prevent a violation of this chapter, to protect a consumer or another licensee, or to assist another state or federal agency in an investigation.

(b) The director may request or issue subpoenas for a licensee's records.

(c) The department may carry out "sting" or undercover investigations in accordance with board-adopted rules if the director believes such action to be appropriate in order to detect and address suspected violations of this chapter.

(d) While an investigation is pending, information obtained by the department in connection with that investigation is confidential unless disclosure of the information is specifically permitted or required by other law.

OCC §1201.609. ACTING WITHOUT LICENSE; CRIMINAL PENALTY

A person who is not exempt under this chapter and who, without first obtaining a license required under this chapter, performs an act that requires a license under this chapter commits an offense. An offense under this section is a Class B misdemeanor. A second or subsequent conviction for an offense under this section is a Class A misdemeanor.

OCC §1201.610. CEASE & DESIST

(a) The director may issue without notice and hearing an order to cease and desist from continuing a particular action or an order to take affirmative action, or both, to enforce compliance with this chapter if the director has reasonable cause to believe that a person has violated or is about to violate any provision of this chapter or a rule adopted under this chapter.

(b) The director may issue an order to any person to cease and desist from violating any law, rule, or written agreement or to take corrective action with respect to any such violations if the violations in any way are related to the sale, financing, or installation of a manufactured home or the providing of goods or services in connection with the sale, financing, or installation of a manufactured home unless the matter that is the basis

of such violation is expressly subject to inspection and regulation by another state agency; provided, however, that if any matter involves a law that is subject to any other administration or interpretation by another agency, the director shall consult with the person in charge of the day-to-day administration of that agency before issuing an order.

(c) An order issued under Subsection (a) or (b) must contain a reasonably detailed statement of the facts on which the order is based. If a person against whom the order is issued requests a hearing before the 31st day after the date the order is issued, the director shall set and give notice of a hearing. The hearing shall be governed by Chapter 2001, Government Code. Based on the findings of fact, conclusions of law, and recommendations of the hearings officer, the board by order may find that a violation has occurred or has not occurred.

(d) If a hearing is not requested under Subsection (c) before the 31st day after the date an order is issued, the order is considered final and not appealable.

(e) The director, after giving notice, may impose against a person who violates a cease and desist order an administrative penalty in an amount not to exceed $1,000 for each day of the violation. In addition to any other remedy provided by law, the director may institute in district court a suit for injunctive relief and for the collection of the administrative penalty. A bond is not required of the director with respect to injunctive relief granted under this subsection.

(f) If a person licensed under this chapter fails to pay an administrative penalty that has become final or fails to comply with an order of the director that has become final, in addition to any other remedy provided by law, the director, after not less than 10 days' notice to the person, may without a prior hearing suspend the person's license. The suspension shall continue until the person has complied with the cease and desist order or paid the administrative penalty. During the period of suspension, the person may not perform any act requiring a license under this chapter, and all compensation received by the person during the period of suspension is subject to forfeiture to the person from whom it was received.

(g) An order of suspension under Subsection (f) may be appealed. An appeal is a contested case governed by Chapter 2001, Government Code. A hearing of an appeal of an order of suspension issued under Subsection (f) shall be held not later than the 15th day after the date of receipt of the notice of appeal. The appellant shall be provided at least three days' notice of the time and place of the hearing.

(h) An order revoking the license of a retailer, broker, installer, or salesperson may provide that the person is prohibited, without obtaining prior written consent of the director, from being a related person of a licensee.

Ⓐ OCC §1201.611. SANCTIONS & PENALTIES

(a) The board shall adopt rules relating to the administrative sanctions that may be enforced against a person regulated by the department.

(b) If a person charged with the violation accepts the determination of the director, the director shall issue an order approving the determination and ordering that the person pay the recommended penalty.

(c) Not later than the 30th day after the date on which the decision is final, the person charged shall:

(1) pay the penalty in full; or

(2) if the person files a petition for judicial review contesting the fact of the violation, the amount of the penalty, or both the fact of the violation and the amount of the penalty:

(A) forward the amount assessed to the department for deposit in an escrow account;

(B) in lieu of payment into escrow, post with the department a supersedeas bond for the amount of the penalty, in a form approved by the director and effective until judicial review of the decision is final; or

(C) without paying the amount of the penalty or posting the supersedeas bond, pursue judicial review.

(d) A person charged with a penalty who is financially unable to comply with Subsection (c)(2) is entitled to judicial review if the person files with the court, as part of the person's petition for judicial review, a sworn statement that the person is unable to meet the requirements of that subsection.

(e) If the person charged does not pay the penalty and does not pursue judicial review, the department or the attorney general may bring an action for the collection of the penalty.

(f) Judicial review of the order of the director assessing the penalty is subject to the substantial evidence rule and shall be instituted by filing a petition with a district court in Travis County.

(g) If, after judicial review, the penalty is reduced or not assessed, the director shall remit to the person charged the appropriate amount, plus accrued interest if the penalty has been paid, or shall execute a release of the bond if a supersedeas bond has been posted. The accrued interest on amounts remitted by the director under this subsection shall be paid at a rate equal to the rate charged on loans to depository institutions by the New York Federal Reserve Bank and shall be paid for the period beginning on the date the assessed penalty is paid to the director and ending on the date the penalty is remitted.

(h) Repealed by H.B. 2019, §85(8), 85th Leg., eff. Sept. 1, 2017.

[~~(h)~~] [~~A penalty collected under this section shall be deposited in the trust fund.~~]

(i) All proceedings conducted under this section and any review or appeal of those proceedings are subject to Chapter 2001, Government Code.

(j) If it appears that a person is in violation of, or is threatening to violate, any provision of this chapter or a rule or order related to the administration and enforcement of the manufactured housing program, the attorney general, on behalf of the director, may institute an action for injunctive relief to restrain the person from continuing the violation and for civil penalties not to exceed $1,000 for each violation and not exceeding $250,000 in the aggregate. A civil action filed under this subsection shall be filed in district court in Travis County. The attorney general and the director may recover reasonable expenses incurred in obtaining injunctive relief under this subsection, including court costs, reasonable attorney's fees, investigative costs, witness fees, and deposition expenses.

2017 Legislation: Amended by H.B. 2019, §85(8), 85th Leg., eff. Sept. 1, 2017.

CHAPTER 1202. INDUSTRIALIZED HOUSING & BUILDINGS

SUBCHAPTER A. GENERAL PROVISIONS

OCC §1202.001. GENERAL DEFINITIONS

In this chapter:

(1) "Commission" means the Texas Commission of Licensing and Regulation.

(2) "Construction site building" means a commercial structure that is:

(A) not open to the public; and

(B) used for any purpose at a commercial site by a person constructing a building, road, bridge, utility, or other infrastructure or improvement to real property.

(3) "Council" means the Texas Industrialized Building Code Council.

(4) "Department" means the Texas Department of Licensing and Regulation.

(4-a) "Executive director" means the executive director of the department.

(5) "Modular component" means a structural part of housing or a building constructed at a location other than the building site in a manner that prevents the construction from being adequately inspected for code compliance at the building site without:

(A) damage; or

(B) removal and reconstruction of a part of the housing or building.

OCC §1202.002. DEFINITION OF INDUSTRIALIZED HOUSING

(a) Industrialized housing is a residential structure that is:

(1) designed for the occupancy of one or more families;

(2) constructed in one or more modules or constructed using one or more modular components built at a location other than the permanent site; and

(3) designed to be used as a permanent residential structure when the module or the modular component is transported to the permanent site and erected or installed on a permanent foundation system.

(b) Industrialized housing includes the structure's plumbing, heating, air conditioning, and electrical systems.

(c) Industrialized housing does not include:

(1) a residential structure that exceeds four stories or 60 feet in height;

(2) housing constructed of a sectional or panelized system that does not use a modular component; or

(3) a ready-built home constructed in a manner in which the entire living area is contained in a single unit or section at a temporary location for the purpose of selling and moving the home to another location.

OCC §1202.003. DEFINITION OF INDUSTRIALIZED BUILDING

(a) An industrialized building is a commercial structure that is:

(1) constructed in one or more modules or constructed using one or more modular components built at a location other than the commercial site; and

(2) designed to be used as a commercial building when the module or the modular component is transported to the commercial site and erected or installed.

(b) An industrialized building includes the structure's plumbing, heating, air conditioning, and electrical systems.

(c) Repealed by Acts 2005, 79th Leg., ch. 714, §5, eff. Sept. 1, 2005.

(d) An industrialized building includes a permanent commercial structure and a commercial structure designed to be transported from one commercial site to another commercial site but does not include:

(1) a commercial structure that exceeds four stories or 60 feet in height; or

(2) a commercial building or structure that is:

(A) installed in a manner other than on a permanent foundation; and

(B) either:

(i) not open to the public; or

(ii) less than 1,500 square feet in total area and used other than as a school or a place of religious worship.

OCC §1202.004. RELOCATABLE EDUCATIONAL FACILITIES

(a) In this section, "relocatable educational facility" means a portable, modular building capable of being relocated, regardless of whether the facility is built at the installation site, that is used primarily as an educational facility for teaching the curriculum required under Section 28.002, Education Code.

(b) A relocatable educational facility that is purchased or leased on or after January 1, 2010, must comply with all provisions applicable to industrialized buildings under this chapter.

Sections 1202.005-1202.050 reserved for expansion

SUBCHAPTER B. TEXAS INDUSTRIALIZED BUILDING CODE COUNCIL

OCC §1202.051. COUNCIL MEMBERSHIP

The Texas Industrialized Building Code Council consists of 12 members appointed by the governor as follows:

(1) three members who represent the industrialized housing and building industries;

(2) three members who represent municipal building officials from municipalities with a population of more than 25,000;

(3) three members who represent general contractors who construct housing or buildings on-site;

(4) one member who is an engineer licensed in this state who acts as a structural engineer;

(5) one member who is an engineer licensed in this state who acts as an electrical engineer; and

(6) one member who is an architect registered in this state.

OCC §1202.052. MEMBERSHIP RESTRICTIONS

An engineer or architect member of the council may not:

(1) be designated as, be employed by, or have an ownership interest in, an entity that is a third-party inspector or design review agency;

(2) have an ownership interest in a business that manufactures or builds industrialized housing or buildings;

(3) in a capacity relating to a matter subject to council review, be employed by or be a paid consultant to a manufacturer or builder of industrialized housing or buildings; or

(4) be an officer, employee, or paid consultant of a trade association that represents the industrialized housing or building industry.

OCC §1202.053. TERMS

Council members serve staggered two-year terms, with the terms of half of the members expiring on February 1 of each even-numbered year and the terms of the other half of the members expiring on February 1 of each odd-numbered year.

OCC §1202.054. PRESIDING OFFICER

The council shall annually elect one of its members as the council's presiding officer.

OCC §1202.055. SECRETARY; PERSONNEL

The executive director shall:

(1) act as secretary of the council; and

(2) provide personnel from the department necessary to perform staff functions for the council.

OCC §1202.056. REIMBURSEMENT

(a) A council member may be reimbursed for actual costs of travel to attend meetings but may not receive a per diem allowance for food or lodging.

(b) The travel costs shall be paid out of fees collected by the department under Section 1202.104.

OCC §1202.057. QUORUM

The vote of at least seven members present at a meeting or the written approval of at least seven members is required for the council to take an action or make a decision.

Sections 1202.058-1202.100 reserved for expansion

SUBCHAPTER C. COUNCIL & COMMISSION POWERS & DUTIES

OCC §1202.101. RULES; ORDERS

(a) The commission shall adopt rules and issue orders as necessary to:

(1) ensure compliance with the purposes of this chapter; and

(2) provide for uniform enforcement of this chapter.

(b) The commission shall adopt rules as appropriate to implement the council's actions, decisions, interpretations, and instructions.

OCC §1202.102. RULES PROVIDING FOR REGISTRATION & REGULATION

The commission by rule shall provide for registration and regulation of manufacturers or builders of industrialized housing or buildings.

OCC §1202.103. REPEALED

OCC §1202.104. FEES

(a) The commission shall set fees, in amounts sufficient to cover the costs of the inspections described by this chapter and the administration of this chapter, for:

(1) the registration of manufacturers or builders of industrialized housing or buildings;

(2) the inspection of industrialized housing or buildings; and

(3) the issuance of decals or insignia required under Section 1202.204.

(b) The fees shall be paid to the comptroller and placed in the general revenue fund, except that a fee for an inspection may be paid directly to an approved third-party inspector who performs the inspection.

(c) The building and permit fees charged by a municipality for an inspection of industrialized housing or buildings to be located in the municipality may not exceed the fees charged for the equivalent inspection of a building constructed on-site.

OCC §1202.105. APPROVAL OF THIRD-PARTY INSPECTORS & DESIGN REVIEW AGENCIES

(a) The council shall establish criteria for the approval of, and approve accordingly, all third-party inspectors and design review agencies.

(b) The executive director shall recommend qualified third-party inspectors and design review agencies to the council.

(c) The executive director shall publish a list of all approved inspectors and design review agencies.

OCC §1202.106. APPLICABILITY OF OTHER LAW

Sections 51.401 and 51.4041 do not apply to this chapter.

OCC §1202.107. LIMITATION ON CERTAIN ACTIONS

(a) Notwithstanding any other law, the commission, executive director, or department may not perform an inspection or investigation, open a complaint, or initiate an administrative or enforcement action against a manufacturer, builder, or third-party inspector of industrialized housing after the second anniversary of the date of the final on-site inspection of the industrialized housing conducted under Section 1202.203.

(b) The commission or executive director may impose a penalty or sanction in an enforcement action against a manufacturer, builder, or third-party inspector of industrialized housing only if the commission, executive director, or department initiates the enforcement action during the period prescribed by Subsection (a).

Sections 1202.108-1202.150 reserved for expansion

SUBCHAPTER D. REQUIREMENTS & STANDARDS FOR INDUSTRIALIZED HOUSING & BUILDINGS

OCC §1202.151. BUILDING CODES

(a) In addition to complying with Subsection (b) or (c), as applicable, industrialized housing and buildings must be constructed to meet or exceed the requirements and standards of the National Electrical Code,

published by the National Fire Protection Association, as that code existed on January 1, 1985.

(b) Industrialized housing and buildings erected or installed in a municipality must be constructed to meet or exceed the requirements and standards of whichever of the following two groups of codes is used by the municipality:

(1) the Uniform Building Code, Uniform Plumbing Code, and Uniform Mechanical Code, published by the International Conference of Building Officials, as those codes existed on January 1, 1985; or

(2) the Standard Building Code, Standard Mechanical Code, Standard Plumbing Code, and Standard Gas Code, published by the Southern Building Code Congress International, Inc., as those codes existed on January 1, 1985.

(c) Industrialized housing and buildings erected or installed outside a municipality or in a municipality that does not use a building code group described by Subsection (b)(1) or (2) must be constructed to meet or exceed the requirements and standards of whichever of those building code groups is selected by the manufacturer of the housing or buildings.

OCC §1202.152. BUILDING CODE AMENDMENT

If a code described by Section 1202.151 is amended after January 1, 1985, the requirements and standards of the amended code shall be used in place of the January 1, 1985, edition if the council determines that use of the amended code is:

(1) in the public interest; and

(2) consistent with the purposes of this chapter.

OCC §1202.153. BUILDING CODE AMENDMENT: MUNICIPALITY OR OTHER POLITICAL SUBDIVISION

(a) A municipality or other political subdivision may not require or enforce, as a prerequisite for granting or approving a building or construction permit or certificate of occupancy, an amendment to a code described by Section 1202.151.

(b) On the petition of a local building official and after a hearing, the council may require a reasonable amendment to a building code group described by Section 1202.151(b)(1) or (2) that the council determines to be essential for public health and safety. The amendment shall be applied uniformly on a statewide basis.

OCC §1202.1535. EFFECT OF BUILDING CODE AMENDMENT

(a) An industrialized building that bears an approved decal or insignia indicating that the building complies with the mandatory building codes and that has not been modified or altered is considered to be in compliance with a new mandatory building code adopted by the council or an amendment to a code approved by the council under Section 1202.152 or 1202.153.

(b) The owner of an industrialized building designed to be transported from one commercial site to another that bears an approved decal or insignia indicating the building complies with the mandatory building codes and that is modified or altered after the date the council adopts a new mandatory building code or the council approves a building code amendment must ensure that the modified or altered building complies with the requirements and standards of the new building code or amendment to the extent required by the most recent edition of the International Existing Building Code adopted by the council.

OCC §1202.154. DESIGN REVIEW

To ensure compliance with the mandatory building codes, the department or approved design review agency shall review all designs, plans, and specifications of industrialized housing and buildings in accordance with council interpretations and instructions.

OCC §1202.155. COUNCIL STAMP OF APPROVAL

(a) The department or approved design review agency shall place the council's stamp of approval on each page of the designs, plans, and specifications of industrialized housing and buildings that:

(1) meet or exceed the code standards and requirements under council interpretations and instructions; and

(2) are approved by the department or design review agency.

(b) Each page of the designs, plans, and specifications must bear the council's stamp of approval if the designs, plans, and specifications satisfy the requirements of Subsection (a)(1) and are approved in accordance with Subsection (a)(2).

OCC §1202.156. COUNCIL DETERMINATION OF CERTAIN QUESTIONS RELATED TO INDUSTRIALIZED HOUSING & BUILDINGS

(a) The council shall determine all questions raised by a municipality in connection with the review of designs, plans, and specifications of industrialized housing and buildings, as authorized by Section 1202.252.

(b) With reference to the standards and requirements of the mandatory building codes, the council shall determine, from an engineering performance standpoint, all questions concerning:

(1) code equivalency; or

(2) alternative materials or methods of construction.

OCC §1202.157. COUNCIL DECISIONS BINDING

The decisions, actions, and interpretations of the council are binding on the department, third-party inspectors, design review agencies, and municipalities and other political subdivisions.

Sections 1202.158-1202.200 reserved for expansion

Subchapter E. Inspections

OCC §1202.201. INSPECTION PROCEDURES

The council may issue instructions to establish procedures for inspecting the construction and installation of industrialized housing and buildings to ensure compliance with approved designs, plans, and specifications.

OCC §1202.202. DEPARTMENT INSPECTIONS

(a) To ensure compliance with the mandatory building codes or approved designs, plans, and specifications, the department shall inspect the construction of industrialized housing and buildings. The executive director may designate approved third-party inspectors to perform the inspections subject to the rules of the commission.

(b) Local building officials may witness department inspections to enable the local officials to make recommendations on inspection procedures to the council.

OCC §1202.203. ON-SITE INSPECTIONS

(a) A municipal building official shall inspect all construction involving industrialized housing and buildings to be located in the municipality to ensure compliance with designs, plans, and specifications, including inspection of:

(1) the construction of the foundation system; and

(2) the erection and installation of the modules or modular components on the foundation.

(b) An approved third-party inspector shall perform on-site inspections of industrialized housing to be located outside the municipality.

(c) An inspection under Subsection (a) shall be conducted:

(1) at the permanent site, if the inspection is of industrialized housing; and

(2) at the commercial site, if the inspection is of industrialized buildings.

(d) If required by commission rule, an approved third-party inspector shall perform on-site inspections of industrialized buildings to be located outside the municipality.

OCC §1202.204. RULES PROVIDING FOR DECALS OR INSIGNIA

(a) The commission by rule shall provide for the placement of decals or insignia on each transportable modular section or modular component to indicate compliance with the mandatory building codes.

(b) The commission by rule shall exempt a construction site building from the requirements of this section.

OCC §1202.205. RECIPROCITY

(a) The commission by rule may authorize an inspection of industrialized housing or buildings constructed in another state to be performed by an inspector of the equivalent regulatory agency of the other state.

(b) The commission by rule may authorize an inspection of industrialized housing or buildings constructed in this state for use in another state.

(c) The commission shall enter into a reciprocity agreement with the equivalent regulatory agency of the other state as necessary to implement this section.

Sections 1202.206-1202.250 reserved for expansion

SUBCHAPTER F. MUNICIPAL AUTHORITY

OCC §1202.251. RESERVATION OF MUNICIPAL AUTHORITY

(a) Municipal authority is specifically and entirely reserved to a municipality, including, as applicable:

(1) land use and zoning requirements;

(2) building setback requirements;

(3) side and rear yard requirements;

(4) site planning and development and property line requirements;

(5) subdivision control; and

(6) landscape architectural requirements.

(b) Except as provided by Section 1202.253, requirements and regulations not in conflict with this chapter or with other state law relating to transportation, erection, installation, or use of industrialized housing or buildings must be reasonably and uniformly applied and enforced without distinctions as to whether the housing or buildings are manufactured or are constructed on-site.

OCC §1202.252. MUNICIPAL REGULATION OF INDUSTRIALIZED HOUSING & BUILDINGS

(a) A municipality that regulates the on-site construction or installation of industrialized housing and buildings may:

(1) require and review, for compliance with mandatory building codes, a complete set of designs, plans, and specifications bearing the council's stamp of approval for each installation of industrialized housing or buildings in the municipality;

(2) require that all applicable local permits and licenses be obtained before construction begins on a building site;

(3) require, in accordance with commission rules, that all modules or modular components bear an approved decal or insignia indicating inspection by the department; and

(4) establish procedures for the inspection of:

(A) the erection and installation of industrialized housing or buildings to be located in the municipality, to ensure compliance with mandatory building codes and commission rules; and

(B) all foundation and other on-site construction, to ensure compliance with approved designs, plans, and specifications.

(b) Procedures described by Subsection (a)(4) may require:

(1) before occupancy, a final inspection or test in accordance with mandatory building codes; and

(2) correction of any deficiency identified by the test or discovered in the final inspection.

OCC §1202.253. MUNICIPAL REGULATION OF SINGLE-FAMILY & DUPLEX INDUSTRIALIZED HOUSING

(a) Single-family or duplex industrialized housing must have all local permits and licenses that are applicable to other single-family or duplex dwellings.

(b) For purposes of this section, single-family or duplex industrialized housing is real property.

(c) A municipality may adopt regulations that require single-family or duplex industrialized housing to:

(1) have a value equal to or greater than the median taxable value for each single-family dwelling located within 500 feet of the lot on which the industrialized housing is proposed to be located, as determined by the most recent certified tax appraisal roll for each county in which the properties are located;

(2) have exterior siding, roofing, roof pitch,[1] foundation fascia, and fenestration compatible with the single-family dwellings located within 500 feet of the lot on which the industrialized housing is proposed to be located;

(3) comply with municipal aesthetic standards, building setbacks, side and rear yard offsets, subdivision control, architectural landscaping, square footage, and other site requirements applicable to single-family dwellings; or

(4) be securely fixed to a permanent foundation.

(d) For purposes of Subsection (c), "value" means the taxable value of the industrialized housing and the lot after installation of the housing.

(e) Except as provided by Subsection (c), a municipality may not adopt a regulation under this section that is more restrictive for industrialized housing than that required for a new single-family or duplex dwelling constructed on-site.

(f) This section does not:

(1) limit the authority of a municipality to adopt regulations to protect historic properties or historic districts; or

(2) affect deed restrictions.

1. **Editor's note:** Acts 2003, 78th Leg., ch. 816, §10.016 enacted an identical subsection (2), except for using "roofing pitch" here.

Sections 1202.254-1202.300 reserved for expansion

SUBCHAPTER G. PROHIBITED PRACTICES & DISCIPLINARY PROCEDURES

OCC §1202.301. PROHIBITED PRACTICES

(a) In this section, "person" means an individual, partnership, company, corporation, association, or other group, however organized.

(b) A person may not construct, sell or offer to sell, lease or offer to lease, or transport over a street or highway of this state any industrialized housing or building, or modular section or component of a modular section, in violation of this chapter or a rule of the commission or order of the commission or executive director.

OCC §1202.302. DENIAL OF CERTIFICATE; DISCIPLINARY ACTION

In addition to imposing sanctions allowed under Section 51.353, the commission may deny, permanently revoke, or suspend for a definite period and specified location or geographic area a certificate of registration if the commission finds that the applicant or registrant:

(1) provided false information on an application or other document filed with the department;

(2) failed to pay a fee or file a report required by the department for the administration or enforcement of this chapter;

(3) engaged in a false, misleading, or deceptive act or practice as described by Subchapter E, Chapter 17, Business & Commerce Code; or

(4) violated:

(A) this chapter;

(B) a rule adopted by the commission or order issued by the commission or the executive director under this chapter; or

(C) a decision, action, or interpretation of the council.

Sections 1202.303-1202.350 reserved for expansion

SUBCHAPTER H. REPEALED

TAX CODE

SELECTED PROVISIONS

TAX CODE
SELECTED PROVISIONS
TABLE OF CONTENTS

TITLE 1. PROPERTY TAX CODE
Subtitle A. General Provisions

TAX CODE

SELECTED PROVISIONS
TABLE OF CONTENTS

TAX CODE

SELECTED PROVISIONS
TABLE OF CONTENTS

TITLE 1. PROPERTY TAX CODE

SUBTITLE A. GENERAL PROVISIONS

CHAPTER 1. GENERAL PROVISIONS

A TAX §1.04. DEFINITIONS

In this title:

(1) "Property" means any matter or thing capable of private ownership.

(2) "Real property" means:

(A) land;

(B) an improvement;

(C) a mine or quarry;

(D) a mineral in place;

(E) standing timber; or

(F) an estate or interest, other than a mortgage or deed of trust creating a lien on property or an interest securing payment or performance of an obligation, in a property enumerated in Paragraphs (A) through (E) of this subdivision.

(3) "Improvement" means:

(A) a building, structure, fixture, or fence erected on or affixed to land;

(B) a transportable structure that is designed to be occupied for residential or business purposes, whether or not it is affixed to land, if the owner of the structure owns the land on which it is located, unless the structure is unoccupied and held for sale or normally is located at a particular place only temporarily; or

(C) for purposes of an entity created under Section 52, Article III, or Section 59, Article XVI, Texas Constitution, the:

(i) subdivision of land by plat;

(ii) installation of water, sewer, or drainage lines; or

(iii) paving of undeveloped land.

(3-a) Notwithstanding anything contained herein to the contrary, a manufactured home is an improvement to real property only if the owner of the home has elected to treat the manufactured home as real property pursuant to Section 1201.2055, Occupations Code, and a [~~certified~~] copy of the statement of ownership [~~and location~~] has been filed with the real property records of the county in which the home is located as provided in Section 1201.2055(d), Occupations Code.

(4) "Personal property" means property that is not real property.

(5) "Tangible personal property" means personal property that can be seen, weighed, measured, felt, or otherwise perceived by the senses, but does not include a document or other perceptible object that constitutes evidence of a valuable interest, claim, or right and has negligible or no intrinsic value.

(6) "Intangible personal property" means a claim, interest (other than an interest in tangible property), right, or other thing that has value but cannot be seen, felt, weighed, measured, or otherwise perceived by the senses, although its existence may be evidenced by a document. It includes a stock, bond, note or account receivable, franchise, license or permit, demand or time deposit, certificate of deposit, share account, share certificate account, share deposit account, insurance policy, annuity, pension, cause of action, contract, and goodwill.

(7) "Market value" means the price at which a property would transfer for cash or its equivalent under prevailing market conditions if:

(A) exposed for sale in the open market with a reasonable time for the seller to find a purchaser;

(B) both the seller and the purchaser know of all the uses and purposes to which the property is adapted and for which it is capable of being used and of the enforceable restrictions on its use; and

(C) both the seller and purchaser seek to maximize their gains and neither is in a position to take advantage of the exigencies of the other.

(8) "Appraised value" means the value determined as provided by Chapter 23 of this code.

(9) "Assessed value" means, for the purposes of assessment of property for taxation, the amount determined by multiplying the appraised value by the applicable assessment ratio, but, for the purposes of determining the debt limitation imposed by Article III, Section 52, of the Texas Constitution, shall mean the market value of the property recorded by the chief appraiser.

(10) "Taxable value" means the amount determined by deducting from assessed value the amount of any applicable partial exemption.

(11) "Partial exemption" means an exemption of part of the value of taxable property.

(12) "Taxing unit" means a county, an incorporated city or town (including a home-rule city), a school

district, a special district or authority (including a junior college district, a hospital district, a district created by or pursuant to the Water Code, a mosquito control district, a fire prevention district, or a noxious weed control district), or any other political unit of this state, whether created by or pursuant to the constitution or a local, special, or general law, that is authorized to impose and is imposing ad valorem taxes on property even if the governing body of another political unit determines the tax rate for the unit or otherwise governs its affairs.

(13) "Tax year" means the calendar year.

(14) "Assessor" means the officer or employee responsible for assessing property taxes as provided by Chapter 26 of this code for a taxing unit by whatever title he is designated.

(15) "Collector" means the officer or employee responsible for collecting property taxes for a taxing unit by whatever title he is designated.

(16) "Possessory interest" means an interest that exists as a result of possession or exclusive use or a right to possession or exclusive use of a property and that is unaccompanied by ownership of a fee simple or life estate in the property. However, "possessory interest" does not include an interest, whether of limited or indeterminate duration, that involves a right to exhaust a portion of a real property.

(17) "Conservation and reclamation district" means a district created under Article III, Section 52, or Article XVI, Section 59, of the Texas Constitution, or under a statute enacted under Article III, Section 52, or Article XVI, Section 59, of the Texas Constitution.

(18) "Clerical error" means an error:

(A) that is or results from a mistake or failure in writing, copying, transcribing, entering or retrieving computer data, computing, or calculating; or

(B) that prevents an appraisal roll or a tax roll from accurately reflecting a finding or determination made by the chief appraiser, the appraisal review board, or the assessor; however, "clerical error" does not include an error that is or results from a mistake in judgment or reasoning in the making of the finding or determination.

(19) "Comptroller" means the Comptroller of Public Accounts of the State of Texas.

2017 Legislation: Amended by H.B. 2019, §79, 85th Leg., eff. Sept. 1, 2017.

SUBTITLE C. TAXABLE PROPERTY & EXEMPTIONS

CHAPTER 11. TAXABLE PROPERTY & EXEMPTIONS

SUBCHAPTER A. TAXABLE PROPERTY

A TAX §11.01. REAL & TANGIBLE PERSONAL PROPERTY

(a) All real and tangible personal property that this state has jurisdiction to tax is taxable unless exempt by law.

(b) This state has jurisdiction to tax real property if located in this state.

(c) This state has jurisdiction to tax tangible personal property if the property is:

(1) located in this state for longer than a temporary period;

(2) temporarily located outside this state and the owner resides in this state; or

(3) used continually, whether regularly or irregularly, in this state.

(d) Tangible personal property that is operated or located exclusively outside this state during the year preceding the tax year and on January 1 of the tax year is not taxable in this state.

(e) For purposes of Subsection (c)(3), property is considered to be used continually, whether regularly or irregularly, in this state if the property is used in this state three or more times on regular routes or for three or more completed assignments occurring in close succession throughout the year. For purposes of this subsection, a series of events are considered to occur in close succession throughout the year if they occur in sequence within a short period at intervals from the beginning to the end of the year.

2017 Legislation: Amended by H.B. 3103, §1, 85th Leg., eff. June 15, 2017.

TAX §11.02. INTANGIBLE PERSONAL PROPERTY

(a) Except as provided by Subsection (b) of this section, intangible personal property is not taxable.

(b) Intangible property governed by Article 4.01, Insurance Code, or by Section 89.003, Finance Code, is taxable as provided by law, unless exempt by law, if this state has jurisdiction to tax those intangibles.

(c) This state has jurisdiction to tax intangible personal property if the property is:

(1) owned by a resident of this state; or

(2) located in this state for business purposes.

SUBTITLE D. APPRAISAL & ASSESSMENT

CHAPTER 21. TAXABLE SITUS

TAX §21.01. REAL PROPERTY

Real property is taxable by a taxing unit if located in the unit on January 1, except as provided by Chapter 41, Education Code.

TAX §21.02. TANGIBLE PERSONAL PROPERTY GENERALLY

(a) Except as provided by Subsections (b) and (e) and by Sections 21.021, 21.04, and 21.05, tangible personal property is taxable by a taxing unit if:

(1) it is located in the unit on January 1 for more than a temporary period;

(2) it normally is located in the unit, even though it is outside the unit on January 1, if it is outside the unit only temporarily;

(3) it normally is returned to the unit between uses elsewhere and is not located in any one place for more than a temporary period; or

(4) the owner resides (for property not used for business purposes) or maintains the owner's principal place of business in this state (for property used for business purposes) in the unit and the property is taxable in this state but does not have a taxable situs pursuant to Subdivisions (1) through (3) of this subsection.

(b) Tangible personal property having taxable situs at the same location as real property detached from a school district and annexed by another school district under Chapter 41, Education Code, is taxable in the tax year in which the detachment and annexation occurs by the same school district by which the real property is taxable in that tax year under Chapter 41, Education Code. For purposes of this subsection and Chapter 41, Education Code, tangible personal property has taxable situs at the same location as real property detached and annexed under Chapter 41, Education Code, if the detachment and annexation of the real property, had it occurred before January 1 of the tax year, would have changed the taxable situs of the tangible personal property determined as provided by Subsection (a) from the school district from which the real property was detached to the school district to which the real property was annexed.

(c) Tangible personal property has taxable situs in a school district that is the result of a consolidation under Chapter 41, Education Code, in the year in which the consolidation occurs if the property would have had taxable situs in the consolidated district in that year had the consolidation occurred before January 1 of that year.

(d) A motor vehicle does not have taxable situs in a taxing unit under Subsection (a)(1) if, on January 1, the vehicle:

(1) has been located for less than 60 days at a place of business of a person who holds a wholesale motor vehicle auction general distinguishing number issued by the Texas Department of Motor Vehicles under Chapter 503, Transportation Code, for that place of business; and

(2) is offered for resale.

(e) In this subsection, "portable drilling rig" includes equipment associated with the drilling rig. A portable drilling rig designed for land-based oil or gas drilling or exploration operations is taxable by each taxing unit in which the rig is located on January 1 if the rig was located in the appraisal district that appraises property for the unit for the preceding 365 consecutive days. If the drilling rig was not located in the appraisal district where it is located on January 1 for the preceding 365 days, it is taxable by each taxing unit in which the owner's principal place of business in this state is located on January 1, unless the owner renders the rig under Chapter 22 to the appraisal district in which the rig is located on January 1, in which event the rig is taxable by each taxing unit in which the rig is located on January 1. If an owner elects to render any portable drilling rig to the appraisal district in which the rig is located on January 1 when the rig otherwise would be taxable at the owner's principal place of business in this state, all the owner's portable drilling rigs are taxable by the taxing units in which each rig is located on January 1. Notwithstanding any other provision of this subsection, if the owner of a portable drilling rig does not have a place of business in this state, the rig is taxable by each taxing unit in which the rig is located on January 1.

TAX §21.021. VESSELS & OTHER WATERCRAFT

(a) A vessel or other watercraft used as an instrumentality of commerce (as defined in Section 21.031(b) of this code) is taxable pursuant to Section 21.02 of this code.

(b) A special-purpose vessel or other watercraft not used as an instrumentality of commerce (as defined in Section 21.031(b) of this code) is deemed to be located

on January 1 for more than a temporary period for purposes of Section 21.02 of this code in the taxing unit in which it was physically located during the year preceding the tax year. If the vessel or watercraft was physically located in more than one taxing unit during the year preceding the tax year, it is deemed to be located for more than a temporary period for purposes of Section 21.02 of this code in the taxing unit in which it was physically located for the longest period during the year preceding the tax year or for 30 days, whichever is longer. If a vessel or other watercraft is not deemed to be located in any taxing unit on January 1 for more than a temporary period pursuant to this subsection, the property is taxable as provided by Subdivisions (2) through (4) of Section 21.02 of this code.

(c) This section applies solely to a determination of taxable situs and does not apply to a determination of jurisdiction to tax under Section 11.01 of this code.

TAX §21.03. INTERSTATE ALLOCATION

(a) If personal property that is taxable by a taxing unit is used continually outside this state, whether regularly or irregularly, the appraisal office shall allocate to this state the portion of the total market value of the property that fairly reflects its use in this state.

(b) The comptroller shall adopt rules:

(1) identifying the kinds of property subject to this section; and

(2) establishing formulas for calculating the proportion of total market value to be allocated to this state.

TAX §21.031. ALLOCATION OF TAXABLE VALUE OF VESSELS & OTHER WATERCRAFT USED OUTSIDE THIS STATE

(a) If a vessel or other watercraft that is taxable by a taxing unit is used continually outside this state, whether regularly or irregularly, the appraisal office shall allocate to this state the portion of the total market value of the vessel or watercraft that fairly reflects its use in this state. The appraisal office shall not allocate to this state the portion of the total market value of the vessel or watercraft that fairly reflects its use in another state or country, in international waters, or beyond the Gulfward boundary of this state.

(b) The appraisal office shall make the allocation as follows:

(1) The allocable portion of the total fair market value of a vessel or other watercraft used as an instrumentality of commerce that is taxable in this state is determined by multiplying the total fair market value by a fraction, the numerator of which is the number of miles the vessel or watercraft was operated in this state during the year preceding the tax year and the denominator of which is the total number of miles the vessel or watercraft was operated during the year preceding the tax year. For purposes of this section, "vessel or other watercraft used as an instrumentality of commerce" means a vessel or other watercraft that is primarily employed in the transportation of cargo, passengers, or equipment, and that is economically employed when it is moving from point to point as a means of transportation.

(2) The allocable portion of the total fair market value of a special-purpose vessel or other watercraft not used as an instrumentality of commerce is determined by multiplying the total fair market value by a fraction, the numerator of which is the number of days the vessel or watercraft was physically located in this state during the year preceding the tax year and the denominator of which is 365. For purposes of this section, "special-purpose vessel or other watercraft not used as an instrumentality of commerce" means a vessel or other watercraft that:

(A) is designed to be transient and customarily is moved from location to location on a more or less regular basis;

(B) is economically employed when operated in a localized area or in a fixed place; and

(C) is not primarily employed to transport cargo, passengers, and equipment but rather to perform some specialized function or operation not requiring constant movement from point to point.

(c) A vessel or other watercraft used as an instrumentality of commerce or a special-purpose vessel or other watercraft not used as an instrumentality of commerce that is used outside this state and is in this state solely to be converted, repaired, stored, or inspected is presumed to be in interstate, international, or foreign commerce and not located in this state for longer than a temporary period for purposes of Sections 11.01 and 21.02.

(d) If the allocation provisions of this section do not fairly reflect the use of a vessel or other watercraft

TAX §21.031

in this state, an alternate allocation formula shall be utilized if the property owner or appraisal office demonstrates that:

(1) the allocation formula specified in this section is arbitrary and unreasonable as applied to the vessel or watercraft; and

(2) the formula or indication of use proposed by the property owner or appraisal office more fairly reflects the vessel or watercraft's use in this state than that specified in this section.

(e) To receive an allocation of value under this section, a property owner must apply for the allocation on a form that substantially complies with the form prescribed by the comptroller. The application must be filed with the chief appraiser for the district in which the property to which the application applies is taxable before the approval of the appraisal records by the appraisal review board as provided by Section 41.12 of this code.

(f) The comptroller shall promulgate forms and may adopt rules consistent with the provisions of this section.

(g) A vessel or other watercraft to be used as an instrumentality of commerce or a special-purpose vessel or other watercraft not to be used as an instrumentality of commerce that is under construction in this state is presumed to be in interstate, international, or foreign commerce and not located in this state for longer than a temporary period for purposes of Sections 11.01 and 21.02.

(h) Tangible personal property in this state is presumed to be in interstate, international, or foreign commerce and not located in this state for longer than a temporary period for purposes of Sections 11.01 and 21.02 if the owner demonstrates to the chief appraiser that the owner intends to incorporate the property in or attach the property to an identified vessel or other watercraft described by Subsection (c) or (g).

TAX §21.04. RAILROAD ROLLING STOCK

(a) A portion of the total market value of railroad rolling stock that is appraised as provided by Subchapter B of Chapter 24 of this code is taxable by each county in which the railroad operates.

(b) The portion of the total market value that is taxable by a county is determined by the provisions of Subchapter B of Chapter 24 of this code.

TAX §21.05. COMMERCIAL AIRCRAFT

(a) If a commercial aircraft that is taxable by a taxing unit is used both in this state and outside this state, the appraisal office shall allocate to this state the portion of the fair market value of the aircraft that fairly reflects its use in this state. The appraisal office shall not allocate to this state the portion of the total market value of the aircraft that fairly reflects its use beyond the boundaries of this state.

(b) The allocable portion of the total fair market value of a commercial aircraft that is taxable in this state is presumed to be the fair market value of the aircraft multiplied by a fraction, the numerator of which is the product of 1.5 and the number of revenue departures by the aircraft from Texas during the year preceding the tax year, and the denominator of which is the greater of (1) 8,760, or (2) the numerator.

(c) During the time in which any commercial aircraft is removed from air transportation service for repair, storage, or inspection, such aircraft is presumed to be in interstate, international, or foreign commerce and not located in this state for longer than a temporary period for purposes of Section 11.01 of this code.

(d) A certificated air carrier shall designate the tax situs of commercial aircraft that land in Texas as either the carrier's principal office in Texas or that Texas airport from which the carrier has the highest number of Texas departures.

(e) For purposes of this subchapter, a commercial aircraft shall mean an instrumentality of air commerce that is:

(1) primarily engaged in the transportation of cargo, passengers, or equipment for others for consideration;

(2) economically employed when it is moving from point to point as a means of transportation; and

(3) operated by a certificated air carrier. A certificated air carrier is one engaged in interstate or intrastate commerce under authority of the U.S. Department of Transportation.

TAX §21.055. BUSINESS AIRCRAFT

(a) If an aircraft is used for a business purpose of the owner, is taxable by a taxing unit, and is used continually outside this state, whether regularly or irregularly, the appraisal office shall allocate to this state the portion of the fair market value of the aircraft that fairly

reflects its use in this state. The appraisal office shall not allocate to this state the portion of the total market value of the aircraft that fairly reflects its use beyond the boundaries of this state.

(b) The allocable portion of the total fair market value of an aircraft described by Subsection (a) is presumed to be the fair market value of the aircraft multiplied by a fraction, the numerator of which is the number of departures by the aircraft from a location in this state during the year preceding the tax year and the denominator of which is the total number of departures by the aircraft from all locations during the year preceding the tax year.

(c) This section does not apply to a commercial aircraft as defined by Section 21.05.

TAX §21.06. INTANGIBLE PROPERTY GENERALLY

(a) Except as provided by Sections 21.07 through 21.09 of this code, intangible property is taxable by a taxing unit if the owner of the property resides in the unit on January 1, unless the property normally is used in this state for business purposes outside the unit. In that event, the intangible property is taxable by each taxing unit in which the property normally is used for business purposes.

(b) Depositing intangible property with an agency of the state pursuant to a law requiring or authorizing the deposit is not using it for a business purpose at the depository.

TAX §21.07. INTANGIBLES OF CERTAIN TRANSPORTATION BUSINESSES

(a) A portion of the total intangible value of a transportation business whose intangibles are appraised as provided by Subchapter A of Chapter 24 of this code is taxable by each county in which the business operates.

(b) The portion of the total value that is taxable as provided by Subsection (a) of this section is determined by the provisions of Subchapter A of Chapter 24 of this code.

TAX §21.08. INTANGIBLES OF CERTAIN FINANCIAL INSTITUTIONS

(a) The taxable situs of intangible property owned by an insurance company incorporated under the laws of this state is determined as provided by Article 4.01, Insurance Code.

(b) The taxable situs of intangible property owned by a savings and loan association is determined as provided by Section 89.003, Finance Code.

A TAX §21.09. ALLOCATION APPLICATION

(a) To receive an allocation authorized by Section 21.03, 21.031, 21.05, or 21.055, a person claiming the allocation must apply for the allocation. To apply for an allocation, a person must file an allocation application form with the chief appraiser in the appraisal district in which the property subject to the claimed allocation has taxable situs.

(b) A person claiming an allocation must apply for the allocation each year the person claims the allocation. A person claiming an allocation must file a completed allocation application form before April [~~May~~] 1 and must provide the information required by the form. If the property was not on the appraisal roll in the preceding year, the deadline for filing the allocation application form is extended to the 30th [~~45th~~] day after the date of receipt of the notice of appraised value required by Section 25.19(a)(3). For good cause shown, the chief appraiser shall extend the deadline for filing an allocation application form by written order for a period not to exceed 30 [~~60~~] days.

(c) The comptroller shall prescribe the contents of the allocation application form and shall ensure that the form requires an applicant to provide the information necessary to determine the validity of the allocation claim.

(d) If the chief appraiser learns of any reason indicating that an allocation previously allowed should be canceled, the chief appraiser shall investigate. If the chief appraiser determines that the property is not entitled to an allocation, the chief appraiser shall cancel the allocation and deliver written notice of the cancellation not later than the fifth day after the date the chief appraiser makes the cancellation. A person may protest the cancellation of an allocation.

(e) The filing of a rendition under Chapter 22 is not a condition of qualification for an allocation.

2017 Legislation: Amended by H.B. 2228, §2, 85th Leg., eff. Jan. 1, 2018.

TAX §21.10. LATE APPLICATION FOR ALLOCATION

(a) The chief appraiser shall accept and approve or deny an application for an allocation under Section 21.09 after the deadline for filing the application has

passed if the application is filed before the date the appraisal review board approves the appraisal records.

(b) If the application is approved, the property owner is liable to each taxing unit for a penalty in an amount equal to 10 percent of the difference between the amount of tax imposed by the taxing unit on the property without the allocation and the amount of tax imposed on the property with the allocation.

(c) The chief appraiser shall make an entry on the appraisal records for the property indicating the property owner's liability for the penalty and shall deliver a written notice of imposition of the penalty, explaining the reason for its imposition, to the property owner.

(d) The tax assessor for a taxing unit that taxes the property shall add the amount of the penalty to the property owner's tax bill, and the tax collector for the unit shall collect the penalty at the time and in the manner the collector collects the tax. The amount of the penalty constitutes a lien against the property against which the penalty is imposed, as if the penalty were a tax, and accrues penalty and interest in the same manner as a delinquent tax.

CHAPTER 22. RENDITIONS & OTHER REPORTS

SUBCHAPTER A. INFORMATION FROM TAXPAYER

TAX §22.01. RENDITION GENERALLY

(a) Except as provided by Chapter 24, a person shall render for taxation all tangible personal property used for the production of income that the person owns or that the person manages and controls as a fiduciary on January 1. A rendition statement shall contain:

(1) the name and address of the property owner;

(2) a description of the property by type or category;

(3) if the property is inventory, a description of each type of inventory and a general estimate of the quantity of each type of inventory;

(4) the physical location or taxable situs of the property; and

(5) the property owner's good faith estimate of the market value of the property or, at the option of the property owner, the historical cost when new and the year of acquisition of the property.

(b) When required by the chief appraiser, a person shall render for taxation any other taxable property that he owns or that he manages and controls as a fiduciary on January 1.

(c) A person may render for taxation any property that he owns or that he manages and controls as a fiduciary on January 1, although he is not required to render it by Subsection (a) or (b) of this section.

(c-1) In this section:

(1) "Secured party" has the meaning assigned by Section 9.102, Business & Commerce Code.

(2) "Security interest" has the meaning assigned by Section 1.201, Business & Commerce Code.

(c-2) With the consent of the property owner, a secured party may render for taxation any property of the property owner in which the secured party has a security interest on January 1, although the secured party is not required to render the property by Subsection (a) or (b). This subsection applies only to property that has a historical cost when new of more than $50,000.

(d) A fiduciary who renders property shall indicate his fiduciary capacity and shall state the name and address of the owner.

(d-1) A secured party who renders property under Subsection (c-2) shall indicate the party's status as a secured party and shall state the name and address of the property owner. A secured party is not liable for inaccurate information included on the rendition statement if the property owner supplied the information or for failure to timely file the rendition statement if the property owner failed to promptly cooperate with the secured party. A secured party may rely on information provided by the property owner with respect to:

(1) the accuracy of information in the rendition statement;

(2) the appraisal district in which the rendition statement must be filed; and

(3) compliance with any provisions of this chapter that require the property owner to supply additional information.

(e) Notwithstanding Subsections (a) and (b), a person is not required to render for taxation cotton that:

(1) the person manages and controls as a fiduciary;

(2) is stored in a warehouse for which an exemption for cotton has been granted under Section 11.437; and

(3) the person intends to transport outside of the state within the time permitted by Article VIII, Section 1-j, of the Texas Constitution for cotton to qualify for an exemption under that section.

(f) Notwithstanding Subsections (a) and (b), a rendition statement of a person who owns tangible personal property used for the production of income located in the appraisal district that, in the owner's opinion, has an aggregate value of less than $20,000 is required to contain only:

(1) the name and address of the property owner;

(2) a general description of the property by type or category; and

(3) the physical location or taxable situs of the property.

(g) A person's good faith estimate of the market value of the property under Subsection (a)(5) is solely for the purpose of compliance with the requirement to render tangible personal property and is inadmissible in any subsequent protest, hearing, appeal, suit, or other proceeding under this title involving the property, except for:

(1) a proceeding to determine whether the person complied with this section;

(2) a proceeding under Section 22.29(b); or

(3) a protest under Section 41.41.

(h) If the property that is the subject of the rendition is regulated by the Public Utility Commission of Texas, the Railroad Commission of Texas, the federal Surface Transportation Board, or the Federal Energy Regulatory Commission, the owner of the property is considered to have complied with the requirements of this section if the owner provides to the chief appraiser, on written request of the chief appraiser, a copy of the annual regulatory report covering the property and sufficient information to enable the chief appraiser to allocate the value of the property among the appropriate taxing units for which the appraisal district appraises property.

(i) Subsection (a) does not apply to a property owner whose property is subject to appraisal by a third party retained by the appraisal district if the property owner provides information substantially equivalent to that required by Subsection (a) regarding the property directly to the third party appraiser.

(j) Subsection (a) does not apply to property that is exempt from taxation.

(k) Notwithstanding Subsections (a) and (b), an individual who has been granted or has applied for an exemption from taxation under Section 11.254 for a motor vehicle the individual owns is not required to render the motor vehicle for taxation.

(*l*) If the information contained in the most recent rendition statement filed by a person in a prior tax year is accurate with respect to the current tax year, the person may comply with the requirements of Subsection (a) by filing a rendition statement on a form prescribed or approved by the comptroller under Section 22.24(c) on which the person has checked the appropriate box to affirm that the information continues to be complete and accurate.

(m) Notwithstanding Subsections (a) and (b), a person is not required to render for taxation personal property appraised under Section 23.24.

TAX §22.02. RENDITION OF PROPERTY LOSING EXEMPTION DURING TAX YEAR OR FOR WHICH EXEMPTION APPLICATION IS DENIED

(a) If an exemption applicable to a property on January 1 terminates during the tax year, the person who owns or acquires the property on the date applicability of the exemption terminates shall render the property for taxation within 30 days after the date of termination.

(b) If the chief appraiser denies an application for an exemption for property described by Section 22.01(a), the person who owns the property on the date the application is denied shall render the property for taxation in the manner provided by Section 22.01 within 30 days after the date of denial.

TAX §22.03. REPORT OF DECREASED VALUE

(a) A person who believes the appraised value of his property decreased during the preceding tax year for any reason other than normal depreciation may file an information report describing the property involved and stating the nature and cause of the decrease.

(b) Except as provided by Subsection (d) of this section, before determining the appraised value of property that is the subject of a completed and timely filed report as provided by Subsection (a) of this section, the chief appraiser must view the property to verify any reported change in appraised value and its cause and nature. The person who views the property shall note on the back of the property owner's report his name, the date he viewed the property, and his determination of any decrease in appraised value and its cause and nature.

(c) The chief appraiser shall deliver a written notice to the property owner of the determination made as provided by Subsection (b) of this section.

(d) Before determining the appraised value of oil and gas property that is the subject of a completed and timely filed report as provided by Subsection (a) of this section, the chief appraiser must review the appraisal of the property to verify any reported change in appraised value and its cause and nature. The person who reviews the appraisal of the property shall note on the back of the property owner's report his name, the date he reviewed the appraisal of the property, and his determination of any decrease in appraised value and its cause and nature.

TAX §22.04. REPORT BY BAILEE, LESSEE, OR OTHER POSSESSOR

(a) When required by the chief appraiser, a person shall file a report listing the name and address of each owner of property that is in his possession or under his management on January 1 by bailment, lease, consignment, or other arrangement.

(b) When required by the chief appraiser, a person who leases or otherwise provides space to another for storage of personal property shall file an information report stating the name and address of each person to whom he leased or otherwise provided storage space on January 1.

(c) This section does not apply to a warehouse for which an exemption for cotton has been granted under Section 11.437.

(d) This section does not apply to a motor vehicle that on January 1 is located at a place of business of a person who holds a wholesale motor vehicle auction general distinguishing number issued by the Texas Department of Motor Vehicles under Chapter 503, Transportation Code, for that place of business, and that:

(1) has not acquired taxable situs under Section 21.02(a)(1) in a taxing unit that participates in the appraisal district because the vehicle is described by Section 21.02(d);

(2) is offered for sale by a dealer who holds a dealer's general distinguishing number issued by the Texas Department of Motor Vehicles under Chapter 503, Transportation Code, and whose inventory of motor vehicles is subject to taxation in the manner provided by Sections 23.121 and 23.122; or

(3) is collateral possessed by a lienholder and offered for sale in foreclosure of a security interest.

TAX §22.05. RENDITION BY RAILROAD

(a) In addition to other reports required by Chapter 24 of this code, a railroad corporation shall render the property the railroad corporation owns or possesses as of January 1.

(b) The rendition shall:

(1) list all real property other than the property covered by Subdivision (2) of this subsection;

(2) list the number of miles of railroad together with the market value per mile, which value shall include right-of-way, roadbed, superstructure, and all buildings and improvements used in the operation of the railroad; and

(3) list all personal property as required by Section 22.01 of this code.

TAX §22.06. REPEALED

TAX §22.07. INSPECTION OF PROPERTY

(a) The chief appraiser or his authorized representative may enter the premises of a business, trade, or profession and inspect the property to determine the existence and market value of tangible personal property used for the production of income and having a taxable situs in the district.

(b) An inspection under this section must be during normal business hours or at a time mutually agreeable to the chief appraiser or his representative and the person in control of the premises.

(c) The chief appraiser may request, either in writing or by electronic means, that the property owner provide a statement containing supporting information indicating how the value rendered under Section 22.01(a)(5) was determined. The statement must:

(1) summarize information sufficient to identify the property, including:

(A) the physical and economic characteristics relevant to the opinion of value, if appropriate; and

(B) the source of the information used;

(2) state the effective date of the opinion of value; and

(3) explain the basis of the value rendered. If the property owner is a business with 50 employees or less,

the property owner may base the estimate of value on the depreciation schedules used for federal income tax purposes.

(d) The property owner shall deliver the statement to the chief appraiser, either in writing or by electronic means, not later than the 21st day after the date the chief appraiser's request is received. The owner's statement is solely for informational purposes and is not admissible in evidence in any subsequent protest, suit, appeal, or other proceeding under this title involving the property other than:

(1) a proceeding to determine whether the property owner has complied with this section;

(2) a proceeding under Section 22.29(b); or

(3) a protest under Section 41.41.

(e) A statement provided under this section is confidential information and may not be disclosed, except as provided by Section 22.27.

(f) Failure to comply with this section in a timely manner is considered to be a failure to timely render under Section 22.01 and penalties as described in Section 22.28 shall be applied by the chief appraiser.

Sections 22.08-22.20 reserved for expansion

SUBCHAPTER B. REQUIREMENTS & PROCEDURES

TAX §22.21. PUBLICIZING REQUIREMENTS

Each year the comptroller and each chief appraiser shall publicize in a manner reasonably designed to notify all property owners the requirements of the law relating to filing rendition statements and property reports and of the availability of forms.

TAX §22.22. METHOD FOR REQUIRING RENDITION OR REPORT

The chief appraiser may require a rendition statement or property report he is authorized to require by this chapter by delivering written notice that the statement or report is required to the person responsible for filing it. He shall attach to the notice a copy of the appropriate form.

A TAX §22.23. FILING DATE

(a) Rendition statements and property reports must be delivered to the chief appraiser after January 1 and not later than April 15, except as provided by Section 22.02.

(b) On written request by the property owner, the chief appraiser shall extend a deadline for filing a rendition statement or property report to May 15. The chief appraiser may further extend the deadline an additional 15 days upon good cause shown in writing by the property owner.

(c) Notwithstanding Subsections (a) and (b), rendition statements and property reports for property located in an appraisal district in which one or more taxing units exempt property under Section 11.251 must be delivered to the chief appraiser not later than April 1. On written request by the property owner, the chief appraiser shall extend the deadline provided by this subsection for filing a rendition statement or property report to May 1. The chief appraiser may further extend the deadline an additional 15 days for good cause shown in writing by the property owner.

(d) Notwithstanding any other provision of this section, rendition statements and property reports for property regulated by the Public Utility Commission of Texas, the Railroad Commission of Texas, the federal Surface Transportation Board, or the Federal Energy Regulatory Commission must be delivered to the chief appraiser not later than April 30, except as provided by Section 22.02. The chief appraiser may extend the filing deadline 15 days for good cause shown in writing by the property owner.

2017 Legislation: Amended by H.B. 2228, §3, 85th Leg., eff. Jan. 1, 2018.

TAX §22.24. RENDITION & REPORT FORMS

(a) A person required to render property or to file a report as provided by this chapter shall use a form that substantially complies with the appropriate form prescribed or approved by the comptroller.

(b) A person filing a rendition or report shall include all information required by Section 22.01.

(c) The comptroller may prescribe or approve different forms for different kinds of property but shall ensure that each form requires a property owner to furnish the information necessary to identify the property and to determine its ownership, taxability, and situs. Each form must include a box that the property owner may check to permit the property owner to affirm that the information contained in the most recent rendition statement filed by the property owner in a prior tax year is accurate with respect to the current tax year in accordance with Section 22.01(*l*). A form may not require but may permit a property owner to furnish information

not specifically required by this chapter to be reported. In addition, a form prescribed or approved under this subsection must contain the following statement in bold type: "If you make a false statement on this form, you could be found guilty of a Class A misdemeanor or a state jail felony under Section 37.10, Penal Code."

(d) Except as required by Section 22.01(a), a rendition or report form shall permit but not require a property owner to state the owner's good faith estimate of the market value of the property.

(e) To be valid, a rendition or report must be sworn to before an officer authorized by law to administer an oath. The comptroller may not prescribe or approve a rendition or report form unless the form provides for the person filing the form to swear that the information provided in the rendition or report is true and accurate to the best of the person's knowledge and belief. This subsection does not apply to a rendition or report filed by a secured party, as defined by Section 22.01, the property owner, an employee of the property owner, or an employee of a property owner on behalf of an affiliated entity of the property owner.

TAX §22.25. PLACE & MANNER OF FILING

A rendition statement or property report required or authorized by this chapter must be filed with the chief appraiser for the district in which the property listed in the statement or report is taxable.

TAX §22.26. SIGNATURE

(a) Each rendition statement or property report required or authorized by this chapter must be signed by an individual who is required to file the statement or report.

(b) When a corporation is required to file a statement or report, an officer of the corporation or an employee or agent who has been designated in writing by the board of directors or by an authorized officer to sign in behalf of the corporation must sign the statement or report.

TAX §22.27. CONFIDENTIAL INFORMATION

(a) Rendition statements, real and personal property reports, attachments to those statements and reports, and other information the owner of property provides to the appraisal office in connection with the appraisal of the property, including income and expense information related to a property filed with an appraisal office and information voluntarily disclosed to an appraisal office or the comptroller about real or personal property sales prices after a promise it will be held confidential, are confidential and not open to public inspection. The statements and reports and the information they contain about specific real or personal property or a specific real or personal property owner and information voluntarily disclosed to an appraisal office about real or personal property sales prices after a promise it will be held confidential may not be disclosed to anyone other than an employee of the appraisal office who appraises property except as authorized by Subsection (b) of this section.

(b) Information made confidential by this section may be disclosed:

(1) in a judicial or administrative proceeding pursuant to a lawful subpoena;

(2) to the person who filed the statement or report or the owner of property subject to the statement, report, or information or to a representative of either authorized in writing to receive the information;

(3) to the comptroller and the comptroller's employees authorized by the comptroller in writing to receive the information or to an assessor or a chief appraiser if requested in writing;

(4) in a judicial or administrative proceeding relating to property taxation to which the person who filed the statement or report or the owner of the property that is a subject of the statement, report, or information is a party;

(5) for statistical purposes if in a form that does not identify specific property or a specific property owner;

(6) if and to the extent the information is required to be included in a public document or record that the appraisal office is required to prepare or maintain;

(7) to a taxing unit or its legal representative that is engaged in the collection of delinquent taxes on the property that is the subject of the information;

(8) to an employee or agent of a taxing unit responsible for auditing, monitoring, or reviewing the operations of an appraisal district; or

(9) to an employee or agent of a school district that is engaged in the preparation of a protest of the comptroller's property value study in accordance with Section 403.303, Government Code.

(c) A person who legally has access to a statement or report or to other information made confidential by

this section or who legally obtains the confidential information commits a Class B misdemeanor if he knowingly:

(1) permits inspection of the statement or report by a person not authorized to inspect it by Subsection (b) of this section; or

(2) discloses the confidential information to a person not authorized to receive the information by Subsection (b) of this section.

(d) No person who directly or indirectly provides information to the comptroller or appraisal office about real or personal property sales prices, either as set forth in Subsection (a) of this section under a promise of confidentiality, or otherwise, shall be liable to any other person as the result of providing such information.

TAX §22.28. PENALTY FOR DELINQUENT REPORT; PENALTY COLLECTION PROCEDURES

(a) Except as otherwise provided by Section 22.30, the chief appraiser shall impose a penalty on a person who fails to timely file a rendition statement or property report required by this chapter in an amount equal to 10 percent of the total amount of taxes imposed on the property for that year by taxing units participating in the appraisal district. The chief appraiser shall deliver by first class mail a notice of the imposition of the penalty to the person. The notice may be delivered with a notice of appraised value provided under Section 25.19, if practicable.

(b) The chief appraiser shall certify to the assessor for each taxing unit participating in the appraisal district that imposes taxes on the property that a penalty imposed under this chapter has become final. The assessor shall add the amount of the penalty to the original amount of tax imposed on the property and shall include that amount in the tax bill for that year. The penalty becomes part of the tax on the property and is secured by the tax lien that attaches to the property under Section 32.01.

(c) A penalty under this chapter becomes final if:

(1) the property owner does not protest under Section 22.30 the imposition of the penalty before the appraisal review board;

(2) the appraisal review board determines a protest brought by the property owner under Section 22.30 by denying a waiver of the penalty and the property owner does not bring an appeal under Chapter 42 or the judgment of the district court sustaining the determination subsequently becomes final; or

(3) a court imposes the penalty under Section 22.29 and the order of the court imposing the penalty subsequently becomes final.

(d) To help defray the costs of administering this chapter, a collector who collects a penalty imposed under Subsection (a) shall remit to the appraisal district that employs the chief appraiser who imposed the penalty an amount equal to five percent of the penalty amount collected.

TAX §22.29. PENALTY FOR FRAUD OR INTENT TO EVADE TAX

(a) The chief appraiser shall impose an additional penalty on the person equal to 50 percent of the total amount of taxes imposed on the property for the tax year of the statement or report by the taxing units participating in the appraisal district if it is finally determined by a court that:

(1) the person filed a false statement or report with the intent to commit fraud or to evade the tax; or

(2) the person alters, destroys, or conceals any record, document, or thing, or presents to the chief appraiser any altered or fraudulent record, document, or thing, or otherwise engages in fraudulent conduct, for the purpose of affecting the course or outcome of an inspection, investigation, determination, or other proceeding before the appraisal district.

(b) Enforcement of this section shall be by a proceeding initiated by the district or county attorney of the county in which the appraisal is established, on behalf of the appraisal district.

(c) In making a determination of liability under this section, the court shall consider:

(1) the person's compliance history with respect to paying taxes and filing statements or reports;

(2) the type, nature, and taxability of the specific property involved;

(3) the type, nature, size, and sophistication of the person's business or other entity for which property is rendered;

(4) the completeness of the person's records;

(5) the person's reliance on advice provided by the appraisal district that may have contributed to the violation;

(6) any change in appraisal district policy during the current or preceding tax year that may affect how property is rendered; and

(7) any other factor the court considers relevant.

(d) The chief appraiser may retain a portion of a penalty collected under this section, not to exceed 20 percent of the amount of the penalty, to cover the chief appraiser's costs of collecting the penalty. The chief appraiser shall distribute the remainder of the penalty to each taxing unit participating in the appraisal district that imposes taxes on the property in proportion to the taxing unit's share of the total amount of taxes imposed on the property by all taxing units participating in the district.

TAX §22.30. WAIVER OF PENALTY

(a) The chief appraiser may waive the penalty imposed by Section 22.28 if the chief appraiser determines that the person exercised reasonable diligence to comply with or has substantially complied with the requirements of this chapter. A written request, accompanied by supporting documentation, stating the grounds on which penalties should be waived must be sent to the chief appraiser before June 1 or not later than the 30th day after the date the person received notification of the imposition of the penalty, whichever is later. The chief appraiser shall make a determination of the penalty waiver request:

(1) based on the information submitted; and

(2) after consideration of the factors described by Subsection (b).

(a-1) If the chief appraiser denies the penalty waiver request, the chief appraiser shall deliver by first class mail written notice of the denial to the property owner. The property owner may protest the imposition of the penalty before the appraisal review board. To initiate a protest, the property owner must file written notice of the protest with the appraisal review board before June 1 or not later than the 30th day after the date the property owner receives the notice of denial, whichever is later.

(b) The appraisal review board shall determine the protest after considering:

(1) the person's compliance history with respect to paying taxes and filing statements or reports;

(2) the type, nature, and taxability of the specific property involved;

(3) the type, nature, size, and sophistication of the person's business or other entity for which property is rendered;

(4) the completeness of the person's records;

(5) the person's reliance on advice provided by the appraisal district that may have contributed to the person's failure to comply and the imposition of the penalty;

(6) any change in appraisal district policy during the current or preceding tax year that may affect how property is rendered; and

(7) any other factors that may have caused the person to fail to timely file a statement or report.

(c) The procedures for a protest before the appraisal review board under this section are governed by the procedures for a taxpayer protest under Subchapter C, Chapter 41. The property owner is entitled to appeal under Chapter 42 an order of the appraisal review board determining a protest brought under this section.

(d) Notwithstanding any other provision of this section, the chief appraiser and a protesting property owner may enter into a settlement agreement on the matter being protested, if both parties agree that there was a mistake.

Sections 22.31-22.40 blank

SUBCHAPTER C. OTHER REPORTS

TAX §22.41. REPORT OF POLITICAL SUBDIVISION ACTIONS AFFECTING REAL PROPERTY VALUES

(a) At the request of the chief appraiser of an appraisal district in which a political subdivision of this state has territory, the governing body of the political subdivision shall deliver a written report to the chief appraiser describing each of the following actions taken by the governing body in the preceding period specified in the request:

(1) a zoning action;

(2) an action that directly restricts the use of real property or a class of real property specified by the action or that exempts real property or a class of real property specified by the action from an existing restriction on the use of the property; or

(3) an action that grants the owner or custodian of real property specified by the action the right or authority to make a change or improvement to the property.

(b) The report is not required to include an action that does not apply to real property in the appraisal district whose chief appraiser requested the report.

(c) The chief appraiser in the request for a report shall specify the period to be covered by the report. The governing body is not required to include in the report an action included in a previous report made to the chief appraiser of the same appraisal district. The governing body must deliver the report to the chief appraiser not later than the 30th day after the date of the request, unless the chief appraiser specifies or agrees to a later date.

(d) As soon as practicable after delivering a report to the chief appraiser under Subsection (c), the governing body making the report shall deliver a copy of the report to the governing body of each taxing unit in which is located property affected by an action included in the report.

SUBTITLE E. COLLECTIONS & DELINQUENCY

CHAPTER 31. COLLECTIONS

TAX §31.01. TAX BILLS

(a) Except as provided by Subsections (f), (i-1), and (k), the assessor for each taxing unit shall prepare and mail a tax bill to each person in whose name the property is listed on the tax roll and to the person's authorized agent. The assessor shall mail tax bills by October 1 or as soon thereafter as practicable. The assessor shall mail to the state agency or institution the tax bill for any taxable property owned by the agency or institution. The agency or institution shall pay the taxes from funds appropriated for payment of the taxes or, if there are none, from funds appropriated for the administration of the agency or institution. The exterior of the tax bill must show the return address of the taxing unit. If the assessor wants the United States Postal Service to return the tax bill if it is not deliverable as addressed, the exterior of the tax bill may contain, in all capital letters, the words "RETURN SERVICE REQUESTED," or another appropriate statement directing the United States Postal Service to return the tax bill if it is not deliverable as addressed.

(b) The county assessor-collector shall mail the tax bill for Permanent University Fund land to the comptroller. The comptroller shall pay all county tax bills on Permanent University Fund land with warrants drawn on the General Revenue Fund and mailed to the county assessors-collectors before February 1.

(c) The tax bill or a separate statement accompanying the tax bill shall:

(1) identify the property subject to the tax;

(2) state the appraised value, assessed value, and taxable value of the property;

(3) if the property is land appraised as provided by Subchapter C, D, E, or H, Chapter 23, state the market value and the taxable value for purposes of deferred or additional taxation as provided by Section 23.46, 23.55, 23.76, or 23.9807, as applicable;

(4) state the assessment ratio for the unit;

(5) state the type and amount of any partial exemption applicable to the property, indicating whether it applies to appraised or assessed value;

(6) state the total tax rate for the unit;

(7) state the amount of tax due, the due date, and the delinquency date;

(8) explain the payment option and discounts provided by Sections 31.03 and 31.05, if available to the unit's taxpayers, and state the date on which each of the discount periods provided by Section 31.05 concludes, if the discounts are available;

(9) state the rates of penalty and interest imposed for delinquent payment of the tax;

(10) include the name and telephone number of the assessor for the unit and, if different, of the collector for the unit;

(11) for real property, state for the current tax year and each of the preceding five tax years:

(A) the appraised value and taxable value of the property;

(B) the total tax rate for the unit;

(C) the amount of taxes imposed on the property by the unit; and

(D) the difference, expressed as a percent increase or decrease, as applicable, in the amount of taxes imposed on the property by the unit compared to the amount imposed for the preceding tax year; and

(12) for real property, state the differences, expressed as a percent increase or decrease, as applicable, in the following for the current tax year as compared to the fifth tax year before that tax year:

(A) the appraised value and taxable value of the property;

(B) the total tax rate for the unit; and

(C) the amount of taxes imposed on the property by the unit.

(c-1) If for any of the preceding six tax years any information required by Subsection (c)(11) or (12) to be included in a tax bill or separate statement is unavailable, the tax bill or statement must state that the information is not available for that year.

(c-2) For a tax bill that includes back taxes on an improvement that escaped taxation in a prior year, the tax bill or separate statement described by Subsection (c) must state that no interest is due on the back taxes if those back taxes are paid not later than the 120th day after the date the tax bill is sent.

(d) Each tax bill shall also state the amount of penalty, if any, imposed pursuant to Sections 23.431, 23.54, 23.541, 23.75, 23.751, 23.87, 23.97, and 23.9804.

(d-1) This subsection applies only to a school district. In addition to stating the total tax rate for the school district, the tax bill or the separate statement shall separately state:

(1) the maintenance and operations rate of the school district;

(2) if the school district has outstanding debt, as defined by Section 26.012, the debt rate of the district;

(3) the maintenance and operations rate of the school district for the preceding tax year;

(4) if for the current tax year the school district imposed taxes for debt, as defined by Section 26.012, the debt rate of the district for the current tax year;

(5) if for the preceding tax year the school district imposed taxes for debt, as defined by Section 26.012, the debt rate of the district for that year; and

(6) the total tax rate of the district for the preceding tax year.

(d-2) to (d-5) Expired.

(e) An assessor may include taxes for more than one taxing unit in the same tax bill, but he shall include the information required by Subsection (c) of this section for the tax imposed by each unit included in the bill.

(f) A collector may provide that a tax bill not be sent until the total amount of unpaid taxes the collector collects on the property for all taxing units the collector serves is $15 or more. A collector may not send a tax bill for an amount of taxes less than $15 if before the tax bill is prepared the property owner files a written request with the collector that a tax bill not be sent until the total amount of unpaid taxes the collector collects on the property is $15 or more. The request applies to all subsequent taxes the collector collects on the property until the property owner in writing revokes the request or the person no longer owns the property.

(g) Except as provided by Subsection (f), failure to send or receive the tax bill required by this section, including a tax bill that has been requested to be sent by electronic means under Subsection (k), does not affect the validity of the tax, penalty, or interest, the due date, the existence of a tax lien, or any procedure instituted to collect a tax.

(h) An assessor who assesses taxes for more than one taxing unit may prepare and deliver separate bills for the taxes of a taxing unit that does not adopt a tax rate for the year before the 60th day after the date the chief appraiser certifies the appraisal roll for the unit under Section 26.01 of this code or, if the taxing unit participates in more than one appraisal district, before the 60th day after the date it receives a certified appraisal roll from any of the appraisal districts in which it participates. If separate tax bills are prepared and delivered under this subsection, the taxing unit or taxing units that failed to adopt the tax rate before the prescribed deadline must pay the additional costs incurred in preparing and mailing the separate bills in addition to any other compensation required or agreed to be paid for the appraisal services rendered.

(i) For a city or town that imposes an additional sales and use tax under Section 321.101(b) of this code, or a county that imposes a sales and use tax under Chapter 323 of this code, the tax bill shall indicate the amount of additional ad valorem taxes, if any, that would have been imposed on the property if additional ad valorem taxes had been imposed in an amount equal to the amount of revenue estimated to be collected from the additional city sales and use tax or from the county sales and use tax, as applicable, for the year determined as provided by Section 26.041 of this code.

(i-1) If an assessor mails a tax bill under Subsection (a) or delivers a tax bill by electronic means under Subsection (k) to a mortgagee of a property, the assessor is not required to mail or deliver by electronic means a copy of the bill to any mortgagor under the mortgage or to the mortgagor's authorized agent.

(j) If a tax bill is mailed under Subsection (a) or delivered by electronic means under Subsection (k) to a mortgagee of a property, the mortgagee shall mail a copy

of the bill to the owner of the property not more than 30 days following the mortgagee's receipt of the bill.

(k) The assessor for a taxing unit shall deliver a tax bill as required by this section by electronic means if on or before September 15 the individual or entity entitled to receive a tax bill under this section and the assessor enter into an agreement for delivery of a tax bill by electronic means. An assessor who delivers a tax bill electronically under this subsection is not required to mail the same bill under Subsection (a). An agreement entered into under this subsection:

(1) must:

(A) be in writing or in an electronic format;

(B) be signed by the assessor and the individual or entity entitled to receive the tax bill under this section;

(C) be in a format acceptable to the assessor;

(D) specify the electronic means by which the tax bill is to be delivered; and

(E) specify the e-mail address to which the tax bill is to be delivered; and

(2) remains in effect for all subsequent tax bills until revoked by an authorized individual in a written revocation filed with the assessor.

(*l*) The comptroller may:

(1) prescribe acceptable media, formats, content, and methods for the delivery of tax bills by electronic means under Subsection (k); and

(2) provide a model form agreement.

TAX §31.02. DELINQUENCY DATE

(a) Except as provided by Subsection (b) of this section and by Sections 31.03 and 31.04 of this code, taxes are due on receipt of the tax bill and are delinquent if not paid before February 1 of the year following the year in which imposed.

(a-1) Expired.

(b) An eligible person serving on active duty in any branch of the United States armed forces during a war or national emergency declared in accordance with federal law may pay delinquent property taxes on property in which the person owns any interest without penalty or interest no later than the 60th day after the date on which the earliest of the following occurs:

(1) the person is discharged from active military service;

(2) the person returns to the state for more than 10 days;

(3) the person returns to non-active duty status in the reserves; or

(4) the war or national emergency ends.

(c) "Eligible person" means a person on active military duty in this state who was transferred out of this state as a result of a war or national emergency declared in accordance with federal law or a person in the reserve forces who was placed on active military duty and transferred out of this state as a result of a war or national emergency declared in accordance with federal law.

(d) A person eligible under Subsection (b) or any co-owner of property that is owned by an eligible person may notify the county tax assessor or collector or central appraisal district for the county in which the property is located of the person's eligibility for exemption under Subsection (b). The county tax assessor or collector or central appraisal district shall provide the forms necessary for those individuals giving notice under this subsection. If the notice is timely given, a taxing unit in the county may not bring suit for delinquent taxes for the tax year in which the notice is given. Failure to file a notice does not affect eligibility for the waiver of penalties and interest.

(e) On verification that notice was properly filed under Subsection (d), a suit for delinquent taxes must be abated without cost to the defendant. The exemptions provided for under this section shall immediately stop all actions against eligible persons until the person's eligibility expires as provided in Subsection (b).

(f) This section applies only to property in which the person eligible for the exemption owned an interest on the date the person was transferred out of this state as described by Subsection (c) or in which the person acquired the interest by gift, devise, or inheritance after that date.

(g) For the purposes of this section, a person is considered to be on active military duty if the person is covered by the Soldiers' and Sailors' Civil Relief Act of 1940 (50 App. U.S.C. Section 501 et seq.) or the Uniformed Services Employment and Reemployment Rights Act of 1994 (38 U.S.C. Section 4301 et seq.), as amended.

(h) Repealed by Acts 2003, 78th Leg., ch. 129, §2, eff. May 28, 2003.

TAX §31.03. SPLIT PAYMENT OF TAXES

(a) The governing body of a taxing unit that collects its own taxes may provide, in the manner required by law for official action by the body, that a person who pays one-half of the unit's taxes before December 1 may pay the remaining one-half of the taxes without penalty or interest before July 1 of the following year.

(b) Except as provided by Subsection (d), the split-payment option, if adopted, applies to taxes for all units for which the adopting taxing unit collects taxes.

(c) If one or more taxing units contract with the appraisal district for collection of taxes, the split-payment option provided by Subsection (a) of this section does not apply to taxes collected by the district unless approved by resolution adopted by a majority of the governing bodies of the taxing units whose taxes the district collects and filed with the secretary of the appraisal district board of directors. After an appraisal district provides for the split-payment option, the option applies to all taxes collected by the district until revoked. It may be revoked in the same manner as provided for adoption.

(d) This subsection applies only to a taxing unit located in a county having a population of not less than 285,000 and not more than 300,000 that borders a county having a population of 3.3 million or more and the Gulf of Mexico. The governing body of a taxing unit that has its taxes collected by another taxing unit that has adopted the split-payment option under Subsection (a) may provide, in the manner required by law for official action by the body, that the split-payment option does not apply to the taxing unit's taxes collected by the other taxing unit.

A TAX §31.031. INSTALLMENT PAYMENTS OF CERTAIN HOMESTEAD TAXES

Subsection (a) was reenacted by S.B. 1047, §1, 85th Leg., eff. Jan. 1, 2018.

(a) This section applies only to:

(1) an individual who is:

(A) disabled or at least 65 years of age; and

(B) qualified for an exemption under Section 11.13(c); or

(2) an individual who is:

(A) a disabled veteran or the unmarried surviving spouse of a disabled veteran; and

(B) qualified for an exemption under Section 11.132 or 11.22.

(a-1) An individual to whom this section applies may pay a taxing unit's taxes imposed on property that the person owns and occupies as a residence homestead in four equal installments without penalty or interest if the first installment is paid before the delinquency date and is accompanied by notice to the taxing unit that the person will pay the remaining taxes in three equal installments. If the delinquency date is February 1, the second installment must be paid before April 1, the third installment must be paid before June 1, and the fourth installment must be paid before August 1. If the delinquency date is a date other than February 1, the second installment must be paid before the first day of the second month after the delinquency date, the third installment must be paid before the first day of the fourth month after the delinquency date, and the fourth installment must be paid before the first day of the sixth month after the delinquency date.

(a-2) Notwithstanding the deadline prescribed by Subsection (a-1) for payment of the first installment, an individual to whom this section applies may pay the taxes in four equal installments as provided by Subsection (a-1) if the first installment is paid and the required notice is provided before the first day of the first month after the delinquency date.

(b) If the individual fails to make a payment, including the first payment, before the applicable date provided by Subsection (a-1), the unpaid installment is delinquent and incurs a penalty of six percent and interest as provided by Section 33.01(c). The penalty provided by Section 33.01(a) does not apply to the unpaid installment.

(c) An individual may pay more than the amount due for each installment and the amount in excess of the amount due shall be credited to the next installment. An individual may not pay less than the total amount due for each installment unless the collector provides for the acceptance of partial payments under this section. If the collector accepts a partial payment, penalties and interest are incurred only by the amount of each installment that remains unpaid on the applicable date provided by Subsection (a-1).

(d) Repealed by Acts 2015, 84th Leg., ch. 226, §6, eff. Sept. 1, 2015.

2017 Legislation: Amended by S.B. 1047, §1, 85th Leg., eff. Jan. 1, 2018.

A

TAX §31.032. INSTALLMENT PAYMENTS OF TAXES ON PROPERTY IN DISASTER AREA

(a) This section applies only to:

(1) real property that:

(A) is:

(i) the residence homestead of the owner or consists of property that is used for residential purposes and that has fewer than five living units; or

(ii) owned or leased by a business entity that had not more than the amount calculated as provided by Subsection (h) in gross receipts in the entity's most recent federal tax year or state franchise tax annual period, according to the applicable federal income tax return or state franchise tax report of the entity;

(B) is located in a disaster area; and

(C) has been damaged as a direct result of the disaster;

(2) tangible personal property that is owned or leased by a business entity described by Subdivision (1)(A)(ii); and

(3) taxes that are imposed on the property by a taxing unit before the first anniversary of the disaster.

(b) A person may pay a taxing unit's taxes imposed on property that the person owns in four equal installments without penalty or interest if the first installment is paid [~~If,~~] before the delinquency date and is [~~, a person pays at least one-fourth of a taxing unit's taxes imposed on property that the person owns,~~] accompanied by notice to the taxing unit that the person will pay the remaining taxes in [~~installments, the person may pay the remaining taxes without penalty or interest in~~] three equal installments. If the delinquency date is February 1, the second [~~first~~] installment must be paid before April 1, the third [~~second~~] installment must be paid before June 1, and the fourth [~~third~~] installment must be paid before August 1. If the delinquency date is a date other than February 1, the second [~~first~~] installment must be paid before the first day of the second month after the delinquency date, the third [~~second~~] installment must be paid before the first day of the fourth month after the delinquency date, and the fourth [~~third~~] installment must be paid before the first day of the sixth month after the delinquency date.

(b-1) Notwithstanding the deadline prescribed by Subsection (b) for payment of the first installment, a person to whom this section applies may pay the taxes in four equal installments as provided by Subsection (b) if the first installment is paid and the required notice is provided before the first day of the first month after the delinquency date.

(c) If the person fails to make a payment before the applicable date provided by Subsection (b), the unpaid installment is delinquent and incurs a penalty of six percent and interest as provided by Section 33.01(c).

(d) A person may pay more than the amount due for each installment and the amount in excess of the amount due shall be credited to the next installment. A person may not pay less than the total amount due for each installment unless the collector provides for the acceptance of partial payments under this section. If the collector accepts a partial payment, penalties and interest are incurred only by the amount of each installment that remains unpaid on the applicable date provided by Subsection (b).

(e) Repealed by Acts 2015, 84th Leg., ch. 226, §6, eff. Sept. 1, 2015.

(f) The comptroller shall adopt rules to implement this section.

(g) In this section:

(1) "Disaster" has the meaning assigned by Section 418.004, Government Code.

(2) "Disaster area" has the meaning assigned by Section 151.350.

(h) For the 2009 tax year, the limit on gross receipts under Subsection (a)(1)(A)(ii) is $5 million. For each subsequent tax year, the comptroller shall adjust the limit to reflect inflation by using the index that the comptroller considers to most accurately report changes in the purchasing power of the dollar for consumers in this state and shall publicize the adjusted limit. Each collector shall use the adjusted limit as calculated by the comptroller under this subsection to determine whether property is owned or leased by a business entity described by Subsection (a)(1)(A)(ii).

2017 Legislation: Amended by S.B. 1047, §2, 85th Leg., eff. Jan. 1, 2018.

TAX §31.035. PERFORMANCE OF SERVICE IN LIEU OF PAYMENT OF TAXES ON HOMESTEAD OF ELDERLY PERSON

(a) The governing body of a taxing unit by order or resolution may permit an individual who is at least 65 years of age to perform service for the taxing unit in lieu of paying taxes imposed by the taxing unit on prop-

erty owned by the individual and occupied as the individual's residence homestead.

(b) The governing body of the taxing unit shall determine:

(1) the number of property owners who will be permitted to perform service for the taxing unit under this section; and

(2) the maximum number of hours of service that a property owner may perform for the taxing unit under this section.

(c) The governing body shall require that each property owner permitted to perform service for the taxing unit under this section execute a contract with the taxing unit. The contract must be executed before the delinquency date and must:

(1) specify:

(A) the nature of the service that the property owner will perform for the taxing unit;

(B) the facility or location where the service will be performed;

(C) the number of hours of service the property owner will perform; and

(D) when the property owner will perform the service; and

(2) set out or describe the provisions of Subsections (d), (e), and (f).

(d) For each hour of service performed for the taxing unit, the property owner receives a credit against the taxes owed in an amount equal to the amount that would be earned by working one hour at the federal hourly minimum wage rate. The contract must require the property owner to perform the service not later than one year after the delinquency date for the taxes against which the property owner receives credit.

(e) Taxes for which the property owner is to receive credit under the contract do not become delinquent on the delinquency date otherwise provided by this chapter as long as the contract is in effect and are considered paid when the service is performed. If the property owner fails to perform the service, or if the taxing unit determines that the service of the property owner is unsatisfactory, the taxing unit shall terminate the contract and notify the property owner of the termination. The unpaid taxes for which the property owner was to receive credit under the contract for service not yet performed become delinquent and incur penalty and interest provided by Section 33.01 on the later of:

(1) the delinquency date otherwise provided by this chapter for the unpaid taxes; or

(2) the first day of the next calendar month that begins at least 21 days after the date the taxing unit delivers notice to the property owner that the contract has been terminated.

(f) While performing service for a taxing unit, the property owner:

(1) is not an employee of the taxing unit; and

(2) is not entitled to any benefit, including workers' compensation coverage, that the taxing unit provides to an employee of the taxing unit.

(g) Property owners performing services for a taxing unit under this section may only supplement or complement the regular personnel of the taxing unit. A taxing unit may not reduce the number of persons the taxing unit employs or reduce the number of hours to be worked by employees of the taxing unit because the taxing unit permits property owners to perform services for the taxing unit under this section.

(h) A person performing service for a taxing unit under this section is not entitled to indemnification from the taxing unit for injury or property damage the person sustains or liability the person incurs in performing service under this section. The taxing unit is not liable for any damages arising from an act or omission of the person in performing service under this section.

TAX §31.036. PERFORMANCE OF TEACHING SERVICES IN LIEU OF PAYMENT OF SCHOOL TAXES ON HOMESTEAD

(a) The governing body of a school district by resolution may permit qualified individuals to perform teaching services for the school district at a junior high school or high school of the district in lieu of paying taxes imposed by the district on property owned and occupied by the individual as a residence homestead.

(b) The governing body of the school district shall determine:

(1) the number of qualified individuals who will be permitted to perform teaching services for the district under this section;

(2) the courses that a qualified individual may teach for the district under this section; and

(3) the amount of the tax credit that a qualified individual may earn.

(c) The governing body shall require that each qualified individual permitted to perform teaching services for the district under this section execute a contract with the district. The contract must be executed before the delinquency date and must:

(1) specify:

(A) the course or courses that the qualified individual will teach for the district;

(B) the high school or junior high school of the district where the qualified individual will perform the teaching services;

(C) the semester in which the qualified individual will perform the teaching services; and

(D) the amount of the tax credit that the qualified individual will receive on successful completion of the individual's contractual obligations; and

(2) set out or describe the provisions of Subsections (d)-(g).

(d) A qualified individual who teaches a course for an entire school semester is entitled to a maximum credit of $500 against the taxes imposed, except that if the qualified individual teaches a course for which a student receives a full year's credit for one semester, the qualified individual is entitled to a maximum credit of $1,000 for each such course taught for one semester by the qualified individual. A qualified individual may not receive credits for teaching more than two courses in any school year.

(e) The district shall terminate the contract if:

(1) the qualified individual fails to perform the teaching services; or

(2) the district determines that the teaching services of the qualified individual are unsatisfactory.

(f) If the contract is terminated under Subsection (e), on the termination date the district may grant the individual a portion of the tax credit based on the portion of the teaching services performed.

(g) While performing teaching services for a school district, the qualified individual:

(1) is not an employee of the district; and

(2) is not entitled to any benefit, including workers' compensation coverage, that the district provides to an employee of the district.

(h) An individual is qualified to perform teaching services for a school district under this section only if the individual holds a baccalaureate or more advanced degree in a field related to each course to be taught and:

(1) is certified as a classroom teacher under Subchapter B, Chapter 21, Education Code; or

(2) obtains a school district teaching permit under Section 21.055, Education Code.

TAX §31.037. PERFORMANCE OF TEACHING SERVICES BY EMPLOYEE IN LIEU OF PAYMENT OF SCHOOL TAXES ON PROPERTY OF BUSINESS ENTITY

(a) The governing body of a school district by resolution may authorize a corporation or other business entity to permit a qualified individual employed by the business entity to perform teaching services in a high school or a junior high school for the school district in lieu of paying taxes imposed by the district on property owned by the business entity.

(b) The governing body of the school district shall determine:

(1) the number of business entities that will be eligible for a tax credit under this section;

(2) the courses that an employee of the business entity may teach for the district under this section; and

(3) the amount of the tax credit that a business entity may earn.

(c) The governing body shall require that each business entity permitted to provide an employee to perform teaching services for the district under this section execute a contract with the district. The contract must be executed before the delinquency date and must:

(1) specify:

(A) the course or courses that the employee will teach for the district;

(B) the high school or junior high school of the district where the employee will perform the teaching services;

(C) the semester in which the employee will perform the teaching services; and

(D) the amount of the tax credit that the business entity will receive on successful completion of the contractual obligations of the business entity and its employee; and

(2) set out or describe the provisions of Subsections (d)-(h).

(d) For each course taught for the entire school semester by an employee of the business entity for the school district, the business entity is entitled to a maximum credit of $500 against the taxes imposed, except that if the employee teaches a course for which a student receives a full year's credit for one semester, the business entity is entitled to a maximum credit of $1,000 for each such course taught for one semester by the employee.

(e) The district shall terminate the contract if:

(1) the employee fails to perform the teaching services; or

(2) the district determines that the teaching services of the employee of the business entity are unsatisfactory.

(f) If the contract is terminated under Subsection (e), on the termination date the district may grant the business entity a portion of the tax credit based on the portion of the teaching services performed.

(g) While performing teaching services for a school district, the employee of the business entity:

(1) is not an employee of the district; and

(2) is not entitled to any benefit, including workers' compensation coverage, that the district provides to an employee of the district.

(h) An individual may not perform teaching services for which a business entity receives a tax credit under this section if the individual enters into a contract with the same school district to provide teaching services for a tax credit for the same tax year under Section 31.036.

(i) An individual is qualified to perform teaching services for a school district under this section only if the individual holds a baccalaureate or more advanced degree in a field related to the course to be taught and:

(1) is certified as a classroom teacher under Subchapter B, Chapter 21, Education Code; or

(2) obtains a school district teaching permit under Section 21.055, Education Code.

TAX §31.04. POSTPONEMENT OF DELINQUENCY DATE

(a) If a tax bill is mailed after January 10, the delinquency date provided by Section 31.02 of this code is postponed to the first day of the next month that will provide a period of at least 21 days after the date of mailing for payment of taxes before delinquent unless the taxing unit has adopted the discounts provided by Section 31.05(c) of this code, in which case the delinquency date is determined by Subsection (d) of this section.

(a-1) If a tax bill is mailed that includes taxes for one or more preceding tax years because the property was erroneously omitted from the tax roll in those tax years, the delinquency date provided by Section 31.02 is postponed to February 1 of the first year that will provide a period of at least 180 days after the date the tax bill is mailed in which to pay the taxes before they become delinquent.

(b) If the delinquency date is postponed as provided by this section, the assessor who mails the bills shall notify the governing body of each taxing unit whose taxes are included in the bills of the postponement.

(c) A payment option provided by Section 31.03 of this code or a discount adopted under Section 31.05(b) of this code does not apply to taxes that are calculated too late for it to be available.

(d) If a taxing unit mails its tax bills after September 30 and adopts the discounts provided by Section 31.05(c) of this code, the delinquency date is postponed to the first day of the next month following the fourth full calendar month following the date the tax bills were mailed.

(e) If the delinquency date for a tax is postponed under Subsection (a) or (a-1), that postponed delinquency date is the date on which penalties and interest begin to be incurred on the tax as provided by Section 33.01.

TAX §31.05. DISCOUNTS

(a) The governing body of a taxing unit may adopt the discounts provided by Subsection (b) or Subsection (c), or both, in the manner required by law for official action by the body. The discounts, if adopted, apply only to that taxing unit's taxes. If a taxing unit adopts both discounts under Subsections (b) and (c), the discounts adopted under Subsection (b) apply unless the tax bills for the unit are mailed after September 30, in which case only the discounts under Subsection (c) apply. A taxing unit that collects taxes for another taxing unit that adopts the discounts may prepare and mail separate tax bills on behalf of the adopting taxing unit and may charge an additional fee for preparing and mailing the separate tax bills and for collecting the taxes imposed by the adopting taxing unit. If under an intergovernmental contract a county assessor-collector collects taxes for a taxing unit that adopts the discounts, the

county assessor-collector may terminate the contract if the county has adopted a discount policy that is different from the discount policy adopted by the adopting taxing unit.

(b) A taxing unit may adopt the following discounts to apply regardless of the date on which it mails its tax bills:

(1) three percent if the tax is paid in October or earlier;

(2) two percent if the tax is paid in November; and

(3) one percent if the tax is paid in December.

(c) A taxing unit may adopt the following discounts to apply when it mails its tax bills after September 30:

(1) three percent if the tax is paid before or during the next full calendar month following the date on which the tax bills were mailed;

(2) two percent if the tax is paid during the second full calendar month following the date on which the tax bills were mailed; and

(3) one percent if the tax is paid during the third full calendar month following the date on which the tax bills were mailed.

(d) The governing body of a taxing unit may rescind a discount adopted by the governing body in the manner required by law for official action by the body. The rescission of a discount takes effect in the tax year following the year in which the discount is rescinded.

TAX §31.06. MEDIUM OF PAYMENT

(a) Except as provided by Section 31.061, taxes are payable only as provided by this section. A collector shall accept United States currency or a check or money order in payment of taxes and shall accept payment by credit card or electronic funds transfer.

(b) Acceptance by a collector of a check or money order or of payment by credit card constitutes payment of a tax as of the date of acceptance if the check, money order, or credit card invoice is duly paid or honored. If the check, money order, or credit card invoice is not duly paid or honored, the collector shall deliver written notice of nonpayment to the person who attempted payment by check, money order, or credit card. Until payment is made in full by cash or by a check, money order, or credit card that is duly paid or honored, the lien securing payment of the tax remains in effect, whether or not the person receives notice of nonpayment.

(c) If a tax is paid by credit card, the collector may collect a fee for processing the payment. The collector shall set the fee in an amount that is reasonably related to the expense incurred by the collector or taxing unit in processing the payment by credit card, not to exceed five percent of the amount of taxes and any penalties or interest being paid. The fee is in addition to the amount of taxes, penalties, or interest.

(d) If a check or money order accepted in payment of taxes or the invoice for a payment of taxes by credit card is not duly paid or honored, the amount of any charge against the taxing unit for processing the check, order, or credit card invoice is added to the amount of tax due in the same manner as penalties and interest are added for taxes that are delinquent. The tax lien on the property also secures payment of the amount of the charge.

TAX §31.061. PAYMENT OF TAXES ASSESSED AGAINST REAL PROPERTY BY CONVEYANCE TO TAXING UNIT OF PROPERTY

(a) An owner of real property may, subject to the approval of the governing body of all of the taxing units, by deed convey the property to the taxing unit that is owed the largest amount of the taxes, penalties, and interest assessed against the property in payment of the taxes, including delinquent taxes, penalties, and interest assessed against the property by each taxing unit. The taxing unit acquiring the property holds title to the property on behalf of each taxing unit. The lien of each taxing unit on the property conveyed is extinguished at the time of the conveyance. The taxing unit acquiring the property may, subject to the approval of the governing body of another taxing unit, by deed convey the property to that taxing unit. The taxing unit acquiring the property holds title to the property on behalf of each taxing unit.

(b) A taxing unit acquiring property under this section may sell the property. The sale may be conducted in a manner provided by Section 34.05. If the taxing unit sells the property within six months after the date the owner conveys the property, the taxing unit shall pay to each taxing unit its proportionate share of the sale proceeds according to each taxing unit's share of the total amount of the taxes, penalties, and interest owed at the time of the acquisition.

(c) A taxing unit that does not sell property acquired under this section within six months after the date the owner conveys the property shall pay to each taxing unit its proportionate share, as determined un-

der Subsection (b), of the appraised market value of the property as shown on the most recent tax roll, less the value of all encumbrances burdening the property. On making the payment provided by this subsection, the taxing unit owns the property outright and not on behalf of each taxing unit. The period during which a taxing unit may hold title to the property on behalf of each taxing unit may be extended subject to the approval of the governing body of each taxing unit.

(d) The collector shall credit against the taxes, penalties, and interest owed each taxing unit:

(1) the taxing unit's share, as determined under Subsection (b), of the sale price if the property is sold within six months after the date the owner conveys the property; or

(2) the taxing unit's share, as determined under Subsection (b), of the appraised market value of the property as shown on the most recent tax roll, less the value of all encumbrances burdening the property, if the property is not sold within six months after the date the owner conveys the property.

(e) The owner remains personally liable to each taxing unit to the extent the amount of the taxes, penalties, and interest owed each taxing unit exceeds the amount credited under Subsection (d). The owner is entitled to a refund from each taxing unit to the extent the amount credited under Subsection (d) exceeds the amount of the taxes, penalties, and interest owed the taxing unit.

(f) A conveyance of property to a taxing unit under this section is voidable by the taxing unit at any time that the taxing unit owns the property and determines that the condition of the property on the date the owner conveyed it was or may have been in violation of a federal or state law, regulation, rule, or order. If the taxing unit voids the conveyance:

(1) the taxing unit shall execute a quitclaim deed of the property to the owner, file the deed in the county records, and give notice of the deed and its filing to the owner;

(2) the collector shall remove the credit against the taxes, penalties, and interest owed each taxing unit made under this section;

(3) a taxing unit that does not acquire the property shall refund the payment made to it by the taxing unit that acquires the property and reinstate the taxes, penalties, and interest owed the taxing unit; and

(4) the lien of each taxing unit is reinstated as of the date it originally attached.

(g) Repealed by Acts 1997, 75th Leg., ch. 1111, §8, eff. Sept. 1, 1997.

TAX §31.07. CERTAIN PAYMENTS ACCEPTED

(a) A person may pay the tax imposed on any one property without simultaneously paying taxes imposed on other property he owns.

(b) A collector shall accept payment of the tax imposed on a property by a taxing unit that has adopted the discounts under Section 31.05 of this code separately from taxes imposed on that property by other taxing units using the same collector, even if the taxes are included in the same bill. The collector may adopt a policy of accepting separate payments in other circumstances. If the tax paid is included in the same bill as other taxes that are not paid, the collector shall send a revised bill or receipt to reflect the tax payment, if a discount applies to the payment, and may send a revised bill or receipt to reflect the tax payment in other circumstances. The sending of a revised bill does not affect the date on which the unpaid taxes become delinquent.

(c) A collector may adopt a policy of accepting partial payments of property taxes. A payment option provided by Section 31.03 of this code or a discount adopted under Section 31.05 of this code does not apply to any portion of a partial payment. If a collector accepts a partial payment on a tax bill that includes taxes for more than one taxing unit, the collector shall allocate the partial payment among all the taxing units included in the bill in proportion to the amount of tax included in the bill for each taxing unit, unless the collector under Subsection (b) has adopted a policy of accepting payments of a taxing unit's taxes separate from the taxes of other taxing units included in the same bill and the taxpayer directs that the partial payment be allocated in specific amounts to one or more specific taxing units. Acceptance of a partial payment does not affect the date that the tax becomes delinquent, but the penalties and interest provided by Section 33.01 of this code are incurred only by the portion of a tax that remains unpaid on the date the tax becomes delinquent.

(d) Notwithstanding Subsection (c), a collector shall accept a partial payment of property taxes on a tax bill that includes taxes for more than one taxing unit if one or more of the taxing units has adopted the dis-

counts under Section 31.05 of this code, the taxpayer directs that the partial payment be allocated first to the payment of the taxes owed one or more of the taxing units that have adopted the discounts, and the amount of the payment is equal to or greater than the amount of the taxes owed the taxing units designated by the taxpayer.

TAX §31.071. CONDITIONAL PAYMENTS

(a) The collector of a taxing unit shall accept conditional payments of taxes before the delinquency date for property taxes that are subject to a pending challenge or protest.

(b) A property owner whose property is subject to a pending protest or challenge may pay the tax due on the amount of value of the property involved in the pending action that is not in dispute or the amount of tax paid on the property in the preceding year, whichever is greater, but not to exceed the amount of tax that would be due on the appraised value that is subject to protest or challenge. The collector of the taxing unit shall provide the property owner with a temporary receipt of taxes paid under this section.

(c) If the property is no longer subject to a challenge, protest, or appeal at any time before the delinquency date, the collector shall apply the amount paid by the property owner under this section to the tax imposed on the property and shall refund the remainder, if any, to the property owner. If the property is still subject to an appeal on the last working day before the delinquency date, or at an earlier date if so requested by the property owner, the collector shall apply the amount paid under this section to the payment required by Section 42.08(b) of this code and shall retain the remainder, if any, until the appeal is completed. When the appeal is completed, the collector shall apply any amount retained under this section to the tax ultimately imposed on the property that is not covered by the payment under Section 42.08(b) and shall refund the remainder, if any, to the property owner.

TAX §31.072. ESCROW ACCOUNTS

(a) The collector for a taxing unit may enter a contract with a property owner under which the property owner deposits money in an escrow account maintained by the collector to provide for the payment of property taxes collected by the collector on any property the person owns.

(b) A contract may not be made before October 1 of the year preceding the tax year for which the account is established. The collector may agree to establish a combined account for more than one item of property having the same owner on the property owner's request. If a collector collects taxes for more than one taxing unit, an account must apply to taxes on the affected property for each of the taxing units.

(c) A contract under this section must require the property owner to make monthly deposits to the escrow account until the amount set in the contract under Subsection (d) of this section accrues in the account or until the tax bill for the property is prepared, whichever occurs earlier.

(d) On request by a property owner to establish an escrow account under this section, the collector shall estimate the amount of taxes to be imposed on the property by the affected taxing units in that year. A contract to establish an escrow account must provide for deposits that would provide, as of the date the collector estimates the tax bill for the property will be prepared, a total deposit that is not less than the amount of taxes estimated by the collector or the amount of taxes imposed on the property by the affected taxing units in the preceding year, whichever is less. The collector may agree to a deposit of a greater amount on the property owner's request.

(e) The county tax assessor-collector shall maintain the escrow account in the county depository. Any other collector shall maintain the escrow account in the depository of the taxing unit or other entity that employs the collector. The collector is not required to maintain a separate account in the depository for each escrow account but shall maintain separate records for each escrow account.

(f) The property owner may withdraw from the collector the money the owner deposited in an escrow account only if the withdrawal is made before the date the tax bill is prepared or October 1 of the tax year, whichever occurs earlier. On and after that date and until the taxes are paid, the collector must agree to a withdrawal by the taxpayer. The property owner may not withdraw less than the total amount deposited in the escrow account.

(g) When the tax bill is prepared for property for which an escrow account is established, the collector shall apply the money in the account to the taxes imposed and deliver a tax receipt to the taxpayer together

with a refund of any amount in the account in excess of the amount of taxes paid. If the amount in the escrow account is not sufficient to pay the taxes in full, the collector shall apply the money to the taxes and deliver to the taxpayer a tax receipt for the partial payment and a tax bill for the unpaid amount. If the escrow account applies to more than one taxing unit or to more than one item of property, the collector shall apply the amount to each taxing unit or item of property in proportion to the amount of taxes imposed unless the contract provides otherwise.

(h) Notwithstanding Subsection (a), if the property owner requesting a collector to establish an escrow account under this section is a disabled veteran as defined by Section 11.22 or a recipient of the Purple Heart, the Congressional Medal of Honor, the Bronze Star Medal, the Silver Star, the Legion of Merit, or a service cross awarded by a branch of the United States armed forces and the escrow account is to be used solely to provide for the payment of property taxes collected by the collector on the property owner's residence homestead, the collector shall enter into a contract with the property owner under this section.

(i) Notwithstanding Subsection (a), if the property owner requesting a collector to establish an escrow account under this section is the owner of a manufactured home and the escrow account is to be used solely to provide for the payment of property taxes collected by the collector on the property owner's manufactured home, the collector shall enter into a contract with the property owner under this section.

TAX §31.073. RESTRICTED OR CONDITIONAL PAYMENTS PROHIBITED

A restriction or condition placed on a check in payment of taxes, penalties, or interest by the maker that limits the amount of taxes, penalties, or interest owed to an amount less than that stated in the tax bill or shown by the tax collector's records is void unless the restriction or condition is authorized by this code.

TAX §31.075. TAX RECEIPT

(a) At the request of a property owner or a property owner's agent, the collector for a taxing unit shall issue a receipt showing the taxable value and the amount of tax imposed by the unit on the property in one or more tax years for which the information is requested, the tax rate for each of those tax years, and the amount of tax paid in each of those years. The receipt must describe the property in the manner prescribed by the comptroller. If the amount of the tax for the current year has not been calculated when the request is made, the collector shall on request issue to the property owner or agent a statement indicating that taxes for the current year have not been calculated.

(b) In any judicial proceeding, including a suit to collect delinquent taxes under Chapter 33 of this code, a tax receipt issued under this section that states that a tax has been paid constitutes prima facie evidence that the tax has been paid as stated by the receipt.

TAX §31.08. TAX CERTIFICATE

(a) At the request of any person, a collector for a taxing unit shall issue a certificate showing the amount of delinquent taxes, penalties, interest, and any known costs and expenses under Section 33.48 due the unit on a property according to the unit's current tax records. If the collector collects taxes for more than one taxing unit, the certificate must show the amount of delinquent taxes, penalties, interest, and any known costs and expenses under Section 33.48 due on the property to each taxing unit for which the collector collects the taxes. The collector shall charge a fee not to exceed $10 for each certificate issued. The collector shall pay all fees collected under this section into the treasury of the taxing unit that employs the collector.

(b) Except as provided by Subsection (c) of this section, if a person transfers property accompanied by a tax certificate that erroneously indicates that no delinquent taxes, penalties, or interest are due a taxing unit on the property or that fails to include property because of its omission from an appraisal roll as described under Section 25.21, the unit's tax lien on the property is extinguished and the purchaser of the property is absolved of liability to the unit for delinquent taxes, penalties, or interest on the property or for taxes based on omitted property. The person who was liable for the tax for the year the tax was imposed or the property was omitted remains personally liable for the tax and for any penalties or interest.

(c) A tax certificate issued through fraud or collusion is void.

TAX §31.081. PROPERTY TAX WITHHOLDING ON PURCHASE OF BUSINESS OR INVENTORY

(a) This section applies only to a person who purchases a business, an interest in a business, or the in-

ventory of a business from a person who is liable under this title for the payment of taxes imposed on personal property used in the operation of that business.

(b) The purchaser shall withhold from the purchase price an amount sufficient to pay all of the taxes imposed on the personal property of the business, plus any penalties and interest incurred, until the seller provides the purchaser with:

(1) a receipt issued by each appropriate collector showing that the taxes due the applicable taxing unit, plus any penalties and interest, have been paid; or

(2) a tax certificate issued under Section 31.08 stating that no taxes, penalties, or interest is due the applicable taxing unit.

(c) A purchaser who fails to withhold the amount required by this section is liable for that amount to the applicable taxing units to the extent of the value of the purchase price, including the value of a promissory note given in consideration of the sale to the extent of the note's market value on the effective date of the purchase, regardless of whether the purchaser has been required to make any payments on that note.

(d) The purchaser may request each appropriate collector to issue a tax certificate under Section 31.08 or a statement of the amount of the taxes, penalties, and interest that are due to each taxing unit for which the collector collects taxes. The collector shall issue the certificate or statement before the 10th day after the date the request is made. If a collector does not timely provide or mail the certificate or statement to the purchaser, the purchaser is released from the duties and liabilities imposed by Subsections (b) and (c) in connection with taxes, penalties, and interest due the applicable taxing unit.

(e) An action to enforce a duty or liability imposed on a purchaser by Subsection (b) or (c) must be brought before the fourth anniversary of the effective date of the purchase. An action to enforce the purchaser's duty or liability is subject to a limitation plea by the purchaser as to any taxes that have been delinquent at least four years as of the date the collector issues the statement under Subsection (d).

(f) This section does not release a person who sells a business or the inventory of a business from any personal liability imposed on the person for the payment of taxes imposed on the personal property of the business or for penalties or interest on those taxes.

(g) For purposes of this section:

(1) a person is considered to have purchased a business if the person purchases the name of the business or the goodwill associated with the business; and

(2) a person is considered to have purchased the inventory of a business if the person purchases inventory of a business, the value of which is at least 50 percent of the value of the total inventory of the business on the date of the purchase.

TAX §31.09. REPEALED

TAX §31.10. REPORTS & REMITTANCES OF OTHER TAXES

(a) Each month the collector of taxes for a taxing unit shall prepare and submit to the governing body of the unit a written report made under oath accounting for all taxes collected for the unit during the preceding month. Reports of collections made in the months of October through January are due on the 25th day of the month following the month that is the subject of the report. Reports of collections made in all other months are due on the 15th day of the month following the month that is the subject of the report. A collector for more than one taxing unit may prepare one report accounting for taxes collected for all units, and he may submit a certified copy of the report as his monthly report to the governing body of each unit.

(b) The collector for a taxing unit shall prepare and submit to the governing body of the unit an annual report made under oath accounting for all taxes of the unit collected or delinquent on property taxed by the unit during the preceding 12-month period. Annual reports are due on the 60th day following the last day of the fiscal year.

(c) Except as otherwise provided by Subsection (d) of this section, at least monthly the collector for a taxing unit shall deposit in the unit's depository all taxes collected for the unit. The governing body of a unit may require deposits to be made more frequently.

(d) If the taxes of a taxing unit are collected by the collector or other officer or employee of another taxing unit or by an appraisal district as provided by the law creating or authorizing creation of the unit or as the result of an election held under Section 6.26 of this code, the entity that collects the taxes shall deposit the taxes in the unit's depository daily, unless the governing body of that unit by official action provides that those deposits may be made less often than daily.

TAX §31.11. REFUNDS OF OVERPAYMENTS OR ERRONEOUS PAYMENTS

(a) If a taxpayer applies to the tax collector of a taxing unit for a refund of an overpayment or erroneous payment of taxes, the collector for the unit determines that the payment was erroneous or excessive, and the auditor for the unit agrees with the collector's determination, the collector shall refund the amount of the excessive or erroneous payment from available current tax collections or from funds appropriated by the unit for making refunds. However, the collector may not make the refund unless:

(1) in the case of a collector who collects taxes for one taxing unit, the governing body of the taxing unit also determines that the payment was erroneous or excessive and approves the refund if the amount of the refund exceeds:

(A) $5,000 for a refund to be paid by a county with a population of two million or more; or

(B) $500 for a refund to be paid by any other taxing unit; or

(2) in the case of a collector who collects taxes for more than one taxing unit, the governing body of the taxing unit that employs the collector also determines that the payment was erroneous or excessive and approves the refund if the amount of the refund exceeds:

(A) $5,000 for a refund to be paid by a county with a population of two million or more; or

(B) $2,500 for a refund to be paid by any other taxing unit.

(b) A taxing unit that determines a taxpayer is delinquent in ad valorem tax payments on property other than the property for which liability for a refund arises or for a tax year other than the tax year for which liability for a refund arises may apply the amount of an overpayment or erroneous payment to the payment of the delinquent taxes if the taxpayer was the sole owner of the property:

(1) for which the refund is sought on January 1 of the tax year in which the taxes that were overpaid or erroneously paid were assessed; and

(2) on which the taxes are delinquent on January 1 of the tax year for which the delinquent taxes were assessed.

(c) Except as provided by Subsection (c-1), an application for a refund must be made within three years after the date of the payment or the taxpayer waives the right to the refund. A taxpayer may apply for a refund by filing:

(1) an application on a form prescribed by the comptroller by rule; or

(2) a written request that includes information sufficient to enable the collector and the auditor for the taxing unit and, if applicable, the governing body of the taxing unit to determine whether the taxpayer is entitled to the refund.

(c-1) The governing body of the taxing unit may extend the deadline provided by Subsection (c) for a single period not to exceed two years on a showing of good cause by the taxpayer.

(d) The collector for a taxing unit shall provide a copy of the refund application form without charge on request of a taxpayer or a taxpayer's representative.

(e) An application for a refund must:

(1) include an affirmation by the taxpayer that the information in the application is true and correct; and

(2) be signed by the taxpayer.

(f) This subsection applies only to a refund that is required to be approved by the governing body of a taxing unit. The presiding officer of the governing body of the taxing unit is not required to sign the application for the refund or any document accompanying the application to indicate the governing body's approval or disapproval of the refund. The collector for the taxing unit shall indicate on the application whether the governing body approved or disapproved the refund and the date of the approval or disapproval.

(g) If a taxpayer submits a payment of taxes that exceeds by $5 or more the amount of taxes owed for a tax year to a taxing unit, the collector for the taxing unit, without charge, shall mail to the taxpayer or the taxpayer's representative a written notice of the amount of the overpayment accompanied by a refund application form.

(h) This section does not apply to an overpayment caused by a change of exemption status or correction of a tax roll. Such an overpayment is covered by Section 26.15 or 42.43, as applicable.

(i) Notwithstanding the other provisions of this section, in the case of an overpayment or erroneous payment of taxes submitted by a taxpayer to a collector who collects taxes for one or more taxing units one of which is a county with a population of two million or more:

(1) a taxpayer is not required to apply to the collector for the refund to be entitled to receive the refund if the amount of the refund is at least $5 but does not exceed $5,000; and

(2) the collector is not required to comply with Subsection (g) unless the amount of the payment exceeds by more than $5,000 the amount of taxes owed for a tax year to a taxing unit for which the collector collects taxes.

(j) If the collector for a taxing unit does not respond to an application for a refund on or before the 90th day after the date the application is filed with the collector, the application is presumed to have been denied.

(k) Not later than the 60th day after the date the collector for a taxing unit denies an application for a refund, the taxpayer may file suit against the taxing unit in district court to compel the payment of the refund. If the collector collects taxes for more than one taxing unit, the taxpayer shall join in the suit each taxing unit on behalf of which the collector denied the refund. If the taxpayer prevails in the suit, the taxpayer may be awarded:

(1) costs of court; and

(2) reasonable attorney's fees in an amount not to exceed the greater of:

(A) $1,500; or

(B) 30 percent of the total amount of the refund determined by the court to be due.

TAX §31.111. REFUNDS OF DUPLICATE PAYMENTS

(a) The collector of a taxing unit who determines that a person erred in making a payment of taxes because the identical taxes were paid by another person shall refund the amount of the taxes to the person who erred in making the payment.

(b) A refund under Subsection (a) shall be made as soon as practicable after the collector discovers the erroneous payment. The refund shall be accompanied by a description of the property subject to the taxes sufficient to identify the property. If the property is assigned an account number, the collector shall include that number.

(c) Each month, the collector shall inform the auditor of each appropriate taxing unit of refunds of taxes made under Subsection (a) during the preceding month.

E

TAX §31.112. REFUNDS OF PAYMENTS MADE TO MULTIPLE LIKE TAXING UNITS

(a) In this section, "like taxing units" has the meaning assigned by Section 72.010(a), Local Government Code.

(b) This section applies only to taxing units described by Section 72.010(b), Local Government Code.

(c) Like taxing units to which a property owner has made tax payments under protest as a result of a dispute or error described by Section 72.010(c), Local Government Code, may enter into an agreement to resolve the dispute or error. An agreement under this subsection:

(1) must establish the correct geographic boundary between the taxing units;

(2) may include an allocation between the taxing units of all or part of the taxes that were paid under protest before the dispute or error was resolved, less any amount that is required to be refunded to the property owner;

(3) must require the taxing units to refund to the property owner any amount by which the amount paid by the owner to the taxing units exceeds the amount due; and

(4) must be in writing.

(d) If a dispute or error described by Section 72.010(c), Local Government Code, is resolved by the agreement of the taxing units, a refund required by Subsection (c)(3) of this section must be made not later than the 90th day after the date on which the agreement is made.

(e) If a dispute or error described by Section 72.010(c), Local Government Code, is not resolved by the agreement of the taxing units and the supreme court enters a final order in a suit under Section 72.010, Local Government Code, determining the amount of taxes owed on the property and the taxing unit or units to which the taxes are owed, a refund required as a result of the order must be made not later than the 180th day after the date the order is entered.

(f) A refund under this section shall be accompanied by:

(1) a description sufficient to identify the property on which the taxes were imposed; and

(2) the tax account number, if applicable.

(g) A collector making a refund under this section shall notify the auditor of each appropriate taxing unit not later than the 30th day after the date the refund is made.

2017 Legislation: Enacted by S.B. 2242, §3, 85th Leg., eff. June 12, 2017.

TAX §31.115. PAYMENT OF TAX UNDER PROTEST

Payment of an ad valorem tax is involuntary if the taxpayer indicates that the tax is paid under protest:

(1) on the instrument by which the tax is paid; or

(2) in a document accompanying the payment.

A TAX §31.12. PAYMENT OF TAX REFUNDS; INTEREST

(a) If a refund of a tax provided by Section 11.431(b), 26.07(g), 26.15(f), 31.11, [~~or~~] 31.111, or 31.112 is paid on or before the 60th day after the date the liability for the refund arises, no interest is due on the amount refunded. If not paid on or before that 60th day, the amount of the tax to be refunded accrues interest at a rate of one percent for each month or part of a month that the refund is unpaid, beginning with the date on which the liability for the refund arises.

(b) For purposes of this section, liability for a refund arises:

(1) if the refund is required by Section 11.431(b), on the date the chief appraiser notifies the collector for the unit of the approval of the late homestead exemption;

(2) if the refund is required by Section 26.07(g), on the date the results of the election to reduce the tax rate are certified;

(3) if the refund is required by Section 26.15(f):

(A) for a correction to the tax roll made under Section 26.15(b), on the date the change in the tax roll is certified to the assessor for the taxing unit under Section 25.25; or

(B) for a correction to the tax roll made under Section 26.15(c), on the date the change in the tax roll is ordered by the governing body of the taxing unit;

(4) if the refund is required by Section 31.11, on the date the auditor for the taxing unit determines that the payment was erroneous or excessive or, if the amount of the refund exceeds the applicable amount specified by Section 31.11(a), on the date the governing body of the unit approves the refund; [~~or~~]

(5) if the refund is required by Section 31.111, on the date the collector for the taxing unit determines that the payment was erroneous; or

(6) if the refund is required by Section 31.112, on the date required by Section 31.112(d) or (e), as applicable.

(c) This section does not apply to a refund in an amount less than $5.

2017 Legislation: Amended by S.B. 2242, §4, 85th Leg., eff. June 12, 2017.

CHAPTER 32. TAX LIENS & PERSONAL LIABILITY

TAX §32.01. TAX LIEN

(a) On January 1 of each year, a tax lien attaches to property to secure the payment of all taxes, penalties, and interest ultimately imposed for the year on the property, whether or not the taxes are imposed in the year the lien attaches. The lien exists in favor of each taxing unit having power to tax the property.

(b) A tax lien on inventory, furniture, equipment, or other personal property is a lien in solido and attaches to all inventory, furniture, equipment, and other personal property that the property owner owns on January 1 of the year the lien attaches or that the property owner subsequently acquires.

(c) If an owner's real property is described with certainty by metes and bounds in one or more instruments of conveyance and part of that property is the owner's residence homestead taxed separately and apart from the remainder of the property, each of the liens under this section that secures the taxes imposed on that homestead and on the remainder of that property extends in solido to all the real property described in the instrument or instruments of conveyance, unless the homestead is identified as a separate parcel and is separately described in the conveyance or another instrument recorded in the real property records.

(d) The lien under this section is perfected on attachment and, except as provided by Section 32.03(b), perfection requires no further action by the taxing unit.

TAX §32.014. TAX LIEN ON MANUFACTURED HOME

(a) If the owner of a manufactured home has elected to treat the home as real property under Section 25.08, the tax lien shall be attached to the land on which the manufactured home is located.

(b) If the owner of a manufactured home does not elect to treat the home as real property with the land on which the manufactured home is located, the tax lien on the manufactured home does not attach to the land on which the home is located.

(c) In this section, "manufactured home" has the meaning assigned by Section 1201.003, Occupations Code.

(d) This section prevails over Chapter 1201, Occupations Code, to the extent of any conflict.

TAX §32.015. TAX LIEN ON MANUFACTURED HOME

(a) On payment of the taxes, penalties, and interest for a year for which a valid tax lien has been recorded on the title records of the department, the collector for the taxing unit shall issue a tax certificate showing no taxes due or a tax paid receipt for such year to the person making payment. When the tax certificate showing no taxes due or tax paid receipt is filed with the department or when no suit to collect a personal property tax lien has been filed and the lien has been delinquent for more than four years, the tax lien is extinguished and canceled and shall be removed from the title records of the manufactured home. The collector for a taxing unit may not refuse to issue a tax paid receipt to the person who offers to pay the taxes, penalties, and interest for a particular year or years, even though taxes may also be due for another year or other years.

(b) In this section, "department" and "manufactured home" have the meanings assigned by Section 1201.003, Occupations Code; however, the term "manufactured home" does not include a manufactured home that has been attached to real property and for which the document of title has been canceled under Section 1201.217 of that code.

TAX §32.02. RESTRICTIONS ON A MINERAL INTEREST TAX LIEN

(a) If a mineral estate is severed from a surface estate and if different persons own the mineral estate and surface estate, the lien resulting from taxes imposed against each interest in the mineral estate exists only for the duration of the interest it encumbers. After an interest in the mineral estate terminates, the lien encumbering it expires and is not enforceable:

(1) against any part of the surface estate not owned by the owner of the interest encumbered by the lien;

(2) against any part of the mineral estate not owned by the owner of the interest encumbered by the lien; or

(3) against the owner of the surface estate as a personal obligation, unless he also owns the interest encumbered by the lien.

(b) Taxes imposed on a severed interest in a mineral estate that has terminated remain the personal liability of the person who owned the interest on January 1 of the year for which the tax was imposed.

A TAX §32.03. RESTRICTIONS ON PERSONAL PROPERTY TAX LIEN

(a) Except as provided by Subsection (a-1), a tax lien may not be enforced against personal property transferred to a buyer in ordinary course of business as defined by Section 1.201(9) of the Business & Commerce Code for value who does not have actual notice of the existence of the lien.

(a-1) With regard to a manufactured home, a tax lien may be recorded at any time not later than six months after the end of the year for which the tax was owed. A tax lien on a manufactured home may be enforced if it has been recorded in accordance with the laws in effect at the time of the recordation of the lien. A properly recorded tax lien may not be enforced against a new manufactured home that is owned by a person who acquired the manufactured home from a retailer as a buyer in the ordinary course of business.

(a-2) A person may not transfer ownership of a manufactured home until all tax liens perfected on the home that have been timely filed with the Texas Department of Housing and Community Affairs have been extinguished or satisfied and released and any personal property taxes on the manufactured home which accrued on each January 1 that falls within the 18 months preceding the date of the sale have been paid. This subsection does not apply to the sale of a manufactured home in inventory.

(b) A bona fide purchaser for value or the holder of a lien recorded on a manufactured home statement of ownership [~~and location~~] is not required to pay any taxes that have not been recorded with the Texas Department of Housing and Community Affairs. In this section, manufactured home has the meaning assigned by Section 32.015(b). Unless a tax lien has been filed timely with the Texas Department of Housing and Community Affairs, no taxing unit, nor anyone acting on its behalf, may use a tax warrant or any other method to attempt to execute or foreclose on the manufactured home.

(c) A taxpayer may designate in writing which tax year will be credited with a particular payment. If a taxpayer pays all the amounts owing for a given year, the taxing unit shall issue a receipt for the payment of the taxes for the designated year.

(d) Notwithstanding any other provision of this section, if a manufactured home was omitted from the tax roll for either or both of the two preceding tax years, the taxing unit may file a tax lien within the 150-day period following the date on which the tax becomes delinquent.

(e) If personal property taxes on a manufactured home have not been levied by the taxing unit, the taxing unit shall provide, upon request, an estimated amount of taxes computed by multiplying the taxable value of the manufactured home, according to the most recent certified appraisal roll for the taxing unit, by the taxing unit's adopted tax rate for the preceding tax year. In order to enable the transfer of the manufactured home, the tax collector shall accept the payment of the estimated personal property taxes and issue a certification to the Texas Department of Housing and Community Affairs that the estimated taxes are being held in escrow until the taxes are levied. Once the taxes are levied, the tax collector shall apply the escrowed sums to the levied taxes. At the time the tax collector accepts the payment of the taxes, the tax collector shall provide notice that the payment of the estimated taxes is an estimate that may be raised once the appraisal rolls for the year are certified and that the new owner may be liable for the payment of any difference between the tax established by the certified appraisal roll and the estimate actually paid.

2017 Legislation: Amended by H.B. 2019, §84, 85th Leg., eff. Sept. 1, 2017.

TAX §32.04. PRIORITIES AMONG TAX LIENS

(a) Whether or not a tax lien provided by this chapter takes priority over a tax lien of the United States is determined by federal law. In the absence of federal law, a tax lien provided by this chapter takes priority over a tax lien of the United States.

(b) Tax liens provided by this chapter have equal priority.

TAX §32.05. PRIORITY OF TAX LIENS OVER OTHER PROPERTY INTERESTS

(a) A tax lien on real property takes priority over a homestead interest in the property.

(b) Except as provided by Subsection (c)(1), a tax lien provided by this chapter takes priority over:

(1) the claim of any creditor of a person whose property is encumbered by the lien;

(2) the claim of any holder of a lien on property encumbered by the tax lien, including any lien held by a property owners' association, homeowners' association, condominium unit owners' association, or council of owners of a condominium regime under a restrictive covenant, condominium declaration, master deed, or other similar instrument that secures regular or special maintenance assessments, fees, dues, interest, fines, costs, attorney's fees, or other monetary charges against the property; and

(3) any right of remainder, right or possibility of reverter, or other future interest in, or encumbrance against, the property, whether vested or contingent.

(b-1) The priority given to a tax lien by Subsection (b) prevails, regardless of whether the debt, lien, future interest, or other encumbrance existed before attachment of the tax lien.

(c) A tax lien provided by this chapter is inferior to:

(1) a claim for any survivor's allowance, funeral expenses, or expenses of the last illness of a decedent made against the estate of a decedent as provided by law;

(2) except as provided by Subsection (b)(2), a recorded restrictive covenant that runs with the land and was recorded before January 1 of the year the tax lien arose; or

(3) a valid easement of record recorded before January 1 of the year the tax lien arose.

(d) In an action brought under Chapter 33 for the enforced collection of a delinquent tax against property, a property owners' association, homeowners' association, condominium unit owners' association, or council of owners of a condominium regime that holds a lien for regular or special maintenance assessments, fees, dues, interest, fines, costs, attorney's fees, or other monetary charges against the property is not a necessary party to the action unless, at the time the action is commenced, notice of the lien in a liquidated amount is evidenced by a sworn instrument duly executed by an authorized person and recorded with the clerk of the county in which the property is located. A tax sale of the property extinguishes the lien held by a property owners' association, homeowners' association, condo-

minium unit owners' association, or council of owners of a condominium regime for all amounts that accrued before the date of sale if:

(1) the holder of the lien is joined as a party to an action brought under Chapter 33 by virtue of a notice of the lien on record at the time the action is commenced; or

(2) the notice of lien is not of record at the time the action is commenced, regardless of whether the holder of the lien is made a party to the action.

(e) The existence of a recorded restrictive covenant, declaration, or master deed that generally provides for the lien held by a property owners' association, homeowners' association, condominium unit owners' association, or council of owners of a condominium regime does not, by itself, constitute actual or constructive notice to a taxing unit of a lien under Subsection (d).

TAX §32.06. PROPERTY TAX LOANS; TRANSFER OF TAX LIEN

(a) In this section:

(1) "Mortgage servicer" has the meaning assigned by Section 51.0001, Property Code.

(2) "Transferee" means a person who is licensed under Chapter 351, Finance Code, or is exempt from the application of that chapter under Section 351.051(c), Finance Code, and who is:

(A) authorized to pay the taxes of another; or

(B) a successor in interest to a tax lien that is transferred under this section.

(a-1) A property owner may authorize another person to pay the taxes imposed by a taxing unit on the owner's real property by executing and filing with the collector for the taxing unit:

(1) a sworn document stating:

(A) the authorization for payment of the taxes;

(B) the name and street address of the transferee authorized to pay the taxes of the property owner;

(C) a description of the property by street address, if applicable, and legal description; and

(D) notice has been given to the property owner that if the property owner is disabled, the property owner may be eligible for a tax deferral under Section 33.06; and

(2) the information required by Section 351.054, Finance Code.

(a-2) Except as provided by Subsection (a-8), a tax lien may be transferred to the person who pays the taxes on behalf of the property owner under the authorization described by Subsection (a-1) for:

(1) taxes that are delinquent at the time of payment; or

(2) taxes that are due but not delinquent at the time of payment if the property is not subject to a recorded mortgage lien.

(a-3) A person who is 65 years of age or older may not authorize a transfer of a tax lien on real property on which the person is eligible to claim an exemption from taxation under Section 11.13(c).

(a-4) The Finance Commission of Texas shall:

(1) prescribe the form and content of an appropriate disclosure statement to be provided to a property owner before the execution of a tax lien transfer;

(2) adopt rules relating to the reasonableness of closing costs, fees, and other charges permitted under this section;

(3) by rule prescribe the form and content of the sworn document under Subsection (a-1) and the certified statement under Subsection (b); and

(4) by rule prescribe the form and content of a request a lender with an existing recorded lien on the property must use to request a payoff statement and the transferee's response to the request, including the period within which the transferee must respond.

(a-5) At the time the transferee provides the disclosure statement required by Subsection (a-4)(1), the transferee must also describe the type and approximate cost range of each additional charge or fee that the property owner may incur in connection with the transfer.

(a-6) Notwithstanding Subsection (f-3), a lender described by Subsection (a-4)(4) may request a payoff statement before the tax loan becomes delinquent. The Finance Commission of Texas by rule shall require a transferee who receives a request for a payoff statement to deliver the requested payoff statement on the prescribed form within a period prescribed by finance commission rule. The prescribed period must allow the transferee at least seven business days after the date the request is received to deliver the payoff statement. The consumer credit commissioner may assess an administrative penalty under Subchapter F, Chapter 14, Finance Code, against a transferee who wilfully fails to provide the payoff statement as prescribed by finance commission rule.

(a-7) A contract between a transferee and a property owner that purports to authorize payment of taxes that are not delinquent or due at the time of the authorization, or that lacks the authorization described by Subsection (a-1), is void.

(a-8) A tax lien may not be transferred to the person who pays the taxes on behalf of the property owner under the authorization described by Subsection (a-1) if the real property:

(1) has been financed, wholly or partly, with a grant or below market rate loan provided by a governmental program or nonprofit organization and is subject to the covenants of the grant or loan; or

(2) is encumbered by a lien recorded under Subchapter A, Chapter 214, Local Government Code.

(a-9) The Finance Commission of Texas may adopt rules to implement Subsection (a-8).

(b) If a transferee authorized to pay a property owner's taxes under Subsection (a-1) pays the taxes and any penalties, interest, and collection costs imposed, the collector shall issue a tax receipt to that transferee. In addition, the collector or a person designated by the collector shall certify that the taxes and any penalties, interest, and collection costs on the subject property have been paid by the transferee on behalf of the property owner and that the taxing unit's tax lien is transferred to that transferee. The collector shall attach to the certified statement the collector's seal of office or sign the statement before a notary public and deliver a tax receipt and the certified statement attesting to the transfer of the tax lien to the transferee within 30 days. The tax receipt and certified statement may be combined into one document. The collector shall identify in a discrete field in the applicable property owner's account the date of the transfer of a tax lien transferred under this section. When a tax lien is released, the transferee shall file a release with the county clerk of each county in which the property encumbered by the lien is located for recordation by the clerk and send a copy to the collector. The transferee may charge the property owner a reasonable fee for filing the release.

(b-1) Not later than the 10th business day after the date the certified statement is received by the transferee, the transferee shall send by certified mail a copy of the sworn document described by Subsection (a-1) to any mortgage servicer and to each holder of a recorded first lien encumbering the property. The copy must be sent, as applicable, to the address shown on the most recent payment invoice, statement, or payment coupon provided by the mortgage servicer to the property owner, or the address of the holder of a recorded first lien as shown in the real property records.

(c) Except as otherwise provided by this section, the transferee of a tax lien is entitled to foreclose the lien in the manner provided by law for foreclosure of tax liens.

(c-1) Repealed by Acts 2013, 83rd Leg., ch. 206, §10, eff. May 29, 2013.

(d) A transferee shall record a tax lien transferred as provided by this section with the certified statement attesting to the transfer of the tax lien as described by Subsection (b) in the deed records of each county in which the property encumbered by the lien is located.

(d-1) A right of rescission described by 12 C.F.R. Section 226.23 applies to a transfer under this section of a tax lien on residential property owned and used by the property owner for personal, family, or household purposes.

(e) A transferee holding a tax lien transferred as provided by this section may not charge a greater rate of interest than 18 percent a year on the funds advanced. Funds advanced are limited to the taxes, penalties, interest, and collection costs paid as shown on the tax receipt, expenses paid to record the lien, plus reasonable closing costs.

(e-1) A transferee of a tax lien may not charge a fee for any expenses arising after the closing of a loan secured by a tax lien transferred under this section, including collection costs, except for:

(1) interest expressly authorized under this section;

(2) the fees for filing the release of the tax lien under Subsection (b);

(3) the fee for providing a payoff statement under Subsection (f-3);

(4) the fee for providing information regarding the current balance owed by the property owner under Subsection (g); and

(5) the fees expressly authorized under Section 351.0021, Finance Code.

(e-2) The contract between the property owner and the transferee may provide for interest for default, in addition to the interest permitted under Subsection (e), if any part of the installment remains unpaid after the 10th day after the date the installment is due, in-

cluding Sundays and holidays. If the lien transferred is on residential property owned and used by the property owner for personal, family, or household purposes, the additional interest may not exceed five cents for each $1 of a scheduled installment.

(f) The holder of a loan secured by a transferred tax lien that is delinquent for 90 consecutive days must send a notice of the delinquency by certified mail on or before the 120th day of delinquency or, if the 120th day is not a business day, on the next business day after the 120th day of delinquency, to any holder of a recorded preexisting lien on the property. The holder or mortgage servicer of a recorded preexisting lien on property encumbered by a tax lien transferred as provided by Subsection (b) is entitled, within six months after the date on which the notice is sent, to obtain a release of the transferred tax lien by paying the transferee of the tax lien the amount owed under the contract between the property owner and the transferee.

(f-1) If an obligation secured by a preexisting first lien on the property is delinquent for at least 90 consecutive days and the obligation has been referred to a collection specialist, the mortgage servicer or the holder of the first lien may send a notice of the delinquency to the transferee of a tax lien. The mortgage servicer or the first lienholder is entitled, within six months after the date on which that notice is sent, to obtain a release of the transferred tax lien by paying the transferee of the tax lien the amount owed under the contract between the property owner and the transferee. The Finance Commission of Texas by rule shall prescribe the form and content of the notice under this subsection.

(f-2) The rights granted by Subsections (f) and (f-1) do not affect a right of redemption in a foreclosure proceeding described by Subsection (k) or (k-1).

(f-3) Notwithstanding any contractual agreement with the property owner, the transferee of a tax lien must provide the payoff information required by this section to the greatest extent permitted by 15 U.S.C. Section 6802 and 12 C.F.R. Part 216. The payoff statement must meet the requirements of a payoff statement defined by Section 12.017, Property Code. A transferee may charge a reasonable fee for a payoff statement that is requested after an initial payoff statement is provided. However, a transferee is not required to release payoff information pursuant to a notice under Subsection (f-1) unless the notice contains the information prescribed by the Finance Commission of Texas.

(f-4) Failure to comply with Subsection (b-1), (f), or (f-1) does not invalidate a tax lien transferred under this section or a deed of trust.

(g) At any time after the end of the six-month period specified by Subsection (f) and before a notice of foreclosure of the transferred tax lien is sent, the transferee of the tax lien may require the property owner to provide written authorization and pay a reasonable fee before providing information regarding the current balance owed by the property owner to the transferee.

(h) A mortgage servicer who pays a property tax loan secured by a tax lien transferred under this section becomes subrogated to all rights in the lien.

(i) A judicial foreclosure of a tax lien transferred under this section may not be instituted within one year from the date on which the lien is recorded in all counties in which the property is located, unless the contract between the owner of the property and the transferee provides otherwise.

(j) After one year from the date on which a tax lien transferred under this section is recorded in all counties in which the property is located, the transferee of the lien may foreclose the lien in the manner provided by Subsection (c) unless the contract between the transferee and the owner of the property encumbered by the lien provides otherwise. The proceeds of a sale following a judicial foreclosure as provided by this subsection shall be applied first to the payment of court costs, then to payment of the judgment, including accrued interest, and then to the payment of any attorney's fees fixed in the judgment. Any remaining proceeds shall be paid to other holders of liens on the property in the order of their priority and then to the person whose property was sold at the tax sale.

(k) Beginning on the date the foreclosure deed is recorded, the person whose property is sold as provided by Subsection (c) or the mortgage servicer of a prior recorded lien against the property is entitled to redeem the foreclosed property from the purchaser or the purchaser's successor by paying the purchaser or successor:

(1) 125 percent of the purchase price during the first year of the redemption period or 150 percent of the purchase price during the second year of the redemption period with cash or cash equivalent funds; and

(2) the amount reasonably spent by the purchaser in connection with the property as costs within the meaning of Section 34.21(g) and the legal judgment rate of return on that amount.

(k-1) The right of redemption provided by Subsection (k) may be exercised on or before the second anniversary of the date on which the purchaser's deed is filed of record if the property sold was the residence homestead of the owner, was land designated for agricultural use, or was a mineral interest. For any other property, the right of redemption must be exercised not later than the 180th day after the date on which the purchaser's deed is filed of record. If a person redeems the property as provided by Subsection (k) and this subsection, the purchaser at the tax sale or the purchaser's successor shall deliver a deed without warranty to the property to the person redeeming the property. If the person who owned the property at the time of foreclosure redeems the property, all liens existing on the property at the time of the tax sale remain in effect to the extent not paid from the sale proceeds.

(*l*) Except as specifically provided by this section, a property owner cannot waive or limit any requirement imposed on a transferee by this section.

TAX §32.065. CONTRACT FOR FORECLOSURE OF TAX LIEN

(a) Section 32.06 does not abridge the right of an owner of real property to enter into a contract for the payment of taxes.

(b) Notwithstanding any agreement to the contrary, a contract entered into under Subsection (a) between a transferee and the property owner under Section 32.06 that is secured by a priority lien on the property shall provide for foreclosure in the manner provided by Section 32.06(c) and:

(1) an event of default;

(2) notice of acceleration; and

(3) recording of the deed of trust or other instrument securing the contract entered into under Subsection (a) in each county in which the property is located.

(b-1) On an event of default and notice of acceleration, the mortgage servicer of a recorded lien encumbering real property may obtain a release of a transferred tax lien on the property by paying the transferee of the tax lien or the holder of the tax lien the amount owed by the property owner to that transferee or holder.

(c) Notwithstanding any other provision of this code, a transferee of a tax lien or the transferee's assignee is subrogated to and is entitled to exercise any right or remedy possessed by the transferring taxing unit, including or related to foreclosure or judicial sale, but is prohibited from exercising a remedy of foreclosure or judicial sale where the transferring taxing unit would be prohibited from foreclosure or judicial sale.

(d) Chapters 342 and 346, Finance Code, and the provisions of Chapter 343, Finance Code, other than Sections 343.203 and 343.205, do not apply to a transaction covered by this section.

(e) If in a contract under this section a person contracts for, charges, or receives a rate or amount of interest that exceeds the rate or amount allowed by this section, the amount of the penalty for which the person is obligated is determined in the manner provided by Chapter 349, Finance Code.

(f) Before accepting an application fee or executing a contract, the transferee shall disclose to the transferee's prospective borrower each type and the amount of possible additional charges or fees that may be incurred by the borrower in connection with the loan or contract under this section.

(g) Repealed by Acts 2007, 80th Leg., ch. 1329, §3, eff. Sept. 1, 2007.

(h) An affidavit of the transferee executed after foreclosure of a tax lien that recites compliance with the terms of Section 32.06 and this section and is recorded in each county in which the property is located:

(1) is prima facie evidence of compliance with Section 32.06 and this section; and

(2) may be relied on conclusively by a bona fide purchaser for value without notice of any failure to comply.

(i) An agreement under this section that attempts to create a lien for the payment of taxes that are not delinquent or due at the time the property owner executes the sworn document under Section 32.06(a-1) is void.

TAX §32.07. PERSONAL LIABILITY FOR TAX

(a) Except as provided by Subsections (b) and (c) of this section, property taxes are the personal obligation of the person who owns or acquires the property on January 1 of the year for which the tax is imposed or would have been imposed had property not been omit-

ted as described under Section 25.21. A person is not relieved of the obligation because he no longer owns the property.

(b) The person in whose name a property is required to be listed by Section 25.13 of this code is personally liable for the taxes imposed on the property.

(c) A qualifying trust as defined by Section 11.13(j) and each trustor of the trust are jointly and severally liable for the tax imposed on the interest of the trust in a residence homestead.

(d) Any person who receives or collects an ad valorem tax or any money represented to be a tax from another person holds the amount so collected in trust for the benefit of the taxing unit and is liable to the taxing unit for the full amount collected plus any accrued penalties and interest on the amount collected.

(e) With respect to an ad valorem tax or other money subject to the provisions of Subsection (d), an individual who controls or supervises the collection of tax or money from another person, or an individual who controls or supervises the accounting for and paying over of the tax or money, and who wilfully fails to pay or cause to be paid the tax or money is liable as a responsible individual for an amount equal to the tax or money, plus all interest, penalties, and costs, not paid or caused to be paid. The liability imposed by this subsection is in addition to any other penalty provided by law. The dissolution of a corporation, association, limited liability company, or partnership does not affect a responsible individual's liability under this subsection.

(f) Venue for suits arising under this section shall be governed by Section 33.41(a).

(g) In this section:

(1) "Responsible individual" includes an officer, manager, director, or employee or a corporation, association, or limited liability company or a member of a partnership who, as an officer, manager, director, employee, or member, is under a duty to perform an act with respect to the collection, accounting, or payment of a tax or money subject to the provisions of Subsection (d).

(2) "Tax" includes any ad valorem tax or money subject to the provisions of Subsection (d), including the penalty and interest computed by reference to the amount of the tax or money.

(h) For purposes of Subsection (a), a person is considered to be an owner of property subject to an installment contract of sale if the person is:

(1) the seller of the property; or

(2) a purchaser of the property who has the duty under the installment contract to pay taxes on the property.

CHAPTER 33. DELINQUENCY

SUBCHAPTER A. GENERAL PROVISIONS

TAX §33.01. PENALTIES & INTEREST

(a) A delinquent tax incurs a penalty of six percent of the amount of the tax for the first calendar month it is delinquent plus one percent for each additional month or portion of a month the tax remains unpaid prior to July 1 of the year in which it becomes delinquent. However, a tax delinquent on July 1 incurs a total penalty of twelve percent of the amount of the delinquent tax without regard to the number of months the tax has been delinquent. A delinquent tax continues to incur the penalty provided by this subsection as long as the tax remains unpaid, regardless of whether a judgment for the delinquent tax has been rendered.

(b) If a person who exercises the split-payment option provided by Section 31.03 of this code fails to make the second payment before July 1, the second payment is delinquent and incurs a penalty of twelve percent of the amount of unpaid tax.

(c) A delinquent tax accrues interest at a rate of one percent for each month or portion of a month the tax remains unpaid. Interest payable under this section is to compensate the taxing unit for revenue lost because of the delinquency. A delinquent tax continues to accrue interest under this subsection as long as the tax remains unpaid, regardless of whether a judgment for the delinquent tax has been rendered.

(d) In lieu of the penalty imposed under Subsection (a), a delinquent tax incurs a penalty of 50 percent of the amount of the tax without regard to the number of months the tax has been delinquent if the tax is delinquent because the property owner received an exemption under:

(1) Section 11.13 and the chief appraiser subsequently cancels the exemption because the residence was not the principal residence of the property owner and the property owner received an exemption for two or more additional residence homesteads for the tax year in which the tax was imposed;

(2) Section 11.13(c) or (d) for a person who is 65 years of age or older and the chief appraiser subse-

quently cancels the exemption because the property owner was younger than 65 years of age; or

(3) Section 11.13(q) and the chief appraiser subsequently cancels the exemption because the property owner was younger than 55 years of age when the property owner's spouse died.

(e) A penalty imposed under Subsection (d) does not apply if:

(1) the exemption was granted by the appraisal district or board and not at the request or application of the property owner or the property owner's agent; or

(2) at any time before the date the tax becomes delinquent, the property owner gives to the chief appraiser of the appraisal district in which the property is located written notice of circumstances that would disqualify the owner for the exemption.

TAX §33.011. WAIVER OF PENALTIES & INTEREST

(a) The governing body of a taxing unit:

(1) shall waive penalties and may provide for the waiver of interest on a delinquent tax if an act or omission of an officer, employee, or agent of the taxing unit or the appraisal district in which the taxing unit participates caused or resulted in the taxpayer's failure to pay the tax before delinquency and if the tax is paid not later than the 21st day after the date the taxpayer knows or should know of the delinquency;

(2) may waive penalties and provide for the waiver of interest on a delinquent tax if:

(A) the property for which the tax is owed is acquired by a religious organization; and

(B) before the first anniversary of the date the religious organization acquires the property, the organization pays the tax and qualifies the property for an exemption under Section 11.20 as evidenced by the approval of the exemption by the chief appraiser under Section 11.45; and

(3) may waive penalties and provide for the waiver of interest on a delinquent tax if the taxpayer submits evidence showing that:

(A) the taxpayer attempted to pay the tax before the delinquency date by mail;

(B) the taxpayer mailed the tax payment to an incorrect address that in a prior tax year was the correct address for payment of the taxpayer's tax;

(C) the payment was mailed to the incorrect address within one year of the date that the former address ceased to be the correct address for payment of the tax; and

(D) the taxpayer paid the tax not later than the 21st day after the date the taxpayer knew or should have known of the delinquency.

(b) If a tax bill is returned undelivered to the taxing unit by the United States Postal Service, the governing body of the taxing unit shall waive penalties and interest if:

(1) the taxing unit does not send another tax bill on the property in question at least 21 days before the delinquency date to the current mailing address furnished by the property owner and the property owner establishes that a current mailing address was furnished to the appraisal district by the property owner for the tax bill before September 1 of the year in which the tax is assessed; or

(2) the tax bill was returned because of an act or omission of an officer, employee, or agent of the taxing unit or the appraisal district in which the taxing unit participates and the taxing unit or appraisal district did not send another tax bill on the property in question at least 21 days before the delinquency date to the proper mailing address.

(c) For the purposes of this section, a property owner is considered to have furnished a current mailing address to the taxing unit or to the appraisal district if the current address is expressly communicated to the appraisal district in writing or if the appraisal district received a copy of a recorded instrument transferring ownership of real property and the current mailing address of the new owner is included in the instrument or in accompanying communications or letters of transmittal.

(d) A request for a waiver of penalties and interest under Subsection (a)(1) or (3), (b), (h), or (j) must be made before the 181st day after the delinquency date. A request for a waiver of penalties and interest under Subsection (a)(2) must be made before the first anniversary of the date the religious organization acquires the property. A request for a waiver of penalties and interest under Subsection (i) must be made before the 181st day after the date the property owner making the request receives notice of the delinquent tax that satisfies the requirements of Section 33.04(c). To be valid, a waiver of penalties or interest under this section must

be requested in writing. If a written request for a waiver is not timely made, the governing body of a taxing unit may not waive any penalties or interest under this section.

(e) Penalties and interest do not accrue during the period that a bill is not sent under Section 31.01(f).

(f) A property owner is not entitled to relief under Subsection (b) of this section if the property owner or the owner's agent furnished an incorrect mailing address to the appraisal district or the taxing unit or to an employee or agent of the district or unit.

(g) Taxes for which penalties and interest have been waived under Subsection (b) of this section must be paid within 21 days of the property owner having received a bill for those taxes at the current mailing address.

(h) The governing body of a taxing unit shall waive penalties and interest on a delinquent tax if:

(1) the tax is payable by electronic funds transfer under an agreement entered into under Section 31.06(a); and

(2) the taxpayer submits evidence sufficient to show that:

(A) the taxpayer attempted to pay the tax by electronic funds transfer in the proper manner before the delinquency date;

(B) the taxpayer's failure to pay the tax before the delinquency date was caused by an error in the transmission of the funds; and

(C) the tax was properly paid by electronic funds transfer or otherwise not later than the 21st day after the date the taxpayer knew or should have known of the delinquency.

(i) The governing body of a taxing unit may waive penalties and interest on a delinquent tax that relates to a date preceding the date on which the property owner acquired the property if:

(1) the property owner or another person liable for the tax pays the tax not later than the 181st day after the date the property owner receives notice of the delinquent tax that satisfies the requirements of Section 33.04(c); and

(2) the delinquency is the result of taxes imposed on:

(A) omitted property entered in the appraisal records as provided by Section 25.21;

(B) erroneously exempted property or appraised value added to the appraisal roll as provided by Section 11.43(i); or

(C) property added to the appraisal roll under a different account number or parcel when the property was owned by a prior owner.

(j) The governing body of a taxing unit may waive penalties and interest on a delinquent tax if the taxpayer submits evidence sufficient to show that the taxpayer delivered payment for the tax before the delinquency date to:

(1) the United States Postal Service for delivery by mail, but an act or omission of the postal service resulted in the taxpayer's payment being postmarked after the delinquency date; or

(2) a private delivery service for delivery, but an act or omission of the private carrier resulted in the taxpayer's payment being received by the taxing unit after the delinquency date.

TAX §33.02. INSTALLMENT PAYMENT OF DELINQUENT TAXES

(a) The collector for a taxing unit may enter into an agreement with a person delinquent in the payment of the tax for payment of the tax, penalties, and interest in installments. The collector for a taxing unit shall, on request by a person delinquent in the payment of the tax on a residence homestead for which the property owner has been granted an exemption under Section 11.13, enter into an agreement with the person for payment of the tax, penalties, and interest in installments if the person has not entered into an installment agreement with the collector for the taxing unit under this section in the preceding 24 months.

(a-1) An installment agreement under this section:

(1) must be in writing;

(2) must provide for payments to be made in monthly installments;

(3) must extend for a period of at least 12 months if the property that is the subject of the agreement is a residence homestead for which the person entering into the agreement has been granted an exemption under Section 11.13; and

(4) may not extend for a period of more than 36 months.

(b) Except as provided by Subsection (b-1), interest and a penalty accrue as provided by Sections

33.01(a) and (c) on the unpaid balance during the period of the agreement.

(b-1) Except as otherwise provided by this subsection, a penalty does not accrue as provided by Section 33.01(a) on the unpaid balance during the period of the agreement if the property that is the subject of the agreement is a residence homestead for which the property owner has been granted an exemption under Section 11.13. If the property owner fails to make a payment as required by the agreement, a penalty accrues as provided by Section 33.01(a) on the unpaid balance as if the owner had not entered into the agreement.

(c) A property owner's execution of an installment agreement under this section is an irrevocable admission of liability for all taxes, penalties, and interest that are subject to the agreement.

(d) Property may not be seized and sold and a suit may not be filed to collect a delinquent tax subject to an installment agreement unless the property owner:

(1) fails to make a payment as required by the agreement;

(2) fails to pay other property taxes collected by the unit when due as required by the collector; or

(3) breaches any other condition of the agreement.

(e) Execution of an installment agreement tolls the limitation periods provided by Section 33.05 of this code for the period during which enforced collection is barred by Subsection (d) of this section.

(f) The collector for a taxing unit must deliver a notice of default to a person who is in breach of an installment agreement under this section and to any other owner of an interest in the property subject to the agreement whose name appears on the delinquent tax roll before the collector may seize and sell the property or file a suit to collect a delinquent tax subject to the agreement.

TAX §33.03. DELINQUENT TAX ROLL

Each year the collector for each taxing unit shall prepare a current and a cumulative delinquent tax roll for the unit.

TAX §33.04. NOTICE OF DELINQUENCY

(a) At least once each year the collector for a taxing unit shall deliver a notice of delinquency to each person whose name appears on the current delinquent tax roll. However, the notice need not be delivered if:

(1) a bill for the tax was not mailed under Section 31.01(f); or

(2) the collector does not know and by exercising reasonable diligence cannot determine the delinquent taxpayer's name and address.

(b) A notice of delinquency under this section must contain the following statement in capital letters: "IF THE PROPERTY DESCRIBED IN THIS DOCUMENT IS YOUR RESIDENCE HOMESTEAD, YOU SHOULD CONTACT THE TAX COLLECTOR FOR (NAME OF TAXING UNIT) REGARDING A RIGHT YOU MAY HAVE TO ENTER INTO AN INSTALLMENT AGREEMENT DIRECTLY WITH THE TAX COLLECTOR FOR (NAME OF TAXING UNIT) FOR THE PAYMENT OF THESE TAXES."

(c) If the delinquency is the result of taxes imposed on property described by Section 33.011(i), the first page of the notice of delinquency must include, in 14-point boldfaced type or 14-point uppercase letters, a statement that reads substantially as follows: "THE TAXES ON THIS PROPERTY ARE DELINQUENT. THE PROPERTY IS SUBJECT TO A LIEN FOR THE DELINQUENT TAXES. IF THE DELINQUENT TAXES ARE NOT PAID, THE LIEN MAY BE FORECLOSED."

TAX §33.045. NOTICE OF PROVISIONS AUTHORIZING DEFERRAL OR ABATEMENT

(a) A tax bill mailed by an assessor or collector under Section 31.01 and any written communication delivered to a property owner by an assessor or collector for a taxing unit or an attorney or other agent of a taxing unit that specifically threatens a lawsuit to collect a delinquent tax assessed against property that may qualify as a residence homestead shall contain the following explanation in capital letters: "IF YOU ARE 65 YEARS OF AGE OR OLDER OR ARE DISABLED, AND YOU OCCUPY THE PROPERTY DESCRIBED IN THIS DOCUMENT AS YOUR RESIDENCE HOMESTEAD, YOU SHOULD CONTACT THE APPRAISAL DISTRICT REGARDING ANY ENTITLEMENT YOU MAY HAVE TO A POSTPONEMENT IN THE PAYMENT OF THESE TAXES."

(b) This section does not apply to a communication that relates to taxes that are the subject of pending litigation.

TAX §33.05. LIMITATION ON COLLECTION OF TAXES

(a) Personal property may not be seized and a suit may not be filed:

(1) to collect a tax on personal property that has been delinquent more than four years; or

(2) to collect a tax on real property that has been delinquent more than 20 years.

(b) A tax delinquent for more than the limitation period prescribed by this section and any penalty and interest on the tax is presumed paid unless a suit to collect the tax is pending.

(c) If there is no pending litigation concerning the delinquent tax at the time of the cancellation and removal, the collector for a taxing unit shall cancel and remove from the delinquent tax roll:

(1) a tax on real property that has been delinquent for more than 20 years;

(2) a tax on personal property that has been delinquent for more than 10 years; and

(3) a tax on real property that has been delinquent for more than 10 years if the property has been owned for at least the preceding eight years by a home-rule municipality in a county with a population of more than 3.3 million.

TAX §33.06. DEFERRED COLLECTION OF TAXES ON RESIDENCE HOMESTEAD OF ELDERLY OR DISABLED PERSON OR DISABLED VETERAN

(a) An individual is entitled to defer collection of a tax, abate a suit to collect a delinquent tax, or abate a sale to foreclose a tax lien if:

(1) the individual:

(A) [~~(1)~~] is 65 years of age or older;

(B) [~~or~~] is disabled as defined by Section 11.13(m); or

(C) is qualified to receive an exemption under Section 11.22; and

(2) the tax was imposed against property that the individual owns and occupies as a residence homestead.

(b) To obtain a deferral, an individual must file with the chief appraiser for the appraisal district in which the property is located an affidavit stating the facts required to be established by Subsection (a). The chief appraiser shall notify each taxing unit participating in the district of the filing. After an affidavit is filed under this subsection, a taxing unit may not file suit to collect delinquent taxes on the property and the property may not be sold at a sale to foreclose the tax lien until the 181st day after the date the individual no longer owns and occupies the property as a residence homestead.

(c) To obtain an abatement of a pending suit, the individual must file in the court in which suit is pending an affidavit stating the facts required to be established by Subsection (a). If no controverting affidavit is filed by the taxing unit filing suit or if, after a hearing, the court finds the individual is entitled to the deferral, the court shall abate the suit until the 181st day after the date the individual no longer owns and occupies the property as a residence homestead. The clerk of the court shall deliver a copy of the judgment abating the suit to the chief appraiser of each appraisal district that appraises the property.

(c-1) To obtain an abatement of a pending sale to foreclose the tax lien, the individual must deliver an affidavit stating the facts required to be established by Subsection (a) to the chief appraiser of each appraisal district that appraises the property, the collector for the taxing unit that requested the order of sale or the attorney representing that unit for the collection of delinquent taxes, and the officer charged with selling the property not later than the fifth day before the date of the sale. After an affidavit is delivered under this subsection, the property may not be sold at a tax sale until the 181st day after the date the individual no longer owns and occupies the property as a residence homestead. If property is sold in violation of this section, the property owner may file a motion to set aside the sale under the same cause number and in the same court as a judgment reference in the order of sale. The motion must be filed during the applicable redemption period as set forth in Section 34.21(a) or, if the property is bid off to a taxing entity, on or before the 180th day following the date the taxing unit's deed is filed of record, whichever is later. This right is not transferable to a third party.

The amended text in subsection (d) is effective for interest that accrues during a deferral or abatement period on or after Jan. 1, 2018. Interest that accrues before Jan. 1, 2018, is governed by the former law in effect at that time. The amended text in subsection (d) will take effect Jan. 1, 2018, only if the constitutional amendment proposed by H.J.R. 21, §1, which will be voted on during the Nov. 7, 2017 general election, is approved by the voters.

(d) A tax lien remains on the property and interest continues to accrue during the period collection of taxes is deferred or abated under this section. The an-

nual interest rate during the deferral or abatement period is five ~~[eight]~~ percent instead of the rate provided by Section 33.01. Interest and penalties that accrued or that were incurred or imposed under Section 33.01 or 33.07 before the date the individual files the deferral affidavit under Subsection (b) or the date the judgment abating the suit is entered, as applicable, are preserved. A penalty under Section 33.01 is not incurred during a deferral or abatement period. The additional penalty under Section 33.07 may be imposed and collected only if the taxes for which collection is deferred or abated remain delinquent on or after the 181st day after the date the deferral or abatement period expires. A plea of limitation, laches, or want of prosecution does not apply against the taxing unit because of deferral or abatement of collection as provided by this section.

(e) Each year the chief appraiser for each appraisal district shall publicize in a manner reasonably designed to notify all residents of the district or county of the provisions of this section and, specifically, the method by which eligible persons may obtain a deferral or abatement.

(f) Notwithstanding the other provisions of this section, if an individual who qualifies for a deferral or abatement of collection of taxes on property as provided by this section dies, the deferral or abatement continues in effect until the 181st day after the date the surviving spouse of the individual no longer owns and occupies the property as a residence homestead if:

(1) the property was the residence homestead of the deceased spouse when the deceased spouse died;

(2) the surviving spouse was 55 years of age or older when the deceased spouse died; and

(3) the property was the residence homestead of the surviving spouse when the deceased spouse died.

(g) If the ownership interest of an individual entitled to a deferral under this section is a life estate, a lien for the deferred tax attaches to the estate of the life tenant, and not to the remainder interest, if the owner of the remainder is an institution of higher education that has not consented to the deferral. In this subsection, "institution of higher education" has the meaning assigned by Section 61.003, Education Code. This subsection does not apply to a deferral for which the individual entitled to the deferral filed the affidavit required by Subsection (b) before September 1, 2011.

2017 Legislation: Amended by H.B. 150, §2, 85th Leg., eff. Jan. 1, 2018; H.B. 217, §§1, 2, 85th Leg. eff. Sept. 1, 2017.

TAX §33.065. DEFERRED COLLECTION OF TAXES ON APPRECIATING RESIDENCE HOMESTEAD

(a) An individual is entitled to defer or abate a suit to collect a delinquent tax imposed on the portion of the appraised value of property the individual owns and occupies as the individual's residence homestead that exceeds the sum of:

(1) 105 percent of the appraised value of the property for the preceding year; and

(2) the market value of all new improvements to the property.

(b) An individual may not obtain a deferral or abatement under this section, and any deferral or abatement previously received expires, if the taxes on the portion of the appraised value of the property that does not exceed the amount provided by Subsection (a) are delinquent.

(c) To obtain a deferral, an individual must file with the chief appraiser for the appraisal district in which the property is located an affidavit stating the facts required to be established by Subsection (a). The chief appraiser shall notify each taxing unit participating in the district of the filing. After an affidavit is filed under this subsection, a taxing unit may not file suit to collect delinquent taxes on the property for which collection is deferred until the individual no longer owns and occupies the property as a residence homestead.

(d) To obtain an abatement, the individual must file in the court in which the delinquent tax suit is pending an affidavit stating the facts required to be established by Subsection (a). If the taxing unit that filed the suit does not file a controverting affidavit or if, after a hearing, the court finds the individual is entitled to the deferral, the court shall abate the suit until the individual no longer owns and occupies the property as the individual's residence homestead. The clerk of the court shall deliver a copy of the judgment abating the suit to the chief appraiser of each appraisal district that appraises the property.

(e) A deferral or abatement under this section applies only to ad valorem taxes imposed beginning with the tax year following the first tax year the individual entitled to the deferral or abatement qualifies the property for an exemption under Section 11.13. For purposes of this subsection, the owner of a residence homestead that is qualified for an exemption under

Section 11.13 on January 1, 1998, is considered to have qualified the property for the first time in the 1997 tax year.

(f) If the collection of delinquent taxes on the property was deferred in a prior tax year and the sum of the amounts described by Subsections (a)(1) and (2) exceeds the appraised value of the property for the current tax year, the amount of taxes the collection of which may be deferred is reduced by the amount calculated by multiplying the taxing unit's tax rate for the current year by the amount by which that sum exceeds the appraised value of the property.

(g) A tax lien remains on the property and interest continues to accrue during the period collection of delinquent taxes is deferred or abated under this section. The annual interest rate during the deferral or abatement period is eight percent instead of the rate provided by Section 33.01. Interest and penalties that accrued or that were incurred or imposed under Section 33.01 or 33.07 before the date the individual files the deferral affidavit under Subsection (c) or the date the judgment abating the suit is entered, as applicable, are preserved. A penalty is not incurred on the delinquent taxes for which collection is deferred or abated during a deferral or abatement period. The additional penalty under Section 33.07 may be imposed and collected only if the delinquent taxes for which collection is deferred or abated remain delinquent on or after the 91st day after the date the deferral or abatement period expires. A plea of limitation, laches, or want of prosecution does not apply against the taxing unit because of deferral or abatement of collection as provided by this section.

(h) Each year the chief appraiser for each appraisal district shall publicize in a manner reasonably designed to notify all residents of the county for which the appraisal district is established of the provisions of this section and, specifically, the method by which an eligible person may obtain a deferral.

(i) In this section:

(1) "New improvement" means an improvement to a residence homestead that is made after the appraisal of the property for the preceding year and that increases the market value of the property. The term does not include ordinary maintenance of an existing structure or the grounds or another feature of the property.

(2) "Residence homestead" has the meaning assigned that term by Section 11.13.

TAX §33.07. ADDITIONAL PENALTY FOR COLLECTION COSTS FOR TAXES DUE BEFORE JUNE 1

(a) A taxing unit or appraisal district may provide, in the manner required by law for official action by the body, that taxes that become delinquent on or after February 1 of a year but not later than May 1 of that year and that remain delinquent on July 1 of the year in which they become delinquent incur an additional penalty to defray costs of collection, if the unit or district or another unit that collects taxes for the unit has contracted with an attorney pursuant to Section 6.30. The amount of the penalty may not exceed the amount of the compensation specified in the contract with the attorney to be paid in connection with the collection of the delinquent taxes.

(b) A tax lien attaches to the property on which the tax is imposed to secure payment of the penalty.

(c) If a penalty is imposed pursuant to this section, a taxing unit may not recover attorney's fees in a suit to collect delinquent taxes subject to the penalty.

(d) If a taxing unit or appraisal district provides for a penalty under this section, the collector shall deliver a notice of delinquency and of the penalty to the property owner at least 30 and not more than 60 days before July 1.

TAX §33.08. ADDITIONAL PENALTY FOR COLLECTION COSTS FOR TAXES DUE ON OR AFTER JUNE 1

(a) This section applies to a taxing unit or appraisal district only if:

(1) the governing body of the taxing unit or appraisal district has imposed the additional penalty for collection costs under Section 33.07; and

(2) the taxing unit or appraisal district, or another taxing unit that collects taxes for the unit, has entered into a contract with an attorney under Section 6.30 for the collection of the unit's delinquent taxes.

(b) The governing body of the taxing unit or appraisal district, in the manner required by law for official action, may provide that taxes that become delinquent on or after June 1 under Section 26.07(f), 26.15(e), 31.03, 31.031, 31.032, 31.04, or 42.42 incur an additional penalty to defray costs of collection. The amount of the penalty may not exceed the amount of the compensation specified in the applicable contract with an attorney under Section 6.30 to be paid in connection with the collection of the delinquent taxes.

(c) After the taxes become delinquent, the collector for a taxing unit or appraisal district that has provided for the additional penalty under this section shall send a notice of the delinquency and the penalty to the property owner. The penalty is incurred on the first day of the first month that begins at least 21 days after the date the notice is sent.

(d) A tax lien attaches to the property on which the tax is imposed to secure payment of the additional penalty.

(e) A taxing unit or appraisal district that imposes the additional penalty under this section may not recover attorney's fees in a suit to collect delinquent taxes subject to the penalty.

TAX §33.09. EXPIRED

TAX §33.10. RESTRICTED OR CONDITIONAL PAYMENTS OF DELINQUENT TAXES, PENALTIES, & INTEREST PROHIBITED

Unless the restriction or condition is authorized by this title, a restriction or condition placed on a check in payment of delinquent taxes by the maker that purports to limit the amount of delinquent taxes owed to an amount less than that stated in the applicable delinquent tax roll, or a restriction or condition placed on a check in payment of penalties and interest on delinquent taxes by the maker that purports to limit the amount of the penalties and interest to an amount less than the amount of penalties and interest accrued on the delinquent taxes, is void.

TAX §33.11. EARLY ADDITIONAL PENALTY FOR COLLECTION COSTS FOR TAXES IMPOSED ON PERSONAL PROPERTY

(a) In order to defray costs of collection, the governing body of a taxing unit or appraisal district in the manner required by law for official action may provide that taxes imposed on tangible personal property that become delinquent on or after February 1 of a year incur an additional penalty on a date that occurs before July 1 of the year in which the taxes become delinquent if:

(1) the taxing unit or appraisal district or another unit that collects taxes for the unit has contracted with an attorney under Section 6.30; and

(2) the taxes on the personal property become subject to the attorney's contract before July 1 of the year in which the taxes become delinquent.

(b) A penalty imposed under Subsection (a) is incurred by the delinquent taxes on the later of:

(1) the date those taxes become subject to the attorney's contract; or

(2) 60 days after the date the taxes become delinquent.

(c) The amount of the penalty may not exceed the amount of the compensation specified in the contract with the attorney to be paid in connection with the collection of the delinquent taxes.

(d) A tax lien attaches to the property on which the tax is imposed to secure payment of the penalty.

(e) If a penalty is provided under this section, a taxing unit or appraisal district may not:

(1) recover attorney's fees in a suit to collect delinquent taxes subject to the penalty; or

(2) impose an additional penalty under Section 33.07 on a delinquent personal property tax.

(f) If the governing body of a taxing unit or appraisal district provides for a penalty under this section, the collector for the taxing unit or appraisal district shall send a notice of the penalty to the property owner. The notice shall state the date on which the penalty is incurred, and the tax collector shall deliver the notice at least 30 and not more than 60 days before that date. If the amount of personal property tax, penalty and interest owed to all taxing units for which the tax collector collects exceeds $10,000 on a single account identified by a unique property identification number, the notice regarding that account must be delivered by certified mail, return receipt requested. All other notices under this section may be delivered by regular first-class mail.

(g) The authority granted to taxing units and appraisal districts under this section is to be construed as an alternative, with regards to delinquent personal property taxes, to the authority given by Section 33.07.

Sections 33.12-33.20 reserved for expansion

SUBCHAPTER B. SEIZURE OF PERSONAL PROPERTY

TAX §33.21. PROPERTY SUBJECT TO SEIZURE

(a) A person's personal property is subject to seizure for the payment of a delinquent tax, penalty, and interest he owes a taxing unit on property.

(b) A person's personal property is subject to seizure for the payment of a tax imposed by a taxing unit on the person's property before the tax becomes delinquent if:

(1) the collector discovers that property on which the tax has been or will be imposed is about to be:

(A) removed from the county; or

(B) sold in a liquidation sale in connection with the cessation of a business; and

(2) the collector knows of no other personal property in the county from which the tax may be satisfied.

(c) Current wages in the possession of an employer are not subject to seizure.

(d) In this subchapter, "personal property" means:

(1) tangible personal property;

(2) cash on hand;

(3) notes or accounts receivable, including rents and royalties;

(4) demand or time deposits; and

(5) certificates of deposit.

TAX §33.22. INSTITUTION OF SEIZURE

(a) At any time after a tax becomes delinquent, a collector may apply for a tax warrant to any court in any county in which the person liable for the tax has personal property. If more than one collector participates in the seizure, all may make a joint application.

(b) A collector may apply at any time for a tax warrant authorizing seizure of property as provided by Subsection (b) of Section 33.21 of this code.

(c) The court shall issue the tax warrant if the applicant shows by affidavit that:

(1) the person whose property the applicant intends to seize is delinquent in the payment of taxes, penalties, and interest in the amount stated in the application; or

(2) taxes in a stated amount have been imposed on the property or taxes in an estimated amount will be imposed on the property, the applicant knows of no other personal property the person owns in the county from which the tax may be satisfied, and the applicant has reason to believe that:

(A) the property owner is about to remove the property from the county; or

(B) the property is about to be sold at a liquidation sale in connection with the cessation of a business.

(d) A collector is entitled to recover attorney's fees in an amount equal to the compensation specified in the contract with the attorney if:

(1) recovery of the attorney's fees is requested in the application for the tax warrant;

(2) the taxing unit served by the collector contracts with an attorney under Section 6.30;

(3) the existence of the contract and the amount of attorney's fees that equals the compensation specified in the contract are supported by the affidavit of the collector; and

(4) the tax sought to be recovered is not subject to the additional penalty under Section 33.07 or 33.08 at the time the application is filed.

(e) If a taxing unit is represented by an attorney who is also an officer or employee of the taxing unit, the collector for the taxing unit is entitled to recover attorney's fees in an amount equal to 15 percent of the total amount of delinquent taxes, penalties, and interest that the property owner owes the taxing unit.

TAX §33.23. TAX WARRANT

(a) A tax warrant shall direct a peace officer in the county and the collector to seize as much of the person's personal property as may be reasonably necessary for the payment of all taxes, penalties, interest, and attorney's fees included in the application and all costs of seizure and sale. The warrant shall direct the person whose property is seized to disclose to the officer executing the warrant the name and the address if known of any other person having an interest in the property.

(b) A bond may not be required of a taxing unit for issuance or delivery of a tax warrant, and a fee or court cost may not be charged for issuance or delivery of a warrant.

(c) After a tax warrant is issued, the collector or peace officer shall take possession of the property pending its sale. The person against whom a tax warrant is issued or another person having possession of property of the person against whom a tax warrant is issued shall surrender the property on demand. Pending the sale of the property, the collector or peace officer may secure the property at the location where it is seized or may move the property to another location.

(d) A person who possesses personal property owned by the person against whom a tax warrant is issued and who surrenders the property on demand is not liable to any person for the surrender. At the time of surrender, the collector shall provide the person surrendering the property a sworn receipt describing the property surrendered.

(e) Subsection (d) does not create an obligation on the part of a person who surrenders property owned by

the person against whom a tax warrant is issued that exceeds or materially differs from that person's obligation to the person against whom the tax warrant is issued.

TAX §33.24. BOND FOR PAYMENT OF TAXES

A person may prevent seizure of property or sale of property seized by delivering to the collector a cash or surety bond conditioned on payment of the tax before delinquency. The bond must be approved by the collector in an amount determined by him, but he may not require an amount greater than the amount of tax if imposed or the collector's reasonable estimate of the amount of tax if not yet imposed.

TAX §33.25. TAX SALE: NOTICE; METHOD; DISPOSITION OF PROCEEDS

(a) After a seizure of personal property, the collector shall make a reasonable inquiry to determine the identity and to ascertain the address of any person having an interest in the property other than the person against whom the tax warrant is issued. The collector shall provide in writing the name and address of each other person the collector identifies as having an interest in the property to the peace officer charged with executing the warrant. The peace officer shall deliver as soon as possible a written notice stating the time and place of the sale and briefly describing the property seized to the person against whom the warrant is issued and to any other person having an interest in the property whose name and address the collector provided to the peace officer. The posting of the notice and the sale of the property shall be conducted:

(1) in a county other than a county to which Subdivision (2) applies, by the peace officer in the manner required for the sale under execution of personal property; or

(2) in a county having a population of three million or more:

(A) by the peace officer or collector, as specified in the warrant, in the manner required for the sale under execution of personal property; or

(B) under an agreement authorized by Subsection (b).

(b) The commissioners court of a county having a population of three million or more by official action may authorize a peace officer or the collector for the county charged with selling property under this subchapter by public auction to enter into an agreement with a person who holds an auctioneer's license to advertise the auction sale of the property and to conduct the auction sale of the property. The agreement may provide for on-line bidding and sale.

(c) The commissioners court of a county that authorizes a peace officer or the collector for the county to enter into an agreement under Subsection (b) may by official action authorize the peace officer or collector to enter into an agreement with a service provider to advertise the auction and to conduct the auction sale of the property or to accept bids during the auction sale of the property under Subsection (b) using the Internet.

(d) The terms of an agreement entered into under Subsection (b) or (c) must be approved in writing by the collector for each taxing unit entitled to receive proceeds from the sale of the property. An agreement entered into under Subsection (b) or (c) is presumed to be commercially reasonable, and the presumption may not be rebutted by any person.

(e) Failure to send or receive a notice required by this section does not affect the validity of the sale or title to the seized property.

(f) The proceeds of a sale of property under this section shall be applied to:

(1) any compensation owed to or any expense advanced by the licensed auctioneer under an agreement entered into under Subsection (b) or a service provider under an agreement entered into under Subsection (c);

(2) all usual costs, expenses, and fees of the seizure and sale, payable to the peace officer conducting the sale;

(3) all additional expenses incurred in advertising the sale or in removing, storing, preserving, or safeguarding the seized property pending its sale;

(4) all usual court costs payable to the clerk of the court that issued the tax warrant; and

(5) taxes, penalties, interest, and attorney's fees included in the application for warrant.

(g) The peace officer or licensed auctioneer conducting the sale shall pay all proceeds from the sale to the collector designated in the tax warrant for distribution as required by Subsection (f).

(h) After a seizure of personal property defined by Sections 33.21(d)(2)-(5), the collector shall apply the seized property toward the payment of the taxes, penal-

ties, interest, and attorney's fees included in the application for warrant and all costs of the seizure as required by Subsection (f).

(i) After a tax warrant is issued, the seizure or sale of the property may be canceled and terminated at any time by the applicant or an authorized agent or attorney of the applicant.

Sections 33.26-33.40 reserved for expansion

SUBCHAPTER C. DELINQUENT TAX SUITS

TAX §33.41. SUIT TO COLLECT DELINQUENT TAX

(a) At any time after its tax on property becomes delinquent, a taxing unit may file suit to foreclose the lien securing payment of the tax, to enforce personal liability for the tax, or both. The suit must be in a court of competent jurisdiction for the county in which the tax was imposed.

(b) A suit to collect a delinquent tax takes precedence over all other suits pending in appellate courts.

(c) In a suit brought under Subsection (a), a taxing unit may foreclose any other lien on the property in favor of the taxing unit or enforce personal liability of the property owner for the other lien.

(d) In a suit brought under this section, a court shall grant a taxing unit injunctive relief on a showing that the personal property on which the taxing unit seeks to foreclose a tax lien is about to be:

(1) removed from the county in which the tax was imposed; or

(2) transferred to another person and the other person is not a buyer in the ordinary course of business, as defined by Section 1.201, Business & Commerce Code.

(e) Injunctive relief granted under Subsection (d) must:

(1) prohibit alienation or dissipation of the property;

(2) order that proceeds from the sale of the property in an amount equal to the taxes claimed to be due be paid into the court registry; or

(3) order any other relief to ensure the payment of the taxes owed.

(f) A taxing unit is not required to file a bond as a condition to the granting of injunctive relief under Subsection (d).

(g) In a petition for relief under Subsection (d), the taxing unit may also seek to secure the payment of taxes for a current tax year that are not delinquent and shall estimate the amount due if those taxes are not yet assessed.

(h) The tax lien attaches to any amounts paid into the court's registry with the same priority as for the property on which taxes are owed.

See also *O'Connor's Texas Appeals*, "Cases given precedence by law," ch. 3-C, §5.1, p. 101.

TAX §33.42. TAXES INCLUDED IN FORECLOSURE SUIT

(a) In a suit to foreclose a lien securing payment of its tax on real property, a taxing unit shall include all delinquent taxes due the unit on the property.

(b) If a taxing unit's tax on real property becomes delinquent after the unit files suit to foreclose a tax lien on the property but before entry of judgment, the court shall include the amount of the tax and any penalty and interest in its judgment.

(c) If a tax required by this section to be included in a suit is omitted from the judgment in the suit, the taxing unit may not enforce collection of the tax at a later time except as provided by Section 34.04(c)(2).

TAX §33.43. PETITION

(a) A petition initiating a suit to collect a delinquent property tax is sufficient if it alleges that:

(1) the taxing unit is legally constituted and authorized to impose and collect ad valorem taxes on property;

(2) tax in a stated amount was legally imposed on each separately described property for each year specified and on each person named if known who owned the property on January 1 of the year for which the tax was imposed;

(3) the tax was imposed in the county in which the suit is filed;

(4) the tax is delinquent;

(5) penalties, interest, and costs authorized by law in a stated amount for each separately assessed property are due;

(6) the taxing unit is entitled to recover each penalty that is incurred and all interest that accrues on delinquent taxes imposed on the property from the date of the judgment to the date of the sale under Section 34.01 or under Section 253.010, Local Government Code, as applicable, if the suit seeks to foreclose a tax lien;

(7) the person sued owned the property on January 1 of the year for which the tax was imposed if the suit seeks to enforce personal liability;

(8) the person sued owns the property when the suit is filed if the suit seeks to foreclose a tax lien;

(9) the taxing unit asserts a lien on each separately described property to secure the payment of all taxes, penalties, interest, and costs due if the suit seeks to foreclose a tax lien;

(10) all things required by law to be done have been done properly by the appropriate officials; and

(11) the attorney signing the petition is legally authorized to prosecute the suit on behalf of the taxing unit.

(b) If the petition alleges that the person sued owns the property on which the taxing unit asserts a lien, the prayer in the petition shall be for foreclosure of the lien and payment of all taxes, penalties, interest, and costs that are due or will become due and that are secured by the lien. If the petition alleges that the person sued owned the property on January 1 of the year for which the taxes were imposed, the prayer shall be for personal judgment for all taxes, penalties, interest, and costs that are due or will become due on the property. If the petition contains the appropriate allegations, the prayer may be for both foreclosure of a lien on the property and personal judgment.

(c) If the suit is for personal judgment against the person who owned personal property on January 1 of the year for which the tax was imposed on the property, the personal property may be described generally.

(d) The petition need not be verified.

(e) The comptroller shall prepare forms for petitions initiating suits to collect delinquent taxes. An attorney representing a taxing unit may use the forms or develop his own form.

TAX §33.44. JOINDER OF OTHER TAXING UNITS

(a) A taxing unit filing suit to foreclose a tax lien on real property shall join other taxing units that have claims for delinquent taxes against all or part of the same property.

(b) For purposes of joining a county, citation may be served on the county tax assessor-collector. For purposes of joining any other taxing unit, citation may be served on the officer charged with collecting taxes for the unit or on the presiding officer or secretary of the governing body of the unit. Citation may be served by certified mail, return receipt requested. A person on whom service is authorized by this subsection may waive the issuance and service of citation in behalf of his taxing unit.

(c) A taxing unit joined in a suit as provided by this section must file its claim for delinquent taxes against the property or its lien on the property is extinguished. The court's judgment in the suit shall reflect the extinguishment of a lien under this subsection.

TAX §33.445. JOINDER OF TAX LIEN TRANSFEREE

(a) A taxing unit acting under Section 33.44(a) shall also join each transferee of a tax lien against the property that may appear of record under Section 32.06. After the joinder, the transferee of the tax lien may file its claim and seek foreclosure in the suit for all amounts owed the transferee that are secured by the transferred tax lien, regardless of when the original transfer of tax lien was recorded or whether the original loan secured by the transferred tax lien is delinquent. In the alternative, the transferee may pay all taxes, penalties, interest, court costs, and attorney's fees owing to the taxing unit that filed the foreclosure suit and each other taxing unit that is joined.

(b) In consideration of the payment by the transferee of those taxes and charges, each joined taxing unit shall transfer its tax lien to the transferee in the form and manner provided by Section 32.06(b) and enter its disclaimer in the suit. The transfer of a tax lien under this subsection does not require authorization by the property owner.

(c) On transfer of all applicable tax liens, the transferee may seek to foreclose the tax liens in the pending suit or in any other manner provided by Section 32.06, regardless of when the original transfer of tax lien was recorded or whether the original loan secured by the transferred tax lien is delinquent. The foreclosure may include all amounts owed to the transferee, including any amount secured by the original transfer of tax lien.

(d) All liens held by a transferee who is joined under this section but fails to act in the manner provided by this section are extinguished, and the court's judgment shall reflect the extinguishment of those liens.

TAX §33.45. PLEADING & ANSWERING TO CLAIMS FILED

A party to the suit must take notice of and plead and answer to all claims and pleadings filed by other parties that have been joined or have intervened, and each citation must so state.

TAX §33.46. PARTITION OF REAL PROPERTY

(a) If suit is filed to foreclose a tax lien on real property owned in undivided interests by two or more persons, one or more of the owners may have the property partitioned in the manner prescribed by law for the partition of real property in district court.

(b) The court shall apportion the taxes, penalties, interest, and costs sued for to the owners of the property in proportion to the interest of each. If an owner pays the taxes, penalties, interest, and costs apportioned to him, the property partitioned to him is free from further claim or lien for the taxes involved in the suit. If an owner refuses to pay the amount apportioned to him, the suit shall proceed against him for that amount.

(c) The court shall allow reasonable attorney's fees and costs of partitioning for each property partitioned. The fee shall be taxed as costs against each owner in proportion to his interest and constitutes a lien against the property until paid.

TAX §33.47. TAX RECORDS AS EVIDENCE

(a) In a suit to collect a delinquent tax, the taxing unit's current tax roll and delinquent tax roll or certified copies of the entries showing the property and the amount of the tax and penalties imposed and interest accrued constitute prima facie evidence that each person charged with a duty relating to the imposition of the tax has complied with all requirements of law and that the amount of tax alleged to be delinquent against the property and the amount of penalties and interest due on that tax as listed are the correct amounts.

(b) If the description of a property in the tax roll or delinquent tax roll is insufficient to identify the property, the records of the appraisal office are admissible to identify the property.

(c) In a suit to collect a tax, a tax receipt issued under Section 31.075 of this code, or an electronic replica of the receipt, that states that a tax has been paid is prima facie evidence that the tax has been paid as stated by the receipt or electronic replica.

TAX §33.475. ATTORNEY AD LITEM REPORT; APPROVAL OF FEES

(a) In a suit to collect a delinquent tax, an attorney ad litem appointed by a court to represent the interests of a defendant served with process by means of citation by publication or posting shall submit to the court a report describing the actions taken by the attorney ad litem to locate and represent the interests of the defendant.

(b) The court may not approve the fees of the attorney ad litem until the attorney ad litem submits the report required by this section and the court determines that the actions taken by the attorney ad litem as described in the report were sufficient to discharge the attorney's duties to the defendant.

TAX §33.48. RECOVERY OF COSTS & EXPENSES

(a) In addition to other costs authorized by law, a taxing unit is entitled to recover the following costs and expenses in a suit to collect a delinquent tax:

(1) all usual court costs, including the cost of serving process and electronic filing fees;

(2) costs of filing for record a notice of lis pendens against property;

(3) expenses of foreclosure sale;

(4) reasonable expenses that are incurred by the taxing unit in determining the name, identity, and location of necessary parties and in procuring necessary legal descriptions of the property on which a delinquent tax is due;

(5) attorney's fees in the amount of 15 percent of the total amount of taxes, penalties, and interest due the unit; and

(6) reasonable attorney ad litem fees approved by the court that are incurred in a suit in which the court orders the appointment of an attorney to represent the interests of a defendant served with process by means of citation by publication or posting.

(b) Each item specified by Subsection (a) of this section is a charge against the property subject to foreclosure in the suit and shall be collected out of the proceeds of the sale of the property or, if the suit is for personal judgment, charged against the defendant.

(c) Fees collected for attorneys and other officials are fees of office, except that fees for contract attorneys representing a taxing unit that is joined or intervenes shall be applied toward the compensation due the attorney under the contract.

(d) A collector who accepts a payment of the court costs and other expenses described by this section shall disburse the amount of the payment as follows:

(1) amounts owing under Subsections (a)(1), (2), (3), and (6) are payable to the clerk of the court in which the suit is pending; and

(2) expenses described by Subsection (a)(4) are payable to the general fund of the taxing unit or to the person or entity who advanced the expense.

See also *O'Connor's Texas COA*, "Taxing unit," ch. 44, §2.2.1(2)(c), p. 1392.

TAX §33.49. LIABILITY OF TAXING UNIT FOR COSTS

(a) Except as provided by Subsection (b), a taxing unit is not liable in a suit to collect taxes for court costs, including any fees for service of process or electronic filing, an attorney ad litem, arbitration, or mediation, and may not be required to post security for costs.

(b) A taxing unit shall pay the cost of publishing citations, notices of sale, or other notices from the unit's general fund as soon as practicable after receipt of the publisher's claim for payment. The taxing unit is entitled to reimbursement from other taxing units that are parties to the suit for their proportionate share of the publication costs on satisfaction of any portion of the tax indebtedness before further distribution of the proceeds. A taxing unit may not pay a word or line rate for publication of citation or other required notice that exceeds the rate the newspaper publishing the notice charges private entities for similar classes of advertising.

See also *O'Connor's Texas Appeals*, "Taxing units," ch. 1-H, §2.2.2(2), p. 68; "School districts & other taxing units," ch. 4-C, §4.1.9, p. 193; *O'Connor's Texas COA*, "Taxing unit," ch. 44, §2.2.1(2)(c), p. 1392.

TAX §33.50. ADJUDGED VALUE

(a) In a suit for foreclosure of a tax lien on property, the court shall determine the market value of the property on the date of trial. The appraised value of the property according to the most recent appraisal roll approved by the appraisal review board is presumed to be its market value on the date of trial, and the person being sued has the burden of establishing that the market value of the property differs from that appraised value. The court shall incorporate a finding of the market value of the property on the date of trial in the judgment.

(b) If the judgment in a suit to collect a delinquent tax is for the foreclosure of a tax lien on property, the order of sale shall specify that the property may be sold to a taxing unit that is a party to the suit or to any other person, other than a person owning an interest in the property or any party to the suit that is not a taxing unit, for the market value of the property stated in the judgment or the aggregate amount of the judgments against the property, whichever is less.

(c) The order of sale shall also specify that the property may not be sold to a person owning an interest in the property or to a person who is a party to the suit other than a taxing unit unless:

(1) that person is the highest bidder at the tax sale; and

(2) the amount bid by that person is equal to or greater than the aggregate amount of the judgments against the property, including all costs of suit and sale.

TAX §33.51. WRIT OF POSSESSION

(a) If the court orders the foreclosure of a tax lien and the sale of real property, the judgment shall provide for the issuance by the clerk of said court of a writ of possession to the purchaser at the sale or to the purchaser's assigns no sooner than 20 days following the date on which the purchaser's deed from the sheriff or constable is filed of record.

(b) The officer charged with executing the writ shall place the purchaser or the purchaser's assigns in possession of the property described in the purchaser's deed without further order from any court and in the manner provided by the writ, subject to any notice to vacate that may be required to be given to a tenant under Section 24.005(b), Property Code.

(c) The writ of possession shall order the officer executing the writ to:

(1) post a written warning that is at least 8½ by 11 inches on the exterior of the front door of the premises notifying the occupant that the writ has been issued and that the writ will be executed on or after a specific date and time stated in the warning that is not sooner than the 10th day after the date the warning is posted; and

(2) on execution of the writ:

(A) deliver possession of the premises to the purchaser or the purchaser's assigns;

(B) instruct the occupants to immediately leave the premises and, if the occupants fail or refuse to comply, physically remove them from the premises;

(C) instruct the occupants to remove, or to allow the purchaser or purchaser's assigns, representatives, or

other persons acting under the officer's supervision to remove, all personal property from the premises; and

(D) place, or have an authorized person place, the removed personal property outside the premises at a nearby location, but not so as to block a public sidewalk, passageway, or street and not while it is raining, sleeting, or snowing.

(d) The writ of possession shall authorize the officer, at the officer's discretion, to engage the services of a bonded or insured warehouseman to remove and store, subject to applicable law, all or part of the personal property at no cost to the purchaser, the purchaser's assigns, or the officer executing the writ. The officer may not require the purchaser or the purchaser's assigns to store the personal property.

(e) The writ of possession shall contain notice to the officer that under Section 7.003, Civil Practice and Remedies Code, the officer is not liable for damages resulting from the execution of the writ if the officer executes the writ in good faith and with reasonable diligence.

(f) The warehouseman's lien on stored property, the officer's duties, and the occupants' rights of redemption as provided by Section 24.0062, Property Code, are all applicable with respect to any personal property that is removed under Subsection (d).

(g) A sheriff or constable may use reasonable force in executing a writ under this section.

(h) If a taxing unit is a purchaser and is entitled to a writ of possession in the taxing unit's name:

(1) a bond may not be required of the taxing unit for issuance or delivery of a writ of possession; and

(2) a fee or court cost may not be charged for issuance or delivery of a writ of possession.

(i) In this section:

(1) "Premises" means all of the property described in the purchaser's deed, including the buildings, dwellings, or other structures located on the property.

(2) "Purchaser" includes a taxing unit to which property is bid off under Section 34.01(j).

TAX §33.52. TAXES INCLUDED IN JUDGMENT

(a) Only taxes that are delinquent on the date of a judgment may be included in the amount recoverable under the judgment by the taxing units that are parties to the suit.

(b) In lieu of stating as a liquidated amount the aggregate total of taxes, penalties, and interest due, a judgment may:

(1) set out the tax due each taxing unit for each year; and

(2) provide that penalties and interest accrue on the unpaid taxes as provided by Subchapter A.

(c) For purposes of calculating penalties and interest due under the judgment, it is presumed that the delinquency date for a tax is February 1 of the year following the year in which the tax was imposed, unless the judgment provides otherwise.

(d) Except as provided by Section 34.05(k), a taxing unit's claim for taxes that become delinquent after the date of the judgment is not affected by the entry of the judgment or a tax sale conducted under that judgment. Those taxes may be collected by any remedy provided by this title.

TAX §33.53. ORDER OF SALE; PAYMENT BEFORE SALE

(a) If judgment in a suit to collect a delinquent tax is for foreclosure of a tax lien, the court shall order the property sold in satisfaction of the amount of the judgment.

(b) On application by a taxing unit that is a party to the judgment, the district clerk shall prepare an order to an officer authorized to conduct execution sales ordering the sale of the property. If more than one parcel of property is included in the judgment, the taxing unit may specify particular parcels to be sold. A taxing unit may request more than one order of sale as necessary to collect all amounts due under the judgment.

(c) An order of sale:

(1) shall be returned to the district clerk as unexecuted if not executed before the 181st day after the date the order is issued; and

(2) may be accompanied by a copy of the judgment and a bill of costs attached to the order and incorporate the terms of the judgment or bill of costs by reference.

(d) A judgment or a bill of costs attached to the order of sale is not required to be certified.

(e) If the owner pays the amount of the judgment before the property is sold, the taxing unit shall:

(1) release the tax lien held by the taxing unit on the property; and

(2) file for record with the clerk of the court in which the judgment was rendered a release of the lien.

TAX §33.54. LIMITATION ON ACTIONS RELATING TO PROPERTY SOLD FOR TAXES

(a) Except as provided by Subsection (b), an action relating to the title to property may not be maintained against the purchaser of the property at a tax sale unless the action is commenced:

(1) before the first anniversary of the date that the deed executed to the purchaser at the tax sale is filed of record; or

(2) before the second anniversary of the date that the deed executed to the purchaser is filed of record, if on the date that the suit to collect the delinquent tax was filed the property was:

(A) the residence homestead of the owner; or

(B) land appraised or eligible to be appraised under Subchapter C or D, Chapter 23.

(b) If a person other than the purchaser at the tax sale or the person's successor in interest pays taxes on the property during the applicable limitations period and until the commencement of an action challenging the validity of the tax sale and that person was not served citation in the suit to foreclose the tax lien, that limitations period does not apply to that person.

(c) When actions are barred by this section, the purchaser at the tax sale or the purchaser's successor in interest has full title to the property, precluding all other claims.

TAX §33.55. EFFECT OF JUDGMENT ON ACCRUAL OF PENALTIES & INTEREST

A judgment for delinquent taxes does not affect the accrual after the date of the judgment of penalties and interest under this chapter on the taxes included in the judgment.

TAX §33.56. VACATION OF JUDGMENT

(a) If, in a suit to collect a delinquent tax, a court renders a judgment for foreclosure of a tax lien on behalf of a taxing unit, any taxing unit that was a party to the judgment may file a petition to vacate the judgment on one or more of the following grounds:

(1) failure to join a person needed for just adjudication under the Texas Rules of Civil Procedure, including a taxing unit required to be joined under Section 33.44(a);

(2) failure to serve a person needed for just adjudication under the Texas Rules of Civil Procedure, including a taxing unit required to be joined under Section 33.44(a);

(3) failure of the judgment to adequately describe the property that is the subject of the suit; or

(4) that the property described in the judgment was subject to multiple appraisals for the tax years included in the judgment.

(b) The taxing unit must file the petition under the same cause number as the delinquent tax suit and in the same court.

(c) The taxing unit may not file a petition if a tax sale of the property has occurred unless:

(1) the tax sale has been vacated by an order of a court;

(2) the property was bid off to a taxing unit under Section 34.01(j) and has not been resold; or

(3) the tax sale or resale purchaser, or the purchaser's heirs, successors, or assigns, consents to the petition.

(d) Consent of the purchaser to a petition may be shown by:

(1) a written memorandum signed by the purchaser and filed with the court;

(2) the purchaser's joinder in the taxing unit's petition;

(3) a statement of the purchaser made in open court on the record in a hearing on the petition; or

(4) the purchaser's signature of approval to an agreed order to grant the petition.

(e) A copy of the petition must be served in a manner authorized by Rule 21a, Texas Rules of Civil Procedure, on each party to the delinquent tax suit.

(f) If the court grants the petition, the court shall enter an order providing that:

(1) the judgment, any tax sale based on that judgment, and any subsequent resale are vacated;

(2) any applicable tax deed or applicable resale deed is canceled;

(3) the delinquent tax suit is revived; and

(4) except in a case in which judgment is vacated under Subsection (a)(4), the taxes, penalties, interest, and attorney's fees and costs, and the liens that secure each of those items, are reinstated.

TAX §33.57. ALTERNATIVE NOTICE OF TAX FORECLOSURE ON CERTAIN PARCELS OF REAL PROPERTY

(a) In this section, "appraised value" means the appraised value according to the most recent appraisal roll approved by the appraisal review board.

(b) This section may be invoked and used by one or more taxing units if there are delinquent taxes, penalties, interest, and attorney's fees owing to a taxing unit on a parcel of real property, and:

(1) the total amount of delinquent taxes, penalties, interest, and attorney's fees owed exceeds the appraised value of the parcel; or

(2) there are 10 or more years for which delinquent taxes are owed on the parcel.

(c) One or more taxing units may file a single petition for foreclosure under this section that includes multiple parcels of property and multiple owners. Alternatively, separate petitions may be filed and docketed separately for each parcel of property. Another taxing unit with a tax claim against the same parcel may intervene in an action for the purpose of establishing and foreclosing its tax lien without further notice to a defendant. The petition must be filed in the county in which the tax was imposed and is sufficient if it is in substantially the form prescribed by Section 33.43 and further alleges that:

(1) the amount owed in delinquent taxes, penalties, interest, and attorney's fees exceeds the appraised value of the parcel; or

(2) there are 10 or more years for which delinquent taxes are owed on the parcel.

(d) Simultaneously with the filing of the petition under this section, a taxing unit shall also file a motion with the court seeking an order approving notice of the petition to each defendant by certified mail in lieu of citation and, if the amount of delinquent taxes, penalties, interest, and attorney's fees alleged to be owed exceeds the appraised value of the parcel, waiving the appointment of an attorney ad litem. The motion must be supported by certified copies of tax records that show the tax years for which delinquent taxes are owed, the amounts of delinquent taxes, penalties, interest, and attorney's fees, and, if appropriate, the appraised value of the parcel.

(e) The court shall approve a motion under Subsection (d) if the documents in support of the motion show that:

(1) the amount of delinquent taxes, penalties, interest, and attorney's fees that are owed exceeds the appraised value of the parcel; or

(2) there are 10 or more years for which delinquent taxes are owed on the parcel.

(f) Before filing a petition under this section, or as soon afterwards as practicable, the taxing unit or its attorney shall determine the address of each owner of a property interest in the parcel for the purpose of providing notice of the pending petition. If the title search, the taxing unit's tax records, and the appraisal district records do not disclose an address of a person with a property interest, consulting the following sources of information is to be considered a reasonable effort by the taxing unit or its attorney to determine the address of a person with a property interest in the parcel subject to foreclosure:

(1) telephone directories, electronic or otherwise, that cover:

(A) the area of any last known address for the person; and

(B) the county in which the parcel is located;

(2) voter registration records in the county in which the parcel is located; and

(3) where applicable, assumed name records maintained by the county clerk of the county in which the parcel is located and corporate records maintained by the secretary of state.

(g) Not later than the 45th day before the date on which a hearing on the merits on a taxing unit's petition is scheduled, the taxing unit or its attorney shall send a copy of the petition and a notice by certified mail to each person whose address is determined under Subsection (f), informing the person of the pending foreclosure action and the scheduled hearing. A copy of each notice shall be filed with the clerk of the court together with an affidavit by the tax collector or by the taxing unit's attorney attesting to the fact and date of mailing of the notice.

(h) In addition to the notice required by Subsection (g), the taxing unit shall provide notice by publication and by posting to all persons with a property interest in the parcel subject to foreclosure. The notice shall be published in the English language once a week for two weeks in a newspaper that is published in the county in which the parcel is located and that has been in general circulation for at least one year immediately

before the date of the first publication, with the first publication to be not less than the 45th day before the date on which the taxing unit's petition is scheduled to be heard. When returned and filed in the trial court, an affidavit of the editor or publisher of the newspaper attesting to the date of publication, together with a printed copy of the notice as published, is sufficient proof of publication under this subsection. If a newspaper is not published in the county in which the parcel is located, publication in an otherwise qualifying newspaper published in an adjoining county is sufficient. The maximum fee for publishing the citation shall be the lowest published word or line rate of that newspaper for classified advertising. The notice by posting shall be in the English language and given by posting a copy of the notice at the courthouse door of the county in which the foreclosure is pending not less than the 45th day before the date on which the taxing unit's petition is scheduled to be heard. Proof of the posting of the notice shall be made by affidavit of the attorney for the taxing unit, or of the person posting it. If the publication of the notice cannot be had for the maximum fee established in this subsection, and that fact is supported by the affidavit of the attorney for the taxing unit, the notice by posting under this subsection is sufficient.

(i) The notice required by Subsections (g) and (h) must include:

(1) a statement that foreclosure proceedings have been commenced and the date the petition was filed;

(2) a legal description, tax account number, and, if known, a street address for the parcel in which the addressee owns a property interest;

(3) the name of the person to whom the notice is addressed and the name of each other person who, according to the title search, has an interest in the parcel in which the addressee owns a property interest;

(4) the date, time, and place of the scheduled hearing on the petition;

(5) a statement that the recipient of the notice may lose whatever property interest the recipient owns in the parcel as a result of the hearing and any subsequent tax sale;

(6) a statement explaining how a person may contest the taxing unit's petition as provided by Subsection (j) and that a person's interest in the parcel may be preserved by paying all delinquent taxes, penalties, interest, attorney's fees, and court costs before the date of the scheduled hearing on the petition;

(7) the name, address, and telephone number of the taxing unit and the taxing unit's attorney of record; and

(8) the name of each other taxing unit that imposes taxes on the parcel, together with a notice that any taxing unit may intervene without further notice and set up its claims for delinquent taxes.

(j) A person claiming a property interest in a parcel subject to foreclosure may contest a taxing unit's petition by filing with the clerk of the court a written response to the petition not later than the seventh day before the date scheduled for hearing on the petition and specifying in the response any affirmative defense of the person. A copy of the response must be served on the taxing unit's attorney of record in the manner required by Rule 21a, Texas Rules of Civil Procedure. The taxing unit is entitled on request to a continuance of the hearing if a written response filed to a notice of the hearing contains an affirmative defense or requests affirmative relief against the taxing unit.

(k) Before entry of a judgment under this section, a taxing unit may remove a parcel erroneously included in the petition and may take a voluntary nonsuit as to one or more parcels of property without prejudicing its action against the remaining parcels.

(*l*) If before the hearing on a taxing unit's petition the taxing unit discovers a deficiency in the provision of notice under this section, the taxing unit shall take reasonable steps in good faith to correct the deficiency before the hearing. A notice provided by Subsections (g)-(i) is in lieu of citation issued and served under Rule 117a, Texas Rules of Civil Procedure. Regardless of the manner in which notice under this section is given, an attorney ad litem may not be appointed for a person with an interest in a parcel with delinquent taxes, penalties, interest, and attorney's fees against the parcel in an amount that exceeds the parcel's appraised value. To the extent of any additional conflict between this section and the Texas Rules of Civil Procedure, this section controls. Except as otherwise provided by this section, a suit brought under this section is governed generally by the Texas Rules of Civil Procedure and by Subchapters C and D of this chapter.

(m) A judgment in favor of a taxing unit under this section must be only for foreclosure of the tax lien against the parcel. The judgment may not include a personal judgment against any person.

(n) A person is considered to have been provided sufficient notice of foreclosure and opportunity to be heard for purposes of a proceeding under this section if the taxing unit follows the procedures required by this section for notice by certified mail or by publication and posting or if one or more of the following apply:

(1) the person had constructive notice of the hearing on the merits by acquiring an interest in the parcel after the date of the filing of the taxing unit's petition;

(2) the person appeared at the hearing on the taxing unit's petition or filed a responsive pleading or other communication with the clerk of the court before the date of the hearing; or

(3) before the hearing on the taxing unit's petition, the person had actual notice of the hearing.

TAX §33.58. ALTERNATIVE NOTICE OF FORECLOSURE FOR PARCELS IN CERTAIN MUNICIPALITIES

(a) This section may be invoked and used by one or more taxing units if there are delinquent taxes, penalties, interest, and attorney's fees owing to a taxing unit on a parcel of real property and there are five or more years for which delinquent taxes are owed on the parcel, if the parcel is located in a municipality having a population of more than 100,000 that is situated in two or more counties, at least two of which have a population of more than one million, and in a subdivision having an average lot size of one-fifth of an acre or less.

(b) If a taxing unit invokes this section, the procedures and other provisions of Section 33.57 apply except as otherwise provided by this section.

(c) Notwithstanding Section 33.57(c), a petition for foreclosure under this section is sufficient if it is in substantially the form prescribed by Section 33.43 and further alleges the grounds for invoking this section provided by Subsection (a).

(d) Notwithstanding Section 33.57(e), a court shall approve a motion under Section 33.57(d) if the documents in support of the motion show that the grounds for invoking this section provided by Subsection (a) exist.

(e) If a taxing unit's petition includes multiple parcels of property and if requested by the taxing unit, the court's order of sale shall provide that the officer conducting the sale shall sell the parcels in solido, regardless of whether the parcels adjoin one another or have common ownership.

(f) If the officer conducting the sale of the property is ordered to sell the property in solido under Subsection (e), the officer shall use, in calculating the minimum bid amount under Section 33.50(b) or (c), as appropriate:

(1) the aggregate of all amounts awarded against the multiple parcels of property as the aggregate amount of the judgments; or

(2) the aggregate of the adjudged market values of the multiple parcels of property as the market value of the property stated in the judgment.

(g) If multiple parcels of property are sold in solido under an order of sale issued under Subsection (e), the amounts prescribed by Section 34.21 that must be paid in redeeming property shall, for the purpose of redeeming an individual parcel of property, be in an amount equal to the taxes, penalties, interest, and attorney's fees adjudged against that individual parcel.

(h) This section expires September 1, 2017.

Sections 33.59-33.70 blank

SUBCHAPTER D. TAX MASTERS

TAX §33.71. MASTERS FOR TAX SUITS

(a) The court may, in delinquent tax suits, for good cause appoint a master in chancery for each case as desired, who shall be a citizen of this state and not an attorney for either party to the action, nor related to either party, who shall perform all of the duties required by the court, be under orders of the court, and have the power the master of chancery has in a court of equity.

(b) The order of reference to the master may specify or limit the master's powers, and may direct the master to report only upon particular issues, or to do or perform particular acts, or to receive and report evidence only, and may fix the time and place for beginning and closing the hearings and for the filing of the master's report.

(c) Subject to the limitations and specifications stated in the order, the master may:

(1) regulate all proceedings in every hearing before the master and do all acts and take all measures necessary or proper for the efficient performance of duties under the order;

(2) require the production of evidence upon all matters embraced in the reference, including the pro-

duction of books, papers, vouchers, documents, and other writings applicable to the case;

(3) rule upon the admissibility of evidence, unless otherwise directed by the order of reference;

(4) put witnesses on oath, and examine them; and

(5) call the parties to the action and examine them upon oath.

(d) When a party requests, the master shall make a record of the evidence offered and excluded in the same manner as provided for a court sitting in the trial of a case.

(e) The clerk of the court shall forthwith furnish the master with a copy of the order of reference.

(f) The parties may procure the attendance of witnesses before the master by the issuance and service of process as provided by law.

(g) A pretrial ruling of a tax master from which a mandamus is sought must be appealed to the referring court before the initiation of mandamus proceedings before the court of appeals.

(h) Notwithstanding any other law or requirement, an attorney appointed a master under this section may practice law in the referring court if otherwise qualified to do so.

TAX §33.72. REPORT TRANSMITTED TO COURT; NOTICE

(a) At the conclusion of any hearing conducted by a master that results in a recommendation of a final judgment or on the request of the referring court, the master shall transmit to the referring court all papers relating to the case, with the master's signed and dated report.

(b) After the master's report has been signed, the master shall give to the parties participating in the hearing notice of the substance of the report. The master's report may contain the master's findings, conclusions, or recommendations. The master's report must be in writing in a form as the referring court may direct. The form may be a notation on the referring court's docket sheet.

(c) If the master's report recommends a final judgment, notice of the right of appeal to the judge of the referring court shall be given to all parties.

A TAX §33.73. COURT ACTION ON MASTER'S REPORT; MASTER'S COMPENSATION

(a) After the master's report is filed, and unless a party has filed a written notice of appeal to the referring court, the court may confirm, modify, correct, reject, reverse, or recommit the report as the court may deem proper and necessary in the particular circumstances of the case.

(b) The court shall award reasonable compensation to the master to be taxed as costs of suit.

(c) The district clerk shall collect the fees taxed as costs of suit and award the fees to the master as required under Subsection (b) in each delinquent tax suit for which a master is appointed under Section 33.71, regardless of the disposition of the suit subject to this subsection. Fees may not be collected or awarded in a suit dismissed by the master unless the master:

(1) held at least one hearing on the suit; or

(2) prepared for the suit for at least a number of hours equivalent to the time typically required to conduct a hearing.

2017 Legislation: Amended by H.B. 3389, §1, 85th Leg., eff. Sept. 1, 2017.

TAX §33.74. APPEAL OF RECOMMENDATION OF FINAL JUDGMENT TO THE REFERRING COURT OR ON REQUEST OF THE REFERRING COURT

(a) Any party is entitled to a hearing by the judge of the referring court, if within 10 days, computed in the manner provided by Rule 4 of the Texas Rules of Civil Procedure, after the master gives the notice required by Section 33.72(c), an appeal of the master's report is filed with the referring court. The first day of the appeal time to the referring court begins on the day after the date on which the master gives the notice.

(b) The notice required by Section 33.72(c) may be given in open court or may be given by first class mail. If the notice is given by first class mail the notice is considered to have been given on the third day after the date of the mailing.

(c) All appeals to the referring court shall be in writing specifying the findings and conclusions of the master that are objected to and the appeal shall be limited to those findings and conclusions.

(d) On appeal to the referring court, the parties may present witnesses as in a hearing de novo only on the issues raised in the appeal.

(e) Notice of any appeal to the referring court shall be given to opposing counsel under Rule 72 of the Texas Rules of Civil Procedure.

(f) If an appeal to the referring court is filed by a party, any other party may file an appeal to the referring

court not later than the seventh day after the date the initial appeal was filed.

(g) The referring court, after notice to the parties, shall hold a hearing on all appeals not later than the 45th day after the date on which the initial appeal was filed with the referring court.

(h) Before a hearing before a master, the parties may waive the right of appeal to the referring court in writing or on the record.

(i) The failure to appeal to the referring court, by waiver or otherwise, a master's report that is approved by the referring court does not deprive any party of the right to appeal to or request other relief from a court of appeals or the supreme court. The date of the signing of an order or judgment by the referring court is the controlling date for the purposes of appeal to or request for other relief from a court of appeals or the supreme court.

TAX §33.75. DECREE OR ORDER OF COURT

If an appeal to the referring court is not filed or the right to an appeal to the referring court is waived, the findings and recommendations of the master become the decree or order of the referring court on the referring court's signing an order or decree conforming to the master's report.

TAX §33.76. JURY TRIAL DEMANDED

(a) In a trial on the merits, if a jury trial is demanded and a jury fee is paid, as prescribed by Rule 216, Texas Rules of Civil Procedure, the master shall refer any matters requiring a jury back to the referring court for a full trial before the referring court and jury. However, the master shall conduct all pretrial work necessary to prepare the case for a jury trial.

(b) The master may require all parties to submit a proposed jury charge or other pretrial order or sanction the parties for failure to present or prepare a proper pretrial order.

TAX §33.77. EFFECT OF MASTER'S REPORT PENDING APPEAL

Pending appeal of the master's report to the referring court, the decisions and recommendations of the master are in full force and effect and are enforceable as an order of the referring court, except for orders providing for incarceration or for the appointment of a receiver.

TAX §33.78. MASTERS MAY NOT BE APPOINTED UNDER TEXAS RULES OF CIVIL PROCEDURE

A court may not appoint a master under Rule 171, Texas Rules of Civil Procedure, in a delinquent tax suit.

TAX §33.79. IMMUNITY

A master appointed under this subchapter has the judicial immunity of a district judge. All existing immunity granted masters by law, express or implied, continues in full force and effect.

TAX §33.80. COURT REPORTER

A court reporter is not required during a hearing held by a master appointed under this subchapter. A party, the master, or the referring court may provide for a reporter during the hearing. The record may be preserved by any other means approved by the master. The referring court or master may tax the expense of preserving the record as costs.

Sections 33.81-33.90 blank

SUBCHAPTER E. SEIZURE OF REAL PROPERTY

TAX §33.91. PROPERTY SUBJECT TO SEIZURE BY MUNICIPALITY

(a) After notice has been provided to a person, the person's real property, whether improved or unimproved, is subject to seizure by a municipality for the payment of delinquent ad valorem taxes, penalties, and interest the person owes on the property and the amount secured by a municipal health or safety lien on the property if:

(1) the property:

(A) is in a municipality;

(B) is less than one acre; and

(C) has been abandoned for at least one year;

(2) the taxes on the property are delinquent for:

(A) each of the preceding five years; or

(B) each of the preceding three years if a lien on the property has been created on the property in favor of the municipality for the cost of remedying a health or safety hazard on the property; and

(3) the tax collector of the municipality determines that seizure of the property under this subchapter for the payment of the delinquent taxes, penalties, and interest, and of a municipal health and safety lien on the property, would be in the best interest of the municipality and the other taxing units after determining that

the sum of all outstanding tax and municipal claims against the property plus the estimated costs under Section 33.48 of a standard judicial foreclosure exceed the anticipated proceeds from a tax sale.

(b) The seizure and sale may not be set aside or voided because of any error in determination.

(c) For purposes of this section, a property is presumed to have been abandoned for at least one year if, during that period, the property has remained vacant and a lawful act of ownership of the property has not been exercised. The tax collector of a municipality may rely on the affidavit of any competent person with personal knowledge of the facts in determining whether a property has been abandoned or vacant. For purposes of this subsection:

(1) property is considered vacant if there is an absence of any activity by the owner, a tenant, or a licensee related to residency, work, trade, business, leisure, or recreation; and

(2) "lawful act of ownership" includes mowing or cutting grass or weeds, repairing or demolishing a structure or fence, removing debris, or other form of property upkeep or maintenance performed by or at the request of the owner of the property.

TAX §33.911. PROPERTY SUBJECT TO SEIZURE BY COUNTY

(a) After notice has been provided to a person, the person's real property, whether improved or unimproved, is subject to seizure by a county for the payment of delinquent ad valorem taxes, penalties, and interest the person owes on the property if:

(1) the property:

(A) is in the county;

(B) is not in a municipality; and

(C) has been abandoned for at least one year;

(2) the taxes on the property are delinquent for each of the preceding five years; and

(3) the county tax assessor-collector determines that seizure of the property under this subchapter for the payment of the delinquent taxes, penalties, and interest would be in the best interest of the county and the other taxing units after determining that the sum of all outstanding tax and county claims against the property plus the estimated costs under Section 33.48 of a standard judicial foreclosure exceed the anticipated proceeds from a tax sale.

(b) The seizure and sale may not be set aside or voided because of any error in determination.

(c) For purposes of this section, a property is presumed to have been abandoned for at least one year if, during that period, the property has remained vacant and a lawful act of ownership of the property has not been exercised. The tax collector of a county may rely on the affidavit of any competent person with personal knowledge of the facts in determining whether a property has been abandoned or vacant. For purposes of this subsection:

(1) property is considered vacant if there is an absence of any activity by the owner, a tenant, or a licensee related to residency, work, trade, business, leisure, or recreation; and

(2) "lawful act of ownership" includes mowing or cutting grass or weeds, repairing or demolishing a structure or fence, removing debris, or other form of property upkeep or maintenance performed by or at the request of the owner of the property.

TAX §33.912. NOTICE

(a) A person is considered to have been provided the notice required by Sections 33.91 and 33.911 if by affidavit or otherwise the collector shows that the assessor or collector for the municipality or county mailed the person each bill for municipal or county taxes required to be sent the person by Section 31.01:

(1) in each of the five preceding years, if the taxes on the property are delinquent for each of those years; or

(2) in each of the three preceding years, if:

(A) the taxes on the property are delinquent for each of those years; and

(B) a lien on the property has been created on the property in favor of the municipality for the cost of remedying a health or safety hazard on the property.

(b) If notice under Subsection (a) is not provided, the notice required by Section 33.91 or 33.911 shall be given by the assessor or the collector for the municipality or county, as applicable, by:

(1) serving, in the manner provided by Rule 21a, Texas Rules of Civil Procedure, a true and correct copy of the application for a tax warrant filed under Section 33.92 to each person known, or constructively known through reasonable inquiry, to own or have an interest in the property;

(2) publishing in the English language a notice of the assessor's intent to seize the property in a newspa-

per published in the county in which the property is located if, after exercising reasonable diligence, the assessor or collector cannot determine ownership or the address of the known owners; or

(3) if required under Subsection (g), posting in the English language a notice of the assessor's intent to seize the property if, after exercising reasonable diligence, the assessor or collector cannot determine ownership or the address of the known owners.

(c) A notice under Subsection (b)(1) shall be provided at the time of filing the application for a tax warrant and must be supported by a certificate of service appearing on the application in the same manner and form as provided by Rule 21a, Texas Rules of Civil Procedure. The notice is sufficient if sent to the person's last known address.

(d) A notice by publication or posting under Subsection (b) must substantially comply with this subsection. The notice must:

(1) be published or posted at least 10 days but not more than 180 days before the date the application for tax warrant under Section 33.92 is filed;

(2) be directed to the owners of the property by name, if known, or, if unknown, to "the unknown owners of the property described below";

(3) state that the assessor or collector intends to seize the property as abandoned property and that the property will be sold at public auction without further notice unless all delinquent taxes, penalties, and interest are paid before the sale of the property; and

(4) describe the property.

(e) A description of the property under Subsection (d)(4) is sufficient if it is the same as the property description appearing on the current tax roll for the county or municipality.

(f) A notice by publication or posting under Subsection (b) may relate to more than one property or to multiple owners of property.

(g) For publishing a notice under Subsection (b)(2), a newspaper may charge a rate that does not exceed the greater of two cents per word or an amount equal to the published word or line rate of that newspaper for the same class of advertising. If notice cannot be provided under Subsection (b)(1) and there is not a newspaper published in the county where the property is located, or a newspaper that will publish the notice for the rate authorized by this subsection, the assessor shall post the notice in writing in three public places in the county. One of the posted notices must be at the door of the county courthouse. Proof of the posting shall be made by affidavit of the person posting the notice or by the attorney for the assessor or collector.

(h) A person is considered to have been provided the notice under Section 33.91 or 33.911 in the manner provided by Subsection (b) if the application for the tax warrant under Section 33.92:

(1) contains the certificate of service as required by Subsection (b)(1);

(2) is accompanied by an affidavit on behalf of the applicable assessor or collector stating the fact of publication under Subsection (b)(2), with a copy of the published notice attached; or

(3) is accompanied by an affidavit of posting on behalf of the applicable assessor or collector under Subsection (g) stating the fact of posting and facts supporting the necessity of posting.

(i) A failure to provide, give, or receive a notice provided under this section does not affect the validity of a sale of the seized property or title to the property.

(j) The costs of publishing notice under this section are chargeable as costs and payable from the proceeds of the sale of the property.

TAX §33.92. INSTITUTION OF SEIZURE

(a) After property becomes subject to seizure under Section 33.91 or 33.911, the collector for a municipality or a county, as appropriate, may apply for a tax warrant to a district court in the county in which the property is located.

(b) The court shall issue the tax warrant if by affidavit the collector shows that the property is subject to seizure under Section 33.91 or 33.911. The collector may show that the property has been abandoned or vacant for at least one year, as required by Section 33.91(a)(1)(C) or 33.911(a)(1)(C) by affidavit of any competent person with personal knowledge of the relevant facts.

(c) The court issuing the tax warrant shall include a statement as to the appraised value of the property according to the most recent appraisal roll approved by the appraisal review board. That value is presumed to be the market value of the property on the date that the warrant is issued.

(d) The collector is entitled, on request in the application, to recover attorney's fees in an amount equal

to the compensation specified in the contract with the attorney for collection of the delinquent taxes, penalties, and interest on the property if:

(1) the taxing unit served by the collector contracts with an attorney under Section 6.30;

(2) the existence of the contract and the amount of attorney's fees that equal the compensation specified in the contract are supported by the affidavit of the collector; and

(3) the delinquent tax sought to be recovered is not subject to an additional penalty under Section 33.07 or 33.08 at the time the application is filed.

TAX §33.93. TAX WARRANT

(a) A tax warrant shall direct the sheriff or a constable in the county and the collector for the municipality or the county to seize the property described in the warrant, subject to the right of redemption, for the payment of the ad valorem taxes, penalties, and interest owing on the property included in the application, any attorney's fees included in the application as provided by Section 33.92(d), the amount secured by a municipal health or safety lien on the property included in the application, and the costs of seizure and sale. The warrant shall direct the person whose property is seized to disclose to a person executing the warrant the name and address if known of any other person having an interest in the property.

(b) A bond may not be required of a municipality or county for issuance or delivery of a tax warrant, and a fee or court cost may not be charged for issuance or delivery of the warrant.

(c) On issuance of a tax warrant, the collector shall take possession of the property pending its sale by the officer charged with selling the property.

TAX §33.94. NOTICE OF TAX SALE

(a) After a seizure of property, the collector for the municipality or county shall make a reasonable inquiry to determine the identity and address of any person, other than the person against whom the tax warrant is issued, having an interest in the property. The collector shall deliver as soon as possible a notice stating the time and place of the sale and briefly describing the property seized to:

(1) the person against whom the warrant is issued, including each person to whom notice was provided under Section 33.912(a);

(2) each person to whom notice was provided under Section 33.912(b)(1); and

(3) any other person the collector determines has an interest in the property if the collector can ascertain the address of the other person.

(b) Failure to send or receive a notice required by this section does not affect the validity of the sale of the seized property or title to the property.

TAX §33.95. PURCHASER

A purchaser for value at or subsequent to the tax sale may conclusively presume the validity of the sale and takes free of any claim of a party with a prior interest in the property subject to the provisions of Section 16.002(b), Civil Practice and Remedies Code, and subject to applicable rights of redemption.

CHAPTER 34. TAX SALES & REDEMPTION

SUBCHAPTER A. TAX SALES

Ⓐ TAX §34.01. SALE OF PROPERTY

(a) Real property seized under a tax warrant issued under Subchapter E, Chapter 33, or ordered sold pursuant to foreclosure of a tax lien shall be sold by the officer charged with selling the property, unless otherwise directed by the taxing unit that requested the warrant or order of sale or by an authorized agent or attorney for that unit. The sale shall be conducted in the manner similar property is sold under execution except as otherwise provided by this subtitle.

(a-1) The commissioners court of a county by official action may authorize the officer charged with selling property under this section to conduct a public auction using online bidding and sale. The commissioners court may adopt rules governing online auctions authorized under this subsection. Rules adopted by the commissioners court under this subsection take effect on the 90th day after the date the rules are published in the real property records of the county.

(b) On receipt of an order of sale of real property, the officer charged with selling the property shall endorse on the order the date and exact time when the officer received the order. The endorsement is a levy on the property without necessity for going upon the ground. The officer shall calculate the total amount due under the judgment, including all taxes, penalties, and interest, plus any other amount awarded by the judgment, court costs, and the costs of the sale. The costs of

a sale include the costs of advertising, and deed recording fees anticipated to be paid in connection with the sale of the property. To assist the officer in making the calculation, the collector of any taxing unit that is party to the judgment may provide the officer with a certified tax statement showing the amount of the taxes included in the judgment that remain due that taxing unit and all penalties, interest, and attorney's fees provided by the judgment as of the date of the proposed sale. If a certified tax statement is provided to the officer, the officer shall rely on the amount included in the statement and is not responsible or liable for the accuracy of the applicable portion of the calculation. A certified tax statement is not required to be sworn to and is sufficient if the tax collector or the collector's deputy signs the statement.

(c) The officer charged with the sale shall give written notice of the sale in the manner prescribed by Rule 21a, Texas Rules of Civil Procedure, as amended, or that rule's successor to each person who was a defendant to the judgment or that person's attorney.

(d) An officer's failure to send the written notice of sale or a defendant's failure to receive that notice is insufficient by itself to invalidate:

(1) the sale of the property; or

(2) the title conveyed by that sale.

(e) A notice of sale under Subsection (c) must substantially comply with this subsection. The notice must include:

(1) a statement of the authority under which the sale is to be made;

(2) the date, time, and location of the sale; and

(3) a brief description of the property to be sold.

(f) A notice of sale is not required to include field notes describing the property. A description of the property is sufficient if the notice:

(1) states the number of acres and identifies the original survey;

(2) as to property located in a platted subdivision or addition, regardless of whether the subdivision or addition is recorded, states the name by which the land is generally known with reference to that subdivision or addition; or

(3) by reference adopts the description of the property contained in the judgment.

(g) For publishing a notice of sale, a newspaper may charge a rate that does not exceed the greater of:

(1) two cents per word; or

(2) an amount equal to the published word or line rate of that newspaper for the same class of advertising.

(h) If there is not a newspaper published in the county of the sale, or a newspaper that will publish the notice of sale for the rate authorized by Subsection (g), the officer shall post the notice in writing in three public places in the county not later than the 20th day before the date of the sale. One of the notices must be posted at the door of the county courthouse.

(i) The owner of real property subject to sale may file with the officer charged with the sale a written request that the property be divided and that only as many portions be sold as necessary to pay the amount due against the property, as calculated under Subsection (b). In the request the owner shall describe the desired portions and shall specify the order in which the portions should be sold. The owner may not specify more than four portions or a portion that divides a building or other contiguous improvement. The request must be delivered to the officer not later than the seventh day before the date of the sale.

(j) If a bid sufficient to pay the lesser of the amount calculated under Subsection (b) or the adjudged value is not received, the taxing unit that requested the order of sale may terminate the sale. If the taxing unit does not terminate the sale, the officer making the sale shall bid the property off to the taxing unit that requested the order of sale, unless otherwise agreed by each other taxing unit that is a party to the judgment, for the aggregate amount of the judgment against the property or for the market value of the property as specified in the judgment, whichever is less. The duty of the officer conducting the sale to bid off the property to a taxing unit under this subsection is self-executing. The actual attendance of a representative of the taxing unit at the sale is not a prerequisite to that duty.

(k) The taxing unit to which the property is bid off takes title to the property for the use and benefit of itself and all other taxing units that established tax liens in the suit. The taxing unit's title includes all the interest owned by the defendant, including the defendant's right to the use and possession of the property, subject only to the defendant's right of redemption. Payments in satisfaction of the judgment and any costs or expenses of the sale may not be required of the purchas-

ing taxing unit until the property is redeemed or resold by the purchasing taxing unit.

(*l*) Notwithstanding that property is bid off to a taxing unit under this section, a taxing unit that established a tax lien in the suit may continue to enforce collection of any amount for which a former owner of the property is liable to the taxing unit, including any post-judgment taxes, penalties, and interest, in any other manner provided by law.

(m) The officer making the sale shall prepare a deed to the purchaser of real property at the sale, to any other person whom the purchaser may specify, or to the taxing unit to which the property was bid off. The taxing unit that requested the order of sale may elect to prepare a deed for execution by the officer. If the taxing unit prepares the deed, the officer shall execute that deed. An officer who executes a deed prepared by the taxing unit is not responsible or liable for any inconsistency, error, or other defect in the form of the deed. As soon as practicable after a deed is executed by the officer, the officer shall either file the deed for recording with the county clerk or deliver the executed deed to the taxing unit that requested the order of sale, which shall file the deed for recording with the county clerk. The county clerk shall file and record each deed filed under this subsection and after recording shall return the deed to the grantee.

(n) The deed vests good and perfect title in the purchaser or the purchaser's assigns to the interest owned by the defendant in the property subject to the foreclosure, including the defendant's right to the use and possession of the property, subject only to the defendant's right of redemption, the terms of a recorded restrictive covenant running with the land that was recorded before January 1 of the year in which the tax lien on the property arose, a recorded lien that arose under that restrictive covenant that was not extinguished in the judgment foreclosing the tax lien, and each valid easement of record as of the date of the sale that was recorded before January 1 of the year the tax lien arose. The deed may be impeached only for fraud.

(o) If a bid sufficient to pay the amount specified by Subsection (p) is not received, the officer making the sale, with the consent of the collector who applied for the tax warrant, may offer property seized under Subchapter E, Chapter 33, to a person described by Section 11.181 or 11.20 for less than that amount. If the property is offered to a person described by Section 11.181 or 11.20, the officer making the sale shall reopen the bidding at the amount of that person's bid and bid off the property to the highest bidder. Consent to the sale by the taxing units entitled to receive proceeds of the sale is not required. The acceptance of a bid by the officer under this subsection is conclusive and binding on the question of its sufficiency. An action to set aside the sale on the grounds that a bid is insufficient may not be sustained, except that a taxing unit that participates in distribution of proceeds of the sale may file an action before the first anniversary of the date of the sale to set aside the sale on the grounds of fraud or collusion between the officer making the sale and the purchaser.

(p) Except as provided by Subsection (o), property seized under Subchapter E, Chapter 33, may not be sold for an amount that is less than the lesser of the market value of the property as specified in the warrant or the total amount of taxes, penalties, interest, costs, and other claims for which the warrant was issued. If a sufficient bid is not received by the officer making the sale, the officer shall bid off the property to a taxing unit in the manner specified by Subsection (j) and subject to the other provisions of that subsection. A taxing unit that takes title to property under this subsection takes title for the use and benefit of that taxing unit and all other taxing units that established tax liens in the suit or that, on the date of the seizure, were owed delinquent taxes on the property.

(q) A sale of property under this section to a purchaser other than a taxing unit:

(1) extinguishes each lien securing payment of the delinquent taxes, penalties, and interest against that property and included in the judgment; and

(2) does not affect the personal liability of any person for those taxes, penalties, and interest included in the judgment that are not satisfied from the proceeds of the sale.

(r) Except as provided by Subsection (a-1) and this subsection, a sale of real property under this section must take place at the county courthouse in the county in which the land is located. The commissioners court of the county may designate an area other than an area at the county courthouse where sales under this section will take place that is in a public place within a reasonable proximity of the county courthouse as determined by the commissioners court and in a location as accessible to the public as the courthouse door. The

commissioners court shall record that designation in the real property records of the county. A designation by a commissioners court under this section is not a ground for challenging or invalidating any sale. A sale must be held at an area designated under this subsection if the sale is held on or after the 90th day after the date the designation is recorded.

(r-1) A sale of real property under this section, other than a sale conducted by means of a public auction using online bidding and sale under Subsection (a-1), must take place between 10 a.m. and 4 p.m. on the first Tuesday of a month or, if the first Tuesday of a month occurs on January 1 or July 4, between 10 a.m. and 4 p.m. on the first Wednesday of the month.

(r-2) A sale of real property conducted by means of a public auction using online bidding and sale under Subsection (a-1) may begin at any time and must conclude at 4 p.m. on the first Tuesday of a month or, if the first Tuesday of a month occurs on January 1 or July 4, at 4 p.m. on the first Wednesday of the month.

(s) To the extent of a conflict between this section and a provision of the Texas Rules of Civil Procedure that relates to an execution, this section controls.

2017 Legislation: Amended by H.B. 1128, §4, 85th Leg., eff. Sept. 1, 2017.

TAX §34.011. BIDDER REGISTRATION

(a) This section applies only to a sale of real property under this chapter conducted in a county in which the commissioners court by order has adopted the provisions of this section.

(b) A commissioners court may require that, to be eligible to bid at a sale of real property under this chapter, a person must be registered as a bidder with the county assessor-collector before the sale begins. The county assessor-collector may adopt rules governing the registration of bidders under this section. The county assessor-collector may require a person registering as a bidder:

(1) to designate the person's name and address;

(2) to provide valid proof of identification;

(3) to provide written proof of authority to bid on behalf of another person, if applicable;

(4) to provide any additional information reasonably required by the county assessor-collector; and

(5) to at least annually execute a statement on a form provided by the county assessor-collector certifying that there are no delinquent ad valorem taxes owed by the person registering as a bidder to the county or to any taxing unit having territory in the county.

(c) The county assessor-collector shall issue a written registration statement to a person who has registered as a bidder under this section. A person is not eligible to bid at a sale of real property under this chapter unless the county assessor-collector has issued a written registration statement to the person before the sale begins.

TAX §34.015. PERSONS ELIGIBLE TO PURCHASE REAL PROPERTY

(a) In this section, "person" does not include a taxing unit or an individual acting on behalf of a taxing unit.

(b) An officer conducting a sale of real property under Section 34.01 may not execute a deed in the name of or deliver a deed to any person other than the person who was the successful bidder. The officer may not execute or deliver a deed to the purchaser of the property unless the purchaser exhibits to the officer an unexpired written statement issued under this section to the person by the county assessor-collector of the county in which the sale is conducted showing that:

(1) there are no delinquent taxes owed by the person to that county; and

(2) for each school district or municipality having territory in the county there are no known or reported delinquent ad valorem taxes owed by the person to that school district or municipality.

(c) On the written request of any person, a county assessor-collector shall issue a written statement stating whether there are any delinquent taxes owed by the person to that county or to a school district or municipality having territory in that county. A request for the issuance of a statement by the county assessor-collector under this subsection must:

(1) sufficiently identify any property subject to taxation by the county or by a school district or municipality having territory in the county, regardless of whether the property is located in the county, that the person owns or formerly owned so that the county assessor-collector and the collector for each school district or municipality having territory in the county may determine whether the property is included on a current or a cumulative delinquent tax roll for the county, the school district, or the municipality under Section 33.03;

(2) specify the address to which the county assessor-collector should send the statement;

(3) include any additional information reasonably required by the county assessor-collector; and

(4) be sworn to and signed by the person requesting the statement.

(d) On receipt of a request under Subsection (c), the county assessor-collector shall send to the collector for each school district and municipality having territory in the county, other than a school district or municipality for which the county assessor-collector is the collector, a request for information as to whether there are any delinquent taxes owed by the person to that school district or municipality. The county assessor-collector shall specify the date by which the collector must respond to the request.

(e) If the county assessor-collector determines that there are delinquent taxes owed to the county, the county assessor-collector shall include in the statement issued under Subsection (c) the amount of delinquent taxes owed by the person to that county. If the county assessor-collector is the collector for a school district or municipality having territory in the county and the county assessor-collector determines that there are delinquent ad valorem taxes owed by the person to the school district or municipality, the assessor-collector shall include in the statement issued under Subsection (c) the amount of delinquent taxes owed by the person to that school district or municipality.

(f) If the county assessor-collector receives a response from the collector for a school district or municipality having territory in the county indicating that there are delinquent taxes owed to that school district or municipality on the person's current or former property for which the person is personally liable, the county assessor-collector shall include in the statement issued under Subsection (c):

(1) the amount of delinquent taxes owed by the person to that school district or municipality; and

(2) the name and address of the collector for that school district or municipality.

(g) If the county assessor-collector determines that there are no delinquent taxes owed by the person to the county or to a school district or municipality for which the county assessor-collector is the collector, the county assessor-collector shall indicate in the statement issued under Subsection (c) that there are no delinquent ad valorem taxes owed by the person to the county or to the school district or municipality.

(h) If the county assessor-collector receives a response from the collector for any school district or municipality having territory in that county indicating that there are no delinquent ad valorem taxes owed by the person to that school district or municipality, the county assessor-collector shall indicate in the statement issued under Subsection (c) that there are no delinquent ad valorem taxes owed by the person to that school district or municipality.

(i) If the county assessor-collector does not receive a response from the collector for any school district or municipality to whom the county assessor-collector sent a request under Subsection (d) as to whether there are delinquent taxes on the person's current or former property owed by the person to that school district or municipality, the county assessor-collector shall indicate in the statement issued under Subsection (c) that there are no reported delinquent taxes owed by the person to that school district or municipality.

(j) To cover the costs associated with the issuance of statements under Subsection (c), a county assessor-collector may charge the person requesting a statement a fee not to exceed $10 for each statement requested.

(k) A statement under Subsection (c) must be issued in the name of the requestor, bear the requestor's name, include the dates of issuance and expiration, and be eligible for recording under Section 12.001(b), Property Code. A statement expires on the 90th day after the date of issuance.

(k-1) If within six months of the date of a sale of real property under Section 34.01, the successful bidder does not exhibit to the officer who conducted the sale an unexpired statement that complies with Subsection (k), the officer who conducted the sale shall provide a copy of the officer's return to the county assessor-collector for each county in which the real property is located. On receipt of the officer's return, the county assessor-collector shall file the copy with the county clerk of the county in which the county assessor-collector serves. The county clerk shall record the return in records kept for that purpose and shall index and cross-index the return in the name of the successful bidder at the auction and each former owner of the property. The chief appraiser of each appraisal district that appraises the real property for taxation may list the successful bidder in the appraisal records of that district as the owner of the property.

(*l*) The deed executed by the officer conducting the sale must name the successful bidder as the grantee and recite that the successful bidder exhibited to that officer an unexpired written statement issued to the person in the manner prescribed by this section, showing that the county assessor-collector of the county in which the sale was conducted determined that:

(1) there are no delinquent ad valorem taxes owed by the person to that county; and

(2) for each school district or municipality having territory in the county there are no known or reported delinquent ad valorem taxes owed by the person to that school district or municipality.

(m) If a deed contains the recital required by Subsection (*l*), it is conclusively presumed that this section was complied with.

(n) A person who knowingly violates this section commits an offense. An offense under this subsection is a Class B misdemeanor.

(o) To the extent of a conflict between this section and any other law, this section controls.

(p) This section applies only to a sale of real property under Section 34.01 that is conducted in:

(1) a county with a population of 250,000 or more in which the commissioners court has not by order adopted the provisions of Section 34.011; or

(2) a county with a population of less than 250,000 in which the commissioners court by order has adopted the provisions of this section.

TAX §34.02. DISTRIBUTION OF PROCEEDS

(a) The proceeds of a tax sale under Section 33.94 or 34.01 shall be applied in the order prescribed by Subsection (b). The amount included under each subdivision of Subsection (b) must be fully paid before any of the proceeds may be applied to the amount included under a subsequent subdivision.

(b) The proceeds shall be applied to:

(1) the costs of advertising the tax sale;

(2) any fees ordered by the judgment to be paid to an appointed attorney ad litem;

(3) the original court costs payable to the clerk of the court;

(4) the fees and commissions payable to the officer conducting the sale;

(5) the expenses incurred by a taxing unit in determining necessary parties and in procuring necessary legal descriptions of the property if those expenses were awarded to the taxing unit by the judgment under Section 33.48(a)(4);

(6) the taxes, penalties, interest, and attorney's fees that are due under the judgment; and

(7) any other amount awarded to a taxing unit under the judgment.

(c) If the proceeds are not sufficient to pay the total amount included under any subdivision of Subsection (b), each participant in the amount included under that subdivision is entitled to a share of the proceeds in an amount equal to the proportion its entitlement bears to the total amount included under that subdivision.

(d) The officer conducting a sale under Section 33.94 or 34.01 shall pay any excess proceeds after payment of all amounts due all participants in the sale as specified by Subsection (b) to the clerk of the court issuing the warrant or order of sale.

(e) In this section, "taxes" includes a charge, fee, or expense that is expressly authorized by Section 32.06 or 32.065.

TAX §34.021. DISTRIBUTION OF EXCESS PROCEEDS IN OTHER TAX FORECLOSURE PROCEEDINGS

A person conducting a sale for the foreclosure of a tax lien under Rule 736 of the Texas Rules of Civil Procedure shall, within 10 days of the sale, pay any excess proceeds after payment of all amounts due all participants in the sale to the clerk of the court that issued the order authorizing the sale. The excess proceeds from such a sale shall be handled according to Sections 34.03 and 34.04 of this code.

TAX §34.03. DISPOSITION OF EXCESS PROCEEDS

(a) The clerk of the court shall:

(1) if the amount of excess proceeds is more than $25, before the 31st day after the date the excess proceeds are received by the clerk, send by certified mail, return receipt requested, a written notice to the former owner of the property, at the former owner's last known address according to the records of the court or any other source reasonably available to the court, that:

(A) states the amount of the excess proceeds;

(B) informs the former owner of that owner's rights to claim the excess proceeds under Section 34.04; and

(C) includes a copy or the complete text of this section and Section 34.04;

(2) regardless of the amount, keep the excess proceeds paid into court as provided by Section 34.02(d) for a period of two years after the date of the sale unless otherwise ordered by the court; and

(3) regardless of the amount, send to the attorney general notice of the deposit and amount of excess proceeds if the attorney general or a state agency represented by the attorney general is named as an in rem defendant in the underlying suit for seizure of the property or foreclosure of a tax lien on the property.

(b) If no claimant establishes entitlement to the proceeds within the period provided by Subsection (a), the clerk shall distribute the excess proceeds to each taxing unit participating in the sale in an amount equal to the proportion its taxes, penalties, and interests bear to the total amount of taxes, penalties, and interest due all participants in the sale.

(c) The clerk shall note on the execution docket in each case the amount of the excess proceeds, the date they were received, and the date they were transmitted to the taxing units participating in the sale. Any local government record data may be stored electronically in addition to or instead of source documents in paper or other media.

TAX §34.04. CLAIMS FOR EXCESS PROCEEDS

(a) A person, including a taxing unit and the Title IV-D agency, may file a petition in the court that ordered the seizure or sale setting forth a claim to the excess proceeds. The petition must be filed before the second anniversary of the date of the sale of the property. The petition is not required to be filed as an original suit separate from the underlying suit for seizure of the property or foreclosure of a tax lien on the property but may be filed under the cause number of the underlying suit.

(b) A copy of the petition shall be served, in the manner prescribed by Rule 21a, Texas Rules of Civil Procedure, as amended, or that rule's successor, on all parties to the underlying action not later than the 20th day before the date set for a hearing on the petition.

(c) At the hearing the court shall order that the proceeds be paid according to the following priorities to each party that establishes its claim to the proceeds:

(1) to the tax sale purchaser if the tax sale has been adjudged to be void and the purchaser has prevailed in an action against the taxing units under Section 34.07(d) by final judgment;

(2) to a taxing unit for any taxes, penalties, or interest that have become due or delinquent on the subject property subsequent to the date of the judgment or that were omitted from the judgment by accident or mistake;

(3) to any other lienholder, consensual or otherwise, for the amount due under a lien, in accordance with the priorities established by applicable law;

(4) to a taxing unit for any unpaid taxes, penalties, interest, or other amounts adjudged due under the judgment that were not satisfied from the proceeds from the tax sale; and

(5) to each former owner of the property, as the interest of each may appear, provided that the former owner:

(A) was a defendant in the judgment;

(B) is related within the third degree by consanguinity or affinity to a former owner that was a defendant in the judgment; or

(C) acquired by will or intestate succession the interest in the property of a former owner that was a defendant in the judgment.

(c-1) Except as provided by Subsections (c)(5)(B) and (C), a former owner of the property that acquired an interest in the property after the date of the judgment may not establish a claim to the proceeds. For purposes of this subsection, a former owner of the property is considered to have acquired an interest in the property after the date of the judgment if the deed by which the former owner acquired the interest was recorded in the real property records of the county in which the property is located after the date of the judgment.

(d) Interest or costs may not be allowed under this section.

(e) An order under this section directing that all or part of the excess proceeds be paid to a party is appealable.

(f) A person may not take an assignment or other transfer of an owner's claim to excess proceeds unless:

(1) the assignment or transfer is taken on or after the 36th day after the date the excess proceeds are deposited in the registry of the court;

(2) the assignment or transfer is in writing and signed by the assignor or transferor;

(3) the assignment or transfer is not the result of an in-person or telephone solicitation;

(4) the assignee or transferee pays the assignor or transferor on the date of the assignment or transfer an amount equal to at least 80 percent of the amount of the assignor's or transferor's claim to the excess proceeds; and

(5) the assignment or transfer document contains a sworn statement by the assignor or transferor affirming:

(A) that the assignment or transfer was given voluntarily;

(B) the date on which the assignment or transfer was made and that the date was not earlier than the 36th day after the date the excess proceeds were deposited in the registry of the court;

(C) that the assignor or transferor has received the notice from the clerk required by Section 34.03;

(D) the nature and specific amount of consideration given for the assignment or transfer;

(E) the circumstances under which the excess proceeds are in the registry of the court;

(F) the amount of the claim to excess proceeds in the registry of the court;

(G) that the assignor or transferor has made no other assignments or transfers of the assignor's or transferor's claim to the excess proceeds;

(H) that the assignor or transferor knows that the assignor or transferor may retain counsel; and

(I) that the consideration was paid in full on the date of the assignment or transfer and that the consideration paid was an amount equal to at least 80 percent of the amount of the assignor's or transferor's claim to the excess proceeds.

(g) An assignee or transferee who obtains excess proceeds without complying with Subsection (f) is liable to the assignor or transferor for the amount of excess proceeds obtained plus attorney's fees and expenses. An assignee or transferee who attempts to obtain excess proceeds without complying with Subsection (f) is liable to the assignor or transferor for attorney's fees and expenses.

(h) An assignee or transferee who files a petition setting forth a claim to excess proceeds must attach a copy of the assignment or transfer document and produce the original of the assignment or transfer document in court at the hearing on the petition. If the original assignment or transfer document is lost, the assignee or transferee must obtain the presence of the assignor or transferor to testify at the hearing. In addition, the assignee or transferee must produce at the hearing the original of any evidence verifying the payment of the consideration given for the assignment or transfer. If the original of any evidence of the payment is lost or if the payment was in cash, the assignee or transferee must obtain the presence of the assignor or transferor to testify at the hearing.

(i) A fee charged by an attorney to obtain excess proceeds for an owner may not be greater than 25 percent of the amount obtained or $1,000, whichever is less. A person who is not an attorney may not charge a fee to obtain excess proceeds for an owner.

(j) The amount of the excess proceeds the court may order be paid to an assignee or transferee may not exceed 125 percent of the amount the assignee or transferee paid the assignor or transferor on the date of the assignment or transfer.

TAX §34.05. RESALE BY TAXING UNIT

(a) If property is sold to a taxing unit that is a party to the judgment, the taxing unit may sell the property at any time by public or private sale. In selling the property, the taxing unit may, but is not required to, use the procedures provided by Section 263.001, Local Government Code, or Section 272.001, Local Government Code. The sale is subject to any right of redemption of the former owner. The redemption period begins on the date the deed to the taxing unit is filed for record.

(b) Property sold pursuant to Subsections (c) and (d) of this section may be sold for any amount. This subsection does not authorize a sale of property in violation of Section 52, Article III, Texas Constitution.

(c) The taxing unit purchasing the property by resolution of its governing body may request the sheriff or a constable to sell the property at a public sale. If the purchasing taxing unit has not sold the property within six months after the date on which the owner's right of redemption terminates, any taxing unit that is entitled to receive proceeds of the sale by resolution of its governing body may request the sheriff or a constable in writing to sell the property at a public sale. On receipt of a request made under this subsection, the sheriff or constable shall sell the property as provided by Subsec-

tion (d), unless the property is sold under Subsection (h) or (i) before the date set for the public sale.

(d) Except as provided by this subsection, all public sales requested as provided by Subsection (c) shall be conducted in the manner prescribed by the Texas Rules of Civil Procedure for the sale of property under execution. The notice of the sale must contain a description of the property to be sold, the number and style of the suit under which the property was sold at the tax foreclosure sale, and the date of the tax foreclosure sale. The description of the property in the notice is sufficient if it is stated in the manner provided by Section 34.01(f). If the commissioners court of a county by order specifies the date or time at which or location in the county where a public sale requested under Subsection (c) shall be conducted, the sale shall be conducted on the date and at the time and location specified in the order. The acceptance of a bid by the officer conducting the sale is conclusive and binding on the question of its sufficiency. An action to set aside the sale on the grounds that the bid is insufficient may not be sustained in court, except that a taxing unit that participates in distribution of proceeds of the sale may file an action before the first anniversary of the date of the sale to set aside the sale on the grounds of fraud or collusion between the officer making the sale and the purchaser. On conclusion of the sale, the officer making the sale shall prepare a deed to the purchaser. The taxing unit that requested the sale may elect to prepare a deed for execution by the officer. If the taxing unit prepares the deed, the officer shall execute that deed. An officer who executes a deed prepared by the taxing unit is not responsible or liable for any inconsistency, error, or other defect in the form of the deed. As soon as practicable after a deed is executed by the officer, the officer shall either file the deed for recording with the county clerk or deliver the executed deed to the taxing unit that requested the sale, which shall file the deed for recording with the county clerk. The county clerk shall file and record each deed under this subsection and after recording shall return the deed to the grantee.

(e) The presiding officer of a taxing unit selling real property under Subsection (h) or (i), under Section 34.051, or under Section 253.010, Local Government Code, or the sheriff or constable selling real property under Subsections (c) and (d) shall execute a deed to the property conveying to the purchaser the right, title, and interest acquired or held by each taxing unit that was a party to the judgment foreclosing tax liens on the property. The conveyance shall be made subject to any remaining right of redemption at the time of the sale.

(f) An action attacking the validity of a resale of property pursuant to this section may not be instituted after the expiration of one year after the date of the resale.

(g) A taxing unit to which property is bid off may recover its costs of upkeep, maintenance, and environmental cleanup from the resale proceeds without further court order.

(h) In lieu of a sale pursuant to Subsections (c) and (d) of this section, the taxing unit that purchased the property may sell the property at a private sale. Consent of each taxing unit entitled to receive proceeds of the sale under the judgment is not required. Property sold under this subsection may not be sold for an amount that is less than the lesser of:

(1) the market value specified in the judgment of foreclosure; or

(2) the total amount of the judgments against the property.

(i) In lieu of a sale pursuant to Subsections (c) and (d) of this section, the taxing unit that purchased the property may sell the property at a private sale for an amount less than required under Subsection (h) of this section with the consent of each taxing unit entitled to receive proceeds of the sale under the judgment. This subsection does not authorize a sale of property in violation of Section 52, Article III, Texas Constitution.

(j) In lieu of a sale pursuant to Subsections (c) and (d), the taxing unit that purchased the property may sell the property at a private sale for an amount equal to or greater than its market value, as shown by the most recent certified appraisal roll, if:

(1) the sum of the amount of the judgment plus post-judgment taxes, penalties, and interest owing against the property exceeds the market value; and

(2) each taxing unit entitled to receive proceeds of the sale consents to the sale for that amount.

(k) A sale under Subsection (j) discharges and extinguishes all liens foreclosed by the judgment and, with the exception of the prorated tax for the current year that is assessed under Section 26.10, the liens for post-judgment taxes that accrued from the date of judg-

ment until the date the taxing unit purchased the property. The presiding officer of a taxing unit selling real property under Subsection (j) shall execute a deed to the property conveying to the purchaser the right, title, and interest acquired or held by each taxing unit that was a party to the judgment foreclosing tax liens on the property. The conveyance is subject to any remaining right of redemption at the time of the sale and to the purchaser's obligation to pay the prorated taxes for the current year as provided by Section 26.10. The deed must recite that the liens foreclosed by the judgment and the post-judgment tax liens are discharged and extinguished by virtue of the conveyance.

(*l*) A taxing unit that does not consent to a sale under Subsection (j) is liable to the taxing unit that purchased the property for a pro rata share of the costs incurred by the purchasing unit in maintaining the property, including the costs of preventing the property from becoming a public nuisance, a danger to the public, or a threat to the public health. The nonconsenting unit's share of the costs described by this subsection is calculated from the date the unit fails to consent to the sale and is equal to the percentage of the proceeds from a sale of the property to which the nonconsenting unit would be entitled multiplied by the costs incurred by the purchasing unit to maintain the property.

TAX §34.051. RESALE BY TAXING UNIT FOR THE PURPOSE OF URBAN REDEVELOPMENT

(a) A municipality is authorized to resell tax foreclosed property for less than the market value specified in the judgment of foreclosure or less than the total amount of the judgments against the property if consent to the conveyance is evidenced by an interlocal agreement between the municipality and each taxing unit that is a party to the judgment, provided, however, that the interlocal agreement complies with the requirements of Subsection (b).

(b) Any taxing unit may enter into an interlocal agreement with the municipality for the resale of tax foreclosed properties to be used for a purpose consistent with the municipality's urban redevelopment plans or the municipality's affordable housing policy. If the tax foreclosed property is resold pursuant to this section to be used for a purpose consistent with the municipality's urban redevelopment plan or affordable housing policy, the deed of conveyance must refer to or set forth the applicable terms of the urban redevelopment plan or affordable housing policy. Any such interlocal agreement should include the following:

(1) a general statement and goals of the municipality's urban redevelopment plans or affordable housing policy, as applicable;

(2) a statement that the interlocal agreement concerns only tax foreclosed property that is either vacant or distressed and has a tax delinquency of six or more years;

(3) a statement that the properties will be used only for a purpose consistent with an urban redevelopment plan or affordable housing policy, as applicable, that is primarily aimed at providing housing for families of low or moderate income;

(4) a statement that the principal goal of the interlocal agreement is to provide an efficient mechanism for returning deteriorated or unproductive properties to the tax rolls, enhancing the value of ownership to the surrounding properties, and improving the safety and quality of life in deteriorating neighborhoods; and

(5) a provision that all properties are sold subject to any right of redemption.

(c) The deed of conveyance of property sold under this section conveys to the purchaser the right, title, and interest acquired or held by each taxing unit that was a party to the judgment of foreclosure, subject to any remaining right of redemption at the time of the sale.

(d) An action attacking the validity of a sale of property pursuant to this section may not be instituted after the expiration of one year after the date of the sale and then only after the unconditional tender into the registry of the court of an amount equal to all taxes, penalties, interest, costs, and post-judgment interest of all judgments on which the original foreclosure sale was based.

TAX §34.06. DISTRIBUTION OF PROCEEDS OF RESALE

(a) The proceeds of a resale of property purchased by a taxing unit at a tax foreclosure sale shall be paid to the purchasing taxing unit.

(b) The proceeds of the resale shall be distributed as required by Subsections (c)-(e).

(c) The purchasing taxing unit shall first retain an amount from the proceeds to reimburse the unit for reasonable costs, as defined by Section 34.21, incurred by the unit for:

(1) maintaining, preserving, and safekeeping the property;

(2) marketing the property for resale; and

(3) costs described by Subsection (f).

(d) After retaining the amount authorized by Subsection (c), the purchasing taxing unit shall then pay all costs of the suit and the sale of the property in the same manner and in the same order of priority as provided by Sections 34.02(b)(1)-(5).

(e) After making the distribution under Subsection (d), any remaining balance of the proceeds shall be paid to each taxing unit participating in the sale in an amount equal to the proportion each participant's taxes, penalties, and interest bear to the total amount of taxes, penalties, and interest adjudged to be due all participants in the sale.

(f) The purchasing taxing unit is entitled to recover from the proceeds of a resale of the property any cost incurred by the taxing unit in inspecting the property to determine whether there is a release or threatened release of solid waste from the property in violation of Chapter 361, Health and Safety Code, or a rule adopted or permit or order issued by the Texas Natural Resource Conservation Commission under that chapter, or a discharge or threatened discharge of waste or a pollutant into or adjacent to water in this state from a point of discharge on the property in violation of Chapter 26, Water Code, or a rule adopted or permit or order issued by the commission under that chapter, and in taking action to remove or remediate the release or threatened release or discharge or threatened discharge regardless of whether the taxing unit:

(1) was required by law to incur the cost; or

(2) obtained the consent of each taxing unit entitled to receive proceeds of the sale under the judgment of foreclosure to incur the cost.

A TAX §34.07. SUBROGATION OF PURCHASER AT VOID SALE

(a) The purchaser at a void or defective tax sale or tax resale is subrogated to the rights of the taxing unit in whose behalf the property was sold or resold to the same extent a purchaser at a void or defective sale conducted in behalf of a judgment creditor is subrogated to the rights of the judgment creditor.

(b) Except as provided by Subsection (c), the purchaser at a void or defective tax sale or tax resale is subrogated to the tax lien of the taxing unit in whose behalf the property was sold or resold to the same extent a purchaser at a void or defective mortgage or other lien foreclosure sale is subrogated to the lien of the lienholder, and the purchaser is entitled to a reforeclosure of the lien to which the purchaser is subrogated.

(c) If the purchaser at a void or defective tax sale or tax resale paid less than the total amount of the judgment against the property, the purchaser is subrogated to the tax lien only in the amount the purchaser paid at the sale or resale.

(d) In lieu of pursuing the subrogation rights provided by this section to which a purchaser is subrogated, a purchaser at a void tax sale or tax resale may elect to file an action against the taxing units to which proceeds of the sale were distributed to recover an amount from each taxing unit equal to the distribution of taxes, penalties, interest, and attorney's fees the taxing unit received. In a suit filed under this subsection, the purchaser may include a claim for, and is entitled to recover, any excess proceeds of the sale that remain on deposit in the registry of the court or, in the alternative, is entitled to have judgment against any party to whom the excess proceeds have been distributed. A purchaser who files a suit authorized by this subsection waives all rights of subrogation otherwise provided by this section. This subsection applies only to an original purchaser at a tax sale or resale and only if that purchaser has not subsequently sold the property to another person.

(e) If the purchaser prevails in a suit filed under Subsection (d), the court shall expressly provide in its final judgment that:

(1) the tax sale is vacated and set aside; and

(2) any lien on the property extinguished by the tax sale is reinstated on the property effective as of the date on which the lien originally attached to the property.

(f) A suit filed against the taxing units under Subsection (d) may not be maintained unless the action is instituted before the first anniversary of the date of sale or resale. In this subsection:

(1) "Date of sale" means the date [~~first Tuesday of the month~~] on which the sheriff or constable conducted the sale of the property under Section 34.01.

(2) "Date of resale" means the date on which the grantor's acknowledgment was taken or, in the case of

multiple grantors, the latest date of acknowledgment by the grantors as shown in the deed.

2017 Legislation: Amended by H.B. 1128, §5, 85th Leg., eff. Sept. 1, 2017.

TAX §34.08. CHALLENGE TO VALIDITY OF TAX SALE

(a) A person may not commence an action that challenges the validity of a tax sale under this chapter unless the person:

(1) deposits into the registry of the court an amount equal to the amount of the delinquent taxes, penalties, and interest specified in the judgment of foreclosure obtained against the property plus all costs of the tax sale; or

(2) files an affidavit of inability to pay under Rule 145, Texas Rules of Civil Procedure.[1]

(b) A person may not commence an action challenging the validity of a tax sale after the time set forth in Section 33.54(a)(1) or (2), as applicable to the property, against a subsequent purchaser for value who acquired the property in reliance on the tax sale. The purchaser may conclusively presume that the tax sale was valid and shall have full title to the property free and clear of the right, title, and interest of any person that arose before the tax sale, subject only to recorded restrictive covenants and valid easements of record set forth in Section 34.01(n) and subject to applicable rights of redemption.

(c) If a person is not barred from bringing an action challenging the validity of a tax sale under Subsection (b) or any other provision of this title or applicable law, the person must bring an action no later than two years after the cause of action accrues to recover real property claimed by another who:

(1) pays applicable taxes on the real property before overdue; and

(2) claims the property under a registered deed executed pursuant to Section 34.01.

(d) Subsection (c) does not apply to a claim based on a forged deed.

1. **Editor's note:** In 2016, TRCP 145 was amended to eliminate the requirement that a party file an affidavit of indigence; now, a party must file a Statement of Inability to Afford Payment of Court Costs. *See* Tex.Sup.Ct. Order, Misc. Docket No. 16-9122 (eff. Sept. 1, 2016).

Sections 34.09-34.20 reserved for expansion

SUBCHAPTER B. REDEMPTION

TAX §34.21. RIGHT OF REDEMPTION

(a) The owner of real property sold at a tax sale to a purchaser other than a taxing unit that was used as the residence homestead of the owner or that was land designated for agricultural use when the suit or the application for the warrant was filed, or the owner of a mineral interest sold at a tax sale to a purchaser other than a taxing unit, may redeem the property on or before the second anniversary of the date on which the purchaser's deed is filed for record by paying the purchaser the amount the purchaser bid for the property, the amount of the deed recording fee, and the amount paid by the purchaser as taxes, penalties, interest, and costs on the property, plus a redemption premium of 25 percent of the aggregate total if the property is redeemed during the first year of the redemption period or 50 percent of the aggregate total if the property is redeemed during the second year of the redemption period.

(b) If property that was used as the owner's residence homestead or was land designated for agricultural use when the suit or the application for the warrant was filed, or that is a mineral interest, is bid off to a taxing unit under Section 34.01(j) or (p) and has not been resold by the taxing unit, the owner having a right of redemption may redeem the property on or before the second anniversary of the date on which the deed of the taxing unit is filed for record by paying the taxing unit:

(1) the lesser of the amount of the judgment against the property or the market value of the property as specified in that judgment, plus the amount of the fee for filing the taxing unit's deed and the amount spent by the taxing unit as costs on the property, if the property was judicially foreclosed and bid off to the taxing unit under Section 34.01(j); or

(2) the lesser of the amount of taxes, penalties, interest, and costs for which the warrant was issued or the market value of the property as specified in the warrant, plus the amount of the fee for filing the taxing unit's deed and the amount spent by the taxing unit as costs on the property, if the property was seized under Subchapter E, Chapter 33, and bid off to the taxing unit under Section 34.01(p).

(c) If real property that was used as the owner's residence homestead or was land designated for agricultural use when the suit or the application for the warrant was filed, or that is a mineral interest, has been resold by the taxing unit under Section 34.05, the owner of the property having a right of redemption may redeem the property on or before the second anniversary of the date on which the taxing unit files for record

the deed from the sheriff or constable by paying the person who purchased the property from the taxing unit the amount the purchaser paid for the property, the amount of the fee for filing the purchaser's deed for record, the amount paid by the purchaser as taxes, penalties, interest, and costs on the property, plus a redemption premium of 25 percent of the aggregate total if the property is redeemed in the first year of the redemption period or 50 percent of the aggregate total if the property is redeemed in the second year of the redemption period.

(d) If the amount paid by the owner of the property under Subsection (c) is less than the amount of the judgment under which the property was sold, the owner shall pay to the taxing unit to which the property was bid off under Section 34.01 an amount equal to the difference between the amount paid under Subsection (c) and the amount of the judgment. The taxing unit shall issue a receipt for a payment received under this subsection and shall distribute the amount received to each taxing unit that participated in the judgment and sale in an amount proportional to the unit's share of the total amount of the aggregate judgments of the participating taxing units. The owner of the property shall deliver the receipt received from the taxing unit to the person from whom the property is redeemed.

(e) The owner of real property sold at a tax sale other than property that was used as the residence homestead of the owner or that was land designated for agricultural use when the suit or the application for the warrant was filed, or that is a mineral interest, may redeem the property in the same manner and by paying the same amounts as prescribed by Subsection (a), (b), (c), or (d), as applicable, except that:

(1) the owner's right of redemption may be exercised not later than the 180th day following the date on which the purchaser's or taxing unit's deed is filed for record; and

(2) the redemption premium payable by the owner to a purchaser other than a taxing unit may not exceed 25 percent.

(f) The owner of real property sold at a tax sale may redeem the real property by paying the required amount as prescribed by this section to the assessor-collector for the county in which the property was sold, if the owner of the real property makes an affidavit stating:

(1) that the period in which the owner's right of redemption must be exercised has not expired; and

(2) that the owner has made diligent search in the county in which the property is located for the purchaser at the tax sale or for the purchaser at resale, and has failed to find the purchaser, that the purchaser is not a resident of the county in which the property is located, that the owner and the purchaser cannot agree on the amount of redemption money due, or that the purchaser refuses to give the owner a quitclaim deed to the property.

(f-1) An assessor-collector who receives an affidavit and payment under Subsection (f) shall accept that the assertions set out in the affidavit are true and correct. The assessor-collector receiving the payment shall give the owner a signed receipt witnessed by two persons. The receipt, when recorded, is notice to all persons that the property described has been redeemed. The assessor-collector shall on demand pay the money received by the assessor-collector to the purchaser. An assessor-collector is not liable to any person for performing the assessor-collector's duties under this subsection in reliance on the assertions contained in an affidavit.

(g) In this section:

(1) "Land designated for agricultural use" means land for which an application for appraisal under Subchapter C or D, Chapter 23, has been finally approved.

(2) "Costs" includes:

(A) the amount reasonably spent by the purchaser for maintaining, preserving, and safekeeping the property, including the cost of:

(i) property insurance;

(ii) repairs or improvements required by a local ordinance or building code or by a lease of the property in effect on the date of the sale;

(iii) discharging a lien imposed by a municipality to secure expenses incurred by the municipality in remedying a health or safety hazard on the property;

(iv) dues or assessments for maintenance paid to a property owners' association under a recorded restrictive covenant to which the property is subject; and

(v) impact or standby fees imposed under the Local Government Code or Water Code and paid to a political subdivision; and

(B) if the purchaser is a taxing unit to which the property is bid off under Section 34.01, personnel and overhead costs reasonably incurred by the purchaser in connection with maintaining, preserving, safekeeping, managing, and reselling the property.

(3) "Purchaser" includes a taxing unit to which property is bid off under Section 34.01.

(4) "Residence homestead" has the meaning assigned by Section 11.13.

(h) The right of redemption does not grant or reserve in the former owner of the real property the right to the use or possession of the property, or to receive rents, income, or other benefits from the property while the right of redemption exists.

(i) The owner of property who is entitled to redeem the property under this section may request that the purchaser of the property, or the taxing unit to which the property was bid off, provide that owner a written itemization of all amounts spent by the purchaser or taxing unit in costs on the property. The owner must make the request in writing and send the request to the purchaser at the address shown for the purchaser in the purchaser's deed for the property, or to the business address of the collector for the taxing unit, as applicable. The purchaser or the collector shall itemize all amounts spent on the property in costs and deliver the itemization in writing to the owner not later than the 10th day after the date the written request is received. Delivery of the itemization to the owner may be made by depositing the document in the United States mail, postage prepaid, addressed to the owner at the address provided in the owner's written request. Only those amounts included in the itemization provided to the owner may be allowed as costs for purposes of redemption.

(j) A quitclaim deed to an owner redeeming property under this section is not notice of an unrecorded instrument. The grantee of a quitclaim deed and a successor or assign of the grantee may be a bona fide purchaser in good faith for value under recording laws.

(k) The inclusion of dues and assessments for maintenance paid to a property owners' association within the definition of "costs" under Subsection (g) may not be construed as:

(1) a waiver of any immunity to which a taxing unit may be entitled from a suit or from liability for those dues or assessments; or

(2) authority for a taxing unit to make an expenditure of public funds in violation of Section 50, 51, or 52(a), Article III, or Section 3, Article XI, Texas Constitution.

TAX §34.22. EVIDENCE OF TITLE TO REDEEM REAL PROPERTY

(a) A person asserting ownership of real property sold for taxes is entitled to redeem the property if he had title to the property or he was in possession of the property in person or by tenant either at the time suit to foreclose the tax lien on the property was instituted or at the time the property was sold. A defect in the chain of title to the property does not defeat an offer to redeem.

(b) A person who establishes title to real property that is superior to the title of one who has previously redeemed the property is entitled to redeem the property during the redemption period by paying the amounts provided by law to the person who previously redeemed the property.

TAX §34.23. DISTRIBUTION OF REDEMPTION PROCEEDS

(a) If the owner of property sold for taxes to a taxing unit redeems the property before the property is resold, the taxing unit shall distribute the redemption proceeds in the manner that proceeds of the resale of property are distributed.

(b) Except as provided by Section 34.21(e), the owner of property sold for taxes to a taxing unit may not redeem the property from the taxing unit after the property has been resold.

SUBTITLE F. REMEDIES

CHAPTER 41. LOCAL REVIEW

SUBCHAPTER A. REVIEW OF APPRAISAL RECORDS BY APPRAISAL REVIEW BOARD

TAX §41.01. DUTIES OF APPRAISAL REVIEW BOARD

(a) The appraisal review board shall:

(1) determine protests initiated by property owners;

(2) determine challenges initiated by taxing units;

(3) correct clerical errors in the appraisal records and the appraisal rolls;

(4) act on motions to correct appraisal rolls under Section 25.25;

(5) determine whether an exemption or a partial exemption is improperly granted and whether land is improperly granted appraisal as provided by Subchapter C, D, E, or H, Chapter 23; and

(6) take any other action or make any other determination that this title specifically authorizes or requires.

(b) The board may not review or reject an agreement between a property owner or the owner's agent and the chief appraiser under Section 1.111(e).

TAX §41.02. ACTION BY BOARD

After making a determination or decision under Section 41.01, the appraisal review board shall by written order direct the chief appraiser to correct or change the appraisal records or the appraisal roll to conform the appraisal records or the appraisal roll to the board's determination or decision.

TAX §41.03. CHALLENGE BY TAXING UNIT

(a) A taxing unit is entitled to challenge before the appraisal review board:

(1) the level of appraisals of any category of property in the district or in any territory in the district, but not the appraised value of a single taxpayer's property;

(2) an exclusion of property from the appraisal records;

(3) a grant in whole or in part of a partial exemption;

(4) a determination that land qualifies for appraisal as provided by Subchapter C, D, E, or H, Chapter 23; or

(5) failure to identify the taxing unit as one in which a particular property is taxable.

(b) If a taxing unit challenges a determination that land qualifies for appraisal under Subchapter H, Chapter 23, on the ground that the land is not located in an aesthetic management zone, critical wildlife habitat zone, or streamside management zone, the taxing unit must first seek a determination letter from the director of the Texas Forest Service. The appraisal review board shall accept the letter as conclusive proof of the type, size, and location of the zone.

TAX §41.04. CHALLENGE PETITION

The appraisal review board is not required to hear or determine a challenge unless the taxing unit initiating the challenge files a petition with the board before June 1 or within 15 days after the date that the appraisal records are submitted to the appraisal review board, whichever is later. The petition must include an explanation of the grounds for the challenge.

TAX §41.05. HEARING ON CHALLENGE

(a) On the filing of a challenge petition, the appraisal review board shall schedule a hearing on the challenge.

(b) The taxing unit initiating the challenge and each taxing unit in which property involved in the challenge is or may be taxable are entitled to an opportunity to appear to offer evidence or argument.

(c) The chief appraiser shall appear at each hearing to represent the appraisal office.

(d) If the challenge relates to a taxable leasehold or other possessory interest in real property that is owned by this state or a political subdivision of this state, the attorney general or a representative of the state agency that owns the real property, if the real property is owned by this state, or a person designated by the political subdivision that owns the real property, as applicable, is entitled to appear at the hearing and offer evidence and argument.

TAX §41.06. NOTICE OF CHALLENGE HEARING

(a) The secretary of the appraisal review board shall deliver to the presiding officer of the governing body of each taxing unit entitled to appear at a challenge hearing written notice of the date, time, and place fixed for the hearing. The secretary shall deliver the notice not later than the 10th day before the date of the hearing.

(b) The secretary shall give the chief appraiser advance notice of the date, time, place, and subject matter of each challenge hearing.

(c) If the challenge relates to a taxable leasehold or other possessory interest in real property that is owned by this state or a political subdivision of this state, the secretary shall deliver notice of the hearing as provided by Subsection (a) to:

(1) the attorney general and the state agency that owns the real property, in the case of real property owned by this state; or

(2) the governing body of the political subdivision, in the case of real property owned by a political subdivision.

TAX §41.07. DETERMINATION OF CHALLENGE

(a) The appraisal review board shall determine each challenge and make its decision by written order.

(b) If on determining a challenge the board finds that the appraisal records are incorrect in some respect raised by the challenge, the board shall refer the matter to the appraisal office and by its order shall direct the chief appraiser to make the reappraisals or corrections in the records that are necessary to conform the records to the requirements of law.

(c) The board shall determine all challenges before approval of the appraisal records as provided by Section 41.12 of this code.

(d) The board shall deliver by certified mail a notice of the issuance of the order and a copy of the order to the taxing unit.

TAX §41.08. CORRECTION OF RECORDS ON ORDER OF BOARD

The chief appraiser shall make the reappraisals or other corrections of the appraisal records ordered by the appraisal review board as provided by this subchapter. The chief appraiser shall submit a copy of the corrected records to the board for its approval as promptly as practicable.

TAX §41.09. CLERICAL ERRORS

At any time before approval of the appraisal records as provided by Section 41.12 of this code, the appraisal review board in writing may correct a clerical error in the records without referring the matter to the appraisal office if the correction will not affect the tax liability of a property owner and if the chief appraiser does not object in writing.

TAX §41.10. CORRECTION OF RECORDS ON RECOMMENDATION OF CHIEF APPRAISER

At any time before approval of the appraisal records as provided by Section 41.12 of this code, the chief appraiser may submit written recommendations to the appraisal review board for corrections in the records. If the board approves a recommended correction and it will not result in an increase in the tax liability of a property owner, the board may make the correction by written order.

A

TAX §41.11. NOTICE TO PROPERTY OWNER OF CHANGE IN RECORDS

(a) Not later than the date the appraisal review board approves the appraisal records as provided by Section 41.12, the secretary of the board shall deliver written notice to a property owner of any change in the records that is ordered by the board as provided by this subchapter and that will result in an increase in the tax liability of the property owner. An owner who receives a notice as provided by this section shall be entitled to protest such action as provided by Section 41.44(a)(2) ~~[41.44(a)(3)]~~.

(b) The secretary shall include in the notice a brief explanation of the procedure for protesting the change.

(c) Failure to deliver notice to a property owner as required by this section nullifies the change in the records to the extent the change is applicable to that property owner.

2017 Legislation: Amended by H.B. 2228, §4, 85th Leg., eff. Jan. 1, 2018.

TAX §41.12. APPROVAL OF APPRAISAL RECORDS BY BOARD

(a) By July 20, the appraisal review board shall:

(1) hear and determine all or substantially all timely filed protests;

(2) determine all timely filed challenges;

(3) submit a list of its approved changes in the records to the chief appraiser; and

(4) approve the records.

(b) The appraisal review board must complete substantially all timely filed protests before approving the appraisal records and may not approve the records if the sum of the appraised values, as determined by the chief appraiser, of all properties on which a protest has been filed but not determined is more than five percent of the total appraised value of all other taxable properties.

(c) The board of directors of an appraisal district established for a county with a population of at least one million by resolution may:

(1) postpone the deadline established by Subsection (a) for the performance of the functions listed in that subsection to a date not later than August 30; or

(2) provide that the appraisal review board may approve the appraisal records if the sum of the appraised values, as determined by the chief appraiser, of all prop-

erties on which a protest has been filed but not determined does not exceed 10 percent of the total appraised value of all other taxable properties.

Sections 41.13-41.20 reserved for expansion

TAX §§41.21 TO 41.27. REPEALED

Sections 41.28-41.40 reserved for expansion

SUBCHAPTER C. TAXPAYER PROTEST

TAX §41.41. RIGHT OF PROTEST

(a) A property owner is entitled to protest before the appraisal review board the following actions:

(1) determination of the appraised value of the owner's property or, in the case of land appraised as provided by Subchapter C, D, E, or H, Chapter 23, determination of its appraised or market value;

(2) unequal appraisal of the owner's property;

(3) inclusion of the owner's property on the appraisal records;

(4) denial to the property owner in whole or in part of a partial exemption;

(5) determination that the owner's land does not qualify for appraisal as provided by Subchapter C, D, E, or H, Chapter 23;

(6) identification of the taxing units in which the owner's property is taxable in the case of the appraisal district's appraisal roll;

(7) determination that the property owner is the owner of property;

(8) a determination that a change in use of land appraised under Subchapter C, D, E, or H, Chapter 23, has occurred; or

(9) any other action of the chief appraiser, appraisal district, or appraisal review board that applies to and adversely affects the property owner.

(b) Each year the chief appraiser for each appraisal district shall publicize in a manner reasonably designed to notify all residents of the district:

(1) the provisions of this section; and

(2) the method by which a property owner may protest an action before the appraisal review board.

TAX §41.411. PROTEST OF FAILURE TO GIVE NOTICE

(a) A property owner is entitled to protest before the appraisal review board the failure of the chief appraiser or the appraisal review board to provide or deliver any notice to which the property owner is entitled.

(b) If failure to provide or deliver the notice is established, the appraisal review board shall determine a protest made by the property owner on any other grounds of protest authorized by this title relating to the property to which the notice applies.

(c) A property owner who protests as provided by this section must comply with the payment requirements of Section 41.4115 or the property owner forfeits the property owner's right to a final determination of the protest.

TAX §41.4115. FORFEITURE OF REMEDY FOR NONPAYMENT OF TAXES

(a) The pendency of a protest under Section 41.411 does not affect the delinquency date for the taxes on the property subject to the protest. However, that delinquency date applies only to the amount of taxes required to be paid under Subsection (b) and, for purposes of Subsection (b), that delinquency date is postponed to the 125th day after the date one or more taxing units first delivered written notice of the taxes due on the property, as determined by the appraisal review board at a hearing under Section 41.44(c-3). If the property owner complies with Subsection (b), the delinquency date for any additional amount of taxes due on the property is determined in the manner provided by Section 42.42(c) for the determination of the delinquency date for additional taxes finally determined to be due in an appeal under Chapter 42, and that additional amount is not delinquent before that date.

(b) Except as provided in Subsection (d), a property owner who files a protest under Section 41.411 must pay the amount of taxes due on the portion of the taxable value of the property subject to the protest that is not in dispute before the delinquency date or the property owner forfeits the right to proceed to a final determination of the protest.

(c) A property owner who pays an amount of taxes greater than that required by Subsection (b) does not forfeit the property owner's right to a final determination of the protest by making the payment. If the property owner files a timely protest under Section 41.411, taxes paid on the property are considered paid under protest, even if paid before the protest is filed.

(d) After filing an oath of inability to pay the taxes at issue, a property owner may be excused from the requirement of prepayment of tax as a prerequisite to the determination of a protest if the appraisal review board,

after notice and hearing, finds that such prepayment would constitute an unreasonable restraint on the property owner's right of access to the board. On the motion of a party, the board shall hold a hearing to review and determine compliance with this section, and the reviewing board may set such terms and conditions on any grant of relief as may be reasonably required by the circumstances. If the board determines that the property owner has not substantially complied with this section, the board shall dismiss the pending protest. If the board determines that the property owner has substantially but not fully complied with this section, the board shall dismiss the pending protest unless the property owner fully complies with the board's determination within 30 days of the determination.

TAX §41.412. PERSON ACQUIRING PROPERTY AFTER JANUARY 1

(a) A person who acquires property after January 1 and before the deadline for filing notice of the protest may pursue a protest under this subchapter in the same manner as a property owner who owned the property on January 1.

(b) If during the pendency of a protest under this subchapter the ownership of the property subject to the protest changes, the new owner of the property on application to the appraisal review board may proceed with the protest in the same manner as the property owner who initiated the protest.

A TAX §41.413. PROTEST BY PERSON LEASING PROPERTY

(a) A person leasing tangible personal property who is contractually obligated to reimburse the property owner for taxes imposed on the property is entitled to protest before the appraisal review board a determination of the appraised value of the property if the property owner does not file a protest relating to the property.

(b) A person leasing real property who is contractually obligated to reimburse the property owner for taxes imposed on the property is entitled to protest before the appraisal review board a determination of the appraised value of the property if the property owner does not file a protest relating to the property. The protest provided by this subsection is limited to a single protest by either the property owner or the lessee.

(c) A person bringing a protest under this section is considered the owner of the property for purposes of the protest. The appraisal review board shall deliver a copy of any notice relating to the protest and of the order determining the protest to the owner of the property and the person bringing the protest.

(d) A [~~The~~] property owner shall [~~timely~~] send to a [~~the~~] person leasing [~~the~~] property under a contract described by this section a copy of any notice of appraised value of the property [~~the property's reappraisal~~] received by the property owner. The property owner must send the notice not later than the 10th day after the date the property owner receives the notice. Failure of the property owner to send a copy of the notice to the person leasing the property does not affect the time within which the person leasing the property may protest the appraised value. This subsection does not apply if the property owner and the person leasing the property have agreed in the contract to waive the requirements of this subsection or that the person leasing the property will not protest the appraised value of the property.

(e) A person leasing property under a contract described by this section may request that the chief appraiser of the appraisal district in which the property is located send the notice described by Subsection (d) to the person. Except as provided by Subsection (f), the chief appraiser shall send the notice to the person leasing the property not later than the fifth day after the date the notice is sent to the property owner if the person demonstrates that the person is contractually obligated to reimburse the property owner for the taxes imposed on the property.

(f) A chief appraiser who receives a request under Subsection (e) is not required to send the notice requested under that subsection if the appraisal district in which the property that is the subject of the notice is located posts the appraised value of the property on the district's Internet website not later than the fifth day after the date the notice is sent to the property owner.

(g) A person leasing property under a contract described by this section may designate another person to act as the agent of the lessee for any purpose under this title. The lessee must make the designation in the manner provided by Section 1.111. An agent designated under this subsection has the same authority and is subject to the same limitations as an agent designated by a property owner under Section 1.111.

2017 Legislation: Amended by H.B. 804, §1, 85th Leg., eff. Sept. 1, 2017.

TAX §41.415[A*]. ELECTRONIC FILING OF NOTICE OF PROTEST

Section 41.415[A] was enacted by Acts 2009, 81st Leg., ch. 1267, §3, enacted May 31, 2009, effective June 19, 2009, without reference to the conflicting enactment made by Acts 2009, 81st Leg., ch. 1370, §1, enacted May 26, 2009, effective Jan. 1, 2011. For harmonizing conflicts, see p. V. The [A*] has been added by the editor to distinguish this §41.415 from the other, which is marked with [B*].*

(a) This section applies only to an appraisal district established for a county having a population of 500,000 or more.

(b) The appraisal district shall implement a system that allows the owner of a property that for the current tax year has been granted a residence homestead exemption under Section 11.13, in connection with the property, to electronically:

(1) file a notice of protest under Section 41.41(a)(1) or (2) with the appraisal review board;

(2) receive and review comparable sales data and other evidence that the chief appraiser intends to use at the protest hearing before the board;

(3) receive, as applicable:

(A) a settlement offer from the district to correct the appraisal records by changing the market value and, if applicable, the appraised value of the property to the value as redetermined by the district; or

(B) a notice from the district that a settlement offer will not be made; and

(4) accept or reject a settlement offer received from the appraisal district under Subdivision (3)(A).

(c) With each notice sent under Section 25.19 to an eligible property owner, the chief appraiser shall include information about the system required by this section, including instructions for accessing and using the system.

(d) A notice of protest filed electronically under this section must include, at a minimum:

(1) a statement as to whether the protest is brought under Section 41.41(a)(1) or under Section 41.41(a)(2);

(2) a statement of the property owner's good faith estimate of the value of the property; and

(3) an electronic mail address that the district may use to communicate electronically with the property owner in connection with the protest.

(e) If the property owner accepts a settlement offer made by the appraisal district, the chief appraiser shall enter the settlement in the appraisal records as an agreement made under Section 1.111(e).

(f) If the property owner rejects a settlement offer, the appraisal review board shall hear and determine the property owner's protest in the manner otherwise provided by this subchapter and Subchapter D.

(g) An appraisal district is not required to make the system required by this section available to an owner of a residence homestead located in an area in which the chief appraiser determines that the factors affecting the market value of real property are unusually complex or to an owner who has designated an agent to represent the owner in a protest as provided by Section 1.111.

(h) An electronic mail address provided by a property owner to an appraisal district under Subsection (d)(3) is confidential and may not be disclosed by the district.

TAX §41.415[B*]. ELECTRONIC FILING OF NOTICE OF PROTEST

Section 41.415[B] was enacted by Acts 2009, 81st Leg., ch. 1370, §1, enacted May 26, 2009, effective Jan. 1, 2011, without reference to the conflicting enactment made by Acts 2009, 81st Leg., ch. 1267, §3, enacted May 31, 2009, effective June 19, 2009. For harmonizing conflicts, see p. V. The [B*] has been added by the editor to distinguish this §41.415 from the other, which is marked with [A*].*

(a) This section applies only to an appraisal district that:

(1) on January 1, 2008, maintained an Internet website accessible to the public; or

(2) after that date established or establishes such an Internet website.

(b) Each appraisal district shall implement a system that allows the owner of a property that for the current tax year has been granted a residence homestead exemption under Section 11.13, in connection with the property, to electronically:

(1) file a notice of protest under Section 41.41(a)(1) or (2) with the appraisal review board;

(2) receive and review comparable sales data and other evidence that the chief appraiser intends to use at the protest hearing before the board;

(3) receive, as applicable:

(A) a settlement offer from the district to correct the appraisal records by changing the market value and, if applicable, the appraised value of the property to the value as redetermined by the district; or

(B) a notice from the district that a settlement offer will not be made; and

(4) accept or reject a settlement offer received from the appraisal district under Subdivision (3)(A).

(c) With each notice sent under Section 25.19 to an eligible property owner, the chief appraiser shall include information about the system required by this section, including instructions for accessing and using the system.

(d) A notice of protest filed electronically under this section must include, at a minimum:

(1) a statement as to whether the protest is brought under Section 41.41(a)(1) or under Section 41.41(a)(2);

(2) a statement of the property owner's good faith estimate of the value of the property; and

(3) an electronic mail address that the district may use to communicate electronically with the property owner in connection with the protest.

(e) If the property owner accepts a settlement offer made by the appraisal district, the chief appraiser shall enter the settlement in the appraisal records as an agreement made under Section 1.111(e).

(f) If the property owner rejects a settlement offer, the appraisal review board shall hear and determine the property owner's protest in the manner otherwise provided by this subchapter and Subchapter D.

(g) An appraisal district is not required to make the system required by this section available to an owner of a residence homestead located in an area in which the chief appraiser determines that the factors affecting the market value of real property are unusually complex.

(h) An electronic mail address provided by a property owner to an appraisal district under Subsection (d)(3) is confidential and may not be disclosed by the district.

(i) Expired.

TAX §41.42. PROTEST OF SITUS

A protest against the inclusion of property on the appraisal records for an appraisal district on the ground that the property does not have taxable situs in that district shall be determined in favor of the protesting party if he establishes that the property is subject to appraisal by another district or that the property is not taxable in this state. The chief appraiser of a district in which the property owner prevails in a protest of situs shall notify the appraisal office of the district in which the property owner has established situs.

TAX §41.43. PROTEST OF DETERMINATION OF VALUE OR INEQUALITY OF APPRAISAL

(a) Except as provided by Subsections (a-1), (a-3), and (d), in a protest authorized by Section 41.41(a)(1) or (2), the appraisal district has the burden of establishing the value of the property by a preponderance of the evidence presented at the hearing. If the appraisal district fails to meet that standard, the protest shall be determined in favor of the property owner.

(a-1) If in the protest relating to a property with a market or appraised value of $1 million or less as determined by the appraisal district the property owner files with the appraisal review board and, not later than the 14th day before the date of the first day of the hearing, delivers to the chief appraiser a copy of an appraisal of the property performed not later than the 180th day before the date of the first day of the hearing by an appraiser certified under Chapter 1103, Occupations Code, that supports the appraised or market value of the property asserted by the property owner, the appraisal district has the burden of establishing the value of the property by clear and convincing evidence presented at the hearing. If the appraisal district fails to meet that standard, the protest shall be determined in favor of the property owner.

(a-2) To be valid, an appraisal filed under Subsection (a-1) must be attested to before an officer authorized to administer oaths and include:

(1) the name and business address of the certified appraiser;

(2) a description of the property that was the subject of the appraisal;

(3) a statement that the appraised or market value of the property:

(A) was, as applicable, the appraised or market value of the property as of January 1 of the current tax year; and

(B) was determined using a method of appraisal authorized or required by Chapter 23; and

TAX §41.43

(4) a statement that the appraisal was performed in accordance with the Uniform Standards of Professional Appraisal Practice.

(a-3) In a protest authorized by Section 41.41(a)(1) or (2), the appraisal district has the burden of establishing the value of the property by clear and convincing evidence presented at the hearing if:

(1) the appraised value of the property was lowered under this subtitle in the preceding tax year;

(2) the appraised value of the property in the preceding tax year was not established as a result of a written agreement between the property owner or the owner's agent and the appraisal district under Section 1.111(e); and

(3) not later than the 14th day before the date of the first day of the hearing, the property owner files with the appraisal review board and delivers to the chief appraiser:

(A) information, such as income and expense statements or information regarding comparable sales, that is sufficient to allow for a determination of the appraised or market value of the property if the protest is authorized by Section 41.41(a)(1); or

(B) information that is sufficient to allow for a determination of whether the property was appraised unequally if the protest is authorized by Section 41.41(a)(2).

(a-4) If the appraisal district has the burden of establishing the value of property by clear and convincing evidence presented at the hearing on a protest as provided by Subsection (a-3) and the appraisal district fails to meet that standard, the protest shall be determined in favor of the property owner.

(a-5) Subsection (a-3)(3) does not impose a duty on a property owner to provide any information in a protest authorized by Section 41.41(a)(1) or (2). That subdivision is merely a condition to the applicability of the standard of evidence provided by Subsection (a-3).

(b) A protest on the ground of unequal appraisal of property shall be determined in favor of the protesting party unless the appraisal district establishes that:

(1) the appraisal ratio of the property is equal to or less than the median level of appraisal of a reasonable and representative sample of other properties in the appraisal district;

(2) the appraisal ratio of the property is equal to or less than the median level of appraisal of a sample of properties in the appraisal district consisting of a reasonable number of other properties similarly situated to, or of the same general kind or character as, the property subject to the protest; or

(3) the appraised value of the property is equal to or less than the median appraised value of a reasonable number of comparable properties appropriately adjusted.

(c) For purposes of this section, evidence includes the data, schedules, formulas, or other information used to establish the matter at issue.

(d) If the property owner fails to deliver, before the date of the hearing, a rendition statement or property report required by Chapter 22 or a response to the chief appraiser's request for information under Section 22.07(c), the property owner has the burden of establishing the value of the property by a preponderance of the evidence presented at the hearing. If the property owner fails to meet that standard, the protest shall be determined in favor of the appraisal district.

Ⓐ TAX §41.44. NOTICE OF PROTEST

(a) Except as provided by Subsections (b), [~~(b-1),~~] (c), (c-1), and (c-2), to be entitled to a hearing and determination of a protest, the property owner initiating the protest must file a written notice of the protest with the appraisal review board having authority to hear the matter protested:

(1) not later than [~~before~~] May 15 [~~1~~] or [~~not later than~~] the 30th day after the date that notice to the property owner was delivered to the property owner as provided by Section 25.19, [~~if the property is a single-family residence that qualifies for an exemption under Section 11.13,~~] whichever is later;

(2) [~~before June 1 or not later than the 30th day after the date that notice was delivered to the property owner as provided by Section 25.19 in connection with any other property, whichever is later;~~]

[~~(3)~~] in the case of a protest of a change in the appraisal records ordered as provided by Subchapter A of this chapter or by Chapter 25, not later than the 30th day after the date notice of the change is delivered to the property owner;

(3) [~~(4)~~] in the case of a determination that a change in the use of land appraised under Subchapter C, D, E, or H, Chapter 23, has occurred, not later than the 30th day after the date the notice of the determination is delivered to the property owner; or

(4) [~~(5)~~] in the case of a determination of eligibility for a refund under Section 23.1243, not later than the 30th day after the date the notice of the determination is delivered to the property owner.

(b) A property owner who files his notice of protest after the deadline prescribed by Subsection (a) of this section but before the appraisal review board approves the appraisal records is entitled to a hearing and determination of the protest if he shows good cause as determined by the board for failure to file the notice on time.

(b-1) Repealed by H.B. 2228, §6, 85th Leg., eff. Jan. 1, 2018.

[~~(b-1)~~] [~~Notwithstanding Subsection (a)(1), an owner of property described by that subsection who files a notice of protest after the deadline prescribed by that subsection but before the appraisal review board approves the appraisal records is entitled to a hearing and determination of the protest if the property owner files the notice before June 1.~~]

(c) A property owner who files notice of a protest authorized by Section 41.411 is entitled to a hearing and determination of the protest if the property owner files the notice prior to the date the taxes on the property to which the notice applies become delinquent. An owner of land who files a notice of protest under Subsection (a)(3) [~~(a)(4)~~] is entitled to a hearing and determination of the protest without regard to whether the appraisal records are approved.

(c-1) A property owner who files a notice of protest after the deadline prescribed by Subsection (a) but before the taxes on the property to which the notice applies become delinquent is entitled to a hearing and determination of the protest if the property owner was continuously employed in the Gulf of Mexico, including employment on an offshore drilling or production facility or on a vessel, for a period of not less than 20 days during which the deadline prescribed by Subsection (a) passed, and the property owner provides the appraisal review board with evidence of that fact through submission of a letter from the property owner's employer or supervisor or, if the property owner is self-employed, a sworn affidavit.

(c-2) A property owner who files a notice of protest after the deadline prescribed by Subsection (a) but before the taxes on the property to which the notice applies become delinquent is entitled to a hearing and determination of the protest if the property owner was serving on full-time active duty in the United States armed forces outside the United States on the day on which the deadline prescribed by Subsection (a) passed and the property owner provides the appraisal review board with evidence of that fact through submission of a valid military identification card from the United States Department of Defense and a deployment order.

(c-3) Notwithstanding Subsection (c), a property owner who files a protest under Section 41.411 on or after the date the taxes on the property to which the notice applies become delinquent, but not later than the 125th day after the property owner, in the protest filed, claims to have first received written notice of the taxes in question, is entitled to a hearing solely on the issue of whether one or more taxing units timely delivered a tax bill. If at the hearing the appraisal review board determines that all of the taxing units failed to timely deliver a tax bill, the board shall determine the date on which at least one taxing unit first delivered written notice of the taxes in question, and for the purposes of this section the delinquency date is postponed to the 125th day after that date.

(d) A notice of protest is sufficient if it identifies the protesting property owner, including a person claiming an ownership interest in the property even if that person is not listed on the appraisal records as an owner of the property, identifies the property that is the subject of the protest, and indicates apparent dissatisfaction with some determination of the appraisal office. The notice need not be on an official form, but the comptroller shall prescribe a form that provides for more detail about the nature of the protest. The form must permit a property owner to include each property in the appraisal district that is the subject of a protest. The comptroller, each appraisal office, and each appraisal review board shall make the forms readily available and deliver one to a property owner on request.

(e) Notwithstanding any other provision of this section, a notice of protest may not be found to be untimely or insufficient based on a finding of incorrect ownership if the notice:

(1) identifies as the property owner a person who is, for the tax year at issue:

(A) an owner of the property at any time during the tax year;

(B) the person shown on the appraisal records as the owner of the property, if that person filed the protest;

(C) a lessee authorized to file a protest; or

(D) an affiliate of or entity related to a person described by this subdivision; or

(2) uses a misnomer of a person described by Subdivision (1).

2017 Legislation: Amended by H.B. 2228, §§5, 6, 85th Leg., eff. Jan. 1, 2018.

Ⓐ TAX §41.45. HEARING ON PROTEST

(a) On the filing of a notice as required by Section 41.44, the appraisal review board shall schedule a hearing on the protest. If more than one protest is filed relating to the same property, the appraisal review board shall schedule a single hearing on all timely filed protests relating to the property. A hearing for a property that is owned in undivided or fractional interests, including separate interests in a mineral in place, shall be scheduled to provide for participation by all owners who have timely filed a protest.

(b) A [~~The~~] property owner initiating a [~~the~~] protest is entitled to [~~an opportunity to~~] appear to offer evidence or argument. A [~~The~~] property owner may offer [~~his~~] evidence or argument by affidavit without personally appearing and may appear by telephone conference call to offer argument. A property owner who appears by telephone conference call must offer any evidence by affidavit. A property owner must submit an affidavit described by this subsection [~~if he attests to the affidavit before an officer authorized to administer oaths and submits the affidavit~~] to the board hearing the protest before the board [~~it~~] begins the hearing on the protest. On receipt of an affidavit, the board shall notify the chief appraiser. The chief appraiser may inspect the affidavit and is entitled to a copy on request.

(b-1) An appraisal review board shall conduct a hearing on a protest by telephone conference call if:

(1) the property owner notifies the board that the property owner intends to appear by telephone conference call in the owner's notice of protest or by written notice filed with the board not later than the 10th day before the date of the hearing; or

(2) the board proposes that the hearing be conducted by telephone conference call and the property owner agrees to the hearing being conducted in that manner.

(b-2) If a property owner elects to have a hearing on a protest conducted by telephone conference call, the appraisal review board shall:

(1) provide a telephone number for the property owner to call to participate in the hearing; and

(2) hold the hearing in a location equipped with telephone equipment that allows each board member and the other parties to the protest who are present at the hearing to hear the property owner offer argument.

(b-3) A property owner is responsible for providing access to a hearing on a protest conducted by telephone conference call to another person that the owner invites to participate in the hearing.

(c) The chief appraiser shall appear at each protest hearing before the appraisal review board to represent the appraisal office.

(d) An appraisal review board consisting of more than three members may sit in panels of not fewer than three members to conduct protest hearings. However, the determination of a protest heard by a panel must be made by the board. If the recommendation of a panel is not accepted by the board, the board may refer the matter for rehearing to a panel composed of members who did not hear the original hearing or, if there are not at least three members who did not hear the original protest, the board may determine the protest. Before determining a protest or conducting a rehearing before a new panel or the board, the board shall deliver notice of the hearing or meeting to determine the protest in accordance with the provisions of this subchapter.

(e) On request made to the appraisal review board before the date of the hearing, a property owner who has not designated an agent under Section 1.111 to represent the owner at the hearing is entitled to one postponement of the hearing to a later date without showing cause. In addition and without limitation as to the number of postponements, the board shall postpone the hearing to a later date if the property owner or the owner's agent at any time shows good cause for the postponement or if the chief appraiser consents to the postponement. The hearing may not be postponed to a date less than five or more than 30 days after the date scheduled for the hearing when the postponement is sought unless the date and time of the hearing as postponed are agreed to by the chairman of the appraisal review board or the chairman's representative, the property owner, and the chief appraiser. A request by a property owner for a postponement under this subsection may be made in writing, including by facsimile transmission or electronic mail, by telephone, or in person to the appraisal review board, a panel of the board, or the

chairman of the board. The chairman or the chairman's representative may take action on a postponement under this subsection without the necessity of action by the full board if the hearing for which the postponement is requested is scheduled to occur before the next regular meeting of the board. The granting by the appraisal review board, the chairman, or the chairman's representative of a postponement under this subsection does not require the delivery of additional written notice to the property owner.

(e-1) A property owner or a person designated by the property owner as the owner's agent to represent the owner at the hearing who fails to appear at the hearing is entitled to a new hearing if the property owner or the owner's agent files, not later than the fourth day after the date the hearing occurred, a written statement with the appraisal review board showing good cause for the failure to appear and requesting a new hearing.

(e-2) For purposes of Subsections (e) and (e-1), "good cause" means a reason that includes an error or mistake that:

(1) was not intentional or the result of conscious indifference; and

(2) will not cause undue delay or other injury to the person authorized to extend the deadline or grant a rescheduling.

(f) A property owner who has been denied a hearing to which the property owner is entitled under this chapter may bring suit against the appraisal review board by filing a petition or application in district court to compel the board to provide the hearing. If the property owner is entitled to the hearing, the court shall order the hearing to be held and may award court costs and reasonable attorney fees to the property owner.

(g) In addition to the grounds for a postponement under Subsection (e), the board shall postpone the hearing to a later date if:

(1) the owner of the property or the owner's agent is also scheduled to appear at a hearing on a protest filed with the appraisal review board of another appraisal district;

(2) the hearing before the other appraisal review board is scheduled to occur on the same date as the hearing set by the appraisal review board from which the postponement is sought;

(3) the notice of hearing delivered to the property owner or the owner's agent by the other appraisal review board bears an earlier postmark than the notice of hearing delivered by the board from which the postponement is sought or, if the date of the postmark is identical, the property owner or agent has not requested a postponement of the other hearing; and

(4) the property owner or the owner's agent includes with the request for a postponement a copy of the notice of hearing delivered to the property owner or the owner's agent by the other appraisal review board.

The amended text in subsection (h) is effective for protests for which notice was filed by a property owner with the appraisal review board on or after Jan. 1, 2018.

(h) Before the hearing on a protest or immediately after the hearing begins, the chief appraiser and the property owner or the owner's agent shall each provide the other with a copy of any written material or material preserved on a [~~any~~] portable device designed to maintain a [~~an electronic, magnetic, or digital~~] reproduction of a document or image that the person intends to offer or submit to the appraisal review board at the hearing. Each person must provide the copy of material in the manner and form prescribed by comptroller rule.

(i) To be valid, an affidavit offered under Subsection (b) must be attested to before an officer authorized to administer oaths and include:

(1) the name of the property owner initiating the protest;

(2) a description of the property that is the subject of the protest; and

(3) evidence or argument.

(j) A statement from the property owner that specifies the determination or other action of the chief appraiser, appraisal district, or appraisal review board relating to the subject property from which the property owner seeks relief constitutes sufficient argument under Subsection (i).

(k) The comptroller shall prescribe a standard form for an affidavit offered under Subsection (b). Each appraisal district shall make copies of the affidavit form available to property owners without charge.

(*l*) A property owner is not required to use the affidavit form prescribed by the comptroller when offering an affidavit under Subsection (b).

(m) If the protest relates to a taxable leasehold or other possessory interest in real property that is owned by this state or a political subdivision of this state, the attorney general or a representative of the state agency

that owns the land, if the real property is owned by this state, or a person designated by the political subdivision that owns the real property, as applicable, is entitled to appear at the hearing and offer evidence and argument.

(n) A property owner does not waive the right to appear in person at a [~~the~~] protest hearing by submitting an affidavit to the appraisal review board or by electing to appear by telephone conference call. The board may consider an [~~the~~] affidavit submitted under this section only if the property owner does not appear in person at the [~~protest~~] hearing [~~in person~~]. For purposes of scheduling the hearing, the property owner must [~~shall~~] state in the affidavit that the property owner does not intend to appear at the hearing or that the property owner intends to appear at the hearing in person or by telephone conference call and that the affidavit may be used only if the property owner does not appear at the hearing in person. If the property owner does not state in the affidavit whether the owner intends to appear at the hearing and has not elected to appear by telephone conference call, the board shall consider the submission of the affidavit as an indication that the property owner does not intend to appear at the hearing. If the property owner states in the affidavit that the owner does not intend to appear at the hearing or does not state in the affidavit whether the owner intends to appear at the hearing and has not elected to appear by telephone conference call, the [~~appraisal review~~] board is not required to consider the affidavit at the scheduled hearing and may consider the affidavit at a hearing designated for the specific purpose of processing affidavits.

The amended text in subsection (o) is effective for protests for which notice was filed by a property owner with the appraisal review board on or after Jan. 1, 2018.

(o) If the chief appraiser uses audiovisual equipment at a hearing on a protest, the appraisal office shall provide audiovisual equipment of the same general type, kind, and character, as prescribed by comptroller rule, for use during the hearing by the property owner or the property owner's agent.

The enacted text in subsection (p) is effective for protests for which notice was filed by a property owner with the appraisal review board on or after Jan. 1, 2018.

(p) The comptroller by rule shall prescribe:

(1) the manner and form, including security requirements, in which a person must provide a copy of material under Subsection (h), which must allow the appraisal review board to retain the material as part of the board's hearing record; and

(2) specifications for the audiovisual equipment provided by an appraisal district for use by a property owner or the property owner's agent under Subsection (o).

2017 Legislation: Amended by H.B. 455, §1, 85th Leg., eff. Sept. 1, 2017; S.B. 1286, §1, 85th Leg., eff. Sept. 1, 2017.

TAX §41.455. POOLED OR UNITIZED MINERAL INTERESTS

(a) If a property owner files protests relating to a pooled or unitized mineral interest that is being produced at one or more production sites located in a single county with the appraisal review boards of more than one appraisal district, the appraisal review board for the appraisal district established for the county in which the production site or sites are located must determine the protest filed with that board and make its decision before another appraisal review board may hold a hearing to determine the protest filed with that other board.

(b) If a property owner files protests relating to a pooled or unitized mineral interest that is being produced at two or more production sites located in more than one county with the appraisal review boards of more than one appraisal district and at least two-thirds of the surface area of the mineral interest is located in the county for which one of the appraisal districts is established, the appraisal review board for that appraisal district must determine the protest filed with that board and make its decision before another appraisal review board may hold a hearing to determine the protest filed with that other board.

(c) A protest determined by an appraisal review board in violation of this section is void.

TAX §41.46. NOTICE OF PROTEST HEARING

(a) The appraisal review board before which a protest hearing is scheduled shall deliver written notice to the property owner initiating a protest of the date, time, and place fixed for the hearing on the protest and of the property owner's entitlement to a postponement of the hearing as provided by Section 41.45 unless the property owner waives in writing notice of the hearing. The board shall deliver the notice not later than the 15th day before the date of the hearing.

(b) The board shall give the chief appraiser advance notice of the date, time, place, and subject matter of each protest hearing.

(c) If the protest relates to a taxable leasehold or other possessory interest in real property that is owned by this state or a political subdivision of this state, the board shall deliver notice of the hearing as provided by Subsection (a) to:

(1) the attorney general and the state agency that owns the real property, in the case of real property owned by this state; or

(2) the governing body of the political subdivision, in the case of real property owned by a political subdivision.

TAX §41.461. NOTICE OF CERTAIN MATTERS BEFORE HEARING

(a) At least 14 days before a hearing on a protest, the chief appraiser shall:

(1) deliver a copy of the pamphlet prepared by the comptroller under Section 5.06(a) to the property owner initiating the protest if the owner is representing himself, or to an agent representing the owner if requested by the agent;

(2) inform the property owner that the owner or the agent of the owner may inspect and may obtain a copy of the data, schedules, formulas, and all other information the chief appraiser plans to introduce at the hearing to establish any matter at issue; and

(3) deliver a copy of the hearing procedures established by the appraisal review board under Section 41.66 to the property owner.

(b) The charge for copies provided to an owner or agent under this section may not exceed the charge for copies of public information as provided under Subchapter F, Chapter 552, Government Code, except:

(1) the total charge for copies provided in connection with a protest of the appraisal of residential property may not exceed $15 for each residence; and

(2) the total charge for copies provided in connection with a protest of the appraisal of a single unit of property subject to appraisal, other than residential property, may not exceed $25.

TAX §41.47. DETERMINATION OF PROTEST

(a) The appraisal review board hearing a protest shall determine the protest and make its decision by written order.

(b) If on determining a protest the board finds that the appraisal records are incorrect in some respect raised by the protest, the board by its order shall correct the appraisal records by changing the appraised value placed on the protesting property owner's property or by making the other changes in the appraisal records that are necessary to conform the records to the requirements of law. If the appraised value of a taxable property interest, other than an interest owned by a public utility or by a cooperative corporation organized to provide utility service, is changed as the result of a protest or challenge, the board shall change the appraised value of all other interests, other than an interest owned by a public utility or by a cooperative corporation organized to provide utility service, in the same property, including a mineral in place, in proportion to the ownership interests.

(c) If the protest is of the determination of the appraised value of the owner's property, the appraisal review board must state in the order the appraised value of the property:

(1) as shown in the appraisal records submitted to the board by the chief appraiser under Section 25.22 or 25.23; and

(2) as finally determined by the board.

(c-1) If, in the case of a determination of eligibility for a refund requested under Section 23.1243, the appraisal review board determines that the dealer is entitled to a refund in excess of the amount, if any, to which the chief appraiser determined the dealer to be entitled, the board shall order the chief appraiser to deliver written notice of the board's determination to the collector and the dealer in the manner provided by Section 23.1243(c).

(d) The board shall deliver by certified mail a notice of issuance of the order and a copy of the order to the property owner and the chief appraiser.

(e) The notice of the issuance of the order must contain a prominently printed statement in upper-case bold lettering informing the property owner in clear and concise language of the property owner's right to appeal the board's decision to district court. The statement must describe the deadline prescribed by Section 42.06(a) of this code for filing a written notice of appeal, and the deadline prescribed by Section 42.21(a) of this code for filing the petition for review with the district court.

Sections 41.48-41.60 reserved for expansion

SUBCHAPTER D. ADMINISTRATIVE PROVISIONS

TAX §41.61. ISSUANCE OF SUBPOENA

(a) If reasonably necessary in the course of a protest provided by this chapter, the appraisal review board on its own motion or at the written request of a party to the protest, may subpoena witnesses or books, records, or other documents of the property owner or appraisal district that relate to the protest.

(b) On the written request of a party to a protest provided by this chapter, the appraisal review board shall issue a subpoena if the requesting party:

(1) shows good cause for issuing the subpoena; and

(2) deposits with the board a sum the board determines is reasonably sufficient to insure payment of the costs estimated to accrue for issuance and service of the subpoena and for compensation of the individual to whom it is directed.

(c) An appraisal review board may not issue a subpoena under this section unless the board holds a hearing at which the board determines that good cause exists for the issuance of the subpoena. The appraisal review board before which a good cause hearing is scheduled shall deliver written notice to the party being subpoenaed and parties to the protest of the date, time, and place of the hearing. The board shall deliver the notice not later than the 5th day before the date of the good cause hearing. The party being subpoenaed must have an opportunity to be heard at the good cause hearing.

TAX §41.62. SERVICE & ENFORCEMENT OF SUBPOENA

(a) A sheriff or constable shall serve a subpoena issued as provided by this subchapter.

(b) If the person to whom a subpoena is directed fails to comply, the issuing board or the party requesting the subpoena may bring suit in the district court to enforce the subpoena. If the district court determines that good cause exists for issuance of the subpoena, the court shall order compliance. The district court may modify the requirements of a subpoena that the court determines are unreasonable. Failure to obey the order of the district court is punishable as contempt.

(c) The county attorney or, if there is no county attorney, the district attorney shall represent the board in a suit to enforce a subpoena.

TAX §41.63. COMPENSATION FOR SUBPOENAED WITNESS

(a) An individual who is not a party to the proceeding and who complies with a subpoena issued as provided by this subchapter is entitled to:

(1) the reasonable costs of producing the documents;

(2) mileage of 15 cents a mile for going to and returning from the place of the proceeding; and

(3) a fee of $10 a day for each whole or partial day that the individual is necessarily present at the proceedings.

(b) The appraisal review board by rule may prescribe greater mileage or fee, but an increase is not effective unless uniformly applicable to all individuals who are entitled to mileage or fee as provided by Subsection (a) of this section.

(c) Compensation authorized as provided by this section is paid by the appraisal office if the subpoena is issued on the motion of the appraisal review board or by the party requesting the subpoena.

(d) Compensation is not payable unless the amount claimed is approved by the appraisal review board that issued the subpoena.

TAX §41.64. INSPECTION OF TAX RECORDS

The appraisal review board may inspect the records or other materials of the appraisal office that are not made confidential under this code. On demand of the board, the chief appraiser shall produce the materials as soon as practicable.

TAX §41.65. REQUEST FOR STATE ASSISTANCE

The appraisal review board may request the comptroller to assist in determining the accuracy of appraisals by the appraisal office or to provide other professional assistance. The appraisal office shall reimburse the costs of providing assistance if the comptroller requests reimbursement.

A TAX §41.66. HEARING PROCEDURES

(a) The appraisal review board shall establish by rule the procedures for hearings it conducts as provided by Subchapters A and C of this chapter. On request made by a property owner in the owner's notice of protest or in a separate writing delivered to the appraisal review board on or before the date the notice of protest

is filed, the property owner is entitled to a copy of the hearing procedures. The copy of the hearing procedures shall be delivered to the property owner not later than the 10th day before the date the hearing on the protest begins and may be delivered with the notice of the protest hearing required under Section 41.46(a). The notice of protest form prescribed by the comptroller under Section 41.44(d) or any other notice of protest form made available to a property owner by the appraisal review board or the appraisal office shall provide the property owner an opportunity to make or decline to make a request under this subsection. The appraisal review board shall post a copy of the hearing procedures in a prominent place in the room in which the hearing is held.

(b) Hearing procedures to the greatest extent practicable shall be informal. Each party to a hearing is entitled to offer evidence, examine or cross-examine witnesses or other parties, and present argument on the matters subject to the hearing. A property owner who is a party to a protest is entitled to elect to present the owner's case at a hearing on the protest either before or after the appraisal district presents the district's case.

(c) A property owner who is entitled as provided by this chapter to appear at a hearing may appear by himself or by his agent. A taxing unit may appear by a designated agent.

(d) Except as provided by Subsection (d-1), hearings conducted as provided by this chapter are open to the public.

(d-1) Notwithstanding Chapter 551, Government Code, the appraisal review board shall conduct a hearing that is closed to the public if the property owner or the chief appraiser intends to disclose proprietary or confidential information at the hearing that will assist the review board in determining the protest. The review board may hold a closed hearing under this subsection only on a joint motion by the property owner and the chief appraiser.

(d-2) Information described by Subsection (d-1) is considered information obtained under Section 22.27.

(e) The appraisal review board may not consider any appraisal district information on a protest that was not presented to the appraisal review board during the protest hearing.

(f) A member of the appraisal review board may not communicate with another person concerning:

(1) the evidence, argument, facts, merits, or any other matters related to an owner's protest, except during the hearing on the protest; or

(2) a property that is the subject of the protest, except during a hearing on another protest or other proceeding before the board at which the property is compared to other property or used in a sample of properties.

(g) At the beginning of a hearing on a protest, each member of the appraisal review board hearing the protest must sign an affidavit stating that the board member has not communicated with another person in violation of Subsection (f). If a board member has communicated with another person in violation of Subsection (f), the member must be recused from the proceeding and may not hear, deliberate on, or vote on the determination of the protest. The board of directors of the appraisal district shall adopt and implement a policy concerning the temporary replacement of an appraisal review board member who has communicated with another person in violation of Subsection (f).

(h) The appraisal review board shall postpone a hearing on a protest if the property owner requests additional time to prepare for the hearing and establishes to the board that the chief appraiser failed to comply with Section 41.461. The board is not required to postpone a hearing more than one time under this subsection.

(i) A hearing on a protest filed by a property owner who is not represented by an agent designated under Section 1.111 shall be set for a time and date certain. If the hearing is not commenced within two hours of the time set for the hearing, the appraisal review board shall postpone the hearing on the request of the property owner.

(j) On the request of a property owner or a designated agent, an appraisal review board shall schedule hearings on protests concerning up to 20 designated properties on the same day. The designated properties must be identified in the same notice of protest, and the notice must contain in boldfaced type the statement "request for same-day protest hearings." A property owner or designated agent may not file more than one request under this subsection with the appraisal review board in the same tax year. The appraisal review board may schedule hearings on protests concerning more than 20 properties filed by the same property owner or designated agent and may use different panels to con-

duct the hearings based on the board's customary scheduling. The appraisal review board may follow the practices customarily used by the board in the scheduling of hearings under this subsection.

(k) If an appraisal review board sits in panels to conduct protest hearings, protests shall be randomly assigned to panels, except that the board may consider the type of property subject to the protest or the ground of the protest for the purpose of using the expertise of a particular panel in hearing protests regarding particular types of property or based on particular grounds. If a protest is scheduled to be heard by a particular panel, the protest may not be reassigned to another panel without the consent of the property owner or designated agent. If the appraisal review board has cause to reassign a protest to another panel, a property owner or designated agent may agree to reassignment of the protest or may request that the hearing on the protest be postponed. The board shall postpone the hearing on that request. A change of members of a panel because of a conflict of interest, illness, or inability to continue participating in hearings for the remainder of the day does not constitute reassignment of a protest to another panel.

(*l*) A property owner, attorney, or agent offering evidence or argument in support of a protest brought under Section 41.41(a)(1) or (2) of this code is not subject to Chapter 1103, Occupations Code, unless the person offering the evidence or argument states that the person is offering evidence or argument as a person holding a license or certificate under Chapter 1103, Occupations Code. A person holding a license or certificate under Chapter 1103, Occupations Code, shall state the capacity in which the person is appearing before the appraisal review board.

(m) An appraisal district or appraisal review board may not make decisions with regard to membership on a panel or chairmanship of a panel based on a member's voting record in previous protests.

(n) A request for postponement of a hearing must contain the mailing address and e-mail address of the person requesting the postponement. An appraisal review board shall respond in writing or by e-mail to a request for postponement of a hearing not later than the seventh day after the date of receipt of the request.

(o) The chairman of an appraisal review board or a member designated by the chairman may make decisions with regard to the scheduling or postponement of a hearing. The chief appraiser or a person designated by the chief appraiser may agree to a postponement of an appraisal review board hearing.

2017 Legislation: Amended by S.B. 1767, §2, 85th Leg., eff. Jan. 1, 2018.

TAX §41.67. EVIDENCE

(a) A member of the appraisal review board may swear witnesses who testify in proceedings under this chapter. All testimony must be given under oath.

(b) Documentary evidence may be admitted in the form of a copy if the appraisal review board conducting the proceeding determines that the original document is not readily available. A party is entitled to an opportunity to compare a copy with the original document on request.

(c) Official notice may be taken of any fact judicially cognizable. A party is entitled to an opportunity to contest facts officially noticed.

(d) Information that was previously requested under Section 41.461 by the protesting party that was not made available to the protesting party at least 14 days before the scheduled or postponed hearing may not be used as evidence in the hearing.

TAX §41.68. RECORD OF PROCEEDING

The appraisal review board shall keep a record of its proceedings in the form and manner prescribed by the comptroller.

TAX §41.69. CONFLICT OF INTEREST

A member of the appraisal review board may not participate in the determination of a taxpayer protest in which he is interested or in which he is related to a party by affinity within the second degree or by consanguinity within the third degree, as determined under Chapter 573, Government Code.

TAX §41.70. PUBLIC NOTICE OF PROTEST & APPEAL PROCEDURES

(a) On or after May 1 but not later than May 15, the chief appraiser shall publish notice of the manner in which a protest under this chapter may be brought by a property owner. The notice must describe how to initiate a protest and must describe the deadlines for filing a protest. The notice must also describe the manner in which an order of the appraisal review board may be appealed. The comptroller by rule shall adopt minimum standards for the form and content of the notice required by this section.

(b) The chief appraiser shall publish the notice in a newspaper having general circulation in the county for which the appraisal district is established. The notice may not be smaller than one-quarter page of a standard-size or tabloid-size newspaper, and may not be published in the part of the paper in which legal notices and classified advertisements appear.

TAX §41.71. EVENING & WEEKEND HEARINGS

An appraisal review board by rule shall provide for hearings on protests in the evening or on a Saturday or Sunday.

CHAPTER 42. JUDICIAL REVIEW

SUBCHAPTER A. IN GENERAL

TAX §42.01. RIGHT OF APPEAL BY PROPERTY OWNER

(a) A property owner is entitled to appeal:

(1) an order of the appraisal review board determining:

(A) a protest by the property owner as provided by Subchapter C of Chapter 41;

(B) a determination of an appraisal review board on a motion filed under Section 25.25;

(C) a determination of an appraisal review board that the property owner has forfeited the right to a final determination of a motion filed under Section 25.25 or of a protest under Section 41.411 for failing to comply with the prepayment requirements of Section 25.26 or 41.4115, as applicable; or

(D) a determination of an appraisal review board of eligibility for a refund requested under Section 23.1243; or

(2) an order of the comptroller issued as provided by Subchapter B, Chapter 24, apportioning among the counties the appraised value of railroad rolling stock owned by the property owner.

(b) A property owner who establishes that the owner did not forfeit the right to a final determination of a motion or of a protest in an appeal under Subsection (a)(1)(C) is entitled to a final determination of the court, as applicable:

(1) of the motion filed under Section 25.25; or

(2) of the protest under Section 41.411 of the failure of the chief appraiser or appraisal review board to provide or deliver a notice to which the property owner is entitled, and, if failure to provide or deliver the notice is established, of a protest made by the property owner on any other grounds of protest authorized by this title relating to the property to which the notice applies.

TAX §42.015. APPEAL BY PERSON LEASING PROPERTY

(a) A person leasing property who is contractually obligated to reimburse the property owner for taxes imposed on the property is entitled to appeal an order of the appraisal review board determining a protest brought by the person under Section 41.413.

(b) A person appealing an order of the appraisal review board under this section is considered the owner of the property for purposes of the appeal. The chief appraiser shall deliver a copy of any notice relating to the appeal to the owner of the property and to the person bringing the appeal.

TAX §42.016. INTERVENTION IN APPEAL BY CERTAIN PERSONS

A person is entitled to intervene in an appeal brought under this chapter and the person has standing and the court has jurisdiction in the appeal if the property that is the subject of the appeal was also the subject of a protest hearing and the person:

(1) owned the property at any time during the tax year at issue;

(2) leased the property at any time during the tax year at issue and the person filed the protest that resulted in the issuance of the order under appeal; or

(3) is shown on the appraisal roll as the owner of the property or as a lessee authorized to file a protest and the person filed the protest that resulted in the issuance of the order under appeal.

TAX §42.02. RIGHT OF APPEAL BY CHIEF APPRAISER

(a) On written approval of the board of directors of the appraisal district, the chief appraiser is entitled to appeal an order of the appraisal review board determining:

(1) a taxpayer protest as provided by Subchapter C, Chapter 41, subject to Subsection (b); or

(2) a taxpayer's motion to change the appraisal roll filed under Section 25.25.

(b) Except as provided by Subsection (c), the chief appraiser may not appeal an order of the appraisal review board determining a taxpayer protest under Subsection (a)(1) if:

TAX §42.02

(1) the protest involved a determination of the appraised or market value of the taxpayer's property and that value according to the order that is the subject of the appeal is less than $1 million; or

(2) for any other taxpayer protest, the property to which the protest applies has an appraised value according to the appraisal roll for the current year of less than $1 million.

(c) On written approval of the board of directors of the appraisal district, the chief appraiser may appeal an order of the appraisal review board determining a taxpayer protest otherwise prohibited by Subsection (b), if the chief appraiser alleges that the taxpayer or a person acting on behalf of the taxpayer committed fraud, made a material misrepresentation, or presented fraudulent evidence in the hearing before the board. In an appeal under this subsection, the court shall first consider whether the taxpayer or a person acting on behalf of the taxpayer committed fraud, made a material misrepresentation, or presented fraudulent evidence to the appraisal review board. If the court does not find by a preponderance of the evidence that the taxpayer or a person acting on behalf of the taxpayer committed fraud, made a material misrepresentation, or presented fraudulent evidence to the appraisal review board, the court shall:

(1) dismiss the appeal; and

(2) award court costs and reasonable attorney's fees to the taxpayer.

TAX §42.03. RIGHT OF APPEAL BY COUNTY

A county may appeal the order of the comptroller issued as provided by Subchapter B, Chapter 24 of this code apportioning among the counties the appraised value of railroad rolling stock.

TAX §42.031. RIGHT OF APPEAL BY TAXING UNIT

(a) A taxing unit is entitled to appeal an order of the appraisal review board determining a challenge by the taxing unit.

(b) A taxing unit may not intervene in or in any other manner be made a party, whether as defendant or otherwise, to an appeal of an order of the appraisal review board determining a taxpayer protest under Subchapter C, Chapter 41, if the appeal was brought by the property owner.

TAX §42.04. INTERVENTION BY STATE OR POLITICAL SUBDIVISION OWNING PROPERTY SUBJECT TO TAXABLE LEASEHOLD

If the challenge or protest relates to a taxable leasehold or other possessory interest in real property that is owned by this state or a political subdivision of this state, the attorney general or a representative of the state agency that owns the real property, if the real property is owned by this state, or a person designated by the political subdivision that owns the real property, as applicable, may intervene in an appeal of an order of an appraisal review board determining a challenge by a taxing unit or a taxpayer protest.

TAX §42.05. COMPTROLLER AS PARTY

The comptroller is an opposing party in an appeal by:

(1) a property owner of an order of the comptroller determining a protest of the appraisal, interstate allocation, or intrastate apportionment of transportation business intangibles; or

(2) a county or a property owner of an order of the comptroller apportioning among the counties the appraised value of railroad rolling stock.

TAX §42.06. NOTICE OF APPEAL

(a) To exercise the party's right to appeal an order of an appraisal review board, a party other than a property owner must file written notice of appeal within 15 days after the date the party receives the notice required by Section 41.47 or, in the case of a taxing unit, by Section 41.07 that the order appealed has been issued. To exercise the right to appeal an order of the comptroller, a party other than a property owner must file written notice of appeal within 15 days after the date the party receives the comptroller's order. A property owner is not required to file a notice of appeal under this section.

(b) A party required to file a notice of appeal under this section other than a chief appraiser who appeals an order of an appraisal review board shall file the notice with the chief appraiser of the appraisal district for which the appraisal review board is established. A chief appraiser who appeals an order of an appraisal review board shall file the notice with the appraisal review board. A party who appeals an order of the comptroller shall file the notice with the comptroller.

(c) If the chief appraiser, a taxing unit, or a county appeals, the chief appraiser, if the appeal is of an order of the appraisal review board, or the comptroller, if the appeal is of an order of the comptroller, shall deliver a copy of the notice to the property owner whose property is involved in the appeal within 10 days after the date the notice is filed.

(d) On the filing of a notice of appeal, the chief appraiser shall indicate where appropriate those entries on the appraisal records that are subject to the appeal.

TAX §42.07. COSTS OF APPEAL

The reviewing court in its discretion may charge all or part of the costs of an appeal taken as provided by this chapter against any of the parties.

TAX §42.08. FORFEITURE OF REMEDY FOR NONPAYMENT OF TAXES

(a) The pendency of an appeal as provided by this chapter does not affect the delinquency date for the taxes on the property subject to the appeal. However, that delinquency date applies only to the amount of taxes required to be paid under Subsection (b). If the property owner complies with Subsection (b), the delinquency date for any additional amount of taxes due on the property is determined by Section 42.42(c), and that additional amount is not delinquent before that date.

(b) Except as provided in Subsection (d), a property owner who appeals as provided by this chapter must pay taxes on the property subject to the appeal in the amount required by this subsection before the delinquency date or the property owner forfeits the right to proceed to a final determination of the appeal. The amount of taxes the property owner must pay on the property before the delinquency date to comply with this subsection is the lesser of:

(1) the amount of taxes due on the portion of the taxable value of the property that is not in dispute;

(2) the amount of taxes due on the property under the order from which the appeal is taken; or

(3) the amount of taxes imposed on the property in the preceding tax year.

(b-1) This subsection applies only to an appeal in which the property owner elects to pay the amount of taxes described by Subsection (b)(1). The appeal filed by the property owner must be accompanied by a statement in writing of the amount of taxes the property owner proposes to pay. The failure to provide the statement required by this subsection is not a jurisdictional error.

(c) A property owner that pays an amount of taxes greater than that required by Subsection (b) does not forfeit the property owner's right to a final determination of the appeal by making the payment. The property owner may pay an additional amount of taxes at any time. If the property owner files a timely appeal under this chapter, taxes paid on the property are considered paid under protest, even if paid before the appeal is filed. If the taxes are subject to the split-payment option provided by Section 31.03, the property owner may comply with Subsection (b) of this section by paying one-half of the amount otherwise required to be paid under that subsection before December 1 and paying the remaining one-half of that amount before July 1 of the following year.

(d) After filing an oath of inability to pay the taxes at issue, a party may be excused from the requirement of prepayment of tax as a prerequisite to appeal if the court, after notice and hearing, finds that such prepayment would constitute an unreasonable restraint on the party's right of access to the courts. On the motion of a party and after the movant's compliance with Subsection (e), the court shall hold a hearing to review and determine compliance with this section, and the reviewing court may set such terms and conditions on any grant of relief as may be reasonably required by the circumstances. If the court determines that the property owner has not substantially complied with this section, the court shall dismiss the pending action. If the court determines that the property owner has substantially but not fully complied with this section, the court shall dismiss the pending action unless the property owner fully complies with the court's determination within 30 days of the determination.

(e) Not later than the 45th day before the date of a hearing to review and determine compliance with this section, the movant must mail notice of the hearing by certified mail, return receipt requested, to the collector for each taxing unit that imposes taxes on the property.

(f) Regardless of whether the collector for the taxing unit receives a notice under Subsection (e), a taxing unit that imposes taxes on the property may intervene in an appeal under this chapter and participate in the proceedings for the limited purpose of determining whether the property owner has complied with this sec-

tion. The taxing unit is entitled to process for witnesses and evidence and to be heard by the court.

TAX §42.09. REMEDIES EXCLUSIVE

(a) Except as provided by Subsection (b) of this section, procedures prescribed by this title for adjudication of the grounds of protest authorized by this title are exclusive, and a property owner may not raise any of those grounds:

(1) in defense to a suit to enforce collection of delinquent taxes; or

(2) as a basis of a claim for relief in a suit by the property owner to arrest or prevent the tax collection process or to obtain a refund of taxes paid.

(b) A person against whom a suit to collect a delinquent property tax is filed may plead as an affirmative defense:

(1) if the suit is to enforce personal liability for the tax, that the defendant did not own the property on which the tax was imposed on January 1 of the year for which the tax was imposed; or

(2) if the suit is to foreclose a lien securing the payment of a tax on real property, that the property was not located within the boundaries of the taxing unit seeking to foreclose the lien on January 1 of the year for which the tax was imposed.

(c) For purposes of this section, "suit" includes a counterclaim, cross-claim, or other claim filed in the course of a lawsuit.

Sections 42.10-42.20 reserved for expansion

SUBCHAPTER B. REVIEW BY DISTRICT COURT

TAX §42.21. PETITION FOR REVIEW

(a) A party who appeals as provided by this chapter must file a petition for review with the district court within 60 days after the party received notice that a final order has been entered from which an appeal may be had or at any time after the hearing but before the 60-day deadline. Failure to timely file a petition bars any appeal under this chapter.

(b) A petition for review brought under Section 42.02 must be brought against the owner of the property involved in the appeal. A petition for review brought under Section 42.031 must be brought against the appraisal district and against the owner of the property involved in the appeal. A petition for review brought under Section 42.01(a)(2) or 42.03 must be brought against the comptroller. Any other petition for review under this chapter must be brought against the appraisal district. A petition for review may not be brought against the appraisal review board. An appraisal district may hire an attorney that represents the district to represent the appraisal review board established for the district to file an answer and obtain a dismissal of a suit filed against the appraisal review board in violation of this subsection.

(c) If an appeal under this chapter is pending when the appraisal review board issues an order in a subsequent year under a protest by the same property owner and that protest relates to the same property that is involved in the pending appeal, the property owner may appeal the subsequent appraisal review board order by amending the original petition for the pending appeal to include the grounds for appealing the subsequent order. The amended petition must be filed with the court in the period provided by Subsection (a) for filing a petition for review of the subsequent order. A property owner may appeal the subsequent appraisal review board order under this subsection or may appeal the order independently of the pending appeal as otherwise provided by this section, but may not do both. A property owner may change the election of remedies provided by this subsection at any time before the end of the period provided by Subsection (a) for filing a petition for review.

(d) An appraisal district is served by service on the chief appraiser at any time or by service on any other officer or employee of the appraisal district present at the appraisal office at a time when the appraisal office is open for business with the public. An appraisal review board is served by service on the chairman of the appraisal review board. Citation of a party is issued and served in the manner provided by law for civil suits generally.

(e) A petition that is timely filed under Subsection (a) or amended under Subsection (c) may be subsequently amended to:

(1) correct or change the name of a party; or

(2) not later than the 120th day before the date of trial, identify or describe the property originally involved in the appeal.

(f) A petition filed by an owner or lessee of property may include multiple properties that are owned or leased by the same person and are of a similar type or are part of the same economic unit and would typically

sell as a single property. If a petition is filed by multiple plaintiffs or includes multiple properties that are not of a similar type, are not part of the same economic unit, or are part of the same economic unit but would not typically sell as a single property, the court may on motion and a showing of good cause sever the plaintiffs or the properties.

(g) A petition filed by an owner or lessee of property may be amended to include additional properties in the same county that are owned or leased by the same person, are of a similar type as the property originally involved in the appeal or are part of the same economic unit as the property originally involved in the appeal and would typically sell as a single property, and are the subject of an appraisal review board order issued in the same year as the order that is the subject of the original appeal. The amendment must be filed within the period during which a petition for review of the appraisal review board order pertaining to the additional properties would be required to be filed under Subsection (a).

(h) The court has jurisdiction over an appeal under this chapter brought on behalf of a property owner or lessee and the owner or lessee is considered to have exhausted the owner's or lessee's administrative remedies regardless of whether the petition correctly identifies the plaintiff as the owner or lessee of the property or correctly describes the property so long as the property was the subject of an appraisal review board order, the petition was filed within the period required by Subsection (a), and the petition provides sufficient information to identify the property that is the subject of the petition. Whether the plaintiff is the proper party to bring the petition or whether the property needs to be further identified or described must be addressed by means of a special exception and correction of the petition by amendment as authorized by Subsection (e) and may not be the subject of a plea to the jurisdiction or a claim that the plaintiff has failed to exhaust the plaintiff's administrative remedies. If the petition is amended to add a plaintiff, the court on motion shall enter a docket control order to provide proper deadlines in response to the addition of the plaintiff.

TAX §42.22[A*]. VENUE

☠ *Section 42.22[A*] was amended by Acts 1993, 73rd Leg., ch. 667, §1, enacted May 29, 1993, effective Sept. 1, 1993, without reference to the conflicting amendment made by Acts 1993, 73rd Leg., ch. 1033, §1, enacted May 29, 1993, effective Sept. 1, 1993. For harmonizing conflicts, see p. V. The [A*] has been added by the editor to distinguish this §42.22 from the other, which is marked with [B*].*

Venue is in the county in which the appraisal review board that issued the order appealed is located, except as provided by Section 42.221. Venue is in Travis County if the order appealed was issued by the comptroller.

TAX §42.22[B*]. VENUE

☠ *Section 42.22[B*] was amended by Acts 1993, 73rd Leg., ch. 1033, §1, enacted May 29, 1993, effective Sept. 1, 1993, without reference to the conflicting amendment made by Acts 1993, 73rd Leg., ch. 667, §1, enacted May 29, 1993, effective Sept. 1, 1993. For harmonizing conflicts, see p. V. The [B*] has been added by the editor to distinguish this §42.22 from the other, which is marked with [A*].*

(a) Except as provided by Subsections (b) and (c), and by Section 42.221, venue is in the county in which the appraisal review board that issued the order appealed is located.

(b) Venue of an action brought under Section 42.01(1) is in the county in which the property is located or in the county in which the appraisal review board that issued the order is located.

(c) Venue is in Travis County if the order appealed was issued by the comptroller.

TAX §42.221. CONSOLIDATED APPEALS FOR MULTICOUNTY PROPERTY

(a) The owner of property of a telecommunications provider, as defined by Section 51.002, Utilities Code, or the owner of property regulated by the Railroad Commission of Texas, the federal Surface Transportation Board, or the Federal Energy Regulatory Commission that runs through or operates in more than one county and is appraised by more than one appraisal district may appeal an order of an appraisal review board relating to the property running through or operating in more than one county to the district court of any county in which a portion of the property is located or operated if the order relating to that portion of the property is appealed.

(b) A petition for review of each appraisal review board order under this section must be filed with the court as provided by Section 42.21.

(c) If only one appeal by the owner of property subject to this section is pending before the court in an appeal from the decision of an appraisal review board of a district other than the appraisal district for that county, any party to the suit may, not earlier than the 30th day before and not later than the 10th day before the date set for the hearing, make a motion to transfer the suit to a district court of the county in which the appraisal review board from which the appeal is taken is located. In the absence of a showing that further appeals under this section will be filed, the court shall transfer the suit.

(d) When the owner files the first petition for review under this section for a tax year, the owner shall include with the petition a list of each appraisal district in which the property is appraised for taxation in that tax year.

(e) The court shall consolidate all the appeals for a tax year relating to a single property subject to this section for which a petition for review is filed with the court and may consolidate other appeals relating to other property subject to this section of the same owner if the property is located in one or more of the counties on the list required by Subsection (d). Except as provided by this subsection, on the motion of the owner of a property subject to this section the court shall grant a continuance to provide the owner with an opportunity to include in the proceeding appeals of appraisal review board orders from additional appraisal districts. The court may not grant a continuance to include an appeal of an appraisal review board order that relates to a property subject to this section in that tax year after the time for filing a petition for review of that order has expired.

(f) This section does not affect the property owner's right to file a petition for review of an individual appraisal district's order relating to a property subject to this section in the district court in the county in which the appraisal review board is located.

(g) On a joint motion or the separate motions of at least 60 percent of the appraisal districts that are defendants in a consolidated suit filed before the 45th day after the date on which the property owner's petitions for review of the appraisal review board orders relating to a property subject to this section for that tax year must be filed, the court shall transfer the suit to a district court of the county named in the motion or motions if that county is one in which one of the appraisal review boards from which an appeal was taken is located.

See also Util. Code §51.002(10).

TAX §42.225. PROPERTY OWNER'S RIGHT TO APPEAL THROUGH ARBITRATION

(a) On motion by a property owner who appeals an appraisal review board order under this chapter, the court shall submit the appeal to nonbinding arbitration. The court shall order the nonbinding arbitration to be conducted in accordance with Chapter 154, Civil Practice and Remedies Code. If the appeal proceeds to trial following an arbitration award or finding under this subsection, either party may introduce the award or finding into evidence. In addition, the court shall award the property owner reasonable attorney fees if the trial was not requested by the property owner and the determination of the appeal results in an appraised value for the owner's property that is equal to or less than the appraised value under the arbitration award or finding. However, the amount of an award of attorney fees under this subsection is subject to the same limitations as those provided by Section 42.29.

(b) On motion by the property owner, the court shall order the parties to an appeal of an appraisal review board order under this chapter to submit to binding arbitration if the appraisal district joins in the motion or consents to the arbitration. A binding arbitration award under this subsection is binding and enforceable in the same manner as a contract obligation.

(c) The court shall appoint an impartial third party to conduct an arbitration under this section. The impartial third party is appointed by the court and serves as provided by Subchapter C, Chapter 154, Civil Practice and Remedies Code.

(d) Each party or counsel for the party may present the position of the party before the impartial third party, who must render a specific arbitration award.

(e) Prior to submission of a case to arbitration the court shall determine matters related to jurisdiction, venue, and interpretation of the law.

(f) Except as provided in this section, an arbitration award may include any remedy or relief that a court could order under this chapter.

See also CPRC ch. 154; *O'Connor's Texas Rules*, "Motion to Compel Statutory Arbitration," ch. 4-C, §3, p. 336.

TAX §42.226. MEDIATION

On motion by a party to an appeal under this chapter, the court shall enter an order requiring the parties to attend mediation. The court may enter an order requiring the parties to attend mediation on its own motion.

TAX §42.227. PRETRIAL SETTLEMENT DISCUSSIONS

(a) A property owner or appraisal district that is a party to an appeal under this chapter may request that the parties engage in settlement discussions, including through an informal settlement conference or a form of alternative dispute resolution. The request must be in writing and delivered to the other party before the date of trial. The court on motion of either party shall enter orders necessary to implement this section, including an order:

(1) specifying the form that the settlement discussions must take; or

(2) changing a deadline to designate experts prescribed by Subsection (c).

(b) On or before the 120th day after the date the written request is delivered under Subsection (a), each party or the party's attorney of record shall attend the settlement discussions and make a good faith effort to resolve the matter under appeal.

(c) If the appraisal district is unable for any reason to attend the settlement discussions on or before the 120th day after the date the written request is delivered under Subsection (a), the deadline to designate experts for the appeal is, notwithstanding a deadline prescribed by the Texas Rules of Civil Procedure:

(1) with regard to all experts testifying for a party seeking affirmative relief, 60 days before the date of trial; and

(2) with regard to all other experts, 30 days before the date of trial.

(d) If a property owner is unable for any reason to attend the settlement discussions on or before the 120th day after the date the written request is delivered under Subsection (a), Section 42.23(d) does not apply to the parties to the appeal.

(e) An appraisal district may not request or require a property owner to waive a right under this title as a condition of attending a settlement discussion.

TAX §42.23. SCOPE OF REVIEW[1]

(a) Review is by trial de novo. The district court shall try all issues of fact and law raised by the pleadings in the manner applicable to civil suits generally.

(b) The court may not admit in evidence the fact of prior action by the appraisal review board or comptroller, except to the extent necessary to establish its jurisdiction.

(c) Any party is entitled to trial by jury on demand.

(d) Each party to an appeal is considered a party seeking affirmative relief for the purpose of discovery regarding expert witnesses under the Texas Rules of Civil Procedure if, on or before the 120th day after the date the appeal is filed, the property owner:

(1) makes a written offer of settlement;

(2) requests alternative dispute resolution; and

(3) designates, in response to an appropriate written discovery request, which cause of action under this chapter is the basis for the appeal.

(e) For purposes of Subsection (d), a property owner may designate a cause of action under Section 42.25 or 42.26 as the basis for an appeal, but may not designate a cause of action under both sections as the basis for the appeal. Discovery regarding a cause of action that is not specifically designated by the property owner under Subsection (d) shall be conducted as provided by the Texas Rules of Civil Procedure. The court may enter a protective order to modify the provisions of this subsection under Rule 192.6 of the Texas Rules of Civil Procedure.

(f) For purposes of a no-evidence motion for summary judgment filed by a party to an appeal under this chapter, the offer of evidence, including an affidavit or testimony, by any person, including the appraisal district, the property owner, or the owner's agent, that was presented at the hearing on the protest before the appraisal review board constitutes sufficient evidence to deny the motion.

(g) For the sole purpose of admitting expert testimony to determine the value of chemical processing property or utility property in an appeal brought under this chapter and for no other purpose under this title, including the rendition of property under Chapter 22, the property is considered to be personal property.

(h) Evidence, argument, or other testimony offered at an appraisal review board hearing by a property

owner or agent is not admissible in an appeal under this chapter unless:

(1) the evidence, argument, or other testimony is offered to demonstrate that there is sufficient evidence to deny a no-evidence motion for summary judgment filed by a party to the appeal or is necessary for the determination of the merits of a motion for summary judgment filed on another ground;

(2) the property owner or agent is designated as a witness for purposes of trial and the testimony offered at the appraisal review board hearing is offered for impeachment purposes; or

(3) the evidence is the plaintiff's testimony at the appraisal review board hearing as to the value of the property.

1. **Editor's note:** In 2015, the Legislature amended §42.23 to give preference to an authorized appraiser's value of real property, but the amendments are not effective until Jan. 1, 2020. For the text of the prospective amendment, see Acts 2015, 84th Leg., ch. 481, §9, eff. Jan. 1, 2020.

TAX §42.24. ACTION BY COURT

In determining an appeal, the district court may:

(1) fix the appraised value of property in accordance with the requirements of law if the appraised value is at issue;

(2) enter the orders necessary to ensure equal treatment under the law for the appealing property owner if inequality in the appraisal of his property is at issue; or

(3) enter other orders necessary to preserve rights protected by and impose duties required by the law.

TAX §42.25. REMEDY FOR EXCESSIVE APPRAISAL

If the court determines that the appraised value of property according to the appraisal roll exceeds the appraised value required by law, the property owner is entitled to a reduction of the appraised value on the appraisal roll to the appraised value determined by the court.

TAX §42.26. REMEDY FOR UNEQUAL APPRAISAL

(a) The district court shall grant relief on the ground that a property is appraised unequally if:

(1) the appraisal ratio of the property exceeds by at least 10 percent the median level of appraisal of a reasonable and representative sample of other properties in the appraisal district;

(2) the appraisal ratio of the property exceeds by at least 10 percent the median level of appraisal of a sample of properties in the appraisal district consisting of a reasonable number of other properties similarly situated to, or of the same general kind or character as, the property subject to the appeal; or

(3) the appraised value of the property exceeds the median appraised value of a reasonable number of comparable properties appropriately adjusted.

(b) If a property owner is entitled to relief under Subsection (a)(1), the court shall order the property's appraised value changed to the value as calculated on the basis of the median level of appraisal according to Subsection (a)(1). If a property owner is entitled to relief under Subsection (a)(2), the court shall order the property's appraised value changed to the value calculated on the basis of the median level of appraisal according to Subsection (a)(2). If a property owner is entitled to relief under Subsection (a)(3), the court shall order the property's appraised value changed to the value calculated on the basis of the median appraised value according to Subsection (a)(3). If a property owner is entitled to relief under more than one subdivision of Subsection (a), the court shall order the property's appraised value changed to the value that results in the lowest appraised value. The court shall determine each applicable median level of appraisal or median appraised value according to law, and is not required to adopt the median level of appraisal or median appraised value proposed by a party to the appeal. The court may not limit or deny relief to the property owner entitled to relief under a subdivision of Subsection (a) because the appraised value determined according to another subdivision of Subsection (a) results in a higher appraised value.

(c) For purposes of establishing the median level of appraisal under Subsection (a)(1), the median level of appraisal in the appraisal district as determined by the comptroller under Section 5.10 is admissible as evidence of the median level of appraisal of a reasonable and representative sample of properties in the appraisal district for the year of the comptroller's determination, subject to the Texas Rules of Evidence and the Texas Rules of Civil Procedure.

(d) For purposes of this section, the value of the property subject to the suit and the value of a comparable property or sample property that is used for comparison must be the market value determined by the

appraisal district when the property is a residence homestead subject to the limitation on appraised value imposed by Section 23.23.

TAX §42.27. REPEALED

TAX §42.28. APPEAL OF DISTRICT COURT JUDGMENT

A party may appeal the final judgment of the district court as provided by law for appeal of civil suits generally, except that an appeal bond is not required of the chief appraiser, the county, the comptroller, or the commissioners court.

TAX §42.29. ATTORNEY'S FEES

(a) A property owner who prevails in an appeal to the court under Section 42.25 or 42.26, in an appeal to the court of a determination of an appraisal review board on a motion filed under Section 25.25, or in an appeal to the court of a determination of an appraisal review board of a protest of the denial in whole or in part of an exemption under Section 11.17, 11.22, 11.23, 11.231, or 11.24 may be awarded reasonable attorney's fees. The amount of the award may not exceed the greater of:

(1) $15,000; or

(2) 20 percent of the total amount by which the property owner's tax liability is reduced as a result of the appeal.

(b) Notwithstanding Subsection (a), the amount of an award of attorney's fees may not exceed the lesser of:

(1) $100,000; or

(2) the total amount by which the property owner's tax liability is reduced as a result of the appeal.

TAX §42.30. ATTORNEY NOTICE OF CERTAIN ENGAGEMENTS

(a) An attorney who accepts an engagement or compensation from a third party to represent a person in an appeal under this chapter shall provide notice to the person represented:

(1) informing the person that the attorney has been retained by a third party to represent the person;

(2) explaining the attorney's ethical obligations to the person in relation to the third party, including the obligation to ensure that the third party does not interfere with the attorney's independent judgment or the attorney-client relationship;

(3) describing the general activities the third party may perform in the appeal;

(4) explaining that compensation will be received by the attorney from the third party; and

(5) informing the person that the person's consent is required before the attorney may accept compensation from the third party.

(b) The attorney shall mail the notice by certified mail to the person represented by the attorney not later than the 30th day after the date the attorney accepts the engagement from the third party.

(c) Notwithstanding the other provisions of this section, an engagement complies with this section if each party related to the engagement, including the person represented in the appeal, the third party, and the attorney, enters into an agreement not later than the 30th day after the date of the filing of the appeal by the attorney that contains the information required by Subsection (a).

(d) A person may void an engagement that does not comply with this section. An attorney who does not comply with this section may be reported to the Office of Chief Disciplinary Counsel for the State Bar of Texas.

Sections 42.31-42.40 reserved for expansion

SUBCHAPTER C. POSTAPPEAL ADMINISTRATIVE PROCEDURES

TAX §42.41. CORRECTION OF ROLLS

(a) Not later than the 45th day after the date an appeal is finally determined, the chief appraiser shall:

(1) correct the appraisal roll and other appropriate records as necessary to reflect the final determination of the appeal; and

(2) certify the change to the assessor for each affected taxing unit.

(b) The assessor for each affected taxing unit shall correct the tax roll and other appropriate records for which the assessor is responsible.

(c) A chief appraiser is irrebutably presumed to have complied with Subsection (a)(2).

TAX §42.42. CORRECTED & SUPPLEMENTAL TAX BILLS

(a) Except as provided by Subsection (b) of this section, if the final determination of an appeal that changes a property owner's tax liability occurs after the tax bill is mailed, the assessor for each affected taxing unit shall prepare and mail a corrected tax bill in the

manner provided by Chapter 31 of this code for tax bills generally. The assessor shall include with the bill a brief explanation of the reason for and effect of the corrected bill.

(b) If the final determination of an appeal that increases a property owner's tax liability occurs after the property owner has paid his taxes, the assessor for each affected taxing unit shall prepare and mail a supplemental tax bill in the manner provided by Chapter 31 for tax bills generally. The assessor shall include with the bill a brief explanation of the reason for and effect of the supplemental bill. The additional tax is due on receipt of the supplemental bill and becomes delinquent if not paid before the delinquency date prescribed by Chapter 31 or before the first day of the next month after the date of mailing that will provide at least 21 days for payment of the tax, whichever is later.

(c) If the final determination of an appeal occurs after the property owner has paid a portion of the tax finally determined to be due as required by Section 42.08, the assessor for each affected taxing unit shall prepare and mail a supplemental tax bill in the form and manner prescribed by Subsection (b). The additional tax is due and becomes delinquent as provided by Subsection (b), but the property owner is liable for penalties and interest on the tax included in the supplemental bill calculated as provided by Section 33.01 as if the tax included in the supplemental bill became delinquent on the original delinquency date prescribed by Chapter 31.

(d) If the property owner did not pay any portion of the taxes imposed on the property because the court found that payment would constitute an unreasonable restraint on the owner's right of access to the courts as provided by Section 42.08(d), after the final determination of the appeal the assessor for each affected taxing unit shall prepare and mail a supplemental tax bill in the form and manner prescribed by Subsection (b). The additional tax is due and becomes delinquent as provided by Subsection (b), but the property owner is liable for interest on the tax included in the supplemental bill calculated as provided by Section 33.01 as if the tax included in the supplemental bill became delinquent on the delinquency date prescribed by Chapter 31.

TAX §42.43. REFUND

(a) If the final determination of an appeal that decreases a property owner's tax liability occurs after the property owner has paid his taxes, the taxing unit shall refund to the property owner the difference between the amount of taxes paid and amount of taxes for which the property owner is liable.

(b) For a refund made under this section, the taxing unit shall include with the refund interest on the amount refunded calculated at an annual rate of 9.5 percent, calculated from the delinquency date for the taxes until the date the refund is made.

(b-1) A taxing unit may not send a refund made under this section before the earlier of:

(1) the 21st day after the final determination of the appeal; or

(2) the date the property owner files the form prescribed by Subsection (i) with the taxing unit.

(c) Notwithstanding Subsection (b), if a taxing unit does not make a refund, including interest, required by this section before the 60th day after the date the chief appraiser certifies a correction to the appraisal roll under Section 42.41, the taxing unit shall include with the refund interest on the amount refunded at an annual rate of 12 percent, calculated from the delinquency date for the taxes until the date the refund is made. A refund is not considered made under this section until sent to the proper person as provided by this section.

(d) A property owner who prevails in a suit to compel a refund, including interest, required by this section that is filed on or after the 180th day after the date the chief appraiser certifies a correction to the appraisal roll is entitled to court costs and reasonable attorney's fees.

(e) Except as provided by Subsection (f) or (g), a taxing unit shall send a refund made under this section to the property owner.

(f) The final judgment in an appeal under this chapter may designate to whom and where a refund is to be sent.

(g) If a form prescribed by the comptroller under Subsection (i) is filed with a taxing unit before the 21st day after the final determination of an appeal that requires a refund be made, the taxing unit shall send the refund to the person and address designated on the form.

(h) A separate form must be filed with a taxing unit under Subsection (g) for each appeal to which the

property owner is a party. A form may be revoked in a written revocation filed with the taxing unit by the property owner.

(i) The comptroller shall prescribe the form necessary to allow a property owner to designate the person to whom a refund must be sent. The comptroller shall include on the form a space for the property owner to designate to whom and where the refund must be sent and provide options to mail the refund to:

(1) the property owner;

(2) the business office of the property owner's attorney of record in the appeal; or

(3) any other individual and address designated by the property owner.

(j) A property owner is not entitled to a refund under this section resulting from the final determination of an appeal of the denial of an exemption under Section 11.31, wholly or partly, unless the property owner is entitled to the refund under Subsection (a) or has entered into a written agreement with the chief appraiser that authorizes the refund as part of an agreement related to the taxation of the property pending a final determination by the Texas Commission on Environmental Quality under Section 11.31.

(k) Not later than the 10th day after the date a property owner and the chief appraiser enter into a written agreement described by Subsection (j), the chief appraiser shall provide to each taxing unit that taxes the property a copy of the agreement. The agreement is void if a taxing unit that taxes the property objects in writing to the agreement on or before the 60th day after the date the taxing unit receives a copy of the agreement.

CHAPTER 43. SUIT AGAINST APPRAISAL OFFICE

TAX §43.01. AUTHORITY TO BRING SUIT

A taxing unit may sue the appraisal district that appraises property for the unit to compel the appraisal district to comply with the provisions of this title, rules of the comptroller, or other applicable law.

TAX §43.02. VENUE

Venue is in the county in which the appraisal district is established.

TAX §43.03. ACTION BY COURT

The court as the evidence warrants shall enter those orders necessary to compel compliance by the appraisal office.

TAX §43.04. SUIT TO COMPEL COMPLIANCE WITH DEADLINES

The governing body of a taxing unit may sue the chief appraiser or members of the appraisal review board, as applicable, for failure to comply with the deadlines imposed by Section 25.22(a), 26.01(a), or 41.12. If the court finds that the chief appraiser or appraisal review board failed to comply for good cause shown, the court shall enter an order fixing a reasonable deadline for compliance. If the court finds that the chief appraiser or appraisal review board failed to comply without good cause, the court shall enter an order requiring the chief appraiser or appraisal review board to comply with the deadline not later than the 10th day after the date the judgment is signed. In a suit brought under this section, the court may enter any other order the court considers necessary to ensure compliance with the court's deadline or the applicable statutory requirements. Failure to obey an order of the court is punishable as contempt.

SELECTED PROVISIONS

TITLE 6. ROADWAYS

Subtitle E. Municipal Streets

Chapter 314. Purchase or Condemnation of Property for Highways by Certain Municipalities

TITLE 6. ROADWAYS

SUBTITLE E. MUNICIPAL STREETS

CHAPTER 314. PURCHASE OR CONDEMNATION OF PROPERTY FOR HIGHWAYS BY CERTAIN MUNICIPALITIES

SUBCHAPTER A. GENERAL PROVISIONS

TRANSP §314.001. APPLICABILITY

This chapter applies only to a municipality with a population of more than 1,000.

Sections 314.002-314.010 reserved for expansion

SUBCHAPTER B. AUTHORITY TO PURCHASE OR CONDEMN PROPERTY

TRANSP §314.011. ACQUISITION OF PROPERTY FOR HIGHWAY IMPROVEMENTS BY MUNICIPALITY

(a) The governing body of a municipality may purchase or condemn property to lay out, construct, improve, or extend any highway within its boundaries.

(b) Costs incurred in making improvements, including the costs of purchase or condemnation of or damage to property and the costs of making assessments or issuing certificates under this chapter, may be paid from any municipal fund available for that purpose.

(c) A municipality may sell property originally purchased for improvements but not used for the improvements on the terms it considers appropriate. The proceeds from the sale shall be deposited in a fund that may be used only to pay for costs described by Subsection (b).

(d) In this section, "highway" includes any street, alley, public place, or square dedicated to public use.

TRANSP §314.012. RESOLUTION

(a) A governing body that determines to proceed under this chapter shall declare its determination by resolution that may:

(1) state the nature, extent, and limits of the improvement to be made; and

(2) describe the real property proposed to be condemned by:

(A) the lot or block number;

(B) the number of front feet;

(C) the name of the owner; or

(D) any other description that substantially identifies the property.

(b) A mistake or omission in the resolution does not invalidate it.

(c) Passage of the resolution is conclusive evidence of the public use and necessity of the proposed improvement.

TRANSP §314.013. SURVEY

(a) On passage of the resolution, the municipal engineer or engineer designated by the governing body shall prepare and submit to the governing body:

(1) a plat showing:

(A) the nature and limits of the proposed improvements;

(B) the location of the proposed improvements; and

(C) the property through which the improvements are to be extended and that is to be condemned for the improvements; and

(2) a written estimate of the total cost of:

(A) the improvements; and

(B) each parcel of property to be condemned.

(b) The governing body shall examine the plat and report and correct any errors. An error or omission does not invalidate the plat or report or a subsequent proceeding held under the plat or report.

Sections 314.014-314.020 reserved for expansion

SUBCHAPTER C. PROCEDURE

TRANSP §314.021. APPOINTMENT OF CONDEMNATION COMMISSION

(a) In addition to qualifying under Section 21.014(a), Property Code, a member of a condemnation commission must be a qualified voter.

(b) If a commissioner dies, becomes disabled, refuses to act, becomes incapacitated, or is absent for more than 30 days from the county, the judge shall promptly, in term time or vacation, appoint a new commissioner having the qualifications prescribed by Subsection (a). An action of the commission taken before the vacancy is valid. After the vacancy is filled, the commission shall proceed and take all actions provided by this chapter as if a vacancy had not occurred.

(c) A commissioner is entitled to receive as compensation not more than $10 for each day the commissioner is employed in the performance of the commissioner's duties.

TRANSP §314.022. NOTICE OF CONDEMNATION

(a) The commission or the clerk, secretary, or recording officer of a municipality shall give written notice of a hearing before the commission to:

(1) each owner of property proposed to be condemned or damaged; and

(2) each person with an interest in or lien on the property.

(b) In addition to the requirements of Section 21.016(a), Property Code, the notice may contain:

(1) a brief statement of the nature and extent of the proposed improvement; and

(2) a description of the property proposed to be condemned.

(c) The description provided by Subsection (b)(2) may be by:

(1) lot and block number;

(2) front feet;

(3) the name of each owner; or

(4) any other description that substantially identifies the property.

(d) Notice of the hearing shall be given by publication for not less than three days in a newspaper of general circulation in the county in which the property is located beginning not later than the 10th day before the date of the hearing.

(e) Notice by publication is valid and binding on each owner or other person with an interest in or lien on the property if it generally notifies the person to appear and be heard without specifically designating the person by name. An error in the name of a person to whom the notice is directed does not invalidate the notice.

(f) A copy of the notice shall be delivered to:

(1) each owner, lienholder, or interested party who is a resident of the county where the property is located;

(2) the agent or attorney of a person described by Paragraph (1); or

(3) the guardian of the owner if the owner is a minor.

(g) The person serving the notice shall make a written return on the notice stating when and how the person served the notice.

(h) The governing body may provide for additional notice, but notice by publication is valid and binding regardless of whether any other notice is given.

(i) The governing body may provide for as many hearings in the course of condemnation proceedings as it determines necessary for whatever purposes it determines necessary.

(j) A notice and a return of a notice shall be filed with the municipality.

TRANSP §314.023. HEARING ON CONDEMNATION

(a) Each owner, lienholder, or other interested party is entitled to appear at the hearing in person or by agent and be heard regarding:

(1) the value of the property proposed to be condemned;

(2) the damages to property not condemned resulting from the improvement;

(3) the legality of the proceedings; or

(4) any right of the owner or other party.

(b) An objection must be in writing and filed with the commission.

(c) The commission may not close the hearing until all interested parties appearing have been heard. At the conclusion of the hearing, the commission shall:

(1) determine the damages due the owners, lienholders, or other interested parties for property taken or damaged;

(2) apportion the damages determined under Subdivision (1) among the owners, lienholders, or other interested parties;

(3) date and sign two copies of a written report; and

(4) file one copy of the report with the clerk, secretary, or recording officer of the municipality and the second copy with the clerk of the court that appointed the commission.

(d) The governing body may record in its minutes the following items relating to a condemnation proceeding:

(1) proceedings of the governing body;

(2) notices issued and returns of the notices;

(3) orders, reports, and other proceedings of the commission; and

(4) certified copies of all orders or proceedings of a court.

(e) A record made under Subsection (d) or a certified copy of the record is prima facie evidence of the facts in the record.

TRANSP §314.024. OBJECTIONS

(a) Not later than the 10th day after the date the commission files a report under Section 314.023 with the court, a party affected by the decision of the commission may file with the court an objection to the decision.

(b) If an objection is not timely filed:

(1) the determinations of the commission become final and binding on the parties and their heirs, successors, and assigns and may not subsequently be questioned in any proceeding; and

(2) the judge shall enter the report in the records of the court and adopt the report as the court's.

(c) The judge may issue process as necessary to enforce a judgment under Subsection (b)(2).

TRANSP §314.025. LAW APPLICABLE

Except as otherwise provided by this chapter, Chapter 21, Property Code, applies to proceedings under this chapter.

TRANSP §314.026. ERRORS

The governing body, the condemnation commission, and the judge before whom a condemnation proceeding is pending shall take all appropriate actions to correct any error or invalidity in the proceeding. An error or omission in a proceeding does not invalidate the proceeding, but a proceeding may be corrected, repeated, or adjourned until the correction is made or omission supplied.

Sections 314.027-314.040 reserved for expansion

SUBCHAPTER D. ASSESSMENTS

TRANSP §314.041. ASSESSMENTS

(a) Except as provided by this section, the governing body may by resolution order an assessment to pay all or part of the costs of making an improvement as described by Section 314.011(b), with reasonable attorney's fees and the costs incurred in making the assessment, against the owner and property if the property is:

(1) adjacent to or in the vicinity of an improvement; and

(2) specially benefited by the improvement.

(b) In its resolution, the governing body may designate:

(1) the property to be assessed; or

(2) a district containing property to be assessed.

(c) The governing body may apportion the costs of the assessment among the owners of the property assessed.

(d) In making an assessment, the governing body may not include the cost of property purchased but not actually used for making the improvement.

(e) An assessment may not be made against:

(1) property or its owner in excess of the special benefit to the property in the enhanced value of the property resulting from the improvement; or

(2) property that is exempt from execution.

(f) The owner of property exempt from assessment under Subsection (e)(2):

(1) shall be assessed an amount equal to the amount the assessment would have been if the property were not exempt; and

(2) is personally liable for the assessment.

TRANSP §314.042. NOTICE TO OWNER OF ASSESSMENT

(a) An assessment may not be made against the property benefited or the owners of the property until after the owners, lienholders, and other interested parties are given a reasonable opportunity to be heard before the governing body or before the commission as provided by Section 314.047.

(b) The governing body or commission shall publish three times before the hearing reasonable notice of the hearing in a newspaper of general circulation in the municipality beginning not later than the 10th day before the date of the hearing.

(c) If an owner is a railway or street railway, the governing body or commission shall also give, not later than the 10th day before the date of the hearing, written notice:

(1) in person to the owner's local agent; or

(2) by mailing the notice through the post office in the municipality to the address of the office of the railway or street railway as it appears on the most recent tax roll of the municipality.

(d) The name of an owner, lienholder, or other interested party need not be specifically set out in the notice required by Subsection (b) or (c), but the real property proposed to be assessed shall be briefly described in the notice by:

(1) lot and block;

(2) number;

(3) front feet;

(4) reference to a plat, report, or record filed in connection with the proceedings; or

(5) any other description reasonably identifying the property.

(e) The governing body or commission may give notice in addition to the notice required by Subsections (b) and (c), but the notice required by those subsections is sufficient.

TRANSP §314.043. NOTICE TO COUNTY CLERK OF ASSESSMENT

(a) A governing body that proposes to assess property abutting an improvement shall file notice with the county clerk of each county in which the property is located. The notice must be signed in the name of the municipality by its clerk, secretary, or mayor or the officer performing the duties of the clerk, secretary, or mayor.

(b) The notice required by Subsection (a) must:

(1) show substantially that the governing body has determined it necessary that the street be improved;

(2) give the name of:

(A) the street and the names of the two cross streets or other approximate lengthwise limits between which the street is to be or has been improved or otherwise identify or designate the street and the portion of the street to be improved; and

(B) the subdivision and affected blocks if the street abuts a subdivision for which a plat has been recorded in the county clerk's office; and

(3) state that a portion of the cost of the improvement is to be or has been specifically assessed as a lien on property abutting the street.

(c) A notice filed under Subsection (a) may include one or more streets or improvements.

(d) A governing body that proposes to assess property not abutting the improvement shall file a notice signed as required by Subsection (a) with the clerk of each county where the property is located.

(e) The notice required by Subsection (d) must:

(1) designate the property proposed to be assessed or the district within which assessments have been or may be made; or

(2) otherwise identify the property against which a lien is proposed to be assessed.

(f) A notice required by Subsection (a) or (d) need not give details or be sworn to or acknowledged. The notice may be filed at any time, and the county clerk with whom the notice is filed shall:

(1) record the notice in the same class of records as a mortgage or deed of trust; and

(2) index the notice in the name of the municipality and in the name or other designation of the street to which the notice relates.

(g) Substantial compliance with this section is sufficient.

(h) In this section, "street" includes any part of a street, alley, highway, public place, or square.

TRANSP §314.044. HEARING ON ASSESSMENT

(a) At a hearing under Section 314.042(a), an owner, lienholder, or other interested party may:

(1) object in writing to an assessment, special benefit to the property, invalidity of the assessment, or any prerequisite to the assessment; and

(2) present testimony in support of the objection.

(b) The governing body or the commission shall determine the amounts, if any, to be assessed.

TRANSP §314.045. LIEN

(a) An assessment creates a lien on property prior to all other liens except a lien for ad valorem taxes.

(b) The lien takes effect on the filing of the notice provided by Section 314.043(a) or (d).

TRANSP §314.046. ASSESSMENTS LEVIED

(a) The governing body may make an assessment only by ordinance.

(b) An assessment may:

(1) be made payable in not more than 16 installments maturing within 15 years; and

(2) bear interest at not more than eight percent a year.

TRANSP §314.047. HEARING ON ASSESSMENT BEFORE CONDEMNATION COMMISSION

(a) The governing body may provide that the condemnation commissioners hold the hearing required under Section 314.042(a).

(b) The commission that holds the hearing:

(1) shall give notice as required by Section 314.042; and

(2) has the powers and duties conferred by this chapter on the governing body except as otherwise provided by this chapter.

(c) At the conclusion of the hearing, the commission shall report in writing its findings to the governing body. The governing body shall:

(1) examine the report and, if it finds the report to be correct, approve the report; and

(2) make an assessment in the proper amount against property and the owner of property found to be benefited by the improvement.

TRANSP §314.048. CERTIFICATES

The municipality may:

(1) issue assignable certificates payable to the municipality or the purchaser of the certificates stating the liability of the property and the owner of the property for the payment of assessments; and

(2) set the terms of the certificates, including the time of payment, conditions of default, and date of maturity.

TRANSP §314.049. ENFORCEMENT OF ASSESSMENT

An assessment may be enforced by:

(1) suit brought by the municipality for the benefit of a holder and owner of an assessment or a certificate issued on the assessment;

(2) suit brought by a holder and owner of an assessment or a certificate issued on the assessment; or

(3) sale of the assessed property in the same manner as nearly as possible as the sale of real property for municipal taxes.

TRANSP §314.050. SUIT ON CERTIFICATE

In a suit to enforce a certificate issued under Section 314.048, the recitals of the certificate are sufficient to allege the proceedings of the governing body in making the improvements, the assessment for the improvements, and all prerequisites to the assessment. The allegations contained in the recitals need not be stated in the pleadings.

TRANSP §314.051. REASSESSMENTS

(a) An error in a proceeding under this chapter, the description of property, or the name of the owner does not invalidate an assessment, and an assessment is in effect against the property and the owner of the property.

(b) A governing body that is advised of an error shall correct the error.

(c) At the request of an interested party, the governing body shall, after notice and hearing that comply with this chapter, reassess an owner or property erroneously assessed in accordance with special benefits as provided by this chapter as to original assessments.

The governing body may set the terms of payment of a reassessment and may issue assignable certificates evidencing the reassessment in the same manner as for an original assessment.

(d) The governing body may not make a reassessment later than six years after the date of the ordinance making the original assessment. If the reassessment is contested in an action at law, the time consumed in the action is not included in computing the six years.

(e) In making a reassessment, the governing body is not required to repeat an action relating to the original assessment, except as required by Subsection (c).

TRANSP §314.052. DEFICIENCY ASSESSMENTS

(a) If, after an assessment is made under this chapter, the amount assessed and apportioned is insufficient to defray all the costs of an improvement:

(1) the governing body may assess the deficiency against property specially benefited and the owners of the property and apportion the deficiency among them, after notice and hearing as provided by this chapter and after complying with each provision of this chapter applicable to original assessments; or

(2) a deficiency assessment may be made after notice and hearing before the commission in the manner provided by Section 314.047.

(b) A municipality may issue assignable certificates evidencing the deficiency assessment.

TRANSP §314.053. SUIT TO SET ASIDE OR CORRECT ASSESSMENT OR REASSESSMENT

(a) A suit to set aside or correct an assessment or reassessment or a proceeding relating to the assessment or reassessment because of an error or invalidity in the assessment or reassessment must be brought by a property owner against whom or whose property an assessment or reassessment has been made not later than the 10th day after the date of the assessment or reassessment.

(b) After the deadline prescribed by Subsection (a), the owner and the owner's heirs, successors, and assigns are barred from bringing an action described by that subsection or objecting to the validity of an assessment, reassessment, or proceeding.

TRANSP §314.054. VALIDITY OF ASSESSMENT

An assessment or reassessment is valid and binding without regard to:

(1) an error, omission, or invalidity in a proceeding of the municipality under this chapter with reference to:

(A) the making of an improvement provided by this chapter;

(B) the taking or condemnation of property for an improvement; or

(C) the determination and payment of damages for property taken or damaged; or

(2) whether as of the date of the assessments the improvement was completed.

WATER CODE

SELECTED PROVISIONS
TABLE OF CONTENTS

TITLE 2. WATER ADMINISTRATION

Subtitle B. Water Rights

Chapter 11. Water Rights

Subchapter A. General Provisions

Subchapter B. Rights in State Water

Subchapter C. Unlawful Use, Diversion, Waste, Etc.

Subchapter D. Permits to Use State Water

SELECTED PROVISIONS
TABLE OF CONTENTS

TITLE 2. WATER ADMINISTRATION

SUBTITLE B. WATER RIGHTS

CHAPTER 11. WATER RIGHTS

SUBCHAPTER A. GENERAL PROVISIONS

WATER §11.001. VESTED RIGHTS NOT AFFECTED

(a) Nothing in this code affects vested private rights to the use of water, except to the extent that provisions of Subchapter G of this chapter might affect these rights.

(b) This code does not recognize any riparian right in the owner of any land the title to which passed out of the State of Texas after July 1, 1895.

A WATER §11.002. DEFINITIONS

The amended text in §11.002 is effective for applications for a new or amended water right received by the Texas Commission on Environmental Quality on or after Sept. 1, 2017. Applications received before Sept. 1, 2017, are governed by the former law in effect at that time.

In this chapter and in Chapter 12 of this code:

(1) "Commission" means the Texas [~~Natural Resource Conservation~~] Commission on Environmental Quality.

(2) "Board" means the Texas Water Development Board.

(3) "Executive director" means the executive director of the Texas [~~Natural Resource Conservation~~] Commission on Environmental Quality.

(4) "Beneficial use" means use of the amount of water which is economically necessary for a purpose authorized by this chapter, when reasonable intelligence and reasonable diligence are used in applying the water to that purpose and shall include conserved water.

(5) "Water right" means a right acquired under the laws of this state to impound, divert, or use state water.

(6) "Appropriator" means a person who has made beneficial use of any water in a lawful manner under the provisions of any act of the legislature before the enactment of Chapter 171, General Laws, Acts of the 33rd Legislature, 1913, as amended, and who has filed with the State Board of Water Engineers a record of his appropriation as required by the 1913 Act, as amended, or a person who makes or has made beneficial use of any water within the limitations of a permit lawfully issued by the commission or one of its predecessors.

(7) Renumbered as subdiv. (6) by Acts 1985, 69th Leg., ch. 795, §1.003, eff. Sept. 1, 1985.

(8) "Conservation" means:

(A) the development of water resources; and

(B) those practices, techniques, and technologies that will reduce the consumption of water, reduce the loss or waste of water, improve the efficiency in the use of water, or increase the recycling and reuse of water so that a water supply is made available for future or alternative uses.

(9) "Conserved water" means that amount of water saved by a holder of an existing permit, certified filing, or certificate of adjudication through practices, techniques, and technologies that would otherwise be irretrievably lost to all consumptive beneficial uses arising from storage, transportation, distribution, or application.

(10) "Surplus water" means water in excess of the initial or continued beneficial use of the appropriator.

(11) "River basin" means a river or coastal basin designated by the board as a river basin under Section 16.051. The term does not include waters originating in the bays or arms of the Gulf of Mexico.

(12) "Agriculture" means any of the following activities:

(A) cultivating the soil to produce crops for human food, animal feed, or planting seed or for the production of fibers;

(B) the practice of floriculture, viticulture, silviculture, and horticulture, including the cultivation of plants in containers or nonsoil media, by a nursery grower;

(C) raising, feeding, or keeping animals for breeding purposes or for the production of food or fiber, leather, pelts, or other tangible products having a commercial value;

(D) raising or keeping equine animals;

(E) wildlife management;

(F) planting cover crops, including cover crops cultivated for transplantation, or leaving land idle for the purpose of participating in any governmental program or normal crop or livestock rotation procedure; and

(G) aquaculture, as defined by Section 134.001, Agriculture Code.

(13) "Agricultural use" means any use or activity involving agriculture, including irrigation.

(14) "Nursery grower" means a person who grows more than 50 percent of the products that the person either sells or leases, regardless of the variety sold, leased, or grown. For the purpose of this definition, "grow" means the actual cultivation or propagation of the product beyond the mere holding or maintaining of the item prior to sale or lease and typically includes activities associated with the production or multiplying of stock such as the development of new plants from cuttings, grafts, plugs, or seedlings.

(15) "Environmental flow analysis" means the application of a scientifically derived process for predicting the response of an ecosystem to changes in instream flows or freshwater inflows.

(16) "Environmental flow regime" means a schedule of flow quantities that reflects seasonal and yearly fluctuations that typically would vary geographically, by specific location in a watershed, and that are shown to be adequate to support a sound ecological environment and to maintain the productivity, extent, and persistence of key aquatic habitats in and along the affected water bodies.

(17) "Environmental flow standards" means those requirements adopted by the commission under Section 11.1471.

(18) "Advisory group" means the environmental flows advisory group.

(19) "Science advisory committee" means the Texas environmental flows science advisory committee.

(20) "Best management practices" means those voluntary efficiency measures developed by the commission and the board that save a quantifiable amount of water, either directly or indirectly, and that can be implemented within a specified time frame.

(21) "Utility commission" means the Public Utility Commission of Texas.

2017 Legislation: Amended by H.B. 3735, §1, 85th Leg., eff. Sept. 1, 2017.

WATER §11.003. STREAMS THAT FORM BOUNDARIES INCLUDED

This chapter applies to all streams or other sources of water supply lying upon or forming a part of the boundaries of this state.

WATER §11.004. COMMISSION TO RECEIVE CERTIFIED COPIES OF JUDGMENTS, ETC.

When any court of record renders a judgment, decree, or order affecting the title to any water right, claim, appropriation, or irrigation facility or affecting any matter over which the commission is given supervision by law, the clerk of the court shall immediately transmit to the commission a certified copy of the judgment, decree, or order.

WATER §11.005. APPLICABILITY TO WORKS UNDER FEDERAL RECLAMATION ACT

This chapter applies to the construction, maintenance, and operation of irrigation works constructed in this state under the federal reclamation act, as amended (43 U.S.C. §371 et seq.), to the extent that this chapter is not inconsistent with the federal act or the regulations made under that act by the secretary of the interior.

SUBCHAPTER B. RIGHTS IN STATE WATER

WATER §11.021. STATE WATER

(a) The water of the ordinary flow, underflow, and tides of every flowing river, natural stream, and lake, and of every bay or arm of the Gulf of Mexico, and the storm water, floodwater, and rainwater of every river, natural stream, canyon, ravine, depression, and watershed in the state is the property of the state.

(b) Water imported from any source outside the boundaries of the state for use in the state and which is transported through the beds and banks of any navigable stream within the state or by utilizing any facilities owned or operated by the state is the property of the state.

WATER §11.022. ACQUISITION OF RIGHT TO USE STATE WATER

The right to the use of state water may be acquired by appropriation in the manner and for the purposes provided in this chapter. When the right to use state water is lawfully acquired, it may be taken or diverted from its natural channel.

WATER §11.023. PURPOSES FOR WHICH WATER MAY BE APPROPRIATED

(a) To the extent that state water has not been set aside by the commission under Section 11.1471(a)(2)

to meet downstream instream flow needs or freshwater inflow needs, state water may be appropriated, stored, or diverted for:

(1) domestic and municipal uses, including water for sustaining human life and the life of domestic animals;

(2) agricultural uses and industrial uses, meaning processes designed to convert materials of a lower order of value into forms having greater usability and commercial value, including the development of power by means other than hydroelectric;

(3) mining and recovery of minerals;

(4) hydroelectric power;

(5) navigation;

(6) recreation and pleasure;

(7) public parks; and

(8) game preserves.

(b) State water also may be appropriated, stored, or diverted for any other beneficial use.

(c) Unappropriated storm water and floodwater may be appropriated to recharge underground freshwater bearing sands and aquifers in the portion of the Edwards underground reservoir located within Kinney, Uvalde, Medina, Bexar, Comal, and Hays counties if it can be established by expert testimony that an unreasonable loss of state water will not occur and that the water can be withdrawn at a later time for application to a beneficial use. The normal or ordinary flow of a stream or watercourse may never be appropriated, diverted, or used by a permittee for this recharge purpose.

(d) When it is put or allowed to sink into the ground, water appropriated under Subsection (c) of this section loses its character and classification as storm water or floodwater and is considered percolating groundwater.

(e) The amount of water appropriated for each purpose mentioned in this section shall be specifically appropriated for that purpose, subject to the preferences prescribed in Section 11.024 of this code. The commission may authorize appropriation of a single amount or volume of water for more than one purpose of use. In the event that a single amount or volume of water is appropriated for more than one purpose of use, the total amount of water actually diverted for all of the authorized purposes may not exceed the total amount of water appropriated.

(f) The water of any arm, inlet, or bay of the Gulf of Mexico may be changed from salt water to sweet or fresh water and held or stored by dams, dikes, or other structures and may be taken or diverted for any purpose authorized by this chapter.

WATER §11.0235. POLICY REGARDING WATERS OF THE STATE

(a) The waters of the state are held in trust for the public, and the right to use state water may be appropriated only as expressly authorized by law.

(b) Maintaining the biological soundness of the state's rivers, lakes, bays, and estuaries is of great importance to the public's economic health and general well-being. The legislature encourages voluntary water and land stewardship to benefit the water in the state, as defined by Section 26.001.

(c) The legislature has expressly required the commission while balancing all other public interests to consider and, to the extent practicable, provide for the freshwater inflows and instream flows necessary to maintain the viability of the state's streams, rivers, and bay and estuary systems in the commission's regular granting of permits for the use of state waters. As an essential part of the state's environmental flows policy, all permit conditions relating to freshwater inflows to affected bays and estuaries and instream flow needs must be subject to temporary suspension if necessary for water to be applied to essential beneficial uses during emergencies.

(d) The legislature has not expressly authorized granting water rights exclusively for:

(1) instream flows dedicated to environmental needs or inflows to the state's bay and estuary systems; or

(2) other similar beneficial uses.

(d-1) to **(d-6)** *Omitted by editor.*

(e) The fact that greater pressures and demands are being placed on the water resources of the state makes it of paramount importance to ensure that these important priorities are effectively addressed by detailing how environmental flow standards are to be developed using the environmental studies that have been and are to be performed by the state and others and specifying in clear delegations of authority how those environmental flow standards will be integrated into the regional water planning and water permitting process.

(f) *Omitted by editor.*

Sections 11.0236-11.0237 omitted by editor

WATER §11.024. APPROPRIATION: PREFERENCES

In order to conserve and properly utilize state water, the public welfare requires not only recognition of beneficial uses but also a constructive public policy regarding the preferences between these uses, and it is therefore declared to be the public policy of this state that in appropriating state water preference shall be given to the following uses in the order named:

(1) domestic and municipal uses, including water for sustaining human life and the life of domestic animals, it being the public policy of the state and for the benefit of the greatest number of people that in the appropriation of water as herein defined, the appropriation of water for domestic and municipal uses shall be and remain superior to the rights of the state to appropriate the same for all other purposes;

(2) agricultural uses and industrial uses, which means processes designed to convert materials of a lower order of value into forms having greater usability and commercial value, including the development of power by means other than hydroelectric;

(3) mining and recovery of minerals;

(4) hydroelectric power;

(5) navigation;

(6) recreation and pleasure; and

(7) other beneficial uses.

WATER §11.025. SCOPE OF APPROPRIATIVE RIGHT

A right to use state water under a permit or a certified filing is limited not only to the amount specifically appropriated but also to the amount which is being or can be beneficially used for the purposes specified in the appropriation, and all water not so used is considered not appropriated.

WATER §11.026. PERFECTION OF AN APPROPRIATION

No right to appropriate water is perfected unless the water has been beneficially used for a purpose stated in the original declaration of intention to appropriate water or stated in a permit issued by the commission or one of its predecessors.

WATER §11.027. RIGHTS BETWEEN APPROPRIATORS

As between appropriators, the first in time is the first in right.

WATER §11.0275. FAIR MARKET VALUE

Whenever the law requires the payment of fair market value for a water right, fair market value shall be determined by the amount of money that a willing buyer would pay a willing seller, neither of which is under any compulsion to buy or sell, for the water in an arms-length transaction and shall not be limited to the amount of money that the owner of the water right has paid or is paying for the water.

WATER §11.029. TITLE TO APPROPRIATION BY LIMITATION

When an appropriator from a source of water supply has used water under the terms of a certified filing or a permit for a period of three years, he acquires title to his appropriation by limitation against any other claimant of water from the same source of water supply and against any riparian owner on the same source of water supply.

WATER §11.030. FORFEITURE OF APPROPRIATION

If any lawful appropriation or use of state water is wilfully abandoned during any three successive years, the right to use the water is forfeited and the water is again subject to appropriation.

WATER §11.031. ANNUAL REPORT

(a) Not later than March 1 of each year, each person who has a water right issued by the commission or who impounded, diverted, or otherwise used state water during the preceding calendar year shall submit a written report to the commission on a form prescribed by the commission. The report shall contain all information required by the commission to aid in administering the water law and in making inventory of the state's water resources. However, with the exception of those persons who hold water rights, no report is required of persons who take water solely for domestic or livestock purposes.

(b) A person who fails to file an annual report with the commission as required by Subsection (a) or fails to timely comply with a request by the commission to make information available under Subsection (d) is liable for a penalty for each day the person fails to file the statement or comply with the request after the applicable deadline in an amount not to exceed:

(1) $100 per day if the person is the holder of a water right authorizing the appropriation of 5,000 acre-feet or less per year; or

(2) $500 per day if the person is the holder of a water right authorizing the appropriation of more than 5,000 acre-feet per year.

(b-1) The state may sue to recover a penalty under Subsection (b).

(c) The commission may waive the requirements of Subsection (a) of this section for a person who has a water right or uses state water in an area of the state where watermaster operations are established.

(d) Each person who has a water right issued by the commission or who impounds, diverts, or otherwise uses state water shall maintain water use information required under Subsection (a) on a monthly basis during the months a water rights holder uses permitted water. The person shall make the information available to the commission on the commission's request. The executive director shall establish a reasonable deadline by which a person must make available information requested by the commission under this subsection.

(e) Except as provided by Subsection (a), the commission may request information maintained under Subsection (d) only during a drought or other emergency shortage of water or in response to a complaint.

(f) Subsection (e) does not affect the authority of a watermaster to obtain water use information under other law.

(g) The commission shall establish a process by which a report required under Subsection (a) may be submitted electronically through the Internet.

WATER §11.032. RECORDS

(a) A person who owns and operates a system of waterworks used for a purpose authorized by this code shall keep a detailed record of daily operations so that the quantity of water taken or diverted each calendar year can be determined.

(b) If the water is used for irrigation, the record must show the number of acres irrigated, the character of the crops grown, and the yield per acre. No survey is required to determine the exact number of acres irrigated.

WATER §11.033. EMINENT DOMAIN

The right to take water necessary for domestic and municipal supply purposes is primary and fundamental, and the right to recover from other uses water which is essential to domestic and municipal supply purposes is paramount and unquestioned in the policy of the state. All political subdivisions of the state and constitutional governmental agencies exercising delegated legislative powers have the power of eminent domain to be exercised as provided by law for domestic, municipal, and manufacturing uses and for other purposes authorized by this code, including the irrigation of land for all requirements of agricultural employment.

WATER §11.034. RESERVOIR SITE: LAND & RIGHTS-OF-WAY

An appropriator who is authorized to construct a dam or reservoir is granted the right-of-way, not to exceed 100 feet wide, and the necessary area for the site, over any public school land, university land, or asylum land of this state and the use of the rock, gravel, and timber on the site and right-of-way for construction purposes, after paying compensation as determined by the commission. An appropriator may acquire the reservoir site and rights-of-way over private land by contract.

WATER §11.035. CONDEMNATION OF PRIVATE PROPERTY

(a) An appropriator may obtain rights-of-way over private land and may obtain the land necessary for pumping plants, intakes, headgates, and storage reservoirs by condemnation.

(b) The party obtaining private property by condemnation shall cause damages to be assessed and paid for as provided by the statutes of this state relating to eminent domain.

(c) If the party exercising the power granted by this section is not a corporation, district, city, or town, he shall apply to the commission for the condemnation.

(d) The executive director shall have the proposed condemnation investigated. After the investigation, the commission may give notice to the party owning the land proposed to be condemned and hold a hearing on the proposed condemnation.

(e) If after a hearing the commission determines that the condemnation is necessary, the executive director may institute condemnation proceedings in the name of the State of Texas for the use and benefit of the party who applied for the condemnation and all others similarly situated.

(f) The parties at whose instance a condemnation suit is instituted shall pay the costs of the suit and condemnation in proportion to the benefits received by each party as fixed by the commission. Before using

any of the condemned rights or property, a party receiving the rights or property shall pay the amount of costs fixed by the commission.

(g) If, after the costs of the condemnation proceedings have been paid, a party seeks to take the benefits of the condemnation proceedings, he shall apply to the commission for the benefits. The commission may grant the application and fix the fees and charges to be paid by the applicant.

WATER §11.036. CONSERVED OR STORED WATER: SUPPLY CONTRACT

(a) A person, association of persons, corporation, or water improvement or irrigation district having in possession and control any storm water, floodwater, or rainwater that is conserved or stored as authorized by this chapter may contract to supply the water to any person, association of persons, corporation, or water improvement or irrigation district having the right to acquire use of the water.

(b) The price and terms of the contract shall be just and reasonable and without discrimination, and the contract is subject to the same revision and control as provided in this code for other water rates and charges. If the contract sets forth explicit expiration provisions, no continuation of the service obligation will be implied.

(c) The terms of a contract may expressly provide that the person using the stored or conserved water is required to develop alternative or replacement supplies prior to the expiration of the contract and may further provide for enforcement of such terms by court order.

(d) If any person uses the stored or conserved water without first entering into a contract with the party that conserved or stored it, the user shall pay for the use at a rate determined by the commission to be just and reasonable, subject to court review as in other cases.

WATER §11.037. WATER SUPPLIERS: RULES & REGULATIONS

(a) Every person, association of persons, corporation, or irrigation district conserving or supplying water for any of the purposes authorized by this chapter shall make and publish reasonable rules and regulations relating to:

(1) the method of supply;

(2) the use and distribution of the water; and

(3) the procedure for applying for the water and for paying for it.

(b) Each person, association of persons, corporation, and district authorized by law to carry out irrigation powers that is conserving or supplying water for any of the purposes authorized by this chapter may make and publish reasonable rules relating to water conservation, as defined by Subdivision (8)(B), Section 11.002, of this code.

WATER §11.038. RIGHTS OF OWNERS OF LAND ADJOINING CANAL, ETC.

(a) A person who owns or holds a possessory interest in land adjoining or contiguous to a canal, ditch, flume, lateral, dam, reservoir, or lake constructed and maintained under the provisions of this chapter and who has secured a right to the use of water in the canal, ditch, flume, lateral, dam, reservoir, or lake is entitled to be supplied from the canal, ditch, flume, lateral, dam, reservoir, or lake with water for agricultural uses, mining, milling, manufacturing, development of power, and stock raising, in accordance with the terms of the person's contract.

(b) If the person, association of persons, or corporation owning or controlling the water and the person who owns or holds a possessory interest in the adjoining land cannot agree on a price for a permanent water right or for the use of enough water for irrigation of the person's land or for agricultural uses, mining, milling, manufacturing, development of power, or stock raising, then the party owning or controlling the water, if the person has any water not contracted to others, shall furnish the water necessary for these purposes at reasonable and nondiscriminatory prices.

WATER §11.039. DISTRIBUTION OF WATER DURING SHORTAGE

(a) If a shortage of water in a water supply not covered by a water conservation plan prepared in compliance with Texas Natural Resource Conservation Commission or Texas Water Development Board rules results from drought, accident, or other cause, the water to be distributed shall be divided among all customers pro rata, according to the amount each may be entitled to, so that preference is given to no one and everyone suffers alike.

(b) If a shortage of water in a water supply covered by a water conservation plan prepared in compliance with Texas Natural Resource Conservation Commission or Texas Water Development Board rules results from drought, accident, or other cause, the person, as-

WATER §11.035

sociation of persons, or corporation owning or controlling the water shall divide the water to be distributed among all customers pro rata, according to:

(1) the amount of water to which each customer may be entitled; or

(2) the amount of water to which each customer may be entitled, less the amount of water the customer would have saved if the customer had operated its water system in compliance with the water conservation plan.

(c) Nothing in Subsection (a) or (b) precludes the person, association of persons, or corporation owning or controlling the water from supplying water to a person who has a prior vested right to the water under the laws of this state.

WATER §11.040. PERMANENT WATER RIGHT

(a) A permanent water right is an easement and passes with the title to land.

(b) A written instrument conveying a permanent water right may be recorded in the same manner as any other instrument relating to a conveyance of land.

(c) The owner of a permanent water right is entitled to use water according to the terms of his contract. If there is no contract, the owner is entitled to use water at a just, reasonable, and nondiscriminatory price.

WATER §11.041. DENIAL OF WATER: COMPLAINT

(a) Any person entitled to receive or use water from any canal, ditch, flume, lateral, dam, reservoir, or lake or from any conserved or stored supply may present to the commission a written petition showing:

(1) that he is entitled to receive or use the water;

(2) that he is willing and able to pay a just and reasonable price for the water;

(3) that the party owning or controlling the water supply has water not contracted to others and available for the petitioner's use; and

(4) that the party owning or controlling the water supply fails or refuses to supply the available water to the petitioner, or that the price or rental demanded for the available water is not reasonable and just or is discriminatory.

(b) If the petition is accompanied by a deposit of $25, the executive director shall have a preliminary investigation of the complaint made and determine whether or not there are probable grounds for the complaint.

(c) If, after preliminary investigation, the executive director determines that probable grounds exist for the complaint, the commission shall enter an order setting a time and place for a hearing on the petition.

(d) The commission may require the complainant to make an additional deposit or execute a bond satisfactory to the commission in an amount fixed by the commission conditioned on the payment of all costs of the proceeding.

(e) At least 20 days before the date set for the hearing, the commission shall transmit by registered mail a certified copy of the petition and a certified copy of the hearing order to the person against whom the complaint is made.

(f) The commission shall hold a hearing on the complaint at the time and place stated in the order. It may hear evidence orally or by affidavit in support of or against the complaint, and it may hear arguments. The utility commission may participate in the hearing if necessary to present evidence on the price or rental demanded for the available water. On completion of the hearing, the commission shall render a written decision.

(g) If, after the preliminary investigation, the executive director determines that no probable grounds exist for the complaint, the executive director shall dismiss the complaint. The commission may either return the deposit or pay it into the State Treasury.

WATER §11.042. DELIVERING WATER DOWN BANKS & BEDS

(a) Under rules prescribed by the commission, a person, association of persons, corporation, water control and improvement district, water improvement district, or irrigation district supplying stored or conserved water under contract as provided in this chapter may use the bank and bed of any flowing natural stream in the state to convey the water from the place of storage to the place of use or to the diversion point of the appropriator.

(a-1) With prior authorization granted under rules prescribed by the commission, a person, association of persons, corporation, water control and improvement district, water improvement district, or irrigation district supplying water imported from a source located

wholly outside the boundaries of this state, except water imported from a source located in the United Mexican States, may use the bed and banks of any flowing natural stream in the state to convey water for use in this state. The authorization must:

(1) allow for the diversion of only the amount of water put into a watercourse or stream, less carriage losses; and

(2) include special conditions adequate to prevent a significant impact to the quality of water in this state.

(b) A person who wishes to discharge and then subsequently divert and reuse the person's existing return flows derived from privately owned groundwater must obtain prior authorization from the commission for the diversion and the reuse of these return flows. The authorization may allow for the diversion and reuse by the discharger of existing return flows, less carriage losses, and shall be subject to special conditions if necessary to protect an existing water right that was granted based on the use or availability of these return flows. Special conditions may also be provided to help maintain instream uses and freshwater inflows to bays and estuaries. A person wishing to divert and reuse future increases of return flows derived from privately owned groundwater must obtain authorization to reuse increases in return flows before the increase.

(c) Except as otherwise provided in Subsection (a) of this section, a person who wishes to convey and subsequently divert water in a watercourse or stream must obtain the prior approval of the commission through a bed and banks authorization. The authorization shall allow to be diverted only the amount of water put into a watercourse or stream, less carriage losses and subject to any special conditions that may address the impact of the discharge, conveyance, and diversion on existing permits, certified filings, or certificates of adjudication, instream uses, and freshwater inflows to bays and estuaries. Water discharged into a watercourse or stream under this chapter shall not cause a degradation of water quality to the extent that the stream segment's classification would be lowered. Authorizations under this section and water quality authorizations may be approved in a consolidated permit proceeding.

(d) Nothing in this section shall be construed to affect an existing project for which water rights and reuse authorizations have been granted by the commission before September 1, 1997.

WATER §11.043. RECORDATION OF CONVEYANCE OF IRRIGATION WORK

(a) A conveyance of a ditch, canal, or reservoir or other irrigation work or an interest in such an irrigation work must be executed and acknowledged in the same manner as a conveyance of real estate. Such a conveyance must be recorded in the deed records of the county in which the ditch, canal, or reservoir is located.

(b) If a conveyance of property covered by Subsection (a) of this section is not made in the prescribed manner, it is null and void against subsequent purchasers in good faith and for valuable consideration.

WATER §11.044. ROADS & HIGHWAYS

(a) An appropriator has the right to construct ditches, canals, or pipelines along or across all roads and highways necessary for the construction of waterworks. Bridges, culverts, or siphons shall be constructed at all road and highway crossings as necessary to prevent any impairment of the uses of the road or highway. Approval of the construction plans and specifications shall be obtained from the owner of the road or highway prior to the installation of conveyance facilities.

(b) If any public road, highway, or public bridge is located on the ground necessary for a damsite, reservoir, or lake, the commissioners court shall change the road and remove the bridge so that it does not interfere with the construction of the proposed dam, reservoir, or lake. The party desiring to construct the dam, reservoir, or lake shall pay the expense of moving the bridge or roadway.

WATER §11.045. DITCHES & CANALS

An appropriator is entitled to construct ditches and canals along or across any stream of water.

WATER §11.046. RETURN SURPLUS WATER

(a) A person who takes or diverts water from a watercourse or stream for the purposes authorized by this code shall conduct surplus water back to the watercourse or stream from which it was taken if the water can be returned by gravity flow and it is reasonably practicable to do so.

(b) In granting an application for a water right, the commission may include conditions in the water right providing for the return of surplus water, in a specific

amount or percentage of water diverted, and the return point on a watercourse or stream as necessary to protect senior downstream permits, certified filings, or certificates of adjudication or to provide flows for instream uses or bays and estuaries.

(c) Except as specifically provided otherwise in the water right, water appropriated under a permit, certified filing, or certificate of adjudication may, prior to its release into a watercourse or stream, be beneficially used and reused by the holder of a permit, certified filing, or certificate of adjudication for the purposes and locations of use provided in the permit, certified filing, or certificate of adjudication. Once water has been diverted under a permit, certified filing, or certificate of adjudication and then returned to a watercourse or stream, however, it is considered surplus water and therefore subject to reservation for instream uses or beneficial inflows or to appropriation by others unless expressly provided otherwise in the permit, certified filing, or certificate of adjudication.

(d) Water appropriated under a permit, certified filing, or certificate of adjudication which is recirculated within a reservoir for cooling purposes shall not be considered to be surplus for purposes of this chapter.

WATER §11.047. FAILURE TO FENCE

If a person, association of persons, corporation, or water improvement or irrigation district that owns or controls a ditch, canal, reservoir, dam, or lake does not keep it securely fenced, there is no cause of action against the owner of livestock that trespass.

WATER §11.048. COST OF MAINTAINING IRRIGATION DITCH

(a) If an irrigation ditch is owned or used by two or more persons, mutual or cooperative companies, or corporations, each party who has an interest in the ditch shall pay his proportionate share of the cost of operating and maintaining the ditch.

(b) If a person who owns a joint interest in a ditch refuses to do or to pay for his proportionate share of the work that is reasonably necessary for the proper maintenance and operation of the ditch, the other owners may, after giving him 10 days written notice, proceed themselves to do his share of the necessary work and recover from him the reasonable expense or value of the work or labor performed. The action for the cost of the work may be brought in any court having jurisdiction over the amount in controversy.

WATER §11.049. EXAMINATION & SURVEY

A person may make any necessary examination and survey in order to select the most advantageous sites for a reservoir and rights-of-way to be used for any of the purposes authorized by this chapter, and for this purpose a person may enter the land or water of any other person.

WATER §11.050. TIDEWATER GATES, ETC.

(a) An appropriator authorized to take water for irrigation, subject to the laws of the United States and the regulations made under its authority, may construct gates or breakwaters, dams, or dikes with gates, in waters wholly in this state, as necessary to prevent pollution of the fresh water of any river, bayou, or stream due to the ebb and flow of the tides of the Gulf of Mexico.

(b) The work shall be done in such a manner that navigation of vessels on the stream is not obstructed, and where any gate is used, the appropriator shall at all times keep a competent person at the gate to allow free navigation.

(c) A dam, dike, or breakwater constructed under this section may not be placed at any point except where Gulf tides ebb and flow and may not be constructed so as to obstruct the flow of fresh water to any appropriator or riparian owner downstream.

WATER §11.051. IRRIGATION: LIEN ON CROPS

(a) A person who constructs a ditch, canal, dam, lake, or reservoir for the purpose of irrigation and who leases, rents, furnishes, or supplies water to any person for irrigation, with or without a contract, has a preference lien superior to every other lien on the irrigated crops. However, when any irrigation district or conservation and reclamation district obtains a water supply under contract with the United States, the board of directors of the district, by resolution entered in its minutes, with the consent of the secretary of the interior, may waive the preference lien in whole or in part.

(b) To enforce the lien, the lienholder has all the rights and remedies prescribed by Articles 5222 through 5239, Revised Civil Statutes of Texas, 1925.

WATER §11.052. ACTIVITIES UNDER THE FEDERAL RECLAMATION ACT

The Secretary of the Interior of the United States is authorized to conduct any activities in this state necessary to perform his duties under the federal reclamation act, as amended (43 U.S.C. Section 371 et seq.).

WATER §11.053. EMERGENCY ORDER CONCERNING WATER RIGHTS

(a) During a period of drought or other emergency shortage of water, as defined by commission rule, the executive director by order may, in accordance with the priority of water rights established by Section 11.027:

(1) temporarily suspend the right of any person who holds a water right to use the water; and

(2) temporarily adjust the diversions of water by water rights holders.

(b) The executive director in ordering a suspension or adjustment under this section shall ensure that an action taken:

(1) maximizes the beneficial use of water;

(2) minimizes the impact on water rights holders;

(3) prevents the waste of water;

(4) takes into consideration the efforts of the affected water rights holders to develop and implement the water conservation plans and drought contingency plans required by this chapter;

(5) to the greatest extent practicable, conforms to the order of preferences established by Section 11.024; and

(6) does not require the release of water that, at the time the order is issued, is lawfully stored in a reservoir under water rights associated with that reservoir.

(c) The commission shall adopt rules to implement this section, including rules:

(1) defining a drought or other emergency shortage of water for purposes of this section; and

(2) specifying the:

(A) conditions under which the executive director may issue an order under this section;

(B) terms of an order issued under this section, including the maximum duration of a temporary suspension or adjustment under this section; and

(C) procedures for notice of, an opportunity for a hearing on, and the appeal to the commission of an order issued under this section.

SUBCHAPTER C. UNLAWFUL USE, DIVERSION, WASTE, ETC.

WATER §11.081. UNLAWFUL USE OF STATE WATER

No person may wilfully take, divert, or appropriate any state water for any purpose without first complying with all applicable requirements of this chapter.

WATER §11.082. UNLAWFUL USE: CIVIL PENALTY

(a) A person who wilfully takes, diverts, or appropriates state water without complying with the applicable requirements of this chapter is also liable to a civil penalty of not more than $5,000 for each day he continues the taking, diversion, or appropriation.

(a-1) Notwithstanding Section 18.002, this section does not apply to a violation of:

(1) Section 18.003 or a permit issued under that section; or

(2) Section 18.004 or an authorization granted under that section.

(b) The state may recover the penalties prescribed in Subsection (a) by suit brought for that purpose in a court of competent jurisdiction. The state may seek those penalties regardless of whether a watermaster has been appointed for the water division, river basin, or segment of a river basin where the unlawful use is alleged to have occurred.

(c) An action to collect the penalty provided in this section must be brought within two years from the date of the alleged violation.

WATER §11.083. OTHER UNLAWFUL TAKING

(a) No person may wilfully open, close, change, or interfere with any headgate or water box without lawful authority.

(b) No person may wilfully use water or conduct water through his ditch or upon his land unless he is entitled to do so.

WATER §11.084. SALE OF PERMANENT WATER RIGHT WITHOUT A PERMIT

No person may sell or offer to sell a permanent water right unless he has perfected a right to appropriate state water by a certified filing, or unless he has obtained a permit from the commission, authorizing the use of the water for the purposes for which the permanent water right is conveyed.

WATER §11.0841. CIVIL REMEDY

(a) Nothing in this chapter affects the right of any private corporation, individual, or political subdivision that has a justiciable interest in pursuing any available common-law remedy to enforce a right or to prevent or seek redress or compensation for the violation of a right or otherwise redress an injury.

(b) A district court may award the costs of litigation, including reasonable attorney fees and expert costs, to any political subdivision of the state, private corporation, or individual that is a water right holder and that prevails in a suit for injunctive relief to redress an unauthorized diversion, impoundment, or use of surface water in violation of this chapter or a rule adopted pursuant to this chapter.

(c) For purposes of this section, the Parks and Wildlife Department has:

(1) the rights of a holder of a water right that is held in the Texas Water Trust, including the right to file suit in a civil court to prevent the unlawful use of such a right;

(2) the right to act in the same manner that a holder of a water right may act to protect the holder's rights in seeking to prevent any person from appropriating water in violation of a set-aside established by the commission under Section 11.1471 to meet instream flow needs or freshwater inflow needs; and

(3) the right to file suit in a civil court to prevent the unlawful use of a set-aside established under Section 11.1471.

WATER §11.0842. ADMINISTRATIVE PENALTY

(a) If a person violates this chapter, a rule or order adopted under this chapter or Section 16.236, or a permit, certified filing, or certificate of adjudication issued under this chapter, the commission may assess an administrative penalty against that person as provided by this section. The commission may assess an administrative penalty for a violation relating to a water division or a river basin or segment of a river basin regardless of whether a watermaster has been appointed for the water division or river basin or segment of the river basin.

(a-1) Notwithstanding Section 18.002, this section does not apply to a violation of:

(1) Section 18.003 or a permit issued under that section; or

(2) Section 18.004 or an authorization granted under that section.

(b) The penalty may be in an amount not to exceed $5,000 for each day the person is in violation of this chapter, the rule or order adopted under this chapter, or the permit, certified filing, or certificate of adjudication issued under this chapter. The penalty may be in an amount not to exceed $1,000 for each day the person is in violation of the rule or order adopted under Section 16.236 of this code. Each day a violation continues may be considered a separate violation for purposes of penalty assessment.

(c) In determining the amount of the penalty, the commission shall consider:

(1) the nature, circumstances, extent, duration, and gravity of the prohibited acts, with special emphasis on the impairment of an existing permit, certified filing, or certificate of adjudication or the hazard or potential hazard created to the health, safety, or welfare of the public;

(2) the impact of the violation on the instream uses, water quality, fish and wildlife habitat, or beneficial freshwater inflows to bays and estuaries;

(3) with respect to the alleged violator:

(A) the history and extent of previous violations;

(B) the degree of culpability, including whether the violation was attributable to mechanical or electrical failures and whether the violation could have been reasonably anticipated and avoided;

(C) demonstrated good faith, including actions taken by the alleged violator to rectify the cause of the violation and to compensate affected persons;

(D) any economic benefit gained through the violation; and

(E) the amount necessary to deter future violations; and

(4) any other matters that justice may require.

(d) If, after examination of a possible violation and the facts surrounding that possible violation, the executive director concludes that a violation has occurred, the executive director shall issue a preliminary report stating the facts on which that conclusion was based, recommending that an administrative penalty under this section be imposed on the person charged, and recommending the amount of the penalty. The executive director shall base the recommended amount of the proposed penalty on the factors provided by Subsec-

tion (c) of this section and shall analyze each factor for the benefit of the commission.

(e) No later than the 10th day after the date on which the report is issued, the executive director shall give written notice of the report to the person charged with the violation. The notice shall include a brief summary of the charges, a statement of the amount of the penalty recommended, and a statement of the right of the person charged to a hearing on the occurrence of the violation, the amount of the penalty, or both the occurrence of the violation and the amount of the penalty.

(f) No later than the 20th day after the date on which notice is received, the person charged may either give to the commission written consent to the executive director's report, including the recommended penalty, or make a written request for a hearing.

(g) If the person charged with the violation consents to the penalty recommended by the executive director or fails to timely respond to the notice, the commission by order shall either assess the penalty or order a hearing to be held on the findings and recommendations in the executive director's report. If the commission assesses the penalty recommended by the report, the commission shall give written notice of its decision to the person charged.

(h) If the person charged requests or the commission orders a hearing, the commission shall call a hearing and give notice of the hearing. As a result of the hearing, the commission by order either may find that a violation has occurred and may assess a penalty, may find that a violation has occurred but that no penalty should be assessed, or may find that no violation has occurred. All proceedings under this subsection are subject to Chapter 2001, Government Code. In making any penalty decision, the commission shall analyze each of the factors provided by Subsection (c) of this section.

(i) The commission shall give notice of its decision to the person charged, and if the commission finds that a violation has occurred and assesses an administrative penalty, the commission shall give written notice to the person charged of its findings, of the amount of the penalty, and of the person's right to judicial review of the commission's order. If the commission is required to give notice of a penalty under this subsection or Subsection (g) of this section, the commission shall file notice of its decision in the Texas Register not later than the 10th day after the date on which the decision is adopted.

(j) Within the 30-day period immediately following the day on which the commission's order is final, as provided by Subchapter F, Chapter 2001, Government Code, the person charged with the penalty shall:

(1) pay the penalty in full;

(2) pay the amount of the penalty and file a petition for judicial review contesting the occurrence of the violation, the amount of the penalty, or both the occurrence of the violation and the amount of the penalty; or

(3) without paying the amount of the penalty, file a petition for judicial review contesting the occurrence of the violation, the amount of the penalty, or both the occurrence of the violation and the amount of the penalty.

(k) Within the 30-day period, a person who acts under Subsection (j)(3) of this section may:

(1) stay enforcement of the penalty by:

(A) paying the amount of the penalty to the court for placement in an escrow account; or

(B) giving to the court a supersedeas bond that is approved by the court for the amount of the penalty and that is effective until all judicial review of the commission's order is final; or

(2) request the court to stay enforcement of the penalty by:

(A) filing with the court a sworn affidavit of the person stating that the person is financially unable to pay the amount of the penalty and is financially unable to give the supersedeas bond; and

(B) giving a copy of the affidavit to the commission by certified mail.

(*l*) If the commission receives a copy of an affidavit under Subsection (k)(2) of this section, it may file with the court within five days after the date the copy is received a contest to the affidavit. The court shall hold a hearing on the facts alleged in the affidavit as soon as practicable and shall stay the enforcement of the penalty on finding that the alleged facts are true. The person who files an affidavit has the burden of proving that the person is financially unable to pay the amount of the penalty and to give a supersedeas bond.

(m) If the person does not pay the amount of the penalty and the enforcement of the penalty is not stayed, the commission may refer the matter to the attorney general for collection of the amount of the penalty.

(n) Judicial review of the order or decision of the commission assessing the penalty shall be under the substantial evidence rule and shall be instituted by filing a petition with a district court in Travis County, as provided by Subchapter G, Chapter 2001, Government Code.

(o) A penalty collected under this section shall be deposited in the state treasury to the credit of the general revenue fund.

(p) Notwithstanding any other provision to the contrary, the commission may compromise, modify, or remit, with or without condition, any penalty imposed under this section.

(q) Payment of an administrative penalty under this section shall be full and complete satisfaction of the violation for which the administrative penalty is assessed and shall preclude any other civil or criminal penalty for the same violation.

WATER §11.0843. FIELD CITATION

(a) Upon witnessing a violation of this chapter or a rule or order or a water right issued under this chapter, the executive director or a person designated by the executive director, including a watermaster or the watermaster's deputy, may issue the alleged violator a field citation alleging that a violation has occurred and providing the alleged violator the option of either:

(1) without admitting to or denying the alleged violation, paying an administrative penalty in accordance with the predetermined penalty amount established under Subsection (b) and taking remedial action as provided in the citation; or

(2) requesting a hearing on the alleged violation in accordance with Section 11.0842.

(b) By rule the commission shall establish penalty amounts corresponding to types of violations of this chapter or rules or orders adopted or water rights issued under this chapter.

(c) A penalty collected under this section shall be deposited in the state treasury to the credit of the general revenue fund.

WATER §11.085. INTERBASIN TRANSFERS

(a) No person may take or divert any state water from a river basin in this state and transfer such water to any other river basin without first applying for and receiving a water right or an amendment to a permit, certified filing, or certificate of adjudication from the commission authorizing the transfer.

(b) The application must include:

(1) the contract price of the water to be transferred;

(2) a statement of each general category of proposed use of the water to be transferred and a detailed description of the proposed uses and users under each category; and

(3) the cost of diverting, conveying, distributing, and supplying the water to, and treating the water for, the proposed users.

(c) The applicant shall provide the information described by Subsection (b) of this section to any person on request and without cost.

(d) Prior to taking action on an application for an interbasin transfer, the commission shall conduct at least one public meeting to receive comments in both the basin of origin of the water proposed for transfer and the basin receiving water from the proposed transfer. Notice shall be provided pursuant to Subsection (g) of this section. Any person may present relevant information and data at the meeting on the criteria which the commission is to consider related to the interbasin transfer.

(e) In addition to the public meetings required by Subsection (d), if the application is contested in a manner requiring an evidentiary hearing under the rules of the commission, the commission shall give notice and hold an evidentiary hearing, in accordance with commission rules and applicable state law. An evidentiary hearing on an application to transfer water authorized under an existing water right is limited to considering issues related to the requirements of this section.

(f) Notice of an application for an interbasin transfer shall be mailed to the following:

(1) all holders of permits, certified filings, or certificates of adjudication located in whole or in part in the basin of origin;

(2) each county judge of a county located in whole or in part in the basin of origin;

(3) each mayor of a city with a population of 1,000 or more located in whole or in part in the basin of origin; and

(4) all groundwater conservation districts located in whole or in part in the basin of origin; and

(5) each state legislator in both basins.

(g) The applicant shall cause the notice of application for an interbasin transfer to be published in two different weeks within a 30-day period in one or more newspapers having general circulation in each county located in whole or in part in the basin of origin or the receiving basin. The published notice may not be smaller than 96.8 square centimeters or 15 square inches with the shortest dimension at least 7.6 centimeters or three inches. The notice of application and public meetings shall be combined in the mailed and published notices.

(h) The notice of application must state how a person may obtain the information described by Subsection (b) of this section.

(i) The applicant shall pay the cost of notice required to be provided under this section. The commission by rule may establish procedures for payment of those costs.

(j) In addition to other requirements of this code relating to the review of and action on an application for a new water right or amended permit, certified filing, or certificate of adjudication, the commission shall:

(1) request review and comment on an application for an interbasin transfer from each county judge of a county located in whole or in part in the basin of origin. A county judge should make comment only after seeking advice from the county commissioners court; and

(2) give consideration to the comments of each county judge of a county located in whole or in part in the basin of origin prior to taking action on an application for an interbasin transfer.

(k) In addition to other requirements of this code relating to the review of and action on an application for a new water right or amended permit, certified filing, or certificate of adjudication, the commission shall weigh the effects of the proposed transfer by considering:

(1) the need for the water in the basin of origin and in the proposed receiving basin based on the period for which the water supply is requested, but not to exceed 50 years;

(2) factors identified in the applicable approved regional water plans which address the following:

(A) the availability of feasible and practicable alternative supplies in the receiving basin to the water proposed for transfer;

(B) the amount and purposes of use in the receiving basin for which water is needed;

(C) proposed methods and efforts by the receiving basin to avoid waste and implement water conservation and drought contingency measures;

(D) proposed methods and efforts by the receiving basin to put the water proposed for transfer to beneficial use;

(E) the projected economic impact that is reasonably expected to occur in each basin as a result of the transfer; and

(F) the projected impacts of the proposed transfer that are reasonably expected to occur on existing water rights, instream uses, water quality, aquatic and riparian habitat, and bays and estuaries that must be assessed under Sections 11.147, 11.150, and 11.152 of this code in each basin. If the water sought to be transferred is currently authorized to be used under an existing permit, certified filing, or certificate of adjudication, such impacts shall only be considered in relation to that portion of the permit, certified filing, or certificate of adjudication proposed for transfer and shall be based on historical uses of the permit, certified filing, or certificate of adjudication for which amendment is sought;

(3) proposed mitigation or compensation, if any, to the basin of origin by the applicant;

(4) the continued need to use the water for the purposes authorized under the existing permit, certified filing, or certificate of adjudication, if an amendment to an existing water right is sought; and

(5) the information required to be submitted by the applicant.

(*l*) The commission may grant, in whole or in part, an application for an interbasin transfer only to the extent that:

(1) the detriments to the basin of origin during the proposed transfer period are less than the benefits to the receiving basin during the proposed transfer period, as determined by the commission based on consideration of the factors described by Subsection (k); and

(2) the applicant for the interbasin transfer has prepared a drought contingency plan and has developed and implemented a water conservation plan that will result in the highest practicable levels of water conservation and efficiency achievable within the jurisdiction of the applicant.

(m) The commission may grant new or amended water rights under this section with or without specific terms or periods of use and with specific conditions under which a transfer of water may occur.

(n) If the transfer of water is based on a contractual sale of water, the new water right or amended permit, certified filing, or certificate of adjudication authorizing the transfer shall contain a condition for a term or period not greater than the term of the contract, including any extension or renewal of the contract.

(o) The parties to a contract for an interbasin transfer may include provisions for compensation and mitigation. If the party from the basin of origin is a government entity, each county judge of a county located in whole or in part in the basin of origin may provide input on the appropriate compensation and mitigation for the interbasin transfer.

(p) A river basin may not be redesignated in order to allow a transfer or diversion of water otherwise in violation of this section.

(q) A person who takes or diverts water in violation of this section is guilty of a misdemeanor and upon conviction is punishable by a fine of not more than $1,000 or by confinement in the county jail for not more than six months.

(r) A person commits a separate offense each day he continues to take or divert water in violation of this section.

(s) Any proposed transfer of all or a portion of a water right under this section is junior in priority to water rights granted before the time application for transfer is accepted for filing.

(t) Any proposed transfer of all or a portion of a water right under this section from a river basin in which two or more river authorities or water districts created under Section 59, Article XVI, Texas Constitution, have written agreements or permits that provide for the coordinated operation of their respective reservoirs to maximize the amount of water for beneficial use within their respective water services areas shall be junior in priority to water rights granted before the time application for transfer is accepted for filing.

(u) An appropriator of water for municipal purposes in the basin of origin may, at the appropriator's option, be a party in any hearings under this section.

(v) The provisions of this section, except Subsection (a), do not apply to:

(1) a proposed transfer which in combination with any existing transfers totals less than 3,000 acre-feet of water per annum from the same permit, certified filing, or certificate of adjudication;

(2) a request for an emergency transfer of water;

(3) a proposed transfer from a basin to its adjoining coastal basin;

(4) a proposed transfer from the part of the geographic area of a county or municipality, or the part of the retail service area of a retail public utility as defined by Section 13.002, that is within the basin of origin for use in that part of the geographic area of the county or municipality, or that contiguous part of the retail service area of the utility, not within the basin of origin; or

(5) a proposed transfer of water that is:

(A) imported from a source located wholly outside the boundaries of this state, except water that is imported from a source located in the United Mexican States;

(B) for use in this state; and

(C) transported by using the bed and banks of any flowing natural stream located in this state.

WATER §11.086. OVERFLOW CAUSED BY DIVERSION OF WATER

(a) No person may divert or impound the natural flow of surface waters in this state, or permit a diversion or impounding by him to continue, in a manner that damages the property of another by the overflow of the water diverted or impounded.

(b) A person whose property is injured by an overflow of water caused by an unlawful diversion or impounding has remedies at law and in equity and may recover damages occasioned by the overflow.

(c) The prohibition of Subsection (a) of this section does not in any way affect the construction and maintenance of levees and other improvements to control floods, overflows, and freshets in rivers, creeks, and streams or the construction of canals for conveying water for irrigation or other purposes authorized by this code. However, this subsection does not authorize any person to construct a canal, lateral canal, or ditch that obstructs a river, creek, bayou, gully, slough, ditch, or other well-defined natural drainage.

(d) Where gullies or sloughs have cut away or intersected the banks of a river or creek to allow floodwaters from the river or creek to overflow the land nearby, the owner of the flooded land may fill the mouth of the

gullies or sloughs up to the height of the adjoining banks of the river or creek without liability to other property owners.

See also *O'Connor's Texas COA*, "Equitable relief," ch. 22-B, §3.4, p. 772; "Overflow of water," ch. 29, §7.8, p. 1037.

WATER §11.087. DIVERSION OF WATER ON INTERNATIONAL STREAM

(a) When storm water or floodwater is released from a dam or reservoir on an international stream and the water is designated for use or storage downstream by a specified user who is legally entitled to receive it, no other person may store, divert, appropriate, or use the water or interfere with its passage downstream.

(b) The commission may make and enforce rules and orders to implement the provisions of this section, including rules and orders designed to:

(1) establish an orderly system for water releases and diversions in order to protect vested rights and to avoid the loss of released water;

(2) prescribe the time that releases of water may begin and end;

(3) determine the proportionate quantities of the released water in transit and the water that would have been flowing in the stream without the addition of the released water;

(4) require each owner or operator of a dam or reservoir on the stream between the point of release and the point of destination to allow free passage of the released water in transit; and

(5) establish other requirements the commission considers necessary to effectuate the purposes of this section.

(c) Orders made by the commission to effectuate its rules under this section shall be mailed by certified mail to each diverter of water and to each reservoir owner on the stream between the point of release and the point of destination of the released water as shown by the records of the commission.

(d) Repealed by Acts 1997, 75th Leg., ch. 1072, §60(a)(1), eff. Sept. 1, 1997.

WATER §11.0871. TEMPORARY DIVERSION OF WATER ON INTERNATIONAL STREAM

(a) The commission may authorize, under conditions stated in an order, a watermaster to provide for the temporary diversion and use by holders of water rights of storm water or floodwater that spills from dams and reservoirs on an international stream and otherwise would flow into the Gulf of Mexico without opportunity for beneficial use.

(b) In an order made by the commission under this section, the commission may not discriminate between holders of water rights from an international stream except to the extent necessary to protect the holders of water rights from the same source of supply.

(c) The commission shall give notice by mail to holders of water rights from an international stream and shall hold an evidentiary hearing before entry of an order under this section.

WATER §11.088. DESTRUCTION OF WATERWORKS

No person may wilfully cut, dig, break down, destroy, or injure or open a gate, bank, embankment, or side of any ditch, canal, reservoir, flume, tunnel or feeder, pump or machinery, building, structure, or other work which is the property of another, or in which another owns an interest, or which is lawfully possessed or being used by another, and which is used for milling, mining, manufacturing, the development of power, domestic purposes, agricultural uses, or stock raising, with intent to:

(1) maliciously injure a person, association, corporation, water improvement or irrigation district;

(2) gain advantage for himself; or

(3) take or steal water or cause water to run out or waste out of the ditch, canal, or reservoir, feeder, or flume for his own advantage or to the injury of a person lawfully entitled to the use of the water or the use or management of the ditch, canal, tunnel, reservoir, feeder, flume, machine, structure, or other irrigation work.

WATER §11.089. JOHNSON GRASS OR RUSSIAN THISTLE

(a) No person who owns, leases, or operates a ditch, canal, or reservoir or who cultivates land abutting a reservoir, ditch, flume, canal, wasteway, or lateral may permit Johnson grass or Russian thistle to go to seed on the waterway within 10 feet of the high-water line if the waterway crosses or lies on the land owned or controlled by him.

(b) The provisions of this section are not applicable in Tom Green, Sterling, Irion, Schleicher, McCullough, Brewster, Menard, Maverick, Kinney, Val Verde, and San Saba counties.

WATER §11.090. POLLUTING & LITTERING

No person may deposit in any canal, lateral, reservoir, or lake, used for a purpose named in this chapter, the carcass of any dead animal, tin cans, discarded buckets or pails, garbage, ashes, bailing or barbed wire, earth, offal, or refuse of any character or any other article which might pollute the water or obstruct the flow of a canal or similar structure.

WATER §11.091. INTERFERENCE WITH DELIVERY OF WATER UNDER CONTRACT

No person may wilfully take, divert, appropriate, or interfere with the delivery of conserved or stored water under Section 11.042 of this code.

WATER §11.092. WASTEFUL USE OF WATER

A person who owns or has a possessory right to land contiguous to a canal or irrigation system and who acquires the right by contract to use the water from it commits waste if he:

(1) permits the excessive or wasteful use of water by any of his agents or employees; or

(2) permits the water to be applied to anything but a beneficial use.

WATER §11.093. ABATEMENT OF WASTE AS PUBLIC NUISANCE

(a) A person who permits an unreasonable loss of water through faulty design or negligent operation of any waterworks using water for a purpose named in this chapter commits waste, and the commission may declare the works causing the waste to be a public nuisance. The commission may take the necessary action to abate the nuisance. Also, any person who may be injured by the waste may sue in the district court having jurisdiction over the works causing the waste to have the operation of the works abated as a public nuisance.

(b) In case of a wasteful use of water defined by Section 11.092 of this code, the commission shall declare the use to be a public nuisance and shall act to abate the nuisance by directing the person supplying the water to close the water gates of the person wasting the water and to keep them closed until the commission determines that the unlawful use of water is corrected.

See also *O'Connor's Texas COA*, "Statutory standing," ch. 22-B, §2.1.2, p. 768; "Equitable relief," ch. 22-B, §3.4, p. 772.

WATER §11.094. PENALTY FOR USE OF WORKS DECLARED PUBLIC NUISANCE

No person may operate or attempt to operate any waterworks or irrigation system or use any water under contract with any waterworks or irrigation system that has been previously declared to be a public nuisance.

WATER §11.096. OBSTRUCTION OF NAVIGABLE STREAMS

No person may obstruct the navigation of any stream which can be navigated by steamboats, keelboats, or flatboats by cutting and felling trees or by building on or across the stream any dike, milldam, bridge, or other obstruction.

WATER §11.097. REMOVAL OF OBSTRUCTIONS FROM NAVIGABLE STREAMS

(a) On its own motion or on written request from a commissioners court, the commission shall investigate a reported natural obstruction in a navigable stream caused by the accumulation of limbs, logs, leaves, other tree parts, or other debris. If making the investigation on request of a commissioners court, the commission must make its investigation not later than the 30th day after the date on which it receives the written request from the commissioners court.

(b) On completion of the investigation, if the commission determines that the obstruction is creating a hazard or is having other detrimental effect on the navigable stream, the commission shall initiate action to remove the obstruction.

(c) In removing an obstruction, the commission may solicit the assistance of federal and state agencies including the Corps of Engineers, Texas National Guard, the Parks and Wildlife Department, and districts and authorities created under Article III, Sections 52(b)(1) and (2), or Article XVI, Section 59, of the Texas Constitution. Also, the commission may enter into contracts for services required to remove an obstruction. However, no river authority may require the removal, relocation, or reconfiguration of a floating structure which was in place before the effective date of this Act and the effective date of any ordinance, rule, resolution, or other act of the river authority mandating such action unless the commission determines the structure is an obstruction to navigation.

SUBCHAPTER D. PERMITS TO USE STATE WATER

WATER §11.121. PERMIT REQUIRED

Except as provided in Sections 11.1405, 11.142, 11.1421, 11.1422, and 18.003, no person may appropriate any state water or begin construction of any work designed for the storage, taking, or diversion of water without first obtaining a permit from the commission to make the appropriation.

A WATER §11.122. AMENDMENTS TO WATER RIGHTS REQUIRED

(a) All holders of permits, certified filings, and certificates of adjudication issued under Section 11.323 of this code shall obtain from the commission authority to change the place of use, purpose of use, point of diversion, rate of diversion, acreage to be irrigated, or otherwise alter a water right. Without obtaining an amendment, the holder of a permit, certified filing, or certificate of adjudication that includes industrial or irrigation use may use or supply water for an agricultural use that was classified as industrial or irrigation before September 1, 2001.

(b) Subject to meeting all other applicable requirements of this chapter for the approval of an application, an amendment, except an amendment to a water right that increases the amount of water authorized to be diverted or the authorized rate of diversion, shall be authorized if the requested change will not cause adverse impact on other water right holders or the environment on the stream of greater magnitude than under circumstances in which the permit, certified filing, or certificate of adjudication that is sought to be amended was fully exercised according to its terms and conditions as they existed before the requested amendment.

Subsections (b-1) and (b-2) were enacted by H.B. 3735, §2, 85th Leg., enacted May 26, 2017, effective Sept. 1, 2017, without reference to the conflicting enactment made by S.B. 1430, §1, 85th Leg., enacted May 21, 2017, effective Sept. 1, 2017. For harmonizing conflicts, see p. V. The enacted text in subsections (b-1) and (b-2) is effective for applications for a new or amended water right received by the Texas Commission on Environmental Quality on or after Sept. 1, 2017. Applications received before Sept. 1, 2017, are governed by the former law in effect at that time.

(b-1) A holder of a water right that begins using desalinated seawater after acquiring the water right has a right to expedited consideration of an application for an amendment to the water right if the amendment:

(1) authorizes the applicant to divert water from a diversion point that is different from or in addition to the point or points from which the applicant was authorized to divert water before the requested amendment;

(2) authorizes the applicant to divert from the different or additional diversion point an amount of water that is equal to or less than the amount of desalinated seawater used by the applicant;

(3) authorizes the applicant to divert from all of the diversion points authorized by the water right an amount of water that is equal to or less than the amount of water the applicant was authorized to divert under the water right before the requested amendment; and

(4) does not authorize the water diverted from the different or additional diversion point to be transferred to another river basin.

(b-2) The executive director or the commission shall prioritize the technical review of an application that is subject to Subsection (b-1) over the technical review of applications that are not subject to that subsection.

Subsections (b-1) and (b-2) were enacted by S.B. 1430, §1, 85th Leg., enacted May 21, 2017, effective Sept. 1, 2017, without reference to the conflicting enactment made by H.B. 3735, §2, 85th Leg., enacted May 26, 2017, effective Sept. 1, 2017. For harmonizing conflicts, see p. V. The enacted text in subsections (b-1) and (b-2) is effective for applications for an amendment to a water right filed with the Texas Commission on Environmental Quality on or after Sept. 1, 2017. Applications filed before Sept. 1, 2017, are governed by the former law in effect at that time.

(b-1) A holder of a water right that begins using desalinated seawater after acquiring the water right has a right to expedited consideration of an application for an amendment to the water right if the amendment:

(1) authorizes the applicant to divert water from a diversion point that is different from or in addition to the point or points from which the applicant was authorized to divert water before the requested amendment;

(2) authorizes the applicant to divert from the different or additional diversion point an amount of water that is equal to or less than the amount of desalinated seawater used by the applicant;

(3) authorizes the applicant to divert from all of the diversion points authorized by the water right an amount of water that is equal to or less than the amount of water the applicant was authorized to divert under the water right before the requested amendment;

(4) authorizes the applicant to divert water from all of the diversion points authorized by the water right at a combined rate that is equal to or less than the combined rate at which the applicant was authorized to divert water under the water right before the requested amendment; and

(5) does not authorize the water diverted from the different or additional diversion point to be transferred to another river basin.

(b-2) The executive director or the commission shall prioritize the technical review of an application that is subject to Subsection (b-1) over the technical review of applications that are not subject to that subsection.

(c) The commission shall adopt rules to effectuate the provisions of this section.

2017 Legislation: Amended by H.B. 3735, §2, 85th Leg., eff. Sept. 1, 2017; S.B. 1430, §1, 85th Leg., eff. Sept. 1, 2017.

WATER §11.123. PERMIT PREFERENCES

The commission shall give preference to applications in the order declared in Section 11.024 of this code and to applications which will effectuate the maximum utilization of water and are calculated to prevent the escape of water without contribution to a beneficial public service.

WATER §11.124. APPLICATION FOR PERMIT

(a) An application to appropriate unappropriated state water must:

(1) be in writing and sworn to;

(2) contain the name and post-office address of the applicant;

(3) identify the source of water supply;

(4) state the nature and purposes of the proposed use or uses and the amount of water to be used for each purpose;

(5) state the location and describe the proposed facilities;

(6) state the time within which the proposed construction is to begin;

(7) state the time required for the application of water to the proposed use or uses; and

(8) contain the name and address of the holder of any lien on:

(A) any water right permit, certified filing, or certificate of adjudication to be granted under the permit for which application is made; or

(B) any land to which that water right permit, certified filing, or certificate of adjudication would be appurtenant.

(b) If the proposed use is irrigation, the application must also contain:

(1) a description of the land proposed to be irrigated; and

(2) an estimate of the total acreage to be irrigated.

(c) If the application is for a seasonal permit, under the provisions of Section 11.137 of this code, the application must also state the months or seasons of the year the water is to be used.

(d) If the application is for a temporary permit under the provisions of Section 11.138 of this code, the application must also state the period of the proposed temporary use.

(e) If the application is for a term permit, the application form used must also state that on expiration of a term permit the applicant does not have an automatic right to renew the permit.

(f) If the application is for a permit to construct a storage reservoir, the application must also contain evidence that the applicant has mailed notice of the application to each member of the governing body of each county and municipality in which the reservoir, or any part of the reservoir, will be located.

A WATER §11.125. MAP OR PLAT

The amended text in §11.125 is effective for applications for a new or amended water right received by the Texas Commission on Environmental Quality on or after Sept. 1, 2017. Applications received before Sept. 1, 2017, are governed by the former law in effect at that time.

(a) The application must be accompanied by a map or plat in the form and containing the information prescribed by the commission [~~drawn on tracing linen on a scale not less than one inch equals 2,000 feet~~].

(b), (c) Repealed by H.B. 3735, §7, 85th Leg., eff. Sept. 1, 2017.

[~~(b)~~] [~~The map or plat must show substantially:~~]

[~~(1)~~] [~~the location and extent of the proposed facilities;~~]

[~~(2)~~] [~~the location of the headgate, intake, pumping plant, or point of diversion by course and distance from permanent natural objects or landmarks;~~]

[~~(3)~~] [~~the location of the main ditch or canal and the locations of the laterals or branches of the main ditch or canal;~~]

[~~(4)~~] [~~the course of the water supply;~~]

[~~(5)~~] [~~the position, waterline, and area of all lakes, reservoirs, or basins intended to be used or created;~~]

[~~(6)~~] [~~the point of intersection of the proposed facilities with any other ditch, canal, lateral, lake, or reservoir; and~~]

[~~(7)~~] [~~the location of any ditch, canal, lateral, reservoir, lake, dam, or other similar facility already existing in the area, drawn in a different colored ink than that used to represent the proposed facilities, and the name of the owner of the existing facility.~~]

[~~(c)~~] [~~The map or plat must also contain:~~]

[~~(1)~~] [~~the name of the proposed facility or enterprise;~~]

[~~(2)~~] [~~the name of the applicant; and~~]

[~~(3)~~] [~~a certificate of the surveyor, giving the date of his survey, his name and post-office address, and the date of the application which the certificate accompanies.~~]

2017 Legislation: Amended by H.B. 3735, §§3, 7, 85th Leg., eff. Sept. 1, 2017.

WATER §11.126. COMMISSION REQUIREMENTS

(a) If the proposed taking or diversion of water for irrigation exceeds nine cubic feet per second, the executive director may require additional information as prescribed by this section.

(b) The executive director may require a continuous longitudinal profile, cross sections of the proposed channel, and the detail plans of any proposed structure, on any scales and with any definition the executive director considers necessary or expedient.

(c) If the application proposes construction of a dam greater than six feet in height either for diversion or storage, the executive director may also require filing a copy of all plans and specifications and a copy of the engineer's field notes of any survey of the lake or reservoir. No work on the project shall proceed until approval of the plans is obtained from the executive director.

(d) If the applicant is a corporation, the commission may require filing a certified copy of its articles of incorporation, a statement of the names and addresses of its directors and officers, and a statement of the amount of its authorized capital stock and its paid-up capital stock.

(e) If the applicant is not a corporation, the commission may require filing a sworn statement showing the name and address of each person interested in the appropriation, the extent of his interest, and his financial condition.

WATER §11.127. ADDITIONAL REQUIREMENTS: DRAINAGE PLANS

If the commission believes that the efficient operation of any existing or proposed irrigation system may be adversely affected by lack of adequate drainage facilities incident to the work proposed to be done by an applicant, the commission may require the applicant to submit to the executive director for approval plans for drainage adequate to guard against any injury which the proposed work may entail.

WATER §11.1271. ADDITIONAL REQUIREMENTS: WATER CONSERVATION PLANS

(a) The commission shall require from an applicant for a new or amended water right the formulation and submission of a water conservation plan and the adoption of reasonable water conservation measures, as defined by Subdivision (8)(B), Section 11.002, of this code.

(b) The commission shall require the holder of an existing permit, certified filing, or certificate of adjudication for the appropriation of surface water in the amount of 1,000 acre-feet a year or more for municipal, industrial, and other uses, and 10,000 acre-feet a year or more for irrigation uses, to develop, submit, and implement a water conservation plan, consistent with the appropriate approved regional water plan, that adopts reasonable water conservation measures as defined by Subdivision (8)(B), Section 11.002, of this code. The requirement for a water conservation plan under this section shall not result in the need for an amendment to an existing permit, certified filing, or certificate of adjudication.

(c) Beginning May 1, 2005, all water conservation plans required under this section must include specific, quantified 5-year and 10-year targets for water savings. The entity preparing the plan shall establish the targets. Targets must include goals for water loss programs and goals for municipal use in gallons per capita per day.

(d) The commission and the board jointly shall identify quantified target goals for water conservation that water suppliers and other entities may use as guidelines in preparing water conservation plans. Goals established under this subsection are not enforceable requirements.

(e) The commission and board jointly shall develop model water conservation programs for different types of water suppliers that suggest best management practices for achieving the highest practicable levels of water conservation and efficiency achievable for each specific type of water supplier.

(f) The commission shall adopt rules:

(1) establishing criteria and deadlines for submission of water conservation plans, including any required amendments, and for submission of implementation reports; and

(2) requiring the methodology and guidance for calculating water use and conservation developed under Section 16.403 to be used in the water conservation plans required by this section.

(g) At a minimum, rules adopted under Subsection (f)(2) must require an entity to report the most detailed level of municipal water use data currently available to the entity. The commission may not adopt a rule that requires an entity to report municipal water use data that is more detailed than the entity's billing system is capable of producing.

WATER §11.1272. ADDITIONAL REQUIREMENT: DROUGHT CONTINGENCY PLANS FOR CERTAIN APPLICANTS & WATER RIGHT HOLDERS

(a) The commission shall by rule require wholesale and retail public water suppliers and irrigation districts to develop drought contingency plans consistent with the appropriate approved regional water plan to be implemented during periods of water shortages and drought.

(b) The wholesale and retail public water suppliers and irrigation districts shall provide an opportunity for public input during preparation of their drought contingency plans and before submission of the plans to the commission.

(c) By May 1, 2005, a drought contingency plan required by commission rule adopted under this section must include specific, quantified targets for water use reductions to be achieved during periods of water shortages and drought. The entity preparing the plan shall establish the targets.

(d) The commission and the board by joint rule shall identify quantified target goals for drought contingency plans that wholesale and retail public water suppliers, irrigation districts, and other entities may use as guidelines in preparing drought contingency plans. Goals established under this subsection are not enforceable requirements.

(e) The commission and the board jointly shall develop model drought contingency programs for different types of water suppliers that suggest best management practices for accomplishing the highest practicable levels of water use reductions achievable during periods of water shortages and drought for each specific type of water supplier.

WATER §11.1273. ADDITIONAL REQUIREMENT: REVIEW OF AMENDMENTS TO CERTAIN WATER MANAGEMENT PLANS

(a) This section applies only to a water management plan consisting of a reservoir operation plan for the operation of two water supply reservoirs that was originally required by a court order adjudicating the water rights for those reservoirs.

(b) Not later than the first anniversary of the date the executive director determines that an application to amend a water management plan is administratively complete, the executive director shall complete a technical review of the plan.

(c) If the executive director submits a written request for additional information to the applicant, the applicant shall submit the requested information to the executive director not later than the 30th day after the date the applicant receives the request or not later than the deadline agreed to by the executive director and the applicant, if applicable. The review period required by Subsection (b) for completing the technical review is tolled until the date the executive director receives the requested information from the applicant.

(d) The commission shall provide an opportunity for public comment and a public hearing on the application, consistent with the process for other water rights applications.

(e) If the commission receives a request for a hearing before the period for submitting public comments and requesting a hearing expires, the commission shall act on the request for a hearing and, if the request is denied, act on the application not later than the 60th day after the date the period expires. If a request for a hearing is not submitted before the period expires, the executive director may act on the application.

Ⓐ WATER §11.128. PAYMENT OF FEE

The amended text in §11.128 is effective for applications for a new or amended water right received by the Texas Commission on Environmental Quality on or after Sept. 1, 2017. Applications received before Sept. 1, 2017, are governed by the former law in effect at that time.

The [~~If the~~] applicant [~~is not exempted from payment of the filing fee under Section 12.112 of this code, he~~] shall pay the filing fee prescribed by Section 5.701 [~~5.701(c)~~] at the time [~~he files~~] the application is filed. The commission may [~~shall~~] not record, file, or consider the application until the executive director certifies to the commission that the fee is paid.

2017 Legislation: Amended by H.B. 3735, §4, 85th Leg., eff. Sept. 1, 2017.

WATER §11.129. REVIEW OF APPLICATION; AMENDMENT

The commission shall determine whether the application, maps, and other materials comply with the requirements of this chapter and the rules of the commission. The commission may require amendment of the application, maps, or other materials to achieve necessary compliance.

WATER §11.130. RECORDING APPLICATIONS

(a) The executive director shall have all applications for appropriations recorded in a well-bound book kept for that purpose in the commission office.

(b) The executive director shall have the applications indexed alphabetically in the name of:

(1) the applicant;

(2) the stream or source from which the appropriation is sought to be made; and

(3) the county in which the appropriation is sought to be made.

WATER §11.131. EXAMINATION & DENIAL OF APPLICATION WITHOUT HEARING

(a) The commission shall make a preliminary examination of the application, and if it appears that there is no unappropriated water in the source of supply or that the proposed appropriation should not be allowed for other reasons, the commission may deny the application.

(b) If the commission denies the application under this section and the applicant elects not to proceed further, the commission may order any part of the fee submitted with the application returned to the applicant.

WATER §11.1311. APPROVAL OF CERTAIN APPLICATIONS WITHOUT HEARING

(a) If a permit for a reservoir project which is listed on the effective date of this section as a recommended project in the current state water plan has been abandoned, voluntarily canceled, or forfeited for failure to commence construction within the time specified by law, and the reservoir project site is owned by a municipality, river authority, other political subdivision, or water supply corporation organized under Chapter 67, the commission may reissue that same permit with a new priority date to the board without notice or hearing, upon submission of an application by the board.

(b) The board may transfer interests in a permit issued under this section to a municipality, river authority, other political subdivision, or water supply corporation organized under Chapter 67 as otherwise provided by law.

(c) A permit issued pursuant to this section shall be administered in accordance with this chapter and as otherwise provided by law.

Ⓐ WATER §11.132. NOTICE

The amended text in §11.132 is effective for applications for a new or amended water right received by the Texas Commission on Environmental Quality on or after Sept. 1, 2017. Applications received before Sept. 1, 2017, are governed by the former law in effect at that time.

(a) Notice shall be given to the persons who in the judgment of the commission may be affected by an application, including those persons listed in Subdivision (2), Subsection (d), of this section. The commission, on the motion of a commissioner or on the request of

the executive director or any affected person, shall hold a public hearing on the application.

(b) If the proposed use is for irrigation, the commission shall include in the notice a general description of the location and area of the land to be irrigated.

(c) In the notice, the commission shall:

(1) state the name and address of the applicant;

(2) state the date the application was filed;

(3) state the purpose and extent of the proposed appropriation of water;

(4) identify the source of supply and the place where the water is to be stored or taken or diverted from the source of supply;

(5) identify any proposed alternative source of water, other than state water, identified by the applicant;

(6) specify the time and location where the commission will consider the application; and

(7) [~~(6)~~] give any additional information the commission considers necessary.

(d) The commission may act on the application without holding a public hearing if:

(1) not less than 30 days before the date of action on the application by the commission, the applicant has published the commission's notice of the application at least once in a newspaper regularly published or circulated within the section of the state where the source of water is located;

(2) not less than 30 days before the date of action on the application by the commission, the commission mails a copy of the notice by first-class mail, postage prepaid, to:

(A) each claimant or appropriator of water from the source of water supply, the record of whose claim or appropriation has been filed with the commission; [~~and~~]

(B) each groundwater conservation district with jurisdiction over the proposed groundwater production, if the applicant proposes to use groundwater from a well located within a groundwater conservation district as an alternative source of water; and

(C) all navigation districts within the river basin concerned; and

(3) within 30 days after the date of the newspaper publication of the commission's notice, a public hearing has not been requested in writing by a commissioner, the executive director, or an affected person who objects to the application.

(e) The inadvertent failure of the commission to mail a notice under Subdivision (2), Subsection (d), of this section to a navigation district that is not a claimant or appropriator of water does not prevent the commission's consideration of the application.

(f) If, on the date specified in the notice prescribed by Subsection (c) of this section, the commission determines that a public hearing must be held, the matter shall be remanded for hearing without the necessity of issuing further notice other than advising all parties of the time and place where the hearing is to convene.

2017 Legislation: Amended by S.B. 864, §1, 85th Leg., eff. Sept. 1, 2017.

WATER §11.133. HEARING

At the time and place stated in the notice, the commission shall hold a hearing on the application. Any person may appear at the hearing in person or by attorney or may enter his appearance in writing. Any person who appears may present objection to the issuance of the permit. The commission may receive evidence, orally or by affidavit, in support of or in opposition to the issuance of the permit, and it may hear arguments.

A WATER §11.134. ACTION ON APPLICATION

The amended text in §11.134 is effective for applications for a new or amended water right received by the Texas Commission on Environmental Quality on or after Sept. 1, 2017. Applications received before Sept. 1, 2017, are governed by the former law in effect at that time.

(a) After the hearing, the commission shall make a written decision granting or denying the application. The application may be granted or denied in whole or in part.

(b) The commission shall grant the application only if:

(1) the application conforms to the requirements prescribed by this chapter and is accompanied by the prescribed fee;

(2) unappropriated water is available in the source of supply;

(3) the proposed appropriation:

(A) is intended for a beneficial use;

(B) does not impair existing water rights or vested riparian rights;

(C) is not detrimental to the public welfare;

(D) considers any applicable environmental flow standards established under Section 11.1471 and, if applicable, the assessments performed under Sections 11.147(d) and (e) and Sections 11.150, 11.151, and 11.152; and

(E) addresses a water supply need in a manner that is consistent with the state water plan and the relevant approved regional water plan for any area in which the proposed appropriation is located, unless the commission determines that conditions warrant waiver of this requirement; and

(4) the applicant has provided evidence that reasonable diligence will be used to avoid waste and achieve water conservation as defined by Section 11.002(8)(B).

(b-1) In determining whether an appropriation is detrimental to the public welfare under Subsection (b)(3)(C), the commission may consider only the factors that are within the jurisdiction and expertise of the commission as established by this chapter.

(c) Beginning January 5, 2002, the commission may not issue a water right for municipal purposes in a region that does not have an approved regional water plan in accordance with Section 16.053(i) unless the commission determines that conditions warrant waiver of this requirement.

2017 Legislation: Amended by H.B. 3735, §5, 85th Leg., eff. Sept. 1, 2017.

WATER §11.135. ISSUANCE OF PERMIT

The amended text in §11.135 is effective for applications for a new or amended water right received by the Texas Commission on Environmental Quality on or after Sept. 1, 2017. Applications received before Sept. 1, 2017, are governed by the former law in effect at that time.

(a) On approval of an application, the commission shall issue a permit to the applicant. The applicant's right to take and use water is limited to the extent and purposes stated in the permit.

(b) The permit shall be in writing and attested by the seal of the commission, and it shall contain substantially the following information:

(1) the name of the person to whom the permit is issued;

(2) the date the permit is issued;

(3) the date the original application was filed;

(4) the use or purpose for which the appropriation is to be made;

(5) the amount or volume of water authorized to be appropriated for each purpose; if use of the appropriated water is authorized for multiple purposes, the permit shall contain a special condition limiting the total amount of water that may actually be diverted for all of the purposes to the amount of water appropriated;

(6) a general description of the source of supply from which the appropriation is proposed to be made, including any alternative source of water that is not state water;

(7) the time within which construction or work must begin and the time within which it must be completed; and

(8) any other information the commission prescribes.

(c) If the appropriation is for irrigation, the commission shall also place in the permit a description and statement of the approximate area of the land to be irrigated.

2017 Legislation: Amended by S.B. 864, §2, 85th Leg., eff. Sept. 1, 2017.

WATER §11.1351. PERMIT RESTRICTIONS

In granting an application, the commission may direct that stream flow restrictions and other conditions and restrictions be placed in the permit being issued to protect the priority of senior water rights.

WATER §11.136. RECORDING OF PERMIT

(a) The commission shall transmit the permit by registered mail to the county clerk of the county in which the appropriation is to be made.

(b) When the county clerk receives the permit and is paid the recording fee (as prescribed by Subchapter B, Chapter 118, Local Government Code[1], he shall file and record the permit in a well-bound book kept for that purpose. He shall index the permit alphabetically in the name of the applicant and of the stream or source of water supply. After he has recorded the permit, the county clerk shall deliver the permit, on demand, to the applicant.

(c) When the permit is filed in the office of the county clerk, it is constructive notice of:

(1) the filing of the application;

(2) the issuance of the permit; and

(3) all the rights arising under the filing of the application and the issuance of the permit.

1. **Editor's note:** So in original. A closing parenthesis probably should appear.

WATER §11.137. SEASONAL PERMITS

(a) The commission may issue seasonal permits in the same manner that it issues regular permits. The provisions of this chapter governing issuance of regular permits apply to issuance of seasonal permits.

(b) The right to take, use, or divert water under seasonal permit is limited to the portion or portions of the calendar year stated in the permit.

(c) In a seasonal permit, the commission shall specify the conditions necessary to fully protect prior appropriations or vested rights on the stream.

WATER §11.138. TEMPORARY PERMITS

(a) The commission may issue temporary permits for beneficial purposes to the extent that they do not interfere with or adversely affect prior appropriations or vested rights on the stream from which water is to be diverted under such temporary permit. The commission may, by appropriate order, authorize any member of the commission to approve and issue temporary permits without notice and hearing if it appears to such issuing party that sufficient water is available at the proposed point of diversion to satisfy the requirements of the temporary permit as well as all existing rights. No temporary permit issued without notice and hearing shall authorize more than 10 acre-feet of water, nor may it be for a term in excess of one year.

(b) The commission may prescribe rules governing notice and procedure for the issuance of temporary permits.

(c) As between temporary permits, the one applied for first has priority.

(d) The commission may not issue a temporary permit for a period exceeding three calendar years.

(e) A temporary permit does not vest in its holder a permanent right to the use of water.

(f) A temporary permit expires and shall be cancelled by the commission in accordance with the terms of the permit.

(g) The commission may prescribe by rule the fees to be paid for issuance of temporary permits, but no fee for issuance or extension of a temporary permit shall exceed $500.

WATER §11.1381. TERM PERMITS

(a) Until a water right is perfected to the full extent provided by Section 11.026 of this code, the commission may issue permits for a term of years for use of state water to which a senior water right has not been perfected.

(b) The commission shall refuse to grant an application for a permit under this section if the commission finds that there is a substantial likelihood that the issuance of the permit will jeopardize financial commitments made for water projects that have been built or that are being built to optimally develop the water resources of the area.

(c) The commission shall refuse to grant an application for a term permit if the holder of the senior appropriative water right can demonstrate that the issuance of the term permit would prohibit the senior appropriative water right holder from beneficially using the senior rights during the term of the term permit. Such demonstration will be made using reasonable projections based on accepted methods.

(d) A permit issued under this section is subordinate to any senior appropriative water rights.

WATER §11.139. EMERGENCY AUTHORIZATIONS

(a) Except as provided by Section 11.148 of this code, the commission may grant an emergency permit, order, or amendment to an existing permit, certified filing, or certificate of adjudication after notice to the governor for an initial period of not more than 120 days if the commission finds that emergency conditions exist which present an imminent threat to the public health and safety and which override the necessity to comply with established statutory procedures and there are no feasible practicable alternatives to the emergency authorization. Such emergency action may be renewed once for not longer than 60 days.

(b) A person desiring to obtain an emergency authorization under this section shall submit to the commission a sworn application containing the following information:

(1) a description of the condition of emergency justifying the granting of the emergency authorization;

(2) a statement setting forth facts which support the findings required under this section;

(3) an estimate of the dates on which the proposed authorization should begin and end;

(4) a description of the action sought and the activity proposed to be allowed, mandated, or prohibited; and

(5) any other statements or information required by the commission.

(c) If the commission finds the applicant's statement made under Subsection (b) of this section to be correct, the commission may grant emergency authorizations under this section without notice and hearing or with such notice and hearing as the commission considers practicable under the circumstances.

(d) If the commission grants an emergency authorization under this section without a hearing, the authorization shall fix a time and place for a hearing to be held before the commission. The hearing shall be held as soon after the emergency authorization is granted as is practicable but not later than 20 days after the emergency authorization is granted.

(e) At the hearing, the commission shall affirm, modify, or set aside the emergency authorization. Any hearing on an emergency authorization shall be conducted in accordance with Chapter 2001, Government Code, and rules of the commission.

(f) If an imminent threat to the public health and safety exists which requires emergency action before the commission can take action as provided by Subsections (a) through (c) of this section and there are no feasible alternatives, the executive director may grant an emergency authorization after notice to the governor. If the executive director issues an emergency authorization under this subsection, the commission shall hold a hearing as provided for in Subsections (d) and (e) of this section. The requirements of Subsection (b) of this section shall be satisfied by the applicant before action is taken by the executive director on the request for emergency authorization.

(g) The requirements of Section 11.132 of this code relating to the time for notice, newspaper notice, and method of giving a person notice do not apply to a hearing held on an application for an emergency authorization under this section, but such general notice of the hearing shall be given as the commission, under Subsections (c) and (e) of this section, considers practicable under the circumstances.

(h) The commission may grant an emergency authorization under this section for the temporary transfer and use of all or part of a permit, certified filing, or certificate of adjudication for other than domestic or municipal use to a retail or wholesale water supplier for public health and safety purposes. In addition to the requirements contained in Subsection (b) of this section, the commission may direct that the applicant will timely pay the amounts for which the applicant may be potentially liable under Subsection (j) of this section and to the extent authorized by law will fully indemnify and hold harmless the state, the executive director, and the commission from any and all liability for the authorization sought. The commission may order bond or other surety in a form acceptable to the commission as a condition for such emergency authorization. The commission may not grant an emergency authorization under this section which would cause a violation of a federal regulation.

(i) In transferring the amount of water requested by the applicant, the executive director or the commission shall allocate the requested amount among two or more permits, certified filings, or certificates of adjudication for other than domestic or municipal use.

(j) The person granted an emergency authorization under Subsection (h) of this section is liable to the owner and the owner's agent or lessee from whom the use is transferred for the fair market value of the water transferred as well as for any damages caused by the transfer of use. If, within 60 days of the termination of the authorization, the parties do not agree on the amount due, or if full payment is not made, either party may file a complaint with the commission to determine the amount due. The commission may use dispute resolution procedures for a complaint filed under this subsection. After exhausting all administrative remedies under this subsection, an owner from whom the use is transferred may file suit to recover or determine the amount due in a district court in the county where the owner resides or has its headquarters. The prevailing party in a suit filed under this subsection is entitled to recover court costs and reasonable attorney's fees.

(k) The commission may prescribe rules and adopt fees which are necessary to carry out the provisions of this section.

(l) An emergency authorization does not vest in the grantee any right to the diversion, impoundment, or use of water and shall expire and be cancelled in accordance with its terms.

WATER §11.140. PERMITS FOR STORAGE FOR PROJECT DEVELOPMENT

The commission may issue permits for storage solely for the purpose of optimum development of projects. The commission may convert these permits to permits for beneficial use if application to have them converted is made to the commission.

WATER §11.1405. DESALINATION OF SEAWATER FOR USE FOR INDUSTRIAL PURPOSES

(a) The commission may issue a permit under this section to authorize a diversion of state water from the Gulf of Mexico or a bay or arm of the Gulf of Mexico for desalination and use for industrial purposes if:

(1) the point of diversion is located less than three miles seaward of any point located on the coast of this state; or

(2) the seawater contains a total dissolved solids concentration based on a yearly average of samples taken monthly at the water source of less than 20,000 milligrams per liter.

(b) A person may divert state water from the Gulf of Mexico or a bay or arm of the Gulf of Mexico for desalination and use for industrial purposes without obtaining a permit if Subsection (a) does not apply.

(c) A person who diverts and uses state water that consists of marine seawater under a permit issued under Subsection (a) or as authorized by Subsection (b) must determine the total dissolved solids concentration of the seawater at the water source by monthly sampling and analysis and provide the data collected to the commission. A person may not begin construction of a facility for the diversion of marine seawater for the purposes provided by this section without obtaining a permit until the person has provided data to the commission based on the analysis of samples taken at the water source over a period of at least one year demonstrating that Subsection (a)(2) does not apply. A person who has begun construction of a facility for the diversion of marine seawater for the purposes provided by this section without obtaining a permit because the person has demonstrated that Subsection (a)(2) does not apply is not required to obtain a permit for the facility if the total dissolved solids concentration of the seawater at the water source subsequently changes so that Subsection (a)(2) applies.

(d) A permit application under this section must be submitted as required by commission rule.

(e) The commission is not required to make a finding of water availability for an application under this section.

(f) The commission shall evaluate whether any proposed diversion under this section is consistent with any applicable environmental flow standards established under Section 11.1471.

(g) The commission may include any provision in a permit issued under this section that the commission considers necessary to comply with the environmental flow standards established under Section 11.1471.

(h) The commission shall adopt rules providing an expedited procedure for acting on an application for a permit under Subsection (a). The rules must provide for notice, an opportunity for the submission of written comment, and an opportunity for a contested case hearing regarding commission actions relating to an application for a permit.

WATER §11.141. DATE OF PRIORITY

When the commission issues a permit, the priority of the appropriation of water and the claimant's right to use the water date from the date of filing of the application.

WATER §11.142. PERMIT EXEMPTIONS

(a) Without obtaining a permit, a person may construct on the person's own property a dam or reservoir with normal storage of not more than 200 acre-feet of water for domestic and livestock purposes. A person who temporarily stores more than 200 acre-feet of water in a dam or reservoir described by this subsection is not required to obtain a permit for the dam or reservoir if the person can demonstrate that the person has not stored in the dam or reservoir more than 200 acre-feet of water on average in any 12-month period. This exemption does not apply to a commercial operation.

☠ *Subsection (b) was amended by Acts 2001, 77th Leg., ch. 966, §2.09, enacted May 28, 2001, effective Sept. 1, 2001, without reference to the conflicting amendment made by Acts 2001, 77th Leg., ch. 1427, §1, enacted May 28, 2001, effective June 17, 2001. For harmonizing conflicts, see p. V.*

(b) Without obtaining a permit, a person may construct on the person's property a dam or reservoir with normal storage of not more than 200 acre-feet of water for fish and wildlife purposes if the property on which the dam or reservoir will be constructed is qualified open-space land, as defined by Section 23.51, Tax Code. This exemption does not apply to a commercial operation.

☠ *Subsection (b) was amended by Acts 2001, 77th Leg., ch. 1427, §1, enacted May 28, 2001, effective June 17, 2001, without reference to the conflicting amendment*

made by Acts 2001, 77th Leg., ch. 966, §2.09, enacted May 28, 2001, effective Sept. 1, 2001. For harmonizing conflicts, see p. V.

(b) Without obtaining a permit, a person may construct on the person's property in an unincorporated area a dam or reservoir with normal storage of not more than 200 acre-feet of water for commercial or noncommercial wildlife management, including fishing, but not including fish farming.

(c) Without obtaining a permit, a person who is drilling and producing petroleum and conducting operations associated with drilling and producing petroleum may take for those purposes state water from the Gulf of Mexico and adjacent bays and arms of the Gulf of Mexico in an amount not to exceed one acre-foot during each 24-hour period.

(d) Without obtaining a permit, a person may construct or maintain a reservoir as part of a surface coal mining operation under Chapter 134, Natural Resources Code, if the water in the reservoir is used solely for:

(1) sediment control; or

(2) compliance with applicable laws, rules, or regulations relating to fire or dust suppression.

WATER §11.1421. PERMIT EXEMPTION FOR MARICULTURE ACTIVITIES

(a) In this section, "mariculture" means the propagation and rearing of aquatic species, including shrimp, other crustaceans, finfish, mollusks, and other similar creatures in a controlled environment using brackish or marine water.

(b) Without obtaining a permit and subject to the requirements and limitations provided by Subsections (c) through (e) of this section, a person who is engaged in mariculture operations on land may take for that purpose state water from the Gulf of Mexico and adjacent bays and arms of the Gulf of Mexico in an amount appropriate to those mariculture activities.

(c) Before a person first takes water under Subsection (b) of this section, the person must give notice to the commission of the proposed appropriation.

(d) Each appropriation of water made under Subsection (b) of this section shall be reported to the commission in the manner provided by the commission's rules.

(e) After notice and hearing, if the commission determines that as a result of low freshwater inflows appropriation of water under Subsection (b) of this section would interfere with natural productivity of bays and estuaries, the commission shall issue an order requiring interruption or reduction of the appropriation.

WATER §11.1422. PERMIT EXEMPTION FOR HISTORIC CEMETERIES

(a) Without obtaining a permit, a tax-exempt nonprofit corporation that owns a cemetery may divert from a river not more than 200 acre-feet of water each year to irrigate the grounds of the cemetery if the cemetery:

(1) borders the river; and

(2) is more than 100 years old.

(b) The executive director or a watermaster who has jurisdiction over the river from which a cemetery diverts water under this section by order may restrict a diversion authorized by this section if the executive director or watermaster determines the diversion will harm a person downstream of the cemetery who acquired a water right before the date this section took effect. The executive director or watermaster shall limit the restriction to the extent of the harm and to the period of the harm.

Ⓐ WATER §11.143. USE OF WATER FROM EXEMPT DAM OR RESERVOIR FOR NONEXEMPT PURPOSES

The amended text in §11.143 is effective for applications for a new or amended water right received by the Texas Commission on Environmental Quality on or after Sept. 1, 2017. Applications received before Sept. 1, 2017, are governed by the former law in effect at that time.

(a) The owner of a dam or reservoir exempted under Section 11.142(a) or (b) who desires to use water from the dam or reservoir for a purpose not described by that subsection shall obtain a permit to do so. The owner may obtain a regular permit, a seasonal permit, or a permit for a term of years. The owner may elect to obtain the permit by proceeding under this section or under the other provisions of this chapter governing issuance of permits.

(b) If the applicant elects to proceed under this section, he shall submit to the commission a sworn application, on a form furnished by the commission, containing the following information:

(1) the name and post-office address of the applicant;

(2) the nature and purpose of the use and the amount of water to be used annually for each purpose;

(3) the major watershed and the tributary (named or unnamed) on which the dam or reservoir is located;

(4) the county in which the dam or reservoir is located;

(5) the approximate distance and direction from the county seat of the county to the location of the dam or reservoir;

(6) the survey or the portion of the survey on which the dam or reservoir is located and, to the best of the applicant's knowledge and belief, the distance and direction of the midpoint of the dam or reservoir from a corner of the survey, which information the executive director may require to be marked on an aerial photograph or map furnished by the commission;

(7) the approximate surface area, to the nearest acre, of the reservoir when it is full and the average depth in feet when it is full; and

(8) the approximate number of square miles in the drainage area above the dam or reservoir.

(c) If the permit is sought for irrigation, the application must also specify:

(1) the total number of irrigable acres in the area;

(2) the number of acres to be irrigated within the area in any one year; and

(3) the approximate distance and direction of the land to be irrigated from the midpoint of the dam or reservoir.

(d) Except as otherwise specifically provided by this subsection, before the commission may approve the application and issue the permit, it shall give notice and hold a hearing as prescribed by this section. The commission may act on the application without holding a public hearing if:

(1) not less than 30 days before the date of action on the application by the commission, the applicant has published the commission's notice of the application at least once in a newspaper regularly published or circulated within the section of the state where the source of water is located;

(2) not less than 30 days before the date of action on the application by the commission, the commission mails a copy of the notice by first-class mail, postage prepaid, to each person whose claim or appropriation has been filed with the commission and whose diversion point is downstream from that described in the application; and

(3) within 30 days after the date of the newspaper publication of the commission's notice, a public hearing is not requested in writing by a commissioner, the executive director, or an affected person who objects to the application.

(e) In the notice, the commission shall:

(1) state the name and post-office address of the applicant;

(2) state the date the application was filed;

(3) state the purpose and extent of the proposed appropriation of water;

(4) identify the source of supply, including any proposed alternative source of water, other than state water, identified by the applicant, and the place where the water is stored; and

(5) specify the time and place of the hearing.

(f) The notice shall be published only once, at least 20 days before the date stated in the notice for the hearing on the application, in a newspaper having general circulation in the county where the dam or reservoir is located. At least 15 days before the date set for the hearing, the commission shall transmit a copy of the notice by first-class mail to each person whose claim or appropriation has been filed with the commission and whose diversion point is downstream from that described in the application. If the notice identifies groundwater from a well located in a groundwater conservation district as a proposed alternative source of water, the notice shall be:

(1) sent to the groundwater conservation district in which the well is located; and

(2) published, at least 20 days before the date stated in the notice for the hearing, in a newspaper having general circulation in each county in which the groundwater district is located.

(g) If on the date specified in the notice prescribed by Subsection (d) of this section, the commission determines that a public hearing must be held, the matter shall be remanded for hearing without the necessity of issuing further notice other than advising all parties of the time and place where the hearing is to convene.

(h) The applicant shall pay the filing fee prescribed by Section 5.701(c) at the time he files the application.

(i) The commission shall approve the application and issue the permit as applied for in whole or part if it determines that:

(1) there is unappropriated water in the source of supply;

(2) the applicant has met the requirements of this section;

(3) the water is to be used for a beneficial purpose;

(4) the proposed use is not detrimental to the public welfare or to the welfare of the locality; and

(5) the proposed use will not impair existing water rights.

2017 Legislation: Amended by S.B. 864, §3, 85th Leg., eff. Sept. 1, 2017.

WATER §11.144. APPROVAL FOR ALTERATIONS

All holders of permits and certified filings shall obtain the approval of the commission before making any alterations, enlargements, extensions, or other changes to any reservoir, dam, main canal, or diversion work on which a permit has been granted or a certified filing recorded. A detailed statement and plans for alterations or changes shall be filed with the commission and approved by the executive director before the alterations or changes are made. This section does not apply to the ordinary maintenance or emergency repair of the facility.

WATER §11.145. WHEN CONSTRUCTION MUST BEGIN

(a) If a permit is for appropriation by direct diversion, construction of the proposed facilities shall begin within the time fixed by the commission, which shall not exceed two years after the date the permit is issued. The appropriator shall work diligently and continuously to the completion of the construction. The commission may, by entering an order of record, extend the time for beginning construction. The commission may establish fees, not to exceed $1,000, for extending the time to begin construction of the proposed facilities.

(b) If the permit contemplates construction of a storage reservoir, construction shall begin within the time fixed by the commission, not to exceed two years after the date the permit is issued. The commission, by entering an order of record, may extend the time for beginning construction. The commission may fix fees, not to exceed $1,000, for extending the time to begin construction of reservoirs.

WATER §11.146. FORFEITURES & CANCELLATION OF PERMIT FOR INACTION

(a) If a permittee fails to begin construction within the time specified in Section 11.145 of this code, he forfeits all rights to the permit, subject to notice and hearing as prescribed by this section.

(b) After beginning construction if the appropriator fails to work diligently and continuously to the completion of the work, the appropriation is subject to cancellation in whole or part, subject to notice and hearing as prescribed by this section.

(c) If the commission believes that an appropriation or permit should be declared forfeited under this section or any other sections of this code, it should give the appropriator or permittee 30 days notice and provide him with an opportunity to be heard.

(d) After the hearing, the commission by entering an order of record may cancel the appropriation in whole or part. The commission shall immediately transmit a certified copy of the cancellation order by certified mail to the county clerk of the county in which the permit is recorded. The county clerk shall record the cancellation order.

(e) Except as provided by Section 11.1381 of this code, if a permit has been issued for the use of water, the water is not subject to a new appropriation until the permit has been cancelled in whole or part as provided by this section.

(f) Except as provided by Subchapter E of this chapter, none of the provisions of this code may be construed as intended to impair, cause, or authorize or may impair, cause, or authorize the forfeiture of any rights acquired by any declaration of appropriation or by any permit if the appropriator has begun or begins the work and development contemplated by his declaration of appropriation or permit within the time provided by the law under which the declaration of appropriation was made or the permit was granted and has prosecuted or continues to prosecute it with all reasonable diligence toward completion.

(g) This section does not apply to a permit for construction of a reservoir designed for the storage of more than 50,000 acre-feet of water.

WATER §11.147. EFFECTS OF PERMIT ON BAYS & ESTUARIES & INSTREAM USES

(a) In this section, "beneficial inflows" means a salinity, nutrient, and sediment loading regime adequate to maintain an ecologically sound environment in the receiving bay and estuary system that is necessary for the maintenance of productivity of economically important and ecologically characteristic sport or commercial fish and shellfish species and estuarine life upon which such fish and shellfish are dependent.

(b) In its consideration of an application for a permit to store, take, or divert water, the commission shall assess the effects, if any, of the issuance of the permit on the bays and estuaries of Texas. For permits issued within an area that is 200 river miles of the coast, to commence from the mouth of the river thence inland, the commission shall include in the permit any conditions considered necessary to maintain beneficial inflows to any affected bay and estuary system, to the extent practicable when considering all public interests and the studies mandated by Section 16.058 as evaluated under Section 11.1491.

(c) For the purposes of making a determination under Subsection (b) of this section, the commission shall consider among other factors:

(1) the need for periodic freshwater inflows to supply nutrients and modify salinity to preserve the sound environment of the bay or estuary, using any available information, including studies and plans specified in Section 11.1491 of this code and other studies considered by the commission to be reliable; together with existing circumstances, natural or otherwise, that might prevent the conditions imposed from producing benefits;

(2) the ecology and productivity of the affected bay and estuary system;

(3) the expected effects on the public welfare of not including in the permit some or all of the conditions considered necessary to maintain the beneficial inflows to the affected bay or estuary system;

(4) the quantity of water requested and the proposed use of water by the applicant, as well as the needs of those who would be served by the applicant;

(5) the expected effects on the public welfare of the failure to issue all or part of the permit being considered; and

(6) for purposes of this section, the declarations as to preferences for competing uses of water as found in Sections 11.024 and 11.033, Water Code, as well as the public policy statement in Section 1.003, Water Code.

(d) In its consideration of an application to store, take, or divert water, the commission shall include in the permit, to the extent practicable when considering all public interests, those conditions considered by the commission necessary to maintain existing instream uses and water quality of the stream or river to which the application applies. In determining what conditions to include in the permit under this subsection, the commission shall consider among other factors:

(1) the studies mandated by Section 16.059; and

(2) any water quality assessment performed under Section 11.150.

(e) The commission shall include in the permit, to the extent practicable when considering all public interests, those conditions considered by the commission necessary to maintain fish and wildlife habitats. In determining what conditions to include in the permit under this subsection, the commission shall consider any assessment performed under Section 11.152.

(e-1) Any permit for a new appropriation of water or an amendment to an existing water right that increases the amount of water authorized to be stored, taken, or diverted must include a provision allowing the commission to adjust the conditions included in the permit or amended water right to provide for protection of instream flows or freshwater inflows. With respect to an amended water right, the provision may not allow the commission to adjust a condition of the amendment other than a condition that applies only to the increase in the amount of water to be stored, taken, or diverted authorized by the amendment. This subsection does not affect an appropriation of or an authorization to store, take, or divert water under a permit or amendment to a water right issued before September 1, 2007. The commission shall adjust the conditions if the commission determines, through an expedited public comment process, that such an adjustment is appropriate to achieve compliance with applicable environmental flow standards adopted under Section 11.1471. The adjustment:

(1) in combination with any previous adjustments made under this subsection may not increase the amount of the pass-through or release requirement for the protection of instream flows or freshwater inflows by more than 12.5 percent of the annualized total of that requirement contained in the permit as issued or of that requirement contained in the amended water right and applicable only to the increase in the amount of water authorized to be stored, taken, or diverted under the amended water right;

(2) must be based on appropriate consideration of the priority dates and diversion locations of any other water rights granted in the same river basin that are subject to adjustment under this subsection; and

(3) must be based on appropriate consideration of any voluntary contributions to the Texas Water Trust, and of any voluntary amendments to existing water rights to change the use of a specified quantity of water to or add a use of a specified quantity of water for instream flows dedicated to environmental needs or bay and estuary inflows as authorized by Section 11.0237(a), that actually contribute toward meeting the applicable environmental flow standards.

(e-2) Any water right holder who makes a contribution or amends a water right as described by Subsection (e-1)(3) is entitled to appropriate credit for the benefits of the contribution or amendment against the adjustment of the holder's water right under Subsection (e-1).

(e-3) Notwithstanding Subsections (b)-(e), for the purpose of determining the environmental flow conditions necessary to maintain freshwater inflows to an affected bay and estuary system, existing instream uses and water quality of a stream or river, or fish and aquatic wildlife habitats, the commission shall apply any applicable environmental flow standard, including any environmental flow set-aside, adopted under Section 11.1471 instead of considering the factors specified by those subsections.

(f) On receipt of an application for a permit to store, take, or divert water, the commission shall send a copy of the permit application and any subsequent amendments to the Parks and Wildlife Department. At its option, the Parks and Wildlife Department may be a party in hearings on applications for permits to store, take, or divert water. In making a final decision on any application for a permit, the commission, in addition to other information, evidence, and testimony presented, shall consider all information, evidence, and testimony presented by the Parks and Wildlife Department and the board.

(g) The failure of the Parks and Wildlife Department to appear as a party does not relieve the commission of the requirements of this section.

Section 11.1471 omitted by editor

WATER §11.148. EMERGENCY SUSPENSION OF PERMIT CONDITIONS & EMERGENCY AUTHORITY TO MAKE AVAILABLE WATER SET ASIDE FOR ENVIRONMENTAL FLOWS

(a) Permit conditions relating to beneficial inflows to affected bays and estuaries and instream uses may be suspended by the commission if the commission finds that an emergency exists and cannot practically be resolved in other ways.

(a-1) State water that is set aside by the commission to meet the needs for freshwater inflows to affected bays and estuaries and instream uses under Section 11.1471(a)(2) may be made available temporarily for other essential beneficial uses if the commission finds that an emergency exists that cannot practically be resolved in another way.

(b) Before the commission suspends a permit condition under Subsection (a) or makes water available temporarily under Subsection (a-1), it must give written notice to the Parks and Wildlife Department of the proposed action. The commission shall give the Parks and Wildlife Department an opportunity to submit comments on the proposed action within 72 hours from such time and the commission shall consider those comments before issuing its order implementing the proposed action.

(c) The commission may suspend the permit condition under Subsection (a) or make water available temporarily under Subsection (a-1) without notice to any other interested party other than the Parks and Wildlife Department as provided by Subsection (b). However, all affected persons shall be notified immediately by publication, and a hearing to determine whether the suspension should be continued shall be held within 15 days of the date on which the order to suspend is issued.

Section 11.1491 omitted by editor

WATER §11.150. EFFECTS OF PERMITS ON WATER QUALITY

In consideration of an application for a permit under this subchapter, the commission shall assess the effects, if any, of the issuance of the permit on water quality in this state.

WATER §11.1501. CONSIDERATION & REVISION OF PLANS

In considering an application for a permit to store, take, or divert surface water, or for an amendment to a permit, certified filing, or certificate of adjudication, the commission shall consider the state water plan and any approved regional water plan for the area or areas in which the water is proposed to be stored, diverted, or used.

WATER §11.151. EFFECTS OF PERMITS ON GROUNDWATER

In considering an application for a permit to store, take, or divert surface water, the commission shall consider the effects, if any, on groundwater or groundwater recharge.

WATER §11.152. ASSESSMENT OF EFFECTS OF PERMITS ON FISH & WILDLIFE HABITATS

In its consideration of an application for a permit to store, take, or divert water in excess of 5,000 acre feet per year, the commission shall assess the effects, if any, on the issuance of the permit on fish and wildlife habitats and may require the applicant to take reasonable actions to mitigate adverse impacts on such habitat. In determining whether to require an applicant to mitigate adverse impacts on a habitat, the commission may consider any net benefit to the habitat produced by the project. The commission shall offset against any mitigation required by the U.S. Fish and Wildlife Service pursuant to 33 C.F.R. Parts 320-330 any mitigation authorized by this section.

WATER §11.153. PROJECTS FOR STORAGE OF APPROPRIATED WATER IN AQUIFERS

(a) In this section, "aquifer storage and recovery project" has the meaning assigned by Section 27.151.

(b) A water right holder or a person who has contracted for the use of water under a contract that does not prohibit the use of the water in an aquifer storage and recovery project may undertake an aquifer storage and recovery project without obtaining any additional authorization under this chapter for the project. A person described by this subsection undertaking an aquifer storage and recovery project must:

(1) obtain any required authorizations under Subchapter G, Chapter 27, and Subchapter N, Chapter 36; and

(2) comply with the terms of the applicable water right.

(c) This section does not preclude the commission from considering an aquifer storage and recovery project to be a component of a project permitted under this chapter that is not required to be based on the continuous availability of historic, normal stream flow.

(d), (e) Repealed by Acts 2015, 84th Leg., ch. 505, §5(1), eff. June 16, 2015.

WATER §11.154. REPEALED

WATER §11.155. AQUIFER STORAGE & RECOVERY REPORTS

The board shall make studies, investigations, and surveys of the aquifers in the state as it considers necessary to determine the occurrence, quantity, quality, and availability of aquifers in which water may be stored and subsequently retrieved for beneficial use. The board shall undertake the studies, investigations, and surveys in the following order of priority:

(1) areas designated by the commission as "priority groundwater management areas" under Section 35.008; and

(2) other areas of the state in a priority to be determined by the board's ranking of where the greatest need exists.

SUBCHAPTER E. CANCELLATION OF PERMITS, CERTIFIED FILINGS, & CERTIFICATES OF ADJUDICATION FOR NONUSE

WATER §11.171. DEFINITIONS

As used in this subchapter:

(1) "Other interested person" means any person other than a record holder who is interested in the permit or certified filing or any person whose direct interest would be served by the cancellation of the permit or certified filing in whole or part.

(2) "Certified filing" means a declaration of appropriation or affidavit that was filed with the State Board of Water Engineers under the provisions of Section 14, Chapter 171, General Laws, Acts of the 33rd Legislature, 1913, as amended.

(3) "Certificate of adjudication" means a certificate issued by the commission under Section 11.323 of this code.

(4) "Permit" means an authorization by the commission granting a person the right to use water.

WATER §11.172. GENERAL PRINCIPLE

A permit, certified filing, or certificate of adjudication is subject to cancellation in whole or part for 10 years nonuse as provided by this subchapter.

WATER §11.173. CANCELLATION IN WHOLE OR IN PART

(a) Except as provided by Subsection (b) of this section, if all or part of the water authorized to be ap-

propriated under a permit, certified filing, or certificate of adjudication has not been put to beneficial use at any time during the 10-year period immediately preceding the cancellation proceedings authorized by this subchapter, then the permit, certified filing, or certificate of adjudication is subject to cancellation in whole or in part, as provided by this subchapter, to the extent of the 10 years nonuse.

(b) A permit, certified filing, or certificate of adjudication or a portion of a permit, certified filing, or certificate of adjudication is exempt from cancellation under Subsection (a):

(1) to the extent of the owner's participation in the Conservation Reserve Program authorized by the Food Security Act, Pub.L. No. 99-198, Secs. 1231-1236, 99 Stat. 1354, 1509-1514 (1985) or a similar governmental program;

(2) if a significant portion of the water authorized to be used pursuant to a permit, certified filing, or certificate of adjudication has been used in accordance with a specific recommendation for meeting a water need included in the regional water plan approved pursuant to Section 16.053;

(3) if the permit, certified filing, or certificate of adjudication:

(A) was obtained to meet demonstrated long-term public water supply or electric generation needs as evidenced by a water management plan developed by the holder; and

(B) is consistent with projections of future water needs contained in the state water plan;

(4) if the permit, certified filing, or certificate of adjudication was obtained as the result of the construction of a reservoir funded, in whole or in part, by the holder of the permit, certified filing, or certificate of adjudication as part of the holder's long-term water planning; or

(5) to the extent the nonuse resulted from:

(A) the implementation of water conservation measures under a water conservation plan submitted by the holder of the permit, certified filing, or certificate of adjudication as evidenced by implementation reports submitted by the holder;

(B) a suspension, adjustment, or other restriction on the use of the water authorized to be appropriated under the permit, certified filing, or certificate of adjudication imposed under an order issued by the executive director; or

(C) an inability to appropriate the water authorized to be appropriated under the permit, certified filing, or certificate of adjudication due to drought conditions.

WATER §11.174. COMMISSION MAY INITIATE PROCEEDINGS

When the commission finds that its records do not show that some portion of the water has been used during the past 10 years, the executive director may initiate proceedings, terminated by public hearing, to cancel the permit, certified filing, or certificate of adjudication in whole or in part.

WATER §11.175. NOTICE

(a) At least 45 days before the date of the hearing, the commission shall send notice of the hearing to the holder of the permit, certified filing, or certificate of adjudication being considered for cancellation in whole or in part. Notice shall be sent by certified mail, return receipt requested, to the last address shown by the records of the commission. The commission shall also send notice by regular mail to all other holders of permits, certified filings, certificates of adjudication, and claims of unadjudicated water rights filed pursuant to Section 11.303 of this code in the same watershed.

(b) The commission shall also have the notice of the hearing published once a week for two consecutive weeks, at least 30 days before the date of the hearing, in a newspaper published in each county in which diversion of water from the source of supply was authorized or proposed to be made and in each county in which the water was authorized or proposed to be used, as shown by the records of the commission. If in any such county no newspaper is published, then the notice may be published in a newspaper having general circulation in the county.

WATER §11.176. HEARING

(a) Except as provided by Subsection (b) of this section, the commission shall hold a hearing and shall give the holder of the permit, certified filing, or certificate of adjudication and other interested persons an opportunity to be heard and to present evidence on any matter pertinent to the questions at issue.

(b) A hearing on the cancellation of a permit, certified filing, or certificate of adjudication as provided by this chapter is unnecessary if the right to such hearing is expressly waived by the affected holder of a permit, certified filing, or certificate of adjudication.

(c) A permit, certified filing, or certificate of adjudication for a term does not vest in the holder of a permit, certified filing, or certificate of adjudication any right to the diversion, impoundment, or use of water for longer than the term of the permit, certified filing, or certificate of adjudication and shall expire and be cancelled in accordance with its terms without further need for notice or hearing.

WATER §11.177. COMMISSION FINDING; ACTION

(a) At the conclusion of the hearing, the commission shall cancel the permit, certified filing, or certificate of adjudication in whole or in part to the extent that it finds that:

(1) the water or any portion of the water appropriated under the permit, certified filing, or certificate of adjudication has not been put to an authorized beneficial use during the 10-year period; and

(2) the holder has not used reasonable diligence in applying the water or the unused portion of the water to an authorized beneficial use or is otherwise unjustified in the nonuse.

(b) In determining what constitutes reasonable diligence or a justified nonuse as used in Subsection (a)(2), the commission shall give consideration to:

(1) whether sufficient water is available in the source of supply to meet all or part of the appropriation during the 10-year period of nonuse;

(2) whether the nonuse is justified by the holder's participation in the federal Conservation Reserve Program or a similar governmental program as provided by Section 11.173(b)(1);

(3) whether the existing or proposed authorized purpose and place of use are consistent with an approved regional water plan as provided by Section 16.053;

(4) whether the permit, certified filing, or certificate of adjudication has been deposited into the Texas Water Bank as provided by Sections 15.7031 and 15.704 or whether it can be shown that the water right or water available under the right is currently being made available for purchase through private marketing efforts; or

(5) whether the permit, certified filing, or certificate of adjudication has been reserved to provide for instream flows or bay and estuary inflows.

WATER §11.183. RESERVOIR

If the holder of a permit, certified filing, or certificate of adjudication has facilities for the storage of water in a reservoir, the commission may allow him to retain the impoundment to the extent of the conservation storage capacity of the reservoir for domestic, livestock, or recreation purposes.

WATER §11.184. MUNICIPAL CERTIFIED FILING

Regardless of other provisions of this subchapter, no portion of a certified filing held by a city, town, village, or municipal water district, authorizing the use of water for municipal purposes, shall be cancelled if water has been put to use under the certified filing for municipal purposes at any time during the 10-year period immediately preceding the institution of cancellation proceedings.

WATER §11.185. EFFECT OF INACTION

Failure to initiate cancellation proceedings under this subchapter does not validate or improve the status of any permit, certified filing, or certificate of adjudication in whole or in part.

WATER §11.186. SUBSEQUENT PROCEEDINGS ON SAME WATER RIGHT

Once cancellation proceedings have been initiated against a particular permit, certified filing, or certificate of adjudication and a hearing has been held, further cancellation proceedings shall not be initiated against the same permit, certified filing, or certificate of adjudication within the five-year period immediately following the date of the hearing.

SUBCHAPTER J. WETLANDS

WATER §11.501. TITLE OF ACT

This Act shall be known and may be cited as the "Wetlands Act."

WATER §11.502. DEFINITION

(1) The definition of the term "wetlands" within the State of Texas, for purposes of the Clean Water Act, 33 U.S.C. 1311, 1344; the Erodible Land and Wetland Conservation and Reserve Program, 16 U.S.C. 3801-3845; the Emergency Wetlands Resources Act of 1986, 16 U.S.C. 3901-3932; the National Environmental Policy Act of 1969, 42 U.S.C. 4321-4370a, all statutory foundation for the Federal Wildlife Service's National Wet-

lands Inventory mapping, including the Water Bank Program for Wetlands Preservation, 16 U.S.C. 1301-1311; the Water Resources development project (wetland areas), 42 U.S.C. 1962d-5e; and the Migratory Bird Conservation Act, 16 U.S.C. 715-715r; and all Texas laws, rules, and regulations adopted pursuant to Chapter 2001, Government Code and interpretation and implementation of any kind whatsoever of both federal and state laws by agencies of the state, including any amendment or revision thereto, relating to wetlands, means an area (including a swamp, marsh, bog, prairie pothole, or similar area) having a predominance of hydric soils that are inundated or saturated by surface or groundwater at a frequency and duration sufficient to support and that under normal circumstances supports the growth and regeneration of hydrophytic vegetation.

(2) The term "hydric soil" means soil that, in its undrained condition, is saturated, flooded, or ponded long enough during a growing season to develop an anaerobic condition that supports the growth and regeneration of hydrophytic vegetation.

(3) The term "hydrophytic vegetation" means a plant growing in: water or a substrate that is at least periodically deficient in oxygen during a growing season as a result of excessive water content.

(4) The term "wetlands" does not include:

(A) irrigated acreage used as farmland;

(B) man-made wetlands of less than one acre; or

(C) man-made wetlands not constructed with wetland creation as a stated objective, including but not limited to impoundments made for the purpose of soil and water conservation which have been approved or requested by soil and water conservation districts.

WATER §11.503. APPLICABILITY TO MAN-MADE WETLANDS

Section 11.502(4)(C) applies only to man-made wetlands, the construction or creation of which commences on or after the effective date of this Act.

WATER §11.504. APPLICABILITY TO CERTAIN MINING-RELATED ACTIVITIES

This Act shall not apply to surface mining and reclamation.

WATER §11.505. APPLICABILITY TO STATE REVOLVING LOAN FUND PROGRAM

This Act shall not apply to the state revolving loan fund program.

WATER §11.506. CONFLICT BETWEEN STATE & FEDERAL LAW

If the state definition conflicts with the federal definition in any manner, the federal definition prevails.

TEXAS RULES OF CIVIL PROCEDURE

SELECTED PROVISIONS

TABLE OF CONTENTS

For the complete Texas Rules of Civil Procedure with annotations, see the current edition of *O'Connor's Texas Rules * Civil Trials*. To order, call 1-800-OCONNOR (1-800-626-6667) or visit www.oconnors.com.

PART II. RULES OF PRACTICE IN DISTRICT & COUNTY COURTS

SECTION 9. EVIDENCE & DISCOVERY

B. DISCOVERY

TRCP 192. PERMISSIBLE DISCOVERY: FORMS & SCOPE; WORK PRODUCT; PROTECTIVE ORDERS; DEFINITIONS

192.1 Forms of Discovery. Permissible forms of discovery are:

(a) requests for disclosure;

(b) requests for production and inspection of documents and tangible things;

(c) requests and motions for entry upon and examination of real property;

(d) interrogatories to a party;

(e) requests for admission;

(f) oral or written depositions; and

(g) motions for mental or physical examinations.

192.2 to 192.7 *Omitted by editor.*

See also *O'Connor's Texas Rules*, "Forms of Discovery," ch. 6-A, §5, p. 494.

SECTION 11. TRIAL OF CAUSES

H. JUDGMENTS

TRCP 310. WRIT OF POSSESSION

When an order foreclosing a lien upon real estate is made in a suit having for its object the foreclosure of such lien, such order shall have all the force and effect of a writ of possession as between the parties to the foreclosure suit and any person claiming under the defendant to such suit by any right acquired pending such suit; and the court shall so direct in the judgment providing for the issuance of such order. The sheriff or other officer executing such order of sale shall proceed by virtue of such order of sale to place the purchaser of the property sold thereunder in possession thereof within thirty days after the day of sale.

PART V. RULES OF PRACTICE IN JUSTICE COURTS

TRCP 500. GENERAL RULES

500.1 Construction of Rules. Unless otherwise expressly provided, in Part V of these Rules of Civil Procedure:

(a) the past, present, and future tense each includes the other;

(b) the term "it" includes a person of either gender or an entity; and

(c) the singular and plural each includes the other.

500.2 Definitions. In Part V of these Rules of Civil Procedure:

(a) "Answer" is the written response that a party who is sued must file with the court after being served with a citation.

(b) "Citation" is the court-issued document required to be served upon a party to inform the party that it has been sued.

(c) "Claim" is the legal theory and alleged facts that, if proven, entitle a party to relief against another party in court.

(d) "Clerk" is a person designated by the judge as a justice court clerk, or the judge if there is no clerk available.

(e) "Counterclaim" is a claim brought by a party who has been sued against the party who filed the lawsuit, for example, a defendant suing a plaintiff.

(f) "County court" is the county court, statutory county court, or district court in a particular county with jurisdiction over appeals of civil cases from justice court.

(g) "Cross-claim" is a claim brought by one party against another party on the same side of a lawsuit. For example, if a plaintiff sues two defendants, the defendants can seek relief against each other by means of a cross-claim.

(h) "Default judgment" is a judgment awarded to a plaintiff when the defendant fails to answer and dispute the plaintiff's claims in the lawsuit.

(i) "Defendant" is a party who is sued, including a plaintiff against whom a counterclaim is filed.

(j) "Defense" is an assertion by a defendant that the plaintiff is not entitled to relief from the court.

(k) "Discovery" is the process through which parties obtain information from each other in order to prepare for trial or enforce a judgment. The term does not refer to any information that a party is entitled to under applicable law.

(l) "Dismissed without prejudice" means a case has been dismissed but has not been finally decided and may be refiled.

(m) "Dismissed with prejudice" means a case has been dismissed and finally decided and may not be refiled.

(n) "Judge" is a justice of the peace.

(o) "Judgment" is a final order by the court that states the relief, if any, a party is entitled to or must provide.

(p) "Jurisdiction" is the authority of the court to hear and decide a case.

(q) "Motion" is a request that the court make a specified ruling or order.

(r) "Notice" is a document prepared and delivered by the court or a party stating that something is required of the party receiving the notice.

(s) "Party" is a person or entity involved in the case that is either suing or being sued, including all plaintiffs, defendants, and third parties that have been joined in the case.

(t) "Petition" is a formal written application stating a party's claims and requesting relief from the court. It is the first document filed with the court to begin a lawsuit.

(u) "Plaintiff" is a party who sues, including a defendant who files a counterclaim.

(v) "Pleading" is a written document filed by a party, including a petition and an answer, that states a claim or defense and outlines the relief sought.

(w) "Relief" is the remedy a party requests from the court, such as the recovery of money or the return of property.

(x) "Serve" and "service" are delivery of citation as required by Rule 501.2, or of a document as required by Rule 501.4.

(y) "Sworn" means signed in front of someone authorized to take oaths, such as a notary, or signed under penalty of perjury. Filing a false sworn document can result in criminal prosecution.

(z) "Third party claim" is a claim brought by a party being sued against someone who is not yet a party to the case.

500.3 Application of Rules in Justice Court Cases.

(a) ***Small Claims Case.*** A small claims case is a lawsuit brought for the recovery of money damages, civil penalties, personal property, or other relief allowed by law. The claim can be for no more than $10,000, excluding statutory interest and court costs but including attorney fees, if any. Small claims cases are governed by Rules 500-507 of Part V of the Rules of Civil Procedure.

(b) ***Debt Claim Case.*** A debt claim case is a lawsuit brought to recover a debt by an assignee of a claim, a debt collector or collection agency, a financial institution, or a person or entity primarily engaged in the business of lending money at interest. The claim can be for no more than $10,000, excluding statutory interest and court costs but including attorney fees, if any. Debt claim cases in justice court are governed by Rules 500-507 and 508 of Part V of the Rules of Civil Procedure. To the extent of any conflict between Rule 508 and the rest of Part V, Rule 508 applies.

(c) ***Repair and Remedy Case.*** A repair and remedy case is a lawsuit filed by a residential tenant under Chapter 92, Subchapter B of the Texas Property Code to enforce the landlord's duty to repair or remedy a condition materially affecting the physical health or safety of an ordinary tenant. The relief sought can be for no more than $10,000, excluding statutory interest and court costs but including attorney fees, if any. Repair and remedy cases are governed by Rules 500-507 and 509 of Part V of the Rules of Civil Procedure. To the extent of any conflict between Rule 509 and the rest of Part V, Rule 509 applies.

(d) ***Eviction Case.*** An eviction case is a lawsuit brought to recover possession of real property under Chapter 24 of the Texas Property Code, often by a landlord against a tenant. A claim for rent may be joined with an eviction case if the amount of rent due and unpaid is not more than $10,000, excluding statutory interest and court costs but including attorney fees, if any. Eviction cases are governed by Rules 500-507 and 510 of Part V of the Rules of Civil Procedure. To the extent of any conflict between Rule 510 and the rest of Part V, Rule 510 applies.

(e) ***Application of Other Rules.*** The other Rules of Civil Procedure and the Rules of Evidence do not apply except:

(1) when the judge hearing the case determines that a particular rule must be followed to ensure that the proceedings are fair to all parties; or

(2) when otherwise specifically provided by law or these rules.

(f) ***Examination of Rules.*** The court must make the Rules of Civil Procedure and the Rules of Evidence available for examination, either in paper form or electronically, during the court's business hours.

500.4 Representation in Justice Court Cases.

(a) ***Representation of an Individual.*** An individual may:

(1) represent himself or herself;

(2) be represented by an authorized agent in an eviction case; or

(3) be represented by an attorney.

(b) ***Representation of a Corporation or Other Entity.*** A corporation or other entity may:

(1) be represented by an employee, owner, officer, or partner of the entity who is not an attorney;

(2) be represented by a property manager or other authorized agent in an eviction case; or

(3) be represented by an attorney.

(c) ***Assisted Representation.*** The court may, for good cause, allow an individual representing himself or herself to be assisted in court by a family member or other individual who is not being compensated.

500.5 Computation of Time; Timely Filing.

(a) ***Computation of Time.*** To compute a time period in these rules:

(1) exclude the day of the event that triggers the period;

(2) count every day, including Saturdays, Sundays, and legal holidays; and

(3) include the last day of the period, but

(A) if the last day is a Saturday, Sunday, or legal holiday, the time period is extended to the next day that is not a Saturday, Sunday, or legal holiday; and

(B) if the last day for filing falls on a day during which the court is closed before 5:00 p.m., the time period is extended to the court's next business day.

(b) ***Timely Filing by Mail.*** Any document required to be filed by a given date is considered timely filed if deposited in the U.S. mail on or before that date, and received within 10 days of the due date. A legible postmark affixed by the United States Postal Service is evidence of the date of mailing.

(c) ***Extensions.*** The judge may, for good cause shown, extend any time period under these rules except those relating to new trial and appeal.

500.6 Judge to Develop the Case. In order to develop the facts of the case, a judge may question a witness or party and may summon any person or party to appear as a witness when the judge considers it necessary to ensure a correct judgment and a speedy disposition.

500.7 Exclusion of Witnesses. The court must, on a party's request, or may, on its own initiative, order witnesses excluded so that they cannot hear the testimony of other witnesses. This rule does not authorize the exclusion of:

(a) a party who is a natural person or the spouse of such natural person;

(b) an officer or employee designated as a representative of a party who is not a natural person; or

(c) a person whose presence is shown by a party to be essential to the presentation of the party's case.

500.8 Subpoenas.

(a) ***Use.*** A subpoena may be used by a party or the judge to command a person or entity to attend and give testimony at a hearing or trial. A person may not be required by subpoena to appear in a county that is more than 150 miles from where the person resides or is served.

(b) ***Who Can Issue.*** A subpoena may be issued by the clerk of the justice court or an attorney authorized to practice in the State of Texas, as an officer of the court.

(c) ***Form.*** Every subpoena must be issued in the name of the "State of Texas" and must:

(1) state the style of the suit and its case number;

(2) state the court in which the suit is pending;

(3) state the date on which the subpoena is issued;

(4) identify the person to whom the subpoena is directed;

(5) state the date, time, place, and nature of the action required by the person to whom the subpoena is directed;

(6) identify the party at whose instance the subpoena is issued, and the party's attorney of record, if any;

(7) state that "Failure by any person without adequate excuse to obey a subpoena served upon that person may be deemed a contempt of court from which the subpoena is issued and may be punished by fine or confinement, or both"; and

(8) be signed by the person issuing the subpoena.

(d) ***Service: Where, by Whom, How.*** A subpoena may be served at any place within the State of Texas by

TRCP 500

any sheriff or constable of the State of Texas, or by any person who is not a party and is 18 years of age or older. A subpoena must be served by delivering a copy to the witness and tendering to that person any fees required by law. If the witness is a party and is represented by an attorney of record in the proceeding, the subpoena may be served on the witness's attorney of record. Proof of service must be made by filing either:

(1) the witness's signed written memorandum attached to the subpoena showing that the witness accepted the subpoena; or

(2) a statement by the person who made the service stating the date, time, and manner of service, and the name of the person served.

(e) ***Compliance Required.*** A person commanded by subpoena to appear and give testimony must remain at the hearing or trial from day to day until discharged by the court or by the party summoning the witness. If a subpoena commanding testimony is directed to a corporation, partnership, association, governmental agency, or other organization, and the matters on which examination is requested are described with reasonable particularity, the organization must designate one or more persons to testify on its behalf as to matters known or reasonably available to the organization.

(f) ***Objection.*** A person commanded to attend and give testimony at a hearing or trial may object or move for a protective order before the court at or before the time and place specified for compliance. A party causing a subpoena to issue must take reasonable steps to avoid imposing undue burden or expense on the person served. In ruling on objections or motions for protection, the court must provide a person served with a subpoena an adequate time for compliance and protection from undue burden or expense. The court may impose reasonable conditions on compliance with a subpoena, including compensating the witness for undue hardship.

(g) ***Enforcement.*** Failure by any person without adequate excuse to obey a subpoena served upon that person may be deemed a contempt of the court from which the subpoena is issued or of a district court in the county in which the subpoena is served, and may be punished by fine or confinement, or both. A fine may not be imposed, nor a person served with a subpoena attached, for failure to comply with a subpoena without proof of service and proof by affidavit of the party requesting the subpoena or the party's attorney of record that all fees due the witness by law were paid or tendered.

500.9 Discovery.

(a) ***Pretrial Discovery.*** Pretrial discovery is limited to that which the judge considers reasonable and necessary. Any requests for pretrial discovery must be presented to the court for approval by written motion. The motion must be served on the responding party. Unless a hearing is requested, the judge may rule on the motion without a hearing. The discovery request must not be served on the responding party unless the judge issues a signed order approving the request. Failure to comply with a discovery order can result in sanctions, including dismissal of the case or an order to pay the other party's discovery expenses.

(b) ***Post-judgment Discovery.*** Post-judgment discovery is not required to be filed with the court. The party requesting discovery must give the responding party at least 30 days to respond to a post-judgment discovery request. The responding party may file a written objection with the court within 30 days of receiving the request. If an objection is filed, the judge must hold a hearing to determine if the request is valid. If the objection is denied, the judge must order the party to respond to the request. If the objection is upheld, the judge may reform the request or dismiss it entirely.

See also CPRC §15.084; Prop. Code §§24.004, 24.0051, 24.011; ***O'Connor's Texas COA***, "Representation," ch. 16-B, §5.1, p. 432; "Unpaid rent," ch. 16-B, §7.6, p. 440; ***O'Connor's Texas Rules***, "Justice Courts," ch. 2-F, §5, p. 172.

TRCP 501. CITATION & SERVICE

501.1 Citation.

(a) ***Issuance.*** When a petition is filed with a justice court to initiate a suit, the clerk must promptly issue a citation and deliver the citation as directed by the plaintiff. The plaintiff is responsible for obtaining service on the defendant of the citation and a copy of the petition with any documents filed with the petition. Upon request, separate or additional citations must be issued by the clerk. The clerk must retain a copy of the citation in the court's file.

(b) ***Form.*** The citation must:

(1) be styled "The State of Texas";

(2) be signed by the clerk under seal of court or by the judge;

(3) contain the name, location, and address of the court;

(4) show the date of filing of the petition;

(5) show the date of issuance of the citation;

(6) show the file number and names of parties;

(7) be directed to the defendant;

(8) show the name and address of attorney for plaintiff, or if the plaintiff does not have an attorney, the address of plaintiff; and

(9) notify defendant that if the defendant fails to file an answer, judgment by default may be rendered for the relief demanded in the petition.

(c) ***Notice.*** The citation must include the following notice to the defendant in boldface type: "You have been sued. You may employ an attorney to help you in defending against this lawsuit. But you are not required to employ an attorney. You or your attorney must file an answer with the court. Your answer is due by the end of the 14th day after the day you were served with these papers. If the 14th day is a Saturday, Sunday, or legal holiday, your answer is due by the end of the first day following the 14th day that is not a Saturday, Sunday, or legal holiday. Do not ignore these papers. If you do not file an answer by the due date, a default judgment may be taken against you. For further information, consult Part V of the Texas Rules of Civil Procedure, which is available online and also at the court listed on this citation."

(d) ***Copies.*** The plaintiff must provide enough copies to be served on each defendant. If the plaintiff fails to do so, the clerk may make copies and charge the plaintiff the allowable copying cost.

16 **501.2 Service of Citation.**

(a) ***Who May Serve.*** No person who is a party to or interested in the outcome of the suit may serve citation in that suit, and, unless otherwise authorized by written court order, only a sheriff or constable may serve a citation in an eviction case, a writ that requires the actual taking of possession of a person, property or thing, or process requiring that an enforcement action be physically enforced by the person delivering the process. Other citations may be served by:

(1) a sheriff or constable;

(2) a process server certified under order of the Supreme Court;

(3) the clerk of the court, if the citation is served by registered or certified mail; or

(4) a person authorized by court order who is 18 years of age or older.

(b) ***Method of Service.*** Citation must be served by:

(1) delivering a copy of the citation with a copy of the petition attached to the defendant in person, after endorsing the date of delivery on the citation; or

(2) mailing a copy of the citation with a copy of the petition attached to the defendant by registered or certified mail, restricted delivery, with return receipt or electronic return receipt requested.

(c) ***Service Fees.*** A plaintiff must pay all fees for service unless the plaintiff has filed a Statement of Inability to Afford Payment of Court Costs with the court. If the plaintiff has filed a Statement, the plaintiff must arrange for the citation to be served by a sheriff, constable, or court clerk.

(d) ***Service on Sunday.*** A citation cannot be served on a Sunday except in attachment, garnishment, sequestration, or distress proceedings.

(e) ***Alternative Service of Citation.*** If the methods under (b) are insufficient to serve the defendant, the plaintiff, or the constable, sheriff, process server certified under order of the Supreme Court, or other person authorized to serve process, may make a request for alternative service. This request must include a sworn statement describing the methods attempted under (b) and stating the defendant's usual place of business or residence, or other place where the defendant can probably be found. The court may authorize the following types of alternative service:

(1) mailing a copy of the citation with a copy of the petition attached by first class mail to the defendant at a specified address, and also leaving a copy of the citation with petition attached at the defendant's residence or other place where the defendant can probably be found with any person found there who is at least 16 years of age; or

(2) mailing a copy of the citation with a copy of the petition attached by first class mail to the defendant at a specified address, and also serving by any other method that the court finds is reasonably likely to provide the defendant with notice of the suit.

(f) ***Service by Publication.*** In the event that service of citation by publication is necessary, the process is governed by the rules in county and district court.

501.3 Duties of Officer or Person Receiving Citation; Return of Service.

(a) ***Endorsement; Execution; Return.*** The officer or authorized person to whom process is delivered must:

(1) endorse on the process the date and hour on which he or she received it;

(2) execute and return the same without delay; and

(3) complete a return of service, which may, but need not, be endorsed on or attached to the citation.

(b) *Contents of Return.* The return, together with any document to which it is attached, must include the following information:

(1) the case number and case name;

(2) the court in which the case is filed;

(3) a description of what was served;

(4) the date and time the process was received for service;

(5) the person or entity served;

(6) the address served;

(7) the date of service or attempted service;

(8) the manner of delivery of service or attempted service;

(9) the name of the person who served or attempted service;

(10) if the person named in (9) is a process server certified under Supreme Court Order, his or her identification number and the expiration date of his or her certification; and

(11) any other information required by rule or law.

(c) *Citation by Mail.* When the citation is served by registered or certified mail as authorized by Rule 501.2(b)(2), the return by the officer or authorized person must also contain the receipt with the addressee's signature.

(d) *Failure to Serve.* When the officer or authorized person has not served the citation, the return must show the diligence used by the officer or authorized person to execute the same and the cause of failure to execute it, and where the defendant is to be found, if ascertainable.

(e) *Signature.* The officer or authorized person who serves or attempts to serve a citation must sign the return. If the return is signed by a person other than a sheriff, constable, or clerk of the court, the return must either be verified or be signed under penalty of perjury. A return signed under penalty of perjury must contain the statement below in substantially the following form:

"My name is ________ (First) ________ (Middle) ________ (Last), my date of birth is ________ (Month) ____ (Day), ____ (Year), and my address is ________ (Street), ________ (City), ________ (State) ________ (Zip Code), ____________ (Country). I declare under penalty of perjury that the foregoing is true and correct.

Executed in ________ County, State of ________, on the ______ day of ______ (Month), ______ (Year).

____
Declarant"

(f) *Alternative Service.* Where citation is executed by an alternative method as authorized by 501.2(e), proof of service must be made in the manner ordered by the court.

(g) *Filing Return.* The return and any document to which it is attached must be filed with the court and may be filed electronically or by fax, if those methods of filing are available.

(h) *Prerequisite for Default Judgment.* No default judgment may be granted in any case until proof of service as provided by this rule, or as ordered by the court in the event citation is executed by an alternative method under 501.2(e), has been on file with the clerk of the court 3 days, exclusive of the day of filing and the day of judgment.

501.4 Service of Papers Other than Citation.

(a) *Method of Service.* Other than a citation or oral motions made during trial or when all parties are present, every notice required by these rules, and every pleading, plea, motion, application to the court for an order, or other form of request, must be served on all other parties in one of the following ways:

(1) *In person.* A copy may be delivered to the party to be served, or the party's duly authorized agent or attorney of record, in person or by agent.

(2) *Mail or courier.* A copy may be sent by courier-receipted delivery or by certified or registered mail, to the party's last known address. Service by certified or registered mail is complete when the document is properly addressed and deposited in the United States mail, postage prepaid.

(3) *Fax.* A copy may be faxed to the recipient's current fax number. Service by fax after 5:00 p.m. local time of the recipient will be deemed to have been served on the following day.

(4) *Email.* A copy may be sent to an email address expressly provided by the receiving party, if the party has consented to email service in writing. Service by email after 5:00 p.m. local time of the recipient will be deemed to have been served on the following day.

(5) *Other.* A copy may be delivered in any other manner directed by the court.

(b) ***Timing.*** If a document is served by mail, 3 days will be added to the length of time a party has to respond to the document. Notice of any hearing requested by a party must be served on all other parties not less than 3 days before the time specified for the hearing.

(c) ***Who May Serve.*** Documents other than a citation may be served by a party to the suit, an attorney of record, a sheriff or constable, or by any other person competent to testify.

(d) ***Certificate of Service.*** The party or the party's attorney of record must include in writing on all documents filed a signed statement describing the manner in which the document was served on the other party or parties and the date of service. A certificate by a party or the party's attorney of record, or the return of the officer, or the sworn statement of any other person showing service of a notice is proof of service.

(e) ***Failure to Serve.*** A party may offer evidence or testimony that a notice or document was not received, or, if service was by mail, that it was not received within 3 days from the date of mailing, and upon so finding, the court may extend the time for taking the action required of the party or grant other relief as it deems just.

TRCP 502. INSTITUTION OF SUIT

502.1 Pleadings and Motions Must Be Written, Signed, and Filed. Except for oral motions made during trial or when all parties are present, every pleading, plea, motion, application to the court for an order, or other form of request must be written and signed by the party or its attorney and must be filed with the court. A document may be filed with the court by personal or commercial delivery, by mail, or electronically, if the court allows electronic filing. Electronic filing is governed by Rule 21.

502.2 Petition.

(a) ***Contents.*** To initiate a lawsuit, a petition must be filed with the court. A petition must contain:

(1) the name of the plaintiff;

(2) the name, address, telephone number, and fax number, if any, of the plaintiff's attorney, if applicable, or the address, telephone number, and fax number, if any, of the plaintiff;

(3) the name, address, and telephone number, if known, of the defendant;

(4) the amount of money, if any, the plaintiff seeks;

(5) a description and claimed value of any personal property the plaintiff seeks;

(6) a description of any other relief requested;

(7) the basis for the plaintiff's claim against the defendant; and

(8) if the plaintiff consents to email service of the answer and any other motions or pleadings, a statement consenting to email service and email contact information.

(b) ***Justice Court Civil Case Information Sheet.*** A justice court civil case information sheet, in the form promulgated by the Supreme Court of Texas, must accompany the filing of a petition and must be signed by the plaintiff or the plaintiff's attorney. The justice court civil case information sheet is for data collection for statistical and administrative purposes and does not affect any substantive right. The court may not reject a pleading because the pleading is not accompanied by a justice court civil case information sheet.

16 **502.3 Fees; Inability to Afford Fees.**

(a) ***Fees and Statement of Inability to Afford Payment of Court Costs.*** On filing the petition, the plaintiff must pay the appropriate filing fee and service fees, if any, with the court. A plaintiff who is unable to afford to pay the fees must file a Statement of Inability to Afford Payment of Court Costs. The Statement must either be sworn to before a notary or made under penalty of perjury. Upon filing the Statement, the clerk must docket the action, issue citation, and provide any other customary services.

(b) ***Supreme Court Form; Contents of Statement.*** The plaintiff must use the form Statement approved by the Supreme Court, or the Statement must include the information required by the Court-approved form. The clerk must make the form available to all persons without charge or request.

(c) ***Certificate of Legal-Aid Provider.*** If the party is represented by an attorney who is providing free legal services because of the party's indigence, without contingency, and the attorney is providing services either directly or by referral from a legal-aid provider described in Rule 145(e)(2), the attorney may file a certificate confirming that the provider screened the party for eligibility under the income and asset guidelines established by the provider. A Statement that is accompanied by the certificate of a legal-aid provider may not be contested under (d).

(d) *Contest.* Unless a certificate is filed under (c), the defendant may file a contest of the Statement at any time within 7 days after the day the defendant's answer is due. If the Statement attests to receipt of government entitlement based on indigence, the Statement may only be contested with regard to the veracity of the attestation. If contested, the judge must hold a hearing to determine the plaintiff's ability to afford the fees. At the hearing, the burden is on the plaintiff to prove the inability to afford fees. The judge may, regardless of whether the defendant contests the Statement, examine the Statement and conduct a hearing to determine the plaintiff's ability to afford fees. If the judge determines that the plaintiff is able to afford the fees, the judge must enter a written order listing the reasons for the determination, and the plaintiff must pay the fees in the time specified in the order or the case will be dismissed without prejudice.

16 **502.4 Venue—Where a Lawsuit May Be Brought.**

(a) *Applicable Law.* Laws specifying the venue—the county and precinct where a lawsuit may be brought—are found in Chapter 15, Subchapter E of the Texas Civil Practice and Remedies Code, which is available online and for examination during the court's business hours.

(b) *General Rule.* Generally, a defendant in a small claims case as described in Rule 500.3(a) or a debt claim case as described in Rule 500.3(b) is entitled to be sued in one of the following venues:

(1) the county and precinct where the defendant resides;

(2) the county and precinct where the incident, or the majority of incidents, that gave rise to the claim occurred;

(3) the county and precinct where the contract or agreement, if any, that gave rise to the claim was to be performed; or

(4) the county and precinct where the property is located, in a suit to recover personal property.

(c) *Non-resident Defendant; Defendant's Residence Unknown.* If the defendant is a non-resident of Texas, or if defendant's residence is unknown, the plaintiff may file the suit in the county and precinct where the plaintiff resides.

(d) *Motion to Transfer Venue.* If a plaintiff files suit in an improper venue, a defendant may challenge the venue selected by filing a motion to transfer venue. The motion must be filed before trial, no later than 21 days after the day the defendant's answer is filed, and must contain a sworn statement that the venue chosen by the plaintiff is improper and a specific county and precinct of proper venue to which transfer is sought. If the defendant fails to name a county and precinct, the court must instruct the defendant to do so and allow the defendant 7 days to cure the defect. If the defendant fails to correct the defect, the motion will be denied, and the case will proceed in the county and precinct where it was originally filed.

(1) *Procedure.*[1]

(A) Judge to Set Hearing. If a defendant files a motion to transfer venue, the judge must set a hearing on the motion.

(B) Response. A plaintiff may file a response to a defendant's motion to transfer venue.

(C) Hearing. The parties may present evidence at the hearing. A witness may testify at a hearing, either in person or, with permission of the court, by means of telephone or an electronic communication system.

(D) Judge's Decision. If the motion is granted, the judge must sign an order designating the court to which the case will be transferred. If the motion is denied, the case will be heard in the court in which the plaintiff initially filed suit.

(E) Review. Motions for rehearing and interlocutory appeals of the judge's ruling on venue are not permitted.

(F) Time for Trial of the Case. No trial may be held until at least the 14th day after the judge's ruling on the motion to transfer venue.

(G) Order. An order granting a motion to transfer venue must state the reason for the transfer and the name of the court to which the transfer is made. When such an order of transfer is made, the judge who issued the order must immediately make out a true and correct transcript of all the entries made on the docket in the case, certify the transcript, and send the transcript, with a certified copy of the bill of costs and the original papers in the case, to the court in the precinct to which the case has been transferred. The court receiving the case must then notify the plaintiff that the case has been received and, if the case is transferred to a different county, that the plaintiff has 14 days after receiving the notice to pay the filing fee in the new court, or file a Statement of Inability to Afford Payment of Court Costs.

The plaintiff is not entitled to a refund of any fees already paid. Failure to pay the fee or file a Statement will result in dismissal of the case without prejudice.

(e) ***Fair Trial Venue Change.*** If a party believes it cannot get a fair trial in a specific precinct or before a specific judge, the party may file a sworn motion stating such, supported by the sworn statements of two other credible persons, and specifying if the party is requesting a change of location or a change of judge. Except for good cause shown, this motion must be filed no less than 7 days before trial. If the party seeks a change of judge, the judge must exchange benches with another qualified justice of the peace, or if no judge is available to exchange benches, the county judge must appoint a visiting judge to hear the case. If the party seeks a change in location, the case must be transferred to the nearest justice court in the county that is not subject to the same or some other disqualification. If there is only one justice of the peace precinct in the county, then the judge must exchange benches with another qualified justice of the peace, or if no judge is available to exchange benches, the county judge must appoint a visiting judge to hear the case. In cases where exclusive jurisdiction is within a specific precinct, as in eviction cases, the only remedy available is a change of judge. A party may apply for relief under this rule only one time in any given lawsuit.

(f) ***Transfer of Venue by Consent.*** On the written consent of all parties or their attorneys, filed with the court, venue must be transferred to the court of any other justice of the peace of the county, or any other county.

502.5 Answer.

(a) ***Requirements.*** A defendant must file with the court a written answer to a lawsuit as directed by the citation and must also serve a copy of the answer on the plaintiff. The answer must contain:

(1) the name of the defendant;

(2) the name, address, telephone number, and fax number, if any, of the defendant's attorney, if applicable, or the address, telephone number, and fax number, if any, of the defendant; and

(3) if the defendant consents to email service, a statement consenting to email service and email contact information.

(b) ***General Denial.*** An answer that denies all of the plaintiff's allegations without specifying the reasons is sufficient to constitute an answer or appearance and does not bar the defendant from raising any defense at trial.

(c) ***Answer Docketed.*** The defendant's appearance must be noted on the court's docket.

(d) ***Due Date.*** Unless the defendant is served by publication, the defendant's answer is due by the end of the 14th day after the day the defendant was served with the citation and petition, but

(1) if the 14th day is a Saturday, Sunday, or legal holiday, the answer is due on the next day that is not a Saturday, Sunday, or legal holiday; and

(2) if the 14th day falls on a day during which the court is closed before 5:00 p.m., the answer is due on the court's next business day.

(e) ***Due Date When Defendant Served by Publication.*** If a defendant is served by publication, the defendant's answer is due by the end of the 42nd day after the day the citation was issued, but

(1) if the 42nd day is a Saturday, Sunday, or legal holiday, the answer is due on the next day that is not a Saturday, Sunday, or legal holiday; and

(2) if the 42nd day falls on a day during which the court is closed before 5:00 p.m., the answer is due on the court's next business day.

16 502.6 Counterclaim; Cross-Claim; Third Party Claim.

(a) ***Counterclaim.*** A defendant may file a petition stating as a counterclaim any claim against a plaintiff that is within the jurisdiction of the justice court, whether or not related to the claims in the plaintiff's petition. The defendant must file a counterclaim petition as provided in Rule 502.2, and must pay a filing fee or provide a Statement of Inability to Afford Payment of Court Costs. The court need not generate a citation for a counterclaim and no answer to the counterclaim need be filed. The defendant must serve a copy of the counterclaim as provided by Rule 501.4.

(b) ***Cross-Claim.*** A plaintiff seeking relief against another plaintiff, or a defendant seeking relief against another defendant may file a cross-claim. The filing party must file a cross-claim petition as provided in Rule 502.2, and must pay a filing fee or provide a Statement of Inability to Afford Payment of Court Costs. A citation must be issued and served as provided by Rule 501.2 on any party that has not yet filed a petition or an answer, as appropriate. If the party filed against has

filed a petition or an answer, the filing party must serve the cross-claim as provided by Rule 501.4.

(c) ***Third Party Claim.*** A defendant seeking to bring another party into a lawsuit who may be liable for all or part of the plaintiff's claim against the defendant may file a petition as provided in Rule 502.2, and must pay a filing fee or provide a Statement of Inability to Afford Payment of Court Costs. A citation must be issued and served as provided by Rule 501.2.

502.7 Amending and Clarifying Pleadings.

(a) ***Amending Pleadings.*** A party may withdraw something from or add something to a pleading, as long as the amended pleading is filed and served as provided by Rule 501.4 not less than 7 days before trial. The court may allow a pleading to be amended less than 7 days before trial if the amendment will not operate as a surprise to the opposing party.

(b) ***Insufficient Pleadings.*** A party may file a motion with the court asking that another party be required to clarify a pleading. The court must determine if the pleading is sufficient to place all parties on notice of the issues in the lawsuit, and may hold a hearing to make that determination. If the court determines a pleading is insufficient, the court must order the party to amend the pleading and set a date by which the party must amend. If a party fails to comply with the court's order, the pleading may be stricken.

1. **Editor's note:** Rule 502.4 does not include a subsection (d)(2). See *O'Connor's Texas Forms*, FORM 1B:17.

TRCP 503. DEFAULT JUDGMENT; PRE-TRIAL MATTERS; TRIAL

503.1 If Defendant Fails to Answer.

(a) ***Default Judgment.*** If the defendant fails to file an answer by the date stated in Rule 502.5, the judge must ensure that service was proper, and may hold a hearing for this purpose. If it is determined that service was proper, the judge must render a default judgment in the following manner:

(1) *Claim Based on Written Document.* If the claim is based on a written document signed by the defendant, and a copy of the document has been filed with the court and served on the defendant, along with a sworn statement from the plaintiff that this is a true and accurate copy of the document and the relief sought is owed, and all payments, offsets or credits due to the defendant have been accounted for, the judge must render judgment for the plaintiff in the requested amount, without any necessity for a hearing. The plaintiff's attorney may also submit affidavits supporting an award of attorney fees to which the plaintiff is entitled, if any.

(2) *Other Cases.* Except as provided in (1), a plaintiff who seeks a default judgment against a defendant must request a hearing, orally or in writing. The plaintiff must appear at the hearing and provide evidence of its damages. If the plaintiff proves its damages, the judge must render judgment for the plaintiff in the amount proven. If the plaintiff is unable to prove its damages, the judge must render judgment in favor of the defendant. With the permission of the court, a party may appear at a hearing by means of telephone or an electronic communication system.

(b) ***Appearance.*** If a defendant files an answer or otherwise appears in a case before a default judgment is signed by the judge, the judge must not enter a default judgment and the case must be set for trial as described in Rule 503.3.

(c) ***Post-answer Default.*** If a defendant who has answered fails to appear for trial, the court may proceed to hear evidence on liability and damages and render judgment accordingly.

(d) ***Notice.*** The plaintiff requesting a default judgment must provide to the clerk in writing the last known mailing address of the defendant at or before the time the judgment is signed. When a default judgment is signed, the clerk must immediately mail written notice of the judgment to the defendant at the address provided by the plaintiff, and note the fact of such mailing on the docket. The notice must state the number and style of the case, the court in which the case is pending, the names of the parties in whose favor and against whom the judgment was rendered, and the date the judgment was signed. Failure to comply with the provisions of this rule does not affect the finality of the judgment.

503.2 Summary Disposition.

(a) ***Motion.*** A party may file a sworn motion for summary disposition of all or part of a claim or defense without a trial. The motion must set out all supporting facts. All documents on which the motion relies must be attached. The motion must be granted if it shows that:

(1) there are no genuinely disputed facts that would prevent a judgment in favor of the party;

TRCP 503

(2) there is no evidence of one or more essential elements of a defense which the defendant must prove to defeat the plaintiff's claim; or

(3) there is no evidence of one or more essential elements of the plaintiff's claim.

(b) *Response.* The party opposing the motion may file a sworn written response to the motion.

(c) *Hearing.* The court must not consider a motion for summary disposition until it has been on file for at least 14 days. The judge may consider evidence offered by the parties at the hearing. By agreement of the parties, the judge may decide the motion and response without a hearing.

(d) *Order.* The judge may enter judgment as to the entire case or may specify the facts that are established and direct such further proceedings in the case as are just.

503.3 Settings and Notice; Postponing Trial.

(a) *Settings and Notice.* After the defendant answers, the case will be set on a trial docket at the discretion of the judge. The court must send a notice of the date, time, and place of this setting to all parties at their address of record no less than 45 days before the setting date, unless the judge determines that an earlier setting is required in the interest of justice. Reasonable notice of all subsequent settings must be sent to all parties at their addresses of record.

(b) *Postponing Trial.* A party may file a motion requesting that the trial be postponed. The motion must state why a postponement is necessary. The judge, for good cause, may postpone any trial for a reasonable time.

503.4 Pretrial Conference.

(a) *Conference Set; Issues.* If all parties have appeared in a lawsuit, the court, at any party's request or on its own, may set a case for a pretrial conference. Reasonable notice must be sent to all parties at their addresses of record. Appropriate issues for the pretrial conference include:

(1) discovery;

(2) the amendment or clarification of pleadings;

(3) the admission of facts and documents to streamline the trial process;

(4) a limitation on the number of witnesses at trial;

(5) the identification of facts, if any, which are not in dispute between the parties;

(6) mediation or other alternative dispute resolution services;

(7) the possibility of settlement;

(8) trial setting dates that are amenable to the court and all parties;

(9) the appointment of interpreters, if needed;

(10) the application of a Rule of Civil Procedure not in Part V or a Rule of Evidence; and

(11) any other issue that the court deems appropriate.

(b) *Eviction Cases.* The court must not schedule a pretrial conference in an eviction case if it would delay trial.

503.5 Alternative Dispute Resolution.

(a) *State Policy.* The policy of this state is to encourage the peaceable resolution of disputes through alternative dispute resolution, including mediation, and the early settlement of pending litigation through voluntary settlement procedures. For that purpose, the judge may order any case to mediation or another appropriate and generally accepted alternative dispute resolution process.

(b) *Eviction Cases.* The court must not order mediation or any other alternative dispute resolution process in an eviction case if it would delay trial.

503.6 Trial.

(a) *Docket Called.* On the day of the trial setting, the judge must call all of the cases set for trial that day.

(b) *If Plaintiff Fails to Appear.* If the plaintiff fails to appear when the case is called for trial, the judge may postpone or dismiss the suit.

(c) *If Defendant Fails to Appear.* If the defendant fails to appear when the case is called for trial, the judge may postpone the case, or may proceed to take evidence. If the plaintiff proves its case, judgment must be awarded for the relief proven. If the plaintiff fails to prove its case, judgment must be rendered against the plaintiff.

TRCP 504. JURY

16 **504.1 Jury Trial Demanded.**

(a) *Demand.* Any party is entitled to a trial by jury. A written demand for a jury must be filed no later than 14 days before the date a case is set for trial. If the demand is not timely, the right to a jury is waived unless the late filing is excused by the judge for good cause.

(b) ***Jury Fee.*** Unless otherwise provided by law, a party demanding a jury must pay a fee of $22.00 or must file a Statement of Inability to Afford Payment of Court Costs at or before the time the party files a written request for a jury.

(c) ***Withdrawal of Demand.*** If a party who demands a jury and pays the fee withdraws the demand, the case will remain on the jury docket unless all other parties present agree to try the case without a jury. A party that withdraws its jury demand is not entitled to a refund of the jury fee.

(d) ***No Demand.*** If no party timely demands a jury and pays the fee, the judge will try the case without a jury.

504.2 Empaneling the Jury.

(a) ***Drawing Jury and Oath.*** If no method of electronic draw has been implemented, the judge must write the names of all prospective jurors present on separate slips of paper as nearly alike as may be, place them in a box, mix them well, and then draw the names one by one from the box. The judge must list the names drawn and deliver a copy to each of the parties or their attorneys.

(b) ***Oath.*** After the draw, the judge must swear the panel as follows: "You solemnly swear or affirm that you will give true and correct answers to all questions asked of you concerning your qualifications as a juror."

(c) ***Questioning the Jury.*** The judge, the parties, or their attorneys will be allowed to question jurors as to their ability to serve impartially in the trial but may not ask the jurors how they will rule in the case. The judge will have discretion to allow or disallow specific questions and determine the amount of time each side will have for this process.

(d) ***Challenge for Cause.*** A party may challenge any juror for cause. A challenge for cause is an objection made to a juror alleging some fact, such as a bias or prejudice, that disqualifies the juror from serving in the case or that renders the juror unfit to sit on the jury. The challenge must be made during jury questioning. The party must explain to the judge why the juror should be excluded from the jury. The judge must evaluate the questions and answers given and either grant or deny the challenge. When a challenge for cause has been sustained, the juror must be excused.

(e) ***Challenges Not for Cause.*** After the judge determines any challenges for cause, each party may select up to 3 jurors to excuse for any reason or no reason at all. But no prospective juror may be excused for membership in a constitutionally protected class.

(f) ***The Jury.*** After all challenges, the first 6 prospective jurors remaining on the list constitute the jury to try the case.

(g) ***If Jury Is Incomplete.*** If challenges reduce the number of prospective jurors below 6, the judge may direct the sheriff or constable to summon others and allow them to be questioned and challenged by the parties as before, until at least 6 remain.

(h) ***Jury Sworn.*** When the jury has been selected, the judge must require them to take substantially the following oath: "You solemnly swear or affirm that you will render a true verdict according to the law and the evidence presented."

504.3 Jury Not Charged. The judge must not charge the jury.

504.4 Jury Verdict for Specific Articles. When the suit is for the recovery of specific articles and the jury finds for the plaintiff, the jury must assess the value of each article separately, according to the evidence presented at trial.

TRCP 505. JUDGMENT; NEW TRIAL

505.1 Judgment.

(a) ***Judgment upon Jury Verdict.*** Where a jury has returned a verdict, the judge must announce the verdict in open court, note it in the court's docket, and render judgment accordingly. The judge may render judgment on the verdict or, if the verdict is contrary to the law or the evidence, judgment notwithstanding the verdict.

(b) ***Case Tried by Judge.*** When a case has been tried before the judge without a jury, the judge must announce the decision in open court, note the decision in the court's docket, and render judgment accordingly.

(c) ***Form.*** A judgment must:

(1) clearly state the determination of the rights of the parties in the case;

(2) state who must pay the costs;

(3) be signed by the judge; and

(4) be dated the date of the judge's signature.

(d) ***Costs.*** The judge must award costs allowed by law to the successful party.

(e) ***Judgment for Specific Articles.*** Where the judgment is for the recovery of specific articles, the

judgment must order that the plaintiff recover such specific articles, if they can be found, and if not, then their value as assessed by the judge or jury with interest at the prevailing post-judgment interest rate.

505.2 Enforcement of Judgment. Justice court judgments are enforceable in the same method as in county and district court, except as provided by law. When the judgment is for personal property, the court may award a special writ for the seizure and delivery of such property to the plaintiff, and may, in addition to the other relief granted in such cases, enforce its judgment by attachment or fine.

505.3 Motion to Set Aside; Motion to Reinstate; Motion for New Trial.

(a) *Motion to Reinstate after Dismissal.* A plaintiff whose case is dismissed may file a motion to reinstate the case no later than 14 days after the dismissal order is signed. The plaintiff must serve the defendant with a copy of the motion no later than the next business day using a method approved under Rule 501.4. The court may reinstate the case for good cause shown.

(b) *Motion to Set Aside Default.* A defendant against whom a default judgment is granted may file a motion to set aside the judgment no later than 14 days after the judgment is signed. The defendant must serve the plaintiff with a copy of the motion no later than the next business day using a method approved under Rule 501.4. The court may set aside the judgment and set the case for trial for good cause shown.

(c) *Motion for New Trial.* A party may file a motion for a new trial no later than 14 days after the judgment is signed. The party must serve all other parties with a copy of the motion no later than the next business day using a method approved under Rule 501.4. The judge may grant a new trial upon a showing that justice was not done in the trial of the case. Only one new trial may be granted to either party.

(d) *Motion Not Required.* Failure to file a motion under this rule does not affect a party's right to appeal the underlying judgment.

(e) *Motion Denied as a Matter of Law.* If the judge has not ruled on a motion to set aside, motion to reinstate, or motion for new trial, the motion is automatically denied at 5:00 p.m. on the 21st day after the day the judgment was signed.

TRCP 506. APPEAL

16 **506.1 Appeal.**

(a) *How Taken; Time.* A party may appeal a judgment by filing a bond, making a cash deposit, or filing a Statement of Inability to Afford Payment of Court Costs with the justice court within 21 days after the judgment is signed or the motion to reinstate, motion to set aside, or motion for new trial, if any, is denied.

(b) *Amount of Bond; Sureties; Terms.* A plaintiff must file a $500 bond. A defendant must file a bond in an amount equal to twice the amount of the judgment. The bond must be supported by a surety or sureties approved by the judge. The bond must be payable to the appellee and must be conditioned on the appellant's prosecution of its appeal to effect and payment of any judgment and all costs rendered against it on appeal.

(c) *Cash Deposit in Lieu of Bond.* In lieu of filing a bond, an appellant may deposit with the clerk of the court cash in the amount required of the bond. The deposit must be payable to the appellee and must be conditioned on the appellant's prosecution of its appeal to effect and payment of any judgment and all costs rendered against it on appeal.

(d) *Statement of Inability to Afford Payment of Court Costs.*

(1) *Filing.* An appellant who cannot furnish a bond or pay a cash deposit in the amount required may instead file a Statement of Inability to Afford Payment of Court Costs. The Statement must be on the form approved by the Supreme Court or include the information required by the Court-approved form and may be the same one that was filed with the petition.

(2) *Contest.* The Statement may be contested as provided in Rule 502.3(d) within 7 days after the opposing party receives notice that the Statement was filed.

(3) *Appeal If Contest Sustained.* If the contest is sustained, the appellant may appeal that decision by filing notice with the justice court within 7 days of that court's written order. The justice court must then forward all related documents to the county court for resolution. The county court must set the matter for hearing within 14 days and hear the contest de novo, as if there had been no previous hearing, and if the appeal is granted, must direct the justice court to transmit to the clerk of the county court the transcript, records, and papers of the case, as provided in these rules.

(4) *If No Appeal or If Appeal Overruled.* If the appellant does not appeal the ruling sustaining the con-

test, or if the county court denies the appeal, the appellant may, within five days, post an appeal bond or make a cash deposit in compliance with this rule.

(e) ***Notice to Other Parties Required.*** If a Statement of Inability to Afford Payment of Court Costs is filed, the court must provide notice to all other parties that the Statement was filed no later than the next business day. Within 7 days of filing a bond or making a cash deposit, an appellant must serve written notice of the appeal on all other parties using a method approved under Rule 501.4.

(f) ***No Default on Appeal Without Compliance with Rule.*** The county court to which an appeal is taken must not render default judgment against any party without first determining that the appellant has fully complied with this rule.

(g) ***No Dismissal of Appeal Without Opportunity for Correction.*** An appeal must not be dismissed for defects or irregularities in procedure, either of form or substance, without allowing the appellant, after 7 days' notice from the court, the opportunity to correct such defect.

(h) ***Appeal Perfected.*** An appeal is perfected when a bond, cash deposit, or Statement of Inability to Afford Payment of Court Costs is filed in accordance with this rule.

(i) ***Costs.*** The appellant must pay the costs on appeal to a county court in accordance with Rule 143a.

506.2 Record on Appeal. When an appeal has been perfected from the justice court, the judge must immediately send to the clerk of the county court a certified copy of all docket entries, a certified copy of the bill of costs, and the original papers in the case.

506.3 Trial De Novo. The case must be tried de novo in the county court. A trial de novo is a new trial in which the entire case is presented as if there had been no previous trial.

16 **506.4 Writ of Certiorari.**

(a) ***Application.*** Except in eviction cases, after final judgment in a case tried in justice court, a party may apply to the county court for a writ of certiorari.

(b) ***Grounds.*** An application must be granted only if it contains a sworn statement setting forth facts showing that either:

(1) the justice court did not have jurisdiction; or

(2) the final determination of the suit worked an injustice to the applicant that was not caused by the applicant's own inexcusable neglect.

(c) ***Bond, Cash Deposit, or Sworn Statement of Indigency to Pay Required.*** If the application is granted, a writ of certiorari must not issue until the applicant has filed a bond, made a cash deposit, or filed a Statement of Inability to Afford Payment of Court Costs that complies with Rule 145.

(d) ***Time for Filing.*** An application for writ of certiorari must be filed within 90 days after the date the final judgment is signed.

(e) ***Contents of Writ.*** The writ of certiorari must command the justice court to immediately make and certify a copy of the entries in the case on the docket, and immediately transmit the transcript of the proceedings in the justice court, together with the original papers and a bill of costs, to the proper court.

(f) ***Clerk to Issue Writ and Citation.*** When the application is granted and the bond, cash deposit, or Statement of Inability to Afford Payment of Court Costs has been filed, the clerk must issue a writ of certiorari to the justice court and citation to the adverse party.

(g) ***Stay of Proceedings.*** When the writ of certiorari is served on the justice court, the court must stay further proceedings on the judgment and comply with the writ.

(h) ***Cause Docketed.*** The action must be docketed in the name of the original plaintiff, as plaintiff, and of the original defendant, as defendant.

(i) ***Motion to Dismiss.*** Within 30 days after the service of citation on the writ of certiorari, the adverse party may move to dismiss the certiorari for want of sufficient cause appearing in the affidavit, or for want of sufficient bond. If the certiorari is dismissed, the judgment must direct the justice court to proceed with the execution of the judgment below.

(j) ***Amendment of Bond or Oath.*** The affidavit or bond may be amended at the discretion of the court in which it is filed.

(k) ***Trial De Novo.*** The case must be tried de novo in the county court and judgment must be rendered as in cases appealed from justice courts. A trial de novo is a new trial in which the entire case is presented as if there had been no previous trial.

TRCP 507. ADMINISTRATIVE RULES FOR JUDGES & COURT PERSONNEL

507.1 Plenary Power. A justice court loses plenary power over a case when an appeal is perfected or if no appeal is perfected, 21 days after the later of the date judgment is signed or the date a motion to set aside, motion to reinstate, or motion for new trial, if any, is denied.

507.2 Forms. The court may provide forms to enable a party to file documents that comply with these rules. No party may be forced to use the court's forms.

507.3 Docket and Other Records.

(a) ***Docket.*** Each judge must keep a civil docket in a permanent record containing the following information:

(1) the title of all suits commenced before the court;

(2) the date when the first process was issued against the defendant, when returnable, and the nature of that process;

(3) the date when the parties, or either of them, appeared before the court, either with or without a citation;

(4) a description of the petition and any documents filed with the petition;

(5) every adjournment, stating at whose request and to what time;

(6) the date of the trial, stating whether the same was by a jury or by the judge;

(7) the verdict of the jury, if any;

(8) the judgment signed by the judge and the date the judgment was signed;

(9) all applications for setting aside judgments or granting new trials and the orders of the judge thereon, with the date;

(10) the date of issuing execution, to whom directed and delivered, and the amount of debt, damages and costs and, when any execution is returned, the date of the return and the manner in which it was executed; and

(11) all stays and appeals that may be taken, and the date when taken, the amount of the bond and the names of the sureties.

(b) ***Other Records.*** The judge must also keep copies of all documents filed; other dockets, books, and records as may be required by law or these rules; and a fee book in which all costs accruing in every suit commenced before the court are taxed.

(c) ***Form of Records.*** All records required to be kept under this rule may be maintained electronically.

507.4 Issuance of Writs. Every writ from the justice courts must be in writing and be issued and signed by the judge officially. The style thereof must be "The State of Texas." It must, except where otherwise specially provided by law or these rules, be directed to the person or party upon whom it is to be served, be made returnable to the court, and note the date of its issuance.

TRCP 508. DEBT CLAIM CASES

508.1 Application. Rule 508 applies to a claim for the recovery of a debt brought by an assignee of a claim, a financial institution, a debt collector or collection agency, or a person or entity primarily engaged in the business of lending money at interest.

508.2 Petition.[1]

(a) ***Contents.*** In addition to the information required by Rule 502.2, a petition filed in a lawsuit governed by this rule must contain the following information:

(1) *Credit Accounts.* In a claim based upon a credit card, revolving credit, or open account, the petition must state:

(A) the account name or credit card name;

(B) the account number (which may be masked);

(C) the date of issue or origination of the account, if known;

(D) the date of charge-off or breach of the account, if known;

(E) the amount owed as of a date certain; and

(F) whether the plaintiff seeks ongoing interest.

(2) *Personal and Business Loans.* In a claim based upon a promissory note or other promise to pay a specific amount as of a date certain, the petition must state:

(A) the date and amount of the original loan;

(B) whether the repayment of the debt was accelerated, if known;

(C) the date final payment was due;

(D) the amount due as of the final payment date;

(E) the amount owed as of a date certain; and

(F) whether plaintiff seeks ongoing interest.

(3) *Ongoing Interest.* If a plaintiff seeks ongoing interest, the petition must state:

(A) the effective interest rate claimed;

(B) whether the interest rate is based upon contract or statute; and

(C) the dollar amount of interest claimed as of a date certain.

(4) *Assigned Debt.* If the debt that is the subject of the claim has been assigned or transferred, the petition must state:

(A) that the debt claim has been transferred or assigned;

(B) the date of the transfer or assignment;

(C) the name of any prior holders of the debt; and

(D) the name or a description of the original creditor.

508.3 Default Judgment.

(a) ***Generally.*** If the defendant does not file an answer to a claim by the answer date or otherwise appear in the case, the judge must promptly render a default judgment upon the plaintiff's proof of the amount of damages.

(b) ***Proof of the Amount of Damages.***

(1) *Evidence Must Be Served or Submitted.* Evidence of plaintiff's damages must either be attached to the petition and served on the defendant or submitted to the court after defendant's failure to answer by the answer date.

(2) *Form of Evidence.* Evidence of plaintiff's damages may be offered in a sworn statement or in live testimony. The evidence offered may include documentary evidence.

(3) *Establishment of the Amount of Damages.* The amount of damages is established by evidence:

(A) that the account or loan was issued to the defendant and the defendant is obligated to pay it;

(B) that the account was closed or the defendant breached the terms of the account or loan agreement;

(C) of the amount due on the account or loan as of a date certain after all payment credits and offsets have been applied; and

(D) that the plaintiff owns the account or loan and, if applicable, how the plaintiff acquired the account or loan.

(4) *Documentary Evidence Offered by Sworn Statement.* Documentary evidence may be considered if it is attached to a sworn statement made by the plaintiff or its representative, a prior holder of the debt or its representative, or the original creditor or its representative, that attests to the following:

(A) the documents were kept in the regular course of business;

(B) it was the regular course of business for an employee or representative with knowledge of the act recorded to make the record or to transmit information to be included in such record;

(C) the documents were created at or near the time or reasonably soon thereafter; and

(D) the documents attached are the original or exact duplicates of the original.

(5) *Consideration of Sworn Statement.* A judge is not required to accept a sworn statement if the source of information or the method or circumstances of preparation indicate lack of trustworthiness. But a judge may not reject a sworn statement only because it is not made by the original creditor or because the documents attested to were created by a third party and subsequently incorporated into and relied upon by the business of the plaintiff.

(c) ***Hearing.*** The judge may enter a default judgment without a hearing if the plaintiff submits sufficient written evidence of its damages and should do so to avoid undue expense and delay. Otherwise, the plaintiff may request a default judgment hearing at which the plaintiff must appear, in person or by telephonic or electronic means, and prove its damages. If the plaintiff proves its damages, the judge must render judgment for the plaintiff in the amount proven. If the plaintiff is unable to prove its damages, the judge must render judgment in favor of the defendant.

(d) ***Appearance.*** If the defendant files an answer or otherwise appears in a case before a default judgment is signed by the judge, the judge must not render a default judgment and must set the case for trial.

(e) ***Post-answer Default.*** If a defendant who has answered fails to appear for trial, the court may proceed to hear evidence on liability and damages and render judgment accordingly.

1. **Editor's note**: Rule 508.2 does not include a subsection (b). *See* Tex. Sup.Ct. Order, Misc. Docket No. 13-9049 (eff. Aug. 31, 2013).

TRCP 509. REPAIR & REMEDY CASES

509.1 Applicability of Rule. Rule 509 applies to a lawsuit filed in a justice court by a residential tenant

under Chapter 92, Subchapter B of the Texas Property Code to enforce the landlord's duty to repair or remedy a condition materially affecting the physical health or safety of an ordinary tenant.

509.2 Contents of Petition; Copies; Forms and Amendments.

(a) ***Contents of Petition.*** The petition must be in writing and must include the following:

(1) the street address of the residential rental property;

(2) a statement indicating whether the tenant has received in writing the name and business street address of the landlord and landlord's management company;

(3) to the extent known and applicable, the name, business street address, and telephone number of the landlord and the landlord's management company, on-premises manager, and rent collector serving the residential rental property;

(4) for all notices the tenant gave to the landlord requesting that the condition be repaired or remedied:

(A) the date of the notice;

(B) the name of the person to whom the notice was given or the place where the notice was given;

(C) whether the tenant's lease is in writing and requires written notice;

(D) whether the notice was in writing or oral;

(E) whether any written notice was given by certified mail, return receipt requested, or by registered mail; and

(F) whether the rent was current or had been timely tendered at the time notice was given;

(5) a description of the property condition materially affecting the physical health or safety of an ordinary tenant that the tenant seeks to have repaired or remedied;

(6) a statement of the relief requested by the tenant, including an order to repair or remedy a condition, a reduction in rent, actual damages, civil penalties, attorney's fees, and court costs;

(7) if the petition includes a request to reduce the rent:

(A) the amount of rent paid by the tenant, the amount of rent paid by the government, if known, the rental period, and when the rent is due; and

(B) the amount of the requested rent reduction and the date it should begin;

(8) a statement that the total relief requested does not exceed $10,000, excluding interest and court costs but including attorney's fees; and

(9) the tenant's name, address, and telephone number.

(b) ***Copies.*** The tenant must provide the court with copies of the petition and any attachments to the petition for service on the landlord.

(c) ***Forms and Amendments.*** A petition substantially in the form promulgated by the Supreme Court is sufficient. A suit may not be dismissed for a defect in the petition unless the tenant is given an opportunity to correct the defect and does not promptly correct it.

509.3 Citation: Issuance; Appearance Date; Answer.

(a) ***Issuance.*** When the tenant files a written petition with a justice court, the judge must immediately issue citation directed to the landlord, commanding the landlord to appear before such judge at the time and place named in the citation.

(b) ***Appearance Date; Answer.*** The appearance date on the citation must not be less than 10 days nor more than 21 days after the petition is filed. For purposes of this rule, the appearance date on the citation is the trial date. The landlord may, but is not required to, file a written answer on or before the appearance date.

509.4 Service and Return of Citation; Alternative Service of Citation.

(a) ***Service and Return of Citation.*** The sheriff, constable, or other person authorized by Rule 501.2 who receives the citation must serve the citation by delivering a copy of it, along with a copy of the petition and any attachments, to the landlord at least 6 days before the appearance date. At least one day before the appearance date, the person serving the citation must file a return of service with the court that issued the citation. The citation must be issued, served, and returned in like manner as ordinary citations issued from a justice court.

(b) ***Alternative Service of Citation.***

(1) If the petition does not include the landlord's name and business street address, or if, after making diligent efforts on at least two occasions, the officer or authorized person is unsuccessful in serving the citation on the landlord under (a), the officer or authorized

person must serve the citation by delivering a copy of the citation, petition, and any attachments to:

(A) the landlord's management company if the tenant has received written notice of the name and business street address of the landlord's management company; or

(B) if (b)(1)(A) does not apply and the tenant has not received the landlord's name and business street address in writing, the landlord's authorized agent for service of process, which may be the landlord's management company, on-premise manager, or rent collector serving the residential rental property.

(2) If the officer or authorized person is unsuccessful in serving citation under (b)(1) after making diligent efforts on at least two occasions at either the business street address of the landlord's management company, if (b)(1)(A) applies, or at each available business street address of the landlord's authorized agent for service of process, if (b)(1)(B) applies, the officer or authorized person must execute and file in the justice court a sworn statement that the officer or authorized person made diligent efforts to serve the citation on at least two occasions at all available business street addresses of the landlord and, to the extent applicable, the landlord's management company, on-premises manager, and rent collector serving the residential rental property, providing the times, dates, and places of each attempted service. The judge may then authorize the officer or authorized person to serve citation by:

(A) delivering a copy of the citation, petition, and any attachments to someone over the age of 16 years, at any business street address listed in the petition, or, if nobody answers the door at a business street address, either placing the citation, petition, and any attachments through a door mail chute or slipping them under the front door, and if neither of these latter methods is practical, affixing the citation, petition, and any attachments to the front door or main entry to the business street address;

(B) within 24 hours of complying with (b)(2)(A), sending by first class mail a true copy of the citation, petition, and any attachments addressed to the landlord at the landlord's business street address provided in the petition; and

(C) noting on the return of the citation the date of delivery under (b)(2)(A) and the date of mailing under (b)(2)(B).

The delivery and mailing to the business street address under (b)(2)(A)-(B) must occur at least 6 days before the appearance date. At least one day before the appearance date, a return of service must be completed and filed in accordance with Rule 501.3 with the court that issued the citation. It is not necessary for the tenant to request the alternative service authorized by this rule.

509.5 Docketing and Trial; Failure to Appear.

(a) ***Docketing and Trial.*** The case must be docketed and tried as other cases. The judge may develop the facts of the case in order to ensure justice.

(b) ***Failure to Appear.***

(1) If the tenant appears at trial and the landlord has been duly served and fails to appear at trial, the judge may proceed to hear evidence. If the tenant establishes that the tenant is entitled to recover, the judge must render judgment against the landlord in accordance with the evidence.

(2) If the tenant fails to appear for trial, the judge may dismiss the lawsuit.

509.6 Judgment: Amount; Form and Content; Issuance and Service; Failure to Comply.

(a) ***Amount.*** Judgment may be rendered against the landlord for failure to repair or remedy a condition at the residential rental property if the total judgment does not exceed $10,000, excluding interest and court costs but including attorney's fees. Any party who prevails in a lawsuit brought under these rules may recover the party's court costs and reasonable attorney's fees as allowed by law.

(b) ***Form and Content.***

(1) The judgment must be in writing, signed, and dated and must include the names of the parties to the proceeding and the street address of the residential rental property where the condition is to be repaired or remedied.

(2) In the judgment, the judge may:

(A) order the landlord to take reasonable action to repair or remedy the condition;

(B) order a reduction in the tenant's rent, from the date of the first repair notice, in proportion to the reduced rental value resulting from the condition until the condition is repaired or remedied;

(C) award a civil penalty of one month's rent plus $500;

(D) award the tenant's actual damages; and

(E) award court costs and attorney's fees, excluding any attorney's fees for a claim for damages relating to a personal injury.

(3) If the judge orders the landlord to repair or remedy a condition, the judgment must include in reasonable detail the actions the landlord must take to repair or remedy the condition and the date when the repair or remedy must be completed.

(4) If the judge orders a reduction in the tenant's rent, the judgment must state:

(A) the amount of the rent the tenant must pay, if any;

(B) the frequency with which the tenant must pay the rent;

(C) the condition justifying the reduction of rent;

(D) the effective date of the order reducing rent;

(E) that the order reducing rent will terminate on the date the condition is repaired or remedied; and

(F) that on the day the condition is repaired or remedied, the landlord must give the tenant written notice, served in accordance with Rule 501.4, that the condition justifying the reduction of rent has been repaired or remedied and the rent will revert to the rent amount specified in the lease.

(c) ***Issuance and Service.*** The judge must issue the judgment. The judgment may be served on the landlord in open court or by any means provided in Rule 501.4 at an address listed in the citation, the address listed on any answer, or such other address the landlord furnishes to the court in writing. Unless the judge serves the landlord in open court or by other means provided in Rule 501.4, the sheriff, constable, or other authorized person who serves the landlord must promptly file a return of service in the justice court.

(d) ***Failure to Comply.*** If the landlord fails to comply with an order to repair or remedy a condition or reduce the tenant's rent, the failure is grounds for citing the landlord for contempt of court under Section 21.002 of the Texas Government Code.

509.7 Counterclaims. Counterclaims and the joinder of suits against third parties are not permitted in suits under these rules. Compulsory counterclaims may be brought in a separate suit. Any potential causes of action, including a compulsory counterclaim, that are not asserted because of this rule are not precluded.

509.8 Appeal: Time and Manner; Perfection; Effect; Costs; Trial on Appeal.

(a) ***Time and Manner.*** Either party may appeal the decision of the justice court to a statutory county court or, if there is no statutory county court with jurisdiction, a county court or district court with jurisdiction by filing a written notice of appeal with the justice court within 21 days after the date the judge signs the judgment. If the judgment is amended in any respect, any party has the right to appeal within 21 days after the date the judge signs the new judgment, in the same manner set out in this rule.

(b) ***Perfection.*** The posting of an appeal bond is not required for an appeal under this rule, and the appeal is considered perfected with the filing of a notice of appeal. Otherwise, the appeal is in the manner provided by law for appeal from a justice court.

(c) ***Effect.*** The timely filing of a notice of appeal stays the enforcement of any order to repair or remedy a condition or reduce the tenant's rent, as well as any other actions.

(d) ***Costs.*** The appellant must pay the costs on appeal to a county court in accordance with Rule 143a.

(e) ***Trial on Appeal.*** On appeal, the parties are entitled to a trial de novo. A trial de novo is a new trial in which the entire case is presented as if there had been no previous trial. Either party is entitled to trial by jury on timely request and payment of a fee, if required. An appeal of a judgment of a justice court under these rules takes precedence in the county court and may be held at any time after the eighth day after the date the transcript is filed in the county court.

509.9 Effect of Writ of Possession. If a judgment for the landlord for possession of the residential rental property becomes final, any order to repair or remedy a condition is vacated and unenforceable.

TRCP 510. EVICTION CASES

510.1 Application. Rule 510 applies to a lawsuit to recover possession of real property under Chapter 24 of the Texas Property Code.

510.2 Computation of Time for Eviction Cases. Rule 500.5 applies to the computation of time in an eviction case. But if a document is filed by mail and not received by the court by the due date, the court may take any action authorized by these rules, including issuing a writ of possession requiring a tenant to leave the property.

510.3 Petition.

(a) ***Contents.*** In addition to the requirements of Rule 502.2, a petition in an eviction case must be sworn to by the plaintiff and must contain:

(1) a description, including the address, if any, of the premises that the plaintiff seeks possession of;

(2) a description of the facts and the grounds for eviction;

(3) a description of when and how notice to vacate was delivered;

(4) the total amount of rent due and unpaid at the time of filing, if any; and

(5) a statement that attorney fees are being sought, if applicable.

(b) ***Where Filed.*** The petition must be filed in the precinct where the premises is located. If it is filed elsewhere, the judge must dismiss the case. The plaintiff will not be entitled to a refund of the filing fee, but will be refunded any service fees paid if the case is dismissed before service is attempted.

(c) ***Defendants Named.*** If the eviction is based on a written residential lease, the plaintiff must name as defendants all tenants obligated under the lease residing at the premises whom plaintiff seeks to evict. No judgment or writ of possession may issue or be executed against a tenant obligated under a lease and residing at the premises who is not named in the petition and served with citation.

(d) ***Claim for Rent.*** A claim for rent within the justice court's jurisdiction may be asserted in an eviction case.

(e) ***Only Issue.*** The court must adjudicate the right to actual possession and not title. Counterclaims and the joinder of suits against third parties are not permitted in eviction cases. A claim that is not asserted because of this rule can be brought in a separate suit in a court of proper jurisdiction.

510.4 Issuance, Service, and Return of Citation.

(a) ***Issuance of Citation; Contents.*** When a petition is filed, the court must immediately issue citation directed to each defendant. The citation must:

(1) be styled "The State of Texas";

(2) be signed by the clerk under seal of court or by the judge;

(3) contain the name, location, and address of the court;

(4) state the date of filing of the petition;

(5) state the date of issuance of the citation;

(6) state the file number and names of parties;

(7) state the plaintiff's cause of action and relief sought;

(8) be directed to the defendant;

(9) state the name and address of attorney for plaintiff, or if the plaintiff does not have an attorney, the address of plaintiff;

(10) state the day the defendant must appear in person for trial at the court issuing citation, which must not be less than 10 days nor more than 21 days after the petition is filed;

(11) notify the defendant that if the defendant fails to appear in person for trial, judgment by default may be rendered for the relief demanded in the petition;

(12) inform the defendant that, upon timely request and payment of a jury fee no later than 3 days before the day set for trial, the case will be heard by a jury;

(13) contain all warnings required by Chapter 24 of the Texas Property Code; and

(14) include the following statement: "For further information, consult Part V of the Texas Rules of Civil Procedure, which is available online and also at the court listed on this citation."

(b) ***Service and Return of Citation.***

(1) *Who May Serve.* Unless otherwise authorized by written court order, citation must be served by a sheriff or constable.

(2) *Method of Service.* The constable, sheriff, or other person authorized by written court order receiving the citation must execute it by delivering a copy with a copy of the petition attached to the defendant, or by leaving a copy with a copy of the petition attached with some person, other than the plaintiff, over the age of 16 years, at the defendant's usual place of residence, at least 6 days before the day set for trial.

(3) *Return of Service.* At least one day before the day set for trial, the constable, sheriff, or other person authorized by written court order must complete and file a return of service in accordance with Rule 501.3 with the court that issued the citation.

(c) ***Alternative Service by Delivery to the Premises.***

(1) *When Allowed.* The citation may be served by delivery to the premises if:

(A) the constable, sheriff, or other person authorized by written court order is unsuccessful in serving the citation under (b);

(B) the petition lists all home and work addresses of the defendant that are known to the plaintiff and states that the plaintiff knows of no other home or work addresses of the defendant in the county where the premises are located; and

(C) the constable, sheriff, or other person authorized files a sworn statement that it has made diligent efforts to serve such citation on at least two occasions at all addresses of the defendant in the county where the premises are located, stating the times and places of attempted service.

(2) *Authorization.* The judge must promptly consider a sworn statement filed under (1)(C) and determine whether citation may be served by delivery to the premises. The plaintiff is not required to make a request or motion for alternative service.

(3) *Method.* If the judge authorizes service by delivery to the premises, the constable, sheriff, or other person authorized by written court order must, at least 6 days before the day set for trial:

(A) deliver a copy of the citation with a copy of the petition attached to the premises by placing it through a door mail chute or slipping it under the front door; if neither method is possible, the officer may securely affix the citation to the front door or main entry to the premises; and

(B) deposit in the mail a copy of the citation with a copy of the petition attached, addressed to defendant at the premises and sent by first class mail.

(4) *Notation on Return.* The constable, sheriff, or other person authorized by written court order must note on the return of service the date the citation was delivered and the date it was deposited in the mail.

510.5 Request for Immediate Possession.

(a) ***Immediate Possession Bond.*** The plaintiff may, at the time of filing the petition or at any time prior to final judgment, file a possession bond to be approved by the judge in the probable amount of costs of suit and damages that may result to defendant in the event that the suit has been improperly instituted, and conditioned that the plaintiff will pay defendant all such costs and damages that are adjudged against plaintiff.

(b) ***Notice to Defendant.*** The court must notify a defendant that the plaintiff has filed a possession bond. The notice must be served in the same manner as service of citation and must inform the defendant that if the defendant does not file an answer or appear for trial, and judgment for possession is granted by default, an officer will place the plaintiff in possession of the property on or after the 7th day after the date defendant is served with the notice.

(c) ***Time for Issuance and Execution of Writ.*** If judgment for possession is rendered by default and a possession bond has been filed, approved, and served under this rule, a writ of possession must issue immediately upon demand and payment of any required fees. The writ must not be executed before the 7th day after the date defendant is served with notice under (b).

(d) ***Effect of Appearance.*** If the defendant files an answer or appears at trial, no writ of possession may issue before the 6th day after the date a judgment for possession is signed or the day following the deadline for the defendant to appeal the judgment, whichever is later.

510.6 Trial Date; Answer; Default Judgment.

(a) ***Trial Date and Answer.*** The defendant must appear for trial on the day set for trial in the citation. The defendant may, but is not required to, file a written answer with the court on or before the day set for trial in the citation.

(b) ***Default Judgment.*** If the defendant fails to appear at trial and fails to file an answer before the case is called for trial, and proof of service has been filed in accordance with Rule 510.4, the allegations of the complaint must be taken as admitted and judgment by default rendered accordingly. If a defendant who has answered fails to appear for trial, the court may proceed to hear evidence and render judgment accordingly.

(c) ***Notice of Default.*** When a default judgment is signed, the clerk must immediately mail written notice of the judgment by first class mail to the defendant at the address of the premises.

16 510.7 Trial.

(a) ***Trial.*** An eviction case will be docketed and tried as other cases. No eviction trial may be held less than 6 days after service under Rule 510.4 has been obtained.

(b) ***Jury Trial Demanded.*** Any party may file a written demand for trial by jury by making a request to the court at least 3 days before the trial date. The demand must be accompanied by payment of a jury fee or

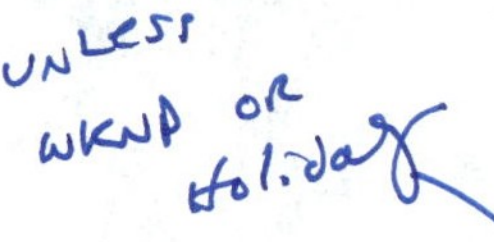

by filing a Statement of Inability to Afford Payment of Court Costs. If a jury is demanded by either party, the jury will be impaneled and sworn as in other cases; and after hearing the evidence it will return its verdict in favor of the plaintiff or the defendant. If no jury is timely demanded by either party, the judge will try the case.

(c) ***Limit on Postponement.*** Trial in an eviction case must not be postponed for more than 7 days total unless both parties agree in writing.

510.8 Judgment; Writ; No New Trial.

(a) ***Judgment upon Jury Verdict.*** Where a jury has returned a verdict, the judge may render judgment on the verdict or, if the verdict is contrary to the law or the evidence, judgment notwithstanding the verdict.

(b) ***Judgment for Plaintiff.*** If the judgment is in favor of the plaintiff, the judge must render judgment for plaintiff for possession of the premises, costs, delinquent rent as of the date of entry of judgment, if any, and attorney fees if recoverable by law.

(c) ***Judgment for Defendant.*** If the judgment is in favor of the defendant, the judge must render judgment for defendant against the plaintiff for costs and attorney fees if recoverable by law.

(d) ***Writ.*** If the judgment or verdict is in favor of the plaintiff, the judge must award a writ of possession upon demand of the plaintiff and payment of any required fees.

(1) *Time to Issue.* Except as provided by Rule 510.5, no writ of possession may issue before the 6th day after the date a judgment for possession is signed or the day following the deadline for the defendant to appeal the judgment, whichever is later. A writ of possession may not issue more than 60 days after a judgment for possession is signed. For good cause, the court may extend the deadline for issuance to 90 days after a judgment for possession is signed.

(2) *Time to Execute.* A writ of possession may not be executed after the 90th day after a judgment for possession is signed.

(3) *Effect of Appeal.* A writ of possession must not issue if an appeal is perfected and, if applicable, rent is paid into the registry, as required by these rules.

(e) ***No Motion for New Trial.*** No motion for new trial may be filed.

16 **510.9 Appeal.**

(a) ***How Taken; Time.*** A party may appeal a judgment in an eviction case by filing a bond, making a cash deposit, or filing a Statement of Inability to Afford Payment of Court Costs with the justice court within 5 days after the judgment is signed.

(b) ***Amount of Security; Terms.*** The justice court judge will set the amount of the bond or cash deposit to include the items enumerated in Rule 510.11. The bond or cash deposit must be payable to the appellee and must be conditioned on the appellant's prosecution of its appeal to effect and payment of any judgment and all costs rendered against it on appeal.

(c) ***Statement of Inability to Afford Payment of Court Costs.***

(1) *Filing.* An appellant who cannot furnish a bond or pay a cash deposit in the amount required may instead file a Statement of Inability to Afford Payment of Court Costs. The Statement must be on the form approved by the Supreme Court or include the information required by the Court-approved form.

(2) *Contest.* The Statement may be contested as provided in Rule 502.3(d) within 5 days after the opposing party receives notice that the Statement was filed.

(3) *Appeal If Contest Sustained.* If the contest is sustained, the appellant may appeal that decision by filing notice with the justice court within 5 days of that court's written order. The justice court must then forward all related documents to the county court for resolution. The county court must set the matter for hearing within 5 days and hear the contest de novo, as if there had been no previous hearing, and, if the appeal is granted, must direct the justice court to transmit to the clerk of the county court the transcript, records, and papers of the case, as provided in these rules.

(4) *If No Appeal or If Appeal Overruled.* If the appellant does not appeal the ruling sustaining the contest, or if the county court denies the appeal, the appellant may, within one business day, post an appeal bond or make a cash deposit in compliance with this rule.

(5) *Payment of Rent in Nonpayment of Rent Appeals.*

(A) Notice. If a defendant appeals an eviction for nonpayment of rent by filing a Statement of Inability to Afford Payment of Court Costs, the justice court must provide to the defendant a written notice at the time the Statement is filed that contains the following information in bold or conspicuous type:

TRCP 510

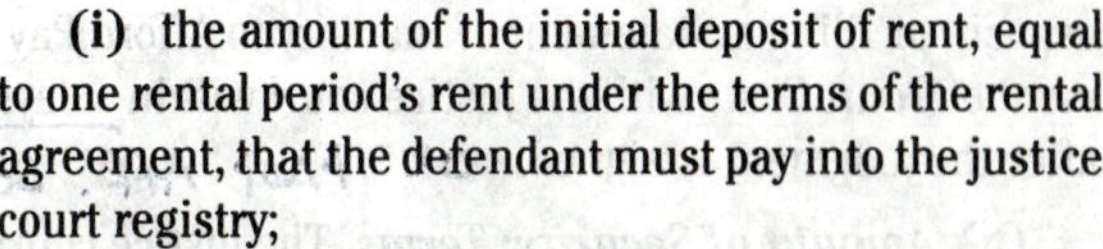

(i) the amount of the initial deposit of rent, equal to one rental period's rent under the terms of the rental agreement, that the defendant must pay into the justice court registry;

(ii) whether the initial deposit must be paid in cash, cashier's check, or money order, and to whom the cashier's check or money order, if applicable, must be made payable;

(iii) the calendar date by which the initial deposit must be paid into the justice court registry, which must be within 5 days of the date the Statement is filed; and

(iv) a statement that failure to pay the required amount into the justice court registry by the required date may result in the court issuing a writ of possession without hearing.

(B) Defendant May Remain in Possession. A defendant who appeals an eviction for nonpayment of rent by filing a Statement of Inability to Afford Payment of Court Costs is entitled to stay in possession of the premises during the pendency of the appeal by complying with the following procedure:

(i) Within 5 days of the date that the defendant files a Statement of Inability to Afford Payment of Court Costs, it must pay into the justice court registry the amount set forth in the notice provided at the time the defendant filed the Statement. If the defendant was provided with notice and fails to pay the designated amount into the justice court registry within 5 days, and the transcript has not been transmitted to the county clerk, the plaintiff is entitled, upon request and payment of the applicable fee, to a writ of possession, which the justice court must issue immediately and without hearing.

(ii) During the appeal process as rent becomes due under the rental agreement, the defendant must pay the designated amount into the county court registry within 5 days of the rental due date under the terms of the rental agreement.

(iii) If a government agency is responsible for all or a portion of the rent, the defendant must pay only that portion of the rent determined by the justice court to be paid during appeal. Either party may contest the portion of the rent that the justice court determines must be paid into the county court registry by filing a contest within 5 days after the judgment is signed. If a contest is filed, the justice court must notify the parties and hold a hearing on the contest within 5 days. If the defendant objects to the justice court's ruling at the hearing, the defendant is required to pay only the portion claimed to be owed by the defendant until the issue is tried in county court.

(iv) If the defendant fails to pay the designated amount into the court registry within the time limits prescribed by these rules, the plaintiff may file a sworn motion that the defendant is in default in county court. The plaintiff must notify the defendant of the motion and the hearing date. Upon a showing that the defendant is in default, the court must issue a writ of possession.

(v) The plaintiff may withdraw any or all rent in the county court registry upon sworn motion and hearing, prior to final determination of the case, showing just cause; dismissal of the appeal; or order of the court after final hearing.

(vi) All hearings and motions under this subparagraph are entitled to precedence in the county court.

(d) *Notice to Other Parties Required.* If a Statement of Inability to Afford Payment of Court Costs is filed, the court must provide notice to all other parties that the Statement was filed no later than the next business day. Within 5 days of filing a bond or making a cash deposit, an appellant must serve written notice of the appeal on all other parties using a method approved under Rule 501.4.

(e) *No Default on Appeal Without Compliance with Rule.* No judgment may be taken by default against the adverse party in the court to which the case has been appealed without first showing substantial compliance with this rule.

(f) *Appeal Perfected.* An appeal is perfected when a bond, cash deposit, or Statement of Inability to Afford Payment of Court Costs is filed in accordance with this rule.

510.10 Record on Appeal; Docketing; Trial De Novo.

(a) *Preparation and Transmission of Record.* Unless otherwise provided by law or these rules, when an appeal has been perfected, the judge must stay all further proceedings on the judgment and must immediately send to the clerk of the county court a certified copy of all docket entries, a certified copy of the bill of costs, and the original papers in the case together with any money in the court registry, including sums tendered pursuant to Rule 510.9(c)(5)(B).

(b) *Docketing; Notice.* The county clerk must docket the case and must immediately notify the par-

ties of the date of receipt of the transcript and the docket number of the case. The notice must advise the defendant that it must file a written answer in the county court within 8 days if one was not filed in the justice court.

(c) *Trial De Novo.* The case must be tried de novo in the county court. A trial de novo is a new trial in which the entire case is presented as if there had been no previous trial. The trial, as well as any hearings and motions, is entitled to precedence in the county court.

510.11 Damages on Appeal. On the trial of the case in the county court the appellant or appellee will be permitted to plead, prove and recover his damages, if any, suffered for withholding or defending possession of the premises during the pendency of the appeal. Damages may include but are not limited to loss of rentals during the pendency of the appeal and attorney fees in the justice and county courts provided, as to attorney fees, that the requirements of Section 24.006 of the Texas Property Code have been met. Only the party prevailing in the county court will be entitled to recover damages against the adverse party. The prevailing party will also be entitled to recover court costs and to recover against the sureties on the appeal bond in cases where the adverse party has executed an appeal bond.

510.12 Judgment by Default on Appeal. An eviction case appealed to county court will be subject to trial at any time after the expiration of 8 days after the date the transcript is filed in the county court. If the defendant has filed a written answer in the justice court, it must be taken to constitute his appearance and answer in the county court and may be amended as in other cases. If the defendant made no answer in writing in the justice court and fails to file a written answer within 8 days after the transcript is filed in the county court, the allegations of the complaint may be taken as admitted and judgment by default may be entered accordingly.

510.13 Writ of Possession on Appeal. The writ of possession, or execution, or both, will be issued by the clerk of the county court according to the judgment rendered, and the same will be executed by the sheriff or constable, as in other cases. The judgment of the county court may not be stayed unless within 10 days from the judgment the appellant files a supersedeas bond in an amount set by the county court pursuant to Section 24.007 of the Texas Property Code.

See also CPRC §15.084; Prop. Code §§24.004, 24.0051, 24.006, 24.0061, 24.007; *O'Connor's Texas Appeals*, "Writ of possession," ch. 4-B, §2.1.2(2)(b), p. 175; "Writ of possession," ch. 4-B, §6.6.5, p. 187; *O'Connor's Texas COA*, "Forcible Detainer—Eviction," ch. 16-B, p. 424; *O'Connor's Texas Rules*, "Eviction," ch. 2-F, §5.2.4, p. 172.

PART VI. RULES RELATING TO ANCILLARY PROCEEDINGS

SECTION 3. EXECUTIONS

TRCP 631. EXECUTION FOR SALE OF PARTICULAR PROPERTY

An execution issued upon a judgment for the sale of particular chattels or personal property or real estate, must particularly describe the property, and shall direct the officer to make the sale by previously giving the public notice of the time and place of sale required by law and these rules.

See also CPRC §§65.013, 65.014.

TRCP 632. EXECUTION FOR DELIVERY OF CERTAIN PROPERTY

An execution issued upon a judgment for the delivery of the possession of a chattel or personal property, or for the delivery of the possession of real property, shall particularly describe the property, and designate the party to whom the judgment awards the possession. The writ shall require the officer to deliver the possession of the property to the party entitled thereto.

See also CPRC §§65.013, 65.014.

TRCP 639. LEVY

In order to make a levy on real estate, it shall not be necessary for the officer to go upon the ground but it shall be sufficient for him to indorse such levy on the writ. Levy upon personal property is made by taking possession thereof, when the defendant in execution is entitled to the possession. Where the defendant in execution has an interest in personal property, but is not entitled to the possession thereof, a levy is made thereon by giving notice thereof to the person who is entitled to the possession, or one of them where there are several.

TRCP 646a. SALE OF REAL PROPERTY

Real property taken by virtue of any execution shall be sold at public auction, at the courthouse door of the county, unless the court orders that such sale be at the place where the real property is situated, on the first Tuesday of the month, between the hours of ten o'clock, a.m. and four o'clock, p.m.

TRCP 647. NOTICE OF SALE OF REAL ESTATE

The time and place of sale of real estate under execution, order of sale, or venditioni exponas, shall be advertised by the officer by having the notice thereof published in the English language once a week for three consecutive weeks preceding such sale, in some newspaper published in said county. The first of said publications shall appear not less than twenty days immediately preceding the day of sale. Said notice shall contain a statement of the authority by virtue of which the sale is to be made, the time of levy, and the time and place of sale; it shall also contain a brief description of the property to be sold, and shall give the number of acres, original survey, locality in the county, and the name by which the land is most generally known, but it shall not be necessary for it to contain field notes. Publishers of newspapers shall charge the legal rate of Two (2) Cents per word for the first insertion of such publication and One (1) Cent per word for such subsequent insertions, or such newspapers shall be entitled to charge for such publication at a rate equal to but not in excess of the published word or line rate of that newspaper for such class of advertising. If there be no newspaper published in the county, or none which will publish the notice of sale for the compensation herein fixed, the officer shall then post such notice in writing in three public places in the county, one of which shall be at the courthouse door of such county, for at least twenty days successively next before the day of sale. The officer making the levy shall give the defendant, or his attorney, written notice of such sale, either in person or by mail, which notice shall substantially conform to the foregoing requirements.

SECTION 8. SEQUESTRATION

TRCP 703. BOND FOR REAL ESTATE

If the property be real estate, the condition of such bond shall be that the defendant will not injure the property, and that he will pay the value of the rents of the same in case he shall be condemned so to do.

TRCP 708. PLAINTIFF MAY REPLEVY

When the defendant fails to replevy the property within ten days after the levy of the writ and service of notice on defendant, the officer having the property in possession shall at any time thereafter and before final judgment, deliver the same to the plaintiff upon his giving bond payable to defendant in a sum of money not less than the amount fixed by the court's order, with sufficient surety or sureties as provided by statute to be approved by such officer. If the property to be replevied be personal property, the condition of the bond shall be that he will have such property, in the same condition as when it is replevied, together with the value of the fruits, hire or revenue thereof, forthcoming to abide the decision of the court, or that he will pay the value thereof, or the difference between its value at the time of replevy and the time of judgment (regardless of the cause of such difference in value, and of the fruits, hire or revenue of the same in case he shall be condemned to do so). If the property be real estate, the condition of such bond shall be that the plaintiff will not injure the property, and that he will pay the value of the rents of the same in case he shall be condemned to do so.

On reasonable notice to the opposing party (which may be less than three days) either party shall have the right to prompt judicial review of the amount of bond required, denial of bond, sufficiency of sureties, and estimated value of the property, by the court which authorized issuance of the writ. The court's determination may be made upon the basis of affidavits, if uncontroverted, setting forth such facts as would be admissible in evidence; otherwise, the parties shall submit evidence. The court shall forthwith enter its order either approving or modifying the requirements of the officer or of the court's prior order, and such order of the court shall supersede and control with respect to such matters.

PART VII. RULES RELATING TO SPECIAL PROCEEDINGS

SECTION 1. PROCEDURES RELATED TO FORECLOSURES OF CERTAIN LIENS

TRCP 735. FORECLOSURES REQUIRING A COURT ORDER

735.1 Liens Affected.

Rule 736 provides the procedure for obtaining a court order, when required, to allow foreclosure of a lien containing a power of sale in the security instrument, dedicatory instrument, or declaration creating the lien, including a lien securing any of the following:

(a) a home equity loan, reverse mortgage, or home equity line of credit under article XVI, sections 50(a)(6), 50(k), and 50(t) of the Texas Constitution;

(b) a tax lien transfer or property tax loan under sections 32.06 and 32.065 of the Tax Code; or

(c) a property owners' association assessment under section 209.0092 of the Property Code.

735.2 Other Statutory and Contractual Foreclosure Provisions Unaltered.

A Rule 736 order does not alter any foreclosure requirement or duty imposed under applicable law or the terms of the loan agreement, contract, or lien sought to be foreclosed. The only issue to be determined in a Rule 736 proceeding is whether a party may obtain an order under Rule 736 to proceed with foreclosure under applicable law and the terms of the loan agreement, contract, or lien sought to be foreclosed.

735.3 Judicial Foreclosure Unaffected.

A Rule 736 order is not a substitute for a judgment for judicial foreclosure, but any loan agreement, contract, or lien that may be foreclosed using Rule 736 procedures may also be foreclosed by judgment in an action for judicial foreclosure.

See also Tex. Const. art. 16, §50; Prop. Code §51.002.

TRCP 736. EXPEDITED ORDER PROCEEDING

736.1 Application.

(a) ***Where Filed.*** An application for an expedited order allowing the foreclosure of a lien listed in Rule 735 to proceed must be filed in a county where all or part of the real property encumbered by the loan agreement, contract, or lien sought to be foreclosed is located or in a probate court with jurisdiction over proceedings involving the property.

(b) ***Style.*** An application must be styled "In re: Order for Foreclosure Concerning [*state: property's mailing address*] under Tex. R. Civ. P. 736."

(c) ***When Filed.*** An application may not be filed until the opportunity to cure has expired under applicable law and the loan agreement, contract, or lien sought to be foreclosed.

(d) ***Contents.*** The application must:

(1) Identify by name and last known address each of the following parties:

(A) "Petitioner"—any person legally authorized to prosecute the foreclosure;

(B) "Respondent"—according to the records of the holder or servicer of the loan agreement, contract, or lien sought to be foreclosed:

(i) for a home equity loan, reverse mortgage, or home equity line of credit, each person obligated to pay the loan agreement, contract, or lien sought to be foreclosed and each mortgagor, if any, of the loan agreement, contract, or lien sought to be foreclosed;

(ii) for a tax lien transfer or property tax loan, each person obligated to pay the loan agreement, contract, or lien sought to be foreclosed, each mortgagor, if any, of the loan agreement, contract, or lien sought to be foreclosed, each owner of the property, and the holder of any recorded preexisting first lien secured by the property;

(iii) for a property owners' association assessment, each person obligated to pay the loan agreement, contract, or lien sought to be foreclosed who has a current ownership interest in the property.

(2) Identify the property encumbered by the loan agreement, contract, or lien sought to be foreclosed by its commonly known street address and legal description.

(3) Describe or state:

(A) the type of lien listed in Rule 735 sought to be foreclosed and its constitutional or statutory reference;

(B) the authority of the party seeking foreclosure, whether as the servicer, beneficiary, lender, investor, property owners' association, or other person with authority to prosecute the foreclosure;

(C) each person obligated to pay the loan agreement, contract, or lien sought to be foreclosed;

(D) each mortgagor, if any, of the loan agreement, contract, or lien sought to be foreclosed who is not a maker or assumer of the underlying debt;

(E) as of a date that is not more than sixty days prior to the date the application is filed:

(i) if the default is monetary, the number of unpaid scheduled payments,

(ii) if the default is monetary, the amount required to cure the default,

(iii) if the default is non-monetary, the facts creating the default, and

(iv) if applicable, the total amount required to pay off the loan agreement, contract, or lien;

(F) that the requisite notice or notices to cure the default has or have been mailed to each person as required under applicable law and the loan agreement, contract, or lien sought to be foreclosed and that the opportunity to cure has expired; and

TRCP 736

(G) that before the application was filed, any other action required under applicable law and the loan agreement, contract, or lien sought to be foreclosed was performed.

(4) For a tax lien transfer or property tax loan, state all allegations required to be contained in the application in accordance with section 32.06(c-1)(1) of the Tax Code.

(5) Conspicuously state:

(A) that legal action is not being sought against the occupant of the property unless the occupant is also named as a respondent in the application; and

(B) that if the petitioner obtains a court order, the petitioner will proceed with a foreclosure of the property in accordance with applicable law and the terms of the loan agreement, contract, or lien sought to be foreclosed.

(6) Include an affidavit of material facts in accordance with Rule 166a(f) signed by the petitioner or the servicer describing the basis for foreclosure and, depending on the type of lien sought to be foreclosed, attach a legible copy of:

(A) the note, original recorded lien, or pertinent part of a property owners' association declaration or dedicatory instrument establishing the lien, and current assignment of the lien, if assigned;

(B) each notice required to be mailed to any person under applicable law and the loan agreement, contract, or lien sought to be foreclosed before the application was filed and proof of mailing of each notice; and

(C) for a tax lien transfer or property tax loan:

(i) the property owner's sworn document required under section 32.06(a-1) of the Tax Code; and

(ii) the taxing authority's certified statement attesting to the transfer of the lien, required under section 32.06(b) of the Tax Code.

736.2 Costs.

All filing, citation, mailing, service, and other court costs and fees are costs of court and must be paid by petitioner at the time of filing an application with the clerk of the court.

736.3 Citation.

(a) *Issuance.*

(1) When the application is filed, the clerk must issue a separate citation for each respondent named in the application and one additional citation for the occupant of the property sought to be foreclosed.

(2) Each citation that is directed to a respondent must state that any response to the application is due the first Monday after the expiration of 38 days from the date the citation was placed in the custody of the U.S. Postal Service in accordance with the clerk's standard mailing procedures and state the date that the citation was placed in the custody of the U.S. Postal Service by the clerk.

(b) *Service and Return.*

(1) The clerk of the court must serve each citation, with a copy of the application attached, by both first class mail and certified mail. A citation directed to a respondent must be mailed to the respondent's last known address that is stated in the application. A citation directed to the occupant of the property sought to be foreclosed must be mailed to Occupant of [*state: property's mailing address*] at the address of the property sought to be foreclosed that is stated in the application.

(2) Concurrently with service, the clerk must complete a return of service in accordance with Rule 107, except that the return of service need not contain a return receipt. For a citation mailed by the clerk in accordance with (b)(1), the date of service is the date and time the citation was placed in the custody of the U.S. Postal Service in a properly addressed, postage prepaid envelope in accordance with the clerk's standard mailing procedures.

(3) The clerk must only charge one fee per respondent or occupant served under this rule.

736.4 Discovery.

No discovery is permitted in a Rule 736 proceeding.

736.5 Response.

(a) *Generally.* A respondent may file a response contesting the application.

(b) *Due Date.* Any response to the application is due the first Monday after the expiration of 38 days from the date the citation was placed in the custody of the U.S. Postal Service in accordance with the clerk's standard mailing procedures, as stated on the citation.

(c) *Form.* A response must be signed in accordance with Rule 57 and may be in the form of a general denial under Rule 92, except that a respondent must affirmatively plead:

(1) why the respondent believes a respondent did not sign a loan agreement document, if applicable, that is specifically identified by the respondent;

TRCP 736

(2) why the respondent is not obligated for payment of the lien;

(3) why the number of months of alleged default or the reinstatement or pay off amounts are materially incorrect;

(4) why any document attached to the application is not a true and correct copy of the original; or

(5) proof of payment in accordance with Rule 95.

(d) ***Other Claims.*** A response may not state an independent claim for relief. The court must, without a hearing, strike and dismiss any counterclaim, cross claim, third party claim, intervention, or cause of action filed by any person in a Rule 736 proceeding.

736.6 Hearing Required When Response Filed.

The court must not conduct a hearing under this rule unless a response is filed. If a response is filed, the court must hold a hearing after reasonable notice to the parties. The hearing on the application must not be held earlier than 20 days or later than 30 days after a request for a hearing is made by any party. At the hearing, the petitioner has the burden to prove by affidavits on file or evidence presented the grounds for granting the order sought in the application.

736.7 Default When No Response Filed.

(a) If no response to the application is filed by the due date, the petitioner may file a motion and proposed order to obtain a default order. For the purposes of obtaining a default order, all facts alleged in the application and supported by the affidavit of material facts constitute prima facie evidence of the truth of the matters alleged.

(b) The court must grant the application by default order no later than 30 days after a motion is filed under (a) if the application complies with the requirements of Rule 736.1 and was properly served in accordance with Rule 736.3. The petitioner need not appear in court to obtain a default order.

(c) The return of service must be on file with the clerk of the court for at least 10 days before the court may grant the application by default.

736.8 Order.

(a) The court must issue an order granting the application if the petitioner establishes the basis for the foreclosure. Otherwise, the court must deny the application.

(b) An order granting the application must describe:

(1) the material facts establishing the basis for foreclosure;

(2) the property to be foreclosed by commonly known mailing address and legal description;

(3) the name and last known address of each respondent subject to the order; and

(4) the recording or indexing information of each lien to be foreclosed.

(c) An order granting or denying the application is not subject to a motion for rehearing, new trial, bill of review, or appeal. Any challenge to a Rule 736 order must be made in a suit filed in a separate, independent, original proceeding in a court of competent jurisdiction.

736.9 Effect of the Order.

An order is without prejudice and has no res judicata, collateral estoppel, estoppel by judgment, or other effect in any other judicial proceeding. After an order is obtained, a person may proceed with the foreclosure process under applicable law and the terms of the lien sought to be foreclosed.

736.10 Bankruptcy.

If a respondent provides proof to the clerk of the court that respondent filed bankruptcy before an order is signed, the proceeding under this rule must be abated so long as the automatic stay is effective.

736.11 Automatic Stay and Dismissal if Independent Suit Filed.

(a) A proceeding or order under this rule is automatically stayed if a respondent files a separate, original proceeding in a court of competent jurisdiction that puts in issue any matter related to the origination, servicing, or enforcement of the loan agreement, contract, or lien sought to be foreclosed prior to 5:00 p.m. on the Monday before the scheduled foreclosure sale.

(b) Respondent must give prompt notice of the filing of the suit to petitioner or petitioner's attorney and the foreclosure trustee or substitute trustee by any reasonable means necessary to stop the scheduled foreclosure sale.

(c) Within ten days of filing suit, the respondent must file a motion and proposed order to dismiss or vacate with the clerk of the court in which the application was filed giving notice that respondent has filed an original proceeding contesting the right to foreclose in a court of competent jurisdiction. If no order has been signed, the court must dismiss a pending proceeding. If an order has been signed, the court must vacate the Rule 736 order.

(d) If the automatic stay under this rule is in effect, any foreclosure sale of the property is void. Within 10 business days of notice that the foreclosure sale was void, the trustee or substitute trustee must return to the buyer of the foreclosed property the purchase price paid by the buyer.

(e) The court may enforce the Rule 736 process under chapters 9 and 10 of the Civil Practices and Remedies Code.

736.12 Attachment of Order to Trustee's Deed.

A conformed copy of the order must be attached to the trustee or substitute trustee's foreclosure deed.

736.13 Promulgated Forms.

The Supreme Court of Texas may promulgate forms that conform to this rule.

See also Tex. Const. art. 16, §50; CPRC §§17.031, 154.028; Prop. Code §51.002.

SECTION 4. PARTITION OF REAL ESTATE

TRCP 756. PETITION

The plaintiff's petition shall state:

(a) The names and residence, if known, of each of the other joint owners, or joint claimants, of such property.

(b) The share or interest which the plaintiff and the other joint owners, or joint claimants, of same own or claim so far as known to the plaintiff.

(c) The land sought to be partitioned shall be so described as that the same may be distinguished from any other and the estimated value thereof stated.

See also Prop. Code §§23.001, 23.002.

TRCP 757. CITATION & SERVICE

Upon the filing of a petition for partition, the clerk shall issue citation for each of the joint owners, or joint claimants, named therein, as in other cases, and such citations shall be served in the manner and for the time provided for the service of citations in other cases.

TRCP 758. WHERE DEFENDANT IS UNKNOWN OR RESIDENCE IS UNKNOWN

If the plaintiff, his agent or attorney, at the commencement of any suit, or during the progress thereof, for the partition of land, shall make affidavit that an undivided portion of the land described in plaintiff's petition in said suit is owned by some person unknown to affiant, or that the place of residence of any known party owning an interest in land sought to be partitioned is unknown to affiant, the Clerk of the Court shall issue citation for publication, conforming to the requirements of Rules 114 and 115, and served in accordance with the directions of Rule 116. In case of unknown residence or party, the affidavit shall include a statement that after due diligence plaintiff and the affiant have been unable to ascertain the name or locate the residence of such party, as the case may be, and in such case it shall be the duty of the court trying the action to inquire into the sufficiency of the diligence so stated before granting any judgment.

TRCP 759. JUDGMENT WHERE DEFENDANT CITED BY PUBLICATION

When the defendant has been duly cited by publication in accordance with the preceding rule, and no appearance is entered within the time prescribed for pleadings, the court shall appoint an attorney to defend in behalf of such owner or owners, and proceed as in other causes where service is made by publication. It shall be the special duty of the court in all cases to see that its decree protects the rights of the unknown parties thereto. The judge of the court shall fix the fee of the attorney so appointed, which shall be entered and collected as costs against said unknown owner or owners.

TRCP 760. COURT SHALL DETERMINE, WHAT

Upon the hearing of the cause, the court shall determine the share or interest of each of the joint owners or claimants in the real estate sought to be divided, and all questions of law or equity affecting the title to such land which may arise.

TRCP 761. APPOINTMENT OF COMMISSIONERS

The court shall determine before entering the decree of partition whether the property, or any part thereof, is susceptible of partition; and, if the court determines that the whole, or any part of such property is susceptible of partition, then the court for that part of such property held to be susceptible of partition shall enter a decree directing the partition of such real es-

tate, describing the same, to be made in accordance with the respective shares or interests of each of such parties entitled thereto, specify in such decree the share or interest of each party, and shall appoint three or more competent and disinterested persons as commissioners to make such partition in accordance with such decree and the law, a majority of which commissioners may act.

TRCP 762. WRIT OF PARTITION

The clerk shall issue a writ of partition, directed to the sheriff or any constable of the county, commanding such sheriff or constable to notify each of the commissioners of their appointment as such, and shall accompany such writ with a certified copy of the decree of the court directing the partition.

TRCP 763. SERVICE OF WRIT OF PARTITION

The writ of partition shall be served by reading the same to each of the persons named therein as commissioners, and by delivering to any one of them the accompanying certified copy of the decree of the court.

TRCP 764. MAY APPOINT SURVEYOR

The court may, should it be deemed necessary, appoint a surveyor to assist the commissioners in making the partition, in which case the writ of partition shall name such surveyor, and shall be served upon him by reading the same to him.

TRCP 765. RETURN OF WRIT

A writ of partition, unless otherwise directed by the court, shall be made returnable twenty days from date of service on the commissioner last served; and the officer serving it shall endorse thereon the time and manner of such service.

TRCP 766. SHALL PROCEED TO PARTITION

The commissioners, or a majority of them, shall proceed to partition the real estate described in the decree of the court, in accordance with the directions contained in such decree and with the provisions of law and these rules.

TRCP 767. MAY CAUSE SURVEY

If the commissioners deem it necessary, they may cause to be surveyed the real estate to be partitioned into several tracts or parcels.

TRCP 768. SHALL DIVIDE REAL ESTATE

The commissioners shall divide the real estate to be partitioned into as many shares as there are persons entitled thereto, as determined by the court, each share to contain one or more tracts or parcels, as the commissioners may think proper, having due regard in the division to the situation, quantity and advantages of each share, so that the shares may be equal in value, as nearly as may be, in proportion to the respective interests of the parties entitled. The commissioners shall then proceed by lot to set apart to each of the parties entitled one of said shares, as determined by the decrees of the court.

TRCP 769. REPORT OF COMMISSIONERS

When the commissioners have completed the partition, they shall report the same in writing and under oath to the court, which report shall show:

(a) The property divided, describing the same.

(b) The several tracts or parcels into which the same was divided by them, describing each particularly.

(c) The number of shares and the land which constitutes each share, and the estimated value of each share.

(d) The allotment of each share.

(e) The report shall be accompanied by such field notes and maps as may be necessary to make the same intelligible.

The clerk shall immediately mail written notice of the filing of the report to all parties.

TRCP 770. PROPERTY INCAPABLE OF DIVISION

Should the court be of the opinion that a fair and equitable division of the real estate, or any part thereof, cannot be made, it shall order a sale of so much as is incapable of partition, which sale shall be for cash, or upon such other terms as the court may direct, and shall be made as under execution or by private or public sale through a receiver, if the court so order, and the proceeds thereof shall be returned into court and be partitioned among the persons entitled thereto, according to their respective interests.

TRCP 771. OBJECTIONS TO REPORT

Either party to the suit may file objections to any report of the commissioners in partition within thirty

days of the date the report is filed, and in such case a trial of the issues thereon shall be had as in other cases. If the report be found to be erroneous in any material respect, or unequal and unjust, the same shall be rejected, and other commissioners shall be appointed by the Court, and the same proceedings had as in the first instance.

SECTION 5. PARTITION OF PERSONAL PROPERTY

TRCP 772. PROCEDURE

An action seeking partition of personal property as authorized by Section 23.001, Texas Property Code, shall be commenced in the same manner as other civil suits, and the several owners or claimants of such property shall be cited as in other cases.

TRCP 773. VALUE ASCERTAINED

The separate value of each article of such personal property, and the allotment in kind to which each owner is entitled, shall be ascertained by the court, with or without a jury.

TRCP 774. DECREE OF COURT EXECUTED

When partition in kind of personal property is ordered by the judgment of the court, a writ shall be issued in accordance with such judgment, commanding the sheriff or constable of the county where the property may be to put the parties forthwith in possession of the property allotted to each respectively.

TRCP 775. PROPERTY SOLD

When personal property will not admit of a fair and equitable partition, the court shall ascertain the proportion to which each owner thereof is entitled, and order the property to be sold, and execution shall be issued to the sheriff or any constable of the county where the property may be describing such property and commanding such officer to sell the same as in other cases of execution, and pay over the proceeds of sale to the parties entitled thereto, in the proportion ascertained by the judgment of the court.

SECTION 6. PARTITION: MISCELLANEOUS PROVISIONS

TRCP 776. CONSTRUCTION

No provision of the statutes or rules relating to partition shall affect the mode of proceeding prescribed by law for the partition of estates of decedents among the heirs and legatees, nor preclude partition in any other manner authorized by the rules of equity, which rules shall govern in proceedings for partition in all respects not provided for by law or these rules.

TRCP 777. PLEADING & PRACTICE

The same rules of pleading, practice and evidence which govern in other civil actions shall govern in suits for partition, when not in conflict with any provisions of the law or these rules relating to partition.

TRCP 778. COSTS

The court shall adjudge the costs in a partition suit to be paid by each party to whom a share has been allotted in proportion to the value of such share.

SECTION 8. TRESPASS TO TRY TITLE

TRCP 783. REQUISITES OF PETITION

The petition shall state:

(a) The real names of the plaintiff and defendant and their residences, if known.

(b) A description of the premises by metes and bounds, or with sufficient certainty to identify the same, so that from such description possession thereof may be delivered, and state the county or counties in which the same are situated.

(c) The interest which the plaintiff claims in the premises, whether it be a fee simple or other estate; and, if he claims an undivided interest, the petition shall state the same and the amount thereof.

(d) That the plaintiff was in possession of the premises or entitled to such possession.

(e) That the defendant afterward unlawfully entered upon and dispossessed him of such premises, stating the date, and withholds from him the possession thereof.

(f) If rents and profits or damages are claimed, such facts as show the plaintiff to be entitled thereto and the amount thereof.

(g) It shall conclude with a prayer for the relief sought.

TRCP 784. THE POSSESSOR SHALL BE DEFENDANT

The defendant in the action shall be the person in possession if the premises are occupied, or some person claiming title thereto in case they are unoccupied.

TRCP 785. MAY JOIN AS DEFENDANTS, WHEN

The plaintiff may join as a defendant with the person in possession, any other person who, as landlord, remainderman, reversioner or otherwise, may claim title to the premises, or any part thereof, adversely to the plaintiff.

TRCP 786. WARRANTOR, ETC., MAY BE MADE A PARTY

When a party is sued for lands, the real owner or warrantor may make himself, or may be made, a party defendant in the suit, and shall be entitled to make such defense as if he had been the original defendant in the action.

TRCP 787. LANDLORD MAY BECOME DEFENDANT

When such action shall be commenced against a tenant in possession, the landlord may enter himself as the defendant, or he may be made a party on motion of such tenant; and he shall be entitled to make the same defense as if the suit had been originally commenced against him.

TRCP 788. MAY FILE PLEA OF "NOT GUILTY" ONLY

The defendant in such action may file only the plea of "not guilty," which shall state in substance that he is not guilty of the injury complained of in the petition filed by the plaintiff against him, except that if he claims an allowance for improvements, he shall state the facts entitling him to the same.

TRCP 789. PROOF UNDER SUCH PLEA

Under such plea of "not guilty" the defendant may give in evidence any lawful defense to the action except the defense of limitations, which shall be specially pleaded.

TRCP 790. ANSWER TAKEN AS ADMITTING POSSESSION

Such plea or any other answer to the merits shall be an admission by the defendant, for the purpose of that action, that he was in possession of the premises sued for, or that he claimed title thereto at the time of commencing the action, unless he states distinctly in his answer the extent of his possession or claim, in which case it shall be an admission to such extent only.

TRCP 791. MAY DEMAND ABSTRACT OF TITLE

After answer filed, either party may, by notice in writing, duly served on the opposite party or his attorney of record, not less than ten days before the trial of the cause, demand an abstract in writing of the claim or title to the premises in question upon which he relies.

TRCP 792. TIME TO FILE ABSTRACT

Such abstract of title shall be filed with the papers of the cause that within thirty days after the service of the notice, or within such further time that the court on good cause shown may grant; and in default thereof, the court may, after notice and hearing prior to the beginning of trial, order that no written instruments which are evidence of the claim or title of such opposite party be given on trial.

TRCP 793. ABSTRACT SHALL STATE, WHAT

The abstract mentioned in the two preceding rules shall state:

(a) The nature of each document or written instrument intended to be used as evidence and its date; or

(b) If a contract or conveyance, its date, the parties thereto and the date of the proof of acknowledgment, and before what officer the same was made; and

(c) Where recorded, stating the book and page of the record.

(d) If not recorded in the county when the trial is had, copies of such instrument, with the names of the subscribing witnesses, shall be included. If such unrecorded instrument be lost or destroyed it shall be sufficient to state the nature of such instrument and its loss or destruction.

TRCP 794. AMENDED ABSTRACT

The court may allow either party to file an amended abstract of title, under the same rules, which authorize the amendment of pleadings so far as they are applicable; but in all cases the documentary evidence of title shall at the trial be confined to the matters contained in the abstract of title.

TRCP 795. RULES IN OTHER CASES OBSERVED

The trial shall be conducted according to the rules of pleading, practice and evidence in other cases in the district court and conformable to the principles of trial by ejectment, except as otherwise provided by these rules.

TRCP 796. SURVEYOR APPOINTED, ETC.

The judge of the court may, either in term time or in vacation, at his own discretion, or on motion of either party to the action appoint a surveyor, who shall survey the premises in controversy pursuant to the order of the court, and report his action under oath to such court. If said report be not rejected for good cause shown, the same shall be admitted as evidence on the trial.

TRCP 797. SURVEY UNNECESSARY, WHEN

Where there is no dispute as to the lines or boundaries of the land in controversy, or where the defendant admits that he is in possession of the lands or tenements included in the plaintiff's claim, or title, an order of survey shall be unnecessary.

TRCP 798. COMMON SOURCE OF TITLE

It shall not be necessary for the plaintiff to deraign title beyond a common source. Proof of a common source may be made by the plaintiff by certified copies of the deeds showing a chain of title to the defendant emanating from and under such common source. Before any such certified copies shall be read in evidence, they shall be filed with the papers of the suit three days before the trial, and the adverse party served with notice of such filing as in other cases. Such certified copies shall not be evidence of title in the defendant unless offered in evidence by him. The plaintiff may make any legal objection to such certified copies, or the originals thereof, when introduced by the defendant.

TRCP 799. JUDGMENT BY DEFAULT

If the defendant, who has been personally served with citation according to law or these rules fails to appear and answer by himself or attorney within the time prescribed by law or these rules for other actions in the district court, then judgment by default may be entered against him and in favor of the plaintiff for the title to the premises, or the possession thereof, or for both, according to the petition, and for all costs, without any proof of title by the plaintiff.

TRCP 800. PROOF EX PARTE

If the defendant has been cited only by publication, and fails to appear and answer by himself, or by attorney of his own selection, or if any defendant, having answered, fails to appear by himself or attorney when the case is called for trial on its merits, the plaintiff shall make such proof as will entitle him prima facie to recover, whereupon the proper judgment shall be entered.

TRCP 801. WHEN DEFENDANT CLAIMS PART ONLY

Where the defendant claims part of the premises only, the answer shall be equivalent to a disclaimer of the balance.

TRCP 802. WHEN PLAINTIFF PROVES PART

Where the defendant claims the whole premises, and the plaintiff shows himself entitled to recover part, the plaintiff shall recover such part and costs.

TRCP 803. MAY RECOVER A PART

When there are two or more plaintiffs or defendants any one or more of the plaintiffs may recover against one or more of the defendants the premises, or any part thereof, or any interest therein, or damages, according to the rights of the parties.

TRCP 804. THE JUDGMENT

Upon the finding of the jury, or of the court where the case is tried by the court, in favor of the plaintiff for the whole or any part of the premises in controversy, the judgment shall be that the plaintiff recover of the defendant the title or possession, or both, as the case may be, of such premises, describing them, and where he recovers the possession, that he have his writ of possession.

TRCP 805. DAMAGES

Where it is alleged and proved that one of the parties is in possession of the premises, the court or jury, if they find for the adverse party, shall assess the damages for the use and occupation of the premises. If special injury to the property be alleged and proved, the damages for such injury shall also be assessed, and the proper judgment shall be entered therefor, on which execution may issue.

TRCP 806. CLAIM FOR IMPROVEMENTS

When the defendant or person in possession has claimed an allowance for improvements in accordance with Sections 22.021-22.024, Texas Property Code, the claim for use and occupation and damages mentioned in the preceding rule shall be considered and acted on in connection with such claim by the defendant or person in possession.

TRCP 807. JUDGMENT WHEN CLAIM FOR IMPROVEMENTS IS MADE

When a claim for improvements is successfully made under Sections 22.021-22.024, Texas Property Code, the judgment shall recite the estimated value of the premises without the improvements, and shall also include the conditions, stipulations and directions contained in Sections 22.021-22.024, Texas Property Code so far as applicable to the case before the court.

TRCP 808. THESE RULES SHALL NOT GOVERN, WHEN

Nothing in Sections 22.001-22.045, Texas Property Code, shall be so construed as to alter, impair or take away the rights of parties, as arising under the laws in force before the introduction of the common law, but the same shall be decided by the principles of the law under which the same accrued, or by which the same were regulated or in any manner affected.

TRCP 809. THESE RULES SHALL NOT GOVERN, WHEN

Nothing in these rules relating to trespass to try title shall be so construed as to alter, impair or take away the rights of parties, as arising under the laws in force before the introduction of the common law, but the same shall be decided by the principles of the law under which the same accrued, or by which the same were regulated or in any manner affected.

SECTION 9. SUITS AGAINST NON-RESIDENTS

TRCP 810. REQUISITES OF PLEADINGS

The petition in actions authorized by Section 17.003, Civil Practice and Remedies Code, shall state the real names of the plaintiff and defendant, and shall describe the property involved with sufficient certainty to identify the same, the interest which the plaintiff claims, and such proceedings shall be had in such action as may be necessary to fully settle and determine the question of right or title in and to said property between the parties to said suit, and to decree the title or right of the party entitled thereto; and the court may issue the appropriate order to carry such decree, judgment or order into effect; and whenever such petition has been duly filed and citation thereon has been duly served by publication as required by Rules 114-116, the plaintiff may, at any time prior to entering the decree by leave of court first had and obtained, file amended and supplemental pleadings that do not subject additional property to said suit without the necessity of reciting the defendants so cited as aforesaid.

TITLE 42. THE PUBLIC HEALTH & WELFARE

Chapter 45. Fair Housing

Subchapter I. Generally

Subchapter II. Prevention of Intimidation

TITLE 42. THE PUBLIC HEALTH & WELFARE

CHAPTER 45. FAIR HOUSING

SUBCHAPTER I. GENERALLY

§3601. DECLARATION OF POLICY

It is the policy of the United States to provide, within constitutional limitations, for fair housing throughout the United States.

History of 42 U.S.C. §3601: Apr. 11, 1968, P.L. 90-284, §801, 82 Stat. 81. See also Prop. Code §301.002.

ANNOTATIONS

Texas Dept. of Hous. & Cmty. Affairs v. Inclusive Cmty. Project, Inc., ___ U.S. ___, 135 S.Ct. 2507, 2521-22 (2015). "Recognition of disparate-impact claims is consistent with the FHA's central purpose. The FHA ... was enacted to eradicate discriminatory practices within a sector of our Nation's economy. [¶] These unlawful practices include zoning laws and other housing restrictions that function unfairly to exclude minorities from certain neighborhoods without any sufficient justification. Suits targeting such practices reside at the heartland of disparate-impact liability. The availability of disparate-impact liability ... has allowed private developers to vindicate the FHA's objectives and to protect their property rights by stopping municipalities from enforcing arbitrary and, in practice, discriminatory ordinances barring the construction of certain types of housing units. Recognition of disparate-impact liability under the FHA also plays a role in uncovering discriminatory intent: It permits plaintiffs to counteract unconscious prejudices and disguised animus that escape easy classification as disparate treatment. In this way disparate-impact liability may prevent segregated housing patterns that might otherwise result from covert and illicit stereotyping."

§3602. DEFINITIONS

As used in this subchapter—

(a) "Secretary" means the Secretary of Housing and Urban Development.

(b) "Dwelling" means any building, structure, or portion thereof which is occupied as, or designed or intended for occupancy as, a residence by one or more families, and any vacant land which is offered for sale or lease for the construction or location thereon of any such building, structure, or portion thereof.

(c) "Family" includes a single individual.

(d) "Person" includes one or more individuals, corporations, partnerships, associations, labor organizations, legal representatives, mutual companies, joint-stock companies, trusts, unincorporated organizations, trustees, trustees in cases under title 11, receivers, and fiduciaries.

(e) "To rent" includes to lease, to sublease, to let and otherwise to grant for a consideration the right to occupy premises not owned by the occupant.

(f) "Discriminatory housing practice" means an act that is unlawful under section 3604, 3605, 3606, or 3617 of this title.

(g) "State" means any of the several States, the District of Columbia, the Commonwealth of Puerto Rico, or any of the territories and possessions of the United States.

(h) "Handicap" means, with respect to a person—

(1) a physical or mental impairment which substantially limits one or more of such person's major life activities,

(2) a record of having such an impairment, or

(3) being regarded as having such an impairment,

but such term does not include current, illegal use of or addiction to a controlled substance (as defined in section 802 of title 21).

(i) "Aggrieved person" includes any person who—

(1) claims to have been injured by a discriminatory housing practice; or

(2) believes that such person will be injured by a discriminatory housing practice that is about to occur.

(j) "Complainant" means the person (including the Secretary) who files a complaint under section 3610 of this title.

(k) "Familial status" means one or more individuals (who have not attained the age of 18 years) being domiciled with—

(1) a parent or another person having legal custody of such individual or individuals; or

(2) the designee of such parent or other person having such custody, with the written permission of such parent or other person.

The protections afforded against discrimination on the basis of familial status shall apply to any person who is pregnant or is in the process of securing legal custody of any individual who has not attained the age of 18 years.

(l) "Conciliation" means the attempted resolution of issues raised by a complaint, or by the investigation of such complaint, through informal negotiations involving the aggrieved person, the respondent, and the Secretary.

(m) "Conciliation agreement" means a written agreement setting forth the resolution of the issues in conciliation.

(n) "Respondent" means—

(1) the person or other entity accused in a complaint of an unfair housing practice; and

(2) any other person or entity identified in the course of investigation and notified as required with respect to respondents so identified under section 3610(a) of this title.

(o) "Prevailing party" has the same meaning as such term has in section 1988 of this title.

History of 42 U.S.C. §3602: Apr. 11, 1968, P.L. 90-284, §802, 82 Stat. 81; Nov. 6, 1978, P.L. 95-598, §331, 92 Stat. 2679; Sept. 13, 1988, P.L. 100-430, §5, 102 Stat. 1619.

See also Prop. Code §§301.003, 301.004.

ANNOTATIONS

Bank of Am. Corp. v. City of Miami, ___ U.S. ___, 137 S.Ct. 1296, ___ (2017). "The FHA permits any aggrieved person to bring a housing-discrimination lawsuit. [¶] [T]he definition of person aggrieved in the original version of the FHA ... showed a congressional intention to define standing as broadly as is permitted by ... the Constitution. [¶] [I]n 1988, when Congress amended the FHA, it retained without significant change the definition of person aggrieved that this Court had broadly construed. [¶] [P's] complaints allege that [Ds] intentionally targeted predatory practices at African-American and Latino neighborhoods and residents.... That unlawful conduct led to a concentration of foreclosures and vacancies in those neighborhoods. Those concentrated foreclosures and vacancies caused stagnation and decline in African-American and Latino neighborhoods. They hindered [P's] efforts to create integrated, stable neighborhoods. And, highly relevant here, they reduced property values, diminishing [P's] property-tax revenue and increasing demand for municipal services. [¶] [P] alleges economic injuries that arguably fall within the FHA's zone of interests, as we have previously interpreted that statute. Principles of *stare decisis* compel our adherence to those precedents in this context." (Internal quotes omitted.)

§3603. EFFECTIVE DATES OF CERTAIN PROHIBITIONS

(a) Application to certain described dwellings.—Subject to the provisions of subsection (b) and section 3607 of this title, the prohibitions against discrimination in the sale or rental of housing set forth in section 3604 of this title shall apply:

(1) Upon enactment of this subchapter, to—

(A) dwellings owned or operated by the Federal Government;

(B) dwellings provided in whole or in part with the aid of loans, advances, grants, or contributions made by the Federal Government, under agreements entered into after November 20, 1962, unless payment due thereon has been made in full prior to April 11, 1968;

(C) dwellings provided in whole or in part by loans insured, guaranteed, or otherwise secured by the credit

of the Federal Government, under agreements entered into after November 20, 1962, unless payment thereon has been made in full prior to April 11, 1968: *Provided*, That nothing contained in subparagraphs (B) and (C) of this subsection shall be applicable to dwellings solely by virtue of the fact that they are subject to mortgages held by an FDIC or FSLIC institution; and

(D) dwellings provided by the development or the redevelopment of real property purchased, rented, or otherwise obtained from a State or local public agency receiving Federal financial assistance for slum clearance or urban renewal with respect to such real property under loan or grant contracts entered into after November 20, 1962.

(2) After December 31, 1968, to all dwellings covered by paragraph (1) and to all other dwellings except as exempted by subsection (b).

(b) Exemptions.—Nothing in section 3604 of this title (other than subsection (c)) shall apply to—

(1) any single-family house sold or rented by an owner: *Provided*, That such private individual owner does not own more than three such single-family houses at any one time: *Provided further*, That in the case of the sale of any such single-family house by a private individual owner not residing in such house at the time of such sale or who was not the most recent resident of such house prior to such sale, the exemption granted by this subsection shall apply only with respect to one such sale within any twenty-four month period: *Provided further*, That such bona fide private individual owner does not own any interest in, nor is there owned or reserved on his behalf, under any express or voluntary agreement, title to or any right to all or a portion of the proceeds from the sale or rental of, more than three such single-family houses at any one time: *Provided further*, That after December 31, 1969, the sale or rental of any such single-family house shall be excepted from the application of this subchapter only if such house is sold or rented (A) without the use in any manner of the sales or rental facilities or the sales or rental services of any real estate broker, agent, or salesman, or of such facilities or services of any person in the business of selling or renting dwellings, or of any employee or agent of any such broker, agent, salesman, or person and (B) without the publication, posting or mailing, after notice, of any advertisement or written notice in violation of section 3604(c) of this title; but nothing in this proviso shall prohibit the use of attorneys, escrow agents, abstractors, title companies, and other such professional assistance as necessary to perfect or transfer the title, or

(2) rooms or units in dwellings containing living quarters occupied or intended to be occupied by no more than four families living independently of each other, if the owner actually maintains and occupies one of such living quarters as his residence.

(c) Business of selling or renting dwellings defined.—For the purposes of subsection (b), a person shall be deemed to be in the business of selling or renting dwellings if—

(1) he has, within the preceding twelve months, participated as principal in three or more transactions involving the sale or rental of any dwelling or any interest therein, or

(2) he has, within the preceding twelve months, participated as agent, other than in the sale of his own personal residence in providing sales or rental facilities or sales or rental services in two or more transactions involving the sale or rental of any dwelling or any interest therein, or

(3) he is the owner of any dwelling designed or intended for occupancy by, or occupied by, five or more families.

History of 42 U.S.C. §3603: Apr. 11, 1968, P.L. 90-284, §803, 82 Stat. 82.
See also Prop. Code §301.041.

§3604. DISCRIMINATION IN THE SALE OR RENTAL OF HOUSING & OTHER PROHIBITED PRACTICES

As made applicable by section 3603 of this title and except as exempted by sections 3603(b) and 3607 of this title, it shall be unlawful—

(a) To refuse to sell or rent after the making of a bona fide offer, or to refuse to negotiate for the sale or rental of, or otherwise make unavailable or deny, a dwelling to any person because of race, color, religion, sex, familial status, or national origin.

(b) To discriminate against any person in the terms, conditions, or privileges of sale or rental of a dwelling, or in the provision of services or facilities in connection therewith, because of race, color, religion, sex, familial status, or national origin.

(c) To make, print, or publish, or cause to be made, printed, or published any notice, statement, or advertisement, with respect to the sale or rental of a dwelling that indicates any preference, limitation, or discrimination based on race, color, religion, sex, handicap, fa-

milial status, or national origin, or an intention to make any such preference, limitation, or discrimination.

(d) To represent to any person because of race, color, religion, sex, handicap, familial status, or national origin that any dwelling is not available for inspection, sale, or rental when such dwelling is in fact so available.

(e) For profit, to induce or attempt to induce any person to sell or rent any dwelling by representations regarding the entry or prospective entry into the neighborhood of a person or persons of a particular race, color, religion, sex, handicap, familial status, or national origin.

(f)(1) To discriminate in the sale or rental, or to otherwise make unavailable or deny, a dwelling to any buyer or renter because of a handicap of—

(A) that buyer or renter,[1]

(B) a person residing in or intending to reside in that dwelling after it is so sold, rented, or made available; or

(C) any person associated with that buyer or renter.

(2) To discriminate against any person in the terms, conditions, or privileges of sale or rental of a dwelling, or in the provision of services or facilities in connection with such dwelling, because of a handicap of—

(A) that person; or

(B) a person residing in or intending to reside in that dwelling after it is so sold, rented, or made available; or

(C) any person associated with that person.

(3) For purposes of this subsection, discrimination includes—

(A) a refusal to permit, at the expense of the handicapped person, reasonable modifications of existing premises occupied or to be occupied by such person if such modifications may be necessary to afford such person full enjoyment of the premises except that, in the case of a rental, the landlord may where it is reasonable to do so condition permission for a modification on the renter agreeing to restore the interior of the premises to the condition that existed before the modification, reasonable wear and tear excepted.[2]

(B) a refusal to make reasonable accommodations in rules, policies, practices, or services, when such accommodations may be necessary to afford such person equal opportunity to use and enjoy a dwelling; or

(C) in connection with the design and construction of covered multifamily dwellings for first occupancy after the date that is 30 months after September 13, 1988, a failure to design and construct those dwellings in such a manner that—

(i) the public use and common use portions of such dwellings are readily accessible to and usable by handicapped persons;

(ii) all the doors designed to allow passage into and within all premises within such dwellings are sufficiently wide to allow passage by handicapped persons in wheelchairs; and

(iii) all premises within such dwellings contain the following features of adaptive design:

(I) an accessible route into and through the dwelling;

(II) light switches, electrical outlets, thermostats, and other environmental controls in accessible locations;

(III) reinforcements in bathroom walls to allow later installation of grab bars; and

(IV) usable kitchens and bathrooms such that an individual in a wheelchair can maneuver about the space.

(4) Compliance with the appropriate requirements of the American National Standard for buildings and facilities providing accessibility and usability for physically handicapped people (commonly cited as "ANSI A117.1") suffices to satisfy the requirements of paragraph (3)(C)(iii).

(5)(A) If a State or unit of general local government has incorporated into its laws the requirements set forth in paragraph (3)(C), compliance with such laws shall be deemed to satisfy the requirements of that paragraph.

(B) A State or unit of general local government may review and approve newly constructed covered multifamily dwellings for the purpose of making determinations as to whether the design and construction requirements of paragraph (3)(C) are met.

(C) The Secretary shall encourage, but may not require, States and units of local government to include in their existing procedures for the review and approval of newly constructed covered multifamily dwellings, de-

terminations as to whether the design and construction of such dwellings are consistent with paragraph (3)(C), and shall provide technical assistance to States and units of local government and other persons to implement the requirements of paragraph (3)(C).

(D) Nothing in this subchapter shall be construed to require the Secretary to review or approve the plans, designs or construction of all covered multifamily dwellings, to determine whether the design and construction of such dwellings are consistent with the requirements of paragraph 3(C).

(6)(A) Nothing in paragraph (5) shall be construed to affect the authority and responsibility of the Secretary or a State or local public agency certified pursuant to section 3610(f)(3) of this title to receive and process complaints or otherwise engage in enforcement activities under this subchapter.

(B) Determinations by a State or a unit of general local government under paragraphs (5)(A) and (B) shall not be conclusive in enforcement proceedings under this subchapter.

(7) As used in this subsection, the term "covered multifamily dwellings" means—

(A) buildings consisting of 4 or more units if such buildings have one or more elevators; and

(B) ground floor units in other buildings consisting of 4 or more units.

(8) Nothing in this subchapter shall be construed to invalidate or limit any law of a State or political subdivision of a State, or other jurisdiction in which this subchapter shall be effective, that requires dwellings to be designed and constructed in a manner that affords handicapped persons greater access than is required by this subchapter.

(9) Nothing in this subsection requires that a dwelling be made available to an individual whose tenancy would constitute a direct threat to the health or safety of other individuals or whose tenancy would result in substantial physical damage to the property of others.

1. **Editor's note:** So in original. The comma probably should be a semicolon.

2. **Editor's note:** So in original. The period probably should be a semicolon.

History of 42 U.S.C. §3604: Apr. 11, 1968, P.L. 90-284, §804, 82 Stat. 83; Aug. 22, 1974, P.L. 93-383, §808(b)(1), 88 Stat. 729; Sept. 13, 1988, P.L. 100-430, §6(a)-(b)(2), (e), 102 Stat. 1620, 1622, 1623, 1636.

See also Prop. Code §§301.021-301.025.

ANNOTATIONS

Texas Dept. of Hous. & Cmty. Affairs v. Inclusive Cmty. Project, Inc., ___ U.S. ___, 135 S.Ct. 2507, 2523 (2015). "[A] disparate-impact claim [brought under 42 U.S.C. §3604 or 3605] that relies on a statistical disparity must fail if the plaintiff cannot point to a defendant's policy or policies causing that disparity. A robust causality requirement ensures that '[r]acial imbalance ... does not, without more, establish a prima facie case of disparate impact' and thus protects defendants from being held liable for racial disparities they did not create. [¶] Courts must therefore examine with care whether a plaintiff has made out a prima facie case of disparate impact and prompt resolution of these cases is important. A plaintiff who fails to allege facts at the pleading stage or produce statistical evidence demonstrating a causal connection cannot make out a prima facie case of disparate impact."

Groome Res. Ltd. v. Parish of Jefferson, 234 F.3d 192, 202 (5th Cir.2000). "The question before this court is whether the activity of regulating discrimination against the disabled in the purchase, sale, or rental of housing can be shown to substantially affect interstate commerce, and therefore be upheld as a legitimate exercise of congressional authority. *At 205-06:* [T]o figure out whether an activity substantially affects interstate commerce, ... we must ask ... whether the regulated activity is an activity economic in nature. [¶] The Parish argues that the activity being regulated is 'wholly non-economic' and presumably non-commercial. We disagree.... [¶] A denial of reasonable accommodations [under §3604(f)(3)(B)] affects a disabled individual's ability to buy, sell, or rent housing. It is an act of discrimination that directly interferes with a commercial transaction, and is an act that can be regulated to facilitate economic activity. *At 209:* [I]n the context of the strong tradition of civil rights enforced through the Commerce Clause—a tradition in which the [Fair Housing Amendments Act of 1988] firmly sits—we have long recognized the broadly defined 'economic' aspect of discrimination. ... As long as there is recognition of an interstate effect, discrimination, even local discrimination, can be regulated under Congress's commerce power."

Elderhaven, Inc. v. City of Lubbock, 98 F.3d 175, 178 (5th Cir.1996). "[W]e reject the suggestion of certain courts that [an FHA] defendant bears the burden

of proof on the question of reasonableness. The text of the [FHA] provides no hint that Congress sought to change the normal rule that a plaintiff bears the burden of proving a violation of law by a preponderance of the evidence."

Simms v. First Gibraltar Bank, 83 F.3d 1546, 1559 (5th Cir.1996). "The FHA does not create a cause of action for bungling a deal, failing to follow industry custom, violating the Equal Credit Opportunity Act, or even making false representations to a government agency. The FHA instead prohibits a lending institution from using race, or any other prohibited factor, as a basis for making a lending decision."

U.S. v. Bob Lawrence Rlty., Inc., 474 F.2d 115, 120-21 (5th Cir.1973). "[D] argues that §3604(e) is unconstitutional [because] Congress does not have authority to enact the statute [and it] violates the 1st Amendment. [¶] This Court will give great deference ... to the congressional determination that §3604(e) will effectuate the purpose of the 13th Amendment by aiding in the elimination of the 'badges and incidents of slavery in the United States.' ... We find that the 13th Amendment empowers Congress to enact §3604(e). [¶] [D also] contends that §3604(e) constitutes an unconstitutional prior restraint by Congress on the right to free speech. [¶] Section 3604(e) regulates commercial activity, not speech. *At 122:* The only 'speech' proscribed by §3604(e) is commercial speech made to gain profit from racial representations. If §3604(e) were to reach a non-commercial statement, a political statement, or a purely informational statement, it would naturally be subject to 1st Amendment attack. However, it doesn't, and so §3604(e) does not violate the 1st Amendment."

§3605. DISCRIMINATION IN RESIDENTIAL REAL ESTATE-RELATED TRANSACTIONS

(a) In general.—It shall be unlawful for any person or other entity whose business includes engaging in residential real estate-related transactions to discriminate against any person in making available such a transaction, or in the terms or conditions of such a transaction, because of race, color, religion, sex, handicap, familial status, or national origin.

(b) "Residential real estate-related transaction" defined.—As used in this section, the term "residential real estate-related transaction" means any of the following:

(1) The making or purchasing of loans or providing other financial assistance—

(A) for purchasing, constructing, improving, repairing, or maintaining a dwelling; or

(B) secured by residential real estate.

(2) The selling, brokering, or appraising of residential real property.

(c) Appraisal exemption.—Nothing in this subchapter prohibits a person engaged in the business of furnishing appraisals of real property to take into consideration factors other than race, color, religion, national origin, sex, handicap, or familial status.

History of 42 U.S.C. §3605: Apr. 11, 1968, P.L. 90-284, §805, 82 Stat. 83; Aug. 22, 1974, P.L. 93-383, §808(b)(2), 88 Stat. 729; Sept. 13, 1988, P.L. 100-430, §6(c), 102 Stat. 1622.

See also Prop. Code §§301.026, 301.042(c).

ANNOTATIONS

Texas Dept. of Hous. & Cmty. Affairs v. Inclusive Cmty. Project, Inc., ___ U.S. ___, 135 S.Ct. 2507, 2523 (2015). See annotation under 42 U.S.C. §3604, p. 1477.

Simms v. First Gibraltar Bank, 83 F.3d 1546, 1559 (5th Cir.1996). See annotation under 42 U.S.C. §3604, this page.

§3606. DISCRIMINATION IN THE PROVISION OF BROKERAGE SERVICES

After December 31, 1968, it shall be unlawful to deny any person access to or membership or participation in any multiple-listing service, real estate brokers' organization or other service, organization, or facility relating to the business of selling or renting dwellings, or to discriminate against him in the terms or conditions of such access, membership, or participation, on account of race, color, religion, sex, handicap, familial status, or national origin.

History of 42 U.S.C. §3606: Apr. 11, 1968, P.L. 90-284, §806, 82 Stat. 84; Aug. 22, 1974, P.L. 93-383, §808(b)(3), 88 Stat. 729; Sept. 13, 1988, P.L. 100-430, §6(b)(1), 102 Stat. 1622.

See also Prop. Code §301.027.

§3607. RELIGIOUS ORGANIZATION OR PRIVATE CLUB EXEMPTION

(a) Nothing in this subchapter shall prohibit a religious organization, association, or society, or any nonprofit institution or organization operated, supervised or controlled by or in conjunction with a religious organization, association, or society, from limiting the sale, rental or occupancy of dwellings which it owns or operates for other than a commercial purpose to persons of

the same religion, or from giving preference to such persons, unless membership in such religion is restricted on account of race, color, or national origin. Nor shall anything in this subchapter prohibit a private club not in fact open to the public, which as an incident to its primary purpose or purposes provides lodgings which it owns or operates for other than a commercial purpose, from limiting the rental or occupancy of such lodgings to its members or from giving preference to its members.

(b)(1) Nothing in this subchapter limits the applicability of any reasonable local, State, or Federal restrictions regarding the maximum number of occupants permitted to occupy a dwelling. Nor does any provision in this subchapter regarding familial status apply with respect to housing for older persons.

(2) As used in this section, "housing for older persons" means housing—

(A) provided under any State or Federal program that the Secretary determines is specifically designed and operated to assist elderly persons (as defined in the State or Federal program); or

(B) intended for, and solely occupied by, persons 62 years of age or older; or

(C) intended and operated for occupancy by persons 55 years of age or older, and—

(i) at least 80 percent of the occupied units are occupied by at least one person who is 55 years of age or older;

(ii) the housing facility or community publishes and adheres to policies and procedures that demonstrate the intent required under this subparagraph; and

(iii) the housing facility or community complies with rules issued by the Secretary for verification of occupancy, which shall—

(I) provide for verification by reliable surveys and affidavits; and

(II) include examples of the types of policies and procedures relevant to a determination of compliance with the requirement of clause (ii). Such surveys and affidavits shall be admissible in administrative and judicial proceedings for the purposes of such verification.

(3) Housing shall not fail to meet the requirements for housing for older persons by reason of:

(A) persons residing in such housing as of September 13, 1988, who do not meet the age requirements of subsections (2)(B) or (C): *Provided*, That new occupants of such housing meet the age requirements of subsections (2)(B) or (C); or

(B) unoccupied units: *Provided*, That such units are reserved for occupancy by persons who meet the age requirements of subsections (2)(B) or (C).

(4) Nothing in this subchapter prohibits conduct against a person because such person has been convicted by any court of competent jurisdiction of the illegal manufacture or distribution of a controlled substance as defined in section 802 of title 21.

(5)(A) A person shall not be held personally liable for monetary damages for a violation of this subchapter if such person reasonably relied, in good faith, on the application of the exemption under this subsection relating to housing for older persons.

(B) For the purposes of this paragraph, a person may only show good faith reliance on the application of the exemption by showing that—

(i) such person has no actual knowledge that the facility or community is not, or will not be, eligible for such exemption; and

(ii) the facility or community has stated formally, in writing, that the facility or community complies with the requirements for such exemption.

History of 42 U.S.C. §3607: Apr. 11, 1968, P.L. 90-284, §807, 82 Stat. 84; Sept. 13, 1988, P.L. 100-430, §6(d), 102 Stat. 1622; Dec. 28, 1995, P.L. 104-76, §§2, 3, 109 Stat. 787.

See also Prop. Code §§301.042(a), (b), 301.043, 301.044.

ANNOTATIONS

City of Edmonds v. Oxford House, Inc., 514 U.S. 725, 728 (1995). "This case presents the question whether a provision in [the city's] zoning code qualifies for §3607(b)(1)'s complete exemption from FHA scrutiny. The provision, governing areas zoned for single-family dwelling units, defines 'family' as 'persons [without regard to number] related by genetics, adoption, or marriage, or a group of five or fewer [unrelated] persons.' [¶] The defining provision at issue describes who may compose a family unit; it does not prescribe '*the* maximum number of occupants' a dwelling unit may house. *At 735:* [R]ules that cap the total number of occupants in order to prevent overcrowding of a dwelling 'plainly and unmistakably[ ]' ... fall within §3607(b)(1)'s absolute exemption from the FHA's governance; rules designed to preserve the family character of a neighborhood, fastening on the composition of households rather than on the total number of occupants living quarters can contain, do not."

§3608. ADMINISTRATION

(a) Authority and responsibility.—The authority and responsibility for administering this Act shall be in the Secretary of Housing and Urban Development.

(b) Assistant Secretary.—The Department of Housing and Urban Development shall be provided an additional Assistant Secretary.

(c) Delegation of authority; appointment of administrative law judges; location of conciliation meetings; administrative review.—The Secretary may delegate any of his functions, duties, and powers to employees of the Department of Housing and Urban Development or to boards of such employees, including functions, duties, and powers with respect to investigating, conciliating, hearing, determining, ordering, certifying, reporting, or otherwise acting as to any work, business, or matter under this subchapter. The person to whom such delegations are made with respect to hearing functions, duties, and powers shall be appointed and shall serve in the Department of Housing and Urban Development in compliance with sections 3105, 3344, 5372, and 7521 of title 5. Insofar as possible, conciliation meetings shall be held in the cities or other localities where the discriminatory housing practices allegedly occurred. The Secretary shall by rule prescribe such rights of appeal from the decisions of his administrative law judges to other administrative law judges or to other officers in the Department, to boards of officers or to himself, as shall be appropriate and in accordance with law.

(d) Cooperation of Secretary and executive departments and agencies in administration of housing and urban development programs and activities to further fair housing purposes.—All executive departments and agencies shall administer their programs and activities relating to housing and urban development (including any Federal agency having regulatory or supervisory authority over financial institutions) in a manner affirmatively to further the purposes of this subchapter and shall cooperate with the Secretary to further such purposes.

(e) Functions of Secretary.—The Secretary of Housing and Urban Development shall—

(1) make studies with respect to the nature and extent of discriminatory housing practices in representative communities, urban, suburban, and rural, throughout the United States;

(2) publish and disseminate reports, recommendations, and information derived from such studies, including an annual report to the Congress—

(A) specifying the nature and extent of progress made nationally in eliminating discriminatory housing practices and furthering the purposes of this subchapter, obstacles remaining to achieving equal housing opportunity, and recommendations for further legislative or executive action; and

(B) containing tabulations of the number of instances (and the reasons therefor) in the preceding year in which—

(i) investigations are not completed as required by section 3610(a)(1)(B) of this title;

(ii) determinations are not made within the time specified in section 3610(g) of this title; and

(iii) hearings are not commenced or findings and conclusions are not made as required by section 3612(g) of this title;

(3) cooperate with and render technical assistance to Federal, State, local, and other public or private agencies, organizations, and institutions which are formulating or carrying on programs to prevent or eliminate discriminatory housing practices;

(4) cooperate with and render such technical and other assistance to the Community Relations Service as may be appropriate to further its activities in preventing or eliminating discriminatory housing practices;

(5) administer the programs and activities relating to housing and urban development in a manner affirmatively to further the policies of this subchapter; and

(6) annually report to the Congress, and make available to the public, data on the race, color, religion, sex, national origin, age, handicap, and family characteristics of persons and households who are applicants for, participants in, or beneficiaries or potential beneficiaries of, programs administered by the Department to the extent such characteristics are within the coverage of the provisions of law and Executive orders referred to in subsection (f) which apply to such programs (and in order to develop the data to be included and made available to the public under this subsection, the Secretary shall, without regard to any other provision of law, collect such information relating to those characteristics as the Secretary determines to be necessary or appropriate).

(f) Provisions of law applicable to Department programs.—The provisions of law and Executive orders to which subsection (e)(6) applies are—

(1) title VI of the Civil Rights Act of 1964 (42 U.S.C. 2000d et seq.);

(2) this subchapter;

(3) section 794 of title 29;

(4) the Age Discrimination Act of 1975 (42 U.S.C. 6101 et seq.);

(5) the Equal Credit Opportunity Act (15 U.S.C. 1691 et seq.);

(6) section 1982 of this title;

(7) section 637(a) of title 15;

(8) section 1735f-5 of title 12;

(9) section 5309 of this title;

(10) section 1701u of title 12;

(11) Executive orders 11063, 11246, 11625, 12250, 12259, and 12432; and

(12) any other provision of law which the Secretary specifies by publication in the Federal Register for the purpose of this subsection.

History of 42 U.S.C. §3608: Apr. 11, 1968, P.L. 90-284, §808, 82 Stat. 84; Mar. 27, 1978, P.L. 95-251, §3, 92 Stat. 184; Oct. 13, 1978, P.L. 95-454, §801(a)(3)(J), 92 Stat. 1222; Sept. 13, 1988, P.L. 100-430, §7, 102 Stat. 1623.

See also Prop. Code §§301.065, 301.066.

§3608a. COLLECTION OF CERTAIN DATA

(a) In general.—To assess the extent of compliance with Federal fair housing requirements (including the requirements established under title VI of Public Law 88-352 (42 U.S.C. 2000d et seq.) and title VIII of Public Law 90-284 (42 U.S.C. 3601 et seq.)), the Secretary of Agriculture shall collect, not less than annually, data on the racial and ethnic characteristics of persons eligible for, assisted, or otherwise benefiting under each community development, housing assistance, and mortgage and loan insurance and guarantee program administered by such Secretary. Such data shall be collected on a building by building basis if the Secretary determines such collection to be appropriate.

(b) Reports to Congress.—The Secretary of Agriculture shall include in the annual report of such Secretary to the Congress a summary and evaluation of the data collected by such Secretary under subsection (a) during the preceding year.

History of 42 U.S.C. §3608a: Feb. 5, 1988, P.L. 100-242, §562, 101 Stat. 1944; Dec. 21, 1995, P.L. 104-66, §1071(e), 109 Stat. 720.

See also Prop. Code §301.065.

§3609. EDUCATION & CONCILIATION; CONFERENCES & CONSULTATIONS; REPORTS

Immediately after April 11, 1968, the Secretary shall commence such educational and conciliatory activities as in his judgment will further the purposes of this subchapter. He shall call conferences of persons in the housing industry and other interested parties to acquaint them with the provisions of this subchapter and his suggested means of implementing it, and shall endeavor with their advice to work out programs of voluntary compliance and of enforcement. He may pay per diem, travel, and transportation expenses for persons attending such conferences as provided in section 5703 of title 5. He shall consult with State and local officials and other interested parties to learn the extent, if any, to which housing discrimination exists in their State or locality, and whether and how State or local enforcement programs might be utilized to combat such discrimination in connection with or in place of, the Secretary's enforcement of this subchapter. The Secretary shall issue reports on such conferences and consultations as he deems appropriate.

History of 42 U.S.C. §3609: Apr. 11, 1968, P.L. 90-284, §809, 82 Stat. 85.

See also Prop. Code §§301.065, 301.066.

§3610. ADMINISTRATIVE ENFORCEMENT; PRELIMINARY MATTERS

(a) Complaints and answers—

(1)(A)(i) An aggrieved person may, not later than one year after an alleged discriminatory housing practice has occurred or terminated, file a complaint with the Secretary alleging such discriminatory housing practice. The Secretary, on the Secretary's own initiative, may also file such a complaint.

(ii) Such complaints shall be in writing and shall contain such information and be in such form as the Secretary requires.

(iii) The Secretary may also investigate housing practices to determine whether a complaint should be brought under this section.

(B) Upon the filing of such a complaint—

(i) the Secretary shall serve notice upon the aggrieved person acknowledging such filing and advising the aggrieved person of the time limits and choice of forums provided under this subchapter;

(ii) the Secretary shall, not later than 10 days after such filing or the identification of an additional respon-

dent under paragraph (2), serve on the respondent a notice identifying the alleged discriminatory housing practice and advising such respondent of the procedural rights and obligations of respondents under this subchapter, together with a copy of the original complaint;

(iii) each respondent may file, not later than 10 days after receipt of notice from the Secretary, an answer to such complaint; and

(iv) the Secretary shall make an investigation of the alleged discriminatory housing practice and complete such investigation within 100 days after the filing of the complaint (or, when the Secretary takes further action under subsection (f)(2) with respect to a complaint, within 100 days after the commencement of such further action), unless it is impracticable to do so.

(C) If the Secretary is unable to complete the investigation within 100 days after the filing of the complaint (or, when the Secretary takes further action under subsection (f)(2) with respect to a complaint, within 100 days after the commencement of such further action), the Secretary shall notify the complainant and respondent in writing of the reasons for not doing so.

(D) Complaints and answers shall be under oath or affirmation, and may be reasonably and fairly amended at any time.

(2)(A) A person who is not named as a respondent in a complaint, but who is identified as a respondent in the course of investigation, may be joined as an additional or substitute respondent upon written notice, under paragraph (1), to such person, from the Secretary.

(B) Such notice, in addition to meeting the requirements of paragraph (1), shall explain the basis for the Secretary's belief that the person to whom the notice is addressed is properly joined as a respondent.

(b) Investigative report and conciliation—

(1) During the period beginning with the filing of such complaint and ending with the filing of a charge or a dismissal by the Secretary, the Secretary shall, to the extent feasible, engage in conciliation with respect to such complaint.

(2) A conciliation agreement arising out of such conciliation shall be an agreement between the respondent and the complainant, and shall be subject to approval by the Secretary.

(3) A conciliation agreement may provide for binding arbitration of the dispute arising from the complaint. Any such arbitration that results from a conciliation agreement may award appropriate relief, including monetary relief.

(4) Each conciliation agreement shall be made public unless the complainant and respondent otherwise agree and the Secretary determines that disclosure is not required to further the purposes of this subchapter.

(5)(A) At the end of each investigation under this section, the Secretary shall prepare a final investigative report containing—

(i) the names and dates of contacts with witnesses;

(ii) a summary and the dates of correspondence and other contacts with the aggrieved person and the respondent;

(iii) a summary description of other pertinent records;

(iv) a summary of witness statements; and

(v) answers to interrogatories.

(B) A final report under this paragraph may be amended if additional evidence is later discovered.

(c) Failure to comply with conciliation agreement.—Whenever the Secretary has reasonable cause to believe that a respondent has breached a conciliation agreement, the Secretary shall refer the matter to the Attorney General with a recommendation that a civil action be filed under section 3614 of this title for the enforcement of such agreement.

(d) Prohibitions and requirements with respect to disclosure of information—

(1) Nothing said or done in the course of conciliation under this subchapter may be made public or used as evidence in a subsequent proceeding under this subchapter without the written consent of the persons concerned.

(2) Notwithstanding paragraph (1), the Secretary shall make available to the aggrieved person and the respondent, at any time, upon request following completion of the Secretary's investigation, information derived from an investigation and any final investigative report relating to that investigation.

(e) Prompt judicial action—

(1) If the Secretary concludes at any time following the filing of a complaint that prompt judicial action is necessary to carry out the purposes of this subchapter, the Secretary may authorize a civil action for appropri-

ate temporary or preliminary relief pending final disposition of the complaint under this section. Upon receipt of such an authorization, the Attorney General shall promptly commence and maintain such an action. Any temporary restraining order or other order granting preliminary or temporary relief shall be issued in accordance with the Federal Rules of Civil Procedure. The commencement of a civil action under this subsection does not affect the initiation or continuation of administrative proceedings under this section and section 3612 of this title.

(2) Whenever the Secretary has reason to believe that a basis may exist for the commencement of proceedings against any respondent under sections 3614(a) and 3614(c) of this title or for proceedings by any governmental licensing or supervisory authorities, the Secretary shall transmit the information upon which such belief is based to the Attorney General, or to such authorities, as the case may be.

(f) Referral for State or local proceedings—

(1) Whenever a complaint alleges a discriminatory housing practice—

(A) within the jurisdiction of a State or local public agency; and

(B) as to which such agency has been certified by the Secretary under this subsection; the Secretary shall refer such complaint to that certified agency before taking any action with respect to such complaint.

(2) Except with the consent of such certified agency, the Secretary, after that referral is made, shall take no further action with respect to such complaint unless—

(A) the certified agency has failed to commence proceedings with respect to the complaint before the end of the 30th day after the date of such referral;

(B) the certified agency, having so commenced such proceedings, fails to carry forward such proceedings with reasonable promptness; or

(C) the Secretary determines that the certified agency no longer qualifies for certification under this subsection with respect to the relevant jurisdiction.

(3)(A) The Secretary may certify an agency under this subsection only if the Secretary determines that—

(i) the substantive rights protected by such agency in the jurisdiction with respect to which certification is to be made;

(ii) the procedures followed by such agency;

(iii) the remedies available to such agency; and

(iv) the availability of judicial review of such agency's action; are substantially equivalent to those created by and under this subchapter.

(B) Before making such certification, the Secretary shall take into account the current practices and past performance, if any, of such agency.

(4) During the period which begins on September 13, 1988, and ends 40 months after September 13, 1988, each agency certified (including an agency certified for interim referrals pursuant to 24 CFR 115.11, unless such agency is subsequently denied recognition under 24 CFR 115.7) for the purposes of this subchapter on the day before September 13, 1988, shall for the purposes of this subsection be considered certified under this subsection with respect to those matters for which such agency was certified on September 13, 1988. If the Secretary determines in an individual case that an agency has not been able to meet the certification requirements within this 40-month period due to exceptional circumstances, such as the infrequency of legislative sessions in that jurisdiction, the Secretary may extend such period by not more than 8 months.

(5) Not less frequently than every 5 years, the Secretary shall determine whether each agency certified under this subsection continues to qualify for certification. The Secretary shall take appropriate action with respect to any agency not so qualifying.

(g) Reasonable cause determination and effect—

(1) The Secretary shall, within 100 days after the filing of the complaint (or, when the Secretary takes further action under subsection (f)(2) with respect to a complaint, within 100 days after the commencement of such further action), determine based on the facts whether reasonable cause exists to believe that a discriminatory housing practice has occurred or is about to occur, unless it is impracticable to do so, or unless the Secretary has approved a conciliation agreement with respect to the complaint. If the Secretary is unable to make the determination within 100 days after the filing of the complaint (or, when the Secretary takes further action under subsection (f)(2) with respect to a complaint, within 100 days after the commencement of such further action), the Secretary shall notify the complainant and respondent in writing of the reasons for not doing so.

(2)(A) If the Secretary determines that reasonable cause exists to believe that a discriminatory housing practice has occurred or is about to occur, the Secretary shall, except as provided in subparagraph (C), immediately issue a charge on behalf of the aggrieved person, for further proceedings under section 3612 of this title.

(B) Such charge—

(i) shall consist of a short and plain statement of the facts upon which the Secretary has found reasonable cause to believe that a discriminatory housing practice has occurred or is about to occur;

(ii) shall be based on the final investigative report; and

(iii) need not be limited to the facts or grounds alleged in the complaint filed under subsection (a).

(C) If the Secretary determines that the matter involves the legality of any State or local zoning or other land use law or ordinance, the Secretary shall immediately refer the matter to the Attorney General for appropriate action under section 3614 of this title, instead of issuing such charge.

(3) If the Secretary determines that no reasonable cause exists to believe that a discriminatory housing practice has occurred or is about to occur, the Secretary shall promptly dismiss the complaint. The Secretary shall make public disclosure of each such dismissal.

(4) The Secretary may not issue a charge under this section regarding an alleged discriminatory housing practice after the beginning of the trial of a civil action commenced by the aggrieved party under an Act of Congress or a State law, seeking relief with respect to that discriminatory housing practice.

(h) **Service of copies of charge.**—After the Secretary issues a charge under this section, the Secretary shall cause a copy thereof, together with information as to how to make an election under section 3612(a) of this title and the effect of such an election, to be served—

(1) on each respondent named in such charge, together with a notice of opportunity for a hearing at a time and place specified in the notice, unless that election is made; and

(2) on each aggrieved person on whose behalf the complaint was filed.

History of 42 U.S.C. §3610: Apr. 11, 1968, P.L. 90-284, §810, as added Sept. 13, 1988, P.L. 100-430, §8(2), 102 Stat. 1625.

See also Prop. Code §§301.081-301.092.

§3611. SUBPOENAS; GIVING OF EVIDENCE

(a) **In general.**—The Secretary may, in accordance with this subsection, issue subpoenas and order discovery in aid of investigations and hearings under this subchapter. Such subpoenas and discovery may be ordered to the same extent and subject to the same limitations as would apply if the subpoenas or discovery were ordered or served in aid of a civil action in the United States district court for the district in which the investigation is taking place.

(b) **Witness fees.**—Witnesses summoned by a subpoena under this subchapter shall be entitled to the same witness and mileage fees as witnesses in proceedings in United States district courts. Fees payable to a witness summoned by a subpoena issued at the request of a party shall be paid by that party or, where a party is unable to pay the fees, by the Secretary.

(c) **Criminal penalties**—

(1) Any person who willfully fails or neglects to attend and testify or to answer any lawful inquiry or to produce records, documents, or other evidence, if it is in such person's power to do so, in obedience to the subpoena or other lawful order under subsection (a), shall be fined not more than $100,000 or imprisoned not more than one year, or both.

(2) Any person who, with intent thereby to mislead another person in any proceeding under this subchapter—

(A) makes or causes to be made any false entry or statement of fact in any report, account, record, or other document produced pursuant to subpoena or other lawful order under subsection (a);

(B) willfully neglects or fails to make or to cause to be made full, true, and correct entries in such reports, accounts, records, or other documents; or

(C) willfully mutilates, alters, or by any other means falsifies any documentary evidence;

shall be fined not more than $100,000 or imprisoned not more than one year, or both.

History of 42 U.S.C. §3611: Apr. 11, 1968, P.L. 90-284, §811, as added Sept. 13, 1988, P.L. 100-430, §8(2), 102 Stat. 1628.

See also Prop. Code §§301.067, 301.133.

§3612. ENFORCEMENT BY SECRETARY

(a) **Election of judicial determination.**—When a charge is filed under section 3610 of this title, a complainant, a respondent, or an aggrieved person on

whose behalf the complaint was filed, may elect to have the claims asserted in that charge decided in a civil action under subsection (o) in lieu of a hearing under subsection (b). The election must be made not later than 20 days after the receipt by the electing person of service under section 3610(h) of this title or, in the case of the Secretary, not later than 20 days after such service. The person making such election shall give notice of doing so to the Secretary and to all other complainants and respondents to whom the charge relates.

(b) Administrative law judge hearing in absence of election.—If an election is not made under subsection (a) with respect to a charge filed under section 3610 of this title, the Secretary shall provide an opportunity for a hearing on the record with respect to a charge issued under section 3610 of this title. The Secretary shall delegate the conduct of a hearing under this section to an administrative law judge appointed under section 3105 of title 5. The administrative law judge shall conduct the hearing at a place in the vicinity in which the discriminatory housing practice is alleged to have occurred or to be about to occur.

(c) Rights of parties.—At a hearing under this section, each party may appear in person, be represented by counsel, present evidence, cross-examine witnesses, and obtain the issuance of subpoenas under section 3611 of this title. Any aggrieved person may intervene as a party in the proceeding. The Federal Rules of Evidence apply to the presentation of evidence in such hearing as they would in a civil action in a United States district court.

(d) Expedited discovery and hearing—

(1) Discovery in administrative proceedings under this section shall be conducted as expeditiously and inexpensively as possible, consistent with the need of all parties to obtain relevant evidence.

(2) A hearing under this section shall be conducted as expeditiously and inexpensively as possible, consistent with the needs and rights of the parties to obtain a fair hearing and a complete record.

(3) The Secretary shall, not later than 180 days after September 13, 1988, issue rules to implement this subsection.

(e) Resolution of charge.—Any resolution of a charge before a final order under this section shall require the consent of the aggrieved person on whose behalf the charge is issued.

(f) Effect of trial of civil action on administrative proceedings.—An administrative law judge may not continue administrative proceedings under this section regarding any alleged discriminatory housing practice after the beginning of the trial of a civil action commenced by the aggrieved party under an Act of Congress or a State law, seeking relief with respect to that discriminatory housing practice.

(g) Hearings, findings and conclusions, and order—

(1) The administrative law judge shall commence the hearing under this section no later than 120 days following the issuance of the charge, unless it is impracticable to do so. If the administrative law judge is unable to commence the hearing within 120 days after the issuance of the charge, the administrative law judge shall notify the Secretary, the aggrieved person on whose behalf the charge was filed, and the respondent, in writing of the reasons for not doing so.

(2) The administrative law judge shall make findings of fact and conclusions of law within 60 days after the end of the hearing under this section, unless it is impracticable to do so. If the administrative law judge is unable to make findings of fact and conclusions of law within such period, or any succeeding 60-day period thereafter, the administrative law judge shall notify the Secretary, the aggrieved person on whose behalf the charge was filed, and the respondent, in writing of the reasons for not doing so.

(3) If the administrative law judge finds that a respondent has engaged or is about to engage in a discriminatory housing practice, such administrative law judge shall promptly issue an order for such relief as may be appropriate, which may include actual damages suffered by the aggrieved person and injunctive or other equitable relief. Such order may, to vindicate the public interest, assess a civil penalty against the respondent—

(A) in an amount not exceeding $10,000 if the respondent has not been adjudged to have committed any prior discriminatory housing practice;

(B) in an amount not exceeding $25,000 if the respondent has been adjudged to have committed one other discriminatory housing practice during the 5-year period ending on the date of the filing of this charge; and

(C) in an amount not exceeding $50,000 if the respondent has been adjudged to have committed 2 or more discriminatory housing practices during the

7-year period ending on the date of the filing of this charge; except that if the acts constituting the discriminatory housing practice that is the object of the charge are committed by the same natural person who has been previously adjudged to have committed acts constituting a discriminatory housing practice, then the civil penalties set forth in subparagraphs (B) and (C) may be imposed without regard to the period of time within which any subsequent discriminatory housing practice occurred.

(4) No such order shall affect any contract, sale, encumbrance, or lease consummated before the issuance of such order and involving a bona fide purchaser, encumbrancer, or tenant without actual notice of the charge filed under this subchapter.

(5) In the case of an order with respect to a discriminatory housing practice that occurred in the course of a business subject to a licensing or regulation by a governmental agency, the Secretary shall, not later than 30 days after the date of the issuance of such order (or, if such order is judicially reviewed, 30 days after such order is in substance affirmed upon such review)—

(A) send copies of the findings of fact, conclusions of law, and the order, to that governmental agency; and

(B) recommend to that governmental agency appropriate disciplinary action (including, where appropriate, the suspension or revocation of the license of the respondent).

(6) In the case of an order against a respondent against whom another order was issued within the preceding 5 years under this section, the Secretary shall send a copy of each such order to the Attorney General.

(7) If the administrative law judge finds that the respondent has not engaged or is not about to engage in a discriminatory housing practice, as the case may be, such administrative law judge shall enter an order dismissing the charge. The Secretary shall make public disclosure of each such dismissal.

(h) Review by Secretary; service of final order—

(1) The Secretary may review any finding, conclusion, or order issued under subsection (g). Such review shall be completed not later than 30 days after the finding, conclusion, or order is so issued; otherwise the finding, conclusion, or order becomes final.

(2) The Secretary shall cause the findings of fact and conclusions of law made with respect to any final order for relief under this section, together with a copy of such order, to be served on each aggrieved person and each respondent in the proceeding.

(i) Judicial review—

(1) Any party aggrieved by a final order for relief under this section granting or denying in whole or in part the relief sought may obtain a review of such order under chapter 158 of title 28.

(2) Notwithstanding such chapter, venue of the proceeding shall be in the judicial circuit in which the discriminatory housing practice is alleged to have occurred, and filing of the petition for review shall be not later than 30 days after the order is entered.

(j) Court enforcement of administrative order upon petition by Secretary—

(1) The Secretary may petition any United States court of appeals for the circuit in which the discriminatory housing practice is alleged to have occurred or in which any respondent resides or transacts business for the enforcement of the order of the administrative law judge and for appropriate temporary relief or restraining order, by filing in such court a written petition praying that such order be enforced and for appropriate temporary relief or restraining order.

(2) The Secretary shall file in court with the petition the record in the proceeding. A copy of such petition shall be forthwith transmitted by the clerk of the court to the parties to the proceeding before the administrative law judge.

(k) Relief which may be granted—

(1) Upon the filing of a petition under subsection (i) or (j), the court may—

(A) grant to the petitioner, or any other party, such temporary relief, restraining order, or other order as the court deems just and proper;

(B) affirm, modify, or set aside, in whole or in part, the order, or remand the order for further proceedings; and

(C) enforce such order to the extent that such order is affirmed or modified.

(2) Any party to the proceeding before the administrative law judge may intervene in the court of appeals.

(3) No objection not made before the administrative law judge shall be considered by the court, unless the failure or neglect to urge such objection is excused because of extraordinary circumstances.

(*l*) Enforcement decree in absence of petition for review.—If no petition for review is filed under subsection (i) before the expiration of 45 days after the date the administrative law judge's order is entered, the administrative law judge's findings of fact and order shall be conclusive in connection with any petition for enforcement—

(1) which is filed by the Secretary under subsection (j) after the end of such day; or

(2) under subsection (m).

(m) Court enforcement of administrative order upon petition of any person entitled to relief.—If before the expiration of 60 days after the date the administrative law judge's order is entered, no petition for review has been filed under subsection (i), and the Secretary has not sought enforcement of the order under subsection (j), any person entitled to relief under the order may petition for a decree enforcing the order in the United States court of appeals for the circuit in which the discriminatory housing practice is alleged to have occurred.

(n) Entry of decree.—The clerk of the court of appeals in which a petition for enforcement is filed under subsection (*l*) or (m) shall forthwith enter a decree enforcing the order and shall transmit a copy of such decree to the Secretary, the respondent named in the petition, and to any other parties to the proceeding before the administrative law judge.

(o) Civil action for enforcement when election is made for such civil action—

(1) If an election is made under subsection (a), the Secretary shall authorize, and not later than 30 days after the election is made the Attorney General shall commence and maintain, a civil action on behalf of the aggrieved person in a United States district court seeking relief under this subsection. Venue for such civil action shall be determined under chapter 87 of title 28.

(2) Any aggrieved person with respect to the issues to be determined in a civil action under this subsection may intervene as of right in that civil action.

(3) In a civil action under this subsection, if the court finds that a discriminatory housing practice has occurred or is about to occur, the court may grant as relief any relief which a court could grant with respect to such discriminatory housing practice in a civil action under section 3613 of this title. Any relief so granted that would accrue to an aggrieved person in a civil action commenced by that aggrieved person under section 3613 of this title shall also accrue to that aggrieved person in a civil action under this subsection. If monetary relief is sought for the benefit of an aggrieved person who does not intervene in the civil action, the court shall not award such relief if that aggrieved person has not complied with discovery orders entered by the court.

(p) Attorney's fees.—In any administrative proceeding brought under this section, or any court proceeding arising therefrom, or any civil action under this section, the administrative law judge or the court, as the case may be, in its discretion, may allow the prevailing party, other than the United States, a reasonable attorney's fee and costs. The United States shall be liable for such fees and costs to the extent provided by section 504 of title 5 or by section 2412 of title 28.

History of 42 U.S.C. §3612: Apr. 11, 1968, P.L. 90-284, §812, as added Sept. 13, 1988, P.L. 100-430, §8(2), 102 Stat. 1629.

See also Prop. Code §§301.093-301.131.

§3613. ENFORCEMENT BY PRIVATE PERSONS

(a) Civil action—

(1)(A) An aggrieved person may commence a civil action in an appropriate United States district court or State court not later than 2 years after the occurrence or the termination of an alleged discriminatory housing practice, or the breach of a conciliation agreement entered into under this subchapter, whichever occurs last, to obtain appropriate relief with respect to such discriminatory housing practice or breach.

(B) The computation of such 2-year period shall not include any time during which an administrative proceeding under this subchapter was pending with respect to a complaint or charge under this subchapter based upon such discriminatory housing practice. This subparagraph does not apply to actions arising from a breach of a conciliation agreement.

(2) An aggrieved person may commence a civil action under this subsection whether or not a complaint has been filed under section 3610(a) of this title and without regard to the status of any such complaint, but if the Secretary or a State or local agency has obtained a conciliation agreement with the consent of an aggrieved person, no action may be filed under this subsection by such aggrieved person with respect to the alleged discriminatory housing practice which forms the basis for such complaint except for the purpose of enforcing the terms of such an agreement.

(3) An aggrieved person may not commence a civil action under this subsection with respect to an alleged discriminatory housing practice which forms the basis of a charge issued by the Secretary if an administrative law judge has commenced a hearing on the record under this subchapter with respect to such charge.

(b) Appointment of attorney by court.—Upon application by a person alleging a discriminatory housing practice or a person against whom such a practice is alleged, the court may—

(1) appoint an attorney for such person; or

(2) authorize the commencement or continuation of a civil action under subsection (a) without the payment of fees, costs, or security, if in the opinion of the court such person is financially unable to bear the costs of such action.

(c) Relief which may be granted—

(1) In a civil action under subsection (a), if the court finds that a discriminatory housing practice has occurred or is about to occur, the court may award to the plaintiff actual and punitive damages, and subject to subsection (d), may grant as relief, as the court deems appropriate, any permanent or temporary injunction, temporary restraining order, or other order (including an order enjoining the defendant from engaging in such practice or ordering such affirmative action as may be appropriate).

(2) In a civil action under subsection (a), the court, in its discretion, may allow the prevailing party, other than the United States, a reasonable attorney's fee and costs. The United States shall be liable for such fees and costs to the same extent as a private person.

(d) Effect on certain sales, encumbrances, and rentals.—Relief granted under this section shall not affect any contract, sale, encumbrance, or lease consummated before the granting of such relief and involving a bona fide purchaser, encumbrancer, or tenant, without actual notice of the filing of a complaint with the Secretary or civil action under this subchapter.

(e) Intervention by Attorney General.—Upon timely application, the Attorney General may intervene in such civil action, if the Attorney General certifies that the case is of general public importance. Upon such intervention the Attorney General may obtain such relief as would be available to the Attorney General under section 3614(e) of this title in a civil action to which such section applies.

History of 42 U.S.C. §3613: Apr. 11, 1968, P.L. 90-284, §813, as added Sept. 13, 1988, P.L. 100-430, §8(2), 102 Stat. 1633.

See also Prop. Code §§301.151-301.156.

ANNOTATIONS

Bank of Am. Corp. v. City of Miami, ___ U.S. ___, 137 S.Ct. 1296, ___ (2017). "It is a well established principle of the common law that in all cases of loss, we are to attribute it to the proximate cause, and not to any remote cause. … A claim for damages under the FHA—which is akin to a tort action, … is no exception to this traditional requirement. [¶] In these cases, the conduct the statute prohibits consists of intentionally lending to minority borrowers on worse terms than equally creditworthy nonminority borrowers and inducing defaults by failing to extend refinancing and loan modifications to minority borrowers on fair terms. [P] alleges that [Ds'] misconduct led to a disproportionate number of foreclosures and vacancies in specific … neighborhoods. These foreclosures and vacancies purportedly harmed [P], which lost property-tax revenue when the value of the properties in those neighborhoods fell and was forced to spend more on municipal services in the affected areas. [¶] We conclude that … foreseeability is [not] sufficient to establish proximate cause under the FHA. … In the context of the FHA, foreseeability alone does not ensure the close connection that proximate cause requires. [¶] Rather, proximate cause under the FHA requires some direct relation between the injury asserted and the injurious conduct alleged." (Internal quotes omitted.)

Texas Dept. of Hous. & Cmty. Affairs v. Inclusive Cmty. Project, Inc., ___ U.S. ___, 135 S.Ct. 2507, 2524 (2015). "[E]ven when courts do find liability under a disparate-impact theory [brought under §3613], their remedial orders must be consistent with the Constitution. Remedial orders in disparate-impact cases should concentrate on the elimination of the offending practice that 'arbitrar[ily] … operate[s] invidiously to discriminate on the basis of rac[e].' If additional measures are adopted, courts should strive to design them to eliminate racial disparities through race-neutral means. Remedial orders that impose racial targets or quotas might raise more difficult constitutional questions."

Havens Rlty. Corp. v. Coleman, 455 U.S. 363, 372 (1982). "[T]he sole requirement for standing to sue under [FHA] §812 [now 42 U.S.C. §3613] is the [U.S. Const.] Art. 3 minima of injury in fact: that the plaintiff

allege that as a result of the defendant's actions he has suffered 'a distinct and palpable injury[ ]'.... *At 373-74:* We [now] address the question of 'tester' standing. [¶] '[T]esters' are individuals who, without an intent to rent or purchase a home or apartment, pose as renters or purchasers for the purpose of collecting evidence of unlawful steering practices. ... Congress has ... conferred on all 'persons' a legal right to truthful information about available housing. [¶] A tester who has been the object of a misrepresentation made unlawful under [FHA] §804(d) [now 42 U.S.C. §3604(d)] has suffered injury in precisely the form the statute was intended to guard against, and therefore has standing to [sue]. That the tester may have approached the real estate agent fully expecting that he would receive false information, and without any intention of buying or renting a home, does not negate the simple fact of injury within the meaning of §804(d)." *See also **Gladstone, Realtors v. Village of Bellwood***, 441 U.S. 91, 109 (1979).

§3614. ENFORCEMENT BY ATTORNEY GENERAL

(a) Pattern or practice cases.—Whenever the Attorney General has reasonable cause to believe that any person or group of persons is engaged in a pattern or practice of resistance to the full enjoyment of any of the rights granted by this subchapter, or that any group of persons has been denied any of the rights granted by this subchapter and such denial raises an issue of general public importance, the Attorney General may commence a civil action in any appropriate United States district court.

(b) On referral of discriminatory housing practice or conciliation agreement for enforcement—

(1)(A) The Attorney General may commence a civil action in any appropriate United States district court for appropriate relief with respect to a discriminatory housing practice referred to the Attorney General by the Secretary under section 3610(g) of this title.

(B) A civil action under this paragraph may be commenced not later than the expiration of 18 months after the date of the occurrence or the termination of the alleged discriminatory housing practice.

(2)(A) The Attorney General may commence a civil action in any appropriate United States district court for appropriate relief with respect to breach of a conciliation agreement referred to the Attorney General by the Secretary under section 3610(c) of this title.

(B) A civil action may be commenced under this paragraph not later than the expiration of 90 days after the referral of the alleged breach under section 3610(c) of this title.

(c) Enforcement of subpoenas.—The Attorney General, on behalf of the Secretary, or other party at whose request a subpoena is issued, under this subchapter, may enforce such subpoena in appropriate proceedings in the United States district court for the district in which the person to whom the subpoena was addressed resides, was served, or transacts business.

(d) Relief which may be granted in civil actions under subsections (a) and (b)—

(1) In a civil action under subsection (a) or (b), the court—

(A) may award such preventive relief, including a permanent or temporary injunction, restraining order, or other order against the person responsible for a violation of this subchapter as is necessary to assure the full enjoyment of the rights granted by this subchapter;

(B) may award such other relief as the court deems appropriate, including monetary damages to persons aggrieved; and

(C) may, to vindicate the public interest, assess a civil penalty against the respondent—

(i) in an amount not exceeding $50,000, for a first violation; and

(ii) in an amount not exceeding $100,000, for any subsequent violation.

(2) In a civil action under this section, the court, in its discretion, may allow the prevailing party, other than the United States, a reasonable attorney's fee and costs. The United States shall be liable for such fees and costs to the extent provided by section 2412 of title 28.

(e) Intervention in civil actions.—Upon timely application, any person may intervene in a civil action commenced by the Attorney General under subsection (a) or (b) which involves an alleged discriminatory housing practice with respect to which such person is an aggrieved person or a conciliation agreement to which such person is a party. The court may grant such appropriate relief to any such intervening party as is authorized to be granted to a plaintiff in a civil action under section 3613 of this title.

History of 42 U.S.C. §3614: Apr. 11, 1968, P.L. 90-284, §814, as added Sept. 13, 1988, P.L. 100-430, §8(2), 102 Stat. 1634.

See also Prop. Code §§301.131-301.133.

ANNOTATIONS

U.S. v. Bob Lawrence Rlty., Inc., 474 F.2d 115, 123 (5th Cir.1973). "[D] urges ... that the Attorney General must prove that [D] participated in an 'individual pattern or practice' to have standing to obtain relief for a 'group pattern or practice'.... [¶] The clear meaning of [42 U.S.C.] §3613 [now 42 U.S.C. §3614] directly refutes [D's] first contention. ... Unless we are to construe the phrase 'group of persons' as totally superfluous, there is no need for each member of the 'group of persons' to be engaged in an 'individual pattern or practice' of violating the [FHA] before the Attorney General has standing to sue. The statute was thus intended to reach the illegal activities of a group of persons even if the individual members of the group of persons were not engaged in an 'individual pattern or practice.' [¶] [D's] second contention that the [group of persons] must have engaged in a conspiracy or concerted action before the Attorney General has standing to sue is also erroneous. *At 124:* To [first] requir[e] proof of a conspiracy ... would be to seriously restrict the congressional intent to stop blockbusting practices [prohibited by 42 U.S.C. §3604(e)] and to unjustifiably restrict the power which Congress gave to the Attorney General to proceed against group patterns or practices. We decline to do so."

§3614-1. INCENTIVES FOR SELF-TESTING & SELF-CORRECTION

(a) Privileged information—

(1) Conditions for privilege.—A report or result of a self-test (as that term is defined by regulation of the Secretary) shall be considered to be privileged under paragraph (2) if any person—

(A) conducts, or authorizes an independent third party to conduct, a self-test of any aspect of a residential real estate related lending transaction of that person, or any part of that transaction, in order to determine the level or effectiveness of compliance with this subchapter by that person; and

(B) has identified any possible violation of this subchapter by that person and has taken, or is taking, appropriate corrective action to address any such possible violation.

(2) Privileged self-test.—If a person meets the conditions specified in subparagraphs (A) and (B) of paragraph (1) with respect to a self-test described in that paragraph, any report or results of that self-test—

(A) shall be privileged; and

(B) may not be obtained or used by any applicant, department, or agency in any—

(i) proceeding or civil action in which one or more violations of this subchapter are alleged; or

(ii) examination or investigation relating to compliance with this subchapter.

(b) Results of self-testing—

(1) In general.—No provision of this section may be construed to prevent an aggrieved person, complainant, department, or agency from obtaining or using a report or results of any self-test in any proceeding or civil action in which a violation of this subchapter is alleged, or in any examination or investigation of compliance with this subchapter if—

(A) the person to whom the self-test relates or any person with lawful access to the report or the results—

(i) voluntarily releases or discloses all, or any part of, the report or results to the aggrieved person, complainant, department, or agency, or to the general public; or

(ii) refers to or describes the report or results as a defense to charges of violations of this subchapter against the person to whom the self-test relates; or

(B) the report or results are sought in conjunction with an adjudication or admission of a violation of this subchapter for the sole purpose of determining an appropriate penalty or remedy.

(2) Disclosure for determination of penalty or remedy.—Any report or results of a self-test that are disclosed for the purpose specified in paragraph (1)(B)—

(A) shall be used only for the particular proceeding in which the adjudication or admission referred to in paragraph (1)(B) is made; and

(B) may not be used in any other action or proceeding.

(c) Adjudication.—An aggrieved person, complainant, department, or agency that challenges a privilege asserted under this section may seek a determination of the existence and application of that privilege in—

(1) a court of competent jurisdiction; or

(2) an administrative law proceeding with appropriate jurisdiction.

History of 42 U.S.C. §3614-1: Apr. 11, 1968, P.L. 90-284, §814A, as added Sept. 30, 1996, P.L. 104-208, §2302(b)(1), 110 Stat. 3009-421.

§3614a. RULES TO IMPLEMENT SUBCHAPTER

The Secretary may make rules (including rules for the collection, maintenance, and analysis of appropriate data) to carry out this subchapter. The Secretary shall give public notice and opportunity for comment with respect to all rules made under this section.

History of 42 U.S.C. §3614a: Apr. 11, 1968, P.L. 90-284, §815, as added Sept. 13, 1988, P.L. 100-430, §8(2), 102 Stat. 1635.

See also Prop. Code §301.062.

§3615. EFFECT ON STATE LAWS

Nothing in this subchapter shall be construed to invalidate or limit any law of a State or political subdivision of a State, or of any other jurisdiction in which this subchapter shall be effective, that grants, guarantees, or protects the same rights as are granted by this subchapter; but any law of a State, a political subdivision, or other such jurisdiction that purports to require or permit any action that would be a discriminatory housing practice under this subchapter shall to that extent be invalid.

History of 42 U.S.C. §3615: Apr. 11, 1968, P.L. 90-284, §816, formerly §815, 82 Stat. 89; Sept. 13, 1988, P.L. 100-430, §8(1), 102 Stat. 1625.

§3616. COOPERATION WITH STATE & LOCAL AGENCIES ADMINISTERING FAIR HOUSING LAWS; UTILIZATION OF SERVICES & PERSONNEL; REIMBURSEMENT; WRITTEN AGREEMENTS; PUBLICATION IN FEDERAL REGISTER

The Secretary may cooperate with State and local agencies charged with the administration of State and local fair housing laws and, with the consent of such agencies, utilize the services of such agencies and their employees and, notwithstanding any other provision of law, may reimburse such agencies and their employees for services rendered to assist him in carrying out this subchapter. In furtherance of such cooperative efforts, the Secretary may enter into written agreements with such State or local agencies. All agreements and terminations thereof shall be published in the Federal Register.

History of 42 U.S.C. §3616: Apr. 11, 1968, P.L. 90-284, §817, formerly §816, 82 Stat. 89; Sept. 13, 1988, P.L. 100-430, §8(1), 102 Stat. 1625.

See also Prop. Code §301.066.

§3616a. FAIR HOUSING INITIATIVES PROGRAM

(a) In general.—The Secretary of Housing and Urban Development (in this section referred to as the "Secretary") may make grants to, or (to the extent of amounts provided in appropriation Acts) enter into contracts or cooperative agreements with, State or local governments or their agencies, public or private nonprofit organizations or institutions, or other public or private entities that are formulating or carrying out programs to prevent or eliminate discriminatory housing practices, to develop, implement, carry out, or coordinate—

(1) programs or activities designed to obtain enforcement of the rights granted by title VIII of the Act of April 11, 1968 (42 U.S.C. 3601 et seq.) (commonly referred to as the Civil Rights Act of 1968), or by State or local laws that provide rights and remedies for alleged discriminatory housing practices that are substantially equivalent to the rights and remedies provided in such title VIII, through such appropriate judicial or administrative proceedings (including informal methods of conference, conciliation, and persuasion) as are available therefor; and

(2) education and outreach programs designed to inform the public concerning rights and obligations under the laws referred to in paragraph (1).

(b) Private enforcement initiatives—

(1) In general.—The Secretary shall use funds made available under this subsection to conduct, through contracts with private nonprofit fair housing enforcement organizations, investigations of violations of the rights granted under title VIII of the Civil Rights Act of 1968 (42 U.S.C. 3601 et seq.), and such enforcement activities as appropriate to remedy such violations. The Secretary may enter into multiyear contracts and take such other action as is appropriate to enhance the effectiveness of such investigations and enforcement activities.

(2) Activities.—The Secretary shall use funds made available under this subsection to conduct, through contracts with private nonprofit fair housing enforcement organizations, a range of investigative and enforcement activities designed to—

(A) carry out testing and other investigative activities in accordance with subsection (b)(1), including building the capacity for housing investigative activities in unserved or underserved areas;

(B) discover and remedy discrimination in the public and private real estate markets and real estate-related transactions, including, but not limited to, the making or purchasing of loans or the provision of other financial assistance sales and rentals of housing and housing advertising;

(C) carry out special projects, including the development of prototypes to respond to new or sophisticated forms of discrimination against persons protected under title VIII of the Civil Rights Act of 1968 (42 U.S.C. 3601 et seq.);

(D) provide technical assistance to local fair housing organizations, and assist in the formation and development of new fair housing organizations; and

(E) provide funds for the costs and expenses of litigation, including expert witness fees.

(c) Funding of fair housing organizations—

(1) In general.—The Secretary shall use funds made available under this section to enter into contracts or cooperative agreements with qualified fair housing enforcement organizations, other private nonprofit fair housing enforcement organizations, and nonprofit groups organizing to build their capacity to provide fair housing enforcement, for the purpose of supporting the continued development or implementation of initiatives which enforce the rights granted under title VIII of the Civil Rights Act of 1968 (42 U.S.C. 3601 et seq.), as amended. Contracts or cooperative agreements may not provide more than 50 percent of the operating budget of the recipient organization for any one year.

(2) Capacity enhancement.—The Secretary shall use funds made available under this section to help establish, organize, and build the capacity of fair housing enforcement organizations, particularly in those areas of the country which are currently underserved by fair housing enforcement organizations as well as those areas where large concentrations of protected classes exist. For purposes of meeting the objectives of this paragraph, the Secretary may enter into contracts or cooperative agreements with qualified fair housing enforcement organizations. The Secretary shall establish annual goals which reflect the national need for private fair housing enforcement organizations.

(d) Education and outreach—

(1) In general.—The Secretary, through contracts with one or more qualified fair housing enforcement organizations, other fair housing enforcement organizations, and other nonprofit organizations representing groups of persons protected under title VIII of the Civil Rights Act of 1968 (42 U.S.C. 3601 et seq.), shall establish a national education and outreach program. The national program shall be designed to provide a centralized, coordinated effort for the development and dissemination of fair housing media products, including—

(A) public service announcements, both audio and video;

(B) television, radio and print advertisements;

(C) posters; and

(D) pamphlets and brochures.

The Secretary shall designate a portion of the amounts provided in subsection (g)(4) for a national program specifically for activities related to the annual national fair housing month. The Secretary shall encourage cooperation with real estate industry organizations in the national education and outreach program. The Secretary shall also encourage the dissemination of educational information and technical assistance to support compliance with the housing adaptability and accessibility guidelines contained in the Fair Housing Act Amendments of 1988.

(2) Regional and local programs.—The Secretary, through contracts with fair housing enforcement organizations, other nonprofit organizations representing groups of persons protected under title VIII of the Civil Rights Act of 1968 (42 U.S.C. 3601 et seq.), State and local agencies certified by the Secretary under section 810(f) of the Fair Housing Act (42 U.S.C. 3610(f)), or other public or private entities that are formulating or carrying out programs to prevent or eliminate discriminatory housing practices, shall establish or support education and outreach programs at the regional and local levels.

(3) Community-based programs.—The Secretary shall provide funding to fair housing organizations and other nonprofit organizations representing groups of persons protected under title VIII of the Civil Rights Act of 1968, or other public or private entities that are formulating or carrying out programs to prevent or eliminate discriminatory housing practices, to support community-based education and outreach activities, including school, church, and community presentations, conferences, and other educational activities.

(e) Program administration—

(1) Not less than 30 days before providing a grant or entering into any contract or cooperative agreement to carry out activities authorized by this section, the Secretary shall submit notification of such proposed grant, contract, or cooperative agreement (including a description of the geographical distribution of such contracts) to the Committee on Banking, Housing, and Urban Affairs of the Senate and the Committee on Banking, Finance and Urban Affairs of the House of Representatives.

(2) Repealed by P.L. 104-66, title I, §1071(d), Dec. 21, 1995, 109 Stat. 720.

(f) Regulations—

(1) The Secretary shall issue such regulations as may be necessary to carry out the provisions of this section.

(2) The Secretary shall, for use during the demonstration authorized in this section, establish guidelines for testing activities funded under the private enforcement initiative of the fair housing initiatives program. The purpose of such guidelines shall be to ensure that investigations in support of fair housing enforcement efforts described in subsection (a)(1) shall develop credible and objective evidence of discriminatory housing practices. Such guidelines shall apply only to activities funded under this section, shall not be construed to limit or otherwise restrict the use of facts secured through testing not funded under this section in any legal proceeding under Federal fair housing laws, and shall not be used to restrict individuals or entities, including those participating in the fair housing initiatives program, from pursuing any right or remedy guaranteed by Federal law. Not later than 6 months after the end of the demonstration period authorized in this section,[1] the Secretary shall submit to Congress the evaluation of the Secretary of the effectiveness of such guidelines in achieving the purposes of this section.

(3) Such regulations shall include provisions governing applications for assistance under this section, and shall require each such application to contain—

(A) a description of the assisted activities proposed to be undertaken by the applicant, together with the estimated costs and schedule for completion of such activities;

(B) a description of the experience of the applicant in formulating or carrying out programs to prevent or eliminate discriminatory housing practices;

(C) available information, including studies made by or available to the applicant, indicating the nature and extent of discriminatory housing practices occurring in the general location where the applicant proposes to conduct its assisted activities, and the relationship of such activities to such practices;

(D) an estimate of such other public or private resources as may be available to assist the proposed activities;

(E) a description of proposed procedures to be used by the applicant for monitoring conduct and evaluating results of the proposed activities; and

(F) any additional information required by the Secretary.

(4) Regulations issued under this subsection shall not become effective prior to the expiration of 90 days after the Secretary transmits such regulations, in the form such regulations are intended to be published, to the Committee on Banking, Housing, and Urban Affairs of the Senate and the Committee on Banking, Finance and Urban Affairs of the House of Representatives.

(5) The Secretary shall not obligate or expend any amount under this section before the effective date of the regulations required under this subsection.

(g) Authorization of appropriations.—There are authorized to be appropriated to carry out the provisions of this section,[2] $21,000,000 for fiscal year 1993 and $26,000,000 for fiscal year 1994, of which—

(1) not less than $3,820,000 for fiscal year 1993 and $8,500,000 for fiscal year 1994 shall be for private enforcement initiatives authorized under subsection (b), divided equally between activities specified under subsection (b)(1) and those specified under subsection (b)(2);

(2) not less than $2,230,000 for fiscal year 1993 and $8,500,000 for fiscal year 1994 shall be for qualified fair housing enforcement organizations authorized under subsection (c)(1);

(3) not less than $2,010,000 for fiscal year 1993 and $4,000,000 for fiscal year 1994 shall be for the creation of new fair housing enforcement organizations authorized under subsection (c)(2); and

(4) not less than $2,540,000 for fiscal year 1993 and $5,000,000 for fiscal year 1994 shall be for education and outreach programs authorized under subsection (d), to be divided equally between activities specified under subsection (d)(1) and those specified under subsections (d)(2) and (d)(3).

Any amount appropriated under this section shall remain available until expended.

(h) Qualified fair housing enforcement organization—

(1) The term "qualified fair housing enforcement organization" means any organization that—

(A) is organized as a private, tax-exempt, nonprofit, charitable organization;

(B) has at least 2 years experience in complaint intake, complaint investigation, testing for fair housing violations and enforcement of meritorious claims; and

(C) is engaged in all the activities listed in paragraph (1)(B) at the time of application for assistance under this section. An organization which is not solely engaged in fair housing enforcement activities may qualify as a qualified fair housing enforcement organization, provided that the organization is actively engaged in each of the activities listed in subparagraph (B).

(2) The term "fair housing enforcement organization" means any organization that—

(A) meets the requirements specified in paragraph (1)(A);

(B) is currently engaged in the activities specified in paragraph (1)(B);

(C) upon the receipt of funds under this section will become engaged in all of the activities specified in paragraph (1)(B); and

(D) for purposes of funding under subsection (b), has at least 1 year of experience in the activities specified in paragraph (1)(B).

(i) Prohibition on use of funds.—None of the funds authorized under this section may be used by the Secretary for purposes of settling claims, satisfying judgments or fulfilling court orders in any litigation action involving either the Department or housing providers funded by the Department. None of the funds authorized under this section may be used by the Department for administrative costs.

(j) Reporting requirements.—Not later than 180 days after the close of each fiscal year in which assistance under this section is furnished, the Secretary shall prepare and submit to the Congress a comprehensive report which shall contain—

(1) a description of the progress made in accomplishing the objectives of this section;

(2) a summary of all the private enforcement activities carried out under this section and the use of such funds during the preceding fiscal year;

(3) a list of all fair housing enforcement organizations funded under this section during the preceding fiscal year, identified on a State-by-State basis;

(4) a summary of all education and outreach activities funded under this section and the use of such funds during the preceding fiscal year; and

(5) any findings, conclusions, or recommendations of the Secretary as a result of the funded activities.

1. **Editor's note:** The phrase "Not later than 6 months after the end of the demonstration period authorized in this section," referred to in subsection (f)(2), probably means the end of the demonstration period under former subsection (e) of this section, which provided that such period was to end Sept. 30, 1992. However, subsection (e) was redesignated (h) and deleted by P.L. 102-550.

2. **Editor's note:** So in original. The comma probably should not appear.

History of 42 U.S.C. §3616a: Feb. 5, 1988, P.L. 100-242, §561, 101 Stat. 1942; Nov. 28, 1990, P.L. 101-625, §953, 104 Stat. 4419; Oct. 28, 1992, P.L. 102-550, §905(b), 106 Stat. 3869; Dec. 21, 1995, P.L. 104-66, §1071(d), 109 Stat. 720.

§3617. INTERFERENCE, COERCION, OR INTIMIDATION

It shall be unlawful to coerce, intimidate, threaten, or interfere with any person in the exercise or enjoyment of, or on account of his having exercised or enjoyed, or on account of his having aided or encouraged any other person in the exercise or enjoyment of, any right granted or protected by section 3603, 3604, 3605, or 3606 of this title.

History of 42 U.S.C. §3617: Apr. 11, 1968, P.L. 90-284, §818, formerly §817, 82 Stat. 89; Sept. 13, 1988, P.L. 100-430, §§8(1), 10, 102 Stat. 1625, 1635.

See also Prop. Code §301.171.

§3618. AUTHORIZATION OF APPROPRIATIONS

There are hereby authorized to be appropriated such sums as are necessary to carry out the purposes of this subchapter.

History of 42 U.S.C. §3618: Apr. 11, 1968, P.L. 90-284, §819, formerly §818, 82 Stat. 89; Sept. 13, 1988, P.L. 100-430, §8(1), 102 Stat. 1625.

§3619. SEPARABILITY

If any provision of this subchapter or the application thereof to any person or circumstances is held invalid, the remainder of the subchapter and the application of the provision to other persons not similarly situated or to other circumstances shall not be affected thereby.

History of 42 U.S.C. §3619: Apr. 11, 1968, P.L. 90-284, §820, formerly §819, 82 Stat. 89; Sept. 13, 1988, P.L. 100-430, §8(1), 102 Stat. 1625.

SUBCHAPTER II. PREVENTION OF INTIMIDATION

§3631. VIOLATIONS; PENALTIES

Whoever, whether or not acting under color of law, by force or threat of force willfully injuries, intimidates or interferes with, or attempts to injure, intimidate or interfere with—

(a) any person because of his race, color, religion, sex, handicap (as such term is defined in section 3602 of this title), familial status (as such term is defined in section 3602 of this title), or national origin and because he is or has been selling, purchasing, renting, financing, occupying, or contracting or negotiating for the sale, purchase, rental, financing or occupation of any dwelling, or applying for or participating in any service, organization, or facility relating to the business of selling or renting dwellings; or

(b) any person because he is or has been, or in order to intimidate such person or any other person or any class of persons from—

(1) participating, without discrimination on account of race, color, religion, sex, handicap (as such term is defined in section 3602 of this title), familial status (as such term is defined in section 3602 of this title), or national origin, in any of the activities, services, organizations or facilities described in subsection (a); or

(2) affording another person or class of persons opportunity or protection so to participate; or

(c) any citizen because he is or has been, or in order to discourage such citizen or any other citizen from lawfully aiding or encouraging other persons to participate, without discrimination on account of race, color, religion, sex, handicap (as such term is defined in section 3602 of this title), familial status (as such term is defined in section 3602 of this title), or national origin, in any of the activities, services, organizations or facilities described in subsection (a), or participating lawfully in speech or peaceful assembly opposing any denial of the opportunity to so participate—shall be fined under title 18 or imprisoned not more than one year, or both; and if bodily injury results from the acts committed in violation of this section or if such acts include the use, attempted use, or threatened use of a dangerous weapon, explosives, or fire shall be fined under title 18 or imprisoned not more than ten years, or both; and if death results from the acts committed in violation of this section or if such acts include kidnapping or an attempt to kidnap, aggravated sexual abuse or an attempt to commit aggravated sexual abuse, or an attempt to kill, shall be fined under title 18 or imprisoned for any term of years or for life, or both.

History of 42 U.S.C. §3631: Apr. 11, 1968, P.L. 90-284, §901, 82 Stat. 89; Aug. 22, 1974, P.L. 93-383, §808(b)(4), 88 Stat. 729; Sept. 13, 1988, P.L. 100-430, §9, 102 Stat. 1635; Sept. 13, 1994, P.L. 103-322, §320103(e), 108 Stat. 2110; Oct. 11, 1996, P.L. 104-294, §604(b)(15), (27), 110 Stat. 3507, 3508.

See also Prop. Code §301.171.

TABLE OF CONTENTS

1. DERIVATION TABLE—PROPERTY CODE TO TRCS

PROPERTY CODE §	TRCS ARTICLE
5.001	1291
5.002	1301
5.003	1290
5.004	1295
5.005	166a
5.006	1293b
5.021	1288
5.022	1292, 1293
5.023	1297
5.024	1298
5.025	1293c
5.026	1293a
5.041	1294
5.042	1289
5.061	1296
5.062	1291a
5.063	1291b
5.081	1301b, §1
5.082	1301b, §1
5.083	1301b, §2
11.001	6630, 6661
11.002	6629
11.003	6626(b)
11.004	6633, 6652
11.005	6655-6657
11.006	6658
12.001	6626(a)
12.002	6626(a)
12.003	6625, 6628, 6634
12.004	6625a
12.005	6638, 6639
12.006	6624
12.007	6640, 6641
12.008	6643a
12.009	6626b
12.010	6644
12.011	6644a
12.012	6662
12.013	6635
12.014	6636
12.015	6637
12.016	6633
13.001	6627
13.002	6646
13.003	6631
13.004	6642, 6643
13.005	6637
21.001	3266a, §1
21.002	3266a, §4
21.003	3269
21.011	3264
21.012	3264
21.013	3264, 3266a, §§2, 3, 5(a), 5(b)
21.014	3264, 3266, ¶2
21.015	3264
21.016	3264
21.017	3269
21.018	3266, ¶6; 3266a, §§2, 3, 5(a), 5(b)
21.019	3265, ¶6
21.020	3265, ¶6
21.021	3268
21.022	3266, ¶8
21.041	3265, ¶1
21.042	3265, ¶¶1-4
21.043	3265, ¶7
21.044	3268
21.045	3270
21.046	3266b, §§1, 2
21.047	3266, ¶¶3-5; 3267
21.048	3265, ¶5; 3266, ¶5
21.061	3266, ¶7
21.062	3268
21.063	3268
21.064	3269
21.065	3271
22.001	7364
22.002	7375
22.003	7391
22.004	7392
22.021	7389, 7393-7396
22.022	7397
22.023	7398, 7399
22.024	7401
22.041	7401A, §§1-3
22.042	7401A, §3
22.043	7401A, §3
22.044	7401A, §4
22.045	7401A, §5
23.001	6082, 6101
23.002	6083, 6102
23.003	6098
23.004	6099, 6100
23.005	6108
24.001	3972, 3974
24.002	3973, 3975
24.003	3975
24.004	3973
24.005	3975a
24.006	3975b
24.007	3992
24.008	3994
25.001	7409
25.002	7417, 7418
41.001	3833

1. DERIVATION TABLE—PROPERTY CODE TO TRCS (CONT'D)

PROPERTY CODE §	TRCS ARTICLE
41.002	3834, 3835, 3839
41.021	3849
41.022	3841-3843
41.023	3845, 3846
41.024	3847, 3848
41.025	3850, 3851
41.026	3851-3853
41.027	3855
41.028	3854
41.029	3856
41.030	3857
42.001	3836(a); 3840
42.002	3836(a)
42.003	3859
42.004	3836(b)-(d)
43.001	3838
51.001	5506
51.002	3810
52.001	5449
52.002	5447
52.003	5447
52.004	5448
52.005	5450
52.006	5449
52.007	5451
52.021	5449(a), §1
52.022	5449(a), §1
52.023	5449(a), §3
52.024	5449(a), §2
52.025	5449(a), §§4, 5
53.001	5452, §§1, 2
53.002	5452, §2
53.003	5456
53.021	5452, §§1, 2
53.022	5452, §1; 5458

PROPERTY CODE §	TRCS ARTICLE
53.023	5452, §1
53.024	5452, §2
53.025	5452, §2
53.026	5452-1
53.051	5452, §1
53.052	5453
53.053	5467
53.054	5455
53.055	5453
53.056	5453
53.057	5453
53.058	5453
53.059	5460
53.081	5463, §1
53.082	5463, §1
53.083	5453, 5454
53.084	5463, §2
53.101	5469
53.102	5469
53.103	5469
53.104	5469
53.105	5469
53.121	5464
53.122	5468
53.123	5459, §1
53.124	5459, §2
53.151	5466
53.152	5470
53.153	5463, §2
53.154	5472
53.155	5471
53.171	5472c, §§1, 4
53.172	5472c, §1
53.173	5472c, §2
53.174	5472c, §3

PROPERTY CODE §	TRCS ARTICLE
53.175	5472c, §4
53.176	5472c, §4a
53.201	5472d, §§1, 7
53.202	5472d, §§1, 2
53.203	5472d, §§1-3
53.204	5472d, §7
53.205	5472d, §1
53.206	5472d, §4
53.207	5472d, §5
53.208	5472d, §6
53.209	5472d, §6
53.210	5472d, §7
53.211	5472d, §8
53.231	5472a
53.232	5472a
53.233	5472a
53.234	5472a
53.235	5472b
53.236	5472b-1, §1
53.237	5472b-1, §§1, 2
53.238	5472b-1, §1
53.239	5472b-1, §2
53.240	5472b-1, §2
54.001	5222
54.002	5222-5224
54.003	5222
54.004	5223
54.005	5225, 5226
54.006	5227
54.007	5232
54.021	5238
54.022	5238
54.023	5238
54.024	5238
54.025	5239

1. DERIVATION TABLE—PROPERTY CODE TO TRCS (CONT'D)

PROPERTY CODE §	TRCS ARTICLE
54.041	5236d, §1
54.042	5236d, §2
54.043	5236d, §§3, 4
54.044	5236d, §§5, 6
54.045	5236d, §7
55.001	5506a, §§1, 4
55.002	5506a, §1
55.003	5506a, §§1-3, 4c
55.004	5506a, §§1, 3
55.005	5506a, §§3, 4
55.006	5506a, §4b
55.007	5506a, §3
55.008	5506a, §4a
56.001	5473, 5474
56.002	5473, 5474
56.003	5473
56.004	5475
56.005	5476b
56.006	5478
56.021	5476a, 5476c
56.022	5476a
56.023	5476c
56.024	5476
56.041	5475, 5476
56.042	5477
56.043	5476c
56.044	5476d
56.045	5476d
57.001	5480
57.002	5480
57.003	5480
57.004	5481
57.005	5482
57.006	5481
58.001	5483
58.002	5483
58.003	5483
58.004	5486
58.005	5483, 5486
58.006	5486, 5488
58.007	5486
58.008	5487
58.009	5485
59.001	5238b, §3
59.002	5238b, §1
59.003	5238b, §2
59.004	5238b, §12
59.005	5238b, §14
59.006	5238b, §10
59.007	5238b, §13
59.008	5238b, §9
59.009	5238b, §11
59.021	5238b, §4
59.022	5238b, §5(a)
59.041	5238b, §5(b)
59.042	5238b, §§6(a), 7, 8(a), (b), (d)
59.043	5238b, §§3, 7
59.044	5238b, §8(a), (c), (d)
59.045	5238b, §6(b), (c)
59.046	5238b, §§3, 6(d)
60.001	5484
60.002	5484
70.001	5503(a), (b)
70.002	5506b, §1
70.003	5502
70.004	5504a(c)
70.005	5504, 5506b, §2
70.006	5504a(a), (b)
70.007	5505, 5506b, §3
70.008	5503(c)
70.101	5500, §1
70.102	5500, §2
70.103	5500, §§1, 2
70.104	5500, §3
70.201	5501
70.202	5501
71.001	3272, §1
71.002	3272, §§1, 2
71.003	3272, §1
71.004	3272, §1
71.005	3272, §1
71.006	3288
71.101	3273
71.102	3274, 3275
71.103	3272, §1
71.104	3276
71.105	3278
71.106	3277
71.107	3279
71.108	3280
71.109	3284
71.201	3282
71.202	3281
71.203	3285
71.301	3286
71.302	3287
71.303	3283
71.304	3289
72.001	3272a, §§1, 10, 10a, 14; 3273
72.101	3272a, §1
72.102	3272a, §1
72.103	3272a, §2
72.104	3272a, §§1, 2

CHARTS & TIMETABLES

1. DERIVATION TABLE—PROPERTY CODE TO TRCS (CONT'D)

PROPERTY CODE §	TRCS ARTICLE
72.105	3272a, §2
72.201	3272a, §3(a)
72.202	3272a, §3(b), (c)
72.203	3272a, §3(d)
72.204	3272a, §3(e), (f)
72.301	3272a, §4(a)
72.302	3272a, §§3(c), 4(b)
72.303	3272a, §3(g)
72.304	3272a, §4(c)
72.305	3272a, §4(d)
72.306	3272a, §11
72.401	3272a, §5(a)
72.402	3272a, §5(b)
72.403	3272a, §5(c)
72.501	3272a, §6(a)
72.502	3272a, §7(a)
72.503	3272a, §7(b)
72.504	3272a, §7(c)
72.505	3272a, §8
72.506	3272a, §6(b)
72.601	3272a, §15
72.602	3272a, §15
72.603	3272a, §15
72.604	3272a, §15
72.701	3272a, §12
72.702	3272a, §9
72.703	3272a, §15
72.704	3272a, §9
72.705	3272a, §13
73.001	3272b, §1
73.002	3272b, §1
73.003	3272b, §§1, 2
73.101	3272b, §3
73.102	3272b, §3
73.103	3272b, §3

PROPERTY CODE §	TRCS ARTICLE
73.104	3272b, §3
73.201	3272b, §4
73.202	3272b, §4
73.203	3272b, §4
73.204	3272b, §7
73.205	3272b, §7
73.206	3272b, §5
73.207	3272b, §5
73.301	3272b, §6
73.302	3272b, §6
73.401	3272b, §5
73.402	3272b, §§5, 6
73.501	3272b, §8
73.502	3272b, §8
73.503	3272b, §9
81.001	1301a, §1
81.002	1301a, §2
81.003	1301a, §23
81.101	1301a, §3
81.102	1301a, §7(B)
81.103	1301a, §§2, 7(A), (C)
81.104	1301a, §§4-6, 7(B)
81.105	1301a, §9
81.106	1301a, §9
81.107	1301a, §6
81.108	1301a, §8
81.109	1301a, §9
81.110	1301a, §§11, 12
81.201	1301a, §§13, 16
81.202	1301a, §13
81.203	1301a, §2
81.204	1301a, §15
81.205	1301a, §19
81.206	1301a, §20
81.207	1301a, §21

PROPERTY CODE §	TRCS ARTICLE
81.208	1301a, §18
81.209	1301a, §14
81.210	1301a, §10
91.001	5236a
91.002	5236c
91.003	5236g
91.004	5236
91.005	5237
92.001	5236e, §1; 5236f, §1; 5236h, §1; 5236i, §1; 5236j, §1
92.002	5236e, §11; 5236f, §17
92.003	5236b
92.004	5236f, §11; 5236h, §9; 5236i, §9; 5236j, §10
92.005	5236f, §10; 5236h, §§10, 11; 5236i, §10; 5236j, §11
92.006	5236e, §7; 5236f, §13; 5236i, §11; 5236j, §14
92.007	5236f, §16; 5236h, §13; 5236i, §14; 5236j, §16
92.051	5236f, §17
92.052	5236f, §§2, 3
92.053	5236f, §3
92.054	5236f, §4
92.055	5236f, §12
92.056	5236f, §§3, 5, 6, 16
92.057	5236f, §7
92.058	5236f, §8
92.059	5236f, §9
92.060	5236f, §1
92.061	5236f, §14
92.101	5236e, §11
92.102	5236e, §1
92.103	5236e, §2(a), (b)

1. DERIVATION TABLE—PROPERTY CODE TO TRCS (CONT'D)

PROPERTY CODE §	TRCS ARTICLE
92.104	5236e, §3(a), (b); 5236h, §4
92.105	5236e, §5
92.106	5236e, §2(b)
92.107	5236e, §6(a)
92.108	5236e, §6(b)
92.109	5236e, §§3(a), 4
92.151	5236h, §1
92.152	5236h, §1
92.153	5236h, §§1-3, 6(b)
92.155	5236h, §5
92.156	5236h, §6(a)
92.157	5236h, §8
92.158	5236h, §7
92.159	5236h, §1
92.160	5236h, §12
92.201	5236i, §§1-3
92.202	5236i, §4
92.203	5236i, §5
92.204	5236i, §6
92.205	5236i, §8
92.206	5236i, §7
92.207	5236i, §1
92.208	5236i, §12
92.251	5236j, §1
92.252	5236j, §15
92.253	5236j, §§12, 13
92.254	5236j, §§1, 2(b)
92.255	5236j, §§1, 2(a), (b)
92.256	5236j, §§1, 3
92.257	5236j, §2(b)
92.258	5236j, §§1, 4, 5
92.259	5236j, §§6, 7
92.260	5236j, §9
92.261	5236j, §8

PROPERTY CODE §	TRCS ARTICLE
92.262	5236j, §1
101.001	7425a
101.002	7425b
111.001	7425b-1
111.002	7425b-2
111.003	7425b-4
111.004	7425b-45
112.001	7425b-7
112.002	7425b-7
112.003	7425b-3
112.031	7425b-3
112.032	7425b-5, 7425b-6
112.033	7425b-7, 7425b-43
112.051	7425b-41
112.052	7425b-42
113.001	7425b-25
113.002	7425b-25
113.003	7425b-25
113.004	7425b-25
113.005	7425b-25
113.006	7425b-25
113.007	7425b-25
113.008	7425b-25
113.009	7425b-15, 7425b-25
113.010	7425b-16
113.011	7425b-25
113.012	7425b-25
113.013	7425b-25
113.014	7425b-25
113.015	7425b-25
113.016	7425b-11
113.017	7425b-25
113.031	7425b-46
113.032	7425b-10
113.033	7425b-12

PROPERTY CODE §	TRCS ARTICLE
113.034	7425b-13
113.035	7425b-14
113.036	7425b-25
113.037	7425b-22
113.051	7425b-38
113.052	7425b-39
113.053	7425b-37
113.054	7425b-40
113.055	7425b-17
113.056	7425b-18
113.071	7425b-26
113.072	7425b-4, 7425b-27
113.073	7425b-28
113.074	7425b-29
113.075	7425b-30
113.076	7425b-31
113.077	7425b-32
113.078	7425b-33
113.079	7425b-34
113.080	7425b-35
113.081	7425b-36
113.101	7425b-48, §4
113.102	7425b-48, §1(a), (b)
113.103	7425b-48, §1(a)
113.104	7425b-48, §2
114.001	7425b-21
114.002	7425b-25
114.003	7425b-25
114.004	7425b-23
114.005	7425b-15
114.006	7425b-16
114.007	7425b-18
114.021	7425b-20
114.022	7425b-25
114.041	7425b-9

1. DERIVATION TABLE—PROPERTY CODE TO TRCS (CONT'D)

PROPERTY CODE §	TRCS ARTICLE
114.042	7425b-8
114.043	7425b-21
114.044	7425b-19
114.045	7425b-19
114.046	7524b-25
115.001	7425b-24
115.002	7425b-24
115.011	7425b-24
115.012	7425b-24
115.013	7425b-25
115.014	7425b-19, 7425b-21
115.015	7425b-19, 7425b-21
121.001	7425d, §1
121.002	7425d, §1
121.003	7425d, §2
121.004	7425d, §3
121.005	7425d, §4
121.051	7425d-1, §1
121.052	7425d-1, §§2, 3
121.053	7425d-1, §2
121.054	7425d-1, §4
121.055	7425d-1, §5
121.056	7425d-1, §6
121.057	7425d-1, §7
121.058	7425d-1, §8
122.001	7425e, §5
122.002	7425e, §4
122.003	7425a-1
122.051	7425e, §1
122.052	7425e, §3
122.053	7425e, §2(a)

PROPERTY CODE §	TRCS ARTICLE
122.054	7425e, §2(b)
141.001	5923-101, §10
141.002	5923-101, §1
141.003	5923-101, §2(a)-(e)
141.004	5923-101, §2(a)
141.005	5923-101, §3
141.006	5923-101, §4(a), (b), (d)-(j)
141.007	5923-101, §5
141.008	5923-101, §6
141.009	5923-101, §7(c), (e), (f)
141.010	5923-101, §7(a), (b), (d)
141.011	5923-101, §4(c)
141.012	5923-101, §8
141.013	5923-101, §9
141.014	5923b, §2
142.001	1994(2)
142.002	1994(1)
142.003	1994(3)
142.004	1994(5)
142.005	1994(6)
142.006	1994(4)
161.001	7425a-2, §1; 7425a-3, §1
161.002	7425a-2, §2(A); 7425a-3, §§2, 3(a)
161.021	7425a-2, §2(A), (B)
161.022	7425a-2, §2(A), (B)
161.023	7425a-2, §2(A)
161.024	7425a-2, §2(A), (B)
161.025	7425a-2, §2(B)

PROPERTY CODE §	TRCS ARTICLE
161.026	7425a-2, §2(B)
161.027	7425a-2, §2(B)
161.028	7425a-2, §2(A), (B)
161.051	7425a-3, §§1, 4
161.052	7425a-3, §§2, 3(a)
161.053	7425a-3, §3(a)
161.054	7425a-3, §§2, 3(a)
161.055	7425a-3, §§2, 3(a)
161.056	7425a-3, §§2, 3(a)
161.057	7425a-3, §3(b)
161.058	7425a-3, §§2, 3(a)
162.001	5472e, §1
162.002	5472e, §1
162.003	5472e, §1
162.004	5472e, §§4, 7
162.031	5472e, §§1, 2
162.032	5472e, §2
162.033	5472e, §3
181.001	7425c, §1(a)-(e)
181.002	7425c, §1(a)
181.003	7425c, §11
181.004	7425c, §13
181.051	7425c, §2
181.052	7425c, §3
181.053	7425c, §8
181.054	7425c, §4
181.055	7425c, §5
181.056	7425c, §6
181.057	7425c, §7
181.058	7425c, §10

2. DISPOSITION TABLE—TRCS TO PROPERTY CODE

TRCS ARTICLE	PROPERTY CODE §
166a	5.005
1288	5.021
1289	5.042
1290	5.003
1291	5.001
1291a	5.062
1291b	5.063
1292	5.022
1293	5.022
1293a	5.026
1293b	5.006
1293c	5.025
1294	5.041
1295	5.004
1296	5.061
1297	5.023
1298	5.024
1301	5.002
1301a, §1	81.001
1301a, §2	81.002, 81.103, 81.203, 81.210*
1301a, §3	81.101
1301a, §4	81.104
1301a, §5	81.104
1301a, §6	81.104, 81.107
1301a, §7(A)	81.103
1301a, §7(B)	81.102, 81.104
1301a, §7(C)	81.103
1301a, §8	81.108
1301a, §9	81.105, 81.106, 81.109
1301a, §10	81.210
1301a, §11	81.110
1301a, §12	81.110
1301a, §13	81.201, 81.202
1301a, §14	81.209
1301a, §15	81.204
1301a, §16	81.201
1301a, §18	81.208
1301a, §19	81.205
1301a, §20	81.206
1301a, §21	81.207
1301a, §23	81.003
1301a, §24	81.210*
1301a, §25	81.210*
1301b, §1	5.081, 5.082
1301b, §2	5.083
1994(1)	142.002
1994(2)	142.001
1994(3)	142.003
1994(4)	142.006
1994(5)	142.004
1994(6)	142.005
3264	21.011-21.016
3265, ¶1	21.041, 21.042
3265, ¶2	21.042
3265, ¶3	21.042
3265, ¶4	21.042
3265, ¶5	21.048
3265, ¶6	21.019, 21.020
3265, ¶7	21.043
3266, ¶1	21.065*
3266, ¶2	21.014
3266, ¶3	21.047, 21.065*
3266, ¶4	21.047
3266, ¶5	21.047, 21.048
3266, ¶6	21.018
3266, ¶7	21.061
3266, ¶8	21.022
3266a, §1	21.001
3266a, §2	21.013, 21.018
3266a, §3	21.013, 21.018
3266a, §4	21.002
3266a, §5(a)	21.013, 21.018
3266a, §5(b)	21.013, 21.018
3266a, §6	21.065*
3266a, §7	21.065*
3266b, §1	21.046
3266b, §1A	21.046
3266b, §2	21.046
3266b, §3	21.065*
3267	21.047
3268	21.021, 21.044, 21.062, 21.063
3269	21.003, 21.017, 21.064
3270	21.045
3271	21.065
3272, §1	71.001-71.005, 71.103
3272, §2	71.002
3272a, §1	72.001, 72.101, 72.102, 72.104, 72.705*
3272a, §2	72.103-72.105, 72.705*
3272a, §3(a)	72.201
3272a, §3(b)	72.202
3272a, §3(c)	72.202, 72.302
3272a, §3(d)	72.203
3272a, §3(e)	72.204
3272a, §3(f)	72.204
3272a, §3(g)	72.303
3272a, §4(a)	72.301
3272a, §4(b)	72.302
3272a, §4(c)	72.304
3272a, §4(d)	72.305
3272a, §5(a)	72.401

* Renumbered

2. DISPOSITION TABLE—TRCS TO PROPERTY CODE (CONT'D)

TRCS ARTICLE	PROPERTY CODE §
3272a, §5(b)	72.402
3272a, §5(c)	72.403
3272a, §6(a)	72.501, 72.705*
3272a, §6(b)	72.506
3272a, §7(a)	72.502
3272a, §7(b)	72.503
3272a, §7(c)	72.504
3272a, §7(d)	72.705*
3272a, §8	72.505
3272a, §9	72.702, 72.704
3272a, §10	72.001
3272a, §10a	72.001
3272a, §11	72.306
3272a, §12	72.701
3272a, §13	72.705
3272a, §14	72.001
3272a, §15	72.601-72.604, 72.703
3272a, §16	72.705*
3272b, §1	73.001-73.003
3272b, §2	73.003
3272b, §3	73.101-73.104
3272b, §4	73.201-73.203
3272b, §5	73.206, 73.207, 73.401, 73.402
3272b, §6	73.301, 73.302, 73.402
3272b, §7	73.204, 73.205
3272b, §8	73.501, 73.502
3272b, §9	73.503
3272b, §10	73.003*
3273	71.101, 72.001
3274	71.102
3275	71.102
3276	71.104
3277	71.106

TRCS ARTICLE	PROPERTY CODE §
3278	71.105
3279	71.107
3280	71.108
3281	71.202, 71.203*
3282	71.201
3283	71.303
3284	71.109
3285	71.203
3286	71.301
3287	71.302
3288	71.006
3289	71.304
3810	51.002
3833	41.001
3834	41.002
3835	41.002
3836(a)	42.001, 42.002
3836(b)	42.004
3836(c)	42.004
3836(d)	42.004
3837	43.001*
3838	43.001
3839	41.002
3840	42.001
3841	41.022
3842	41.022
3843	41.022
3844	41.030*
3845	41.023
3846	41.023
3847	41.024
3848	41.024
3849	41.021
3850	41.025
3851	41.025, 41.026

TRCS ARTICLE	PROPERTY CODE §
3852	41.026
3853	41.026
3854	41.028
3855	41.027
3856	41.029
3857	41.030
3858	41.030*
3859	42.003
3973	24.001, 24.002, 24.004
3974	24.001
3975	24.002, 24.003
3975a	24.005
3975b	24.006
3992	24.007
3994	24.008
5222	54.001-54.003
5223	54.002, 54.004
5224	54.002
5225	54.005
5226	54.005
5227	54.006
5232	54.007
5236	91.004
5236a	91.001
5236b	92.003
5236c	91.002
5236d, §1	54.041
5236d, §2	54.042
5236d, §3	54.043
5236d, §4	54.043
5236d, §5	54.044
5236d, §6	54.044
5236d, §7	54.045
5236d, §8	54.045*

* Renumbered

2. DISPOSITION TABLE—TRCS TO PROPERTY CODE (CONT'D)

TRCS ARTICLE	PROPERTY CODE §
5236e, §1	92.001, 92.102
5236e, §2(a)	92.103
5236e, §2(b)	92.103, 92.106
5236e, §3(a)	92.104, 92.109
5236e, §3(b)	92.104
5236e, §4	92.109
5236e, §5	92.105
5236e, §6(a)	92.107
5236e, §6(b)	92.108
5236e, §7	92.006
5236e, §8	92.109*
5236e, §9	92.109*
5236e, §10	92.109*
5236e, §11	92.002, 92.101
5236e, §12	92.109*
5236f, §1	92.001, 92.060
5236f, §2	92.052
5236f, §3	92.052, 92.053, 92.056
5236f, §4	92.054
5236f, §5	92.056
5236f, §6	92.056
5236f, §7	92.057
5236f, §8	92.058
5236f, §9	92.059
5236f, §10	92.005
5236f, §11	92.004
5236f, §12	92.055
5236f, §13	92.006
5236f, §14	92.061
5236f, §15	92.061*
5236f, §16	92.007, 92.056
5236f, §17	92.002, 92.051
5236g	91.003
5236h, §1	92.001, 92.151-92.153, 92.159
5236h, §2	92.153
5236h, §3	92.153
5236h, §4	92.104
5236h, §5	92.155
5236h, §6(a)	92.156
5236h, §6(b)	92.153
5236h, §7	92.158
5236h, §8	92.157
5236h, §9	92.004
5236h, §10	92.005
5236h, §11	92.005
5236h, §12	92.160
5236h, §13	92.007
5236i, §1	92.001, 92.201, 92.207
5236i, §2	92.201
5236i, §3	92.201
5236i, §4	92.202
5236i, §5	92.203
5236i, §6	92.204
5236i, §7	92.206
5236i, §8	92.205
5236i, §9	92.004
5236i, §10	92.005
5236i, §11	92.006
5236i, §12	92.208
5236i, §13	92.208*
5236i, §14	92.007
5236j, §1	92.001, 92.251, 92.254-92.256, 92.258, 92.262*
5236j, §2(a)	92.255
5236j, §2(b)	92.254, 92.255, 92.257
5236j, §3	92.256
5236j, §4	92.258
5236j, §5	92.258
5236j, §6	92.259
5236j, §7	92.259
5236j, §8	92.261
5236j, §9	92.260
5236j, §10	92.004
5236j, §11	92.005
5236j, §12	92.253
5236j, §13	92.253
5236j, §14	92.006
5236j, §15	92.252, 92.262*
5236j, §16	92.007
5236j, §17	92.262*
5237	91.005
5238	54.021, 54.022-54.024
5238b, §1	59.002
5238b, §2	59.003
5238b, §3	59.001, 59.043, 59.046
5238b, §4	59.021
5238b, §5(a)	59.022
5238b, §5(b)	59.041
5238b, §6(a)	59.042
5238b, §6(b)	59.045
5238b, §6(c)	59.045
5238b, §6(d)	59.046
5238b, §7	59.042, 59.043
5238b, §8(a)	59.042, 59.044
5238b, §8(b)	59.042
5238b, §8(c)	59.044
5238b, §8(d)	59.042, 59.044
5238b, §9	59.008
5238b, §10	59.006
5238b, §11	59.009
5238b, §12	59.004
5238b, §13	59.007

* Renumbered

2. DISPOSITION TABLE—TRCS TO PROPERTY CODE (CONT'D)

TRCS ARTICLE	PROPERTY CODE §
5238b, §14	59.005
5238b, §15	59.046*
5239	54.025
5447	52.002, 52.003
5448	52.004
5449	52.001, 52.006
5449(a), §1	52.021, 52.022
5449(a), §2	52.024
5449(a), §3	52.023
5449(a), §4	52.025
5449(a), §5	52.025
5450	52.005
5451	52.007
5452, §1	53.001, 53.021-53.023, 53.051
5452, §2	53.001, 53.002, 53.021, 53.024, 53.025
5452-1	53.026
5453	53.052, 53.055-53.058, 53.083
5454	53.083
5455	53.054
5456	53.003
5458	53.022
5459, §1	53.123
5459, §2	53.124
5460	53.059
5463, §1	53.081, 53.082
5463, §2	53.084, 53.153
5464	53.121
5466	53.151
5467	53.053
5468	53.122
5469	53.101-53.105
5470	53.152
5471	53.155

TRCS ARTICLE	PROPERTY CODE §
5472	53.154
5472a	53.231-53.234, 53.240*
5472b	53.235
5472b-1, §1	53.236-53.238
5472b-1, §2	53.237, 53.239, 53.240
5472c, §1	53.171, 53.172
5472c, §2	53.173
5472c, §3	53.174
5472c, §4	53.171, 53.175
5472c, §4a	53.176
5472d, §1	53.201-53.203, 53.205
5472d, §2	53.202, 53.203
5472d, §3	53.203
5472d, §4	53.206
5472d, §5	53.207
5472d, §6	53.208, 53.209
5472d, §7	53.201, 53.204, 53.210
5472d, §8	53.211
5472e, §1	162.001-162.003, 162.031
5472e, §2	162.031, 162.032
5472e, §3	162.033
5472e, §4	162.004
5472e, §5	162.033*
5472e, §6	162.033*
5472e, §7	162.004
5473	56.001-56.003
5474	56.001, 56.002
5475	56.004, 56.041
5476	56.024, 56.041
5476a	56.021, 56.022
5476b	56.005
5476c	56.021, 56.023, 56.043

TRCS ARTICLE	PROPERTY CODE §
5476d	56.044, 56.045
5477	56.042
5478	56.006
5479	56.045*
5480	57.001-57.003
5481	57.004, 57.006
5482	57.005
5483	58.001-58.003, 58.005
5484	60.001, 60.002
5485	58.009
5486	58.004-58.007
5487	58.008
5488	58.006
5500, §1	70.101, 70.103, 70.202*
5500, §2	70.102, 70.103
5500, §3	70.104
5500, §4	70.202*
5501	70.201, 70.202
5502	70.003
5503(a)	70.001
5503(b)	70.001
5503(c)	70.008
5504	70.005
5504a(a)	70.006
5504a(b)	70.006
5504a(c)	70.004
5505	70.007
5506	51.001
5506a, §1	55.001-55.004
5506a, §2	55.003
5506a, §3	55.003-55.005, 55.007
5506a, §4	55.001, 55.005
5506a, §4a	55.008

* Renumbered

2. DISPOSITION TABLE—TRCS TO PROPERTY CODE (CONT'D)

TRCS ARTICLE	PROPERTY CODE §
5506a, §4b	55.006
5506a, §4c	55.003
5506b, §1	70.002
5506b, §2	70.005
5506b, §3	70.007
5923b, §1	141.014*
5923b, §2	141.014, 141.014*
5923b, §4	141.014*
5923-101, §1	141.002
5923-101, §2(a)	141.003, 141.004
5923-101, §2(b)	141.003
5923-101, §2(c)	141.003
5923-101, §2(d)	141.003
5923-101, §2(e)	141.003
5923-101, §3	141.005
5923-101, §4(a)	141.006
5923-101, §4(b)	141.006
5923-101, §4(c)	141.011
5923-101, §4(d)	141.006
5923-101, §4(e)	141.006
5923-101, §4(f)	141.006
5923-101, §4(g)	141.006
5923-101, §4(h)	141.006
5923-101, §4(i)	141.006
5923-101, §4(j)	141.006
5923-101, §5	141.007
5923-101, §6	141.008
5923-101, §7(a)	141.010
5923-101, §7(b)	141.010
5923-101, §7(c)	141.009
5923-101, §7(d)	141.010
5923-101, §7(e)	141.009
5923-101, §7(f)	141.009
5923-101, §8	141.012
5923-101, §9	141.013

TRCS ARTICLE	PROPERTY CODE §
5923-101, §10	141.001
6082	23.001
6083	23.002, 23.005*
6085	23.005*
6098	23.003
6099	23.004
6100	23.004
6101	23.001
6102	23.002, 23.005*
6108	23.005
6624	12.006
6625	12.003
6625a	12.004
6626(a)	12.001, 12.002
6626(b)	11.003
6626b	12.009
6627	13.001
6628	12.003
6629	11.002
6630	11.001
6631	13.003
6633	11.004, 12.016
6634	12.003
6635	12.013
6636	12.014
6637	12.015, 13.005
6638	12.005
6639	12.005
6640	12.007
6641	12.007
6642	13.004
6643	13.004
6643a	12.008
6644	12.010
6644a	12.011

TRCS ARTICLE	PROPERTY CODE §
6646	13.002
6652	11.004
6653	11.006*
6654	11.006*
6655	11.005
6656	11.005
6657	11.005
6658	11.006
6659	11.006*
6660	11.006*
6661	11.001
6662	12.012, 12.012*
7364	22.001
7375	22.002
7389	22.021, 22.045*
7391	22.003
7392	22.004
7393	22.021
7394	22.021
7395	22.021
7396	22.021
7397	22.022
7398	22.023
7399	22.023
7401	22.024
7401A, §1	22.041
7401A, §2	22.041
7401A, §3	22.041-22.043
7401A, §4	22.044
7401A, §5	22.045
7409	25.001
7417	25.002
7418	25.002
7425a	101.001
7425a-1	122.003

* Renumbered

2. DISPOSITION TABLE—TRCS TO PROPERTY CODE (CONT'D)

TRCS ARTICLE	PROPERTY CODE §
7425a-2, §1	161.001
7425a-2, §2(A)	161.002, 161.021-161.024, 161.028
7425a-2, §2(B)	161.021, 161.022, 161.024-161.028
7425a-2, §3	161.058*
7425a-3, §1	161.001, 161.051
7425a-3, §2	161.002, 161.052, 161.054-161.056, 161.058
7425a-3, §3(a)	161.002, 161.052-161.056, 161.058
7425a-3, §3(b)	161.057
7425a-3, §4	161.051
7425b	101.002
7425b-1	111.001
7425b-2	111.002
7425b-3	112.003, 112.031
7425b-4	111.003, 113.072
7425b-5	112.032
7425b-6	112.032
7425b-7	112.001, 112.002, 112.033
7425b-8	114.042
7425b-9	114.041
7425b-10	113.032
7425b-11	113.016
7425b-12	113.033
7425b-13	113.034
7425b-14	113.035
7425b-15	113.009, 114.005
7425b-16	113.010, 114.006
7425b-17	113.055
7425b-18	113.056, 114.007
7425b-19	114.044, 114.045, 115.014, 115.015
7425b-20	114.021
7425b-21	114.001, 114.043, 115.014, 115.015

TRCS ARTICLE	PROPERTY CODE §
7425b-22	113.037
7425b-23	114.004
7425b-24	115.001, 115.002, 115.011, 115.012
7425b-25	113.001-113.009, 113.011-113.015, 113.017, 113.036, 113.104,* 114.002, 114.003, 114.022, 114.046, 115.013
7425b-26	113.071
7425b-27	113.072
7425b-28	113.073
7425b-29	113.074
7425b-30	113.075
7425b-31	113.076
7425b-32	113.077
7425b-33	113.078
7425b-34	113.079
7425b-35	113.080
7425b-36	113.081
7425b-37	113.053
7425b-38	113.051
7425b-39	113.052
7425b-40	113.054
7425b-41	112.051
7425b-42	112.052
7425b-43	112.033
7425b-44	112.052*
7425b-45	111.004
7425b-46	113.031, 113.031*
7425b-47	111.004*
7425b-48, §1(a)	113.102, 113.103
7425b-48, §1(b)	113.102
7425b-48, §2	113.104
7425b-48, §3	113.104*
7425b-48, §4	113.101
7425b-48, §5	113.104*

TRCS ARTICLE	PROPERTY CODE §
7425b-48, §6	113.104*
7425b-48a	113.104*
7425c, §1(a)	181.001, 181.002
7425c, §1(b)	181.001
7425c, §1(c)	181.001
7425c, §1(d)	181.001
7425c, §1(e)	181.001
7425c, §2	181.051
7425c, §3	181.052
7425c, §4	181.054
7425c, §5	181.055
7425c, §6	181.056
7425c, §7	181.057
7425c, §8	181.053
7425c, §9	181.058*
7425c, §10	181.058
7425c, §11	181.003
7425c, §12	181.004*
7425c, §13	181.004
7425c, §14	181.058*
7425c, §15	181.058*
7425d, §1	121.001, 121.002
7425d, §2	121.003
7425d, §3	121.004
7425d, §4	121.005
7425d, §5	121.058*
7425d-1, §1	121.051
7425d-1, §2	121.052, 121.053
7425d-1, §3	121.052
7425d-1, §4	121.054
7425d-1, §5	121.055
7425d-1, §6	121.056
7425d-1, §7	121.057
7425d-1, §8	121.058
7425e, §1	122.051

* Renumbered

2. DISPOSITION TABLE—TRCS TO PROPERTY CODE (CONT'D)

TRCS ARTICLE	PROPERTY CODE §
7425e, §2(a)	122.053
7425e, §2(b)	122.054
7425e, §3	122.052
7425e, §4	122.002
7425e, §5	122.001

3. ATTORNEY FEES IN PROPERTY-LAW PROCEEDINGS

	CAUSE OF ACTION/SITUATION	AUTHORITY	MISCELLANEOUS
Condemnation			
1	Condemnor did not make bona fide offer to acquire voluntarily under PROP §21.0113	PROP §21.047(d)	Court must award attorney fees, costs, and other professional fees directly related to violation.
2	Condemnor refused to produce information on specific property owned by requestor	PROP §21.025(f)	Court may award requestor's reasonable fees incurred to compel production of information.
3	Dismissal of condemnation proceedings	PROP §21.019(b), (c)	Court's allowance for attorney, appraiser, and photographer fees, as well as other expenses, depends on which party moves to dismiss.
4	Dismissal of condemnation proceedings involving Texas Department of Transportation	PROP §21.0195(c)	Court must make allowance to property owner for (1) fees as part of expenses incurred in connection with condemnation and (2) use and damage caused.
Condominiums			
5	Declarations, bylaws, or rules—enforcement	PROP §82.161(b)	Prevailing party is entitled to fees and costs.
6	Declarations, bylaws, or rules—unit owner's violation	PROP §82.117(4)	Owner is liable for costs incurred to obtain compliance, including fees.
Construction Defect			
7	Construction defect—actions subject to RCLA	PROP §27.004(g)(6)	Claimant may recover fees and other economic damages proximately caused by defect.
8	Construction defect—failure to cure imminent threat	PROP §27.004(m)	Owner of residence may recover attorney fees and costs, reasonable cost of repairs, and other damages.
9	Construction defect—frivolous suit	PROP §27.0031	Plaintiff is liable for fees and costs.
Landlord/Tenant			
10	Application fee or deposit—bad-faith failure to return	PROP §92.354	Landlord is liable for fees, $100, and three times amount wrongfully retained.
11	Disclosure of information about ownership and management—incorrect information	PROP §92.205(a)(2)-(4)	Tenant may recover fees, actual costs, one month's rent plus $100, and court costs.
12	Disclosure of ownership and management—suit under PROP ch. 92, subch. E	PROP §92.005	Prevailing party may recover fees and court costs. No fees in suit for disclosure if suit relates to property damage, personal injury, or criminal acts.
13	Disclosure of ownership and management—suit under PROP ch. 92, subch. E filed in bad faith or to harass	PROP §92.004	Plaintiff is liable to defendant for fees and one month's rent plus $100.
14	Forcible entry and detainer—eviction suit	PROP §24.006(b), (c)	To recover fees, landlord must send written demand to vacate. Alternatively, landlord is entitled to recover fees without notice if written lease provides for such recovery. Prevailing tenant is entitled to recover fees if lease provides that either party can recover fees or if landlord gives required notice. Prevailing party is entitled to recover all court costs. PROP §24.006(d).
15	Forcible entry and detainer—tenant fails to pay rent during appeal	PROP §24.0054(b)	Tenant must pay fees in filing motion and all unpaid rent.
16	Landlord violation—closes rental unit and violates reoccupancy and move-out rules	PROP §92.055(e)	Landlord is liable to tenant for fees and one month's rent plus $100.

3. ATTORNEY FEES IN PROPERTY-LAW PROCEEDINGS (CONT'D)

	CAUSE OF ACTION/SITUATION	AUTHORITY	MISCELLANEOUS
	Landlord/Tenant (continued)		
17	Landlord violation—failure to install or rekey security devices	PROP §92.164(a)(3), (4)	Tenant who files suit without serving request for compliance may obtain judgment for fees, as well as court costs and actual damages. Tenant who files suit after serving request for compliance may obtain judgment for fees, actual damages, punitive damages, civil penalty of one month's rent plus $500, and court costs. Fees are not recoverable in suits for property damage, personal injury, or wrongful death. Even if request has not been served, court can order landlord to comply if tenant still occupies dwelling.
18	Landlord violation—occupancy limits	PROP §92.010(c)	Prevailing party in suit to enjoin landlord may recover fees and court costs. In addition, prevailing plaintiff may recover $500 for each violation.
19	Landlord violation—prohibits tenant from summoning police or emergency assistance in response to family violence	PROP §92.015(c)	Tenant is entitled to recover fees, civil penalty of one month's rent, actual damages, court costs, and injunctive relief.
20	Landlord violation—refusal to rekey, change, add, repair, or replace security device	PROP §92.165(3)(B)-(F)	Tenant may obtain judgment for fees, as well as actual damages, punitive damages, civil penalty of one month's rent plus $500, and court costs. Fees are not recoverable in suits for property damage, personal injury, or wrongful death.
21	Landlord violation—removes door, window, or landlord-supplied furniture, fixtures, or appliances	PROP §92.0081(h)(2) (residential), §93.002(g)(2) (commercial)	Tenant may recover fees, as well as actual damages, court costs, and either civil penalty of one month's rent plus $1,000 (residential) or greater of one month's rent or $500 (commercial). Any delinquent rents or other sums owed by tenant will be deducted.
22	Landlord violation—tenant's right to make cash rental payments	PROP §92.011(c)	Prevailing party in suit to enjoin may recover fees and court costs. In addition, prevailing tenant may recover greater of one month's rent or $500 for each violation.
23	Landlord violation—tenant's right to vacate after certain decisions related to military service	PROP §92.017(h)	Landlord is liable for fees, actual damages, and civil penalty of one month's rent plus $500.
24	Landlord violation—tenant's right to vacate after certain sex offenses or stalking	PROP §92.0161(f)	Landlord is liable for fees, actual damages, and civil penalty of one month's rent plus $500.
25	Landlord violation—tenant's right to vacate after family violence	PROP §92.016(e)	Landlord is liable for fees, actual damages, and civil penalty of one month's rent plus $500.
26	Landlord violation—unlawfully excludes tenant	PROP §92.0081(h)(2) (residential), §93.002(g)(2) (commercial)	Tenant may recover fees, as well as actual damages, court costs, and either civil penalty of one month's rent plus $1,000 (residential) or greater of one month's rent or $500 (commercial). Any delinquent rents or other sums owed by tenant will be deducted.
27	Manufactured-home tenancies—landlord's violation of PROP ch. 94	PROP §94.301	Landlord is liable for fees, actual damages, civil penalty of two months' rent plus $500, and costs.
28	Manufactured-home tenancies—tenant's suit filed in bad faith or to harass	PROP §94.302	Tenant is liable for fees, two months' rent plus $500, and costs.
29	Reentry—tenant makes bad-faith claim	PROP §92.009(k) (residential), §93.003(k) (commercial)	Landlord may recover fees, actual damages, greater of one month's rent or $500, and court costs. Any sums for which landlord is liable will be deducted.

3. ATTORNEY FEES IN PROPERTY-LAW PROCEEDINGS (CONT'D)

	CAUSE OF ACTION/SITUATION	AUTHORITY	MISCELLANEOUS
	Landlord/Tenant (continued)		
30	Repairs—affidavit for delay submitted in bad faith or landlord fails to continue diligent efforts to repair	PROP §92.0562(f) (residential), §94.158(f) (manufactured home)	Landlord is liable for fees (excluding fees for cause of action relating to personal injury), civil penalty of one month's rent plus $1,000, actual damages, and court costs.
31	Repairs—landlord breaches duty to repair	PROP §92.0563(a) (residential), §94.159(a) (manufactured home)	Landlord is liable for fees (excluding fees for cause of action relating to personal injury), civil penalty of one month's rent plus $500, actual damages, and court costs.
32	Repairs—landlord contracts with tenant to waive duty to repair	PROP §92.0563(b) (residential), §94.159(b) (manufactured home)	Landlord is liable for fees, civil penalty of one month's rent plus $2,000, and actual damages.
33	Repairs—new landlord violates duty to repair	PROP §92.0562(g)(5) (residential), §94.158(g)(5) (manufactured home)	New landlord is liable for fees, civil penalty of one month's rent plus $2,000, and actual damages.
34	Repairs—suit under PROP ch. 92, subch. B	PROP §92.005(a)	Prevailing party may recover fees and court costs.
35	Repairs—suit under PROP ch. 92, subch. B filed in bad faith or to harass	PROP §92.004	Plaintiff is liable for fees and one month's rent plus $100.
36	Repairs—withholding rent	PROP §92.058(c) (residential), §94.160(c) (manufactured home)	Prevailing party shall recover fees (in litigation).
37	Retaliation—against tenant	PROP §92.333 (residential), §94.254 (manufactured home)	Tenant may recover fees, civil penalty of one month's rent plus $500, actual damages, and court costs. Any delinquent rents or other sums owed by tenant will be deducted.
38	Retaliation—tenant's suit filed in bad faith	PROP §92.334(b) (residential), §94.255(b) (manufactured home)	Landlord may recover fees, civil penalty of one month's rent plus $500, and court costs.
39	Revocation of certificate of occupancy	PROP §92.023	Landlord is liable for tenant's security deposit, pro rata portion of rent paid in advance, tenant's actual damages, and costs and fees arising from any related cause of action against landlord.
40	Security deposit—bad-faith failure to provide written description of damages	PROP §92.109(b) (residential), §93.011(b) (commercial), §94.109(b) (manufactured home)	Landlord is liable for fees and forfeits right to withhold any portion of deposit or bring suit against tenant for damages to premises.
41	Security deposit—bad-faith retention	PROP §92.109(a) (residential), §93.011(a) (commercial), §94.109(a) (manufactured home)	Landlord is liable for fees and $100 plus three times the portion of deposit wrongfully withheld.
42	Security deposit—withholding last month's rent	PROP §92.108(b) (residential), §93.010(b) (commercial), §94.108(b) (manufactured home)	Tenant who in bad faith withholds rent is liable for fees and three times the rent wrongfully withheld.
43	Security devices—suit under PROP ch. 92, subch. D filed in bad faith or to harass	PROP §92.004	Plaintiff is liable for fees and one month's rent plus $100.
44	Smoke alarm—failure to install, inspect, or repair	PROP §92.260(5)	Tenant may recover fees in action for court order directing landlord to comply with request and may recover fees and civil penalty of one month's rent plus $100 if landlord does not comply with written request within seven days.

3. ATTORNEY FEES IN PROPERTY-LAW PROCEEDINGS (CONT'D)

	Cause of Action/Situation	Authority	Miscellaneous
	Landlord/Tenant (continued)		
45	Smoke alarm—suit under PROP ch. 92, subch. F	PROP §92.005	Prevailing party may recover fees and court costs, unless suit relates to property damage, personal injury, or criminal acts.
46	Smoke alarm—suit under PROP ch. 92, subch. F filed in bad faith	PROP §92.004	Plaintiff is liable for fees and one month's rent plus $100.
47	Smoke alarm—tenant disables or fails to replace batteries	PROP §92.2611(e)	Landlord shall have judgment against tenant for fees, civil penalty of one month's rent plus $100, and court costs.
48	Utilities—interruption due to landlord's nonpayment	PROP §92.301(b)(6), (7)	Tenant may recover fees, actual damages, and court costs. Fees are not recoverable in suits for personal injury.
49	Utilities—landlord interrupts and tenant files suit in bad faith	PROP §92.0091(j)	Landlord may recover fees, actual damages, greater of one month's rent or $500, and court costs. Any sums owed by landlord will be deducted.
50	Utilities—landlord interrupts when paid by tenant or furnished as incident of tenancy	PROP §92.008(f)(2) (residential), §93.002(g)(2) (commercial)	Tenant may recover fees, actual damages, one month's rent plus $1,000 (residential) or greater of one month's rent or $500 (commercial), and court costs. Any delinquent rents or other sums owed by tenant will be deducted.
	Liens		
51	Agricultural—suit to foreclose	PROP §70.409	Prevailing agricultural producer may recover fees, court costs, and interest on lien funds.
52	Aircraft repair and maintenance—suit to foreclose	PROP §70.306	Prevailing party may be awarded fees.
53	Assignment of rents to lienholder—assignor does not turn over proceeds collected to assignee	PROP §64.060(b)	Assignee may recover fees and costs to extent of agreement with assignor and not prohibited by law, and proceeds assignor was obligated to turn over to assignee.
54	Commercial real-estate broker's—broker's failure to execute, acknowledge, and return subordination agreement or release lien	PROP §62.141(d)	Court may award fees, court costs, and actual damages. If broker acted with gross negligence or in bad faith, court may assess a civil penalty not to exceed three times the amount of claimed commission.
55	Commercial real-estate broker's—suit to enforce commission agreement	PROP §62.142(b)	Court may award fees, court costs, and actual damages. If owner or tenant acted with gross negligence or in bad faith, court may assess a civil penalty not to exceed three times the amount of claimed commission.
56	Commercial real-estate broker's—suit to foreclose	PROP §62.063	Prevailing party is entitled to fees, costs, and prejudgment interest.
57	Garageman's—suit concerning possession	PROP §70.008	Prevailing party may be awarded fees.
58	Mechanic's—proceeding to foreclose lien or enforce claim against bond, or proceeding to declare lien invalid or unenforceable	PROP §53.156	Court must award equitable and just attorney fees and court costs. Court may order payment of costs and fees when lien or claim arises from residential construction contract.

3. ATTORNEY FEES IN PROPERTY-LAW PROCEEDINGS (CONT'D)

	CAUSE OF ACTION/SITUATION	AUTHORITY	MISCELLANEOUS
	Liens (continued)		
59	Residential landlord's—willful violation	PROP §54.046	Tenant is entitled to fees, actual damages, return of property seized or proceeds if sold, and sum of one month's rent and $1,000. Any sums owed by tenant will be deducted.
60	Warehouseman's	PROP §24.0062(k)	Prevailing party is entitled to fees, actual damages, court costs, and any property withheld or its value if sold.
	Nuisances		
61	Abatement	CPRC §§125.064(a), 125.068	Suit may be brought by district, county, or city attorney, AG, or private citizen. Prevailing party may recover fees and costs.
62	Public-health nuisance	LGOVT §232.035(c), (d)	Governmental entity may recover fees, court costs, and investigative costs. Subdivider may also be liable for fees, costs, investigative costs, and a civil penalty of $10,000-$15,000.
63	Unincorporated area—public nuisance	H&SC §343.013(b)	County, property owner, neighborhood resident, or neighborhood organization may recover attorney fees and court costs if court grants injunction.
	Property Tax		
64	Appeal to district court to reduce excessive or unequal appraisal value of property	TAX §42.29(b); *see* ***Martinez***, 339 S.W.3d 184, 192 (Dal. 2011, no pet.) (§42.29 allows no discretion in awarding fees)	Prevailing property owner may recover fees. Fees cannot exceed lesser of $100,000 or total amount by which property owner's tax liability is reduced.
65	Assignee or transferee illegally obtaining or attempting to illegally obtain excess tax-sale proceeds	TAX §34.04(g)	Assignor or transferor may recover fees, expenses, and excess proceeds.
66	Suit to collect delinquent tax	TAX §33.48(a)(5), (6)	Taxing unit is entitled to fees in the amount of 15% of total amount of taxes, penalties, and interest due, as well as reasonable attorney ad litem fees if approved by court.
67	Suit to compel refund by property owner	TAX §42.43(d)	Prevailing property owner is entitled to recover fees and court costs only if suit is filed on or after 180th day after certified correction to appraisal roll.
68	Suit to compel refund of overpayment or erroneous payment	TAX §31.11(k)	Prevailing property owner may be awarded fees not to exceed greater of $1,500 or 30% of total refund determined by court to be due, plus court costs.
	Restrictive Covenants		
69	Breach of restrictive covenant of master mixed-use associations	PROP §215.010	Prevailing party is entitled to reasonable fees, costs, and actual damages.
70	Breach of restrictive covenant of real property	PROP §5.006(a)	Prevailing plaintiff is entitled to fees, costs, and claim.
71	Homeowners' association denies a member access to or copies of association books or records	PROP §209.005(n), (o)	Prevailing party may recover fees and court costs.
72	Homeowners' association's enforcement of restrictions and bylaws	PROP §209.008	Homeowners' association may collect fees and costs.

3. ATTORNEY FEES IN PROPERTY-LAW PROCEEDINGS (CONT'D)

	CAUSE OF ACTION/SITUATION	AUTHORITY	MISCELLANEOUS
	Restrictive Covenants (continued)		
73	Homeowners' association's failure to timely disclose information	PROP §207.004(b)(1)	Homeowner may recover fees, judgment of not more than $500, and court costs.
74	Land-use-restriction violation	PROP §203.005(a)	County may recover fees and court costs.
75	Master mixed-use association's enforcement of restrictive covenant	PROP §215.009(b)	Prevailing association may recover fees and costs.
76	Purchaser of foreclosed property from homeowners' association fails to deliver title when original lot owner redeems property	PROP §209.011(f)	Prevailing original owner or lienholder may recover fees.
	Takings		
77	Challenging governmental action	GOVT §2007.026	Prevailing party may recover fees and court costs.
78	Failure to prepare takings impact assessment	GOVT §2007.044(c)	Prevailing private-real-property owner may recover fees and court costs.
	Trusts		
79	Proceeding under PROP trust provisions	PROP §114.064	Court may award fees and court costs.
80	Trustee's breach of fiduciary duty involving charitable trust	PROP §123.006(a)	AG may recover fees and actual costs.
	Water		
81	Determination and recovery of fair market value of water transferred under emergency authorization	WATER §11.139(j)	Prevailing party is entitled to recover fees and court costs. Owner may recover damages and fair market value of transferred water.
82	Failure to construct water or sewer facilities—suit by governmental entity	LGOVT §232.035(c)	Subdivider must pay fees, penalties, court costs, and investigative costs.
83	Failure to construct water or sewer facilities in economically distressed area—suit by governmental entity	LGOVT §§232.079(b), 232.080(a)(3)	Subdivider may be liable for fees, court costs, penalties, litigation costs, and investigative costs.
84	Failure to construct water or sewer facilities in economically distressed area—suit by private person	LGOVT §232.038	Purchaser may recover fees, permanent improvement value, actual expenses, and court costs.
85	Notice of water- or sewer-service supplier to purchaser of unimproved real estate	WATER §13.257(m), (n)	Purchaser may recover fees plus either all costs related to purchase plus interest or damages up to $5,000.
86	Unauthorized diversion, impoundment, or use of surface water	WATER §11.0841(b)	Political subdivision of state, private corporation, or individual that is a water-right holder and prevails in suit for injunctive relief may recover fees and litigation and expert costs.
87	Violation of laws relating to water wells, drilled or mined shafts, and radioactive materials	WATER §7.354	Court may award fees and costs.
88	Violation of restrictions on use of real property when necessary to sustain taxable property values in district	WATER §54.237(c)	Prevailing water district is entitled to fees, court costs, and damages.

3. ATTORNEY FEES IN PROPERTY-LAW PROCEEDINGS (CONT'D)

	CAUSE OF ACTION/SITUATION	AUTHORITY	MISCELLANEOUS
		Miscellaneous	
89	Abandoned property—suit to compel delivery or to file property report	PROP §74.709(e)	AG may recover fees in addition to property accrued or penalty or interest due.
90	Adverse possession	CPRC §16.034(a)	Fees and costs may be awarded when prevailing party recovers possession from person in unlawful actual possession; fees and costs must be awarded when claim by person in possession is groundless and in bad faith.
91	Arbitration award	CPRC §171.048(c)	Fees shall be awarded by arbitrator if included in agreement to arbitrate or provided by law.
92	Collection of judgment	CPRC §31.002(e)	Judgment creditor may be awarded fees and costs. Fees and costs mandatory if judgment creditor is successful in obtaining turnover relief. ***Great Global Assur.***, 904 S.W.2d 771, 776 (C.C. 1995, no writ).
93	Contract—oral or written	CPRC §38.001(8)	Prevailing plaintiff may recover fees, claim, and costs. Fees not recoverable against political subdivisions of the state. ***Base-Seal***, 901 S.W.2d 783, 786-87 (Beau. 1995, denied).
94	Contract—seller's failure to provide annual accounting statement	PROP §5.077(c), (d)	Seller is liable for fees, as well as $100/statement or $250/day after Jan. 31 that seller does not comply, depending on number of transactions.
95	Contract—seller's failure to transfer title after final payment under executory contract	PROP §5.079(b)	Seller is liable for fees, as well as $250/day for 31st through 90th day seller does not comply and $500/day thereafter.
96	Contract for motor vehicle—lienholder's failure to release lien after payment in full	FIN §348.409	Lienholder is liable for fees, costs, interest, and three times the difference between amount buyer paid and amount holder sought.
97	Contract lien—filing false affidavit by title-insurance company for release	PROP §12.017(i)	Prevailing party may recover fees and court costs, in addition to actual damages when affidavit negligently filed; AG may recover penalties when affidavit knowingly filed.
98	Debt-collection-law violation—suit	FIN §392.403(b), (c)	Prevailing plaintiff is entitled to fees and costs reasonably related to amount of work performed. Defendant may recover fees reasonably related to work performed and costs for suit brought in bad faith or for harassment.
99	Deceptive trade practices	B&CC §17.50(c), (d)	Fees and costs shall be awarded to prevailing consumer, or to prevailing defendant if suit found to be (1) groundless in fact or law, (2) brought in bad faith, or (3) brought for purpose of harassment.
100	Declaratory judgment	CPRC §37.009	Court may award equitable and just fees and costs.
101	Deed in lieu of foreclosure on certain residential real-estate transactions—AG action	B&CC §21A.003(b)	AG may recover expenses, including fees and court costs, and civil penalties.
102	Deed in lieu of foreclosure on certain residential real estate voidable	B&CC §21A.002(d)	Prevailing party may recover fees.
103	Texas Fair Housing Act—discriminatory housing practices	PROP §301.153	Plaintiff may recover fees, court costs, and actual and punitive damages.

3. ATTORNEY FEES IN PROPERTY-LAW PROCEEDINGS (CONT'D)

	CAUSE OF ACTION/SITUATION	AUTHORITY	MISCELLANEOUS
Miscellaneous (continued)			
104	Fraud in real-estate or stock transaction	B&CC §27.01(e)	Party defrauded by false representation or false promise regarding real estate or stock may recover fees, expert-witness fees, and costs.
105	Fraudulent court record, lien, or claim against property	CPRC §§12.002(b), 12.006(b)	Violator may be liable to each injured person for fees, court costs, greater of $10,000 or actual damages, exemplary damages, and other expenses incurred in bringing action.
106	Fraudulent transfer	B&CC §24.013	Court may award fees and costs.
107	Freight—overcharges, lost, or damaged	CPRC §38.001(4), (5)	Prevailing plaintiff may recover fees, claim, and costs. Fees not recoverable against political subdivisions of the state. ***Base-Seal***, 901 S.W.2d at 786-87.
108	Labor performed	CPRC §38.001(2)	Prevailing plaintiff may recover fees, claim, and costs. Fees not recoverable against political subdivisions of the state. ***Base-Seal***, 901 S.W.2d at 786-87.
109	Lease—unconscionability	B&CC §2A.108(d)	Fees shall be awarded to prevailing lessee, or to lessor if lessee is found to have brought or maintained groundless action.
110	Livestock—killed or injured	CPRC §38.001(6)	Prevailing plaintiff may recover fees, claim, and costs. Fees not recoverable against political subdivisions of the state. ***Base-Seal***, 901 S.W.2d at 786-87.
111	Loans and financed transactions—violation of FIN tit. 4	FIN §§349.001(a)(2), (b)(2), 349.003(b), 349.202(c), 349.203(b)(2), 349.403(e)(2)	Reasonable attorney fees set by trial court.
112	Manufactured homes—repossession	FIN §347.404(b)	Creditor may recover fees, costs, and damages from owner of real property who unlawfully refuses to allow creditor to repossess and move manufactured home.
113	Materials furnished	CPRC §38.001(3)	Prevailing plaintiff may recover fees, claim, and costs. Fees not recoverable against political subdivisions of the state. ***Base-Seal***, 901 S.W.2d at 786-87.
114	Mineral interest—disclosure in offer to purchase	PROP §5.151(d)	Prevailing party may recover reasonable fees and court costs in suit against purchaser for not giving required notice.
115	Municipal-services plan—enforcement (population less than 1.6 million)	LGOVT §43.056(*l*)(6)	Resident in annexed area may bring mandamus action and collect fees and costs.
116	Possessory lien—recovery of rental charges	FIN §347.403	Owner of real property may recover fees, actual damages, and court costs.
117	Prompt payment to contractor—action to enforce	PROP §28.005(b)	Court may award fees and costs.
118	Real Estate License Act violation	OCC §1101.610(a)	Claimant may recover claims, including fees, interest, and court costs.
119	Residential Mortgage Loan Company Licensing and Registration Act violation	FIN §156.402(a)	Mortgage applicant may recover fees, costs, and actual damages.

3. ATTORNEY FEES IN PROPERTY-LAW PROCEEDINGS (CONT'D)

CAUSE OF ACTION/SITUATION		AUTHORITY	MISCELLANEOUS
Miscellaneous (continued)			
120	Services rendered	CPRC §38.001(1)	Prevailing plaintiff may recover fees, claim, and costs. Fees not recoverable against political subdivisions of the state. ***Base-Seal***, 901 S.W.2d at 786-87.
121	Sewage-disposal-systems violation	H&SC §§366.092, 366.0923	State or authorized agent may recover fees, investigative costs, court costs, and civil penalty.
122	Unauthorized use of deceased person's name, voice, signature, photograph, or likeness	PROP §26.013(a)(4)	Owner of infringed property right may recover fees, costs, and expenses.
123	Vehicle Storage Facility Act violation	OCC §2303.301	Texas Department of Licensing and Regulation or AG may recover fees, court costs, injunctive relief, and civil penalties.
124	Wrongful sequestration	CPRC §62.044(b) (compulsory counterclaim), §62.045(a) (consumer goods)	In consumer-goods case in which writ is dissolved, defendant or party in possession of goods is entitled to fees and damages.

Legend:

AG	Attorney General
B&CC	Business & Commerce Code
CPRC	Civil Practice & Remedies Code
FIN	Finance Code
GOVT	Government Code
H&SC	Health & Safety Code
LGOVT	Local Government Code
OCC	Occupations Code
PROP	Property Code
TAX	Tax Code
WATER	Water Code

4. Statutes of Limitations in Property-Law Proceedings

	Cause of Action	Authority	Limitations Period	Discovery Rule	Miscellaneous
Contracts & Commercial					
1	Breach of contract for sale	B&CC §2.725(a)	4 years; in original agreement, parties may reduce to not less than 1 year but cannot extend.	Does not apply. B&CC §2.725(b).	Cause accrues on breach regardless of knowledge of breach. B&CC §2.725(b).
2	Breach of warranty in contract for sale	B&CC §2.725(a)	4 years; in original agreement, parties may reduce to not less than 1 year but cannot extend.	Does not apply. ***Martinez***, 940 S.W.2d 139, 147 (E.P. 1996), *aff'd sub nom.* ***Childs***, 974 S.W.2d 31 (Tex.1998).	Breach of warranty occurs when tender of delivery is made, except when warranty explicitly extends to future performance of goods and discovery of breach must await the time of such performance. B&CC §2.725(b).
3	Default under a lease contract, including breach of warranty or indemnity	B&CC §2A.506(a)	4 years; in original nonconsumer lease, parties may reduce to not less than 1 year but cannot expand.	Contained in statute. B&CC §2A.506(b).	Cause accrues when the act or omission on which the default or breach of warranty is based is or should have been discovered by the aggrieved party. B&CC §2A.506(b).
4	Deceptive trade practices under B&CC §17.50	B&CC §17.565	2 years.	Contained in statute. *See also* ***KPMG***, 988 S.W.2d 746, 749 (Tex.1999).	Action must be brought within 2 years after date on which the false, misleading, or deceptive act or practice occurred or within 2 years after consumer discovered or should have discovered the occurrence. Limitations period may be extended for 180 days if D knowingly engaged in conduct to induce P to refrain from or postpone action.
5	Breach of contract	CPRC §16.004(a), (c) or §16.051 (residual limitations)	4 years; parties may agree to a lesser period not shorter than 2 years. CPRC §16.070(a).	May apply when special relationship (e.g., fiduciary) exists. *See* ***Harrison***, 888 S.W.2d 532, 538 (C.C. 1994, no writ).	Without an allegation of fraudulent concealment, cause accrues at time of breach. ***Matthiessen***, 900 S.W.2d 792, 796 (S.A. 1995, denied).
6	Against a carrier of property for overcharges	CPRC §16.006(b)	3 years.		Cause accrues on delivery or tender of property by carrier. CPRC §16.006(e). Period extended 6 months if written claim for overcharges presented within 3-year period. CPRC §16.006(c).

4. STATUTES OF LIMITATIONS IN PROPERTY-LAW PROCEEDINGS (CONT'D)

	Cause of Action	Authority	Limitations Period	Discovery Rule	Miscellaneous
	Contracts & Commercial (continued)				
7	Misappropriation of trade secrets	CPRC §16.010(a)	3 years.	Contained in statute. *See also* ***Southwestern Energy Prod.***, 491 S.W.3d 699, 722 (Tex.2016).	Misappropriation of trade secrets continuing over time is single cause of action. CPRC §16.010(b). Cause accrues when trade secret is actually used. ***Southwestern Energy Prod.***, 491 S.W.3d at 721; ***Computer Assocs.***, 918 S.W.2d 453, 455 (Tex.1996). "Use" means commercial use by which the offending party seeks to profit from the use of the secret. ***Southwestern Energy Prod.***, 491 S.W.3d at 722.
8	Usury—violation of FIN subtit. A	FIN §305.006(a)	4 years.		Cause accrues on date that usurious interest was contracted for, charged, or received.
9	Usury—violation of FIN subtit. B	FIN §349.402	4 years from date of loan or retail installment or 2 years from date of violation, whichever is later.		Cause relating to open-ended credit transaction must be brought within 2 years from date of violation.
10	Unfair insurance practices	INS §541.162(a)	2 years from date unfair act or practice occurred or 2 years from date person discovered or should have discovered the unfair act or practice.	Contained in statute.	Period extended 180 days if delay caused by defendant's attempt to induce plaintiff to refrain from or postpone action. INS §541.162(b). Person seeking damages must give defendant 60 days' written notice of suit. INS §541.154(a).

4. STATUTES OF LIMITATIONS IN PROPERTY-LAW PROCEEDINGS (CONT'D)

	Cause of Action	Authority	Limitations Period	Discovery Rule	Miscellaneous
Debt Collection					
11	Enforcement of note payable at definite time	B&CC §3.118(a)	6 years after due date stated in note or, if due date is accelerated, within 6 years after accelerated date.		
12	Against guarantor for collection of debt	CPRC §16.004(a)(3)	4 years.		When lender can sue guarantor without first suing maker, guarantor cannot defend by showing that limitations barred claim against maker. ***Ocean Transp.***, 878 S.W.2d 256, 267 (C.C. 1994, denied).
13	On a debt	CPRC §16.004(a)(3)	4 years.		Limitations period for collection of debt runs from date money was borrowed. *See **Halleman***, 775 S.W.2d 869, 870 (S.A. 1989, no writ). Limitations period on partner's liability for partnership debt runs from date creditor can proceed against partner's assets (i.e., generally when 90-day satisfaction period expires). ***American Star Energy & Minerals***, 457 S.W.3d 427, 431 (Tex.2015). Limitations period on promissory note that is payable at definite time begins to run on maturity date. ***Edlund***, 842 S.W.2d 719, 726 (Dal. 1992, denied). If demand is integral part of cause of action, limitations period does not run until demand is made, unless it is waived or unreasonably delayed. ***Intermedics***, 683 S.W.2d 842, 845-46 (Hous. [1st] 1984, ref'd n.r.e.).

4. STATUTES OF LIMITATIONS IN PROPERTY-LAW PROCEEDINGS (CONT'D)

	Cause of Action	Authority	Limitations Period	Discovery Rule	Miscellaneous
Governmental Entities					
14	Against incorporated city or town for passing ordinance or adopting order closing and abandoning public street or alley in city or town or public road or thoroughfare in county	CPRC §16.005(a)	2 years.		Cause accrues when order or ordinance is passed or adopted. CPRC §16.005(b).
15	Taxpayer's suit to recover taxes paid under protest	TAX §112.052(b)	91 days after protest payment made.		Period to contest franchise taxes may be extended when taxpayer is given extension to file annual report.
16	Property owner's suit to set aside or correct property assessment made by municipality for road improvements	TRANSP §312.045(a)	20 days after assessment.		After limitations period has expired, property owner can neither file any action to set aside or correct assessment, nor may she raise defense alleging invalidity of assessment. TRANSP §312.045(b).
Real & Personal Property					
17	Void contract for deed when purchasing colonias	B&CC §21A.003(e)	4 years after deed recorded.		
18	Set aside sale of property seized under Tax Code	CPRC §16.002(b)	1 year after property sold.		
19	Trespass by permanent injury to land	CPRC §16.003(a)	2 years.	Applies. ***Waddy***, 834 S.W.2d 97, 102 (Hous. [1st] 1992, denied).	Cause accrues upon discovery of first actionable injury. ***Walton***, 65 S.W.3d 262, 271 (E.P. 2001, denied).
20	Specific performance of contract for conveyance of real property	CPRC §16.004(a)(1)	4 years.	Applies. *See* ***McCord***, 200 S.W.2d 885, 888 (East. 1947, no writ).	Cause accrues when there is a failure to perform. ***F.D. Stella Prods.***, 875 S.W.2d 462, 464 (Aus. 1994, no writ).
21	Damages or penalty on penal clause of bond to convey real property	CPRC §16.004(a)(2)	4 years.		
22	Against surveyor for injury caused by error in survey	CPRC §16.011(a) (surveyor's statute of repose)	10 years after survey completed.	Does not apply to statutes of repose. ***Galbraith***, 290 S.W.3d 863, 868 (Tex.2009).	If written claim for damages is presented within 10-year period, period extended for 2 years from that date. CPRC §16.011(b).
23	Adverse possession—property held under title or color of title	CPRC §16.024	3 years.		

4. STATUTES OF LIMITATIONS IN PROPERTY-LAW PROCEEDINGS (CONT'D)

	CAUSE OF ACTION	AUTHORITY	LIMITATIONS PERIOD	DISCOVERY RULE	MISCELLANEOUS
Real & Personal Property (continued)					
24	Adverse possession—property cultivated, used, or enjoyed by person who pays taxes and claims the property under registered deed	CPRC §16.025(a)	5 years.		Does not apply to claim based on forged deed or deed executed under forged power of attorney. CPRC §16.025(b).
25	Inverse condemnation	*See* CPRC §16.026	10 years.		Covered by 10-year adverse-possession statute. ***Bragg***, 421 S.W.3d 118, 134 (S.A. 2013, denied).
26	Adverse possession—property cultivated, used, or enjoyed	CPRC §16.026(a)	10 years.		Limitations period begins on the date the adverse possessor actually and visibly appropriates the claimed land. ***Brown***, ___ S.W.3d ___ (Texark. 2017, n.p.h.) (No. 06-16-00078-CV; 5-17-17). Adverse possessor is limited to 160 acres unless property is enclosed. CPRC §16.026(b); *see also id.* §16.031 (certain exemptions for lands that are entirely surrounded by claimant).
27 17	Adverse possession—property held in peaceable and exclusive possession that is cultivated, used, or enjoyed by cotenant heir who pays all property taxes	CPRC §16.0265	5 years after other cotenant heir files affidavit of heirship and adverse possession.		Adverse possessor is limited to 160 acres unless property is enclosed. CPRC §16.0265(h).
28	Adverse possession—property cultivated, used, or enjoyed	CPRC §16.027 (statute of repose)	25 years regardless of legal disability.		
29	Adverse possession—property held in good faith and under recorded instrument purporting to convey	CPRC §16.028(a) (statute of repose)	25 years regardless of legal disability.		
30	Recovery of (or interest in) real property conveyed by instrument with technical defect	CPRC §16.033(a)	2 years after day instrument was filed for record.		Does not apply to forged instrument. CPRC §16.033(b).
31	Recovery of real property under lien or foreclosure of lien	CPRC §16.035(a)	4 years.		Statute applies to installment notes. *See* ***Palmer***, 831 S.W.2d 479, 481-82 (Texark. 1992, no writ). Parties may enter written extension agreement to suspend running of statute for 4 years. CPRC §16.036.

4. STATUTES OF LIMITATIONS IN PROPERTY-LAW PROCEEDINGS (CONT'D)

	CAUSE OF ACTION	AUTHORITY	LIMITATIONS PERIOD	DISCOVERY RULE	MISCELLANEOUS
Real & Personal Property (continued)					
32	Division of property not divided on divorce or annulment	FAM §9.202(a)	2 years from date former spouse communicates repudiation of other spouse's ownership interest.		Limitations tolled while a Texas court does not have jurisdiction over spouses or property. FAM §9.202(b). Section 9.202 (former FAM §3.90) does not bar otherwise valid partition under Prop. Code. ***Mayes***, 11 S.W.3d 440, 457 (Hous. [14th] 2000, denied).
33	Recovery of unpaid wages due under minimum-wage laws	LAB §62.202	2 years from date wages are due and payable.		
34	Violation of buyer of mineral interest to properly notify seller	PROP §5.151(e)	2 years from date conveyance executed.		
35	Improper transfer of nonexempt personal property	PROP §42.004(b)	2 years after transaction for creditor; 1 year after judgment for unliquidated or contingent claim.		
36	Deficiency judgment after lien-foreclosure sale	PROP §51.003(a)	2 years from date of foreclosure sale.		
37	Deed-of-trust foreclosure after deed in lieu of foreclosure	PROP §51.006(b)	4 years from date deed is executed and foreclosed.		
38	Foreclosure of mechanic's, contractor's, or materialman's lien	PROP §53.158	2 years after date claimant may file lien affidavit (1 year for residential construction project) or 1 year after completion, termination, or abandonment of contractual work, whichever is later.		
39	Action on bond to indemnify mechanic's, contractor's, or materialman's lien or claim	PROP §53.175(a)	1 year after notice is served or lien claim becomes unenforceable.		
40	Action on bond to pay mechanic's, contractor's, or materialman's lien or claim	PROP §53.208(d)	1 year if bond is recorded when lien is filed; 2 years if bond is not recorded when lien is filed.		

4. STATUTES OF LIMITATIONS IN PROPERTY-LAW PROCEEDINGS (CONT'D)

	CAUSE OF ACTION	AUTHORITY	LIMITATIONS PERIOD	DISCOVERY RULE	MISCELLANEOUS
Real & Personal Property (continued)					
41	Foreclosure of broker's lien	PROP §62.062(a)	2 years from recording of lien.		Broker claiming lien to collect deferred commission must bring suit within the earlier of (1) 2 years after commission becomes payable, or (2) the later of 10 years after lien is recorded or broker records subsequent renewal of the lien. PROP §62.062(b).
42	Claim of excess proceeds arising from foreclosure of possessory lien	PROP §70.007(b)	2 years after excess is paid to treasurer.		Excess becomes part of county's general fund if claim is not made on time.
43	Enforcement of agricultural lien	PROP §70.405	1 year after date of attachment.		
44	Recovery of escheated property	PROP §71.301(a) (personal property), §71.303(a) (real property)	4 years for personal property; 2 years for real property.		Cause accrues on date of final judgment of escheat proceeding.
45	Recovery of property loaned to museum	PROP §80.007(a)	2 years. *See* CPRC §16.003.		Action subject to 15-year statute of repose. PROP §80.007(b).
46	Discriminatory housing practice	PROP §301.151(a)	2 years after occurrence or termination of discriminatory practice, or breach of conciliation agreement, whichever occurs last.		Period does not include any time during which an administrative hearing is pending on the complaint (only applies to occurrence and termination of practice). PROP §301.151(b).
Torts					
47	Breach of duty of good faith and fair dealing in denial of insurance coverage	CPRC §16.003(a)	2 years.	Does not apply when there has been an outright and express denial of a claim. ***Davis***, 843 S.W.2d 777, 778 (Texark. 1992, no writ).	Cause accrues at denial of coverage. ***Davis***, 843 S.W.2d at 778.
48	Conversion of personal property	CPRC §16.003(a)	2 years.	Applies when possession initially lawful and no demand made. ***Wells Fargo***, 360 S.W.3d 691, 702 (Dal. 2012, no pet.).	Generally, cause accrues at time of unlawful taking. ***Wells Fargo***, 360 S.W.3d at 700. If possession is initially lawful, cause accrues at earlier of demand and refusal or when unequivocal acts of conversion occur. *Id.*
49	Forcible detainer	CPRC §16.003(a)	2 years.		
50	Forcible entry and detainer	CPRC §16.003(a)	2 years.		

4. STATUTES OF LIMITATIONS IN PROPERTY-LAW PROCEEDINGS (CONT'D)

	CAUSE OF ACTION	AUTHORITY	LIMITATIONS PERIOD	DISCOVERY RULE	MISCELLANEOUS
	Torts (continued)				
51	Negligence	CPRC §16.003(a)	2 years.	Generally does not apply. *See* ***Darr Equip.***, 824 S.W.2d 710, 712 (Amar. 1992, denied).	Cause normally accrues when duty of ordinary care is breached. ***Bell***, 899 S.W.2d 749, 753 (Amar. 1995, denied).
52	Nuisance	CPRC §16.003(a)	2 years.	Applies to permanent nuisance. ***Schneider***, 147 S.W.3d 264, 270, 279 (Tex.2004).	Cause accrues when injury first occurs or is discovered if permanent, or anew upon each injury if temporary. ***Schneider***, 147 S.W.3d at 270; *see* ***Town of Dish***, ___ S.W.3d ___ (Tex.2017) (No. 15-0613; 5-19-17). Limitations will not bar suit to abate continuing nuisance. *See* ***Yalamanchili***, 316 S.W.3d 33, 39 (Hous. [14th] 2010, denied).
53	On bond of executor, administrator, or guardian	CPRC §16.004(b)	4 years after death, resignation, removal, or discharge of executor, administrator, or guardian.		
54	Suit against architect, engineer, interior designer, or landscape architect who designs, plans, or inspects the construction of improvements or equipment attached to real property	CPRC §16.008(a) (statute of repose)	10 years after substantial completion of improvements or beginning of operation of equipment.	Does not apply to statutes of repose. ***Galbraith***, 290 S.W.3d 863, 868 (Tex.2009).	If written claim for damages, contribution, or indemnity is presented within 10-year period, period extended for 2 years from that date. CPRC §16.008(c).
55	Suit against person who constructs or repairs improvement to real property	CPRC §16.009(a) (statute of repose)	10 years after substantial completion of improvement.	Does not apply to statutes of repose. ***Galbraith***, 290 S.W.3d 863, 868 (Tex.2009).	If written claim for damages, contribution, or indemnity is presented within 10-year period, period extended for 2 years from that date. CPRC §16.009(c). Does not apply to materialmen, suppliers, or others not directly involved in the construction or repair. ***Petro Stopping Ctrs.***, 906 S.W.2d 618, 620 (E.P. 1995, no writ).

4. STATUTES OF LIMITATIONS IN PROPERTY-LAW PROCEEDINGS (CONT'D)

	Cause of Action	Authority	Limitations Period	Discovery Rule	Miscellaneous
	Wills, Trusts & Estates				
56	Declaration and establishment of a trust and recovery of title to trust property or damages for conversion	*See* CPRC §16.051 (residual limitations)	4 years.		Covered under residual limitations. ***Hicks***, 422 S.W.2d 613, 614 (Waco 1967, ref'd n.r.e.).
57	Admission of domestic will to probate	EST §256.003(a)	4 years from death of testator.		Time may be extended by showing no default for failing to present in 4 years, thereby allowing probate of will as muniment of title, but administration is not possible after 4 years. *See* EST §§257.052, 301.002.
58	Contest of validity of will admitted to probate	EST §256.204	2 years after will admitted to probate.		Incapacitated persons have 2 years from removal of disability to contest probate. If fraud or forgery discovered, then 2 years after date of discovery.
59	Application for letters testamentary or letters of administration	EST §301.002(a); *see id.* §501.006(a)	For domestic will: 4 years from death of testator or intestate. For foreign will: no limitations period.		Section 301.002(a) does not apply where administration is necessary to (1) receive or recover property due the estate, or (2) prevent real property in the estate from becoming a danger to health, safety, or welfare of general public and the applicant is home-rule municipality that is a creditor of the estate. EST §301.002(b).
60	Admission of foreign will to ancillary probate	EST §501.001	No limitations period.		Will may be admitted at any time if (1) will affects property in Texas, and (2) proof is presented that will stands probated or otherwise established in any U.S. state or foreign nation.
61	Trustee-removal suit	*See* PROP (Trust) §113.082(a)	No limitations period.		Trustee-removal suit is not the same as breach-of-fiduciary-duty suit. 4-year limitations period of CPRC §16.004(a)(5) does not apply. ***Ditta***, 298 S.W.3d 187, 192 (Tex.2009).

Legend:

B&CC	Business & Commerce Code
CPRC	Civil Practice & Remedies Code
EST	Estates Code
FAM	Family Code
FIN	Finance Code
INS	Insurance Code
LAB	Labor Code
PROP	Property Code
TAX	Tax Code
TRANSP	Transportation Code

5. STATUTORY INJUNCTIONS CHART

The following chart lists statutory injunctions available to private litigants. The chart does not list statutory injunctions available (1) only to the Attorney General or another governmental agency or unit or (2) during the appeal of a case decided by a district court. Although a statutory injunction may not exist for your cause, an equitable one may. *See* CPRC §65.011; TRCP 680-693a.

	STATUTE	WHAT MAY BE ENJOINED	PETITIONER	OTHER RELIEF
		Agriculture Code		
1	AGRIC §72.044(a)	Noncompliance with AGRIC §72.025(c) order to clean premises quarantined for Mexican fruit fly	Resident of county in which Mexican fruit-fly control is conducted.	
2	AGRIC §72.044(b)	Noncompliance with AGRIC ch. 72's Mexican fruit-fly provisions	Resident of Texas.	
3	AGRIC §161.131	Noncompliance with AGRIC ch. 161's animal-disease and pest-control provisions (other than provisions governing animal-shipment inspections, veterinarian's diseased-animal reports, and livestock-market regulations)	Citizen of Texas.	
4	AGRIC §164.022(f)	Texas Animal Health Commission order for scabies dipping of cattle or sheep	Person who owns, controls, or cares for animals. *See* AGRIC §164.021(a).	
5	AGRIC §167.106(a)	Noncompliance with AGRIC ch. 167's tick-eradication provisions	Resident of Texas.	
6	AGRIC §167.106(c)	Livestock caretaker or owner's noncompliance with tick-eradication order to dip livestock	Resident of county where tick eradication is conducted.	
7	AGRIC §251.004(b)	Agricultural operation conducted for one year or more	Any person.	Damages sustained from agricultural operation conducted in violation of federal, state, or local law. AGRIC §251.004(c).
		Business & Commerce Code		
8	B&CC §§16.102(b), 16.104(a)	Infringement of registered trademark or service mark	Registrant.	Damages (treble if intentionally), surrender or destruction of infringing mark, attorney fees. B&CC §§16.102(c)-(e), 16.104(b), (c).
9	B&CC §16.103(c)	Dilution of famous mark	Owner of mark.	If dilution is willful, owner may receive treble damages, attorney fees, and destruction of diluting items. B&CC §§16.102(c), (d), 16.104(b), (c).
10	B&CC §17.50(b)	DTPA violation	Consumer.	Economic damages (treble if knowingly), mental-anguish damages (treble if intentionally), attorney fees, costs. B&CC §17.50(b)-(d).

5. STATUTORY INJUNCTIONS CHART (CONT'D)

	STATUTE	WHAT MAY BE ENJOINED	PETITIONER	OTHER RELIEF
		Business & Commerce Code (continued)		
11	B&CC §21A.003	Violation of B&CC ch. 21 by executing contract for deed in sales of colonias	Attorney General.	Civil penalty of $500 per violation, attorney fees and costs, additional orders to make purchaser whole.
12	B&CC §24.008(a)(3)(A)	Disposition of fraudulently transferred asset by debtor or transferee	Creditor.	Avoidance of transfer, attachment of asset. B&CC §24.008(a)(1), (2).
13	B&CC §57.401(a)	Violation of B&CC ch. 57's agricultural, construction, industrial, mining, forestry, landscaping, and outdoor-power-equipment-dealer agreements	Dealer.	Damages, attorney fees, costs.
		Civil Practice & Remedies Code		
14	CPRC §12.003(a)	Making or using fraudulent court record or fraudulent lien or claim against property	(1) Fraudulent judgment lien—person against whom judgment was rendered; (2) fraudulent lien or claim against property—obligor, debtor, or owner. CPRC §12.003(a)(7), (8).	Greater of $10,000 or actual damages, exemplary damages, attorney fees, costs. CPRC §12.002(b).
15	CPRC §16.012(a)(2)(E)	Defective product	Claimant. *See* CPRC §§16.012(a)(1), 82.001.	Damages. CPRC §16.012(a)(2)(A)-(D).
16	CPRC §31.002(a)	Property in possession of judgment debtor	Judgment creditor.	Attorney fees, costs. CPRC §31.002(e).
17	CPRC §65.011	General injunction statute. Allows injunctions for (1) acts prejudicial to applicant, (2) acts relating to pending litigation that would render litigation ineffectual, (3) statutes or equity principles, (4) clouds on real-property titles, and (5) irreparable injury to property irrespective of other remedies at law.	Applicant.	
18	CPRC §65.012(a)	Subsurface drilling or mining operations	Adjacent landowner who has injury to her surface or minerals.	
19	CPRC §65.013	Judgment or legal proceeding	Complainant.	
20	CPRC §65.014(a)	Execution of judgment	Defendant.	
21	CPRC §65.015	Closing of street	Owner or lessee of property abutting part of closed street.	
22	CPRC §106.002(a)	Discrimination based on race, religion, color, sex, or national origin by state officer or employee	Injured person.	Attorney fees, costs. CPRC §106.002(b).
23	CPRC §125.002(e)	Common nuisance	Individual. CPRC §125.002(a).	
24	CPRC §§125.064, 125.065	Public nuisance by criminal combination or street gang	Resident of Texas.	
25	CPRC §171.086(a)(3)	Destruction of subject matter of controversy, books, or records before arbitration	Party supporting arbitration.	

5. Statutory Injunctions Chart (cont'd)

Statute		What May Be Enjoined	Petitioner	Other Relief
Code of Criminal Procedure				
26	CCP art. 59.06(k)(2)	Waste of income from property that has increased in value because of notoriety of a crime	Crime victim who is suing notorious defendant for damages.	
Education Code				
27	EDUC §44.004(e)	Collection of taxes by school district in violation of notice requirements for its budget meeting	Person who owns taxable property in school district.	
Finance Code				
28	FIN §156.402(b)	Violation of Residential Mortgage Loan Company and Originator Licensing and Registration Act	Injured mortgage applicant.	Actual damages, attorney fees, costs. FIN §156.402(a).
29	FIN §157.027(b)	Violation of Mortgage Banker Registration and Residential Mortgage Loan Originator License Act	Injured mortgage applicant.	Actual damages, attorney fees, costs. FIN §157.027(a).
30	FIN §347.404(b)	Unlawful refusal of real-property owner to allow creditor to repossess manufactured home	Creditor of manufactured-home buyer.	Actual and exemplary damages, attorney fees, costs.
Government Code				
31	GOVT §442.012(a)	Adversely affecting historic structures, landmarks, monuments, and markers	Resident of Texas.	Costs, deposition expenses, expert-witness and attorney fees. *See* GOVT §442.012(c).
32	GOVT §551.142(a)	Violation of GOVT ch. 551's open-meeting requirements by members of governmental body	Interested person.	Costs, attorney fees. GOVT §551.142(b).
33	GOVT §552.3215(b)	Violation of GOVT ch. 552's public-information-availability provisions by governmental body	Complainant. GOVT §552.3215(e).	Declaratory relief, costs, attorney fees. GOVT §§552.3215(b), 552.323(a).
34	GOVT §554.003(a)	Retaliation against whistleblowing public employee by governmental entity	Public employee.	Actual damages; costs; attorney fees; reinstatement of position, lost wages, fringe benefits, seniority. GOVT §554.003(a), (b).
35	GOVT §3151.101	Construction of structure that would obstruct view of state capitol	Any person.	
Health & Safety Code				
36	H&SC §365.015(a)	Illegal dumping of litter or solid waste	Person affected.	Investigative costs, attorney fees, costs. H&SC §365.015(c).
37	H&SC §711.007	Maintenance or location of cemetery (1) in violation of H&SC chs. 711 and 712's provisions regulating cemeteries, or (2) in manner that is offensive to surrounding community	Owner of residence near cemetery or owner of plot. H&SC §711.007(b)(5).	
38	H&SC §712.026(a)	Lack of maintenance of perpetual-care cemetery	Group of at least five plot owners. H&SC §712.026(b).	Costs, attorney fees. H&SC §712.026(c).
39	H&SC §714.002	Operation of feed pen or slaughterhouse near cemetery in county with more than 525,000 people	Cemetery or plot owner.	

5. Statutory Injunctions Chart (cont'd)

	Statute	What May Be Enjoined	Petitioner	Other Relief
Health & Safety Code (continued)				
40	H&SC §773.094	Unauthorized disclosure of emergency-care records or confidential communications	Aggrieved person.	Damages.
41	H&SC §821.057	Violation of H&SC ch. 821's provisions governing animal euthanasia	Any person.	
42	H&SC §822.115	Violation of H&SC ch. 822's provisions governing ownership of dangerous wild animals	Person harmed or threatened with harm.	
43	H&SC §823.007	Violation of H&SC ch. 823's animal-shelters provisions	Any person.	
Insurance Code				
44	INS §541.152(a)(2)	Unfair methods of competition or unfair or deceptive acts in insurance business	Person who has sustained actual damages. INS §541.151.	Damages (treble if knowingly), attorney fees, costs, and other relief the court deems proper. INS §541.152(a)(1), (3), (b).
45	INS §541.252(2)	Unfair methods of competition or unfair or deceptive acts in insurance business that harm insurance-buying public (class action)	Person who has sustained actual damages (on behalf of the class). INS §541.251(a).	Actual damages, costs, attorney fees, and other relief the court determines is proper. INS §541.252(1), (3).
46	INS §2211.213	Violation of agreements made pursuant to issuance of public securities to raise funds for residential-property insurance	Any party of interest.	Writ of mandamus.
Local Government Code				
47	LGOVT §89.004(c)	Action by county	Any person.	Damages.
48	LGOVT §232.008(f)	Cancellation or closing of roadway or easement in subdivision outside municipality	Person who owns a lot that (1) abuts path to be closed or (2) uses path to connect to nearest public highway or common amenity of subdivision.	Damages. LGOVT §232.008(g).
49	LGOVT §233.036	Construction of structure in violation of building or set-back line	Owner of real property in county.	Mandamus, abatement.
50	LGOVT §235.024	Discharge of firearms in subdivision located in unincorporated area	Any person.	
51	LGOVT §235.044	Hunting with bows and arrows in subdivision located in unincorporated area	Any person.	
52	LGOVT §352.051(h)	Violation of LGOVT §352.051's restricted-fireworks provisions	Affected party.	
53	LGOVT §352.081(g)	Violation of LGOVT §352.081's outdoor-burning provisions	Any person.	
54	LGOVT §392.101(b)	Violation of obligee's rights under Housing Authorities Law	Obligee.	Mandamus, possession of housing project, appointment of receiver for housing project, or accounting by housing authority. LGOVT §§392.101(a), 392.102(a)(2), (3).

5. STATUTORY INJUNCTIONS CHART (CONT'D)

	STATUTE	WHAT MAY BE ENJOINED	PETITIONER	OTHER RELIEF
		Natural Resources Code		
55	NatRes §52.097	Drilling for oil and gas under state contract in riverbeds and channels or condemning adjoining land to facilitate drilling. *See* NatRes §§52.071, 52.093.	Complaining party.	
56	NatRes §85.244	Enforcement or adoption by Railroad Commission of rule or order concerning oil and gas conservation or waste	Interested person. NatRes §85.241.	
57	NatRes §91.182	Production or possession of gas injected for storage by one who is not injector	Storer.	
58	NatRes §134.186	Violation of Texas Surface Coal Mining and Reclamation Act	Affected person. NatRes §134.182(a).	Damages, costs, expert-witness and attorney fees. NatRes §§134.182(b), 134.186.
59	NatRes §152.105	Use of forest pest-control measures by Texas Forest Service on landowner's forest	Landowner.	
60	NatRes §191.173	Violation of Antiquities Code of Texas	Citizen of Texas.	
		Occupations Code		
61	OCC §1201.222(d)	Violation of OCC §1201.222's provisions governing installations for manufactured homes that are considered to be real property	Purchaser in county of violation.	
62	OCC §1303.354(c)	Disciplinary action against residential service company by Texas Real Estate Commission during appeal of commission's decision. *See* OCC §§1303.351, 1303.354(c).	Adversely affected person. OCC §1303.354(a).	
		Property Code		
63	PROP §5.207	Violation of prohibition on collecting private transfer fee	Attorney General.	Declaratory relief, civil penalty for double fee collected; pattern or practice (penalty up to $250,000).
64	PROP §§21.003, 21.064	Condemnation of property or entering property under eminent-domain authority	Property owner.	Damages to owner. PROP §21.064(b).
65	PROP §51.007(e)	Foreclosure sale of real property by trustee	Party.	
66	PROP §92.010(c)	Exceeding occupancy limit of leased dwelling	Individual (or entity on individual's behalf) who owns or leases dwelling within 3,000 feet of dwelling in violation.	Attorney fees, costs, $500 for each violation of PROP §92.010.
67	PROP §92.011(c)	Nonacceptance of cash rental payments by residential landlord if cash payments are permitted by lease	Tenant (or entity on tenant's behalf).	Attorney fees, costs, greater of one month's rent or $500 for each violation of PROP §92.011.
68	PROP §92.015(c)	Landlord's violation of tenant's right to summon emergency assistance	Tenant.	One month's rent, damages, attorney fees, costs.

5. STATUTORY INJUNCTIONS CHART (CONT'D)

	STATUTE	WHAT MAY BE ENJOINED	PETITIONER	OTHER RELIEF
		Property Code (continued)		
69	PROP §92.333	Retaliation by residential landlord for tenant's exercising of rights	Tenant.	Declaratory relief, one month's rent plus $500, property, actual and statutory damages, moving costs, actual expenses, attorney fees, costs, less any delinquent rents or other sums owed to landlord.
70	PROP §94.007(c)	Nonacceptance of cash rental payments by manufactured-home landlord if cash payments are permitted by lease	Tenant (or entity on tenant's behalf).	
71	PROP §94.254	Retaliation by manufactured-home landlord for tenant's exercising of rights	Tenant.	Declaratory relief, one month's rent plus $500, actual and statutory damages, court costs, attorney fees, less any delinquent sums owed to landlord.
72	PROP §209.007(d)	Violation of restrictive covenants by residential-property owner or nonpayment of property owners' association's assessments. *See* PROP §209.006(a).	Property owners' association.	Attorney fees, costs. PROP §209.008.
73	PROP §301.153	Discriminatory housing practice	Aggrieved person. PROP §301.151(a).	Actual and punitive damages, attorney fees, costs.
		Tax Code		
74	TAX §23.12(e)	(1) Failure by chief appraiser to establish or adhere to equitable and uniform inventory-appraisal procedures or (2) inequitable enforcement or verification of inventory-audit procedures	Inventory owner.	
75	TAX §26.04(g)	Adoption of tax rate by taxing unit's assessor who has not complied in good faith with TAX §26.04's computation and publication requirements	Owner of taxable property in taxing unit.	
76	TAX §26.05(e)	Collection of taxes by taxing unit that has not complied in good faith with TAX §26.05's tax-rate-adoption requirements	Owner of taxable property in taxing unit.	
77	TAX §112.101	Assessment or collection of state tax or fee by public official whose duty it is to collect tax or fee	Applicant.	

5. STATUTORY INJUNCTIONS CHART (CONT'D)

	STATUTE	WHAT MAY BE ENJOINED	PETITIONER	OTHER RELIEF
		Transportation Code		
78	TRANSP §203.033	Denial of previously existing access to state highway by Texas Transportation Commission	Owner or lessee of real property that adjoins part of highway to which access is denied.	Damages. *See* TRANSP §§203.033, 203.034(b).
79	TRANSP §251.058(a)	Closing, abandoning, or vacating any part of public road by Texas Transportation Commission	Owner of property (1) that abuts portion of road or (2) whose only ingress or egress is supplied by road.	Damages. TRANSP §251.058(c).
80	TRANSP §396.002(a)	Violation of TRANSP ch. 396's provisions governing automobile-wrecking-and-salvage yards and junkyards	Any person.	
		Water Code		
81	WATER §7.351(a)	Violation of H&SC ch. 401's radioactive-materials provisions (Texas Radiation Control Act)	Affected person.	
82	WATER §11.0841(b)	Unauthorized diversion, impoundment, or use of surface water	Water-right holder.	Costs, expert-witness and attorney fees.
83	WATER §11.334	Injury to water right by decision of Texas Natural Resource Conservation Commission under the auspices of Water Rights Adjudication Act	Injured person.	
84	WATER §36.119(b)	Drilling or operating well without permit or producing groundwater in violation of district rule	Landowner or person who has right to produce groundwater from land adjacent to or within ½ mile of well.	Damages. WATER §36.119(c).
85	WATER §51.429(b)	Creation of water-control-and-improvement district, issuance of its bonds, or contracting with U.S. for reclamation projects	Affected party.	
86	WATER §58.459(b)	Creation of irrigation district, issuance of its bonds, or contracting with U.S. for reclamation projects	Affected party.	

Legend:

AGRIC	Agriculture Code	INS	Insurance Code
B&CC	Business & Commerce Code	LGOVT	Local Government Code
CCP	Code of Criminal Procedure	NatRes	Natural Resources Code
CPRC	Civil Practice & Remedies Code	OCC	Occupations Code
DTPA	Deceptive Trade Practices Act	PROP	Property Code
EDUC	Education Code	TAX	Tax Code
FIN	Finance Code	TRANSP	Transportation Code
GOVT	Government Code	TRCP	Texas Rules of Civil Procedure
H&SC	Health & Safety Code	WATER	Water Code

6. CONDEMNATION PROCEDURE TIMETABLE

STEP	ACTION	DEADLINE	RULE	DUE	DONE
1a	Condemnor sends landowner's bill of rights to property owner.	At or before first representation of eminent-domain authority and again no later than 7 days before Step 3	PROP §21.0112		
1b	Condemnor makes initial offer to purchase property. ❶		PROP §§21.0111(a), (c), 21.0113(b)(1), 21.012; ***Hubenak***, 141 S.W.3d 172, 184 (Tex.2004)		
1c	Condemnor provides all appraisal reports prepared in the 10 years preceding the date of offer.	At Step 1b	PROP §21.0111(a)		
1d	Condemnee discloses all appraisal reports used in determining owner's opinion of value.	No later than 10 days after receipt of report, or 3 business days before Step 8, if report will be used	PROP §21.0111(b)		
2	Condemnor obtains appraisal of value and damages to owner's remaining property.	Before Step 3	PROP §21.0113(b)(4)		
3	Condemnor makes final offer to acquire property voluntarily. ❷	Step 1b + 30 days	PROP §§21.0113(b)(2), (3), 21.012(b)(6)		
4a	If no agreement, condemnor files a condemnation petition in county court at law, district court, or probate court. ❸	At least 14 days after Step 3	PROP §§21.001, 21.0113(b)(7), 21.012(a), 21.013		
4b	Condemnor sends copy of petition by certified mail to condemnee.	At Step 4a	PROP §21.012(c)		

❶ If condemning for ground or surface water, condemnor must first prepare a drought-contingency plan, implement a water-conservation plan, make a bona fide effort to obtain practicable alternative water supplies and to acquire the water rights to be condemned by voluntary purchase or lease, and show that the political subdivision needs the water rights for its domestic needs for the next ten-year period. Prop. Code §21.0121.

❷ Condemnor seeking to acquire property through eminent domain may not include a confidentiality provision in an offer or agreement to acquire the property from condemnee. Prop. Code §21.0111(c).

❸ Condemnor should file the petition in the county court at law in which condemnee resides if part of the property is located in the county. Prop. Code §21.013(a). If condemnee does not reside in a county where part of the property is located, then any county in which part of the property is located is appropriate venue. *Id.* If the property is located in a county where there are no county courts at law, then the condemnor must file the petition in the district court. *Id.* §21.013(c). However, some counties have special rules that designate certain courts for eminent-domain actions. *E.g.*, Gov't Code §25.0173(a) (Bexar County Probate Court has jurisdiction over all statutory and inverse condemnations), §25.0635(d) (Denton County Probate Court has jurisdiction over all statutory and inverse condemnations); Travis Cty. Loc. R. 2.15 (county courts) (Probate Court handles eminent-domain cases until there is objection to award).

6. CONDEMNATION PROCEDURE TIMETABLE (CONT'D)

STEP	ACTION	DEADLINE	RULE	DUE	DONE
5	Judge appoints 3 special commissioners to conduct hearing and assess damages. ❹		PROP §§21.014(a), (b), 21.015		
6	Commissioners schedule hearing.	At least 20 days after Step 5	PROP §21.015		
7	Commissioners provide notice of hearing.	At least 20 days before Step 8	PROP §21.016		
8	Commissioners hold hearing.		PROP §§21.014(c), 21.015		
9	Commissioners rule on damages and costs.		PROP §§21.041, 21.042, 21.047		
10	Commissioners file a dated and signed written decision in court in which condemnor filed condemnation petition. ❺	No later than next working day after Step 9	PROP §21.048		
11	Judge informs clerk of decision.	No later than next working day after Step 10	PROP §21.049		
12	Clerk sends notice of decision to condemnor and condemnee.	No later than next working day after Step 10	PROP §21.049		
13a	Any party who is displeased with the commissioners' findings or a condemnee who otherwise objects to the condemnation must file written and specific objections. ❻	By 1st Monday after 20th day after Step 10	PROP §21.018(a); *see* PROP §21.061		
13b	If no party objects to commissioners' findings, court adopts findings as judgment, records the judgment, and issues process necessary to enforce judgment.	After 1st Monday after 20th day after Step 10	PROP §21.061; *see* PROP §21.018		

❹ Special commissioners are disinterested real-property owners who reside in the county where the property is located. Prop. Code §21.014(a). The judge will give preference to real-property owners agreed on by the parties. *Id.* The judge will allow a reasonable period to strike one of the commissioners appointed by the court. *Id.* If a person does not serve as a commissioner or is struck by a party, the judge shall appoint a replacement. *Id.*

❺ The written decision includes damages, accrued costs of the proceedings, and the party against whom costs are adjudged. Prop. Code §21.048.

❻ If objections to the findings of the special commissioners are filed, the court will serve citation on the other parties. Prop. Code §21.018(b).

6. CONDEMNATION PROCEDURE TIMETABLE (CONT'D)

STEP	ACTION	DEADLINE	RULE	DUE	DONE
14a	If condemnee did not participate in the commissioners' hearing, she may raise in her written statement that condemnor failed to negotiate in good faith. ❼	At or after Step 13a	*See* ***Hubenak***, 141 S.W.3d at 179-80		
14b	If court determines that condemnor failed to negotiate in good faith, then the court must abate the proceedings for a reasonable time to allow condemnor to satisfy the unable-to-agree requirement. ❽		***Hubenak***, 141 S.W.3d at 184		
14c	If after a reasonable time condemnor fails to make a good-faith offer, then the court should dismiss the condemnation proceeding.		***Hubenak***, 141 S.W.3d at 184		
15	Condemnor may take possession of property after commission issues its decision pending trial, if condemnor satisfies prerequisites. ❾		PROP §21.021(a)		
16a	Condemnor or condemnee may file a motion to dismiss proceedings. ❿	Anytime after Step 4	PROP §§21.019, 21.0195		

❼ Condemnee cannot raise the issue of failure to negotiate in good faith during the administrative phase. Condemnee may raise the issue during the trial phase; however, if condemnee participates in the commission hearing, she waives the right to complain at trial that condemnor did not make a good-faith effort to agree. ***Hubenak v. San Jacinto Gas Transmission Co.***, 141 S.W.3d 172, 179 (Tex.2004). If condemnee withdraws the commissioners' award from the court registry during the trial phase, she may appeal only the amount of damages awarded by the commission. *See* ***Religious of the Sacred Heart v. City of Houston***, 836 S.W.2d 606, 613 (Tex.1992); ***State v. Jackson***, 388 S.W.2d 924, 925-26 (Tex.1965).

❽ If the court determines condemnor did not make a bona fide offer to acquire the property before filing the petition, the court will abate the suit, order condemnor to make a bona fide offer, and order condemnor to pay costs, reasonable attorney fees, and other professional fees. Prop. Code §21.047(d).

❾ Condemnor may take possession of property only if it (1) pays the owner the damages assessed by the commissioners or deposits the same amount with the court, (2) deposits the same amount or a surety bond of the same amount to secure any damages awarded by the court above that of the commissioners, and (3) executes a bond with two or more solvent sureties to secure any costs awarded by the court above that of the commissioners. Prop. Code §21.021(a). However, if condemnor is the state, a county, a municipal corporation, an irrigation district, a water-improvement district, or a water-power-control district, only the first requirement applies. *Id.* §21.021(c).

❿ Condemnor may seek to dismiss the action (or amend the description of the condemned property and abandon part of the land or rights that it had previously sought to condemn) (1) if such action would not prejudice condemnee or (2) if condemnor is the Texas Department of Transportation and if the property owner's interest is not materially affected by the dismissal. *See* Prop. Code §21.0195(b); ***Murray v. Devco, Ltd.***, 731 S.W.2d 555, 557-58 (Tex.1987); ***State v. Nelson***, 334 S.W.2d 788, 790 (Tex.1960).

6. CONDEMNATION PROCEDURE TIMETABLE (CONT'D)

STEP	ACTION	DEADLINE	RULE	DUE	DONE
16b	Upon dismissal, court makes allowance to property owner. ⓫	After Step 16a	PROP §§21.019(b), (c), 21.0195(c), 21.044		
16c	If condemnor files another condemnation petition after moving to dismiss first proceeding to condemn substantially the same property interest, court will enter original commissioners' award and award triple expenses allowed to owner prior to dismissal.		PROP §21.020		
16d	If court holds that condemnor does not have a right to condemn property and condemnor has possession of property, then writ of possession is issued to condemnee; court may award damages that resulted from temporary possession and may order such damages be paid out of any condemnor's deposit of the special commissioners' award to secure possession.		PROP §§21.044(a), 21.062		
17	Trial before appropriate court with jurisdiction to determine right to condemn property and/or assess damages.				
18	If court holds that condemnor has right to condemn property, court enters judgment awarding condemnee amount of damages, including interest if any is due. Judgment of court vests legal title in property with condemnor. ⓬		*See* PROP §21.065; ***Dixon***, 250 S.W.2d 636, 637-38 (Dal. 1952, ref'd n.r.e.)		

⓫ The court's discretion in making an allowance to a property owner varies depending on the circumstances of the case. If the court grants a motion to dismiss made by condemnor, it must make an allowance to the property owner for fees and expenses. Prop. Code §21.019(b). However, if the motion to dismiss is made by a property owner seeking judicial denial of the right to condemn, then the court may, but is not required to, make an allowance for fees and expenses. *Id.* §21.019(c). Additionally, if condemnor is the Texas Department of Transportation and the proceeding is dismissed on the department's motion or because of its failure to bring the proceeding properly, then the court must make an allowance for the value of the department's use of the property while in its possession, any damage caused by the condemnation, and any other expenses and fees incurred by the property owner. *Id.* §21.0195(c).

⓬ Condemnor generally receives a vested right only for the purpose for which it condemned the property. *See* Prop. Code §21.045. If condemnor petitioned for a right-of-way or easement, then title remains with condemnee and condemnor receives a vested right only in the right-of-way or easement. *See id.*; ***Brunson v. State***, 418 S.W.2d 504, 506 (Tex.1967). However, when a governmental entity condemns an entire fee simple for a purpose that when fully stated includes the actual use of the interest, the condemnation remains valid as long as the actual use is for a public purpose. ***City of Arlington v. Golddust Twins Rlty. Corp.***, 41 F.3d 960, 965 (5th Cir.1994).

6. CONDEMNATION PROCEDURE TIMETABLE (CONT'D)

STEP	ACTION	DEADLINE	RULE	DUE	DONE
19	If condemnor is an entity with eminent-domain authority, written notice must be provided to condemnee of right to repurchase if eminent domain is canceled, no actual progress is made toward public use, or property becomes unnecessary for public use in next 10 years.	After Step 13b or 18	PROP §§21.023, 21.101(a), (b), 21.102		
20a	If public use for the condemnation is canceled, no actual progress is made toward public use, or property becomes unnecessary for public use in next 10 years, condemnor sends written notice to prior owner of right to repurchase property at price paid to owner at time property was acquired by eminent domain.	No later than 180 days after cancellation	PROP §§21.101(a), (b), 21.102, 21.103(a), (b)		
20b	Condemnee requests determination by condemnor on whether eminent domain was canceled, actual progress was made toward public use, or property became unnecessary for public use.	Step 13b or 18 + 10 years	PROP §§21.101(b), 21.1021(a), (b)		
20c	Condemnor responds to request for determination.	No later than 90 days after receipt of request in Step 20b	PROP §21.1021(c)		
20d	Prior owner notifies condemnor of intent to repurchase property. [13]	No later than 180 days after Step 20a or 20c	PROP §21.103(a)		
20e	Condemnor makes offer to sell property.	As soon as practicable after Step 20d	PROP §21.103(b)		
20f	Prior owner purchases property.	No later than 90 days after Step 20e	PROP §21.103(b)		

[13] The right to repurchase ends one year after the notice period set out in Property Code §21.102 if condemnor (1) is required to give notice under that section, (2) makes a good-faith effort to locate and provide notice to each entitled person before the expiration of the deadline for giving notice under Property Code §21.102, and (3) does not receive a response to any notice provided under Property Code §21.102 within the time limits prescribed by Property Code §21.103. Prop. Code §21.1022.

Legend:
PROP Property Code

7. EVICTION TIMETABLE

STEP	ACTION	DEADLINE	RULE	DUE	DONE
1a	Tenant in default/breach of contract	At least 3 days' notice to vacate unless lease states otherwise.	PROP §24.005(a)		
1b	Tenant holds over	At least 3 days' notice to vacate unless lease states otherwise and must comply with PROP §91.001.	PROP §24.005(a)		
2a	Termination of tenancy—lease provision for notice	Lease provision controls.	PROP §91.001(e)		
2b	Termination of tenancy—no lease provision for notice	Depends on rent-paying period. ❶	PROP §91.001(b), (c)		
3	Attorney-fees notice	10 days' notice in forcible-detainer case if lease does not provide for attorney fees.	PROP §24.006(a)		
4	Lease or applicable law gives tenant right to respond to proposed eviction	Notice to vacate cannot be given until time for tenant to respond has expired.	PROP §24.005(e)		
5	File suit with J.P. ❷		PROP §24.004; *see* TRCP 510.3 ❸		
6	Citation and service of process ❹		TRCP 510.4; *see* TRCP 501.2(b)		
7	Trial	At least 6 days after Step 6. TRCP 510.7(a).	TRCP 510.7 ❺		

❶ If the rent-paying period is at least one month, the lease terminates on the later of (1) the date given in the notice or (2) one month after the notice is given. Prop. Code §91.001(b). If the rent-paying period is less than one month, the lease terminates on the later of (1) the date given in the notice or (2) one rental period after the notice. *Id.* §91.001(c).

❷ Exclusive original jurisdiction is in justice court in the county and precinct where the property is located, except when a suit is based on a deed executed in violation of Business & Commerce Code ch. 21. *See* Prop. Code §24.004.

❸ Plaintiff must name as defendants all tenants obligated under the lease residing at the premises whom plaintiff seeks to evict. No judgment or writ of possession may issue against any tenant residing at the premises who is not named in the petition and served with citation. TRCP 510.3(c). The petition should list all home and work addresses of every defendant that are known to plaintiff and should state that plaintiff knows of no other home or work addresses of defendant in the county where the premises are located. *See* TRCP 510.4(c)(1)(B).

❹ Unless otherwise authorized by written court order, the citation must be served by a constable or sheriff. TRCP 510.4(b)(1). Service is to be made by in-hand delivery to defendant or a person over 16 at defendant's usual place of residence. TRCP 510.4(b)(2). Upon motion supported by sworn statement of the constable, sheriff, or other authorized process server, the trial court may order alternative service. Alternative service methods include placing a copy through a mail chute or under a front door, or if neither is possible, affixing it to the front door. The person serving process must also send a copy of the citation and petition to the address by first-class mail. *See* TRCP 510.4(c).

❺ Jury demand must be made and jury fee must be paid or Statement of Inability to Afford Payment of Court Costs must be filed within three days of date of trial. TRCP 510.7(b). The trial may be postponed for no more than seven days unless both parties agree in writing. TRCP 510.7(c).

Only issue in F&D suit is right to possession, except suit for delinquent rent may be added R510.

7. EVICTION TIMETABLE (CONT'D)

STEP	ACTION	DEADLINE	RULE	DUE	DONE
8	**Appeal**—For the procedure for appealing the J.P.'s judgment, see timetable 8, "Eviction Appeal," p. 1543.				
9	**Writ of possession**—For the deadlines for a writ of possession, see timetable 10, "Writ of Possession & Warehouseman's Lien," p. 1547.				

Legend:

J.P.	Justice of the Peace
PROP	Property Code
TRCP	Texas Rules of Civil Procedure

See also ***O'Connor's Texas COA***, "Forcible Detainer—Eviction," ch. 16-B, p. 424.

8. EVICTION APPEAL TIMETABLE

STEP	ACTION	DEADLINE	RULE	DUE	DONE
1	J.P. signs judgment ❶		TRCP 510.8		
2	Party appeals to county court by filing appeal bond or cash deposit with J.P. ❷	Step 1 + 5 days ❸	TRCP 510.9		
3	Tenant who files appeal bond pays into J.P. registry amount of rent to be paid in one rental pay period	Step 2 + 5 days	PROP §24.0053(a-3)		
4	**Appealing by sworn statement**—If party is unable to pay costs or file a bond or deposit, see timetable 9, "Eviction Appeal by Statement of Inability to Pay," p. 1545.				
5	**Writ of possession**—If no bond, deposit, or sworn statement is timely filed, see timetable 10, "Writ of Possession & Warehouseman's Lien," p. 1547. ❹				
6	J.P. stays proceedings and files transcript, original papers, and money in registry with county-court clerk	Immediately after Step 2	TRCP 510.10(a)		
7	County-court clerk notifies parties of receipt of transcript ❺	Immediately after Step 6	TRCP 510.10(b)		
8	Party appealing serves adverse party with notice of appeal filed	Step 2 + 5 days ❸	TRCP 510.9(d); *see* TRCP 21a, 501.4		
9	Defendant files answer (if pleaded orally in J.P.)	Step 6 + 8 days ❸	TRCP 510.12		
10	Landlord may file motion to withdraw money deposited into J.P. registry	Before final determination, dismissal of appeal, or order of court after final hearing	PROP §24.0053(a-4)		

❶ A judgment for residential eviction for nonpayment of rent must note the amount of rent to be paid each rental period while an appeal is pending. Prop. Code §24.0053(a).

❷ The bond or cash deposit is to be made payable to the adverse party with the condition that the party will prosecute the appeal with effect or pay all costs and damages. TRCP 510.9(b).

❸ Count all days starting on the day after the judgment and include the last day, but if the deadline falls on a Saturday, Sunday, legal holiday, or day the court closes before 5:00 p.m., the deadline to file is the next day that the court is open. TRCP 500.5(a); *see* TRCP 510.2. If a document is filed by mail and not received by the court by the due date, the court may take any action authorized by the Texas Rules of Civil Procedure, including issuing a writ of possession requiring a tenant to leave the property. TRCP 510.2.

❹ If the tenant appeals and does not timely pay amount of rent equal to one rental pay period into the J.P. court registry, the landlord may obtain a writ of possession. Regardless of whether a writ of possession is issued, the J.P. must transmit the transcript and appeal documents to the county court. Prop. Code §24.0053(a-3).

❺ The clerk's written notice must also advise defendant of the need to file a written answer in the county court within 8 days if one was not filed in the J.P. court. TRCP 510.10(b).

8. EVICTION APPEAL TIMETABLE (CONT'D)

STEP	ACTION	DEADLINE	RULE	DUE	DONE
11	County court may enter judgment by default	If no written answer filed, and after Step 6 + 8 days	TRCP 510.12; *see* TRCP 510.9(e)		
12	County court conducts trial de novo ❻	Step 6 + anytime after 8 days	TRCP 510.10(c)		

❻ The trial, as well as any hearings and motions, is entitled to precedence in the county court. TRCP 510.10(c).

Legend:

J.P. Justice of the Peace
PROP Property Code
TRCP Texas Rules of Civil Procedure

See also ***O'Connor's Texas COA***, "Appeal," ch. 16-B, §6.6, p. 439.

9. EVICTION APPEAL BY STATEMENT OF INABILITY TO PAY TIMETABLE

STEP	ACTION	DEADLINE	RULE	DUE	DONE
1	J.P. signs judgment ❶		TRCP 510.8		
2	Appealing party files Statement of Inability to Afford Payment of Court Costs ❷	Step 1 + 5 days ❸	PROP §24.0052(a); TRCP 502.3, 510.9(c)		
3	J.P. provides tenant written notice of requirements for making rent deposit to J.P. registry	At Step 2	PROP §24.0053(a-1)		
4	J.P. or clerk sends written notice to adverse party via first-class mail	Step 2 + 1 day ❸	TRCP 510.9(d)		
5a	Tenant retains possession during appeal by paying rent into J.P. registry	• Initially, Step 2 + 5 days ❸ (into J.P. registry) • Then, rent due date + 5 days ❸ (into county-court registry)	PROP §24.0053(a-2), (b); TRCP 510.9(c)(5)(B)		
5b	Tenant loses possession (without hearing) while appealing by failing to timely pay initial rent deposit into J.P. registry and landlord requests writ of possession	Step 5a not satisfied + 1 day	PROP §24.0054(a)		
5c	Transcript sent to county court for trial de novo even though writ of possession was issued and tenant is no longer in possession ❹	After Step 5b	PROP §24.0054(a-2)		
6a	Landlord files sworn motion in county court after tenant defaults on rent ❹	Any day after rent becomes delinquent under the deadline listed in Step 5a	PROP §24.0054(a-4); TRCP 510.9(c)(5)(B)(iv)		

❶ A judgment for residential eviction for nonpayment of rent must note the amount of rent to be paid each rental period while an appeal is pending. Prop. Code §24.0053(a).

❷ In 2016, Texas Rules of Civil Procedure 502.3 and 510.9 were amended, in conjunction with Texas Rule of Civil Procedure 145, to require a plaintiff who is unable to afford court costs to file a Statement of Inability to Afford Payment of Court Costs. *See* Tex.Sup.Ct. Order, Misc. Docket No. 16-9122 (eff. Sept. 1, 2016). Instead of a sworn statement of inability to pay costs or an affidavit of indigence, a plaintiff must now use a form Statement approved by the Supreme Court or file a statement that includes the information required by the Court-approved form. *See* TRCP 502.3(b). Property Code §24.0052(a), however, still refers to the filing of a pauper's affidavit and lists the required contents of the affidavit. Prop. Code §24.0052(a). That information is now included in the Court-approved Statement. An electronic version of the Court-approved Statement can be found on the Texas Office of Court Administration website, www.txcourts.gov/rules-forms/forms.

❸ Count all days starting on the day after the judgment, but if the deadline falls on a Saturday, Sunday, or legal holiday, the deadline to file is the next day that the court is open. TRCP 4, 500.5, 510.2.

❹ Tenant has lost possession of premises during appeal, but the appeal has not been lost.

9. EVICTION APPEAL BY STATEMENT OF INABILITY TO PAY TIMETABLE (CONT'D)

STEP	ACTION	DEADLINE	RULE	DUE	DONE
6b	Landlord notifies tenant of motion and hearing date ❺	After Step 5b	PROP §24.0054(a-4)		
6c	County court hears motion on default		PROP §24.0054(b); TRCP 510.9(c)(5)(B)(iv)		
6d	County court issues writ of restitution/possession upon showing of default	Step 6c + showing of default without cure	PROP §24.0054(b); *see* TRCP 510.9(c)(5)(B)(iv)		
7	Adverse party contests Statement ❻	Step 2 + 5 days ❸	PROP §24.0052(d); TRCP 510.9(c)(2)		
8	J.P. hears contest and rules on it ❼	Step 7 + 5 days ❸	PROP §24.0052(d); TRCP 502.3(d), 510.9(c)(3)		
9	If J.P. approves the sworn statement, the appeal proceeds without bond or cash deposit. See Step 6, timetable 8, "Eviction Appeal," p. 1543. If J.P. disapproves the sworn statement, tenant may appeal the denial of the sworn statement to the county court. TRCP 510.9(c)(4). Tenant may, within one business day, file an appeal bond or cash deposit. *Id.* For appeal by filing a bond or cash deposit, see Step 2, timetable 8, "Eviction Appeal," p. 1543.				
10	Tenant appeals disapproval of sworn statement	Disapproval of sworn statement + 5 days ❸	TRCP 510.9(c)(3)		
11	County court hears contest of sworn statement de novo	Step 10 + 5 days	TRCP 510.9(c)(3), 510.10(c)		
12	If the county court approves the sworn statement, appellant may proceed without bond or cash deposit. See Step 6, timetable 8, "Eviction Appeal," p. 1543. If the county court disapproves the sworn statement, appellant may, within one business day, proceed only after payment of bond or cash deposit. TRCP 510.9(c)(4). See Step 2, timetable 8, "Eviction Appeal," p. 1543.				

❸ Count all days starting on the day after the judgment, but if the deadline falls on a Saturday, Sunday, or legal holiday, the deadline to file is the next day that the court is open. TRCP 4, 500.5, 510.2.

❺ If tenant cures the default on or before the day of the hearing, the appeal continues. Prop. Code §24.0054(b). After tenant cures the first default, tenant will not be entitled to cure another default. *Id.* §24.0054(c); *see id.* §24.0054(b); *see also* TRCP 510.9 (rule contains no "cure" language for defaults).

❻ A sworn statement accompanied by a certificate confirming that a legal-aid provider screened the party cannot be contested. TRCP 502.3(c).

❼ At the hearing, tenant has the burden to prove by competent evidence the inability to afford payment of the costs of appeal or file an appeal bond or cash deposit. *See* Prop. Code §24.0052(d); TRCP 502.3(d).

Legend:

J.P.	Justice of the Peace
PROP	Property Code
TRCP	Texas Rules of Civil Procedure

10. WRIT OF POSSESSION & WAREHOUSEMAN'S LIEN TIMETABLE

STEP	ACTION	DEADLINE	RULE	DUE	DONE
1	J.P. signs judgment ❶		TRCP 510.8(a)-(c)		
2	Court notifies tenant of default judgment via first-class mail	County court's entry of default + 48 hours	PROP §24.0061(c)		
3	Writ of possession issued if (1) no appeal bond, cash deposit, or sworn statement filed, (2) sworn statement filed but rent deposit not timely paid and landlord requests writ, (3) sworn statement disapproved and no appeal bond or cash deposit filed, or (4) county court finds uncured noncompliance with rent requirements during appeal ❷	• Step 1 + 6 days ❸ • If sworn statement filed in nonpayment-of-rent case, date of filing + 6 days if no deposit into registry • If sworn statement disapproved, date of disapproval + 5 days • If rent not paid during appeal, date motion was sustained See Steps 9 and 12, timetable 9, "Eviction Appeal by Statement of Inability to Pay," p. 1546.	PROP §§24.0054(a)-(c), 24.0061(a), (b); TRCP 510.5, 510.8(d); *see* TRCP 507.4, 510.3(c)		
4a	Officer posts notice of impending execution of writ	Anytime after Step 3	PROP §24.0061(d)(1)		
4b	Officer executes writ	Notice posted + at least 24 hours	PROP §24.0061(d)(2)		
5	Officer gives tenant notice if property is to be removed to warehouse	• If in person, when writ executed • If by first-class mail, within 72 hours after writ executed	PROP §24.0062(b)		
6	Tenant demands property while property is being removed from tenant's premises	During removal of property and before warehouseman permanently leaves premises (all requested property returned without charge)	PROP §24.0062(d)		
7	Tenant demands certain listed items	Storage of listed items + 30 days (if costs reasonably attributable to items redeemed are paid) ❹	PROP §24.0062(e)		

❶ A judgment for residential eviction for nonpayment of rent must note the amount of rent to be paid each rental period while an appeal is pending. Prop. Code §24.0053(a).

❷ A writ of possession may not be issued more than 60 days after a judgment for possession is signed. TRCP 510.8(d)(1). For good cause, a court may extend the deadline for issuance to 90 days after a judgment for possession is signed. *Id.*

❸ A writ of possession may not be issued before the sixth day after the date on which the judgment for possession is rendered unless a possession bond has been filed and approved and a judgment for possession is granted by default. Prop. Code §24.0061(b). Possession-bond requirements are contained in Texas Rule of Civil Procedure 510.5.

❹ The warehouseman has a lien on the property in the amount of any reasonable storage and moving charges incurred. Prop. Code §24.0062(a). The lien does not attach until the property is actually stored. *Id.*

10. WRIT OF POSSESSION & WAREHOUSEMAN'S LIEN TIMETABLE (CONT'D)

STEP	ACTION	DEADLINE	RULE	DUE	DONE
8	Tenant demands all property after stored in warehouse	On payment by tenant before property sold	PROP §24.0062(g)		
9	Tenant brings suit on grounds that warehouseman's moving or storage charges are not reasonable	Before sale of listed items (if demand and payment are timely or charges are not reasonable) ❹	PROP §24.0062(h), (i)		
10	Tenant demands all remaining property	During period of Step 7 and before sale of property (warehouseman returns property if all costs on all property are paid)	PROP §24.0062(g)		

❹ The warehouseman has a lien on the property in the amount of any reasonable storage and moving charges incurred. Prop. Code §24.0062(a). The lien does not attach until the property is actually stored. *Id.*

Legend:

J.P.	Justice of the Peace
PROP	Property Code
TRCP	Texas Rules of Civil Procedure

See also ***O'Connor's Texas COA***, "Writ of possession," ch. 16-B, §3.1, p. 429.

INDEX

INDEX

INDEX

INDEX

Notes